The 1996 Information Please Sports Almanac

Now in its 7th year as America's
favorite sports reference book.
Ranked as one of journalism's
"50 Basic Reference Books"
by *The Essential Researcher*.

With Year in Review essays by many of the country's top sports writers:

Tony Barnhart
Atlanta Constitution
on College Sports

Mark Blaudschun
The Boston Globe
on College Football

Jerry Crasnick
The Denver Post
on Baseball

Eric Duhatschek
Calgary Herald
on Hockey

Bernard Fernandez
The Philadelphia Daily News
on Boxing

Tom Gaffney
Akron Beacon Journal
on Bowling

Paul Gardner
Soccer America
on Soccer

Mike Harris
Associated Press
on Auto Racing

Philip Hersh
Chicago Tribune
on the Olympic Games
and International Sports

Michelle Hiskey
The Atlanta Constitution
on Ballpark & Arenas

David Moore
Dallas Morning News
on Pro Basketball

Scott Ostler
San Francisco Chronicle
on The Year in Sports

Marino Parascenzo
Pittsburgh Post-Gazette
on Golf

Diane Pucin
The Philadelphia Inquirer
on Tennis

Richard Sandomir
The New York Times
on Business & Media

Sharon Smith
Author and commentator
on Horse Racing

Vito Stellino
The Baltimore Sun
on Pro Football

Gene Wojciechowski
Los Angeles Times
on College Basketball

Plus an exclusive cartoon by 1995 Pulitzer Prize-winner **Mike Luckovich** of the *Atlanta Constitution*. Additional articles provided by **Clark Booth** on the Boston Garden, **Jim Callis** on College Baseball, **Dean Caparaz** on Women's Soccer, **Bill Center** on the America's Cup, **Neil Koepke** on College Hockey, **Bob Ley** on the Class of '95, **Wendy Parker** on Women's College Basketball, **Dave Supleve** on CFL Football, **Ian Thomsen** on the Rugby World Cup, **Nathan Ward** on upcoming Anniversaries, **David Whitford** on Labor Issues and **Mike Woitalla** on College Soccer.

"This is a remarkable book—complete, accurate and interesting. After my over 60 years announcing sports, I should know a great record book. This is certainly it."
—Red Barber (1908-92)

The Champions of 1995

Auto Racing

NASCAR Circuit
Daytona 500................................Sterling Marlin
Winston 500 ....Mark Martin
Coca-Cola 600 ....Bobby Labonte
Southern 500 ....Jeff Gordon

IndyCar Circuit
Indianapolis 500 ....Jacques Villeneuve
PPG Cup Champion ....Jacques Villeneuve

Formula One Circuit
World Driving Championship ....Michael Schumacher

Baseball

World Series ....Atlanta def. Cleveland 4 games to 2
MVP..Tom Glavine, Atlanta, P

All-Star Game......................NL 3, AL 2 at Arlington, TX
MVP...Jeff Conine, Florida, DH

College World Series............................Cal St. Fullerton
MVP ....Mark Kotsay, Cal St. Fullerton, OF

College Basketball

Men's NCAA Final Four
Championship..............................UCLA 89, Arkansas 78
Semifinals...................................UCLA 74, Oklahoma St. 61
Arkansas 75, North Carolina 68
MVP..Ed O'Bannon, UCLA, F

Women's NCAA Final Four
Championship..............................UConn 70, Tennesee 64
Semifinals...................................UConn 87, Stanford 60
Tennessee 73, Georgia 51
MVP ....Rebecca Lobo, UConn, F

Pro Basketball

NBA Finals.................Houston def. Orlando 4 games to 0
MVP...Hakeem Olajuwon, Houston, C
Eastern Final.............Orlando def. Indiana 4 games to 3
Western Final......Houston def. San Antonio 4 games to 3
All-Star Game ....West 139, East 112 at Phoenix
MVP...Mitch Richmond, Sacramento, F

Bowling

Men's Major Championships
PBA National ....Scott Alexander
BPAA U.S. Open ....Dave Husted
Tournament of Champions ....Mike Aulby
ABC Masters ....Mike Aulby

Women's Major Championships
Sam's Town Invitational (1994).....Tish Johnson
WIBC Queens ....Sandy Postman
BPAA U.S. Open ....Cheryl Daniels

College Football (1994)

National Champions
AP and Coaches ....Nebraska (13-0)

Major Bowls
Orange......................................Nebraska 24, Miami 17
Rose..Penn St. 38, Oregon 20
Sugar...Florida St. 23, Florida 17
Fiesta...Colorado 41, Notre Dame 24
Cotton..USC 55, Texas Tech 14

Pro Football (1994)

Super Bowl XXIX ....San Francisco 49, San Diego 26
MVP ....Steve Young, San Francisco, QB
AFC Championship.............San Diego 17, Pittsburgh 13
NFC Championship ....San Fransico 38, Dallas 28
Pro Bowl ....AFC 41, NFC 13
MVP ....Marshall Faulk, Indianapolis, RB

Golf

Men's Major Championships
Masters......................................Ben Crenshaw
U.S. Open ....Corey Pavin
British Open ....John Daly
PGA Championships.....................Steve Elkington

Seniors Major Championships
The Tradition...............................Jack Nicklaus
PGA Seniors................................Ray Floyd
U.S. Senior Open ....Tom Weiskopf
Senior Players Championship .........J.C. Snead

Women's Major Championships
Nabisco Dinah Shore ....Nanci Bowen
LPGA Championship ....Kelly Robbins
U.S. Women's Open ....Annika Sorenstam
du Marier Classic ....Jenny Lidback

National Team Competition
Ryder Cup (Men) ....Europe 14½, United States 13½

Hockey

Stanley Cup.............New Jersey def. Detroit 4 game to 0
MVP ....Claude Lemieux, New Jersey, RW
Western Final ....Detroit def. Chicago 4 games to 1
Eastern Final...New Jersey def. Philadelphia 4 games to 2
All-Star Game ....cancelled
NCAA Div. 1 Final ....Boston Univ. 6, Maine 2
MVP..Chris O'Sullivan, Boston Univ., LW
World Championship...................Finland 4, Sweden 1

Horse Racing

Triple Crown Champions
Kentucky Derby ....Thunder Gulch (Gary Stevens)
Preakness.............................Timber Country (Pat Day)
Belmont...............................Thunder Gulch (Gary Stevens)

Harness Racing
Hambletonian ....Tagliabue (John Campbell)

Soccer

World Youth Championship.............................Argentina
U-20 World Championship..................Argentina 2, Brazil 0
U-17 World Championship ....Ghana 3, Brazil 2
Women's World Championship........Norway 2, Germany 0
US Cup '95 ....USA
Copa America ....Uruguay 1, Brazil 1
(Uruguay wins on penalty kicks, 5-3)

Tennis

Men's Grand Slam Championships
Australian Open ....Andre Agassi
French Open ....Thomas Muster
Wimbledon ....Pete Sampras
U.S. Open ....Pete Sampras

Women's Grand Slam Championships
Australian Open ....Mary Pierce
French Open ....Steffi Graf
Wimbledon ....Steffi Graf
U.S. Open ....Steffi Graf

Yachting

America's Cup Final
Black Magic I (NZE) def. Young America (USA) 5 races to 0

Miscellaneous Champions

Little League World Series ....Taiwan
Rugby World Cup ....South Africa
Tour de France............................Miguel Induráin (SPA)
Tour du Pont ....Lance Armstrong (USA)
World Chess Championships ....Garry Kasparov (RUS)

THE 1996
INFORMATION PLEASE®
SPORTS
ALMANAC

Mike Meserole

EDITOR

Assistant Editor
Gerry Brown

Production by **Working Media, Inc.**
Linda Bean-Pardee, Andy Gluck, Madeleine Newell, John Perry

Research assistance by
**Bob Baggett, Mike Coffey,
Brian Miller, Pat Page,
Adam Polgreen, Ed Ryan**
and **Howie Schwab**

HOUGHTON MIFFLIN COMPANY
Boston   New York

The Information Please Sports Almanac

ISSN: 1045-4980
ISBN: 0-395-66567-1

Front Cover photographs: **Ripken**: 1995 Doug Pensinger/Allsport USA; **O'Neal and Olajuwan**: 1995 Allsport USA; **Steve Young**: 1995 Martin Venegas/Allsport USA; **Tyson and King:** 1995 Al Bello/Allsport USA; **Graf**: 1995 AP Photo Color; **Villeneuve**: 1995 Allsport USA.

Spine photograph: **O'Bannon**: 1995 Wide World Photos, Inc.

Back cover photographs: **Gallacher**: 1995 Wide World Photos, Inc.; **Agassi and Sampras**: 1995 AP Photocolor; **Lemieux**: 1995 Bruce Bennett Studios; **Stevens and Lukas**: 1995 Wide World Photos, Inc.; **Lobo**: 1995 Matthew Stockman/Allsport USA.

Comments and Suggestions

Comments and suggestions from readers are invited. Because of the many letters received, however, its not possible to respond personally to every correspondent. Nevertheless, all letters are welcome and each will be carefully considered. **The Information Please Sports Almanac** does not rule on bets or wagers. Address all correspondence to INSO Corp., 31 St. James Avenue, Boston, Massachusetts 02116-4104.

Additional copies of The **1996 Information Please Sports Almanac** may be ordered directly by mail from:

Customer Service Department
Houghton Mifflin Company
181 Ballardvale St.
P.O. Box 7050
Wilmington, MA 01887-7050

Phone toll-free (800) 225-3362 for price and shipping information. In Massachusetts, phone (617) 272-1500.

Printed in the United States of America

WPC 10 9 8 7 6 5

CONTENTS

Y ou can't put a book like this together without a lot of help. A *lot* of help. Production designers, writers, fact-checkers, photography researchers, mailroom personnel, overnight delivery people, a strong local pizza joint, friends and readers who write in with helpful suggestions.

My thanks to everybody who assisted in the making of this seventh edition of The Sports Almanac.

I would especially like to thank my right hand man— assistant editor Gerry Brown, whose expertise, thoroughness and good humor under pressure were a godsend. Gerry, along with fact-checkers Adam Polgreen and Brian Miller are all veterans of Jack Grinold's Northeastern University sports information office. You trained them well, Jack. Thanks. And Go, Huskies!

The IPSA also benefited from a new production/design team this year— Working Media, Inc. of Boston, which is also responsible for the production and editorial content of the new *1996 Information Please Entertainment Almanac*. Thanks to them all, especially John Perry and the peripatetic Andy Gluck.

Thanks also to Steve Lewers, Marnie Patterson, Mark Caleb and Chris Leonesio at Houghton Mifflin; to Jim Murphy and Paul Schaefer at Western Publishing; to Steve Vana-Paxhia and our new keepers at Inso Corp. (love that air conditioning on the weekends); to Bill Trippe, Patty Guzikowski, Robert Heywood and everyone else who is working on the electronic versions of the IPSA.

Photos for the book wouldn't have been possible without the assistance of Nat Andriani at Wide World Photos, Jonathan Braun and Jamie Calsyn at Allsport, Susan Williams at Agence France-Presse, and Sarah Partridge at Bettmann.

Additional help was asked for and graciously supplied— often at the 11th hour— by Jim Callis and Allan Simpson at *Baseball America*; Paul Kennedy and Mike Woitalla at *Soccer America*; Sean Mullin and Joe Sullivan at *The Boston Globe*; Rick Campbell and Gary Johnson at the NCAA; Terry Lyons of the NBA; Leslie Hammond of the NFL; Phil Pritchard and Jeff Davis at the Hockey Hall of Fame; Peggy Hendershot and Howard Bass at Thoroughbred Racing Communications, Inc.; Larry Barber at the MEAC; and many, many others.

Finally, thanks to Charley and Marcia Monagan, Michael and Lynn Michaud, Bruce and Allie Delventhal and my family for their continued support.

That's it. Dig in.

—Mike Meserole

Boston
Nov. 1, 1995

Major League Cities & Teams

As of Oct. 31, 1995, there were 128 major league teams playing or scheduled to play baseball, basketball, football and hockey in 54 cities in the United States and Canada. Listed below are the cities and the teams that play there.

Anaheim
AL   California Angels
NHL   Mighty Ducks of Anaheim

Arlington
AL   Texas Rangers

Atlanta
NL   Braves
NBA   Hawks
NFL   Falcons

Baltimore
AL   Orioles
CFL   Football Club

Boston
AL   Red Sox
NBA   Celtics
NFL   N.E. Patriots (Foxboro)
NHL   Bruins

Birmingham
CFL   Barracudas

Buffalo
NFL   Bills (Orchard Park)
NHL   Sabres

Calgary
CFL   Stampeders
NHL   Flames

Charlotte
NBA   Hornets
NFL   Carolina Panthers

Chicago
AL   White Sox
NL   Cubs
NBA   Bulls
NFL   Bears
NHL   Blackhawks

Cincinnati
NL   Reds
NFL   Bengals

Cleveland
AL   Indians
NBA   Cavaliers
NFL   Browns

Dallas
NBA   Mavericks
NFL   Cowboys (Irving)
NHL   Stars

Denver
NL   Colorado Rockies
NBA   Nuggets
NFL   Broncos
NHL   Colorado Avalanche

Detroit
AL   Tigers
NBA   Pistons (Auburn Hills)
NFL   Lions (Pontiac)
NHL   Red Wings

East Rutherford
NBA   New Jersey Nets
NFL   New York Giants
NFL   New York Jets
NHL   New Jersey Devils

Edmonton
CFL   Eskimos
NHL   Oilers

Green Bay
NFL   Packers

Hamilton
CFL   Tiger-Cats

Hartford
NHL   Whalers

Houston
NL   Astros
NBA   Rockets
NFL   Oilers

Indianapolis
NBA   Pacers
NFL   Colts

Jacksonville
NFL   Jaguars

Kansas City
AL   Royals
NFL   Chiefs

Los Angeles
NL   Dodgers
NBA   Clippers
NBA   Lakers (Inglewood)
NHL   Kings (Inglewood)

Memphis
CFL   Mad Dogs

Miami
NL   Florida Marlins
NBA   Heat
NFL   Dolphins
NHL   Florida Panthers

Milwaukee
AL   Brewers
NBA   Bucks

Minneapolis
AL   Minn. Twins
NBA   Minn. Timberwolves
NFL   Minn. Vikings

Montreal
NL   Expos
NHL   Canadiens

New Orleans
NFL   Saints

New York
AL   Yankees
NL   Mets
NBA   Knicks
NHL   Rangers

Oakland
AL   Athletics
NBA   Golden St. Warriors
NFL   Raiders

Orlando
NBA   Magic

Ottawa
CFL   Rough Riders
NHL   Senators

Philadelphia
NL   Phillies
NBA   76ers
NFL   Eagles
NHL   Flyers

Phoenix
NBA   Suns
NFL   Arizona Cardinals (Tempe)
MLB   Arizona DiamondBacks (1998)

Pittsburgh
NL   Pirates
NFL   Steelers
NHL   Penguins

Portland
NBA   Trail Blazers

Regina
CFL   Saskatchewan Roughriders

Sacramento
NBA   Kings

St. Louis
NL   Cardinals
NFL   Rams
NHL   Blues

Salt Lake City
NBA   Utah Jazz

San Antonio
CFL   Texans
NBA   Spurs

San Diego
NL   Padres
NFL   Chargers

San Francisco
NL   Giants
NFL   49ers

San Jose
NHL   Sharks

Seattle
AL   Mariners
NBA   SuperSonics
NFL   Seahawks

Shreveport
CFL   Pirates

Tampa
NFL   Buccaneers
NHL   Lightning
MLB   Devil Rays (1998)

Toronto
AL   Blue Jays
CFL   Argonauts
NBA   Raptors
NHL   Maple Leafs

Uniondale
NHL   New York Islanders

Vancouver
CFL   B.C. Lions
NBA   Grizzlies
NHL   Canucks

Washington
NBA   Bullets (Landover)
NFL   Redskins
NHL   Capitals (Landover)

Winnipeg
NHL   Jets
CFL   Blue Bombers

Baseball paid the price for its 1994-95 players' strike with shrinking attendance figures. On the final day of the season, acting commissioner Bud Selig's Brewers drew less than 15,000 in Milwaukee.

UPDATES

Could Be Worse

In the wake of baseball's 232-day players' strike and owner lockouts in the NHL and NBA, be thankful for what you got.

Cheer up! A year ago last fall, three of the four major sports were either in the middle of a strike or preparing for one.

Things look a whole lot better now. Hockey and basketball have both settled, guaranteeing peace for, oh, at least a couple of years. And baseball, having paid a steep price during the summer in declining revenues and waning popularity, now has a powerful incentive to come to terms as quickly as possible on a new Basic Agreement. You'd think so, anyway.

Keep those happy thoughts in mind while you work your way through the following sport-by-sport rundown of recent developments in the labor wars. With any luck, next year's roundup will be a short one.

Baseball

Well, it could have been a lot worse. That's one way to think about the 1995 baseball season. In the afterglow of the World Series it's hard to do, but try to remember just for a moment how gloomy things were last winter, how hopeless the prospects for the coming season.

As the year began, the strike was entering its fifth month and counting. Richard Ravitch, the owners' chief negotiator, had just quit. With Ravitch out of the way, the owners had gone ahead and unilaterally

imposed a salary cap, effectively ending all hope of compromise on the strike's central issue. Veteran federal mediator W.J. Usery, appointed by Labor Secretary Robert Reich in October, looked on helplessly.

During the fall, President Clinton had invited acting commissioner Bud Selig and union chief Donald Fehr to the White House, to no effect. In late January, the president reentered the game, setting a Feb. 6 deadline for progress toward a settlement. The day before the deadline, the owners did away with salary arbitration, significantly widening the gap between them and the players. On Feb. 7, a chastened president begged both sides to accept binding arbitration. He might as well have asked Newt Gingrich for a tax increase. The players were willing but the owners, to no one's surprise, refused.

By that point, perhaps the only people in the world looking forward to Opening Day were the replacement players, who shortly afterwards began streaming into camps in Florida and Arizona. Even the cancellation of the World Series— unthinkable until it happened— paled in comparison with the thought of has-beens, never-weres and never-will-bes masquerading in Major League uniforms.

It was left to the courts, in the person of Federal judge Sonia Sotomayor, to salvage what the owners and players seemed so intent on destroying. On March 31, responding favorably to a request for an injunction by the National Labor Relations Board,

---

David Whitford writes for *Inc.* magazine and is the author of *Playing Hardball: The High Stakes Battle for Baseball's New Franchises.*

Federal mediator **W.J. Usery** (left) meeting in the Oval Office with **President Clinton** and Labor Secretary **Robert Reich** on Feb. 6, to discuss the status of negotiations to end the baseball strike. Despite the President's best efforts to settle the impasse, it continued for nearly two more months.

Judge Sotomayor tossed out the salary cap, reinstated salary arbitration and otherwise ordered both parties to comply with all the terms of the 1990 Basic Agreement— until such time as they could agree on a new one. And with that, three and a half weeks late on April 25, baseball embarked on an abbreviated 144-game schedule.

In seven previous work stoppages since 1972, baseball's paying customers had shown an amazing capacity to forgive and forget. Not this time. During the more than eight months the strike lasted, a lot of fans who hadn't thought so before learned that they could live without baseball. In most cities, near-empty stadiums greeted the players upon their return, and those few fans who did bother to show up weren't shy about venting their disgust— like the wise guys at New York's Shea Stadium who rushed the field during the home opener, scattering dollar bills at the players' feet. The message: Welcome back, you greedy bastards. Overall, attendance in 1995 declined by more than 20 percent compared to the last full season in 1993, despite the artificial

pennant fever generated by baseball's new multi-tier playoff system.

Which brings us to Nov. 1, 1995, and the disturbing fact that baseball still is without a Basic Agreement. Remember, nothing was ever settled, only postponed. Not only that, but all progress toward a new Basic Agreement ceased as soon as the games resumed, with both sides passing the summer in a state of denial.

In September, the owners introduced their new lead negotiator, Randy Levine, fresh from a two-year stint as New York City labor relations commissioner.

Never mind Fehr and the rest— if Levine is to succeed where his predecessors failed, he first must quell the discord in his own camp, still deeply divided among small-market and big-market teams. Not a problem, according to Levine. "I don't have a fear," he says. "Maybe I'm charming."

There is one thing the players and owners agree on. They are opposed to a measure in the Budget Reconciliation Bill called the executive compensation amendment. The bill would affect every pro sport and would limit employers from deducting employees' salaries to $1 million in hopes of raising $12-14 billion over the next five years. The amendment would allow Social Security beneficiaries to increase the amount of money they earn without affecting their benefits.

Meanwhile, as the year came to a close, the future of several teams was in doubt. After 42 years of ownership, Anheuser-Busch announced on Oct. 25 that it was selling the St. Louis Cardinals in order to focus on its core products of beer, theme parks and aluminum cans. The Cards are valued at $110 million, but with Busch Stadium and four garages, they could sell for more than $200 million.

In Pittsburgh, the Pirates were still on the block after a $1 million deposit by newspaper heir Kevin McClatchy was rejected. Cable mogul John Rigas and Pittsburgh Penguins owner Harold Baldwin said they are working together to keep the team in the city. Both men had their individual attempts rejected, but believe they can forge a deal collectively.

According to *The Washington Post*, Houston Astros owner Drayton McLane had a $150 million agreement to sell his team to the Virginia Baseball Stadium Authority, although Selig denied the agreement was made. The team would play at RFK Stadium for a year before a facility in northern Virginia would be completed.

Despite several unstable franchises and the fragile labor situation, baseball appeared close to signing a five-year TV deal with NBC, Fox, ESPN and TNT for a reported $1.15 billion.

According to *The New York Times* and *USA Today*, Fox would pay up to $120 million a year for a Saturday afternoon Game of the Week, two All-Star Games, three World Series and half the League Championship Series. NBC would pay $100 million per year for three All-Star Games, two World Series, half the LCS's, but no regular season games.

On cable, ESPN and TNT will put up a combined $200 million to share the playoff games that Fox and NBC don't want and after 1997, TNT will join ESPN in regular season coverage.

The deal marked a significant about face for NBC Sports president Dick Ebersol, who only four months before had savaged base-

ball as a double-dealing partner in The Baseball Network (see page 566).

Hockey

"Was it worth losing so much of the season? I don't know," said Hartford Whalers GM Jim Rutherford when the NHL owners' lockout finally ended on Jan. 11. What, exactly, did the 103-day shutdown achieve? Hard to say. The owners got a rookie salary cap starting at $850,000 and reaching $1.075 million by 2000; a few more restrictions on free agency; and a rejiggered arbitration system that in some cases lets the clubs walk away from outlandish awards. And that's it.

And the players? They didn't win anything, except in the negative sense of not losing on the issue most dear to them: A comprehensive salary cap. If anything could be said to have caused the lockout, it was the owners' lust for a cap. They hoped new commissioner Gary Bettman could do for them what he had done almost a decade earlier for the NBA as that league's vice president in the mid-1980s— devise a workable salary cap and convince the players to go for it.

But in asking for so much from the players, the owners had overlooked, or chosen to ignore, a crucial fact: the NHL was not in trouble. Yes, there were sharp revenue disparities among the franchises, with gross receipts ranging from a high of more than $55 million for the New York Rangers to a low of fewer than $15 million for the Winnipeg Jets.

[The Jets, who nearly left Manitoba before the 1995-96 season (see page 381) were sold to Minneapolis businessmen Richard Burke and Steve Gluckstern for $68 million on Oct. 18 and will move to Minnesota next season.

In late 1994, the NHL players did not see revenue disparities as their problem, choosing instead to focus on the big picture. During the just-completed 1993-94 season, the New York Rangers had won the Stanley Cup for the first time in more than five decades, greatly increasing the sport's public awareness. League-wide attendance and revenues had both reached record levels. And over the summer, the Fox network had christened the league's coming-of-age with a five-year, $155-million national broadcast deal.

NBA Players' Association president **Buck Williams** of the Trail Blazers (center), union vice president **Charles Smith** of the Knicks (left) and union chief **Simon Gourdine** at a Sept. 13 news conference in Chicago, announcing ratification of a new, six-year labor agreement with the NBA.

Years ago, when the NBA players agreed to a salary cap, they had no choice. It was give in or go down with the league. But absent a compelling reason to compromise, the NHL players balked, and the result was a damaging strike that came perilously close to wiping out the entire season.

Basketball

On Oct. 27, 1994, the NBA players and owners signed a no-strike, no-lockout agreement. It wasn't a settlement— that would have to wait— but at least it allowed the 1994-95 season to start on time, thereby preserving the NBA's perfect-attendance record (it's still the only pro sports league yet to suffer a work stoppage). Nice NBA, sane NBA, reasonable NBA— not like those other leagues that can never stop bickering.

Fast-forward to June 23, 1995. The season is over, Houston repeats as champion, and the players have gathered in Chicago to approve the new contract hammered out by NBA commissioner David Stern and the president of their union, Simon Gourdine. A sense of urgency prevails: the owners want a signed agreement before the college draft, only five days away. And everything falls apart.

From the players' point of view, there are appealing aspects to the proposed agreement, namely higher average salaries and a fifty-fold increase in licensing revenue. But for the veterans, especially, there's a deal-breaker: in the second year of the six-year deal, clubs that exceed the salary cap by re-signing their own players would have to pay a 100 percent luxury tax on the amount over the cap. Top players and their agents decide that's unacceptable. Led by Michael Jordan and Patrick Ewing, they undertake to invalidate the agreement by decertifying the union.

On June 29, Utah Jazz owner Larry Miller warns: "If the players continue down this path, they're taking us down the exact same road baseball and hockey went down." The next day, Miller votes with the other owners to lock out the players, even though they're all on vacation anyway. And it's welcome to the labor wars, NBA.

While the dissidents gather support for

Football

The NFL was supposed to be the exception to the rule— a tranquil zone untouched by the raging pro sports labor wars. That's because prior to the 1994 season the owners and players had worked out a salary-cap arrangement both felt they could live with: 64 percent of league revenues, divided by the number of teams in the league. But then San Francisco 49ers president Carmen Policy found a way to pry the cap loose last year to accommodate Deion Sanders. When the Niners went on to win the Super Bowl, well, let's just say it gave a lot of people ideas.

Enter Jerry Jones, the renegade owner of the Dallas Cowboys. Because he happens to own the lease on Texas Stadium, Jones draws refreshment from a gushing revenue stream denied most of his league brethren. He gets all the dollars from parking, concessions, luxury boxes, stadium advertising, even rent for stadium events other than football games— a total of $37.3 million in 1994, according to *Financial World* magazine, or about five times the league average in that revenue category.

On top of all that, Jones went out this past fall and signed a pair of precedent-shattering long-term sponsorship deals with PepsiCo ($25 million) and Nike (at least $14 million).

So what did Jones do with all that money? Why, he went out and bought Deion Sanders, of course. A seven-year deal worth $35 million, sliced, diced and tenderized in such a way as to somehow stuff it all in under the cap.

When Harold Henderson, the NFL's executive vice president for labor relations, saw that Sanders would earn the NFL minimum salary of $178,000 for the first three years, never mind the $12.5 million signing bonus, he was not amused. "The CBA (collective bargaining agreement) is completely undermined if contracts for superstars are structured with artificial, substandard salaries and outsized bonuses," Henderson fumed. The NFL, which earlier had filed a $300 million suit against the Cowboys protesting the Pepsi and Nike deals, then ordered Jones to restructure Sanders' contract (but allowed Sanders to play).

"This is not about Deion," a wounded Jones shot back. "What this is about is sticking it to the Cowboys. They're trying to intimidate the Cowboys. They're trying to be a bully." ❑

Wide World Photos

Deion Sanders takes the field in Atlanta for his first game as a Dallas Cowboy on Oct. 29. The All-Pro defensive back played most of the game on defense and four plays on offense as Dallas beat the Falcons, 28-13, to improve their record to 7-1.

decertification, a weakened NBA Players Association presses negotiations with the owners. The parties reach a new, improved agreement in early August that includes unrestricted free agency after three years and does not contain a luxury tax.

The National Labor Relations Board, meanwhile, schedules an election for early September, in which some 400 NBA players will have a chance to vote yes (for the union and, by extension, the contract), or no (against the union and the contract). As election day approaches, the outcome is anybody's guess.

"We are absolutely, flat-out petrified," says Stern, who warns that a vote to decertify will lead the league to ruin.

When the votes are tallied on Sept. 12, it's a rout: 226-134, in favor of the union. One day later the player reps overwhelmingly approve the new contract, and are joined the following week by the grateful owners. Camps open, the season begins on time, and the NBA's streak continues.

by Todd Archer

AUTO RACING

Heading into the final race of the NASCAR season, Jeff Gordon was poised to supplant Dale Earnhardt as Winston Cup champion. All the rising star had to do was finish somewhere other than last at Atlanta, where he won in March, and he would pick up his first title.

"I think we can do that," Gordon said.

Gordon all but secured the championship with a fifth-place in the Dura-Lube 500 at Phoenix International Raceway. Earnhardt was third, but gained only 15 points. Ricky Rudd won the race, stretching his streak of winning at least one race to 13 years, second only to Earnhardt's 14.

In Formula One, Germany's Michael Schumacher, 26, became the youngest driver ever to win consecutive World Driving Championships. Schumacher won the Pacific Grand Prix in Aida, Japan, overcoming the blocking tactics of rival Damon Hill, who finished third and refused to shake Schumacher's hand on the podium.

BASEBALL

Less than a year after Michael Jordan returned to Chicago and the Bulls, the Windy City prepared for the return for another one of their favorites. Cubs second baseman Ryne Sandberg, the 1984 National League MVP, will be back in uniform (No. 23, same as Jordan) at Wrigley Field next season, ending his retirement. Sandberg said goodbye June 13, 1994, walking away in the second year of a four-year, $17 million contract. A nine-time Gold Glove winner, Sandberg has a .298 career average, 245 home runs and 905 RBI in 14 seasons.

On Oct. 30, Davey Johnson was replaced as manager of the Cincinnati Reds by Ray Knight, a favorite of owner Marge Schott. Johnson wasn't out of work for long, however, signing on as skipper of the Baltimore Orioles the same day.

Tony La Russa left the Oakland A's for the National League's St. Louis Cardinals and took pitching coach Dave Duncan along with him.

Todd Archer is a correspondant for *The Boston Globe.*

The free agent class of 1995 looks to be a strong one, and could be even more so if the owners and players ever reach a new bargaining agreement. The biggest names to file for free agency by the end of October were second baseman Roberto Alomar and outfielders Jose Canseco, Ron Gant and Rickey Henderson.

Dwight Gooden finished his one-year suspension from baseball for substance abuse and signed with the New York Yankees, rejoining his former Mets teammate Darryl Strawberry.

The Yankees lost manager Buck Showalter, however, when he rejected a two-year extension from owner George Steinbrenner. Showalter served the longest stretch— four full seasons and 581 games— of any Yankee manager under Steinbrenner. Also gone in New York is general manager Gene Michael, who was replaced by Houston GM Bob Watson.

In Detroit, Sparky Anderson resigned as manager and GM Joe Klein's was reassigned. San Diego GM took over Klein's job and Showalter was expected to replace Anderson.

COLLEGE BASKETBALL

Mike Krzyzewski returned to his coaching duties at Duke after sitting out most of the 1994-95 season with a bad back.

Elsewhere, Notre Dame prepared for its first season as a member of the Big East Conference and Conference USA got ready for its inaugural season as a conglomeration of the former Metro and Great Midwest conferences (see 435).

PRO BASKETBALL

While the NBA was able to reach a settlement with the players union over the summer, it approached opening night of the 1995-96 season still unable to hammer out a new deal with league referees. The refs wanted a 21 percent boost in pay rather than the league's proposed 15 percent increase. The NBA was prepared to use replacement officials if no agreement was reached.

The new collective bargaining agreement with the players mostly affected the rookies. No. 1 pick Joe Smith's average salary with Golden State will be $2.83 million for three seasons, compared to that of 1994 No. 1 Glenn Robinson, who averages $6.82 million a year from the Milwaukee Bucks.

The summer lockout forced teams to act quickly on free agent signings and trades. The most notable addition was made by the Chicago Bulls, who traded center Will Perdue to San Antonio for rebounding champion and social misfit Dennis Rodman. Dan Majerle (Cleveland) and Hot Rod Williams (Phoenix) switched teams and the Cavaliers also sent All-Star point guard Mark Price to Washington.

After settling tampering charges with New York, Miami introduced Pat Riley as their head coach, president and part-owner in hopes of extracting themselves from the shadow of upstate rival Orlando.

The Magic lost NBA scoring champion and league poster-boy Shaquille O'Neal for six to eight weeks when he broke his right thumb on Oct. 24, in an exhibition game against the Heat. He will be replaced by backup center Jon Koncak.

BOWLING

Venezuela's Amleto Monacelli started off the PBA's Fall Tour by winning the Japan Cup in Tokyo. Dave D'Entremont was the runner-up for the second straight year. Jason Couch won for the second time this season with a 256-223 victory over Richard Wolfe at the Indianapolis Open. Brian Voss (Greater Detroit Open) and Danny Wiseman (Great Lakes Open) won the next two events before Walter Ray Williams Jr. took the Rochester Open for his 16th career title.

Mike Aulby, who owned the '95 Winter tour, failed to win one of the first five fall tournaments.

On Oct. 6, Cheryl Daniels kicked off the Ladies Pro Bowlers Tour fall season with a 235-180 win over Tish Johson at the PBAA Women's U.S. Open at Bloomington, Minn. It was Daniels' first major victory in Daniels' 16-year career.win in.

BOXING

A fractured right thumb forced Mike Tyson to postpone his Nov. 4 bout with 20-to-1 underdog Buster Mathis Jr.

Tyson initially hurt the thumb in early October, but aggravated the injury a few days before the fight and announced on Oct. 31 that he would be sidelined for four to six weeks.

With Tyson out of the picture, the MGM Grand hotel in Las Vegas called off the entire card, which included three world championship fights. Fox network, which had paid $10 million to carry the bout on free TV, was left scrambling to fill the air time. Tyson's setback, however, was pay-per-view's gain as the Riddick Bowe-Evander Holyfield rubber match, which was also scheduled for Nov. 4, suddenly had the Las Vegas spotlight to itself.

Elsewhere, many were questioning the sport's existence.

In the Philippines, two boxers died in a week. On Oct. 16, junior flyweight Restituto Espineli died from head injuries he suffered in a bout with Marlon Carillo. The 19-year-old Espineli turned pro in June in hopes of earning enough money to support his family. He earned only $240 in his fight with Carillo.

A week later in Manila, flyweight Marvin Corpuz also died from head injuries. In the eighth round of his fight with Allan Llaneta. Corpuz told his corner he wanted to quit, but the crowd urged him on with chants of "No surrender, No surrender." Corpuz collapsed in the ring after the bout and was dead the next day.

In Glasgow, Scotland, James Murray died on Oct. 13, less than two days after he was knocked out in the 12th round of a bantamweight fight with Drew Docherty. Murray had a blood clot removed from his brain, but he never recovered. He was the fourth boxer in Britain to die from injuries since 1980 and the second in 18 months. Super bantamweight Bradley Stone died after suffering a brain hemorrhage in April 1994.

COLLEGE FOOTBALL

The world of agents and players clashed one more time. At Southern California, defensive end Israel Ifeanyi, linebacker Errick Herrin and running back Shawn Walters were suspended for their dealings with agent, Robert Troy Caron. USC went a step further and filed suit against Caron, who paid the school a $50,000 settlement.

While powerhouses Florida State and Nebraska continued to win, another perennial power, Miami of Florida, floundered under first-year coach Butch Davis. Humiliated by UCLA, 31-8, in their opener, the Hurricanes entered October without a win over a Division 1-A opponent. It was worse in their intra-state battle with Florida St. The Seminoles won, 41-17.

COLLEGE FOOTBALL

Wildcats Stun Irish, Big Ten

by Mark Blaudschun
The Boston Globe

The 1995 college football season began with a bang that made Notre Dame fans whimper and the rest of college football fans blink in disbelief.

The season had not even reached Labor Day and Notre Dame was already 0-1 and ostensibly out of the national championship race. It wasn't that the Irish lost. But rather whom they lost to.

Would you believe Northwestern? At Notre Dame. And convincingly, which the 17-15 score really didn't indicate. "I told the team this was going to happen," said Northwestern coach Gary Barnett, making it sound like it was something that happened every day, rather than once in 33 years, which was the last time the Wildcats had beaten the Irish.

What it was, however, was a trend for a season that followed some familiar steps and took some new uncharted ones.

For traditionalists among you, having Florida State and Nebraska ranked 1-2 in the polls at midseason was no surprise. The two winningest college football teams in the 1990s were still winning week after week.

And in late October, the teams traded spots in the polls after the Cornhuskers pummeled Colorado, 44-21. Not that the Seminoles actually deserved to be dropped. They just didn't play that weekend.

Nebraska had its share of controversy, but no one created a bigger stir than Heisman Trophy candidate Lawrence Phillips, who was indefinitely suspended from the team for assaulting his former girlfriend Sept. 10. After receiving counseling, Phillips was reinstated by coach Tom Osborne Oct. 24. and was scheduled to play Nov. 4 against Iowa State, adding to Nebraska's troubling off-field reputation.

Northwestern, ranked No. 6 with a 7-1 record heading into November, had no worries. During the first two months of the season, the Wildcats only stumbled once, a stunning, 30-28, loss to Miami of Ohio on Sept. 16. Meanwhile, their Big Ten ledger included victories over Michigan (19-13, at Ann Arbor), Wisconsin (35-0) and Illinois (17-14).

The other Cinderella story was in Kansas, where going into the final week of October,

Wide World Photos

Northwestern quarterback **Steve Schnur** (right) hugs cornerback **Rodney Ray** after the Wildcats shocked Notre Dame, 17-15, at South Bend.

Kansas and Kansas State, two teams who as recently as seven years ago, were incapable of winning six games between them for an entire season, were each 6-0 and ranked in the Top 10.

Even when Kansas State stumbled on Oct. 21, with a 49-25 loss to Nebraska, Kansas rolled on, whipping Oklahoma, 38-17 at Norman (for the first time in 20 years), which gave the Jayhawks their best start since 1968.

The season at halftime also included a milestone. Legendary Grambling State coach Eddie Robinson won the 400th game of his 53-year career on Oct. 7, when the Tigers mauled Mississippi Valley State, 42-6, for their third victory in the Southwestern Athletic Conference. A tearful Robinson, who has been coaching at Grambling since 1941, took a congratulatory call from President Clinton.

The monster team in the Big Ten was Ohio State, which ran off successive wins against Notre Dame (45-26) at home and Penn State (28-25) and Wisconsin (27-16) on the road to move up to No. 5 in the AP Poll.

Speaking of Notre Dame, the Irish had another jolt, when coach Lou Holtz went into the hospital Sept. 12 for spinal surgery to correct a disc problem that could have left him paralyzed if untreated. In typical Holtz fashion, however, he returned 10 days later.

Miami's tradition, built on cockiness and talent, seemed ready to take a fall when the NCAA concluded its investigation into the program. On Oct. 31, school officials admitted to six of the 10 NCAA charges, including falsification of Pell Grant applications, but denied the most serious charge—lack of institutional control.

For the first time in a long time the race for the Heisman Trophy is wide open. Nebraska's Lawrence Phillips was the preseason favorite, but his off-the-field problems ended his chances.

Phillips' teammate, quaterback Tommie Frazier, has picked up the slack and made his way into contention. Iowa State's Troy Davis leads the nation in rushing. Florida St. has two hopefuls in running back Warrick Dunn and quarterback Danny Kanell. USC wide receiver Keyshawn Johnson might have seen his hopes disappear when the Trojans were spanked by Notre Dame, 38-10. The Ohio State duo of quarterback Bobby Hoying and running back Eddie George and Northwestern's running back Darnell Autry are the candidates from the Big Ten. Tennessee's sophomore quarterback Peyton Manning is another contender.

In a 42-26 loss to Duke, Wake Forest quarterback Rusty LaRue completed an NCAA record 55 passes in 78 attempts for 478 yards. Houston's David Klingler held the previous mark of 48 completions.

Finally, Prairie View lost its 54th straight game, adding to its all-time record for consecutive losses through October.

PRO FOOTBALL

The Raiders are back in Oakland for the first time in a decade, winning games and getting involved in lawsuits. What else is new. Raiders owner Al Davis filed a $200 million antitrust suit against the NFL, charging that the league blocked the Raiders' relocation to Oakland from Los Angeles for the 1994 season. Davis also objects to the NFL asking for a $4 million yearly share of personal seat license money and other revenues the team receives from the Oakland Coliseum. Alameda County and the Oakland Coliseum Authority joined Davis in the suit.

Dan Marino, who earlier in the season surpassed Fran Tarkenton's completions record, missed two games after having arthoscopic knee surgery on Oct. 9. That sent the Dolphins, who were a preseason possibility to represent the AFC in the Super Bowl, into a tailspin. They lost a 27-24 overtime decision to Indianapolis in Marino's last start and followed that with losses to winless New Orleans and the New York Jets. Marino returned Oct. 29 against the Bills and the Dolphins returned to the win column, 23-6.

Marino's old teammate, Keith Jackson, finally reported to the Green Bay Packers on Oct. 20 after trying to force a trade. The Dolphins sent the tight end to Green Bay for a second-round draft pick in the offseason.

In the Canadian Football League, Calgary Stampeders quarterback Doug Flutie, a four-time league MVP, had elbow surgery on Sept. 5 to repair a torn tendon. In eight games, Flute was 212 of 316 for 2,659 yards and 16 touchdowns. His backup Jeff Garcia led the Stamps to the North Division regular-season title. The Baltimore Stallions, who lost in the Grey Cup final to the B.C. Lions in 1994, won the All-American team South Division.

GOLF

He was not one of the favorites entering the PGA season finale. Probably not even considered a long shot, but after playing mistake-free golf at a very difficult Southern Hills Country Club in Tulsa, Okla., Billy Mayfair did what many expected Greg Norman or Corey Pavin or Ernie Els to do, he won the Tour Championship.

It was a bad year all around for the U.S. in match play. Not only did the U.S. lose the Ryder Cup to Europe earlier in the fall (see page 821), but the team of Ben Crenshaw, Peter Jacobsen and Lee Janzen finished last in their group at the Dunhill Cup at St. Andrews. Scotland won the championship for the first time, beating Zimbabwe in the final, 2-1.

HOCKEY

He is simply the Magnificent One. Mario Lemieux of Pittsburgh Penguins, forced from the game for a year because of Hodgkins disease and a bad back, punctuated his return to regular duty in the NHL by scoring the 500th goal of his career with a hat trick against the New York Islanders on Oct. 26.

The goal came in the 605th game of Lemieux' 11-year career. Only Wayne

Cowboys Roll As 49ers Falter

by Vito Stellino
The Baltimore Sun

The Dallas Cowboys, who specialized in winning football games and making big bucks, dominated the first half of the 1995 season on and off the field.

With their Big Three of Troy Aikman, Emmitt Smith and Michael Irvin leading the NFL, the Cowboys— foiled in their bid for a third straight title by the San Francisco 49ers last year— started out 7-1 before their bye week for the best record in the NFC.

At the half, Aikman was the league's top passer with a 68.3 completion percentage and a 103.2 quaterback rating. Smith had rushed for 979 yards in 189 attempts and scored 14 touchdowns. And Irvin had 58 catches for 908 yards and five TDs.

By contrast, their chief rivals, the 49ers, lost a pair of early season games to the Detroit Lions and the Indianapolis Colts when their field goal kicker, Doug Brien, missed critical attempts. If that wasn't bad enough, the 49ers later lost to the New Orleans Saints, 11-7, to fall to 5-3.

Super Bowl MVP Steve Young injured his throwing shoulder against the Colts and was on the shelf for a month. Backup Elvis Grbac, had a terrific opening game, routing the Rams, 44-10, but he struggled the following week against the Saints. The lone highlight for the 49ers that day was Jerry Rice. The wide receiver added to his growing list of accomplishments by overtaking James Lofton in the record book for receiving yardage (14,040).

"It was great breaking the record," said Rice, who made eight catches in the game for 108 yards. "But the worst thing is the loss. Losing is hard to deal with."

A once certain fourth straight NFC title game between the Cowboys and 49ers became muddled.

Cowboys owner Jerry Jones became the central figure in the sport. He infuriated his fellow owners when he made his own marketing deals outside the umbrella of NFL Properties so he didn't have to share the revenue with the other teams.

The league responded by suing Jones for $300 million, but that didn't slow Jones down. He then signed cornerback Deion Sanders to a seven-year $35 million deal that featured a

Wide World Photos

San Francisco struggled through the first half of the 1995 regular season with a 5-3 record, but that didn't stop **Jerry Rice** from becoming the NFL's all-time leader in receiving yardage on Oct. 29.

$12.9 million signing bonus and the minimum salary of $178,000 the first three years.

Because the NFL felt the deal violated the salary cap, Sanders was ruled ineligible, although the league acquiesced and allowed Prime Time to play Oct. 29 against the Falcons. He allowed only one reception caught a 6-yard pass from Aikman and narrowly missed a 42-yard scoring throw.

Meanwhile, the AFC was wide open.

The Kansas City Chiefs showed there's life after Joe Montana by posting the best record in the conference (7-1) in the first half of the season with Steve Bono at quarterback. The Raiders, who moved back to Oakland from Los Angeles, were right behind them at 6-2.

Every other team in the conference lost at least three games in the first half of the season, including four teams— Miami, San Diego, Pittsburgh, and Cleveland— that were supposed to be Super Bowl contenders.

But the most disappointing team in the AFC had to be the New England Patriots, who started out 2-6 after quarterback Drew Bledsoe led them to the playoffs in 1994.

To the surprise of many the expansion teams in Carolina and Jacksonville, with identical 3-5 records, were better than expected. The Panthers set an expansion record by beating the Patriots, 20-17, for their third straight win.

Gretzky reached the milestone faster.

The Montreal Canadiens measure yearly success by Stanley Cups. Winless after four games and having allowed 20 goals, their 24th championship seemed miles away on Oct. 17, so management fired coach Jacques Demers and general manager Serge Savard in an attempt to save the season.

Demers was in his fourth year as the Habs' coach. In his first season, he delivered a Stanley Cup, but since then the team has gone downhill. Savard brought Montreal championships in 1986 and '93, but several ill-fated trades and draft picks hurt his standing. Montreal dipped into its rich history for a new coach and general manager, hiring Mario Tremblay and Rejean Houle, and the team responded with six straight wins to enter November with a 6-4 record.

St. Louis Blues coach Mike Keenan pulled his latest stunt on Oct. 23, when he stripped All-Star forward Brett Hull of his team captaincy, for objecting to Keenan's benching of recently acquired forward Dale Hawerchuk. Shayne Corson, acquired in an offseason trade, was named Hull's replacement.

Said Hull: "I'm still the captain of this team. I don't play for him [Keenan], I play for the guys."

The chances of duplicating the U.S. Olympic hockey team's 1980 "Miracle on Ice," became very remote on Sept. 29, when the NHL board of governors approved a plan to let league players participate in the 1998 Winter Games in Nagano, Japan and a quadrennial World Cup tournament to replace the old Canada Cup.

Among the countries to be stocked by NHL players for both tournaments are the U.S., Canada, Russia, Sweden, Finland and thr Czech Republic.

As part of the deal worked out with the NHL Players Association, both the league and the union agreed to waive the reopener clause in their collective bargaining agreement, thus buying peace on the NHL labor front until the year 2000.

HORSE RACING

If not for Cigar's tremendous run of 12 straight victories, Thunder Gulch might have received more acclaim in 1995. Winner of the Kentucky Derby, Belmont, Swaps and Travers, the 3-year-old colt's career came to an abrupt end on Oct. 7, when he fractured his left front leg running fifth in the Jockey Club Gold Cup at Belmont Park. Cigar won the race.

Thunder Gulch earned $2.9 million and won seven of 10 starts in 1995. He joined Shut Out, Whirlaway and Twenty Grand as the only horses to win the Derby, Belmont and Travers.

SOCCER

After floating in limbo for more than a year, Major League Soccer, the United States' first attempt at Division I soccer since the North American Soccer League folded in 1984., had its official unveiling in New York on Oct. 17. The 10-team league will begin play on April 6, 1996 and be made up of two conferences of five teams each.

The Eastern Conference will have teams in Foxboro, Mass. (New England Revolution), Columbus, Ohio (Crew), East Rutherford, N.J. (NY/NJ Metrostars), Tampa (Mutiny) and Washington, D.C. (United). The Western Conference will have teams in Dallas (Burn), Denver (Colorado Rapids), Kansas City (Wiz), Los Angeles (Galaxy) and San Jose (Clash).

U.S. national team stars Alexi Lalas, John Harkes, Tab Ramos and Roy Wegerle have signed to play with the Revolution, United, Metrostars and Rapids, respectively.

While the MLS acquired most of the attention, the A-League crowned its champion when the Seattle Sounders defeated the Atlanta Ruckus, 2-1, in a shootout. In the Continental Indoor Soccer League, Monterrey La Raza defeated the Sacramento Knights, 10-7, in the third and final game.

Elsewhere, Virginia coach Bruce Arena was named head coach of the 1996 U.S. men's Olympic team on Oct. 24. Arena has coached the Cavaliers to an NCAA-record four consecutive NCAA national championships.

TENNIS

Because of a chest-muscle injury, Andre Agassi lost his top-ranking on the ATP Tour to friend and rival Pete Sampras, who will take over No. 1 no matter how he fares at the Paris Open. Agassi had to pull out of the Eurocard Open, allowing Thomas Muster to gain his tour-leading 12th win of the season and first not on clay. Agassi hoped to return for the Nov. 14-19 ATP Tour Championship.

HORSE RACING

Cigar Lights Up Breeders'

by Sharon Smith

The words "wet track" and "excuse" are often heard in the same sentence around racetracks, so the monsoon-like rainstorm that hit Belmont Park a few hours before the 1995 Breeders' Cup had everybody wondering how they might have to apply the sentence to Cigar.

Although Cigar was going to be an Eclipse Award winner and Horse of the Year regardless of his race in the Classic, those honors might be tarnished by excuses. But there's another phrase often heard at the track— a good horse can run on anything. They can't always, but a great horse can. Cigar's mud-spattered 2½ length victory over L'Carrierre and Unaccounted For left no doubt about which word applies.

"This is the greatest horse I've ever seen," said jockey Jerry Bailey, who has won four of the last five Classics. Cigar's time of 1:59⅗ was the fastest ever for the race. He ended the season undefeated in 12 starts.

"He's done everything to rank him with the all-time greats," said Bill Mott, the trainer of the 5-year-old bay owned by Allen Paulson.

Two records loom on the horizon: Citation's 16 straight wins and Alysheba's all-time money-earning mark of $6.5 million. With the Classic victory worth $1.5 million, Cigar set a new single-season earnings record with $4,819,800.

But the most impressive win of Breeders' Cup Day was that of Inside Information, who beat stablemate Heavenly Prize by 13½ lengths in the Distaff. Lakeway was third, Serena's Song unplaced.

"A colossal victory," announced race caller Tom Durkin as Inside Information skipped under the wire more than a second faster than any previous Distaff winner had run. It might have been colossal enough for Horse of the Year honors in a Cigarless season. She'll have to settle for an Eclipse Award.

The Breeders' Cup usually determines 2-year-old champions, but the 1995 winners may not collect the trophies. My Flag, daughter of the great Personal Ensign, won the filly race, but third place finisher Golden Attraction may still hold on for the Eclipse.

The Juvenile winner Unbridled's Song beat two good colts in Hennessey and Editor's

Wide World Photos

Jockey **Jerry Bailey** indicates "We're No. 1" as he and **Cigar** cross the finish line at Belmont after winning the Breeders' Cup Classic on Oct. 28.

Note, but he may not overcome the season-long record of the absent Maria's Mon. Both My Flag and Unbridled's Song won their races in stakes-record time, proving that a muddy track is not necessarily a slow one.

The Sprint did not produce a record, but it did produce only the second field horse ever to win a Breeder's Cup race— the mare Desert Stormer, a victor over Mr. Greeley and Lit de Justice in a race that lacked a standout.

No records either on the wet turf course. Northern Spur won a dramatic stretch duel over co-favorite Freedom Cry in the $2 million Turf, and the 3-year-old Irish filly Ridgewood Pearl outlasted Fastness in the Mile.

Two apparent losers for the day were trainer D. Wayne Lukas and Belmont Park itself, but losing is relative. Lukas failed to win a race with his seven entries, but his trainees came home with two seconds, two thirds, a fourth, a fifth and more than $716,000.

Soggy Belmont Park drew 37,246 fans— the smallest crowd in Breeders' Cup history. But they saw seven perfectly run races, each won by a good horse. They also saw the best horse ever to run in a Breeders' Cup. That's a win by anybody's standards.

Sharon Smith has covered horse racing for ESPN, NBC and *Horse Illustrated*.

Steffi Graf won all three of the Grand Slam tournaments she entered in 1995— a back injury forced her from competing in the Australian Open— but her off-court troubles, involving her father may be an opponent that's too tough to beat.

Peter Graf is in a German prison for tax evasion, while his daughter, the world's co-No.1, was forced to turn her books over to German authorities. She has since turned management of her finances over to the U.S. firm of Price Waterhouse. In her last tournament in October, Graf lost to South African qualifier Mariaan de Swardt, 2-6, 6-4, 6-1, in the second round of the Brighton (England) International Championships.

Monica Seles, who had a busy summer returning to tournament tennis for the first time in more than two years, was named to the U.S. Fed Cup team that was scheduled to play Spain for the Cup in November.

Meanwhile, If Seles and Graf meet in the U.S. Open final again, they will play on Sunday, the same day as the men's singles final. The new scheduling is part of a new five-year agreement between CBS Sports and the USTA. In the past, the women's final was played on Saturday in between the two men's semifinal matches .

More good news for the women came on Oct. 11, when the WTA announced a three-year, $12 million deal making Corel Corp. the tour's world sponsor. The women's tour had been without a sponsor since Kraft pulled the plug in 1993.

BALLPARKS & ARENAS

It seems every team is seeking a new stadium, complete with luxury boxes and club seating to boost revenue. Baseball teams would like to capitalize on the success stadia like Camden Yards and Jacobs Field.

In Milwaukee, owner Bud Selig wants to build a replica of Ebbetts Field, costing close to $250 million. After an all-night session, the Wisconsin state senate voted, 16-15, to raise taxes to help build the stadium. The state Assembly made it a reality by passing the measure, 61-37.

The Seattle Mariners gave their fans a taste of baseball post-season with a thrilling ride that ended in Game 6 of the American League Championship Series. Despite the team's success and the rocking Kingdome, the state Legislature, unlike Wisconsin, rejected a plan to give money, but did allow

county residents to vote on a tax increase of one-tenth of a penny per dollar to finance the proposed $285 million retractable roof stadium.

King County residents voted down the tax increase, forcing the state to take another look at helping finance the stadium. The Mariners have agreed to kick in $45 million toward the construction of the stadium, but if there is no agreement they said they would put the team up for sale.

The city of St. Louis celebrated when the Rams moved into town from Los Angeles. Their mood was tempered a bit when the scheduled opening of the TransWorld Dome was delayed. The Rams were supposed to christen the new stadium Oct. 22 against San Francisco, but it was not ready in time, forcing the game to be played at Busch Stadium.

INTERNATIONAL SPORTS

At the World Gymnastics Championships in Sabae, Japan in October, the U.S. women took a bronze in the team competition, but only national champion Dominique Moceanu won an individual medal with a silver in the balance beam. The Romanian women won the gold medal while China placed second.

In the men's competition, China cruised to the team gold medal, followed by host Japan and Romania. The U.S. finished a disappointing ninth.

Miguel Induráin has owned the Tour de France for five straight years. In fact, Spain's Big Mig has so dominated cycling's biggest event, that organizers decided to rearrange the race stages. Instead of holding the first time trial before the Tour enters the mountains, organizers have moved the trial between two testing days in the Alps in a move to reward strong climbers instead of time-trial specialists like Induráin.

In order to accommodate the Summer Olympics in Atlanta, where professional riders will be allowed to race for the first time, the Tour will be moved up a week to June 29 and will begin in the Dutch city of Den Bosch.

HALLS OF FAME

The Track and Field Hall of Fame's Class of '95 includes distance runner Marty Liquori, Olympic gold medalists, Florence Griffith Joyner, Valerie Briscoe-Hooks and Louise Ritter, 1992 Olympic team coach Mel Rosen and the late distance runner Don Lash.

COLLEGE FOOTBALL

AP Top 25 Poll
(as of Oct. 30, 1995)

Sportswriters and broadcasters poll, including games through Oct. 28, 1995. First place votes in parentheses, followed by record, total points (based on 25 for 1st, 24 for 2nd, etc.) and preseason rank.

	Record	Pts	Preseason		Record	Pts	Preseason
1 Nebraska. (23)	8-0-0	1501	2	14 USC	6-1-1	759	7
2 Florida St. (31)	7-0-0	1498	1	15 Washington	5-2-1	554	24t
3 Florida (2)	7-0-0	1417	5	16 Alabama	6-2-0	544	10
4 Ohio St. (6)	8-0-0	1412	12	17 Texas A&M	5-2-0	512	3
5 Tennessee	7-1-0	1299	8	18 Arkansas	6-2-0	544	44
6 Northwestern	7-1-0	1216	NR	19 Oregon	6-2-0	457	27
7 Michigan	7-1-0	1180	14	20 Syracuse	6-1-0	354	38
8 Notre Dame	7-2-0	1042	9	21 Auburn	5-3-0	330	6
9 Kansas St.	7-1-0	1038	29	22 UCLA	6-2-0	328	16
10 Colorado	6-2-0	860	13	23 Texas Tech	5-2-0	307	35
11 Kansas	7-1-0	833	NR	24 Virginia	6-3-0	305	17
12 Penn State	6-2-0	828	4	25 Oklahoma	5-2-1	172	15
13 Texas	5-1-1	764	18				

Others receiving votes: Virginia Tech (72); Baylor (20); San Diego St. (20); Stanford (18); Iowa (11); Toledo (10); Army (1); Clemson (1).

TRANSACTIONS

Player Moves
Since the end of the 1994 and 1994-95 seasons.

NFL

	'95 team	'94 team		'95 team	'94 team
Eric Allen, CB	New Orleans	Philadelphia	Eric Metcalf, RB	Atlanta	Cleveland
Morten Andersen, K	Atlanta	New Orleans	Rob Moore, WR	Arizona	NY Jets
Trace Armstrong, DE	Miami	Chicago	Bryce Paup, LB	Buffalo	Green Bay
Mark Brunell, QB	Jacksonville	Green Bay	Michael Dean Perry, DT	Denver	Cleveland
Steve Emtman, DE	Miami	Indianapolis	Kelvin Pritchett, DE	Jacksonville	Detroit
Craig Erickson, QB	Indianapolis	Tampa Bay	Andre Rison, WR	Cleveland	Atlanta
Eric Green, TE	Miami	Pittsburgh	Deion Sanders, DB	Dallas	San Francisco
Alvin Harper, WR	Tampa Bay	Dallas	Pat Swilling, LB	Oakland	Detroit
Jeff Lageman, DE	Jacksonville	NY Jets	Henry Thomas, DT	Detroit	Minnesota
Lamar Lathon, LB	Carolina	Houston	Herschel Walker, RB	NY Giants	Philadelphia
Mark Ingram, WR	Green Bay	Miami	Ricky Watters, RB	Philadelphia	San Francisco
David Meggett, RB	NE Patriots	NY Giants			

NBA

	'95 team	'94 team		'95 team	'94 team
B.J. Armstrong, G	Golden State	Chicago	Vernon Maxwell, G	Philadelphia	Houston
Dana Barros, G	Boston	Philadelphia	Robert Pack, G	Washington	Denver
Mark Bryant, F	Houston	Portland	Will Perdue, C	San Antonio	Chicago
Rex Chapman, G	Miami	Washington	Mark Price, G	Washington	Cleveland
Richard Dumas, F	Philadelphia	Phoenix	Dennis Rodman, F	Chicago	San Antonio
Kendall Gill, G	Charlotte	Seattle	Rodney Rogers, F	LA Clippers	Denver
Hersey Hawkins, G	Seattle	Charlotte	Otis Thorpe, F	Detroit	Portland
Don MacLean, F	Denver	Washington	Dominique Wilkins, F	Greece	Boston
Chris Morris, F	Utah	New Jersey	Hot Rod Williams, F/C	Phoenix	Cleveland
Dan Majerle, G/F	Cleveland	Phoenix			

NHL

	'95 team	'94 team		'95 team	'94 team
Brian Bellows, LW	Tampa Bay	Montreal	Larry Murphy, D	Toronto	Pittsburgh
Wendel Clark, LW	NY Islanders	Quebec	Petr Nedved, C	Pittsburgh	NY Rangers
Shayne Corson, LW	St. Louis	Edmonton	Brian Noonan, RW	St. Louis	NY Rangers
Geoff Courtnall, LW	St. Louis	Vancouver	Joel Otto, C	Philadelphia	Calgary
Steve Duchesne, D	Ottawa	St. Louis	Chris Pronger, D	St. Louis	Hartford
Grant Fuhr, G	St. Louis	Los Angeles	Luc Robitaille, LW	NY Rangers	Pittsburgh
Dale Hawerchuk, C	St. Louis	Buffalo	Kjell Samuelsson, D	Philadelphia	Pittsburgh
Curtis Joseph, G	Edmonton	St. Louis	Ulf Samuelsson, D	NY Rangers	Pittsburgh
Claude Lemieux, RW	Colorado	New Jersey	Brendan Shanahan, LW	Hartford	St. Louis
Alexander Mogilny, RW	Vancouver	Buffalo	Kevin Stevens, LW	Boston	Pittsburgh
Joe Mullen, RW	Boston	Pittsburgh	Sergei Zubov, D	Pittsburgh	NY Rangers

TENNIS

Late 1995 Tournament Results

Men's Tour

Finals	Tournament	Winner	Earnings	Loser	Score
Oct. 1	Davidoff Swiss Indoors (Basel)	Jim Courier	$137,000	J. Siemerink	67 76 57 62 75
Oct. 1	Championship of Sicily	Francisco Clavet	43,000	J. Burillo	67 63 76
Oct. 8	Kuala Lumpur Open (Malaysia)	Marcelo Rios	55,000	M. Philippoussis	76 62
Oct. 8	Toulouse Grand Prix (France)	Arnaud Boetsch	54,000	J. Courier	64 67 60
Oct. 15	Seiko Super Tennis (Tokyo)	Michael Chang	153,000	M. Philippoussis	63 64
Oct. 15	Czech Indoors (Ostrava)	Wayne Ferreira	54,000	M. Washington	36 64 63
Oct. 15	Eisenberg Israel Open	Jan Kroslak	54,000	J. Sanchez	63 64
Oct. 22	Lyon Grand Prix (France)	Wayne Ferreira	80,000	P. Sampras	76 57 63
Oct. 22	CA Tennis Trophy (Vienna)	Filip DeWulf	66,000	T. Muster	75 62 16 75
Oct. 22	Salem Open (Beijing)	Michael Chang	43,000	R. Furlan	75 63
Oct. 29	Eurocard Open (Essen)	Thomas Muster	315,000	M. Washington	76 26 63 64
Oct. 29	Hellman's Cup (Santiago)	Slave Dosedel	29,000	M. Rios	76 63

Remaining ATP Events (7): Paris Open (Nov. 5); Topper Open (Nov. 5); Stockholm Open (Nov. 12); Kremlin Cup (Nov. 12); South American Open (Nov. 12); ATP Tour Singles Championships (Nov. 19); ATP Tour Double Championships (Nov. 26).

Women's Tour

Finals	Tournament	Winner	Earnings	Loser	Score
Oct. 1	Sparkassen Cup (Leipzig)	Anke Huber	$79,000	M. Maleeva	walkover
Oct. 8	Wismilak Open (Surabaya)	Shi-Ting Wang	17,000	J.Q. Yi	61 61
Oct. 15	Porsche Grand Prix (Filderstadt)	Iva Majoli	79,000	G. Sabatini	64 76
Oct. 22	Brighton International (England)	Mary Joe Fernandez	79,000	A. Coetzer	64 75

Remaining WTA Events (6): Bank of the West Classic (Nov. 5); Bell Challenge (Nov. 5); Advanta Championships (Nov. 12); WTA Tour Championships (Nov. 19.); Volvo Women's Open (Nov. 19); Fed Cup final (Nov. 26).

GOLF

Late 1995 Tournament Results

PGA Tour

Last Rd	Tournament	Winner	Earnings	Runner-Up
Oct. 1	Buick Southern Open	Fred Funk (272)	$180,000	L. Roberts & J. Morse (273)
Oct. 8	WDW/Oldsmobile Classic	Brad Bryant (198)#	216,000	H. Sutton & T. Tryba
Oct. 15	Las Vegas Invitational	Jim Furyk (331)	270,000	B. Mayfair (332)
Oct. 22	Texas Open	Duffy Waldorf (268)	198,000	J. Leonard (274)
Oct. 29	PGA Tour Championship	Billy Mayfair (280)	540,000	S. Elkington & C. Pavin (283)

#rain-shortened.
Remaining Events (7): Kapalua International (Nov. 2-5); PGA Grand Slam (Nov. 7-8); World Cup of Golf (Nov. 9-12); Shark Shootout (Nov. 16-19); Skins Game (Nov. 25-26); JC Penney Classic (Nov. 30-Dec. 3); Diners Club Matches (Dec. 7-10).

European PGA Tour

Last Rd	Tournament	Winner	Earnings	Runner-Up
Oct. 1	Smurfit European Open	Bernhard Langer (280)*	£167,911	B. Lane (280)
Oct. 8	German Masters	Anders Forsband (264)	108,330	B. Langer (266)
Oct. 15	World Matchplay	Ernie Els (3 & 1)	170,000	S. Elkington
Oct. 22	Alfred Dunhill Cup	Scotland (2-1)	300,000	Zimbabwe
Oct. 29	Volvo Masters	Alexander Cejka (282)	125,000	C. Montgomerie (284)

Remaining Events (3): World Open Championship (Nov. 2-5); World Cup of Golf (Nov. 9-12); The Johnnie Walker World Championship (Dec. 14-17).

Seniors Tour

Last Rd	Tournament	Winner	Earnings	Runner-Up
Oct. 1	Vantage Championship	Hale Irwin (199)	$225,000	D. Stockton (203)
Oct. 8	TransAmerica Championship	Lee Trevino (201)	97,500	B. Summerhays (204)
Oct. 15	Raley's Gold Rush	Don Bies (205)	105,000	L.Trevino (206)
Oct. 22	Ralph's Classic	John Bland (201)	120,000	J. Colbert (202)
Oct. 29	Maui Kaanapali Classic	Bob Charles (204)*	90,000	D. Stockton (204)

***Playoffs: Kaanapali Classic**— Charles won on the 3rd hole.
Remaining Events (4): Emerald Coast Classic (Nov. 3-5); Senior Tour Championship (Nov. 9-12); Diners Club Matches (Dec. 8-10); Lexus Challenge (Dec. 16-17).

LPGA

Last Rd	Tournament	Winner	Earnings	Runner-Up
Oct. 1	Fieldcrest Cannon Classic	Gail Graham (273)	$75,000	T. Green (275)
Oct. 8	World Invitational	Michelle McGann (283)	144,000	M. Hirase (287)
Oct. 15	World Championship of Golf	Annika Sorenstam (282)*	117,500	L. Davies (282)
Oct. 29	Nichirei International	USA (19)	396,000	Japan (17)

*Playoffs: World Championship— Sorenstam won one the 1st hole.

Remaining Events (4): Toray Japan Queens Cup (Nov. 3-5); JC Penney Classic (Nov. 30-Dec. 3); Diners Club Matches (Dec. 8-10); Wendy's Three-Tour Challenge (Dec. 17-18).

Team Competition

Alfred Dunhill Cup

at St. Andrews, Scotland (Oct. 19-22)
Scotland def. Zimbabwe, 2-1

Semifinals (Scotland def. Ireland, 2-1): Colin Montgomerie (SCOT) def. Darren Clarke (IRE), 70-72; Andrew Coltart (SCOT) def. Philip Walton (IRE), 75-76; Ronan Rafferty (IRE) def. Sam Torrance (SCOT), 73-74.

Semifinals (Zimbabwe def. Spain, 2-1): Miguel Angel Jimenez (SPA) def. Tony Johnstone (ZIM). 70-71; Nick Price (ZIM) def. Jose Rivero (SPA), 69-70; Mark McNulty (ZIM) def. Ignacio Garrido (Spain), 73-DQ.

Final (Scotland def. Zimbabwe, 2-1): Andrew Coltart (SCOT) def. Tony Johnstone (ZIM), 67-71; Sam Torrance (SCOT) def. Mark McNulty (ZIM), 68-70; Nick Price (ZIM) def. Colin Montgomerie (SCOT), 68-74.

THOROUGHBRED RACING

Breeders' Cup

Results from the seven Breeders' Cup races held Saturday, Oct. 28, 1995, at Belmont Park in Elmont, N.Y.

	Time	Top 3 Finishers	Jockeys	Trainers	Money Won
Sprint 6 furlongs)	1:09	1 Desert Stormer 2 Mr. Greeley 3 Lit de Justice	Kent Desormeaux Julie Krone Corey Nakatani	Frank Lyons Nick Zito Jenine Sahadi	$520,000 200,000 120,000
Juv. Fil 1 ⅟₁₆ miles)	1:42⅖	1 My Flag 2 Cara Rafaela 3 Golden Attraction	Jerry Bailey Pat Day Gary Stevens	Shug McGaughey D. Wayne Lukas D. Wayne Lukas	$520,000 200,000 120,000
Distaff (1 ⅛ miles)	1:46	1 Inside Information 2 Heavenly Prize 3 Lakeway	Mike Smith Pat Day Kent Desormeaux	Shug McGaughey Shug McGaughey Gary Jones	$520,000 200,000 120,000
Mile	1:43⅗	1 Ridgewood Pearl 2 Fastness 3 Sayyedati	John Murtagh Gary Stevens Corey Nakatani	John Oxx Jenine Sahadi Clive Brittain	$520,000 200,000 120,000
Juvenile (1 ⅟₁₆ miles)	1:41⅗	1 Unbridled's Song 2 Hennessy 3 Editor's Note	Mike Smith Donna Barton Jerry Bailey	James Ryerson D. Wayne Lukas D. Wayne Lukas	$520,000 200,000 120,000
Turf (1 ½ miles)	2:42	1 Northern Spur 2 Freedom Cry 3 Carnegie	Chris McCarron Oliver Peslier Thierry Jarnet	Ron McAnally Andre Fabre Andre Fabre	$1,040,000 400,000 240,000
Classic (1 ¼ miles)	2:59⅖	1 Cigar 2 L'Carriere 3 Unaccounted For	Jerry Bailey Jorge Chavez Pat Day	Bill Mott H. James Bond Scotty Schulhofer	$1,560,000 650,000 360,000

Other Late 1995 Major Stakes Races

Date	Race	Location	Miles	Winner	Jockey	Purse
Sept. 30	Super Derby XVI	La. Downs	1 ¼	Mecke	Jerry Bailey	$750,000
Sept. 30	My Dear Girl Stakes	Calder	1 ⅟₁₆	Effectivenss	Gary Boulanger	350,000
Sept. 30	In Reality Stakes	Calder	1 ⅟₁₆	Seacliff	Rene Douglas	350,000
Oct. 1	L'Arc de Triomphe	Longchamp	1 ½ (T)	Lammtarra	Frankie Dettori	7,000,000*
Oct. 6	Meadowlands Cup	Meadowlands	1 ⅛	Peaks and Valleys	Julie Krone	500,000
Oct. 6	Frizzette Stakes	Belmont	1 ⅟₁₆	Golden Attraction	Gary Stevens	250,000
Oct. 6	Beldame Stakes	Belmont	1 ⅛	Serena's Song	Gary Stevens	250,000
Oct. 6	Turf Classic	Belmont	1 ½ (T)	Turk Passer	John Velazquez	500,000
Oct. 6	Jockey Club Gold Cup	Belmont	1 ¼	Cigar	Jerry Bailey	750,000
Oct. 6	Champagne Stakes	Belmont	1 ⅟₁₆	Maria's Mon	Robbie Davis	500,000
Oct. 7	Goodwood Handicap	Santa Anita	1 ⅛	Soul of the Matter	Kent Desmormeaux	250,000
Oct. 8	Oak Tree Invitational	Santa Anita	1 ½ (T)	Northern Spur (IRE)	Chris McCarron	300,000
Oct. 8	Spinster Stakes	Keeneland	1 ⅛	Inside Information	Mike Smith	300,000
Oct. 15	Rothmans International	Woodbine	1 ½ (T)	Lassigny	Pat Day	1,000,000

* L'Arc de Triomphe purse is paid in francs.

Remaining major events (6): Hollywood Derby (Nov. 26); Japan Cup (Nov. 26); Hollywood Turf Cup (Dec. 10); Hollywood Starlet Stakes (Dec. 16); Hollywood Futurity (Dec. 17).

HARNESS RACING

Late 1995 Major Stakes Races

Date	Race	Raceway	Winner	Driver	Purse
Sept. 20	BC 3 & up Open Trot	Delaware, Ohio	Panifesto	Luc Ouellette	$300,000
Sept. 20	BC 3 & up Filly and Mare Trot	Delaware, Ohio	CR Kay Suzie	Rod Allen	300,000
Sept. 22	BC 3 & up Open Pace	Northfield Park	Thatll Be Me	Roger Mayotte	300,000
Sept. 22	BC 3 & up Filly and Mare Pace	Northfield Park	Ellamony	Mike Saftic	250,000
Oct. 7	Kentucky Futurity	The Red Mile	CR Track Master	Mike Allen	151,600
Oct. 20	BC 2-Yr-Old Colt Pace	Garden St. Park	John Street North	Jack Moiseyev	500,000
Oct. 20	BC 2-Yr-Old Filly trot	Garden St. Park	Continentalvictory	Mike Lachance	300,000
Oct. 21	BC 2-Yr-Old Colt trot	Garden St. Park	Armbro Officer	Steve Condren	347,800
Oct. 21	BC 2-Yr-Old Filly Pace	Garden St. Park	Paige Nicole Q	John Campbell	470,300

Remaining Events (7): BC 3-Yr-Old Colt Pace (Nov. 3); BC 3-Yr-Old Filly Pace (Nov. 3); BC 3-Yr-Old Colt Trot (Nov. 3); BC 3-Yr-Old Filly Trot (Nov. 3); Governor's Cup (Nov. 18); Gold Smith Maid (Nov. 24); Provincial Cup (Dec. 3).

AUTO RACING

Late 1995 Results

NASCAR

Date	Event	Location	Winner (Pos.)	Avg.mph	Earnings	Pole	Qual.mph
Oct. 8	UAW-GM 500	Charlotte	Mark Martin (5)	145.358	$105,650	R. Rudd	180.578
Oct. 22	AC Delco 400	Rockinham	Ward Burton (3)	114,778	70,250	H. Stricklin	155.379
Oct. 29	Dura-Libe 500	Phoenix	Ricky Rudd (29)	102.128	78,260	B. Elliott	130.020†

†track record
Winning Cars: Ford Thunderbird (2)— Martin, Rudd; Pontiac Grand Prix (1) — Burton.
Remaining Races (2): Slick-50 500 (Oct. 30); Hooters 500 (Nov. 13)

IndyCar

IndyCar Season ended Oct. 3rd. (see Auto Racing chapter).

Formula 1

Date	Event	Location	Winner (Pos.)	Time	Avg.mph	Pole	Qual.mph
Oct. 29	Japanese GP	Suzuka, Japan	Michael Schumacher (1)	1:36:52.930	119.256	M. Schumacher	133.820

Winning Constructors: Benneton-Ford (2).
Remaining Races (1): Australian Grand Prix (Nov. 12).

BOWLING

1995 Fall Tour Results

PBA

Final	Event	Winner	Earnings	Final	Runner-Up
Sept. 24	Japan Cup (Tokyo)	Ameleto Monacelli	$50,000	232-215	Dave D'Entremont
Oct. 4	Indianapolis Open	Jason Couch	17,500	256-223	Richard Wolfe
Oct. 11	Greatern Detroit Open	Brian Voss	17,500	247-188	Justin Hromek
Oct. 18	Great Lakes Open	Danny Wiseman	17,500	232-191	John Mazza
Oct. 25	Rochester Open	Walter Ray Williams Jr.	17,500	235-232	David Traber

Remaining Events (2): Dick Weber Classic (Oct. 28-Nov. 1); Touring Players Championship (Nov. 4-8).

Seniors

Final	Event	Winner	Earnings	Final	Runner-Up
Sept. 19	Naples Senior Open	Tommy Evans	$10,000	223-218	John Handegard
Sept. 26	St. Pete/Clearwater PBA Open	Don Helling	15,000	245-193	Lary Laub
Oct. 4	Palm Beach PBA Senior Classic	John Hricsina	10,000	255-249	Avery LaBlanc

Season completed.

LPBT

Final	Event	Winner	Earnings	Final	Runner-Up
Oct. 6	PBAA Women's U.S. Open	Cheryl Daniels	$18,000	235-180	Tish Johnson
Oct. 12	Brunswick Three Rivers Open	Sandra Jo Shiery	12,000	234-195	Tammy Turner
Oct. 19	Columbia 300 Delaware Open	Marianne DiRupo	12,800	279-185	CherylDaniels
Oct. 26	Hammer Eastern Open	Kim Adler	12,000	247-186	Anne Marie Duggan

Remaining Events (4): Lady Ebonite Classic (Oct. 29-Nov. 2); Hammer Players Championship (Nov. 4-9); Sam's Town Invitational (Nov. 12-18).

Doug Pensinger/Allsport

THE CLASS
OF '95

Top Personalities of the Year
by Bob Ley

Oh, what a banquet t'would be to gather these sixteen folk to celebrate their inclusion in our annual assessment. The editors of *The Sports Almanac* would take pains to insure Jerry Jones not sell dinner rights to Nike, and we would set enough places for all the Ryder Cup golfers, who would happily finish the champagne Steve Young leaves untouched.

And as these figures communed, there would be stories of vision and grace from Nelson Mandela and Hakeem Olajuwon; tales of recovery and rededication, from Mike Tyson and Monica Seles; modest recollections of supremacy from guys named Maddux, Ripken and Sampras. Tom Osborne would find good in each person, and Steve Sampson would wonder at his place in this company. And should there be a question when the check arrives, everyone would nominate David Stern to negotiate the matter. Bon appetit.

The Sports Almanac Class of '95

(in alphabetical order)

Andre Agassi/Pete Sampras	Rebecca Lobo	Cal Ripken Jr.
Europe's Ryder Cup Team	D. Wayne Lukas	David Stern
Steffi Graf/Monica Seles	Greg Maddux	Mike Tyson
Michael Johnson	Nelson Mandela	U.S. Soccer
Jerry Jones	Hakeem Olajuwon	Steve Young
	Tom Osborne	

Bob Ley is the principal reporter for ESPN's Emmy Award-winning "Outside The Lines" series and has been a SportsCenter anchor since the sports cable network started in 1979.

Andre Agassi/Pete Sampras

Digital logic dictates a need for a No. 1, so these rivals and friends traded the label as world's best. Agassi ended Sampras' 82-week reign in April, and ceded it back in November, after an injury.

Agassi admits Sampras had a more satisfying year, with a four-set win in their final at the U.S. Open. Sampras also became only the 4th man to amass three U.S. and three Wimbledon titles. Agassi proved conclusively his image has substance. And still they found time for the Davis Cup team.

Europe's Ryder Cup Team

They were given virtually no chance, a conventional wisdom that seemed haughty the final Sunday, as Europe teed off, trailing the host U.S. squad, 9-7. But the Ryder Cup defies expectation, as millionaires play for nothing but pride, amid wrenching tension.

While American household names wilted, Europeans such as David Gilford, Howard Clark and Phillip Walton rose to the occasion. By day's end, Seve Ballesteros was in tears, and the Ryder Cup heading east on the Concorde. Back home.

Gary M. Prior/Allsport

Steffi Graf/Monica Seles

They are linked in accomplishment and travail. But Seles seems ascendant, and Graf a haunted No. 1, an unlikely scenario when the year began. Graf's three-set U.S. Open win over Seles was her 3rd Grand Slam singles title of the year and 18th of her career.

But recurring back and foot problems threatened to disrupt Graf's game, while a tax investigation saw her father jailed, and Graf's concentration tested. Meanwhile, Seles' re-emergence from a two-year recovery proved her game has matured, as has she.

Allsport

Michael Johnson

The rest of the world recognizes the 28-year-old Johnson as a once-in-a-generation athlete. America is just starting to notice. It may take the '96 Olympics to insure that, but already his track accomplishments are epochal.

Sprinters have won at 100 and 200 meters, but Johnson is perfecting the hellish 200/400 double, winning both events at the 1995 World Championships, and warming to an unprecedented Olympic possibility. If Atlanta race schedules are juggled, Johnson is poised to write history.

Dallas Cowboys

Jerry Jones

In six short years, Jerry Jones has caused a shift in the NFL balance of power on and off the field. Blinded by the glare of his two Super Bowl rings, the Cowboys' owner has hacked a trail through the league's salary cap jungle and its hidebound socialist economics.

For his troubles, Jones inherited not the wind, but Deion Sanders— though it took a federal judge to insure Prime Time could play— and a $300 million NFL lawsuit, attacking the enterprise shown by America's Team in dealing with Nike, Pepsi and others.

Matthew Stockman

Rebecca Lobo

Imagine a national championship athlete who had to be told to be more selfish and demand the ball. That, more than anything, is a window on Rebecca Lobo's psyche, in a year that propelled her sport to new heights.

The Connecticut forward, a Rhodes Scholarship candidate, was the catalyst in her team's perfect season. By year's end, she was considering offers from three different pro leagues, beginning to enjoy endorsement monies, and poised to lift her sport's profile even higher.

Doug Pensinger/Allsport

D. Wayne Lukas

His successes of the 1980's a distant memory, D. Wayne Lukas answered the critics who ascribed his training success merely to volume. From the 1994 Preakness through the '95 Belmont, five straight Triple Crown races went to Lucas-trained horses. An unprecedented run.

The 1995 sweep came with two horses, Thunder Gulch and Timber Country. Another first. A winless Breeders' Cup hurt, but not much. His seven steeds got 2 seconds, 2 thirds, a fourth, a fifth and won $716,000.

Atlanta Braves

Greg Maddux

His excellence is so expected, the Braves an October fixture, how surprising it was that the 1995 World Series was Maddux' first. His unprecedented fourth straight Cy Young Award was an anti-climax, after a season of clinical pitching for the World Champions.

Looking younger than his 29 years, Maddux simply got better as the year passed, especially away from home. Eight complete games on the road, and 4-0 with a 0.29 ERA in September. A quiet, unassuming star, whose personality belies his dominance.

David Rogers/Allsport

Nelson Mandela

Symbols are important in both sports and politics. Their poetic convergence arrived with South Africa's World Cup rugby championship on June 24 in Johannesburg. President Nelson Mandela embraced a symbol he once reviled— the national rugby team— a side with one black player.

Under apartheid, the Springboks were the exclusive passion of white South Africans. Mandela urged the new South Africa to back "our boys," and (clad in a team jersey) he cheered their upset win over New Zealand.

Houston Rockets

Hakeem Olajuwon

Already validated as a champion, he knew that staying on top was tougher. Hakeem Olajuwon mastered that and joined an elite group of the NBA's great centers. Where the David Robinsons and Shaquille O'Neals can only knock on the door.

In a tumultuous year for the Houston Rockets, Olajuwon was a rock. He sparked playoff comebacks from 2-1 and 3-1 deficits and then averaged 32.8 ppg in the sweep of Shaq's Magic, to prove there was no torch-passing on the horizon.

Univ. of Nebraska

Tom Osborne

The year began with his first national championship in 22 years at Nebraska. As he chased a second, Tom Osborne found himself scrutinized more for off-field personnel decisions than his Saturday play calls.

Discipline problems are nothing new in big time college football, but Nebraska had seemed different. Now, Osborne was under fire for first dismissing and then welcoming back one-time Heisman candidate Lawrence Phillips. While Osborne had good reasons, winning another title seemed to be one of them.

Baltimore Orioles

Cal Ripken Jr.

What was so special about a record we could set our watch to? Cal Ripken Jr.'s longevity was remarkable, his milestone as expected as his name on the daily lineup card.

The answer arrived as Ripken equaled Lou Gehrig. The unveiling of the 2,130 numeral produced tangible chills and immediate understanding of the history involved. Game 2,131 was a celebration of family and work ethic. Ripken's spontaneous lap of gratitude amid a 22-minute ovation was the singular baseball moment in an imperfect season.

Jonathan Daniel/Allsport

David Stern

Lionized as the Smartest Man in Sports, Stern needed to prove it again, lest his globally-profitable NBA follow the other major sports into labor hell. Stern produced, with a congenial public face and serious private muscle.

He negotiated not one, but two labor contracts with the players even as superstars Michael Jordan and Patrick Ewing led a move to decertify the union. Bottom line: signed labor deal, union intact and no regular season work stoppage. Smart guy.

Wide World Photos

Mike Tyson

Despite the broken right thumb that cancelled his second comeback fight, it is only a matter of time before Mike Tyson owns at least one heavyweight title belt. His release from prison and return to the ring in 1995 breathed life into the aging division.

Tyson generated over $96 million worldwide in his 89-second bout with the ill-equipped Peter McNeeley. But he remained unrepentant over his conviction, the most visible personification of the growing issue of athletes' violence against women.

J. Brett Whitesell

U.S. Soccer

The sacking of Bora Milutinovic left U.S. soccer lurching, just months after World Cup '94. Assistant coach Steve Sampson was a stopgap pick. Until several international coaches turned down the gig. A funny thing happened while serving as caretaker.

Sampson unleashed his players' creativity and offense. What followed was a U.S. Cup title, followed by seismic results in South America's Copa. The USA's 3-0 win over Argentina stoked soccer panic in that country, and gave this one hope for France '98.

Mike Powell/Allsport

Steve Young

With plenty of time left in Super Bowl XXIX, Steve Young began cackling on the sidelines about "getting that monkey off my back." He removed the metaphorical ape with a mythical game against San Diego. A game not even Joe Montana ever enjoyed.

As his six TD passes made the 49ers the NFL's first 5-time Super Bowl winner, Young punctuated an historic year. An unparalleled 4th straight season leading the league in passing, with the highest career rating, But most importantly, a ring to call his own.

Also Receiving Votes
(In alphabetical order)

Mark Allen (triathalon)
Mike Aulby (bowling)
Albert Belle (baseball)
Atlanta Braves (baseball)
Bonnie Blair (speed skating)
Cigar (horse racing)
Cleveland Indians (baseball)
UConn Women's Basketball Team
John Daly (golf)
Mark Davis (fishing)
Dale Earnhardt (auto racing)
Dick Ebersol (TV and radio)
Jonathan Edwards (track and field)
Michael Eisner (TV and radio)
Tommie Frazier (college football)
Tom Glavine (baseball)
Jeff Gordon (auto racing)
Jim Harrick (college basketball)
Orel Hershiser (baseball)
Houston Rockets (basketball)
Miguel Induráin (cycling)
Roy Jones Jr. (boxing)
Michael Jordan (basketball)
Garry Kasparov (chess)
Betsy King (golf)
Don King (boxing)

Phil Knight (business)
Mark Kotsay (college baseball)
Jacques Lemaire (hockey)
Claude Lemieux (hockey)
Eric Lindros (hockey)
Mickey Mantle (baseball)
Dan Marino (football)
Noureddine Morceli (track and field)
New Jersey Devils (hockey)
New Zealand's America's Cup Team
Ed O'Bannon (college basketball)
Shaquille O'Neal (basketball)
Ivan Pedroso (track and field)
Jerry Rice (football)
San Francisco 49ers (football)
Deion Sanders (football)
Vreni Schneider (skiing)
Michael Schumacher (auto racing)
Hon. Sonia Sotamayor (baseball)
Picabo Street (skiing)
Thunder Gulch (horse racing)
Alberto Tomba (skiing)
Gwen Torrence (track and field)
Jacques Villeneuve (auto racing)
Lenny Wilkens (basketball)
Tiger Woods (golf)

Mike Luckovich for The Sports Almanac

THE YEAR IN REVIEW

Up To Here

If nothing else, 1995 was a test to see just where the boundaries of audacity were in sports and how fed up fans have gotten.

Early in the Mike Tyson vs. Peter McNeeley fight, somewhere in the first three seconds when McNeeley was still giving a fine account of himself, hope hovered in the Las Vegas night air. This might be it!

Finally in 1995, we might have a major event that delivered what it promised, repaid the fans for their investment of time, money and enthusiasm, and restored their faith in the integrity of big-time sports.

Alas, McNeeley, a rising young tomato can, was felled by a flurry of Tyson warmup punches and it became apparent that the young man not only had a glass chin, but a glass manager as well.

Vinny Vecchione, McNeeley's manager and possibly his life-insurance agent, couldn't find a towel so he threw himself in the ring and had his "fighter" disqualified after 89 seconds.

"I talked the talk and I walked the walk," McNeeley crowed, although what he actually did was kiss the canvas and cash the check.

No, it wasn't a real fight, just as '95 wasn't a real year in sports. It was merely a test to see where the boundaries were. How far could the performers and purveyors of sport push the limits of taste, credibility, commercialism, artistry, audacity and even poetry? And how much guff could fans in the stands put up with before putting down

their overpriced cup of beer, vaulting the front rail and charging the mound— as one fed-up denizen of Wrigley Field fan did when Chicago Cubs reliever Randy Myers gave up an inopportune home run late in the season.

Boomer Esiason, New York Jets' quarterback, unintentionally summed up the spirit of '95 when he was asked to explain one of several Jets loses.

"Last night was what it was," Boomer boomed, "and you take it for what it is, which is what it was."

So it was with 1995. It was what it was, and nowhere was the *was* more *is* than in baseball, where a strike and then the threat of another strike were ugly bookends for a strange and finally wonderful season.

The players were still on strike when spring training opened, so the owners forged ahead with their threat to turn the national pastime over to roving gangs of replacement players.

Actual big-league uniforms were issued to has-beens, washouts, minor leaguers and assorted desperadoes. The California Angels signed a vacationing FBI agent, who was cut before he could even steal any signs.

Reds' owner Marge Schott dredged up pitcher Pedro Borbon, who was merely 15 years and 50 pounds beyond his playing days. Rumor has it Borbon demonstrated his conditioning by beating Marge in wind

---

Scott Ostler is a sports columnist for the *San Francisco Chronicle*.

Mike Luckovich is the Pulitzer Prize-winning editorial cartoonist for the *Atlanta Constitution*.

Trainer **Vinny Vecchione** (left) moments after jumping into the ring during the first round of the Mike Tyson-Peter McNeeley fight on Aug. 19, to save his fighter from being beaten to a pulp by Tyson. A month later, Chicago relief pitcher **Randy Myers** threw a high, hard one at Cubs' fan John Murray, who jumped from the stands and rushed Myers to register a complaint about a late inning gopher ball.

sprints, two out of three.

"The gulf between us is wide," sighed player's union leader Donald Fehr, and owners' main man Bud Selig said the negotiations were "a journey fraught with heartbreaks."

"I got your gulf and your journey right here," Joe Fan scoffed.

A federal judge eventually ended the eight-month strike on March 31, by ordering the owners to let the real players come back to work, but the fans seethed on, channeling their anger into a grass-roots apathy. It became a time once foretold by Yogi Berra when he said, "If the fans don't want to come out to the ballpark, nobody's going to stop them."

Fans marked games with New York Yankees broadcaster Phil Rizzuto's favorite scorebook symbol: WW— Wasn't Watching. Attendance plummeted and the average player salary skidded to $1,084,000, barely above baseball's poverty line.

And still the players didn't get it. When Chicago White Sox management juggled pregame routines so that fans could watch players like Frank Thomas take batting practice, the Big Hurt did the Big Whine over the inconvenience.

"It's our profession," Thomas pouted, "it's not the Barnum and Bailey Circus."

No, but there were clowns. Too many to mention here.

During the abbreviated, 144-game season, however, some true baseball heroes stepped forward. Foremost among them was Cal Ripken Jr., who sailed past Lou Gehrig's ironman consecutive game streak of 2,130. More importantly, Cal helped rebuild baseball's image with a million autographs, handshakes and smiles, the same currency with which Babe Ruth originally purchased the hearts of American fans.

Ripken's record-breaking moment came one month after the heart-breaking death of Mickey Mantle. After finally facing up to decades of industrial-strength debauchery, the Mick had given up drinking and taken up thinking. At age 63, he had become a man and a hero.

"Don't be like me," the humbled Hall of Famer told the world. "God gave me the ability to play baseball and I wasted it. I'm going to spend the rest of my life trying to make up."

And he did. When his liver gave out, Mantle received a transplant, but soon after he was done in by what his doctors called "the most aggressive cancer we've ever seen." That figures. Mickey Mantle, king of the big swing, wasn't going to be taken out by any wimpy cancer.

Heroes were in short supply in '95. Even old heroes couldn't seem to cut it anymore. Duke Snider and Willie McCovey were nailed for failing to report income from autograph shows, thus joining Darryl Strawberry and Pete Rose in the IRS Hall of Shame.

Strawberry also tested positive for cocaine and was sentenced to three months of home confinement. And his former New York Mets teammate Dwight Gooden sat out the entire season under a substance-abuse suspension.

By the end of the year they had been reunited by none other than George Steinbrenner, in his new role as the major league's Father Flanagan.

"Yankee Stadium is now the halfway house that Ruth built," joked Al Trautwig, one of the team's play-by play announcers.

Kidding aside, the ugliest lawbreakers in '95 were the wife-beaters, who seemed to come out of the woodwork. Robert Parish's ex-wife told gruesome tales about the Chief, and Warren Moon's wife said he choked her unconscious and chased her in his car. Atlanta Braves' manager Bobby Cox was arrested for slapping his wife around, and dozens of other athletes, pro and college, were nailed for illegal use of hands.

No. 1 on the spousal-abuse hit list was O.J. Simpson, who was found not guilty on Oct. 3 in the ghastly murders of his ex-wife and her friend, but was tarnished by the revelations of his physical and psychological abuse of Nicole Simpson.

Simpson's fame, apparently, was no handicap at the trial. According to a *Newsweek* pre-trial survey of the jury, nine of the 12 said it was highly unlikely Simpson would have committed the crimes, because he had been a great football player. Thus the Heisman had become a get-out-of-jail-free trophy.

Equating football prowess with morality was a stretch, as was illustrated at the University of Nebraska, where the defending national champions of college football were a study in priorities.

Nebraska's long-time team mascot Herbie the Husker was fired because school officials deemed him a marketing liability. But star running back Lawrence Phillips was allowed back on the team shortly after being arrested for throwing an ex-girlfriend to the floor and dragging her down three flights of stairs.

"The thing people have got to understand," Nebraska coach Tom Osborne said of Phillips' reinstatement, "is that there's a consistent philosophy here."

That's what we were afraid of, Tom.

Although the Cornhuskers later welcomed Herbie back, it was a tough year for mascots. In the minor leagues, Sir Slap Shot of hockey's Atlanta Knights was punched out by an opposing team coach and Davey Cricket of baseball's Lubbock Crickets was ejected by an ump who ordered, "Get that bug off the field!"

Major league mascots found themselves on the disabled list about as often as NFL quarterbacks. During the playoffs, the Seattle Mariner Moose collided with the left-field wall at the Kingdome while rollerblading and broke his (its?) right ankle and Slider of the Cleveland Indians tumbled out of the stands at Jacobs Field and tore up his right knee. And in Denver, Rocky the Mountain Lion of the NBA Nuggets broke three bones in his back trying a trampoline-propelled dunk during an exhibition game.

But the mascot mishap of the year happened in pregame ceremonies before the Mighty Ducks of Anaheim home opener against Vancouver on Oct. 18. That's when Wild Wing, the team's cavorting canvasback, stumbled while attempting to jump through a wall of fire and turned himself into duck flambé. Luckily, he escaped unhurt. Unluckily, the Mighty Ducks a l'Orange County went on to lose by six goals.

Big-time college football could have used more mascots to distract the fans from the scandals. Alabama was slapped with three years' probation by the NCAA, and the Miami of Florida program was a veritable Mardi Gras of misdeeds. There were reports of drug-test coverups, under-the-table payments, racial disharmony, cash bounties for injuring opponents, and a threat by rap star Luther Campbell to squeal on cheaters within the program unless Luther's pal Ryan Campbell was given the

It was not a good year for sports mascots, particularly **Wild Wing** of the NHL's Mighty Ducks, who caught fire during an opening night mishap at the Pond in Anaheim. Fortunately Wing escaped unhurt.

starting quarterback job.

At least the college teams didn't strike, as major league baseball and hockey did, and NBA basketall threatened to do.

The NHL labor dispute was actually a boon to the fans. It wiped out the first 36 games of the 1994-95 season for each team, but the remaining 48-game schedule that meant each game actually meant something.

The NBA avoided a strike over the summer, but was plagued with a bumper crop of whiners, slackers, head cases and malcontents. Exhibit A was the New Jersey Nets, the league's Jerky Boys, led by center Derrick Coleman, who flaunted team rules and referred to Jazz forward Karl Malone as an Uncle Tom, probably because Malone regularly attends his team's practices.

The NBA's poster dude for rotten 'tude was the San Antonio Spurs' Dennis Rodman, who fell off a motorcycle, missed practices and games, and posed naked for one magazine and in leather hot pants for another.

Rodman assumed it was his offbeat attire and neon hairstyles that put people off. But what fans and teammates didn't dig was Rodman emotionally abandoning his team during the playoffs, turning his back on huddles, blasting his coach and hoisting up absurd three-point shots.

Fans who waded through the NBA's garbage, though, were eventually rewarded with a wonderful, if brief, Finals, where solid citizen Hakeem Olajuwon led the Houston Rockets to their second title in a row. The Rockets, a team assembled like a ransom note, were sizable underdogs, but they stunned Shaquille O'Neal and the Orlando Magic in four straight.

Olajuwon set new standards for charm, enthusiasm and clutch postseason play. He didn't get the big off-court money that went to guys like Shaq and Rodman, but he did land contracts to endorse (seriously) water and rice. There's a lesson there somewhere.

The lesson in the NFL was that somebody had better pull the plug on this AFC-NFC alignment before any more innocent fans die of boredom.

The AFC's annual sacrifice to the Super Bowl volcano was the San Diego Chargers. The NFC sent the supercharged San

Francisco 49ers. So laughable was the mismatch that the biggest game-week story in Miami was a love-boat gambling cruise featuring 200 naked showgirls, a nude limbo contest and a swimming pool filled with Jello-O.

"No, we don't want a love-boat story," one newspaper editor barked at his Super Bowl reporter. "That would be Jello-O journalism."

Whoever won the limbo contest, they didn't go as low as the Chargers, who ducked under six Steve Young touchdown passes in the 49-26 drubbing— the AFC's 11th consecutive Super Bowl superloss. Dealignment, anyone?

The 49ers proved a tough act for themselves to follow. They faltered early in the '95 regular season, largely because Young hurt his shoulder and defensive demon and morale booster Deion Sanders defected to the Dallas Cowboys after a hard recruiting rush from Cowboys owner Jerry Jones— who had to make side deals with Nike, Pepsi, American Express and Toys R Us in order to raise the funds to sign him.

Deion, who played cheap for the '49ers, said it was time to go for the money, which was in keeping with the spirit of the year.

Call it smart business or crass and heartless cashing in, but players and owners made an undignified dash for the dough in '95. Georgia Frontiere moved her Rams to St. Louis and Al Davis took his Raiders back to Oakland, both owners grabbing huge up-front payoffs. Never before has sports incompetence been so richly rewarded.

Years of mediocre football and worse marketing had driven away Southern California football fans, giving Frontiere and Davis a convenient excuse to flee to cities waving big checks.

Davis' gift to the loyal Oakland fans was to nearly double the Raiders' average ticket price to a major-league-sports high $51, on top of a hefty Personal Seat License fee. Many fans granted Davis license to kiss their personal seats.

Franchise movement is nothing new, of course. That's why it's fitting that the Atlanta Braves won the 1995 World Series. In doing so the Braves became the first team to win the Series in three different cities, having already done so in Boston in 1914 and Milwaukee in 1957.

Elsewhere, money chipped away at the

The Year of the Boobs

The reason women can't golf very well, CBS golf commentator Ben Wright told a newspaper interviewer, is that their breasts interfere with their swings.

"Boobs get in the way," Wright explained.

And he is absolutely correct. The same problem plagues women in nearly every sport, as was demonstrated graphically in 1995.

Boobs got in the way. The boobs were men like Ben Wright, Bill Koch, Gunter Parche, Peter Graf and Ma Junren.

Not that women didn't frequently overcome the handicap of male boob-ism.

Betsy King earned her way into the LPGA Hall of Fame, the only sports hall where admission is based soley on achieving objective standards. No man could get in her way.

Rebecca Lobo led the University of Connecticut to a 35-0 season and was named NCAA Player of the Year in basketball. U.S. speed skater Bonnie Blair and Swiss alpine skier Vreni Schneider each retired at the top of her sport. American skier Picabo Street starred on the World Cup circuit. And when even the President of the United States was unable to end the baseball strike, it was a woman— federal judge Sonia Sotomayor— who finally stepped in and ordered the owners to play ball.

Not that men could be blamed for everything. After Jeff Tarango stormed off a Wimbledon sidecourt in mid-match to protest a chair umpire's alleged dishonesty, Benedicte Tarango helped her husband incur $63,000 in fines when she slapped the ump in the face.

"Women are so emotional," Jeff explained, cooly.

But about those men.

Wright set the tone when he took shots at lesbians and women golfers in an interview with a Wilmington, Del., newspaper then denied saying any of it. Who can trust a female reporter, right Ben?

Gunter Parche, the bratwurst-for-brains German fan who stabbed Monica Seles in 1993, continued to be a big winner. He got another favorable court ruling in Hamburg

David McNew/Reuters/Archive Photos

The all-women crew of **Mighty Mary** in action during the America's Cup races off San Diego.

and still has served no time for the crime. And his original scheme— to help his heroine Steffi Graf win tournaments by eliminating her chief opponent— continued to bear fruit.

Before Seles' return to the tour in August, Graf had won six of the 10 available Grand Slam titles in her absence, and then beat the still-rusty Monica on the way to a U.S. Open victory.

Meanwhile, Steffi's father and money manager, Peter Graf, was jailed in Germany, denied bail and charged with evading millions in taxes on Steffi's income, thus placing a huge emotional and financial burden on Fraulein Forehand.

Martina Navratilova became the first woman honored in the rafters of a major sports arena, when her tennis jersey was hoisted to the heavens at Madison Square Garden— up there with the championship banners and retired numbers of the Knicks and Rangers. However, as soon as Martina's tournament ended, her shirt was hauled down, on orders from a Garden exec. A guy.

Ma Junren is the male Chinese coach and guru who pushed his women runners to incredible record times two years ago. But his methods were so maniacal— and very possibly unethical and illegal— that 17 of his top runners bolted the team.

Boobism reached its apex off the coast of San Diego in the America's Cup yacht racing.

For the first 143 years of the Cup, women were not allowed to compete, probably due to an adminstrative oversight. To celebrate the falling of the gender barrier in '95, what would be cooler than a boat sailed by an all-female crew?

Advertisers lept aboard *Mighty Mary*, as did millions of new yachting fans, male and female.

"I'm dedicated to a principle," said Bill Koch, chief of the U.S. sailing group, "and we're gonna see it through, one way or another."

Koch apparently had his fingers crossed behind his back, because when *Mighty Mary* had some troubles in early races, Koch gave up on his principles and on helmswoman, J.J. Isler, replacing her with Dave Dellenbaugh, who, true to his first name, is a man.

Imagine a simliar occurence on, say, the U.S. women's gymnastics team.

Okay, girls, we're trailing the Romanians in the standings for the all-around gold medal, so we're going to make a slight change. Please welcome your new teammate, Dave, and give him some help with his leotard and lipstick.

Even if the *Mighty Mary* crew requested the change, as insiders insist, Koch blew a great opportunity and betrayed the pioneering spirit of the venture. Fact is, none of the American boats had a chance to beat New Zealand— Dennis Conner couldn't win even one race against them.

Knowing that, Koch should have stood by his women. They wouldn't have won the Cup, but they would have won a lot of hearts.

Sometimes, we guys don't have a clue.

Wide World Photos

Al Davis returned the Raiders to Oakland in 1995 and promptly rewarded a grateful citizenry with the highest average ticket prices in the NFL.

subtle charms of sport. In San Francisco, the 49ers played in 3Com Park— the city and the team having sold naming rights for their bleak and frigid stadium to the highest bidder, a computer firm.

As one scribe noted, "In California, 3Com Park is the worst place to watch or play a sport since Candlestick Park."

But let's forget money and pay our last respects to the artistry of the year.

Runners of the year were Michael Johnson in track and field and Cigar in horse racing. Johnson set his sights on dominating the 1996 Olympics in Atlanta after he won an unprecedented 100 and 200-meter double at the World Track and Field Championships. And 5-year-old Cigar won 12 straight races, including the Breeders' Cup Classic, to clinch Horse of the Year.

It was a season of wonderful comebacks. Michael Jordan bailed on baseball and came back to the Chicago Bulls, spicing up the second half of the NBA season before the rust from his absence finally caught up with him.

Monica Seles was comebacker of the year, returning to tennis after 28 months of physical and mental recuperation from a stabbing. She looked and sounded better than ever, pushing old rival Steffi Graf to the limit at the U.S. Open.

UCLA's basketball program returned from decades of wandering in the wilderness, to win the NCAA title. Tyson came back strong after being paroled from the slammer, although who could really tell from his coming-out bout? Tyson probably had tougher fights over who would control the channel clicker in the prison's TV room.

Golfer Corey Pavin, who has less distance off the tee than your Aunt Gladys, won his first major at the U.S. Open and John Daly came out of nowhere to win his second at the British Open. But the most dramatic individual win belonged to Ben Crenshaw at the Masters. Ben's coach and mentor, Harvey Penick, the Confucius of golf, died four days before the Masters began, and his spirit was with Crenshaw at Augusta. When Crenshaw holed the winning putt on the 18th, he dropped to his knees and sobbed.

More tears were shed at the Ryder Cup, by Curtis Strange. He needed one par over the last three holes of the last day to enable the U.S. to hold on to the Cup, but he went bogey-bogey-bogey and Europe won.

Tennis provided the best on-going rivalry of the year in Andre Agassi and Pete Sampras. Andre cut his hair and beat Pete in Australia, but Sampras won his third straight Wimbledon and beat Andre in the U.S. Open final to stake a solid claim as No. 1.

And sailing, a riveting spectator sport to tens of people, gave us unexpected thrills at the America's Cup competition off San Diego. In thick fog, the aircraft carrier USS Abraham Lincoln drifted onto the course and became the only object in the race that was larger than Dennis Conners' ego.

Stormy weather added an interesting twist to the competition. One ferocious gust ripped the main mast off a French boat, and big waves snapped the *oneAustralia* in half as if it were a mere Exxon oil tanker.

These accidents occurred in what sailors call "confused seas." But the seas weren't confused, they knew exactly what they were doing. They had a chance to wreck a few $3 million boats and grabbed it.

In 1995, such power to strike back was a sports fan's dream. ◻

Wide World Photos

LIKE FATHER, LIKE SON

Seattle outfielder **Jay Buhner** and his 1½-year-old son **Chase** check out Dad's handiwork in a mirror as the two prepare for "Buhner Buzz Night" at the Kingdome on Aug. 23. The Mariners gave away free tickets to anyone showing up with a bald head or were willing to have their heads shaved.

EXTRA POINTS

EXTRA POINTS
by Charles A. Monagan

Peter Schumacher/The Herald-Sun (Durham (N.C.)

A NIGHT TO DISMEMBER ▲

Violence broke out during "Strike Out Domestic Violence Night" at a May 22 Class A minor-league game between the host Durham Bulls and the Winston-Salem Warthogs. The game at New Durham Athletic Park started with a beanball war and then erupted into a dugout-clearing half-hour brawl. Ten players were ejected and a Warthog player was knocked out and hospitalized. The crowd of 4,371, many wearing badges decrying violence in the home, stood and cheered as the players fought.

STATUE TAKES LIBERTIES

The 9-foot, 800-pound statue of Babe Ruth at the entrance to Baltimore's Oriole Park at Camden Yards shows the Bambino holding a right-handed fielder's glove at his hip. Ruth, of course, batted left, fielded left and was even called "Lefty" as a kid. "Oh, well," explained artist Susan Luery.

Charles A. Monagan has been the editor of *Connecticut* magazine since 1989.

HEAD CASES

A Virginia study found that soccer players who frequently head the ball may be damaging themselves and tend to have lower I.Q.s than their non-heading teammates. Testing of 60 players by psychologist Adrienne Witol revealed those who headed the ball 10 or more times a game had I.Q.s of 103, while those heading once or less a game came in at 112. What Dr. Witol failed to mention was that players who head the ball all the time may just be dumber to begin with.

NO DEAL. PERIOD.

The women's pro tennis tour turned down an offer from Tambrands, makers of Tampax, to sponsor the tour. Bad for the image, the female pros decided, although Virginia Slims cigarettes had been just fine.

HEADLINE OF THE YEAR

"Nice Hat, Ugly Tie"
—*The Phila. Daily News*, on the Feb. 23 game that saw Eric Lindros score a hat trick but the Flyers blow a 6-3 lead vs. Quebec.

QUOTES OF THE YEAR, PART I

"We can pitch him inside now."

—Red Sox pitcher Roger Clemens, after Cal Ripken Jr. broke Lou Gehrig's consecutive game record.

"Buy them books."

—Bulls coach Phil Jackson, asked what he'd tell parents who bought expensive No. 45 Bulls' jerseys for their kids, only to see Michael Jordan return to No. 23.

"Negotiators should be locked in a room with no windows or air conditioning, and should be fed baked beans, fried cheese, hard-boiled eggs and chocolate kisses. In eight hours they'll be pleading 'Play ball!'"

—U.S. Rep. James Traficant of Ohio, offering his solution to the baseball strike.

"We need more cohesion rather than Stalinistic purges where you operated under a level of fear. We all need to join hands and sing 'Kumbaya.'"

—Denver Nuggets forward Brian Williams, speaking of his new coach, noted disciplinarian Bernie Bickerstaff.

Gary Newkirk/Allsport
Ben Wright

LPGA Tour
Nancy Lopez

"Women are handicapped by having boobs."

—CBS golf analyst Ben Wright, as quoted in a Delaware newspaper, on why men can swing clubs better than women. Wright denied making the comment.

"How does he know? He doesn't have any."

—LPGA Hall of Famer Nancy Lopez, on Wright's alleged comment.

Mike Powell/Allsport

HIGH FIVE ▲

Sergey Bubka (above) won his fifth straight world championship in the pole vault.

New Zealand bumped off Dennis Connor and *Young America* to take the America's Cup final in five straight races.

Stanford University won five NCAA championships in 1994-95.

Cyclist Miguel Indurain won his fifth consecutive Tour de France.

Horses trained by D. Wayne Lukas won five straight Triple Crown races.

THE JERRY LEWIS AWARD FOR EFFECTIVE FUNDRAISING

To Indianapolis deejay Adam Smasher, who attempted to raise $30,000 from listeners to pay an NCAA fine that had been levied against Indiana University coach Bob Knight. Smasher raised $167.

THE DR. SEUSS AWARD FOR MEDICAL REPORTING

To the reporter who, during a press conference regarding Mickey Mantle's newly transplanted liver, asked, "Is the donor still alive?"

THE MONEYED CLASSES

After police were called in to an Orlando Waffle House to investigate a 4:30 a.m. disturbance involving the Magic's Brian Shaw, the Sonics' Gary Payton and the Mavericks' Jason Kidd, Shaw threatened to buy the restaurant so he could fire the employees who'd called the police.

Clive Brunskil/Allsport

AFP Photo

THE AGASSI AND THE ECSTACY ▲

Some very close personal fans of Andre Agassi got together over the summer at Centre Court Wimbledon. No sign of the Brooke Shields look-alikes.

THE MAN ON "THE X-FILES," THE ONE WHO SMOKES MARLBOROS? DOESN'T HE WEAR NIKES?

As surely and menacingly as a crafty government operation, Nike seems to be penetrating society in all sorts of ways in all sorts of places. Evidence:

—Boris Becker on his feeling that Andre Agassi at Wimbledon always gets to play on Centre Court at 2 p.m.: "I think Nike has something to do with it."

—In early September, Dallas Cowboys' owner Jerry Jones seemed to become possessed by Nike and its swooshy logo. At the team's home opener, the logo hung from the speakers suspended over midfield, from portals, scoreboards, stadium employees caps and shirts and even on napkins—all to emphasize the team's new arrangement with the sneaker company. Jones even took to wearing a swoosh in his lapel.

—In Australia, Nike is accused of glorifying violence and corrupting youth. In one TV ad for Nike, Australian Rules football star Wayne Carey describes his various injuries over the years and finishes by saying, "I'm not saying I'd die for my team, but I'd be willing to go into an extended coma."

ANAGRAM OF THE YEAR

Me Idiot

—NHL goon Tie Domi of the Toronto Maple Leafs.

PRICE CHECK

Official Ryder Cup T-shirt	$25.00
Pay-Per-View charge for 89-second Tyson-McNeeley bout	$39.95
Super Bowl XXIX sweatshirt with appliquéd lettering	$79.98
Daily expense allowance for Miami Heat coach Pat Riley	$300.00
Bat autographed by Cal Ripken	$449.00
Price of a courtside ticket for a 1995-96 Knicks game	$1,000.00
Personal seat license fee for all season ticket holders of the St. Louis Rams	$4,500.00
Product endorsement fee Reebok agreed to pay Shaquille O'Neal	$20,000,000.00
Amount Malcolm Glazer agreed to pay for Tampa Bay Bucs franchise	$192,000,000.00

Wide World Photos

New Bucs' owner **Malcolm Glazer.**

QUOTES OF THE YEAR, PART II

"I ain't doing a damn thing, and I don't start 'til noon."

—Former NFL coach Bum Phillips, on how his retirement is going.

"Cleveland got the better of the deal. They didn't get anybody."

—Cincinnati manager Davey Johnson, on a trade of replacement players which sent five players to his team for future considerations.

"No. The owners took it all."

—Rangers forward Nick Kypreos, to a U.S. customs agent when asked if he had anything to declare upon leaving his native Canada following the NHL lockout.

"I'm going to give 110 percent on every play. You can't give any more than that."

—Illinois quarterback Johnny Johnson, on his plans for the 1995 Big Ten season.

"It was an organizational decision to blow him off."

—Orioles spokesman John Maroon, after Kato Kaelin asked the team for free tickets, a press pass and a chance to throw out the first pitch at a game.

Kansas City Chiefs

Marcus Allen

UPI/Bettmann

Marcus Garvey

"I think you mean to refer to Marcus Allen, not Marcus Garvey."

—ABC News anchor Peter Jennings, correcting Cynthia McFadden during coverage of the O.J. Simpson trial.

"Can ya shoot the rock?"

—ESPN's Dick Vitale, questioning President Clinton at a Villanova-Georgetown game.

NCAA Photos

BRUINATION ▲

Australian softball star Tanya Harding (no, not Tonya Harding the infamous ice skater-turned-pop singer) joined the UCLA varsity in mid-March, pitched 18 games, won 17, hit .444 and pitched the Bruins to the NCAA championship. Two days after the title game, she packed her bags and headed back home, registering incompletes in her three classes. "There was nothing unethical," said a UCLA spokesman.

MAYBE THEY STUDIED AT KNIGHT SCHOOL

Nice girls' basketball game between the Lincoln Park Academy in Fort Pierce, Fla., and St. Edward's of Vero Beach. The game was called with a little over a minute left when the Lincoln Park coach refused to leave the floor after having been ejected. To that point, 47 personal fouls and six technicals had been called in the game. *After* that point, Lincoln Park players tossed their chairs onto the floor and tore up the visitors' lockers room, ripping shower curtains and destroying benches.

WRINKLED FINGERS DEPT.

Frenchman Guy Delage jumped into the ocean last winter off the Cape Verde Islands with the intention of swimming to Barbados, 2,335 miles away. When he got there, 55 days later, practically no one believed he had swum much of the way, and instead had spent quite a bit of time either on board or being pulled along by his 15-foot, sail-powered raft. "I did nothing superhuman or extraordinary," he admitted upon arrival.

NEWS FROM OLYMPUS

—Ballroom dancing has been added as a demonstration sport for the 1996 Summer Games in Atlanta. Look for treading water, diaper changing and raking the leaves to join the roster soon.

—The U.S. Olympic Committee came down hard on a 10-table coffee shop in New York call the Olympic Restaurant. The USOC didn't like the fact that the restaurant, which has been around since 1980, displayed the Olympics' five-ringed symbol and thus infringed on McDonald's $40 million rights as the official fast-food sponsor for the Games. The restaurant removed the rings, but it'll take a little longer than that for the USOC to remove the egg from its face.

—"Wheel of Fortune" and "Jeopardy" have been named as the official TV game shows of the '96 Summer Olympics.

Wide World Photos

BASEBALL: WINNING BACK THE FANS

—Early in the season, Chicago White Sox fan Michael Robelli wrote a letter to his favorite team complaining about the strike and saying he would forgive all if the White Sox would send him an autographed baseball. Here is the reply he got from Sox marketing VP Rob Gallas:

"Dear Mr. Robelli: We receive thousands of letters every year from all over the country. Many are outrageous. Congratulations! Your letter made it to the top of the list. So you want an autographed ball and you will return to baseball. Do us a favor. Stay away."

—Major League Baseball decided that kids' teams using big-league nicknames should pay for the privilege. For example a youth-league team calling itself the Dodgers would have to buy licensed equipment at an added cost of $6 per uniform. "If you don't protect your trademark, you risk losing it," explained a spokesman for the owners.

—Asked with other players to hand out hats before the Padres post-strike opener, pitcher Andy Benes complained, "I'm not accustomed to being in a public area handing out hats before I start a game. It wouldn't be something I would choose to do on my own."

Reuters/Archive Photos

SHOT FROM A GRASSY KNOLL ▲

—Norma Early was a little late in ducking an errant shot off the club of former President George Bush at the Bob Hope Desert Classic on February 15. Her glasses were shattered and stitches were needed to close the cut on her nose. Later in the round, Bush hit another spectator, John C. Rynd, in the calf.

LET NO SPOT GO UNSPOILED

Ads on jockeys, ads behind home plate—it makes you wonder what they'll think of next. Well, a Connecticut company is successfully selling golf courses on the idea of placing advertisements at the bottom of golf holes.

OVER/UNDER

Overweight: Former Formula One race car champion Nigel Mansell missed two races in his new McLaren MP4/10 when he couldn't fit into the car's cockpit.

Underachiever: Austrian tennis star Thomas Muster. After winning the French Open, he didn't even enter Wimbledon.

Overreacted: Vernon Maxwell. The hot-headed Rockets guard went into the stands in Portland and punched a heckling fan.

Underemployed: Lawrence Taylor. The retired New York Giant linebacker hammed it up with the legendary Bam Bam Bigelow in a pay-per-view Wrestlemania match.

Over the top: Georgia Frontiere. The Rams owner's 48-seat luxury suite in St. Louis includes her baby grand piano.

Underestimated: The U.S. national team upset heavily-favored Argentina, 3-0, in the Copa America soccer tournament.

Overcoached: Mike Hoban. The 16-year-old was selected to try a three-point shot for $1 million at the NBA All-Star festivities. Coached by local hero Dan Majerle of the Suns, he threw up an air ball.

Underwhelming: Blue Jays' 2nd baseman Roberto Alomar sat out six of the team's last seven games to protect his .300 batting average.

Overed when he should have undered: Art Schlister. The former Ohio State and pro QB was sentenced to 24 months in jail for stealing from friends to fuel his gambling habit.

NO WONDER NOBODY'S EVER SEEN JERRY JONES AT THE HARNESS TRACK

The winner of this year's Hambletonian was a 4-1 shot named Tagliabue, who is the son of Super Bowl, but no relation to the commissioner of the NFL.

Tagliabue
Son of Super Bowl

Meadowlands

Tagliabue
Lord of Super Bowl

NFL

Wide World Photos

FUN COUPLES ▲

Wimbledon crybaby Jeff Tarango and his umpire-slapping wife Benedicte (above).
Pat Riley and Dave Checketts
Michael Schumacher and Damon Hill
Don King and Seth Abraham
Albert Belle and Hannah Storm
Jerry Rice and Deion Sanders
Dennis Rodman and Madonna
Gwen Torrence and Merlene Ottey
Johnnie Cochran and Christopher Darden

NO REQUIEM FOR THESE HEAVYWEIGHTS

Former undisputed heavyweight champion Riddick Bowe elevated the WBO belt to semi-legitimacy on March 11 when he beat up Herbie Hide for the title. That means there were a total of 18 current or former heavyweight champions fighting in 1995.

Here's the list: Trevor Berbick, Riddick Bowe, Frank Bruno, George Foreman, Herbie Hide, Larry Holmes, Evander Holyfield, Lennox Lewis, Michael Moorer, Oliver McCall, Tommy Morrison, Bonecrusher Smith, Bruce Seldon, Leon Spinks, Tony Tubbs, Tony Tucker, Mike Tyson and Tim Witherspoon.

TENNIS, ANYONE?

According to Pollstar, the rock band, Package Featuring John McEnroe, had the lowest grossing concert ($824) in the country the first week of June.

Wide World Photos

YER OUTTA HERE!

Thirty of 111 big league head coaching and managing jobs opened up between Nov. 1, 1994 and Oct. 31, 1995. That's 27 percent of the work force. Note that with the NBA expanding by two teams in 1995-96, the number of masterminds in jeopardy grows to 113.

NFL

Pete Carroll, Jets (fired)
Tom Flores, Seahawks (fired)
Chuck Knox, Rams (fired)
Rich Kotite, Eagles (fired)
Jack Pardee, Oilers (fired)
Wade Phillips, Broncos (fired)
Art Shell, Raiders (fired)

NBA

Don Chaney, Pistons (fired)
Chris Ford, Celtics (fired)
Dan Issel, Nuggets (quit)
Kevin Loughery, Heat (fired)
Don Nelson, Warriors (quit)
Pat Riley, Knicks (quit)

NHL

George Burnett, Oilers (fired)
Jacques Demers, Canadiens (fired)
Lorne Henning, Islanders (fired)
Dave King, Flames (fired)
Barry Melrose, Kings (fired)
John Muckler, Sabres (GM only)
Roger Neilson, Panthers (fired)
John Paddock, Jets (GM only)
Brian Sutter, Bruins (fired)
Darryl Sutter, Blackhawks (quit)

Baseball

Sparky Anderson, Tigers (quit)
Davey Johnson, Reds (fired)
Gene Lamont, White Sox (fired)
Tony La Russa, Athletics (quit)
Phil Regan, Orioles (fired)
Buck Showalter, Yankees (quit)
Joe Torre, Cardinals (fired)

OVER BEFORE THEY STARTED

Tyson vs. McNeeley (89 seconds)
Super Bowl XXIX (Rice scores at 1:24)
Indianapolis 500 for Team Penske
Hakeem vs. Shaq, "The War on the Floor" (cancelled when Olajuwon hurt his back)
NBA Finals (Rockets sweep)
Stanley Cup finals (Devils sweep)
America's Cup final (New Zealand sweeps)
Ki-Jana Carter's rookie year (top pick of NFL draft tears up left knee on third play of first exhibition game with Bengals)
Jacques Demers' 4th season as coach of the Canadiens (fired after 0-4 start)

WHY RICKEY HENDERSON WILL NEVER GET A 23-MINUTE STANDING OVATION

On the same day that Cal Ripken played in his 2,131st consecutive game for the Orioles, Oakland's Rickey Henderson, with his team still in the race for an AL wild-card berth, sat out his game because, as he put it, "My head is puzzled."

FORGET CAL RIPKEN'S STREAK

Let's hear it for streakmeister Michael Porter. A junior at Prairie View A&M, Porter has never won a football game in high school or in college. His Davis High School team in Dallas lost 30 in a row while he was there (as part of a national-record 80 straight losses) and at Prairie View he was on hand to see his team lose a record 51st game in a row (a convincing 64-0 rout at the hands of Grambling State). Mel Kiper Jr. says the kid's a lock to get drafted by the 1976 Tampa Bay Bucs.

FORGET RIPKEN'S STREAK II

The Harlem Globetrotters finally lost a game after 24 years and 8,829 straight wins. The streak ended in Vienna, Austria, with a 91-85 loss to a team led by Kareem Abdul-Jabbar, who in the closing moments of the game reportedly drop-kicked a three from the half-court line and then befuddled the 'Trotters when he used a basketball with an elastic band attached to it.

OH, AND SPEAKING OF RIPKEN'S STREAK

Here are three major league baseball records that no one will break. Ever.
Cy Young's 750 career complete games.
Owen Wilson's single-season mark of 36 triples in 1912.
And Johnny Vander Meer's back-to-back no-hitters in 1938.

Speedskater **Bonnie Blair** takes a final victory lap at the Calgary Olympic oval after participation in her last race on March 18. She won the first of her five Olympic gold medals at Calgary in 1988.

CALENDAR

NOV '94

Sun	Mon	Tue	Wed	Thu	Fri	Sat
			1	2	3	4	5
6	7	8	9	10	11	12
13	14	15	16	17	18	19
20	21	22	23	24	25	26
27	28	29	30			

Senior Partners

NOV. 5— Of the five oldest boxers to challenge for a world championship, the oldest— George Foreman— is the only one to actually win:

1. **George Foreman** won heavy weight title, knocking out champion Michael Moorer at 2:03 of 10th round on Nov. 5, 1994 in Las Vegas. AGE: 45 years, 9 months and 26 days.

2. **Archie Moore** knocked out in 5th round by Floyd Patterson in bout for vacant heavyweight title on Nov. 30, 1956 in Chicago. AGE: 42 years, 11 months and 17 days.

3. **Larry Holmes** lost unanimous 12-round decision to heavyweight champion Evander Holyfield on June 19, 1992 in Las Vegas. AGE: 42 years, 7 months and 16 days *(see Apr. 8, 1995).*

4. **George Foreman** lost unanimous 12-round decision to heavyweight champion Evander Holyfield on Apr. 19, 1991 in Atlantic City. AGE: 42 years, 3 months and 9 days.

5. **Archie Moore** knocked out in 9th round by heavyweight champion Rocky Marciano on Sept. 21, 1955 in New York. AGE: 41 years, 9 months and 8 days.

Election Day

NOV. 8— Republicans gain control of Congress and majority of state governorships. Newly-elected House members include former NFL All-Pro wide-receiver **Steve Largent** (R., Okla.) and former Oklahoma quarterback **J.C. Watts** (R., Okla.). Former baseball pitcher **Jim Bunning** (R., Ky.), wins re-election as does Sen. **Herb Kohl** (D., Wisc.), owner of the NBA's Milwaukee Bucks. In Texas, Rangers' general partner **George W. Bush** wins governor's race.

1 Chicago Bulls retire Michael Jordan's uniform no.23 in 2-hour ceremony at the United Center.
United Baseball League announces plans for 10-team league to begin play in 1996. Eight franchises will be located in U.S. and one each in Canada and Mexico.

2 NFL announces divisional assignments for 1995 expansion teams. Carolina Panthers will play in NFC West and Jacksonville Jaguars in AFC Central.

3 Glenn Robinson signs most lucrative rookie contract in NBA history, inking $68.15 million, 10-year pact with Milwaukee Bucks. League's 1994 No. 1 draft pick ends holdout one day before regular season opener.

4 Dwight Gooden suspended by Major League Baseball for 1995 season because of repeated drug violations. The New York Mets pitcher had served a 60-day suspension for cocaine use during the '94 season.

5 George Foreman KO's Michael Moorer in 10th round to become, at age 45, the oldest heavyweight champion in history. Victory comes 20 years after Foreman lost title to Muhammad Ali in Zaire.

6 Mexico's German Silva recovers from making wrong turn late in the race to win closest-ever New York City Marathon. Silva edges countryman Benjamin Paredes by two seconds with time of 2:11:21. Kenya's Tegla Loroupe wins women's race in 2:27:37.

10 Interim Commissioner Bud Selig appoints Boston Red Sox CEO John Harrington chairman of baseball's six-member owners negotiating team. As players' strike enters 91st day, Selig denies move reduces role of chief negotiator Richard Ravitch.

12 Prairie View A&M breaks all-time NCAA record for longest Div. I losing streak. Jackson St. hands the Panthers their 45th straight defeat, 52-7. Prairie View hasn't won since beating Mississippi Valley St., 21-12 on Oct. 28, 1989.

13 New England QB Drew Bledsoe sets NFL single-game passing records with 45 completions and 70 attempts. Patriots come from behind to beat Minnesota, 26-20, in overtime.
Michael Schumacher of Germany edges Britain's Damon Hill by one point (92-91) for Formula One World Championship at season-ending Australian Grand Prix. Former F1 and IndyCar champion Nigel Mansell wins race which ends for Schumacher and Hill when they collide on 35th lap.

14 Houston Oilers fire head coach Jack Pardee and offensive coordinator Kevin Gilbride. The Oilers, who at 1-9 have the NFL's worst record, name defensive coordinator Jeff Fisher as Pardee's successor.
L.A. Kings president Bruce McNall faces up to 45 years in prison after Federal prosecutors charge him with defrauding six banks to obtain nearly $236 million in loans from Jan. 1983 to Apr. 1994. McNall is expected to plead guilty to one count of conspiracy, two counts of bank fraud and one count of wire fraud. He will be arraigned on Nov. 28.

15 Martina Navratilova reaches end of 19-year pro tennis singles career with 4-6, 2-6 loss to Gabriela Sabatini in first round of Virginia Slims Championships in New York. Navratilova won a record 167 singles titles, including 18 in Grand Slam events.

16 Chris Webber ends bitter contract dispute with Golden St., signing a one-year deal for $2.1 million amid rumors that he will be traded. Webber, last season's NBA Rookie of the Year, became a restricted free agent after exercising a one-year "out clause" in his 15-year, $74 million contract with the Warriors.
Major League Soccer announces plans to delay the start of its inaugural season until 1996.

Al Bello/Allsport

George Forman leans against the ropes on Nov. 5 as referee **Joe Cortez** counts out heavyweight champion **Michael Moorer**. The knockout made Foreman the oldest heavyweight titlist ever at age 45.

17 Golden St. trades Chris Webber to Washington for Tom Gugliotta and first round draft choices in 1996, 1998, and 2000. Bullets also sign top pick Juwan Howard to 12-year, $41.3 million deal, reuniting two-fifths of Michigan Fab Five.

NHL further reduces 1994-95 regular season schedule to 60 games per team as negotiators meet in Boston on 48th day of lockout.

NCAA places the University of Mississippi football program on four years probation for recruiting violations. Ole Miss is banned from postseason play during the 1995 and '96 seasons and TV games in '95.

Federal grand jury indicts eight, including former Baylor basketball coach Darrel Johnson and three former assistants, for conspiring with junior college officials to commit mail and wire fraud in order to gain eligibility for incoming transfers for the 1993-94 season. Johnson was fired by Baylor on Nov. 16.

Fox network announces $25 million deal to underwrite new 1995 World Golf Tour headed by PGA Tour star Greg Norman. Proposed eight-event tour would include Top 30 players on Sony World Rankings plus 10 sponsor invitees. PGA Tour not receptive.

18 Roy Jones Jr. wins IBF super middleweight title with unanimous decision over James Toney in battle of unbeatens. Jones improves his record to 26-0 while Toney drops to 44-1-2.

19 Undefeated Alabama snaps Auburn's 21-game unbeaten streak with 21-14 victory before 83,091 at Legion Field in Birmingham.

Colorado head coach Bill McCartney abruptly announces resignation following Buffaloes' 41-20 victory over winless Iowa State. Citing family reasons, he will step down at the end of the season.

20 North Carolina wins ninth straight NCAA Div. I women's soccer championship, blanking Notre Dame, 5-0, in Portland, Ore.

Gabriela Sabatini ends 2½ year drought by winning Virginia Slims Championship with 6-3, 6-2, 6-4 victory over Lindsay Davenport in New York. Pete Sampras defeats Boris Becker in four sets in ATP World Championship final in Frankfurt, Germany.

22 Houston Astros re-sign National League MVP Jeff Bagwell to four-year, $27.5 million contract, making him baseball's fourth highest-paid player behind Barry Bonds, Frank Thomas and Cecil Fielder.

25 No. 1 Nebraska beats Oklahoma, 13-3, to finish unbeaten regular season and earn fourth straight Orange Bowl berth.

UMass shocks top-ranked Arkansas in college basketball season opener, winning Tipoff Classic 104-80 in Springfield, Mass.

27 B.C. Lions keep Grey Cup in Canada, beating Baltimore, 26-23, on Lui Passaglia's last-second 38-yard field goal.

28 Bill Walsh resigns as head football coach at Stanford after second straight losing season. The former 49ers boss and Pro Football Hall of Famer returned to Palo Alto for second tour of duty in 1992.

Colorado names assistant Rick Neuheisel as head football coach, passing over assistant head coach Bob Simmons.

30 Major League owners agree with federal mediator W.J. Usery to push back deadline for implementing salary cap from Dec. 5 to Dec. 15. With the baseball strike entering its fifth month, owners also postpone deadline for offering arbitration to Dec. 17.

DEC '94

Sun	Mon	Tue	Wed	Thu	Fri	Sat
				1	2	3
4	5	6	7	8	9	10
11	12	13	14	15	16	17
18	19	20	21	22	23	24
25	26	27	28	29	30	31

Loss Leaders

DEC. 7— The L.A. Clippers victory over Milwaukee ends their run at two of the NBA's ugliest team records— consecutive losses at the start of a season (17) and overall consecutive losses (24).

Here are the all-time losers in major pro team sports:

From start of season: *AL Baseball* (0-21)—Baltimore, 1988. *NBA* (0-17)—Miami, 1988. *NFL* (0-14)—Tampa Bay, 1976; New Orleans, 1980; Baltimore, 1981 and New England, 1990. *NHL* (0-11)—NY Rangers, 1943. *NL Baseball* (0-10)—Atlanta Braves, 1988.

Overall: *NFL* (24 in a row)—Tampa Bay, Sept. 12, 1976 to Dec. 11, 1977. *NBA* (24 in a row)—Cleveland, Mar. 19 to Nov. 5, 1982. *NL Baseball* (23 in a row)—Phila. Phillies (July 29 to Aug. 20, 1961). *AL Baseball* (21 in a row)— Baltimore, Apr. 4-28, 1988. *NHL* (17 in a row)— Washington, Feb. 18 to Mar. 26, 1975 and San Jose, Jan. 4 to Feb. 12, 1993.

Swap Meet

DEC. 28— The 12-player deal between San Diego and Houston was the biggest major league trade since 1957 when the Detroit Tigers and Kansas City Athletics pulled off the biggest swap in major league history. Here are the players involved in each deal.

1995: 12 players— Padres get Ken Caminiti, Andujar Cedeno, Steve Finley, Roberto Petagine, Brian Williams and a minor leaguer to be named later. Astros get Derek Bell, Doug Brocail, Ricky Guttierez, Pedro Martinez, Phil Plantier and Craig Shipley.

1957: 13 players— Tigers get Billy Martin, Mickey McDermott, Tom Morgan, Lou Skizas, Tim Thompson and Guz Zernial. K.C. A's get Kent Hadley, Frank House, Duke Maas, Jim McManus, Jim Small, Bill Tuttle and John Tsitouris.

1 **PGA Tour commissioner** Tim Finchem says Greg Norman is backing off support of proposed World Golf Tour for 1995.

Wayne Gretzky's "Ninety-Nine All-Stars," made up of 20 locked out NHL luminaries, lose to IHL Detroit Vipers, 4-3, in tune-up for six-game Scandinavian tour.

Seattle Seahawks defensive tackle Mike Frier is paralyzed after breaking his neck in a Kirkland, Wash. car crash that also injures teammates Chris Warren (two cracked ribs) and Lamar Smith (broken foot).

3 **No. 6 Florida claims** second straight SEC Championship Game, beating previously undefeated and third-ranked Alabama, 24-23, at the Georgia Dome.

Sweden clinches its fifth Davis Cup and first since 1987 with doubles victory over Russia in Moscow.

American cyclist Greg LeMond, three-time winner of the Tour de France, announces retirement. His decision comes after being diagnosed with a rare muscular disease known as mitochondrial myopathy which, though not life threatening, prevents him from competing at a world-class level.

Kansas topples No. 1 UMass, 81-75, at the inaugural John Wooden Classic in Anaheim.

4 **Minor league outfielder** Michael Jordan tops *Forbes* magazine Super 40 list of top-earning athletes for third straight year with his $10,000 salary and $30 million in endorsements. See "Business and Media" for complete list.

6 **CBS extends** TV rights for NCAA men's basketball tournament through 2002. The new deal, worth $1.725 billion over the next eight years, replaces seven-year, $1 billion agreement set to expire in 1997.

7 **Previously winless** Los Angeles Clippers (0-16) beat Milwaukee, 96-94, in overtime to avoid tying the 1988 Miami Heat for the worst start in NBA history.

San Antonio Spurs suspend NBA bad boy Dennis Rodman indefinitely without pay when he fails to report to practice after a month-long leave of absence.

Italian sportswear company Fila files $6 million damage suit against tennis star Monica Seles, claiming she reneged on a contract. Seles was stabbed on April 30, 1993 and has yet to return to the women's pro tour.

8 **Federal grand jury** indicts San Francisco outfielder Darryl Strawberry and his agent Eric Goldschmidt for failing to report more than $500,000 in personal appearance and card show earnings from 1986-90.

NHL All-Star Game becomes latest casualty of lockout as league cancels game scheduled for Jan. 21 at San Jose Arena.

9 **Jose Canseco traded** by Texas Rangers to Boston Red Sox for centerfielder Otis Nixon and minor league pitcher Luis Ortiz.

10 **Heisman Trophy** goes to Colorado junior running back Rashaan Salaam, who outpoints Penn St. back Ki-Jana Carter and QB Steve McNair of Div. I-AA Alcorn St. Salaam is only the fourth Div. I-A player to gain 2,000 yards in one season.

Art Monk sets NFL record of 178 straight games with a reception when he makes a five-yard catch on N.Y. Jets first play from scrimmage in an 18-7 loss to Detroit.

11 **San Francisco 49ers** pummel San Diego Chargers 38-15, in Super Bowl preview at Jack Murphy Stadium.

Virginia wins unprecedented fourth consecutive NCAA men's Div. I soccer title, beating Indiana, 1-0, on goal by senior striker A.J. Wood.

Bruce Bennett Studios

Wayne Gretzky (center) and his "Ninety-Nine All-Stars" toured Europe in December during the third month of the NHL owners lockout. The Gretzkys posted a record of 5-2 in seven games.

12 **NHL Board of Governors** vote unanimously to instruct commissioner Gary Bettman to cancel 1994-95 season if 50-game schedule becomes impossible.

Dennis Rodman's debut helps San Antonio even record at 9-9. NBA rebound champion returns after two suspensions and a leave of absence as Spurs rout Washington, 122-101.

14 **Bruce McNall pleads** guilty to bank fraud charges. L.A. Kings president faces maximum of 45 years in prison and a $1.75 million fine. He will be sentenced July 6.

Chicago White Sox trade 1993 AL Cy Young award-winner Jack McDowell to N.Y. Yankees for a minor league pitcher and player to be named later. In the NL, Philadelphia signs free agent switch-hitter Gregg Jefferies to four-year, $20 million contract.

Gretzky All-Stars finish European tour with 5-2 record, after 8-5 win in Freiberg, Germany.

15 **Major League owners** vote 25-3 to give Executive Counsel power to declare impasse and implement salary cap if no agreement is reached in player strike negotiations by Dec. 22.

16 **Sooners and Cowboys** name new head football coaches as Oklahoma signs Louisville's Howard Schnellenberger (five years, $125,000 per year) and Oklahoma St. inks Colorado assistant head coach Bob Simmons (five years, $110,000 per year).

17 **Minnesota wide receiver** Cris Carter sets NFL single-season reception record of 119 with eight catches against Detroit. New mark eclipses previous high of 112 set by Green Bay's Sterling Sharpe.

18 **Buffalo Bills lose** shot at fifth straight Super Bowl appearance as visiting New England eliminates them from playoff hunt with 41-17 pasting.

20 **Ivan Lendl quits** men's tennis tour at age 34 after 17-year career. Recurring back problems force the four-time No. 1 player to retire.

21 **Texas software magnate** John Moores buys 80 percent of San Diego Padres for $80 million. A syndicate headed by TV producer Tom Werner bought the team for $75 million in 1990.

22 **Baseball owners declare** impasse in strike negotiations and impose salary cap which would be $34,243,314 (with a floor $26,149,000) per team. Plan would also eliminate salary arbitration. Players union says it will file unfair labor practice charge with National Labor Relations Board.

Major League umpires join players in filing unfair practices charge with National Labor Relations Board, charging American and National Leagues with failing to bargain in good faith. The umpires' current contract expires on Dec. 31.

24 **L.A. Rams lose** to Washington, 24-21, in what may or may not be their final NFL home game in Anaheim. Club plans relocation to St. Louis in 1995.

29 **NHL commissioner** Gary Bettman says Jan. 16 is latest date new season can start. With 10-day training camps necessary, agreement to end lockout must be reached by Jan. 7.

Two also-rans from the AFC West fire head coaches as Seattle dismisses GM-coach Tom Flores after three seasons and Denver axes Wade Phillips after two.

30 **Jockeys' Guild** and Thoroughbred Racing Association reach agreement on new three-year contract. Deal comes less than 48 hours before jockeys planned a nationwide walkout over accident benefits.

JAN '95

Sun	Mon	Tue	Wed	Thu	Fri	Sat
1	2	3	4	5	6	7
8	9	10	11	12	13	14
15	16	17	18	19	20	21
22	23	24	25	26	27	28
29	30	31				

Hall of Fame Month

JAN. 9— Mike Schmidt's elevation to Cooperstown is one of several Hall of Fame elections for the month:

Bowling (Jan. 30)— Walter Ray Williams Jr. and David Ozio.

Boxing (Jan. 17)— Cus D'Amato, Max Baer, Wilfredo Gomez, Masahiko (Fighting) Harada and 11 others.

College Football (Jan. 18)— Jim Brown, Paul Robeson, Mike Singletary and 10 others.

Pro Football (Jan. 28)— Steve Largent, Kellen Winslow, Lee Roy Selmon, Henry Jordan and Jim Finks.

Tennis (Jan. 24)— Chris Evert.

All the Moves

JAN. 17— The Los Angeles Rams' decision to move east to St. Louis for the 1995 NFL season comes 49 years after the club migrated west from Cleveland. Over the last six decades, L.A. has figured in a dozen major league franchise comings and goings:

1946—NFL Rams arrive from Cleveland.

1958—National League Dodgers arrive from Brooklyn.

1960— NBA Lakers arrive from Minneapolis; L.A. Chargers arrive as charter team in AFL.

1961— LA (now California) Angels arrive as expansion team in American League; AFL Chargers move to San Diego.

1966— AL Angels move to Anaheim.

1967— L.A. Kings arrive as expansion team in NHL.

1980—NFL Rams move to Anaheim.

1982—NFL Raiders arrive from Oakland.

1984—NBA Clippers arrive from San Diego.

1995—NFL Rams announce they will move to St. Louis.

(See Aug. 7 for L.A. Raiders announcement that they will move back to Oakland in '95.)

1 **Top-ranked Nebraska** rallies in fourth quarter to beat No. 3 Miami, 24-17, in Orange Bowl. Victory clinches first national title in 22-year tenure of Cornhuskers' coach Tom Osborne.

2 **No. 2 Penn St. defeats** No. 12 Oregon, 38-20, in Rose Bowl but finishes distant second to Nebraska in final AP Poll. In other major bowl action, No. 4 Colorado routs Notre Dame in Fiesta, No. 7 Florida St. beats No. 5 Florida in Sugar, and No. 6 Alabama tops No. 13 Ohio St. in Citrus.

3 **NFL penalizes** expansion Carolina Panthers $150,000 and two draft picks for prematurely discussing head coach's job with Pittsburgh defensive coordinator Dom Capers. Steelers fined $50,000 for allowing Capers to negotiate before end of season.

4 **Sen. Daniel Moynihan** (D., N.Y.) introduces bill to repeal baseball's 73-year-old anti-trust exemption.

5 **N.Y. Jets dismiss** head coach Pete Carroll (6-10) after first season and replace him with Rich Kotite (7-9), who was fired by Philadelphia on Dec. 26.

6 **Lenny Wilkens lights up** 939th regular season NBA victory to pass Red Auerbach as league's all-time winningest coach. Atlanta defeats Washington, 112-90.

7 **Latest offer** by NHL Board of Governors to players union drops payroll tax plan but increases age of unrestricted free agency from 30 to 32. Owners give union until noon on Jan. 10 to accept offer or season will be cancelled.

8 **NHL players reject** owners' latest offer in unanimous vote. Union boss Bob Goodenow and commissioner Gary Bettman agree to meet Jan. 9 in their first face-to-face talks since Dec. 6.

9 **Mike Schmidt voted** into Baseball Hall of Fame in first year of eligibility. Former Philadelphia slugger (548 HRs) receives 96.5 percent of vote and is only player elected.

10 **NHL owners reject** players' unrestricted free agency proposal (one year at age 32, five years at 31) and offer counter proposal (three years at 32, three at 31). **L.A. Rams fire** head coach Chuck Knox after ending season with seven-game losing streak and 4-12 record. Knox ranks 6th in all-time wins with 193 in 22 years.

11 **NHL lockout ends** after 103 days as players union agrees to owners' final contract offer. Six-year deal includes rookie salary cap and option to reopen negotiations in 1998. Regular season will run 48 games and open Jan. 20.

12 **Dennis Erickson leaves** Miami of Florida to sign five-year, $5 million contract as head coach of the Seattle Seahawks. **College juniors** Rashaan Salaam of Colorado, Ki-Jana Carter of Penn St. and Warren Sapp of Miami-FL are among 33 underclassmen eligible for NFL's 1995 college draft. (See page 164 for complete list.) **Thoroughbred racing's** Eclipse awards announced with Holy Bull (top 3-year-old) and D. Wayne Lukas (top trainer) among 15 winners (see Jan. 27).

13 **NHL players ratify** collective bargaining agreement, a week before opening of abbreviated 1994-1995 schedule. Regular season will run through May 3. **Baseball Executive Council** approves guidelines for signing temporary replacement players. Replacements will come from six-year minor league free agents, current minor leaguers and recently released or retired players. **First entirely female crew** in America's Cup history sails Mighty Mary to victory over Dennis Conner and Stars & Stripes as defender trials begin.

Mike Powell/Allsport

San Francisco running back **Ricky Watters** jumps into the arms of lineman **Steve Wallace** after scoring one of his three touchdowns in the Niners' 49-26 victory over San Diego in the Super Bowl.

15 All-California battle set for Super Bowl XXIX as San Francisco and San Diego win NFL conference title games. The 49ers beat Dallas, 38-28, and the Chargers, who upset Pittsburgh, 17-13, will meet Jan. 29 in Miami.

Denver Nuggets' Dan Issel, citing personal reasons, abruptly resigns in his third season as head coach. Assistant Gene Littles is named interim coach.

16 No. 2 Connecticut defeats No. 1 Tennessee, 71-66, in women's college basketball showdown in Storrs, Conn.

Earthquake, measuring 7.2 on the Richter scale, jolts Kobe, Japan killing 5,373 and injuring 26,800.

17 Los Angeles Rams owner Georgia Frontiere officially announces she will move franchise to St. Louis for 1995 season. NFL owners will vote on whether to approve shift on Mar. 15 in Phoenix.

18 Jim Brown finally elected to College Football Hall of Fame. Vote comes 38 years after the All-America running back's graduation from Syracuse. Paul Robeson, Billy Sims, Mike Singletary and Frank Kush are among 12 others honored.

20 N.Y. Rangers raise 1994 Stanley Cup banner to rafters of Madison Square Garden as shortened NHL regular season begins.

22 Duke basketball coach Mike Krzyzewski will miss remainder of 1994-95 season as he recovers from Oct. 22 back surgery and a bout with exhaustion that landed him in the hospital for four days (Jan. 6-9).

23 Carolina Panthers name Pittsburgh defensive coordinator Dom Capers as team's first head coach.

24 Prosecution delivers opening statements in O.J. Simpson double murder trial.

Salt Lake City; Ostersund, Sweden; Quebec City and Sion, Switzerland named four finalists for 2002 Winter Games. International Olympic Committee will announce decision on June 16.

25 Oakland Athletics sold to Bay Area businessmen Steve Schott and Ken Hoffmann for $85 million and guarantee to keep team in city for 10 years.

26 President Clinton orders baseball owners and players union back to the bargaining table saying: settle strike by Feb. 6 or we'll settle it for you.

Mark Messier inks two-year pact with N.Y. Rangers for nearly $6 million a year. Team captain's old contract contained clause allowing him to renegotiate if he led club to first Stanley Cup since 1940.

27 Mary Pierce wins first major tennis title with 6-2, 6-3 victory over top-seeded Arantxa Sanchez Vicario at Australian open.

Holy Bull collects 241 of 246 votes cast to win the Eclipse award as Horse of the Year. The big grey, who won eight of 10 starts in 1994, placed 12th in the Kentucky Derby and passed up the Preakness, Belmont and Breeders' Cup.

28 Andre Agassi dethrones top-seeded Pete Sampras 4-6, 6-1, 7-6 (8-6), 6-4, to win Australian Open in his debut Down Under.

Congressman Steve Largent elected to Pro Football Hall of Fame along with Kellen Winslow, Lee Roy Selmon, Henry Jordan and Jim Finks.

29 MVP Steve Young throws record six touchdown passes to lead S.F. 49ers past San Diego, 49-26, for record fifth Super Bowl title.

31 Denver Broncos name 49ers offensive coordinator Mike Shanahan as head coach.

FEB '95

Sun	Mon	Tue	Wed	Thu	Fri	Sat
			1	2	3	4
5	6	7	8	9	10	11
12	13	14	15	16	17	18
19	20	21	22	23	24	25
26	27	28				

Initiation Inflation

FEB. 15— Steve Beuerlein, Jacksonville's first NFL expansion draft pick, will cost $2,083,300 to sign for the 1995 season

That's nearly four times the $550,000 that Dallas paid for the 36 veterans they picked in the 1960 NFL expansion draft.

Dallas joined the league for a franchise fee of $50,000. Thirty-five years later, Jacksonville and Carolina were obliged to pay $140 million each.

The escalating cost of membership in the NFL:

1960— Dallas and the Minnesota Vikings join for $50,000 each (plus $550,000 apiece for 36 players from dispersal drafts). Dallas will begin play in 1960, Minnesota in '61.

1965— The Atlanta Falcons join for a franchise fee of $8.5 million, while the Miami Dolphins become the AFL's first expansion team for $7.5 million.

1966— The New Orleans Saints join the NFL for $8.5 million.

1967— The Cincinnati Bengals join the AFL for $8.5 million.

1974— The Seattle Seahawks and Tampa Bay Buccaneers join for $16 million each.

1994— The Carolina Panthers and Jacksonville Jaguars join for $140 million each.

Earnhardt's Luck

FEB. 19— The Daytona 500 just isn't Dale Earnhardt's race. Despite entering 1995 with seven Winston Cup titles and 63 career wins, he has now failed to win NASCAR's biggest event for 17 years.

Year	Year	Year
1979—8th	1985—32nd	1991—5th
1980—4th	1986—14th	1992—9th
1981—5th	1987—5th	1993—2nd
1982—36th	1988—10th	1994—7th
1983—35th	1989—3rd	1995—2nd
1984—2nd	1990—5th	

1 **Latest proposal** by baseball owners removes demands for salary cap and reduction of players' salaries to 50 percent of total revenues. Players union not impressed.

John Stockton passes Magic Johnson as NBA all-time assist leader. Utah guard sets new mark of 9,927. His 16 assists help lead Jazz past Denver, 129-88.

2 **L.A. Raiders fire** sixth-year head coach Art Shell after missing the playoffs with 9-7 record and replace him with assistant Mike White.

Philadelphia Eagles name S.F. 49ers defensive coordinator Ray Rhodes as head coach.

5 **Colts running back** Marshall Faulk gains 180 yards to break O.J. Simpson's Pro Bowl rushing record as AFC routs NFC, 41-13, in Honolulu.

USA beats France, 4-1, in first round of 1995 Davis Cup. Americans will face Italy in second round at Palermo.

6 **President Clinton extends** deadline for ending baseball strike one day, after mediator W.J. Usery appeals for more time to reach agreement.

Phoenix Suns lose forward Danny Manning for rest of season after he tears anterior cruciate ligament in left knee at practice.

Darryl Strawberry suspended for 60 days by commissioner's office and has contract with S.F. Giants terminated for violation of baseball's drug aftercare program.

Arantxa Sánchez Vicario reaches No. 1, becoming only the sixth top-ranked player on the WTA tour since 1975. She follows Chris Evert (262 weeks), Martina Navratilova (331), Tracy Austin (22), Steffi Graf (277) and Monica Seles (113).

7 **White House meeting** between players and owners fails to advance baseball talks, leading frustrated President Clinton to ask Congress to impose binding arbitration. Meanwhile, mediator W.J. Usery's settlement proposal— which includes a payroll tax— is embraced by the owners and attacked by the players.

More than 150 students stage halftime sit-in forcing suspension of college basketball game between No. 5 UMass and Rutgers at Piscataway, N.J. Oncourt protest comes after a report discloses that Rutgers president Francis L. Lawrence told a November faculty meeting that disadvantaged students lacked "genetic and hereditary background" to score well on college admissions tests.

8 **NBA suspends** Houston guard Vernon Maxwell for 10 games and fines him $20,000 for going into the stands and punching a heckler on Feb. 6 in Portland.

9 **Darryl Strawberry pleads** guilty to tax evasion. Recently-released San Francisco outfielder didn't pay $75,000-$120,000 between 1986 and '90.

Philadelphia Flyers trade right wing Mark Recchi to Montreal for left wing Gilbert Dionne, center John LeClair and defenseman Eric Desjardins.

10 **St. Louis Rams name** Oregon's Rich Brooks as head coach. Brooks, the 1994 Pac-10 Coach of the Year, led the Ducks to their first Rose Bowl since 1958.

FIFA cancels World Youth Soccer Championship scheduled for Nigeria Mar. 11-26. Cases of meningitis and cholera had been reported in two of four competition sites. Tournament will later be moved to Qatar and scheduled for Apr. 13-28.

11 **Holy Bull retired** after breaking down in backstretch of Donn Handicap at Gulfstream Park in Florida. The 1994 Horse of the Year suffers strained ligaments in his left front leg. Injury is not life-threatening.

Seventeen-year-old Nicole Bobek wins women's title at U.S. Figure Skating Championships in Providence, R.I. Todd Eldredge, 23, wins his third men's crown.

Wide World Photos

Sterling Marlin celebrates after winning his second straight Daytona 500. In 19 seasons on the NASCAR circuit, Marlin has won only twice— both times in stock car racing's biggest race.

12 UConn basketball makes history as men join women atop weekly AP and USA Today/Coaches polls. No school's men's and women's hoop teams have ever claimed No. 1 at the same time before.
MVP Mitch Richmond scores 23 points as West routs East, 139-112, in NBA All-Star game at Phoenix.
Bonnie Blair breaks own world record in 500-meter World Cup speed skating race at Calgary. Five-time Olympic gold medalist lowers mark to 38.69 seconds.

13 Don Nelson resigns as head coach and GM of Golden St. after injuries and divisive Chris Webber trade result in 14-31 record at the All-Star break. Assistant Bob Lanier takes over as coach.
NBA approves sale of Miami Heat to family of Carnival Cruise Lines founder Ted Arison, who bought out partners Billy Cunningham and Lewis Schaffel.

14 Houston Rockets acquire guard Clyde Drexler and forward Tracy Murray of Portland for forward Otis Thorpe and a conditional 1995 first round draft pick.
Lukewarm Miami Heat dumps coach Kevin Loughery in favor of assistant Alvin Gentry.

15 Jacksonville Jaguars make Arizona quarterback Steve Beuerlein top pick in first NFL expansion draft since 1976. Carolina Panthers select New England defensive back Rod Smith first.

17 Detroit Tigers manager Sparky Anderson, saying, "There ain't no place in our game for replacement players," takes unpaid leave of absence.

18 Pittsburgh Penguins stopped two games short of best NHL start ever, losing at Hartford, 4-2. The Pens record falls to 12-1-1.
Golden St. trades forward Tom Gugliotta to Minnesota for rookie forward Donyell Marshall.

19 Sterling Marlin becomes first driver to win back-to-back Daytona 500s since Richard Petty repeated in 1973-74.

20 Denver Nuggets GM Bernie Bickerstaff replaces interim coach Gene Littles. The Nuggets were 3-13 since resignation of Dan Issel on Dec. 15.
Steffi Graf regains women's No. 1 ranking in her 1995 debut, beating Mary Pierce 6-2, 6-2 in Paris Open.

22 Four-time Olympic diving champion Greg Louganis reveals he has AIDS. His taped interview with Barbara Walters airs Feb. 24 and earns highest ratings of the season for ABC-TV's "20/20."

24 Evander Holyfield cleared to return to competitive boxing after Nevada State Athletic Commission votes 4-1 to lift his medical suspension. Holyfield was diagnosed with heart problems after losing his title to Michael Moorer on Apr. 22, 1994.

26 Gerald McClellan undergoes emergency brain surgery to remove a blood clot after suffering 10th round knockout the night before in WBC super middleweight bout with Nigel Benn in London.

27 Baseball strike enters 200th day as talks resume for first time since Feb. 7. Meetings in Scottsdale, Ariz., last 5½ hours but yield no meaningful progress .
Speed skater Dan Jansen wins Sullivan Award as nation's top amateur athlete of 1994. A veteran of four Winter Olympics, Jansen finally won a gold medal at Lillehammer in the 1,000 meters.

28 Green Bay All-Pro wide receiver Sterling Sharpe is released by Packers. Sharpe, who had two vertebrae fused on Feb. 3 and will miss the 1995 season, refused club's offer to reduce non-guaranteed $3.2 million salary to $200,000.

MAR '95

Sun	Mon	Tue	Wed	Thu	Fri	Sat
			1	2	3	4
5	6	7	8	9	10	11
12	13	14	15	16	17	18
19	20	21	22	23	24	25
26	27	28	29	30	31	

Bonnie Blur

MAR. 19— Bonnie Blair retires from competitive speed skating the day after her 31st birthday. She steps down as the nation's most decorated female Olympian with five gold medals and one bronze since 1988. She also leaves as the fastest woman on skates with three world records in the 500-meter sprint:

Time	Date	Location
39.10*	Feb. 22, 1988	Calgary
38.99	Mar. 26, 1994	Calgary
38.69	Feb. 12, 1995	Calgary

*World and Olympic record.

Balls, Strikes and Lockouts

MAR. 31— Baseball's latest work stoppage comes to a close (but not a resolution) after 232 days— a U.S. major team sport record. Here is a list of all previous strikes and lockouts:

Major League Baseball

Year	Cause	Days	Dates
1972	Strike	13	4/1 to 4/13
1973	Lockout	17	2/8 to 2/25
1976	Lockout	17	3/1 to 3/17
1980	Strike	8	4/1 to 4/8
1981	Strike	50	6/12 to 7/31
1985	Strike	2	8/6 to 8/7
1990	Lockout	32	2/15 to 3/18
1994-95	Strike	232	8/12 to 3/31

NBA Basketball
None

NFL Football

Year	Cause	Days	Dates
1982	Strike	57	9/21 to 11/17
1987	Strike	34	9/22 to 10/22

NHL Hockey

Year	Cause	Days	Dates
1992	Strike	10	4/1 to 4/10
1994-95	Lockout	103	10/1 to 1/11

1 **Replacement baseball** games begin as California Angels beat Arizona St., 13-5, before 1,300 fans at Tempe's Diablo Stadium.

3 **NFL free agent signings** include return specialist Mel Gray with Houston (2 years, $2.4 million) and running back David Meggett with New England (5 years, $10 million).
UMass completes Feb. 7 suspended game, beating Rutgers, 77-62, before a crowd of 445 at the Spectrum in Philadelphia.
TNT fires former N.Y. Giants linebacker Lawrence Taylor as NFL analyst in the wake of Taylor's announcement that he will participate in an Apr. 2 pay-per-view World Wrestling Federation match.

4 **Pernell Whitaker steps up** in weight to win unanimous decision against WBA junior middleweight champion Julio Cesar Vasquez in Atlantic City. Whitaker, the reigning WBC welterweight champ, has now won titles in four weight classes (135, 140, 147 and 154 lbs.). He will relinquish newly-won belt on Mar. 8 and return to welterweight division.
George Foreman stripped of WBA heavyweight title after scheduling his first defense against Germany's Axel Schulz on Apr. 22. Since Foreman was unranked when he beat Michael Moorer on Nov. 5, 1994, he had to fight the WBA's No. 1 challenger Tony Tucker within four months.

5 **Worst accident** in America's Cup history results in sinking of oneAustralia as 75-foot carbon-fiber boat breaks in half in rough seas of San Diego. All 17 crew member are rescued.
Jacques Villenueve of Canada wins inaugural Grand Prix of Miami in IndyCar season opener .

7 **Veterans Committee elects** former players Richie Ashburn, Leon Day and Vic Willis and ex-NL president William Hulbert to Baseball Hall of Fame.
Seattle businessman John McCaw Jr. assumes controlling interest in both NHL Vancouver Canucks and NBA-expansion Vancouver Grizzlies in corporate restructuring of Northwest Entertainment Group.

8 **Tampa Bay Bucs sign** free agent wide receiver Alvin Harper to four-year deal worth reported $10 million.
Gerald McClellan regains consciousness for first time since Feb. 26 emergency brain surgery. McClellan lost WBC super middleweight title to Nigel Benn on Feb. 25.

9 **Major League Baseball** expands to Phoenix and Tampa. Arizona Diamondbacks and Tampa Bay Devil Rays will each pay $130 million initiation fee and begin play in 1998.
Boston Celtics threaten to sue The Wall Street Journal for $100 million after newspaper reports that cocaine was probably a factor in 1993 death of Reggie Lewis.
Canadian Elvis Stojko successfully defends men's World figure skating championship in Birmingham, England. American Todd Eldredge takes silver medal.

10 **Michael Jordan** announces retirement from baseball.

11 **Picabo Street becomes** first American skier to capture World Cup season downhill title, winning her fifth downhill race of the season.
Riddick Bowe knocks down Herbie Hide seven times before finally knocking him out at 2:25 of the sixth round to win WBO heavyweight title in Las Vegas.
China's Chen Lu, the Olympic bronze medalist at Lillehammer, wins women's title at World Figure Skating Championships. Surya Bonaly of France is second and America's Nicole Bobek is third.

Wide World Photos

Crew members of *oneAustralia* scramble to abandon ship during their America's Cup race against Team New Zealand on March 5. The $3 million yacht broke apart and sank within two minutes.

Pan American Games open in Mar Del Plata, Argentina. U.S. men's gymnastics team wins gold medal.

12 UCLA and UConn top men's and women's final basketball polls before NCAA Div. I tournaments.

United States wins four gold medals in final day of World Indoor Track and Field Championships at Barcelona.

14 Doug Swingley wins Iditarod Trail Sled Dog race in record time. Montana rancher's nine-dog team completes the 1,160-mile course in 9 days, 2 hours, 42 minutes and 19 seconds.

15 NFL owners reject proposed move of L.A. Rams to St. Louis. Rams threaten to file suit after losing vote, 21-3 with six owners abstaining *(see Apr. 12)*.

16 Upsets mark start of NCAA Div. I men's basketball tournament. Manhattan surprises Oklahoma, 77-67, and Miami of Ohio stuns Arizona, 71-62.

18 He's back! Michael Jordan announces he will end retirement and rejoin the Chicago Bulls on Mar. 19.

Alberto Tomba wins third World Cup season title, adding men's giant slalom to overall and slalom championships.

19 Wearing No. 45, Michael Jordan returns to NBA after 17 months, scoring 19 points in Chicago Bulls' 103-96 overtime loss to Indiana.

San Antonio Spurs' Dennis Rodman, the NBA's leading rebounder, separates right shoulder in motorcycle accident and is expected to miss 2-4 weeks.

Vreni Schneider clinches third World Cup overall title with victory in women's slalom at Bormio, Italy.

22 NFL raises salary cap to $37.1 million for 1995 season. Cap was $34.6 million in 1994.

25 He's back, too! Former heavyweight champion Mike Tyson is released from an Indiana prison after serving three years for rape.

UCLA and North Carolina reach NCAA Final Four. The Bruins beat UConn, 102-96, while the Tar Heels down Kentucky, 74-61.

Undefeated Connecticut is joined by Tennessee, Stanford and Georgia in Women's NCAA Final Four.

26 Arkansas and Oklahoma St. round out Final Four. The Razorbacks beat Virginia 68-61, and the Cowboys rout UMass, 68-54.

United States collects a record 424 medals, including 169 golds, as Pan American games come to a close.

27 NHL suspends Buffalo head coach John Muckler for three games without pay and fines him $10,000 for attacking a heckler after the Sabres' 6-1 loss to Tampa Bay on Mar. 19 in Buffalo.

28 Michael Jordan breaks Madison Square Garden record for points in a game with 55 in 113-111 victory over Knicks. Jordan set previous high of 50 in 1986.

29 Baseball players union executive board votes to end strike and return to work under the terms and conditions of the previous basic agreement with the owners if a federal judge grants the National Labor Relations Board's request for an injunction on Mar. 31.

31 Federal judge Sonia Sotomayor of U.S. District Court in Manhattan issues injunction against baseball owners in move that effectively ends the 232-day strike.

Near-capacity crowd of 47,563 fills new Coors Field in Denver to see exhibition game between Colorado Rockies and N.Y. Yankees. Replacement Rockies roll, 4-1.

Bowling Green center Brian Holzinger wins Hobey Baker Award as college hockey's top player.

APRIL '95

Sun	Mon	Tue	Wed	Thu	Fri	Sat
						1
2	3	4	5	6	7	8
9	10	11	12	13	14	15
16	17	18	19	20	21	22
23/30	24	25	26	27	28	29

Into the Sunset

As the month progressed five aging headliners decided to call it a career:

Bo Jackson, 32— baseball; outfielder and DH; 8 seasons with Royals, White Sox and Angels; 141 HR, 415 RBI and .250 average. Won the 1985 Heisman Trophy while at Auburn and played several seasons with the Los Angeles Raiders (Apr. 3).

Joe Montana, 38— football; quarter-back; 15 seasons with 49ers and Chiefs; career 92.3 passing rating with 3,409 completions, 40,551 yards, 273 TD passes and 139 interceptions; three-time Super Bowl MVP; NFL regular-season MVP in 1989 and 1990 (Apr. 18).

Jack Morris, 39— baseball; RHP; 18 seasons with Tigers, Twins, Blue Jays and Indians; 254-186 record with 3.90 ERA; MVP of 1991 World Series, but no Cy Young awards (Apr. 18).

Goose Gossage, 43— baseball; RHP; 22 seasons with White Sox, Pirates, Yankees, Padres, Cubs, Giants, Rangers, A's and Mariners; 124-107 record with 310 saves and 3.01 ERA (Apr. 19).

Jeff Reardon, 39— baseball; RHP; 16 seasons with Mets, Expos, Twins, Red Sox, Braves, Reds, and Yankees; 73-77 record with 366 saves and 3.16 ERA; ranks second in career saves (Apr. 20).

National Passed Time?

APR. 24— Baseball has slipped to a 35-year low in popularity, according to a polll taken by ABC News.

Asked "What is your favorite sport to watch?" a national sample of 1,026 adults favored football by a 3-to-1 margin over baseball. In fact, baseball finished in third behind second place basketball.

A Gallup poll taken on Dec. 13, 1960 placed baseball first, followed by football and basketball.

1 **UCLA beats** Oklahoma St., 74-61, and Arkansas downs North Carolina, 75-68, to reach final of the NCAA basketball tournament in Seattle.
Boston University claims 4th NCAA hockey title with 6-2 win over Hockey East rival Maine at Providence.

2 **Baseball strike officially ends** as owners accept players' offer to return to work without new collective bargaining agreement. Spring Training camps open Apr. 7. Opening Day for revised 144-game regular season set for Apr. 25.
Unbeaten UConn tops Tennessee, 70-64, in Minneapolis to go 35-0 and win its first women's NCAA basketball title.

3 **UCLA dethrones** Arkansas, 89-78, to win its 11th NCAA basketball title and first since 1975. Bruins' senior forward Ed O'Bannon named MVP.
German judge upholds two-year suspended sentence of Gunter Parche for stabbing tennis star Monica Seles on Apr. 30, 1993 in Hamburg.

4 **America's Cup** defense committee allows *Young America*, *Mighty Mary* and *Stars & Stripes* to compete in unprecedented three-boat, 12-race defender final starting Apr. 10 off San Diego.

5 **Montreal Expos deal** high-priced pitchers Ken Hill (to St. Louis) and John Wetteland (to N.Y. Yankees) for minor leaguers and cash.
Kansas City Royals trade outfielder Brian McRae to Chicago Cubs for two minor league pitchers.
Montreal Canadiens send center and captain Kirk Muller to N.Y. Islanders for center Pierre Turgeon in five-player deal.
Jerry Tarkanian, Class of 1956, returns to Fresno St. as head basketball coach. The 64-year-old Tarkanian, who has previously coached at Long Beach St. and UNLV, is the NCAA's all-time winningest Division I coach by percentage (.837) with a record of 625-122.
Winnipeg GM John Paddock resigns as head coach, naming assistant Terry Simpson to take his place.

6 **Expos continue** financially-motivated housecleaning by trading outfielder Marquis Grissom to Atlanta for outfielders Roberto Kelly and Tony Tarasco and a minor league pitcher.
Royals send Cy Young Award winner and outspoken union activist David Cone to Toronto for three minor leaguers in another cost-cutting move.
Edmonton Oilers fire first-year head coach George Burnett, assigning interim job to assistant Ron Low.

7 **UCLA's Ed O'Bannon** outpolls Shawn Respert of Michigan St. and Randolph Childress of Wake Forest to win Wooden Award as college basketball's Player of the Year.

8 **Oliver McCall outpoints** former heavyweight champion Larry Holmes in first defense of WBC title. Holmes becomes second-oldest boxer to fight for the heavyweight championship, stepping into Las Vegas ring at age 45 years, 5 months, and 5 days.

9 **Ben Crenshaw cards** final round 68 to win second Masters green jacket one week after death of friend and mentor Harvey Penick.

10 **Andre Agassi reaches** No. 1 ranking on ATP Tour computer for first time, ending Pete Sampras' 101-week stay at the top. Agassi defeated Sampras to win Lipton Championship on Mar. 26 in Key Biscayne.

12 **NFL owners vote** to give L.A. Rams permission to move to St. Louis. Approval comes after Rams agree to pay league $30 million relocation fee and $17 million in personal seat license revenue. Final vote is 23-6 with L.A. Raiders abstaining.

Stephen Dunn/Allsport

Senior point guard **Tyus Edney**, who got UCLA to the NCAA final but then missed most of the game with a sprained right wrist, helps cut down the net after the Bruins' 89-78 win over Arkansas.

13 Spring Training games begin with replacement umpires as Major League umps walk picket line seeking 53 percent raise.

14 Charles Grantham resigns as executive director of NBA players union, citing irreconcilable differences over internal matters. He is replaced by general counsel Simon Gourdine.
Bora Milutinovic is forced out as head coach of U.S. National Soccer Team after four years at the helm. He is succeeded by assistant Steve Sampson.

17 Defending champions Cosmas Ndeti of Kenya and Uta Pippig of Germany repeat as winners in 99th Boston Marathon. Ndeti's third straight victory ties him with Clarence DeMar (1922-24) and Bill Rodgers (1978-80) as only three-peaters in race history.

18 Joe Montana retires from pro football at age 38, making announcement before crowd of 20,000 well-wishers in San Francisco. Montana, who played the last two seasons in Kansas City, led the 49ers to four Super Bowl titles in 13 years.

19 Skier Vreni Schneider of Switzerland quits alpine circuit at age 30 after a career in which she won 55 World Cup races, three World Cup overall titles, three world championships and three Olympic gold medals.

20 *Black Magic 1* of New Zealand beats *oneAustralia* to clinch best-of-nine challenger series in six races .

21 Barry Melrose fired by L.A. Kings, who are in danger of missing NHL playoffs with 13-21-7 record. Team president Rogie Vachon becomes interim coach.

22 Cincinnati Bengals trade up to select Penn St. junior running back Ki-Jana Carter as top overall pick at NFL Draft in New York *(see page 241).*

George Foreman defends his IBF heavyweight title in Las Vegas in a controversial majority decision over Germany's Axel Schulz. At age 46, Foreman is 20 years older than Schulz.

23 Moment of silence observed at arenas and stadiums across the country in memory of 168 who died in Apr. 19 car bomb explosion that destroyed a federal office building in Oklahoma City.
Howard Cosell dies at 77. Legendary sportscaster succumbs after four-year battle with stomach cancer.

24 Lenny Wilkens named head coach of U.S. Olympic men's basketball team.
Darryl Strawberry avoids prison for tax evasion but gets three years probation, six months of house confinement and a $350,000 fine. He is free to resume baseball career on June 24.

25 Baseball finally returns after 257 days as 1995 regular season begins in Miami with Marlins losing 8-7 to L.A. Dodgers. Locked-out major league umpires picket use of replacement umps.

26 *Stars & Stripes* rallies to beat *Mighty Mary* in stunning final-leg comeback. Winning skipper Dennis Conner advances to fifth America's Cup final.

28 Replacement umps locked out in Toronto as Ontario Labor Relations Board rules they can't work at SkyDome.

29 Detroit Pistons name TV analyst Doug Collins head coach and GM three days after Don Chaney and GM Billy McKinney were forced out.
Dennis Conner announces deal with PACT'95 syndicate to sail *Young America* instead of *Stars & Stripes* in America's Cup final against New Zealand.

MAY '95

Sun	Mon	Tue	Wed	Thu	Fri	Sat
	1	2	3	4	5	6
7	8	9	10	11	12	13
14	15	16	17	18	19	20
21	22	23	24	25	26	27
28	29	30	31			

Ancient Arenas

With a feeble 3-2 loss to New Jersey in the first round of the Stanley Cup Playoffs on May 14, the Boston Bruins closed the book on professional sports in **the Boston Garden**, one of the most storied structures in the history of sports in North America (see page 549).

Here is a list of the oldest active arenas in sports:

Baseball	**built**
Fenway Park, Boston	1912
Tiger Stadium, Detroit	1912

Pro Hockey
Montreal Forum, Montreal......................1924

Pro Basketball
L.A. Sports Arena, L.A. Clippers............1959

Pro Football
Soldier Field, Chicago...........................1924

College Football
IA-Dodd/Grant, Ga. Tech.....................1913
IAA-Franklin Field, Penn.......................1895

College Basketball
Matthews Arena, Northeastern................1909

The Longest Shots

MAY 6— When **Thunder Gulch**, a 24-1 shot, won the 121st Kentucky Derby, he became one of the biggest long-shots to win the run for the roses. Below are listed the biggest odds-beaters in Derby history:

Odds	Horse	Year
91-1	Donerail	1913
35-1	Gallahadion	1940
30-1	Proud Clarion	1967
30-1	Exterminator	1918
25-1	Dark Star	1953
24-1	Stone Street	1908
24-1	**Thunder Gulch**	1995
21-1	Gato Del Sol	1982
21-1	Bold Venture	1936
19-1	Zev	1923
18-1	Ferndinand	1986

1 Owners end 120-day lockout of major league umpires with five-year agreement that increases salary scale to $75,000 for a rookie to $225,000 for a 30-year veteran, plus postseason bonuses.

3 Pittsburgh forward Jaromir Jagr becomes first European to win scoring title as abbreviated NHL regular season ends. Jagr ties Eric Lindros of Philadelphia with 70 points but takes Art Ross Trophy with more goals (32 to 29). Lindros missed last two games with an eye injury.
N.Y. Islanders fire first-year coach Lorne Henning after finishing in NHL Atlantic Division cellar.

4 Gary Moeller resigns as head football coach at Michigan six days after a drunken outburst in a suburban Detroit restaurant led to his arrest for disorderly conduct and assault and battery. Moeller was 44-13-3 in five years with the Wolverines.

6 Thunder Gulch, a 24-1 longshot, wins 121st Kentucky Derby by 2¼ lengths. Favorite Timber Country finishes third.
America's Cup final begins off San Diego with *Black Magic* of New Zealand beating *Young America* by 2:45 in first race of best-of-nine series.
Oscar De La Hoya wins IBF lightweight title, stopping champion Rafael Ruelas in 2nd round at Las Vegas. Ruelas's brother Gabriel, the WBC jr. lightweight champ, TKO's Jimmy Garcia in 11th round. Garcia in critical condition after undergoing surgery for blood clot in brain.

7 American cyclist Lance Armstrong wins 12-day Tour DuPont, beating defending champion Viatcheslav Ekimov of Russia by two minutes after 1,130 miles.

8 Flying Dutchman Arie Luyendyk turns in fastest lap in history of Indianapolis Motor Speedway with clocking of 234.107 mph. Old record was 233.433 mph, set by Jim Crawford in 1992.

9 Dennis Erickson denies reports that he tried to cover up players' drug-testing results while head football coach at Miami-FL.

11 Chicago Bulls fined $25,000 for failing to clear Michael Jordan's uniform number change with NBA before May 10 playoff game against Orlando. Jordan, who switched from No. 45 back to his old No. 23, was fined $5,000.
High school center Kevin Garnett of Chicago's Farragut Academy declares for NBA draft. If selected, he would become the first high-schooler taken since Darryl Dawkins (Philadelphia 76ers) and Bill Willoughby (Atlanta Hawks) in 1975.

12 Golf commentator Ben Wright of CBS Sports is quoted in *The News Journal* of Wilmington, Del., as saying "lesbians in the sport hurt women's golf" and that women golfers are handicapped by having breasts.

13 *Black Magic* **completes rout** of *Young America*, as New Zealand sweeps America's Cup best-of-nine final in five straight races. Defeat is only the second for U.S. in 144-year history of race.
Recently-deposed heavyweight champions Michael Moorer and Lennox Lewis score easy victories in Sacramento doubleheader. Moorer decisions Melvin Foster and Lewis knocks out Lionel Butler in 5th round.
Winnipeg Jets accept conditional offer from Minneapolis businessman Richard Burke to buy club for $68 million.

14 Scott Brayton wins Indianapolis 500 pole position and $100,000 bonus with top qualifying speed of 231.604 mph. Front row will also include Lola-Menard teammate Arie Luyendyk and Scott Goodyear.

Agence France-Presse

The legs of driver **Stan Fox** dangle from his car after being hit by **Eddie Cheever** (No. 14) on the first lap of the Indianapolis 500. The car in the foreground is driven by Paul Tracy.

16 NHL reprimands referee Andy Van Hellemond for "a glaring error in judgement" in his decision to disallow a Quebec goal in the Nordiques' 3-2 overtime loss to the N.Y. Rangers in Game 4 of their Eastern Conference quarterfinal series.
Michigan appoints Lloyd Carr interim head football coach. Carr an was assistant head coach under Gary Moeller. (see May 4).

17 Canned in Boston: head coaches Chris Ford of the Celtics and Brian Sutter of the Bruins.
NBA announces Grant Hill of Detroit and Jason Kidd of Dallas are first co-Rookies of Year since Dave Cowens and Geoff Petrie in 1971.
NCAA adopts overtime for Div. I-A bowl games.

18 Orlando eliminates Chicago from NBA playoffs. Series defeat first for Jordan-led Bulls since 1990.
Walt Disney Co. buys 25 percent of California Angels and will assume role of managing general partner with an option to buy remainder of club after majority owner Gene Autry's death.
Winnipeg Jets sale to Minneapolis businessman Richard Burke called off as local Spirit of Manitoba group emerges with plan to buy team and build new arena for $111 million (Canadian funds).

19 Baseball owners and players reach two year agreement regarding welfare and pension contributions. Deal ensures All-Star Game will be played on July 11.
Golden St. names Rick Adelman head coach. Adelman led Portland to the NBA finals in 1990.
Boxer Jimmy Garcia dies 13 days after brain surgery following his TKO loss to WBC super featherweight champ Gabriel Ruelas.

20 Timber Country wins 120th Preakness Stakes. Kentucky Derby winner Thunder Gulch finishes third.

Evander Holyfield rallies for unanimous 10-round decision over Ray Mercer in first fight since losing heavyweight title to Michael Moorer on April 22, 1994.

21 Penske Racing team shut out of 33-car Indianapolis 500 field as two-time winners Al Unser Jr. and Emerson Fittipaldi fail in last ditch bids to qualify.
Golden St. wins No. 1 pick in NBA draft lottery. L.A. Clippers and Philadelphia round out top three.

23 San Antonio center David Robinson beats out NBA scoring champion Shaquille O'Neal of Orlando for MVP award. Robinson gets 73 of 105 first place votes.
Driver Nigel Mansell fired by McLaren Formula One racing team after lackluster Grand Prix performances at San Marino (10th) and Spain (DNF).

24 NFL owners adopt plan to build 67,500-seat, $200 million stadium for L.A. Raiders at Hollywood Park in Inglewood by 1997 season.

25 Quebec Nordiques sold to COMSAT Entertainment Group of Denver for $75 million (see Aug. 10).
Women's basketball stars Rebecca Lobo and Sheryl Swoopes head list of 11 players named to U.S. women's national team after seven-day trials.

26 Ken Griffey Jr. breaks right wrist when he hits Kingdome wall making circus catch against Baltimore. Mariners star expected to be out three months.

28 Canadian Jacques Villeneuve wins Indianapolis 500 when countryman Scott Goodyear is black-flagged for refusing to take penalty after passing pace car on a restart.

29 Pacers top Magic, 94-93, with a 16-foot Rik Smits buzzer-beater in a game that saw four lead changes in the final 13.3 seconds and evened their best-of-seven Eastern Conference finals at 2-2.

JUNE '95

Sun	Mon	Tue	Wed	Thu	Fri	Sat
				1	2	3
4	5	6	7	8	9	10
11	12	13	14	15	16	17
18	19	20	21	22	23	24
25	26	27	28	29	30	

Dubious Debuts

Both 1995-96 NBA expansion teams named head coaches this month when the Toronto Raptors hired Detroit assistant Brendan Malone (June 2) and the Vancouver Grizzlies tabbed Atlanta assistant Brian Winters (June 19).

Judging from the performances of first-year teams since 1961-62, both coaches are in for long seasons.

Season		Record
1961-62	Chicago Packers (Jim Pollard)	18-62
1966-67	Chicago Bulls (Red Kerr)	33-48
1967-68	San Diego Rockets (Jack McMahon)	15-67
1967-68	Seattle SuperSonics (Al Bianci)	23-59
1968-69	Milwaukee Bucks (Larry Costello)	27-55
1968-69	Phoenix Suns (Red Kerr)	16-66
1970-71	Buffalo Braves (Dolph Schayes)	22-60
1970-71	Cleveland Cavaliers (Bill Fitch)	15-67
1970-71	Portland Trail Blazers (Rolland Todd)	29-53
1974-75	New Orleans Jazz (three coaches)	23-59
1980-81	Dallas Mavericks (Dick Motta)	15-67
1988-89	Charlotte Hornets (Dick Harter)	20-62
1988-89	Miami Heat (Ron Rothstein)	15-67
1989-90	Orlando Magic (Matt Guokas)	18-64
1989-90	Minn. Timberwolves (Bill Musselman)	22-60

2 Chicago White Sox, trailing Cleveland by 10 games in AL Central, fire manager Gene Lamont and name 3B coach Terry Bevington to replace him.
Race car driver Stan Fox, who suffered severe head injuries in Indy 500 wall crash that involved six cars on the first lap, regains consciousness five days after race.

3 NL Triple Crown leader Matt Williams fouls ball off right foot, fracturing the second metatarsal bone. Williams will be sidelined for six weeks.
IBF orders heavyweight champion George Foreman to fight rematch with Axel Schulz or forfeit his title.

6 Major League Soccer commissioner Alan Rothenberg announces 10-team outdoor league will kick off inaugural 32-game regular season on April 6, 1996.

7 NBA Finals open in Orlando with Rockets beating Magic 120-118 in overtime. Magic blows three-point lead in last 10.5 seconds of regulation when Nick Anderson misses four straight free throws and Houston's Kenny Smith hits Finals' record seventh 3-pointer.

8 Hall of Fame outfielder Mickey Mantle, 63, is in critical condition at Dallas hospital after receiving liver transplant.
Florida Panthers fire head coach Roger Neilson.

10 D. Wayne Lukas saddles winner in record fifth straight Triple Crown race as favored Thunder Gulch takes Belmont Stakes. Lukas is first trainer to win Triple Crown with two different horses in same year.
Cal-State Fullerton wins third College World Series, beating USC, 11-5. Titans' CF/P Mark Kotsay hits 2 HRs, drives in 5 and closes door in relief.
Steffi Graf wins her fourth French Open singles title, defeating Arantxa Sanchez Vicario in three sets.

11 Thomas Muster wins French Open in straight sets over Michael Chang. The clay court specialist will pass up Wimbledon, where he has lost four times in the first round.

12 U.S. Supreme Court rejects appeal by 18 current and former NFL players who sought to nullify $200 million settlement of eight-year antitrust lawsuit. Ruling ends litigation that followed 24-day player strike in 1987 and allows for distribution of remaining $138 million in settlement funds.

13 NCAA fines Indiana University record $30,000 for basketball coach Bob Knight's obscenity-laden tirade against volunteer worker after Hoosiers first round tournament loss to Missouri.
Buffalo general manager John Muckler steps down after four years as head coach of the Sabres.

14 Houston sweeps Orlando to repeat as NBA champions. Hakeem Olajuwon wins second straight Finals' MVP award.

15 Pat Riley quits as New York coach with a year left on his contract. Knicks front office had offered him a five-year, $15 million extension but Riley wanted more control over personnel decisions.
Norway eliminates defending champion U.S. soccer team 1-0 in semifinals of Women's World Championship in Sweden.

16 Salt Lake City selected by International Olympic Committee as site for 2002 Winter Olympics. Utah capital receives 54 of 89 votes, becoming first city since Sapporo, Japan to win on first ballot.
Joe Torre fired as manager in St. Louis. Cardinals (20-27) name farm director Mike Jorgensen to replace him.

18 Corey Pavin wins first major golf championship with two-stroke victory over Greg Norman to capture U.S. Open at Shinnecock Hills CC in New York.
Norway wins Women's World Championship of soccer with 2-0 win over Germany in Stockholm.

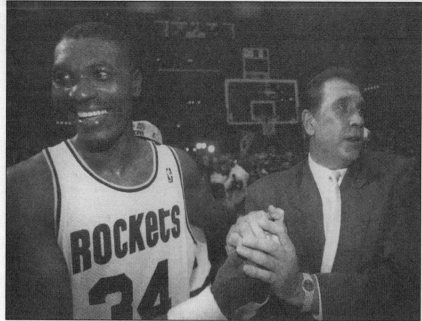

Wide World Photos

Two-time playoff MVP **Hakeem Olajuwon** (left) and coach **Rudy Tomjanovich** congratulate each other at midcourt following the Houston Rockets' four-game sweep of Orlando in the NBA Finals.

19 **Boston Celtics** general manager M.L. Carr names himself head coach.

Chicago Blackhawks coach Darryl Sutter resigns after three seasons, citing personal reasons.

20 **Penguins' captain** Mario Lemieux announces he will return for 60 to 70 games of 1995-96 NHL season after taking year off to rest ailing back and recover from radiation treatments for Hodgkin's disease.

21 **NBA and players union** reach new collective bargaining agreement. Six-year deal increases players' share of revenues to 57 percent and ups salary cap to nearly $24 million per team. Pact also includes a luxury tax and limits on rookie salaries.

NHL owners approve sale and transfer of Quebec Nordiques to Denver-based COMSAT Entertainment Group for $75 million.

22 **Seven fans suffer** minor injuries when two 30-pound acoustic tiles fall 50 feet from facing of fifth deck at Skydome during Blue Jays-Brewers game. Jays lose 9-0.

23 **Al Davis signs** letter of intent to return Raiders to Oakland after 13 years in Los Angeles. Homecoming deal worth $225 million and includes $100 million to modernize Oakland Coliseum, $10 million for a new practice facility and $54 million in relocation loans.

NBA contract on hold as players defer ratification of agreement negotiated by union leadership. Owners, meanwhile, approve deal 28-0.

Former NCAA chief Dick Schultz named executive director of U.S. Olympic Committee.

24 **New Jersey Devils** complete sweep of Detroit Red Wings to win Stanley Cup. Right wing Claude Lemieux is named Conn Smythe winner as MVP.

South Africa beats New Zealand, 15-12 in overtime, to win Rugby World Cup in Johannesburg.

First selections in NBA expansion draft are guards B.J. Armstrong of Chicago (by Toronto) and Greg Anthony of New York (by Vancouver).

25 **Betsy King qualifies** for LPGA Hall of Fame by winning the ShopRite Classic in Somers Point, N.J. Victory is the 30th of her career.

26 **U.S. Supreme Court** upholds random drug-testing program in Vernonia, Ore. The 6-to-3 decision allows public high school officials to require student-athletes to submit to random urinalysis as a condition of being allowed to play interscholastic sports.

28 **Golden St. makes** Maryland center Joe Smith first overall choice in NBA draft as sophomores are first four picks. Chicago high school star Kevin Garnett is taken fifth by Minnesota.

29 **New York files** tampering charges against Miami for comments by Heat executives on their interest on hiring Pat Riley. Riley quit as Knicks coach on June 15 but still has a year to go on his contract.

Heavyweight champion George Foreman relinquishes IBF title rather than accept organization's mandate that he give Germany's Axel Schulz a rematch.

Chicago Blackhawks name minor league coach Craig Hartsburg to replace Daryl Sutter.

30 **NBA moves to lock out** players and suspend operations until a new collective bargaining agreement is reached. Lockout is first labor action in league history.

Eddie Murray singles off Minnesota's Mike Trombley in 6th inning to become 20th player in baseball history to reach 3,000 hits.

JULY '95

Sun	Mon	Tue	Wed	Thu	Fri	Sat
						1
2	3	4	5	6	7	8
9	10	11	12	13	14	15
16	17	18	19	20	21	22
23 / 30	24 / 31	25	26	27	28	29

Leading Men

JULY 20— The New England Patriots made quarterback Drew Bledsoe the highest-paid player in NFL history, putting four quarterbacks at the top of pro football's financial heap.

NFL's Top 5 Salaries

	Avg.
Drew Bledsoe, Patriots	$6.0 mil.
Troy Aikman, Cowboys	5.8 mil.*
Steve Young, 49ers	5.0 mil.
John Elway, Broncos	4.6 mil.
Reggie White, Packers	4.2 mil.

*Aikman's 8-year, $50 million contract with Dallas includes some deferred money while Bledsoe's 7-year, $42 million deal with New England does not.

While You Were Gone

Before Monica Seles was stabbed in the back on April 30, 1993, at a tournament in Hamburg, Germany, she had won seven out of the last nine women's Grand Slam singles titles. Her attacker, an unemployed lathe operator and Steffi Graf fan named Gunter Parche said he did it so Graf could again be the top-ranked women's player in the world.

Since the assault, Graf has won six of 10 Grand Slam events and indeed regained her No. 1 rank.

Before The Stabbing

	1991	1992	1993
Aussie	Seles	Seles	Seles
French	Seles	Seles	—
Wimble	Graf	Graf	—
U.S	Seles	Seles	—

After the Stabbing

	1993	1994	1995
Aussie	—	Graf	Pierce
French	Graf	Vicario	Graf
Wimble	Graf	Martinez	Graf
U.S	Graf	Vicario	

(Graf beat Seles for 1995 U.S. Open title, see Sept. 9.)

1 **American Jeff Tarango** becomes first player in 109-year history of Wimbledon to be defaulted after quitting during a match. He storms off after accusing chair umpire Bruno Rebeuh of favoritism. Tarango's wife, Benedicte, chases down Rebeuh afterward and slaps his face.

2 **Toronto 2nd baseman** Roberto Alomar is removed from Blue Jays home game against Baltimore following death threat. Tricia Miller, 31, is apprehended with a loaded .22-caliber pistol and arrested at SkyDome hotel where Alomar lives.
   Tom Weiskopf wins U.S. Senior Open by four strokes over Jack Nicklaus. Nicklaus beat Weiskopf by a stroke for 1993 U.S. Senior Open.

3 **Indy Racing League** announces point system that will guarantee Indianapolis 500 starting spots to IRL's Top 25 drivers in 1996, leaving final eight berths up for grabs.

5 **New York Islanders** name former Boston Bruins coach and ESPN analyst Mike Milbury as sixth head coach.

6 **Philadelphia center** Eric Lindros wins Hart Trophy as MVP in NHL. Other major awards go to defenseman Paul Coffey (Norris), goaltender Dominik Hasek (Vezina), and rookie Peter Forsberg (Calder).
   Veteran NBA head coach Don Nelson gets N.Y. Knicks' job 5 months after resigning at Golden St. Nelson ranks 6th all-time in regular-season victories with 817.
   Boston acquires reliever Rick Aguilera (191 career saves) from Minnesota for pitching prospect Frank Rodriguez and player to be named later.

7 **Top-seeded Andre Agassi** bounced from Wimbledon in 4-set semifinal loss to Boris Becker. No. 2 seed Pete Sampras survives 5-set semi against Goran Ivanisevic.

8 **Steffi Graf wins** sixth Wimbledon singles title, beating Arantxa Sanchez Vicario 4-6, 6-1, 7-5. Third set features 32-point, 20-minute 11th game.
   Ottawa makes defenseman Bryan Berard only 3rd American to be first overall selection in NHL draft.

9 **Pete Sampras becomes** first U.S. man to win 3 straight Wimbledon singles titles, defeating Boris Becker 6-7 (5-7), 6-2, 6-4, 6-2.

11 **National League wins** 66th All-Star Game, beating AL, 3-2. Florida's Jeff Conine earns MVP nod with game-winning blast in 8th. National TV rating of 13.9 is lowest since the game moved to prime time in 1967.
   Baseball approves plan to speed up ballgames starting July 28. Average game time is currently 2 hours, 59 minutes in AL and 2:48 in NL.

12 **Noureddine Morceli** of Algeria betters his own world record in 1,500 meters by more than a second with clocking of 3:27.37 at Nice, France.

14 **Ramon Martinez throws** 22nd no-hitter in Dodgers history with 7-0 victory over Florida.
   U.S. National Team upsets Argentina 3-0 at Copa America soccer tournament in Uruguay. Victory is first ever by Yanks over Argentines.

16 **Annika Sorenstam** of Sweden becomes 6th foreigner to win U.S. Women's Open, with one stroke victory over Meg Mallon. Win is also her first on LPGA Tour.

17 **United States advances** to semifinals of Copa America, beating Mexico, 4-1, in penalty kicks after scoreless tie in regulation.
   Calgary Flames name former Minnesota and Quebec coach Pierre Page as their ninth head coach.

18 **Italian cyclist** Fabio Casartelli dies from head injuries after crashing into a concrete barrier at 55 mph on mountain descent during 15th stage of Tour de France. His death is 3rd since Tour began in 1903 and first since '67.

David Canon/Allsport

British Open champion **John Daly** barely has time to hug his wife Paulette before a streaker darts across the hallowed turf at St. Andrews. Daly beat Italy's Costantino Rocca in a four-hole playoff.

19 **Cincinnati Bengals** sign NFL's No. 1 draft pick Ki-Jana Carter to 7-year contract worth $19.2 million. Deal includes record $7.25 million rookie signing bonus.

20 **World Cup champion** Brazil blanks U.S. soccer team, 1-0, in Copa America semifinals. Brazilians will play Uruguay in championship match.
Patriots sign quarterback Drew Bledsoe to richest contract in NFL history. Seven-year, $42 million pact includes a record signing-bonus of $11.5 million.
Baseball Hall of Famers Duke Snider and Willie McCovey plead guilty to tax evasion charges stemming from unreported autograph and memorabilia income.
WTA announces Monica Seles will be co-ranked No. 1 with Steffi Graf when she returns to the tour on Aug. 14 at the Canadian Open in Toronto.

21 **Deion Sanders** traded by Cincinnati to S.F. Giants in eight-player deal that sends pitchers Mark Portugal and Dave Burba and outfielder Darren Lewis to Reds.
Raiders move back to Oakland approved by NFL owners at meeting in Chicago. Margin is 23-0 with 5 owners abstaining (including Raiders' Al Davis) and the 49ers and Cardinals leaving before the vote.

23 **John Daly wins** British Open at St. Andrews, capturing 2nd major championship by 4 strokes in 4-hole playoff with Costantino Rocca.
Miguel Induráin pedals to record fifth straight Tour de France. Spaniard joins Jacques Anquetil, Eddy Merckx and Bernard Hinault as only 5-time winners.
U.S. advances to Fed Cup final with 3-2 victory over France. Spain beats Germany, 3-2, in other semifinal.
Uruguay surprises Brazil to win Copa America soccer title in Montevideo. Hosts win 5-3 on penalty kicks after 1-1 tie in regulation.

25 **Houston Oilers sign** QB Steve McNair to 7-year, $28.4 million contract. Incentives could push value to a rookie-record $30 million.

26 **National Labor Relations Board** orders vote on decertification of NBA players union by late August or early September. Vote will be referendum on the collective bargaining agreement reached June 21.
Los Angeles Kings name New Jersey assistant Larry Robinson as their 18th head coach.

27 **St. Louis Blues trade** winger Brendan Shanahan to Hartford Whalers for defenseman Chris Pronger.

28 **N.Y. Yankees obtain** pitcher David Cone from Toronto for three minor leaguers and send Danny Tartabull to Oakland for Ruben Sierra.
N.Y. Mets trade Bobby Bonilla to Baltimore for minor league outfielders Alex Ochoa and Damon Buford.

29 **Monica Seles ends** 820-day exile from tennis, beating Martina Navratilova, 6-3, 6-2, in Atlantic City exhibition.
Apparent world record set in long jump as Cuba's Ivan Pedroso leaps 29 feet, 4¾ inches at altitude in Sestriere, Italy. Record is disallowed by IAAF on Aug. 4 after videotape reveals an Italian official blocking wind gauge.

31 **Trade deadline spurs** deals for pitching, as Colorado acquires Bret Saberhagen from the Mets, Seattle gets Andy Benes from the Padres, Los Angeles gets Kevin Tapani from the Twins and Cincinnati gets David Wells from the Tigers.
Walt Disney Co. announces acquisition of Capital Cities/ABC in deal valued at $19 billion. Merger brings together Disney, ABC Sports, ESPN, and ESPN2.

AUG '95

Sun	Mon	Tue	Wed	Thu	Fri	Sat
		1	2	3	4	5
6	7	8	9	10	11	12
13	14	15	16	17	18	19
20	21	22	23	24	25	26
27	28	29	30	31		

Tide's Out

AUG. 2— Alabama became the latest Southeastern Conference school to be penalized by the NCAA, receiving a 3-year probation in August. Seven of the league's 12 schools have been slapped with penalties since 1990.

	Program	Length
Alabama	football	1995-97
Auburn	football	1992-95
Tennessee	football	1992-93
Florida	football	1991-92
Kentucky	basketball	1990-92
S. Carolina	basketball	1991-92
Mississippi	football	1995-98

Crime Ring

AUG. 17— Former heavyweight champion Mike Tyson, who made his return to boxing after serving 2½ years on a rape conviction, leads a list of several well-known pugilists who have spent time in jail.

Heavyweights	Crime
Trevor Berbick	rape
Mitch Green	various offenses
Sonny Liston	armed robbery
Ron Lyle	armed robbery
Mike Tyson	rape

Bowled Over

AUG. 18— The Freedom Bowl became the ninth college bowl game to be canned since 1958, when it was officially discontinued.

Bowl	Years Played
Bluegrass	1958
Aviation	1961
Mercy	1961
Gotham	1961-62
Garden State	1978-81
Cherry	1984-85
Bluebonnet	1959-87
All-American	1977-90
Freedom	1984-95

1 Doctors treating Mickey Mantle, who received a liver transplant on June 8, reveal the Hall of Famer has cancer in his right lung.

2 NCAA places Alabama football on probation for three years following an investigation that found the Crimson Tide guilty of violations that included improper bank loans to a former player. 'Bama faces a one-year ban from post-season play (1995) and a cut in their overall scholarship limit for two seasons (1995-96).
Boston Bruins acquire left wing Kevin Stevens and center Shawn McEachern from Pittsburgh for forwards Bryan Smolinski and Glen Murray and a third-round draft choice.
Steffi Graf's father and manager, Peter, is arrested in Germany on suspicion of tax evasion. Prosecutors in Manheim stated that Graf failed to file a return for four years and paid only $5 million in taxes on her $25 million income.

3 Senate Judiciary committee votes, 9-8, to partially repeal baseball's anti-trust exemption. The measure now faces a vote by the full Senate, which is not expected to come until late in the year.
Jerry Jones, owner of the Dallas Cowboys, signs a controversial 10-year, $25 million deal with Pepsi to make it the official cola of Texas Stadium, despite the NFL's sponsorship agreement with Coca-Cola.

4 Darryl Strawberry returns to the major leagues after troubles with cocaine and tax evasion and goes 1-for-4 in his Yankee debut in a 4-1 win over Detroit.

5 Dale Earnhardt charges from the middle of the pack to edge Rusty Wallace and win NASCAR's second Brickyard 400 at Indianapolis Motor Speedway.
Tagliabue captures Harness Racing's Hambletonian after heavily-favored filly CR Kay Suzie breaks stride in the first heat and fails to qualify for the final.

6 Canadian sprinters Donovan Bailey (9.97) and Bruny Surin (10.03) finish 1-2 in the 100 meter finals of the World Track and Field Championships in Göteborg, Sweden.

7 NBC spends a record $1.27 billion and lands the much-desired broadcast rights to both the 2000 Summer Olympics in Sydney ($715 million) and the 2002 Winter Games in Salt Lake City ($555 million).
Great Britain's Jonathan Edwards breaks the world triple jump record and the 60-foot barrier with his leap of 60-¼, while Americans Gwen Torrence (100 meters) and Dan O'Brien (decathlon) win gold medals at the World Track and Field Championships in Göteborg, Sweden.
Owner Al Davis signs a 16-year agreement that brings the Raiders back to Oakland after 13 years.

8 NBA owners and the players union come to a tentative collective bargaining agreement, effectively ending the five-week old owners' lockout. The union will officially vote on the deal Aug. 30.

9 American Michael Johnson wins the 400 meter dash, running the second-fastest time (43.39) in history at the World Track and Field Championships in Göteborg, Sweden.

10 Los Angeles Dodgers are forced to forfeit a game against St. Louis in ninth inning after fans shower the field with souvenir baseballs and other debris. It is the first forfeit in major league baseball since 1979.
American Gwen Torrence is disqualified for running out of her lane after apparently winning the 200-meter dash with her time of 21.77 at the World Track and Field Championships in Göteborg, Sweden. Jamaica's Merlene Ottey is awarded the victory after a U.S. appeal is unanimously rejected.

Agence-France-Presse

Monica Seles returns a backhand shot to Kimberly Po on Aug. 15 in the first round of the du Maurier Open in Toronto. Seles won easily in her first WTA tournament match since being stabbed in 1993.

11 **Michael Johnson wins** the 200 meter dash in 19.79 seconds at Göteborg, Sweden and makes history, becoming the first man to record victories in both the 200 and 400 meter sprints at the World Track and Field Championships

Legendary harness driver Herve Filion surrenders to authorities and pleads not guilty to charges that he took part in a scheme to fix a race at Yonkers Raceway on June 26.

12 **Raiders make their return** to Oakland, beating the St. Louis Rams, 27-22, in an exhibition meeting between the recently-departed Los Angeles neighbors before an estimated 45,000 fans at Oakland Coliseum.

13 **Hall of Famer Mickey Mantle**, 63, dies after a short battle with lung cancer in Dallas.

Australia's Steve Elkington birdies the first hole of a sudden-death playoff to defeat Colin Montgomerie to win the PGA championship at Pacific Palisades, Calif.

Michael Johnson leads the U.S. 4x400 meter relay team to victory, winning his third gold medal on the final day of the World Track and Field Championships.

15 **Monica Seles returns** to the WTA Tour after a 28-month abscence following her 1993 stabbing with a first-round win (6-0, 6-3) over Kimberly Po at du Maurier Ltd. Open in Toronto.

Seattle Mariners activate all-star center fielder Ken Griffey following his 2½-month stay on the disabled list (broken wrist). The Mariners also get speedster Vince Coleman from Kansas City for a player to be named later.

18 **Cincinnati's Ki-Jana Carter**, the topl pick in the 1995 NFL Draft, ends his season before it begins when he tears the anterior cruciate ligament in his left knee on the third play of an exhibition against Detroit.

19 **Mike Tyson makes his return** to the ring after more than four years, beating Peter McNeeley on a first-round disqualification. McNeeley's trainer Vinny Vecchione ends the fight after 89 seconds, stepping into the ring when his fighter is knocked down for the second time.

Thunder Gulch, winner of the Kentucky Derby and Belmont Stakes, takes the $750,000 Travers Stakes at Saratoga, setting the stage for a horse of the year showdown with Cigar at the Breeders' Cup in October.

20 **Monica Seles** makes her return to professional tennis a successful one, defeating Amanda Coetzer, 6-0, 6-1 in the final of the du Maurier Ltd. Open in Toronto.

23 **Alabama AD Hootie Ingram** announces he will be voluntarily reassigned in the wake of the university football program's recent NCAA-imposed probation.

25 **Jim Brown and Paul Robeson** lead list of 13 inducted into new College Football Hall of Fame at South Bend, Ind.

26 **Michigan rallies** from 17-0 deficit to defeat Virginia, 18-17, on freshman quarterback Scott Dreisbach's 15-yard TD pass as time expires at Ann Arbor.

Taiwan dominates Spring, Texas, in the final of the Little League World Series as the 10-run mercy rule is invoked when they lead 17-3 after four innings.

27 **Tiger Woods wins** his second straight U.S. Amateur Golf Championship by two strokes at Newport, R.I.

28 **Nevada boxing comissioners** agree to release trainer Vinny Vecchione's $179,820 share of the purse from the Aug. 19 Mike Tyson-Peter McNeeley fight.

31 **New York Rangers acquire** left-wing Luc Robitaille and defenseman Ulf Samuelsson from Pittsburgh for defenseman Sergei Zubov and center Petr Nedved.

SEPT '95

Sun	Mon	Tue	Wed	Thu	Fri	Sat
					1	2
3	4	5	6	7	8	9
10	11	12	13	14	15	16
17	18	19	20	21	22	23
24	25	26	27	28	29	30

Dynamic Duos

Detroit infielders Alan Trammell and Lou Whitaker set an AL record when they played in their 1,915th game together on Sept. 13. Cubs Ron Santo and Billy Williams hold the all-time major league record with 2,015 games together. Here are some other great partnerships:

Doc Blanchard and Glenn Davis: the fullback and halfback were 3-time All-Americas with Army from 1944-46 and won back-to-back Heisman Trophies.

Eddie Arcaro & Ben A. Jones: the jockey and trainer won Triple Crowns with Whirlaway in 1941 and Citation in 1948.

Martina Navratilova & Pam Shriver: this doubles team won 79 titles together including 20 Grand Slams from 1981-92.

Magic Johnson & Kareem Abdul-Jabbar: the guard and center teamed to bring 5 NBA titles to Los Angeles in the 1980's.

Steve Young & Jerry Rice: the 49ers pair have connected on an NFL record 67 touchdowns.

John Madden & Pat Summerall: the broadcasting tandem entered their 15th season doing NFL games together in 1995 and remain the best in the business.

Ironmen of Sports

The longest consecutive-game playing streaks.

	Gm
baseball: Cal Ripken Jr.	2131+
(since 5/30/82)	
hockey: Doug Jarvis	964
(10/8/75-10/10/87)	
basketball: Randy Smith	906
(2/18/72-3/13/83)	
football: Jim Marshall	282
(9/25/60 to 12/16/79)	

1 **Miami Heat settle** tampering case with New York Knicks, giving them $1 million and a first round pick for the right to negotiate with coach Pat Riley.

NCAA modifies its anti-celebration rule to permit end zone prayers after it was challenged by Liberty University.

Doug Flutie, of the CFL's Calgary Stampeders, announces he will undergo surgery to repair a torn tendon in his throwing arm. The four-time league MVP is expected to miss rest of season.

2 **Pat Riley named** president and head coach of the Miami Heat for an estimated $15 million over five years.

Northwestern stuns Notre Dame, 17-15, at South Bend. The 28-point underdogs last beat the Irish in 1962 when Ara Parseghian coached the Wildcats.

Frank Bruno beats Oliver McCall to capture the WBC heavyweight title on a 12-round unanimous decision in Wembley, England.

4 **Dallas Cowboys owner** Jerry Jones continues to challenge NFL Properties, signing a seven-year sponsorship deal worth a reported $14 million with Nike to, among other things, build a theme park near Texas Stadium and outfit Cowboys coaches and players.

5 **Cal Ripken ties** Lou Gehrig's record of 2,130 consecutive games played. Ripken homers in Baltimore's 8-0 win over California.

6 **Cal Ripken plays** in his 2,131st consecutive game, breaking Lou Gehrig's 56-year-old record. Ripken receives a 22-minute standing ovation and goes 2-for-4, hitting a home run as the Orioles beat the Angels, 4-2.

Seattle wide-receiver Brian Blades is formally charged with manslaughter by Florida prosecutors in the July 5 shooting death of his cousin.

8 **Cleveland Indians clinch** the AL Central for their first title since 1954, beating Baltimore, 3-2 at Jacobs Field.

9 **Steffi Graf wins** her fourth U.S. Open singles title, beating Monica Seles 7-6 (8-6), 0-6, 6-3 in one hour, 52 minutes at Flushing Meadows, N.Y. It is Graf's third grand slam title of 1995.

10 **Pete Sampras defeats** top seed Andre Agassi, 6-4, 6-3, 4-6, 7-5 for his third U.S. Open singles title in two hours, 28 minutes at Flushing Meadows, N.Y. Sampras becomes only the fourth player to win three U.S. Opens and three Wimbledon singles titles.

Nebraska running back Lawrence Phillips is arrested for attacking girlfriend and dismissed from the team. Two days later, coach Tom Osborne hints he may allow his Heisman candidate to return.

Jacques Villeneuve finishes in 11th place but still clinches his first IndyCar PPG Cup Championship at the Bank of America 300 in Monterey, Calif. Rookie Gil de Ferran grabs his first IndyCar win.

11 **Dallas Cowboys sign** flamboyant cornerback Deion Sanders to a seven-year, $35 million deal that includes a record $13 million signing bonus.

Hockey Hall of Fame announces it will induct long-time Canadiens star defenseman Larry Robinson and former N.Y. Islanders general manager Bill Torrey among others at a Nov. 20 ceremony in Toronto.

12 **NBA Players resolve** lockout and put the upcoming NBA season back on schedule by rejecting a bid to decertify their union by a 226-134 vote.

Notre Dame football coach Lou Holtz undergoes 4½ hours of surgery at the Mayo Clinic to relieve pressure on his spinal cord. Holtz is expected to return to sidelines in three weeks.

13 **Atlanta beats** Colorado, 9-7, and Philadelphia loses to Montreal, 5-4, to give the Braves their first NL East title and their fourth division championship of the 1990's.

Agence-France-Presse

Deion Sanders (right) and Dallas owner **Jerry Jones** at their Sept. 11 news conference where it was announced that the Cowboys had made Sanders the highest-paid defensive player in NFL history.

NBA Player representatives, needing 21 votes to ratify the new collective bargaining agreement with the owners, approve the measure 25-2, clearing another hurdle to starting the 1995-96 season on schedule.

Harlem Globetrotters lose their first game in 24 years when they are defeated Kareem Abdul-Jabbar-led team of professionals 91-85 in Vienna, Austria. The Trotters had won 8,829 straight.

14 Don King staggers rival TVKO, striking a deal with the Fox network worth an estimated $10 million to televise the upcoming Mike Tyson-Buster Mathis Jr. fight on "free" TV. King scoops the competition, putting his fight directly up against TVKO's pay-per-view Evander Holyfield-Riddick Bowe bout on Nov. 4.

15 NBA owners vote 24-5 to approve the new collective bargaining agreement with the players, ending the lockout which began on July 1.

18 NFL Properites files a $300 million suit against Dallas Cowboys owner Jerry Jones in response to his recent marketing deals with Pepsi-Cola and Nike.

19 NCAA approves Baylor University's self-imposed television and postseason sanctions following revelations of academic fraud involving the men's basketball team.

20 Los Angeles Kings sold to Denver investor Philip Anschutz and LA developer Edward Roski. The bankrupt Kings went for an estimated $100 million in a deal that must be approved by U.S. Bankruptcy Court.

Detroit Pistons acquire forward Otis Thorpe from the Portland Trail Blazers for forward Billy Curley and the rights to guard Randolph Childress.

Jeff Tarango's three-week suspension is reduced to two weeks by the ATP Tour hearing an appeal about his outburst at Wimbledon. His $20,000 fine is upheld.

21 John Vander Wal of the Colorado Rockies sets the major league record for pinch hits in a season with his 26th, coming off the bench to homer in the seventh inning against San Francisco's Sergio Valdez.

24 Europe rallies on the final day of competition to upset the United States and win golf's 31st Ryder Cup, 14½ to 13½ at Oak Hill in Rochester, N.Y.

Todd Martin, replacing an injured Andre Agassi, beats Thomas Enqvist, 7-5, 7-5, 7-6 (6-2) as the U.S. defeats Sweden, 4-1, for a spot in the Davis Cup finals. The U.S. will face Russia, who rallies from 0-2 deficit to beat Germany, 3-2 for their finals berth.

28 Randy Myers, a pitcher for the Chicago Cubs, knocks down and pins a fan who charged the mound at Wrigley Field. John Murray, a 27-year-old bond trader, jumped onto the field and rushed Myers after the lefthander allowed a home run.

Seattle Mariners ownership sets an Oct. 30 deadline for a stadium agreement, saying they will sell the club if a deal for a new ballpark is not reached.

29 Jury begins deliberation in O.J. Simpson's double murder trial after hearing 8 months and 5 days of testimony.

NHL and NHLPA make a deal that allows league players to participate in 1998 Winter Olympics. The NHL will suspend play for 16 days for the Games at Nagano, Japan.

Hakeem Olajuwon cancels his pay-per-view battle with Shaquille O'Neal scheduled for Sept. 30 after the Rocket center aggravates a back injury in practice.

30 Cleveland slugger Albert Belle clubs his 50th home run of the season, becoming the first player in major-league history to hit 50 home runs and 50 doubles in the same season.

OCT '95

Sun	Mon	Tue	Wed	Thu	Fri	Sat
1	2	3	4	5	6	7
8	9	10	11	12	13	14
15	16	17	18	19	20	21
22	23	24	25	26	27	28
29	30	31				

Undertime

After 253 days in court, the jury in the O.J. Simpson trial deliberated for less than four hours before reaching a decision. Here are some events this year that took somewhat longer to decide.

	Time
World Chess Champ. Game 3	3:40
Ripken passes Gehrig night	3:57
World Series Game 3	4:09
NFL Draft (first round)	5:39
Ironman Triathalon	8:21

High Five

Eddie Robinson finished October with a combined NCAA Div. 1 and 1-AA football record 401 wins. Consider the Top 5:

	Yrs	Record
Eddie Robinson	53	401-147-15
Bear Bryant	38	323-85-17
Pop Warner	44	319-106-32
Amos A. Stagg	57	314-199-35
Joe Paterno	30	275-71-3

Expansion

The Rockies set an expansion record when they qualified for the playoffs in only their third year. (thank you, Wildcard). Below is a rundown of baseball's expansion teams with inaugural seasons and first postseasons.

	debut	1st post.	span
California	1961	1979	19
Texas	1961	—	35+
Houston	1962	1980	19
N.Y. Mets	1962	1969	8
Kansas City	1969	1976	8
Milwaukee	1969	1982	14
Montreal	1969	1981	13
San Diego	1969	1984	16
Seattle	1977	1995	19
Toronto	1977	1985	9
Colorado	1993	1995	3
Florida	1993	—	3+

1 **Colorado Rockies capture** the NL Wild Card berth when they come from behind to beat the San Francisco Giants, 10-9.
Jacksonville beats Houston, 17-16, in final minutes for its first NFL win.
Ernie Irvan returns to NASCAR, placing 6th at the Tyson Holly Farms 400.

2 **Seattle beats** California, 9-1, in their one-game playoff for the AL West title. Randy Johnson pitches a 3-hitter, lifting the M's to their first ever post-season.
Dennis Rodman takes his act to Chicago when he is traded from San Antonio for center Will Perdue.
Detroit manager Sparky Anderson, Montreal Expos' GM Kevin Malone and Padres GM Randy Smith's all announce their resignations.

3 **O.J. Simpson goes free** when a Los Angeles jury finds him not guilty of double murder.
Claude Lemeiux goes to Colorado, Steve Thomas heads to New Jersey and Wendel Clark is sent to the N.Y. Islanders in a three-way swap of NHL forwards.

4 **Golden Warriors sign** NBA No. 1 draft pick Joe Smith to a three-year deal worth $8.5 million.

5 **Monica Seles and Martina Navratilova** are among seven players named to the U.S. team by captain Billie Jean King for the Nov. 25 Fed Cup final against Spain.

6 **Cincinnati and Cleveland** complete sweeps of their divisional series opponents. The Reds club the Dodgers, 10-1, and the Indians pound Boston, 8-2.
Colorado Avalanche debuts in Denver with a 3-2 victory over Detroit as NHL season gets underway.
Cowboys owner Jerry Jones continues his NFL mutiny, inking a deal with American Express.

7 **Eddie Robinson wins** his milestone 400th game as football coach at Grambling State as the Tigers beat Miss. Valley St., 42-6.
Phoenix Suns trade all-star forward Dan Majerle, Antonio Lang, and a future first round pick to Cleveland for foward/center Hot Rod Williams.
Cigar wins his 11th straight race with a strong finish in the Jockey Club Gold Cup. Thunder Gulch suffered a career-ending foot fractured and finished fifth.
Atlanta Braves beat Colorado, 10-4, to advance to the NLCS against Cincinnati.

8 **Seattle Mariners rally** in the bottom of the eleventh to beat New York, 6-5, in Game 5 of their divisonal series, advancing to face Cleveland in the ALCS.
Miami quarterback Dan Marino breaks the NFL career completion mark, with his 3,687th pass in the Dolphins' 27-24 loss to Indianapolis. Marino injures his knee and hip and is expected to miss two weeks.

10 **Don King's** mail fraud trial starts with opening arguments in New York.

11 **CBS moves** the women's final of U.S. Open tennis championship to Sunday as part of their new broadcasting agreement. WTA Tour signs a three-year sponsorship deal with Corel, a software company.

12 **Wisconsin Legislature approves** the building of a new tax-funded $250 million stadium for the Milwaukee Brewers.

14 **Atlanta Braves beat** Cincinnati, 6-0, to complete their four-game sweep of the Reds in the NLCS and advance to the World Series.

15 **Carolina Panthers earn** the first win in franchise history, downing the New York Jets, 26-15.

16 **San Francisco quarterback** Steve Young to miss four weeks after injuring his throwing shoulder when he is sacked six times in the 49ers' 18-17 loss to the Colts.

Wide World Photos

O.J. Simpson, flanked by attorneys **F. Lee Bailey** (left) and **Johnnie Cochran**, reacts as he is found not guilty of murdering his ex-wife Nicole Brown Simpson and her friend Ron Goldman.

17 Cleveland beats Seattle, 4-0, in Game 6 of the ALCS, to claim their first AL Pennant since 1954 and advance to the World Series against Atlanta.
Montreal Canadiens clean house, firing head coach Jacques Demers and GM Serge Savard. The duo helped bring a Stanley Cup to Montreal in 1993.
Marv Levy, head coach of the 4-time AFC champion Buffalo Bills, is listed in good condition after undergoing surgery for prostate cancer.

18 Winnipeg Jets sold to American businessmen Richard Burke and Steven Gluckstern for $68 million and are most likely headed to Minnesota at end of season.

20 Baltimore fires manager Phil Regan after just one season as the Orioles skipper. Team GM Roland Hemond announces his resignation.

21 Greg Maddux pitches a 2-hitter to lead Atlanta to a 3-2 win over Cleveland in Game 1 of the World Series.
Mario Tremblay named head coach of the Montreal Canadiens and Rejean Houle is tabbed as the Habs new GM.

22 Michael Schumacher captures his second consecutive Formula One title with his win over Damon Hill in the Pacific Grand Prix at Aida, Japan.

23 Tony La Russa, longtime Oakland A's skipper, is named manager of St. Louis Cardinals.
Seattle's King County council votes, 10-3, to approve a plan to build a $320 million retractable dome for the Mariners.

24 Detroit trades Ray Sheppard to the San Jose Sharks for Igor Larionov.
Nebraska's Lawrence Phillips, suspended on Sept. 10 for assaulting ex-girlfriend, returns to practice.

Shaquille O'Neal is expected to miss 6-8 weeks after breaking his thumb in an exhibition win over Miami.
Virginia's Bruce Arena is named to coach the U.S. Olympic soccer team.

25 Anheuser Busch announces plans to sell the St. Louis Cardinals and Busch stadium.

26 Buck Showalter quits as manager of the New York Yankees, rejecting a two-year, $1.05 million deal.
Mario Lemieux notches his 500th career goal, scoring a hat trick in a 7-5 Pittsburgh win over the Islanders.

28 Atlanta Braves beat Cleveland, 1-0 in Game 6 for their first World Series title since 1957. Series MVP Tom Glavine and closer Mark Wohlers combine to throw a one-hitter. Dave Justice hits the game-winning homer off Jim Poole in the sixth inning.
Cigar's victory in the Classic highlights the Breeders' Cup at a soggy Belmont Park. Cigar covered the last quarter mile in an amazing 22⅗ seconds, putting a lock on his bid for Horse of the Year. Trainer D. Wayne Lukas finishes his incredible year on a down note when none of his horses finished first.

29 Jerry Rice surpasses James Lofton as the NFL career receiving yardage leader on a 13-yard pass from Elvis Grbac in San Francisco's 11-7 loss at New Orleans. Rice finished the day with 14,040 career yards.

30 Ray Knight is named manager of the Cincinnati Reds replacing Davey Johnson. Johnson is hired the same day as the Baltimore Orioles new skipper.

31 Ryne Sandberg ends his 16-month retirement, inking a one-year deal with the Cubs.
Mike Tyson cancels his Nov. 4 bout with Buster Mathis Jr. after breaking his thumb while sparring.

JANUARY

1 Major bowl games (2): Orange (Miami); Rose (Pasadena).
2 Fiesta bowl (Tempe).
6 NCAA Convention begins (Dallas).
6 NFL playoffs (2): AFC/NFC semifinal games.
7 NFL playoffs (2): AFC/NFC semifinal games.
14 NFL playoffs (2): AFC/NFC championship games.
15 Australian Open tennis begins (Melbourne).
21 NHL All-Star Game (Boston).
28 Super Bowl XXX (Tempe, Ariz.).

FEBRUARY

3 24 hours at Daytona begins (Daytona Beach).
4 NFL Pro Bowl (Honolulu).
9 Davis Cup first round begins (eight sites).
11 NBA All-Star Game (San Antonio).
12 Westminster Dog Show begins (New York).
14 Figure Skating Championships (San Jose).
18 Daytona 500 (Daytona Beach).

MARCH

1 World Cup '98 Soccer qualifying begins.
2 Iditarod Trail Sled Dog race begins (Anchorage to Nome).
8 NCAA Indoor Track & Field Championships begin (Indianapolis).
10 NFL Annual Meeting begins (W. Palm Beach, Fla.).
14 NCAA Men's Division I Basketball tournament begins.
15 NCAA Women's Division I Basketball tournament begins.
18 World Figure Skating Championships begin (Edmonton).
21 NCAA Women's Div. I Swimming & Diving finals begin. (Ann Arbor, Mich.)
25 LPGA Dinah Shore golf begins (Rancho Mirage, Calif.)
28 NCAA Div. I Hockey Final Four begins (Cincinnati).
28 NCAA Men's Div. I Swimming & Diving finals begin. (Austin, Tex.)
29 NCAA Women's Basketball Final Four begins (Charlotte).
30 NCAA Men's Basketball Final Four begins (E. Rutherford, N.J.).
31 Baseball Opening Night.*

APRIL

5 Davis Cup second round begins (four sites).
11 Masters golf begins (Augusta).
14 NHL regular season ends.
15 Boston Marathon.
15 World Gymnastics Team Champ. begin (San Juan, Puerto Rico).
16 NHL Stanley Cup playoffs begin.
20 NFL Draft begins (New York).
21 NBA regular season ends.
25 NBA playoffs begin.
25 PBA Tournament of Champions bowling begins (Lake Zurich, Ill.)
27 Women's Fed Cup tennis first round begins.
30 ABC Masters Bowling begins (Salt Lake City).

MAY

1 Tour DuPont cycling race begins (Eastern U.S.).
4 Kentucky Derby (Louisville).
9 LPGA McDonald's Championship golf begins (Wilmington, Del.).
18 Preakness Stakes (Baltimore).
25 NCAA Men's Div. I Lacrosse Final Four begins (College Park, Md.).
26 Indianapolis 500.
27 French Open tennis begins (Paris).
29 NCAA Men's and Women's Track & Field Championships begin (Eugene, Ore.).
30 U.S. Women's Open golf begins (Southern Pines, N.C.).
31 NCAA College World Series begins (Omaha, Neb.).

* tentative dates

JUNE

5 U.S. Gymnastics Championships begin (Knoxville).
6 PBA National Championship (Toledo).
8 Belmont Stakes (Elmont, N.Y.).
13 U.S. Open golf begins (Birmingham, Mich.).
14 U.S. Track & Field Olympic Trials (Atlanta).
15 24 Hours of Le Mans auto racing begins (France).
22 NHL Draft (St. Louis).
24 Wimbledon tennis begins.
26 NBA Draft (TBA).
29 Tour de France cycling begins (through July 21).

JULY

4 U.S. Senior Open golf begins (Cleveland).
9 Baseball All Star Game (Philadelphia).
13 Women's Fed Cup tennis semifinals begin.
18 British Open golf begins (Royal Lytham).
19 Summer Olympics begin (Atlanta).

AUGUST

3 Hambletonian harness race (E. Rutherford, N.J.).
4 Summer Olympics end (Atlanta).
8 PGA Championship golf begins (Louisville).
10 All-American Soap Box Derby (Akron, Ohio).
19 Little League World Series begins (Williamsport, Pa.).
22 LPGA du Maurier Classic begins (Canada).
24 Triathalon World Championship (Cleveland).
26 U.S. Open tennis begins (Flushing, N.Y.).

SEPTEMBER

1 NFL regular season opens.
20 Davis Cup tennis semifinal round begins (two sites).
20 Solheim Cup golf begins (Chepstow, Wales).
23 Women's Fed Cup tennis finals begins.
29 Baseball regular season ends.

OCTOBER

1 Baseball playoffs begin (first round).
4 U.S. Women's Open bowling.*
8 Baseball League Championship Series begin.
12 College Football: Florida State at Miami and Oklahoma vs. Texas (Dallas).
19 World Series begins (in city of AL champion).
26 Ironman Triathlon Championship (Hawaii).

NOVEMBER

2 Breeders' Cup horse racing (Toronto).
2 Nebraska at Oklahoma.*
3 New York City Marathon.
18 ATP Men's Tennis Championship begins (Frankfurt).
18 WTA Tour Tennis Championships begin (New York).
23 College Football: Auburn at Alabama, Michigan at Ohio St., USC at UCLA and Yale at Harvard.
29 Davis Cup tennis final begins.
30 College football: Florida at Florida State and Notre Dame at USC.

DECEMBER

6 National Finals Rodeo begins (Las Vegas).
6 NCAA Women's Soccer Final Four (Santa Clara, Calif.)
7 College Football: SEC Championship Game (Atlanta); Army vs. Navy (Philadelphia).
8 CFL Grey Cup (Hamilton, Ont.).
8 Heisman Trophy winner announced (New York).
13 NCAA Men's Soccer Final Four (Richmond, Va.).
21 NCAA Div. I-AA Football Championship (Huntington, W.Va.).
23 NFL regular season ends.
28 NFL Playoffs begin.

* tentative dates

Atlanta catcher **Javier Lopez** leaps into the waiting arms of relief pitcher **Mark Wohlers** after the final out of the 1995 World Series gave the Braves their first championship since 1957.

BASEBALL

Good Show

Atlanta defeats Cleveland in six games as the World Series returns and baseball temporarily forgets its labor miseries.

Here's a novel concept: The 28 major-league baseball clubs compete from April to October for the privilege of qualifying for postseason play. The best two teams meet in the World Series and the winner is treated to the mother of all parades.

Purists can only hope that baseball finds the idea appealing enough to make it an annual occurrence.

Well...it was just a thought.

Perhaps the 1995 World Series failed to restore baseball to its station as America's national pastime, but it certainly served as a comforting port between labor-related storms. The Atlanta Braves beat the Cleveland Indians in this politically incorrect Classic and did it in six games that were tense and, for the most part, entertaining. Some fans actually found it in their hearts to forgive owners and players for bringing the industry to its knees with their incessant bickering in 1994 and '95.

"I hope this will be a tremendous shot in the arm for the game," said Cleveland manager Mike Hargrove. If the respective parties can manage to pull it off again next year, they just might be on to something.

The 1995 season didn't begin in earnest until March 31, when the longest work stoppage in professional sports history ended with no settlement, no labor peace and no guarantee that Donald Fehr and Bud Selig

could prevent the same, sordid scenario from transpiring all over again.

Major-league players agreed to end their nearly eight-month-old strike when U.S. District Court Judge Sonia Sotomayor issued an injunction restoring the terms of the old collective bargaining agreement. Owners responded by abandoning their scheme to use replacement players and cleared the way for training camps to open in Florida and Arizona.

Bye-bye, Matt Stark. Hello, Don Mattingly.

The parties were unable to salvage the '95 season in its entirety, however. Owners and players agreed to reduce the schedule from 162 games to 144 with Opening Day pushed back to April 26.

For several clubs, it was a season to remember. The Indians, reborn as a powerhouse, won 100 games and finished 30 games ahead of Kansas City in the American League's Central Division. The Seattle Mariners beat California in a one-game playoff to win the AL West and earn their first post-season berth in 19 years. The Colorado Rockies christened a new ballpark, Coors Field, and set a record by making the playoffs in their third year of operation.

A handful of individuals also stood above the crowd. Albert Belle of Cleveland became the first player in history to accumulate 50 homers and 50 doubles in a season. Mo Vaughn, Belle's principal rival for the AL MVP Award, carried the Boston Red Sox on his broad shoulders for much of the summer.

Jerry Crasnick is the national baseball writer for *The Denver Post* and a columnist for *Baseball America*.

Atlanta owner **Ted Turner** (left) with pitcher and World Series Most Valuable Player **Tom Glavine** in the champions' locker room after eliminating Cleveland on Oct. 28. Glavine had two wins in the Series and gave up only two runs and four hits in 14 innings while striking out 11. Back in 1988, he was 7-17 for a Braves club that finished dead last in the NL West with record of 56-106.

Vaughn provided leadership in the clubhouse, and showed that caring and community service aren't outmoded concepts.

Tony Gwynn won his sixth National League batting title, despite playing two months with a fractured toe. Greg Maddux became the first pitcher since Walter Johnson to finish with an ERA below 1.80 in consecutive seasons. And Colorado's Blake Street Bombers— Dante Bichette, Andres Galarraga, Larry Walker and Vinny Castilla— became the first four teammates to hit 30 homers in a season since Steve Garvey, Ron Cey, Reggie Smith and Dusty Baker of the 1977 Los Angeles Dodgers.

The Dodgers' Ramon Martinez pitched the season's only no-hitter with a 7-0 victory over Florida. His brother Pedro carried a no-hitter into the 10th inning against San Diego before surrendering a hit to Bip Roberts.

On June 30, Eddie Murray, Cleveland's 39-year-old switch-hitting stoic, became only the 20th player to collect 3,000 hits, with a single (batting from the left side) off Minnesota's Mike Trombley. Even more amazing, Murray conducted a press conference after the game.

"It was nice," he said, "but 3,000 is just a number. It's not something that I focused on. I've never looked at personal goals that way." Next stop: join Hank Aaron and Willie Mays as the only players to get 3,000 hits and 500 home runs. By season's end, Murray had only 21 homers to go.

Mickey Mantle, the only switch-hitter to ever hit 500 HRs, died on Aug. 13 at age 63. Cancer killed him two months after a well-publicized liver transplant and an emotional July 11 press conference in Dallas in which the gaunt, former Yankee great atoned for wasting his talents and disregarding his health and announced plans to set up an national organ donor program.

At the All-Star Game in Arlington, Texas, the next night, the National League recorded only three hits, but made them count. Jeff Conine, Craig Biggio and Mike Piazza all hit home runs, and the Nationals beat the Americans, 3-2.

Conine hit a Steve Ontiveros slider 410 feet into the left-field stands to break a 2-2 tie in the eighth. He became the 10th player to homer in his first All-Star at bat and was named MVP of the game.

Baseball's most charismatic newcomer spoke very little English, but performed with an intensity and flair that transcended cultural barriers. Hideo Nomo, formerly of the Kintetsu Buffaloes of the Japanese major leagues, burst on the scene with his funky delivery and hellacious forkball. Dodger Stadium, once home to Fernando-mania, fell under the spell of Nomo-mania. And baseball fans in Nomo's native Japan woke up at 4:30 a.m. to catch his starts on television.

"I can't tell you how exciting it gets at Dodger Stadium when he takes a shutout into the seventh or eighth inning and everybody starts buzzing," said Piazza, the Dodgers' catcher. "I get pumped up myself. The game really needs him."

Amid so much negative fallout from the strike, the game needed all the goodwill it could muster. At times, the tenson between players and "fans" reached the boiling point. That anger manifested itself in a number of ways. Chili Davis angrily confronted a fan in Milwaukee. Chuck Knoblauch clashed with an autograph-seeker in a hotel lobby. The Pirates handed out souvenir pennants, and the crowd responded by littering the field with them. And in a gesture straight out of the Abby Hoffman playbook, three men wearing "Greed" T-shirts ran onto the field at a Mets game, threw $1 bills at the players, then stood at second base with their fists raised in protest.

The ugliest and most frightening display of unrest occurred in Detroit, when fans threw beer, whiskey and soda bottles, cigarette lighters, baseballs, batteries and a metal napkin dispenser at Cleveland center fielder Kenny Lofton.

While overall attendance plunged more than 20 percent— from an average per-game crowd of 31,611 in 1994 to 25,257 in '95— baseball's caretakers could at least take heart in the knowledge that the season ended on an upswing. With the new wild-card system in place, teams that might have been eliminated in August remained in the hunt in September.

Purists bashed the expanded playoff format for watering down the regular season. But the Rockies and Yankees, who qualified

Ripken Passes Gehrig, Takes Victory Lap

Cal Ripken entered the baseball record books as the only contestant in a 13-year marathon.

He reached the end of the line on a warm summer night in Baltimore and punctuated his journey with the simplest and most eloquent of gestures: A quarter-mile jog around Camden Yards, shaking hands all the way.

Ripken, the Baltimore Orioles' shortstop and blue-collar iron man, played in his 2,131st consecutive game on Sept. 6 to eclipse Lou Gehrig's standard for stamina. The crowd of 46,272 poured out its heart in appreciation and Ripken responded with the most dramatic victory lap since speed skater Dan Jansen circled the oval at the 1994 Winter Olympics with his infant daughter in his arms.

During a 22-minute, 15-second delay in the fifth inning, Ripken received eight curtain calls from the crowd. On his impromptu tour of the grounds, he shook hands with children, rambunctious teenagers, stunned security guards, the Oriole bullpen and the visiting Angels.

Ripken welcomed anyone with an outstretched palm and a love for the game into his circle of friends.

It might be overstating the case to say Ripken saved baseball. But he gave a sport with labor woes, attendance problems and a cloudy future a very welcome respite.

In a heartfelt postgame speech, Ripken paid tribute to four major influences in his life: His father, Cal Sr., his mother, Violet, his wife, Kelly, and former teammate Eddie Murray, "who showed me how to play this game, day in and day out."

Ripken acknowledged the contribution of Gehrig, whose record had stood for 56 years, four months and six days. A plaque at Yankee Stadium honors Gehrig as "a man, a gentleman and a great ballplayer, whose amazing record of 2,130 consecutive games should stand for all time."

The plaque, in place since July 4, 1941, has suddenly become obsolete.

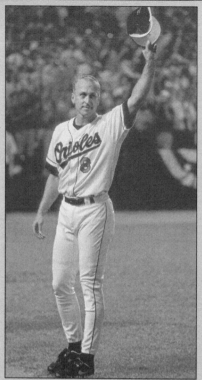

Cal Ripken Jr. waves to the capacity crowd at Camden Yards in Baltimore during one of eight curtain calls he received on Sept. 6, after officially breaking Lou Gehrig's consecutive game streak.

With Hall of Famers Joe DiMaggio and Brooks Robinson among the onlookers, Ripken spoke with a slight tremble in his voice.

"Tonight, I stand here overwhelmed, as my name is linked with the great and courageous Lou Gehrig," Ripken said. "I'm truly humbled to have our names spoken in the same breath.

"I know that if Lou Gehrig is looking down on tonight's activities, he isn't concerned about someone playing one more consecutive game than he did. Instead, he's viewing tonight as just another example of what is good and right about the great American game."

Ripken's pursuit of Gehrig evoked an innocence and earnestness that were missing in a period of bitterness and labor discord in baseball. For months, The Streak was a peripheral issue in negotiations between owners and players. Ripken vowed not to cross the picket line, but the union feared his streak might go down in flames if he failed to participate in replacement games.

Mercifully, that scenario failed to materialize. But as Ripken approached the record, a few unthinking observers suggested that he stop at 2,130 and settle for a tie as a tribute to Gehrig. His teammates sprang to his defense.

"What, Hank Aaron is supposed to stop at 714 [homers]?" wondered Brady Anderson. "Pete Rose is supposed to stop when he gets close to Ty Cobb? Whose record did Lou Gehrig break? Everett Scott? The nerve of the guy."

Ripken hit a home run in the tying game and went deep off California's Shawn Boskie in the record-breaker. His place in history then became secure when Orioles second baseman Manny Alexander caught a pop-up by Damion Easley to make Baltimore's 4-2 victory over California official. As Ripken ran off the field in the bottom of the fifth inning, the capacity crowd stood and erupted in applause.

John Tesh's theme song, "Day One," played over the loudspeakers. The Orioles dropped the banner on the B & O Warehouse in right field from 2130 to 2131. And Ripken's teammates burst out of the dugout to congratulate him.

Ripken celebrated the moment by tearing off his uniform and handing it to his wife. He embraced his two-year-old son Ryan and kissed his daughter Rachel, 5.

Ripken's iron man streak began on May 30, 1982. During his pursuit of Gehrig, he appeared in 19,231 out of a possible 19,395 innings.

The Baltimore players were in awe of Ripken's feat. Bobby Bonilla brought a camcorder to the park to record the proceedings. Mike Mussina called it "the most impressive athletic accomplishment in our lifetime."

President Clinton and Vice President Gore were in attendance. But it was left to Brooks Robinson, Baltimore's Hall of Fame third baseman and a local treasure, to put Ripken's status in perspective.

"People say I'm Mr. Oriole," Robinson said. "But they're wrong. Cal Ripken is Mr. Oriole."

as wild cards, liked the setup just fine. And the Royals, Cubs, Rangers and Astros enjoyed the fun while it lasted.

"The wild card has energized baseball," said Atlanta general manager John Schuerholz.

The first two rounds of the postseason were thrilling for fans, gut-wrenching for players, and murder on mascots.

Two members of the costumed crowd cavorted their way onto the disabled list in October. The Mariner Moose suffered a compound fracture of the right ankle when he crashed into the outfield wall at the Kingdome in a rollerblading mishap. Then Slider, the Moose's Cleveland counterpart, tore ligaments in his right knee when he took a plunge off the outfield wall at Jacobs Field.

"I always wanted to see Slider fall," said the Indians' Hargrove. "But I never wanted to see him hurt himself."

Amid the unpredictability and gore, baseball watchers could take solace in one development: The game's two best teams qualified for the World Series.

Cleveland won its first pennant in 41 years by sweeping Boston in the divisional playoffs, then beating Seattle four games to two in the Championship Series. Atlanta beat Colorado in the opening round before sweeping Cincinnati out of the NLCS.

The Indians, known for their offense, also cut a swath through the opposition with their pitching. They outscored Boston, 17-6, over three games, and held Vaughn and Jose Canseco hitless in 27 at bats.

Against the Mariners, the Cleveland staff compiled an ERA of 1.64. Seattle scored a total of 12 runs, the fewest-ever for a six-game ALCS, and managed to hit a measly .184 as a team. Tribe starters Orel Hershiser, Dennis Martinez, Charles Nagy and Ken Hill were superb.

Seattle entered the ALCS on an adrenaline rush. After Randy Johnson beat California in a one-game playoff to qualify for the postseason, the Mariners rode emotion, Johnson's left arm and the bat of third baseman Edgar Martinez to a dramatic first-round victory over New York.

The Mariners looked dead after losing the first two games in New York. To compound their anguish, they were pelted with everything from pretzels to batteries by a hostile Yankee Stadium crowd.

But the Mariners rallied to win three straight at home to close out the series and ruin Don Mattingly's first trip to the postseason. In Game 5, Martinez's double in the 11th inning scored Joey Cora and Ken Griffey Jr. to give Seattle a 6-5 victory.

The Kingdome, a mausoleum in the worst of times, suddenly crackled with energy. It was crammed with 57,000 fans chanting wildly and waving signs with the Mariners' new mantra: Refuse to Lose. The more the home team won, the more the fans pumped up the volume.

Martinez, the AL batting champion, hit .571 against New York. Reggie Jackson, now a member of the Yankees' front office, proclaimed him "the best hitter in baseball."

But the Indians figured out a way to stifle Martinez in the next round— limiting him to 2 hits in 23 at bats.

In the deciding game of the ALCS, Dennis Martinez beat Johnson, 4-0, for his first postseason victory. It had been a long wait: Martinez, 40, broke into the major leagues with Baltimore in 1976.

Hershiser, 2-0 with a 1.29 ERA, was named MVP of the LCS. But a strong case could have been made for Lofton. He hit .458, stole five bases, and chased down everything in center field.

Atlanta took a more methodical and less stressful route to the Series. The Braves figured to have their hands full in the NLCS against Cincinnati, which was fresh off an opening-round sweep of Los Angeles. But it was no contest.

The Atlanta staff— led by starters Maddux, Tom Glavine, John Smoltz and Steve Avery— compiled a 1.15 ERA against the Reds. The Braves made Cincinnati cleanup man Reggie Sanders look especially feeble. A .306 hitter during the regular season with 28 homers and 99 RBI, Sanders batted just .125 (2-for-16) and struck out 10 times.

The Braves won two extra-inning games in Cincinnati before bored, less-than-capacity crowds. Then they put the Reds away in Atlanta. Outfielder Mike Devereaux, acquired from the Chicago White Sox for depth in the stretch drive, hit .308 with five RBI to win the series MVP award.

The Braves received a tougher challenge from Colorado in the first round. The Rockies held the lead in all four games, but an overworked bullpen did them in each time.

Wide World Photos

Otto Greule/Allsport

Aces **Greg Maddux** of the Braves (left) and **Orel Hershiser** of the Indians opposed each other two times in the Series. Maddux hurled a two-hitter in Game 1 with Atlanta winning, 3-2. Hershiser then came back to take Game 5, giving up five hits and two runs in eight innings as Cleveland won 5-4.

"We gave them a fight for their money," Larry Walker said. "Go over there and ask them and they'll admit it. We just fell a little short."

The World Series was full of subplots. Atlanta hadn't won the Series since 1957 and Cleveland hadn't been here at all since 1954.

Belle, no media darling, tried to evict a TV reporter from the Indians' dugout. David Justice ripped Braves fans for their lack of enthusiasm. And Mike Hargrove experienced the thrill of being second-guessed on a nightly basis.

But the overriding theme was pitching. In a fitting climax to the festivities, Glavine and closer Mark Wohlers combined on the fifth one-hitter in World Series history to give the Braves a 1-0 victory and the city of Atlanta its first major league championship on the eve of hosting the Summer Olympics.

The Cleveland lineup, which terrorized American League pitching all year, hit .179

(35-for-195) against Atlanta. It was the eighth lowest batting average ever for a World Series participant— and the lowest since Oakland batted .177 against the Dodgers in 1988.

Maddux set the tone with a complete-game two-hitter to win the Series opener, 3-2. How dominant was the 29-year-old righthander? He allowed just four balls to leave the infield in nine innings. Both Cleveland hits— singles by Jim Thome and Lofton— went to the opposite field and both of their runs were unearned.

"That's as well-pitched a game as I've ever seen," Hargrove said. "He doesn't have overpowering stuff as far as throwing the ball by you. But he is everything you would want a pitcher to be."

Glavine wasn't quite as effective in Game 2, but he was good enough. He combined with three Atlanta relievers on a six-hit, 4-3 Braves victory. Javier Lopez broke open a tie game with a two-run homer in the sixth

Otto Greule/Allsport

After ripping into hometown fans for their luke-warm support, Braves outfielder **David Justice** became everybody's Georgia Peach when he homered in the bottom of the sixth inning for the only run Atlanta needed in Game 6.

inning and picked Manny Ramirez off first base with a snap throw to kill a Cleveland threat in the eighth.

After two straight losses in Atlanta, the Indians were starting to think negative thoughts. They began to hear comparisons to '54, when Al Rosen, Larry Doby and a pitching staff led by Bob Lemon, Early Wynn and Bob Feller won 111 games and then fell to the New York Giants in four straight.

To Cleveland's everlasting relief, there would be no sweep this time. In the marathon game of the Series, Murray drove in pinch-runner Alvaro Espinoza in the 11th inning of Game 3 to give the home team a 7-6 win before a frigid, frenzied crowd at Jacobs Field.

The game was deemed so crucial by Hargrove that he used his closer, Jose Mesa, for three innings and a whopping 51 pitches. Atlanta manager Bobby Cox did the same, calling on Wohlers for 2⅔ innings and 40 pitches.

Hargrove held a team meeting before the game and told his players not to worry about Games 4, 5 or 6. Just take them one at a time.

"Basically we said, 'If we're going to go down, let's go down fighting,'" said catcher Sandy Alomar Jr.

Atlanta's pitchers regained the upper hand in Game 4. Avery and three relievers combined on a six-hitter and the Braves won, 5-2. Luis Polonia broke a 1-1 tie with an RBI double off Hill, and Justice added a two-run single to give the Braves a cushion.

In Game 5, Hershiser was placed in the strange position of having to redeem himself. People questioned Hershiser's competitiveness after he voluntarily lifted himself because of mechanical problems in Game 1.

"It was the first time I've been involved in anything controversial in a World Series—maybe in my whole career," Hershiser said. "I felt it was important to go back out there and show the intensity and leadership I was brought here for."

Hershiser responded to the challenge. He outpitched Maddux, and the Indians sent the Series back to Atlanta with a 5-4 victory.

By the time Game 6 rolled around, off-field proceedings were generating as much news as the events between the lines. Belle issued an apology to NBC reporter Hannah Storm for verbally assaulting her in the dugout in Cleveland before Game 3. And the fans at Fulton County Stadium booed Justice on general principle. Among other things, Justice had said Atlanta fans "will probably burn our houses down if we don't win."

Justice won over his antagonists with one memorable swing— a sixth-inning homer to right off lefty Jim Poole for the game's only run. As it turned out, five of the six games in the Series were decided by a single run.

Glavine's arm stiffened after 109 pitches and eight innings, and he gave way to Wohlers. The Indians went down quietly in the ninth, with Carlos Baerga flying to Marquis Grissom in center field to end the game and the Series.

After the champagne stopped flowing in the Braves' clubhouse, Maddux— the perennial Cy Young Award winner— paid tribute to Glavine. "What you saw tonight was a great pitcher throw a great game at a great time," Maddux said.

For Atlanta and for baseball. ❐

THE 1996 SPORTS ALMANAC — INFORMATION PLEASE

BASEBALL STATISTICS

THE SEASON IN REVIEW
1995
LEAGUE LEADERS • POST SEASON

SEC A

PAGE 83

Final Major League Standings

Division champions (*) and Wild Card† winners are noted. Number of seasons listed after each manager refers to current tenure with club.

American League

East Division

	W	L	Pct	GB	Home	Road
* Boston	86	58	.597	—	42-30	44-28
† New York	79	65	.549	7	46-26	33-39
Baltimore	71	73	.493	15	36-36	35-37
Detroit	60	84	.417	26	35-37	25-47
Toronto	56	88	.389	30	29-43	27-45

1995 Managers: Bos— Kevin Kennedy (1st season); **NY**— Buck Showalter (4th); **Bal**— Phil Regan (1st); **Det**— Sparky Anderson (17th); **Tor**— Cito Gaston (7th)
1994 Standings: 1. New York (70-43); 2. Baltimore (63-49); 3. Toronto (55-60); 4. Boston (54-61); 5. Detroit (53-62).

Central Division

	W	L	Pct	GB	Home	Road
* Cleveland	100	44	.694	—	54-18	46-26
Kansas City	70	74	.486	30	35-37	35-37
Chicago	68	76	.472	32	38-34	30-42
Milwaukee	65	79	.451	35	33-39	32-40
Minnesota	56	88	.389	44	29-43	27-45

1995 Managers: Cle— Mike Hargrove (5th season); **KC**— Bob Boone (1st); **Chi**— replaced Gene Lamont (4th, 11-20) with Terry Bevington (57-56) on June 2; **Mil**— Phil Garner (4th); **Min**— Tom Kelly (10th).
1994 Standings: 1. Chicago (67-46); 2. Cleveland (66-47); 3. Kansas City (64-51); 4. Minnesota (53-60); 5. Milwaukee (53-62).

West Division

	W	L	Pct	GB	Home	Road
* Seattle	79	66	.545	—	46-27	33-39
California	78	67	.538	—	39-33	39-34
Texas	74	70	.514	4	41-31	33-39
Oakland	67	77	.465	11	38-34	29-43

1995 Managers: Sea— Lou Piniella (3rd); **Cal**— Marcel Lacheman (2nd); **Tex**— Johhny Oates (1st); **Oak**— Tony La Russa (10th).
1994 Standings: 1. Texas (52-62); 2. Oakland (51-63); 3. Seattle (49-63); 4. California (47-68).

National League

East Division

	W	L	Pct	GB	Home	Road
* Atlanta	90	54	.625	—	44-28	46-26
Philadelphia	69	75	.479	21	35-37	34-38
New York	69	75	.479	21	40-32	29-43
Florida	67	76	.469	22½	35-37	30-42
Montreal	66	78	.458	24	31-41	35-37

1995 Managers: Atl— Bobby Cox (6th season); **Phi**— Jim Fregosi (5th); **NY**— Dallas Green (3rd); **Fla**— Rene Lacheman (3rd); **Mon**— Felipe Alou (4th).
1994 Standings: 1. Montreal (74-40); 2. Atlanta (68-46); 3. New York (55-58); 4. Philadelphia (54-61); 5. Florida (51-64).

Central Division

	W	L	Pct	GB	Home	Road
* Cincinnati	85	59	.590	—	44-28	41-31
Houston	76	68	.528	9	36-36	40-32
Chicago	73	71	.507	12	34-38	39-33
St. Louis	62	81	.434	22½	39-33	23-48
Pittsburgh	58	86	.403	27	31-41	27-45

1995 Managers: Cin— Davey Johnson (3rd season); **Hou**— Terry Collins (2nd); **Chi**— Jim Riggleman (1st); **St.L**— replaced Joe Torre (6th, 20-27) with Mike Jorgensen (42-54) on June 16; **Pit**— Jim Leyland (10th).
1994 Standings: 1. Cincinnati (66-48); 2. Houston (66-49); 3. Pittsburgh (53-61) and St. Louis (53-61); 5. Chicago (49-64).

West Division

	W	L	Pct	GB	Home	Road
* Los Angeles	78	66	.542	—	39-33	39-33
† Colorado	77	67	.535	1	44-28	33-39
San Diego	70	74	.486	8	40-32	30-42
San Francisco	67	77	.465	11	37-35	30-42

1995 Managers: LA— Tommy Lasorda (20th season); **Col**— Don Baylor (3rd); **SD**— Bruce Bochy (1st); **SF**— Dusty Baker (3rd).
1994 Standings: 1. Los Angeles (58-56); 2. San Francisco (55-60); 3. Colorado (53-64); 4. San Diego (47-70).

Baseball's Eight Work Stoppages

Year	Work Stoppage	Games Missed	Length	Dates	Issue
1972	Strike	86	13 days	April 1-13	Pensions
1973	Lockout	0	17 days	February 8-25	Salary arbitration
1976	Lockout	0	17 days	March 1-17	Free agency
1980	Strike	0	8 days	April 1-8	Free-agent compensation
1981	Strike	712	50 days	June 12-July 31	Free-agent compensation
1985	Strike	0	2 days	August 6-7	Salary arbitration
1990	Lockout	0	32 days	Feb. 15-March 18	Salary arbitration and salary cap
1994	Strike	920	232 days	Aug. 12-March 31	Salary cap and revenue sharing

Wide World Photos

Albert Belle
HRs, RBIs, Runs, Doubles,
Total Bases

Wide World Photos

Edgar Martinez
Batting Average

Wide World Photos

Mike Mussina
Wins

Wide World Photos

Randy Johnson
ERA, Strikeouts
Winning Pct.

American League Leaders
Batting

	Bat	Gm	AB	R	H	Avg	TB	2B	3B	HR	RBI	BB	Int BB	SO	SB	Slg Pct	OB Pct
Edgar Martinez, Sea	R	145	511	121	182	.356	321	52	0	29	113	116	19	87	4	.628	.479
Chuck Knoblauch, Min	R	136	538	107	179	.333	262	34	8	11	63	78	3	95	46	.487	.424
Tim Salmon, Cal	R	143	537	111	177	.330	319	34	3	34	105	91	2	111	5	.594	.429
Wade Boggs, NY	L	126	460	76	149	.324	194	22	4	5	63	74	5	50	1	.422	.412
Eddie Murray, Cle	S	113	436	68	141	.323	225	21	0	21	82	39	5	65	5	.516	.375
B.J. Surhoff, Mil	L	117	415	72	133	.320	204	26	3	13	73	37	4	43	7	.492	.378
Chili Davis, Cal	S	119	424	81	135	.318	218	23	0	20	86	89	12	79	3	.514	.429
Albert Belle, Cle	R	143	546	121	173	.317	377	52	1	50	126	73	5	80	5	.690	.401
Carlos Baerga, Cle	S	135	557	87	175	.314	252	28	2	15	90	35	6	31	11	.452	.355
Kirby Puckett, Min	R	137	538	83	169	.314	277	39	0	23	99	56	18	89	3	.515	.379
Jim Thome, Cle	L	137	452	92	142	.314	252	29	3	25	73	97	3	113	4	.558	.438
Kevin Seitzer, Mil	R	132	492	56	153	.311	207	33	3	5	69	64	2	57	2	.421	.395
Wally Joyner, KC	L	131	465	69	144	.310	208	28	0	12	83	69	10	65	3	.447	.394
Kenny Lofton, Cle	L	118	481	93	149	.310	218	22	13	7	53	40	6	49	54	.453	.362
Rafael Palmeiro, Bal	L	143	554	89	172	.310	323	30	2	39	104	62	5	65	3	.583	.380

Home Runs

Belle, Cle	50
Buhner, Sea	40
F. Thomas, Chi	40
McGwire, Oak	39
Palmeiro, Bal	39
Vaughn, Bos	39
Gaetti, KC	35
Salmon, Cal	34
Edmonds, Cal	33
Tettleton, Tex	32

Runs Batted In

Belle, Cle	126
Vaughn, Bos	126
Buhner, Sea	121
E. Martinez, Sea	113
T. Martinez, Sea	111
F. Thomas, Chi	111
Edmonds, Cal	107
Ramirez, Cle	107
Salmon, Cal	105
Palmeiro, Bal	104

Hits

Johnson, Chi	186
E. Martinez, Sea	182
Knoblauch, Min	179
Salmon, Cal	177
Baerga, Cle	175
Nixon, Tex	174
Belle, Clev	173
B. Williams, NY	173
Palmeiro, Balt	172
Puckett, Minn	169

Stolen Bases

	SB	CS
Lofton, Cle	54	15
Goodwin, KC	50	18
Nixon, Tex	50	21
Knoblauch, Min	46	18
Coleman, KC-Sea	42	16
Johnson, Chi	40	6
Javier, Oak	36	5
Henderson, Oak	32	10
Alomar, Tor	30	3

Triples

Lofton, Cle	13
Johnson, Chi	12
Anderson, Bal	10
B. Williams, NY	9
Knoblauch, Min	8
Alomar, Tor	7
Vina, Mil	7
7 tied with 6 each.	

Doubles

Belle, Cle	52
E. Martinez, Sea	52
Puckett, Min	39
Valentin, Bos	37
T. Martinez, Sea	35
Knoblauch, Min	34
Salmon, Cal	34
Three tied with 33 each	

Runs

Belle, Cle	121
E. Martinez, Sea	121
Edmonds, Cal	120
Phillips, Cal	120
Salmon, Cal	111
Anderson, Bal	108
Valentin, Bos	108
Knoblauch, Min	107

Total Bases

Belle, Cle	377
Palmeiro, Bal	323
E. Martinez, Sea	321
Salmon, Cal	319
Vaughn, Bos	316
Edmonds, Cal	299
F. Thomas, Chi	299
T. Martinez, Sea	286

On Base Pct.

E. Martinez, Sea	.479
F. Thomas, Chi	.454
Thome, Cle	.438
Salmon, Cal	.429
Davis, Cal	.429
Knoblauch, Min	.424
Naehring, Bos	.415

Slugging Pct.

Belle, Cle	.690
E. Martinez, Sea	.628
F. Thomas, Chi	.606
Salmon, Cal	.594
Palmeiro, Bal	.583
Vaughn, Bos	.575
Buhner, Sea	.566

Walks

F. Thomas, Chi	136
E. Martinez, Sea	116
Phillips, Cal	113
Tettleton, Tex	107
Thome, Cle	97
Salmon, Cal	91
Davis, Cal	89

Strikeouts

Vaughn, Bos	150
Gil, Tex	147
Phillips, Cal	135
Edmonds, Cal	130
Blowers, Sea	128
Buhner, Sea	120
Fielder, Det	116

Pitching

	Arm	W	L	ERA	Gm	GS	CG	ShO	Sv	IP	H	R	ER	HR	HB	BB	SO	WP
Randy Johnson, Sea	L	18	2	2.48	30	30	6	3	0	214.1	159	65	59	12	6	65	294	5
Tim Wakefield, Bos	R	16	8	2.95	27	27	6	1	0	195.1	163	76	64	22	9	68	119	11
Dennis Martinez, Cle	R	12	5	3.08	28	28	3	2	0	187.0	174	71	64	17	12	46	99	3
Mike Mussina, Bal	L	19	9	3.29	32	32	7	4	0	221.2	187	86	81	24	1	50	158	2
Kenny Rogers, Tex	R	17	7	3.38	31	31	3	1	0	208.0	192	87	78	26	2	76	141	8
David Cone, NY	R	18	8	3.57	30	30	6	2	0	229.1	195	95	91	24	6	88	191	11
Kevin Brown, Bal	R	10	9	3.60	26	26	3	1	0	172.1	155	73	69	10	9	48	117	3
Jim Abbott, Cal	L	11	8	3.70	30	30	4	1	0	197.0	209	93	81	14	2	64	86	1
Mark Gubicza, KC	R	12	14	3.75	33	33	3	2	0	213.1	222	97	89	21	6	62	81	4
Al Leiter, Tor	L	11	11	3.64	28	28	2	1	0	183.0	162	80	77	15	6	108	153	14
Alex Fernandez, Chi	R	12	8	3.80	30	30	5	2	0	203.2	200	98	86	19	0	65	159	3
Jack McDowell, NY	R	15	10	3.93	30	30	8	2	0	217.2	210	106	95	25	5	78	157	9
Kevin Appier, KC	R	15	10	3.89	31	31	4	1	0	201.1	163	90	87	14	8	80	185	5
Orel Hershiser, Cle	R	16	6	3.87	26	26	1	1	0	167.1	151	76	73	21	5	51	111	3
Andy Pettitte*, NY	L	12	9	4.17	31	26	3	0	0	175.0	182	86	81	15	1	63	114	8

Wins

Mussina, Bal	19-9
Johnson, Sea	18-2
Cone, Tor-NY	18-8
Rogers, Tex	17-7
Hershiser, Cle	16-6
Nagy, Cle	16-6
Wakefield, Bos	16-8
Hanson, Bos	15-5
Langston, Cal	15-7
Appier, KC	15-10
McDowell, NY	15-10
Finley, Cal	15-12

Losses

Gross, Tex	9-15
Bere, Chi	8-15
Moore, Det	5-15
Gubicza, KC	12-14
Guzman, Tor	4-14
Hentgen, Tor	10-14
Radke, Min	11-14
Lira, Det	9-13
Belcher, Sea	10-12
Bones, Mil	10-12
Finley, Cal	15-12
Gordon, Kan	12-12

Saves

	Sv	BS
Mesa, Cle	46	2
Smith, Cal	37	4
Aguilera, Min-Bos	32	4
Hernandez, Chi	32	10
Montgomery, KC	31	7
Wetteland, NY	31	6
Eckersley, Oak	29	9
Fetters, Mil	22	5
Jones, Bal	22	3
Russell, Tex	20	4
Ayala, Sea	19	8

Strikeouts

Johnson, Sea	294
Stottlemyre, Oak	205
Finley, Cal	195
Cone, Tor-NY	191
Appier, KC	185
Fernandez, Chi	159
Mussina, Bal	158
McDowell, NY	157
Leiter, Tor	153
Pavlik, Tex	149
Langston, Cal	142
Rogers, Tex	140

Appearances

Orosco, Bal	65
McDowell, Tex	64
Ayala, Sea	63
Belinda, Bos	63
Wickman, NY	63
Four tied at 62 each.	

Innings

Cone, Tor-NY	229.1
Mussina, Bal	221.2
McDowell, NY	217.2
Johnson, Sea	214.1
Gubicza, KC	213.1
Stottlemyre, Oak	209.2
Rogers, Tex	208.0
Fernandez, Chi	203.2
Finley, Cal	203.0
Sparks, Mil	202.0

HRs Given Up

Radke, Min	32
Gross, Tex	27
Bones, Mil	26
Rogers, Tex	26
Stottlemyre, Oak	26
Darwin, Tor-Tex	25
McDowell, NY	25

Walks

Leiter, Tor	108
Bere, Chi	106
Alvarez, Chi	93
Finley, Cal	93
Hentgen, Tor	90
Pavlik, Tex	90
Two tied with 89 each.	

Complete Games

McDowell, NY	8
Erickson, Min-Bal	7
Mussina, Bal	7
Cone, Tor-NY	6
Johnson, Sea	6
Wakefield, Bos	6
Fernandez, Chi	5

Shutouts

Mussina, Bal	4
Johnson, Sea	3
Six tied with 2 each.	

Wild Pitches

Leiter, Tor	14
Bergman, Det	13
Finley, Cal	13
Cone, Tor-NY	11
Hurtado, Tor	11
Stottlemyre, Oak	11
Wakefield, Bos	11

Hit Batters

Clemens, Bos	14
Martinez, Cle	12
K. Brown, Bal	9
Wakefield, Bos	9
Appier, KC	8
Gross, Tex	8
Lira, Det	8
Roberson, Mil	8

Team Leaders

Batting

	Avg	AB	R	H	HR	RBI	SB
New York	.290	3986	670	1155	139	632	55
Cleveland	.291	5028	840	1461	207	803	132
Chicago	.280	5060	755	1417	146	712	110
Boston	.280	4997	791	1399	175	754	99
Minnesota	.279	5005	703	1398	120	662	105
California	.277	5019	801	1390	186	761	57
New York	.276	4947	749	1365	122	709	50
Seattle	.276	4996	796	1377	182	767	110
Milwaukee	.266	5000	740	1329	128	700	105
Texas	.265	4913	691	1304	138	651	90
Oakland	.264	4915	730	1296	169	694	112
Baltimore	.262	4837	704	1267	173	668	92
Kansas City	.260	4903	629	1275	119	578	120
Toronto	.260	5036	642	1309	140	613	75
Detroit	.247	4865	654	1204	159	619	73

Pitching

	ERA	W	Sv	CG	ShO	HR	BB	SO
Cleveland	3.83	100	50	10	10	135	445	926
Chicago	3.96	67	20	13	9	115	377	754
Baltimore	4.31	71	29	19	10	149	523	930
Boston	4.39	86	39	7	9	127	476	888
Kansas City	4.49	70	37	11	10	142	503	763
Seattle	4.50	79	39	9	8	149	591	1068
California	4.52	78	42	8	9	163	486	901
New York	4.56	79	35	18	5	159	535	908
Texas	4.66	74	34	14	4	152	514	838
Milwaukee	4.82	65	31	7	4	146	603	699
Chicago	4.85	68	36	12	4	164	617	892
Toronto	4.88	56	22	16	8	145	654	894
Oakland	4.93	67	34	8	4	153	556	890
Detroit	5.49	60	38	5	3	170	536	729
Minnesota	5.76	56	27	7	2	210	533	790

Wide World Photos

Tony Gwynn
Batting Average, Hits

Wide World Photos

Dante Bichette
Hrs, RBIs, Hits, Total Bases

Los Angeles Dodgers

Hideo Nomo
Strikeouts, Shutouts

Wide World Photos

Greg Maddux
ERA, Wins, Complete
Games, Shutouts, Win Pct.

National League Leaders
Batting

	Bat	Gm	AB	R	H	Avg	TB	2B	3B	HR	RBI	BB	Int BB	SO	SB	Slg Pct	OB Pct
Tony Gwynn, SD	L	135	535	82	197	.368	259	33	1	9	90	35	10	15	17	.484	.404
Mike Piazza, LA	R	112	434	82	150	.346	263	17	0	32	93	39	10	80	1	.606	.400
Dante Bichette, Col	R	139	579	102	197	.340	359	38	2	40	128	22	5	96	1	.620	.364
Derek Bell, Hou	R	112	452	63	151	.334	200	21	2	8	86	33	2	71	27	.442	.385
Mark Grace, Chi	L	143	552	97	180	.326	285	51	3	16	92	65	9	46	6	.516	.395
Barry Larkin, Cin	R	131	496	98	158	.319	244	29	6	15	66	61	2	49	51	.492	.394
Vinny Castilla, Col	R	139	527	82	163	.309	297	34	2	32	90	30	2	87	2	.564	.347
David Segui, NY-Mon	S	130	456	68	141	.309	210	25	4	12	90	40	5	47	2	.461	.367
Gregg Jefferies, Phi	S	114	480	69	147	.306	215	31	2	11	56	35	5	26	9	.448	.349
Larry Walker, Col	L	131	494	96	151	.306	300	31	5	36	101	49	13	72	16	.607	.381
Reggie Sanders, Cin	R	133	484	91	148	.306	280	36	6	28	99	69	4	122	36	.579	.397
Craig Biggio, Hou	R	141	553	123	167	.302	267	30	2	22	77	80	1	85	33	.483	.406
Ken Caminiti, SD	S	143	526	74	159	.302	270	33	0	26	94	69	8	94	12	.513	.380
Jeff Conine, Fla	R	133	483	72	146	.302	251	26	2	25	105	66	5	94	2	.520	.379
Brett Butler, NY-LA	L	129	513	78	154	.300	193	18	9	1	38	67	2	51	32	.376	.377
Orlando Merced, Pit	L	132	487	75	146	.300	228	29	4	15	83	52	9	74	7	.468	.365

Home Runs

Bichette, Col	40
Sosa, Chi	36
Walker, Col	36
Bonds, SF	33
Castilla, Col	32
Karros, LA	32
Piazza, LA	32
Galarraga, Col	31
Gant, Cin	29
R. Sanders, Cin	28

Runs Batted In

Bichette, Col	128
Sosa, Chi	119
Galarraga, Col	106
Conine, Fla	105
Karros, LA	105
Bonds, SF	104
Walker, Col	101
R. Sanders, Cin	99
Caminiti, SD	94
Two tied with 93 each.	

Hits

Bichette, Col	197
Gwynn, SD	197
Grace, Chi	180
Biggio, Hou	167
Finley, SD	167
McRae, Chi	167
Karros, LA	164
Castilla, Col	163
Caminiti, SD	159
Larkin, Cin	158

Stolen Bases

	SB	CS
Veras, Fla	56	21
Larkin, Cin	51	5
DeShields, LA	39	14
Finley, SD	36	12
R. Sanders, Cin	36	12
Young, Col	35	12
Sosa, Chi	34	7
Biggio, Hou	33	8
Two tied with 32 each.		

Triples

Butler, NY-LA	9
Young, Col	9
Finley, SD	8
Gonzalez, Hou -Chi	8
Sanders, Cin -SF	8
Six tied with 7 each.	

Doubles

Grace, Chi	51
Bichette, Col	38
McRae, Chi	38
R. Sanders, Cin	36
Cordero, Mtl	35
Lankford, Stl	35
Three tied with 34 each.	

Runs

Biggio, Hou	123
Bonds, SF	109
Finley, SD	104
Bichette, Col	102
Larkin, Cin	98
Grace, Chi	97
Walker, Col	96
McRae, Chi	92

Total Bases

Bichette, Col	359
Walker, Col	300
Castilla, Col	297
Karros, LA	295
Bonds, SF	292
Grace, Chi	285
Galarraga, Col	283
Sosa, Chi	282

On Base Pct.

Bonds, SF	.431
Biggio, Hou	.406
Gwynn, SD	.404
Weiss, Col	.403
Piazza, LA	.400
Bagwell, Hou	.399
R. Sanders, Cin	.397
Grace, Chi	.395

Slugging Pct.

Bichette, Col	.620
Walker, Col	.607
Piazza, LA	.606
R. Sanders, Cin	.579
Bonds, SF	.577
Castilla, Col	.564
Gant, Cin	.554

Walks

Bonds, SF	120
Weiss, Col	98
Biggio, Hou	80
Veras, Fla	80
Bagwell, Hou	79
Gant, Cin	74

Strikeouts

Galarraga, Col	146
Sosa, Chi	134
R. Sanders, Cin	122
Karros, LA	115
Brogna, NY	111
Three tied with 110 each.	

Pitching

	Arm	W	L	ERA	Gm	GS	CG	ShO	Sv	IP	H	R	ER	HR	HB	BB	SO	WP
Greg Maddux, Atl............	R	19	2	1.63	28	28	10	3	0	209.2	147	39	38	8	4	23	181	1
Hideo Nomo*, L.A.	R	13	6	2.54	28	28	4	3	0	191.1	124	63	54	14	5	78	236	19
Andy Ashby, S.D.............	R	12	10	2.94	31	31	2	2	0	192.2	180	79	63	17	11	62	149	7
Ismael Valdes, L.A.	L	13	11	3.05	33	27	6	2	1	197.2	168	76	67	17	1	51	150	1
Joey Hamilton, S.D.........	R	6	9	3.08	31	30	2	2	0	204.1	189	89	70	17	11	56	123	2
Tom Glavine, Atl............	L	16	7	3.08	29	29	3	1	0	198.2	182	76	68	9	5	66	127	3
John Smoltz, Atl...............	R	12	7	3.18	29	29	2	1	0	192.2	166	76	68	15	4	72	193	13
Frank Castillo, Chi............	R	11	10	3.21	29	29	2	2	0	188.0	179	75	67	22	6	52	135	3
Pete Schourek, Cin..........	L	18	7	3.22	29	29	2	0	0	190.1	158	72	68	17	8	45	160	1
Jaime Navarro, Chi.........	R	14	6	3.28	29	29	1	1	0	200.1	194	79	73	19	3	56	128	1
Mike Hampton, Hou	L	9	8	3.35	24	24	0	0	0	150.2	141	73	56	13	4	49	115	3
Denny Neagle, Pit	L	13	8	3.43	31	31	5	1	0	209.2	221	91	80	20	3	45	150	6
Pat Rapp, Fla	R	14	7	3.44	28	28	3	2	0	167.1	158	72	64	10	7	76	102	7
John Smiley, Cin............	L	12	5	3.46	28	27	1	0	0	176.2	173	72	68	11	4	39	124	5
Shane Reynolds, Hou ......R	R	10	11	3.47	30	30	3	2	0	189.1	196	87	73	15	2	37	175	7

Four tied with 11 each.

Wins

Maddux, Atl...............19-2
Schourek, Cin.............18-7
R. Martinez, LA 17-7
Glavine, Atl.................16-7
Navarro, Chi...............14-6
Rapp, Fla 14-7
P. Martinez, Mon.......14-10
Burkett, Fla 14-14
Nomo, LA 13-6
Neagle, Pit................13-8
Valdes, LA.................13-11
Fassero, Mon...........13-14

Losses

Wagner, Pit.................5-16
Candiotti, LA 7-14
Fassero, Mon............13-14
Burkett, Fla 14-14
Mulholland, SF 5-13
Avery, Atl...................7-13
Trachsel, Chi 7-13
Kile, Hou...................4-12
Leiter, SF 10-12
Quantrill, Phi 11-12

Four tied with 11 each.

Saves

	SV	BS
Franco, NY 30	30	6
Myers, Chi................38	38	7
Henke, St.L 36	36	2
Beck, SF 33	33	10
Slocumb, Phi............32	32	6
Worrell, LA...............32	32	4
Hoffman, SD..............31	31	8
Rojas, Mon...............30	30	9
Franco, NY...............29	29	7
Brantley, Cin.............28	28	5
Wohlers, Atl..............25	25	4

Strikeouts

Nomo, LA 236
Smoltz, Atl...................193
Maddux, Atl.................181
Reynolds, Hou 175
P. Martinez, Mon 174
Fassero, Mon..............164
Schourek, Cin.............160
Ashby, SD...................150
Neagle, Pit.................150
Valdes, LA...................150
Foster, Chi..................146
Drabek, Hou...............143

Appearances

Leskanic, Col 76
Veres, Hou 72
Reed, Col 71
Perez, Fla 69
Holmes, Col 68
Jones, Hou 68
Perez, Chi 68

Innings

Maddux, Atl 209.2
Neagle, Pitt 209.2
Martinez, LA............206.1
Hamilton, SD 204.1
Navarro, Chi............200.1
Glavine, Atl..............198.2
Valdes, LA................197.2
B. Jones, NY.............195.2
Leiter, SF 195.2
Martinez, Mon..........194.2

HRs Given Up

Foster, Chi.................32
Mulholland, SF 25
Trachsel, Chi..............25
Bautista, SF................24
Milacki, NY 23
Avery, Atl..................22
Burkett, Fla................22
Castillo, Chi...............22

Walks

R. Martinez, LA...........81
Nomo, LA...................78
Rapp, Fla...................76
Trachsel, Chi..............76
Mimbs, Phi................75
Fassero, Mon.............74
Kile, Hou...................73

Complete Games

Maddux, Atl 10
Leiter, SF 7
Valdes, LA 6
Neagle, Pit 5
Burkett, Fla 4
Green, Phi 4
R. Martinez, LA.............4
Nomo, LA....................4

Shutouts

Maddux, Atl 3
Nomo, LA......................3
10 tied with 2 each.

Wild Pitches

Nomo, LA 19
Carrasco, Cin 15
Smoltz, Atl.................13
Borland, Phi...............12
Ericks, Pit...................11
Klye, Hou...................11
Three tied with 9 each.

Hit Batters

Leiter, SF 17
Kile, Hou 12
Ashby, SD 11
Hamilton, SD 11
P. Martinez, Mon 11
Saberhagen, NY-Col......10
Three tied with 9 each.

Team Leaders

Batting

	Avg	AB	R	H	HR	RBI	SB
Colorado........	.282	4994	785	1406	200	749	125
Houston.........	.275	5097	747	1403	109	694	176
San Diego	.272	4950	668	1345	116	618	124
Cincinnati......	.270	4903	747	1326	161	694	190
New York.......	.267	4958	657	1323	125	617	58
Chicago	.265	4963	693	1315	158	648	105
Los Angeles...	.264	4942	634	1300	140	593	127
Philadelphia...	.262	4950	615	1296	94	576	72
Florida	.262	4886	673	1278	144	636	131
Pittsburgh......	.259	4937	629	1281	125	587	84
Montreal........	.259	4905	621	1268	118	572	120
San Francisco	.253	4971	652	1256	152	610	138
Atlanta	.250	4814	645	1202	168	618	73
St. Louis.........	.247	4779	563	1182	107	533	79

Pitching

	ERA	W	Sv	CG	ShO	HR	BB	SO
Atlanta..........	3.44	90	34	18	11	107	436	1087
Los Angeles...	3.66	78	37	16	11	125	462	1060
New York	3.88	69	36	9	9	133	401	901
Cincinnati......	4.03	85	38	8	10	131	424	903
Houston.........	4.06	76	32	6	8	118	460	1056
St. Louis........	4.09	62	38	4	6	135	445	842
Montreal........	4.11	66	42	7	9	128	416	950
Chicago	4.13	73	45	6	12	162	518	926
San Diego.......	4.13	70	35	6	10	142	512	1047
Philadelphia...	4.21	69	41	8	8	134	538	980
Florida	4.27	67	29	12	7	139	562	994
Pittsburgh......	4.70	58	29	11	7	130	477	871
San Francisco.	4.86	67	34	12	5	173	505	801
Colorado........	4.97	77	43	1	1	160	512	891

1995 All-Star Game

66th Baseball All-Star Game. **Date:** July 11 at The Ballpark in Arlington, Texas; **Managers:** Felipe Alou, Montreal (NL) and Buck Showalter, New York (AL); **Most Valuable Player:** PH Jeff Conine (NL): 1-for-1, game-winning pinch hit HR in 8th.

National League

	AB	R	H	BI	BB	SO	Avg
Len Dykstra, Phi, cf	2	0	0	0	1	0	.000
Sammy Sosa, Chi, cf	1	0	0	0	0	0	.000
Tony Gwynn, SD, rf	2	0	0	0	0	0	.000
Reggie Sanders, Cin, rf	1	0	0	0	0	1	.000
Raul Mondesi, Mon, rf	1	0	0	0	0	0	.000
Barry Bonds, SF, lf	3	0	0	0	0	1	.000
Dante Bichette, Col, lf	1	0	0	0	0	1	.000
Mike Piazza, LA, c	3	1	1	1	0	0	.333
Darren Daulton, Phi, c	0	0	0	0	0	0	—
Fred McGriff, Atl, 1b	3	0	0	0	0	2	.000
Mark Grace, Chi, 1b	0	0	0	0	0	0	—
Ron Gant, Cin, dh	2	0	0	0	1	0	.000
Jeff Conine, Fla, dh	1	1	1	1	0	0	1.000
Barry Larkin, Cin, ss	3	0	0	0	0	0	.000
Jose Offerman, LA, ss	0	0	0	0	0	0	—
Vinny Castilla, Col, 3b	2	0	0	0	0	1	.000
Bobby Bonilla, NY, 3b	1	0	0	0	0	1	.000
Craig Biggio, Hou, 2b	2	1	1	1	0	0	.500
Mickey Morandini, Phi, 2b	1	0	0	0	0	1	.000
TOTALS	29	3	3	3	1	9	.103

American League

	AB	R	H	BI	BB	SO	Avg
Kenny Lofton, Cle, cf	3	0	0	0	0	1	.000
Jim Edmonds, Cal, cf	1	0	0	0	0	1	.000
Carlos Baerga, Cle, 2b	3	1	3	0	0	0	1.000
Roberto Alomar, Tor, 2b	1	0	0	0	0	0	.000
Edgar Martinez, Sea, dh	3	0	0	0	0	1	.000
Tino Martinez, Sea, dh	1	0	1	0	0	0	1.000
Frank Thomas, Chi, 1b	2	1	1	2	0	0	.500
Mo Vaughn, Bos, 1b	2	0	0	0	0	2	.000
Albert Belle, Cle, lf	3	0	0	0	0	1	.000
Paul O'Neill, NY, lf	1	0	0	0	0	0	.000
Cal Ripken, Bal, ss	3	0	2	0	0	0	.667
Gary DiSarcina, Cal, ss	1	0	0	0	0	0	.000
Wade Boggs, NY, 3b	2	0	1	0	0	0	.500
Kevin Seitzer, Mil, 3b	2	0	0	0	0	0	.000
Kirby Puckett, Min, rf	2	0	0	0	0	1	.000
Manny Ramirez, Cle, rf	0	0	0	0	2	0	—
Ivan Rodriguez, Tex, c	3	0	0	0	0	1	.000
Mike Stanley, NY, c	1	0	0	0	0	0	.000
TOTALS	34	2	8	2	2	8	.235

	1	2	3	4	5	6	7	8	9	R	H	E
National League	0	0	0	0	0	1	1	1	0 —	3	3	0
American League	0	0	0	2	0	0	0	0	0 —	2	8	0

LOB— American 7, National 0. **2B**— Baerga (AL). **HR**— Thomas (off Smiley), Piazza (off Rogers), Conine (off Ontiveros), Biggio (off D. Martinez). **SB**— Alomar, AL. **CS**— Dykstra, NL; Baerga, AL. **SF**— Rodriguez, AL. **GIDP**— none **DP**— none.

NL Pitching	IP	H	R	ER	BB	SO	NP
Hideo Nomo, LA	2.0	1	0	0	0	3	25
John Smiley, Cin	2.0	2	2	2	0	0	24
Tyler Green, Phi	1.0	2	0	0	0	1	12
Denny Neagle, Pit	1.0	1	0	0	0	1	17
Carlos Perez, Mon	0.1	1	0	0	1	0	12
Heathcliff Slocumb, Phi (W)	1.0	1	0	0	0	1	15
Tom Henke, St.L	0.2	0	0	0	0	1	9
Randy Myers, Chi (S)	1.0	0	0	0	1	0	20
TOTALS	9.0	8	2	2	2	7	134

AL Pitching	IP	H	R	ER	BB	SO	NP
Randy Johnson, Sea	2.0	0	0	0	1	3	27
Kevin Appier, KC	2.0	0	0	0	0	1	19
Dennis Martinez, Cle	2.0	1	1	1	0	0	20
Kenny Rogers, Tex	1.0	1	1	1	0	2	21
Steve Ontiveros, Oak (L)	0.2	1	1	1	0	0	8
David Wells, Det	0.1	0	0	0	0	1	4
Jose Mesa, Cle	1.0	0	0	0	0	1	8
TOTALS	9.0	3	3	3	1	5	107

Umpires— Durwood Merrill (AL) plate; Charlie Williams (NL) 1b; Al Clark (AL) 2b; Mike Winters (NL) 3b; Ted Hendry (AL) lf; Ed Rapuano (NL) rf. **Attendance**— 50,920. **Time**— 2:40. **TV Rating**— 13.9/25 share (ABC).

Home Attendance

Overall 1995 regular season attendance in Major League Baseball was 50,464,375 in 1,998 games for an average per game crowd of 25,257; numbers in parentheses indicate ranking in 1994; HD indicates home dates.

American League

Based on tickets sold.

	Attendance	HD	Average
1 Baltimore (2)	3,098,475	72	43,034
2 Cleveland (4)	2,842,725	71	40,038
3 Toronto (1)	2,826,483	72	39,257
4 Boston (7)	2,164,378	72	30,061
5 Texas (3)	1,985,910	72	27,582
6 California (10)	1,748,680	72	24,287
7 New York (6)	1,705,257	70	24,361
8 Seattle (8)	1,640,992	73	22,479
9 Chicago (5)	1,609,773	71	22,673
10 Kansas City (9)	1,232,969	70	17,614
11 Detroit (14)	1,180,979	71	16,634
12 Oakland (13)	1,174,310	71	16,540
13 Milwaukee (12)	1,087,560	71	15,318
14 Minnesota (11)	1,057,667	72	14,690
AL Totals	25,356,158	1000	25,356

National League

Based on tickets sold.

	Attendance	HD	Average
1 Colorado (1)	3,390,037	72	47,084
2 Los Angeles (3)	2,766,251	72	38,420
3 Atlanta (2)	2,561,831	72	35,581
4 Philadelphia (4)	2,043,588	71	28,783
5 Chicago (7)	1,918,265	71	27,018
6 Cincinnati (8)	1,843,649	71	25,967
7 St. Louis (5)	1,748,709	72	24,288
8 Florida (6)	1,700,466	71	24,292
9 Houston (10)	1,363,801	71	19,208
10 Montreal (11)	1,309,618	72	18,189
11 New York (12)	1,273,183	71	17,932
12 San Francisco (9)	1,241,497	72	17,243
13 San Diego (14)	1,041,805	72	14,673
14 Pittsburgh (13)	905,517	72	12,936
NL Totals	25,108,217	998	25,153

AL Team by Team Statistics

At least 120 at bats or 25 innings pitched during the regular season, unless otherwise indicated. Players who competed for more than one AL team are listed with their final club. Players traded from the NL are listed with AL team only if they have 120 AB or 25 IP. Note that (*) indicates rookie and PTBN indicates player to be named.

Baltimore Orioles

Batting (135 AB)	Avg	AB	R	H	HR	RBI	SB
Bobby Bonilla	.333	237	47	79	10	46	0
Rafael Palmeiro	.310	554	89	172	39	104	3
Harold Baines	.299	385	60	115	24	63	0
Curtis Goodwin*	.263	289	40	76	1	24	22
Cal Ripken	.262	550	71	144	17	88	0
Brady Anderson	.262	554	108	145	16	64	26
Jeff Manto	.256	254	31	65	17	38	0
Chris Hoiles	.250	352	53	88	19	58	1
Jeff Huson	.248	161	24	40	1	19	5
Kevin Bass	.244	295	32	72	5	32	8
Jeffrey Hammonds	.242	178	18	43	4	23	4
Bret Barberie	.241	237	32	57	2	25	3
Manny Alexander*	.236	242	35	57	3	23	11

Acquired: P Erickson from Min. for P Scott Klingenbeck (July 7). OF Bonilla from N.Y. Mets for OF Damon Buford (July 28).
Claimed: P Oquist off waivers (Aug. 16).

Pitching (40 IP)	ERA	W-L	Gm	IP	BB	SO
Jesse Orosco	3.26	2-4	65	49.2	27	58
Mike Mussina	3.29	19-9	32	221.2	50	158
Kevin Brown	3.60	10-9	26	172.1	48	117
Ben McDonald	4.16	3-6	14	80.0	38	62
Mike Oquist	4.17	2-1	27	54.0	41	27
Rick Krivda*	4.54	2-7	13	75.1	25	53
Scott Erickson	4.81	13-10	32	196.1	67	106
Doug Jones	5.01	0-4	52	46.2	16	42
Jamie Moyer	5.21	8-6	27	115.2	30	65
Armando Benitez*	5.66	1-5	44	47.2	37	56
Arthur Rhodes	6.21	2-5	19	75.1	48	77

Saves: Jones (22); Orosco (3); Benitez (2); Lee and Clark (1).
Complete games: Erickson and Mussina (7); Brown (3); McDonald and Krivda (1). **Shutouts:** Mussina (4); Erickson (2); Brown (1).

Boston Red Sox

Batting (135 AB)	Avg	AB	R	H	HR	RBI	SB
Troy O'Leary	.308	399	60	123	10	49	5
Tim Naehring	.307	433	61	133	10	57	0
Jose Canseco	.306	396	64	121	24	81	4
Mo Vaughn	.300	550	98	165	39	126	11
John Valentin	.298	520	108	155	27	102	20
Mike Greenwell	.297	481	67	143	15	76	9
Willie McGee	.285	200	32	57	2	15	5
Lee Tinsley	.284	341	61	97	7	41	18
Luis Alicea	.270	419	64	113	6	44	13
Bill Haselman	.243	152	22	37	5	23	0
Mike Macfarlane	.225	364	45	82	15	51	2

Acquired: P Aguilera from Min. for P Frank Rodriguez (July 6).
Signed: Free agent P Maddux (May 30); Free agent OF McGee (June 6).

Pitching (40 IP)	ERA	W-L	Gm	IP	BB	SO
Rick Aguilera	2.60	3-3	52	55.1	13	52
Tim Wakefield	2.95	16-8	27	195.1	68	119
Stan Belinda	3.10	8-1	63	69.2	28	57
Mike Maddux	3.61	4-1	36	89.2	15	65
Rheal Cormier	4.07	7-5	48	115.0	31	69
Joe Hudson	4.11	0-1	39	46.0	23	29
Roger Clemens	4.18	10-5	23	140.0	60	132
Eric Hanson	4.24	15-5	29	186.2	59	139
Vaughn Eshelman	4.85	6-3	23	81.2	36	41
Zane Smith	5.61	8-8	24	110.2	23	47

Saves: Aguilera (32); Belinda (10); Ryan (7); Maddux and Hudson (1). **Complete games:** Wakefield (6); Hanson (1). **Shutouts:** Hanson and Wakefield (1).

California Angels

Batting (120 AB)	Avg	AB	R	H	HR	RBI	SB
Tim Salmon	.330	537	111	177	34	105	5
Garret Anderson*	.321	374	50	120	16	69	6
Chili Davis	.318	424	81	135	20	86	3
Gary DiSarcina	.307	362	61	111	5	41	7
Jim Edmonds	.290	558	120	162	33	107	1
J.T. Snow	.289	544	80	157	24	102	2
Mike Aldrete	.268	149	19	40	4	24	0
Rex Hudler	.265	223	30	59	6	27	12
Tony Phillips	.261	525	119	137	27	61	13
Greg Myers	.260	273	35	71	9	38	0
Jorge Fabregas	.247	227	24	56	1	22	0
Jose Lind	.236	140	9	33	0	7	0
Spike Owen	.229	218	17	50	1	28	3
Damion Easley	.216	357	35	77	4	35	5

Acquired: P Habyan from St.L for OF Mark Sweeney and PTBN (July 8); P Abbott and P Tim Fortugno from Chi. AL for P Andrew Lorraine (July 27); P Springer from Phi. for OF Kevin Flora (Aug. 15); OF Aldrete from Oak. for OF Demond Smith (Aug. 25).

Pitching (40 IP)	ERA	W-L	Gm	IP	BB	SO
Bob Patterson	4.07	2-3	47	42.0	15	30
Troy Percival*	1.95	3-2	62	74.0	26	94
Bob Patterson	3.04	5-2	62	53.1	13	41
Lee Smith	3.47	0-5	52	49.1	25	43
Jim Abbott	3.70	11-8	30	197.0	64	86
Mike James*	3.88	3-0	46	55.2	26	36
Chuck Finley	4.21	15-12	32	203.0	93	195
Mark Langston	4.63	15-7	31	200.1	64	142
Mike Butcher	4.73	6-1	40	51.1	31	29
Mike Harkey	5.44	8-9	26	127.1	47	56
Shawn Boskie	5.64	7-7	20	111.2	25	51
Brian Anderson	5.87	6-8	18	99.2	30	45
Mike Bielecki	5.97	4-6	22	75.1	31	45
Russ Springer	6.10	1-2	19	51.2	25	38

Saves: Smith (37); Percival (3); James (1). **Complete games:** Abbott (4), Finley and Langston (2); Harkey, Boskie and Anderson (1). **Shutouts:** Abbott, Finley and Langston (1).

Chicago White Sox

Batting (120 AB)	Avg	AB	R	H	HR	RBI	SB
Frank Thomas	.353	399	106	141	38	101	2
Julio Franco	.319	433	72	138	20	98	8
Darrin Jackson	.312	369	43	115	10	51	7
Ozzie Guillen	.288	365	46	105	1	39	5
Robin Ventura	.282	401	57	113	18	78	3
Mike Lavalliere	.281	139	6	39	1	24	0
Lance Johnson	.277	412	56	114	3	54	26
Joey Cora	.276	312	55	86	2	30	8
Norberto Martin*	.275	131	19	36	1	16	4
Tim Raines	.266	384	80	102	10	52	13
Ron Karkovice	.213	207	33	44	11	29	0

Pitching (40 IP)	ERA	W-L	Gm	IP	BB	SO
Jose DeLeon	3.36	3-2	42	67.0	31	67
Alex Fernandez	3.80	12-8	30	203.2	65	159
Roberto Hernandez	3.92	3-7	60	59.2	28	84
Dave Righetti	4.20	3-2	10	49.1	18	29
Wilson Alvarez	4.32	8-11	29	175.0	93	118
Kirk McCaskill	4.89	6-4	55	81.0	33	50
Brian Keyser*	4.97	5-6	23	92.1	27	48
Jose DeLeon	5.19	5-3	38	67.2	28	53
Jason Bere	7.19	8-15	27	137.2	106	110

Saves: Hernandez (32); McCaskill (2); Scott Radinsky (1). **Complete games:** Fernandez (5); Alvarez (3); Bere (1). **Shutouts:** Fernandez (2).

Cleveland Indians

Batting (120 AB)

	Avg	AB	R	H	HR	RBI	SB
Albert Belle	.357	412	90	147	36	101	9
Eddie Murray	.323	436	68	141	21	82	5
Albert Belle	.317	546	121	173	50	126	5
Herb Perry*	.315	162	23	51	3	23	1
Carlos Baerga	.314	557	87	175	15	90	11
Jim Thome	.314	452	92	142	25	73	4
Kenny Lofton	.310	481	93	149	7	53	54
Manny Ramirez	.308	484	85	149	31	107	6
Sandy Alomar	.300	203	32	61	10	35	3
Omar Vizquel	.266	542	87	144	6	56	29
Tony Peña	.262	263	25	69	5	28	1
Alvaro Espinoza	.252	143	15	36	2	17	0
Paul Sorrento	.235	323	50	76	25	79	1
Wayne Kirby	.207	188	29	39	1	14	10

Acquired: P Hill from St.L for IF David Bell (July 27).

Pitching (25 IP)

	ERA	W-L	Gm	IP	BB	SO
Jose Mesa	1.13	3-0	62	64.0	17	58
Julian Tavarez*	2.44	10-2	57	85.0	21	68
Eric Plunk	2.67	6-2	56	64.0	27	71
Paul Assenmacher	2.82	6-2	47	38.1	12	40
Chad Ogea*	3.05	8-3	20	106.1	29	57
Dennis Martinez	3.08	12-5	28	187.0	46	99
Jim Poole	3.75	3-3	42	50.1	17	41
Orel Hershiser	3.87	16-6	26	167.1	51	111
Ken Hill	3.98	4-1	12	74.2	32	48
Charles Nagy	4.55	16-6	29	178.0	61	139
Mark Clark	5.27	9-7	22	124.2	42	68
Jason Grimsley	6.09	0-0	15	34.0	32	25
Bud Black	6.85	4-2	11	47.1	16	34

Saves: Mesa (46); Plunk (2); Alan Embree (1). **Complete games:** Martinez (3); Nagy and Clark (2); Hershiser, Ogea, and Hill (1). **Shutouts:** Martinez (2); Nagy and Hershiser (1).

Detroit Tigers

Batting (120 AB)

	Avg	AB	R	H	HR	RBI	SB
Lou Whitaker*	.293	249	36	73	14	44	4
Travis Fryman	.275	567	79	156	15	81	4
Alan Trammell	.269	223	28	60	2	23	3
Chad Curtis	.268	586	96	157	21	67	27
Kirk Gibson	.260	227	37	59	9	35	9
John Flaherty	.243	354	39	86	11	40	0
Cecil Fielder	.243	494	70	120	31	82	0
Scott Fletcher	.231	182	19	42	1	17	1
Ron Tingley	.226	124	14	28	4	18	0
Bobby Higginson*	.224	410	61	92	14	43	6
Chris Gomez	.223	431	49	96	11	50	4
Danny Bautista	.203	271	28	55	7	27	4

Traded: P Groom to Fla. for PTBN (Aug. 7).

Pitching (25 IP)

	ERA	W-L	Gm	IP	BB	SO
David Wells	3.04	10-3	18	130.1	37	83
Mike Christopher*	3.82	4-0	36	61.1	14	34
Felipe Lira*	4.31	9-13	37	146.1	56	89
John Doherty	5.10	5-9	48	113.0	37	46
Sean Bergman	5.12	7-10	28	135.1	67	86
Brian Bohanon	5.54	1-1	52	105.2	41	63
Jose Lima*	6.11	3-9	15	73.2	18	37
Joe Boever	6.39	5-7	60	98.2	44	71
Brian Maxcy*	6.88	4-5	41	52.1	31	20
C.J. Nitkowski*	7.09	1-4	11	39.1	20	13
Buddy Groom	7.52	1-3	23	40.2	26	23
Mike Moore	7.53	5-15	25	132.2	68	64

Saves: Doherty (6); Dwayne Henry (5); Boever (3); Bohanon, Christopher and Ben Blomdahl (1). **Complete games:** Bergman (1). **Shutouts:** Bergman (1).

Kansas City Royals

Batting (135 AB)

	Avg	AB	R	H	HR	RBI	SB
Keith Lockhart*	.321	274	41	88	6	33	8
Wally Joyner	.310	465	69	144	12	83	3
Tom Goodwin	.288	480	72	138	4	28	50
Johnny Damon*	.282	188	32	53	3	23	7
Juan Samuel	.263	205	31	54	12	39	6
Gary Gaetti	.261	514	76	134	35	96	3
Michael Tucker*	.260	177	23	46	4	17	2
Greg Gagne	.256	430	58	110	6	49	3
Brent Mayne	.251	307	23	77	1	27	0
Jon Nunnally*	.244	303	51	74	14	42	6
David Howard	.243	255	23	62	0	19	6
Pat Borders	.231	143	14	33	4	13	0
Bob Hamelin	.168	208	20	35	7	25	0

Traded: C Borders to Hou. for PTBN (Aug. 11).
Acquired: P Fleming from Sea. for P Bob Milacki (July 7); IF Samuel from Det. for C Phil Hiatt (Sept. 8).

Pitching (40 IP)

	ERA	W-L	Gm	IP	BB	SO
Jeff Montgomery	3.43	2-3	54	65.2	25	49
Chris Haney	3.65	3-4	16	81.1	33	31
Mark Gubicza	3.75	12-14	33	213.1	62	81
Kevin Appier	3.89	15-10	31	201.1	80	185
Mike Magnante	4.23	1-1	28	44.2	16	28
Hipolito Pichardo	4.36	8-4	44	64.0	30	43
Tom Gordon	4.43	12-12	31	189.0	89	119
Rusty Meacham	4.98	4-3	49	59.2	19	30
Jason Jacome	5.36	4-6	15	84.0	21	39
Billy Brewer	5.56	2-4	48	45.1	20	31
Melvin Bunch*	5.63	1-3	13	40.0	14	19
Dave Fleming	5.96	1-6	25	80.0	53	40
Dilson Torres*	6.09	1-2	24	44.1	17	28

Saves: Montgomery (31); Olson (3), Meacham (2); Pichardo and Jim Converse (1). **Complete games:** Appier (4), Gubicza (3), Gordon (2), Jacome (1). **Shutouts:** Gubicza (2); Appier (1).

Milwaukee Brewers

Batting (120 AB)

	Avg	AB	R	H	HR	RBI	SB
B.J. Surhoff	.320	415	72	133	13	73	7
John Jaha	.313	316	59	99	20	65	2
Kevin Seitzer	.311	492	56	153	5	69	2
Dave Nilsson	.278	263	41	73	12	53	2
Jeff Cirillo	.277	328	57	91	9	39	7
Joe Oliver	.273	337	43	92	12	51	2
Darryl Hamilton	.271	398	54	108	5	44	11
Fernando Vina	.257	288	46	74	3	29	6
Matt Mieske	.251	267	42	67	12	48	2
David Hulse	.251	339	46	85	3	47	15
Mike Matheny	.247	166	13	41	0	21	2
Greg Vaughn	.224	392	67	88	17	59	10
Jose Valentin	.219	338	62	74	11	49	16
Pat Listach	.219	334	35	73	0	25	13

Pitching (34 IP)

	ERA	W-L	Gm	IP	BB	SO
Mark Kiefer*	3.44	4-1	24	49.2	27	41
Scott Karl*	4.14	6-7	25	124.0	50	59
Ricky Bones	4.63	10-12	32	200.1	83	77
Steve Sparks*	4.63	9-11	33	202.0	86	96
Brian Givens*	4.95	5-7	19	107.1	54	73
Angel Miranda	5.23	4-5	30	74.0	49	45
Bill Wegman	5.35	5-7	37	70.2	21	50
Sid Roberson*	5.76	6-4	26	84.1	37	40
Bob Scanlan	6.59	4-7	17	83.1	44	29

Saves: Mike Fetters (22); Graeme Lloyd (4); Wegman (2); Miranda, Ron Rightnowar, Rob Dibble and Kevin Wickander (1). **Complete games:** Bones and Sparks (3), Karl (1). **Shutouts:** none.

Minnesota Twins

Batting (120 AB)	Avg	AB	R	H	HR	RBI	SB
Chuck Knoblauch	.333	538	107	179	11	63	46
Kirby Puckett	.314	538	83	169	23	99	3
Pedro Munoz	.301	376	45	113	18	58	0
Jeff Reboulet	.292	216	39	63	4	23	1
Matt Merullo	.282	195	19	55	1	27	0
Marty Cordova*	.277	512	81	142	24	84	20
Pat Meares	.269	390	57	105	12	49	10
Scott Stahoviak*	.266	263	28	70	3	23	5
Matt Walbeck	.257	393	40	101	1	44	3
Scott Leius	.247	372	51	92	4	45	2
Dan Masteller*	.237	198	21	47	3	21	1
Rich Becker*	.237	392	45	93	2	33	8

Acquired: P Rodriguez from Bos. for P Aguilera (July 6); P Kligenbeck from Balt. for P Erickson (July 7); P Parra, IF Ron Coomer and P Greg Hansell from LA for P Tapani and P Guthrie (July 31)

Pitching (40 IP)	ERA	W-L	Gm	IP	BB	SO
Rich Robertson	3.83	2-0	25	51.2	31	38
Mark Guthrie	4.46	5-3	36	42.1	16	48
Kevin Tapani	4.92	6-11	20	133.2	34	88
Dave Stevens	5.07	5-4	56	65.2	32	47
Eddie Guardado	5.12	4-9	51	91.1	45	71
Brad Radke	5.32	11-14	29	181.0	47	75
Mike Trombley	5.62	4-8	20	97.2	42	68
Frank Rodriguez*	6.13	5-8	25	105.2	57	59
Pat Mahomes	6.37	4-10	47	94.2	47	67
Erik Schullstrom*	6.89	0-0	37	47.0	22	21
Scott Klingenbeck*	7.12	2-4	24	79.2	42	42
Jose Parra*	7.59	1-5	12	61.2	22	29

Saves: Stevens (10); Mahomes (3); Guardado (2). **Complete games:** Radke (2); LaTroy Hawkins (1). **Shutout:** Radke (1).

New York Yankees

Batting (120 AB)	Avg	AB	R	H	HR	RBI	SB
Wade Boggs	.324	460	76	149	5	63	1
Bernie Williams	.307	563	93	173	18	82	8
Paul O'Neill	.300	460	82	138	22	96	1
Don Mattingly	.288	458	59	132	7	49	0
Dion James	.287	209	22	60	2	26	4
Randy Velarde	.278	367	60	102	7	46	5
Jim Leyritz	.269	264	37	71	7	37	1
Mike Stanley	.268	399	63	107	18	83	1
Ruben Sierra	.263	479	73	126	19	86	5
Luis Polonia	.261	238	37	62	2	15	10
Gerald Williams	.247	182	33	45	6	28	4
Tony Fernandez	.245	384	57	94	5	45	6
Pat Kelly	.237	270	32	64	4	29	8

Traded: OF Polonia to Atl. for minor leaguer (Aug. 11).
Acquired: OF Sierra from Oak. for OF Danny Tartabull (July 28); P Cone from Tor. for 3 minor league pitchers (July 28).

Pitching (40 IP)	ERA	W-L	Gm	IP	BB	SO
Bobby Witt	5.04	8-10	24	135.2	70	111
John Wetteland	2.93	1-5	60	61.1	14	66
Rick Honeycutt	2.96	5-1	52	45.2	10	21
David Cone	3.57	18-8	30	229.1	88	191
Jack McDowell	3.93	15-10	30	217.2	78	157
Scott Kamieniecki	4.01	7-6	17	89.2	49	43
Bob Wickman	4.05	2-4	63	80.0	33	51
Andy Pettitte*	4.17	12-9	31	175.0	63	114
Sterling Hitchcock	4.70	11-10	27	168.1	68	121
Bob MacDonald	4.86	1-1	33	46.1	22	41
Steve Howe	4.96	6-3	56	49.0	17	28
Mariano Rivera*	5.51	5-3	19	67.0	30	51
Melido Perez	5.58	5-5	13	69.1	31	44

Saves: Wetteland (31); Howe and Honeycutt (2); Ausanio and Wickman (1). **Complete games:** McDowell (8), Cone (6), Hitchcock (4); Pettitte (3), Kamieniecki and Perez (1). **Shutouts:** Cone and McDowell (2); Hitchcock (1).

Oakland Athletics

Batting (120 AB)	Avg	AB	R	H	HR	RBI	SB
Rickey Henderson	.300	407	67	122	9	54	32
Geronimo Berroa	.278	546	87	152	22	88	7
Terry Steinbach	.278	406	43	113	15	65	1
Stan Javier	.278	442	81	123	8	56	36
Mark McGwire	.274	317	75	87	39	90	1
Mike Bordick	.264	428	46	113	8	44	11
Scott Brosius	.263	388	69	102	17	46	4
Jason Giambi*	.256	176	27	45	6	25	2
Brent Gates	.254	524	60	133	5	56	3
Danny Tartabull	.236	280	34	66	8	35	0
Mike Gallego	.233	120	11	28	0	8	0
Craig Paquette	.226	283	42	64	13	49	5

Acquired: OF Tartabull from N.Y. Yankees for OF Sierra (July 28).

Pitching (25 IP)	ERA	W-L	Gm	IP	BB	SO
Jim Corsi	2.20	2-4	38	45.0	26	26
Steve Ontiveros	4.37	9-6	22	129.2	38	77
Todd Stottlemyre	4.55	14-7	31	209.2	80	205
Doug Johns*	4.61	5-3	11	54.2	26	25
Dennis Eckersley	4.83	4-6	52	50.1	11	40
Todd Van Poppel	4.88	4-8	36	138.1	56	122
Ariel Prieto*	4.97	2-6	14	58.0	32	37
Carlos Reyes	5.09	4-6	40	69.0	28	48
S. Wojciechowski*	5.18	2-3	14	48.2	28	13
Mark Acre	5.71	1-2	43	52.0	28	47
Ron Darling	6.23	4-7	21	104.0	46	69
Dave Stewart	6.89	3-7	16	81.0	39	58

Saves: Eckersley (29); Corsi (2); Mike Mohler (1). **Complete games:** Stottlemyre and Ontiveros (2); Prieto and Johns (1). **Shutouts:** Ontiveros and Johns (1).

Seattle Mariners

Batting (120 AB)	Avg	AB	R	H	HR	RBI	SB
Edgar Martinez	.356	511	121	182	29	113	4
Joey Cora	.297	427	64	127	3	39	18
Tino Martinez	.293	519	92	152	31	111	0
Luis Sojo	.289	339	50	98	7	39	4
Vince Coleman	.288	455	66	131	5	29	42
Rich Amaral	.282	238	45	67	2	19	21
Dan Wilson	.278	399	40	111	9	51	2
Doug Strange	.271	155	19	42	2	21	0
Jay Buhner	.262	470	86	123	40	121	0
Warren Newson	.261	157	34	41	5	15	2
Ken Griffey	.258	260	52	67	17	42	4
Mike Blowers	.257	439	59	113	23	96	2
Alex Diaz	.248	270	44	67	3	27	18
Darren Bragg*	.234	145	20	34	3	12	9
Alex Rodriguez*	.232	142	15	33	5	19	4
Felix Fermin	.195	200	21	39	0	15	2

Acquired: P Belcher from Cin. for P Roger Salkeld (May 15); P Torres from S.F. for 2 minor leaguers. (May 20); OF Newson from Chi. AL for PTBN (July 18); P Benes from S.D. for P Ron Villone and OF Marc Newfield (July 31); OF Coleman from K.C. for P Jim Converse.

Pitching (25 IP)	ERA	W-L	Gm	IP	BB	SO
Norm Charlton	1.51	2-1	30	47.2	16	58
Jeff Nelson	2.17	7-3	62	78.2	27	96
Randy Johnson	2.48	18-2	30	214.1	65	294
Bill Risley	3.13	2-1	45	60.1	18	65
Bob Wolcott*	4.42	3-2	7	36.2	14	19
Bobby Ayala	4.44	6-5	63	71.0	30	77
Tim Belcher	4.52	10-12	28	179.1	88	96
Chris Bosio	4.92	10-8	31	170.0	69	85
Rafael Carmona*	5.66	2-4	15	47.2	34	28
Bob Wells*	5.75	4-3	30	76.2	39	38
Andy Benes	5.86	7-2	12	63.0	33	45
Salomon Torres	6.00	3-8	16	72.0	42	45

Saves: Ayala (19); Charlton (14); Nelson (2); Risley, Carmona and Lee Guetterman (1). **Complete games:** Johnson (6), Belcher and Torres (1). **Shutouts:** Johnson (3).

Texas Rangers

Batting (120 AB)	Avg	AB	R	H	HR	RBI	SB
Ivan Rodriguez	.303	492	56	149	12	67	0
Will Clark	.302	454	85	137	16	92	0
Juan Gonzalez	.295	352	57	104	27	82	0
Otis Nixon	.295	589	87	174	0	45	50
Jeff Frye	.278	313	38	87	4	29	3
Rusty Greer	.271	417	58	113	13	61	3
Candy Maldonado ...	.263	190	28	50	9	30	1
Mark McLemore	.261	467	73	122	5	41	21
Mickey Tettleton	.238	429	76	102	32	78	0
Mike Pagliarulo	.232	241	27	56	4	27	0
Benji Gil*	.219	415	36	91	9	46	2

Acquired: P Cook from Clev. for minor leaguer (June 22). P Witt from Fla. for P Wilson Heredia (Aug. 8). OF Maldonado from Tor. for PTBN (Aug. 31).

Pitching (25 IP)	ERA	W-L	Gm	IP	BB	SO
Ed Vosberg	3.00	5-5	44	36.0	16	36
Jeff Russell	3.03	1-0	37	32.2	9	21
Kenny Rogers	3.38	17-7	31	208.0	76	140
Roger McDowell	4.02	7-4	64	85.0	34	49
Matt Whiteside	4.08	5-4	40	53.0	19	46
Darren Oliver	4.22	4-2	17	49.0	32	39
Roger Pavlik	4.37	10-10	31	191.2	90	149
Dennis Cook	4.53	0-2	46	57.2	26	53
Bobby Witt	4.55	3-4	10	61.1	21	46
Bob Tewksbury	4.58	8-7	21	129.2	20	53
Kevin Gross	5.54	9-15	31	183.2	89	106
Terry Burrows	6.45	2-2	28	44.2	19	22
Danny Darwin	7.45	3-10	20	99.0	31	58

Saves: Russell (20), McDowell and Vosberg (4), Whiteside (3), Cook (2). **Complete games:** Gross and Tewksbury (4), Rogers (3), Pavlik (2), Darwin and Witt (1). **Shutouts:** Pavlik, Rogers and Tewksbury (1).

Toronto Blue Jays

Batting (120 AB)	Avg	AB	R	H	HR	RBI	SB
Roberto Alomar	.300	517	71	155	13	66	30
John Olerud	.291	492	72	143	8	54	0
Shawn Green*	.288	379	52	109	15	54	1
Devon White	.283	427	61	121	10	53	11
Paul Molitor	.270	525	63	142	15	60	12
Joe Carter	.253	558	70	141	25	76	12
Ed Sprague	.244	521	77	127	18	74	0
Alex Gonzalez*	.243	367	51	89	10	42	4
Sandy Martinez*	.241	191	12	46	2	25	0
Domingo Cedeno	.236	161	18	38	4	14	0
Michael Huff	.232	138	14	32	1	9	1
Randy Knorr	.212	132	18	28	3	16	0
Lance Parrish	.202	178	15	36	4	22	0

Pitching (25 IP)	ERA	W-L	Gm	IP	BB	SO
Mike Timlin	2.14	4-3	31	42.0	17	36
Tim Crabtree*	3.09	0-2	31	32.0	13	21
Tony Castillo	3.22	1-5	55	72.2	24	38
Al Leiter	3.64	11-11	28	183.0	108	153
Woody Williams	3.69	1-2	23	53.2	28	41
Ken Robinson*	3.69	1-2	21	39.0	22	31
Paul Menhart*	4.92	1-4	21	78.2	47	50
Pat Hentgen	5.11	10-14	30	200.2	90	135
Edwin Hurtado*	5.45	5-2	14	77.2	40	33
Juan Guzman	6.32	4-14	24	135.1	73	94
Giovanni Carrara*	7.21	2-4	12	48.2	25	27
Danny Cox	7.40	1-3	24	45.0	33	38

Saves: Castillo (13), Timlin (5). **Complete games:** Guzman (3), Hentgen and Leiter (2), Carrara and Hurtado (1). **Shutout:** Leiter (1).

Players Who Played in Both Leagues in 1995

While all individual major league statistics count on career records, players cannot transfer their stats from one league to the other if they are traded during the regular season. Here are the combined stats for batters with 160 at bats and pitchers with 78 innings pitched, who played in both leagues in 1995.

Batters (170 AB)

	BA	AB	R	H	HR	RBI	SB
Bobby Bonilla	.329	554	96	182	28	99	0
NY (NL)	.325	317	49	103	18	53	0
BAL.	.333	237	47	79	10	46	0
Pat Borders	.208	178	15	37	4	13	0
KC	.231	143	14	33	4	13	0
HOU	.114	35	1	4	0	0	0
M. Devereaux	.299	388	55	116	11	63	8
CHI (AL)	.306	333	48	102	10	55	6
ATL.	.255	55	7	14	1	8	2
Dave Gallagher	.306	173	13	53	1	14	0
CAL	.188	16	1	3	0	2	0.
PHI	.318	157	12	50	1	12	0
Dave Hollins	.225	218	48	49	7	26	1
PHI	.229	205	46	47	7	25	1
BOS.	.154	13	2	2	0	1	0
Derrick May	.282	319	44	90	9	50	5
MIL.	.248	113	15	28	1	9	0.
HOU.	.301	206	29	62	8	41	5
Lois Polonia	.261	291	43	76	2	17	13
NY (AL)	.261	238	37	62	2	15	10
ATL.	.264	53	6	14	0	2	3
A. Van Slyke	.224	277	32	62	6	24	7
BAL.	.159	63	6	10	3	8	0
PHI	.243	214	26	52	3	16	7
Mark Whiten	.241	320	51	77	12	47	8
BOS.	.185	108	13	20	1	10	1
PHI	.269	212	38	57	11	37	7

Pitchers (78 IP)

	ERA	W-L	G	IP	BB	SO
Andy Benes	4.76	11-9	31	181.2	78	171
SD	4.17	4-7	19	118.2	45	126
SEA	5.86	7-2	12	63.0	33	45
Sid Fernandez	4.56	6-5	19	92.2	38	110
BAL.	7.39	0-4	8	28.0	17	31
PHI	3.34	6-1	11	64.2	21	79
Ken Hill	4.62	10-8	30	185.0	77	98
ST.L.	5.06	6-7	18	110.1	45	50
CLE.	3.98	4-1	12	74.2	32	48
Jason Jacome	6.34	4-10	20	105.0	36	50
NY (NL)	10.29	0-4	5	21.0	15	11
KC	5.36	4-6	15	84.0	21	39
Mike Maddux	4.10	5-1	44	98.2	18	69
PIT	9.00	1-0	8	9.0	3	4
BOS.	3.61	4-1	36	89.2	15	65
Russ Springer	5.29	1-2	33	78.1	35	70
CAL	6.10	1-2	19	51.2	25	38
PHI	3.71	0-0	14	26.2	10	32
Kevin Tapani	4.96	10-13	33	190.2	48	131
MIN.	4.92	6-11	20	133.2	34	88
LA.	5.05	4-2	13	57.0	14	43
David Wells	3.24	16-8	29	203.0	53	133
DET.	3.04	10-3	18	130.1	37	83
CIN.	3.59	6-5	11	72.2	16	50
Bobby Witt	4.13	5-11	29	172.0	68	111
FLA.	3.90	2-7	19	110.2	47	95
TEX.	4.55	3-4	10	61.1	21	46

NL Team by Team Statistics

At least 120 at bats or 25 innings pitched during the regular season unless otherwise indicated. Players who competed for more than one NL team are listed with their final club. Players traded from the AL are listed with NL team only if they have 120 AB or 25 IP. Note that (*) indicates rookie.

Atlanta Braves

Batting (120 AB)	Avg	AB	R	H	HR	RBI	SB
Javier Lopez	.315	333	37	105	14	51	0
Ryan Klesko	.310	329	48	102	23	70	5
Fred McGriff	.280	528	85	148	27	93	3
Chipper Jones*	.265	524	87	139	23	86	8
Marquis Grissom	.258	551	80	142	12	42	29
Mark Lemke	.253	399	42	101	5	38	2
David Justice	.253	411	73	104	24	78	4
Dwight Smith	.252	131	16	33	3	21	0
Charlie O'Brien	.227	198	18	45	9	23	0
Rafael Belliard	.222	180	12	40	0	7	2
Jeff Blauser	.211	431	60	91	12	31	8
Mike Kelly	.190	137	26	26	3	17	7

Acquired: P Pena from Fla. for P Chris Seelbach

Pitching (25 IP)	ERA	W-L	Gm	IP	BB	SO
Hector Carrasco*	2.24	5-6	45	56.1	30	41
Greg Maddux	1.63	19-2	28	209.2	23	181
Mark Wohlers	2.09	7-3	65	64.2	24	90
Alejandro Peña	2.61	2-0	27	31.0	7	39
Greg McMichael	2.79	7-2	67	80.2	32	74
Tom Glavine	3.08	16-7	29	198.2	66	127
Pedro Borbón Jr.*	3.09	2-2	41	32.0	17	33
John Smoltz	3.18	12-7	29	192.2	72	193
Brad Clontz*	3.65	8-1	59	69.0	22	55
Kent Mercker	4.15	7-8	29	143.0	61	102
Steve Avery	4.67	7-13	29	173.1	52	141

Saves: Wohlers (25); Clontz (4); McMichael and Borbon Jr. (2)
Complete games: Maddux (10); Avery and Glavine (3); Smoltz (2) **Shutouts:** Maddux (3); Avery, Glavine and Smoltz (1).

Chicago Cubs

Batting (120 AB)	Avg	AB	R	H	HR	RBI	SB
Mark Grace	.326	552	97	180	16	92	6
Shawon Dunston	.296	477	58	141	14	69	10
Brian McRae	.288	580	92	167	12	48	27
Rey Sanchez	.278	428	57	119	3	27	6
Luis Gonzalez	.276	471	69	130	13	69	6
Scott Bullett*	.273	150	19	41	3	22	8
Sammy Sosa	.268	564	89	151	36	119	34
Scott Servais	.265	264	38	70	13	47	2
Ozzie Timmons*	.263	171	30	45	8	28	3
Todd Zeile	.246	426	50	105	14	52	1
Jose Hernandez	.245	245	37	60	13	40	1
Mark Parent	.234	265	30	62	18	38	0
Howard Johnson	.195	169	26	33	7	22	1

Acquired: IF Zeile from St.L for P Mike Morgan (June 16). OF Gonzalez and C Servais from Hou. for C Rick Wilkens (June 28). C Paremt from Pitt. for PTBN (Aug. 31).

Pitching (25 IP)	ERA	W-L	Gm	IP	BB	SO
Frank Castillo	3.21	11-10	29	188.0	52	135
Mike Walker	3.22	1-3	42	44.2	24	20
Jamie Navarro	3.28	14-6	29	200.1	56	128
Mike Perez	3.66	2-6	68	71.1	27	49
Anthony Young	3.70	3-4	32	41.1	14	15
Randy Myers	3.88	1-2	57	55.2	28	59
Jim Bullinger	4.14	12-8	24	150.0	65	93
Kevin Foster	4.51	12-11	30	167.2	65	146
Turk Wendell	4.92	3-1	43	60.1	24	50
Steve Trachsel	5.15	7-13	30	160.2	76	117

Saves: Myers (38); Perez and Young (2); Walker and Terry Adams (1) **Complete games:** Trachsel and Castillo (2); Navarro and Bullinger (1). **Shutouts:** Castillo (2); Bullinger and Navarro (1).

Cincinnati Reds

Batting (135 AB)	Avg	AB	R	H	HR	RBI	SB
Mark Lewis	.339	171	25	58	3	30	0
Barry Larkin	.319	496	98	158	15	66	51
Reggie Sanders	.306	484	91	148	28	99	36
Thomas Howard	.302	281	42	85	3	26	17
Jerome Walton	.290	162	32	47	8	22	10
Mariano Duncan	.287	265	36	76	6	36	1
Benito Santiago	.286	266	40	76	11	44	2
Eddie Taubensee	.284	218	32	62	9	44	2
Hal Morris	.279	359	53	100	11	51	1
Ron Gant	.276	410	79	113	29	88	23
Bret Boone	.267	513	63	137	15	68	5
Jeff Branson	.260	331	43	86	12	45	2
Darren Lewis	.250	472	66	118	1	24	32
Lenny Harris	.208	197	32	41	2	16	10

Acquired: OF Lewis, P Burba and P Portugal from S.F. for OF Deion Sanders (July 21). P Wells from Det. for P Nitkowski (July 31)

Pitching (40 IP)	ERA	W-L	Gm	IP	BB	SO
Mike Jackson	2.39	6-1	40	49.0	19	41
Jeff Brantley	2.82	3-2	56	70.1	20	62
Pete Schourek	3.22	18-7	29	190.1	45	160
John Smiley	3.46	12-5	28	176.2	39	124
David Wells	3.59	6-5	11	72.2	16	50
Tim Pugh	3.84	6-5	28	98.1	32	38
Dave Burba	3.97	10-4	52	106.2	51	96
Mark Portugal	4.01	11-10	31	181.2	56	96
Hector Carrasco	4.12	2-7	64	87.1	46	64
Jose Rijo	4.17	5-4	14	69.0	22	62
Xavier Hernandez	4.60	7-2	59	90.0	31	84
Kevin Jarvis*	5.70	3-4	19	79.0	32	33
Chuck McElroy	6.02	3-4	44	40.1	15	27

Saves: Brantley (28); Carrasco (5); Hernandez (3); Jackson (2) **Complete games:** Wells (3); Schourek (2); Jarvis, Portugal, and Smiley (1) **Shutout:** Jarvis (1).

Colorado Rockies

Batting (120 AB)	Avg	AB	R	H	HR	RBI	SB
Dante Bichette	.340	579	102	197	40	128	13
Eric Young	.317	366	68	116	6	36	35
Vinny Castilla	.309	527	82	163	32	90	2
Larry Walker	.306	494	96	151	36	101	16
Andres Galarraga	.280	554	89	155	31	106	12
Mike Kingery	.269	350	66	94	8	37	13
Jason Bates*	.267	322	42	86	8	46	3
Ellis Burks	.266	278	41	74	14	49	7
Joe Girardi	.262	462	63	121	8	55	3
Walt Weiss	.260	427	65	111	1	25	15

Acquired: P Saberhagen from N.Y. Mets for P Acevedo and a minor leaguer (July 31)

Pitching (60 IP)	ERA	W-L	Gm	IP	BB	SO
Steve Reed	2.14	5-2	71	84.0	21	79
Darren Holmes	3.24	6-1	68	66.2	28	61
Curtis Leskanic	3.40	6-3	76	98.0	33	107
Bret Saberhagen	4.18	7-6	25	153.0	33	100
Kevin Ritz	4.21	11-11	31	173.1	65	120
Bill Swift	4.94	9-3	19	105.2	43	68
Brian Rekar*	4.98	4-6	15	85.0	24	60
Roger Bailey*	4.98	7-6	39	81.1	39	33
Armando Reynoso	5.32	7-7	20	93.0	36	40
Marvin Freeman	5.89	3-7	22	94.2	41	61
Juan Acevedo	6.44	4-6	17	65.2	20	40

Saves: Holmes (14); Bruce Ruffin (11); Leskanic (10); Reed (3); Mike Muñoz (2). **Complete games:** Saberhagen (3); Rekar (1). **Shutouts:** none.

Florida Marlins

Batting (120 AB)

	Avg	AB	R	H	HR	RBI	SB
Gary Sheffield	.324	213	46	69	16	46	19
Jeff Conine	.302	483	72	146	25	105	2
Terry Pendleton	.290	513	70	149	14	78	1
Jesus Tavarez*	.289	190	31	55	2	13	7
Greg Colbrunn	.277	528	70	146	23	89	11
Alex Arias	.269	216	22	58	3	26	1
Quilvio Veras*	.261	440	86	115	5	32	56
Andre Dawson	.257	226	30	58	8	37	0
Jerry Browne	.255	184	21	47	1	17	1
Kurt Abbott	.255	420	60	107	17	60	4
Charles Johnson*	.251	315	40	79	11	39	0
Tommy Gregg	.237	156	20	37	6	20	3
Chuck Carr	.227	308	54	70	2	20	25
Steve Decker	.226	133	12	30	3	13	1

Traded: P Witt to Tex. for P Wilson Heredia (Aug. 8).
Claimed: P Banks on waivers (Aug. 10)

Pitching (25 IP)

	ERA	W-L	Gm	IP	BB	SO
Robb Nen	3.29	0-7	62	65.2	23	68
Terry Mathews	3.38	4-4	57	84.2	25	72
Pat Rapp	3.44	14-7	28	167.1	76	102
Richie Lewis	3.75	0-1	21	36.0	15	32
Chris Hammond	3.80	9-6	25	161.0	47	126
Randy Veres	3.88	4-4	47	48.2	22	31
Bobby Witt	3.90	2-7	19	110.2	47	95
John Burkett	4.30	14-14	30	188.1	57	126
Mark Gardner	4.49	5-5	39	102.1	43	87
Yorkis Perez	5.21	2-6	69	46.2	28	47
Willie Banks	5.66	2-6	25	90.2	58	62
Dave Weathers	5.98	4-5	28	90.1	52	60

Saves: Nen (23); Mathews (3); Gardner, Perez and Veres (1).
Complete games: Burkett (4); Hammond and Rapp (3).
Shutouts: Hammond and Rapp (2).

Houston Astros

Batting (120 AB)

	Avg	AB	R	H	HR	RBI	SB
Derek Bell	.334	452	63	151	8	86	27
John Cangelosi	.318	201	46	64	2	18	21
Dave Magadan	.313	348	44	109	2	51	2
Brian Hunter*	.302	321	52	97	2	28	24
Craig Biggio	.302	553	123	167	22	77	33
Derrick May	.301	206	29	62	8	41	5
Tony Eusebio	.299	368	46	110	6	58	0
Jeff Bagwell	.290	448	88	130	21	87	12
Ricky Gutierrez	.276	156	22	43	0	12	5
Craig Shipley	.263	232	23	61	3	24	6
Orlando Miller*	.262	324	36	85	5	36	3
James Mouton	.262	298	42	78	4	27	25
Mike Simms	.256	121	14	31	9	24	1
Milt Thompson	.220	132	14	29	2	19	4
Rick Wilkins	.203	202	30	41	7	19	0

Acquired: OF May from Milw. for PTBN (June 21). C Wilkins from Chi. NL for OF Luis Gonzalez and C Scott Servais (June 28). P Tabaka from S.D. for OF Phil Plantier (July 19).

Pitching (25 IP)

	ERA	W-L	Gm	IP	BB	SO
Dave Veres	2.26	5-1	72	103.1	30	94
Todd Jones	3.07	6-5	68	99.2	52	96
Dean Hartgraves*	3.22	2-0	40	36.1	16	24
Jeff Tabaka	3.23	1-0	34	30.2	17	25
Mike Hampton	3.35	9-8	24	150.2	49	115
Shane Reynolds	3.47	10-11	30	189.1	37	175
Doug Brocail	4.19	6-4	36	77.1	22	39
Greg Swindell	4.47	10-9	33	153.0	39	96
Doug Drabek	4.77	10-9	31	185.0	54	143
Jim Dougherty*	4.92	8-4	56	67.2	25	49
Darryl Kile	4.96	4-12	25	127.0	73	113

Saves: Jones (15); Mike Henneman (8); Brocail and Verez (1).
Complete games: Reynolds (3); Drabek (2); Swindell (1).
Shutouts: Reynolds (2); Drabek and Swindell (1).

Los Angeles Dodgers

Batting (120 AB)

	Avg	AB	R	H	HR	RBI	SB
Mike Piazza	.346	434	82	150	32	93	1
Brett Butler	.300	513	78	154	1	38	32
Eric Karros	.298	551	83	164	32	105	4
Dave Hansen	.287	181	19	52	1	14	0
Jose Offerman	.287	429	69	123	4	33	2
Raul Mondesi	.285	536	91	153	26	88	27
Chad Fonville*	.278	320	43	89	0	16	20
Roberto Kelly	.278	504	58	140	7	57	19
Tim Wallach	.266	327	24	87	9	38	0
Delino DeShields	.256	425	66	109	8	37	39
Billy Ashley	.237	215	17	51	8	27	0

Acquired: OF Kelly from Mon. for IF Jeff Treadway and OF Henry Rodriguez (May 23). P Tapani and P Mark Guthrie from Minn. for P Jose Parra, IF Ron Coomer and P Greg Hansell (July 31). OF Butler from N.Y. Mets for 2 minor leaguers (Aug. 18).

Pitching (25 IP)

	ERA	W-L	Gm	IP	BB	SO
Todd Worrell	2.02	4-1	59	62.1	19	61
Hideo Nomo*	2.54	13-6	28	191.1	78	236
John Cummings	3.00	3-1	35	39.0	10	21
Ismael Valdes	3.05	13-11	33	197.2	51	150
Tom Candiotti	3.50	7-14	30	190.1	58	141
Ramon Martinez	3.66	17-7	30	206.1	81	138
Pedro Astacio	4.24	7-8	48	104.0	29	80
Antonio Osuna*	4.43	2-4	39	44.2	20	46
Kevin Tapani	5.05	4-2	13	57.0	14	43
Rudy Seanez	6.75	1-3	37	34.2	18	29

Saves: Worrell (32); Jim Bruske (1). **Complete games:** Valdes (6); Martinez and Nomo (4); Candiotti (1) **Shutouts:** Nomo (3); Martinez and Valdes (2) and Candiotti (1).

Montreal Expos

Batting (120 AB)

	Avg	AB	R	H	HR	RBI	SB
Sean Berry	.318	314	38	100	14	55	3
David Segui	.309	456	68	141	12	68	2
Rondell White	.295	474	87	140	13	57	25
Will Cordero	.286	514	64	147	10	49	9
Darrin Fletcher	.286	350	42	100	11	45	0
Moises Alou	.273	344	48	94	14	58	4
Mike Lansing	.255	467	47	119	10	62	27
Tony Tarasco	.249	438	64	109	14	40	24
Mark Grudzielanek*	.245	269	27	66	1	20	8
Henry Rodriguez	.239	138	13	33	2	15	0
Tim Laker	.234	141	17	33	3	20	0
Shane Andrews*	.214	220	27	47	8	31	1

Traded: P Shaw to Chi. AL for P Jose DeLeon (Aug. 28).
Acquired: IF Segui from N.Y. Mets for P Reid Cornelius (June 8).

Pitching (25 IP)

	ERA	W-L	Gm	IP	BB	SO
Greg Harris	2.61	2-3	45	48.1	16	47
Butch Henry	2.84	7-9	21	126.2	28	60
Kirk Rueter	3.23	5-3	9	47.1	9	28
Pedro Martinez	3.51	14-10	30	194.2	66	174
Carlos Perez*	3.69	10-8	28	141.1	28	106
Tim Scott	3.98	2-0	62	63.1	23	57
Mel Rojas	4.12	1-4	59	67.2	29	61
Gill Heredia	4.31	5-6	40	119.0	21	74
Jeff Fassero	4.33	13-14	30	189.0	74	164
Jeff Shaw	4.62	1-6	50	62.1	26	45
Tavo Alvarez*	6.75	1-5	8	37.1	16	27

Saves: Rojas (30); Scott, Dave Leiper and Willie Fraser (2); Heredia (1). **Complete games:** Martinez and Perez (2); Rueter and Fassero (1). **Shutouts:** Martinez (2); Perez and Rueter (1).

New York Mets

Batting (120 AB)	Avg	AB	R	H	HR	RBI	SB
Bobby Bonilla	.325	317	49	103	18	53	0
Tim Bogar	.290	145	17	42	1	21	1
Rico Brogna	.289	495	72	143	22	76	0
Jose Vizcaino	.287	509	66	146	3	56	8
Joe Orsulak	.283	290	41	82	1	37	1
Chris Jones	.280	182	33	51	8	31	2
Todd Hundley	.280	275	39	77	15	51	1
Edgardo Alfonzo*	.278	335	26	93	4	41	1
Jeff Kent	.278	472	65	131	20	65	3
Carl Everett*	.260	289	48	75	12	54	2
Ryan Thompson	.251	267	39	67	7	31	3
Damon Buford	.235	136	24	32	4	12	7
Kelly Stinnett	.219	196	23	43	4	18	2

Acquired: P Cornelius from Mon. for IF David Segui; OF Buford from Balt. for OF Bonilla (July 28).

Pitching (25 IP)	ERA	W-L	Gm	IP	BB	SO
John Franco	2.44	5-3	48	51.2	17	41
Jason Isringhausen*	2.81	9-2	14	93.0	31	55
Doug Henry	2.96	3-6	51	67.0	25	62
Blas Minor	3.66	4-2	35	46.2	13	43
Pete Harnisch	3.68	2-8	18	110.0	24	82
Jerry DiPoto	3.78	4-6	58	78.2	29	49
Bill Pulsipher*	3.98	5-7	17	126.2	45	81
Bobby Jones	4.19	10-10	30	195.2	53	127
Dave Mlicki	4.26	9-7	29	160.2	54	123
Reid Cornelius*	5.54	3-7	18	66.2	30	39

Saves: Franco (29); Henry (4); DiPoto (2) and Minor (1)
Complete games: Jones (3); Pulsipher (2); Isringhausen (1).
Shutout: Jones (1).

Philadelphia Phillies

Batting (120 AB)	Avg	AB	R	H	HR	RBI	SB
Dave Gallagher	.318	157	12	50	1	12	0
Jim Eisenreich	.316	377	46	119	10	55	10
Gregg Jefferies	.306	480	69	147	11	56	9
Mickey Morandini	.283	494	65	140	6	49	9
Charlie Hayes	.276	529	58	146	11	85	5
Mark Whiten	.269	212	38	57	11	37	7
Lenny Webster	.267	150	18	40	4	14	0
Lenny Dykstra	.264	254	37	67	2	18	10
Darren Daulton	.249	342	44	85	9	55	3
Andy Van Slyke	.243	214	26	52	3	16	7
Dave Hollins	.229	205	46	47	7	25	1
Kevin Stocker	.218	412	42	90	1	32	6

Traded: OF Gallagher to Cal. for OF Kevin Flora (Aug. 9).
Acquired: OF Van Slyke from Bal. for P Gene Harris (June 18). OF Whiten from Bos. for IF Hollins (July 24).

Pitching (35 IP)	ERA	W-L	Gm	IP	BB	SO
Rickey Bottalico*	2.46	5-3	62	87.2	42	87
Heathcliff Slocumb	2.89	5-6	61	65.1	35	63
Mike Williams	3.29	3-3	33	87.2	29	57
Sid Fernandez	3.34	6-1	11	64.2	21	79
Curt Schilling	3.57	7-5	17	116.0	26	114
Toby Borland	3.77	1-3	50	74.0	37	59
David West	3.79	3-2	8	38.0	19	25
Jeff Juden	4.02	2-4	13	62.2	31	47
Michael Mimbs*	4.15	9-7	35	136.2	75	93
Paul Quantrill	4.67	11-12	33	179.1	44	103
Tyler Green*	5.31	8-9	26	140.2	66	85
Omar Olivares	6.91	1-4	16	41.2	23	22
Tommy Greene	8.29	0-5	11	50.0	20	24

Saves: Slocumb (32); Borland (6); Bottalico and Steve Frey (1).
Complete games: Green (4); Mimbs (2); Juden (1) **Shutouts:**
Green (2); Mimbs (1).

Pittsburgh Pirates

Batting (120 AB)	Avg	AB	R	H	HR	RBI	SB
Orlando Merced	.300	487	75	146	15	83	7
Carlos Garcia	.294	367	41	108	6	50	8
Nelson Liriano	.286	259	29	74	5	38	2
Al Martin	.282	439	70	124	13	41	20
Dave Clark	.281	196	30	55	4	24	3
Jacob Brumfield	.271	402	64	109	4	26	22
Jeff King	.265	445	61	118	18	87	7
Jay Bell	.262	530	79	139	13	55	2
Steve Pegues*	.246	171	17	42	6	16	1
Midre Cummings*	.243	152	13	37	2	15	1
Kevin Young	.232	181	13	42	6	22	1
Angelo Encarnacion*	.226	159	18	36	2	10	1
Mark Johnson	.208	221	32	46	13	28	5

Pitching (25 IP)	ERA	W-L	Gm	IP	BB	SO
Denny Neagle	3.43	13-8	31	209.2	45	150
Dan Plesac	3.58	4-4	58	60.1	27	57
Jason Christiansen*	4.15	1-3	63	56.1	34	53
Mike Dyer	4.34	4-5	55	74.2	30	53
John Ericks	4.58	3-9	19	106.0	50	80
Dan Miceli	4.66	4-4	58	58.0	28	56
Rick White	4.75	2-3	15	55.0	18	29
Paul Wagner	4.80	5-16	33	165.0	72	120
Jeff McCurry*	5.02	1-4	55	61.0	30	27
Esteban Loaiza*	5.16	8-9	32	172.2	55	85
Steve Parris*	5.38	6-6	15	82.0	33	61
Jim Gott	6.03	2-4	25	31.1	12	19
Jon Lieber	6.32	4-7	21	72.2	14	45

Saves: Miceli (21); Plesac (3); McCurry (1). **Complete games:** Neagle (5); Wagner (3); Ericks, Loaiza and Parris (1). **Shutouts:** Neagle, Parris and Wagner (1).

St. Louis Cardinals

Batting (120 AB)	Avg	AB	R	H	HR	RBI	SB
John Mabry*	.307	388	35	119	5	41	0
Bernard Gilkey	.298	480	73	143	17	69	12
Brian Jordan	.296	490	83	145	22	81	24
Ray Lankford	.277	483	81	134	25	82	24
David Bell*	.250	144	13	36	2	19	1
Danny Sheaffer	.231	208	24	48	5	30	0
Scott Cooper	.230	374	29	86	3	40	0
Tripp Cromer*	.226	345	36	78	5	18	0
Darnell Coles	.225	138	13	31	3	16	0
Tom Pagnozzi	.215	219	17	47	2	15	0
Jose Oquendo	.209	220	31	46	2	17	1
Ozzie Smith	.199	156	16	31	0	11	4
Jose Oliva*	.142	183	15	26	7	20	0

Acquired: P Morgan from Chi. NL for IF Todd Zeile (June 16). IF Bell from Clev. for P Hill (July 27). IF Oliva from Atl. for minor leaguer (Aug. 25). OF Mark Sweeney and PTBN from Cal. for P Habyan (July 8);

Pitching (25 IP)	ERA	W-L	Gm	IP	BB	SO
Tony Fossas	1.47	3-0	58	36.2	10	40
Tom Henke	1.82	1-1	52	54.1	18	48
John Habyan	2.88	3-2	31	40.2	15	35
Rich DeLucia	3.39	8-7	56	82.1	36	76
Mike Morgan	3.56	7-7	21	131.1	34	61
Jeff Parrett	3.64	4-7	59	76.2	28	71
Tom Urbani	3.70	3-5	24	82.2	21	52
Donovan Osborne	3.81	4-6	19	113.1	34	82
Rene Arocha	3.99	3-5	41	49.2	18	25
Mark Petkovsek	4.00	6-6	26	137.1	35	71
John Frascatore*	4.41	1-1	14	32.2	16	21
Allen Watson	4.96	7-9	21	114.1	41	49
Ken Hill	5.06	6-7	18	110.1	45	50
Vicente Palacios	5.80	2-3	20	40.1	19	34
Danny Jackson	5.90	2-12	19	100.2	48	52

Saves: Henke (36); T.J. Mathews (2). **Complete games:** Morgan and Petkovsek (1). **Shutout:** Petkovsek (1).

San Diego Padres

Batting (120 AB)	Avg	AB	R	H	HR	RBI	SB
Tony Gwynn	.368	535	82	197	9	90	17
Scott Livingstone	.337	196	26	66	5	32	2
Bip Roberts	.304	296	40	90	2	25	20
Ken Caminiti	.302	526	74	159	26	94	12
Steve Finley	.297	562	104	167	10	44	36
Brad Ausmus	.293	328	44	96	5	34	16
Eddie Williams	.260	296	35	77	12	47	0
Jody Reed	.256	445	58	114	4	40	6
Phil Plantier	.255	216	33	55	9	34	1
Brian Johnson	.251	207	20	52	3	29	0
Andujar Cedeno	.210	390	42	82	6	31	5
Melvin Nieves*	.205	234	32	48	14	38	2

Traded: P Benes to Sea. for OF Marc Newfield and P Ron Villone (July 31).
Acquired: OF Plantier from Hou. for P Jeff Tabaka (July 19).

Pitching (25 IP)	ERA	W-L	Gm	IP	BB	SO
Andy Ashby	2.94	12-10	31	192.2	62	150
Bryce Florie*	3.01	2-2	47	68.2	38	68
Joey Hamilton	3.08	6-9	31	204.1	56	123
Doug Bochtler*	3.57	4-4	34	45.1	19	45
Trevor Hoffman	3.88	7-4	55	53.1	14	52
Andy Benes	4.17	4-7	19	118.2	45	126
Scott Sanders	4.30	5-5	17	90.0	31	88
Willie Blair	4.34	7-5	40	114.0	45	83
Fernando Valenzuela	4.98	8-3	29	90.1	34	57
Glenn Dishman*	5.01	4-8	19	97.0	34	43
Andres Berumen*	5.68	2-3	37	44.1	36	42
Brian Williams	6.00	3-10	44	72.0	38	75
Dustin Hermanson*	6.82	3-1	26	31.2	22	19

Saves: Hoffman (31); Berumen, Bochtler, Florie and Ron Villone (1). **Complete games:** Ashby and Hamilton (2) **Shutouts:** Ashby and Hamilton (2).

San Francisco Giants

Batting (120 AB)	Avg	AB	R	H	HR	RBI	SB
Matt Williams	.336	283	53	95	23	65	2
Mark Carreon	.301	396	53	119	17	65	0
Barry Bonds	.294	506	109	149	33	104	31
Deion Sanders	.268	343	48	92	6	28	24
Steve Scarsone	.266	233	33	62	11	29	3
Glenallen Hill	.264	497	71	131	24	86	25
Kurt Manwaring	.251	379	21	95	4	36	1
Royce Clayton	.244	509	56	124	5	58	24
Robby Thompson	.223	336	51	75	8	23	1
Mike Benjamin	.220	186	19	41	3	12	11
John Patterson	.205	205	27	42	1	14	4
J.R. Phillips*	.195	231	27	45	9	28	1

Acquired: OF Sanders and P Service from Cin. for P Mark Portugal, P Dave Burba and OF Darren Lewis (July 21).

Pitching (25 IP)	ERA	W-L	Gm	IP	BB	SO
Mark Dewey	3.13	1-0	27	31.2	17	32
Scott Service	3.19	3-1	28	31.0	20	30
W. VanLandingham	3.67	6-3	18	122.2	40	95
Mark Leiter	3.82	10-12	30	195.2	55	129
Trevor Wilson	3.92	3-4	17	82.2	38	38
Shawn Barton*	4.26	4-1	52	44.1	19	22
Rod Beck	4.45	5-6	60	58.2	21	42
Jamie Brewington*	4.54	6-4	13	75.1	45	45
Sergio Valdez	4.75	4-5	13	66.1	17	29
Luis Aquino	5.10	0-3	34	42.1	13	26
Chris Hook*	5.50	5-1	45	52.1	29	40
Terry Mulholland	5.80	5-13	29	149.0	38	65
Jose Bautista	6.44	3-8	52	100.2	26	45
Joe Rosselli*	8.70	2-1	9	30.0	20	7

Saves: Beck (33); Hook (2); Barton (1). **Complete games:** Leiter (7); Mulholland (2); Valdez and VanLandingham (1). **Shutout:** Leiter (1).

3,000 HITS	**IN A PINCH**	**NO-HITTER**	**BOTH HANDS**

Cleveland Indians	Colorado Rockies	Los Angeles Dodgers	Montreal Expos
Eddie Murray	**John Vander Wal**	**Ramon Martinez**	**Greg A. Harris**

Collected 3,000th hit of his 19-year career with a 6th inning single off Twins' Mike Tombley at Minnesota on June 30...gets hit batting left-handed...2nd switch-hitter to reach 3,000 (Pete Rose was the 1st)...2,045 hits from left side of plate, 955 from right side...Indians win game, 4-1.

Slugged solo home run for single-season record 26th pinch hit...blow came in 7th inning off Giants' Sergio Valdez at San Francisco on Sept. 21...batted for pitcher Steve Reed...ended season with 29 pinch hits...broke record of 25 set in 1976 by Rockies' coach Jose Morales...Giants win, 5-3.

Hurled only no-hitter of 1995 major league season and first of his career on July 14...shut out Florida Marlins, 7-0, in front of 30,988 at Dodger Stadium ...faced 28 batters...walked one and struck out eight...finished game with 9-6 record...catcher was Mike Piazza.

First pitcher in modern baseball history to throw with both hands in a single game...faced four batters in scoreless relief stint in bottom of 9th inning on Sept. 28 against Cincinnati...pitched righty, lefty, righty and got 3 ground outs and a walk...used special six-finger glove.

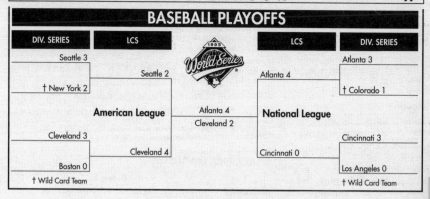

BASEBALL PLAYOFFS

| DIV. SERIES | LCS | | LCS | DIV. SERIES |

Seattle 3

† New York 2

Seattle 2

American League

Cleveland 3

Boston 0

Cleveland 4

Atlanta 4
Cleveland 2

Atlanta 4

Cincinnati 0

National League

Atlanta 3

† Colorado 1

Cincinnati 3

Los Angeles 0

† Wild Card Team

† Wild Card Team

Divisional Series Summaries

AMERICAN LEAGUE

Indians, 3-0

Date	Winner	Home Field
Oct. 3	Indians, 5-4 (13 inn.)	at Cleveland
Oct. 4	Indians, 4-0	at Cleveland
Oct. 6	Indians, 8-2	at Boston

Game 1

Tuesday, Oct. 3, at Cleveland

	1 2 3	4 5 6	7 8 9	0 1 2 3	R	H	E
Boston	0 0 2	0 0 0	0 1 0	0 1 0 0	4	11	2
Cleveland	0 0 0	0 0 3	0 0 0	0 1 0 1	5	10	2

Win: Hill, Cle. (1-0) **Loss:** Smith, Bos. (0-1)
2B: Boston— Alicea; Cleveland— Belle. **HR:** Boston— Valentin (1), Naehring (1), Alicea (1); Cleveland— Belle (1), Peña (1). **RBI:** Boston— Valentin 2, Naehring, Alicea; Cleveland— Belle 3, Murray, Pena. **SB:** Boston— Alicea (1); Cleveland— Vizquel (1).
Attendance: 44,218. **Time:** 5:01.

Game 2

Wednesday, Oct 4, at Cleveland

	1 2 3	4 5 6	7 8 9	R	H	E
Boston	0 0 0	0 0 0	0 0 0	0	3	2
Cleveland	0 0 0	0 2 0	0 2 x	4	4	1

Win: Hershiser, Cle. (1-0). **Loss:** Hanson, Bos. (0-1).
2B: Cleveland— Vizquel. **3B:** Cleveland— Murray. **HR:** Cleveland— Murray (1). **RBI:** Cleveland— Vizquel 2, Murray 2. **SB:** Boston— Hosey (1).
Attendance: 44,264. **Time:** 2:33.

Game 3

Friday, Oct. 6, at Boston

	1 2 3	4 5 6	7 8 9	R	H	E
Cleveland	0 2 1	0 0 5	0 0 0	8	11	1
Boston	0 0 0	1 0 0	0 0 1	2	7	2

Win: Nagy, Cle. (1-0). **Loss:** Wakefield, Bos. (0-1).
2B: Cleveland— Alomar, Baerga; Boston— Valentin. **HR:** Cleveland— Thome (1). **RBI:** Cleveland— Thome 3, Vizquel 2, Alomar, Baerga, Sorrento. Boston— McGee, MacFarlane.
Attendance: 34,211. **Time:** 3:18.

Mariners, 3-2

Date	Winner	Home Field
Oct. 3	Yankees, 9-6	at New York
Oct. 4	Yankees, 7-5 (15 inn.)	at New York
Oct. 6	Mariners, 7-4	at Seattle
Oct. 7	Mariners, 11-8	at Seattle
Oct. 8	Mariners, 6-5 (11 inn.)	at Seattle

Game 1

Tuesday, Oct. 3, at New York

	1 2 3	4 5 6	7 8 9	R	H	E
Seattle	0 0 1	0 0 1	2 0 2	6	9	0
New York	0 0 2	0 0 2	4 1 x	9	13	0

Win: Cone, N.Y. (1-0). **Loss:** J. Nelson, Sea. (0-1).
2B: New York— Boggs, B. Williams, Mattingly. **HR:** Seattle— Griffey 2 (2); New York— Boggs (1), Sierra (1). **RBI:** Seattle— Griffey 3, E. Martinez, T. Martinez, D. Wilson; New York — Boggs 2, B. Williams 2, Sierra 2, Mattingly, Stanley, O'Neill.
Attendance: 57,178. **Time:** 3:39.

Game 2

Wednesday, Oct 4, at New York

	1 2 3	4 5 6	7 8 9	0 1 2	3 4 5	R	H	E
Seattle	0 0 1	0 0 1	2 0 0	0 0 1	0 0 0	5	16	2
New York	0 0 0	0 1 2	1 0 0	0 0 1	0 0 2	7	11	0

Win: M. Rivera, N.Y. (1-0). **Loss:** Belcher, Sea. (0-1).
2B: Seattle— E. Martinez, Buhner, Cora; New York— B. Williams 2, Sierra; **HR:** New York— O'Neill (1), Sierra (2), Mattingly (1), Leyritz (1); Seattle— Coleman (1), Griffey (3). **RBI:** Seattle— Griffey 2, Coleman, Sojo, T. Martinez; New York— Sierra 2, Leyritz 2, B. Williams, O'Neill, Mattingly.
Attendance: 57,216. **Time:** 5:13.

Game 3

Friday, Oct. 6, at Seattle

	1 2 3	4 5 6	7 8 9	R	H	E
New York	0 0 0	1 0 0	1 2 0	4	6	2
Seattle	0 0 0	0 2 4	1 0 x	7	7	0

Win: R. Johnson, Sea. (1-0). **Loss:** McDowell, N.Y. (0-1).
3B: Seattle— Coleman. **HR:** Seattle— T. Martinez (1); New York— B. Williams 2 (2), Stanley (1). **RBI:** Seattle— T. Martinez 3, Blowers, Buhner, Sojo; New York— B. Williams 2, Kelly, Stanley. **SB:** Seattle—Coleman (1), Cora (1), Griffey (1); New York— B. Williams.
Attendance: 57,944 (59,166). **Time:** 3:04.

Baseball Playoffs (Cont.)
AMERICAN LEAGUE

Game 4
Saturday, Oct. 7, at Seattle

	1	2	3	4	5	6	7	8	9	R	H	E
New York	3	0	2	0	0	0	0	1	2	8	14	1
Seattle	0	0	4	0	1	1	0	5	x	11	16	0

Win: Charlton, Sea. (1-0). **Save:** Risley, Sea. (1). **Loss:** Wetteland, N.Y. (0-1).

2B: New York— Boggs, Sierra, Mattingly 2. **HR:** New York— O'Neill (2); Seattle— Griffey (4), E. Martinez 2 (2), Buhner (1). **RBI:** New York— O'Neill 2, Boggs, Sierra, Stanley; Seattle— E. Martinez 7, Buhner, Griffey, Sojo.
Attendance: 57,180. **Time:** 4:08.

Game 5
Sunday, Oct. 9, at Seattle

	1	2	3	4	5	6	7	8	9	10	11	R	H	E
New York	0	0	0	2	0	2	0	0	0	0	1	5	6	0
Seattle	0	0	1	1	0	0	0	2	0	0	2	6	15	0

Win: R. Johnson, Sea. (2-0). **Loss:** McDowell, N.Y. (0-2).
2B: New York— Mattingly, Fernandez 2; Seattle— E. Martinez 2, T. Martinez. **HR:** New York— O'Neill (3); Seattle— Cora (1), Griffey (5). **RBI:** New York— O'Neill 2, Mattingly 2, Velarde; Seattle— E. Martinez 2, Buhner, Cora, Griffey.
Attendance: 57,411. **Time:** 4:19.

NATIONAL LEAGUE

⚾ Braves, 3-1

Date	Winner	Home Field
Oct. 3	Braves, 5-4	at Colorado
Oct. 4	Braves, 7-4	at Colorado
Oct. 6	Rockies, 7-5 (10)	at Atlanta
Oct. 7	Braves, 10-4	at Atlanta

Game 1
Tuesday, Oct. 3, at Colorado

	1	2	3	4	5	6	7	8	9	R	H	E
Atlanta	0	0	1	0	0	2	0	1	1	5	12	1
Colorado	0	0	0	3	0	0	0	1	0	4	13	4

Win: A. Pena, Atl. (1-0). **Save:** Wohlers, Atl. (1). **Loss:** Leskanic, Col. (0-1).
2B: Atlanta— Grissom; Colorado— Young, Burks, Castilla. **HR:** Atlanta— Grissom (1), Jones 2 (2); Colorado— Castilla (1). **RBI:** Atlanta— Jones 2, Grissom, Polonia, D. Smith; Colorado— Burks 2, Castilla. **SB:** Atlanta— Polonia (1).
Attendance: 50,040. **Time:** 3:19.

Game 2
Wednesday, Oct. 4, at Colorado

	1	2	3	4	5	6	7	8	9	R	H	E
Atlanta	1	0	1	1	0	0	0	0	4	7	13	1
Colorado	0	0	0	0	0	3	0	1	0	4	8	2

Win: A. Pena, Atl. (2-0). **Save:** Wohlers, Atl. (2). **Loss:** M. Munoz, Col. (0-1).
2B: Atlanta— Jones, D. Smith; Colorado— Bichette 2, Galarraga. **HR:** Atlanta— Grissom 2 (3); Colorado— Walker (1) **RBI:** Atlanta— Grissom 2, McGriff, J. Lopez, Mordecai; Colorado— L. Walker 3, Galarraga.
Attendance: 50,063. **Time:** 3:08.

Game 3
Friday, Oct. 6, at Atlanta

	1	2	3	4	5	6	7	8	9	10	R	H	E
Colorado	1	0	2	0	0	2	0	0	0	2	7	9	0
Atlanta	0	0	0	3	0	0	1	0	1	0	5	11	0

Win: Holmes, Col. (1-0). **Save:** M. Thompson, Col. (1). **Loss:** Wohlers, Atl. (0-1).
2B: Colorado— Bichette. Atlanta— Klesko, Mordecai. **HR:** Colorado— E. Young (1), Castilla (2). **RBI:** Colorado— Castilla 3, E. Young 2, Gallaraga; Atlanta— J. Lopez 2, Klesko, Mordecai, Polonia **SB:** Colorado—L. Walker (1), Weiss (1); Atlanta— Grissom (1).
Attendance: 51,300. **Time:** 3:16.

Playoff Series

The AL and NL League Championship Series began in 1969 with a Best of 5 format, then changed to Best of 7 in 1985. The '95 season was the first year for wild card teams and the new Best of 3 Divisional Series.

Game 4
Saturday, Oct. 7, at Atlanta

	1	2	3	4	5	6	7	8	9	R	H	E
Colorado	0	0	3	0	0	1	0	0	0	4	11	1
Atlanta	0	4	2	1	3	0	0	x		10	15	0

Win: Maddux, Atl. (1-0). **Loss:** Saberhagen, Col. (0-1).
2B: Atlanta— Grissom, Lemke, Jones. **HR:** Colorado— Bichette (1), Castilla (3); Atlanta— McGriff 2 (2). **RBI:** Colorado— Bichette 3, Castilla 1; Atlanta— McGriff 5, Jones 2, Lemke, Grissom. **SB:** Colorado— E. Young (1); Atlanta— Grissom (2).
Attendance: 50,027. **Time:** 2:38.

⚾ Reds, 3-0

Date	Winner	Home Field
Oct. 3	Reds, 7-2	at Los Angeles
Oct. 4	Reds, 5-4	at Los Angeles
Oct. 6	Reds, 10-1	at Cincinnati

Game 1
Tuesday, Oct. 3, at Los Angeles

	1	2	3	4	5	6	7	8	9	R	H	E
Cincinnati	4	0	0	3	0	0	0	0	—	7	12	0
Los Angeles	0	0	1	1	0	0	0	0	—	2	8	0

Win: Schourek, Cin. (1-0). **Loss:** R. Martinez, LA (0-1).
2B: Cincinnati— Howard, R. Sanders, Morris, Boone, Branson. **HR:** Cincinnati— Santiago (1); Los Angeles— Piazza (1). **RBI:** Cincinnati— Santiago 3, Branson 2, Morris 2; Los Angeles— Butler, Piazza. **SB:** Cincinnati— Larkin.
Attendance: 44,199. **Time:** 3:15.

Game 2
Wednesday, Oct 4, at Los Angeles

	1	2	3	4	5	6	7	8	9	R	H	E
Cincinnati	0	0	0	2	0	0	0	1	2	5	6	0
Los Angeles	1	0	0	1	0	0	0	0	2	4	14	2

Win: Burba, Cin. (1-0). **Save:** J. Brantley, Cin. (1). **Loss:** Osuna, LA (0-1).
2B: Los Angeles— Karros. **HR:** Cincinnati— R. Sanders (1); Los Angeles— Karros 2 (2). **RBI:** Cincinnati— R. Sanders 2, Larkin, M. Lewis, Duncan; Los Angeles— Karros 4. **SB:** Cincinnati— R. Sanders 2 (2), Morris (1), Duncan (1).
Attendance: 46,051. **Time:** 3:21.

Game 3
Friday, Oct. 6, at Cincinnati

	1	2	3	4	5	6	7	8	9	R	H	E
Los Angeles	0	0	0	1	0	0	0	0	0	1	9	1
Cincinnati	0	0	2	1	0	4	3	0	x	10	11	2

Win: D. Wells, Cin. (1-0). **Loss:** Nomo, LA (0-1). **HR:** Los Angeles— Piazza; Cincinnati— M. Jackson. **2B:** Los Angeles— Gant (1), Boone (1), M. Lewis (1). **RBI:** Los Angeles— Mondesi; Cincinnati— M. Lewis 4, M. Jackson 3, Gant 2, Boone. **SB:** Cincinnati— Larkin 2 (4), Boone (1).
Attendance: 53,276. **Time:** 3:27.

American League Championship Series

Indians, 4-2

Date	Winner	Home Field
Oct. 10	Mariners, 3-2	at Seattle
Oct. 11	Indians, 5-2	at Seattle
Oct. 13	Mariners, 5-2 (11 inn.)	at Cleveland
Oct. 14	Indians, 7-0	at Cleveland
Oct. 15	Indians, 3-2	at Cleveland
Oct. 17	Indians, 4-0	at Seattle

Most Valuable Player

Orel Hershiser, Cleveland, P

Hershiser's victories in Games 2 and 5 earned him his second LCS MVP award. His first came with Los Angeles in 1988.

W-L	ERA	Gm	IP	H	BB	SO
2-0	1.29	2	14.0	9	3	15

Game 1

Tuesday, Oct. 10, at Seattle

	1 2 3	4 5 6	7 8 9	R	H	E
Cleveland	0 0 1	0 0 0	1 0 0	2	10	1
Seattle	0 2 0	0 0 0	1 0 x	3	7	0

Win: Wolcott, Sea. (1-0). **Loss:** Martinez, Cle. (0-1).
2B: Cleveland— Sorrento; Seattle— Cora, Griffey, Buhner, Sojo. **3B:** Cleveland— Lofton. **HR:** Cleveland— Belle (1); Seattle— Blowers (1). **RBI:** Cleveland— Belle, Thome; Seattle— Blowers 2, Sojo.
Attendance: 57,065. **Time:** 3:07.

Game 2

Wednesday, Oct. 11, at Seattle

	1 2 3	4 5 6	7 8 9	R	H	E
Cleveland	0 0 0	0 2 2	0 1 0	5	12	0
Seattle	0 0 0	0 0 1	0 0 1	2	6	1

Win: Hershiser, Cle. (1-0). **Loss:** Belcher, Sea. (0-1).
3B: Cleveland— Alomar. **HR:** Cleveland— Ramirez 2 (2); Seattle— Griffey (1), Buhner (1). **RBI:** Cleveland— Baerga 2, Ramirez 2, Alomar; Seattle— Griffey, Buhner. **SB:** Cleveland— Vizquel (1); Seattle— Coleman (1).
Attendance: 58,144. **Time:** 3:14.

Game 3

Friday, Oct. 13, at Cleveland

	1 2 3	4 5 6	7 8 9	10 11	R	H	E
Seattle	0 1 1	0 0 0	0 0 0	0 3	5	9	1
Cleveland	0 0 0	1 0 0	0 0 0	0 2	4	2	2

Win: Charlton, Sea. (1-0). **Loss:** Tavarez, Cle. (0-1).
3B: Cleveland— Lofton. **HR:** Seattle— Buhner 2 (3). **RBI:** Seattle— Buhner 4; Cleveland— Lofton, Vizquel. **SB:** Seattle— Cora (1), Griffey (1); Cleveland— Lofton (1).
Attendance: 43,643. **Time:** 3:18.

Game 4

Saturday, Oct. 14, at Cleveland

	1 2 3	4 5 6	7 8 9	R	H	E
Seattle	0 0 0	0 0 0	0 0 0	0	6	1
Cleveland	3 1 2	0 0 1	0 0 x	7	9	0

Win: K. Hill, Cle. (1-0). **Loss:** Benes, Sea. (0-1).
2B: Seattle— Buhner; Cleveland— Vizquel. **HR:** Cleveland— Murray (1), Thome (1). **RBI:** Cleveland— Murray 2, Thome 2, Lofton, Vizquel, Baerga; Seattle— Coleman (2), Griffey (2); Cleveland— Lofton (2), Kirby (1).
Attendance: 43,686. **Time:** 3:30.

Game 5

Sunday, Oct. 15, at Cleveland

	1 2 3	4 5 6	7 8 9	R	H	E
Seattle	0 0 1	0 1 0	0 0 0	2	5	2
Cleveland	1 0 0	0 0 2	0 0 x	3	10	4

Win: Hershiser, Cle. (2-0). **Save:** Mesa, Cle. (1). **Loss:** Bosio, Sea. (0-1).
2B: Seattle— Griffey, Diaz; Cleveland— Murray, Alomar. **3B:** Cleveland— Thome (2). **RBI:** Seattle— Griffey; Cleveland— Murray, Thome 2. **SB:** Seattle— Cora (2), Coleman (3); Cleveland— Lofton 2 (4), Vizquel 2 (3).
Attendance: 43,607. **Time:** 3:37.

Game 6

Tuesday, Oct. 17, at Seattle

	1 2 3	4 5 6	7 8 9	R	H	E
Cleveland	0 0 0	0 1 0	0 3 0	4	8	0
Seattle	0 0 0	0 0 0	0 0 0	0	4	1

Win: D. Martinez, Cle. (1-1). **Loss:** Johnson, Sea. (0-1).
2B: Cleveland— Belle, Peña; Seattle— Sojo. **HR:** Cleveland— Baerga (1). **RBI:** Cleveland— Lofton, Baerga. **SB:** Cleveland— Lofton (5); Seattle— Coleman (4), E. Martinez (1).
Attendance: 58,489. **Time:** 2:54.

ALCS Composite Box Score
Cleveland Indians

Batting	LCS vs Seattle							Overall AL Playoffs						
	Avg	AB	R	H	HR	RBI	BB	SO	Avg	AB	R	H	HR	RBI	BB	SO
Kenny Lofton, cf	.458	24	4	11	0	3	4	6	.351	37	5	13	0	3	5	9
Carlos Baerga, 2b	.400	25	3	10	1	4	2	3	.359	39	5	14	1	5	2	4
Tony Peña, c	.333	6	1	2	0	0	1	0	.375	8	2	3	1	1	1	0
Manny Ramirez, rf	.286	21	2	6	2	2	2	5	.182	33	3	6	2	2	3	7
Sandy Alomar, c	.267	15	0	4	0	1	1	3	.231	26	1	6	0	2	1	2
Jim Thome, 3b	.267	15	4	4	2	5	3	3	.214	28	5	6	3	8	3	9
Eddie Murray, dh	.250	24	2	6	1	3	2	3	.297	37	5	11	2	6	4	4
Albert Belle, lf	.222	18	1	4	1	1	3	5	.241	29	4	7	2	4	7	8
Wayne Kirby rf-lf	.200	5	2	1	0	0	0	0	.333	6	2	2	0	0	0	0
Paul Sorrento, 1b	.154	13	2	2	0	0	1	3	.217	23	4	5	0	1	4	6
Alvaro Espinoza, 3b	.125	8	1	1	0	0	0	2	.111	9	1	1	0	0	0	3
Omar Vizquel, ss	.087	23	2	2	0	2	5	2	.114	35	4	4	0	6	7	4
Herb Perry, 1b	.000	8	0	0	0	0	1	3	.000	9	0	0	0	0	1	3
Ruben Amaro, pr	.000	1	0	0	0	0	0	0	.000	1	0	0	0	0	0	0
TOTALS	.257	206	23	53	7	21	25	37	.243	320	40	78	11	38	38	59

ALCS Composite Box Score (Cont.)

Cleveland Indians

Pitching	ERA	W-L	Sv	Gm	IP	H	BB	SO	ERA	W-L	Sv	Gm	IP	H	BB	SO
Ken Hill	0.00	1-0	0	1	7.0	5	3	6	0.00	2-0	0	2	8.1	6	3	8
Paul Assenmacher	0.00	0-0	0	3	1.1	0	1	2	0.00	0-0	0	6	3.0	0	1	5
Jim Poole	0.00	0-0	0	1	1.0	0	0	2	3.38	0-0	0	2	2.2	2	1	4
Chad Ogea	0.00	0-0	0	1	0.2	1	0	2	0.00	0-0	0	1	0.2	1	0	2
Alan Embree	0.00	0-0	0	1	0.1	0	0	1	0.00	0-0	0	1	0.1	0	0	1
Charles Nagy	1.12	0-0	0	1	8.0	5	0	6	1.20	1-0	0	2	15.0	9	5	12
Orel Hershiser	1.29	2-0	0	2	14.0	9	3	15	0.84	3-0	0	3	21.1	12	5	22
Dennis Martinez	2.03	1-1	0	2	13.1	10	3	7	2.33	1-1	0	3	19.1	15	3	9
Jose Mesa	2.25	0-0	1	4	4.0	3	1	1	1.50	0-0	1	6	6.0	3	3	1
Julian Tavarez	2.70	0-1	0	4	3.1	3	1	2	4.50	0-1	0	7	6.0	8	1	5
Eric Plunk	9.00	0-0	0	3	2.0	1	3	2	5.40	0-0	0	4	3.1	2	4	3
TOTALS	1.64	4-2	1	6	55	37	15	46	1.67	7-2	1	37	86	58	26	72

Wild Pitches— LCS (none); OVERALL (Hershiser 2, Ogea). **Hit Batters—** LCS (Hershiser, Nagy); OVERALL (Hershiser, Martinez, Nagy).

Seattle Mariners

Batting	LCS vs Cleveland								Overall AL Playoffs							
	Avg	AB	R	H	HR	RBI	BB	SO	Avg	AB	R	H	HR	RBI	BB	SO
Alex Diaz, ph-lf	.429	7	0	3	0	0	1	1	.400	10	0	4	0	0	2	2
Ken Griffey, cf	.333	21	2	7	1	2	4	4	.364	44	11	16	6	9	6	8
Jay Buhner, rf	.304	23	5	7	3	5	2	8	.383	47	7	18	4	8	4	12
Luis Sojo, ss	.250	20	2	5	0	1	0	2	.250	40	2	10	0	4	0	5
Jeff Blowers, 3b	.222	18	1	4	1	2	0	4	.194	36	1	7	1	3	3	11
Joey Cora, 2b	.174	23	2	4	0	0	1	0	.238	42	9	10	1	1	4	0
Tino Martinez, 1b	.136	22	0	3	0	0	3	7	.273	44	4	12	1	5	6	11
Vince Coleman, lf	.100	20	2	2	0	2	2	6	.163	43	6	7	1	1	4	10
Edgar Martinez, dh	.087	23	0	2	0	0	2	5	.318	44	6	14	2	10	8	7
Dan Wilson, c	.000	16	0	0	0	0	0	4	.061	33	0	2	0	1	2	10
Doug Strange, ph-3b	.000	4	0	0	0	0	0	2	.000	8	0	0	0	0	1	3
Rich Amaral, ph	.000	2	0	0	0	0	0	1	.000	2	0	0	0	0	0	1
Alex Rodriguez, ph	.000	1	0	0	0	0	0	1	.000	2	1	0	0	0	0	1
Chris Widger, c	.000	1	0	0	0	0	0	1	.000	4	0	0	0	0	0	4
Felix Fermin, 2b-ss	—	0	0	0	0	0	0	0	.000	1	0	0	0	0	0	1
Warren Newson, ph	—	—	—	—	—	—	—	—	.000	1	0	0	0	0	0	0
TOTALS	.184	201	12	37	5	10	15	46	.249	401	47	100	16	43	40	87

Pitching	ERA	W-L	Sv	Gm	IP	H	BB	SO	ERA	W-L	Sv	Gm	IP	H	BB	SO
Norm Charlton	0.00	1-0	1	3	6.0	1	1	5	1.35	2-0	2	7	13.1	5	4	14
Jeff Nelson	0.00	0-0	0	3	3.0	3	5	3	2.08	0-1	0	6	8.2	10	8	10
Bill Risley	0.00	0-0	0	3	2.2	1	2	2	3.18	0-0	0	7	5.2	4	1	3
Randy Johnson	2.35	0-1	0	2	15.1	12	2	13	2.49	2-1	0	4	25.1	17	8	29
Bobby Ayala	2.45	0-0	0	2	3.2	3	3	3	10.38	0-0	0	4	4.1	9	4	3
Bob Wolcott	2.57	1-0	0	1	7.0	8	5	2	2.57	1-0	0	1	7.0	8	5	2
Bob Wells	3.00	0-0	0	1	3.0	2	2	2	4.50	0-0	0	2	4.0	4	3	2
Chris Bosio	3.38	0-1	0	1	5.1	7	2	3	7.62	0-1	0	3	13.0	17	6	5
Tim Belcher	6.35	0-0	0	1	5.2	9	2	1	6.30	0-2	0	3	10.0	13	7	1
Andy Benes	23.14	0-1	0	1	2.1	6	2	3	8.36	0-1	0	3	14.0	16	11	11
TOTALS	3.33	2-4	1	6	54.0	53	25	37	4.53	5-6	3	11	105.1	103	57	80

Wild Pitches— LCS (none); OVERALL (Charlton). **Hit Batters—** LCS (Charlton); OVERALL (Charlton, Nelson, Risley).

Score by Innings

	1	2	3	4	5	6	7	8	9	10	11		R	H	E
Cleveland	4	1	3	2	0	1	1	5	0	0	0	—	23	53	7
Seattle	0	3	2	0	1	1	1	0	3	1	—		12	37	6

DP: Cleveland 4; Seattle 7. **LOB:** Cleveland 44; Seattle 49. **2B:** Cleveland— Alomar, Belle, Peña, Sorrento, Vizquel; Seattle— Buhner (2), Griffey (2), Sojo (2), Cora, Diaz. **3B:** Cleveland— Lofton (2), Alomar. **SB:** Cleveland— Lofton (5), Vizquel (3), Kirby; Seattle— Coleman (4), Griffey (2), E. Martinez. **CS:** Cleveland— Perry; Seattle— Griffey, E. Martinez. **S:** Cleveland— Kirby; Seattle— Strange. **SF:** Cleveland— Vizquel, Lofton.

Umpires: Dave Phillips, Derryl Cousins, Rick Reed, Dale Ford, Tim McClelland, Drew Coble.

National League Championship Series

🦅 Braves, 4-0

Date	Winner	Home Field
Oct. 10	Braves, 2-1	at Cincinnati
Oct. 11	Braves, 6-2	at Cincinnati
Oct. 13	Braves, 5-2	at Atlanta
Oct. 14	Braves, 6-0	at Atlanta

Most Valuable Player

Mike Devereaux, Atlanta, RF

Avg	AB	R	H	HR	RBI	BB	SO
.308	13	2	4	1	5	1	2

Game 1

Tuesday, Oct. 10, at Cincinnati

	1 2 3	4 5 6	7 8 9	0 1	R	H	E
Atlanta	0 0 0	0 0 0	0 0 1	0 1	2	7	0
Cincinnati	0 0 0	1 0 0	0 0 0	0 0	1	8	0

Win: Wohlers, Atl. (1-0). **Save:** McMichael, Atl. (1) **Loss:** Jackson, Cin. (0-1).
2B: Cincinnati— Howard, Larkin, Morris. **3B:** Cincinnati— Larkin. **RBI:** Atlanta— Justice, Deveraux.
Attendance: 40,382. **Time:** 3:18.

Game 2

Wednesday, Oct. 11, at Cincinnati

	1 2 3	4 5 6	7 8 9	R	H	E
Atlanta	1 0 0	1 0 0	0 0 4	6	11	1
Cincinnati	0 0 0	0 2 0	0 0 0	2	9	1

Win: McMichael, Atl. (1-0) **Loss:** Portugal, Cin. (0-1).
2B: Atlanta— McGriff 3, Devereaux; Cincinnati— Larkin. **HR:** Atlanta— Lopez. **RBI:** Atlanta— Lopez 3, Jones, Devereaux; Cincinnati— Harris. **SB:** Atlanta— Smoltz (1); Cincinnati— Larkin (1), Morris (1), Harris (1), Branson (1).
Attendance: 44,624. **Time:** 3:26.

Game 3

Friday, Oct. 13, at Atlanta

	1 2 3	4 5 6	7 8 9	R	H	E
Cincinnati	0 0 0	0 0 0	0 1 1	2	8	0
Atlanta	0 0 0	0 0 3	2 0 x	5	12	1

Win: Maddux, Atl. (1-0). **Loss:** Wells, Cin. (0-1).
2B: Cincinnati— Branson; Atlanta— McGriff. **HR:** Atlanta— Jones (1), O'Brien (1). **RBI:** Cincinnati— Howard, Morris; Atlanta— O'Brien 3, Jones 2. **SB:** Atlanta— Jones (1).
Attendance: 51,424. **Time:** 2:42.

Game 4

Saturday, Oct. 14, at Atlanta

	1 2 3	4 5 6	7 8 9	R	H	E
Cincinnati	0 0 0	0 0 0	0 0 0	0	3	1
Atlanta	0 0 1	0 0 0	5 0 x	6	12	1

Win: Avery, Atl. (1-0). **Loss:** Schourek, Cin. (0-1).
2B: Atlanta— J. Lopez, Grissom. **3B:** Atlanta— Grissom. **HR:** Atlanta— Devereaux (1). **RBI:** Atlanta— Devereaux 3, Lemke, Polonia.
Attendance: 52,067. **Time:** 2:54.

NLCS Composite Box Score
Atlanta Braves

Batting		LCS vs Cincinnati							Overall NL Playoffs							
	Avg	AB	R	H	HR	RBI	BB	SO	Avg	AB	R	H	HR	RBI	BB	SO
Luis Polonia, pr-lf	.500	2	0	1	0	1	0	0	.400	5	0	2	0	3	0	1
Steve Avery, p	.500	2	0	1	0	0	0	0	.500	2	0	1	0	0	0	0
Chipper Jones, 3b	.438	16	3	7	1	3	3	1	.412	34	7	14	3	7	5	3
Fred McGriff, 1b	.438	16	5	7	0	0	3	0	.382	34	9	13	2	6	5	3
Charlie O'Brien, c	.400	5	1	2	1	3	0	1	.300	10	1	3	1	3	1	2
Javier Lopez, c	.357	14	2	5	1	4	0	4	.391	23	2	9	1	6	0	4
John Smoltz, p	.333	3	0	1	0	0	0	1	.200	5	0	1	0	0	0	1
Mike Devereaux, rf	.308	13	2	4	1	5	1	2	.278	18	3	5	1	5	1	2
Rafael Belliard, ss	.273	11	1	3	0	0	0	3	.188	16	2	3	0	0	0	4
Dave Justice, rf	.273	11	1	3	0	1	2	1	.250	24	3	6	0	1	7	3
Marquis Grissom, cf	.263	19	2	5	0	0	1	4	.400	40	7	16	3	4	1	7
Mark Lemke, 2b	.167	18	2	3	0	1	1	0	.189	37	5	7	0	2	2	3
Ryan Klesko, lf	.000	7	0	0	0	0	3	4	.318	22	5	7	0	1	3	7
Jeff Blauser, ss	.000	4	0	0	0	0	0	2	.000	10	0	0	0	0	2	5
Greg Maddux, p	.000	3	0	0	0	0	0	1	.111	9	1	1	0	0	0	2
Mike Mordecai, ph-ss	.000	2	0	0	0	0	0	1	.400	5	1	2	0	0	0	1
Dwight Smith	.000	2	0	0	0	0	0	0	.400	5	0	2	0	0	0	0
Tom Glavine, p	.000	1	0	0	0	0	1	0	.250	4	0	1	0	0	1	1
TOTALS	.282	149	19	42	4	17	16	22	.307	303	46	93	11	41	28	49

Pitching		LCS vs Cincinnati							Overall NL Playoffs							
	ERA	W-L	Sv	Gm	IP	H	BB	SO	ERA	W-L	Sv	Gm	IP	H	BB	SO
Steve Avery	0.00	1-0	0	2	6.0	2	3	6	1.35	1-0	0	3	6.2	3	4	7
Alejandro Peña	0.00	0-0	0	3	3.0	2	1	4	0.00	2-0	0	6	6.0	5	2	6
Greg McMichael	0.00	1-0	1	3	2.2	1	1	2	2.25	1-0	1	6	4.0	1	3	3
Brad Clontz	0.00	0-0	0	1	0.1	1	0	0	0.00	0-0	0	2	1.2	1	0	2
Greg Maddux	1.12	1-0	0	1	8.0	7	2	4	3.27	2-0	0	3	22.0	26	4	11
Tom Glavine	1.29	0-0	0	1	7.0	7	2	5	1.93	0-0	0	2	14.0	12	3	8
Mark Wohlers	1.80	1-0	4	5	5.0	2	0	8	3.52	1-1	2	7	7.2	8	2	12
John Smoltz	2.57	0-0	0	1	7.0	7	2	2	4.97	0-0	0	2	12.2	12	3	8
Pedro Borbon Jr.	—	—	—	—	—	—	—	—	0.00	0-0	0	1	1.0	1	0	3
Kent Mercker	—	—	—	—	—	—	—	—	0.00	0-0	0	1	0.1	0	0	0
TOTALS	1.15	4-0	1	4	39.0	28	11	31	2.72	7-1	3	32	76.0	69	21	60

Wild Pitches— LCS (Maddux); OVERALL (Maddux, Smoltz). **Hit Batters—** LCS (Glavine, Maddux); OVERALL (Maddux 2, Glavine, Peña, Smoltz).

NLCS Composite Box Score (Cont.)
Cincinnati Reds

Batting	Avg	AB	R	H	HR	RBI	BB	SO	Avg	AB	R	H	HR	RBI	BB	SO
		LCS vs Atlanta								**Overall NL Playoffs**						
Lenny Harris, ph	1.000	2	0	2	0	1	0	0	1.000	2	0	2	0	1	0	0
Eddie Taubensee, c	.500	2	0	1	0	0	0	0	.500	2	0	1	0	0	0	0
David Wells, p	.500	2	0	1	0	0	0	0	.400	5	0	2	0	0	0	1
Barry Larkin, ss	.389	18	1	7	0	0	1	1	.387	31	3	12	0	1	2	3
Thomas Howard, ph	.250	8	0	2	0	1	2	0	.167	18	0	3	0	1	2	2
Mark Lewis, 3b	.250	4	0	1	0	0	1	1	.333	6	2	2	1	5	2	1
Benito Santiago, c	.231	13	0	3	0	0	2	3	.273	22	2	6	1	3	5	6
Bret Boone, 2b	.214	14	1	3	0	0	1	2	.250	24	5	6	1	1	2	5
Ron Gant, lf	.188	16	1	3	0	1	0	3	.207	29	4	6	1	3	0	6
Hal Morris, 1b	.167	12	0	2	0	0	2	0	.318	22	5	7	0	3	4	2
Reggie Sanders, rf	.125	16	0	2	0	0	2	10	.138	29	3	4	1	2	3	19
Jeff Branson, ph-3b	.111	9	2	1	0	0	0	2	.188	16	2	3	0	0	1	3
Jerome Walton, cf-lf	.000	7	0	0	0	0	1	2	.000	10	0	0	0	0	1	3
Pete Schourek, p	.000	5	0	0	0	0	0	4	.000	7	0	0	0	0	0	5
Mariano Duncan, ph	.000	3	0	0	0	0	1	1	.333	6	1	2	0	1	1	1
Eric Anthony, ph	.000	1	0	0	0	0	1	1	.000	1	0	0	0	0	1	1
Darren Lewis, cf	.000	1	0	0	0	0	0	0	.000	4	0	0	0	0	0	1
John Smiley, p	.000	1	0	0	0	0	0	0	.000	3	0	0	0	0	0	1
Mike Jackson, p	—	—	—	—	—	—	—	—	1.000	1	0	1	0	3	0	0
TOTALS	.209	134	5	28	0	4	12	31	.239	238	27	57	5	26	25	59

Pitching	ERA	W-L	Sv	Gm	IP	H	BB	SO	ERA	W-L	Sv	Gm	IP	H	BB	SO
Ken Hill	0.00	1-0	0	1	7.0	5	3	6	0.00	2-0	0	2	8.1	6	3	8
Jeff Brantley	0.00	0-0	0	2	2.2	0	2	4	3.18	0-0	1	5	5.2	5	2	3
Dave Burba	0.00	0-0	0	1	2.0	3	4	0	0.00	0-0	0	3	4.2	5	5	0
Hector Carrasco	0.00	0-0	0	1	1.1	1	0	3	0.00	0-0	0	1	1.1	1	0	3
Pete Schourek	1.26	0-1	0	2	14.1	14	3	13	1.69	1-1	0	3	21.1	19	6	18
John Smiley	3.60	0-0	0	1	5.0	5	0	2	3.27	0-0	0	2	11.0	14	0	2
David Wells	4.50	0-1	0	1	6.0	8	2	3	2.19	1-1	0	2	12.1	14	3	11
Mike Jackson	23.14	0-1	0	3	2.1	5	4	1	9.00	0-1	0	6	6.0	9	4	2
Xavier Hernandez	27.00	0-0	0	1	0.2	3	1	0	27.00	0-0	0	1	0.2	3	1	0
Mark Portugal	36.00	0-1	0	1	3.0	3	1	0	36.00	0-1	0	1	1.0	3	1	0
TOTALS	4.62	0-4	0	4	37.0	42	16	22	3.52	3-4	1	24	64.0	73	21	39

Wild Pitches— LCS (Burba, Portugal, Schourek); OVERALL (Burba, Portugal, Schourek). **Hit Batters—** LCS (none); OVERALL (Wells). **Balks—** LCS (none); OVERALL (Jackson).

Score by Innings

	1	2	3	4	5	6	7	8	9	10	11	R	H	E
Atlanta	1	0	1		1	0	3		7	0	1	—19	42	3
Cincinnati	0	0	1		0	2	0		0	1	1	—5	28	2

DP: Atlanta 8, Cincinnati 4. **LOB:** Atlanta 36, Cincinnati 28. **2B:** Atlanta— McGriff (4), Devereaux, Lopez; Cincinnati— Larkin (2), Howard, Morris, Branson. **3B:** Atlanta— Grissom; Cincinnati— Larkin. **HR:** Atlanta— Jones, O'Brien, Lopez, Devereaux. **SB:** Atlanta— Smoltz, Jones; Cincinnati— Larkin, Morris, Branson, Harris. **CS:** Atlanta— Klesko; Cincinnati— Howard, Sanders, Larkin. **S:** Atlanta— Polonia; Cincinnati— Branson. **SF:** Cincinnati— Howard. **Umpires:** Ed Runge, Jim Quick, Dana DeMuth, Gerry Davis, Randy Marsh, Jerry Crawford.

WORLD SERIES

⚾ Braves, 4-2

Date	Winner	Home Field
Oct. 21	Braves, 3-2	Atlanta
Oct. 22	Braves, 4-3	Atlanta
Oct. 24	Indians, 7-6 (11 inn.)	Cleveland
Oct. 25	Braves, 5-2	Cleveland
Oct. 26	Indians, 5-4	Cleveland
Oct. 28	Braves, 1-0	Atlanta

Most Valuable Player
Tom Glavine, Atlanta
Pitcher

W-L	ERA	Gm	IP	H	BB	SO
2-0	1.29	2	14.0	4	6	11

Game 1
Saturday, Oct. 21, at Atlanta

	1	2	3	4	5	6	7	8	9	R	H	E
Cleveland	1	0	0	0	0	0	0	0	1	2	2	0
Atlanta	0	1	0	0	0	2	0	x		3	3	2

Win: Maddux, Atl. (1-0). **Loss:** Hershiser, Cle. (0-1).
HR: Atlanta— McGriff (1). **RBI:** Cleveland— Baerga; Atlanta— McGriff, Polonia, Belliard. **SB:** Cleveland— Lofton 2 (2).
Attendance: 51,876. **Time:** 2:37.

Game 2
Sunday, Oct. 22, at Atlanta

	1	2	3	4	5	6	7	8	9	R	H	E
Cleveland	0	2	0	0	0	0	1	0	0	3	6	2
Atlanta	0	0	2	0	0	2	0	0	x	4	8	2

Win: Glavine, Atl. (1-0). **Save:** Wohlers, Atl. (1). **Loss:** D. Martinez, Cle. (0-1).
2B: Atlanta— Jones. **HR:** Cleveland— Murray (1); Atlanta— Lopez (1). **RBI:** Cleveland— Murray 2; Atlanta— Lopez 2, Jones, Justice. **SB:** Cleveland— Lofton 2 (4), Vizquel (1).
Attendance: 51,877. **Time:** 3:17.

Game 3
Tuesday, Oct. 24 at Cleveland

	1 2 3	4 5 6	7 8 9	0 1	R	H	E
Atlanta	1 0 0	0 0 1	1 3 0	0 0	6	12	1
Cleveland	2 0 2	0 0 0	1 1 0	0 1	7	12	2

Win: Mesa, Cle. (0-1). **Loss:** A. Peña (0-1).
2B: Atlanta— Grissom, Jones; Cleveland— Lofton, Baerga, Alomar. **3B—** Cleveland— Vizquel. **HR:** Atlanta— McGriff (2), Klesko (1). **RBI:** Atlanta— McGriff 2, Devereaux, Justice, Klesko, Polonia; Cleveland— Baerga 3, Alomar, Belle, Murray, Vizquel. **SB:** Atlanta— Polonia (1), McGriff (1); Cleveland— Lofton (5), Ramirez (1).
Attendance: 43,584. **Time:** 4:09.

Game 4
Wednesday, Oct. 25, at Cleveland

	1 2 3	4 5 6	7 8 9	R	H	E
Atlanta	0 0 0	0 0 1	3 0 1	5	11	1
Cleveland	0 0 0	0 0 1	0 0 1	2	6	0

Win: Avery, Atl. (1-0). **Save:** Borbon, Atl. (1). **Loss:** Hill, Cle. (0-1).
2B: Atlanta— Polonia, McGriff, Lopez; Cleveland— Sorrento, Thome. **HR:** Atlanta— Klesko (2); Cleveland— Belle (1), Ramirez (1). **RBI:** Atlanta— Justice 2, Klesko, Polonia, Lopez; Cleveland— Belle, Ramirez. **SB:** Atlanta— Grissom 2 (2).
Attendance: 43,578. **Time:** 3:14.

Game 5
Thursday, Oct. 26, at Cleveland

	1 2 3	4 5 6	7 8 9	R	H	E
Atlanta	0 0 0	1 1 0	0 0 2	4	7	0
Cleveland	2 0 0	0 0 2	0 1 x	5	8	1

Win: Hershiser, Cle. (1-1). **Save:** Mesa, Cle. (1). **Loss:** Maddux, Atl. (1-1).
2B: Atlanta— Jones, McGriff; Cleveland— Baerga, Alomar. **HR:** Atlanta— Polonia (1), Klesko (3); Cleveland— Belle (2), Thome (1). **RBI:** Atlanta— Klesko 2, Grissom, Polonia; Cleveland— Belle 2, Thome 2, Ramirez.
Attendance: 43,595. **Time:** 2:33.

Game 6
Saturday, Oct. 28, at Atlanta

	1 2 3	4 5 6	7 8 9	R	H	E
Cleveland	0 0 0	0 0 0	0 0 0	0	1	1
Atlanta	0 0 0	0 0 1	0 0 x	1	6	0

Win: Glavine, Atl. (2-0). **Save:** Wohlers, Atl. (2). **Loss:** Poole (0-1).
2B: Atlanta— Justice. **HR:** Atlanta— Justice (1). **RBI:** Atlanta— Justice. **SB:** Cleveland— Lofton (6); Atlanta— Grissom (3).
Attendance: 51,875. **Time:** 3:02.

World Series Composite Box Score
Atlanta Braves

Batting	WS vs Cleveland								Overall Playoffs							
	Avg	AB	R	H	HR	RBI	BB	SO	Avg	AB	R	H	HR	RBI	BB	SO
Dwight Smith, ph	.500	2	0	1	0	0	0	0	.429	7	0	3	0	1	1	0
Marquis Grissom, cf	.360	25	3	9	0	1	1	3	.385	65	10	25	3	5	2	10
Mike Mordecai, ph-ss	.333	3	0	1	0	0	0	1	.375	8	1	3	0	2	0	2
Ryan Klesko, dh-lf	.313	16	4	5	3	4	3	4	.316	38	9	12	3	5	6	11
Chipper Jones, 3b	.286	21	3	6	0	1	4	3	.364	55	10	20	3	8	9	8
Luis Polonia, ph-lf	.286	14	3	4	1	4	1	3	.316	19	3	6	1	7	1	4
Mark Lemke, 2b	.273	22	1	6	0	0	3	2	.220	59	6	13	0	2	5	5
Fred McGriff, 1b	.261	23	5	6	2	3	3	7	.333	57	14	19	4	9	8	8
Dave Justice, rf	.250	20	3	5	1	5	5	1	.250	44	6	11	1	6	12	4
Mike Devereaux, lf-rf	.250	4	0	1	0	1	0	1	.273	22	3	6	1	6	3	3
Javier Lopez, ph-c	.176	17	1	3	1	3	1	1	.300	40	3	12	2	9	1	5
Rafael Belliard, ss	.000	16	0	0	0	1	0	4	.094	32	2	3	0	1	0	8
Charlie O'Brien, c	.000	0	0	0	0	0	0	0	.231	13	1	3	1	3	1	3
Tom Glavine, p	.000	4	0	0	0	0	1	2	.125	8	0	1	0	0	2	3
Greg Maddux, p	.000	3	0	0	0	0	0	0	.083	12	1	1	0	0	0	3
Steve Avery, p	.000	0	0	0	0	0	0	0	.500	2	0	1	0	0	0	0
John Smoltz, p	.000	0	0	0	0	0	0	0	.200	5	0	1	0	0	0	1
Jeff Blauser, ss	—	0	0	0	0	0	0	0	.000	10	0	0	0	0	2	5
TOTALS	.244	193	23	47	8	23	25	34	.282	496	69	140	19	64	53	83

Pitching	ERA	W-L	Sv	Gm	IP	H	BB	SO	ERA	W-L	Sv	Gm	IP	H	BB	SO
Pedro Borbon Jr.	0.00	0-0		1	1.0	0	0	2	0.00	0-0		2	2.0	1	0	5
Tom Glavine	1.29	2-0	0	2	14.0	6		11	1.61	2-0	0	4	28.0	16	9	19
Steve Avery	1.50	1-0		1	6.0	3	5	3	1.42	2-0	0	4	12.2	6	9	10
Mark Wohlers	1.80	0-0	2	4	5.0	3	3	3	2.83	1-1	4	11	12.2	12	5	15
Greg Maddux	2.25	1-1	0	2	16.0	9	3	8	2.84	3-1	0	5	38.0	35	7	19
Brad Clontz	2.70	0-0		2	3.1	0	2	2	1.80	0-0	0	4	5.0	3	0	4
Greg McMichael	2.70	0-0		3	3.1	2	2	2	2.50	1-0	1	9	7.1	4	5	5
Kent Mercker	4.50	0-0		1	2.0	1	2	2	3.91	0-0	0	2	2.1	1	2	2
Alejandro Peña	9.00	0-1		2	1.0	3	2	1	1.28	2-1	0	8	7.0	8	4	6
John Smoltz	15.43	0-0		1	2.1	6	2	4	6.60	0-0	0	3	15.0	18	5	12
TOTALS	2.67	4-2	3		54.0	35	25	37	2.70	11-3	6	14	130.0	104	46	97

Wild Pitches—WS (none); OVERALL (Maddux, Smoltz). **Hit Batters**— WS (none); OVERALL (Maddux 2, Glavine, A. Peña, Smoltz). **Balk**— WS (Avery); OVERALL— (Avery).

World Series Composite Box Score (Cont.)
Cleveland Indians

| | WS vs Atlanta | | | | | | | | Overall Playoffs | | | | | | | |
Batting	Avg	AB	R	H	HR	RBI	BB	SO	Avg	AB	R	H	HR	RBI	BB	SO
Alvaro Espinoza, pr-3b	.500	2	1	1	0	0	0	0	.182	11	2	2	0	0	0	3
Albert Belle, lf	.235	17	4	4	2	4	7	5	.239	46	8	11	4	8	14	13
Manny Ramirez, rf	.222	18	2	4	1	2	4	5	.196	51	5	10	3	4	7	12
Jim Thome, ph-3b	.211	19	1	4	1	2	2	5	.213	47	4	10	4	10	5	14
Kenny Lofton, cf	.200	25	6	5	0	0	3	1	.290	62	11	18	0	3	8	10
Sandy Alomar, c	.200	15	0	3	0	1	0	2	.220	41	1	9	0	3	1	4
Carlos Baerga, 2b	.192	26	1	5	0	4	1	1	.292	65	6	19	1	9	3	5
Paul Sorrento, ph-1b	.182	11	0	2	0	0	0	4	.206	34	4	7	0	1	4	10
Omar Vizquel, ss	.174	23	3	4	0	1	3	5	.138	58	7	8	0	7	10	9
Tony Peña, c	.167	6	0	1	0	0	0	1	.286	14	2	4	1	1	1	0
Eddie Murray, 1b-dh	.105	19	1	2	1	3	5	4	.232	56	6	13	3	9	9	8
Wayne Kirby, ph-rf	.000	1	0	0	0	0	0	1	.286	7	2	2	0	0	0	1
Hebert Perry, 1b	.000	5	0	0	0	0	0	2	.000	14	0	0	0	0	1	5
Dennis Martinez, p	.000	3	0	0	0	0	0	1	.000	3	0	0	0	0	0	1
Ruben Amaro, ph-rf	.000	2	0	0	0	0	0	0	.000	3	1	0	0	0	0	1
Orel Hershiser, p	.000	2	0	0	0	0	0	0	.000	2	0	0	0	0	0	0
Jim Poole, p	.000	1	0	0	0	0	0	0	.000	1	0	0	0	0	0	0
TOTALS	.179	195	19	35	5	17	25	37	.219	515	59	113	16	55	63	96

Pitching	ERA	W-L	Sv	Gm	IP	H	BB	SO	ERA	W-L	Sv	Gm	IP	H	BB	SO
Julian Tavarez	0.00	0-0	0	5	4.1	3	2	1	2.62	0-1	0	12	10.1	11	3	6
Orel Hershiser	2.57	1-1	0	2	14.0	8	4	13	1.53	4-1	0	5	35.1	20	9	35
Alan Embree	2.70	0-0	0	4	3.1	2	2	2	2.43	0-0	0	5	3.2	2	2	3
Dennis Martinez	3.48	0-1	0	2	10.1	12	8	5	2.73	1-2	0	5	29.2	27	11	14
Jim Poole	3.86	0-1	0	2	2.1	1	0	1	3.60	0-1	0	4	5.0	3	1	5
Ken Hill	4.26	0-1	0	2	6.1	7	4	1	1.84	2-1	0	4	14.2	10	7	9
Jose Mesa	4.50	1-0	1	2	4.0	5	1	4	2.70	1-0	2	8	10.0	8	4	5
Charles Nagy	6.43	0-0	0	1	7.0	8	1	4	2.86	1-0	0	3	22.0	17	6	16
Paul Assenmacher	6.75	0-0	0	4	1.1	1	3	3	2.09	0-0	0	10	4.1	1	4	8
TOTALS	3.57	2-4	1	6	53.0	47	25	34	2.47	9-6	2	15	135.0	99	47	101

Wild Pitches— WS (none); OVERALL (Burba, Portugal, Schourek). **Hit Batters—** WS (Martinez, Tavarez); OVERALL (Martinez 2, Hershiser, Nagy, Tavarez).

Score by Innings

	1	2	3	4	5	6	7	8	9	10	11		R	H	E
Cleveland	5	2	2	0	0	3	2	2	2	0	1	—	19	35	6
Atlanta	1	1	2	1	1	5	6	3	3	0	0	—	23	47	6

DP: Cleveland 8, Atlanta 2. **LOB:** Cleveland 39, Atlanta 44. **2B:** Cleveland— Alomar (2), Baerga (2), Lofton, Sorrento, Thome; Atlanta— Jones (3), Lopez (2), McGriff (2), Grissom, Justice, Polonia. **3B:** Cleveland— Vizquel. **HR:** Cleveland— Belle (2), Murray, Ramirez, Thome; Atlanta— Klesko (3), McGriff (2), Justice, Lopez, Polonia. **SB:** Cleveland— Lofton (6), Vizquel, Ramirez; Atlanta—Grissom (3), McGriff. Polonia. **CS:** Cleveland— Lofton, Espinoza, Belle; Atlanta— Grissom, Lemke. **S:** Atlanta— Belliard (2), Mordecai, O'Brien, Lemke. **SF:** Atlanta— Jones.

Umpires: Harry Wendelstedt (NL), James McKean (AL), Bruce Froemming (NL), John Hirschbeck (AL), Frank Pulli (NL), Joe Brinkman (AL).

The **Atlanta Braves** celebrate their first world championship since moving from Milwaukee in 1966.

COLLEGE

Final *Baseball America* Top 25

Final 1995 Division I Top 25, voted on by the editors of *Baseball America* and released June 11, following the NCAA College World Series. Given are final records and winning percentage (including all postseason games); records in College World Series and team eliminated by (DNP indicates team did not play in tourney); head coach (career years and record including 1995 postseason) preseason ranking and rank before start of CWS.

	Record	Pct	CWS Recap	Head Coach	Rank	Rank
1 CS-Fullerton	57-9	.864	4-0	Augie Garrido (27 yrs: 1107-508-7)	15	1
2 USC	49-21	.700	4-2 (CS-Fullerton)	Mike Gillespie (9 yrs: 348-214-1)	6	10
3 Florida St.	53-16	.768	1-2 (USC)	Mike Martin (16 yrs: 867-296-3)	2	3
4 Miami	48-17	.738	2-2 (USC)	Jim Morris (14 yrs: 601-275-1)	7	7
5 Tennessee	54-16	.771	2-2 (CS-Fullerton)	Rod Delmonico (6 yrs: 255-120)	12	15
6 Clemson	54-14	.794	0-2 (Stanford)	Jack Leggett (16 yrs: 488-319)	4	2
7 Oklahoma	42-16	.724	0-2 (USC)	Larry Cochell (29 yrs: 1002-560-2)	3	12
8 Texas Tech	51-14	.785	DNP	Larry Hays (25 yrs: 1018-574-2)	NR	8
9 Auburn	50-13	.794	DNP	Hal Baird (16 yrs: 564-297)	10	6
10 Stanford	40-25	.615	1-2 (Tennessee)	Mark Marquess (19 yrs: 776-410-4)	1	16
11 Oklahoma St.	46-19	.708	DNP	Gary Ward (18 yrs: 908-292-1)	9	4
12 Rice	43-19	.694	DNP	Wayne Graham (4 yrs: 142-84)	16	14
13 Wichita St.	53-17	.757	DNP	Gene Stephenson (18 yrs: 1004-309-3)	5	11
14 Alabama	42-23	.646	DNP	Jim Wells (6 yrs: 234-112)	NR	20
15 LSU	39-25	.723	DNP	Skip Bertman (12 yrs: 576-220-1)	8	5
16 Texas A&M	44-22	.667	DNP	Mark Johnson (11 yrs: 494-198-1)	23	NR
17 Long Beach St.	39-25	.609	DNP	Dave Snow (11 yrs: 456-223-3)	19	NR
18 Mississippi	40-22	.645	DNP	Don Kessinger (5 yrs: 161-123)	20	23
19 Central Florida	49-13	.790	DNP	Jay Bergman (19 yrs: 714-419-3)	NR	13
20 Pepperdine	36-19	.655	DNP	Pat Harrison (1 yr: 36-19)	17	NR
21 Texas	44-19	.698	DNP	Cliff Gustafson (28 yrs: 1338-349-2)	11	9
22 Florida Int'l	50-11	.820	DNP	Danny Price (16 yrs: 633-320)	NR	21
23 Fresno St.	41-22	.651	DNP	Bob Bennett (27 yrs: 1048-575-7)	NR	18
24 Lamar	38-24	.613	DNP	Jim Gilligan (19 yrs: 664-395-6)	NR	NR
25 North Carolina	39-23	.629	DNP	Mike Roberts (18 yrs: 676-349-3)	NR	NR

College World Series

CWS Seeds: 1. CS-Fullerton (53-9); **2.** Florida State (52-14); **3.** Miami-FL (46-15); **4.** Clemson (54-12); **5.** Tennessee (52-14); **6.** USC (45-19); **7.** Oklahoma (42-14); **8.** Stanford (39-23).

Bracket One

June 2— Florida St 3 ....Oklahoma 2
June 2— Miami-FL 15 ....USC 10
June 4— Miami-FL 4................................Florida St. 2
June 4— USC 9 ....Oklahoma 4 (out)
June 6— USC 16 ....Florida St. 11 (out)
June 7— USC 7 ....Miami-FL 5 (out)
June 9— USC 7 ....Miami-FL 3 (out)

Bracket Two

June 3— CS-Fullerton 6 ....Stanford 5
June 3— Tennessee 3 ....Clemson 1
June 5— CS-Fullerton 11 ....Tennessee 1
June 5— Stanford 8....................................Clemson 3 (out)
June 6— Tennessee 6 ....Stanford 2 (out)
June 8— CS-Fullerton 11 ....Tennessee 0 (out)

CWS Championship Game

Saturday, June 10, at Rosenblatt Stadium in Omaha.

	1	2	3	4	5	6	7	8	9	R	H	E
USC	0	3	2	0	0	0	0	0	0	5	8	3
CS-Fullerton	3	4	0	0	0	4	0	x	—	11	12	1

Win: CSF— Ted Silva (18-1). **Loss:** USC— Brian Cooper (8-3). **Starters:** CSF— Silva; USC— Cooper. **Strikeouts:** CSF— Silva 5, Mark Kotsay 2; USC— Seth Etherton 3. **WP:** USC— Etherton. **2B:** USC— Ernie Diaz, Geoff Jenkins. **HR:** USC— Walter Dawkins (9), Diaz (9), Jenkins (23); CSF— Kotsay 2 (21), Tony Martinez (7), Tony Miranda (12). **RBI:** USC— Diaz 3, Dawkins, Jenkins; CSF— Kotsay 5, Martinez 3, Miranda 2, C.J. Ankrum (5). **SB:** USC— Jacque Jones (7). CSF— Ankrum (6), Joe Fraser (12), Jack Jones (19), Martinez (12).
Attendance— 22,027. **Time**—3:01.

Most Outstanding Player

Mark Kotsay, CS-Fullerton, OF/LHP

Avg	AB	R	H	2B	3B	HR	RBI	SB
.563	16	7	9	2	0	3	10	0

W	L	ERA	G	Sv	IP	H	BB	SO
0	0	0.00	2	1	3.1	5	0	4

All-Tournament Team

C— Brian Loyd, CS-Fullerton. **1B**— Doug Mientkiewicz, Florida State. **2B**— Wes Rachels, USC. **3B**— Tony Martinez, CS-Fullerton. **SS**— Alex Cora, Miami. **OF**— J.D. Drew, Florida State; Geoff Jenkins, USC; Mark Kotsay, CS-Fullerton. **DH**— Scott Schroeffel, Tennessee. **P**— Randy Flores, USC; Ted Silva, CS-Fullerton.

Annual Awards

Chosen by *Baseball America*, *Collegiate Baseball* and the American Baseball Coaches Association.

Players of the Year

Todd Helton, Tennessee ....ABCA, *BA*, co-*CB*
Mark Kotsay, CS-Fullerton ....co-*CB*

Coaches of the Year

Rod Delmonico, Tennessee ....*BA*
Augie Garrido, CS-Fullerton ....ABCA, *CB*

Kotsay Leads CS-Fullerton to College Title

by Jim Callis

Maybe the College World Series should be renamed "The Mark Kotsay Show." For the second straight year Cal State Fullerton star Mark Kotsay was the headliner in Omaha, leading the Titans to the 1995 national championship.

As a freshman in 1994, Kotsay went 6-for-13 and tied a CWS record with seven RBI in one game as Fullerton finished in a third-place tie. Those heroics, however, paled in comparison to his '95 performance.

In an opening 6-5 win over Stanford, Kotsay doubled and scored the tying run, sacrificed to set up the go-ahead run and retired the last five Cardinal hitters for the save. In the second round, he sacrificed to set up the first run, hit a grand slam in the second inning to put the game out of reach then added three more singles in an 11-1 stomping of Tennessee.

In the semifinal rematch with the Volunteers, Kotsay walked during a seven-run first inning and added an RBI double in the fifth of an 11-0 demolition of the SEC representatives.

And he was just warming up. Kotsay decided the June 10 championship game against Southern California with the first two swings of his bat.

He hit a three-run home run over the 26-foot-high center-field wall in the first inning, then added a two-run shot to right in the second to snap a 3-3 tie. When starter Ted Silva's back stiffened, Kotsay came on to record the last five outs in the 11-5 win. Afterward, Trojans coach Mike Gillespie called Kotsay "The Messiah."

Along the way, Kotsay established career CWS records for batting average (.517), slugging percentage (1.103) and grand slams (two), and tied standards for career home runs (four) as well as championship-game homers (two) and RBI (five).

About the only thing Kotsay can't do is explain what happens to him when he steps into the batter's box at Rosenblatt Stadium.

"I don't know," said Kotsay, a sophomore center fielder and lefthander from Santa Fe Springs, Calif., who is expected to be one of the frontline stars on the 1996 U.S. Olympic team. "Coming in, I had a lot of confidence from last

Bill Setliff

Cal State Fullerton's **Mark Kotsay** watches one of his two home runs go over the fence in the Titans' 11-5 championship game victory over Southern Cal in the College World Series.

year. Maybe at the College World Series I'm more focused. Maybe it's a feeling I get."

He starred at the plate and on the mound all season— batting .422 with 21 homers and 90 RBI, while going 2-1 with 11 saves and a 0.31 ERA. Asked if there was anything Kotsay didn't accomplish in 1995, Fullerton coach Augie Garrido said, "Well, he didn't drive the team bus."

Despite his heroics, Kotsay wasn't the Player of the Year choice of either *Baseball America* or the American Baseball Coaches Association, who both make their selections before the CWS.

Both awards went to another two-way star, Tennessee junior first baseman-lefthander Todd Helton. Taken by the Colorado Rockies as the eighth overall pick in the June amateur draft, Helton batted .407, hit 20 homers and drove in 92, in addition to posting an 8-2 record, a 1.66 ERA, 12 saves and four complete-game victories in four starts.

Jim Callis is the managing editor of *Baseball America*.

Consensus All-America Team

NCAA Division I players cited most frequently by the following four selectors: the American Baseball Coaches Assn. (ABCA), *Baseball America*, *Collegiate Baseball*, and the National Collegiate Baseball Writers Assn. (NCBWA). Holdover from the 1994 All-America first team are in **bold** type.

First Team

Pos		Cl	Avg	HR	RBI
C	A.J. Hinch, Stanford	Jr.	.371	8	56
1B	Todd Helton, Tennesse	Jr.	.413	19	89
2B	Jason Totman, Texas Tech	Sr.	.435	5	53
SS	Gabe Alvarez, USC	Jr.	.358	12	55
3B	Clint Bryant, Auburn	Jr.	.422	16	93
OF	**Jose Cruz Jr.**, Rice	Jr.	.377	16	76
OF	Darin Erstad, Nebraska	Jr.	.410	19	76
OF	Mark Kotsay, CS-Fullerton	So.	.413	18	80
DH	Steve Hacker, SW Mo. St.	Jr.	.409	37	95

		Cl	W-L	Sv	ERA
P	Matt Morris, Seton Hall	Jr.	10-3	0	2.68
P	Mark Redman, Oklahoma	Jr.	15-2	0	2.16
P	Ted Silva, CS-Fullerton	Jr.	16-1	6	2.67
P	Ryan Halla, Auburn	Jr.	16-3	0	3.07
P	Jamey Price, Mississippi	Sr.	11-6	0	1.72
P	Evan Thomas, Fla. Int'l	Jr.	15-2	0	1.70

Second Team

Pos		Cl	Avg	HR	RBI
C	Javier Flores, Oklahoma	So.	.365	10	53
1B	Sean Casey, Richmond	Jr.	.461	14	70
2B	Marlon Anderson, So. Ala.	Jr.	.362	7	46
SS	Mark Bellhorn, Auburn	Jr.	.342	12	60
3B	Toby Kominek, Cent. Mich.	Jr.	.460	6	70
OF	Geoff Jenkins, USC	Jr.	.389	19	69
OF	Mark Wulfert, New Mex.	Sr.	.438	15	80
OF	Shane Monahan, Clemson	Jr.	.396	12	52
OF	David Dellucci, Miss.	Sr.	.410	17	63
DH	Tal Light, Okla. St.	Jr.	.335	26	104

		Cl	W-L	Sv	ERA
P	Jonathan Johnson, FSU	Jr.	11-3	0	2.95
P	Kyle Peterson, Stanford	Fr.	13-1	1	2.96
P	Scott Winchester, Clemson	Jr.	4-2	14	0.60
P	David Yocum, FSU	So.	12-2	0	2.38
P	Scott Schultz, LSU	Sr.	11-4	0	3.46

NCAA Division I Leaders

Batting

Average

(At least 75 AB)	Cl	Gm	AB	H	Avg
Sean Casey, Richmond	Jr.	55	193	89	.461
Todd Tatlock, Indiana St.	Sr.	58	213	98	.460
Garrett Newbart, Columbia	Jr.	39	155	71	.458
Bart Teal, Columbia	Sr.	35	118	54	.458
Doug Spofford, UNH	Sr.	41	113	51	.451

Home Runs

(At least 15)	Cl	Gm	HR	Avg
Steve Hacker, SW Mo. St.	Jr.	58	37*	0.64
Matt Berger, Louisville	So.	52	22	0.42
Toby Kominek, Cent. Mich.	Jr.	60	25	0.42
Mike Miller, Hofstra	Sr.	48	20	0.42
Tal Light, Okla. St.	Jr.	63	26	0.41

Runs Batted In

(At least 50)	Cl	Gm	RBI	Avg
Tal Light, Okla. St.	Jr.	63	104*	1.65
Steve Hacker, SW Mo. St.	Jr.	58	95	1.64
Mark Wulfert, New Mexico	Sr.	49	80	1.63
Ryan Topham, Notre Dame	Jr.	55	79	1.44
Mark Quinn, Rice	Sr.	62	89	1.44

Pitching

Earned Run Avg.

(At least 50 inn.)	Cl	Gm	IP	ERA
Joseph Burns, Fla. Int'l.	Sr.	12	67.1	1.20
Curt Schnur, Delware	Sr.	16	104.0	1.21
Jay Tessmer, Miami-FL	Sr.	45	75.1	1.31
Brett Wheeler, Old Dominon	So.	10	61.0	1.48
Greg Wooten, Portland St.	So.	18	119.0	1.51

Wins

	Cl	Gm	IP	W-L
Ted Silva, Cal St. Fullerton	Jr.	29	152.2	18-1
Ryan Halla, Auburn	Jr.	24	146.2	16-3
Evan Thomas, Fla. Int'l	Jr.	20	127.0	15-2
Mark Redman, Oklahoma	Jr.	20	141.2	15-3
Tedde Campbell, Pitt	Sr.	26	135.0	15-4

Strikeouts (per 9 inn.)

(At least 50 inn.)	Cl	IP	SO	Avg
J. O'Shaughnessy, N'eastern	So.	54.2	82	13.5
Matt Seely, Murray St.	Sr.	58.1	80	12.3
Scott Downs, Kentucky	Fr.	76.1	102	12.0
Scott Schultz, LSU	Sr.	117.0	150	11.5
Billy Koch, Clemson	So.	87.0	111	11.5

Other College World Series

Participants' final records in parentheses.

NCAA Div. II

at Montgomery, Ala. (May 27-June 3)

Participants: Ashland, OH (36-20); Bloomsburg, PA (37-21); UC Davis (31-32); Central Missouri St. (49-10); Florida Southern (51-10); Georgia College (49-19-1); New Haven, CT (31-7); Valdosta St., GA (41-22).
Championship: Fla. Southern def. Georgia Col., 15-0.

NCAA Div. III

at Salem, Va. (May 25-30)

Participants: Carthage, WI (39-8-1); Cortland St., NY (30-13); Eastern Conn. St. (28-12); LaVerne, CA (39-9); Marietta, OH (46-9); Methodist, NC (36-19-1); Wm. Patterson, NJ (36-9); WI-Oshkosh (39-5).
Championship: LaVerne def. Methodist, 5-3.

NAIA

at Sioux City, Iowa (May 26-June 1)

Participants: Bellevue, NE (57-13); Birmingham-Southern, AL (43-18); Cumberland, TN (49-19); Lewis-Clark St., ID (57-16); Col. of St. Francis, IL (49-17); St. Mary's, TX (46-12); SE Oklahoma (47-14); Wilmington College, DE (37-16).
Championship: Bellevue def. Cumberland, 8-5.

NJCAA Div. I

at Grand Junction, Colo. (May 27-June 2)

Participants: Allegany, MD (46-4); Dixie, UT (40-21); Indian Hills, Iowa (38-13); Indian River, FL (46-14); Middle Georgia (56-12); Odessa, TX (49-12); St. Louis-Meramec, MO (39-17); Seminole, OK (52-6); Triton, IL (42-13); Volunteer St., TN (41-23).
Championship: Middle Ga. def. Indian River, 11-6.

MLB Amateur Draft

Top 50 selections at the 31st Amateur Draft held June 1-3, 1995. Selections 1-28 are first round picks.

Top 50 Picks

No		Pos
1 California	Darin Erstad, Nebraska	OF
2 San Diego	Ben Davis, HS—Malverne, Pa.	C
3 Seattle	Jose Cruz Jr., Rice	OF
4 Chi-NL	Kerry Wood, HS—Grand Prairie, Tex.	P
5 Oakland	Ariel Prieto, Palm Sprgs/Western League	P
6 Florida	Jamie Jones, HS—San Diego, Calif.	OF
7 Texas	Jonathan Johnson, Florida State	P
8 Colorado	Todd Helton, Tennessee	1B/P
9 Milwaukee	Geoff Jenkins, USC	OF
10 Pittsburgh	Chad Hermansen, HS—Henderson, Nev.	SS
11 Detroit	Mike Drumright, Wichita St.	P
12 St. Louis	Matt Morris, Seton Hall	P
13 Minnesota	Mark Redman, Oklahoma	P
14 Phila.	Reggie Taylor, HS—Newberry, S.C.	OF
15 Boston	Andy Yount, HS—Kingwood, Tex.	P
16 San Fran.	Joe Fontenot, HS-Lafayette, La.	P
17 Toronto	Roy Halladay, HS—Arvada, Col.	P
18 NY Mets	Ryan Jaroncyk, HS—Escondido, Calif.	SS
19 Kansas City	Juan LeBron, HS—Arroyo, P.R.	OF
20 Los Angeles	David Yocum, Florida State	P
21 Baltimore	Alvie Shepherd, Nebraska	P
22 Houston	Tony McKnight, HS—Texarkana, Ark.	P
23 Cleveland	David Miller, Clemson	1B
24 **a**-Boston	Corey Jenkins, HS—Columbia, S.C.	OF
25 Chicago-AL	Jeff Liefer, Long Beach St.	3B

No		Pos
26 Atlanta	Chad Hutchinson, HS—Encinitas, Calif.	P
27 NY Yankees	Shea Morenz, Texas	OF
28 Montreal	Michael Barrett, HS—Atlanta, Ga.	SS
29 **c**-St. Louis	Chris Haas, HS—Paducah, Ky.	3B
30 **b**-Phila.	Dave Coggin, HS—Upland, Calif.	P
31 California	Jarrod Washburn, Wisc.-Oshkosh	P
32 San Diego	Gabe Alvarez, USC	SS
33 Seattle	Shane Monahan, Clemson	OF
34 Chicago-NL	Brian McNichol, James Madison	P
35 Oakland	Mark Bellhorn, Auburn	SS
36 Florida	Nate Rolison, HS—Petal, Miss.	1B
37 Texas	Phill Lowery, HS—Petalima, Calif.	P
38 Colorado	Ben Petrick, HS—Hillsboro, OR	C
39 Milwaukee	Mike Pasqualicchio, Lamar	P
40 Pittsburgh	Garrett Long, HS—Houston, Tex.	1B
41 Detroit	Brian Powell, Georgia	P
42 **b**-Phila.	Marlon Anderson, South Alabama	2B
43 Minnesota	Jason Bell, Oklahoma St.	P
44 **c**-St. Louis	Jason Wolf, HS—Hialeah, Fla.	SS
45 Boston	Jose Olmeda, HS—Fajardo, P.R.	SS
46 San Fran.	Jason Brester, HS—Burlington, WA	P
47 Toronto	Craig Wilson, HS—Hunt. Beach, Calif.	C
48 NY Mets	Brett Herbison, HS—Elgin, Ill.	P/SS
49 Kansas City	Carlos Beltram, HS—Manati, P.R.	OF
50 Los Angles	Darrin Babineaux, SW Louisiana	P

Acquired picks: **a**—from Cincinnati for signing Type B free agent Damon Berryhill; **b**—from St. Louis for signing Type A free agent Danny Jackson; **c**—from Philadelphia for signing Type A free agent Gregg Jefferies.

Minor League Triple A Final Standings

All playoff series are Best of 5 games.

International League

Eastern Division

	W	L	Pct	GB
Rochester (Orioles)	73	69	.514	—
Ottawa (Expos)	72	70	.507	1
Pawtucket (Red Sox)	70	71	.496	2½
Scranton/W-B (Phillies)	70	72	.493	3
Syracuse (Blue Jays)	59	82	.418	13½

Western Division

	W	L	Pct	GB
Norfolk (Mets)	86	56	.606	—
Richmond (Braves)	75	66	.532	10½
Columbus (Yankees)	71	68	.511	13½
Toledo (Tigers)	71	71	.500	15
Charlotte (Marlins)	59	81	.421	26

Playoffs: FIRST ROUND— Norfolk def. Richmond (3-2); Ottawa def. Rochester (3-2). CHAMPIONSHIP— Ottawa def. Norfolk (3-1).

Pacific Coast League

	W	L	Pct	GB
†Tucson (Astros)	87	56	.608	—
* Vancouver (Angels)	81	60	.574	5
†Salt Lake (Twins)	79	65	.549	8½
* Colo. Springs (Rockies)	77	66	.538	10
Albuquerque (Dodgers)	75	69	.521	12½
Edmonton (Athletics)	68	76	.472	19½
Tacoma (Mariners)	68	76	.472	19½
Phoenix (Giants)	62	82	.431	25½
Las Vegas (Padres)	61	83	.424	26½
Calgary (Pirates)	58	83	.411	28

*first half divisional champion; †second half divisional champion.
Playoffs: FIRST ROUND— Salt Lake def. Vancouver (3-1); Colorado Springs def. Tucson (3-1). CHAMPIONSHIP— Colorado Springs def. Salt Lake (3-2).

American Association

	W	L	Pct	GB
Indianapolis (Reds)	88	56	.611	—
Buffalo (Indians)	82	62	.569	6
Omaha (Royals)	76	68	.528	12
Louisville (Cardinals)	74	70	.514	14
Iowa (Cubs)	69	74	.483	18½
Nashville (White Sox)	68	76	.472	20
New Orleans (Brewers)	63	79	.444	24
Oklahoma City (Rangers)	54	89	.378	33½

Playoffs: FIRST ROUND— Louisville def. Indianapolis (3-0); Buffalo def. Omaha (3-1). CHAMPIONSHIP— Louisville def. Buffalo (3-2).

Japanese Leagues

Final Standings

Central League

	W	L	T	Pct	GB
Yakult Swallows	82	48	0	.631	—
Hiroshima Carp	74	56	1	.569	8
Yomiuri Giants	72	58	1	.554	10
Yokohama BayStars	66	64	0	.508	16
Chunichi Dragons	50	80	0	.385	32
Hanshin Tigers	46	84	0	.354	36

Pacific League

	W	L	T	Pct	GB
Orix Blue Wave	82	47	1	.636	—
Chiba Lotte Marines	69	58	3	.543	12
Seibu Lions	67	57	6	.540	12½
Nippon Ham Fighters	59	68	3	.465	22
Fukuoka Daiei Hawks	52	72	4	.429	26½
Kintetsu Buffaloes	49	78	3	.386	32

Japan series (Best of 7): Yakult def. Orix (4-1).

THE 1996 INFORMATION PLEASE SPORTS ALMANAC

BASEBALL
STATISTICS

THROUGH THE YEARS
1876-1995
WORLD SERIES • ALL-TIMERS

SEC
B

PAGE
109

The World Series

The World Series began in 1903 when Pittsburgh of the older National League (founded in 1876) invited Boston of the American League (founded in 1901) to play a best-of-9 game series to determine which of the two league champions was the best. Boston was the surprise winner, 5 games to 3. The 1904 NL champion New York Giants refused to play Boston the following year, so there was no series. Giants' owner John T. Brush and his manager John McGraw both despised AL president Ban Johnson and considered the junior circuit to be a minor league. By the following year, however, Brush and Johnson had smoothed out their differences and the Giants agreed to play Philadelphia in a best-of-7 game series. Since then the World Series has been a best-of-7 format, except from 1919-21 when it returned to best-of-9.

After surviving two world wars and an earthquake in 1989, the World Series was cancelled for only the second time in 1994 when the players went out on strike Aug. 12 to protest the owners' call for revenue sharing and a salary cap. On Sept. 14, with no hope of reaching a labor agreement to end the 34-day strike, the owners called off the remainder of the regular season and the entire postseason. The strike ended after 232 days on Mar. 31, 1995.

In the chart below, the National League teams are listed in CAPITAL letters. Also, each World Series champion's wins and losses are noted in parentheses after the Series score in games.

Multiple champions: New York Yankees (22); Philadelphia-Oakland A's and St. Louis Cardinals (9); Brooklyn-Los Angeles Dodgers (6); Boston Red Sox, Cincinnati Reds, New York-San Francisco Giants and Pittsburgh Pirates (5); Detroit Tigers (4); Baltimore Orioles, Boston-Milwaukee-Atlanta Braves and Washington Senators-Minnesota Twins (3); Chicago Cubs, Chicago White Sox, Cleveland Indians, New York Mets and Toronto Blue Jays (2).

Year	Winner	Manager	Series	Loser	Manager
1903	Boston Red Sox	Jimmy Collins	5-3 (LWLLWWWW)	PITTSBURGH	Fred Clarke
1904	Not held				
1905	NY GIANTS	John McGraw	4-1 (WLWWW)	Philadelphia A's	Connie Mack
1906	Chicago White Sox	Fielder Jones	4-2 (WLWLWW)	CHICAGO CUBS	Frank Chance
1907	CHICAGO CUBS	Frank Chance	4-0-1 (TWWWW)	Detroit	Hughie Jennings
1908	CHICAGO CUBS	Frank Chance	4-1 (WWLWW)	Detroit	Hughie Jennings
1909	PITTSBURGH	Fred Clarke	4-3 (WLWLWLW)	Detroit	Hughie Jennings
1910	Philadelphia A's	Connie Mack	4-1 (WWWLW)	CHICAGO CUBS	Frank Chance
1911	Philadelphia A's	Connie Mack	4-2 (LWWWLW)	NY GIANTS	John McGraw
1912	Boston Red Sox	Jake Stahl	4-3-1 (WTLWWLLW)	NY GIANTS	John McGraw
1913	Philadelphia A's	Connie Mack	4-1 (WWWLW)	NY GIANTS	John McGraw
1914	BOSTON BRAVES	George Stallings	4-0	Philadelphia A's	Connie Mack
1915	Boston Red Sox	Bill Carrigan	4-1 (LWWWW)	PHILA. PHILLIES	Pat Moran
1916	Boston Red Sox	Bill Carrigan	4-1 (WWLWW)	BKLN. DODGERS	Wilbert Robinson
1917	Chicago White Sox	Pants Rowland	4-2 (WWLLWW)	NY GIANTS	John McGraw
1918	Boston Red Sox	Ed Barrow	4-2 (WLWWLW)	CHICAGO CUBS	Fred Mitchell
1919	CINCINNATI	Pat Moran	5-3 (WWLWWLLW)	Chicago White Sox	Kid Gleason
1920	Cleveland	Tris Speaker	5-2 (WLLWWWW)	BKLN. DODGERS	Wilbert Robinson
1921	NY GIANTS	John McGraw	5-3 (LLWWLWWW)	NY Yankees	Miller Huggins
1922	NY GIANTS	John McGraw	4-0-1 (WTWWW)	NY Yankees	Miller Huggins
1923	NY Yankees	Miller Huggins	4-2 (LWLWWW)	NY GIANTS	John McGraw
1924	Washington	Bucky Harris	4-3 (LWLWLWW)	NY GIANTS	John McGraw
1925	PITTSBURGH	Bill McKechnie	4-3 (LWLLWWW)	Washington	Bucky Harris
1926	ST.L. CARDINALS	Rogers Hornsby	4-3 (LWWLWLW)	NY Yankees	Miller Huggins
1927	NY Yankees	Miller Huggins	4-0	PITTSBURGH	Donie Bush
1928	NY Yankees	Miller Huggins	4-0	ST.L. CARDINALS	Bill McKechnie
1929	Philadelphia A's	Connie Mack	4-1 (WWLWW)	CHICAGO CUBS	Joe McCarthy
1930	Philadelphia A's	Connie Mack	4-2 (WWLLWW)	ST.L. CARDINALS	Gabby Street
1931	ST.L. CARDINALS	Gabby Street	4-3 (LWWLWLW)	Philadelphia A's	Connie Mack
1932	NY Yankees	Joe McCarthy	4-0	CHICAGO CUBS	Charlie Grimm
1933	NY GIANTS	Bill Terry	4-1 (WWLWW)	Washington	Joe Cronin
1934	ST.L. CARDINALS	Frankie Frisch	4-3 (WLWLWLW)	Detroit	Mickey Cochrane
1935	Detroit	Mickey Cochrane	4-2 (LWWWLW)	CHICAGO CUBS	Charlie Grimm
1936	NY Yankees	Joe McCarthy	4-2 (LWWWLW)	NY GIANTS	Bill Terry
1937	NY Yankees	Joe McCarthy	4-1 (WWWLW)	NY GIANTS	Bill Terry
1938	NY Yankees	Joe McCarthy	4-0	CHICAGO CUBS	Gabby Hartnett
1939	NY Yankees	Joe McCarthy	4-0	CINCINNATI	Bill McKechnie

World Series (Cont.)

Year	Winner	Manager	Series	Loser	Manager
1940	CINCINNATI	Bill McKechnie	4-3 (LWLWLWW)	Detroit	Del Baker
1941	NY Yankees	Joe McCarthy	4-1 (WLWWW)	BKLN. DODGERS	Leo Durocher
1942	ST.L. CARDINALS	Billy Southworth	4-1 (LWWWW)	NY Yankees	Joe McCarthy
1943	NY Yankees	Joe McCarthy	4-1 (WLWWW)	ST.L. CARDINALS	Billy Southworth
1944	ST.L. CARDINALS	Billy Southworth	4-2 (LWWLWW)	St. Louis Browns	Luke Sewell
1945	Detroit	Steve O'Neill	4-3 (LWLWLWL)	CHICAGO CUBS	Charlie Grimm
1946	ST.L. CARDINALS	Eddie Dyer	4-3 (LWLWLWW)	Boston Red Sox	Joe Cronin
1947	NY Yankees	Bucky Harris	4-3 (WLWWLLW)	BKLN. DODGERS	Burt Shotton
1948	Cleveland	Lou Boudreau	4-2 (LWWWLW)	BOSTON BRAVES	Billy Southworth
1949	NY Yankees	Casey Stengel	4-1 (WLWWW)	BKLN. DODGERS	Burt Shotton
1950	NY Yankees	Casey Stengel	4-0	PHILA. PHILLIES	Eddie Sawyer
1951	NY Yankees	Casey Stengel	4-2 (LWWLW)	NY GIANTS	Leo Durocher
1952	NY Yankees	Casey Stengel	4-3 (LWLWLWW)	BKLN. DODGERS	Charlie Dressen
1953	NY Yankees	Casey Stengel	4-2 (WWLLWW)	BKLN. DODGERS	Charlie Dressen
1954	NY GIANTS	Leo Durocher	4-0	Cleveland	Al Lopez
1955	BKLN. DODGERS	Walter Alston	4-3 (LLWWWLW)	NY Yankees	Casey Stengel
1956	NY Yankees	Casey Stengel	4-3 (LLWWWLW)	BKLN. DODGERS	Walter Alston
1957	MILW. BRAVES	Fred Haney	4-3 (WLWWLWW)	NY Yankees	Casey Stengel
1958	NY Yankees	Casey Stengel	4-3 (LLWLWWW)	MILW. BRAVES	Fred Haney
1959	LA DODGERS	Walter Alston	4-2 (LWWWLW)	Chicago White Sox	Al Lopez
1960	PITTSBURGH	Danny Murtaugh	4-3 (WLLWWWW)	NY Yankees	Casey Stengel
1961	NY Yankees	Ralph Houk	4-1 (WLWWW)	CINCINNATI	Fred Hutchinson
1962	NY Yankees	Ralph Houk	4-3 (WLWLWLW)	SF GIANTS	Alvin Dark
1963	LA DODGERS	Walter Alston	4-0	NY Yankees	Ralph Houk
1964	ST.L. CARDINALS	Johnny Keane	4-3 (WLWWLLW)	NY Yankees	Yogi Berra
1965	LA DODGERS	Walter Alston	4-3 (LLWWWLW)	Minnesota	Sam Mele
1966	Baltimore	Hank Bauer	4-0	LA DODGERS	Walter Alston
1967	ST.L. CARDINALS	Red Schoendienst	4-3 (WLLWWLW)	Boston Red Sox	Dick Williams
1968	Detroit	Mayo Smith	4-3 (LWLWLWW)	ST.L. CARDINALS	Red Schoendienst
1969	NY METS	Gil Hodges	4-1 (LWWWW)	Baltimore	Earl Weaver
1970	Baltimore	Earl Weaver	4-1 (WWWLW)	CINCINNATI	Sparky Anderson
1971	PITTSBURGH	Danny Murtaugh	4-3 (LLWWWLW)	Baltimore	Earl Weaver
1972	Oakland A's	Dick Williams	4-3 (WWLWLLW)	CINCINNATI	Sparky Anderson
1973	Oakland A's	Dick Williams	4-3 (WLWLLWW)	NY METS	Yogi Berra
1974	Oakland A's	Alvin Dark	4-1 (WLWWW)	LA DODGERS	Walter Alston
1975	CINCINNATI	Sparky Anderson	4-3 (LWWLWLW)	Boston Red Sox	Darrell Johnson
1976	CINCINNATI	Sparky Anderson	4-0	NY Yankees	Billy Martin
1977	NY Yankees	Billy Martin	4-2 (WLWWLW)	LA DODGERS	Tommy Lasorda
1978	NY Yankees	Bob Lemon	4-2 (LLWWWW)	LA DODGERS	Tommy Lasorda
1979	PITTSBURGH	Chuck Tanner	4-3 (LWLLWWW)	Baltimore	Earl Weaver
1980	PHILA. PHILLIES	Dallas Green	4-2 (WWLLWW)	Kansas City	Jim Frey
1981	LA DODGERS	Tommy Lasorda	4-2 (LLWWWW)	NY Yankees	Bob Lemon
1982	ST.L. CARDINALS	Whitey Herzog	4-3 (LWWLLWW)	Milwaukee Brewers	Harvey Kuenn
1983	Baltimore	Joe Altobelli	4-1 (LWWWW)	PHILA. PHILLIES	Paul Owens
1984	Detroit	Sparky Anderson	4-1 (WLWWW)	SAN DIEGO	Dick Williams
1985	Kansas City	Dick Howser	4-3 (LLWLWWW)	ST.L. CARDINALS	Whitey Herzog
1986	NY METS	Davey Johnson	4-3 (LLWWWLW)	Boston Red Sox	John McNamara
1987	Minnesota	Tom Kelly	4-3 (WWLLLWW)	ST.L. CARDINALS	Whitey Herzog
1988	LA DODGERS	Tommy Lasorda	4-1 (WWLWW)	Oakland A's	Tony La Russa
1989	Oakland A's	Tony La Russa	4-0	SF GIANTS	Roger Craig
1990	CINCINNATI	Lou Piniella	4-0	Oakland A's	Tony La Russa
1991	Minnesota	Tom Kelly	4-3 (WWLLLWW)	ATLANTA BRAVES	Bobby Cox
1992	Toronto	Cito Gaston	4-2 (LWWWLW)	ATLANTA BRAVES	Bobby Cox
1993	Toronto	Cito Gaston	4-2 (WLWLWW)	PHILA. PHILLIES	Jim Fregosi
1994	Not held				
1995	ATLANTA BRAVES	Bobby Cox	4-2 (WWLWLW)	Cleveland	Mike Hargrove

Most Valuable Players

Currently selected by media panel made up of representatives of CBS Sports, CBS Radio, AP, UPI, and World Series official scorers. Presented by *Sport* magazine from 1955-88 and by Major League Baseball since 1989. Winner who did not play for World Series champions is in **bold** type.

Multiple winners: Bob Gibson, Reggie Jackson and Sandy Koufax (2).

Year		Year		Year	
1955	Johnny Podres, Bklyn, P	1960	**Bobby Richardson**, NY, 2B	1965	Sandy Koufax, LA, P
1956	Don Larsen, NY, P	1961	Whitey Ford, NY, P	1966	Frank Robinson, Bal., OF
1957	Lew Burdette, Mil., P	1962	Ralph Terry, NY, P	1967	Bob Gibson, St.L., P
1958	Bob Turley, NY, P	1963	Sandy Koufax, LA, P	1968	Mickey Lolich, Det., P
1959	Larry Sherry, LA, P	1964	Bob Gibson, St.L., P	1969	Donn Clendenon, NY, 1B

Year		Year		Year	
1970	Brooks Robinson, Bal., 3B	1980	Mike Schmidt, Phi., 3B	1988	Orel Hershiser, LA, P
1971	Roberto Clemente, Pit., OF	1981	Pedro Guerrero, LA, OF;	1989	Dave Stewart, Oak., P
1972	Gene Tenace, Oak., C		Ron Cey, LA, 3B;	1990	Jose Rijo, Cin., P
1973	Reggie Jackson, Oak., OF		& Steve Yeager, LA, C	1991	Jack Morris, Min., P
1974	Rollie Fingers, Oak., P	1982	Darrell Porter, St.L., C	1992	Pat Borders, Tor., C
1975	Pete Rose, Cin., 3B	1983	Rick Dempsey, Bal., C	1993	Paul Molitor, Tor., DH/1B/3B
1976	Johnny Bench, Cin., C	1984	Alan Trammell, Det., SS	1994	Series not held.
1977	Reggie Jackson, NY, OF	1985	Bret Saberhagen, KC, P	1995	Tom Glavine, Atl., P
1978	Bucky Dent, NY, SS	1986	Ray Knight, NY, 3B		
1979	Willie Stargell, Pit., 1B	1987	Frank Viola, Min., P		

All-Time World Series Leaders
CAREER

World Series leaders through 1995. Years listed indicate number of World Series appearances.

Hitting

Games

	Yrs	Gm
Yogi Berra, NY Yankees	14	75
Mickey Mantle, NY Yankees	12	65
Elston Howard, NY Yankees-Boston	10	54
Hank Bauer, NY Yankees	9	53
Gil McDougald, NY Yankees	8	53

At Bats

	Yrs	AB
Yogi Berra, NY Yankees	14	259
Mickey Mantle, NY Yankees	12	230
Joe DiMaggio, NY Yankees	10	199
Frankie Frisch, NY Giants-St.L. Cards	8	197
Gil McDougald, NY Yankees	8	190

Batting Avg. (minimum 50 AB)

	AB	H	Avg
Pepper Martin, St.L. Cards	55	23	.418
Lou Brock, St. Louis	87	34	.391
Thurman Munson, NY Yankees	67	25	.373
George Brett, Kansas City	51	19	.373
Hank Aaron, Milw. Braves	55	20	.364

World Series Appearances

In the 91 years that the World Series has been contested, American League teams have won 53 championships while National League teams have won 38.

The following teams are ranked by number of appearances through the 1995 World Series; (*) indicates AL teams.

	App	W	L	Pct.	Last Series	Last Title
NY Yankees*	33	22	11	.667	1981	1978
Bklyn/LA Dodgers	18	6	12	.333	1988	1988
NY/SF Giants	16	5	11	.313	1989	1954
St.L. Cardinals	15	9	6	.600	1987	1982
Phi/KC/Oak.A's*	14	9	5	.643	1990	1989
Chicago Cubs	10	2	8	.200	1945	1908
Boston Red Sox*	9	5	4	.556	1986	1918
Cincinnati Reds	9	5	4	.556	1990	1990
Detroit Tigers*	9	4	5	.444	1984	1984
Pittsburgh Pirates	7	5	2	.714	1979	1979
St.L/Bal.Orioles*	7	3	4	.429	1983	1983
Wash/Min.Twins*	6	3	3	.500	1991	1991
Bos/Mil/Atl.Braves	7	3	4	.429	1995	1995
Chi.White Sox*	4	2	2	.500	1959	1917
Phi.Phillies	5	1	4	.200	1993	1980
Cle.Indians*	4	2	2	.500	1995	1948
NY Mets	3	2	1	.667	1986	1986
Tor. Blue Jays*	2	2	0	1.000	1993	1993
KC Royals*	2	1	1	.500	1985	1985
Sea/Mil.Brewers*	1	0	1	.000	1982	—
SD Padres	1	0	1	.000	1984	—

Hits

	AB	H	Avg
Yogi Berra, NY Yankees	259	71	.274
Mickey Mantle, NY Yankees	230	59	.257
Frankie Frisch, NYG-St.L. Cards	197	58	.294
Joe DiMaggio, NY Yankees	199	54	.271
Hank Bauer, NY Yankees	188	46	.245
Pee Wee Reese, Brooklyn	169	46	.272

Runs

	Gm	R
Mickey Mantle, NY Yankees	65	42
Yogi Berra, NY Yankees	75	41
Babe Ruth, Boston Red Sox-NY Yankees	41	37
Lou Gehrig, NY Yankees	34	30
Joe DiMaggio, NY Yankees	51	27

Home Runs

	AB	HR
Mickey Mantle, NY Yankees	230	18
Babe Ruth, Boston Red Sox-NY Yankees	129	15
Yogi Berra, NY Yankees	259	12
Duke Snider, Brooklyn-LA	133	11
Lou Gehrig, NY Yankees	119	10
Reggie Jackson, Oakland-NY Yankees	98	10

Runs Batted In

	Gm	RBI
Mickey Mantle, NY Yankees	65	40
Yogi Berra, NY Yankees	75	39
Lou Gehrig, NY Yankees	34	35
Babe Ruth, Boston Red Sox-NY Yankees	41	33
Joe DiMaggio, NY Yankees	51	30

Stolen Bases

	Gm	SB
Lou Brock, St. Louis	21	14
Eddie Collins, Phi. A's-Chisox	34	14
Frank Chance, Chi. Cubs	20	10
Davey Lopes, Los Angeles	23	10
Phil Rizzuto, NY Yankees	52	10

Total Bases

	Gm	TB
Mickey Mantle, NY Yankees	65	123
Yogi Berra, NY Yankees	75	117
Babe Ruth, Boston Red Sox-NY Yankees	41	96
Lou Gehrig, NY Yankees	34	87
Joe DiMaggio, NY Yankees	51	84

Slugging Pct. (50 AB)

	AB	Pct
Reggie Jackson, Oakland-NY Yankees	98	.755
Babe Ruth, Boston Red Sox-NY Yankees	129	.744
Lou Gehrig, NY Yankees	119	.731
Al Simmons, Phi. A's-Cincinnati	73	.658
Lou Brock, St. Louis	87	.655

All-Time World Series Leaders (Cont.)
Pitching

Games

	Yrs	Gm
Whitey Ford, NY Yankees	11	22
Rollie Fingers, Oakland	3	16
Allie Reynolds, NY Yankees	6	15
Bob Turley, NY Yankees	5	15
Clay Carroll, Cincinnati	3	14

Innings Pitched

	Gm	IP
Whitey Ford, NY Yankees	22	146
Christy Mathewson, NY Giants	11	102
Red Ruffing, NY Yankees	10	86
Chief Bender, Philadelphia A's	10	85
Waite Hoyt, NY Yankees-Phi. A's	12	84

Wins

	Gm	W-L
Whitey Ford, NY Yankees	22	10-8
Bob Gibson, St. Louis	9	7-2
Allie Reynolds, NY Yankees	15	7-2
Red Ruffing, NY Yankees	10	7-2
Lefty Gomez, NY Yankees	7	6-0
Chief Bender, Philadelphia A's	10	6-4
Waite Hoyt, NY Yankees-Phi. A's	12	6-4

Complete Games

	GS	CG	W-L
Christy Mathewson, NY Giants	11	10	5-5
Chief Bender, Philadelphia A's	10	9	6-4
Bob Gibson, St. Louis	9	8	7-2
Whitey Ford, NY Yankees	22	7	10-8
Red Ruffing, NY Yankees	10	7	7-2

Strikeouts

	Gm	IP	SO
Whitey Ford, NY Yankees	22	146	94
Bob Gibson, St. Louis	9	81	92
Allie Reynolds, NY Yankees	15	77	62
Sandy Koufax, Los Angeles	8	57	61
Red Ruffing, NY Yankees	10	86	61

ERA (minimum 25 IP)

	Gm	IP	ERA
Jack Billingham, Cincinnati	7	25	0.36
Harry Brecheen, St. Louis	7	33	0.83
Babe Ruth, Boston Red Sox	3	31	0.87
Sherry Smith, Brooklyn	3	30	0.89
Sandy Koufax, Los Angeles	8	57	0.95

Bases on Balls

	Gm	IP	BB
Whitey Ford, NY Yankees	22	146	34
Allie Reynolds, NY Yankees	15	77	32
Art Nehf, NY Giants-Chi. Cubs	12	79	32
Jim Palmer, Baltimore	9	65	31
Bob Turley, NY Yankees	15	54	29

Saves

	Gm	IP	Sv
Rollie Fingers, Oakland	16	33	6
Allie Reynolds, NY Yankees	15	77	4
Johnny Murphy, NY Yankees	8	16	4
Seven pitchers tied with 3 each.			

Losses

	Gm	W-L
Whitey Ford, NY Yankees	22	10-8
Christy Mathewson, NY Giants	11	5-5
Joe Bush, Phi. A's-Bosox-NY Yankees	9	2-5
Rube Marquard, NY Giants-Brooklyn	11	2-5
Eddie Plank, Philadelphia A's	7	2-5
Schoolboy Rowe, Detroit	8	2-5

Shutouts

	GS	CG	ShO
Christy Mathewson, NY Giants	11	10	4
Three Finger Brown, Chi. Cubs	7	5	3
Whitey Ford, NY Yankees	22	7	3
Seven pitchers tied with 2 each.			

League Championship Series

Division play came to the major leagues in 1969 when both the American and National Leagues expanded to 12 teams. With an East and West Division in each league, League Championship Series (LCS) became necessary to determine the NL and AL pennant winners. In the charts below, the East Division champions are noted by the letter E and the West Division champions by W. Also, each playoff winner's wins and losses are noted in parentheses after the series score. The LCS changed from best-of-5 to best-of-7 in 1985. Each league's LCS was cancelled in 1994 due to the players' strike.

National League

Multiple champions: Cincinnati and LA Dodgers (5); Atlanta, NY Mets, Philadelphia and St. Louis (3); Pittsburgh (2).

Year	Winner	Manager	Series	Loser	Manager
1969	E- New York	Gil Hodges	3-0	W- Atlanta	Lum Harris
1970	W- Cincinnati	Sparky Anderson	3-0	E- Pittsburgh	Danny Murtaugh
1971	E- Pittsburgh	Danny Murtaugh	3-1 (LWWW)	W- San Francisco	Charlie Fox
1972	W- Cincinnati	Sparky Anderson	3-2 (LWLWW)	E- Pittsburgh	Bill Virdon
1973	E- New York	Yogi Berra	3-2 (LWLWL)	W- Cincinnati	Sparky Anderson
1974	W- Los Angeles	Walter Alston	3-1 (WWLW)	E- Pittsburgh	Danny Murtaugh
1975	W- Cincinnati	Sparky Anderson	3-0	E- Pittsburgh	Danny Murtaugh
1976	W- Cincinnati	Sparky Anderson	3-0	E- Philadelphia	Danny Ozark
1977	W- Los Angeles	Tommy Lasorda	3-1 (LWWW)	E- Philadelphia	Danny Ozark
1978	W- Los Angeles	Tommy Lasorda	3-1 (WWLW)	E- Philadelphia	Danny Ozark
1979	E- Pittsburgh	Chuck Tanner	3-0	W- Cincinnati	John McNamara
1980	E- Philadelphia	Dallas Green	3-2 (WLLWW)	W- Houston	Bill Virdon
1981	W- Los Angeles	Tommy Lasorda	3-2 (WLLWW)	E- Montreal	Jim Fanning

Year	Winner	Manager	Series	Loser	Manager
1982	E- St. Louis	Whitey Herzog	3-0	W- Atlanta	Joe Torre
1983	E- Philadelphia	Paul Owens	3-1 (WLWW)	W- Los Angeles	Tommy Lasorda
1984	W- San Diego	Dick Williams	3-2 (LLWWW)	E- Chicago	Jim Frey
1985	E- St. Louis	Whitey Herzog	4-2 (LLWWWW)	W- Los Angeles	Tommy Lasorda
1986	E- New York	Davey Johnson	4-2 (LWWLWW)	W- Houston	Hal Lanier
1987	E- St. Louis	Whitey Herzog	4-3 (WLWLLWW)	W- San Francisco	Roger Craig
1988	W- Los Angeles	Tommy Lasorda	4-3 (LWLWWLW)	E- New York	Davey Johnson
1989	W- San Francisco	Roger Craig	4-1 (WLWWW)	E- Chicago	Don Zimmer
1990	W- Cincinnati	Lou Piniella	4-2 (LWWWLW)	E- Pittsburgh	Jim Leyland
1991	W- Atlanta	Bobby Cox	4-3 (LWWLLWW)	E- Pittsburgh	Jim Leyland
1992	W- Atlanta	Bobby Cox	4-3 (WWWLLLW)	E- Pittsburgh	Jim Leyland
1993	E- Philadelphia	Jim Fregosi	4-2 (WLLWWW)	W- Atlanta	Bobby Cox
1994	Not held				
1995	E- Atlanta	Bobby Cox	4-0	C- Cincinnati	Davey Johnson

NLCS Most Valuable Players

Winners who did not play for NLCS champions are in **bold** type. **Multiple winner:** Steve Garvey (2).

Year		Year		Year	
1977	Dusty Baker, LA, OF	1984	Steve Garvey, SD, 1B	1990	Rob Dibble, Cin., P
1978	Steve Garvey, LA, 1B	1985	Ozzie Smith, St.L., SS		& Randy Myers, Cin., P
1979	Willie Stargell, Pit., 1B	1986	**Mike Scott**, Hou., P	1991	Steve Avery, Atl., P
1980	Manny Trillo, Phi., 2B	1987	**Jeff Leonard**, SF, OF	1992	John Smoltz, Atl., P
1981	Burt Hooton, LA, P	1988	Orel Hershiser, LA, P	1993	Curt Schilling, Phi., P
1982	Darrell Porter, St.L., C	1989	Will Clark, SF, 1B	1994	LCS not held.
1983	Gary Matthews, Phi., OF			1995	Mike Devereaux, Atl., OF

American League

Multiple champions: Oakland (6); Baltimore (5); NY Yankees (4); Boston, Kansas City, Minnesota and Toronto (2).

Year	Winner	Manager	Series	Loser	Manager
1969	E- Baltimore	Earl Weaver	3-0	W- Minnesota	Billy Martin
1970	E- Baltimore	Earl Weaver	3-0	W- Minnesota	Bill Rigney
1971	E- Baltimore	Earl Weaver	3-0	W- Oakland	Dick Williams
1972	W- Oakland	Dick Williams	3-2 (WWLLW)	E- Detroit	Billy Martin
1973	W- Oakland	Dick Williams	3-2 (LWWLW)	E- Baltimore	Earl Weaver
1974	W- Oakland	Alvin Dark	3-1 (LWWW)	E- Baltimore	Earl Weaver
1975	E- Boston	Darrell Johnson	3-0	W- Oakland	Alvin Dark
1976	E- New York	Billy Martin	3-2 (WLWLW)	W- Kansas City	Whitey Herzog
1977	E- New York	Billy Martin	3-2 (LWLWW)	W- Kansas City	Whitey Herzog
1978	E- New York	Bob Lemon	3-1 (WLWW)	W- Kansas City	Whitey Herzog
1979	E- Baltimore	Earl Weaver	3-1 (WWLW)	W- California	Jim Fregosi
1980	W- Kansas City	Jim Frey	3-0	E- New York	Dick Howser
1981	E- New York	Bob Lemon	3-0	W- Oakland	Billy Martin
1982	E- Milwaukee	Harvey Kuenn	3-2 (LLWWW)	W- California	Gene Mauch
1983	E- Baltimore	Joe Altobelli	3-1 (LWWW)	W- Chicago	Tony La Russa
1984	E- Detroit	Sparky Anderson	3-0	W- Kansas City	Dick Howser
1985	W- Kansas City	Dick Howser	4-3 (LLWLWWW)	E- Toronto	Bobby Cox
1986	E- Boston	John McNamara	4-3 (LWLLWWW)	W- California	Gene Mauch
1987	W- Minnesota	Tom Kelly	4-1 (WWLWW)	E- Detroit	Sparky Anderson
1988	W- Oakland	Tony La Russa	4-0	E- Boston	Joe Morgan
1989	W- Oakland	Tony La Russa	4-1 (WWLWW)	E- Toronto	Cito Gaston
1990	W- Oakland	Tony La Russa	4-0	E- Boston	Joe Morgan
1991	W- Minnesota	Tom Kelly	4-1 (WLWWW)	E- Toronto	Cito Gaston
1992	E- Toronto	Cito Gaston	4-2 (LWWWLW)	W- Oakland	Tony La Russa
1993	E- Toronto	Cito Gaston	4-2 (WWLLWW)	W- Chicago	Gene Lamont
1994	Not held				
1995	C- Cleveland	Mark Hargrove	4-2 (LWLWWW)	W-Seattle	Lou Piniella

ALCS Most Valuable Players

Winner who did not play for ALCS champions is in **bold** type. **Multiple winner:** Dave Stewart (2).

Year		Year		Year	
1980	Frank White, KC, 2B	1986	Marty Barrett, Bos., 2B	1991	Kirby Puckett, Min., OF
1981	Graig Nettles, NY, 3B	1987	Gary Gaetti, Min., 3B	1992	Roberto Alomar, Tor., 2B
1982	**Fred Lynn**, Cal., OF	1988	Dennis Eckersley, Oak., P	1993	Dave Stewart, Tor., P
1983	Mike Boddicker, Bal., P	1989	Rickey Henderson, Oak., OF	1994	LCS not held.
1984	Kirk Gibson, Det., OF	1990	Dave Stewart, Oak., P	1995	Orel Hershiser, Cle., P
1985	George Brett, KC, 3B				

Other Playoffs

Seven times from 1946-80, playoffs were necessary to decide league or division championships when two teams tied for first place at the end of the regular season. In the strike year of 1981, there were playoffs between the first and second half-season champions in both leagues. In 1995, the 1994–95 players' strike shortened the regular season to 144 games.

National League

Year	NL	W	L	Manager	Year	NL West	W	L	Manager
1946	Brooklyn	96	58	Leo Durocher	1980	Houston	92	70	Bill Virdon
	St. Louis	96	58	Eddie Dyer		Los Angeles	92	70	Tommy Lasorda
	Playoff: (Best-of-3) St. Louis, 2-0					Playoff: (1 game) Houston, 7-1 (at LA)			
	NL	**W**	**L**	**Manager**		**NL East**	**W**	**L**	**Manager**
1951	Brooklyn	96	58	Charlie Dressen	1981	(1st Half) Phila	34	21	Dallas Green
	New York	96	58	Leo Durocher		(2nd Half) Montreal	30	23	Jim Fanning
	Playoff: (Best-of-3) New York, 2-1 (WLW)					Playoff: (Best-of-5) Montreal, 3-2 (WWLLW)			
	NL	**W**	**L**	**Manager**		**NL West**	**W**	**L**	**Manager**
1959	Milwaukee	86	68	Fred Haney		(1st Half) Los Ang	36	21	Tommy Lasorda
	Los Angeles	86	68	Walter Alston		(2nd Half) Houston	33	20	Bill Virdon
	Playoff: (Best-of-3) Los Angeles, 2-0					Playoff: (Best-of-5) Los Angeles, 3-2 (LLWWW)			
	NL	**W**	**L**	**Manager**					
1962	Los Angeles	101	61	Walter Alston					
	San Francisco	101	61	Alvin Dark					
	Playoff: (Best-of-3) San Francisco, 2-1 (WLW)								

American League

Year	AL	W	L	Manager	Year	AL East	W	L	Manager
1948	Boston	96	58	Joe McCarthy	1981	(1st Half) N.Y.	34	22	Bob Lemon
	Cleveland	96	58	Lou Boudreau		(2nd Half) Milw.	31	22	Buck Rodgers
	Playoff: (1 game) Cleveland, 8-3 (at Boston)					Playoff: (Best-of-5) New York, 3-2 (WWLLW)			
	AL East	**W**	**L**	**Manager**		**AL West**	**W**	**L**	**Manager**
1978	Boston	99	63	Don Zimmer		(1st Half) Oakland	37	23	Billy Martin
	New York	99	63	Bob Lemon		(2nd Half) Kan.City	30	23	Jim Frey
	Playoff: (1 game) New York, 5-4 (at Boston)					Playoff: (Best-of-5), Oakland, 3-0			
						AL West	**W**	**L**	**Manager**
					1995	Seattle	78	66	Lou Piniella
						California	78	66	Marcel Lachemann
						Playoff: (1 game) Seattle, 9-1 (at Seattle)			

Regular Season League & Division Winners

Regular season National and American League pennant winners from 1900-68, as well as West and East divisional champions from 1969-93. In 1994, both leagues went to three divisions—West, Central and East. However, due to the 1994 players' strike that resulted in the cancelling of the season after games played on Aug. 11, division leaders at the time of the strike are not considered official champions by either league. Note that (*) indicates 1994 divisional champion is unofficial and that **GA** column indicates games ahead of the second place club. See page 119 for NL Pennant winners before 1900.

National League

Multiple pennant winners: Brooklyn-LA (19); New York-SF Giants (17); St. Louis (15); Chicago (10); Cincinnati and Pittsburgh (9); Boston-Milwaukee-Atlanta (7); Philadelphia (5); New York Mets (3). **Multiple division winners:** WEST—Los Angeles (8); Cincinnati (7); Atlanta (5); San Francisco (3); Houston (2). EAST—Pittsburgh (9); Philadelphia (6); NY Mets (4); St. Louis (3); Chicago (2).

Year		W	L	Pct	GA	Year		W	L	Pct	GA
1900	Brooklyn	82	54	.603	4½	1920	Brooklyn	93	61	.604	7
1901	Pittsburgh	90	49	.647	7½	1921	New York	94	59	.614	4
1902	Pittsburgh	103	36	.741	27½	1922	New York	93	61	.604	7
1903	Pittsburgh	91	49	.650	6½	1923	New York	95	58	.621	4½
1904	New York	106	47	.693	13	1924	New York	93	60	.608	1½
1905	New York	105	48	.686	9	1925	Pittsburgh	95	58	.621	8½
1906	Chicago	116	36	.763	20	1926	St. Louis	89	65	.578	2
1907	Chicago	107	45	.704	17	1927	Pittsburgh	94	60	.610	1½
1908	Chicago	99	55	.643	1	1928	St. Louis	95	59	.617	2
1909	Pittsburgh	110	42	.724	6½	1929	Chicago	98	54	.645	10½
1910	Chicago	104	50	.675	13	1930	St. Louis	92	62	.597	2
1911	New York	99	54	.647	7½	1931	St. Louis	101	53	.656	13
1912	New York	103	48	.682	10	1932	Chicago	90	64	.584	4
1913	New York	101	51	.664	12½	1933	New York	91	61	.599	5
1914	Boston	94	59	.614	10½	1934	St. Louis	95	58	.621	2
1915	Philadelphia	90	62	.592	7	1935	Chicago	100	54	.649	4
1916	Brooklyn	94	60	.610	2½	1936	New York	92	62	.597	5
1917	New York	98	56	.636	10	1937	New York	95	57	.625	3
1918	Chicago	84	45	.651	10½	1938	Chicago	89	63	.586	2
1919	Cincinnati	96	44	.686	9	1939	Cincinnati	97	57	.630	4½

Year		W	L	Pct	GA	Year		W	L	Pct	GA
1940	Cincinnati	100	53	.654	12	1976	West—Cincinnati	102	60	.630	10
1941	Brooklyn	100	54	.649	2½		East—Philadelphia	101	61	.623	9
1942	St. Louis	106	48	.688	2	1977	West—Los Angeles	98	64	.605	10
1943	St. Louis	105	49	.682	18		East—Philadelphia	101	61	.623	5
1944	St. Louis	105	49	.682	14½	1978	West—Los Angeles	95	67	.586	2½
1945	Chicago	98	56	.636	3		East—Philadelphia	90	72	.556	1½
1946	St. Louis†	98	58	.628	2	1979	West—Cincinnati	90	71	.559	1½
1947	Brooklyn	94	60	.610	5		East—Pittsburgh	98	64	.605	2
1948	Boston	91	62	.595	6½						
1949	Brooklyn	97	57	.630	1	1980	West—Houston	93	70	.571	1
							East—Philadelphia	91	71	.562	1
1950	Philadelphia	91	63	.591	2	1981	West—Los Angeles†	63	47	.573	—
1951	New York†	98	59	.624	1		East—Montreal†	60	48	.556	—
1952	Brooklyn	96	57	.627	4½	1982	West—Atlanta	89	73	.549	1
1953	Brooklyn	105	49	.682	13		East—St. Louis	92	70	.568	3
1954	New York	97	57	.630	5	1983	West—Los Angeles	91	71	.562	3
1955	Brooklyn	98	55	.641	13½		East—Philadelphia	90	72	.556	6
1956	Brooklyn	93	61	.604	1	1984	West—San Diego	92	70	.568	12
1957	Milwaukee	95	59	.617	8		East—Chicago	96	65	.596	6½
1958	Milwaukee	92	62	.597	8	1985	West—Los Angeles	95	67	.586	5½
1959	Los Angeles†	88	68	.564	2		East—St. Louis	101	61	.623	3
						1986	West—Houston	96	66	.593	10
1960	Pittsburgh	95	59	.617	7		East—N.Y. Mets	108	54	.667	21½
1961	Cincinnati	93	61	.604	4	1987	West—San Francisco	90	72	.556	6
1962	San Francisco†	103	62	.624	1		East—St. Louis	95	67	.586	3
1963	Los Angeles	99	63	.611	6	1988	West—Los Angeles	94	67	.584	7
1964	St. Louis	93	69	.574	1		East—N.Y. Mets	100	60	.625	15
1965	Los Angeles	97	65	.599	2	1989	West—San Francisco	92	70	.568	3
1966	Los Angeles	95	67	.586	1½		East—Chicago	93	69	.574	6
1967	St. Louis	101	60	.627	10½						
1968	St. Louis	97	65	.599	9	1990	West—Cincinnati	91	71	.562	5
1969	West—Atlanta	93	69	.574	3		East—Pittsburgh	95	67	.586	4
	East—N.Y. Mets	100	62	.617	8	1991	West—Atlanta	94	68	.580	1
							East—Pittsburgh	98	64	.605	14
1970	West—Cincinnati	102	60	.630	14½	1992	West—Atlanta	98	64	.605	8
	East—Pittsburgh	89	73	.549	5		East—Pittsburgh	96	66	.593	9
1971	West—San Francisco	90	72	.556	1	1993	West—Atlanta	104	58	.642	1
	East—Pittsburgh	97	65	.599	7		East—Philadelphia	97	65	.599	3
1972	West—Cincinnati	95	59	.617	10½	1994	West—Los Angeles*	58	56	.509	3½
	East—Pittsburgh	96	59	.619	11		Central—Cincinnati*	66	48	.579	½
1973	West—Cincinnati	99	63	.611	3½		East—Montreal*	74	40	.649	6
	East—N.Y. Mets	82	79	.509	1½	1995	West—Los Angeles	78	66	.542	1
1974	West—Los Angeles	102	60	.630	4		Central—Cincinnati	85	59	.590	9
	East—Pittsburgh	88	74	.543	1½		East—Atlanta	90	54	.625	21
1975	West—Cincinnati	108	54	.667	20						
	East—Pittsburgh	92	69	.571	6½						

†**Regular season playoffs: 1946**—St. Louis def. Brooklyn (2 games to 1); **1951**—New York def. Brooklyn (2 games to 1); **1959**—Los Angeles def. Milwaukee (2 games to none); **1962**—San Francisco def. Los Angeles (2 games to 1); **1981**—East: Montreal def. Philadelphia (3 games to 2) and West: Los Angeles def. Houston (3 games to 2).

American League

Multiple pennant winners: NY Yankees (32); Philadelphia-Oakland A's (15); Boston (10); Detroit (9); Baltimore and Washington-Minnesota (6); Chicago (5); Cleveland (3); KC Royals and Toronto (2). **Multiple division winners:** WEST—Oakland (10); Kansas City (6); Minnesota (4); California (3); Chicago (2). EAST—Baltimore (7); Boston, NY Yankees and Toronto (5); Detroit (3).

Year		W	L	Pct	GA	Year		W	L	Pct	GA
1901	Chicago	83	53	.610	4	1916	Boston	91	63	.591	2
1902	Philadelphia	83	53	.610	5	1917	Chicago	100	54	.649	9
1903	Boston	91	47	.659	14½	1918	Boston	75	51	.595	2½
1904	Boston	95	59	.617	1½	1919	Chicago	88	52	.629	3½
1905	Philadelphia	92	56	.622	2	1920	Cleveland	98	56	.636	2
1906	Chicago	93	58	.616	3	1921	New York	98	55	.641	4½
1907	Detroit	92	58	.613	1½	1922	New York	94	60	.610	1
1908	Detroit	90	63	.588	½	1923	New York	98	54	.645	16
1909	Detroit	98	54	.645	3½	1924	Washington	92	62	.597	2
1910	Philadelphia	102	48	.680	14½	1925	Washington	96	55	.636	8½
1911	Philadelphia	101	50	.669	13½	1926	New York	91	63	.591	3
1912	Boston	105	47	.691	14	1927	New York	110	44	.714	19
1913	Philadelphia	96	57	.627	6½	1928	New York	101	53	.656	2½
1914	Philadelphia	99	53	.651	8½	1929	Philadelphia	104	46	.693	18
1915	Boston	101	50	.669	2½						

Regular Season League & Division Winners (Cont.)
American League

Year		W	L	Pct	GA
1930	Philadelphia	102	52	.662	8
1931	Philadelphia	107	45	.704	13½
1932	New York	107	47	.695	13
1933	Washington	99	53	.651	7
1934	Detroit	101	53	.656	7
1935	Detroit	93	58	.616	3
1936	New York	102	51	.667	19½
1937	New York	102	52	.662	13
1938	New York	99	53	.651	9½
1939	New York	106	45	.702	17
1940	Detroit	90	64	.584	1
1941	New York	101	53	.656	17
1942	New York	103	51	.669	9
1943	New York	98	56	.636	13½
1944	St. Louis	89	65	.578	1
1945	Detroit	88	65	.575	1½
1946	Boston	104	50	.675	12
1947	New York	97	57	.630	12
1948	Cleveland†	97	58	.626	1
1949	New York	97	57	.630	1
1950	New York	98	56	.636	3
1951	New York	98	56	.636	5
1952	New York	95	59	.617	2
1953	New York	99	52	.656	8½
1954	Cleveland	111	43	.721	8
1955	New York	96	58	.623	3
1956	New York	97	57	.630	9
1957	New York	98	56	.636	8
1958	New York	92	62	.597	10
1959	Chicago	94	60	.610	5
1960	New York	97	57	.630	8
1961	New York	109	53	.673	8
1962	New York	96	66	.593	5
1963	New York	104	57	.646	10½
1964	New York	99	63	.611	1
1965	Minnesota	102	60	.630	7
1966	Baltimore	97	63	.606	9
1967	Boston	92	70	.568	1
1968	Detroit	103	59	.636	12
1969	West—Minnesota	97	65	.599	9
	East—Baltimore	109	53	.673	19
1970	West—Minnesota	98	64	.605	9
	East—Baltimore	108	54	.667	15
1971	West—Oakland	101	60	.627	16
	East—Baltimore	101	57	.639	12
1972	West—Oakland	93	62	.600	5½
	East—Detroit	86	70	.551	½

Year		W	L	Pct	GA
1973	West—Oakland	94	68	.580	6
	East—Baltimore	97	65	.599	8
1974	West—Oakland	90	72	.556	5
	East—Baltimore	91	71	.562	2
1975	West—Oakland	98	64	.605	7
	East—Boston	95	65	.594	4½
1976	West—Kansas City	90	72	.556	2½
	East—New York	97	62	.610	10½
1977	West—Kansas City	102	60	.630	8
	East—New York	100	62	.617	2½
1978	West—Kansas City	92	70	.568	5
	East—New York†	100	63	.613	1
1979	West—California	88	74	.543	3
	East—Baltimore	102	57	.642	8
1980	West—Kansas City	97	65	.599	14
	East—New York	103	59	.636	3
1981	West—Oakland†	64	45	.587	—
	East—New York†	59	48	.551	—
1982	West—California	93	69	.574	3
	East—Milwaukee	95	67	.586	1
1983	West—Chicago	99	63	.611	20
	East—Baltimore	98	64	.605	6
1984	West—Kansas City	84	78	.519	3
	East—Detroit	104	58	.642	15
1985	West—Kansas City	91	71	.562	1
	East—Toronto	99	62	.615	2
1986	West—California	92	70	.568	5
	East—Boston	95	66	.590	5½
1987	West—Minnesota	85	77	.525	2
	East—Detroit	98	64	.605	2
1988	West—Oakland	104	58	.642	13
	East—Boston	89	73	.549	1
1989	West—Oakland	99	63	.611	7
	East—Toronto	89	73	.549	2
1990	West—Oakland	103	59	.636	9
	East—Boston	88	74	.543	2
1991	West—Minnesota	95	67	.586	8
	East—Toronto	91	71	.562	7
1992	West—Oakland	96	66	.593	6
	East—Toronto	96	66	.593	4
1993	West—Chicago	94	68	.580	8
	East—Toronto	95	67	.586	7
1994	West—Texas*	52	62	.456	1
	Central—Chicago*	67	46	.593	1
	East—New York*	70	43	.619	6½
1995	West—Seattle†	79	66	.545	1
	Central—Cleveland	100	44	.694	30
	East—Boston	86	58	.597	7

†**Regular season playoffs: 1948**—Cleveland def. Boston, 2-1 (one game); **1978**—New York def. Boston, 5-4 (one game); **1981**—East: New York def. Milwaukee (3 games to 2) and West: Oakland def. Kansas City (3 games to none); **1995**—Seattle def. California, 9-1 (one game).

The All-Star Game

Baseball's first All-Star Game was held on July 6, 1933, before 47,595 at Comiskey Park in Chicago. From that year on, the All-Star Game has matched the best players in the American League against the best in the National. From 1959-62, two All-Star Games were played. The only year an All-Star Game wasn't played was 1945, when World War II travel restrictions made it necessary to cancel the meeting. The NL leads the series, 39-26-1. In the chart below, the American League is listed in **bold** type.

The All-Star Game MVP Award is named after Arch Ward, the *Chicago Tribune* sports editor who founded the game in 1933. First given at the two All-Star games in 1962, the name of the award was changed to the Commissioner's Trophy in 1970 and back to the Ward Memorial Award in 1985. **Multiple winners:** Gary Carter, Steve Garvey and Willie Mays (2).

Year		Host	AL Manager	NL Manager	MVP
1933	**American,** 4-2	Chicago (AL)	Connie Mack	John McGraw	No award
1934	**American,** 9-7	New York (NL)	Joe Cronin	Bill Terry	No award
1935	**American,** 4-1	Cleveland	Mickey Cochrane	Frankie Frisch	No award
1936	National, 4-3	Boston (NL)	Joe McCarthy	Charlie Grimm	No award

The All-Star Game (Cont.)

Year		Host	AL Manager	NL Manager	MVP
1937	**American,** 8-3	Washington	Joe McCarthy	Bill Terry	No award
1938	National, 4-1	Cincinnati	Joe McCarthy	Bill Terry	No award
1939	**American,** 3-1	New York (AL)	Joe McCarthy	Gabby Hartnett	No award
1940	National, 4-0	St. Louis (NL)	Joe Cronin	Bill McKechnie	No award
1941	**American,** 7-5	Detroit	Del Baker	Bill McKechnie	No award
1942	**American,** 3-1	New York (NL)	Joe McCarthy	Leo Durocher	No award
1943	**American,** 5-3	Philadelphia (AL)	Joe McCarthy	Billy Southworth	No award
1944	National, 7-1	Pittsburgh	Joe McCarthy	Billy Southworth	No award
1945	Not held				
1946	**American,** 12-0	Boston (AL)	Steve O'Neill	Charlie Grimm	No award
1947	**American,** 2-1	Chicago (NL)	Joe Cronin	Eddie Dyer	No award
1948	**American,** 5-2	St. Louis (AL)	Bucky Harris	Leo Durocher	No award
1949	**American,** 11-7	Brooklyn	Lou Boudreau	Billy Southworth	No award
1950	National, 4-3 (14)	Chicago (AL)	Casey Stengel	Burt Shotton	No award
1951	National, 8-3	Detroit	Casey Stengel	Eddie Sawyer	No award
1952	National, 3-2 (5, rain)	Philadelphia (NL)	Casey Stengel	Leo Durocher	No award
1953	National, 5-1	Cincinnati	Casey Stengel	Charlie Dressen	No award
1954	**American,** 11-9	Cleveland	Casey Stengel	Walter Alston	No award
1955	National, 6-5 (12)	Milwaukee	Al Lopez	Leo Durocher	No award
1956	National, 7-3	Washington	Casey Stengel	Walter Alston	No award
1957	**American,** 6-5	St. Louis	Casey Stengel	Walter Alston	No award
1958	**American,** 4-3	Baltimore	Casey Stengel	Fred Haney	No award
1959-a	National, 5-4	Pittsburgh	Casey Stengel	Fred Haney	No award
1959-b	**American,** 5-3	Los Angeles	Casey Stengel	Fred Haney	No award
1960-a	National, 5-3	Kansas City	Al Lopez	Walter Alston	No award
1960-b	National, 6-0	New York	Al Lopez	Walter Alston	No award
1961-a	National, 5-4 (10)	San Francisco	Paul Richards	Danny Murtaugh	No award
1961-b	TIE, 1-1 (9, rain)	Boston	Paul Richards	Danny Murtaugh	No award
1962-a	National, 3-1	Washington	Ralph Houk	Fred Hutchinson	Maury Wills, LA (NL), SS
1962-b	**American,** 9-4	Chicago (NL)	Ralph Houk	Fred Hutchinson	Leon Wagner, LA (AL), OF
1963	National, 5-3	Cleveland	Ralph Houk	Alvin Dark	Willie Mays, SF, OF
1964	National, 7-4	New York (NL)	Al Lopez	Walter Alston	Johnny Callison, Phi., OF
1965	National, 6-5	Minnesota	Al Lopez	Gene Mauch	Juan Marichal, SF, P
1966	National, 2-1 (10)	St. Louis	Sam Mele	Walter Alston	Brooks Robinson, Bal., 3B
1967	National, 2-1 (15)	California	Hank Bauer	Walter Alston	Tony Perez, Cin., 3B
1968	National, 1-0	Houston	Dick Williams	Red Schoendienst	Willie Mays, SF, OF
1969	National, 9-3	Washington	Mayo Smith	Red Schoendienst	Willie McCovey, SF, 1B
1970	National, 5-4 (12)	Cincinnati	Earl Weaver	Gil Hodges	Carl Yastrzemski, Bos., OF-1B
1971	**American,** 6-4	Detroit	Earl Weaver	Sparky Anderson	Frank Robinson, Bal., OF
1972	National, 4-3 (10)	Atlanta	Earl Weaver	Danny Murtaugh	Joe Morgan, Cin., 2B
1973	National, 7-1	Kansas	Dick Williams	Sparky Anderson	Bobby Bonds, SF, OF
1974	National, 7-2	Pittsburgh	Dick Williams	Yogi Berra	Steve Garvey, LA, 1B
1975	National, 6-3	Milwaukee	Alvin Dark	Walter Alston	Bill Madlock, Chi. (NL), 3B & Jon Matlack, NY (NL), P
1976	National, 7-1	Philadelphia	Darrell Johnson	Sparky Anderson	George Foster, Cin., OF
1977	National, 7-5	New York (AL)	Billy Martin	Sparky Anderson	Don Sutton, LA, P
1978	National, 7-3	San Diego	Billy Martin	Tommy Lasorda	Steve Garvey, LA, 1B
1979	National, 7-6	Seattle	Bob Lemon	Tommy Lasorda	Dave Parker, Pit, OF
1980	National, 4-2	Los Angeles	Earl Weaver	Chuck Tanner	Ken Griffey, Cin., OF
1981	National, 5-4	Cleveland	Jim Frey	Dallas Green	Gary Carter, Mon., C
1982	National, 4-1	Montreal	Billy Martin	Tommy Lasorda	Dave Concepcion, Cin., SS
1983	**American,** 13-3	Chicago (AL)	Harvey Kuenn	Whitey Herzog	Fred Lynn, Cal., OF
1984	National, 3-1	San Francisco	Joe Altobelli	Paul Owens	Gary Carter, Mon., C
1985	National, 6-1	Minnesota	Sparky Anderson	Dick Williams	LaMarr Hoyt, SD, P
1986	**American,** 3-2	Houston	Dick Howser	Whitey Herzog	Roger Clemens, Bos., P
1987	National, 2-0 (13)	Oakland	John McNamara	Davey Johnson	Tim Raines, Mon., OF
1988	**American,** 2-1	Cincinnati	Tom Kelly	Whitey Herzog	Terry Steinbach, Oak., C
1989	**American,** 5-3	California	Tony La Russa	Tommy Lasorda	Bo Jackson, KC, OF
1990	**American,** 2-0	Chicago (NL)	Tony La Russa	Roger Craig	Julio Franco, Tex., 2B
1991	**American,** 4-2	Toronto	Tony La Russa	Lou Piniella	Cal Ripken Jr., Bal., SS
1992	**American,** 13-6	San Diego	Tom Kelly	Bobby Cox	Ken Griffey Jr., Sea., OF
1993	**American,** 9-3	Baltimore	Cito Gaston	Bobby Cox	Kirby Puckett, Min., OF
1994	National, 8-7 (10)	Pittsburgh	Cito Gaston	Jim Fregosi	Fred McGriff, Atl., 1B
1995	National, 3-2	Texas	Buck Showalter	Felipe Alou	Jeff Conine, Fla., PH

Major League Franchise Origins

Here is what the current 28 teams in Major League Baseball have to show for the years they have put in as members of the National League (NL) and American League (AL). Pennants and World Series championships are since 1901.

National League

	1st Year	Pennants & World Series	Franchise Stops
Atlanta Braves...............1876		7 NL (1914,48,57-58,91-92,95) 3 WS (1914,57,95)	• Boston (1876-1952) Milwaukee (1953-65) Atlanta (1966—)
Chicago Cubs.....................1876		10 NL (1906-08,10,18,29,32,35,38,45) 2 WS (1907-08)	• Chicago (1876—)
Cincinnati Reds.................1876		9 NL (1919,39-40,61,70,72,75-76,90) 5 WS (1919,40,75-76,90)	• Cincinnati (1876-80) Cincinnati (1890—)
Colorado Rockies.............1993		None	• Denver (1993—)
Florida Marlins.................1993		None	• Miami (1993—)
Houston Astros.................1962		None	• Houston (1962—)
Los Angeles Dodgers........1890		18 NL (1916,20,41,47,49,52-53,55-56,59,63, 65-66,74,77-78, 81,88) 6 WS (1955,59,63,65,81,88)	• Brooklyn (1890-1957) Los Angeles (1958—)
Montreal Expos.................1969		None	• Montreal (1969—)
New York Mets.................1962		3 NL (1969,73,86) 2 WS (1969,86)	• New York (1962—)
Philadelphia Phillies.........1883		5 NL (1915,50,80,83,93) 1 WS (1980)	• Philadelphia (1883—)
Pittsburgh Pirates.............1887		7 NL (1903,09,25,27,60,71,79) 5 WS (1909,25,60,71,79)	• Pittsburgh (1887—)
St. Louis Cardinals............1892		15 NL (1926,28,30-31,34,42-44,46,64, 67-68,82,85,87) 9 WS (1926,31,34,42,44,46,64,67,82)	• St. Louis (1892—)
San Diego Padres..............1969		1 NL (1984)	• San Diego (1969—)
San Francisco Giants........1883		16 NL (1905,11-13,17,21-24,33,36-37,51, 54,62,89) 5 WS (1905,21-22,33,54)	• New York (1883-1957) San Francisco (1958—)

American League

	1st Year	Pennants & World Series	Franchise Stops
Baltimore Orioles.............1901		7 AL (1944,66,69-71,79,83) 3 WS (1966,70,83)	• Milwaukee (1901) St. Louis (1902-53) Baltimore (1954—)
Boston Red Sox.................1901		9 AL (1903,12,15-16,18,46,67,75,86) 5 WS (1903,12,15-16,18)	• Boston (1901—)
California Angels..............1961		None	• Los Angeles (1961-65) Anaheim, CA (1966—)
Chicago White Sox...........1901		4 AL (1906,17,19,59) 2 WS (1906,17)	• Chicago (1901—)
Cleveland Indians..............1901		4 AL (1920,48,54,95) 2 WS (1920,48)	• Cleveland (1901—)
Detroit Tigers.....................1901		9 AL (1907-09,34-35,40,45,68,84) 4 WS (1935,45,68,84)	• Detroit (1901—)
Kansas City Royals...........1969		2 AL (1980,85) 1 WS (1985)	• Kansas City (1969—)
Milwaukee Brewers.........1969		1 AL (1982)	• Seattle (1969) Milwaukee (1970—)
Minnesota Twins...............1901		6 AL (1924-25,33,65,87,91) 3 WS (1924,87,91)	• Washington, DC (1901-60) Bloomington, MN (1961-81) Minneapolis (1982—)
New York Yankees...........1901		33 AL (1921-23,26-28,32,36-39,41-43,47, 49-53,55-58,60-64,76-78,81) 22 WS (1923,27-28,32,36-39,41,43,47,49-53, 56,58,61-62,77-78)	• Baltimore (1901-02) New York (1903—)
Oakland Athletics.............1901		14 AL (1905,10-11,13-14,29-31,72-74,88-90) 9 WS (1910-11,13,29-30,72-74,89)	• Philadelphia (1901-54) Kansas City (1955-67) Oakland (1968—)

	1st Year	Pennants & World Series	
Seattle Mariners	1977	None	**Franchise Stops**
			• Seattle (1977—)
Texas Rangers	1961	None	• Washington, DC (1961-71)
			Arlington, TX (1972—)
Toronto Blue Jays	1977	2 AL (1992-93)	• Toronto (1977—)
		2 WS (1992-93)	

The Growth of Major League Baseball

The National League (founded in 1876) and the American League (founded in 1901) were both eight-team circuits at the turn of the century and remained that way until expansion finally came to Major League Baseball in the 1960s. The AL added two teams in 1961 and the NL did the same a year later. Both leagues went to 12 teams and split into two divisions in 1969. The AL then grew by two more teams in 1977, but the NL didn't follow suit until adding its 13th and 14th clubs in 1993.

Expansion Timetable (Since 1901)

1961—Los Angeles Angels (now California) and Washington Senators (now Texas Rangers) join AL; **1962**—Houston Colt .45s (now Astros) and New York Mets join NL; **1969**—Kansas City Royals and Seattle Pilots (now Milwaukee Brewers) join AL, while Montreal Expos and San Diego Padres join NL; **1977**—Seattle Mariners and Toronto Blue Jays join AL; **1993**—Colorado Rockies and Florida Marlins join NL; **1995**—New franchises awarded to Phoenix and St. Petersburg, Fla. The Arizona Diamondbacks and Tampa Bay Devil Rays will begin play in 1998, which leagues they join will be decided later.

City and Nickname Changes
National League

1953—Boston Braves move to Milwaukee; **1958**—Brooklyn Dodgers move to Los Angeles and New York Giants move to San Francisco; **1965**—Houston Colt .45s renamed Astros; **1966**—Milwaukee Braves move to Atlanta.
  Other nicknames: Boston (Beaneaters and Doves through 1908, and Bees from 1936-40); **Brooklyn** (Superbas through 1926, then Robins from 1927-31; then Dodgers from 1932-57); **Cincinnati** (Red Legs from 1944-45, then Redlegs from 1954-60, then Reds since 1961); **Philadelphia** (Blue Jays from 1943-44).

American League

1902—Milwaukee Brewers move to St. Louis and become Browns; **1903**—Baltimore Orioles move to New York and become Highlanders; **1913**—NY Highlanders renamed Yankees; **1954**—St. Louis Browns move to Baltimore and become Orioles; **1955**—Philadelphia Athletics move to Kansas City; **1961**—Washington Senators move to Bloomington, Minn., and become Minnesota Twins; **1965**—LA Angels renamed California Angels; **1966**—California Angels move to Anaheim; **1968**—KC Athletics move to Oakland and become A's; **1970**—Seattle Pilots move to Milwaukee and become Brewers; **1972**—Washington Senators move to Arlington, Texas, and become Rangers; **1982**—Minnesota Twins move to Minneapolis; **1987**—Oakland A's renamed Athletics.
  Other nicknames: Boston (Pilgrims, Puritans, Plymouth Rocks and Somersets through 1906); **Cleveland** (Broncos, Blues, Naps and Molly McGuires through 1914); **Washington** (Senators through 1904, then Nationals from 1905-44, then Senators again from 1945-60).

National League Pennant Winners from 1876-99

Founded in 1876, the National League played 24 seasons before the turn of the century and its eventual rivalry with the younger American League. **Multiple winners:** Boston (8); Chicago (6); Baltimore (3); Brooklyn and New York (2).

Year		Year		Year		Year	
1876	Chicago	1882	Chicago	1888	New York	1894	Baltimore
1877	Boston	1883	Boston	1889	New York	1895	Baltimore
1878	Boston	1884	Providence	1890	Brooklyn	1896	Baltimore
1879	Providence	1885	Chicago	1891	Boston	1897	Boston
1880	Chicago	1886	Chicago	1892	Boston	1898	Boston
1881	Chicago	1887	Detroit	1893	Boston	1899	Brooklyn

Champions of Leagues That No Longer Exist

A Special Baseball Records Committee appointed by the commissioner found in 1968 that four extinct leagues qualified for major league status—the American Association (1882-91), the Union Association (1884), the Players' League (1890) and the Federal League (1914-15). The first years of the American League (1900) and Federal League (1913) were not recognized.

American Association

Year	Champion	Manager	Year	Champion	Manager	Year	Champion	Manager
1882	Cincinnati	Pop Snyder	1886	St. Louis	Charlie Comiskey	1889	Brooklyn	Bill McGunnigle
1883	Philadelphia	Lew Simmons	1887	St. Louis	Charlie Comiskey	1890	Louisville	Jack Chapman
1884	New York	Jim Mutrie	1888	St. Louis	Charlie Comiskey	1891	Boston	Arthur Irwin
1885	St. Louis	Charlie Comiskey						

Union Association			**Players' League**			**Federal League**		
Year	Champion	Manager	Year	Champion	Manager	Year	Champion	Manager
1884	St. Louis	Henry Lucas	1890	Boston	King Kelly	1914	Indianapolis	Bill Phillips
						1915	Chicago	Joe Tinker

Annual Batting Leaders (since 1900)
Batting Average
National League

Multiple winners: Honus Wagner (8); Rogers Hornsby and Stan Musial (7); Tony Gwynn (6); Roberto Clemente and Bill Madlock (4); Pete Rose and Paul Waner (3); Hank Aaron, Richie Ashburn, Jake Daubert, Tommy Davis, Ernie Lombardi, Willie McGee, Lefty O'Doul, Dave Parker and Edd Roush (2).

Year		Avg	Year		Avg	Year		Avg
1900	Honus Wagner, Pit	.381	1932	Lefty O'Doul, Bklyn	.368	1964	Roberto Clemente, Pit	.339
1901	Jesse Burkett, St.L	.382	1933	Chuck Klein, Phi	.368	1965	Roberto Clemente, Pit	.329
1902	Ginger Beaumont, Pit	.357	1934	Paul Waner, Pit	.362	1966	Matty Alou, Pit	.342
1903	Honus Wagner, Pit	.355	1935	Arkie Vaughan, Pit	.385	1967	Roberto Clemente, Pit	.357
1904	Honus Wagner, Pit	.349	1936	Paul Waner, Pit	.373	1968	Pete Rose, Cin	.335
1905	Cy Seymour, Cin	.377	1937	Joe Medwick, St.L	.374	1969	Pete Rose, Cin	.348
1906	Honus Wagner, Pit	.339	1938	Ernie Lombardi, Cin	.342			
1907	Honus Wagner, Pit	.350	1939	Johnny Mize, St.L	.349	1970	Rico Carty, Atl	.366
1908	Honus Wagner, Pit	.354				1971	Joe Torre, St.L	.363
1909	Honus Wagner, Pit	.339	1940	Debs Garms, Pit	.355	1972	Billy Williams, Chi	.333
			1941	Pete Reiser, Bklyn	.343	1973	Pete Rose, Cin	.338
1910	Sherry Magee, Phi	.331	1942	Ernie Lombardi, Bos	.330	1974	Ralph Garr, Atl	.353
1911	Honus Wagner, Pit	.334	1943	Stan Musial, St.L	.357	1975	Bill Madlock, Chi	.354
1912	Heinie Zimmerman, Chi	.372	1944	Dixie Walker, Bklyn	.357	1976	Bill Madlock, Chi	.339
1913	Jake Daubert, Bklyn	.350	1945	Phil Cavarretta, Chi	.355	1977	Dave Parker, Pit	.338
1914	Jake Daubert, Bklyn	.329	1946	Stan Musial, St.L	.365	1978	Dave Parker, Pit	.334
1915	Larry Doyle, NY	.320	1947	Harry Walker, St.L-Phi	.363	1979	Keith Hernandez, St.L	.344
1916	Hal Chase, Cin	.339	1948	Stan Musial, St.L	.376			
1917	Edd Roush, Cin	.341	1949	Jackie Robinson, Bklyn	.342	1980	Bill Buckner, Chi	.324
1918	Zack Wheat, Bklyn	.335				1981	Bill Madlock, Pit	.341
1919	Edd Roush, Cin	.321	1950	Stan Musial, St.L	.346	1982	Al Oliver, Mon	.331
			1951	Stan Musial, St.L	.355	1983	Bill Madlock, Pit	.323
1920	Rogers Hornsby, St.L	.370	1952	Stan Musial, St.L	.336	1984	Tony Gwynn, SD	.351
1921	Rogers Hornsby, St.L	.397	1953	Carl Furillo, Bklyn	.344	1985	Willie McGee, St.L	.353
1922	Rogers Hornsby, St.L	.401	1954	Willie Mays, NY	.345	1986	Tim Raines, Mon	.334
1923	Rogers Hornsby, St.L	.384	1955	Richie Ashburn, Phi	.338	1987	Tony Gwynn, SD	.370
1924	Rogers Hornsby, St.L	.424	1956	Hank Aaron, Mil	.328	1988	Tony Gwynn, SD	.313
1925	Rogers Hornsby, St.L	.403	1957	Stan Musial, St.L	.351	1989	Tony Gwynn, SD	.336
1926	Bubbles Hargrave, Cin	.353	1958	Richie Ashburn, Phi	.350			
1927	Paul Waner, Pit	.380	1959	Hank Aaron, Mil	.355	1990	Willie McGee, St.L	.335
1928	Rogers Hornsby, Bos	.387				1991	Terry Pendleton, Atl	.319
1929	Lefty O'Doul, Phi	.398	1960	Dick Groat, Pit	.325	1992	Gary Sheffield, SD	.330
			1961	Roberto Clemente, Pit	.351	1993	Andres Galarraga, Col	.370
1930	Bill Terry, NY	.401	1962	Tommy Davis, LA	.346	1994	Tony Gwynn, SD	.394
1931	Chick Hafey, St.L	.349	1963	Tommy Davis, LA	.326	1995	Tony Gwynn, SD	.368

American League

Multiple winners: Ty Cobb (12); Rod Carew (7); Ted Williams (6); Wade Boggs (5); Harry Heilmann (4); George Brett, Nap Lajoie, Tony Oliva and Carl Yastrzemski (3); Luke Appling, Joe DiMaggio, Ferris Fain, Jimmie Foxx, Edgar Martinez, Pete Runnels, Al Simmons, George Sisler and Mickey Vernon (2).

Year		Avg	Year		Avg	Year		Avg
1901	Nap Lajoie, Phi	.422	1924	Babe Ruth, NY	.378	1947	Ted Williams, Bos	.343
1902	Ed Delahanty, Wash	.376	1925	Harry Heilmann, Det	.393	1948	Ted Williams, Bos	.369
1903	Nap Lajoie, Cle	.355	1926	Heinie Manush, Det	.378	1949	George Kell, Det	.343
1904	Nap Lajoie, Cle	.381	1927	Harry Heilmann, Det	.398			
1905	Elmer Flick, Cle	.306	1928	Goose Goslin, Wash	.379	1950	Billy Goodman, Bos	.354
1906	George Stone, St.L	.358	1929	Lew Fonseca, Cle	.369	1951	Ferris Fain, Phi	.344
1907	Ty Cobb, Det	.350				1952	Ferris Fain, Phi	.327
1908	Ty Cobb, Det	.324	1930	Al Simmons, Phi	.381	1953	Mickey Vernon, Wash	.337
1909	Ty Cobb, Det	.377	1931	Al Simmons, Phi	.390	1954	Bobby Avila, Clev	.341
			1932	Dale Alexander, Det-Bos	.367	1955	Al Kaline, Det	.340
1910	Ty Cobb, Det	.385	1933	Jimmie Foxx, Phi	.356	1956	Mickey Mantle, NY	.353
1911	Ty Cobb, Det	.420	1934	Lou Gehrig, NY	.363	1957	Ted Williams, Bos	.388
1912	Ty Cobb, Det	.410	1935	Buddy Myer, Wash	.349	1958	Ted Williams, Bos	.328
1913	Ty Cobb, Det	.390	1936	Luke Appling, Chi	.388	1959	Harvey Kuenn, Det	.353
1914	Ty Cobb, Det	.368	1937	Charlie Gehringer, Det	.371			
1915	Ty Cobb, Det	.369	1938	Jimmie Foxx, Bos	.349	1960	Pete Runnels, Bos	.320
1916	Tris Speaker, Cle	.386	1939	Joe DiMaggio, NY	.381	1961	Norm Cash, Det	.361
1917	Ty Cobb, Det	.383				1962	Pete Runnels, Bos	.326
1918	Ty Cobb, Det	.382	1940	Joe DiMaggio, NY	.352	1963	Carl Yastrzemski, Bos	.321
1919	Ty Cobb, Det	.384	1941	Ted Williams, Bos	.406	1964	Tony Oliva, Min	.323
			1942	Ted Williams, Bos	.356	1965	Tony Oliva, Min	.321
1920	George Sisler, St.L	.407	1943	Luke Appling, Chi	.328	1966	Frank Robinson, Bal	.316
1921	Harry Heilmann, Det	.394	1944	Lou Boudreau, Clev	.327	1967	Carl Yastrzemski, Bos	.326
1922	George Sisler, St.L	.420	1945	Snuffy Stirnweiss, NY	.309	1968	Carl Yastrzemski, Bos	.301
1923	Harry Heilmann, Det	.403	1946	Mickey Vernon, Wash	.353	1969	Rod Carew, Min	.332

Year		Avg	Year		Avg	Year		Avg
1970	Alex Johnson, Cal	.329	1980	George Brett, KC	.390	1990	George Brett, KC	.329
1971	Tony Oliva, Min	.337	1981	Carney Lansford, Bos	.336	1991	Julio Franco, Tex	.341
1972	Rod Carew, Min	.318	1982	Willie Wilson, KC	.332	1992	Edgar Martinez, Sea	.343
1973	Rod Carew, Min	.350	1983	Wade Boggs, Bos	.361	1993	John Olerud, Tor	.363
1974	Rod Carew, Min	.364	1984	Don Mattingly, NY	.343	1994	Paul O'Neill, NY	.359
1975	Rod Carew, Min	.359	1985	Wade Boggs, Bos	.368	1995	Edgar Martinez, Sea	.356
1976	George Brett, KC	.333	1986	Wade Boggs, Bos	.357			
1977	Rod Carew, Min	.388	1987	Wade Boggs, Bos	.363			
1978	Rod Carew, Min	.333	1988	Wade Boggs, Bos	.366			
1979	Fred Lynn, Bos	.333	1989	Kirby Puckett, Min	.339			

Home Runs
National League

Multiple winners: Mike Schmidt (8); Ralph Kiner (7); Gavvy Cravath and Mel Ott (6); Hank Aaron, Chuck Klein, Willie Mays, Johnny Mize, Cy Williams and Hack Wilson (4); Willie McCovey (3); Ernie Banks, Johnny Bench, George Foster, Rogers Hornsby, Tim Jordan, Dave Kingman, Eddie Mathews, Dale Murphy, Bill Nicholson, Dave Robertson, Wildfire Schulte and Willie Stargell (2).

Year		Avg	Year		HR	Year		HR
1900	Herman Long, Bos	12	1932	Chuck Klein, Phi	38	1963	Hank Aaron, Mil	44
1901	Sam Crawford, Cin	16		& Mel Ott, NY	38		& Willie McCovey, SF	44
1902	Tommy Leach, Pit	6	1933	Chuck Klein, Phi	28	1964	Willie Mays, SF	47
1903	Jimmy Sheckard, Bklyn	9	1934	Rip Collins, St.L	35	1965	Willie Mays, SF	52
1904	Harry Lumley, Bklyn	9		& Mel Ott, NY	35	1966	Hank Aaron, Atl	44
1905	Fred Odwell, Cin	9	1935	Wally Berger, Bos	34	1967	Hank Aaron, Atl	39
1906	Tim Jordan, Bklyn	12	1936	Mel Ott, NY	33	1968	Willie McCovey, SF	36
1907	Dave Brain, Bos	10	1937	Joe Medwick, St.L	31	1969	Willie McCovey, SF	45
1908	Tim Jordan, Bklyn	12		& Mel Ott, NY	31			
1909	Red Murray, NY	7	1938	Mel Ott, NY	36	1970	Johnny Bench, Cin	45
			1939	Johnny Mize, St.L	28	1971	Willie Stargell, Pit	48
1910	Fred Beck, Bos	10				1972	Johnny Bench, Cin	40
	& Wildfire Schulte, Chi	10	1940	Johnny Mize, St.L	43	1973	Willie Stargell, Pit	44
1911	Wildfire Schulte, Chi	21	1941	Dolf Camilli, Bklyn	34	1974	Mike Schmidt, Phi	36
1912	Heinie Zimmerman, Chi	14	1942	Mel Ott, NY	30	1975	Mike Schmidt, Phi	38
1913	Gavvy Cravath, Phi	19	1943	Bill Nicholson, Chi	29	1976	Mike Schmidt, Phi	38
1914	Gavvy Cravath, Phi	19	1944	Bill Nicholson, Chi	33	1977	George Foster, Cin	52
1915	Gavvy Cravath, Phi	24	1945	Tommy Holmes, Bos	28	1978	George Foster, Cin	40
1916	Cy Williams, Chi	12	1946	Ralph Kiner, Pit	23	1979	Dave Kingman, Chi	48
	& Dave Robertson, NY	12	1947	Ralph Kiner, Pit	51			
1917	Gavvy Cravath, Phi	12		& Johnny Mize, NY	51	1980	Mike Schmidt, Phi	48
	& Dave Robertson, NY	12	1948	Ralph Kiner, Pit	40	1981	Mike Schmidt, Phi	31
1918	Gavvy Cravath, Phi	8		& Johnny Mize, NY	40	1982	Dave Kingman, NY	37
1919	Gavvy Cravath, Phi	12	1949	Ralph Kiner, Pit	54	1983	Mike Schmidt, Phi	40
			1950	Ralph Kiner, Pit	47	1984	Dale Murphy, Atl	36
1920	Cy Williams, Phi	15	1951	Ralph Kiner, Pit	42		& Mike Schmidt, Phi	36
1921	George Kelly, NY	23	1952	Ralph Kiner, Pit	37	1985	Dale Murphy, Atl	37
1922	Rogers Hornsby, St.L	42		& Hank Sauer, Chi	37	1986	Mike Schmidt, Phi	37
1923	Cy Williams, Phi	41	1953	Eddie Mathews, Mil	47	1987	Andre Dawson, Chi	49
1924	Jack Fournier, Bklyn	27	1954	Ted Kluszewski, Cin	49	1988	Darryl Strawberry, NY	39
1925	Rogers Hornsby, St.L	39	1955	Willie Mays, NY	51	1989	Kevin Mitchell, SF	47
1926	Hack Wilson, Chi	21	1956	Duke Snider, Bklyn	43			
1927	Cy Williams, Phi	30	1957	Hank Aaron, Mil	44	1990	Ryne Sandberg, Chi	40
	& Hack Wilson, Chi	30	1958	Ernie Banks, Chi	47	1991	Howard Johnson, NY	38
1928	Jim Bottomley, St.L	31	1959	Eddie Mathews, Mil	46	1992	Fred McGriff, SD	35
	& Hack Wilson, Chi	31	1960	Ernie Banks, Chi	41	1993	Barry Bonds, SF	46
1929	Chuck Klein, Phi	43	1961	Orlando Cepeda, SF	46	1994	Matt Williams, SF	43
1930	Hack Wilson, Chi	56	1962	Willie Mays, SF	49	1995	Dante Bichette, Col	40
1931	Chuck Klein, Phi	31						

American League

Multiple winners: Babe Ruth (12); Harmon Killebrew (6); Home Run Baker, Harry Davis, Jimmie Foxx, Hank Greenberg, Reggie Jackson, Mickey Mantle and Ted Williams (4); Lou Gehrig and Jim Rice (3); Dick Allen, Tony Armas, Jose Canseco, Joe DiMaggio, Larry Doby, Cecil Fielder, Juan Gonzalez, Frank Howard, Wally Pipp, Al Rosen and Gorman Thomas (2).

Year		HR	Year		HR	Year		HR
1901	Nap Lajoie, Phi	14	1908	Sam Crawford, Det	7	1914	Home Run Baker, Phi	9
1902	Socks Seybold, Phi	16	1909	Ty Cobb, Det	9	1915	Braggo Roth, Chi-Cle	7
1903	Buck Freeman, Bos	13	1910	Jake Stahl, Bos	10	1916	Wally Pipp, NY	12
1904	Harry Davis, Phi	10	1911	Home Run Baker, Phi	11	1917	Wally Pipp, NY	9
1905	Harry Davis, Phi	8	1912	Home Run Baker, Phi	10	1918	Babe Ruth, Bos	11
1906	Harry Davis, Phi	12		& Tris Speaker, Bos	10		& Tilly Walker, Phi	11
1907	Harry Davis, Phi	8	1913	Home Run Baker, Phi	12	1919	Babe Ruth, Bos	29

Annual Batting Leaders (Cont.)
Home Runs
American League

Year		HR	Year		HR	Year		HR
1920	Babe Ruth, NY	54	1948	Joe DiMaggio, NY	39	1974	Dick Allen, Chi	32
1921	Babe Ruth, NY	59	1949	Ted Williams, Bos	43	1975	Reggie Jackson, Oak	36
1922	Ken Williams, St.L	39					& George Scott, Mil	36
1923	Babe Ruth, NY	41	1950	Al Rosen, Cle	37	1976	Graig Nettles, NY	32
1924	Babe Ruth, NY	46	1951	Gus Zernial, Chi-Phi	33	1977	Jim Rice, Bos	39
1925	Bob Meusel, NY	33	1952	Larry Doby, Cle	32	1978	Jim Rice, Bos	46
1926	Babe Ruth, NY	47	1953	Al Rosen, Cle	43	1979	Gorman Thomas, Mil	45
1927	Babe Ruth, NY	60	1954	Larry Doby, Cle	32			
1928	Babe Ruth, NY	54	1955	Mickey Mantle, NY	37	1980	Reggie Jackson, NY	41
1929	Babe Ruth, NY	46	1956	Mickey Mantle, NY	52		& Ben Oglivie, Mil	41
			1957	Roy Sievers, Wash	42	1981	Tony Armas, Oak	22
1930	Babe Ruth, NY	49	1958	Mickey Mantle, NY	42		Dwight Evans, Bos	22
1931	Lou Gehrig, NY	46	1959	Rocky Colavito, Cle	42		Bobby Grich, Cal	22
	& Babe Ruth, NY	46		& Harmon Killebrew, Wash	42		& Eddie Murray, Bal	22
1932	Jimmie Foxx, Phi	58				1982	Reggie Jackson, Cal	39
1933	Jimmie Foxx, Phi	48	1960	Mickey Mantle, NY	40		& Gorman Thomas, Mil	39
1934	Lou Gehrig, NY	49	1961	Roger Maris, NY	61	1983	Jim Rice, Bos	39
1935	Jimmie Foxx, Phi	36	1962	Harmon Killebrew, Min	48	1984	Tony Armas, Bos	43
	& Hank Greenberg, Det	36	1963	Harmon Killebrew, Min	45	1985	Darrell Evans, Det	40
1936	Lou Gehrig, NY	49	1964	Harmon Killebrew, Min	49	1986	Jesse Barfield, Tor	40
1937	Joe DiMaggio, NY	46	1965	Tony Conigliaro, Bos	32	1987	Mark McGwire, Oak	49
1938	Hank Greenberg, Det	58	1966	Frank Robinson, Bal	49	1988	Jose Canseco, Oak	42
1939	Jimmie Foxx, Bos	35	1967	Harmon Killebrew, Min	44	1989	Fred McGriff, Tor	36
				& Carl Yastrzemski, Bos	44			
1940	Hank Greenberg, Det	41	1968	Frank Howard, Wash	44	1990	Cecil Fielder, Det	51
1941	Ted Williams, Bos	37	1969	Harmon Killebrew, Min	49	1991	Jose Canseco, Oak	44
1942	Ted Williams, Bos	36					& Cecil Fielder, Det	44
1943	Rudy York, Det	34	1970	Frank Howard, Wash	44	1992	Juan Gonzalez, Tex	43
1944	Nick Etten, NY	22	1971	Bill Melton, Chi	33	1993	Juan Gonzalez, Tex	46
1945	Vern Stephens, St.L	24	1972	Dick Allen, Chi	37	1994	Ken Griffey Jr., Sea	40
1946	Hank Greenberg, Det	44	1973	Reggie Jackson, Oak	32	1995	Albert Belle, Cle	50
1947	Ted Williams, Bos	32						

Runs Batted In
National League

Multiple winners: Hank Aaron, Rogers Hornsby, Sherry Magee, Mike Schmidt and Honus Wagner (4); Johnny Bench, George Foster, Joe Medwick, Johnny Mize and Heinie Zimmerman (3); Ernie Banks, Jim Bottomley, Orlando Cepeda, Gavvy Cravath, George Kelly, Chuck Klein, Willie McCovey, Dale Murphy, Stan Musial, Bill Nicholson and Hack Wilson (2).

Year		RBI	Year		RBI	Year		RBI
1900	Elmer Flick, Phi	110	1923	Irish Meusel, NY	125	1949	Ralph Kiner, Pit	127
1901	Honus Wagner, Pit	126	1924	George Kelly, NY	136	1950	Del Ennis, Phi	126
1902	Honus Wagner, Pit	91	1925	Rogers Hornsby, St.L	143	1951	Monte Irvin, NY	121
1903	Sam Mertes, NY	104	1926	Jim Bottomley, St.L	120	1952	Hank Sauer, Chi	121
1904	Bill Dahlen, NY	80	1927	Paul Waner, Pit	131	1953	Roy Campanella, Bklyn	142
1905	Cy Seymour, Cin	121	1928	Jim Bottomley, St.L	136	1954	Ted Kluszewski, Cin	141
1906	Jim Nealon, Pit	83	1929	Hack Wilson, Chi	159	1955	Duke Snider, Bklyn	136
	& Harry Steinfeldt, Chi	83				1956	Stan Musial, St.L	109
1907	Sherry Magee, Phi	85	1930	Hack Wilson, Chi	190	1957	Hank Aaron, Mil	132
1908	Honus Wagner, Pit	109	1931	Chuck Klein, Phi	121	1958	Ernie Banks, Chi	129
1909	Honus Wagner, Pit	100	1932	Don Hurst, Phi	143	1959	Ernie Banks, Chi	143
			1933	Chuck Klein, Phi	120			
1910	Sherry Magee, Phi	123	1934	Mel Ott, NY	135	1960	Hank Aaron, Mil	126
1911	Wildfire Schulte, Chi	121	1935	Wally Berger, Bos	130	1961	Orlando Cepeda, SF	142
1912	Heinie Zimmerman, Chi	103	1936	Joe Medwick, St.L	138	1962	Tommy Davis, LA	153
1913	Gavvy Cravath, Phi	128	1937	Joe Medwick, St.L	154	1963	Hank Aaron, Mil	130
1914	Sherry Magee, Phi	103	1938	Joe Medwick, St.L	122	1964	Ken Boyer, St.L	119
1915	Gavvy Cravath, Phi	115	1939	Frank McCormick, Cin	128	1965	Deron Johnson, Cin	130
1916	Heinie Zimmerman, Chi-NY	83	1940	Johnny Mize, St.L	137	1966	Hank Aaron, Atl	127
1917	Heinie Zimmerman, NY	102	1941	Dolph Camilli, Bklyn	120	1967	Orlando Cepeda, St.L	111
1918	Sherry Magee, Cin	76	1942	Johnny Mize, NY	110	1968	Willie McCovey, SF	105
1919	Hy Myers, Bklyn	73	1943	Bill Nicholson, Chi	128	1969	Willie McCovey, SF	126
			1944	Bill Nicholson, Chi	122			
1920	Rogers Hornsby, St.L	94	1945	Dixie Walker, Bklyn	124	1970	Johnny Bench, Cin	148
	& George Kelly, NY	94	1946	Enos Slaughter, St.L	130	1971	Joe Torre, St.L	137
1921	Rogers Hornsby, St.L	126	1947	Johnny Mize, NY	138	1972	Johnny Bench, Cin	125
1922	Rogers Hornsby, St.L	152	1948	Stan Musial, St.L	131	1973	Willie Stargell, Pit	119

Year	RBI	Year	RBI	Year	RBI
1974 Johnny Bench, Cin	129	1982 Dale Murphy, Atl	109	1988 Will Clark, SF	109
1975 Greg Luzinski, Phi	120	& Al Oliver, Mon	109	1989 Kevin Mitchell, SF	125
1976 George Foster, Cin	121	1983 Dale Murphy, Atl	121		
1977 George Foster, Cin	149	1984 Gary Carter, Mon	106	1990 Matt Williams, SF	122
1978 George Foster, Cin	120	& Mike Schmidt, Phi	106	1991 Howard Johnson, NY	117
1979 Dave Winfield, SD	118	1985 Dave Parker, Cin	125	1992 Darren Daulton, Phi	109
		1986 Mike Schmidt, Phi	119	1993 Barry Bonds, SF	123
1980 Mike Schmidt, Phi	121	1987 Andre Dawson, Chi	137	1994 Jeff Bagwell, Hou	116
1981 Mike Schmidt, Phi	91			1995 Dante Bichette, Col	128

American League

Multiple winners: Babe Ruth (6); Lou Gehrig (5); Ty Cobb, Hank Greenberg and Ted Williams (4); Sam Crawford, Cecil Fielder, Jimmie Foxx, Jackie Jensen, Harmon Killebrew, Vern Stephens and Bobby Veach (3); Home Run Baker, Albert Belle, Cecil Cooper, Harry Davis, Joe DiMaggio, Buck Freeman, Nap Lajoie, Roger Maris, Jim Rice, Al Rosen, and Bobby Veach (2).

Year	RBI	Year	RBI	Year	RBI
1901 Nap Lajoie, Phi	125	1933 Jimmie Foxx, Phi	163	1964 Brooks Robinson, Bal	118
1902 Buck Freeman, Bos	121	1934 Lou Gehrig, NY	165	1965 Rocky Colavito, Cle	108
1903 Buck Freeman, Bos	104	1935 Hank Greenberg, Det	170	1966 Frank Robinson, Bal	122
1904 Nap Lajoie, Cle	102	1936 Hal Trosky, Cle	162	1967 Carl Yastrzemski, Bos	121
1905 Harry Davis, Phi	83	1937 Hank Greenberg, Det	183	1968 Ken Harrelson, Bos	109
1906 Harry Davis, Phi	96	1938 Jimmie Foxx, Bos	175	1969 Harmon Killebrew, Min	140
1907 Ty Cobb, Det	116	1939 Ted Williams, Bos	145		
1908 Ty Cobb, Det	108			1970 Frank Howard, Wash	126
1909 Ty Cobb, Det	107	1940 Hank Greenberg, Det	150	1971 Harmon Killebrew, Min	119
		1941 Joe DiMaggio, NY	125	1972 Dick Allen, Chi	113
1910 Sam Crawford, Det	120	1942 Ted Williams, Bos	137	1973 Reggie Jackson, Oak	117
1911 Ty Cobb, Det	144	1943 Rudy York, Det	118	1974 Jeff Burroughs, Tex	118
1912 Home Run Baker, Phi	133	1944 Vern Stephens, St.L	109	1975 George Scott, Mil	109
1913 Home Run Baker, Phi	126	1945 Nick Etten, NY	111	1976 Lee May, Bal	109
1914 Sam Crawford, Det	104	1946 Hank Greenberg, Det	127	1977 Larry Hisle, Min	119
1915 Sam Crawford, Det	112	1947 Ted Williams, Bos	114	1978 Jim Rice, Bos	139
& Bobby Veach, Det	112	1948 Joe DiMaggio, NY	155	1979 Don Baylor, Cal	139
1916 Del Pratt, St.L	103	1949 Ted Williams, Bos	159		
1917 Bobby Veach, Det	103	& Vern Stephens, Bos	159	1980 Cecil Cooper, Mil	122
1918 Bobby Veach, Det	78			1981 Eddie Murray, Bal	78
1919 Babe Ruth, Bos	114	1950 Walt Dropo, Bos	144	1982 Hal McRae, KC	133
		& Vern Stephens, Bos	144	1983 Cecil Cooper, Mil	126
1920 Babe Ruth, NY	137	1951 Gus Zernial, Chi-Phi	129	& Jim Rice, Bos	126
1921 Babe Ruth, NY	171	1952 Al Rosen, Cle	105	1984 Tony Armas, Bos	123
1922 Ken Williams, St.L	155	1953 Al Rosen, Cle	145	1985 Don Mattingly, NY	145
1923 Babe Ruth, NY	131	1954 Larry Doby, Cle	126	1986 Joe Carter, Cle	121
1924 Goose Goslin, Wash	129	1955 Ray Boone, Det	116	1987 George Bell, Tor	134
1925 Bob Meusel, NY	138	& Jackie Jensen, Bos	116	1988 Jose Canseco, Oak	124
1926 Babe Ruth, NY	145	1956 Mickey Mantle, NY	130	1989 Ruben Sierra, Tex	119
1927 Lou Gehrig, NY	175	1957 Roy Sievers, Wash	114		
1928 Lou Gehrig, NY	142	1958 Jackie Jensen, Bos	122	1990 Cecil Fielder, Det	132
& Babe Ruth, NY	142	1959 Jackie Jensen, Bos	112	1991 Cecil Fielder, Det	133
1929 Al Simmons, Phi	157			1992 Cecil Fielder, Det	124
		1960 Roger Maris, NY	112	1993 Albert Belle, Cle	129
1930 Lou Gehrig, NY	174	1961 Roger Maris, NY	142	1994 Kirby Puckett, Min	112
1931 Lou Gehrig, NY	184	1962 Harmon Killebrew, Min	126	1995 Albert Belle, Cle	126
1932 Jimmie Foxx, Phi	169	1963 Dick Stuart, Bos	118	& Mo Vaughn, Bos	126

Batting Triple Crown Winners

Players who led either league in Batting Average, Home Runs and Runs Batted In over a single season.

National League

	Year	Avg	HR	RBI
Paul Hines, Providence	1878	.358	4	50
Hugh Duffy, Boston	1894	.438	18	145
Heinie Zimmerman, Chicago	1912	.372	14	103
Rogers Hornsby, St. Louis	1922	.401	42	152
Rogers Hornsby, St. Louis	1925	.403	39	143
Chuck Klein, Philadelphia	1933	.368	28	120
Joe Medwick, St. Louis	1937	.374	31*	154

*Tied for league lead in HRs with Mel Ott, NY.

American League

	Year	Avg	HR	RBI
Nap Lajoie, Philadelphia	1901	.422	14	125
Ty Cobb, Detroit	1909	.377	9	115
Jimmie Foxx, Philadelphia	1933	.356	48	163
Lou Gehrig, New York	1934	.363	49	165
Ted Williams, Boston	1942	.356	36	137
Ted Williams, Boston	1947	.343	32	114
Mickey Mantle, New York	1956	.353	52	130
Frank Robinson, Baltimore	1966	.316	49	122
Carl Yastrzemski, Boston	1967	.326	44*	121

*Tied for league lead in HRs with Harmon Killebrew, Min.

Annual Batting Leaders (Cont.)
Stolen Bases
National League

Multiple winners: Max Carey (10); Lou Brock (8); Vince Coleman and Maury Wills (6); Honus Wagner (5); Bob Bescher, Kiki Cuyler, Willie Mays and Tim Raines (4); Bill Bruton, Frankie Frisch and Pepper Martin (3); George Burns, Frank Chance, Augie Galan, Marquis Grissom, Stan Hack, Sam Jethroe, Davey Lopes, Omar Moreno, Pete Reiser and Jackie Robinson (2).

Year		SB	Year		SB	Year		SB
1900	Patsy Donovan, St.L	45	1930	Kiki Cuyler, Chi	37	1962	Maury Wills, LA	104
	& George Van Haltren, NY	45	1931	Frankie Frisch, St.L	28	1963	Maury Wills, LA	40
1901	Honus Wagner, Pit	49	1932	Chuck Klein, Phi	20	1964	Maury Wills, LA	53
1902	Honus Wagner, Pit	42	1933	Pepper Martin, St.L	26	1965	Maury Wills, LA	94
1903	Frank Chance, Chi	67	1934	Pepper Martin, St.L	23	1966	Lou Brock, St.L	74
	& Jimmy Sheckard, Bklyn	67	1935	Augie Galan, Chi	22	1967	Lou Brock, St.L	52
1904	Honus Wagner, Pit	53	1936	Pepper Martin, St.L	23	1968	Lou Brock, St.L.	62
1905	Art Devlin, NY	59	1937	Augie Galan, Chi	23	1969	Lou Brock, St.L	53
	& Billy Maloney, Chi	59	1938	Stan Hack, Chi	16			
1906	Frank Chance, Chi	57	1939	Stan Hack, Chi	17	1970	Bobby Tolan, Cin	57
1907	Honus Wagner, Pit	61		& Lee Handley, Pit	17	1971	Lou Brock, St.L	64
1908	Honus Wagner, Pit	53				1972	Lou Brock, St.L	63
1909	Bob Bescher, Cin	54	1940	Lonny Frey, Cin	22	1973	Lou Brock, St.L	70
			1941	Danny Murtaugh, Phi	18	1974	Lou Brock, St.L	118
1910	Bob Bescher, Cin	70	1942	Pete Reiser, Bklyn	20	1975	Davey Lopes, LA	77
1911	Bob Bescher, Cin	81	1943	Arky Vaughan, Bklyn	20	1976	Davey Lopes, LA	63
1912	Bob Bescher, Cin	67	1944	Johnny Barrett, Pit	28	1977	Frank Taveras, Pit	70
1913	Max Carey, Pit	61	1945	Red Schoendienst, St.L.	26	1978	Omar Moreno, Pit	71
1914	George Burns, NY	62	1946	Pete Reiser, Bklyn	34	1979	Omar Moreno, Pit	77
1915	Max Carey, Pit	36	1947	Jackie Robinson, Bklyn	29			
1916	Max Carey, Pit	63	1948	Richie Ashburn, Phi	32	1980	Ron LeFlore, Mon	97
1917	Max Carey, Pit	46	1949	Jackie Robinson, Bklyn	37	1981	Tim Raines, Mon	71
1918	Max Carey, Pit	58				1982	Tim Raines, Mon	78
1919	George Burns, NY	40	1950	Sam Jethroe, Bos	35	1983	Tim Raines, Mon	90
			1951	Sam Jethroe, Bos	35	1984	Tim Raines, Mon	75
1920	Max Carey, Pit	52	1952	Pee Wee Reese, Bklyn	30	1985	Vince Coleman, St.L	110
1921	Frankie Frisch, NY	49	1953	Bill Bruton, Mil	26	1986	Vince Coleman, St.L	107
1922	Max Carey, Pit	51	1954	Bill Bruton, Mil	34	1987	Vince Coleman, St.L	109
1923	Max Carey, Pit	51	1955	Bill Bruton, Mil	25	1988	Vince Coleman, St.L	81
1924	Max Carey, Pit	49	1956	Willie Mays, NY	40	1989	Vince Coleman, St.L	65
1925	Max Carey, Pit	46	1957	Willie Mays, NY	38			
1926	Kiki Cuyler, Pit	35	1958	Willie Mays, SF	31	1990	Vince Coleman, St.L	77
1927	Frankie Frisch, St.L	48	1959	Willie Mays, SF	27	1991	Marquis Grissom, Mon	76
1928	Kiki Cuyler, Chi	37				1992	Marquis Grissom, Mon	78
1929	Kiki Cuyler, Chi	43	1960	Maury Wills, LA	50	1993	Chuck Carr, Fla	58
			1961	Maury Wills, LA	35	1994	Craig Biggio, Hou	39
						1995	Quilvio Veras, Fla	56

American League

Multiple winners: Rickey Henderson (11); Luis Aparicio (9); Bert Campaneris, George Case and Ty Cobb (6); Ben Chapman, Eddie Collins, Kenny Lofton and George Sisler (4); Bob Dillinger, Minnie Minoso and Bill Werber (3); Elmer Flick, Tommy Harper, Clyde Milan, Johnny Mostil, Bill North and Snuffy Stirnweiss (2).

Year		SB	Year		SB	Year		SB
1901	Frank Isbell, Chi	52	1920	Sam Rice, Wash	63	1939	George Case, Wash	51
1902	Topsy Hartsel, Phi	47	1921	George Sisler, St.L	35	1940	George Case, Wash	35
1903	Harry Bay, Cle	45	1922	George Sisler, St.L	51	1941	George Case, Wash	33
1904	Elmer Flick, Cle	42	1923	Eddie Collins, Chi	47	1942	George Case, Wash	44
1905	Danny Hoffman, Phi	46	1924	Eddie Collins, Chi	42	1943	George Case, Wash	61
1906	John Anderson, Wash	39	1925	Johnny Mostil, Chi	43	1944	Snuffy Stirnweiss, NY	55
	& Elmer Flick, Cle	39	1926	Johnny Mostil, Chi	35	1945	Snuffy Stirnweiss, NY	33
1907	Ty Cobb, Det	49	1927	George Sisler, St.L	27	1946	George Case, Cle	28
1908	Patsy Dougherty, Chi	47	1928	Buddy Myer, Bos	30	1947	Bob Dillinger, St.L	34
1909	Ty Cobb, Det	76	1929	Charlie Gehringer, Det	28	1948	Bob Dillinger, St.L	28
						1949	Bob Dillinger, St.L	20
1910	Eddie Collins, Phi	81	1930	Marty McManus, Det	23			
1911	Ty Cobb, Det	83	1931	Ben Chapman, NY	61	1950	Dom DiMaggio, Bos	15
1912	Clyde Milan, Wash	88	1932	Ben Chapman, NY	38	1951	Minnie Minoso, Cle-Chi	31
1913	Clyde Milan, Wash	75	1933	Ben Chapman, NY	27	1952	Minnie Minoso, Chi	22
1914	Fritz Maisel, NY	74	1934	Bill Werber, Bos	40	1953	Minnie Minoso, Chi	25
1915	Ty Cobb, Det	96	1935	Bill Werber, Bos	29	1954	Jackie Jensen, Bos	22
1916	Ty Cobb, Det	68	1936	Lyn Lary, St.L	37	1955	Jim Rivera, Chi	25
1917	Ty Cobb, Det	55	1937	Ben Chapman, Wash-Bos	35	1956	Luis Aparicio, Chi	21
1918	George Sisler, St.L	45		& Bill Werber, Phi	35	1957	Luis Aparicio, Chi	28
1919	Eddie Collins, Chi	33	1938	Frank Crosetti, NY	27			

Year		SB	Year		SB	Year		SB
1958	Luis Aparicio, Chi	29	1972	Bert Campaneris, Oak	52	1986	Rickey Henderson, NY	87
1959	Luis Aparicio, Chi	56	1973	Tommy Harper, Bos	54	1987	Harold Reynolds, Sea	60
			1974	Bill North, Oak	54	1988	Rickey Henderson, NY	93
1960	Luis Aparicio, Chi	51	1975	Mickey Rivers, CA	70	1989	R. Henderson, NY-Oak	77
1961	Luis Aparicio, Chi	53	1976	Bill North, Oak	75			
1962	Luis Aparicio, Chi	31	1977	Freddie Patek, KC	53	1990	Rickey Henderson, Oak	65
1963	Luis Aparicio, Bal	40	1978	Ron LeFlore, Det	68	1991	Rickey Henderson, Oak	58
1964	Luis Aparicio, Bal	57	1979	Willie Wilson, KC	83	1992	Kenny Lofton, Cle	66
1965	Bert Campaneris, KC	51				1993	Kenny Lofton, Cle	70
1966	Bert Campaneris, KC	52	1980	Rickey Henderson, Oak	100	1994	Kenny Lofton, Cle	60
1967	Bert Campaneris, KC	55	1981	Rickey Henderson, Oak	56	1995	Kenny Lofton, Cle	54
1968	Bert Campaneris, Oak	62	1982	Rickey Henderson, Oak	130			
1969	Tommy Harper, Sea	73	1983	Rickey Henderson, Oak	108			
			1984	Rickey Henderson, Oak	66			
1970	Bert Campaneris, Oak	42	1985	Rickey Henderson, NY	80			
1971	Amos Otis, KC	52						

30 Homers & 30 Stolen Bases in One Season
National League

	Year	Gm	HR	SB
Willie Mays, NY Giants	1956	152	36	40
Willie Mays, NY Giants	1957	152	35	38
Hank Aaron, Milwaukee	1963	161	44	31
Bobby Bonds, San Francisco	1969	158	32	45
Bobby Bonds, San Francisco	1973	160	39	43
Dale Murphy, Atlanta	1983	162	36	30
Eric Davis, Cincinnati	1987	129	37	50
Howard Johnson, NY Mets	1987	157	36	32
Darryl Strawberry, NY Mets	1987	154	39	36
Howard Johnson, NY Mets	1989	153	36	41
Ron Gant, Atlanta	1990	152	32	33
Barry Bonds, Pittsburgh	1990	151	33	52
Ron Gant, Atlanta	1991	154	32	34
Howard Johnson, NY Mets	1991	156	38	30

	Year	Gm	HR	SB
Barry Bonds, Pittsburgh	1992	140	34	39
Sammy Sosa, Chicago	1993	159	33	36
Barry Bonds, San Francisco	1995	144	33	31
Sammy Sosa, Chicago	1995	144	36	34

American League

	Year	Gm	HR	SB
Kenny Williams, St. Louis	1922	153	39	37
Tommy Harper, Milwaukee	1970	154	31	38
Bobby Bonds, New York	1975	145	32	30
Bobby Bonds, California	1977	158	37	41
Bobby Bonds, Chicago-Texas	1978	156	31	43
Joe Carter, Cleveland	1987	149	32	31
Jose Canseco, Oakland	1988	158	42	40

Consecutive Game Streaks
Regular season games through 1995.

Games Played
Active streak in **bold** type.

Gm		Dates of Streak	
2153	**Cal Ripken Jr.,** Bal	5/30/82 to	—
2130	Lou Gehrig, NY	6/1/25 to	4/30/39
1307	Everett Scott, Bos-NY	6/20/16 to	5/5/25
1207	Steve Garvey, LA-SD	9/3/75 to	7/29/83
1117	Billy Williams, Cubs	9/22/63 to	9/2/70
1103	Joe Sewell, Cle	9/13/22 to	4/30/30
895	Stan Musial, St.L	4/15/52 to	8/23/57
829	Eddie Yost, Wash	4/30/49 to	5/11/55
822	Gus Suhr, Pit	9/11/31 to	6/4/37
798	Nellie Fox, Chisox	8/8/55 to	9/3/60
745	Pete Rose, Cin-Phi	9/2/78 to	8/23/83
740	Dale Murphy, Atl	9/26/81 to	7/8/86
730	Richie Ashburn, Phi	6/7/50 to	4/13/55
717	Ernie Banks, Cubs	8/28/56 to	6/22/61
678	Pete Rose, Cin	9/28/73 to	5/7/78

Others

Gm		Gm	
673	Earl Averill	565	Aaron Ward
652	Frank McCormick	540	Candy LaChance
648	Sandy Alomar Sr.	535	Buck Freeman
618	Eddie Brown	533	Fred Luderus
585	Roy McMillan	511	Clyde Milan
577	George Pinckney	511	Charlie Gehringer
574	Steve Brodie	508	Vada Pinson

Hitting

	Gm	Year
Joe DiMaggio, New York (AL)	56	1941
Willie Keeler, Baltimore (NL)	44	1897
Pete Rose, Cincinnati (NL)	44	1978
Bill Dahlen, Chicago (NL)	42	1894
George Sisler, St. Louis (AL)	41	1922
Ty Cobb, Detroit (AL)	40	1911
Paul Molitor, Milwaukee (AL)	39	1987
Tommy Holmes, Boston (NL)	37	1945
Billy Hamilton, Philadelphia (NL)	36	1894
Fred Clarke, Louisville (NL)	35	1895
Ty Cobb, Detroit (AL)	35	1917
Ty Cobb, Detroit (AL)	34	1912
George Sisler, St. Louis (AL)	34	1925
George McQuinn, St. Louis (AL)	34	1938
Dom DiMaggio, Boston (AL)	34	1949
Benito Santiago, San Diego (NL)	34	1987
George Davis, New York (NL)	33	1893
Hal Chase, New York (AL)	33	1907
Rogers Hornsby, St. Louis (NL)	33	1922
Heinie Manush, Washington (AL)	33	1933
Ed Delahanty, Philadelphia (NL)	31	1899
Nap Lajoie, Cleveland (AL)	31	1906
Sam Rice, Washington, (AL)	31	1924
Willie Davis, Los Angeles (NL)	31	1969
Rico Carty, Atlanta (NL)	31	1970
Ken Landreaux, Minnesota (AL)	31	1980

Annual Pitching Leaders (since 1900)
Winning Percentage
At least 15 wins, except in strike years of 1981 and 1994 (when the minimum was 10).

National League

Multiple winners: Ed Reulbach and Tom Seaver (3); Larry Benton, Harry Brecheen, Jack Chesbro, Paul Derringer, Freddie Fitzsimmons, Don Gullet, Claude Hendrix, Carl Hubbell, Sandy Koufax, Bill Lee, Christy Mathewson, Don Newcombe and Preacher Roe (2).

Year		W-L	Pct	Year		W-L	Pct
1900	Jesse Tannehill, Pittsburgh	20-6	.769	1950	Sal Maglie, New York	18-4	.818
1901	Jack Chesbro, Pittsburgh	21-10	.677	1951	Preacher Roe, Brooklyn	22-3	.880
1902	Jack Chesbro, Pittsburgh	28-6	.824	1952	Hoyt Wilhelm, New York	15-3	.833
1903	Sam Leever, Pittsburgh	25-7	.781	1953	Carl Erskine, Brooklyn	20-6	.769
1904	Joe McGinnity, New York	35-8	.814	1954	Johnny Antonelli, New York	21-7	.750
1905	Christy Mathewson, New York	31-8	.795	1955	Don Newcombe, Brooklyn	20-5	.800
1906	Ed Reulbach, Chicago	19-4	.826	1956	Don Newcombe, Brooklyn	27-7	.794
1907	Ed Reulbach, Chicago	17-4	.810	1957	Bob Buhl, Milwaukee	18-7	.720
1908	Ed Reulbach, Chicago	24-7	.774	1958	Warren Spahn, Milwaukee	22-11	.667
1909	Howie Camnitz, Pittsburgh	25-6	.806		& Lew Burdette, Milwaukee	20-10	.667
	& Christy Mathewson, New York	25-6	.806	1959	Roy Face, Pittsburgh	18-1	.947
1910	King Cole, Chicago	20-4	.833	1960	Ernie Broglio, St. Louis	21-9	.700
1911	Rube Marquard, New York	24-7	.774	1961	Johnny Podres, Los Angeles	18-5	.783
1912	Claude Hendrix, Pittsburgh	24-9	.727	1962	Bob Purkey, Cincinnati	23-5	.821
1913	Bert Humphries, Chicago	16-4	.800	1963	Ron Perranoski, Los Angeles	16-3	.842
1914	Bill James, Boston	26-7	.788	1964	Sandy Koufax, Los Angeles	19-5	.792
1915	Grover Alexander, Phila.	31-10	.756	1965	Sandy Koufax, Los Angeles	26-8	.765
1916	Tom Hughes, Boston	16-3	.842	1966	Juan Marichal, San Francisco	25-6	.806
1917	Ferdie Schupp, New York	21-7	.750	1967	Dick Hughes, St. Louis	16-6	.727
1918	Claude Hendrix, Chicago	19-7	.731	1968	Steve Blass, Pittsburgh	18-6	.750
1919	Dutch Ruether, Cincinnati	19-6	.760	1969	Tom Seaver, New York	25-7	.781
1920	Burleigh Grimes, Brooklyn	23-11	.676	1970	Bob Gibson, St. Louis	23-7	.767
1921	Bill Doak, St. Louis	15-6	.714	1971	Don Gullet, Cincinnati	16-6	.727
1922	Pete Donohue, Cincinnati	18-9	.667	1972	Gary Nolan, Cincinnati	15-5	.750
1923	Dolf Luque, Cincinnati	27-8	.771	1973	Tommy John, Los Angeles	16-7	.696
1924	Emil Yde, Pittsburgh	16-3	.842	1974	Andy Messersmith, Los Angeles	20-6	.769
1925	Bill Sherdel, St. Louis	15-6	.714	1975	Don Gullet, Cincinnati	15-4	.789
1926	Ray Kremer, Pittsburgh	20-6	.769	1976	Steve Carlton, Philadelphia	20-7	.741
1927	Larry Benton, Boston-NY	17-7	.708	1977	John Candelaria, Pittsburgh	20-5	.800
1928	Larry Benton, New York	25-9	.735	1978	Gaylord Perry, San Diego	21-6	.778
1929	Charlie Root, Chicago	19-6	.760	1979	Tom Seaver, Cincinnati	16-6	.727
1930	Freddie Fitzsimmons, NY	19-7	.731	1980	Jim Bibby, Pittsburgh	19-6	.760
1931	Paul Derringer, St. Louis	18-8	.692	1981	Tom Seaver, Cincinnati	14-2	.875
1932	Lon Warneke, Chicago	22-6	.786	1982	Phil Niekro, Atlanta	17-4	.810
1933	Ben Cantwell, Boston	20-10	.667	1983	John Denny, Philadelphia	19-6	.760
1934	Dizzy Dean, St. Louis	30-7	.811	1984	Rick Sutcliffe, Chicago	16-1	.941
1935	Bill Lee, Chicago	20-6	.769	1985	Orel Hershiser, Los Angeles	19-3	.864
1936	Carl Hubbell, New York	26-6	.813	1986	Bob Ojeda, New York	18-5	.783
1937	Carl Hubbell, New York	22-8	.733	1987	Dwight Gooden, New York	15-7	.682
1938	Bill Lee, Chicago	22-9	.710	1988	David Cone, New York	20-3	.870
1939	Paul Derringer, Cincinnati	25-7	.781	1989	Mike Bielecki, Chicago	18-7	.720
1940	Freddie Fitzsimmons, Bklyn	16-2	.889	1990	Doug Drabek, Pittsburgh	22-6	.786
1941	Elmer Riddle, Cincinnati	19-4	.826	1991	John Smiley, Pittsburgh	20-8	.714
1942	Larry French, Brooklyn	15-4	.789		& Jose Rijo, Cincinnati	15-6	.714
1943	Mort Cooper, St. Louis	21-8	.724	1992	Bob Tewksbury, St. Louis	16-5	.762
1944	Ted Wilks, St. Louis	17-4	.810	1993	Mark Portugal, Houston	18-4	.818
1945	Harry Brecheen, St. Louis	14-4	.778	1994	Marvin Freeman, Colorado	10-2	.833
1946	Murray Dickson, St. Louis	15-6	.714	1995	Greg Maddux, Atlanta	19-2	.905
1947	Larry Jansen, New York	21-5	.808				
1948	Harry Brecheen, St. Louis	20-7	.741				
1949	Preacher Roe, Brooklyn	15-6	.714				

Note: In 1984, Sutcliffe was also 4-5 with Cleveland for a combined AL-NL record of 20-6 (.769).

American League

Multiple winners: Lefty Grove (5); Chief Bender and Whitey Ford (3); Johnny Allen, Eddie Cicotte, Roger Clemens, Mike Cuellar, Lefty Gomez, Catfish Hunter, Walter Johnson, Jim Palmer, Pete Vuckovich and Smokey Joe Wood (2).

Year		W-L	Pct	Year		W-L	Pct
1901	Clark Griffith, Chicago	24-7	.774	1904	Jack Chesbro, New York	41-12	.774
1902	Bill Bernhard, Phila-Cleve	18-5	.783	1905	Andy Coakley, Philadelphia	20-7	.741
1903	Cy Young, Boston	28-9	.757	1906	Eddie Plank, Philadelphia	19-6	.760

Year		W-L	Pct	Year		W-L	Pct
1907	Wild Bill Donovan, Detroit	25-4	.862	1953	Ed Lopat, New York	16-4	.800
1908	Ed Walsh, Chicago	40-15	.727	1954	Sandy Consuegra, Chicago	16-3	.842
1909	George Mullin, Detroit	29-8	.784	1955	Tommy Byrne, New York	16-5	.762
1910	Chief Bender, Philadelphia	23-5	.821	1956	Whitey Ford, New York	19-6	.760
1911	Chief Bender, Philadelphia	17-5	.773	1957	Dick Donovan, Chicago	16-6	.727
1912	Smokey Joe Wood, Boston	34-5	.872		& Tom Sturdivant, New York	16-6	.727
1913	Walter Johnson, Washington	36-7	.837	1958	Bob Turley, New York	21-7	.750
1914	Chief Bender, Philadelphia	17-3	.850	1959	Bob Shaw, Chicago	18-6	.750
1915	Smokey Joe Wood, Boston	15-5	.750	1960	Jim Perry, Cleveland	18-10	.643
1916	Eddie Cicotte, Chicago	15-7	.682	1961	Whitey Ford, New York	25-4	.862
1917	Reb Russell, Chicago	15-5	.750	1962	Ray Herbert, Chicago	20-9	.690
1918	Sad Sam Jones, Boston	16-5	.762	1963	Whitey Ford, New York	24-7	.774
1919	Eddie Cicotte, Chicago	29-7	.806	1964	Wally Bunker, Baltimore	19-5	.792
1920	Jim Bagby, Cleveland	31-12	.721	1965	Mudcat Grant, Minnesota	21-7	.750
1921	Carl Mays, New York	27-9	.750	1966	Sonny Siebert, Cleveland	16-8	.667
1922	Joe Bush, New York	26-7	.788	1967	Joe Horlen, Chicago	19-7	.731
1923	Herb Pennock, New York	19-6	.760	1968	Denny McLain, Detroit	31-6	.838
1924	Walter Johnson, Washington	23-7	.767	1969	Jim Palmer, Baltimore	16-4	.800
1925	Stan Coveleski, Washington	20-5	.800	1970	Mike Cuellar, Baltimore	24-8	.750
1926	George Uhle, Cleveland	27-11	.711	1971	Dave McNally, Baltimore	21-5	.808
1927	Waite Hoyt, New York	22-7	.759	1972	Catfish Hunter, Oakland	21-7	.750
1928	General Crowder, St. Louis	21-5	.808	1973	Catfish Hunter, Oakland	21-5	.808
1929	Lefty Grove, Philadelphia	20-6	.769	1974	Mike Cuellar, Baltimore	22-10	.688
1930	Lefty Grove, Philadelphia	28-5	.848	1975	Mike Torrez, Baltimore	20-9	.690
1931	Lefty Grove, Philadelphia	31-4	.886	1976	Bill Campbell, Minnesota	17-5	.773
1932	Johnny Allen, New York	17-4	.810	1977	Paul Splittorff, Kansas City	16-6	.727
1933	Lefty Grove, Philadelphia	24-8	.750	1978	Ron Guidry, New York	25-3	.893
1934	Lefty Gomez, New York	26-5	.839	1979	Mike Caldwell, Milwaukee	16-6	.727
1935	Eldon Auker, Detroit	18-7	.720	1980	Steve Stone, Baltimore	25-7	.781
1936	Monte Pearson, New York	19-7	.731	1981	Pete Vuckovich, Milwaukee	14-4	.778
1937	Johnny Allen, Cleveland	15-1	.938	1982	Pete Vuckovich, Milwaukee	18-6	.750
1938	Red Ruffing, New York	21-7	.750		& Jim Palmer, Baltimore	15-5	.750
1939	Lefty Grove, Boston	15-4	.789	1983	Rich Dotson, Chicago	22-7	.759
1940	Schoolboy Rowe, Detroit	16-3	.842	1984	Doyle Alexander, Toronto	17-6	.739
1941	Lefty Gomez, New York	15-5	.750	1985	Ron Guidry, New York	22-6	.786
1942	Ernie Bonham, New York	21-5	.808	1986	Roger Clemens, Boston	24-4	.857
1943	Spud Chandler, New York	20-4	.833	1987	Roger Clemens, Boston	20-9	.690
1944	Tex Hughson, Boston	18-5	.783	1988	Frank Viola, Minnesota	24-7	.774
1945	Hal Newhouser, Detroit	25-9	.735	1989	Bret Saberhagen, Kansas City	23-6	.793
1946	Boo Ferriss, Boston	25-6	.806	1990	Bob Welch, Oakland	27-6	.818
1947	Allie Reynolds, New York	19-8	.704	1991	Scott Erickson, Minnesota	20-8	.714
1948	Jack Kramer, Boston	18-5	.783	1992	Mike Mussina, Baltimore	18-5	.783
1949	Ellis Kinder, Boston	23-6	.793	1993	Jimmy Key, New York	18-6	.750
1950	Vic Raschi, New York	21-8	.724	1994	Jason Bere, Chicago	12-2	.857
1951	Bob Feller, Cleveland	22-8	.733	1995	Randy Johnson, Seattle	18-2	.900
1952	Bobby Shantz, Philadelphia	24-7	.774				

Earned Run Average

Earned Run Averages were based on at least 10 complete games pitched (1900-50), at least 154 innings pitched (1950-60), and at least 162 innings pitched since 1961 in the AL and 1962 in the NL. In the strike year of 1981, '94 and '95 qualifiers had to pitch at least as many innings as the total number of games their team played that season.

National League

Multiple winners: Grover Alexander, Sandy Koufax and Christy Mathewson (5); Carl Hubbell, Greg Maddux, Tom Seaver, Warren Spahn and Dazzy Vance (3); Bill Doak, Ray Kremer, Dolf Luque, Howie Pollet, Nolan Ryan, Bill Walker and Bucky Walters (2).

Year		ERA	Year		ERA	Year		ERA
1900	Rube Waddell, Pit	2.37	1909	Christy Mathewson, NY	1.14	1917	Grover Alexander, Phi	1.86
1901	Jesse Tannehill, Pit	2.18	1910	George McQuillan, Phi	1.60	1918	Hippo Vaughn, Chi	1.74
1902	Jack Taylor, Chi	1.33	1911	Christy Mathewson, NY	1.99	1919	Grover Alexander, Chi	1.72
1903	Sam Leever, Pit	2.06	1912	Jeff Tesreau, NY	1.96	1920	Grover Alexander, Chi	1.91
1904	Joe McGinnity, NY	1.61	1913	Christy Mathewson, NY	2.06	1921	Bill Doak, St.L	2.59
1905	Christy Mathewson, NY	1.27	1914	Bill Doak, St.L	1.72	1922	Rosy Ryan, NY	3.01
1906	Three Finger Brown, Chi	1.04	1915	Grover Alexander, Phi	1.22	1923	Dolf Luque, Cin	1.93
1907	Jack Pfiester, Chi	1.15	1916	Grover Alexander, Phi	1.55	1924	Dazzy Vance, Bklyn	2.16
1908	Christy Mathewson, NY	1.43						

Annual Pitching Leaders (Cont.)
Earned Run Average
National League

Year		ERA	Year		ERA	Year		ERA
1925	Dolf Luque, Cin	2.63	1950	Jim Hearn, St.L-NY	2.49	1975	Randy Jones, SD	2.24
1926	Ray Kremer, Pit	2.61	1951	Chet Nichols, Bos	2.88	1976	John Denny, St.L	2.52
1927	Ray Kremer, Pit	2.47	1952	Hoyt Wilhelm, NY	2.43	1977	John Candelaria, Pit	2.34
1928	Dazzy Vance, Bklyn	2.09	1953	Warren Spahn, Mil	2.10	1978	Craig Swan, NY	2.43
1929	Bill Walker, NY	3.09	1954	Johnny Antonelli, NY	2.30	1979	J.R. Richard, Hou	2.71
1930	Dazzy Vance, Bklyn	2.61	1955	Bob Friend, Pit	2.83	1980	Don Sutton, LA	2.21
1931	Bill Walker, NY	2.26	1956	Lew Burdette, Mil	2.70	1981	Nolan Ryan, Hou	1.69
1932	Lon Warneke, Chi	2.37	1957	Johnny Podres, Bklyn	2.66	1982	Steve Rogers, Mon	2.40
1933	Carl Hubbell, NY	1.66	1958	Stu Miller, SF	2.47	1983	Atlee Hammaker, SF	2.25
1934	Carl Hubbell, NY	2.30	1959	Sam Jones, SF	2.83	1984	Alejandro Peña, LA	2.48
1935	Cy Blanton, Pit	2.58	1960	Mike McCormick, SF	2.70	1985	Dwight Gooden, NY	1.53
1936	Carl Hubbell, NY	2.31	1961	Warren Spahn, Mil	3.02	1986	Mike Scott, Hou	2.22
1937	Jim Turner, Bos	2.38	1962	Sandy Koufax, LA	2.54	1987	Nolan Ryan, Hou	2.76
1938	Bill Lee, Chi	2.66	1963	Sandy Koufax, LA	1.88	1988	Joe Magrane, St.L	2.18
1939	Bucky Walters, Cin	2.29	1964	Sandy Koufax, LA	1.74	1989	Scott Garrelts, SF	2.28
1940	Bucky Walters, Cin	2.48	1965	Sandy Koufax, LA	2.04	1990	Danny Darwin, Hou	2.21
1941	Elmer Riddle, Cin	2.24	1966	Sandy Koufax, LA	1.73	1991	Dennis Martinez, Mon	2.39
1942	Mort Cooper, St.L	1.78	1967	Phil Niekro, Atl	1.87	1992	Bill Swift, SF	2.08
1943	Howie Pollet, St.L	1.75	1968	Bob Gibson, St.L	1.12	1993	Greg Maddux, Atl	2.36
1944	Ed Heusser, Cin	2.38	1969	Juan Marichal, SF	2.10	1994	Greg Maddux, Atl	1.56
1945	Hank Borowy, Chi	2.13	1970	Tom Seaver, NY	2.81	1995	Greg Maddux, Atl	1.63
1946	Howie Pollet, St.L	2.10	1971	Tom Seaver, NY	1.76			
1947	Warren Spahn, Bos	2.33	1972	Steve Carlton, Phi	1.97			
1948	Harry Brecheen, St.L	2.24	1973	Tom Seaver, NY	2.08			
1949	Dave Koslo, NY	2.50	1974	Buzz Capra, Atl	2.28			

Note: In 1945, Borowy had a 3.13 ERA in 18 games with New York (AL) for a combined ERA of 2.65.

American League

Multiple winners: Lefty Grove (9); Walter Johnson (5); Roger Clemens (4); Spud Chandler, Stan Coveleski, Red Faber, Whitey Ford, Lefty Gomez, Ron Guidry, Addie Joss, Hal Newhouser, Jim Palmer, Gary Peters, Luis Tiant and Ed Walsh (2).

Year		ERA	Year		ERA	Year		ERA
1901	Cy Young, Bos	1.62	1933	Monte Pearson, Cle	2.33	1965	Sam McDowell, Cle	2.18
1902	Ed Siever, Det	1.91	1934	Lefty Gomez, NY	2.33	1966	Gary Peters, Chi	1.98
1903	Earl Moore, Cle	1.77	1935	Lefty Grove, Bos	2.70	1967	Joe Horlen, Chi	2.06
1904	Addie Joss, Cle	1.59	1936	Lefty Grove, Bos	2.81	1968	Luis Tiant, Cle	1.60
1905	Rube Waddell, Phi	1.48	1937	Lefty Gomez, NY	2.33	1969	Dick Bosman, Wash	2.19
1906	Doc White, Chi	1.52	1938	Lefty Grove, Bos	3.08	1970	Diego Segui, Oak	2.56
1907	Ed Walsh, Chi	1.60	1939	Lefty Grove, Bos	2.54	1971	Vida Blue, Oak	1.82
1908	Addie Joss, Cle	1.16	1940	Bob Feller, Cle	2.61	1972	Luis Tiant, Bos	1.91
1909	Harry Krause, Phi	1.39	1941	Thornton Lee, Chi	2.37	1973	Jim Palmer, Bal	2.40
1910	Ed Walsh, Chi	1.27	1942	Ted Lyons, Chi	2.10	1974	Catfish Hunter, Oak	2.49
1911	Vean Gregg, Cle	1.81	1943	Spud Chandler, NY	1.64	1975	Jim Palmer, Bal	2.09
1912	Walter Johnson, Wash	1.39	1944	Dizzy Trout, Det	2.12	1976	Mark Fidrych, Det	2.34
1913	Walter Johnson, Wash	1.09	1945	Hal Newhouser, Det	1.81	1977	Frank Tanana, Cal	2.54
1914	Dutch Leonard, Bos	1.01	1946	Hal Newhouser, Det	1.94	1978	Ron Guidry, NY	1.74
1915	Smokey Joe Wood, Bos	1.49	1947	Spud Chandler, NY	2.46	1979	Ron Guidry, NY	2.78
1916	Babe Ruth, Bos	1.75	1948	Gene Bearden, Cle	2.43	1980	Rudy May, NY	2.47
1917	Eddie Cicotte, Chi	1.53	1949	Mel Parnell, Bos	2.77	1981	Steve McCatty, Oak	2.32
1918	Walter Johnson, Wash	1.27	1950	Early Wynn, Cle	3.20	1982	Rick Sutcliffe, Cle	2.96
1919	Walter Johnson, Wash	1.49	1951	Saul Rogovin, Det-Chi	2.78	1983	Rick Honeycutt, Tex	2.42
1920	Bob Shawkey, NY	2.45	1952	Allie Reynolds, NY	2.06	1984	Mike Boddicker, Bal	2.79
1921	Red Faber, Chi	2.48	1953	Ed Lopat, NY	2.42	1985	Dave Stieb, Tor	2.48
1922	Red Faber, Chi	2.80	1954	Mike Garcia, Cle	2.64	1986	Roger Clemens, Bos	2.48
1923	Stan Coveleski, Cle	2.76	1955	Billy Pierce, Chi	1.97	1987	Jimmy Key, Tor	2.76
1924	Walter Johnson, Wash	2.72	1956	Whitey Ford, NY	2.47	1988	Allan Anderson, Min	2.45
1925	Stan Coveleski, Wash	2.84	1957	Bobby Shantz, NY	2.45	1989	Bret Saberhagen, KC	2.16
1926	Lefty Grove, Phi	2.51	1958	Whitey Ford, NY	2.01	1990	Roger Clemens, Bos	1.93
1927	Wilcy Moore, NY	2.28	1959	Hoyt Wilhelm, Bal	2.19	1991	Roger Clemens, Bos	2.62
1928	Garland Braxton, Wash	2.51	1960	Frank Baumann, Chi	2.67	1992	Roger Clemens, Bos	2.41
1929	Lefty Grove, Phi	2.81	1961	Dick Donovan, Wash	2.40	1993	Kevin Appier, KC	2.56
1930	Lefty Grove, Phi	2.54	1962	Hank Aguirre, Det	2.21	1994	Steve Ontiveros, Oak	2.65
1931	Lefty Grove, Phi	2.06	1963	Gary Peters, Chi	2.33	1995	Randy Johnson, Sea	2.48
1932	Lefty Grove, Phi	2.84	1964	Dean Chance, LA	1.65			

Note: In 1940, Ernie Bonham of NY had a 1.90 ERA and 10 complete games, but appeared in only a total of 12 games and 99 innings.

Strikeouts
National League

Multiple winners: Dazzy Vance (7); Grover Alexander (6); Steve Carlton, Christy Mathewson and Tom Seaver (5); Dizzy Dean, Sandy Koufax and Warren Spahn (4); Don Drysdale, Sam Jones and Johnny Vander Meer (3); David Cone, Dwight Gooden, Bill Hallahan, J.R. Richard, Robin Roberts, Nolan Ryan and Hippo Vaughn (2).

Year		SO	Year		SO	Year		SO
1900	Rube Waddell, Pit	130	1933	Dizzy Dean, St.L	199	1964	Bob Veale, Pit	250
1901	Noodles Hahn, Cin	239	1934	Dizzy Dean, St.L	195	1965	Sandy Koufax, LA	382
1902	Vic Willis, Bos	225	1935	Dizzy Dean, St.L	190	1966	Sandy Koufax, LA	317
1903	Christy Mathewson, NY	267	1936	Van Lingle Mungo, Bklyn	238	1967	Jim Bunning, Phi	253
1904	Christy Mathewson, NY	212	1937	Carl Hubbell, NY	159	1968	Bob Gibson, St.L	268
1905	Christy Mathewson, NY	206	1938	Clay Bryant, Chi	135	1969	Ferguson Jenkins, Chi	273
1906	Fred Beebe, Chi-St.L	171	1939	Claude Passeau, Phi-Chi	137			
1907	Christy Mathewson, NY	178		& Bucky Walters, Cin	137	1970	Tom Seaver, NY	283
1908	Christy Mathewson, NY	259				1971	Tom Seaver, NY	289
1909	Orval Overall, Chi	205	1940	Kirby Higbe, Phi	137	1972	Steve Carlton, Phi	310
			1941	John Vander Meer, Cin	202	1973	Tom Seaver, NY	251
1910	Earl Moore, Phi	185	1942	John Vander Meer, Cin	186	1974	Steve Carlton, Phi	240
1911	Rube Marquard, NY	237	1943	John Vander Meer, Cin	174	1975	Tom Seaver, NY	243
1912	Grover Alexander, Phi	195	1944	Bill Voiselle, NY	161	1976	Tom Seaver, NY	235
1913	Tom Seaton, Phi	168	1945	Preacher Roe, Pit	148	1977	Phil Niekro, Atl	262
1914	Grover Alexander, Phi	214	1946	Johnny Schmitz, Chi	135	1978	J.R. Richard, Hou	303
1915	Grover Alexander, Phi	241	1947	Ewell Blackwell, Cin	193	1979	J.R. Richard, Hou	313
1916	Grover Alexander, Phi	167	1948	Harry Brecheen, St.L	149			
1917	Grover Alexander, Phi	201	1949	Warren Spahn, Bos	151	1980	Steve Carlton, Phi	286
1918	Hippo Vaughn, Chi	148				1981	F. Valenzuela, LA	180
1919	Hippo Vaughn, Chi	141	1950	Warren Spahn, Bos	191	1982	Steve Carlton, Phi	286
			1951	Don Newcombe, Bklyn	164	1983	Steve Carlton, Phi	275
1920	Grover Alexander, Chi	173		& Warren Spahn, Bos	164	1984	Dwight Gooden, NY	276
1921	Burleigh Grimes, Bklyn	136	1952	Warren Spahn, Bos	183	1985	Dwight Gooden, NY	268
1922	Dazzy Vance, Bklyn	134	1953	Robin Roberts, Phi	198	1986	Mike Scott, Hou	306
1923	Dazzy Vance, Bklyn	197	1954	Robin Roberts, Phi	185	1987	Nolan Ryan, Hou	270
1924	Dazzy Vance, Bklyn	262	1955	Sam Jones, Chi	198	1988	Nolan Ryan, Hou	228
1925	Dazzy Vance, Bklyn	221	1956	Sam Jones, Chi	176	1989	Jose DeLeon, St.L	201
1926	Dazzy Vance, Bklyn	140	1957	Jack Sanford, Phi	188			
1927	Dazzy Vance, Bklyn	184	1958	Sam Jones, St.L	225	1990	David Cone, NY	233
1928	Dazzy Vance, Bklyn	200	1959	Don Drysdale, LA	242	1991	David Cone, NY	241
1929	Pat Malone, Chi	166				1992	John Smoltz, Atl	215
			1960	Don Drysdale, LA	246	1993	Jose Rijo, Cin	227
1930	Bill Hallahan, St.L	177	1961	Sandy Koufax, LA	269	1994	Andy Benes, SD	189
1931	Bill Hallahan, St.L	159	1962	Don Drysdale, LA	232	1995	Hideo Nomo, LA	236
1932	Dizzy Dean, St.L	191	1963	Sandy Koufax, LA	306			

American League

Multiple winners: Walter Johnson (12); Nolan Ryan (9); Bob Feller and Lefty Grove (7); Rube Waddell (6); Sam McDowell (5); Randy Johnson (4); Lefty Gomez, Mark Langston and Camilo Pascual (3); Len Barker, Tommy Bridges, Jim Bunning, Roger Clemens, Hal Newhouser, Allie Reynolds, Herb Score, Ed Walsh and Early Wynn (2).

Year		SO	Year		SO	Year		SO
1901	Cy Young, Bos	158	1920	Stan Coveleski, Cle	133	1939	Bob Feller, Cle	246
1902	Rube Waddell, Phi	210	1921	Walter Johnson, Wash	143			
1903	Rube Waddell, Phi	302	1922	Urban Shocker, St.L	149	1940	Bob Feller, Cle	261
1904	Rube Waddell, Phi	349	1923	Walter Johnson, Wash	130	1941	Bob Feller, Cle	260
1905	Rube Waddell, Phi	287	1924	Walter Johnson, Wash	158	1942	Tex Hughson, Bos	113
1906	Rube Waddell, Phi	196	1925	Lefty Grove, Phi	116		& Bobo Newsom, Wash	113
1907	Rube Waddell, Phi	232	1926	Lefty Grove, Phi	194	1943	Allie Reynolds, Cle	151
1908	Ed Walsh, Chi	269	1927	Lefty Grove, Phi	174	1944	Hal Newhouser, Det	187
1909	Frank Smith, Chi	177	1928	Lefty Grove, Phi	183	1945	Hal Newhouser, Det	212
			1929	Lefty Grove, Phi	170	1946	Bob Feller, Cle	348
1910	Walter Johnson, Wash	313				1947	Bob Feller, Cle	196
1911	Ed Walsh, Chi	255	1930	Lefty Grove, Phi	209	1948	Bob Feller, Cle	164
1912	Walter Johnson, Wash	303	1931	Lefty Grove, Phi	175	1949	Virgil Trucks, Det	153
1913	Walter Johnson, Wash	243	1932	Red Ruffing, NY	190			
1914	Walter Johnson, Wash	225	1933	Lefty Gomez, NY	163	1950	Bob Lemon, Cle	170
1915	Walter Johnson, Wash	203	1934	Lefty Gomez, NY	158	1951	Vic Raschi, NY	164
1916	Walter Johnson, Wash	228	1935	Tommy Bridges, Det	163	1952	Allie Reynolds, NY	160
1917	Walter Johnson, Wash	188	1936	Tommy Bridges, Det	175	1953	Billy Pierce, Chi	186
1918	Walter Johnson, Wash	162	1937	Lefty Gomez, NY	194	1954	Bob Turley, Bal	185
1919	Walter Johnson, Wash	147	1938	Bob Feller, Cle	240	1955	Herb Score, Cle	245

Annual Pitching Leaders (Cont.)
Strikeouts
American League

Year		SO	Year		SO	Year		SO
1956	Herb Score, Cle	263	1970	Sam McDowell, Cle	304	1984	Mark Langston, Sea	204
1957	Early Wynn, Cle	184	1971	Mickey Lolich, Det	308	1985	Bert Blyleven, Cle-Min	206
1958	Early Wynn, Chi	179	1972	Nolan Ryan, Cal	329	1986	Mark Langston, Sea	245
1959	Jim Bunning, Det	201	1973	Nolan Ryan, Cal	383	1987	Mark Langston, Sea	262
			1974	Nolan Ryan, Cal	367	1988	Roger Clemens, Bos	291
1960	Jim Bunning, Det	201	1975	Frank Tanana, Cal	269	1989	Nolan Ryan, Tex	301
1961	Camilo Pascual, Min	221	1976	Nolan Ryan, Cal	327			
1962	Camilo Pascual, Min	206	1977	Nolan Ryan, Cal	341	1990	Nolan Ryan, Tex	232
1963	Camilo Pascual, Min	202	1978	Nolan Ryan, Cal	260	1991	Roger Clemens, Bos	241
1964	Al Downing, NY	217	1979	Nolan Ryan, Cal	223	1992	Randy Johnson, Sea	241
1965	Sam McDowell, Cle	325				1993	Randy Johnson, Sea	308
1966	Sam McDowell, Cle	225	1980	Len Barker, Cle	187	1994	Randy Johnson, Sea	204
1967	Jim Lonborg, Bos	246	1981	Len Barker, Cle	127	1995	Randy Johnson, Sea	294
1968	Sam McDowell, Cle	283	1982	Floyd Bannister, Sea	209			
1969	Sam McDowell, Cle	279	1983	Jack Morris, Det	232			

Pitching Triple Crown Winners

Pitchers who led either league in Earned Run Average, Wins and Strikeouts over a single season.

National League

	Year	ERA	W-L	SO
Tommy Bond, Bos	1877	2.11	40-17	170
Hoss Radbourn, Prov	1884	1.38	60-12	441
Tim Keefe, NY	1888	1.74	35-12	333
John Clarkson, Bos	1889	2.73	49-19	284
Amos Rusie, NY	1894	2.78	36-13	195
Christy Mathewson, NY	1905	1.27	31-8	206
Christy Mathewson, NY	1908	1.43	37-11	259
Grover Alexander, Phi	1915	1.22	31-10	241
Grover Alexander, Phi	1916	1.55	33-12	167
Grover Alexander, Phi	1917	1.86	30-13	201
Hippo Vaughn, Chi	1918	1.74	22-10	148
Grover Alexander, Chi	1920	1.91	27-14	173
Dazzy Vance, Bklyn	1924	2.16	28-6	262
Bucky Walters, Cin	1939	2.29	27-11	137
Sandy Koufax, LA	1963	1.88	25-5	306
Sandy Koufax, LA	1965	2.04	26-8	382
Sandy Koufax, LA	1966	1.73	27-9	317

	Year	ERA	W-L	SO
Steve Carlton, Phi	1972	1.97	27-10	310
Dwight Gooden, NY	1985	1.53	24-4	268

Ties: In 1894, Rusie tied for league lead in wins with Jouett Meekin, NY (36-10); in 1939, Walters tied for league lead in strikeouts with Claude Passeau, Phi-Chi; in 1963, Koufax tied for the league lead in wins with Juan Marichal, SF.

American League

	Year	ERA	W-L	SO
Cy Young, Bos	1901	1.62	33-10	158
Rube Waddell, Phi	1905	1.48	26-11	287
Walter Johnson, Wash	1913	1.09	36-7	243
Walter Johnson, Wash	1918	1.27	23-13	162
Walter Johnson, Wash	1924	2.72	23-7	158
Lefty Grove, Phi	1930	2.54	28-5	209
Lefty Grove, Phi	1931	2.06	31-4	175
Lefty Gomez, NY	1934	2.33	26-5	158
Lefty Gomez, NY	1937	2.33	21-11	194
Hal Newhouser, Det	1945	1.81	25-9	212

Perfect Games

Sixteen pitchers have thrown perfect games (27 up, 27 down) in major league history. However, the games pitched by Harvey Haddix and Ernie Shore are not considered to be official.

National League

	Game	Date	Score
Lee Richmond	Wor. vs Cle.	6/12/1880	1-0
Monte Ward	Prov. vs Bos.	6/17/1880	5-0
Harvey Haddix	Pit. at Mil.	5/26/1959	0-1*
Jim Bunning	Phi. at NY	6/21/1964	6-0
Sandy Koufax	LA vs. Chi.	9/9/1965	1-0
Tom Browning	Cin. vs LA	9/16/1988	1-0
Dennis Martinez	Mon. at LA	7/28/1991	2-0

American League

	Game	Date	Score
Cy Young	Bos. vs Phi.	5/5/1904	3-0
Addie Joss	Cle. vs Chi.	10/2/1908	1-0
Ernie Shore	Bos. vs Wash.	6/23/1917	4-0*
Charlie Robertson	Chi. at Det.	4/30/1922	2-0
Catfish Hunter	Oak. vs Min.	5/8/1968	4-0
Len Barker	Cle. vs Tor.	5/15/1981	3-0
Mike Witt	Cal. at Tex.	9/30/1984	1-0
Kenny Rogers	Tex. vs Cal.	6/28/1994	4-0

*Haddix pitched 12 perfect innings before losing in the 13th. Braves' lead-off batter Felix Mantilla reached on a throwing error by Pirates 3B Don Hoak, Eddie Mathews sacrificed Mantilla to 2nd, Hank Aaron was walked intentionally, and Joe Adcock hit a 3-run HR. Adcock, however, passed Aaron on the bases and was only credited with a 1-run double.

*Babe Ruth started for Boston, walking Senators' lead-off batter Ray Morgan, then was thrown out of game by umpire Brick Owens for arguing the call. Shore came on in relief. Morgan was caught stealing and Shore retired the next 26 batters in a row. While technically not a perfect game—since he didn't start—Shore gets credit anyway.

World Series

Pitcher	Game	Date	Score
Don Larsen	NY vs Bklyn	10/8/1956	2-0

No-Hit Games

Nine innings or more, including perfect games, since 1876. Losing pitchers in **bold** type.

Multiple no-hitters: Nolan Ryan (7); Sandy Koufax (4); Larry Cocoran, Bob Feller and Cy Young (3); Jim Bunning, Steve Busby, Carl Erskine, Bob Forsch, Pud Galvin, Ken Holtzman, Addie Joss, Hub Leonard, Jim Maloney, Christy Mathewson, Allie Reynolds, Warren Spahn, Bill Stoneham, Virgil Trucks and Johnny Vander Meer (2).

National League

Year	Date	Pitcher	Result	Year	Date	Pitcher	Result
1876	7/15	George Bradley	St.L vs Har, 2-0	1956	5/12	Carl Erskine	Bklyn vs NY, 3-0
1880	6/12	Lee Richmond	Wor vs Cle,1-0		9/25	Sal Maglie	Bklyn vs Phi, 5-0
			(perfect game)	1960	5/15	Don Cardwell	Chi vs St.L, 4-0
	6/17	John M. Ward	Prov vs Buf, 5-0		8/18	Lew Burdette	Mil vs Phi, 1-0
	8/19	Larry Cocoran	Chi vs Bos, 6-0		9/16	Warren Spahn	Mil vs Phi, 4-0
	8/20	Pud Galvin	Buf at Wor, 1-0	1961	4/28	Warren Spahn	Mil vs SF, 1-0
1882	9/20	Larry Cocoran	Chi vs Wor, 1-0	1962	6/30	Sandy Koufax	LA vs NY, 5-0
1883	7/25	Old Hoss Radbourn	Prov at Cle, 8-0	1963	5/11	Sandy Koufax	LA vs SF, 1-0
	9/13	Hugh Daily	Cle at Phi, 1-0		5/17	Don Nottebart	Hou vs Phi, 4-1
1884	6/27	Larry Cocoran	Chi vs Prov, 6-0		6/15	Juan Marichal	SF vs Hou, 1-0
	8/4	Pud Galvin	Buf at Det, 18-0	1964	4/23	**Ken Johnson**	Hou vs Cin, 0-1
1885	7/27	John Clarkson	Chi vs Prov, 4-0		6/4	Sandy Koufax	LA at Phi, 3-0
	8/29	Charlie Ferguson	Phi vs Prov, 1-0		6/21	Jim Bunning	Phi at NY, 6-0
1891	6/22	Tom Lovett	Bklyn vs NY, 4-0				(perfect game)
	7/31	Amos Ruise	NY vs Bklyn, 11-0	1965	8/19	Jim Maloney	Cin at Chi, 1-0 (10)
1892	8/6	John Stivetts	Bos vs Bklyn, 11-0		9/9	Sandy Koufax	LA vs Chi, 1-0
	8/22	Ben Sanders	Lou vs Bal, 6-2				(perfect game)
	10/22	Bumpus Jones	Cin vs Pit, 7-1	1967	6/18	Don Wilson	Hou vs Atl, 2-0
			(1st major league game)	1968	7/29	George Culver	Cin at Phi, 6-1
1893	8/16	Bill Hawke	Bal vs Wash, 5-0		9/17	Gaylord Perry	SF vs St.L, 1-0
1897	9/18	Cy Young	Cle vs Cin, 6-0		9/18	Ray Washburn	St.L at SF, 2-0
1898	4/22	Ted Breitenstein	Cin vs Pit, 11-0				(next day, same park)
	4/22	Jim Hughes	Bal vs Bos, 8-0	1969	4/17	Bill Stoneman	Mon at Phi, 7-0
	7/8	Frank Donahue	Phi vs Bos, 5-0		4/30	Jim Maloney	Cin vs Hou, 10-0
	8/21	Walter Thornton	Chi vs Bklyn, 2-0		5/1	Don Wilson	Hou at Cin, 4-0
1899	5/25	Deacon Phillippe	Lou vs NY, 7-0		8/19	Ken Holtzman	Chi vs Atl, 3-0
1900	7/12	Noodles Hahn	Cin vs Phi, 4-0		9/20	Bob Moose	Pit at NY, 4-0
1901	7/15	Christy Mathewson	NY vs St.L, 5-0	1970	6/12	Dock Ellis	Pit at SD, 2-0
1903	9/18	Chick Fraser	Phi at Chi, 10-0		7/20	Bill Singer	LA vs Phi, 5-0
1905	6/13	Christy Mathewson	NY at Chi, 1-0	1971	6/3	Ken Holtzman	Chi at Cin, 1-0
1906	5/1	John Lush	Phi at Bklyn, 1-0		6/23	Rick Wise	Phi at Cin, 4-0
	7/20	Mal Eason	Bklyn at St.L, 2-0		8/14	Bob Gibson	St.L at Pit, 11-0
1907	5/8	Frank Pfeffer	Bos vs Cin, 6-0	1972	4/16	Burt Hooton	Chi vs Phi, 4-0
	9/20	Nick Maddox	Pit vs Bkn, 2-1		9/2	Milt Pappas	Chi vs SD, 8-0
1908	7/4	Hooks Wiltse	NY vs Phi, 1-0 (10)		10/2	Bill Stoneman	Mon vs NY, 7-0
	9/5	Nap Rucker	Bklyn vs Bos, 6-0	1973	8/5	Phil Niekro	Atl vs SD, 9-0
1912	9/6	Jeff Tesreau	NY at Phi, 3-0	1975	8/24	Ed Halicki	SF vs NY, 6-0
1914	9/9	George Davis	Bos vs Phi, 7-0	1976	7/9	Larry Dierker	Hou vs Mon, 6-0
1915	4/15	Rube Marquard	NY vs Bklyn, 2-0		8/9	John Candelaria	Pit vs LA, 2-0
	8/31	Jimmy Lavender	Chi at N.Y, 2-0		9/29	John Montefusco	SF vs Atl, 9-0
1916	6/16	Tom Hughes	Bos vs. Pit, 2-0	1978	6/16	Bob Forsch	St.L vs Phi, 5-0
1917	5/2	Fred Toney	Cin at Chi, 1-0 (10)		6/16	Tom Seaver	Cin vs St.L, 4-0
1919	5/11	Hod Eller	Cin at St.L, 6-0	1979	4/7	Ken Forsch	Hou vs Atl, 6-0
1922	5/7	Jesse Barnes	NY vs Phi, 6-0	1980	6/27	Jerry Reuss	LA at SF, 4-0
1924	7/17	Jesse Haines	St.L vs Bos, 5-0	1981	5/10	Charlie Lea	Mon vs SF, 4-0
1925	9/17	Dazzy Vance	Bklyn vs Phi, 10-1		9/26	Nolan Ryan	Hou vs LA, 5-0
1929	5/8	Carl Hubbell	NY vs Pit, 2-0	1983	9/26	Bob Forsch	St.L vs Mon, 3-0
1934	9/21	Paul Dean	St.L vs Bklyn, 3-0	1986	9/25	Mike Scott	Hou vs SF, 2-0
1938	6/11	Johnny Vander Meer	Cin vs Bos, 3-0	1988	9/16	Tom Browning	Cin vs LA, 1-0
	6/15	Johnny Vander Meer	Cin at Bklyn, 6-0				(perfect game)
			(consecutive starts)	1990	6/29	Fernando Valenzuela	LA vs St.L, 6-0
1940	4/30	Tex Carleton	Bklyn at Cin, 3-0		8/15	Terry Mulholland	Phi vs SF, 6-0
1941	8/30	Lon Warneke	St.L at Cin, 2-0	1991	5/23	Tommy Greene	Phi at Mon, 2-0
1944	4/27	Jim Tobin	Bos vs Bklyn, 2-0		7/28	Dennis Martinez	Mon at LA, 2-0
	5/15	Clyde Shoun	Cin vs Bos, 1-0				(perfect game)
1946	4/23	Ed Head	Bklyn at NY, 5-0		9/11	Kent Mercker (6),	Atl vs SD, 1-0
1947	6/18	Ewell Blackwell	Cin vs Bos, 6-0			Mark Wohlers (2)	(combined no-hitter)
1948	9/9	Rex Barney	Bklyn at NY, 2-0			& Alejandro Peña (1)	
1950	6/11	Vern Bickford	Bos vs Bklyn, 7-0	1992	8/17	Kevin Gross	LA vs SF, 2-0
1951	5/6	Cliff Chambers	Pit at Bos, 3-0	1993	9/8	Darryl Kile	Hou vs NY, 7-1
1952	6/19	Carl Erskine	Bklyn vs Chi, 5-0	1994	4/8	Kent Mercker	Atl at LA, 6-0
1954	6/12	Jim Wilson	Mil vs Phi, 2-0	1995	7/14	Ramon Martinez	LA vs Fla, 7-0
1955	5/12	Sam Jones	Chi vs Pit, 4-0				

No-Hit Games (Cont.)
American League

Year	Date	Pitcher	Result
1902	9/20	Jimmy Callahan	Chi vs Det, 3-0
1904	5/5	Cy Young	Bos vs Phi, 3-0 (perfect game)
	8/17	Jesse Tannehill	Bos vs Chi, 6-0
1905	7/22	Weldon Henley	Phi at St. L, 6-0
	9/6	Frank Smith	Chi at Det, 15-0
	9/27	Bill Dinneen	Bos vs Chi, 2-0
1908	6/30	Cy Young	Bos at NY, 8-0
	9/18	Dusty Rhoades	Cle vs Bos, 2-0
	9/20	Frank Smith	Chi vs Phi, 1-0
	10/2	Addie Joss	Cle vs Chi, 1-0 (perfect game)
1910	4/20	Addie Joss	Cle at Chi, 1-0
	5/12	Chief Bender	Phi vs Cle, 4-0
1911	7/19	Smokey Joe Wood	Bos vs St. L, 5-0
	8/27	Ed Walsh	Chi vs Bos, 5-0
1912	7/4	George Mullin	Det vs St. L, 7-0
	8/30	Earl Hamilton	St. L at Det, 5-1
1914	5/31	Joe Benz	Chi vs Cle, 6-1
1916	6/16	Rube Foster	Bos vs NY, 2-0
	8/26	Joe Bush	Phi vs Cle, 5-0
	8/30	Hub Leonard	Bos vs St. L, 4-0
1917	4/14	Ed Cicotte	Chi at St. L, 11-0
	4/24	George Mogridge	NY at Bos, 2-1
	5/5	Ernie Koob	St. L vs Chi, 1-0
	5/6	Bob Groom	St. L vs Chi, 3-0
	6/23	Babe Ruth (0) & Ernie Shore (9)	Bos vs Wash, 4-0 (combined no-hitter)
1918	6/3	Hub Leonard	Bos at Det, 5-0
1919	9/10	Ray Caldwell	Cle at NY, 3-0
1920	7/1	Walter Johnson	Wash at Bos, 1-0
1922	4/30	Charlie Robertson	Chi at Det, 2-0 (perfect game)
1923	9/4	Sam Jones	NY at Phi, 2-0
	9/7	Howard Ehmke	Bos at Phi, 4-0
1926	8/21	Ted Lyons	Chi at Bos, 6-0
1931	4/29	Wes Ferrell	Cle vs St. L, 9-0
	8/8	Bob Burke	Wash vs Bos, 5-0
1935	8/31	Vern Kennedy	Chi vs Cle, 5-0
1937	6/1	Bill Dietrich	Chi vs St. L, 8-0
1938	8/27	Monte Pearson	NY vs Det, 13-0
1940	4/16	Bob Feller	Cle at Chi, 1-0 (Opening Day)
1945	9/9	Dick Fowler	Phi vs St. L, 1-0
1946	4/30	Bob Feller	Cle vs NY, 1-0
1947	7/10	Don Black	Cle vs Phi, 3-0
	9/3	Bill McCahan	Phi vs Wash, 3-0
1948	6/30	Bob Lemon	Cle at Det, 2-0
1951	7/1	Bob Feller	Cle vs Det, 2-1
	7/12	Allie Reynolds	NY vs Cle, 1-0
	9/28	Allie Reynolds	NY vs Bos, 8-0
1952	5/15	Virgil Trucks	Det vs Wash, 1-0
	8/25	Virgil Trucks	Det at NY, 1-0
1953	5/6	Bobo Holloman	St. L vs Phi, 6-0 (first major league start)
1956	7/14	Mel Parnell	Bos vs Chi, 4-0
	10/8	Don Larsen	NY vs Bklyn, 2-0 (perfect W. Series game)
1957	8/20	Bob Keegan	Chi vs Wash, 6-0
1958	7/20	Jim Bunning	Det at Bos, 3-0
	9/2	Hoyt Wilhelm	Bal vs NY, 1-0
1962	5/5	Bo Belinsky	LA vs Bal, 2-0
	6/26	Earl Wilson	Bos vs LA, 2-0
	8/1	Bill Monbouquette	Bos at Chi, 1-0
	8/26	Jack Kralick	Min vs KC, 1-0
1965	9/16	Dave Morehead	Bos vs Cle, 2-0
1966	6/10	Sonny Siebert	Cle vs Wash, 2-0
1967	4/30	**Steve Barber & Stu Miller**	Bal vs Det, 1-2
	8/25	Dean Chance	Min at Cle, 2-1
	9/10	Joel Horlen	Chi vs Det, 6-0
1968	4/27	Tom Phoebus	Bal vs Bos, 6-0
	5/8	Catfish Hunter	Oak vs Min, 4-0 (perfect game)
1969	8/13	Jim Palmer	Bal vs Oak, 8-0
1970	7/3	Clyde Wright	Cal vs Oak, 4-0
	9/21	Vida Blue	Oak vs Min, 6-0
1973	4/27	Steve Busby	KC at Det, 3-0
	5/15	Nolan Ryan	Cal at KC, 3-0
	7/15	Nolan Ryan	Cal at Det, 6-0
	7/30	Jim Bibby	Tex at Oak, 6-0
1974	6/19	Steve Busby	KC at Mil, 2-0
	7/19	Dick Bosman	Cle at Oak, 4-0
	9/28	Nolan Ryan	Cal at Min, 4-0
1975	6/1	Nolan Ryan	Cal vs Bal, 1-0
	9/28	Blue (5) Abbott & Lindblad (1), and Fingers (2)	Oak vs Cal, 5-0 (combined no-hitter)
1976	7/28	John Odom (5) & Francisco Barrios (4)	Chi at Oak, 2-1 (combined no-hitter)
1977	5/14	Jim Colborn	KC vs Tex, 6-0
	5/30	Dennis Eckersley	Cle vs Cal, 1-0
	9/22	Bert Blyleven	Tex at Cal, 6-0
1981	5/15	Len Barker	Cle vs Tor, 3-0 (perfect game)
1983	7/4	Dave Righetti	NY vs Bos, 4-0
	9/29	Mike Warren	Oak vs Chi, 3-0
1984	4/7	Jack Morris	Det at Chi, 4-0
	9/30	Mike Witt	Cal at Tex, 1-0 (perfect game)
1986	9/19	Joe Cowley	Chi at Cal, 7-1
1987	4/15	Juan Nieves	Mil at Bal, 7-0
1990	6/2	Mark Langston (7) & Mike Witt (2)	Cal vs Sea, 1-0 (combined no-hitter)
	6/2	Randy Johnson	Sea vs Det, 2-0
	6/11	Nolan Ryan	Tex at Oak, 5-0
	6/29	Dave Stewart	Oak at Tor, 5-0
	9/2	Dave Stieb	Tor at Cle, 3-0
1991	5/1	Nolan Ryan	Tex vs Tor, 3-0
	7/13	Bob Milacki (6), Mike Flanagan (1), Mark Williamson (1) & Gregg Olson (1)	Bal at Oak, 2-0 (combined no-hitter)
	8/11	Wilson Alvarez	Chi at Bal, 7-0
	8/26	Bret Saberhagen	KC vs Chi, 7-0
1993	4/22	Chris Bosio	Sea vs Bos, 7-0
	9/4	Jim Abbott	NY vs Cle, 4-0
1994	4/27	Scott Erickson	Min vs Mil, 6-0
	7/28	Kenny Rogers	Tex vs Cal, 4-0 (perfect game)

All-Time Major League Leaders

Based on statistics compiled by *The Baseball Encyclopedia* (9th ed.); through 1995 regular season.

CAREER

Players active in 1995 in **bold** type.

Batting

Note that (*) indicates left-handed hitter and (†) indicates switch-hitter.

Batting Average

		Yrs	AB	H	Avg
1	Ty Cobb*	24	11,429	4191	.367
2	Rogers Hornsby	23	8,137	2930	.358
3	Joe Jackson*	13	4,981	1774	.356
4	Ed Delahanty	16	7,509	2597	.346
5	Tris Speaker*	22	10,197	3514	.345
6	Ted Williams*	19	7,706	2654	.344
7	Billy Hamilton*	14	6,284	2163	.344
8	Willie Keeler*	19	8,585	2947	.343
9	Dan Brouthers*	19	6,711	2296	.342
10	Babe Ruth*	22	8,399	2873	.342
11	Harry Heilmann	17	7,787	2660	.342
12	Pete Browning	13	4,820	1646	.341
13	Bill Terry*	14	6,428	2193	.341
14	George Sisler*	15	8,267	2812	.340
15	Lou Gehrig*	17	8,001	2721	.340
16	Jesse Burkett*	16	8,413	2853	.339
17	Nap Lajoie	21	9,592	3244	.338
18	**Tony Gwynn***	14	7,144	2401	.336
19	Riggs Stephenson	14	4,508	1515	.336
20	**Wade Boggs***	14	7,599	2541	.334
21	Al Simmons	20	8,761	2927	.334
22	Paul Waner*	20	9,459	3152	.333
23	Eddie Collins*	25	9,951	3313	.333
24	Stan Musial*	22	10,972	3630	.331
25	Sam Thompson*	14	6,005	1986	.331

Hits

		Yrs	AB	H	Avg
1	Pete Rose†	24	14,053	4256	.303
2	Ty Cobb*	24	11,429	4191	.367
3	Hank Aaron	23	12,364	3771	.305
4	Stan Musial*	22	10,972	3630	.331
5	Tris Speaker*	22	10,197	3514	.345
6	Carl Yastrzemski*	23	11,988	3419	.285
7	Honus Wagner	21	10,443	3418	.327
8	Eddie Collins*	25	9,951	3313	.333
9	Willie Mays	22	10,881	3283	.302
10	Nap Lajoie	21	9,592	3244	.338
11	George Brett*	21	10,349	3154	.305
12	Paul Waner*	20	9,459	3152	.333
13	Robin Yount	20	11,008	3142	.285
14	**Dave Winfield**	22	11,003	3110	.283
15	**Eddie Murray†**	19	10,603	3071	.290
16	Rod Carew*	19	9,315	3053	.328
17	Lou Brock*	19	10,332	3023	.293
18	Al Kaline	22	10,116	3007	.297
19	Cap Anson	22	9,108	3000	.329
	Roberto Clemente	18	9,454	3000	.317
21	Sam Rice*	20	9,269	2987	.322
22	Sam Crawford*	19	9,580	2964	.309
23	Willie Keeler*	19	8,585	2947	.343
24	Frank Robinson	21	10,006	2943	.294
25	Jake Beckley*	20	9,527	2931	.308

Players Active in 1995

		Yrs	AB	H	Avg
1	Tony Gwynn*	14	7,144	2401	.336
2	Wade Boggs*	14	7,599	2541	.334
3	Frank Thomas	6	2,764	893	.323
4	Kirby Puckett	12	7,244	2304	.318
5	Edgar Martinez	9	2,777	868	.313
6	Kenny Lofton*	5	2,159	673	.312
7	Hal Morris*	8	2,394	737	.308
8	Don Mattingly*	14	7,003	2153	.307
9	Mark Grace*	8	4,356	1333	.306
10	Jeff Bagwell	5	2,523	771	.306
11	Paul Molitor	18	9,135	2789	.305
12	Carlos Baerga†	6	3,185	971	.305
13	Mike Greenwell*	11	4,328	1313	.303

Players Active in 1995

		Yrs	AB	H	Avg
1	Dave Winfield*	22	11,003	3110	.283
2	Eddie Murray†	19	10,603	3071	.290
3	Paul Molitor	18	9,135	2789	.305
4	Andre Dawson	20	9,869	2758	.279
5	Wade Boggs*	14	7,599	2541	.334
6	Tony Gwynn*	14	7,144	2401	.336
7	Ozzie Smith†	18	9,169	2396	.261
8	Cal Ripken Jr.	15	8,577	2371	.276
9	Lou Whitaker*	19	8,569	2369	.276
10	Rickey Henderson†	17	8,063	2338	.290
11	Alan Trammell	19	8,095	2320	.287
12	Kirby Puckett	12	7,244	2304	.318
13	Tim Raines†	17	7,766	2295	.296

Games Played

1	Pete Rose	3562
2	Carl Yastrzemski	3308
3	Hank Aaron	3298
4	Ty Cobb	3034
5	Stan Musial	3026
6	Willie Mays	2992
7	**Dave Winfield**	2973
8	Rusty Staub	2951
9	Brooks Robinson	2896
10	Robin Yount	2856
11	Al Kaline	2834
12	Eddie Collins	2826
13	Reggie Jackson	2820
14	**Eddie Murray**	2819
15	Frank Robinson	2808
16	Tris Speaker	2789
	Honus Wagner	2789
18	Tony Perez	2777
19	Mel Ott	2734
20	George Brett	2707

At Bats

1	Pete Rose	14,053
2	Hank Aaron	12,364
3	Carl Yastrzemski	11,988
4	Ty Cobb	11,429
5	Robin Yount	11,008
6	**Dave Winfield**	11,003
7	Stan Musial	10,972
8	Willie Mays	10,881
9	Brooks Robinson	10,654
10	**Eddie Murray**	10,603
11	Honus Wagner	10,441
12	George Brett	10,349
13	Lou Brock	10,332
14	Luis Aparicio	10,230
15	Tris Speaker	10,197
16	Al Kaline	10,116
17	Rabbit Maranville	10,078
18	Frank Robinson	10,006
19	Eddie Collins	9,951
20	Andre Dawson	9,869

Total Bases

1	Hank Aaron	6856
2	Stan Musial	6134
3	Willie Mays	6066
4	Ty Cobb	5863
5	Babe Ruth	5793
6	Pete Rose	5752
7	Carl Yastrzemski	5539
8	Frank Robinson	5373
9	**Dave Winfield**	5219
10	**Eddie Murray**	5108
11	Tris Speaker	5103
12	Lou Gehrig	5059
13	George Brett	5044
14	Mel Ott	5041
15	Jimmie Foxx	4956
16	Ted Williams	4884
17	Honus Wagner	4868
18	Al Kaline	4852
19	Reggie Jackson	4834
20	**Andre Dawson**	4763

All-Time Major League Leaders (Cont.)
Batting

Home Runs

		Yrs	AB	HR	AB/HR
1	Hank Aaron	23	12,364	755	16.4
2	Babe Ruth*	22	8,399	714	11.8
3	Willie Mays	22	10,881	660	16.5
4	Frank Robinson	21	10,006	586	17.1
5	Harmon Killebrew	22	8,147	573	14.2
6	Reggie Jackson*	21	9,864	563	17.5
7	Mike Schmidt	18	8,352	548	15.2
8	Mickey Mantle†	18	8,102	536	15.1
9	Jimmie Foxx	20	8,134	534	15.2
10	Ted Williams*	19	7,706	521	14.8
	Willie McCovey*	22	8,197	521	15.7
12	Ed Mathews*	17	8,537	512	16.7
	Ernie Banks	19	9,421	512	18.4
14	Mel Ott*	22	9,456	511	18.5
15	Lou Gehrig*	17	8,001	493	16.2
16	Eddie Murray†	19	10,603	479	22.1
17	Willie Stargell*	21	7,927	475	16.7
	Stan Musial*	22	10,972	475	23.1
19	Dave Winfield	22	11,003	465	23.7
20	Carl Yastrzemski*	23	11,988	452	26.5
21	Dave Kingman	16	6,677	442	15.1
22	Andre Dawson	20	9,869	436	22.6
23	Billy Williams*	18	9,350	426	22.0
24	Darrell Evans	21	8,973	414	21.7
25	Duke Snider	18	7,161	407	17.6

Runs Batted In

		Yrs	Gm	RBI	P/G
1	Hank Aaron	23	3298	2297	.70
2	Babe Ruth*	22	2503	2211	.88
3	Lou Gehrig*	17	2164	1990	.92
4	Ty Cobb*	24	3034	1961	.65
5	Stan Musial*	22	3026	1951	.64
6	Jimmie Foxx	20	2317	1921	.83
7	Willie Mays	22	2992	1903	.64
8	Mel Ott*	22	2732	1861	.68
9	Carl Yastrzemski*	23	3308	1844	.56
10	Ted Williams*	19	2292	1839	.80
11	Dave Winfield	22	2973	1833	.62
12	Al Simmons*	20	2215	1827	.82
13	Eddie Murray†	19	2819	1820	.65
14	Frank Robinson	21	2808	1812	.65
15	Honus Wagner*	21	2786	1732	.62
16	Cap Anson*	22	2276	1715	.75
17	Reggie Jackson*	21	2820	1702	.60
18	Tony Perez	23	2777	1652	.59
19	Ernie Banks	19	2528	1636	.65
20	Goose Goslin*	18	2287	1609	.70
21	Nap Lajoie	21	2475	1599	.65
22	Mike Schmidt	18	2404	1595	.66
	George Brett*	21	2707	1595	.59
24	Rogers Hornsby*	23	2259	1584	.70
	Harmon Killebrew	22	2435	1584	.65

Players Active in 1995

		Yrs	AB	HR	AB/HR
1	Eddie Murray†	19	10,603	479	22.1
2	Dave Winfield	22	11,003	465	23.7
3	Andre Dawson	20	9,869	436	22.6
4	Joe Carter	13	6,797	327	20.8
	Cal Ripken Jr.	15	8,577	327	26.2
6	Lance Parrish	19	7,067	324	21.8
7	Harold Baines*	16	7,871	301	26.1
8	Jose Canseco	11	4,711	300	15.7
9	Darryl Strawberry*	13	4,843	297	16.3
10	Barry Bonds*	10	5,020	292	17.2
	Gary Gaetti	15	7,203	292	24.7
12	Fred McGriff*	10	4,512	289	15.6
13	Mark McGwire	10	3,659	277	13.2
14	Chili Davis†	15	7,087	270	26.2
15	Kirk Gibson	17	5,798	255	22.7

Players Active in 1995

		Yrs	Gm	RBI	P/G
1	Dave Winfield	22	2973	1833	.62
2	Eddie Murray†	19	2819	1820	.65
3	Andre Dawson	20	2553	1577	.62
4	Cal Ripken Jr.	15	2218	1267	.57
5	Harold Baines*	16	2178	1261	.58
6	Joe Carter	13	1731	1173	.68
7	Chili Davis†	15	1968	1100	.56
8	Don Mattingly*	14	1783	1099	.62
9	Kirby Puckett	12	1780	1085	.61
10	Lou Whitaker*	19	2377	1084	.46
11	Tim Wallach	16	2109	1083	.51
12	Gary Gaetti	15	1964	1075	.55
13	Lance Parrish	19	1986	1070	.54
14	Paul Molitor	18	2260	1036	.46
15	Alan Trammell	19	2219	987	.44

Runs

1	Ty Cobb	2245
2	Babe Ruth	2174
	Hank Aaron	2174
4	Pete Rose	2165
5	Willie Mays	2062
6	Stan Musial	1949
7	Lou Gehrig	1888
8	Tris Speaker	1882
9	Mel Ott	1859
10	Frank Robinson	1829
11	Eddie Collins	1820
12	Carl Yastrzemski	1816
13	Ted Williams	1798
14	Charlie Gehringer	1774
15	Jimmie Foxx	1751
16	Honus Wagner	1735
17	Willie Keeler	1727
18	Cap Anson	1719
	Rickey Henderson	1719
20	Jesse Burkett	1718

Extra Base Hits

1	Hank Aaron	1477
2	Stan Musial	1377
3	Babe Ruth	1356
4	Willie Mays	1323
5	Lou Gehrig	1190
6	Frank Robinson	1186
7	Carl Yastrzemski	1157
8	Ty Cobb	1139
9	Tris Speaker	1132
10	George Brett	1119
11	Ted Williams	1117
	Jimmie Foxx	1117
13	Dave Winfield	1093
14	Reggie Jackson	1075
15	Mel Ott	1071
16	Eddie Murray	1045
17	Pete Rose	1041
18	Andre Dawson	1035
19	Mike Schmidt	1015
20	Rogers Hornsby	1011

Slugging Average

1	Babe Ruth	.690
2	Ted Williams	.634
3	Lou Gehrig	.632
4	Jimmie Foxx	.609
5	Hank Greenberg	.605
6	Joe DiMaggio	.579
7	Rogers Hornsby	.577
8	Johnny Mize	.562
9	Stan Musial	.559
10	Willie Mays	.557
11	Mickey Mantle	.557
12	Hank Aaron	.555
13	Ralph Kiner	.548
14	Hack Wilson	.545
15	Chuck Klein	.543
16	Duke Snider	.540
17	Frank Robinson	.537
18	Al Simmons	.535
19	Dick Allen	.534
20	Earl Averill	.533

Stolen Bases

1	**Rickey Henderson**	1149
2	Lou Brock	938
3	Billy Hamilton	915
4	Ty Cobb	892
5	**Tim Raines**	777
6	Eddie Collins	743
7	**Vince Coleman**	740
7	Max Carey	738
8	Honus Wagner	720
10	Joe Morgan	689
11	Arlie Latham	679
12	Willie Wilson	668
13	Bert Campaneris	649
14	Tom Brown	627
15	George Davis	615
16	Dummy Hoy	597
17	Maury Wills	586
18	Hugh Duffy	583
	George Van Haltren	583
20	**Ozzie Smith**	573

Walks

1	Babe Ruth	2056
2	Ted Williams	2019
3	Joe Morgan	1865
4	Carl Yastrzemski	1845
5	Mickey Mantle	1734
6	Mel Ott	1708
7	Eddie Yost	1614
8	Darrell Evans	1605
9	Stan Musial	1599
10	Pete Rose	1566
11	Harmon Killebrew	1559
12	**Rickey Henderson**	1550
13	Lou Gehrig	1508
14	Mike Schmidt	1507
15	Eddie Collins	1503
16	Willie Mays	1463
17	Jimmie Foxx	1452
18	Eddie Mathews	1444
19	Frank Robinson	1420
20	Hank Aaron	1402

Strikeouts

1	Reggie Jackson	2597
2	Willie Stargell	1936
3	Mike Schmidt	1883
4	Tony Perez	1867
5	Dave Kingman	1816
6	Bobby Bonds	1757
7	Dale Murphy	1748
8	Lou Brock	1730
9	Mickey Mantle	1710
10	Harmon Killebrew	1699
11	Dwight Evans	1697
12	**Dave Winfield**	1686
13	Lee May	1570
14	Dick Allen	1556
15	Willie McCovey	1550
16	Dave Parker	1537
17	Frank Robinson	1532
18	**Lance Parrish**	1527
19	Willie Mays	1526
20	Rick Monday	1513

Pitching

Note that (*) indicates left-handed pitcher. Active pitcher leaders are listed for wins, strikeouts and saves.

Wins

		Yrs	GS	W	L	Pct
1	Cy Young	22	815	511	316	.618
2	Walter Johnson	21	666	416	279	.599
3	Christy Mathewson	17	551	373	188	.665
	Grover Alexander	20	598	373	208	.642
5	Warren Spahn*	21	665	363	245	.597
6	Kid Nichols	15	561	361	208	.634
	Pud Galvin	14	682	361	308	.540
8	Tim Keefe	14	594	342	225	.603
9	Steve Carlton*	24	709	329	244	.574
10	Eddie Plank*	17	527	327	193	.629
11	John Clarkson	12	518	326	177	.648
12	Don Sutton	23	756	324	256	.559
13	Nolan Ryan	27	773	324	292	.526
14	Phil Niekro	24	716	318	274	.537
15	Gaylord Perry	22	690	314	265	.542
16	Old Hoss Radbourn	12	503	311	194	.616
	Tom Seaver	20	647	311	205	.603
18	Mickey Welch	13	549	308	209	.596
19	Lefty Grove*	17	456	300	141	.680
	Early Wynn	23	612	300	244	.551
21	Tommy John*	26	700	288	231	.555
22	Bert Blyleven	22	685	287	250	.534
23	Robin Roberts	19	609	286	245	.539
24	Tony Mullane	13	505	285	220	.564
25	Ferguson Jenkins	19	594	284	226	.557
26	Jim Kaat*	25	625	283	237	.544
27	Red Ruffing	22	536	273	225	.548
28	Burleigh Grimes	19	495	270	212	.560
29	Jim Palmer	19	521	268	152	.638
30	Bob Feller	18	484	266	162	.621

Strikeouts

		Yrs	IP	SO	P/9
1	Nolan Ryan	27	5387.0	5714	9.54
2	Steve Carlton*	24	5217.1	4136	7.13
3	Bert Blyleven	22	4970.1	3701	6.70
4	Tom Seaver	20	4782.2	3640	6.85
5	Don Sutton	23	5282.1	3574	6.09
6	Gaylord Perry	22	5350.1	3534	5.94
7	Walter Johnson	21	5923.2	3508	5.33
8	Phil Niekro	24	5404.1	3342	5.57
9	Ferguson Jenkins	19	4500.2	3192	6.38
10	Bob Gibson	17	3884.1	3117	7.22
11	Jim Bunning	17	3760.1	2855	6.83
12	Mickey Lolich*	16	3638.1	2832	7.01
13	Cy Young	22	7354.2	2796	3.42
14	Frank Tanana*	21	4186.2	2773	5.96
15	Warren Spahn*	21	5243.2	2583	4.43
16	Bob Feller	18	3827.0	2581	6.07
17	Jerry Koosman*	19	3839.1	2556	5.99
18	Tim Keefe	14	5061.1	2527	4.50
19	Christy Mathewson	17	4781.0	2502	4.71
20	Don Drysdale	14	3432.0	2486	6.52
21	Jack Morris	18	3824.2	2478	5.83
22	Jim Kaat*	25	4530.1	2461	4.89
23	Sam McDowell*	15	2492.1	2453	8.86
24	Luis Tiant	19	3486.1	2416	6.24
25	Sandy Koufax*	12	2324.1	2396	9.28
26	Charlie Hough	25	3799.1	2363	5.60
27	Robin Roberts	19	4688.2	2357	4.52
28	Early Wynn	23	4564.0	2334	4.60
29	**Roger Clemens**	12	2533.1	2333	8.29
30	Rube Waddell*	13	2961.1	2316	7.04

Pitchers Active in 1995

		Yrs	GS	W	L	Pct
1	Dennis Martinez	20	527	231	176	.568
2	Dennis Eckersley	21	361	192	159	.547
3	Roger Clemens	12	348	182	98	.650
4	Frank Viola*	14	414	175	147	.543
5	Mark Langston*	12	379	166	140	.542
6	Scott Sanderson	18	403	163	141	.536
7	Mike Moore	14	440	161	176	.478
8	Fernando Valenzuela*	15	375	158	133	.543
9	Jimmy Key*	12	314	152	93	.620
10	Greg Maddux	10	297	150	93	.617
	Orel Hershiser	13	329	150	108	.581

Pitchers Active in 1995

		Yrs	IP	SO	P/9
1	Roger Clemens	12	2533.1	2333	8.29
2	Dennis Eckersley	21	3133.0	2285	6.56
3	Mark Langston*	12	2648.2	2252	7.65
4	Dennis Martinez	20	3748.1	2022	4.86
5	Fernando Valenzuela*	15	2669.1	1918	6.47
6	Frank Viola*	14	2806.0	1826	5.86
7	David Cone	10	1922.0	1741	8.15
8	Mike Moore	14	2831.1	1667	5.30
9	Sid Fernandez*	13	1770.2	1624	8.26
10	Scott Sanderson	18	2543.1	1604	5.68

All-Time Major League Leaders (Cont.)
Pitching

Winning Pct.

		Yrs	W-L	Pct
1	Bob Caruthers	9	218-97	.692
2	Dave Foutz	11	147-66	.690
3	Whitey Ford*	16	236-106	.690
4	Lefty Grove*	17	300-141	.680
5	Vic Raschi	10	132-66	.667
6	Christy Mathewson	17	373-188	.665
7	Larry Corcoran	8	177-90	.663
8	Sam Leever	13	194-101	.658
9	Sal Maglie	10	119-62	.657
10	Sandy Koufax*	12	165-87	.655
11	Johnny Allen	13	142-75	.654
12	Ron Guidry*	14	170-91	.651
13	**Roger Clemens**	12	182-98	.650
14	Lefty Gomez*	14	189-102	.649
15	Dwight Gooden	11	157-85	.649

Losses

		Yrs	GS	W	L	Pct
1	Cy Young	22	815	511	**316**	.618
2	Pud Galvin	14	682	361	**308**	.540
3	Nolan Ryan	27	773	324	**292**	.526
4	Walter Johnson	21	666	416	**279**	.599
5	Phil Niekro	24	716	318	**274**	.537
6	Gaylord Perry	22	690	314	**265**	.542
7	Jack Powell	16	517	245	**256**	.489
	Don Sutton	23	756	324	**256**	.559
9	Eppa Rixey*	21	552	266	**251**	.515
10	Bert Blyleven	22	685	287	**250**	.534
11	Robin Roberts	19	609	286	**245**	.539
	Warren Spahn*	21	665	363	**245**	.597
13	Early Wynn	23	612	300	**244**	.551
	Steve Carlton*	24	709	329	**244**	.574
15	Jim Kaat*	25	625	283	**237**	.544

Appearances

1	Hoyt Wilhelm	1070
2	Kent Tekulve	1050
3	Rich Gossage	1002
4	Lindy McDaniel	987
5	Rollie Fingers	944
6	**Lee Smith**	943
7	Gene Garber	931
8	Cy Young	906
9	**Dennis Eckersley**	901
10	Sparky Lyle	899
11	Jim Kaat	898
12	Jeff Reardon	880
13	Don McMahon	874
14	Phil Niekro	864
15	Charlie Hough	858

Innings Pitched

1	Cy Young	7356.0
2	Pud Galvin	5941.1
3	Walter Johnson	5923.2
4	Phil Niekro	5403.1
5	Nolan Ryan	5387.0
6	Gaylord Perry	5350.1
7	Don Sutton	5280.1
8	Warren Spahn	5243.2
9	Steve Carlton	5217.1
10	Grover Alexander	5189.2
11	Kid Nichols	5084.0
12	Tim Keefe	5061.1
13	Bert Blyleven	4970.1
14	Mickey Welch	4802.0
15	Tom Seaver	4782.2

Earned Run Avg.

1	Ed Walsh	1.82
2	Addie Joss	1.88
3	Three Finger Brown	2.06
4	Monte Ward	2.10
5	Christy Mathewson	2.13
6	Rube Waddell	2.16
7	Walter Johnson	2.17
8	Orval Overall	2.24
9	Tommy Bond	2.25
10	Will White	2.28
11	Ed Reulbach	2.28
12	Jim Scott	2.32
13	Eddie Plank	2.34
14	Larry Corcoran	2.36
15	Eddie Cicotte	2.37

Shutouts

1	Walter Johnson	110
2	Grover Alexander	90
3	Christy Mathewson	80
4	Cy Young	76
5	Eddie Plank	69
6	Warren Spahn	63
7	Nolan Ryan	61
	Tom Seaver	61
9	Bert Blyleven	60
10	Don Sutton	58
11	Three Finger Brown	57
	Pud Galvin	57
	Ed Walsh	57
14	Bob Gibson	56
15	Steve Carlton	55

Walks Allowed

1	Nolan Ryan	2795
2	Steve Carlton	1833
3	Phil Niekro	1809
4	Early Wynn	1775
5	Bob Feller	1764
6	Bobo Newsom	1732
7	Amos Rusie	1704
8	Charlie Hough	1665
9	Gus Weyhing	1566
10	Red Ruffing	1541
11	Bump Hadley	1442
12	Warren Spahn	1434
13	Earl Whitehill	1431
14	Tony Mullane	1409
15	Sad Sam Jones	1396

HRs Allowed

1	Robin Roberts	505
2	Ferguson Jenkins	484
3	Phil Niekro	482
4	Don Sutton	472
5	Frank Tanana	448
6	Warren Spahn	434
7	Bert Blyleven	430
8	Steve Carlton	414
9	Gaylord Perry	399
10	Jim Kaat	395
11	Jack Morris	389
12	Charlie Hough	383
13	Tom Seaver	380
14	Jim Hunter	374
15	Jim Bunning	372

Saves

1	**Lee Smith**	471	11	**Randy Myers**	243	
2	Jeff Reardon	367	12	Sparky Lyle	238	
3	Rollie Fingers	341	13	Hoyt Wilhelm	227	
4	**Dennis Eckersley**	323	14	Gene Garber	218	
5	**Tom Henke**	311		**Jeff Montgomery**	218	
6	Rich Gossage	310	16	Doug Jones	217	
7	Bruce Sutter	300	17	Dave Smith	216	
8	John Franco	295	18	**Rick Aguilera**	211	
9	Dave Righetti	252	19	Bobby Thigpen	201	
10	Dan Quisenberry	244	20	Roy Face	193	

21	Mitch Williams	192
22	**Steve Bedrosian**	184
	Kent Tekulve	184
24	**Jeff Russell**	183
25	Tug McGraw	180
26	Ron Perranoski	179
27	**Bryan Harvey**	177
28	Lindy McDaniel	172
29	**Gregg Olson**	164
30	**Roger McDowell**	155
	Jay Howell	155

SINGLE SEASON

Through 1995 regular season.

Batting

Home Runs

		Year	Gm	AB	HR
1	Roger Maris, NY-AL	1961	162	590	61
2	Babe Ruth, NY-AL	1927	151	540	60
3	Babe Ruth, NY-AL	1921	152	540	59
4	Hank Greenberg, Det	1938	155	556	58
	Jimmie Foxx, Phi-AL	1932	154	585	58
6	Hack Wilson, Chi-NL	1930	155	585	56
7	Babe Ruth, NY-AL	1920	142	458	54
	Mickey Mantle, NY-AL	1961	153	514	54
	Babe Ruth, NY-AL	1928	154	536	54
	Ralph Kiner, Pit	1949	152	549	54
11	Mickey Mantle, NY-AL	1956	150	533	52
	Willie Mays, SF	1965	157	558	52
	George Foster, Cin	1977	158	615	52
14	Ralph Kiner, Pit	1947	152	565	51
	Cecil Fielder, Det	1990	159	573	51
	Willie Mays, NY-AL	1955	152	580	51
	Johnny Mize, NY-NL	1947	154	586	51
18	Jimmie Foxx, Bos-AL	1938	149	565	50
	Albert Belle, Cle	1995	143	546	50

Hits

		Year	AB	H	Avg
1	George Sisler, StL-AL	1920	631	257	.407
2	Bill Terry, NY-NL	1930	633	254	.401
	Lefty O'Doul, Phi-NL	1929	638	254	.398
4	Al Simmons, Phi-AL	1925	658	253	.384
5	Rogers Hornsby, StL-NL	1922	623	250	.401
6	Chuck Klein, Phi-NL	1930	648	250	.386
7	Ty Cobb, Det	1911	591	248	.420
8	George Sisler, StL-AL	1922	586	246	.420
9	Babe Herman, Bklyn	1930	614	241	.393
	Heinie Manush, StL-AL	1928	638	241	.378
11	Wade Boggs, Bos	1985	653	240	.368
12	Rod Carew, Min	1977	616	239	.388
13	Don Mattingly, NY-AL	1986	677	238	.352
14	Harry Heilmann, Det	1921	602	237	.394
	Paul Waner, Pit	1927	623	237	.380
	Joe Medwick, StL-NL	1937	633	237	.374
17	Jack Tobin, StL-AL	1921	671	236	.352
18	Rogers Hornsby, StL-NL	1921	592	235	.397

Batting Average

From 1900-49

		Year	AB	H	Avg
1	Rogers Hornsby, StL-NL	1924	536	227	.424
2	Nap Lajoie, Phi-AL	1901	543	229	.422
3	George Sisler, StL-AL	1922	586	246	.420
4	Ty Cobb, Det	1911	591	248	.420
5	Ty Cobb, Det	1912	533	227	.410
6	Joe Jackson, Cle	1911	571	233	.408
7	George Sisler, StL-AL	1920	631	257	.407
8	Ted Williams, Bos-AL	1941	456	185	.406
9	Rogers Hornsby, StL-NL	1925	504	203	.403
10	Harry Heilmann, Det	1923	524	211	.403

Since 1950

		Year	AB	H	Avg
1	Tony Gwynn, SD	1994	419	175	.394
2	George Brett, KC	1980	449	175	.390
3	Ted Williams, Bos	1957	420	163	.388
4	Rod Carew, Min	1977	616	239	.388
5	Andres Galarraga, Col	1993	470	174	.370
6	Tony Gwynn, SD	1987	589	218	.370
7	Tony Gwynn, SD	1995	535	197	.368
8	Wade Boggs, Bos	1985	653	240	.368
9	Wade Boggs, Bos	1988	584	214	.366
10	Rico Carty, Atl	1970	478	175	.366

Total Bases

From 1900-49

		Year	TB
1	Babe Ruth, New York-AL	1921	457
2	Rogers Hornsby, St. Louis-NL	1922	450
3	Lou Gehrig, New York-AL	1927	447
4	Chuck Klein, Philadelphia-NL	1930	445
5	Jimmie Foxx, Philadelphia-AL	1932	438
6	Stan Musial, St. Louis-NL	1948	429
7	Hack Wilson, Chicago-NL	1930	423
8	Chuck Klein, Philadelphia-NL	1932	420
9	Lou Gehrig, New York-AL	1930	419
10	Joe DiMaggio, New York-AL	1937	418

Since 1950

		Year	TB
1	Jim Rice, Boston	1978	406
2	Hank Aaron, Milwaukee	1959	400
3	George Foster, Cincinnati	1977	388
	Don Mattingly, New York-AL	1986	388
5	Willie Mays, New York-NL	1955	382
	Willie Mays, San Francisco	1962	382
	Jim Rice, Boston	1977	382
8	Frank Robinson, Cincinnati	1962	380
9	Ernie Banks, Chicago-NL	1958	379
10	Duke Snider, Brooklyn	1954	378

Runs Batted In

From 1900-49

		Year	Avg	HR	RBI
1	Hack Wilson, Chi-NL	1930	.356	56	190
2	Lou Gehrig, NY-AL	1931	.341	46	184
3	Hank Greenberg, Det	1937	.337	40	183
4	Lou Gehrig, NY-AL	1927	.373	47	175
	Jimmie Foxx, Bos-AL	1938	.349	50	175
6	Lou Gehrig, NY-AL	1930	.379	41	174
7	Babe Ruth, NY-AL	1921	.378	59	171
8	Chuck Klein, Phi-NL	1930	.386	40	170
	Hank Greenberg, Det	1935	.328	36	170
10	Jimmie Foxx, Phi-AL	1932	.364	58	169

Since 1950

		Year	Avg	HR	RBI
1	Tommy Davis, LA-NL	1962	.346	27	153
2	George Foster, Cin	1977	.320	52	149
3	Johnny Bench, Cin	1970	.293	45	148
4	Al Rosen, Cle	1953	.336	43	145
	Don Mattingly, NY-AL	1985	.324	35	145
6	Walt Dropo, Bos-AL	1950	.322	34	144
	Vern Stephens, Bos-AL	1950	.295	30	144
8	Ernie Banks, Chi-NL	1959	.304	45	143
9	Roy Campanella, Bklyn	1953	.312	41	142
	Orlando Cepeda, SF	1961	.311	46	142
	Roger Maris, NY-AL	1961	.269	61	142

All-Time Major League Leaders (Cont.)
Batting

Runs

		Year	Runs
1	Babe Ruth, New York-AL	1921	177
2	Lou Gehrig, New York-AL	1936	167
3	Babe Ruth, New York-AL	1928	163
	Lou Gehrig, New York-AL	1931	163
5	Babe Ruth, New York-AL	1920	158
	Babe Ruth, New York-AL	1927	158
	Chuck Klein, Philadelphia-NL	1930	158
8	Rogers Hornsby, Chicago-NL	1929	156
9	Kiki Cuyler, Chicago-NL	1930	155
10	Lefty O'Doul, Philadelphia-NL	1929	152
	Woody English, Chicago-NL	1930	152
	Al Simmons, Philadelphia-AL	1930	152
	Chuck Klein, Philadelphia-NL	1932	152
14	Babe Ruth, New York-AL	1923	151
	Jimmie Foxx, Philadelphia-AL	1932	151
	Joe DiMaggio, New York-AL	1937	151
17	Babe Ruth, New York-AL	1930	150
	Ted Williams, Boston-AL	1940	150
19	Lou Gehrig, New York-AL	1927	149
	Babe Ruth, New York-AL	1931	149

Walks

		Year	BB
1	Babe Ruth, New York-AL	1923	170
2	Ted Williams, Boston-AL	1947	162
	Ted Williams, Boston-AL	1949	162
4	Ted Williams, Boston-AL	1946	156
5	Eddie Yost, Washington	1956	151
6	Eddie Joost, Philadelphia-AL	1949	149
7	Babe Ruth, New York-AL	1920	148
	Eddie Stanky, Brooklyn	1945	148
	Jimmy Wynn, Houston	1969	148
10	Jimmy Sheckard, Chicago-NL	1911	147

Extra Base Hits

		Year	EBH
1	Babe Ruth, New York-AL	1921	119
2	Lou Gehrig, New York-AL	1927	117
3	Chuck Klein, Philadelphia-NL	1930	107
4	Chuck Klein, Philadelphia-NL	1932	103
	Hank Greenberg, Detroit	1937	103
	Stan Musial, St. Louis-NL	1948	103
	Albert Belle, Cleveland	1995	103
8	Rogers Hornsby, St. Louis-NL	1922	102
9	Lou Gehrig, New York-AL	1930	100
	Jimmie Foxx, Philadelphia-AL	1933	100

Slugging Percentage
From 1900-49

		Year	Pct
1	Babe Ruth, New York-AL	1920	.847
2	Babe Ruth, New York-AL	1921	.846
3	Babe Ruth, New York-AL	1927	.772
4	Lou Gehrig, New York-AL	1927	.765
5	Babe Ruth, New York-AL	1923	.764
6	Rogers Hornsby, St. Louis-NL	1925	.756
7	Jimmie Foxx, Philadelphia-AL	1932	.749
8	Babe Ruth, New York-AL	1924	.739
9	Babe Ruth, New York-AL	1926	.737
10	Ted Williams, Boston-AL	1941	.735

Since 1950

		Year	Pct
1	Jeff Bagwell, Houston	1994	.750
2	Ted Williams, Boston	1957	.731
3	Frank Thomas, Chicago-AL	1994	.729
4	Albert Belle, Cleveland	1994	.714
5	Mickey Mantle, New York-AL	1956	.705

Stolen Bases

		Year	SB
1	Rickey Henderson, Oakland	1982	130
2	Lou Brock, St. Louis	1974	118
3	Vince Coleman, St. Louis	1985	110
4	Vince Coleman, St. Louis	1987	109
5	Rickey Henderson, Oakland	1983	108
6	Vince Coleman, St. Louis	1986	107
7	Maury Wills, Los Angeles-NL	1962	104
8	Rickey Henderson, Oakland	1980	100
9	Ron LeFlore, Montreal	1980	97
10	Ty Cobb, Detroit	1915	96
11	Omar Moreno, Pittsburgh	1980	96
12	Maury Wills, Los Angeles	1965	94
13	Rickey Henderson, New York-AL	1988	93
14	Tim Raines, Montreal	1983	90
15	Clyde Milan, Washington	1912	88
16	Rickey Henderson, New York-AL	1986	87
17	Ty Cobb, Detroit	1911	83
	Willie Wilson, Kansas City	1979	83
19	Bob Bescher, Cincinnati	1911	81
	Eddie Collins, Philadelphia-AL	1910	81
	Vince Coleman, St. Louis	1988	81

Strikeouts

		Year	SO
1	Bobby Bonds, San Francisco	1970	189
2	Bobby Bonds, San Francisco	1969	187
3	Rob Deer, Milwaukee	1987	186
4	Pete Incaviglia, Texas	1986	185
5	Cecil Fielder, Detroit	1990	182
6	Mike Schmidt, Philadelphia	1975	180
7	Rob Deer, Milwaukee	1986	179
8	Dave Nicholson, Chicago-AL	1963	175
	Gorman Thomas, Milwaukee	1979	175
	Jose Canseco, Oakland	1986	175
	Rob Deer, Detroit	1991	175

Pinch Hits

Career pinch hits in parentheses.

		Year	PH	
1	John Vander Wal, Colorado	1995	26	(54)
2	Jose Morales, Montreal	1976	25	(123)
3	Dave Philley, Baltimore	1961	24	(93)
	Vic Davalillo, St. Louis	1970	24	(95)
	Rusty Staub, New York-NL	1983	24	(100)
6	Four tied with 22 each.			

Note: The all-time career pinch hit leader is Manny Mota (150).

Four Home Runs in One Game
National League

	Date	H/A	Inn
Bobby Lowe, Boston	5/30/1894	H	9
Ed Delahanty, Philadelphia	7/13/1896	A	9
Chuck Klein, Philadelphia	7/10/1936	A	10
Gil Hodges, Brooklyn	8/31/1950	H	9
Joe Adcock, Milwaukee	7/31/1954	A	9
Willie Mays, San Francisco	4/30/1961	A	9
Mike Schmidt, Philadelphia	4/17/1976	A	10
Bob Horner, Atlanta	7/6/1986	H	9
Mark Whiten, St. Louis	9/7/1993	A	9

American League

	Date	H/A	Inn
Lou Gehrig, New York	6/3/1932	A	9
Pat Seerey, Chicago	7/18/1948	A	11
Rocky Colavito, Cleveland	6/10/1959	A	9

Pitching
Wins

From 1900-49

		Year	W	L	Pct
1	Jack Chesbro, NY-AL	1904	41	12	.774
2	Ed Walsh, Chi-AL	1908	40	15	.727
3	Christy Mathewson, NY-NL	1908	37	11	.771
4	Walter Johnson, Wash	1913	36	7	.837
5	Joe McGinnity, NY-NL	1904	35	8	.814
6	Smokey Joe Wood, Bos-AL	1912	34	5	.872
7	Cy Young, Bos-AL	1901	33	10	.767
	Grover Alexander, Phi-NL	1916	33	12	.733
	Christy Mathewson, NY-NL	1904	33	12	.733
10	Cy Young, Bos-AL	1902	32	11	.744

Since 1950

		Year	W	L	Pct
1	Denny McLain, Det	1968	31	6	.838
2	Robin Roberts, Phi-NL	1952	28	7	.800
3	Bob Welch, Oak	1990	27	6	.818
	Don Newcombe, Bklyn	1956	27	7	.794
	Sandy Koufax, LA	1966	27	9	.750
	Steve Carlton, Phi	1972	27	10	.730
7	Sandy Koufax, LA	1965	26	8	.765
	Juan Marichal, SF	1968	26	9	.743

Note: 11 pitchers tied with 25 wins, including Marichal twice.

Earned Run Average

From 1900-49

		Year	ShO	ERA
1	Dutch Leonard, Bos-AL	1914	7	1.01
2	Three Finger Brown,	1906	10	1.04
3	Walter Johnson, Wash	1913	11	1.09
4	Christy Mathewson, NY-NL	1909	8	1.14
5	Jack Pfiester, Chi-NL	1907	3	1.15
6	Addie Joss, Cle	1908	9	1.16
7	Carl Lundgren, Chi-NL	1907	7	1.17
8	Grover Alexander, Phi-NL	1915	12	1.22
9	Cy Young, Bos-AL	1908	3	1.26
10	Three pitchers tied at 1.27			

Since 1950

		Year	ShO	ERA
1	Bob Gibson, St.L	1968	13	1.12
2	Dwight Gooden, NY-NL	1985	8	1.53
3	Greg Maddux, Atl	1994	3	1.56
4	Luis Tiant, Cle	1968	9	1.60
5	Greg Maddux, Atl	1995	3	1.63
6	Dean Chance, LA-AL	1964	11	1.65
7	Nolan Ryan, Cal	1981	3	1.69
8	Sandy Koufax, LA	1966	5	1.73
9	Sandy Koufax, LA	1964	7	1.74
9	Ron Guidry, NY-AL	1978	9	1.74
10	Tom Seaver, NY-NL	1971	4	1.76

Winning Pct.

		Year	W-L	Pct
1	Roy Face, Pit	1959	18-1	.947
2	Rick Sutcliffe, Chi-NL*	1984	16-1	.941
3	Johnny Allen, Cle	1937	15-1	.938
4	Greg Maddux, Atl	1995	19-2	.904
5	Randy Johnson, Sea	1995	18-2	.900
6	Ron Guidry, NY-AL	1978	25-3	.893
7	Freddie Fitzsimmons, Bklyn	1940	16-2	.889
8	Lefty Grove, Phi-AL	1931	31-4	.886
9	Bob Stanley, Bos	1978	15-2	.882
10	Preacher Roe, Bklyn	1951	22-3	.880
11	Tom Seaver, Cin	1981	14-2	.875
12	Smokey Joe Wood, Bos-AL	1912	34-5	.872

*Sutcliffe began 1984 with Cleveland and was 4-5 before being traded to the Cubs; his overall winning pct. was .769 (20-6).

Strikeouts

		Year	SO	P/G
1	Nolan Ryan, Cal	1973	383	10.57
2	Sandy Koufax, LA	1965	382	10.24
3	Nolan Ryan, Cal	1974	367	9.92
4	Rube Waddell, Phi-AL	1904	349	8.12
5	Bob Feller, Cle	1946	348	8.45
6	Nolan Ryan, Cal	1977	341	10.26
7	Nolan Ryan, Cal	1972	329	10.43
8	Nolan Ryan, Cal	1976	327	10.36
9	Sam McDowell, Cle	1965	325	10.71
10	Sandy Koufax, LA	1966	317	8.83

Appearances

		Year	App	Sv
1	Mike Marshall, LA	1974	106	21
2	Kent Tekulve, Pit	1979	94	31
3	Mike Marshall, LA	1973	92	31
4	Kent Tekulve, Pit	1978	91	31
5	Wayne Granger, Cin	1969	90	27
	Mike Marshall, Min	1979	90	32
	Kent Tekulve, Phi	1987	90	3

Saves

		Year	App	Sv
1	Bobby Thigpen, Chi-AL	1990	77	57
2	Randy Myers, Chi-NL	1993	73	53
3	Dennis Eckersley, Oak	1992	69	51
4	Dennis Eckersley, Oak	1990	63	48
	Rod Beck, SF	1993	76	48
6	Lee Smith, St.L	1991	67	47

Innings Pitched (since 1920)

		Year	IP	W-L
1	Wilbur Wood, Chi-AL	1972	377	24-17
2	Mickey Lolich, Det	1971	376	25-14
3	Bob Feller, Cle	1946	371	26-15
4	Grover Alexander, Chi-NL	1920	363	27-14
5	Wilbur Wood, Chi-AL	1973	359	24-20

Shutouts

		Year	ShO	ERA
1	Grover Alexander, Phi-NL	1916	16	1.55
2	Jack Coombs, Phi-AL	1910	13	1.30
	Bob Gibson, St.L	1968	13	1.12
4	Christy Mathewson, NY-NL	1908	12	1.43
	Grover Alexander, Phi-NL	1915	12	1.22

Walks Allowed

		Year	BB	SO
1	Bob Feller, Cle	1938	208	240
2	Nolan Ryan, Cal	1977	204	341
3	Nolan Ryan, Cal	1974	202	367
4	Bob Feller, Cle	1941	194	260
5	Bobo Newsom, St.L-AL	1938	192	226

Home Runs Allowed

		Year	HRs
1	Bert Blyleven, Minnesota	1986	50
2	Robin Roberts, Philadelphia	1956	46
	Bert Blyleven, Minnesota	1987	46
4	Pedro Ramos, Washington	1957	43
5	Denny McLain, Detroit	1966	42

All-Time Winningest Managers

Top 20 Major League career victories through the 1995 season. Career, regular season and postseason (playoffs and World Series) records are noted along with AL and NL pennants and World Series titles won. Managers active during 1995 season in **bold** type.

		Career			Regular Season			Postseason			
	Yrs	W	L	Pct	W	L	Pct	W	L	Pct	Titles
1 Connie Mack	53	**3755**	3967	.486	3731	3948	.486	24	19	.558	9 AL, 5 WS
2 John McGraw	33	**2810**	1987	.586	2784	1959	.587	26	28	.482	10 NL, 3 WS
3 **Sparky Anderson**	26	**2238**	1855	.547	2194	1834	.545	34	21	.618	4 NL, 1 AL, 3 WS
4 Bucky Harris	29	**2168**	2228	.493	2157	2218	.493	11	10	.524	3 AL, 2 WS
5 Joe McCarthy	24	**2155**	1346	.616	2125	1333	.615	30	13	.698	1 NL, 8 AL, 7 WS
6 Walter Alston	23	**2063**	1634	.558	2040	1613	.558	23	21	.523	7 NL, 4 WS
7 Leo Durocher	24	**2015**	1717	.540	2008	1709	.540	7	8	.467	3 NL, 1 WS
8 Casey Stengel	25	**1942**	1868	.510	1905	1842	.508	37	26	.587	10 AL, 7 WS
9 Gene Mauch	26	**1907**	2044	.483	1902	2037	.483	5	7	.417	—None—
10 Bill McKechnie	25	**1904**	1737	.523	1896	1723	.524	8	14	.364	4 NL, 2 WS
11 Ralph Houk	20	**1627**	1539	.514	1619	1531	.514	8	8	.500	3 AL, 2 WS
12 Fred Clarke	19	**1609**	1189	.575	1602	1181	.576	7	8	.467	4 NL, 1 WS
13 Dick Williams	21	**1592**	1474	.519	1571	1451	.520	21	23	.477	3 AL, 1 NL, 2 WS
14 **Tommy Lasorda**	20	**1589**	1434	.526	1558	1404	.526	31	30	.508	4 NL, 2 WS
15 Earl Weaver	17	**1506**	1080	.582	1480	1060	.583	26	20	.565	4 AL, 1 WS
16 Clark Griffith	20	**1491**	1367	.522	1491	1367	.522	0	0	.000	1 AL (1901)
17 Miller Huggins	17	**1431**	1149	.555	1413	1134	.555	18	15	.545	6 AL, 3 WS
18 Al Lopez	17	**1412**	1012	.583	1410	1004	.584	2	8	.200	2 AL
19 Jimmy Dykes	21	**1406**	1541	.477	1406	1541	.477	0	0	.000	—None—
20 Wilbert Robertson	19	**1402**	1407	.499	1399	1398	.500	3	9	.250	2 NL

Notes: John McGraw's postseason record also includes two World Series tie games (1912,'22); Miller Huggins postseason record also includes one World Series tie game (1922).

Where They Managed

Alston—Brooklyn/Los Angeles NL (1954-76); **Anderson**—Cincinnati NL (1970-78), Detroit AL (1979-95); **Clarke**—Louisville NL (1897-99), Pittsburgh NL (1900-15); **Durocher**—Brooklyn NL (1939-46,48), New York NL (1948-55), Chicago NL (1966-72), Houston NL (1972-73); **Dykes**—Chicago AL (1934-46), Philadelphia AL (1951- 53), Baltimore AL (1954), Cincinnati NL (1958), Detroit AL (1959-60), Cleveland AL (1960-61); **Griffith**—Chicago AL (1901-02), New York AL (1903-08), Cincinnati NL (1909-11), Washington AL (1912-20); **Harris**—Washington AL (1924-28,35-42,50-54), Detroit AL (1929-33,55-56), Boston AL (1934), Philadelphia NL (1943), New York AL (1947-48); **Houk**—New York AL (1961-63,66-73), Detroit AL (1974-78), Boston AL (1981-84); **Huggins**—St. Louis NL (1913-17), New York AL (1918-29); **Lasorda**—Los Angeles NL (1976—); **Lopez**—Cleveland AL (1951-56), Chicago AL (1957-65,68-69).

Mack—Pittsburgh NL (1894-96), Philadelphia AL (1901-50); **Mauch**—Philadelphia NL (1960-68), Montreal NL (1969-75), Minnesota AL (1976-80), California AL (1981-82,85-87); **McCarthy**—Chicago NL (1926-30), New York AL (1931-46), Boston AL (1948-50); **McGraw**—Baltimore NL (1899), Baltimore AL (1901-02), New York NL (1902-32); **McKechnie**—Newark FL (1915), Pittsburgh NL (1922-26), St. Louis NL (1928-29), Boston NL (1930- 37), Cincinnati NL (1938-46); **Robertson**—Baltimore AL (1902), Brooklyn NL (1914-31); **Stengel**—Brooklyn NL (1934-36), Boston NL (1938-43), New York AL (1949-60), New York NL (1962-65); **Weaver**—Baltimore AL (1968-82,85-86); **Williams**—Boston AL (1967-69), Oakland AL (1971-73), California AL (1974-76), Montreal NL (1977-81), San Diego NL (1982-85), Seattle AL (1986-88).

Regular Season Winning Pct.

Minimum of 750 victories.

	Yrs	W	L	Pct	Pen
1 Joe McCarthy	24	2125	1333	.615	9
2 Charlie Comiskey	12	838	541	.608	4
3 Frank Selee	16	1284	862	.598	5
4 Billy Southworth	13	1044	704	.597	4
5 Frank Chance	11	946	648	.593	4
6 John McGraw	33	2784	1959	.587	10
7 Al Lopez	17	1410	1004	.584	2
8 Earl Weaver	17	1480	1060	.583	4
9 Cap Anson	20	1296	947	.578	5
10 Davey Johnson	10	799	589	.576	1
11 Fred Clarke	19	1602	1181	.576	4
12 Steve O'Neill	14	1040	821	.559	1
13 Walter Alston	23	2040	1613	.558	7
14 Bill Terry	10	823	661	.555	3
15 Miller Huggins	17	1413	1134	.555	6
16 Billy Martin	16	1253	1013	.553	2
17 Harry Wright	18	1000	825	.548	3
18 Charlie Grimm	19	1287	1067	.547	3
19 Sparky Anderson	26	2194	1834	.545	5
20 Hugh Jennings	15	1163	984	.542	3

World Series Victories

	App	W	L	T	Pct	WS
1 Casey Stengel	10	37	26	0	.587	7
2 Joe McCarthy	9	30	13	0	.698	7
3 John McGraw	9	26	28	2	.482	2
4 Connie Mack	8	24	19	0	.558	5
5 Walter Alston	7	20	20	0	.500	4
6 Miller Huggins	6	18	15	1	.544	3
7 **Sparky Anderson**	5	16	12	0	.571	3
8 **Tommy Lasorda**	4	12	11	0	.522	2
Dick Williams	4	12	14	0	.462	2
10 Frank Chance	4	11	9	1	.548	2
Bucky Harris	3	11	10	0	.524	2
Billy Southworth	4	11	11	0	.500	2
Earl Weaver	4	11	13	0	.458	1
14 Whitey Herzog	3	10	11	0	.476	1
15 Bill Carrigan	2	8	2	0	.800	2
Danny Murtaugh	2	8	6	0	.571	2
Ralph Houk	3	8	8	0	.500	2
Bill McKechnie	4	8	14	0	.364	2
Tom Kelly	2	8	6	0	.571	2
20 Seven tied with 7 wins each.						

Active Managers' Records

Regular season games only; through 1995.

National League

	Yrs	W	L	Pct
1 Tommy Lasorda, LA 20		1558	1404	.526
2 Tony La Russa, St.L.........17		1320	1183	.527
3 Bobby Cox, Atl 14		1115	962	.537
4 Jim Fregosi, Phi.............12		794	843	.485
5 Jim Leyland, Pit 10		778	774	.501
6 Dallas Green, NY 7		395	406	.493
7 Rene Lacheman, Fla 7		389	512	.432
8 Felipe Alou, Mon 4		304	241	.558
9 Dusty Baker, SF.............3		225	196	.534
10 Don Baylor, Col 3		197	226	.466
11 Jim Riggleman, Chi..........4		185	250	.425
12 Terry Collins, Hou 2		142	117	.548
13 Bruce Bochy, SD 1		70	74	.486
14 Ray Knight, Cin..............0		0	0	.000

American League

	Yrs	W	L	Pct
1 Davey Johnson, Cin 10		799	589	.576
2 Tom Kelly, Min 10		707	707	.500
3 Lou Piniella, Sea 9		689	633	.521
4 Cito Gaston, Tor 7		537	463	.537
5 Johnny Oates, Tex 4		365	340	.518
6 Mike Hargrove, Cle..........5		350	316	.526
7 Phil Garner, Mil 4		279	304	.479
8 Kevin Kennedy, Bos..........3		224	196	.533
9 Marcel Lacheman, Cal 2		108	111	.493
10 Bob Boone, KC 1		70	74	.486
11 Terry Bevington, Chi..........1		57	56	.504
12 Detroit				
13 New York				
14 Oakland				

Annual Awards

MOST VALUABLE PLAYER

There have been three different Most Valuable Player awards in baseball since 1911—the Chalmers Award (1911-14), presented by the Detroit-based automobile company; the League Award (1922-29), presented by the National and American Leagues; and the Baseball Writers' Award (since 1931), presented by the Baseball Writers' Association of America. Statistics for winning players are provided below. Stats for winning pitchers before advent of Cy Young Award are on page 142.

Multiple winners: NL—Barry Bonds, Roy Campanella, Stan Musial and Mike Schmidt (3); Ernie Banks, Johnny Bench, Rogers Hornsby, Carl Hubbell, Willie Mays, Joe Morgan and Dale Murphy (2). **AL**—Yogi Berra, Joe DiMaggio, Jimmie Foxx and Mickey Mantle (3); Mickey Cochrane, Lou Gehrig, Hank Greenberg, Walter Johnson, Roger Maris, Hal Newhouser, Cal Ripken Jr., Frank Thomas and Ted Williams (2). **NL & AL**—Frank Robinson (2, one in each).

Chalmers Award

National League

Year		Pos	HR	RBI	Avg
1911	Wildfire Schulte, Chi ....OF		21	121	.300
1912	Larry Doyle, NY 2B		10	90	.330
1913	Jake Daubert, Bklyn.............1B		2	52	.350
1914	Johnny Evers, Bos 2B		1	40	.279

American League

Year		Pos	HR	RBI	Avg
1911	Ty Cobb, Det ....OF		8	144	.420
1912	Tris Speaker, Bos ....OF		10	98	.383
1913	Walter Johnson, Wash..........P		—	—	—
1914	Eddie Collins, Phi 2B		2	85	.344

League Award

National League

Year		Pos	HR	RBI	Avg
1922	No selection				
1923	No selection				
1924	Dazzy Vance, Bklyn................P		—	—	—
1925	Rogers Hornsby, St.L 2B-Mgr		39	143	.403
1926	Bob O'Farrell, St.L................C		7	68	.293
1927	Paul Waner, Pit ....OF		9	131	.380
1928	Jim Bottomley, St.L...............1B		31	136	.325
1929	Rogers Hornsby, Chi.............2B		39	149	.380

American League

Year		Pos	HR	RBI	Avg
1922	George Sisler, St.L................1B		8	105	.420
1923	Babe Ruth, NY....................OF		41	131	.393
1924	Walter Johnson, Wash...........P		—	—	—
1925	Roger Peckinpaugh, Wash ....SS		4	64	.294
1926	George Burns, Cle.................1B		4	114	.358
1927	Lou Gehrig, NY...................1B		47	175	.373
1928	Mickey Cochrane, Phi C		10	57	.293
1929	No selection				

Most Valuable Player

National League

Year		Pos	HR	RBI	Avg
1931	Frankie Frisch, St.L................2B		4	82	.311
1932	Chuck Klein, Phi ....OF		38	137	.348
1933	Carl Hubbell, NY..................P		—	—	—
1934	Dizzy Dean, St.L...................P		—	—	—
1935	Gabby Hartnett, Chi..............C		13	91	.344
1936	Carl Hubbell, NY..................P		—	—	—
1937	Joe Medwick, St.L................OF		31	154	.374
1938	Ernie Lombardi, Cin C		19	95	.342
1939	Bucky Walters, Cin ....P		—	—	—
1940	Frank McCormick, Cin 1B		19	127	.309
1941	Dolf Camilli, Bklyn 1B		34	120	.285
1942	Mort Cooper, St.L.................P		—	—	—
1943	Stan Musial, St.L.................OF		13	81	.357
1944	Marty Marion, St.L................SS		6	63	.267
1945	Phil Cavarretta, Chi 1B		6	97	.355

American League

Year		Pos	HR	RBI	Avg
1931	Lefty Grove, Phi ....P		—	—	—
1932	Jimmie Foxx, Phi 1B		58	169	.364
1933	Jimmie Foxx, Phi 1B		48	163	.356
1934	Mickey Cochrane, Det.....C-Mgr		2	76	.320
1935	Hank Greenberg, Det 1B		36	170	.328
1936	Lou Gehrig, NY...................1B		49	152	.354
1937	Charlie Gehringer, Det 2B		14	96	.371
1938	Jimmie Foxx, Bos.................1B		50	175	.349
1939	Joe DiMaggio, NY ....OF		30	126	.381
1940	Hank Greenberg, Det...........OF		41	150	.340
1941	Joe DiMaggio, NY ....OF		30	125	.357
1942	Joe Gordon, NY..................2B		18	103	.322
1943	Spud Chandler, NY ....P		—	—	—
1944	Hal Hewhouser, Det...............P		—	—	—
1945	Hal Newhouser, Det ....P		—	—	—

Annual Awards (Cont.)
Most Valuable Player

National League					American League				
Year	Pos	HR	RBI	Avg	Year	Pos	HR	RBI	Avg
1946 Stan Musial, St.L	1B-OF	16	103	.365	1946 Ted Williams, Bos	OF	38	123	.342
1947 Bob Elliott, Bos	3B	22	113	.317	1947 Joe DiMaggio, NY	OF	20	97	.315
1948 Stan Musial, St.L	OF	39	131	.376	1948 Lou Boudreau, Cle	SS-Mgr	18	106	.355
1949 Jackie Robinson, Bklyn	2B	16	124	.342	1949 Ted Williams, Bos	OF	43	159	.343
1950 Jim Konstanty, Phi	P	—	—	—	1950 Phil Rizzuto, NY	SS	7	66	.324
1951 Roy Campanella, Bklyn	C	33	108	.325	1951 Yogi Berra, NY	C	27	88	.294
1952 Hank Sauer, Chi	OF	37	121	.270	1952 Bobby Shantz, Phi	P	—	—	—
1953 Roy Campanella, Bklyn	C	41	142	.312	1953 Al Rosen, Cle	3B	43	145	.336
1954 Willie Mays, NY	OF	41	110	.345	1954 Yogi Berra, NY	C	22	125	.307
1955 Roy Campanella, Bklyn	C	32	107	.318	1955 Yogi Berra, NY	C	27	108	.272
1956 Don Newcombe, Bklyn	P	—	—	—	1956 Mickey Mantle, NY	OF	52	130	.353
1957 Hank Aaron, Mil	OF	44	132	.322	1957 Mickey Mantle, NY	OF	34	94	.365
1958 Ernie Banks, Chi	SS	47	129	.313	1958 Jackie Jensen, Bos	OF	35	122	.286
1959 Ernie Banks, Chi	SS	45	143	.304	1959 Nellie Fox, Chi	2B	2	70	.306
1960 Dick Groat, Pit	SS	2	50	.325	1960 Roger Maris, NY	OF	39	112	.283
1961 Frank Robinson, Cin	OF	37	124	.323	1961 Roger Maris, NY	OF	61	142	.269
1962 Maury Wills, LA	SS	6	48	.299	1962 Mickey Mantle, NY	OF	30	89	.321
1963 Sandy Koufax, LA	P	—	—	—	1963 Elston Howard, NY	C	28	85	.287
1964 Ken Boyer, St.L	3B	24	119	.295	1964 Brooks Robinson, Bal	3B	28	118	.317
1965 Willie Mays, SF	OF	52	112	.317	1965 Zoilo Versalles, Min	SS	19	77	.273
1966 Roberto Clemente, Pit	OF	29	119	.317	1966 Frank Robinson, Bal	OF	49	122	.316
1967 Orlando Cepeda, St.L	1B	25	111	.325	1967 Carl Yastrzemski, Bos	OF	44	121	.326
1968 Bob Gibson, St.L	P	—	—	—	1968 Denny McLain, Det	P	—	—	—
1969 Willie McCovey, SF	1B	45	126	.320	1969 Harmon Killebrew, Min	3B-1B	49	140	.276
1970 Johnny Bench, Cin	C	45	148	.293	1970 Boog Powell, Bal	1B	35	114	.297
1971 Joe Torre, St.L	3B	24	137	.363	1971 Vida Blue, Oak	P	—	—	—
1972 Johnny Bench, Cin	C	40	125	.270	1972 Dick Allen, Chi	1B	37	113	.308
1973 Pete Rose, Cin	OF	5	64	.338	1973 Reggie Jackson, Oak	OF	32	117	.293
1974 Steve Garvey, LA	1B	21	111	.312	1974 Jeff Burroughs, Tex	OF	25	118	.301
1975 Joe Morgan, Cin	2B	17	94	.327	1975 Fred Lynn, Bos	OF	21	105	.331
1976 Joe Morgan, Cin	2B	27	111	.320	1976 Thurman Munson, NY	C	17	105	.302
1977 George Foster, Cin	OF	52	149	.320	1977 Rod Carew, Min	1B	14	100	.388
1978 Dave Parker, Pit	OF	30	117	.334	1978 Jim Rice, Bos	OF-DH	46	139	.315
1979 Keith Hernandez, St.L	1B	11	105	.344	1979 Don Baylor, Cal	OF-DH	36	139	.296
& Willie Stargell, Pit	1B	32	82	.281					
1980 Mike Schmidt, Phi	3B	48	121	.286	1980 George Brett, KC	3B	24	118	.390
1981 Mike Schmidt, Phi	3B	31	91	.316	1981 Rollie Fingers, Mil	P	—	—	—
1982 Dale Murphy, Atl	OF	36	109	.281	1982 Robin Yount, Mil	SS	29	114	.331
1983 Dale Murphy, Atl	OF	36	121	.302	1983 Cal Ripken Jr., Bal	SS	27	102	.318
1984 Ryne Sandberg, Chi	2B	19	84	.314	1984 Willie Hernandez, Det	P	—	—	—
1985 Willie McGee, St.L	OF	10	82	.353	1985 Don Mattingly, NY	1B	35	145	.324
1986 Mike Schmidt, Phi	3B	37	119	.290	1986 Roger Clemens, Bos	P	—	—	—
1987 Andre Dawson, Chi	OF	49	137	.287	1987 George Bell, Tor	OF	47	134	.308
1988 Kirk Gibson, LA	OF	25	76	.290	1988 Jose Canseco, Oak	OF	42	124	.307
1989 Kevin Mitchell, SF	OF	47	125	.291	1989 Robin Yount, Mil	OF	21	103	.318
1990 Barry Bonds, Pit	OF	33	114	.301	1990 Rickey Henderson, Oak	OF	28	61	.325
1991 Terry Pendleton, Atl	3B	22	86	.319	1991 Cal Ripken Jr., Bal	SS	34	114	.323
1992 Barry Bonds, Pit	OF	34	103	.311	1992 Dennis Eckersley, Oak	P	—	—	—
1993 Barry Bonds, SF	OF	46	123	.336	1993 Frank Thomas, Chi	1B	41	128	.317
1994 Jeff Bagwell, Hou	1B	39	116	.368	1994 Frank Thomas, Chi	1B	38	101	.353

MVP Pitchers' Statistics

Pitchers have been named Most Valuable Player on 23 occasions, 10 times in the NL and 13 in the AL. Four have been relief pitchers—Jim Konstanty, Rollie Fingers, Willie Hernandez and Dennis Eckersley.

National League					American League				
Year	Gm	W-L	SV	ERA	Year	Gm	W-L	SV	ERA
1924 Dazzy Vance, Bklyn	35	28-6	0	2.16	1913 Walter Johnson, Wash	47	36-7	2	1.09
1933 Carl Hubbell, NY	45	23-12	5	1.66	1924 Walter Johnson, Wash	38	23-7	0	2.72
1934 Dizzy Dean, St.L	50	30-7	7	2.66	1931 Lefty Grove, Phi	41	31-4	5	2.06
1936 Carl Hubbell, NY	42	26-6	3	2.31	1943 Spud Chandler, NY	30	20-4	0	1.64
1939 Bucky Walters, Cin	39	27-11	0	2.29	1944 Hal Hewhouser, Det	47	29-9	2	2.22
1942 Mort Cooper, St.L	37	22-7	0	1.78	1945 Hal Newhouser, Det	40	25-9	2	1.81
1950 Jim Konstanty, Phi	74	16-7	22	2.66	1952 Bobby Shantz, Phi	33	24-7	0	2.48

CY YOUNG AWARD

Voted on by the Baseball Writers Association of America. One award was presented from 1956-66, two since 1967. Pitchers who won the MVP and Cy Young awards in the same season are in **bold** type.

Multiple winners: NL—Steve Carlton (4); Sandy Koufax, Greg Maddux and Tom Seaver (3); Bob Gibson (2). **AL**—Jim Palmer and Roger Clemens (3); Denny McLain (2). **NL & AL**—Gaylord Perry (2, one in each).

NL and AL Combined

Year	National League	Gm	W-L	SV	ERA	Year	American League	Gm	W-L	SV	ERA
1956	**Don Newcombe**, Bklyn	38	27-7	0	3.06	1958	Bob Turley, NY	33	21-7	1	2.97
1957	Warren Spahn, Mil	39	21-11	3	2.69	1959	Early Wynn, Chi	37	22-10	0	3.17
1960	Vernon Law, Pit	35	20-9	0	3.08	1961	Whitey Ford, NY	39	25-4	0	3.21
1962	Don Drysdale, LA	43	25-9	1	2.83	1964	Dean Chance, LA	46	20-9	4	1.65
1963	**Sandy Koufax**, LA	40	25-5	0	1.88						
1965	Sandy Koufax, LA	43	26-8	2	2.04						
1966	Sandy Koufax, LA	41	27-9	0	1.73						

Separate League Awards

National League					American League				
Year	Gm	W-L	SV	ERA	Year	Gm	W-L	SV	ERA
1967 Mike McCormick, SF	40	22-10	0	2.85	1967 Jim Lonborg, Bos	39	22-9	0	3.16
1968 **Bob Gibson**, St.L	34	22-9	0	1.12	1968 **Denny McLain**, Det	41	31-6	0	1.96
1969 Tom Seaver, NY	36	25-7	0	2.21	1969 Denny McLain, Det	42	24-9	0	2.80
					& Mike Cuellar, Bal	39	23-11	0	2.38
1970 Bob Gibson, St.L	34	23-7	0	3.12	1970 Jim Perry, Min	40	24-12	0	3.03
1971 Ferguson Jenkins, Chi	39	24-13	0	2.77	1971 **Vida Blue**, Oak	39	24-8	0	1.82
1972 Steve Carlton, Phi	41	27-10	0	1.97	1972 Gaylord Perry, Cle	41	24-16	1	1.92
1973 Tom Seaver, NY	36	19-10	0	2.08	1973 Jim Palmer, Bal	38	22-9	1	2.40
1974 Mike Marshall, LA	106	15-12	21	2.42	1974 Catfish Hunter, Oak	41	25-12	0	2.49
1975 Tom Seaver, NY	36	22-9	0	2.38	1975 Jim Palmer, Bal	39	23-11	1	2.09
1976 Randy Jones, SD	40	22-14	0	2.74	1976 Jim Palmer, Bal	40	22-13	0	2.51
1977 Steve Carlton, Phi	36	23-10	0	2.64	1977 Sparky Lyle, NY	72	13-5	26	2.17
1978 Gaylord Perry, SD	37	21-6	0	2.72	1978 Ron Guidry, NY	35	25-3	0	1.74
1979 Bruce Sutter, Chi	62	6-6	37	2.23	1979 Mike Flanagan, Bal	39	23-9	0	3.08
1980 Steve Carlton, Phi	38	24-9	0	2.34	1980 Steve Stone, Bal	37	25-7	0	3.23
1981 Fernando Valenzuela, LA	25	13-7	0	2.48	1981 **Rollie Fingers**, Mil	47	6-3	28	1.04
1982 Steve Carlton, Phi	38	23-11	0	3.10	1982 Pete Vuckovich, Mil	30	18-6	0	3.34
1983 John Denny, Phi	36	19-6	0	2.37	1983 LaMarr Hoyt, Chi	36	24-10	0	3.66
1984 Rick Sutcliffe, Chi	20*	16-1	0	2.69	1984 **Willie Hernandez**, Det	80	9-3	32	1.92
1985 Dwight Gooden, NY	35	24-4	0	1.53	1985 Bret Saberhagen, KC	32	20-6	0	2.87
1986 Mike Scott, Hou	37	18-10	0	2.22	1986 **Roger Clemens**, Bos	33	24-4	0	2.48
1987 Steve Bedrosian, Phi	65	5-3	40	2.83	1987 Roger Clemens, Bos	36	20-9	0	2.97
1988 Orel Hershiser, LA	35	23-8	1	2.26	1988 Frank Viola, Min	35	24-7	0	2.64
1989 Mark Davis, SD	70	4-3	44	1.85	1989 Bret Saberhagen, KC	36	23-6	0	2.16
1990 Doug Drabek, Pit	33	22-6	0	2.76	1990 Bob Welch, Oak	35	27-6	0	2.95
1991 Tom Glavine, Atl	34	20-11	0	2.55	1991 Roger Clemens, Bos	35	18-10	0	2.62
1992 Greg Maddux, Chi	35	20-11	0	2.18	1992 **Dennis Eckersley**, Oak	69	7-1	51	1.91
1993 Greg Maddux, Atl	36	20-10	0	2.36	1993 Jack McDowell, Chi	34	22-10	0	3.37
1994 Greg Maddux, Atl	25	16-6	0	1.56	1994 David Cone, KC	23	16-5	0	2.94

*NL games only, Sutcliffe pitched 15 games with Cleveland before being traded to the Cubs.

ROOKIE OF THE YEAR

Voted on by the Baseball Writers Assn. of America. One award was presented from 1947-48. Two awards (one for each league) have been presented since 1949. Winner who was also named MVP is in **bold** type.

NL and AL Combined

Year		Pos	Year		Pos
1947	Jackie Robinson, Brooklyn	1B	1948	Alvin Dark, Boston-NL	SS

National League

Year		Pos	Year		Pos	Year		Pos
1949	Don Newcombe, Bklyn	P	1954	Wally Moon, St.L	OF	1960	Frank Howard, LA	OF
1950	Sam Jethroe, Bos	OF	1955	Bill Virdon, St.L	OF	1961	Billy Williams, Chi	OF
1951	Willie Mays, NY	OF	1956	Frank Robinson, Cin	OF	1962	Ken Hubbs, Chi	2B
1952	Joe Black, Bklyn	P	1957	Jack Sanford, Phi	P	1963	Pete Rose, Cin	2B
1953	Jim Gilliam, Bklyn	2B	1958	Orlando Cepeda, SF	1B	1964	Richie Allen, Phi	3B
			1959	Willie McCovey, SF	1B	1965	Jim Lefebvre, LA	2B

Annual Awards (Cont.)
Rookie of the Year
National League

Year		Pos	Year		Pos	Year		Pos
1966	Tommy Helms, Cin	3B	1976	Butch Metzger, SD	P	1985	Vince Coleman, St.L	OF
1967	Tom Seaver, NY	P		& Pat Zachry, Cin	P	1986	Todd Worrell, St.L	P
1968	Johnny Bench, Cin	C	1977	Andre Dawson, Mon	OF	1987	Benito Santiago, SD	C
1969	Ted Sizemore, LA	2B	1978	Bob Horner, Atl	3B	1988	Chris Sabo, Cin	3B
			1979	Rick Sutcliffe, LA	P	1989	Jerome Walton, Chi	OF
1970	Carl Morton, Mon	P						
1971	Earl Williams, Atl	C	1980	Steve Howe, LA	P	1990	David Justice, Atl	OF
1972	Jon Matlack, NY	P	1981	Fernando Valenzuela, LA	P	1991	Jeff Bagwell, Hou	1B
1973	Gary Matthews, SF	OF	1982	Steve Sax, LA	2B	1992	Eric Karros, LA	1B
1974	Bake McBride, St.L	OF	1983	Darryl Strawberry, NY	OF	1993	Mike Piazza, LA	C
1975	John Montefusco, SF	P	1984	Dwight Gooden, NY	P	1994	Raul Mondesi, LA	OF

American League

Year		Pos	Year		Pos	Year		Pos
1949	Roy Sievers, St.L	OF	1965	Curt Blefary, Bal	OF	1980	Joe Charboneau, Cle	OF-DH
			1966	Tommie Agee, Chi	OF	1981	Dave Righetti, NY	P
1950	Walt Dropo, Bos	1B	1967	Rod Carew, Min	2B	1982	Cal Ripken Jr., Bal	SS-3B
1951	Gil McDougald, NY	3B	1968	Stan Bahnsen, NY	P	1983	Ron Kittle, Chi	OF
1952	Harry Byrd, Phi	P	1969	Lou Piniella, KC	OF	1984	Alvin Davis, Sea	1B
1953	Harvey Kuenn, Det	SS				1985	Ozzie Guillen, Chi	SS
1954	Bob Grim, NY	P	1970	Thurman Munson, NY	C	1986	Jose Canseco, Oak	OF
1955	Herb Score, Cle	P	1971	Chris Chambliss, Cle	1B	1987	Mark McGwire, Oak	1B
1956	Luis Aparicio, Chi	SS	1972	Carlton Fisk, Bos	C	1988	Walt Weiss, Oak	SS
1957	Tony Kubek, NY	INF-OF	1973	Al Bumbry, Bal	OF	1989	Gregg Olson, Bal	P
1958	Albie Pearson, Wash	OF	1974	Mike Hargrove, Tex	1B			
1959	Bob Allison, Wash	OF	1975	**Fred Lynn**, Bos	OF	1990	Sandy Alomar Jr., Cle	C
			1976	Mark Fidrych, Det	P	1991	Chuck Knoblauch, Min	2B
1960	Ron Hansen, Bal	SS	1977	Eddie Murray, Bal	DH-1B	1992	Pat Listach, Mil	SS
1961	Don Schwall, Bos	P	1978	Lou Whitaker, Det	2B	1993	Tim Salmon, Cal	OF
1962	Tom Tresh, NY	SS-OF	1979	John Castino, Min	3B	1994	Bob Hamelin, KC	DH
1963	Gary Peters, Chi	P		& Alfredo Griffin, Tor	SS			
1964	Tony Oliva, Min	OF						

MANAGER OF THE YEAR

Voted on by the Baseball Writers Association of America. Two awards (one for each league) presented since 1983. Note that (*) indicates manager's team won division championship and (†) indicates unofficial division won in 1994.

Multiple winners: Tony La Russa (3); Sparky Anderson, Bobby Cox, Tommy Lasorda and Jim Leyland (2).

National League   American League

Year		Improvement			Year		Improvement		
1983	Tommy Lasorda, LA	88-74	to	91-71*	1983	Tony La Russa, Chi	87-75	to	99-63*
1984	Jim Frey, Chi	71-91	to	96-75*	1984	Sparky Anderson, Det	92-70	to	104-58*
1985	Whitey Herzog, St. L	84-78	to	101-61*	1985	Bobby Cox, Tor	89-73	to	99-62*
1986	Hal Lanier, Hou	83-79	to	96-66*	1986	John McNamara, Bos	81-81	to	95-66*
1987	Buck Rodgers, Mon	78-83	to	91-71	1987	Sparky Anderson, Det	87-75	to	98-64*
1988	Tommy Lasorda, LA	73-89	to	94-67*	1988	Tony La Russa, Oak	81-81	to	104-58*
1989	Don Zimmer, Chi	77-85	to	93-69*	1989	Frank Robinson, Bal	54-107	to	87-75
1990	Jim Leyland, Pit	74-88	to	95-67*	1990	Jeff Torborg, Chi	69-92	to	94-68
1991	Bobby Cox, Atl	65-97	to	94-68*	1991	Tom Kelly, Min	74-88	to	95-67*
1992	Jim Leyland, Pit	98-64*	to	96-66*	1992	Tony La Russa, Oak	84-78	to	96-66*
1993	Dusty Baker, SF	72-90	to	103-59	1993	Gene Lamont, Chi	86-76	to	94-68*
1994	Felipe Alou, Mon	94-68	to	74-40†	1994	Buck Showalter, NY	88-74	to	70-43†

George Steinbrenner's Managerial Merry-Go-Round

As managing general partner of the New York Yankees since 1973, George Steinbrenner has changed managers 20 times in 23 years. In that time, the Yankees have won four AL pennants (1976-78 and '81) and two World Series (1977-78). Note that (*) indicates interim status. Managers with multiple hitches are Billy Martin (5), and Bob Lemon, Gene Michael and Lou Piniella (2).

Tenure		W-L	Tenure		W-L	Tenure		W-L
Ralph Houk	1973	80-82	Gene Michael	1981	48-34	Lou Piniella	1986-87	179-145
Bill Virdon	1974-75	142-124	Bob Lemon	1981-82	17-22	Billy Martin	1988	40-28
Billy Martin	1975-78*	279-192	Gene Michael	1982	44-42	Lou Piniella	1988	45-48
Dick Howser	1978	0-1	Clyde King	1982	29-33	Dallas Green	1989	56-65
Bob Lemon	1978-79	82-51	Billy Martin	1983	91-71	Bucky Dent	1989-90	36-53
Billy Martin	1979	55-40	Yogi Berra	1984-85	93-85	Stump Merrill	1990-91	120-155
Dick Howser	1980	103-59	Billy Martin	1985	91-54	Buck Showalter	1992-95	313-268

COLLEGE BASEBALL

College World Series

The NCAA Division I College World Series has been held in Kalamazoo, Mich. (1947-48), Wichita, Kan. (1949) and Omaha, Neb. (since 1950).

Multiple winners: USC (11); Arizona St. (5); Texas (4); Arizona, CS-Fullerton and Minnesota (3); California, LSU, Miami-FL, Michigan, Oklahoma and Stanford (2).

Year	Winner	Coach	Score	Runner-up	Year	Winner	Coach	Score	Runner-up
1947	California	Clint Evans	8-7	Yale	1973	USC	Rod Dedeaux	4-3	Ariz. St.
1948	USC	Sam Barry	9-2	Yale	1974	USC	Rod Dedeaux	7-3	Miami, FL
1949	Texas	Bibb Falk	10-3	W. Forest	1975	Texas	Cliff Gustafson	5-1	S. Carolina
1950	Texas	Bibb Falk	3-0	Wash. St.	1976	Arizona	Jerry Kindall	7-1	E. Michigan
1951	Oklahoma	Jack Baer	3-2	Tennessee	1977	Arizona St.	Jim Brock	2-1	S. Carolina
1952	Holy Cross	Jack Barry	8-4	Missouri	1978	USC	Rod Dedeaux	10-3	Ariz. St.
1953	Michigan	Ray Fisher	7-5	Texas	1979	CS-Fullerton	Augie Garrido	2-1	Arkansas
1954	Missouri	Hi Simmons	4-1	Rollins	1980	Arizona	Jerry Kindall	5-3	Hawaii
1955	Wake Forest	Taylor Sanford	7-6	W. Mich.	1981	Arizona St.	Jim Brock	7-4	Okla. St.
1956	Minnesota	Dick Siebert	12-1	Arizona	1982	Miami-FL	Ron Fraser	9-3	Wichita St.
1957	California	Geo. Wolfman	1-0	Penn St.	1983	Texas	Cliff Gustafson	4-3	Alabama
1958	USC	Rod Dedeaux	8-7	Missouri	1984	CS-Fullerton	Augie Garrido	3-1	Texas
1959	Oklahoma St.	Toby Greene	5-3	Arizona	1985	Miami-FL	Ron Fraser	10-6	Texas
1960	Minnesota	Dick Siebert	2-1	USC	1986	Arizona	Jerry Kindall	10-2	Fla. St.
1961	USC	Rod Dedeaux	1-0	Okla. St.	1987	Stanford	M. Marquess	9-5	Okla. St.
1962	Michigan	Don Lund	5-4	S. Clara	1988	Stanford	M. Marquess	9-4	Ariz. St.
1963	USC	Rod Dedeaux	5-2	Arizona	1989	Wichita St.	G.Stephenson	5-3	Texas
1964	Minnesota	Dick Siebert	5-1	Missouri	1990	Georgia	Steve Webber	2-1	Okla. St.
1965	Arizona St.	Bobby Winkles	2-1	Ohio St.	1991	LSU	Skip Bertman	6-3	Wichita St.
1966	Ohio St.	Marty Karow	8-2	Okla. St.	1992	Pepperdine	Andy Lopez	3-2	CS-Fullerton
1967	Arizona St.	Bobby Winkles	11-2	Houston	1993	LSU	Skip Bertman	8-0	Wichita St.
1968	USC	Rod Dedeaux	4-3	So. Ill.	1994	Oklahoma	Larry Cochell	13-5	Ga. Tech
1969	Arizona St.	Bobby Winkles	10-1	Tulsa	1995	CS-Fullerton	Augie Garrido	11-5	USC
1970	USC	Rod Dedeaux	2-1	Fla. St.					
1971	USC	Rod Dedeaux	7-2	So. Ill.					
1972	USC	Rod Dedeaux	1-0	Ariz. St.					

Most Outstanding Players

The Most Outstanding Player has been selected every year of the College World Series since 1949. Winners who did not play for the CWS champion are listed in **bold** type. No player has won the award more than once.

Year		Year		Year	
1949	**Charles Teague**, W. Forest, 2B	1966	Steve Arlin, Ohio St., P	1982	Dan Smith, Miami-FL, P
1950	**Ray VanCleef**, Rutgers, CF	1967	Ron Davini, Ariz. St., C	1983	Calvin Schiraldi, Texas, P
1951	**Sidney Hatfield**, Tenn., P-1B	1968	Bill Seinsoth, USC, 1B	1984	John Fishel, CS-Fullerton, LF
1952	James O'Neill, Holy Cross, P	1969	John Dolinsek, Ariz. St., LF	1985	Greg Ellena, Miami-FL, LF
1953	**J.L. Smith**, Texas, P	1970	**Gene Ammann**, Fla. St., P	1986	Mike Senne, Arizona, DH
1954	**Tom Yewcic**, Mich. St., C	1971	**Jerry Tabb**, Tulsa, 1B	1987	Paul Carey, Stanford, RF
1955	**Tom Borland**, Okla. St., P	1972	Russ McQueen, USC, P	1988	Lee Plemel, Stanford, P
1956	Jerry Thomas, Minn., P	1973	**Dave Winfield**, Minn., P-OF	1989	Greg Brummett, Wich. St., P
1957	**Cal Emery**, Penn St., P-1B	1974	George Milke, USC, P		
1958	Bill Thom, USC, P	1975	Mickey Reichenbach, Texas, 1B	1990	Mike Rebhan, Georgia, P
1959	Jim Dobson, Okla. St., 3B	1976	Steve Powers, Arizona, P-DH	1991	Gary Hymel, LSU, C
1960	John Erickson, Minn., 2B	1977	Bob Horner, Ariz. St., 3B	1992	**Phil Nevin**, CS-Fullerton, 3B
1961	**Littleton Fowler**, Okla. St., P	1978	Rod Boxberger, USC, P	1993	Todd Walker, LSU, 2B
1962	**Bob Garibaldi**, Santa Clara, P	1979	Tony Hudson, CS-Fullerton, P	1994	Chip Glass, Oklahoma, OF
1963	Bud Hollowell, USC, C			1995	Mark Kotsay, CS-Fullerton, OF
1964	**Joe Ferris**, Maine, P	1980	Terry Francona, Arizona, LF		
1965	Sal Bando, Ariz. St., 3B	1981	Stan Holmes, Ariz. St., LF		

Annual Awards
Golden Spikes Award

First presented in 1978 by USA Baseball, honoring the nation's best amateur player. Alex Fernandez, the 1990 winner, has been the only junior college player chosen.

Year		Year		Year	
1978	Bob Horner, Ariz. St, 2B	1984	Oddibe McDowell, Ariz. St., OF	1990	Alex Fernandez, Miami-Dade, P
1979	Tim Wallach, CS-Fullerton, 1B	1985	Will Clark, Miss. St., 1B	1991	Mike Kelly, Ariz. St., OF
1980	Terry Francona, Arizona, OF	1986	Mike Loynd, Fla. St., P	1992	Phil Nevin, CS-Fullerton, 3B
1981	Mike Fuentes, Fla. St., OF	1987	Jim Abbott, Michigan, P	1993	Darren Dreifort, Wichita St., P
1982	Augie Schmidt, N. Orleans, SS	1988	Robin Ventura, Okla. St., 3B	1994	Jason Varitek, Ga. Tech, C
1983	Dave Magadan, Alabama, 1B	1989	Ben McDonald, LSU, P	1995	TBA (Nov. 14.)

Annual Awards (Cont.)
Baseball America Player of the Year

Presented to the College Player of the Year since 1981 by *Baseball America*.

Year		Year		Year	
1981	Mike Sodders, Ariz. St., 3B	1986	Casey Close, Michigan, OF	1991	David McCarty, Stanford, 1B
1982	Jeff Ledbetter, Fla. St., OF/P	1987	Robin Ventura, Okla. St., 3B	1992	Phil Nevin, CS-Fullerton, 3B
1983	Dave Magadan, Alabama, 1B	1988	John Olerud, Wash. St., 1B/P	1993	Brooks Kieschnick, Texas, DH/P
1984	Oddibe McDowell, Ariz. St., OF	1989	Ben McDonald, LSU, P	1994	Jason Varitek, Ga. Tech, C
1985	Pete Incaviglia, Okla. St., OF	1990	Mike Kelly, Ariz. St., OF	1995	Todd Helton, Tenn., 1B/P

Dick Howser Trophy

Presented to the College Player of the Year since 1987 by the American Baseball Coaches Association. Named after the late two-time All-America shortstop and college coach at Florida St., Howser was also a major league manager with Kansas City and the New York Yankees.

Multiple winner: Brooks Kieschnick (2).

Year		Year		Year	
1987	Mike Fiore, Miami-FL, OF	1990	Paul Ellis, UCLA, C	1993	Brooks Kieschnick, Texas, DH/P
1988	Robin Ventura, Okla. St., 3B	1991	Bobby Jones, Fresno St., P	1994	Jason Varitek, Ga. Tech, C
1989	Scott Bryant, Texas, DH	1992	Brooks Kieschnick, Texas, DH/P	1995	Todd Helton, Tenn., 1B/P

Baseball America Coach of the Year

Presented to the College Player of the Year since 1981 by *Baseball America*.

Multiple winner: Dave Snow and Gene Stephenson (2).

Year		Year		Year	
1981	Ron Fraser, Miami-FL	1987	Mark Marquess, Stanford	1993	Gene Stephenson, Wichita St.
1982	Gene Stephenson, Wichita St.	1988	Jim Brock, Arizona St.	1994	Jim Morris, Miami-FL
1983	Barry Shollenberger, Alabama	1989	Dave Snow, Long Beach St.	1995	Rob Delmonico, Tennessee
1984	Augie Garrido, CS-Fullerton	1990	Steve Webber, Georgia		
1985	Ron Polk, Mississippi St.	1991	Jim Hendry, Creighton		
1986	Skip Bertman, LSU	1992	Andy Lopez, Pepperdine		
	& Dave Snow, Loyola-CA				

All-Time Winningest Coaches

Coaches active in 1995 in **bold** type.

Top 10 Winning Percentage

(Minimum 10 years in Division I)

		Yrs	W	L	T	Pct
1	John Barry	40	619	147	6	.806
2	W.J. Disch	29	465	115	0	.802
3	**Cliff Gustafson**	28	1388	349	2	.799
4	Harry Carlson	17	143	41	0	.777
5	**Gene Stephenson**	18	1004	309	3	.764
6	**Gary Ward**	18	908	292	1	.756
7	George Jacobs	11	76	25	0	.752
	Bobby Winkles	13	524	173	0	.752
9	**Mike Martin**	16	867	296	3	.745
10	Frank Sancet	23	831	283	8	.744

Top 10 Victories

		Yrs	W	L	T	Pct
1	Cliff Gustafson	28	1388	349	2	.799
2	Rod Dedeaux	45	1332	571	11	.699
3	Ron Fraser	30	1271	438	9	.742
4	Bobo Brayton	33	1162	523	8	.690
	Al Ogletree	38	1162	661	10	.637
6	Bill Wilhelm	36	1161	536	10	.683
7	Jack Stallings	35	1127	697	5	.618
8	Augie Garrido	27	1107	508	7	.685
9	Chuck Hartman	36	1103	535	3	.673
10	Jim Brock	23	1100	440	0	.714

Other NCAA Champions
Divison II

Multiple winner: Florida Southern (8); Cal Poly Pomona (3); CS-Northridge, Jacksonville St., Tampa, Troy St., UC-Irvine and UC-Riverside (2).

Year		Year		Year		Year	
1968	Chapman, CA	1975	Florida Southern	1982	UC-Riverside	1989	Cal Poly SLO
1969	Illinois St.	1976	Cal Poly Pomona	1983	Cal Poly Pomona	1990	Jacksonville St., AL
1970	CS-Northridge	1977	UC-Riverside	1984	CS-Northridge	1991	Jacksonville St., AL
1971	Florida Southern	1978	Florida Southern	1985	Florida Southern	1992	Tampa
1972	Florida Southern	1979	Valdosta St., GA	1986	Troy St., AL	1993	Tampa
1973	UC-Irvine	1980	Cal Poly Pomona	1987	Troy St., AL	1994	Central Missouri St.
1974	UC-Irvine	1981	Florida Southern	1988	Florida Southern	1995	Florida Southern

Divison III

Multiple winner: Marietta (3); CS-Stanislaus, Eastern Conn. St., Glassboro St., Ithaca and Montclair St. (2).

Year		Year		Year		Year	
1976	CS-Stanislaus	1981	Marietta, OH	1986	Marietta, OH	1991	Southern Maine
1977	CS-Stanislaus	1982	Eastern Conn. St.	1987	Montclair St., NJ	1992	Wm. Paterson, NJ
1978	Glassboro St., NJ	1983	Marietta, OH	1988	Ithaca, NY	1993	Montclair St., NJ
1979	Glassboro St., NJ	1984	Ramapo, NJ	1989	NC-Wesleyan	1994	Wisconsin-Oshkosh
1980	Ithaca, NY	1985	Wisconsin-Oshkosh	1990	Eastern Conn. St.	1995	La Verne, CA

Head coach **Tom Osborne** is carried off the field New Year's Night after Nebraska defeated Miami, 24-17, to win the Orange Bowl and clinch Osborne's first national championship.

COLLEGE FOOTBALL

Finally!

After 22 seasons, Tom Osborne and Nebraska land the big one, rallying to win the Orange Bowl and claim the national title.

He was like Ahab, chasing Moby Dick with a stoic look on his face and a sharpened harpoon in his hand. Don't let Nebraska coach Tom Osborne tell you that after 22 seasons at the helm this business of winning his first national championship was "not that big a deal."

Don't let him tell you that as the top-ranked Cornhuskers prepared for their New Year's Night Orange Bowl battle with No. 3 Miami he didn't work a little harder and study film a little more closely looking for an edge against the favored Hurricanes.

Osborne needed an edge. He had inherited the Nebraska program from Bob Devaney in 1973 after the Huskers had won back-to-back national titles in 1970-71 and finished fourth in 1972 after whipping Notre Dame, 40-6, in the Orange Bowl. Since then, however, the postseason waters had yielded very few big fish for the Big Red.

Entering 1995, Osborne's teams had won 210 regular season games, but were 8-13 in bowl games. Worse than that, they were 1-7 in the Orange Bowl, 0-3 against Miami and riding a seven-game January 1st losing streak— including the 18-16 loss to Florida State in a 1994 showdown for the national title.

Now they faced Miami again at the Orange Bowl, where the hometown

Hurricanes had lost only two games in the last 10 years and where, on Jan. 1, 1984, the Canes had upset another unbeaten and top-ranked Nebraska team, 31-30, to win their first of four national titles.

This time, Miami jumped in front 10-0 by the end of the first quarter and entered the fourth with a 17-9 lead. It looked bad for Nebraska. After all, the Canes were the nation's top defensive team and prided themselves on owning the fourth quarter. But that's just when the edge Osborne had been counting on— Nebraska's superior conditioning— revealed itself.

"We had 23 or 24 December practices and had really conditioned ourselves hard," said Osborne. "We felt the fourth quarter would be ours."

Much less winded than their hosts, the Huskers dominated the final 15 minutes— moving the ball 102 yards on offense (83 yards on the ground) while the defense pushed Miami backwards for minus 37 yards. Inspired by the return of previously disabled quarterback Tommie Frazier and helped by Corey Schlesinger touchdown runs of 15 and 14 yards, Nebraska won, 24-17, to finish the season at 13-0.

Meanwhile, No. 2 Penn State, the undefeated Big Ten champion, was a 17-point favorite to beat No. 12 Oregon in the Rose Bowl, which had been rescheduled for Monday, Jan. 2, in deference to the opening round of the NFL playoffs. The Nittany Lions had been the nation's top-ranked team the last two weeks in October, but fell

Mark Blaudschun has been the national college football and basketball writer for *The Boston Globe* since 1990.

Simon Bruty/Allsport

Nebraska tight end **Mack Gilman** (right) is bowled over by Miami linebacker Ray Lewis after catching a 19-yard scoring pass from quarterback Brook Berringer at 7:06 of the second quarter. The touchdown pulled the Cornhuskers to within 10-7 at halftime of the Orange Bowl.

a notch after Nebraska's 24-7 victory over No. 2 Colorado on Oct. 29.

Back in 1992, before Penn State had ever played a game in the Big 10, head coach Joe Paterno figured PSU would fare much better in its new surroundings than it had as an independent. Mindful that three of his four unbeaten teams (in 1968, 1969 and 1973) had not won national championships, Paterno said, "I'm sure that with the prestige of the Big 10 Conference and the clout of the Rose Bowl, if we are unbeaten in the Big 10 and win the Rose Bowl, something like that won't happen."

No such luck, Joe.

Penn State beat Oregon as expected, 38-20, but finished a distant second to Nebraska in both the final Associated Press media poll and the final *USA Today*/CNN coaches poll.

Since the two best teams in the country did not play each other, naturally there was some debate as to the identity of the No. 1 college football team in 1994.

"Frankly, nobody deserves a national championship more than Tom Osborne," said Paterno prior to the bowls. "I will not be unhappy if Nebraska wins the national title, if that's the way it turns out." After the final polls were released, Paterno could only add, "We deserve it as much as they do."

Osborne's public utterances after beating Miami were not much different than after the Huskers beat Big Eight rival Colorado. "I know everybody wants me to say, 'Gee, everything's different,'" said Osborne. "But I feel about the same as after any game we won. I felt good about the way we played after we lost [to Florida State] last year."

Junior defensive tackle Christian Peter, who led Nebraska in regular season sacks with seven, was more to the point: "We got

149

the monkey off our backs," he said. "We got Miami in Miami. Case closed."

The preseason favorite for No. 1 was the University of Florida, which looked like the Team of the Decade in September, scoring 174 points in lopsided wins over New Mexico State (70-21) and SEC East rivals Kentucky (73-7) and Tennessee (31-0).

By Oct. 15, the Gators were 5-0 when they entertained No. 6 Auburn in Gainesville. Such was the hype surrounding coach Steve Spurrier's squad that even though the visiting Tigers were 6-0 and had yet to lose or even tie a game in two seasons under coach Terry Bowden, nobody gave them a chance.

Auburn entered The Swamp as a 17-point underdog and exited with a wild, come-from-behind, 36-33 victory that culminated in an eight-yard touchdown pass from Patrick Nix to Frank Sanders with 30 seconds left. The Tigers, serving the second year of a two-year NCAA probation, kept their winning streak alive until Nov. 12 when Georgia tied them in Athens, 23-23. A week later, they finally lost to unbeaten Alabama, 21-14, in Birmingham and ended their first two seasons under Bowden at 20-1-1.

Florida, meanwhile, reeled off four more victories before running into another Bowden, Terry's father Bobby and defending national champion Florida State at Tallahassee on Nov. 26. The Gators built a 31-3 lead over three quarters then watched their 28-point advantage disappear as the Seminoles salvaged a stunning 31-31 tie.

A week later, Florida bounced back to derail Alabama, 24-23, in the SEC championship game, clinching a Sugar Bowl berth and a rare same-season rematch with Florida State. The second time around, FSU had the lead going into the fourth quarter and held on to win, 23-17. The Seminoles (10-1-1) ended the season ranked fifth in both polls, the eighth straight year they've finished in the final Top 5.

Back to mid-October. In the wake of Auburn's victory over then-No. 1 Florida, the top three ranked teams in the AP poll were Penn State, Colorado and Nebraska. Of the three, the Cornhuskers had done the least heavy lifting, cruising past West Virginia, Texas Tech, UCLA and Pacific and rallying to beat Wyoming by 10

Coalition Gives Way to New Bowl Alliance

The face of college football changed dramatically in 1992 when the Bowl Coalition was formed to bring order out of chaos.

Made up of four major bowls (the Cotton, Fiesta, Orange and Sugar), five major conferences (the ACC, Big East, Big Eight, SEC and SWC) and one major independent (Notre Dame), the Coalition's mission was to arrange a national championship game without screwing up the bowl system with a playoff.

It also hoped to eliminate all the behind-closed-doors wheeling and dealing that had elevated bowl representatives into power brokers, who were extending invitations to schools before Halloween when there were still three or four regular season games to be played.

"We controlled the inventory," said Big East commissioner Mike Tranghese. "So we felt we should have more of a say in how things were done. Besides, the old way was absolutely crazy."

The new way was to wait until the first week in December to issue bowl invitations, thus creating the best possible matchups between conference champions.

There were two potential glitches. First of all, the Big Eight, SEC and SWC champions were committed to the Orange, Sugar and Cotton bowls, respectively. If teams from any of those conferences ended the regular season ranked No. 1 and No. 2, they couldn't meet.

Secondly, the Rose Bowl was not a Coalition member. The only way the Big Ten and Pac-10 champions could play for the national title was if they were the two top ranked teams in the country after the regular season and that hasn't been the case since 1968.

As it happened, Tranghese & Co. went two-for-three. Coalition teams met for the national championship in the 1993 Sugar Bowl (No. 2 Alabama beat No. 1 Miami) and the 1994 Orange Bowl (No. 2 Florida State beat No. 1 Nebraska). Last year, with No. 2 Penn State committed to the Rose Bowl, top-ranked Nebraska was obliged to play No. 3 Miami.

The new Bowl Alliance, which was formed on Aug. 4, 1994 and begins a six-year run this season, will involve the same five conference champions that the old Coalition did, as well as Notre Dame (provided the Irish are ranked in the Top 10). However, for the first

The **Fiesta Bowl** will host a national championship game between the top two teams in the country on Jan. 2, 1996, unless a Big Ten or Pac-10 team ranks first or second in the final regular season polls.

time in a generation the champions of the Big Eight, SEC and SWC will not be automatically locked into any one bowl.

Instead, the six qualifiers will be divided up between the Fiesta, Orange and Sugar bowls according to their national rank— the fourth and sixth ranked teams playing on Dec. 31 each year, the third and fifth ranked teams meeting on Jan. 1, and the No. 1 and No. 2 teams squaring off for the national championship on Jan. 2.

The title game will rotate among the Big Three bowls for the next three years, with the Fiesta playing host at the conclusion of the 1995 regular season followed by the Sugar and then the Orange.

Odd bowl out in this arrangement is the Cotton, which couldn't come up with the $100 million needed to make the Big Three. The Fiesta Bowl won the bidding war with an offer of approximately $115 million over six years, while the Sugar and Orange bowls qualified with bids of slightly more than $100 million each through 2000.

Per-team payouts will be enormous, dwarfing the $6.5 million Penn State and Oregon each picked up at the 1995 Rose Bowl. The two teams who play for all the marbles in the 1996 Fiesta Bowl will be paid approximately

$8.5 million each. The combatants in the Sugar and Orange bowls won't do poorly either, walking away with a little more than $8 million apiece.

The Alliance, however, is still missing one ally: the Rose Bowl, whose contract with the Big Ten and Pac-10 runs through 2000.

"Not having the Rose Bowl as part of the mix could create a problem" concedes Tranghese. "But we've built in a window of opportunity after three years where they could join, if the Pac-10 and Big 10 agree."

The addition of the Big Ten and Pac-10 champions as well as the Rose Bowl would complete the field.

"If you can get all the conference champions involved in this, you won't hear any more talk about a playoff," says one conference commissioner. "With the No. 1 playing No. 2 every year you won't need one."

In February, the NCAA removed another traditional roadblock to settling the national championship on the field when it announced that starting this year all bowl games will be required to use the tiebreaker.

Unlike the NFL, the NCAA's tiebreaker gives each team four downs to score from its opponent's 25-yard line. Both teams go at it until one side scores and the other doesn't.

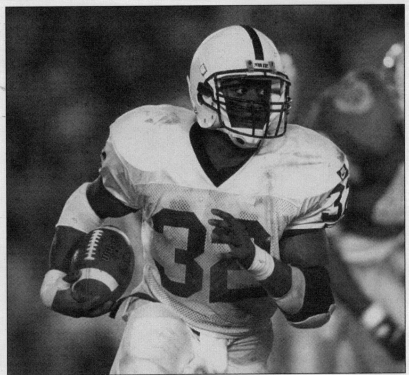

Junior running back **Ki-Jana Carter** of Penn State, who led the second-ranked Nittany Lions to an undefeated record, a Big Ten championship and a Rose Bowl victory over Oregon, finished second in the Heisman Trophy voting but was the overall first round pick in the 1995 NFL draft.

before getting into the Big Eight portion of their schedule.

They had also encountered some unexpected adversity when blood clots were discovered behind starting quarterback Frazier's right knee four games into the season. Surgery was necessary to correct the problem on Oct. 6, and the talented junior appeared to be lost for the year when doctors put him on blood thinners and prohibited strenuous physical activity for three to six months.

With Frazier on the shelf, the Huskers called on junior backup Brook Berringer and went right on winning.

The key victory came in the most anticipated game of the season— the Halloween weekend collision with Colorado in Lincoln. The Buffaloes (7-0) were on a run of their own and had attracted considerable No. 1 attention, thanks to three straight early-sea-

son victories over Wisconsin, Michigan and Texas.

A win over the Cornhuskers would move Colorado closer to, if not past, Penn State in the polls and put the Buffs in ideal position to win their second national title in four seasons under coach Bill McCartney. Colorado was confident. Maybe a little *too* confident. After their 35-21 win over Kansas State on Oct. 22, word got back to Nebraska that Buffs' quarterback Kordell Stewart had been running his mouth as well as his offense.

"He came in after that game and said, 'Okay, let's have some fun with the Nebraska defense next week,'" said Christian Peter of the Huskers. "That got back to us real quick. It wasn't a wise thing to say."

After fuming all week, Nebraska went out and roasted the Buffaloes, beating them for the third year in a row, 24-7. Berringer passed for 142 yards and a touchdown while sophomore tailback Lawrence Phillips rushed for 86 yards to offset the 134 yards piled up by Heisman Trophy front-runner Rashaan Salaam. The win catapulted the Huskers to the top of the AP poll as they inherited most of Colorado's support and edged Penn State in first-place votes (33-28), despite the Nittany Lions' 63-14 rout of Ohio State.

Colorado slipped to No. 7, but could still boast of the season's most spectacular play.

In an intersectional game against then-No. 4 Michigan on Sept. 24th in Ann Arbor, the Buffs were trailing the Wolverines, 26-21, with six seconds to go. They had the ball on their own 36 yard line with no timeouts. In the huddle, Colorado quarterback Stewart called "Jet Rocket Left," a desperation Hail Mary pass to wide receiver Michael Westbrook. Westbrook's assignment was to tip the ball toward the end zone, where it would hopefully be caught by a teammate.

Only it didn't work out that way. Stewart threw the ball as far as he could, but Westbrook had drifted too deep into the Michigan end zone. Amazingly, when he saw the ball coming down, Westbrook was behind all the Wolverine defenders and instead of tipping the ball, he leaped up and caught it for the 27-26 Colorado victory.

After the game someone asked Stewart if he remembered the 1984 Doug Flutie to Gerard Phelan pass that enabled Boston College to pull out a 47-45 late season win over Miami at the Orange Bowl.

"Sure," said Stewart. "That was the greatest play ever. It made history...Until today. Now history has happened twice."

While "The Play" left the state of Michigan in shock, it was nothing compared to the jolt the state of Colorado got on Nov. 19 when McCartney announced that he would resign after the Buffaloes' bowl game. He was the winningest coach in school history (92-55-5), but he said he needed to get away from the grind of college football and spend more time with his family.

On Nov. 28, Colorado officials bypassed 46-year-old black assistant head coach Bob Simmons and gave McCartney's job to Rick Neuheisel, 33, the team's quarterbacks and receivers coach. McCartney had recommended either Simmons or offensive coordinator Elliott Uzelac. Not surprisingly, Neuheisel's elevation was blasted by the Rev. Jesse Jackson and others, who pointed out that despite several qualified African-American candidates on college and pro coaching staffs, only three of the 107 schools in Division I-A had black head coaches.

Simmons, who elected to downplay the controversy, was named head coach at Oklahoma State on Dec. 16. By the end of the year, there were five black head coaches in Division I-A— Simmons, Jim Caldwell at Wake Forest, Ron Cooper at Louisville, Ron Dickerson at Temple and Tyrone Willingham at Stanford.

On the Heisman Trophy front, Colorado junior Salaam went from longshot on Labor Day to shoo-in by Thanksgiving, never rushing for less than 100 yards in any game and exceeding 200 yards on four occasions. A 259-yard effort against Iowa State in the final game of the regular season made him only the fourth player in NCAA history to gain 2,000 yards in one season. The others— Marcus Allen, Mike Rozier and Barry Sanders—all won Heismans. Salaam led the nation not only in rushing yards (2,055), but also in all-purpose yards (2,349) and scoring (144 points).

Salaam's primary competition for Player of the Year came from junior running back Ki-Jana Carter and senior quarterback Kerry Collins of Penn State, and record-setting Division I-AA senior quarterback Steve McNair of Alcorn State. Collins led the nation in passing efficiency with a rating of 172.9, while Carter was second in scoring, fourth in rushing and fifth in all-purpose running. McNair had the year's loftiest stats— 304 completions for 4,863 yards and 44 touchdowns, as well as a Division I-record 527.18 yards a game in total offense. He also benefited from a rave cover story in the Sept. 26th issue of *Sports Illustrated* ("Hand Him the Heisman"), but voters held his weak, I-AA competition against him.

Salaam won the award easily, receiving 400 first place votes— 73 more than Carter, McNair and Collins combined. After the bowl games, Salaam and Carter were among 33 juniors who gave up their senior year of eligibility and declared for the NFL draft. Carter was the overall first selection

Mike Powell/Allsport

Colorado running back **Rashaan Salaam** ran away with the Heisman Trophy as a junior after becoming only the fourth player in NCAA history to rush for over 2,000 yards in a single season.

and went to Cincinnati, while Salaam, the 21st pick, was chosen by Chicago. Seniors McNair and Collins were the third and fifth picks, respectively— McNair going to Houston and Collins to Carolina.

If there was a mystery during the season it was "What Happened to Notre Dame?" After finishing No. 2 in 1993, the Irish were a consensus Top 5 choice in most 1994 preseason publications. The positive vibes emanating from South Bend centered around sophomore quarterback Ron Powlus, who missed the entire 1993 season with a cracked right collarbone and was making his college debut with more publicity and pressure than almost any player in the history of the game. Television analysts said he was going to lead ND to a couple of national titles and maybe win one or two Heismans before he was through.

Powlus opened the season with four touchdown passes in a 42-15 romp over Northwestern. Still, for once in his life, coach Lou Holtz was right when he said his team wasn't that good. They were inexperienced along the offensive line as well as at

quarterback. They also had injury problems for most of the season.

Notre Dame lost its second start, dropping a 26-24 decision to Michigan on a last second field goal at home. By Oct. 8, the Irish were 4-1, but had slipped to eighth in the AP poll. Then the roof fell in. In their next six games, the Irish went 2-3-1 with losses to Boston College (30-10), Brigham Young (21-14) and Florida State (23-16) and a tie with Southern Cal (17-17).

By the time the regular season ended, Notre Dame was barely above .500 and getting hammered in the press and on the radio talk shows for accepting a Bowl Coalition arrangement that sent them to the Fiesta Bowl to face Colorado. The Irish were hammered again in Tempe, losing 41-24, to end the season at 6-5-1. It was their worst record since going 5-6 the year Holtz arrived in 1986.

Three coaches with national titles to their credit and one with three Super Bowl rings all quit the ranks or took new jobs in 1994. Dennis Erickson left Miami after six seasons and two titles to accept a five-year, $5 million offer to revive the NFL's Seattle Seahawks. Howard Schnellenberger, who led Miami to its first title in 1983, walked away from the relative quiet of Louisville for the fast lane at Oklahoma. And former San Francisco 49ers mastermind Bill Walsh joined McCartney of Colorado in retirement after a three-year comeback at Stanford ended with a disappointing 3-7-1 season.

Two venerable bowls faced oblivion of one kind or another at the close of the season as the Bowl Coalition gave way to the Bowl Alliance (see page 150).

Following Southern Cal's 55-14 rout of Texas Tech, the Cotton Bowl ceased to be a major bowl game for the first time since its inception in 1937. Meanwhile, the Orange Bowl game will be leaving Miami's inner city for to the suburbs after one more New Year's in the national spotlight. Organizers will abandon the Orange Bowl stadium after 62 years for Joe Robbie Stadium in 1997.

And finally, after 22 years and 269 games, Tom Osborne could enter a new season without wondering if he'd ever win a national championship. He and Nebraska won it all in 1994 .

Capt. Ahab's chase was over.   ❑

THE 1996 SPORTS ALMANAC
INFORMATION PLEASE

COLLEGE FOOTBALL
S T A T I S T I C S

SEC
A

THE SEASON IN REVIEW
1994-1995
TOP 25 • BOWLS • STANDINGS

PAGE
155

Final AP Top 25 Poll

Voted on by panel of 62 sportswriters & broadcasters following Jan. 2, 1995 bowl games: winning team receives the Bear Bryant Trophy, given since 1983; first place votes in parentheses, records, total points (based on 25 for 1st, 24 for 2nd, etc.) bowl game result, head coach and career record, preseason rank (released on Aug. 21) and final regular season rank (released Dec. 4, 1994).

		Final Record	Points	Bowl Game	Head Coach	Aug.19 Rank	Dec.4 Rank
1	Nebraska (51½)	13-0-0	1539½	won Orange	Tom Osborne (22 yrs: 219-47-3)	4	1
2	Penn St. (10½)	12-0-0	1497½	won Rose	Joe Paterno (29 yrs: 269-69-3)	9	2
3	Colorado	11-1-0	1410	won Fiesta	Bill McCartney (13 yrs: 93-55-5)	8	4
4	Florida St	10-1-1	1320	won Sugar	Bobby Bowden (29 yrs: 249-79-4)	3	7
5	Alabama	12-1-0	1312	won Citrus	Gene Stallings (12 yrs: 79-55-2)	12	6
6	Miami-FL	10-2-0	1249	lost Orange	Dennis Erickson (13 yrs: 113-40-1)	6	3
7	Florida	10-2-1	1153	lost Sugar	Steve Spurrier (8 yrs: 69-25-2)	1	5
8	Texas A&M	10-0-1	1117	on probation	R.C. Slocum (6 yrs: 59-12-2)	15	8
9	Auburn	9-1-1	1110	on probation	Terry Bowden (11 yrs: 84-37-2)	11	9
10	Utah	10-2-0	955	won Freedom	Ron McBride (5 yrs: 34-26-0)	42t	14
11	Oregon	9-4-0	810	lost Rose	Rich Brooks (18 yrs: 91-109-4)	NR	12
12	Michigan	8-4-0	732	won Holiday	Gary Moeller (8 yrs: 50-37-6)	5	20
13	USC	8-3-1	691	won Cotton	John Robinson (9 yrs: 83-22-3)	17	21
14	Ohio St	9-4-0	672	lost Citrus	John Cooper (18 yrs: 135-67-6)	20	13
15	Virginia	9-3-0	648	won Independence	George Welsh (22 yrs: 144-105-4)	29	18
16	Colorado St	10-2-0	630	lost Holiday	Sonny Lubick (6 yrs: 36-27-0)	NR	10
17	N.C. State	9-3-0	511	won Peach	Mike O'Cain (2 yrs: 16-8-0)	NR	23
18	BYU	10-3-0	500	won Copper	LaVell Edwards (23 yrs: 207-76-3)	27	22
19	Kansas St	9-3-0	496	lost Aloha	Bill Snyder (6 yrs: 36-31-1)	31	11
20	Arizona	8-4-0	364	lost Freedom	Dick Tomey (18 yrs: 117-81-7)	7	15
21	Washington St	8-4-0	344	won Alamo	Mike Price (14 yrs: 81-77-0)	NR	24
22	Tennessee	8-4-0	303	won Gator	Phillip Fulmer (3 yrs: 21-6-1)	13	26
23	Boston College	7-4-1	236	won Aloha	Dan Henning (1 yr: 7-4-1)	30	28
24	Mississippi St	8-4-0	160	lost Peach	Jackie Sherrill (17 yrs: 130-65-4)	36	16
25	Texas	8-4-0	90	won Sun	John Mackovic (10 yrs: 63-50-2)	18	NR

Other teams receiving votes: 26. **Virginia Tech** (8-4-0, 75 points, lost Gator); 27. **North Carolina** (8-4-0, 65 pts, lost Sun); 28. **Wisconsin** (7-4-1, 54 pts, won Hall of Fame); 29. **Illinois** (7-5-0, 45 pts, won Liberty); 30. **Washington** (7-4-0, 41 pts, ineligible for bowl); 31. **Duke** (8-4-0, 9 pts, lost Hall of Fame); 32. **Syracuse** (7-4-0, 7 pts, no bowl); 33. **Air Force** (8-4-0, 2 pts, no bowl) and **South Carolina** (7-5-0, 2 pts, won Carquest).

AP Preseason and Final Regular Season Polls

First place votes in parentheses.

Top 25 (Aug.19, 1994)

		Pts
1	Florida (15)	1416
2	Notre Dame (13)	1414
3	Florida St. (10)	1407
4	Nebraska (18)	1398
5	Michigan (2)	1283
6	Miami-FL (1)	1190
7	Arizona (2)	1070
8	Colorado	1057
9	Penn St.	1012
10	Wisconsin	932
11	Auburn	924
12	Alabama (1)	923
13	Tennessee	793
14	UCLA	661
15	Texas A&M	603
16	Oklahoma	560
17	USC	557
18	Texas	527
19	North Carolina	526
20	Ohio St	320
21	Illinois	249
22	Virginia Tech	235
23	Washington	181
24	West Virginia	121
25	Clemson	113

Top 25 (Dec. 4, 1994)

		Pts
1	Nebraska (38)	1526
2	Penn St. (24)	1511
3	Miami-FL	1398
4	Colorado	1345
5	Florida	1313
6	Alabama	1217
7	Florida St	1211
8	Texas A&M	1081
9	Auburn	1059
10	Colorado St	968
11	Kansas St	943
12	Oregon	916
13	Ohio St	751
14	Utah	700
15	Arizona	625
16	Mississippi St	560
17	Virginia Tech	486
18	Virginia	416
19	North Carolina	402
20	Michigan	372
21	USC	355
22	BYU	237
23	N.C. State	222
24	Washington St	186
25	Duke	99

1994-95 Bowl Games

Listed by bowls matching highest-ranked teams as of final regular season AP poll (released Dec. 4, 1994). Texas A&M (No. 8) and Auburn (No. 9) were on probation and ineligible for postseason play.

Bowl		Winner	Regular Season		Loser	Regular Season	Score	Date	Attendance
Orange	# 1	Nebraska	12-0-0	# 3	Miami-FL	10-1-0	24-17	Jan. 1	81,753
Rose	# 2	Penn St.	11-0-0	#12	Oregon	9-3-0	38-20	Jan. 2	102,247
Fiesta	# 4	Colorado	10-1-0		Notre Dame	6-4-1	41-24	Jan. 2	73,968
Sugar	# 7	Florida St.	9-1-1	# 5	Florida	10-1-1	23-17	Jan. 2	76,224
Citrus	# 6	Alabama	11-1-0	#13	Ohio St.	9-3-0	24-17	Jan. 2	71,195
Holiday	#20	Michigan	7-4-0	#10	Colorado St.	10-1-0	24-14	Dec. 30	59,453
Aloha		Boston College	6-4-1	#11	Kansas St.	9-2-0	12-7	Dec. 25	44,862
Freedom	#14	Utah	9-2-0	#15	Arizona	8-3-0	16-13	Dec. 27	27,477
Peach	#23	N.C. State	8-3-0	#16	Miss. St.	7-4-0	28-24	Jan. 1	64,902
Gator		Tennessee	7-4-0	#17	Virginia Tech	8-3-0	45-23	Dec. 30	62,200
Independence	#18	Virginia	8-3-0		TCU	7-4-0	20-10	Dec. 28	27,242
Sun		Texas	7-4-0	#19	North Carolina	8-3-0	35-31	Dec. 30	50,612
Cotton		USC	7-3-1		Texas Tech	6-5-0	55-14	Jan. 2	70,218
Copper	#21	BYU	9-3-0		Oklahoma	6-5-0	31-6	Dec. 29	45,122
Alamo	#22	Washington St.	7-4-0		Baylor	7-4-0	10-3	Dec. 31	44,106
Hall/Fame		Wisconsin	6-4-1	#25	Duke	8-3-0	34-20	Jan. 2	61,384
Carquest		South Carolina	6-5-0		West Virginia	7-5-0	24-21	Jan. 2	50,833
Liberty		Illinois	6-5-0		East Carolina	7-4-0	30-0	Dec. 31	33,280
Las Vegas		UNLV	6-5-0		Central Mich.	9-2-0	52-24	Dec. 15	17,562

Per Team Payouts

Rose ($6.5 million each); **Federal Express Orange** ($4.5 million); **USF&G Insurance Sugar** ($4.45 million); **Mobil Cotton** and **IBM OS/2 Fiesta** ($3 million); **CompUSA Florida Citrus** ($2.5 million); **Thrifty Car Rental Holiday** ($1.7 million); **Outback Steakhouse Gator** ($1.5 million); **Peach** ($1.13 million); **Sun** ($1.1 million); **Carquest** and **Hall of Fame** ($1 million); **Builders Square Alamo, Jeep Eagle Aloha, Weiser Lock Copper, Poulan/Weed Eater Independence** and **St. Jude Liberty** ($750,000); **Freedom** ($700,000); **Las Vegas** ($228,000).

Final Bowl Coalition Poll

Combined point totals of the final regular season AP media and USA/CNN coaches' polls to determine bowl match-ups and released Dec. 4, 1994.

Although Texas A&M and Auburn were on probation and ineligible for the coaches' poll, their AP points totals were doubled in the coalition poll.

		AP Poll		Coaches		Total
		No.	Pts	No.	Pts	Pts
1	Nebraska	1	(1526)	1	(1532)	3058
2	Penn St	2	(1511)	2	(1505)	3016
3	Miami-FL	3	(1398)	3	(1406)	2804
4	Colorado	4	(1345)	5	(1317)	2662
5	Florida	5	(1313)	4	(1325)	2638
6	Alabama	6	(1217)	6	(1235)	2452
7	Florida St	7	(1211)	7	(1218)	2429
8	Texas A&M	8	(1081)	—		2162
9	Auburn	9	(1059)	—		2118
10	Kansas St	11	(943)	8	(1076)	2019
11	Oregon	12	(916)	9	(1051)	1967
12	Colorado St	10	(968)	10	(976)	1944
13	Ohio St	13	(751)	11	(915)	1666
14	Utah	14	(700)	12	(792)	1492
15	Arizona	15	(625)	13	(766)	1391
16	Va. Tech	17	(486)	15	(641)	1127
17	N. Carolina	19	(402)	14	(693)	1095
18	Miss. St	16	(560)	17	(523)	1083
19	Virginia	18	(416)	16	(572)	988
20	Michigan	20	(372)	18	(460)	832
21	BYU	22	(237)	19	(454)	691
22	USC	21	(355)	22	(305)	660
23	N.C. State	23	(222)	20	(376)	598
24	Duke	25	(99)	21	(352)	451
25	Wash. St	24	(186)	23	(261)	447

Bowl MVPs

Most Valuable Player, Offensive and Defensive Players of the Game, and Team MVP selections in all 19 bowl games of the 1994 season.

		Pos
Alamo	Off— Chad Davis, Wash. St.	QB
	Def— Ron Childs, Wash. St.	LB
Aloha	MVP— Mike Mamula, Boston Col.	LB
Carquest	MVP— Steve Taneyhill, S. Carolina	QB
Copper	MVP— John Walsh, BYU	QB
Cotton	Off— Keyshawn Johnson, USC	WR
	Def— John Herpin, USC	CB
Fiesta	Off— Kordell Stewart, Colo.	QB
	Def— Shannon Clavelle, Colo.	DT
Fla. Citrus	MVP— Sherman Williams, Alabama	RB
Freedom	Team— Cal Beck, Utah	KR
	Team— Tedy Bruschi, Arizona	DE
Gator	MVP— James Stewart, Tennessee	RB
Hall of Fame	MVP— Terrell Fletcher, Wisconsin	RB
Holiday	Off— Anthoney Hill, Colo. St.	QB
	& Todd Collins, Michigan	QB
	Def— Matt Dyson, Michigan	LB
Independence	Off— Mike Groh, Virginia	QB
	Def— Mike Frederick, Virginia	DE
Las Vegas	MVP— Henry Bailey, UNLV	WR
Liberty	MVP— Johnny Johnson, Illinois	QB
Orange	Team— Tommie Frazier, Nebraska	QB
	Team— Chris T. Jones, Miami-FL	WR
Peach	Off— Tremayne Stephens, N.C. St.	TB
	& Tim Rogers, Miss. St.	PK
	Def— Carl Reeves, N.C. State	DT
	Damien Covington, N.C. State	LB
	& Larry Williams, Miss. St.	DL
Rose	Team— Danny O'Neil, Oregon	QB
	Team— Ki-Jana Carter, Penn St.	RB
Sugar	MVP— Warrick Dunn, Florida St.	TB
Sun	MVP— Priest Holmes, Texas	RB

The Top Two

Opponents' records and AP rank are day of game.

Nebraska Cornhuskers (13-0-0)

Date	AP Rank	Opponent	Result
Aug. 28	#4	vs #24 West Virginia* (0-0)	31- 0
Sept. 3	#2	OPEN DATE	
Sept. 8	#1	at Texas Tech (1-0)	42-16
Sept. 17	#2	#13 UCLA (2-0)	49-21
Sept. 24	#2	Pacific (2-1)	70-21
Oct. 1	#2	Wyoming (2-2)	42-32
Oct. 8	#2	Oklahoma St. (3-1)	32- 3
Oct. 15	#2	at #16 Kansas St. (4-0)	17- 6
Oct. 22	#3	at Missouri (2-4)	42- 7
Oct. 29	#3	#2 Colorado (7-0)	24- 7
Nov. 5	#1	Kansas (5-3)	45-17
Nov. 12	#1	at Iowa St. (0-8-1)	28-12
Nov. 19	#1	OPEN DATE	
Nov. 25	#1	at Oklahoma (6-4)	13- 3
Jan. 1	#1	vs #3 Miami-FL‡ (10-1)	24-17

*Kickoff Classic (at East Rutherford, N.J.) †Orange Bowl (at Miami)

Regular Season Statistics

Passing (5 Att)
	Att	Cmp	Pct	Yds	TD	Rate
Brook Berringer	151	94	62.3	1295	10	149.5
Matt Turman	12	6	50.0	81	1	134.2
Tommie Frazier	44	19	43.2	273	4	116.2

Interceptions: Berringer 5, Frazier 2.

Top Receivers
	No	Yds	Avg	Long	TD
Abdul Muhammad	23	360	15.7	44	2
Lawrence Phillips	22	172	7.8	27	0
Reggie Baul	17	300	17.7	51-td	3
Mark Gilman	17	196	11.5	48	1
Eric Alford	14	271	19.4	46-td	4

Top Rushers
	Car	Yds	Avg	Long	TD
Lawrence Phillips	286	1722	6.0	74-td	16
Cory Schlesinger	63	456	7.2	41	4
Clinton Childs	62	395	6.4	30-td	5
Damon Benning	67	367	5.5	23	5
Jeff Makovicka	47	321	6.8	50	2
Brook Berringer	71	279	3.9	28	6
Tommie Frazier	33	248	7.5	58-td	6

Most Touchdowns
	TD	Run	Rec	Ret	Pts
Lawrence Phillips	16	16	0	0	96
Tommie Frazier	6	6	0	0	40*
Brook Berringer	6	6	0	0	36
Damon Benning	5	5	0	0	30
Clinton Childs	5	5	0	0	30

*Includes two 2-pt. conversion runs.

Kicking
	FG/Att	Lg	PAT/Att	Pts
Darin Erstad	3/8	48	10/10	21*
Tom Sieler	4/6	35	40/42	52

*Includes one 2-pt. conversion catch.

Punting (10 or more)
	No	Yds	Long	Blk	Avg
Darin Erstad	50	2130	73	0	42.6

Most Interceptions
Barron Miles 5

Most Sacks
Christian Peter 7

Orange Bowl

Sunday night, Jan. 1, 1995 at Miami.

#1 Nebraska (Big 8)	0	7	2	15	**24**
#3 Miami-FL (Big East)	10	0	7	0	**17**

Favorite: Miami-FL by 1 **Attendance:** 81,753 (record)
Field: Grass **Time:** 3:44
Weather: 74, Mixed **TV Rating:** 18.9/31 share (NBC)

Touchdowns: NEB— Cory Schlesinger (2), Mark Gilman; MIA— Jonathan Harris, Trent Jones. **Field Goal:** MIA— Dane Prewitt (44 yds). **Top Rusher:** Lawrence Phillips, NEB (19 for 96 yds). **Top Passer:** Frank Costa, MIA (18 of 35 for 248 yds, 2 TDs, 1 INT).

Penn St. Nittany Lions (12-0-0)

Date	AP Rank	Opponent	Result
Sept. 4	#9	North Texas* (0-0)	76-14
Sept. 3	#9	at Minnesota (0-0)	56- 3
Sept. 10	#8	#14 USC (1-0)	38-14
Sept. 17	#6	Iowa (2-0)	61-21
Sept. 24	#5	Rutgers (2-1)	55-27
Oct. 1	#4	at Temple (2-1)*	48-21
Oct. 8	#4	OPEN DATE	
Oct. 15	#3	at #5 Michigan (4-1)	31-24
Oct. 22	#1	OPEN DATE	
Oct. 29	#1	#21 Ohio St. (6-2)	63-14
Nov. 5	#2	at Indiana (5-3)	35-29
Nov. 12	#2	at Illinois (6-3)	35-31
Nov. 19	#2	Northwestern (3-6-1)	45-17
Nov. 26	#2	Michigan St. (5-5)	59-31
Jan. 2	#2	vs #12 Oregon† (9-3)	38-20

*at Franklin Field in Philadelphia †Rose Bowl (at Pasadena)

Regular Season Statistics

Passing (5 Att)
	Att	Cmp	Pct	Yds	TD	Rate
Kerry Collins	264	176	66.7	2679	21	172.9
Wally Richardson	33	16	48.5	177	0	93.5

Interceptions: Collins 7.

Top Receivers
	No	Yds	Avg	Long	TD
Bobby Engram	52	1029	19.8	63	7
Freddie Scott	47	973	20.7	82-td	9
Kyle Brady	27	365	13.5	41	2
Mike Archie	22	215	9.8	47	2
Brian Milne	15	78	5.2	14	0
Ki-Jana Carter	14	123	8.8	32	0

Top Rushers
	Car	Yds	Avg	Long	TD
Ki-Jana Carter	198	1539	7.8	80-td	23
Mike Archie	52	303	5.8	35-td	5
Brian Milne	56	267	4.8	49	8
Jon Witman	49	241	4.9	17	5
Stephen Pitts	33	189	5.7	26	0

Most Touchdowns
	TD	Run	Rec	Ret	Pts
Ki-Jana Carter	23	23	0	0	138
Freddie Scott	9	0	9	0	58*
Brian Milne	8	8	0	0	48
Mike Archie	7	5	2	0	44†
Bobby Engram	7	7	0	0	42
Jon Witman	6	5	1	0	36

*Includes two 2-pt. conversion catches.
†Includes one 2-pt. conversion catch.

Kicking
	FG/Att	Lg	PAT/Att	Pts
Brett Conway	10/12	49	62/63	92

Punting (10 or more)
	No	Yds	Long	Blk	Avg
Darrell Kania	23	849	52	0	36.9
Joe Jurevicius	15	553	51	0	36.9

Most Interceptions
Brian Miller 4

Most Sacks
Willie Smith 7

Rose Bowl

Monday afternoon, Jan. 2, 1995 at Pasadena

#2 Penn St. (Big 10)	7	7	14	10	**38**
#12 Oregon (Pac-10)	7	0	7	6	**20**

Favorite: Penn St. by 17 **Attendance:** 102,247
Field: Grass **Time:** 3:41
Weather: 67, Sunny **TV Rating:** 18.2/30 share (ABC)

Touchdowns: PSU— Ki-Jana Carter (3), Brian Milne, Jon Witman; ORE— Cristin McLemore, Ricky Whittle, Josh Wilcox. **Field Goal:** PSU— Brett Conway (43 yds). **Top Rusher:** Carter, PSU (21 for 156 yds, TD runs of 83, 17, 3). **Top Passer:** Danny O'Neil (41 of 61 for 456 yds, 2 TDs, 2 INTs).

Other Division I-A Final Polls

USA Today/CNN Coaches Poll

Voted on by panel of 62 Division I-A head coaches; winning team receives the Sears Trophy (originally the McDonald's Trophy, 1991-93); first place votes in parentheses with total points (based on 25 for 1st, 24 for 2nd, etc.).

	Pts		Pts
1 Nebraska (54)	1542	14 Colorado St	690
2 Penn St. (8)	1496	15 USC	670
3 Colorado	1387	16 Kansas St	657
4 Alabama	1345	17 N.C. State	627
5 Florida St	1325	18 Tennessee	517
6 Miami-FL	1231	19 Washington St	453
7 Florida	1182	20 Arizona	402
8 Utah	1034	21 North Carolina	312
9 Ohio St	846	22 Boston College	301
10 BYU	840	23 Texas	250
11 Oregon	834	24 Virginia Tech	188
12 Michigan	797	25 Mississippi St	149
13 Virginia	777		

Other teams receiving votes: Wisconsin (96 pts); Illinois (91); Duke (51); Syracuse (20); Air Force (19); South Carolina (14); Bowling Green (4); West Virginia (2); TCU (1). **Teams on probation** (and ineligible to receive votes): Auburn, Texas A&M and Washington.

NFF/Hall of Fame Poll

Voted on by panel of 62 members of the National Football Foundation and College Hall of Fame; winning team receives the NFF's MacArthur Bowl, given since 1959: first place votes in parentheses with total points (based on 25 for 1st, 24 for 2nd, etc.).

	Pts		Pts
1 Nebraska (48)	1536	14 USC	688
2 Penn St. (14)	1502	15 BYU	686
3 Alabama	1364	16 Michigan	667
4 Colorado	1350	17 N.C. State	650
5 Florida St	1316	18 Arizona	504
6 Miami-FL	1222	19 Tennessee	426
7 Florida	1204	20 Washington St	398
8 Utah	1032	21 Boston College	282
9 Oregon	958	22 Mississippi St	280
10 Ohio St	904	23 North Carolina	270
11 Virginia	794	24 Virginia Tech	228
12 Colorado St	730	25 Texas	122
13 Kansas St	706		

Teams on probation (and ineligible to receive votes): Auburn, Texas A&M and Washington.

FWAA Poll

Voted on by five-man panel comprised of Ed Sherman and Andy Bagnato of the *Chicago Tribune*; Mark Blaudschun of *The Boston Globe*; Ivan Maisel of *Newsday*; and Gene Wojciechowski of the *LA Times*. Each selector selects three teams in order of preference (three points for 1st, two for 2nd and one for 3rd); winning team receives the Grantland Rice Award, given since 1954.

	1st	2nd	3rd	Pts
1 Nebraska	5	0	0 —	15
2 Penn St.	0	5	0 —	10
3 Colorado	0	0	5 —	5

NY Times Computer Ratings

Based on an analysis of each team's scores with emphasis on three factors: who won, by what margin, and against what quality of opposition. Computer balances lop-sided scores, notes home field advantage and gives late-season games more weight than those played earlier in the schedule. The top team is assigned a rating of 1.000, ratings of all other teams reflect their strength relative to strength of No.1 team.

	Rating		Rating
1 Penn St.	1.000	14 Virginia	.772
2 Nebraska	.979	15 Colorado St	.761
3 Florida St	.940	16 Oregon	.743
4 Colorado	.917	17 Kansas St	.737
5 Florida	.883	18 N.C. State	.734
6 Texas A&M	.872	19 Ohio St	.729
7 Alabama	.864	20 BYU	.723
8 Miami-FL	.858	21 Illinois	.719
9 Tennessee	.832	22 Boston College	.717
10 Auburn	.822	Wisconsin	.717
11 Utah	.818	24 Washington St	.714
12 Michigan	.804	25 Texas	.709
13 USC	.800		

Top 30 Teams Over Last 5 Years

Division I-A schools with the best overall winning percentage over the last five seasons (1990-94), through the bowl games of Jan. 2, 1995.

National champions: 1990— Colorado (AP, FWAA, NFF) and Georgia Tech (UPI); 1991— Miami-FL (AP) and Washington (FWAA, NFF, USA Today/CNN); 1992— Alabama; 1993— Florida St; 1994— Nebraska.

	Overall Record	Bowls Record	Overall Win Pct
1 Florida St	54- 7-1	5-0-0	.879
2 Miami-FL	52- 8-0	2-3-0	.867
3 Texas A&M	51- 8-2	1-3-0	.852
4 Nebraska	51- 9-1	1-4-0	.844
5 Alabama	52-10-2	4-1-0	.828
6 Colorado	47-10-4	3-2-0	.803
Penn State	49-12-0	3-2-0	.803
8 Florida	49-12-1	2-2-0	.798
9 Washington	45-13-0	2-1-0	.776
10 Notre Dame	46-13-3	3-2-0	.766
11 Michigan	43-13-3	4-1-0	.754
12 Tennessee	44-14-3	3-2-0	.746
13 Ohio State	42-16-3	1-4-0	.713
14 Auburn	38-15-3	1-0-0	.705
15 Syracuse	40-16-3	3-0-0	.703
16 North Carolina	40-18-1	1-2-0	.686
17 N.C.State	41-19-1	2-3-0	.680
18 Fresno State	40-19-2	1-2-0	.672
19 BYU	42-20-2	1-3-1	.672
20 Virginia	39-19-1	1-3-0	.669
21 Clemson	38-19-1	2-1-0	.664
22 Oklahoma	37-19-2	2-1-0	.655
23 Kansas State	35-21-1	1-1-0	.623
Central Michigan	33-19-5	0-2-0	.623
25 Texas	34-22-1	1-1-0	.605
Georgia	34-22-1	2-0-0	.605
27 Arizona	35-23-1	1-3-0	.602
28 Iowa	34-23-2	0-2-1	.593
29 Air Force	36-25-0	2-1-0	.590
30 West Virginia	33-23-2	0-2-0	.586

☞ See pages 168-170 for list of all national championship teams since 1869. Also, see pages 172-186 for every Associated Press final Top 20 poll since 1936.

NCAA Division I-A Final Standings

Standings based on conference games only; overall records include postseason games.

Atlantic Coast Conference

	Conference				Overall			
	W	L	T	PF	PA	W	L	T	PF	PA
*Florida St.	8	0	0	331	102	10	1	1	428	200
*N.C.State	6	2	0	205	188	9	3	0	305	275
*N.Carolina	5	3	0	239	191	8	4	0	374	267
*Duke	5	3	0	257	216	8	4	0	380	281
*Virginia	5	3	0	224	149	9	3	0	370	195
Clemson	4	4	0	116	109	5	6	0	164	188
Maryland	2	6	0	192	282	4	7	0	270	326
Wake Forest	1	7	0	84	301	3	8	0	143	373
GeorgiaTech	0	8	0	116	226	1	10	0	185	319

Bowls (3-2): Florida St. (won Sugar); N.C. State (won Peach); Duke (lost Hall of Fame); North Carolina (lost Sun); Virginia (won Independence).

Big East Conference

	Conference				Overall			
	W	L	T	PF	PA	W	L	T	PF	PA
*Miami-FL	7	0	0	191	51	10	2	0	365	143
*Virginia Tech	5	2	0	196	119	8	4	0	327	247
Syracuse	4	3	0	151	176	7	4	0	256	259
*West Virginia	4	3	0	160	167	7	6	0	296	286
*Boston Col	3	1	0	138	100	7	4	1	271	169
Rutgers	2	4	1	156	177	5	5	1	241	261
Pittsburgh	2	5	0	156	201	3	8	0	246	307
Temple	0	7	0	154	311	2	9	0	244	417

Bowls (1-3): Miami-FL (lost Orange); Virginia Tech (lost Gator); West Virginia (lost Carquest); Boston College (won Aloha).

Big Eight Conference

	Conference				Overall			
	W	L	T	PF	PA	W	L	T	PF	PA
*Nebraska	7	0	0	201	55	13	0	0	459	162
*Colorado	6	1	0	234	124	11	1	0	439	235
*Kansas St	5	2	0	167	129	9	3	0	312	168
*Oklahoma	4	3	0	147	145	6	6	0	224	269
Kansas	3	4	0	169	188	6	5	0	314	242
Missouri	2	5	0	133	197	3	8	1	208	325
Oklahoma St	0	6	1	86	184	3	7	1	180	254
Iowa St	0	6	1	132	247	0	10	1	192	363

Bowls (2-2): Nebraska (won Orange); Colorado (won Fiesta); Kansas St. (lost Aloha); Oklahoma (lost Copper).

Big Ten Conference

	Conference				Overall			
	W	L	T	PF	PA	W	L	T	PF	PA
*Penn St	8	0	0	385	170	12	0	0	564	252
*Ohio St	6	2	0	190	149	9	4	0	336	211
*Michigan	5	3	0	220	177	8	4	0	330	268
*Wisconsin	4	3	1	212	156	7	4	1	357	238
*Illinois	4	4	0	194	136	7	5	0	309	156
Michigan St	4	4	0	205	219	5	6	0	280	267
Iowa	3	4	1	200	254	5	5	1	307	324
Indiana	3	5	0	172	239	6	5	0	294	285
Purdue	2	4	2	215	269	4	5	2	336	346
Northwestern	2	6	0	140	258	3	7	1	210	351
Minnesota	1	7	0	183	289	3	8	0	256	348

Bowls (4-1): Penn St. (won Rose); Ohio St.(lost Citrus); Michigan (won Holiday); Wisconsin (won Hall of Fame); Illinois (won Liberty).

Big West Conference

	Conference				Overall			
	W	L	T	PF	PA	W	L	T	PF	PA
*UNLV	5	1	0	160	133	7	5	0	315	329
Nevada	5	1	0	216	127	9	2	0	414	272
SW Louisiana	5	1	0	151	95	6	5	0	221	264
Pacific	4	2	0	161	134	6	5	0	252	275
Northern Ill	3	3	0	185	165	4	7	0	301	294
San Jose St	3	3	0	127	138	3	8	0	200	377
Utah St	2	4	0	134	157	3	8	0	209	313
N. Mexico St	2	4	0	136	185	3	8	0	235	422
Louisiana Tech	1	5	0	69	112	3	8	0	164	274
Arkansas St	0	6	0	63	156	1	10	0	123	316

Tiebreaker: Since UNLV, SW Louisiana and Nevada did not all play each other, the conference title was decided in two steps: 1. UNLV and Nevada both defeated San Jose St. (the highest-finishing common opponent) while SW Louisiana did not; and 2. UNLV beat Nevada, 32-27 (Nov. 19).

Bowl (1-0): UNLV (won Las Vegas).

Mid-American Conference

	Conference				Overall			
	W	L	T	PF	PA	W	L	T	PF	PA
*Central Mich	8	1	0	320	188	9	3	0	400	315
Bowl. Green	7	1	0	279	133	9	2	0	391	174
Western Mich	5	3	0	194	146	7	4	0	274	189
Miami-OH	5	3	0	221	163	5	5	1	262	260
Ball St	5	3	1	241	231	5	5	1	276	296
Toledo	4	3	1	268	219	6	4	1	352	324
Eastern Mich	5	4	0	244	212	5	6	0	247	285
Kent	2	7	0	120	237	2	9	0	140	293
Akron	1	8	0	131	331	1	10	0	145	404
Ohio Univ	0	9	0	66	224	0	11	0	82	259

Bowl (0-1): Central Michigan (lost Las Vegas).

Pacific-10 Conference

	Conference				Overall			
	W	L	T	PF	PA	W	L	T	PF	PA
*Oregon	7	1	0	199	108	9	4	0	349	250
*USC	6	2	0	233	147	8	3	1	356	243
*Arizona	6	2	0	186	139	8	4	0	278	190
*Wash. St	5	3	0	139	111	8	4	0	192	136
Washington	4	4	0	198	177	7	4	0	295	233
UCLA	3	5	0	176	213	5	6	0	239	295
California	3	5	0	130	205	4	7	0	212	248
Oregon St	2	6	0	141	172	4	7	0	223	239
Stanford	2	6	0	220	264	3	7	1	327	359
Arizona St	2	6	0	174	260	3	8	0	242	347

Bowls (2-2): Oregon (lost Rose); Arizona (lost Freedom); USC (won Cotton); Washington St. (won Alamo).

Conference Bowling Results

Postseason records for 1994 season.

	W-L		W-L
Big Ten	4-1	Big West	1-0
ACC	3-2	Big East	1-3
SEC	3-2	SWC	1-3
WAC	2-1	Mid-American	0-1
Big Eight	2-2	Independents	0-2
Pac-10	2-2		

NCAA Division I-A Final Standings (Cont.)

Southeastern Conference

		Conference					Overall			
Eastern	**W**	**L**	**T**	**PF**	**PA**	**W**	**L**	**T**	**PF**	**PA**
*Florida	8	1	0	365	136	10	2	1	538	228
*Tennessee.........	5	3	0	261	138	8	4	0	363	208
*S. Carolina	4	4	0	170	186	7	5	0	300	276
Georgia	3	4	1	193	253	6	4	1	351	283
Vanderbilt	2	6	0	117	223	5	6	0	203	277
Kentucky...........	0	8	0	86	311	1	10	0	149	405

		Conference					Overall			
Western	**W**	**L**	**T**	**PF**	**PA**	**W**	**L**	**T**	**PF**	**PA**
*Alabama..........	8	1	0	205	144	12	1	0	305	190
Auburn	6	1	1	239	166	9	1	1	359	199
*Mississippi St	5	3	0	217	203	8	4	0	373	262
LSU	3	5	0	190	208	4	7	0	270	271
Arkansas	2	6	0	133	156	4	7	0	212	213
Mississippi.........	2	6	0	133	185	4	7	0	246	205

SEC Championship: Florida beat Alabama, 24-23 (Dec. 3).
Bowls (3-2): Florida (lost Sugar); Tennessee (won Gator); South Carolina (won Carquest); Alabama (won Citrus); Mississippi St. (lost Peach).

Southwest Conference

		Conference					Overall			
	W	**L**	**T**	**PF**	**PA**	**W**	**L**	**T**	**PF**	**PA**
Texas A&M......	6	0	1	198	93	10	0	1	319	147
*Baylor	4	3	0	220	197	7	5	0	362	277
*Texas	4	3	0	223	172	8	4	0	366	291
*TCU	4	3	0	170	176	7	5	0	302	301
*Texas Tech........	4	3	0	195	94	6	6	0	312	246
Rice.................	4	3	0	130	114	5	6	0	206	203
Houston...........	1	6	0	95	267	1	10	0	115	402
SMU	0	6	1	115	233	1	9	1	197	343

Bowls (1-3): Baylor (lost Alamo); Texas (won Sun); TCU (lost Independence); Texas Tech (lost Cotton).

Western Athletic Conference

		Conference					Overall			
	W	**L**	**T**	**PF**	**PA**	**W**	**L**	**T**	**PF**	**PA**
*Colorado St......	7	1	0	276	210	10	2	0	400	269
*Utah................	6	2	0	278	164	10	2	0	426	210
*BYU	6	2	0	260	228	10	3	0	385	300
Air Force	6	2	0	278	202	8	4	0	377	285
Wyoming	4	4	0	211	234	6	6	0	319	341
New Mexico	4	4	0	254	240	5	7	0	401	384
Fresno St	3	4	1	259	279	5	7	1	376	426
San Diego St....	2	6	0	237	265	4	7	0	332	339
UTEP	1	6	1	149	299	3	7	1	217	359
Hawaii	0	8	0	137	218	3	8	1	260	273

Bowls (2-1): Colorado St. (lost Holiday); Utah (won Freedom); BYU (won Copper).

I-A Independents

	W	**L**	**T**	**PF**	**PA**
*East Carolina.................	7	5	0	303	263
*Notre Dame	6	5	1	342	280
Louisville	6	5	0	255	253
Memphis	6	5	0	163	159
Southern Mississippi	6	5	0	278	261
Army	4	7	0	215	252
Navy	3	8	0	188	399
NE Louisiana..................	3	8	0	242	384
Tulsa	3	8	0	244	304
Cincinnati......................	2	8	1	159	301
Tulane...........................	1	10	0	135	358

Bowls (0-2): East Carolina (lost Liberty); Notre Dame (lost Fiesta).

On Probation

Auburn of the SEC, Texas A&M of the SWC and Washington of the Pac-10 were all on NCAA probation and ineligible for postseason play in 1994.

NCAA Division I-A Individual Leaders

REGULAR SEASON
Total Offense

			Rushing				Passing			Total Offense			
	Cl	**Car**	**Gain**	**Loss**	**Net**	**Att**	**Yds**	**Plays**	**Yds**	**YdsPP**	**TDR**	**YdsPG**
Mike Maxwell, Nevada...........	Jr.	30	40	79	–39	447	3537	477	3498	7.33	32	318.00
Eric Zeier, Georgia	Sr.	21	104	43	61	433	3396	454	3457	7.61	25	314.27
Stoney Case, New Mexico	Sr.	140	714	182	532	409	3117	549	3649	6.65	33	304.08
Steve Stenstrom, Stanford	Sr.	65	125	233	–108	333	2822	398	2714	6.82	19	301.56
John Walsh, BYU..................	Jr.	77	81	320	–239	463	3712	540	3473	6.43	29	289.42
Mike McCoy, Utah	Sr.	75	287	218	69	381	3035	456	3104	6.81	29	282.18
Craig Whelihan, Pacific	Sr.	24	57	69	–12	326	2318	350	2306	6.59	18	256.22
Marcus Crandell, E.Car	So.	71	203	107	96	401	2687	472	2783	5.90	22	253.00
Anthony Hill, Colo. St...........	Sr.	93	328	165	163	290	2552	383	2715	7.09	21	246.82
Kordell Stewart, Colorado	Sr.	122	818	179	639	237	2071	359	2710	7.55	17	246.36

Games: All played 11, except Case and Walsh (12); Stenstrom and Whelihan (9). **Note:** TDR indicates Touchdowns Responsible For.

All-Purpose Running

	Cl	**Gm**	**Rush**	**Rec**	**PR**	**KOR**	**Total Yds**	**YdsPG**
Rashaan Salaam, Colorado	Jr.	11	2055	294	0	0	2349	213.55
Brian Pruitt, Central Mich	Sr.	11	1890	69	0	330	2289	208.09
Andre Davis, TCU	Jr.	11	1494	522	0	0	2016	183.27
Napoleon Kaufman, Washington	Sr.	11	1390	199	8	229	1826	166.00
Ki-Jana Carter, Penn St	Jr.	11	1539	123	0	81	1743	158.45
Chris Darkins, Minnsota	Jr.	11	1443	299	0	0	1742	158.36
Lawrence Phillips, Nebraska..............	So.	12	1722	172	0	0	1894	157.83
Terrell Fletcher, Wisconsin................	Sr.	11	1235	172	0	314	1721	156.45
Alex Van Dyke, Nevada....................	Jr.	11	1	1246	5	451	1703	154.82
Terrell Willis, Rutgers......................	So.	11	1080	71	0	546	1697	154.27

Colorado

Nevada

Penn St.

Penn St.

Rashaan Salaam
Rushing, Scoring,
All-Purpose Running

Mike Maxwell
Total Offense

Ki-Jana Carter
Top NFL draft pick

Kerry Collins
Passing Efficiency

Passing Efficiency

(Minimum 15 attempts per game)

	Cl	Gm	Att	Cmp	Cmp Pct	Int	Int Pct	Yds	Yds/ Att	TD	TD Pct	Rating Points
Kerry Collins, Penn St	Sr.	11	264	176	66.67	7	2.65	2679	10.15	21	7.95	172.9
Terry Dean, Florida	Jr.	10	180	109	60.56	10	5.56	1492	8.29	20	11.11	155.7
Jay Barker, Alabama	Sr.	12	226	139	61.50	5	2.21	1996	8.83	14	6.19	151.7
Danny Wuerffel, Florida	So.	12	212	132	62.26	9	4.25	1754	8.27	18	8.49	151.3
Rob Johnson, USC	Sr.	9	255	170	66.67	6	2.35	2210	8.67	12	4.71	150.3
Mike McCoy, Utah	Sr.	11	381	247	64.83	11	2.89	3035	7.97	28	7.35	150.2
Max Knake, TCU	Jr.	11	316	184	58.23	7	2.22	2624	8.30	24	7.59	148.6
Steve Stenstrom, Stanford	Sr.	9	333	217	65.17	6	1.80	2822	8.47	16	4.80	148.6
Todd Collins, Michigan	Sr.	11	264	172	65.15	7	2.65	2356	8.92	11	4.17	148.6
Ryan Henry, Bowling Green	So.	11	293	174	59.39	11	3.75	2368	8.08	25	8.53	147.9
Kordell Stewart, Colorado	Sr.	11	237	147	62.03	3	1.27	2071	8.74	10	4.22	146.8
John Gustin, Wyoming	Sr.	12	306	181	59.15	13	4.25	2757	9.01	17	5.56	144.7
Mike Groh, Virginia	Jr.	11	216	138	63.89	7	3.24	1711	7.92	13	6.02	143.8
Scott Milanovich, Maryland	Jr.	11	333	229	68.77	9	2.70	2394	7.19	20	6.01	143.6
John Walsh, BYU	Jr.	12	463	284	61.34	14	3.02	3712	8.02	29	6.26	143.3

Rushing

	Cl	Car	Yds	TD	YdsPG
Rashaan Salaam, Colorado	Jr.	298	2055	24	186.82
Brian Pruitt, Cent. Mich	Sr.	292	1890	20	171.82
Lawrence Phillips, Nebraska	So.	286	1722	16	143.50
Ki-Jana Carter, Penn St	Jr.	198	1539	23	139.91
Andre Davis, TCU	Jr.	260	1494	7	135.82
Alex Smith, Indiana	Fr.	265	1475	10	134.09
Chris Darkins, Minnesota	Jr.	277	1443	11	131.18
Napoleon Kaufman, Wash	Sr.	255	1390	9	126.36
Billy West, Pittsburgh	So.	252	1358	6	123.45
R. Christopherson, Wyoming	Sr.	300	1455	10	121.25

Games: All played 11, except Christopherson and Phillips (12).

Receptions

	Cl	Ct	Yds	TD	CPG
Alex Van Dyke, Nevada	Jr.	98	1246	10	8.91
Randy Gatewood, UNLV	Sr.	88	1203	6	8.00
Mick Rossley, SMU	Sr.	83	857	4	7.55
Geroy Simon, Maryland	So.	77	891	5	7.00
Wes Caswell, Tulsa	So.	74	893	3	6.73
Kevin Jordan, UCLA	Jr.	73	1228	7	6.64
Jamie Asher, Louisville	Sr.	70	794	1	6.36
Andre Wallace, West. Mich	Sr.	68	758	7	6.18
Justin Armour, Stanford	Sr.	67	1092	7	6.09
Marcus Harris, Wyoming	So.	71	1431	11	5.92

Games: All played 11, except Harris (12).

Scoring

Non-Kickers

	Cl	TD	Pts	P/Gm
Rashaan Salaam, Colorado	Jr.	24	144	13.09
Ki-Jana Carter, Penn St	Jr.	23	138	12.55
Brian Pruitt, Central Mich	Sr.	22	132	12.00
Rodney Thomas, Texas A&M	Sr.	16	96	8.73
Tyrone Wheatley, Michigan	Sr.	13	78	8.67
Anthony Shelman, Louisville	Sr.	15	90	8.18
Lawrence Phillips, Nebraska	So.	16	96	8.00
Jack Jackson, Florida	Jr.	16	96	8.00
James Stewart, Miami-FL	Jr.	12	72	8.00
Mike Alstott, Purdue	Jr.	14	86*	7.82
Casey McBeth, Toledo	Sr.	14	86*	7.82

*Includes one 2-point conversion.

Games: All played 11, except Jackson and Phillips (12); Stewart and Wheatley (9).

Kickers

	Cl	FG/Att	PAT/Att	Pts
Judd Davis, Florida	Sr.	14/16	65/65	107
Brian Leaver, Bowl.Green	Sr.	21/24	42/43	105
Remy Hamilton, Michigan	So.	24/29	23/25	95
Steve McLaughlin, Ariz	Sr.	23/29	26/26	95
Brett Conway, Penn St	So.	10/12	62/63	92
Kanon Parkman, Georgia	Jr.	17/22	40/41	91
Nick Garritano, UNLV	Sr.	21/26	24/25	87
Rafael Garcia, Virginia	So.	17/22	34/34	85
Kyle Bryant, Texas A&M	Fr.	17/25	31/34	82
Phil Dawson, Texas	Fr.	14/19	38/38	80
Johan Lyssand, Fresno St	Fr.	14/18	38/38	80
Neil Voskeritchian, Colo	Jr.	10/17	50/51	80

Games: All played 11, except Davis (12); Dawson (10).

NCAA Division I-A Individual Leaders (Cont.)

Field Goals

	Cl	FG/Att	Pct	LG
Remy Hamilton, Michigan	So.	24/29	.828	42
Steve McLaughlin, Ariz	Sr.	23/29	.793	54
Brian Leaver, Bowl. Green	Sr.	21/24	.875	51
Nick Garritano, UNLV	Sr.	21/26	.808	54*
John Wales, Washington	So.	18/25	.720	47*
Ryan Williams, Va. Tech	Sr.	17/21	.810	50
Mike Chalberg, Minn.	Jr.	17/23	.739	44
Kanon Parkman, Georgia	Jr.	17/22	.773	46
Rafael Garcia, Virgina	So.	17/22	.773	50
Jon Baker, Ariz. St	Sr.	17/24	.708	48
Marty Kent, La. Tech	Fr.	17/24	.708	45
Kyle Bryant, Texas A&M	Fr.	1/25	.680	61†

*Did it twice. †Longest field goal of season (Sept. 24, vs So. Miss.).

Games: All played 11, except Williams and Chalberg (10).

Interceptions

	Cl	No	Yds	TD	LG
Aaron Beasley, West Va.	Jr.	10	133	2	63
Brian Robinson, Auburn	Jr.	8	140	1	41
Ronde Barber, Virginia	Fr.	8	56	0	35
Demetrice Martin, Mich. St	Jr.	7	41	0	35
Alundis Brice, Ole Miss	Sr.	7	29	0	26

Games: All played 11, except Beasley (12).

Punting
(Minimum of 3.6 per game)

	Cl	No	Yds	Avg
Todd Sauerbrun, West Va	Sr.	72	3486	48.42
Jason Bender, Georgia Tech	Sr.	55	2503	45.51
Brad Maynard, Ball St	Jr.	59	2684	45.49
Brian Lambert, NE Louisiana	Sr.	55	2479	45.07
Gary Layton, Miami-OH	Sr.	55	2477	45.04

Punt Returns
(Minimum of 1.2 per game)

	Cl	No	Yds	TD	Avg
Steve Clay, Eastern Mich.	Jr.	14	278	1	19.86
Nilo Silvan, Tennessee	Jr.	15	272	0	18.13
Ray Peterson, S. Diego St	Jr.	12	190	2	15.83
Kevin Alexander, Utah St	Jr.	14	199	1	14.21
Eddie Kennison, LSU	So.	36	439	1	12.19

Kickoff Returns
(Minimum of 1.2 per game)

	Cl	No	Yds	TD	Avg
Eric Moulds, Miss. St	Jr.	13	426	0	32.77
David Dunn, Fresno St.	Sr.	35	1037	0	28.94
Marcus Wall, N. Carolina	Jr.	27	743	1	27.52
Parrish Foster, N. Mex. St	Sr.	14	385	0	27.50
Derrick Mason, Mich. St	So.	36	966	1	26.83

NCAA Division I-A Team Leaders
REGULAR SEASON

Scoring Offense

	Gm	Record	Pts	Avg
Penn St	11	11-0-0	526	47.8
Florida	12	10-1-1	521	43.4
Nevada	11	9-2-0	414	37.6
Utah	11	9-2-0	410	37.3
Florida St	11	9-1-1	405	36.8
Nebraska	12	12-0-0	435	36.3
Colorado	11	10-1-0	398	36.2
Bowling Green	11	9-2-0	391	35.5
Colorado St	11	10-1-0	386	35.1
Central Michigan	11	9-2-0	376	34.2

Scoring Defense

	Gm	Record	Pts	Avg
Miami-FL	11	10-1-0	119	10.8
Nebraska	12	12-0-0	145	12.1
Washington St.	11	7-4-0	133	12.1
Texas A&M	11	10-0-1	147	13.4
Kansas St	11	9-2-0	156	14.2
Illinois	11	6-5-0	156	14.2
Alabama	12	11-1-0	173	14.4
Memphis	11	6-5-0	159	14.5
Boston College	11	6-4-1	162	14.7
Ohio St	12	9-3-0	187	15.6

Total Offense

	Gm	Plays	Yds	Avg	TD	YdsPG
Penn St	11	749	5722	7.6	68	520.18
Nevada	11	901	5581	6.2	55	507.36
Colorado	11	773	5448	7.0	52	495.27
Florida St	11	853	5314	6.2	52	483.09
Nebraska	12	897	5734	6.4	59	477.83
New Mexico	12	937	5664	6.0	51	472.00
Georgia	11	754	5135	6.8	41	466.82
Florida	12	851	5553	6.5	62	462.75
BYU	12	955	5489	5.7	45	457.42
Wyoming	12	929	5468	5.9	38	455.67

Note: Touchdowns scored by rushing and passing only.

Total Defense

	Gm	Plays	Yds	Avg	TD	YdsPG
Miami-FL	11	702	2430	3.5	9	220.9
Washington St	11	732	2519	3.4	13	229.0
Memphis	11	729	2774	3.8	15	252.2
Nebraska	12	765	3106	4.1	18	258.8
Texas A&M	11	758	2920	3.9	17	265.5
Boston College	11	697	2927	4.2	19	266.1
Florida St	11	754	2937	3.9	19	267.0
Western Mich	11	726	3047	4.2	23	277.0
Illinois	11	700	3138	4.5	16	285.3
Arizona	11	688	3140	4.6	19	285.5

Note: Opponents' TDs scored by rushing and passing only.

Single Game Highs
INDIVIDUAL

Rushing Yards

Yds
356 Brian Pruitt, Central Mich. vs Toledo (Nov. 5)
325 Andre Davis, TCU at New Mexico vs (Sept. 10)
317 Rashaan Salaam, Colorado at Texas (Oct. 1)

Rushing & Passing Yards

Yds
494 Eric Zeier, Georgia vs South Carolina (Sept. 3)
468 Derrick Taite, Miss. St. vs Tulane (Oct. 22)
464 Stoney Case, New Mexico vs TCU (Sept. 10)

Passes Completed

No
40 Danny Kanell, Florida St. vs Florida (Nov. 26)
39 Steve Taneyhill, S. Carolina vs E. Carolina (Oct. 8)
37 Steve Stenstrom, Stanford at Notre Dame (Oct. 1)
37 Stoney Case, New Mexico vs TCU (Sept. 10)

Passes Attempted

Att
62 Stoney Case, New Mexico vs TCU (Sept. 10)
59 Steve Stenstrom, Stanford at Notre Dame (Oct. 1)
59 Tim Gutierrez, San Diego St. vs Air Force (Oct. 1)

Passing Yards

Yds
485 Eric Zeier, Georgia vs South Carolina (Sept. 3)
466 Derrick Taite, Miss St. vs Tulane (Oct. 22)
451 Steve Taneyhill, S. Carolina vs E. Carolina (Oct. 8)

Receiving Yards

Yds
363 Randy Gatewood, UNLV vs Idaho (Sept. 17)
260 Marcus Harris, Wyoming vs Oct. 15
235 Charlie Jones, Fresno St. vs Oct. 15

Receptions

No
23 Randy Gatewood, UNLV vs Idaho (Sept. 17)
17 Curtis Shearer, San Diego St. vs Air Force (Oct. 1)
15 Brent Tillman, Wyoming vs San Diego St. (Oct. 22)
15 Alex Van Dyke, Nevada at Fresno St. (Nov. 5)

TEAM

Points Scored

Pts
73 Florida (73-7) vs Kentucky (Sept. 10)
72 Kansas (72-0) vs Ala-Birmingham* (Sept. 24)
70 Nebraska (70-21) vs Pacific (Sept. 24)
70 Florida (70-21) vs New Mexico St. (Sept. 3)
66 Mississippi St. (66-22) vs Tulane (Oct. 22)
66 Utah (66-0) vs Idaho St.* (Sept. 10)
65 Tennessee (65-0) at Vanderbilt (Nov. 26)
63 Penn St. (63-14) vs Ohio St. (Oct. 29)
63 Texas (63-35) at Baylor (Nov. 24)
62 Nevada (62-35) at Fresno St. (Nov. 5)
62 NE Louisiana (62-37) vs Weber St.* (Oct. 1)
62 Wisconsin (62-13) vs Indiana (Sept. 24)

*Division I-AA opponent.

Annual Awards

Player of the Year

Rashaan Salaam, Colorado........Camp, Heisman, UPI, *TSN*
Kerry Collins, Penn St. ....Maxwell

Position Players of the Year

Davey O'Brien Award (Top QB)......................Kerry Collins
Johnny Unitas Award (Senior QB) ....Jay Barker
Doak Walker Award (Top RB)..................Rashaan Salaam
UPI Back of Year ....Kerry Collins
Biletnikoff Award (Top Receiver)..................Bobby Engram
Lou Groza (Top PK)...........................Steve McLaughlin
Outland Trophy (Top Int. Lineman) ....Zach Wiegert
UPI Lineman of Year ....Zach Wiegert
Lombardi Award (Top Lineman)......................Warren Sapp
FWAA Top Defensive Player.......................Warren Sapp
Butkus Award (Top LB)...............................Dana Howard
Thorpe Award (Top DB).............................Chris Hudson

Coaches of the Year

Rich Brooks, Oregon ....FWAA, *The Sporting News*
Fred Goldsmith, Duke ....Dodd
Sonny Lubick, Colorado St..UPI
Tom Osborne, Nebraska ....AFCA
Joe Paterno, Penn St..Camp

Heisman Trophy Vote

Presented since 1935 by the Downtown Athletic Club of New York City and named after former college coach and DAC athletic director John W. Heisman. Voting done by national media and former Heisman winners. Each ballot allows for three names (points based on 3 for 1st, 2 for 2nd and 1 for 3rd).

Top 10 Vote-Getters

	Pos	1st	2nd	3rd	Pts
Rashaan Salaam, Colo........	RB	400	229	85	1743
Ki-Jana Carter, Penn St	RB	115	205	146	901
Steve McNair, Alcorn St	QB	111	85	152	655
Kerry Collins, Penn St	QB	101	117	102	639
Jay Barker, Alabama	QB	36	58	71	295
Warren Sapp, Miami-FL......	DT	17	37	67	192
Eric Zeier, Georgia	QB	7	15	32	83
Lawrence Phillips, Neb	RB	1	8	21	40
Napoleon Kaufman, Wash......	RB	3	3	12	27
Zach Wiegert, Nebraska	OT	1	7	10	27

Note: All players were seniors except juniors Carter, Salaam and Sapp, and sophomore Phillips.

Consensus All-America Team

NCAA Division I-A players cited most frequently by the following five selectors: AFCA (Kodak), AP, FWAA, UPI and Walter Camp Foundation. Holdover from 1993 All-America team are in **bold** type; (*) indicates unanimous selection.

Offense

Pos	Class	Hgt	Wgt
WR—Jack Jackson, Florida	Jr.	5-9	171
WR—Michael Westbrook, Colorado	Sr.	6-4	210
TE—Pete Mitchell, Boston College..........	Sr.	6-2	238
L—Zach Wiegert*, Nebraska................	Sr.	6-5	300
L—Tony Boselli, USC..........................	Sr.	6-8	305
L—Korey Stringer, Ohio St..................	Jr.	6-5	315
L—Brenden Stai, Nebraska................	Sr.	6-4	300
C—Cory Raymer, Wisconsin	Sr.	6-4	290
QB—Kerry Collins, Penn St	Sr.	6-5	235
RB—Rashaan Salaam*, Colorado	Jr.	6-1	210
RB—Ki-Jana Carter*, Penn St................	Sr.	5-10	212
PK—Steve McLaughlin, Arizona..........	Sr.	6-1	175
KR—Leeland McElroy, Texas A&M........	So.	5-11	200

Defense

Pos	Class	Hgt	Wgt
L—Warren Sapp*, Miami-FL................	Jr.	6-3	284
L—Tedy Bruschi, Arizona	Jr.	6-1	255
L—Luther Elliss, Utah	Sr.	6-6	288
L—Kevin Carter, Florida	Sr.	6-6	265
LB—Dana Howard*, Illinois	Sr.	6-0	235
LB—Ed Stewart, Nebraska..................	Sr.	6-1	215
LB—Derrick Brooks, Florida St..............	Sr.	6-1	226
B—Clifton Abraham, Flordia St	Sr.	5-9	185
B—Bobby Taylor, Notre Dame............	Jr.	6-3	201
B—Chris Hudson, Colorado	Sr.	5-11	195
B—Brian Robinson, Auburn	Jr.	6-3	194
B—Tony Bouie, Arizona.....................	Sr.	5-10	183
P—Todd Sauerbrun*, West Va............	Sr.	6-0	205

Underclassmen Who Declared For 1995 NFL Draft

Thirty-three players— all juniors who have been out of high school for at least three seasons— forfeited the remainder of their college eligibility and declared for the NFL Draft in 1995. NFL teams drafted 22 underclassmen. Players listed in alphabetical order; first round selections in **bold** type.

	Pos	Drafted By	Overall Pick
Derrick Alexander, Fla. St	DE	Minnesota	11
Toney Bates, Iowa	DE	Not selected	—
Greg Black, N. Carolina	DT	Not selected	—
Blake Brockermeyer, Texas	OT	Carolina	29
Devin Bush, Fla. St	DB	Atlanta	26
Ki-Jana Carter, Penn St	RB	Cincinnati	1
Shannon Clavelle, Colorado	DE	Buffalo	185
Lee DeRamus, Wisconsin	WR	New Orleans	184
Brian Easter, Arizona St	LB	Not selected	—
Brian Fitzgerald, N.C. State	RB	Not selected	—
Elliott Fortune, Ga. Tech	DT	Not selected	—
Che Foster, Michigan	RB	Not selected	—
Profail Grier, Utah St	RB	Not selected	—
Brandell Jackson, Baylor	RB	Not selected	—
Jack Jackson, Florida	WR	Chicago	116
Trezelle Jenkins, Michigan	OT	Kansas City	31
Curtis Johnson, N. Carolina	RB	Not selected	—
Greg Landry, Boston College	OG	Not selected	—

	Pos	Drafted By	Overall Pick
Ty Law, Michigan	DB	New England	23
Mike Mamula, Boston College	DE	Philadelphia	7
Curtis Martin, Pittsburgh	RB	New England	74
Lovell Pinkney, Texas	TE	St. Louis	115
Craig Powell, Ohio St	LB	Cleveland	30
Brian Robinson, Auburn	DB	Not selected	—
Rashaan Salaam, Colorado	RB	Chicago	21
Warren Sapp, Miami-FL	DT	Tampa Bay	12
James Stewart, Miami-FL	RB	Minnesota	157
Korey Stringer, Ohio St	OT	Minnesota	24
Lorenzo Styles, Ohio St	LB	Atlanta	77
Bobby Taylor, Notre Dame	DB	Philadelphia	50
Johnny Thomas, Arizona St	WR	St. Louis	240
Tamarick Vanover, Fla. St.*	WR	Kansas City	81
John Walsh, BYU	QB	Cincinnati	213

*Vanover left Florida St. after his sophomore season in 1993.

NCAA Division I-AA Final Standings

Standings based on conference games only; overall records include postseason games.

American West Conference

	Conference					Overall				
	W	L	T	PF	PA	W	L	T	PF	PA
Cal Poly-SLO	3	0	0	92	50	7	4	0	304	334
CS-Sacramento	2	1	0	73	65	5	5	0	255	214
Southern Utah	1	2	0	82	82	4	7	0	252	342
CS-Northridge	0	3	0	48	98	3	7	0	246	290

Playoffs: No teams invited.
Note: Cal Poly moved up to Div. I-AA in 1994.

Ivy League

	Conference					Overall				
	W	L	T	PF	PA	W	L	T	PF	PA
Penn	7	0	0	147	53	9	0	0	233	68
Princeton	4	3	0	133	117	7	3	0	201	184
Brown	4	3	0	151	143	7	3	0	229	197
Cornell	3	4	0	130	139	6	4	0	193	190
Columbia	3	4	0	160	176	5	4	1	240	230
Yale	3	4	0	117	120	5	5	0	224	195
Harvard	2	5	0	124	168	4	6	0	209	254
Dartmouth	2	5	0	92	138	4	6	0	166	187

Playoffs: League does not play postseason games.

Big Sky Conference

	Conference					Overall				
	W	L	T	PF	PA	W	L	T	PF	PA
*Boise St	6	1	0	202	126	13	2	0	433	291
*Montana	5	2	0	256	180	11	3	0	473	294
*Idaho	5	2	0	302	165	9	3	0	493	289
Northern Ariz	4	3	0	201	194	7	4	0	391	273
Idaho St	4	3	0	165	241	6	5	0	269	369
Weber St	2	5	0	174	205	5	6	0	308	300
Eastern Wash	2	5	0	152	198	4	7	0	300	294
Montana St	0	7	0	137	280	3	8	0	253	341

*Playoffs (5-3): Boise St. (3-1); Montana (2-1); Idaho (0-1).

Metro Atlantic Athletic Conference

	Conference					Overall				
	W	L	T	PF	PA	W	L	T	PF	PA
St. John's	6	1	0	162	99	10	1	0	260	147
Marist	6	1	0	188	93	7	3	0	257	163
Duquesne	4	3	0	103	94	6	4	0	138	141
Georgetown	4	3	0	160	104	5	4	0	184	132
Iona	3	4	0	135	161	3	6	0	181	228
Siena	2	5	0	133	176	2	7	0	146	249
Canisius	2	5	0	107	118	2	8	0	132	183
St. Peter's	1	6	0	87	230	1	8	0	113	308

Note: Former independents Duquesne and Marist joined conference in 1994.
Playoffs: No teams invited.

Gateway Athletic Conference

	Conference					Overall				
	W	L	T	PF	PA	W	L	T	PF	PA
*Northern Iowa	6	0	0	141	75	8	4	0	271	204
Western Ill	4	2	0	143	128	8	3	0	356	222
Eastern Ill	4	2	0	128	100	6	5	0	253	232
Illinois St	3	3	0	120	83	5	5	1	254	191
Indiana St	2	4	0	94	110	5	6	0	246	174
SW Missouri St	2	4	0	109	143	4	7	0	217	263
Southern Ill	0	6	0	89	185	1	10	0	156	351

*Playoffs (0-1): Northern Iowa (0-1).

Mid-Eastern Athletic Conference

	Conference					Overall				
	W	L	T	PF	PA	W	L	T	PF	PA
†S.C. State	6	0	0	232	124	10	2	0	423	258
Delaware St	4	2	0	203	129	7	4	0	301	256
N. Car. A&T	3	3	0	131	163	6	5	0	261	269
Beth-Cookman	3	3	0	148	128	5	6	0	254	261
Florida A&M	2	4	0	135	121	6	5	0	232	188
Morgan St	2	4	0	85	200	3	8	0	182	420
Howard	1	5	0	95	164	4	7	0	224	280

* **Playoffs:** No teams invited.
† **Heritage Bowl:** South Carolina St. beat SWAC champion Grambling St., 31-27 (Dec. 30).

Ohio Valley Conference

	Conference				Overall			
	W	L	T	PF	PA	W	L	T	PF	PA
*Eastern Ky...........8	0	0	277	101	10	3	0	399	195
*Mid. Tenn. St.......7	1	0	293	92	8	3	1	401	229
SE Missouri St....5	3	0	158	151	7	5	0	218	229
Tennessee St.......4	4	0	177	174	5	6	0	231	247
Murray St...........4	4	0	201	194	5	6	0	262	321
Tenn-Martin........3	5	0	116	168	6	5	0	207	214
Tenn. Tech..........3	5	0	179	182	5	6	0	236	213
Austin Peay St 2	6	0	191	201	3	8	0	292	272
Morehead St 0	8	0	76	405	0	11	0	98	556

*Playoffs (1-2): Eastern Kentucky (1-1); Middle Tennessee St. (0-1).

Patriot League

	Conference				Overall			
	W	L	T	PF	PA	W	L	T	PF	PA
Lafayette 5	0	0	175	55	5	6	0	230	202
Lehigh 3	2	0	139	127	5	5	1	307	314
Holy Cross............3	2	0	107	93	3	8	0	175	327
Bucknell................2	3	0	101	167	5	6	0	272	311
Colgate 2	3	0	100	79	3	8	0	174	253
Fordham 0	5	0	66	167	0	11	0	146	315

Playoffs: League does not play postseason games.

Pioneer League

	Conference				Overall			
	W	L	T	PF	PA	W	L	T	PF	PA
Dayton 4	1	0	144	75	8	2	0	328	170
Butler 4	1	0	160	99	7	3	0	275	202
Drake...................3	2	0	95	85	7	3	0	217	115
Valparaiso............2	3	0	97	121	7	3	0	243	182
San Diego 2	3	0	115	137	6	4	0	296	283
Evansville 0	5	0	72	166	4	6	0	218	288

Playoffs: No teams invited.

Southern Conference

	Conference				Overall			
	W	L	T	PF	PA	W	L	T	PF	PA
*Marshall 7	1	0	316	135	12	2	0	560	215
*Appalachian St....6	2	0	236	130	9	4	0	363	209
W.Carolina...........5	3	0	250	199	6	5	0	312	296
Ga.Southern........5	3	0	253	186	6	5	0	333	270
E.Tenn. St............4	4	0	220	228	6	5	0	306	266
The Citadel...........4	4	0	281	295	6	5	0	384	343
Tenn-Chatt 2	6	0	194	307	3	8	0	282	426
Furman 2	6	0	195	249	3	8	0	253	325
VMI 1	7	0	100	316	1	10	0	153	433

*Playoffs (3-2): Marshall (2-1); Appalachian St. (1-1).

Southland Conference

	Conference				Overall			
	W	L	T	PF	PA	W	L	T	PF	PA
*North Texas 5	0	1	178	122	7	4	1	343	261
*McNeese St.........5	1	0	163	94	10	3	0	341	233
S.F. Austin St.......4	1	1	166	94	6	3	2	311	198
Northwestern St...3	3	0	175	110	5	6	0	266	228
Sam Houston St ...1	5	0	62	181	6	5	0	200	225
Nicholls St...........1	5	0	104	158	5	6	0	255	227
SW Texas St........1	5	0	97	186	4	7	0	223	307

*Playoffs (1-2): North Texas (0-1); McNeese St. (1-1).

Southwestern Athletic Conference

	Conference				Overall			
	W	L	T	PF	PA	W	L	T	PF	PA
†Grambling St......6	1	0	289	158	9	3	0	479	260
*Alcorn St.............6	1	0	334	199	8	3	1	523	427
Southern-BR 5	2	0	184	89	6	5	0	253	147
Jackson St...........4	3	0	214	173	7	4	0	336	269
Alabama St..........3	4	0	152	196	6	5	0	269	304
Tex. Southern.......2	5	0	156	212	4	7	0	225	335
Miss. Valley St.....2	5	0	118	181	3	7	0	180	246
Prairie View 0	7	0	64	303	0	11	0	100	508

Tiebreaker: Grambling St. beat Alcorn St., 62-56 (Sept. 3).

*Playoffs (0-1): Alcorn St. (0-1).

†Heritage Bowl: Grambling St. lost to MEAC champion South Carolina St., 31-27 (Dec. 30).

Yankee Conference

Mid-Atlantic	Conference				Overall			
	W	L	T	PF	PA	W	L	T	PF	PA
*James Madison...6	2	0	225	133	10	3	0	388	224
Wm. & Mary.......6	2	0	198	140	8	3	0	274	210
Delaware 5	3	0	216	155	7	3	1	360	280
Villanova 2	6	0	172	214	5	6	0	246	248
Northeastern 2	6	0	128	171	2	9	0	175	270
Richmond 1	7	0	127	245	3	8	0	185	313

Tiebreaker: James Madison beat William & Mary, 33-7 (Oct. 22).

New England	Conference				Overall			
	W	L	T	PF	PA	W	L	T	PF	PA
*New Hampshire ..8	0	0	213	147	10	2	0	299	209
*Boston Univ 6	2	0	272	189	9	3	0	396	252
Massachusetts......4	4	0	154	179	5	6	0	208	221
Connecticut 4	4	0	195	189	4	7	0	240	264
Maine.................2	6	0	130	187	3	8	0	181	249
Rhode Island 2	6	0	137	218	2	9	0	208	320

*Playoffs (1-3): James Madison (1-1); New Hampshire (0-1); Boston University (0-1).

I-AA Independents

	W	L	T	PF	PA
*Youngstown St 14	0	1	418	152
Hofstra 8	1	1	371	162
Robert Morris 7	1	1	240	154
Towson St 8	2	0	364	159
Monmouth 7	2	0	202	111
St. Mary's-CA 7	3	0	249	178
*Troy St.............................8	4	0	430	326
Alabama-Birmingham........7	4	0	301	258
Central Florida 7	4	0	399	263
Wagner............................6	5	0	299	243
Liberty 5	6	0	353	290
Western Kentucky..............5	6	0	255	291
Samford 4	6	1	275	359
Central Connecticut St........4	6	0	187	291
Davidson...........................3	7	0	140	165
Buffalo..............................3	8	0	156	331
St. Francis-PA....................2	7	1	159	218
Charleston Southern 0	11	0	218	516

Note: Monmouth and Robert Morris joined Div. I-AA as independents in 1994.

*Playoffs (4-1): Youngstown St. (4-0); Troy St. (0-1).

Division I-AA Adds 23

With the beginning of the 1993-94 academic year, all NCAA Division I schools had to classify all sports in Division I. As a result, 23 schools upgraded their football programs to Div. I-AA: eight from Div. II and 15 from Div. III.

NCAA Division I-AA Regular Season Leaders

INDIVIDUALS

Passing Efficiency

(Minimum 15 attempts per game)

	Cl	Gm	Att	Cmp	Cmp Pct	Int	Int Pct	Yds	Yds/ Att	TD	TD Pct	Rating Points
Dave Dickenson, Montana	Jr.	9	336	229	68.15	6	1.79	3053	9.09	24	7.14	164.5
Todd Donnan, Marshall	Sr.	11	288	182	63.19	8	2.78	2403	8.34	28	9.72	159.8
Brian Brennan, Idaho	Fr.	10	200	116	58.00	4	2.00	1766	8.83	18	9.00	157.9
Mitch Maher, North Texas	Sr.	10	319	202	63.32	12	3.76	2840	8.90	25	7.84	156.4
Steve McNair, Alcorn St	Sr.	11	530	304	57.36	17	3.21	4863	9.18	44	8.30	155.4

Total Offense

	Cl	Rush	Pass	Total	YdsPG
Steve McNair, Alcorn St	Sr.	936	4863	5799	527.18
Dave Dickenson, Mont	Jr.	55	3053	3108	345.33
Jeff Lewis, No. Ariz	Jr.	32	3355	3387	307.91
Mitch Maher, N. Texas	Sr.	175	2840	3015	301.50
Robert Dougherty, BU	Sr.	92	3173	3265	296.82

Games: All played 11, except Dickenson (9), Maher (10).

Rushing

	Cl	Car	Yds	TD	YdsPG
Arnold Mickens, Butler	Jr.	409	2255	18	225.50
Tim Hall, Robert Morris	Jr.	154	1336	11	148.44
Don Wilkerson, SW Texas St	Sr.	302	1569	9	142.64
Thomas Haskins, VMI	So.	258	1509	11	137.18
Rene Ingoglia, UMass	Jr.	258	1505	14	136.82

Games: All played 11, except Hall (9); and Mickens (10).

Receptions

	Cl	Ct	Yds	TD	CPG
Jeff Johnson, E. Tenn. St	Sr.	73	857	8	8.11
Ray Marshall, St. Peter's	Sr.	69	797	4	7.67
Derrick Ingram, UAB	Sr.	83	1457	13	7.55
Heston Sutman, C. Conn. St	Sr.	70	1018	7	7.00
Tim McNair, Alcorn St	Sr.	74	1230	13	6.73

Games: All played 11, except Johnson and Marshall (9); and Sutman (10).

Interceptions

	Cl	No	Yds	TD	LG
Joseph Vaughn, CS-N'ridge	Sr.	9	265	4	81
Brian Clark, Hofstra	Jr.	9	56	0	19
Chris Hanson, Cornell	Sr.	8	83	0	38
Jason Wilson, St. Fran-PA	Sr.	8	52	1	52
Shayne Snider, Valparaiso	Sr.	8	49	0	23

Games: All played 10.

Scoring
Non-Kickers

	Cl	TD	XPt	Pts	P/Gm
Michael Hicks, S.Car. St	Jr.	22	0	132	12.0
Arnold Mickens, Butler	Jr.	18	0	108	10.8
Brian McCarty, Towson St	Sr.	17	0	102	10.2
Chris Parker, Marshall	Jr.	18	2	110*	10.0
Wayne Chrebet, Hofstra	Sr.	16	2	98	9.8

Games: All played 10, except Hicks and Parker (11).

Kickers

	Cl	FG/Att	PAT/Att	Pts
Ryan Woolverton, Idaho	Jr.	14/22	54/56	96
Charlie Pierce, Cent. Fla	So.	14/16	47/47	89
John Coursey, J. Madison	So.	15/23	37/37	82
Daniel Whitehead, Liberty	Sr.	13/16	40/40	79
Garth Petrilli, Mid Tenn	Sr.	13/18	40/42	79

Games: All played 11.

Field Goals

	Cl	FG/Att	Pct	LG
Matt Waller, No. Iowa	So.	17/26	.654	50
Jim Richter, Furman	Jr.	16/19	.842	49
John Coursey, J. Madison	So.	15/23	.652	46
Andy Glockner, Penn	Sr.	14/20	.700	44
Bob Warden, Brown	Sr.	14/16	.875	40
Charlie Pierce, Cent.Fla	So.	14/16	.875	48
Ryan Woolverton, Idaho	Jr.	14/22	.636	52

Games: All played 11, except Glockner (9) and Warden (10).

Punt/Kickoff Leaders

Punting	Cl	No	Yds	Avg
Scott Holmes, Samford	Jr.	49	2099	42.84

Punt Returns	Cl	No	Yds	TD	Avg
Mark Orlando, Towson St	Sr.	19	377	1	19.8

Kickoff Returns	Cl	No	Yds	TD	Avg
Errin Hatwood, St. John's	Sr.	12	401	1	33.4

TEAMS

Scoring Offense

	Gm	Record	Pts	Avg
Alcorn St	11	8-2-1	503	45.7
Idaho	11	9-2-0	472	42.9
Marshall	11	10-1-0	459	41.7
Grambling St	11	9-1-0	452	41.1
Montana	11	9-2-0	411	37.4
Hofstra	10	8-1-1	371	37.1
Troy St	11	8-3-0	404	36.7
Towson St	10	8-2-0	364	36.4
Central Florida	11	7-4-0	399	36.3
South Carolina St.	11	9-2-0	392	35.6

Scoring Defense

	Gm	Record	Pts	Avg
Penn	9	9-0-0	68	7.6
Youngstown St.	11	10-0-1	94	8.5
Drake	10	7-3-0	115	11.5
Monmouth	9	7-2-0	111	12.3
St. John's	10	8-1-0	133	13.3
Southern-Baton Rouge	11	6-5-0	147	13.4
Marshall	11	10-1-0	152	13.8
Eastern Kentucky	11	9-2-0	154	14.0
Duquesne	10	6-4-0	141	14.1
Georgetown	9	5-4-0	132	14.7

NCAA Playoffs

Division I-AA

First Round (Nov. 25-26)

Appalachian St. 17 ....OT........at New Hampshire 10
at Boise St. 24 ....North Texas 20
at Eastern Kentucky 30 ....Boston University 23
at James Madison 45...Troy St. 26
at Marshall 49...........................Middle Tennessee St. 14
at McNeese St. 38...Idaho 21
at Montana 23.....................................Northern Iowa 20
at Youngstown St. 63.....................................Alcorn St. 20

Quarterfinals (Dec. 3)

at Boise St. 17 ....Appalachian St. 14
at Marshall 28 ....OT ....James Madison 21
at Montana 30...McNeese St. 28
at Youngstown St. 18 ....Eastern Kentucky 15

Semifinals (Dec. 10)

at Boise St. 28 ....Marshall 24
at Youngstown St. 28 ....Montana 9

Championship Game

Dec. 17 at Huntington, W. Va. (Att: 27,674)
Youngstown St. 28 ....Boise St. 14
(14-0-1)   (13-2-0)

Division II

First Round (Nov. 19)

at Ferris St. (Mich.) 43 ....West Chester (Pa.) 40
at Indiana (Pa.) 35 ....Grand Valley St. (Mich.) 27
at North Alabama 17 ....Carson-Newman (Tenn.) 13
at North Dakota 18..NE Missouri St. 6
North Dakota St. 18 ....3OT...at Pittsburg St. (Kan.) 12
at Texas A&M-Kingsville 43................Western St. (Colo.) 7
at Portland St. (Ore.) 29......................Angelo St. (Tex.) 0
at Valdosta St. (Ga.) 14 ....Albany St. (Ga.) 7

Quarterfinals (Nov. 26)

Indiana (Pa.) 21 ....at Ferris St. 17
at North Alabama 27..........2OT...............Valdosta St. 24
at North Dakota 14...................................North Dakota St. 7
at Texas A&M-Kingsville 21 ....Portland St. 16

Semifinals (Dec. 3)

at North Alabama 35 ....North Dakota 7
at Texas A&M-Kingsville 46......................Indiana (Pa.) 20

Championship Game

Dec. 10 at Florence, Ala. (Att: 13,526)
North Alabama 16 ....Texas A&M-Kingsville 10
(13-1-0)   (12-2-0)

Division I-AA, II and III Awards

Players of the Year

Payton Award (Div. I-AA) ....Steve McNair, QB
Alcorn St. (Sr.)
Hill Trophy (Div. II) ....Chris Hatcher, QB
Valdosta St. (Sr.)
Gagliardi Trophy (Div. III)..................Carey Bender, RB
Coe College (Sr.)

Coaches of the Year

Eddie Robinson Award.........Jim Tressel, Youngstown St.
AFCA (NCAA Div. I-AA)....Jim Tressel, Youngstown St.
AFCA (College Div. I) .....Bobby Wallace, No. Alabama
AFCA (College Div. II)..................Pete Schmidt, Albion

Division III

First Round (Nov. 19)

at Albion (Mich.) 28 ....Augustana (Ill.) 21
at Ithaca (N.Y.) 10 ....2OT........Buffalo St. (N.Y.) 7
Mount Union (Ohio) 28......................at Allegheny (Pa.) 19
at Plymouth St. (N.H.) 19 ....Merchant Marine (N.Y.) 18
at St. John's (Minn.) 51 ....La Verne (Calif.) 12
Wartburg (Iowa) 22 ....at Central (Iowa) 21
Wash. & Jeff. (Pa.) 28 ....at Trinity (Tex.) 0
Widener (Pa.) 14 ....at Dickinson (Pa.) 0

Quarterfinals (Nov. 26)

at Albion 34...Mount Union 33
Ithaca 22...at Plymouth St. 7
at St. John's (Minn.) 42................................Wartburg 14
at Washington & Jefferson 37.........................Widener 21

Semifinals (Dec. 3)

Albion 19 ....at St. John's (Minn.) 16
Washington & Jefferson 23 ....at Ithaca 19

Amos Alonzo Stagg Bowl

Dec. 10 at Salem, Va. (Att: 7,168)
Albion 38 ....Washington & Jefferson 15
(13-0-0)   (11-2-0)

NAIA Playoffs

Division I

First Round (Nov. 19)

at Arkansas-Pine Bluff 21 ....Central St. (Ohio) 14
Langston (Okla.) 56 ....at Arkansas Tech 42
at Northeastern St. (Okla.) 14.........Moorhead St. (Minn.) 7
at Western Montana 48 ....Glenville St. (W.Va.) 38

Semifinals (Dec. 3)

at Northeastern St. 3...Langston 0
at Arkansas-Pine Bluff 60.....OT ....Western Montana 53

Championship

Dec. 10 at Pine Bluff, Ark. (Att: 12,000)
Northeastern St. 13 ....Arkansas-Pine Bluff 12
(11-2-0)   (9-4-0)

Division II

First Round (Nov. 19)

at Hardin-Simmons (Tex.) 49...................Missouri Valley 21
at Lambuth (Tenn.) 48...........................Evangel (Mo.) 19
at Minot St. (N.D.) 20 ....Sioux Falls (S.D.) 13
at Northwestern (Iowa) 38 ....Trinity (Ill.) 20
Pacific Luth. (Wash.) 34 ....at Midland Luth. (Neb.) 14
at Tiffin (Ohio) 41 ....Eureka (Ill.) 14
Western Washington 21 ....at Linfield (Ore) 2
at Westminster (Pa.) 41 ....Findlay (Ohio) 30

Quarterfinals (Dec. 3)

Lambuth 57..at Hardin-Simmons 54
at Northwestern (Iowa) 28..............................Minot St. 26
at Pacific Lutheran 25.................Western Washington 20
at Westminster 42 ....Tiffin 14

Semifinals (Dec. 10)

at Pacific Lutheran 28......................Northwestern (Iowa) 7
at Westminster 46 ....Lambuth 6

Championship

Dec. 17 at Portland, Ore. (Att: 4,357)
Westminster 27 ....Pacific Lutheran 14
(12-2-0)   (11-2-0)

COLLEGE FOOTBALL
S T A T I S T I C S

THROUGH THE YEARS
1869-1995

BOWLS • ALL-TIME LEADERS

THE 1996 INFORMATION PLEASE SPORTS ALMANAC

SEC B

PAGE 168

National Champions

Over the last 125 years, there have been 25 major selectors of national champions by way of polls (11), mathematical rating systems (10) and historical research (4). The best-known and most widely circulated of these surveys, the Associated Press poll of sportswriters and broadcasters, first appeared during the 1936 season. Champions prior to 1936 have been determined by retro polls and ratings and historical research.

The Early Years (1869-1935)

National champions based on the Dickinson mathematical system (DS) and three historical retro polls taken by the College Football Researchers Association (CFRA), the National Championship Foundation (NCF) and the Helms Athletic Foundation (HF). The CFRA and NCF polls start in 1869, college football's inaugural year, while the Helms poll begins in 1883, the first season the game adopted a point system for scoring. Frank Dickinson, an economics professor at Illinois, introduced his system in 1926 and retro-picked winners in 1924 and '25. Bowl game results were counted in the Helms selections, but not in the other three.

Multiple champions: Yale (18); Princeton (17); Harvard (9); Michigan (7); Notre Dame and Penn (4); Alabama, Cornell, Illinois, Pittsburgh and USC (3); California, Georgia Tech, Minnesota and Penn St. (2).

Year		Record	Year		Record	Year		Record
1869	Princeton	1-1-0	1880	Yale (CFRA)	4-0-1	1890	Harvard	11-0-0
1870	Princeton	1-0-0		& Princeton (NCF)	4-0-1	1891	Yale	13-0-0
1871	No games played		1881	Yale	5-0-1	1892	Yale	13-0-0
1872	Princeton	1-0-0	1882	Yale	8-0-0	1893	Princeton	11-0-0
1873	Princeton	1-0-0	1883	Yale	8-0-0	1894	Yale	16-0-0
1874	Yale	3-0-0	1884	Yale	8-0-1	1895	Penn	14-0-0
1875	Princeton (CFRA)	2-0-0	1885	Princeton	9-0-0	1896	Princeton (CFRA)	10-0-1
	& Harvard (NCF)	4-0-0	1886	Yale	9-0-1		& Lafayette (NCF)	11-0-1
1876	Yale	3-0-0	1887	Yale	9-0-0	1897	Penn	15-0-0
1877	Yale	3-0-1	1888	Yale	13-0-0	1898	Harvard	11-0-0
1878	Princeton	6-0-0	1889	Princeton	10-0-0	1899	Princeton (CFRA)	12-1-0
1879	Princeton	4-0-1					& Harvard (NCF, HF)	10-0-1

Year		Record	Bowl Game	Head Coach	Outstanding Player
1900	Yale	12-0-0	No bowl	Malcolm McBride	Perry Hale, HB
1901	Harvard (CFRA)	12-0-0	No bowl	Bill Reid	Bob Kernan, HB
	& Michigan (NCF, HF)	11-0-0	Won Rose	Hurry Up Yost	Neil Snow, E
1902	Michigan	11-0-0	No bowl	Hurry Up Yost	Boss Weeks, QB
1903	Princeton	11-0-0	No bowl	Art Hillebrand	John DeWitt, G
1904	Penn (CFRA, HF)	12-0-0	No bowl	Carl Williams	Andy Smith, FB
	& Michigan (NCF)	10-0-0	No bowl	Hurry Up Yost	Willie Heston, HB
1905	Chicago	10-0-0	No bowl	Amos Alonzo Stagg	Walter Eckersall, QB
1906	Princeton	9-0-1	No bowl	Bill Roper	Cap Wister, E
1907	Yale	9-0-1	No bowl	Bill Knox	Tad Jones, HB
1908	Penn (CFRA, HF)	11-0-1	No bowl	Sol Metzger	Hunter Scarlett, E
	& LSU (NCF)	10-0-0	No bowl	Edgar Wingard	Doc Fenton, QB
1909	Yale	12-1-0	No bowl	Howard Jones	Ted Coy, FB
1910	Harvard (CFRA, HF)	8-0-1	No bowl	Percy Haughton	Percy Wendell, HB
	& Pittsburgh (NCF)	9-0-0	No bowl	Joe Thompson	Ralph Galvin, C
1911	Princeton (CFRA, HF)	8-0-2	No bowl	Bill Roper	Sam White, E
	& Penn St. (NCF)	8-0-1	No bowl	Bill Hollenback	Dexter Very, E
1912	Harvard (CFRA, HF)	9-0-0	No bowl	Percy Haughton	Charley Brickley, HB
	& Penn St. (NCF)	8-0-0	No bowl	Bill Hollenback	Dexter Very, E
1913	Harvard	9-0-0	No bowl	Percy Haughton	Eddie Mahan, FB
1914	Army	9-0-0	No bowl	Charley Daly	John McEwan, C
1915	Cornell	9-0-0	No bowl	Al Sharpe	Charley Barrett, QB
1916	Pittsburgh	8-0-0	No bowl	Pop Warner	Bob Peck, C
1917	Georgia Tech	9-0-0	No bowl	John Heisman	Ev Strupper, HB
1918	Pittsburgh (CFRA, HF)	4-1-0	No bowl	Pop Warner	Tom Davies, HB
	& Michigan (NCF)	5-0-0	No bowl	Hurry Up Yost	Frank Steketee, FB
1919	Harvard (CFRA-tie, HF)	9-0-1	Won Rose	Bob Fisher	Eddie Casey, HB
	Illinois (CFRA-tie)	6-1-0	No bowl	Bob Zuppke	Chuck Carney, E
	& Notre Dame (NCF)	9-0-0	No bowl	Knute Rockne	George Gipp, HB

National Champions (Cont.)

Year		Record	Bowl Game	Head Coach	Outstanding Player
1920	**California**	9-0-0	Won Rose	Andy Smith	Dan McMillan, T
1921	**California** (CFRA)	9-0-1	Tied Rose	Andy Smith	Brick Muller, E
	& Cornell (NCF, HF)	8-0-0	No bowl	Gil Dobie	Eddie Kaw, HB
1922	**Princeton** (CFRA)	8-0-0	No bowl	Bill Roper	Herb Treat, T
	California (NCF)	9-0-0	No bowl	Andy Smith	Brick Muller, E
	& Cornell (HF)	8-0-0	No bowl	Gil Dobie	Eddie Kaw, HB
1923	**Illinois** (CFRA, HF)	8-0-0	No bowl	Bob Zuppke	Red Grange, HB
	& Michigan (NCF)	8-0-0	No bowl	Hurry Up Yost	Jack Blott, C
1924	**Notre Dame**	10-0-0	Won Rose	Knute Rochne	"The Four Horsemen"*
1925	**Alabama** (CFRA, HF)	10-0-0	Won Rose	Wallace Wade	Johnny Mack Brown, HB
	& Dartmouth (DS)	8-0-0	No bowl	Jesse Hawley	Swede Oberlander, HB
1926	**Alabama** (CFRA, HF)	9-0-1	Tied Rose	Wallace Wade	Hoyt Winslett, E
	& Stanford (DS)	10-0-1	Tied Rose	Pop Warner	Ted Shipkey, E
1927	**Yale** (CFRA)	7-1-0	No bowl	Tad Jones	Bill Webster, G
	& Illinois (NCF, HF, DS)	7-0-1	No bowl	Bob Zuppke	Bob Reitsch, C
1928	**Georgia Tech** (CFRA, NCF, HF)	10-0-0	Won Rose	Bill Alexander	Pete Pund, C
	& USC (DS)	9-0-1	No bowl	Howard Jones	Jesse Hibbs, T
1929	**Notre Dame**	9-0-0	No bowl	Knute Rockne	Frank Carideo, QB
1930	**Alabama** (CFRA)	10-0-0	Won Rose	Wallace Wade	Fred Sington, T
	& Notre Dame (NCF, HF, DS)	10-0-0	No bowl	Knute Rockne	Marchy Schwartz, HB
1931	**USC**	10-1-0	Won Rose	Howard Jones	John Baker, G
1932	**USC** (CFRA, NCF, HF)	10-0-0	Won Rose	Howard Jones	Ernie Smith, T
	& Michigan (DS)	8-0-0	No bowl	Harry Kipke	Harry Newman, QB
1933	**Michigan**	8-0-0	No bowl	Harry Kipke	Chuck Bernard, C
1934	**Minnesota**	8-0-0	No bowl	Bernie Bierman	Pug Lund, HB
1935	**Minnesota** (CFRA, NCF, HF)	8-0-0	No bowl	Bernie Bierman	Dick Smith, T
	& SMU (DS)	12-1-0	Lost Rose	Matty Bell	Bobby Wilson, HB

*Notre Dame's **Four Horsemen** were Harry Stuhldreher (QB), Jim Crowley (HB), Don Miller (HB-P) and Elmer Layden (FB).

The Media Poll Years (since 1936)

National champions according to seven media and coaches' polls: Associated Press (since 1936), United Press (1950-57), International News Service (1952-57), United Press International (1958-92), Football Writers Association of America (since 1954), National Football Foundation and Hall of Fame (since 1959) and USA Today/CNN (since 1991). In 1991, the American Football Coaches Association switched outlets for its poll from UPI to USA Today/CNN.

After 29 years of releasing its final Top 20 poll in early December, AP named its 1965 national champion following that season's bowl games. AP returned to a pre-bowls final vote in 1966 and '67, but has polled its writers and broadcasters after the bowl games since the 1968 season. The FWAA has selected its champion after the bowl games since the 1955 season, the NFF-Hall of Fame since 1971, UPI after 1974 and USA Today/CNN since 1982.

The Associated Press changed the name its national championship award from the AP Trophy to the Bear Bryant Trophy after the legendary Alabama coach's death in 1983. The Football Writers' trophy is called the Grantland Rice Award (after the celebrated sportswriter) and the NFF-Hall of Fame trophy is called the MacArthur Bowl (in honor of Gen. Douglas MacArthur).

Multiple champions: Notre Dame (9); Alabama (7); Ohio St. and Oklahoma (6); USC (5); Miami-FL and Minnesota (4); Michigan St., Nebraska and Texas (3); Army, Georgia Tech, Penn St. and Pittsburgh (2).

Year		Record	Bowl Game	Head Coach	Outstanding Player
1936	**Minnesota**	7-1-0	No bowl	Bernie Bierman	Ed Widseth, T
1937	**Pittsburgh**	9-0-1	No bowl	Jock Sutherland	Marshall Goldberg, HB
1938	**TCU**	11-0-0	Won Sugar	Dutch Meyer	Davey O'Brien, QB
1939	**Texas A&M**	11-0-0	Won Sugar	Homer Norton	John Kimbrough, FB
1940	**Minnesota**	8-0-0	No Bowl	Bernie Bierman	George Franck, HB
1941	**Minnesota**	8-0-0	No bowl	Bernie Bierman	Bruce Smith, HB
1942	**Ohio St.**	9-1-0	No bowl	Paul Brown	Gene Fekete, FB
1943	**Notre Dame**	9-1-0	No bowl	Frank Leahy	Angelo Bertelli, QB
1944	**Army**	9-0-0	No bowl	Red Blaik	Glenn Davis, HB
1945	**Army**	9-0-0	No bowl	Red Blaik	Doc Blanchard, FB
1946	**Notre Dame**	8-0-1	No bowl	Frank Leahy	Johnny Lujack, QB
1947	**Notre Dame**	9-0-0	No bowl	Frank Leahy	Johnny Lujack, QB
1948	**Michigan**	9-0-0	No bowl	Bennie Oosterbaan	Dick Rifenburg, E
1949	**Notre Dame**	10-0-0	No bowl	Frank Leahy	Leon Hart, E
1950	**Oklahoma**	10-1-0	Lost Sugar	Bud Wilkinson	Leon Heath, FB
1951	**Tennessee**	10-0-0	Lost Sugar	Bob Neyland	Hank Lauricella, TB
1952	**Michigan St.** (AP, UP)	9-0-0	No bowl	Biggie Munn	Don McAuliffe, HB
	& Georgia Tech (INS)	12-0-0	Won Sugar	Bobby Dodd	Hal Miller, T
1953	**Maryland**	10-1-0	Lost Orange	Jim Tatum	Bernie Faloney, QB
1954	**Ohio St.** (AP, INS)	10-0-0	Won Rose	Woody Hayes	Howard Cassady, HB
	& UCLA (UP, FW)	9-0-0	No bowl	Red Sanders	Jack Ellena, T
1955	**Oklahoma**	11-0-0	Won Orange	Bud Wilkinson	Jerry Tubbs, C
1956	**Oklahoma**	10-0-0	No bowl	Bud Wilkinson	Tommy McDonald, HB

National Champions (Cont.)

Year		Record	Bowl Game	Head Coach	Outstanding Player
1957	**Auburn** (AP)	10-0-0	No bowl	Shug Jordan	Jimmy Phillips, E
	& **Ohio St.** (UP, FW, INS)	9-1-0	Won Rose	Woody Hayes	Bob White, FB
1958	**LSU** (AP, UPI)	11-0-0	Won Sugar	Paul Dietzel	Billy Cannon, HB
	& **Iowa** (FW)	8-1-1	Won Rose	Forest Evashevski	Randy Duncan, QB
1959	**Syracuse**	11-0-0	Won Cotton	Ben Schwartzwalder	Ernie Davis, HB
1960	**Minnesota** (AP, UPI, NFF)	8-2-0	Lost Rose	Murray Warmath	Tom Brown, G
	& **Mississippi** (FW)	10-0-1	Won Sugar	Johnny Vaught	Jake Gibbs, QB
1961	**Alabama** (AP, UPI, NFF)	11-0-0	Won Sugar	Bear Bryant	Billy Neighbors, T
	& **Ohio St.** (FW)	8-0-1	No bowl	Woody Hayes	Bob Ferguson, HB
1962	**USC**	11-0-0	Won Rose	John McKay	Hal Bedsole, E
1963	**Texas**	11-0-0	Won Cotton	Darrell Royal	Scott Appleton, T
1964	**Alabama** (AP, UPI),	10-1-0	Lost Orange	Bear Bryant	Joe Namath, QB
	Arkansas (FW)	11-0-0	Won Cotton	Frank Broyles	Ronnie Caveness, LB
	& **Notre Dame** (NFF)	9-1-0	No bowl	Ara Parseghian	John Huarte, QB
1965	**Alabama** (AP, FW-tie)	9-1-1	Won Orange	Bear Bryant	Paul Crane, C
	& **Michigan St.** (UPI, NFF, FW-tie)	10-1-0	Lost Rose	Duffy Daugherty	George Webster, LB
1966	**Notre Dame** (AP, UPI, FW, NFF-tie)	9-0-1	No bowl	Ara Parseghian	Jim Lynch, LB
	& **Michigan St.** (NFF-tie)	9-0-1	No bowl	Duffy Daugherty	Bubba Smith, DE
1967	**USC**	10-1-0	Won Rose	John McKay	O.J. Simpson, HB
1968	**Ohio St.**	10-0-0	Won Rose	Woody Hayes	Rex Kern, QB
1969	**Texas**	11-0-0	Won Cotton	Darrell Royal	James Street, QB
1970	**Nebraska** (AP, FW)	11-0-1	Won Orange	Bob Devaney	Jerry Tagge, QB
	Texas (UPI, NFF-tie)	10-1-0	Lost Cotton	Darrell Royal	Steve Worster, RB
	& **Ohio St.** (NFF-tie)	9-1-0	Lost Rose	Woody Hayes	Jim Stillwagon, MG
1971	**Nebraska**	13-0-0	Won Orange	Bob Devaney	Johnny Rodgers, WR
1972	**USC**	12-0-0	Won Rose	John McKay	Charles Young, TE
1973	**Notre Dame** (AP, FW, NFF)	11-0-0	Won Sugar	Ara Parseghian	Mike Townsend, DB
	& **Alabama** (UPI)	11-1-0	Lost Sugar	Bear Bryant	Buddy Brown, OT
1974	**Oklahoma** (AP)	11-0-0	No bowl	Barry Switzer	Joe Washington, RB
	& **USC** (UPI, FW, NFF)	10-1-1	Won Rose	John McKay	Anthony Davis, RB
1975	**Oklahoma**	11-1-0	Won Orange	Barry Switzer	Lee Roy Selmon, DT
1976	**Pittsburgh**	12-0-0	Won Sugar	Johnny Majors	Tony Dorsett, RB
1977	**Notre Dame**	11-1-0	Won Cotton	Dan Devine	Ross Browner, DE
1978	**Alabama** (AP, FW, NFF)	11-1-0	Won Sugar	Bear Bryant	Marty Lyons, DT
	& **USC** (UPI)	12-1-0	Won Rose	John Robinson	Charles White, RB
1979	**Alabama**	12-0-0	Won Sugar	Bear Bryant	Jim Bunch, OT
1980	**Georgia**	12-0-0	Won Sugar	Vince Dooley	Herschel Walker, RB
1981	**Clemson**	12-0-0	Won Orange	Danny Ford	Jeff Davis, LB
1982	**Penn St.**	11-1-0	Won Sugar	Joe Paterno	Todd Blackledge, QB
1983	**Miami-FL**	11-1-0	Won Orange	H. Schnellenberger	Bernie Kosar, QB
1984	**BYU**	13-0-0	Won Holiday	LaVell Edwards	Robbie Bosco, QB
1985	**Oklahoma**	11-1-0	Won Orange	Barry Switzer	Brian Bosworth, LB
1986	**Penn St.**	12-0-0	Won Fiesta	Joe Paterno	D.J. Dozier, RB
1987	**Miami-FL**	12-0-0	Won Orange	Jimmy Johnson	Steve Walsh, QB
1988	**Notre Dame**	12-0-0	Won Fiesta	Lou Holtz	Tony Rice, QB
1989	**Miami-FL**	11-1-0	Won Sugar	Dennis Erickson	Craig Erickson, QB
1990	**Colorado** (AP, FW, NFF)	11-1-1	Won Orange	Bill McCartney	Eric Bieniemy, RB
	& **Georgia Tech** (UPI)	11-0-1	Won Citrus	Bobby Ross	Shawn Jones, QB
1991	**Miami-FL** (AP)	12-0-0	Won Orange	Dennis Erickson	Gino Torretta, QB
	& **Washington** (USA, FW, NFF)	12-0-0	Won Rose	Don James	Steve Emtman, DT
1992	**Alabama**	13-0-0	Won Sugar	Gene Stallings	Eric Curry, DE
1993	**Florida St.**	12-1-0	Won Orange	Bobby Bowden	Charlie Ward, QB
1994	**Nebraska**	13-0-0	Won Orange	Tom Osborne	Zach Wiegert, OT

Number 1 vs. Number 2

Since the Associated Press writers poll started keeping track of such things in 1936, the No.1 and No.2 ranked teams in the country have met 29 times; 19 during the regular season and 10 in bowl games. Since the first showdown in 1943, the No.1 team has beaten the No.2 team 17 times, lost 10 and there have been two ties. Each showdown is listed below with the date, the match-up, each team's record going into the game, the final score, the stadium and site.

Date	Match-up		Stadium	Date	Match-up		Stadium
Oct. 9 1943	#1 Notre Dame (2-0) #2 Michigan (3-0)	35 12	Michigan (Ann Arbor)	Nov. 10 1945	#1 Army (6-0) #2 Notre Dame (5-0-1)	48 0	Yankee (New York)
Nov. 20 1943	#1 Notre Dame (8-0) #2 Iowa Pre-Flight (8-0)	14 13	Notre Dame (South Bend)	Dec. 1 1945	#1 Army (8-0) #2 Navy (7-0-1)	32 13	Municipal (Philadelphia)
Dec. 2 1944	#1 Army (8-0) #2 Navy (6-2)	23 7	Municipal (Baltimore)	Nov. 9 1946	#1 Army (7-0) #2 Notre Dame (5-0)	0 0	Yankee (New York)

Date	Match-up		Stadium
Jan. 1 1963	#1 USC (10-0)	42	ROSE BOWL
	#2 Wisconsin (8-1)	37	(Pasadena)
Oct. 12 1963	#2 Texas (3-0)	28	Cotton Bowl
	#1 Oklahoma (2-0)	7	(Dallas)
Jan. 1 1964	#1 Texas (10-0)	28	COTTON BOWL
	#2 Navy (9-1)	6	(Dallas)
Nov. 19 1966	#1 Notre Dame (8-0)	10	Spartan
	#2 Michigan St. (9-0)	10	(East Lansing)
Sept. 28 1968	#1 Purdue (1-0)	37	Notre Dame
	#2 Notre Dame (1-0)	22	(South Bend)
Jan. 1 1969	#1 Ohio St. (9-0)	27	ROSE BOWL
	#2 USC (9-0-1)	16	(Pasadena)
Dec. 6 1969	#1 Texas (9-0)	15	Razorback
	#2 Arkansas (9-0)	14	(Fayetteville)
Nov. 25 1971	#1 Nebraska (10-0)	35	Owen Field
	#2 Oklahoma (9-0)	31	(Norman)
Jan. 1 1972	#1 Nebraska (12-0)	38	ORANGE BOWL
	#2 Alabama (11-0)	6	(Miami)
Jan. 1 1979	#2 Alabama (10-1)	14	SUGAR BOWL
	#1 Penn St. (11-0)	7	(New Orleans)
Sept. 26 1981	#1 USC (2-0)	28	Coliseum
	#2 Oklahoma (1-0)	24	(Los Angeles)
Jan. 1 1983	#2 Penn St. (10-1)	27	SUGAR BOWL
	#1 Georgia (11-0)	23	(New Orleans)

Date	Match-up		Stadium
Oct. 19 1985	#1 Iowa (5-0)	12	Kinnick
	#2 Michigan (5-0)	10	(Iowa City)
Sept. 27 1986	#2 Miami-FL (3-0)	28	Orange Bowl
	#1 Oklahoma (2-0)	16	(Miami)
Jan. 2 1987	#2 Penn St. (11-0)	14	FIESTA BOWL
	#1 Miami-FL (11-0)	10	(Tempe)
Nov. 21 1987	#2 Oklahoma (10-0)	17	Memorial
	#1 Nebraska (10-0)	7	(Lincoln)
Jan. 1 1988	#2 Miami-FL (11-0)	20	ORANGE BOWL
	#1 Oklahoma (11-0)	14	(Miami)
Nov. 26 1988	#1 Notre Dame (10-0)	27	Coliseum
	#2 USC (10-0)	10	(Los Angeles)
Sept. 16 1989	#1 Notre Dame (1-0)	24	Michigan
	#2 Michigan (0-0)	19	(Ann Arbor)
Nov. 16 1991	#2 Miami-FL (8-0)	17	Doak Campbell
	#1 Florida St. (10-0)	16	(Tallahassee)
Jan. 1 1993	#2 Alabama (12-0-0)	34	SUGAR BOWL
	#1 Miama-FL (11-0-0)	13	(New Orleans)
Nov. 13 1993	#2 Notre Dame (9-0)	31	Notre Dame
	#1 Florida St. (9-0)	24	(South Bend)
Jan. 1 1994	#1 Florida St. (11-1)	18	ORANGE BOWL
	#2 Nebraska (11-0)	16	(Miami)

Top 50 Rivalries

Top Division I series records, including games through the 1994 season. Note that the Boston College-Holy Cross series ended after the 1986 season with BC ahead 48-31-0. Notre Dame and Miami-FL concluded their series in 1990 with Notre Dame ahead 15-7-1. And Arkansas and Texas ended their series in 1992 with Texas ahead 54-19-0. The series between Miami-FL and Florida was suspended after the 1987 season and formally cancelled in 1991 with Florida in front 25-24-0. Penn St. and Pitt played each other annually from 1935-92 and 91 times from 1893-1992 with Penn St. leading 47-41-4. They are not scheduled to meet again until 1997.

	Gm	Series Leader		Gm	Series Leader
Air Force-Army	29	Air Force (17-11-1)	Kentucky-Tennessee	90	Tennessee (58-23-9)
Air Force-Navy	27	Air Force (18-9-0)	Lafayette-Lehigh	130	Lafayette (71-54-5)
Alabama-Auburn	59	Alabama (34-24-1)	LSU-Tulane	92	LSU (63-22-7)
Alabama-Tennessee	77	Alabama (42-27-8)	Michigan-Michigan St	87	Michigan (57-25-5)
Arizona-Arizona St	68	Arizona (39-28-1)	Michigan-Notre Dame	26	Michigan (15-10-1)
Army-Navy	95	Army (45-43-7)	Michigan-Ohio St	91	Michigan (51-34-6)
Auburn-Georgia	98	Auburn (46-44-8)	Minnesota-Wisconsin	104	Minnesota (57-39-8)
Baylor-TCU	101	Tied (47-47-7)	Mississippi-Miss.St	91	Ole Miss (52-33-6)
BYU-Utah	70	Utah (42-24-4)	Nebraska-Oklahoma	75	Oklahoma (39-33-3)
California-Stanford	97	Stanford (47-39-11)	N. Mexico-N. Mex. St	84	New Mexico (54-25-5)
Cincinnati-Miami,OH	99	Miami (53-39-7)	N.Carolina-N.C.State	84	N.Carolina (54-24-6)
The Citadel-VMI	54	Tied (26-26-2)	Notre Dame-Purdue	66	Notre Dame (43-21-2)
Clemson-S. Carolina	92	Clemson (54-34-4)	Notre Dame-USC	66	Notre Dame (38-23-5)
Colorado-Nebraska	53	Nebraska (37-14-2)	Oklahoma-Okla.St	89	Oklahoma (71-11-7)
Colo. St.-Wyoming	84	Colorado St. (43-36-5)	Oklahoma-Texas	89	Texas (52-33-4)
Duke-North Carolina	80	N.Carolina (41-35-4)	Oregon-Oregon St	98	Oregon (48-40-10)
Florida-Florida St	38	Florida (23-13-2)	Penn St.-Pittsburgh	92	Penn St.(47-41-4)
Florida-Georgia	73	Georgia (44-27-2)	Pittsburgh-West Va	87	Pitt (55-29-3)
Florida St.-Miami,FL	38	Miami (23-15-0)	Princeton-Yale	117	Yale (63-44-10)
Georgia-Georgia Tech	89	Georgia (49-35-5)	Richmond-Wm.& Mary	104	Wm.& Mary (52-47-5)
Harvard-Yale	111	Yale (61-42-8)	Tennessee-Vanderbilt	88	Tennessee (57-26-5)
Indiana-Purdue	97	Purdue (58-33-6)	Texas-Texas A&M	101	Texas (64-32-5)
Iowa-Iowa St	42	Iowa (30-12-0)	UCLA-USC	64	USC (34-23-7)
Kansas-Missouri	103	Missouri (48-46-9)	Utah-Utah St	92	Utah (61-27-4)
Kansas-Kansas St	92	Kansas (61-26-5)	Washington-Wash.St	87	Washington (55-26-6)

Associated Press Final Polls

The Associated Press introduced its weekly college football poll of sportswriters (later, sportswriters and broadcasters) in 1936. The final AP poll was released at the end of the regular season until 1965, when bowl results were included for one year. After a two-year return to regular season games only, the final poll has come out after the bowls since 1968.

1936

Final poll released Nov. 30. Top 20 regular season results after that: **Dec. 5**—#8 Notre Dame tied USC, 13-13; #17 Tennessee tied Ole Miss, 0-0; #18 Arkansas over Texas, 6-0. **Dec. 12**—#16 TCU over #6 Santa Clara, 9-0.

	As of Nov. 30	Head Coach	After Bowls
1 Minnesota	7-1-0	Bernie Bierman	same
2 LSU	9-0-1	Bernie Moore	9-1-1
3 Pittsburgh	7-1-1	Jock Sutherland	8-1-1
4 Alabama	8-0-1	Frank Thomas	same
5 Washington	7-1-1	Jimmy Phelan	7-2-1
6 Santa Clara	7-0-0	Buck Shaw	8-1-0
7 Northwestern	7-1-0	Pappy Waldorf	same
8 Notre Dame	6-2-0	Elmer Layden	6-2-1
9 Nebraska	7-2-0	Dana X. Bible	same
10 Penn	7-1-0	Harvey Harman	same
11 Duke	9-1-0	Wallace Wade	same
12 Yale	7-1-0	Ducky Pond	same
13 Dartmouth	7-1-1	Red Blaik	same
14 Duquesne	7-2-0	John Smith	8-2-0
15 Fordham	5-1-2	Jim Crowley	same
16 TCU	7-2-2	Dutch Meyer	9-2-2
17 Tennessee	6-2-1	Bob Neyland	6-2-2
18 Arkansas	6-3-0	Fred Thomsen	7-3-0
Navy	6-3-0	Tom Hamilton	same
20 Marquette	7-1-0	Frank Murray	7-2-0

Key Bowl Games

Sugar—#6 Santa Clara over #2 LSU, 21-14; **Rose**—#3 Pitt over #5 Washington, 21-0; **Orange**—#14 Duquesne over Mississippi St., 13-12; **Cotton**—#16 TCU over #20 Marquette, 16-6.

1937

Final poll released Nov. 29. Top 20 regular season results after that: **Dec. 4**—#18 Rice over SMU, 15-7.

	As of Nov. 29	Head Coach	After Bowls
1 Pittsburgh	9-0-1	Jock Sutherland	same
2 California	9-0-1	Stub Allison	10-0-1
3 Fordham	7-0-1	Jim Crowley	same
4 Alabama	9-0-0	Frank Thomas	9-1-0
5 Minnesota	6-2-0	Bernie Bierman	same
6 Villanova	8-0-1	Clipper Smith	same
7 Dartmouth	7-0-2	Red Blaik	same
8 LSU	9-1-0	Bernie Moore	9-2-0
9 Notre Dame	6-2-1	Elmer Layden	same
Santa Clara	8-0-0	Buck Shaw	9-0-0
11 Nebraska	6-1-2	Biff Jones	same
12 Yale	6-1-1	Ducky Pond	same
13 Ohio St.	6-2-0	Francis Schmidt	same
14 Holy Cross	8-0-2	Eddie Anderson	same
Arkansas	6-2-2	Fred Thomsen	same
16 TCU	4-2-2	Dutch Meyer	same
17 Colorado	8-0-0	Bunnie Oakes	8-1-0
18 Rice	4-3-2	Jimmy Kitts	6-3-2
19 North Carolina	7-1-1	Ray Wolf	same
20 Duke	7-2-1	Wallace Wade	same

Key Bowl Games

Rose—#2 Cal over #4 Alabama, 13-0; **Sugar**—#9 Santa Clara over #8 LSU, 6-0; **Cotton**—#18 Rice over #17 Colorado, 28-14; **Orange**—Auburn over Michigan St., 6-0.

1938

Final poll released Dec. 5. Top 20 regular season results after that: **Dec. 26**—#14 Cal over Georgia Tech, 13-7.

	As of Dec. 5	Head Coach	After Bowls
1 TCU	10-0-0	Dutch Meyer	11-0-0
2 Tennessee	10-0-0	Bob Neyland	11-0-0
3 Duke	9-0-0	Wallace Wade	9-1-0
4 Oklahoma	10-0-0	Tom Stidham	10-1-0
5 Notre Dame	8-1-0	Elmer Layden	same
6 Carnegie Tech	7-1-0	Bill Kern	7-2-0
7 USC	8-2-0	Howard Jones	9-2-0
8 Pittsburgh	8-2-0	Jock Sutherland	same
9 Holy Cross	8-1-0	Eddie Anderson	same
10 Minnesota	6-2-0	Bernie Bierman	same
11 Texas Tech	10-0-0	Pete Cawthon	10-1-0
12 Cornell	5-1-1	Carl Snavely	same
13 Alabama	7-1-1	Frank Thomas	same
14 California	9-1-0	Stub Allison	10-1-0
15 Fordham	6-1-2	Jim Crowley	same
16 Michigan	6-1-1	Fritz Crisler	same
17 Northwestern	4-2-2	Pappy Waldorf	same
18 Villanova	8-0-1	Clipper Smith	same
19 Tulane	7-2-1	Red Dawson	same
20 Dartmouth	7-2-0	Red Blaik	same

Key Bowl Games

Sugar—#1 TCU over #6 Carnegie Tech, 15-7; **Orange**—#2 Tennessee over #4 Oklahoma, 17-0; **Rose**—#7 USC over #3 Duke, 7-3; **Cotton**—St. Mary's over #11 Texas Tech 20-13.

1939

Final poll released Dec. 11. Top 20 regular season results after that: None.

	As of Dec. 11	Head Coach	After Bowls
1 Texas A&M	10-0-0	Homer Norton	11-0-0
2 Tennessee	10-0-0	Bob Neyland	10-1-0
3 USC	7-0-2	Howard Jones	8-0-2
4 Cornell	8-0-0	Carl Snavely	same
5 Tulane	8-0-1	Red Dawson	8-1-1
6 Missouri	8-1-0	Don Faurot	8-2-0
7 UCLA	6-0-4	Babe Horrell	same
8 Duke	8-1-0	Wallace Wade	same
9 Iowa	6-1-1	Eddie Anderson	same
10 Duquesne	8-0-1	Buff Donelli	same
11 Boston College	9-1-0	Frank Leahy	9-2-0
12 Clemson	8-1-0	Jess Neely	9-1-0
13 Notre Dame	7-2-0	Elmer Layden	same
14 Santa Clara	5-1-3	Buck Shaw	same
15 Ohio St.	6-2-0	Francis Schmidt	same
16 Georgia Tech	7-2-0	Bill Alexander	8-2-0
17 Fordham	6-2-0	Jim Crowley	same
18 Nebraska	7-1-1	Biff Jones	same
19 Oklahoma	6-2-1	Tom Stidham	same
20 Michigan	6-2-0	Fritz Crisler	same

Key Bowl Games

Sugar—#1 Texas A&M over #5 Tulane, 14-13; **Rose**—#3 USC over #2 Tennessee, 14-0; **Orange**—#16 Georgia Tech over #6 Missouri, 21-7; **Cotton**—#12 Clemson over #11 Boston College, 6-3.

1940

Final poll released Dec. 2. Top 20 regular season results after that: **Dec. 7**—#16 SMU over Rice, 7-6.

	As of Dec. 2	Head Coach	After Bowls
1 Minnesota	8-0-0	Bernie Bierman	same
2 Stanford	9-0-0	Clark Shaughnessy	10-0-0
3 Michigan	7-1-0	Fritz Crisler	same
4 Tennessee	10-0-0	Bob Neyland	10-1-0
5 Boston College	10-0-0	Frank Leahy	11-0-0
6 Texas A&M	8-1-0	Homer Norton	9-1-0
7 Nebraska	8-1-0	Biff Jones	8-2-0
8 Northwestern	6-2-0	Pappy Waldorf	same
9 Mississippi St.	9-0-1	Allyn McKeen	10-0-1
10 Washington	7-2-0	Jimmy Phelan	same
11 Santa Clara	6-1-1	Buck Shaw	same
12 Fordham	7-1-0	Jim Crowley	7-2-0
13 Georgetown	8-1-0	Jack Hagerty	8-2-0
14 Penn	6-1-1	George Munger	same
15 Cornell	6-2-0	Carl Snavely	same
16 SMU	7-1-1	Matty Bell	8-1-1
17 Hardin-Simmons	9-0-0	Warren Woodson	same
18 Duke	7-2-0	Wallace Wade	same
19 Lafayette	9-0-0	Hooks Mylin	same
20 —			

Note: Only 19 teams ranked.

Key Bowl Games

Rose—#2 Stanford over #7 Nebraska, 21-13; **Sugar**—#5 Boston College over #4 Tennessee, 19-13; **Cotton**—#6 Texas A&M over #12 Fordham, 13-12; **Orange**—#9 Mississippi St. over #13 Georgetown, 14-7.

1941

Final poll released Dec. 1. Top 20 regular season results after that: **Dec. 6**—#4 Texas over Oregon, 71-7; #9 Texas A&M over #19 Washington St., 7-0; #16 Mississippi St. over San Francisco, 26-13.

	As of Dec. 1	Head Coach	After Bowls
1 Minnesota	8-0-0	Bernie Bierman	same
2 Duke	9-0-0	Wallace Wade	9-1-0
3 Notre Dame	8-0-1	Frank Leahy	same
4 Texas	7-1-1	Dana X. Bible	8-1-1
5 Michigan	6-1-1	Fritz Crisler	same
6 Fordham	7-1-0	Jim Crowley	8-1-0
7 Missouri	8-1-0	Don Faurot	8-2-0
8 Duquesne	8-0-0	Buff Donelli	same
9 Texas A&M	8-1-0	Homer Norton	9-2-0
10 Navy	7-1-1	Swede Larson	same
11 Northwestern	5-3-0	Pappy Waldorf	same
12 Oregon St.	7-2-0	Lon Stiner	8-2-0
13 Ohio St.	6-1-1	Paul Brown	same
14 Georgia	8-1-1	Wally Butts	9-1-1
15 Penn	7-1-1	George Munger	same
16 Mississippi St.	7-1-1	Allyn McKeen	8-1-1
17 Mississippi	6-2-1	Harry Mehre	same
18 Tennessee	8-2-0	John Barnhill	same
19 Washington St.	6-3-0	Babe Hollingbery	6-4-0
20 Alabama	8-2-0	Frank Thomas	9-2-0

Note: 1942 Rose Bowl moved to Durham, N.C., for one year after outbreak of World War II.

Key Bowl Games

Rose—#12 Oregon St. over #2 Duke, 20-16; **Sugar**—#6 Fordham over #7 Missouri, 2-0; **Cotton**—#20 Alabama over #9 Texas A&M, 29-21; **Orange**—#14 Georgia over TCU, 40-26.

1942

Final poll released Nov. 30. Top 20 regular season results after that: **Dec. 5**—#6 Notre Dame tied Great Lakes Naval Station, 13-13; #13 UCLA over Idaho, 40-13; #14 William & Mary over Oklahoma, 14-7; #17 Washington St. lost to Texas A&M, 21-0; #18 Mississippi St. over San Francisco, 19-7. **Dec. 12**—#13 UCLA over USC, 14-7.

	As of Nov. 30	Head Coach	After Bowls
1 Ohio St.	9-1-0	Paul Brown	same
2 Georgia	10-1-0	Wally Butts	11-1-0
3 Wisconsin	8-1-1	Harry Stuhldreher	same
4 Tulsa	10-0-0	Henry Frnka	10-1-0
5 Georgia Tech	9-1-0	Bill Alexander	9-2-0
6 Notre Dame	7-2-1	Frank Leahy	7-2-2
7 Tennessee	8-1-1	John Barnhill	9-1-1
8 Boston College	8-1-0	Denny Myers	8-2-0
9 Michigan	7-3-0	Fritz Crisler	same
10 Alabama	7-3-0	Frank Thomas	8-3-0
11 Texas	8-2-0	Dana X. Bible	9-2-0
12 Stanford	6-4-0	Marchie Schwartz	same
13 UCLA	5-3-0	Babe Horrell	7-4-0
14 William & Mary	8-1-1	Carl Voyles	9-1-1
15 Santa Clara	7-2-0	Buck Shaw	same
16 Auburn	6-4-1	Jack Meagher	same
17 Washington St.	6-1-2	Babe Hollingbery	6-2-2
18 Mississippi St.	7-2-0	Allyn McKeen	8-2-0
19 Minnesota	5-4-0	George Hauser	same
Holy Cross	5-4-1	Ank Scanlon	same
Penn St.	6-1-1	Bob Higgins	same

Key Bowl Games

Rose—#2 Georgia over #13 UCLA, 9-0; **Sugar**—#7 Tennessee over #4 Tulsa, 14-7; **Cotton**—#11 Texas over #5 Georgia Tech, 14-7; **Orange**—#10 Alabama over #8 Boston College, 37-21.

1943

Final poll released Nov. 29. Top 20 regular season results after that: **Dec. 11**—#10 March Field over #19 Pacific, 19-0.

	As of Nov. 29	Head Coach	After Bowls
1 Notre Dame	9-1-0	Frank Leahy	same
2 Iowa Pre-Flight	9-1-0	Don Faurot	same
3 Michigan	8-1-0	Fritz Crisler	same
4 Navy	8-1-0	Billick Whelchel	same
5 Purdue	9-0-0	Elmer Burnham	same
6 Great Lakes Naval Station	10-2-0	Tony Hinkle	same
7 Duke	8-1-0	Eddie Cameron	same
8 Del Monte Pre-Flight	7-1-0	Bill Kern	same
9 Northwestern	6-2-0	Pappy Waldorf	same
10 March Field	8-1-0	Paul Schissler	9-1-0
11 Army	7-2-1	Red Blaik	same
12 Washington	4-0-0	Ralph Welch	4-1-0
13 Georgia Tech	7-3-0	Bill Alexander	8-3-0
14 Texas	7-1-0	Dana X. Bible	7-1-1
15 Tulsa	6-0-1	Henry Frnka	6-1-1
16 Dartmouth	6-1-0	Earl Brown	same
17 Bainbridge Navy Training School	7-0-0	Joe Maniaci	same
18 Colorado College	7-0-0	Hal White	same
19 Pacific	7-1-0	Amos A. Stagg	7-2-0
20 Penn	6-2-1	George Munger	same

Key Bowl Games

Rose—USC over #12 Washington, 29-0; **Sugar**—#13 Georgia Tech over #15 Tulsa, 20-18; **Cotton**—#14 Texas tied Randolph Field, 7-7; **Orange**—LSU over Texas A&M, 19-14.

Associated Press Final Polls (Cont.)

1944

Final poll released Dec. 4. Top 20 regular season results after that: **Dec. 10**—#3 Randolph Field over #10 March Field, 20-7; #18 Fort Pierce over Kessler Field, 34-7; Morris Field over #20 Second Air Force, 14-7.

	As of Dec. 4	Head Coach	After Bowls
1 Army	9-0-0	Red Blaik	same
2 Ohio St.	9-0-0	Carroll Widdoes	same
3 Randolph Field	10-0-0	Frank Tritico	12-0-0
4 Navy	6-3-0	Oscar Hagberg	same
5 Bainbridge Navy Training School	10-0-0	Joe Maniaci	same
6 Iowa Pre-Flight	10-1-0	Jack Meagher	same
7 USC	7-0-2	Jeff Cravath	8-0-2
8 Michigan	8-2-0	Fritz Crisler	same
9 Notre Dame	8-2-0	Ed McKeever	same
10 March Field	7-0-2	Paul Schissler	7-1-2
11 Duke	5-4-0	Eddie Cameron	6-4-0
12 Tennessee	7-0-1	John Barnhill	7-1-1
13 Georgia Tech	8-2-0	Bill Alexander	8-3-0
14 Norman Pre-Flight	6-0-0	John Gregg	same
15 Illinois	5-4-1	Ray Eliot	same
16 El Toro Marines	8-1-0	Dick Hanley	same
17 Great Lakes Naval Station	9-2-1	Paul Brown	same
18 Fort Pierce	8-0-0	Hamp Pool	9-0-0
19 St.Mary's Pre-Flight	4-4-0	Jules Sikes	same
20 Second Air Force	10-2-1	Bill Reese	10-4-1

Key Bowl Games

Treasury—#3 Randolph Field over #20 Second Air Force, 13-6; **Rose**—#7 USC over #12 Tennessee, 25-0; **Sugar**—#11 Duke over Alabama, 29-26; **Orange**—Tulsa over #13 Georgia Tech, 26-12; **Cotton**—Oklahoma A&M over TCU, 34-0.

1945

Final poll released Dec. 3. Top 20 regular season results after that: None.

	As of Dec. 3	Head Coach	After Bowls
1 Army	9-0-0	Red Blaik	same
2 Alabama	9-0-0	Frank Thomas	10-0-0
3 Navy	7-1-0	Oscar Hagberg	same
4 Indiana	9-0-1	Bo McMillan	same
5 Oklahoma A&M	8-0-0	Jim Lookabaugh	9-0-0
6 Michigan	7-3-0	Fritz Crisler	same
7 St. Mary's-CA	7-1-0	Jimmy Phelan	7-2-0
8 Penn	6-2-0	George Munger	same
9 Notre Dame	7-2-1	Hugh Devore	same
10 Texas	9-1-0	Dana X. Bible	10-1-0
11 USC	7-3-0	Jeff Cravath	7-4-0
12 Ohio St.	7-2-0	Carroll Widdoes	same
13 Duke	6-2-0	Eddie Cameron	same
14 Tennessee	8-1-0	John Barnhill	same
15 LSU	7-2-0	Bernie Moore	same
16 Holy Cross	8-1-0	John DeGrosa	8-2-0
17 Tulsa	8-2-0	Henry Frnka	8-3-0
18 Georgia	8-2-0	Wally Butts	9-2-0
19 Wake Forest	4-3-1	Peahead Walker	5-3-1
20 Columbia	8-1-0	Lou Little	same

Key Bowl Games

Rose—#2 Alabama over #11 USC, 34-14; **Sugar**— #5 Oklahoma A&M over #7 St. Mary's, 33-13; **Cotton**—#10 Texas over Missouri, 40-27; **Orange**—Miami-FL over #16 Holy Cross, 13-6.

1946

Final poll released Dec. 2. Top 20 regular season results after that: None.

	As of Dec. 2	Head Coach	After Bowls
1 Notre Dame	8-0-1	Frank Leahy	same
2 Army	9-0-1	Red Blaik	same
3 Georgia	10-0-0	Wally Butts	11-0-0
4 UCLA	10-0-0	Bert LaBrucherie	10-1-0
5 Illinois	7-2-0	Ray Eliot	8-2-0
6 Michigan	6-2-1	Fritz Crisler	same
7 Tennessee	9-1-0	Bob Neyland	9-2-0
8 LSU	9-1-0	Bernie Moore	9-1-1
9 North Carolina	8-1-1	Carl Snavely	8-2-1
10 Rice	8-2-0	Jess Neely	9-2-0
11 Georgia Tech	8-2-0	Bobby Dodd	9-2-0
12 Yale	7-1-1	Howard Odell	same
13 Penn	6-2-0	George Munger	same
14 Oklahoma	7-3-0	Jim Tatum	8-3-0
15 Texas	8-2-0	Dana X. Bible	same
16 Arkansas	6-3-1	John Barnhill	6-3-2
17 Tulsa	9-1-0	J.O. Brothers	same
18 N.C. State	8-2-0	Beattie Feathers	8-3-0
19 Delaware	9-0-0	Bill Murray	10-0-0
20 Indiana	6-3-0	Bo McMillan	same

Key Bowl Games

Sugar—#3 Georgia over #9 N.Carolina, 20-10; **Rose**—#5 Illinois over #4 UCLA, 45-14; **Orange**—#10 Rice over #7 Tennessee, 8-0; **Cotton**—#8 LSU tied #16 Arkansas, 0-0.

1947

Final poll released Dec. 8. Top 20 regular season results after that: None.

	As of Dec. 8	Head Coach	After Bowls
1 Notre Dame	9-0-0	Frank Leahy	same
2 Michigan	9-0-0	Fritz Crisler	10-0-0
3 SMU	9-0-1	Matty Bell	9-0-2
4 Penn St.	9-0-0	Bob Higgins	9-0-1
5 Texas	9-1-0	Blair Cherry	10-1-0
6 Alabama	8-2-0	Red Drew	8-3-0
7 Penn	7-0-1	George Munger	same
8 USC	7-1-1	Jeff Cravath	7-2-1
9 North Carolina	8-2-0	Carl Snavely	same
10 Georgia Tech	9-1-0	Bobby Dodd	10-1-0
11 Army	5-2-2	Red Blaik	same
12 Kansas	8-0-2	George Sauer	8-1-2
13 Mississippi	8-2-0	Johnny Vaught	9-2-0
14 William & Mary	9-1-0	Rube McCray	9-2-0
15 California	9-1-0	Pappy Waldorf	same
16 Oklahoma	7-2-1	Bud Wilkinson	same
17 N.C. State	5-3-1	Beattie Feathers	same
18 Rice	6-3-1	Jess Neely	same
19 Duke	4-3-2	Wallace Wade	same
20 Columbia	7-2-0	Lou Little	same

Key Bowl Games

Rose—#2 Michigan over #8 USC, 49-0; **Cotton**—#3 SMU tied #4 Penn St., 13-13; **Sugar**—#5 Texas over #6 Alabama, 27-7; **Orange**—#10 Georgia Tech over #12 Kansas, 20-14.

Note: An unprecedented "Who's No. 1?" poll was conducted by AP after the Rose Bowl game, pitting Notre Dame against Michigan. The Wolverines won the vote, 226-119, but AP ruled that the Irish would be the No. 1 team of record.

1948

Final poll released Nov. 29. Top 20 regular season results after that: **Dec. 3**—#12 Vanderbilt over Miami-FL, 33-6. **Dec. 4**—#2 Notre Dame tied USC, 14-14; #11 Clemson over The Citadel, 20-0.

	As of Nov.29	Head Coach	After Bowls
1 Michigan	9-0-0	Bennie Oosterbaan	same
2 Notre Dame	9-0-0	Frank Leahy	9-0-1
3 North Carolina	9-0-1	Carl Snavely	9-1-1
4 California	10-0-0	Pappy Waldorf	10-1-0
5 Oklahoma	9-1-0	Bud Wilkinson	10-1-0
6 Army	8-0-1	Red Blaik	same
7 Northwestern	7-2-0	Bob Voigts	8-2-0
8 Georgia	9-1-0	Wally Butts	9-2-0
9 Oregon	9-1-0	Jim Aiken	9-2-0
10 SMU	8-1-1	Matty Bell	9-1-1
11 Clemson	9-0-0	Frank Howard	11-0-0
12 Vanderbilt	7-2-1	Red Sanders	8-2-1
13 Tulane	9-1-0	Henry Frnka	same
14 Michigan St.	6-2-2	Biggie Munn	same
15 Mississippi	8-1-0	Johnny Vaught	same
16 Minnesota	7-2-0	Bernie Bierman	same
17 William & Mary	6-2-2	Rube McCray	7-2-2
18 Penn St.	7-1-1	Bob Higgins	same
19 Cornell	8-1-0	Lefty James	same
20 Wake Forest	6-3-0	Peahead Walker	6-4-0

Note: Big Nine "no-repeat" rule kept Michigan from Rose Bowl.

Key Bowl Games

Sugar—#5 Oklahoma over #3 North Carolina, 14-6; **Rose**—#7 Northwestern over #4 Cal, 20-14; **Orange**—Texas over #8 Georgia, 41-28; **Cotton**—#10 SMU over #9 Oregon, 21-13.

1949

Final poll released Nov. 28. Top 20 regular season results after that: **Dec. 2**—#14 Maryland over Miami-FL, 13-0. **Dec. 3**—#1 Notre Dame over SMU, 27-20; #10 Pacific over Hawaii, 75-0.

	As of Nov. 28	Head Coach	After Bowls
1 Notre Dame	9-0-0	Frank Leahy	10-0-0
2 Oklahoma	10-0-0	Bud Wilkinson	11-0-0
3 California	10-0-0	Pappy Waldorf	10-1-0
4 Army	9-0-0	Red Blaik	same
5 Rice	9-1-0	Jess Neely	10-1-0
6 Ohio St.	6-1-2	Wes Fesler	7-1-2
7 Michigan	6-2-1	Bennie Oosterbaan	same
8 Minnesota	7-2-0	Bernie Bierman	same
9 LSU	8-2-0	Gaynell Tinsley	8-3-0
10 Pacific	10-0-0	Larry Siemering	11-0-0
11 Kentucky	9-2-0	Bear Bryant	9-3-0
12 Cornell	8-1-0	Lefty James	same
13 Villanova	8-1-0	Jim Leonard	same
14 Maryland	7-1-0	Jim Tatum	9-1-0
15 Santa Clara	7-2-1	Len Casanova	8-2-1
16 North Carolina	7-3-0	Carl Snavely	7-4-0
17 Tennessee	7-2-1	Bob Neyland	same
18 Princeton	6-3-0	Charlie Caldwell	same
19 Michigan St.	6-3-0	Biggie Munn	same
20 Missouri	7-3-0	Don Faurot	7-4-0
Baylor	8-2-0	Bob Woodruff	same

Key Bowl Games

Sugar—#2 Oklahoma over #9 LSU, 35-0; **Rose**—#6 Ohio St. over #3 Cal, 17-14; **Cotton**—#5 Rice over #16 North Carolina, 27-13; **Orange**—#15 Santa Clara over #11 Kentucky, 21-13.

1950

Final poll released Nov. 27. Top 20 regular season results after that: **Nov. 30**—#3 Texas over Texas A&M, 17-0. **Dec. 1**—#15 Miami-FL over Missouri, 27—9. **Dec. 2**—#1 Oklahoma over Okla. A&M, 41-14; Navy over #2 Army, 14-2; #4 Tennessee over Vanderbilt, 43-0; #16 Alabama over Auburn, 34-0; #19 Tulsa over Houston, 28-21; #20 Tulane tied LSU, 14-14. **Dec. 9**—#3 Texas over LSU, 21-6.

	As of Nov. 27	Head Coach	After Bowls
1 Oklahoma	9-0-0	Bud Wilkinson	10-1-0
2 Army	8-1-0	Red Blaik	same
3 Texas	7-1-0	Blair Cherry	9-2-0
4 Tennessee	9-1-0	Bob Neyland	11-1-0
5 California	9-0-1	Pappy Waldorf	9-1-1
6 Princeton	9-0-0	Charlie Caldwell	same
7 Kentucky	10-1-0	Bear Bryant	11-1-0
8 Michigan St.	8-1-0	Biggie Munn	same
9 Michigan	5-3-1	Bennie Oosterbaan	6-3-1
10 Clemson	8-0-1	Frank Howard	9-0-1
11 Washington	8-2-0	Howard Odell	same
12 Wyoming	9-0-0	Bowden Wyatt	10-0-0
13 Illinois	7-2-0	Ray Eliot	same
14 Ohio St.	6-3-0	Wes Fesler	same
15 Miami-FL	8-0-1	Andy Gustafson	9-1-1
16 Alabama	8-2-0	Red Drew	9-2-0
17 Nebraska	6-2-1	Bill Glassford	same
18 Wash. & Lee	8-2-0	George Barclay	8-3-0
19 Tulsa	8-1-1	J.O. Brothers	9-1-1
20 Tulane	6-2-0	Henry Frnka	6-2-1

Key Bowl Games

Sugar—#7 Kentucky over #1 Oklahoma, 13-7; **Cotton**—#4 Tennessee over #3 Texas, 20-14; **Rose**—#9 Michigan over #5 Cal, 14-6; **Orange**—#10 Clemson over #15 Miami-FL, 15-14.

1951

Final poll released Dec. 3. Top 20 regular season results after that: None.

	As of Dec. 3	Head Coach	After Bowls
1 Tennessee	10-0-0	Bob Neyland	10-1-0
2 Michigan St.	9-0-0	Biggie Munn	same
3 Maryland	9-0-0	Jim Tatum	10-0-0
4 Illinois	8-0-1	Ray Eliot	9-0-1
5 Georgia Tech	10-0-1	Bobby Dodd	11-0-1
6 Princeton	9-0-0	Charlie Caldwell	same
7 Stanford	9-1-0	Chuck Taylor	9-2-0
8 Wisconsin	7-1-1	Ivy Williamson	8-2-1
9 Baylor	8-1-1	George Sauer	same
10 Oklahoma	8-2-0	Bud Wilkinson	same
11 TCU	6-4-0	Dutch Meyer	6-5-0
12 California	8-2-0	Pappy Waldorf	same
13 Virginia	8-1-0	Art Guepe	same
14 San Francisco	9-0-0	Joe Kuharich	same
15 Kentucky	7-4-0	Bear Bryant	8-4-0
16 Boston Univ.	6-4-0	Buff Donelli	same
17 UCLA	5-3-1	Red Sanders	same
18 Washington St.	7-3-0	Forest Evashevski	same
19 Holy Cross	8-2-0	Eddie Anderson	same
Clemson	7-2-0	Frank Howard	7-3-0

Key Bowl Games

Sugar—#3 Maryland over #1 Tennessee, 28-13; **Rose**—#4 Illinois over #7 Stanford, 40-7; **Orange**—#5 Georgia Tech over #9 Baylor, 17-14; **Cotton**—#15 Kentucky over #11 TCU, 20-7.

Associated Press Final Polls (Cont.)

1952

Final poll released Dec. 1. Top 20 regular season results after that: **Dec. 6**—#15 Florida over #20 Kentucky, 27-20.

		As of Dec. 1	Head Coach	After Bowls
1	Michigan St.	9-0-0	Biggie Munn	same
2	Georgia Tech	11-0-0	Bobby Dodd	12-0-0
3	Notre Dame	7-2-1	Frank Leahy	same
4	Oklahoma	8-1-1	Bud Wilkinson	same
5	USC	9-1-0	Jess Hill	10-1-0
6	UCLA	8-1-0	Red Sanders	same
7	Mississippi	8-0-2	Johnny Vaught	8-1-2
8	Tennessee	8-1-1	Bob Neyland	8-2-1
9	Alabama	9-2-0	Red Drew	10-2-0
10	Texas	8-2-0	Ed Price	9-2-0
11	Wisconsin	6-2-1	Ivy Williamson	6-3-1
12	Tulsa	8-1-1	J.O. Brothers	8-2-1
13	Maryland	7-2-0	Jim Tatum	same
14	Syracuse	7-2-0	Ben Schwartzwalder	7-3-0
15	Florida	6-3-0	Bob Woodruff	8-3-0
16	Duke	8-2-0	Bill Murray	same
17	Ohio St.	6-3-0	Woody Hayes	same
18	Purdue	4-3-2	Stu Holcomb	same
19	Princeton	8-1-0	Charlie Caldwell	same
20	Kentucky	5-3-2	Bear Bryant	5-4-2

Note: Michigan St. would officially join Big Ten in 1953.

Key Bowl Games

Sugar—#2 Georgia Tech over #7 Ole Miss, 24-7; **Rose**—#5 USC over #11 Wisconsin, 7-0; **Cotton**—#10 Texas over #8 Tennessee, 16-0; **Orange**—#9 Alabama over #14 Syracuse, 61-6.

1953

Final poll released Nov. 30. Top 20 regular season results after that: **Dec. 5**—#2 Notre Dame over SMU, 40-14.

		As of Nov. 30	Head Coach	After Bowls
1	Maryland	10-0-0	Jim Tatum	10-1-0
2	Notre Dame	8-0-1	Frank Leahy	9-0-1
3	Michigan St.	8-1-0	Biggie Munn	9-1-0
4	Oklahoma	8-1-1	Bud Wilkinson	9-1-1
5	UCLA	8-1-0	Red Sanders	8-2-0
6	Rice	8-2-0	Jess Neely	9-2-0
7	Illinois	7-1-1	Ray Eliot	same
8	Georgia Tech	8-2-1	Bobby Dodd	9-2-1
9	Iowa	5-3-1	Forest Evashevski	same
10	West Virginia	8-1-0	Art Lewis	8-2-0
11	Texas	7-3-0	Ed Price	same
12	Texas Tech	10-1-0	DeWitt Weaver	11-1-0
13	Alabama	6-2-3	Red Drew	6-3-3
14	Army	7-1-1	Red Blaik	same
15	Wisconsin	6-2-1	Ivy Williamson	same
16	Kentucky	7-2-1	Bear Bryant	same
17	Auburn	7-2-1	Shug Jordan	7-3-1
18	Duke	7-2-1	Bill Murray	same
19	Stanford	6-3-1	Chuck Taylor	same
20	Michigan	6-3-0	Bennie Oosterbaan	same

Key Bowl Games

Orange—#4 Oklahoma over #1 Maryland, 7-0; **Rose**—#3 Michigan St. over #5 UCLA, 28-20; **Cotton**—#6 Rice over #13 Alabama, 28-6; **Sugar**—#8 Georgia Tech over #10 West Virginia, 42-19.

1954

Final poll released Nov. 29. Top 20 regular season results after that: **Dec. 4**—#4 Notre Dame over SMU, 26-14.

		As of Nov. 29	Head Coach	After Bowls
1	Ohio St.	9-0-0	Woody Hayes	10-0-0
2	UCLA	9-0-0	Red Sanders	same
3	Oklahoma	10-0-0	Bud Wilkinson	same
4	Notre Dame	8-1-0	Terry Brennan	9-1-0
5	Navy	7-2-0	Eddie Erdelatz	8-2-0
6	Mississippi	9-1-0	Johnny Vaught	9-2-0
7	Army	7-2-0	Red Blaik	same
8	Maryland	7-2-1	Jim Tatum	same
9	Wisconsin	7-2-0	Ivy Williamson	same
10	Arkansas	8-2-0	Bowden Wyatt	8-3-0
11	Miami-FL	8-1-0	Andy Gustafson	same
12	West Virginia	8-1-0	Art Lewis	same
13	Auburn	7-3-0	Shug Jordan	8-3-0
14	Duke	7-2-1	Bill Murray	8-2-1
15	Michigan	6-3-0	Bennie Oosterbaan	same
16	Virginia Tech	8-0-1	Frank Moseley	same
17	USC	8-3-0	Jess Hill	8-4-0
18	Baylor	7-3-0	George Sauer	7-4-0
19	Rice	7-3-0	Jess Neely	same
20	Penn St.	7-2-0	Rip Engle	same

Note: PCC and Big Seven "no-repeat" rules kept UCLA and Oklahoma from Orange and Rose bowls, respectively.

Key Bowl Games

Rose—#1 Ohio St. over #17 USC, 20-7; **Sugar**—#5 Navy over #6 Ole Miss, 21-0; **Cotton**—Georgia Tech over #10 Arkansas, 14-6; **Orange**—#14 Duke over Nebraska, 34-7.

1955

Final poll released Nov. 28. Top 20 regular season results after that: None.

		As of Nov. 28	Head Coach	After Bowls
1	Oklahoma	10-0-0	Bud Wilkinson	11-0-0
2	Michigan St.	8-1-0	Duffy Daugherty	9-1-0
3	Maryland	10-0-0	Jim Tatum	10-1-0
4	UCLA	9-1-0	Red Sanders	9-2-0
5	Ohio St.	7-2-0	Woody Hayes	same
6	TCU	9-1-0	Abe Martin	9-2-0
7	Georgia Tech	8-1-1	Bobby Dodd	9-1-1
8	Auburn	8-1-1	Shug Jordan	8-2-1
9	Notre Dame	8-2-0	Terry Brennan	same
10	Mississippi	9-1-0	Johnny Vaught	10-1-0
11	Pittsburgh	7-3-0	John Michelosen	7-4-0
12	Michigan	7-2-0	Bennie Oosterbaan	same
13	USC	6-4-0	Jess Hill	same
14	Miami-FL	6-3-0	Andy Gustafson	same
15	Miami-OH	9-0-0	Ara Parseghian	same
16	Stanford	6-3-1	Chuck Taylor	same
17	Texas A&M	7-2-1	Bear Bryant	same
18	Navy	6-2-1	Eddie Erdelatz	same
19	West Virginia	8-2-0	Art Lewis	same
20	Army	6-3-0	Red Blaik	same

Note: Big Ten "no-repeat" rule kept Ohio St. from Rose Bowl.

Key Bowl Games

Orange—#1 Oklahoma over #3 Maryland, 20-6; **Rose**—#2 Michigan St. over #4 UCLA, 17-14; **Cotton**—#10 Ole Miss over #6 TCU, 14-13; **Sugar**—#7 Georgia Tech over #11 Pitt, 7-0; **Gator**—Vanderbilt over #8 Auburn, 25-13.

1956

Final poll released Dec. 3. Top 20 regular season results after that: **Dec. 8**—#13 Pitt over #6 Miami-FL, 14-7.

	As of Dec. 3	Head Coach	After Bowls
1 Oklahoma	10-0-0	Bud Wilkinson	same
2 Tennessee	10-0-0	Bowden Wyatt	10-1-0
3 Iowa	8-1-0	Forest Evashevski	9-1-0
4 Georgia Tech	9-1-0	Bobby Dodd	10-1-0
5 Texas A&M	9-0-1	Bear Bryant	same
6 Miami-FL	8-0-1	Andy Gustafson	8-1-1
7 Michigan	7-2-0	Bennie Oosterbaan	same
8 Syracuse	7-1-0	Ben Schwartzwalder	7-2-0
9 Michigan St.	7-2-0	Duffy Daugherty	same
10 Oregon St.	7-2-1	Tommy Prothro	7-3-1
11 Baylor	8-2-0	Sam Boyd	9-2-0
12 Minnesota	6-1-2	Murray Warmath	same
13 Pittsburgh	6-2-1	John Michelosen	7-3-1
14 TCU	7-3-0	Abe Martin	8-3-0
15 Ohio St.	6-3-0	Woody Hayes	same
16 Navy	6-1-2	Eddie Erdelatz	same
17 G. Washington	7-1-1	Gene Sherman	8-1-1
18 USC	8-2-0	Jess Hill	same
19 Clemson	7-1-2	Frank Howard	7-2-2
20 Colorado	7-2-1	Dallas Ward	8-2-1

Note: Big Seven "no-repeat" rule kept Oklahoma from Orange Bowl and Texas A&M was on probation.

Key Bowl Games

Sugar—#11 Baylor over #2 Tennessee, 13-7; **Rose**— #3 Iowa over #10 Oregon St., 35-19; **Gator**—#4 Georgia Tech over #13 Pitt, 21-14; **Cotton**—#14 TCU over #8 Syracuse, 28-27; **Orange**—#20 Colorado over #19 Clemson, 27-21.

1957

Final poll released Dec. 2. Top 20 regular season results after that: **Dec. 7**—#10 Notre Dame over SMU, 54-21.

	As of Dec. 2	Head Coach	After Bowls
1 Auburn	10-0-0	Shug Jordan	same
2 Ohio St.	8-1-0	Woody Hayes	9-1-0
3 Michigan St.	8-1-0	Duffy Daugherty	same
4 Oklahoma	9-1-0	Bud Wilkinson	10-1-0
5 Navy	8-1-1	Eddie Erdelatz	9-1-1
6 Iowa	7-1-1	Forest Evashevski	same
7 Mississippi	8-1-1	Johnny Vaught	9-1-1
8 Rice	7-3-0	Jess Neely	7-4-0
9 Texas A&M	8-2-0	Bear Bryant	8-3-0
10 Notre Dame	6-3-0	Terry Brennan	7-3-0
11 Texas	6-3-1	Darrell Royal	6-4-1
12 Arizona St.	10-0-0	Dan Devine	same
13 Tennessee	7-3-0	Bowden Wyatt	8-3-0
14 Mississippi St.	6-2-1	Wade Walker	same
15 N.C. State	7-1-2	Earle Edwards	same
16 Duke	6-2-1	Bill Murray	6-3-2
17 Florida	6-2-1	Bob Woodruff	same
18 Army	7-2-0	Red Blaik	same
19 Wisconsin	6-3-0	Milt Bruhn	same
20 VMI	9-0-1	John McKenna	same

Note: Auburn on probation, ineligible for bowl game.

Key Bowl Games

Rose—#2 Ohio St. over Oregon, 10-7; **Orange**—#4 Oklahoma over #16 Duke, 48-21; **Cotton**—#5 Navy over #8 Rice, 20-7; **Sugar**—#7 Ole Miss over #11 Texas, 39-7; **Gator**—#13 Tennessee over #9 Texas A&M, 3-0.

1958

Final poll released Dec. 1. Top 20 regular season results after that: None.

	As of Dec. 1	Head Coach	After Bowls
1 LSU	10-0-0	Paul Dietzel	11-0-0
2 Iowa	7-1-1	Forest Evashevski	8-1-1
3 Army	8-0-1	Red Blaik	same
4 Auburn	9-0-1	Shug Jordan	same
5 Oklahoma	9-1-0	Bud Wilkinson	10-1-0
6 Air Force	9-0-1	Ben Martin	9-0-2
7 Wisconsin	7-1-1	Milt Bruhn	same
8 Ohio St.	6-1-2	Woody Hayes	same
9 Syracuse	8-1-0	Ben Schwartzwalder	8-2-0
10 TCU	8-2-0	Abe Martin	8-2-1
11 Mississippi	8-2-0	Johnny Vaught	9-2-0
12 Clemson	8-2-0	Frank Howard	8-3-0
13 Purdue	6-1-2	Jack Mollenkopf	same
14 Florida	6-3-1	Bob Woodruff	6-4-1
15 South Carolina	7-3-0	Warren Giese	same
16 California	7-3-0	Pete Elliott	7-4-0
17 Notre Dame	6-4-0	Terry Brennan	same
18 SMU	6-4-0	Bill Meek	same
19 Oklahoma St.	7-3-0	Cliff Speegle	8-3-0
20 Rutgers	8-1-0	John Stiegman	same

Key Bowl Games

Sugar—#1 LSU over #12 Clemson, 7-0; **Rose**—#2 Iowa over #16 Cal, 38-12; **Orange**—#5 Oklahoma over #9 Syracuse, 21-6; **Cotton**—#6 Air Force tied #10 TCU, 0-0.

1959

Final poll released Dec. 7. Top 20 regular season results after that: None.

	As of Dec. 7	Head Coach	After Bowls
1 Syracuse	10-0-0	Ben Schwartzwalder	11-0-0
2 Mississippi	9-1-0	Johnny Vaught	10-1-0
3 LSU	9-1-0	Paul Dietzel	9-2-0
4 Texas	9-1-0	Darrell Royal	9-2-0
5 Georgia	9-1-0	Wally Butts	10-1-0
6 Wisconsin	7-2-0	Milt Bruhn	7-3-0
7 TCU	8-2-0	Abe Martin	8-3-0
8 Washington	9-1-0	Jim Owens	10-1-0
9 Arkansas	8-2-0	Frank Broyles	9-2-0
10 Alabama	7-1-2	Bear Bryant	7-2-2
11 Clemson	8-2-0	Frank Howard	9-2-0
12 Penn St.	8-2-0	Rip Engle	9-2-0
13 Illinois	5-3-1	Ray Eliot	same
14 USC	8-2-0	Don Clark	same
15 Oklahoma	7-3-0	Bud Wilkinson	same
16 Wyoming	9-1-0	Bob Devaney	same
17 Notre Dame	5-5-0	Joe Kuharich	same
18 Missouri	6-4-0	Dan Devine	6-5-0
19 Florida	5-4-1	Bob Woodruff	same
20 Pittsburgh	6-4-0	John Michelosen	same

Note: Big Seven "no-repeat" rule kept Oklahoma from Orange Bowl.

Key Bowl Games

Cotton—#1 Syracuse over #4 Texas, 23-14; **Sugar**— #2 Ole Miss over #3 LSU, 21-0; **Orange**—#5 Georgia over #18 Missouri, 14-0; **Rose**—#8 Washington over #6 Wisconsin, 44-8; **Bluebonnet**—#11 Clemson over #7 TCU, 23-7; **Gator**—#9 Arkansas over Georgia Tech, 14-7; **Liberty**—#12 Penn St. over #10 Alabama, 7-0.

Associated Press Final Polls (Cont.)

AP ranked only 10 teams from 1962-67.

1960

Final poll released Nov. 28. Top 20 regular season results after that: **Dec. 3**—UCLA over #10 Duke, 27-6.

	As of Nov. 28	Head Coach	After Bowls
1 Minnesota	8-1-0	Murray Warmath	8-2-0
2 Mississippi	9-0-1	Johnny Vaught	10-0-1
3 Iowa	8-1-0	Forest Evashevski	same
4 Navy	9-1-0	Wayne Hardin	9-2-0
5 Missouri	9-1-0	Dan Devine	10-1-0
6 Washington	9-1-0	Jim Owens	10-1-0
7 Arkansas	8-2-0	Frank Broyles	8-3-0
8 Ohio St.	7-2-0	Woody Hayes	same
9 Alabama	8-1-1	Bear Bryant	8-1-2
10 Duke	7-2-0	Bill Murray	8-3-0
11 Kansas	7-2-1	Jack Mitchell	same
12 Baylor	8-2-0	John Bridgers	8-3-0
13 Auburn	8-2-0	Shug Jordan	same
14 Yale	9-0-0	Jordan Olivar	same
15 Michigan St.	6-2-1	Duffy Daugherty	same
16 Penn St.	6-3-0	Rip Engle	7-3-0
17 New Mexico St.	10-0-0	Warren Woodson	11-0-0
18 Florida	8-2-0	Ray Graves	9-2-0
19 Syracuse	7-2-0	Ben Schwartzwalder	same
Purdue	4-4-1	Jack Mollenkopf	same

Key Bowl Games

Rose—#6 Washington over #1 Minnesota, 17-7; **Sugar**—#2 Ole Miss over Rice, 14-6; **Orange**—#5 Missouri over #4 Navy, 21-14; **Cotton**—#10 Duke over #7 Arkansas, 7-6; **Bluebonnet**—#9 Alabama tied Texas, 3-3.

1961

Final poll released Dec. 4. Top 20 regular season results after that: None.

	As of Dec. 4	Head Coach	After Bowls
1 Alabama	10-0-0	Bear Bryant	11-0-0
2 Ohio St.	8-0-1	Woody Hayes	same
3 Texas	9-1-0	Darrell Royal	10-1-0
4 LSU	9-1-0	Paul Dietzel	10-1-0
5 Mississippi	9-1-0	Johnny Vaught	9-2-0
6 Minnesota	7-2-0	Murray Warmath	8-2-0
7 Colorado	9-1-0	Sonny Grandelius	9-2-0
8 Michigan St.	7-2-0	Duffy Daugherty	same
9 Arkansas	8-2-0	Frank Broyles	8-3-0
10 Utah St.	9-0-1	John Ralston	9-1-1
11 Missouri	7-2-1	Dan Devine	same
12 Purdue	6-3-0	Jack Mollenkopf	same
13 Georgia Tech	7-3-0	Bobby Dodd	7-4-0
14 Syracuse	7-3-0	Ben Schwartzwalder	8-3-0
15 Rutgers	9-0-0	John Bateman	same
16 UCLA	7-3-0	Bill Barnes	7-4-0
17 Rice	7-3-0	Jess Neely	7-4-0
Penn St.	7-3-0	Rip Engle	8-3-0
Arizona	8-1-1	Jim LaRue	same
20 Duke	7-3-0	Bill Murray	same

Note: Ohio St. faculty council turned down Rose Bowl invitation citing concern with OSU's overemphasis on sports.

Key Bowl Games

Sugar—#1 Alabama over #9 Arkansas, 10-3; **Cotton**—#3 Texas over #5 Ole Miss, 12-7; **Orange**—#4 LSU over #7 Colorado, 25-7; **Rose**—#6 Minnesota over #16 UCLA, 21-3; **Gotham**—Baylor over #10 Utah St., 24-9.

1962

Final poll released Dec. 3. Top 10 regular season results after that: None.

	As of Dec. 3	Head Coach	After Bowls
1 USC	10-0-0	John McKay	11-0-0
2 Wisconsin	8-1-0	Milt Bruhn	8-2-0
3 Mississippi	9-0-0	Johnny Vaught	10-0-0
4 Texas	9-0-1	Darrell Royal	9-1-1
5 Alabama	9-1-0	Bear Bryant	10-1-0
6 Arkansas	9-1-0	Frank Broyles	9-2-0
7 LSU	8-1-1	Charlie McClendon	9-1-1
8 Oklahoma	8-2-0	Bud Wilkinson	8-3-0
9 Penn St.	9-1-0	Rip Engle	9-2-0
10 Minnesota	6-2-1	Murray Warmath	same

Key Bowl Games

Rose—#1 USC over #2 Wisconsin, 42-37; **Sugar**—#3 Ole Miss over #6 Arkansas, 17-13; **Cotton**—#7 LSU over #4 Texas, 13-0; **Orange**—#5 Alabama over #8 Oklahoma, 17-0; **Gator**—Florida over #9 Penn St., 17-7.

1963

Final poll released Dec. 9. Top 10 regular season results after that: **Dec. 14**—#8 Alabama over Miami-FL, 17-12.

	As of Dec. 9	Head Coach	After Bowls
1 Texas	10-0-0	Darrell Royal	11-0-0
2 Navy	9-1-0	Wayne Hardin	9-2-0
3 Illinois	7-1-1	Pete Elliott	8-1-1
4 Pittsburgh	9-1-0	John Michelosen	same
5 Auburn	9-1-0	Shug Jordan	9-2-0
6 Nebraska	9-1-0	Bob Devaney	10-1-0
7 Mississippi	7-0-2	Johnny Vaught	7-1-2
8 Alabama	7-2-0	Bear Bryant	9-2-0
9 Michigan St.	6-2-1	Duffy Daugherty	same
10 Oklahoma	8-2-0	Bud Wilkinson	same

Key Bowl Games

Cotton—#1 Texas over #2 Navy, 28-6; **Rose**—#3 Illinois over Washington, 17-7; **Orange**—#6 Nebraska over #5 Auburn, 13-7; **Sugar**—#8 Alabama over #7 Ole Miss, 12-7.

1964

Final poll released Nov. 30. Top 10 regular season results after that: **Dec. 5**—Florida over #7 LSU, 20-6.

	As of Nov. 30	Head Coach	After Bowls
1 Alabama	10-0-0	Bear Bryant	10-1-0
2 Arkansas	10-0-0	Frank Broyles	11-0-0
3 Notre Dame	9-1-0	Ara Parseghian	same
4 Michigan	8-1-0	Bump Elliott	9-1-0
5 Texas	9-1-0	Darrell Royal	10-1-0
6 Nebraska	9-1-0	Bob Devaney	9-2-0
7 LSU	7-1-1	Charlie McClendon	8-2-1
8 Oregon St.	8-2-0	Tommy Prothro	8-3-0
9 Ohio St.	7-2-0	Woody Hayes	same
10 USC	7-3-0	John McKay	same

Key Bowl Games

Orange—#5 Texas over #1 Alabama, 21-17; **Cotton**—#2 Arkansas over #6 Nebraska, 10-7; **Rose**—#4 Michigan over #8 Oregon St., 34-7; **Sugar**—#7 LSU over Syracuse, 13-10.

1965

Final poll taken after bowl games for the first time.

	After Bowls	Head Coach	Regular Season
1 Alabama	9-1-1	Bear Bryant	8-1-1
2 Michigan St.	10-1-0	Duffy Daugherty	10-0-0
3 Arkansas	10-1-0	Frank Broyles	10-0-0
4 UCLA	8-2-1	Tommy Prothro	7-1-1
5 Nebraska	10-1-0	Bob Devaney	10-0-0
6 Missouri	8-2-1	Dan Devine	7-2-1
7 Tennessee	8-1-2	Doug Dickey	6-1-2
8 LSU	8-3-0	Charlie McClendon	7-3-0
9 Notre Dame	7-2-1	Ara Parseghian	same
10 USC	7-2-1	John McKay	same

Key Bowl Games

Rankings below reflect final regular season poll, released Nov. 29. No bowls for then #8 USC or #9 Notre Dame. **Rose**—#5 UCLA over #1 Michigan St., 14-12; **Cotton**—LSU over #2 Arkansas, 14-7; **Orange**—#4 Alabama over #3 Nebraska, 39-28; **Sugar**—#6 Missouri over Florida, 20-18; **Bluebonnet**—#7 Tennessee over Tulsa, 27-6; **Gator**—Georgia Tech over #10 Texas Tech, 31-21.

1966

Final poll released Dec. 5, returning to pre-bowl status. Top 10 regular season results after that: None.

	As of Dec. 5	Head Coach	After Bowls
1 Notre Dame	9-0-1	Ara Parseghian	same
2 Michigan St.	9-0-1	Duffy Daugherty	same
3 Alabama	10-0-0	Bear Bryant	11-0-0
4 Georgia	9-1-0	Vince Dooley	10-1-0
5 UCLA	9-1-0	Tommy Prothro	same
6 Nebraska	9-1-0	Bob Devaney	9-2-0
7 Purdue	8-2-0	Jack Mollenkopf	9-2-0
8 Georgia Tech	9-1-0	Bobby Dodd	9-2-0
9 Miami-FL	7-2-1	Charlie Tate	8-2-1
10 SMU	8-2-0	Hayden Fry	8-3-0

Key Bowl Games

Sugar—#3 Alabama over #6 Nebraska, 34-7; **Cotton**—#4 Georgia over #10 SMU, 24-9; **Rose**—#7 Purdue over USC, 14-13; **Orange**—Florida over #8 Georgia Tech, 27-12; **Liberty**—#9 Miami-FL over Virginia Tech, 14-7.

1967

Final poll released Nov. 27. Top 10 regular season results after that: **Dec. 2**—#2 Tennessee over Vanderbilt, 41-14; #3 Oklahoma over Oklahoma St., 38-14; #8 Alabama over Auburn, 7-3.

	As of Nov. 27	Head Coach	After Bowls
1 USC	9-1-0	John McKay	10-1-0
2 Tennessee	8-1-0	Doug Dickey	9-2-0
3 Oklahoma	8-1-0	Chuck Fairbanks	10-1-0
4 Indiana	9-1-0	John Pont	9-2-0
5 Notre Dame	8-2-0	Ara Parseghian	same
6 Wyoming	10-0-0	Lloyd Eaton	10-1-0
7 Oregon St.	7-2-1	Dee Andros	same
8 Alabama	7-1-1	Bear Bryant	8-2-1
9 Purdue	8-2-0	Jack Mollenkopf	same
10 Penn St.	8-2-0	Joe Paterno	8-2-1

Key Bowl Games

Rose—#1 USC over #4 Indiana, 14-3; **Orange**—#3 Oklahoma over #2 Tennessee, 26-24; **Sugar**—LSU over #6 Wyoming, 20-13; **Cotton**—Texas A&M over #8 Alabama, 20-16; **Gator**—#10 Penn St. tied Florida St. 17-17.

1968

Final poll taken after bowl games for first time since close of 1965 season.

	After Bowls	Head Coach	Regular Season
1 Ohio St.	10-0-0	Woody Hayes	9-0-0
2 Penn St.	11-0-0	Joe Paterno	10-0-0
3 Texas	9-1-1	Darrell Royal	8-1-1
4 USC	9-1-1	John McKay	9-0-1
5 Notre Dame	7-2-1	Ara Parseghian	same
6 Arkansas	10-1-0	Frank Broyles	9-1-0
7 Kansas	9-2-0	Pepper Rodgers	9-1-0
8 Georgia	8-1-2	Vince Dooley	8-0-2
9 Missouri	8-3-0	Dan Devine	7-3-0
10 Purdue	8-2-0	Jack Mollenkopf	same
11 Oklahoma	7-4-0	Chuck Fairbanks	7-3-0
12 Michigan	8-2-0	Bump Elliott	same
13 Tennessee	8-2-1	Doug Dickey	8-1-1
14 SMU	8-3-0	Hayden Fry	7-3-0
15 Oregon St.	7-3-0	Dee Andros	same
16 Auburn	7-4-0	Shug Jordan	6-4-0
17 Alabama	8-3-0	Bear Bryant	8-2-0
18 Houston	6-2-2	Bill Yeoman	same
19 LSU	8-3-0	Charlie McClendon	7-3-0
20 Ohio Univ.	10-1-0	Bill Hess	10-0-0

Key Bowl Games

Rankings below reflect final regular season poll, released Dec. 2. No bowls for then #7 Notre Dame and #11 Purdue. **Rose**—#1 Ohio St. over #2 USC, 27-16; **Orange**—#3 Penn St. over #6 Kansas, 15-14; **Sugar**—#9 Arkansas over #4 Georgia, 16-2; **Cotton**—#5 Texas over #8 Tennessee, 36-13; **Bluebonnet**—#20 SMU over #10 Oklahoma, 28-27; **Gator**—#16 Missouri over #12 Alabama, 35-10.

1969

Final poll taken after bowl games.

	After Bowls	Head Coach	Regular Season
1 Texas	11-0-0	Darrell Royal	10-0-0
2 Penn St.	11-0-0	Joe Paterno	10-0-0
3 USC	10-0-1	John McKay	9-0-1
4 Ohio St.	8-1-0	Woody Hayes	same
5 Notre Dame	8-2-1	Ara Parseghian	8-1-1
6 Missouri	9-2-0	Dan Devine	9-1-0
7 Arkansas	9-2-0	Frank Broyles	9-1-0
8 Mississippi	8-3-0	Johnny Vaught	7-3-0
9 Michigan	8-3-0	Bo Schembechler	8-2-0
10 LSU	9-1-0	Charlie McClendon	same
11 Nebraska	9-2-0	Bob Devaney	8-2-0
12 Houston	9-2-0	Bill Yeoman	8-2-0
13 UCLA	8-1-1	Tommy Prothro	same
14 Florida	9-1-1	Ray Graves	8-1-1
15 Tennessee	9-2-0	Doug Dickey	9-1-0
16 Colorado	8-3-0	Eddie Crowder	7-3-0
17 West Virginia	10-1-0	Jim Carlen	9-1-0
18 Purdue	8-2-0	Jack Mollenkopf	same
19 Stanford	7-2-1	John Ralston	same
20 Auburn	8-3-0	Shug Jordan	8-2-0

Key Bowl Games

Rankings below reflect final regular season poll, released Dec. 8. No bowls for then #4 Ohio St., #8 LSU and #10 UCLA.

Cotton—#1 Texas over #9 Notre Dame, 21-17; **Orange**—#2 Penn St. over #6 Missouri, 10-3; **Sugar**—#13 Ole Miss over #3 Arkansas, 27-22; **Rose**—#5 USC over #7 Michigan, 10-3.

Associated Press Final Polls (Cont.)

Final polls taken after bowl games.

1970

	After Bowls	Head Coach	Regular Season
1 Nebraska	11-0-1	Bob Devaney	10-0-1
2 Notre Dame	10-1-0	Ara Parseghian	9-0-1
3 Texas	10-1-0	Darrell Royal	10-0-0
4 Tennessee	11-1-0	Bill Battle	10-1-0
5 Ohio St.	9-1-0	Woody Hayes	9-0-0
6 Arizona St.	11-0-0	Frank Kush	10-0-0
7 LSU	9-3-0	Charlie McClendon	9-2-0
8 Stanford	9-3-0	John Ralston	8-3-0
9 Michigan	9-1-0	Bo Schembechler	same
10 Auburn	9-2-0	Shug Jordan	8-2-0
11 Arkansas	9-2-0	Frank Broyles	same
12 Toledo	12-0-0	Frank Lauterbur	11-0-0
13 Georgia Tech	9-3-0	Bud Carson	8-3-0
14 Dartmouth	9-0-0	Bob Blackman	same
15 USC	6-4-1	John McKay	same
16 Air Force	9-3-0	Ben Martin	9-2-0
17 Tulane	8-4-0	Jim Pittman	7-4-0
18 Penn St.	7-3-0	Joe Paterno	same
19 Houston	8-3-0	Bill Yeoman	7-3-0
20 Oklahoma	7-4-1	Chuck Fairbanks	7-4-0
Mississippi	7-4-0	Johnny Vaught	7-3-0

Key Bowl Games

Rankings below reflect final regular season poll, released Dec. 7. No bowls for then #4 Arkansas and #7 Michigan. **Cotton**—#6 Notre Dame over #1 Texas, 24-11; **Rose**—#12 Stanford over #2 Ohio St., 27-17; **Orange**—#3 Nebraska over #8 LSU, 17-12; **Sugar**— #5 Tennessee over #11 Air Force, 34-13; **Peach**—#9 Ariz. St. over N. Carolina, 48-26.

1971

	After Bowls	Head Coach	Regular Season
1 Nebraska	13-0-0	Bob Devaney	12-0-0
2 Oklahoma	11-1-0	Chuck Fairbanks	10-1-0
3 Colorado	10-2-0	Eddie Crowder	9-2-0
4 Alabama	11-1-0	Bear Bryant	11-0-0
5 Penn St.	11-1-0	Joe Paterno	10-1-0
6 Michigan	11-1-0	Bo Schembechler	11-0-0
7 Georgia	11-1-0	Vince Dooley	10-1-0
8 Arizona St.	11-1-0	Frank Kush	10-1-0
9 Tennessee	10-2-0	Bill Battle	9-2-0
10 Stanford	9-3-0	John Ralston	8-3-0
11 LSU	9-3-0	Charlie McClendon	8-3-0
12 Auburn	9-2-0	Shug Jordan	9-1-0
13 Notre Dame	8-2-0	Ara Parseghian	same
14 Toledo	12-0-0	John Murphy	11-0-0
15 Mississippi	10-2-0	Billy Kinard	9-2-0
16 Arkansas	8-3-1	Frank Broyles	8-2-1
17 Houston	9-3-0	Bill Yeoman	9-2-0
18 Texas	8-3-0	Darrell Royal	8-2-0
19 Washington	8-3-0	Jim Owens	same
20 USC	6-4-1	John McKay	same

Key Bowl Games

Rankings below reflect final regular season poll, released Dec. 6.
Orange—#1 Nebraska over #2 Alabama, 38-6; **Sugar**—#3 Oklahoma over #5 Auburn, 40-22; **Rose**—#16 Stanford over #4 Michigan, 13-12; **Gator**—#6 Georgia over N.Carolina, 7-3; **Bluebonnet**—#7 Colorado over #15 Houston, 29-17; **Fiesta**—#8 Ariz. St. over Florida St., 45-38; **Cotton**—#10 Penn St. over #12 Texas, 30-6.

1972

	After Bowls	Head Coach	Regular Season
1 USC	12-0-0	John McKay	11-0-0
2 Oklahoma	11-1-0	Chuck Fairbanks	10-1-0
3 Texas	10-1-0	Darrell Royal	9-1-0
4 Nebraska	9-2-1	Bob Devaney	8-2-1
5 Auburn	10-1-0	Shug Jordan	9-1-0
6 Michigan	10-1-0	Bo Schembechler	same
7 Alabama	10-2-0	Bear Bryant	10-1-0
8 Tennessee	10-2-0	Bill Battle	9-2-0
9 Ohio St.	9-2-0	Woody Hayes	9-1-0
10 Penn St.	10-2-0	Joe Paterno	10-1-0
11 LSU	9-2-1	Charlie McClendon	9-1-1
12 North Carolina	11-1-0	Bill Dooley	10-1-0
13 Arizona St.	10-2-0	Frank Kush	9-2-0
14 Notre Dame	8-3-0	Ara Parseghian	8-2-0
15 UCLA	8-3-0	Pepper Rodgers	same
16 Colorado	8-4-0	Eddie Crowder	8-3-0
17 N.C. State	8-3-1	Lou Holtz	7-3-1
18 Louisville	9-1-0	Lee Corso	same
19 Washington St.	7-4-0	Jim Sweeney	same
20 Georgia Tech	7-4-1	Bill Fulcher	6-4-1

Key Bowl Games

Rankings below reflect final regular season poll, released Dec. 4. No bowl for then #8 Michigan.
Rose—#1 USC over #3 Ohio St., 42-17; **Sugar**—#2 Oklahoma over #5 Penn St., 14-0; **Cotton**—#7 Texas over #4 Alabama, 17-13; **Orange**—#9 Nebraska over #12 Notre Dame, 40-6; **Gator**—#6 Auburn over #13 Colorado, 24-3; **Bluebonnet**—#11 Tennessee over #10 LSU, 24-17.

1973

	After Bowls	Head Coach	Regular Season
1 Notre Dame	11-0-0	Ara Parseghian	10-0-0
2 Ohio St.	10-0-1	Woody Hayes	9-0-1
3 Oklahoma	10-0-1	Barry Switzer	same
4 Alabama	11-1-0	Bear Bryant	11-0-0
5 Penn St.	12-0-0	Joe Paterno	11-0-0
6 Michigan	10-0-1	Bo Schembechler	same
7 Nebraska	9-2-1	Tom Osborne	8-2-1
8 USC	9-2-1	John McKay	9-1-1
9 Arizona St.	11-1-0	Frank Kush	10-1-0
Houston	11-1-0	Bill Yeoman	10-1-0
11 Texas Tech	11-1-0	Jim Carlen	10-1-0
12 UCLA	9-2-0	Pepper Rodgers	same
13 LSU	9-3-0	Charlie McClendon	9-2-0
14 Texas	8-3-0	Darrell Royal	8-2-0
15 Miami-OH	11-0-0	Bill Mallory	10-0-0
16 N.C. State	9-3-0	Lou Holtz	8-3-0
17 Missouri	8-4-0	Al Onofrio	7-4-0
18 Kansas	7-4-1	Don Fambrough	7-3-1
19 Tennessee	8-4-0	Bill Battle	8-3-0
20 Maryland	8-4-0	Jerry Claiborne	8-3-0
Tulane	9-3-0	Bennie Ellender	9-2-0

Key Bowl Games

Rankings below reflect final regular season poll, released Dec. 3. No bowls for then #2 Oklahoma (probation), #5 Michigan and #9 UCLA.
Sugar—#3 Notre Dame over #1 Alabama, 24-23; **Rose**—#4 Ohio St. over #7 USC, 42-21; **Orange**—#6 Penn St. over #13 LSU, 16-9; **Cotton**—#12 Nebraska over #8 Texas, 19-3; **Fiesta**—#10 Ariz. St. over Pitt, 28-7; **Bluebonnet**—#14 Houston over #17 Tulane, 47-7.

1974

	After Bowls	Head Coach	Regular Season
1 Oklahoma	11-0-0	Barry Switzer	same
2 USC	10-1-1	John McKay	9-1-1
3 Michigan	10-1-0	Bo Schembechler	same
4 Ohio St.	10-2-0	Woody Hayes	10-1-0
5 Alabama	11-1-0	Bear Bryant	11-0-0
6 Notre Dame	10-2-0	Ara Parseghian	9-2-0
7 Penn St.	10-2-0	Joe Paterno	9-2-0
8 Auburn	10-2-0	Shug Jordan	9-2-0
9 Nebraska	9-3-0	Tom Osborne	8-3-0
10 Miami-OH	10-0-1	Dick Crum	9-0-1
11 N.C. State	9-2-1	Lou Holtz	9-2-0
12 Michigan St.	7-3-1	Denny Stolz	same
13 Maryland	8-4-0	Jerry Claiborne	8-3-0
14 Baylor	8-4-0	Grant Teaff	8-3-0
15 Florida	8-4-0	Doug Dickey	8-3-0
16 Texas A&M	8-3-0	Emory Ballard	same
17 Mississippi St.	9-3-0	Bob Tyler	8-3-0
Texas	8-4-0	Darrell Royal	8-3-0
19 Houston	8-3-1	Bill Yeoman	8-3-0
20 Tennessee	7-3-2	Bill Battle	6-3-2

Key Bowl Games

Rankings below reflect final regular season poll, released Dec. 2. No bowls for #1 Oklahoma (probation) and then #4 Michigan.

Orange—#9 Notre Dame over #2 Alabama, 13-11; **Rose**—#5 USC over #3 Ohio St., 18-17; **Gator**—#6 Auburn over #11 Texas, 27-3; **Cotton**—#7 Penn St. over #12 Baylor, 41-20; **Sugar**—#8 Nebraska over #18 Florida, 13-10; **Liberty**—Tennessee over #10 Maryland, 7-3.

1975

	After Bowls	Head Coach	Regular Season
1 Oklahoma	11-1-0	Barry Switzer	10-1-0
2 Arizona St.	12-0-0	Frank Kush	11-0-0
3 Alabama	11-1-0	Bear Bryant	10-1-0
4 Ohio St.	11-1-0	Woody Hayes	11-0-0
5 UCLA	9-2-1	Dick Vermeil	8-2-1
6 Texas	10-2-0	Darrell Royal	9-2-0
7 Arkansas	10-2-0	Frank Broyles	9-2-0
8 Michigan	8-2-2	Bo Schembechler	8-1-2
9 Nebraska	10-2-0	Tom Osborne	10-1-0
10 Penn St.	9-3-0	Joe Paterno	9-2-0
11 Texas A&M	10-2-0	Emory Bellard	10-1-0
12 Miami-OH	11-1-0	Dick Crum	10-1-0
13 Maryland	9-2-1	Jerry Claiborne	8-2-1
14 California	8-3-0	Mike White	same
15 Pittsburgh	8-4-0	Johnny Majors	7-4-0
16 Colorado	9-3-0	Bill Mallory	9-2-0
17 USC	8-4-0	John McKay	7-4-0
18 Arizona	9-2-0	Jim Young	same
19 Georgia	9-3-0	Vince Dooley	9-2-0
20 West Virginia	9-3-0	Bobby Bowden	8-3-0

Key Bowl Games

Rankings below reflect final regular season poll, released Dec. 1. Texas A&M was unbeaten and ranked 2nd in that poll, but lost to #18 Arkansas, 31-6, in its final regular season game on Dec.6.

Rose—#11 UCLA over #1 Ohio St., 23-10; **Liberty**—#17 USC over #2 Texas A&M, 20-0; **Orange**—#3 Oklahoma over #5 Michigan, 14-6; **Sugar**—#4 Alabama over #8 Penn St., 13-6; **Fiesta**—#7 Ariz. St. over #6 Nebraska, 17-14; **Bluebonnet**—#9 Texas over #10 Colorado, 38-21; **Cotton**—#18 Arkansas over #12 Georgia, 31-10.

1976

	After Bowls	Head Coach	Regular Season
1 Pittsburgh	12-0-0	Johnny Majors	11-0-0
2 USC	11-1-0	John Robinson	10-1-0
3 Michigan	10-2-0	Bo Schembechler	10-1-0
4 Houston	10-2-0	Bill Yeoman	9-2-0
5 Oklahoma	9-2-1	Barry Switzer	8-2-1
6 Ohio St.	9-2-1	Woody Hayes	8-2-1
7 Texas A&M	10-2-0	Emory Bellard	9-2-0
8 Maryland	11-1-0	Jerry Claiborne	11-0-0
9 Nebraska	9-3-1	Tom Osborne	8-3-1
10 Georgia	10-2-0	Vince Dooley	10-1-0
11 Alabama	9-3-0	Bear Bryant	8-3-0
12 Notre Dame	9-3-0	Dan Devine	8-3-0
13 Texas Tech	10-2-0	Steve Sloan	10-1-0
14 Oklahoma St.	9-3-0	Jim Stanley	8-3-0
15 UCLA	9-2-1	Terry Donahue	9-1-1
16 Colorado	8-4-0	Bill Mallory	8-3-0
17 Rutgers	11-0-0	Frank Burns	same
18 Kentucky	8-4-0	Fran Curci	7-4-0
19 Iowa St.	8-3-0	Earle Bruce	same
20 Mississippi St.	9-2-0	Bob Tyler	same

Key Bowl Games

Rankings below reflect final regular season poll, released Nov. 29. No bowl for then #20 Miss. St. (probation).

Sugar—#1 Pitt over #5 Georgia, 27-3; **Rose**—#3 USC over #2 Michigan, 14-6; **Cotton**—#6 Houston over #4 Maryland, 30-21; **Liberty**—#16 Alabama over #7 UCLA, 36-6; **Fiesta**—#8 Oklahoma over Wyoming, 41-7; **Bluebonnet**—#13 Nebraska over #9 Texas Tech, 27-24; **Sun**—#10 Texas A&M over Florida, 37-14; **Orange**—#11 Ohio St. over #12 Colorado, 27-10.

1977

	After Bowls	Head Coach	Regular Season
1 Notre Dame	11-1-0	Dan Devine	10-1-0
2 Alabama	11-1-0	Bear Bryant	10-1-0
3 Arkansas	11-1-0	Lou Holtz	10-1-0
4 Texas	11-1-0	Fred Akers	11-0-0
5 Penn St.	11-1-0	Joe Paterno	10-1-0
6 Kentucky	10-1-0	Fran Curci	same
7 Oklahoma	10-2-0	Barry Switzer	10-1-0
8 Pittsburgh	9-2-1	Jackie Sherrill	8-2-1
9 Michigan	10-2-0	Bo Schembechler	10-1-0
10 Washington	8-4-0	Don James	7-4-0
11 Ohio St.	9-3-0	Woody Hayes	9-2-0
12 Nebraska	9-3-0	Tom Osborne	8-3-0
13 USC	8-4-0	John Robinson	7-4-0
14 Florida St.	10-2-0	Bobby Bowden	9-2-0
15 Stanford	9-3-0	Bill Walsh	8-3-0
16 San Diego St.	10-1-0	Claude Gilbert	same
17 North Carolina	8-3-1	Bill Dooley	8-2-1
18 Arizona St.	9-3-0	Frank Kush	9-2-0
19 Clemson	8-3-1	Charley Pell	8-2-1
20 BYU	9-2-0	LaVell Edwards	same

Key Bowl Games

Rankings below reflect final regular season poll, released Nov. 28. No bowl for then #7 Kentucky (probation).

Cotton—#5 Notre Dame over #1 Texas, 38-10; **Orange**—#6 Arkansas over #2 Oklahoma, 31-6; **Sugar**—#3 Alabama over #9 Ohio St., 35-6; **Rose**—#13 Washington over #4 Michigan, 27-20; **Fiesta**—#8 Penn St. over #15 Ariz. St., 42-30; **Gator**—#10 Pitt over #11 Clemson, 34-3.

Associated Press Final Polls (Cont.)

Final polls taken after bowl games.

1978

	After Bowls	Head Coach	Regular Season
1 Alabama	11-1-0	Bear Bryant	10-1-0
2 USC	12-1-0	John Robinson	11-1-0
3 Oklahoma	11-1-0	Barry Switzer	10-1-0
4 Penn St.	11-1-0	Joe Paterno	11-0-0
5 Michigan	10-2-0	Bo Schembechler	10-1-0
6 Clemson	11-1-0	Charley Pell	10-1-0
7 Notre Dame	9-3-0	Dan Devine	8-3-0
8 Nebraska	9-3-0	Tom Osborne	9-2-0
9 Texas	9-3-0	Fred Akers	8-3-0
10 Houston	9-3-0	Bill Yeoman	9-2-0
11 Arkansas	9-2-1	Lou Holtz	9-2-0
12 Michigan St.	8-3-0	Darryl Rogers	same
13 Purdue	9-2-1	Jim Young	8-2-1
14 UCLA	8-3-1	Terry Donahue	8-3-0
15 Missouri	8-4-0	Warren Powers	7-4-0
16 Georgia	9-2-1	Vince Dooley	9-1-1
17 Stanford	8-4-0	Bill Walsh	7-4-0
18 N.C. State	9-3-0	Bo Rein	8-3-0
19 Texas A&M	8-4-0	Emory Bellard (4-2) & Tom Wilson (4-2)	7-4-0
20 Maryland	9-3-0	Jerry Claiborne	9-2-0

Key Bowl Games

Rankings below reflect final regular season poll, released Dec. 4. No bowl for then #12 Michigan St. (probation).
Sugar—#2 Alabama over #1 Penn St., 14-7; **Rose**—#3 USC over #5 Michigan, 17-10; **Orange**—#4 Oklahoma over #6 Nebraska, 31-24; **Gator**—#7 Clemson over #20 Ohio St., 17-15; **Fiesta**—#8 Arkansas tied #15 UCLA, 10-10; **Cotton**—#10 Notre Dame over #9 Houston, 35-34.

1980

	After Bowls	Head Coach	Regular Season
1 Georgia	12-0-0	Vince Dooley	11-0-0
2 Pittsburgh	11-1-0	Jackie Sherrill	10-1-0
3 Oklahoma	10-2-0	Barry Switzer	9-2-0
4 Michigan	10-2-0	Bo Schembechler	9-2-0
5 Florida St.	10-2-0	Bobby Bowden	10-1-0
6 Alabama	10-2-0	Bear Bryant	9-2-0
7 Nebraska	10-2-0	Tom Osborne	9-2-0
8 Penn St.	10-2-0	Joe Paterno	9-2-0
9 Notre Dame	9-2-1	Dan Devine	9-1-1
10 North Carolina	11-1-0	Dick Crum	10-1-0
11 USC	8-2-1	John Robinson	same
12 BYU	12-1-0	LaVell Edwards	11-1-0
13 UCLA	9-2-0	Terry Donahue	same
14 Baylor	10-2-0	Grant Teaff	10-1-0
15 Ohio St.	9-3-0	Earle Bruce	9-2-0
16 Washington	9-3-0	Don James	9-2-0
17 Purdue	9-3-0	Jim Young	8-3-0
18 Miami-FL	9-3-0	H. Schnellenberger	8-3-0
19 Mississippi St.	9-3-0	Emory Bellard	9-2-0
20 SMU	8-4-0	Ron Meyer	8-3-0

Key Bowl Games

Rankings below reflect final regular season poll, released Dec. 8.
Sugar—#1 Georgia over #7 Notre Dame, 17-10; **Orange**—#4 Oklahoma over #2 Florida St., 18-17; **Gator**—#3 Pitt over #18 S. Carolina, 37-9; **Rose**—#5 Michigan over #16 Washington, 23-6; **Cotton**—#9 Alabama over #6 Baylor, 30-2; **Sun**—#8 Nebraska over #17 Miss. St., 31-17; **Fiesta**—#10 Penn St. over #11 Ohio St., 31-19; **Bluebonnet**—#13 N. Carolina over Texas, 16-7.

1979

	After Bowls	Head Coach	Regular Season
1 Alabama	12-0-0	Bear Bryant	11-0-0
2 USC	11-0-1	John Robinson	10-0-1
3 Oklahoma	11-1-0	Barry Switzer	10-1-0
4 Ohio St.	11-1-0	Earle Bruce	11-0-0
5 Houston	11-1-0	Bill Yeoman	10-1-0
6 Florida St.	11-1-0	Bobby Bowden	11-0-0
7 Pittsburgh	11-1-0	Jackie Sherrill	10-1-0
8 Arkansas	10-2-0	Lou Holtz	10-1-0
9 Nebraska	10-2-0	Tom Osborne	10-1-0
10 Purdue	10-2-0	Jim Young	9-2-0
11 Washington	9-3-0	Don James	8-3-0
12 Texas	9-3-0	Fred Akers	9-2-0
13 BYU	11-1-0	LaVell Edwards	11-0-0
14 Baylor	8-4-0	Grant Teaff	7-4-0
15 North Carolina	8-3-1	Dick Crum	7-3-1
16 Auburn	8-3-0	Doug Barfield	same
17 Temple	10-2-0	Wayne Hardin	9-2-0
18 Michigan	8-4-0	Bo Schembechler	8-3-0
19 Indiana	8-4-0	Lee Corso	7-4-0
20 Penn St.	8-4-0	Joe Paterno	7-4-0

Key Bowl Games

Rankings below reflect final regular season poll, released Dec. 3. No bowl for then #17 Auburn (probation).
Sugar—#2 Alabama over #6 Arkansas, 24-9; **Rose**—#3 USC over #1 Ohio St., 17-16; **Orange**—#5 Oklahoma over #4 Florida St., 24-7; **Sun**—#13 Washington over #11 Texas, 14-7; **Cotton**—#8 Houston over #7 Nebraska, 17-14; **Fiesta**—#10 Pitt over Arizona, 16-10.

1981

	After Bowls	Head Coach	Regular Season
1 Clemson	12-0-0	Danny Ford	11-0-0
2 Texas	10-1-1	Fred Akers	9-1-1
3 Penn St.	10-2-0	Joe Paterno	9-2-0
4 Pittsburgh	11-1-0	Jackie Sherrill	10-1-0
5 SMU	10-1-0	Ron Meyer	same
6 Georgia	10-2-0	Vince Dooley	10-1-0
7 Alabama	9-2-1	Bear Bryant	9-1-1
8 Miami-FL	9-2-0	H. Schnellenberger	same
9 North Carolina	10-2-0	Dick Crum	9-2-0
10 Washington	10-2-0	Don James	9-2-0
11 Nebraska	9-3-0	Tom Osborne	9-2-0
12 Michigan	9-3-0	Bo Schembechler	8-3-0
13 BYU	11-2-0	LaVell Edwards	10-2-0
14 USC	9-3-0	John Robinson	9-2-0
15 Ohio St.	9-3-0	Earle Bruce	8-3-0
16 Arizona St.	9-2-0	Darryl Rogers	same
17 West Virginia	9-3-0	Don Nehlen	8-3-0
18 Iowa	8-4-0	Hayden Fry	8-3-0
19 Missouri	8-4-0	Warren Powers	7-4-0
20 Oklahoma	7-4-1	Barry Switzer	6-4-1

Key Bowl Games

Rankings below reflect final regular season poll, released Nov. 30. No bowl for then #5 SMU (probation), #9 Miami-FL (probation), and #17 Ariz. St. (probation).
Orange—#1 Clemson over #4 Nebraska, 22-15; **Sugar**—#10 Pitt over #2 Georgia, 24-20; **Cotton**—#6 Texas over #3 Alabama, 14-12; **Fiesta**—#7 Penn St. over #8 USC, 26-10; **Gator**—#11 N. Carolina over Arkansas, 31-27; **Rose**—#12 Washington over #13 Iowa, 28-0.

1982

	After Bowls	Head Coach	Regular Season
1 Penn St.	11-1-0	Joe Paterno	10-1-0
2 SMU	11-0-1	Bobby Collins	10-0-1
3 Nebraska	12-1-0	Tom Osborne	11-1-0
4 Georgia	11-1-0	Vince Dooley	11-0-0
5 UCLA	10-1-1	Terry Donahue	9-1-1
6 Arizona St.	10-2-0	Darryl Rogers	9-2-0
7 Washington	10-2-0	Don James	9-2-0
8 Clemson	9-1-1	Danny Ford	same
9 Arkansas	9-2-1	Lou Holtz	8-2-1
10 Pittsburgh	9-3-0	Foge Fazio	9-2-0
11 LSU	8-3-1	Jerry Stovall	8-2-1
12 Ohio St.	9-3-0	Earle Bruce	8-3-0
13 Florida St.	9-3-0	Bobby Bowden	8-3-0
14 Auburn	9-3-0	Pat Dye	8-3-0
15 USC	8-3-0	John Robinson	same
16 Oklahoma	8-4-0	Barry Switzer	8-3-0
17 Texas	9-3-0	Fred Akers	9-2-0
18 North Carolina	8-4-0	Dick Crum	7-4-0
19 West Virginia	9-3-0	Don Nehlen	9-2-0
20 Maryland	8-4-0	Bobby Ross	8-3-0

Key Bowl Games

Rankings below reflect final regular season poll, released Dec. 6. No bowl for then #7 Clemson (probation) and #15 USC (probation).
Sugar—#2 Penn St. over #1 Georgia, 27-23; **Orange**—#3 Nebraska over #13 LSU, 21-20; **Cotton**—#4 SMU over #6 Pitt, 7-3; **Rose**—#5 UCLA over #19 Michigan, 24-14; **Aloha**—#9 Washington over #16 Maryland, 21-20; **Fiesta**—#11 Ariz. St. over #12 Oklahoma, 32-21; **Bluebonnet**—#14 Arkansas over Florida, 28-24.

1983

	After Bowls	Head Coach	Regular Season
1 Miami-FL	11-1-0	H. Schnellenberger	10-1-0
2 Nebraska	12-1-0	Tom Osborne	12-0-0
3 Auburn	11-1-0	Pat Dye	10-1-0
4 Georgia	10-1-1	Vince Dooley	9-1-1
5 Texas	11-1-0	Fred Akers	11-0-0
6 Florida	9-2-1	Charley Pell	8-2-1
7 BYU	11-1-0	LaVell Edwards	10-1-0
8 Michigan	9-3-0	Bo Schembechler	9-2-0
9 Ohio St.	9-3-0	Earle Bruce	8-3-0
10 Illinois	10-2-0	Mike White	10-1-0
11 Clemson	9-1-1	Danny Ford	same
12 SMU	10-2-0	Bobby Collins	10-1-0
13 Air Force	10-2-0	Ken Hatfield	9-2-0
14 Iowa	9-3-0	Hayden Fry	9-2-0
15 Alabama	8-4-0	Ray Perkins	7-4-0
16 West Virginia	9-3-0	Don Nehlen	8-3-0
17 UCLA	7-4-1	Terry Donahue	6-4-1
18 Pittsburgh	8-3-1	Foge Fazio	8-2-1
19 Boston College	9-3-0	Jack Bicknell	9-2-0
20 East Carolina	8-3-0	Ed Emory	same

Key Bowl Games

Rankings below reflect final regular season poll, released Dec. 5. No bowl for then #12 Clemson (probation).
Orange—#5 Miami-FL over #1 Nebraska, 31-30; **Cotton**—#7 Georgia over #2 Texas, 10-9; **Sugar**— #3 Auburn over #8 Michigan, 9-7; **Rose**—UCLA over #4 Illinois, 45-9; **Holiday**—#9 BYU over Missouri, 21-17; **Gator**—#11 Florida over #10 Iowa, 14-6; **Fiesta**—#14 Ohio St. over #15 Pitt, 28-23.

1984

	After Bowls	Head Coach	Regular Season
1 BYU	13-0-0	LaVell Edwards	12-0-0
2 Washington	11-1-0	Don James	10-1-0
3 Florida	9-1-1	Charley Pell & Galen Hall (9-0)	(0-1-0) same
4 Nebraska	10-2-0	Tom Osborne	9-2-0
5 Boston College	10-2-0	Jack Bicknell	9-2-0
6 Oklahoma	9-2-1	Barry Switzer	9-1-1
7 Oklahoma St.	10-2-0	Pat Jones	9-2-0
8 SMU	10-2-0	Bobby Collins	9-2-0
9 UCLA	9-3-0	Terry Donahue	8-3-0
10 USC	9-3-0	Ted Tollner	8-3-0
11 South Carolina	10-2-0	Joe Morrison	10-1-0
12 Maryland	9-3-0	Bobby Ross	8-3-0
13 Ohio St.	9-3-0	Earle Bruce	9-2-0
14 Auburn	9-4-0	Pat Dye	8-4-0
15 LSU	8-3-1	Bill Arnsparger	8-2-1
16 Iowa	8-4-1	Hayden Fry	7-4-1
17 Florida St.	7-3-2	Bobby Bowden	7-3-1
18 Miami-FL	8-5-0	Jimmy Johnson	8-4-0
19 Kentucky	9-3-0	Jerry Claiborne	8-3-0
20 Virginia	8-2-2	George Welsh	7-2-2

Key Bowl Games

Rankings below reflect final regular season poll, released Dec. 3. No bowl for then #3 Florida (probation).
Holiday—#1 BYU over Michigan, 24-17; **Orange**—#4 Washington over #2 Oklahoma, 28-17; **Sugar**—#5 Nebraska over #11 LSU, 28-10; **Rose**—#18 USC over #6 Ohio St., 20-17; **Gator**—#9 Okla. St. over #7 S. Carolina, 21-14; **Cotton**—#8 BC over Houston, 45-28; **Aloha**—#10 SMU over #17 Notre Dame, 27-20.

1985

	After Bowls	Head Coach	Regular Season
1 Oklahoma	11-1-0	Barry Switzer	10-1-0
2 Michigan	10-1-1	Bo Schembechler	9-1-1
3 Penn St.	11-1-0	Joe Paterno	11-0-0
4 Tennessee	9-1-2	Johnny Majors	8-1-2
5 Florida	9-1-1	Galen Hall	same
6 Texas A&M	10-2-0	Jackie Sherrill	9-2-0
7 UCLA	9-2-1	Terry Donahue	8-2-1
8 Air Force	12-1-0	Fisher DeBerry	11-1-0
9 Miami-FL	10-2-0	Jimmy Johnson	10-1-0
10 Iowa	10-2-0	Hayden Fry	10-1-0
11 Nebraska	9-3-0	Tom Osborne	9-2-0
12 Arkansas	10-2-0	Ken Hatfield	9-2-0
13 Alabama	9-2-1	Ray Perkins	8-2-1
14 Ohio St.	9-3-0	Earle Bruce	8-3-0
15 Florida St.	9-3-0	Bobby Bowden	8-3-0
16 BYU	11-3-0	LaVell Edwards	11-2-0
17 Baylor	9-3-0	Grant Teaff	8-3-0
18 Maryland	9-3-0	Bobby Ross	8-3-0
19 Georgia Tech	9-2-1	Bill Curry	8-2-1
20 LSU	9-2-1	Bill Arnsparger	9-1-1

Key Bowl Games

Rankings below reflect final regular season poll, released Dec. 9. No bowl for then #6 Florida (probation).
Orange—#3 Oklahoma over #1 Penn St., 25-10; **Sugar**—#8 Tennessee over #2 Miami-FL, 35-7; **Rose**—#13 UCLA over #4 Iowa, 45-28; **Fiesta**—#5 Michigan over #7 Nebraska, 27-23; **Bluebonnet**—#10 Air Force over Texas, 24-16; **Cotton**—#11 Texas A&M over #16 Auburn, 36-16.

Associated Press Final Polls (Cont.)

Final polls taken after bowl games.

1986

	After Bowls	Head Coach	Regular Season
1 Penn St.	12-0-0	Joe Paterno	11-0-0
2 Miami-FL	11-1-0	Jimmy Johnson	11-0-0
3 Oklahoma	11-1-0	Barry Switzer	10-1-0
4 Arizona St.	10-1-1	John Cooper	9-1-1
5 Nebraska	10-2-0	Tom Osborne	9-2-0
6 Auburn	10-2-0	Pat Dye	9-2-0
7 Ohio St.	10-3-0	Earle Bruce	9-3-0
8 Michigan	11-2-0	Bo Schembechler	11-1-0
9 Alabama	10-3-0	Ray Perkins	9-3-0
10 LSU	9-3-0	Bill Arnsparger	9-2-0
11 Arizona	9-3-0	Larry Smith	8-3-0
12 Baylor	9-3-0	Grant Teaff	8-3-0
13 Texas A&M	9-3-0	Jackie Sherrill	9-2-0
14 UCLA	8-3-1	Terry Donahue	7-3-1
15 Arkansas	9-3-0	Ken Hatfield	9-2-0
16 Iowa	9-3-0	Hayden Fry	8-3-0
17 Clemson	8-2-2	Danny Ford	7-2-2
18 Washington	8-3-1	Don James	8-2-1
19 Boston College	9-3-0	Jack Bicknell	8-3-0
20 Virginia Tech	9-2-1	Bill Dooley	8-2-1

Key Bowl Games

Rankings below reflect final regular season poll, released Dec. 1.
Fiesta—#2 Penn St. over #1 Miami-FL, 14-10; **Orange**—#3 Oklahoma over #9 Arkansas, 42-8; **Rose**— #7 Ariz. St. over #4 Michigan, 22-15; **Sugar**—#6 Nebraska over #5 LSU, 30-15; **Cotton**—#11 Ohio St. over #8 Texas A&M, 28-12; **Citrus**—#10 Auburn over USC, 16-7; **Sun**—#13 Alabama over #12 Washington, 28-6.

1987

	After Bowls	Head Coach	Regular Season
1 Miami-FL	12-0-0	Jimmy Johnson	11-0-0
2 Florida St.	11-1-0	Bobby Bowden	10-1-0
3 Oklahoma	11-1-0	Barry Switzer	11-0-0
4 Syracuse	11-0-1	Dick MacPherson	11-0-0
5 LSU	10-1-1	Mike Archer	9-1-1
6 Nebraska	10-2-0	Tom Osborne	10-1-0
7 Auburn	9-1-2	Pat Dye	9-1-1
8 Michigan St.	9-2-1	George Perles	8-2-1
9 UCLA	10-2-0	Terry Donahue	9-2-0
10 Texas A&M	10-2-0	Jackie Sherrill	9-2-0
11 Oklahoma St.	10-2-0	Pat Jones	9-2-0
12 Clemson	10-2-0	Danny Ford	9-2-0
13 Georgia	9-3-0	Vince Dooley	8-3-0
14 Tennessee	10-2-1	Johnny Majors	9-2-1
15 South Carolina	8-4-0	Joe Morrison	8-3-0
16 Iowa	10-3-0	Hayden Fry	9-3-0
17 Notre Dame	8-4-0	Lou Holtz	8-3-0
18 USC	8-4-0	Larry Smith	8-3-0
19 Michigan	8-4-0	Bo Schembechler	7-4-0
20 Arizona St.	7-4-1	John Cooper	6-4-1

Key Bowl Games

Rankings below reflect final regular season poll, released Dec. 7.
Orange—#2 Miami-FL over #1 Oklahoma, 20-14; **Fiesta**—#3 Florida St. over #5 Nebraska, 31-28; **Sugar**—#4 Syracuse tied #6 Auburn, 16-16; **Gator**—#7 LSU over #9 S.Carolina, 30-13; **Rose**—#8 Mich. St. over #16 USC, 20-17; **Aloha**—#10 UCLA over Florida, 20-16; **Cotton**—#13 Texas A&M over #12 Notre Dame, 35-10.

1988

	After Bowls	Head Coach	Regular Season
1 Notre Dame	12-0-0	Lou Holtz	11-0-0
2 Miami-FL	11-1-0	Jimmy Johnson	10-1-0
3 Florida St.	11-1-0	Bobby Bowden	10-1-0
4 Michigan	9-2-1	Bo Schembechler	8-2-1
5 West Virginia	11-1-0	Don Nehlen	11-0-0
6 UCLA	10-2-0	Terry Donahue	9-2-0
7 USC	10-2-0	Larry Smith	10-1-0
8 Auburn	10-2-0	Pat Dye	10-1-0
9 Clemson	10-2-0	Danny Ford	9-2-0
10 Nebraska	11-2-0	Tom Osborne	11-1-0
11 Oklahoma St.	10-2-0	Pat Jones	9-2-0
12 Arkansas	10-2-0	Ken Hatfield	10-1-0
13 Syracuse	10-2-0	Dick MacPherson	9-2-0
14 Oklahoma	9-3-0	Barry Switzer	9-2-0
15 Georgia	9-3-0	Vince Dooley	8-3-0
16 Washington St.	9-3-0	Dennis Erickson	8-3-0
17 Alabama	9-3-0	Bill Curry	8-3-0
18 Houston	9-3-0	Jack Pardee	9-2-0
19 LSU	8-4-0	Mike Archer	8-3-0
20 Indiana	8-3-1	Bill Mallory	7-3-1

Key Bowl Games

Rankings below reflect final regular season poll, released Dec. 5.
Fiesta—#1 Notre Dame over #3 West Va., 34-21; **Orange**—#2 Miami-FL over #6 Nebraska, 23-3; **Sugar**—#4 Florida St. over #7 Auburn, 13-7; **Rose**—#11 Michigan over #5 USC, 22-14; **Cotton**—#9 UCLA over #8 Arkansas, 17-3; **Citrus**—#13 Clemson over #10 Oklahoma, 13-6.

1989

	After Bowls	Head Coach	Regular Season
1 Miami-FL	11-1-0	Dennis Erickson	10-1-0
2 Notre Dame	12-1-0	Lou Holtz	11-1-0
3 Florida St.	10-2-0	Bobby Bowden	9-2-0
4 Colorado	11-1-0	Bill McCartney	11-0-0
5 Tennessee	11-1-0	Johnny Majors	10-1-0
6 Auburn	10-2-0	Pat Dye	9-2-0
7 Michigan	10-2-0	Bo Schembechler	10-1-0
8 USC	9-2-1	Larry Smith	8-2-1
9 Alabama	10-2-0	Bill Curry	10-1-0
10 Illinois	10-2-0	John Mackovic	9-2-0
11 Nebraska	10-2-0	Tom Osborne	10-1-0
12 Clemson	10-2-0	Danny Ford	9-2-0
13 Arkansas	10-2-0	Ken Hatfield	10-1-0
14 Houston	9-2-0	Jack Pardee	same
15 Penn St.	8-3-1	Joe Paterno	7-3-1
16 Michigan St.	8-4-0	George Perles	7-4-0
17 Pittsburgh	8-3-1	Mike Gottfried & Paul Hackett (1-0)	(7-3-1) 7-3-1
18 Virginia	10-3-0	George Welsh	10-2-0
19 Texas Tech	9-3-0	Spike Dykes	8-3-0
20 Texas A&M	8-4-0	R.C. Slocum	8-3-0

Key Bowl Games

Rankings below reflect final regular season poll, released Dec. 11. No bowl for then #13 Houston (probation).
Orange—#4 Notre Dame over #1 Colorado, 21-6; **Sugar**—#2 Miami-FL over #7 Alabama, 33-25; **Rose**—#12 USC over #3 Michigan, 17-10; **Fiesta**—#5 Florida St. over #6 Nebraska, 41-17; **Cotton**—#8 Tennessee over #10 Arkansas, 31-27; **Hall of Fame**—#9 Auburn over #21 Ohio St., 31-14; **Citrus**—#11 Illinois over #15 Virginia, 31-21.

1990

	After Bowls	Head Coach	Regular Season
1 Colorado	11-1-1	Bill McCartney	10-1-1
2 Georgia Tech	11-0-1	Bobby Ross	10-0-1
3 Miami-FL	10-2-0	Dennis Erickson	9-2-0
4 Florida St.	10-2-0	Bobby Bowden	9-2-0
5 Washington	10-2-0	Don James	9-2-0
6 Notre Dame	9-3-0	Lou Holtz	9-2-0
7 Michigan	9-3-0	Gary Moeller	8-3-0
8 Tennessee	9-2-2	Johnny Majors	8-2-2
9 Clemson	10-2-0	Ken Hatfield	9-2-0
10 Houston	10-1-0	John Jenkins	same
11 Penn St.	9-3-0	Joe Paterno	9-2-0
12 Texas	10-2-0	David McWilliams	10-1-0
13 Florida	9-2-0	Steve Spurrier	same
14 Louisville	10-1-1	H. Schnellenberger	9-1-1
15 Texas A&M	9-3-1	R.C. Slocum	8-3-1
16 Michigan St.	8-3-1	George Perles	7-3-1
17 Oklahoma	8-3-0	Gary Gibbs	same
18 Iowa	8-4-0	Hayden Fry	8-3-0
19 Auburn	8-3-1	Pat Dye	7-3-1
20 USC	8-4-1	Larry Smith	8-3-1

Key Bowl Games

Rankings below reflect final regular season poll, released Dec. 3. No bowl for then #9 Houston (probation), #11 Florida (probation) and #20 Oklahoma (probation).
Orange—#1 Colorado over #5 Notre Dame, 10-9; **Citrus**—#2 Ga. Tech over #19 Nebraska, 45-21; **Cotton**—#4 Miami-FL over #3 Texas, 46-3; **Blockbuster**—#6 Florida St. over #7 Penn St., 24-17; **Rose**—#8 Washington over #17 Iowa, 46-34; **Sugar**—#10 Tennessee over Virginia, 23-22; **Gator**—#12 Michigan over #15 Ole Miss, 35-3.

1991

	After Bowls	Head Coach	Regular Season
1 Miami-FL	12-0-0	Dennis Erickson	11-0-0
2 Washington	12-0-0	Don James	11-0-0
3 Penn St.	11-2-0	Joe Paterno	10-2-0
4 Florida St.	11-2-0	Bobby Bowden	10-2-0
5 Alabama	11-1-0	Gene Stallings	10-1-0
6 Michigan	10-2-0	Gary Moeller	10-1-0
7 Florida	10-2-0	Steve Spurrier	10-1-0
8 California	10-2-0	Bruce Snyder	9-2-0
9 East Carolina	11-1-0	Bill Lewis	10-1-0
10 Iowa	10-1-1	Hayden Fry	10-1-0
11 Syracuse	10-2-0	Paul Pasqualoni	9-2-0
12 Texas A&M	10-2-0	R.C. Slocum	10-1-0
13 Notre Dame	10-3-0	Lou Holtz	9-3-0
14 Tennessee	9-3-0	Johnny Majors	9-2-0
15 Nebraska	9-2-1	Tom Osborne	9-1-1
16 Oklahoma	9-3-0	Gary Gibbs	8-3-0
17 Georgia	9-3-0	Ray Goff	8-3-0
18 Clemson	9-2-1	Ken Hatfield	9-1-1
19 UCLA	9-3-0	Terry Donahue	8-3-0
20 Colorado	8-3-1	Bill McCartney	8-2-1

Key Bowl Games

Rankings below reflect final regular season poll, taken Dec. 2. **Orange**—#1 Miami-FL over #11 Nebraska, 22-0; **Rose**—#2 Washington over #4 Michigan, 34-14; **Sugar**—#18 Notre Dame over #3 Florida, 39-28; **Cotton**—#5 Florida St. over #9 Texas A&M, 10-2; **Fiesta**—#6 Penn St. over #10 Tennessee, 42-17; **Holiday**—#7 Iowa tied BYU, 13-13; **Blockbuster**—#8 Alabama over #15 Colorado, 30-25; **Citrus**—#14 California over #13 Clemson, 37-13; **Peach**—#12 East Carolina over #21 N.C. State, 37-34.

1992

	After Bowls	Head Coach	Regular Season
1 Alabama	13-0-0	Gene Stallings	12-0-0
2 Florida St.	11-1-0	Bobby Bowden	0-1-0
3 Miami-FL	11-1-0	Dennis Erickson	11-0-0
4 Notre Dame	10-1-1	Lou Holtz	9-1-1
5 Michigan	9-0-3	Gary Moeller	8-0-3
6 Syracuse	10-2-0	Paul Pasqualoni	9-2-0
7 Texas A&M	12-1-0	R.C. Slocum	12-0-0
8 Georgia	10-2-0	Ray Goff	9-2-0
9 Stanford	10-3-0	Bill Walsh	9-3-0
10 Florida	9-4-0	Steve Spurrier	8-4-0
11 Washington	9-3-0	Don James	9-2-0
12 Tennessee	9-3-0	Johnny Majors (5-3) & Phillip Fulmer (4-0)	8-3-0
13 Colorado	9-2-1	Bill McCartney	9-1-1
14 Nebraska	9-3-0	Tom Osborne	9-2-0
15 Washington St.	9-3-0	Mike Price	8-3-0
16 Mississippi	9-3-0	Billy Brewer	8-3-0
17 N.C. State	9-3-1	Dick Sheridan	9-2-1
18 Ohio St.	8-3-1	John Cooper	8-2-1
19 North Carolina	9-3-0	Mack Brown	8-3-0
20 Hawaii	11-2-0	Bob Wagner	10-2-0

Key Bowl Games

Rankings below reflect final regular season poll, taken Dec. 5. **Sugar**—#2 Alabama over #1 Miami-FL, 34-13; **Orange**—#3 Florida St. over #11 Nebraska, 27-14; **Cotton**—#5 Notre Dame over #4 Texas A&M, 28-3; **Fiesta**—#6 Syracuse over #10 Colorado, 26-22; **Rose**—#7 Michigan over #9 Washington, 38-31; **Citrus**—#8 Georgia over #15 Ohio St., 21-14.

1993

	After Bowls	Head Coach	Regular Season
1 Florida St	12-1-0	Bobby Bowden	11-1-0
2 Notre Dame	11-1-0	Lou Holtz	10-1-0
3 Nebraska	11-1-0	Tom Osborne	11-0-0
4 Auburn	11-0-0	Terry Bowden	11-0-0
5 Florida	11-2-0	Steve Spurrier	10-2-0
6 Wisconsin	10-1-1	Barry Alvarez	9-1-1
7 West Virginia	11-1-0	Don Nehlen	11-0-0
8 Penn St	10-2-0	Joe Paterno	9-2-0
9 Texas A&M	10-2-0	R.C. Slocum	10-1-0
10 Arizona	10-2-0	Dick Tomey	9-2-0
11 Ohio St	10-1-1	John Cooper	9-1-1
12 Tennessee	9-2-1	Phillip Fulmer	9-1-1
13 Boston College	9-3-0	Tom Coughlin	8-3-0
14 Alabama	9-3-1	Gene Stallings	8-3-1
15 Miami-FL	9-3-0	Dennis Erickson	9-2-0
16 Colorado	8-3-1	Bill McCartney	7-3-1
17 Oklahoma	9-3-0	Gary Gibbs	8-3-0
18 UCLA	8-4-0	Terry Donahue	8-3-0
19 North Carolina	10-3-0	Mack Brown	10-2-0
20 Kansas St	9-2-1	Bill Snyder	8-2-1

Key Bowl Games

Rankings below reflect final regular season poll, taken Dec. 5. No bowl for then #5 Auburn (probation).
Orange—#1 Florida St. over #2 Nebraska, 18-16; **Sugar**—#8 Florida over #3 West Virginia, 41-7; **Cotton**—#4 Notre Dame over #7 Texas A&M, 24-21; **Citrus**—#13 Penn St. over #6 Tennessee, 31-13; **Rose**—#9 Wisconsin over #14 UCLA, 21-16; **Fiesta**—#16 Arizona over #10 Miami-FL, 29-0; **Holiday**—#11 Ohio St. over BYU, 28-21; **Gator**—#18 Alabama over #12 North Carolina, 24-10; **Carquest**—#15 Boston College over Virginia, 31-13.

Associated Press Final Polls (Cont.)

Final poll taken after bowl games.

1994

	After Bowls	Head Coach	Regular Season
1	Nebraska	13-0-0	Tom Osborne	12-0-0
2	Penn St	12-0-0	Joe Paterno	11-0-0
3	Colorado	11-1-0	Bill McCartney	10-1-0
4	Florida St	10-1-1	Bobby Bowden	9-1-1
5	Alabama	12-1-0	Gene Stallings	11-1-0
6	Miami-FL	10-2-0	Dennis Erickson	10-1-0
7	Florida	10-2-1	Steve Spurrier	10-1-1
8	Texas A&M	10-0-1	R.C. Slocum	same
9	Auburn	9-1-1	Terry Bowden	same
10	Utah	10-2-0	Ron McBride	9-2-0
11	Oregon	9-4-0	Rich Brooks	9-3-0
12	Michigan	8-4-0	Gary Moeller	7-4-0
13	USC	8-3-1	John Robinson	7-3-1
14	Ohio St	9-4-0	John Cooper	9-3-0
15	Virginia	9-3-0	George Welsh	8-3-0
16	Colorado St	10-2-0	Sonny Lubick	10-1-0
17	N.C. State	9-3-0	Mike O'Cain	8-3-0
18	BYU	10-3-0	LaVell Edwards	9-3-0
19	Kansas St	9-3-0	Bill Snyder	9-2-0
20	Arizona	8-4-0	Dick Tomey	8-3-0

Key Bowl Games

Rankings below reflect final regular season poll, taken Dec. 4. No bowls for then #8 Texas A&M (probation) and #9 Auburn (probation).

Orange— #1 Nebraska over #3 Miami-FL, 24-17; **Rose**— #2 Penn St. over #12 Oregon, 38-20; **Fiesta**— #4 Colorado over Notre Dame, 41-24; **Sugar**— #7 Florida St. over #5 Florida, 23-17; **Citrus**— #6 Alabama over #13 Ohio St., 24-17; **Freedom**— #14 Utah over #15 Arizona, 16-13.

All-Time AP Top 20

The composite AP Top 20 from the 1936 season through the 1994 season, based on the final rankings of each year. The final AP poll has been taken after the bowl games in 1965 and since 1968. Team point totals are based on 20 points for all 1st place finishes, 19 for each 2nd, etc. Also listed are the number of times each team has been named national champion by AP and times ranked in the final Top 10 and Top 20.

		Final AP		
	Pts	No.1	Top 10	Top 20
1 Notre Dame	614	8	34	42
2 Oklahoma	558	6	29	41
3 Alabama	541	6	30	40
Michigan	541	1	32	42
5 Ohio St.	456	3	21	37
6 Nebraska	446	3	24	34
7 USC	405	3	20	35
8 Texas	393	2	19	30
9 Penn St	362	2	20	30
10 Tennessee	357	1	17	31
11 UCLA	293	0	14	27
12 Auburn	271	1	14	25
13 LSU	260	1	14	23
14 Arkansas	259	0	13	23
15 Miami-FL	256	4	13	19
16 Georgia	238	1	13	20
Michigan St	238	1	12	19
18 Florida St	201	1	10	14
19 Texas A&M	199	1	11	19
20 Pittsburgh	194	2	10	16
Washington	194	0	10	16

The Bowl Alliance

Division I-A football remains the only NCAA sport on any level that does not have a sanctioned national champion. To that end, the Bowl Coalition was formed in 1992 in an attempt to keep the bowl system intact while forcing an annual championship game between the regular season's two top-ranked teams.

The Coalition, which lasted for three seasons, consolidated the resources of four major bowl games (the Cotton, Fiesta, Orange and Sugar), the champions of five major conferences (the ACC, Big East, Big Eight, Southeastern and Southwest) and the national following of independent Notre Dame. It worked two out of three years with No. 1 vs. No. 2 showdowns in the 1993 Sugar Bowl and 1994 Orange Bowl.

The Bowl Alliance, which begins a six-year run with the 1995 season, is an updated version of the Coalition.

Member conferences: ACC, Big East, Big Eight, Big 10, Pac-10, SEC, SWC and independent Notre Dame. Note that SWC ceases operation on June 30, 1996 when Baylor, Texas, Texas A&M and Texas Tech join the Big Eight which then becomes the Big 12. **Major bowls** (3): Fiesta, Orange and Sugar. **Major bowl automatic berths:** *1995 season*— FIESTA (No. 1 vs. No. 2), ORANGE (No. 3 vs. No. 5), SUGAR (No. 4 vs. No. 6); *1996 season*— SUGAR (No. 1 vs. No. 2), FIESTA (No. 3 vs. No. 5), ORANGE (No. 4 vs. No. 6); *1997 season*— ORANGE (No. 1 vs. No. 2), SUGAR (No. 3 vs. No. 5), FIESTA (No. 4 vs. No. 6). **Annual bowl dates:** Dec. 31 (No. 4 vs. No. 6); Jan. 1 (No. 3 vs. No. 5); and Jan. 2 (No. 1 vs. No. 2). **Missing ingredients:** the champions of the Big Ten and Pac-10, and the Rose Bowl game.

Pool of teams for six slots (ranked according to combined AP media and *USA Today*/CNN coaches' polls at the end of the regular season)**:** ACC champion, Big East champ, Big Eight champ, SEC champ, SWC champ and Notre Dame (provided the Irish are ranked in either Top 10). If Notre Dame doesn't qualify, it's at-large slot would be filled by an eligible Division I-A team that met the following requirements: a) had at least eight wins, b) is ranked in the Top 12 of the AP media or *USA Today*/CNN coaches' polls, and c) is ranked no lower in either poll than the lowest ranked conference champion.

Non-Alliance matchups (in order of importance)**:** ALAMO (fourth pick from Big Eight/SWC pool vs. fourth pick from Big 10); ALOHA (fifth pick from Big Eight/SWC pool vs. at-large opponent); CARQUEST (third pick from Big East vs. fifth pick from SEC); CITRUS (second pick from Big 10 vs. second pick from SEC); COPPER (second pick from WAC vs. sixth pick from Big Eight/SWC pool); COTTON (first choice of either WAC champ or second pick from Pac-10 vs. second pick from Big Eight/SWC pool); OUTBACK (third pick from Big 10 vs. third pick from SEC); HOLIDAY (second choice of either WAC champ or second pick from Pac- 10 vs. third pick from Big Eight/SWC pool); INDEPENDENCE (at-large vs. at-large); LAS VEGAS (Big West champ vs. Mid-American champ); LIBERTY (team with best record from independent from Cincinnati, East Carolina, Memphis, Southern Miss. and Tulane vs. at-large opponent); PEACH (third pick from ACC vs. fourth pick from SEC); ROSE (Big 10 champion vs. Pac-10 champ). **Note:** Big Eight/SWC pool includes Big Eight and SWC teams with at least six victories.

Bowl Games

From Jan. 1, 1902 through Jan. 2, 1995. Corporate title sponsors and automatic berths updated through Aug. 15, 1995.

Rose Bowl

City: Pasadena, Calif. **Stadium:** Rose Bowl. **Capacity:** 100,225. **Playing surface:** Grass. **First game:** Jan. 1, 1902.
Playing sites: Tournament Park (1902, 1916-22), Rose Bowl (1923-41 and since 1943) and Duke Stadium in Durham, N.C. (1942, due to wartime restrictions following Japan's attack at Pearl Harbor on Dec. 7, 1941).
Automatic berths: Pacific Coast Conference champion vs. opponent selected by PCC (1924-45 seasons); Big Ten champion vs. Pac-10 champion (since 1946 season).
Multiple wins: USC (19); Michigan (7); Washington (6); Ohio St., Stanford and UCLA (5); Alabama (4); Illinois and Michigan St. (3); California and Iowa (2).

Year		Year		Year	
1902*	Michigan 49, Stanford 0	1944	USC 29, Washington 0	1973	USC 42, Ohio St. 17
1916	Washington St. 14, Brown 0	1945	USC 25, Tennessee 0	1974	Ohio St. 42, USC 21
1917	Oregon 14, Penn 0	1946	Alabama 34, USC 14	1975	USC 18, Ohio St. 17
1918	Mare Island 19, Camp Lewis 7	1947	Illinois 45, UCLA 14	1976	UCLA 23, Ohio St. 10
1919	Great Lakes 17, Mare Island 0	1948	Michigan 49, USC 0	1977	USC 14, Michigan 6
1920	Harvard 7, Oregon 6	1949	Northwestern 20, California 14	1978	Washington 27, Michigan 20
1921	California 28, Ohio St. 0			1979	USC 17, Michigan 10
1922	0-0, California vs Wash. & Jeff.	1950	Ohio St. 17, California 14		
1923	USC 14, Penn St. 0	1951	Michigan 14, California 6	1980	USC 17, Ohio St. 16
1924	14-14, Navy vs Washington	1952	Illinois 40, Stanford 7	1981	Michigan 23, Washington 6
1925	Notre Dame 27, Stanford 10	1953	USC 7, Wisconsin 0	1982	Washington 28, Iowa 0
1926	Alabama 20, Washington 19	1954	Michigan St. 28, UCLA 20	1983	UCLA 24, Michigan 14
1927	7-7, Alabama vs Stanford	1955	Ohio St. 20, USC 7	1984	UCLA 45, Illinois 9
1928	Stanford 7, Pittsburgh 6	1956	Michigan St. 17, UCLA 14	1985	USC 20, Ohio St. 17
1929	Georgia Tech 8, California 7	1957	Iowa 35, Oregon St. 19	1986	UCLA 45, Iowa 28
1930	USC 47, Pittsburgh 14	1958	Ohio St. 10, Oregon 7	1987	Arizona St. 22, Michigan 15
1931	Alabama 24, Washington St. 0	1959	Iowa 38, California 12	1988	Michigan St. 20, USC 17
1932	USC 21, Tulane 12			1989	Michigan 22, USC 14
1933	USC 35, Pittsburgh 0	1960	Washington 44, Wisconsin 8		
1934	Columbia 7, Stanford 0	1961	Washington 17, Minnesota 7	1990	USC 17, Michigan 10
1935	Alabama 29, Stanford 13	1962	Minnesota 21, UCLA 3	1991	Washington 46, Iowa 34
1936	Stanford 7, SMU 0	1963	USC 42, Wisconsin 37	1992	Washington 34, Michigan 14
1937	Pittsburgh 21, Washington 0	1964	Illinois 17, Washington 7	1993	Michigan 38, Washington 31
1938	California 13, Alabama 0	1965	Michigan 34, Oregon St. 7	1994	Wisconsin 21, UCLA 16
1939	USC 7, Duke 3	1966	UCLA 14, Michigan St. 12	1995	Penn St. 38, Oregon 20
1940	USC 14, Tennessee 0	1967	Purdue 14, USC 13		
1941	Stanford 21, Nebraska 13	1968	USC 14, Indiana 3		
1942	Oregon St. 20, Duke 16	1969	Ohio St. 27, USC 16		
1943	Georgia 9, UCLA 0	1970	USC 10, Michigan 3		
		1971	Stanford 27, Ohio St. 17		
		1972	Stanford 13, Michigan 12		

*January game since 1902.

Fiesta Bowl

City: Tempe, Ariz. **Stadium:** Sun Devil. **Capacity:** 73,655. **Playing surface:** Grass. **First game:** Dec. 27, 1971. **Playing site:** Sun Devil Stadium (since 1971). **Corporate title sponsors:** Sunkist Citrus Growers (1986-91) and IBM OS/2 (1993-95) and Frito-Lay Tostitos (beginning in 1996).
Automatic berths: Two of first five picks from 8-team Bowl Coalition pool (1992-94 seasons). New Bowl Alliance matchups starting with 1995 season: #1 vs. #2 on Jan. 2, 1996; #3 vs. #5 on Jan. 1, 1997; and #4 vs. #6 on Dec. 31, 1997.
Multiple wins: Arizona St. and Penn St. (5); Florida St. (2).

Year		Year		Year	
1971†	Arizona St. 45, Florida St. 38	1979	Pittsburgh 16, Arizona 10	1988	Florida St. 31, Nebraska 28
1972	Arizona St. 49, Missouri 35			1989	Notre Dame 34, West Va. 21
1973	Arizona St. 28, Pittsburgh 7	1980	Penn St. 31, Ohio St. 19		
1974	Oklahoma St. 16, BYU 6	1982*	Penn St. 26, USC 10	1990	Florida St. 41, Nebraska 17
1975	Arizona St. 17, Nebraska 14	1983	Arizona St. 32, Oklahoma 21	1991	Louisville 34, Alabama 7
1976	Oklahoma 41, Wyoming 7	1984	Ohio St. 28, Pittsburgh 23	1992	Penn St. 42, Tennessee 17
1977	Penn St. 42, Arizona St. 30	1985	UCLA 39, Miami-FL 37	1993	Syracuse 26, Colorado 22
1978	10-10, Arkansas vs UCLA	1986	Michigan 27, Nebraska 23	1994	Arizona 29, Miami-FL 0
		1987	Penn St. 14, Miami-FL 10	1995	Colorado 41, Notre Dame 24

†December game from 1971-80.　　*January game since 1982.

NCAA Approves Tiebreakers in Bowl Games

The NCAA tiebreaker system has been approved for Division I-A bowl games beginning with the 1995 postseason. Unlike sudden-death overtime in the NFL, the NCAA tiebreaking procedure gives both teams a chance to score after regulation time has expired. Each team gets an offensive series beginning on the opponent's 25-yard line. A team's possession ends when it scores, turns the ball over or fails to convert a fourth-down play. This untimed procedure is repeated until the score is no longer tied at the end of an overtime period, which consists of one possession per team.

Bowl Games (Cont.)

Sugar Bowl

City: New Orleans, La. **Stadium:** Louisiana Superdome. **Capacity:** 77,450. **Playing surface:** AstroTurf. **First game:** Jan. 1, 1935. **Playing sites:** Tulane Stadium (1935-74) and Superdome (since 1975). **Corporate title sponsors:** USF&G Financial Services (1987-95) and Nokia cellular telephones of Finland (starting in 1995).

Automatic berths: SEC champion vs. at-large opponent (1976-91 seasons); SEC champion vs. one of first five picks from 8-team Bowl Coalition pool (1992-94 seasons). New Bowl Alliance matchups starting with 1995 season: #4 vs. #6 on Dec. 31, 1995; #1 vs. #2 on Jan. 2, 1997; and #3 vs. #5 on Jan. 1, 1998.

Multiple wins: Alabama (8); Mississippi (5); Georgia Tech, Oklahoma and Tennessee (4); LSU and Nebraska (3); Florida St., Georgia, Notre Dame, Pittsburgh, Santa Clara and TCU (2).

Year		Year		Year	
1935*	Tulane 20, Temple 14	1956	Georgia Tech 7, Pittsburgh 0	1977*	Pittsburgh 27, Georgia 3
1936	TCU 3, LSU 2	1957	Baylor 13, Tennessee 7	1978	Alabama 35, Ohio St. 6
1937	Santa Clara 21, LSU 14	1958	Mississippi 39, Texas 7	1979	Alabama 14, Penn St. 7
1938	Santa Clara 6, LSU 0	1959	LSU 7, Clemson 0		
1939	TCU 15, Carnegie Tech 7			1980	Alabama 24, Arkansas 9
		1960	Mississippi 21, LSU 0	1981	Georgia 17, Notre Dame 10
1940	Texas A&M 14, Tulane 13	1961	Mississippi 14, Rice 6	1982	Pittsburgh 24, Georgia 20
1941	Boston College 19, Tennessee 13	1962	Alabama 10, Arkansas 3	1983	Penn St. 27, Georgia 23
1942	Fordham 2, Missouri 0	1963	Mississippi 17, Arkansas 13	1984	Auburn 9, Michigan 7
1943	Tennessee 14, Tulsa 7	1964	Alabama 12, Mississippi 7	1985	Nebraska 28, LSU 10
1944	Georgia Tech 20, Tulsa 18	1965	LSU 13, Syracuse 10	1986	Tennessee 35, Miami-FL 7
1945	Duke 29, Alabama 26	1966	Missouri 20, Florida 18	1987	Nebraska 30, LSU 15
1946	Okla. A&M 33, St.Mary's 13	1967	Alabama 34, Nebraska 7	1988	16-16, Syracuse vs Auburn
1947	Georgia 20, N.Carolina 10	1968	LSU 20, Wyoming 13	1989	Florida St. 13, Auburn 7
1948	Texas 27, Alabama 7	1969	Arkansas 16, Georgia 2		
1949	Oklahoma 14, N.Carolina 6			1990	Miami-FL 33, Alabama 25
		1970	Mississippi 27, Arkansas 22	1991	Tennessee 23, Virginia 22
1950	Oklahoma 35, LSU 0	1971	Tennessee 34, Air Force 13	1992	Notre Dame 39, Florida 28
1951	Kentucky 13, Oklahoma 7	1972	Oklahoma 40, Auburn 22	1993	Alabama 34, Miami-FL 13
1952	Maryland 28, Tennessee 13	1972†	Oklahoma 14, Penn St. 0	1994	Florida 41, West Va. 7
1953	Georgia Tech 24, Mississippi 7	1973	Notre Dame 24, Alabama 23	1995	Florida St. 23, Florida 17
1954	Georgia Tech 42, West Va. 19	1974	Nebraska 13, Florida 10		
1955	Navy 21, Mississippi 0	1975	Alabama 13, Penn St. 6		

*January game from 1935-72 and since 1977.   †Game played on Dec. 31 from 1972-75.

Orange Bowl

City: Miami, Fla. **Stadium:** Orange Bowl. **Capacity:** 74,475. **Playing surface:** Grass. **First game:** Jan. 1, 1935. **Playing sites:** Orange Bowl (since 1935); game moves to Joe Robbie Stadium Dec. 31, 1996. **Corporate title sponsor:** Federal Express (since 1989).

Automatic berths: Big 8 champion vs. at-large opponent (1953-63 seasons and 1975-91 seasons); Big 8 champion vs. one of first five picks from 8-team Bowl Coalition pool (1992-94 seasons). New Bowl Alliance matchups starting with 1995 season: #3 vs. #5 on Jan. 1, 1996; #4 vs. #6 on Dec. 31, 1996; and #1 vs. #2 on Jan. 2, 1998.

Multiple wins: Oklahoma (11); Nebraska (6); Miami-FL (5); Alabama (4); Georgia Tech and Penn St. (3); Clemson, Colorado, Florida State, Georgia, LSU, Notre Dame and Texas (2).

Year		Year		Year	
1935*	Bucknell 26, Miami-FL 0	1956	Oklahoma 20, Maryland 6	1977	Ohio St. 27, Colorado 10
1936	Catholic U. 20, Mississippi 19	1957	Colorado 27, Clemson 21	1978	Arkansas 31, Oklahoma 6
1937	Duquesne 13, Mississippi St. 12	1958	Oklahoma 48, Duke 21	1979	Oklahoma 31, Nebraska 24
1938	Auburn 6, Michigan St. 0	1959	Oklahoma 21, Syracuse 6		
1939	Tennessee 17, Oklahoma 0			1980	Oklahoma 24, Florida St. 7
		1960	Georgia 14, Missouri 0	1981	Oklahoma 18, Florida St. 17
1940	Georgia Tech 21, Missouri 7	1961	Missouri 21, Navy 14	1982	Clemson 22, Nebraska 15
1941	Mississippi St. 14, Georgetown 7	1962	LSU 25, Colorado 7	1983	Nebraska 31, LSU 20
1942	Georgia 40, TCU 26	1963	Alabama 17, Oklahoma 0	1984	Miami-FL 31, Nebraska 30
1943	Alabama 37, Boston College 21	1964	Nebraska 13, Auburn 7	1985	Washington 28, Oklahoma 17
1944	LSU 19, Texas A&M 14	1965†	Texas 21, Alabama 17	1986	Oklahoma 25, Penn St. 10
1945	Tulsa 26, Georgia Tech 12	1966	Alabama 39, Nebraska 28	1987	Oklahoma 42, Arkansas 8
1946	Miami-FL 13, Holy Cross 6	1967	Florida 27, Georgia Tech 12	1988	Miami-FL 20, Oklahoma 14
1947	Rice 8, Tennessee 0	1968	Oklahoma 26, Tennessee 24	1989	Miami-FL 23, Nebraska 3
1948	Georgia Tech 20, Kansas 14	1969	Penn St. 15, Kansas 14		
1949	Texas 41, Georgia 28			1990	Notre Dame, 21, Colorado 6
		1970	Penn St. 10, Missouri 3	1991	Colorado 10, Notre Dame 9
1950	Santa Clara 21, Kentucky 13	1971	Nebraska 17, LSU 12	1992	Miami-FL 22, Nebraska 0
1951	Clemson 15, Miami-FL 14	1972	Nebraska 38, Alabama 6	1993	Florida St. 27, Nebraska 14
1952	Georgia Tech 17, Baylor 14	1973	Nebraska 40, Notre Dame 6	1994	Florida St. 18, Nebraska 16
1953	Alabama 61, Syracuse 6	1974	Penn St. 16, LSU 9	1995	Nebraska 24, Miami-FL 17
1954	Oklahoma 7, Maryland 0	1975	Notre Dame 13, Alabama 11		
1955	Duke 34, Nebraska 7	1976	Oklahoma 14, Michigan 6		

*January game since 1935.   †Night game since 1965.

Cotton Bowl

City: Dallas, Tex. **Stadium:** Cotton Bowl. **Capacity:** 68,250. **Playing surface:** Grass. **First game:** Jan 1, 1937. **Playing sites:** Fair Park Stadium (1937) and Cotton Bowl (since 1938). **Corporate title sponsor:** Mobil Corporation (1988-95).

Automatic berths: SWC champion vs. at-large opponent (1941-91 seasons); SWC champion vs. one of first five picks from 8-team Bowl Coalition pool (1992-1994 seasons). New Bowl Alliance matchup starting with 1995 season: first choice of WAC champion or second pick from Pac-10 vs. second pick from Big 12 (Big Eight/SWC).

Multiple wins: Texas (9); Notre Dame (5); Texas A&M (4); Rice (3); Alabama, Arkansas, Georgia, Houston, LSU, Penn St., SMU, Tennessee and TCU (2).

Year	Year	Year
1937* TCU 16, Marquette 6	1957 TCU 28, Syracuse 27	1977 Houston 30, Maryland 21
1938 Rice 28, Colorado 14	1958 Navy 20, Rice 7	1978 Notre Dame 38, Texas 10
1939 St. Mary's 20, Texas Tech 13	1959 0-0, TCU vs Air Force	1979 Notre Dame 35, Houston 34
1940 Clemson 6, Boston College 3	1960 Syracuse 23, Texas 14	1980 Houston 17, Nebraska 14
1941 Texas A&M 13, Fordham 12	1961 Duke 7, Arkansas 6	1981 Alabama 30, Baylor 2
1942 Alabama 29, Texas A&M 21	1962 Texas 12, Mississippi 7	1982 Texas 14, Alabama 12
1943 Texas 14, Georgia Tech 7	1963 LSU 13, Texas 0	1983 SMU 7, Pittsburgh 3
1944 7-7, Texas vs Randolph Field	1964 Texas 28, Navy 6	1984 Georgia 10, Texas 9
1945 Oklahoma A&M 34, TCU 0	1965 Arkansas 10, Nebraska 7	1985 Boston College 45, Houston 28
1946 Texas 40, Missouri 27	1966 LSU 14, Arkansas 7	1986 Texas A&M 36, Auburn 16
1947 0-0, Arkansas vs LSU	1966† Georgia 24, SMU 9	1987 Ohio St. 28, Texas A&M 12
1948 13-13, SMU vs Penn St.	1968* Texas A&M 20, Alabama 16	1988 Texas A&M 35, Notre Dame 10
1949 SMU 21, Oregon 13	1969 Texas 36, Tennessee 13	1989 UCLA 17, Arkansas 3
1950 Rice 27, N. Carolina 13	1970 Texas 21, Notre Dame 17	1990 Tennessee 31, Arkansas 27
1951 Tennessee 20, Texas 14	1971 Notre Dame 24, Texas 11	1991 Miami-FL 46, Texas 3
1952 Kentucky 20, TCU 7	1972 Penn St. 30, Texas 6	1992 Florida St. 10, Texas A&M 2
1953 Texas 16, Tennessee 0	1973 Texas 17, Alabama 13	1993 Notre Dame 28, Texas A&M 3
1954 Rice 28, Alabama 6	1974 Nebraska 19, Texas 3	1994 Notre Dame 24, Texas A&M 21
1955 Georgia Tech 14, Arkansas 6	1975 Penn St. 41, Baylor 20	1995 USC 55, Texas Tech 14
1956 Mississippi 14, TCU 13	1976 Arkansas 31, Georgia 10	

*January game from 1937-66 and since 1968.   †Game played on Dec. 31, 1966.

Florida Citrus Bowl

City: Orlando, Fla. **Stadium:** Florida Cirtus Bowl. **Capacity:** 73,000. **Playing surface:** Grass. **First game:** Jan. 1, 1947. **Name change:** Tangerine Bowl (1947-82) and Florida Citrus Bowl (since 1983). **Playing sites:** Tangerine Bowl (1947-72, 1974-82), Ben Hill Griffin Stadium in Gainesville (1973), Orlando Stadium (1983-85) and Florida Citrus Bowl (since 1986). The Tangerine Bowl, Orlando Stadium and Florida Citrus Bowl are all the same stadium. **Corporate title sponsors:** Florida Department of Cirtus (since 1983) and CompUSA (since 1992).

Automatic berths: Championship game of Atlantic Coast Regional Conference (1964-67 seasons); Mid-American Conference champion vs. Southern Conference champion (1968-75 seasons); ACC champion vs. at-large opponent (1987-91 seasons); second pick from SEC vs. second pick from Big 10 (1992-94 seasons). New Bowl Alliance matchup starting with 1995 season: second pick from SEC vs. second pick from Big 10.

Multiple wins: East Texas St., Miami-OH and Toledo (3); Auburn, Catawba, Clemson, East Carolina (2).

Year	Year	Year
1947* Catawba 31, Maryville 6	1963 Western Ky. 27, Coast Guard 0	1980 Florida 35, Maryland 20
1948 Catawba 7, Marshall 0	1964 E. Carolina 14, Massachusetts 13	1981 Missouri 19, Southern Miss. 17
1949 21-21, Murray St. vs Sul Ross St.	1965 E. Carolina 31, Maine 0	1982 Auburn 33, Boston College 26
1950 St. Vincent 7, Emory & Henry 6	1966 Morgan St. 14, West Chester 6	1983 Tennessee 30, Maryland 23
1951 M. Harvey 35, Emory & Henry 14	1967 Tenn-Martin 25, West Chester 8	1984 17-17, Florida St. vs Georgia
1952 Stetson 35, Arkansas St. 20	1968 Richmond 49, Ohio U. 42	1985 Ohio St. 10, BYU 7
1953 E. Texas St. 33, Tenn. Tech 0	1969 Toledo 56, Davidson 33	1987* Auburn 16, USC 7
1954 7-7, E. Texas St. vs Arkansas St.	1970 Toledo 40, Wm. & Mary 12	1988 Clemson 35, Penn St. 10
1955 Neb.-Omaha 7, Eastern Ky. 6	1971 Toledo 28, Richmond 3	1989 Clemson 13, Oklahoma 6
1956 6-6, Juniata vs Missouri Valley	1972 Tampa 21, Kent St. 18	1990 Illinois 31, Virginia 21
1957 W. Texas St. 20, So. Miss. 13	1973 Miami-OH 16, Florida 7	1991 Georgia Tech 45, Nebraska 21
1958 E. Texas St. 10, So. Miss. 9	1974 Miami-OH 21, Georgia 10	1992 California 37, Clemson 13
1958† E. Texas St. 26, Mo. Valley 7	1975 Miami-OH 20, S. Carolina 7	1993 Georgia 21, Ohio St. 14
	1976 Oklahoma 49, BYU 21	1994 Penn St. 31, Tennessee 13
1960* Mid. Tenn. 21, Presbyterian 12	1977 Florida St. 40, Texas Tech 17	1995 Alabama 24, Ohio St. 17
1960† Citadel 27, Tenn. Tech 0	1978 N.C. State 30, Pittsburgh 17	
1961 Lamar 21, Middle Tenn. 14	1979 LSU 34, Wake Forest 10	
1962 Houston 49, Miami-OH 21		

*January game from 1947-58, in 1960 and since 1987.   †December game from 1958 and 1960-85.

Bowl Games (Cont.)

Gator Bowl

City: Jacksonville, Fla. **Stadium:** New Gator Bowl. **Capacity:** 73,000. **Playing surface:** Grass. **First game:** Jan. 1, 1946. **Playing sites:** Gator Bowl (1946-93), Ben Hill Griffin Stadium in Gainesville (1994) and New Gator Bowl (beginning in 1995). **Corporate title sponsors:** Mazda Motors of America, Inc. (1986-91), Outback Steakhouse, Inc. (1992-94) and Toyota Motor Co. (starting in 1995).

Automatic berths: Third pick from SEC vs. sixth pick from 8-team Bowl Coalition pool (1992-94 seasons). New Bowl Alliance matchup starting with 1995 season: second pick from ACC vs. second pick from Big East.

Multiple wins: Florida (6); Auburn and Clemson (4); Florida St., North Carolina and Tennessee (3); Georgia, Georgia Tech, Maryland, Oklahoma, Pittsburgh, and Texas Tech (2).

Year	Year	Year
1946* Wake Forest 26, S. Carolina 14	1962 Florida 17, Penn St. 7	1980 Pittsburgh 37, S. Carolina 9
1947 Oklahoma 34, N.C. State 13	1963 N. Carolina 35, Air Force 0	1981 N. Carolina 31, Arkansas 27
1948 20-20, Maryland vs Georgia	1965* Florida St. 36, Oklahoma 19	1982 Florida St. 31, West Va. 12
1949 Clemson 24, Missouri 23	1965† Georgia Tech 31, Texas Tech 21	1983 Florida 14, Iowa 6
	1966 Tennessee 18, Syracuse 12	1984 Oklahoma St. 21, S. Carolina 14
1950 Maryland 20, Missouri 7	1967 17-17, Florida St. vs Penn St.	1985 Florida St. 34, Oklahoma St. 23
1951 Wyoming 20, Wash. & Lee 7	1968 Missouri 35, Alabama 10	1986 Clemson 27, Stanford 21
1952 Miami-FL 14, Clemson 0	1969 Florida 14, Tennessee 13	1987 LSU 30, S. Carolina 13
1953 Florida 14, Tulsa 13		1989* Georgia 34, Michigan St. 27
1954 Texas Tech 35, Auburn 13	1971* Auburn 35, Mississippi 28	1989† Clemson 27, West Va. 7
1954† Auburn 33, Baylor 13	1971† Georgia 7, N. Carolina 3	
1955 Vanderbilt 25, Auburn 13	1972 Auburn 24, Colorado 3	1991* Michigan 35, Mississippi 3
1956 Georgia Tech 21, Pittsburgh 14	1973 Texas Tech 28, Tennessee 19	1991† Oklahoma 48, Virginia 14
1957 Tennessee 3, Texas A&M 0	1974 Auburn 27, Texas 3	1992 Florida 27, N.C. State 10
1958 Mississippi 7, Florida 3	1975 Maryland 13, Florida 0	1993 Alabama 24, N. Carolina 10
	1976 Notre Dame 20, Penn St. 9	1994 Tennessee 45, Va. Tech 23
1960* Arkansas 14, Georgia Tech 7	1977 Pittsburgh 34, Clemson 3	
1960† Florida 13, Baylor 12	1978 Clemson 17, Ohio St. 15	
1961 Penn St. 30, Georgia Tech 15	1979 N. Carolina 17, Michigan 15	

*January game from 1946-54, 1960, 1965, 1971, 1989 and 1991.
†December game from 1954-58, 1960-63, 1965-69, 1971-87, 1989 and since 1991.

Holiday Bowl

City: San Diego, Calif. **Stadium:** San Diego/Jack Murphy. **Capacity:** 62,860. **Playing surface:** Grass. **First game:** Dec. 22, 1978. **Playing sites:** San Diego/Jack Murphy Stadium (since 1978). **Corporate title sponsors:** Sea World (1986-90), Thrifty Car Rental (1991-94) and Chrysler-Plymouth Division of Chrysler Corp. (starting in 1995).

Automatic berths: WAC champion vs. at-large opponent (1978-84, 1986-90 seasons); WAC champ vs. second pick from Big 10 (1991 season); WAC champ vs. third pick from Big 10 (1992-94 seasons). New Bowl Alliance matchup starting with 1995 season: second choice of WAC champion or second pick from Pac-10 vs. third pick from Big 12 (Big Eight/SWC).

Multiple wins: BYU (4); Iowa and Ohio St. (2).

Year	Year	Year
1978† Navy 23, BYU 16	1984 BYU 24, Michigan 17	1990 Texas A&M 65, BYU 14
1979 Indiana 38, BYU 37	1985 Arkansas 18, Arizona St. 17	1991 13-13, Iowa vs BYU
1980 BYU 46, SMU 45	1986 Iowa 39, San Diego St. 38	1992 Hawaii 27, Illinois 17
1981 BYU 38, Washington St. 36	1987 Iowa 20, Wyoming 19	1993 Ohio St. 28, BYU 21
1982 Ohio St. 47, BYU 17	1988 Oklahoma St. 62, Wyoming 14	1994 Michigan 24, Colo. St. 14
1983 BYU 21, Missouri 17	1989 Penn St. 50, BYU 39	

†December game since 1978.

Bowl Matchups of Unbeaten Teams

Date	Bowl	Winner	Head Coach	Score	Loser	Head Coach
1/1/21	Rose	California (8-0)	Andy Smith	28-0	Ohio St. (7-0)	John Wilce
1/2/22	Rose	Wash. & Jeff. (10-0)	Greasy Neale	0-0	California (9-0)	Andy Smith
1/1/27	Rose	Stanford (10-0)	Pop Warner	7-7	Alabama (9-0)	Wallace Wade
1/1/31	Rose	Alabama (9-0)	Wallace Wade	24-0	Washington St. (9-0)	Babe Hollingbery
1/2/39	Orange	Tennessee (10-0)	Bob Neyland	17-0	Oklahoma (10-0)	Tom Stidham
1/1/41	Sugar	Boston College (10-0)	Frank Leahy	19-13	Tennessee (10-0)	Bob Neyland
1/1/52	Sugar	Maryland (9-0)	Jim Tatum	28-13	Tennessee (10-0)	Bob Neyland
1/2/56	Orange	Oklahoma (10-0)	Bud Wilkinson	20-6	Maryland (10-0)	Jim Tatum
1/1/72	Orange	Nebraska (12-0)	Bob Devaney	38-6	Alabama (11-0)	Bear Bryant
12/31/73	Sugar	Notre Dame (10-0)	Ara Parseghian	24-23	Alabama (11-0)	Bear Bryant
1/2/87	Fiesta	Penn St. (11-0)	Joe Paterno	14-10	Miami-FL (11-0)	Jimmy Johnson
1/1/88	Orange	Miami-FL (11-0)	Jimmy Johnson	20-14	Oklahoma (11-0)	Barry Switzer
1/2/89	Fiesta	Notre Dame (11-0)	Lou Holtz	34-21	West Va. (11-0)	Don Nehlen
1/1/93	Sugar	Alabama (12-0)	Gene Stallings	34-13	Miami-FL. (11-0)	Dennis Erickson

Outback Bowl

City: Tampa, Fla. **Stadium:** Tampa. **Capacity:** 74,300. **Playing surface:** Grass. **First game:** Dec. 23, 1986. **Name change:** Hall of Fame Bowl (1986-95) and Outback Bowl (starting in 1995). **Playing site:** Tampa Stadium (since 1986). **Corporate title sponsor:** Outback Steakhouse, Inc. (starting in 1995).

Automatic berths: Fourth pick from ACC vs. fourth pick from Big 10 (1993-94 seasons); New Bowl Alliance matchup starting with 1995 season: third pick from Big 10 vs. third pick from SEC.

Multiple wins: Michigan and Syracuse (2).

Year		Year		Year	
1986†	Boston College 27, Georgia 24	1990	Auburn 31, Ohio St. 14	1993	Tennessee 38, Boston Col. 23
1988*	Michigan 28, Alabama 24	1991	Clemson 30, Illinois 0	1994	Michigan 42, N.C. State 7
1989	Syracuse 23, LSU 10	1992	Syracuse 24, Ohio St. 17	1995	Wisconsin 34, Duke 20

†December game in 1986. *January game since 1988.

Peach Bowl

City: Atlanta, Ga. **Stadium:** Georgia Dome. **Capacity:** 71,230. **Playing surface:** AstroTurf. **First game:** Dec. 30, 1968. **Playing sites:** Grant Field (1968-70), Atlanta-Fulton County Stadium (1971-92) and Georgia Dome (since 1993).

Automatic berths: Third pick from ACC vs. at-large opponent (1992 season); third pick from ACC vs. fourth pick from SEC (1993-94 seasons). New Bowl Alliance matchup starting with 1995 season: third pick from ACC vs. fourth pick from SEC.

Multiple wins: N.C. State (4); West Virginia (3).

Year		Year		Year	
1968†	LSU 31, Florida St. 27	1977	N.C. State 24, Iowa St. 14	1986	Va. Tech 25, N.C. State 24
1969	West Va. 14, S. Carolina 3	1978	Purdue 41, Georgia Tech 21	1988*	Tennessee 27, Indiana 22
1970	Arizona St. 48, N. Carolina 26	1979	Baylor 24, Clemson 18	1988†	N.C. State 28, Iowa 23
1971	Mississippi 41, Georgia Tech 18	1981*	Miami-FL 20, Va. Tech 10	1989	Syracuse 19, Georgia 18
1972	N.C. State 49, West Va. 13	1981†	West Va. 26, Florida 6	1990	Auburn 27, Indiana 23
1973	Georgia 17, Maryland 16	1982	Iowa 28, Tennessee 22	1992*	E. Carolina 37, N.C. State 34
1974	6-6, Vanderbilt vs Texas Tech	1983	Florida St. 28, N. Carolina 3	1993	N. Carolina 21, Miss. St.17
1975	West Va. 13, N.C. State 10	1984	Virginia 27, Purdue 24	1993†	Clemson 14, Kentucky 13
1976	Kentucky 21, N. Carolina 0	1985	Army 31, Illinois 29	1995*	N.C. State 24, Miss. St. 24

†December game from 1968-79, 1981-86, 1988-90, and 1993. *January game in 1981, 1988, 1992-93 and since 1995.

Sun Bowl

City: El Paso, Tex. **Stadium:** Sun Bowl. **Capacity:** 51,120. **Playing surface:** AstroTurf. **First game:** Jan. 1, 1936. **Name changes:** Sun Bowl (1936-85), John Hancock Sun Bowl (1986-88), John Hancock Bowl (1989-93) and Sun Bowl (since 1994). **Playing sites:** Kidd Field (1936-62) and Sun Bowl (since 1963). **Corporate title sponsor:** John Hancock Financial Services (1986-93).

Automatic berths: Eighth pick from 8-team Boal Coalition pool vs. at-large opponent (1992); Seventh and eighth picks from 8-team Bowl Coalition pool (1993-94 seasons). New Bowl Alliance matchup starting with 1995 season: third pick from Pac-10 vs. fifth pick from Big-10.

Multiple wins: Texas Western/UTEP (5); Alabama and Wyoming (3); Nebraska, New Mexico St., North Carolina, Oklahoma, Pittsburgh, Southwestern-Texas, Texas, West Texas St. and West Virginia (2).

Year		Year		Year	
1936*	14-14, Hardin-Simmons vs New Mexico St.	1954	Tex. Western 37, So. Miss. 14	1974	Miss. St. 26, N. Carolina 24
1937	Hardin-Simmons 34, Texas Mines 6	1955	Tex. Western 47, Florida St. 20	1975	Pittsburgh 33, Kansas 19
1938	West Va. 7, Texas Tech 6	1956	Wyoming 21, Texas Tech 14	1977*	Texas A&M 37, Florida 14
1939	Utah 26, New Mexico 0	1957	Geo. Wash. 13, Tex. Western 0	1977†	Stanford 24, LSU 14
1940	0-0, Catholic U. vs Arizona St.	1958	Louisville 34, Drake 20	1978	Texas 42, Maryland 0
1941	W. Reserve 26, Arizona St. 13	1958*	Wyoming 14, Hardin-Simmons 6	1979	Washington 14, Texas 7
1942	Tulsa 6, Texas Tech 0	1959	New Mexico St. 28, N. Texas 8	1980	Nebraska 31, Miss. St. 17
1943	Second Air Force 13, Hardin-Simmons 7	1960	New Mexico St. 20, Utah St. 13	1981	Oklahoma 40, Houston 14
1944	SW Texas 7, New Mexico 0	1961	Villanova 17, Wichita 9	1982	N. Carolina 26, Texas 10
1945	SW Texas 35, U. of Mexico 0	1962	West Texas 15, Ohio U. 14	1983	Alabama 28, SMU 7
1946	New Mexico 34, Denver 24	1963	Oregon 21, SMU 14	1984	Maryland 28, Tennessee 27
1947	Cincinnati 18, Va. Tech 6	1964	Georgia 7, Texas Tech 0	1985	13-13, Georgia vs Arizona
1948	Miami-OH 13, Texas Tech 12	1965	Texas Western 13, TCU 12	1986	Alabama 28, Washington 6
1949	West Va. 21, Texas Mines 12	1966	Wyoming 28, Florida St. 20	1987	Oklahoma St. 35, West Va. 33
1950	Tex. Western 33, Georgetown 20	1967	UTEP 14, Mississippi 7	1988	Alabama 29, Army 28
1951	West Texas 14, Cincinnati 13	1968	Auburn 34, Arizona 10	1989	Pittsburgh 31, Texas A&M 28
1952	Texas Tech 25, Pacific 14	1969	Nebraska 45, Georgia 6	1990	Michigan St. 17, USC 16
1953	Pacific 26, Southern Miss. 7	1970	Georgia Tech 17, Texas Tech 9	1991	UCLA 6, Illinois 3
		1971	LSU 33, Iowa St. 15	1992	Baylor 20, Arizona 15
		1972	N. Carolina 32, Texas Tech 28	1993	Oklahoma 41, Texas Tech 10
		1973	Missouri 34, Auburn 17	1994	Texas 35, N. Carolina 31

*January game from 1936-58 and in 1977. †December game from 1958-75 and since 1977.

Bowl Games (Cont.)

Alamo Bowl

City: San Antonio, Tex. **Stadium:** Alamodome. **Capacity:** 65,000. **Playing surface:** Turf. **First game:** Dec. 31, 1993. **Playing site:** Alamodome (since 1993). **Corporate title sponsor:** Builders Square (since 1993).
   Automatic berths: third pick from SWC vs. fourth pick from Pac-10 (1993-94 seasons). New Bowl Alliance matchup starting with 1995 season: fourth pick from Big 10 vs. fourth pick from Big 12 (Big Eight/SWC).
   Multiple wins: None.

Year		Year	
1993†	California 37, Iowa 3	1994	Washington St. 10, Baylor 3

†December game since 1993.

Copper Bowl

City: Tucson, Ariz. **Stadium:** Arizona. **Capacity:** 56,165. **Playing surface:** Grass. **First game:** Dec. 31, 1989. **Playing site:** Arizona Stadium (since 1989). **Corporate title sponsors:** Domino's Pizza (1990-91) and Weiser Lock (since 1992).
   Automatic berths: third pick from WAC vs. at-large opponent (1992 season); third pick from WAC vs. fourth pick from Big Eight (1993-94 seasons). New Bowl Alliance matchup starting with 1995 season: second pick from WAC vs. sixth pick from Big 12 (Big Eight/SWC).
   Multiple wins: None.

Year		Year		Year	
1989†	Arizona 17, N.C. State 10	1991	Indiana 24, Baylor 0	1993	Kansas St. 52, Wyoming 17
1990	California 17, Wyoming 15	1992	Washington St. 31, Utah 28	1994	BYU 31, Oklahoma 6

†December game since 1989.

Liberty Bowl

City: Memphis, Tenn. **Stadium:** Liberty Bowl Memorial. **Capacity:** 62,920. **Playing surface:** Grass. **First game:** Dec. 19, 1959. **Playing sites:** Municipal Stadium in Philadelphia (1959-63), Convention Hall in Atlantic City, N.J. (1964), Memphis Memorial Stadium (1965-75) and Liberty Bowl Memorial Stadium (since 1976). Memphis Memorial Stadium renamed Liberty Bowl Memorial in 1976. **Corporate title sponsor:** St. Jude's Hospital (since 1993).
   Automatic berths: Commander-in-Chief's Trophy winner (Army, Navy or Air Force) vs. at-large opponenent (1989-92 seasons); none (1993 season); first pick from independent group of Cincinnati, East Carolina, Memphis, Southern Miss. and Tulane vs. at-large opponent (for the 1994 and '95 seasons).
   Multiple wins: Mississippi (4); Penn St. and Tennessee (3); Air Force, Alabama and N.C. State (2).

Year		Year		Year	
1959†	Penn St. 7, Alabama 0	1971	Tennessee 14, Arkansas 13	1983	Notre Dame 19, Boston Col. 18
1960	Penn St. 41, Oregon 12	1972	Georgia Tech 31, Iowa St. 30	1984	Auburn 21, Arkansas 15
1961	Syracuse 15, Miami-FL 14	1973	N.C. State 31, Kansas 18	1985	Baylor 21, LSU 7
1962	Oregon St. 6, Villanova 0	1974	Tennessee 7, Maryland 3	1986	Tennessee 21, Minnesota 14
1963	Mississippi St. 16, N.C. State 12	1975	USC 20, Texas A&M 0	1987	Georgia 20, Arkansas 17
1964	Utah 32, West Virginia 6	1976	Alabama 36, UCLA 6	1988	Indiana 34, S. Carolina 10
1965	Mississippi 13, Auburn 7	1977	Nebraska 21, N. Carolina 17	1989	Mississippi 42, Air Force 29
1966	Miami-FL 14, Virginia Tech 7	1978	Missouri 20, LSU 15	1990	Air Force 23, Ohio St. 11
1967	N.C. State 14, Georgia 7	1979	Penn St. 9, Tulane 6	1991	Air Force 38, Mississippi St. 15
1968	Mississippi 34, Virginia Tech 17	1980	Purdue 28, Missouri 25	1992	Mississippi 13, Air Force 0
1969	Colorado 47, Alabama 33	1981	Ohio St. 31, Navy 28	1993	Louisville 18, Michigan St. 7
1970	Tulane 17, Colorado 3	1982	Alabama 21, Illinois 15	1994	Illinois 30, E. Carolina 0

†December game since 1959.

Bluebonnet Bowl
Discontinued in 1988.

Years: 1959-87. **City:** Houston, Tex. **Name changes:** Bluebonnet Bowl (1959-67, 1977-87); Astro-Bluebonnet Bowl (1968-76). **Playing sites:** Rice Stadium (1959-67, 1985-86), Astrodome (1968-84, 1987). **Dates:** December game every year.
   Automatic berths: None.
   Multiple wins: Texas (3); Baylor, Colorado, Houston and Tennessee (2).

Year		Year		Year	
1959	Clemson 23, TCU 7	1969	Houston 36, Auburn 7	1979	Purdue 27, Tennessee 22
1960	3-3, Alabama vs Texas	1970	24-24, Alabama vs Oklahoma	1980	N. Carolina 16, Texas 7
1961	Kansas 33, Rice 7	1971	Colorado 29, Houston 17	1981	Michigan 33, UCLA 14
1962	Missouri 14, Georgia Tech 10	1972	Tennessee 24, LSU 17	1982	Arkansas 28, Florida 24
1963	Baylor 14, LSU 7	1973	Houston 47, Tulane 7	1983	Oklahoma St. 24, Baylor 14
1964	Tulsa 14, Mississippi 7	1974	31-31, Houston vs N.C. State	1984	West Va. 31, TCU 14
1965	Tennessee 27, Tulsa 6	1975	Texas 38, Colorado 21	1985	Air Force 24, Texas 16
1966	Texas 19, Mississippi 0	1976	Nebraska 27, Texas Tech 24	1986	Baylor 21, Colorado 9
1967	Colorado 31, Miami-FL 21	1977	USC 47, Texas A&M 28	1987	Texas 32, Pittsburgh 27
1968	SMU 28, Oklahoma 27	1978	Stanford 25, Georgia 22		

Carquest Bowl

City: Miami, Fla. **Stadium:** Joe Robbie. **Capacity:** 74,915. **Playing surface:** Grass. **First game:** Dec. 28, 1990.
Name change: Blockbuster Bowl (1990-93) and Carquest Bowl (since 1994) **Playing site:** Joe Robbie Stadium (since 1990). **Corporate title sponsors:** Blockbuster Video (1990-93) and Carquest Auto Parts (since 1993).
    Automatic berths: Penn St. vs. seventh pick from 8-team Bowl Coalition pool (1992 season); third pick from Big East vs. fifth pick from SEC (1993-94 seasons). New Bowl Alliance matchup starting with 1995 season: third pick from Big East vs. fifth pick from SEC.

Year	Year	Year
1990† Florida St. 24, Penn St. 17	1993* Stanford 24, Penn St. 3	1995 S. Carolina 24, West Va. 21
1991 Alabama 30, Colorado 25	1994 Boston College 31, Virginia 13	

†December game from 1990-91. *January game since 1993.

Aloha Bowl

City: Honolulu, Hawaii. **Stadium:** Aloha. **Capacity:** 50,000. **Playing surface:** AstroTurf. **First game:** Dec. 25, 1982.
Playing site: Aloha Stadium (since 1982). **Corporate title sponsor:** Jeep Eagle Division of Chrysler (since 1987).
    Automatic berths: second pick from WAC vs. third pick from Big Eight (1992-93 seasons); third pick from Big Eight vs. at-large opponent (1994 season) New Bowl Alliance matchup starting with 1995 season: fifth pick from Big 12 (Big Eight/SWC) vs. at-large opponent.

Year	Year	Year
1982† Washington 21, Maryland 20	1987 UCLA 20, Florida 16	1992 Kansas 23, BYU 20
1983 Penn St. 13, Washington 10	1988 Washington St. 24, Houston 22	1993 Colorado 41, Fresno St. 30
1984 SMU 27, Notre Dame 20	1989 Michigan St. 33, Hawaii 13	1994 Boston Col. 12, Kansas St. 7
1985 Alabama 24, USC 3	1990 Syracuse 28, Arizona 0	
1986 Arizona 30, N. Carolina 21	1991 Georgia Tech 18, Stanford 17	

†December game since 1982.

Las Vegas Bowl

City: Las Vegas, Nev. **Stadium:** Sam Boyd Stadium. **Capacity:** 33,215. **Playing surface:** AstroTurf. **First game:** Dec. 18, 1992. **Playing site:** Silver Bowl (since 1992);
    Automatic berths: Mid-American champion vs. Big West champion (since 1992 season).
    Note: the MAC and Big West champs have met in a bowl game since 1981, originally in Fresno at the California Bowl (1981-88, 1992) and California Raisin Bowl (1989-91). The results from 1981-91 are included below.
    Multiple wins: Fresno St. (4); Bowling Green, San Jose St. and Toledo (2).

Year	Year	Year
1981† Toledo 27, San Jose St. 25	1986 San Jose St. 37, Miami-OH 7	1991 Bowling Green 28, Fresno St. 21
1982 Fresno St. 29, Bowling Green 28	1987 E. Michigan 30, San Jose St. 27	1992 Bowling Green 35, Nevada 34
1983 Northern Ill. 20, CS-Fullerton 13	1988 Fresno St. 35, W. Michigan 30	1993 Utah St. 42, Ball St. 33
1984 UNLV 30, Toledo 13	1989 Fresno St. 27, Ball St. 6	1994 UNLV 52, C. Michigan 24
1985 Fresno St. 51, Bowling Green 7	1990 San Jose St. 48, C. Michigan 24	

†December game since 1981. **Note:** Toledo later ruled winner of 1984 game by forfeit when UNLV was found to have used ineligible players.

Independence Bowl

City: Shreveport, La. **Stadium:** Independence. **Capacity:** 50,460. **Playing surface:** Grass. **First game:** Dec. 13, 1976. **Playing sites:** Independence Stadium (since 1976). **Corporate title sponsor:** Poulan/Weed Eater (since 1990).
    Automatic berths: None (since 1976 season).
    Multiple wins: Air Force and Southern Miss (2).

Year	Year	Year
1976† McNeese St. 20, Tulsa 16	1983 Air Force 9, Mississippi 3	1990 34-34, La. Tech vs Maryland
1977 La. Tech 24, Louisville 14	1984 Air Force 23, Va. Tech 7	1991 Georgia 24, Arkansas 15
1978 E. Carolina 35, La. Tech 13	1985 Minnesota 20, Clemson 13	1992 Wake Forest 39, Oregon 35
1979 Syracuse 31, McNeese St. 7	1986 Mississippi 20, Texas Tech 17	1993 Va. Tech 45, Indiana 10
1980 Southern Miss 16, McNeese St. 14	1987 Washington 24, Tulane 12	1994 Virginia 20, TCU 10
1981 Texas A&M 33, Oklahoma St.16	1988 Southern Miss 38, UTEP 18	
1982 Wisconsin 14, Kansas St. 3	1989 Oregon 27, Tulsa 24	

†December game since 1976.

Freedom Bowl

Discontinued in 1995.

Years: 1984-94. **City:** Anaheim, Calif. **Playing site:** Anaheim Stadium. **Dates:** December game every year.
    Automatic berths: Third pick from Pac-10 vs. at-large opponent (1992 season); Third pick from Pac-10 vs. fourth pick from WAC (1993 season); second pick from WAC vs. third pick from Pac-10 (1994 season).
    Multiple wins: Washington (2).

Year	Year	Year
1984† Iowa 55, Texas 17	1988 BYU 20, Colorado 17	1992 Fresno St. 24, USC 7
1985 Washington 20, Colorado 17	1989 Washington 34, Florida 7	1993 USC 28, Utah 21
1986 UCLA 31, BYU 10	1990 Colorado St. 32, Oregon 31	1994 Utah 16, Arizona 13
1987 Arizona St. 33, Air Force 28	1991 Tulsa 28, San Diego St. 17	

All-Time Winningest Division I-A Teams

Schools classified as Divison I-A for at least 10 years; through 1994 season (including bowl games).

Top 25 Winning Percentage

		Yrs	Gm	W	L	T	Pct	Bowls App	Bowls Record	1994 Season Bowl	1994 Season Record
1	Notre Dame	106	987	729	216	42	.760	20	13-7-0	lost Fiesta	6-5-1
2	Michigan	115	1029	747	246	36	.743	26	13-13-0	won Holiday	8-4-0
3	Alabama	100	985	703	238	44	.736	47	27-17-3	won Citrus	12-1-0
4	Oklahoma	100	963	665	246	52	.718	32	20-11-1	lost Copper	6-6-0
5	Texas	102	1004	695	277	32	.708	35	17-16-2	won Sun	8-4-0
6	Ohio St	105	990	668	269	53	.702	27	13-14-0	lost Citrus	9-4-0
7	USC	102	948	638	257	53	.701	37	24-13-0	won Cotton	8-3-1
8	Nebraska	105	1016	686	290	40	.695	33	15-18-0	won Orange	13-0-0
9	Penn St	108	1018	686	291	41	.694	31	19-10-2	won Rose	12-0-0
10	Tennessee	98	977	644	280	53	.686	35	19-16-0	won Gator	8-4-0
11	Central Michigan	94	782	489	257	36	.648	5	3-2-0	lost Las Vegas	9-2-0
12	Florida St	48	520	326	177	17	.643	24	15-7-2	won Sugar	10-1-1
13	Washington	105	932	569	314	49	.637	21	12-8-1	on probation	7-4-0
14	Army	105	976	592	334	50	.632	3	2-1-0	none	4-7-0
15	Miami-OH	106	907	551	313	43	.631	7	5-2-0	none	5-5-1
16	Georgia	101	986	595	337	54	.631	31	15-13-3	none	6-4-1
17	LSU	101	955	577	332	46	.628	28	11-16-1	none	4-7-0
18	Arizona St	82	734	447	263	24	.625	15	9-5-1	none	3-8-0
19	Auburn	102	950	567	336	47	.622	23	12-9-2	on probation	9-1-1
20	Colorado	105	953	568	349	36	.615	19	7-12-0	won Fiesta	11-1-0
21	Miami-FL	68	702	421	262	19	.613	21	10-11-0	lost Orange	10-2-0
22	Bowling Green	76	694	398	244	52	.611	5	2-3-0	none	9-2-0
23	Michigan St	98	903	526	334	43	.606	11	5-6-0	none	5-6-0
24	Texas A&M	100	968	559	361	48	.602	20	10-10-0	on probation	10-0-1
25	UCLA	76	765	442	286	37	.602	19	10-8-1	none	5-6-0

Top 50 Victories

		Wins			Wins			Wins
1	Michigan	747	18	Auburn	567	35	Maryland	509
2	Notre Dame	729	19	West Virginia	564	36	Vanderbilt	507
3	Alabama	703	20	Texas A&M	559	37	Boston College	504
4	Texas	695	21	Minnesota	558	38	Illinois	503
5	Nebraska	686	22	Georgia Tech	556	39	Florida	501
	Penn St	686		North Carolina	556	40	Kentucky	491
7	Ohio St	668	24	Arkansas	554	41	Central Michigan	489
8	Oklahoma	665	25	Miami-OH	551	42	Wisconsin	485
9	Tennessee	644	26	Navy	549	43	Kansas	483
10	USC	638	27	Rutgers	535		Stanford	483
11	Georgia	595	28	California	534		Utah	483
12	Army	592	29	Clemson	531	46	Tulsa	477
13	Syracuse	590	30	Michigan St	526	47	Baylor	475
14	LSU	577	31	Virginia Tech	521		Purdue	475
15	Pittsburgh	570	32	Mississippi	517	49	Iowa	470
16	Washington	569	33	Missouri	510	50	Arizona	467
17	Colorado	568		Virginia	510			

Note: Division I-AA schools with 500 or more wins through 1994: Yale (778); Princeton (713); Harvard (705); Penn (703); Fordham (671); Dartmouth (595); Lafayette (568); Cornell (554); Holy Cross (525); Delaware and Lehigh (514).

Most Bowl Appearances

		Overall App	W	L	T	Big Four W	L	T
1	Alabama	47	27	17	3	18	12	1
2	USC	37	24	13	0	20	8	0
3	Tennessee	35	19	16	0	7	9	0
	Texas	35	17	16	2	12	10	1
5	Nebraska	33	15	18	0	10	13	0
6	Oklahoma	32	20	11	1	15	6	0
7	Penn St	31	19	10	2	7	5	1
	Georgia	31	15	13	3	7	6	0
9	LSU	28	11	16	1	7	10	1
10	Arkansas	27	9	15	3	4	10	1
	Ohio St	27	12	15	0	7	8	0
12	Michigan	26	13	13	0	7	11	0
13	Georgia Tech	25	17	8	0	9	3	0
	Mississippi	25	14	11	0	6	5	0
15	Auburn	23	12	9	2	2	4	1
	Florida St	23	14	7	2	5	2	0
17	Florida	22	10	12	0	2	4	0
18	Washington	21	12	8	1	7	6	1
	Texas A&M	21	11	10	0	5	6	0
	Miami-FL	21	10	11	0	7	5	0
21	Notre Dame	20	13	7	0	11	5	0
	Texas Tech	20	4	15	1	0	2	0

Note: The "Big Four" bowls are the Rose, Orange, Sugar and Cotton. Only Alabama, Georgia, Georgia Tech, Notre Dame and Penn State have won all four.

Major Conference Champions

Atlantic Coast Conference

Founded in 1953 when charter members all left Southern Conference to form ACC. **Charter members** (7): Clemson, Duke, Maryland, North Carolina, North Carolina St., South Carolina and Wake Forest. **Admitted later** (3): Virginia in 1953 (began play in '54); Georgia Tech in 1978 (began play in '83); Florida St. (began play in '92). **Withdrew later** (1): South Carolina in 1971.

Current playing membership (9): Clemson, Duke, Florida St., Georgia Tech, Maryland, North Carolina, N.C. State, Virginia and Wake Forest.

Multiple titles: Clemson (13); Maryland (8); Duke and N.C. State (7); North Carolina (5); Florida St. (3).

Year		Year		Year		Year	
1953	Duke (4-0)	1963	North Carolina (6-1)	1973	N.C. State (6-0)	1984	Maryland (5-0)
	& Maryland (3-0)		& N.C. State (6-1)	1974	Maryland (6-0)	1985	Maryland (6-0)
1954	Duke (4-0)	1964	N.C. State (5-2)	1975	Maryland (5-0)	1986	Clemson (5-1-1)
1955	Maryland (4-0)	1965	Clemson (5-2)	1976	Maryland (5-0)	1987	Clemson (6-1)
	& Duke (4-0)		& N.C. State (5-2)	1977	North Carolina (5-0-1)	1988	Clemson (6-1)
1956	Clemson (4-0-1)	1966	Clemson (6-1)	1978	Clemson (6-0)	1989	Virginia (6-1)
1957	N.C. State (5-0-1)	1967	Clemson (6-0)	1979	N.C. State (5-1)		& Duke (6-1)
1958	Clemson (5-1)	1968	N.C. State (6-1)	1980	North Carolina (6-0)	1990	Georgia Tech (6-0-1)
1959	Clemson (6-1)	1969	South Carolina (6-0)	1981	Clemson (6-0)	1991	Clemson (6-0-1)
1960	Duke (5-1)	1970	Wake Forest (5-1)	1982	Clemson (6-0)	1992	Florida St. (8-0)
1961	Duke (5-1)	1971	North Carolina (6-0)	1983	Clemson (7-0) †	1993	Florida St. (8-0)
1962	Duke (6-0)	1972	North Carolina (6-0)		& Maryland (5-0)	1994	Florida St. (8-0)

†On probation, ineligible for championship.

Big East Conference

Founded in 1991 when charter members all gave up independent football status to form Big East. **Charter members** (8): Boston College, Miami of Florida, Pittsburgh, Rutgers, Syracuse, Temple, Virginia Tech and West Virginia. **Note:** Temple and Virginia Tech are Big East members in football only.

Current playing membership (8): Boston College, Miami-FL, Pittsburgh, Rutgers, Syracuse, Temple, Virginia Tech and West Virginia.

Conference champion: For 1991 and '92, team with highest ranking in final regular season *USA Today*/CNN coaches poll won title. Championship decided by full 7-game round robin schedule sine 1993.

Multiple titles: Miami-FL (3).

Year		Year		Year		Year	
1991	Miami-FL (2-0, #1)	1992	Miami-FL (4-0, #1)	1993	West Virginia (7-0)	1994	Miami-FL (7-0)
	& Syracuse (5-0, #16)						

Big Eight Conference

Originally founded in 1907 as Missouri Valley Intercollegiate Athletic Assn. **Charter members** (5): Iowa, Kansas, Missouri, Nebraska and Washington University of St. Louis. **Admitted later** (6): Drake and Iowa St. (then Ames College) in 1908; Kansas St. in 1913; Grinnell in 1919; Oklahoma in 1920; Oklahoma St. (then Oklahoma A&M) in 1925. **Withdrew later** (1): Iowa in 1911. **Note:** Iowa belonged to both the MVIAA and Western Conference from 1907-10.

Big Six founded in 1928 when charter members left MVIAA. **Charter members** (6): Iowa St., Kansas, Kansas St., Missouri, Nebraska and Oklahoma. **Admitted later** (6): Colorado in 1947 (began play in '48); Oklahoma St. in 1957 (began play in '60); Baylor, Texas, Texas A&M, and Texas Tech in 1994 (all four will begin play in '96). Renamed **Big Seven** in 1948, **Big Eight** in 1958, and will become **Big 12** in 1996.

Current playing membership (8): Colorado, Iowa St., Kansas, Kansas St., Missouri, Nebraska, Oklahoma and Oklahoma St.

Multiple titles: Nebraska (40); Oklahoma (33); Missouri (12); Kansas (6); Colorado (5); Iowa St. and Oklahoma St. (2).

Year		Year		Year		Year	
1907	Iowa (1-0)	1917	Nebraska (2-0)	1930	Kansas (4-1)	1944	Oklahoma (4-0-1)
	& Nebraska (1-0)	1918	Vacant (WW I)	1931	Nebraska (5-0)	1945	Missouri (5-0)
1908	Kansas (4-0)	1919	Missouri (4-0-1)	1932	Nebraska (5-0)	1946	Oklahoma (4-1)
1909	Missouri (4-0-1)			1933	Nebraska (5-0)		& Kansas (4-1)
		1920	Oklahoma (4-0-1)	1934	Kansas St. (5-0)	1947	Kansas (4-0-1)
1910	Nebraska (2-0)	1921	Nebraska (3-0)	1935	Nebraska (4-0-1)		& Oklahoma (4-0-1)
1911	Iowa St. (2-0-1)	1922	Nebraska (5-0)	1936	Nebraska (5-0)	1948	Oklahoma (5-0)
	& Nebraska (2-0-1)	1923	Nebraska (3-0-2)	1937	Nebraska (3-0-2)	1949	Oklahoma (5-0)
1912	Iowa St. (2-0)		& Kansas (3-0-3)	1938	Oklahoma (5-0)		
	& Nebraska (2-0)	1924	Missouri (5-1)	1939	Missouri (5-0)	1950	Oklahoma (6-0)
1913	Missouri (4-0)	1925	Missouri (5-1)			1951	Oklahoma (6-0)
	& Nebraska (3-0)	1926	Okla. A&M (3-0-1)	1940	Nebraska (5-0)	1952	Oklahoma (5-0-1)
1914	Nebraska (3-0)	1927	Missouri (5-1)	1941	Missouri (5-0)	1953	Oklahoma (6-0)
1915	Nebraska (4-0)	1928	Nebraska (4-0)	1942	Missouri (4-0-1)	1954	Oklahoma (6-0)
1916	Nebraska (3-1)	1929	Nebraska (3-0-2)	1943	Oklahoma (5-0)	1955	Oklahoma (6-0)

Major Conference Champions (Cont.)
Big Eight Conference

Year		Year		Year		Year	
1956	Oklahoma (6-0)	1968	Kansas (6-1)	1976	Colorado (5-2),	1984	Oklahoma (6-1)
1957	Oklahoma (6-0)		& Oklahoma (6-1)		Oklahoma (5-2)		& Nebraska (6-1)
1958	Oklahoma (6-0)	1969	Missouri (6-1)		& Oklahoma St. (5-2)	1985	Oklahoma (7-0)
1959	Oklahoma (5-1)		& Nebraska (6-1)	1977	Oklahoma (7-0)	1986	Oklahoma (7-0)
				1978	Nebraska (6-1)	1987	Oklahoma (7-0)
1960	Missouri (7-0)	1970	Nebraska (7-0)		& Oklahoma (6-1)	1988	Nebraska (7-0)
1961	Colorado (7-0)	1971	Nebraska (7-0)	1979	Oklahoma (7-0)	1989	Colorado (7-0)
1962	Oklahoma (7-0)	1972	Nebraska (5-1-1)*				
1963	Nebraska (7-0)	1973	Oklahoma (7-0)	1980	Oklahoma (7-0)	1990	Colorado (7-0)
1964	Nebraska (6-1)	1974	Oklahoma (7-0)	1981	Nebraska (7-0)	1991	Nebraska (6-0-1)
1965	Nebraska (6-1)	1975	Nebraska (6-1)	1982	Nebraska (7-0)		& Colorado (6-0-1)
1966	Nebraska (6-1)		& Oklahoma (6-1)	1983	Nebraska (7-0)	1992	Nebraska (7-0)
1967	Oklahoma (7-0)					1993	Nebraska (7-0)
						1994	Nebraska (7-0)

*Oklahoma (6-1) forfeited title in 1972.

Big Ten Conference

Originally founded in 1895 as the Intercollegiate Conference of Faculty Representatives, better known as the Western Conference. **Charter members** (7): Chicago, Illinois, Michigan, Minnesota, Northwestern, Purdue and Wisconsin. **Admitted later** (5): Indiana and Iowa in 1899; Ohio St. in 1912; Michigan St. in 1950 (began play in '53); Penn St. in 1990 (began play in '93). **Withdrew later** (2): Michigan in 1907 (rejoined in '17); Chicago in 1940. **Note:** Iowa belonged to both the Western and Missouri Valley conferences from 1907-10.

Unofficially called **Big Ten** from 1912 until Chicago withdrew after 1939 season, then **Big Nine** from 1940 until Michigan St. began conference play in 1953. Formally renamed **Big Ten** in 1984 and has kept name with Penn St. as 11th member.

Current playing membership (11): Illinois, Indiana, Iowa, Michigan, Michigan St., Minnesota, Northwestern, Ohio St., Penn St., Purdue and Wisconsin.

Multiple titles: Michigan (37); Ohio St. (26); Minnesota (18); Illinois (14); Iowa and Wisconsin (9); Purdue (7); Chicago and Michigan St. (6); Northwestern (5); Indiana (2).

Year		Year		Year		Year	
1896	Wisconsin (2-0-1)	1920	Ohio St. (5-0)	1944	Ohio St. (6-0)	1972	Ohio St. (7-1)
1897	Wisconsin (3-0)	1921	Iowa (5-0)	1945	Indiana (5-0-1)		& Michigan (7-1)
1898	Michigan (3-0)	1922	Iowa (5-0)	1946	Illinois (6-1)	1973	Ohio St. (7-0-1)
1899	Chicago (4-0)		& Michigan (4-0)	1947	Michigan (6-0)		& Michigan (7-0-1)
		1923	Illinois (5-0)	1948	Michigan (6-0)	1974	Ohio St. (7-1)
1900	Iowa (3-0-1)		& Michigan (4-0)	1949	Ohio St. (4-1-1)		& Michigan (7-1)
	& Minnesota (3-0-1)	1924	Chicago (3-0-3)		& Michigan (4-1-1)	1975	Ohio St. (8-0)
1901	Michigan (4-0)	1925	Michigan (5-1)			1976	Michigan (7-1)
	& Wisconsin (2-0)	1926	Michigan (5-0)	1950	Michigan (4-1-1)		& Ohio St. (7-1)
1902	Michigan (5-0)		& Northwestern (5-0)	1951	Illinois (5-0-1)	1977	Michigan (7-1)
1903	Michigan (3-0-1),	1927	Illinois (5-0)	1952	Wisconsin (4-1-1)		& Ohio St. (7-1)
	Minnesota (3-0-1)		& Minnesota (3-0-1)		& Purdue (4-1-1)	1978	Michigan (7-1)
	& Northwestern (1-0-2)	1928	Illinois (4-1)	1953	Michigan St. (5-1)		& Michigan St. (7-1)
1904	Minnesota (3-0)	1929	Purdue (5-0)		& Illinois (5-1)	1979	Ohio St. (8-0)
	& Michigan (2-0)			1954	Ohio St. (7-0)		
1905	Chicago (7-0)	1930	Michigan (5-0)	1955	Ohio St. (6-0)	1980	Michigan (8-0)
1906	Wisconsin (3-0),		& Northwestern (5-0)	1956	Iowa (5-1)	1981	Iowa (6-2)
	Minnesota (2-0)	1931	Purdue (5-1),	1957	Ohio St. (7-0)		& Ohio St. (6-2)
	& Michigan (1-0)		Michigan (5-1)	1958	Iowa (5-1)	1982	Michigan (8-1)
1907	Chicago (4-0)		& Northwestern (5-1)	1959	Wisconsin (5-2)	1983	Illinois (9-0)
1908	Chicago (5-0)	1932	Michigan (6-0)			1984	Ohio St. (7-2)
1909	Minnesota (3-0)		& Purdue (5-0-1)	1960	Minnesota (5-1)	1985	Iowa (7-1)
		1933	Michigan (5-0-1)		& Iowa (5-1)	1986	Michigan (7-1)
1910	Illinois (4-0)		& Minnesota (2-0-4)	1961	Ohio St. (6-0)		& Ohio St. (7-1)
	& Minnesota (2-0)	1934	Minnesota (5-0)	1962	Wisconsin (6-1)	1987	Michigan St. (7-0-1)
1911	Minnesota (3-0-1)	1935	Minnesota (5-0)	1963	Illinois (5-1-1)	1988	Michigan (7-0-1)
1912	Wisconsin (6-0)		& Ohio St. (5-0)	1964	Michigan (6-1)	1989	Michigan (8-0)
1913	Chicago (7-0)	1936	Northwestern (6-0)	1965	Michigan St. (7-0)		
1914	Illinois (6-0)	1937	Minnesota (5-0)	1966	Michigan St. (7-0)	1990	Iowa (6-2),
1915	Minnesota (3-0-1)	1938	Minnesota (4-1)	1967	Indiana (6-1),		Michigan (6-2),
	& Illinois (3-0-2)	1939	Ohio St. (5-1)		Purdue (6-1)		Michigan St. (6-2)
1916	Ohio St. (4-0)				& Minnesota (6-1)		& Illinois (6-2)
1917	Ohio St. (4-0)	1940	Minnesota (6-0)	1968	Ohio St. (7-0)	1991	Michigan (8-0)
1918	Illinois (4-0),	1941	Minnesota (5-0)	1969	Ohio St. (6-1)	1992	Michigan (6-0-2)
	Michigan (2-0)	1942	Ohio St. (5-1)		& Michigan (6-1)	1993	Wisconsin (6-1-1)
	& Purdue (1-0)	1943	Purdue (6-0)				& Ohio St. (6-1-1)
1919	Illinois (6-1)		& Michigan (6-0)	1970	Ohio St. (7-0)	1994	Penn St. (8-0)
				1971	Michigan (8-0)		

Big West Conference

Originally founded in 1969 as Pacific Coast Athletic Assn. **Charter members** (7): Cal-Santa Barbara, Cal St.-Los Angeles, Fresno St., Long Beach St., Pacific, San Diego St. and San Jose St. **Admitted later** (9): Cal St.-Fullerton in 1974; Utah St. in 1977 (began play in '78); Nevada-Las Vegas in 1982; New Mexico St. in 1983 (began play in '84); Nevada-Reno in 1991 (began play in '92); Arkansas St., Louisiana Tech, Northern Illinois and SW Louisiana in 1992 (all four began play in '93 in football only). **Withdrew later** (7): UC-Santa Barbara in 1972; CS-Los Angeles in 1974; San Diego St. in 1976; Fresno St. in 1991 (left for WAC after '91 season); Long Beach St. in 1991 (dropped football after '91 season); San Jose St. and UNLV in 1994 (both will leave for WAC after '95 season). Renamed **Big West** in 1988.

Current playing membership (11): Arkansas St., CS-Fullerton, Louisiana Tech., Nevada, New Mexico St., Northern Illinois, Pacific, San Jose St., SW Louisiana, UNLV and Utah St.

Multiple titles: San Jose St. (8); Fresno St. (6); San Diego St. (5); Long Beach St. and Utah St. (3); CS-Fullerton St. (2).

Year		Year		Year		Year	
1969	San Diego St. (6-0)	1976	San Jose St. (4-0)	1983	CS-Fullerton (5-1)	1991	Fresno St. (6-1)
1970	Long Beach St. (5-1)	1977	Fresno St. (4-0)	1984	CS-Fullerton (6-1)†		& San Jose St. (6-1)
	& San Diego St. (5-1)	1978	San Jose St. (4-1)	1985	Fresno St. (7-0)	1992	Nevada (5-1)
1971	Long Beach St. (5-1)		& Utah St. (4-1)	1986	San Jose St. (7-0)	1993	Utah St. (5-1)
1972	San Diego St. (4-0)	1979	Utah St. (4-0-1)*	1987	San Jose St. (7-0)		& SW Louisiana (5-1)
1973	San Diego St. (3-0-1)	1980	Long Beach St. (5-0)	1988	Fresno St. (7-0)	1994	UNLV (5-1)
1974	San Diego St. (4-0)	1981	San Jose St. (5-0)	1989	Fresno St. (5-0)		
1975	San Jose St. (5-0)	1982	Fresno St. (6-0)	1990	San Jose St. (7-0)		

*San Jose St. (4-0-1) forfeited share of title in 1979.   †UNLV (7-0) forfeited title in 1984.

Mid-American Conference

Founded in 1946. **Charter members** (6): Butler, Cincinnati, Miami of Ohio, Ohio University, Western Michigan and Western Reserve (Miami and WMU began play in '48). **Admitted later** (9): Kent St. (now Kent) and Toledo in 1951 (Toledo began play in '52); Bowling Green in 1952; Marshall in 1954; Central Michigan and Eastern Michigan in 1972 (CMU began play in '75, EMU in '76); Ball St. and Northern Illinois in 1973 (both began play in '75); Akron in 1991 (began play in '92). **Withdrew later** (5): Butler in 1950; Cincinnati in 1953; Western Reserve in 1955; Marshall in 1969; Northern Ill. in 1986.

Current playing membership (10): Akron, Ball St., Bowling Green, Central Michigan, Eastern Michigan, Kent, Miami-OH, Ohio University, Toledo and Western Michigan.

Multiple titles: Miami-OH (15); Bowling Green (10); Toledo (7); Ohio University (5); Central Michigan and Cincinnati (4); Ball St. (3); Western Michigan (2).

Year		Year		Year		Year	
1947	Cincinnati (3-1)	1959	Bowling Green (6-0)	1970	Toledo (5-0)	1984	Toledo (7-1-1)
1948	Miami-OH (4-0)	1960	Ohio Univ. (6-0)	1971	Toledo (5-0)	1985	Bowling Green (9-0)
1949	Cincinnati (4-0)	1961	Bowling Green (5-1)	1972	Kent St. (4-1)	1986	Miami-OH (6-2)
1950	Miami-OH (4-0)	1962	Bowling Green (5-0-1)	1973	Miami-OH (5-0)	1987	Eastern Mich. (7-1)
1951	Cincinnati (3-0)	1963	Ohio Univ. (5-1)	1974	Miami-OH (5-0)	1988	Western Mich. (7-1)
1952	Cincinnati (3-0)	1964	Bowling Green (5-1)	1975	Miami-OH (6-0)	1989	Ball St. (6-1-1)
1953	Ohio Univ. (5-0-1)	1965	Bowling Green (5-1)	1976	Ball St. (4-1)	1990	Central Mich. (7-1)
	& Miami-OH (3-0-1)		& Miami-OH (5-1)	1977	Miami-OH (5-0)		& Toledo (7-1)
1954	Miami-OH (4-0)	1966	Miami-OH (5-1)	1978	Ball St. (8-0)	1991	Bowling Green (8-0)
1955	Miami-OH (5-0)		& Western Mich. (5-1)	1979	Central Mich. (8-0-1)	1992	Bowling Green (8-0)
1956	Bowling Green (5-0-1)	1967	Toledo (5-1)	1980	Central Mich. (7-2)	1993	Ball St. (7-0-1)
	& Miami-OH (4-0-1)		& Ohio Univ. (5-1)	1981	Toledo (8-1)	1994	Central Mich. (8-1)
1957	Miami-OH (5-0)	1968	Ohio Univ. (6-0)	1982	Bowling Green (7-2)		
1958	Miami-OH (5-0)	1969	Toledo (5-0)	1983	Northern Ill. (8-1)		

Pacific-10 Conference

Originally founded in 1915 as Pacific Coast Conference. **Charter members** (4): California, Oregon, Oregon St. and Washington. **Admitted later** (6): Washington St. in 1917; Stanford in 1918; Idaho and USC (Southern Cal) in 1922; Montana in 1924; UCLA in 1928. **Withdrew later** (1): Montana in 1950.

The **PCC** dissolved in 1959 and the **AAWU** (Athletic Assn. of Western Universities) was founded. **Charter members** (5): California, Stanford, UCLA, USC and Washington. **Admitted later** (5): Washington St. in 1962, Oregon and Oregon St. in 1964, Arizona and Arizona St. in 1978. Conference renamed **Pac-8** in 1968 and **Pac-10** in 1978.

Current playing membership (10): Arizona, Arizona St., California, Oregon, Oregon St., Stanford, UCLA, USC, Washington and Washington St.

Multiple titles: USC (29); UCLA (16); California (13); Washington (13); Stanford (11); Oregon (5); Oregon St. (4); Washington St. (2).

Year		Year		Year		Year	
1916	Washington (3-0-1)	1923	California (5-0)	1930	Washington St. (6-0)	1936	Washington (6-0-1)
1917	Washington St. (3-0)	1924	Stanford (3-0-1)	1931	USC (7-0)	1937	California (6-0-1)
1918	California (3-0)	1925	Washington (5-0)	1932	USC (6-0)	1938	USC (6-1)
1919	Oregon (2-1)	1926	Stanford (4-0)	1933	Oregon (4-1)		& California (6-1)
	& Washington (2-1)	1927	USC (4-0-1)		& Stanford (4-1)	1939	USC (5-0-2)
			& Stanford (4-0-1)	1934	Stanford (5-0)		& UCLA (5-0-3)
1920	California (3-0)	1928	USC (4-0-1)	1935	California (4-1),	1940	Stanford (7-0)
1921	California (5-0)	1929	USC (6-1)		Stanford (4-1)	1941	Oregon St. (7-2)
1922	California (3-0)				& UCLA (4-1)		

Major Conference Champions (Cont.)
Pacific-10 Conference

Year		Year		Year		Year	
1942	UCLA (6-1)	1957	Oregon (6-2)	1969	USC (6-0)	1983	UCLA (6-1-1)
1943	USC (4-0)		& Oregon St. (6-2)	1970	Stanford (6-1)	1984	USC (7-1)
1944	USC (3-0-2)	1958	California (6-1)	1971	Stanford (6-1)	1985	UCLA (6-2)
1945	USC (5-1)	1959	Washington (3-1),	1972	USC (7-0)	1986	Arizona St. (5-1-1)
1946	UCLA (7-0)		USC (3-1)	1973	USC (7-0)	1987	USC (7-1)
1947	USC (6-0)		& UCLA (3-1)	1974	USC (6-0-1)		& UCLA (7-1)
1948	California (6-0)			1975	UCLA (6-1)	1988	USC (8-0)
	& Oregon (6-0)	1960	Washington (4-0)		& California (6-1)	1989	USC (6-0-1)
1949	California (7-0)	1961	UCLA (3-1)	1976	USC (7-0)		
		1962	USC (4-0)	1977	Washington (6-1)	1990	Washington (7-1)
1950	California (5-0-1)	1963	Washington (4-1)	1978	USC (6-1)	1991	Washington (8-0)
1951	Stanford (6-1)	1964	Oregon St. (3-1)	1979	USC (6-0-1)	1992	Washington (6-2)
1952	USC (6-0)		& USC (3-1)				& Stanford (6-2)
1953	UCLA (6-1)	1965	UCLA (4-0)	1980	Washington (6-1)	1993	UCLA (6-2),
1954	UCLA (6-0)	1966	USC (4-1)	1981	Washington (6-2)		Arizona (6-2)
1955	UCLA (6-0)	1967	USC (6-1)	1982	UCLA (5-1-1)		& USC (6-2)
1956	Oregon St. (6-1-1)	1968	USC (6-0)			1994	Oregon (7-1)

Southeastern Conference

Founded in 1933 when charter members all left Southern Conference to form SEC. **Charter members** (13): Alabama, Auburn, Florida, Georgia, Georgia Tech, Kentucky, LSU (Louisiana St.), Mississippi, Mississippi St., Sewanee, Tennessee, Tulane and Vanderbilt. **Admitted later** (2): Arkansas and South Carolina in 1990 (both began play in '92). **Withdrew later** (3): Sewanee in 1940; Georgia Tech in 1964; Tulane in 1966.
   Current playing membership (12): Alabama, Arkansas, Auburn, Florida, Georgia, Kentucky, LSU, Mississippi, Mississippi St., South Carolina, Tennessee and Vanderbilt. **Note:** Conference title decided by championship game between Western and Eastern division winners since 1992.
   Multiple titles: Alabama (20); Tennessee (11); Georgia (10); LSU (7); Mississippi (6); Auburn and Georgia Tech (5); Florida (4); Kentucky and Tulane (3).

Year		Year		Year		Year	
1933	Alabama (5-0-1)	1948	Georgia (6-0)	1965	Alabama (6-1-1)	1981	Georgia (6-0)
1934	Tulane (8-0)	1949	Tulane (5-1)	1966	Alabama (6-0)		& Alabama (6-0)
	& Alabama (7-0)	1950	Kentucky (5-1)		& Georgia (6-0)	1982	Georgia (6-0)
1935	LSU (5-0)	1951	Georgia Tech (7-0)	1967	Tennessee (6-0)	1983	Auburn (6-0)
1936	LSU (6-0)		& Tennessee (5-0)	1968	Georgia (5-0-1)	1984	Florida (5-0-1)*
1937	Alabama (6-0)	1952	Georgia Tech (6-0)	1969	Tennessee (5-1)	1985	Florida (5-1)†
1938	Tennessee (7-0)	1953	Alabama (4-0-3)				& Tennessee (5-1)
1939	Tennessee (6-0),	1954	Mississippi (5-1)	1970	LSU (5-0)	1986	LSU (5-1)
	Georgia Tech (6-0)	1955	Mississippi (5-1)	1971	Alabama (7-0)	1987	Auburn (5-0-1)
	& Tulane (5-0)	1956	Tennessee (6-0)	1972	Alabama (7-1)	1988	Auburn (6-1)
		1957	Auburn (7-0)	1973	Alabama (8-0)		& LSU (6-1)
1940	Tennessee (5-0)	1958	LSU (6-0)	1974	Alabama (6-0)	1989	Alabama (6-1),
1941	Mississippi St. (4-0-1)	1959	Georgia (7-0)	1975	Alabama (6-0)		Tennessee (6-1)
1942	Georgia (6-1)			1976	Georgia (5-1)		& Auburn (6-1)
1943	Georgia Tech (3-0)				& Kentucky (5-1)		
1944	Georgia Tech (4-0)	1960	Mississippi (5-0-1)	1977	Alabama (7-0)	1990	Florida (6-1)†
1945	Alabama (6-0)	1961	Alabama (7-0)		& Kentucky (6-0)		& Tennessee (5-1-1)
1946	Georgia (5-0)		& LSU (6-0)	1978	Alabama (6-0)	1991	Florida (7-0)
	& Tennessee (5-0)	1962	Mississippi (6-0)	1979	Alabama (6-0)	1992	Alabama (9-0)
1947	Mississippi (6-1)	1963	Mississippi (5-0-1)	1980	Georgia (6-0)	1993	Florida (8-1)
		1964	Alabama (8-0)			1994	Florida (8-1)

*Title vacated.   †On probation, ineligible for championship.

Southwest Conference

Founded in 1914 as Southwest Athletic Conference. **Charter members** (8): Arkansas, Baylor, Oklahoma, Oklahoma A&M (now Oklahoma St.), Rice, Southwestern, Texas, Texas A&M. **Admitted later** (5): SMU (Southern Methodist) in 1918; Phillips in 1920; TCU (Texas Christian) in 1923; Texas Tech in 1956 (began play in 1960); Houston in 1971 (began play in 1976). **Withdrew later** (9): Southwestern in 1917; Oklahoma in 1920; Phillips in 1921; Oklahoma A&M in 1925; Arkansas in 1990 (left for SEC after '91 season); Baylor, Texas, Texas A&M and Texas Tech in 1994 (all will leave for Big 12 after '95 season); Rice, SMU and TCU in 1994 (all will leave for WAC after '95 season) and Houston in 1994 (will leave for new Conference USA after '95 season).
   Current playing membership (8): Baylor, Houston, Rice, SMU, Texas, Texas A&M, TCU and Texas Tech.
   Multiple titles: Texas (24); Texas A&M (18); Arkansas (14); SMU (10); TCU (8); Rice (6); Baylor and Houston (4).

Year		Year		Year		Year	
1914	No champion	1918	No champion	1922	Baylor (5-0)	1926	SMU (5-0)
1915	Oklahoma (3-0)	1919	Texas A&M (4-0)	1923	SMU (5-0)	1927	Texas A&M (4-0-1)
1916	No champion	1920	Texas (5-0)	1924	Baylor (4-0-1)	1928	Texas (5-1)
1917	Texas A&M (2-0)	1921	Texas A&M (3-0-2)	1925	Texas A&M (4-1)	1929	TCU (4-0-1)

Year		Year		Year		Year	
1930	Texas (4-1)	1948	SMU (5-0-1)	1963	Texas (7-0)	1979	Houston (7-1)
1931	SMU (5-0-1)	1949	Rice (6-0)	1964	Arkansas (7-0)		& Arkansas (7-1)
1932	TCU (6-0)			1965	Arkansas (7-0)		
1933	Arkansas (4-1)*	1950	Texas (6-0)	1966	SMU (6-1)	1980	Baylor (8-0)
1934	Rice (5-1)	1951	TCU (5-1)	1967	Texas A&M (6-1)	1981	SMU (7-1)
1935	SMU (6-0)	1952	Texas (6-0)	1968	Arkansas (6-1)	1982	SMU (7-0-1)
1936	Arkansas (5-1)	1953	Rice (5-1)		& Texas (6-1)	1983	Texas (8-0)
1937	Rice (4-1-1)		& Texas (5-1)	1969	Texas (7-0)	1984	SMU (6-2)
1938	TCU (6-0)	1954	Arkansas (5-1)				& Houston (6-2)
1939	Texas A&M (6-0)	1955	TCU (5-1)	1970	Texas (7-0)	1985	Texas A&M (7-1)
		1956	Texas A&M (6-0)	1971	Texas (7-0)	1986	Texas A&M (7-1)
1940	Texas A&M (5-1)	1957	Rice (5-1)	1972	Texas (7-0)	1987	Texas A&M (6-1)
	& SMU (5-1)	1958	TCU (5-1)	1973	Texas (7-0)	1988	Arkansas (7-0)
1941	Texas A&M (5-1)	1959	Texas (5-1),	1974	Baylor (6-1)	1989	Arkansas (7-1)
1942	Texas (5-1)		TCU (5-1)	1975	Arkansas (6-1),		
1943	Texas (5-0)		& Arkansas (5-1)		Texas (6-1)	1990	Texas (8-0)
1944	TCU (3-1-1)	1960	Arkansas (6-1)		& Texas A&M (6-1)	1991	Texas A&M (8-0)
1945	Texas (5-1)	1961	Texas (6-1)	1976	Houston (7-1)	1992	Texas A&M (7-0)
1946	Rice (5-1)		& Arkansas (6-1)		& Texas Tech (7-1)	1993	Texas A&M (7-0)
	& Arkansas (5-1)	1962	Texas (6-0-1)	1977	Texas (8-0)	1994	Texas A&M (6-0-1)
1947	SMU (5-0-1)			1978	Houston (7-1)		*Title vacated.

Western Athletic Conference

Founded in 1962 when charter members left the Skyline and Border Conferences to form the WAC. **Charter members** (6): Arizona (independent); Arizona St. (from Border); BYU (Brigham Young), New Mexico, Utah and Wyoming (from Skyline). **Admitted later** (12): Colorado St. and UTEP (Texas-El Paso) in 1967 (both began play in '68); San Diego St. in 1978; Hawaii in 1979; Air Force in 1980; Fresno St. in 1991 (began play in '92); Rice, San Jose St., SMU (Southern Methodist), TCU (Texas Christian), Tulsa and UNLV (Nevada - Las Vegas) in 1994 (all will begin play in '96). **Withdrew later** (2): Arizona and Arizona St. in 1978.

    Current playing membership (10): Air Force, BYU, Colorado St., Fresno St., Hawaii, New Mexico, San Diego St., UTEP, Utah and Wyoming.

    Multiple titles: BYU (17); Arizona St. (7); Wyoming (7); New Mexico (3); Arizona and Fresno St. (2).

Year		Year		Year		Year	
1962	New Mexico (2-1-1)	1970	Arizona St. (7-0)	1978	BYU (5-1)	1988	Wyoming (8-0)
1963	New Mexico (3-1)	1971	Arizona St. (7-0)	1979	BYU (7-0)	1989	BYU (7-1)
1964	Utah (3-1),	1972	Arizona St. (5-1)				
	New Mexico (3-1)	1973	Arizona St. (6-1)	1980	BYU (6-1)	1990	BYU (7-1)
	& Arizona (3-1)		& Arizona (6-1)	1981	BYU (7-1)	1991	BYU (7-0-1)
1965	BYU (4-1)	1974	BYU (6-0-1)	1982	BYU (7-1)	1992	Hawaii (6-2),
1966	Wyoming (5-0)	1975	Arizona St. (7-0)	1983	BYU (7-0)		BYU (6-2)
1967	Wyoming (5-0)	1976	BYU (6-1)	1984	BYU (8-0)		& Fresno St. (6-2)
1968	Wyoming (6-1)		& Wyoming (6-1)	1985	Air Force (7-1)	1993	BYU (6-2),
1969	Arizona St. (6-1)	1977	Arizona St. (6-1)		& BYU (7-1)		Fresno St. (6-2)
			& BYU (6-1)	1986	San Diego St. (7-1)		& Wyoming (6-2)
				1987	Wyoming (8-0)	1994	Colorado St. (7-1)

Ivy League

First called the "Ivy League" in 1937 by sportswriter Caswell Adams of the *New York Herald Tribune*. Unofficial conference of 10 eastern teams was occasionally referred to as the "Old 10" and included: Army, Brown, Columbia, Cornell, Dartmouth, Harvard, Navy, Pennsylvania, Princeton and Yale. Army and Navy were dropped from the group after 1940. **League formalized** in 1954 for play beginning in 1956. **Charter members** (8): Brown, Columbia, Cornell, Dartmouth, Harvard, Pennsylvania, Princeton, and Yale. League downgraded from Division I to Division I-AA after 1977 season. **Current playing membership:** the same.

    Multiple titles: Dartmouth (16); Yale (12); Penn (9); Harvard (8); Princeton (7); Cornell (3).

Year		Year		Year		Year	
1955	Princeton (6-1)	1967	Yale (7-0)	1976	Brown (6-1)	1985	Penn (6-1)
1956	Yale (7-0)	1968	Harvard (6-0-1)		& Yale (6-1)	1986	Penn (7-0)
1957	Princeton (6-1)		& Yale (6-0-1)	1977	Yale (6-1)	1987	Harvard (6-1)
1958	Dartmouth (6-1)	1969	Dartmouth (6-1),	1978	Dartmouth (6-1)	1988	Penn (6-1)
1959	Penn (6-1)		Yale (6-1)	1979	Yale (6-1)		& Cornell (6-1)
			& Princeton (6-1)	1980	Yale (6-1)	1989	Princeton (6-1)
1960	Yale (7-0)			1981	Yale (6-1)		& Yale (6-1)
1961	Columbia (6-1)	1970	Dartmouth (7-0)		& Dartmouth (6-1)		
	& Harvard (6-1)	1971	Cornell (6-1)	1982	Harvard (5-2),	1990	Cornell (6-1)
1962	Dartmouth (7-0)		& Dartmouth (6-1)		Penn (5-2)		& Dartmouth (6-1)
1963	Dartmouth (5-2)	1972	Dartmouth (5-1-1)		& Dartmouth (5-2)	1991	Dartmouth (6-0-1)
	& Princeton (5-2)	1973	Dartmouth (6-1)	1983	Harvard (5-1-1)	1992	Dartmouth (6-1)
1964	Princeton (7-0)	1974	Harvard (6-1)		& Penn (5-1-1)		& Princeton (6-1)
1965	Dartmouth (7-0)		& Yale (6-1)	1984	Penn (7-0)	1993	Penn (7-0)
1966	Dartmouth (6-1),	1975	Harvard (6-1)			1994	Penn (7-0)
	Harvard (6-1)						
	& Princeton (6-1)						

Longest Division I Streaks

Winning Streaks

(Including bowl games)

No		Seasons	Spoiler	Score
47	Oklahoma	1953-57	Notre Dame	7-0
39	Washington	1908-14	Oregon St.	0-0
37	Yale	1890-93	Princeton	6-0
37	Yale	1887-89	Princeton	10-0
35	Toledo	1969-71	Tampa	21-0
34	Penn	1894-96	Lafayette	6-4
31	Oklahoma	1948-50	Kentucky	13-7*
31	Pittsburgh	1914-18	Cleve. Naval	10-9
31	Penn	1896-98	Harvard	10-0
30	Texas	1968-70	Notre Dame	24-11*
29	Miami-FL	1990-93	Alabama	34-13*
29	Michigan	1901-03	Minnesota	6-6
28	Alabama	1991-93	Tennessee	17-17
28	Alabama	1978-80	Mississippi St.	6-3
28	Oklahoma	1973-75	Kansas	23-3
28	Michigan St.	1950-53	Purdue	6-0
27	Nebraska	1901-04	Colorado	6-0
26	Cornell	1921-24	Williams	14-7
26	Michigan	1903-05	Chicago	2-0
25	BYU	1983-85	UCLA	27-24
25	Michigan	1946-49	Army	21-7
25	Army	1944-46	Notre Dame	0-0
25	USC	1931-33	Oregon St.	0-0

***Note:** Kentucky beat Oklahoma in 1951 Sugar Bowl, Notre Dame beat Texas in 1971 Cotton Bowl and Alabama beat Miami-FL in 1993 Sugar Bowl.

Unbeaten Streaks

(Including bowl games)

No	W-T		Seasons	Spoiler	Score
63	59-4	Washington	1907-17	California	27-0
56	55-1	Michigan	1901-05	Chicago	2-0
50	46-4	California	1920-25	Olympic Club	15-0
48	47-1	Oklahoma	1953-57	N. Dame	7-0
48	47-1	Yale	1885-89	Princeton	10-0
47	42-5	Yale	1879-85	Princeton	6-5
44	42-2	Yale	1894-96	Princeton	24-6
42	39-3	Yale	1904-08	Harvard	4-0
39	37-2	N. Dame	1946-50	Purdue	28-14
37	36-1	Oklahoma	1972-75	Kansas	23-3
37	37-0	Yale	1890-93	Princeton	6-0
35	35-0	Toledo	1967-71	Tampa	21-0
35	34-1	Minnesota	1903-05	Wisconsin	16-12

Losing Streaks

No		Seasons	Victim	Score
46	Prairie View	1989–	current streak	
44	Columbia	1983-88	Princeton	16-14
34	Northwestern	1979-82	No. Illinois	31-6
28	Virginia	1958-60	Wm. & Mary	21-6
28	Kansas St.	1945-48	Arkansas St.	37-6
27	Eastern Mich.	1980-82	Kent St.	9-7
27	New Mexico St.	1988-90	CS-Fullerton	43-9

Note: Virginia ended its losing streak in the opening game of the 1961 season.

Annual NCAA Division I-A Leaders

Note that Oklahoma A&M is now Oklahoma St. and Texas Mines is now UTEP.

Rushing

Individual championship decided on Rushing Yards (1937-69), and on Yards Per Game (since 1970).

Multiple winners: Marshall Faulk, Art Lupino, Ed Marinaro, Rudy Mobley, Jim Pilot and O.J. Simpson (2).

Year		Car	Yards
1937	Byron (Whizzer) White, Colorado	181	1121
1938	Len Eshmont, Fordham	132	831
1939	John Polanski, Wake Forest	137	882
1940	Al Ghesquiere, Detroit	146	957
1941	Frank Sinkwich, Georgia	209	1103
1942	Rudy Mobley, Hardin-Simmons	187	1281
1943	Creighton Miller, Notre Dame	151	911
1944	Red Williams, Minnesota	136	911
1945	Bob Fenimore, Oklahoma A&M	142	1048
1946	Rudy Mobley, Hardin-Simmons	227	1262
1947	Wilton Davis, Hardin-Simmons	193	1173
1948	Fred Wendt, Texas Mines	184	1570
1949	John Dottley, Ole Miss	208	1312
1950	Wilford White, Arizona St	199	1502
1951	Ollie Matson, San Francisco	245	1566
1952	Howie Waugh, Tulsa	164	1372
1953	J.C. Caroline, Illinois	194	1256
1954	Art Luppino, Arizona	179	1359
1955	Art Luppino, Arizona	209	1313
1956	Jim Crawford, Wyoming	200	1104
1957	Leon Burton, Arizona St	117	1126
1958	Dick Bass, Pacific	205	1361
1959	Pervis Atkins, New Mexico St	130	971
1960	Bob Gaiters, New Mexico St	197	1338
1961	Jim Pilot, New Mexico St	191	1278
1962	Jim Pilot, New Mexico St	208	1247
1963	Dave Casinelli, Memphis St	219	1016
1964	Brian Piccolo, Wake Forest	252	1044
1965	Mike Garrett, USC	267	1440
1966	Ray McDonald, Idaho	259	1329
1967	O.J. Simpson, USC	266	1415
1968	O.J. Simpson, USC	355	1709
1969	Steve Owens, Oklahoma	358	1523

Year		Car	Yards	P/Gm
1970	Ed Marinaro, Cornell	285	1425	158.3
1971	Ed Marinaro, Cornell	356	1881	209.0
1972	Pete VanValkenburg, BYU	232	1386	138.6
1973	Mark Kellar, Northern Ill	291	1719	156.3
1974	Louie Giammona, Utah St.	329	1534	153.4
1975	Ricky Bell, USC	357	1875	170.5
1976	Tony Dorsett, Pittsburgh	338	1948	177.1
1977	Earl Campbell, Texas	267	1744	158.5
1978	Billy Sims, Oklahoma	231	1762	160.2
1979	Charles White, USC	293	1803	180.3
1980	George Rogers, S. Carolina	297	1781	161.9
1981	Marcus Allen, USC	403	2342	212.9
1982	Ernest Anderson, Okla. St.	353	1877	170.6
1983	Mike Rozier, Nebraska	275	2148	179.0
1984	Keith Byars, Ohio St.	313	1655	150.5
1985	Lorenzo White, Mich. St.	386	1908	173.5
1986	Paul Palmer, Temple	346	1866	169.6
1987	Ickey Woods, UNLV	259	1658	150.7
1988	Barry Sanders, Okla. St.	344	2628	238.9
1989	Anthony Thompson, Ind	358	1793	163.0
1990	Gerald Hudson, Okla. St.	279	1642	149.3
1991	Marshall Faulk, S. Diego St.	201	1429	158.8
1992	Marshall Faulk, S. Diego St.	265	1630	163.0
1993	LeShon Johnson, No. Ill.	327	1976	179.6
1994	Rashaan Salaam, Colorado	298	2055	186.8

All-Purpose Running

Championship decided on Running Yards Per Game.

Multiple winners: Marcus Allen, Pervis Atkins, Ryan Benjamin, Louie Giammona, Tom Harmon, Art Lupino, Napolean McCallum, O.J. Simpson, Charles White and Gary Wood (2).

Year		Yards	P/Gm	Year		Yards	P/Gm
1937	Byron (Whizzer) White, Colorado	1970	246.3	1966	Frank Quayle, Virginia	1616	161.6
1938	Parker Hall, Ole Miss	1420	129.1	1967	O.J. Simpson, USC	1700	188.9
1939	Tom Harmon, Michigan	1208	151.0	1968	O.J. Simpson, USC	1966	196.6
				1969	Lynn Moore, Army	1795	179.5
1940	Tom Harmon, Michigan	1312	164.0				
1941	Bill Dudley, Virginia	1674	186.0	1970	Don McCauley, North Carolina	2021	183.7
1942	Complete records not available			1971	Ed Marinaro, Cornell	1932	214.7
1943	Stan Koslowski, Holy Cross	1411	176.4	1972	Howard Stevens, Louisville	2132	213.2
1944	Red Williams, Minnesota	1467	163.0	1973	Willard Harrell, Pacific	1777	177.7
1945	Bob Fenimore, Oklahoma A&M	1577	197.1	1974	Louie Giammona, Utah St	1984	198.4
1946	Rudy Mobley, Hardin-Simmons	1765	176.5	1975	Louie Giammona, Utah St	2045	185.9
1947	Wilton Davis, Hardin-Simmons	1798	179.8	1976	Tony Dorsett, Pittsburgh	2021	183.7
1948	Lou Kusserow, Columbia	1737	193.0	1977	Earl Campbell, Texas	1855	168.6
1949	Johnny Papit, Virginia	1611	179.0	1978	Charles White, USC	2096	174.7
				1979	Charles White, USC	1941	194.1
1950	Wilford White, Arizona St.	2065	206.5				
1951	Ollie Matson, San Francisco	2037	226.3	1980	Marcus Allen, USC	1794	179.4
1952	Billy Vessels, Oklahoma	1512	151.2	1981	Marcus Allen, USC	2559	232.6
1953	J.C. Caroline, Illinois	1470	163.3	1982	Carl Monroe, Utah	2036	185.1
1954	Art Luppino, Arizona	2193	219.3	1983	Napoleon McCallum, Navy	2385	216.8
1955	Jim Swink, TCU	1702	170.2	1984	Keith Byars, Ohio St	2284	207.6
	& Art Luppino, Arizona	1702	170.2	1985	Napoleon McCallum, Navy	2330	211.8
1956	Jack Hill, Utah St.	1691	169.1	1986	Paul Palmer, Temple	2633	239.4
1957	Overton Curtis, Utah St.	1608	160.8	1987	Eric Wilkerson, Kent St	2074	188.6
1958	Dick Bass, Pacific	1878	187.8	1988	Barry Sanders, Oklahoma St.	3250	295.5
1959	Pervis Atkins, New Mexico St	1800	180.0	1989	Mike Pringle, CS-Fullerton	2690	244.6
1960	Pervis Atkins, New Mexico St	1613	161.3	1990	Glyn Milburn, Stanford	2222	202.0
1961	Jim Pilot, New Mexico St	1606	160.6	1991	Ryan Benjamin, Pacific	2995	249.6
1962	Gary Wood, Cornell	1395	155.0	1992	Ryan Benjamin, Pacific	2597	236.1
1963	Gary Wood, Cornell	1508	167.6	1993	LeShon Johnson, Northern Ill.	2082	189.3
1964	Donny Anderson, Texas Tech	1710	171.0	1994	Rashaan Salaam, Colorado	2349	213.5
1965	Floyd Little, Syracuse	1990	199.0				

Total Offense

Individual championship decided on Total Yards (1937-69), and on Yards Per Game (since 1970).

Multiple winners: Johnny Bright, Bob Fenimore and Jim McMahon (2).

Year		Plays	Yards	Year		Plays	Yards	
1937	Byron (Whizzer) White, Colorado	224	1596	1967	Sal Olivas, New Mexico St	368	2184	
1938	Davey O'Brien, TCU	291	1847	1968	Greg Cook Cincinnati	507	3210	
1939	Kenny Washington, UCLA	259	1370	1969	Dennis Shaw, San Diego St	388	3197	
1940	Johnny Knolla, Creighton	298	1420	**Year**		**Plays**	**Yards**	**P/Gm**
1941	Bud Schwenk, Washington-MO	354	1928	1970	Pat Sullivan, Auburn	333	2856	285.6
1942	Frank Sinkwich, Georgia	341	2187	1971	Gary Huff, Florida St	386	2653	241.2
1943	Bob Hoernschemeyer, Indiana	355	1648	1972	Don Strock, Va. Tech	480	3170	288.2
1944	Bob Fenimore, Oklahoma A&M	241	1758	1973	Jesse Freitas, San Diego St.	410	2901	263.7
1945	Bob Fenimore, Oklahoma A&M	203	1641	1974	Steve Joachim, Temple	331	2227	222.7
1946	Travis Bidwell, Auburn	339	1715	1975	Gene Swick, Toledo	490	2706	246.0
1947	Fred Enke, Arizona	329	1941	1976	Tommy Kramer, Rice	562	3272	297.5
1948	Stan Heath, Nevada-Reno	233	1992	1977	Doug Williams, Grambling	377	3229	293.5
1949	Johnny Bright, Drake	275	1950	1978	Mike Ford, SMU	459	2957	268.8
				1979	Marc Wilson, BYU	488	3580	325.5
1950	Johnny Bright, Drake	320	2400					
1951	Dick Kazmaier, Princeton	272	1827	1980	Jim McMahon, BYU	540	4627	385.6
1952	Ted Marchibroda, Detroit	305	1813	1981	Jim McMahon, BYU	487	3458	345.8
1953	Paul Larson, California	262	1572	1982	Todd Dillon, Long Beach St	585	3587	326.1
1954	George Shaw, Oregon	276	1536	1983	Steve Young, BYU	531	4346	395.1
1955	George Welsh, Navy	203	1348	1984	Robbie Bosco, BYU	543	3932	327.7
1956	John Brodie, Stanford	295	1642	1985	Jim Everett, Purdue	518	3589	326.3
1957	Bob Newman, Washington St	263	1444	1986	Mike Perez, San Jose St	425	2969	329.9
1958	Dick Bass, Pacific	218	1440	1987	Todd Santos, San Diego St.	562	3688	307.3
1959	Dick Norman, Stanford	319	2018	1988	Scott Mitchell, Utah	589	4299	390.8
				1989	Andre Ware, Houston	628	4661	423.7
1960	Billy Kilmer, UCLA	292	1889					
1961	Dave Hoppmann, Iowa St	320	1638	1990	David Klingler, Houston	704	5221	474.6
1962	Terry Baker, Oregon St	318	2276	1991	Ty Detmer, BYU	478	4001	333.4
1963	George Mira, Miami-FL	394	2318	1992	Jimmy Klingler, Houston	544	3768	342.6
1964	Jerry Rhome, Tulsa	470	3128	1993	Chris Vargas, Nevada	535	4332	393.8
1965	Bill Anderson, Tulsa	580	3343	1994	Mike Maxwell, Nevada	477	3498	318.0
1966	Virgil Carter, BYU	388	2545					

Annual NCAA Division I-A Leaders (Cont.)

Passing

Individual championship decided on Completions (1937-69), on Completions Per Game (1970-78), and on Passing Efficiency rating points (since 1979).

Multiple winners: Elvis Grbac, Don Heinrich, Jim McMahon, Davey O'Brien and Don Trull (2).

Year		Cmp	Pct	TD	Yds
1937	Davey O'Brien, TCU	94	.402	—	969
1938	Davey O'Brien, TCU	93	.557	—	1457
1939	Kay Eakin, Arkansas	78	.404	—	962
1940	Billy Sewell, Wash. St	86	.494	—	1023
1941	Bud Schwenk, Wash.-MO	114	.487	—	1457
1942	Ray Evans, Kansas	101	.505	—	1117
1943	Johnny Cook, Georgia	73	.465	—	1007
1944	Paul Rickards, Pittsburgh	84	.472	—	997
1945	Al Dekdebrun, Cornell	90	.464	—	1227
1946	Travis Tidwell, Auburn	79	.500	5	943
1947	Charlie Conerly, Ole Miss	133	.571	18	1367
1948	Stan Heath, Nev-Reno	126	.568	22	2005
1949	Adrian Burk, Baylor	110	.576	14	1428
1950	Don Heinrich, Washington	134	.606	14	1846
1951	Don Klosterman, Loyola-CA	159	.505	9	1843
1952	Don Heinrich, Washington	137	.507	13	1647
1953	Bob Garrett, Stanford	118	.576	17	1637
1954	Paul Larson, California	125	.641	10	1537
1955	George Welsh, Navy	94	.627	8	1319
1956	John Brodie, Stanford	139	.579	12	1633
1957	Ken Ford, H-Simmons	115	.561	14	1254
1958	Buddy Humphrey, Baylor	112	.574	7	1316
1959	Dick Norman, Stanford	152	.578	11	1963
1960	Harold Stephens, H-Simm	145	.566	3	1254
1961	Chon Gallegos, S. Jose St	117	.594	14	1480
1962	Don Trull, Baylor	125	.546	11	1627
1963	Don Trull, Baylor	174	.565	12	2157
1964	Jerry Rhome, Tulsa	224	.687	32	2870
1965	Bill Anderson, Tulsa	296	.582	30	3464
1966	John Eckman, Wichita St	195	.426	7	2339
1967	Terry Stone, N. Mexico	160	.476	9	1946

Year		Cmp	Pct	TD	Yds
1968	Chuck Hixson, SMU	265	.566	21	3103
1969	John Reaves, Florida	222	.561	24	2896

Year		Cmp	P/Gm	TD	Yds
1970	Sonny Sixkiller, Wash	186	18.6	15	2303
1971	Brian Sipe, S. Diego St.	196	17.8	17	2532
1972	Don Strock, Va. Tech	228	20.7	16	3243
1973	Jesse Freitas, S. Diego St.	227	20.6	21	2993
1974	Steve Bartkowski, Cal	182	16.5	12	2580
1975	Craig Penrose, S. Diego St.	198	18.0	15	2660
1976	Tommy Kramer, Rice	269	24.5	21	3317
1977	Guy Benjamin, Stanford	208	20.8	19	2521
1978	Steve Dils, Stanford	247	22.5	22	2943

Year		Cmp	TD	Yds	Rating
1979	Turk Schonert, Stanford	148	19	1922	163.0
1980	Jim McMahon, BYU	284	47	4571	176.9
1981	Jim McMahon, BYU	272	30	3555	155.0
1982	Tom Ramsey, UCLA	191	21	2824	153.5
1983	Steve Young, BYU	306	33	3902	168.5
1984	Doug Flutie, BC	233	27	3454	152.9
1985	Jim Harbaugh, Michigan	139	18	1913	163.7
1986	V. Testaverde, Miami-FL	175	26	2557	165.8
1987	Don McPherson, Syracuse	129	22	2341	164.3
1988	Timm Rosenbach, Wash. St.	199	23	2791	162.0
1989	Ty Detmer, BYU	265	32	4560	175.6
1990	Shawn Moore, Virginia	144	21	2262	160.7
1991	Elvis Grbac, Michigan	152	24	1955	169.0
1992	Elvis Grbac, Michigan	112	15	1465	154.2
1993	Trent Dilfer, Fresno St.	217	28	3276	173.1
1994	Kerry Collins, Penn St.	176	21	2679	172.9

Receptions

Championship decided on Passes Caught (1937-69), and on Catches Per Game (since 1970). Touchdown totals unavailable in 1939 and 1941-45.

Multiple winners: Neil Armstrong, Hugh Campell, Manny Hazard, Reid Mosely, Jason Phillips and Howard Twilley (2).

Year		No	TD	Yds
1937	Jim Benton, Arkansas	47	7	754
1938	Sam Boyd, Baylor	32	5	537
1939	Ken Kavanaugh, LSU	30	—	467
1940	Eddie Bryant, Virginia	30	2	222
1941	Hank Stanton, Arizona	50	—	820
1942	Bill Rogers, Texas A&M	39	—	432
1943	Neil Armstrong, Okla. A&M	39	—	317
1944	Reid Moseley, Georgia	32	—	506
1945	Reid Moseley, Georgia	31	—	662
1946	Neil Armstrong, Okla. A&M	32	1	479
1947	Barney Poole, Ole Miss	52	8	513
1948	Red O'Quinn, Wake Forest	39	7	605
1949	Art Weiner, N. Carolina	52	7	762
1950	Gordon Cooper, Denver	46	8	569
1951	Dewey McConnell, Wyoming	47	9	725
1952	Ed Brown, Fordham	57	6	774
1953	John Carson, Georgia	45	4	663
1954	Jim Hanifan, California	44	7	569
1955	Hank Burnine, Missouri	44	2	594
1956	Art Powell, San Jose St	40	5	583
1957	Stuart Vaughan, Utah	53	5	756
1958	Dave Hibbert, Arizona	61	4	606
1959	Chris Burford, Stanford	61	6	756
1960	Hugh Campbell, Wash. St	66	10	881
1961	Hugh Campbell, Wash. St	53	5	723

Year		No	TD	Yds
1962	Vern Burke, Oregon St	69	10	1007
1963	Lawrence Elkins, Baylor	70	8	873
1964	Howard Twilley, Tulsa	95	13	1178
1965	Howard Twilley, Tulsa	134	16	1779
1966	Glenn Meltzer, Wichita St.	91	4	1115
1967	Bob Goodridge, Vanderbilt	79	6	1114
1968	Ron Sellers, Florida St.	86	12	1496
1969	Jerry Hendren, Idaho	95	12	1452

Year		No	P/Gm	TD	Yds
1970	Mike Mikolayunas, Davidson	87	8.7	8	1128
1971	Tom Reynolds, San Diego St	67	6.7	7	1070
1972	Tom Forzani, Utah St.	85	7.7	8	1169
1973	Jay Miller, BYU	100	9.1	8	1181
1974	D. McDonald, San Diego St	86	7.8	7	1157
1975	Bob Farnham, Brown	56	6.2	2	701
1976	Billy Ryckman, La. Tech	77	7.0	10	1382
1977	W. Tolleson, W. Carolina	73	6.6	7	1101
1978	Dave Petzke, Northern Ill	91	8.3	11	1217
1979	Rick Beasley, Appalach. St.	74	6.7	12	1205
1980	Dave Young, Purdue	67	6.1	8	917
1981	Pete Harvey, N. Texas St	66	6.3	3	743
1982	Vincent White, Stanford	68	6.8	8	677
1983	Keith Edwards, Vanderbilt	97	8.8	8	909
1984	David Williams, Illinois	101	9.2	8	1278
1985	Rodney Carter, Purdue	98	8.9	4	1099
1986	Mark Templeton, L. Beach St	99	9.0	2	688

Year		No	P/Gm	TD	Yds	Year		No	P/Gm	TD	Yds
1987	Jason Phillips, Houston	99	9.0	3	875	1991	Fred Gilbert, Houston	106	9.6	7	957
1988	Jason Phillips, Houston	108	9.8	15	1444	1992	Sherman Smith, Houston	103	9.4	6	923
1989	Manny Hazard, Houston	142	12.9	22	1689	1993	Chris Penn, Tulsa	105	9.6	12	1578
1990	Manny Hazard, Houston	78	7.8	9	946	1994	Alex Van Dyke, Nevada	98	8.9	10	1246

Scoring

Championship decided on Total Points (1937-69), and on Points Per Game (since 1970).
Multiple winners: Tom Harmon and Billy Sims (2).

Year		TD	XP	FG	Pts	Year		TD	XP	FG	Pts	
1937	Byron (Whizzer) White, Colo	16	23	1	122	1967	Leroy Keyes, Purdue	19	0	0	114	
1938	Parker Hall, Ole Miss	11	7	0	73	1968	Jim O'Brien, Cincinnati	12	31	13	142	
1939	Tom Harmon, Michigan	14	15	1	102	1969	Steve Owens, Oklahoma	23	0	0	138	
1940	Tom Harmon, Michigan	16	18	1	117	**Year**		**TD**	**XP**	**FG**	**Pts**	**P/Gm**
1941	Bill Dudley, Virginia	18	23	1	134	1970	Brian Bream, Air Force	20	0	0	120	12.0
1942	Bob Steuber, Missouri	18	13	0	121		& Gary Kosins, Dayton	18	0	0	108	12.0
1943	Steve Van Buren, LSU	14	14	0	98	1971	Ed Marinaro, Cornell	24	4	0	148	16.4
1944	Glenn Davis, Army	20	0	0	120	1972	Harold Henson, Ohio St.	20	0	0	120	12.0
1945	Doc Blanchard, Army	19	1	0	115	1973	Jim Jennings, Rutgers	21	2	0	128	11.6
1946	Gene Roberts, Tenn-Chatt	18	9	0	117	1974	Bill Marek, Wisconsin	19	0	0	114	12.7
1947	Lou Gambino, Maryland	16	0	0	96	1975	Pete Johnson, Ohio St	25	0	0	150	13.6
1948	Fred Wendt, Texas Mines	20	32	0	152	1976	Tony Dorsett, Pitt	22	2	0	134	12.2
1949	George Thomas, Oklahoma	19	3	0	117	1977	Earl Campbell, Texas	19	0	0	114	10.4
						1978	Billy Sims, Oklahoma	20	0	0	120	10.9
1950	Bobby Reynolds, Nebraska	22	25	0	157	1979	Billy Sims, Oklahoma	22	0	0	132	12.0
1951	Ollie Matson, San Francisco	21	0	0	126							
1952	Jackie Parker, Miss. St.	16	24	0	120	1980	Sammy Winder, So. Miss	20	0	0	120	10.9
1953	Earl Lindley, Utah St.	13	3	0	81	1981	Marcus Allen, USC	23	0	0	138	12.5
1954	Art Luppino, Arizona	24	22	0	166	1982	Greg Allen, Fla. St.	21	0	0	126	11.5
1955	Jim Swink, TCU	20	5	0	125	1983	Mike Rozier, Nebraska	29	0	0	174	14.5
1956	Clendon Thomas, Oklahoma	18	0	0	108	1984	Keith Byars, Ohio St	24	0	0	144	13.1
1957	Leon Burton, Ariz. St.	16	0	0	96	1985	Bernard White, B. Green	19	0	0	114	10.4
1958	Dick Bass, Pacific	18	8	0	116	1986	Steve Bartalo, Colo.	19	0	0	114	10.4
1959	Pervis Atkins, N. Mexico St.	17	5	0	107	1987	Paul Hewitt, S. Diego St	24	0	0	144	12.0
						1988	Barry Sanders, Okla. St	39	0	0	234	21.3
1960	Bob Gaiters, N. Mexico St.	23	7	0	145	1989	Anthony Thompson, Ind	25	4	0	154	14.0
1961	Jim Pilot, N. Mexico St.	21	12	0	138							
1962	Jerry Logan, W. Texas St.	13	32	0	110	1990	Stacey Robinson, No. Ill	19	6	0	120	10.9
1963	Cosmo Iacavazzi, Princeton	14	0	0	84	1991	Marshall Faulk, S.D. St.	23	2	0	140	15.6
	& Dave Casinelli, Memphis St.	14	0	0	84	1992	Garrison Hearst, Georgia	21	0	0	126	11.5
1964	Brian Piccolo, Wake Forest	17	9	0	111	1993	Bam Morris, Texas Tech	22	2	0	134	12.2
1965	Howard Twilley, Tulsa	16	31	0	127	1994	Rashaan Salaam, Colo	24	0	0	144	13.1
1966	Ken Hebert, Houston	11	41	2	113							

All-Time NCAA Division I-A Leaders

Through the 1994 regular season. The NCAA does not recognize active players among career Per Game leaders.

CAREER

Passing

(Minimum 500 Completions)

Passing Efficiency	Years	Rating
1 Ty Detmer, BYU	1988-91	162.7
2 Jim McMahon, BYU	1977-78,80-81	156.9
3 Steve Young, BYU	1982,84-86	149.8
4 Robbie Bosco, BYU	1981-83	149.4
5 Chuck Long, Iowa	1981-85	147.8

Yards Gained	Years	Yards
1 Ty Detmer, BYU	1988-91	15,031
2 Todd Santos, San Diego St	1984-87	11,425
3 Eric Zeier, Georgia	1991-94	11,153
4 Alex Van Pelt, Pittsburgh	1989-92	10,913
5 Kevin Sweeney, Fresno St.	1983-86	10,623

Completions	Years	No
1 Ty Detmer, BYU	1988-91	958
2 Todd Santos, San Diego St	1984-87	910
3 Brian McClure, Bowling Green	1982-85	900
4 Erik Wilhelm, Oregon St.	1985-88	870
5 Alex Van Pelt, Pittsburgh	1989-92	845

Receptions

Catches	Years	No
1 Aaron Turner, Pacific	1989-92	266
2 Terance Mathis, New Mexico	1985-87,89	263
3 Mark Templeton, Long Beach St	1983-86	262
4 Howard Twilley, Tulsa	1963-65	261
5 David Williams, Illinois	1983-85	245

Catches Per Game	Years	No	P/Gm
1 Manny Hazard, Houston	1989-90	220	10.5
2 Howard Twilley, Tulsa	1963-65	261	10.0
3 Jason Phillips, Houston	1987-88	207	9.4
4 Bryan Reeves, Nevada	1991-93	234	7.6
5 David Williams, Illinois	1983-85	245	7.4

Yards Gained	Years	No	Yards
1 Ryan Yarborough, Wyoming	1990-93	229	4357
2 Aaron Turner, Pacific	1989-92	266	4345
3 Terance Mathis, N. Mexico	1985-87,89	263	4254
4 Marc Zeno, Tulane	1984-87	236	3725
5 Ron Sellers, Florida St	1966-68	212	3598

All-Time NCAA Division I-A Leaders (Cont.)

Rushing

Yards Gained	Years	Yards
1 Tony Dorsett, Pittsburgh	1973-76	6082
2 Charles White, USC	1976-79	5598
3 Herschel Walker, Georgia	1980-82	5259
4 Archie Griffin, Ohio St.	1972-75	5177
5 Darren Lewis, Texas A&M	1987-90	5012

Yards Per Game	Years	Yards	P/Gm
1 Ed Marinaro, Cornell	1969-71	4715	174.6
2 O.J. Simpson, USC	1967-68	3124	164.4
3 Herschel Walker, Georgia	1980-82	5259	159.4
4 LeShon Johnson, No. Ill.	1992-93	3314	150.6
5 Marshall Faulk, S. Diego St.	1991-93	4589	148.0

Total Offense

Yards Gained	Years	Yards
1 Ty Detmer, BYU	1988-91	14,665
2 Doug Flutie, Boston College	1981-84	11,317
3 Eric Zeier, Georgia	1991-94	10,841
4 Alex Van Pelt, Pittsburgh	1989-92	10,814
5 Stoney Case, New Mexico	1991-94	10,651

Yards Per Game	Years	Yards	P/Gm
1 Chris Vargas, Nevada	1992-93	6,417	320.9
2 Ty Detmer, BYU	1988-91	14,665	318.8
3 Mike Perez, San Jose St.	1986-87	6,182	309.1
4 Doug Gaynor, L. Beach St.	1984-85	6,710	305.0
5 Tony Eason, Illinois	1981-82	6,589	299.5

All-Purpose Running

Yards Gained	Years	Yards
1 Napoleon McCallum, Navy	1981-85	7172
2 Darrin Nelson, Stanford	1977-78,80-81	6885
3 Terance Mathis, N. Mexico	1985-87,89	6691
4 Tony Dorsett, Pittsburgh	1973-76	6615
5 Paul Palmer, Temple	1983-86	6609

Yards Per Game	Years	Yards	P/Gm
1 Ryan Benjamin, Pacific	1990-92	5706	237.8
2 Sheldon Canley, S. Jose St.	1988-90	5146	205.8
3 Howard Stevens, Louisville	1971-72	3873	193.7
4 O.J. Simpson, USC	1967-68	3666	192.9
5 Ed Marinaro, Cornell	1969-71	4940	183.0

Scoring
NON-KICKERS

Points	Years	TD	Xpt	FG	Pts
1 Anthony Thompson, Ind.	1986-89	65	4	0	394
2 Marshall Faulk, S.D. St.	1991-93	62	4	0	376
3 Tony Dorsett, Pittsburgh	1973-76	59	2	0	356
4 Glenn Davis, Army	1943-46	59	0	0	354
5 Art Luppino, Arizona	1953-56	48	49	0	337

Touchdown Catches	Years	No
1 Aaron Turner, Pacific	1989-92	43
2 Ryan Yarborough, Wyoming	1990-93	42
3 Clarkston Hines, Duke	1986-89	38
4 Terance Mathis, N. Mexico	1985-87,89	36
5 Elmo Wright, Houston	1968-70	34

Points Per Game	Years	Pts	P/Gm
1 Marshall Faulk, S.Diego St.	1991-93	376	12.1
2 Ed Marinaro, Cornell	1969-71	318	11.8
3 Bill Burnett, Arkansas	1968-70	294	11.3
4 Steve Owens, Oklahoma	1967-69	336	11.2
5 Eddie Talboom, Wyoming	1948-50	303	10.8

KICKERS

Points	Years	FG	XP	Pts
1 Roman Anderson, Hou	1988-91	70	213	423
2 Carlos Huerta, Mia-FL	1988-91	73	178	397
3 Jason Elam, Hawaii	1988-89, 91-92	79	158	395
4 Derek Schmidt, Fla. St	1984-87	73	174	393
5 Luis Zendejas, Ariz. St	1981-84	78	134	368
6 Jeff Jaeger, Wash	1983-86	80	118	358
7 John Lee, UCLA	1982-85	79	116	353
Max Zendejas, Arizona	1982-85	77	122	353
Kevin Butler, Georgia	1981-84	77	122	353
10 Derek Mahoney, Fresno St	1990-93	45	216	351

Touchdowns Rushing	Years	No
1 Anthony Thompson, Indiana	1986-89	64
2 Marshall Faulk, S.Diego St.	1991-93	57
3 Steve Owens, Oklahoma	1967-69	56
4 Tony Dorsett, Pittsburgh	1973-76	55
5 Ed Marinaro, Cornell	1969-71	50

Touchdowns Passing	Years	No
1 Ty Detmer, BYU	1988-91	121
2 David Klingler, Houston	1988-91	91
3 Troy Kopp, Pacific	1989-92	87
4 Jim McMahon, BYU	1977-78,80-81	84
5 Joe Adams, Tenn. St	1977-80	81

Field Goals	Years	No
1 Jeff Jaeger, Washington	1983-86	80
2 John Lee, UCLA	1982-85	79
Jason Elam, Hawaii	1988-89, 91-92	79
4 Philip Doyle, Alabama	1987-90	78
Luis Zendejas, Arizona St	1981-84	78

Miscellaneous

Interceptions	Years	No
1 Al Brosky, Illinois	1950-52	29
2 John Provost, Holy Cross	1972-74	27
Martin Bayless, Bowling Green	1980-83	27
4 Tom Curtis, Michigan	1967-69	25
Tony Thurman, Boston College	1981-84	25
Tracy Saul, Texas Tech	1989-92	25

Punt Return Average*	Years	Avg
1 Jack Mitchell, Oklahoma	1946-48	23.6
2 Gene Gibson, Cincinnati	1949-50	20.5
3 Eddie Macon, Pacific	1949-51	18.9
4 Jackie Robinson, UCLA	1939-40	18.8
Two tied at 17.7 each.		

*At least 1.2 punt returns per game.

Punting Average*	Years	Avg
1 Todd Sauerbrun, West Va.	1991-94	46.3
2 Reggie Roby, Iowa	1979-82	45.6
3 Greg Montgomery, Mich. St	1985-87	45.4

*At least 150 punts kicked.

Kickoff Return Average*	Years	Avg
1 Forrest Hall, San Francisco	1946-47	36.2
2 Anthony Davis, USC	1972-74	35.1
3 Overton Curtis, Utah St	1957-58	31.0

*At least 1.2 kickoff returns per game.

SINGLE SEASON

Rushing

Yards Gained	Year	Gm	Car	Yards
Barry Sanders, Okla. St	1988	11	344	2628
Marcus Allen, USC	1981	11	403	2342
Mike Rozier, Nebraska	1983	12	275	2148
Rashaan Salaam, Colorado	1994	11	298	2055
LeShon Johnson, No. Ill.	1993	11	327	1976

Yards Per Game	Year	Gm	Yards	P/Gm
Barry Sanders, Okla. St	1988	11	2628	238.9
Marcus Allen, USC	1981	11	2342	212.9
Ed Marinaro, Cornell	1971	9	1881	209.0
Rashaan Salaam, Colorado	1994	11	2055	186.8
Charles White, USC	1979	10	1803	180.3

Total Offense

Yards Gained	Year	Gm	Plays	Yards
David Klingler, Houston	1990	11	704	5221
Ty Detmer, BYU	1990	12	635	5022
Andre Ware, Houston	1989	11	628	4661
Jim McMahon, BYU	1980	12	540	4627
Ty Detmer, BYU	1989	12	497	4433

Yards Per Game	Year	Gm	Yards	P/Gm
David Klingler, Houston	1990	11	5221	474.6
Andre Ware, Houston	1989	11	4661	423.7
Ty Detmer, BYU	1990	12	5022	418.5
Steve Young, BYU	1983	11	4346	395.1
Chris Vargas, Nevada	1993	11	4332	393.8

All-Purpose Running

Yards Gained	Year	Yards
Barry Sanders, Okla. St.	1988	3250
Ryan Benjamin, Pacific	1991	2995
Mike Pringle, CS-Fullerton	1989	2690
Paul Palmer, Temple	1986	2633
Ryan Benjamin, Pacific	1992	2597

Yards Per Game	Year	Yards	P/Gm
Barry Sanders, Okla. St	1988	3250	295.5
Ryan Benjamin, Pacific	1991	2995	249.6
Byron (Whizzer) White, Colo	1937	1970	246.3
Mike Pringle, CS-Fullerton	1989	2690	244.6
Paul Palmer, Temple	1986	2633	239.4

Passing

Passing Efficiency (Minimum 15 Attempts Per Game)	Year	Rating
Jim McMahon, BYU	1980	176.9
Ty Detmer, BYU	1989	175.6
Trent Dilfer, Fresno St.	1993	173.1
Kerry Collins, Penn St.	1994	172.9
Jerry Rhome, Tulsa	1964	172.6

Yards Gained	Year	Yards
Ty Detmer, BYU	1990	5188
David Klingler, Houston	1990	5140
Andre Ware, Houston	1989	4699
Jim McMahon, BYU	1980	4571
Ty Detmer, BYU	1989	4560

Completions	Year	Att	No
David Klingler, Houston	1990	643	374
Andre Ware, Houston	1989	578	365
Ty Detmer, BYU	1990	562	361
Robbie Bosco, BYU	1985	511	338
Chris Vargas, Nevada	1993	490	331

Receptions

Catches	Year	Gm	No
Manny Hazard, Houston	1989	11	142
Howard Twilley, Tulsa	1965	10	134
Jason Phillips, Houston	1988	11	108
Fred Gilbert, Houston	1991	11	106
Chris Penn, Tulsa	1993	11	105

Catches Per Game	Year	No	P/Gm
Howard Twilley, Tulsa	1965	134	13.4
Manny Hazard, Houston	1989	142	12.9
Jason Phillips, Houston	1988	108	9.8
Fred Gilbert, Houston	1991	106	9.6
Chris Penn, Tulsa	1993	105	9.6
Jerry Hendren, Idaho	1969	95	9.5
Howard Twilley, Tulsa	1964	95	9.5

Yards Gained	Year	No	Yards
Howard Twilley, Tulsa	1965	134	1779
Manny Hazard, Houston	1989	142	1689
Aaron Turner, Pacific	1991	92	1604
Chris Penn, Tulsa	1993	106	1578
Chuck Hughes, UTEP*	1965	80	1519

*UTEP was Texas Western in 1965.

Scoring

Points	Year	TD	Xpt	FG	Pts
Barry Sanders, Okla. St	1988	39	0	0	234
Mike Rozier, Nebraska	1983	29	0	0	174
Lydell Mitchell, Penn St	1971	29	0	0	174
Art Luppino, Arizona	1954	24	22	0	166
Bobby Reynolds, Nebraska	1950	22	25	0	157

Points Per Game	Year	Pts	P/Gm
Barry Sanders, Okla. St.	1988	234	21.3
Bobby Reynolds, Nebraska	1950	157	17.4
Art Luppino, Arizona	1954	166	16.6
Ed Marinaro, Cornell	1971	148	16.4
Lydell Mitchell, Penn St	1971	174	15.8

Touchdowns Rushing	Year	No
Barry Sanders, Okla. St.	1988	37
Mike Rozier, Nebraska	1983	29
Ed Marinaro, Cornell	1971	24
Anthony Thompson, Indiana	1988	24
Anthony Thompson, Indiana	1989	24
Rashaan Salaam, Colorado	1994	24

Touchdowns Passing	Year	No
David Klingler, Houston	1990	54
Jim McMahon, BYU	1980	47
Andre Ware, Houston	1989	46
Ty Detmer, BYU	1990	41
Dennis Shaw, San Diego St.	1969	39

Touchdown Catches	Year	No
Manny Hazard, Houston	1989	22
Desmond Howard, Michigan	1991	19
Tom Reynolds, San Diego St.	1969	18
Dennis Smith, Utah	1989	18
Aaron Turner, Pacific	1991	18

Field Goals	Year	No
John Lee, UCLA	1984	29
Paul Woodside, West Virginia	1982	28
Luis Zendejas, Arizona St	1983	28
Fuad Reveiz, Tennessee	1982	27
Three tied with 25 each.		

All-Time NCAA Division I-A Leaders (Cont.)

Miscellaneous

Interceptions	Year	No		Punt Return Average*	Year	Avg
Al Worley, Washington	1968	14		Bill Blackstock, Tennessee	1951	25.9
George Shaw, Oregon	1951	13		George Sims, Baylor	1948	25.0
Eight tied with 12 each.				Gene Derricotte, Michigan	1947	24.8
				*At least 1.2 returns per game.		

Punting Average*	Year	Avg		Kickoff Return Average*	Year	Avg
Reggie Roby, Iowa	1981	49.8		Paul Allen, BYU	1961	40.1
Kirk Wilson, UCLA	1956	49.3		Leeland McElroy, Texas A&M	1993	39.3
Todd Sauerbrun, West Virginia	1984	48.4		Forrest Hall, San Francisco	1946	38.2
Zack Jordan, Colorado	1950	48.2		Tony Ball, Tenn-Chattanooga	1977	36.4
Ricky Anderson, Vanderbilt	1984	48.2		*At least 1.2 kickoff returns per game.		
*Qualifiers for championship.						

SINGLE GAME

Rushing

Yards Gained	Opponent	Year	Yds
Tony Sands, Kansas	Missouri	1991	396
Marshall Faulk, San Diego St.	Pacific	1991	386
Anthony Thompson, Indiana	Wisconsin	1989	377
Rueben Mayes, Wash.St.	Oregon	1984	357
Mike Pringle, CS-Fullerton	N. Mex. St.	1989	357

Total Offense

Yards Gained	Opponent	Year	Yds
David Klingler, Houston	Arizona St.	1990	732
Matt Vogler, TCU	Houston	1990	696
David Klingler, Houston	TCU	1990	625
Scott Mitchell, Utah	Air Force	1988	625
Jimmy Klinger, Houston	Rice	1992	612

Passing

Yards Gained	Opponent	Year	Yds
David Klingler, Houston	Arizona St.	1990	716
Matt Vogler, TCU	Houston	1990	690
Scott Mitchell, Utah	Air Force	1988	631
Jeremy Leach, New Mexico	Utah	1989	622
Dave Wilson, Illinois	Ohio St.	1980	621

Completions	Opponent	Year	No
David Klingler, Houston	SMU	1990	48
Jimmy Klingler, Houston	Rice	1992	46
Sandy Schwab, Northwestern	Michigan	1982	45
Chuck Hartlieb, Iowa	Indiana	1988	44
Jim McMahon, BYU	Colo. St.	1981	44
Matt Vogler, TCU	Houston	1990	44

Receptions

Catches	Opponent	Year	No
Randy Gatewood, UNLV	Idaho	1994	23
Miller, BYU	New Mexico	1973	22
Rick Eber, Tulsa	Idaho St.	1967	20
Howard Twilley, Tulsa	Colo. St.	1965	19
Ron Fair, Arizona St	Wash.St.	1989	19
Manny Hazard, Houston	TCU	1989	19
Manny Hazard, Houston	Texas	1989	19

Yards Gained	Opponent	Year	Yds
Randy Gatewood, UNLV	Idaho	1994	363
Chuck Hughes, UTEP*	N. Texas St.	1965	349
Rick Eber, Tulsa	Idaho St.	1967	322
Harry Wood, Tulsa	Idaho St.	1967	318
Jeff Evans, N. Mexico St	So.Ill.	1978	316
*UTEP was Texas Western in 1965.			

Longest Plays (since 1941)

Rushing	Opponent	Year	Yds
Gale Sayers, Kansas	Nebraska	1963	99
Max Anderson, Ariz. St.	Wyoming	1967	99
Ralph Thompson, W. Texas St	Wich. St.	1970	99
Kelsey Finch, Tennessee	Florida	1977	99
Eleven tied at 98 each.			

Passing	Opponent	Year	Yds
Fred Owens			
to Jack Ford, Portland	St. Mary's	1947	99
Bo Burris			
to Warren McVea, Houston	Wash. St.	1966	99
Colin Clapton			
to Eddie Jenkins, Holy Cross	Boston U.	1970	99
Terry Peel			
to Robert Ford, Houston	Syracuse	1970	99
Terry Peel			
to Robert Ford, Houston	S. Diego St.	1972	99
Cris Collinsworth			
to Derrick Gaffney, Florida	Rice	1977	99
Scott Ankrom			
to James Maness, TCU	Rice	1984	99
Gino Torretta			
to Horace Copeland, Miami-FL	Ark.	1991	99
John Paci			
to Thomas Lewis, Indiana	Penn St.	1993	99

Field Goals	Opponent	Year	Yds
Steve Little, Arkansas	Texas	1977	67
Russell Erxleben, Texas	Rice	1977	67
Joe Williams, Wichita St	So. Ill.	1978	67

Scoring

Points	Opponent	Year	Pts
Howard Griffith, Illinois	So. Ill.	1990	48
Marshall Faulk, S. Diego St.	Pacific	1991	44
Jim Brown, Syracuse	Colgate	1956	43
Showboat Boykin, Ole Miss	Miss. St.	1951	42
Fred Wendt, UTEP*	N. Mex. State	1948	42
*UTEP was Texas Mines in 1948.			

Touchdowns Rushing	Opponent	Year	No
Howard Griffith, Illinois	So. Ill	1990	8
Showboat Boykin, Ole Miss	Miss. St.	1951	7
Note: Griffith's TD runs (5-51-7-41-5-18-5-3).			

Touchdowns Passing	Opponent	Year	No
David Klingler, Houston	E. Wash.	1990	11
Dennis Shaw, S. Diego St.	N. Mex. St.	1969	9
Note: Klingler's TD passes (5-48-29-7-3-7-40-8-7-8-51).			

Touchdown Catches	Opponent	Year	No
Tim Delaney, S. Diego St	N. Mex. St.	1969	6
Note: Delaney TD catches (2-22-34-31-30-9).			

Field Goals	Opponent	Year	No
Dale Klein, Nebraska	Missouri	1985	7
Mike Prindle, W. Mich	Marshall	1984	7
Note: Klein's FGs (32-22-43-44-29-43-43); Prindle's FGs (32-44-42-23-48-41-27).			

Extra Points (Kick)	Opponent	Year	No
Terry Leiweke, Houston	Tulsa	1968	13
Derek Mahoney, Fresno St	New Mexico	1991	13

Annual Awards

Heisman Trophy

Originally presented in 1935 as the DAC Trophy by the Downtown Athletic Club of New York City to the best college football player east of the Mississippi. In 1936, players across the country were eligible and the award was renamed the Heisman Trophy following the death of former college coach and DAC athletic director John W. Heisman. Top three vote getters for each year are listed with point totals.

Multiple winner: Archie Griffin (2).

Winners in junior year (12): Doc Blanchard (1945), Ty Detmer (1990); Archie Griffin (1974), Desmond Howard (1991), Vic Janowicz (1950), Rashaan Salaam (1994), Barry Sanders (1988), Billy Sims (1978), Roger Staubach (1963), Doak Walker (1948), Herschel Walker (1982), Andre Ware (1989).

Winners on AP national champions (8): Angelo Bertelli (Notre Dame, 1943); Doc Blanchard (Army, 1945); Tony Dorsett (Pittsburgh, 1976); Leon Hart (Notre Dame, 1949); Johnny Lujack (Notre Dame, 1947); Davey O'Brien (TCU, 1938); Bruce Smith (Minnesota, 1941); Charlie Ward (Florida St., 1993).

Year		Points
1935	**Jay Berwanger,** Chicago, HB	84
	2nd—Monk Meyer, Army, HB	29
	3rd—Bill Shakespeare, Notre Dame, HB	23
	4th—Pepper Constable, Princeton, FB	20
1936	**Larry Kelley,** Yale, E.	219
	2nd—Sam Francis, Nebraska, FB	47
	3rd—Ray Buivid, Marquette, HB	43
	4th—Sammy Baugh, TCU, HB	39
1937	**Clint Frank,** Yale, HB	524
	2nd—Byron (Whizzer) White, Colo., HB	264
	3rd—Marshall Goldberg, Pitt, HB	211
	4th—Alex Wojciechowicz, Fordham, C	85
1938	**Davey O'Brien,** TCU, QB	519
	2nd—Marshall Goldberg, Pitt, HB	294
	3rd—Sid Luckman, Columbia, QB	154
	4th—Bob MacLeod, Dartmouth, HB	78
1939	**Nile Kinnick,** Iowa, HB	651
	2nd—Tom Harmon, Michigan, HB	405
	3rd—Paul Christman, Missouri, QB	391
	4th—George Cafego, Tennessee, QB	296
1940	**Tom Harmon,** Michigan, HB	1303
	2nd—John Kimbrough, Texas A&M, FB	841
	3rd—George Franck, Minnesota, HB	102
	4th—Frankie Albert, Stanford, QB	90
1941	**Bruce Smith,** Minnesota, HB	554
	2nd—Angelo Bertelli, N.Dame, HB	345
	3rd—Frankie Albert, Stanford, QB	336
	4th—Frank Sinkwich, Georgia, HB	249
1942	**Frank Sinkwich,** Georgia, TB	1059
	2nd—Paul Governali, Columbia, QB	218
	3rd—Clint Castleberry, Ga.Tech, HB	99
	4th—Mike Holovak, Boston College, FB	95
1943	**Angelo Bertelli,** Notre Dame, QB	648
	2nd—Bob Odell, Penn, HB	177
	3rd—Otto Graham, Northwestern, QB	140
	4th—Creighton Miller, Notre Dame, HB	134
1944	**Les Horvath,** Ohio St., TB-QB	412
	2nd—Glenn Davis, Army, HB	287
	3rd—Doc Blanchard, Army, FB	237
	4th—Don Whitmire, Navy, T	115
1945	**Doc Blanchard,** Army, FB	860
	2nd—Glenn Davis, Army, HB	638
	3rd—Bob Fenimore, Oklahoma A&M, HB	187
	4th—Herman Wedermeyer, St. Mary's, HB	152
1946	**Glenn Davis,** Army, HB	792
	2nd—Charlie Trippi, Georgia, HB	435
	3rd—Johnny Lujack, Notre Dame, QB	379
	4th—Doc Blanchard, Army, FB	267
1947	**Johnny Lujack,** Notre Dame, QB	742
	2nd—Bob Chappius, Michigan, HB	555
	3rd—Doak Walker, SMU, HB	196
	4th—Charlie Conerly, Mississippi, QB	186
1948	**Doak Walker,** SMU, HB	778
	2nd—Charlie Justice, N. Carolina, HB	443
	3rd—Chuck Bednarik, Penn, C	336
	4th—Jackie Jensen, California, HB	143

Year		Points
1949	**Leon Hart,** Notre Dame, E	995
	2nd—Charlie Justice, N. Carolina, HB	272
	3rd—Doak Walker, SMU, HB	229
	4th—Arnold Galiffa, Army QB	196
1950	**Vic Janowicz,** Ohio St., HB	633
	2nd—Kyle Rote, SMU, HB	280
	3rd—Reds Bagnell, Penn, HB	231
	4th—Babe Parilli, Kentucky, QB	214
1951	**Dick Kazmaier,** Princeton, TB	1777
	2nd—Hank Lauricella, Tennessee, HB	424
	3rd—Babe Parilli, Kentucky, QB	344
	4th—Bill McColl, Stanford, E	313
1952	**Billy Vessels,** Oklahoma, HB	525
	2nd—Jack Scarbath, Maryland, QB	367
	3rd—Paul Giel, Minnesota, HB	329
	4th—Donn Moomaw, UCLA, C	257
1953	**Johnny Lattner,** Notre Dame, HB	1850
	2nd—Paul Giel, Minnesota, HB	1794
	3rd—Paul Cameron, UCLA, HB	444
	4th—Bernie Faloney, Maryland, QB	258
1954	**Alan Ameche,** Wisconsin, FB	1068
	2nd—Kurt Burris, Oklahoma, C	838
	3rd—Howard Cassady, Ohio St., HB	810
	4th—Ralph Guglielmi, Notre Dame, QB	691
1955	**Howard Cassady,** Ohio St., HB	2219
	2nd—Jim Swink, TCU, HB	742
	3rd—George Welsh, Navy, QB	383
	4th—Earl Morrall, Michigan St., QB	323
1956	**Paul Hornung,** Notre Dame, QB	1066
	2nd—Johnny Majors, Tennessee, HB	994
	3rd—Tommy McDonald, Oklahoma, HB	973
	4th—Jerry Tubbs, Oklahoma, C	724
1957	**John David Crow,** Texas A&M, HB	1183
	2nd—Alex Karras, Iowa, T	693
	3rd—Walt Kowalczyk, Mich. St., HB	630
	4th—Lou Michaels, Kentucky, T	330
1958	**Pete Dawkins,** Army, HB	1394
	2nd—Randy Duncan, Iowa, QB	1021
	3rd—Billy Cannon, LSU, HB	975
	4th—Bob White, Ohio St., HB	365
1959	**Billy Cannon,** LSU, HB	1929
	2nd—Richie Lucas, Penn St., QB	613
	3rd—Don Meredith, SMU, QB	286
	4th—Bill Burrell, Illinois, G	196
1960	**Joe Bellino,** Navy, HB	1793
	2nd—Tom Brown, Minnesota, G	731
	3rd—Jake Gibbs, Mississippi, QB	453
	4th—Ed Dyas, Auburn, HB	319
1961	**Ernie Davis,** Syracuse, HB	824
	2nd—Bob Ferguson, Ohio St., HB	771
	3rd—Jimmy Saxton, Texas, HB	551
	4th—Sandy Stephens, Minnesota, QB	543
1962	**Terry Baker,** Oregon St., QB	707
	2nd—Jerry Stovall, LSU, HB	618
	3rd—Bobby Bell, Minnesota, T	429
	4th—Lee Roy Jordan, Alabama, C	321

Annual Awards (Cont.)
Heisman Trophy

Year		Points
1963	**Roger Staubach,** Navy, QB	1860
	2nd—Billy Lothridge, Ga.Tech, QB	504
	3rd—Sherman Lewis, Mich. St., HB	369
	4th—Don Trull, Baylor, QB	253
1964	**John Huarte,** Notre Dame, QB	1026
	2nd—Jerry Rhome, Tulsa, QB	952
	3rd—Dick Butkus, Illinois, C	505
	4th—Bob Timberlake, Michigan, QB	361
1965	**Mike Garrett,** USC, HB	926
	2nd—Howard Twilley, Tulsa, E	528
	3rd—Jim Grabowski, Illinois, FB	481
	4th—Donny Anderson, Texas Tech, HB	408
1966	**Steve Spurrier,** Florida, QB	1679
	2nd—Bob Griese, Purdue, QB	816
	3rd—Nick Eddy, Notre Dame, HB	456
	4th—Gary Beban, UCLA, QB	318
1967	**Gary Beban,** UCLA, QB	1968
	2nd—O.J. Simpson, USC, HB	1722
	3rd—Leroy Keyes, Purdue, HB	1366
	4th—Larry Csonka, Syracuse, FB	136
1968	**O.J. Simpson,** USC, HB	2853
	2nd—Leroy Keyes, Purdue, HB	1103
	3rd—Terry Hanratty, Notre Dame, QB	387
	4th—Ted Kwalick, Penn St., TE	254
1969	**Steve Owens,** Oklahoma, HB	1488
	2nd—Mike Phipps, Purdue, QB	1344
	3rd—Rex Kern, Ohio St., QB	856
	4th—Archie Manning, Mississippi, QB	582
1970	**Jim Plunkett,** Stanford, QB	2229
	2nd—Joe Theismann, Notre Dame, QB	1410
	3rd—Archie Manning, Mississippi, QB	849
	4th—Steve Worster, Texas, RB	398
1971	**Pat Sullivan,** Auburn, QB	1597
	2nd—Ed Marinaro, Cornell, RB	1445
	3rd—Greg Pruitt, Oklahoma, RB	586
	4th—Johnny Musso, Alabama, RB	365
1972	**Johnny Rodgers,** Nebraska, FL	1310
	2nd—Greg Pruitt, Oklahoma, RB	966
	3rd—Rich Glover, Nebraska, MG	652
	4th—Bert Jones, LSU, QB	351
1973	**John Cappelletti,** Penn St., RB	1057
	2nd—John Hicks, Ohio St., OT	524
	3rd—Roosevelt Leaks, Texas, RB	482
	4th—David Jaynes, Kansas, QB	394
1974	**Archie Griffin,** Ohio St., RB	1920
	2nd—Anthony Davis, USC, RB	819
	3rd—Joe Washington, Oklahoma, RB	661
	4th—Tom Clements, Notre Dame, QB	244
1975	**Archie Griffin,** Ohio St., RB	1800
	2nd—Chuck Muncie, California, RB	730
	3rd—Ricky Bell, USC, RB	708
	4th—Tony Dorsett, Pitt, RB	616
1976	**Tony Dorsett,** Pittsburgh, RB	2357
	2nd—Ricky Bell, USC, RB	1346
	3rd—Rob Lytle, Michigan, RB	413
	4th—Terry Miller, Oklahoma St., RB	197
1977	**Earl Campbell,** Texas, RB	1547
	2nd—Terry Miller, Oklahoma, RB	812
	3rd—Ken MacAfee, Notre Dame, TE	343
	4th—Doug Williams, Grambling, QB	266
1978	**Billy Sims,** Oklahoma, RB	827
	2nd—Chuck Fusina, Penn St., QB	750
	3rd—Rick Leach, Michigan, QB	435
	4th—Charles White, USC, RB	354
1979	**Charles White,** USC, RB	1695
	2nd—Billy Sims, Oklahoma, RB	773
	3rd—Marc Wilson, BYU, QB	589
	4th—Art Schlichter, Ohio St., QB	251

Year		Points
1980	**George Rogers,** South Carolina, RB	1128
	2nd—Hugh Green, Pittsburgh, DE	861
	3rd—Herschel Walker, Georgia, RB	683
	4th—Mark Herrmann, Purdue, QB	405
1981	**Marcus Allen,** USC, RB	1797
	2nd—Herschel Walker, Georgia, RB	1199
	3rd—Jim McMahon, BYU, QB	706
	4th—Dan Marino, Pitt, QB	256
1982	**Herschel Walker,** Georgia, RB	1926
	2nd—John Elway, Stanford, QB	1231
	3rd—Eric Dickerson, SMU, RB	465
	4th—Anthony Carter, Michigan, WR	142
1983	**Mike Rozier,** Nebraska, RB	1801
	2nd—Steve Young, BYU, QB	1172
	3rd—Doug Flutie, Boston College, QB	253
	4th—Turner Gill, Nebraska, QB	190
1984	**Doug Flutie,** Boston College, QB	2240
	2nd—Keith Byers, Ohio St., RB	1251
	3rd—Robbie Bosco, BYU, QB	443
	4th—Bernie Kosar, Miami-FL, QB	320
1985	**Bo Jackson,** Auburn, RB	1509
	2nd—Chuck Long, Iowa, QB	1464
	3rd—Robbie Bosco, BYU, QB	459
	4th—Lorenzo White, Michigan St., RB	391
1986	**Vinny Testaverde,** Miami-FL, QB	2213
	2nd—Paul Palmer, Temple, RB	672
	3rd—Jim Harbaugh, Michigan, QB	458
	4th—Brian Bosworth, Oklahoma, LB	395
1987	**Tim Brown,** Notre Dame, WR	1442
	2nd—Don McPherson, Syracuse, QB	831
	3rd—Gordie Lockbaum, Holy Cross, WR-DB	657
	4th—Lorenzo White, Michigan St., RB	632
1988	**Barry Sanders,** Oklahoma St., RB	1878
	2nd—Rodney Peete, USC, QB	912
	3rd—Troy Aikman, UCLA, QB	582
	4th—Steve Walsh, Miami-FL, QB	341
1989	**Andre Ware,** Houston, QB	1073
	2nd—Anthony Thompson, Ind., RB	1003
	3rd—Major Harris, West Va., QB	709
	4th—Tony Rice, Notre Dame, QB	523
1990	**Ty Detmer,** BYU, QB	1482
	2nd—Rocket Ismail, Notre Dame, FL	1177
	3rd—Eric Bieniemy, Colorado, RB	798
	4th—Shawn Moore, Virginia, QB	465
1991	**Desmond Howard,** Michigan, WR	2077
	2nd—Casey Weldon, Florida St., QB	503
	3rd—Ty Detmer, BYU, QB	445
	4th—Steve Emtman, Washington, DT	357
1992	**Gino Torretta,** Miami-FL, QB	1400
	2nd—Marshall Faulk, S. Diego St., RB	1080
	3rd—Garrison Hearst, Georgia, RB	982
	4th—Marvin Jones, Florida St., LB	392
1993	**Charlie Ward,** Florida St., QB	2310
	2nd—Heath Shuler, Tennessee, QB	688
	3rd—David Palmer, Alabama, RB	292
	4th—Marshall Faulk, S. Diego St., RB	250
1994	**Rashaan Salaam,** Colorado, RB	1743
	2nd—Ki-Jana Carter, Penn St., RB	901
	3rd—Steve McNair, Alcorn St., QB	655
	4th—Kerry Collins, Penn St., QB	639

Five Or More Heismans

Notre Dame (7)—Bertelli (1943), Brown (1987), Hart (1949), Hornung (1956), Huarte (1964), Lattner (1953) and Lujack (1947). **Ohio St.** (5)—Cassady (1955), Griffin (1974-75), Horvath (1944) and Janowicz (1950).

Maxwell Award

First presented in 1937 by the Maxwell Memorial Football Club of Philadelphia, the award is named after Robert (Tiny) Maxwell, a Philadelphia native who was a standout lineman at the University of Chicago at the turn of the century. Like the Heisman, the Maxwell is given to the outstanding college player in the nation. Both awards have gone to the same player in the same season 30 times. Those players are preceded by (#). Glenn Davis of Army and Doak Walker of SMU won both but in different years.

Multiple winner: Johnny Lattner (2).

Year	Year	Year
1937 #Clint Frank, Yale, HB	1957 Bob Reifsnyder, Navy, T	1977 Ross Browner, Notre Dame, DE
1938 #Davey O'Brien, TCU, QB	1958 #Pete Dawkins, Army, HB	1978 Chuck Fusina, Penn St., QB
1939 #Nile Kinnick, Iowa, HB	1959 Rich Lucas, Penn St., QB	1979 #Charles White, USC, RB
1940 #Tom Harmon, Michigan, HB	1960 #Joe Bellino, Navy, HB	1980 Hugh Green, Pitt, DE
1941 Bill Dudley, Virginia, HB	1961 Bob Ferguson, Ohio St., HB	1981 #Marcus Allen, USC, RB
1942 Paul Governali, Columbia, QB	1962 #Terry Baker, Oregon St., QB	1982 #Herschel Walker, Georgia, RB
1943 Bob Odell, Penn, HB	1963 #Roger Staubach, Navy, QB	1983 #Mike Rozier, Nebraska, RB
1944 Glenn Davis, Army, HB	1964 Glenn Ressler, Penn St., G	1984 #Doug Flutie, Boston Col., QB
1945 #Doc Blanchard, Army, FB	1965 Tommy Nobis, Texas, LB	1985 Chuck Long, Iowa, QB
1946 Charley Trippi, Georgia, HB	1966 Jim Lynch, Notre Dame, LB	1986 #V. Testaverde, Miami-FL, QB
1947 Doak Walker, SMU, HB	1967 #Gary Beban, UCLA, QB	1987 Don McPherson, Syracuse, QB
1948 Chuck Bednarik, Penn, C	1968 #O.J. Simpson, USC, HB	1988 #Barry Sanders, Okla. St., RB
1949 #Leon Hart, Notre Dame, E	1969 Mike Reid, Penn St., DT	1989 Anthony Thompson, Indiana, RB
1950 Reds Bagnell, Penn, HB	1970 #Jim Plunkett, Stanford, QB	1990 #Ty Detmer, BYU, QB
1951 #Dick Kazmaier, Princeton, TB	1971 Ed Marinaro, Cornell, RB	1991 #Desmond Howard, Mich., WR
1952 Johnny Lattner, Notre Dame, HB	1972 Brad Van Pelt, Michigan St., DB	1992 #Gino Torretta, Miami-FL, QB
1953 #Johnny Lattner, N. Dame, HB	1973 #John Cappelletti, Penn St., RB	1993 #Charlie Ward, Florida St., QB
1954 Ron Beagle, Navy, E	1974 Steve Joachim, Temple, QB	1994 Kerry Collins, Penn St., QB
1955 #Howard Cassady, Ohio St., HB	1975 #Archie Griffin, Ohio St., RB	
1956 Tommy McDonald, Okla., HB	1976 #Tony Dorsett, Pitt, RB	

Outland Trophy

First presented in 1946 by the Football Writers Association of America, honoring the the nation's outstanding interior lineman. The award is named after its benefactor, Dr. John H. Outland (Kansas, Class of 1898). Players listed in **bold** type helped lead their team to a national championship (according to AP).

Multiple winner: Dave Rimington (2). **Winners in junior year:** Ross Browner (1976), Steve Emtman (1991) and Rimington (1981).

Year	Year	Year
1946 **George Connor**, N. Dame, T	1963 **Scott Appleton**, Texas, T	1980 Mark May, Pittsburgh, OT
1947 Joe Steffy, Army, G	1964 Steve DeLong, Tennessee, T	1981 Dave Rimington, Nebraska, C
1948 Bill Fischer, Notre Dame, G	1965 Tommy Nobis, Texas, G	1982 Dave Rimington, Nebraska, C
1949 Ed Bagdon, Michigan St., G	1966 Loyd Phillips, Arkansas, T	1983 Dean Steinkuhler, Nebraska, G
1950 Bob Gain, Kentucky, T	1967 **Ron Yary**, USC, T	1984 Bruce Smith, Virginia Tech, DT
1951 Jim Weatherall, Oklahoma, T	1968 Bill Stanfill, Georgia, T	1985 Mike Ruth, Boston College, NG
1952 Dick Modzelewski, Maryland, T	1969 Mike Reid, Penn St., DT	1986 Jason Buck, BYU, DT
1953 J.D. Roberts, Oklahoma, G	1970 Jim Stillwagon, Ohio St., MG	1987 Chad Hennings, Air Force, DT
1954 Bill Brooks, Arkansas, G	1971 **Larry Jacobson**, Neb., DT	1988 Tracy Rocker, Auburn, DT
1955 Calvin Jones, Iowa, G	1972 Rich Glover, Nebraska, MG	1989 Mohammed Elewonibi, BYU, G
1956 Jim Parker, Ohio St., G	1973 John Hicks, Ohio St., OT	1990 Russell Maryland, Miami-FL, NT
1957 Alex Karras, Iowa, T	1974 Randy White, Maryland, DT	1991 Steve Emtman, Washington, DT
1958 Zeke Smith, Auburn, G	1975 **Lee Roy Selmon**, Okla., DT	1992 Will Shields, Nebraska, G
1959 Mike McGee, Duke, T	1976 Ross Browner, Notre Dame, DE	1993 Rob Waldrop, Arizona, NG
1960 **Tom Brown**, Minnesota, G	1977 Brad Shearer, Texas, DT	1994 **Zach Weigert**, Nebraska, OT
1961 Merlin Olsen, Utah St., T	1978 Greg Roberts, Oklahoma, G	
1962 Bobby Bell, Minnesota, T	1979 Jim Richter, N.C. State, C	

Butkus Award

First presented in 1985 by the Downtown Athletic Club of Orlando, Fla., to honor the nation's outstanding linebacker. The award is named after Dick Butkus, two-time consensus All-America at Illinois and six-time All-Pro with the Chicago Bears.

Multiple winner: Brian Bosworth (2).

Year	Year	Year
1985 Brian Bosworth, Oklahoma	1989 Percy Snow, Michigan St.	1992 Marvin Jones, Florida St.
1986 Brian Bosworth, Oklahoma	1990 Alfred Williams, Colorado	1993 Trev Alberts, Nebraska
1987 Paul McGowan, Florida St.	1991 Erick Anderson, Michigan	1994 Dana Howard, Illinois
1988 Derrick Thomas, Alabama		

Annual Awards (Cont.)

Lombardi Award

First presented in 1970 by the Rotary Club of Houston, honoring the nation's best lineman. The award is named after pro football coach Vince Lombardi, who, as a guard, was a member of the famous "Seven Blocks of Granite" at Fordham in the 1930s. The Lombardi and Outland awards have gone to the same player in the same year nine times. Those players are preceded by (#). Ross Browner of Notre Dame won both, but in different years.

Year	Year	Year
1970 #Jim Stillwagon, Ohio St., MG	1979 Brad Budde, USC, G	1987 Chris Spielman, Ohio St., LB
1971 Walt Patulski, Notre Dame, DE		1988 #Tracy Rocker, Auburn, DT
1972 #Rich Glover, Nebraska, MG	1980 Hugh Green, Pitt, DE	1989 Percy Snow, Michigan St., LB
1973 #John Hicks, Ohio St., OT	1981 Kenneth Sims, Texas, DT	
1974 #Randy White, Maryland, DT	1982 #Dave Rimington, Neb., C	1990 Chris Zorich, Notre Dame, NT
1975 #Lee Roy Selmon, Okla., DT	1983 #Dean Steinkuhler, Neb., G	1991 #Steve Emtman, Wash., DT
1976 Wilson Whitley, Houston, DT	1984 Tony Degrate, Texas, DT	1992 Marvin Jones, Florida St., LB
1977 Ross Browner, Notre Dame, DE	1985 Tony Casillas, Oklahoma, NG	1993 Aaron Taylor, Notre Dame, OT
1978 Bruce Clark, Penn St., DT	1986 Cornelius Bennett, Alabama, LB	1994 Warren Sapp, Miami-FL, DT

O'Brien Quarterback Award

First presented in 1977 as the O'Brien Memorial Trophy, the award went to the outstanding player in the Southwest. In 1981, however, the Davey O'Brien Educational and Charitable Trust of Ft. Worth renamed the prize the O'Brien National Quarterback Award and now honors the nation's best quarterback. The award is named after 1938 Heisman Trophy-winning QB Davey O'Brien of Texas Christian.
Multiple winners: Ty Detmer and Mike Singletary (2).

Memorial Trophy

Year	Year	Year
1977 Earl Campbell, Texas, RB	1979 Mike Singletary, Baylor, LB	1980 Mike Singletary, Baylor, LB
1978 Billy Sims, Oklahoma, RB		

National QB Award

Year	Year	Year
1981 Jim McMahon, BYU	1986 Vinny Testaverde, Miami,FL	1991 Ty Detmer, BYU
1982 Todd Blackledge, Penn St.	1987 Don McPherson, Syracuse	1992 Gino Torretta, Miami-FL
1983 Steve Young, BYU	1988 Troy Aikman, UCLA	1993 Charlie Ward, Florida St.
1984 Doug Flutie, Boston College	1989 Andre Ware, Houston	1994 Kerry Collins, Penn St.
1985 Chuck Long, Iowa	1990 Ty Detmer, BYU	

Thorpe Award

First presented in 1986 by the Jim Thorpe Athletic Club of Oklahoma City to honor the nation's outstanding defensive back. The award is named after Jim Thorpe—Olympic champion, two-time consensus All-America HB at Carlisle, and pro football pioneer.

Year	Year	Year
1986 Thomas Everett, Baylor	1989 Mike Carrier, USC	1992 Deon Figures, Colorado
1987 Bennie Blades, Miami-FL	1990 Darryl Lewis, Arizona	1993 Antonio Langham, Alabama
& Rickey Dixon, Oklahoma	1991 Terrell Buckley, Florida St.	1994 Chris Hudson, Colorado
1988 Deion Sanders, Florida St.		

Payton Award

First presented in 1987 by the Sports Network and Division I-AA sports information directors to honor the nation's outstanding Division I-AA player. The award is named after Walter Payton, the NFL's all-time leading rusher who was an All-America RB at Jackson St.

Year	Year	Year
1987 Kenny Gamble, Colgate, RB	1990 Walter Dean, Grambling, RB	1993 Doug Nussmeier, Idaho, QB
1988 Dave Meggett, Towson St., RB	1991 Jamie Martin, Weber St., QB	1994 Steve McNair, Alcorn St., QB
1989 John Friesz, Idaho, QB	1992 Michael Payton, Marshall, QB	

Hill Trophy

First presented in 1986 by the Harlon Hill Awards Committee in Florence, AL, to honor the nation's outstanding Division II player. The award is named after three-time NFL All-Pro Harlon Hill who played college ball at North Alabama.
Multiple winner: Johnny Bailey (3).

Year	Year	Year
1986 Jeff Bentrim, N.Dakota St., QB	1989 Johnny Bailey, Texas A&I, RB	1992 Ronald Moore, Pittsburg St., RB
1987 Johnny Bailey, Texas A&I, RB	1990 Chris Simdorn, N. Dakota St., QB	1993 Roger Graham, New Haven, RB
1988 Johnny Bailey, Texas A&I, RB	1991 Ronnie West, Pittsburg St., WR	1994 Chris Hatcher, Valdosta St., QB

All-Time Winningest Division I-A Coaches

Minimum of 10 years in Division I-A through 1994 season. Regular season and bowl games included. Coaches active in 1994 in **bold** type.

Top 25 Winning Percentage

	Yrs	W	L	T	Pct
1 Knute Rockne	13	105	12	5	.881
2 Frank Leahy	13	107	13	9	.864
3 George Woodruff	12	142	25	2	.846
4 Barry Switzer	16	157	29	4	.837
5 Percy Haughton	13	96	17	6	.832
6 Bob Neyland	21	173	31	12	.829
7 Hurry Up Yost	29	196	36	12	.828
8 Bud Wilkinson	17	145	29	4	.826
9 **Tom Osborne**	22	219	47	3	.820
10 Jock Sutherland	20	144	28	14	.812
11 Bob Devaney	16	136	30	7	.806
12 Frank Thomas	19	141	33	9	.795
13 **Joe Paterno**	29	269	69	3	.793
14 Henry Williams	23	141	34	12	.786
15 Gil Dobie	33	180	45	15	.781
16 Bear Bryant	38	323	85	17	.780
17 Fred Folsom	19	106	28	6	.779
18 Bo Schembechler	27	234	65	8	.775
19 Fritz Crisler	18	116	32	9	.768
20 Charley Moran	18	122	33	12	.766
21 Wallace Wade	24	171	49	10	.765
22 Frank Kush	22	176	54	1	.764
23 Dan McGugin	30	197	55	19	.762
24 Jim Crowley	13	78	21	10	.761
25 Andy Smith	17	116	32	13	.761

Top 25 Victories

	Yrs	W	L	T	Pct
1 Bear Bryant	38	323	85	17	.780
2 Pop Warner	44	319	106	32	.733
3 Amos Alonzo Stagg	57	314	199	35	.605
4 **Joe Paterno**	29	269	69	3	.793
5 **Bobby Bowden**	29	249	79	4	.756
6 Woody Hayes	33	238	72	10	.759
7 Bo Schembechler	27	234	65	8	.775
8 **Tom Osborne**	22	219	47	3	.820
9 **LaVell Edwards**	23	207	76	3	.729
Jess Neely	40	207	176	19	.539
11 **Hayden Fry**	33	205	158	10	.563
12 Warren Woodson	31	203	95	14	.673
13 Vince Dooley	25	201	77	10	.715
Eddie Anderson	39	201	128	15	.606
15 **Lou Holtz**	25	199	89	7	.686
16 Dana X. Bible	33	198	72	23	.715
17 Dan McGugin	30	197	55	19	.762
18 Hurry Up Yost	29	196	36	12	.828
19 Howard Jones	29	194	64	21	.733
20 **Jim Sweeney**	30	191	140	4	.576
21 Johnny Vaught	25	190	61	12	.745
22 John Heisman	36	185	70	17	.711
23 Darrell Royal	23	184	60	5	.749
24 Gil Dobie	33	180	45	15	.781
Carl Snavely	32	180	96	16	.644

Note: Eddie Robinson of Division I-AA Grambling (1941-42, 1945—) is the all-time NCAA leader in coaching wins with a 397-143-15 record and .729 winning pct. over 52 seasons.

Where They Coached

Anderson—Loras (1922-24), DePaul (1925-31), Holy Cross (1933-34), Iowa (1939-42), Holy Cross (1950-64); **Bible**—Mississippi College (1913-15), LSU (1916), Texas A&M (1917, 1919-28), Nebraska (1929-36), Texas (1937-46); **Bowden**—Samford (1959-62), West Virginia (1970-75), Florida St. (1976—); **Bryant**—Maryland (1945), Kentucky (1946-53), Texas A&M (1954-57), Alabama (1958-82); **Crisler**—Minnesota (1930-31), Princeton (1932-37), Michigan (1938-47); **Crowley**—Michigan St. (1929-32), Fordham (1933-41); **Devaney**—Wyoming (1957-61), Nebraska (1962-72); **Dobie**—North Dakota St. (1906-07), Washington (1908-16), Navy (1917-19), Cornell (1920-35), Boston College (1936-38); **V. Dooley**—Georgia (1964-88); **Edwards**—BYU (1972—); **Folsom**—Colorado (1895-99, 1901-02), Dartmouth (1903-06), Colorado (1908-15).

Fry—SMU (1962-72), North Texas (1973-78), Iowa (1979—); **Haughton**—Cornell (1899-1900), Harvard (1908-16), Columbia (1923-24); **Hayes**—Denison (1946-48), Miami-OH (1949-50), Ohio St. (1951-78); **Heisman**—Oberlin (1892), Akron (1893), Oberlin (1894), Auburn (1895-99), Clemson (1900-03), Georgia Tech (1904-19), Penn (1920-22), Washington & Jefferson (1923), Rice (1924-27); **Holtz**—William & Mary (1969-71), N.C. State (1972-75), Arkansas (1977-83), Minnesota (1984-85), Notre Dame (1986—); **Jones**—Syracuse (1908), Yale (1909), Ohio St. (1910), Yale (1913), Iowa (1916-23), Duke (1924), USC (1925-40); **Kush**—Arizona St. (1958-79); **Leahy**—Boston College (1939- 40), Notre Dame (1941-43, 1946-53); **McGugin**—Vanderbilt (1904-17, 1919-34); **Moran**—Texas A&M (1909-14), Centre (1919-23), Bucknell (1924-26), Catawba (1930-33).

Neely—Rhodes (1924-27), Clemson (1931-39), Rice (1940-66); **Neyland**—Tennessee (1926-34, 1936-40, 1946-52); **Osborne**—Nebraska (1973—); **Paterno**—Penn St. (1966—); **Rockne**—Notre Dame (1918-30); **Royal**—Mississippi St. (1954-55), Washington (1956), Texas (1957-76); **Schembechler**—Miami-OH (1963-68), Michigan (1969-89); **Smith**—Penn (1909-12), Purdue (1913-15), California (1916-25); **Snavely**—Bucknell (1927-33), North Carolina (1934-35), Cornell (1936-44), North Carolina (1945-52), Washington-MO (1953-58); **Stagg**—Springfield College (1890-91), Chicago (1892-1932), Pacific (1933-46); **Sutherland**—Lafayette (1919-23), Pittsburgh (1924-38); **Sweeney**—Montana St. (1963-67), Washington St. (1968-75), Fresno St. (1976—); **Switzer**—Oklahoma (1973-88).

Thomas—Chattanooga (1925-28), Alabama (1931-42, 1944-46); **Vaught**—Mississippi (1947-70); **Wade**—Alabama (1923-30), Duke (1931-41, 1946-50); **Warner**—Georgia (1895-96), Cornell (1897-98), Carlisle (1899-1903), Cornell (1904-06), Carlisle (1907-13), Pittsburgh (1915-23), Stanford (1924-32), Temple (1933-38); **Wilkinson**—Oklahoma (1947-63); **Williams**—Army (1891), Minnesota (1900-21); **Woodruff**—Penn (1892-1901), Illinois (1903), Carlisle (1905); **Woodson**—Central Arkansas (1935-39), Hardin-Simmons (1941-42, 1946-51), Arizona (1952-56), New Mexico St. (1958-67), Trinity-TX (1972-73); **Yost**—Ohio Wesleyan (1897), Nebraska (1898), Kansas (1899), Stanford (1900), Michigan (1901-23, 1925-26).

Winningest Division I-A Coaches (Cont.)

All-Time Bowl Appearances

Coaches active in 1994 in **bold** type.

		Overall			Big Four		
		App	W	L	T	W	L	T
1	Bear Bryant	29	15	12	2	12	8	0
2	**Joe Paterno**	25	16	8	1	7	4	0
	Tom Osborne	22	9	13	0	6	8	0
4	Vince Dooley	20	8	10	2	3	5	0
5	**Lou Holtz**	19	10	7	2	5	3	0
	LaVell Edwards	19	6	12	1	0	0	0
7	**Bobby Bowden**	18	14	3	1	5	2	0
	Johnny Vaught	18	10	8	0	6	4	0
9	Bo Schembechler	17	5	12	0	2	10	0
10	**Johnny Majors**	16	9	7	0	4	0	0
	Darrell Royal	16	8	7	1	6	6	0
12	Don James	15	10	5	0	5	2	0
13	**Hayden Fry**	14	5	8	1	0	4	0
14	Bobby Dodd	13	9	4	0	6	1	0
	Barry Switzer	13	8	5	0	6	3	0
	Charlie McClendon	13	7	6	0	4	2	0
17	**Terry Donahue**	12	8	3	1	4	1	0
	Earle Bruce	12	7	5	0	1	2	0
	Woody Hayes	12	6	6	0	5	5	0
	Shug Jordan	12	5	7	0	0	2	0

Active Coaches' Victories

Minimum 5 years in Division I-A.

		Yrs	W	L	T	Pct
1	Joe Paterno, Penn St.	29	**269**	69	3	.793
2	Bobby Bowden, Fla. St	29	**249**	79	4	.756
3	Tom Osborne, Nebraska	22	**219**	47	3	.820
4	LaVell Edwards, BYU	23	**207**	76	6	.729
5	Hayden Fry, Iowa	33	**205**	158	10	.563
6	Lou Holtz, Notre Dame	25	**199**	89	7	.686
7	Jim Sweeney, Fresno St	30	**191**	140	4	.576
8	Johnny Majors, Pitt	27	**179**	121	10	.594
9	Don Nehlen, West Va	24	**163**	97	8	.623
10	Bill Mallory, Indiana	24	**161**	113	4	.586
11	Al Molde, Western Mich	24	**159**	92	8	.629
12	Jim Wacker, Minnesota	24	**153**	115	3	.570
13	Terry Donahue, UCLA	19	**144**	69	8	.670
	George Welsh, Virginia	22	**144**	105	4	.585
15	John Cooper, Ohio St	18	**135**	67	6	.663
16	Jackie Sherrill, Miss. St	19	**130**	65	4	.663
17	Ken Hatfield, Rice	16	**118**	68	3	.632
18	Dick Tomey, Arizona	18	**117**	81	7	.588
19	Larry Smith, Missouri	18	**113**	88	7	.560
20	Danny Ford, Arkansas	14	**105**	41	5	.712

Note: The "Big Four" bowls are the Rose, Orange, Sugar and Cotton. Only one coach, Joe Paterno of Penn St., has won each of them—three Orange Bowls (1969, 70 74); two Cotton Bowls (1972, 75); one Sugar Bowl (1983) and one Rose Bowl (1995).

AFCA Coach of the Year

First presented in 1935 by the American Football Coaches Association.

Multiple winners: Joe Paterno (4), Bear Bryant (3), John McKay and Darrell Royal (2).

Year

1935 Pappy Waldorf, Northwestern
1936 Dick Harlow, Harvard
1937 Hooks Mylin, Lafayette
1938 Bill Kern, Carnegie Tech
1939 Eddie Anderson, Iowa

1940 Clark Shaughnessy, Stanford
1941 Frank Leahy, Notre Dame
1942 Bill Alexander, Georgia Tech
1943 Amos Alonzo Stagg, Pacific
1944 Carroll Widdoes, Ohio St.
1945 Bo McMillin, Indiana
1946 Red Blaik, Army
1947 Fritz Crisler, Michigan
1948 Bennie Oosterbaan, Michigan
1949 Bud Wilkinson, Oklahoma

1950 Charlie Caldwell, Princeton
1951 Chuck Taylor, Stanford
1952 Biggie Munn, Michigan St.
1953 Jim Tatum, Maryland
1954 Red Sanders, UCLA
1955 Duffy Daugherty, Michigan St.

Year

1956 Bowden Wyatt, Tennessee
1957 Woody Hayes, Ohio St.
1958 Paul Dietzel, LSU
1959 Ben Schwartzwalder, Syracuse

1960 Murray Warmath, Minnesota
1961 Bear Bryant, Alabama
1962 John McKay, USC
1963 Darrell Royal, Texas
1964 Frank Broyles, Arkansas
     & Ara Parseghian, Notre Dame
1965 Tommy Prothro, UCLA
1966 Tom Cahill, Army
1967 John Pont, Indiana
1968 Joe Paterno, Penn St.
1969 Bo Schembechler, Michigan

1970 Charlie McClendon, LSU
     & Darrell Royal, Texas
1971 Bear Bryant, Alabama
1972 John McKay, USC
1973 Bear Bryant, Alabama
1974 Grant Teaff, Baylor

Year

1975 Frank Kush, Arizona St.
1976 Johnny Majors, Pittsburgh
1977 Don James, Washington
1978 Joe Paterno, Penn St.
1979 Earle Bruce, Ohio St.

1980 Vince Dooley, Georgia
1981 Danny Ford, Clemson
1982 Joe Paterno, Penn St.
1983 Ken Hatfield, Air Force
1984 LaVell Edwards, BYU
1985 Fisher DeBerry, Air Force
1986 Joe Paterno, Penn St.
1987 Dick MacPherson, Syracuse
1988 Don Nehlen, West Virginia
1989 Bill McCartney, Colorado

1990 Bobby Ross, Georgia Tech
1991 Bill Lewis, East Carolina
1992 Gene Stallings, Alabama
1993 Barry Alvarez, Wisconsin
1994 Tom Osborne, Nebraska

FWAA Coach of the Year

First presented in 1957 by the Football Writers Association of America. The FWAA and AFCA awards have both gone to the same coach in the same season 25 times. Those double winners are preceded by (#).

Multiple winners: Woody Hayes and Joe Paterno (3); Lou Holtz, Johnny Majors and John McKay (2).

Year

1957 #Woody Hayes, Ohio St.
1958 #Paul Dietzel, LSU
1959 #Ben Schwartzwalder, Syracuse

1960 #Murray Warmath, Minnesota
1961 Darrell Royal, Texas
1962 #John McKay, USC
1963 #Darrell Royal, Texas

Year

1964 #Ara Parseghian, Notre Dame
1965 #Duffy Daugherty, Michigan St.
1966 #Tom Cahill, Army
1967 #John Pont, Indiana
1968 Woody Hayes, Ohio St.
1969 #Bo Schembechler, Michigan

1970 Alex Agase, Northwestern
1971 Bob Devaney, Nebraska

Year

1972 #John McKay, USC
1973 Johnny Majors, Pitt
1974 #Grant Teaff, Baylor
1975 Woody Hayes, Ohio St.
1976 #Johnny Majors, Pitt
1977 Lou Holtz, Arkansas
1978 #Joe Paterno, Penn St.
1979 #Earle Bruce, Ohio St.

Year	Year	Year
1980 #Vince Dooley, Georgia	1985 #Fisher DeBerry, Air Force	1990 #Bobby Ross, Georgia Tech
1981 #Danny Ford, Clemson	1986 #Joe Paterno, Penn St.	1991 Don James, Washington
1982 #Joe Paterno, Penn St.	1987 #Dick MacPherson, Syracuse	1992 #Gene Stallings, Alabama
1983 Howard Schnellenberger, Miami-FL	1988 Lou Holtz, Notre Dame	1993 Terry Bowden, Auburn
1984 #LaVell Edwards, BYU	1989 #Bill McCartney, Colorado	1994 Rich Brooks, Oregon

Active Division I-AA Coaches

Minimum of 5 years as a Division I-A and/or Division I-AA through 1994 season.

Top 5 Winning Percentage

	Yrs	W	L	T	Pct
1 Terry Allen, Northen Iowa	6	55	19	0	.743
2 Roy Kidd, Eastern Ky	31	257	91	8	.733
3 Eddie Robinson, Gram	52	397	143	15	.729
4 Jim Tressel, Yngstwn St	9	84	33	2	.714
5 Tubby Raymond, Del	29	239	95	3	.714

Top 5 Victories

	Yrs	W	L	T	Pct
1 Eddie Robinson, Gram	52	397	143	15	.729
2 Roy Kidd, Eastern Ky	31	257	91	8	.733
3 Tubby Raymond, Del	29	239	95	3	.714
4 Carmen Cozza, Yale	30	174	104	5	.624
5 Ron Randleman, S.Hous.St	26	161	110	6	.592

Division I-AA Coach of the Year

First presented in 1983 by the American Football Coaches Association.
Multiple winners: Mark Duffner and Erk Russell (2).

Year	Year	Year
1983 Rey Dempsey, Southern Ill.	1987 Mark Duffner, Holy Cross	1991 Mark Duffner, Holy Cross
1984 Dave Arnold, Montana St.	1988 Jimmy Satterfield, Furman	1992 Charlie Taafe, Citadel
1985 Dick Sheridan, Furman	1989 Erk Russell, Ga. Southern	1993 Dan Allen, Boston Univ.
1986 Erk Russell, Ga. Southern	1990 Tim Stowers, Ga. Southern	1994 Jim Tressel, Youngstown St.

NCAA PLAYOFFS

Division I-AA

Established in 1978 as a four-team playoff. Tournament field increased to eight teams in 1981, 12 teams in 1982 and 16 teams in 1986. Automatic berths have been awarded to champions of the Big Sky, Gateway, Ohio Valley, Southern, Southland and Yankee conferences since 1992.
Multiple winners: Georgia Southern (4); Youngstown St. (3); Eastern Kentucky (2).

Year	Winner	Score	Loser	Year	Winner	Score	Loser
1978	Florida A&M	35-28	Massachusetts	1987	NE Louisiana	43-42	Marshall, WV
1979	Eastern Kentucky	30-7	Lehigh, PA	1988	Furman, SC	17-12	Georgia Southern
				1989	Georgia Southern	37-34	S.F. Austin St.
1980	Boise St., ID	31-29	Eastern Kentucky				
1981	Idaho St.	34-23	Eastern Kentucky	1990	Georgia Southern	36-13	Nevada-Reno
1982	Eastern Kentucky	17-14	Delaware	1991	Youngstown St.	25-17	Marshall
1983	Southern Illinois	43-7	Western Carolina	1992	Marshall	31-28	Youngstown St.
1984	Montana St.	19-6	Louisiana Tech	1993	Youngstown St.	17-5	Marshall
1985	Georgia Southern	44-42	Furman, SC	1994	Youngstown St.	28-14	Boise St.
1986	Georgia Southern	48-21	Arkansas St.				

Division II

Established in 1973 as an eight-team playoff. Tournament field increased to 16 teams in 1988. From 1964-72, eight qualifying NCAA College Division member institutions competed in four regional bowl games, but there was no tournament and no national championship until 1973.
Multiple winners: North Dakota St. (5); North Alabama, Southwest Texas St. and Troy St. (2).

Year	Winner	Score	Loser	Year	Winner	Score	Loser
1973	Louisiana Tech	34-0	Western Kentucky	1984	Troy St., AL	18-17	North Dakota St.
1974	Central Michigan	54-14	Delaware	1985	North Dakota St.	35-7	North Alabama
1975	Northern Michigan	16-14	Western Kentucky	1986	North Dakota St.	27-7	South Dakota
1976	Montana St.	24-13	Akron, OH	1987	Troy St., AL	31-17	Portland St., OR
1977	Lehigh, PA	33-0	Jacksonville St., AL	1988	North Dakota St.	35-21	Portland St., OR
1978	Eastern Illinois	10-9	Delaware	1989	Mississippi Col.	3-0	Jacksonville St., AL
1979	Delaware	38-21	Youngstown St., OH				
1980	Cal Poly-SLO	21-13	Eastern Illinois	1990	North Dakota St.	51-11	Indiana, PA
1981	SW Texas St.	42-13	North Dakota St.	1991	Pittsburg St., KS	23-6	Jacksonville St., AL
1982	SW Texas St.	34-9	UC-Davis	1992	Jacksonville St., AL	17-13	Pittsburg St., KS
1983	North Dakota St.	41-21	Central St., OH	1993	North Alabama	41-34	Indiana, PA
				1994	North Alabama	16-10	Tex. A&M (Kings.)

NCAA Playoffs (Cont.)

Division III

Established in 1973 as a four-team playoff. Tournament field increased to eight teams in 1975 and 16 teams in 1985. From 1969-72, four qualifying NCAA College Division member institutions competed in two regional bowl games, but there was no tournament and no national championship until 1973.

Multiple winners: Augustana (4); Ithaca (3); Dayton, Widener and Wittenberg (2).

Year	Winner	Score	Loser	Year	Winner	Score	Loser
1973	Wittenberg, OH	41-0	Juniata, PA	1984	Augustana, IL	21-12	Central, IA
1974	Central, IA	10-8	Ithaca, NY	1985	Augustana, IL	20-7	Ithaca, NY
1975	Wittenberg, OH	28-0	Ithaca, NY	1986	Augustana, IL	31-3	Salisbury St., MD
1976	St. John's, MN	31-28	Towson St., MD	1987	Wagner, NY	19-3	Dayton, OH
1977	Widener, PA	39-36	Wabash, IN	1988	Ithaca, NY	39-24	Central, IA
1978	Baldwin-Wallace	24-10	Wittenberg, OH	1989	Dayton, OH	17-7	Union, NY
1979	Ithaca, NY	14-10	Wittenberg, OH				
1980	Dayton, OH	63-0	Ithaca, NY	1990	Allegheny, PA*	21-14	Lycoming, PA
1981	Widener, PA	17-10	Dayton, OH	1991	Ithaca, NY	34-20	Dayton, OH
1982	West Georgia	14-0	Augustana, IL	1992	WI-La Crosse	16-12	Wash. & Jeff., PA
1983	Augustana, IL	21-17	Union, NY	1993	Mt. Union, OH	34-24	Rowan, NJ
				1994	Albion, MI	38-15	Wash. & Jeff., PA

*Overtime

NAIA PLAYOFFS

Division I

Established in 1956 as two-team playoff. Tournament field increased to four teams in 1958, eight teams in 1978 and 16 teams in 1987 before cutting back to eight teams in 1989. The title game has ended in a tie four times (1956, '64, '84 and '85).

Multiple winners: Texas A&I (7); Carson-Newman (5); Central Arkansas (3); Abilene Christian, Central St-OH, Central St-OK, Elon, Pittsburg St. and St. John's-MN (2).

Year	Winner	Score	Loser	Year	Winner	Score	Loser
1956	Montana St.	0-0	St. Joseph's, IN	1976	Texas A&I	26-0	Central Arkansas
1957	Pittsburg St., KS	27-26	Hillsdale, MI	1977	Abilene Christian	24-7	SW Oklahoma
1958	NE Oklahoma	19-13	Northern Arizona	1978	Angelo St., TX	34-14	Elon, NC
1959	Texas A&I	20-7	Lenoir-Rhyne, NC	1979	Texas A&I	20-14	Central St., OK
1960	Lenoir-Rhyne, NC	15-14	Humboldt St., CA	1980	Elon, NC	17-10	NE Oklahoma
1961	Pittsburg St., KS	12-7	Linfield, OR	1981	Elon, NC	3-0	Pittsburg St., KS
1962	Central St., OK	28-13	Lenoir-Rhyne, NC	1982	Central St., OK	14-11	Mesa, CO
1963	St. John's, MN	33-27	Prairie View, TX	1983	Car-Newman, TN	36-28	Mesa, CO
1964	Concordia, MN	7-7	Sam Houston, TX	1984	Car-Newman, TN	19-19	Central Arkansas
1965	St. John's, MN	33-0	Linfield, OR	1985	Hillsdale, MI	10-10	Central Arkansas
1966	Waynesburg, PA	42-21	WI-Whitewater	1986	Car-Newman, TN	17-0	Cameron, OK
1967	Fairmont St., WV	28-21	Eastern Wash.	1987	Cameron, OK	30-2	Car-Newman, TN
1968	Troy St., AL	43-35	Texas A&I	1988	Car-Newman, TN	56-21	Adams St., CO
1969	Texas A&I	32-7	Concordia, MN	1989	Car-Newman, TN	34-20	Emporia St., KS
1970	Texas A&I	48-7	Wofford, SC	1990	Central St., OH	38-16	Mesa, CO
1971	Livingston, AL	14-12	Arkansas Tech	1991	Central Arkansas	19-16	Central St., OH
1972	East Texas St.	21-18	Car-Newman, TN	1992	Central St., OH	19-16	Gardner-Webb, NC
1973	Abilene Christian	42-14	Elon, NC	1993	E. Central, OK	49-35	Glenville St., WV
1974	Texas A&I	34-23	Henderson St., AR	1994	N'eastern St., OK	13-12	Ark-Pine Bluff
1975	Texas A&I	37-0	Salem, WV				

Division II

Established in 1970 as four-team playoff. Tournament field increased to eight teams in 1978 and 16 teams in 1987. The title game has ended in a tie twice (1981 and '87).

Multiple winners: Westminster (6); Linfield and Pacific Lutheran (3); Concordia-MN, Findlay, Northwestern-IA and Texas Lutheran (2).

Year	Winner	Score	Loser	Year	Winner	Score	Loser
1970	Westminster, PA	21-16	Anderson, IN	1983	Northwestern, IA	25-21	Pacific Lutheran
1971	Calif. Lutheran	20-14	Westminster, PA	1984	Linfield, OR	33-22	Northwestern, IA
1972	Missouri Southern	21-14	Northwestern, IA	1985	WI-La Crosse	24-7	Pacific Lutheran
1973	Northwestern, IA	10-3	Glenville St., WV	1986	Linfield, OR	17-0	Baker, KS
1974	Texas Lutheran	42-0	Missouri Valley	1987	Pacific Lutheran	16-16	WI-Stevens Pt.*
1975	Texas Lutheran	34-8	Calif.Lutheran	1988	Westminster, PA	21-14	WI-La Crosse
1976	Westminster, PA	20-13	Redlands, CA	1989	Westminster, PA	51-30	WI-La Crosse
1977	Westminster, PA	17-9	Calif.Lutheran				
1978	Concordia, MN	7-0	Findlay, OH	1990	Peru St., NE	17-7	Westminster, PA
1979	Findlay, OH	51-6	Northwestern, IA	1991	Georgetown-KY	28-20	Pacific Lutheran
				1992	Findlay, OH	26-13	Linfield, OR
1980	Pacific Lutheran	38-10	Wilmington, OH	1993	Pacific Lutheran	50-20	Westminster, PA
1981	Austin College, TX	24-24	Concordia, MN	1994	Westminster, PA	27-7	Pacific Lutheran
1982	Linfield, OR	33-15	Wm. Jewell, MO				

*Wisconsin-Stevens Point forfeited its entire 1987 schedule due to its use of an ineligible player.

Mike Powell/Allsport

Super Bowl MVP **Steve Young** raises his fist and helmet in triumph after throwing a record six touchdown passes to lead San Francisco to a 49-26 rout of San Diego in Miami on Jan. 29.

PRO FOOTBALL

PRO FOOTBALL
by Vito Stellino

Gold Rush

*Steve Young leads 49ers to their 5th Super Bowl title as
NFC championship game is once again the pivotal contest.*

While the NFL celebrated its 75th anniversary in 1994 by selecting an all-time team and dressing the hired help in "throwback" uniforms, two of the league's glamour teams fought it out for a place in the sport's history books.

The San Francisco 49ers and Dallas Cowboys each entered the season with a shot at becoming the first team to win five Super Bowls. The defending champions from Texas were also in position to become the first club to three-peat.

In what turned out to be the two most important games of the season, the 49ers prevailed— beating the Cowboys, 21-14, at Candlestick Park on Nov. 13 to secure home field advantage for the playoffs and then winning again, 38-28, two months later in the NFC championship game.

As usual, the Super Bowl was a dud. Not only did the Niners take the field as the heaviest favorite [18 points] in the game's 29-year history, they exceeded expectations by rolling over the San Diego Chargers by 23 points in a 49-26 blowout at Miami's Joe Robbie Stadium. Quarterback Steve Young was the Super Bowl MVP, completing 24 of 36 passes and throwing a record six touchdown passes— three of them to the redoubtable Jerry Rice.

The victory gave San Francisco its fifth title

in 14 seasons and the first of the post-Joe Montana era, while the defeat was the 11th in a row for the AFC and the 13th loss in the last 14 years. The last time the AFC won back-to-back Super Bowls, the Los Angeles Rams had just moved to Anaheim and the Raiders hadn't left Oakland yet.

The rout was no reflection on the Chargers, who looked great during the regular season in their old powder blue uniforms. Led by quarterback Stan Humphries and second-year running back Natrone Means, they rebounded from an 8-8 record in 1993 to go 11-5 and reach their first Super Bowl.

Given the lopsided outcome of the Super Bowl, the showdown for the NFC title was the season's pivotal game. The 49ers jumped out to a 21-0 lead early in the first quarter, sparked by a 44-yard interception return for a touchdown by cornerback Eric Davis on the third play of the game. Aided by two Young TD passes, the Niners led at halftime, 31-14, then held off the Cowboys in the second half. In addition, the San Francisco defense held Dallas running back Emmitt Smith to 74 yards rushing and roughed up quarterback Troy Aikman with four sacks and three interceptions.

"I feel like *this* was the Super Bowl," said flamboyant San Francisco cornerback Deion Sanders. "I was brought here for this one game."

Sanders was one of several key veterans— including Ken Norton Jr., Rickey Jackson, Gary Plummer and Toi Cook—

Vito Stellino is the national pro football writer for *The Baltimore Sun* and has covered six Super Bowl championship teams in Pittsburgh and Washington since 1974.

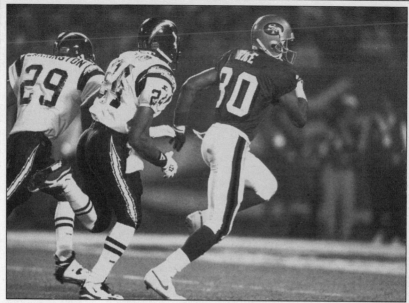

Jerry Rice of the 49ers outruns San Diego safeties **Darren Carrington** (left) and **Stanley Richard** for a 44-yard touchdown on the third play of Super Bowl XXIX. Rice caught 10 passes and scored three times in the game to become the all-time Super Bowl leader in receptions and points scored.

acquired by the 49ers, whose front office figured out how to manipulate the NFL's new salary cap (see sidebar).

The Niners signed Sanders on Sept. 15. Ten days before that, Rice, the club's most enduring star at age 32, opened the season with three touchdown receptions against the Raiders which enabled him to break Jim Brown's all-time NFL career touchdown record of 126. By the end of the regular season Rice had upped his career TD total to 139, moved into second place on the all-time reception list (behind Art Monk) with 820, made All-Pro for the seventh time in 10 years, and was named to the 75th anniversary All-Time All-NFL team.

Beating Dallas and then winning it all in Super Bowl XXIX allowed Rice's battery mate Young and head coach George Seifert to emerge from the long shadows cast by Montana and former coach Bill Walsh.

At the start of the season, Seifert already had a Super Bowl victory to his credit and had posted 50 victories faster than any other coach in NFL history. Bay Area fans, however, were not as impressed with his 68-21 career record and .764 winning

percentage as they might have been. Instead, they focused on the fact that the 49ers had lost three out of the last four NFC championship games.

Young was even more unappreciated. By the end of the '94 regular season, he had led the league in passing for four straight years, surpassed Montana as both the NFL's single season and career passing efficiency leader and received his second MVP award. Still, he had never won the big one and his detractors were quick to point out that he had been outdueled by Montana in the second game of the season when the Kansas City Chiefs beat the 49ers, 24-17, at Arrowhead Stadium.

When Young was handed the Vince Lombardi Trophy after beating San Diego, he cradled it like a baby in both arms.

"I'll always remember this," he said. "I hope there's more to come."

Seifert called Young one of the greatest quarterbacks in league history, adding: "Joe Montana established a standard and Steve Young has maintained it."

To practically no one's surprise, Montana retired on April 18, saying that he had "lost the drive to do what's necessary to compete in the NFL." The announcement was made not in Kansas City where he had led the Chiefs to two straight playoff appearances, but in San Francisco where he had led the 49ers to four Super Bowl championship seasons in the 1980s.

A crowd of 20,000 hero worshippers attended the public event near City Hall, many chanting "One more year, one more year" —even if it meant with the Chiefs.

Hearing a fan yell, "We love you, Joe," master of ceremonies and former coach Bill Walsh replied: "You weren't saying that [after we drafted him] in 1979. Then you were saying, "Where'd you get this guy who looks like a Swedish placekicker?"

Sixteen years later, how did the 38-year-old Montana measure up to the NFL's all-time greats? Just fine. The four quarterbacks on the 75th anniversary All-NFL team were Montana, Sammy Baugh, Otto Graham and Johnny Unitas.

John Madden, the peerless TV analyst and former Raiders coach, went one step further: "I'll say it without any disclaimer," he told the crowd at Joe's retirement rally. "This guy is the greatest quarterback who ever played the game."

Conspicuous by his absence on the stage with Montana was Young, who had not been invited to join several ex-teammates and front office brass. If he felt left out, he didn't say so, calling Montana "the greatest I've ever seen."

Meanwhile in Dallas, the Cowboys could only think of what might have been.

They ran into the usual pitfalls that have plagued previous teams trying to win three straight Super Bowls— injuries and critical turnovers. Tackle Erik Williams was lost for the season in an Oct. 24th auto accident and Emmitt Smith was never the same after pulling a hamstring on Dec. 19 against New Orleans. Quarterback Troy Aikman was bothered by thumb and knee injuries and also suffered a concussion.

What may have hurt the Cowboys the most, however, was the clash of egos between owner Jerry Jones and Jimmy Johnson, who was paid $2 million to walk away as head coach on March 29, 1994. Jones hired former University of Oklahoma coach Barry Switzer to replace Johnson.

After getting Dallas back to the NFC title game, Switzer short-circuited his team's comeback attempt in the fourth quarter shortly after Dallas had cut the deficit to 38-28. Complaining that Deion Sanders had interfered with Cowboys' wide receiver Michael Irvin on a pass from Aikman down the left sideline, the energetic Switzer bumped an official and drew a 15-yard penalty for unsportsmanlike conduct. End of drive.

Nobody will ever know if the Cowboys would have won with Johnson, but it's a fact they didn't win without him.

Jones said he had no second thoughts about forcing Johnson out, but conceded, "If anybody's going to get the blame, it's me."

While the 49ers and Cowboys dominated the NFC, the Chargers and Pittsburgh Steelers were the class of the AFC.

With Humphries passing for 3,209 regular season yards and Means rushing for 1,350, the Chargers got off to a 6-0 start then hung on to win their second AFC West title in three years under coach Bobby Ross. In the playoffs, they recorded back-to-back victories over Miami and Pittsburgh on the final drive of each game.

San Diego beat the Dolphins, 22-21, on Jan. 8 when Miami placekicker Pete Stoyanovich's 48-yard field goal attempt sailed wide right with one second left on the clock. A week later, the Steelers fell, 17-13, in the AFC title game when linebacker Dennis Gibson batted away a fourth down Neil O'Donnell-to-Barry Foster pass from the Charger 3-yard line with 1:08 to go.

The Chargers-Dolphins game featured two blown calls in the second half that added fuel to an already burning debate over the quality of the officiating in the league. Late in the third quarter refs awarded a touchdown to Means of San Diego when he was pushed out of bounds well short of the end zone. Then in the fourth, they took a touchdown away from Miami's Shawn Jefferson even though he had both feet in bounds after catching the ball in the end zone.

While owners turned down a proposal to bring instant replay back just for the play-offs, the issue will remain a hot topic of conversation if officials continue to make highly visible bad calls in 1995.

Elsewhere, the NFC champion didn't have the Buffalo Bills to kick around in the Super Bowl this time. The only team to lose four straight Super Bowls, the Bills failed to make

Joe Montana announcing his retirement on April 18 before a crowd of 20,000 in San Francisco. Although he played his last two seasons in Kansas City, the 38-year-old quarterback and third-round pick in the 1979 NFL draft led the 49ers to four Super Bowl titles in his 14 years with the club.

it back for a fifth try as they struggled to a 7-9 finish. The Bills were victimized by age and free agency and their defense ranked 23rd out of 28 against the pass.

Another perennial playoff team that missed the cut was the Houston Oilers, who went from sharing the league's best record (12-4) in 1993 to outright possession of the worst (2-14) a year later. The 10-win nose-dive from one full season to another broke the previous record of nine, set 30 years ago by the New York Giants, who went from 11-3 in 1963 to 2-10-2 in '64.

Houston never overcame the loss of quarterback Warren Moon, who was traded to Minnesota after the Oilers made the ill-advised decision to go with backup Cody Carlson. The result was that Jack Pardee was the only head coach fired during the season.

Once the season ended, however, six other coaches— Pete Carroll (Jets), Tom Flores (Seahawks), Chuck Knox (Rams), Rich Kotite (Eagles), Wade Phillips (Broncos) and Art Shell (Raiders), were shown the door. Kotite resurfaced with the Jets and the Raiders promoted assistant Mike White. Otherwise, San Francisco lost

offensive coordinator Mike Shanahan to the Broncos and defensive coordinator Ray Rhodes to the Eagles, while the Seahawks (Dennis Erickson) and Rams (Rich Brooks) reached into the college ranks.

The team that made the most positive turnaround was the New England Patriots, who improved by five victories to go 10-6 and reach the playoffs for the first time in eight seasons. Led by second-year quarterback Drew Bledsoe and Coach of the Year Bill Parcells, the Pats sold out every home game for the first time since 1972. They were ousted from the playoffs in the wild card round, losing, 20-17, in Cleveland.

League officials successfully tinkered with the game to decrease field goals and increase touchdowns in 1994.

The kickoffs were moved back from the 35 to the 30-yard line and the defense was given the ball at the spot of the kick rather than at the line of scrimmage after a missed field goal attempt. The league also decided to strictly enforce the rule forbidding defensive backs from touching receivers more than five yards off the line of scrimmage.

The result was that field goals dropped

from 673 to 640 while touchdowns went up from 906 to 1020 and overall points increased from 37.4 per game to 40.5. Meanwhile, passing yardage jumped from 401.3 yards to 427.3 per game and the number of returned kickoffs increased from 1381 to 1842. The average kickoff return jumped from 19.5 yards to 21.3 yards a kick and there were 16 kickoffs returned for touchdowns compared to just four in 1993.

Another popular change was the introduction of the two-point conversion as teams made 61 of 111 attempts.

Individual regular season league leaders included Emmitt Smith with 22 touchdowns, Detroit running back Barry Sanders with 1,883 yards rushing, San Diego placekicker John Carney with 34 field goals and 135 points, Pittsburgh linebacker Kevin Greene with 14 sacks, and Minnesota wide receiver Cris Carter with an NFL-record 122 catches.

Carter broke the one-year old mark of 112 set by Sterling Sharpe of Green Bay. Sharpe had 94 catches and a league-leading 18 touchdown grabs in 1994, but will have to sit out the entire '95 season after undergoing surgery on Feb. 3 to fuse the top two vertebrae in his neck. Saying "research indicates [that] no player who has had that type of surgery has returned," Packers general manager released Sharpe on Feb. 28 after Sharpe refused to reduce his non-guaranteed $3.2 million salary to $200,000.

Among the year's other record-breakers were Bledsoe of the Patriots, who had 70 passing attempts and 45 completions in a single game— a come-from-behind overtime win over Minnesota on Nov. 13; Robert Bailey of the Los Angeles Rams, who returned a punt 103 yards for a touchdown against New Orleans on Oct. 23; Tyrone Hughes of New Orleans, who gained 304 yards on seven kickoff returns and scored two touchdowns in the same game; Mel Gray of Detroit, who reached 7,650 yards in career kickoff returns; and Monk of the New York Jets, who ended the season with at least one catch in 181 consecutive games.

Indianapolis running back Marshall Faulk, the second pick of the 1994 college draft, ran off with the Rookie of the Year award, finishing third among AFC rushers with 1,282 yards and tying San Diego running back Natrone Means in AFC

49ers Find Way Around Salary Cap

Back on Sept. 15, 1994, when All-Pro free agent and unemployed outfielder Deion Sanders decided to ignore more lucrative long-term offers and sign a one-year deal with the San Francisco 49ers, New Orleans Saints' owner Tom Benson thundered, "What kind of Mickey Mouse organization do we have out there?"

Now you know, Tom: a *winning* Mickey Mouse organization. One that made the Saints and most other NFL teams look like Goofy.

A big reason the 49ers won Super Bowl XXIX was the creative way team president Carmen Policy and staff accountant Dominic Corsell were able to maneuver around the NFL's new salary cap which was supposed to rein in the league's biggest spenders.

"We could have said, 'Well, because of the cap, we're not going to be competitive for the next two or three years,'" Policy said. "Instead, we decided to use it as an opportunity."

Knowing he had to slash $18 million from his payroll to get under the $34.6 million limit mandated by the cap, Policy traded or let go of expendable veterans like Bill Romanowski, Tom Rathman, Steve Bono and Ted Washington. He then went about holding on to the 49ers' star players.

Policy told team owner Eddie DeBartolo that the only way to beat the cap was to invest $10 to $12 million in signing key veterans to hefty bonuses before the cap was implemented on Dec. 23, 1993. Any money spent frontloading contracts prior to the deadline would not count against the cap.

The 49ers weren't the only team to use this strategy, but they were the most successful at it.

Once Policy and football operations coordinator Dwight Clark had tied up all their key veterans, they set about fortifying the 49er defense which had been picked apart in two straight NFC championship games by Dallas. In addition to Sanders, they signed linebackers Gary Plummer, Rickey Jackson and Ken Norton Jr., end Richard Dent and cornerback Toi Cook.

This is where the creative accounting came into play. With Corsell crunching the numbers, several contracts were restructured to turn base salary figures into signing bonuses that could be pro-rated in future years. It also

San Francisco president and chief strategist **Carmen Policy** (right) stands quietly and confidently in the background as team owner **Eddie DeBartolo Jr.** cradles the 49ers' unprecedented fifth Vince Lombardi Trophy and accepts the congratulations of President Clinton after Super Bowl XXIX.

helped that perennial All-Pro wide receiver Jerry Rice was more than happy to give up $170,000 in incentive bonus money to help land Sanders.

"You kidding?" asked Rice. "Just $170,000 *not* to have Deion guarding me twice a year? That's cheap."

The 49ers also had to convince potential recruits to play for them for less money than other teams were offering. The pitch was simple: play for us and you've got a great shot at winning the Super Bowl.

Jackson and Cook both signed for the $162,000 minimum, although Jackson wound up making $1 million because he was a starter and the team reached the Super Bowl. The 49ers can count his $828,000 in bonus money against their 1995 cap number.

As Cook said: "It's not like we took $162,000 to go play for the Rams or Cincinnati."

Sanders turned down a four-year $17 million offer from the Saints to sign with the Niners for one year and $1.134 million. He also received a $750,000 bonus when San Francisco qualified for the Super Bowl.

Along the way, the 49ers couldn't resist gloating a bit. When the Saints lost a 24-13 decision to the Niners at Candlestick Park on Sept. 25, they put Mickey Mouse hats in Benson's box and played "The Mickey Mouse Club" theme song when Sanders wrapped up the victory by running 58 yards for a touchdown with an intercepted pass.

According to DeBartolo, the rift with Benson has since been healed.

The Saints weren't the only team complaining, though. There is little doubt that Nike gave Sanders a better endorsement deal to sign with the 49ers. And there were more objections when Sega signed Sanders to a video game deal that will pay him twice as much if he stays with the 49ers in 1995 ($2.5 million) than if he leaves.

Policy, meanwhile, brushes off all the criticism. "I don't know if I'd call it professional jealousy," he said. "But I might call it professional frustration."

DeBartolo added that, despite suggestions to the contrary, the team didn't mortgage the future. It only has to count about $1.5 million in 1994 bonuses toward the 1995 salary cap, which the NFL increased in March by almost $2.5 million to $37.1 million per team.

"We didn't sell our soul to the devil," DeBartolo said.

They just beat the devil out of the cap.

World Wide Photos

Detroit running back **Barry Sanders** led the NFL in rushing for the third time in six years, running for a career-high 1,883 yards.

touchdowns with 12.

Defensive tackle Tim Bowens of Miami, the 20th pick of the draft, was the year's top defensive rookie, while the overall No. 1 selection, defensive tackle Dan Wilkinson of Cincinnati, struggled in his first season.

One of the more noteworthy aspects of the 1994 season was that the NFL was the picture of tranquility in an otherwise turbulent world of professional team sports. Playing the second season of a seven-year contract that includes a salary cap and doesn't run out until 1999, the NFL had none of the difficulties of Major League Baseball (232-day strike), NHL hockey (103-day lockout) and NBA basketball (expired collective bargaining agreement).

Despite complaints by some veterans who were forced to take paycuts, Gene Upshaw, the head of the NFL Players Association, argued the cap was a good tradeoff for free agency. Originally $34.6 million per team for 1994, the cap rose to $37.1 million per team in 1995.

The blue chip free agents also were able to get big contracts despite the cap. Andre Rison, who played with Atlanta from 1990-94, became the highest paid wide receiver in NFL history when he signed a five-year,

$17 million deal with the Cleveland Browns on March 24. (See "Updates" for list of 1995 free agent signings.)

Aging players with hefty salaries like Chris Doleman, Michael Dean Perry, Tom Rathman and Gary Clark were ignored in the league's first expansion draft since 1976 on Feb. 15. The Jacksonville Jaguars selected Arizona quarterback Steve Beuerlein with the first pick, spending $15.5 million on 31 players. New England cornerback Rod Smith was the first choice of the Carolina Panthers, who laid out $9.35 million for 35 players.

Carolina traded the No. 1 pick of the 1995 college draft to the Cincinnati Bengals, who took Penn State running back Ki-Jana Carter. In return the Panthers got the Bengals' first and second round choices and plucked quarterback and Carter teammate Kerry Collins with the fifth overall pick. The three remaining Top 5 selections were No. 2 Tony Boselli of USC (to Jacksonville), No. 3 quarterback Steve McNair of Alcorn St. (to Houston) and No. 4 wide receiver Michael Westbrook of Colorado (to Washington).

Finally, the NFL will play the 1995 regular season without a team in Los Angeles for the first time in 49 years (see "Ballparks and Arenas").

On Jan. 17, the Rams announced their intention to flee the empty confines of Anaheim Stadium for a new 65,000-seat indoor facility in St. Louis. NFL owners gave their approval on April 12 but only after the Rams agreed to pay the league a $29 million relocation fee and 34 percent ($17 million) of its seat licensing agreement with St. Louis.

The Raiders made public their plans to return to Oakland on June 23, despite an NFL offer to build them a new ballpark next to Hollywood Park race track and guarantee the place two Super Bowls.

Oakland and Alameda County officials approved of plans calling for $85 million in renovations to the Oakland Coliseum on July 12 and NFL owners, loath to take Raider boss Al Davis to court, okayed the move on July 14.

"I'm glad to be going back home," said Davis. "The roar of the Oakland crowd will live with me forever."

Or at least until a better offer comes along.   ❑

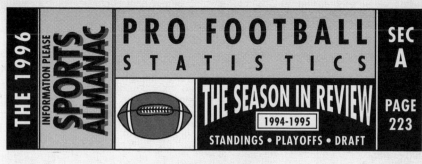

Final NFL Standings

Division champions (*) and Wild Card playoff qualifiers (†) are noted; division champions with two best records received first round byes. Number of seasons listed after each head coach refers to latest tenure with club through 1994 season.

American Football Conference

Eastern Division

	W	L	T	PF	PA	vs Div	vs AFC
*Miami	10	6	0	389	327	5-3-0	8-4-0
†New England	10	6	0	351	312	4-4-0	6-6-0
Indianapolis	8	8	0	307	320	4-4-0	8-6-0
Buffalo	7	9	0	340	356	3-5-0	6-6-0
NY Jets	6	10	0	264	320	4-4-0	5-7-0

1994 Head coaches: Mia— Don Shula (25th season); **NE—** Bill Parcells (2nd); **Ind—** Ted Marchibroda (3rd); **Buf—** Marv Levy (9th season); **NY—** Pete Carroll (1st).
1993 Standings: 1. Buffalo (12-4); 2. Miami (9-7); 3. NY Jets (8-8); 4. New England (5-11); 5. Indianapolis (4-12).

Central Division

	W	L	T	PF	PA	vs Div	vs AFC
*Pittsburgh	12	4	0	316	234	6-0-0	10-2-0
†Cleveland	11	5	0	340	204	4-2-0	8-4-0
Cincinnati	3	13	0	276	406	1-5-0	2-10-0
Houston	2	14	0	226	352	1-5-0	2-10-0

1994 Head coaches: Pit— Bill Cowher (3rd season); **Cle—** Bill Belichick (4th); **Cin—** David Shula (3rd); **Hou—** replaced Jack Pardee (5th, 1-9) with defensive coordinator Jeff Fisher (1-5) on Nov. 14.
1993 Standings: 1. Houston (12-4); 2. Pittsburgh (9-7); 3. Cleveland (7-9); 4. Cincinnati (3-13).

Western Division

	W	L	T	PF	PA	vs Div	vs AFC
*San Diego	11	5	0	381	306	6-2-0	9-3-0
†Kansas City	9	7	0	319	298	4-4-0	6-6-0
LA Raiders	9	7	0	303	327	4-4-0	6-6-0
Denver	7	9	0	347	396	4-4-0	6-6-0
Seattle	6	10	0	287	323	2-6-0	4-10-0

1994 Head coaches: SD— Bobby Ross (3rd season); **KC—** Marty Schottenheimer (6th); **LA—** Art Shell (6th); **Den—** Wade Phillips (2nd); **Sea—** Tom Flores (3rd).
1993 Standings: 1. Kansas City (11-5); 2. LA Raiders (10-6); 3. Denver (9-7); 4. San Diego (8-8); 5. Seattle (6-10).

National Football Conference

Eastern Division

	W	L	T	PF	PA	vs Div	vs NFC
*Dallas	12	4	0	414	248	7-1-0	9-3-0
NY Giants	9	7	0	279	305	6-2-0	6-6-0
Arizona	8	8	0	235	267	4-4-0	5-7-0
Philadelphia	7	9	0	308	308	3-5-0	6-6-0
Washington	3	13	0	320	412	0-8-0	2-12-0

1994 Head coaches: Dal— Barry Switzer (1st season); **NY—** Dan Reeves (2nd); **Ariz—** Buddy Ryan (1st); **Phi—** Rich Kotite (4th); **Wash—** Norv Turner (1st).
1993 Standings: 1. Dallas (12-4); 2. NY Giants (11-5); 3. Philadelphia (8-8); 4. Phoenix (7-9); 5. Washington (4-12).

Central Division

	W	L	T	PF	PA	vs Div	vs NFC
*Minnesota	10	6	0	356	314	4-4-0	8-4-0
†Green Bay	9	7	0	382	287	6-2-0	8-4-0
†Detroit	9	7	0	357	342	4-4-0	7-5-0
†Chicago	9	7	0	271	307	3-5-0	6-6-0
Tampa Bay	6	10	0	251	351	2-6-0	5-9-0

1994 Head coaches: Det— Wayne Fontes (7th season); **Min—** Dennis Green (3rd); **GB—** Mike Holmgren (3rd); **Chi—** Dave Wannstedt (2nd); **TB—** Sam Wyche (3rd).
1993 Standings: 1. Detroit (10-6); 2. Minnesota (9-7); 3. Green Bay (9-7); 4. Chicago (7-9); 5. Tampa Bay (5-11).

Western Division

	W	L	T	PF	PA	vs Div	vs NFC
*San Francisco	13	3	0	505	296	6-0-0	10-2-0
New Orleans	7	9	0	348	407	4-2-0	6-6-0
Atlanta	7	9	0	317	385	2-4-0	6-6-0
LA Rams	4	12	0	286	365	0-6-0	2-10-0

1994 Head coaches: SF— George Seifert (6th season); **NO—** Jim Mora (9th); **Atl—** June Jones (1st); **LA—** Chuck Knox (3rd).
1993 Standings: 1. San Francisco (10-6); 2. New Orleans (8-8); 3. Atlanta (6-10); 4. LA Rams (5-11).

Playoff Tiebreakers

Divisional Championship— AFC: Miami (10-6) qualified over New England (10-6) by winning both regular season games.
Wild Card berths— AFC: Kansas City (9-7) qualified over the LA Raiders (9-7) by winning both regular season games. NFC: Green Bay (9-7) qualified over NY Giants (9-7) with better conference record; Detroit (9-7) over NY Giants with head-to-head victory; Chicago (9-7) over NY Giants with better record against common opponents.

NFL Regular Season Individual Leaders

(* indicates rookies)

Passing Efficiency

(Minimum of 224 attempts)

AFC	Att	Cmp	Cmp Pct	Yds	Avg Gain	TD	Long	Int	Sack	Yds Lost	Rating
Dan Marino, Mia	615	385	62.6	4453	7.24	30	64-td	17	18	113	89.2
John Elway, Den	494	307	62.1	3490	7.06	16	63	10	46	303	85.7
Jim Kelly, Buf	448	285	63.6	3114	6.95	22	83-td	17	34	244	84.6
Joe Montana, KC	493	299	60.6	3283	6.66	16	57-td	9	19	132	83.6
Stan Humphries, SD	453	264	58.3	3209	7.08	17	99-td	12	25	223	81.6
Jeff Hostetler, LA	455	263	57.8	3334	7.33	20	77-td	16	41	232	80.8
Neil O'Donnell, Pit	370	212	57.3	2443	6.60	13	60-td	9	35	250	78.9
Boomer Esiason, NY	440	255	58.0	2782	6.32	17	69	13	19	134	77.3
Jeff Blake, Cin	306	156	51.0	2154	7.04	14	76	9	19	120	76.9
Drew Bledsoe, NE	691	400	57.9	4555	6.59	25	62-td	27	22	139	73.6
Vinny Testaverde, Cle	376	207	55.1	2575	6.85	16	81-td	18	12	83	70.7
Rick Mirer, Sea	381	195	51.2	2151	5.65	11	51	7	27	145	70.2
David Klingler, Cin	231	131	56.7	1327	5.74	6	56	9	24	165	65.7
Billy Joe Tolliver, Hou	240	121	50.4	1287	5.36	6	44	7	27	166	62.6

NFC	Att	Cmp	Cmp Pct	Yds	Avg Gain	TD	Long	Int	Sack	Yds Lost	Rating
Steve Young, SF	461	324	70.3	3969	8.61	35	69-td	10	31	163	112.8
Brett Favre, GB	582	363	62.4	3882	6.67	33	49	14	31	188	90.7
Jim Everett, NO	540	346	64.1	3855	7.14	22	78-td	18	21	164	84.9
Troy Aikman, Dal	361	233	64.5	2676	7.41	13	90	12	14	59	84.9
Jeff George, Atl	524	322	61.5	3734	7.13	23	85-td	18	32	206	83.3
Craig Erickson, TB	399	225	56.4	2919	7.32	16	71-td	10	22	129	82.5
Warren Moon, Min	601	371	61.7	4264	7.09	18	65-td	19	29	235	79.9
Steve Walsh, Chi	343	208	60.6	2078	6.06	10	50	8	11	52	77.9
Randall Cunningham, Phi	490	265	54.1	3229	6.59	16	93	13	43	333	74.4
Chris Miller, LA	317	173	54.6	2104	6.64	16	54	14	28	193	73.6
Dave Brown, NY	350	201	57.4	2536	7.25	12	53	16	42	248	72.5
Jay Schroeder, Ariz	238	133	55.9	1510	6.34	4	48-td	7	11	85	68.4
Scott Mitchell, Det	246	119	48.4	1456	5.92	10	34	11	12	63	62.0
Steve Beuerlein, Ariz	255	130	51.0	1545	6.06	5	63	9	20	129	61.6
Heath Shuler*, Wash	265	120	45.3	1658	6.26	10	81-td	12	12	83	59.6

Receptions

AFC	No	Yds	Avg	Long	TD
Ben Coates, NE	96	1174	12.2	62-td	7
Andre Reed, Buf	90	1303	14.5	83-td	8
Tim Brown, LA	89	1309	14.7	77-td	9
Shannon Sharpe, Den	87	1010	11.6	44	4
Brian Blades, Sea	81	1086	13.4	45	4
Rob Moore, NY	78	1010	12.9	41-td	6
Glyn Milburn, Den	77	549	7.1	33	3
Michael Timpson, NE	74	941	12.7	37	3
Irving Fryar, Mia	73	1270	17.4	54-td	7
Carl Pickens, Cin	71	1127	15.9	70-td	11
Webster Slaughter, Hou	68	846	12.4	57	2
Haywood Jeffires, Hou	68	783	11.5	50	6

NFC	No	Yds	Avg	Long	TD
Cris Carter, Min	122	1256	10.3	65-td	7
Jerry Rice, SF	112	1499	13.4	69-td	13
Terance Mathis, Atl	111	1342	12.1	81	11
Sterling Sharpe, GB	94	1119	11.9	49	18
Jake Reed, Min	85	1175	13.8	59	4
Quinn Early, NO	82	894	10.9	33	4
Andre Rison, Atl	81	1088	13.4	69-td	8
Michael Irvin, Dal	79	1241	15.7	65-td	6
Fred Barnett, Phi	78	1127	14.4	54	5
Edgar Bennett, GB	78	546	7.0	40	4
Michael Haynes, NO	77	985	12.8	78-td	5
Larry Centers, Ariz	77	647	8.4	36	2

Rushing

AFC	Car	Yds	Avg	Long	TD
Chris Warren, Sea	333	1545	4.6	41	9
Natrone Means, SD	343	1350	3.9	25	12
Marshall Faulk*, Ind	314	1282	4.1	52	11
Thurman Thomas, Buf	287	1093	3.8	29	7
Harvey Williams, LA	282	983	3.5	28	4
Johnny Johnson, NY	240	931	3.9	90	3
Leroy Hoard, Cle	209	890	4.3	39	5
Bernie Parmalee, Mia	216	868	4.0	47-td	6
Barry Foster, Pit	216	851	3.9	29-td	5
Bam Morris, Pit	198	836	4.2	20	7
Lorenzo White, Hou	191	757	4.0	33	3
Marcus Allen, KC	189	709	3.8	36-td	7

NFC	Car	Yds	Avg	Long	TD
Barry Sanders, Det	331	1883	5.7	85	7
Emmitt Smith, Dal	368	1484	4.0	46	21
Rodney Hampton, NY	327	1075	3.3	27-td	6
Terry Allen, Min	255	1031	4.0	45	8
Jerome Bettis, LA	319	1025	3.2	19	3
Errict Rhett, TB	284	1011	3.6	27	7
Lewis Tillman, Chi	275	899	3.3	25-td	7
Ricky Watters, SF	239	877	3.7	23	6
Ron Moore, Ariz	232	780	3.4	24	4
Craig Heyward, Atl	183	779	4.3	17	7
Ricky Ervins, Wash	185	650	3.5	49	3
Edgar Bennett, GB	178	623	3.5	39-td	5

San Francisco 49ers
Steve Young
Passing Efficiency

Minnesota Vikings
Cris Carter
Receptions

Detroit Lions
Barry Sanders
Rushing

Dallas Cowboys
Emmitt Smith
Touchdowns

All-Purpose Running

AFC	Rush	Rec	Ret	Total	NFC	Rush	Rec	Ret	Total
Glyn Milburn, Den	201	549	1172	1922	Brian Mitchell, Wash	311	236	1930	2477
Chris Warren, Sea	1545	323	0	1868	Barry Sanders, Det	1883	283	0	2166
Marshall Faulk*, Ind	1282	522	0	1804	Emmitt Smith, Dal	1484	341	0	1825
Tim Brown, LA	0	1309	487	1796	Tyrone Hughes, NO	6	0	1699	1705
Natrone Means, SD	1350	235	0	1585	Kevin Williams, Dal	20	181	1497	1698
Harvey Williams, LA	983	391	153	1527	Herschel Walker, Phi	528	500	581	1609
Rocket Ismail, LA	31	513	923	1467	Ricky Watters, SF	877	719	0	1596
Thurman Thomas, Buf	1093	349	0	1442	Jerry Rice, SF	93	1499	0	1592
Andre Reed, Buf	87	1303	0	1390	Dexter Carter, SF	34	99	1426	1559
Leroy Hoard, Cle	890	445	30	1365	Mel Gray, Det	0	0	1509	1509
Eric Metcalf, Cle	329	436	558	1323	Qadry Ismail, Min	0	696	807	1503
Andre Coleman, SD	0	0	1293	1293	Dave Meggett, NY	298	293	871	1462

Note: Returns (Ret) includes kickoffs, punts, fumbles and interceptions returned.

Scoring

(†) point total includes 2-point conversions.

Touchdowns

AFC	TD	Rush	Rec	Ret	Pts
Marshall Faulk*, Ind	12	11	1	0	72
Natrone Means, SD	12	12	0	0	72
Chris Warren, Sea	11	9	2	0	68†
Carl Pickens, Cin	11	0	11	0	66
Tim Brown, LA	9	0	9	0	54
Leroy Hoard, Cle	9	5	4	0	54
Leonard Russell, Den	9	9	0	0	54
Thurman Thomas, Buf	9	7	2	0	54
Marion Butts, NE	8	8	0	0	48
Andre Reed, Buf	8	0	8	0	48
Irving Fryar, Mia	7	0	7	0	46†
Marcus Allen, KC	7	7	0	0	44†
Keith Jackson, Mia	7	0	7	0	44†
Bernie Parmalee, Mia	7	6	1	0	44†
Harvey Williams, LA	7	4	3	0	44†

NFC	TD	Rush	Rec	Ret	Pts
Emmitt Smith, Dal	22	21	1	0	132
Sterling Sharpe, GB	18	0	18	0	108
Jerry Rice, SF	15	2	13	0	92†
Terance Mathis, Atl	11	0	11	0	70†
Herman Moore, Det	11	0	11	0	66
Ricky Watters, SF	11	6	5	0	66
Brent Jones, SF	9	0	9	0	56†
Edgar Bennett, GB	9	5	4	0	54
Terry Allen, Min	8	8	0	0	50†
Andre Rison, Atl	8	0	8	0	50†
Alvin Harper, Dal	8	0	8	0	48
Craig Heyward, Atl	8	7	1	0	48
Barry Sanders, Det	8	7	1	0	48
Herschel Walker, Phi	8	5	2	1	48

Kickers

AFC	PAT	FG	Long	Pts
John Carney, SD	33/33	34/38	50	135
Jason Elam, Den	29/29	30/37	54	119
Matt Bahr, NE	36/36	27/34	48	117
Steve Christie, Buf	38/38	24/28	52	110
Matt Stover, Cle	32/32	26/28	45	110
Doug Pelfrey, Cin	24/25	28/33	54	108
Pete Stoyanovich, Mia	35/35	24/31	50	107
Lin Elliott, KC	30/30	25/30	49	105
Gary Anderson, Pit	32/32	24/29	50	104
Jeff Jaeger, LA	31/31	22/28	51	97
Nick Lowery, NY	26/27	20/23	49	86
Dean Biasucci, Ind	37/37	16/24	50	85
John Kasay, Sea	25/26	20/24	50	85

NFC	PAT	FG	Long	Pts
Fuad Reveiz, Min	30/30	34/39	51	132
Morten Andersen, NO	32/32	28/39	48	116
Chris Boniol, Dal	48/48	22/29	47	114
Doug Brien, SF	60/62	15/20	48	105
Chris Jacke, GB	41/43	19/26	50	98
Eddie Murray, Phi	33/33	21/25	42	96
Norm Johnson, Atl	32/32	21/25	50	95
Jason Hanson, Det	39/40	18/27	49	93
Chip Lohmiller, Wash	30/32	20/28	54	90
Michael Husted, TB	20/20	23/35	53	89
Kevin Butler, Chi	24/24	21/29	52	87
Tony Zendejas, LA	28/28	18/23	47	82
Greg Davis, Ariz	17/17	20/26	51	77

NFL Regular Season Individual Leaders (Cont.)

Interceptions

AFC	No	Yds	Long	TD
Eric Turner, Cle	9	199	93-td	1
Ray Buchanan, Ind	8	221	90-td	3
Darren Perry, Pit	7	112	42	0
Terry McDaniel, LA	7	103	35	2
Maurice Hurst, NE	7	68	24	0

NFC	No	Yds	Long	TD
Aeneas Williams, Ariz	9	89	43	0
Merton Hanks, SF	7	93	38	0
Deion Sanders, SF	6	303	93-td	3
Greg Jackson, Phi	6	86	55-td	1

Seven tied with 5 INTs each.

Sacks

AFC	No
Kevin Greene, Pittsburgh	14
Leslie O'Neal, San Diego	12½
Neil Smith, Kansas City	11½
Chris Mims, San Diego	11
Derrick Thomas, Kansas City	11

NFC	No
Ken Harvey, Washington	13½
John Randle, Minnesota	13½
Charles Haley, Dallas	12½
Chuck Smith, Atlanta	11
Darion Conner, New Orleans	10½
Sean Jones, Green Bay	10½

Punting

AFC	No	Yds	Long	Avg	In 20
Jeff Gossett, LA	77	3377	65	43.9	19
Lee Johnson, Cin	79	3461	64	43.8	19
Rick Tuten, Sea	91	3905	64	42.9	33
Tom Rouen, Den	76	3258	59	42.9	23
Rich Camarillo, Hou	96	4115	58	42.9	35

NFC	No	Yds	Long	Avg	In 20
Sean Landeta, LA	78	3494	62	44.8	23
Reggie Roby, Wash	82	3639	65	44.4	21
Gregg Montgomery, Det	63	2782	64	44.2	19
Tommy Barnhardt, NO	67	2920	57	43.6	14
Mike Saxon, Min	77	3301	67	42.9	28

Punt Returns

AFC	No	Yds	Avg	Long	TD
Darrien Gordon, SD	36	475	13.2	90-td	2
Tim Brown, LA	40	487	12.2	48	0
Corey Sawyer, Cin	26	307	11.8	82-td	1
Jeff Burris, Buf	32	332	10.4	57	0
Eric Metcalf, Cle	35	348	9.9	92-td	2

NFC	No	Yds	Avg	Long	TD
Brian Mitchell, Wash	32	452	14.1	78-td	2
David Meggett, NY	26	323	12.4	68-td	2
Mel Gray, Det	21	233	11.1	24	0
Vernon Turner, TB	21	218	10.4	80-td	1
Jeff Sydner, Phi	40	381	9.5	49	0

Kickoff Returns

AFC	No	Yds	Avg	Long	TD
Randy Baldwin, Cle	28	753	26.9	85-td	1
Andre Coleman, SD	49	1293	26.4	90-td	2
Jon Vaughn, Sea.-KC	33	829	25.1	93-td	2
Butler By'not'e, Den*	24	545	22.7	41	0
Ron Dickerson, KC	21	472	22.5	62	0

NFC	No	Yds	Avg	Long	TD
Mel Gray, Det	45	1276	28.4	102-td	3
Herschel Walker, Phi	21	581	27.7	94-td	1
Kevin Williams, Dal	43	1148	26.7	87-td	1
Brian Mitchell, Wash	58	1478	25.5	86	0
Nate Lewis, Chi	35	874	25.0	55	0

Single Game Highs

(*) indicates overtime game.

Passing

AFC	Att/Cmp	Yds	TD
Dan Marino, Mia vs NE (9/4)	42/33	473	5
Dan Marino, Mia at Min (9/25)	54/29	431	5
Drew Bledsoe, NE vs Min (11/13)*	70/45	426	3
Drew Bledsoe, NE at Mia (9/4)	51/32	421	4
Joe Montana, KC at Den (10/17)	54/34	393	3

NFC	Att/Cmp	Yds	TD
Warren Moon, Min vs NO (11/6)	57/33	420	3
Warren Moon, Min vs NYJ (11/20)	50/33	400	2
John Friesz, Wash at NYG (9/18)	50/32	381	2
Jim Everett, NO vs Wash (9/11)	46/31	376	2
Brett Favre, GB at Det (12/4)	43/29	366	3

Rushing

AFC	Car	Yds	TD
Chris Warren, Sea at Hou (12/11)	30	185	1
Barry Foster, Pit vs Ind (9/18)	31	179	1
Lorenzo White, Hou vs NYG (11/21)	27	156	0
Bernie Parmalee, Mia vs Raiders (10/16)*	30	150	0
Bam Morris, Pit at NYG (10/23)	29	146	1

NFC	Car	Yds	TD
Barry Sanders, Det vs TB (11/13)	26	237	0
Barry Sanders, Det at Dal (9/19)*	40	194	0
Errict Rhett, TB vs Wash (12/4)	40	192	1
Barry Sanders, Det vs GB (12/4)	20	188	1
Emmitt Smith, Dal at Pit (9/4)	31	171	1

Reception Yards

AFC	No	Yds	TD
Irving Fryar, Mia vs NE (9/4)	5	211	3
Andre Reed, Buf vs GB (11/20)	15	191	2
Carl Pickens, Cin vs Hou (11/13)	11	188	3
Cedric Tillman, Den vs Atl (11/20)	8	175	0
Tony Martin, SD vs SF (12/11)	9	172	1

NFC	No	Yds	TD
Torrance Small, NO at Den (12/24)	6	200	2
Henry Ellard, Wash vs NYG (9/18)	10	197	1
Andre Rison, Atl at Det (9/4)*	14	193	2
Henry Ellard, Wash at Ariz (12/11)	8	191	1
Fred Barnett, Phi vs Hou (10/24)	5	187	1

NFL Bests

Longest Field Goal
54 yds .... Jason Elam, Den at SD (10/23)
54 yds .... Chip Lohmiller, Wash vs Phi (10/30)
54 yds .... Doug Pelfrey, Cin vs Phi (12/24)

Longest Run from Scrimmage
91 yds .... Herschel Walker, Phi at Atl (11/27), TD

Longest Pass Play
99 yds .... Humphries to Martin, SD at Sea (9/18), TD

Longest Interception Return
99 yds .... Stanley Richard, SD at Den (9/4), TD

Longest Punt Return
103 yds .... Robert Bailey, Rams at N.O. (10/23), TD

Longest Kickoff Return
102 yds .... Mel Gray, Det vs Chi (10/23), TD

NFL Regular Season Team Leaders

Offense

AFC	Points For	Avg	Rush	Yardage Pass	Total	Avg
Miami	389	24.3	1658	4420	6078	379.9
New England	351	21.9	1332	4444	5776	361.0
Kansas City	319	19.9	1732	3960	5692	355.8
Denver	347	21.7	1470	4017	5487	342.9
Buffalo	340	21.3	1831	3413	5244	327.8
San Diego	381	23.8	1852	3368	5220	326.3
Pittsburgh	316	19.8	2180	2964	5144	321.5
Cleveland	340	21.3	1657	3175	4832	302.0
Cincinnati	276	17.3	1556	3236	4792	299.5
Los Angeles	303	18.9	1512	3267	4779	298.7
New York	264	16.5	1566	3137	4703	293.9
Seattle	287	17.9	2084	2568	4652	290.8
Houston	226	14.1	1682	2799	4481	280.1
Indianapolis	307	19.2	2060	2353	4413	275.8

NFC	Points For	Avg	Rush	Yardage Pass	Total	Avg
San Francisco	505	31.6	1897	4163	6060	378.8
Minnesota	356	22.3	1524	4324	5848	365.5
Atlanta	317	19.8	1249	4112	5361	335.1
Dallas	414	25.9	1953	3368	5321	332.6
Green Bay	382	23.9	1543	3773	5316	332.3
New Orleans	348	21.8	1336	3846	5182	323.9
Philadelphia	308	19.3	1761	3364	5125	320.3
Detroit	357	22.3	2080	2922	5002	312.6
Washington	320	20.0	1415	3378	4793	299.6
Tampa Bay	251	15.7	1489	3265	4754	297.1
Los Angeles	286	17.9	1389	3358	4747	296.7
Chicago	271	16.9	1588	3091	4679	292.4
Arizona	235	14.7	1560	3047	4607	287.9
New York	279	17.4	1754	2562	4316	269.8

Defense

AFC	Points Opp	Avg	Rush	Yardage Pass	Total	Avg
Pittsburgh	234	14.6	1452	2874	4326	270.4
Cleveland	204	12.8	1669	3157	4826	301.6
Houston	352	22.0	2120	2795	4915	307.2
Los Angeles	327	20.4	1543	3400	4943	308.9
Kansas City	298	18.6	1734	3266	5000	312.5
San Diego	306	19.1	1404	3658	5062	316.4
Cincinnati	406	25.4	1906	3248	5154	322.1
Buffalo	356	22.3	1515	3660	5175	323.4
New England	312	19.5	1760	3447	5207	325.4
Miami	327	20.4	1430	3794	5224	326.5
Indianapolis	320	20.0	1646	3679	5325	332.8
New York	320	20.0	1809	3529	5338	333.6
Seattle	323	20.2	1952	3397	5349	334.3
Denver	396	24.8	1752	4155	5907	369.2

NFC	Points Opp	Avg	Rush	Yardage Pass	Total	Avg
Dallas	248	15.5	1561	2752	4313	269.6
Arizona	267	16.7	1370	3038	4408	275.5
Philadelphia	308	19.3	1616	3094	4710	294.4
Minnesota	314	19.6	1090	3652	4742	296.4
Green Bay	287	17.9	1363	3401	4764	297.8
San Francisco	296	18.5	1338	3501	4839	302.4
New York	305	19.1	1728	3222	4950	309.4
Chicago	307	19.2	1922	3087	5009	313.1
Los Angeles	365	22.8	1781	3389	5170	323.1
Tampa Bay	351	21.9	1964	3372	5336	333.5
Detroit	342	21.4	1859	3546	5405	337.8
New Orleans	407	25.4	1758	3811	5569	348.1
Washington	412	25.8	1975	3634	5609	350.6
Atlanta	385	24.1	1693	4136	5829	364.3

Takeaways / Giveaways

AFC	Takeaways Int	Fum	Tot	Giveaways Int	Fum	Tot	Net Diff
Pittsburgh	17	14	31	9	8	14	+14
Kansas City	12	26	38	14	12	26	+12
NY Jets	17	21	38	18	10	28	+10
San Diego	17	15	32	14	9	23	+9
New England	22	18	40	27	11	38	+2
Seattle	19	11	30	9	19	28	+2
Miami	23	9	32	18	14	32	0
Indianapolis	18	10	28	14	17	31	-3
Cleveland	18	13	31	21	14	35	-4
Denver	12	14	26	13	18	31	-5
LA Raiders	12	13	25	16	14	30	-5
Buffalo	16	12	28	21	13	34	-6
Houston	14	12	26	17	25	42	-16
Cincinnati	10	8	18	19	22	41	-23
TOTALS	227	196	423	230	206	436	-13

NFC	Takeaways Int	Fum	Tot	Giveaways Int	Fum	Tot	Net Diff
San Francisco	23	12	35	11	13	24	+11
Green Bay	21	12	33	14	8	22	+11
Philadelphia	14	21	35	14	12	26	+9
NY Giants	16	16	32	18	7	25	+7
Arizona	23	13	36	19	10	29	+7
Dallas	22	9	31	14	10	24	+7
Minnesota	18	16	34	20	14	34	0
New Orleans	17	14	31	18	14	31	-1
Detroit	12	11	23	14	10	24	-1
Tampa Bay	9	12	21	16	7	23	-2
Atlanta	22	11	33	25	11	36	-3
Chicago	12	10	22	16	10	26	-4
L.A. Rams	14	6	20	18	13	31	-11
Washington	17	6	23	27	13	40	-17
TOTALS	247	162	409	244	152	396	+13

Overall Club Rankings

Combined AFC and NFC rankings by yards gained on offense and yards given up on defense.

	Offense Rush	Pass	Rank	Defense Rush	Pass	Rank
Arizona	17	22	25	4	4	3
Atlanta	28	5	7	14	27	27
Buffalo	8	10	10	8	23	17
Chicago	15	21	23	24	5	13
Cincinnati	18	18	18	23	9	15
Cleveland	14	19	16	13	7	7
Dallas	5	12†	8	10	1	1
Denver	23	6	6	17	28	28
Detroit	3	24	15	22	19	24
Green Bay	19	9	9	3	15	6
Houston	12	25	26	28	2	9
Indianapolis	4	28	27	12	24	20
Kansas City	11	7	5	16	10	12
LA Raiders	21	16	19	9	14	10
LA Rams	25	15	21	20	12	16
Miami	13	2	1	6	25	19
Minnesota	20	3	3	1	21	5
New England	27	1	4	19	16	18
New Orleans	26	8	12	18	26	25
NY Giants	10	27	28	15	8	11
NY Jets	16	20	22	21	18	22
Philadelphia	9	14	14	11	6	4
Pittsburgh	1	23	13	7	3	2
San Diego	7	12†	11	5	22	14
San Francisco	6	4	2	2	17	8
Seattle	2	26	24	25	13	23
Tampa Bay	22	17	20	26	11	21
Washington	24	11	17	27	20	26

AFC Team by Team Statistics

Players with more than one team during the regular season are listed with second club; (*) indicates rookies.

Buffalo Bills

Passing (5 Att)	Att	Cmp	Pct	Yds	TD	Rate
Jim Kelly	448	285	63.6	3114	22	84.6
Frank Reich	93	56	60.2	568	1	63.4

Interceptions: Kelly 17, Reich 4.

Top Receivers	No	Yds	Avg	Long	TD
Andre Reed	90	1303	14.5	83-td	8
Thurman Thomas	50	349	7.0	28	2
Pete Metzelaars	49	428	8.7	35-td	5
Bill Brooks	42	482	11.5	32	2
Don Beebe	40	527	13.2	72-td	4

Top Rushers	Car	Yds	Avg	Long	TD
Thurman Thomas	287	1093	3.8	29	7
Kenneth Davis	91	381	4.2	60	2
Carwell Gardner	41	135	3.3	13	4
Andre Reed	10	87	8.7	20	0
Jim Kelly	25	77	3.1	18	1

Most Touchdowns	TD	Run	Rec	Ret	Pts
Thurman Thomas	9	7	2	0	54
Andre Reed	8	0	8	0	48
Pete Metzelaars	5	0	5	0	30
Don Beebe	4	0	4	0	24
Carwell Gardner	4	4	0	0	24

2-pt Conversions: None.

Kicking	PAT/Att	FG/Att	Lg	Pts
Steve Christie	38/38	24/28	52	110

Punts (10 or more)	No	Yds	Long	Avg	In 20
Chris Mohr	67	2799	71	41.8	13

Most Interceptions		Most Sacks	
Matt Darby	4	Bruce Smith	10

Cleveland Browns

Passing (5 Att)	Att	Cmp	Pct	Yds	TD	Rate
Vinny Testaverde	376	207	55.1	2575	16	70.7
Mark Rypien	128	59	46.1	694	4	63.7

Interceptions: Testaverde 18, Rypien 3.

Top Receivers	No	Yds	Avg	Long	TD
Derrick Alexander*	48	828	17.3	81-td	2
Eric Metcalf	47	436	9.3	57-td	3
Leroy Hoard	45	445	9.9	65-td	4
Mark Carrier	29	452	15.6	43	5
Brian Kinchen	24	232	9.7	38	1

Top Rushers	Car	Yds	Avg	Long	TD
Leroy Hoard	209	890	4.3	39	5
Eric Metcalf	93	329	3.5	37-td	2
Earnest Byner	75	219	2.9	15	2
Randy Baldwin	23	78	3.4	16	0
Tommy Vardell	15	48	3.2	9	0

Most Touchdowns	TD	Run	Rec	Ret	Pts
Leroy Hoard	9	5	4	0	54
Eric Metcalf	7	2	3	2	42
Mark Carrier	6	1	5	0	36
Derrick Alexander*	2	0	2	0	14

Three tied with 2 TDs each.

2-pt Conversions: Tom Tupa (3), Alexander.

Kicking	PAT/Att	FG/Att	Lg	Pts
Matt Stover	32/32	26/28	45	110

Punts (10 or more)	No	Yds	Long	Avg	In 20
Tom Tupa	80	3211	65	40.1	27

Most Interceptions		Most Sacks	
Eric Turner	9	Rob Burnett	10

Cincinnati Bengals

Passing (5 Att)	Att	Cmp	Pct	Yds	TD	Rate
Jeff Blake	306	156	51.0	2154	14	76.9
David Klingler	231	131	56.7	1327	6	65.7

Interceptions: Blake 9, Klingler 9.

Top Receivers	No	Yds	Avg	Long	TD
Carl Pickens	71	1127	15.9	70-td	11
Darnay Scott*	46	866	18.8	76	5
Tony McGee	40	492	12.3	54	1
Derrick Fenner	36	276	7.7	29	1
Steve Broussard	34	218	6.4	25	0

Top Rushers	Car	Yds	Avg	Long	TD
Derrick Fenner	141	468	3.3	21	1
Steve Broussard	94	403	4.3	37-td	2
Harold Green	76	223	2.9	22	1
Jeff Blake	37	204	5.5	16	1
Darnay Scott*	10	106	10.6	23	0

Most Touchdowns	TD	Run	Rec	Ret	Pts
Carl Pickens	11	0	11	0	66
Darnay Scott	5	0	5	0	30
Steve Broussard	2	2	0	0	14
Derrick Fenner	2	1	1	0	12
Harold Green	2	1	1	0	12

2-pt Conversions: Jeff Blake, Broussard.

Kicking	PAT/Att	FG/Att	Lg	Pts
Doug Pelfrey	24/25	28/33	54	108

Punts (10 or more)	No	Yds	Long	Avg	In 20
Lee Johnson	79	3461	64	43.8	19

Most Interceptions		Most Sacks	
Louis Oliver	3	Alfred Williams	9½

Denver Broncos

Passing (5 Att)	Att	Cmp	Pct	Yds	TD	Rate
John Elway	494	307	62.1	3490	16	85.7
Hugh Millen	131	81	61.8	893	2	77.6

Interceptions: Elway 10, Millen 3.

Top Receivers	No	Yds	Avg	Long	TD
Shannon Sharpe	87	1010	11.6	44	4
Glyn Milburn	77	549	7.1	33	3
Anthony Miller	60	1107	18.5	76	5
Leonard Russell	38	227	6.0	19	0
Cedric Tillman	28	455	16.3	63	1

Top Rushers	Car	Yds	Avg	Long	TD
Leonard Russell	190	620	3.3	22-td	9
John Elway	58	235	4.1	22	4
Glyn Milburn	58	201	3.5	20	1
Derrick Clark*	56	168	3.0	12	3
Rod Bernstine	17	91	5.4	24	0

Most Touchdowns	TD	Run	Rec	Ret	Pts
Leonard Russell	9	9	0	0	54
Anthony Miller	5	0	5	0	32
Shannon Sharpe	4	0	4	0	28
Glyn Milburn	4	1	3	0	24
John Elway	4	4	0	0	24

2-pt Conversions: Sharpe (2), Miller.

Kicking	PAT/Att	FG/Att	Lg	Pts
Jason Elam	29/29	30/37	54	119

Punts (10 or more)	No	Yds	Long	Avg	In 20
Tom Rouen	76	3258	59	42.9	23

Most Interceptions		Most Sacks	
Three tied with 2 INTs each.		Simon Fletcher	7

Houston Oilers

Passing (5 Att)

	Att	Cmp	Pct	Yds	TD	Rate
Bucky Richardson ..181	94	51.9	1202	6	70.3	
Billy Joe Tolliver 240	121	50.4	1287	6	62.6	
Cody Carlson 132	59	44.7	727	1	52.2	

Interceptions: Tolliver 7, Richardson, 6 Carlson 4.

Top Receivers

	No	Yds	Avg	Long	TD
Webster Slaughter..............68	846	12.4	57	2	
Haywood Jeffires 68	783	11.5	50	6	
Ernest Givins.....................36	521	14.5	76-td	1	
Lorenzo White 21	188	9.0	41	1	
Pat Coleman 20	298	14.9	81	1	
Gary Brown 18	194	10.8	24	1	

Top Rushers

	Car	Yds	Avg	Long	TD
Lorenzo White 191	757	4.0	33	3	
Gary Brown 169	648	3.8	18	4	
Bucky Richardson..............30	217	7.2	18	1	
Billy Joe Tolliver 12	37	3.1	10	2	
Cody Carlson 10	17	1.7	6	0	

Most Touchdowns

	TD	Run	Rec	Ret	Pts
Haywood Jeffires 6	0	6	0	42	
Gary Brown 5	4	1	0	30	
Lorenzo White 4	3	1	0	24	
Billy Joe Tolliver 2	2	0	0	12	
Webster Slaughter..............2	0	2	0	12	
Ernest Givins.....................2	0	1	1	12	

2-pt Conversions: Jeffires (3), Reggie Brown.

Kicking

	PAT/Att	FG/Att	Lg	Pts
Al Del Greco 18/18	16/20	50	66	

Punts (10 or more)

	No	Yds	Long	Avg	In20
Rich Camarillo 96	4115	58	42.9	35	

Most Interceptions | **Most Sacks**

Darryll Lewis ....5 | Lamar Lathon 8½

Indianapolis Colts

Passing (5 Att)

	Att	Cmp	Pct	Yds	TD	Rate
Jim Harbaugh 202	125	61.9	1440	9	85.8	
Don Majkowski 152	84	55.3	1010	6	69.8	
Browning Nagle 21	8	38.1	69	0	27.7	

Interceptions: Harbaugh 6, Majkowski 7, Nagle 1.

Top Receivers

	No	Yds	Avg	Long	TD
Floyd Turner.....................52	593	11.4	28	6	
Marshall Faulk* 52	522	10.0	85-td	1	
Sean Dawkins...................51	742	14.5	49	5	
Roosevelt Potts 26	251	9.7	30	1	
Kerry Cash 16	190	11.9	24	1	

Top Rushers

	Car	Yds	Avg	Long	TD
Marshall Faulk* 314	1282	4.1	52	11	
Roosevelt Potts 77	336	4.4	52	1	
Jim Harbaugh 39	223	5.7	41	0	
Ronald Humphrey 18	85	4.7	27	0	
Lamont Warren* 18	80	4.4	34	0	

Most Touchdowns

	TD	Run	Rec	Ret	Pts
Marshall Faulk* 12	11	1	0	72	
Floyd Turner.....................6	0	6	0	36	
Sean Dawkins...................5	0	5	0	30	
Don Majkowski 3	3	0	0	18	
Ray Buchanan 3	0	0	3	18	

2-pt Conversions: None.

Kicking

	PAT/Att	FG/Att	Lg	Pts
Dean Biasucci.........................37/37	16/24	50	85	

Punts (10 or more)

	No	Yds	Long	Avg	In20
Rohn Stark.......................73	3092	60	42.4	22	

Most Interceptions | **Most Sacks**

Ray Buchanan ....8 | Tony Bennett...................9

Kansas City Chiefs

Passing (5 Att)

	Att	Cmp	Pct	Yds	TD	Rate
Joe Montana.........493	299	60.6	3283	16	83.6	
Steve Bono...........117	66	56.4	796	4	74.6	

Interceptions: Montana 9, Bono 4.

Top Receivers

	No	Yds	Avg	Long	TD
Kimble Anders 67	525	7.8	30	1	
Willie Davis......................51	822	16.1	62-td	5	
J.J. Birden 48	637	13.3	44	4	
Marcus Allen 42	349	8.3	38	0	
Lake Dawson*...................37	537	14.5	50	2	

Top Rushers

	Car	Yds	Avg	Long	TD
Marcus Allen 189	709	3.8	36-td	7	
Greg Hill*......................141	574	4.1	20	1	
Kimble Anders 62	231	3.7	19	2	
Donnell Bennett* 46	178	3.9	17	2	
Jon Vaughn 27	96	3.6	16	1	
SEA.............................27	96	3.6	16	1	
KC.............................0	0	0.0	0	0	

Signed: Vaughn (Nov. 30).

Most Touchdowns

	TD	Run	Rec	Ret	Pts
Marcus Allen 7	7	0	0	44	
Willie Davis......................5	0	5	0	32	
Jon Vaughn 4	1	1	2	26	
SEA.............................3	1	1	1	18	
KC.............................1	0	0	1	6	
J.J. Birden 4	0	4	0	26	

2-pt Conversions: Allen, Birden, W. Davis, Vaughn (with Sea.).

Kicking

	PAT/Att	FG/Att	Lg	Pts
Lin Elliott 30/30	25/30	49	105	

Punts (10 or more)

	No	Yds	Long	Avg	In20
Louie Aguiar.....................85	3582	61	42.1	15	

Most Interceptions | **Most Sacks**

Charles Mincy ....3 | Neil Smith...................11½

Los Angeles Raiders

Passing (5 Att)

	Att	Cmp	Pct	Yds	TD	Rate
Vince Evans 33	18	54.5	222	2	95.8	
Jeff Hostetler 455	263	57.8	3334	20	80.8	

Interceptions: Hostetler 16, Evans 0.

Top Receivers

	No	Yds	Avg	Long	TD
Tim Brown 89	1309	14.7	77-td	9	
Harvey Williams 47	391	8.3	27-td	3	
Rocket Ismail 34	513	15.1	42	5	
Andrew Glover 33	371	11.2	27-td	2	
Tom Rathman 26	194	7.5	18	0	

Top Rushers

	Car	Yds	Avg	Long	TD
Harvey Williams 282	983	3.5	28	4	
Jeff Hostetler 46	159	3.5	14	2	
Tom Rathman 28	118	4.2	14	0	
Tyrone Montgomery 36	97	2.7	15	0	
Calvin Jones*....................22	93	4.2	10	0	

Most Touchdowns

	TD	Run	Rec	Ret	Pts
Tim Brown 9	0	9	0	54	
Harvey Williams 7	4	3	0	44	
Rocket Ismail 5	0	5	0	30	
Terry McDaniel 3	0	0	3	18	

Three tied with two TDs each.

2-pt Conversion: H. Williams.

Kicking

	PAT/Att	FG/Att	Lg	Pts
Jeff Jaeger 31/31	22/28	51	97	

Punts (10 or more)

	No	Yds	Long	Avg	In20
Jeff Gossett......................77	3377	65	43.9	19	

Most Interceptions | **Most Sacks**

Terry McDaniel ....7 | Chester McGlockton 9½

Miami Dolphins

Passing (5 Att)	Att	Cmp	Pct	Yds	TD	Rate
Dan Marino	615	385	62.6	4453	30	89.2
Bernie Kosar	12	7	58.3	80	1	71.5

Interceptions: Marinio 17, Kosar 1.

Top Receivers	No	Yds	Avg	Long	TD
Irving Fryar	73	1270	17.4	54-td	7
Keith Jackson	59	673	11.4	35	7
Keith Byars	49	418	8.5	34	5
Mark Ingram	44	506	11.5	64-td	6
O.J. McDuffie	37	488	13.2	30	3

Top Rushers	Car	Yds	Avg	Long	TD
Bernie Parmalee	216	868	4.0	47-td	6
Irving Spikes*	70	312	4.5	40	2
Terry Kirby	60	233	3.9	30	2
Mark Higgs	19	68	3.6	21	0
Keith Byars	19	64	3.4	12	2

Most Touchdowns	TD	Run	Rec	Ret	Pts
Irving Fryar	7	0	7	0	46
Bernie Parmalee	7	6	1	0	44
Keith Jackson	7	0	7	0	44
Keith Byars	7	2	5	0	42
Mark Ingram	6	0	6	0	36

2-pt Conversions: Fryar (2), Aaron Craver, K. Jackson, Terry Kirby, Parmalee.

Kicking	PAT/Att	FG/Att	Lg	Pts
Pete Stoyanovich	35/35	24/31	50	107

Punts (10 or more)	No	Yds	Long	Avg	In20
Jim Arnold	46	1810	53	39.3	14
John Kidd	21	848	58	40.4	3
SD	7	246	53	35.1	1
MIA	14	602	58	43.0	2

Signed: Kidd (Nov. 30).

Most Interceptions		Most Sacks	
Troy Vincent	5	Jeff Cross	9½

New York Jets

Passing (5 Att)	Att	Cmp	Pct	Yds	TD	Rate
Boomer Esiason	440	255	58.0	2782	17	77.3
Jack Trudeau	91	50	54.9	496	1	55.9
Glenn Foley*	8	5	62.5	45	0	38.0

Interceptions: Esiason 13, Trudeau 4, Foley 1.

Top Receivers	No	Yds	Avg	Long	TD
Rob Moore	78	1010	12.9	41-td	6
Johnny Mitchell	58	749	12.9	55	4
Art Monk	46	581	12.6	69	3
Johnny Johnson	42	303	7.2	24	2
Richie Anderson	25	212	8.5	27-td	1

Top Rushers	Car	Yds	Avg	Long	TD
Johnny Johnson	240	931	3.9	90	3
Richie Anderson	43	207	4.8	55	1
Brad Baxter	60	170	2.8	13	4
Adrian Murrell	33	160	4.8	19	0
Boomer Esiason	28	59	2.1	15	0

Most Touchdowns	TD	Run	Rec	Ret	Pts
Rob Moore	6	0	6	0	40
Johnny Johnson	5	3	2	0	30
Brad Baxter	4	4	0	0	24
Johnny Mitchell	4	0	4	0	24
Art Monk	3	0	3	0	18

2-pt Conversions: Moore (2).

Kicking	PAT/Att	FG/Att	Lg	Pts
Nick Lowery	26/27	20/23	49	86

Punts (10 or more)	No	Yds	Long	Avg	In20
Brian Hansen	84	3534	64	42.1	25

Most Interceptions		Most Sacks	
James Hasty	5	Jeff Lageman	6½
Marcus Turner	5		

New England Patriots

Passing (5 Att)	Att	Cmp	Pct	Yds	TD	Rate
Drew Bledsoe	691	400	57.9	4555	25	73.6
Scott Zolak	8	5	62.5	28	0	68.8

Interceptions: Bledsoe 27, Zolak 0.

Top Receivers	No	Yds	Avg	Long	TD
Ben Coates	96	1174	12.2	62-td	7
Michael Timpson	74	941	12.7	37	3
Leroy Thompson	65	465	7.2	27-td	5
Vincent Brisby	58	904	15.6	43	5
Kevin Turner	52	471	9.1	32	2
Ray Crittenden	28	379	13.5	32	3

Top Rushers	Car	Yds	Avg	Long	TD
Marion Butts	243	703	2.9	26	8
Leroy Thompson	102	312	3.1	13	2
Kevin Turner	36	111	3.1	13	1
Sam Gash	30	86	2.9	10	0

Most Touchdowns	TD	Run	Rec	Ret	Pts
Marion Butts	8	8	0	0	48
Ben Coates	7	0	7	0	42
Leroy Thompson	7	2	5	0	42
Vincent Brisby	5	0	5	0	30

Three tied with 3 TDs each.

2-pt Conversions: None.

Kicking	PAT/Att	FG/Att	Lg	Pts
Matt Bahr	36/36	27/34	48	117
Pat O'Neill*	0/0	0/1	0	0

Punts (10 or more)	No	Yds	Long	Avg	In20
Pat O'Neill*	69	2841	67	41.2	25

Most Interceptions		Most Sacks	
Maurice Hurst	7	Chris Slade	9½

Pittsburgh Steelers

Passing (5 Att)	Att	Cmp	Pct	Yds	TD	Rate
Mike Tomczak	93	54	58.1	804	4	100.8
Neil O'Donnell	370	212	57.3	2443	13	78.9

Interceptions: O'Donnell 9, Tomczak 0.

Top Receivers	No	Yds	Avg	Long	TD
John L. Williams	51	378	7.4	23	2
Eric Green	46	618	13.4	46	4
Charles Johnson*	38	577	15.2	84-td	3
Yancey Thigpen	36	546	15.2	60-td	4
Bam Morris*	22	204	9.3	49	0

Top Rushers	Car	Yds	Avg	Long	TD
Barry Foster	216	851	3.9	29-td	5
Bam Morris*	198	836	4.2	20	7
John L. Williams	68	317	4.7	23	1
Neil O'Donnell	31	80	2.6	18	1

Most Touchdowns	TD	Run	Rec	Ret	Pts
Bam Morris*	7	7	0	0	42
Barry Foster	5	5	0	0	30
Yancey Thigpen	4	0	4	0	24
Eric Green	4	0	4	0	24
John L. Williams	3	1	2	0	18
Charles Johnson	3	0	3	0	18

2-pt Conversion: Dwight Stone.

Kicking	PAT/Att	FG/Att	Lg	Pts
Gary Anderson	32/32	24/29	50	104

Punts (10 or more)	No	Yds	Long	Avg	In20
Mark Royals	97	3849	64	39.7	35

Most Interceptions		Most Sacks	
Darren Perry	7	Kevin Greene	14

San Diego Chargers

Passing (5 Att)

	Att	Cmp	Pct	Yds	TD	Rate
Gale Gilbert	67	41	61.2	410	3	87.3
Stan Humphries	453	264	58.3	3209	17	81.6

Interceptions: Humphries 12, Gilbert 1.

Top Receivers

	No	Yds	Avg	Long	TD
Mark Seay	58	645	11.1	49-td	6
Ronnie Harmon	58	615	10.6	35	1
Tony Martin	50	885	17.7	99-td	7
Shawn Jefferson	43	627	14.6	52-td	3
Natrone Means	39	235	6.0	22	0

Top Rushers

	Car	Yds	Avg	Long	TD
Natrone Means	343	1350	3.9	25	12
Eric Bieniemy	73	295	4.0	36	0
Ronnie Harmon	25	94	3.8	15-td	1
Rodney Culver	8	63	7.9	22	0
Shawn Jefferson	3	40	13.3	22	0

Most Touchdowns

	TD	Run	Rec	Ret	Pts
Natrone Means	12	12	0	0	72
Tony Martin	7	0	7	0	42
Mark Seay	6	0	6	0	36
Shawn Jefferson	3	0	3	0	18

Five tied with two TDs each.

2-pt Conversions: Ronnie Harmon (3).

Kicking

	PAT/Att	FG/Att	Lg	Pts
John Carney	33/33	34/38	50	135

Punts (10 or more)

	No	Yds	Long	Avg	In20
Bryan Wagner	65	2705	59	41.6	20

Most Interceptions
Darrien Gordon 4
Stanley Richard 4

Most Sacks
Leslie O'Neal 12½

Seattle Seahawks

Passing (5 Att)

	Att	Cmp	Pct	Yds	TD	Rate
Stan Gelbaugh	11	7	63.6	80	1	115.7
Rick Mirer	381	195	51.2	2151	11	70.2
Dan McGwire	105	51	48.6	578	1	60.7

Interceptions: Mirer 7, McGwire 2, Gelbaugh 0.

Top Receivers

	No	Yds	Avg	Long	TD
Brian Blades	81	1086	13.4	45	4
Kelvin Martin	56	681	12.2	32	1
Chris Warren	41	323	7.9	51	2
Paul Green	30	208	6.9	20	1
Steve Smith	11	142	12.9	25	1

Top Rushers

	Car	Yds	Avg	Long	TD
Chris Warren	333	1545	4.6	41	9
Rick Mirer	34	153	4.5	14	0
Mack Strong	27	114	4.2	14	0
Steve Smith	26	80	3.1	12	0
Tracy Johnson	12	44	3.7	14	2

Most Touchdowns

	TD	Run	Rec	Ret	Pts
Chris Warren	11	9	2	0	68
Brian Blades	4	0	4	0	26
Steve Smith	3	2	1	0	18
Mack Strong	2	2	0	0	12
Tracy Johnson	2	2	0	0	12

2-pt Conversions: Blades, Rick Tuten, C. Warren.

Kicking

	PAT/Att	FG/Att	Lg	Pts
John Kasay	25/26	20/24	50	85

Punts (10 or more)

	No	Yds	Long	Avg	In20
Rick Tuten	91	3905	64	42.9	33

Most Interceptions
Four tied with 3 INTs each.

Most Sacks
Michael Sinclair 4½

NFC Team by Team Statistics

Players with more than one team during the regular season are listed with second club; (*) indicates rookies.

Arizona Cardinals

Passing (5 Att)

	Att	Cmp	Pct	Yds	TD	Rate
Jay Schroeder	238	133	55.9	1510	4	68.4
Steve Beuerlein	255	130	51.0	1545	5	61.6
Jim McMahon	43	23	53.5	219	1	46.6

Interceptions: Beuerlein 9, Schroeder 7, McMahon 3.

Top Receivers

	No	Yds	Avg	Long	TD
Larry Centers	77	647	8.4	36	2
Ricky Proehl	51	651	12.8	63	5
Gary Clark	50	771	15.4	45	1
Randal Hill	38	544	14.3	51	0

Top Rushers

	Car	Yds	Avg	Long	TD
Ron Moore	232	780	3.4	24	4
Larry Centers	115	336	2.9	17	5
Mark Higgs	62	195	3.1	21	0
MIA	19	68	3.6	21	0
ARIZ	43	127	3.0	16	0

Signed: Higgs (Nov. 17).

Most Touchdowns

	TD	Run	Rec	Ret	Pts
Larry Centers	7	5	2	0	42
Ron Moore	5	4	1	0	32
Ricky Proehl	5	0	5	0	30

2-pt Conversion: R. Moore.

Kicking

	PAT/Att	FG/Att	Lg	Pts
Greg Davis	17/17	20/26	51	77
Todd Peterson	4/4	2/4	35	10

Acquired: Peterson (Oct. 12). **Waived:** Peterson (Oct. 24).

Punts (10 or more)

	No	Yds	Long	Avg	In20
Jeff Feagles	98	3997	54	40.8	33

Most Interceptions
Aeneas Williams 9

Most Sacks
Eric Swann 7

Atlanta Falcons

Passing (5 Att)

	Att	Cmp	Pct	Yds	TD	Rate
Jeff George	524	322	61.5	3734	23	83.3
Bobby Hebert	103	52	50.5	610	2	51.0

Interceptions: George 18, Hebert 6.

Top Receivers

	No	Yds	Avg	Long	TD
Terance Mathis	111	1342	12.1	81	11
Andre Rison	81	1088	13.4	69-td	8
Ricky Sanders	67	599	8.9	28	1
Bert Emanuel*	46	649	14.1	85-td	4
Craig Heyward	32	335	10.5	34	1

Top Rushers

	Car	Yds	Avg	Long	TD
Craig Heyward	183	779	4.3	17	7
Erric Pegram	103	358	3.5	25	1
Jeff George	30	66	2.2	10	0
Bobby Hebert	9	43	4.8	20	0

Most Touchdowns

	TD	Run	Rec	Ret	Pts
Terance Mathis	11	0	11	0	70
Andre Rison	8	0	8	0	50
Craig Heyward	8	7	1	0	48
Bert Emanuel*	4	0	4	0	24

2-pt Conversions: Mathis (2), Rison.

Kicking

	PAT/Att	FG/Att	Lg	Pts
Norm Johnson	32/32	21/25	50	95

Punts (10 or more)

	No	Yds	Long	Avg	In20
Harold Alexander	71	2836	61	39.9	12

Most Interceptions
D.J. Johnson 5

Most Sacks
Chuck Smith 11

Chicago Bears

Passing (5 Att)	Att	Cmp	Pct	Yds	TD	Rate
Erik Kramer	158	99	62.7	1129	8	79.9
Steve Walsh	343	208	60.6	2078	10	77.9

Interceptions: Walsh 8, Kramer 8.

Top Receivers	No	Yds	Avg	Long	TD
Jeff Graham	68	944	13.9	76-td	4
Curtis Conway	39	546	14.0	85-td	2
Raymont Harris*	39	236	6.1	18	0
Lewis Tillman	27	222	8.2	39	0
Tom Waddle	25	244	9.8	22	1

Top Rushers	Car	Yds	Avg	Long	TD
Lewis Tillman	275	899	3.3	25-td	7
Raymont Harris*	123	464	3.8	13	1
Robert Green	25	122	4.9	14	0
Curtis Conway	6	31	5.2	12	0
Bob Christian	7	29	4.1	8	0

Most Touchdowns	TD	Run	Rec	Ret	Pts
Lewis Tillman	7	7	0	0	42
Jeff Graham	5	0	4	1	32
Chris Gedney	3	0	3	0	18
Keith Jennings	3	0	3	0	18
Curtis Conway	2	0	2	0	14
Robert Green	2	0	2	0	12

2-pt Conversions: Conway, Graham.

Kicking	PAT/Att	FG/Att	Lg	Pts
Kevin Butler	24/24	21/29	52	87

Punts (10 or more)	No	Yds	Long	Avg	In20
Chris Gardocki	76	2871	57	37.8	23

Most Interceptions		Most Sacks	
Donnell Woolford	5	Trace Armstrong	7½

Detroit Lions

Passing (5 Att)	Att	Cmp	Pct	Yds	TD	Rate
Dave Krieg	212	131	61.8	1629	14	101.7
Scott Mitchell	246	119	48.4	1456	10	62.0

Interceptions: Mitchell 11, Krieg 3.

Top Receivers	No	Yds	Avg	Long	TD
Herman Moore	72	1173	16.3	51-td	11
Brett Perriman	56	761	13.6	39	4
Barry Sanders	44	283	6.4	22	1
Rodney Holman	17	163	9.6	18	0
Ron Hall	10	106	10.6	18	0

Top Rushers	Car	Yds	Avg	Long	TD
Barry Sanders	331	1883	5.7	85	7
Brett Perriman	9	86	9.6	25	0
Derrick Moore	27	52	1.9	12	4
Dave Krieg	23	35	1.5	15	0
Scott Mitchell	15	24	1.6	7	1

Most Touchdowns	TD	Run	Rec	Ret	Pts
Herman Moore	11	0	11	0	66
Barry Sanders	8	7	1	0	48
Brett Perriman	4	0	4	0	28
Derrick Moore	4	4	0	0	24

Three tied with three TDs each.

2-pt Conversions: Perriman (2).

Kicking	PAT/Att	FG/Att	Lg	Pts
Jason Hanson	39/40	18/27	49	93

Punts (10 or more)	No	Yds	Long	Avg	In20
Greg Montgomery	63	2782	64	44.2	19

Most Interceptions		Most Sacks	
Robert Massey	4	Broderick Thomas	7

Dallas Cowboys

Passing (5 Att)	Att	Cmp	Pct	Yds	TD	Rate
Rodney Peete	56	33	58.9	470	4	102.5
Jason Garrett	31	16	51.6	315	2	95.5
Troy Aikman	361	233	64.5	2676	13	84.9

Interceptions: Aikman 12, Peete 1, Garrett 1.

Top Receivers	No	Yds	Avg	Long	TD
Michael Irvin	79	1241	15.7	65-td	6
Emmitt Smith	50	341	6.8	68	1
Jay Novacek	47	475	10.1	27	2
Daryl Johnston	44	325	7.4	24	2
Alvin Harper	33	821	24.9	90	8

Top Rushers	Car	Yds	Avg	Long	TD
Emmitt Smith	368	1484	4.0	46	21
Lincoln Coleman	64	180	2.8	13	1
Daryl Johnston	40	138	3.5	9-td	2
Blair Thomas	43	137	3.2	13	2
NE	19	67	3.5	13	1
DAL	24	70	2.9	11	1

Signed: Thomas (Nov. 30).

Most Touchdowns	TD	Run	Rec	Ret	Pts
Emmitt Smith	22	21	1	0	132
Alvin Harper	8	0	8	0	48
Michael Irvin	6	0	6	0	36
Daryl Johnston	4	2	2	0	24

Three tied with two TDs each.

2-pt Conversions: None.

Kicking	PAT/Att	FG/Att	Lg	Pts
Chris Boniol*	48/48	22/29	47	114

Punts (10 or more)	No	Yds	Long	Avg	In20
John Jett	70	2935	58	41.9	26

Most Interceptions		Most Sacks	
James Washington	5	Charles Haley	12½
Darren Woodson	5		

Green Bay Packers

Passing (5 Att)	Att	Cmp	Pct	Yds	TD	Rate
Brett Favre	582	363	62.4	3882	33	90.7
Mark Brunell	27	12	44.4	95	0	53.8

Interceptions: Favre 14, Brunell 0.

Top Receivers	No	Yds	Avg	Long	TD
Sterling Sharpe	94	1119	11.9	49	18
Edgar Bennett	78	546	7.0	40	4
Robert Brooks	58	648	11.2	35	4
Reggie Cobb	35	299	8.5	37-td	1
Ed West	31	377	12.2	26	2

Top Rushers	Car	Yds	Avg	Long	TD
Edgar Bennett	178	623	3.5	39-td	5
Reggie Cobb	153	579	3.8	30	3
Brett Favre	42	202	4.8	36-td	2
LeShon Johnson*	26	99	3.8	43	0

Most Touchdowns	TD	Run	Rec	Ret	Pts
Sterling Sharpe	18	0	18	0	108
Edgar Bennett	9	5	4	0	54
Robert Brooks	6	0	4	2	36
Reggie Cobb	4	3	1	0	24
Anthony Morgan	4	0	4	0	24

2-pt Conversion: Ed West.

Kicking	PAT/Att	FG/Att	Lg	Pts
Chris Jacke	41/43	19/26	50	98

Punts (10 or more)	No	Yds	Long	Avg	In20
Craig Hentrich	81	3351	70	41.4	24

Most Interceptions		Most Sacks	
Terrell Buckley	5	Sean Jones	10½

Los Angeles Rams

Passing (5 Att)	Att	Cmp	Pct	Yds	TD	Rate
Chris Chandler	176	108	61.4	1352	7	93.8
Chris Miller	317	173	54.6	2104	16	73.6
Tommy Maddox	19	10	52.6	141	0	37.3

Interceptions: Miller 14, Chandler 2, Maddox 2.

Top Receivers	No	Yds	Avg	Long	TD
Johnny Bailey	58	516	8.9	28	0
Willie Anderson	46	945	20.5	72-td	5
Jessie Hester	45	644	14.3	41	3
Troy Drayton	32	276	8.6	22-td	6
Jerome Bettis	31	293	9.5	34	1

Top Rushers	Car	Yds	Avg	Long	TD
Jerome Bettis	319	1025	3.2	19	3
Chris Miller	20	100	5.0	16	0
Chris Chandler	18	61	3.4	22	1
Todd Kinchen	1	44	44.0	44-td	1
Johnny Bailey	11	35	3.2	9	1

Most Touchdowns	TD	Run	Rec	Ret	Pts
Troy Drayton	6	0	6	0	36
Willie Anderson	5	0	5	0	30
Jerome Bettis	4	3	1	0	28
Todd Kinchen	4	1	3	0	24
Jessie Hester	3	0	3	0	18
Isaac Bruce*	3	0	3	0	18

2-pt Conversions: Bettis (2).

Kicking	PAT/Att	FG/Att	Lg	Pts
Tony Zendejas	28/28	18/23	47	82

Punts (10 or more)	No	Yds	Long	Avg	In20
Sean Landeta	78	3494	62	44.8	23

Most Interceptions		Most Sacks	
Darryl Henley	3	Robert Young	6½
Marquez Pope	3		

Minnesota Vikings

Passing (5 Att)	Att	Cmp	Pct	Yds	TD	Rate
Warren Moon	601	371	61.7	4264	18	79.9
Brad Johnson	37	22	59.5	150	0	68.5
Sean Salisbury	34	16	47.1	156	0	48.2

Interceptions: Moon 19, Johnson 0, Salisbury 1.

Top Receivers	No	Yds	Avg	Long	TD
Cris Carter	122	1256	10.3	65-td	7
Jake Reed	85	1175	13.8	59	4
Qadry Ismail	45	696	15.5	65-td	5
Amp Lee	45	368	8.2	35	2
Andrew Jordan*	35	336	9.6	25	0
Adrian Cooper	32	363	11.3	34	0

Top Rushers	Car	Yds	Avg	Long	TD
Terry Allen	255	1031	4.0	45	8
Scottie Graham	64	207	3.2	11	2
Robert Smith	31	106	3.4	14-td	1
Amp Lee	29	104	3.6	16	0

Most Touchdowns	TD	Run	Rec	Ret	Pts
Terry Allen	8	8	0	0	50
Cris Carter	7	0	7	0	46
Qadry Ismail	5	0	5	0	30
Jake Reed	4	0	4	0	24
Dewayne Washington*	3	0	0	3	18
Anthony Parker	3	0	0	3	18

2-pt Conversions: Carter (2), Allen, Andrew Jordan.

Kicking	PAT/Att	FG/Att	Lg	Pts
Fuad Reveiz	30/30	34/39	51	132

Punts (10 or more)	No	Yds	Long	Avg	In20
Mike Saxon	77	3301	67	42.9	28

Most Interceptions		Most Sacks	
Vencie Glenn	4	John Randle	13½
Anthony Parker	4		

New Orleans Saints

Passing (5 Att)	Att	Cmp	Pct	Yds	TD	Rate
Wade Wilson	28	20	71.4	172	0	87.2
Jim Everett	540	346	64.1	3855	22	84.9

Interceptions: Everett 18, Wilson 0.

Top Receivers	No	Yds	Avg	Long	TD
Quinn Early	82	894	10.9	33	4
Michael Haynes	77	985	12.8	78-td	5
Torrance Small	49	719	14.7	75-td	5
Derek Brown	44	428	9.7	37	1
Irv Smith	41	330	8.0	19	3
Wesley Walls	38	406	10.7	31	4

Top Rushers	Car	Yds	Avg	Long	TD
Mario Bates*	151	579	3.8	40	6
Derek Brown	146	489	3.3	16	3
Lorenzo Neal	30	90	3.0	12	1

Most Touchdowns	TD	Run	Rec	Ret	Pts
Mario Bates*	6	6	0	0	36
Torrance Small	5	0	5	0	32
Michael Haynes	5	0	5	0	30
Wesley Walls	4	0	4	0	26

Three tied with 4 TDs each.

2-pt Conversions: Small, Walls.

Kicking	PAT/Att	FG/Att	Lg	Pts
Morten Andersen	32/32	28/39	48	116

Punts (10 or more)	No	Yds	Long	Avg	In20
Tommy Barnhardt	67	2920	57	43.6	14

Most Interceptions		Most Sacks	
Vinnie Clark	5	Darion Conner	10½
ATL	4		
NO.	1		
Jimmy Spencer	5		

Signed: Clark (Nov. 23).

New York Giants

Passing (5 Att)	Att	Cmp	Pct	Yds	TD	Rate
Dave Brown	350	201	57.4	2536	12	72.5
Kent Graham	53	24	45.3	295	3	66.2

Interceptions: Brown 16, Graham 2.

Top Receivers	No	Yds	Avg	Long	TD
Mike Sherrard	53	825	15.6	55	6
Chris Calloway	43	666	15.5	51-td	2
Dave Meggett	32	293	9.2	34	0
Howard Cross	31	364	11.7	40	4
Aaron Pierce	20	214	10.7	29	4

Top Rushers	Car	Yds	Avg	Long	TD
Rodney Hampton	327	1075	3.3	27-td	6
Dave Meggett	91	298	3.3	26-td	4
Dave Brown	60	196	3.3	21	2
Chris Calloway	8	77	9.6	20	0
Gary Downs*	15	51	3.4	8	0

Most Touchdowns	TD	Run	Rec	Ret	Pts
Rodney Hampton	6	6	0	0	38
Dave Meggett	4	0	2	2	36
Mike Sherrard	6	0	6	0	36
Aaron Pierce	4	0	4	0	24
Howard Cross	4	0	4	0	24

2-pt Conversion: Hampton.

Kicking	PAT/Att	FG/Att	Lg	Pts
David Treadwell	22/23	11/17	41	55
Brad Daluiso	5/5	11/11	52	38

Punts (10 or more)	No	Yds	Long	Avg	In20
Mike Horan	85	3521	63	41.4	25

Most Interceptions		Most Sacks	
John Booty	3	Keith Hamilton	6½
Phillippi Sparks	3	Erik Howard	6½

Philadelphia Eagles

Passing (5 Att)	Att	Cmp	Pct	Yds	TD	Rate
Bubby Brister	76	51	67.1	507	2	89.1
R. Cunningham	490	265	54.1	3229	16	74.4

Interceptions: Cunningham 13, Brister 1.

Top Receivers	No	Yds	Avg	Long	TD
Fred Barnett	78	1127	14.4	54	5
Calvin Williams	58	813	14.0	53	3
Herschel Walker	50	500	10.0	93	2
James Joseph	43	344	8.0	35-td	2
Maurice Johnson	21	204	9.7	22	2

Top Rushers	Car	Yds	Avg	Long	TD
Herschel Walker	113	528	4.7	91-td	5
Charlie Garner*	109	399	3.7	28-td	3
Vaughn Hebron	82	325	4.0	19	2
R. Cunningham	65	288	4.4	22	3
James Joseph	60	203	3.4	34-td	1

Most Touchdowns	TD	Run	Rec	Ret	Pts
Herschel Walker	8	5	2	1	48
Fred Barnett	5	0	5	0	30

Four tied with 3 TDs each.

2-pt Conversions: None.

Kicking	PAT/Att	FG/Att	Lg	Pts
Eddie Murray	33/33	21/25	42	96

Punts (10 or more)	No	Yds	Long	Avg	In20
Bryan Barker	66	2696	67	40.8	20
Mitch Berger*	25	951	57	38.0	8

Most Interceptions
Greg Jackson 6

Most Sacks
William Fuller 9½

San Francisco 49ers

Passing (5 Att)	Att	Cmp	Pct	Yds	TD	Rate
Steve Young	461	324	70.3	3969	35	112.8
Elvis Grbac	50	35	70.0	393	2	98.2

Interceptions: Young 10, Grbac 1.

Top Receivers	No	Yds	Avg	Long	TD
Jerry Rice	112	1499	13.4	69-td	13
Ricky Watters	66	719	10.9	65-td	5
Brent Jones	49	670	13.7	69-td	9
John Taylor	41	531	13.0	35	5
Nate Singleton	21	294	14.0	43-td	2

Top Rushers	Car	Yds	Avg	Long	TD
Ricky Watters	239	877	3.7	23	6
William Floyd*	87	305	3.5	26	6
Steve Young	58	293	5.1	27	7
Marc Logan	33	143	4.3	22	1
Derek Loville	31	99	3.2	13	0

Most Touchdowns	TD	Run	Rec	Ret	Pts
Jerry Rice	15	2	13	0	92
Ricky Watters	11	6	5	0	66
Brent Jones	9	0	9	0	56
Steve Young	7	7	0	0	42
William Floyd*	6	6	0	0	36
John Taylor	5	0	5	0	30

2-pt Conversions: Jones, Rice.

Kicking	PAT/Att	FG/Att	Lg	Pts
Doug Brien*	60/62	15/20	48	105

Punts (10 or more)	No	Yds	Long	Avg	In20
Klaus Wilmsmeyer	54	2235	60	41.4	18

Most Interceptions
Merton Hanks 7
Deion Sanders 6

Most Sacks
Dana Stubblefield 8½

Tampa Bay Buccaneers

Passing (5 Att)	Att	Cmp	Pct	Yds	TD	Rate
Casey Weldon	9	7	77.8	63	0	95.8
Craig Erickson	399	225	56.4	2919	16	82.5
Trent Dilfer*	82	38	46.3	433	1	36.3

Interceptions: Erickson 10, Dilfer 6, Weldon 0.

Top Receivers	No	Yds	Avg	Long	TD
Lawrence Dawsey	46	673	14.6	46	1
Courtney Hawkins	37	438	11.8	32	5
Charles Wilson	31	652	21.0	71-td	6
Anthony McDowell	29	193	6.7	19	1
Jackie Harris	26	337	13.0	48-td	3

Top Rushers	Car	Yds	Avg	Long	TD
Errict Rhett*	284	1011	3.6	27	7
Vince Workman	79	291	3.7	18	0
Craig Erickson	26	68	2.6	17	1
Anthony McDowell	21	58	2.8	8	0

Most Touchdowns	TD	Run	Rec	Ret	Pts
Errict Rhett*	7	7	0	0	44
Charles Wilson	6	0	6	0	36
Courtney Hawkins	5	0	5	0	30
Jackie Harris	3	0	3	0	18

2-pt Conversions: Horace Copeland, J. Harris, Rhett.

Kicking	PAT/Att	FG/Att	Lg	Pts
Michael Husted	20/20	23/35	53	89

Punts (10 or more)	No	Yds	Long	Avg	In20
Dan Stryzinski	72	2800	53	38.9	20

Most Interceptions
Martin Mayhew 2
Hardy Nickerson 2

Most Sacks
Brad Culpepper 4

Washington Redskins

Passing (5 Att)	Att	Cmp	Pct	Yds	TD	Rate
John Friesz	180	105	58.3	1266	10	77.7
Gus Frerotte*	100	46	46.0	600	5	61.3
Heath Shuler*	265	120	45.3	1658	10	59.6

Interceptions: Shuler 12, Friesz 9, Frerotte 5.

Top Receivers	No	Yds	Avg	Long	TD
Henry Ellard	74	1397	18.9	73-td	6
Ricky Ervins	51	293	5.7	21	1
Desmond Howard	40	727	18.2	81-td	5
Brian Mitchell	26	236	9.1	46-td	1
Tydus Winans*	19	344	18.1	51	2

Top Rushers	Car	Yds	Avg	Long	TD
Ricky Ervins	185	650	3.5	49	3
Brian Mitchell	78	311	4.0	33	0
Reggie Brooks	100	297	3.0	15	2
Heath Shuler	26	103	4.0	26	0
Cedric Smith	10	48	4.8	13	0

Most Touchdowns	TD	Run	Rec	Ret	Pts
Henry Ellard	6	0	6	0	36
Desmond Howard	5	0	5	0	32
James Jenkins	4	0	4	0	24
Ricky Ervins	4	3	1	0	24
Brian Mitchell	3	0	1	2	20
Ethan Horton	3	0	3	0	18

2-pt Conversions: Howard, Mitchell, Tydus Winans.

Kicking	PAT/Att	FG/Att	Lg	Pts
Chip Lohmiller	30/32	20/28	54	90

Punts (10 or more)	No	Yds	Long	Avg	In20
Reggie Roby	82	3639	65	44.4	21

Most Interceptions
Andre Collins 4

Most Sacks
Ken Harvey 13½

NFL PLAYOFFS

| 1ST ROUND | SEMIFINALS | FINAL | | FINAL | SEMIFINALS | 1ST ROUND |

- † Kansas City 17
- Miami 27
- Miami 21
- San Diego 22
- San Diego 17
- † New England 13
- † Cleveland 20
- Cleveland 9
- **AFC**
- Pittsburgh 13
- San Diego 26
- San Francisco 49
- Pittsburgh 29
- **NFC**
- Dallas 28
- Dallas 35
- San Francisco 38
- Chicago 15
- San Francisco 44
- Green Bay 9
- † Detroit 12
- † Green Bay 16
- † Chicago 35
- Minnesota 18

Jan. 29, 1995
Joe Robbie Stadium, Miami

† Wild Card Team

† Wild Card Team

Game Summaries

Team records listed in parentheses indicate records before game.

WILD CARD ROUND

AFC

● Dolphins, 27-17

Kansas City (9-7)	14	3	0	0—	**17**
Miami (10-6)	7	10	10	0—	**27**

Date— Dec. 31. **Att**— 67,487. **Time**— 2:47.

1st Quarter: KC— Derrick Walker 1-yd pass from Joe Montana (Lin Elliott kick), 6:28. MIA— Bernie Parmalee 1-yd run (Pete Stoyanovich kick), 12:40. KC— Kimble Anders 57-yd pass from Montana (Elliott kick), 14:20.

2nd Quarter: MIA— Stoyanovich 40-yd FG, 2:45. KC— Elliott 21-yd FG, 8:48. MIA— Ronnie Williams 1-yd pass from Dan Marino (Stoyanovich kick), 14:38.

3rd Quarter: MIA— Irving Fryar 7-yd pass from Marino (Stoyanovich kick), 3:02. MIA— Stoyanovich 40-yd FG, 13:14.

● Browns, 20-13

New England (10-6)	0	10	0	3—	**13**
Cleveland (11-5)	3	7	7	3—	**20**

Date— Jan. 1. **Att**— 78,512. **Time**— 2:57.

1st Quarter: CLE— Matt Stover 30-yd FG, 7:20.

2nd Quarter: NE— Leroy Thompson 13-yd pass from Drew Bledsoe (Matt Bahr kick), 4:12. CLE— Mark Carrier 5-yd pass from Vinny Testaverde (Stover kick), 7:57. NE— Bahr 23-yd FG, 14:30.

3rd Quarter: CLE— Leroy Hoard 10-yd run (Stover kick), 12:39.

4th Quarter: CLE— Stover 21-yd FG, 11:24. NE— Bahr 33-yd FG, 13:30.

NFC

● Packers, 16-12

Detroit (9-7)	0	0	3	9—	**12**
Green Bay (9-7)	7	3	3	3—	**16**

Date— Dec. 31. **Att**— 58,125. **Time**— 3:07.

1st Quarter: GB— Dorsey Levens 3-yd run (Chris Jacke kick), 7:24.

2nd Quarter: GB— Jacke 51-yd FG, 12:04.

3rd Quarter: DET— Jason Hanson 38-yd FG, 9:22. GB— Jacke 32-yd FG, 14:49.

4th Quarter: DET— Brett Perriman 3-yd pass from Dave Krieg (Hanson kick), 1:25. GB— Jacke 28-yd FG, 9:25. DET— Safety (punter Craig Hentrich forced out of end zone), 15:00.

● Bears, 35-18

Chicago (9-7)	0	14	7	14—	**35**
Minnesota (10-6)	3	6	3	6—	**18**

Date— Jan. 1. **Att**— 60,347. **Time**— 3:14.

1st Quarter: MIN— Fuad Reveiz 29-yd FG, 6:59.

2nd Quarter: CHI— Lewis Tillman 1-yd run (Kevin Butler kick), 3:14. CHI— Keith Jennings 9-yd pass from Steve Walsh (Butler kick), 6:57. MIN— Cris Carter 4-yd pass from Warren Moon (pass failed), 14:41.

3rd Quarter: CHI— Raymont Harris 29-yd run (Butler kick), 2:03. MIN— Reveiz 48-yd FG, 14:55.

4th Quarter: CHI— Jeff Graham 21-yd pass from S. Walsh (Butler kick), 2:18. MIN— Amp Lee 11-yd pass from Moon (pass failed), 9:24. CHI— Kevin Miniefield 48-yd fumble return (Butler kick), 11:55.

NFL Playoffs (Cont.)
DIVISIONAL SEMIFINALS

AFC

🏈 Steelers, 29-9

| Cleveland (12-5) | 0 | 3 | 0 | 6— **9** |
| Pittsburgh (12-4) | 3 | 21 | 3 | 2— **29** |

Date— Jan. 7. **Att**— 58,185. **Time**— 2:56.

1st Quarter: PIT— Gary Anderson 39-yd FG, 9:38.

2nd Quarter: PIT— Eric Green 2-yd pass from Neil O'Donnell (Anderson kick), 0:48. PIT— John L. Williams 26-yd run (Anderson kick), 5:57. CLE— Matt Stover 22-yd FG, 12:23. PIT— Yancey Thigpen 9-yd pass from O'Donnell (Anderson kick), 14:44.

3rd Quarter: PIT— Anderson 40-yd FG, 12:25.

4th Quarter: CLE— Keenan McCardell 20-yd pass from Vinny Testaverde (pass failed), 9:07. PIT— Safety (Carnell Lake tackled Testaverde in end zone), 12:15.

🏈 Chargers, 22-21

| Miami (11-6) | 7 | 14 | 0 | 0— **21** |
| San Diego (11-5) | 0 | 6 | 9 | 7— **22** |

Date— Jan. 8. **Att**— 63,381. **Time**— 3:03.

1st Quarter: MIA— Keith Jackson 8-yd pass from Dan Marino (Pete Stoyanovich kick), 12:36.

2nd Quarter: SD— John Carney 20-yd FG, 4:24. MIA— K. Jackson 9-yd pass from Marino (Stoyanovich kick), 7:39. SD— Carney 21-yd FG, 12:13. MIA— Mike Williams 16-yd pass from Marino (Stoyanovich kick), 14:33.

3rd Quarter: SD— Safety (Reuben Davis tackled Bernie Parmalee in end zone), 8:06. SD— Natrone Means 24-yd run (Carney kick), 12:18.

4th Quarter: SD— Mark Seay 8-yd pass from Stan Humphries (Carney kick), 14:25.

NFC

🏈 49ers, 44-15

| Chicago (10-7) | 3 | 0 | 0 | 12— **15** |
| San Francisco (13-3) | 7 | 23 | 7 | 7— **44** |

Date— Jan. 7. **Att**— 64,644. **Time**— 3:03.

1st Quarter: CHI— Kevin Butler 39-yd FG, 3:58. SF— William Floyd 2-yd run (Doug Brien kick), 11:19.

2nd Quarter: SF— Brent Jones 8-yd pass from Steve Young (kick failed), 0:44. SF— Floyd 4-yd run (Brien kick), 8:56. SF— Brien 36-yd FG, 12:15. SF— S. Young 6-yd run (Brien kick), 13:43.

3rd Quarter: SF— Floyd 1-yd run (Brien kick), 8:01.

4th Quarter: CHI— Jim Flanigan 2-yd pass from Erik Kramer (pass failed), 0:49. SF— Adam Walker 1-yd run (Brien kick), 3:09. CHI— Lewis Tillman 1-yd run (pass failed), 9:16.

🏈 Cowboys, 35-9

| Green Bay (10-7) | 3 | 6 | 0 | 0— **9** |
| Dallas (12-4) | 14 | 14 | 0 | 7— **35** |

Date— Jan. 8. **Att**— 64,745. **Time**— 3:20.

1st Quarter: DAL— Emmitt Smith 5-yd run (Chris Boniol kick), 3:53. GB— Chris Jacke 50-yd FG, 7:28. DAL— Alvin Harper 94-yd pass from Troy Aikman (Boniol kick), 11:20.

2nd Quarter: DAL— Blair Thomas 1-yd run (Boniol kick), 8:15. GB— Edgar Bennett 1-yd run (pass failed), 10:29. Dal— Scott Galbraith 1-yd pass from Aikman (Boniol kick), 14:49.

4th Quarter: DAL— B. Thomas 2-yd run (Boniol kick), 3:32.

CONFERENCE CHAMPIONSHIPS

AFC

🏈 Chargers, 17-13

| San Diego (12-5) | 0 | 3 | 7 | 7— **17** |
| Pittsburgh (13-4) | 7 | 3 | 3 | 0— **13** |

Date— Jan. 15. **Att**— 61,545. **Time**— 2:54.

1st Quarter: PIT— John L. Williams 16-yd pass from Neil O'Donnell (Gary Anderson kick), 7:32.

2nd Quarter: SD— John Carney 20-yd FG, 11:19. PIT— Anderson 39-yd FG, 14:51.

3rd Quarter: PIT— Anderson 23-yd FG, 4:23. SD— Alfred Pupunu 43-yd pass from Stan Humphries (Carney kick), 6:57.

4th Quarter: SD— Tony Martin 43-yd pass from Humphries (Carney kick), 9:47.

NFC

🏈 49ers, 38-28

| Dallas (13-4) | 7 | 7 | 7 | 7— **28** |
| San Francisco (14-3) | 21 | 10 | 7 | 0— **38** |

Date— Jan. 15. **Att**— 69,125. **Time**— 3:26.

1st Quarter: SF— Eric Davis 44-yd interception return (Doug Brien kick), 1:02. SF— Ricky Watters 29-yd pass from Steve Young (Brien kick), 4:19. SF— William Floyd 1-yd run (Brien kick), 7:27. DAL— Michael Irvin 44-yd pass from Troy Aikman (Chris Boniol kick), 12:46.

2nd Quarter: SF— Brien 34-yd FG, 9:06. DAL— Emmitt Smith 4-yd run (Boniol kick), 13:04. SF— Jerry Rice 28-yd pass from S. Young (Brien kick), 14:52.

3rd Quarter: DAL— E. Smith 1-yd run (Boniol kick), 3:12. SF— S. Young 3-yd run (Brien kick), 8:21.

4th Quarter: DAL— Irvin 10-yd pass from Aikman (Boniol kick); 6:31.

Super Bowl XXIX
Sunday, Jan. 29 at Joe Robbie Stadium in Miami

San Diego (13-5)......................7   3   8   8— **26**
San Francisco (15-3)...............14   14   14   7— **49**

1st: SF— Jerry Rice 44-yd pass from Steve Young (Doug Brien kick), 1:24. *Drive:* 59 yards in 3 plays. SF— Ricky Watters 51-yd pass from Young (Brien kick), 4:55. *Drive:* 79 yards in 4 plays. SD— Natrone Means 1-yd run (John Carney kick), 12:16. *Drive:* 78 yds in 13 plays.

2nd: SF— William Floyd 5-yd pass from Young (Brien kick), 1:58. *Drive:* 70 yards in 10 plays. SF— Watters 8-yd pass from Young (Brien kick), 10:16. *Drive:* 49 yards in 9 plays. SD— Carney 31-yd FG, 13:16. *Drive:* 62 yards in 8 plays.

3rd: SF— Watters 9-yd run (Brien kick), 5:25. *Drive:* 62 yards in 7 plays. SF— Rice 15-yd pass from Young (Brien kick), 11:42. *Drive:* 67 yards in 10 plays. SD— Andre Coleman 98-yd kickoff return (2-pt conversion, Mark Seay pass from Stan Humphries), 11:59.

4th: SF— Rice 7-yd pass from Young (Brien kick), 1:11. *Drive:* 32 yards in 6 plays. SD— Tony Martin 30-yd pass from Humphries (2-pt conversion, Alfred Pupunu from Humphries), 12:35. *Drive:* 67 yards in 8 plays.

Favorite: 49ers by 18   **Attendance:** 74,107
Field: Grass   **Time:** 3:36
Weather: Overcast   **TV Rating:** 41.3/62 share (ABC)

MVP: Steve Young, San Francisco, QB

Team Statistics

	Chargers	49ers
Touchdowns	3	7
Rushing	1	1
Passing	1	6
Returns	1	0
Time of possession	28:29	31:31
First downs	20	28
Rushing	5	10
Passing	14	17
Penalties	1	1
3rd down efficiency	6-16	7-13
4th down efficiency	0-4	0-0
Total offense (net yards)	354	449
Plays	76	73
Average gain	4.7	6.2
Carries/yards	19/67	32/133
Passing yards	287	316
Completions/attempts	27/55	25/38
Times sacked/yards lost	2/18	3/15
Return yardage	243	76
Punt returns/yards	3/1	2/12
Kickoff returns/yards	8/242	4/48
Interceptions/yards	0/0	3/16
Fumbles/lost	1/0	2/0
Penalties/yards	6/63	3/18
Punts/average	4/49	5/40
Punts blocked	0	0

Individual Statistics

San Diego Chargers

Passing	Att	Cmp	Pct	Yds	TD	Int
Stan Humphries	49	24	49.0	275	1	2
Gale Gilbert	6	3	50.0	30	0	1
TOTAL	55	27	49.0	305	1	3

Receiving	No	Yds	Avg	Long	TD
Ronnie Harmon	8	68	8.5	20	0
Mark Seay	7	75	10.7	22	0
Alfred Pupunu	4	48	12.0	23	0
Tony Martin	3	59	19.7	30-td	1
Shawn Jefferson	2	15	7.5	9	0
Three tied with one each.					
TOTAL	27	305	11.3	33	1

Rushing	Car	Yds	Avg	Long	TD
Natrone Means	13	33	2.5	11	1
Shawn Jefferson	1	10	10.0	10	0
Ronnie Harmon	2	10	5.0	10	0
Gale Gilbert	1	8	8.0	8	0
Eric Bieniemy	1	3	3.0	3	0
Stan Humphries	1	3	3.0	3	0
TOTAL	19	67	3.5	11	1

Field Goals	20-29	30-29	40-49	50-59	Total
John Carney	0-0	1-1	0-0	0-0	1-1

Punting	No	Yds	Long	Avg	In 20
Bryan Wagner	4	195	55	48.8	0

Punt Returns	FC	Ret	Yds	Long	Avg	TD
Darrien Gordon	2	1	1	1	1.0	0

Kickoff Returns	No	Yds	Long	Avg	TD
Andre Coleman	8	242	98-td	30.3	1

Sacks		Most Tackles	
Raylee Johnson	2	Dennis Gibson	9
Junior Seau	1	Junior Seau	9

San Francisco 49ers

Passing	Att	Cmp	Pct	Yds	TD	Int
Steve Young	36	24	66.7	325	6	0
Bill Musgrave	1	1	100.0	6	0	0
Elvis Grbac	1	0	0.0	0	0	0
TOTAL	38	25	65.8	331	6	0

Receiving	No	Yds	Avg	Long	TD
Jerry Rice	10	149	14.9	44-td	3
John Taylor	4	43	10.8	16	0
William Floyd	4	26	6.5	9	1
Ricky Watters	3	61	20.3	51-td	2
Brent Jones	2	41	20.5	33	0
Two tied with one each.					
TOTAL	25	331	13.2	51	6

Rushing	Car	Yds	Avg	Long	TD
Steve Young	5	49	9.8	21	0
Ricky Watters	15	47	3.1	13	1
William Floyd	9	32	3.6	6	0
Jerry Rice	1	10	10.0	10	0
Dexter Carter	2	−5	−2.5	1	0
TOTAL	32	133	4.2	21	1

Field Goals	20-29	30-29	40-49	50-59	Total
Doug Brien	0-0	0-0	0-1	0-0	0-1

Punting	No	Yds	Long	Avg	In 20
Klaus Wilmsmeyer	5	199	46	39.8	2

Punt Returns	FC	Ret	Yds	Long	Avg	TD
Dexter Carter	0	2	12	11	6.0	0

Kickoff Returns	No	Yds	Long	Avg	TD
Dexter Carter	4	48	18	12.0	0

Interceptions	No	Yds	Long	Avg	TD
Deion Sanders	1	15	15	15.0	0
Toi Cook	1	1	1	1.0	0
Eric Davis	1	0	0	0.0	0

Sacks		Most Tackles	
Dana Stubblefield	1	Tim McDonald	8

Super Bowl Finalists' Playoff Statistics

San Francisco (3-0)

Passing (5 Att)

	Att	Cmp	Pct	Yds	TD	Rate
Steve Young	87	53	60.9	623	9	117.2
Bill Musgrave	1	1	100.0	6	0	91.7
Elvis Grbac	5	2	40.0	47	0	74.6
TOTAL	93	56	60.2	676	9	114.8

Interceptions: None.

Receiving

	No	Yds	Avg	Long	TD
Jerry Rice	16	233	14.6	44-td	4
John Taylor	10	125	12.5	17	0
Brent Jones	10	104	10.4	33	1
Ricky Watters	7	108	15.4	51-td	3
William Floyd	7	42	6.0	9	1
Ted Popson	4	15	3.8	6	0
Two tied with 1 catch each.					
TOTAL	56	676	12.1	51-td	9

Rushing

	Car	Yds	Avg	Long	TD
Ricky Watters	40	174	4.4	15	1
Steve Young	20	128	6.4	24	2
William Floyd	26	77	3.0	64	4
John Taylor	1	15	15.0	15	0
Dexter Carter	5	15	3.0	23	0
Jerry Rice	1	10	10.0	10	0
Adam Walker	3	3	1.0	2	1
Elvis Grbac	4	-5	-1.2	0	0
TOTAL	100	417	4.2	24	8

Touchdowns

	TD	Run	Rec	Ret	Pts
William Floyd	5	4	1	0	30
Jerry Rice	4	0	4	0	24
Ricky Watters	4	1	3	0	24
Steve Young	2	2	0	0	12
Three tied with 1 TD each.					
TOTAL	18	8	9	1	108

Kicking

	PAT/Att	FG/Att	Lg	Pts
Doug Brien	17/18	2/3	36	23

Punts

	No	Yds	Long	Avg	In20
Klaus Wilmsmeyer	12	454	46	37.8	5

Most Interceptions
Eric Davis ... 4

Most Sacks
Tim Harris ... 4½

San Diego (2-1)

Passing (5 Att)

	Att	Cmp	Pct	Yds	TD	Rate
Stan Humphries	114	63	55.3	716	4	67.7
Gale Gilbert	6	3	50.0	30	0	25.0
TOTAL	120	66	55.0	746	4	64.1

Interceptions: Humphries 5, Gilbert 1.

Receiving

	No	Yds	Avg	Long	TD
Ronnie Harmon	16	117	7.3	20	0
Mark Seay	13	136	10.5	22	1
Alfred Pupunu	10	137	13.7	43-td	1
Tony Martin	9	164	18.2	43-td	2
Shawn Jefferson	7	75	10.7	16	0
Natrone Means	6	39	6.5	15	0
Rodney Culver	2	23	11.5	18	0
Three tied with 1 catch each.					
TOTAL	66	746	11.3	43-td	4

Rushing

	Car	Yds	Avg	Long	TD
Natrone Means	57	241	4.2	24-td	2
Eric Bieniemy	5	36	7.2	17	0
Ronnie Harmon	5	22	4.4	10	0
Rodney Culver	6	14	2.3	6	0
Shawn Jefferson	2	13	6.5	10	0
Gale Gilbert	1	8	8.0	8	0
Stan Humphries	7	1	0.1	3	0
TOTAL	83	335	4.0	24-td	2

Touchdowns

	TD	Run	Rec	Ret	Pts
Tony Martin	2	0	2	0	12
Natrone Means	2	2	0	0	12
Alfred Pupunu	1	0	1	0	8*
Mark Seay	1	0	1	0	8*
Andre Coleman	1	0	0	1	6
TOTAL	7	2	4	1	46*

*Includes 2-pt Conversions.

Kicking

	PAT/Att	FG/Att	Lg	Pts
John Carney	5/5	4/4	31	17

Punts

	No	Yds	Long	Avg	In20
Bryan Wagner	11	474	55	43.1	2

Most Interceptions
None

Most Sacks
Raylee Johnson ... 2

49ers' 1994 Schedule

Date	Regular Season	Result	W-L
Sept. 5*	LA Raiders (0-0)	W, 44-14	1-0
Sept.11	at Kansas City (1-0)	L, 17-24	1-1
Sept.18	at LA Rams (1-1)	W, 34-19	2-1
Sept.25	New Orleans (1-2)	W, 24-13	3-1
Oct. 2	Philadelphia (2-1)	L, 8-40	3-2
Oct. 9	at Detroit (2-3)	W, 27-21	4-2
Oct. 16	at Atlanta (4-2)	W, 42-3	5-2
Oct. 23	Tampa Bay (2-4)	W, 41-16	6-2
Oct. 30	OPEN DATE	—	—
Nov. 6	at Washington (2-7)	W, 37-22	7-2
Nov. 13	Dallas (8-1)	W, 21-14	8-2
Nov. 20	LA Rams (4-6)	W, 31-27	9-2
Nov. 28*	at New Orleans (4-7)	W, 35-14	10-2
Dec. 4	Atlanta (6-6)	W, 50-14	11-2
Dec. 11	at San Diego (9-4)	W, 38-15	12-2
Dec. 17	Denver (7-7)	W, 42-19	13-2
Dec. 26*	at Minnesota (9-6)	L, 14-21	13-3

Date	Playoffs	Result	W-L
Jan. 1	Bye	—	—
Jan. 8	Chicago (9-7)	W, 44-15	14-3
Jan. 15	Dallas (13-4)	W, 38-28	15-3
Jan. 29	vs San Diego (13-5)	W, 49-26	16-3

Chargers' 1994 Schedule

Date	Regular Season	Result	W-L
Sept. 4	at Denver (0-0)	W, 37-34	1-0
Sept. 11	Cincinnati (0-1)	W, 27-10	2-0
Sept. 18	at Seattle (2-0)	W, 24-10	3-0
Sept. 25	at LA Raiders (1-2)	W, 26-24	4-0
Oct. 2	OPEN DATE	—	—
Oct. 9	Kansas City (3-1)	W, 20-6	5-0
Oct. 16	at New Orleans (2-4)	W, 36-22	6-0
Oct. 23	Denver (1-5)	L, 15-20	6-1
Oct. 30	Seattle (3-4)	W, 35-15	7-1
Nov. 6	at Atlanta (4-4)	L, 9-10	7-2
Nov. 13	at Kansas City (6-3)	W, 14-13	8-2
Nov. 20	at New England (4-6)	L, 17-23	8-3
Nov. 27	LA Rams (4-7)	W, 31-17	9-3
Dec. 5*	LA Raiders (6-6)	L, 17-24	9-4
Dec. 11	San Francisco (11-2)	L, 15-38	9-5
Dec. 18	at NY Jets (6-8)	W, 21-6	10-5
Dec. 24	Pittsburgh (12-3)	W, 37-34	11-5

Date	Playoffs	Result	W-L
Jan. 1	Bye	—	—
Jan. 8	Miami (10-6)	W, 22-21	12-5
Jan. 15	Pittsburgh (13-4)	W, 17-13	13-5
Jan. 29	vs San Francisco (15-3)	L, 26-49	13-6

Note: (*) indicates Monday night game; listed records of opponents are day of game.

NFL Pro Bowl

45th NFL Pro Bowl Game and 25th AFC-NFC contest (NFC leads series, 14-11). **Date:** Feb. 5 at Aloha Stadium in Honolulu. **Coaches:** Bill Cowher, Pittsburgh (AFC) and Barry Switzer, Dallas (NFC). **Player of the Game:** RB Marshall Faulk of Indianapolis, who rushed for a record 180 yards and caught 2 passes for 27 yards. Faulk broke O.J. Simpson's Pro Bowl rushing mark of 112 yards set in 1973.

AFC	0	17	3	21—**41**
NFC	10	0	3	0—**13**

1st Quarter: NFC— Fuad Reveiz 28-yd FG, 6:55. NFC— Cris Carter 51-yd pass from Steve Young (Reveiz kick), 9:09.

2nd Quarter: AFC— Eric Green 22-yd pass from John Elway (John Carney kick), 0:43. AFC— Carney 22-yd FG, 7:28. AFC— Leroy Hoard 4-yd run (Carney kick), 12:53.

3rd Quarter: NFC— Reveiz 49-yd FG, 4:58. AFC— Carney 23-yd FG, 13:24.

4th Quarter: AFC— Chris Warren 11-yd run (Carney kick), 2:31. AFC— Green 16-yd pass from Jeff Hostetler (Carney kick), 8:17. AFC— Marshall Faulk 49-yd run (Carney kick), 12:31.

Attendance—49,121; **Time**—3:11; **TV Rating**—11.8/20 share (ABC).

STARTING LINEUPS

As voted on by NFL players and coaches.

American Conference

Pos Offense	Pos Defense
WR–Tim Brown, LA	E–Bruce Smith, Buf.
WR–Andre Reed, Buf.	E–Leslie O'Neal, SD
TE–Ben Coates, NE	T–Cortez Kennedy, Sea
T–Richmond Webb, Mia.	T–Michael D. Perry, Cle.
T–Bruce Armstrong, NE	LB–Junior Seau, SD
G–Keith Sims, Mia.	LB–Derrick Thomas, KC
G–Steve Wisniewski, LA	LB–Greg Lloyd, Pit.
C–Dermontti Dawson, Pit.	CB–Rod Woodson, Pit.
QB–Dan Marino, Mia.	CB–Terry McDaniel, LA
RB–Marshall Faulk, Ind.	S–Carnell Lake, Pit.
RB–Natrone Means, SD	S–Eric Turner, Cle.
K–John Carney, SD	P–Rick Tuten, Sea.
KR–Eric Metcalf, Cle.	ST–Steve Tasker, Buf.

Note: OG Wisniewski and QB Marino were injured and unable to play.

National Conference

Pos Offense	Pos Defense
WR–Jerry Rice, SF	E–Reggie White, GB
WR–Cris Carter, Min.	E–Charles Haley, Dal.
TE–Brent Jones, SF	L–John Randle, Min.
T–William Roaf, NO	L–Leon Lett, Dal.
T–Lomas Brown, Det.	LB–Ken Harvey, Wash.
G–Nate Newton, Dal.	LB–Bryce Paup, GB
G–Randall McDaniel, Min.	LB–Chris Spielman, Det.
C–Mark Stepnoski, Dal.	CB–Deion Sanders, SF
QB–Steve Young, SF	CB–Aeneas Williams, Ariz.
RB–Emmitt Smith, Dal.	S–Darren Woodson, Dal.
RB–Barry Sanders, Det.	S–Merton Hanks, SF
K–Fuad Reveiz, Min.	P–Reggie Roby, Wash.
KR–Mel Gray, Det.	ST–Elbert Shelley, Atl.

Note: RB Smith and DE White were injured and unable to play.

Reserves

Offense: WR— Irving Fryar, Mia. and Rob Moore, NY; **TE**— Shannon Sharpe, Den.; **T**— Gary Zimmerman, Den.; **G**— Duval Love, Pit.; **C**— Bruce Matthews, Hou.; **QB**— John Elway, Den. and Drew Bledsoe, NE; **RB**— Chris Warren, Sea.; **FB**— Leroy Hoard, Cle.

Defense: E— Neil Smith, KC; **T**— Chester McGlockton, LA; **LB**— Kevin Greene, Pit. and Bryan Cox, Mia.; **CB**— Dale Carter, KC; **S**— Steve Atwater, Den.

Replacements: OFFENSE— TE Eric Green, Pit. for Sharpe; G Kevin Gogan, LA for Wisniewski; QB Jeff Hostetler, LA for Marino. DEFENSE— DE Rob Burnett, Cle. for N. Smith. NEED PLAYER— Pepper Johnson, Cle., LB.

Reserves

Offense: WR— Sterling Sharpe, GB and Michael Irvin, Dal.; **TE**— Jay Novacek, Dal.; **T**— Mark Tuinei, Dal.; **G**— Jesse Sapolu, SF; **C**— Bart Oates, SF; **QB**— Troy Aikman, Dal. and Warren Moon, Min.; **RB**— Jerome Bettis, LA; **FB**— Daryl Johnston, Dal.

Defense: E— William Fuller, Phi.; **T**— Dana Stubblefield, SF; **LB**— Seth Joyner, Ariz. and Jesse Tuggle, Atl.; **CB**— Eric Allen, Phi.; **S**— Tim McDonald, SF.

Replacements: OFFENSE— WR Terance Mathis, Atl. for Sharpe; RB Ricky Watters, SF for E. Smith; DEFENSE— DE Wayne Martin, NO for White. NEED PLAYER— Jack Del Rio, Min., LB.

Annual Awards

The NFL does not sanction any postseason awards for players or coaches, but many are given out. Among the presenters for the 1994 regular season were AP, UPI, *The Sporting News* and the Pro Football Writers of America. MVP awards are also given out by the Maxwell Club of Philadelphia (Bert Bell Trophy) and the NFL Players Association.

Most Valuable Player | **Selectors**
NFL Steve Young, San Fran., QB...AP, Max, PFWA, *TSN*
AFC Dan Marino, Miami, QB ....NFLPA
NFC Barry Sanders, Detroit, RB.........................NFLPA

Offensive Players of the Year
NFL Barry Sanders, Detroit, RB ....AP
AFC Dan Marino, Miami, QB.................................UPI
NFC Steve Young, San Francisco, QB.....................UPI

Defensive Players of the Year
NFL Deion Sanders, San Francisco, CB...................AP
AFC Greg Lloyd, Pittsburgh, LB.............................UPI
NFC Charles Haley, Dallas, DE ....UPI

Rookies of the Year | **Selectors**
NFL Marshall Faulk, Indianapolis, RB ....PFWA, *TSN*
AFC Marshall Faulk, Indianapolis, RB.....................UPI
NFC Bryant Young, San Francisco, DT ....UPI
Offense Marshall Faulk, Indianapolis ....AP
Defense Tim Bowens, Miami, DT ....AP

Coaches of the Year | **Selectors**
NFL Bill Parcells, New England.....................AP, PFWA
  George Seifert, San Francisco............................*TSN*
AFC Bill Parcells, New England................................UPI
NFC Dave Wannstedt, Chicago ....UPI

1994 All-NFL Team

The 1994 All-NFL team combining the All-Pro selections of the Associated Press and the Pro Football Writers of America (PFWA). Holdovers from the 1993 All-NFL team in **bold** type.

Offense

Pos		Selectors
WR —	**Jerry Rice**, San Francisco	AP, PFWA
WR —	Cris Carter, Miami	AP, PFWA
TE —	Ben Coates, New England	AP, PFWA
T —	William Roaf, New Orleans	AP, PFWA
T —	Richmond Webb, Miami	AP, PFWA
G —	**Randall McDaniel**, Minnesota	AP, PFWA
G —	Nate Newton, Dallas	AP, PFWA
C —	**Dermontti Dawson**, Pittsburgh	AP, PFWA
QB —	**Steve Young**, San Francisco	AP, PFWA
RB —	Barry Sanders, Detroit	AP, PFWA
RB —	**Emmitt Smith**, Dallas	AP, PFWA

Defense

Pos		Selectors
DE —	**Bruce Smith**, Buffalo	AP, PFWA
DE —	Charles Haley, San Francisco	AP, PFWA
DT —	**John Randle**, Minnesota	AP, PFWA
DT —	**Cortez Kennedy**, Seattle	AP
DT —	Chester McClockton, LA Raiders	PFWA
LB —	**Greg Lloyd**, Pittsburgh	AP, PFWA
LB —	Kevin Greene, Pittsburgh	AP, PFWA
LB —	**Junior Seau**, San Diego	AP, PFWA
LB —	Chris Spielman, Detroit	PFWA
CB —	**Deion Sanders**, Atlanta	AP, PFWA
CB —	**Rod Woodson**, Pittsburgh	AP, PFWA
S —	Eric Turner, Cleveland	AP, PFWA
S —	Darren Woodson, Dallas	AP, PFWA

Specialists

Pos		Selectors	Pos		Selectors
PK —	John Carney, San Diego	AP	KR —	Mel Gray, Detroit	AP, PFWA
PK —	Fuad Reveiz, Minnesota	PFWA	PR —	Brian Mitchell, Washington	PFWA
P —	Reggie Roby, Washington	AP, PFWA	ST —	**Steve Tasker**, Buffalo	PFWA

1995 Expansion Draft

Complete selection lists of 1995 NFL expansion draft, held Feb. 15, 1995, in New York City. Carolina and Jacksonville had 36 picks apiece from a pool made up of six players from each of the league's 28 established teams. The Jaguars won coin toss to pick first. Note that (*) indicates restricted free agent.

Jacksonville Jaguars

		1994 Team	Pos	Yrs
1	Steve Beuerlein	Arizona	QB	9
3	Corey Raymond*	NY Giants	DB	4
5	Jeff Novak	Miami	OT	2
7	John Duff	LA Raiders	DE	2
9	Keith Goganious*	Buffalo	LB	4
11	Mark Williams	Green Bay	LB	1
13	Al Jackson	Philadelphia	DB	1
15	Mark Tucker	Arizona	C	3
17	Paul Frase	NY Jets	DE	7
19	Tom Myslinski	Chicago	G	3
21	Willie Jackson	Dallas	WR	1
23	Othello Henderson	New Orleans	DB	3
25	Santo Stephens	Cincinnati	LB	3
27	Darren Carrington	San Diego	S	7
29	Michael Davis	Houston	DB	1
31	Dave Thomas	Dallas	DB	3
33	Mazio Royster	Tampa Bay	RB	4
35	Le'Shai Maston	Houston	LB	3
37	Charles Davenport*	Pittsburgh	WR	4
39	Monty Grow	Kansas City	DB	1
41	Marcus Wilson	Green Bay	RB	4
43	Brant Boyer	Miami	LB	1
45	Harry Colon	Detroit	DB	5
47	Derek Brown	NY Giants	TE	4
49	James Williams	New Orleans	LB	6
51	Eugene Chung	New England	G	4
53	Reggie Cobb	Green Bay	RB	6
55	Desmond Howard	Washington	WR	4
57	Kelvin Martin	Seattle	WR	9
59	Cedric Tillman*	Denver	WR	7
61	Rogerick Green	Tampa Bay	CB	4

Note: Jaguars passed on picks 63-71.

Carolina Panthers

		1994 Team	Pos	Yrs
2	Rod Smith*	New England	DB	4
4	Harry Boatswain	San Francisco	OT	5
6	Kurt Haws	Washington	TE	1
8	Tyrone Rodgers*	Seattle	DE	4
10	Mark Thomas*	San Francisco	DE	4
12	Tim McKyer	Pittsburgh	DB	9
14	Curtis Whitley*	San Diego	OL	4
16	Howard Griffith	LA Rams	RB	3
18	Greg Kragen	Kansas City	NT	11
20	Cary Brabham	LA Raiders	DB	2
22	Dave Garnett	Minnesota	LB	3
24	Andre Powell	NY Giants	LB	3
26	Dewell Brewer	Indianapolis	RB	2
28	Bob Christian	Chicago	RB	3
30	Fred Foggie	Pittsburgh	DB	2
32	Mark Carrier	Cleveland	WR	9
34	Mark Rodenhauser	Detroit	C	8
36	Steve Hawkins	New England	WR	1
38	Brian O'Neal	Philadelphia	FB	1
40	Derrick Lassic	Dallas	RB	3
42	Richard Buchanan	LA Rams	WR	3
44	Doug Pederson*	Miami	QB	3
46	Vince Marrow	Buffalo	TE	1
48	Larry Ryans	Detroit	WR	2
50	Baron Rollins	New Orleans	G	2
52	William Sims	Minnesota	LB	2
54	Paul Butcher	Indianapolis	LB	9
56	Jack Trudeau	NY Jets	QB	10
58	Charles Swann	Denver	WR	2
60	David Mims	Atlanta	WR	1
62	Shawn Price	Tampa Bay	DE	3
64	Eric Guliford	Minnesota	WR	3
66	Bill Goldberg	Atlanta	DL	1
68	Eric Ball	Cincinnati	RB	7
70	Mike Teeter*	Houston	DT	4

Note: Panthers passed on 72nd pick.

1995 College Draft

First and second round selections at the 60th annual NFL College Draft held April 22-23, 1995, in New York City. Eleven underclassmen were among the first 64 players chosen and are listed in CAPITAL letters.

First Round

	Team		Pos
1	**a**-Cincinnati	KI-JANA CARTER, Penn St.	RB
2	Jacksonville	Tony Boselli, USC	OT
3	Houston	Steve McNair, Alcorn St.	QB
4	Washington	Michael Westbrook, Colorado	WR
5	**b**-Carolina	Kerry Collins, Penn St.	QB
6	St. Louis	Kevin Carter, Florida	DE
7	**c**-Philadelphia	MIKE MAMULA, Boston Col.	DE
8	Seattle	Joey Galloway, Ohio St.	WR
9	NY Jets	Kyle Brady, Penn St.	TE
10	**d**-San Francisco	J.J. Stokes, UCLA	WR
11	**e**-Minnesota	DERRICK ALEXANDER, Fla. St.	DE
12	**f**-Tampa Bay	WARREN SAPP, Miami-FL.	DT
13	New Orleans	Mark Fields, Wash. St.	LB
14	Buffalo	Ruben Brown, Pittsburgh	OG
15	Indianapolis	Ellis Johnson, Florida	DT
16	**g**-NY Jets	Hugh Douglas, Central (OH) St.	DE
17	NY Giants	Tyrone Wheatley, Michigan	RB
18	Los Angeles	Napoleon Kaufman, Washington	RB
19	**h**-Jacksonville	James Stewart, Tennessee	RB
20	Detroit	Luther Elliss, Utah	DT
21	Chicago	RASHAAN SALAAM, Colorado	RB
22	**i**-Carolina	Tyrone Poole, Ft. Valley St.	CB
23	New England	TY LAW, Michigan	CB
24	Minnesota	KOREY STRINGER, Ohio St.	OT
25	Miami	Billy Milner, Houston	OT
26	**j**-Atlanta	DEVIN BUSH, Florida St.	S
27	Pittsburgh	Mark Bruener, Washington	TE
28	**k**-Tampa Bay	Derrick Brooks, Florida St.	LB
29	**l**-Carolina	BLAKE BROCKERMEYER, Texas	OT
30	**m**-Cleveland	CRAIG POWELL, Ohio St.	LB
31	**n**-Kansas City	TREZELLE JENKINS, Michigan	OT
32	**o**-Green Bay	Craig Newsome, Arizona St.	CB

Acquired picks: a— from Carolina; **b—** from Cincinnati; **c—** from Tampa Bay; **d—** from Atlanta thru Cleveland; **e—** from Denver thru Atlanta; **f—** from Philadelphia; **g—** from Arizona; **h—** from Kansas City; **j—** from Green Bay; **j—** from Cleveland; **k—** from Dallas; **l—** from San Diego; **m—** from San Francisco; **n—** Jacksonville; **o—** from Carolina.

Second Round

	Team		Pos
33	**a**-NY Jets	Matt O'Dwyer, Northwestern	OG
34	**b**-San Diego	Terrance Shaw, S.F. Austin St.	DB
35	Houston	Anthony Cook, S. Carolina St.	DT
36	**c**-Carolina	Shawn King, NE Louisiana	DE
37	Washington	Cory Raymer, Wisconsin	C
38	St. Louis	Zack Wiegert, Nebraska	OT
39	Seattle	Christian Fauria, Colorado	TE
40	**d**-Jacksonville	Brian DeMarco, Mich. St.	OT
41	**e**-Atlanta	Ronald Davis, Tennessee	CB
42	**f**-Minnesota	Orlando Thomas, SW Louisiana	S
43	**g**-Tampa Bay	Melvin Johnson, Kentucky	S
44	New Orleans	Ray Zellars, Notre Dame	FB
45	Buffalo	Todd Collins, Michigan	QB
46	**h**-Dallas	Sherman Williams, Alabama	RB
47	Arizona	Frank Sanders, Auburn	WR
48	Indianapolis	Ken Dilger, Illinois	TE
49	Los Angeles	Barret Robbins, TCU	C
50	**i**-Philadelphia	BOBBY TAYLOR, Notre Dame	DB
51	**j**-San Diego	Terrell Fletcher, Wisconsin	RB
52	Chicago	Patrick Riley, Miami-FL	DT
53	**k**-Miami	Andrew Greene, Indiana	OG
54	NY Giants	Scott Gragg, Montana	OT
55	Minnesota	Corey Fuller, Florida St.	DB
56	**l**-Chicago	Todd Sauerbrun, West Va.	P
57	New England	Ted Johnson, Colorado	LB
58	**m**-Philadelphia	Barrett Brooks, Kansas St.	OT
59	Dallas	Kendall Watkins, Miss. St.	TE
60	Pittsburgh	Kordell Stewart, Colorado	QB
61	San Diego	Jimmy Oliver, TCU	WR
62	**n**-St. Louis	Jesse James, Miss. St.	OG
63	**o**-Dallas	Shane Hannah, Mich. St.	OG
—	Carolina	forfeited selection	
64	Jacksonville	Bryan Schwartz, Augustana	LB

Acquired picks: a— from Jacksonville; **b—** from Carolina; **c—** from Cincinnati; **d—** from NY Jets; **e—** from Tampa Bay thru Dallas; **f—** from Denver; **g—** from Philadelphia; **h—** from Atlanta; **i—** from Kansas City; **j—** from Detroit; **k—** from Green Bay; **l—** from Miami; **m—** from Cleveland; **n—**from San Francisco; **o—** from Philadelphia thru Tampa Bay.

Head Coaching Changes For 1995

As of May 1, 1995, eight new head coaches were in place for the start of the '95 regular season. The list includes Carolina and Jacksonville, the NFL's first two expansion teams since Seattle and Tampa Bay took the field in 1976.

AFC	Old Coach	Why Left?	New Coach	Hired	Old Job
Denver	Wade Phillips	Fired (Dec. 29)	Mike Shanahan	Jan. 31	Off. Coord., NFL 49ers
LA Raiders	Art Shell	Fired (Feb. 2)	Mike White	Feb. 2	Ast., NFL Raiders
NY Jets	Pete Carroll	Fired (Jan. 5)	Rich Kotite	Jan. 5	Coach, NFL Eagles
Seattle	Tom Flores	Fired (Dec. 29)	Dennis Erickson	Jan.12	Coach, U. of Miami
Jacksonville	None	Expansion team	Tom Coughlin	2/21/94	Coach, Boston College

NFC	Old Coach	Why Left?	New Coach	Hired	Old Job
Philadelphia	Rich Kotite	Fired (Dec. 26)	Ray Rhodes	Feb. 2	Def. Coord., NFL 49ers
St. Louis	Chuck Knox	Fired (Jan. 9)	Rich Brooks	Feb.10	Coach, U. of Oregon
Carolina	None	Expansion team	Dom Capers	Jan. 23	Def. Coord., NFL Steelers

Franchise Moves in 1995

As of July 21, 1995.

	Team	Old City	New City	Announced Move	Approved by NFL	New Playground	Capacity
AFC	Raiders	Los Angeles*	Oakland	June 23	July 21	Oakland Coliseum	54,587
NFC	Rams	L.A./Anaheim†	St. Louis	Jan.17	April 12	New Domed Stadium	65,900

* Raiders moved from Oakland to Los Angeles in 1982.
† Rams moved from Cleveland to Los Angeles in 1946 and from L.A. to Anaheim in 1980.

Canadian Football League
Final 1994 Standings

Division champions (*) and other playoff qualifiers (†) are noted. Number of seasons listed after each head coach refers to latest tenure with club through 1994 season.

Western Division

	W	L	T	Pts	PF	PA	vs Div
*Calgary	15	3	0	30	698	355	8-2-0
†Edmonton	13	5	0	26	518	401	7-3-0
†B.C. Lions	11	6	1	23	604	456	5-4-1
†Saskatchewan	11	7	0	22	512	454	4-6-0
Sacramento	9	8	1	19	436	436	3-6-1
Las Vegas	5	13	0	10	447	622	2-8-0

Head Coaches: Calg— Wally Buono (5th season); **Edm**— Ron Lancaster (4th); **BC**— Dave Ritchie (2nd); **Sask**— Ray Jauch (1st); **Sac**— Kay Stephenson (2nd); **LV**— Ron Meyer (1st).
1993 Standings: 1. Calgary (15-3); 2. Edmonton (12-6); 3. Saskatchewan (11-7); 4. B.C. Lions (10-8); 5. Sacramento (6-12).

Eastern Division

	W	L	T	Pts	PF	PA	vs Div
*Winnipeg	13	5	0	26	651	572	9-1-0
†Baltimore	12	6	0	24	561	431	8-2-0
†Toronto	7	11	0	14	504	578	5-5-0
†Ottawa	4	14	0	8	480	647	3-7-0
Hamilton	4	14	0	8	435	562	3-7-0
Shreveport	3	15	0	6	330	661	2-8-0

Head Coaches: Win—Cal Murphy (3rd season); **Bal**— Don Matthews (1st); **Tor**— Bill O'Billovich (2nd); **Ott**— Adam Rita (1st); **Ham**— John Gregory (4th); **Shrv**— Forrest Gregg (1st).
1993 Standings: 1. Winnipeg (14-4); 2. Hamilton (6-12); 3. Ottawa (4-14); 4. Toronto (3-15).

All-CFL Team

The All-CFL team as selected by a Football Writers of Canada panel.

Pos	Offense	Pos	Defense
WR	Paul Masotti, Tor.	E	Tim Cofield, Ham.
WR	Rod Harris, Sac.	E	Will Johnson, Calg.
T	Shar Pourdanesh, Bal.	T	Bennie Goods, Edm.
T	Chris Walby, Win.	T	Rodney Harding, Tor.
G	Pierre Vercheval, Tor.	LB	Willie Pless, Edm.
G	Rocco Romano, Calg.	LB	Ron Goetz, Sask.
C	Mike Anderson, Sask.	LB	Calvin Tiggle, Tor.
QB	Doug Flutie, Calg.	CB	Less Browne, BC
FB	Sean Millington, BC	CB	Irvin Smith, Bal.
RB	Mike Pringle, Bal.	HB	Charles Gordon, BC
SB	Allen Pitts, Calg.	HB	Robert Holland, Edm.
SB	Gerald Wilcox, Win.	S	Greg Knox, Calg.

Specialists

PK— Mark McLoughlin, Calg.
P— Josh Miller, Bal.
Special Teams— Henry Williams, Edm.

CFL Playoffs

Division Semifinals (Nov. 13-14)

Western: B.C. Lions 24 .... at Edmonton 23
at Calgary 36 .... Saskatchewan 3

Eastern: at Baltimore 34 .... Toronto 15
at Winnipeg 26 .... Ottawa 16

Division Championships (Nov. 20)

Western: B.C. Lions 37 .... at Calgary 36
Eastern: Baltimore 14 .... at Winnipeg 12

82nd Grey Cup Championship

Nov. 27, at B.C. Place, Vancouver (Att: 55,097)

Baltimore (15-4)	0	17	3	3 — 23	
B.C. Lions (14-6)	3	7	10	6 — 26	

Most Outstanding Player: Karl Anthony, Baltimore, DB (1 INT, 1 TD for 36 yds off lateral; 3 tackles). **Most Outstanding Canadian:** Lui Passaglia, B.C. Lions, PK/P (FG— 4 for 6; good from 47, 42, 27, 37 yds; missed from 49, 37 yds. Punts— 7 for 267 yds, 38.1 avg.)

Regular Season Individual Leaders
Passing Efficiency

(Minimum of 400 attempts)

	Att	Cmp	Cmp Pct	Yds	Avg Gain	TD	Long	Int	Rating
Doug Flutie, Calg.	659	403	61.2	5726	8.69	48	106-td	19	118.2
Matt Dunigan, Win.	431	252	58.5	3965	9.20	31	88-td	16	114.3
Tracy Ham, Bal.	519	280	53.9	4348	8.38	30	83-td	13	107.4
Tom Burgess, Sask.	451	243	53.9	3442	7.63	19	67-td	14	96.6
Kent Austin, BC	551	317	57.5	4193	7.61	24	61-td	22	96.3

Rushing

	Car	Yds	Avg	Long	TD
Mike Pringle, Bal.	308	1972	6.4	83-td	13
Cory Philpot, BC	201	1451	7.2	92-td	13
Blaise Bryant, Win.	232	1289	5.6	65-td	10
Troy Mills, Sac.	178	1230	6.9	40	7
Mike Saunders, Sask.	234	1205	5.1	49	8

Touchdowns

	TD	Rush	Rec	Ret	Pts
Allen Pitts, Calg.	21	0	21	0	126
Tony Stewart, Calg.	19	14	5	0	114
Gerald Alphin, Win.	18	0	18	0	108
Chris Armstrong, Bal.	18	0	18	0	108
Mike Pringle, Bal.	16	13	3	0	96

Other Individual Leaders

Points (Kicking)	213	Troy Westwood, Win.
Passing Yards	5726	Doug Flutie, Calg.
Receptions	126	Allen Pitts, Calg.
Yds from Scrimmage	2414	Mike Pringle, Bal.
Interceptions	11	Less Browne, BC
Sacks	17	Will Johnson, Calg.
Punting Average	44.0	Bjorn Nittmo, Shrv.

Most Outstanding Awards

Player	Doug Flutie, Calgary, QB
Canadian	Gerald Wilcox, Winnipeg, SB
Offensive Lineman	Shar Pourdanesh, Baltimore, OT
Defensive Player	Willie Pless, Edmonton, LB
Rookie	Matt Goodwin, Baltimore, DB
Coach	Don Matthews, Baltimore

CFL Eyes More U.S. Expansion

by Dave Supleve

The Canadian Football League is having an identity crisis.

It has grown from eight teams to 13 in the last three seasons, but all five of the new clubs are located in the United States. In 1995, with the addition of new franchises in Memphis and Birmingham, Ala., the *Canadian* Football League is over one third American.

And this comes one season after a CFL expansion team in Baltimore caused a national uproar when it almost made off with the league's Holy Grail, the Grey Cup.

Not that Canadian football fans have anything against American players. College stars from the States who have either been unable or unwilling to play in the NFL have always been welcome in the CFL. The league's Most Outstanding Player Award dates from Billy Vessels in 1953 to fellow Heisman Trophy winner Doug Flutie, who has been honored in each of the last four seasons.

But Americans, or "imports" as they are known up here, have always been rationed. In 1936, the Western Canada Rugby Football Union, a forerunner of the CFL, restricted member teams to just five imports and only players who had lived in Canada for a full year could participate in the Grey Cup.

Six decades later, the 37-man rosters of Canadian-based CFL teams are limited to a maximum of 17 imports. American teams, however, are under no such restraints and are not obligated to carry any Canadian players.

Which is why the 1994 Grey Cup game, won by the British Columbia Lions on a last second, 37-yard field goal by 40-year-old Vancouver native Lui Passaglia, stirred such partisan feelings among Canadian fans.

"The thought that we might lose the Cup brought out a patriotism similar to the way the country felt when Team Canada played the Russians [in hockey] in 1972," said Saskatchewan Roughriders GM Alan Ford.

Oddly enough, Baltimore, more than any of the Canadian teams, epitomized the CFL's identity dilemma in 1994. Christened the "CFL Colts," in tribute to the city's love affair with the

World Wide Photos

Vancouver native **Lui Passaglia** jumps into the arms of teammate **Darren Flutie** after kicking the winning field goal in the B.C. Lions' 26-23 victory over Baltimore in the 1994 Grey Cup.

departed Colts of the NFL, Baltimore was barred by a court order from using the nickname. Two weeks into the 1995 season the NFL agreed to let Baltimore take the nickname 'Stallions' which had been copyrighted for a possible NFL expansion team in St. Louis.

Meanwhile, CFL commissioner Larry Smith, a tireless 44-year-old lawyer who spent nine seasons as a slotback with the now-defunct Montreal Alouettes, continued to pursue his master plan of making the CFL a 16-team league by the turn of the century with eight clubs on both sides of the border.

The good news was that the Memphis Mad Dogs, owned by Federal Express founder Fred Smith, and the equally-well funded Birmingham Barracudas, coached by Jack Pardee, have joined the league.

On the negative side, the Sacramento Gold Miners decided to move to San Antonio where they became the Texans and the Las Vegas Posse had to suspend operations.

In Canada, no teams moved or folded up during the offseason, but Hamilton and Ottawa almost went under and community-owned Winnipeg was on the ropes for awhile.

Dave Supleve covers the CFL for the *Winnipeg Free Press*.

PRO FOOTBALL STATISTICS

THE 1996 INFORMATION PLEASE SPORTS ALMANAC

SEC B

THROUGH THE YEARS
1920-1995
SUPER BOWLS • NFL LEADERS

PAGE 244

The Super Bowl

The first AFL-NFL World Championship Game, as it was originally called, was played seven months after the two leagues agreed to merge in June of 1966. It became the Super Bowl (complete with roman numerals) by the third game in 1969. The Super Bowl winner has been presented the Vince Lombardi Trophy since 1971. Lombardi, whose Green Bay teams won the first two title games, died in 1970. NFL champions (1966-69) and NFC champions (since 1970) are listed in CAPITAL letters.

Multiple winners: San Francisco (5); Dallas and Pittsburgh (4); Oakland-LA Raiders and Washington (3); Green Bay, Miami and NY Giants (2).

Bowl	Date	Winner	Head Coach	Score	Loser	Head Coach	Site
I	1/15/67	GREEN BAY	Vince Lombardi	35-10	Kansas City	Hank Stram	Los Angeles
II	1/14/68	GREEN BAY	Vince Lombardi	33-14	Oakland	John Rauch	Miami
III	1/12/69	NY Jets	Weeb Ewbank	16- 7	BALTIMORE	Don Shula	Miami
IV	1/11/70	Kansas City	Hank Stram	23- 7	MINNESOTA	Bud Grant	New Orleans
V	1/17/71	Baltimore	Don McCafferty	16-13	DALLAS	Tom Landry	Miami
VI	1/16/72	DALLAS	Tom Landry	24- 3	Miami	Don Shula	New Orleans
VII	1/14/73	Miami	Don Shula	14- 7	WASHINGTON	George Allen	Los Angeles
VIII	1/13/74	Miami	Don Shula	24- 7	MINNESOTA	Bud Grant	Houston
IX	1/12/75	Pittsburgh	Chuck Noll	16- 6	MINNESOTA	Bud Grant	New Orleans
X	1/18/76	Pittsburgh	Chuck Noll	21-17	DALLAS	Tom Landry	Miami
XI	1/ 9/77	Oakland	John Madden	32-14	MINNESOTA	Bud Grant	Pasadena
XII	1/15/78	DALLAS	Tom Landry	27-10	Denver	Red Miller	New Orleans
XIII	1/21/79	Pittsburgh	Chuck Noll	35-31	DALLAS	Tom Landry	Miami
XIV	1/20/80	Pittsburgh	Chuck Noll	31-19	LA RAMS	Ray Malavasi	Pasadena
XV	1/25/81	Oakland	Tom Flores	27-10	PHILADELPHIA	Dick Vermeil	New Orleans
XVI	1/24/82	SAN FRANCISCO	Bill Walsh	26-21	Cincinnati	Forrest Gregg	Pontiac, MI
XVII	1/30/83	WASHINGTON	Joe Gibbs	27-17	Miami	Don Shula	Pasadena
XVIII	1/22/84	LA Raiders	Tom Flores	38- 9	WASHINGTON	Joe Gibbs	Tampa
XIX	1/20/85	SAN FRANCISCO	Bill Walsh	38-16	Miami	Don Shula	Stanford
XX	1/26/86	CHICAGO	Mike Ditka	46-10	New England	Raymond Berry	New Orleans
XXI	1/25/87	NY GIANTS	Bill Parcells	39-20	Denver	Dan Reeves	Pasadena
XXII	1/31/88	WASHINGTON	Joe Gibbs	42-10	Denver	Dan Reeves	San Diego
XXIII	1/22/89	SAN FRANCISCO	Bill Walsh	20-16	Cincinnati	Sam Wyche	Miami
XXIV	1/28/90	SAN FRANCISCO	George Seifert	55-10	Denver	Dan Reeves	New Orleans
XXV	1/27/91	NY GIANTS	Bill Parcells	20-19	Buffalo	Marv Levy	Tampa
XXVI	1/26/92	WASHINGTON	Joe Gibbs	37-24	Buffalo	Marv Levy	Minneapolis
XXVII	1/31/93	DALLAS	Jimmy Johnson	52-17	Buffalo	Marv Levy	Pasadena
XXVIII	1/30/94	DALLAS	Jimmy Johnson	30-13	Buffalo	Marv Levy	Atlanta
XXIX	1/29/95	SAN FRANCISCO	George Seifert	49-26	San Diego	Bobby Ross	Miami

Pete Rozelle Award (MVP)

The Most Valuable Player in the Super Bowl. Currently selected by an 11-member panel made up of national pro football writers and broadcasters chosen by the NFL. Presented by *Sport* magazine from 1967-89 and by the NFL since 1990. Named after former NFL commissioner Pete Rozelle in 1990. Winner who did not play for Super Bowl champion is in **bold** type.

Multiple winners: Joe Montana (3); Terry Bradshaw and Bart Starr (2).

Bowl		Bowl		Bowl	
I	Bart Starr, Green Bay, QB	XI	Fred Biletnikoff, Oakland, WR	XX	Richard Dent, Chicago, DE
II	Bart Starr, Green Bay, QB	XII	Harvey Martin, Dallas, DE	XXI	Phil Simms, NY Giants, QB
III	Joe Namath, NY Jets, QB		& Randy White, Dallas, DT	XXII	Doug Williams, Washington, QB
IV	Len Dawson, Kansas City, QB	XIII	Terry Bradshaw, Pittsburgh, QB	XXIII	Jerry Rice, San Francisco, WR
V	**Chuck Howley, Dallas, LB**	XIV	Terry Bradshaw, Pittsburgh, QB	XXIV	Joe Montana, San Francisco, QB
VI	Roger Staubach, Dallas, QB	XV	Jim Plunkett, Oakland, QB	XXV	Ottis Anderson, NY Giants, RB
VII	Jake Scott, Miami, S	XVI	Joe Montana, San Francisco, QB	XXVI	Mark Rypien, Washington, QB
VIII	Larry Csonka, Miami, RB	XVII	John Riggins, Washington, RB	XXVII	Troy Aikman, Dallas, QB
IX	Franco Harris, Pittsburgh, RB	XVIII	Marcus Allen, LA Raiders, RB	XXVIII	Emmitt Smith, Dallas, RB
X	Lynn Swann, Pittsburgh, WR	XIX	Joe Montana, San Francisco, QB	XXIX	Steve Young, San Francisco, QB

All-Time Super Bowl Leaders

Through Jan. 29, 1995; participants in Super Bowl XXIX in **bold** type.

CAREER
Passing Efficiency

Ratings based on performance standards established for completion percentage, average gain, touchdown percentage and interception percentage. Quarterbacks are allocated points according to how their statistics measure up to those standards. Minimum 25 passing attempts.

	Gm	Att	Cmp	Cmp%	Yards	Avg Gain	TD	TD%	Int	Int%	Rating
1 Phil Simms, NYG	1	25	22	88.0	268	10.72	3	12.0	0	0.0	150.9
2 **Steve Young**, SF	2	39	26	66.7	345	8.85	6	15.4	0	0.0	134.1
3 Doug Williams, Wash	1	29	18	62.1	340	11.72	4	13.8	1	3.4	128.1
4 Joe Montana, SF	4	122	83	68.0	1142	9.36	11	9.0	0	0.0	127.8
5 Jim Plunkett, Oak-LA	2	46	29	63.0	433	9.41	4	8.7	0	0.0	122.8
6 Troy Aikman, Dal	2	57	41	71.9	480	8.42	4	7.0	1	1.8	113.2
7 Terry Bradshaw, Pit	4	84	49	58.3	932	11.10	9	10.7	4	4.8	112.6
8 Roger Staubach, Dal	4	98	61	62.2	734	7.49	8	8.2	4	4.1	95.4
9 Ken Anderson, Cin	1	34	25	73.5	300	8.82	2	5.9	2	5.9	95.2
10 Bart Starr, GB	2	47	29	61.7	452	9.62	3	6.4	1	2.1	95.1

Passing Yards

	Gm	Att	Cmp	Pct	Yds
1 Joe Montana, SF	4	122	83	68.0	1142
2 Terry Bradshaw, Pit	4	84	49	58.3	932
3 Jim Kelly, Buf	4	145	81	55.9	829
4 Roger Staubach, Dal	4	98	61	62.2	734
5 John Elway, Den	3	101	46	45.5	669
6 Fran Tarkenton, Min	3	89	46	51.7	489
7 Troy Aikman, Dal	2	57	41	71.9	480
8 Bart Starr, GB	2	47	29	61.7	452
9 Jim Plunkett, Raiders	2	46	29	63.0	433
10 Joe Theismann, Wash	2	58	31	53.4	386
11 Len Dawson, KC	2	44	28	63.6	353
12 **Steve Young**, SF	2	26	39	66.7	345
13 Doug Williams, Wash	1	29	18	62.1	340
14 Dan Marino, Mia	1	50	29	58.0	318
15 Ken Anderson, Cin	1	34	25	73.5	300

Receptions

	Gm	No	Yds	Avg	TD
1 **Jerry Rice**, SF	3	28	512	18.3	7
2 Andre Reed, Buf	4	27	323	12.0	0
3 Roger Craig, SF	3	20	212	10.6	3
4 Thurman Thomas, Buf	4	20	144	7.2	0
5 Lynn Swann, Pit	4	16	364	22.8	3
6 Chuck Foreman, Min	3	15	139	9.3	0
7 Cliff Branch, Raiders	3	14	181	12.9	3
8 Don Beebe, Buf	3	12	171	14.3	2
Preston Pearson, Bal-Pit-Dal	5	12	105	8.8	0
Jay Novacek, Dal	2	12	98	8.2	1
Kenneth Davis, Buf	4	12	72	6.0	0
12 John Stallworth, Pit	4	11	268	24.4	3
Michael Irvin, Dal	2	11	180	16.4	2
Dan Ross, Cin	1	11	104	9.5	2
15 Six tied with 10 catches each.					

Super Bowl Appearances

Through Super Bowl XXIX, ten NFL teams have yet to play for the Vince Lombardi Trophy. In alphabetical order, they are: Arizona, Atlanta, Carolina, Cleveland, Detroit, Houston, Jacksonville, New Orleans, Seattle and Tampa Bay. Of the 20 teams that have participated, Dallas has the most appearances (7) and San Francisco has the most titles (5).

App	W	L	Pct	PF	PA
7 Dallas	4	3	.571	194	115
5 San Francisco	5	0	1.000	188	89
5 Washington	3	2	.600	122	103
5 Miami	2	3	.400	74	103
4 Pittsburgh	4	0	1.000	103	73
4 Oak/LA Raiders	3	1	.750	111	66
4 Buffalo	0	4	.000	73	139
4 Denver	0	4	.000	50	163
4 Minnesota	0	4	.000	34	95
2 Green Bay	2	0	1.000	68	24
2 NY Giants	2	0	1.000	59	39
2 Baltimore Colts	1	1	.500	23	29
2 Kansas City	1	1	.500	33	42
2 Cincinnati	0	2	.000	37	46
1 Chicago	1	0	1.000	46	10
1 NY Jets	1	0	1.000	16	7
1 LA Rams	0	1	.000	19	31
1 New England	0	1	.000	10	46
1 Philadelphia	0	1	.000	10	27
1 San Diego	0	1	.000	26	49

Rushing

	Gm	Car	Yds	Avg	TD
1 Franco Harris, Pit	4	101	354	3.5	4
2 Larry Csonka, Mia	3	57	297	5.2	2
3 Emmitt Smith, Dal	2	52	240	4.6	3
4 John Riggins, Wash	2	64	230	3.6	2
5 Timmy Smith, Wash	1	22	204	9.3	2
Thurman Thomas, Buf	4	52	204	3.9	4
7 Roger Craig, SF	3	52	201	3.9	2
8 Marcus Allen, Raiders	1	20	191	9.5	2
9 Tony Dorsett, Dal	2	31	162	5.2	1
10 Mark van Eeghen, Raiders	2	37	153	4.1	0
11 Kenneth Davis, Buf	4	30	145	4.8	0
12 Rocky Bleier, Pit	4	44	144	3.3	0
13 Walt Garrison, Dal	2	26	139	5.3	0
14 Clarence Davis, Raiders	1	16	137	8.6	0
15 Duane Thomas, Dal	2	37	130	3.5	1

All-Purpose Running

	Gm	Rush	Rec	Ret	Total
1 **Jerry Rice**, SF	3	15	512	0	527
2 Franco Harris, Pit	4	354	114	0	468
3 Roger Craig, SF	3	201	212	0	413
4 Lynn Swann, Pit	4	-7	364	34	391
5 Thurman Thomas, Buf	4	204	144	0	348
6 Andre Reed, Buf	3	0	323	0	323
7 Larry Csonka, Mia	3	297	17	0	314
8 Fulton Walker, Mia	2	0	0	298	298
9 Emmitt Smith, Dal	2	240	53	0	293
10 Ricky Sanders, Wash	2	-3	234	46	277

All-Time Super Bowl Leaders (cont.)
Scoring

Points

		Gm	TD	FG	PAT	Pts
1	**Jerry Rice**, SF	3	7	0	0	42
2	Roger Craig, SF	3	4	0	0	24
	Franco Harris, Pit	4	4	0	0	24
	Thurman Thomas, Buf	4	4	0	0	24
5	Ray Wersching, SF	2	0	5	7	22
6	Don Chandler, GB	2	0	4	8	20
7	Cliff Branch, Raiders	3	3	0	0	18
	John Stallworth, Pit	4	3	0	0	18
	Emmitt Smith, Dal	2	3	0	0	18
	Lynn Swann, Pit	4	3	0	0	18
	Ricky Watters, SF	1	3	0	0	18
12	Chris Bahr, Raiders	2	0	3	8	17
13	Matt Bahr, Pit-NYG	2	0	3	6	15
	Mike Cofer, SF	2	0	2	9	15
	Uwe von Schamann, Mia	2	0	4	3	15

Touchdowns

		Gm	Rush	Rec	Ret	TD
1	**Jerry Rice**, SF	3	0	7	0	7
2	Roger Craig, SF	3	2	2	0	4
	Franco Harris, Pit	4	4	0	0	4
	Thurman Thomas, Buf	4	4	0	0	4
5	Cliff Branch, Raiders	3	0	3	0	3
	Emmitt Smith, Dal	2	3	0	0	3
	John Stallworth, Pit	4	0	3	0	3
	Lynn Swann, Pit	4	0	3	0	3
	Ricky Watters, SF	1	1	2	0	3
10	Twenty-three tied with 2 TDs each.					

Marcus Allen, Raiders; Ottis Anderson, NYG; Pete Banaszak, Raiders; Don Beebe, Buf.; Gary Clark, Wash.; Larry Csonka, Mia.; John Elway, Den.; Michael Irvin, Dal.; Butch Johnson, Dal.; Jim Kiick, Mia.; Max McGee, GB; Jim McMahon, Chi.; Bill Miller, Raiders; Joe Montana, SF; Elijah Pitts, GB; Tom Rathman, SF; John Riggins, Wash.; Gerald Riggs, Wash.; Dan Ross, Cin.; Ricky Sanders, Wash.; Timmy Smith, Wash.; **John Taylor**, SF and Duane Thomas, Dal.

Punting
(Minimum 10 Punts)

		Gm	No	Yds	Avg.
1	Jerrel Wilson, KC	2	11	511	46.5
2	Ray Guy, Raiders	3	14	587	41.9
3	Larry Seiple, Mia	3	15	620	41.3
4	Mike Eischeid, Oak-Min	3	17	698	41.1
5	Danny White, Dal	2	10	406	40.6

Interceptions

		Gm	No	Yds	TD
1	Chuck Howley, Dal	2	3	63	0
	Rod Martin, Raiders	2	3	44	0
3	Randy Beverly, NYJ	1	2	0	0
	Mel Blount, Pit	4	2	23	0
	Brad Edwards, Wash	1	2	56	0
	Thomas Everett, Dal	1	2	22	0
	Jake Scott, Mia	3	2	63	0
	Mike Wagner, Pit	3	2	45	0
	James Washington, Dal	2	2	25	0
	Barry Wilburn, Wash	1	2	11	0
	Eric Wright, SF	4	2	25	0

Punt Returns
(Minimum 4 returns)

		Gm	No	Yds	Avg.	TD
1	**John Taylor**, SF	3	6	94	15.7	0
2	Neal Colzie, Oak	1	4	43	10.8	0
3	Dana McLemore, SF	1	5	51	10.2	0
4	Mike Fuller, Cin	1	4	35	8.8	0
5	Mike Nelms, Wash	1	6	52	8.7	0

Kickoff Returns
(Minimum 4 returns)

		Gm	No	Yds	Avg.	TD
1	Fulton Walker, Mia	2	8	283	35.4	1
2	**Andre Coleman**, SD	1	8	242	30.3	1
3	Larry Anderson, Pit	2	8	207	25.9	0
4	Darren Carrington, Den	1	6	146	24.3	1
5	Jim Duncan, Bal	1	4	90	22.5	0

Sacks

		Gm	No
1	Charles Haley, SF-Dal	4	3½
2	Leonard Marshall, NYG	2	3
	Danny Stubbs, SF	2	3
	Jeff Wright, Buf	4	3
5	Jim Jeffcoat, Dal	2	2½
	Dexter Manley, Wash	3	2½

Four or More Super Bowl Wins
San Francisco 49ers (5)

Year	Bowl	Head Coach	Quarterback	MVP	Opponent	Score	Site
1982	XVI	Bill Walsh	Joe Montana	Montana	Cincinnati	26-21	Pontiac
1985	XIX	Bill Walsh	Joe Montana	Montana	Miami	38-16	Stanford
1989	XXIII	Bill Walsh	Joe Montana	Jerry Rice	Cincinnati	20-16	Miami
1990	XXIV	George Seifert	Joe Montana	Montana	Denver	55-10	New Orleans
1995	XXIX	George Seifert	Steve Young	Young	San Diego	49-26	Miami

Dallas Cowboys (4)

Year	Bowl	Head Coach	Quarterback	MVP	Opponent	Score	Site
1972	VI	Tom Landry	Roger Staubach	Staubach	Miami	24-3	New Orleans
1978	XII	Tom Landry	Roger Staubach	Harvey Martin & Randy White	Denver	27-10	New Orleans
1993	XXVII	Jimmy Johnson	Troy Aikman	Aikman	Buffalo	52-17	Pasadena
1994	XXVIII	Jimmy Johnson	Troy Aikman	Emmitt Smith	Buffalo	30-13	Atlanta

Pittsburgh Steelers (4)

Year	Bowl	Head Coach	Quarterback	MVP	Opponent	Score	Site
1975	IX	Chuck Noll	Terry Bradshaw	Franco Harris	Minnesota	16-6	New Orleans
1976	X	Chuck Noll	Terry Bradshaw	Lynn Swann	Dallas	21-17	Miami
1979	XIII	Chuck Noll	Terry Bradshaw	Bradshaw	Dallas	35-31	Miami
1980	XIV	Chuck Noll	Terry Bradshaw	Bradshaw	LA Rams	31-19	Pasadena

SINGLE GAME

Passing

Yards Gained

Yards Gained	Year	Att/Cmp	Yds
Joe Montana, SF vs Cin	1989	36/23	357
Doug Williams, Wash vs Den	1988	29/18	340
Joe Montana, SF vs Mia	1985	35/24	331
Steve Young, SF vs SD	1995	24/36	325
Terry Bradshaw, Pit vs Dal	1979	30/17	318
Dan Marino, Mia vs SF	1985	50/29	318
Terry Bradshaw, Pit vs Rams	1980	21/14	309
John Elway, Den vs NYG	1987	37/22	304
Ken Anderson, Cin vs SF	1982	34/25	300
Joe Montana, SF vs Den	1990	29/22	297

Touchdown Passes	Year	TD	Int
Steve Young, SF vs SD	1995	6	0
Joe Montana, SF vs Den	1990	5	0
Terry Bradshaw, Pit vs Dal	1979	4	1
Doug Williams, Wash vs Den	1988	4	1
Troy Aikman, Dal vs Buf	1993	4	0
Roger Staubach, Dal vs Pit	1979	3	1
Jim Plunkett, Raiders vs Phi	1981	3	0
Joe Montana, SF vs Mia	1985	3	0
Phil Simms, NYG vs Den	1987	3	0

Rushing

Yards Gained	Year	Car	Yds	TD
Timmy Smith, Wash vs Den	1988	22	204	2
Marcus Allen, Raiders vs Wash	1984	20	191	2
John Riggins, Wash vs Mia	1983	38	166	1
Franco Harris, Pit vs Min	1975	34	158	1
Larry Csonka, Mia vs Min	1974	33	145	2
Clarence Davis, Raiders vs Min.	1977	16	137	0
Thurman Thomas, Buf vs NYG	1991	15	135	1
Emmitt Smith, Dal vs Buf	1994	30	132	2
Matt Snell, NYJ vs Bal	1969	30	121	1
Tom Matte, Bal vs NYJ	1969	11	116	0
Larry Csonka, Mia vs Wash	1973	15	112	1
Emmitt Smith, Dal vs Buf	1993	22	108	1
Ottis Anderson, NYG vs Buf	1991	21	102	1
Tony Dorsett, Dal vs Pit	1979	16	96	0
Duane Thomas, Dal vs Mia	1972	19	95	1

Scoring

Points	Year	TD	FG	PAT	Pts
Roger Craig, SF vs Mia	1985	3	0	0	18
Jerry Rice, SF vs Den	1990	3	0	0	18
Jerry Rice, SF vs SD	1995	3	0	0	18
Ricky Watters, SF vs SD	1995	3	0	0	18
Don Chandler, GB vs Raiders	1968	0	4	3	15

Touchdowns	Year	TD	Rush	Rec
Roger Craig, SF vs Mia	1985	3	1	2
Jerry Rice, SF vs Den	1990	3	0	3
Jerry Rice, SF vs SD	1995	3	0	3
Ricky Watters, SF vs SD	1995	3	1	2
Max McGee, GB vs KC	1967	2	0	2
Elijah Pitts, GB vs KC	1967	2	2	0
Bill Miller, Raiders vs GB	1968	2	0	2
Larry Csonka, Mia vs Min	1974	2	2	0
Pete Banaszak, Raiders vs Min.	1977	2	2	0
John Stallworth, Pit vs Dal	1979	2	0	2
Franco Harris, Pit vs Rams	1980	2	2	0
Cliff Branch, Raiders vs Phi	1981	2	0	2
Dan Ross, Cin vs SF	1982	2	0	2
Marcus Allen, Raiders vs Wash	1984	2	2	0
Jim McMahon, Chi vs NE	1986	2	2	0
Ricky Sanders, Wash vs Den	1988	2	0	2
Timmy Smith, Wash vs Den	1988	2	2	0
Tom Rathman, SF vs Den	1990	2	2	0
Gerald Riggs, Wash vs Buf	1992	2	2	0
Michael Irvin, Dal vs Buf	1993	2	0	2
Emmitt Smith, Dal vs Buf	1994	2	2	0

Receptions

Catches	Year	No	Yds	TD
Dan Ross, Cin vs SF	1982	11	104	2
Jerry Rice, SF vs Cin	1989	11	215	1
Tony Nathan, Mia vs SF	1985	10	83	0
Jerry Rice, SF vs SD	1995	10	149	3
Ricky Sanders, Wash vs Den	1988	9	193	2
George Sauer, NYJ vs Bal	1969	8	133	0
Roger Craig, SF vs Cin	1989	8	101	0
Andre Reed, Buf vs NYG	1991	8	62	0
Andre Reed, Buf vs Dal	1993	8	152	0
Ronnie Harmon, SD vs SF	1995	8	68	0

Yards Gained	Year	No	Yds	TD
Jerry Rice, SF vs Cin	1989	11	215	1
Ricky Sanders, Wash vs Den	1988	9	193	2
Lynn Swann, Pit vs Dal	1976	4	161	1
Andre Reed, Buf vs Dal	1993	8	152	0
Jerry Rice, SF vs SD	1995	10	149	3
Jerry Rice, SF vs Den	1990	7	148	3
Max McGee, GB vs KC	1967	7	138	2
George Sauer, NYJ vs Bal	1969	8	133	0
Willie Gault, Chi vs NE	1986	4	129	0
Lynn Swann, Pit vs Dal	1979	7	124	1

All-Purpose Running

Yards Gained	Year	Run	Rec	Tot
Andre Coleman, SD vs SF	1995	0	0	242*
Ricky Sanders, Wash vs Den	1988	193	–4	235†
Jerry Rice, SF vs Cin	1989	215	5	220
Timmy Smith, Wash vs Den	1988	204	9	213
Marcus Allen, Raiders vs Wash	1984	191	18	209
Stephen Starring, NE vs Chi	1986	0	39	192#
Fulton Walker, Mia vs Wash	1983	0	0	190$
Thurman Thomas, Buf vs NYG	1991	135	55	190
John Riggins, Wash vs Mia	1983	166	15	181
Roger Craig, SF vs Cin	1989	74	101	175

*Coleman gained all his yards on eight kickoff returns.
†Sanders also returned three kickoffs for 48 yards.
#Starring also returned seven kickoffs for 153 yards.
$Walker gained all his yards on four kickoff returns.

Interceptions

	Year	No	Yds	TD
Rod Martin, Raiders vs Phi	1981	3	44	0

Six tied with two interceptions each.

Punting

(Minimum 4 punts)

	Year	No	Yds	Avg
Bryan Wagner, SD vs SF	1995	4	195	48.8
Jerrel Wilson, KC vs Min	1970	4	194	48.5
Jim Miller, SF vs Cin	1982	4	185	46.3

Punt Returns

(Minimum 3 returns)

	Year	No	Yds	Avg
John Taylor, SF vs Cin	1989	3	56	18.7
John Taylor, SF vs Den	1990	3	38	12.7
Kelvin Martin, Dal vs Buf	1993	3	35	11.7

Kickoff Returns

(Minimum 3 returns)

	Year	No	Yds	Avg
Fulton Walker, Mia vs Wash	1983	4	109	47.5
Larry Anderson, Pit vs Rams	1980	5	162	32.4
Rick Upchurch, Den vs Dal	1978	3	94	31.3

Super Bowl Playoffs

The Super Bowl forced the NFL to set up pro football's first guaranteed multiple-game playoff format. Over the years, the NFL-AFL merger, the creation of two conferences comprised of three divisions each and the proliferation of Wild Card entries has seen the postseason field grow from four teams (1966), to six (1967-68), to eight (1969-77), to 10 (1978-81, 1983-89), to the present 12 (since 1990).

In 1982, when a 57-day players' strike shortened the regular season to just nine games, playoff berths were extended to 16 teams (eight from each conference) and a 15-game tournament was played.

Note that in the following year-by-year summary, records of finalists include all games leading up to the Super Bowl; (*) indicates Wild Card teams.

1966 Season

AFL Playoffs

Championship ....Kansas City 31, at Buffalo 7

NFL Playoffs

Championship ....Green Bay 34, at Dallas 27

Super Bowl I
Jan. 15, 1967
Memorial Coliseum, Los Angeles
Favorite: Packers by 14   Attendance: 61,946

Kansas City (12-2-1) ....0 10 0 0— **10**
Green Bay (13-2) ....7 7 14 7— **35**
MVP: Green Bay QB Bart Starr (16 for 23, 250 yds, 2 TD, 1 Int)

1967 Season

AFL Playoffs

Championship ....at Oakland 40, Houston 7

NFL Playoffs

Eastern Conference.....................at Dallas 52, Cleveland 14
Western Conference.................at Green Bay 28, LA Rams 7
Championship...........................at Green Bay 21, Dallas 17

Super Bowl II
Jan. 14, 1968
Orange Bowl, Miami
Favorite: Packers by 13½   Attendance: 75,546

Green Bay (11-4-1) ....3 13 10 7— **33**
Oakland (14-1) ....0 7 0 7— **14**
MVP: Green Bay QB Bart Starr (13 for 24, 202 yds, 1 TD)

1968 Season

AFL Playoffs

Western Div. Playoff ....at Oakland 41, Kansas City 6
AFL Championship ....at NY Jets 27, Oakland 23

NFL Playoffs

Eastern Conference....................at Cleveland 31, Dallas 20
Western Conference ....at Baltimore 24, Minnesota 14
NFL Championship ....Baltimore 34, at Cleveland 0

Super Bowl III
Jan. 12, 1969
Orange Bowl, Miami
Favorite: Colts by 18   Attendance: 75,389

NY Jets (12-3) ....0 7 6 3— **16**
Baltimore (15-1) ....0 0 0 7— **7**
MVP: NY Jets QB Joe Namath (17 for 28, 206 yds)

1969 Season

AFL Playoffs

Inter-Division ....*Kansas City 13, at NY Jets 6
.............................at Oakland 56, *Houston 7
AFL Championship ....Kansas City 17, at Oakland 7

NFL Playoffs

Eastern Conference....................Cleveland 38, at Dallas 14
Western Conference ....at Minnesota 23, LA Rams 20
NFL Championship ....at Minnesota 27, Cleveland 7

Super Bowl IV
Jan. 11, 1970
Tulane Stadium, New Orleans
Favorite: Vikings by 12   Attendance: 80,562

Minnesota (14-2) ....0 0 7 0— **7**
Kansas City (13-3)....................3 13 7 0— **23**
MVP: KC QB Len Dawson (12 for 17, 142 yds, 1 TD, 1 Int)

1970 Season

AFC Playoffs

First Round............................at Baltimore 17, Cincinnati 0
.................................at Oakland 21, *Miami 14
Championship.......................at Baltimore 27, Oakland 17

NFC Playoffs

First Round ....at Dallas 5, *Detroit 0
...................San Francisco 17, at Minnesota 14
Championship....................Dallas 17, at San Francisco 10

Super Bowl V
Jan. 17, 1971
Orange Bowl, Miami
Favorite: Cowboys by 2½   Attendance: 79,204

Baltimore (13-2-1).....................0 6 0 10— **16**
Dallas (12-4) ....3 10 0 0— **13**
MVP: Dallas LB Chuck Howley (2 Interceptions for 22 yds)

1971 Season

AFC Playoffs

First Round ....Miami 27, at Kansas City 24 (OT)
.............................*Baltimore 20, at Cleveland 3
Championship ....at Miami 21, Baltimore 0

NFC Playoffs

First Round ....Dallas 20, at Minnesota 12
...............at San Francisco 24, *Washington 20
Championship......................at Dallas 14, San Francisco 3

Super Bowl VI
Jan. 16, 1972
Tulane Stadium, New Orleans
Favorite: Cowboys by 6   Attendance: 81,023

Dallas (13-3) ....3 7 7 7— **24**
Miami (12-3-1) ....0 3 0 0— **3**
MVP: Dallas QB Roger Staubach (12 for 19, 119 yds, 2 TD)

1972 Season

AFC Playoffs

First Round ....at Pittsburgh 13, Oakland 7
...............................at Miami 20, *Cleveland 14
Championship.........................Miami 21, at Pittsburgh 17

NFC Playoffs

First Round ....*Dallas 30, at San Francisco 28
........................at Washington 16, Green Bay 3
Championship..........................at Washington 26, Dallas 3

Super Bowl VII

Jan. 14, 1973
Memorial Coliseum, Los Angeles
Favorite: Redskins by 1½   Attendance: 90,182

Miami (16-0).............................7   7   0   0— **14**
Washington (13-3) 0   0   0   7— **7**
MVP: Miami safety Jake Scott (2 Interceptions for 63 yds)

1973 Season

AFC Playoffs

First Round...........................at Oakland 33, *Pittsburgh 14
...............................at Miami 34, Cincinnati 16
Championship ....at Miami 27, Oakland 10

NFC Playoffs

First Round....................at Minnesota 27, *Washington 20
...............................at Dallas 27, LA Rams 16
Championship ....Minnesota 27, at Dallas 10

Super Bowl VIII

Jan. 13, 1974
Rice Stadium, Houston
Favorite: Dolphins by 6½   Attendance: 71,882

Minnesota (14-2) 0   0   0   7— **7**
Miami (12-4).............................14   3   7   0— **24**
MVP: Miami FB Larry Csonka (33 carries, 145 yds, 2 TD)

1974 Season

AFC Playoffs

First Round................................at Oakland 28, Miami 26
...............................at Pittsburgh 32, *Buffalo 14
Championship ....Pittsburgh 24, at Oakland 13

NFC Playoffs

First Round ....at Minnesota 30, St.Louis 14
...............................at LA Rams 19, *Washington 10
Championship ....at Minnesota 14, LA Rams 10

Super Bowl IX

Jan. 12, 1975
Tulane Stadium, New Orleans
Favorite: Steelers by 3   Attendance: 80,997

Pittsburgh (12-3-1) 0   2   7   7— **16**
Minnesota (12-4) 0   0   0   6— **6**
MVP: Pittsburgh RB Franco Harris (34 carries, 158 yds, 1 TD)

1975 Season

AFC Playoffs

First Round ....at Pittsburgh 28, Baltimore 10
...............................at Oakland 31, *Cincinnati 28
Championship ....at Pittsburgh 16, Oakland 10

NFC Playoffs

First Round..............................at LA Rams 35, St. Louis 23
...............................*Dallas 17, at Minnesota 14
Championship..............................Dallas 37, at LA Rams 7

Super Bowl X

Jan. 18, 1976
Orange Bowl, Miami
Favorite: Steelers by 6½   Attendance: 80,187

Dallas (12-4)..............................7   3   0   7— **17**
Pittsburgh (14-2).......................7   0   0   14— **21**
MVP: Pittsburgh WR Lynn Swann (4 catches, 161 yds, 1 TD)

1976 Season

AFC Playoffs

First Round.....................at Oakland 24, *New England 21
............................Pittsburgh 40, at Baltimore 14
Championship ....at Oakland 24, Pittsburgh 7

NFC Playoffs

First Round......................at Minnesota 35, *Washington 20
...............................LA Rams 14, at Dallas 12
Championship ....at Minnesota 24, LA Rams 13

Super Bowl XI

Jan. 9, 1977
Rose Bowl, Pasadena
Favorite: Raiders by 4½   Attendance: 103,438

Oakland (15-1) 0   16   3   13— **32**
Minnesota (13-2-1) 0   0   7   7— **14**
MVP: Oakland WR Fred Biletnikoff (4 catches, 79 yds)

1977 Season

AFC Playoffs

First Round................................at Denver 34, Pittsburgh 21
...............................*Oakland 37, at Baltimore 31 (OT)
Championship ....at Denver 20, Oakland 17

NFC Playoffs

First Round ....at Dallas 37, *Chicago 7
...............................Minnesota 14, at LA Rams 7
Championship ....at Dallas 23, Minnesota 6

Super Bowl XII

Jan. 15, 1978
Louisiana Superdome, New Orleans
Favorite: Cowboys by 6   Attendance: 75,583

Dallas (14-2)..............................10   3   7   7— **27**
Denver (14-2) 0   0   10   0— **10**
MVPs: Dallas DE Harvey Martin and DT Randy White
(Cowboys' defense forced 8 turnovers)

A Year Later...

Super Bowl champions who did not qualify for the playoffs the following season.

Season		Record	Finish	Season		Record	Finish
1968	Green Bay	6-7-1	3rd in NFL Central	1982	San Francisco	3-6-0*	11th in overall NFC
1970	Kansas City	7-5-2	2nd in AFC West	1987	NY Giants	6-9-0*	5th in NFC East
1980	Pittsburgh	9-7-0	3rd in AFC Central	1988	Washington	7-9-0	3rd in NFC East
1981	Oakland	7-9-0	4th in AFC West	1991	NY Giants	8-8-0	4th in NFC East

*Seasons when player strikes interrupted schedule.

Super Bowl Playoffs (Cont.)

1978 Season

AFC Playoffs

First Round ....*Houston 17, at *Miami 9
Second Round ....Houston 31, at New England 14
.........................at Pittsburgh 33, Denver 10
Championship ....at Pittsburgh 34, Houston 5

NFC Playoffs

First Round.......................at *Atlanta 14, *Philadelphia 13
Second Round ....at Dallas 27, Atlanta 20
.........................at LA Rams 34, Minnesota 10
Championship..............................Dallas 28, at LA Rams 0

Super Bowl XIII
Jan. 21, 1979
Orange Bowl, Miami
Favorite: Steelers by 3½   Attendance: 79,484

Pittsburgh (16-2).....................7 14   0 14— **35**
Dallas (14-4).............................7   7   3 14— **31**
MVP: Pittsburgh QB Terry Bradshaw (17 for 30, 318 yds, 4 TD, 1 Int)

1979 Season

AFC Playoffs

First Round ....at *Houston 13, *Denver 7
Second Round ....Houston 17, at San Diego 14
.........................at Pittsburgh 34, Miami 14
Championship ....at Pittsburgh 27, Houston 13

NFC Playoffs

First Round.......................at *Philadelphia 27, *Chicago 17
Second Round ....at Tampa Bay 24, Philadelphia 17
.........................LA Rams 21, at Dallas 19
Championship..............................LA Rams 9, at Tampa Bay 0

Super Bowl XIV
Jan. 20, 1980
Rose Bowl, Pasadena
Favorite: Steelers by 10½   Attendance: 103,985

LA Rams (11-7)...........................7   6   6   0— **19**
Pittsburgh (14-4)........................3   7   7 14— **31**
MVP: Pittsburgh QB Terry Bradshaw (14 for 21, 309 yds, 2 TD, 3 Int)

1980 Season

AFC Playoffs

First Round ....at *Oakland 27, *Houston 7
Second Round ....at San Diego 20, Buffalo 14
.........................Oakland 14, at Cleveland 12
Championship ....Oakland 34, at San Diego 27

NFC Playoffs

First Round ....at *Dallas 34, *LA Rams 13
Second Round ....at Philadelphia 31, Minnesota 16
.........................Dallas 30, at Atlanta 27
Championship ....at Philadelphia 20, Dallas 7

Super Bowl XV
Jan. 25, 1981
Louisiana Superdome, New Orleans
Favorite: Eagles by 3   Attendance: 76,135

Oakland (14-5) 14   0 10   3— **27**
Philadelphia (14-4) 0   3   0   7— **10**
MVP: Oakland QB Jim Plunkett (13 for 21, 261 yds, 3 TD)

1981 Season

AFC Playoffs

First Round ....*Buffalo 31, at *NY Jets 27
Second Round ....San Diego 41, at Miami 38 (OT)
.........................at Cincinnati 28, Buffalo 21
Championship ....at Cincinnati 27, San Diego 7

NFC Playoffs

First Round ....*NY Giants 27, at *Philadelphia 21
Second Round ....at Dallas 38, Tampa Bay 0
.........................at San Francisco 38, NY Giants 24
Championship....................at San Francisco 28, Dallas 27

Super Bowl XVI
Jan. 24, 1982
Pontiac Silverdome, Pontiac, Mich.
Favorite: Pick'em   Attendance: 81,270

San Francisco (15-3).................7 13   0   6— **26**
Cincinnati (14-4).........................0   0   7 14— **21**
MVP: San Francisco QB Joe Montana (14 for 22, 157 yds, 1 TD; 6 carries, 18 yds, 1 TD)

1982 Season

A 57-day players' strike shortened the regular season from 16 games to nine. The playoff format was changed to a 16-team tournament open to the top eight teams in each conference.

AFC Playoffs

First Round ....at LA Raiders 27, Cleveland 10
.........................at Miami 28, New England 3
.........................NY Jets 44, at Cincinnati 17
.........................San Diego 31, at Pittsburgh 28
Second Round ....NY Jets 17, at LA Raiders 14
.........................at Miami 34, San Diego 13
Championship ....at Miami 14, NY Jets 0

NFC Playoffs

First Round ....at Washington 31, Detroit 7
.........................at Dallas 30, Tampa Bay 17
.........................at Green Bay 41, St. Louis 16
.........................at Minnesota 30, Atlanta 24
Second Round ....at Washington 21, Minnesota 7
.........................at Dallas 37, Green Bay 26
Championship.....................at Washington 31, Dallas 17

Super Bowl XVII
Jan. 30, 1983
Rose Bowl, Pasadena
Favorite: Dolphins by 3   Attendance: 103,667

Miami (10-2)..........................7 10   0   0— **17**
Washington (11-1) ....0 10   3 14— **27**
MVP: Washington RB John Riggins (38 carries, 166 yds, 1 TD; 1 catch, 15 yds)

Most Popular Playing Sites
Stadiums hosting more than one Super Bowl.

No		Years
5	Orange Bowl (Miami)	1968-69, 71, 76, 79
5	Rose Bowl (Pasadena)	1977, 80, 83, 87, 93
4	Superdome (N. Orleans)	1978, 81, 86, 90
3	Tulane Stadium (N. Orleans)	1970, 72, 75
2	Joe Robbie Stadium (Miami)	1989, 95
2	LA Memorial Coliseum	1967, 73
2	Tampa Stadium	1984, 91

1983 Season

AFC Playoffs

First Round ....at *Seattle 31, *Denver 7
Second Round ....Seattle 27, at Miami 20
......................at LA Raiders 38, Pittsburgh 10
Championship ....at LA Raiders 30, Seattle 14

NFC Playoffs

First Round ....*LA Rams 24, at *Dallas 17
Second Round ....at San Francisco 24, Detroit 23
......................at Washington 51, LA Rams 7
Championship ....at Washington 24, San Francisco 21

Super Bowl XVIII

Jan. 22, 1984
Tampa Stadium, Tampa
Favorite: Redskins by 3   Attendance: 72,920

Washington (16-2)	0	3	6	0—	**9**
LA Raiders (14-4)	7	14	14	3—	**38**

MVP: LA Raiders RB Marcus Allen (20 carries, 191 yds,
2 TD; 2 catches, 18 yds)

1984 Season

AFC Playoffs

First Round............................at *Seattle 13, *LA Raiders 7
Second Round ....at Miami 31, Seattle 10
...........................Pittsburgh 24, at Denver 17
Championship...........................at Miami 45, Pittsburgh 28

NFC Playoffs

First Round ....*NY Giants 16, at *LA Rams 13
Second Round...............at San Francisco 21, NY Giants 10
.......................Chicago 23, at Washington 19
Championship...................at San Francisco 23, Chicago 0

Super Bowl XIX

Jan. 20, 1985
Stanford Stadium, Stanford, Calif.
Favorite: 49ers by 3   Attendance: 84,059

Miami (16-2)	10	6	0	0—	**16**
San Francisco (17-1)	7	21	10	0—	**38**

MVP: San Francisco QB Joe Montana (24 for 35, 331
yds, 2 TD; 5 carries, 59 yards, 1 TD)

1985 Season

AFC Playoffs

First Round ....*New England 26, at *NY Jets 14
Second Round...........................at Miami 24, Cleveland 21
...........................New England 27, at LA Raiders 20
Championship ....New England 31, at Miami 14

NFC Playoffs

First Round................at *NY Giants 17, *San Francisco 3
Second Round...............................at LA Rams 20, Dallas 0
.......................at Chicago 21, NY Giants 0
Championship ....at Chicago 24, LA Rams 0

Super Bowl XX

Jan. 26, 1986
Louisiana Superdome, New Orleans
Favorite: Bears by 10   Attendance: 73,818

Chicago Bears (17-1)	13	10	21	2—	**46**
New England (14-5)	3	0	0	7—	**10**

MVP: Chicago DE Richard Dent (Bears defense: 7 sacks, 6
turnovers, 1 safety and gave up just 123 total yards)

1986 Season

AFC Playoffs

First Round ....at *NY Jets 35, *Kansas City 15
Second Round...............at Cleveland 23, NY Jets 20 (OT)
.....................at Denver 22, New England 17
Championship ....Denver 23, at Cleveland 20 (OT)

NFC Playoffs

First Round ....at *Washington 19, *LA Rams 7
Second Round...................Washington 27, at Chicago 13
......................at NY Giants 49, San Francisco 3
Championship ....at NY Giants 17, Washington 0

Super Bowl XXI

Jan. 25, 1987
Rose Bowl, Pasadena
Favorite: Giants by 9½   Attendance: 101,063

Denver (13-5)	10	0	0	10—	**20**
NY Giants (16-2)	7	2	17	13—	**39**

MVP: NY Giants QB Phil Simms (22 for 25, 268 yds, 3
TD; 3 carries, 25 yds)

1987 Season

A 24-day players' strike shortened the regular season to 15
games with replacement teams playing for three weeks.

AFC Playoffs

First Round ....at *Houston 23, *Seattle 20 (OT)
Second Round ....at Cleveland 38, Indianapolis 21
...............................at Denver 34, Houston 10
Championship ....at Denver 38, Cleveland 33

NFC Playoffs

First Round ....*Minnesota 44, at *New Orleans 10
Second Round...............Minnesota 36, at San Francisco 24
.....................Washington 21, at Chicago 17
Championship ....at Washington 17, Minnesota 10

Super Bowl XXII

Jan. 31, 1988
San Diego/Jack Murphy Stadium
Favorite: Broncos by 3½   Attendance: 73,302

Washington (13-4)	0	35	0	7—	**42**
Denver (12-4-1)	10	0	0	0—	**10**

MVP: Washington QB Doug Williams (18 for 29, 340
yds, 4 TD, 1 Int)

1988 Season

AFC Playoffs

First Round...........................*Houston 24, at *Cleveland 23
Second Round ....at Buffalo 17, Houston 10
...............................at Cincinnati 21, Seattle 13
Championship ....at Cincinnati 21, Buffalo 10

NFC Playoffs

First Round ....at *Minnesota 28, *LA Rams 17
Second Round...............at San Francisco 34, Minnesota 9
.......................at Chicago 20, Philadelphia 12
Championship...................San Francisco 28, at Chicago 3

Super Bowl XXIII

Jan. 22, 1989
Joe Robbie Stadium, Miami
Favorite: 49ers by 7   Attendance: 75,129

Cincinnati (17-1)	0	3	10	3—	**16**
San Francisco (14-5)	3	0	3	14—	**20**

MVP: San Francisco WR Jerry Rice (11 catches, 215 yds,
1 TD; 1 carry, 5 yds)

Super Bowl Playoffs (Cont.)

1989 Season

AFC Playoffs

First Round ....*Pittsburgh 26, at *Houston 23
Second Round..........................at Cleveland 34, Buffalo 30
.............................at Denver 24, Pittsburgh 23
Championship ....at Denver 37, Cleveland 21

NFC Playoffs

First Round ....*LA Rams 21, at *Philadelphia 7
Second Round.................LA Rams 19, NY Giants 13 (OT)
................at San Francisco 41, Minnesota 13
Championship ....at San Francisco 30, LA Rams 3

Super Bowl XXIV

Jan. 28, 1990
Louisiana Superdome, New Orleans
Favorite: 49ers by 12½   Attendance: 72,919

San Francisco (17-2)...............13 14 14 14— **55**
Denver (13-6) 3   0   7   0— **10**
MVP: San Francisco QB Joe Montana (22 for 29, 297 yds, 5 TD, 0 Int)

1990 Season

AFC Playoffs

First Round..........................at *Miami 17, *Kansas City 16
..........................at Cincinnati 41, *Houston 14
Second Round..........................at Buffalo 44, Miami 34
.............................at LA Raiders 20, Cincinnati 10
Championship ....at Buffalo 51, LA Raiders 3

NFC Playoffs

First Round....................*Washington 20, at *Philadelphia 6
..........................at Chicago 16, *New Orleans 6
Second Round ....at San Francisco 28, Washington 10
.............................at NY Giants 31, Chicago 3
Championship...............NY Giants 15, at San Francisco 13

Super Bowl XXV

Jan. 27, 1991
Tampa Stadium, Tampa
Favorite: Bills by 7   Attendance: 73,813

Buffalo (15-4)..............................3   9   0   7— **19**
NY Giants (16-3)........................3   7   7   3— **20**
MVP: NY Giants RB Ottis Anderson (21 carries, 102 yds, 1 TD; 1 catch, 7 yds)

1991 Season

AFC Playoffs

First Round ....at *Kansas City 10, *LA Raiders 6
...................................at Houston 17, *NY Jets 10
Second Round ....at Denver 26, Houston 24
.............................at Buffalo 37, Kansas City 14
Championship.................................at Buffalo 10, Denver 7

NFC Playoffs

First Round........................*Atlanta 27, at New Orleans 20
.............................*Dallas 17, at *Chicago 13
Second Round ....at Washington 24, Atlanta 7
.............................at Detroit 38, Dallas 6
Championship.......................at Washington 41, Detroit 10

Super Bowl XXVI

Jan. 26, 1992
Hubert Humphrey Metrodome, Minneapolis
Favorite: Redskins by 7   Attendance: 63,130

Washington (16-2) ....0 17 14   6— **37**
Buffalo (15-3) 0   0 10 14— **24**
MVP: Washington QB Mark Rypien (18 for 33, 292 yds, 2 TD, 1 Int)

1992 Season

AFC Playoffs

First Round.......................at *Buffalo 41, *Houston 38 (OT)
.......................at San Diego 17, *Kansas City 0
Second Round ....Buffalo 24, at Pittsburgh 3
.............................at Miami 31, San Diego 0
Championship.................................Buffalo 29, at Miami 10

NFC Playoffs

First Round ....*Washington 24, at Minnesota 7
..............*Philadelphia 36, at *New Orleans 20
Second Round ....at San Francisco 20, Washington 13
.........................at Dallas 34, Philadelphia 10
Championship....................Dallas 30, at San Francisco 20

Super Bowl XXVII

Jan. 31, 1993
Rose Bowl, Pasadena
Favorite: Cowboys by 7   Attendance: 98,374

Buffalo (14-5) 7   3   7   0— **17**
Dallas (15-3)..........................14 14   3 21— **52**
MVP: Dallas QB Troy Aikman (22 for 30, 273 yds, 4 TD, 0 Int)

1993 Season

AFC Playoffs

First Round...............at Kansas City 27, *Pittsburgh 24 (OT)
.......................at *LA Raiders 42, *Denver 24
Second Round..........................at Buffalo 29, LA Raiders 23
.......................Kansas City 28, at Houston 20
Championship......................at Buffalo 30, Kansas City 13

NFC Playoffs

First Round ....*Green Bay 28, at Detroit 24
...................at *NY Giants 17, *Minnesota 10
Second Round.................at San Francisco 44, NY Giants 3
.............................at Dallas 27, Green Bay 17
Championship....................at Dallas 38, San Francisco 21

Super Bowl XXVIII

Jan. 30, 1994
Georgia Dome, Atlanta
Favorite: Cowboys by 10½   Attendance: 72,817

Dallas (15-4) 6   0 14 10— **30**
Buffalo (14-5) ....3 10   0   0— **13**
MVP: Dallas RB Emmitt Smith (30 carries, 132 yds, 2 TDs; 4 catches, 26 yds)

1994 Season

AFC Playoffs

First Round ....at Miami 27, *Kansas City 17
................at *Cleveland 20, *New England 13
Second Round........................at Pittsburgh 29, Cleveland 9
...........................at San Diego 22, Miami 21
Championship....................San Diego 17, at Pittsburgh 13

NFC Playoffs

First Round ....at *Green Bay 16, *Detroit 12
...........................*Chicago 25, at Minnesota 18
Second Round.................at San Francisco 44, Chicago 15
...............................at Dallas 35, Green Bay 9
Championship....................at San Francisco 38, Dallas 28

Super Bowl XXIX

Jan. 29, 1995
Joe Robbie Stadium, Miami
Favorite: 49ers by 18   Attendance: 74,107

San Diego (13-5) 7	3	8	8—	**26**
San Francisco (15-3)................14	14	14	7—	**49**

MVP: San Francisco QB Steve Young (24 for 36, 325 yds, 6 TD, 0 Int.)

Before the Super Bowl

The first NFL champion was the Akron Pros in 1920, when the league was called the American Professional Football Association (APFA) and the title went to the team with the best regular season record. The APFA changed its name to the National Football League in 1922.

The first playoff game with the championship at stake came in 1932, when the Chicago Bears (6-1-6) and Portsmouth (Ohio) Spartans (6-1-4) ended the regular season tied for first place. The Bears won the subsequent playoff, 9-0. Due to a snowstorm and cold weather, the game was moved from Wrigley Field to an improvised 80-yard dirt field at Chicago Stadium, making it the first indoor title game as well.

The NFL Championship Game decided the league title until the NFL merged with the AFL and the first Super Bowl was played following the 1966 season.

NFL Champions, 1920-32

Winning player-coaches noted by position.
Multiple winners: Canton-Cleveland Bulldogs and Green Bay (3); Chicago Staleys/Bears (2).

Year	Champion	Head Coach
1920	Akron Pros	Fritz Pollard, HB & Elgie Tobin, QB
1921	Chicago Staleys	George Halas, E
1922	Canton Bulldogs	Guy Chamberlin, E
1923	Canton Bulldogs	Guy Chamberlin, E
1924	Cleveland Bulldogs	Guy Chamberlin, E
1925	Chicago Cardinals	Norm Barry
1926	Frankford Yellow Jackets	Guy Chamberlin, E
1927	New York Giants	Earl Potteiger, QB
1928	Providence Steam Roller	Jimmy Conzelman, HB
1929	Green Bay Packers	Curly Lambeau, QB
1930	Green Bay Packers	Curly Lambeau
1931	Green Bay Packers	Curly Lambeau
1932	Chicago Bears	Ralph Jones
	(Bears beat Portsmouth-OH in playoff, 9-0)	

NFL-NFC Championship Game

NFL Championship games from 1933-69 and NFC Championship games since the completion of the NFL-AFL merger following the 1969 season.
Multiple winners: Green Bay (8); Chicago Bears, Dallas and Washington (7); NY Giants and San Francisco (5); Cleveland Browns, Detroit, Minnesota, and Philadelphia (4); Baltimore (3); Cleveland-LA Rams (2).

Season	Winner	Head Coach	Score	Loser	Head Coach	Site
1933	Chicago Bears	George Halas	23-21	New York	Steve Owen	Chicago
1934	New York	Steve Owen	30-13	Chicago Bears	George Halas	New York
1935	Detroit	Potsy Clark	26- 7	New York	Steve Owen	Detroit
1936	Green Bay	Curly Lambeau	21- 6	Boston Redskins	Ray Flaherty	New York
1937	Washington Redskins	Ray Flaherty	28-21	Chicago Bears	George Halas	Chicago
1938	New York	Steve Owen	23-17	Green Bay	Curly Lambeau	New York
1939	Green Bay	Curly Lambeau	27- 0	New York	Steve Owen	Milwaukee
1940	Chicago Bears	George Halas	73- 0	Washington	Ray Flaherty	Washington
1941	Chicago Bears	George Halas	37- 9	New York	Steve Owen	Chicago
1942	Washington	Ray Flaherty	14- 6	Chicago Bears	Hunk Anderson & Luke Johnsos	Washington
1943	Chicago Bears	Hunk Anderson & Luke Johnsos	41-21	Washington	Arthur Bergman	Chicago
1944	Green Bay	Curly Lambeau	14- 7	New York	Steve Owen	New York
1945	Cleveland Rams	Adam Walsh	15-14	Washington	Dudley DeGroot	Cleveland
1946	Chicago Bears	George Halas	24-14	New York	Steve Owen	New York
1947	Chicago Cardinals	Jimmy Conzelman	28-21	Philadelphia	Greasy Neale	Chicago
1948	Philadelphia	Greasy Neale	7- 0	Chicago Cardinals	Jimmy Conzelman	Philadelphia
1949	Philadelphia	Greasy Neale	14- 0	Los Angeles Rams	Clark Shaughnessy	Los Angeles
1950	Cleveland Browns	Paul Brown	30-28	Los Angeles	Joe Stydahar	Cleveland
1951	Los Angeles	Joe Stydahar	24-17	Cleveland	Paul Brown	Los Angeles
1952	Detroit	Buddy Parker	17- 7	Cleveland	Paul Brown	Cleveland
1953	Detroit	Buddy Parker	17-16	Cleveland	Paul Brown	Detroit
1954	Cleveland	Paul Brown	56-10	Detroit	Buddy Parker	Cleveland
1955	Cleveland	Paul Brown	38-14	Los Angeles	Sid Gillman	Los Angeles
1956	New York	Jim Lee Howell	47- 7	Chicago Bears	Paddy Driscoll	New York

NFL-NFC Championship Game (Cont.)

Season	Winner	Head Coach	Score	Loser	Head Coach	Site
1957	Detroit	George Wilson	59-14	Cleveland	Paul Brown	Detroit
1958	Baltimore	Weeb Ewbank	23-17*	New York	Jim Lee Howell	New York
1959	Baltimore	Weeb Ewbank	31-16	New York	Jim Lee Howell	Baltimore
1960	Philadelphia	Buck Shaw	17-13	Green Bay	Vince Lombardi	Philadelphia
1961	Green Bay	Vince Lombardi	37- 0	New York	Allie Sherman	Green Bay
1962	Green Bay	Vince Lombardi	16- 7	New York	Allie Sherman	New York
1963	Chicago	George Halas	14-10	New York	Allie Sherman	Chicago
1964	Cleveland	Blanton Collier	27- 0	Baltimore	Don Shula	Cleveland
1965	Green Bay	Vince Lombardi	23-12	Cleveland	Blanton Collier	Green Bay
1966	Green Bay	Vince Lombardi	34-27	Dallas	Tom Landry	Dallas
1967	Green Bay	Vince Lombardi	21-17	Dallas	Tom Landry	Green Bay
1968	Baltimore	Don Shula	34- 0	Cleveland	Blanton Collier	Cleveland
1969	Minnesota	Bud Grant	27- 7	Cleveland	Blanton Collier	Minnesota
1970	Dallas	Tom Landry	17-10	San Francisco	Dick Nolan	San Francisco
1971	Dallas	Tom Landry	14- 3	San Francisco	Dick Nolan	Dallas
1972	Washington	George Allen	26- 3	Dallas	Tom Landry	Washington
1973	Minnesota	Bud Grant	27-10	Dallas	Tom Landry	Dallas
1974	Minnesota	Bud Grant	14-10	Los Angeles	Chuck Knox	Minnesota
1975	Dallas	Tom Landry	37- 7	Los Angeles	Chuck Knox	Los Angeles
1976	Minnesota	Bud Grant	24-13	Los Angeles	Chuck Knox	Minnesota
1977	Dallas	Tom Landry	23- 6	Minnesota	Bud Grant	Dallas
1978	Dallas	Tom Landry	28- 0	Los Angeles	Ray Malavasi	Los Angeles
1979	Los Angeles	Ray Malavasi	9- 0	Tampa Bay	John McKay	Tampa Bay
1980	Philadelphia	Dick Vermeil	20- 7	Dallas	Tom Landry	Philadelphia
1981	San Francisco	Bill Walsh	28-27	Dallas	Tom Landry	San Francisco
1982	Washington	Joe Gibbs	31-17	Dallas	Tom Landry	Washington
1983	Washington	Joe Gibbs	24-21	San Francisco	Bill Walsh	Washington
1984	San Francisco	Bill Walsh	23- 0	Chicago	Mike Ditka	San Francisco
1985	Chicago	Mike Ditka	24- 0	Los Angeles	John Robinson	Chicago
1986	New York	Bill Parcells	17- 0	Washington	Joe Gibbs	New York
1987	Washington	Joe Gibbs	17-10	Minnesota	Jerry Burns	Washington
1988	San Francisco	Bill Walsh	28- 3	Chicago	Mike Ditka	Chicago
1989	San Francisco	George Seifert	30- 3	Los Angeles	John Robinson	San Francisco
1990	New York	Bill Parcells	15-13	San Francisco	George Seifert	San Francisco
1991	Washington	Joe Gibbs	41-10	Detroit	Wayne Fontes	Washington
1992	Dallas	Jimmy Johnson	30-20	San Francisco	George Seifert	San Francisco
1993	Dallas	Jimmy Johnson	38-21	San Francisco	George Seifert	Dallas
1994	San Francisco	George Seifert	38-28	Dallas	Barry Switzer	San Francisco

*Sudden death overtime

NFL-NFC Championship Game Appearances

App		W	L	Pct	PF	PA	App		W	L	Pct	PF	PA
16	NY Giants	5	11	.313	240	322	10	Green Bay	8	2	.800	223	116
15	Dallas Cowboys	7	8	.467	323	292	6	Minnesota	4	2	.667	108	80
13	Chicago Bears	7	6	.538	286	245	6	Detroit	4	2	.667	139	141
12	Boston-Wash.Redskins	7	5	.583	222	255	5	Philadelphia	4	1	.800	79	48
12	Cleveland-LA Rams	3	9	.250	123	270	4	Baltimore Colts	3	1	.750	88	60
11	San Francisco	5	6	.455	235	199	2	Chicago Cardinals	1	1	.500	28	28
11	Cleveland Browns	4	7	.364	224	253	1	Tampa Bay	0	1	.000	0	9

AFL-AFC Championship Game

AFL Championship games from 1960-69 and AFC Championship games since the completion of the NFL-AFL merger following the 1969 season.

Multiple winners: Buffalo (6); Miami (5); Denver, Oakland-LA Raiders and Pittsburgh (4); Dallas Texans-KC Chiefs (3); Cincinnati, Houston and San Diego (2).

Season	Winner	Head Coach	Score	Loser	Head Coach	Site
1960	Houston	Lou Rymkus	24-16	LA Chargers	Sid Gillman	Houston
1961	Houston	Wally Lemm	10- 3	SD Chargers	Sid Gillman	San Diego
1962	Dallas	Hank Stram	20-17*	Houston	Pop Ivy	Houston
1963	San Diego	Sid Gillman	51-10	Boston Patriots	Mike Holovak	San Diego
1964	Buffalo	Lou Saban	20- 7	San Diego	Sid Gillman	Buffalo
1965	Buffalo	Lou Saban	23- 0	San Diego	Sid Gillman	San Diego
1966	Kansas City	Hank Stram	31- 7	Buffalo	Joel Collier	Buffalo
1967	Oakland	John Rauch	40- 7	Houston	Wally Lemm	Oakland
1968	NY Jets	Webb Ewbank	27-23	Oakland	John Rauch	New York
1969	Kansas City	Hank Stram	17- 7	Oakland	John Madden	Oakland

Season	Winner	Head Coach	Score	Loser	Head Coach	Site
1970	Baltimore	Don McCafferty	27-17	Oakland	John Madden	Baltimore
1971	Miami	Don Shula	21- 0	Baltimore	Don McCafferty	Miami
1972	Miami	Don Shula	21-17	Pittsburgh	Chuck Noll	Pittsburgh
1973	Miami	Don Shula	27-10	Oakland	John Madden	Miami
1974	Pittsburgh	Chuck Noll	24-13	Oakland	John Madden	Oakland
1975	Pittsburgh	Chuck Noll	16-10	Oakland	John Madden	Pittsburgh
1976	Oakland	John Madden	24- 7	Pittsburgh	Chuck Noll	Oakland
1977	Denver	Red Miller	20-17	Oakland	John Madden	Denver
1978	Pittsburgh	Chuck Noll	34- 5	Houston	Bum Phillips	Pittsburgh
1979	Pittsburgh	Chuck Noll	27-13	Houston	Bum Phillips	Pittsburgh
1980	Oakland	Tom Flores	34-27	San Diego	Don Coryell	San Diego
1981	Cincinnati	Forrest Gregg	27- 7	San Diego	Don Coryell	Cincinnati
1982	Miami	Don Shula	14- 0	NY Jets	Walt Michaels	Miami
1983	LA Raiders	Tom Flores	30-14	Seattle	Chuck Knox	Los Angeles
1984	Miami	Don Shula	45-28	Pittsburgh	Chuck Noll	Miami
1985	NE Patriots	Raymond Berry	31-14	Miami	Don Shula	Miami
1986	Denver	Dan Reeves	23-20*	Cleveland	Marty Schottenheimer	Cleveland
1987	Denver	Dan Reeves	38-33	Cleveland	Marty Schottenheimer	Denver
1988	Cincinnati	Sam Wyche	21-10	Buffalo	Marv Levy	Cincinnati
1989	Denver	Dan Reeves	37-21	Cleveland	Bud Carson	Denver
1990	Buffalo	Marv Levy	51- 3	LA Raiders	Art Shell	Buffalo
1991	Buffalo	Marv Levy	10- 7	Denver	Dan Reeves	Buffalo
1992	Buffalo	Marv Levy	29-10	Miami	Don Shula	Miami
1993	Buffalo	Marv Levy	30-13	Kansas City	Marty Schottenheimer	Buffalo
1994	San Diego	Bobby Ross	17-13	Pittsburgh	Bill Cowher	Pittsburgh

*Sudden death overtime

AFL-AFC Championship Game Appearances

App		W	L	Pct	PF	PA	App		W	L	Pct	PF	PA
12	Oakland-LA Raiders	4	8	.333	228	264	4	Dallas Texans/KC Chiefs	3	1	.750	81	61
8	Buffalo	6	2	.750	180	92	3	Cleveland	0	3	.000	74	98
8	Pittsburgh	4	4	.500	166	148	2	Cincinnati	2	0	1.000	48	17
8	LA-San Diego Chargers	2	6	.250	128	161	2	Baltimore Colts	1	1	.500	27	38
7	Miami	5	2	.714	152	115	2	Boston-NE Patriots	1	1	.500	41	65
6	Houston	2	4	.333	76	140	2	NY Jets	1	1	.500	27	37
5	Denver	4	1	.800	125	101	1	Seattle	0	1	.000	14	30

NFL Divisional Champions

The NFL adopted divisional play for the first time in 1967, splitting both conferences into two four-team divisions—the Capitol and Century divisions in the East and the Central and Coastal divisions in the West. Merger with the AFL in 1970 increased NFL membership to 26 teams and made it necessary for the league to realign. Two 13-team conferences—the AFC and NFC—were formed by moving established NFL clubs in Baltimore, Cleveland and Pittsburgh to the AFC and rearranging both conferences into Eastern, Central and Western divisions.

Division champions are listed below; teams that went on to win the Super Bowl are in **bold** type. Note that in 1980, Oakland won the Super Bowl as a wild card team; and in 1982, the players' strike shortened the regular season to nine games and eliminated divisional play for one season.

Multiple champions (since 1970): **AFC**—Miami and Pittsburgh (11); Oakland-LA Raiders (9); Denver (7); Buffalo and Cleveland (6); Baltimore-Indianapolis Colts, Cincinnati and San Diego (5); Houston, Kansas City and New England (2). **NFC**—San Francisco (14); Dallas and Minnesota (12); LA Rams (8); Chicago (6); Washington (5); Detroit and NY Giants (3); Philadelphia, St. Louis Cardinals and Tampa Bay (2).

American Football League

Season	East	West
1966	Buffalo	Kansas City

Season	East	West
1967	Houston	Oakland
1968	**NY Jets**	Oakland
1969	NY Jets	Oakland

Note: Kansas City, an AFL Wild Card team, won the Super Bowl in 1969.

National Football League

Season	East		West
1966	Dallas		**Green Bay**

Season	Capitol	Century	Central	Coastal
1967	Dallas	Cleveland	**Green Bay**	LA Rams
1968	Dallas	Cleveland	Minnesota	Baltimore
1969	Dallas	Cleveland	Minnesota	LA Rams

American Football Conference

Season	East	Central	West
1970	**Baltimore**	Cincinnati	Oakland
1971	Miami	Cleveland	Kansas City
1972	**Miami**	Pittsburgh	Oakland
1973	**Miami**	Cincinnati	Oakland
1974	Miami	**Pittsburgh**	Oakland
1975	Baltimore	**Pittsburgh**	Oakland
1976	Baltimore	Pittsburgh	**Oakland**
1977	Baltimore	Pittsburgh	Denver

National Football Conference

Season	East	Central	West
1970	Dallas	Minnesota	San Francisco
1971	**Dallas**	Minnesota	San Francisco
1972	Washington	Green Bay	San Francisco
1973	Dallas	Minnesota	LA Rams
1974	St. Louis	Minnesota	LA Rams
1975	St. Louis	Minnesota	LA Rams
1976	Dallas	Minnesota	LA Rams
1977	**Dallas**	Minnesota	LA Rams

NFL Divisional Champions (Cont.)

American Football Conference

Season	East	Central	West
1978	New England	Pittsburgh	Denver
1979	Miami	Pittsburgh	San Diego
1980	Buffalo	Cleveland	San Diego
1981	Miami	Cincinnati	San Diego
1982	—	—	—
1983	Miami	Pittsburgh	LA Raiders
1984	Miami	Pittsburgh	Denver
1985	Miami	Cleveland	LA Raiders
1986	New England	Cleveland	Denver
1987	Indianapolis	Cleveland	Denver
1988	Buffalo	Cincinnati	Seattle
1989	Buffalo	Cleveland	Denver
1990	Buffalo	Cincinnati	LA Raiders
1991	Buffalo	Houston	Denver
1992	Miami	Pittsburgh	San Diego
1993	Buffalo	Houston	Kansas City
1994	Miami	Pittsburgh	San Diego

National Football Conference

Season	East	Central	West
1978	Dallas	Minnesota	LA Rams
1979	Dallas	Tampa Bay	LA Rams
1980	Philadelphia	Minnesota	Atlanta
1981	Dallas	Tampa Bay	San Francisco
1982			
1983	Washington	Detroit	San Francisco
1984	Washington	Chicago	San Francisco
1985	Dallas	Chicago	LA Rams
1986	NY Giants	Chicago	San Francisco
1987	Washington	Chicago	San Francisco
1988	Philadelphia	Chicago	San Francisco
1989	NY Giants	Minnesota	San Francisco
1990	NY Giants	Chicago	San Francisco
1991	Washington	Detroit	New Orleans
1992	Dallas	Minnesota	San Francisco
1993	Dallas	Detroit	San Francisco
1994	Dallas	Minnesota	San Francisco

Note: Oakland, an AFC Wild Card team, won the Super Bowl in 1980.

Overall Postseason Games

The postseason records of all NFL teams, ranked by number of playoff games participated in from 1933 through the 1994 season.

Gm		W	L	Pct	PF	PA
46	Dallas Cowboys	28	18	.609	1102	836
36	Oakland-LA Raiders	21	15	.583	855	659
35	Boston-Wash. Redskins	21	14	.600	738	625
33	Cleveland-LA Rams	13	20	.394	501	697
32	San Francisco 49ers	21	11	.656	843	605
32	New York Giants	14	18	.438	529	593
31	Minnesota Vikings	13	18	.419	553	646
30	Miami Dolphins	17	13	.567	675	596
30	Cleveland Browns	11	19	.367	596	702
29	Pittsburgh Steelers	17	12	.586	651	571
28	Chicago Bears	14	14	.500	579	552
24	Buffalo Bills	13	11	.542	563	520
22	Green Bay Packers	15	7	.682	486	357
22	Houston Oilers	9	13	.409	371	533

Gm		W	L	Pct	PF	PA
19	Denver Broncos	9	10	.474	380	502
17	Philadelphia Eagles	8	9	.471	287	288
17	Dallas Texans/KC Chiefs	8	9	.471	284	360
17	LA-San Diego Chargers	7	10	.412	312	393
16	Balt-Indianapolis Colts	8	8	.500	285	300
14	Detroit Lions	7	7	.500	305	299
12	Cincinnati Bengals	5	7	.417	246	257
11	New York Jets	5	6	.455	216	200
11	Boston-NE Patriots	4	7	.364	208	278
7	Seattle Seahawks	3	4	.429	128	139
6	Atlanta Falcons	2	4	.333	119	144
5	Chi-St. L. Cardinals	1	4	.200	81	134
4	Tampa Bay Buccaneers	1	3	.250	41	94
4	New Orleans Saints	0	4	.000	56	123

All-Time Postseason Leaders

Through Super Bowl XXIX, Jan. 29, 1995; participants in 1994 season playoffs in **bold** type.

CAREER

Passing Efficiency

Ratings based on performance standards established for completion percentage, average gain, touchdown percentage and interception percentage. Minimum 150 passing attempts.

	Gm	Cmp%	Yds	TD	Int	Rtg
1 Bart Starr	10	61.0	1753	15	3	104.8
2 Troy Aikman	9	68.9	2312	17	8	103.8
3 Steve Young	15	65.4	1884	14	5	99.5
4 Joe Montana	23	62.7	5772	45	21	95.6
5 Kenny Anderson	6	66.3	1321	9	6	93.5
6 Joe Theismann	10	60.7	1782	11	7	91.4
7 Dan Marino	12	56.8	3178	27	14	85.6
8 Warren Moon	10	64.3	2870	17	14	84.9
9 Ken Stabler	13	57.8	2641	19	13	84.2
10 Bernie Kosar	9	56.1	1943	16	10	83.3

Receptions

Catches	Gm	No	Yds	Avg
1 Jerry Rice	18	100	1539	15.5
2 Cliff Branch	22	73	1289	17.7
3 Fred Biletnikoff	19	70	1167	16.7

Rushing

Yards Gained	Gm	Car	Yds	Avg
1 Franco Harris	19	400	1556	3.89
2 Tony Dorsett	17	302	1383	4.58
3 Marcus Allen	14	234	1216	5.20

Scoring

Points	Gm	TD	FG	PAT	Pts
1 George Blanda	19	0	22	49	115
2 Matt Bahr	14	0	21	40	103
3 Jerry Rice	18	17	0	0	102
Franco Harris	19	17	0	0	102

Touchdowns	Gm	Run	Rec	Ret	No
1 Jerry Rice	18	0	17	0	17
Franco Harris	19	16	1	0	17
3 Thurman Thomas	16	12	3	0	15

Field Goals	Gm	Att	FG	Pct
1 George Blanda	19	39	22	.564
2 Matt Bahr	14	25	21	.840
3 Toni Fritsch	14	28	20	.714

Champions Of Leagues That No Longer Exist

No professional league in American sports has had to contend with more pretenders to the throne than the NFL. Seven times in as many decades a rival league has risen up to challenge the NFL and six of them went under in less than five seasons. Only the fourth American Football League (1960-69) succeeded, forcing the older league to sue for peace and a full partnership in 1966.

Of the six leagues that didn't make it, only the All-America Football Conference (1946-49) lives on—the Cleveland Browns and San Francisco 49ers joined the NFL after the AAFC folded in 1949. The champions of leagues past are listed below.

American Football League I

Year		Head Coach
1926	Philadelphia Quakers (7-2)	Bob Folwell

Note: Philadelphia was challenged to a postseason game by the 7th place New York Giants (8-4-1) of the NFL. The Giants won, 31-0, in a snowstorm.

American Football League II

Year		Head Coach
1936	Boston Shamrocks (8-3)	George Kenneally
1937	Los Angeles Bulldogs (8-0)	Gus Henderson

Note: Boston was scheduled to play 2nd place Cleveland (5-2-2) in the '36 championship game, but the Shamrock players refused to participate because they were owed pay for past games.

American Football League III

Year		Head Coach
1940	Columbus Bullies (8-1-1)	Phil Bucklew
1941	Columbus Bullies (5-1-2)	Phil Bucklew

All-America Football Conference

Year	Winner	Head Coach	Score	Loser	Head Coach	Site
1946	Cleveland Browns	Paul Brown	14-9	NY Yankees	Ray Flaherty	Cleveland
1947	Cleveland Browns	Paul Brown	14-3	NY Yankees	Ray Flaherty	New York
1948	Cleveland Browns	Paul Brown	49-7	Buffalo Bills	Red Dawson	Cleveland
1949	Cleveland Browns	Paul Brown	21-7	S.F. 49ers	Buck Shaw	Cleveland

World Football League

Year	Winner	Head Coach	Score	Loser	Head Coach	Site
1974	Birmingham Americans	Jack Gotta	22-21	Florida Blazers	Jack Pardee	Birmingham
1975	WFL folded Oct. 22.					

United States Football League

Year	Winner	Head Coach	Score	Loser	Head Coach	Site
1983	Michigan Panthers	Jim Stanley	24-22	Philadelphia Stars	Jim Mora	Denver
1984	Philadelphia Stars	Jim Mora	23-3	Arizona Wranglers	George Allen	Tampa
1985	Baltimore Stars	Jim Mora	28-24	Oakland Invaders	Charlie Sumner	E. Rutherford

Defunct Leagues

AFL I (1926): Boston Bulldogs, Brooklyn Horseman, Chicago Bulls, Cleveland Panthers, Los Angeles Wildcats, New York Yankees, Newark Bears, Philadelphia Quakers, Rock Island Independents.

AFL II (1936-37): Boston Shamrocks (1936-37); Brooklyn Tigers (1936); Cincinnati Bengals (1937); Cleveland Rams (1936); Los Angeles Bulldogs (1937); New York Yankees (1936-37); Pittsburgh Americans (1936-37); Rochester Tigers (1936-37).

AFL III (1940-41): Boston Bears (1940); Buffalo Indians (1940-41); Cincinnati Bengals (1940-41); Columbus Bullies (1940-41); Milwaukee Chiefs (1940-41); New York Yankees (1940) renamed Americans (1941).

AAFC (1946-49): Brooklyn Dodgers (1946-48) merged to become Brooklyn-New York Yankees (1949); Buffalo Bisons (1946) renamed Bills (1947-49); Chicago Rockets (1946-48) renamed Hornets (1949); Cleveland Browns (1946-49); Los Angeles Dons (1946-49); Miami Seahawks (1946) became Baltimore Colts (1947-49); New York Yankees (1946-48) merged to become Brooklyn-New York Yankees (1949); San Francisco 49ers (1946-49).

WFL (1974-75): Birmingham Americans (1974) renamed Vulcans (1975); Chicago Fire (1974) renamed Winds (1975); Detroit Wheels (1974); Florida Blazers (1974) became San Antonio Wings (1975); The Hawaiians (1974-75); Houston Texans (1974) became Shreveport (La.) Steamer (1974-75); Jacksonville Sharks (1974) renamed Express (1975); Memphis Southmen (1974) also known as Grizzlies (1975); New York Stars (1974) became Charlotte Hornets (1974-75); Philadelphia Bell (1974-75); Portland Storm (1974) renamed Thunder (1975); Southern California Sun (1974-75).

USFL (1983-85): Arizona Wranglers (1983-84) merged with Oklahoma to become Arizona Outlaws (1985); Birmingham Stallions (1983-85); Boston Breakers (1983) became New Orleans Breakers (1984) and then Portland Breakers (1985); Chicago Blitz (1983-84); Denver Gold (1983-85); Houston Gamblers (1984-85); Jacksonville Bulls (1984-85); Los Angeles Express (1983-85); Memphis Showboats (1984-85). Michigan Panthers (1983-84) merged with Oakland (1985); New Jersey Generals (1983-85); Oakland Invaders (1983-85); Oklahoma Outlaws (1984) merged with Arizona to become Arizona Outlaws (1985); Philadelphia Stars (1983-84) became Baltimore Stars (1985); Pittsburgh Maulers (1984); San Antonio Gunslingers (1984-85); Tampa Bay Bandits (1983-85); Washington Federals (1983-84) became Orlando Renegades (1985).

NFL Pro Bowl

A postseason All-Star game between the new league champion and a team of professional all-stars was added to the NFL schedule in 1939. In the first game at Wrigley Field in Los Angeles, the NY Giants beat a team made up of players from NFL teams and two independent clubs in Los Angeles (the LA Bulldogs and Hollywood Stars). An all-NFL All-Star team provided the opposition over the next four seasons, but the game was cancelled in 1943.

The Pro Bowl was revived in 1951 as a contest between conference all-star teams: American vs National (1951-53), Eastern vs Western (1954-70), and AFC vs NFC (since 1971). The NFC leads the current series with the AFC, 14-11.

The MVP trophy was named the Dan McGuire Award in 1984 after the late SF 49ers publicist and *Honolulu Advertiser* sports columnist.

Year	Winner	Score	Loser
1939	NY Giants	13-10	All-Stars
1940	Green Bay	16- 7	All-Stars
1940	Chicago Bears	28-14	All-Stars
1942	Chicago Bears	35-24	All-Stars
1942	All-Stars	17-14	Washington
1943-50		No game	

Year	Winner	MVP
1951	American, 28-27	Otto Graham, Cle., QB
1952	National, 30-13	Dan Towler, LA, HB
1953	National, 27-7	Don Doll, Det., DB
1954	East, 20-9	Chuck Bednarik, Phi., LB
1955	West, 26-19	Billy Wilson, SF, E
1956	East, 31-30	Ollie Matson, Cards, HB
1957	West, 19-10	Back—Bert Rechichar, Bal.
		Line—Ernie Stautner, Pit.
1958	West, 26-7	Back—Hugh McElhenny, SF
		Line—Gene Brito, Wash.
1959	East, 28-21	Back—Frank Gifford, NY
		Line—Doug Atkins, Chi.
1960	West, 38-21	Back—Johnny Unitas, Bal.
		Line—Big Daddy Lipscomb, Pit.
1961	West, 35-31	Back—Johnny Unitas, Bal.
		Line—Sam Huff, NY
1962	West, 31-30	Back—Jim Brown, Cle.
		Line—Henry Jordan, GB
1963	East, 30-20	Back—Jim Brown, Cle.
		Line—Big Daddy Lipscomb, Pit.
1964	West, 31-17	Back—Johnny Unitas, Bal.
		Line—Gino Marchetti, Bal.
1965	West, 34-14	Back—Fran Tarkenton, Min.
		Line—Terry Barr, Det.
1966	East, 36-7	Back—Jim Brown, Cle.
		Line—Dale Meinhart, St.L.
1967	East, 20-10	Back—Gale Sayers, Chi.
		Line—Floyd Peters, Phi.
1968	West, 38-20	Back—Gale Sayers, Chi.
		Line—Dave Robinson, GB

Year	Winner	MVP
1969	West, 10-7	Back—Roman Gabriel, LA
		Line—Merlin Olsen, LA
1970	West, 16-13	Back—Gale Sayers, Chi.
		Line—George Andrie, Dal.
1971	NFC, 27-6	Back—Mel Renfro, Dal.
		Line—Fred Carr, GB
1972	AFC, 26-13	Off—Jan Stenerud, KC
		Def—Willie Lanier, KC
1973	AFC, 33-28	O.J. Simpson, Buf., RB
1974	AFC, 15-13	Garo Yepremian, Mia., PK
1975	NFC, 17-10	James Harris, LA Rams, QB
1976	NFC, 23-20	Billy Johnson, Hou., KR
1977	AFC, 24-14	Mel Blount, Pit., CB
1978	NFC, 14-13	Walter Payton, Chi., RB
1979	NFC, 13-7	Ahmad Rashad, Min., WR
1980	NFC, 37-27	Chuck Muncie, NO, RB
1981	NFC, 21-7	Eddie Murray, Det., PK
1982	AFC, 16-13	Kellen Winslow, SD, WR
		& Lee Roy Selmon, TB, DE
1983	NFC, 20-19	Dan Fouts, SD, QB
		& John Jefferson, GB, WR
1984	NFC, 45-3	Joe Theismann, Wash., QB
1985	AFC, 22-14	Mark Gastineau, NYJ, DE
1986	NFC, 28-24	Phil Simms, NYG, QB
1987	AFC, 10-6	Reggie White, Phi., DE
1988	AFC, 15-6	Bruce Smith, Buf., DE
1989	NFC, 34-3	Randall Cunningham, Phi., QB
1990	NFC, 27-21	Jerry Gray, LA Rams, CB
1991	AFC, 23-21	Jim Kelly, Buf., QB
1992	NFC, 21-15	Michael Irvin, Dal., WR
1993	AFC, 23-20 (OT)	Steve Tasker, Buf., Sp. Teams
1994	NFC, 17-3	Andre Rison, Atl., WR
1995	AFC, 41-13	Marshall Faulk, Ind., RB

Playing sites: Wrigley Field in Los Angeles (1939); Gilmore Stadium in Los Angeles (both games); Polo Grounds in New York (Jan., 1942); Shibe Park in Philadelphia (Dec., 1942); Memorial Coliseum in Los Angeles (1951-72 and 1979); Texas Stadium in Irving, TX (1973); Arrowhead Stadium in Kansas City (1974); Orange Bowl in Miami (1975); Superdome in New Orleans (1976); Kingdome in Seattle (1977); Tampa Stadium in Tampa (1978) and Aloha Stadium in Honolulu (since 1980).

AFL All-Star Game

The AFL did not play an All-Star game after its first season in 1960 but did stage All-Star games from 1962-70. All-Star teams from the Eastern and Western divisions played each other every year except 1966 with the West winning the series, 6-2. In 1966, the league champion Buffalo Bills met an elite squad made up of the best players from the league's other eight clubs and lost, 30-19.

Year	Winner	MVP
1962	West, 47-27	Cotton Davidson, Oak., QB
1963	West, 21-14	Off—Curtis McClinton, Dal.
		Def—Earl Faison, SD
1964	West, 27-24	Off—Keith Lincoln, SD
		Def—Archie Matsos, Oak.
1965	West, 38-14	Off—Keith Lincoln, SD
		Def—Willie Brown, Den.
1966	All-Stars 30	Off—Joe Namath, NY
	Buffalo 19	Def—Frank Buncom, SD

Year	Winner	MVP
1967	East, 30-23	Off—Babe Parilli, Bos.
		Def—Verlon Biggs, NY
1968	East, 25-24	Off—Joe Namath, NY
		& Don Maynard, NY
		Def—Speedy Duncan, SD
1969	West, 38-25	Off—Len Dawson, KC
		Def—George Webster, Hou.
1970	West, 26-3	John Hadl, SD, QB

Playing sites: Balboa Stadium in San Diego (1962-64); Jeppesen Stadium in Houston (1965); Rice Stadium in Houston (1966); Oakland Coliseum (1967); Gator Bowl in Jacksonville (1968-69) and Astrodome in Houston (1970).

NFL Franchise Origins

Here is what the current 30 teams in the National Football League have to show for the years they have put in as members of the American Professional Football Association (APFA), the NFL, the All-America Football Conference (AAFC) and the American Football League (AFL). Years given for league titles indicate seasons championships were won.

American Football Conference

	First Season	League Titles	Franchise Stops
Buffalo Bills	1960 (AFL)	2 AFL (1964-65)	• Buffalo (1960-72) Orchard Park, NY (1973—)
Cincinnati Bengals	1968 (AFL)	None	• Cincinnati (1968—)
Cleveland Browns	1946 (AAFC)	4 AAFC (1946-49) 4 NFL (1950,54-55,64)	• Cleveland (1946—)
Denver Broncos	1960 (AFL)	None	• Denver (1960—)
Houston Oilers	1960 (AFL)	2 AFL (1960-61)	• Houston (1960—)
Indianapolis Colts	1953 (NFL)	3 NFL (1958-59,68) 1 Super Bowl (1970)	• Baltimore (1953-83) Indianapolis (1984—)
Jacksonville Jaguars	1995 (NFL)	None	• Jacksonville, FL (1995—)
Kansas City Chiefs	1960 (AFL)	3 AFL (1962,66,69) 1 Super Bowl (1969)	• Dallas (1960-62) Kansas City (1963—)
Miami Dolphins	1966 (AFL)	2 Super Bowls (1972-73)	• Miami (1966—)
New England Patriots	1960 (AFL)	None	• Boston (1960-70) Foxboro, MA (1971—)
New York Jets	1960 (AFL)	1 AFL (1968) 1 Super Bowl (1968)	• New York (1960-83) E. Rutherford, NJ (1984—)
Oakland Raiders	1960 (AFL)	1 AFL (1967) 3 Super Bowls (1976,80,83)	• Oakland (1960-81, 1995—) Los Angeles (1982-94)
Pittsburgh Steelers	1933 (NFL)	4 Super Bowls (1974-75,78-79)	• Pittsburgh (1933—)
San Diego Chargers	1960 (AFL)	1 AFL (1963)	• Los Angeles (1960) San Diego (1961—)
Seattle Seahawks	1976 (NFL)	None	• Seattle (1976—)

National Football Conference

	First Season	League Titles	Franchise Stops
Arizona Cardinals	1920 (APFA)	2 NFL (1925,47)	• Chicago (1920-59) St. Louis (1960-87) Tempe, AZ (1988—)
Atlanta Falcons	1966 (NFL)	None	• Atlanta (1966—)
Carolina Panthers	1995 (NFL)	None	• Clemson, SC (1995) Charlotte, NC (1996)
Chicago Bears	1920 (APFA)	8 NFL (1921, 32-33,40-41,43, 46,63) 1 Super Bowl (1985)	• Decatur, IL (1920) Chicago (1921—)
Dallas Cowboys	1960 (NFL)	4 Super Bowls (1971,77,92-93)	• Dallas (1960-70) Irving, TX (1971—)
Detroit Lions	1930 (NFL)	4 NFL (1935,52-53,57)	• Portsmouth, OH (1930-33) Detroit (1934-74) Pontiac, MI (1975—)
Green Bay Packers	1921 (APFA)	11 NFL (1929-31,36,39,44, 61-62,65-67) 2 Super Bowls (1966-67)	• Green Bay (1921—)
Minnesota Vikings	1961 (NFL)	1 NFL (1969)	• Bloomington, MN (1961-81) Minneapolis, MN (1982—)
New Orleans Saints	1967 (NFL)	None	• New Orleans (1967—)
New York Giants	1925 (NFL)	4 NFL (1927,34,38,56) 2 Super Bowls (1986,90)	• New York (1925-73,75) New Haven, CT (1973-74) E. Rutherford, NJ (1976—)
Philadelphia Eagles	1933 (NFL)	3 NFL (1948-49,60)	• Philadelphia (1933—)
St. Louis Rams	1937 (NFL)	2 NFL (1945,51)	• Cleveland (1937-45) Los Angeles (1946-79) Anaheim (1980-94) St. Louis (1995—)
San Francisco 49ers	1946 (AAFC)	5 Super Bowls (1981,84,88-89,94)	• San Francisco (1946—)
Tampa Bay Buccaneers	1976 (NFL)	None	• Tampa, FL (1976—)
Washington Redskins	1932 (NFL)	2 NFL (1937,42) 3 Super Bowls (1982,87,91)	• Boston (1932-36) Washington, DC (1937—)

The Growth of the NFL

Of the 14 franchises that comprised the American Professional Football Association in 1920, only two remain—the Arizona Cardinals (then the Chicago Cardinals) and the Chicago Bears (originally the Decatur-IL Staleys). Green Bay joined the APFC in 1921 and the league changed its name to the NFL in 1922. Since then, 54 NFL clubs have come and gone, five rival leagues have expired and two other leagues have been swallowed up.

The NFL merged with the **All-America Football Conference** (1946-49) following the 1949 season and adopted three of its seven clubs—the Baltimore Colts, Cleveland Browns and San Francisco 49ers. The four remaining AAFC teams—the Brooklyn/NY Yankees, Buffalo Bills, Chicago Hornets and Los Angeles Dons—did not survive. After the 1950 season, the financially troubled Colts were sold back to the NFL. The league folded the team and added its players to the 1951 college draft pool. A new Baltimore franchise, also named the Colts, joined the NFL in 1953.

The formation of the **American Football League** (1960-69) was announced in 1959 with ownership lined up in eight cities—Boston, Buffalo, Dallas, Denver, Houston, Los Angeles, Minneapolis and New York. Set to begin play in the autumn of 1960, the AFL was stunned early that year when Minneapolis withdrew to accept an offer to join the NFL as an expansion team in 1961. The new league responded by choosing Oakland to replace Minneapolis and inherit the departed team's draft picks. Since no AFL team actually played in Minneapolis, it is not considered the original home of the Oakland Raiders.

In 1966, the NFL and AFL agreed to a merger that resulted in the first Super Bowl (originally called the AFL-NFL World Championship Game) following the '66 league playoffs. In 1970, the now 10-member AFL officially joined the NFL, forming a 26-team league made up of two conferences of three divisions each.

Expansion/Merger Timetable

For teams currently in NFL.

1921—Green Bay Packers; **1925**—New York Giants; **1930**—Portsmouth-OH Spartans (now Detroit Lions); **1932**—Boston Braves (now Washington Redskins); **1933**—Philadelphia Eagles and Pittsburgh Pirates (now Steelers); **1937**—Cleveland Rams (now Los Angeles); **1950**—added AAFC's Cleveland Browns and San Francisco 49ers; **1953**—Baltimore Colts (now Indianapolis).

1960—Dallas Cowboys; **1961**—Minnesota Vikings; **1966**—Atlanta Falcons; **1967**—New Orleans Saints; **1970**—added AFL's Boston Patriots (now New England), Buffalo Bills, Cincinnati Bengals (1968 expansion team), Denver Broncos, Houston Oilers, Kansas City Chiefs, Miami Dolphins (1966 expansion team), New York Jets, Oakland Raiders and San Diego Chargers (the AFL-NFL merger divided the league into two 13-team conferences with old-line NFL clubs Baltimore, Cleveland and Pittsburgh moving to the AFC); **1976**—Seattle Seahawks and Tampa Bay Buccaneers (Seattle was originally in the NFC West and Tampa Bay in the AFC West, but were switched to their current divisions in 1977). **1995**—Carolina Panthers and Jacksonville Jaguars.

City and Nickname Changes

1921—Decatur Staleys move to Chicago; **1922**—Chicago Staleys renamed Bears; **1933**—Boston Braves renamed Redskins; **1937**—Boston Redskins move to Washington; **1934**—Portsmouth (Ohio) Spartans move to Detroit and become Lions; **1941**—Pittsburgh Pirates renamed Steelers; **1943**—Philadelphia and Pittsburgh merge for one season and become Phil-Pitt, or the "Steagles"; **1944**—Chicago Cardinals and Pittsburgh merge for one season and become Card-Pitt; **1946**—Cleveland Rams move to Los Angeles.

1960—Chicago Cardinals move to St. Louis; **1961**—Los Angeles Chargers (AFL) move to San Diego; **1963**—New York Titans (AFL) renamed Jets and Dallas Texans (AFL) move to Kansas City and become Chiefs; **1971**—Boston Patriots become New England Patriots; **1982**—Oakland Raiders move to Los Angeles; **1984**—Baltimore Colts move to Indianapolis; **1988**—St. Louis Cardinals move to Phoenix; **1994**—Phoenix Cardinals become Arizona Cardinals. **1995**—L.A. Rams move to St. Louis and L.A. Raiders move back to Oakland.

Defunct NFL Teams

Teams that once played in the APFA and NFL, but no longer exist.

Akron-OH—Pros (1920-25) and Indians (1926); **Baltimore**—Colts (1950); **Boston**—Bulldogs (1926) and Yanks (1944-48); **Brooklyn**—Lions (1926), Dodgers (1930-43) and Tigers (1944); **Buffalo**—All-Americans (1921-23), Bisons (1924-25), Rangers (1926), Bisons (1927,1929); **Canton-OH**—Bulldogs (1920-23,1925-26); **Chicago**—Tigers (1920); **Cincinnati**—Celts (1921) and Reds (1933-34); **Cleveland**—Tigers (1920), Indians (1921), Indians (1923), Bulldogs (1924-25,1927) and Indians (1931); **Columbus-OH**—Panhandles (1920-22) and Tigers (1923-26); **Dallas**—Texans (1952); **Dayton-OH**—Triangles (1920-29).

Detroit—Heralds (1920-21), Panthers (1925-26) and Wolverines (1928); **Duluth-MN**—Kelleys (1923-25) and Eskimos (1926-27); **Evansville-IN**—Crimson Giants (1921-22); **Frankford-PA**—Yellow Jackets (1924-31); **Hammond-IN**—Pros (1920-26); **Hartford**—Blues (1926); **Kansas City**—Blues (1924) and Cowboys (1925-26); **Kenosha-WI**—Maroons (1924); **Los Angeles**—Buccaneers (1926); **Louisville**—Brecks (1921-23) and Colonels (1926); **Marion-OH**—Oorang Indians (1922-23); **Milwaukee**—Badgers (1922-26); **Minneapolis**—Marines (1922-24) and Red Jackets (1929-30); **Muncie-IN**—Flyers (1920-21).

New York—Giants (1921), Yankees (1927-28), Bulldogs (1949) and Yankees (1950-51); **Newark-NJ**—Tornadoes (1930); **Orange-NJ**—Tornadoes (1929); **Pottsville-PA**—Maroons (1925-28); **Providence-RI**—Steam Roller (1925-31); **Racine-WI**—Legion (1922-24) and Tornadoes (1926); **Rochester-NY**—Jeffersons (1920-25); **Rock Island-IL**—Independents (1920-26); **Staten Island-NY**—Stapletons (1929-32); **St. Louis**—All-Stars (1923) and Gunners (1934); **Toledo-OH**—Maroons (1922-23); **Tonawanda-NY**—Kardex (1921), also called Lumbermen; **Washington**—Senators (1921).

Annual NFL Leaders

Individual leaders in NFL (1932-69), NFC (since 1970), AFL (1960-69) and AFC (since 1970).

Passing
NFL-NFC

Since 1932, the NFL has used several formulas to determine passing leadership, from Total Yards alone (1932-37), to the current rating system—adopted in 1973—that takes Completions, Completion Pct., Yards Gained, TD Passes, Interceptions, Interception Pct. and other factors into account. The quarterbacks listed below all led the league according to the system in use at the time.

Multiple winners: Sammy Baugh (6); Joe Montana and Roger Staubach (5); Steve Young (4); Arnie Herber, Sonny Jurgensen, Bart Starr, and Norm Van Brocklin (3); Ed Danowski, Otto Graham, Cecil Isbell, Milt Plum and Bob Waterfield (2).

Year		Att	Cmp	Yds	TD	Year		Att	Cmp	Yds	TD
1932	Arnie Herber, GB	101	37	639	9	1963	Y.A.Tittle, NY	367	221	3145	36
1933	Harry Newman, NY	136	53	973	11	1964	Bart Starr, GB	272	163	2144	15
1934	Arnie Herber, GB	115	42	799	8	1965	Rudy Bukich, Chi	312	176	2641	20
1935	Ed Danowski, NY	113	57	794	10	1966	Bart Starr, GB	251	156	2257	14
1936	Arnie Herber, GB	173	77	1239	11	1967	Sonny Jurgensen, Wash	508	288	3747	31
1937	Sammy Baugh, Wash	171	81	1127	8	1968	Earl Morrall, Bal	317	182	2909	26
1938	Ed Danowski, NY	129	70	848	7	1969	Sonny Jurgensen, Wash	442	274	3102	22
1939	Parker Hall, Cle. Rams	208	106	1227	9						
						1970	John Brodie, SF	378	223	2941	24
1940	Sammy Baugh, Wash	177	111	1367	12	1971	Roger Staubach, Dal	211	126	1882	15
1941	Cecil Isbell, GB	206	117	1479	15	1972	Norm Snead, NY	325	196	2307	17
1942	Cecil Isbell, GB	268	146	2021	24	1973	Roger Staubach, Dal	286	179	2428	23
1943	Sammy Baugh, Wash	239	133	1754	23	1974	Sonny Jurgensen, Wash	167	107	1185	11
1944	Frank Filchock, Wash	147	84	1139	13	1975	Fran Tarkenton, Min	425	273	2994	25
1945	Sammy Baugh, Wash	182	128	1669	11	1976	James Harris, LA	158	91	1460	8
	& Sid Luckman, Chi. Bears	217	117	1725	14	1977	Roger Staubach, Dal	361	210	2620	18
1946	Bob Waterfield, LA	251	127	1747	18	1978	Roger Staubach, Dal	413	231	3190	25
1947	Sammy Baugh, Wash	354	210	2938	25	1979	Roger Staubach, Dal	461	267	3586	27
1948	Tommy Thompson, Phi	246	141	1965	25						
1949	Sammy Baugh, Wash	255	145	1903	18	1980	Ron Jaworski, Phi	451	257	3529	27
						1981	Joe Montana, SF	488	311	3565	19
1950	Norm Van Brocklin, LA	233	127	2061	18	1982	Joe Theismann, Wash	252	161	2033	13
1951	Bob Waterfield, LA	176	88	1566	13	1983	Steve Bartkowski, Atl	432	274	3167	22
1952	Norm Van Brocklin, LA	205	113	1736	14	1984	Joe Montana, SF	432	279	3630	28
1953	Otto Graham, Cle	258	167	2722	11	1985	Joe Montana, SF	494	303	3653	27
1954	Norm Van Brocklin, LA	260	139	2637	13	1986	Tommy Kramer, Min	372	208	3000	24
1955	Otto Graham, Cle	185	98	1721	15	1987	Joe Montana, SF	398	266	3054	31
1956	Ed Brown, Chi. Bears	168	96	1667	11	1988	Wade Wilson, Min	332	204	2746	15
1957	Tommy O'Connell, Cle	110	63	1229	9	1989	Don Majkowski, GB	599	353	4318	27
1958	Eddie LeBaron, Wash	145	79	1365	11						
1959	Charlie Conerly, NY	194	113	1706	14	1990	Joe Montana, SF	520	321	3944	26
						1991	Steve Young, SF	279	180	2517	17
1960	Milt Plum, Cle	250	151	2297	21	1992	Steve Young, SF	402	268	3465	25
1961	Milt Plum, Cle	302	177	2416	16	1993	Steve Young, SF	462	314	4023	29
1962	Bart Starr, GB	285	178	2438	12	1994	Steve Young, SF	461	324	3969	35

Note: In 1945, **Sammy Baugh** and **Sid Luckman** tied with 8 points on an inverse rating system.

AFL-AFC

Multiple winners: Dan Marino (5); Ken Anderson and Len Dawson (4); Bob Griese, Daryle Lamonica, Warren Moon and Ken Stabler (2).

Year		Att	Cmp	Yds	TD	Year		Att	Cmp	Yds	TD
1960	Jack Kemp, LA	406	211	3018	20	1978	Terry Bradshaw, Pit	368	207	2915	28
1961	George Blanda, Hou	362	187	3330	36	1979	Dan Fouts, SD	530	332	4082	24
1962	Len Dawson, Dal	310	189	2759	29						
1963	Tobin Rote, SD	286	170	2510	20	1980	Brian Sipe, Cle	554	337	4132	30
1964	Len Dawson, KC	354	199	2879	30	1981	Ken Anderson, Cin	479	300	3753	29
1965	John Hadl, SD	348	174	2798	20	1982	Ken Anderson, Cin	309	218	2495	12
1966	Len Dawson, KC	284	159	2527	26	1983	Dan Marino, Mia	296	173	2210	20
1967	Daryle Lamonica, Oak	425	220	3228	30	1984	Dan Marino, Mia	564	362	5084	48
1968	Len Dawson, KC	224	131	2109	17	1985	Ken O'Brien, NY	488	297	3888	25
1969	Greg Cook, Cin	197	106	1854	15	1986	Dan Marino, Mia	623	378	4746	44
						1987	Bernie Kosar, Cle	389	241	3033	22
1970	Daryle Lamonica, Oak	356	179	2516	22	1988	Boomer Esiason, Cin	388	223	3572	28
1971	Bob Griese, Mia	263	145	2089	19	1989	Dan Marino, Mia	550	308	3997	24
1972	Earl Morrall, Mia	150	83	1360	11						
1973	Ken Stabler, Oak	260	163	1997	14	1990	Warren Moon, Hou	584	362	4689	33
1974	Ken Anderson, Cin	328	213	2667	18	1991	Jim Kelly, Buf	474	304	3844	33
1975	Ken Anderson, Cin	377	228	3169	21	1992	Warren Moon, Hou	346	224	2521	18
1976	Ken Stabler, Oak	291	194	2737	27	1993	John Elway, Den	551	348	4030	25
1977	Bob Griese, Mia	307	180	2252	22	1994	Dan Marino, Mia	615	385	4453	30

Annual NFL Leaders (Cont.)

Receptions

NFL-NFC

Multiple winners: Don Hutson (8); Raymond Berry, Tom Fears, Pete Pihos, Sterling Sharpe and Billy Wilson (3); Dwight Clark, Ahmad Rashad, Jerry Rice and Charley Taylor (2).

Year		No	Yds	Avg	TD	Year		No	Yds	Avg	TD
1932	Ray Flaherty, NY	21	350	16.7	3	1963	Bobby Joe Conrad, St.L.	73	967	13.2	10
1933	Shipwreck Kelly, Bklyn	22	246	11.2	3	1964	Johnny Morris, Chi. Bears	93	1200	12.9	10
1934	Joe Carter, Phi.	16	238	14.9	4	1965	Dave Parks, SF	80	1344	16.8	12
	& Red Badgro, NY	16	206	12.9	1	1966	Charley Taylor, Wash.	72	1119	15.5	12
1935	Tod Goodwin, NY	26	432	16.6	4	1967	Charley Taylor, Wash.	70	990	14.1	9
1936	Don Hutson, GB	34	536	15.8	8	1968	Clifton McNeil, SF	71	994	14.0	7
1937	Don Hutson, GB	41	552	13.5	7	1969	Dan Abramowicz, NO.	73	1015	13.9	7
1938	Gaynell Tinsley, Chi. Cards	41	516	12.6	1						
1939	Don Hutson, GB	34	846	24.9	6	1970	Dick Gordon, Chi	71	1026	14.5	13
						1971	Bob Tucker, NY	59	791	13.4	4
1940	Don Looney, Phi	58	707	12.2	4	1972	Harold Jackson, Phi	62	1048	16.9	4
1941	Don Hutson, GB	58	739	12.7	10	1973	Harold Carmichael, Phi.	67	1116	16.7	9
1942	Don Hutson, GB	74	1211	16.4	17	1974	Charle Young, Phi.	63	696	11.0	3
1943	Don Hutson, GB	47	776	16.5	11	1975	Chuck Foreman, Min	73	691	9.5	9
1944	Don Hutson, GB	58	866	14.9	9	1976	Drew Pearson, Dal.	58	806	13.9	6
1945	Don Hutson, GB	47	834	17.7	9	1977	Ahmad Rashad, Min.	51	681	13.4	2
1946	Jim Benton, LA	63	981	15.6	6	1978	Rickey Young, Min.	88	704	8.0	5
1947	Jim Keane, Chi. Bears	64	910	14.2	10	1979	Ahmad Rashad, Min.	80	1156	14.5	9
1948	Tom Fears, LA	51	698	13.7	4						
1949	Tom Fears, LA	77	1013	13.2	9	1980	Earl Cooper, SF	83	567	6.8	4
						1981	Dwight Clark, SF	85	1105	13.0	4
1950	Tom Fears, LA	84	1116	13.3	7	1982	Dwight Clark, SF	60	913	12.2	5
1951	Elroy Hirsch, LA.	66	1495	22.7	17	1983	Roy Green, St.L.	78	1227	15.7	14
1952	Mac Speedie, Cle	62	911	14.7	5		Charlie Brown, Wash.	78	1225	15.7	8
1953	Pete Pihos, Phi	63	1049	16.7	10		& Earnest Gray, NY	78	1139	14.6	5
1954	Pete Pihos, Phi	60	872	14.5	10	1984	Art Monk, Wash.	106	1372	12.9	7
	& Billy Wilson, SF	60	830	13.8	5	1985	Roger Craig, SF	92	1016	11.0	6
1955	Pete Pihos, Phi	62	864	13.9	7	1986	Jerry Rice, SF	86	1570	18.3	15
1956	Billy Wilson, SF	60	889	14.8	5	1987	J.T. Smith, St.L	91	1117	12.3	8
1957	Billy Wilson, SF	52	757	14.6	6	1988	Henry Ellard, LA	86	1414	16.4	10
1958	Raymond Berry, Bal	56	794	14.2	9	1989	Sterling Sharpe, GB	90	1423	15.8	12
	& Pete Retzlaff, Phi	56	766	13.7	2						
1959	Raymond Berry, Bal	66	959	14.5	14	1990	Jerry Rice, SF	100	1502	15.0	13
						1991	Michael Irvin, Dal	93	1523	16.4	8
1960	Raymond Berry, Bal	74	1298	17.5	10	1992	Sterling Sharpe, GB	108	1461	13.5	13
1961	Red Phillips, LA	78	1092	14.0	5	1993	Sterling Sharpe, GB	112	1274	11.4	11
1962	Bobby Mitchell, Wash.	72	1384	19.2	11	1994	Cris Carter, Min.	122	1256	10.3	7

AFL-AFC

Multiple winners: Lionel Taylor (5); Lance Alworth, Haywood Jeffires, Lydell Mitchell and Kellen Winslow (3); Fred Biletnikoff, Todd Christensen and Al Toon (2).

Year		No	Yds	Avg	TD	Year		No	Yds	Avg	TD
1960	Lionel Taylor, Den	92	1235	13.4	12	1978	Steve Largent, Sea	71	1168	16.5	8
1961	Lionel Taylor, Den	100	1176	11.8	4	1979	Joe Washington, Bal	82	750	9.1	3
1962	Lionel Taylor, Den	77	908	11.8	4						
1963	Lionel Taylor, Den	78	1101	14.1	10	1980	Kellen Winslow, SD	89	1290	14.5	9
1964	Charley Hennigan, Hou	101	1546	15.3	8	1981	Kellen Winslow, SD	88	1075	12.2	10
1965	Lionel Taylor, Den	85	1131	13.3	6	1982	Kellen Winslow, SD	54	721	13.4	6
1966	Lance Alworth, SD	73	1383	18.9	13	1983	Todd Christensen, LA	92	1247	13.6	12
1967	George Sauer, NY	75	1189	15.9	6	1984	Ozzie Newsome, Cle	89	1001	11.2	5
1968	Lance Alworth, SD	68	1312	19.3	10	1985	Lionel James, SD	86	1027	11.9	6
1969	Lance Alworth, SD	64	1003	15.7	4	1986	Todd Christensen, LA	95	1153	12.1	8
						1987	Al Toon, NY	68	976	14.4	5
1970	Marlin Briscoe, Buf	57	1036	18.2	8	1988	Al Toon, NY	93	1067	11.5	5
1971	Fred Biletnikoff, Oak	61	929	15.2	9	1989	Andre Reed, Buf	88	1312	14.9	9
1972	Fred Biletnikoff, Oak	58	802	13.8	7						
1973	Fred Willis, Hou	57	371	6.5	1	1990	Haywood Jeffires, Hou	74	1048	14.2	8
1974	Lydell Mitchell, Bal	72	544	7.6	2		& Drew Hill, Hou	74	1019	13.8	5
1975	Reggie Rucker, Cle	60	770	12.8	3	1991	Haywood Jeffires, Hou	100	1181	11.8	7
	& Lydell Mitchell, Bal	60	544	9.1	4	1992	Haywood Jeffires, Hou	90	913	10.1	9
1976	MacArthur Lane, KC	66	686	10.4	1	1993	Reggie Langhorne, Ind	85	1038	12.2	3
1977	Lydell Mitchell, Bal	71	620	8.7	4	1994	Ben Coates, NE	96	1174	12.2	7

Rushing
NFL-NFC

Multiple winners: Jim Brown (8); Walter Payton (5); Steve Van Buren (4); Eric Dickerson, Barry Sanders and Emmitt Smith (3); Cliff Battles, John Brockington, Larry Brown, Bill Dudley, Leroy Kelly, Bill Paschal, Joe Perry, Gale Sayers and Whizzer White (2).

Year		Car	Yds	Avg	TD	Year		Car	Yds	Avg	TD
1932	Cliff Battles, Bos	148	576	3.9	3	1964	Jim Brown, Cle	280	1446	5.2	7
1933	Jim Musick, Bos	173	809	4.7	5	1965	Jim Brown, Cle	289	1544	5.3	17
1934	Beattie Feathers, Chi. Bears	119	1004	8.4	8	1966	Gale Sayers, Chi	229	1231	5.4	8
1935	Doug Russell, Chi. Cards	140	499	3.6	0	1967	Leroy Kelly, Cle	235	1205	5.1	11
1936	Tuffy Leemans, NY	206	830	4.0	2	1968	Leroy Kelly, Cle	248	1239	5.0	16
1937	Cliff Battles, Wash	216	874	4.0	5	1969	Gale Sayers, Chi	236	1032	4.4	8
1938	Whizzer White, Pit	152	567	3.7	4						
1939	Bill Osmanski, Chi. Bears	121	699	5.8	7	1970	Larry Brown, Wash	237	1125	4.7	5
						1971	John Brockington, GB	216	1105	5.1	4
1940	Whizzer White, Det	146	514	3.5	5	1972	Larry Brown, Wash	285	1216	4.3	8
1941	Pug Manders, Bklyn	111	486	4.4	5	1973	John Brockington, GB	265	1144	4.3	3
1942	Bill Dudley, Pit	162	696	4.3	5	1974	Lawrence McCutcheon, LA	236	1109	4.7	3
1943	Bill Paschal, NY	147	572	3.9	10	1975	Jim Otis, St.L	269	1076	4.0	5
1944	Bill Paschal, NY	196	737	3.8	9	1976	Walter Payton, Chi	311	1390	4.5	13
1945	Steve Van Buren, Phi	143	832	5.8	15	1977	Walter Payton, Chi	339	1852	5.5	14
1946	Bill Dudley, Pit	146	604	4.1	3	1978	Walter Payton, Chi	333	1395	4.2	11
1947	Steve Van Buren, Phi	217	1008	4.6	13	1979	Walter Payton, Chi	369	1610	4.4	14
1948	Steve Van Buren, Phi	201	945	4.7	10						
1949	Steve Van Buren, Phi	263	1146	4.4	11	1980	Walter Payton, Chi	317	1460	4.6	6
						1981	George Rogers, NO	378	1674	4.4	13
1950	Marion Motley, Cle	140	810	5.8	3	1982	Tony Dorsett, Dal	177	745	4.2	5
1951	Eddie Price, NY Giants	271	971	3.6	7	1983	Eric Dickerson, LA	390	1808	4.6	18
1952	Dan Towler, LA	156	894	5.7	10	1984	Eric Dickerson, LA	379	2105	5.6	14
1953	Joe Perry, SF	192	1018	5.3	10	1985	Gerald Riggs, Atl	397	1719	4.3	10
1954	Joe Perry, SF	173	1049	6.1	8	1986	Eric Dickerson, LA	404	1821	4.5	11
1955	Alan Ameche, Bal	213	961	4.5	9	1987	Charles White, LA	324	1374	4.2	11
1956	Rick Casares, Chi. Bears	234	1126	4.8	12	1988	Herschel Walker, Dal	361	1514	4.2	5
1957	Jim Brown, Cle	202	942	4.7	9	1989	Barry Sanders, Det	280	1470	5.3	14
1958	Jim Brown, Cle	257	1527	5.9	17						
1959	Jim Brown, Cle	290	1329	4.6	14	1990	Barry Sanders, Det	255	1304	5.1	13
						1991	Emmitt Smith, Dal	365	1563	4.3	12
1960	Jim Brown, Cle	215	1257	5.8	9	1992	Emmitt Smith, Dal	373	1713	4.6	18
1961	Jim Brown, Cle	305	1408	4.6	8	1993	Emmitt Smith, Dal	283	1486	5.3	9
1962	Jim Taylor, GB	272	1474	5.4	19	1994	Barry Sanders, Det	331	1883	5.7	7
1963	Jim Brown, Cle	291	1863	6.4	12						

Note: Jim Brown led the NFL in rushing eight of his nine years in the league. The one season he didn't win (1962) he finished fourth (996 yds) behind Jim Taylor, John Henry Johnson of Pittsburgh (1,141 yds) and Dick Bass of the LA Rams (1,033 yds).

AFL-AFC

Multiple winners: Earl Campbell and O.J. Simpson (4); Thurman Thomas (3); Cookie Gilchrist, Eric Dickerson, Floyd Little, Jim Nance and Curt Warner (2).

Year		Car	Yds	Avg	TD	Year		Car	Yds	Avg	TD
1960	Abner Haynes, Dal	157	875	5.6	9	1978	Earl Campbell, Hou	302	1450	4.8	13
1961	Billy Cannon, Hou	200	948	4.7	6	1979	Earl Campbell, Hou	368	1697	4.6	19
1962	Cookie Gilchrist, Buf	214	1096	5.1	13						
1963	Clem Daniels, Oak	215	1099	5.1	3	1980	Earl Campbell, Hou	373	1934	5.2	13
1964	Cookie Gilchrist, Buf	230	981	4.3	6	1981	Earl Campbell, Hou	361	1376	3.8	10
1965	Paul Lowe, SD	222	1121	5.0	7	1982	Freeman McNeil, NY	151	786	5.2	6
1966	Jim Nance, Bos	299	1458	4.9	11	1983	Curt Warner, Sea	335	1449	4.3	13
1967	Jim Nance, Bos	269	1216	4.5	7	1984	Earnest Jackson, SD	296	1179	4.0	8
1968	Paul Robinson, Cin	238	1023	4.3	8	1985	Marcus Allen, LA	380	1759	4.6	11
1969	Dickie Post, SD	182	873	4.8	6	1986	Curt Warner, Sea	319	1481	4.6	13
						1987	Eric Dickerson, Ind	223	1011	4.5	5
1970	Floyd Little, Den	209	901	4.3	3	1988	Eric Dickerson, Ind	388	1659	4.3	14
1971	Floyd Little, Den	284	1133	4.0	6	1989	Christian Okoye, KC	370	1480	4.0	12
1972	O.J. Simpson, Buf	292	1251	4.3	6						
1973	O.J. Simpson, Buf	332	2003	6.0	12	1990	Thurman Thomas, Buf	271	1297	4.8	11
1974	Otis Armstrong, Den	263	1407	5.3	9	1991	Thurman Thomas, Buf	288	1407	4.9	7
1975	O.J. Simpson, Buf	329	1817	5.5	16	1992	Barry Foster, Pit	390	1690	4.3	11
1976	O.J. Simpson, Buf	290	1503	5.2	8	1993	Thurman Thomas, Buf	355	1315	3.7	6
1977	Mark van Eeghen, Oak	324	1273	3.9	7	1994	Chris Warren, Sea	333	1545	4.6	9

Note: Eric Dickerson was traded to Indianapolis from the NFC's LA Rams during the 1987 season. In three games with the Rams, he carried the ball 60 times for 277 yds, a 4.6 avg and 1 TD. His official AFC statistics above came in nine games with the Colts.

Annual NFL Leaders (Cont.)

Scoring

NFL-NFC

Multiple winners: Don Hutson (5); Dutch Clark, Pat Harder, Paul Hornung, Chip Lohmiller and Mark Moseley (3); Kevin Butler, Mike Cofer, Fred Cox, Jack Manders, Chester Marcol, Eddie Murray, Gordy Soltau and Doak Walker (2).

Year		TD	FG	PAT	Pts	Year		TD	FG	PAT	Pts
1932	Dutch Clark, Portsmouth	6	3	10	55	1964	Lenny Moore, Bal	20	0	0	120
1933	Glenn Presnell, Portsmouth	6	6	10	64	1965	Gale Sayers, Chi	22	0	0	132
	& Ken Strong, NY	6	5	13	64	1966	Bruce Gossett, LA	0	28	29	113
1934	Jack Manders, Chi. Bears	3	10	31	79	1967	Jim Bakken, St.L	0	27	36	117
1935	Dutch Clark, Det	6	1	16	55	1968	Leroy Kelly, Cle	20	0	0	120
1936	Dutch Clark, Det	7	4	19	73	1969	Fred Cox, Min	0	26	43	121
1937	Jack Manders, Chi. Bears	5	8	15	69						
1938	Clarke Hinkle, GB	7	3	7	58	1970	Fred Cox, Min	0	30	35	125
1939	Andy Farkas, Wash	11	0	2	68	1971	Curt Knight, Wash	0	29	27	114
						1972	Chester Marcol, GB	0	33	29	128
1940	Don Hutson, GB	7	0	15	57	1973	David Ray, LA	0	30	40	130
1941	Don Hutson, GB	12	1	20	95	1974	Chester Marcol, GB	0	25	19	94
1942	Don Hutson, GB	17	1	33	138	1975	Chuck Foreman, Min	22	0	0	132
1943	Don Hutson, GB	12	3	26	117	1976	Mark Moseley, Wash	0	22	31	97
1944	Don Hutson, GB	9	0	31	85	1977	Walter Payton, Chi	16	0	0	96
1945	Steve Van Buren, Phi	18	0	2	110	1978	Frank Corral, LA	0	29	31	118
1946	Ted Fritsch, GB	10	9	13	100	1979	Mark Moseley, Wash	0	25	39	114
1947	Pat Harder, Chi. Cards	7	7	39	102						
1948	Pat Harder, Chi. Cards	6	7	53	110	1980	Eddie Murray, Det	0	27	35	116
1949	Gene Roberts, NY Giants	17	0	0	102	1981	Rafael Septien, Dal	0	27	40	121
	& Pat Harder, Chi. Cards	8	3	45	102		& Eddie Murray, Det	0	25	46	121
						1982	Wendell Tyler, LA	13	0	0	78
1950	Doak Walker, Det	11	8	38	128	1983	Mark Moseley, Wash	0	33	62	161
1951	Elroy Hirsch, LA	17	0	0	102	1984	Ray Wersching, SF	0	25	56	131
1952	Gordy Soltau, SF	7	6	34	94	1985	Kevin Butler, Chi	0	31	51	144
1953	Gordy Soltau, SF	6	10	48	114	1986	Kevin Butler, Chi	0	28	36	120
1954	Bobby Walston, Phi	11	4	36	114	1987	Jerry Rice, SF	23	0	0	138
1955	Doak Walker, Det	7	9	27	96	1988	Mike Cofer, SF	0	27	40	121
1956	Bobby Layne, Det	5	12	33	99	1989	Mike Cofer, SF	0	29	49	136
1957	Sam Baker, Wash	1	14	29	77						
	& Lou Groza, Cle	0	15	32	77	1990	Chip Lohmiller, Wash	0	30	41	131
1958	Jim Brown, Cle	18	0	0	108	1991	Chip Lohmiller, Wash	0	31	56	149
1959	Paul Hornung, GB	7	7	31	94	1992	Chip Lohmiller, Wash	0	30	30	120
							& Morten Andersen, NO	0	29	33	120
1960	Paul Hornung, GB	15	15	41	176	1993	Jason Hanson, Det	0	34	28	130
1961	Paul Hornung, GB	10	15	41	146	1994	Emmitt Smith, Dal	22	0	0	132
1962	Jim Taylor, GB	19	0	0	114		& Fuad Reveiz, Min	0	34	30	132
1963	Don Chandler, NY	0	18	52	106						

AFL-AFC

Multiple winners: Gino Cappelletti (5); Gary Anderson (3); Jim Breech, Roy Gerela, Gene Mingo, Nick Lowery, John Smith, Pete Stoyanovich and Jim Turner (2).

Year		TD	FG	PAT	Pts	Year		TD	FG	PAT	Pts
1960	Gene Mingo, Den	6	18	33	123	1980	John Smith, NE	0	26	51	129
1961	Gino Cappelletti, Bos	8	17	48	147	1981	Nick Lowery, KC	0	26	37	115
1962	Gene Mingo, Den	4	27	32	137		& Jim Breech, Cin	0	22	49	115
1963	Gino Cappelletti, Bos	2	22	35	113	1982	Marcus Allen, LA	14	0	0	84
1964	Gino Cappelletti, Bos	7	25	36	155	1983	Gary Anderson, Pit	0	27	38	119
1965	Gino Cappelletti, Bos	9	17	27	132	1984	Gary Anderson, Pit	0	24	45	117
1966	Gino Cappelletti, Bos	6	16	35	119	1985	Gary Anderson, Pit	0	33	40	139
1967	George Blanda, Oak	0	20	56	116	1986	Tony Franklin, NE	0	32	44	140
1968	Jim Turner, NY	0	34	43	145	1987	Jim Breech, Cin	0	24	25	97
1969	Jim Turner, NY	0	32	33	129	1988	Scott Norwood, Buf	0	32	33	129
						1989	David Treadwell, Den	0	27	39	120
1970	Jan Stenerud, KC	0	30	26	116						
1971	Garo Yepremian, Mia	0	28	33	117	1990	Nick Lowery, KC	0	34	37	139
1972	Bobby Howfield, NY	0	27	40	121	1991	Pete Stoyanovich, Mia	0	31	28	121
1973	Roy Gerela, Pit	0	29	36	123	1992	Pete Stoyanovich, Mia	0	30	34	124
1974	Roy Gerela, Pit	0	20	33	93	1993	Jeff Jaeger, LA	0	35	27	132
1975	O.J. Simpson, Buf	23	0	0	138	1994	John Carney, SD	0	34	33	135
1976	Toni Linhart, Bal	0	20	49	109						
1977	Errol Mann, Oak	0	20	39	99						
1978	Pat Leahy, NY	0	22	41	107						
1979	John Smith, NE	0	23	46	115						

All-Time NFL Leaders

Through 1994 regular season.

CAREER

Players active in 1994 in **bold** type.

Passing Efficiency

Ratings based on performance standards established for completion percentage, average gain, touchdown percentage and interception percentage. Quarterbacks are allocated points according to how their statistics measure up to those stardards. Minimum 1500 passing attempts.

		Yrs	Att	Cmp	Cmp%	Yards	Avg Gain	TD	TD%	Int	Int%	Rating
1	**Steve Young**	10	2429	1546	63.6	19,869	8.18	140	5.8	68	2.8	96.8
2	Joe Montana	15	5391	3409	63.2	40,551	7.52	273	5.1	139	2.6	92.3
3	**Dan Marino**	12	6049	3604	59.6	45,173	7.47	328	5.4	185	3.1	88.2
4	**Jim Kelly**	9	3942	2397	60.8	29,527	7.49	201	5.1	143	3.6	85.8
5	Roger Staubach	11	2958	1685	57.0	22,700	7.67	153	5.2	109	3.7	83.4
6	**Dave Krieg**	15	4390	2562	58.4	32,114	7.32	231	5.3	166	3.8	83.0
7	Neil Lomax	8	3153	1817	57.6	22,771	7.22	136	4.3	90	2.9	82.7
8	Sonny Jurgensen	18	4262	2433	57.1	32,224	7.56	255	6.0	189	4.4	82.63
9	Len Dawson	19	3741	2136	57.1	28,711	7.67	239	6.4	183	4.9	82.56
10	**Brett Favre**	4	1580	983	62.2	10,412	6.59	70	4.4	53	3.4	82.2
11	Ken Anderson	16	4475	2654	59.3	32,838	7.34	197	4.4	160	3.6	81.9
12	**Bernie Kosar**	10	3225	1896	58.8	22,394	6.94	120	3.7	82	2.5	81.82
13	**Jeff Hostetler**	9	1505	864	57.4	10,985	7.30	54	3.6	38	2.5	81.78
14	Danny White	13	2950	1761	59.7	21,959	7.44	155	5.3	132	4.5	81.7
15	**Boomer Esiason**	11	4291	2440	56.9	31,874	7.43	207	4.8	153	3.6	81.64
16	**Troy Aikman**	6	2281	1424	62.4	16,303	7.15	82	3.6	78	3.4	81.62
17	Bart Starr	16	3149	1808	57.4	24,718	7.85	152	4.8	138	4.4	80.5
18	Ken O'Brien	10	3602	2110	58.6	25,094	6.97	128	3.6	98	2.7	80.44
19	Fran Tarkenton	18	6467	3686	57.0	47,003	7.27	342	5.3	266	4.1	80.35
20	**Warren Moon**	11	5147	3003	58.3	37,949	7.37	214	4.2	185	3.6	80.3
21	Dan Fouts	15	5604	3297	58.8	43,040	7.68	254	4.5	242	4.3	80.2
22	Tony Eason	8	1564	911	58.2	11,142	7.12	61	3.9	51	3.3	79.7
23	**Randall Cunningham**	10	3241	1805	55.7	22,272	6.87	147	4.5	100	3.1	79.4
24	Mark Rypien	7	2335	1303	55.8	16,622	7.12	105	4.5	78	3.3	79.3
25	**Jim Everett**	9	3817	2193	57.5	27,613	7.23	164	4.3	141	3.7	79.0

Note: The NFL does not recognize records from the All-American Football Conference (1946-49). If it did, **Otto Graham** would rank 4th (after Marino) with the following stats: 10 Yrs; 2,626 Att; 1,464 Comp; 55.8 Comp Pct; 23,584 Yards; 8.98 Avg Gain; 174 TD; 6.6 TD Pct; 135 Int; 5.1 Int Pct; and 86.6 Rating Pts.

Touchdown Passes

		No
1	Fran Tarkenton	342
2	**Dan Marino**	328
3	Johnny Unitas	290
4	**Joe Montana**	273
5	Sonny Jurgensen	255
6	Dan Fouts	254
7	John Hadl	244
8	Len Dawson	239
9	George Blanda	236
10	**Dave Krieg**	231
11	John Brodie	214
	Warren Moon	214
13	Terry Bradshaw	212
	Y.A. Tittle	212
15	Jim Hart	209
16	**Boomer Esiason**	207
17	Roman Gabriel	201
	Jim Kelly	201
19	**John Elway**	199
	Phil Simms	199
21	Ken Anderson	197
22	Joe Ferguson	196
	Bobby Layne	196
	Norm Snead	196
25	Ken Stabler	194
26	Steve DeBerg	193
27	Bob Griese	192
28	Sammy Baugh	187
	Craig Morton	183
30	Steve Grogan	182
31	Ron Jaworski	179
32	Babe Parilli	178
33	Charlie Conerly	173
	Joe Namath	173
	Norm Van Brocklin	173
36	Charley Johnson	170
37	**Jim Everett**	164
	Daryle Lamonica	164
	Jim Plunkett	164
40	Earl Morrall	161
41	Joe Theismann	160
42	Tommy Kramer	159
43	Steve Bartkowski	156
44	Danny White	155
45	Brian Sipe	154

Note: The NFL does not recognize records from the All-American Football Conference (1946-49). If it did, **Y.A. Tittle** would rank 8th (after Hadl) with 242 TDs and **Otto Graham** would rank 33rd (after Parilli) with 174 TDs.

Passes Intercepted

		No
1	George Blanda	277
2	John Hadl	268
3	Fran Tarkenton	266
4	Norm Snead	253
	Johnny Unitas	253
6	Jim Hart	247
7	Bobby Layne	243
8	Dan Fouts	242
9	John Brodie	224
10	Ken Stabler	222
11	Y.A. Tittle	221
12	Joe Namath	220
	Babe Parilli	220
14	Terry Bradshaw	210
15	Joe Ferguson	209
16	Steve Grogan	208
17	Sammy Baugh	203
	Steve DeBerg	203
19	Jim Plunkett	198
20	Tobin Rote	191

All-Time NFL Leaders (Cont.)

Passing Yards

		Yrs	Att	Comp	Pct	Yards
1	Fran Tarkenton	18	6467	3686	57.0	47,003
2	Dan Marino	12	6409	3604	59.6	45,173
3	Dan Fouts	15	5604	3297	58.8	43,040
4	Joe Montana	15	5391	3409	63.2	40,551
5	Johnny Unitas	18	5186	2830	54.6	40,239
6	Warren Moon	11	5147	3003	58.3	37,949
7	John Elway	12	5384	3030	56.3	37,736
8	Jim Hart	19	5076	2593	51.1	34,665
9	Steve DeBerg	16	4965	2844	57.3	33,872
10	John Hadl	16	4687	2363	50.4	33,503
11	Phil Simms	14	4647	2576	55.4	33,462
12	Ken Anderson	16	4475	2654	59.3	32,838
13	Sonny Jurgensen	18	4262	2433	57.1	32,224
14	Dave Krieg	15	4390	2562	58.4	32,114
15	Boomer Esiason	11	4291	2440	56.9	31,874
16	John Brodie	17	4491	2469	55.0	31,548
17	Norm Snead	15	4353	2276	52.3	30,797
18	Joe Ferguson	18	4519	2369	52.4	29,817
19	Jim Kelly	9	3942	2397	60.8	29,527
20	Roman Gabriel	16	4498	2366	52.6	29,444
21	Len Dawson	19	3741	2136	57.1	28,711
22	Y.A. Tittle	15	3817	2118	55.5	28,339
23	Ron Jaworski	16	4117	2187	53.1	28,190
24	Terry Bradshaw	14	3901	2025	51.9	27,989
25	Ken Stabler	15	3793	2270	59.8	27,938

Note: The NFL does not recognize records from the All-American Football Conference (1946-49). If it did, **Y.A. Tittle** would rank 12th (after Simms) with the following stats: 17 Yrs; 4,395 Att; 2,427 Comp; 55.2 Pct; and 33,070 Yards.

Receptions

		Yrs	No	Yards	Avg	TD
1	Art Monk	15	934	12,607	13.5	68
2	Jerry Rice	10	820	13,275	16.2	131
3	Steve Largent	14	819	13,089	16.0	100
4	James Lofton	16	764	14,004	18.3	75
5	Charlie Joiner	18	750	12,146	16.2	65
6	Andre Reed	10	676	9,536	14.1	66
7	Henry Ellard	12	667	11,158	16.7	54
8	Gary Clark	10	662	10,331	15.6	63
	Ozzie Newsome	13	662	7,980	12.1	47
10	Charley Taylor	13	649	9,110	14.0	79
11	Drew Hill	14	634	9,831	15.5	60
12	Don Maynard	15	633	11,834	18.7	88
13	Raymond Berry	13	631	9,275	14.7	68
14	Sterling Sharpe	7	598	8,134	13.6	65
15	Harold Carmichael	14	590	8,985	15.2	79
16	Fred Biletnikoff	14	589	8,974	15.2	76
17	Mark Clayton	11	582	8,974	15.4	84
18	Harold Jackson	16	579	10,372	17.9	76
19	Lionel Taylor	10	567	7,195	12.7	45
20	Roger Craig	11	566	4,911	8.7	17
21	Wes Chandler	11	559	8,966	16.0	56
	Roy Green	14	559	8,965	16.0	66
23	Stanley Morgan	14	557	10,716	19.2	72
24	Eric Martin	10	553	8,161	14.8	49
25	J.T. Smith	13	544	6,974	12.8	35

Rushing

		Yrs	Car	Yards	Avg	TD
1	Walter Payton	13	3838	16,726	4.4	110
2	Eric Dickerson	11	2996	13,259	4.4	90
3	Tony Dorsett	12	2936	12,739	4.3	77
4	Jim Brown	9	2359	12,312	5.2	106
5	Franco Harris	13	2949	12,120	4.1	91
6	John Riggins	14	2916	11,352	3.9	104
7	O.J. Simpson	11	2404	11,236	4.7	61
8	Ottis Anderson	14	2562	10,273	4.0	81
9	Marcus Allen	13	2485	10,018	4.0	98
10	Earl Campbell	8	2187	9,407	4.3	74
11	Thurman Thomas	7	2018	8,724	4.3	48
12	Barry Sanders	6	1763	8,672	4.9	62
13	Jim Taylor	10	1941	8,597	4.4	83
14	Joe Perry	14	1737	8,378	4.8	53
15	Roger Craig	11	1991	8,189	4.1	56
16	Gerald Riggs	10	1989	8,188	4.1	69
17	Larry Csonka	11	1891	8,081	4.3	64
18	Freeman McNeil	12	1798	8,074	4.5	38
19	Herschel Walker	9	1907	7,996	4.2	60
20	James Brooks	12	1685	7,962	4.7	49
21	Mike Pruitt	11	1844	7,378	4.0	51
22	Leroy Kelly	10	1727	7,274	4.2	74
23	Emmitt Smith	5	1630	7,183	4.4	71
24	George Rogers	7	1692	7,176	4.2	54
25	Ernest Byner	11	1737	6,882	4.0	50

Note: The NFL does not recognize records from the All-American Football Conference (1946-49). If it did, **Joe Perry** would rank 10th (after Allen) with the following stats: 16 Yrs; 1,929 Att; 9,723 Yards; 5.0 Avg; and 71 TD.

All-Purpose Running

		Rush	Rec	Ret	Total
1	Walter Payton	16,726	4,538	539	21,803
2	Tony Dorsett	12,739	3,554	33	16,326
3	Jim Brown	12,312	2,499	648	15,459
4	Eric Dickerson	13,259	2,137	15	15,411
5	James Brooks	7,962	3,621	3,327	14,910
6	Marcus Allen	10,018	4,845	-6	14,857
7	Herschel Walker	7,996	4,387	2257	14,640
8	Franco Harris	12,120	2,287	215	14,622
9	O.J. Simpson	11,236	2,142	990	14,368
10	James Lofton	246	14,004	27	14,277
11	Bobby Mitchell	2,735	7,954	3,389	14,078
12	Jerry Rice	511	13,275	6	13,792
13	John Riggins	11,352	2,090	-7	13,435
14	Steve Largent	83	13,089	224	13,396
15	Ottis Anderson	10,273	3,062	29	13,364
16	Drew Hill	19	9,831	3,487	13,337
17	Greg Pruitt	5,672	3,069	4,521	13,262
18	Roger Craig	8,189	4,911	43	13,143
19	Henry Ellard	50	11,158	1,891	13,099
20	Art Monk	332	12,607	10	12,949
21	Ollie Matson	5,173	3,285	4,426	12,884
22	Timmy Brown	3,862	3,399	5,423	12,684
23	Lenny Moore	5,174	6,039	1,238	12,451
24	Don Maynard	70	11,834	475	12,379
25	Charlie Joiner	22	12,146	199	12,367

Note: The NFL does not recognize records from the All-American Football Conference (1946-49). If it did, **Joe Perry** would rank 23rd (after Timmy Brown) with the following stats: 9,723 Rush; 2,021 Rec; 788 Ret; 12,532 Total in 16 years.

Years played: Allen (13), Anderson (14), Brooks (12), J. Brown (9), T. Brown (10), Craig (11), Dickerson (11), Dorsett (12), Ellard (12), Harris (13), Hill (14), Joiner (18), Largent (14), Lofton (16), Matson (14), Maynard (15), Mitchell (11), Monk (15), Moore (12), Payton (13), Pruitt (12), Rice (10), Riggins (14), Simpson (11) and Walker (9).

Scoring

Points

		Yrs	TD	FG	PAT	Total
1	George Blanda	26	9	335	943	2002
2	Jan Stenerud	19	0	373	580	1699
3	Nick Lowery	16	0	349	512	1559
4	Pat Leahy	18	0	304	558	1470
5	Jim Turner	16	1	304	521	1439
6	Mark Moseley	16	0	300	482	1382
7	Jim Bakken	17	0	282	534	1380
8	Fred Cox	15	0	282	519	1365
9	Eddie Murray	15	0	295	465	1350
10	Lou Groza	17	1	234	641	1349
11	Gary Anderson	13	0	309	416	1343
12	Matt Bahr	16	0	277	495	1326
13	Morten Andersen	13	0	302	412	1318
14	Jim Breech	14	0	243	517	1246
15	Chris Bahr	14	0	241	490	1213
16	Norm Johnson	13	0	243	476	1205
17	Gino Cappelletti	11	42	176	350	1130†
18	Ray Wersching	15	0	222	456	1122
19	Don Cockroft	13	0	216	432	1080
20	Garo Yepremian	14	0	210	444	1074
21	Bruce Gossett	11	0	219	374	1031
22	Kevin Butler	10	0	220	342	1002
23	Sam Baker	15	2	179	428	977
24	Rafael Septien	10	0	180	420	960
25	Lou Michaels	13	1	187	386	955†

†Cappelletti's total includes four 2-point conversions, and Michaels' total includes one safety.

Note: The NFL does not recognize records from the All-American Football Conference (1946-49). If it did, **Lou Groza** would move up to 3rd (after Stenerud) with the following stats: 21 Yrs; 1 TD; 264 FG, 810 PAT; 1,608 Pts.

Touchdowns

		Yrs	Rush	Rec	Ret	Total
1	Jerry Rice	10	8	131	0	139
2	Jim Brown	9	106	20	0	126
3	Walter Payton	13	110	15	0	125
4	Marcus Allen	13	98	21	1	120
5	John Riggins	14	104	12	0	116
6	Lenny Moore	12	63	48	2	113
7	Don Hutson	11	3	99	3	105
8	Steve Largent	14	1	100	0	101
9	Franco Harris	13	91	9	0	100
10	Eric Dickerson	11	90	6	0	96
11	Jim Taylor	10	83	10	0	93
12	Tony Dorsett	12	77	13	1	91
	Bobby Mitchell	11	18	65	8	91
14	Leroy Kelly	10	74	13	3	90
	Charley Taylor	13	11	79	0	90
16	Don Maynard	15	0	88	0	88
17	Lance Alworth	11	2	85	0	87
18	Ottis Anderson	14	81	5	0	86
	Paul Warfield	13	1	85	0	86
20	Mark Clayton	11	0	84	1	85
	Tommy McDonald	12	0	84	1	85
22	Pete Johnson	8	76	6	0	82
23	Art Powell	10	0	81	1	82
24	Herschel Walker	9	60	18	2	80
25	Harold Carmichael	14	0	79	0	79

Note: The NFL does not recognize records from the All-American Football Conference (1946-49). If it did, **Joe Perry** would rank 22nd (after Clayton and McDonald) with the following stats: 16 Yrs; 71 Rush; 12 Rec; 1 Ret; 84 TDs.

Interceptions

		Yrs	No	Yards	TD
1	Paul Krause	16	81	1185	3
2	Emlen Tunnell	14	79	1282	4
3	Dick (Night Train) Lane	14	68	1207	5
4	Ken Riley	15	65	596	5
5	Ronnie Lott	14	63	730	5

Sacks (unofficial)

		Yrs	No
1	Deacon Jones	14	172
2	Jack Youngblood	14	150½
3	Alan Page	15	148
4	Reggie White	10	145
5	Lawrence Taylor	13	142

Kickoff Returns

Minimum 75 returns.

		Yrs	No	Yards	Avg	TD
1	Gale Sayers	7	91	2781	30.6	6
2	Lynn Chandnois	7	92	2720	29.6	3
3	Abe Woodson	9	193	5538	28.7	5
4	Buddy Young	6	90	2514	27.9	2
5	Travis Williams	5	102	2801	27.5	6

Punting

Minimum 300 punts.

		Yrs	No	Yards	Avg
1	Sammy Baugh	16	338	15,245	45.1
2	Tommy Davis	11	511	22,833	44.7
3	Yale Lary	11	503	22,279	44.3
4	Rohn Stark	13	985	43,162	43.8
	Horace Gillom	7	385	16,872	43.8
	Jerry Norton	11	358	15,671	43.8

Punt Returns

Minimum 75 returns.

		Yrs	No	Yards	Avg	TD
1	George McAfee	8	112	1431	12.8	2
	Jack Christiansen	8	85	1084	12.8	8
3	Claude Gibson	5	110	1381	12.6	3
4	Bill Dudley	9	124	1515	12.2	3
5	Rick Upchurch	9	248	3008	12.1	8

Safeties

		Yrs	No
1	Ted Hendricks	15	4
	Doug English	10	4
3	Thirteen players tied with three.		

Long-Playing Records

Seasons	Games	Consecutive Games
No	**No**	**No**
1 George Blanda, QB-K 26	1 George Blanda, QB-K 340	1 Jim Marshall, DE 282
2 Earl Morrall, QB 21	2 Jim Marshall, DE 282	2 Mick Tingelhoff, C 240
3 Jim Marshall, DE 20	3 Jan Stenerud, K 263	3 Jim Bakken, K 234

All-Time NFL Leaders (Cont.)

SINGLE SEASON

Passing

Yards Gained	Year	Att	Cmp	Pct	Yds	Efficiency	Year	Att/Cmp	TD	Rtg
Dan Marino, Mia	1984	564	362	64.2	5084	Steve Young, SF	1994	461/324	35	112.8
Dan Fouts, SD	1981	609	360	59.1	4802	Joe Montana, SF	1989	386/271	26	112.4
Dan Marino, Mia	1986	623	378	60.7	4746	Milt Plum, Cle	1960	250/151	21	110.4
Dan Fouts, SD	1980	589	348	59.1	4715	Sammy Baugh, Wash	1945	182/128	11	109.9
Warren Moon, Hou	1991	655	404	61.7	4690	Dan Marino, Mia	1984	564/362	48	108.9
Warren Moon, Hou	1990	584	362	62.0	4689	Sid Luckman, Bears	1943	202/110	28	107.5
Neil Lomax, St.L	1984	560	345	61.6	4614	Steve Young, SF	1992	402/268	25	107.0
Drew Bledsoe, NE	1994	691	400	57.9	4555	Bart Starr, GB	1966	251/156	14	105.0
Lynn Dicky, GB	1983	484	286	59.7	4458	Y.A. Tittle, NYG	1963	367/221	36	104.8
Dan Marino, Mia	1994	615	385	62.6	4353	Roger Staubach, Dal	1971	211/126	15	104.8

Receptions

Catches	Year	No	Yds
Cris Carter, Min	1994	122	1256
Jerry Rice, SF	1994	112	1499
Sterling Sharpe, GB	1993	112	1274
Terance Mathis, Atl	1994	111	1342
Sterling Sharpe, GB	1992	108	1461
Art Monk, Wash	1984	106	1372
Charley Hennigan, Hou	1964	101	1546
Jerry Rice, SF	1990	100	1502
Haywood Jeffires, Hou	1991	100	1181
Lionel Taylor, Den	1961	100	1176

Rushing

Yards Gained	Year	Car	Yds	Avg
Eric Dickerson, LA Rams	1984	379	2105	5.6
O.J. Simpson, Buf	1973	332	2003	6.0
Earl Campbell, Hou	1980	373	1934	5.2
Barry Sanders, Det	1994	331	1883	5.7
Jim Brown, Cle	1963	291	1863	6.4
Walter Payton, Chi	1977	339	1852	5.5
Eric Dickerson, LA Rams	1986	404	1821	4.5
O.J. Simpson, Buf	1975	329	1817	5.5
Eric Dickerson, LA Rams	1983	390	1808	4.6
Marcus Allen, LA Raiders	1985	390	1759	4.6

Scoring

Points

	Year	TD	PAT	FG	Pts
Paul Hornung, GB	1960	15	41	15	176
Mark Moseley, Wash	1983	0	62	33	161
Gino Cappelletti, Bos	1964	7	38	25	155
Chip Lohmiller, Wash	1991	0	56	31	149
Gino Cappelletti, Bos	1961	8	48	17	147
Paul Hornung, GB	1961	10	41	15	146
Jim Turner, Jets	1968	0	43	34	145
John Riggins, Wash	1983	24	0	0	144
Kevin Butler, Chi	1985	0	51	31	144
Tony Franklin, NE	1986	0	44	32	140

Touchdowns

	Year	Rush	Rec	Ret	Total
John Riggins, Wash	1983	24	0	0	24
O.J. Simpson, Buf	1975	16	7	0	23
Jerry Rice, SF	1987	1	22	0	23
Gale Sayers, Chi	1966	14	6	2	22
Chuck Foreman, Min	1975	13	9	0	22
Emmitt Smith, Dal	1994	21	1	0	22
Jim Brown, Cle	1965	17	4	0	21
Joe Morris, NY Giants	1985	21	0	0	21
Lenny Moore, Bal	1964	16	3	1	20
Leroy Kelly, Cle	1968	16	4	0	20
Eric Dickerson, LA Rams	1983	18	2	0	20

Note: The NFL regular season schedule grew from 12 games (1947-60) to 14 (1961-77) to 16 (1978-present). The AFL regular season schedule was always 14 games (1960-69).

Touchdowns Rushing

	Year	No
John Riggins, Washington	1983	24
Joe Morris, NY Giants	1985	21
Emmitt Smith, Dallas	1994	21
Jim Taylor, Green Bay	1962	19
Earl Campbell, Houston	1979	19
Chuck Muncie, San Diego	1981	19
Eric Dickerson, LA Rams	1983	18
George Rogers, Washington	1986	18
Emmitt Smith, Dallas	1992	18
Jim Brown, Cleveland	1958	17
Jim Brown, Cleveland	1965	17

Touchdowns Receiving

	Year	No
Jerry Rice, San Francisco	1987	22
Mark Clayton, Miami	1984	18
Sterling Sharpe, Green Bay	1994	18
Don Hutson, Green Bay	1942	17
Elroy (Crazylegs) Hirsch, LA Rams	1951	17
Bill Groman, Houston	1961	17
Jerry Rice, San Francisco	1989	17
Art Powell, Oakland	1963	16
Jerry Rice, San Francisco	1986	15
Jerry Rice, San Francisco	1993	15
Andre Rison, Atlanta	1993	15

Touchdowns Passing

	Year	No
Dan Marino, Miami	1984	48
Dan Marino, Miami	1986	44
George Blanda, Houston	1961	36
Y.A. Tittle, NY Giants	1963	36
Steve Young, San Francisco	1994	35
Y.A. Tittle, NY Giants	1962	33
Dan Fouts, San Diego	1981	33
Warren Moon, Houston	1990	33
Jim Kelly, Buffalo	1991	33
Brett Favre, Green Bay	1994	33

Field Goals

	Year	Att	No
Ali Haji-Sheikh, NY Giants	1983	42	35
Jeff Jaeger, LA Rams	1993	44	35
Nick Lowery, Kansas City	1990	37	34
Jim Turner, NY Jets	1968	46	34
Jason Hanson, Detroit	1993	43	34
John Carney, San Diego	1994	38	34
Fuad Reveiz, Minnesota	1994	39	34
Gary Anderson, Pittsburgh	1985	42	33
Mark Moseley, Washington	1983	47	33
Chester Marcol, Green Bay	1972	48	33

Interceptions

	Year	No
Dick (Night Train) Lane, Detroit	1952	14
Dan Sandifer, Washington	1948	13
Spec Sanders, NY Yanks	1950	13
Lester Hayes, Oakland	1980	13

Punting

Qualifiers	Year	Avg
Sammy Baugh, Washington	1940	51.4
Yale Lary, Detroit	1963	48.9
Sammy Baugh, Washington	1941	48.7

Kickoff Returns

	Year	Avg
Travis Williams, Green Bay	1967	41.1
Gale Sayers, Chicago	1967	37.7
Ollie Matson, Chicago Cards	1958	35.5

Punt Returns

	Year	Avg
Herb Rich, Baltimore	1950	23.0
Jack Christiansen, Detroit	1952	21.5
Dick Christy, NY Titans	1961	21.3
Bob Hayes, Dallas	1968	20.8

Sacks (unofficial)

	Year	No		Year	No
Coy Bacon, Cincinnati	1976	26	Reggie White, Philadelphia	1987	21
Mark Gastineau, NY Jets	1984	22	Chris Doleman, Minnesota	1989	21

SINGLE GAME

Passing

Yards Gained	Date	Yds
Norm Van Brocklin, LA vs NY Yanks	9/28/51	554
Warren Moon, Hou at KC	12/16/90	527
Dan Marino, Mia vs NYJ	10/23/88	521
Phil Simms, NYG vs Cin	10/13/85	513
Vince Ferragamo, Rams vs Chi	12/26/82	509

Completions	Date	No
Drew Bledsoe, NE vs Min	11/13/94	45
Richard Todd, NYJ vs SF	9/21/80	42
Warren Moon, Hou vs Dal	11/10/91	41
Ken Anderson, Cin vs SD	12/20/82	40
Phil Simms, NYG vs Cin	10/13/85	40

Receptions

Catches	Date	No
Tom Fears, LA vs GB	12/ 3/50	18
Clark Gaines, NYJ vs SF	9/21/80	17
Sonny Randle, St.L vs NYG	11/ 4/62	16
Six tied with 15 each.		

Yards Gained	Date	Yds
Flipper Anderson, LA Rams vs NO	11/26/89	336
Stephone Paige, KC vs SD	12/22/85	309
Jim Benton, Cle vs Det	11/22/45	303
Cloyce Box, Det vs Bal	12/ 3/50	302
John Taylor, SF vs LA Rams	12/11/89	286

Rushing

Yards Gained	Date	Yds
Walter Payton, Chi vs Min	11/20/77	275
O.J. Simpson, Buf vs Det	11/25/76	273
O.J. Simpson, Buf vs NE	9/16/73	250
Willie Ellison, LA Rams vs NO	12/ 5/71	247
Cookie Gilchrist, Buf vs NYJ	12/ 8/63	243

All-Purpose Running

	Date	Yds
Billy Cannon, Hou vs NY Titans	12/10/61	373
Lionel James, SD vs Raiders	11/10/85	345
Timmy Brown, Phi vs St.L	12/16/62	341
Gale Sayers, Chi vs Min	12/18/66	339
Gale Sayers, Chi vs SF	12/12/65	336

Scoring

Points

	Date	Pts
Ernie Nevers, Chi. Cards vs Chi. Bears	11/28/29	40
Dub Jones, Cle vs Chi. Bears	11/25/51	36
Gale Sayers, Chi vs SF	12/12/65	36
Paul Hornung, GB vs Bal	10/ 8/61	33
Bob Shaw, Chi. Cards vs Bal	10/ 2/50	30
Jim Brown, Cle vs Bal	11/ 1/59	30
Abner Haynes, Dal. Texans vs Oak	11/26/61	30
Billy Cannon, Hou vs NY Titans	12/10/61	30
Cookie Gilchrist, Buf vs NY Jets	12/ 8/63	30
Kellen Winslow, SD vs Oak	11/22/81	30
Jerry Rice, SF at Atl	10/14/90	30

Note: Nevers celebrated Thanksgiving, 1929, by scoring all the Chicago Cardinals' points on six rushing TDs and four PATs. The Cards beat Red Grange and the Chicago Bears, 40-6.

Touchdowns Passing

	Date	No
Sid Luckman, Chi. Bears vs NYG	11/14/43	7
Adrian Burk, Phi vs Wash	10/17/54	7
George Blanda, Hou vs NY Titans	11/19/61	7
Y.A. Tittle, NYG vs Wash	10/28/62	7
Joe Kapp, Min vs Bal	9/28/69	7

Touchdowns Receiving

	Date	No
Bob Shaw, Chi. Cards vs Bal	10/ 2/50	5
Kellen Winslow, SD vs Oak	11/22/81	5
Jerry Rice, SF at Atl	10/14/90	5

Touchdowns Rushing

	Date	No
Ernie Nevers, Chi. Cards vs Chi. Bears	11/28/29	6
Jim Brown, Cle vs Bal	11/ 1/59	5
Cookie Gilchrist, Buf vs NY Jets	12/ 8/63	5

Field Goals

	Date	No
Jim Bakken, St.L vs Pit	9/24/67	7
Rich Karlis, Min vs Rams	11/ 5/89	7
Eight players tied with 6 FGs.		

Note: Bakken was 7-for-9, Karlis 7-for-7.

Extra Point Kicks

	Date	No
Pat Harder, Cards vs NYG	10/17/48	9
Bob Waterfield, LA vs Bal	10/22/50	9
Charlie Gogolak, Wash vs NYG	11/27/66	9

All-Time NFL Leaders (Cont.)
LONGEST PLAYS

Passing (all for TDs)	Date	Yds
Frank Filchock to Andy Farkas, Wash vs Pit	10/15/39	99
George Izo to Bobby Mitchell, Wash vs Cle	9/15/63	99
Karl Sweetan to Pat Studstill, Det vs Bal	10/16/66	99
Sonny Jurgensen to Gerry Allen, Wash vs Chi	9/15/68	99
Jim Plunkett to Cliff Branch, LA Raiders vs Wash	10/2/83	99
Ron Jaworski to Mike Quick, Phi vs Atl	11/10/85	99
Stan Humphries to Tony Martin, SD at Sea	9/18/94	99

Runs from Scrimmage (all for TDs)	Date	Yds
Tony Dorsett, Dal vs Min	1/3/83	99
Andy Uram, GB vs Chi. Cards	10/8/39	97
Bob Gage, Pit vs Bears	12/4/49	97

Field Goals	Date	Yds
Tom Dempsey, NO vs Det	11/8/70	63
Steve Cox, Cle vs Cin	10/21/84	60
Morten Andersen, NO vs Chi	10/27/91	60

Punt Returns (all for TDs)	Date	Yds
Robert Bailey, Rams at NO	10/23/94	103
Gil LeFebvre, Cin vs Bklyn	12/3/33	98
Charlie West, Min vs Wash	11/3/68	98
Dennis Morgan, Dal vs St.L	10/13/74	98
Terance Mathis, NYJ vs Dal	11/4/90	98

Kickoff Returns (all for TDs)	Date	Yds
Al Carmichael, GB vs Chi. Bears	10/7/56	106
Noland Smith, KC vs Den	12/17/67	106
Roy Green, St.L vs Dal	10/21/79	106

Interception Returns (for TDs)	Date	Yds
Vencie Glenn, SD vs Den	11/29/87	103
Louis Oliver, Mia vs Buf	10/4/92	103
Six players tied with 102-yd returns.		

Chicago College All-Star Game

On Aug. 31, 1934, a year after sponsoring Major League Baseball's first All-Star Game, *Chicago Tribune* sports editor Arch Ward presented the first Chicago College All-Star Game at Soldier Field. A crowd of 79,432 turned out to see an all-star team of graduated college seniors battle the 1933 NFL champion Chicago Bears to a scoreless tie. The preseason game was played annually at Soldier Field until it was cancelled in 1977. The NFL champs won the series, 32-9-1.

Year		Year		Year	
1934	Chi. Bears 0, All-Stars 0	1950	All-Stars 17, Philadelphia 7	1965	Cleveland 24, All-Stars 16
1935	Chi. Bears 5, All-Stars 0	1951	Cleveland 33, All-Stars 0	1966	Green Bay 38, All-Stars 0
1936	Detroit 7, All-Stars 0	1952	LA Rams 10, All-Stars 7	1967	Green Bay 27, All-Stars 0
1937	All-Stars 6, Green Bay 0	1953	Detroit 24, All-Stars 10	1968	Green Bay 34, All-Stars 17
1938	All-Stars 28, Washington 16	1954	Detroit 31, All-Stars 6	1969	NY Jets 26, All-Stars 24
1939	NY Giants 9, All-Stars 0	1955	All-Stars 30, Cleveland 27		
		1956	Cleveland 26, All-Stars 0	1970	Kansas City 24, All-Stars 3
1940	Green Bay 45, All-Stars 28	1957	NY Giants 22, All-Stars 12	1971	Baltimore 24, All-Stars 17
1941	Chi. Bears 37, All-Stars 13	1958	All-Stars 35, Detroit 19	1972	Dallas 20, All-Stars 7
1942	Chi. Bears 21, All-Stars 0	1959	Baltimore 29, All-Stars 0	1973	Miami 14, All-Stars 3
1943	All-Stars 27, Washington 7			1974	No Game (NFLPA Strike)
1944	Chi. Bears 24, All-Stars 21	1960	Baltimore 32, All-Stars 7	1975	Pittsburgh 21, All-Stars 14
1945	Green Bay 19, All-Stars 7	1961	Philadelphia 28, All-Stars 14	1976	Pittsburgh 24, All-Stars 0*
1946	All-Stars 16, LA Rams 0	1962	Green Bay 42, All-Stars 20		
1947	All-Stars 16, Chi. Bears 0	1963	All-Stars 20, Green Bay 17	*Downpour flooded field, game called
1948	Chi. Cards 28, All-Stars 0	1964	Chi. Bears 28, All-Stars 17	with 1:22 left in 3rd quarter.
1949	Philadelphia 38, All-Stars 0				

Number One Draft Choices

In an effort to blunt the dominance of the Chicago Bears and New York Giants in the 1930s and distribute talent more evenly throughout the league, the NFL established the college draft in 1936. The first player chosen in the first draft was Jay Berwanger, who was also college football's first Heisman Trophy winner. In all, 16 Heisman winners have also been the NFL's No.1 draft choice. They are noted in **bold** type. The American Football League (formed in 1960) held its own draft for six years before agreeing to merge with the NFL and select players in a common draft starting in 1967.

Year	Team		Year	Team	
1936	Philadelphia	**Jay Berwanger**, HB, Chicago	1953	San Francisco	Harry Babcock, E, Georgia
1937	Philadelphia	Sam Francis, FB, Nebraska	1954	Cleveland	Bobby Garrett, QB, Stanford
1938	Cleveland Rams	Corbett Davis, FB, Indiana	1955	Baltimore	George Shaw, QB, Oregon
1939	Chicago Cards	Ki Aldrich, C, TCU	1956	Pittsburgh	Gary Glick, DB, Colo. A&M
			1957	Green Bay	**Paul Hornung**, QB, N. Dame
1940	Chicago Cards	George Cafego, HB, Tennessee	1958	Chicago Cards	King Hill, QB, Rice
1941	Chicago Bears	**Tom Harmon**, HB, Michigan	1959	Green Bay	Randy Duncan, QB, Iowa
1942	Pittsburgh	Bill Dudley, HB, Virginia			
1943	Detroit	**Frank Sinkwich**, HB, Georgia	1960	NFL—LA Rams	**Billy Cannon**, HB, LSU
1944	Boston Yanks	**Angelo Bertelli**, QB, N. Dame		AFL—No choice	
1945	Chicago Cards	Charley Trippi, HB, Georgia	1961	NFL—Minnesota	Tommy Mason, HB, Tulane
1946	Boston Yanks	Frank Dancewicz, QB, N. Dame		AFL—Buffalo	Ken Rice, G, Auburn
1947	Chicago Bears	Bob Fenimore, HB, Okla. A&M	1962	NFL—Washington	**Ernie Davis**, HB, Syracuse
1948	Washington	Harry Gilmer, QB, Alabama		AFL—Oakland	Roman Gabriel, QB, N.C. State
1949	Philadelphia	Chuck Bednarik, C, Penn	1963	NFL—LA Rams	**Terry Baker**, QB, Oregon St.
				AFL—Kan.City	Buck Buchanan, DT, Grambling
1950	Detroit	**Leon Hart**, E, Notre Dame	1964	NFL—San Fran	Dave Parks, E, Texas Tech
1951	NY Giants	Kyle Rote, HB, SMU		AFL—Boston	Jack Concannon, QB, Boston Col.
1952	LA Rams	Bill Wade, QB, Vanderbilt			

Year	Team		Year	Team	
1965	NFL—NY Giants	Tucker Frederickson, HB, Auburn	1980	Detroit	**Billy Sims**, RB, Oklahoma
	AFL—Houston	Lawrence Elkins, E, Baylor	1981	New Orleans	**George Rogers**, RB, S. Carolina
1966	NFL—Atlanta	Tommy Nobis, LB, Texas	1982	New England	Kenneth Sims, DT, Texas
	AFL—Miami	Jim Grabowski, FB, Illinois	1983	Baltimore	John Elway, QB, Stanford
1967	Baltimore	Bubba Smith, DT, Michigan St.	1984	New England	Irving Fryar, WR, Nebraska
1968	Minnesota	Ron Yary, T, USC	1985	Buffalo	Bruce Smith, DE, Va. Tech
1969	Buffalo	**O.J. Simpson**, RB, USC	1986	Tampa Bay	**Bo Jackson**, RB, Auburn
			1987	Tampa Bay	**V. Testaverde**, QB, Miami-FL
1970	Pittsburgh	Terry Bradshaw, QB, La.Tech	1988	Atlanta	Aundray Bruce, LB, Auburn
1971	New England	**Jim Plunkett**, QB, Stanford	1989	Dallas	Troy Aikman, QB, UCLA
1972	Buffalo	Walt Patulski, DE, Notre Dame			
1973	Houston	John Matuszak, DE, Tampa	1990	Indianapolis	Jeff George, QB, Illinois
1974	Dallas	Ed (Too Tall) Jones, Tenn. St.	1991	Dallas	Russell Maryland, DL, Miami-FL
1975	Atlanta	Steve Bartkowski, QB, Calif.	1992	Indianapolis	Steve Emtman, DL, Washington
1976	Tampa Bay	Lee Roy Selmon, DE, Oklahoma	1993	New England	Drew Bledsoe, QB, Washington St.
1977	Tampa Bay	Ricky Bell, RB, USC	1994	Cincinnati	Dan Wilkinson, DT, Ohio St.
1978	Houston	**Earl Campbell**, RB, Texas	1995	Cincinnati	Ki-Jana Carter, RB, Penn St.
1979	Buffalo	Tom Cousineau, LB, Ohio St.			

All-Time Winningest NFL Coaches

NFL career victories through the 1994 season. Career, regular season and playoff records are noted along with NFL, AFL and Super Bowl titles won. Coaches active during 1994 season in **bold** type.

		Career				Regular Season				Playoffs			
		Yrs	W	L	T	Pct	W	L	T	Pct	W	L	Pct.	League Titles
1	Don Shula	32	**338**	165	6	.670	319	149	6	.679	19	16	.543	2 Super Bowls and 1 NFL
2	George Halas	40	**324**	151	31	.671	318	148	31	.671	6	3	.667	5 NFL
3	Tom Landry	29	**270**	178	6	.601	250	162	6	.605	20	16	.556	2 Super Bowls
4	Curly Lambeau	33	**229**	134	22	.623	226	132	22	.624	3	2	.600	6 NFL
5	Chuck Noll	23	**209**	156	1	.572	193	148	1	.566	16	8	.667	4 Super Bowls
6	**Chuck Knox**	22	**193**	158	1	.550	186	147	1	.558	7	11	.389	—None—
7	Paul Brown	21	**170**	108	6	.609	166	100	6	.621	4	8	.333	3 NFL
8	Bud Grant	18	**168**	108	5	.607	158	96	5	.620	10	12	.455	1 NFL
9	Steve Owen	23	**153**	108	17	.581	132	100	17	.595	2	8	.200	2 NFL
10	Joe Gibbs	12	**140**	65	0	.683	124	60	0	.674	16	5	.762	3 Super Bowls
11	**Dan Reeves**	14	**138**	92	1	.600	130	85	1	.604	8	7	.553	—None—
12	Hank Stram	17	**136**	100	10	.573	131	97	10	.571	5	3	.625	1 Super Bowl and 3 AFL
13	Weeb Ewbank	20	**134**	130	7	.507	130	129	7	.502	4	1	.800	1 Super Bowl, 2 NFL, and 1 AFL
14	**Marv Levy**	14	**127**	96	0	.570	117	90	0	.565	10	6	.625	—None—
15	Sid Gillman	18	**123**	104	7	.541	122	99	7	.550	1	5	.167	1 AFL
16	George Allen	12	**118**	54	5	.681	116	47	5	.705	2	7	.222	—None—
17	Don Coryell	14	**114**	89	1	.561	111	83	1	.572	3	6	.333	—None—
18	John Madden	10	**112**	39	7	.731	103	32	7	.750	9	7	.563	1 Super Bowl
	Mike Ditka	11	**112**	68	0	.622	106	62	0	.631	6	6	.500	1 Super Bowl
20	**Marty Schottenheimer**	11	**108**	72	1	.599	103	63	1	.620	5	9	.357	—None—
21	Buddy Parker	15	**107**	76	9	.581	104	75	9	.577	3	1	.750	2 NFL
22	Vince Lombardi	10	**105**	35	6	.740	96	34	6	.728	9	1	.900	2 Super Bowls and 5 NFL
	Tom Flores	12	**105**	90	0	.538	97	87	0	.527	8	3	.727	2 Super Bowls
24	Bill Walsh	10	**102**	63	1	.617	92	59	1	.609	10	4	.714	3 Super Bowls
25	**Bill Parcells**	10	**100**	70	1	.588	92	66	1	.582	8	4	.667	2 Super Bowls

Notes: The NFL does not recognize records from the All-American Football Conference (1946-49). If it did, **Paul Brown** (52-4-3 in four AAFC seasons) would move up to 5th on the all-time list with the following career stats— 25 Yrs; 222 Wins; 112 Losses; 9 Ties; .660 Pct; 9-8 playoff record; and 4 AAFC titles.

The NFL also considers the Playoff Bowl or "Runner-up Bowl" (officially: the Bert Bell Benefit Bowl) as a post-season exhibition game. The Playoff Bowl was contested every year from 1960-69 in Miami between Eastern and Western Conference second place teams. While the games did not count, six of the coaches above went to the Playoff Bowl at least once and came away with the following records— Allen (2-0), Brown (0-1), Grant (0-1), Landry (1-2), Lombardi (1-1) and Shula (2-0).

Where They Coached

Allen— LA Rams (1966-70), Washington (1971-77); **Brown**— Cleveland (1950-62), Cincinnati (1968-75); **Coryell**— St. Louis (1973-77), San Diego (1978-86); **Ditka**— Chicago (1982-92); **Ewbank**— Baltimore (1954-62), NY Jets (1963-73); **Flores**— Oakland-LA Raiders (1979-87), Seattle (1992-94) **Gibbs**— Washington (1981-92); **Gillman**— LA Rams (1955-59), LA-San Diego Chargers (1960-69), Houston (1973-74).
Grant— Minnesota (1967-83,1985); **Halas**— Chicago Bears (1920-29,33-42,46-55,58-67); **Knox**— LA Rams (1973-77, 1992-94), Buffalo (1978-82), Seattle (1983-91); **Lambeau**— Green Bay (1921-49), Chicago Cards (1950-51), Washington (1952-53); **Landry**— Dallas (1960-88); **Levy**— Kansas City (1978-82), Buffalo (1986—); **Lombardi**— Green Bay (1959-67), Washington (1969); **Madden**— Oakland (1969-78).
Noll— Pittsburgh (1969-91); **Owen**— NY Giants (1931-53); **Parcells**— NY Giants (1983-90), New England (1993—); **Parker**— Chicago Cards (1949), Detroit (1951-56), Pittsburgh (1957-64); **Reeves**— Denver (1981-92), NY Giants (1993—); **Schottenheimer**— Cleveland (1984-88), Kansas City (1989—); **Shula**— Baltimore (1963-69), Miami (1970—); **Stram**— Dallas-Kansas City (1960-74), New Orleans (1976-77); **Walsh**— San Francisco (1979-88).

All-Time Winningest NFL Coaches (Cont.)

Top Winning Percentages

Minimum of 84 NFL victories, including playoffs.

		Yrs	W	L	T	Pct
1	George Seifert	6	84	24	0	.778
2	Vince Lombardi	10	105	35	6	.740
3	John Madden	10	112	39	7	.731
4	Joe Gibbs	12	140	65	0	.683
5	George Allen	12	118	54	5	.681
6	George Halas	40	324	151	31	.671
7	Don Shula	32	338	165	6	.670
8	Curly Lambeau	33	229	134	22	.623
9	Mike Ditka	11	112	68	0	.622
10	Bill Walsh	10	102	63	1	.617
11	Paul Brown	21	170	108	6	.609
12	Bud Grant	18	168	108	5	.607
13	Tom Landry	29	270	178	6	.601
14	Dan Reeves	14	138	92	1	.600
15	Marty Schottenheimer	11	108	72	1	.599
16	Bill Parcells	10	100	70	1	.588
17	Steve Owen	23	153	108	17	.581
18	Buddy Parker	15	107	76	9	.581
19	Hank Stram	17	136	100	10	.573
20	Chuck Noll	23	209	156	1	.572
21	Jim Mora	9	84	63	0	.571
22	Marv Levy	14	127	96	0	.570
23	Don Coryell	14	114	89	1	.561
24	Jimmy Conzelman	15	89	68	17	.560
25	Chuck Knox	22	193	158	1	.550

Note: If AAFC records are included, **Paul Brown** moves to 8th with a percentage of .660 (25 yrs, 222-112-9) and Buck Shaw would be 10th at .619 (8 yrs, 91-55-5).

Active Coaches' Victories

Through 1994 season, including playoffs.

		Yrs	W	L	T	Pct
1	Don Shula, Miami	32	338	165	6	.670
2	Dan Reeves, NY Giants	14	138	92	1	.600
3	Marv Levy, Buffalo	14	127	96	0	.570
4	Marty Schottenheimer, KC	11	108	72	1	.599
5	Bill Parcells, New England	10	100	70	1	.588
6	George Seifert, San Fran.	6	84	24	0	.778
	Jim Mora, New Orleans	9	84	63	0	.571
8	Sam Wyche, Tampa Bay	11	80	100	0	.444
9	Ted Marchibroda, Ind.	8	62	63	0	.496
10	Wayne Fontes, Detroit	7	52	53	0	.495
11	Buddy Ryan, Arizona	6	51	46	1	.526
12	Rich Kotite, NY Jets	4	37	29	0	.561
13	Bill Cowher, Pittsburgh	3	33	19	0	.635
	Bobby Ross, San Diego	3	33	20	0	.623
15	Bill Belichick, Cleveland	4	32	34	0	.485
16	Dennis Green, Minnesota	3	30	21	0	.588
17	Mike Holmgren, Green Bay	3	29	23	0	.558
18	Dave Wannstedt, Chicago	2	17	17	0	.500
19	Barry Switzer, Dallas	1	13	5	0	.722
20	David Shula, Cincinnati	3	11	37	0	.229
21	Mike Shanahan, Denver	2	8	12	0	.400
22	June Jones, Atlanta	1	7	9	0	.438
23	Norv Turner, Washington	1	3	13	0	.188
24	Jeff Fisher, Houston	1	1	5	0	.167
25	Rich Brooks, St. Louis	0	0	0	0	.000
	Dom Capers, Carolina	0	0	0	0	.000
	Tom Coughlin, Jacksonville	0	0	0	0	.000
	Dennis Erickson, Seattle	0	0	0	0	.000
	Ray Rhodes, Philadelphia	0	0	0	0	.000
	Mike White, Oakland	0	0	0	0	.000

Annual Awards
Most Valuable Player

Unlike other major pro team sports, the NFL does not sanction an MVP award. It gave out the Joe F. Carr Trophy (Carr was NFL president from 1921-39) for nine years but discontinued it in 1947. Since then, four principal MVP awards have been given out: UPI (1953-69), AP (since 1957), the Maxwell Club of Philadelphia's Bert Bell Trophy (since 1959) and the Pro Football Writers Assn. (since 1976). UPI switched to AFC and NFC Player of the Year awards in 1970.

Multiple winners (more than one season): Jim Brown (4); Johnny Unitas and Y.A. Tittle (3); Earl Campbell, Randall Cunningham, Otto Graham, Don Hutson, Joe Montana, Walter Payton, Ken Stabler, Joe Theismann and Steve Young (2).

Year		Awards
1938	Mel Hein, NY Giants, C	Carr
1939	Parker Hall, Cleveland Rams, HB	Carr
1940	Ace Parker, Brooklyn, HB	Carr
1941	Don Hutson, Green Bay, E	Carr
1942	Don Hutson, Green Bay, E	Carr
1943	Sid Luckman, Chicago Bears, QB	Carr
1944	Frank Sinkwich, Detroit, HB	Carr
1945	Bob Waterfield, Cleveland Rams, QB	Carr
1946	Bill Dudley, Pittsburgh, HB	Carr
1947-52	No award	
1953	Otto Graham, Cleveland Browns, QB	UPI
1954	Joe Perry, San Francisco, FB	UPI
1955	Otto Graham, Cleveland, QB	UPI
1956	Frank Gifford, NY Giants, HB	UPI
1957	Y.A. Tittle, San Francisco, QB	UPI
	& Jim Brown, Cleveland, FB	AP
1958	Jim Brown, Cleveland, FB	UPI
	& Gino Marchetti, Baltimore, DE	AP
1959	Johnny Unitas, Baltimore, QB	UPI, Bell
	& Charley Conerly, NY Giants, QB	AP
1960	Norm Van Brocklin, Phi., QB	UPI, AP (tie), Bell
	& Joe Schmidt, Detroit, LB	AP (tie)
1961	Paul Hornung, Green Bay, HB	UPI, AP, Bell
1962	Y.A. Tittle, NY Giants, QB	UPI
	Jim Taylor, Green Bay, FB	AP
	& Andy Robustelli, NY Giants, DE	Bell

Year		Awards
1963	Jim Brown, Cleveland, FB	UPI, Bell
	& Y.A. Tittle, NY Giants, QB	AP
1964	Johnny Unitas, Baltimore, QB	UPI, AP, Bell
1965	Jim Brown, Cleveland, FB	UPI, AP
	& Pete Retzlaff, Philadelphia, TE	Bell
1966	Bart Starr, Green Bay, QB	UPI, AP
	& Don Meredith, Dallas, QB	Bell
1967	Johnny Unitas, Baltimore, QB	UPI, AP, Bell
1968	Earl Morrall, Baltimore, QB	UPI, AP
	& Leroy Kelly, Cleveland, RB	Bell
1969	Roman Gabriel, LA Rams, QB	UPI, AP, Bell
1970	John Brodie, San Francisco, QB	AP
	& George Blanda, Oakland, QB-PK	Bell
1971	Alan Page, Minnesota, DT	AP
	& Roger Staubach, Dallas, QB	Bell
1972	Larry Brown, Washington, RB	AP, Bell
1973	O.J. Simpson, Buffalo, RB	AP, Bell
1974	Ken Stabler, Oakland, QB	AP, Bell
	& Merlin Olsen, LA Rams, DT	Bell
1975	Fran Tarkenton, Minnesota, QB	AP, Bell
1976	Bert Jones, Baltimore, QB	AP, PFWA
	& Ken Stabler, Oakland, QB	Bell
1977	Walter Payton, Chicago, RB	AP, PFWA
	& Bob Griese, Miami, QB	Bell
1978	Terry Bradshaw, Pittsburgh, QB	AP, Bell
	& Earl Campbell, Houston, RB	PFWA
1979	Earl Campbell, Houston, RB	AP, Bell, PFWA

Year		Awards	Year		Awards
1980	Brian Sipe, Cleveland, QB	AP, PFWA	1987	Jerry Rice, San Francisco, WR	Bell, PFWA
	& Ron Jaworski, Philadelphia, QB	Bell		& John Elway, Denver, QB	AP
1981	Ken Anderson, Cincinnati, QB	AP, Bell, PFWA	1988	Boomer Esiason, Cincinnati, QB	AP, PFWA
1982	Mark Moseley, Washington, PK	AP		& Randall Cunningham, Phila, QB	Bell
	Joe Theismann, Washington, QB	Bell	1989	Joe Montana, San Francisco, QB	AP, Bell, PFWA
	& Dan Fouts, San Diego, QB	PFWA	1990	Randall Cunningham, Phila., QB	Bell, PFWA
1983	Joe Theismann, Washington, QB	AP, PFWA		& Joe Montana, San Francisco, QB	AP
	& John Riggins, Washington, RB	Bell	1991	Thurman Thomas, Buffalo, RB	AP, PFWA
1984	Dan Marino, Miami, QB	AP, Bell, PFWA		& Barry Sanders, Detroit, RB	Bell
1985	Marcus Allen, LA Raiders, RB	AP, PFWA	1992	Steve Young, San Francisco, QB	AP, Bell, PFWA
	& Walter Payton, Chicago, RB	Bell	1993	Emmitt Smith, Dallas, RB	AP, Bell, PFWA
1986	Lawrence Taylor, NY Giants, LB	AP, Bell, PFWA	1994	Steve Young, San Francisco, QB	AP, Bell, PFWA

NFC Player of the Year

Given out by UPI since 1970. Offensive and defensive players honored since 1983. Rookie winners are in **bold** type.

Multiple winners: Eric Dickerson and Mike Singletary (3); Charles Haley, Walter Payton, Lawrence Taylor, Reggie White and Steve Young (2).

Year		Pos	Year		Pos
1970	John Brodie, San Francisco	QB	1986	Off—Eric Dickerson, Los Angeles	RB
1971	Alan Page, Minnesota	DT		Def—Lawrence Taylor, New York	LB
1972	Larry Brown, Washington	RB	1987	Off—Jerry Rice, San Francisco	WR
1973	John Hadl, Los Angeles	QB		Def—Reggie White, Philadelphia	DE
1974	Jim Hart, St. Louis	QB	1988	Off—Roger Craig, San Francisco	RB
1975	Fran Tarkenton, Minnesota	QB		Def—Mike Singletary, Chicago	LB
1976	Chuck Foreman, Minnesota	RB	1989	Off—Joe Montana, San Francisco	QB
1977	Walter Payton, Chicago	RB		Def—Keith Millard, Minnesota	DT
1978	Archie Manning, New Orleans	QB	1990	Off—Randall Cunningham, Philadelphia	QB
1979	**Ottis Anderson**, St. Louis	RB		Def—Charles Haley, San Francisco	LB
1980	Ron Jaworski, Philadelphia	QB	1991	Off—Mark Rypien, Washington	QB
1981	Tony Dorsett, Dallas	RB		Def—Reggie White, Philadelphia	DE
1982	Mark Moseley, Washington	PK	1992	Off—Steve Young, San Francisco	QB
1983	Off—**Eric Dickerson**, Los Angeles	RB		Def—Chris Doleman, Minnesota	DE
	Def—Lawrence Taylor, New York	LB	1993	Off—Emmitt Smith, Dallas	RB
1984	Off—Eric Dickerson, Los Angeles	RB		Def—Eric Allen, Philadelphia	CB
	Def—Mike Singletary, Chicago	LB	1994	Off—Steve Young, San Francisco	QB
1985	Off—Walter Payton, Chicago	RB		Def—Charles Haley, Dallas	DE
	Def—Mike Singletary, Chicago	LB			

AFL-AFC Player of the Year

Presented by UPI to the top player in the AFL (1960-69) and AFC (since 1970). Offensive and defensive players have been honored since 1983. Rookie winners are in **bold** type.

Multiple winners: O.J. Simpson and Bruce Smith (3); Cornelius Bennett, George Blanda, John Elway, Dan Fouts, Daryle Lamonica, Dan Marino and Curt Warner (2).

Year		Pos	Year		Pos
1960	**Abner Haynes**, Dallas Texans	HB	1984	Off—Dan Marino, Miami	QB
1961	George Blanda, Houston	QB		Def—Mark Gastineau, New York	DE
1962	Cookie Gilchrist, Buffalo	FB	1985	Off—Marcus Allen, Los Angeles	RB
1963	Lance Alworth, San Diego	FL		Def—Andre Tippett, New England	LB
1964	Gino Cappelletti, Boston	FL-PK	1986	Off—Curt Warner, Seattle	RB
1965	Paul Lowe, San Diego	HB		Def—Rulon Jones, Denver	DE
1966	Jim Nance, Boston	FB	1987	Off—John Elway, Denver	QB
1967	Daryle Lamonica, Oakland	QB		Def—Bruce Smith, Buffalo	DE
1968	Joe Namath, New York	QB	1988	Off—Boomer Esiason, Cincinnatti	QB
1969	Daryle Lamonica, Oakland	QB		Def—Bruce Smith, Buffalo	DE
1970	George Blanda, Oakland	QB-PK		& Cornelius Bennett, Buffalo	LB
1971	Otis Taylor, Kansas City	WR	1989	Off—Christian Okoye, Kansas City	RB
1972	O.J. Simpson, Buffalo	RB		Def—Michael Dean Perry, Cleveland	NT
1973	O.J. Simpson, Buffalo	RB	1990	Off—Warren Moon, Houston	QB
1974	Ken Stabler, Oakland	QB		Def—Bruce Smith, Buffalo	DE
1975	O.J. Simpson, Buffalo	RB	1991	Off—Thurman Thomas, Buffalo	RB
1976	Bert Jones, Baltimore	QB		Def—Cornelius Bennett, Buffalo	LB
1977	Craig Morton, Denver	QB	1992	Off—Barry Foster, Pittsburgh	RB
1978	**Earl Campbell**, Houston	RB		Def—Junior Seau, San Diego	LB
1979	Dan Fouts, San Diego	QB	1993	Off—John Elway, Denver	QB
1980	Brian Sipe, Cleveland	QB		Def—Rod Woodson, Pittsburgh	CB
1981	Ken Anderson, Cincinnati	QB	1994	Off—Dan Marino, Miami	QB
1982	Dan Fouts, San Diego	QB		Def—Greg Lloyd, Pittsburgh	LB
1983	Off—**Curt Warner**, Seattle	RB			
	Def—Rod Martin, Los Angeles	LB			

Annual Awards (Cont.)

NFL-NFC Rookie of the Year

Presented by UPI to the top rookie in the NFL (1955-69) and NFC (since 1970). Players who were the overall first pick in the NFL draft are in **bold** type.

Year		Pos	Year		Pos	Year		Pos
1955	Alan Ameche, Bal	FB	1970	Bruce Taylor, SF	DB	1985	Jerry Rice, SF	WR
1956	Lenny Moore, Bal	HB	1971	John Brockington, GB	RB	1986	Reuben Mayes, NO	RB
1957	Jim Brown, Cle	FB	1972	Chester Marcol, GB	PK	1987	Robert Awalt, St.L	TE
1958	Jimmy Orr, Pit	FL	1973	Charle Young, Phi	TE	1988	Keith Jackson, Phi	TE
1959	Boyd Dowler, GB	FL	1974	John Hicks, NY	G	1989	Barry Sanders, Det	RB
1960	Gail Cogdill, Det	FL	1975	Mike Thomas, Wash	RB	1990	Mark Carrier, Chi	S
1961	Mike Ditka, Chi	TE	1976	Sammy White, Min	WR	1991	Lawrence Dawsey, TB	WR
1962	Ronnie Bull, Chi	FB	1977	Tony Dorsett, Dal	RB	1992	Robert Jones, Dal	LB
1963	Paul Flatley, Min	FL	1978	Bubba Baker, Det	DE	1993	Jerome Bettis, LA	RB
1964	Charley Taylor, Wash	HB	1979	Ottis Anderson, St.L	RB	1994	Bryant Young, SF	DT
1965	Gale Sayers, Chi	HB	1980	**Billy Sims**, Det	RB			
1966	Johnny Roland, St.L	HB	1981	**George Rogers**, NO	RB			
1967	Mel Farr, Det	RB	1982	Jim McMahon, Chi	QB			
1968	Earl McCullough, Det	FL	1983	Eric Dickerson, LA	RB			
1969	Calvin Hill, Dal	RB	1984	Paul McFadden, Phi	PK			

AFL-AFC Rookie of the Year

Presented by UPI to the top rookie in the AFL (1960-69) and AFC (since 1970). Players who were the overall first pick in the AFL or NFL draft are in **bold** type.

Year		Pos	Year		Pos	Year		Pos
1960	Abner Haynes, Dal	HB	1972	Franco Harris, Pit	RB	1984	Louis Lipps, Pit	WR
1961	Earl Faison, SD	DE	1973	Boobie Clark, Cin	RB	1985	Kevin Mack, Cle	RB
1962	Curtis McClinton, Dal	HB	1974	Don Woods, SD	RB	1986	Leslie O'Neal, SD	DE
1963	Billy Joe, Den	FB	1975	Robert Brazile, Hou	LB	1987	Shane Conlan, Buf	LB
1964	Matt Snell, NY	FB	1976	Mike Haynes, NE	DB	1988	John Stephens, NE	RB
1965	Joe Namath, NY	QB	1977	A.J. Duhe, Mia	DE	1989	Derrick Thomas, KC	LB
1966	Bobby Burnett, Buf	HB	1978	**Earl Campbell**, Hou	RB			
1967	George Webster, Hou	LB	1979	Jerry Butler, Buf	WR	1990	Richmond Webb, Mia	OT
1968	Paul Robinson, Cin	RB				1991	Mike Croel, Den	LB
1969	Greg Cook, Cin	QB	1980	Joe Cribbs, Buf	RB	1992	Dale Carter, KC	CB
			1981	Joe Delaney, KC	RB	1993	Rick Mirer, Sea	QB
1970	Dennis Shaw, Buf	QB	1982	Marcus Allen, LA	RB	1994	Marshall Faulk, Ind	RB
1971	**Jim Plunkett**, NE	QB	1983	Curt Warner, Sea	RB			

NFL-NFC Coach of the Year

Presented by UPI to the top coach in the NFL (1955-69) and NFC (since 1970). Records indicate how much coach's team improved over one season.

Multiple winners: George Allen, Leeman Bennett, Mike Ditka, George Halas, Tom Landry, Jack Pardee, Allie Sherman, Don Shula and Bill Walsh (2).

Year		Improvement	Year		Improvement
1955	Joe Kuharich, Washington	3-9 to 8-4	1976	Jack Pardee, Chicago	4-10 to 7-7
1956	Buddy Parker, Detroit	3-9 to 9-3	1977	Leeman Bennett, Atlanta	4-10 to 7-7
1957	Paul Brown, Cleveland	5-7 to 9-2-1	1978	Dick Vermeil, Philadelphia	5-9 to 9-7
1958	Weeb Ewbank, Baltimore	7-5 to 9-3	1979	Jack Pardee, Washington	8-8 to 10-6
1959	Vince Lombardi, Green Bay	1-10-1 to 7-5	1980	Leeman Bennett, Atlanta	6-10 to 12-4
1960	Buck Shaw, Philadelphia	7-5 to 10-2	1981	Bill Walsh, San Francisco	6-10 to 13-3
1961	Allie Sherman, New York	6-4-2 to 10-3-1	1982	Joe Gibbs, Washington	8-8 to 8-1
1962	Allie Sherman, New York	10-3-1 to 12-2	1983	John Robinson, Los Angeles	2-7 to 9-7
1963	George Halas, Chicago	9-5 to 11-1-2	1984	Bill Walsh, San Francisco	10-6 to 15-1
1964	Don Shula, Baltimore	8-6 to 12-2	1985	Mike Ditka, Chicago	10-6 to 15-1
1965	George Halas, Chicago	5-9 to 9-5	1986	Bill Parcells, New York	10-6 to 14-2
1966	Tom Landry, Dallas	7-7 to 10-3-1	1987	Jim Mora, New Orleans	7-9 to 12-3
1967	George Allen, Los Angeles	8-6 to 11-1-2	1988	Mike Ditka, Chicago	11-4 to 12-4
1968	Don Shula, Baltimore	11-1-2 to 13-1	1989	Lindy Infante, Green Bay	4-12 to 10-6
1969	Bud Grant, Minnesota	8-6 to 12-2	1990	Jimmy Johnson, Dallas	1-15 to 7-9
1970	Alex Webster, New York	6-8 to 9-5	1991	Wayne Fontes, Detroit	6-10 to 12-4
1971	George Allen, Washington	6-8 to 9-4-1	1992	Dennis Green, Minnesota	8-8 to 11-5
1972	Dan Devine, Green Bay	4-8-2 to 10-4	1993	Dan Reeves, New York	6-10 to 11-5
1973	Chuck Knox, Los Angeles	6-7-1 to 12-2	1994	Dave Wannstedt, Chicago	7-9 to 9-7
1974	Don Coryell, St. Louis	4-9-1 to 10-4			
1975	Tom Landry, Dallas	8-6 to 10-4			

AFL-AFC Coach of the Year

Presented by UPI to the top coach in the AFL (1960-69) and AFC (since 1970). Records indicate how much coach's team improved over one season. The AFC began play in 1960.

Multiple winners: Chuck Knox, Marv Levy, Dan Reeves, Sam Rutigliano, Lou Saban, and Don Shula (2)

Year		Improvement	Year		Improvement
1960	Lou Rymkus, Houston	10-4	1978	Walt Michaels, New York	3-11 to 8-8
1961	Wally Lemm, Houston	10-4 to 10-3-1	1979	Sam Rutigliano, Cleveland	8-8 to 9-7
1962	Jack Faulkner, Denver	3-11 to 7-7			
1963	Al Davis, Oakland	1-13 to 10-4	1980	Sam Rutigliano, Cleveland	9-7 to 11-5
1964	Lou Saban, Buffalo	7-6-1 to 12-2	1981	Forrest Gregg, Cincinnati	6-10 to 12-4
1965	Lou Saban, Buffalo	12-2 to 10-3-1	1982	Tom Flores, Los Angeles	7-9 to 8-1
1966	Mike Holovak, Boston	4-8-2 to 8-4-2	1983	Chuck Knox, Seattle	4-5 to 9-7
1967	John Rauch, Oakland	8-5-1 to 13-1	1984	Chuck Knox, Seattle	9-7 to 12-4
1968	Hank Stram, Kansas City	9-5 to 12-2	1985	Raymond Berry, New England	9-7 to 11-5
1969	Paul Brown, Cincinnati	3-11 to 4-9-1	1986	Marty Schottenheimer, Cleveland	8-8 to 12-4
			1987	Ron Meyer, Indianapolis	3-13 to 9-6
1970	Don Shula, Miami	3-10-1 to 10-4	1988	Marv Levy, Buffalo	7-8 to 12-4
1971	Don Shula, Miami	10-4 to 10-3-1	1989	Dan Reeves, Denver	8-8 to 11-5
1972	Chuck Noll, Pittsburgh	6-8 to 11-3			
1973	John Ralston, Denver	5-9 to 7-5-2	1990	Art Shell, Los Angeles	8-8 to 12-4
1974	Sid Gillman, Houston	1-13 to 7-7	1991	Dan Reeves, Denver	5-11 to 12-4
1975	Ted Marchibroda, Baltimore	2-12 to 10-4	1992	Bobby Ross, San Diego	4-12 to 11-5
1976	Chuck Fairbanks, New England	3-11 to 11-3	1993	Marv Levy, Buffalo	11-5 to 12-4
1977	Red Miller, Denver	9-5 to 12-2	1994	Bill Parcells, New England	5-11 to 10-6

CANADIAN FOOTBALL

The Grey Cup

Earl Grey, the Governor-General of Canada (1904-11) donated a trophy in 1909 for the Rugby Football Championship of Canada. The trophy, which later became known as the Grey Cup, was originally open to competition for teams registered with the Canada Rugby Union. Since 1954, the Cup has gone to the champion of the Canadian Football League (CFL).

Overall multiple winners: Toronto Argonauts (12); Edmonton Eskimos (11); Winnipeg Blue Bombers (9); Hamilton Tiger-Cats and Ottawa Rough Riders (7); Hamilton Tigers (5); Montreal Alouettes and University of Toronto (4); B.C. Lions, Calgary Stampeders and Queen's University (3); Ottawa Senators, Sarnia Imperials, Saskatchewan Roughriders and Toronto Balmy Beach (2).

CFL multiple winners (since 1954): Edmonton (11); Winnipeg (7); Hamilton (6); Ottawa (5); B.C. Lions and Montreal (3); Calgary, Saskatchewan and Toronto (2).

Year	Cup Final	Year	Cup Final
1909	Univ. of Toronto 26, Toronto Parkdale 6	1934	Sarnia Imperials 20, Regina Roughriders 12
1910	Univ. of Toronto 16, Hamilton Tigers 7	1935	Winnipeg 'Pegs 18, Hamilton Tigers 12
1911	Univ. of Toronto 14, Toronto Argonauts 7	1936	Sarnia Imperials 26, Ottawa Rough Riders 20
1912	Hamilton Alerts 11, Toronto Argonauts 4	1937	Toronto Argonauts 4, Winnipeg Blue Bombers 3
1913	Hamilton Tigers 44, Toronto Parkdale 2	1938	Toronto Argonauts 30, Winnipeg Blue Bombers 7
1914	Toronto Argonauts 14, Univ. of Toronto 2	1939	Winnipeg Blue Bombers 8, Ottawa Rough Riders 7
1915	Hamilton Tigers 13, Toronto Rowing 7		
1916-19	Not held (WWI)	1940	Gm 1: Ottawa Rough Riders 8, Toronto B-Beach 2
			Gm 2: Ottawa Rough Riders 12, Toronto B-Beach 5
1920	Univ. of Toronto 16, Toronto Argonauts 3	1941	Winnipeg Blue Bombers 18, Ottawa Rough Riders 16
1921	Toronto Argonauts 23, Edmonton Eskimos 0	1942	Toronto RACF 8, Winnipeg RACF 5
1922	Queens Univ. 13, Edmonton Elks 1	1943	Hamilton Wildcats 23, Winnipeg RACF 14
1923	Queens Univ. 54, Regina Roughriders 0	1944	Montreal HMCS 7, Hamilton Wildcats 6
1924	Queens Univ. 11, Toronto Balmy Beach 3	1945	Toronto Argonauts 35, Winnipeg Blue Bombers 0
1925	Ottawa Senators 24, Winnipeg Tigers 1	1946	Toronto Argonauts 28, Winnipeg Blue Bombers 6
1926	Ottawa Senators 10, Univ. of Toronto 7	1947	Toronto Argonauts 10, Winnipeg Blue Bombers 9
1927	Toronto Balmy Beach 9, Hamilton Tigers 6	1948	Calgary Stampeders 12, Ottawa Rough Riders 7
1928	Hamilton Tigers 30, Regina Roughriders 0	1949	Montreal Alouettes 28, Calgary Stampeders 15
1929	Hamilton Tigers 14, Regina Roughriders 3		
		1950	Toronto Argonauts 13, Winnipeg Blue Bombers 0
1930	Toronto Balmy Beach 11, Regina Roughriders 6	1951	Ottawa Rough Riders 21, Saskatch. Roughriders 14
1931	Montreal AAA 22, Regina Roughriders 0	1952	Toronto Argonauts 21, Edmonton Eskimos 11
1932	Hamilton Tigers 25, Regina Roughriders 6	1953	Hamilton Tiger-Cats 12, Winnipeg Blue Bombers 6
1933	Toronto Argonauts 4, Sarnia Imperials 3		

Year	Winner	Head Coach	Score	Loser	Head Coach	Site
1954	Edmonton	Frank (Pop) Ivy	26-25	Montreal	Doug Walker	Toronto
1955	Edmonton	Frank (Pop) Ivy	34-19	Montreal	Doug Walker	Vancouver
1956	Edmonton	Frank (Pop) Ivy	50-27	Montreal	Doug Walker	Toronto
1957	Hamilton	Jim Trimble	32-7	Winnipeg	Bud Grant	Toronto
1958	Winnipeg	Bud Grant	35-28	Hamilton	Jim Trimble	Vancouver
1959	Winnipeg	Bud Grant	21-7	Hamilton	Jim Trimble	Toronto
1960	Ottawa	Frank Clair	16-6	Edmonton	Eagle Keys	Vancouver
1961	Winnipeg	Bud Grant	21-14 (OT)	Hamilton	Jim Trimble	Toronto

Canadian Football (Cont.)

The Grey Cup

Year	Winner	Head Coach	Score	Loser	Head Coach	Site
1962	Winnipeg	Bud Grant	28-27*	Hamilton	Jim Trimble	Toronto
1963	Hamilton	Ralph Sazio	21-10	B.C. Lions	Dave Skrien	Vancouver
1964	B.C. Lions	Dave Skrien	34-24	Hamilton	Ralph Sazio	Toronto
1965	Hamilton	Ralph Sazio	22-16	Winnipeg	Bud Grant	Toronto
1966	Saskatchewan	Eagle Keys	29-14	Ottawa	Frank Clair	Vancouver
1967	Hamilton	Ralph Sazio	24- 1	Saskatchewan	Eagle Keys	Ottawa
1968	Ottawa	Frank Clair	24-21	Calgary	Jerry Williams	Toronto
1969	Ottawa	Frank Clair	29-11	Saskatchewan	Eagle Keys	Montreal
1970	Montreal	Sam Etcheverry	23-10	Calgary	Jim Duncan	Toronto
1971	Calgary	Jim Duncan	14-11	Toronto	Leo Cahill	Vancouver
1972	Hamilton	Jerry Williams	13-10	Saskatchewan	Dave Skrien	Hamilton
1973	Ottawa	Jack Gotta	22-18	Edmonton	Ray Jauch	Toronto
1974	Montreal	Marv Levy	20- 7	Edmonton	Ray Jauch	Vancouver
1975	Edmonton	Ray Jauch	9- 8	Montreal	Marv Levy	Calgary
1976	Ottawa	George Brancato	23-20	Saskatchewan	John Payne	Toronto
1977	Montreal	Marv Levy	41- 6	Edmonton	Hugh Campbell	Montreal
1978	Edmonton	Hugh Campbell	20-13	Montreal	Joe Scannella	Toronto
1979	Edmonton	Hugh Campbell	17- 9	Montreal	Joe Scannella	Montrea
1980	Edmonton	Hugh Campbell	48-10	Hamilton	John Payne	Toronto
1981	Edmonton	Hugh Campbell	26-23	Ottawa	George Brancato	Montreal
1982	Edmonton	Hugh Campbell	32-16	Toronto	Bob O'Billovich	Toronto
1983	Toronto	Bob O'Billovich	18-17	B.C. Lions	Don Matthews	Vancouver
1984	Winnipeg	Cal Murphy	47-17	Hamilton	Al Bruno	Edmonton
1985	B.C. Lions	Don Matthews	37-24	Hamilton	Al Bruno	Montreal
1986	Hamilton	Al Bruno	39-15	Edmonton	Jack Parker	Vancouver
1987	Edmonton	Joe Faragalli	38-36	Toronto	Bob O'Billovich	Vancouver
1988	Winnipeg	Mike Riley	22-21	B.C. Lions	Larry Donovan	Ottawa
1989	Saskatchewan	John Gregory	43-40	Hamilton	Al Bruno	Toronto
1990	Winnipeg	Mike Riley	50-11	Edmonton	Joe Faragalli	Vancouver
1991	Toronto	Adam Rita	36-21	Calgary	Wally Buono	Winnipeg
1992	Calgary	Wally Buono	24-10	Winnipeg	Urban Bowman	Toronto
1993	Edmonton	Ron Lancaster	33-23	Winnipeg	Cal Murphy	Calgary
1994	B.C. Lions	Dave Ritchie	26-23	Baltimore	Don Matthews	Vancouver

*Halted by fog in 4th quarter, final 9:29 played the following day.

CFL Most Outstanding Player

Regular season Player of the Year as selected by The Football Reporters of Canada since 1953.
Multiple winners: Doug Flutie (4); Russ Jackson and Jackie Parker (3); Dieter Brock, Ron Lancaster (2).

Year		Year		Year	
1953	Billy Vessels, Edmonton, RB	1968	Bill Symons, Toronto, RB	1982	Condredge Holloway, Tor., QB
1954	Sam Etcheverry, Montreal, QB	1969	Russ Jackson, Ottawa, QB	1983	Warren Moon, Edmonton, QB
1955	Pat Abbruzzi, Montreal, RB			1984	Willard Reaves, Winnipeg, RB
1956	Hal Patterson, Montreal, E-DB	1970	Ron Lancaster, Saskatch., QB	1985	Merv Fernandez, B.C. Lions, WR
1957	Jackie Parker, Edmonton, RB	1971	Don Jonas, Winnipeg, QB	1986	James Murphy, Winnipeg, WR
1958	Jackie Parker, Edmonton, QB	1972	Garney Henley, Hamilton, WR	1987	Tom Clements, Winnipeg, QB
1959	Johnny Bright, Edmonton, RB	1973	Geo. McGowan, Edmonton, WR	1988	David Williams, B.C. Lions, WR
		1974	Tom Wilkinson, Edmonton, QB	1989	Tracy Ham, Edmonton, QB
1960	Jackie Parker, Edmonton, QB	1975	Willie Burden, Calgary, RB		
1961	Bernie Faloney, Hamilton, QB	1976	Ron Lancaster, Saskatch., QB	1990	Mike Clemons, Toronto, RB
1962	George Dixon, Montreal, RB	1977	Jimmy Edwards, Hamilton, RB	1991	Doug Flutie, B.C. Lions, QB
1963	Russ Jackson, Ottawa, QB	1978	Tony Gabriel, Ottawa, TE	1992	Doug Flutie, Calgary, QB
1964	Lovell Coleman, Calgary, RB	1979	David Green, Montreal, RB	1993	Doug Flutie, Calgary, QB
1965	George Reed, Saskatchewan, RB			1994	Doug Flutie, Calgary, QB
1966	Russ Jackson, Ottawa, QB	1980	Dieter Brock, Winnipeg, QB		
1967	Peter Liske, Calgary, QB	1981	Dieter Brock, Winnipeg, QB		

CFL Most Outstanding Rookie

Regular season Rookie of the Year as selected by The Football Reporters of Canada since 1972.

Year		Year		Year	
1972	Chuck Ealey, Hamilton, QB	1980	William Miller, Winnipeg, RB	1988	Orville Lee, Ottawa, RB
1973	Johnny Rodgers, Montreal, WR	1981	Vince Goldsmith, Saskatch., LB	1989	Stephen Jordan, Hamilton, DB
1974	Sam Cvijanovich, Toronto, LB	1982	Chris Issac, Ottawa, QB		
1975	Tom Clements, Ottawa, QB	1983	Johnny Shepherd, Hamilton, RB	1990	Reggie Barnes, Ottawa, RB
1976	John Sciarra, B.C. Lions, QB	1984	Dwaine Wilson, Montreal, RB	1991	Jon Volpe, B.C. Lions, RB
1977	Leon Bright, B.C. Lions, WR	1985	Mike Gray, B.C. Lions, DT	1992	Mike Richardson, Winnipeg, RB
1978	Joe Poplawski, Winnipeg, WR	1986	Harold Hallman, Calgary, DT	1993	Michael O'Shea, Hamilton, DT
1979	Brian Kelly, Edmonton, WR	1987	Gill Fenerty, Toronto, RB	1994	Matt Goodwin, Baltimore, DB

UCLA forward **Ed O'Bannon** throws a left-handed shot over the reach of Arkansas center **Dwight Stewart** during the Bruins' 89-78 win against the Razorbacks in the NCAA championship game.

COLLEGE BASKETBALL

COLLEGE BASKETBALL
by Gene Wojciechowski

Back On Top

*Two decades and five head coaches after its last NCAA title,
UCLA finally wins its first championship of the post-Wooden era.*

They came.
They saw.
They resigned.
That's how it was at UCLA after John Wooden retired in 1975. First there was Gene Bartow. Then Gary Cunningham. Then Larry Brown. Then Larry Farmer. Then Walt Hazzard. Trapped deep in the shadows of Wooden's 10 national championship banners, none of them lasted longer than four seasons at Westwood. Three of them lasted just half that time.

Then came Jim Harrick. By UCLA standards, he was an outsider. Hired away from Pepperdine in 1988, Harrick wasn't even the school's first choice. Or second. Or, depending on the source, not even the third.

Harrick won games, but he didn't win admirers. His critics said he couldn't recruit, couldn't coach and couldn't keep his mouth shut. In other words, he wasn't John Wooden Jr.

In 1992, the same season Harrick insisted he deserved a similar salary as, among others, Bob Knight, Indiana humiliated UCLA by nearly 30 points in the NCAA tournament. In 1993, Michigan eliminated the Bruins in the second round. A year later, Tulsa shocked UCLA in the first round.

Only UCLA chancellor Charles Young and

athletic director Peter Dalis will ever know for sure how close Harrick came to receiving a pink slip. But this much is certain: another first-round loss in 1995 and Harrick would be exploring the exciting world of aluminum siding sales.

Instead, Harrick and the Bruins, who entered the NCAAs ranked No. 1 in the country, not only won their first game of the tournament, but their second, their third, their fourth, their fifth and then, against the defending national champion Arkansas Razorbacks, their sixth. Suddenly Harrick had his own legacy and UCLA had another banner to hang next to the 10 faded reminders of the Wooden years.

Wooden, now 84, was in Seattle the night of April 3 when the Bruins defied Arkansas and logic. Seated 30 or so yards away from the Kingdome court, Wooden watched calmly as the Bruins defeated the Razorbacks, 89-78. But afterward, he admitted that he too had his doubts about UCLA's chances.

"To be honest, I didn't think they could win it without [Tyus] Edney," Wooden said. "He makes that team run."

Magical seasons don't come about without a few miracles. And for the Bruins it was Edney, the 5-foot-10, senior point guard, who provided the magic in two of the most memorable games of the tournament.

Miracle No. 1 (West Regional, second round): With only 4.8 seconds separating the top-seeded Bruins from another early

Gene Wojciechowski is the national college basketball and football reporter for the *Los Angeles Times* and a columnist for *The Sporting News*.

UCLA head coach **Jim Harrick** (right) with former Bruins coach **John Wooden**. Harrick is the sixth man to succeed Wooden, but the first to bring home an NCAA championship since the legendary Wizard of Westwood retired in 1975 after winning the last of his 10 national titles.

round exit, Edney takes the inbounds pass against No. 8 seed Missouri, weaves his way through the Tigers' ill-conceived defense, smooches the ball off the smudged glass and then watches as the shot falls through the net for a 75-74 victory.

It was a play the Bruins had frequently tried in practice, based on Harrick's vivid recollection of Jerry West going the length of the floor in three seconds for a basket against the Celtics in Game 3 of the 1962 NBA Finals.

"This is a crazy business," said Harrick in a hallway outside the UCLA locker room. "One point makes all the difference. The whole state of Missouri is down tonight because its team lost by one point.

"I know if we had lost…well, I don't want to answer that."

Miracle No. 2 (Final Four, championship game): After spraining his right wrist in the 74-61 semifinal win against Oklahoma State, Edney missed Sunday's practice and was considered iffy for the final. During warmups he took one shot— a five-foot air-ball— and then returned to the Bruin bench.

"Can you play?" asked Harrick.

"It's going to be a long night," Edney replied. "I don't think I can play, but I'll give it a shot."

Edney started the game, but he was useless. He couldn't dribble. He couldn't pass. He couldn't shoot. He couldn't be what UCLA needed most. He couldn't be Tyus.

He lasted two minutes and 37 seconds.

And that's when the miracle happened. Reduced to a six-man rotation against the deep roster of Arkansas, the Bruins played as if it were nothing to lose your starting point guard minutes before tip-off. They inserted defensive specialist Cameron Dollar in Edney's place, hoped for the best…and got it.

Senior forward Ed O'Bannon, who plays with a dead man's ligament in his surgically repaired left knee, scored 30 points, had 17 rebounds, three steals, three assists and never left the floor. When the game was over he was named the tournament's Most Outstanding Player.

Freshman off-guard Toby Bailey scored 26 and had nine rebounds. Senior center George Zidek scored 14, but even more important, helped limit Arkansas All-American Corliss Williamson to a dreadful three-of-16 from the field.

Stephen Dunn/Allsport

Senior guard and team MVP **Tyus Edney** drives past **Travis Knight** of UConn en route to a 102-96 victory in the West Regional final. He later sprained his right wrist against Oklahoma State and missed all but 2:37 of the title game.

In the end, Arkansas had more players, but UCLA had more heart.

"We don't have a Walton, we don't have an Alcindor, we don't have a Goodrich, and tonight, we didn't have an Edney," Charles O'Bannon said. "But we have a team of guys with big hearts and a lot of faith. We knew we'd be successful."

Standing on the makeshift stage used to present the NCAA championship trophy, Ed O'Bannon was handed a microphone.

"Yo!" O'Bannon yelled to the Kingdome audience of 38,540 fans. "I want you to hear this. This is the real MVP. Give it up for Tyus. He got us here. That's the man. That's the real MVP."

Watching from a few feet away was Harrick. At last he had his national title. And for the first time since Wooden left 20 years earlier, a Bruin coach had his own identity.

"Sometimes these things work in your favor," he said, remembering the failures of the past. "Our players deserve a lot of credit, but I'd like to give emotion or divine intervention a little credit, too."

While regular season losses to Pac-10 rivals Oregon and California kept UCLA (31-2) from going undefeated, women's national champion Connecticut, led by consensus Player of the Year Rebecca Lobo, went 35-0 and beat Tennessee 70-64 to win its first title (see page 297).

Arkansas returned to defend its men's championship after reaching the Final Four for the third time in six seasons. Despite a handful of regular season upsets and a 95-93 overtime loss to Kentucky in the SEC tournament final, the Razorbacks won 32 games overall. Their most bizarre win was a 96-94 overtime escape against Syracuse in the second round of the NCAAs, made possible in the last 4.3 seconds of regulation when Lawrence Moten of the Orangemen received a technical foul for calling a timeout he didn't have with Syracuse ahead 82-81.

As usual, there were rumors about Arkansas coach Nolan Richardson jumping to the NBA. Also as usual, he stayed put. Smart move. The Razorbacks had one of the best recruiting classes of 1995. Of course, with juniors Williamson and Scotty Thurman leaving early for the pros, Richardson will need all the help he can get.

Also back in the Final Four was North Carolina, which last won the national title in 1993. The Tar Heels (28-6) were ranked No. 1 for six weeks during the regular season and featured two gifted sophomores, swingman Jerry Stackhouse and center Rasheed Wallace. With coach Dean Smith's blessings, both Stackhouse and Wallace made themselves available for the NBA draft at season's end.

Thanks to the backboard-breaking Bryant (Big Country) Reeves and the sometimes under-appreciated efforts of coach Eddie Sutton, Oklahoma State found itself among the elite for the first time since 1951.

All told, the four coaches had taken teams to a combined 65 NCAA tournaments and the four contending schools had reached the Final Four a total of 38 times.

As always, the tournament included its share of shockers, beginning with the decision by the Men's Basketball Committee to ignore Georgia Tech, Iowa, George Washington and New Mexico State— all programs with 18 or more victories. A miffed Bobby Cremins questioned the committee's logic and later turned down an invitation to play in the NIT, the first time that's happened since 1987.

Once the tournament began, there were assorted scoreboard double takes. Arizona lost in the first round for the third time in four seasons. No. 13 seed Manhattan beat No. 4 seed Oklahoma. No. 14 seed Old Dominion defeated No. 3 seed Villanova in triple overtime. And Arkansas barely beat No. 15 seed Texas Southern.

However, nothing compared to the belly flop of the Big Ten conference. Of the six teams invited, only Purdue reached the second round. The most notable victim was Jud Heathcote's Michigan State team, which had been seeded third in the Southeast region. The loss ended Heathcote's 24-year coaching career, 19 of them at East Lansing. He left with 417 victories and one national championship— won in 1979 with Magic Johnson.

The tournament's most heartwarming story involved Mount St. Mary's and its coach Jim Phelan of the little-regarded Northeast conference. In 40 years at the school Phelan had won 720 games (second only to Carolina's Smith), but had never been to the Division I tournament. Finally, in 1994-95 the Mountaineers won 17 games and earned the conference's automatic bid. Phelan and his team enjoyed every second of their brief appearance, even if it did include a 113-67 dusting by No. 1 seed Kentucky in the Southeast Regional.

In victory, UCLA joined the 1982 North Carolina club and the 1992 Duke squad as the only teams in the last 17 years to enter the tournament ranked No. 1 in the country and emerge as champions.

Six different teams held the AP No. 1 ranking during the 17-week regular season that stretched from Nov. 22 to March 13: Arkansas (week 1), Massachusetts (week 2 and weeks 8-11), North Carolina (weeks 3-7 and week 12), Connecticut (week 13), Kansas (week 14) and UCLA (weeks 15-17). UConn's one week at the top from Feb. 13-19 marked the first time in polling history that the same school had the No. 1 men's and women's teams in the country.

There are other stories to tell, including the dizzying fall of Rollie Massimino at Nevada-Las Vegas. Massimino was done in partly by his own greed and by UNLV's Gang That Couldn't Shoot Straight— former school president Robert Maxson,

Doug Pensinger/Allsport

Oklahoma State center **Bryant Reeves** ducks under Alabama center **Roy Rogers** during the Cowboys' 66-52 win in the second round of the NCAA East Regional. Reeves led OSU to its first Final Four appearance since 1951.

former legal counsel Brad Booke and athletic director Jim Weaver.

It was Maxson, Booke and Weaver who helped arrange a secret supplemental contract for Massimino that added another $375,000 annually to a Board of Regents-approved $511,000 deal. The supplemental contract didn't stay secret for long and Massimino immediately found himself at the center of a major controversy.

After initially saying he planned to fulfill the remainder of his original contract, which ran through the 1996-97 season, Massimino instructed his lawyers to negotiate a settlement with the school and resigned less than a month before the start of the season. Former UNLV assistant coach Tim Grgurich was hired to succeed Massimino.

Meanwhile, Indiana coach Bob Knight added to his list of temper tantrum incidents. This time he tore into a volunteer news conference moderator named Rance Pugmire with an obscenity-peppered tirade after the Hoosiers' 65-60 loss to Missouri in the opening round of the tournament. The Men's Basketball Committee publicly reprimanded Knight on June 13, fining I.U. a record $30,000 (which will be deducted from its share of NCAA basketball revenue) and recommending that future outbursts by Knight in the tournament result in a suspension of one or more games.

Knight issued a reprimand of his own the next day, proposing an eight-year "purity plan" that would require the nine-member committee to be without sin in the eyes of the NCAA. In other words, if your school broke any NCAA rules during your watch, you're off the committee.

"I even have a suggested name for the rule: the John 8:7 Rule, which I have slightly paraphrased to read, 'Let him who is without sin cast the first reprimand,'" said Knight in his statement.

Also reprimanded for unprofessional behavior during the tournament was Memphis coach Larry Finch, whose school was fined a mere $2,500. Finch criticized the officiating after the Tigers were beaten by Arkansas in the Midwest region semifinals.

Meanwhile, North Carolina's Smith and Clemson's Rick Barnes didn't exactly do themselves proud in the ACC tournament. Near the end of their quarterfinal game, Smith and Barnes had to be separated at midcourt after a nose-to-nose argument about a hard foul called against Clemson. ACC commissioner Gene Corrigan called the incident a "sorry spectacle" and fined each coach $2,500, payable to the charity of their choice.

Also notable on the sidelines was the absence of several high-profile coaches who either resigned or missed more than a few games because of health and stress-related reasons. Among the missing were George Raveling of Southern Cal, Mike Krzyzewski of Duke, Gary Williams of Maryland and Grgurich of UNLV (see sidebar).

Grgurich's old boss at Las Vegas, Jerry Tarkanian, made his unexpected return to the college ranks on April 5 when he took the reins at Fresno State. Tarkanian, the winningest coach by percentage in NCAA history (.837), had been in self-imposed retirement after a failed 20-game fling with the NBA's San Antonio Spurs in 1992.

Whenever he was asked about a possible comeback, Tark would say he missed the players, the assistants and the practices, but not the games. "Too much pressure," he said. It wasn't until Gary Colson resigned at Fresno State that the 64-year-old Tarkanian

Coaches Find Stress Harder To Handle

It began with Southern Cal's George Raveling and eventually grew into a conga line of coaches who no longer could, or would, handle the pressures of college basketball.

Raveling's awakening came in the aftermath of a near-fatal automobile accident on Sept. 25, 1994 in Los Angeles. Laid up in a hospital for six weeks with a broken pelvis and clavicle, nine broken ribs and a collapsed lung, the 57-year-old Raveling realized just how little he enjoyed his job. A man true to himself, the longtime coach (22 years in Division I) announced his resignation on Nov. 14.

Duke's Mike Krzyzewski was next. Krzyzewski, 48, the supposed poster boy for keeping things in perspective, returned from offseason back surgery much too quickly and was a mess by early January. Overwhelmed by pain and stress-related exhaustion, he left the team on Jan. 6— missing his first game as a head coach in 20 years— and later that month told the Blue Devils he was done for the season.

Nevada-Las Vegas coach Tim Grgurich, who was hired on Oct. 22, 1994 to replace Rollie Massimino, burned out after several months of 20-hour workdays. He won two of his first seven games before being hospitalized for exhaustion on Jan. 6— the same day Krzyzewski checked into Duke University Hospital for more rest and back treatment.

Grgurich, 52, officially resigned five months after he took the UNLV job. Howie Landa, the 63-year-old assistant who took over for Grgurich, was also forced to quit after seven games because of health-related concerns.

Then there was Iona's Jerry Welsh, who coached at Division III Potsdam State (N.Y.) for 22 successful years then quit on Feb. 4 after less than four seasons in Division I. The reason: stress and exhaustion.

"It just doesn't seem like there's anyplace to hide," said Louisiana State's Dale Brown, who began the 1994-95 season as one of only 10 active Division I basketball coaches with at least 23 seasons of service at the same school. "If you're on the bottom, you get fired. I've seen seven football coaches get fired at LSU and one of them had a 70-percent winning record. If you're on top, you either quit or burn out. If you're in the middle, nobody's happy

Otto Creule/Allsport

A pensive **George Raveling** sits between Southern Cal assistants **Jack Ferting** (left) and **Charlie Parker** during the 1993-94 season. Raveling left behind his stress filled coaching job at USC for the relative ease of the broadcast booth after a September 1994 auto accident.

and you don't last very long.

"We've just lost perspective— all of us," he said. "This is a game, but it's turned into much more than that. It's become a multi-billion— I used to say multi-million— dollar business, but we forget we're still dealing with teenagers."

Raveling had considered retirement from coaching for several seasons. But the auto accident, followed by considerable rehabilitation time, forced him to reassess his future. He decided that big-time coaching wasn't worth the tradeoff and chose instead to pursue a career in broadcasting. He remains active in both the Black Coaches Association and the National Association of Basketball Coaches.

Krzyzewski was a victim of his own high standards and, who knows, maybe guilt. In his haste to return to a young Blue Devil team, Krzyzewski basically ignored his doctor's advice and was back on the sidelines only 10 days after surgery to repair a displaced disk. He didn't last long. On Jan. 22, he informed the school he wouldn't return for the remainder of the season.

The rumors started shortly thereafter. Coach K had cancer. He was getting a divorce. He was addicted to painkillers. He had hit one of his players during a practice and had been suspended by the university. He was quitting for good. He was leaving for the NBA.

Krzyzewski held a press conference on March 6 to address his status. He said he would return for the 1995-96 season, but added that he had learned his lesson.

"I never had [suffered exhaustion] before in my life," he said. "And you can be damn sure I never will again. It's revealing to me. It shows me that you can have limits, no matter who the hell you are."

One treatment gaining popularity is early retirement.

Kentucky's Rick Pitino, 42, figures he'll be out of the business within 10 years. And John Calipari, 35, of UMass has said he can't see himself coaching at age 55 or 60.

When asked what advice he'd give a frazzled colleague, Calipari points to Dean Smith, college basketball's all-time winningest coach with 830 victories and two NCAA championships in 34 seasons at North Carolina.

Says Calipari: "Dean said it best: 'If you treat this stuff like life and death, then you're going to die a lot.'"

World Wide Photos

Sophomore center **Joe Smith** of Maryland shared player of the year honors with Ed O'Bannon and Shawn Respert. He was also the first teenager since Magic Johnson to be made the first overall selection of the NBA draft.

decided he wanted one more chance.

"I wasn't really [looking]," he said, "but Fresno is like my old town. It's my alma mater. They've got the best fans in the country, them and Kentucky."

There were 40 candidates for the Bulldogs' job, one of 36 that opened up during the offseason, but Tarkanian was the only one to receive an on-campus interview. Under heavy pressure from alums and fans, Fresno State president John Welty and athletic director Gary Cunningham offered Tarkanian a three-year package worth a reported $600,000. To ease the fears of those faculty members who were quick to remind Welty of Tarkanian's history with the NCAA enforcement office, the school also hired a compliance officer and inserted the standard contract clause about adhering to NCAA rules.

"Everybody knows [NCAA officials] were picking on me," Tarkanian said. "But that's

over with. It shouldn't have any effect on what I'm doing here."

Ed O'Bannon shared Player of the Year honors with senior guard Shawn Respert of Michigan State and sophomore forward Joe Smith of Maryland. They were joined on the first team of the consensus All-America squad by Stackhouse of North Carolina and senior guard Damon Stoudamire of Arizona.

Sophomores were the top four picks of the NBA draft on June 28. Smith, the first teenager since Magic Johnson to be the overall No. 1 pick, went to the Golden State Warriors, followed in order by Alabama forward Antonio McDyess (to the L.A. Clippers and then traded to Denver), Stackhouse (to Philadelphia) and North Carolina center Wallace (to Washington). A record 10 underclassmen, including high school senior Kevin Garnett of Farragut Academy in Chicago, went in the first round (see page 293).

O'Bannon, whose knee problems scared off some NBA teams, was chosen ninth by the New Jersey Nets. The 10th pick, by Miami, was TCU center Kurt Thomas, who became only the third player to lead the NCAA in both scoring and rebounding with per game averages of 28.9 points and 14.6 boards in 1994-95.

Finally, there was one more controversy. During an Atlantic 10 conference game between UMass and Rutgers at Piscataway, N.J., on Feb. 7, more than 150 protesters conducted a sit-in to draw national attention to racially insensitive remarks made by Rutgers president Francis Lawrence three months earlier. In short, Lawrence suggested that African-Americans lacked the "genetic and hereditary background" to score well on college admissions tests.

Oops. Lawrence later apologized for the remarks and found an ally in Temple coach John Chaney, a longtime spokesman for the Black Coaches Association.

"I know that everybody makes mistakes," said Chaney. "Mr. Lawrence made a mistake. All of us make mistakes, but I also know the man has made great contributions to education, to Rutgers, to diversity, and I'm willing to go on."

The UMass-Rutgers game was eventually completed on March 3 at the Spectrum in Philadelphia. The Minutemen won, 77-62, before 445 onlookers.   ❑

284

THE 1996

COLLEGE BASKETBALL
S T A T I S T I C S

THE SEASON IN REVIEW
1994-1995
TOP 25 • NCAA'S • STANDINGS

SEC
A

PAGE
285

Final Regular Season AP Men's Top 25 Poll
Taken **before** start of NCAA tournament.

The sportswriters & broadcasters poll: first place votes in parentheses; records through Sunday, March 12, 1995; total points (based on 25 for 1st, 24 for 2nd, etc.); record in NCAA tourney and team lost to; head coach (career years and record including 1995 postseason), and preseason ranking. Teams in **bold** type went on to reach NCAA Final Four.

		Mar.12 Record	Points	NCAA Recap	Head Coach	Preseason Rank
1	**UCLA** (64)	25-2	1624	6-0	Jim Harrick (16 yrs: 335-152)	6
2	Kentucky (1)	25-4	1552	3-1 (N. Carolina)	Rick Pitino (13 yrs: 283-117)	4
3	Wake Forest	24-5	1473	2-1 (Oklahoma St.)	Dave Odom (9 yrs: 154-108)	24
4	**North Carolina**	24-5	1347	4-1 (Arkansas)	Dean Smith (34 yrs: 830-236)	2
5	Kansas	23-5	1344	2-1 (Virginia)	Roy Williams (7 yrs: 184-51)	11
6	**Arkansas**	27-6	1322	5-1 (UCLA)	Nolan Richardson (15 yrs: 371-119)	1
7	Massachusetts	26-4	1256	3-1 (Oklahoma St.)	John Calipari (7 yrs: 158-69)	3
8	Connecticut	25-4	1123	3-1 (UCLA)	Jim Calhoun (23 yrs: 438-233)	19
9	Villanova	25-7	1095	0-1 (Old Dominion)	Steve Lappas (7 yrs: 109-101)	22
10	Maryland	24-7	986	2-1 (UConn)	Gary Williams (17 yrs: 312-205)	7
11	Michigan St	22-5	972	0-1 (Weber St.)	Jud Heathcote (24 yrs: 417-275)	20
12	Purdue	24-6	929	1-1 (Memphis)	Gene Keady (17 yrs: 360-161)	32
13	Virginia	22-8	854	3-1 (Arkansas)	Jeff Jones (5 yrs: 105-57)	14
14	**Oklahoma St**	23-9	736	4-1 (UCLA)	Eddie Sutton (25 yrs: 553-109)	21
15	Arizona	23-7	700	0-1 (Miami-OH)	Lute Olson (22 yrs: 481-187)	5
16	Arizona St	22-8	638	2-1 (Kentucky)	Bill Frieder (15 yrs: 299-162)	42t
17	Oklahoma	23-8	497	0-1 (Manhattan)	Kelvin Sampson (12 yrs: 199-157)	40
18	Mississippi St	20-7	492	2-1 (UCLA)	Richard Williams (9 yrs: 138-122)	30t
19	Utah	27-5	466	1-1 (Miss. St.)	Rick Majerus (11 yrs: 223-96)	50
20	Alabama	22-9	306	1-1 (Oklahoma St.)	David Hobbs (3 yrs: 59-33)	18
21	Western Kentucky	26-3	248	1-1 (Kansas)	Matt Kilcullen (7 yrs: 89-101)	45
22	Georgetown	19-9	220	2-1 (N. Carolina)	John Thompson (23 yrs: 524-200)	15
23	Missouri	19-8	202	1-1 (UCLA)	Norm Stewart (34 yrs: 660-319)	54t
24	Iowa St	22-10	194	1-1 (N. Carolina)	Tim Floyd (9 yrs: 185-94)	26
25	Syracuse	19-9	103	1-1 (Arkansas)	Jim Boeheim (19 yrs: 454-150)	12

Others receiving votes: 26. Oregon (19-8, 99 pts); 27. **Texas** (22-6, 75); 28. **Stanford** (19-8, 44); 29. **Tulsa** (22-7, 42); 30. **Cincinnati** (21-11, 36); 31. **Memphis** (22-9, 32); 32. **Indiana** (19-11, 22); 33. **Florida.** (17-12, 16); 34. **Penn** (22-5, 12); 35. **Georgia Tech.** (18-12, 10) and **Saint Louis** (22-7, 10); 37. **New Mexico St.** (23-9, 7) and **Xavier-OH** (23-4, 7); 39. **Illinois** (19-11, 6); 40. **Ball St.** (19-10, 5); 41. **Providence** (16-12, 4) and **Southern Ill.** (23-8, 4); 43. **Minnesota** (19-11, 3) and **Utah St.** (21-7, 3); 45. **Santa Clara** (21-6, 2) and **Tulane** (22-9, 2); 47. **BYU** (22-9, 1), **Col. of Charleston** (23-5, 1), **Long Beach St.** (20-9, 1), **Manhattan** (25-4, 1), and **Nicholls St.** (25-5, 1).

NCAA Men's Division I Tournament Seeds

	WEST		MIDWEST		SOUTHEAST		EAST
1	UCLA (25-2)	1	Kansas (23-5)	1	Kentucky (25-4)	1	Wake Forest (24-5)
2	UConn (25-4)	2	Arkansas (27-6)	2	North Carolina (24-5)	2	UMass (26-4)
3	Maryland (24-7)	3	Purdue (24-6)	3	Michigan St, (22-5)	3	Villanova (25-7)
4	Utah (27-5)	4	Virginia (22-8)	4	Oklahoma (23-8)	4	Oklahoma St. (23-9)
5	Mississippi St. (20-7)	5	Arizona (23-7)	5	Arizona St. (22-8)	5	Alabama (22-9)
6	Oregon (19-8)	6	Memphis (22-9)	6	Georgetown (19-9)	6	Tulsa (22-7)
7	Cincinnati (21-11)	7	Syracuse (19-9)	7	Iowa St. (22-10)	7	NC-Charlotte (19-8)
8	Missouri (19-8)	8	Western Ky. (26-3)	8	BYU (22-9)	8	Minnesota (19-11)
9	Indiana (19-11)	9	Michigan (17-13)	9	Tulane (22-9)	9	Saint Louis (22-7)
10	Temple (19-10)	10	Southern Ill. (23-8)	10	Florida (17-12)	10	Stanford (19-8)
11	Texas (22-6)	11	Louisville (19-13)	11	Xavier-OH (23-4)	11	Illinois (19-11)
12	Santa Clara (21-6)	12	Miami-OH (22-6)	12	Ball St. (19-10)	12	Penn (22-5)
13	Long Beach St. (20-9)	13	Nicholls St. (24-5)	13	Manhattan (25-4)	13	Drexel (22-7)
14	Gonzaga (21-8)	14	WI-Green Bay (22-7)	14	Weber St. (20-8)	14	Old Dominion (20-11)
15	Tenn-Chatt. (19-10)	15	Texas Southern (22-6)	15	Murray St. (21-8)	15	St. Peter's (19-10)
16	Florida Int'l. (11-18)	16	Colgate (17-12)	16	Mt. St. Mary's (17-12)	16	N. Car. A&T (15-14)

1995 NCAA BASKETBALL MEN'S DIVISION I

NCAA Final Four · SEATTLE 1995

MIDWEST

1ST ROUND March 16-17	2ND ROUND March 18-19	REGIONALS March 23-26
1 Kansas 82		
16 Colgate 68	Kansas 75	
8 Western Ky. 82		
9 Michigan (OT) 76	Western Ky. 70	Kansas 58
5 Arizona 62		
12 Miami-OH 71	Miami-OH 54	
4 Virginia 96		Virginia 67
13 Nicholls St. 72	Virginia 60	
6 Memphis 77		Virginia 61
11 Louisville 56	Memphis 75	
3 Purdue 49		
14 WI-Green Bay 48	Purdue 73	Memphis 91 (OT)
7 Syracuse 96		
10 Southern Ill. 92	Syracuse 94	
2 Arkansas 79		Arkansas 96
15 TX Southern 78	Arkansas 96 (OT)	

KANSAS CITY — Arkansas 68 → Arkansas 75

SOUTHEAST

1ST ROUND March 16-17	2ND ROUND March 18-19	REGIONALS March 23-26
1 Kentucky 113		
16 Mt. St. Mary's 67	Kentucky 82	
8 BYU 70		
9 Tulane 76	Tulane 60	Kentucky 97
5 Arizona St. 81		
12 Ball St. 66	Arizona St. 64	
4 Oklahoma 67		Arizona St. 73
13 Manhattan 77	Manhattan 54	
6 Georgetown 68		Kentucky 61
11 Xavier-OH 63	Georgetown 53	
3 Michigan St. 72		
14 Weber St. 79	Weber St. 51	Georgetown 64
7 Iowa St. 64		
10 Florida 61	Iowa St. 51	
2 N. Carolina 80		N. Carolina 74
15 Murray St. 70	N. Carolina 73	

BIRMINGHAM — N. Carolina 68 → N. Carolina 74

EAST

1ST ROUND March 16-17	2ND ROUND March 18-19	REGIONALS March 23-26
1 Wake Forest 79		
16 N.C. A&T 47	Wake Forest 64	
8 Minnesota 61		
9 St. Louis (OT) 64	St. Louis 59	Wake Forest 66
5 Alabama 91		
12 Penn (OT) 85	Alabama 52	
4 Oklahoma St. 73		Oklahoma St. 71
13 Drexel 49	Oklahoma St. 66	
6 Tulsa 68		Oklahoma St. 68
11 Illinois 62	Tulsa 64	
3 Villanova 81		
14 ODU (3OT) 89	ODU 52	Tulsa 51
7 NC-Charlotte 68		
10 Stanford 70	Stanford 53	
2 UMass 68		UMass 76
15 St. Peter's 51	UMass 75	

EAST RUTHERFORD — UMass 54 → Oklahoma St. 61

WEST

1ST ROUND March 16-17	2ND ROUND March 18-19	REGIONALS March 23-26
1 UCLA 92		
16 Florida Int'l 56	UCLA 75	
8 Missouri 65		
9 Indiana 60	Missouri 74	UCLA 86
5 Miss. St. 75		
12 Santa Clara 67	Miss. St. 78	
4 Utah 76		Miss. St. 67
13 Long Beach St. 64	Utah 64	
6 Oregon 73		UCLA 102
11 Texas 90	Texas 68	
3 Maryland 87		
14 Gonzaga 63	Maryland 82	Maryland 89
7 Cincinnati 77		
10 Temple 71	Cincinnati 91	
2 UConn 100		UConn 99
15 Tenn-Chatt. 71	UConn 96	

OAKLAND — UConn 96 → UCLA 74

NATIONAL CHAMPIONSHIP

UCLA 89
Arkansas 78

FINAL FOUR

at the Seattle Kingdome

Semifinals: April 1
Final: April 3

NCAA Men's Championship Game

57th NCAA Division I Championship Game. **Date:** Monday, April 3, at the Seattle Kingdome. **Coaches:** Nolan Richardson of Arkansas and Jim Harrick of UCLA. **Favorite:** UCLA by 3. **Attendance:** 38,540; **Officials:** Jim Burr, Ted Valentine and John Cahill; **TV Rating:** 19.3/30 share (CBS).

Arkansas 78

	Min	FG M-A	FT M-A	Pts	Reb O-T	A	PF
Scotty Thurman	32	2-9	0-0	5	0-3	1	2
Corliss Williamson	33	3-16	6-10	12	2-4	6	1
Elmer Martin	6	1-2	0-0	3	1-3	1	2
Clint McDaniel	35	5-10	3-4	16	1-3	1	5
Corey Beck	25	4-6	1-2	11	2-3	2	3
Dwight Stewart	22	5-10	1-2	12	2-5	0	4
Alex Dillard	15	2-4	0-0	6	1-2	1	1
Darnell Robinson	10	2-3	0-0	4	0-2	0	3
Davor Rimac	12	1-1	0-0	2	1-2	3	0
Lee Wilson	7	3-4	1-2	7	0-0	0	1
Landis Williams	1	0-0	0-0	0	0-0	0	0
Reggie Garrett	2	0-0	0-0	0	0-0	0	0
TOTALS	200	28-65	12-20	78	10-27	15	22

Three-point FG: 10-28 (McDaniel 3-7, Beck 2-3, Dillard 2-3, Martin 1-2, Stewart 1-5, Thurman 1-7, Robinson 0-1); **Team Rebounds:** 4; **Blocked Shots:** 4 (Robinson 2, Beck, Wilson); **Turnovers:** 18 (Williamson 3, Beck 2, Dillard 2, Martin 2, Rimac 2, Robinson 2, Stewart 2, Thurman 2, McDaniel); **Steals:** 15 (McDaniel 4, Williamson 4, Beck 3, Rimac 2, Martin, Thurman). **Percentages:** 2-Pt FG (.486), 3-Pt FG (.357), Total FG (.431), Free Throws (.600).

UCLA 89

	Min	FG M-A	FT M-A	Pts	Reb O-T	A	PF
Ed O'Bannon	40	10-21	9-11	30	6-17	3	2
Charles O'Bannon	36	4-10	3-4	11	4-9	6	1
George Zidek	29	5-8	4-7	14	4-6	0	4
Toby Bailey	39	12-20	1-2	26	4-9	3	3
Tyus Edney	3	0-0	0-0	0	0-0	0	0
Cameron Dollar	36	1-4	4-5	6	0-3	8	4
J.R. Henderson	17	1-5	0-0	2	1-2	1	1
TOTALS	200	33-68	21-29	89	19-46	21	15

Three-point FG: 2-7 (E.O'Bannon 1-4, Bailey 1-2, Dollar 0-1); **Team Rebounds:** 4; **Blocked Shots:** 4 (C.O'Bannon 2, Dollar, Henderson); **Turnovers:** 20 (E.O'Bannon 5, Bailey 3, Dollar -3, Henderson 3, C.O'Bannon 3, Zidek 2, Edney); **Steals:** 11 (Dollar 4, E.O'Bannon, Bailey 2, C.O'Bannon 2). **Percentages:** 2-Pt FG (.508), 3-Pt FG (.286), Total FG (.485), Free Throws (.724).

Arkansas (SEC)		39	39—	78
UCLA (Pac-10)		40	49—	89

Final USA Today/CNN Coaches Poll

Taken **after** NCAA Tournament.

Voted on by a panel of 34 Division I head coaches following the NCAA tournament: first place votes in parentheses with total points (based on 25 for 1st, 24 for 2nd, etc.). Schools on major probation are ineligible to be ranked.

		After NCAAs		Before NCAAs	
		W-L	Pts	W-L	Rank
1	UCLA (34)	31-2	850	25-2	1
2	Arkansas	32-7	815	27-6	6
3	North Carolina	28-6	777	24-5	5
4	Oklahoma St	27-10	742	23-9	14
5	Kentucky	28-5	685	25-4	2
6	Connecticut	28-5	653	25-4	8
7	Massachusetts	29-5	643	26-4	7
8	Virginia	25-9	610	22-8	15
9	Wake Forest	26-6	590	24-5	3
10	Kansas	25-6	532	23-5	4
11	Maryland	26-8	513	24-7	10
12	Mississippi St	22-8	395	20-7	19
13	Arizona St	24-9	388	22-8	16
14	Memphis	24-10	349	22-9	38
15	Tulsa	24-8	327	22-7	45t
16	Georgetown	21-10	260	19-9	26
17	Syracuse	20-10	226	19-9	22
18	Missouri	20-9	220	19-8	23
19	Purdue	25-7	196	24-6	11
20	Michigan St	22-6	175	22-5	9
21	Alabama	23-10	165	22-9	21
22	Utah	28-6	144	27-5	17
23	Villanova	25-8	126	25-7	12
24	Texas	23-7	119	22-6	29
25	Arizona	23-8	115	23-7	13

Others receiving votes: 26. **Iowa State** (23-11, 88 pts); 27. **Miami-OH** (23-7, 70); 28. **Virginia Tech** (won NIT, 25-10, 51); 29. **Western Ky.** (27-4, 43); 30. **Manhattan** (26-5, 36); 31. **Oklahoma** (23-9, 32); 32. **Stanford** (20-9, 30); 33. **Minnesota** (19-12, 21); 34. **Penn** (22-6, 18); 35. **Tulane** (23-10, 14); 36. **Cincinnati** (22-12, 10); 37. **Weber St.** (21-9, 9); 38. **BYU** (22-10, 4); 39. **Ohio University** (24-10, 3) and **Oregon** (19-9, 3); 41. **Marquette** (runner-up NIT, 21-12, 2) and **Saint Louis** (23-8, 2); 43. **Texas Tech** (20-10, 1).

THE FINAL FOUR

The Kingdome in Seattle (April 1-3)

Most Outstanding Player

Ed O'Bannon, UCLA senior forward. SEMIFINAL— 36 minutes, 15 points, 8 rebounds, 4 steals; FINAL— 40 minutes, 30 points, 17 rebounds, 3 assists, 3 steals.

All-Tournament Team

O'Bannon and guard Toby Bailey of UCLA; forward Corliss Williamson and guard Clint McDaniel of Arkansas; and center Bryant Reeves of Oklahoma St.

Semifinal—Game One

West Regional champion UCLA vs. East Regional champ Oklahoma St.; Saturday, April 1 (5:42 p.m. tipoff). Coaches: Jim Harrick, UCLA and Eddie Sutton, Oklahoma St. Favorite: UCLA by 4 ½.

Oklahoma St. (Big 8)	37	24—	61
UCLA (Pac-10)	37	37—	74

High scorers— Bryant Reeves, Okla. St. (25) and Tyus Edney, UCLA (21); **Att**— 38,540; **TV Rating—** 11.6/27 share (CBS).

Semifinal—Game Two

Midwest Regional champion Arkansas vs. Southeast Regional champ North Carolina; Saturday, April 1 (8:12 p.m. tipoff). Coaches: Nolan Richardson, Arkansas and Dean Smith, North Carolina. Favorite: North Carolina by 2.

Arkansas (SEC)	34	41—	75
North Carolina (ACC)	38	30—	68

High scorers— Corliss Williamson, Ark. (21) and Donald Williams, N. Carolina (19); **Att**— 38,540; **TV Rating**— 13.3/25 share (CBS).

NCAA Finalists' Tournament and Season Statistics

At least 10 games played during the overall season.

UCLA (31-2)

| | | NCAA TOURNAMENT | | | | | | OVERALL SEASON | | | | |
| | | | | Per Game | | | | | | Per Game | | |
	Gm	FG%	TPts	Pts	Reb	Ast	Gm	FG%	TPts	Pts	Reb	Ast
Ed O'Bannon	6	.500	115	19.2	9.0	1.5	33	.533	673	20.4	8.3	2.5
Toby Bailey	6	.525	82	13.7	5.0	1.7	33	.484	347	10.5	4.8	1.9
Tyus Edney	6	.524	76	12.7	1.8	6.3	32	.497	456	14.3	3.1	6.8
Charles O'Bannon	6	.565	69	11.5	5.2	3.2	33	.554	449	13.6	6.1	3.3
George Zidek	6	.511	57	9.5	3.2	0.3	33	.553	350	10.6	5.4	0.5
J.R. Henderson	6	.581	57	9.5	3.0	1.0	33	.547	305	9.2	4.2	1.3
Kris Johnson	3	.545	15	5.0	3.0	0.3	21	.420	54	2.6	1.7	0.3
Cameron Dollar	6	.357	25	4.2	3.3	3.5	33	.354	112	3.4	1.9	3.1
Ike Nwankwo	3	.500	10	3.3	2.0	0.3	23	.571	63	2.7	1.6	0.1
omm'A Givens	3	.750	6	2.0	0.7	0.0	25	.381	41	1.6	1.3	0.1
Bob Myers	3	.500	4	1.3	1.0	0.0	18	.167	6	0.3	0.5	0.1
Kevin Dempsey	3	.333	2	0.7	1.0	0.0	14	.474	24	1.7	0.8	0.4
UCLA	6	.523	518	86.3	37.0	17.8	33	.513	2889	87.5	40.4	19.8
OPPONENTS	6	.413	432	72.0	34.7	15.2	33	.408	2438	73.9	36.0	14.8

Three-pointers: NCAA TOURNEY— E. O'Bannon (9-for-28), Edney (6-12), Bailey (3-12), Dempsey (0-1), Johnson (0-1), C. O'Bannon (0-2), Dollar (0-3), Team (18-59 for .305 Pct.); OVERALL— E. O'Bannon (55-for-127), Edney (25-66), Bailey (20-73), C. O'Bannon (6-29), Dempsey (3-9), Henderson (3-10), Zidek (2-5), Burns (2-6), Dollar (2-16), Myers (0-2), Johnson (0-3), Team (118-346 for .341 Pct.).

ARKANSAS (32-7)

| | | NCAA TOURNAMENT | | | | | | OVERALL SEASON | | | | |
| | | | | Per Game | | | | | | Per Game | | |
	Gm	FG%	TPts	Pts	Reb	Ast	Gm	FG%	TPts	Pts	Reb	Ast
Corliss Williamson	6	.527	125	20.8	8.7	2.7	39	.550	770	19.7	7.5	2.3
Scotty Thurman	6	.411	83	13.8	4.0	2.5	37	.458	571	15.4	3.9	2.3
Dwight Stewart	6	.478	61	10.2	5.0	1.2	30	.373	220	7.3	4.7	1.8
Clint McDaniel	6	.385	57	9.5	3.7	1.7	37	.460	424	11.5	3.1	2.4
Corey Beck	6	.394	46	7.7	3.7	4.2	39	.493	308	7.9	4.8	5.3
Lee Wilson	6	.652	41	6.8	2.7	0.2	37	.674	150	4.1	2.4	0.7
Alex Dillard	6	.324	33	5.5	1.8	1.2	39	.384	265	6.8	1.5	1.2
Davor Rimac	6	.350	19	3.2	1.3	1.3	35	.396	130	3.7	1.5	0.8
Darnell Robinson	6	.278	13	2.2	2.8	1.5	37	.411	236	6.4	3.8	0.9
Elmer Martin	6	.400	10	1.7	1.8	0.7	35	.301	64	1.8	1.9	0.5
Reggie Garrett	5	.500	4	0.8	0.2	0.6	33	.480	182	5.5	2.2	1.3
Landis Williams	1	.000	0	0.0	0.0	0.0	18	.639	53	2.9	1.1	0.3
Kareem Reid	0						18	.526	34	1.9	0.4	0.4
ARKANSAS	6	.440	492	82.0	37.8	16.5	39	.464	3416	87.6	39.2	18.5
OPPONENTS	6	.437	481	80.2	43.7	16.3	39	.437	3115	79.9	40.6	16.2

Three-pointers: NCAA TOURNEY— Thurman (17-for-44), Stewart (12-32), McDaniel (9-27), Beck (8-11), Dillard (7-23), Martin (2-6), Robinson (0-5), Garrett (0-1), Team (60-165 for .364 Pct.); OVERALL— Thurman (102-for-239), Dillard (63-161), McDaniel (55-139), Stewart (39-112), Rimac (35-84), Beck (24-49), Garrett (14-32), Robinson (14-40), Martin (11-39), Reid (2-7), Engskov (1-5), Williamson (1-6), Merritt (0-2), Williams (0-2), Team (361-917 for .394 Pct.).

UCLA's Schedule

Reg. Season (25-2)

W	CS-Northridge	83-60
W	Kentucky	82-81
W	CS-Fullerton	99-65
W	at LSU	92-72
W	Geo. Mason	137-100
W	N.C. State	88-80
L	at Oregon	72-82
W	at Oregon St.	87-78
W	Washington	75-57
W	Washington St.	91-78
W	at Arizona	71-61
W	at Arizona St.	85-72
W	Stanford	77-74
L	California	93-100
W	at USC	73-69
W	Notre Dame	92-55
W	at Washington	74-66
W	at Washington St.	98-83
W	Arizona St. (OT)	82-77
W	Arizona	72-70
W	at Stanford	88-77
W	at California	104-88
W	Duke	100-77
W	USC	85-66
W	at Louisville	91-73
W	Oregon St.	86-67
W	Oregon	94-78

NCAA Tourney (6-0)

W	Florida Int'l	92-56
W	Missouri	75-74
W	Miss. St.	86-67
W	Connecticut	102-96
W	Oklahoma St.	74-61
W	Arkansas	89-78

Note: the Pac-10 does not have a postseason tournament

Arkansas' Schedule

Reg. Season (25-5)

L	UMass	80-104
W	Georgetown	97-79
W	Jackson St.	103-87
W	at Missouri	94-71
W	Centenary	121-94
W	at SMU	78-66
W	Murray St.	94-69
W	Fla. A&M	97-57
W	Tulsa	82-63
W	Oklahoma	86-84
W	Cincinnati	84-75
W	Iowa	101-92
L	at Mississippi	71-76
W	Tennessee	97-79
W	Miss. St.	79-74
L	at Auburn	90-104
W	Georgia	84-82
W	at S. Carolina	88-73
L	Alabama	70-88
W	Kentucky	94-92
W	LSU	105-81
L	at Miss. St.	62-83
W	Memphis	88-87
W	at Vanderbilt (OT)	97-94
W	at Alabama	86-80
W	Mississippi	85-70
W	at LSU	92-90
W	Montevallo	122-64
W	at Florida	94-85
W	Auburn	68-66

SEC Tourney (2-1)

W	Vanderbilt	73-72
W	Alabama	69-58
L	Kentucky (OT)	93-95

NCAA Tourney (5-1)

W	TX-Southern	79-78
W	Syracuse (OT)	96-94
W	Memphis (OT)	96-91
W	Virginia	68-61
W	N. Carolina	75-68
L	UCLA	78-89

Final NCAA Men's Division I Standings

Conference records include regular season games only. Overall records include all postseason tournament games.

American West Conference

	Conference			Overall		
	W	L	Pct	W	L	Pct
Southern Utah	6	0	1.000	17	11	.607
CS-Northridge	4	2	.667	8	20	.286
Sacramento St.	2	4	.333	6	21	.222
CAL Poly SLO	0	6	.000	1	26	.037

Conf. Tourney Final: Southern Utah 83, CS-Northridge 82.

Atlantic Coast Conference

	Conference			Overall		
	W	L	Pct	W	L	Pct
*Wake Forest	12	4	.750	26	6	.813
*North Carolina	12	4	.750	28	6	.824
*Maryland	12	4	.750	26	8	.765
*Virginia	12	4	.750	25	9	.735
Georgia Tech	8	8	.500	18	12	.600
†Clemson	5	11	.313	15	13	.536
Florida St.	5	11	.313	12	15	.444
N.C. State	4	12	.250	12	15	.444
Duke	2	14	.125	13	18	.419

Conf. Tourney Final: Wake Forest 82, North Carolina 80 (OT).
* **NCAA Tourney (11-4):** Maryland (2-1), North Carolina (4-1), Virginia (3-1), Wake Forest (2-1).
†**NIT Tourney (0-1):** Clemson (0-1). Georgia Tech turned down NIT bid.

Atlantic 10 Conference

	Conference			Overall		
	W	L	Pct	W	L	Pct
*Massachusetts	13	3	.813	29	5	.853
*Temple	10	6	.625	19	11	.633
†George Washington	10	6	.625	18	14	.563
†St. Joseph's	9	7	.563	17	12	.586
†St. Bonaventure	9	7	.563	18	13	.581
West Virginia	7	9	.438	13	13	.500
Rutgers	7	9	.438	13	15	.464
Duquesne	5	11	.313	10	18	.357
Rhode Island	2	14	.125	7	20	.259

Conf. Tourney Final: UMass 63, Temple 44.
* **NCAA Tourney (3-2):** UMass (3-1), Temple (0-1).
†**NIT Tourney (1-3):** George Washington (0-1), St. Bonaventure (1-1), St. Joseph's (0-1).

Big East Conference

	Conference			Overall		
	W	L	Pct	W	L	Pct
*Connecticut	16	2	.889	28	5	.848
*Villanova	14	4	.778	25	8	.758
*Syracuse	12	6	.667	20	10	.667
*Georgetown	11	7	.611	21	10	.677
†Miami-FL	9	9	.500	15	13	.536
†Providence	7	11	.389	17	13	.567
†Seton Hall	7	11	.389	16	14	.533
†St. John's	7	11	.389	14	14	.500
Pittsburgh	5	13	.278	10	18	.357
Boston College	2	16	.111	9	19	.321

Conf. Tourney Final: Villanova 94, UConn 78.
* **NCAA Tourney (6-4):** UConn (3-1), Syracuse (1-1), Georgetown (2-1), Villanova (0-1).
†**NIT Tourney (1-4):** Miami-FL (0-1), Providence (1-1), St. John's (0-1), Seton Hall (0-1).

Big Eight Conference

	Conference			Overall		
	W	L	Pct	W	L	Pct
*Kansas	11	3	.786	25	6	.806
*Oklahoma St.	10	4	.714	27	10	.730
*Oklahoma	9	5	.643	23	9	.719
*Missouri	8	6	.571	20	9	.690
*Iowa St.	6	8	.429	23	11	.676
†Colorado	5	9	.357	15	13	.536
†Nebraska	4	10	.286	18	14	.563
Kansas St.	3	11	.214	12	15	.444

Conf. Tourney Final: Oklahoma St. 62, Iowa St. 53.
* **NCAA Tourney (8-5):** Iowa St. (1-1), Kansas (2-1), Missouri (1-1), Oklahoma (1-1), Oklahoma St. (4-1).
†**NIT Tourney (1-2):** Colorado (0-1), Nebraska (1-1).

Big Sky Conference

	Conference			Overall		
	W	L	Pct	W	L	Pct
*Weber St.	11	3	.786	21	9	.700
†Montana	11	3	.786	21	9	.700
Montana St.	8	6	.571	21	8	.724
Idaho St.	7	7	.500	18	10	.643
Boise St.	7	7	.500	17	10	.630
Idaho	6	8	.429	12	15	.444
Northern Arizona	4	10	.286	8	18	.308
Eastern Washington	2	12	.143	6	20	.231

Conf. Tourney Final: Weber St. 84, Montana 62.
* **NCAA Tourney (1-1):** Weber St. (1-1).
†**NIT Tourney (0-1):** Montana (0-1).

Big South Conference

	Conference			Overall		
	W	L	Pct	W	L	Pct
NC-Greensboro	14	2	.875	23	6	.793
Charleston Southern	12	4	.750	19	10	.655
MD-Balt. County	10	6	.625	13	14	.481
Radford	9	7	.563	16	12	.571
Liberty	7	9	.438	12	16	.429
NC-Asheville	7	9	.438	11	16	.407
Towson St.	6	10	.375	12	15	.444
Winthrop	4	12	.250	7	20	.259
Coastal Carolina	3	13	.188	6	20	.231

Conf. Tourney Final: Charleston Southern 68, NC-Greensboro 67.

Big Ten Conference

	Conference			Overall		
	W	L	Pct	W	L	Pct
*Purdue	15	3	.833	25	7	.781
*Michigan St.	14	4	.778	22	6	.786
*Indiana	11	7	.611	19	12	.613
*Michigan	11	7	.611	17	14	.548
*Illinois	10	8	.556	19	12	.613
*Minnesota	10	8	.556	19	12	.613
†Iowa	9	9	.500	21	12	.636
†Penn St.	9	9	.500	21	11	.656
Wisconsin	7	11	.389	13	14	.481
Ohio St.	2	16	.111	6	22	.214
Northwestern	1	17	.056	5	22	.185

Conf. Tourney Final: Big Ten has no tournament.
* **NCAA Tourney (1-6):** Michigan (0-1), Purdue (1-1), Indiana (0-1), Michigan St. (0-1), Minnesota (0-1), Illinois (0-1).
†**NIT Tourney (6-2):** Iowa (2-1), Penn St. (4-1).

Final NCAA Men's Division I Standings (Cont.)

Big West Conference

	Conference			Overall		
	W	L	Pct	W	L	Pct
†Utah St.	14	4	.778	21	8	.724
†New Mexico St.	13	5	.722	25	10	.714
*Long Beach St.	13	5	.722	20	10	.667
Nevada	12	6	.667	18	11	.621
Pacific	9	9	.500	14	13	.519
UC-Santa Barbara	8	10	.444	13	14	.481
UNLV	7	11	.389	12	16	.429
UC-Irvine	6	12	.333	13	16	.448
CS-Fullerton	5	13	.278	7	20	.259
San Jose St.	3	15	.167	4	23	.148

Conf. Tourney Final: Long Beach St. 76, Nevada 69 (OT).
NCAA Tourney (0-1): Long Beach St. (0-1).
†**NIT Tourney (2-2):** New Mexico St. (2-1), Utah St. (0-1).

Colonial Athletic Association

	Conference			Overall		
	W	L	Pct	W	L	Pct
*Old Dominion	12	2	.857	21	12	.636
NC-Wilmington	10	4	.714	16	11	.593
James Madison	9	5	.643	16	13	.552
East Carolina	7	7	.500	18	11	.621
American	7	7	.500	9	19	.321
William & Mary	6	8	.429	8	19	.296
Richmond	3	11	.214	8	20	.286
George Mason	2	12	.143	7	20	.259

Conf. Tourney Final: Old Dominion 80, James Madison 75.
NCAA Tourney (1-1): Old Dominion (1-1).

Great Midwest Conference

	Conference			Overall		
	W	L	Pct	W	L	Pct
*Memphis	9	3	.750	24	10	.706
*Saint Louis	8	4	.667	23	8	.742
*Cincinnati	7	5	.583	22	12	.647
†Marquette	7	5	.583	21	12	.636
†DePaul	6	6	.500	17	11	.607
Ala-Birmingham	5	7	.417	14	16	.467
Dayton	0	12	.000	7	20	.259

Conf. Tourney Final: Cincinnati 67, Saint Louis 65.
NCAA Tourney (4-3): Cincinnati (1-1), Memphis (2-1), Saint Louis (1-1).
†**NIT Tourney (4-2):** DePaul (0-1), Marquette (4-1).

Ivy League

	Conference			Overall		
	W	L	Pct	W	L	Pct
*Penn	14	0	1.000	22	6	.786
Princeton	10	4	.714	16	10	.615
Dartmouth	10	4	.714	13	13	.500
Brown	8	6	.571	13	13	.500
Yale	5	9	.357	9	17	.346
Cornell	4	10	.286	9	17	.346
Harvard	4	10	.286	6	20	.231
Columbia	1	13	.071	4	22	.154

Conf. Tourney Final: Ivy League has no tournament.
NCAA Tourney (0-1): Penn (0-1).

Metro Conference

	Conference			Overall		
	W	L	Pct	W	L	Pct
*NC-Charlotte	8	4	.667	19	9	.679
*Tulane	7	5	.583	23	10	.697
*Louisville	7	5	.583	19	14	.576
†Virginia Tech	6	6	.500	25	10	.714
†South Mississippi	6	6	.500	17	13	.567
†South Florida	5	7	.417	18	12	.600
VCU	3	9	.250	16	14	.533

Conf. Tourney Final: Louisville 78, Southern Miss. 64.
NCAA Tourney (1-3): Louisville (0-1), NC-Charlotte (0-1), Tulane (1-1).
†**NIT Tourney (7-2):** South Florida (2-1), Southern Miss. (0-1), Virginia Tech (5-0).

Metro Atlantic Conference

	Conference			Overall		
	W	L	Pct	W	L	Pct
*Manhattan	12	2	.857	26	5	.839
*St. Peter's	10	4	.714	19	11	.633
†Canisius	10	4	.714	21	14	.600
Fairfield	6	8	.429	13	15	.464
Iona	6	8	.429	10	17	.370
Loyola-MD	5	9	.357	9	18	.333
Siena	5	9	.357	8	19	.296
Niagara	2	12	.143	5	25	.167

Conf. Tourney Final: St. Peter's 80, Manhattan 78 (OT).
NCAA Tourney (1-2): Manhattan (1-1), St. Peter's (0-1).
†**NIT Tourney (3-2):** Canisius (3-2).

Mid-American Conference

	Conference			Overall		
	W	L	Pct	W	L	Pct
*Miami-OH	16	2	.889	23	7	.767
†Ohio University	13	5	.722	24	10	.706
†Eastern Michigan	12	6	.667	20	10	.667
*Ball St.	11	7	.611	19	11	.633
Bowling Green	10	8	.556	16	11	.593
Toledo	10	8	.556	16	11	.593
Western Michigan	9	9	.500	14	13	.519
Kent	5	13	.278	8	19	.296
Akron	4	14	.222	8	18	.308
Central Michigan	0	18	.000	3	23	.115

Conf. Tourney Final: Ball St. 77, Eastern Michigan 70.
NCAA Tourney (1-2): Ball St. (0-1), Miami-OH (1-1).
†**NIT Tourney (1-2):** Eastern Mich. (0-1), Ohio Univ. (1-1).

Mid-Continent Conference

	Conference			Overall		
	W	L	Pct	W	L	Pct
Valparaiso	14	4	.778	20	8	.714
Western Illinois	13	5	.722	20	8	.714
Buffalo	12	6	.667	18	10	.643
Youngstown St.	10	8	.556	18	10	.643
Eastern Illinois	10	8	.556	16	13	.552
Troy St.	10	8	.556	11	16	.407
MO Kansas City	7	11	.389	7	19	.269
Central Conn. St.	6	12	.333	8	18	.308
Chicago St.	6	12	.333	6	20	.231
NE Illinois	2	16	.111	4	22	.154

Conf. Tourney Final: Valparaiso 88, Western Illinois 85 (3 OT).

Mid-Eastern Athletic Conference

	Conference			Overall		
	W	L	Pct	W	L	Pct
†Coppin St.	15	1	.938	21	10	.677
South Carolina St.	11	5	.688	15	13	.536
*N. Carolina A&T	10	6	.625	15	15	.500
MD-Eastern Shore	9	7	.563	13	14	.481
Bethune Cookman	9	7	.563	12	16	.429
Howard	8	8	.500	9	18	.333
Morgan St.	5	11	.313	5	22	.185
Delaware St.	3	13	.188	7	21	.250
Florida A&M	2	14	.125	5	22	.185

Conf. Tourney Final: N. Carolina A&T 66, Coppin St. 64.
* NCAA Tourney (0-1): N. Carolina A&T (0-1).
†NIT Tourney (1-1): Coppin St. (1-1).

Midwestern Collegiate Conference

	Conference			Overall		
	W	L	Pct	W	L	Pct
*Xavier-OH	14	0	1.000	23	5	.821
*WI-Green Bay	11	4	.733	22	8	.733
Illinois-Chicago	11	4	.733	18	9	.667
Detroit Mercy	9	5	.643	13	15	.464
Butler	8	7	.533	15	12	.556
La Salle	7	7	.500	13	14	.481
Northern Illinois	7	8	.467	19	10	.655
Wright St.	6	8	.429	13	17	.433
Cleveland St.	3	11	.214	10	17	.370
Loyola-IL	2	13	.133	5	22	.185
WI-Milwaukee	2	13	.133	3	24	.111

Conf. Tourney Final: Wisconsin-Green Bay 73, Wright St. 59.
* NCAA Tourney (0-2): WI-Green Bay (0-1), Xavier-OH (0-1).

Missouri Valley Conference

	Conference			Overall		
	W	L	Pct	W	L	Pct
*Tulsa	15	3	.833	24	8	.750
*Southern Illinois	13	5	.722	23	9	.719
†Illinois St.	13	5	.722	20	13	.606
†Bradley	12	6	.667	20	10	.667
Evansville	11	7	.611	18	9	.667
SW Missouri St.	9	9	.500	16	11	.593
Drake	9	9	.500	12	15	.444
Wichita St.	6	12	.333	13	14	.481
Northern Iowa	4	14	.222	8	20	.286
Creighton	4	14	.222	7	19	.269
Indiana St.	3	15	.167	7	19	.269

Conf. Tourney Final: Southern Illinois 77, Tulsa 62.
* NCAA Tourney (2-2): Tulsa (2-1), Southern Ill. (0-1).
†NIT Tourney (2-2): Bradley (1-1), Illinois St. (1-1).

North Atlantic Conference

	Conference			Overall		
	W	L	Pct	W	L	Pct
*Drexel	12	4	.750	22	8	.733
New Hampshire	11	5	.688	19	9	.679
Northeastern	10	6	.625	18	11	.621
Vermont	7	9	.438	14	13	.519
Boston University	7	9	.438	15	16	.484
Delaware	7	9	.438	12	15	.444
Hartford	7	9	.438	11	16	.407
Maine	6	10	.375	11	16	.407
Hofstra	5	11	.313	10	18	.357

Conf. Tourney Final: Drexel 72, Northeastern 52.
* NCAA Tourney (0-1) Drexel (0-1)

Northeast Conference

	Conference			Overall		
	W	L	Pct	W	L	Pct
Rider	13	5	.722	18	11	.621
Marist	12	6	.667	17	11	.607
*Mt. St. Mary's	12	6	.667	17	13	.567
Fairleigh Dickinson	11	7	.611	16	12	.571
Monmouth	11	7	.611	13	14	.481
Wagner	9	9	.500	10	17	.370
LIU Brooklyn	8	10	.444	11	17	.393
St. Francis-PA	7	11	.389	12	16	.429
St. Francis-NY	5	13	.278	9	18	.333
Robert Morris	2	16	.111	4	23	.148

Conf. Tourney Final: Mount St. Mary's 69, Rider 62.
* NCAA Tourney (0-1): Mount St. Mary's (0-1).

Ohio Valley Conference

	Conference			Overall		
	W	L	Pct	W	L	Pct
Tennessee St.	11	5	.688	17	10	.630
*Murray St.	11	5	.688	21	9	.700
Morehead St.	10	6	.625	15	12	.556
Tennessee Tech	9	7	.563	13	14	.481
Austin Peay St.	8	8	.500	13	16	.448
SE Missouri St.	7	9	.438	13	14	.481
Eastern Kentucky	6	10	.375	9	19	.321
Middle Tenn St.	5	11	.313	12	15	.444
Tennessee-Martin	5	11	.313	7	20	.259

Conf. Tourney Final: Murray St. 92, Austin Peay St. 84.
* NCAA Tourney (0-1): Murray St. (0-1)

Pacific-10 Conference

	Conference			Overall		
	W	L	Pct	W	L	Pct
*UCLA	16	2	.889	31	2	.939
*Arizona	13	5	.722	23	8	.742
*Arizona St.	12	6	.667	24	9	.727
*Oregon	11	7	.611	19	9	.676
*Stanford	10	8	.556	20	9	.690
†Washington St.	10	8	.556	18	12	.600
Oregon St.	6	12	.333	9	18	.333
California	5	13	.278	13	14	.481
Washington	5	13	.278	9	18	.333
USC	2	16	.111	7	21	.250

Conf. Tourney Final: Pac-10 has no tournament.
* NCAA Tourney (9-4): Arizona (0-1), Arizona St. (2-1), Oregon (0-1), Stanford (1-1), UCLA (6-0).
†NIT Tourney (2-1): Washington St. (2-1).

Patriot League

	Conference			Overall		
	W	L	Pct	W	L	Pct
*Colgate	11	3	.786	17	13	.567
Bucknell	11	3	.786	13	14	.481
Navy	10	4	.714	20	9	.690
Holy Cross	9	5	.643	15	12	.556
Fordham	6	8	.429	11	17	.393
Lehigh	5	9	.357	11	16	.407
Army	4	10	.286	12	16	.429
Lafayette	0	14	.000	2	25	.074

Note: Colgate and Bucknell were regular season co-champions.
Conf. Tourney Final: Colgate 68, Navy 63.
* NCAA Tourney (0-1): Colgate (0-1).

Final NCAA Men's Division I Standings (Cont.)

Southeastern Conference

Eastern Div.	Conference			Overall		
	W	L	Pct	W	L	Pct
*Kentucky	14	2	.875	28	5	.848
†Georgia	9	7	.563	18	10	.643
*Florida	8	8	.500	17	13	.567
Vanderbilt	6	10	.375	13	15	.464
South Carolina	5	11	.313	10	17	.370
Tennessee	4	12	.250	11	16	.407

Western Div.	Conference			Overall		
	W	L	Pct	W	L	Pct
*Arkansas	12	4	.750	32	7	.821
*Mississippi St.	12	4	.750	22	8	.733
*Alabama	10	6	.625	23	10	.697
†Auburn	7	9	.438	16	13	.552
LSU	6	10	.375	12	15	.444
Mississippi	3	13	.188	8	19	.296

Conf. Tourney Final: Kentucky 95, Arkansas 93 (OT).
• NCAA Tourney (11-5): Alabama (1-1), Arkansas (5-1), Florida (0-1), Kentucky (3-1), Mississippi St. (2-1).
†NIT Tourney (0-2): Auburn (0-1), Georgia (0-1).

Southern Conference

Northern Div.	Conference			Overall		
	W	L	Pct	W	L	Pct
Marshall	10	4	.714	18	9	.667
East Tennessee St.	9	5	.643	14	14	.500
Davidson	7	7	.500	14	13	.519
VMI	6	8	.429	10	17	.370
Appalachian St.	4	10	.286	9	20	.310

Southern Div.	Conference			Overall		
	W	L	Pct	W	L	Pct
*Tenn-Chattanooga	11	3	.786	19	11	.633
Western Carolina	8	6	.571	14	14	.500
The Citadel	6	8	.429	11	16	.407
Furman	6	8	.429	10	17	.370
Georgia Southern	3	11	.214	8	20	.286

Conf. Tourney Final: Tenn-Chattanooga 63, Western Carolina 61.
• NCAA Tourney (0-1): Tenn-Chattanooga (0-1).

Southland Conference

	Conference			Overall		
	W	L	Pct	W	L	Pct
NE Louisiana	15	3	.833	19	9	.679
*Nicholls St.	17	1	.944	24	6	.800
Texas-San Antonio	11	7	.611	15	13	.536
NE Louisiana	11	7	.611	14	18	.438
North Texas	9	9	.500	14	13	.519
Stephen F. Austin St.	9	9	.500	14	14	.500
Northwestern St.	8	10	.444	13	14	.481
SW Texas St.	7	11	.389	12	14	.462
McNeese St.	7	11	.389	11	16	.407
Texas-Arlington	7	11	.389	10	17	.370
Sam Houston St.	4	14	.222	7	19	.269

Conf. Tourney Final: Nicholls St. 98, NE Louisiana 87.
• NCAA Tourney (0-1): Nicholls St. (0-1).

Best in Show

Conferences with at least two wins in 1995 NCAA's; number of tournament teams in parentheses.

	W-L		W-L
ACC (4)	11-4	Big East (4)	6-4
SEC (5)	11-5	Great Midwest (3)	4-3
Pac-10 (5)	9-4	Atlantic 10 (2)	3-2
Big Eight (5)	8-5	Mo. Valley (2)	2-2

Southwest Conference

	Conference			Overall		
	W	L	Pct	W	L	Pct
*Texas	11	3	.786	23	7	.767
†Texas Tech	11	3	.786	20	10	.667
TCU	8	6	.571	16	11	.593
Rice	8	6	.571	15	13	.536
Texas A&M	7	7	.500	14	16	.467
Houston	5	9	.357	9	19	.321
Baylor	3	11	.214	9	19	.321
SMU	3	11	.214	7	20	.259

Conf. Tourney Final: Texas 107, Texas Tech 104 (OT).
• NCAA Tourney (1-1): Texas (1-1).
†NIT Tourney (0-1): Texas Tech (0-1).

Southwestern Athletic Conference

	Conference			Overall		
	W	L	Pct	W	L	Pct
*Texas Southern	12	2	.857	22	7	.759
Miss. Valley St.	10	4	.714	17	11	.607
Alabama St.	8	6	.571	10	15	.400
Southern-BR	7	7	.500	13	13	.500
Jackson St.	7	7	.500	12	19	.387
Grambling St.	5	9	.357	11	17	.393
Alcorn St.	4	10	.286	7	19	.269
Prairie View A&M	3	11	.214	5	21	.192

Conf. Tourney Final: Texas Southern 75, Miss. Valley St. 62.
• NCAA Tourney (0-1): Texas Southern (0-1).

Sun Belt Conference

	Conference			Overall		
	W	L	Pct	W	L	Pct
*Western Kentucky	17	1	.944	27	4	.871
New Orleans	13	5	.722	20	11	.645
Jacksonville	12	6	.667	18	9	.667
Texas-Pan Am.	10	8	.556	14	14	.500
Ark-Little Rock	9	9	.500	17	12	.586
Louisiana Tech	9	9	.500	14	13	.519
South Alabama	7	11	.389	9	18	.333
Lamar	6	12	.333	11	16	.407
SW Louisiana	4	14	.222	7	22	.241
Arkansas St.	3	15	.167	8	20	.286

Conf. Tourney Final: Western Kentucky 82, Ark-Little Rock 79.
• NCAA Tourney (1-1): Western Kentucky (1-1).

Trans America Athletic Conference

	Conference			Overall		
	W	L	Pct	W	L	Pct
†Col. of Charleston	15	1	.938	23	6	.793
Samford	11	5	.688	16	11	.593
Stetson	11	5	.688	15	12	.556
Mercer	8	8	.500	15	14	.517
SE Louisiana	7	9	.438	12	16	.429
Central Florida	7	9	.438	11	16	.407
Centenary	7	9	.438	10	17	.370
Georgia St.	6	10	.375	11	17	.393
*Florida Int'l	4	12	.250	11	19	.367
Campbell	4	12	.250	8	18	.308
Florida Atlantic	0	0	.000	9	18	.333

Note: Fla. Atlantic will play first full TAAC schedule in 1995-96.
Conf. Tourney Final: Florida International 68, Mercer 57.
• NCAA Tourney (0-1): Florida International (0-1).
†NIT Tourney (0-1): College of Charleston (0-1).

West Coast Conference

	Conference			Overall		
	W	L	Pct	W	L	Pct
*Santa Clara	12	2	.857	21	7	.750
Portland	10	4	.714	21	8	.724
St. Mary's	10	4	.714	18	10	.643
*Gonzaga	7	7	.500	21	9	.700
San Diego	5	9	.357	11	16	.407
Loyola-CA	4	10	.286	13	15	.464
San Francisco	4	10	.286	10	19	.345
Pepperdine	4	10	.286	8	19	.296

Conf. Tourney Final: Gonzaga 80, Portland 67.
* **NCAA Tourney (0-2):** Gonzaga (0-1), Santa Clara (0-1).

Western Athletic Conference

	Conference			Overall		
	W	L	Pct	W	L	Pct
*Utah	15	3	.833	28	6	.824
*BYU	13	5	.722	22	10	.688
†UTEP	13	5	.722	20	10	.667
New Mexico	9	9	.500	15	15	.500
Wyoming	9	9	.500	13	15	.464
Hawaii	8	10	.444	16	13	.552
Colorado St.	7	11	.389	17	14	.548
Fresno St.	7	11	.389	13	15	.464
San Diego St.	5	13	.278	11	17	.393
Air Force	4	14	.222	8	20	.286

Conf. Tourney Final: Utah 67, Hawaii 54.
* **NCAA Tourney (1-2):** BYU (0-1), Utah (1-1).
† **NIT Tourney (1-1):** UTEP (1-1).

Division I Independents

	W	L	Pct
Notre Dame	15	12	.556
Oral Roberts	10	17	.370

Annual Awards
Player of the Year

Joe Smith, Maryland	AP, Naismith, UPI
Ed O'Bannon, UCLA	USBWA, Wooden
Shawn Respert, Michigan St.	NABC, TSN

Wooden Award Voting

Presented since 1977 by the Los Angeles Athletic Club and named after the former Purdue All-America and UCLA coach John Wooden. Voting done by 984-member panel of national media; candidates must have a cumulative college grade point average of 2.0 (out of 4.0).

		Cl	Pos	Pts
1	Ed O'Bannon, UCLA	Sr.	F	4396
2	Shawn Respert, Michigan St	Sr.	G	3247
3	Randolph Childress, W. Forest	Sr.	G	3224
4	Jerry Stackhouse, N. Carolina	So.	F	2887
5	Corliss Williamson, Arkansas	Jr.	F	2511
6	Damon Stoudamire, Arizona	Sr.	G	1975
7	Rasheed Wallace, N. Carolina	So.	F	1949
8	Kerry Kittles, Villanova	Jr.	F/G	1693
9	Lou Roe, UMass	Sr.	F	1653
10	Ray Allen, UConn	So.	F/G	979

Other nominees (5): Alan Henderson, Indiana (947 pts); Lawrence Moten, Syracuse (640); Jacque Vaughn, Kansas (594); Gary Trent, Ohio Univ. (577); Mario Bennett, Ariz. St. (503).

Note: Bryant Reeves (Sr., C) of Oklahoma St., Joe Smith (So., F/C) of Maryland and Kurt Thomas (Sr., C) of TCU were ineligible due to grade point averages below 2.0.

Consensus All-America Team

The NCAA Division I players cited most frequently by the following All-America selectors: AP, U.S. Basketball Writers, National Assn. of Basketball Coaches and UPI. There were no holdovers from the 1993-94 first team; (*) indicates unanimous first team selection.

First Team

	Class	Hgt	Pos
Joe Smith, Maryland*	So.	6-10	F/C
Ed O'Bannon, UCLA*	Sr.	6-8	F
Shawn Respert, Michigan St.*	Sr.	6-3	G
Damon Stoudamire, Arizona*	Sr.	5-11	G
Jerry Stackhouse, North Carolina*	So.	6-6	F

Second Team

	Class	Hgt	Pos
Randolph Childress, Wake Forest	Sr.	6-2	G
Corliss Williamson, Arkansas	Jr.	6-7	F
Kerry Kittles, Villanova	Jr.	6-5	G/F
Rasheed Wallace, North Carolina	So.	6-10	C
Lou Roe, Massachusetts	Sr.	6-7	F

Third Team

	Class	Hgt	Pos
Bryant Reeves, Oklahoma St	Sr.	7-0	C
Tim Duncan, Wake Forest	So.	6-10	C
Ray Allen, Connecticut	So.	6-5	F/G
Kurt Thomas, TCU	Sr.	6-9	C
Lawrence Moten, Syracuse	Sr.	6-5	G

Underclassmen in NBA Draft

Fourteen Division 1 players (10 juniors and four sophomores), one junior college player and one high school senior forfeited the remainder of their college eligibility and declared for the 1995 NBA draft which took place in Toronto on June 28. See page 358 for entire draft list.

Players are listed in alphabetical order; first round selections in **bold** type.

	Cl	Drafted by	Overall Pick
Cory Alexander, Virginia	Jr.	San Antonio	29
Mario Bennett, Ariz. St.	Jr.	Phoenix	27
Chris Carr, Southern Ill.	Jr.	Phoenix	56
Michael Evans, Okaloosa (Fla.)	JC	Not drafted	–
Kevin Garnett, Farragut Acad.	HS	Minnesota	5
Rashard Griffith, Wisc.	So.	Milwaukee	38
Antonio McDyess, Alabama	So.	LA Clippers*	2
Joe Smith, Maryland	So.	Golden St.	1
Jerry Stackhouse, N. Car.	So.	Philadelphia	3
Scotty Thurman, Arkansas	Jr.	Not drafted	–
Gary Trent, Ohio Univ.	Jr.	Milwaukee*	11
David Vaughn, Memphis	Jr.	Orlando	25
Darroll Wright, Mo. Western	Jr.	Not drafted	–
Rasheed Wallace, N.Car.	So.	Washington	4
Corliss Williamson, Ark.	Jr.	Sacramento	13

* McDyess traded to Denver and Trent traded to Portland.
Note: Juniors John Wallace of Syracuse and Rodrick Rhodes of Kentucky declared for the draft then withdrew their names before June 28.

Coaches of the Year

Jim Harrick, UCLA	NABC, Naismith
Kelvin Sampson, Oklahoma	AP, USBWA
Leonard Hamilton, Miami-FL	UPI
Jud Heathcote, Michigan St	*The Sporting News*

NCAA Men's Division I Leaders

Includes games through NCAA and NIT tourneys.

INDIVIDUAL

Scoring

	Cl	Gm	FG%	3Pt/Att	FT%	Reb	Ast	Stl	Blk	Pts	Avg	Hi
Kurt Thomas, TCU	Sr.	27	54.8	3/12	71.4	393	32	51	66	781	**28.9**	45
Frankie King, Western Carolina	Sr.	28	47.9	52/134	83.2	204	94	42	13	743	**26.5**	41
Kenny Sykes, Grambling St.	Sr.	26	42.9	82/220	76.7	107	80	36	2	684	**26.3**	50
Sherell Ford, IL-Chicago	Sr.	27	47.2	47/113	76.5	283	39	44	52	707	**26.2**	37
Tim Roberts, Southern-BR	Jr.	26	40.9	108/313	73.1	123	30	28	3	680	**26.2**	56
Kareem Townes, La Salle	Sr.	27	43.8	103/284	80.6	88	50	75	4	699	**25.9**	52
Joe Griffin, LIU-Brooklyn	Sr.	28	49.5	11/31	66.4	229	57	42	7	723	**25.8**	46
Shawn Respert, Michigan St	Sr.	28	47.3	119/251	86.8	111	85	38	1	716	**25.6**	40
Rob Feaster, Holy Cross	Sr.	27	44.7	55/168	73.9	186	54	44	24	672	**24.9**	42
Shannon Smith, WI-Milwaukee	Jr.	27	39.4	51/157	79.1	148	26	44	8	661	**24.5**	38
Mark Lueking, Army	Jr.	28	41.0	98/243	87.1	65	75	21	1	682	**24.4**	43
Otis Jones, Air Force	Sr.	28	43.0	71/210	76.0	130	73	39	2	670	**23.9**	42
Ryan Minor, Oklahoma	Jr.	32	48.6	69/176	82.3	269	69	70	22	756	**23.6**	36
Alan Henderson, Indiana	Sr.	31	59.7	2/10	63.4	302	54	42	64	729	**23.5**	35
Ronnie Henderson, LSU	So.	27	42.9	68/212	73.4	142	59	35	16	630	**23.3**	40
Scott Drapeau, UNH	Sr.	28	52.9	21/65	70.7	273	54	26	26	648	**23.1**	34
Tucker Neale, Colgate	Sr.	30	45.0	84/224	76.9	138	73	41	5	692	**23.1**	41
Gary Trent, Ohio Univ.	Jr.	33	52.7	8/35	64.2	423	79	20	26	757	**22.9**	33
Joe Wilbert, Texas A&M	Sr.	30	53.5	4/14	72.2	226	51	19	22	687	**22.9**	38
Damon Stoudamire, Arizona	Sr.	30	47.6	112/241	82.6	128	220	52	1	684	**22.8**	45

Rebounds

	Cl	Gm	No	Avg
Kurt Thomas, TCU	Sr.	27	393	14.6
Malik Rose, Drexel	Jr.	30	404	13.5
Gary Trent, Ohio Univ.	Jr.	33	423	12.8
Dan Callahan, Northeastern	Jr.	29	364	12.6
Tim Duncan, Wake Forest	So.	32	401	12.5
Adonal Foyle, Colgate	Fr.	30	371	12.4
Tunji Awojobi, Boston Univ.	So.	31	378	12.2
Kareem Carpenter, Eastern Mich.	Sr.	29	343	11.8
Marcus Mann, Miss. Valley St.	Jr.	27	317	11.7
Chris Ensminger, Valparaiso	Jr.	28	315	11.3
Javan Rouzan, S.F. Austin St.	Jr.	28	312	11.1
Harry Harrison, Idaho	Jr.	26	283	10.9
Reggie Jackson, Nicholls St	Jr.	30	325	10.8
Rashard Griffith, Wisconsin	So.	26	281	10.8
Larry Sykes, Xavier-OH	Sr.	27	291	10.8

Assists

	Cl	Gm	No	Avg
Nelson Haggerty, Baylor	Sr.	28	284	10.1
Curtis McCants, George Mason	So.	27	251	9.3
Raimonds Miglinieks, UC-Irvine	Jr.	29	245	8.4
Eric Snow, Michigan St.	Sr.	28	217	7.8
Jacque Vaughn, Kansas	So.	31	238	7.7
Anthony Foster, S. Alabama	Sr.	27	203	7.5
Tony Miller, Marquette	Sr.	33	248	7.5
Hassan Sanders, Southern -BR	Jr.	24	179	7.5
Ray Washington, Nicholls St.	Jr.	29	213	7.3
Damon Stoudamire, Arizona	Sr.	30	220	7.3
Eathan O'Bryant, Nevada	Jr.	29	211	7.3
Marcell Capers, Arizona St.	Jr.	33	233	7.1
Dominick Young, Fresno St.	So.	28	197	7.0
Roderick Anderson, Texas	Sr.	30	211	7.0
Andre Owens, Oklahoma St.	Jr.	37	256	6.9
Donminic Ellison, Wash. St.	So.	28	192	6.9

Field Goal Percentage

Minimum 5 Field Goals made per game.

	Cl	Gm	FT	FTA	Pct
Shane Kline-Ruminski, B. Green	Sr.	26	181	265	.683
George Spain, Davidson	Sr.	27	141	210	.671
Rasheed Wallace, N. Carolina	So.	34	238	364	.654
Erick Dampier, Miss St	So.	30	153	239	.640
Alexander Koul, G. Washington	Fr.	32	160	253	.632
Joe McNaull, L. Beach St	Sr.	30	156	248	.629
Mark Hendrickson, Wash St	Jr.	30	183	292	.627
Darnell McCulloch, Fresno St	So.	28	152	244	.623
Lorenzo Coleman, Tenn Tech	So.	27	168	270	.622
Chuckie Robinson, E. Carolina	Sr.	29	181	293	.618

3-Pt Field Goal Percentage

Minimum 1.5 Three-Point FG made per game.

	Cl	Gm	FG	FGA	Pct
Brian Jackson, Evansville	Jr.	27	53	95	.558
Scott Kegler, Penn	Sr.	28	58	114	.509
Chris Westlake, WI-Green Bay	Sr.	30	87	174	.500
Dante Calabria, N. Carolina	Jr.	33	66	133	.496
Malik Hightower, Marshall	Sr.	27	46	95	.484
Jeremy Lake, Montana	Sr.	30	76	157	.484
Dion Cross, Stanford	Sr.	29	82	171	.480
Shawn Respert, Mich. St.	Sr.	28	119	251	.474
Daryl Christopher, So. Utah	Jr.	27	53	112	.473
Rob Wooster, St. Francis-PA	Jr.	28	82	174	.471

Free Throw Percentage

Minimum 2.5 Free Throws made per game.

	Cl	Gm	FT	FTA	Pct
Greg Bibb, Tenn Tech	Jr.	27	106	117	.906
Scott Hartzell, NC-Greensboro	Jr.	29	97	108	.898
Marcus Brown, Murray St	Jr.	30	189	211	.896
Keith Cornett, TX-Arlington	Jr.	27	70	79	.886
Arlando Johnson, Eastern Ky	Sr.	28	123	139	.885
Danny Basile, Marist	Jr.	28	74	84	.881
Steve Nash, Santa Clara	Jr.	27	153	174	.879
John Rillie, Gonzaga	Sr	30	87	99	.879

3-Pt Field Goals Per Game

	Cl	Gm	No	Avg
Mitch Taylor, Southern-BR	Jr.	25	109	4.4
Shawn Respert, Mich. St.	Sr.	28	119	4.3
Tim Roberts, Southern-BR	Jr.	26	108	4.2
Randy Rutherford, Okla. St.	Sr.	37	146	3.9
Kareem Townes, La Salle	Sr.	27	103	3.8
LaZelle Durden, Cincinnati	Sr.	34	127	3.7
Damon Stoudamire, Arizona	Sr.	30	112	3.7
Aundre Branch, Baylor	Sr.	28	104	3.7

Joe Collins Photo

Kurt Thomas
Scoring & Rebounds

Baylor

Nelson Haggerty
Assists

Evansville

Brian Jackson
3-Pt FG Pct.

Texas

Roderick Anderson
Steals

Blocked Shots

	Cl	Gm	No	Avg
Keith Closs, Central Conn. St	Fr.	26	139	5.3
Theo Ratliff, Wyoming	Sr.	28	144	5.1
Adonal Foyle, Colgate	Fr.	30	147	4.9
Pascal Fleury, Md-Balt. County	Sr.	27	124	4.6
Lorenzo Coleman, Tenn. Tech	So.	27	122	4.5
Tim Duncan, Wake Forest	So.	32	135	4.2
Brian Gilpin, Dartmouth	So.	26	92	3.5
Mario Bennett, Ariz. St	Jr.	33	115	3.5
Peter Aluma, Liberty	So.	28	97	3.5
Four tied at 3.4 each.				

Steals

	Cl	Gm	No	Avg
Roderick Anderson, Texas	Sr.	30	101	3.37
Greg Black, Texas-Pan Am	Sr.	28	94	3.36
Nate Langley, George Mason	So.	26	87	3.35
Ray Washington, Nicholls St.	Sr.	29	88	3.0
Clarence Ceasar, LSU	Sr.	22	66	3.0
Allen Iverson, Georgetown	Fr.	30	89	3.0
Shandue McNeill, St. Bona	So.	31	90	2.9
Dominick Young, Fresno St	So.	28	81	2.9
Erick Strickland, Nebraska	Jr.	31	89	2.9
Gerald Walker, San Fran.	Jr.	28	80	2.9

Single Game Highs
Individual Points

No		Opponent	Date
56	Tim Roberts, South-BR	Faith Baptist	12/2
52	Kareem Townes, La Salle	Loyola-IL	2/4
50	Kenny Sykes, Grambling	Southern-BR	1/8
48	Mitch Taylor, South-BR	La. Christian	12/1
46	Joe Griffin, LIU	Marist	2/16
45	Kurt Thomas, TCU	IL-Chicago	12/3
45	LaZelle Durden, Cinn.	Wyoming	12/17
45	Damon Stoudamire, Ariz.	Stanford	1/14
45	Randy Rutherford, Okla. St.	Kansas	3/5
44	Kerry Kittles, Villanova	Boston Col.	2/28

Team Points

No		Opponent	Date
156	S. Alabama	Prairie View (NCAA I)	12/2
148	Geo. Mason	Troy St. (NCAA I)	12/10
140	Geo. Mason	Macalester (NCAA III)	11/29
140	Southern Utah	S. Alabama (NCAA I)	12/10
140	Nicholls St.	Faith Baptist (NCCAA)	12/17
140	Troy St.	Chicago St. (NCAA I)	1/23
138	Murray St.	Campbellsville (NAIA I)	11/30
137	UCLA	George Mason (NCAA I)	12/22
Three tied with 132 points each.			

TEAM
Scoring Offense

	Gm	W-L	Pts	Avg
TCU	27	16-11	2529	93.7
Southern-Baton Rouge	26	13-13	2425	93.3
Texas	30	23-7	2787	92.9
George Mason	27	7-20	2499	92.6
Troy St	27	11-16	2468	91.4
Nicholls St	30	24-6	2709	90.3
Texas Tech	30	20-10	2664	88.8
Stephen F. Austin St.	28	14-14	2461	87.9
Arkansas	39	32-7	3416	87.6
UCLA	33	31-2	2889	87.5
Kentucky	33	28-5	2884	87.4
Murray St	30	21-9	2509	86.9
Maryland	34	26-8	2946	86.6
Connecticut	33	28-5	2837	86.0

Scoring Defense

	Gm	W-L	Pts	Avg
Princeton	26	16-10	1501	57.7
Wisconsin-Green Bay	30	22-8	1767	58.9
Temple	30	19-11	1792	59.7
Miami-OH	30	23-7	1827	60.9
Manhattan	31	26-5	1929	62.2
Clemson	28	15-13	1749	62.5
Saint Louis	31	23-8	1940	62.6
College of Charleston	29	23-6	1819	62.7
Wake Forest	32	26-6	2011	62.8
Texas-Pan Am	28	14-14	1769	63.2
SW Missouri St	27	16-11	1707	63.2
Tennessee	27	11-16	1711	63.4
Louisiana Tech	27	14-13	1718	63.6
Evansville	27	18-9	1719	63.7

Scoring Margin

	Off	Def	Margin
Kentucky	87.4	69.0	+18.4
Massachusetts	80.9	65.7	+15.2
Penn	82.2	67.5	+14.7
UCLA	87.5	73.9	+13.6
Montana St	84.2	70.8	+13.4
Evansville	77.0	63.7	+13.3
Saint Louis	75.8	62.6	+13.2
Manhattan	75.3	62.2	+13.1
Kansas	83.0	70.0	+13.0
Oklahoma St.	77.3	64.3	+13.0
Maryland	86.6	73.9	+12.7
Utah	77.6	64.9	+12.7
Nicholls St	90.3	78.0	+12.3
Texas	92.9	80.8	+12.1

Other Men's 1995 Tournaments

NIT Tournament

The 58th annual National Invitation Tournament had a 32-team field. First three rounds played on home courts of higher seeded teams. Semifinal, Third Place and Championship games played March 27 and 29 at Madison Square Garden in New York.

1st Round

at Bradley 86	2OT	Eastern Michigan 85
at Canisius 83		Seton Hall 71
Coppin St. 75	OT	at St. Joseph's 68
Illinois St. 93	OT	at Utah St. 87
at Iowa 96		DePaul 87
Marquette 68		at Auburn 61
at Nebraska 69		Georgia 61
at New Mexico St. 97		Colorado 83
at Ohio Univ. 83		George Washington 71
at Penn St. 62		Miami-FL 56
at Providence 72		Col. of Charleston 67
at St. Bonaventure 75		Southern Miss. 70
at South Florida 74		St. John's 67
at UTEP 90		Montana 60
at Virginia Tech 62		Clemson 54
at Washington St. 94		Texas Tech 82

2nd Round

Canisius 55		at Bradley 53
at Iowa 66		Ohio Univ. 62
at Marquette 70		St. Bonaventure 61
at New Mexico St. 92	OT	UTEP 89
Penn St. 65		at Nebraska 59
at South Florida 75		Coppin St. 59
Virginia Tech 91		at Providence 78
Washington St. 83		at Illinois St. 80

Quarterfinals

at Canisius 89		Washington St. 80
at Marquette 57	OT	South Florida 50
Penn St. 67		at Iowa 64
at Virginia Tech 64		New Mexico St. 61

Semifinals

Marquette 87		Penn St. 79
Virginia Tech 71		Canisius 59

Third Place

Penn St. 66		Canisius 62

Championship

Virginia Tech 65	OT	Marquette 64

Most Valuable Players

NIT
Shawn Smith
Virginia Tech guard

NCAA Division II
William Wilson
CS-Riverside forward

NCAA Division III
Ernie Peavy
WI-Platteville guard

NAIA Division I	**NAIA Division II**
James Cason	Mark Galloway
Birmingham-Southern center	Bethel (Ind.) guard

NCAA Division II

The eight regional winners of the 48-team field: NORTHEAST— New Hampshire College (27-5); EAST— Indiana, Pa. (28-1); SOUTH ATLANTIC— Norfolk St., Va. (26-5); SOUTH— Alabama A&M (29-2); SOUTH CENTRAL— Central Missouri (24-7); GREAT LAKES— Southern Indiana (26-4); NORTH CENTRAL— Morningside, Iowa (24-7); WEST— Cal St. Riverside (24-5).

After a 15-year run in Springfield, Mass., the Elite Eight was played March 22-25, in Louisville, Ky. There was no Third Place game.

Quarterfinals

Indiana-PA 90		Central Missouri 79
CS-Riverside 71		Morningside 58
Norfolk St. 85		Alabama A&M 67
Southern Ind. 108		N.H. College 93

Semifinals

CS-Riverside 73		Indiana-PA 69
Southern Ind. 89		Norfolk St. 81

Championship

Southern Ind. 71		CS-Riverside 63

NCAA Division III

For the first time, 64 teams played into the 32-team Division III field. The four sectional winners: ATLANTIC— Rowan, N.J. (26-3); NORTHEAST— Trinity, Conn. (25-3); MIDWEST— Manchester, Ind. (30-0); SOUTH— Wisconsin-Platteville (29-0).

The Final Four was played March 17-18, in Buffalo, N.Y.

Semifinals

WI-Platteville 82		Trinity 59
Manchester 79		Rowan 66

Third Place

Rowan 105		Trinity 72

Championship

WI-Platteville 69		Manchester 55

NAIA Division I

The quarterfinalists, in alphabetical order, after two rounds of the 32-team NAIA tournament: Arkansas Tech (28-5); Belmont, Tenn. (36-1); Birmingham-Southern, Ala. (32-2); Georgia Southwestern (30-4); The Master's, Calif. (31-4); Montana St. Northern (17-18); Oklahoma City (30-2); Pfeiffer, N.C. (23-7).

All tournament games played, March 14-20, at the Mabee Center in Tulsa. There was no Third Place game.

Quarterfinals: Arkansas Tech 87, Montana St-Northern 67; Belmont 91, The Master's 72; Birm-Southern 109, GA-Southwestern 76; Pfeiffer 92, Oklahoma City 78.

Semifinals: Birm-Southern 90, Belmont 80; Pfeiffer 68, Arkansas Tech 58.

Championship: Birm-Southern 92, Pfeiffer 76.

NAIA Division II

The semifinalists, in alphabetical order, after two rounds of the 32-team NAIA tournament: Bethel, Ind. (36-2); Northern St., S.D. (29-4); Northwest Nazarene, Id. (26-6); William Jewell, Mo. (29-9).

All tournament games played, March 8-14, at Nampa, Idaho. There was no Third Place game.

Semifinals: Bethel 96, William Jewell 87; NW Nazarene 67, Northern St. 62.

Championship: Bethel 103, NW Nazarene 95 (OT).

Ending Is Perfection For UConn

by Wendy Parker

They will go down in history as the second women's Division I basketball team to go undefeated and win an NCAA national championship, but the Connecticut Huskies accomplished so much more than a perfect 35-0 season in 1995.

For the first time in the short history of the women's tournament, everybody from the coach on down to the last player off the bench emerged as celebrities in a sport that has been perpetually overshadowed by high-profile men's college and professional teams.

There have been individuals, such as USC phenom Cheryl Miller a decade ago and Texas Tech's Sheryl Swoopes in 1993, who have gotten considerable ink and prime time television exposure for their basketball exploits. But Connecticut, located in the backyard of the New York City media market and feasting off a press corps more alert to the accomplishments of women athletes, might have changed all that.

A full month after their dramatic, come-from-behind, 70-64 win over Tennessee in the NCAA title game in Minneapolis, the Huskies still were the object of their fans' adulation. Nearly 100,000 crammed the streets of downtown Hartford on April 29 for a victory parade.

The week after bringing home the trophy, UConn players were the darlings of the network TV talk show circuit. While Player of the Year Rebecca Lobo traded one-liners with David Letterman, her teammates were showing Kathie Lee Gifford and Regis Philbin how to throw a bounce pass.

Lobo, a smooth 6-4 forward with a consistent perimeter shot and a 4.0 grade-point average, attracted most of the notice. She concluded her career as the Big East's all-time leading scorer, rebounder and shot blocker, but her exemplary off-the-court demeanor and willingness to serve as a role model for youngsters triggered much of UConn's appeal. The nation subsequently found out about her reading profiles in *Sports Illustrated*, *People* and *Newsweek*.

"I'd like to thank Rebecca Lobo for giving me the opportunity to go around the country and tell people that I'm Rebecca Lobo's coach," Geno Auriemma said after the season.

Robert Benson

The UConn starting five (clockwise from bottom): **Pam Webber, Kara Wolters, Jamelle Elliott, Jennifer Rizzotti** and **Rebecca Lobo.**

Auriemma and the Huskies grabbed the No. 1 spot in the polls on Jan. 16 when they defeated No. 1 Tennessee, 77-66 at sold-out Gampel Pavilion in Storrs.

Seven weeks later, they met again in the NCAA final before 18,023 at the Target Center. With Lobo in foul trouble early (three fouls in the first seven minutes), the Lady Vols took a 38-32 halftime lead and were well-positioned to win their fourth national championship in nine years.

The second half, however, was a different story. With their dream season on the line, UConn outhustled the SEC champs on the boards, stopped their lethal transition game in its tracks and pressured Vols' coach Pat Summitt into the fatal decision to pound the ball inside.

Lobo recovered to lead all scorers with 17 points, but it was gutty, 5-foot-5 junior point guard Jennifer Rizzotti who reversed Tennessee's momentum in the final five minutes— scoring on two long drives that helped erase a nine-point Vols lead. Her rebound and coast-to-coast layup with 1:51 left gave UConn the lead for good at 63-61.

"I hope they get the recognition they deserve for this," said Auriemma, after the title was won. "It couldn't have happened to a nicer bunch of kids."

Wendy Parker covers women's college basketball for the *Atlanta Journal-Constitution*.

Final Regular Season AP Women's Top 25 Poll

Taken **before** start of NCAA tournament.

The sportswriters & broadcasters poll: first place votes in parentheses; records through Sunday, March 12, 1995; total points (based on 25 for 1st, 24 for 2nd, etc.); record in NCAA tourney and team lost to; head coach (career years and record including 1995 postseason), and preseason ranking. Teams in **bold** type went on to reach NCAA Final Four.

		Mar.12 Record	Points	NCAA Recap	Head Coach	Preseason Rank
1	**Connecticut** (32)	29-0	800	6-0	Geno Auriemma (10 yrs: 227-81)	4
2	Colorado	27-2	746	3-1 (Georgia)	Ceal Barry (16 yrs: 323-163)	11
3	**Tennessee**	29-2	742	5-1 (UConn)	Pat Summitt (21 yrs: 564-129)	1
4	**Stanford**	26-2	695	4-1 (UConn)	Tara VanDerveer (17 yrs: 403-113)	5
5	Texas Tech	30-3	647	3-1 (Tennessee)	Marsha Sharp (13 yrs: 302-106)	9
6	Vanderbilt	26-6	644	2-1 (Purdue)	Jim Foster (17 yrs: 353-153)	12
7	Penn St.	25-4	584	1-1 (N.C. State)	Rene Portland (19 yrs: 438-140)	10
8	Louisiana Tech	26-4	583	2-1 (Virginia)	Leon Barmore (13 yrs: 366-61)	3
9	Western Kentucky	26-3	557	2-1 (Tennessee)	Paul Sanderford (13 yrs: 324-98)	21
10	Virginia	24-4	522	3-1 (UConn)	Debbie Ryan (18 yrs: 413-140)	7
11	North Carolina	28-4	504	2-1 (Stanford)	Sylvia Hatchell (20 yrs: 444-181)	6
12	**Georgia**	24-4	443	4-1 (Tennessee)	Andy Landers (16 yrs: 389-119)	19
13	Alabama	20-8	391	2-1 (UConn)	Rick Moody (6 yrs: 126-56)	8
14	Washington	23-8	364	2-1 (Texas Tech)	Chris Gobrecht (16 yrs: 311-168)	17
15	Arkansas	22-6	317	1-1 (Washington)	Gary Blair (10 yrs: 248-64)	NR
16	Purdue	21-7	306	3-1 (Stanford)	Lin Dunn (24 yrs: 427-246)	2
17	Florida	23-8	281	1-1 (Virginia)	Carol Ross (5 yrs: 97-50)	14
18	George Washington	24-5	276	2-1 (Colorado)	Joe McKeown (8 yrs: 176-65)	18
19	Mississippi	21-7	193	0-1 (Drake)	Van Chancellor (17 yrs: 405-132)	24
20	Duke	21-8	186	1-1 (Alabama)	Gail Goestenkors (3 yrs: 50-35)	NR
21	Oregon St.	20-7	158	1-1 (Western Ky.)	Aki Hill (17 yrs: 274-206)	31
22	San Diego St.	24-5	116	0-1 (Montana)	Beth Burns (6 yrs: 108-68)	37t
23	Kansas	20-10	95	0-1 (Wisconsin)	Marian Washington (22 yrs: 410-242)	15
24	N.C. State	19-9	58	2-1 (Georgia)	Kay Yow (24 yrs: 488-192)	NR
25	Old Dominion	27-5	27	0-1 (Florida Int'l)	Wendy Larry (11 yrs: 209-114)	NR

Others receiving votes: 26. **Florida Int'l** (26-4, 19 pts); 27. **Utah** (23-6, 18); 28. **Oklahoma** (21-8, 17) and **USC** (18-9, 17); 30. **San Francisco** (24-4, 16); 31. **Oregon** (18-9, 15); 32. **Drake** (24-5, 10); 33. **DePaul** (20-8, 9) and **Southern Miss.** (21-8, 9); 35. **SMU** (20-9, 7) and **Wisconsin** (19-8, 7); 37. **Memphis** (21-7, 6) and **Ohio St.** (17-13, 6); 39. **Seton Hall** (23-8, 4); 40. **Toledo** (24-6, 3).

NCAA Women's Division I Leaders

Includes games through NCAA and WNIT tourneys.

Scoring

	Cl	Gm	Pts	Avg
Koko Lahanas, CS-Fullerton	Jr.	29	778	26.8
Latasha Byears, DePaul	Jr.	28	740	26.4
Cornelia Gayden, LSU	Sr.	27	697	25.8
Kim Mays, Eastern Ky	Sr.	28	719	25.7
Anita Maxwell, N. Mexico St.	Jr.	29	738	25.4
DeShawne Blocker, E. Tenn.	Sr.	30	730	24.3
Gray Harris, SE Missouri	Jr.	26	630	24.2
Korie Hlede, Duquesne	Fr.	26	628	24.2
Patty Stoffey, Loyola-MD	Sr.	29	697	24.0
Shannon Johnson, S. Carolina	Jr.	27	646	23.9
Melissa Gower, L. Beach St.	Sr.	27	637	23.6
Sha Hopson, Grambling St.	Sr.	28	655	23.4
Angela Aycock, Kansas	Sr.	31	716	23.1
Amy Burnett, Wyoming	Sr.	27	614	22.7
Carolyn Aldridge, Tenn St.	Sr.	29	657	22.7

Rebounds

	Cl	Gm	No	Avg
Tera Sheriff, Jackson St.	Sr.	29	401	13.8
Rene Doctor, Coppin St.	Sr.	25	344	13.8
Melissa Gower, L. Beach St.	Sr.	27	352	13.0
Oberon Pitterson, Western Ill	Sr.	28	354	12.6
Dana Wynne, Seton Hall	So.	33	415	12.6
Joskeen Garner, Northwestern St.	Jr.	30	376	12.5
Niamh Darcy, VCU	Sr.	30	363	12.1
Scherrie Jackson, Beth-Cookman	So.	25	298	11.9
Stephaine Minor, Murray St.	So.	21	245	11.7
Carrie Coffman, Bradley	Sr.	26	302	11.6

Assists

	Cl	Gm	No	Avg
Andrea Nagy, Florida Int'l	Sr.	32	315	9.8
Dayna Smith, Rhode Island	Jr.	27	239	8.9
Tina Nicholson, Penn St.	Jr.	31	250	8.1
Tabitha Truesdale, Texas Tech	Sr.	37	281	7.6
Tiffany Martin, Georgia Tech	So.	30	220	7.3
Lori Goerlitz, Marquette	Sr.	31	222	7.2
Dani Maziur, New Orleans	Jr.	27	191	7.1
Boky Vidic, Oregon St.	Jr.	29	203	7.0
Gretchen Hollifield, Wake Forest	Jr.	21	147	7.0
Gwynn Hobbs, UNLV	Sr.	26	180	6.9
Heather Fiore, Canisius	So.	27	185	6.9

High-Point Games

No		Opponent	Date
51	Carolyn Aldridge, Tennessee	W. Forest	12/2
51	Keri Chaconas, George Mason	E. Carolina	2/17
49	Cornelia Gayden, LSU	Jackson St.	2/9
48	Koko Lahanas, CS-Fullerton	Cal Poly-SLO	2/14
46	Corneila Gayden, LSU	S. Carolina	1/14

1995 NCAA BASKETBALL WOMEN'S DIVISION I

MIDWEST — DES MOINES

1ST ROUND March 16-17	2ND ROUND March 18-19	REGIONALS March 23-25
1 Colorado 83	Colorado 78	Colorado 79 (OT)
16 Holy Cross 49		
8 Utah 47	SW Mo. St. 34	
9 SW Mo. St. 49		
5 Drake 87	Drake 93	G. Washington 61
12 Mississippi (OT) 81		
4 G. Washington 87	G. Washington 96	
13 DePaul 79		
		Colorado 79
6 Oregon 65	Louisville 68	Georgia 98
11 Louisville 67		
3 Georgia 81	Georgia 81	
14 Indiana 64		
7 N.C. State 77	N.C. State 76	N.C. State 79
10 Marquette 62		
2 Penn St. 75	Penn St. 74	Georgia 82
15 Jackson St. 62		

Georgia 51

MIDEAST — KNOXVILLE

1ST ROUND March 16-17	2ND ROUND March 18-19	REGIONALS March 23-25
1 Tennessee 96	Tennessee 70	Tennessee 87
16 Fla. A&M 59		
8 Old Dominion 76	Fla. Int'l 44	
9 Fla. Int'l 81		
5 Oregon St. 88	Oregon St. 78	Western Ky. 65
12 Tenn. St. (OT) 75		
4 Western Ky. 77	Western Ky. 85	
13 Toledo 63		
		Tennessee 80
6 Arkansas 67	Arkansas 50	Washington 52
11 San Francisco 58		
3 Washington 73	Washington 54	
14 Ohio 56		
7 Kansas 72	Wisconsin 65	Texas Tech 67
10 Wisconsin 73		
2 Texas Tech 87	Texas Tech 88	Texas Tech 59
15 Tulane 72		

Tennessee 73

EAST — STORRS, CONN.

1ST ROUND March 16-17	2ND ROUND March 18-19	REGIONALS March 23-25
1 UConn 105	UConn 91	UConn 87
16 Maine 75		
8 Va. Tech 62	Va. Tech 45	
9 St. Joseph's 52		
5 Duke 76	Duke 120 (4OT)	Alabama 56
12 Oklahoma St. 64		
4 Alabama 82	Alabama 121	
13 Mt. St. Mary's 55		
		UConn 87
6 Florida 89	Florida 67	Virginia 63
11 Radford 49		
3 Virginia 71	Virginia 72	
14 Dartmouth 68		
7 Oklahoma 90	Oklahoma 36	La. Tech 62
10 Loyola-MD 55		
2 La. Tech 90	La. Tech 48	Virginia 63
15 Furman 52		

UConn 87

WEST — LOS ANGELES

1ST ROUND March 16-17	2ND ROUND March 18-19	REGIONALS March 23-25
1 Vanderbilt 90	Vanderbilt 95	Vanderbilt 66
16 Northern Ill. 44		
8 Memphis 74	Memphis 68	
9 USC 72		
5 San Diego St. 46	Montana 51	Purdue 67
12 Montana 57		
4 Purdue 74	Purdue 62	
13 Portland 59		
		Purdue 58
6 Seton Hall 73	Seton Hall 45	N. Carolina 71
11 S.F. Austin 63		
3 N. Carolina 89	N. Carolina 59	
14 Western Ill. 48		
7 So. Miss. 95	SMU 73	Stanford 81
10 SMU (OT) 96		
2 Stanford 88	Stanford 95	Stanford 69
15 UC-Irvine 55		

Stanford 60

NATIONAL CHAMPIONSHIP

UConn 70
Tennessee 64

FINAL FOUR
at the Target Center in Minneapolis

Semifinals: April 1
Final: April 2

WOMEN'S FINAL FOUR
at Target Center in Minneapolis (April 1-2).

Semifinals
Connecticut 87 ....Stanford 60
Tennessee 73 ....Georgia 51

Championship
Connecticut 70.......................................Tennessee 64

Final Records: UConn (35-0), Tennessee (34-3), Georgia (28-5); Stanford (30-3).

Most Outstanding Player: Rebecca Lobo, UConn senior forward. SEMIFINAL— 37 minutes, 17 points, 9 rebounds, 3 assists, 3 steals, 2 blocked shots, 1 foul; FINAL— 28 minutes, 17 points, 8 rebounds, 2 assists, 2 blocked shots, 4 fouls.

All-Tournament Team: Lobo, center Kara Wolters, forward Jamelle Elliott and guard Jennifer Rizzotti of UConn; and forward Nikki McCray of Tennessee.

NCAA Championship Game
Tennessee 64

	Min	FG M-A	FT M-A	Pts	Reb O-T	A	F
Nikki McCray	31	3-12	1-2	7	3-5	4	2
Pashen Thompson	10	1-1	2-2	4	3-3	1	2
Dana Johnson	33	3-11	3-3	9	3-10	0	2
Michelle Marciniak	30	3-11	1-3	8	0-0	5	3
Latina Davis	31	5-12	0-1	11	3-5	1	4
Vonda Ward	16	2-5	2-2	6	1-2	1	3
Tiffani Johnson	21	3-7	1-1	7	2-5	1	3
Michelle Johnson	13	2-3	0-0	5	0-3	1	2
Laurie Milligan	10	1-3	2-2	4	0-0	2	0
Abby Conklin	5	1-1	0-0	3	1-1	0	1
TOTALS	200	24-66	12-16	64	16-34	16	22

Three-point FG: 4-14 (Conklin 1-1, M. Johnson 1-2, Davis 1-4, Marciniak 1-6, McCray 0-1); **Team Rebounds:** 3; **Blocked Shots:** 1 (T. Johnson); **Turnovers:** 14 (Marciniak 3, McCray 3, Conklin 2, T. Johnson 2, Davis, D. Johnson, Milligan, Thompson); **Steals:** 6 (D. Johnson 2, Marciniak 2, Davis, McCray). **Percentages:** 2-Pt FG (.385); 3-Pt FG (.286); Total FG (.364); Free Throws (.750).

Connecticut 70

	Min	FG M-A	FT M-A	Pts	Reb O-T	A	F
Jamelle Elliott	39	5-7	3-4	13	2-7	3	3
Rebecca Lobo	28	5-10	7-8	17	2-8	2	4
Kara Wolters	31	4-9	2-4	10	1-3	0	4
Jennifer Rizzotti	32	6-8	2-2	15	0-3	3	3
Pam Webber	17	0-1	0-0	0	1-1	2	1
Nykesha Sales	33	4-12	1-4	10	2-6	3	3
Carla Berube	20	1-6	3-5	5	2-3	2	0
TOTALS	200	25-53	18-27	70	10-31	15	18

Three-point FG: 2-10 (Rizzotti 1-2, Sales 1-4, Berube 0-1, Webber 0-1, Lobo 0-2); **Team Rebounds:** 12; **Blocked Shots:** 4 (Lobo 2, Wolters 2); **Turnovers:** 16 (Elliott 5, Rizzotti 4, Berube 3, Lobo 2, Sales, Wolters); **Steals:** 7 (Rizzotti 3, Sales 3, Elliott). **Percentages:** 2-Pt FG (.535); 3-Pt FG (.200); Total FG (.472); Free Throws (.667).

Tennessee (SEC) ....38 26— **64**
Connecticut (Big East) ....32 38— **70**

Technical Fouls: None. **Officials:** Dee Kantner, Larry Sheppard. **Attendance:** 18,038. **TV Rating:** 5.7/15 share (CBS).

Final *USA Today*/CNN Coaches Poll
Taken **after** NCAA tournament.

Voted on by panel of 40 women's coaches and media following the NCAA tournament: first place votes in parentheses with final overall records.

		W-L			W-L
1	UConn (40)	35-0	14	Alabama	22-9
2	Tennessee	34-3	15	G. Washington	26-6
3	Stanford	30-3	16	Penn St	26-5
4	Georgia	28-5	17	Duke	22-9
5	Colorado	30-3	18	Florida	24-9
6	Virginia	27-5	19	N.C. State	21-10
7	Texas Tech	33-4	20	Arkansas	23-7
8	Vanderbilt	28-7	21	Oregon St	21-8
9	Purdue	24-8	22	Mississippi	21-8
10	Louisiana Tech	28-5	23	Kansas	20-11
11	N. Carolina	30-5	24	Drake	25-6
12	Western Ky.	28-4	25	Montana	26-7
13	Washington	25-9			

Annual Awards
Player of the Year
Rebecca Lobo, UConn......................AP, Naismith, USBWA, Wade, WBCA, WBNS

Note: The Wade Trophy is awarded for academics and community service as well as player performance.

Coaches of the Year
Geno Auriemma, UConn ....AP, Naismith, USBWA
Gary Blair, Arkansas ....WBCA, WBNS

Consensus All-America Team
The NCAA Division I players cited most frequently by the Associated Press, U.S. Basketball Writers Assn., the Women's Basketball Coaches Assn. and the Women's Basketball News Service. Holdovers from the 1993-94 All-America first team are in **bold** type; (*) indicates unanimous first team selection.

First Team
		Class	Hgt	Pos
Niesa Johnson, Alabama		Sr.	5-9	G
Rebecca Lobo, UConn*		Sr.	6-4	F
Nikki McCray, Tennessee*		Sr.	5-11	F
Wendy Palmer, Virginia		Jr.	6-2	F
Charlotte Smith, N. Carolina		Sr.	6-0	F

Second Team
		Class	Hgt	Pos
Angela Aycock, Kansas		Sr.	6-2	G/F
Dana Johnson, Tennessee		Sr.	6-2	F
Vickie Johnson, La. Tech		Jr.	5-9	G/F
Andrea Nagy, Florida Int'l		Sr.	5-7	G
Shelley Sheetz, Colorado		Sr.	5-6	G

Other Women's Tournaments
WNIT (Mar. 25 at Amarillo, Texas): Final— Texas A&M 85, Northwestern St. (La.) 81.

NCAA Division II (Mar. 25 at Fargo, N.D.): Final— North Dakota St. 98, Portland St. 85.

NCAA Division III (Mar. 18 at Eau Claire, WI): Final— Capital (Ohio) 59, Wisconsin-Oshkosh 55.

NAIA Division I (Mar. 21 at Jackson, Tenn.): Final— Southern Nazarene (Okla.) 78, SE Oklahoma 77.

NAIA Division II (Mar. 14 at Monmouth, Ore.): Final— Western Oregon 75, Northwest Nazarene 67.

THE 1996 INFORMATION PLEASE SPORTS ALMANAC

COLLEGE BASKETBALL STATISTICS

SEC B

THROUGH THE YEARS

1901-1995

NCAA'S • ALL-TIME LEADERS

PAGE 301

National Champions

The Helms Foundation of Los Angeles, under the direction of founder Bill Schroeder, selected national college basketball champions from 1942-82 and researched retroactive picks from 1901-41. The first NIT tournament and then the NCAA tournament have settled the national championship since 1938, but there are four years (1939, '40, '44 and '54) where the Helms selections differ.

Multiple champions (1901-37): Chicago, Columbia and Wisconsin (3); Kansas, Minnesota, Notre Dame, Penn, Pittsburgh, Syracuse and Yale (2).

Multiple champions (since 1938): UCLA (11); Kentucky (6); Indiana (5); North Carolina (3); Cincinnati, Duke, Kansas, Louisville, N.C. State, Oklahoma A&M (now Oklahoma St.) and San Francisco (2).

Year		Record	Head Coach	Outstanding Player
1901	Yale	10-4	No coach	G.M. Clark, F
1902	Minnesota	11-0	Louis Cooke	W.C. Deering, F
1903	Yale	15-1	W.H. Murphy	R.B. Hyatt, F
1904	Columbia	17-1	No coach	Harry Fisher, F
1905	Columbia	19-1	No coach	Harry Fisher, F
1906	Dartmouth	16-2	No coach	George Grebenstein, F
1907	Chicago	22-2	Joseph Raycroft	John Schommer, C
1908	Chicago	21-2	Joseph Raycroft	John Schommer, C
1909	Chicago	12-0	Joseph Raycroft	John Schommer, C
1910	Columbia	11-1	Harry Fisher	Ted Kiendl, F
1911	St. John's-NY	14-0	Claude Allen	John Keenan, F/C
1912	Wisconsin	15-0	Doc Meanwell	Otto Stangel, F
1913	Navy	9-0	Louis Wenzell	Laurence Wild, F
1914	Wisconsin	15-0	Doc Meanwell	Gene Van Gent, C
1915	Illinois	16-0	Ralph Jones	Ray Woods, G
1916	Wisconsin	20-1	Doc Meanwell	George Levis, F
1917	Washington St	25-1	Doc Bohler	Roy Bohler, G
1918	Syracuse	16-1	Edmund Dollard	Joe Schwarzer, G
1919	Minnesota	13-0	Louis Cooke	Arnold Oss, F
1920	Penn	22-1	Lon Jourdet	George Sweeney, F
1921	Penn	21-2	Edward McNichol	Danny McNichol, G
1922	Kansas	16-2	Phog Allen	Paul Endacott, G
1923	Kansas	17-1	Phog Allen	Paul Endacott, G
1924	North Carolina	25-0	Bo Shepard	Jack Cobb, F
1925	Princeton	21-2	Al Wittmer	Art Loeb, G
1926	Syracuse	19-1	Lew Andreas	Vic Hanson, F
1927	Notre Dame	19-1	George Keogan	John Nyikos, C
1928	Pittsburgh	21-0	Doc Carlson	Chuck Hyatt, F
1929	Montana St.	36-2	Schubert Dyche	John (Cat) Thompson, F
1930	Pittsburgh	23-2	Doc Carlson	Chuck Hyatt, F
1931	Northwestern	16-1	Dutch Lonborg	Joe Reiff, C
1932	Purdue	17-1	Piggy Lambert	John Wooden, G
1933	Kentucky	20-3	Adolph Rupp	Forest Sale, F
1934	Wyoming	26-3	Willard Witte	Les Witte, G
1935	NYU	19-1	Howard Cann	Sid Gross, F
1936	Notre Dame	22-2-1	George Keogan	John Moir, F
1937	Stanford	25-2	John Bunn	Hank Luisetti, F

Year		Record	Winner	Head Coach	Outstanding Player
1938	Temple	23-2	NIT	James Usilton	Meyer Bloom, G
1939	Oregon	29-5	NCAA	Howard Hobson	Slim Wintermute, C
	& LIU-Brooklyn (Helms)	24-0	NIT	Clair Bee	Irv Torgoff, F
1940	Indiana	20-3	NCAA	Branch McCracken	Marv Huffman, G
	& USC (Helms)	20-3	*	Sam Barry	Ralph Vaughn, F
1941	Wisconsin	20-3	NCAA	Bud Foster	Gene Englund, F

*USC was beaten by Kansas in the West regional of the NCAA tournament.

National Champions (Cont.)

Year	Winner	Record	Winner	Head Coach	Outstanding Player
1942	Stanford	27-4	NCAA	Everett Dean	Jim Pollard, F
1943	Wyoming	31-2	NCAA	Everett Shelton	Kenny Sailors, G
1944	Utah	21-4	NCAA	Vadal Peterson	Arnie Ferrin, F
	& Army (Helms)	15-0	**	Ed Kelleher	Dale Hall, F
1945	Oklahoma A&M	27-4	NCAA	Hank Iba	Bob Kurland, C
1946	Oklahoma A&M	31-2	NCAA	Hank Iba	Bob Kurland, C
1947	Holy Cross	27-3	NCAA	Doggie Julian	George Kaftan, F
1948	Kentucky	36-3	NCAA	Adolph Rupp	Ralph Beard, G
1949	Kentucky	32-2	NCAA	Adolph Rupp	Alex Groza, C
1950	CCNY	24-5	NCAA & NIT	Nat Holman	Irwin Dambrot, G
1951	Kentucky	32-2	NCAA	Adolph Rupp	Bill Spivey, C
1952	Kansas	28-3	NCAA	Phog Allen	Clyde Lovellette, C
1953	Indiana	23-3	NCAA	Branch McCracken	Don Schlundt, C
1954	La Salle	26-4	NCAA	Ken Loeffler	Tom Gola, F
	& Kentucky (Helms)	25-0	***	Adolph Rupp	Cliff Hagan, G
1955	San Francisco	28-1	NCAA	Phil Woolpert	Bill Russell, C
1956	San Francisco	29-0	NCAA	Phil Woolpert	Bill Russell, C
1957	North Carolina	32-0	NCAA	Frank McGuire	Lennie Rosenbluth, F
1958	Kentucky	23-6	NCAA	Adolph Rupp	Vern Hatton, G
1959	California	25-4	NCAA	Pete Newell	Darrall Imhoff, C
1960	Ohio St	25-3	NCAA	Fred Taylor	Jerry Lucas, C
1961	Cincinnati	27-3	NCAA	Ed Jucker	Bob Wiesenhahn, F
1962	Cincinnati	29-2	NCAA	Ed Jucker	Paul Hogue, C
1963	Loyola-IL	29-2	NCAA	George Ireland	Jerry Harkness, F
1964	UCLA	30-0	NCAA	John Wooden	Walt Hazzard, G
1965	UCLA	28-2	NCAA	John Wooden	Gail Goodrich, G
1966	Texas Western	28-1	NCAA	Don Haskins	Bobby Joe Hill, G
1967	UCLA	30-0	NCAA	John Wooden	Lew Alcindor, C
1968	UCLA	29-1	NCAA	John Wooden	Lew Alcindor, C
1969	UCLA	29-1	NCAA	John Wooden	Lew Alcindor, C
1970	UCLA	28-2	NCAA	John Wooden	Sidney Wicks, F
1971	UCLA	29-1	NCAA	John Wooden	Sidney Wicks, F
1972	UCLA	30-0	NCAA	John Wooden	Bill Walton, C
1973	UCLA	30-0	NCAA	John Wooden	Bill Walton, C
1974	N.C. State	30-1	NCAA	Norm Sloan	David Thompson, F
1975	UCLA	28-3	NCAA	John Wooden	Dave Meyers, F
1976	Indiana	32-0	NCAA	Bob Knight	Scott May, F
1977	Marquette	25-7	NCAA	Al McGuire	Butch Lee, G
1978	Kentucky	30-2	NCAA	Joe B. Hall	Jack Givens, F
1979	Michigan St	26-6	NCAA	Jud Heathcote	Magic Johnson, G
1980	Louisville	33-3	NCAA	Denny Crum	Darrell Griffith, G
1981	Indiana	26-9	NCAA	Bob Knight	Isiah Thomas, G
1982	North Carolina	32-2	NCAA	Dean Smith	James Worthy, F
1983	N.C. State	26-10	NCAA	Jim Valvano	Sidney Lowe, G
1984	Georgetown	34-3	NCAA	John Thompson	Patrick Ewing, C
1985	Villanova	25-10	NCAA	Rollie Massimino	Ed Pinckney, C
1986	Louisville	32-7	NCAA	Denny Crum	Pervis Ellison, C
1987	Indiana	30-4	NCAA	Bob Knight	Steve Alford, G
1988	Kansas	27-11	NCAA	Larry Brown	Danny Manning, C
1989	Michigan	30-7	NCAA	Steve Fisher	Glen Rice, F
1990	UNLV	35-5	NCAA	Jerry Tarkanian	Larry Johnson, F
1991	Duke	32-7	NCAA	Mike Krzyzewski	Christian Laettner, F/C
1992	Duke	34-2	NCAA	Mike Krzyzewski	Christian Laettner, C
1993	North Carolina	34-4	NCAA	Dean Smith	Eric Montross, C
1994	Arkansas	31-3	NCAA	Nolan Richardson	Corliss Williamson, F
1995	UCLA	31-2	NCAA	Jim Harrick	Ed O'Bannon, F

**Army did not lift its policy against postseason play until accepting a bid to the 1961 NIT.
***Unbeaten Kentucky turned down a bid to the 1954 NCAA tournament after the NCAA declared seniors Cliff Hagan, Frank Ramsey and Lou Tsioropoulos ineligible for postseason play.

The Red Cross Benefit Games, 1943-45

For three seasons during World War II, the NCAA and NIT champions met in a benefit game at Madison Square Garden in New York to raise money for the Red Cross. The NCAA champs won all three games.

Year	Winner	Score	Loser
1943	Wyoming (NCAA)	52-47	St. John's (NIT)
1944	Utah (NCAA)	43-36	St. John's (NIT)
1945	Oklahoma A&M (NCAA)	52-44	DePaul (NIT)

NCAA Final Four

The NCAA basketball tournament began in 1939 under the sponsorship of the National Association of Basketball Coaches, but was taken over by the NCAA in 1940. From 1939-51, the winners of the Eastern and Western Regionals played for the national championship, while regional runners-up shared third place. The concept of a Final Four originated in 1952 when four teams qualified for the first national semifinals. Consolation games to determine overall third place were held between regional finalists from 1946-51 and then national semifinalists from 1952-81. Consolation games were discontinued in 1982.

Multiple champions: UCLA (11); Indiana and Kentucky (5); North Carolina (3); Cincinnati, Duke, Kansas, Louisville, N.C. State, Oklahoma A&M (now Oklahoma St.) and San Francisco (2).

Year	Champion	Runner-up	Score	Final Two	Third Place	
1939	Oregon	Ohio St.	46-33	@ Evanston, IL	Oklahoma	Villanova
1940	Indiana	Kansas	60-42	@ Kansas City	Duquesne	USC
1941	Wisconsin	Washington St.	39-34	@ Kansas City	Arkansas	Pittsburgh
1942	Stanford	Dartmouth	53-38	@ Kansas City	Colorado	Kentucky
1943	Wyoming	Georgetown	46-34	@ New York	DePaul	Texas
1944	Utah	Dartmouth	42-40 (OT)	@ New York	Iowa St.	Ohio St.
1945	Oklahoma A&M	NYU	49-45	@ New York	Arkansas	Ohio St.

Year	Champion	Runner-up	Score	Final Two	Third Place	Fourth Place
1946	Oklahoma A&M	North Carolina	43-40	@ New York	Ohio St.	California
1947	Holy Cross	Oklahoma	58-47	@ New York	Texas	CCNY
1948	Kentucky	Baylor	58-42	@ New York	Holy Cross	Kansas St.
1949	Kentucky	Oklahoma A&M	46-36	@ Seattle	Illinois	Oregon St.
1950	CCNY	Bradley	71-68	@ New York	N.C. State	Baylor
1951	Kentucky	Kansas St.	68-58	@ Minneapolis	Illinois	Oklahoma A&M

Year	Champion	Runner-up	Score	Third Place	Fourth Place	Final Four
1952	Kansas	St. John's	80-63	Illinois	Santa Clara	@ Seattle
1953	Indiana	Kansas	69-68	Washington	LSU	@ Kansas City
1954	La Salle	Bradley	92-76	Penn St.	USC	@ Kansas City
1955	San Francisco	La Salle	77-63	Colorado	Iowa	@ Kansas City
1956	San Francisco	Iowa	83-71	Temple	SMU	@ Evanston, IL
1957	North Carolina	Kansas	54-53 (3OT)	San Francisco	Michigan St.	@ Kansas City
1958	Kentucky	Seattle	84-72	Temple	Kansas St.	@ Louisville
1959	California	West Virginia	71-70	Cincinnati	Louisville	@ Louisville
1960	Ohio St.	California	75-55	Cincinnati	NYU	@ San Francisco
1961	Cincinnati	Ohio St.	70-65 (OT)	St. Joseph's-PA	Utah	@ Kansas City
1962	Cincinnati	Ohio St.	71-59	Wake Forest	UCLA	@ Louisville
1963	Loyola-IL	Cincinnati	60-58 (OT)	Duke	Oregon St.	@ Louisville
1964	UCLA	Duke	98-83	Michigan	Kansas St.	@ Kansas City
1965	UCLA	Michigan	91-80	Princeton	Wichita St.	@ Portland, OR
1966	Texas Western	Kentucky	72-65	Duke	Utah	@ College Park, MD
1967	UCLA	Dayton	79-64	Houston	North Carolina	@ Louisville
1968	UCLA	North Carolina	78-55	Ohio St.	Houston	@ Los Angeles
1969	UCLA	Purdue	92-72	Drake	North Carolina	@ Louisville
1970	UCLA	Jacksonville	80-69	New Mexico St.	St. Bonaventure	@ College Park, MD
1971	UCLA	Villanova	68-62	Western Ky.	Kansas	@ Houston
1972	UCLA	Florida St.	81-76	North Carolina	Louisville	@ Los Angeles
1973	UCLA	Memphis St.	87-66	Indiana	Providence	@ St. Louis
1974	N.C. State	Marquette	76-64	UCLA	Kansas	@ Greensboro, NC
1975	UCLA	Kentucky	92-85	Louisville	Syracuse	@ San Diego
1976	Indiana	Michigan	86-68	UCLA	Rutgers	@ Philadelphia
1977	Marquette	North Carolina	67-59	UNLV	NC-Charlotte	@ Atlanta
1978	Kentucky	Duke	94-88	Arkansas	Notre Dame	@ St. Louis
1979	Michigan St.	Indiana St.	75-64	DePaul	Penn	@ Salt Lake City
1980	Louisville	UCLA	59-54	Purdue	Iowa	@ Indianapolis
1981	Indiana	North Carolina	63-50	Virginia	LSU	@ Philadelphia

Year	Champion	Runner-up	Score	Third Place		Final Four
1982	North Carolina	Georgetown	63-62	Houston	Louisville	@ New Orleans
1983	N.C. State	Houston	54-52	Georgia	Louisville	@ Albuquerque
1984	Georgetown	Houston	84-75	Kentucky	Virginia	@ Seattle
1985	Villanova	Georgetown	66-64	Memphis St.	St. John's	@ Lexington
1986	Louisville	Duke	72-69	Kansas	LSU	@ Dallas
1987	Indiana	Syracuse	74-73	Providence	UNLV	@ New Orleans
1988	Kansas	Oklahoma	83-79	Arizona	Duke	@ Kansas City
1989	Michigan	Seton Hall	80-79 (OT)	Duke	Illinois	@ Seattle
1990	UNLV	Duke	103-73	Arkansas	Georgia Tech	@ Denver
1991	Duke	Kansas	72-65	North Carolina	UNLV	@ Indianapolis
1992	Duke	Michigan	71-51	Cincinnati	Indiana	@ Minneapolis
1993	North Carolina	Michigan	77-71	Kansas	Kentucky	@ New Orleans
1994	Arkansas	Duke	76-72	Arizona	Florida	@ Charlotte
1995	UCLA	Arkansas	89-78	North Carolina	Oklahoma St.	@ Seattle

Note: Five teams have had their standing in the Final Four vacated for using ineligible players: 1961—St. Joseph's-PA (3rd place); 1971—Villanova (Runner-up) and Western Kentucky (3rd place); 1980—UCLA (Runner-up); 1985—Memphis St. (3rd place).

Most Outstanding Player

A Most Outstanding Player has been selected every year of the NCAA tournament. Winners who did not play for the tournament champion are listed in **bold** type. The 1939 and 1951 winners are unofficial and not recognized by the NCAA.

Multiple winners: Lew Alcindor (3); Alex Groza, Bob Kurland, Jerry Lucas and Bill Walton (2).

Year		Year		Year	
1939	**Jimmy Hull**, Ohio St.	1958	**Elgin Baylor**, Seattle	1977	Butch Lee, Marquette
1940	Marv Huffman, Indiana	1959	**Jerry West**, West Virginia	1978	Jack Givens, Kentucky
1941	John Kotz, Wisconsin	1960	Jerry Lucas, Ohio St.	1979	Magic Johnson, Michigan St.
1942	Howie Dallmar, Stanford	1961	Jerry Lucas, Ohio St.	1980	Darrell Griffith, Louisville
1943	Kenny Sailors, Wyoming	1962	Paul Hogue, Cincinnati	1981	Isiah Thomas, Indiana
1944	Arnie Ferrin, Utah	1963	**Art Heyman**, Duke	1982	James Worthy, N. Carolina
1945	Bob Kurland, Okla. A&M	1964	Walt Hazzard, UCLA	1983	Akeem Olajuwon, Houston
1946	Bob Kurland, Okla. A&M	1965	**Bill Bradley**, Princeton	1984	Patrick Ewing, Georgetown
1947	George Kaftan, Holy Cross	1966	**Jerry Chambers**, Utah	1985	Ed Pinckney, Villanova
1948	Alex Groza, Kentucky	1967	Lew Alcindor, UCLA	1986	Pervis Ellison, Louisville
1949	Alex Groza, Kentucky	1968	Lew Alcindor, UCLA	1987	Keith Smart, Indiana
1950	Irwin Dambrot, CCNY	1969	Lew Alcindor, UCLA	1988	Danny Manning, Kansas
1951	Bill Spivey, Kentucky	1970	Sidney Wicks, UCLA	1989	Glen Rice, Michigan
1952	Clyde Lovellette, Kansas	1971	**Howard Porter**, Villanova	1990	Anderson Hunt, UNLV
1953	**B.H. Born**, Kansas	1972	Bill Walton, UCLA	1991	Christian Laettner, Duke
1954	Tom Gola, La Salle	1973	Bill Walton, UCLA	1992	Bobby Hurley, Duke
1955	Bill Russell, San Francisco	1974	David Thompson, N.C. State	1993	Donald Williams, N. Carolina
1956	**Hal Lear**, Temple	1975	Richard Washington, UCLA	1994	Corliss Williamson, Arkansas
1957	**Wilt Chamberlain**, Kansas	1976	Kent Benson, Indiana	1995	Ed O'Bannon, UCLA

Note: Howard Porter (1971) was declared ineligible by the NCAA after the tournament and his award was vacated.

Final Four All-Decade Teams

To celebrate the 50th anniversary of the NCAA tournament in 1989, five All-Decade teams were selected by a blue ribbon panel of coaches and administrators. An All-Time Final Four team was also chosen.

Selection panel: Vic Bubas, Denny Crum, Wayne Duke, Dave Gavitt, Joe B. Hall, Jud Heathcote, Hank Iba, Pete Newell, Dean Smith, John Thompson and John Wooden.

All-1950s

	Years
Elgin Baylor, Seattle	1958
Wilt Chamberlain, Kansas	1957
Tom Gola, La Salle	1954
K.C. Jones, San Francisco	1955
Clyde Lovellette, Kansas	1952
Oscar Robertson, Cinn.	1959-60
Guy Rodgers, Temple	1958
Lennie Rosenbluth, N. Carolina	1957
Bill Russell, San Francisco	1955-56
Jerry West, West Virginia	1959

All-1970s

	Years
Kent Benson, Indiana	1976
Larry Bird, Indiana St.	1979
Jack Givens, Kentucky	1978
Magic Johnson, Mich. St.	1979
Marques Johnson, UCLA	1975-76
Scott May, Indiana	1976
David Thompson, N.C. State	1974
Bill Walton, UCLA	1972-74
Sidney Wicks, UCLA	1969-71
Keith Wilkes, UCLA	1972-74

All-Time Team

	Years
Lew Alcindor, UCLA	1967-69
Larry Bird, Indiana St.	1979
Wilt Chamberlain, Kansas	1957
Magic Johnson, Mich. St.	1979
Michael Jordan, N. Carolina	1982

All-1940s

	Years
Ralph Beard, Kentucky	1948-49
Howie Dallmar, Stanford	1942
Dwight Eddleman, Illinois	1949
Arnie Ferrin, Utah	1944
Alex Groza, Kentucky	1948-49
George Kaftan, Holy Cross	1947
Bob Kurland, Okla. A&M	1945-46
Jim Pollard, Stanford	1942
Kenny Sailors, Wyoming	1943
Gerry Tucker, Oklahoma	1947

All-1960s

	Years
Lew Alcindor, UCLA	1967-69
Bill Bradley, Princeton	1965
Gail Goodrich, UCLA	1964-65
John Havlicek, Ohio St	1961-62
Elvin Hayes, Houston	1967
Walt Hazzard, UCLA	1964
Jerry Lucas, Ohio St	1960-61
Jeff Mullins, Duke	1964
Cazzie Russell, Michigan	1965
Charlie Scott, N. Carolina	1968-69

All-1980s

	Years
Steve Alford, Indiana	1987
Johnny Dawkins, Duke	1986
Patrick Ewing, Georgetown	1982-84
Darrell Griffith, Louisville	1980
Michael Jordan, N. Carolina	1982
Rodney McCray, Louisville	1980
Akeem Olajuwon, Houston	1983-84
Ed Pinckney, Villanova	1985
Isiah Thomas, Indiana	1981
James Worthy, N. Carolina	1982

Note: Lew Alcindor later changed his name to Kareem Abdul-Jabbar; Keith Wilkes later changed his first name to Jamaal; and Akeem Olajuwon later changed the spelling of his first name to Hakeem.

Collegiate Commissioners Association Tournament

The Collegiate Commissioners Association staged an eight-team tournament for teams that didn't make the NCAA tournament in 1974 and '75.

Most Valuable Players: 1974—Kent Benson, Indiana: 1975—Bob Elliot, Arizona.

Year	Winner	Score	Loser	Site	Year	Winner	Score	Loser	Site
1974	Indiana	85-60	USC	St. Louis	1975	Drake	83-76	Arizona	Louisville

NCAA Tournament Appearances

Through 1995; listed are schools with most appearances, overall tournament records, times reaching Final Four, and number of NCAA championships.

App		W-L	F4	Championships	App		W-L	F4	Championships
37	Kentucky	66-34	10	5 (1948-49, 51, 58, 78)	18	Ohio St.	31-17	8	1 (1960)
31	UCLA	74-24	15	11 (1964-65,67-3,75,95)	18	Houston	26-23	5	None
29	N. Carolina	67-29	12	3 (1957, 82, 93)	18	Princeton	11-22	1	None
25	Louisville	43-27	7	2 (1980, 86)	18	Michigan	40-17	6	1 (1989)
24	Notre Dame	25-28	1	None	18	Connecticut	15-19	0	None
24	Indiana	50-19	7	5 (1940, 53, 76, 81, 87)	18	BYU	11-21	0	None
24	Kansas	51-24	10	2 (1952, 88)	17	N.C. State	27-16	3	2 (1974,83)
23	St. John's	23-25	2	None	17	West Va.	11-17	1	None
22	Villanova	35-22	3	1 (1985)	17	Utah	20-20	3	1 (1944)
22	Syracuse	30-23	2	None	17	Illinois	21-18	4	None
21	Kansas St.	27-25	4	None	16	Iowa	22-18	3	None
21	Arkansas	35-21	6	1 (1994)	16	Missouri	13-16	0	None
20	DePaul	20-23	2	None	16	Oregon St.	12-19	2	None
19	Duke	56-17	11	2 (1991-92)	16	Penn	13-18	1	None
19	Marquette	27-20	2	1 (1977)	16	Western Ky.	15-17	1	None
19	Georgetown	33-18	4	1 (1984)					
19	Temple	22-19	2	None					

Note: Although all NCAA tournament appearances are included above, the NCAA has officially voided the records of Villanova (4-1) in 1971, UCLA (5-1) in 1980, Oregon St. (2-3) from 1980-82, N.C. State (0-2) from 1987-88 and Kentucky (2-1) in 1988.

All-Time NCAA Division I Tournament Leaders

Through 1995; minimum of six games; **Last** column indicates final year played.

CAREER

Scoring

	Points	Yrs	Last	Gm	Pts
1	Christian Laettner, Duke	4	1992	23	407
2	Elvin Hayes, Houston	3	1968	13	358
3	Danny Manning, Kansas	4	1988	16	328
4	Oscar Robertson, Cincinnati	3	1960	10	324
5	Glen Rice, Michigan	4	1989	13	308
6	Lew Alcindor, UCLA	3	1969	12	304
7	Bill Bradley, Princeton	3	1965	9	303
8	Austin Carr, Notre Dame	3	1971	7	289
9	Juwan Howard, Michigan	3	1994	16	280
10	Calbert Cheaney, Indiana	4	1993	13	279

	Average	Yrs	Last	Pts	Avg
1	Austin Carr, Notre Dame	3	1971	289	41.3
2	Bill Bradley, Princeton	3	1965	303	33.7
3	Oscar Robertson, Cincinnati	3	1960	324	32.4
4	Jerry West, West Virginia	3	1960	275	30.6
5	Bob Pettit, LSU	2	1954	183	30.5
6	Dan Issel, Kentucky	3	1970	176	29.3
	Jim McDaniels, Western Ky	2	1971	176	29.3
8	Dwight Lamar, SW Louisiana	2	1973	175	29.2
9	Bo Kimble, Loyola-CA	3	1990	204	29.1
10	David Robinson, Navy	3	1987	200	28.6

Rebounds

	Total	Yrs	Last	Gm	No
1	Elvin Hayes, Houston	3	1968	13	222
2	Lew Alcindor, UCLA	3	1969	12	201
3	Jerry Lucas, Ohio St.	3	1962	12	197
4	Bill Walton, UCLA	3	1974	12	176
5	Christian Laettner, Duke	4	1992	23	169
6	Paul Hogue, Cincinnati	3	1962	12	160
7	Sam Lacey, New Mexico St.	3	1970	11	157
8	Derrick Coleman, Syracuse	4	1990	14	155
9	Akeem Olajuwon, Houston	3	1984	15	153
10	Patrick Ewing, Georgetown	4	1985	18	144

	Average	Yrs	Last	Reb	Avg
1	Johnny Green, Michigan St.	2	1959	118	19.7
2	Artis Gilmore, Jacksonville	2	1971	115	19.2
3	Paul Silas, Creighton	3	1964	111	18.5
4	Len Chappell, Wake Forest	2	1962	137	17.1
5	Elvin Hayes, Houston	3	1968	222	17.1
6	Lew Alcindor, UCLA	3	1969	201	16.8
7	Jerry Lucas, Ohio St.	3	1962	197	16.4
8	Bill Walton, UCLA	3	1974	176	14.7
9	Sam Lacey, New Mexico St.	3	1970	157	14.3
10	Bob Lanier, St. Bonaventure	3	1970	85	14.2

3-Pt Field Goals

	Total	Yrs	Last	Gm	No
1	Bobby Hurley, Duke	4	1993	20	42
2	Jeff Fryer, Loyola-CA	3	1990	7	38
3	Glen Rice, Michigan	4	1989	13	35
4	Anderson Hunt, UNLV	3	1991	15	34
5	Dennis Scott, Georgia Tech	3	1990	8	33

Assists

	Total	Yrs	Last	Gm	No
1	Bobby Hurley, Duke	4	1993	20	145
2	Sherman Douglas, Syracuse	4	1989	14	106
3	Greg Anthony, UNLV	3	1991	15	100
4	Mark Wade, UNLV	2	1987	8	93
	Rumeal Robinson, Michigan	3	1990	11	93

SINGLE TOURNAMENT

Scoring

	Points	Year	Gm	Pts
1	Glen Rice, Michigan	1989	6	184
2	Bill Bradley, Princeton	1965	5	177
3	Elvin Hayes, Houston	1968	5	167
4	Danny Manning, Kansas	1988	6	163
5	Hal Lear, Temple	1956	5	160
	Jerry West, West Virginia	1959	5	160

	Average	Year	Gm	Pts	Avg
1	Austin Carr, Notre Dame	1970	3	158	52.7
2	Austin Carr, Notre Dame	1971	3	125	41.7
3	Jerry Chambers, Utah	1966	4	143	35.8
	Bo Kimble, Loyola-CA	1990	4	143	35.8
5	Bill Bradley, Princeton	1965	5	177	35.4
6	Clyde Lovellette, Kansas	1952	4	141	35.3

All-Time NCAA Division I Tourney Leaders (Cont.)

Rebounds

	Total	Year	Gm	No	Avg
1	Elvin Hayes, Houston	1968	5	97	19.4
2	Artis Gilmore, Jacksonville	1970	5	93	18.6
3	Elgin Baylor, Seattle	1958	5	91	18.2
4	Sam Lacey, New Mexico St.	1970	5	90	18.0
5	Clarence Glover, Western Ky	1971	5	89	17.8

Assists

	Total	Year	Gm	No	Avg
1	Mark Wade, UNLV	1987	5	61	12.2
2	Rumeal Robinson, Michigan	1989	6	56	9.3
3	Sherman Douglas, Syracuse	1987	6	49	8.2
4	Bobby Hurley, Duke	1992	6	47	7.8
5	Michael Jackson, Georgetown	1985	6	45	7.5

SINGLE GAME

Scoring

	Points	Year	Pts
1	Austin Carr, Notre Dame vs Ohio Univ	1970	61
2	Bill Bradley, Princeton vs Wichita St.	1965	58
3	Oscar Robertson, Cincinnati vs Arkansas	1958	56
4	Austin Carr, Notre Dame vs Kentucky	1970	52
	Austin Carr, Notre Dame vs TCU	1971	52
6	David Robinson, Navy vs Michigan	1987	50
7	Elvin Hayes, Houston vs Loyola-IL	1968	49
8	Hal Lear, Temple vs SMU	1956	48
9	Austin Carr, Notre Dame vs Houston	1971	47
10	Dave Corzine, DePaul vs Louisville	1978	46
11	Bob Houbregs, Washington vs Seattle	1953	45
	Austin Carr, Notre Dame vs Iowa	1970	45
	Bo Kimble, Loyola-CA vs New Mexico St.	1990	45
14	Seven players tied with 44 each.		

Rebounds

	Total	Year	No
1	Fred Cohen, Temple vs UConn	1956	34
2	Nate Thurmond, Bowling Green vs Miss. St.	1963	31
3	Jerry Lucas, Ohio St. vs Kentucky	1961	30
4	Toby Kimball, UConn vs St. Joseph's-PA	1965	29
5	Elvin Hayes, Houston vs Pacific	1966	28

Assists

	Total	Year	No
1	Mark Wade, UNLV vs Indiana	1987	18
2	Sam Crawford, N. Mexico St. vs Nebraska	1993	16
3	Kenny Patterson, DePaul vs Syracuse	1985	15
4	Keith Smart, Indiana vs Auburn	1987	15
5	Five players tied with 14 each.		

SINGLE FINAL FOUR GAME

Letters in the **Year** column indicate the following: C for Consolation Game, F for Final and S for Semifinal.

Scoring

	Points	Year	Pts
1	Bill Bradley, Princeton vs Wichita St.	1965-C	58
2	Hal Lear, Temple vs SMU	1956-C	48
3	Bill Walton, UCLA vs Memphis St	1973-F	44
4	Bob Houbregs, Washington vs LSU	1953-C	42
	Jack Egan, St. Joseph's-PA vs Utah	1961-C	42*
	Gail Goodrich, UCLA vs Michigan	1965-C	42
7	Jack Givens, Kentucky vs Duke	1978-F	41
8	Oscar Robertson, Cincinnati vs L'ville	1959-C	39
	Al Wood, N. Carolina vs Virginia	1981-S	39
10	Jerry West, West Va. vs Louisville	1959-S	38
	Jerry Chambers, Utah vs Texas Western	1966-S	38
	Freddie Banks, UNLV vs Indiana	1987-S	38

* Four overtimes.

Rebounds

	Total	Year	No
1	Bill Russell, San Francisco vs Iowa	1956-F	27
2	Elvin Hayes, Houston vs UCLA	1967-S	24
3	Bill Russell, San Francisco vs SMU	1956-S	23
4	Four players tied with 22 each.		

Assists

	Total	Year	No
1	Mark Wade, UNLV vs Indiana	1987-S	18
2	Rumeal Robinson, Michigan vs Illinois	1989-S	12
3	Michael Jackson, G'town vs St. John's	1985-S	11
4	Milt Wagner, Louisville vs LSU	1986-S	11
5	Rumeal Robinson, Mich. vs Seton Hall	1989-F	11*

*Overtime.

Teams in both NCAA and NIT

Fourteen teams played in both the NCAA and NIT tournaments from 1940-52. Colorado (1940), Utah (1944), Kentucky (1949) and BYU (1951) won one of the titles, while CCNY won two in 1950, beating Bradley in both championship games.

Year		NIT	NCAA
1940	Colorado	Won Final	Lost 1st Rd
	Duquesne	Lost Final	Lost 2nd Rd
1944	Utah	Lost 1st Rd	Won Final
1949	Kentucky	Lost 2nd Rd	Won Final
1950	CCNY	Won Final	Won Final
	Bradley	Lost Final	Lost Final
1951	BYU	Won Final	Lost 2nd Rd
	St. John's	Lost 3rd Rd	Lost 2nd Rd
	N.C. State	Lost 2nd Rd	Lost 2nd Rd
	Arizona	Lost 2nd Rd	Lost 1st Rd
1952	St. John's	Lost Final	Lost 2nd Rd
	Dayton	Lost 1st Rd	Lost Final
	Duquesne	Lost 2nd Rd	Lost 2nd Rd
	Saint Louis	Lost 2nd Rd	Lost 2nd Rd

Most Popular Final Four Sites

The NCAA has staged its Men's Division I championship—the Final Two (1939-51) and Final Four (since 1952)—at 29 different arenas and indoor stadiums in 24 different cities. The following facilities have all hosted the event more than once.

No	Arena	Years
9	Municipal Auditorium (KC)	1940-42, 53-55, 57, 61, 64
7	Madison Sq. Garden (NYC)	1943-48, 50
6	Freedom Hall (Louisville)	1958-59, 62-63, 67, 69
3	Kingdome (Seattle)	1984, 89, 95
	Superdome (New Orleans)	1982, 87, 93
2	Cole Field House (College Park, Md.)	1966, 70
	Edmundson Pavilion (Seattle)	1949, 52
	LA Sports Arena	1968, 72
	St. Louis Arena	1973, 78
	Spectrum (Philadelphia)	1976, 81

NIT Championship

The National Invitation Tournament began under the sponsorship of the Metropolitan New York Basketball Writers Association in 1938. The NIT is now administered by the Metropolitan Intercollegiate Basketball Association. All championship games have been played at Madison Square Garden.

Multiple winners: St. John's (5); Bradley (4); BYU, Dayton, Kentucky, LIU-Brooklyn, Providence, Temple, Virginia and Virginia Tech (2).

Year	Winner	Score	Loser	Year	Winner	Score	Loser
1938	Temple	60-36	Colorado	1968	Dayton	61-48	Kansas
1939	LIU-Brooklyn	44-32	Loyola-IL	1969	Temple	89-76	Boston College
1940	Colorado	51-40	Duquesne	1970	Marquette	65-53	St. John's
1941	LIU-Brooklyn	56-42	Ohio Univ.	1971	North Carolina	84-66	Georgia Tech
1942	West Virginia	47-45	Western Ky.	1972	Maryland	100-69	Niagara
1943	St. John's	48-27	Toledo	1973	Virginia Tech	92-91 (OT)	Notre Dame
1944	St. John's	47-39	DePaul	1974	Purdue	97-81	Utah
1945	DePaul	71-54	Bowling Green	1975	Princeton	80-69	Providence
1946	Kentucky	46-45	Rhode Island	1976	Kentucky	71-67	NC-Charlotte
1947	Utah	49-45	Kentucky	1977	St. Bonaventure	94-91	Houston
1948	Saint Louis	65-52	NYU	1978	Texas	101-93	N.C. State
1949	San Francisco	48-47	Loyola-IL	1979	Indiana	53-52	Purdue
1950	CCNY	69-61	Bradley	1980	Virginia	58-55	Minnesota
1951	BYU	62-43	Dayton	1981	Tulsa	86-84 (OT)	Syracuse
1952	La Salle	75-64	Dayton	1982	Bradley	67-58	Purdue
1953	Seton Hall	58-46	St. John's	1983	Fresno St.	69-60	DePaul
1954	Holy Cross	71-62	Duquesne	1984	Michigan	83-63	Notre Dame
1955	Duquesne	70-58	Dayton	1985	UCLA	65-62	Indiana
1956	Louisville	93-80	Dayton	1986	Ohio St.	73-63	Wyoming
1957	Bradley	84-83	Memphis St.	1987	Southern Miss.	84-80	La Salle
1958	Xavier-OH	78-74 (OT)	Dayton	1988	Connecticut	72-67	Ohio St.
1959	St. John's	76-71 (OT)	Bradley	1989	St. John's	73-65	Saint Louis
1960	Bradley	88-72	Providence	1990	Vanderbilt	74-72	Saint Louis
1961	Providence	62-59	Saint Louis	1991	Stanford	78-72	Oklahoma
1962	Dayton	73-67	St. John's	1992	Virginia	81-76 (OT)	Notre Dame
1963	Providence	81-66	Canisius	1993	Minnesota	62-61	Georgetown
1964	Bradley	86-54	New Mexico	1994	Villanova	80-73	Vanderbilt
1965	St. John's	55-51	Villanova	1995	Virginia Tech	65-64 (OT)	Marquette
1966	BYU	97-84	NYU				
1967	Southern Illinois	71-56	Marquette				

Most Valuable Player

A Most Valuable Player has been selected every year of the NIT tournament. Winners who did not play for the tournament champion are listed in **bold** type.

Multiple winners: None. However, Tom Gola is the only player to be named MVP in both the NIT (1952) and NCAA (1954) tournaments.

Year		Year		Year	
1938	Don Shields, Temple	1958	Hank Stein, Xavier-OH	1978	Ron Baxter, Texas
1939	**Bill Lloyd**, St. John's	1959	Tony Jackson, St. John's		& Jim Krivacs, Texas
1940	Bob Doll, Colorado	1960	**Lenny Wilkens**, Providence	1979	Clarence Carter, Indiana
1941	**Frank Baumholtz**, Ohio U.	1961	Vin Ernst, Providence		& Ray Tolbert, Indiana
1942	Rudy Baric, West Virginia	1962	Bill Chmielewski, Dayton	1980	Ralph Sampson, Virginia
1943	Harry Boykoff, St. John's	1963	Ray Flynn, Providence	1981	Greg Stewart, Tulsa
1944	Bill Kotsores, St. John's	1964	Lavern Tart, Bradley	1982	Mitchell Anderson, Bradley
1945	George Mikan, DePaul	1965	Ken McIntyre, St. John's	1983	Ron Anderson, Fresno St.
1946	**Ernie Calverley**, Rhode Island	1966	**Bill Melchionni**, Villanova	1984	Tim McCormick, Michigan
1947	Vern Gardner, Utah	1967	Walt Frazier, So. Illinois	1985	Reggie Miller, UCLA
1948	Ed Macauley, Saint Louis	1968	Don May, Dayton	1986	Brad Sellers, Ohio St.
1949	Don Lofgan, San Francisco	1969	**Terry Driscoll**, Boston College	1987	Randolph Keys, So. Miss.
1950	Ed Warner, CCNY	1970	Dean Meminger, Marquette	1988	Phil Gamble, Connecticut
1951	Roland Minson, BYU	1971	Bill Chamberlain, N. Carolina	1989	Jayson Williams, St. John's
1952	Tom Gola, La Salle	1972	Tom McMillen, Maryland	1990	Scott Draud, Vanderbilt
	& Norm Grekin, La Salle	1973	**John Shumate**, Notre Dame	1991	Adam Keefe, Stanford
1953	Walter Dukes, Seton Hall	1974	**Mike Sojourner**, Utah	1992	Bryant Stith, Virginia
1954	Togo Palazzi, Holy Cross	1975	**Ron Lee**, Oregon	1993	Voshon Lenard, Minnesota
1955	**Maurice Stokes**, St. Francis-PA	1976	**Cedric Maxwell**, NC-Charlotte	1994	**Doremus Bennerman**, Siena
1956	Charlie Tyra, Louisville	1977	Greg Sanders, St. Bonaventure	1995	Shawn Smith, Va. Tech
1957	**Win Wilfong**, Memphis St.				

All-Time Winningest Division I Teams

Top 25 Winning Percentage

Division I schools with best winning percentages through 1994-95 season (including tournament games). Years in Division I only; minimum 20 years. NCAA tournament columns indicate years in tournament, record and number of championships.

		First Year	Yrs	Games	Won	Lost	Tied	Pct	—NCAA Tourney—		
									Yrs	W-L	Titles
1	Kentucky	1903	92	2135	1616	518	1	.757	37	66-34	5
2	UNLV	1959	37	1047	779	268	0	.744	12	30-11	1
3	North Carolina	1911	85	2203	1626	577	0	.738	29	67-29	3
4	UCLA	1920	76	1939	1351	588	0	.697	31	74-24	11
5	St. John's	1908	88	2174	1508	666	0	.694	23	23-25	0
6	Kansas	1899	97	2270	1567	703	0	.690	24	51-24	2
7	Western Kentucky	1915	76	1952	1331	621	0	.682	16	15-17	0
8	Syracuse	1901	94	2064	1403	661	0	.680	22	30-23	0
9	Duke	1906	90	2201	1474	727	0	.670	19	56-17	2
10	DePaul	1924	72	1748	1166	582	0	.667	20	20-23	0
11	Arkansas	1924	72	1865	1230	635	0	.660	21	35-21	1
12	Notre Dame	1898	90	2120	1389	730	1	.655	24	25-28	0
13	Louisville	1912	81	1952	1277	675	0	.654	25	43-27	2
14	Indiana	1901	95	2101	1369	732	0	.652	24	50-19	5
15	Weber St.	1963	33	933	605	328	0	.6484	11	5-12	0
16	Temple	1895	99	2215	1435	780	0	.6478	19	22-19	0
17	La Salle	1931	65	1658	1069	589	0	.645	11	11-10	1
18	Utah	1909	87	2007	1290	717	0	.643	17	20-20	1
19	Illinois	1906	90	1994	1281	713	0	.6424	17	21-18	0
20	Purdue	1897	97	2043	1311	732	0	.6417	14	17-14	0
21	Penn	1897	95	2206	1408	796	2	.639	16	13-18	0
22	Villanova	1921	75	1894	1206	688	0	.637	22	35-22	1
23	Houston	1946	50	1389	884	505	0	.6364	18	26-23	0
24	North Carolina St.	1913	83	2009	1277	732	0	.6356	17	27-16	2
25	UTEP	1947	49	1319	830	489	0	.629	14	14-13	1

Top 35 Victories

Division I schools with most victories through 1994-95 (including postseason tournaments). Minimum 20 years in Division I.

	Wins		Wins		Wins		Wins
1 North Carolina	1626	10 Notre Dame	1389	19 Utah	1290	28 Montana St.	1229
2 Kentucky	1616	11 Indiana	1369	20 Bradley	1284	Cincinnati	1229
3 Kansas	1567	12 UCLA	1351	21 Illinois	1281	30 Arizona	1226
4 St. John's	1508	13 Washington	1332	22 N.C. State	1277	31 USC	1218
5 Duke	1474	14 Western Ky.	1331	Louisville	1277	32 Alabama	1215
6 Temple	1435	15 Princeton	1313	24 Washington St.	1270	33 Kansas St.	1207
7 Oregon St.	1430	16 Purdue	1311	25 Texas	1263	34 Villanova	1206
8 Penn	1408	17 Fordham	1303	26 Ohio St	1236	35 St. Joseph's-PA	1201
9 Syracuse	1403	18 West Virginia	1292	27 Arkansas	1230	36 Iowa	1200

Top 50 Single-Season Victories

Division I schools with most victories in a single season through 1994-95 (including postseason tournaments). NCAA champions in **bold** type.

	Year	Record		Year	Record		Year	Record
1 UNLV	1987	37-2	18 **N. Carolina**	1957	32-0	37 Indiana	1975	31-1
Duke	1986	37-3	**Indiana**	1976	32-0	Wyoming	1943	31-2
3 **Kentucky**	1948	36-3	**Kentucky**	1949	32-2	**Okla. A&M**	1946	31-2
4 Georgetown	1985	35-3	**Kentucky**	1951	32-2	Seton Hall	1953	31-2
Arizona	1988	35-3	N. Carolina	1982	32-2	Houston	1968	31-2
Kansas	1986	35-4	Temple	1988	32-2	Rutgers	1976	31-2
Oklahoma	1988	35-4	Arkansas	1978	32-3	**UCLA**	1995	31-2
UNLV	1990	35-5	Bradley	1986	32-3	Houston	1983	31-3
9 UNLV	1991	34-1	Louisville	1983	32-4	**Arkansas**	1994	31-3
Duke	1992	34-2	Kentucky	1986	32-4	Memphis St	1985	31-4
Kentucky	1947	34-3	N. Carolina	1987	32-4	St. John's	1985	31-4
Georgetown	1984	34-3	Temple	1987	32-4	Indiana	1993	31-4
Arkansas	1991	34-4	Bradley	1950	32-5	LSU	1981	31-5
N. Carolina	1993	34-4	Marshall	1947	32-5	St. John's	1986	31-5
15 Indiana St	1979	33-1	Houston	1984	32-5	Illinois	1989	31-5
Louisville	1980	33-3	Bradley	1951	32-6	Michigan	1993	31-5
UNLV	1986	33-5	**Louisville**	1986	32-7	Oklahoma	1985	31-6
			Duke	1991	32-7	Connecticut	1990	31-6
			Arkansas	1995	32-7	Syracuse	1987	31-7
						Seton Hall	1989	31-7

Associated Press Final Polls

The Associated Press introduced its weekly college basketball poll of sportswriters (later, sportswriters and broadcasters) during the 1948-49 season.

Since the NCAA Division I tournament has determined the national champion since 1939, the final AP poll ranks the nation's best teams through the regular season and conference tournaments.

Except for four seasons (see page 321), the final AP poll has been released prior to the NCAA and NIT tournaments and has gone from a Top 10 (1949 and 1963-67) to a Top 20 (1950-62 and 1968-89) to a Top 25 (since 1990).

Tournament champions are in **bold** type.

1949

		Before Tourns	Head Coach	Final Record
1	**Kentucky**	29-1	Adolph Rupp	32-2
2	Oklahoma A&M	21-4	Hank Iba	23-5
3	Saint Louis	22-3	Eddie Hickey	22-4
4	Illinois	19-3	Harry Combes	21-4
5	Western Ky.	25-3	Ed Diddle	25-4
6	Minnesota	18-3	Ozzie Cowles	same
7	Bradley	25-6	Forddy Anderson	27-8
8	**San Francisco**	21-5	Pete Newell	25-5
9	Tulane	24-4	Cliff Wells	same
10	Bowling Green	21-6	Harold Anderson	24-7

NCAA Final Four (at Edmundson Pavilion, Seattle): **Third Place**—Illinois 57, Oregon St. 53. **Championship**—Kentucky 46, Oklahoma A&M 36.

NIT Final Four (at Madison Square Garden): **Semifinals**—San Francisco 49, Bowling Green 39; Loyola-IL 55, Bradley 50. **Third Place**—Bowling Green 82, Bradley 77. **Championship**—San Francisco 48, Loyola-IL 47.

1950

		Before Tourns	Head Coach	Final Record
1	Bradley	28-3	Forddy Anderson	32-5
2	Ohio St.	21-3	Tippy Dye	22-4
3	Kentucky	25-4	Adolph Rupp	25-5
4	Holy Cross	27-2	Buster Sheary	27-4
5	N.C. State	25-5	Everett Case	27-6
6	Duquesne	22-5	Dudey Moore	23-6
7	UCLA	24-5	John Wooden	24-7
8	Western Ky.	24-5	Ed Diddle	25-6
9	St. John's	23-4	Frank McGuire	24-5
10	La Salle	20-3	Ken Loeffler	21-4
11	Villanova	25-4	Al Severance	same
12	San Francisco	19-6	Pete Newell	19-7
13	LIU-Brooklyn	20-4	Clair Bee	20-5
14	Kansas St.	17-7	Jack Gardner	same
15	Arizona	26-4	Fred Enke	26-5
16	Wisconsin	17-5	Bud Foster	same
17	San Jose St.	21-7	Walter McPherson	same
18	Washington St.	19-13	Jack Friel	same
19	Kansas	14-11	Phog Allen	same
20	Indiana	17-5	Branch McCracken	same

Note: Unranked **CCNY**, coached by Nat Holman, won both the NCAAs and NIT. The Beavers entered the postseason at 17-5 and had a final record of 24-5.

NCAA Final Four (at Madison Square Garden): **Third Place**—N. Carolina St. 53, Baylor 41. **Championship**—CCNY 71, Bradley 68.

NIT Final Four (at Madison Square Garden): **Semifinals**—Bradley 83, St. John's 72; CCNY 62, Duquesne 52. **Third Place**—St. John's 69, Duquesne 67 (OT). **Championship**—CCNY 69, Bradley 61.

1951

		Before Tourns	Head Coach	Final Record
1	**Kentucky**	28-2	Adolph Rupp	32-2
2	Oklahoma A&M	27-4	Hank Iba	29-6
3	Columbia	22-0	Lou Rossini	22-1
4	Kansas St.	22-3	Jack Gardner	25-4
5	Illinois	19-4	Harry Combes	22-5
6	Bradley	32-6	Forddy Anderson	same
7	Indiana	19-3	Branch McCracken	same
8	N.C. State	29-4	Everett Case	30-7
9	St. John's	22-3	Frank McGuire	26-5
10	Saint Louis	21-7	Eddie Hickey	22-8
11	BYU	22-8	Stan Watts	26-10
12	Arizona	24-4	Fred Enke	24-6
13	Dayton	24-4	Tom Blackburn	27-5
14	Toledo	23-8	Jerry Bush	same
15	Washington	22-5	Tippy Dye	24-6
16	Murray St.	21-6	Harlan Hodges	same
17	Cincinnati	18-3	John Wiethe	18-4
18	Siena	19-8	Dan Cunha	same
19	USC	21-6	Forrest Twogood	same
20	Villanova	25-6	Al Severance	25-7

NCAA Final Four (at Williams Arena, Minneapolis): **Third Place**—Illinois 61, Oklahoma St. 46. **Championship**—Kentucky 68, Kansas St. 58.

NIT Final Four (at Madison Sq. Garden): **Semifinals**—Dayton 69, St. John's 62 (OT); BYU 69, Seton Hall 59. **Third Place**—St. John's 70, Seton Hall 68 (2 OT). **Championship**—BYU 62, Dayton 43.

1952

		Before Tourns	Head Coach	Final Record
1	Kentucky	28-2	Adolph Rupp	29-3
2	Illinois	19-3	Harry Combes	22-4
3	Kansas St.	19-5	Jack Gardner	same
4	Duquesne	21-1	Dudey Moore	23-4
5	Saint Louis	22-6	Eddie Hickey	23-8
6	Washington	25-6	Tippy Dye	same
7	Iowa	19-3	Bucky O'Connor	same
8	**Kansas**	24-3	Phog Allen	28-3
9	West Virginia	23-4	Red Brown	same
10	St. John's	23-4	Frank McGuire	25-5
11	Dayton	24-3	Tom Blackburn	28-5
12	Duke	24-6	Harold Bradley	same
13	Holy Cross	23-3	Buster Sheary	24-4
14	Seton Hall	25-2	Honey Russell	25-3
15	St. Bonaventure	19-5	Ed Melvin	21-6
16	Wyoming	27-6	Everett Shelton	28-7
17	Louisville	20-5	Peck Hickman	20-6
18	Seattle	29-7	Al Brightman	29-8
19	UCLA	19-10	John Wooden	19-12
20	SW Texas St.	30-1	Milton Jowers	same

Note: Unranked **La Salle**, coached by Ken Loefler, won the NIT. The Explorers entered the postseason at 21-7 and had a final record of 25-7.

NCAA Final Four (at Edmundson Pavillion, Seattle): **Semifinals**—St. John's 61, Illinois 59; Kansas 74, Santa Clara 59. **Third Place**—Illinois 67, Santa Clara 64. **Championship**—Kansas 80, St. John's 63.

NIT Final Four (at Madison Sq. Garden): **Semifinals**—La Salle 59, Duquesne 46; Dayton 69, St. Bonaventure 62. **Third Place**—St. Bonaventure 48, Duquesne 34. **Championship**—La Salle 75, Dayton 64.

Associated Press Final Polls (Cont.)

Taken **before** NCAA and NIT tournaments

1953

	Before Tourns	Head Coach	Final Record
1 Indiana	18-3	Branch McCracken	23-3
2 La Salle	25-2	Ken Loeffler	25-3
3 Seton Hall	28-2	Honey Russell	31-2
4 Washington	27-2	Tippy Dye	30-3
5 LSU	22-1	Harry Rabenhorst	24-3
6 Kansas	16-5	Phog Allen	19-6
7 Oklahoma A&M	22-6	Hank Iba	23-7
Kansas St.	17-4	Jack Gardner	same
9 Western Ky.	25-5	Ed Diddle	25-6
10 Illinois	18-4	Harry Combes	same
11 Oklahoma City	18-4	Doyle Parrick	18-6
12 N.C. State	26-6	Everett Case	same
13 Notre Dame	17-4	John Jordan	19-5
14 Louisville	21-5	Peck Hickman	22-6
Seattle	27-3	Al Brightman	29-4
16 Miami-OH	17-5	Bill Rohr	17-6
17 Eastern Ky.	16-8	Paul McBrayer	16-9
18 Duquesne	18-7	Dudey Moore	21-8
Navy	16-4	Ben Carnevale	16-5
20 Holy Cross	18-5	Buster Sheary	20-6

NCAA Final Four (at Municipal Auditorium, Kansas City): **Semifinals**—Indiana 80, LSU 67; Kansas 79, Washington 53. **Third Place**—Washington 88, LSU 69. **Championship**—Indiana 69, Kansas 68.
NIT Final Four (at Madison Sq. Garden): **Semifinals**—Seton Hall 74, Manhattan 56; St. John's 64, Duquesne 55. **Third Place**—Duquesne 81, Manhattan 67. **Championship**—Seton Hall 58, St. John's 46.

1955

	Before Tourns	Head Coach	Final Record
1 San Francisco	23-1	Phil Woolpert	28-1
2 Kentucky	22-2	Adolph Rupp	23-3
3 La Salle	22-4	Ken Loeffler	26-5
4 N.C. State	28-4	Everett Case	same
5 Iowa	17-5	Bucky O'Connor	19-7
6 Duquesne	19-4	Dudey Moore	22-4
7 Utah	23-3	Jack Gardner	24-4
8 Marquette	22-2	Jack Nagle	24-3
9 Dayton	23-3	Tom Blackburn	25-4
10 Oregon St.	21-7	Slats Gill	22-8
11 Minnesota	15-7	Ozzie Cowles	same
12 Alabama	19-5	Johnny Dee	same
13 UCLA	21-5	John Wooden	same
14 G. Washington	24-6	Bill Reinhart	same
15 Colorado	16-5	Bebe Lee	19-6
16 Tulsa	20-6	Clarence Iba	21-7
17 Vanderbilt	16-6	Bob Polk	same
18 Illinois	17-5	Harry Combes	same
19 West Virginia	19-10	Fred Schaus	19-11
20 Saint Louis	19-7	Eddie Hickey	20-8

NCAA Final Four (at Municipal Auditorium, Kansas City): **Semifinals**—La Salle 76, Iowa 73; San Francisco 62, Colorado 50. **Third Place**—Colorado 75, Iowa 74. **Championship**—San Francisco 77, La Salle 63.
NIT Final Four (at Madison Square Garden): **Semifinals**—Dayton 79, St. Francis-PA 73 (OT); Duquesne 65, Cincinnati 51. **Third Place**—Cincinnati 96, St. Francis-PA 91 (OT). **Championship**—Duquesne 70, Dayton 58.

1954

	Before Tourns	Head Coach	Final Record
1 Kentucky	25-0	Adolph Rupp	same*
2 Indiana	19-3	Branch McCracken	20-4
3 Duquesne	24-2	Dudey Moore	26-3
4 Western Ky.	28-1	Ed Diddle	29-3
5 Oklahoma A&M	23-4	Hank Iba	24-5
6 Notre Dame	20-2	John Jordan	22-3
7 Kansas	16-5	Phog Allen	same
8 Holy Cross	23-2	Buster Sheary	26-2
9 LSU	21-3	Harry Rabenhorst	21-5
10 La Salle	21-4	Ken Loeffler	26-4
11 Iowa	17-5	Bucky O'Connor	same
12 Duke	22-6	Harold Bradley	same
13 Colorado A&M	22-5	Bill Strannigan	22-7
14 Illinois	17-5	Harry Combes	same
15 Wichita	27-3	Ralph Miller	27-4
16 Seattle	26-1	Al Brightman	26-2
17 N.C. State	26-6	Everett Case	28-7
18 Dayton	24-6	Tom Blackburn	25-7
Minnesota	17-5	Ozzie Cowles	same
20 Oregon St.	19-10	Slats Gill	same
UCLA	18-7	John Wooden	same
USC	17-12	Forrest Twogood	19-14

*Kentucky turned down invitation to NCAA tournament after NCAA declared seniors Cliff Hagan, Frank Ramsey and Lou Tsioropoulos ineligible for postseason play.

NCAA Final Four (at Municipal Auditorium, Kansas City): **Semifinals**—La Salle 69, Penn St. 54; Bradley 74, USC 72. **Third Place**—Penn St. 70, USC 61. **Championship**—La Salle 92, Bradley 76.
NIT Final Four (at Madison Square Garden): **Semifinals**—Duquesne 66, Niagara 51; Holy Cross 75, Western Ky. 69. **Third Place**—Niagara 71, Western Ky. 65. **Championship**—Holy Cross 71, Duquesne 62.

1956

	Before Tourns	Head Coach	Final Record
1 San Francisco	25-0	Phil Woolpert	29-0
2 N.C. State	24-3	Everett Case	24-4
3 Dayton	23-3	Tom Blackburn	25-4
4 Iowa	17-5	Bucky O'Connor	20-6
5 Alabama	21-3	Johnny Dee	same
6 Louisville	23-3	Peck Hickman	26-3
7 SMU	22-2	Doc Hayes	25-4
8 UCLA	21-5	John Wooden	22-6
9 Kentucky	19-5	Adolph Rupp	20-6
10 Illinois	18-4	Harry Combes	same
11 Oklahoma City	18-6	Abe Lemons	20-7
12 Vanderbilt	19-4	Bob Polk	same
13 North Carolina	18-5	Frank McGuire	same
14 Holy Cross	22-4	Roy Leenig	22-5
15 Temple	23-3	Harry Litwack	27-4
16 Wake Forest	19-9	Murray Greason	same
17 Duke	19-7	Harold Bradley	same
18 Utah	21-5	Jack Gardner	22-6
19 Oklahoma A&M	18-8	Hank Iba	18-9
20 West Virginia	21-8	Fred Schaus	21-9

NCAA Final Four (at McGaw Hall, Evanston, IL): **Semifinals**—Iowa 83, Temple 76; San Francisco 76, SMU 68. **Third Place**—Temple 90, SMU 81. **Championship**—San Francisco 83, Iowa 71.
NIT Final Four (at Madison Square Garden): **Semifinals**—Dayton 89, St. Francis-NY 58; Louisville 89, St. Joseph's-PA 79. **Third Place**—St. Joseph's-PA 93, St. Francis-NY 82. **Championship**—Louisville 93, Dayton 80.

1957

	Before Tourns	Head Coach	Final Record
1 North Carolina	27-0	Frank McGuire	32-0
2 Kansas	21-2	Dick Harp	24-3
3 Kentucky	22-4	Adolph Rupp	23-5
4 SMU	21-3	Doc Hayes	22-4
5 Seattle	24-2	John Castellani	24-3
6 Louisville	21-5	Peck Hickman	same
7 West Va.	25-4	Fred Schaus	25-5
8 Vanderbilt	17-5	Bob Polk	same
9 Oklahoma City	17-8	Abe Lemons	19-9
10 Saint Louis	19-7	Eddie Hickey	19-9
11 Michigan St.	14-8	Forddy Anderson	16-10
12 Memphis St.	21-5	Bob Vanatta	24-6
13 California	20-4	Pete Newell	21-5
14 UCLA	22-4	John Wooden	same
15 Mississippi St.	17-8	Babe McCarthy	same
16 Idaho St.	24-2	John Grayson	25-4
17 Notre Dame	18-7	John Jordan	20-8
18 Wake Forest	19-9	Murray Greason	same
19 Canisius	20-5	Joe Curran	22-6
20 Oklahoma A&M	17-9	Hank Iba	same

Note: Unranked **Bradley**, coached by Chuck Orsborn, won the NIT. The Braves entered the tourney at 19-7 and had a final record of 22-7.

NCAA Final Four (at Municipal Auditorium, Kansas City): **Semifinals**—North Carolina 74, Michigan St. 70 (3 OT); Kansas 80, San Francisco 56. **Third Place**—San Francisco 67, Michigan St. 60. **Championship**—North Carolina 54, Kansas 53 (3 OT).

NIT Final Four (at Madison Square Garden): **Semifinals**—Memphis St. 80, St. Bonaventure 78; Bradley 78, Temple 66. **Third Place**—Temple 67, St. Bonaventure 50. **Championship**—Bradley 84, Memphis St. 83.

1958

	Before Tourns	Head Coach	Final Record
1 West Virginia	26-1	Fred Schaus	26-2
2 Cincinnati	24-2	George Smith	25-3
3 Kansas St.	20-3	Tex Winter	22-5
4 San Francisco	24-1	Phil Woolpert	25-2
5 Temple	24-2	Harry Litwack	27-3
6 Maryland	20-6	Bud Millikan	22-7
7 Kansas	18-5	Dick Harp	same
8 Notre Dame	22-4	John Jordan	24-5
9 Kentucky	19-6	Adolph Rupp	23-6
10 Duke	18-7	Harold Bradley	same
11 Dayton	23-3	Tom Blackburn	25-4
12 Indiana	12-10	Branch McCracken	13-11
13 North Carolina	19-7	Frank McGuire	same
14 Bradley	20-6	Chuck Orsborn	20-7
15 Mississippi St.	20-5	Babe McCarthy	same
16 Auburn	16-6	Joel Eaves	same
17 Michigan St.	16-6	Forddy Anderson	same
18 Seattle	18-8	John Castellani	24-7
19 Oklahoma St.	19-7	Hank Iba	21-8
20 N.C. State	18-6	Everett Case	same

Note: Unranked **Xavier-OH**, coached by Jim McCafferty, won the NIT. The Musketeers entered the tourney at 15-11 and had a final record of 19-11.

NCAA Final Four (at Freedom Hall, Louisville): **Semifinals**—Kentucky 61, Temple 60; Seattle 73, Kansas St. 51. **Third Place**—Temple 67, Kansas St. 57. **Championship**—Kentucky 84, Seattle 72.

NIT Final Four (at Madison Square Garden): **Semifinals**—Dayton 80, St. John's 56; Xavier-OH 72, St. Bonaventure 53. **Third Place**—St. Bonaventure 84, St. John's 69. **Championship**—Xavier-OH 78, Dayton 74 (OT).

1959

	Before Tourns	Head Coach	Final Record
1 Kansas St.	24-1	Tex Winter	25-2
2 Kentucky	23-2	Adolph Rupp	24-3
3 Mississippi St.	24-1	Babe McCarthy	same*
4 Bradley	23-3	Chuck Orsborn	25-4
5 Cincinnati	23-3	George Smith	26-4
6 N.C. State	22-4	Everett Case	same
7 Michigan St.	18-3	Forddy Anderson	19-4
8 Auburn	20-2	Joel Eaves	same
9 North Carolina	20-4	Frank McGuire	20-5
10 West Virginia	25-4	Fred Schaus	29-5
11 California	21-4	Pete Newell	25-4
12 Saint Louis	20-5	John Benington	20-6
13 Seattle	23-6	Vince Cazzetta	same
14 St. Joseph's-PA	22-3	Jack Ramsay	22-5
15 St. Mary's-CA	18-5	Jim Weaver	19-6
16 TCU	19-5	Buster Brannon	20-6
17 Oklahoma City	20-6	Abe Lemons	20-7
18 Utah	21-5	Jack Gardner	21-7
19 St. Bonaventure	20-2	Eddie Donovan	20-3
20 Marquette	22-4	Eddie Hickey	23-6

*Mississippi St. turned down invitation to NCAA tournament because it was an integrated event.

Note: Unranked **St. John's**, coached by Joe Lapchick, won the NIT. The Redmen entered the tourney at 16-6 and had a final record of 20-6.

NCAA Final Four (at Freedom Hall, Louisville): **Semifinals**—West Virginia 94, Louisville 79; California 64, Cincinnati 58. **Third Place**—Cincinnati 98, Louisville 85. **Championship**—California 71, West Virginia 70.

NIT Final Four (at Madison Square Garden): **Semifinals**—Bradley 59, NYU 57; St. John's 76, Providence 55. **Third Place**—NYU 71, Providence 57. **Championship**—St. John's 76, Bradley 71 (OT).

1960

	Before Tourns	Head Coach	Final Record
1 Cincinnati	25-1	George Smith	28-2
2 California	24-1	Pete Newell	28-2
3 Ohio St.	21-3	Fred Taylor	25-3
4 Bradley	24-2	Chuck Orsborn	27-2
5 West Virginia	24-4	Fred Schaus	26-5
6 Utah	24-2	Jack Gardner	26-3
7 Indiana	20-4	Branch McCracken	same
8 Utah St.	22-4	Cecil Baker	24-5
9 St. Bonaventure	19-3	Eddie Donovan	21-5
10 Miami-FL	23-3	Bruce Hale	23-4
11 Auburn	19-3	Joel Eaves	same
12 NYU	19-4	Lou Rossini	22-5
13 Georgia Tech	21-5	Whack Hyder	22-6
14 Providence	21-4	Joe Mullaney	24-5
15 Saint Louis	19-7	John Benington	19-8
16 Holy Cross	20-5	Roy Leenig	20-6
17 Villanova	19-5	Al Severance	20-6
18 Duke	15-10	Vic Bubas	17-11
19 Wake Forest	21-7	Bones McKinney	same
20 St. John's	17-7	Joe Lapchick	17-8

NCAA Final Four (at the Cow Palace, San Fran.): **Semifinals**—Ohio St. 76, NYU 54; California 77, Cincinnati 69. **Third Place**—Cincinnati 95, NYU 71. **Championship**—Ohio St. 75, California 55.

NIT Final Four (at Madison Square Garden): **Semifinals**—Bradley 82, St. Bonaventure 71; Providence 68, Utah St. 62. **Third Place**—Utah St. 99, St. Bonaventure 93. **Championship**—Bradley 88, Providence 72.

Associated Press Final Polls (Cont.)

Taken **before** NCAA and NIT tournaments

1961

		Before Tourns	Head Coach	Final Record
1	Ohio St.	24-0	Fred Taylor	27-1
2	**Cincinnati**	23-3	Ed Jucker	27-3
3	St. Bonaventure	22-3	Eddie Donovan	24-4
4	Kansas St.	22-3	Tex Winter	23-4
5	North Carolina	19-4	Frank McGuire	same
6	Bradley	21-5	Chuck Orsborn	same
7	USC	20-6	Forrest Twogood	21-8
8	Iowa	18-6	S. Scheuerman	same
9	West Virginia	23-4	George King	same
10	Duke	22-6	Vic Bubas	same
11	Utah	21-6	Jack Gardner	23-8
12	Texas Tech	14-9	Polk Robison	15-10
13	Niagara	16-4	Taps Gallagher	16-5
14	Memphis St.	20-2	Bob Vanatta	20-3
15	Wake Forest	17-10	Bones McKinney	19-11
16	St. John's	20-4	Joe Lapchick	20-5
17	St. Joseph's-PA	22-4	Jack Ramsay	25-5
18	Drake	19-7	Maury John	same
19	Holy Cross	19-4	Roy Leenig	22-5
20	Kentucky	18-8	Adolph Rupp	19-9

Note: Unranked **Providence**, coached by Joe Mullaney, won the NIT. The Friars entered the tourney at 20-5 and had a final record of 24-5.

NCAA Final Four (at Municipal Auditorium, Kansas City): **Semifinals**—Ohio St. 95, St. Joseph's-PA 69; Cincinnati 82, Utah 67. **Third Place**—St. Joseph's-PA 127, Utah 120 (4 OT). **Championship**—Cincinnati 70, Ohio St. 65 (OT).

NIT Final Four (at Madison Square Garden) **Semifinals**—St. Louis 67, Dayton 60; Providence 90, Holy Cross 83 (OT). **Third Place**—Holy Cross 85, Dayton 67. **Championship**—Providence 62, St. Louis 59.

1962

		Before Tourns	Head Coach	Final Record
1	Ohio St.	23-1	Fred Taylor	26-2
2	**Cincinnati**	25-2	Ed Jucker	29-2
3	Kentucky	22-2	Adolph Rupp	23-3
4	Mississippi St.	19-6	Babe McCarthy	same
5	Bradley	21-6	Chuck Orsborn	21-7
6	Kansas St.	22-3	Tex Winter	same
7	Utah	23-3	Jack Gardner	same
8	Bowling Green	21-3	Harold Anderson	same
9	Colorado	18-6	Sox Walseth	19-7
10	Duke	20-5	Vic Bubas	same
11	Loyola-IL	21-3	George Ireland	23-4
12	St. John's	19-4	Joe Lapchick	21-5
13	Wake Forest	18-8	Bones McKinney	22-9
14	Oregon St.	22-4	Slats Gill	24-5
15	West Virginia	24-5	George King	24-6
16	Arizona St.	23-3	Ned Wulk	23-4
17	Duquesne	20-5	Red Manning	22-7
18	Utah St.	21-5	Ladell Andersen	22-7
19	UCLA	16-9	John Wooden	18-11
20	Villanova	19-6	Jack Kraft	21-7

Note: Unranked **Dayton**, coached by Tom Blackburn, won the NIT. The Flyers entered the tourney at 20-6 and had a final record of 24-6.

NCAA Final Four (at Freedom Hall, Louisville): **Semifinals**—Ohio St. 84, Wake Forest 68; Cincinnati 72, UCLA 70. **Third Place**—Wake Forest 82, UCLA 80. **Championship**—Cincinnati 71, Ohio St. 59.

NIT Final Four (at Madison Square Garden): **Semifinals**—Dayton 98, Loyola-IL 82; St. John's 76, Duquesne 65. **Third Place**—Loyola-IL 95, Duquesne 84. **Championship**—Dayton 73, St. John's 84.

1963

AP ranked only 10 teams from the 1962-63 season through 1967-68.

		Before Tourns	Head Coach	Final Record
1	Cincinnati	23-1	Ed Jucker	26-2
2	Duke	24-2	Vic Bubas	27-3
3	**Loyola-IL**	24-2	George Ireland	29-2
4	Arizona St.	24-2	Ned Wulk	26-3
5	Wichita	19-7	Ralph Miller	19-8
6	Mississippi St.	21-5	Babe McCarthy	22-6
7	Ohio St.	20-4	Fred Taylor	same
8	Illinois	19-5	Harry Combes	20-6
9	NYU	17-3	Lou Rossini	18-5
10	Colorado	18-6	Sox Walseth	19-7

Note: Unranked **Providence**, coached by Joe Mullaney, won the NIT. The Friars entered the tourney at 21-4 and had a final record of 24-4.

NCAA Final Four (at Freedom Hall, Louisville): **Semifinals**—Loyola-IL 94, Duke 75; Cincinnati 80, Oregon St. 46. **Third Place**—Duke 85, Oregon St. 63. **Championship**—Loyola-IL 60, Cincinnati 58 (OT).

NIT Final Four (at Madison Square Garden): **Semifinals**—Providence 70, Marquette 64; Canisius 61, Villanova 46. **Third Place**—Marquette 66, Villanova 58. **Championship**—Providence 81, Canisius 66.

1964

AP ranked only 10 teams from the 1962-63 season through 1967-68.

		Before Tourns	Head Coach	Final Record
1	UCLA	26-0	John Wooden	30-0
2	Michigan	20-4	Dave Strack	23-5
3	Duke	23-4	Vic Bubas	26-5
4	Kentucky	21-4	Adolph Rupp	21-6
5	Wichita	22-5	Ralph Miller	23-6
6	Oregon St.	25-3	Slats Gill	25-4
7	Villanova	22-3	Jack Kraft	24-4
8	Loyola-IL	20-5	George Ireland	22-6
9	DePaul	21-3	Ray Meyer	21-4
10	Davidson	22-4	Lefty Driesell	same

Note: Unranked **Bradley**, coached by Chuck Orsborn, won the NIT. The Braves entered the tourney at 20-6 and finished with a record of 23-6.

NCAA Final Four (at Municipal Auditorium, Kansas City): **Semifinals**—Duke 91, Michigan 80; UCLA 90, Kansas St. 84. **Third Place**—Michigan 100, Kansas St. 90. **Championship**—UCLA 98, Duke 83.

NIT Final Four (12 at Madison Square Garden): **Semifinals**—New Mexico 72, NYU 65; Bradley 67, Army 52. **Third Place**—Army 60, NYU 59. **Championship**—Bradley 86, New Mexico 54.

Undefeated National Champions

The 1964 UCLA team is one of only seven NCAA champions to win the title with an undefeated record.

Year		W-L	Year		W-L
1956	San Francisco	29-0	1972	UCLA	30-0
1957	North Carolina	32-0	1973	UCLA	30-0
1964	UCLA	30-0	1976	Indiana	32-0
1967	UCLA	30-0			

1965

AP ranked only 10 teams from the 1962-63 season through 1967-68.

		Before Tourns	Head Coach	Final Record
1	Michigan	21-3	Dave Strack	24-4
2	UCLA	24-2	John Wooden	28-2
3	St. Joseph's-PA	25-1	Jack Ramsay	26-3
4	Providence	22-1	Joe Mullaney	24-2
5	Vanderbilt	23-3	Roy Skinner	24-4
6	Davidson	24-2	Lefty Driesell	same
7	Minnesota	19-5	John Kundla	same
8	Villanova	21-4	Jack Kraft	23-5
9	BYU	21-5	Stan Watts	21-7
10	Duke	20-5	Vic Bubas	same

Note: Unranked **St. John's**, coached by Joe Lapchick, won the NIT. The Redmen entered the tourney at 17-8 and finished with a record of 21-8.

NCAA Final Four (at Memorial Coliseum, Portland, OR): **Semifinals**—Michigan 93, Princeton 76; UCLA 108, Wichita St. 89. **Third Place**—Princeton 118, Wichita St. 82. **Championship**—UCLA 91, Michigan 80.

NIT Final Four (at Madison Square Garden): **Semifinals**—Villanova 91, NYU 69; St. John's 67, Army 60. **Third Place**—Army 75, NYU 74. **Championship**—St. John's 55, Villanova 51.

1966

AP ranked only 10 teams from the 1962-63 season through 1967-68.

		Before Tourns	Head Coach	Final Record
1	Kentucky	24-1	Adolph Rupp	27-2
2	Duke	23-3	Vic Bubas	26-4
3	Texas Western	23-1	Don Haskins	28-1
4	Kansas	22-3	Ted Owens	23-4
5	St. Joseph's-PA	22-4	Jack Ramsay	24-5
6	Loyola-IL	22-2	George Ireland	22-3
7	Cincinnati	21-5	Tay Baker	21-7
8	Vanderbilt	22-4	Roy Skinner	same
9	Michigan	17-7	Dave Strack	18-8
10	Western Ky.	23-2	Johnny Oldham	25-3

Note: Unranked **BYU**, coached by Stan Watts, won the NIT. The Cougars entered the tourney at 17-5 and had a final record of 20-5.

NCAA Final Four (at Cole Fieldhouse, College Park, MD): **Semifinals**—Kentucky 83, Duke 79; Texas Western 85, Utah 78. **Third Place**—Duke 79, Utah 77. **Championship**—Texas Western 72, Kentucky 65.

NIT Final Four (at Madison Square Garden): **Semifinals**—BYU 66, Army 60; NYU 69, Villanova 63. **Third Place**—Villanova 76, Army 65. **Championship**—BYU 97, NYU 84.

1967

AP ranked only 10 teams from the 1962-63 season through 1967-68.

		Before Tourns	Head Coach	Final Record
1	UCLA	26-0	John Wooden	30-0
2	Louisville	23-3	Peck Hickman	23-5
3	Kansas	22-3	Ted Owens	23-4
4	North Carolina	24-4	Dean Smith	26-6
5	Princeton	23-2	B. van Breda Kolff	25-3
6	Western Ky.	23-2	Johnny Oldham	23-3
7	Houston	23-3	Guy Lewis	27-4
8	Tennessee	21-5	Ray Mears	21-7
9	Boston College	19-2	Bob Cousy	21-3
10	Texas Western	20-5	Don Haskins	22-6

Note: Unranked **Southern Illinois**, coached by Jack Hartman, won the NIT. The Salukis entered the tourney at 20-2 and had a final record of 24-2.

NCAA Final Four (at Freedom Hall, Louisville): **Semifinals**—Dayton 76, N. Carolina 62; UCLA 73, Houston 58. **Third Place**—Houston 84, N. Carolina 62. **Championship**—UCLA 79, Dayton 64.

NIT Final Four (at Madison Square Garden): **Semifinals**—Marquette 83, Marshall 78; Southern Ill. 79, Rutgers 70. **Third Place**—Rutgers 93, Marshall 76. **Championship**—Southern Ill. 71, Marquette 56.

1968

AP ranked only 10 teams from the 1962-63 season through 1967-68.

		Before Tourns	Head Coach	Final Record
1	Houston	28-0	Guy Lewis	31-2
2	UCLA	25-1	John Wooden	29-1
3	St. Bonaventure	22-0	Larry Weise	23-2
4	North Carolina	25-3	Dean Smith	28-4
5	Kentucky	21-4	Adolph Rupp	22-5
6	New Mexico	23-3	Bob King	23-5
7	Columbia	21-4	Jack Rohan	23-5
8	Davidson	22-4	Lefty Driesell	24-5
9	Louisville	20-6	John Dromo	21-7
10	Duke	21-5	Vic Bubas	22-6

Note: Unranked **Dayton**, coached by Don Donoher, won the NIT. The Flyers entered the tourney at 17-9 and had a final record of 21-9.

NCAA Final Four (at the Sports Arena, Los Angeles): **Semifinals**—N. Carolina 80, Ohio St. 66; UCLA 101, Houston 69. **Third Place**—Ohio St. 89, Houston 85. **Championship**—UCLA 78, N. Carolina 55.

NIT Final Four (at Madison Square Garden): **Semifinals**—Dayton 76, Notre Dame 74 (OT); Kansas 58, St. Peter's 46. **Third Place**—Notre Dame 81, St. Peter's 78. **Championship**—Dayton 61, Kansas 48.

Highest-Rated College Games on TV

The dozen highest-rated college basketball games seen on U.S. television have been NCAA tournament championship games, led by the 1979 Michigan State-Indiana State final that featured Magic Johnson and Larry Bird.

Listed below are the finalists (winning team first), date of game, TV network, and TV rating and audience share (according to Nielson Media Research).

		Date	Net	Rtg/Sh			Date	Net	Rtg/Sh
1	Michigan St.-Indiana St.	3/26/79	NBC	24.1/38	7	N. Carolina-Georgetown	3/29/82	CBS	21.6/31
2	Villanova-Georgetown	4/1/85	CBS	23.3/33	8	UCLA-Kentucky	3/31/75	NBC	21.3/33
3	Duke-Michigan	4/6/92	CBS	22.7/35	9	Michigan-Seton Hall	4/3/89	CBS	21.3/33
4	N.C. State-Houston	4/4/83	CBS	22.3/32	10	Louisville-Duke	3/32/86	CBS	20.7/31
5	N. Carolina-Michigan	4/5/93	CBS	22.2/34	11	Indiana-N. Carolina	3/30/81	NBC	20.7/29
6	Arkansas-Duke	4/4/94	CBS	21.6/33	12	UCLA-Memphis St.	3/26/73	NBC	20.5/32

Associated Press Final Polls (Cont.)

Taken **before** NCAA, NIT and Collegiate Commissioner's Assn. (1974-75) tournaments; (*) indicates on probation.

1969

	Before Tourns	Head Coach	Final Record
1 UCLA	25-1	John Wooden	29-1
2 La Salle	23-1	Tom Gola	same*
3 Santa Clara	26-1	Dick Garibaldi	27-2
4 North Carolina	25-3	Dean Smith	27-5
5 Davidson	24-2	Lefty Driesell	26-3
6 Purdue	20-4	George King	23-5
7 Kentucky	22-4	Adolph Rupp	23-5
8 St. John's	22-4	Lou Carnesecca	23-6
9 Duquesne	19-4	Red Manning	21-5
10 Villanova	21-4	Jack Kraft	21-5
11 Drake	23-4	Maury John	26-5
12 New Mexico St.	23-3	Lou Henson	24-5
13 South Carolina	20-6	Frank McGuire	21-7
14 Marquette	22-4	Al McGuire	24-5
15 Louisville	20-5	John Dromo	21-6
16 Boston College	21-3	Bob Cousy	24-4
17 Notre Dame	20-6	Johnny Dee	20-7
18 Colorado	20-6	Sox Walseth	21-7
19 Kansas	20-6	Ted Owens	20-7
20 Illinois	19-5	Harvey Schmidt	same

Note: Unranked **Temple**, coached by Harry Litwak, won the NIT. The Owls entered the tourney at 18-8 and finished with a record of 22-8.

NCAA Final Four (at Freedom Hall, Louisville): **Semifinals**—Purdue 92, N. Carolina 65; UCLA 85, Drake 82. **Third Place**—Drake 104, N. Carolina 84. **Championship**—UCLA 92, Purdue 72.

NIT Final Four (at Madison Square Garden): **Semifinals**—Temple 63, Tennessee 58; Boston College 73, Army 61. **Third Place**—Tennessee 64, Army 52. **Championship**—Temple 89, Boston College 76.

1971

	Before Tourns	Head Coach	Final Record
1 UCLA	25-1	John Wooden	29-1
2 Marquette	26-0	Al McGuire	28-1
3 Penn	26-0	Dick Harter	28-1
4 Kansas	25-1	Ted Owens	27-3
5 USC	24-2	Bob Boyd	24-2
6 South Carolina	23-4	Frank McGuire	23-6
7 Western Ky.	20-5	John Oldham	24-6
8 Kentucky	22-4	Adolph Rupp	22-6
9 Fordham	25-1	Digger Phelps	26-3
10 Ohio St.	19-5	Fred Taylor	20-6
11 Jacksonville	22-3	Tom Wasdin	22-4
12 Notre Dame	19-7	Johnny Dee	20-9
13 North Carolina	22-6	Dean Smith	26-6
14 Houston	20-6	Guy Lewis	22-7
15 Duquesne	21-3	Red Manning	21-4
16 Long Beach St.	21-4	Jerry Tarkanian	23-5
17 Tennessee	20-6	Ray Mears	21-7
18 Villanova	19-5	Jack Kraft	23-6
19 Drake	20-7	Maury John	21-8
20 BYU	18-9	Stan Watts	18-11

NCAA Final Four (at the Astrodome, Houston): **Semifinals**—Villanova 92, Western Ky. 89 (2 OT); UCLA 68, Kansas 60. **Third Place**—Western Ky. 77, Kansas 75. **Championship**—UCLA 68, Villanova 62.

NIT Final Four (at Madison Square Garden): **Semifinals**—N. Carolina 73, Duke 69; Ga. Tech 76, St. Bonaventure 71 (2 OT). **Third Place**—St. Bonaventure 92, Duke 88 (OT). **Championship**—N. Carolina 84, Ga. Tech 66.

1970

	Before Tourns	Head Coach	Final Record
1 Kentucky	25-1	Adolph Rupp	26-2
2 UCLA	24-2	John Wooden	28-2
3 St. Bonaventure	22-1	Larry Weise	25-3
4 Jacksonville	23-1	Joe Williams	27-2
5 New Mexico St.	23-2	Lou Henson	27-3
6 South Carolina	25-3	Frank McGuire	25-3
7 Iowa	19-4	Ralph Miller	20-5
8 Marquette	22-3	Al McGuire	26-3
9 Notre Dame	20-6	Johnny Dee	21-8
10 N.C. State	22-6	Norm Sloan	23-7
11 Florida St.	23-3	Hugh Durham	23-3
12 Houston	24-3	Guy Lewis	25-5
13 Penn	25-1	Dick Harter	25-2
14 Drake	21-6	Maury John	22-7
15 Davidson	22-4	Terry Holland	22-5
16 Utah St.	20-6	Ladell Andersen	22-7
17 Niagara	21-5	Frank Layden	22-7
18 Western Ky.	22-2	John Oldham	22-3
19 Long Beach St.	23-3	Jerry Tarkanian	24-5
20 USC	18-8	Bob Boyd	18-8

NCAA Final Four (at Cole Fieldhouse, College Park, MD): **Semifinals**—Jacksonville 91, St. Bonaventure 83; UCLA 93, New Mexico St. 77. **Third Place**—N. Mexico St. 79, St. Bonaventure 73. **Championship**—UCLA 80, Jacksonville 69.

NIT Final Four (at Madison Square Garden): **Semifinals**—St. John's 60, Army 59; Marquette 101, LSU 79. **Third Place**—Army 75, LSU 68. **Championship**—Marquette 65, St. John's 53.

1972

	Before Tourns	Head Coach	Final Record
1 UCLA	26-0	John Wooden	30-0
2 North Carolina	23-4	Dean Smith	26-5
3 Penn	23-2	Chuck Daly	25-3
4 Louisville	23-4	Denny Crum	26-5
5 Long Beach St.	23-3	Jerry Tarkanian	25-4
6 South Carolina	22-4	Frank McGuire	24-5
7 Marquette	24-2	Al McGuire	25-4
8 SW Louisiana	23-3	Beryl Shipley	25-4
9 BYU	21-4	Stan Watts	21-5
10 Florida St.	23-5	Hugh Durham	27-6
11 Minnesota	17-6	Bill Musselman	18-7
12 Marshall	23-3	Carl Tacy	23-4
13 Memphis St.	21-6	Gene Bartow	21-7
14 Maryland	23-5	Lefty Driesell	27-5
15 Villanova	19-6	Jack Kraft	20-8
16 Oral Roberts	25-1	Ken Trickey	26-2
17 Indiana	17-7	Bob Knight	17-8
18 Kentucky	20-6	Adolph Rupp	21-7
19 Ohio St.	18-6	Fred Taylor	same
20 Virginia	21-6	Bill Gibson	21-7

NCAA Final Four (at the Sports Arena, Los Angeles): **Semifinals**—Florida St. 79, N. Carolina 75; UCLA 96, Louisville 77. **Third Place**—N. Carolina 105, Louisville 91. **Championship**—UCLA 81, Florida St. 76.

NIT Final Four (at Madison Square Garden): **Semifinals**—Maryland 91, Jacksonville 77; Niagara 69, St. John's 67. **Third Place**—Jacksonville 83, St. John's 80. **Championship**—Maryland 100, Niagara 69.

1973

	Before Tourns	Head Coach	Final Record
1 UCLA	26-0	John Wooden	30-0
2 N.C. State	27-0	Norm Sloan	same*
3 Long Beach St.	24-2	Jerry Tarkanian	26-3
4 Providence	24-2	Dave Gavitt	27-4
5 Marquette	23-3	Al McGuire	25-4
6 Indiana	19-5	Bob Knight	22-6
7 SW Louisiana	23-2	Beryl Shipley	24-5
8 Maryland	22-6	Lefty Driesell	23-7
9 Kansas St.	22-4	Jack Hartman	23-5
10 Minnesota	20-4	Bill Musselman	21-5
11 North Carolina	22-7	Dean Smith	25-8
12 Memphis St.	21-5	Gene Bartow	24-6
13 Houston	23-3	Guy Lewis	23-4
14 Syracuse	22-4	Roy Danforth	24-5
15 Missouri	21-5	Norm Stewart	21-6
16 Arizona St.	18-7	Ned Wulk	19-9
17 Kentucky	19-7	Joe B. Hall	20-8
18 Penn	20-5	Chuck Daly	21-7
19 Austin Peay	21-5	Lake Kelly	22-7
20 San Francisco	22-4	Bob Gaillard	23-5

*N.C. State was ineligible for NCAA tournament for using improper methods to recruit David Thompson.

Note: Unranked **Virginia Tech**, coached by Don DeVoe, won the NIT. The Hokies entered the tourney at 18-5 and finished with a record of 22-5.

NCAA Final Four (at The Arena, St. Louis): **Semifinals**—Memphis St. 98, Providence 85; UCLA 70, Indiana 59. **Third Place**—Indiana 97, Providence 79. **Championship**—UCLA 87, Memphis St. 66.

NIT Final Four (at Madison Square Garden): **Semifinals**—Va. Tech 74, Alabama 73; Notre Dame 78, N. Carolina 71. **Third Place**—N. Carolina 88, Alabama 69. **Championship**—Va. Tech 92, Notre Dame 91 (OT).

1975

	Before Tourns	Head Coach	Final Record
1 Indiana	29-0	Bob Knight	31-1
2 UCLA	23-3	John Wooden	28-3
3 Louisville	24-2	Denny Crum	28-3
4 Maryland	22-4	Lefty Driesell	24-5
5 Kentucky	22-4	Joe B. Hall	26-5
6 North Carolina	21-7	Dean Smith	23-8
7 Arizona St.	23-3	Ned Wulk	25-4
8 N.C. State	22-6	Norm Sloan	22-6
9 Notre Dame	18-8	Digger Phelps	19-10
10 Marquette	23-3	Al McGuire	23-4
11 Alabama	22-4	C.M. Newton	22-5
12 Cincinnati	21-5	Gale Catlett	23-6
13 Oregon St.	18-10	Ralph Miller	19-12
14 Drake	16-10	Bob Ortegel	19-10
15 Penn	23-4	Chuck Daly	23-5
16 UNLV	22-4	Jerry Tarkanian	24-5
17 Kansas St.	18-8	Jack Hartman	20-9
18 USC	18-7	Bob Boyd	18-8
19 Centenary	25-4	Larry Little	same
20 Syracuse	20-7	Roy Danforth	23-9

NCAA Final Four (at San Diego Sports Arena): **Semifinals**—Kentucky 95, Syracuse 79; UCLA 75, Louisville 74 (OT). **Third Place**—Louisville 96, Syracuse 88 (OT). **Championship**—UCLA 92, Kentucky 85.

NIT Championship (at Madison Sq. Garden): Princeton 80, Providence 69. No Top 20 teams played in NIT.

CCA Championship (at Freedom Hall, Louisville): Drake 83, Arizona 76. No.14 Drake and No.18 USC were only Top 20 teams in CCA.

1974

	Before Tourns	Head Coach	Final Record
1 N.C. State	26-1	Norm Sloan	30-1
2 UCLA	23-3	John Wooden	26-4
3 Notre Dame	24-2	Digger Phelps	26-3
4 Maryland	23-5	Lefty Driesell	same
5 Providence	26-3	Dave Gavitt	28-4
6 Vanderbilt	23-3	Roy Skinner	23-5
7 Marquette	22-4	Al McGuire	26-5
8 North Carolina	22-5	Dean Smith	22-6
9 Long Beach St.	24-2	Lute Olson	same
10 Indiana	20-5	Bob Knight	23-5
11 Alabama	22-4	C.M. Newton	same
12 Michigan	21-4	Johnny Orr	22-5
13 Pittsburgh	23-3	Buzz Ridl	25-4
14 Kansas	21-5	Ted Owens	23-7
15 USC	22-4	Bob Boyd	24-5
16 Louisville	21-6	Denny Crum	21-7
17 New Mexico	21-6	Norm Ellenberger	22-7
18 South Carolina	22-4	Frank McGuire	22-5
19 Creighton	22-6	Eddie Sutton	23-7
20 Dayton	19-7	Don Donoher	20-9

NCAA Final Four (at Greensboro, NC, Coliseum): **Semifinals**—N.C. State 80, UCLA 77 (2 OT); Marquette 64, Kansas 51. **Third Place**—UCLA 78, Kansas 61. **Championship**—N.C. State 76, Marquette 64.

NIT Final Four (at Madison Square Garden): **Semifinals**—Purdue 78, Jacksonville 63; Utah 117, Boston Col. 93. **Third Place**—Boston Col. 87, Jacksonville 77. **Championship**—Purdue 87, Utah 81.

CCA Final Four (at The Arena, St. Louis): **Semifinals**—Indiana 73, Toledo 72; USC 74, Bradley 73. **Championship**—Indiana 85, USC 60.

1976

	Before Tourns	Head Coach	Final Record
1 Indiana	27-0	Bob Knight	32-0
2 Marquette	25-1	Al McGuire	27-2
3 UNLV	28-1	Jerry Tarkanian	29-2
4 Rutgers	28-0	Tom Young	31-2
5 UCLA	24-3	Gene Bartow	28-4
6 Alabama	22-4	C.M. Newton	23-5
7 Notre Dame	22-5	Digger Phelps	23-6
8 North Carolina	25-3	Dean Smith	25-4
9 Michigan	21-6	Johnny Orr	25-7
10 Western Mich.	24-2	Eldon Miller	25-3
11 Maryland	22-6	Lefty Driesell	same
12 Cincinnati	25-5	Gale Catlett	25-6
13 Tennessee	21-5	Ray Mears	21-6
14 Missouri	24-4	Norm Stewart	26-5
15 Arizona	22-8	Fred Snowden	24-9
16 Texas Tech	24-5	Gerald Myers	25-6
17 DePaul	19-8	Ray Meyer	20-9
18 Virginia	18-11	Terry Holland	18-12
19 Centenary	22-5	Larry Little	same
20 Pepperdine	21-5	Gary Colson	22-6

NCAA Final Four (at the Spectrum, Phila.); **Semifinals**—Michigan 86, Rutgers 70; Indiana 65, UCLA 51. **Third Place**—UCLA 106, Rutgers 92. **Championship**—Indiana 86, Michigan 68.

NIT Championship (at Madison Square Garden): Kentucky 71, NC-Charlotte 67. No Top 20 teams played in NIT.

Associated Press Final Polls (Cont.)

Taken **before** NCAA and NIT Tournaments; (*) indicates on probation.

1977

	Before Tourns	Head Coach	Final Record
1 Michigan	24-3	Johnny Orr	26-4
2 UCLA	24-3	Gene Bartow	25-4
3 Kentucky	24-3	Joe B. Hall	26-4
4 UNLV	25-2	Jerry Tarkanian	29-3
5 North Carolina	24-4	Dean Smith	28-5
6 Syracuse	25-3	Jim Boeheim	26-4
7 Marquette	20-7	Al McGuire	25-7
8 San Francisco	29-1	Bob Gaillard	29-2
9 Wake Forest	20-7	Carl Tacy	22-8
10 Notre Dame	21-6	Digger Phelps	22-7
11 Alabama	23-4	C.M. Newton	25-6
12 Detroit	24-3	Dick Vitale	25-4
13 Minnesota	24-3	Jim Dutcher	same*
14 Utah	22-6	Jerry Pimm	23-7
15 Tennessee	22-5	Ray Mears	22-6
16 Kansas St.	23-6	Jack Hartman	24-7
17 NC-Charlotte	25-3	Lee Rose	28-5
18 Arkansas	26-1	Eddie Sutton	26-2
19 Louisville	21-6	Denny Crum	21-7
20 VMI	25-3	Charlie Schmaus	26-4

NCAA Final Four (at the Omni, Atlanta): **Semifinals**—Marquette 51, NC-Charlotte, 49; N. Carolina 84, UNLV 83. **Third Place**—UNLV 106, NC-Charlotte 94. **Championship**—Marquette 67, N. Carolina 59.

NIT Championship (at Madison Square Garden): St. Bonaventure 94, Houston 91. No.11 Alabama was only Top 20 team in NIT.

1978

	Before Tourns	Head Coach	Final Record
1 Kentucky	25-2	Joe B. Hall	30-2
2 UCLA	24-2	Gary Cunningham	25-3
3 DePaul	25-2	Ray Meyer	27-3
4 Michigan St.	23-4	Jud Heathcote	25-5
5 Arkansas	28-3	Eddie Sutton	32-3
6 Notre Dame	20-6	Digger Phelps	23-8
7 Duke	23-6	Bill Foster	27-7
8 Marquette	24-3	Hank Raymonds	24-4
9 Louisville	22-6	Denny Crum	23-7
10 Kansas	24-4	Ted Owens	24-5
11 San Francisco	22-5	Bob Gaillard	23-6
12 New Mexico	24-3	Norm Ellenberger	24-4
13 Indiana	20-7	Bob Knight	21-8
14 Utah	22-5	Jerry Pimm	23-6
15 Florida St.	23-5	Hugh Durham	23-6
16 North Carolina	23-7	Dean Smith	23-8
17 Texas	22-5	Abe Lemons	26-5
18 Detroit	24-3	Dave Gaines	25-4
19 Miami-OH	18-8	Darrell Hedric	19-9
20 Penn	19-7	Bob Weinhauer	20-8

NCAA Final Four (at the Checkerdome, St. Louis): **Semifinals**—Kentucky 64, Arkansas 59; Duke 90, Notre Dame 86. **Third Place**—Arkansas 71, Notre Dame 69. **Championship**—Kentucky 94, Duke 88.

NIT Championship (at Madison Square Garden): Texas 101, N.C. State 93. No.17 Texas and No.18 Detroit were only Top 20 teams in NIT.

1979

	Before Tourns	Head Coach	Final Record
1 Indiana St.	29-0	Bill Hodges	33-1
2 UCLA	23-4	Gary Cunningham	25-5
3 Michigan St.	21-6	Jud Heathcote	26-6
4 Notre Dame	22-5	Digger Phelps	24-6
5 Arkansas	23-4	Eddie Sutton	25-5
6 DePaul	22-5	Ray Meyer	26-6
7 LSU	22-5	Dale Brown	23-6
8 Syracuse	25-3	Jim Boeheim	26-4
9 North Carolina	23-5	Dean Smith	23-6
10 Marquette	21-6	Hank Raymonds	22-7
11 Duke	22-7	Bill Foster	22-8
12 San Francisco	21-6	Dan Belluomini	22-7
13 Louisville	23-7	Denny Crum	24-8
14 Penn	21-5	Bob Weinhauer	25-7
15 Purdue	23-7	Lee Rose	27-8
16 Oklahoma	20-9	Dave Bliss	21-10
17 St. John's	18-10	Lou Carnesecca	21-11
18 Rutgers	21-8	Tom Young	22-9
19 Toledo	21-6	Bob Nichols	22-7
20 Iowa	20-7	Lute Olson	20-8

NCAA Final Four (at Special Center, Salt Lake City): **Semifinals**—Michigan St. 101, Penn 67; Indiana St. 76, DePaul 74. **Third Place**—DePaul 96, Penn 93. **Championship**—Michigan St. 75, Indiana St. 64.

NIT Championship (at Madison Square Garden): Indiana 53, Purdue 52. No.15 Purdue was only Top 20 team in NIT.

1980

	Before Tourns	Head Coach	Final Record
1 DePaul	26-1	Ray Meyer	26-2
2 Louisville	28-3	Denny Crum	33-3
3 LSU	24-5	Dale Brown	26-6
4 Kentucky	28-5	Joe B. Hall	29-6
5 Oregon St.	26-3	Ralph Miller	26-4
6 Syracuse	25-3	Jim Boeheim	26-4
7 Indiana	20-7	Bob Knight	21-8
8 Maryland	23-6	Lefty Driesell	24-7
9 Notre Dame	20-7	Digger Phelps	20-8
10 Ohio St.	24-5	Eldon Miller	21-8
11 Georgetown	24-5	John Thompson	26-6
12 BYU	24-4	Frank Arnold	24-5
13 St. John's	24-4	Lou Carnesecca	24-5
14 Duke	22-8	Bill Foster	24-9
15 North Carolina	21-7	Dean Smith	21-8
16 Missouri	23-5	Norm Stewart	25-6
17 Weber St.	26-2	Neil McCarthy	26-3
18 Arizona St.	21-6	Ned Wulk	22-7
19 Iona	28-4	Jim Valvano	29-5
20 Purdue	19-9	Lee Rose	23-10

NCAA Final Four (at Market Square Arena, Indianapolis): **Semifinals**—Louisville 80, Iowa 72; UCLA 67, Purdue 62; **Championship**—Louisville 59, UCLA 54.

NIT Championship (at Madison Square Garden): Virginia 58, Minnesota 55. No Top 20 teams played in NIT.

1981

	Before Tourns	Head Coach	Final Record
1 DePaul	27-1	Ray Meyer	27-2
2 Oregon St.	26-1	Ralph Miller	26-2
3 Arizona St.	24-3	Ned Wulk	24-4
4 LSU	28-3	Dale Brown	31-5
5 Virginia	25-3	Terry Holland	29-4
6 North Carolina	25-7	Dean Smith	29-8
7 Notre Dame	22-5	Digger Phelps	23-6
8 Kentucky	22-5	Joe B. Hall	22-6
9 Indiana	21-9	Bob Knight	26-9
10 UCLA	20-6	Larry Brown	20-7
11 Wake Forest	22-6	Carl Tacy	22-7
12 Louisville	21-8	Denny Crum	21-9
13 Iowa	21-6	Lute Olson	21-7
14 Utah	24-4	Jerry Pimm	25-5
15 Tennessee	20-7	Don DeVoe	21-8
16 BYU	22-6	Frank Arnold	25-7
17 Wyoming	23-5	Jim Brandenburg	24-6
18 Maryland	20-9	Lefty Driesell	21-10
19 Illinois	20-7	Lou Henson	21-8
20 Arkansas	22-7	Eddie Sutton	24-8

NCAA Final Four (at the Spectrum, Phila.): **Semifinals**—N. Carolina 78, Virginia 65; Indiana 67, LSU 49. **Third Place**—Virginia 78, LSU 74. **Championship**—Indiana 63, N. Carolina 50.

NIT Championship (at Madison Square Garden): Tulsa 86, Syracuse 84. No Top 20 teams played in NIT.

1983

	Before Tourns	Head Coach	Final Record
1 Houston	27-2	Guy Lewis	31-3
2 Louisville	29-3	Denny Crum	32-4
3 St. John's	27-4	Lou Carnesecca	28-5
4 Virginia	27-4	Terry Holland	29-5
5 Indiana	23-5	Bob Knight	24-6
6 UNLV	28-2	Jerry Tarkanian	28-3
7 UCLA	23-5	Larry Farmer	23-6
8 North Carolina	26-7	Dean Smith	28-8
9 Arkansas	25-3	Eddie Sutton	26-4
10 Missouri	26-7	Norm Stewart	26-8
11 Boston College	24-6	Gary Williams	25-7
12 Kentucky	22-7	Joe B. Hall	23-8
13 Villanova	22-7	Rollie Massimino	24-8
14 Wichita St.	25-3	Gene Smithson	same*
15 Tenn-Chatt.	26-3	Murray Arnold	26-4
16 N.C. State	20-10	Jim Valvano	26-10
17 Memphis St.	22-7	Dana Kirk	23-8
18 Georgia	21-9	Hugh Durham	24-10
19 Oklahoma St.	24-6	Paul Hansen	24-7
20 Georgetown	21-9	John Thompson	22-10

NCAA Final Four (at The Pit, Albuquerque, NM): **Semifinals**—N.C. State 67, Georgia 60; Houston 94, Louisville 81. **Championship**—N.C. State 54, Houston 52.

NIT Championship (at Madison Square Garden): Fresno St. 69, DePaul 60. No Top 20 teams played in NIT.

1982

	Before Tourns	Head Coach	Final Record
1 North Carolina	27-2	Dean Smith	32-2
2 DePaul	26-1	Ray Meyer	26-2
3 Virginia	29-3	Terry Holland	30-4
4 Oregon St.	23-4	Ralph Miller	25-5
5 Missouri	26-3	Norm Stewart	27-4
6 Georgetown	26-6	John Thompson	30-7
7 Minnesota	22-5	Jim Dutcher	23-6
8 Idaho	26-2	Don Monson	27-3
9 Memphis St.	23-4	Dana Kirk	24-5
10 Tulsa	24-5	Nolan Richardson	24-6
11 Fresno St.	26-2	Boyd Grant	27-3
12 Arkansas	23-5	Eddie Sutton	23-6
13 Alabama	23-6	Wimp Sanderson	24-7
14 West Virginia	26-3	Gale Catlett	27-4
15 Kentucky	22-7	Joe B. Hall	22-8
16 Iowa	20-7	Lute Olson	21-8
17 Ala-Birmingham	23-5	Gene Bartow	25-6
18 Wake Forest	20-8	Carl Tacy	21-9
19 UCLA	21-6	Larry Farmer	21-6
20 Louisville	20-9	Denny Crum	23-10

NCAA Final Four (at the Superdome, New Orleans): **Semifinals**—N. Carolina 68, Houston 63; Georgetown 50, Louisville 46. **Championship**—N. Carolina 63, Georgetown 62.

NIT Championship (at Madison Square Garden): Bradley 67, Purdue 58. No Top 20 teams played in NIT.

1984

	Before Tourns	Head Coach	Final Record
1 North Carolina	27-2	Dean Smith	28-3
2 Georgetown	29-3	John Thompson	34-3
3 Kentucky	26-4	Joe B. Hall	29-5
4 DePaul	26-2	Ray Meyer	27-3
5 Houston	28-4	Guy Lewis	32-5
6 Illinois	24-4	Lou Henson	26-5
7 Oklahoma	29-4	Billy Tubbs	29-5
8 Arkansas	25-6	Eddie Sutton	25-7
9 UTEP	27-3	Don Haskins	27-4
10 Purdue	22-6	Gene Keady	22-7
11 Maryland	23-7	Lefty Driesell	24-8
12 Tulsa	27-3	Nolan Richardson	27-4
13 UNLV	27-5	Jerry Tarkanian	29-6
14 Duke	24-9	Mike Krzyzewski	24-10
15 Washington	22-6	Marv Harshman	24-7
16 Memphis St.	24-6	Dana Kirk	26-7
17 Oregon St.	22-6	Ralph Miller	22-7
18 Syracuse	22-8	Jim Boeheim	23-9
19 Wake Forest	21-8	Carl Tacy	23-9
20 Temple	25-4	John Chaney	26-5

NCAA Final Four (at the Kingdome, Seattle): **Semifinals**—Houston 49, Virginia 47 (OT); Georgetown 53, Kentucky 40. **Championship**—Georgetown 84, Houston 75.

NIT Championship (at Madison Square Garden): Michigan 83, Notre Dame 63. No Top 20 teams played in NIT.

Associated Press Final Polls (Cont.)

Taken **before** NCAA and NIT Tournaments; (*) indicates on probation.

1985

		Before Tourns	Head Coach	Final Record
1	Georgetown	30-2	John Thompson	35-3
2	Michigan	25-3	Bill Frieder	26-4
3	St. John's	27-3	Lou Carnesecca	31-4
4	Oklahoma	28-5	Billy Tubbs	31-6
5	Memphis St.	27-3	Dana Kirk	31-4
6	Georgia Tech	24-7	Bobby Cremins	27-8
7	North Carolina	24-8	Dean Smith	27-9
8	Louisiana Tech	27-2	Andy Russo	29-3
9	UNLV	27-3	Jerry Tarkanian	28-4
10	Duke	22-7	Mike Krzyzewski	23-8
11	VCU	25-5	J.D. Barnett	26-6
12	Illinois	24-8	Lou Henson	26-9
13	Kansas	25-7	Larry Brown	26-8
14	Loyola-IL	25-5	Gene Sullivan	27-6
15	Syracuse	21-8	Jim Boeheim	22-9
16	N.C. State	20-9	Jim Valvano	23-10
17	Texas Tech	23-7	Gerald Myers	23-8
18	Tulsa	23-7	Nolan Richardson	23-8
19	Georgia	21-8	Hugh Durham	22-9
20	LSU	19-9	Dale Brown	19-10

Note: Unranked **Villanova**, coached by Rollie Massimino, won the NCAAs. The Wildcats entered the tourney at 19-10 and had a final record of 25-10.

NCAA Final Four (at Rupp Arena, Lexington, KY): **Semifinals**— Georgetown 77, St. John's 59; Villanova 52, Memphis St. 45. **Championship**—Villanova 66, Georgetown 64.

NIT Championship (at Madison Square Garden): UCLA 65, Indiana 62. No Top 20 teams played in NIT.

1986

		Before Tourns	Head Coach	Final Record
1	Duke	32-2	Mike Krzyzewski	37-3
2	Kansas	31-3	Larry Brown	35-4
3	Kentucky	29-3	Eddie Sutton	32-4
4	St. John's	30-4	Lou Carnesecca	31-5
5	Michigan	27-4	Bill Frieder	28-5
6	Georgia Tech	25-6	Bobby Cremins	27-7
7	Louisville	26-7	Denny Crum	32-7
8	North Carolina	26-5	Dean Smith	28-6
9	Syracuse	25-5	Jim Boeheim	26-6
10	Notre Dame	23-5	Digger Phelps	23-6
11	UNLV	31-4	Jerry Tarkanian	33-5
12	Memphis St.	27-5	Dana Kirk	28-6
13	Georgetown	23-7	John Thompson	24-8
14	Bradley	31-2	Dick Versace	32-3
15	Oklahoma	25-8	Billy Tubbs	26-9
16	Indiana	21-7	Bob Knight	21-8
17	Navy	27-4	Paul Evans	30-5
18	Michigan St.	21-7	Jud Heathcote	23-8
19	Illinois	21-9	Lou Henson	22-10
20	UTEP	27-5	Don Haskins	27-6

NCAA Final Four (at Reunion Arena, Dallas): **Semifinals**—Duke 71, Kansas 67; Louisville 88, LSU 77. **Championship**—Louisville 72, Duke 69.

NIT Championship (at Madison Square Garden): Ohio St. 73, Wyoming 63. No Top 20 teams played in NIT.

1987

		Before Tourns	Head Coach	Final Record
1	UNLV	33-1	Jerry Tarkanian	37-2
2	North Carolina	29-3	Dean Smith	32-4
3	Indiana	24-4	Bob Knight	30-4
4	Georgetown	26-4	John Thompson	29-5
5	DePaul	26-2	Joey Meyer	28-3
6	Iowa	27-4	Tom Davis	30-5
7	Purdue	24-4	Gene Keady	25-5
8	Temple	31-3	John Chaney	32-4
9	Alabama	26-4	Wimp Sanderson	28-5
10	Syracuse	26-6	Jim Boeheim	31-7
11	Illinois	23-7	Lou Henson	23-8
12	Pittsburgh	24-7	Paul Evans	25-8
13	Clemson	25-5	Cliff Ellis	25-6
14	Missouri	24-9	Norm Stewart	24-10
15	UCLA	24-6	Walt Hazzard	25-7
16	New Orleans	25-3	Benny Dees	26-4
17	Duke	22-8	Mike Krzyzewski	24-9
18	Notre Dame	22-7	Digger Phelps	24-8
19	TCU	23-6	Jim Killingsworth	24-7
20	Kansas	23-10	Larry Brown	25-11

NCAA Final Four (at the Superdome, New Orleans): **Semifinals**—Syracuse 77, Providence 63; Indiana 97, UNLV 93. **Championship**—Indiana 74, Syracuse 73.

NIT Championship (at Madison Square Garden): Southern Miss. 84, La Salle 80. No Top 20 teams played in NIT.

1988

		Before Tourns	Head Coach	Final Record
1	Temple	29-1	John Chaney	32-2
2	Arizona	31-2	Lute Olson	35-3
3	Purdue	27-3	Gene Keady	29-4
4	Oklahoma	30-3	Billy Tubbs	35-4
5	Duke	24-6	Mike Krzyzewski	28-7
6	Kentucky	25-5	Eddie Sutton	27-6
7	North Carolina	24-6	Dean Smith	27-7
8	Pittsburgh	23-6	Paul Evans	24-7
9	Syracuse	25-8	Jim Boeheim	26-9
10	Michigan	24-7	Bill Frieder	26-8
11	Bradley	26-4	Stan Albeck	26-5
12	UNLV	27-5	Jerry Tarkanian	28-6
13	Wyoming	26-5	Benny Dees	26-6
14	N.C. State	24-7	Jim Valvano	24-8
15	Loyola-CA	27-3	Paul Westhead	28-4
16	Illinois	22-9	Lou Henson	23-10
17	Iowa	22-9	Tom Davis	24-10
18	Xavier-OH	26-3	Pete Gillen	26-4
19	BYU	25-5	Ladell Andersen	26-6
20	Kansas St.	22-8	Lon Kruger	25-9

Note: Unranked **Kansas**, coached by Larry Brown, won the NCAAs. The Jayhawks entered the tourney at 21-11 and had a final record of 27-11.

NCAA Final Four (at Kemper Arena, Kansas City): **Semifinals**—Kansas 66, Duke 59; Oklahoma 86, Arizona 78. **Championship**—Kansas 83, Oklahoma 79.

NIT Championship (at Madison Square Garden): Connecticut 72, Ohio St. 67. No Top 20 teams played in NIT.

1989

	Before Tourns	Head Coach	Final Record
1 Arizona	27-3	Lute Olson	29-4
2 Georgetown	26-4	John Thompson	29-5
3 Illinois	27-4	Lou Henson	31-5
4 Oklahoma	28-5	Billy Tubbs	30-6
5 North Carolina	27-7	Dean Smith	29-8
6 Missouri	27-7	Norm Stewart & Rich Daly	29-8
7 Syracuse	27-7	Jim Boeheim	30-8
8 Indiana	25-7	Bob Knight	27-8
9 Duke	24-7	Mike Krzyzewski	28-8
10 **Michigan**	24-7	Bill Frieder & Steve Fisher	30-7
11 Seton Hall	26-6	P.J. Carlesimo	31-7
12 Louisville	22-8	Denny Crum	24-9
13 Stanford	26-6	Mike Montgomery	26-7
14 Iowa	22-9	Tom Davis	23-10
15 UNLV	26-7	Jerry Tarkanian	29-8
16 Florida St.	22-7	Pat Kennedy	22-8
17 West Virginia	25-4	Gale Catlett	26-5
18 Ball State	28-2	Rick Majerus	29-3
19 N.C. State	20-8	Jim Valvano	22-9
20 Alabama	23-7	Wimp Sanderson	23-8

NCAA Final Four (at The Kingdome, Seattle): **Semifinals**—Seton Hall 95, Duke 78; Michigan 83, Illinois 81. **Championship**—Michigan 80, Seton Hall 79 (OT).

NIT Championship (at Madison Square Garden): St. John's 73, St. Louis 65. No Top 20 teams played in NIT.

1991

	Before Tourns	Head Coach	Final Record
1 UNLV	30-0	Jerry Tarkanian	34-1
2 Arkansas	31-3	Nolan Richardson	34-4
3 Indiana	27-4	Bob Knight	29-5
4 North Carolina	25-5	Dean Smith	29-6
5 Ohio St.	25-3	Randy Ayers	27-4
6 **Duke**	26-7	Mike Krzyzewski	32-7
7 Syracuse	26-5	Jim Boeheim	26-6
8 Arizona	26-6	Lute Olson	28-7
9 Kentucky	22-6	Rick Pitino	same*
10 Utah	28-3	Rick Majerus	30-4
11 Nebraska	26-7	Danny Nee	26-8
12 Kansas	22-7	Roy Williams	27-8
13 Seton Hall	22-8	P.J. Carlesimo	25-9
14 Oklahoma St.	22-7	Eddie Sutton	24-8
15 New Mexico St.	23-5	Neil McCarthy	23-6
16 UCLA	23-8	Jim Harrick	23-9
17 E. Tennessee St.	28-4	Alan LaForce	28-5
18 Princeton	24-2	Pete Carril	24-3
19 Alabama	21-9	Wimp Sanderson	23-10
20 St. John's	20-8	Lou Carnesecca	23-9
21 Mississippi St.	20-8	Richard Williams	20-9
22 LSU	20-9	Dale Brown	20-10
23 Texas	22-8	Tom Penders	23-9
24 DePaul	20-8	Joey Meyer	20-9
25 Southern Miss	21-7	M.K. Turk	21-8

NCAA Final Four (at the Hoosier Dome, Indianapolis): **Semifinals**—Kansas 79, North Carolina 73; Duke 79, UNLV 77. **Championship**—Duke 72, Kansas 65.

NIT Championship (at Madison Square Garden): Stanford 78, Oklahoma 72. No Top 25 teams played in NIT.

1990

	Before Tourns	Head Coach	Final Record
1 Oklahoma	26-4	Billy Tubbs	27-5
2 **UNLV**	29-5	Jerry Tarkanian	35-5
3 Connecticut	28-5	Jim Calhoun	31-6
4 Michigan St.	26-5	Jud Heathcote	28-6
5 Kansas	29-4	Roy Williams	30-5
6 Syracuse	24-6	Jim Boeheim	26-7
7 Arkansas	26-4	Nolan Richardson	30-5
8 Georgetown	23-6	John Thompson	24-7
9 Georgia Tech	24-6	Bobby Cremins	28-7
10 Purdue	21-7	Gene Keady	22-8
11 Missouri	26-5	Norm Stewart	26-6
12 La Salle	29-1	Speedy Morris	30-2
13 Michigan	22-7	Steve Fisher	23-8
14 Arizona	24-6	Lute Olson	25-7
15 Duke	24-8	Mike Krzyzewski	29-9
16 Louisville	26-7	Denny Crum	27-8
17 Clemson	24-8	Cliff Ellis	26-9
18 Illinois	21-7	Lou Henson	21-8
19 LSU	22-8	Dale Brown	23-9
20 Minnesota	20-8	Clem Haskins	23-9
21 Loyola-CA	23-5	Paul Westhead	26-6
22 Oregon St.	22-6	Jim Anderson	22-7
23 Alabama	24-8	Wimp Sanderson	26-9
24 New Mexico St.	26-4	Neil McCarthy	26-5
25 Xavier-OH	26-4	Pete Gillen	28-5

NCAA Final Four (at McNichols Sports Arena, Denver): **Semifinals**—Duke 97, Arkansas 83; UNLV 90, Georgia Tech 81. **Championship**—UNLV 103, Duke 73.

NIT Championship (at Madison Square Garden): Vanderbilt 74, St. Louis 72. No Top 25 teams played in NIT.

1992

	Before Tourns	Head Coach	Final Record
1 **Duke**	28-2	Mike Krzyzewski	34-2
2 Kansas	26-4	Roy Williams	27-5
3 Ohio St.	23-5	Randy Ayers	26-6
4 UCLA	25-4	Jim Harrick	28-5
5 Indiana	23-6	Bob Knight	27-7
6 Kentucky	26-6	Rick Pitino	29-7
7 UNLV	26-2	Jerry Tarkanian	same*
8 USC	23-5	George Raveling	24-6
9 Arkansas	25-7	Nolan Richardson	26-8
10 Arizona	24-6	Lute Olson	24-7
11 Oklahoma St.	26-7	Eddie Sutton	28-8
12 Cincinnati	25-4	Bob Huggins	29-5
13 Alabama	25-8	Wimp Sanderson	26-9
14 Michigan St.	21-7	Jud Heathcote	22-8
15 Michigan	20-8	Steve Fisher	25-9
16 Missouri	20-8	Norm Stewart	21-9
17 Massachusetts	28-4	John Calipari	30-5
18 North Carolina	21-9	Dean Smith	23-10
19 Seton Hall	21-8	P.J. Carlesimo	23-9
20 Florida St.	20-9	Pat Kennedy	22-10
21 Syracuse	21-9	Jim Boeheim	22-10
22 Georgetown	21-9	John Thompson	22-10
23 Oklahoma	21-8	Billy Tubbs	21-9
24 DePaul	20-8	Joey Meyer	20-9
25 LSU	20-9	Dale Brown	21-10

NCAA Final Four (at the Metrodome, Minneapolis): **Semifinals**—Michigan 76, Cincinnati 72; Duke 81, Indiana 78. **Championship**—Duke 71, Michigan 51.

NIT Championship (at Madison Square Garden): Virginia 81, Notre Dame 76 (OT). No Top 25 teams played in NIT.

Associated Press Final Polls (Cont.)

Taken **before** NCAA and NIT Tournaments; (*) indicates on probation.

1993

		Before Tourns	Head Coach	Final Record
1	Indiana	28-3	Bob Knight	31-4
2	Kentucky	26-3	Rick Pitino	30-4
3	Michigan	26-4	Steve Fisher	31-5
4	**North Carolina**	28-4	Dean Smith	34-4
5	Arizona	24-3	Lute Olson	24-4
6	Seton Hall	27-6	P.J. Carlesimo	28-7
7	Cincinnati	24-4	Bob Huggins	27-5
8	Vanderbilt	26-5	Eddie Fogler	28-6
9	Kansas	25-6	Roy Williams	29-7
10	Duke	23-7	Mike Krzyzewski	24-8
11	Florida St.	22-9	Pat Kennedy	25-10
12	Arkansas	20-8	Nolan Richardson	22-9
13	Iowa	22-8	Tom Davis	23-9
14	Massachusetts	23-6	John Calipari	24-7
15	Louisville	20-8	Denny Crum	22-9
16	Wake Forest	19-8	Dave Odom	21-9
17	New Orleans	26-3	Tim Floyd	26-4
18	Georgia Tech	19-10	Bobby Cremins	19-11
19	Utah	23-6	Rick Majerus	24-7
20	Western Ky.	24-5	Ralph Willard	26-6
21	New Mexico	24-6	Dave Bliss	24-7
22	Purdue	18-9	Gene Keady	18-10
23	Oklahoma St.	19-8	Eddie Sutton	20-9
24	New Mexico St.	25-7	Neil McCarthy	26-8
25	UNLV	21-7	Rollie Massimino	21-8

NCAA Final Four (at the Superdome, New Orleans): **Semifinals**—North Carolina 78, Kansas 68; Michigan 81, Kentucky 78 (OT). **Championship**—North Carolina 77, Michigan 71.

NIT Championship (at Madison Square Garden): Minnesota 62, Georgetown 61. No. 25 UNLV was only Top 25 team played in NIT.

1994

		Before Tourns	Head Coach	Final Record
1	North Carolina	27-6	Dean Smith	28-7
2	**Arkansas**	25-3	Nolan Richardson	31-3
3	Purdue	26-4	Gene Keady	29-5
4	Connecticut	27-4	Jim Calhoun	29-5
5	Missouri	25-3	Norm Stewart	28-4
6	Duke	23-5	Mike Krzyzewski	28-6
7	Kentucky	26-6	Rick Pitino	27-7
8	Massachusetts	27-6	John Calipari	28-7
9	Arizona	25-5	Lute Olson	29-6
10	Louisville	26-5	Denny Crum	28-6
11	Michigan	21-7	Steve Fisher	24-8
12	Temple	22-7	John Chaney	23-8
13	Kansas	25-7	Roy Williams	27-8
14	Florida	25-7	Lon Kruger	29-8
15	Syracuse	21-6	Jim Boeheim	23-7
16	California	22-7	Todd Bozeman	22-8
17	UCLA	21-6	Jim Harrick	21-7
18	Indiana	19-8	Bob Knight	21-9
19	Oklahoma St.	23-9	Eddie Sutton	24-10
20	Texas	25-7	Tom Penders	26-8
21	Marquette	22-8	Kevin O'Neill	24-9
22	Nebraska	20-9	Danny Nee	20-10
23	Minnesota	20-11	Clem Haskins	21-12
24	Saint Louis	23-5	Charlie Spoonhour	23-6
25	Cincinnati	22-9	Bob Huggins	22-10

NCAA Final Four (at the Charlotte Coliseum): **Semifinals**— Arkansas 91, Arizona 82; Duke 70, Florida 65. **Championship**— Arkansas 76, Duke 72.

NIT Championship (at Madison Square Garden): Villanova 80, Vanderbilt 73. No top 25 teams played in NIT.

1995

		Before Tourns	Head Coach	Final Record
1	UCLA	25-2	Jim Harrick	31-2
2	Kentucky	25-4	Rick Pitino	28-5
3	Wake Forest	24-5	Dave Odom	26-6
4	North Carolina	24-5	Dean Smith	28-6
5	Kansas	23-5	Roy Williams	25-6
6	Arkansas	27-6	Nolan Richardson	32-7
7	Massachusetts	26-4	John Calipari	26-5
8	Connecticut	25-4	Jim Calhoun	28-5
9	Villanova	25-7	Steve Lappas	25-8
10	Maryland	24-7	Gary Williams	26-8
11	Michigan St.	22-5	Jud Heathcote	22-6
12	Purdue	24-6	Gene Keady	25-7
13	Virginia	22-8	Jeff Jones	25-9
14	Oklahoma St.	23-9	Eddie Sutton	27-10
15	Arizona	23-7	Lute Olson	23-8
16	Arizona St.	22-8	Bill Frieder	24-9
17	Oklahoma	23-8	Kelvin Sampson	23-9
18	Mississippi St.	20-7	Richard Williams	22-8
19	Utah	27-5	Rick Majerus	28-6
20	Alabama	22-9	David Hobbs	23-1
21	Western Ky.	26-3	Matt Kilcullen	27-4
22	Georgetown	19-9	John Thompson	21-10
23	Missouri	19-8	Norm Stewart	20-9
24	Iowa St.	22-10	Tim Floyd	23-11
25	Syracuse	19-9	Jim Boeheim	20-10

NCAA Final Four (at the Kingdome, Seattle): **Semifinals**— UCLA 74, Oklahoma St. 61; Arkansas 75, North Carolina 68. **Championship**— UCLA 89, Arkansas 78.

NIT Championship (at Madison Square Garden): Virginia Tech 65, Marquette 64 (OT). No top 25 teams played in NIT.

All Time AP Top 20

The composite AP Top 20 from the 1948-49 season through 1994-95, based on the final regular season rankings of each year. The final AP poll has been taken before the NCAA and NIT tournaments each season since 1949 except in 1953 and '54 and again in 1974 and '75 when the final poll came out after the postseason. Team point totals are based on 20 points for all 1st place finishes, 19 for each 2nd, etc.).

		Pts	No.1	Top10	Top20
1	Kentucky	533	7	30	35
2	North Carolina	450	4	25	32
3	UCLA	414	7	21	30
4	Duke	304	2	17	26
5	Indiana	290	4	16	22
6	Kansas	257	0	14	21
7	Louisville	233	0	11	22
8	Notre Dame	195	0	13	17
9	Michigan	191	2	10	14
10	N.C. State	176	1	9	16
11	UNLV	173	2	8	13
12	Cincinnati	172	2	8	12
13	Marquette	165	0	11	14
14	Illinois	162	0	8	17
15	Arkansas	158	0	9	13
16	Ohio St	149	2	9	10
17	Kansas St	147	1	8	12
18	Syracuse	144	0	9	14
19	DePaul	141	2	8	10
20	Bradley	139	1	7	10

AP Post-Tournament Final Polls

The final AP Top 20 poll has been released **after** the NCAA and NIT tournaments four times— in 1953 and '54 and again in 1974 and '75. Those four polls are listed below; teams that were not included in the last regular season polls are in CAPITAL italic letters.

	1953	Final Record		1954	Final Record		1974	Final Record		1975	Final Record
1	Indiana	23-3	1	Kentucky	25-0	1	N.C. State	30-1	1	UCLA	28-3
2	Seton Hall	31-2	2	La Salle	26-4	2	UCLA	26-4	2	Kentucky	26-5
3	Kansas	19-6	3	Holy Cross	26-2	3	Marquette	26-5	3	Indiana	31-1
4	Washington	30-3	4	Indiana	20-4	4	Maryland	23-5	4	Louisville	28-3
5	LSU	24-3	5	Duquesne	26-3	5	Notre Dame	26-3	5	Maryland	24-5
6	La Salle	25-3	6	Notre Dame	22-3	6	Michigan	22-5	6	Syracuse	23-9
7	*ST. JOHN'S*	17-6	7	*BRADLEY*	19-13	7	Kansas	23-7	7	N.C. State	22-6
8	Okla. A&M	23-7	8	Western Ky.	29-3	8	Providence	28-4	8	Arizona St.	25-4
9	Duquesne	21-8	9	*PENN ST.*	18-6	9	Indiana	23-5	9	North Carolina	23-8
10	Notre Dame	19-5	10	Okla. A&M	24-5	10	Long Beach St.	24-2	10	Alabama	22-5
11	Illinois	18-4	11	USC	19-14	11	*PURDUE*	22-8	11	Marquette	23-4
12	Kansas St.	17-4	12	*GEO. WASH.*	23-3	12	North Carolina	22-6	12	*PRINCETON*	22-8
13	Holy Cross	20-6	13	Iowa	17-5	13	Vanderbilt	23-5	13	Cincinnati	23-6
14	Seattle	29-4	14	LSU	21-5	14	Alabama	22-4	14	Notre Dame	19-10
15	*WAKE FOREST*	22-7	15	Duke	22-6	15	*UTAH*	22-8	15	Kansas St.	20-9
16	*SANTA CLARA*	20-7	16	*NIAGARA*	24-6	16	Pittsburgh	25-4	16	Drake	19-10
17	Western Ky.	25-6	17	Seattle	26-2	17	USC	24-5	17	UNLV	24-5
18	N.C. State	26-6	18	Kansas	16-5	18	*ORAL ROBERTS*	23-6	18	Oregon St.	19-12
19	*DEPAUL*	19-9	19	Illinois	17-5	19	South Carolina	22-5	19	*MICHIGAN*	19-8
20	*SW MISSOURI*	24-4	20	*MARYLAND*	23-7	20	Dayton	20-9	20	Penn	23-5

Pre-Tournament Records

1953— St. John's (Al DeStefano, 14-5); Wake Forest (Murray Greason, 21-6); Santa Clara (Bob Feerick, 18-6); DePaul (Ray Meyer, 18-7); SW Missouri St. (Bob Vanatta, 19-4 before NAIA tourney). **1954**— Bradley (Forddy Anderson, 15-12); Penn St. (Elmer Gross, 14-5); George Washington (Bill Reinhart, 23-2); Niagara (Taps Gallagher, 22-5); Maryland (Bud Millikan, 23-7). **1974**— Purdue (Fred Schaus, 18-8); Utah (Bill Foster, 19-7); Oral Roberts (Ken Trickey, 21-5). **1975**— Princeton (Pete Carril, 18-8); Michigan (Johnny Orr, 19-7).

Division I Winning Streaks

Full Season
(Including tournaments)

No		Seasons	Broken by	Score
88	UCLA	1971-74	Notre Dame	71-70
60	San Francisco	1955-57	Illinois	62-33
47	UCLA	1966-68	Houston	71-69
45	UNLV	1990-91	Duke	79-77
44	Texas	1913-17	Rice	24-18
43	Seton Hall	1939-41	LIU-Bklyn	49-26
43	LIU-Brooklyn	1935-37	Stanford	45-31
41	UCLA	1968-69	USC	46-44
39	Marquette	1970-71	Ohio St.	60-59
37	Cincinnati	1962-63	Wichita St.	65-64
37	North Carolina	1957-58	West Virginia	75-64
36	N.C. State	1974-75	Wake Forest	83-78
35	Arkansas	1927-29	Texas	26-25

Regular Season
(Not including tournaments)

No		Seasons	Broken by	Score
76	UCLA	1971-74	Notre Dame	71-70
57	Indiana	1975-77	Toledo	59-57
56	Marquette	1970-72	Detroit	70-49
54	Kentucky	1952-55	Georgia Tech	59-58
51	San Francisco	1955-57	Illinois	62-33
48	Penn	1970-72	Temple	57-52
47	Ohio St.	1960-62	Wisconsin	86-67
44	Texas	1913-17	Rice	24-18
43	UCLA	1966-68	Houston	71-69
43	LIU-Brooklyn	1935-37	Stanford	45-31
42	Seton Hall	1939-41	LIU-Bklyn	49-26

All-Time Highest Scoring Teams

SINGLE SEASON
Scoring

	Year	Gm	Pts	Avg
Loyola-CA	1990	32	3918	122.4
Loyola-CA	1989	31	3486	112.5
UNLV	1976	31	3426	110.5
Loyola-CA	1988	32	3528	110.3
UNLV	1977	32	3426	107.1

SINGLE GAME
Scoring

	Score	Opponent	Date
Loyola-CA	186-140	US Int'l	1/5/91
Loyola-CA	181-150	US Int'l	1/31/89
Oklahoma	173-101	US Int'l	11/29/89
Oklahoma	172-112	Loyola-CA	12/15/90
Arkansas	166-101	US Int'l	12/9/89

Annual NCAA Division I Leaders
Scoring

The NCAA did not begin keeping individual scoring records until the 1947-48 season. All averages include postseason games where applicable.

Multiple winners: Pete Maravich and Oscar Robertson (3); Darrell Floyd, Harry Kelly, Frank Selvy and Freeman Williams (2).

Year	Gm	Pts	Avg	Year	Gm	Pts	Avg
1948 Murray Wier, Iowa	19	399	21.0	1972 Dwight Lamar, SW La	29	1054	36.3
1949 Tony Lavelli, Yale	30	671	22.4	1973 Bird Averitt, Pepperdine	25	848	33.9
				1974 Larry Fogle, Canisius	25	835	33.4
1950 Paul Arizin, Villanova	29	735	25.3	1975 Bob McCurdy, Richmond	26	855	32.9
1951 Bill Mlkvy, Temple	25	731	29.2	1976 Marshall Rodgers, Texas-Pan Am	25	919	36.8
1952 Clyde Lovellette, Kansas	28	795	28.4	1977 Freeman Williams, Portland St.	26	1010	38.8
1953 Frank Selvy, Furman	25	738	29.5	1978 Freeman Williams, Portland St.	27	969	35.9
1954 Frank Selvy, Furman	29	1209	41.7	1979 Lawrence Butler, Idaho St	27	812	30.1
1955 Darrell Floyd, Furman	25	897	35.9				
1956 Darrell Floyd, Furman	28	946	33.8	1980 Tony Murphy, Southern-BR	29	932	32.1
1957 Grady Wallace, S. Carolina	29	906	31.2	1981 Zam Fredrick, S. Carolina	27	781	28.9
1958 Oscar Robertson, Cincinnati	28	984	35.1	1982 Harry Kelly, Texas Southern	29	862	29.7
1959 Oscar Robertson, Cincinnati	30	978	32.6	1983 Harry Kelly, Texas Southern	29	835	28.8
				1984 Joe Jakubick, Akron	27	814	30.1
1960 Oscar Robertson, Cincinnati	30	1011	33.7	1985 Xavier McDaniel, Wichita St	31	844	27.2
1961 Frank Burgess, Gonzaga	26	842	32.4	1986 Terrance Bailey, Wagner	29	854	29.4
1962 Billy McGill, Utah	26	1009	38.8	1987 Kevin Houston, Army	29	953	32.9
1963 Nick Werkman, Seton Hall	22	650	29.5	1988 Hersey Hawkins, Bradley	31	1125	36.3
1964 Howie Komives, Bowling Green	23	844	36.7	1989 Hank Gathers, Loyola-CA	31	1015	32.7
1965 Rick Barry, Miami-FL	26	973	37.4				
1966 Dave Schellhase, Purdue	24	781	32.5	1990 Bo Kimble, Loyola-CA	32	1131	35.3
1967 Jimmy Walker, Providence	28	851	30.4	1991 Kevin Bradshaw, US Int'l	28	1054	37.6
1968 Pete Maravich, LSU	26	1138	43.8	1992 Brett Roberts, Morehead St	29	815	28.1
1969 Pete Maravich, LSU	26	1148	44.2	1993 Greg Guy, Texas-Pan Am	19	556	29.3
				1994 Glenn Robinson, Purdue	34	1030	30.3
1970 Pete Maravich, LSU	31	1381	44.5	1995 Kurt Thomas, TCU	27	781	28.9
1971 Johnny Neumann, Ole Miss	23	923	40.1				

Note: Sixteen underclassmen have won the title. **Sophomores** (4)—Robertson (1958), Maravich (1968), Neumann (1971) and Fogle (1974); **Juniors** (12)—Selvy (1953), Floyd (1955), Robertson (1959), Werkman (1963), Maravich (1969), Lamar (1972), Williams (1977), Kelly (1982), Bailey (1986), Gathers (1989), Guy (1993) and Robinson (1994).

Rebounds

The NCAA did not begin keeping individual rebounding records until the 1950-51 season. From 1956-62, the championship was decided on highest percentage of recoveries out of all rebounds made by both teams in all games. All averages include postseason games where applicable.

Multiple winners: Artis Gilmore, Jerry Lucas, Xavier McDaniel, Kermit Washington and Leroy Wright (2).

Year	Gm	No	Avg	Year	Gm	No	Avg
1951 Ernie Beck, Penn	27	556	20.6	1974 Marvin Barnes, Providence	32	597	18.7
1952 Bill Hannon, Army	17	355	20.9	1975 John Irving, Hofstra	21	323	15.4
1953 Ed Conlin, Fordham	26	612	23.5	1976 Sam Pellom, Buffalo	26	420	16.2
1954 Art Quimby, Connecticut	26	588	22.6	1977 Glenn Moseley, Seton Hall	29	473	16.3
1955 Charlie Slack, Marshall	21	538	25.6	1978 Ken Williams, N. Texas	28	411	14.7
1956 Joe Holup, G. Washington	26	604	.256	1979 Monti Davis, Tennessee St	26	421	16.2
1957 Elgin Baylor, Seattle	25	508	.235				
1958 Alex Ellis, Niagara	25	536	.262	1980 Larry Smith, Alcorn State	26	392	15.1
1959 Leroy Wright, Pacific	26	652	.238	1981 Darryl Watson, Miss. Valley St.	27	379	14.0
				1982 LaSalle Thompson, Texas	27	365	13.5
1960 Leroy Wright, Pacific	17	380	.234	1983 Xavier McDaniel, Wichita St.	28	403	14.4
1961 Jerry Lucas, Ohio St.	27	470	.198	1984 Akeem Olajuwon, Houston	37	500	13.5
1962 Jerry Lucas, Ohio St.	28	499	.211	1985 Xavier McDaniel, Wichita St.	31	460	14.8
1963 Paul Silas, Creighton	27	557	20.6	1986 David Robinson, Navy	35	455	13.0
1964 Bob Pelkington, Xavier-OH	26	567	21.8	1987 Jerome Lane, Pittsburgh	33	444	13.5
1965 Toby Kimball, Connecticut	23	483	21.0	1988 Kenny Miller, Loyola-IL	29	395	13.6
1966 Jim Ware, Oklahoma City	29	607	20.9	1989 Hank Gathers, Loyola-CA	31	426	13.7
1967 Dick Cunningham, Murray St.	22	479	21.8				
1968 Neal Walk, Florida	25	494	19.8	1990 Anthony Bonner, St. Louis	33	456	13.8
1969 Spencer Haywood, Detroit	22	472	21.5	1991 Shaquille O'Neal, LSU	28	411	14.7
				1992 Popeye Jones, Murray St.	30	431	14.4
1970 Artis Gilmore, Jacksonville	28	621	22.2	1993 Warren Kidd, Mid. Tenn. St.	26	386	14.8
1971 Artis Gilmore, Jacksonville	26	603	23.2	1994 Jerome Lambert, Baylor	24	355	14.8
1972 Kermit Washington, American	23	455	19.8	1995 Kurt Thomas, TCU	27	393	14.6
1973 Kermit Washington, American	22	439	20.0				

Note: Only three players have ever led the NCAA in scoring and rebounding in the same season: Xavier McDaniel of Wichita St. (1985), Hank Gathers of Loyola-Marymount (1989) and Kurt Thomas of TCU (1995).

Assists

The NCAA did not begin keeping individual assist records until the 1983-84 season. All averages include postseason games where applicable.

Multiple winner: Avery Johnson (2).

Year		Gm	No	Avg
1984	Craig Lathen, IL-Chicago	29	274	9.45
1985	Rob Weingard, Hofstra	24	228	9.50
1986	Mark Jackson, St. John's	36	328	9.11
1987	Avery Johnson, Southern-BR	31	333	10.74
1988	Avery Johnson, Southern-BR	30	399	13.30
1989	Glenn Williams, Holy Cross	28	278	9.93
1990	Todd Lehmann, Drexel	28	260	9.29
1991	Chris Corchiani, N.C. State	31	299	9.65
1992	Van Usher, Tennessee Tech	29	254	8.76
1993	Sam Crawford, N. Mexico St	34	310	9.12
1994	Jason Kidd, California	30	272	9.06
1995	Nelson Haggerty, Baylor	28	284	10.14

Blocked Shots

The NCAA did not begin keeping individual blocked shots records until the 1985-86 season. All averages include postseason games where applicable.

Multiple winner: David Robinson (2).

Year		Gm	No	Avg
1986	David Robinson, Navy	35	207	5.91
1987	David Robinson, Navy	32	144	4.50
1988	Rodney Blake, St. Joe's-PA	29	116	4.00
1989	Alonzo Mourning, G'town	34	169	4.97
1990	Kenny Green, Rhode Island	26	124	4.77
1991	Shawn Bradley, BYU	34	177	5.21
1992	Shaquille O'Neal, LSU	30	157	5.23
1993	Theo Ratliff, Wyoming	28	124	4.43
1994	Grady Livingston, Howard	26	115	4.42
1995	Keith Closs, Cen. Conn. St.	26	139	5.35

All-Time NCAA Division I Individual Leaders

Through 1994-95; includes regular season and tournament games; **Last** column indicates final year played.

CAREER

Scoring

	Points	Yrs	Last	Gm	Pts
1	Pete Maravich, LSU	3	1970	83	3667
2	Freeman Williams, Port. St.	4	1978	106	3249
3	Lionel Simmons, La Salle	4	1990	131	3217
4	Alphonzo Ford, Miss. Val. St.	4	1993	109	3165
5	Harry Kelly, Texas-Southern	4	1983	110	3066
6	Hersey Hawkins, Bradley	4	1988	125	3008
7	Oscar Robertson, Cincinnati	3	1960	88	2973
8	Danny Manning, Kansas	4	1988	147	2951
9	Alfredrick Hughes, Loyola-IL	4	1985	120	2914
10	Elvin Hayes, Houston	3	1968	93	2884
11	Larry Bird, Indiana St.	3	1979	94	2850
12	Otis Birdsong, Houston	4	1977	116	2832
13	Kevin Bradshaw, US Int'l	4	1991	111	2804
14	Allan Houston, Tennessee	4	1993	128	2801
15	Hank Gathers, USC/Loyola-CA	4	1990	117	2723
16	Reggie Lewis, N'eastern	4	1987	122	2708
17	Daren Queenan, Lehigh	4	1988	118	2703
18	Byron Larkin, Xavier-OH	4	1988	121	2696
19	David Robinson, Navy	4	1987	127	2669
20	Wayman Tisdale, Oklahoma	3	1985	104	2661

	Average	Yrs	Last	Pts	Avg
1	Pete Maravich, LSU	3	1970	3667	44.2
2	Austin Carr, Notre Dame	3	1971	2560	34.6
3	Oscar Robertson, Cinn	3	1960	2973	33.8
4	Calvin Murphy, Niagara	3	1970	2548	33.1
5	Dwight Lamar, SW La	2	1973	1862	32.7
6	Frank Selvy, Furman	3	1954	2538	32.5
7	Rick Mount, Purdue	3	1970	2323	32.3
8	Darrell Floyd, Furman	3	1956	2281	32.1
9	Nick Werkman, Seton Hall	3	1964	2273	32.0
10	Willie Humes, Idaho St.	2	1971	1510	31.5
11	William Averitt, Pepperdine	2	1973	1541	31.4
12	Elgin Baylor, Idaho/Seattle	3	1958	2500	31.3
13	Elvin Hayes, Houston	3	1968	2884	31.0
14	Freeman Williams, Port. St.	4	1978	3249	30.7
15	Larry Bird, Indiana St.	3	1979	2850	30.3
16	Bill Bradley, Princeton	3	1965	2503	30.2
17	Rich Fuqua, Oral Roberts	2	1973	1617	29.9
18	Wilt Chamberlain, Kansas	2	1958	1433	29.9
19	Rick Barry, Miami-FL	3	1965	2298	29.8
20	Doug Collins, Illinois St.	3	1973	2240	29.1

	Field Goal Pct.	Yrs	Last	FG	FGA	Pct
1	Ricky Nedd, Appalach. St.	4	1994	412	597	.690
2	Stephen Scheffler, Purdue	4	1990	408	596	.685
3	Steve Johnson, Ore. St.	4	1981	828	1222	.678
4	Murray Brown, Fla. St.	4	1980	566	847	.668
5	Lee Campbell, SW Mo. St.	3	1990	411	618	.665
6	Warren Kidd, M. Tenn. St.	3	1993	496	747	.664
7	Joe Senser, West Chester	4	1979	476	719	.662
8	Kevin McGee, UC-Irvine	2	1982	552	841	.656
9	O. Phillips, Pepperdine	2	1983	404	618	.654
10	Bill Walton, UCLA	3	1974	747	1147	.651

Note: minimum 400 FGs made.

	Free Throw Pct.	Yrs	Last	FT	FTA	Pct
1	Greg Starrick, Ky/So. Ill	4	1972	341	375	.909
2	Jack Moore, Nebraska	4	1982	446	495	.901
3	Steve Henson, Kansas St.	4	1990	361	401	.900
4	Steve Alford, Indiana	4	1987	535	596	.898
5	Bob Lloyd, Rutgers	3	1967	543	605	.898
6	Jim Barton, Dartmouth	4	1989	394	440	.895
7	Tommy Boyer, Arkansas	3	1963	315	353	.892
8	Rob Robbins, N. Mexico	4	1991	309	348	.888
9	Sean Miller, Pitt	4	1992	317	358	.885
10	Ron Perry, Holy Cross	4	1980	680	768	.885
	Joe Dykstra, Western Ill	4	1983	587	663	.885

Note: minimum 300 FTs made.

	3-Pt Field Goals	Yrs	Last	Gm	3FG
1	Doug Day, Radford	4	1993	117	401
2	Ronnie Schmitz, Missouri-KC	4	1993	112	378
3	Mark Alberts, Akron	4	1993	107	375
4	Jeff Fryer, Loyola-CA	4	1990	112	363
5	Dennis Scott, Ga. Tech	3	1990	99	351

	3-Pt Field Goal Pct.	Yrs	Last	3FG	Att	Pct
1	Tony Bennett, Wisc-GB	4	1992	290	584	.497
2	Keith Jennings, E. Tenn. St.	4	1991	223	452	.493
3	Kirk Manns, Michigan St.	4	1990	212	446	.475
4	Tim Locum, Wisconsin	4	1991	227	481	.472
5	David Olson, Eastern Ill	4	1992	262	562	.466

Note: minimum 200 3FGs made.

All-Time NCAA Division I Individual Leaders (Cont.)

Rebounds

Total (before 1973)	Yrs	Last	Gm	No
1 Tom Gola, La Salle	4	1955	118	2201
2 Joe Holup, G. Washington	4	1956	104	2030
3 Charlie Slack, Marshall	4	1956	88	1916
4 Ed Conlin, Fordham	4	1955	102	1884
5 Dickie Hemric, Wake Forest	4	1955	104	1802
6 Paul Silas, Creighton	3	1964	81	1751
7 Art Quimby, Connecticut	4	1955	80	1716
8 Jerry Harper, Alabama	4	1956	93	1688
9 Jeff Cohen, Wm. & Mary	4	1961	103	1679
10 Steve Hamilton, Morehead St.	4	1958	102	1675

Total (since 1973)	Yrs	Last	Gm	No
1 Derrick Coleman, Syracuse	4	1990	143	1537
2 Ralph Sampson, Virginia	4	1983	132	1511
3 Pete Padgett, Nevada-Reno	4	1976	104	1464
4 Lionel Simmons, La Salle	4	1990	131	1429
5 Anthony Bonner, St. Louis	4	1990	133	1424
6 Tyrone Hill, Xavier-OH	4	1990	126	1380
7 Popeye Jones, Murray St.	4	1992	123	1374
8 Michael Brooks, La Salle	4	1980	114	1372
9 Xavier McDaniel, Wichita St.	4	1985	117	1359
10 John Irving, Ariz./Hofstra	4	1977	103	1348

Average (before 1973)	Yrs	Last	No	Avg
1 Artis Gilmore, Jacksonville	2	1971	1224	22.7
2 Charlie Slack, Marshall	4	1956	1916	21.8
3 Paul Silas, Creighton	3	1964	1751	21.6
4 Leroy Wright, Pacific	3	1960	1442	21.5
5 Art Quimby, Connecticut	4	1955	1716	21.5

Note: minimum 800 rebounds.

Average (since 1973)	Yrs	Last	No	Avg
1 Glenn Mosley, Seton Hall	4	1977	1263	15.2
2 Bill Campion, Manhattan	3	1975	1070	14.2
3 Pete Padgett, Nevada-Reno	4	1976	1464	14.1
4 Bob Warner, Maine	4	1976	1304	13.6
5 Shaquille O'Neal, LSU	3	1992	1217	13.5

Note: minimum 650 rebounds.

Assists

Total	Yrs	Last	Gm	No
1 Bobby Hurley, Duke	4	1993	140	1076
2 Chris Corchiani, N.C. State	4	1991	124	1038
3 Keith Jennings, E. Tenn. St.	4	1991	127	983
4 Sherman Douglas, Syracuse	4	1989	138	960
5 Tony Miller, Marquette	4	1995	123	956
6 Greg Anthony, Portland/UNLV	4	1991	138	950
7 Gary Payton, Oregon St.	4	1990	120	939
8 Orlando Smart, San Fran	4	1994	116	902
9 Andre LaFleur, N'eastern	4	1987	128	894
10 Jim Les, Bradley	4	1986	118	884

Average	Yrs	Last	No	Avg
1 A. Johnson, Cameron/Southern	3	1988	838	8.91
2 Sam Crawford, N. Mexico St.	2	1993	592	8.84
3 Mark Wade, Okla/UNLV	3	1987	693	8.77
4 Chris Corchiani, N.C. State	4	1991	1038	8.37
5 Taurence Chisholm, Delaware	4	1988	877	7.97
6 Van Usher, Tennessee Tech	3	1992	676	7.95
7 Anthony Manuel, Bradley	3	1989	855	7.92
8 Gary Payton, Oregon St.	4	1990	938	7.82
9 Orlando Smart, San Fran	4	1994	902	7.78
10 Tony Miller, Marquette	4	1995	956	7.77

Note: minimum 550 assists.

Blocked Shots

Average	Yrs	Last	No	Avg
1 David Robinson, Navy	2	1987	351	5.24
2 Shaquille O'Neal, LSU	3	1992	412	4.58
3 Theo Ratliff, Wyoming	4	1995	425	3.83
4 Alonzo Mourning, Georgetown	4	1992	453	3.78
5 Lorenzo Williams, Stetson	2	1991	234	3.71

Note: minimum 200 blocked shots.

Steals

Average	Yrs	Last	No	Avg
1 Mookie Blaylock, Oklahoma	2	1989	281	3.80
2 Ronn McMahon, Eastern Wash	3	1990	225	3.52
3 Jason Kidd, California	2	1994	204	3.46
4 Eric Murdock, Providence	4	1991	376	3.21
5 Van Usher, Tennessee Tech	3	1992	270	3.18

Note: minimum 200 steals.

2000 Points/1000 Rebounds

For a combined total of 4000 or more.

	Gm	Pts	Reb	Total
1 Tom Gola, La Salle	118	2462	2201	4663
2 Lionel Simmons, La Salle	131	3217	1429	4646
3 Elvin Hayes, Houston	93	2884	1602	4486
4 Dickie Hemric, W. Forest	104	2587	1802	4389
5 Oscar Robertson, Cinn.	88	2973	1338	4311
6 Joe Holup, G. Washington	104	2226	2030	4256
7 Harry Kelly, TX-Southern	110	3066	1085	4151
8 Danny Manning, Kansas	147	2951	1187	4138
9 Larry Bird, Indiana St.	94	2850	1247	4097
10 Elgin Baylor, Col.Idaho/Seattle	80	2500	1559	4059
11 Michael Brooks, La Salle	114	2628	1372	4000

Years Played— Baylor (1956-58); **Bird** (1977-79); **Brooks** (1977-80); **Gola** (1952-55); **Hayes** (1966-68); **Hemric** (1952-55); **Holup** (1953-56); **Kelly** (1980-83); **Manning** (1985-88); **Robertson** (1958-60); **Simmons** (1987-90).

SINGLE SEASON

Scoring

Points	Year	Gm	Pts
1 Pete Maravich, LSU	1970	31	1381
2 Elvin Hayes, Houston	1968	33	1214
3 Frank Selvy, Furman	1954	29	1209
4 Pete Maravich, LSU	1969	26	1148
5 Pete Maravich, LSU	1968	26	1138
6 Bo Kimble, Loyola-CA	1990	32	1131
7 Hersey Hawkins, Bradley	1988	31	1125
8 Austin Carr, Notre Dame	1970	29	1106
9 Austin Carr, Notre Dame	1971	29	1101
10 Otis Birdsong, Houston	1977	36	1090

Average	Year	Gm	Pts	Avg
1 Pete Maravich, LSU	1970	31	1381	44.5
2 Pete Maravich, LSU	1969	26	1148	44.2
3 Pete Maravich, LSU	1968	26	1138	43.8
4 Frank Selvy, Furman	1954	29	1209	41.7
5 Johnny Neumann, Ole Miss	1971	23	923	40.1
6 Freeman Williams, Port. St.	1977	26	1010	38.8
7 Billy McGill, Utah	1962	26	1009	38.8
8 Calvin Murphy, Niagara	1968	24	916	38.2
9 Austin Carr, Notre Dame	1970	29	1106	38.1
10 Austin Carr, Notre Dame	1971	29	1101	38.0

Scoring

Field Goal Pct.

		Year	FG	FGA	Pct
1	Steve Johnson, Oregon St.	1981	235	315	.746
2	Dwayne Davis, Florida	1989	179	248	.722
3	Keith Walker, Utica	1985	154	216	.713
4	Steve Johnson, Oregon St.	1980	211	297	.710
5	Oliver Miller, Arkansas	1991	254	361	.704

Free Throw Pct.

		Year	FT	FTA	Pct
1	Craig Collins, Penn St.	1985	94	98	.959
2	Rod Foster, UCLA	1982	95	100	.950
3	Carlos Gibson, Marshall	1978	84	89	.944
4	Danny Basile, Marist	1994	84	89	.944
5	Jim Barton, Dartmouth	1986	65	69	.942

3-Pt Field Goal Pct.

		Year	3FG	Att	Pct
1	Glenn Tropf, Holy Cross	1988	52	82	.634
2	Sean Wightman, W. Mich	1992	48	76	.632
3	Keith Jennings, E. Tenn. St.	1991	84	142	.592
4	Dave Calloway, Monmouth	1989	48	82	.585
5	Steve Kerr, Arizona	1988	114	199	.573

Assists

Average

		Year	Gm	No	Avg
1	Avery Johnson, Southern-BR	1988	30	399	13.3
2	Anthony Manuel, Bradley	1988	31	373	12.0
3	Avery Johnson, Southern-BR	1987	31	333	10.7
4	Mark Wade, UNLV	1987	38	406	10.7
5	Glenn Williams, Holy Cross	1989	28	278	9.9

Rebounds

Average (before 1973)

		Year	Gm	No	Avg
1	Charlie Slack, Marshall	1955	21	538	25.6
2	Leroy Wright, Pacific	1959	26	652	25.1
3	Art Quimby, Connecticut	1955	25	611	24.4
4	Charlie Slack, Marshall	1956	22	520	23.6
5	Ed Conlin, Fordham	1953	26	612	23.5

Average (since 1973)

		Year	Gm	No	Avg
1	Kermit Washington, American	1973	25	511	20.4
2	Marvin Barnes, Providence	1973	30	571	19.0
3	Marvin Barnes, Providence	1974	32	597	18.7
4	Pete Padgett, Nevada	1973	26	462	17.8
5	Jim Bradley, Northern Ill	1973	24	426	17.8

Blocked Shots

Average

		Year	Gm	No	Avg
1	David Robinson, Navy	1986	35	207	5.91
2	Shaquille O'Neal, LSU	1992	30	157	5.23
3	Shawn Bradley, BYU	1991	34	177	5.21
4	Cedric Lewis, Maryland	1991	28	143	5.11
5	Shaquille O'Neal, LSU	1991	28	140	5.00
	Alonzo Mourning, G'town	1992	32	160	5.00

Steals

Average

		Year	Gm	No	Avg
1	Darron Brittman, Chicago St.	1986	28	139	4.96
2	Aldwin Ware, Florida A&M	1988	29	142	4.90
3	Ronn McMahon, East Wash.	1990	29	130	4.48
4	Jim Paguaga, St. Francis-NY	1986	28	120	4.29
5	Marty Johnson, Towson St.	1988	30	124	4.13

SINGLE GAME

Scoring

Points vs Div. I Team

		Year	Pts
1	Kevin Bradshaw, US Int'l vs Loyola-CA	1991	72
2	Pete Maravich, LSU vs Alabama	1970	69
3	Calvin Murphy, Niagara vs Syracuse	1969	68
4	Jay Handlan, Wash. & Lee vs Furman	1951	66
	Pete Maravich, LSU vs Tulane	1969	66
	Anthony Roberts, Oral Rbts vs N.C. A&T	1977	66
7	Anthony Roberts, Oral Rbts vs Ore	1977	65
	Scott Haffner, Evansville vs Dayton	1989	65
9	Pete Maravich, LSU vs Kentucky	1970	64
10	Johnny Neumann, Ole Miss vs LSU	1971	63
	Hersey Hawkins, Bradley vs Detroit	1988	63

Points vs Non-Div. I Team

		Year	Pts
1	Frank Selvy, Furman vs Newberry	1954	100
2	Paul Arizin, Villanova vs Phi. NAMC	1949	85
3	Freeman Williams, Port. St. vs Rocky Mt	1978	81
4	Bill Mlkvy, Temple vs Wilkes	1951	73
5	Freeman Williams, Port. St. vs So. Ore	1977	71

Note: Bevo Francis of Division II Rio Grande (Ohio) scored an overall collegiate record 113 points against Hillsdale in 1954. He also scored 84 against Alliance and 82 against Bluffton that same season.

Assists

		Year	No
1	Tony Fairley, Baptist vs Armstrong St.	1987	22
	Avery Johnson, Southern-BR vs TX-South.	1988	22
	Sherman Douglas, Syracuse vs Providence	1989	22
4	Mark Wade, UNLV vs Navy	1986	21
	Kelvin Scarborough, N. Mexico vs Hawaii	1987	21
	Anthony Manuel, Bradley vs UC-Irvine	1987	21
	Avery Johnson, Southern-BR vs Ala. St.	1988	21

3-Pt Field Goals

		Year	No
1	Dave Jamerson, Ohio U. vs Charleston	1989	14
	Askia Jones, Kansas St. vs Fresno St.	1994	14
3	Gary Bosserd, Niagara vs Siena	1987	12
	Darrin Fitzgerald, Butler vs Detroit	1987	12
	Al Dillard, Arkansas vs Delaware St.	1993	12
	Mitch Taylor, South-BR vs La. Christian	1995	12

Rebounds

Total (before 1973)

		Year	No
1	Bill Chambers, Wm. & Mary vs Virginia	1953	51
2	Charlie Slack, Marshall vs M. Harvey	1954	43
3	Tom Heinsohn, Holy Cross vs BC	1955	42
4	Art Quimby, UConn vs BU	1955	40
5	Three players tied with 39 each.		

Total (since 1973)

		Year	No
1	David Vaughn, Oral Roberts vs Brandeis	1973	34
2	Robert Parish, Centenary vs So. Miss	1973	33
3	Durand Macklin, LSU vs Tulane	1976	32
	Jervaughn Scales, South-BR vs Grambling	1994	32
5	Jim Bradley, Northern Ill. vs WI-Milw.	1973	31
	Calvin Natt, NE La. vs Ga. Southern	1976	31

Blocked Shots

		Year	No
1	David Robinson, Navy vs NC-Wilmington	1986	14
2	Shawn Bradley, BYU vs Eastern Ky	1990	14
3	Jim McIlvaine, Marquette vs No. Ill	1993	13
	Keith Closs, C. Conn. St. vs St. Fran-PA	1995	13
5	Ten players tied with 12 each.		

Steals

		Year	No
1	Mookie Blaylock, Oklahoma vs Centenary	1987	13
	Mookie Blaylock, Oklahoma vs Loyola-CA	1988	13
3	Kenny Robertson, Cleve. St. vs Wagner	1988	12
	Terry Evans, Oklahoma vs Florida A&M	1993	12
5	Eight players tied with 11 each.		

Annual Awards

UPI picked the first national Division I Player of the Year in 1955. Since then, the U.S. Basketball Writers Assn. (1959), the Commonwealth Athletic Club of Kentucky's Adolph Rupp Trophy (1961), the Atlanta Tip-Off Club (1969), the National Assn. of Basketball Coaches (1975), and the LA Athletic Club's John Wooden Award (1977) have joined in.

Since 1977, the first year all six awards were given out, the same player has won all of them in the same season eight times: Marques Johnson in 1977, Larry Bird in 1979, Ralph Sampson in both 1982 and '83, Michael Jordan in 1984, David Robinson in 1987, Lionel Simmons in 1990, Calbert Cheaney in 1993 and Glenn Robinson in 1994.

United Press International

Voted on by a panel of UPI college basketball writers and first presented in 1955.
Multiple winners: Oscar Robertson, Ralph Sampson and Bill Walton (3); Lew Alcindor and Jerry Lucas (2).

Year		Year		Year	
1955	Tom Gola, La Salle	1970	Pete Maravich, LSU	1985	Chris Mullin, St. John's
1956	Bill Russell, San Francisco	1971	Austin Carr, Notre Dame	1986	Walter Berry, St. John's
1957	Chet Forte, Columbia	1972	Bill Walton, UCLA	1987	David Robinson, Navy
1958	Oscar Robertson, Cincinnati	1973	Bill Walton, UCLA	1988	Hersey Hawkins, Bradley
1959	Oscar Robertson, Cincinnati	1974	Bill Walton, UCLA	1989	Danny Ferry, Duke
		1975	David Thompson, N.C. State		
1960	Oscar Robertson, Cincinnati	1976	Scott May, Indiana	1990	Lionel Simmons, La Salle
1961	Jerry Lucas, Ohio St.	1977	Marques Johnson, UCLA	1991	Shaquille O'Neal, LSU
1962	Jerry Lucas, Ohio St.	1978	Butch Lee, Marquette	1992	Jim Jackson, Ohio St.
1963	Art Heyman, Duke	1979	Larry Bird, Indiana St.	1993	Calbert Cheaney, Indiana
1964	Gary Bradds, Ohio St.			1994	Glenn Robinson, Purdue
1965	Bill Bradley, Princeton	1980	Mark Aguirre, DePaul	1995	Joe Smith, Maryland
1966	Cazzie Russell, Michigan	1981	Ralph Sampson, Virginia		
1967	Lew Alcindor, UCLA	1982	Ralph Sampson, Virginia		
1968	Elvin Hayes, Houston	1983	Ralph Sampson, Virginia		
1969	Lew Alcindor, UCLA	1984	Michael Jordan, N. Carolina		

U.S. Basketball Writers Association

Voted on by the USBWA and first presented in 1959.
Multiple winners: Ralph Sampson and Bill Walton (3); Lew Alcindor, Jerry Lucas and Oscar Robertson (2).

Year		Year		Year	
1959	Oscar Robertson, Cincinnati	1972	Bill Walton, UCLA	1985	Chris Mullin, St. John's
		1973	Bill Walton, UCLA	1986	Walter Berry, St. John's
1960	Oscar Robertson, Cincinnati	1974	Bill Walton, UCLA	1987	David Robinson, Navy
1961	Jerry Lucas, Ohio St.	1975	David Thompson, N.C. State	1988	Hersey Hawkins, Bradley
1962	Jerry Lucas, Ohio St.	1976	Adrian Dantley, Notre Dame	1989	Danny Ferry, Duke
1963	Art Heyman, Duke	1977	Marques Johnson, UCLA		
1964	Walt Hazzard, UCLA	1978	Phil Ford, North Carolina	1990	Lionel Simmons, La Salle
1965	Bill Bradley, Princeton	1979	Larry Bird, Indiana St.	1991	Larry Johnson, UNLV
1966	Cazzie Russell, Michigan			1992	Christian Laettner, Duke
1967	Lew Alcindor, UCLA	1980	Mark Aguirre, DePaul	1993	Calbert Cheaney, Indiana
1968	Elvin Hayes, Houston	1981	Ralph Sampson, Virginia	1994	Glenn Robinson, Purdue
1969	Lew Alcindor, UCLA	1982	Ralph Sampson, Virginia	1995	Ed O'Bannon, UCLA
		1983	Ralph Sampson, Virginia		
1970	Pete Maravich, LSU	1984	Michael Jordan, N. Carolina		
1971	Sidney Wicks, UCLA				

Rupp Trophy

Voted on by AP sportswriters and broadcasters and first presented in 1961 by the Commonwealth Athletic Club of Kentucky in the name of former University of Kentucky coach Adolph Rupp.
Multiple winners: Ralph Sampson (3); Lew Alcindor, Jerry Lucas, David Thompson and Bill Walton (2).

Year		Year		Year	
1961	Jerry Lucas, Ohio St.	1973	Bill Walton, UCLA	1985	Patrick Ewing, Georgetown
1962	Jerry Lucas, Ohio St.	1974	David Thompson, N.C. State	1986	Walter Berry, St. John's
1963	Art Heyman, Duke	1975	David Thompson, N.C. State	1987	David Robinson, Navy
1964	Gary Bradds, Ohio St.	1976	Scott May, Indiana	1988	Hersey Hawkins, Bradley
1965	Bill Bradley, Princeton	1977	Marques Johnson, UCLA	1989	Sean Elliott, Arizona
1966	Cazzie Russell, Michigan	1978	Butch Lee, Marquette		
1967	Lew Alcindor, UCLA	1979	Larry Bird, Indiana St.	1990	Lionel Simmons, La Salle
1968	Elvin Hayes, Houston			1991	Shaquille O'Neal, LSU
1969	Lew Alcindor, UCLA	1980	Mark Aguirre, DePaul	1992	Christian Laettner, Duke
		1981	Ralph Sampson, Virginia	1993	Calbert Cheaney, Indiana
1970	Pete Maravich, LSU	1982	Ralph Sampson, Virginia	1994	Glenn Robinson, Purdue
1971	Austin Carr, Notre Dame	1983	Ralph Sampson, Virginia	1995	Joe Smith, Maryland
1972	Bill Walton, UCLA	1984	Michael Jordan, N. Carolina		

Naismith Award

Voted on by a panel of coaches, sportswriters and broadcasters and first presented in 1969 by the Atlanta Tip-Off Club in 1969 in the name of the inventor of basketball, Dr. James Naismith.
Multiple winners: Ralph Sampson and Bill Walton (3).

Year		Year		Year	
1969	Lew Alcindor, UCLA	1978	Butch Lee, Marquette	1987	David Robinson, Navy
1970	Pete Maravich, LSU	1979	Larry Bird, Indiana St.	1988	Danny Manning, Kansas
1971	Austin Carr, Notre Dame	1980	Mark Aguirre, DePaul	1989	Danny Ferry, Duke
1972	Bill Walton, UCLA	1981	Ralph Sampson, Virginia	1990	Lionel Simmons, La Salle
1973	Bill Walton, UCLA	1982	Ralph Sampson, Virginia	1991	Larry Johnson, UNLV
1974	Bill Walton, UCLA	1983	Ralph Sampson, Virginia	1992	Christian Laettner, Duke
1975	David Thompson, N.C. State	1984	Michael Jordan, N. Carolina	1993	Calbert Cheaney, Indiana
1976	Scott May, Indiana	1985	Patrick Ewing, Georgetown	1994	Glenn Robinson, Purdue
1977	Marques Johnson, UCLA	1986	Johnny Dawkins, Duke	1995	Joe Smith, Maryland

National Association of Basketball Coaches

Voted on by the National Assn. of Basketball Coaches and presented by the Eastman Kodak Co. from 1975-94.
Multiple winner: Ralph Sampson (2).

Year		Year		Year	
1975	David Thompson, N.C. State	1982	Ralph Sampson, Virginia	1990	Lionel Simmons, La Salle
1976	Scott May, Indiana	1983	Ralph Sampson, Virginia	1991	Larry Johnson, UNLV
1977	Marques Johnson, UCLA	1984	Michael Jordan, N. Carolina	1992	Christian Laettner, Duke
1978	Phil Ford, North Carolina	1985	Patrick Ewing, Georgetown	1993	Calbert Cheaney, Indiana
1979	Larry Bird, Indiana St.	1986	Walter Berry, St. John's	1994	Glenn Robinson, Purdue
1980	Michael Brooks, La Salle	1987	David Robinson, Navy	1995	Shawn Respert, Mich. St.
1981	Danny Ainge, BYU	1988	Danny Manning, Kansas		
		1989	Sean Elliott, Arizona		

Wooden Award

Voted on by a panel of coaches, sportswriters and broadcasters and first presented in 1977 by the Los Angeles Athletic Club in the name of former Purdue All-America and UCLA coach John Wooden. Unlike the other five Player of the Year awards, candidates for the Wooden must have a minimum grade point average of 2.00 (out of 4.00).
Multiple winner: Ralph Sampson (2).

Year		Year		Year	
1977	Marques Johnson, UCLA	1983	Ralph Sampson, Virginia	1990	Lionel Simmons, La Salle
1978	Phil Ford, North Carolina	1984	Michael Jordan, N. Carolina	1991	Larry Johnson, UNLV
1979	Larry Bird, Indiana St.	1985	Chris Mullin, St. John's	1992	Christian Laettner, Duke
1980	Darrell Griffith, Louisville	1986	Walter Berry, St. John's	1993	Calbert Cheaney, Indiana
1981	Danny Ainge, BYU	1987	David Robinson, Navy	1994	Glenn Robinson, Purdue
1982	Ralph Sampson, Virginia	1988	Danny Manning, Kansas	1995	Ed O'Bannon, UCLA
		1989	Sean Elliott, Arizona		

Players of the Year and Top Draft Picks

Consensus college Players of the Year and first overall selections in NBA Draft since the abolition of the NBA's Territorial Draft in 1966. Top draft picks who became Rookie of the Year are in **bold** type; (*) indicates top draft pick chosen as junior and (**) indicates top draft pick chosen as sophomore.

Year	Player of the Year	Top Draft Pick	Year	Player of the Year	Top Draft Pick
1966	Cazzie Russell, Mich.	Cazzie Russell, NY	1982	Ralph Sampson, Va.	James Worthy, LAL*
1967	Lew Alcindor, UCLA	Jimmy Walker, Det.	1983	Ralph Sampson, Va.	**Ralph Sampson**, Hou.
1968	Elvin Hayes, Houston	Elvin Hayes, SD	1984	Michael Jordan, N. Caro.	Akeem Olajuwon, Hou.
1969	Lew Alcindor, UCLA	**Lew Alcindor**, Milw.	1985	Patrick Ewing, G'town	**Patrick Ewing**, NY
1970	Pete Maravich, LSU	Bob Lanier, Det.		& Chris Mullin, St. John's	
1971	Sidney Wicks, UCLA	Austin Carr, Cle.	1986	Walter Berry, St. John's	Brad Daugherty, Cle.
1972	Bill Walton, UCLA	LaRue Martin, Port.	1987	David Robinson, Navy	**David Robinson**, SA
1973	Bill Walton, UCLA	Doug Collins, Phi.	1988	Hersey Hawkins, Bradley	Danny Manning, LAC
1974	Bill Walton, UCLA	Bill Walton, Port.		& Danny Manning, Kan.	
1975	David Thompson, N.C. St.	David Thompson, Atl.	1989	Sean Elliott, Arizona	Pervis Ellison, Sac.
1976	Scott May, Indiana	John Lucas, Hou.		& Danny Ferry, Duke	
1977	Marques Johnson, UCLA	Kent Benson, Ind.	1990	Lionel Simmons, La Salle	**Derrick Coleman**, NJ
1978	Butch Lee, Marquette	Mychal Thompson, Port.	1991	Shaquille O'Neal, LSU	**Larry Johnson**, Char.
	& Phil Ford, N. Caro.		1992	Christian Laettner, Duke	**Shaquille O'Neal**, Orl.*
1979	Larry Bird, Indiana St.	Magic Johnson, LAL**	1993	Calbert Cheaney, Ind.	**Chris Webber**, Orl**
1980	Mark Aguirre, DePaul	Joe Barry Carroll, G. St.	1994	Glenn Robinson, Purdue	Glenn Robinson, Mil*
1981	Ralph Sampson, Virginia	Mark Aguirre, Dal.	1995	Ed O'Bannon, UCLA	Joe Smith, G. St.**
	& Danny Ainge, BYU			& Joe Smith, Maryland	

All-Time Winningest Division I Coaches

Minimum of 10 seasons as Division I head coach; regular season and tournament games included; coaches active during 1994-95 in **bold** type.

Top 30 Winning Percentage

	Yrs	W	L	Pct
1 Jerry Tarkanian	24	625	122	.837
2 Clair Bee	21	412	87	.826
3 Adolph Rupp	41	876	190	.822
4 John Wooden	29	664	162	.804
5 **Dean Smith**	34	830	236	.779
6 Harry Fisher	13	147	44	.770
7 Frank Keaney	27	387	117	.768
8 George Keogan	24	385	117	.767
9 Jack Ramsay	11	231	71	.765
10 Vic Bubas	10	213	67	.761
11 **Nolan Richardson**	15	371	119	.757
12 **Jim Boeheim**	19	454	150	.752
13 **John Chaney**	23	520	175	.748
14 Chick Davies	21	314	106	.748
15 Ray Mears	21	399	135	.747
16 Al McGuire	20	405	143	.739
17 Everett Case	18	376	133	.739
18 Phog Allen	48	746	264	.739
19 **Bob Knight**	30	659	235	.737
20 Walter Meanwell	22	280	101	.735
21 **Denny Crum**	24	565	212	.727
22 Lew Andreas	22	355	134	.726
23 **Eddie Sutton**	25	553	209	.726
24 Lou Carnesecca	24	526	200	.725
25 **John Thompson**	23	524	200	.724
26 Fred Schaus	12	251	96	.723
27 Cam Henderson	35	630	243	.722
28 Hugh Greer	17	290	112	.721
29 Joe Lapchick	20	335	130	.720
30 **Lute Olson**	22	481	187	.720

Top 30 Victories

	Yrs	W	L	Pct
1 Adolph Rupp	41	876	190	.822
2 **Dean Smith**	34	830	236	.779
3 Hank Iba	41	767	338	.694
4 Ed Diddle	42	759	302	.715
5 Phog Allen	48	746	264	.739
6 Ray Meyer	42	724	354	.672
7 **Don Haskins**	34	665	298	.691
8 John Wooden	29	664	162	.804
9 **Norm Stewart**	34	660	319	.674
10 **Bob Knight**	30	659	235	.737
11 **Lefty Driesell**	33	657	302	.685
Ralph Miller	38	657	382	.632
13 Marv Harshman	40	654	449	.593
14 **Lou Henson**	33	645	318	.670
15 **Gene Bartow**	33	631	339	.651
16 Cam Henderson	35	630	243	.722
17 Jerry Tarkanian	24	625	122	.837
18 Norm Sloan	37	624	393	.614
19 Slats Gill	36	599	392	.604
20 Abe Lemons	34	597	344	.634
21 Guy Lewis	30	592	279	.680
22 **Denny Crum**	24	565	212	.727
23 **Gary Colson**	34	563	384	.570
24 Tony Hinkle	41	557	393	.586
25 **Eddie Sutton**	25	553	209	.726
26 Glenn Wilkes	36	551	436	.558
27 Frank McGuire	30	549	236	.699
28 Harry Miller	34	534	374	.588
29 Lou Carnesecca	24	526	200	.725
30 **Tom Young**	31	524	328	.615

Note: Clarence **(Bighouse) Gaines** of Division II Winston-Salem St. (1947-93) retired after the 1992-93 season to finish his 47-year career ranked No. 2 on the all-time NCAA list of all coaches regardless of division. His record is 828-446 with a .650 winning percentage.

Where They Coached

Allen—Baker (1906-08), Kansas (1908-09), Haskell (1909), Central Mo. St. (1913-19), Kansas (1920-56); **Andreas**—Syracuse (1925-43; 45-50); **Bartow**—Central Mo. St. (1962-64), Valparaiso (1965-70), Memphis (1971-74), Illinois (1975), UCLA (1976-77), UAB (1979—); **Bee**—Rider (1929-31), LIU-Brooklyn (1932-45, 46-51); **Boeheim**—Syracuse (1977—); **Bubas**—Duke (1960-69); **Carnesecca**—St. John's (1966-70, 74-92); **Case**—N.C. State (1947-64); **Chaney**—Cheyney (1973-82), Temple (1983—); **Colson**—Valdosta St. (1959-68), Pepperdine (1969-79), New Mexico (1981-88), Fresno St. (1991—); **Crum**—Louisville (1972—); **Davies**—Duquesne (1925-43, 47-48); **Diddle**—Western Ky. (1923-64); **Driesell**—Davidson (1961-69), Maryland (1970-86), J. Madison (1989—); **Enke**—Louisville (1924-25), Arizona (1926-61); **Fisher**—Columbia (1907-16), Army (1922-23, 25).

Gill—Oregon St. (1929-64); **Greer**—Connecticut (1947-63); **Harshman**—Pacific Lutheran (1946-58), Wash. St. (1959-71), Washington (1972-85); **Haskins**—UTEP (1962—); **Henderson**—Muskingum (1920-22), Davis & Elkins (1923-35), Marshall (1936-55); **Henson**—Hardin-Simmons (1963-66), N. Mexico St. (1967-75), Illinois (1976—); **Hinkle**—Butler (1927-42, 46-70); **Iba**—NW Missouri St. (1930-33), Colorado (1934), Oklahoma St. (1935-70); **Keaney**—Rhode Island (1921-48); **Knight**—Army (1966-71), Indiana (1972—); **Koegan**—St. Louis (1916), Allegheny (1919), Valparaiso (1920-21), Notre Dame (1924-43).

Lapchick—St. John's (1937-47, 57-65); **Lemons**—Okla. City (1956-73), Pan American (1974-76), Texas (1977-82), Okla. City (1984-90); **Lewis**— Houston (1957-86); **A. McGuire**—Belmont Abbey (1958-64), Marquette (1965-77); **F. McGuire**—St. John's (1948-52), North Carolina (1953-61), South Carolina (1965-80); **Meanwell**—Wisconsin (1912-17, 21-34), Missouri (1918-20); **Mears**—Wittenberg (1957-62), Tennessee (1963-77); **Meyer**—DePaul (1943-84); **H. Miller**—Western St. (1953-58), Fresno St. (1961-65), E. New Mexico (1966-70), North Texas (1971), Wichita St. (1972-78), S.F. Austin (1979-88); **R. Miller**—Wichita St. (1952-64), Iowa (1965-70), Oregon St. (1971-89); **Olson**—Long Beach St. (1974), Iowa (1975-83), Arizona (1984—).

Ramsay—St. Joseph's-PA (1956-66); **Richardson**—Tulsa (1981-85), Arkansas (1986—); **Rupp**—Kentucky (1931-72); **Schaus**—West Va. (1955-60), Purdue (1973-78); **Sloan**—Presbyterian (1952-55), Citadel (1957-60), Florida (1961-66), N.C. State (1967-80), Florida (1981-89); **Smith**—North Carolina (1962—); **Stewart**—No. Iowa (1962-67), Missouri (1968—); **Sutton**—Creighton (1970-74), Arkansas (1975-85), Kentucky (1986-89), Oklahoma St. (1991—); **Tarkanian**—Long Beach St. (1969-73), UNLV (1974-92); **Thompson**—Georgetown (1973—); **Wilkes**—Stetson (1958-93); **Wooden**— Indiana St. (1947-48), UCLA (1949-75).

Most NCAA Tournaments

Through 1995; listed are number of appearances, overall tournament record, times reaching Final Four, and number of NCAA championships.

App		W-L	F4	Championships
25	Dean Smith	60-25	10	2 (1982, 93)
20	Adolph Rupp	30-18	6	4 (1948-49,51, 58)
19	Bob Knight	40-16	5	3 (1976, 81, 87)
19	Denny Crum	37-19	6	2 (1980, 86)
18	Lou Carnesecca	17-20	1	None
18	John Thompson	31-17	3	1 (1984)
18	Eddie Sutton	27-18	2	None
18	Lou Henson	19-19	2	None
16	John Wooden	47-10	12	10 (1964-65, 67-73, 75)
16	Jerry Tarkanian	37-16	4	1 (1990)
16	Jim Boeheim	22-16	1	None
16	Lute Olson	20-17	3	None
15	Digger Phelps	17-17	1	None
15	Norm Stewart	12-15	0	None
14	Don Haskins	14-13	1	1 (1966)
14	Guy Lewis	26-18	5	None
13	Dale Brown	15-14	2	None
13	Ray Meyer	14-16	2	None

Active Coaches' Victories

Minimum five seasons in Division I.

		Yrs	W	L	Pct
1	Dean Smith, N. Carolina	34	830	236	.779
2	Jim Phelan, Mt. St. Mary's	41	737	392	.653
3	Don Haskins, UTEP	34	665	298	.691
4	Norm Stewart, Missouri	34	660	319	.674
5	Bob Knight, Indiana	30	659	235	.737
6	Lefty Driesell, J. Madison	33	657	302	.685
7	Lou Henson, Illinois	33	645	318	.670
8	Gene Bartow, UAB	33	631	339	.651
9	Jerry Tarkanian, Fresno St.	24	625	122	.837
10	Denny Crum, Louisville	24	565	212	.727
11	Eddie Sutton, Okla. St.	25	553	209	.726
12	Eldon Miller, N. Iowa	33	528	377	.583
13	John Thompson, Georgetown	23	524	200	.723
14	John Chaney, Temple	23	520	175	.748
15	Pete Carril, Princeton	29	503	266	.654
16	Bill Foster, Va. Tech	28	494	303	.620
17	Lute Olson, Arizona	22	481	187	.720
18	Bob Hallberg, IL-Chicago	24	474	255	.650
19	Gale Catlett, West Va.	23	459	226	.670
20	Tom Davis, Iowa	24	458	250	.647

Annual Awards

UPI picked the first national Division I Coach of the Year in 1955. Since then, The U.S. Basketball Writers Assn. (1959), AP (1967), the National Assn. of Basketball Coaches (1969), and the Atlanta Tip-Off Club (1987) have joined in. Since 1987, the first year all five awards were given out, no coach has won all of them in the same season.

United Press International

Voted on by a panel of UPI college basketball writers and first presented in 1955.

Multiple winners: John Wooden (6); Bob Knight, Ray Meyer, Adolph Rupp, Norm Stewart, Fred Taylor and Phil Woolpert (2).

Year		Year		Year	
1955	Phil Woolpert, San Francisco	1970	John Wooden, UCLA	1985	Lou Carnesecca, St. John's
1956	Phil Woolpert, San Francisco	1971	Al McGuire, Marquette	1986	Mike Krzyzewski, Duke
1957	Frank McGuire, North Carolina	1972	John Wooden, UCLA	1987	John Thompson, Georgetown
1958	Tex Winter, Kansas St.	1973	John Wooden, UCLA	1988	John Chaney, Temple
1959	Adolph Rupp, Kentucky	1974	Digger Phelps, Notre Dame	1989	Bob Knight, Indiana
1960	Pete Newell, California	1975	Bob Knight, Indiana	1990	Jim Calhoun, Connecticut
1961	Fred Taylor, Ohio St.	1976	Tom Young, Rutgers	1991	Rick Majerus, Utah
1962	Fred Taylor, Ohio St.	1977	Bob Gaillard, San Francisco	1992	Perry Clark, Tulane
1963	Ed Jucker, Cincinnati	1978	Eddie Sutton, Arkansas	1993	Eddie Fogler, Vanderbilt
1964	John Wooden, UCLA	1979	Bill Hodges, Indiana St.	1994	Norm Stewart, Missouri
1965	Dave Strack, Michigan			1995	Leonard Hamilton, Miami-FL
1966	Adolph Rupp, Kentucky	1980	Ray Meyer, DePaul		
1967	John Wooden, UCLA	1981	Ralph Miller, Oregon St.		
1968	Guy Lewis, Houston	1982	Norm Stewart, Missouri		
1969	John Wooden, UCLA	1983	Jerry Tarkanian, UNLV		
		1984	Ray Meyer, DePaul		

U.S. Basketball Writers Association

Voted on by the USBWA and first presented in 1959.

Multiple winners: John Wooden (5); Bob Knight (3); Lou Carnesecca, John Chaney, Ray Meyer and Fred Taylor (2).

Year		Year		Year	
1959	Eddie Hickey, Marquette	1972	John Wooden, UCLA	1986	Dick Versace, Bradley
1960	Pete Newell, California	1973	John Wooden, UCLA	1987	John Chaney, Temple
1961	Fred Taylor, Ohio St.	1974	Norm Sloan, N.C. State	1988	John Chaney, Temple
1962	Fred Taylor, Ohio St.	1975	Bob Knight, Indiana	1989	Bob Knight, Indiana
1963	Ed Jucker, Cincinnati	1976	Bob Knight, Indiana		
1964	John Wooden, UCLA	1977	Eddie Sutton, Arkansas	1990	Roy Williams, Kansas
1965	Butch van Breda Kolff, Princeton	1978	Ray Meyer, DePaul	1991	Randy Ayers, Ohio St.
1966	Adolph Rupp, Kentucky	1979	Dean Smith, North Carolina	1992	Perry Clark, Tulane
1967	John Wooden, UCLA			1993	Eddie Fogler, Vanderbilt
1968	Guy Lewis, Houston	1980	Ray Meyer, DePaul	1994	Charlie Spoonhour, St. Louis
1969	Maury John, Drake	1981	Ralph Miller, Oregon St.	1995	Kelvin Sampson, Oklahoma
		1982	John Thompson, Georgetown		
1970	John Wooden, UCLA	1983	Lou Carnesecca, St. John's		
1971	Al McGuire, Marquette	1984	Gene Keady, Purdue		
		1985	Lou Carnesecca, St. John's		

Annual Awards (Cont.)

Associated Press

Voted on by AP sportswriters and broadcasters and first presented in 1967.
Multiple winners: John Wooden (5); Bob Knight (3); Guy Lewis, Ray Meyer, Ralph Miller and Eddie Sutton (2).

Year		Year		Year	
1967	John Wooden, UCLA	1977	Bob Gaillard, San Francisco	1987	Tom Davis, Iowa
1968	Guy Lewis, Houston	1978	Eddie Sutton, Arkansas	1988	John Chaney, Temple
1969	John Wooden, UCLA	1979	Bill Hodges, Indiana St.	1989	Bob Knight, Indiana
1970	John Wooden, UCLA	1980	Ray Meyer, DePaul	1990	Jim Calhoun, Connecticut
1971	Al McGuire, Marquette	1981	Ralph Miller, Oregon St.	1991	Randy Ayers, Ohio St.
1972	John Wooden, UCLA	1982	Ralph Miller, Oregon St.	1992	Roy Williams, Kansas
1973	John Wooden, UCLA	1983	Guy Lewis, Houston	1993	Eddie Fogler, Vanderbilt
1974	Norm Sloan, N.C. State	1984	Ray Meyer, DePaul	1994	Norm Stewart, Missouri
1975	Bob Knight, Indiana	1985	Bill Frieder, Michigan	1995	Kelvin Sampson, Oklahoma
1976	Bob Knight, Indiana	1986	Eddie Sutton, Kentucky		

National Association of Basketball Coaches

Voted on by NABC membership and first presented in 1969.
Multiple winner: John Wooden (3).

Year		Year		Year	
1969	John Wooden, UCLA	1979	Ray Meyer, DePaul	1987	Rick Pitino, Providence
1970	John Wooden, UCLA	1980	Lute Olson, Iowa	1988	John Chaney, Temple
1971	Jack Kraft, Villanova	1981	Ralph Miller, Oregon St.	1989	P.J. Carlesimo, Seton Hall
1972	John Wooden, UCLA		& Jack Hartman, Kansas St.	1990	Jud Heathcote, Michigan St.
1973	Gene Bartow, Memphis St.	1982	Don Monson, Idaho	1991	Mike Krzyzewski, Duke
1974	Al McGuire, Marquette	1983	Lou Carnesecca, St. John's	1992	George Raveling, USC
1975	Bob Knight, Indiana	1984	Marv Harshman, Washington	1993	Eddie Fogler, Vanderbilt
1976	Johnny Orr, Michigan	1985	John Thompson, Georgetown	1994	Nolan Richardson, Arkansas
1977	Dean Smith, North Carolina	1986	Eddie Sutton, Kentucky		& Gene Keady, Purdue
1978	Bill Foster, Duke			1995	Jim Harrick, UCLA
	& Abe Lemons, Texas				

Naismith Award

Voted on by a panel of coaches, sportswriters and broadcasters and first presented by the Atlanta Tip-Off Club in 1987 in the name of the inventor of basketball, Dr. James Naismith.
Multiple winner: Mike Krzyzewski (2).

Year		Year		Year	
1987	Bob Knight, Indiana	1990	Bobby Cremins, Georgia Tech	1993	Dean Smith, North Carolina
1988	Larry Brown, Kansas	1991	Randy Ayers, Ohio St.	1994	Nolan Richardson, Arkansas
1989	Mike Krzyzewski, Duke	1992	Mike Krzyzewski, Duke	1995	Jim Harrick, UCLA

Other Men's Champions

The NCAA has sanctioned national championship tournaments for Divison II since 1957 and Division III since 1975. The NAIA sanctioned a single tournament from 1937-91, then split into two divisions in 1992.

NCAA Div. II Finals

Multiple winners: Kentucky Wesleyan (6); Evansville (5); CS-Bakersfield, North Alabama and Virginia Union (2).

Year	Winner	Score	Loser	Year	Winner	Score	Loser
1957	Wheaton, IL	89-65	Ky. Wesleyan	1977	Tennessee-Chatt.	71-62	Randolph-Macon
1958	South Dakota	75-53	St. Michael's, VT	1978	Cheyney, PA	47-40	WI-Green Bay
1959	Evansville, IN	83-67	SW Missouri St.	1979	North Alabama	64-50	WI-Green Bay
1960	Evansville, IN	90-69	Chapman, CA	1980	Virginia Union	80-74	New York Tech
1961	Wittenberg, OH	42-38	SE Missouri St.	1981	Florida Southern	73-68	Mt. St. Mary's, MD
1962	Mt. St. Mary's, MD	58-57*	CS-Sacramento	1982	Dist. of Columbia	73-63	Florida Southern
1963	South Dakota St.	42-40	Wittenberg, OH	1983	Wright St., OH	92-73	Dist. of Columbia
1964	Evansville, IN	72-59	Akron, OH	1984	Central Mo. St.	81-77	St. Augustine's, NC
1965	Evansville, IN	85-82*	Southern Illinois	1985	Jacksonville St.	74-73	South Dakota St.
1966	Ky. Wesleyan	54-51	Southern Illinois	1986	Sacred Heart, CT	93-87	SE Missouri St.
1967	Winston-Salem, NC	77-74	SW Missouri St.	1987	Ky. Wesleyan	92-74	Gannon, PA
1968	Ky. Wesleyan	63-52	Indiana St.	1988	Lowell, MA	75-72	AK-Anchorage
1969	Ky. Wesleyan	75-71	SW Missouri St.	1989	N.C. Central	73-46	SE Missouri St.
1970	Phila. Textile	76-65	Tennessee St.	1990	Ky. Wesleyan	93-79	CS-Bakersfield
1971	Evansville, IN	97-82	Old Dominion, VA	1991	North Alabama	79-72	Bridgeport, CT
1972	Roanoke, VA	84-72	Akron, OH	1992	Virginia Union	100-75	Bridgeport, CT
1973	Ky. Wesleyan	78-76*	Tennessee St.	1993	CS-Bakersfield	85-72	Troy St., AL
1974	Morgan St., MD	67-52	SW Missouri St.	1994	CS-Bakersfield	92-86	Southern Ind.
1975	Old Dominion, VA	76-74	New Orleans	1995	Southern Indiana	71-63	CS-Riverside
1976	Puget Sound, WA	83-74	Tennessee-Chatt.				

*Overtime

NCAA Div. III Finals

Multiple winners: North Park (5); Potsdam St., Scranton, WI-Platteville and WI-Whitewater (2).

Year	Winner	Score	Loser	Year	Winner	Score	Loser
1975	LeMoyne-Owen, TN	57-54	Glassboro St., NJ	1986	Potsdam St., NY	76-73	LeMoyne-Owen, TN
1976	Scranton, PA	60-57	Wittenberg, OH	1987	North Park, IL	106-100	Clark, MA
1977	Wittenberg, OH	79-66	Oneonta St., NY	1988	Ohio Wesleyan	92-70	Scranton, PA
1978	North Park, IL	69-57	Widener, PA	1989	WI-Whitewater	94-86	Trenton St., NJ
1979	North Park, IL	66-62	Potsdam St., NY	1990	Rochester, NY	43-42	DePauw, IN
1980	North Park, IL	83-76	Upsala, NJ	1991	WI-Platteville	81-74	Franklin Marshall
1981	Potsdam St., NY	67-65*	Augustana, IL	1992	Calvin, MI	62-49	Rochester, NY
1982	Wabash, IN	83-62	Potsdam St., NY	1993	Ohio Northern	71-68	Augustana, IL
1983	Scranton, PA	64-63	Wittenberg, OH	1994	Lebanon Valley, PA	66-59*	NYU
1984	WI-Whitewater	103-86	Clark, MA	1995	WI-Platteville	69-55	Manchester, IN
1985	North Park, IL	72-71	Potsdam St., NY				

*Overtime

NAIA Finals, 1937-91

Multiple winners: Grand Canyon, Hamline, Kentucky St. and Tennessee St. (3); Central Missouri, Central St., Fort Hays St. and SW Missouri St. (2).

Year	Winner	Score	Loser	Year	Winner	Score	Loser
1937	Central Missouri	35-24	Morningside, IA	1965	Central St., OH	85-51	Oklahoma Baptist
1938	Central Missouri	45-30	Roanoke, VA	1966	Oklahoma Baptist	88-59	Georgia Southern
1939	Southwestern, KS	32-31	San Diego St.	1967	St. Benedict's	71-65	Oklahoma Baptist
1940	Tarkio, MO	52-31	San Diego St.	1968	Central St., OH	51-48	Fairmont St., WV
1941	San Diego St.	36-32	Murray St., KY	1969	Eastern New Mexico	99-76	MD-Eastern Shore
1942	Hamline, MN	33-31	SE Oklahoma	1970	Kentucky St.	79-71	Central Wash.
1943	SE Missouri St.	34-32	NW Missouri St.	1971	Kentucky St.	102-82	Eastern Michigan
1944	Not held			1972	Kentucky St.	71-62	WI-Eau Claire
1945	Loyola-LA	49-36	Pepperdine, CA	1973	Guilford, NC	99-96	MD-Eastern Shore
1946	Southern Illinois	49-40	Indiana St.	1974	West Georgia	97-79	Alcorn St., MS
1947	Marshall, WV	73-59	Mankato St., MN	1975	Grand Canyon, AZ	65-54	M'western St., TX
1948	Louisville, KY	82-70	Indiana St.	1976	Coppin St., MD	96-91	Henderson St., AR
1949	Hamline, MN	57-46	Regis, CO	1977	Texas Southern	71-44	Campbell, NC
1950	Indiana St.	61-47	East Central, OK	1978	Grand Canyon, AZ	79-75	Kearney St., NE
1951	Hamline, MN	69-61	Millikin, IL	1979	Drury, MO	60-54	Henderson St., AR
1952	SW Missouri St.	73-64	Murray St., KY	1980	Cameron, OK	84-77	Alabama St.
1953	SW Missouri St.	79-71	Hamline, MN	1981	Beth. Nazarene, OK	86-85*	AL-Huntsville
1954	St. Benedict's, KS	62-56	Western Illinois	1982	SC-Spartanburg	51-38	Biola, CA
1955	East Texas St.	71-54	SE Oklahoma	1983	Charleston, SC	57-53	WV-Wesleyan
1956	McNeese St., LA	60-55	Texas Southern	1984	Fort Hays St., KS	48-46*	WI-Stevens Pt.
1957	Tennessee St.	92-73	SE Oklahoma	1985	Fort Hays St., KS	82-80*	Wayland Bapt., TX
1958	Tennessee St.	85-73	Western Illinois	1986	David Lipscomb, TN	67-54	AR-Monticello
1959	Tennessee St.	97-87	Pacific-Luth., WA	1987	Washburn, KS	79-77	West Virginia St.
1960	SW Texas St.	66-44	Westminster, PA	1988	Grand Canyon, AZ	88-86*	Auburn-Montg., AL
1961	Grambling, LA	95-75	Georgetown, KY	1989	St. Mary's, TX	61-58	East Central, OK
1962	Prairie View, TX	62-53	Westminster, PA	1990	Birm-Southern, AL	88-80	WI-Eau Claire
1963	Pan American, TX	73-62	Western Carolina	1991	Oklahoma City	77-74	Central Arkansas
1964	Rockhurst, MO	66-56	Pan American, TX				

*Overtime

NAIA Div. I Finals

NAIA split tournament into two divisions in 1992.
Multiple winner: Oklahoma City (2).

Year	Winner	Score	Loser
1992	Oklahoma City	82-73*	Central Arkansas
1993	Hawaii Pacific	88-83	Okla. Baptist
1994	Oklahoma City	99-81	Life, GA
1995	Birm-Southern	92-76	Pfeiffer, NC

*Overtime

NAIA Div. II Finals

NAIA split tournament into two divisions in 1992.

Year	Winner	Score	Loser
1992	Grace, IN	85-79*	Northwestern-IA
1993	Williamette, OR	63-56	Northern St., SD
1994	Eureka, IL	98-95*	Northern St., SD
1995	Bethel, IN	103-95*	NW Nazarene, ID

*Overtime

Player of the Year and NBA MVP

College basketball Players of the Year who have gone on to win the NBA's Most Valuable Player award.
Bill Russell: COLLEGE—San Francisco (1956); PROS—Boston Celtics (1958, 1961, 1962, 1963 and 1965).
Oscar Robertson: COLLEGE—Cincinnati (1958, 1959 and 1960); PROS—Cincinnati Royals (1964).
Kareem Abdul-Jabbar: COLLEGE—UCLA (1967 and 1968); PROS—Milwaukee Bucks (1971 and 1972) and LA Lakers (1974, 1976, 1977 and 1980).
Bill Walton: COLLEGE—UCLA (1972, 1973 and 1974); PROS—Portland Trail Blazers (1978).
Larry Bird: COLLEGE—Indiana St. (1979); PROS—Boston Celtics (1984, 1985, and 1986).
Michael Jordan: COLLEGE—North Carolina (1984); PROS—Chicago Bulls (1988, 1991 and 1992).
David Robinson: COLLEGE—Navy (1987); PROS—San Antonio Spurs (1995).

WOMEN

NCAA Final Four

Replaced the Association of Intercollegiate Athletics for Women (AIAW) tournament in 1982 as the official playoff for the national championship.

Multiple winners: Tennessee (3); Louisiana Tech, Stanford and USC (2).

Year	Champion	Head Coach	Score	Runner-up	Third Place	
1982	Louisiana Tech	Sonya Hogg	76-62	Cheyney	Maryland	Tennessee
1983	USC	Linda Sharp	69-67	Louisiana Tech	Georgia	Old Dominion
1984	USC	Linda Sharp	72-61	Tennessee	Cheyney	Louisiana Tech
1985	Old Dominion	Marianne Stanley	70-65	Georgia	NE Louisiana	Western Ky.
1986	Texas	Jody Conradt	97-81	USC	Tennessee	Western Ky.
1987	Tennessee	Pat Summitt	67-44	Louisiana Tech	Long Beach St.	Texas
1988	Louisiana Tech	Leon Barmore	56-54	Auburn	Long Beach St.	Tennessee
1989	Tennessee	Pat Summitt	76-60	Auburn	Louisiana Tech	Maryland
1990	Stanford	Tara VanDerveer	88-81	Auburn	Louisiana Tech	Virginia
1991	Tennessee	Pat Summitt	70-67 (OT)	Virginia	Connecticut	Stanford
1992	Stanford	Tara VanDerveer	78-62	Western Kentucky	SW Missouri St.	Virginia
1993	Texas Tech	Marsha Sharp	84-82	Ohio St.	Iowa	Vanderbilt
1994	North Carolina	Sylvia Hatchell	60-59	Louisiana Tech	Alabama	Purdue
1995	Connecticut	Geno Auriemma	70-64	Tennessee	Georgia	Stanford

Final Four sites: 1982 (Norfolk, Va.), **1983** (Norfolk, Va.), **1984** (Los Angeles), **1985** (Austin), **1986** (Lexington), **1987** (Austin), **1988** (Tacoma), **1989** (Tacoma), **1990** (Knoxville), **1991** (New Orleans), **1992** (Los Angeles), **1993** (Atlanta), **1994** (Richmond), **1995** (Minneapolis).

Most Outstanding Player

A Most Outstanding Player has been selected every year of the NCAA tournament. Winner who did not play for the tournament champion is listed in **bold** type.

Multiple winner: Cheryl Miller (2).

Year		Year		Year	
1982	Janice Lawrence, La. Tech	1987	Tonya Edwards, Tennessee	1992	Molly Goodenbour, Stanford
1983	Cheryl Miller, USC	1988	Erica Westbrooks, La. Tech	1993	Sheryl Swoopes, Texas Tech
1984	Cheryl Miller, USC	1989	Bridgette Gordon, Tennessee	1994	Charlotte Smith, N. Carolina
1985	Tracy Claxton, Old Dominion	1990	Jennifer Azzi, Stanford	1995	Rebecca Lobo, Connecticut
1986	Clarissa Davis, Texas	1991	**Dawn Staley,** Virginia		

All-Time NCAA Division I Tournament Leaders

Through 1994-95; minimum of six games; **Last** column indicates final year played

CAREER

Scoring

	Points	Yrs	Last	Pts	Avg
1	Bridgette Gordon, Tenn	4	1989	388	21.6
2	Cheryl Miller, USC	4	1986	333	20.8
3	Janice Lawrence, La. Tech	3	1984	312	22.3
4	Penny Toler, L. Beach St	4	1989	291	22.4
5	Dawn Staley, Virginia	4	1992	274	18.3
6	Cindy Brown, L. Beach St	4	1987	263	21.9
7	Venus Lacy, La. Tech	3	1990	263	18.8
8	Clarissa Davis, Texas	3	1989	261	21.8
9	Janet Harris, Georgia	4	1985	254	19.5
10	Val Whiting, Stanford	4	1993	249	15.6

Rebounds

	Average	Yrs	Last	No	Avg
1	Cheryl Miller, USC	4	1986	170	10.6
2	Sheila Frost, Tennessee	4	1989	162	9.0
3	Val Whiting, Stanford	4	1993	161	10.1
4	Venus Lacy, La. Tech	3	1990	148	10.6
5	Bridgette Gordon, Tenn	4	1989	142	7.9
6	Kirsten Cummings, L. Beach St.	4	1985	136	10.5
7	Nora Lewis, La. Tech	3	1989	130	9.3
8	Pam McGee, USC	3	1984	127	9.8
9	Daedra Charles, Tenn	3	1991	125	9.6
	Paula McGee, USC	3	1984	125	9.6

SINGLE GAME

Scoring

		Year	Pts
1	Lorri Bauman, Drake vs Maryland	1982	50
2	Sheryl Swoopes, Texas Tech vs Ohio St.	1993	47
3	Barbara Kennedy, Clemson vs Penn St.	1982	43
4	LaTaunya Pollard, L. Beach St. vs Howard	1982	40
	Cindy Brown, L. Beach St. vs Ohio St.	1987	40
6	Kerry Bascom, UConn vs Toledo	1991	39
	Portia Hill, S.F. Austin St. vs Arkansas	1990	39
	Delmonica DeHorney, Ark. vs Stanford	1990	39
9	LaTaunya Pollard, L. Beach St. vs USC	1983	37
	Teresa Edwards, Georgia vs Tennessee	1986	37

Rebounds

		Year	No
1	Cheryl Taylor, Tenn. Tech vs Georgia	1985	23
	Charlotte Smith, N. Car. vs La. Tech	1994	23
3	Daedra Charles, Tenn. vs SW Missouri	1991	22
4	Cherie Nelson, USC vs Western Ky	1987	21
5	Alison Lang, Oregon vs Missouri	1982	20
	Shelda Arceneaux, S.D. St. vs L. Beach St.	1984	20
	Tracy Claxton, ODU vs Georgia	1985	20
	Brigette Combs, West. Ky. vs West Va.	1989	20
	Tandreia Green, West. Ky. vs West Va.	1989	20
10	Six tied with 19 each.		

Associated Press Final Top 10 Polls

The Associated Press weekly women's college basketball poll was begun by Mel Greenberg of *The Philadelphia Inquirer* during the 1976-77 season. The Association of Intercollegiate Athletics for Women (AIAW) Tournament determined the Division I national champion for 1972-81. The NCAA began its women's Division I tournament in 1982. The final AP Polls were taken **before** the NCAA tournament. Eventual national champions are in **bold** type.

1977
1 **Delta St.**
2 Immaculata
3 St. Joseph's-PA
4 CS-Fullerton
5 Tennessee
6 Tennessee Tech
7 Wayland Baptist
8 Montclair St.
9 S.F. Austin St.
10 N.C. State

1978
1 Tennessee
2 Wayland Baptist
3 N.C. State
4 Montclair St.
5 **UCLA**
6 Maryland
7 Queens-NY
8 Valdosta St.
9 Delta St.
10 LSU

1979
1 **Old Dominion**
2 Louisiana Tech
3 Tennessee
4 Texas
5 S.F. Austin St.
6 UCLA
7 Rutgers
8 Maryland
9 Cheyney
10 Wayland Baptist

1980
1 **Old Dominion**
2 Tennessee
3 Louisiana Tech
4 South Carolina
5 S.F. Austin St.
6 Maryland
7 Texas
8 Rutgers
9 Long Beach St.
10 N.C. State

1981
1 **Louisiana Tech**
2 Tennessee
3 Old Dominion
4 USC
5 Cheyney
6 Long Beach St.
7 UCLA
8 Maryland
9 Rutgers
10 Kansas

1982
1 **Louisiana Tech**
2 Cheyney
3 Maryland
4 Tennessee
5 Texas
6 USC
7 Old Dominion
8 Rutgers
9 Long Beach St.
10 Penn St.

1983
1 **USC**
2 Louisiana Tech
3 Texas
4 Old Dominion
5 Cheyney
6 Long Beach St.
7 Maryland
8 Penn St.
9 Georgia
10 Tennessee

1984
1 Texas
2 Louisiana Tech
3 Georgia
4 Old Dominion
5 **USC**
6 Long Beach St.
7 Kansas St.
8 LSU
9 Cheyney
10 Mississippi

1985
1 Texas
2 NE Louisiana
3 Long Beach St.
4 Louisiana Tech
5 **Old Dominion**
6 Mississippi
7 Ohio St.
8 Georgia
9 Penn St.
10 Auburn

1986
1 **Texas**
2 Georgia
3 USC
4 Louisiana Tech
5 Western Ky.
6 Virginia
7 Auburn
8 Long Beach St.
9 LSU
10 Rutgers

1987
1 Texas
2 Auburn
3 Louisiana Tech
4 Long Beach St.
5 Rutgers
6 Georgia
7 **Tennessee**
8 Mississippi
9 Iowa
10 Ohio St.

1988
1 Tennessee
2 Iowa
3 Auburn
4 Texas
5 **Louisiana Tech**
6 Ohio St.
7 Long Beach St.
8 Rutgers
9 Maryland
10 Virginia

1989
1 **Tennessee**
2 Auburn
3 Louisiana Tech
4 Stanford
5 Maryland
6 Texas
7 Long Beach St.
8 Iowa
9 Colorado
10 Georgia

1990
1 **Louisiana Tech**
2 Stanford
3 Washington
4 Tennessee
5 UNLV
6 S.F. Austin St.
7 Georgia
8 Texas
9 Auburn
10 Iowa

1991
1 Penn St.
2 Virginia
3 Georgia
4 **Tennessee**
5 Purdue
6 Auburn
7 N.C. State
8 LSU
9 Arkansas
10 Western Ky.

1992
1 Virginia
2 Tennessee
3 **Stanford**
4 S.F. Austin St.
5 Mississippi
6 Miami-FL
7 Iowa
8 Maryland
9 Penn St.
10 SW Missouri St.

1993
1 Vanderbilt
2 Tennessee
3 Ohio St.
4 Iowa
5 **Texas Tech**
6 Stanford
7 Auburn
8 Penn St.
9 Virginia
10 Colorado

1994
1 Tennessee
2 Penn St.
3 Connecticut
4 **North Carolina**
5 Colorado
6 Louisiana Tech
7 USC
8 Purdue
9 Texas Tech
10 Virginia

1995
1 **Connecticut**
2 Colorado
3 Tennessee
4 Stanford
5 Texas Tech
6 Vanderbilt
7 Penn St.
8 Louisiana Tech
9 Western Ky.
10 Virginia

All-Time Winningest Division I Teams

Division I schools with best winning percentages and most victories through 1994-95 (including postseason tournaments).

Top 10 Winning Percentage

		Yrs	W	L	Pct
1	Louisiana Tech	21	583	117	.833
2	Tennessee	21	564	129	.814
3	Texas	21	575	133	.812
4	Mount St. Mary's	21	427	132	.764
5	Montana	21	442	148	.749
6	S.F. Austin St.	23	539	185	.744
	Long Beach St.	33	588	202	.744
8	Mississippi	21	483	171	.739
9	UNLV	21	438	157	.736
10	Rutgers	20	445	164	.731

Top 10 Victories

		Yrs	W	L	Pct
1	Long Beach St.	33	588	202	.744
2	Louisiana Tech	21	583	117	.833
3	James Madison	70	576	310	.650
4	Texas	21	575	133	.812
5	Tennessee	21	564	129	.814
6	Tennessee Tech	25	555	217	.719
7	S.F. Austin St.	23	539	185	.744
8	Old Dominion	26	530	205	.721
9	Ohio St.	30	510	207	.711
10	Southern Illinois	36	493	243	.670

Annual NCAA Division I Leaders

All averages include postseason games

Scoring

Multiple winner: Andrea Congreaves (2).

Year		Gm	Pts	Avg
1982	Barbara Kennedy, Clemson	31	908	29.3
1983	LaTaunya Pollard, L. Beach St	31	907	29.3
1984	Deborah Temple, Delta St.	28	873	31.2
1985	Anucha Browne, Northwestern	28	855	30.5
1986	Wanda Ford, Drake	30	919	30.6
1987	Tresa Spaulding, BYU	28	810	28.9
1988	LeChandra LeDay, Grambling	28	850	30.4
1989	Patricia Hoskins, Miss. Valley	27	908	33.6
1990	Kim Perrot, SW Louisiana	28	839	30.0
1991	Jan Jensen, Drake	30	888	29.6
1992	Andrea Congreaves, Mercer	28	925	33.0
1993	Andrea Congreaves, Mercer	26	805	31.0
1994	Kristy Ryan, CS-Sacramento	26	727	28.0
1995	Koko Lahanas, CS-Fullerton	29	778	26.8

Rebounds

Multiple winner: Patricia Hoskins (2).

Year		Gm	No	Avg
1982	Anne Donovan, Old Dominion	28	412	14.7
1983	Deborah Mitchell, Miss. Col	28	447	16.0
1984	Joy Kellog, Oklahoma City	23	373	16.2
1985	Rosina Pearson, Beth-Cookman	26	480	18.5
1986	Wanda Ford, Drake	30	506	16.9
1987	Patricia Hoskins, Miss. Valley	28	476	17.0
1988	Katie Beck, East Tenn. St.	25	441	17.6
1989	Patricia Hoskins, Miss. Valley	27	440	16.3
1990	Pam Hudson, Northwestern St	29	438	15.1
1991	Tarcha Hollis, Grambling	29	443	15.3
1992	Christy Greis, Evansville	28	383	13.7
1993	Ann Barry, Nevada	25	355	14.2
1994	DeShawne Blocker, E. Tenn. St.	26	450	17.3
1995	Tera Sheriff, Jackson St	29	401	13.8

Note: Wanda Ford (1986) and Patricia Hoskins (1989) each led the country in scoring and rebounds in the same year.

All-Time NCAA Division I Individual Leaders

Through 1994-95; includes regular season and tournament games; **Last** column indicates final year played.

CAREER

Scoring

	Average	Yrs	Last	Pts	Avg
1	Patricia Hoskins, Miss.Valley St.	4	1989	3122	28.4
2	Sandra Hodge, New Orleans	4	1984	2860	26.7
3	Lorri Bauman, Drake	4	1984	3115	26.0
4	Valorie Whiteside, Aplach. St.	4	1988	2944	25.4
5	Joyce Walker, LSU	4	1984	2906	24.8
6	Tarcha Hollis, Grambling	4	1991	2058	24.2
7	Karen Pelphrey, Marshall	4	1986	2746	24.1
8	Erma Jones, Bethune-Cookman	3	1984	2095	24.1
9	Cheryl Miller, USC	4	1986	3018	23.6
10	Chris Starr, Nevada	4	1986	2356	23.3

Rebounds

	Average	Yrs	Last	Reb	Avg
1	Wanda Ford, Drake	4	1986	1887	16.1
2	Patricia Hoskins, Miss.Valley St.	4	1989	1662	15.1
3	Tarcha Hollis, Grambling	4	1991	1185	13.9
4	Katie Beck, East Tenn. St.	4	1988	1404	13.4
5	Marilyn Stephens, Temple	4	1984	1519	13.0
6	Cheryl Taylor, Tenn. Tech	4	1987	1532	12.8
7	Olivia Bradley, West Virginia	4	1985	1484	12.7
8	Judy Mosley, Hawaii	4	1990	1441	12.6
9	Chana Perry, NE La./S. Diego St.	4	1989	1286	12.5
10	Three players tied at 12.2 each.				

SINGLE SEASON

Scoring

	Average	Year	Gm	Pts	Avg
1	Patricia Hoskins, Miss.Valley St.	1989	27	908	33.6
2	Andrea Congreaves, Mercer	1992	28	925	33.0
3	Deborah Temple, Delta St.	1984	28	873	31.2
4	Andrea Congreaves, Mercer	1993	26	805	31.0
5	Wanda Ford, Drake	1986	30	919	30.6
6	Anucha Browne, Northwestern	1985	28	855	30.5
7	LeChandra LeDay, Grambling	1988	28	850	30.4
8	Kim Perrot, SW Louisiana	1990	28	839	30.0
9	Tina Hutchinson, San Diego St.	1984	30	898	29.9
10	Jan Jensen, Drake	1991	30	888	29.6

SINGLE GAME

Scoring

	Average	Year	Pts
1	Cindy Brown, Long Beach St. vs San Jose St.	1987	60
2	Lorri Bauman, Drake vs SW Missouri St.	1984	58
	Kim Perrot, SW La. vs SE La.	1990	58
4	Patricia Hoskins, Miss.Valley St. vs South-BR	1989	55
	Patricia Hoskins, Miss.Valley St. vs Ala. St.	1989	55
6	Wanda Ford, Drake vs SW Missouri St.	1986	54
7	Chris Starr, Nevada vs CS-Sacramento	1983	53
	Felisha Edwards, NE La. vs Southern Miss	1991	53
	Sheryl Swoopes, Texas Tech vs Texas	1993	53
10	Three players tied at 52 points each.		

Winningest Active Division I Coaches

Minimum of five seasons as Division I head coach; regular season and tournament games included.

Top 10 Winning Percentage

		Yrs	W	L	Pct
1	Leon Barmore, La. Tech	13	366	61	.857
2	Sonja Hogg, Baylor	12	320	69	.823
3	Bill Sheahan, Mt. St. Mary's	14	321	70	.821
4	Pat Summitt, Tennessee	21	564	129	.814
5	Robin Selvig, Montana	17	408	100	.803
6	Gary Blair, Arkansas	10	248	64	.795
7	Vivian Stringer, Rutgers	23	520	135	.794
8	Jody Conradt, Texas	26	654	178	.786
9	Tara VanDerveer, Stanford	17	403	113	.781
10	Joe Ciampi, Auburn	18	426	121	.779

Top 12 Victories

		Yrs	W	L	Pct
1	Jody Conradt, Texas	26	654	178	.786
2	Pat Summitt, Tennessee	21	564	129	.814
3	Vivian Stringer, Rutgers	23	520	135	.794
4	Sue Gunter, LSU	25	501	229	.686
5	Kay Yow, N.C. State	24	488	192	.718
6	Marynell Meadors, Florida St.	25	487	271	.642
7	Theresa Grentz, Illinois	21	461	154	.750
8	Sylvia Hatchell, N. Carolina	20	444	181	.710
9	Rene Portland, Penn St.	19	438	140	.758
10	Kay James, So. Miss.	23	428	192	.690
11	Lin Dunn, Purdue	24	427	246	.634
12	Joe Ciampi, Auburn	18	426	121	.779

Annual Awards

The Broderick Award was first given out to the Women's Division I or Large School Player of the Year in 1977. Since then, the National Assn. for Girls and Women in Sports (1978), the Women's Basketball Coaches Assn. (1983) and the Atlanta Tip-Off Club (1983) and the Associated Press (1995) have joined in.

Since 1983, the first year as many as four awards were given out, the same player has won all of them in the same season twice: Cheryl Miller of USC in 1985 and Rebecca Lobo of Connecticut in 1995.

Associated Press

Voted on by AP sportswriters and broadcasters and first presented in 1995.

Year
1995 Rebecca Lobo, Connecticut

Broderick Award

Voted on by a national panel of women's collegiate athletic directors and first presented by the late Thomas Broderick, an athletic outfitter, in 1977. Honda has presented the award since 1987. Basketball Player of the Year is one of 10 nominated for Collegiate Woman Athlete of the Year; (*) indicates player also won Athlete of the Year.
Multiple winners: Nancy Lieberman, Cheryl Miller and Dawn Staley (2).

Year	**Year**	**Year**
1977 Lucy Harris, Delta St.*	1984 Cheryl Miller, USC*	1990 Jennifer Azzi, Stanford
1978 Anne Meyers, UCLA*	1985 Cheryl Miller, USC	1991 Dawn Staley, Virginia
1979 Nancy Lieberman, Old Dominion*	1986 Kamie Ethridge, Texas*	1992 Dawn Staley, Virginia
1980 Nancy Lieberman, Old Dominion*	1987 Katrina McClain, Georgia	1993 Sheryl Swoopes, Texas Tech
1981 Lynette Woodward, Kansas	1988 Teresa Weatherspoon, La. Tech*	1994 Lisa Leslie, USC
1982 Pam Kelly, La. Tech.	1989 Bridgette Gordon, Tennessee	1995 Rebecca Lobo, Connecticut
1983 Anne Donovan, Old Dominion		

Wade Trophy

Voted on by the National Assn. for Girls and Women in Sports (NAGWS) and awarded for academics and community service as well as player performance. First presented in 1978 in the name of former Delta St. coach Margaret Wade.
Multiple winner: Nancy Lieberman (2).

Year	**Year**	**Year**
1978 Carol Blazejowski, Montclair St.	1984 Janice Lawrence, La. Tech	1990 Jennifer Azzi, Stanford
1979 Nancy Lieberman, Old Dominion	1985 Cheryl Miller, USC	1991 Daedra Charles, Tennessee
1980 Nancy Lieberman, Old Dominion	1986 Kamie Ethridge, Texas	1992 Susan Robinson, Penn St.
1981 Lynette Woodward, Kansas	1987 Shelly Pennefather, Villanova	1993 Karen Jennings, Nebraska
1982 Pam Kelly, La. Tech	1988 Teresa Weatherspoon, La. Tech	1994 Carol Ann Shudlick, Minnesota
1983 LaTaunya Pollard, L. Beach St.	1989 Clarissa Davis, Texas	1995 Rebecca Lobo, Connecticut

Naismith Trophy

Voted on by a panel of coaches, sportwriters and broadcasters and first presented in 1983 by the Atlanta Tip-Off Club in the name of the inventor of basketball, Dr. James Naismith.
Multiple winners: Cheryl Miller (3); Clarissa Davis and Dawn Staley (2).

Year	**Year**	**Year**
1983 Anne Donovan, Old Dominion	1988 Sue Wicks, Rutgers	1993 Sheryl Swoopes, Texas Tech
1984 Cheryl Miller, USC	1989 Clarissa Davis, Texas	1994 Lisa Leslie, USC
1985 Cheryl Miller, USC	1990 Jennifer Azzi, Stanford	1995 Rebecca Lobo, Connecticut
1986 Cheryl Miller, USC	1991 Dawn Staley, Virgina	
1987 Clarissa Davis, Texas	1992 Dawn Staley, Virginia	

Annual Awards (Cont.)

Women's Basketball Coaches Association

Voted on by the WBCA and first presented by Champion athletic outfitters in 1983.
Multiple winners: Cheryl Miller and Dawn Staley (2).

Year	Year	Year
1983 Anne Donovan, Old Dominion	1988 Michelle Edwards, Iowa	1992 Dawn Staley, Virginia
1984 Janice Lawrence, La. Tech	1989 Clarissa Davis, Texas	1993 Sheryl Swoopes, Texas Tech
1985 Cheryl Miller, USC	1990 Venus Lacey, La. Tech	1994 Lisa Leslie, USC
1986 Cheryl Miller, USC	1991 Dawn Staley, Virgina	1995 Rebecca Lobo, Connecticut
1987 Katrina McClain, Georgia		

Coach of the Year Award

Voted on by the Women's Basketball Coaches Assn. and first presented by Converse athletic outfitters in 1983.
Multiple winners: Jody Conradt and Vivian Stringer (2).

Year	Year	Year
1983 Pat Summitt, Tennessee	1988 Vivian Stringer, Iowa	1992 Ferne Labati, Miami-FL
1984 Jody Conradt, Texas	1989 Tara VanDerveer, Stanford	1993 Vivian Stringer, Iowa
1985 Jim Foster, St. Joseph's-PA	1990 Kay Yow, N.C. State	1994 Marsha Sharp, Texas Tech
1986 Jody Conradt, Texas	1991 Rene Portland, Penn St.	1995 Gary Blair, Arkansas
1987 Theresa Grentz, Rutgers		

Other Women's Champions

The NCAA has sanctioned national championship tournaments for Division II and Division III since 1982. The NAIA sanctioned a single tournament from 1981-91, then split in to two divisions in 1992.

NCAA Div. II Finals

Multiple winners: North Dakota St. (4); Cal Poly Pomona (3); Delta St. (2).

Year	Winner	Score	Loser
1982	Cal Poly Pomona	93-74	Tuskegee, AL
1983	Virginia Union	73-60	Cal Poly Pomona
1984	Central Mo. St.	80-73	Virginia Union
1985	Cal Poly Pomona	80-69	Central Mo. St.
1986	Cal Poly Pomona	70-63	North Dakota St.
1987	New Haven, CT	77-75	Cal Poly Pomona
1988	Hampton, VA	65-48	West Texas St.
1989	Delta St., MS	88-58	Cal Poly Pomona
1990	Delta St., MS	77-43	Bentley, MA
1991	North Dakota St.	81-74	SE Missouri St.
1992	Delta St., MS	65-63	North Dakota St.
1993	North Dakota St.	95-63	Delta St., MS
1994	North Dakota St.	89-56	CS-San Bernadino
1995	North Dakota St.	98-85	Portland St.

NCAA Div. III Finals

Multiple winners: Capital and Elizabethtown (2).

Year	Winner	Score	Loser
1982	Elizabethtown, PA	67-66*	NC-Greensboro
1983	North Central, IL	83-71	Elizabethtown, PA
1984	Rust College, MS	51-49	Elizabethtown, PA
1985	Scranton, PA	68-59	New Rochelle, NY
1986	Salem St., MA	89-85	Bishop, TX
1987	WI-Stevens Pt.	81-74	Concordia, MN
1988	Concordia, MN	65-57	St. John Fisher, NY
1989	Elizabethtown, PA	66-65	CS-Stanislaus
1990	Hope, MI	65-63	St. John Fisher
1991	St. Thomas, MN	73-55	Muskingum, OH
1992	Alma, MI	79-75	Moravian, PA
1993	Central Iowa	71-63	Capital, OH
1994	Capital, OH	82-63	Washington, MO
1995	Capital, OH	59-55	WI-Oshkosh

*Overtime

AIAW Finals

The Association of Intercollegiate Athletics for Women Large College tournament determined the women's national champion for 10 years until supplanted by the NCAA.

In 1982, most Division I teams entered the first NCAA tournament rather than the last one staged by the AIAW.

Year	Winner	Score	Loser
1972	Immaculata, PA	52-48	West Chester, PA
1973	Immaculata, PA	59-52	Queens College, NY
1974	Immaculata, PA	68-53	Mississippi College
1975	Delta St., MS	90-81	Immaculata, PA
1976	Delta St., MS	69-64	Immaculata, PA
1977	Delta St., MS	68-55	LSU
1978	UCLA	90-74	Maryland
1979	Old Dominion	75-65	Louisiana Tech
1980	Old Dominion	68-53	Tennessee
1981	Louisiana Tech	79-59	Tennessee
1982	Rutgers	83-77	Texas

NAIA Finals

Multiple winners: One tournament—SW Oklahoma (4); Div. I tourney—Arkansas Tech and Southern Nazarene (2); Div. II tourney—Northern St. (2).

Year	Winner	Score	Loser
1981	Kentucky St.	73-67	Texas Southern
1982	SW Oklahoma	80-45	Mo. Southern
1983	SW Oklahoma	80-68	AL-Huntsville
1984	NC-Asheville	72-70*	Portland, OR
1985	SW Oklahoma	55-54	Saginaw Val., MI
1986	Francis Marion, SC	75-65	Wayland Baptist, TX
1987	SW Oklahoma	60-58	North Georgia
1988	Oklahoma City	113-95	Claflin, SC
1989	So. Nazarene	98-96	Claflin, SC
1990	SW Oklahoma	82-75	AR-Monticello
1991	Ft. Hays St., KS	57-53	SW Oklahoma
1992	I—Arkansas Tech	84-68	Wayland Baptist, TX
	II—Northern St., SD	82-71	Tarleton St., TX
1993	I—Arkansas Tech	76-75	Union, TN
	II—No. Montana	71-68	Northern St., SD
1994	I—So. Nazarene	97-74	David Lipscomb, TN
	II—Northern St., SD	48-45	Western Oregon
1995	I—So. Nazarene	78-77	SE Oklahoma
	II—Western Oregon	75-67	NW Nazarene, ID

*Overtime

Wide World Photos

Former University of Houston teammates **Hakeem Olajuwon** (left) and **Clyde Drexler** celebrate the Houston Rockets' 113-101 victory over Orlando to clinch the 1995 NBA championship.

PRO BASKETBALL

Sweep Dreams

*Hakeem Olajuwon and the Rockets rout Orlando in 4 games
to cap a remarkable campaign in defense of their NBA title.*

It had been easy to dismiss Houston as a one-year champion, a product of some metaphysical glitch or inferior competition. The league, after all, was still spinning from the loss of Michael Jordan when the Rockets ascended to the throne.

This lack of respect drove the Rockets during the 1994-95 season. Much like the Detroit Pistons four years earlier, Houston was determined to prove its title was no fluke. Those who dismissed the Rockets or ignored their accomplishments had to be slam-dunked to their senses.

The defining— or perhaps, the redefining— moment came with the Rockets' sweep of Shaquille O'Neal and the Orlando Magic in the NBA Finals.

"Never underestimate the heart of a champion," Houston coach Rudy Tomjanovich shouted after the Rockets 113-101 victory in Game 4 yielded a second consecutive championship. "You can't take anything away from last year's team, but this year with a new team we did what no one had ever done before."

What the Rockets did was unprecedented. Houston became the first team in league history to defeat four 50-win teams on the way to the championship. They became the first team to win a title without having the home court advantage in any of its four playoff rounds. And they overcame deficits

of 2-1 to Utah in the first round and a 3-1 chasm to Phoenix in the second round.

Each step along this improbable way, Houston began to earn the respect for which it hungered. When it was over, the Rockets took their place next to the Boston Celtics, Los Angeles Lakers, Chicago Bulls and Pistons as the only franchises in league history to win back-to-back titles. Center Hakeem Olajuwon cemented his claim to being the sport's best player, Tomjanovich proved he belonged with the best in his profession and guard Clyde Drexler earned the championship that eluded him and Olajuwon when they were teammates at the University of Houston 13 years earlier.

The Rockets were 29-17 on Feb. 14 when they traded starting power forward Otis Thorpe to Portland for Drexler. They went 18-18 from there and finished the regular season at 47-35, good for only a No. 6 seed in the tough Western Conference.

Carl Herrera, who was expected to step in for Thorpe, played just six minutes in the first round of the playoffs due to a dislocated shoulder. Vernon Maxwell, the volatile Rockets' guard who was fined $20,000 and suspended 10 games for punching out a fan in Portland on Feb. 8, was later granted a leave of absence one game into the postseason when he complained about his lack of minutes since Drexler's arrival. He never returned.

Houston made up for this with a combative spirit and a team concept. With teams concentrating on Olajuwon and Drexler,

---

David Moore has been the national pro basketball writer for *The Dallas Morning News* since 1989. He is also an NBA analyst for ESPN.

Allsport USA

All-Star centers **Hakeem Olajuwon** of Houston (left) and **Shaquille O'Neal** of Orlando jump for the opening tap in Game 3 of the NBA finals. Olajuwon, 32, led the playoffs in scoring and won his second straight postseason MVP award. O'Neal, 23, was the regular season scoring champion.

Robert Horry, Sam Cassell, Kenny Smith and Mario Elie all came up big for the Rockets at crucial times. This allowed the Rockets to win a record nine playoff games on the road and resulted in 11 victories in their final 13 games.

"They have no choice but to give us respect," Horry said of the Rockets critics as champagne streamed down his face for the second consecutive year.

Still, the heart and indomitable soul of the Rockets' success was Olajuwon. He averaged 35.3 points, 12.5 rebounds, 5 assists and 4.2 blocked shots against San Antonio's David Robinson, the league's regular-season Most Valuable Player, during the Western Conference Finals. Tomjanovich called it a legendary performance. Olajuwon followed that by averaging 32.8 points, 11.5 rebounds and 5.5 assists against O'Neal, the regular sea-

son scoring champion, in the finals. That effort allowed him to join Jordan as the only players to be named the MVP of the finals in consecutive years.

"Everybody in the league respects Hakeem," Magic forward Horace Grant said. "He's one of those guys you like playing against, even when he beats you. He never throws an elbow or a cheap shot. He plays hard. He plays everywhere. He's awesome."

Olajuwon's emergence as the sport's dominant player was a welcome sight to the NBA hierarchy. The humble, gracious way in which Olajuwon carried himself served as a needed counterpoint to the brash, obnoxious antics of some of the league's young stars.

Minnesota's Isaiah Rider and Christian Laettner, New Jersey's Derrick Coleman and Chris Morris, Golden State's Latrell Sprewell all came to epitomize the selfish, petulant player who puts his own needs and emotions above those of the team.

The leader of this disturbing movement was Coleman. The Nets star showed no regard for authority or his status as one of the league's best players. When rookie coach Butch Beard instituted a dress code, Coleman presented him with a blank check and told Beard to go ahead and fill out the amount he would owe in fines for violating it. Coleman consistently ignored instruction, skipped practices and fought with teammates and club officials. He called Utah forward Karl Malone an "Uncle Tom" and generally alienated anyone he came across.

The overall climate became so bad that former stars such as Magic Johnson and Kareem Abdul-Jabbar were compelled to rip the league's younger generation. Orlando's Anfernee Hardaway tried to distance himself from his peers by pleading not to be lumped in that group while Phoenix forward Charles Barkley, once the league's *enfant terrible*, took a swipe at Coleman and Co.

"A lot of people misunderstand," Olajuwon said. "A role model is not someone who's trying to be one. You don't try. You believe in some principles, fundamental principles, where you are the same person at home that you are in public. If you act one way at home and another way when you're in public, that's when there's pressure. There's no consistency.

"The consistency is in being yourself."

San Antonio's Dennis Rodman was consistantly bizarre. The NBA's rebel without a cause challenged the Spurs' authority throughout a tumultuous nine months in which he was granted a month-long leave of absence in November— during which he reportedly saw a psychiatrist— and missed time late in the season after hurting his shoulder in a motorcycle accident. Rodman changed hair colors, pierced body parts and added tatoos with an eclectic fury that often overshadowed his accomplishments as the league's best rebounder and the success of his team.

During the season Rodman appeared naked, on his knees and bound in chains on the cover of *Gentleman's Quarterly*. He was later featured on the May 29 cover of *Sports Illustrated* wearing a skimpy black outfit complete with a silver-studded dog collar and an exotic bird perched on his hand.

The Second Coming Shows A Little Rust

Two words ended the speculation and set the stage for arguably the most anticipated comeback in sports history.

"I'm back."

With that brief statement, released through his agent on March 18, Michael Jordan ended his 17-month retirement from basketball and acknowledged his return to the Chicago Bulls, the NBA and the sport that made him an icon.

His timing was perfect. The NBA's television ratings were down. A Jan. 30 *Sports Illustrated* cover story had blasted the league's overabundance of whining young millionaires. And a lengthy front page report in the March 9 edition of *The Wall Street Journal* had speculated about a possible drug link in the 1993 death of Boston Celtics star Reggie Lewis.

The comeback began to take shape when the 32-year-old Jordan decided to end his quixotic baseball career after one year in Double A and a .202 batting average. Faced with the uncertainty of the ongoing Major League players' strike, he left the Chicago White Sox spring training camp on March 2 and announced his retirement eight days later.

At that point it was just a matter of time. Two days before Jordan's return, President Clinton alluded to the comeback at a White House press conference.

"As of today, the economy has produced 6.1 million jobs since I became President," said Mr. Clinton. "And if Michael Jordan goes back to the Bulls, it'll be six million, one hundred thousand and one new jobs."

Chicago Tribune columnist Bob Greene, who co-wrote the book *Hang Time* with Jordan, said Jordan was coming back because he couldn't resist the challenge.

"People are going to say he's 32 years-old; he's too old; he's been away from the game too long..." Greene told Chicago radio station WBBM. "That's precisely the kind of thing that drives him...Those are fighting words."

His first game back, a nationally-televised, 103-96 overtime road loss to the Pacers on March 19, was one of the highest rated games in NBA history. Jordan, who was scoreless the first 16 minutes, ended up with 19 points after missing 21 of 28 shots from the field.

There were moments from Jordan's 17 regular season games that reaffirmed his greatness. He hit a game-winning shot from the top of the key in his fourth game back to beat Atlanta. He had 55

Michael Jordan officially ended his retirement from pro basketball on March 19 with a new uniform number and 19 points against the Indiana Pacers. He went on to average 26.9 points in 17 regular season games and 31.5 points per game in the playoffs where the Bulls lost in the second round.

points at Madison Square Garden to defeat the New York Knicks on March 28. He ended up averaging 26.9 points a game, which lowered his regular season career average to 32.2.

But the playoffs had always been Jordan's ultimate stage. In his first postseason game in nearly two years, Jordan had 48 points, nine rebounds and eight assists in an overtime victory over the Charlotte Hornets.

"I felt like a shark in the water who saw blood," Jordan said. "I had to attack."

Jordan scored 10 points in overtime, going four-for-four from the field, with two rebounds, a blocked shot and a scintillating assist to Toni Kukoc to ice the game with 1:31 remaining.

"I think he got to the point where he just broke us down in the overtime," Hornets coach Allan Bristow said. "He could do anything he wanted to at that time of the game."

But as the playoffs wore on, it became clear that Jordan, despite averaging 31.5 points a game, was not as numbingly brilliant night in and night out as he had been in the past. His effort in Game 1 of the Bulls second round series with Orlando, when he was held to 19 points and committed two turnovers in the final 10 seconds, underlined the difference.

"No. 45 didn't explode like No. 23 used to,"

Magic guard Nick Anderson said, referring to Jordan's number change upon his return.

His mystique fading amidst whispers that he had lost a step, Jordan dusted off his old No. 23 jersey (which the Bulls had retired on Nov. 1, 1994) for Game 2 in Orlando. For one evening, at least, the clothes did make the man. Jordan erupted for 38 points, 22 of them coming in the second half, and led the Bulls to a 10-point win.

To some, Jordan's switching from No. 45 (his Birmingham Barons baseball uniform number) to No. 23 (which he wore in leading the Bulls to three consecutive NBA titles) was a gimmick. To others, it was symbolic. To the NBA, it was a violation that resulted in a $100,000 fine for the club.

Jordan's mystique took its final hit a few days later when Orlando's 108-102 victory at the United Center knocked the Bulls out of the playoffs. It was the first time a Chicago team with Jordan had lost a playoff series since 1990.

"My intentions were to come back and win it all," said Jordan, who failed to score, shot an air ball from 15-feet and turned the ball over twice in the final six minutes of that decisive game.

"We weren't the same team we were 18 months ago. But the fun part is trying to live up to the accomplishments of the past."

Although San Antonio forward **Dennis Rodman** led the NBA in rebounding for the fourth season in a row, he received more publicity for frequently changing his hair color, posing for bizarre magazine covers and taking his shoes off whenever he was benched in the playoffs by Spurs coach Bob Hill.

But it was his strained relationship with Spurs' coach Bob Hill, which flared up during the playoffs when he avoided team huddles and took his shoes off after being benched, that left his future with the club in doubt.

"I don't think anyone understands me," Rodman said. "All you need to understand is that when Dennis Rodman steps on the floor, that's it. Don't make me out to be a devil or a pirate. If you make me out to be anything, make me out as a guy who is out there busting his butt every night."

Pat Riley, Don Nelson and Chris Webber didn't occupy the same abnormal plane as Rodman, but their celebrated breakups did generate dicussion.

One theory going into the season was that the New York Knicks had been wound so tight, for so long, that they could break. Riley, who set a maniacal, obsessive tone for the team, always refuted that premise. But as the season wore on, it became clear that Riley's dictatorial ways began to wear on the Knicks. When New York was eliminated in

the second round of the playoffs by Indiana, it became clear something had to give.

It was Riley. Not only did he turn down a five-year, $15 million extension, he fired off a press release on June 15, saying he would not complete the final year of his contract. Riley, who had sought an ownership share of the corporately-owned Knicks, blamed a lack of control over personnel for his decision to leave. Team president Dave Checketts was incensed, pointing out no move was made during Riley's four-year tenure that didn't meet his approval.

The New York media vilified Riley as he flew off to vacation in Greece. When the Miami Heat made public overtones to Riley, the Knicks responded by filing a tampering charge with the league. Ironically, the Knicks coaching search led them to the only figure with a more discussed breakup than Riley's.

In February, Nelson ended a six-and-a-half year relationship with the Golden State Warriors. An ugly rift with Webber, the 1993-94 Rookie of the Year who refused to re-sign with the Warriors and was traded to

Washington on Nov. 17 for third year forward Tom Gugliotta and three No. 1 picks, led to his downfall.

For most of his career, Nelson had been revered as an innovator. He reached 800 victories quicker than any coach other than Red Auerbach and received the Coach of the Year award an unprecedented three times. But after his inexplicable episode with Webber, Nelson found himself reviled in some circles. A steady stream of former players began to call his methods into question. Nelson, who spent 32 of his 54 years in the NBA as a player, coach and/or general manager, was being portrayed as a Machiavelli with a clipboard.

"I just think it's sad to see a guy with his talents and caliber of success being dragged down by the bad stuff of our game," said Seattle coach George Karl, who was dragged down for a second consecutive year by a talented SuperSonics team that failed to advance past the first round of the playoffs. "Nellie really represents what has become an entire package of disrespect in our game. It just goes to show no matter how big you are, you can be dissed by the game."

Ten days after he traded Webber, Nelson blacked out and found himself laying on the floor of a Detroit hotel room. Suffering from viral pneumonia, he coached the next eight games before putting himself on the disabled list. He spent five days in the hospital and 13 days at home before he returned to the Golden State bench. One month later, he stepped down as what had been a promising season for the Warriors disintegrated into a Shakespearean tragedy.

But there were also some uplifting stories. Jordan's return to the NBA in March (see sidebar) sparked an interest in the league that survived beyond the Bulls' second-round elimination. With Nick Van Exel at the point and an improving Vlade Divac in the middle, the Los Angeles Lakers returned to playoff prominence. Coach Dick Motta came out of retirement to team with rookie Jason Kidd and propel the Dallas Mavericks to the biggest turnaround (23 games) in the league. Orlando provided a glimpse of their awesome future, the Cleveland Cavaliers overcame a numbing succession of injuries to make the playoffs and Toronto and Vancouver laid the groundwork to enter the league for the 1995-96 season.

Two major milestones were achieved in 1995. On Jan. 6, Atlanta's Lenny Wilkens won his 939th regular season game to pass Auerbach as the winningest coach in NBA history. Wilkens savored the feat by puffing on a cigar in tribute to the former Celtics mastermind.

"This record stood for 28 years," Auerbach said. "He's a super guy. He's a Hall of Fame player. He's a great coach and a good friend. Hey, who else would you want to break it?"

The honors didn't end there for Wilkens. In April he was named to coach the U.S. Olympic basketball team in 1996 and finished the season with 968 victories. Next stop: 1,000 wins.

On Feb. 1, Utah's John Stockton passed Magic Johnson's record of 9,921 career assists to become the league's all-time leader. The accomplishment gave the 32-year-old Stockton a sense of pride, but the attention showered upon him during the pursuit was a nuisance.

"I enjoy playing the game," said Stockton, who had to be begged by the Jazz public relations department to talk to the local media the day before he set the record. "The other stuff to me is the work part of it."

Individually, Detroit's Grant Hill captured the imagination of the public, was the leading vote-getter for the All-Star Game and shared the Rookie of the Year award with Kidd of the Mavs. Robinson led the Spurs to the NBA's best record (62-20) and garnered his first MVP trophy. Stockton led the league in assists for the eighth straight season. Rodman was the rebounding leader for the fourth year in a row. And Del Harris, who was recycled by the Lakers, beat out Cleveland's Mike Fratello in the voting for Coach of the Year.

Also, scoring increased slightly due to rule changes that limited hand-checking and moved in the three-point line to a uniform 22 feet from the basket.

All this set the stage for the playoffs. The Sonics weren't the only marquee team to fall by the wayside. The Suns were eliminated in the second round by Houston for the second consecutive year. Afterwards, Barkley once again threatened to retire.

Indiana's Reggie Miller enhanced his reputation as a big-time player by shooting the legs out from under an aging Knicks team

Wide World Photos

Atlanta's **Lenny Wilkens** puffs on a victory cigar after supplanting Red Auerbach as the NBA's all-time winningest regular season coach. Wilkens' 939th triumph came at the Omni on Jan. 6, with a 112-90 decision over Washington.

in the second round. His most dramatic performance was in Game 1 where he scored eight points in 11 seconds for the win after New York led by six with 18.7 seconds remaining. The series went seven with Indiana taking the final game, 97-95, when Patrick Ewing missed a layup at the buzzer.

But the most exciting game of the playoffs came in Game 4 of the Eastern Conference final between the Pacers and the Magic where the lead changed hands four times in the last 13.3 seconds. Pacers center Rik Smits hit a 14-foot jumper as time expired to give Indiana a pulsating 94-93 victory.

"I've never been involved in a game like that," Pacer coach Larry Brown said. "I don't remember even watching one like that."

Indiana's playoff run was dramatic. But the team that commanded the most attention, other than Houston, was Orlando.

O'Neal and Hardaway gave indications they could be the Abdul-Jabbar and Johnson of the '90s. A team that had failed to win a playoff game in its brief history disposed of Boston, Chicago and Indiana on its way to the finals. The Magic grew up more quickly than many expected and served notice their potential is close to being a deadly reality. Being swept by Houston in the Finals did little to dampen that enthusiasm.

"This is our first time," O'Neal said. "This is a learning experience. I'm going to get here again before I retire. I'm going to get here many times."

The inability to reach a collective bargaining agreement, the threat of decertification of the Players Association and the owners decision to impose a lockout on July 1 created an uncertain off-season (see "Updates" chapter). Before these events, however, hope sprung eternal in the form of the NBA draft.

A record 10 underclassmen were selected in the first round. Of the first five players drafted, none was older than 20. The youngest was Kevin Garnett. A 19-year-old forward from Farragut Academy in Chicago, Garnett was taken by Minnesota with the fifth pick and became the fifth player to jump from high school to the NBA without first honing his skills on the college level. He joins Darryl Dawkins, Moses Malone, Bill Willoughby and Shawn Kemp in that select group.

"I don't think I'm the average 19-year-old," said Garnett on draft night. "If given the chance, I'm going to prove to all of you that I'm man enough to take what's given out and mature enough to give it back."

One day later, Garnett seemed to say all the right things about hard work and taking advice when he met with Timberwolves' officials and the Minnesota media. But there were a few raised eyebrows when Garnett said he looked up to Rider and respected him as a player.

What did coach Bill Blair have to say about the petulant Rider being a role model for an impressionable player just out of high school?

"We're going to get him another role model," Blair said.

Unfortunately for the 'Wolves, Olajuwon is already taken. Besides, he and the Rockets have something else in mind.

"This team is like the heart and soul of the city of Houston," Rockets owner Les Alexander said. "Now, the only thing to do is try for a three-peat." ❑

PRO BASKETBALL
S T A T I S T I C S

THE SEASON IN REVIEW
1994-1995
STANDINGS • PLAYOFFS • DRAFT

THE 1996 SPORTS ALMANAC INFORMATION PLEASE

SEC
A

PAGE
345

Final NBA Standings

Division champions (*) and playoff qualifiers (†) are noted. Number of seasons listed after each head coach refers to current tenure with club.

Western Conference
Midwest Division

	W	L	Pct	GB	–Per Game– For	Opp
* San Antonio	62	20	.756	—	106.6	100.6
† Utah	60	22	.732	2	106.4	98.4
† Houston	47	35	.573	15	103.5	101.4
† Denver	41	41	.500	21	101.3	100.5
Dallas	36	46	.439	26	103.2	106.1
Minnesota	21	61	.256	41	94.2	103.2

Head Coaches: SA— Bob Hill (1st season); **Utah—** Jerry Sloan (7th); **Hou—** Rudy Tomjanovich (4th); **Den—** Dan Issel (3rd, 18-16) resigned Jan. 15 and was replaced first by assistant Gene Littles (3-13) and then GM Bernie Bickerstaff (20-12) on Feb. 20; **Dal—** Dick Motta (1st)—Bill Blair (1st).
1993-94 Standings: 1. Houston (58-24); 2. San Antonio (55-27); 3. Utah (53-29); 4. Denver (42-40); 5. Minnesota (20-62); 6. Dallas (13-69).

Pacific Division

	W	L	Pct	GB	–Per Game– For	Opp
* Phoenix	59	23	.720	—	110.6	106.8
† Seattle	57	25	.695	2	110.4	102.2
† LA Lakers	48	34	.585	11	105.1	105.3
† Portland	44	38	.537	15	103.1	99.2
Sacramento	39	43	.476	20	98.2	99.2
Golden St	26	56	.317	33	105.7	111.1
LA Clippers	17	65	.207	42	96.7	105.8

Head Coaches: Pho— Paul Westphal (3rd season); **Sea—** George Karl (4th); **LAL—** Del Harris (1st); **Port—** P.J. Carlesimo (1st); **Sac—** Garry St. Jean (3rd); **G.St.—** Don Nelson (7th, 14-31) resigned Feb. 13 and was replaced by assistant Bob Lanier (12-25); **LAC—** Bill Fitch (1st).
1993-94 Standings: 1. Seattle (63-19); 2. Phoenix (56-26); 3. Golden St. (50-32); 4. Portland (47-35); 5. LA Lakers (33-49); 6. Sacramento (28-54); 7. LA Clippers (27-55).

Eastern Conference
Atlantic Division

	W	L	Pct	GB	–Per Game– For	Opp
* Orlando	57	25	.695	—	110.9	103.8
† New York	55	27	.671	2	98.2	95.1
† Boston	35	47	.427	22	102.8	104.7
Miami	32	50	.390	25	101.1	102.8
New Jersey	30	52	.366	27	98.1	101.2
Philadelphia	24	58	.293	33	95.4	100.4
Washington	21	61	.256	36	100.5	106.1

Head Coaches: Orl— Brian Hill (2nd season); **NY—** Pat Riley (4th); **Bos—** Chris Ford (5th); **Mia—** replaced Kevin Loughery (4th, 17-29) with assistant Alvin Gentry (15-21) on Feb. 14; **NJ—** Butch Beard (1st); **Phi—** John Lucas (1st); **Wash—** Jim Lynam (1st).
1993-94 Standings: 1. New York (57-25); 2. Orlando (50-32); 3. New Jersey (45-37); 4. Miami (42-40); 5. Boston (32-50); 6. Philadelphia (25-57); 7. Washington (24-58).

Central Division

	W	L	Pct	GB	–Per Game– For	Opp
* Indiana	52	30	.634	—	99.2	95.5
† Charlotte	50	32	.610	2	100.6	97.3
† Chicago	47	35	.573	5	101.5	96.7
† Cleveland	43	39	.524	9	90.5	89.8
† Atlanta	42	40	.512	10	96.6	95.3
Milwaukee	34	48	.415	18	99.3	103.7
Detroit	28	54	.341	24	98.2	105.5

Head Coaches: Ind— Larry Brown (2nd season); **Char—** Allan Bristow (4th); **Chi—** Phil Jackson (6th); **Cle—** Mike Fratello (2nd); **Atl—** Lenny Wilkens (2nd); **Mil—** Mike Dunleavy (3rd); **Det—** Don Chaney (2nd).
1993-94 Standings: 1. Atlanta (57-25); 2. Chicago (55-27); 3. Indiana (47-35); 4. Cleveland (47-35); 5. Charlotte (41-41); 6. Detroit (20-62); 7. Milwaukee (20-62).

Overall Conference Standings

Sixteen teams— eight from each conference— qualify for the NBA Playoffs; (*) indicates division champions.

Western Conference

	W	L	Home	Away	Div	Conf
1 San Antonio*	62	20	33-8	29-12	20-6	41-13
2 Phoenix*	59	23	32-9	27-14	23-7	39-15
3 Utah	60	22	33-8	27-14	17-9	36-18
4 Seattle	57	25	32-9	25-16	16-14	34-20
5 LA Lakers	48	34	29-12	19-22	15-15	30-24
6 Houston	47	35	25-16	22-19	13-13	27-27
7 Portland	44	38	26-15	18-23	17-13	28-26
8 Denver	41	41	23-18	18-23	13-13	27-27
Sacramento	39	43	27-14	12-29	17-13	25-29
Dallas	36	46	19-22	17-24	11-15	23-31
Golden St	26	56	13-28	11-30	11-19	19-35
Minnesota	21	61	13-28	8-33	4-22	12-42
LA Clippers	17	65	13-28	4-37	6-24	10-44

Eastern Conference

	W	L	Home	Away	Div	Conf
1 Orlando*	57	25	39-2	18-23	18-10	39-17
2 Indiana*	52	30	33-8	19-22	18-10	35-21
3 New York	55	27	29-12	26-15	23-5	37-19
4 Charlotte	50	32	29-12	21-20	17-11	36-20
5 Chicago	47	35	28-13	19-22	16-12	35-21
6 Cleveland	43	39	26-15	17-24	17-11	33-23
7 Atlanta	42	40	24-17	18-23	9-19	28-28
8 Boston	35	47	20-21	15-26	14-14	24-32
Milwaukee	34	48	22-19	12-29	13-15	26-30
Miami	32	50	22-19	10-31	9-19	25-31
New Jersey	30	52	20-21	10-31	13-15	21-35
Detroit	28	54	22-19	6-35	8-20	21-35
Philadelphia	24	58	14-27	10-31	12-16	16-40
Washington	21	61	13-28	8-33	9-19	16-40

1995 NBA All-Star Game
West, 139-112

45th NBA All-Star Game. **Date:** Feb. 12, at America West Arena in Phoenix; **Coaches:** Paul Westphal, Phoenix (West) and Brian Hill, Orlando (East); **MVP:** Mitch Richmond, Sacramento (22 minutes, 23 points).

Starters chosen by fan vote (Detroit's Grant Hill was first rookie to lead all players in votes received with 1,289,585); bench chosen by conference coaches vote. Team replacements: EAST— none; WEST— Denver center Dikembe Mutombo for LA Lakers forward Cedric Ceballos (torn ligament right thumb).

Eastern Conference

Starters		Min	FG M-A	Pts	Rb	A
C	Shaquille O'Neal, Orl	26	9-16	22	7	1
F	Scottie Pippen, Chi	30	5-15	12	7	3
G	Anfernee Hardaway, Orl	31	4-9	12	5	11
F	Grant Hill, Det	20	5-8	10	0	3
G	Reggie Miller, Ind	23	3-9	9	0	2
Bench						
G	Joe Dumars, Det	21	5-8	11	0	6
C	Alonzo Mourning, Char	19	4-9	10	8	1
C	Patrick Ewing, NY	22	4-7	10	3	1
F	Larry Johnson, Char	20	2-3	7	4	2
F	Dana Barros, Phi	11	2-5	5	1	3
F	Tyrone Hill, Cle	6	1-1	2	4	0
F	Vin Baker, Mil	11	0-2	2	2	0
	Totals	240	44-92	**112**	41	33

Three-Point FG: 8-22 (Miller 3-6, Pippen 2-6, Johnson 1-1, Dumars 1-2, Barros 1-3, Mourning 0-1, O'Neal 0-1, Hardaway 0-2); **Free Throws:** 16-28 (Hardaway 4-6, O'Neal 4-7, Ewing 2-2, Johnson 2-2, Mourning 2-3, Baker 2-4, G.Hill 0-4); **Percentages:** FG (.478), Three-Pt. FG (.364), Free Throws (.571); **Turnovers:** 20 (Ewing 5, Pippen 4, Hardaway 3, O'Neal 2, Baker, Dumars, G.Hill, Johnson, Miller, Mourning); **Steals:** 10 (O'Neal 3, G.Hill 2, Pippen 2, Dumars, Ewing, Miller); **Blocked Shots:** 6 (O'Neal 2, Baker, Miller, Mourning, Pippen); **Fouls:** 17 (Mourning 4, Ewing 3, G.Hill 2, O'Neal 2, Baker, Dumars, Hardaway, T.Hill, Pippen); **Team Rebounds:** 8.

Western Conference

Starters		Min	FG M-A	Pts	Rb	A
F	Charles Barkley, Pho	23	7-12	15	9	2
F	Shawn Kemp, Sea	23	4-6	13	2	2
C	Hakeem Olajuwon, Hou	25	6-13	13	11	1
G	Dan Majerle, Pho	20	4-12	10	5	3
G	Latrell Sprewell, G.St.	22	4-9	9	4	4
Bench						
G	Mitch Richmond, Sac	22	10-13	23	4	2
F	Karl Malone, Utah	16	6-6	15	3	1
C	Dikembe Mutombo, Den	20	6-8	12	8	1
C	David Robinson, SA	14	3-5	10	3	2
F	Detlef Schrempf, Sea	18	4-11	9	4	5
G	Gary Payton, Sea	23	3-10	6	5	15
G	John Stockton, Utah	14	2-6	4	1	6
	Totals	240	59-111	**139**	59	44

Three-Point FG: 8-27 (Richmond 3-3, Majerle 2-7, Olajuwon 1-1, Barkley 1-4, Schrempf 1-4, Sprewell 0-2, Payton 0-3, Stockton 0-3); **Free Throws:** 13-19 (Kemp 5-6, Robinson 4-6, Malone 3-4, Sprewell 1-1, Olajuwon 0-2); **Percentages:** FG (.532), Three-Pt. FG (.296), Free Throws (.684); **Turnovers:** 15 (Kemp 4, Olajuwon 3, Payton 3, Barkley 2, Malone, Robinson, Sprewell); **Steals:** 15 (Sprewell 3, Payton 3, Barkley 2, Olajuwon 2, Robinson 2, Stockton 2, Kemp); **Blocked Shots:** 7 (Mutombo 4, Olajuwon 2, Robinson); **Fouls:** 17 (Kemp 5, Mutombo 3, Robinson 2, Schrempf 2, Olajuwon 2, Barkley, Majerle, Payton); **Team Rebounds:** 10.

	1	2	3	4	F
East	28	28	25	31	112
West	31	41	32	35	139

Halftime— West, 72-56; **Third Quarter—** West, 104-81; **Technical Fouls—** none; **Officials—** Dick Bavetta, Steve Javie, Jack Nies; **Attendance—** 18,755; **Time—** 2:19; **TV Rating—** 10.7/17 share (NBC).

NBA Regular Season Team Leaders

Offense
— Per Game —

WEST	Pts	Reb	Ast	FG%	3Pt%	FT%
Phoenix	110.6	41.8	26.8	.482	.369	.756
Seattle	110.4	41.5	25.8	.491	.376	.758
San Antonio	106.6	45.0	23.4	.484	.375	.738
Utah	106.4	40.1	27.5	.512	.376	.781
Golden State	105.7	42.3	24.6	.468	.341	.704
LA Lakers	105.1	42.0	25.3	.463	.352	.735
Houston	103.5	40.5	25.1	.480	.368	.749
Dallas	103.2	48.1	23.7	.440	.322	.734
Portland	103.1	46.3	22.5	.451	.365	.697
Denver	101.3	42.0	22.4	.479	.356	.738
Sacramento	98.2	41.4	22.2	.468	.346	.711
LA Clippers	96.7	38.3	22.0	.444	.315	.710
Minnesota	94.2	36.3	21.7	.449	.313	.775

— Per Game —

EAST	Pts	Reb	Ast	FG%	3Pt%	FT%
Orlando	110.9	44.0	27.8	.502	.370	.669
Boston	102.8	42.4	21.7	.464	.368	.753
Chicago	101.5	41.5	24.0	.476	.373	.726
Miami	101.1	41.0	21.7	.467	.367	.736
Charlotte	100.6	39.4	25.3	.474	.397	.777
Washington	100.5	39.8	21.3	.460	.343	.724
Milwaukee	99.3	39.9	21.2	.459	.366	.712
Indiana	99.2	40.7	22.9	.477	.380	.751
Detroit	98.2	38.6	22.8	.461	.354	.741
New York	98.2	41.5	25.1	.467	.368	.734
New Jersey	98.1	46.1	23.0	.436	.319	.759
Atlanta	96.6	41.2	21.4	.447	.341	.724
Philadelphia	95.4	40.9	19.1	.448	.379	.737
Cleveland	90.5	40.0	20.4	.441	.385	.760

Defense
— Per Game —

WEST	Pts	Reb	Ast	FG%	3Pt%	FT%
Utah	98.4	37.1	20.9	.453	.382	.741
Sacramento	99.2	41.6	22.2	.453	.304	.741
Portland	99.2	38.8	21.8	.456	.372	.754
Denver	100.5	39.4	21.8	.456	.347	.750
San Antonio	100.6	40.5	22.9	.454	.341	.714
Houston	101.4	43.3	23.7	.453	.376	.751
Seattle	102.2	39.9	22.5	.453	.343	.735
LA Lakers	105.3	45.8	26.9	.468	.352	.708
Dallas	106.1	41.9	24.3	.488	.366	.734
LA Clippers	105.8	44.1	23.4	.496	.370	.750
Phoenix	106.8	42.3	26.2	.477	.340	.744
Golden State	111.1	45.4	28.6	.488	.355	.720
Minnesota	113.2	42.4	25.2	.474	.377	.731

— Per Game —

EAST	Pts	Reb	Ast	FG%	3Pt%	FT%
Cleveland	89.8	37.8	22.1	.461	.357	.757
New York	95.1	40.7	19.3	.437	.341	.736
Atlanta	95.3	42.0	21.1	.463	.347	.726
Indiana	95.5	39.1	22.0	.456	.364	.726
Chicago	96.7	40.5	20.9	.457	.349	.738
Charlotte	97.3	42.3	23.1	.454	.333	.740
Philadelphia	100.4	42.2	24.3	.465	.363	.763
New Jersey	101.2	42.6	22.3	.461	.374	.721
Miami	102.8	41.4	22.7	.471	.361	.740
Orlando	103.8	41.0	24.2	.457	.378	.741
Milwaukee	103.7	40.9	25.6	.493	.395	.729
Boston	104.7	41.5	24.4	.484	.358	.720
Detroit	105.5	43.6	24.5	.476	.363	.722
Washington	106.1	44.2	23.9	.480	.383	.765

Orlando Magic

Shaquille O'Neal
Scoring

Utah Jazz

John Stockton
Assists

Chicago Bulls

Scottie Pippen
Steals

Sacramento Kings

Spud Webb
Free Throw Pct.

NBA Regular Season Individual Leaders

Minimum of 70 games or 1400 points, 800 rebounds, 400 assists, 100 blocked shots, 300 field goals, 125 steals, 125 free throws made and 50 three-point field goals; (*) indicates rookie.

Scoring

	Gm	Min	FG	FG%	3Pt/Att	FT	FT%	Reb	Ast	Stl	Blk	Pts	Avg	Hi
Shaquille O'Neal, Orl	79	2923	930	.583	0/5	455	.533	901	214	73	192	2315	**29.3**	46
Hakeem Olajuwon, Hou	72	2853	798	.517	3/16	406	.756	775	255	133	242	2005	**27.8**	47
David Robinson, SA	81	3074	788	.530	6/20	656	.774	877	236	134	262	2238	**27.6**	43
Karl Malone, Utah	82	3126	830	.536	11/41	516	.742	871	285	129	85	2187	**26.7**	45
Jamal Mashburn, Dal	80	2980	683	.436	113/344	447	.739	331	298	82	8	1926	**24.1**	50
Patrick Ewing, NY	79	2920	730	.503	6/21	420	.750	867	212	68	159	1886	**23.9**	46
Charles Barkley, Pho	68	2382	554	.486	74/219	379	.748	756	276	110	45	1561	**23.0**	45
Mitch Richmond, Sac	82	3172	668	.446	156/424	375	.843	357	311	91	29	1867	**22.8**	44
Glen Rice, Mia	82	3014	667	.475	185/451	312	.855	378	192	112	14	1831	**22.3**	56
Glenn Robinson*, Mil	80	2958	636	.451	86/268	397	.796	513	197	115	22	1755	**21.9**	38
Clyde Drexler, Port-Hou	76	2728	571	.461	147/408	364	.824	480	362	136	45	1653	**21.8**	41
Scottie Pippen, Chi	79	3014	634	.480	109/316	315	.716	639	409	232	89	1692	**21.4**	40
Clifford Robinson, Port	75	2725	597	.452	142/383	265	.694	423	198	79	82	1601	**21.3**	33
Alonzo Mourning, Char	77	2941	571	.519	11/34	490	.761	761	111	49	225	1643	**21.3**	36
Anfernee Hardaway, Orl	77	2901	585	.512	87/249	356	.769	336	551	130	26	1613	**20.9**	39
Gary Payton, Sea	82	3015	685	.509	70/232	249	.716	281	583	204	13	1689	**20.6**	33
Latrell Sprewell, G.St.	69	2771	490	.418	90/326	350	.781	256	279	112	46	1420	**20.6**	40
Dana Barros, Phi	82	3318	571	.490	197/425	347	.899	274	619	149	4	1686	**20.6**	50
Isaiah Rider, Min	75	2645	558	.447	139/396	277	.817	249	245	69	23	1532	**20.4**	42
Grant Hill*, Det	70	2678	508	.477	4/27	374	.732	445	353	124	62	1394	**19.9**	33
Reggie Miller, Ind	81	2665	505	.462	195/470	383	.897	210	242	98	16	1588	**19.6**	40
Detlef Schrempf, Sea	82	2886	521	.523	93/181	437	.839	508	310	93	35	1572	**19.2**	33
Larry Johnson, Char	81	3234	585	.480	81/210	274	.774	585	369	78	28	1525	**18.8**	39
Shawn Kemp, Sea	82	2679	545	.547	2/7	438	.749	893	149	102	122	1530	**18.7**	42
Sean Elliott, SA	81	2858	502	.468	136/333	326	.807	287	206	78	38	1466	**18.1**	32
C. Weatherspoon, Phi	76	2991	543	.439	4/21	283	.751	526	215	115	67	1373	**18.1**	31

Rebounds

	Gm	Off	Def	Total	Avg
Dennis Rodman, SA	49	274	549	823	16.8
Dikembe Mutombo, Den	82	319	710	1029	12.5
Shaquille O'Neal, Orl	79	328	573	901	11.4
Patrick Ewing, NY	79	157	710	867	11.0
Tyrone Hill, Cle	70	269	496	765	10.9
Shawn Kemp, Sea	82	318	575	893	10.9
David Robinson, SA	81	234	643	877	10.8
Hakeem Olajuwon, Hou	72	172	603	775	10.8
Karl Malone, Utah	82	156	715	871	10.6
Popeye Jones, Dal	80	329	515	844	10.6
Vlade Divac, LAL	80	261	568	829	10.4
Vin Baker, Mil	82	289	557	846	10.3
Alonzo Mourning, Char	77	200	561	761	9.9
Horace Grant, Orl	74	223	492	715	9.7
Loy Vaught, LAC	80	261	511	772	9.7

Assists

	Gm	No	Avg
John Stockton, Utah	82	1011	12.3
Kenny Anderson, NJ	72	680	9.4
Tim Hardaway, G.St.	62	578	9.3
Rod Strickland, Port	64	562	8.8
Tyrone Bogues, Char	78	675	8.7
Nick Van Exel, LAL	80	660	8.3
Avery Johnson, SA	82	670	8.2
Pooh Richardson, LAC	80	632	7.9
Mookie Blaylock, Atl	80	616	7.7
Jason Kidd*, Dal	79	607	7.7
Dana Barros, Phi	82	619	7.5
Mark Jackson, Ind	82	616	7.5
Scott Skiles, Wash	62	452	7.3
Anfernee Hardaway, Orl	77	551	7.2
Gary Payton, Sea	82	583	7.1

NBA Regular Season Individual Leaders (Cont.)

Field Goal Pct.

	Gm	FG	Att	Avg
Chris Gatling, G.St.	58	324	512	.633
Shaquille O'Neal, Orl	78	930	1594	.583
Horace Grant, Orl	73	401	707	.567
Otis Thorpe, Port	69	385	681	.565
Dale Davis, Ind	73	324	576	.563
Gheorghe Muresan, Wash	72	303	541	.560
Dikembe Mutombo, Den	81	349	628	.556
Shawn Kemp, Sea	81	545	997	.547
Danny Manning, Pho	46	340	622	.547
Olden Polynice, Sac	80	376	691	.544

Free Throw Pct.

	Gm	FG	Att	Avg
Spud Webb, Sac	75	226	242	.934
Mark Price, Cle	47	148	162	.914
Dana Barros, Phi	81	347	386	.899
Reggie Miller, Ind	80	383	427	.897
Tyrone Bogues, Char	77	160	180	.889
Scott Skiles, Wash	62	179	202	.886
Mahmoud Abdul Rauf, Den	73	138	156	.885
B.J. Armstrong, Chi	81	206	233	.884
Jeff Hornacek, Utah	80	284	322	.882
Keith Jennings, G.St.	79	134	153	.876

3-Point Field Goal Pct.

	Gm	FG	Att	Avg
Steve Kerr, Chi	81	89	170	.524
Detlef Schrempf, Sea	81	93	181	.514
Dana Barros, Phi	81	197	425	.464
Hubert Davis, NY	81	131	288	.455
John Stockton, Utah	81	102	227	.449
Hersey Hawkins, Char	81	131	298	.440
Wesley Person*, Pho	77	116	266	.436
Kenny Smith, Hou	80	142	331	.429
B.J. Armstrong, Chi	81	108	253	.427
Dell Curry, Char	68	154	361	.427

Game High Points

	Opp	Date	FG-FT—Pts
Glen Rice, Mia	vs. Orl	4/15	20- 9—56
Michael Jordan, Chi	at NY	3/28	21-10—55
Willie Burton, Mia	at Phi.	12/13	12-24—53
Jim Jackson, Dal	at Den.	11/26	17-16—50*
Jamal Mashburn, Dal	at Chi.	11/12	19- 9—50
Cedric Ceballos, LAL	vs. Min	12/20	21- 5—50
Dana Barros, Phi	at Hou.	3/14	21- 2—50
Hakeem Olajuwon, Hou	vs. SA	1/13	21- 5—47
Shaquille O'Neal, Orl	at Char.	11/9	20- 6—46
Patrick Ewing, NY	vs. Bos.	3/7	18-10—46
Shaquille O'Neal, Orl	vs. LAL	3/8	20- 6—46

*Overtime.

Blocked Shots

	Gm	No	Avg
Dikembe Mutombo, Den	82	321	3.91
Hakeem Olajuwon, Hou	72	242	3.36
Shawn Bradley, Phi	82	274	3.34
David Robinson, SA	81	262	3.23
Alonzo Mourning, Char	77	225	2.92
Shaquille O'Neal, Orl	79	192	2.43
Vlade Divac, LAL	80	174	2.18
Patrick Ewing, NY	79	159	2.01
Bo Outlaw, LAC	81	151	1.86
Oliver Miller, Det	64	116	1.81
Elden Campbell, LAL	73	132	1.81

Steals

	Gm	No	Avg
Scottie Pippen, Chi	79	232	2.94
Mookie Blaylock, Atl	80	200	2.50
Gary Payton, Sea	82	204	2.49
John Stockton, Utah	82	194	2.37
Nate McMillan, Sea	80	165	2.06
Eddie Jones*, LAL	64	131	2.05
Jason Kidd*, Dal	79	151	1.91
Elliot Perry, Pho	82	156	1.90
Hakeem Olajuwon, Hou	72	133	1.85
Dana Barros, Phi	82	149	1.82

Rookie Leaders

Scoring	Gm	FG	FT	Pts	Avg
Glenn Robinson, Mil	80	636	397	1755	21.9
Grant Hill, Det	70	508	374	1394	19.9
Juwan Howard, Wash	65	455	194	1104	17.0
Lamond Murray, LAC	81	439	199	1142	14.1
Eddie Jones, LAL	64	342	122	897	14.0

Field Goal Pct.	Gm	FG	Att	Pct
Michael Smith, Sac	82	220	406	.542
Eric Montross, Bos	78	307	575	.534
Greg Minor, Bos	63	155	301	.515
Brian Grant, Sac	80	413	809	.511
Juwan Howard, Wash	65	455	931	.489

Rebounds	Gm	Off	Def	Tot	Avg
Juwan Howard, Wash	65	184	361	545	8.4
Brian Grant, Sac	80	207	391	598	7.5
Clifford Rozier, G.St.	66	200	286	486	7.4
Eric Montross, Bos	78	196	370	566	7.3
Glenn Robinson, Mil	80	169	344	513	6.4
Grant Hill, Det	70	125	320	445	6.4

Assists	Gm	No	Avg
Jason Kidd, Dal	79	607	7.7
Grant Hill, Det	70	353	5.0
Jalen Rose, Den	81	389	4.8
Khalid Reeves, Mia	67	288	4.3
Chris Childs, NJ	53	219	4.1

Personal Fouls

Shawn Bradley, Phi	338
Shawn Kemp, Sea	337
Lorenzo Williams, Dal	306
Vlade Divac, LAL	305
Christian Laettner, Minn	302

Disqualifications

Shawn Bradley, Phi	18
Eric Montross*, Bos	10
Shawn Kemp, Sea	9
Four tied with 8 each.	

Turnovers

Glenn Robinson*, Mil	313
Scottie Pippen, Chi	271
John Stockton, Utah	267
Shawn Kemp, Sea	259
Patrick Ewing, NY	256

Triple Doubles

Jason Kidd*, Dal	4
Chris Webber, Wash	3
Mookie Blaylock, Atl	2
Dikembe Mutombo, Den	2
17 tied with 1 each.	

Minutes Played

Vin Baker, Mil	3361
Dana Barros, Phi	3318
Larry Johnson, Char	3234
Mitch Richmond, Sac	3172
Karl Malone, Utah	3126

Assist/Turnover Ratio

Muggsy Bogues, Char	5.11
Vinny Del Negro, SA	4.04
John Stockton, Utah	3.79
Pooh Richardson, LAC	3.70
Sedale Threatt, LAL	3.54

Team by Team Statistics

At least 15 games played. Players who competed for more than one team during the regular season are listed with their final club; (*) indicates rookies.

Atlanta Hawks

	Gm	FG%	TPts	Pts	Reb	Ast
Mookie Blaylock	80	.425	1373	17.2	4.9	7.7
Steve Smith	80	.426	1305	16.3	3.5	3.4
MIA	2	.379	41	20.5	3.0	3.5
ATL	78	.427	1264	16.2	3.5	3.4
Stacey Augmon	76	.453	1053	13.9	4.8	2.6
Ken Norman	74	.453	938	12.7	4.9	1.3
Grant Long	81	.478	939	11.6	7.5	1.6
MIA	2	.417	16	8.0	5.5	2.0
ATL	79	.479	923	11.7	7.5	1.6
Craig Ehlo	49	.453	477	9.7	3.0	2.3
Andrew Lang	82	.473	794	9.7	5.6	0.9
Tyrone Corbin	81	.442	502	6.2	3.2	0.8
Morlon Wiley	43	.427	137	3.2	1.0	1.7
DAL	38	.423	130	3.4	1.0	1.8
ATL	5	.500	7	1.4	0.8	1.2
Greg Anderson	51	.548	148	2.9	3.7	0.3
Jon Koncak	62	.412	179	2.9	3.0	0.8
Ennis Whatley	27	.453	70	2.6	1.1	2.0
Jim Les	24	.289	50	2.1	1.1	1.8
Doug Edwards	38	.458	67	1.8	1.3	0.3

Triple Doubles: Blaylock (2). **3-pt FG leader:** Blaylock (199). **Steals leader:** Blaylock (200). **Blocks leader:** Lang (144).

Acquired: G Smith, F Long and future 2nd round draft pick from Miami for F/C Kevin Willis and future 1st round pick (Nov. 7). **Signed:** G Wiley (Mar. 4) as free agent.

Boston Celtics

	Gm	FG%	TPts	Pts	Reb	Ast
Dee Brown	77	.480	1192	15.5	3.9	4.5
Dominique Wilkins	77	.424	1370	17.8	5.2	2.2
Dino Radja	66	.490	1133	17.2	8.7	1.7
Dee Brown	79	.447	1236	15.6	3.2	3.8
Sherman Douglas	65	.475	954	14.7	2.6	6.9
Eric Montross*	78	.534	781	10.0	7.3	0.5
Rick Fox	53	.481	464	8.8	2.9	2.6
Xavier McDaniel	68	.451	587	8.6	4.4	1.6
David Wesley	51	.409	378	7.4	2.3	5.2
Pervis Ellison	55	.507	375	6.8	5.6	0.6
Derek Strong	70	.453	441	6.3	5.4	0.6
Greg Minor*	63	.515	377	6.0	2.2	1.1
Acie Earl	30	.382	66	2.2	1.5	0.1
Jay Humphries	18	.235	20	1.1	0.7	1.1
UTAH	12	.160	10	0.8	0.8	0.8
BOS	6	.444	10	1.7	0.5	1.7

Triple Doubles: none. **3-pt FG leader:** Brown (126). **Steals leader:** Brown (110). **Blocks leader:** Radja (86).

Acquired: G Humphries and 1995 2nd round draft pick from Utah for G/F Blue Edwards (Feb 3)

Individual Game Highs

Most Field Goals Made

21	Cedric Ceballos, LAL vs. Min. (12/20)
21	Hakeem Olajuwon, Hou. vs. SA (1/13)
21	Dana Barros, Phi. at Hou. (3/14)
21	Michael Jordan, Chi. at NY (3/28)

Most 3-Pt Field Goals Made

11	Joe Dumars, Det. vs. Min. (11/8)

Charlotte Hornets

	Gm	FG%	TPts	Pts	Reb	Ast
Alonzo Mourning	77	.519	1643	21.3	9.9	1.4
Larry Johnson	81	.480	1525	18.8	7.2	4.6
Hersey Hawkins	82	.482	1172	14.3	3.8	3.2
Dell Curry	69	.441	935	13.6	2.4	1.6
Scott Burrell	65	.467	750	11.5	5.7	2.5
Tyrone Bogues	78	.477	862	11.1	3.3	8.7
Michael Adams	29	.453	188	6.5	1.0	3.3
Kenny Gattison	21	.470	125	6.0	3.6	0.8
Greg Sutton	53	.409	263	5.0	1.1	1.7
Robert Parish	81	.427	389	4.8	4.3	0.5
Darrin Hancock*	46	.562	153	3.3	1.2	0.7
David Wingate	52	.410	122	2.3	1.2	1.1
Joe Wolf	63	.469	90	1.4	2.0	0.6

Triple Doubles: Johnson (1). **3-pt FG leader:** Curry (154). **Steals leader:** Hawkins (122). **Blocks leader:** Mourning (225).

Chicago Bulls

	Gm	FG%	TPts	Pts	Reb	Ast
Michael Jordan	17	.411	457	26.9	6.9	5.3
Scottie Pippen	79	.480	1692	21.4	8.1	5.2
Toni Kukoc	81	.504	1271	15.7	5.4	4.6
B.J. Armstrong	82	.468	1150	14.0	2.3	3.0
Steve Kerr	82	.527	674	8.2	1.5	1.8
Will Perdue	78	.553	621	8.0	6.7	1.2
Ron Harper	77	.426	530	6.9	2.3	2.0
Luc Longley	55	.447	358	6.5	4.8	1.3
Bill Wennington	73	.492	363	5.0	2.6	0.5
Pete Myers	71	.415	318	4.5	2.0	2.1
Larry Krystkowiak	19	.389	83	4.4	3.1	1.4
Jud Buechler	57	.492	217	3.8	1.7	0.9
Corie Blount	68	.476	238	3.5	3.5	0.9
Dickey Simpkins*	59	.424	206	3.5	2.6	0.6

Triple Doubles: Kukoc (1), Pippen (1). **3-pt FG leader:** Pippen (109). **Steals leader:** Pippen (232). **Blocks leader:** Pippen (89).

Cleveland Cavaliers

	Gm	FG%	TPts	Pts	Reb	Ast
Mark Price	48	.413	757	15.8	2.3	7.0
Tyrone Hill	70	.504	963	13.8	10.9	0.8
Terrell Brandon	67	.448	889	13.3	2.8	5.4
John Williams	74	.452	929	12.6	6.9	2.6
Chris Mills	80	.420	986	12.3	4.6	1.9
Bobby Phills	80	.414	878	11.0	3.3	2.3
Danny Ferry	82	.446	614	7.5	1.7	1.2
Tony Campbell	78	.411	469	6.0	2.0	0.9
Michael Cage	82	.521	407	5.0	6.9	0.7
John Battle	28	.377	116	4.1	0.4	1.3
Fred Roberts	21	.389	80	3.8	1.6	0.4
Steve Colter	57	.396	196	3.4	1.0	1.8
Greg Dreiling	58	.412	110	1.9	2.0	0.4

Triple Doubles: Phills (1). **3-pt FG leader:** Price (103). **Steals leader:** Phills (115). **Blocks leader:** Williams (101).

Dallas Mavericks

	Gm	FG%	TPts	—Per Game— Pts	Reb	Ast
Jim Jackson	51	.472	1309	25.7	5.1	3.7
Jamal Mashburn	80	.436	1926	24.1	4.1	3.7
Roy Tarpley	55	.479	691	12.6	8.2	1.1
Jason Kidd*	79	.385	922	11.7	5.4	7.7
Popeye Jones	80	.443	825	10.3	10.6	2.0
George McCloud	42	.439	402	9.6	3.5	1.3
Lucious Harris	79	.459	751	9.5	2.8	1.7
Scott Brooks	59	.458	341	5.8	1.1	2.0
HOU	28	.538	96	3.4	0.5	0.8
DAL	31	.433	245	7.9	1.7	3.0
Doug Smith	63	.417	320	5.1	2.3	0.7
Tony Dumas*	58	.384	264	4.6	1.1	1.0
Lorenzo Williams	82	.477	328	4.0	8.4	1.5
Donald Hodge	54	.407	209	3.9	2.3	0.8
Terry Davis	46	.434	140	3.0	3.4	0.2

Triple Doubles: Kidd (4). **3-pt FG leader:** Mashburn (113).
Steals leader: Kidd (151). **Blocks leader:** Williams (148).
   Acquired: G Brooks from Houston for G Morlon Wiley and 1995 2nd round draft pick (Feb. 23).

Denver Nuggets

	Gm	FG%	TPts	—Per Game— Pts	Reb	Ast
Mahmoud Abdul Rauf	73	.470	1165	16.0	1.9	3.6
Reggie Williams	74	.459	993	13.4	4.4	3.1
Rodney Rogers	80	.488	979	12.2	4.8	2.0
Robert Pack	42	.430	507	12.1	2.7	6.9
Dikembe Mutombo	82	.556	946	11.5	12.5	1.4
Dale Ellis	81	.453	918	11.3	2.7	0.7
Bryant Stith	81	.472	911	11.2	3.3	1.9
Jalen Rose*	81	.454	663	8.2	2.7	4.8
Brian Williams	63	.589	498	7.9	4.7	0.8
Tom Hammonds	70	.535	410	5.9	3.2	0.5
Reggie Slater*	25	.494	120	4.8	2.3	0.5
Cliff Levingston	57	.423	129	2.3	2.2	0.5
Greg Grant	14	.303	31	2.2	0.6	3.1

Triple Doubles: Mutombo (2), Pack (1), R. Williams (1). **3-pt FG leader:** D. Ellis (106). **Steals leader:** R. Williams (114). **Blocks leader:** Mutombo (321).

Detroit Pistons

	Gm	FG%	TPts	—Per Game— Pts	Reb	Ast
Joe Dumars	69	.452	1410	20.4	2.2	3.8
Grant Hill*	70	.477	1394	19.9	6.4	5.0
Joe Dumars	67	.430	1214	18.1	2.4	5.5
Terry Mills	72	.447	1118	15.5	7.8	2.2
Allan Houston	76	.463	1101	14.5	2.2	2.2
Oliver Miller	64	.555	545	8.5	7.4	1.5
Rafael Addison	79	.476	656	8.3	3.1	1.4
Lindsey Hunter	42	.374	314	7.5	1.8	3.8
Mark West	67	.556	500	7.5	6.1	0.3
Johnny Dawkins	50	.463	325	6.5	2.3	4.1
Mark Macon	55	.381	276	5.0	1.4	1.1
Negele Knight	47	.397	199	4.2	1.3	2.7
PORT	3	.467	18	6.0	1.0	3.7
DET	44	.392	181	4.1	1.3	2.6
Eric Leckner	57	.527	225	3.9	3.1	0.2
Bill Curley*	53	.433	143	2.7	2.3	0.5
Ivano Newbill*	34	.356	40	1.2	2.4	0.5

Triple Doubles: Hill (1). **3-pt FG leader:** Houston (158).
Steals leader: Hill (124). **Blocks leader:** Miller (116).
   Acquired: G Knight (Dec. 30) as free agent.

Golden State Warriors

	Gm	FG%	TPts	—Per Game— Pts	Reb	Ast
Latrell Sprewell	69	.418	1420	20.6	3.7	4.0
Tim Hardaway	62	.427	1247	20.1	3.1	9.3
Chris Mullin	25	.489	476	19.0	4.6	5.0
Chris Gatling	58	.633	796	13.7	7.6	0.9
Donyell Marshall*	72	.394	906	12.6	5.6	1.5
MIN	40	.374	431	10.8	4.9	1.4
G.St.	32	.413	475	14.8	6.5	1.5
Ricky Pierce	27	.437	338	12.5	2.4	1.5
Rony Seikaly	36	.516	435	12.1	7.4	1.3
Victor Alexander	50	.515	502	10.0	5.8	1.2
Carlos Rogers	49	.529	438	8.9	5.7	0.8
Keith Jennings	80	.447	589	7.4	1.9	4.7
Ryan Lorthridge*	37	.475	272	7.4	1.9	2.7
Tim Legler	24	.522	176	7.3	1.7	1.1
Clifford Rozier*	66	.485	448	6.8	7.4	0.7
David Wood	78	.469	428	5.5	3.1	0.8
Dwayne Morton*	41	.388	167	4.1	1.4	0.4

Triple Doubles: Mullin (1). **3-pt FG leader:** Hardaway (168).
Steals leader: Sprewell (112). **Blocks leader:** Marshall (88).
   Acquired: F Marshall from Minnesota for F Tom Gugliotta (Feb. 18).

Houston Rockets

	Gm	FG%	TPts	—Per Game— Pts	Reb	Ast
Hakeem Olajuwon	72	.517	2005	27.8	10.8	3.5
Clyde Drexler	76	.461	1653	21.8	6.3	4.8
PORT	41	.428	904	22.0	5.7	5.1
HOU	35	.506	749	21.4	7.0	4.4
Vernon Maxwell	64	.394	854	13.3	2.6	4.3
Kenny Smith	81	.484	842	10.4	1.9	4.0
Robert Horry	64	.447	652	10.2	5.1	3.4
Sam Cassell	82	.427	783	9.5	2.6	4.9
Mario Elie	81	.499	710	8.8	2.4	2.3
Carl Herrera	61	.523	415	6.8	4.6	0.7
Chucky Brown	41	.603	249	6.1	4.6	0.7
Pete Chilcutt	68	.445	358	5.3	4.7	1.0
Tracy Murray	54	.408	258	4.8	1.1	0.4
PORT	29	.412	170	5.9	1.3	0.5
HOU	25	.400	88	3.5	0.9	0.2
Tim Breaux*	42	.372	128	3.0	0.8	0.4
Zan Tabak*	37	.453	75	2.0	1.5	0.1

Triple Doubles: Drexler (1), Olajuwon (1). **3-pt FG leader:** Drexler (147). **Steals leader:** Drexler (136). **Blocks leader:** Olajuwon (242).
   Acquired: G Drexler and F Murray from Portland for F Otis Thorpe, the rights to F Marcello Nicola and a conditional 1995 1st round draft pick (Feb 14).

Dream Team III

The 10-man NBA All-Star roster announced on July 30 to represent the USA at the 1996 Summer Olympics, scheduled to run from July 20-Aug. 3, in Atlanta. Two more players will be named in 1996. The team will be coached by Lenny Wilkens of the Atlanta Hawks and assistants Bobby Cremins of Ga. Tech, Clem Haskins of Minnesota and Jerry Sloan of the Utah Jazz.

   Centers: Hakeem Olajuwon, Houston; Shaquille O'Neal, Orlando; David Robinson, San Antonio.

   Forwards: Grant Hill, Detroit; Karl Malone, Utah; Scottie Pippen, Chicago; Glenn Robinson, Milwaukee.

   Guards: Anfernee Hardaway, Orlando; Reggie Miller, Indiana; John Stockton, Utah.

   Note: Malone, Pippen, D. Robinson and Stockton were all on the 1992 Olympic team.

Indiana Pacers

	Gm	FG%	TPts	Pts	Reb	Ast
Reggie Miller	81	.462	1588	19.6	2.6	3.0
Rik Smits	78	.526	1400	17.9	7.7	1.4
Derrick McKey	81	.493	1075	13.3	4.9	3.4
Dale Davis	74	.563	786	10.6	9.4	0.8
Byron Scott	80	.455	802	10.0	1.9	1.4
Mark Jackson	82	.422	624	7.6	3.7	7.5
Antonio Davis	44	.445	335	7.6	6.4	0.6
Sam Mitchell	81	.487	529	6.5	3.0	0.8
Vern Fleming	55	.495	251	4.6	1.6	2.0
Haywoode Workman	69	.375	292	4.2	1.6	2.8
Duane Ferrell	56	.480	231	4.1	1.6	0.6
LaSalle Thompson	38	.415	112	2.9	2.3	0.5
John Williams	34	.357	100	2.9	1.8	0.8

Triple Doubles: none. **3-pt FG leader:** Miller (195). **Steals leader:** McKey (125). **Blocks leader:** D. Davis (116).

Los Angeles Clippers

	Gm	FG%	TPts	Pts	Reb	Ast
Loy Vaught	80	.514	1401	17.5	9.7	1.7
Lamond Murray*	81	.402	1142	14.1	4.4	1.6
Malik Sealy	60	.435	778	13.0	3.6	1.8
Pooh Richardson	80	.394	874	10.9	3.3	7.9
Terry Dehere	80	.407	835	10.4	1.9	2.8
Tony Massenburg	80	.469	741	9.3	5.7	0.8
Eric Piatkowski*	81	.441	566	7.0	1.6	1.0
Elmore Spencer	19	.441	132	6.9	3.4	1.3
Gary Grant	33	.470	205	6.2	1.1	2.8
Michael Smith	29	.470	153	5.3	1.9	0.7
Bo Outlaw	81	.523	422	5.2	3.9	1.0
Matt Fish*	26	.476	123	4.7	3.2	0.7
Eric Riley	40	.448	177	4.4	2.8	0.3
Harold Ellis	69	.481	252	3.7	1.3	0.6
Randy Woods	62	.316	124	2.0	0.7	2.2

Triple Doubles: Richardson (1). **3-pt FG leader:** Richardson (87). **Steals leader:** Richardson (129). **Blocks leader:** Outlaw (151).

Los Angeles Lakers

	Gm	FG%	TPts	Pts	Reb	Ast
Cedric Ceballos	58	.509	1261	21.7	8.0	1.8
Nick Van Exel	80	.420	1348	16.9	2.8	8.3
Vlade Divac*	80	.507	1277	16.0	10.4	4.1
Eddie Jones*	64	.460	897	14.0	3.9	2.0
Elden Campbell	73	.459	913	12.5	6.1	1.3
Anthony Peeler	73	.432	756	10.4	2.3	1.7
Sedale Threatt	59	.497	558	9.5	2.1	4.2
Lloyd Daniels	30	.383	208	6.9	2.1	1.3
PHI	5	.333	23	4.6	1.4	0.8
LAL	25	.390	185	7.4	2.2	1.4
George Lynch	56	.468	341	6.1	3.3	1.1
Tony Smith	61	.427	340	5.6	1.8	1.7
Sam Bowie	67	.442	306	4.6	4.3	1.8
Anthony Miller*	46	.530	189	4.1	3.3	0.8
Antonio Harvey	59	.438	179	3.0	1.7	0.4
Kurt Rambis	26	.514	44	1.7	1.3	0.6

Triple Doubles: Divac (1). **3-pt FG leader:** Van Exel (183). **Steals leader:** Jones (131). **Blocks leader:** Divac (174). **Signed:** G Daniels (Feb. 22) as free agent.

Miami Heat

	Gm	FG%	TPts	Pts	Reb	Ast
Glen Rice	82	.475	1831	22.3	4.6	2.3
Kevin Willis	67	.466	1154	17.2	10.9	1.3
ATL	2	.390	42	21.0	18.0	1.5
MIA	65	.469	1112	17.1	10.7	1.3
Billy Owens	70	.491	1002	14.3	7.2	3.5
Bimbo Coles	68	.430	679	10.0	2.8	6.1
Khalid Reeves*	67	.443	619	9.2	2.8	4.3
Matt Geiger	74	.536	617	8.3	5.6	0.7
Kevin Gamble	77	.489	566	7.4	1.6	1.5
Ledell Eackles	54	.439	395	7.3	1.8	1.3
Harold Miner	45	.403	329	7.3	2.6	1.5
John Salley	75	.499	547	7.2	4.5	1.6
Keith Askins	50	.391	229	4.6	4.0	0.8
Brad Lohaus	61	.420	267	4.4	1.7	0.7
Kevin Pritchard	19	.406	44	2.3	0.6	1.8
PHI	5	.000	1	0.2	0.2	2.2
MIA	14	.448	43	3.1	0.8	1.6

Triple Doubles: Owens (1). **3-pt FG leader:** Rice (185). **Steals leader:** Rice (112). **Blocks leader:** Salley (85). **Acquired:** F/C Willis and future 1st round draft pick from Atlanta for G Steve Smith, F Grant Long and future 2nd round draft pick (Nov. 7). **Signed:** G Pritchard (Mar. 6) as free agent.

Milwaukee Bucks

	Gm	FG%	TPts	Pts	Reb	Ast
Glenn Robinson*	80	.451	1755	21.9	6.4	2.5
Vin Baker	82	.483	1451	17.7	10.3	3.6
Todd Day	82	.424	1310	16.0	3.9	1.6
Eric Murdock	75	.415	977	13.0	2.9	6.4
Marty Conlon	82	.532	815	9.9	5.2	1.3
Johnny Newman	82	.463	634	7.7	2.1	1.1
Lee Mayberry	82	.422	474	5.8	1.0	3.4
Eric Mobley*	46	.591	180	3.9	3.3	0.5
Jon Barry	52	.425	191	3.7	0.9	1.6
Alton Lister	60	.493	167	2.8	3.9	0.2
Ed Pinckney	62	.495	140	2.3	3.4	0.3
Aaron Williams	15	.333	24	1.6	1.3	0.0

Triple Doubles: Baker (1). **3-pt FG leader:** Day (163). **Steals leader:** Robinson (115). **Blocks leader:** Baker (116).

Minnesota Timberwolves

	Gm	FG%	TPts	Pts	Reb	Ast
Isaiah Rider	75	.447	1532	20.4	3.3	3.3
Christian Laettner	81	.489	1322	16.3	7.6	2.9
Doug West	71	.461	919	12.9	3.2	2.6
Tom Gugliotta	77	.443	976	12.7	7.4	3.6
WASH	6	.398	96	16.0	8.8	3.0
G.St.	40	.443	435	10.9	7.4	3.1
MIN	31	.454	445	14.4	7.2	4.5
Sean Rooks	80	.470	868	10.9	6.1	1.2
Darrick Martin	34	.408	254	7.5	1.9	3.9
Winston Garland	73	.415	448	6.1	2.3	4.4
Stacey King	50	.467	266	5.3	3.3	0.5
Pat Durham	59	.494	302	5.1	1.6	0.9
Chris Smith	64	.439	320	5.0	1.1	2.3
Greg Foster	78	.472	385	4.9	3.3	0.5
CHI	17	.477	104	6.1	3.2	0.9
MIN	61	.470	281	4.6	3.4	0.4
Charles Shackleford	21	.600	94	4.5	3.2	0.4
Andres Guibert	17	.340	45	2.6	2.6	0.6
Mike Brown	27	.250	35	1.3	1.7	0.4

Triple Doubles: none. **3-pt FG leader:** Rider (139). **Steals leader:** Gugliotta (132). **Blocks leader:** Laettner (87). **Acquired:** F Gugliotta from Golden State for F Donyell Marshall (Feb. 18).

New Jersey Nets

	Gm	FG%	TPts	—Per Game— Pts	Reb	Ast
Derrick Coleman	56	.424	1146	20.5	10.6	3.3
Kenny Anderson	72	.399	1267	17.6	3.5	9.4
Armon Gilliam	82	.503	1212	14.8	7.5	1.2
Chris Morris	71	.410	950	13.4	5.7	2.1
Benoit Benjamin	61	.510	675	11.1	7.2	0.6
P.J. Brown	80	.446	651	8.1	6.1	1.7
Rex Walters	80	.439	523	6.5	1.2	1.5
Chris Childs*	53	.380	308	5.8	1.3	4.1
Jayson Williams	75	.461	363	4.8	5.7	0.5
Sean Higgins	57	.385	268	4.7	1.4	0.5
Eric Floyd	48	.335	197	4.1	1.1	2.6
Rick Mahorn	58	.523	198	3.4	2.8	0.4
Dwayne Schintzius	43	.380	88	2.0	1.9	0.3

Triple Doubles: none. **3-pt FG leader:** Morris (106). **Steals leader:** Anderson (103). **Blocks leader:** Brown (135).

New York Knickerbockers

	Gm	FG%	TPts	—Per Game— Pts	Reb	Ast
Patrick Ewing	79	.503	1886	23.9	11.0	2.7
John Starks	80	.395	1223	15.3	2.7	5.1
Charles Smith	76	.471	966	12.7	4.3	1.6
Derek Harper	80	.446	919	11.5	2.4	5.7
Charles Oakley	50	.489	506	10.1	8.9	2.5
Hubert Davis	82	.480	820	10.0	1.3	1.8
Anthony Mason	77	.566	765	9.9	8.4	3.1
Greg Anthony	61	.437	372	6.1	1.0	2.6
Anthony Bonner	58	.456	221	3.8	4.5	1.4
Herb Williams	56	.456	187	3.3	2.4	0.5
Monty Williams*	41	.451	137	3.3	2.4	1.2

Triple Doubles: none. **3-pt FG leader:** Starks (217). **Steals leader:** Starks (92). **Blocks leader:** Ewing (159).

Orlando Magic

	Gm	FG%	TPts	—Per Game— Pts	Reb	Ast
Shaquille O'Neal	79	.583	2315	29.3	11.4	2.7
Anfernee Hardaway	77	.512	1613	20.9	4.4	7.2
Nick Anderson	76	.476	1200	15.8	4.4	4.1
Dennis Scott	62	.439	802	12.9	2.4	2.1
Horace Grant	74	.567	948	12.8	9.7	2.3
Donald Royal	70	.475	635	9.1	4.0	2.8
Brian Shaw	78	.389	502	6.4	3.1	5.2
Anthony Bowie	77	.480	427	5.5	1.8	2.1
Jeff Turner	49	.410	199	4.1	2.0	0.8
Anthony Avent	71	.430	258	3.6	4.1	0.6
Brooks Thompson*	38	.395	116	3.1	0.6	1.1
Tree Rollins	51	.476	61	1.2	1.9	0.2

Triple Doubles: Hardaway (1). **3-pt FG leader:** Anderson (179). **Steals leader:** Hardaway (130). **Blocks leader:** O'Neal (192).

Heisman to Hoops

Charlie Ward, the Heisman Trophy-winning quarterback who led Florida State to its first national championship in 1994, passed up pro football for the NBA in 1995. A two-time All-ACC pick in basketball, the 6-foot-1 Ward was drafted in the first round by the New York Knicks. He played in only 10 games, however.

His stats:

Gm	Min	FT%	FG%	3Pt/Att	Pts	Avg	Reb	Ast	Stl
10	44	.700	.211	1/10	16	1.6	6	4	2

Philadelphia 76ers

	Gm	FG%	TPts	—Per Game— Pts	Reb	Ast
Dana Barros	82	.490	1686	20.6	3.3	7.5
Jeff Malone	19	.507	350	18.4	2.9	1.5
C. Weatherspoon	76	.439	1373	18.1	6.9	2.8
Willie Burton	53	.401	812	15.3	3.1	1.8
Sharone Wright*	79	.465	904	11.4	6.0	0.6
Shawn Bradley	82	.455	778	9.5	8.0	0.6
Jeff Grayer	47	.428	389	8.3	3.2	1.6
Scott Williams	77	.475	491	6.4	6.3	0.8
Greg Graham	50	.426	251	5.0	1.2	1.3
Alaa Abdelnaby	54	.511	256	4.7	2.1	0.2
SAC	51	.532	254	5.0	2.1	0.3
PHI	3	.091	2	0.7	2.7	0.0
Derrick Alston*	64	.465	299	4.7	3.4	0.5
B.J. Tyler*	55	.381	195	3.5	1.1	3.2
Jaren Jackson	21	.368	70	3.3	2.0	0.9
Tim Perry	42	.346	76	1.8	2.1	0.3

Triple Doubles: Barros (1). **3-pt FG leader:** Barros (197). **Steals leader:** Barros (149). **Blocks leader:** Bradley (274). **Signed:** C/F Abdelnaby (Mar. 24) as free agent.

Phoenix Suns

	Gm	FG%	TPts	—Per Game— Pts	Reb	Ast
Charles Barkley	68	.486	1561	23.0	11.1	4.1
Danny Manning	46	.457	822	17.9	6.0	3.3
Dan Majerle	82	.425	1281	15.6	4.6	4.1
Kevin Johnson	47	.470	730	15.5	2.4	7.7
A.C. Green	82	.504	916	11.2	8.2	1.5
Wesley Person*	78	.484	814	10.4	2.6	1.3
Wayman Tisdale	65	.484	650	10.0	3.8	0.7
Elliot Perry	82	.520	795	9.7	1.8	4.8
Danny Ainge	74	.460	571	7.7	1.5	2.8
Richard Dumas	15	.507	82	5.5	1.9	0.5
Trevor Ruffin	49	.426	233	4.8	0.5	1.0
Dan Schayes	69	.508	303	4.4	3.0	0.3
Joe Kleine	75	.449	280	3.7	3.5	0.5

Triple Doubles: none. **3-pt FG leader:** Majerle (199). **Steals leader:** Perry (156). **Blocks leader:** Manning (57).

Portland Trail Blazers

	Gm	FG%	TPts	—Per Game— Pts	Reb	Ast
Clifford Robinson	75	.452	1601	21.3	5.6	2.6
Rod Strickland	64	.466	1211	18.9	5.0	8.8
Otis Thorpe	70	.565	937	13.4	8.0	1.6
HOU	36	.563	479	13.3	8.9	1.6
PORT	34	.568	458	13.5	6.9	1.6
Buck Williams	82	.512	757	9.2	8.2	1.0
James Robinson	71	.409	651	9.2	1.9	2.5
Harvey Grant	75	.461	683	9.1	3.8	1.1
Terry Porter	35	.393	312	8.9	2.3	3.8
Jerome Kersey	63	.415	508	8.1	4.1	1.3
Aaron McKie*	45	.444	293	6.5	2.9	2.0
Chris Dudley	82	.406	447	5.5	9.3	0.4
Mark Bryant	49	.526	244	5.0	3.3	0.6
Steve Henson	37	.430	119	3.2	0.7	2.3
James Edwards	28	.386	75	2.7	1.5	0.3

Triple Doubles: Strickland (1). **3-pt FG leader:** C. Robinson (142). **Steals leader:** Strickland (123). **Blocks leader:** Dudley (126).

Acquired: F Thorpe, the rights to F Marcello Nicola and a conditional 1995 1st round draft pick from Houston for G Clyde Drexler and F Tracy Murray (Feb. 14).

Sacramento Kings

	Gm	FG%	TPts	—Per Game— Pts	Reb	Ast
Mitch Richmond	82	.446	1867	22.8	4.4	3.8
Walt Williams	77	.446	1259	16.4	4.5	4.1
Brian Grant*	80	.511	1058	13.2	7.5	1.2
Spud Webb	76	.438	878	11.6	2.3	6.2
Olden Polynice	81	.544	877	10.8	9.0	0.8
Michael Smith*	82	.542	567	6.9	5.9	0.8
Lionel Simmons	58	.420	327	5.6	3.4	1.5
Randy Brown	67	.432	317	4.7	1.6	2.0
Bobby Hurley	68	.363	285	4.2	1.0	3.3
Duane Causwell	58	.517	209	3.6	3.0	0.3
Trevor Wilson	15	.450	47	3.1	1.7	0.8
Henry Turner	30	.404	68	2.3	0.9	0.2
Doug Lee	22	.360	43	2.0	0.2	0.2

Triple Doubles: none. **3-pt FG leader:** Richmond (156).
Steals leader: Williams (123). **Blocks leader:** Grant (116).

San Antonio Spurs

	Gm	FG%	TPts	—Per Game— Pts	Reb	Ast
David Robinson	81	.530	2238	27.6	10.8	2.9
Sean Elliott	81	.468	1466	18.1	3.5	2.5
Avery Johnson	82	.519	1101	13.4	2.5	8.2
Vinny Del Negro	75	.486	938	12.5	2.6	3.0
Chuck Person	81	.423	872	10.8	3.2	1.3
Dennis Rodman	49	.571	349	7.1	16.8	2.0
J.R. Reid	81	.508	563	7.0	4.9	0.7
Terry Cummings	76	.483	520	6.8	5.0	0.8
Doc Rivers	63	.358	321	5.1	1.7	2.6
NY	3	.308	19	6.3	3.0	2.7
SA	60	.360	302	5.0	1.7	2.6
Willie Anderson	38	.469	185	4.9	1.4	1.4
Moses Malone	17	.371	49	2.9	2.7	0.4
Howard Eisley*	49	.328	120	2.4	1.0	1.9
MIN	34	.352	113	3.3	1.2	2.3
SA	15	.176	7	0.5	0.4	1.2
Jack Haley	31	.426	73	2.4	0.9	0.1
Chris Whitney	25	.298	42	1.7	0.5	1.1
Julius Nwosu*	23	.321	31	1.3	1.0	0.1

Triple Doubles: none. **3-pt FG leader:** Person (172). **Steals
leader:** Robinson (134). **Blocks leader:** Robinson (262).
Signed: G Rivers (Dec. 26) and G Eisley (Feb. 26) as free
agents.

Seattle Supersonics

	Gm	FG%	TPts	—Per Game— Pts	Reb	Ast
Gary Payton	82	.509	1689	20.6	3.4	7.1
Detlef Schrempf	82	.523	1572	19.2	6.2	3.8
Shawn Kemp	82	.547	1530	18.7	10.9	1.8
Kendall Gill	73	.457	1002	13.7	4.0	2.6
Sam Perkins	82	.466	1043	12.7	4.9	1.6
Vincent Askew	71	.492	703	9.9	2.5	2.5
Sarunas Marciulionis	66	.473	612	9.3	1.0	1.7
Nate McMillan	80	.418	419	5.3	3.8	5.3
Byron Houston	39	.458	132	3.4	1.4	0.2
Ervin Johnson	64	.443	199	3.1	4.5	0.3
Bill Cartwright	29	.391	69	2.4	3.0	0.3
Dontonio Wingfield*	20	.353	46	2.3	1.5	0.2
Steve Scheffler	18	.522	39	2.2	1.3	0.2

Triple Doubles: none. **3-pt FG leader:** Perkins (136). **Steals
leader:** Payton (204). **Blocks leader:** Kemp (122).

Utah Jazz

	Gm	FG%	TPts	—Per Game— Pts	Reb	Ast
Karl Malone	82	.536	2187	26.7	10.6	3.5
Jeff Hornacek	81	.514	1337	16.5	2.6	4.3
John Stockton	82	.542	1206	14.7	3.1	12.3
David Benoit	71	.486	740	10.4	5.2	0.8
Antoine Carr	78	.531	746	9.6	3.4	0.9
Felton Spencer	34	.488	317	9.3	7.6	0.5
Blue Edwards	67	.461	459	6.9	1.9	1.1
BOS	31	.426	220	7.1	2.1	1.5
UTAH	36	.495	239	6.6	1.8	0.8
Tom Chambers	81	.457	503	6.2	2.6	0.9
Adam Keefe	75	.577	461	6.1	4.4	0.4
Walter Bond	23	.464	107	4.7	1.4	1.0
DET	5	.250	10	2.0	1.0	1.4
UTAH	18	.500	97	5.4	1.5	0.9
Bryon Russell	63	.437	283	4.5	2.2	0.5
John Crotty	80	.403	295	3.7	1.2	2.6
Jamie Watson*	60	.500	195	3.3	1.2	1.0
James Donaldson	43	.595	110	2.6	2.5	0.3

Triple Doubles: none. **3-pt FG leader:** Stockton (102).
Steals leader: Stockton (194). **Blocks leader:** Malone (85).
Acquired: G/F Edwards from Boston for G Jay Humphries and
1995 2nd round draft pick (Feb 3). **Signed:** G Bond (Jan. 10) as
free agent.

Washington Bullets

	Gm	FG%	TPts	—Per Game— Pts	Reb	Ast
Chris Webber	54	.495	1085	20.1	9.6	4.7
Juwan Howard*	65	.489	1104	17.0	8.4	2.5
Calbert Cheaney	78	.453	1293	16.6	4.1	2.3
Rex Chapman	45	.397	731	16.2	2.5	2.8
Scott Skiles	62	.455	805	13.0	2.6	7.3
Don MacLean	39	.438	430	11.0	4.2	1.3
Gheorghe Muresan	73	.560	730	10.0	6.7	0.5
Mitchell Butler	76	.421	597	7.9	2.2	1.2
Kevin Duckworth	40	.442	283	7.1	4.9	0.5
Doug Overton	82	.416	576	7.0	1.7	3.0
Anthony Tucker*	62	.457	243	3.9	2.7	1.1
Larry Stewart	40	.461	102	2.6	1.7	0.5
Kenny Walker	24	.429	57	2.4	2.0	0.3
Jim McIlvaine*	55	.479	96	1.7	1.9	0.2

Triple Doubles: Webber (3). **3-pt FG leader:** Cheaney and
Skiles (96). **Steals leader:** Webber (83). **Blocks leader:**
Muresan (127).
Acquired: F Webber from Golden State for F Tom Gugliotta
and three future 1st round draft picks (Nov. 17).

More Individual Game Highs
(*) indicates overtime.

Most Assists
22* .... Tim Hardaway, G.St. vs. Orl. (12/16)

Most Offensive Rebounds
30 .... Dennis Rodman, SA at Hou. (2/21)

Most Blocked Shots
11 .... Dikembe Mutombo, Den. at Dal. (11/8)

Most Steals
8* .... Pooh Richardson, LAC at Orl. (12/30)
8 .... Scottie Pippen, Chi. vs. Mil. (3/17)
8 .... Latrell Sprewell, G.St. at Orl. (3/26)

NBA PLAYOFFS

| FIRST ROUND | SEMIFINALS | FINAL | | FINAL | SEMIFINALS | FIRST ROUND |

The **1995 NBA** *Finals*

San Antonio 3
Denver 0
San Antonio 4
Seattle 1
LA Lakers 3
LA Lakers 2
San Antonio 2

Phoenix 3
Portland 0
Phoenix 3
Utah 2
Houston 3
Houston 4
Houston 4

WESTERN CONFERENCE

Houston 4
Orlando 0

EASTERN CONFERENCE

Orlando 3
Boston 1
Orlando 4
Charlotte 1
Chicago 3
Chicago 2
Orlando 4

Indiana 3
Atlanta 0
Indiana 4
New York 3
Cleveland 1
New York 3
Indiana 3

Series Summaries
WESTERN CONFERENCE

FIRST ROUND (Best of 5)

	W-L	Avg.	Leading Scorer
Houston	3 2	108.0	Olajuwon (35.0)
Utah	2 3	104.0	Malone (30.2)

Date	Winner	Home Court
Apr. 27	Jazz, 102-100	at Utah
Apr. 29	Rockets, 140-126	at Utah
May 3	Jazz, 95-82	at Houston
May 5	Rockets, 123-106	at Houston
May 7	Rockets, 95-91	at Utah

	W-L	Avg.	Leading Scorer
Phoenix	3 0	116.3	Barkley (33.7)
Portland	0 3	101.7	Strickland (23.3)

Date	Winner	Home Court
Apr. 28	Suns, 129-102	at Phoenix
Apr. 30	Suns, 103-94	at Phoenix
May 2	Suns, 117-109	at Portland

	W-L	Avg.	Leading Scorer
San Antonio	3 0	108.3	Robinson (19.0) & Elliott (19.0)
Denver	0 3	93.0	Stith (16.7)

Date	Winner	Home Court
Apr. 28	Spurs, 104-88	at San Antonio
Apr. 30	Spurs, 122-96	at San Antonio
May 2	Spurs, 99-95	at Denver

	W-L	Avg.	Leading Scorer
LA Lakers	3 1	93.5	Van Exel (24.8)
Seattle	1 3	97.3	Kemp (24.8)

Date	Winner	Home Court
Apr. 27	Sonics, 96-71	at Seattle
Apr. 30	Lakers, 84-82	at Seattle
May 1	Lakers, 105-101	at Los Angeles
May 4	Lakers, 114-110	at Los Angeles

SEMIFINALS (Best of 7)

	W-L	Avg.	Leading Scorer
Houston	4 3	109.1	Olajuwon (29.6)
Phoenix	3 4	108.7	Johnson (27.9)

Date	Winner	Home Court
May 9	Suns, 130-108	at Phoenix
May 11	Suns, 118-94	at Phoenix
May 13	Rockets, 118-85	at Houston
May 14	Suns, 114-110	at Houston
May 16	Rockets, 103-97 (OT)	at Phoenix
May 18	Rockets, 116-103	at Houston
May 20	Rockets, 115-114	at Phoenix

	W-L	Avg.	Leading Scorer
San Antonio	4 2	94.7	Robinson (30.0)
LA Lakers	2 4	88.8	Campbell (18.7)

Date	Winner	Home Court
May 6	Spurs, 110-94	at San Antonio
May 8	Spurs, 97-90 (OT)	at San Antonio
May 12	Lakers, 92-85	at Los Angeles
May 14	Spurs, 80-71	at Los Angeles
May 16	Lakers, 98-96 (OT)	at San Antonio
May 18	Spurs, 100-88	at Los Angeles

CHAMPIONSHIP (Best of 7)

	W-L	Avg.	Leading Scorer
Houston	4 2	99.0	Olajuwon (35.3)
San Antonio	2 4	97.3	Robinson (23.8)

Date	Winner	Home Court
May 22	Rockets, 94-93	at San Antonio
May 24	Rockets, 106-96	at San Antonio
May 26	Spurs, 107-102	at Houston
May 28	Spurs, 103-81	at Houston
May 30	Rockets, 111-90	at San Antonio
June 1	Rockets, 100-95	at Houston

EASTERN CONFERENCE

FIRST ROUND (Best of 5)

	W-L	Avg.	Leading Scorer
Orlando	3 1	98.3	O'Neal (22.5)
Boston	1 3	86.3	Wilkins (19.0)

Date	Winner	Home Court
Apr. 28	Magic, 124-77	at Orlando
Apr. 30	Celtics, 99-92	at Orlando
May 3	Magic, 82-77	at Boston
May 5	Magic, 95-92	at Boston

	W-L	Avg.	Leading Scorer
Chicago	3 1	96.3	Jordan (32.3)
Charlotte	1 3	92.5	Mourning (22.0)

Date	Winner	Home Court
Apr. 28	Bulls, 108-100 (OT)	at Charlotte
Apr. 30	Hornets, 106-89	at Charlotte
May 2	Bulls, 103-80	at Chicago
May 4	Bulls, 85-84	at Chicago

	W-L	Avg.	Leading Scorer
Indiana	3 0	100.0	Miller (31.7)
Atlanta	0 3	89.3	Smith (19.0)

Date	Winner	Home Court
Apr. 27	Pacers, 90-82	at Indiana
Apr. 29	Pacers, 105-97	at Indiana
May 2	Pacers, 105-89	at Atlanta

	W-L	Avg.	Leading Scorer
New York	3 1	90.8	Ewing (18.5)
Cleveland	1 3	82.5	Price (15.0)

Date	Winner	Home Court
Apr. 27	Knicks, 103-79	at New York
Apr. 29	Cavaliers, 90-84	at New York
May 1	Knicks, 83-80	at Cleveland
May 4	Knicks, 93-80	at Cleveland

SEMIFINALS (Best of 7)

	W-L	Avg.	Leading Scorer
Orlando	4 2	100.7	O'Neal (24.3)
Chicago	2 4	99.8	Jordan (31.0)

Date	Winner	Home Court
May 7	Magic, 94-91	at Orlando
May 10	Bulls, 104-94	at Orlando
May 12	Magic, 110-101	at Chicago
May 14	Bulls, 106-95	at Chicago
May 16	Magic, 103-95	at Orlando
May 18	Magic, 108-102	at Chicago

	W-L	Avg.	Leading Scorer
Indiana	4 3	93.3	Miller (22.6)
			& Smits (22.6)
New York	3 4	94.7	Ewing (19.3)

Date	Winner	Home Court
May 7	Pacers, 107-105	at New York
May 9	Knicks, 96-77	at New York
May 11	Pacers, 97-95 (OT)	at Indiana
May 13	Pacers, 98-84	at Indiana
May 17	Knicks, 96-95	at New York
May 19	Knicks, 92-82	at Indiana
May 21	Pacers, 97-95	at New York

CHAMPIONSHIP (Best of 7)

	W-L	Avg.	Leading Scorer
Orlando	4 3	103.7	O'Neal (27.3)
Indiana	3 4	103.4	Miller (25.9)

Date	Winner	Home Court
May 23	Magic, 105-101	at Orlando
May 25	Magic, 119-114	at Orlando
May 27	Pacers, 105-100	at Indiana
May 29	Pacers, 94-93	at Indiana
May 31	Magic, 108-106	at Orlando
June 2	Pacers, 123-96	at Indiana
June 4	Magic, 105-81	at Orlando

NBA FINALS (Best of 7)

	W-L	Avg.	Leading Scorer
Houston	4 0	114.0	Olajuwon (32.8)
Orlando	0 4	107.0	O'Neal (28.0)

Date	Winner	Home Court
June 7	Rockets, 120-118 (OT)	at Orlando
June 9	Rockets, 117-106	at Orlando
June 11	Rockets, 106-103	at Houston
June 14	Rockets, 113-101	at Houston

Most Valuable Player

Hakeem Olajuwon, Houston, C
32.8 pts, 11.5 rebs, 2.0 blocks, 5.5 assists.

Final Playoff Standings

(Ranked by victories)

	Gm	W	L	Pct	For	Opp
Houston	22	15	7	.682	107.0	104.2
Orlando	21	11	10	.524	102.4	101.1
Indiana	17	10	7	.588	98.6	97.5
San Antonio	15	9	6	.600	98.5	93.7
Phoenix	10	6	4	.600	111.0	106.9
New York	11	6	5	.545	93.3	89.4
Chicago	10	5	5	.500	98.4	97.4
Los Angeles	10	5	5	.500	90.7	95.7
Utah	5	2	3	.400	104.0	108.0
Boston	4	1	3	.250	86.3	98.3
Charlotte	4	1	3	.250	92.5	96.3
Cleveland	4	1	3	.250	82.5	90.8
Seattle	4	1	3	.250	97.3	93.5
Atlanta	3	0	3	.000	89.3	100.0
Denver	3	0	3	.000	93.0	108.3
Portland	3	0	3	.000	101.7	116.3

Bombs Away!

A total of 47 three-point field goals records were set during the 1995 playoffs, including new marks for three-pointers made in a 3-game series (13 by Reggie Miller, Indiana vs. Atlanta); a 4-game series (14 by Nick Van Exel, LA Lakers vs. Seattle); a 7-game series (28 by Dennis Scott, Orlando vs. Indiana) and a 4-game NBA finals (11 by Robert Horry of Houston and Anfernee Hardaway of Orlando).

NBA Playoff Leaders

Scoring

	Gm	FG	FT	Pts	Avg
Hakeem Olajuwon, Hou	22	306	111	725	33.0
Michael Jordan, Chi	10	120	64	315	31.5
Karl Malone, Utah	5	48	54	151	30.2
Charles Barkley, Pho	10	91	66	257	25.7
Shaquille O'Neal, Orl	21	195	149	539	25.7
Reggie Miller, Ind	17	138	104	434	25.5
David Robinson, SA	15	129	121	380	25.3
Kevin Johnson, Pho	10	86	71	248	24.8
Shawn Kemp, Sea	4	33	32	99	24.8
Rod Strickland, Port	3	27	14	70	23.3
Alonzo Mourning, Char	4	24	36	88	22.0
Larry Johnson, Char	4	31	20	83	20.8
Clyde Drexler, Hou	22	155	110	450	20.5
Rik Smits, Ind	17	127	86	341	20.1
Nick Van Exel, LAL	10	67	45	200	20.0
Anfernee Hardaway, Orl	21	144	84	412	19.6
Patrick Ewing, NY	11	80	48	209	19.0
Steve Smith, Atl	3	17	16	57	19.0
Dominique Wilkins, Bos	4	26	16	76	19.0
Dee Brown, Bos	4	26	14	75	18.8
Detlef Schrempf, Sea	4	23	19	75	18.8

High-Point Games

	Date	FG-FT	—Pts
Michael Jordan, Chi at Char	4/28	18-11	—48*
Charles Barkley, Pho at Port	5/2	16-11	—47
Kevin Johnson, Pho vs Hou	5/20	12-21	—46
Hakeem Olajuwon, Hou at Utah	4/27	20-5	—45
Kevin Johnson, Pho at Hou	5/14	18-5	—43
Hakeem Olajuwon, Hou vs SA	5/26	19-4	—43

*Overtime.

Rebounds

	Gm	Off	Def	Tot	Avg
Dennis Rodman, SA	16	69	138	207	14.8
Charles Barkley, Pho	10	39	95	134	13.4
Alonzo Mourning, Char	4	14	39	53	13.3
Karl Malone, Utah	5	15	51	66	13.2
David Robinson, SA	15	57	125	182	12.1

Assists

	Gm	No	Avg
Rod Strickland, Port	3	37	12.3
John Stockton, Utah	5	51	10.2
Kevin Johnson, Phoenix	10	93	9.3
Avery Johnson, SA	15	125	8.3
Sherman Douglas, Bos	4	33	8.3

NBA Finalists' Composite Box Scores
Houston Rockets (15-7)

		Overall Playoffs		Per Game				Finals vs Orlando		Per Game		
	Gm	FG%	TPts	Pts	Reb	Ast	Gm	FG%	TPts	Pts	Reb	Ast
Hakeem Olajuwon	22	.531	725	33.0	10.3	4.5	4	.483	131	32.8	11.5	5.5
Clyde Drexler	22	.481	450	20.5	7.0	5.0	4	.450	86	21.5	9.5	6.8
Robert Horry	22	.445	288	13.1	7.0	3.5	4	.434	71	17.8	10.0	3.8
Sam Cassell	22	.438	243	11.0	1.9	4.0	4	.429	57	14.3	1.8	3.0
Kenny Smith	22	.438	238	10.8	2.2	4.5	4	.379	30	7.5	1.8	4.0
Mario Elie	22	.504	201	9.1	2.8	2.5	4	.649	65	16.3	4.3	3.3
Pete Chilcutt	20	.484	90	4.5	2.9	0.9	3	—	0	0.0	0.0	0.0
Chucky Brown	21	.447	94	4.5	3.1	0.3	4	.455	12	3.0	2.8	0.0
Vernon Maxwell	1	.143	3	3.0	3.0	1.0	0	—	0	0.0	0.0	0.0
Carl Herrera	1	1.000	2	2.0	0.0	1.0	0	—	0	0.0	0.0	0.0
Zan Tabak	8	.400	6	0.8	0.1	0.1	0	—	0	0.0	0.0	0.0
Charles Jones	19	.385	14	0.7	2.3	0.0	4	.500	4	1.0	1.8	0.0
ROCKETS	22	.483	2354	107.0	39.1	25.2	4	.472	456	114.0	43.3	26.3
OPPONENTS	22	.467	2293	104.2	43.8	23.0	4	.466	428	107.0	46.0	27.5

Three-pointers: PLAYOFFS— Smith (46-for-104), Horry (44-110), Drexler (30-99), Elie (28-65), Cassell (24-60), Chilcutt (14-36), Olajuwon (2-4), Brown (1-2), Maxwell (0-2), Jones (0-1), Team (189-483 for .391 pct.); FINALS— Horry (11-for-29), Elie (8-14), Smith (8-19), Cassell (7-15), Drexler (2-13), Olajuwon (1-1), Brown (0-1), Team (37-92 for .402 pct.).

Orlando Magic (11-10)

		Overall Playoffs		Per Game				Finals vs Houston		Per Game		
	Gm	FG%	TPts	Pts	Reb	Ast	Gm	FG%	TPts	Pts	Reb	Ast
Shaquille O'Neal	21	.577	539	25.7	11.9	3.3	4	.595	112	28.0	12.5	6.3
Anfernee Hardaway	21	.472	412	19.6	3.8	7.7	4	.500	102	25.5	4.8	8.0
Dennis Scott	21	.413	308	14.7	3.0	2.1	4	.310	42	10.5	3.5	2.3
Nick Anderson	21	.448	298	14.2	4.8	3.1	4	.360	49	12.3	8.5	4.3
Horace Grant	21	.540	287	13.7	10.4	1.9	4	.532	54	13.5	12.0	1.5
Brian Shaw	21	.390	138	6.6	3.0	3.1	4	.426	50	12.5	3.3	3.3
Brooks Thompson	3	.750	12	4.0	0.7	1.0	0	—	0	0.0	0.0	0.0
Sam Bowie	17	.500	55	3.2	0.7	1.1	4	.600	13	3.3	0.5	1.5
Jeff Turner	18	.425	49	2.7	1.4	0.6	4	.200	6	1.5	1.0	0.5
Donald Royal	18	.333	37	2.1	1.1	0.5	1	—	0	0.0	0.0	0.0
Anthony Avent	7	.429	9	1.3	1.1	0.0	0	—	0	0.0	0.0	0.0
Tree Rollins	14	.600	7	0.5	0.4	0.0	0	—	0	0.0	0.0	0.0
MAGIC	21	.482	2151	102.4	40.2	23.2	4	.466	428	107.0	46.0	27.5
OPPONENTS	21	.453	2124	101.1	41.4	23.3	4	.472	456	114.0	43.3	26.3

Three-pointers: PLAYOFFS— Scott (56-for-151), Anderson (41-107), Hardaway (40-99), Shaw (22-57), Turner (11-22), Bowie (5-7), Thompson (3-4), Grant (0-2), Avent (0-1), Team (178-450 for .396 pct.); FINALS— Hardaway (11-for-24), Shaw (10-26), Anderson (10-31), Scott (7-29), Turner (2-6), Bowie (1-2), Team (41-118 for .347 pct.).

Annual Awards

Most Valuable Player

The Maurice Podoloff Trophy; voting by 105-member panel of local and national pro basketball writers and broadcasters. Each ballot has five entries; points awarded on 10-7-5-3-1 basis.

	1st	2nd	3rd	4th	5th	Pts
David Robinson, SA	73	17	8	4	0	901
Shaquille O'Neal, Orl	12	45	30	5	5	605
Karl Malone, Utah	14	23	38	11	8	532
Patrick Ewing, NY	2	4	9	39	20	230
Hakeem Olajuwon, Hou	1	4	9	13	25	147

Also receiving votes: Charles Barkley, Pho. (96 pts); Scottie Pippen, Chi. (83 pts); John Stockton, Utah (47 pts); Gary Payton, Sea. (34 pts); Anfernee Hardaway, Orl. (23 pts); Michael Jordan, Chi (12 pts); Dennis Rodman, SA (9 pts); Jason Kidd, Dal (7 pts); Clyde Drexler, Port-Hou. (3 pts) and Cedric Ceballos, LAL (1 pt).

All-NBA Teams

Voting by a 105-member panel of local and national pro basketball writers and broadcasters. Each ballot has entries for three teams; points awarded on 5-3-1 basis. First Team repeaters from 1993-94 are in **bold** type.

First Team	1st	Pts
F **Karl Malone**, Utah	102	519
F **Scottie Pippen**, Chicago	73	451
C David Robinson, San Antonio	86	479
G **John Stockton**, Utah	73	447
G Anfernee Hardaway, Orlando	55	394

Second Team	1st	Pts
F Charles Barkley, Phoenix	31	363
F Shawn Kemp, Seattle	0	161
C Shaquille O'Neal, Orlando	15	311
G Gary Payton, Seattle	40	342
G Mitch Richmond, Sacramento	25	253

Third Team	1st	Pts
F Dennis Rodman, San Antonio	1	113
F Detlef Schrempf, Seattle	1	95
C Hakeem Olajuwon, Houston	3	102
G Reggie Miller, Indiana	2	158
G Clyde Drexler, Portland-Houston	4	73

All-Defensive Teams

Voting by NBA's 27 head coaches. Each ballot has entries for two teams; two points given for 1st team, one for 2nd. Coaches cannot vote for own players. First Team repeaters from 1993-94 are in **bold** type.

First Team	1st	Pts
F **Scottie Pippen**, Chicago	22	46
F Dennis Rodman, San Antonio	15	35
C David Robinson, San Antonio	10	27
G **Gary Payton**, Seattle	19	43
G **Mookie Blaylock**, Atlanta	11	32

Second Team	1st	Pts
F Horace Grant, Chicago	6	18
F Derrick McKey, Indiana	3	13
C Dikembe Mutombo, Denver	10	26
G John Stockton, Utah	4	14
G Nate McMillan, Seattle	2	13

Coach of the Year

The Red Auerbach Trophy; voting by 105-member panel of local and national pro basketball writers and broadcasters. Each ballot has one entry.

	Votes	Improvement
Del Harris, LA Lakers	62	33-49 to 48-34
Mike Fratello, Cleveland	15	47-35 to 43-39
Bob Hill, San Antonio	12	55-27 to 62-20

Also receiving votes: Jerry Sloan, Utah (11); Dick Motta, Dal (5).

Rookie of the Year

The Eddie Gottlieb Trophy; voting by 105-member panel of local and national pro basketball writers and broadcasters. Each ballot has one entry.

	Pos	Votes
Grant Hill, Detroit	F	43
Jason Kidd, Dallas	G	43
Glenn Robinson, Milwaukee	F	15

Also receiving votes: Eddie Jones, LAL (2 pts); Brian Grant, Sac (1 pt) and Juwan Howard, Wash. (1 pt)

All-Rookie Team

Voting by NBA's 27 head coaches. Each ballot has entries for two five-man teams, regardless of position; two points given for 1st team, one for 2nd. Coaches cannot vote for their own players. First team votes in parentheses.

First Team	College	Pts
Jason Kidd, Dallas (26)	California	52
Grant Hill, Detroit (25)	Duke	51
Glenn Robinson, Milwaukee (25)	Purdue	50
Eddie Jones, LA Lakers (21)	Temple	45
Brian Grant, Sacramento (17)	Xavier-OH	42

Second Team	College	Pts
Juwan Howard, Washington (12)	Michigan	38
Eric Montross, Boston (6)	N. Carolina	31
Wesley Person, Phoenix	Auburn	24
Jalen Rose, Denver	Michigan	16
Donyell Marshall, Golden State (1)	UConn	14
Sharone Wright, Philadelphia	Clemson	14

Other Awards

Defensive Player of the Year— Dikembe Mutombo, Denver; **Most Improved Player—** Dana Barros, Philadelphia; **Sixth Man Award—** Anthony Mason, New York; **Court Vision Award** (assists and steals divided by turnovers)— Muggsy Bogues, Charlotte; **IBM Award** (for contributing most to team's success)— David Robinson, San Antonio; **Executive of the Year** (chosen by *The Sporting News*)— Jerry West, LA Lakers.

1995 European Championship

The European Basketball Championship, held in Athens, Greece from June 21 to July 2, 1995.

Quarterfinals

Croatia 71		Italy 61
Greece 66		Spain 64
Lithuania 82		Russia 71
Yugoslavia 104		France 86

Semifinals

Lithuania 90		Croatia 80
Yugoslavia 60		Greece 52

Third Place

Croatia 73		Greece 68

Championship

Yugoslavia 96		Lithuania 90

Most Valuable Player

Sarunas Marciulionis, Lithuania, guard

All-Tournament

First Team (picked by media): **G—** Marciulionis, Lithuania; **C—** Vlade Divac; Yugoslavia and Arvydas Sabonis, Lithuania, **F—** Fanis Christodoulou, Greece and Toni Kukoc, Croatia.

1995 Expansion Draft

Complete selection lists of 1995 NBA expansion draft held June 24 in Secaucus, N.J. Toronto had 14 picks and Vancouver had 13 from a pool of players remaining after each of the league's 27 established teams protected eight players each. No team could lose more than one player from its roster. Toronto won right to pick first after losing coin toss for the sixth pick in the college draft.

Toronto Raptors

	Player	1994-95 team	Pos	Yrs
1	B.J. Armstrong	Chicago	G	6
3	Tony Massenburg	LA Clippers	F	3
5	Andres Guibert	Minnesota	F	2
7	Keith Jennings	Golden State	G	3
9	Dontonio Wingfield	Seattle	F	1
11	Doug Smith	Dallas	F	4
13	Jerome Kersey	Portland	F	11
15	Zan Tabak	Houston	C	1
17	Willie Anderson	San Antonio	G/F	7
19	Ed Pinckney	Milwaukee	F	10
21	Acie Earl	Boston	C	2
23	B.J. Tyler	Philadelphia	G	1
25	John Salley	Miami	F	9
27	Oliver Miller	Detroit	C	3

Vancouver Grizzlies

	Player	1994-95 team	Pos	Yrs
2	Greg Anthony	New York	G	4
4	Rodney Dent	Orlando	F	1
6	Antonio Harvey	LA Lakers	F/C	2
8	Reggie Slater	Denver	F	1
10	Trevor Ruffin	Phoenix	G	1
12	Derrick Phelps	Sacramento	G	1
14	Larry Stewart	Washington	F	4
16	Kenny Gattison	Charlotte	F	9
18	Byron Scott	Indiana	G	12
20	Gerald Wilkins	Cleveland	G	10
22	Benoit Benjamin	New Jersey	C	10
24	Doug Edwards	Atlanta	F	2
26	Blue Edwards	Utah	G/F	6

1995 College Draft

First and second round picks at the 49th annual NBA college draft held June 28, 1995, at SkyDome in Toronto. The order of the first 11 positions determined by a draft lottery held May 21, in Secaucus, N.J. Positions 12 through 29 reflect regular season records in reverse order. Vancouver won expansion team coin toss with Toronto for sixth pick. Underclassmen selected are noted in CAPITAL letters.

First Round

	Team		Pos
1	Golden State	JOE SMITH, Maryland	C
2	a-LA Clippers	ANTONIO McDYESS, Alabama	F
3	Philadelphia	JERRY STACKHOUSE, N. Carolina	G
4	Washington	RASHEED WALLACE, N. Carolina	F
5	Minnesota	KEVIN GARNETT, Farragut Acad.	C
6	Vancouver	Bryant Reeves, Oklahoma St.	C
7	Toronto	Damon Stoudamire, Arizona	G
8	bd-Portland	Shawn Respert, Michigan St.	G
9	New Jersey	Ed O'Bannon, UCLA	F
10	Miami	Kurt Thomas, TCU	F
11	b-Milwaukee	Gary Trent, Ohio	F
12	Dallas	Cherokee Parks, Duke	C
13	Sacramento	CORLISS WILLIAMSON, Arkansas	F
14	Boston	Eric Williams, Providence	F
15	a-Denver	Brent Barry, Oregon St.	G
16	c-Atlanta	Alan Henderson, Idiana	F
17	Cleveland	Bobby Sura, Florida St.	G
18	d-Detroit	Theo Ratliff, Wyoming	F
19	d-Detroit	Randolph Childress, Wake Forest	G
20	Chicago	Jason Caffey, Alabama	F
21	Phoenix	Michael Finley, Wisconsin	F
22	Charlotte	George Zidek, UCLA	C
23	Indiana	Travis Best, Georgia Tech	G
24	Dallas	Loren Meyer, Iowa St.	C
25	Orlando	DAVID VAUGHN, Memphis	F
26	Seattle	Sherell Ford, Illinois-Chicago	F
27	Phoenix	MARIO BENNETT, Arizona St.	F
28	Utah	Greg Ostertag, Kansas	C
29	San Antonio	CORY ALEXANDER, Virginia	G

Second Round

	Team		Pos
30	e-Detroit	Lou Roe, Massachusetts	F
31	f-Chicago	Dragan Tarlac, Greece	F
32	Washington	Terrence Rencher, Texas	G
33	g-Boston	Junior Burrough, Virginia	F
34	Golden State	Andrew DeClerq, Florida	F
35	Toronto	Jimmy King, Michigan	G
36	Vancouver	Lawrence Moten, Syracuse	G
37	h-LA Lakers	Frankie King, W. Carolina	G
38	i-Milwaukee	RASHARD GRIFFITH, Wisconsin	C
39	j-Cleveland	Donny Marshall, Connecticut	F
40	k-Golden St.	Dwayne Whitfield, Jackson St.	F
41	l-Houston	Erik Meek, Duke	C
42	m-Atlanta	Donnie Boyce, Colorado	G
43	no-Milwaukee	Eric Snow, Michigan St.	G
44	Denver	Anthony Pelle, Fresno St.	C
45	Atlanta	Troy Brown, Providence	F
46	p-Miami	George Banks, UTEP	F
47	q-Sacramento	Tyus Edney, UCLA	G
48	r-Minnesota	Mark Davis, Texas Tech	F
49	s-Minnesota	Jerome Allen, Penn	G
50	t-Golden St.	Martin Lewis, Seward CC	F
51	u-Sacramento	Dejan Bodiroga, Italy	F
52	Indiana	Fred Hoiberg, Iowa St.	G
53	v-LA Clippers	Constantin Popa, Miami	C
54	o-Seattle	Eurelijas Zukauskas, Lithuania	C
55	w-Golden St.	Michael McDonald, New Orleans	G
56	Phoenix	CHRIS CARR, So. Illinois	G
57	x-Atlanta	Cuonzo Martin, Purdue	G
58	y-Detroit	Don Reid, Georgetown	F

Acquired Picks

FIRST ROUND: **a-** LA Clippers traded third-year player Randy Woods and the rights to McDyess to Denver for second-year player Rodney Rogers and the rights to Barry; **b-** Portland sent the rights to Respert to Milwaukee for the rights to Trent and a No. 1 pick in 1996; **c-** Atlanta exercised option to take Miami's '95 first pick; **d-** Portland gave Detroit the 18th and 19th picks for the eighth overall pick.
SECOND ROUND: **e-** from LA Clippers; **f-** from Minnesota; **g-** from Philadelphia via Utah; **h-** from Detroit via Washington; **i-** from Milwaukee via LA Lakers; **j-** from Miami; **k-** from Milwaukee via LA Lakers; **l-** from Dallas; **m-** from Sacramento; **n-** from Boston; **o-** Milwaukee traded the rights to Snow to Seattle for the rights to Zukaukas and a second round pick in 1996; **p-** from Cleveland; **q-** from Portland via Golden St.; **r-** from Chicago; **s-** from Houston; **t-** from LA Lakers via Seattle; **u-** from Charlotte; **v-** from New York; **w-** from Orlando via Seattle; **x-** for Utah; **y-** from San Antonio via Houston and Portland.

The NBA Finals

Although the National Basketball Association traces its first championship back to the 1946-47 season, the league was then called the Basketball Association of America (BAA). It did not become the NBA until after the 1948-49 season when the BAA and the National Basketball League (NBL) agreed to merge.

In the chart below, the Eastern finalists (representing the NBA Eastern Division from 1947-70, and the NBA Eastern Conference since 1971) are listed in CAPITAL letters. Also, each NBA champion's wins and losses are noted in parentheses after the series score.

Multiple winners: Boston (16); Minneapolis-LA Lakers (11); Chicago Bulls, Phi-SF-Golden St. Warriors and Syracuse Nationals-Phi. 76ers (3); Detroit, Houston and New York (2).

Year	Winner	Head Coach	Series	Loser	Head Coach
1947	PHILADELPHIA WARRIORS	Eddie Gottlieb	4-1 (WWWLW)	Chicago Stags	Harold Olsen
1948	Baltimore Bullets	Buddy Jeannette	4-2 (LWWWLW)	PHILA. WARRIORS	Eddie Gottlieb
1949	Minneapolis Lakers	John Kundla	4-2 (WWWLLW)	WASH. CAPITOLS	Red Auerbach
1950	Minneapolis Lakers	John Kundla	4-2 (WLWLW)	SYRACUSE	Al Cervi
1951	Rochester	Les Harrison	4-3 (WWWLLLW)	NEW YORK	Joe Lapchick
1952	Minneapolis Lakers	John Kundla	4-3 (WLWLWLW)	NEW YORK	Joe Lapchick
1953	Minneapolis Lakers	John Kundla	4-1 (LWWWW)	NEW YORK	Joe Lapchick
1954	Minneapolis Lakers	John Kundla	4-3 (WLWLWLW)	SYRACUSE	Al Cervi
1955	SYRACUSE	Al Cervi	4-3 (WWLLLWW)	Ft. Wayne Pistons	Charley Eckman
1956	PHILADELPHIA WARRIORS	George Senesky	4-1 (WWLWW)	Ft. Wayne Pistons	Charley Eckman
1957	BOSTON	Red Auerbach	4-3 (LWLWWLW)	St. Louis Hawks	Alex Hannum
1958	St. Louis Hawks	Alex Hannum	4-2 (WLWLWW)	BOSTON	Red Auerbach
1959	BOSTON	Red Auerbach	4-0	Mpls. Lakers	John Kundla
1960	BOSTON	Red Auerbach	4-3 (WLWLWLW)	St. Louis Hawks	Ed Macauley
1961	BOSTON	Red Auerbach	4-1 (WWLWW)	St. Louis Hawks	Paul Seymour
1962	BOSTON	Red Auerbach	4-3 (WLLWLWW)	LA Lakers	Fred Schaus
1963	BOSTON	Red Auerbach	4-2 (WWLWLW)	LA Lakers	Fred Schaus
1964	BOSTON	Red Auerbach	4-1 (WWLWW)	SF Warriors	Alex Hannum
1965	BOSTON	Red Auerbach	4-1 (WWLWW)	LA Lakers	Fred Schaus
1966	BOSTON	Red Auerbach	4-3 (LWWWLLW)	LA Lakers	Fred Schaus
1967	PHILADELPHIA 76ERS	Alex Hannum	4-2 (WWLWWW)	SF Warriors	Bill Sharman
1968	BOSTON	Bill Russell	4-2 (WLWLWW)	LA Lakers	B.van Breda Kolff
1969	BOSTON	Bill Russell	4-3 (LLWWLWW)	LA Lakers	B.van Breda Kolff
1970	NEW YORK	Red Holzman	4-3 (WLWLWLW)	LA Lakers	Joe Mullaney
1971	Milwaukee	Larry Costello	4-0	BALT. BULLETS	Gene Shue
1972	LA Lakers	Bill Sharman	4-1 (LWWWW)	NEW YORK	Red Holzman
1973	NEW YORK	Red Holzman	4-1 (LWWWW)	LA Lakers	Bill Sharman
1974	BOSTON	Tommy Heinsohn	4-3 (WLWLWLW)	Milwaukee	Larry Costello
1975	Golden St. Warriors	Al Attles	4-0	WASH. BULLETS	K.C. Jones
1976	BOSTON	Tommy Heinsohn	4-2 (WWLLWW)	Phoenix	John MacLeod
1977	Portland	Jack Ramsay	4-2 (LLWWWW)	PHILA. 76ERS	Gene Shue
1978	WASHINGTON BULLETS	Dick Motta	4-3 (LWLWLWW)	Seattle	Lenny Wilkens
1979	Seattle	Lenny Wilkens	4-1 (LWWWW)	WASH. BULLETS	Dick Motta
1980	LA Lakers	Paul Westhead	4-2 (WLWWLW)	PHILA. 76ERS	Billy Cunningham
1981	BOSTON	Bill Fitch	4-2 (WLWLWW)	Houston	Del Harris
1982	LA Lakers	Pat Riley	4-2 (WLWWLW)	PHILA. 76ERS	Billy Cunningham
1983	PHILADELPHIA 76ERS	Billy Cunningham	4-0	LA Lakers	Pat Riley
1984	BOSTON	K.C. Jones	4-3 (LWLWLWW)	LA Lakers	Pat Riley
1985	LA Lakers	Pat Riley	4-2 (LWWLWW)	BOSTON	K.C. Jones
1986	BOSTON	K.C. Jones	4-2 (WWWLWW)	Houston	Bill Fitch
1987	LA Lakers	Pat Riley	4-2 (WWLWLW)	BOSTON	K.C. Jones
1988	LA Lakers	Pat Riley	4-3 (LWWLLWW)	DETROIT PISTONS	Chuck Daly
1989	DETROIT PISTONS	Chuck Daly	4-0	LA Lakers	Pat Riley

NBA Finals (Cont.)

Year	Winner	Head Coach	Series	Loser	Head Coach
1990	DETROIT	Chuck Daly	4-1 (WLWWW)	Portland	Rick Adelman
1991	CHICAGO	Phil Jackson	4-1 (LWWWW)	LA Lakers	Mike Dunleavy
1992	CHICAGO	Phil Jackson	4-2 (WLWLWW)	Portland	Rick Adelman
1993	CHICAGO	Phil Jackson	4-2 (WWLWLW)	Phoenix	Paul Westphal
1994	Houston	Rudy Tomjanovich	4-3 (WLWLLWW)	NEW YORK	Pat Riley
1995	Houston	Rudy Tomjanovich	4-0	Orlando	Brian Hill

Note: Four finalists were led by player-coaches: **1948**—Buddy Jeannette (guard) of Baltimore; **1950**—Al Cervi (guard) of Syracuse; **1968**—Bill Russell (center) of Boston; **1969**—Bill Russell (center) of Boston.

Most Valuable Player

Selected by an 11-member media panel. Winner who did not play for the NBA champion is in **bold** type.

Multiple winners: Magic Johnson and Michael Jordan (3); Kareem Abdul-Jabbar, Larry Bird, Hakeem Olajuwon and Willis Reed (2).

Year		Year		Year	
1969	**Jerry West**, LA Lakers, G	1978	Wes Unseld, Washington, C	1987	Magic Johnson, LA Lakers, G
		1979	Dennis Johnson, Seattle, G	1988	James Worthy, LA Lakers, F
1970	Willis Reed, New York, C	1980	Magic Johnson, LA Lakers, G/C	1989	Joe Dumars, Detroit, G
1971	Lew Alcindor, Milwaukee, C	1981	Cedric Maxwell, Boston, F		
1972	Wilt Chamberlain, LA Lakers, C	1982	Magic Johnson, LA Lakers, G	1990	Isiah Thomas, Detroit, G
1973	Willis Reed, New York, C	1983	Moses Malone, Philadelphia, C	1991	Michael Jordan, Chicago, G
1974	John Havlicek, Boston, F	1984	Larry Bird, Boston, F	1992	Michael Jordan, Chicago, G
1975	Rick Barry, Golden State, F	1985	K. Abdul-Jabbar, LA Lakers, C	1993	Michael Jordan, Chicago, G
1976	Jo Jo White, Boston, G	1986	Larry Bird, Boston, F	1994	Hakeem Olajuwon, Houston, C
1977	Bill Walton, Portland, C			1995	Hakeem Olajuwon, Houston, C

Note: Lew Alcindor changed his name to Kareem Abdul-Jabbar after the 1970-71 season.

All-Time NBA Playoff Leaders

Through the 1995 playoffs.

CAREER

Years listed indicate number of playoff appearances. Players active in 1995 in **bold** type.

Points

		Yrs	Gm	Pts	Avg
1	Kareem Abdul-Jabbar	18	237	5762	24.3
2	Jerry West	13	153	4457	29.1
3	**Michael Jordan**	10	121	4165	34.4
4	Larry Bird	12	164	3897	23.8
5	John Havlicek	13	172	3776	22.0
6	Magic Johnson	12	186	3640	19.6
7	Elgin Baylor	12	134	3623	27.0
8	Wilt Chamberlain	13	160	3607	22.5
9	Kevin McHale	13	169	3182	18.8
10	Dennis Johnson	13	180	3116	17.3
11	Julius Erving	11	141	3088	21.9
12	**Hakeem Olajuwon**	10	107	3023	28.3
13	James Worthy	9	143	3022	21.1
14	Sam Jones	12	154	2909	18.9
15	**Robert Parish**	15	182	2818	15.5
16	Bill Russell	13	165	2673	16.2
17	**Clyde Drexler**	12	116	2465	21.3
18	Byron Scott	12	175	2400	13.7
19	**Charles Barkley**	9	95	2315	24.4
20	Isiah Thomas	9	111	2261	20.4

Scoring Average

Minimum of 25 games or 700 points.

		Yrs	Gm	Pts	Avg
1	**Michael Jordan**	10	121	4165	34.4
2	Jerry West	13	153	4457	29.1
3	**Hakeem Olajuwon**	10	107	3023	28.3
4	**Karl Malone**	10	79	2169	27.5
5	Elgin Baylor	12	134	3623	27.0
6	George Gervin	9	59	1592	27.0
7	**Dominique Wilkins**	9	55	1421	25.8
8	Bob Pettit	9	88	2240	25.5
9	Rick Barry	7	74	1833	24.8
10	**Reggie Miller**	6	48	1182	24.6
11	Bernard King	5	28	687	24.5
12	Alex English	10	68	1661	24.4
13	**Charles Barkley**	9	95	2315	24.4
14	Kareem Abdul-Jabbar	18	237	5762	24.3
15	Paul Arizin	8	49	1186	24.2
16	**David Robinson**	5	43	1037	24.1
17	Larry Bird	12	164	3897	23.8
18	George Mikan	9	91	2141	23.5
19	Bob Love	6	47	1076	22.9
20	Elvin Hayes	10	96	2194	22.9

Field Goals

		Yrs	FG	Att	Pct
1	Kareem Abdul-Jabbar	18	2356	4422	.533
2	Jerry West	13	1622	3460	.469
3	**Michael Jordan**	10	1531	3066	.499
4	Larry Bird	12	1458	3090	.472
5	John Havlicek	13	1451	3329	.436
7	Wilt Chamberlain	13	1425	2728	.522
7	Elgin Baylor	12	1388	3161	.439
8	Magic Johnson	12	1276	2513	.508
9	James Worthy	9	1267	2329	.544
10	**Hakeem Olajuwon**	10	1208	2276	.531

Free Throws

		Yrs	FT	Att	Pct
1	Jerry West	13	1213	1507	.805
2	Kareem Abdul-Jabbar	18	1050	1419	.740
3	Magic Johnson	12	1040	1241	.838
4	**Michael Jordan**	10	1006	1208	.833
5	Larry Bird	12	901	1012	.891
6	John Havlicek	13	874	1046	.836
7	Elgin Baylor	12	847	1101	.769
8	Kevin McHale	13	766	972	.788
9	Wilt Chamberlain	13	757	1627	.465
10	Dennis Johnson	13	756	943	.802

Assists

		Yrs	Gm	No	Avg
1	Magic Johnson	12	186	2320	12.5
2	Larry Bird	12	164	1062	6.5
3	Dennis Johnson	13	180	1006	5.6
4	Isiah Thomas	9	111	987	8.9
5	John Stockton	11	89	980	11.0

Rebounds

		Yrs	Gm	No	Avg
1	Bill Russell	13	165	4104	24.9
2	Wilt Chamberlain	13	160	3913	24.5
3	Kareem Abdul-Jabbar	18	237	2481	10.5
4	Wes Unseld	12	119	1777	14.9
5	Robert Parish	15	182	1761	9.7

Appearances

	No		No
Kareem Abdul-Jabbar	18	Hal Greer	13
Robert Parish	15	John Havlicek	13
Dolph Schayes	15	Kevin McHale	13
Paul Silas	14	Dennis Johnson	13
Wilt Chamberlain	13	Bill Russell	13
Maurice Cheeks	13	Chet Walker	13
Bob Cousy	13	Jerry West	13

Games Played

	No		No
K. Abdul-Jabbar	237	Kevin McHale	169
Danny Ainge	193	Michael Cooper	168
Magic Johnson	186	Bill Russell	165
Robert Parish	182	Larry Bird	164
Dennis Johnson	180	Paul Silas	163
Byron Scott	175	Wilt Chamberlain	160
John Havlicek	170	Sam Jones	154

SINGLE GAME

Points

	Date	FG-FT—Pts
Michael Jordan, Chi at Bos*	4/20/86	22-19—63
Elgin Baylor, LA at Bos	4/14/62	22-17—61
Wilt Chamberlain, Phi vs Syr	3/22/62	22-12—56
Michael Jordan, Chi at Mia	4/29/92	20-16—56
Charles Barkley, Pho vs G.St.	5/4/94	23- 7—56
Rick Barry, SF vs Phi	4/18/67	22-11—55
Michael Jordan, Chi vs Cle	5/1/88	24- 7—55
Michael Jordan, Chi vs Pho	4/16/93	21-13—55

*Double overtime.

Field Goals

	Date	FG	Att
Wilt Chamberlain, Phi vs Syr	3/14/60	24	42
John Havlicek, Bos vs Atl	4/1/73	24	36
Michael Jordan, Chi vs Cle	5/1/88	24	45
Seven tied with 22 each.			

Miscellaneous

3-Pt Field Goals

	Date	No
Dan Majerle, Pho vs Sea	6/1/93	8
Eight tied with 7 each.		

Assists

	Date	No
Magic Johnson, LA vs Pho	5/15/84	24
John Stockton, Utah at LA Lakers	5/17/88	24
Magic Johnson, LA Lakers at Port	5/3/85	23
Doc Rivers, Atl vs Bos	5/16/88	22
Four tied with 21 each.		

Rebounds

	Date	No
Wilt Chamberlain, Phi vs Bos	4/5/67	41
Bill Russell, Bos vs Phi	3/23/58	40
Bill Russell, Bos vs St.L	3/29/60	40
Bill Russell, Bos vs LA*	4/18/62	40
Three tied with 39 each.		

*Overtime.

Appearances in NBA Finals

Standings of all NBA teams that have reached the NBA Finals since 1947.

App		Titles	Last Won
24	Minneapolis-LA Lakers	11	1988
19	Boston Celtics	16	1986
8	Syracuse Nats-Phila. 76ers	3	1983
7	New York Knicks	2	1973
6	Phila-SF-Golden St. Warriors	3	1975
5	Ft. Wayne-Detroit Pistons	2	1990
4	Houston Rockets	2	1995
4	St. Louis Hawks	1	1958
4	Baltimore-Washington Bullets	1	1978
3	Chicago Bulls	3	1993
3	Portland Trail Blazers	1	1977
2	Milwaukee Bucks	1	1971
2	Seattle SuperSonics	1	1979
2	Phoenix Suns	0	—
1	Baltimore Bullets	1	1948
1	Chicago Stags	0	—
1	Orlando Magic	0	—
1	Rochester Royals	0	—
1	Washington Capitols	0	—

Change of address: The St. Louis Hawks now play in Atlanta and the Rochester Royals are now the Sacramento Kings.

Teams now defunct: Baltimore Bullets (1947-55), Chicago Stags (1946-50) and Washington Capitols (1946-51).

NBA FINALS

Points

Series		Year	Pts
4-Gm	Hakeem Olajuwon, Hou vs Orl	1995	131
5-Gm	Jerry West, LA vs Bos	1965	169
6-Gm	Michael Jordan, Chi vs Pho	1993	246
7-Gm	Elgin Baylor, LA vs Bos	1962	284

Field Goals

Series		Year	No
4-Gm	Hakeem Olajuwon, Hou vs Orl	1995	56
5-Gm	Michael Jordan, Chi vs LAL	1991	63
6-Gm	Michael Jordan, Chi vs Pho	1993	101
7-Gm	Elgin Baylor, LA vs Bos	1962	101

Assists

Series		Year	No
4-Gm	Bob Cousy, Bos vs Mpls	1959	51
5-Gm	Magic Johnson, LAL vs Chi	1991	62
6-Gm	Magic Johnson, LAL vs Bos	1985	84
7-Gm	Magic Johnson, LA vs Bos	1984	95

Rebounds

Series		Year	No
4-Gm	Bill Russell, Bos vs Mpls	1959	118
5-Gm	Bill Russell, Bos vs St.L	1961	144
6-Gm	Wilt Chamberlain, Phi vs SF	1967	171
7-Gm	Bill Russell, Bos vs LA	1962	189

The National Basketball League

Formed in 1937 by three corporations— General Electric and the Firestone and Goodyear rubber companies of Akron, Ohio— who were interested in moving up from their midwestern industrial league origins and backing a fully professional league. The NBL started with 13 previously independent teams in 1937-38 and although GE, Firestone and Goodyear were gone by late 1942, ran 12 years before merging with the three-year-old Basketball Association of America in 1949 to form the NBA.

Multiple champions: Akron Firestone Non-Skids, Fort Wayne Zollner Pistons, Oshkosh All-Stars (2).

Year	Winner	Series	Loser	Year	Winner	Series	Loser
1938	Goodyear Wingfoots	2-1	Oshkosh All-Stars	1944	Ft. Wayne Pistons	3-0	Sheboygan Redskins
1939	Firestone Non-Skids	3-2	Oshkosh All-Stars	1945	Ft. Wayne Pistons	3-2	Sheboygan Redskins
1940	Firestone Non-Skids	3-2	Oshkosh All-Stars	1946	Rochester Royals	3-0	Sheboygan Redskins
1941	Oshkosh All-Stars	3-0	Sheboygan Redskins	1947	Chicago Gears	3-2	Rochester Royals
1942	Oshkosh All-Stars	2-1	Ft. Wayne Pistons	1948	Minneapolis Lakers	3-1	Rochester Royals
1943	Sheboygan Redskins	2-1	Ft. Wayne Pistons	1949	Anderson Packers	3-0	Oshkosh All-Stars

NBA All-Star Game

The NBA staged its first All-Star Game before 10,094 at Boston Garden on March 2, 1951. From that year on, the game has matched the best players in the East against the best in the West. Winning coaches are listed first. East leads series, 28-16.

Multiple MVP winners: Bob Pettit (4); Oscar Robertson (3); Bob Cousy, Julius Erving, Magic Johnson, Karl Malone and Isiah Thomas (2).

Year		Host	Coaches	Most Valuable Player
1951	East 111, West 94	Boston	Joe Lapchick, John Kundla	Ed Macauley, Boston
1952	East 108, West 91	Boston	Al Cervi, John Kundla	Paul Arizin, Philadelphia
1953	West 79, East 75	Ft. Wayne	John Kundla, Joe Lapchick	George Mikan, Minneapolis
1954	East 98, West 93 (OT)	New York	Joe Lapchick, John Kundla	Bob Cousy, Boston
1955	East 100, West 91	New York	Al Cervi, Charley Eckman	Bill Sharman, Boston
1956	West 108, East 94	Rochester	Charley Eckman, George Senesky	Bob Pettit, St. Louis
1957	East 109, West 97	Boston	Red Auerbach, Bobby Wanzer	Bob Cousy, Boston
1958	East 130, West 118	St. Louis	Red Auerbach, Alex Hannum	Bob Pettit, St. Louis
1959	West 124, East 108	Detroit	Ed Macauley, Red Auerbach	Bob Pettit, St. Louis
				& Elgin Baylor, Minneapolis
1960	East 125, West 115	Philadelphia	Red Auerbach, Ed Macauley	Wilt Chamberlain, Philadelphia
1961	West 153, East 131	Syracuse	Paul Seymour, Red Auerbach	Oscar Robertson, Cincinnati
1962	West 150, East 130	St. Louis	Fred Schaus, Red Auerbach	Bob Pettit, St. Louis
1963	East 115, West 108	Los Angeles	Red Auerbach, Fred Schaus	Bill Russell, Boston
1964	East 111, West 107	Boston	Red Auerbach, Fred Schaus	Oscar Robertson, Cincinnati
1965	East 124, West 123	St. Louis	Red Auerbach, Alex Hannum	Jerry Lucas, Cincinnati
1966	East 137, West 94	Cincinnati	Red Auerbach, Fred Schaus	Adrian Smith, Cincinnati
1967	West 135, East 120	San Francisco	Fred Schaus, Red Auerbach	Rick Barry, San Francisco
1968	East 144, West 124	New York	Alex Hannum, Bill Sharman	Hal Greer, Philadelphia
1969	East 123, West 112	Baltimore	Gene Shue, Richie Guerin	Oscar Robertson, Cincinnati
1970	East 142, West 135	Philadelphia	Red Holzman, Richie Guerin	Willis Reed, New York
1971	West 108, East 107	San Diego	Larry Costello, Red Holzman	Lenny Wilkens, Seattle
1972	West 112, East 110	Los Angeles	Bill Sharman, Tom Heinsohn	Jerry West, Los Angeles
1973	East 104, West 84	Chicago	Tom Heinsohn, Bill Sharman	Dave Cowens, Boston
1974	West 134, East 123	Seattle	Larry Costello, Tom Heinsohn	Bob Lanier, Detroit
1975	East 108, West 102	Phoenix	K.C. Jones, Al Attles	Walt Frazier, New York
1976	East 123, West 109	Philadelphia	Tom Heinsohn, Al Attles	Dave Bing, Washington
1977	West 125, East 124	Milwaukee	Larry Brown, Gene Shue	Julius Erving, Philadelphia
1978	East 133, West 125	Atlanta	Billy Cunningham, Jack Ramsay	Randy Smith, Buffalo
1979	West 134, East 129	Detroit	Lenny Wilkens, Dick Motta	David Thompson, Denver
1980	East 144, West 136 (OT)	Washington	Billy Cunningham, Lenny Wilkens	George Gervin, San Antonio
1981	East 123, West 120	Cleveland	Billy Cunningham, John MacLeod	Nate Archibald, Boston
1982	East 120, West 118	New Jersey	Bill Fitch, Pat Riley	Larry Bird, Boston
1983	East 132, West 123	Los Angeles	Billy Cunningham, Pat Riley	Julius Erving, Philadelphia
1984	East 154, West 145 (OT)	Denver	K.C. Jones, Frank Layden	Isiah Thomas, Detroit
1985	West 140, East 129	Indiana	Pat Riley, K.C. Jones	Ralph Sampson, Houston
1986	West 139, East 132	Dallas	K.C. Jones, Pat Riley	Isiah Thomas, Detroit
1987	West 154, East 149 (OT)	Seattle	Pat Riley, K.C. Jones	Tom Chambers, Seattle
1988	East 138, West 133	Chicago	Mike Fratello, Pat Riley	Michael Jordan, Chicago
1989	West 143, East 134	Houston	Pat Riley, Lenny Wilkens	Karl Malone, Utah
1990	East 130, West 113	Miami	Chuck Daly, Pat Riley	Magic Johnson, LA Lakers
1991	East 116, West 114	Charlotte	Chris Ford, Rick Adelman	Charles Barkley, Philadelphia
1992	West 153, East 113	Orlando	Don Nelson, Phil Jackson	Magic Johnson, LA Lakers
1993	West 135, East 132 (OT)	Salt Lake City	Paul Westphal, Pat Riley	Karl Malone, Utah
				& John Stockton, Utah
1994	East 127, West 118	Minneapolis	Lenny Wilkens, George Karl	Scottie Pippen, Chicago
1995	West 139, East 112	Phoenix	Paul Westphal, Brian Hill	Mitch Richmond, Sacramento

NBA Franchise Origins

Here is what the current 29 teams in the National Basketball Association have to show for the years they have put in as members of the National Basketball League (NBL), Basketball Association of America (BAA), the NBA, and the American Basketball Association (ABA). League titles are noted by year won.

Western Conference

	First Season		League Titles	Franchise Stops
Dallas Mavericks	1980-81	(NBA)	None	• Dallas (1980—)
Denver Nuggets	1967-68	(ABA)	None	• Denver (1967—)
Golden St. Warriors	1946-47	(BAA)	1 BAA (1947)	• Philadelphia (1946-62)
			2 NBA (1956,75)	San Francisco (1962-71)
				Oakland (1971—)
Houston Rockets	1967-68	(NBA)	2 NBA (1994,95)	• San Diego (1967-71)
				Houston (1971—)
Los Angeles Clippers	1970-71	(NBA)	None	• Buffalo (1970-78)
				San Diego (1978-84)
				Los Angeles (1984—)
Los Angeles Lakers	1947-48	(NBL)	1 NBL (1947)	• Minneapolis (1947-60)
			1 BAA (1949)	Los Angeles (1960-67)
			10 NBA (1950,52-54,72,	Inglewood, CA (1967—)
			80,82,85,87-88)	
Minnesota Timberwolves	1989-90	(NBA)	None	• Minneapolis (1989—)
Phoenix Suns	1968-69	(NBA)	None	• Phoenix (1968—)
Portland Trail Blazers	1970-71	(NBA)	1 NBA (1977)	• Portland (1970—)
Sacramento Kings	1945-46	(NBL)	1 NBL (1946)	• Rochester, NY (1945-58)
			1 NBA (1951)	Cincinnati (1958-72)
				KC-Omaha (1972-75)
				Kansas City (1975-85)
				Sacramento (1985—)
San Antonio Spurs	1967-68	(ABA)	None	• Dallas (1967-73)
				San Antonio (1973—)
Seattle SuperSonics	1967-68	(NBA)	1 NBA (1979)	• Seattle (1967—)
Utah Jazz	1974-75	(NBA)	None	• New Orleans (1974-79)
				Salt Lake City (1979—)
Vancouver Grizzlies	1995-96	(NBA)	None	• Vancouver (1995—)

Eastern Conference

	First Season		League Titles	Franchise Stops
Atlanta Hawks	1946-47	(NBL)	1 NBA (1958)	• Tri-Cities (1946-51)
				Milwaukee (1951-55)
				St. Louis (1955-68)
				Atlanta (1968—)
Boston Celtics	1946-47	(BAA)	16 NBA (1957,59-66,68-69	• Boston (1946—)
			74,76,81,84,86)	
Charlotte Hornets	1988-89	(NBA)	None	• Charlotte (1988—)
Chicago Bulls	1966-67	(NBA)	3 NBA (1991-92)	• Chicago (1966—)
Cleveland Cavaliers	1970-71	(NBA)	None	• Cleveland (1970-74)
				Richfield, OH (1974-94)
				Cleveland (1994—)
Detroit Pistons	1941-42	(NBL)	2 NBL (1944-45)	• Ft. Wayne, IN (1941-57)
			2 NBA (1989-90)	Detroit (1957-78)
				Pontiac, MI (1978-88)
				Auburn Hills, MI (1988—)
Indiana Pacers	1967-68	(ABA)	3 ABA (1970,72-73)	• Indianapolis (1967—)
Miami Heat	1988-89	(NBA)	None	• Miami (1988—)
Milwaukee Bucks	1968-69	(NBA)	1 NBA (1971)	• Milwaukee (1968—)
New Jersey Nets	1967-68	(ABA)	2 ABA (1974,76)	• Teaneck, NJ (1967-68)
				Commack, NY (1968-69)
				W. Hempstead, NY (1969-71)
				Uniondale, NY (1971-77)
				Piscataway, NJ (1977-81)
				E. Rutherford, NJ (1981—)
New York Knicks	1946-47	(BAA)	2 NBA (1970,73)	• New York (1946—)
Orlando Magic	1989-90	(NBA)	None	• Orlando, FL (1989—)
Philadelphia 76ers	1949-50	(NBA)	3 NBA (1955,67,83)	• Syracuse, NY (1949-63)
				Philadelphia (1963—)
Toronto Raptors	1995-96	(NBA)	None	• Toronto (1995—)
Washington Bullets	1961-62	(NBA)	1 NBA (1978)	• Chicago (1961-63)
				Baltimore (1963-73)
				Landover, MD (1973—)

Note: The Tri-Cities Blackhawks represented Moline and Rock Island, Ill., and Davenport, Iowa.

The Growth of the NBA

Of the 11 franchises that comprised the Basketball Association of America (BAA) at the start of the 1946-47 season, only three remain—the Boston Celtics, New York Knickerbockers and Golden State Warriors (originally Philadelphia Warriors).

Just before the start of the 1948-49 season, four teams from the more established **National Basketball League** (NBL)—the Ft. Wayne Pistons (now Detroit), Indianapolis Jets, Minneapolis Lakers (now Los Angeles) and Rochester Royals (now Sacramento Kings)—joined the BAA.

A year later, the six remaining NBL franchises—Anderson (Ind.), Denver, Sheboygan (Wisc.), the Syracuse Nationals (now Philadelphia 76ers), Tri-Cities Blackhawks (now Atlanta Hawks) and Waterloo (Iowa)—joined along with the new Indianapolis Olympians and the BAA became the 17-team **National Basketball Association**.

The NBA was down to 10 teams by the 1950-51 season and slipped to eight by 1954-55 with Boston, New York, Philadelphia and Syracuse in the Eastern Division, and Ft. Wayne, Milwaukee (formerly Tri-Cities), Minneapolis and Rochester in the West.

By 1960, five of those surviving eight teams had moved to other cities but by the end of the decade the NBA was a 14-team league. It also had a rival, the **American Basketball Association**, which began play in 1967 with a red, white and blue ball, a three-point line and 11 teams. After a nine-year run, the ABA merged four clubs—the Denver Nuggets, Indiana Pacers, New York Nets and San Antonio Spurs—with the NBA following the 1975-76 season. The NBA adopted the three-point play in 1979-80.

Expansion/Merger Timetable
For teams currently in NBA.

1948—Added NBL's Ft. Wayne Pistons (now Detroit), Minneapolis Lakers (now Los Angeles) and Rochester Royals (now Sacramento Kings); **1949**—Syracuse Nationals (now Philadelphia 76ers) and Tri-Cities Blackhawks (now Atlanta Hawks).

1961—Chicago Packers (now Washington Bullets); **1966**—Chicago Bulls; **1967**—San Diego Rockets (now Houston) and Seattle SuperSonics; **1968**—Milwaukee Bucks and Phoenix Suns.

1970—Buffalo Braves (now Los Angeles Clippers), Cleveland Cavaliers and Portland Trail Blazers; **1974**—New Orleans Jazz (now Utah); **1976**—added ABA's Denver Nuggets, Indiana Pacers, New York Nets (now New Jersey) and San Antonio Spurs.

1980—Dallas Mavericks; **1988**—Charlotte Hornets and Miami Heat; **1989**—Minnesota Timberwolves and Orlando Magic.

1995—Toronto Raptors and Vancouver Grizzlies.

City and Nickname Changes

1951—Tri-Cities Blackhawks, who divided home games between Moline and Rock Island, Ill., and Davenport, Iowa, move to Milwaukee and become the Hawks; **1955**—Milwaukee Hawks move to St. Louis; **1957**—Ft. Wayne Pistons move to Detroit, while Rochester Royals move to Cincinnati.

1960—Minneapolis Lakers move to Los Angeles; **1962**—Chicago Packers renamed Zephyrs, while Philadelphia Warriors move to San Francisco; **1963**—Chicago Zephyrs move to Baltimore and become Bullets, while Syracuse Nationals move to Philadelphia and become 76ers; **1968**—St. Louis Hawks move to Atlanta.

1971—San Diego Rockets move to Houston, while San Francisco Warriors move to Oakland and become Golden State Warriors; **1972**—Cincinnati Royals move to Midwest, divide home games between Kansas City, Mo., and Omaha, Neb., and become Kings; **1973**—Baltimore Bullets move to Landover, Md., outside Washington and become Capital Bullets; **1974**—Capital Bullets renamed Washington Bullets; **1975**—KC-Omaha Kings settle in Kansas City; **1977**—New York Nets move from Uniondale, N.Y., to Piscataway, N.J. (later East Rutherford) and become New Jersey Nets; **1978**—Buffalo Braves move to San Diego and become Clippers.

1980—New Orleans Jazz move to Salt Lake City and become Utah Jazz; **1984**—San Diego Clippers move to Los Angeles; **1985**—Kansas City Kings move to Sacramento.

Defunct NBA Teams
Teams that once played in the BAA and NBA, but no longer exist.

Anderson (Ind.)—Packers (1949-50); **Baltimore**—Bullets (1947-55); **Chicago**—Stags (1946-50); **Cleveland**—Rebels (1946-47); **Denver**—Nuggets (1949-50); **Detroit**—Falcons (1946-47); **Indianapolis**—Jets (1948-49) and Olympians (1949-53). **Pittsburgh**—Ironmen (1946-47); **Providence**—Steamrollers (1946-49); **St. Louis**—Bombers (1946-50); **Sheboygan (Wisc.)**—Redskins (1949-50); **Toronto**—Huskies (1946-47); **Washington**—Capitols (1946-51); **Waterloo (Iowa)**—Hawks (1949-50).

ABA Teams (1967-76)

Anaheim—Amigos (1967-68, moved to LA); **Baltimore**—Claws (1975, never played); **Carolina**—Cougars (1969-74, moved to St. Louis); **Dallas**—Chaparrals (1967-73, called Texas Chaparrals in 1970-71, moved to San Antonio); **Denver**—Rockets (1967-76, renamed Nuggets in 1974-76); **Miami**—Floridians (1968-72, called simply Floridians in 1970-72).

Houston—Mavericks (1967-69, moved to North Carolina); **Indiana**—Pacers (1967-76); **Kentucky**—Colonels (1967-76); **Los Angeles**—Stars (1968-70, moved to Utah); **Memphis**—Pros (1970-75, renamed Tams in 1972 and Sounds in 1974, moved to Baltimore); **Minnesota**—Muskies (1967-68, moved to Miami) and Pipers (1968-69, moved back to Pittsburgh); **New Jersey**—Americans (1967-68, moved to New York).

New Orleans—Buccaneers (1967-70, moved to Memphis); **New York**—Nets (1968-76); **Oakland**—Oaks (1967-69, moved to Washington); **Pittsburgh**—Pipers (1967-68, moved to Minnesota), Pipers (1969-72, renamed Condors in 1970); **St. Louis**—Spirits of St. Louis (1974-76); **San Antonio**—Spurs (1973-76); **San Diego**—Conquistadors (1972-75, renamed Sails in 1975); **Utah**—Stars (1970-75); **Virginia**—Squires (1970-76); **Washington**—Caps (1969-70, moved to Virginia).

Annual NBA Leaders
Scoring

Decided by total points from 1947-69, and per game average since 1970.
Multiple winners: Wilt Chamberlain and Michael Jordan (7); George Gervin (4); Neil Johnston, Bob McAdoo and George Mikan (3); Kareem Abdul-Jabbar, Paul Arizin, Adrian Dantley and Bob Pettit (2).

Year		Gm	Pts	Avg	Year		Gm	Pts	Avg
1947	Joe Fulks, Phi	60	1389	23.2	1972	Kareem Abdul-Jabbar, Mil	81	2822	34.8
1948	Max Zaslofsky, Chi	48	1007	21.0	1973	Nate Archibald, KC-Omaha	80	2719	34.0
1949	George Mikan, Mpls	60	1698	28.3	1974	Bob McAdoo, Buf	74	2261	30.6
					1975	Bob McAdoo, Buf	82	2831	34.5
1950	George Mikan, Mpls	68	1865	27.4	1976	Bob McAdoo, Buf	78	2427	31.1
1951	George Mikan, Mpls	68	1932	28.4	1977	Pete Maravich, NO	73	2273	31.1
1952	Paul Arizin, Phi	66	1674	25.4	1978	George Gervin, SA	82	2232	27.2
1953	Neil Johnston, Phi	70	1564	22.3	1979	George Gervin, SA	80	2365	29.6
1954	Neil Johnston, Phi	72	1759	24.4					
1955	Neil Johnston, Phi	72	1631	22.7	1980	George Gervin, SA	78	2585	33.1
1956	Bob Pettit, St.L	72	1849	25.7	1981	Adrian Dantley, Utah	80	2452	30.7
1957	Paul Arizin, Phi	71	1817	25.6	1982	George Gervin, SA	79	2551	32.3
1958	George Yardley, Det	72	2001	27.8	1983	Alex English, Den	82	2326	28.4
1959	Bob Pettit, St.L	72	2105	29.2	1984	Adrian Dantley, Utah	79	2418	30.6
					1985	Bernard King, NY	55	1809	32.9
1960	Wilt Chamberlain, Phi	72	2707	37.6	1986	Dominique Wilkins, Atl	78	2366	30.3
1961	Wilt Chamberlain, Phi	79	3033	38.4	1987	Michael Jordan, Chi	82	3041	37.1
1962	Wilt Chamberlain, Phi	80	4029	50.4	1988	Michael Jordan, Chi	82	2868	35.0
1963	Wilt Chamberlain, SF	80	3586	44.8	1989	Michael Jordan, Chi	81	2633	32.5
1964	Wilt Chamberlain, SF	80	2948	36.9					
1965	Wilt Chamberlain, SF-Phi	73	2534	34.7	1990	Michael Jordan, Chi	82	2753	33.6
1966	Wilt Chamberlain, Phi	79	2649	33.5	1991	Michael Jordan, Chi	82	2580	31.5
1967	Rick Barry, SF	78	2775	35.6	1992	Michael Jordan, Chi	80	2404	30.1
1968	Dave Bing, Det	79	2142	27.1	1993	Michael Jordan, Chi	78	2541	32.6
1969	Elvin Hayes, SD	82	2327	28.4	1994	David Robinson, SA	80	2383	29.8
1970	Jerry West, LA	74	2309	31.2	1995	Shaquille O'Neal, Orl	79	2315	29.3
1971	Lew Alcindor, Mil	82	2596	31.7					

Note: Lew Alcindor changed his name to Kareem Abdul-Jabbar after the 1970-71 season.

Rebounds

Decided by total rebounds from 1951-69 and per game average since 1970.
Multiple winners: Wilt Chamberlain (11); Moses Malone (6); Dennis Rodman and Bill Russell (4); Elvin Hayes and Hakeem Olajuwon (2).

Year		Gm	No	Avg	Year		Gm	No	Avg
1951	Dolph Schayes, Syr	66	1080	16.4	1973	Wilt Chamberlain, LA	82	1526	18.6
1952	Larry Foust, Ft. Wayne	66	880	13.3	1974	Elvin Hayes, Cap*	81	1463	18.1
	& Mel Hutchins, Mil	66	880	13.3	1975	Wes Unseld, Wash	73	1077	14.8
1953	George Mikan, Mpls	70	1007	14.4	1976	Kareem Abdul-Jabbar, LA	82	1383	16.9
1954	Harry Gallatin, NY	72	1098	15.3	1977	Bill Walton, Port	65	934	14.4
1955	Neil Johnston, Phi	72	1085	15.1	1978	Len Robinson, NO	82	1288	15.7
1956	Bob Pettit, St.L	72	1164	16.2	1979	Moses Malone, Hou	82	1444	17.6
1957	Maurice Stokes, Roch	72	1256	17.4					
1958	Bill Russell, Bos	69	1564	22.7	1980	Swen Nater, SD	81	1216	15.0
1959	Bill Russell, Bos	70	1612	23.0	1981	Moses Malone, Hou	80	1180	14.8
					1982	Moses Malone, Hou	81	1188	14.7
1960	Wilt Chamberlain, Phi	72	1941	27.0	1983	Moses Malone, Phi	78	1194	15.3
1961	Wilt Chamberlain, Phi	79	2149	27.2	1984	Moses Malone, Phi	71	950	13.4
1962	Wilt Chamberlain, Phi	80	2052	25.7	1985	Moses Malone, Phi	79	1031	13.1
1963	Wilt Chamberlain, SF	80	1946	24.3	1986	Bill Laimbeer, Det	82	1075	13.1
1964	Bill Russell, Bos	78	1930	24.7	1987	Charles Barkley, Phi	68	994	14.6
1965	Bill Russell, Bos	78	1878	24.1	1988	Michael Cage, LA Clippers	72	938	13.0
1966	Wilt Chamberlain, Phi	79	1943	24.6	1989	Hakeem Olajuwon, Hou	82	1105	13.5
1967	Wilt Chamberlain, Phi	81	1957	24.2					
1968	Wilt Chamberlain, Phi	82	1952	23.8	1990	Hakeem Olajuwon, Hou	82	1149	14.0
1969	Wilt Chamberlain, LA	81	1712	21.1	1991	David Robinson, SA	82	1063	13.0
					1992	Dennis Rodman, Det	82	1530	18.7
1970	Elvin Hayes, SD	82	1386	16.9	1993	Dennis Rodman, Det	62	1232	18.3
1971	Wilt Chamberlain, LA	82	1493	18.2	1994	Dennis Rodman, SA	79	1132	17.3
1972	Wilt Chamberlain, LA	82	1572	19.2	1995	Dennis Rodman, SA	49	823	16.8

*The Baltimore Bullets moved to Landover, MD in 1973-74 and became first the Capital Bullets, then the Washington Bullets in 1974-75.

Annual NBA Leaders (Cont.)

Assists

Decided by total assists from 1952-69 and per game average since 1970.
Multiple winners: Bob Cousy and John Stockton (8); Oscar Robertson (6); Magic Johnson and Kevin Porter (4); Andy Phillip and Guy Rodgers (2).

Year		No	Year		No	Year		Avg
1947	Ernie Calverley, Prov	202	1964	Oscar Robertson, Cin	868	1980	M.R. Richardson, NY	10.1
1948	Howie Dallmar, Phi	120	1965	Oscar Robertson, Cin	861	1981	Kevin Porter, Wash	9.1
1949	Bob Davies, Roch	321	1966	Oscar Robertson, Cin	847	1982	Johnny Moore, SA	9.6
1950	Dick McGuire, NY	386	1967	Guy Rodgers, Chi	908	1983	Magic Johnson, LA	10.5
1951	Andy Phillip, Phi	414	1968	Wilt Chamberlain, Phi	702	1984	Magic Johnson, LA	13.1
1952	Andy Phillip, Phi	539	1969	Oscar Robertson, Cin	772	1985	Isiah Thomas, Det	13.9
1953	Bob Cousy, Bos	547				1986	Magic Johnson, Lakers	12.6
1954	Bob Cousy, Bos	518	Year		Avg	1987	Magic Johnson, Lakers	12.2
1955	Bob Cousy, Bos	557	1970	Lenny Wilkens, Sea	9.1	1988	John Stockton, Utah	13.8
1956	Bob Cousy, Bos	642	1971	Norm Van Lier, Chi	10.1	1989	John Stockton, Utah	13.6
1957	Bob Cousy, Bos	478	1972	Jerry West, LA	9.7			
1958	Bob Cousy, Bos	463	1973	Nate Archibald, KC-O	11.4	1990	John Stockton, Utah	14.5
1959	Bob Cousy, Bos	557	1974	Ernie DiGregorio, Buf	8.2	1991	John Stockton, Utah	14.2
1960	Bob Cousy, Bos	715	1975	Kevin Porter, Wash	8.0	1992	John Stockton, Utah	13.7
1961	Oscar Robertson, Cin	690	1976	Slick Watts, Sea	8.1	1993	John Stockton, Utah	12.0
1962	Oscar Robertson, Cin	899	1977	Don Buse, Ind	8.5	1994	John Stockton, Utah	12.6
1963	Guy Rodgers, SF	825	1978	Kevin Porter, Det-NJ	10.2	1995	John Stockton, Utah	12.3
			1979	Kevin Porter, Det	13.4			

Field Goal Percentage

Multiple winners: Wilt Chamberlain (9); Artis Gilmore (4); Neil Johnston (3); Bob Feerick, Johnny Green, Alex Groza, Cedric Maxwell, Kevin McHale, Ken Sears and Buck Williams (2).

Year		Pct	Year		Pct	Year		Pct
1947	Bob Feerick, Wash	.401	1963	Wilt Chamberlain, SF	.528	1980	Cedric Maxwell, Bos	.609
1948	Bob Feerick, Wash	.340	1964	Jerry Lucas, Cin	.527	1981	Artis Gilmore, Chi.	.670
1949	Arnie Risen, Roch	.423	1965	W.Chamberlain, SF-Phi	.510	1982	Artis Gilmore, Chi.	.652
1950	Alex Groza, Indpls	.478	1966	Wilt Chamberlain, Phi	.540	1983	Artis Gilmore, SA	.626
1951	Alex Groza, Indpls	.470	1967	Wilt Chamberlain, Phi	.683	1984	Artis Gilmore, SA	.631
1952	Paul Arizin, Phi	.448	1968	Wilt Chamberlain, Phi	.595	1985	James Donaldson, LAC	.637
1953	Neil Johnston, Phi	.452	1969	Wilt Chamberlain, LA	.583	1986	Steve Johnson, SA	.632
1954	Ed Macauley, Bos	.486	1970	Johnny Green, Cin	.559	1987	Kevin McHale, Bos	.604
1955	Larry Foust, Ft.W	.487	1971	Johnny Green, Cin	.587	1988	Kevin McHale, Bos	.604
1956	Neil Johnston, Phi	.457	1972	Wilt Chamberlain, LA	.649	1989	Dennis Rodman, Det.	.595
1957	Neil Johnston, Phi	.447	1973	Wilt Chamberlain, LA	.727			
1958	Jack Twyman, Cin	.452	1974	Bob McAdoo, Buf	.547	1990	Mark West, Pho	.625
1959	Ken Sears, NY	.490	1975	Don Nelson, Bos	.539	1991	Buck Williams, Port.	.602
1960	Ken Sears, NY	.477	1976	Wes Unseld, Wash	.561	1992	Buck Williams, Port.	.604
1961	Wilt Chamberlain, Phi.	.509	1977	K. Abdul-Jabbar, LA	.579	1993	Cedric Ceballos, Pho	.576
1962	Walt Bellamy, Chi	.519	1978	Bobby Jones, Den	.578	1994	Shaquille O'Neal, Orl	.599
			1979	Cedric Maxwell, Bos	.584	1995	Chris Gatling, G.St	.633

Free Throw Percentage

Multiple winners: Bill Sharman (7); Rick Barry (6); Larry Bird (4); Dolph Schayes (3); Larry Costello, Ernie DiGregorio, Bob Feerick, Kyle Macy, Calvin Murphy, Mark Price, Oscar Robertson and Larry Siegfried (2).

Year		Pct	Year		Pct	Year		Pct
1947	Fred Scolari, Wash	.811	1963	Larry Costello, Syr	.881	1980	Rick Barry, Hou	.935
1948	Bob Feerick, Wash	.788	1964	Oscar Robertson, Cin	.853	1981	Calvin Murphy, Hou	.958
1949	Bob Feerick, Wash	.859	1965	Larry Costello, Phi	.877	1982	Kyle Macy, Pho	.899
1950	Max Zaslofsky, Chi	.843	1966	Larry Siegfried, Bos	.881	1983	Calvin Murphy, Hou	.920
1951	Joe Fulks, Phi	.855	1967	Adrian Smith, Cin	.903	1984	Larry Bird, Bos	.888
1952	Bob Wanzer, Roch	.904	1968	Oscar Robertson, Cin	.873	1985	Kyle Macy, Pho	.907
1953	Bill Sharman, Bos	.850	1969	Larry Siegfried, NY	.864	1986	Larry Bird, Bos	.896
1954	Bill Sharman, Bos	.844				1987	Larry Bird, Bos	.910
1955	Bill Sharman, Bos	.897	1970	Flynn Robinson, Mil	.898	1988	Jack Sikma, Mil	.922
1956	Bill Sharman, Bos	.867	1971	Chet Walker, Chi	.859	1989	Magic Johnson, LAL	.911
1957	Bill Sharman, Bos	.905	1972	Jack Marin, Bal	.894			
1958	Dolph Schayes, Syr	.904	1973	Rick Barry, G.St.	.902	1990	Larry Bird, Bos	.930
1959	Bill Sharman, Bos	.932	1974	Ernie DiGregorio, Buf	.902	1991	Reggie Miller, Ind	.918
1960	Dolph Schayes, Syr	.892	1975	Rick Barry, G.St.	.904	1992	Mark Price, Cle	.947
1961	Bill Sharman, Bos	.921	1976	Rick Barry, G.St.	.923	1993	Mark Price, Cle	.948
1962	Dolph Schayes, Syr	.896	1977	Ernie DiGregorio, Buf	.945	1994	M. Abdul-Rauf, Den	.956
			1978	Rick Barry, G.St.	.924	1995	Spud Webb, Sac	.934
			1979	Rick Barry, Hou	.947			

Blocked Shots

Decided by per game average since 1973-74 season.

Multiple winners: Kareem Abdul-Jabbar and Mark Eaton (4); George Johnson and Hakeem Olajuwon (3); Manute Bol and Dikembe Mutombo (2).

Year		Gm	No	Avg
1974	Elmore Smith, LA	81	393	4.85
1975	Kareem Abdul-Jabbar, Mil	65	212	3.26
1976	Kareem Abdul-Jabbar, LA	82	338	4.12
1977	Bill Walton, Port.	65	211	3.25
1978	George Johnson, NJ	81	274	3.38
1979	Kareem Abdul-Jabbar, LA	80	316	3.95
1980	Kareem Abdul-Jabbar, LA	82	280	3.41
1981	George Johnson, SA	82	278	3.39
1982	George Johnson, SA	75	234	3.12
1983	Tree Rollins, Atl	80	343	4.29
1984	Mark Eaton, Utah	82	351	4.28
1985	Mark Eaton, Utah	82	456	5.56
1986	Manute Bol, Wash	80	397	4.96
1987	Mark Eaton, Utah	79	321	4.06
1988	Mark Eaton, Utah	82	304	3.71
1989	Manute Bol, G.St.	80	345	4.31
1990	Akeem Olajuwon, Hou	82	376	4.59
1991	Hakeem Olajuwon, Hou	56	221	3.95
1992	David Robinson, SA	68	305	4.49
1993	Hakeem Olajuwon, Hou	82	342	4.17
1994	Dikembe Mutombo, Den	82	336	4.10
1995	Dikembe Mutombo, Den	82	321	3.91

Note: Akeem Olajuwon changed the spelling of his first name to Hakeem during the 1990-91 season.

Steals

Decided by per game average since 1973-74 season.

Multiple winners: Michael Jordan, Micheal Ray Richardson and Alvin Robertson (3); Magic Johnson and John Stockton (2).

Year		Gm	No	Avg
1974	Larry Steele, Port	81	217	2.68
1975	Rick Barry, G.St.	80	228	2.85
1976	Slick Watts, Sea	82	261	3.18
1977	Don Buse, Ind	81	281	3.47
1978	Ron Lee, Pho	82	225	2.74
1979	M.L. Carr, Det	80	197	2.46
1980	Micheal Ray Richardson, NY	82	265	3.23
1981	Magic Johnson, LA	37	127	3.43
1982	Magic Johnson, LA	78	208	2.67
1983	Micheal Ray Richardson, G.St-NJ	64	182	2.84
1984	Rickey Green, Utah	81	215	2.65
1985	Micheal Ray Richardson, NJ	82	243	2.96
1986	Alvin Robertson, SA	82	301	3.67
1987	Alvin Robertson, SA	81	260	3.21
1988	Michael Jordan, Chi	82	259	3.16
1989	John Stockton, Utah	82	263	3.21
1990	Michael Jordan, Chi	82	227	2.77
1991	Alvin Robertson, SA	81	246	3.04
1992	John Stockton, Utah	82	244	2.98
1993	Michael Jordan, Chi	78	221	2.83
1994	Nate McMillan, Sea	73	216	2.96
1995	Scottie Pippen, Chi	79	232	2.94

All-Time NBA Regular Season Leaders

Through the 1994-95 regular season.

CAREER

Players active in 1994-95 in **bold** type.

Points

		Yrs	Gm	Pts	Avg
1	Kareem Abdul-Jabbar	20	1560	38,387	24.6
2	Wilt Chamberlain	14	1045	31,419	30.1
3	**Moses Malone**	19	1329	27,409	20.6
4	Elvin Hayes	16	1303	27,313	21.0
5	Oscar Robertson	14	1040	26,710	25.7
6	John Havlicek	16	1270	26,395	20.8
7	Alex English	15	1193	25,613	21.5
8	**Dominique Wilkins**	13	984	25,389	25.8
9	Jerry West	14	932	25,192	27.0
10	Adrian Dantley	15	955	23,177	24.3
11	Elgin Baylor	14	846	23,149	27.4
12	**Robert Parish**	19	1494	22,883	15.3
13	**Michael Jordan**	10	684	21,998	32.2
14	Larry Bird	13	897	21,791	24.3
15	Hal Greer	15	1122	21,586	19.2
16	**Karl Malone**	10	816	21,237	26.0
17	Walt Bellamy	14	1043	20,941	20.1
18	Bob Pettit	11	792	20,880	26.4
19	George Gervin	10	791	20,708	26.2
20	**Tom Chambers**	14	1094	20,024	18.3
21	**Hakeem Olajuwon**	11	828	19,904	24.0
22	Bernard King	14	874	19,655	22.5
23	Walter Davis	15	1033	19,521	18.9
24	Dolph Schayes	16	1059	19,249	18.2
25	Bob Lanier	14	959	19,248	20.1
26	Gail Goodrich	14	1031	19,181	18.6
27	**Charles Barkley**	11	819	19,091	23.3
28	Reggie Theus	13	1026	19,015	18.5
29	Chet Walker	13	1032	18,831	18.2
30	Isiah Thomas	13	979	18,822	19.2

Scoring Average

Minimum of 400 games or 10,000 points.

		Yrs	Gm	Pts	Avg
1	**Michael Jordan**	10	684	21,998	32.2
2	Wilt Chamberlain	14	1045	31,419	30.1
3	Elgin Baylor	14	846	23,149	27.4
4	Jerry West	14	932	25,192	27.0
5	Bob Pettit	11	792	20,880	26.4
6	George Gervin	10	791	20,708	26.2
7	**Karl Malone**	10	816	21,237	26.0
8	**Dominique Wilkins**	13	984	25,309	25.8
9	Oscar Robertson	14	1040	26,710	25.7
10	Kareem Abdul-Jabbar	20	1560	38,387	24.6
11	Larry Bird	13	897	21,791	24.3
12	Adrian Dantley	15	955	23,177	24.3
13	Pete Maravich	10	658	15,948	24.2
14	**Hakeem Olajuwon**	11	828	19,904	24.0
15	**Patrick Ewing**	10	759	18,077	23.8
16	**Charles Barkley**	11	819	19,091	23.3
17	Rick Barry	10	794	18,395	23.2
18	Paul Arizin	10	713	16,266	22.8
19	George Mikan	9	520	11,764	22.6
20	Bernard King	14	874	19,655	22.5
21	David Thompson	8	509	11,264	22.1
22	Bob McAdoo	14	852	18,787	22.1
23	Julius Erving	11	836	18,364	22.0
24	**Chris Mullin**	10	653	14,243	21.8
25	Alex English	15	1193	25,613	21.5
26	Elvin Hayes	16	1303	27,313	21.0
27	Billy Cunningham	9	654	13,626	20.8
28	**Clyde Drexler**	12	902	18,789	20.8
29	John Havlicek	16	1270	26,395	20.8
30	**Moses Malone**	19	1329	27,409	20.6

All-Time NBA Regular Season Leaders (Cont.)

NBA-ABA Top 20
Points

All-Time combined regular season scoring leaders, including ABA service (1968-76). NBA players with ABA experience are listed in CAPITAL letters. Players active during 1994-95 are in **bold** type.

		Yrs	Pts	Avg
1	Kareem Abdul-Jabbar	20	38,387	24.6
2	Wilt Chamberlain	14	31,419	30.1
3	JULIUS ERVING	16	30,026	24.2
4	MOSES MALONE	21	29,580	20.3
5	DAN ISSEL	15	27,482	22.6
6	Elvin Hayes	16	27,313	21.0
7	Oscar Robertson	14	26,710	25.7
8	GEORGE GERVIN	14	26,595	25.1
9	John Havlicek	16	26,395	20.8
10	Alex English	15	25,613	21.5
11	Dominique Wilkins	13	25,389	25.8
12	RICK BARRY	14	25,279	24.8
13	Jerry West	14	25,192	27.0
14	ARTIS GILMORE	17	24,941	18.8
15	Adrian Dantley	15	23,177	24.3
16	Elgin Baylor	14	23,149	27.4
17	Robert Parish	19	22,883	15.3
18	Michael Jordan	10	21,998	32.2
19	Larry Bird	13	21,791	24.3
20	Hal Greer	15	21,586	19.2

ABA Totals: BARRY (4 yrs, 226 gm, 6884 pts, 30.5 avg); ERVING (5 yrs, 407 gm, 11,662 pts, 28.7 avg); GERVIN (4 yrs, 269 gm, 5887 pts, 21.9 avg); GILMORE (5 yrs, 420 gm, 9362 pts, 22.3 avg); ISSEL (6 yrs, 500 gm, 12,823 pts, 25.6 avg); MALONE (2 yrs, 126 gm, 2171 pts, 17.2 avg).

Field Goals

		Yrs	FG	Att	Pct
1	Kareem Abdul-Jabbar	20	15,837	28,307	.559
2	Wilt Chamberlain	14	12,681	23,497	.540
3	Elvin Hayes	16	10,976	24,272	.452
4	Alex English	15	10,659	21,036	.507
5	John Havlicek	16	10,513	23,930	.439
6	Dominique Wilkins	13	9,516	20,504	.464
7	Oscar Robertson	14	9,508	19,620	.485
8	Moses Malone	19	9,435	19,225	.491
9	Robert Parish	19	9,424	17,530	.538
10	Jerry West	14	9,016	19,032	.474

Note: If field goals made in the ABA are included, consider these NBA-ABA totals: Julius Erving (11,818), Dan Issel (10,431), George Gervin (10,368), Moses Malone (10,277), Rick Barry (9,695) and Artis Gilmore (9,403).

Free Throws

		Yrs	FT	Att	Pct
1	Moses Malone	19	8531	11,090	.769
2	Oscar Robertson	14	7694	9,185	.838
3	Jerry West	14	7160	8,801	.814
4	Dolph Schayes	16	6979	8,273	.844
5	Adrian Dantley	15	6832	8,351	.818
6	Kareem Abdul-Jabbar	20	6712	9,304	.721
7	Bob Pettit	11	6182	8,119	.761
8	Wilt Chamberlain	14	6057	11,862	.511
9	Elgin Baylor	14	5763	7,391	.780
10	Dominique Wilkins	13	5721	7,046	.812

Note: If free throws made in the ABA are included, consider these totals: Moses Malone (9,018), Dan Issel (6,591), Julius Erving (6,256) and Artis Gilmore (6,132).

Assists

		Yrs	Gm	No	Avg
1	John Stockton	11	898	10,394	11.6
2	Magic Johnson	12	874	9921	11.4
3	Oscar Robertson	14	1040	9887	9.5
4	Isiah Thomas	13	979	9061	9.3
5	Maurice Cheeks	15	1101	7392	6.7
6	Lenny Wilkens	15	1077	7211	6.7
7	Bob Cousy	14	924	6955	7.5
8	Guy Rodgers	12	892	6917	7.8
9	Nate Archibald	13	876	6476	7.4
10	John Lucas	14	928	6454	7.0

Rebounds

		Yrs	Gm	No	Avg
1	Wilt Chamberlain	14	1045	23,924	22.9
2	Bill Russell	13	963	21,620	22.5
3	Kareem Abdul-Jabbar	20	1560	17,440	11.2
4	Elvin Hayes	16	1303	16,279	12.5
5	Moses Malone	19	1329	16,212	12.2
6	Nate Thurmond	14	964	14,464	15.0
7	Robert Parish	19	1494	14,323	9.6
8	Walt Bellamy	14	1043	14,241	13.7
9	Wes Unseld	13	984	13,769	14.0
10	Jerry Lucas	11	829	12,942	15.6

Note: If rebounds pulled down in the ABA are included, consider the following totals: Moses Malone (17,834) and Artis Gilmore (16,330).

Years Played

		Yrs	Career	Gm
1	Kareem Abdul-Jabbar	20	1969-89	1560
2	Robert Parish	19	1976—	1494
	Moses Malone	19	1976—	1329
4	James Edwards	18	1977—	1140
5	Four tied with 16 each.			

Note: If ABA records are included, consider the following year totals: Moses Malone (21, 1974—); Artis Gilmore (17, 1971-88); Caldwell Jones (17, 1973-90); Julius Erving (16, 1971-87); Dan Issel (15, 1970-85); Billy Paultz (15, 1970-85).

Games Played

		Yrs	Career	Gm
1	Kareem Abdul-Jabbar	20	1970-89	1560
2	Robert Parish	19	1976—	1494
3	Moses Malone	19	1976—	1329
4	Elvin Hayes	16	1969-84	1303
5	John Havlicek	16	1963-78	1270

Note: If ABA records are included, consider the following game totals: Moses Malone (1,455); Artis Gilmore (1,329); Caldwell Jones (1,299); Julius Erving (1,243); Dan Issel (1,218); Billy Paultz (1,124).

Personal Fouls

		Yrs	Gm	Fouls	DQ
1	Kareem Abdul-Jabbar	20	1560	4657	48
2	Robert Parish	19	1494	4323	86
3	Elvin Hayes	16	1303	4193	53
4	James Edwards	18	1140	3981	95
5	Jack Sikma	14	1107	3879	80

Note: If ABA records are included, consider the following personal foul totals: Artis Gilmore (4,529) and Caldwell Jones (4,436).

Disqualifications

		Yrs	Gm	No
1	Vern Mikkelsen	10	699	127
2	Walter Dukes	8	553	121
3	Charlie Share	8	555	105
4	Paul Arizin	10	713	101
5	Darryl Dawkins	14	726	100

SINGLE SEASON

Scoring Average

		Season	Avg
1	Wilt Chamberlain, Phi	1961-62	50.4
2	Wilt Chamberlain, SF	1962-63	44.8
3	Wilt Chamberlain, Phi	1960-61	38.4
4	Elgin Baylor, LA	1961-62	38.3
5	Wilt Chamberlain, Phi	1959-60	37.6
6	Michael Jordan, Chi	1986-87	37.1
7	Wilt Chamberlain, SF	1963-64	36.9
8	Rick Barry, SF	1966-67	35.6
9	Michael Jordan, Chi	1987-88	35.0
10	Elgin Baylor, LA	1960-61	34.8
	Kareem Abdul-Jabbar, Mil	1971-72	34.8

Field Goal Pct.

		Season	Pct
1	Wilt Chamberlain, LA	1972-73	.727
2	Wilt Chamberlain, SF	1966-67	.683
3	Artis Gilmore, Chi	1980-81	.670
4	Artis Gilmore, Chi	1981-82	.652
5	Wilt Chamberlain, LA	1971-72	.649

Free Throw Pct.

		Season	Pct
1	Calvin Murphy, Hou	1980-81	.958
2	Mahmond Abdul-Rauf, Den	1993-94	.956
3	Mark Price, Cle	1992-93	.948
4	Mark Price, Cle	1991-92	.947
	Rick Barry, Hou	1978-79	.947

3-Pt Field Goal Pct.

		Season	Pct
1	Steve Kerr, Chi	1994-95	.524
2	Jon Sundvold, Mia	1988-89	.522
3	Detlef Schrempf, Sea	1994-95	.514
4	Steve Kerr, Cle	1989-90	.507
5	Craig Hodges, Mil-Pho	1987-88	.491

Assists

		Season	Avg
1	John Stockton, Utah	1989-90	14.5
2	John Stockton, Utah	1990-91	14.2
3	Isiah Thomas, Det	1984-85	13.9
4	John Stockton, Utah	1987-88	13.8
5	John Stockton, Utah	1991-92	13.7
6	John Stockton, Utah	1988-89	13.6
7	Kevin Porter, Det	1978-79	13.4
8	Magic Johnson, LA Lakers	1983-84	13.1
9	Magic Johnson, LA Lakers	1988-89	12.8
10	Magic Johnson, LA Lakers	1984-85	12.6
	John Stockton, Utah	1993-94	12.6

Rebounds

		Season	Avg
1	Wilt Chamberlain, Phi	1960-61	27.2
2	Wilt Chamberlain, Phi	1959-60	27.0
3	Wilt Chamberlain, Phi	1961-62	25.7
4	Bill Russell, Bos	1963-64	24.7
5	Wilt Chamberlain, Phi	1965-66	24.6

Blocked Shots

		Season	Avg
1	Mark Eaton, Utah	1984-85	5.56
2	Manute Bol, Wash	1985-86	4.96
3	Elmore Smith, LA	1973-74	4.85
4	Mark Eaton, Utah	1985-86	4.61
5	Hakeem Olajuwon, Hou	1989-90	4.59

Steals

		Season	Avg
1	Alvin Robertson, SA	1985-86	3.67
2	Don Buse, Ind	1976-77	3.47
3	Magic Johnson, LA Lakers	1980-81	3.43
4	Micheal Ray Richardson, NY	1979-80	3.23
5	Alvin Robertson, SA	1986-87	3.21

SINGLE GAME

Points

	Date	FG-FT	Pts
Wilt Chamberlain, Phi vs NY	3/2/62	36-28	100
Wilt Chamberlain, Phi vs LA***	12/8/61	31-16	78
Wilt Chamberlain, Phi vs Chi	1/13/62	29-15	73
David Thompson, Den at Det	4/9/78	28-17	73
Wilt Chamberlain, SF at LA	11/3/62	29-14	72
Elgin Baylor, LA at NY	11/15/60	28-15	71
David Robinson, SA at LAC	4/24/94	26-18	71
Wilt Chamberlain, SF at Syr	3/10/63	27-16	70
Michael Jordan, Chi at Cle*	3/28/90	23-21	69
Wilt Chamberlain, Phi at Chi	12/16/67	30- 8	68
Pete Maravich, NO vs NYK	2/25/77	26-16	68
Wilt Chamberlain, Phi vs NY	3/9/61	27-13	67
Wilt Chamberlain, Phi at St. L	2/17/62	26-15	67
Wilt Chamberlain, Phi vs NY	2/25/62	25-17	67
Wilt Chamberlain, SF vs LA	1/11/63	28-11	67
Wilt Chamberlain, LA vs Pho	2/9/69	29- 8	66
Wilt Chamberlain, Phi at Cin	2/13/62	24-17	65
Wilt Chamberlain, Phi at St. L	2/27/62	25-15	65
Wilt Chamberlain, Phi vs LA	2/7/66	28- 9	65
Elgin Baylor, Mpls vs Bos	11/8/59	25-14	64
Rick Barry, G.St. vs Port	3/26/74	30- 4	64
Michael Jordan, Chi vs Orl	1/16/93	27- 9	64

*Overtime; ***Triple overtime.
Note: Wilt Chamberlain's 100-point game vs New York was
played at Hershey, Pa.

Field Goals

	Date	FG	Att
Wilt Chamberlain, Phi vs NY	3/2/62	36	63
Wilt Chamberlain, Phi vs LA***	12/8/61	31	62
Wilt Chamberlain, Phi at Chi	12/16/67	30	40
Rick Barry, G.St. vs Port	2/26/74	30	45
Wilt Chamberlain made 29 four times.			

***Triple overtime.

Free Throws

	Date	FT	Att
Wilt Chamberlain, Phi vs NY	3/2/62	28	32
Adrian Dantley, Utah vs Hou	1/4/84	28	29
Adrian Dantley, Utah vs Den	11/25/83	27	31
Adrian Dantley, Utah vs Dal	10/31/80	26	29
Michael Jordan, Chi vs NJ	2/26/87	26	27

3-Pt Field Goals

	Date	No
Brian Shaw, Mia at Mil	4/8/93	10
Joe Dumars, Det vs Min	11/8/94	10
Dale Ellis, Sea vs LA Clippers	4/20/90	9
Michael Adams, Den at LA Clippers	4/12/91	9
Seven tied with 8 each.		

All-Time NBA Regular Season Leaders (Cont.)

Assists

	Date	No
Scott Skiles, Orl vs Den	12/30/90	30
Kevin Porter, NJ vs Hou	2/24/78	29
Bob Cousy, Bos vs Mpls	2/27/59	28
Guy Rodgers, SF vs St.L	3/14/63	28
John Stockton, Utah vs SA	1/15/91	28

Rebounds

	Date	No
Wilt Chamberlain, Phi vs Bos	11/24/60	55
Bill Russell, Bos vs Syr	2/5/60	51
Bill Russell, Bos vs Phi	11/16/57	49
Bill Russell, Bos vs Det	3/11/65	49
Wilt Chamberlain, Phi vs Syr	2/6/60	45
Wilt Chamberlain, Phi vs LA	1/21/61	45

Blocked Shots

	Date	No
Elmore Smith, LA vs Port	10/28/73	17
Manute Bol, Wash vs Atl	1/25/86	15
Manute Bol, Wash vs Ind	2/26/87	15
Shaquille O'Neal, Orl at NJ	11/20/93	15

Steals

	Date	No
Larry Kenon, San Antonio at KC	12/26/76	11

11 different players tied with 10 each, including Alvin Robertson who had 10 steals in a game four times.

All-Time Winningest NBA Coaches

Top 25 NBA career victories through the 1994-95 season. Career, regular season and playoff records are noted along with NBA titles won. Coaches active during 1994-95 season in **bold** type.

		Yrs	Career			Regular Season			Playoffs			
			W	L	Pct	W	L	Pct	W	L	Pct	NBA Titles
1	Red Auerbach	20	1037	548	.654	938	479	.662	99	69	.589	9 (1957, 59-66)
2	Lenny Wilkens	22	1028	878	.539	968	814	.543	60	64	.484	1 (1979)
3	Dick Motta	23	948	979	.492	892	909	.495	56	70	.444	1 (1978)
4	Bill Fitch	22	917	993	.480	862	942	.478	55	51	.519	1 (1981)
5	Jack Ramsay	21	908	841	.519	864	783	.525	44	58	.431	1 (1977)
6	Pat Riley	13	893	374	.705	756	299	.717	137	75	.646	4 (1982,85,87-88)
7	Don Nelson	18	868	665	.566	817	604	.575	51	61	.455	None
8	Cotton Fitzsimmons	19	839	791	.515	805	745	.519	34	46	.425	None
9	Gene Shue	22	814	908	.473	784	861	.477	30	47	.390	None
10	Red Holzman	18	754	652	.536	696	604	.535	58	48	.547	2 (1970, 73)
	John MacLeod	18	754	711	.515	707	657	.518	47	54	.465	None
12	Doug Moe	15	661	579	.533	628	529	.543	33	50	.398	None
13	Chuck Daly	12	638	427	.599	564	379	.598	74	48	.607	2 (1989-90)
14	K.C. Jones	10	603	309	.661	522	252	.674	81	57	.587	2 (1984,86)
15	Al Attles	14	588	548	.518	557	518	.518	31	30	.508	1 (1975)
16	Larry Brown	12	572	446	.562	533	407	.567	39	39	.500	None
17	Billy Cunningham	8	520	235	.689	454	196	.698	66	39	.629	1 (1983)
18	Alex Hannum	12	518	446	.536	471	412	.533	47	34	.580	2 (1958, 67)
19	Jerry Sloan	10	487	350	.582	458	314	.593	29	36	.446	None
20	John Kundla	11	485	338	.589	423	302	.583	62	36	.633	5 (1949-50, 52-54)
21	Kevin Loughery	17	480	683	.413	474	662	.417	6	21	.222	None
22	Tommy Heinsohn	9	474	296	.616	427	263	.619	47	33	.588	2 (1974,76)
23	Larry Costello	10	467	323	.591	430	300	.589	37	23	.617	1 (1971)
24	Mike Fratello	10	433	355	.549	414	327	.559	19	28	.404	None
25	Del Harris	10	406	411	.497	380	375	.503	26	36	.419	None

Note: The NBA does not recognize records from the National Basketball League (1937-49), the American Basketball League (1961-62) or the American Basketball Assn. (1968-76), so the following NBL, ABL and ABA overall coaching records are not included above: NBL—**John Kundla** (51-19 and a title in 1 year). ABA—**Larry Brown** (249-129 in 4 yrs), **Alex Hannum** (194-164 and one title in 4 yrs), **K.C. Jones** (30-58 in 1 yr); **Kevin Loughery** (189-95 and one title in 3 yrs).

Where They Coached

Attles—Golden St. (1970-80,80-83); **Auerbach**—Washington (1946-49); Tri-Cities (1949-50); Boston (1950-66); **Brown**—Denver (1976-79), New Jersey (1981-83), San Antonio (1988-92), LA Clippers (1992-93), Indiana (1993—); **Costello**—Milwaukee (1968-76), Chicago (1978-79); **Cunningham**—Philadelphia (1977-85); **Daly**—Cleveland (1981-82), Detroit (1983-92), New Jersey (1992-94); **Fitch**—Cleveland (1970-79), Boston (1979-83), Houston (1983-88), New Jersey (1989-92), LA Clippers (1994—); **Fitzsimmons**—Phoenix (1970-72), Atlanta (1972-76), Buffalo (1977-78), Kansas City (1978-84), San Antonio (1984-86), Phoenix (1988-92); **Fratello**—Atlanta (1980-90), Cleveland (1993—).
Hannum—St. Louis (1957-58), Syracuse (1960-63), San Francisco (1963-66), Phila. 76ers (1966-68), Houston (1970-71); **Harris**—Houston (1979-83), Milwaukee (1987-92), LA Lakers (1994—); **Heinsohn**—Boston (1969-77); **Holzman**—Milwaukee-St. Louis Hawks (1954-57), NY Knicks (1968-77,78-82); **Jones**—Washington (1973-76), Boston (1983-88), Seattle (1990-92); **Kundla**—Minneapolis (1948-57,58-59); **Loughery**—Philadelphia (1972-73), NY-NJ Nets (1976-81), Atlanta (1981-83), Chicago (1983-85), Washington (1985-88), Miami (1991-95); **MacLeod**—Phoenix (1973-87), Dallas (1987-89), NY Knicks (1990-91); **Moe**—San Antonio (1976-80), Denver (1981-90), Philadelphia (1992-93). **Motta**—Chicago (1968-76), Washington (1976-80), Dallas (1980-87), Sacramento (1990-91), Dallas (1994—); **Nelson**—Milwaukee (1976-87), Golden St. (1988-95), New York (1995—); **Ramsay**—Philadelphia (1968-72), Buffalo (1972-76), Portland (1976-86), Indiana (1986-89); **Riley**—LA Lakers (1981-90), New York (1991-95); **Shue**—Baltimore (1967-73), Philadelphia (1973-77), San Diego Clippers (1978-80), Washington (1980-86), LA Clippers (1987-89); **Sloan**—Chicago (1979-82), Utah (1988—); **Wilkens**—Seattle (1969-72), Portland (1974-76), Seattle (1977-85), Cleveland (1986-93), Atlanta (1993—).

Top Winning Percentages

Minimum of 350 victories, including playoffs; coaches active during 1994-95 season in **bold** type.

		Yrs	W	L	Pct
1	**Pat Riley**	13	893	374	.705
2	**Phil Jackson**	6	408	178	.696
3	Billy Cunningham	8	520	235	.689
4	K.C. Jones	10	603	309	.661
5	Red Auerbach	20	1037	548	.654
6	Tommy Heinsohn	9	474	296	.616
7	Chuck Daly	12	638	427	.599
8	Larry Costello	10	467	323	.591
9	John Kundla	11	485	338	.589
10	**Jerry Sloan**	10	487	350	.582
11	Bill Sharman	7	368	267	.580
12	Al Cervi	9	359	267	.573
13	**Don Nelson**	18	868	665	.566
14	Joe Lapchick	9	356	277	.562
15	**Larry Brown**	12	572	446	.562
16	**Mike Fratello**	10	433	355	.549
17	Bill Russell	8	375	317	.542
18	**Lenny Wilkens**	22	1028	878	.539
19	Alex Hannum	12	518	446	.537
20	Red Holzman	18	754	651	.536
21	Doug Moe	15	661	579	.533
22	Richie Guerin	8	353	325	.521
23	Jack Ramsay	21	908	841	.519
24	Al Attles	14	588	548	.518
25	Cotton Fitzsimmons	19	839	791	.515
26	John MacLeod	18	754	711	.515

Active Coaches' Victories

Through 1994-95 season, including playoffs.

		Yrs	W	L	Pct
1	Lenny Wilkens, Atlanta	22	1028	878	.539
2	Dick Motta, Dallas	23	948	979	.492
3	Bill Fitch, LA Clippers	22	917	993	.480
4	Pat Riley, Miami	13	893	374	.705
5	Don Nelson, New York	18	868	665	.566
6	Larry Brown, Indiana	12	572	446	.562
7	Jerry Sloan, Utah	10	487	350	.582
8	Mike Fratello, Cleveland	10	433	355	.549
9	Phil Jackson, Chicago	6	408	178	.696
10	Del Harris, LA Lakers	10	406	411	.497
11	George Karl, Seattle	8	343	291	.541
12	Rick Adelman, Golden St.	6	327	187	.636
13	Jim Lynam, Washington	8	275	338	.449
14	Bernie Bickerstaff, Denver	6	233	230	.503
15	Rudy Tomjanovich, Houston	4	212	121	.637
16	Paul Westphal, Phoenix	2	202	88	.697
17	Mike Dunleavy, Milwaukee	5	196	237	.453
18	Bob Hill, San Antonio	5	197	189	.510
19	Allan Bristow, Charlotte	4	171	170	.501
20	Doug Collins, Detroit	3	150	126	.543
21	John Lucas, Philadelphia	3	124	115	.519
22	Brian Hill, Orlando	2	118	70	.628
23	Gary St. Jean, Sacramento	3	92	154	.374
24	P.J. Carlesimo, Portland	1	44	41	.518
25	Butch Beard, New Jersey	1	30	52	.366
26	Bill Blair, Minnesota	1	21	61	.256
27	M.L. Carr, Boston	0	0	0	.000
	Brendan Malone, Toronto	0	0	0	.000
	Brian Winters, Vancouver	0	0	0	.000

Annual Awards
Most Valuable Player

The Maurice Podoloff Trophy for regular season MVP. Named after the first commissioner (then president) of the NBA. Winners first selected by the NBA players (1956-80) then a national panel of pro basketball writers and broadcasters (since 1981). Winners' scoring averages are provided; (*) indicates led league.

Multiple winners: Kareem Abdul-Jabbar (6); Bill Russell (5); Wilt Chamberlain (4); Larry Bird, Magic Johnson, Michael Jordan and Moses Malone (3); Bob Pettit (2).

Year		Avg
1956	Bob Pettit, St. Louis, F	25.7*
1957	Bob Cousy, Boston, G	20.6
1958	Bill Russell, Boston, C	16.6
1959	Bob Pettit, St. Louis, F	29.2*
1960	Wilt Chamberlain, Philadelphia, C	37.6*
1961	Bill Russell, Boston, C	16.9
1962	Bill Russell, Boston, C	18.9
1963	Bill Russell, Boston, C	16.8
1964	Oscar Robertson, Cincinnati, G	31.4
1965	Bill Russell, Boston, C	14.1
1966	Wilt Chamberlain, Philadelphia, C	33.5*
1967	Wilt Chamberlain, Philadelphia, C	24.1
1968	Wilt Chamberlain, Philadelphia, C	24.3
1969	Wes Unseld, Baltimore, C	13.8
1970	Willis Reed, New York, C	21.7
1971	Lew Alcindor, Milwaukee, C	31.7*
1972	Kareem Abdul-Jabbar, Milwaukee, C	34.8*
1973	Dave Cowens, Boston, C	20.5
1974	Kareem Abdul-Jabbar, LA, C	27.0
1975	Bob McAdoo, Buffalo, F	34.5*

Year		Avg
1976	Kareem Abdul-Jabbar, LA, C	27.7
1977	Kareem Abdul-Jabbar, LA, C	26.2
1978	Bill Walton, Portland, C	18.9
1979	Moses Malone, Houston, C	24.8
1980	Kareem Abdul-Jabbar, LA, C	24.8
1981	Julius Erving, Philadelphia, F	24.6
1982	Moses Malone, Houston, C	31.1
1983	Moses Malone, Philadelphia, C	24.5
1984	Larry Bird, Boston, F	24.2
1985	Larry Bird, Boston, F	28.7
1986	Larry Bird, Boston, F	25.8
1987	Magic Johnson, LA Lakers, G	23.9
1988	Michael Jordan, Chicago, G	35.0*
1989	Magic Johnson, LA Lakers, G	22.5
1990	Magic Johnson, LA Lakers, G	22.3
1991	Michael Jordan, Chicago, G	31.5*
1992	Michael Jordan, Chicago, G	30.1*
1993	Charles Barkley, Phoenix, F	25.6
1994	Hakeem Olajuwon, Houston, C	27.3
1995	David Robinson, San Antonio, C	27.6

Note: Lew Alcindor changed his name to Kareem Abdul-Jabbar after the 1970-71 season.

Annual Awards (Cont.)
Rookie of the Year

The Eddie Gottlieb Trophy for outstanding rookie of the regular season. Named after the pro basketball pioneer and owner-coach of the first NBA champion Philadelphia Warriors. Winners selected by a national panel of pro basketball writers and broadcasters. Winners' scoring averages provided; (*) indicated led league; winners who were also named MVP are in **bold** type.

Year		Avg	Year		Avg
1953	Don Meineke, Ft. Wayne, F	10.8	1975	Keith Wilkes, Golden St., F	14.2
1954	Ray Felix, Baltimore, C	17.6	1976	Alvan Adams, Phoenix, C	19.0
1955	Bob Pettit, Milwaukee Hawks, F	20.4	1977	Adrian Dantley, Buffalo, F	20.3
1956	Maurice Stokes, Rochester, F/C	16.8	1978	Walter Davis, Phoenix, G	24.2
1957	Tommy Heinsohn, Boston, F	16.2	1979	Phil Ford, Kansas City, G	15.9
1958	Woody Sauldsberry, Philadelphia, F/C	12.8			
1959	Elgin Baylor, Minneapolis, F	24.9	1980	Larry Bird, Boston, F	21.3
			1981	Darrell Griffith, Utah, G	20.6
1960	**Wilt Chamberlain**, Philadelphia, C	37.6*	1982	Buck Williams, New Jersey, F	15.5
1961	Oscar Robertson, Cincinnati, G	30.5	1983	Terry Cummings, San Diego, F	23.7
1962	Walt Bellamy, Chicago Packers, C	31.6	1984	Ralph Sampson, Houston, C	21.0
1963	Terry Dischinger, Chicago Zephyrs, F	25.5	1985	Michael Jordan, Chicago, G	28.2
1964	Jerry Lucas, Cincinnati, F/C	17.7	1986	Patrick Ewing, New York, C	20.0
1965	Willis Reed, New York, C	19.5	1987	Chuck Person, Indiana, F	18.8
1966	Rick Barry, San Francisco, F	25.7	1988	Mark Jackson, New York, G	13.6
1967	Dave Bing, Detroit, G	20.0	1989	Mitch Richmond, Golden St., G	22.0
1968	Earl Monroe, Baltimore, G	24.3			
1969	**Wes Unseld**, Baltimore, C	13.8	1990	David Robinson, San Antonio, C	24.3
			1991	Derrick Coleman, New Jersey, F	18.4
1970	Lew Alcindor, Milwaukee Bucks, C	28.8	1992	Larry Johnson, Charlotte, F	19.2
1971	Dave Cowens, Boston, C	17.0	1993	Shaquille O'Neal, Orlando, C	23.4
	& Geoff Petrie, Portland, F	24.8	1994	Chris Webber, Golden St., F	17.5
1972	Sidney Wicks, Portland, F	24.5	1995	Grant Hill, Detroit, F	19.9
1973	Bob McAdoo, Buffalo, C/F	18.0		& Jason Kidd, Dallas, G	11.7
1974	Ernie DiGregorio, Buffalo, G	15.2			

Note: The Chicago Packers changed their name to the Zephyrs after 1961-62 season. Also, Lew Alcindor changed his name to Kareem Abdul-Jabbar after the 1970-71 season.

Sixth Man Award

Awarded to the Best Player Off the Bench for the regular season. Winners selected by a national panel of pro basketball writers and broadcasters.
   Multiple winners: Kevin McHale, Ricky Pierce and Detlef Schrempf (2).

Year		Year		Year	
1983	Bobby Jones, Phi., F	1988	Roy Tarpley, Dal., F	1992	Detlef Schrempf, Ind., F
1984	Kevin McHale, Bos., F	1989	Eddie Johnson, Pho., F	1993	Cliff Robinson, Port., F
1985	Kevin McHale, Bos., F	1990	Ricky Pierce, Mil., G/F	1994	Dell Curry, Char., G
1986	Bill Walton, Bos., F/C	1991	Detlef Schrempf, Ind., F	1995	Anthony Mason, NY, F
1987	Ricky Pierce, Mil., G/F				

Number One Draft Choices

Overall first choices in the NBA draft since the abolition of the territorial draft in 1966. Players who became Rookie of the Year are in **bold** type. The draft lottery began in 1985.

Year		Overall 1st Pick	Year		Overall 1st Pick
1966	New York	Cazzie Russell, Michigan	1982	LA Lakers	James Worthy, N. Carolina
1967	Detroit	Jimmy Walker, Providence	1983	Houston	**Ralph Sampson**, Virginia
1968	San Diego	Elvin Hayes, Houston	1984	Houston	Akeem Olajuwon, Houston
1969	Milwaukee	**Lew Alcindor**, UCLA	1985	New York	**Patrick Ewing**, Georgetown
			1986	Cleveland	Brad Daugherty, N. Carolina
1970	Detroit	Bob Lanier, St. Bonaventure	1987	San Antonio	**David Robinson**, Navy
1971	Cleveland	Austin Carr, Notre Dame	1988	LA Clippers	Danny Manning, Kansas
1972	Portland	LaRue Martin, Loyola-Chicago	1989	Sacramento	Pervis Ellison, Louisville
1973	Philadelphia	Doug Collins, Illinois St.			
1974	Portland	Bill Walton, UCLA	1990	New Jersey	**Derrick Coleman**, Syracuse
1975	Atlanta	David Thompson, N.C. State	1991	Charlotte	**Larry Johnson**, UNLV
1976	Houston	John Lucas, Maryland	1992	Orlando	**Shaquille O'Neal**, LSU
1977	Milwaukee	Kent Benson, Indiana	1993	Orlando	**Chris Webber**, Michigan
1978	Portland	Mychal Thompson, Minnesota	1994	Milwaukee	Glenn Robinson, Purdue
1979	LA Lakers	Magic Johnson, Michigan St.	1995	Golden St.	Joe Smith, Maryland
1980	Golden St	Joe Barry Carroll, Purdue			
1981	Dallas	Mark Aguirre, DePaul			

Note: Lew Alcindor changed his name to Kareem Abdul-Jabbar after the 1970-71 season; Akeem Olajuwon changed his first name to Hakeem in 1991; and David Robinson joined NBA for 1989-90 season after fulfilling military obligation.

Defensive Player of the Year

Awarded to the Best Defensive Player for the regular season. Winners selected by a national panel of pro basketball writers and broadcasters.

Multiple winners: Mark Eaton, Sidney Moncrief, Hakeem Olajuwon and Dennis Rodman (2).

Year		Year		Year	
1983	Sidney Moncrief, Mil., G	1988	Michael Jordan, Chi., G	1992	David Robinson, SA, C
1984	Sidney Moncrief, Mil., G	1989	Mark Eaton, Utah, C	1993	Hakeem Olajuwon, Hou., C
1985	Mark Eaton, Utah, C	1990	Dennis Rodman, Det., F	1994	Hakeem Olajuwon, Hou., C
1986	Alvin Robertson, SA, G	1991	Dennis Rodman, Det., F	1995	Dikembe Mutombo, Den., C
1987	Michael Cooper, LAL, F				

Most Improved Player

Awarded to the Most Improved Player for the regular season. Winners selected by a national panel of pro basketball writers and broadcasters.

Year		Year		Year	
1986	Alvin Robertson, SA, G	1990	Rony Seikaly, Mia., C	1993	Mahmoud Abdul-Rauf, Den., G
1987	Dale Ellis, Sea., G	1991	Scott Skiles, Orl., G	1994	Don MacLean, Wash., F
1988	Kevin Duckworth, Port., C	1992	Pervis Ellison, Wash., C	1995	Dana Barros, Phi., G
1989	Kevin Johnson, Pho., G				

Coach of the Year

The Red Auerbach Trophy for outstanding coach of the year. Renamed in 1967 for the former Boston coach who led the Celtics to nine NBA titles. Winners selected by a national panel of pro basketball writers and broadcasters. Previous season and winning season records are provided; (*) indicates division title.

Multiple winners: Don Nelson (3); Bill Fitch, Cotton Fitzsimmons, Pat Riley and Gene Shue (2).

Year		Improvement	Year		Improvement
1963	Harry Gallatin, St. L	29-51 to 48-32	1980	Bill Fitch, Bos	29-53 to 61-21*
1964	Alex Hannum, SF	31-49 to 48-32*	1981	Jack McKinney, Ind	37-45 to 44-38
1965	Red Auerbach, Bos	59-21* to 61-18*	1982	Gene Shue, Wash	39-43 to 43-39
1966	Dolph Schayes, Phi	40-40 to 55-25*	1983	Don Nelson, Mil	55-27* to 51-31*
1967	Johnny Kerr, Chi	Expan. to 33-48	1984	Frank Layden, Utah	30-52 to 45-37*
1968	Richie Guerin, St. L	39-42 to 56-26*	1985	Don Nelson, Mil	50-32* to 59-23*
1969	Gene Shue, Balt	36-46 to 57-25*	1986	Mike Fratello, Atl	34-48 to 50-32
1970	Red Holzman, NY	54-28 to 60-22*	1987	Mike Schuler, Port	40-42 to 49-33
1971	Dick Motta, Chi	39-43 to 51-31	1988	Doug Moe, Den	37-45 to 54-28*
1972	Bill Sharman, LA	48-34* to 69-13*	1989	Cotton Fitzsimmons, Pho	28-54 to 55-27
1973	Tommy Heinsohn, Bos	56-26* to 68-14*	1990	Pat Riley, LA Lakers	57-25* to 63-19*
1974	Ray Scott, Det	40-42 to 52-30	1991	Don Chaney, Hou	41-41 to 52-30
1975	Phil Johnson, KC-Omaha	33-49 to 44-38	1992	Don Nelson, GS	44-38 to 55-27
1976	Bill Fitch, Cle	40-42 to 49-33*	1993	Pat Riley, NY	51-31 to 60-22
1977	Tom Nissalke, Hou	40-42 to 49-33*	1994	Lenny Wilkens, Atl	43-39 to 57-25*
1978	Hubie Brown, Atl	31-51 to 41-41	1995	Del Harris, LA Lakers	33-49 to 48-34
1979	Cotton Fitzsimmons, KC	31-51 to 48-34*			

World Championships

The World Basketball Championships for men and women have been played regularly at four-year intervals (give or take a year) since 1970. The men's tournament began in 1950 and the women's in 1953. The Federation Internationale de Basketball Amateur (FIBA), which governs the World and Olympic tournaments, was founded in 1932. FIBA first allowed professional players from the NBA to participate in 1994.

MEN

Multiple wins: Soviet Union, USA and Yugoslavia (3); Brazil (2).

Year	
1950	**Argentina**, United States, Chile
1954	**United States**, Brazil, Philippines
1959	**Brazil**, United States, Chile
1963	**Brazil**, Yugoslavia, Soviet Union
1967	**Soviet Union**, Yugoslavia, Brazil
1970	**Yugoslavia**, Brazil, Soviet Union
1974	**Soviet Union**, Yugoslavia, United States
1978	**Yugoslavia**, Soviet Union, Brazil
1982	**Soviet Union**, United States, Yugoslavia
1986	**United States**, Soviet Union, Yugoslavia
1990	**Yugoslavia**, Soviet Union, United States
1994	**United States**, Russia, Croatia
1998	at Athens (August)

WOMEN

Multiple wins: Soviet Union (6); USA (5).

Year	
1953	**United States**, Chile, France
1957	**United States**, Soviet Union, Czechoslovakia
1959	**Soviet Union**, Bulgaria, Czechoslovakia
1964	**Soviet Union**, Czechoslovakia, Bulgaria
1967	**Soviet Union**, South Korea, Czechoslovakia
1971	**Soviet Union**, Czechoslovakia, Brazil
1975	**Soviet Union**, Japan, Czechoslovakia
1979	**United States**, South Korea, Canada
1983	**Soviet Union**, United States, China
1986	**United States**, Soviet Union, Canada
1990	**United States**, Yugoslavia, Cuba
1994	**Brazil**, China, United States
1998	at Berlin (July)

American Basketball Association
ABA Finals

The American Basketball Assn. began play in 1967-68 as a 10-team rival of the 21-year-old NBA. The ABA, which introduced the three-point basket, a multi-colored ball and the All-Star Game Slam Dunk Contest, lasted nine seasons before folding following the 1975-76 season. Four ABA teams—Denver, Indiana, New York and San Antonio—survived to enter the NBA in 1976-77. The NBA also adopted the three-point basket (in 1979-80) and the All-Star Game Slam Dunk Contest. The older league, however, refused to take in the ABA ball.

Multiple winners: Indiana (3); New York (2).

Year	Winner	Head Coach	Series	Loser	Head Coach
1968	Pittsburgh Pipers	Vince Cazetta	4-3 (WLLWLWW)	New Orleans Bucs	Babe McCarthy
1969	Oakland Oaks	Alex Hannum	4-1 (WLWWW)	Indiana Pacers	Bob Leonard
1970	Indiana Pacers	Bob Leonard	4-2 (WWLWLW)	Los Angeles Stars	Bill Sharman
1971	Utah Stars	Bill Sharman	4-3 (WWLLWLW)	Kentucky Colonels	Frank Ramsey
1972	Indiana Pacers	Bob Leonard	4-2 (WLWLWW)	New York Nets	Lou Carnesecca
1973	Indiana Pacers	Bob Leonard	4-3 (WLLWWLW)	Kentucky Colonels	Joe Mullaney
1974	New York Nets	Kevin Loughery	4-1 (WWWLW)	Utah Stars	Joe Mullaney
1975	Kentucky Colonels	Hubie Brown	4-1 (WWWLW)	Indiana Pacers	Bob Leonard
1976	New York Nets	Kevin Loughery	4-2 (WLWLWW)	Denver Nuggets	Larry Brown

Most Valuable Player

Winners' scoring averages provided; (*) indicates led league.

Multiple winners: Julius Erving (3); Mel Daniels (2).

Year		Avg
1968	Connie Hawkins, Pittsburgh, C	26.8*
1969	Mel Daniels, Indiana, C	24.0
1970	Spencer Haywood, Denver, C	30.0*
1971	Mel Daniels, Indiana, C	21.0
1972	Artis Gilmore, Kentucky, C	23.8
1973	Billy Cunningham, Carolina, F	24.1
1974	Julius Erving, New York, F	27.4*
1975	George McGinnis, Indiana, F	29.8*
	& Julius Erving, New York, F	27.9
1976	Julius Erving, New York, F	29.3*

Rookie of the Year

Winners' scoring averages provided; (*) indicates led league. Rookies who were also named Most Valuable Player are in bold type.

Year		Avg
1968	**Mel Daniels, Minnesota, C**	22.2
1969	Warren Armstrong, Oakland, G	21.5
1970	**Spencer Haywood, Denver, C**	30.0*
1971	Dan Issel, Kentucky, C	29.8*
	& Charlie Scott, Virginia, G	27.1
1972	**Artis Gilmore, Kentucky, C**	23.8
1973	Brian Taylor, New York, G	15.3
1974	Swen Nater, Virginia-SA, C	14.1
1975	Marvin Barnes, St. Louis, C	24.0
1976	**David Thompson, Denver, C**	26.0

Note: Warren Armstrong changed his name to Warren Jabali after the 1970-71 season.

Coach of the Year

Previous season and winning season records are provided; (*) indicates division title.

Multiple winner: Larry Brown (3).

Year		Improvement
1968	Vince Cazetta, Pittsburgh	54-24*
1969	Alex Hannum, Oakland	22-56 to 60-18*
1970	Joe Belmont, Denver	44-34 to 51-33*
	& Bill Sharman, LA Stars	33-45 to 43-41
1971	Al Bianchi, Virginia	44-40 to 55-29*
1972	Tom Nissalke, Dallas	30-54 to 42-42
1973	Larry Brown, Carolina	35-49 to 57-27*
1974	Babe McCarthy, Kentucky	56-28 to 53-31
	& Joe Mullaney, Utah	55-29* to 51-33*
1975	Larry Brown, Denver	37-47 to 65-19*
1976	Larry Brown, Denver	65-19* to 60-24*

Scoring Leaders

Scoring championship decided by per game point average every season.

Multiple winner: Julius Erving (3).

Year		Gm	Avg	Pts
1968	Connie Hawkins, Pittsburgh	70	1875	26.8
1969	Rick Barry, Oakland	35	1190	34.0
1970	Spencer Haywood, Denver	84	2519	30.0
1971	Dan Issel, Kentucky	83	2480	29.8
1972	Charlie Scott, Virginia	73	2524	34.6
1973	Julius Erving, Virginia	71	2268	31.9
1974	Julius Erving, New York	84	2299	27.4
1975	George McGinnis, Indiana	79	2353	29.8
1976	Julius Erving, New York	84	2462	29.3

ABA All-Star Game

The ABA All-Star Game was an Eastern Division vs Western Division contest from 1968-75. League membership had dropped to seven teams by 1976, the ABA's last season, so the team in first place at the break (Denver) played an All-Star team made up from the other six clubs.

Series: East won 5, West 3 and Denver 1.

Year	Result	Host	Coaches	Most Valuable Player
1968	East 126, West 120	Indiana	Jim Pollard, Babe McCarthy	Larry Brown, New Orleans
1969	West 133, East 127	Louisville	Alex Hannum, Gene Rhodes	John Beasley, Dallas
1970	West 128, East 98	Indiana	Babe McCarthy, Bob Leonard	Spencer Haywood, Denver
1971	East 126, West 122	Carolina	Al Bianchi, Bill Sharman	Mel Daniels, Indiana
1972	East 142, West 115	Louisville	Joe Mullaney, Ladell Andersen	Dan Issel, Kentucky
1973	West 123, East 111	Utah	Ladell Andersen, Larry Brown	Warren Jabali, Denver
1974	East 128, West 112	Virginia	Babe McCarthy, Joe Mullaney	Artis Gilmore, Kentucky
1975	East 151, West 124	San Antonio	Kevin Loughery, Larry Brown	Freddie Lewis, St. Louis
1976	Denver 144, ABA 138	Denver	Larry Brown, Kevin Loughery	David Thompson, Denver

Coach **Jacques Lemaire** and playoff MVP **Claude Lemieux** are all French-Canadian smiles after leading the New Jersey Devils to an improbable Stanley Cup victory against Detroit.

HOCKEY

HOCKEY

by Eric Duhatschek

Raising Hell

The New Jersey Devils trap their way to a Stanley Cup sweep after an owners' lockout cuts NHL regular season to 48 games.

They almost didn't drop the puck. A 103-day lockout by National Hockey League owners kept the ice men on ice until mid-January, the longest regular season work stoppage in major professional sports history. For almost four months, it looked as if the 1994-95 season would go into the record books as a "DNP."

Even when the owners and players union finally hammered out a new collective bargaining agreement on Jan. 11— after passing several "final" deadlines issued by commissioner Gary Bettman— the lockout cast a shadow over everything else that followed.

The abridged 1995 schedule consisted of just 48-games— the fewest since the 1941-42 season— and made every night meaningful. The playoff race in the Western Conference went down to the final week, with all seven clubs that hadn't already clinched a berth still alive for the three remaining slots. In the East, only hapless Ottawa (9-34-5) was out of it with two weeks to go.

On the down side, there was no regular season competition between conferences. That meant that no one in the East got to see the Los Angeles Kings' Wayne Gretzky, still the greatest star in the league at age 34. And no city west of Pittsburgh was visited by the NHL's two youngest phenoms:

22-year-old Most Valuable Player Eric Lindros of the Flyers (see sidebar) and scoring champion Jaromir Jagr, 23, of the Penguins.

By the time Bettman finally handed over the Stanley Cup it was summer (June 24) and the recipients were the New Jersey Devils, who emerged as fitting champions of a quirky, off-center season. Geographically, only a Holland Tunnel traffic jam separates the Devils from the New York Rangers, their metropolitan rivals and the 1994 Cup holders. Psychologically, however, there's a world of difference between the two organizations.

The Rangers are one of the NHL's most storied franchises. The Devils one of its most ignominious. The Rangers joined the league in 1926 and Madison Square Garden has been their mailing address ever since. The Devils began life as the Kansas City Scouts in 1974, moved to Denver and became the Colorado Rockies in 1976, then headed back east in 1982 and didn't stop until they reached Exit 16W off the New Jersey Turnpike.

Even before staging a Stanley Cup parade around the Meadowlands parking lot in East Rutherford, the Devils were threatening to relocate again — this time to Nashville— as a result of a lease dispute with the New Jersey Sports and Exposition Authority and a $20 million offer to set up shop in Opreyland. After lengthy discussions with state officials, however, Devils owner John McMullen agreed on July 13 to stay put for

Eric Duhatschek has covered the NHL for the *Calgary Herald* since 1980. He is also a columnist for *The Hockey News.*

New Jersey captain **Scott Stevens** lifts the Stanley Cup triumphantly over his head following the Devils' 5-2 win over Detroit in Game 4 at the Meadowlands. The Devils, a 1974 expansion club with previous franchise stops in Kansas City and Denver, had never been to the Cup final before.

the 1995-96 season and through 2007 as well, if a renegotiated lease containing new revenues from luxury suites and advertising is approved by Sept. 15.

In their first 15 years, the Scouts/Rockies/Devils missed the playoffs 13 times. They were so inept that even Gretzky, that most cautious of interview subjects, called them a "Mickey Mouse franchise" after a 13-4 loss to the Oilers on Nov. 19, 1983. The defeat was the Devils' 18th loss in the first 20 games of their second season in New Jersey.

It may have been the most quoted phrase that ever tumbled out of the Great One's mouth and it was gleefully voiced again by 19,040 Devils' fans the night their heroes clinched the championship by sweeping the favored Detroit Red Wings in four games.

But winning the Cup didn't gain the Devils the respect of the hockey establishment. Their playing style, dictated by Hall of Fame forward-turned-defensive genius Jacques Lemaire, who played on eight Stanley Cup winners in Montreal from 1968-79, choked off opponents' offensive creativity.

Employing a strategy commonly known as the "neutral-zone trap," the Devils smothered, interfered, held and otherwise stretched the rule book to its limits.

To hear some people discuss it, the trap is a revolutionary concept that has changed the entire face of hockey. Actually, there is little new in the trap. It's simply a passive forechecking system that requires players to read and react to the play. If an opponent doesn't have puck control in the zone, a trap allows you to forecheck aggressively. If they do control the puck, then the defending team circles one forechecker into the zone and keeps the remaining four players in the neutral zone, hoping the congestion forces a turnover.

More than anything, the trap is a disciplined style that requires players with good hockey sense. In sticking to its game plan, New Jersey dispatched a quartet of opponents— Boston, Pittsburgh, Philadelphia and Detroit— all of whom entered the playoffs with better regular-season records.

There was a certain symmetry in the fact

that the Devils, the fifth seed in the Eastern Conference, eliminated in successive series a fourth-, a third-, a second- and a top-seeded club. They relied on a team concept that included a brilliant coach in Lemaire; a rugged leader in Scott Stevens, the league's highest-paid defenseman ($17 million over four years); a pair of Montreal Canadiens' rejects in Claude (Pepe) Lemieux and Stephane Richer; and 1994 Rookie of the Year Martin Brodeur, the lowest-paid goaltender in the NHL at $140,000.

One could argue that Lemaire, who became the franchise's 15th coach in 20 years on June 28, 1993, was also the Devils' MVP.

"The minute he came here we became a team," said Lemieux. "We believe in him and we believe in the system."

At first blush, Lemieux seemed an unlikely candidate to win the Conn Smythe Trophy as MVP of the playoffs. The 34-year-old winger scored only six goals during the regular season, but his postseason resumé suggested he could raise his game to a higher level. As a rookie with Montreal in 1986, Lemieux paced the Cup champion Canadiens with 10 playoff goals and was runner-up to goaltender Patrick Roy in the Smythe vote.

Opponents' dislike for Lemieux is legendary. The Bruins' Cam Neely once called him a "gutless puke." Lemieux is an exasperating player to play against. There are at least two documented cases in which he bit an opposing player during a melee and even when resting on the Devils' bench he's been known to take swings at unsuspecting passers-by.

Lemieux's ability to annoy isn't restricted to opposing players either.

"He does it with the coach too," quipped Lemaire, "but I'm getting older and I can deal with it now."

For all that, in the playoffs Lemaire gave Lemieux the task of shadowing the NHL's top power forwards: Neely, Jagr, Lindros and Keith Primeau of Detroit. Not only did Lemieux shut them all down, he outscored them, 13-7, and tilted the ice in the Devils' favor.

Afterwards, Lemieux addressed the issue of New Jersey's defensive style, saying it was time for critics to give the Devils their due: "We've been jabbed by so many people...but you can put all that in the garbage now. You can stuff that. I'm sorry,

Eric Lindros NHL's New Hart Throb

Mario Lemieux, missed the entire 1995 season, recovering from a bad back and the aftereffects of his two-year battle with Hodgkin's disease.

Wayne Gretzky, the most prolific scorer in National Hockey League history, struggled through a disappointing regular season, missed the playoffs and barely cracked the Top 20 in scoring.

The time was right for a new star to emerge, to take the torch from Gretzky's hands and carry the league towards the year 2000.

That new star was Eric Lindros, the 22-year-old captain of the Philadelphia Flyers.

The most highly-touted young player of the 1990's, Lindros finally started to fulfill the enormous potential forecast for him when the Quebec Nordiques made him the first overall pick of the 1991 NHL draft.

Lindros gained immediate notoriety when he refused to play the 1991-92 season for the small market Nordiques. Instead, he skated for the Canadian Olympic team which won a silver medal at the 1992 Winter Games in Albertville.

The following June, the Flyers forked over a small fortune in acquiring the 6-foot-4, 225-pound center some 90 minutes before the start of the '92 NHL draft. It took six players (including the rights to eventual 1995 Rookie of the Year Peter Forsberg of Sweden), two No. 1 draft picks and $15 million to pry Lindros loose. Shortly afterward, Philadelphia signed him to a six-year contract worth $2.5 million a year.

In his first two seasons, Lindros's kamikaze playing style caused him to miss a total of 42 games with various knee injuries, but he provided enough glimpses to indicate that he was the real deal.

When the lockout ended and the 1995 season finally got underway, the Flyers played their first 10 games like they were going to miss the playoffs for the sixth straight season and Lindros continued his maddening flashes of brilliance and inconsistency.

Things started to change for the better on Feb. 9, when Flyers' general manager Bob Clarke engineered the most significant trade of the season. In exchange for sending high scoring right wing Mark Recchi to Montreal, the Flyers acquired defenseman Eric Desjardins and for-

Philadelphia captain and league most valuable player **Eric Lindros** (center) and his 'Legion of Doom' linemates **Mikael Renberg** (left) and **John LeClair**. After LeClair's arrival from Montreal on Feb. 9, the Flyers rose from sixth to first in their division and Lindros just missed winning the scoring title.

wards John LeClair and Gilbert Dionne from the Canadiens.

LeClair, who is 6-foot-2 and 220 pounds, was installed on Lindros's left side and took the pressure off Lindros to be constantly on the lookout for the big hit. Along with right wing Mikael Renberg, they formed the NHL's premier line, the "Legion of Doom," and all three finished in the Top 10 in scoring. The day of the trade the Flyers were sixth in the Atlantic Division standings with a record of 3-6-1. After the trade, they went 25-10-3, won the division by eight points and were the only team to win two games against Stanley Cup champion New Jersey.

Lindros was healthy for all but the final two games of the regular-season when a fluke accident cost him the Art Ross Trophy as the league's leading scorer. On April 30, he caught a puck in the left eye when a slapshot he took against the New York Rangers hit opposing defenseman Jeff Beukeboom in the hip and caromed back into his face. It took five stitches to close the wound and Lindros didn't get medical clearance to play again until the Flyers' fourth game of the opening playoff round.

The injury allowed Jaromir Jagr of Pittsburgh to catch Lindros and become the first European player to win an NHL scoring championship.

They actually finished in a tie with 70 points each, but Jagr won the title by having the most goals (32 to 29). The Ross Trophy had been decided on goals on two previous occasions: in 1962 when Bobby Hull beat out Andy Bathgate, and in 1980 when Marcel Dionne edged Gretzky.

Like Gretzky in '80, Lindros lost the scoring race but won the Hart Trophy as the league's most valuable player. Thanks to contract bonuses, the award bumped his salary to $4.1 million per season for the next three years.

Discussing the emergence of Lindros, Pierre Page, the man who traded him from Quebec to Philadelphia, commented: "After Eric's slow start, I think Bobby Clarke was losing patience.

"The easiest thing to do with a skilled player who isn't producing is to get mad at him. But Clarkie saw the problem. Everybody was running at Eric, so he went out and got him some big guys to help out."

The trade with the Canadiens turned No. 88 into No. 1.

"He's more controlled now, so he does everything with a purpose," said Buffalo GM John Muckler. He has learned his body is an advantage for him when he has the puck and he doesn't have to run all over the ice hitting people."

but we held it in for so long— if people don't like our style, too bad. We have the Cup. They can go watch a show somewhere else."

Lemieux's teammate of 10 years, Richer, grew up idolizing fellow Quebecker Guy Lafleur and pulled on a Canadiens sweater for the first time during Lafleur's last season with the club in 1984-85. Groomed to replace the two-time MVP, Richer found the role difficult to bear and welcomed the 1991 trade that sent him to New Jersey for Devils captain Kirk Muller.

Richer shares Lemieux's outspoken ways and alienated many of his peers by breaking ranks with the players' association during the lockout, saying that the majority of players would be willing to settle if they could vote privately on the owners' proposal.

Guy Carbonneau, his old teammate in Montreal and a key NHLPA spokesman, blistered his ears in an angry phone call.

"My timing was bad," admitted Richer, "but I didn't feel I could just sit and wait."

In the end, Richer finished second to Detroit's Sergei Fedorov in playoff scoring with 21 points and all was forgiven. In New Jersey anyway.

Brodeur, harkens back to the great Montreal goaltenders' tradition: from Jacques Plante to Ken Dryden to Roy. The son of Denis Brodeur, a former Canadiens' photographer, he is cool beyond his 23 years. His minuscule 1.67 goals-against average over the 20-game postseason provided a solid last-line of defense on the rare occasions that the Devils gave up a scoring chance.

The Devils also benefited from a pair of key midseason acquisitions by general manager Lou Lamoriello, who sent center Cory Millen to Dallas for center Neal Broten on Feb. 27, and acquired defenseman Shawn Chambers in a four-player deal with Tampa Bay on March 14.

Lamoriello, who became New Jersey's president and GM in 1987, actually made his biggest deal of the season on July 11, 1994. That's the day he opened up the club's notoriously tight purse strings and re-signed Stevens for $17.05 million over four years. The contract matched a St. Louis offer and kept the Devils' captain from leaving as a free agent.

Meanwhile, the Red Wings were fighting the same Ghosts of Stanley Cups Past that the Rangers finally exorcised in 1994. With New York ending its 54-year dry spell, Detroit had become the NHL team with the longest stretch— 40 years— since winning its last championship.

Until they crashed in the finals, the Red Wings flew through the first three rounds of the playoffs in 14 games— two more than the minimum— and Scotty Bowman looked like a cinch to become the first coach to lead three different teams to a Stanley Cup title.

Detroit, the regular season points leader for the second straight season, beat Dallas in five games, San Jose in four and Chicago in five. The second-round meeting with the upstart Sharks brought the Red Wings a measure of revenge after being upset in the first round of the playoffs in 1994. This time the Sharks had no bite, losing by tennis scores of 6-0, 6-2, 6-2 and 6-2. The Western Conference final was much more of a challenge as the Wings struggled to outscore the Blackhawks, 13-12, and leaned on the steady goaltending of Mike Vernon to win three games in overtime.

In the final, however, the Red Wings ran out of wins long before their fans ran out of octopi to throw on the ice at Joe Louis Arena. The picture of confidence entering the series, Detroit lost the first two games at home and never recovered. The bigger, more physical Devils held them to a combined 35 shots in both games and rallied from a 2-1 deficit midway through the third period of Game 2 to win, 4-2. When the series resumed in New Jersey, the Wings went down meekly in back-to-back 5-2 losses.

"The fact is, we just ran into a team that we couldn't handle," said Bowman, who was beaten by his protégé, Lemaire. "They're a big, strong team. They have depth, a real good goaltender and they hold teams to two goals or less about 90 percent of the time. Do that and winning [the Cup] is no fluke."

Elsewhere, the 1995 irregular season represented a changing of the NHL guard. The 1994 finalists, the Rangers and Vancouver, barely scraped into the playoffs, while the '93 finalists, Montreal and Los Angeles, missed them altogether. After contributing more than a dozen players to the four semifinalists through various ill-advised trades, the Canadiens sat out the postseason for the first time since 1970— a catastrophic development in the province of Quebec,

NHL commissioner **Gary Bettman** (left) and players' union chief **Bob Goodenow** meet the press on Jan.11 after signing a new six-year collective bargaining agreement in New York. The settlement ended the 103-day owners' lockout and the regular season had to be reduced to only 48 games.

which considers itself the cradle of hockey.

The rest of the country didn't fare much better. Only four of the eight Canadian-based teams qualified for postseason play and three of them— Quebec, Calgary and Toronto—lost in the first round to lower-seeded opponents. The only team to advance to the second round, Vancouver, was swept by Chicago. The last time there were no Canadian teams in the Stanley Cup final four was 1980.

And there was more unsettling news. As the playoffs got underway in May, the Quebec Nordiques and Winnipeg Jets were headed for relocation in the United States.

The Nordiques, who went from missing the playoffs in 1994 to the best overall record in the Eastern Conference (30-13-5) in 1995, were sold to COMSAT Entertainment Group of Denver for $75 million (U.S. funds) on May 25. Three months later they were rechristened the Colorado Avalanche.

The debt-ridden Jets, who failed to reach the playoffs for the second straight year, accepted a conditional offer on May 13 from Minneapolis businessman Richard Burke to buy the club for $68 million (U.S.). The deal was voided on May 18, however, when a local group named the Spirit of Manitoba emerged with a plan to save the franchise by raising $111 million (Canadian) to buy the team and finance a new arena.

Back in 1991, team owner Barry Shenkarow had promised to sell the club to community interests for $32 million (Canadian) before signing a deal with outsiders. Unfortunately, after an enthusiastic start, the Spirit of Manitoba failed in its efforts to raise the money by an agreed-to deadline of Aug. 15.

By then the Jets were committed to playing the 1995-96 NHL season in Winnipeg, but appeared destined to move to Minneapolis after that.

The future of the six remaining Canadian teams is anything but secure. Without some sort of currency relief, only Montreal, Toronto and Vancouver will ultimately be able to compete with their American counterparts. In mid-1995, the Canadian dollar

Bruce Bennett/BBS

The French **fleur-de-lis** shoulder patch made its final NHL appearance on May 16 when the Quebec Nordiques were eliminated from the playoffs by the New York Rangers. Nine days later, the Nords were sold and moved to Denver where they became the Colorado Avalanche.

was trading at around 75 cents. That, figured in with the fact that Calgary, Edmonton and Ottawa each operate in cities of less than 700,000 people, will hinder their chances of fielding competitive teams in the years ahead.

Currency relief was one of the issues the players and owners tried to address in the collective bargaining talks that wiped out the first half of the season. Both sides spent the better part of two months trying to fine tune separate versions of a "luxury tax," designed to aid the small-market teams. In the end, both proposals were scrapped in favor of a system that included an entry-level salary cap; plus new restrictions on arbitration and free agency that effectively tie a player, for a minimum of five years, to the team that drafts him.

The deal runs through Sept. 15, 2000, with either side having the right to re-open the deal in June, 1998.

Negotiations were extremely acrimonious and frequently descended into name-calling. Early on, players' boss Bob Goodenow suggested it was "absolutely clear the NHL is not interested in the fans, the game or the small-market clubs." For his part, NHL com-

missioner Gary Bettman said he was "baffled" at the players' lack of movement and that all the union wanted was to maintain the status quo.

So it went for the better part of three months, with the dialogue getting more vitriolic every day. When the two sides finally settled, perhaps Flames' captain Joe Nieuwendyk said it best: "Nobody wins in this situation. We lost. They lost. The fans lost."

One of the reasons for the 11th-hour settlement was the fact that the NHL had signed a five-year, $155 million deal with Fox Network on Sept. 13, marking their first long-term contract with a major U.S. network since the 1970s.

Curiously, the primary casualties of the 1995 season were the nine coaches who were fired from April 5 to June 19.

In theory, the truncated schedule was supposed to provide a measure of stability for the men who are hired to be fired. Not quite. Two general managers who also coached, John Paddock of Winnipeg and John Muckler of Buffalo, kicked themselves upstairs. Chicago's Darryl Sutter retired to spend more time with his two-year-old son Christopher, who has Down's Syndrome. The other six, including Sutter's brother Brian, were pushed, creating openings in Boston, Calgary, Edmonton, Florida, Los Angeles and the New York Islanders (see page 417).

One survivor was Mike Keenan, who bolted the New York Rangers after just one season on July 15, 1994, signed a five-year, $9 million deal with St. Louis two days later and was forced by the league to pay a mere $100,000 fine for breaking his contract with the Rangers. The Blues, who added a half-dozen pricey players to their roster, had the second best record in the West, but were knocked out of the playoffs in the first round by Vancouver.

Finally, this positive note for the coming season: Mario Lemieux will be back. The Pittsburgh captain and two-time playoff MVP announced on June 20 that he would return for all 42 home games and at least half of the Pens' road schedule in 1995-96. Lemieux returns after taking 12 months off due to a recurring bad back and fatigue brought on by radiation treatments for Hodgkin's disease.

While Mario was away, Claude stood in as the playoffs' Mr. Lemieux. ❏

HOCKEY STATISTICS

THE 1996 SPORTS ALMANAC · INFORMATION PLEASE

THE SEASON IN REVIEW 1995

NHL · WORLD · U.S. COLLEGES

SEC A

PAGE 383

Final NHL Standings

Division champions (*) and playoff qualifiers (†) are noted. Number of seasons listed after each head coach refers to current tenure with club through 1994-95 season.

Western Conference

Central Division

	W	L	T	Pts	Goals For	Opp	Dif
* Detroit	33	11	4	70	180	117	+63
†St. Louis	28	15	5	61	178	135	+43
†Chicago	24	19	5	53	156	115	+41
†Toronto	21	19	8	50	135	146	-11
†Dallas	17	23	8	42	136	135	+1
Winnipeg	16	25	7	39	157	177	-20

Head Coaches: Det— Scotty Bowman (2nd season); **St.L**— Mike Keenan (1st); **Chi**— Darryl Sutter (3rd); **Tor**— Pat Burns (3rd); **Dal**— Bob Gainey (5th); **Win**— GM-coach John Paddock (4th, 9-18-6) replaced himself with assistant Terry Simpson (7-7-1) on Apr. 5.

1993-94 Standings: 1. Detroit (46-30-8, 100 points); 2. Toronto (43-29-12, 98 pts); 3. Dallas (42-29-13, 97 pts); 4. St. Louis (40-33-11, 91 pts); 5. Chicago (39-36-9, 87 pts); 6. Winnipeg (24-51-9, 57 pts).

Pacific Division

	W	L	T	Pts	Goals For	Opp	Dif
* Calgary	24	17	7	55	163	135	+28
†Vancouver	18	18	12	48	153	148	+5
†San Jose	19	25	4	42	129	161	-32
Los Angeles	16	23	9	41	142	174	-32
Edmonton	17	27	4	38	136	183	-47
Anaheim	16	27	5	37	125	164	-39

Head Coaches: Calg— Dave King (3rd season); **Van**— Rick Ley (1st); **SJ**— Kevin Constantine (2nd); **LA**— fired Barry Melrose (3rd, 13-21-7) on Apr. 21 and replaced him with team president Rogie Vachon (3-2-2); **Edm**— fired George Burnett (1st, 12-20-3) on Apr. 6 and replaced him with assistant Ron Low (5-7-1); **Ana**— Ron Wilson (2nd).

1993-94 Standings: 1. Calgary (42-29-13, 97 points); 2. Vancouver (41-40-3, 85 pts); 3. San Jose (33-35-16, 82 pts); 4. Anaheim (33-46-5, 71 pts); 5. Los Angeles (27-45-12, 66 pts); 6. Edmonton (25-45-14, 64 pts).

Eastern Conference

Northeast Division

	W	L	T	Pts	Goals For	Opp	Dif
* Quebec	30	13	5	65	185	134	+51
†Pittsburgh	29	16	3	61	181	158	+23
†Boston	27	18	3	57	150	127	+23
†Buffalo	22	19	7	51	130	119	+11
Hartford	19	24	5	43	127	141	-14
Montreal	18	23	7	43	125	148	-23
Ottawa	9	34	5	23	117	174	-57

Head Coaches: Que— Marc Crawford (1st season); **Pit**— Eddie Johnston (2nd); **Bos**— Brian Sutter (3rd); **Buf**— John Muckler (4th); **Hart**— Paul Holmgren (1st); **Mon**— Jacques Demers (3rd); **Ott**— Rick Bowness (3rd).

1993-94 Standings: 1. Pittsburgh (44-27-13, 101 points); 2. Boston (42-29-13, 97 pts); 3. Montreal (41-29-14, 96 pts); 4. Buffalo (43-32-9, 95 pts); 5. Quebec (34-42-8, 76 pts); 6. Hartford (27-48-9, 63 pts); 7. Ottawa (14-61-9, 37 pts).

Atlantic Division

	W	L	T	Pts	Goals For	Opp	Dif
* Philadelphia	28	16	4	60	150	132	+18
†New Jersey	22	18	8	52	136	121	+15
†Washington	22	18	8	52	136	120	+16
†NY Rangers	22	23	3	47	139	134	+5
Florida	20	22	6	46	115	127	-12
Tampa Bay	17	28	3	37	120	144	-24
NY Islanders	15	28	5	35	126	158	-32

Head Coaches: Phi— Terry Murray (1st season); **NJ**— Jacques Lemaire (2nd); **Wash**— Jim Schoenfeld (2nd); **NYR**— Colin Campbell (1st); **Fla**— Roger Neilson (2nd); **TB**— Terry Crisp (3rd); **NYI**— Lorne Henning (1st).

1993-94 Standings: 1. NY Rangers (52-24-8, 112 points); 2. New Jersey (47-25-12, 106 pts); 3. Washington (39-35-10, 88 pts); 4. NY Islanders (36-36-12, 84 pts); 5. Florida (33-34-17, 83 pts); 6. Philadelphia (35-39-10, 80 pts); 7. Tampa Bay (30-43-11, 71 pts).

The NHL's Two Work Stoppages

Year	Work Stoppage	Games Missed	Length	Dates	Issue
1991-92	Strike	None	10 days	April 1-10	Free agency and licensing rights
1994-95	Lockout	468	103 days	Oct. 1-Jan. 11	Salary cap and luxury tax

1995 All-Star Game Cancelled

The 1995 NHL All-Star Game scheduled for Jan. 21 in San Jose was cancelled on Dec. 8, 1994. It marked the first time since 1947 that the game had been called off for something other than a midseason series against the Russians.

Quebec Nordiques Become Colorado Avalanche

On June 21, the NHL board of governors approved the $75 Million (U.S.) sale of the Nordiques to COMSAT Denver. The renamed Avalanche will move from the Northeast Division to the Pacific Division in time for the 1995-96 season.

Home & Away, Division Records

Sixteen teams— eight from each conference— qualify for the Stanley Cup Playoffs; (*) indicates division champions.

Western Conference

		Pts	Home	Away	Div
1	Detroit*	70	17-4-3	16-7-1	17-5-2
2	Calgary*	55	15-7-2	9-10-5	13-8-3
3	St. Louis	61	16-6-2	12-9-3	13-8-3
4	Chicago	53	11-10-3	13-9-2	7-13-4
5	Toronto	50	15-7-2	6-12-6	10-10-4
6	Vancouver	48	10-8-6	8-10-6	14-4-6
7	San Jose	42	10-13-1	9-12-3	10-12-2
8	Dallas	42	9-10-5	8-13-3	8-15-1
	Los Angeles	41	7-11-6	9-12-3	5-15-4
	Winnipeg	39	10-10-4	6-15-3	9-13-2
	Edmonton	38	11-12-1	6-15-3	9-13-2
	Anaheim	37	11-9-4	5-18-1	11-10-3

Eastern Conference

		Pts	Home	Away	Div
1	Quebec*	65	19-1-4	11-12-1	14-6-4
2	Philadelphia*	60	16-7-1	12-9-3	16-6-2
3	Pittsburgh	61	18-5-1	11-11-2	15-8-1
4	Boston	57	15-7-2	12-11-1	15-7-2
5	New Jersey	52	14-4-6	8-14-2	12-8-4
6	Washington	52	15-6-3	7-12-5	11-9-4
7	Buffalo	51	15-8-1	7-11-6	8-10-6
8	NY Rangers	47	11-10-3	11-13-0	11-11-2
	Florida	46	9-12-3	11-10-3	7-13-4
	Hartford	43	12-10-2	7-14-3	13-10-1
	Montreal	43	15-5-4	3-18-3	8-12-4
	Tampa Bay	37	10-14-0	7-14-3	7-14-3
	NY Islanders	35	10-11-3	5-17-2	9-12-3
	Ottawa	23	5-16-3	4-18-2	1-21-2

Game-Winning Goals in Overtime

A total of 101 games were tied after regulation during the abbreviated 1995 regular season, but only 26 were resolved in overtime. Teams play one five-minute overtime period during then regular season; (*) indicates rookie.

	Date	Time	Score
Peter Douris, Ana vs Edm	1/23	4:20	Ana., 5-4
Adam Oates, Bos vs NJ	1/23	3:43	Bos., 1-0
Ray Ferraro, NYI at Phi	2/2	1:43	NYI, 5-4
Brett Hull, St.L at Win	2/2	3:32	St.L., 5-4
Tony Amonte, Chi at Calg	2/2	2:25	Chi., 4-3
Theoren Fleury, Calg vs Dal	2/2	4:34	Calg., 3-2
Donald Brashear*, Mon vs NYI	2/2	1:54	Mon., 3-2
Darren Turcotte, Hart vs Bos	2/2	2:59	Hart., 3-2
Brian Bradley, TB at Ott	3/2	3:55	TB, 3-2
Larry Murphy, Pit at Bos	3/4	4:36	Pit., 4-3
Robert Kron, Hart vs TB	3/4	1:11	Hart., 3-2
Yuri Khmylev, Buf at Fla	3/14	0:54	Buf., 2-1
Troy Murray, Ott vs Buf	3/18	3:42	Ott., 4-3
Eric Lindros, Phi at Fla	3/18	2:13	Phil, 4-3
Stephane Richer, NJ vs Bos	3/19	1:36	NJ, 4-3
Owen Nolan, Que vs Fla	3/20	2:33	Que., 5-4
Fred Knipscheer*, Bos at TB	3/24	3:32	Bos., 4-3
Geoff Sanderson, Hart at Wash	3/26	2:16	Hart., 4-3
Petr Klima, TB vs Mon	3/27	2:23	TB, 3-2
Jeff Friesen, SJ vs Win	3/28	4:27	SJ, 6-5
Stephan Lebeau, Ana vs Edm	4/5	4:09	Ana., 4-3
Darren Turcotte, Hart vs Mon	4/14	2:04	Hart., 4-3
Rod Brind'Amour, Phi vs Pit	4/16	1:30	Phi., 4-3
John LeClair, Phi at NJ	4/22	0:54	Phi., 4-3
Murray Craven, Chi vs Van	4/25	2:00	Chi., 4-3
Zdeno Ciger, Edm vs St.L	4/27	3:19	Edm., 3-2

Hat Tricks

Players scored three or more goals in one game a total of 48 times during the abbreviated 1995 regular season. Eric Lindros of Philadelphia, Bernie Nicholls of Chicago and Owen Nolan of Quebec led the way with three hat tricks each. Nicholls scored four goals in a game twice.

Five Goals	Date	Score
Alexei Zhamnov, Win at LA	Apr.1	Tied, 7-7

Four Goals	Date	Score
Sergei Fedorov, Det vs LA	Feb. 12	Tied, 4-4
Brett Hull, St.L vs Det	Apr. 16	Blues, 6-5
Bernie Nicholls, Chi at Van	Feb. 5	Blackhawks, 9-4
Bernie Nicholls, Chi at LA	Feb. 28	Blackhawks, 8-4
Luc Robitaille, Pit vs Hart	Feb. 16	Penguins, 5-2

Three Goals	Date	Score
Jason Arnott, Edm vs Calg	Mar. 20	Oilers, 5-2
Donald Audette, Buf vs Ott	Mar. 30	Sabres, 7-0
Josef Beranek, Phi vs NYI	Feb. 2	Islanders, 5-4
Peter Bondra, Wash vs Hart	Apr. 21	Capitals, 6-3
Pavel Bure, Van vs Ana	Apr. 11	Canucks, 5-0
Igor Chibirev, Hart at Pit	Apr. 5	Whalers, 4-4
Wendel Clark, Que at Bos	Feb. 9	Nordiques, 4-3
Russ Courtnall, Van vs Edm	Apr. 22	Canucks, 6-1
Alexandre Daigle, Ott vs Que	Mar. 26	Nordiques, 11-4
Nelson Emerson, Win at SJ	Mar. 28	Sharks, 6-5
Tony Granato, LA vs Edm	Apr. 3	Kings, 7-2
Adam Graves, NYR vs Ott	Jan. 30	Rangers, 6-2
Todd Harvey*, Dal vs Tor	Apr. 22	Stars, 6-4
Brett Hull, St.L vs Dal	Feb. 4	Blues, 7-4
Jaromir Jagr, Pit vs Bos	Feb. 14	Penguins, 5-3
Uwe Krupp, Que vs TB	Mar. 1	Nordiques, 8-2
Steve Larouche*, Ott vs Mon	Apr. 3	Canadiens, 5-4

Three Goals	Date	Score
John LeClair, Phi at TB	Feb. 14	Flyers, 5-2
John LeClair, Phi at Mon	Feb. 25	Flyers, 7-0
Eric Lindros, Phi at Que	Feb. 23	Tied, 6-6
Eric Lindros, Phi vs NYI	Mar. 18	Flyers, 4-3
Eric Lindros, Phi vs Mon	Mar. 20	Flyers, 8-4
Cam Neely, Bos vs Phi	Jan. 22	Bruins, 4-1
Cam Neely, Bos vs NYR	Apr. 23	Bruins, 5-4
Bernie Nicholls, Chi vs SJ	Mar. 21	Blackhawks, 7-3
Joe Nieuwendyk, Calg vs SJ	Apr. 10	Flames, 8-3
Owen Nolan, Que vs NJ	Mar. 6	Nordiques, 6-3
Owen Nolan, Que at NYR	Mar. 30	Nordiques, 5-4
Owen Nolan, Que vs Ott	Apr. 2	Nordiques, 7-5
Brian Noonan, NYR at Hart	Mar. 1	Rangers, 5-2
David Oliver, Edm at Dal	Apr. 22	Tied, 4-4
Steven Rice, Hart at Fla	Mar. 29	Tied, 4-4
Geoff Sanderson, Hart vs Mon	Feb. 15	Whalers, 4-1
Ray Sheppard, Det vs Van	Jan. 24	Red Wings, 6-3
Bryan Smolinski, Bos vs NJ	Mar. 2	Bruins, 7-2
Ronnie Stern, Calg at Dal	Mar. 12	Tied, 4-4
German Titov, Calg vs Tor	Feb. 4	Flames, 4-1
Rick Tocchet, LA vs Det	Feb. 4	Kings, 4-3
Pierre Turgeon, Mon vs Wash	Apr. 17	Canadiens, 5-2
Alexei Yashin, Ott vs Wash	Feb. 23	Tied, 5-5
Scott Young, Que at Ott	Mar. 26	Nordiques, 11-4
Alexei Zhamnov, Win at St.L	Feb. 11	Jets, 3-2

Pittsburgh Penguins

Jaromir Jagr
Scoring

Philadelphia Flyers

Eric Lindros
Scoring

Detroit Red Wings

Paul Coffey
Defenseman Points

Buffalo Sabres

Dominik Hasek
Goals Against Avg.

NHL Regular Season Individual Leaders

(*) indicates rookie eligible for Calder Trophy.

Scoring

	Pos	Gm	G	A	Pts	+/-	PM	PP	SH	GW	GT	Shots	Pct
Jaromir Jagr, Pittsburgh	RW	48	32	38	70†	+23	37	8	3	7	0	192	16.7
Eric Lindros, Philadelphia	C	46	29	41	70	+27	60	7	0	4	1	144	20.1
Alexei Zhamnov, Winnipeg	C	48	30	35	65	+5	20	9	0	4	0	155	19.4
Joe Sakic, Quebec	C	47	19	43	62	+7	30	3	2	5	0	157	12.1
Ron Francis, Pittsburgh	C	44	11	48	59	+30	18	3	0	1	0	94	11.7
Theoren Fleury, Calgary	RW	47	29	29	58	+6	112	9	2	5	0	173	16.8
Paul Coffey, Detroit	D	45	14	44	58	+18	72	4	1	2	0	181	7.7
Mikael Renberg, Philadelphia	RW	47	26	31	57	+20	20	8	0	4	0	143	18.2
John LeClair, Mon-Phi	LW	46	26	28	54	+20	30	6	0	7	0	131	19.8
Mark Messier, Rangers	C	46	14	39	53	+8	40	3	3	2	0	126	11.1
Adam Oates, Boston	C	48	12	41	53	−11	8	4	1	2	0	109	11.0
Bernie Nicholls, Chicago	C	48	22	29	51	+4	32	11	2	5	0	114	19.3
Keith Tkachuk, Winnipeg	LW	48	22	29	51	−4	152	7	2	2	1	129	17.1
Brett Hull, St. Louis	RW	48	29	21	50	+13	10	9	3	6	0	200	14.5
Joe Nieuwendyk, Calgary	C	46	21	29	50	+11	33	3	0	4	0	122	17.2
Sergei Fedorov, Detroit	C	42	20	30	50	+6	24	7	3	5	0	147	13.6
Peter Forsberg*, Quebec	C	47	15	35	50	+17	16	3	0	3	0	86	17.4
Owen Nolan, Quebec	RW	46	30	19	49	+21	46	13	2	8	0	137	21.9
Teemu Selanne, Winnipeg	RW	45	22	26	48	+1	2	8	2	1	1	167	13.2
Mark Recchi, Phi-Mon	RW	49	16	32	48	−9	28	9	0	3	0	121	13.2
Wayne Gretzky, LA	C	48	11	37	48	−20	6	3	0	1	0	142	7.7

†Jagr won scoring title on first tie breaker (total goals).

Goals

Bondra, Wash	34
Jagr, Pit	32
Nolan, Que	30
Sheppard, Det	30
Zhamnov, Win	30
Hull, St.L	29
Fleury, Calg	29
Lindros, Phi	29
Neely, Bos	27
LeClair, Phi-Mon	26
Renberg, Phi	26
Audette, Buf	24
Turgeon, NYI-Mon	24
Four tied with 23 each.	

Assists

Francis, Pit	48
Coffey, Det	44
Sakic, Que	43
Lindros, Phi	41
Oates, Bos	41
Messier, NYR	39
Jagr, Pit	38
Juneau, Wash	38
Gretzky, LA	37
Forsberg*, Que	35
Housley, Calg	35
Zhamnov, Win	35
Chelios, Chi	33
Weight, Edm	33

Defensemen Points

Coffey, Det	58
Bourque, Bos	43
Housley, Calg	43
Leetch, NYR	41
Chelios, Chi	38
Duchesne, St.L	38
Murphy, Pit	38
Suter, Chi	37
Zubov, NYR	36
Galley, Phi-Buf	32
Gill, Tor	32

Power Play Goals

Neely, Bos	16
Audette, Buf	13
Nolan, Que	13
Bondra, Wash	12
Mogilny, Buf	12
Nicholls, Chi	11
Sheppard, Det	11
Yashin, Ott	11
Oliver*, Edm	10
Nine tied with 9 each.	

Rookie Points

Forsberg, Que	50
Kariya, Ana	39
Oliver, Edm	30
Laperriere, St.L	27
Marchant, Edm	27
Czerkawski, Bos	26
Friesen, SJ	25
Harvey, Dal	20
Oksiuta, Edm-Van	20
Krivokrasov, Chi	19
Savage, Mon	19

Short-Handed Goals

Bondra, Wash	6
Presley, Buf	5
Fedorov, Det	3
Gilchrist, Dal	3
Hull, St.L	3
Jagr, Pit	3
Konowalchuk, Wash	3
Messier, NYR	3
Young, Que	3
Zamuner, TB	3

Plus/Minus

Francis, Pit	+30
Duchesne, St.L	+29
Leschyshyn, Que	+29
Lindros, Phi	+27
Jagr, Pit	+23
Gilbert, St.L	+22
Norton, St.L	+22

Penalty Minutes

Ciccone, TB	225
Churla, Dal	186
Marchment, Edm	184
Berube, Wash	173
Ray, Buf	173
Peluso, NJ	167

NHL Regular Season Individual Leaders (Cont.)

Goaltending

(Minimum 25 games)

	Gm	Min	GAA	GA	Shots	Sv%	EN	SO	Record	Offense G	A	Pts	PM
Dominik Hasek, Buffalo	41	2416	2.11	85	1221	.930	2	5	19-14-7	0	0	0	2
Rick Tabaracci, Wash-Calg	13	596	2.11	21	240	.913	0	0	3-3-3	0	2	2	2
Jim Carey*, Washington	28	1604	2.13	57	654	.913	2	4	18-6-3	0	0	0	0
Chris Osgood, Detroit	19	1087	2.26	41	496	.917	0	1	14-5-0	0	0	0	2
Ed Belfour, Chicago	42	2450	2.28	93	990	.906	4	5	22-15-3	0	3	3	11
Jocelyn Thibault, Quebec	18	898	2.34	35	423	.917	0	1	12-2-2	0	0	0	0
Dominic Roussel, Philadelphia	19	1075	2.34	42	486	.914	1	1	11-7-0	0	0	0	6
Glenn Healy, NY Rangers	17	888	2.36	35	377	.907	0	1	8-6-1	0	2	2	2
Blaine Lacher*, Boston	35	1965	2.41	79	805	.902	0	4	19-11-2	0	1	1	4
Andy Moog, Dallas	31	1770	2.44	72	846	.915	1	2	10-12-7	0	1	1	14
Martin Brodeur, New Jersey	40	2184	2.45	89	908	.908	1	3	19-11-6	0	2	2	2
John Vanbiesbrouck, Florida	37	2087	2.47	89	908	.902	4	4	14-15-4	0	1	1	6
Olaf Kolzig, Washington	14	724	2.49	30	305	.902	4	0	2-8-2	0	0	0	4
Mike Vernon, Detroit	30	1807	2.52	76	710	.893	0	1	19-6-4	0	0	0	8
Chris Terreri, New Jersey	15	734	2.53	31	309	.900	0	0	3-7-2	0	0	0	0

Wins

Wregget, Pit	25
Belfour, Chi	22
Kidd, Calg	22
Joseph, St.L	20
Brodeur, NJ	19
Hasek, Buf	19
Lacher*, Bos	19
Vernon, Det	19
Carey*, Wash	18
McLean, Van	18

Shutouts

Belfour, Chi	5
Hasek, Buf	5
Carey*, Wash	4
Irbe, SJ	4
Lacher*, Bos	4
Vanbiesbrouck, Fla	4
Brodeur, NJ	3
Kidd, Calg	3
Seven tied with 2 each.	

Save Pct.

Hasek, Buf	.930
Osgood, Det	.917
Thibault, Que	.917
Rhodes, Tor	.916
Moog, Dal	.915
Roussel, Phi	.914
Vanbiesbrouck, Fla	.914
Carey*, Wash	.913
Tabaracci, Wash-Calg	.913
Burke, Hart	.912

Losses

Beaupre, Ott	25
Hebert, Ana	20
Ranford, Edm	20
Roy, Mon	20
Burke, Hart	19
Irbe, SJ	19
Puppa, TB	19
Richter, NYR	17
Cheveldae, Win	16

Team Goaltending

WESTERN	GAA	Mins	GA	Shots	Sv%	EN	SO	EASTERN	GAA	Mins	GA	Shots	Sv%	EN	SO
Chicago	2.37	2909	115	1195	.904	4	5	Buffalo	2.45	2920	119	1458	.918	2	5
Detroit	2.42	2900	117	1206	.903	0	2	Washington	2.46	2922	120	1192	.899	6	4
Calgary	2.77	2922	135	1408	.904	7	3	New Jersey	2.48	2926	121	1218	.901	1	3
Dallas	2.77	2925	135	1388	.903	2	4	Florida	2.61	2916	127	1366	.907	5	6
St. Louis	2.78	2912	135	1356	.900	0	1	Boston	2.62	2911	127	1168	.891	2	4
Toronto	3.00	2920	146	1532	.905	8	0	Philadelphia	2.73	2906	132	1289	.898	2	2
Vancouver	3.02	2942	148	1421	.896	2	1	Quebec	2.76	2908	134	1455	.908	1	3
San Jose	3.33	2904	161	1517	.894	6	5	NY Rangers	2.78	2895	134	1263	.894	2	3
Anaheim	3.38	2913	164	1586	.897	6	2	Hartford	2.90	2914	141	1474	.904	7	0
Los Angeles	3.57	2925	174	1668	.896	7	0	Tampa Bay	2.97	2906	144	1325	.891	5	2
Winnipeg	3.63	2923	177	1545	.885	4	0	Montreal	3.04	2921	148	1532	.903	3	1
Edmonton	3.77	2912	183	1469	.875	3	2	NY Islanders	3.26	2909	158	1448	.891	3	1
								Pittsburgh	3.27	2901	158	1578	.900	2	0
								Ottawa	3.58	2913	174	1561	.889	6	1

Power Play/Penalty Killing

Power play and penalty killing conversions. Power play: No— number of opportunities; GF— goals for; Pct— percentage. Penalty killing: No— number of times shorthanded; GA— goals against; Pct— percentage of penalties killed; SH— shorthanded goals for.

WESTERN	Power Play No	GF	Pct	Penalty Killing No	GA	Pct	SH	EASTERN	Power Play No	GF	Pct	Penalty Killing No	GA	Pct	SH
Chicago	212	52	24.5	228	36	84.2	7	Quebec	186	45	24.2	203	38	81.3	9
Detroit	215	52	24.2	206	28	86.4	5	Boston	211	46	21.8	183	24	86.9	3
Vancouver	238	47	19.7	236	39	83.5	7	NY Rangers	200	40	20.0	211	34	83.9	5
Winnipeg	219	42	19.2	235	40	83.0	7	Washington	226	45	19.9	220	34	84.5	13
Calgary	211	39	18.5	249	37	85.1	7	Philadelphia	204	40	19.6	193	37	80.8	2
Los Angeles	200	35	17.5	221	42	81.0	5	Pittsburgh	221	42	19.0	229	46	79.9	8
Toronto	218	37	17.0	185	28	84.9	5	Buffalo	242	45	18.6	220	32	85.5	13
St. Louis	220	36	16.4	233	46	80.3	7	Hartford	174	30	17.2	185	37	80.0	3
Edmonton	259	42	16.2	233	52	77.7	8	Montreal	172	28	16.3	191	37	80.6	1
Dallas	248	39	15.7	218	34	84.4	4	NY Islanders	178	28	15.7	213	46	78.4	4
San Jose	203	24	11.8	208	39	81.3	6	Ottawa	215	31	14.4	199	39	80.4	1
Anaheim	202	23	11.4	193	47	75.6	4	Tampa Bay	177	25	14.1	205	32	84.4	6
								New Jersey	164	22	13.4	149	28	81.2	3
								Florida	222	29	13.1	191	32	83.2	1

Team by Team Statistics

High scorers and goaltenders with at least 10 games played. Players who competed for more than one team during the regular season are listed with their final club; (*) indicates rookies eligible for Calder Trophy.

Mighty Ducks of Anaheim

Top Scorers	Gm	G	A	Pts	+/-	PM	PP
Paul Kariya*	47	18	21	39	-17	4	7
Shaun Van Allen	45	8	21	29	-4	32	1
Stephan Lebeau	38	8	16	24	+6	12	1
Todd Krygier	35	11	11	22	+1	10	1
Peter Douris	46	10	11	21	+4	12	0
Patrik Carnback	41	6	15	21	-8	32	0
Bobby Dollas	45	7	13	20	-3	12	3
Bob Corkum	44	10	9	19	-7	25	0
Joe Sacco	41	10	8	18	-8	23	2
Steve Rucchin*	43	6	11	17	-7	23	0
Mike Sillinger	28	4	11	15	+4	8	2
DET	13	2	6	8	+3	2	0
ANA	15	2	5	7	+1	6	2
Oleg Tverdovsky*	36	3	9	12	-6	14	1
Valeri Karpov*	30	4	7	11	-4	6	0
Milos Holan*	25	2	8	10	+4	14	1
PHI	0	0	0	0	E	0	0
ANA	25	2	8	10	+3	14	1
Jason York*	24	1	9	10	+2	10	0
DET	10	1	2	3	E	2	0
ANA	14	0	7	7	+2	8	0
Garry Valk	36	3	6	9	-4	34	0
Tom Kurvers	22	4	3	7	-13	6	1

Acquired: D Holan from Phi. for C Anatoli Semenov (Mar. 8); RW Sillinger and D York from Det. for D Mark Ferner, LW Stu Grimson and '96 6th-round pick (Apr. 4).

Goalies (5 Gm)	Gm	Min	GAA	Sv%	Record
Guy Hebert	39	2092	3.13	.904	12-20-4
Mikhail Shtalenkov	18	810	3.63	.891	4-7-1
ANAHEIM	48	2913	3.38	.897	16-27-5

Shutouts: Hebert (2). **Assists:** none. **PM:** Hebert (2) and Shtalenkov (2).

Boston Bruins

Top Scorers	Gm	G	A	Pts	+/-	PM	PP
Adam Oates	48	12	41	53	-11	8	4
Ray Bourque	46	12	31	43	+3	20	9
Cam Neely	42	27	14	41	+7	72	16
Bryan Smolinski	44	18	13	31	-3	31	6
Mariusz Czerkawski*	47	12	14	26	+4	31	1
Mats Naslund	34	8	14	22	-4	4	2
Don Sweeney	47	3	19	22	+6	24	1
Ted Donato	47	10	10	20	+3	10	1
Jozef Stumpel	44	5	13	18	+4	8	1
Steve Heinze	36	7	9	16	E	23	0
Alexei Kasatonov	44	2	14	16	-2	33	0
Brent Hughes	44	6	6	12	+6	139	0
Steve Leach	35	5	6	11	-3	68	1
Jon Rohloff*	34	3	8	11	+1	39	0
Dave Reid	38	5	5	10	+8	10	0
Sandy Moger*	18	2	6	8	-1	6	2
Glen Murray	35	5	2	7	-11	46	0
David Shaw	44	3	4	7	-9	36	1
John Gruden*	38	0	6	6	+3	22	0
Jamie Huscroft	34	0	6	6	-3	103	0
Fred Knipscheer*	16	3	1	4	+1	2	0

Acquired: G Billington from Ott. for future considerations (Apr. 7).

Goalies (5 Gm)	Gm	Min	GAA	Sv%	Record
Blaine Lacher*	35	1965	2.41	.902	19-11-2
Vincent Riendeau	11	565	2.87	.878	3-6-1
Craig Billington	17	845	3.62	.866	5-7-2
OTT	9	472	4.07	.867	0-6-2
BOS	8	373	3.06	.864	5-1-0
BOSTON	48	2911	2.62	.891	27-18-3

Shutouts: Lacher (4). **Assists:** Lacher (1). **PM:** Billington (4), Lacher (4), Riendeau (2).

Buffalo Sabres

Top Scorers	Gm	G	A	Pts	+/-	PM	PP
Alexander Mogilny	44	19	28	47	E	36	12
Donald Audette	46	24	13	37	-3	27	13
Garry Galley	47	3	29	32	+4	30	2
PHI	33	2	20	22	E	20	1
BUF	14	1	9	10	+4	10	1
Pat LaFontaine	22	12	15	27	+2	4	6
Yuri Khmylev	48	8	17	25	+8	14	2
Derek Plante	47	3	19	22	-4	12	2
Doug Bodger	44	3	17	20	-3	47	2
Wayne Presley	46	14	5	19	+5	41	0
Dale Hawerchuk	23	5	11	16	-2	2	2
Dave Hannan	42	4	12	16	+3	32	0
Alexei Zhitnik	32	4	10	14	-6	61	3
LA	11	2	5	7	-3	27	2
BUF	21	2	5	7	-3	34	1
Jason Dawe	42	7	4	11	-6	19	0
Craig Simpson	24	4	7	11	-5	26	1
Richard Smehlik	39	4	7	11	+5	46	0
Bob Sweeney	45	5	4	9	-6	18	1
Scott Pearson	42	3	5	8	-14	74	0
EDM	28	1	4	5	-11	54	0
BUF	14	2	1	3	-3	20	0

Acquired: D Charlie Huddy, G Stauber, D Zhitnik and future pick from LA for D Philippe Boucher, G Grant Fuhr and two others (Feb. 14); D Galley from Phi. for D Petr Svoboda (Apr. 7); RW Pearson from Edm. for D Ken Sutton (Apr. 7).

Goalies (5 Gm)	Gm	Min	GAA	Sv%	Record
Dominik Hasek	41	2416	2.11	.930	19-14-7
Robb Stauber	7	333	3.96	.859	2-3-0
LA	1	16	7.50	.667	0-0-0
BUF	6	317	3.79	.867	2-3-0
BUFFALO	48	2920	2.45	.918	22-19-7

Shutouts: Hasek (5). **Assists:** none. **PM:** Hasek (2).

Calgary Flames

Top Scorers	Gm	G	A	Pts	+/-	PM	PP
Theoren Fleury	47	29	29	58	+6	112	9
Joe Nieuwendyk	46	21	29	50	+11	33	3
Phil Housley	43	8	35	43	+17	18	3
Robert Reichel	48	18	17	35	-2	28	5
Zarley Zalapski	48	4	24	28	+9	46	1
Steve Chiasson	45	2	23	25	+10	39	1
German Titov	40	12	12	24	+6	16	3
Joel Otto	47	8	13	21	+8	130	0
Wes Walz	39	6	12	18	+7	11	4
Paul Kruse	45	11	5	16	+13	141	0
Sheldon Kennedy	30	7	8	15	+5	45	1
Ronnie Stern	39	9	4	13	+4	163	1
Kevin Dahl	34	4	8	12	+8	38	0
Kelly Kisio	12	7	4	11	+2	6	5
Mike Sullivan	38	4	7	11	-2	14	0
Nikolai Borschevsky	27	0	10	10	+10	0	0
TOR	19	0	5	5	+3	0	0
CALG	8	0	5	5	+7	0	0
James Patrick	43	0	10	10	-3	14	0

Acquired: RW Borschevsky from Tor. for '96 6th-round pick (Apr. 6); G Tabaracci from Wash. for future draft pick (Apr. 7).

Goalies (5 Gm)	Gm	Min	GAA	Sv%	Record
Rick Tabaracci	13	596	2.11	.913	3-3-3
WASH	8	394	2.44	.891	1-3-2
CALG	5	202	1.49	.946	2-0-1
Trevor Kidd	43	2463	2.61	.909	22-14-6
Andrei Trefilov*	6	236	4.07	.877	0-3-0
CALGARY	48	2922	2.77	.904	24-17-7

Shutouts: Kidd (3). **Assists:** Tabaracci (2), Kidd (1). **PM:** Tabaracci (2), Kidd (2).

Chicago Blackhawks

Top Scorers	Gm	G	A	Pts	+/-	PM	PP
Bernie Nicholls	48	22	29	51	+4	32	11
Joe Murphy	40	23	18	41	+7	89	7
Chris Chelios	48	5	33	38	+17	72	3
Gary Suter	48	10	27	37	+14	42	5
Tony Amonte	48	15	20	35	+7	41	6
Jeremy Roenick	33	10	24	34	+5	14	5
Patrick Poulin	45	15	15	30	+13	53	4
Denis Savard	43	10	15	25	−3	18	2
TB	31	6	11	17	−6	10	1
CHI	12	4	4	8	+3	8	1
Sergei Krivokrasov*	41	12	7	19	+9	33	6
Jeff Shantz	45	6	12	18	+11	33	0
Brent Sutter	47	7	8	15	+6	51	1
Dirk Graham	40	4	9	13	+2	42	1
Eric Weinrich	48	3	10	13	+1	33	1
Steve Smith	47	1	12	13	+6	128	0
Murray Craven	16	4	3	7	+2	2	1
Brent Grieve	24	1	5	6	+2	23	0
Jim Cummins	37	4	1	5	−6	158	0
TB	10	1	0	1	−3	41	0
CHI	27	3	1	4	−3	117	0
Gerald Diduck	35	2	3	5	−5	63	1
VAN	22	1	3	4	−8	15	1
CHI	13	1	0	1	+3	48	0

Acquired: RW Cummins and two others from TB for LW Paul Ysebaert and RW Rich Sutter (Feb. 22); C Savard from TB for '96 6th-round pick (Apr. 6); D Diduck from Van. for RW Bogdan Savenko and '95 3rd-round pick (Apr. 7).

Goalies (5 Gm)	Gm	Min	GAA	Sv%	Record
Ed Belfour	42	2450	2.28	.906	22-15-3
Jeff Hackett	7	328	2.38	.913	1-3-2
CHICAGO	48	2909	2.37	.904	24-19-5

Shutouts: Belfour (5). **Assists:** Belfour (3). **PM:** Belfour (11).

Dallas Stars

Top Scorers	Gm	G	A	Pts	+/-	PM	PP
Dave Gagner	48	14	28	42	+2	42	7
Mike Modano	30	12	17	29	+7	8	4
Kevin Hatcher	47	10	19	29	−4	66	3
Mike Donnelly	44	12	15	27	−4	33	3
LA	9	1	1	2	−7	4	0
DAL	35	11	14	25	+3	29	3
Corey Millen	45	5	18	23	+6	36	1
NJ	17	2	3	5	+2	8	0
DAL	28	3	15	18	+4	28	1
Trent Klatt	47	12	10	22	−2	26	5
Greg Adams	43	8	13	21	−3	16	3
VAN	31	5	10	15	+1	12	2
DAL	12	3	3	6	−4	4	1
Todd Harvey*	40	11	9	20	−3	67	2
Mike Kennedy*	44	6	12	18	+4	33	2
Grant Ledyard	38	5	13	18	+6	20	4
Paul Broten	47	7	9	16	−7	36	0
Derian Hatcher	43	5	11	16	+3	105	2
Dean Evason	47	8	7	15	+3	48	1
Brent Gilchrist	32	9	4	13	−3	16	1
Paul Cavallini	44	1	11	12	+8	28	0
Peter Zezel	30	6	5	11	−6	19	0
Craig Ludwig	47	2	9	9	−6	61	0

Acquired: LW Donnelly for '96 4th-round pick. (Feb. 17); C Millen from NJ for C Neal Broten. (Feb. 27); LW Adams, RW Dan Kesa and '95 5th-round pick from Van. for RW Russ Courtnall (Apr. 7).

Goalies (5 Gm)	Gm	Min	GAA	Sv%	Record
Andy Moog	31	1770	2.44	.915	10-12-7
Darcy Wakaluk	15	754	3.18	.883	4-8-0
Mike Torchia*	6	327	3.30	.895	3-2-1
DALLAS	48	2925	2.77	.903	17-23-8

Shutouts: Moog (2) and Wakaluk (2). **Assists:** Moog (1). **PM:** Moog (14) and Wakaluk (4).

Detroit Red Wings

Top Scorers	Gm	G	A	Pts	+/-	PM	PP
Paul Coffey	45	14	44	58	+18	72	4
Sergei Fedorov	42	20	30	50	+6	24	7
Dino Ciccarelli	42	16	27	43	+12	39	6
Keith Primeau	45	15	27	42	+17	99	1
Ray Sheppard	43	30	10	40	+11	17	11
Steve Yzerman	47	12	26	38	+6	40	4
Vyacheslav Kozlov	46	13	20	33	+12	45	5
Nicklas Lidstrom	43	10	16	26	+15	6	7
Doug Brown	45	9	12	21	+14	16	1
Bob Errey	43	8	13	21	+13	58	0
SJ	13	2	2	4	+4	27	0
DET	30	6	11	17	+9	31	0
Slava Fetisov	18	3	12	15	+1	2	3
NJ	4	0	1	1	−2	0	0
DET	14	3	11	14	+3	2	3
Vladimir Konstantinov	47	3	11	14	+10	101	0
Shawn Burr	42	6	8	14	+13	60	0
Darren McCarty	31	5	8	13	+5	88	1
Martin Lapointe	39	4	6	10	+1	73	0
Greg Johnson	22	3	5	8	+1	14	2
Kris Draper	36	2	6	8	+1	22	0
Bob Rouse	48	1	7	8	+14	36	0
Mark Howe	18	1	5	6	−3	10	0

Acquired: LW Errey from SJ for '95 5th-round pick. (Feb. 27); D Fetisov from NJ for '95 3rd-round pick (Apr. 3).

Goalies (5 Gm)	Gm	Min	GAA	Sv%	Record
Chris Osgood	19	1087	2.26	.917	14-5-0
Mike Vernon	30	1807	2.52	.893	19-6-4
DETROIT	48	2900	2.42	.903	33-11-4

Shutouts: Osgood (1) and Vernon (1). **Assists:** none. **PM:** Vernon (8) and Osgood (2).

Edmonton Oilers

Top Scorers	Gm	G	A	Pts	+/-	PM	PP
Doug Weight	48	7	33	40	−17	69	1
Jason Arnott	42	15	22	37	−14	128	7
Shayne Corson	48	12	24	36	−17	86	2
David Oliver*	44	16	14	30	−11	20	10
Todd Marchant*	45	13	14	27	−3	32	3
Kelly Buchberger	48	7	17	24	E	82	2
Scott Thornton	47	10	12	22	−4	89	0
Igor Kravchuk	36	7	11	18	−15	29	3
Mike Stapleton	46	6	11	17	−12	21	3
Luke Richardson	46	3	10	13	−6	40	1
Jiri Slegr	31	2	10	12	−5	46	1
VAN	19	1	5	6	E	32	0
EDM	12	1	5	6	−5	14	1
Kirk Maltby	47	8	3	11	−11	49	0
Dean Kennedy	40	2	8	10	+2	25	0
Fredrik Olausson	33	0	10	10	−4	20	0
Boris Mironov	29	1	7	8	−9	40	0
Ken Sutton	24	4	3	7	−3	42	0
BUF	12	1	2	3	−2	30	0
EDM	12	3	1	4	−1	12	0
Peter White*	9	2	4	6	+1	0	2
Bryan Marchment	40	1	5	6	−11	184	0
Zdeno Ciger	5	2	2	4	−1	0	1

Acquired: D Sutton from Buf. for RW Scott Pearson (Apr. 7); D Slegr from Van. for RW Roman Oksiuta (Apr. 7).

Goalies (5 Gm)	Gm	Min	GAA	Sv%	Record
Bill Ranford	40	2203	3.62	.883	15-20-3
Fred Brathwaite*	14	601	3.99	.863	2-5-1
EDMONTON	48	2912	3.77	.875	17-27-4

Shutouts: Ranford (2). **Assists:** Ranford (2). **PM:** Ranford (2).

Florida Panthers

Top Scorers	Gm	G	A	Pts	+/-	PM	PP
Jesse Belanger	47	15	14	29	–5	18	6
Stu Barnes	41	10	19	29	+7	8	1
Scott Mellanby	48	13	12	25	–16	90	4
Gord Murphy	46	6	16	22	–14	24	5
Dave Lowry	45	10	10	20	–3	25	2
Jody Hull	46	11	8	19	–1	8	0
Bill Lindsay	48	10	9	19	+1	46	0
Tom Fitzgerald	48	3	13	16	–3	31	0
Brian Skrudland	47	5	9	14	E	88	1
Johan Garpenlov	40	4	10	14	+1	2	0
SJ	13	1	1	2	–3	2	0
FLA	27	3	9	12	+4	0	0
Mike Hough	48	6	7	13	+1	38	0
Jason Woolley	34	4	9	13	–1	18	1
Gaetan Duchesne	46	3	9	12	–3	16	0
SJ	33	2	7	9	–6	16	0
FLA	13	1	2	3	+3	0	0
Rob Niedermayer	48	4	6	10	–13	36	1
Bob Kudelski	26	6	3	9	+2	2	3
Brian Benning	24	1	7	8	–6	18	1
Magnus Svensson	19	2	5	7	+5	10	1
Andrei Lomakin	31	1	6	7	–5	6	1
Paul Laus	37	0	7	7	+12	138	0
Geoff Smith	47	2	4	6	–5	22	0

Acquired: LW Garpenlov from SJ for '98 5th-round pick (Mar. 3); LW Duchesne from SJ for '95 6th-round pick (Apr. 7).

Goalies (5 Gm)	Gm	Min	GAA	Sv%	Record
John Vanbiesbrouck	37	2087	2.47	.914	14-15-4
Mark Fitzpatrick	15	819	2.64	.900	6-7-2
FLORIDA	48	2916	2.61	.907	20-22-6

Shutouts: Vanbiesbrouck (4). **Assists:** Vanbiesbrouck (1). **PM:** Vanbiesbrouck (6).

Hartford Whalers

Top Scorers	Gm	G	A	Pts	+/-	PM	PP
Andrew Cassels	46	7	30	37	–3	18	1
Darren Turcotte	47	17	18	35	+1	22	3
Geoff Sanderson	46	18	14	32	–10	24	4
Steven Rice	40	11	10	21	+2	61	4
Paul Ranheim	47	6	14	20	–3	10	0
Frantisek Kucera	48	3	17	20	+3	30	0
Jimmy Carson	38	9	10	19	+5	29	4
Robert Kron	37	10	8	18	–3	10	1
Andrei Nikolishin*	39	8	10	18	+7	10	1
Adam Burt	46	7	11	18	E	65	3
Glen Wesley	48	2	14	16	–6	50	1
Chris Pronger	43	5	9	14	–12	54	3
Jocelyn Lemieux	41	6	5	11	–7	32	0
Ted Drury	34	3	6	9	–3	21	0
Mark Janssens	46	2	5	7	–8	93	0
Brian Glynn	43	1	6	7	–2	32	0
Kevin Smyth*	16	1	5	6	–3	13	0
Igor Chibirev	8	3	1	4	+1	0	0
Kelly Chase	28	0	4	4	+1	141	0
Glen Featherstone	19	2	1	3	–7	50	0
NYR	6	1	0	1	E	18	0
HART	13	1	1	2	–7	32	0
Jim Storm	6	0	3	3	+2	0	0
Scott Daniels*	12	0	2	2	+1	55	0

Acquired: D Featherstone, D Michael Stewart, '95 1st-round pick and '96 4th-round pick from NYR for RW Pat Verbeek (Mar 23).

Goalies (5 Gm)	Gm	Min	GAA	Sv%	Record
Sean Burke	42	2418	2.68	.912	17-19-4
Jeff Reese	11	477	3.27	.889	2-5-1
HARTFORD	48	2914	2.90	.904	19-24-5

Shutouts: none. **Assists:** Burke (1). **PM:** Burke (8).

Los Angeles Kings

Top Scorers	Gm	G	A	Pts	+/-	PM	PP
Wayne Gretzky	48	11	37	48	–20	6	3
Rick Tocchet	36	18	17	35	–8	70	7
Dan Quinn	44	14	17	31	–3	32	2
Jari Kurri	38	10	19	29	–17	24	2
Tony Granato	33	13	11	24	+9	68	2
Darryl Sydor	48	4	19	23	–2	36	3
Marty McSorley	41	3	18	21	–14	83	1
John Druce	43	15	5	20	–3	20	3
Randy Burridge	40	4	15	19	–4	10	2
WASH	2	0	0	0	E	2	0
LA	38	4	15	19	–4	8	2
Michel Petit	40	5	12	17	+4	84	2
Eric Lacroix*	45	9	7	16	+2	54	2
Pat Conacher	48	7	9	16	–9	12	0
Robert Lang	36	4	8	12	–7	4	0
Rob Blake	24	4	7	11	–16	38	4
Kevin Todd	33	3	8	11	–5	12	0
Gary Shuchuk	22	3	6	9	–2	6	0
Rob Cowie	32	2	7	9	–6	20	0
Chris Snell*	32	2	7	9	–7	22	0
Yanic Perreault*	26	2	5	7	+3	20	0
Philippe Boucher	15	2	4	6	+3	4	0
BUF	9	1	4	5	+6	0	0
LA	6	1	0	1	–3	4	0

Acquired: LW Burridge from Wash. for LW Warren Rychel (Feb. 10); D Boucher, G Fuhr and two others for D Charlie Huddy, G Robb Stauber, D Alexei Zhitnik and future pick (Feb. 14).

Goalies (5 Gm)	Gm	Min	GAA	Sv%	Record
Kelly Hrudey	35	1894	3.14	.910	14-13-5
Jamie Storr*	5	263	3.88	.888	1-3-1
Grant Fuhr	17	878	4.03	.873	2-9-3
BUF	3	180	4.00	.859	1-2-0
LA	14	698	4.04	.876	1-7-3
LOS ANGELES	48	2925	3.57	.896	16-23-9

Shutouts: none. **Assists:** none. **PM:** Fuhr (2).

Montreal Canadiens

Top Scorers	Gm	G	A	Pts	+/-	PM	PP
Mark Recchi	49	16	32	48	–9	28	9
PHI	10	2	3	5	–6	12	1
MON	39	14	29	43	–3	16	8
Pierre Turgeon	49	24	23	47	E	14	5
NYI	34	13	14	27	–12	10	3
MON	15	11	9	20	+12	4	2
Vincent Damphousse	48	10	30	40	+15	42	4
Benoit Brunet	45	7	18	25	+7	16	1
Vladimir Malakhov	40	4	17	21	–3	46	1
NYI	26	3	13	16	–1	32	1
MON	14	1	4	5	–2	14	0
Mike Keane	48	10	10	20	+5	15	1
Brian Savage*	37	12	7	19	+5	27	0
Brian Bellows	41	8	8	16	–7	8	1
Patrice Brisebois	35	4	8	12	–2	26	0
Yves Racine	47	4	7	11	–1	42	2
Lyle Odelein	48	3	7	10	–13	152	0
J.J. Daigneault	45	3	5	8	+2	40	0
Turner Stevenson*	41	6	1	7	E	86	0
Bryan Fogarty	21	5	2	7	–3	34	3
Oleg Petrov	12	2	5	7	–7	4	0
Ed Ronan	30	1	4	5	–7	12	0
Peter Popovic	33	0	5	5	–10	8	0

Acquired: RW Recchi and '95 3rd-round pick from Phi. for D Eric Desjardins, LW Gilbert Dionne and LW John LeClair (Feb. 9); C Turgeon and D Malakhov from NYI for C Kirk Muller, D Mathieu Schneider and C Craig Darby (Apr. 5).

Goalies (5 Gm)	Gm	Min	GAA	Sv%	Record
Patrick Roy	43	2566	2.97	.906	17-20-6
Ron Tugnutt	7	346	3.12	.895	1-3-1
MONTREAL	48	2921	3.04	.903	18-23-7

Shutouts: Roy (1), Tugnutt (1); **Assists:** Roy (1); **PM:** Roy (20).

New Jersey Devils

Top Scorers	Gm	G	A	Pts	+/-	PM	PP
Stephane Richer	45	23	16	39	+8	10	1
Neal Broten	47	8	24	32	+1	24	2
DAL	17	0	4	4	–8	4	0
NJ	30	8	20	28	+9	20	2
John MacLean	46	17	12	29	+13	32	2
Bill Guerin	48	12	13	25	+6	72	4
Scott Stevens	48	2	20	22	+4	56	1
Shawn Chambers	45	4	17	21	+2	12	2
TB	24	2	12	14	E	6	1
NJ	21	2	5	7	+2	6	1
Bobby Holik	48	10	10	20	+9	18	0
Claude Lemieux	45	6	13	19	+2	86	1
Scott Niedermayer	48	4	15	19	+19	18	4
Tom Chorske	42	10	8	18	–4	16	0
Brian Rolston*	40	7	11	18	+5	17	2
Bob Carpenter	41	5	11	16	–1	19	0
Bruce Driver	41	4	12	16	–1	18	1
Tommy Albelin	48	5	10	15	+9	20	2
Sergei Brylin*	26	6	8	14	+12	8	0
Randy McKay	33	5	7	12	+10	44	0
Mike Peluso	46	2	9	11	+5	167	0
Danton Cole	38	4	5	9	–1	14	1
TB	26	3	3	6	–1	6	1
NJ	12	1	2	3	E	8	0

Acquired: C Broten from Dal. for C Corey Millen (Feb. 27); D Chambers and RW Cole from TB for C Alexander Semak and RW Ben Hankinson (Mar. 14).

Goalies (5 Gm)	Gm	Min	GAA	Sv%	Record
Martin Brodeur	40	2184	2.45	.902	19-11-6
Chris Terreri	15	734	2.53	.900	3-7-2
NEW JERSEY	48	2926	2.48	.901	22-18-8

Shutouts: Brodeur (3). **Assists:** Brodeur (2). **PM:** Brodeur (2).

New York Islanders

Top Scorers	Gm	G	A	Pts	+/-	PM	PP
Ray Ferraro	47	22	21	43	+1	30	2
Mathieu Schneider	43	8	21	29	–8	79	3
MON	30	5	15	20	–3	49	2
NYI	13	3	6	9	–5	30	1
Kirk Muller	45	11	16	27	–18	47	4
MON	33	8	11	19	–21	33	3
NYI	12	3	5	8	+3	14	1
Patrick Flatley	45	7	20	27	+9	12	1
Steve Thomas	47	11	15	26	–14	60	3
Derek King	43	10	16	26	–5	41	7
Zigmund Palffy*	33	10	7	17	+3	6	1
Marty McInnis	41	9	7	16	–1	8	0
Scott Lachance	26	6	7	13	+2	26	3
Travis Green	42	5	7	12	–10	25	0
Dennis Vaske	41	1	11	12	+3	53	0
Bob Beers	22	2	7	9	–8	6	1
Brent Severyn	28	2	4	6	–2	71	1
FLA	9	1	1	2	–3	37	1
NYI	19	1	3	4	+1	34	0
Brad Dalgarno	22	3	2	5	–8	14	1
Chris Marinucci*	12	1	4	5	–1	2	0
Ron Sutter	27	1	4	5	–8	21	0

Acquired: D Severyn from Fla. for '95 4th-round pick (Mar. 3); C Muller, D Schneider and C Craig Darby from Mon. for C Pierre Turgeon and D Vladimir Malakhov (Apr. 5).

Goalies (5 Gm)	Gm	Min	GAA	Sv%	Record
Tommy Salo*	6	358	3.02	.905	1-5-0
Tommy Soderstrom	26	1350	3.11	.902	8-12-3
Jamie McLennan*	21	1185	3.39	.876	6-11-2
NY ISLANDERS	48	2909	3.26	.891	15-28-5

Shutouts: Soderstrom (1). **Assists:** Salo (1). **PM:** McLellan (2) and Soderstrom (2).

New York Rangers

Top Scorers	Gm	G	A	Pts	+/-	PM	PP
Mark Messier	46	14	39	53	+8	40	3
Brian Leetch	48	9	32	41	E	18	3
Sergei Zubov	38	10	26	36	–2	18	6
Pat Verbeek	48	17	16	33	–2	71	7
HART	29	7	11	18	E	53	3
NYR	19	10	5	15	–2	18	4
Adam Graves	47	17	14	31	+9	51	9
Steve Larmer	47	14	15	29	+8	16	3
Alexei Kovalev	48	13	15	28	–6	30	1
Brian Noonan	45	14	13	27	–3	26	7
Petr Nedved	46	11	12	23	–1	26	1
Sergei Nemchinov	47	7	6	13	–6	16	0
Alexander Karpovtsev	47	4	8	12	–4	30	1
Troy Loney	30	5	4	9	–2	23	2
NYI	26	5	4	9	E	23	2
NYR	4	0	0	0	–2	0	0
Jay Wells	43	2	7	9	E	36	0
Nathan LaFayette	39	4	4	8	+3	2	0
VAN	27	4	4	8	+2	2	0
NYR	12	0	0	0	+1	0	0
Stephane Matteau	41	3	5	8	–8	25	0
Kevin Lowe	44	1	7	8	–2	58	1

Acquired: RW Verbeek from Hart. for D Glen Featherstone, D Michael Stewart, '95 1st-round pick and '96 4th-round pick (Mar. 23); C LaFayette from Van. for G Corey Hirsch (Apr. 7). **Claimed:** LW Loney on waivers from NYI (Apr. 7).

Goalies (5 Gm)	Gm	Min	GAA	Sv%	Record
Glenn Healy	17	888	2.36	.907	8-6-1
Mike Richter	35	1993	2.92	.890	14-17-2
NY RANGERS	48	2895	2.78	.894	22-23-3

Shutouts: Richter (2) and Healy (1). **Assists:** Healy (2). **PM:** Richter (2) and Healy (2).

Ottawa Senators

Top Scorers	Gm	G	A	Pts	+/-	PM	PP
Alexei Yashin	47	21	23	44	–20	20	11
Alexandre Daigle	47	16	21	37	–22	14	4
Sylvain Turgeon	33	11	8	19	–1	29	2
Martin Straka	37	5	13	18	–1	16	0
PIT	31	4	12	16	E	16	0
OTT	6	1	1	2	–1	0	0
Steve Larouche*	18	8	7	15	–5	6	2
Sean Hill	45	1	14	15	–11	30	0
Rob Gaudreau	36	5	9	14	–16	8	0
Michel Picard	24	5	8	13	–1	14	1
Scott Levins	24	5	6	11	+4	51	0
Dave McIlwain	43	5	6	11	–26	22	1
Radek Bonk*	42	3	8	11	–5	28	1
Randy Cunneyworth	48	5	5	10	–19	68	2
Pat Elynuik	41	3	7	10	–11	51	0
Troy Mallette	23	3	5	8	+6	35	0
Chris Dahlquist	46	1	7	8	–30	36	1
Phil Bourque	38	4	3	7	–17	20	0
Pavol Demitra*	16	4	3	7	–4	0	1
Kerry Huffman	37	2	4	6	–17	46	2
Dave Archibald	14	2	2	4	–7	19	0
Stanislav Neckar*	48	1	3	4	–20	37	0
Dennis Vial	27	0	4	4	E	65	0

Acquired: C Straka from Pit. for C Troy Murray and D Norm Maciver (Apr. 7).

Goalies (5 Gm)	Gm	Min	GAA	Sv%	Record
Don Beaupre	37	2101	3.37	.897	7-25-3
Darrin Madeley	6	315	3.43	.895	2-3-0
OTTAWA	48	2913	3.58	.889	9-34-5

Shutouts: Beaupre (1). **Assists:** none. **PM:** Beaupre (10).

Philadelphia Flyers

Top Scorers	Gm	G	A	Pts	+/-	PM	PP
Eric Lindros	46	29	41	70	+27	60	7
Mikael Renberg	47	26	31	57	+20	20	8
John LeClair	46	26	28	54	+20	30	6
MON	9	1	4	5	-1	10	1
PHI	37	25	24	49	+21	20	5
Rod Brind'Amour	48	12	27	39	-4	33	4
Eric Desjardins	43	5	24	29	+12	14	1
MON	9	0	6	6	+2	2	0
PHI	34	5	18	23	+10	12	1
Dmitri Yushkevich	40	5	9	14	-4	47	3
Kevin Dineen	40	8	5	13	-1	39	4
Chris Therien*	48	3	10	13	+8	38	1
Brent Fedyk	30	8	4	12	-2	14	3
Craig MacTavish	45	3	9	12	+2	23	0
Anatoli Semenov	41	4	6	10	-12	10	2
ANA	15	3	4	7	-12	4	2
PHI	26	1	2	3	-2	6	0
Shjon Podein	44	3	7	10	-2	33	0
Kevin Haller	36	2	7	9	+16	48	0
Gilbert Dionne	26	0	9	9	-4	4	0
MON	6	0	3	3	-3	2	0
PHI	20	0	6	6	-1	2	0
Karl Dykhuis	33	2	6	8	+7	37	1
Petr Svoboda	37	0	8	8	-5	70	0
BUF	26	0	5	5	-5	60	0
PHI	11	0	3	3	E	10	0

Acquired: D Desjardins, LW Dionne and LW LeClair from Mon. for RW Mark Recchi and '95 3rd-round pick (Feb. 9); C Semenov from Ana. for D Milos Holan (Mar. 8); D Svoboda from Buf. for D Garry Galley (Apr. 7).

Goalies (5 Gm)	Gm	Min	GAA	Sv%	Record
Dominic Roussel	19	1075	2.34	.914	11-7-0
Ron Hextall	31	1824	2.89	.890	17-9-4
PHILADELPHIA	48	2906	2.73	.898	28-16-4

Shutouts: Roussel (1) and Hextall (1). **Assists:** Hextall (1). **PM:** Hextall (13) and Roussel (6).

Quebec Nordiques

Top Scorers	Gm	G	A	Pts	+/-	PM	PP
Joe Sakic	47	19	43	62	+7	30	3
Peter Forsberg*	47	15	35	50	+17	16	3
Owen Nolan	46	30	19	49	+21	46	13
Scott Young	48	18	21	39	+9	14	3
Mike Ricci	48	15	21	36	+5	40	9
Wendel Clark	37	12	18	30	-1	45	5
Valeri Kamensky	40	10	20	30	+3	22	5
Bob Bassen	47	12	15	27	+14	33	0
Andrei Kovalenko	45	14	10	24	-4	31	1
Uwe Krupp	44	6	17	23	+14	20	3
Adam Deadmarsh*	48	9	8	17	+16	56	0
Curtis Leschyshyn	44	2	13	15	+29	20	0
Sylvain Lefebvre	48	2	11	13	+13	17	0
Claude Lapointe	29	4	8	12	+5	41	0
Chris Simon	29	3	9	12	+14	106	0
Martin Rucinsky	20	3	6	9	+5	14	0
Craig Wolanin	40	3	6	9	+12	40	0
Adam Foote	35	0	7	7	+17	52	0
Bill Huard	33	3	3	6	E	77	0
OTT	26	1	1	2	-2	64	0
QUE	7	2	2	4	+2	13	0
Paul MacDermid	14	3	1	4	+3	22	0

Acquired: RW Huard from Ott. for D Mika Stromberg and '95 4th-round pick (Apr. 7).

Goalies (5 Gm)	Gm	Min	GAA	Sv%	Record
Jocelyn Thibault	18	898	2.34	.917	12-2-2
Stephane Fiset	32	1879	2.78	.910	17-10-3
QUEBEC	48	2908	2.76	.908	30-13-5

Shutouts: Fiset (2) and Thibault (1). **Assists:** Fiset (3). **PM:** Fiset (2).

Pittsburgh Penguins

Top Scorers	Gm	G	A	Pts	+/-	PM	PP
Jaromir Jagr	48	32	38	70	+23	37	8
Ron Francis	44	11	48	59	+30	18	3
Tomas Sandstrom	47	21	23	44	+1	42	4
Luc Robitaille	46	23	19	42	+10	37	5
Larry Murphy	48	13	25	38	+12	18	4
Joe Mullen	45	16	21	37	+15	6	5
John Cullen	46	13	24	37	-4	66	2
Kevin Stevens	27	15	12	27	E	51	6
Shawn McEachern	44	13	13	26	+4	22	1
Norm Maciver	41	4	16	20	-2	16	2
OTT	28	4	7	11	-9	10	2
PIT	13	0	9	9	+7	6	0
Troy Murray	46	4	12	16	-2	39	0
OTT	33	4	10	14	-1	16	0
PIT	13	0	2	2	-1	23	0
Ulf Samuelsson	44	1	15	16	+11	113	0
Chris Joseph	33	5	10	15	+3	46	3
Len Barrie*	48	3	11	14	-4	66	0
Mike Hudson	40	2	9	11	-1	34	0
Kjell Samuelsson	41	1	6	7	+8	54	0
Greg Hawgood	21	1	4	5	+2	25	1
Markus Naslund	14	2	2	4	E	2	0
Greg Andrusak*	7	0	4	4	-1	6	0

Acquired: C Murray and D Maciver from Ott. for C Martin Straka (Apr. 7).

Goalies (5 Gm)	Gm	Min	GAA	Sv%	Record
Ken Wregget	38	2208	3.21	.903	25-9-2
Wendell Young	10	497	3.26	.894	3-6-0
PITTSBURGH	48	2901	3.27	.900	29-16-3

Shutouts: none. **Assists:** none. **PM:** Wregget (14) and Young (2).

St. Louis Blues

Top Scorers	Gm	G	A	Pts	+/-	PM	PP
Brett Hull	48	29	21	50	+13	10	9
Brendan Shanahan	45	20	21	41	+7	136	6
Steve Duchesne	47	12	26	38	+29	36	1
Esa Tikkanen	43	12	23	35	+13	22	5
Adam Creighton	48	14	20	34	+17	74	3
Jeff Norton	48	3	27	30	+22	72	0
SJ	20	1	9	10	+1	39	0
ST.L	28	2	18	20	+21	33	0
Al MacInnis	32	8	20	28	+19	43	2
Ian Laperriere*	37	13	14	27	+12	85	1
Glenn Anderson	36	12	14	26	+9	37	0
Greg Gilbert	46	11	14	25	+22	11	0
Todd Elik	35	9	14	23	+8	22	4
SJ	22	7	10	17	+3	18	4
ST.L	13	2	4	6	+5	4	0
Bill Houlder	41	5	13	18	+16	20	1
Denis Chasse*	47	7	9	16	+12	133	1
Guy Carbonneau	42	5	11	16	+11	16	1
Patrice Tardif*	27	3	10	13	+4	29	1
Dave Roberts*	19	6	5	11	+2	10	3
Vitali Karamnov	26	3	7	10	+7	14	0
Doug Lidster	37	2	7	9	+9	12	1
Craig Johnson*	15	3	3	6	+4	4	0

Acquired: D Norton from SJ for C Craig Janney and '97 4th-round pick (Mar. 6); C Elik from SJ for RW Kevin Miller (Mar. 23).

Goalies (5 Gm)	Gm	Min	GAA	Sv%	Record
Jon Casey	19	872	2.75	.900	7-5-4
Curtis Joseph	36	1914	2.79	.902	20-10-1
ST. LOUIS	48	2912	2.78	.900	28-15-5

Shutouts: Joseph (1). **Assists:** Joseph (1). **PM:** none.

San Jose Sharks

Top Scorers	Gm	G	A	Pts	+/-	PM	PP
Ulf Dahlen	46	11	23	34	−2	11	4
Craig Janney	35	7	20	27	−1	10	3
ST.L	8	2	5	7	+3	0	1
SJ	27	5	15	20	−4	10	2
Jeff Friesen*	48	15	10	25	−8	14	5
Ray Whitney	39	13	12	25	−7	14	4
Sandis Ozolinsh	48	9	16	25	−6	30	3
Sergei Makarov	43	10	14	24	−4	40	1
Igor Larionov	33	4	20	24	−3	14	0
Kevin Miller	36	8	12	20	+4	13	1
ST.L	15	2	5	7	+4	0	0
SJ	21	6	7	13	E	13	1
Pat Falloon	46	12	7	19	−4	25	0
Tom Pederson	47	5	11	16	−14	31	0
Chris Tancill	26	3	11	14	+1	10	0
Jamie Baker	43	7	4	11	−7	22	0
Mike Rathje	42	2	7	9	−1	29	0
Andrei Nazarov*	26	3	5	8	−1	94	0
Jeff Odgers	48	4	3	7	−8	117	0
Jim Kyte	18	2	5	7	−7	33	0
Jayson More	45	0	6	6	+7	71	0
Ilya Byakin	13	0	5	5	−9	14	0
Michal Sykora*	16	0	4	4	+6	10	0

Acquired: C Janney from St.L. for D Jeff Norton and '97 4th-round pick (Mar. 6); LW Miller from St.L. from C Todd Elik (Mar. 23).

Goalies (5 Gm)	Gm	Min	GAA	Sv%	Record
Wade Flaherty	18	852	3.10	.903	5-6-1
Arturs Irbe	38	2043	3.26	.895	14-19-3
SAN JOSE	48	2904	3.33	.894	19-25-4

Shutouts: Irbe (4) and Flaherty (1). **Assists:** Flaherty (1). **PM:** Irbe (4).

Tampa Bay Lightning

Top Scorers	Gm	G	A	Pts	+/-	PM	PP
Brian Bradley	46	13	27	40	−6	42	3
Paul Ysebaert	44	12	16	28	+3	18	0
CHI	15	4	5	9	+4	6	0
TB	29	8	11	19	−1	12	0
Chris Gratton	46	7	20	27	−2	89	2
Petr Klima	47	13	13	26	−13	26	4
John Tucker	46	12	13	25	−10	14	2
Roman Hamrlik	48	12	11	23	−18	86	7
Alexander Semak	41	7	11	18	−7	25	0
NJ	19	2	6	8	−4	13	0
TB	22	5	5	10	−3	12	0
Alexander Selivanov*	43	10	6	16	−2	14	4
Rob Zamuner	43	9	6	15	−3	24	0
Marc Bureau	48	2	12	14	−8	30	0
Mikael Andersson	36	4	7	11	−3	4	0
Enrico Ciccone	41	2	4	6	+3	225	0
Marc Bergevin	44	2	4	6	−6	51	0
Cory Cross*	43	1	5	6	−6	41	0
Eric Charron*	45	1	4	5	+1	26	0
Bob Halkidis	31	1	4	5	−10	46	0
DET	4	0	1	1	+2	6	0
TB	27	1	3	4	−12	40	0
Jason Wiemer*	36	1	4	5	−2	44	0

Acquired: LW Ysebaert and RW Rich Sutter from Chi. for RW Jim Cummins and two others. (Feb. 22); C Semak and RW Ben Hankinson from NJ for D Shawn Chambers and RW Danton Cole (Mar. 14). **Claimed:** D Halkidis on waivers from Det. (Feb. 9).

Goalies (5 Gm)	Gm	Min	GAA	Sv%	Record
Darren Puppa	36	2013	2.68	.905	14-19-2
J.C. Bergeron	17	883	3.33	.869	3-9-1
TAMPA BAY	48	2906	2.97	.891	17-28-3

Shutouts: Puppa (1) and Bergeron (1). **Assists:** Puppa (1). **PM:** Puppa (2) and Bergeron (2).

Toronto Maple Leafs

Top Scorers	Gm	G	A	Pts	+/-	PM	PP
Mats Sundin	47	23	24	47	−5	14	9
Dave Andreychuk	48	22	16	38	−7	34	8
Mike Ridley	48	10	27	37	+1	14	2
Doug Gilmour	44	10	23	33	−5	26	3
Todd Gill	47	7	25	32	−8	64	3
Randy Wood	48	13	11	24	+7	34	1
Mike Gartner	38	12	8	20	E	6	2
Dmitri Mironov	33	5	12	17	+6	28	2
Benoit Hogue	45	9	7	16	E	34	2
NYI	33	6	4	10	E	34	1
TOR	12	3	3	6	E	0	1
Dave Ellett	33	5	10	15	−6	26	3
Paul DiPietro	34	5	6	11	−9	10	0
MON	22	4	5	9	−3	4	0
TOR	12	1	1	2	−6	6	0
Mike Craig	37	5	5	10	−21	12	1
Jamie Macoun	46	2	8	10	−6	75	1
Tie Domi	40	4	5	9	−5	159	0
WIN	31	4	4	8	−6	128	0
TOR	9	0	1	1	+1	31	0
Kenny Jonsson*	39	2	7	9	−8	16	0
Garth Butcher	45	1	7	8	−5	59	0
Warren Rychel	33	1	6	7	−4	120	0
LA	7	0	0	0	−5	19	0
TOR	26	1	6	7	+1	101	0

Acquired: LW Rychel from LA via Wash. for future pick (Feb. 10); LW Hogue and two future picks from NYI for G Eric Fichaud (Apr. 6); C DiPietro from Mon. for future pick (Apr. 6); RW Domi from Win. for C Mike Eastwood and '95 3rd-round pick (Apr. 7).

Goalies (5 Gm)	Gm	Min	GAA	Sv%	Record
Damian Rhodes*	13	760	2.68	.916	6-6-1
Felix Potvin	36	2144	2.91	.907	15-13-7
TORONTO	48	2920	3.00	.905	21-19-8

Shutouts: none. **Assists:** none. **PM:** Potvin (4) and Rhodes (4).

Vancouver Canucks

Top Scorers	Gm	G	A	Pts	+/-	PM	PP
Pavel Bure	44	20	23	43	−8	47	6
Trevor Linden	48	18	22	40	−5	40	9
Russ Courtnall	45	11	24	35	+2	17	2
DAL	32	7	10	17	−8	13	2
VAN	13	4	14	18	+10	4	0
Geoff Courtnall	45	16	18	34	+2	81	7
Josef Beranek	51	13	18	31	−7	30	3
PHI	14	5	5	10	+3	2	1
VAN	37	8	13	21	−10	28	2
Jeff Brown	33	8	23	31	−2	16	3
Sergio Momesso	48	10	15	25	−2	65	6
Cliff Ronning	41	6	19	25	−4	27	3
Martin Gelinas	46	13	10	23	+8	36	1
Roman Oksiuta*	38	16	4	20	−12	10	6
EDM	26	11	2	13	−14	8	5
VAN	12	5	2	7	+2	2	1
Christian Ruuttu	45	7	11	18	+14	29	0
CHI	20	2	5	7	+3	6	0
VAN	25	5	6	11	11	23	0
Jyrki Lumme	36	5	12	17	+4	26	3
Dave Babych	40	3	11	14	−13	18	1
Bret Hedican	45	2	11	13	−3	34	0
Mike Peca*	33	6	6	12	−6	30	2

Acquired: C Beranek from Phi. for LW Shawn Antoski (Feb. 15); LW Ruuttu from Van. for rights to LW Murray Craven (Mar. 10); RW Oksiuta from Edm. for D Jiri Slegr (Apr. 7); RW R. Courtnall from Dal. for LW Greg Adams, RW Dan Kesa, and '95 5th-round pick (Apr. 7).

Goalies (5 Gm)	Gm	Min	GAA	Sv%	Record
Kirk McLean	40	2374	2.75	.904	18-12-10
Kay Whitmore	11	558	3.98	.867	0-6-2
VANCOUVER	48	2942	3.02	.896	18-18-12

Shutouts: McLean (1). **Assists:** McLean (1). **PM:** Whitmore (7) and McLean (4).

Washington Capitals

Top Scorers	Gm	G	A	Pts	+/-	PM	PP
Peter Bondra	47	34	9	43	+9	24	12
Joe Juneau	44	5	38	43	-1	8	3
Michal Pivonka	46	10	23	33	+3	50	4
Calle Johansson	46	5	26	31	-6	35	4
Dmitri Khristich	48	12	14	26	E	41	8
Steve Konowalchuk	46	11	14	25	+7	44	3
Kelly Miller	48	10	13	23	+5	6	2
Dale Hunter	45	8	15	23	-4	101	3
Keith Jones	40	14	6	20	-2	65	1
Sylvain Cote	47	5	14	19	+2	53	1
Jim Johnson	47	0	13	13	+6	43	0
Mark Tinordi	42	3	9	12	-5	71	2
Dave Poulin	29	4	5	9	+2	10	0
Mike Eagles	40	3	4	7	-11	48	0
WIN	27	2	1	3	-13	40	0
WASH	13	1	3	4	+2	8	0
Sergei Gonchar*	31	2	5	7	+4	22	0
Joe Reekie	48	1	6	7	+10	97	0
Craig Berube	43	2	4	6	-5	173	0
Rob Pearson	32	0	6	6	-6	96	0
Igor Ulanov	22	1	4	5	+1	29	0
WIN	19	1	3	4	-2	27	0
WASH	3	0	1	1	+3	2	0

Acquired: C Eagles and D Ulanov from Win. for '95 3rd and 5th-round picks (Apr. 3).

Goalies (5 Gm)	Gm	Min	GAA	Sv%	Record
Jim Carey*	28	1604	2.13	.913	18-6-3
Rick Tabaracci	8	394	2.44	.891	1-3-2
Olaf Kolzig*	14	724	2.49	.902	2-8-2
WASHINGTON	48	2922	2.46	.899	22-18-8

Shutouts: Carey (4). **Assists:** none. **PM:** Kolzig (4).

Winnipeg Jets

Top Scorers	Gm	G	A	Pts	+/-	PM	PP
Alexei Zhamnov	48	30	35	65	+5	20	9
Keith Tkachuk	48	22	29	51	-4	152	7
Teemu Selanne	45	22	26	48	+1	2	8
Nelson Emerson	48	14	23	37	-12	26	4
Igor Korolev	45	8	22	30	+1	10	1
Dallas Drake	43	8	18	26	-6	30	0
Stephane Quintal	43	6	17	23	E	78	3
Teppo Numminen	42	5	16	21	+12	16	2
Mike Eastwood	49	8	11	19	-9	36	0
TOR	36	5	5	10	-12	32	0
WIN	13	3	6	9	+3	4	0
Dave Manson	44	3	15	18	-20	139	2
Thomas Steen	31	5	10	15	-13	14	2
Darryl Shannon	40	5	9	14	+1	48	0
Ed Olczyk	33	4	9	13	-1	12	2
NYR	20	2	1	3	-2	4	1
WIN	13	2	8	10	+1	8	1
Randy Gilhen	44	5	6	11	-17	52	0
Darrin Shannon	19	5	3	8	-6	14	3
Kris King	48	4	2	6	E	85	0
Neil Wilkinson	40	1	4	5	-26	75	0
Michal Grosek*	24	2	2	4	-3	21	0
Greg Brown	9	0	3	3	+1	17	0

Acquired: LW Olczyk from NYR for '95 5th-round pick (Apr. 7); C Eastwood and '95 3rd-round pick from Tor. for RW Tie Domi (Apr. 7).

Goalies (5 Gm)	Gm	Min	GAA	Sv%	Record
Nikolai Khabibulin*	26	1339	3.41	.895	8-9-4
Tim Cheveldae	30	1571	3.70	.881	8-16-3
WINNIPEG	48	2923	3.63	.885	16-25-7

Shutouts: none. **Assists:** Khabibulin (1) and Cheveldae (1). **PM:** Khabibulin (4) and Cheveldae (2).

World Championship

The 48th World Hockey Championships, held in Galve and Stockholm, Sweden from April 23 to May 7, 1995. Top four teams in Groups A and B after preliminary round-robin advanced to quarterfinals.

Final Round Robin Standings

(Overall records in parentheses)

Group A	Gm	W-L-T	Pts	GF	GA
*Russia (5-1-0)	5	5-0-0	10	24	8
*Italy (3-2-1)	5	3-1-1	7	14	11
*France (3-3-0)	5	3-2-0	6	14	11
*Canada (4-3-1)	5	2-2-1	5	15	14
Germany (1-4-0)	5	1-4-0	2	10	20
Switzerland (0-5-0)	5	0-5-0	0	10	24

Group B	Gm	W-L-T	Pts	GF	GA
*United States (3-1-2)	5	3-0-2	8	17	11
*Finland (6-1-1)	5	3-1-1	7	22	14
*Sweden (5-2-1)	5	3-1-1	7	17	9
*Czech Republic (4-4-0)	5	3-2-0	6	14	9
Norway (1-4-0)	5	1-4-0	2	9	18
Austria (0-5-0)	5	0-5-0	0	9	27

Note: Finland beat Sweden, 6-3, in round robin.

Quarterfinals

Canada 4	United States 1
Czech Republic 2	Russia 0
Finland 5	France 0
Sweden 7	Italy 0

Semifinals

Finland 3	Czech Republic 0
Sweden 3 ...... OT	Canada 2

Third Place: Canada 4 .... Czech Republic 1

Championship: Finland 4 .... Sweden 1

Leading Scorers

	Gm	G	A	Pts	PM
Andrew McKim, Canada	8	6	7	13	4
Ville Peltonen, Finland	8	6	5	11	4
Saku Koivu, Finland	8	5	5	10	18
Andreas Johansson, Sweden	8	3	6	9	8
Mikael Johansson, Sweden	8	3	6	9	4
Iain Fraser, Canada	8	2	7	9	8
Sergei Berezin, Russia	6	7	1	8	4
Jon Morris, USA	6	3	5	8	4
Christian Pouget, France	6	2	6	8	4
Raimo Helminen, Finland	8	1	7	8	2

Leading Goaltenders

	Gm	Min	GA	Avg	Sv%
Michael Rosati, Ita	5	132	3	1.36	.972
Thomas Ostlund, Swe	8	368	9	1.47	.914
Roman Turek, Cze	7	359	9	1.50	.939
Alexei Cherviakov, Rus	6	180	5	1.67	.923
Jarmo Myllys, Fin	7	420	12	1.71	.917

Position MVPs

(Selected by tournament officials)

Goalie— Jarmo Myllys, Finland; **Defenseman**— Christer Olsson, Sweden; **Forward**— Saku Koivu, Finland.

All-Tournament Team

(Selected by media)

G— Roman Turek, Czech Republic; **D**— Tommy Sjodin, Sweden and Timo Jutila, Finland; **C**— Saku Koivu, Finland; **LW**— Ville Peltonen, Finland; **RW**— Jere Lehtinen, Finland.

STANLEY CUP PLAYOFFS

| FIRST ROUND | SEMIFINALS | FINAL | | FINAL | SEMIFINALS | FIRST ROUND |

WESTERN CONFERENCE   EASTERN CONFERENCE

1995 STANLEY CUP CHAMPIONSHIP

Western Conference:
- Detroit 4 / Dallas 1 → Detroit 4
- Calgary 3 / San Jose 4 → San Jose 0
- Detroit 4
- St. Louis 3 / Vancouver 4 → Vancouver 0
- Chicago 4 / Toronto 3 → Chicago 4
- Chicago 1
- WESTERN CONFERENCE: Detroit 4

Eastern Conference:
- Quebec 2 / NY Rangers 4 → NY Rangers 0
- Philadelphia 4 / Buffalo 1 → Philadelphia 4
- Philadelphia 2
- Pittsburgh 4 / Washington 3 → Pittsburgh 1
- New Jersey 4 / Boston 1 → New Jersey 4
- New Jersey 4
- EASTERN CONFERENCE: New Jersey 4

FINAL: New Jersey 4 / Detroit 0

Series Summaries

WESTERN CONFERENCE

FIRST ROUND (Best of 7)

	W-L	GF	Leading Scorers
Detroit	4-1	17	Coffey (1-6-7)
Dallas	1-4	10	K. Hatcher (2-1-3), Broten (1-2-3) & Evason (1-2-3)

Date	Winner	Home Ice
May 7	Red Wings, 4-3	at Detroit
May 9	Red Wings, 4-1	at Detroit
May 11	Red Wings, 5-1	at Dallas
May 14	Stars, 4-1	at Dallas
May 15	Red Wings, 3-1	at Detroit

	W-L	GF	Leading Scorers
San Jose	4-3	26	Dahlen (4-3-7)
Calgary	3-4	35	& Janney (3-4-7) Fleury (7-7-14)

Date	Winner	Home Ice
May 7	Sharks, 5-4	at Calgary
May 9	Sharks, 5-4 (OT)	at Calgary
May 11	Flames, 9-2	at San Jose
May 13	Flames, 6-4	at San Jose
May 15	Flames, 5-0	at Calgary
May 17	Sharks, 5-3	at San Jose
May 19	Sharks, 5-4 (2 OT)	at Calgary

Shutout: Kidd, Calg.

	W-L	GF	Leading Scorers
Vancouver	4-3	27	Shanahan (4-5-9)
St. Louis	3-4	27	Bure (7-5-12)

Date	Winner	Home Ice
May 7	Blues, 2-1	at St. Louis
May 9	Canucks, 5-3	at St. Louis
May 11	Canucks, 6-1	at Vancouver
May 13	Blues, 5-2	at Vancouver
May 15	Canucks, 6-5 (OT)	at St. Louis
May 17	Blues, 8-2	at Vancouver
May 19	Canucks, 5-3	at St. Louis

	W-L	GF	Leading Scorers
Chicago	4-3	22	Savard (2-6-8)
Toronto	3-4	20	& Nicholls (0-8-8) Sundin (5-4-9)

Date	Winner	Home Ice
May 7	Maple Leafs, 5-3	at Chicago
May 9	Maple Leafs, 3-0	at Chicago
May 11	Blackhawks, 3-2	at Toronto
May 13	Blackhawks, 3-1	at Toronto
May 15	Blackhawks, 4-2	at Chicago
May 17	Maple Leafs, 5-4 (OT)	at Toronto
May 19	Blackhawks, 5-2	at Chicago

Shutout: Felix Potvin, Tor.

SEMIFINALS (Best of 7)

	W-L	GF	Leading Scorers
Chicago	4-0	11	Savard (1-3-4)
Vancouver	0-4	6	Five tied with 2 pts

Date	Winner	Home Ice
May 21	Blackhawks, 2-1 (OT)	at Chicago
May 23	Blackhawks, 2-0	at Chicago
May 25	Blackhawks, 3-2 (OT)	at Vancouver
May 27	Blackhawks, 4-3 (OT)	at Vancouver

Shutout: Belfour, Chi.

	W-L	GF	Leading Scorers
Detroit	4-0	24	Fedorov (4-7-11)
San Jose	0-4	6	Larionov (0-3-3)

Date	Winner	Home Ice
May 21	Red Wings, 6-0	at Detroit
May 23	Red Wings, 6-2	at Detroit
May 25	Red Wings, 6-2	at San Jose
May 27	Red Wings, 6-2	at San Jose

Shutout: Vernon, Det.

CHAMPIONSHIP (Best of 7)

	W-L	GF	Leading Scorers
Detroit	4-1	13	Lindstrom (1-4-5)
Chicago	1-4	12	Savard (4-2-6)

Date	Winner	Home Ice
June 1	Red Wings, 2-1 (OT)	at Detroit
June 4	Red Wings, 3-2	at Detroit
June 6	Red Wings, 4-3 (2 OT)	at Chicago
June 8	Blackhawks, 5-2	at Chicago
June 11	Red Wings, 2-1 (2OT)	at Detroit

EASTERN CONFERENCE

FIRST ROUND (Best of 7)

	W-L	GF	Leading Scorers
New Jersey	4-1	14	Richer (2-6-8)
Boston	1-4	5	Bourque (0-3-3)

Date	Winner	Home Ice
May 7	Devils, 5-0	at Boston
May 8	Devils, 3-0	at Boston
May 10	Bruins, 3-2	at New Jersey
May 12	Devils, 1-0 (OT)	at New Jersey
May 14	Devils, 3-2	at Boston

Shutouts: Martin Brodeur, NJ (3).

	W-L	GF	Leading Scorers
NY Rangers	4-2	25	Kovalev (4-5-9)
			& Leetch (2-7-9)
Quebec	2-4	19	Bassen (2-4-6),
			Forsberg (2-4-6)
			& Young (3-3-6)

Date	Winner	Home Ice
May 6	Nordiques, 5-4	at Quebec
May 8	Rangers, 8-3	at Quebec
May 10	Rangers, 4-3	at New York
May 12	Rangers, 3-2 (OT)	at New York
May 14	Nordiques, 4-2	at Quebec
May 16	Rangers, 4-2	at New York

	W-L	GF	Leading Scorers
Philadelphia	4-1	18	Brind'Amr. (3-5-8)
Buffalo	1-4	13	Mogilny (3-2-5)

Date	Winner	Home Ice
May 7	Flyers, 4-3 (OT)	at Philadelphia
May 8	Flyers, 3-1	at Philadelphia
May 10	Sabres, 3-1	at Buffalo
May 12	Flyers, 4-2	at Buffalo
May 14	Flyers, 6-4	at Philadelphia

	W-L	GF	Leading Scorers
Pittsburgh	4-3	29	Francis (3-11-14)
Washington	3-4	26	Bondra (5-3-8),
			Hunter (4-4-8),
			Jones (4-4-8)
			& Juneau (2-6-8)

Date	Winner	Home Ice
May 6	Capitals, 5-4	at Pittsburgh
May 8	Penguins, 5-3	at Pittsburgh
May 10	Capitals, 6-2	at Washington
May 12	Capitals, 6-2	at Washington
May 14	Penguins, 6-5 (OT)	at Pittsburgh
May 16	Penguins, 7-1	at Washington
May 18	Penguins, 3-0	at Pittsburgh

Shutout: Wregget, Pit.

SEMIFINALS (Best of 7)

	W-L	GF	Leading Scorers
Philadelphia	4-0	18	Renberg (3-4-7)
NY Rangers	0-4	10	Leetch (4-1-5)
			& Messier (1-4-5)

Date	Winner	Home Ice
May 21	Flyers, 5-4 (OT)	at Philadelphia
May 22	Flyers, 4-3 (OT)	at Philadelphia
May 24	Flyers, 5-2	at NY Rangers
May 26	Flyers, 4-1	at NY Rangers

	W-L	GF	Leading Scorers
New Jersey	4-1	17	Lemieux (6-1-7)
Pittsburgh	1-4	8	Francis (3-2-5)

Date	Winner	Home Ice
May 20	Penguins, 3-2	at Pittsburgh
May 22	Devils, 4-2	at Pittsburgh
May 24	Devils, 5-1	at New Jersey
May 26	Devils, 2-1 (OT)	at New Jersey
May 28	Devils, 4-1	at Pittsburgh

CHAMPIONSHIP (Best of 7)

	W-L	GF	Leading Scorers
New Jersey	4-2	20	McKay (4-3-7)
Philadelphia	2-4	14	Lindros (2-3-5)

Date	Winner	Home Ice
June 3	Devils, 4-1	at Philadelphia
June 5	Devils, 5-2	at Philadelphia
June 7	Flyers, 3-2 (OT)	at New Jersey
June 10	Flyers, 4-2	at New Jersey
June 11	Devils, 3-2	at Philadelphia
June 13	Devils, 4-2	at New Jersey

STANLEY CUP FINAL (Best of 7)

	W-L	GF	Leading Scorers
New Jersey	4-0	16	Broten (3-3-6)
Detroit	0-4	7	Fedorov (3-2-5)

Date	Winner	Home Ice
June 17	Devils, 2-1	at Detroit
June 20	Devils, 4-2	at Detroit
June 22	Devils, 5-2	at New Jersey
June 24	Devils, 5-2	at New Jersey

Conn Smythe Trophy (MVP)

Claude Lemieux, New Jersey, RW
20 games, 13 goals, 3 assists, 16 points

Stanley Cup Leaders

Scoring

	Pos	Gm	G	A	Pts	+/-	PM
Sergei Fedorov, Det	C	17	7	17	24	+13	6
Stephane Richer, NJ	R	19	6	15	21	+9	2
Neal Broten, NJ	C	20	7	12	19	+13	6
Ron Francis, Pit	C	12	6	13	19	+3	4
Denis Savard, Chi	C	16	7	11	18	+12	10
Paul Coffey, Det	D	18	6	12	18	+4	10
John MacLean, NJ	R	20	5	13	18	+8	14
Claude Lemieux, NJ	R	20	13	3	16	+12	20
Vyacheslav Kozlov, Det	L	18	9	7	16	+12	10
Nicklas Lidstrom, Det	D	18	4	12	16	+4	8
Jaromir Jagr, Pit	C	12	10	5	15	+3	6
Rod Brind'Amour, Phi	L	15	6	9	15	+5	8
Eric Lindros, Phi	C	12	4	11	15	+7	18
Larry Murphy, Pit	D	12	2	13	15	+3	0
Theoren Fleury, Calg	R	7	7	7	14	+8	2

Goaltending

(Minimum 420 minutes)

	Gm	Min	W-L	ShO	GAA
Martin Brodeur, NJ	20	1222	16-4	3	1.67
Ed Belfour, Chi	16	1014	9-7	1	2.19
Mike Vernon, Det	18	1063	12-6	1	2.31
Ron Hextall, Phi	15	897	10-5	0	2.81
Felix Potvin, Tor	7	424	3-4	1	2.83
Ken Wregget, Pit	11	661	5-6	1	3.00

Goals

Lemieux, NJ	13
Jagr, Pit	10
Ciccarelli, Det	9
Kozlov, Det	9
Murphy, Chi	9
McKay, NJ	8

Assists

Fedorov, Det	17
Richer, NJ	15
MacLean, NJ	13
Francis, Pit	13
Murphy, Pit	13
Three tied at 12 each.	

Wins

Brodeur, NJ	16-4
Vernon, Det	12-6
Hextall, Phi	10-5
Belfour, Chi	9-7
Wregget, Pit	5-6

Save Pct.

Brodeur, NJ	.927
Belfour, Chi	.923
Potvin, Tor	.920
Wregget, Pit	.905
Hextall, Phi	.904

Power Play Goals

Ciccarelli, Det	6
Rathje, SJ	5
Nine tied with three each.	

Overtime Goals

Chelios, Chi	2
16 tied with one each.	

Final Stanley Cup Standings

	Gm	W	L	For	Opp	Dif
New Jersey	20	16	4	67	34	+33
Detroit	18	12	6	61	44	+17
Philadelphia	15	10	5	50	43	+7
Chicago	16	9	7	45	39	+6
Pittsburgh	12	5	7	37	43	-6
NY Rangers	10	4	6	35	37	-2
Vancouver	11	4	7	33	38	-5
San Jose	11	4	7	32	59	-27
Calgary	7	3	4	35	26	+9
St. Louis	7	3	4	27	27	E
Toronto	7	3	4	20	22	-2
Washington	7	3	4	26	29	-3
Quebec	6	2	4	19	25	-6
Buffalo	5	1	4	13	18	-5
Dallas	5	1	4	10	17	-7
Boston	5	1	4	5	14	-9

Plus/Minus

Brown, Det	+14
Desjardins, Phi	+13
Driver, NJ	+13
Fedorov, Det	+13
Broten, NJ	+13

Penalty Minutes

Anderson, St.L	49
Odjick, Van	47
Kaminski, Wash	36
G. Courtnall, Van	34
Samuelsson, Pit	32

Finalists' Composite Box Scores
New Jersey Devils (16-4)

		Overall Playoffs							Finals vs Detroit						
Top Scorers	Pos	Gm	G	A	Pts	+/-	PM	PP	S	Gm	G	A	Pts	+/-	PM	PP	S
Stephane Richer	R	19	6	15	21	+9	2	3	55	4	2	2	4	+1	2	1	10
Neal Broten	C	20	7	12	19	+13	6	1	47	4	3	3	6	+5	4	0	10
John MacLean	R	20	5	13	18	+8	14	2	57	4	1	4	5	+5	0	0	10
Claude Lemieux	R	20	13	3	16	+12	20	0	65	4	2	0	2	+2	4	0	12
Randy McKay	R	19	8	4	12	+5	11	2	30	4	1	0	1	E	0	0	3
Scott Niedermayer	D	20	4	7	11	+11	10	2	53	4	1	3	4	+5	0	0	6
Bill Guerin	R	20	3	8	11	+6	30	1	28	4	0	4	4	+4	12	0	5
Shawn Chambers	D	20	4	5	9	+2	2	2	36	4	2	1	3	+3	0	0	5
Bobby Holik	L	20	4	4	8	+7	22	2	33	4	1	1	2	E	8	1	7
Tommy Albelin	D	20	1	7	8	+5	2	0	17	4	0	2	2	+1	2	0	5
Scott Stevens	D	20	1	7	8	+10	24	0	54	4	0	2	2	+5	4	0	5
Bruce Driver	D	17	1	6	7	+13	8	1	19	4	1	2	3	+4	0	1	6
Tom Chorske	L	17	1	5	6	-2	4	0	21	3	0	2	2	+1	0	0	5
Bob Carpenter	L	17	1	4	5	-1	6	1	21	4	0	1	1	+1	2	0	9
Brian Rolston	C	6	2	1	3	+6	4	1	12	2	0	1	1	+2	0	0	2
Jim Dowd	C	11	2	1	3	+3	8	0	12	1	1	1	2	+2	0	0	1
Sergei Brylin	L	12	1	2	3	+1	4	0	15	4	0	0	0	+1	2	0	2
Valeri Zelepukin	L	18	1	2	3	+1	12	0	13	4	0	0	3	+4	0	0	0
Mike Peluso	L	20	1	2	3	+4	8	0	10	4	0	0	0	E	0	0	3

Overtime goals— OVERALL (Broten, McKay); FINALS (none). **Shorthanded goals—** OVERALL (Richer); FINALS (none). **Power Play conversions—** 3 for 15 (20.0%).

Goaltending	Gm	Min	GAA	GA	SA	Sv%	W-L	Gm	Min	GAA	GA	SA	Sv%	W-L
Martin Brodeur	20	1222	1.67	34	463	.927	16-4	4	240	1.75	7	75	.907	4-0
Chris Terreri	1	8	0.00	0	2	1.000	0-0							
TOTAL	20	1232	1.66	34	465	.927	16-4	4	240	1.75	7	75	.907	4-0

Empty Net Goals— OVERALL (0); **Shutouts—** OVERALL (Brodeur 3), FINALS (none); **Assists—** OVERALL (Brodeur 1), FINALS (none); **Penalty Minutes:** OVERALL (Brodeur 6), FINALS (Brodeur 2).

Detroit Red Wings (12-6)

Top Scorers	Pos	Gm	G	A	Pts	+/-	PM	PP	S	Gm	G	A	Pts	+/-	PM	PP	S
				Overall Playoffs									**Finals vs New Jersey**				
Sergei Fedorov	C	17	7	17	24	+13	6	3	53	4	3	2	5	+1	0	1	12
Paul Coffey	D	18	6	12	18	+4	10	2	74	4	1	1	2	-3	0	0	13
Vyacheslav Kozlov	C	18	9	7	16	+12	10	1	45	4	1	0	1	-1	0	1	2
Nicklas Lidstrom	D	18	4	12	16	+4	8	3	37	4	0	2	2	-6	0	0	5
Steve Yzerman	C	15	4	8	12	-2	0	2	37	4	1	0	1	-7	0	1	6
Doug Brown	R	18	4	8	12	+14	2	0	27	4	0	3	3	+1	2	0	2
Dino Ciccarelli	R	16	9	2	11	-4	22	6	49	4	1	1	2	-5	6	1	6
Keith Primeau	L	17	5	4	9	-2	45	2	34	3	0	0	0	-3	8	0	4
Viacheslav Fetisov	D	18	0	8	8	+1	14	0	31	4	0	3	3	-5	0	0	5
Ray Sheppard	R	17	4	3	7	-6	5	2	41	3	0	1	1	-3	0	0	4
Bob Errey	L	18	1	5	6	E	30	1	18	4	0	0	0	-7	4	0	1
Kris Draper	C	18	4	1	5	-2	12	0	22	4	0	0	0	-3	4	0	3
Darren McCarty	R	18	3	2	5	+3	14	0	31	4	0	0	0	-3	4	0	2
Bob Rouse	D	18	0	3	3	+2	8	0	16	4	0	0	0	-2	0	0	2
Vlad. Konstantinov	D	18	1	1	2	+6	22	0	25	4	0	0	0	-1	8	0	3
Shawn Burr	L	16	0	2	2	-2	6	0	20	4	0	0	0	-1	0	0	1
Stu Grimson	L	11	0	1	1	E	26	0	3	2	0	0	0	-1	2	0	0
Martin LaPointe	R	2	0	1	1	+1	8	0	0	2	0	1	1	+1	8	0	0
Tim Taylor	C	6	0	1	1	-4	12	0	11	2	0	0	0	-1	2	0	3
Mike Ramsey	D	15	0	1	1	+2	4	0	7	2	0	0	0	-2	0	0	1

Overtime goals— OVERALL (Kozlov, Lidstrom, Konstantinov); FINALS (none). **Shorthanded goals—** OVERALL (Coffey, Brown, Draper); FINALS (Coffey); **Power Play conversions—** 4 for 19 (21.1%).

Goaltending	Gm	Min	GAA	GA	SA	Sv%	W-L	Gm	Min	GAA	GA	SA	Sv%	W-L
Chris Osgood	2	68	**1.76**	2	25	.920	0-0	1	32	**1.88**	1	11	.909	0-0
Mike Vernon	18	1063	**2.31**	41	370	.889	12-6	4	206	**4.08**	14	97	.856	0-4
TOTAL	18	1133	**2.33**	44	396	.889	12-6	4	238	**3.75**	16	108	.852	0-4

Empty Net Goals— OVERALL (1), FINALS (1); **Shutouts—** OVERALL (Vernon 1), FINALS (none); **Assists—** OVERALL (none); **Penalty Minutes:** OVERALL (none).

1995 NHL Draft

First and second round selections at the 33rd annual NHL entry draft held July 8, 1995, in Edmonton. The order of the first 10 positions determined by a draft lottery held June 4, in New York. Positions 11 through 26 reflect regular season records in reverse order. League and national affiliations are listed below.

First Round

Team		Pos
1 Ottawa	Bryan Berard, Detroit	D
2 NY Islanders	Wade Redden, Brandon	D
3 Los Angeles	Aki-Petteri Berg, Kiekko (FIN)	D
4 Anaheim	Chad Kilger, Kingston	C
5 Tampa Bay	Daymond Langkow, Tri-City	C
6 Edmonton	Steve Kelly, Prince Albert	C
7 Winnipeg	Shane Doan, Kamloops	R
8 Montreal	Terry Ryan, Tri-City	L
9 a-Boston	Kyle McLaren, Tacoma	D
10 Florida	Radek Dvorak, Budejovice (CZE)	L
11 Dallas	Jarome Iginla, Kamloops	C
12 San Jose	Teemu Riihijarvi, Espoo (FIN)	L
13 b-Hartford	Jean-Sebastien Giguere, Halifax	G
14 c-Buffalo	Jay McKee, Niagara Falls	D
15 Toronto	Jeff Ware, Oshawa	D
16 Buffalo	Martin Biron, Beauport	G
17 Washington	Brad Church, Prince Albert	L
18 New Jersey	Petr Sykora, Detroit Vipers	C
19 Chicago	Dimitri Nabokov, Krylja Sovetov (RUS)	C
20 Calgary	Denis Gauthier, Drummondville	D
21 Boston	Sean Brown, Belleville	D
22 Philadelphia	Brian Boucher, Tri-City	G
23 d-Washington	Mikka Elomo, Kjekko (FIN)	R
24 Pittsburgh	Alexei Morozov, Krylja Sovetov (RUS)	R
25 Colorado	Marc Denis, Chicoutimi	G
26 Detroit	Maxim Kuznetsov, Moscow Dynamo (RUS)	D

Second Round

Team		Pos
27 Ottawa	Marc Moro, Kingston	D
28 NY Islanders	Jan Hlavac, Sparta (CZE)	L
29 Anaheim	Brian Wesenberg, Guelph	R
30 Tampa Bay	Mike McBain, Red Deer	D
31 Edmonton	Georges Laraque, St. Jean	R
32 Winnipeg	Marc Chouinard, Beauport	C
33 Los Angeles	Donald MacLean, Beauport	C
34 e-Winnipeg	Jason Doig, Laval	D
35 Hartford	Sergei Fedotov, Dynamo (RUS)	D
36 Florida	Aaron MacDonald, Swift Current	G
37 Dallas	Patrick Cote, Beauport	L
38 San Jose	Peter Roed, White Bear Lake HS	C
39 NY Rangers	Christian Dube, Sherbrooke	C
40 Vancouver	Chris McAllister, Saskatoon	D
41 NY Islanders	Denis Smith, Windsor	D
42 Buffalo	Mark Dutiaume, Brandon	L
43 Washington	Dwayne Hay, Guelph	L
44 New Jersey	Nathan Perrott, Oshawa	R
45 Chicago	Christian Laflamme, Beauport	D
46 Calgary	Pavel Smirnov, Molot Perm (RUS)	L
47 Boston	Paxton Schafer, Medicine Hat	G
48 Philadelphia	Shane Kenny, Owen Sound	D
49 St. Louis	Jochen Hecht, Mannheim (GER)	C
50 f-Los Angeles	Pavel Rosa, Litvinov (CZE)	R
51 Colorado	Nic Beaudoin, Detroit	L
52 Detroit	Philippe Audet, Granby	L

Acquired picks: FIRST ROUND: **a—** from Hartford; **b—** from NY Rangers; **c—** from Vancouver; **d—** St. Louis; SECOND ROUND: **e—** from Montreal; **f—** from Pittsburgh

Affiliations: Czech Republic— Budejovice, Litvinov, Sparta; **Finland—** Espoo, Kiekko; **Germany—** Mannheim; **IHL** (International Hockey League)— Detroit Vipers; **OHL** (Ontario Hockey League)— Belleville, Detroit, Guelph, Kingston, Niagara Falls, Oshawa, Owen Sound, Windsor; **QMJHL** (Quebec Major Jr. Hockey League)— Beauport, Chicoutimi, Drummondville, Granby, Halifax, Laval, St. Jean, Sherbrooke; **Russia—** Dynamo-Moscow, Krylja Sovetov, Molot-Perm; **U.S. High School—** White Bear Lake H.S. (Minn.); **WHL** (Western Hockey League)— Brandon, Kamloops, Kelowna, Medicine Hat, Oshawa, Prince Albert, Red Deer, Saskatoon, Swift Current, Tacoma, Tri-City.

Annual Awards

Except for the Vezina Trophy and Adams Award, voting is done by a 50-member panel of the Pro Hockey Writers Assn., while full PHWA membership voted for Masterton Trophy. Vezina Trophy voted on by NHL general managers and Adams Award by NHL broadcasters. Points awarded on 5-3-1 basis.

Hart Trophy

For Most Valuable Player.

	Pos	1st	2nd	3rd	Pts
Eric Lindros, Phi	C	10	4	1—	63
Jaromir Jagr, Pit	C	2	4	5—	27
Dominik Hasek, Buf	G	3	2	2—	23
Paul Coffey, Det	D	0	4	3—	15

Calder Trophy

For Rookie of the Year.

	Pos	1st	2nd	3rd	Pts
Peter Forsberg, Que	C	13	2	0—	71
Jim Carey, Wash	G	2	9	4—	41
Paul Kariya, Ana	C	0	4	9—	21
Jeff Friesen, S.J.	L	0	0	2—	2

Norris Trophy

For Best Defenseman.

	1st	2nd	3rd	Pts
Paul Coffey, Det	12	3	0—	69
Chris Chelios, Chi	2	9	2—	39
Ray Bourque, Bos	1	1	12—	20
Larry Murphy, Pit	0	2	1—	7

Vezina Trophy

For Outstanding Goaltender.

	1st	2nd	3rd	Pts
Dominik Hasek, Buf	17	6	1—	104
Ed Belfour, Chi	2	4	3—	25
Jim Carey, Wash	1	4	8—	25
Mike Vernon, Det	3	1	3—	21
Ken Wregget, Pit	1	2	0—	11
John Vanbiesbrouck, Fla	1	1	3—	11

Lady Byng Trophy

For Sportsmanship and Gentlemanly Play.

	Pos	1st	2nd	3rd	Pts
Ron Francis, Pit	C	6	6	2—	50
Adam Oates, Bos	C	6	3	1—	40
Alexei Zhamnov, Win	C	2	3	3—	22
Brett Hull, St.L	R	1	0	4—	9
Mikael Renberg, Phi	L	0	2	3—	9
Teemu Selanne, Win	R	0	1	2—	5

Selke Trophy

For Best Defensive Forward.

	Pos	1st	2nd	3rd	Pts
Ron Francis, Pit	C	7	4	3—	50
Esa Tikkanen, St.L	L	4	8	2—	46
Joel Otto, Calg	C	3	2	2—	23
Sergei Fedorov, Det	C	1	0	1—	6
Brian Skrudland, Fla	C	0	1	2—	5
Wayne Presley, Buf	R	0	0	5—	5

Adams Award

For Coach of the Year.

	1st	2nd	3rd	Pts
Marc Crawford, Que	34	20	9—	239
Scotty Bowman, Det	17	21	12—	160
Terry Murray, Phi	9	18	19—	112
Ed Johnston, Pit	3	3	7—	31
Mike Keenan, St.L	2	4	2—	24
Jim Schoenfeld, Wash	3	2	2—	23

Bruce Bennett Studios

Pittsburgh center **Ron Francis** after winning the Lady Byng and Selke trophies on July 6.

Other Awards

Lester Pearson Award (NHL Players Assn. MVP)— Eric Lindros, Philadelphia; **Jennings Trophy** (goaltenders with a minimum of 13 games played for team with fewest goals against)— Ed Belfour, Chicago; **Masterton Trophy** (for perseverance and dedication to hockey)— Pat LaFontaine, Buffalo; **Executive of the Year** (chosen by *The Hockey News*)— Bob Clarke, Philadelphia.

All-NHL

Voting by Pro Hockey Writers' Association (PHWA). Holdover from 1993-94 All-NHL first team in **bold** type.

First Team		1st	2nd	3rd	Pts
G	**Dominik Hasek, Buf**	14	1	0—	73
D	Paul Coffey, Det	15	0	0—	75
D	Chris Chelios, Chi	11	3	1—	65
C	Eric Lindros, Phi	15	0	0—	75
R	Jaromir Jagr, Pit	14	0	1—	71
L	John LeClair, Mon-Phi	7	7	0—	56

Second Team		1st	2nd	3rd	Pts
G	Ed Belfour, Chi	1	8	3—	32
D	Ray Bourque, Bos	2	11	2—	45
D	Larry Murphy, Pit	2	5	6—	31
C	Alexei Zhamnov, Win	0	10	3—	33
R	Theoren Fleury, Calg	0	11	2—	35
L	Keith Tkachuk, Win	7	6	1—	54

All-Rookie Team

Voting by PHWA. Vote totals not released.

Pos		Pos	
G	Jim Carey, Wash.	C	Peter Forsberg, Que.
D	Kenny Jonsson, Tor.	F	Paul Kariya, Ana.
D	Chris Therien, Phi.	F	Jeff Friesen, SJ

U.S. Division I College Hockey

Final regular season standings; overall records, including all postseason tournament games, in parentheses.

Central Collegiate Hockey Assn.

	W	L	T	Pts	GF	GA
* Michigan (30-8-1)	22	4	1	45	151	74
Bowling Green (25-11-2)	18	7	2	38	135	101
* Michigan St. (25-12-3)	17	7	3	37	128	79
* Lake Superior (23-12-6)	14	9	4	32	114	78
Miami-OH (18-15-6)	13	8	6	32	88	87
Ferris St. (12-20-4)	9	14	4	22	82	111
Western Mich. (17-18-5)	9	14	4	22	87	102
IL-Chicago (11-22-4)	8	16	3	19	99	132
Notre Dame (11-23-1)	7	19	1	15	77	126
Ohio St. (7-29-2)	3	22	2	8	76	142

Note: Affiliate team Alaska-Fairbanks (11-21-1) was 5-10 vs CCHA during regular season.
Conf. Tourney Final: Lake Superior St. 5, Michigan St. 3.
NCAA Tourney (2-3): Michigan (1-1), Lake Superior St. (1-1), Michigan St. (0-1).

Eastern Collegiate Athletic Conf.

	W	L	T	Pts	GF	GA
* Clarkson (23-10-4)	14	5	3	31	116	70
Brown (15-12-3)	13	7	2	28	78	76
Harvard (14-14-2)	12	9	1	25	79	68
Colgate (20-16-1)	12	9	1	25	98	78
Vermont (19-14-2)	11	9	2	24	85	61
* RPI (19-14-4)	10	9	3	23	75	78
Princeton (17-13-4)	9	10	3	21	81	83
St. Lawrence (15-17-1)	10	12	0	20	83	110
Cornell (11-15-4)	8	10	4	20	72	76
Union (9-16-4)	6	12	4	16	70	87
Dartmouth (9-16-2)	7	13	2	16	80	111
Yale (6-13-3)	6	13	3	15	65	84

Conf. Tourney Final: RPI 5, Princeton 1.
NCAA Tourney (0-2): Clarkson (0-1), RPI (0-1).

Hockey East Association

	W	L	SW	Pts	GF	GA
* Maine (32-6-6)	15	3	6	1	88	104	63
* Boston Univ. (31-6-3)	16	5	3	2	88	131	82
* New Hamp. (22-10-4)	14	5	4	0	78	113	85
Northeastern (16-14-5)	11	8	5	5	70	98	89
UMass-Lowell (17-19-4)	11	12	1	1	58	105	116
Providence (14-17-6)	7	11	6	3	50	102	103
Merrimack (14-18-5)	7	12	5	3	48	74	91
Boston College (11-22-2)	8	14	2	1	45	86	119
UMass-Amherst (6-28-2)	3	21	0	0	15	64	129

Tiebreaker: Maine was 1-0-2 vs. BU during regular HEA season.
Note: Teams receive 5 points for a win, 2 for a tie and an extra point for a shootout win (SW).

Conf. Tourney Final: Boston University 3, Providence 2.
NCAA Tourney (5-2): BU (3-0), Maine (2-1), UNH (0-1).

Western Collegiate Hockey Assn.

	W	L	T	Pts	GF	GA
* Colorado Col. (30-12-1)	22	9	1	45	155	108
* Wisconsin (24-15-4)	17	11	4	38	128	112
* Denver (25-15-2)	18	12	2	38	131	115
* Minnesota (25-14-5)	16	11	5	37	121	95
St. Cloud St. (17-20-1)	15	16	1	31	126	113
North Dakota (18-18-3)	14	15	3	31	120	141
Minn-Duluth (16-18-4)	13	15	4	30	124	127
Michigan Tech (15-20-4)	12	17	3	27	109	140
Northern Mich. (13-24-3)	10	19	3	23	110	136
AK-Anchorage (11-25-0)	10	22	0	20	106	142

Conf. Tourney Final: Wisconsin 4, Colorado College 3 (OT).
NCAA Tourney (4-4): Minnesota (2-1), Denver (1-1), Wisconsin (1-1), Colorado College (0-1).

NCAA Top 10 Poll

Taken **before** final two rounds of league tournaments.

Final weekly regular season Top 10 poll conducted by *The Record* of Troy, N.Y. and taken March 12, before semifinals and finals of league tournaments. Voting panel made up of 21 Division I coaches, eight national media correspondents and one pro scout. First place votes in parentheses; teams in **bold** type went on to reach NCAA tournament Final Four.

	League	W	L	T	Pts
1 **Maine** (18)	HEA	28	4	6	284
2 **Michigan** (7)	CCHA	28	6	1	265
3 **Boston Univ.** (4)	HEA	26	6	3	252
4 Colorado Col. (1)	WCHA	29	10	1	218
5 Bowling Green	CCHA	24	10	2	153
6 Denver	WCHA	24	12	2	137
7 Clarkson	ECAC	21	8	4	91
8 Michigan St	CCHA	23	10	3	87
9 New Hampshire	HEA	22	9	4	84
10 **Minnesota**	WCHA	21	12	5	47

Also receiving votes: 11. **Wisconsin** (17 pts); 12. **Lake Superior St.** (11 pts); 13. **Colgate** (3 pts); 14. **RPI** (1 pt).

Leading Scorers

Including postseason games.

West	Cl	Pos	Gm	G	A	Pts
Brendan Morrison, Mich.	So.	C	39	23	53	76
Brian Holzinger, B. Green	Sr.	C	38	35	34	69
Brian Bonin, Minnesota	Jr.	C	44	32	31	63
Mike Knuble, Michigan	Sr.	R	34	38	22	60
Peter Geronazzo, Colo. Col.	Jr.	R	43	29	28	57
Colin Schmidt, Colo. Col.	Jr.	C	43	26	31	57
Rem Murray, Mich. St.	Sr.	L	40	20	36	56
Max Williams, Wisconsin	Jr.	R	43	26	26	52
Brian Felsner, LSS	So.	L	44	24	27	51
Anson Carter, Mich. St.	Jr.	C	39	34	17	51
Jay McNeill, Colo. Col	Jr.	C	43	33	18	51
Kevin Hilton, Michigan	Jr.	C	37	20	31	51
Steve Guolla, Mich. St.	Sr.	L	40	16	35	51

East	Cl	Pos	Gm	G	A	Pts
Martin St. Louis, Vermont	So.	L	35	23	48	71
Eric Perrin, Vermont	So.	C	35	28	39	67
Greg Bullock, Lowell	So.	C	40	25	40	65
Marko Tuomainen, Clark.	Sr.	R	37	23	37	60
Mike Harder, Colgate	So.	R	36	22	36	58
Chris O'Sullivan, BU	So.	C	40	23	33	56
Patrice Robitaille, Clarkson	Sr.	L	37	30	26	56
Chris DeProfio, Colgate	Jr.	C	35	21	34	55
Mike Grier, BU	So.	R	37	29	26	55
Jeff Tory, Maine	Jr.	D	40	13	42	55

Leading Goaltenders

Including postseason games; minimum 15 games.

West	Cl	Record	Sv%	GAA
Marty Turco, Mich	Fr.	27-7-1	.894	2.76
Jeff Callinan, Minn	Sr.	23-11-5	.892	2.78
John Grahame, LSS	Fr.	16-7-3	.887	2.79
Sinuhe Wallinheimo, DU	Jr.	16-10-1	.904	2.84
Chuck Thuss, Miami-OH	Sr.	16-10-6	.901	2.87

East	Cl	Record	Sv%	GAA
Blair Allison, Maine	Jr.	32-6-6	.887	2.68
Tim Thomas, Vermont	So.	18-14-2	.914	2.69
Tom Noble, BU	Fr.	15-2-0	.890	2.75
Derek Herlofsky, BU	Sr.	16-4-3	.875	2.90
Mike Tamburro, RPI	Jr.	13-8-4	.914	2.93

Terriers Back As NCAA Top Dogs

by Neil Koepke

NCAA Photos

Boston University captain **Jacques Joubert** shows off championship trophy after BU's 6-2 victory over Maine at Providence Civic Center.

From the first day of practice in early October, Boston University was a team on a mission.

"Without a doubt, our goal from the start of the season was to win the national championship," said senior center Jacques Joubert, the Terriers' captain.

Winning the NCAA title was the only way BU's returning lettermen could erase the memory of the 1994 championship game, a humiliating 9-1 loss to Lake Superior State.

"We just didn't show up," Joubert said of the biggest rout in an NCAA final since 1961. "We wanted to prove that it was just a fluke."

With a wealth of talent returning at every position, Boston University was the preseason favorite to win its fourth national title and first in 17 years. But after two losses and two ties against fellow Hockey East power Maine early in the schedule, the Terriers spent most of the season playing in the shadow of the Black Bears, who entered the postseason ranked No. 1 in the country

The inability to beat Maine served as an early reality check for BU, which had a record of 7-3-3 on Dec. 3.

"We were floundering and had to change our style," said coach Jack Parker. "We were too offensive-minded. We told our players they had to start playing defense and they accepted the challenge."

Over the last three months of the regular season, the Terriers were virtually unbeatable. They went 18-3, won the final Beanpot tournament at the old Boston Garden and gained a national audience through the exploits of right wing Mike Grier, a 6-foot-1, 237-pound sophomore whom *Sports Illustrated* tabbed as possibly the NHL's "first American-born-and-trained black offensive star." Grier, who scored 29 goals in 37 games, made first team All-America and was a finalist in the Hobey Baker Award voting won by Bowling Green senior center Brian Holzinger.

The anticipated showdown between BU and Maine was put off when Providence upset the Black Bears, 7-3, in the Hockey East tournament semifinals. Boston then beat the Friars, 3-2, for the championship.

In the NCAAs, however, the Terriers confronted both their demons and triumphed by identical 6-2 scores. First, they avenged the 1994 title game debacle by beating Lake State in the quarterfinals. Then, after putting away Minnesota in the semifinals at the Final Four in Providence, BU defeated Maine in the first All-East final since 1985.

Sophomore left wing Chris O'Sullivan, a defenseman-turned-forward who led the Terriers in scoring for the season with 56 points, had two goals in the final and was named the tournament's Most Outstanding Player.

Maine reached the title game after outlasting Michigan, 4-3, in triple overtime— a game that will be considered one of the greatest in NCAA tournament history. It came to an end just 28 seconds into the third extra period when sophomore center Dan Shermerhorn of the Black Bears scored on a face-off. The Wolverines were making their third Final Four appearance in four years.

"The entire season was treading water waiting to get back to this tournament," said Parker, who has coached the Terriers for 22 years. "I'm glad the kids had the opportunity to redeem themselves."

Neil Koepke is the national college hockey writer for the *Lansing* (Mich.) *State Journal.*

NCAA Division I Tournament

Regional Seeds

West	East
1 **Michigan** (28-7-1)	1 **Boston U.** (28-6-3)
2 Colorado Col. (30-11-1)	2 **Maine** (29-5-6)
3 Minnesota (23-13-5)	3 New Hampshire (22-9-4)
4 Wisconsin (23-14-4)	4 Clarkson (23-9-4)
5 Michigan St. (25-11-3)	5 Lake Superior (22-11-6)
6 RPI (19-13-4)	6 Denver (24-14-2)

West Regional

At Dane County Coliseum in Madison, Wisc., March 24-25. Single elimination, two second round winners advance.

First Round

Minnesota 3 ....RPI 0
Wisconsin 5.................................Michigan St. 3
(Byes: Colorado College and Michigan)

Second Round

Minnesota 5 ....Colorado College 2
Michigan 4 ....Wisconsin 3
(Michigan and Minnesota advance)

East Regional

At the Worcester (Mass.) Centrum, March 24-25. Single elimination, two second round winners advance.

First Round

Denver 9 ....New Hampshire 2
Lake Superior St. 5.............................Clarkson 4
(Byes: Boston University and Maine)

Second Round

Maine 4 ....Denver 2
Boston University 6...............Lake Superior St. 2
(BU and Maine advance)

Hobey Baker Award

For College Player of the Year. Presented since 1981 by the Decathlon Athletic Club of Bloomington, Minn. Voting done by 18-member panel of national media, coaches and pro scouts. Vote totals not released.

		Cl	Pos
Winner: Brian Holzinger, Bowl. Green		Sr.	F
Runner-up: Chris Imes, Maine		Sr.	D

Division I All-America

Regional university first team selections as chosen by the American Hockey Coaches Association. Holdover from 1993-94 All-America first teams in **bold** type.

West Team

Pos		Yr	Hgt	Wgt
G	Chuck Thuss, Miami-OH	Sr.	6-0	185
D	Kelly Perrault, Bowling Green	So.	6-0	185
D	Brian Rafalski, Wisconsin	Sr.	5-9	180
F	Brian Bonin, Minnesota	Jr.	5-10	182
F	Brian Holzinger, Bowling Green	Sr.	5-11	185
F	Brendan Morrison, Michigan	So.	5-11	176

East Team

Pos		Yr	Hgt	Wgt
G	Blair Allison, Maine	Jr.	5-11	185
D	Chris Imes, Maine	Sr.	5-11	195
D	**Brian Mueller**, Clarkson	Sr.	6-0	235
F	Greg Bullock, UMass-Lowell	So.	5-11	177
F	Mike Grier, Boston Univ.	So.	6-0	242
F	Martin St. Louis, Vermont	So.	5-7	150

THE FINAL FOUR

At Providence (R.I.) Civic Center, March 30 and April 1. Single elimination; no consolation game.

Semifinals

Maine 4 ....3OT ....Michigan 3
Boston University 7 ....Minnesota 3

Championship

Boston University 6 ....Maine 2

Final records: Boston University (31-6-3); Maine (32-6-6); Michigan (29-8-1); Minnesota (25-14-5).

Outstanding Player: Chris O'Sullivan, Boston University sophomore left wing; SEMIFINAL— 1 goal; FINAL— 2 goals.

All-Tournament Team: O'Sullivan, forward Shawn Bates and defenseman Kaj Linna of Boston University; forward Dan Shermerhorn, defenseman Chris Imes and goaltender Blair Allison of Maine.

Championship Game

Boston University, 6-2

Saturday, April 1, 1995, at Providence (R.I.) Civic Center; Attendance: 12,155; TV Rating: 0.8/2 share (ESPN).

Maine (Hockey East)	0	1	1	—	2
Boston University (Hockey East)	1	2	3	—	6

Scoring

1st Period: BU— Steve Thornton (unassisted), 14:57.
2nd Period: BU— Chris O'Sullivan (Mike Grier, Thornton) 7:27; BU— Jacques Joubert (Kaj Linna, Mike Prendergast) 9:15; UM— Tim Lovell (Tony Frenette, Jamie Thompson), 14:51.
3rd Period: UM— Trevor Roenick (Jacque Rodrigue, Jeff Tory) 0:31; BU— Mike Sylvia (Shawn Bates, Jay Pandolfo) 5:23; BU— O'Sullivan (Rich Brennan, Grier) 8:30; BU— Bob Lachance (Thornton) 18:47.

Goaltenders

Saves: BU— Tom Noble (23 shots/21 saves); UM—Blair Allison (39 shots/33 saves).

Other NCAA Tournaments

Division II

Two teams selected from limited national field. Championship decided in two games.

Final Two

March 17-18 at Erie, Pa.
Championship: GAME ONE— Bemidji St. (Minn.) 6, Mercyhurst (Pa.) 2; GAME TWO— Bemidji St. 5, Mercyhurst 4.
Final records: Bemidji St. (24-7-2), Mercyhurst (23-3-2).

Division III

Final Four

March 24-25 at Middlebury, Vt.
Semifinals— Fredonia St. 4, WI-Superior 3; Middlebury 3, WI-River Falls 1. **Third Place—** WI-River Falls 6, WI-Superior 5 (OT). **Championship—** Middlebury 1, Fredonia St. 0.
Final records: Middlebury (22-2-2); Fredonia St. (25-5-4); WI-River Falls (19-10-4); WI-Superior (23-9-1).

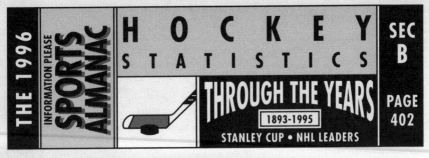

THE 1996 INFORMATION PLEASE SPORTS ALMANAC

HOCKEY STATISTICS

THROUGH THE YEARS
1893-1995
STANLEY CUP • NHL LEADERS

SEC B

PAGE 402

The Stanley Cup

The Stanley Cup was originally donated to the Canadian Amateur Hockey Association by Sir Frederick Arthur Stanley, Lord Stanley of Preston and 16th Earl of Derby, who had become interested in the sport while Governor General of Canada from 1888 to 1893. Stanley wanted the trophy to be a challenge cup, contested for each year by the best amateur hockey teams in Canada.

In 1893, the Cup was presented without a challenge to the AHA champion Montreal Amateur Athletic Association team. Every year since, however, there has been a playoff. In 1914, Cup trustees limited the field challenging for the trophy to the champion of the eastern professional National Hockey Association (NHA, organized in 1910) and the western professional Pacific Coast Hockey Association (PCHA, organized in 1912).

The NHA disbanded in 1917 and the National Hockey League (NHL) was formed. From 1918 to 1926, the NHL and PCHA champions played for the Cup with the Western Canada Hockey League (WCHL) champion joining in a three-way challenge in 1923 and '24. The PCHA disbanded in 1924, while the WCHL became the Western Hockey League (WHL) for the 1925-26 season and folded the following year. The NHL playoffs have decided the winner of the Stanley Cup ever since.

Champions, 1893-1917

Multiple winners: Montreal Victorias and Montreal Wanderers (4); Montreal Amateur Athletic Association and Ottawa Silver Seven (3); Montreal Shamrocks, Ottawa Senators, Quebec Bulldogs and Winnipeg Victorias (2).

Year		Year		Year	
1893	Montreal AAA	1901	Winnipeg Victorias	1909	Ottawa Senators
1894	Montreal AAA	1902	Montreal AAA	1910	Montreal Wanderers
1895	Montreal Victorias	1903	Ottawa Silver Seven	1911	Ottawa Senators
1896	(Feb.) Winnipeg Victorias	1904	Ottawa Silver Seven	1912	Quebec Bulldogs
	(Dec.) Montreal Victorias	1905	Ottawa Silver Seven	1913	Quebec Bulldogs
1897	Montreal Victorias	1906	Montreal Wanderers	1914	Toronto Blueshirts (NHA)
1898	Montreal Victorias	1907	(Jan.) Kenora Thistles	1915	Vancouver Millionaires (PCHA)
1899	Montreal Shamrocks		(Mar.) Montreal Wanderers	1916	Montreal Canadiens (NHA)
1900	Montreal Shamrocks	1908	Montreal Wanderers	1917	Seattle Metropolitans (PCHA)

Champions Since 1918

Multiple winners: Montreal Canadiens (23); Toronto Arenas-St.Pats-Maple Leafs (13); Detroit Red Wings (7); Boston Bruins and Edmonton Oilers (5); NY Islanders, NY Rangers and Ottawa Senators (4); Chicago Blackhawks (3); Philadelphia Flyers, Pittsburgh Penguins and Montreal Maroons (2).

Year	Winner	Head Coach	Series	Loser	Head Coach
1918	Toronto Arenas	Dick Carroll	3-2 (WLWLW)	Vancouver (PCHA)	Frank Patrick
1919	No Decision: (see below).				
1920	Ottawa	Pete Green	3-2 (WWLLW)	Seattle (PCHA)	Pete Muldoon
1921	Ottawa	Pete Green	3-2 (LWWLW)	Vancouver (PCHA)	Frank Patrick
1922	Toronto St.Pats	Eddie Powers	3-2 (LWLWW)	Vancouver (PCHA)	Frank Patrick
1923	Ottawa	Pete Green	3-1 (WLWW)	Vancouver (PCHA)	Frank Patrick
			2-0	Edmonton (WCHL)	K.C. McKenzie
1924	Montreal	Leo Dandurand	2-0	Vancouver (PCHA)	Frank Patrick
			2-0	Calgary (WCHL)	Eddie Oatman
1925	Victoria (WCHL)	Lester Patrick	3-1 (WWLW)	Montreal	Leo Dandurand
1926	Montreal Maroons	Eddie Gerard	3-1 (WWLW)	Victoria (WHL)	Lester Patrick
1927	Ottawa	Dave Gill	2-0 (TWTW)	Boston	Art Ross
1928	NY Rangers	Lester Patrick	3-2 (LWLWW)	Montreal Maroons	Eddie Gerard
1929	Boston	Cy Denneny	2-0	NY Rangers	Lester Patrick
1930	Montreal	Cecil Hart	2-0	Boston	Art Ross
1931	Montreal	Cecil Hart	3-2 (WLLWW)	Chicago	Art Duncan
1932	Toronto	Dick Irvin	3-0	NY Rangers	Lester Patrick
1933	NY Rangers	Lester Patrick	3-1 (WWLW)	Toronto	Dick Irvin
1934	Chicago	Tommy Gorman	3-1 (WWLW)	Detroit	Jack Adams
1935	Montreal Maroons	Tommy Gorman	3-0	Toronto	Dick Irvin
1936	Detroit	Jack Adams	3-1 (WWLW)	Toronto	Dick Irvin

Note: The 1919 Finals were cancelled after five games due to an influenza epidemic with Montreal and Seattle (PCHA) tied at 2-2-1.

Year	Winner	Head Coach	Series	Loser	Head Coach
1937	Detroit	Jack Adams	3-2 (LWLWW)	NY Rangers	Lester Patrick
1938	Chicago	Bill Stewart	3-1 (WLWW)	Toronto	Dick Irvin
1939	Boston	Art Ross	4-1 (WLWWW)	Toronto	Dick Irvin
1940	NY Rangers	Frank Boucher	4-2 (WWLLWW)	Toronto	Dick Irvin
1941	Boston	Cooney Weiland	4-0	Detroit	Jack Adams
1942	Toronto	Hap Day	4-3 (LLLWWWW)	Detroit	Jack Adams
1943	Detroit	Ebbie Goodfellow	4-0	Boston	Art Ross
1944	Montreal	Dick Irvin	4-0	Chicago	Paul Thompson
1945	Toronto	Hap Day	4-3 (WWWWLLLW)	Detroit	Jack Adams
1946	Montreal	Dick Irvin	4-1 (WWWLW)	Boston	Dit Clapper
1947	Toronto	Hap Day	4-2 (LWWWLW)	Montreal	Dick Irvin
1948	Toronto	Hap Day	4-0	Detroit	Tommy Ivan
1949	Toronto	Hap Day	4-0	Detroit	Tommy Ivan
1950	Detroit	Tommy Ivan	4-3 (WLWLLWW)	NY Rangers	Lynn Patrick
1951	Toronto	Joe Primeau	4-1 (WLWWW)	Montreal	Dick Irvin
1952	Detroit	Tommy Ivan	4-0	Montreal	Dick Irvin
1953	Montreal	Dick Irvin	4-1 (WLWWW)	Boston	Lynn Patrick
1954	Detroit	Tommy Ivan	4-3 (WWLWLW)	Montreal	Dick Irvin
1955	Detroit	Jimmy Skinner	4-3 (WWLLWLW)	Montreal	Dick Irvin
1956	Montreal	Toe Blake	4-1 (WWLWW)	Detroit	Jimmy Skinner
1957	Montreal	Toe Blake	4-1 (WWWLW)	Boston	Milt Schmidt
1958	Montreal	Toe Blake	4-2 (WLWLW)	Boston	Milt Schmidt
1959	Montreal	Toe Blake	4-1 (WWLWW)	Toronto	Punch Imlach
1960	Montreal	Toe Blake	4-0	Toronto	Punch Imlach
1961	Chicago	Rudy Pilous	4-2 (WLWLW)	Detroit	Sid Abel
1962	Toronto	Punch Imlach	4-2 (WWLLWW)	Chicago	Rudy Pilous
1963	Toronto	Punch Imlach	4-1 (WWLWW)	Detroit	Sid Abel
1964	Toronto	Punch Imlach	4-3 (WLLWLWW)	Detroit	Sid Abel
1965	Montreal	Toe Blake	4-3 (WWLLWW)	Chicago	Billy Reay
1966	Montreal	Toe Blake	4-2 (LLWWWW)	Detroit	Sid Abel
1967	Toronto	Punch Imlach	4-2 (LWWLWW)	Montreal	Toe Blake
1968	Montreal	Toe Blake	4-0	St. Louis	Scotty Bowman
1969	Montreal	Claude Ruel	4-0	St. Louis	Scotty Bowman
1970	Boston	Harry Sinden	4-0	St. Louis	Scotty Bowman
1971	Montreal	Al MacNeil	4-3 (LLWWLWW)	Chicago	Billy Reay
1972	Boston	Tom Johnson	4-2 (WWLWLW).	NY Rangers	Emile Francis
1973	Montreal	Scotty Bowman	4-2 (WWLWLW)	Chicago	Billy Reay
1974	Philadelphia	Fred Shero	4-2 (LWWLWW)	Boston	Bep Guidolin
1975	Philadelphia	Fred Shero	4-2 (WWLLWW)	Buffalo	Floyd Smith
1976	Montreal	Scotty Bowman	4-0	Philadelphia	Fred Shero
1977	Montreal	Scotty Bowman	4-0	Boston	Don Cherry
1978	Montreal	Scotty Bowman	4-2 (WWLWW)	Boston	Don Cherry
1979	Montreal	Scotty Bowman	4-1 (LWWW)	NY Rangers	Fred Shero
1980	NY Islanders	Al Arbour	4-2 (WLWLW)	Philadelphia	Pat Quinn
1981	NY Islanders	Al Arbour	4-1 (WWWLW)	Minnesota	Glen Sonmor
1982	NY Islanders	Al Arbour	4-0	Vancouver	Roger Neilson
1983	NY Islanders	Al Arbour	4-0	Edmonton	Glen Sather
1984	Edmonton	Glen Sather	4-1 (WLWWW)	NY Islanders	Al Arbour
1985	Edmonton	Glen Sather	4-1 (LWWWW)	Philadelphia	Mike Keenan
1986	Montreal	Jean Perron	4-1 (LWWWW)	Calgary	Bob Johnson
1987	Edmonton	Glen Sather	4-3 (WWLWLLW)	Philadelphia	Mike Keenan
1988	Edmonton	Glen Sather	4-0	Boston	Terry O'Reilly
1989	Calgary	Terry Crisp	4-2 (WLLWWW)	Montreal	Pat Burns
1990	Edmonton	John Muckler	4-1 (WLWWW)	Boston	Mike Milbury
1991	Pittsburgh	Bob Johnson	4-2 (LWLWWW)	Minnesota	Bob Gainey
1992	Pittsburgh	Scotty Bowman	4-0	Chicago	Mike Keenan
1993	Montreal	Jacques Demers	4-1 (LWWWW)	Los Angeles	Barry Melrose
1994	NY Rangers	Mike Keenan	4-3 (LWWWLLW)	Vancouver	Pat Quinn
1995	New Jersey	Jacques Lemaire	4-0	Detroit	Scotty Bowman

M.J. O'Brien Trophy

Donated by Canadian mining magnate M.J. O'Brien, whose son Ambrose founded the National Hockey Association in 1910. Originally presented to the NHA champion until the league's demise in 1917, the trophy then passed to the NHL champion through 1927. It was awarded to the NHL's Canadian Division winner from 1927-38 and the Stanley Cup runner-up from 1939-50 before being retired in 1950.

NHA winners included the Montreal Wanderers (1910), original Ottawa Senators (1911 and '15), Quebec Bulldogs (1912 and '13), Toronto Blueshirts (1914) and Montreal Canadiens (1916 and '17).

Conn Smythe Trophy

The Most Valuable Player of the Stanley Cup Playoffs, as selected by the Pro Hockey Writers Assn. Presented since 1965 by Maple Leaf Gardens Limited in the name of the former Toronto coach, GM and owner, Conn Smythe. Winners who did not play for the Cup champion are in **bold** type.

Multiple winners: Wayne Gretzky, Mario Lemieux, Bobby Orr, Bernie Parent and Patrick Roy (2).

Year		Year		Year	
1965	Jean Beliveau, Mon., C	1976	**Reggie Leach**, Phi., RW	1987	**Ron Hextall**, Phi., G
1966	**Roger Crozier**, Det., G	1977	Guy Lafleur, Mon., RW	1988	Wayne Gretzky, Edm., C
1967	Dave Keon, Tor., C	1978	Larry Robinson, Mon., D	1989	Al MacInnis, Calg., D
1968	**Glenn Hall**, St.L., G	1979	Bob Gainey, Mon., LW		
1969	Serge Savard, Mon., D			1990	Bill Ranford, Edm., G
		1980	Bryan Trottier, NYI, C	1991	Mario Lemieux, Pit., C
1970	Bobby Orr, Bos., D	1981	Butch Goring, NYI, C	1992	Mario Lemieux, Pit., C
1971	Ken Dryden, Mon., G	1982	Mike Bossy, NYI, RW	1993	Patrick Roy, Mon., G
1972	Bobby Orr, Bos., D	1983	Billy Smith, NYI, G	1994	Brian Leetch, NYR, D
1973	Yvan Cournoyer, Mon., RW	1984	Mark Messier, Edm., LW	1995	Claude Lemieux, NJ, RW
1974	Bernie Parent, Phi., G	1985	Wayne Gretzky, Edm., C		
1975	Bernie Parent, Phi., G	1986	Patrick Roy, Mon., G		

Note: Ken Dryden (1971) and Patrick Roy (1986) are the only players to win as rookies.

All-Time Stanley Cup Playoff Leaders

CAREER

Stanley Cup Playoff leaders through 1995. Years listed indicate number of playoff appearances. Players active in 1995 in **bold** type; (DNP) indicates active player did not participate in 1995 playoffs.

Scoring

Points

		Yrs	Gm	G	A	Pts
1	**Wayne Gretzky** (DNP)	14	180	110	236	346
2	**Mark Messier**	15	210	102	170	272
3	**Jari Kurri** (DNP)	12	174	102	120	222
4	**Glenn Anderson**	14	214	92	117	209
5	Bryan Trottier	17	221	71	113	184
6	Jean Beliveau	17	162	79	97	176
7	**Paul Coffey**	13	155	53	119	172
8	Denis Savard	14	153	65	105	170
9	Denis Potvin	14	185	56	108	164
10	Mike Bossy	10	129	85	75	160
	Gordie Howe	20	157	68	92	160
	Bobby Smith	13	184	64	96	160
13	**Doug Gilmour**	11	130	48	104	152
14	Stan Mikita	18	155	59	91	150
15	Brian Propp	13	160	64	84	148
16	Larry Robinson	20	227	28	116	144
17	Jacques Lemaire	11	145	61	78	139
	Ray Bourque	16	157	33	106	139
19	Phil Esposito	15	130	61	76	137
20	Guy Lafleur	14	128	58	76	134
21	Steve Larmer	13	140	56	75	131
22	Bobby Hull	14	119	62	67	129
	Henri Richard	18	180	49	80	129
24	Yvan Cournoyer	12	147	64	63	127
25	Maurice Richard	15	133	82	44	126

Goals

		Yrs	Gm	G
1	**Wayne Gretzky** (DNP)	14	180	110
2	**Jari Kurri** (DNP)	12	174	102
	Mark Messier	15	210	102
4	**Glenn Anderson**	14	214	92
5	Mike Bossy	10	129	85
6	Maurice Richard	15	133	82
7	Jean Beliveau	17	162	79
8	Bryan Trottier	17	221	71
9	Gordie Howe	20	157	68
10	**Dino Ciccarelli**	13	124	67
11	Denis Savard	14	153	65
12	Yvan Cournoyer	12	147	64
	Brian Propp	13	160	64
	Bobby Smith	13	184	64
15	Bobby Hull	14	119	62

Assists

		Yrs	Gm	A
1	**Wayne Gretzky** (DNP)	14	180	236
2	**Mark Messier**	15	210	170
3	**Jari Kurri** (DNP)	12	174	120
4	**Paul Coffey**	13	155	119
5	**Glenn Anderson**	14	214	117
6	Larry Robinson	20	227	116
7	Bryan Trottier	17	221	113
8	Denis Potvin	14	185	108
9	**Ray Bourque**	16	157	106
10	Denis Savard	14	153	105
11	**Doug Gilmour**	11	130	104
12	Jean Beliveau	17	162	97
13	Bobby Smith	13	184	96
14	Gordie Howe	20	157	92
15	Stan Mikita	18	155	91

Goaltending

Wins

		Gm	W-L	Pct	GAA
1	Billy Smith	132	88-36	.710	2.73
2	Ken Dryden	112	80-32	.714	2.40
3	**Grant Fuhr** (DNP)	119	77-36	.681	3.06
4	Jacques Plante	112	71-37	.657	2.17
5	**Patrick Roy** (DNP)	114	70-42	.625	2.46
6	**Andy Moog**	116	61-48	.560	3.05
7	Turk Broda	102	58-42	.580	1.98
8	Mike Vernon	99	55-39	.585	2.89
9	Terry Sawchuk	106	54-48	.529	2.54
10	Glenn Hall	115	49-65	.430	2.79
11	**Tom Barrasso**	84	47-34	.580	3.15
	Gerry Cheevers	88	47-35	.573	2.69
13	Tony Esposito	99	45-53	.459	3.07
14	Gump Worsley	70	41-25	.621	2.82
15	Bernie Parent	71	38-33	.535	2.43

Shutouts

		Gm	GAA	No
1	Clint Benedict	48	1.80	15
	Jacques Plante	112	2.17	15
3	Turk Broda	102	1.98	13
4	Terry Sawchuk	106	2.54	12
5	Ken Dryden	112	2.40	10

Goaltending
Goals Against Average
Minimum of 50 games played.

		Gm	Min	GA	GAA
1	George Hainsworth	52	3486	112	1.93
2	Turk Broda	101	6348	211	1.98
3	Jacques Plante	112	6651	241	2.17
4	Ken Dryden	112	6846	274	2.40
5	Bernie Parent	71	4302	174	2.43
6	Patrick Roy (DNP)	114	6964	285	2.46
7	Harry Lumley	76	4759	199	2.51
8	Johnny Bower	74	4350	184	2.54
9	Terry Sawchuk	106	6311	267	2.54
10	Frankie Brimsek	68	4365	186	2.56

Note: Clint Benedict had an average of 1.80 but played in only 48 games.

Games Played

		Yrs	Gm
1	Billy Smith, NY Islanders	13	132
2	Grant Fuhr, Edm-Buf (DNP)	10	119
3	Andy Moog, Edm-Bos-Dal	14	116
4	Glenn Hall, Det-Chi-St. L	17	115
5	Patrick Roy, Montreal (DNP)	9	114

Appearances in Cup Final
Standings of all teams that have reached the Stanley Cup championship round, since 1918.

App		Cups	Last Won
32	Montreal Canadiens	23*	1993
21	Toronto Maple Leafs	13†	1967
19	Detroit Red Wings	7	1955
17	Boston Bruins	5	1972
10	New York Rangers	4	1994
10	Chicago Blackhawks	3	1961
6	Edmonton Oilers	5	1990
6	Philadelphia Flyers	2	1975
5	New York Islanders	4	1983
5	Vancouver Millionaires (PCHA)	0	—
4	(original) Ottawa Senators	4	1927
3	Montreal Maroons	2	1935
3	St. Louis Blues	0	—
2	Pittsburgh Penguins	2	1992
2	Calgary Flames	1	1989
2	Victoria Cougars (WCHL-WHL)	1	1925
2	Minnesota North Stars	0	—
2	Seattle Metropolitans (PCHA)	0	—
2	Vancouver Canucks	0	—
1	New Jersey Devils	1	1995
1	Buffalo Sabres	0	—
1	Calgary Tigers (WCHL)	0	—
1	Edmonton Eskimos (WCHL)	0	—
1	Los Angeles Kings	0	—

*Les Canadiens also won the Cup in 1916 for a total of 24. Also, their final with Seattle in 1919 was cancelled due to an influenza epidemic that claimed the life of the Habs' Joe Hall.

†Toronto has won the Cup under three nicknames—Arenas (1918), St. Pats (1922) and Maple Leafs (1932,42,45,47-49,51,62-64,67).

Teams now defunct (6): Calgary Tigers, Edmonton Eskimos, Montreal Maroons, (original) Ottawa Senators, Seattle, Vancouver Millionaires and Victoria. Edmonton (1923) and Calgary (1924) represented the WCHL and later the WHL, while Vancouver (1918,1921-24) and Seattle (1919-20) played out of the PCHA.

Miscellaneous
Championships

		Yrs	Cups
1	Henri Richard, Montreal	18	11
2	Yvan Cournoyer, Montreal	15	10
	Jean Beliveau, Montreal	17	10
4	Claude Provost, Montreal	14	9
5	Jacques Lemaire, Montreal	11	8
	Maurice Richard, Montreal	15	8
	Red Kelly, Detroit-Toronto	19	8

Years in Playoffs

		Yrs	Gm
1	Gordie Howe, Detroit-Hartford	20	157
	Larry Robinson, Montreal-Los Angeles	20	227
3	Red Kelly, Detroit-Toronto	19	164
4	Henri Richard, Montreal	18	180
	Stan Mikita, Chicago	18	155

Games Played

		Yrs	Gm
1	Larry Robinson, Montreal-Los Angeles	20	227
2	Bryan Trottier, NY Isles-Pittsburgh	17	221
3	Glenn Anderson, Edm-Tor-NYR-St. L	14	214
4	Mark Messier, Edm-NY Rangers	15	210
5	Kevin Lowe, Edm-NY Rangers	15	202

Penalty Minutes

		Yrs	Gm	Min
1	Dale Hunter, Que-Wash	15	140	637
2	Chris Nilan, Mon-NYR-Bos-Mon	12	111	541
3	Willi Plett, Atl-Calg-Min-Bos	10	83	466
4	Dave Williams, Tor-Van-LA	12	83	455
5	Tim Hunter, Calg-Van	12	132	426

SINGLE SEASON
Scoring
Points

		Year	Gm	G	A	Pts
1	Wayne Gretzky, Edm	1985	18	17	30	47
2	Mario Lemieux, Pit	1991	23	16	28	44
3	Wayne Gretzky, Edm	1988	19	12	31	43
4	Wayne Gretzky, LA	1993	24	15	25	40
5	Wayne Gretzky, Edm	1983	16	12	26	38
6	Paul Coffey, Edm	1985	18	12	25	37
7	Mike Bossy, NYI	1981	18	17	18	35
	Wayne Gretzky, Edm	1984	19	13	22	35
	Doug Gilmour, Tor	1993	21	10	25	35
10	Mario Lemieux, Pit	1992	15	16	18	34
	Mark Messier, Edm	1988	19	11	23	34
	Mark Recchi, Pit	1991	24	10	24	34
	Wayne Gretzky, Edm	1987	21	5	29	34
14	Brian Leetch, NYR	1994	23	11	23	34
15	Kevin Stevens, Pit	1991	24	17	16	33
	Rick Middleton, Bos	1983	17	11	22	33

Goals

		Year	Gm	No
1	Reggie Leach, Philadelphia	1976	16	19
	Jari Kurri, Edmonton	1985	18	19
3	Newsy Lalonde, Montreal	1919	10	17
	Mike Bossy, NY Islanders	1981	18	17
	Wayne Gretzky, Edmonton	1985	18	17
	Steve Payne, Minnesota	1981	19	17
	Mike Bossy, NY Islanders	1982	19	17
	Mike Bossy, NY Islanders	1983	19	17
	Kevin Stevens, Pittsburgh	1991	24	17
10	Six tied with 16 goals each.			

All-Time Stanley Cup Playoff Leaders (Cont.)

Assists

		Year	Gm	No
1	Wayne Gretzky, Edmonton	1988	19	31
2	Wayne Gretzky, Edmonton	1985	18	30
3	Wayne Gretzky, Edmonton	1987	21	29
4	Mario Lemieux, Pittsburgh	1991	23	28
5	Wayne Gretzky, Edmonton	1983	16	26
6	Paul Coffey, Edmonton	1985	18	25
	Doug Gilmour, Toronto	1993	21	25
	Wayne Gretzky, Los Angeles	1993	24	25
9	Al MacInnis, Calgary	1989	22	24
	Mark Recchi, Pittsburgh	1991	24	24

Goaltending

Wins

		Year	Gm	Min	W-L
1	Grant Fuhr, Edm	1988	19	1136	16-2
	Patrick Roy, Mon	1993	20	1293	16-4
	Martin Brodeur, NJ	1995	20	1222	16-4
	Mike Vernon, Calg	1989	22	1381	16-5
	Tom Barrasso, Pit	1992	21	1233	16-5
	Bill Ranford, Edm	1990	22	1401	16-6
	Mike Richter, NYR	1994	23	1417	16-7
8	Six tied with 15 wins each.				

Shutouts

		Year	Gm	No
1	Clint Benedict, Mon. Maroons	1926	8	4
	Terry Sawchuk, Detroit	1952	8	4
	Clint Benedict, Mon. Maroons	1928	9	4
	Dave Kerr, NY Rangers	1937	9	4
	Frank McCool, Toronto	1945	13	4
	Ken Dryden, Montreal	1977	14	4
	Bernie Parent, Philadelphia	1975	17	4
	Mike Richter, NY Rangers	1994	23	4
	Kirk McLean, Vancouver	1994	24	4

Goals Against Average

Minimum of eight games played.

		Year	Gm	Min	GA	GAA
1	Terry Sawchuk, Det	1952	8	480	5	0.63
2	Clint Benedict, Mon-M	1928	9	555	8	0.89
3	Turk Broda, Tor	1951	9	509	9	1.06
4	Dave Kerr, NYR	1937	9	553	10	1.11
5	Jacques Plante, Mon	1960	8	489	11	1.35
6	Rogie Vachon, Mon	1969	8	507	12	1.42
7	Jacques Plante, St.L	1969	10	589	14	1.43
8	Frankie Brimsek, Bos	1939	12	863	18	1.50
9	Chuck Gardiner, Chi	1934	8	602	12	1.50
10	Ken Dryden, Mon	1977	14	849	22	1.55

Note: Average determined by games played through 1942-43 season and by minutes played since then.

SINGLE SERIES

Scoring

Points

	Year	Rd	G-A—Pts
Rick Middleton, Bos vs Buf	1983	DF	5-14—19
Wayne Gretzky, Edm vs Chi	1985	CF	4-14—18
Mario Lemieux, Pit vs Wash	1992	DSF	7-10—17
Barry Pedersen, Bos vs Buf	1983	DF	7-9—16
Doug Gilmour, Tor vs SJ	1994	CSF	3-13—16
Jari Kurri, Edm vs Chi	1985	CF	12-3—15
Tim Kerr, Phi vs Pit	1989	DF	10-5—15
Mario Lemieux, Pit vs Bos	1991	CF	6-9—15
Wayne Gretzky, Edm vs LA	1987	DSF	2-13—15

Goals

	Year	Rd	No
Jari Kurri, Edm vs Chi	1985	CF	12
Newsy Lalonde, Mon vs Ott	1919	SF*	11
Tim Kerr, Phi vs Pit	1989	DF	10
Five tied with nine each.			

*NHL final prior to Stanley Cup series with Seattle.

Assists

	Year	Rd	No
Rick Middleton, Bos vs Buf	1983	DF	14
Wayne Gretzky, Edm vs Chi	1985	CF	14
Wayne Gretzky, Edm vs LA	1987	DSF	13
Doug Gilmour, Tor vs SJ	1994	CSF	13
Four tied with 11 each.			

SINGLE GAME

Scoring

Points

	Date	G	A	Pts
Patrik Sundstrom, NJ vs Wash	4/22/88	3	5	8
Mario Lemieux, Pit vs Phi	4/25/89	3	5	8
Wayne Gretzky, Edm at Calg	4/17/83	4	3	7
Wayne Gretzky, Edm at Win	4/25/85	3	4	7
Wayne Gretzky, Edm vs LA	4/9/87	1	6	7

Goals

	Date	No
Newsy Lalonde, Mon vs Ott	3/1/19	5
Maurice Richard, Mon vs Tor	3/23/44	5
Darryl Sittler, Tor vs Phi	4/22/76	5
Reggie Leach, Phi vs Bos	5/6/76	5
Mario Lemieux, Pit vs Phi	4/25/89	5

Assists

	Date	No
Mikko Leinonen, NYR vs Phi	4/8/82	6
Wayne Gretzky, Edm vs LA	4/9/87	6
Ten players tied with five each.		

Ten Longest Playoff Overtime Games

The 10 longest overtime games in Stanley Cup history. Note the following Series initials: SF (semifinals), DSF (division semifinal). QF (quarterfinal) and Final (Cup Final). Series winners are in **bold** type; (*) indicates deciding game of series.

		OTs	Elapsed Time	Goal Scorer	Date	Series	Location
1	**Detroit** 1, Montreal Maroons 0	6	116:30	Mud Bruneteau	3/24/36	SF, Gm 1	Montreal
2	**Toronto** 1, Boston 0	6	104:46	Ken Doraty	4/3/33	SF, Gm 5	Toronto
3	Toronto 3, **Detroit** 2	4	70:18	Jack McLean	3/23/43	SF, Gm 2	Detroit
4	**Montreal** 2, NY Rangers 1	4	68:52	Gus Rivers	3/28/30	SF, Gm 1	Montreal
5	**NY Islanders** 3, Washington 2	4	68:47	Pat LaFontaine	4/18/87	DSF, Gm 7*	Washington
6	Buffalo 1, **New Jersey** 0	4	65:43	Dave Hannan	4/27/94	QF, Gm 6	Buffalo
7	**Montreal** 3, Detroit 2	4	61:09	Maurice Richard	3/27/51	SF, Gm 1	Detroit
8	**NY Americans** 3, NY Rangers 2	4	60:40	Lorne Carr	3/27/38	QF, Gm 3*	New York
9	**NY Rangers** 4, Montreal 3	3	59:32	Fred Cook	3/26/32	SF, Gm 2	Montreal
10	**Boston** 2, NY Rangers 1	3	59:25	Mel Hill	3/21/39	SF, Gm 1	New York

NHL All-Star Game

Three benefit NHL All-Star games were staged in the 1930s for forward Ace Bailey and the families of Howie Morenz and Babe Siebert. Bailey, of Toronto, suffered a fractured skull on a career-ending check by Boston's Eddie Shore. Morenz, the Montreal Canadiens' legend, died of a heart attack at age 35 after a severely broken leg ended his career. And Siebert, who played with both Montreal teams, drowned at age 35.

The All-Star Game was revived at the start of the 1947-48 season as an annual exhibition match between the defending Stanley Cup champion and All-Stars from the league's other five teams. The format has changed several times since then. The game was moved to midseason in 1966-67 and became an East vs. West contest. The Eastern (Wales, 1975-93) Conference leads the series, 13-5.

Benefit Games

Date	Occasion		Host	Coaches
2/14/34	Ace Bailey Benefit	Toronto 7, All-Stars 3	Toronto	Dick Irvin, Lester Patrick
11/3/37	Howie Morenz Memorial	All-Stars 6, Montreals* 5	Montreal	Jack Adams, Cecil Hart
10/29/39	Babe Siebert Memorial	All-Stars 5, Canadiens 2	Montreal	Art Ross, Pit Lepine

*Combined squad of Montreal Canadiens and Montreal Maroons.

All-Star Games

Multiple MVP winners: Mario Lemieux (3); Wayne Gretzky, Bobby Hull and Frank Mahovlich (2).

Year		Host	Coaches	Most Valuable Player
1947	All-Stars 4, Toronto 3	Toronto	Dick Irvin, Hap Day	No award
1948	All-Stars 3, Toronto 1	Chicago	Tommy Ivan, Hap Day	No award
1949	All-Stars 3, Toronto 1	Toronto	Tommy Ivan, Hap Day	No award
1950	Detroit 7, All-Stars 1	Detroit	Tommy Ivan, Lynn Patrick	No award
1951	1st Team 2, 2nd Team 2	Toronto	Joe Primeau, Hap Day	No award
1952	1st Team 1, 2nd Team 1	Detroit	Tommy Ivan, Dick Irvin	No award
1953	All-Stars 3, Montreal 1	Montreal	Lynn Patrick, Dick Irvin	No award
1954	All-Stars 2, Detroit 2	Detroit	King Clancy, Jim Skinner	No award
1955	Detroit 3, All-Stars 1	Detroit	Jim Skinner, Dick Irvin	No award
1956	All-Stars 1, Montreal 1	Montreal	Jim Skinner, Toe Blake	No award
1957	All-Stars 5, Montreal 3	Montreal	Milt Schmidt, Toe Blake	No award
1958	Montreal 6, All-Stars 3	Montreal	Toe Blake, Milt Schmidt	No award
1959	Montreal 6, All-Stars 1	Montreal	Toe Blake, Punch Imlach	No award
1960	All-Stars 2, Montreal 1	Montreal	Punch Imlach, Toe Blake	No award
1961	All-Stars 3, Chicago 1	Chicago	Sid Abel, Rudy Pilous	No award
1962	Toronto 4, All-Stars 1	Toronto	Punch Imlach, Rudy Pilous	Eddie Shack, Tor., RW
1963	All-Stars 3, Toronto 3	Toronto	Sid Abel, Punch Imlach	Frank Mahovlich, Tor., LW
1964	All-Stars 3, Toronto 2	Toronto	Sid Abel, Punch Imlach	Jean Beliveau, Mon., C
1965	All-Stars 5, Montreal 2	Montreal	Billy Reay, Toe Blake	Gordie Howe, Det., RW
1966	No game (see below)			
1967	Montreal 3, All-Stars 0	Montreal	Toe Blake, Sid Abel	Henri Richard, Mon., C
1968	Toronto 4, All-Stars 3	Toronto	Punch Imlach, Toe Blake	Bruce Gamble, Tor., G
1969	West 3, East 3	Montreal	Scotty Bowman, Toe Blake	Frank Mahovlich, Det., LW
1970	East 4, West 1	St. Louis	Claude Ruel, Scotty Bowman	Bobby Hull, Chi., LW
1971	West 2, East 1	Boston	Scotty Bowman, Harry Sinden	Bobby Hull, Chi., LW
1972	East 3, West 2	Minnesota	Al MacNeil, Billy Reay	Bobby Orr, Bos., D
1973	East 5, West 4	NY Rangers	Tom Johnson, Billy Reay	Greg Polis, Pit., LW
1974	West 6, East 4	Chicago	Billy Reay, Scotty Bowman	Garry Unger, St.L., C
1975	Wales 7, Campbell 1	Montreal	Bep Guidolin, Fred Shero	Syl Apps Jr., Pit., C
1976	Wales 7, Campbell 5	Philadelphia	Floyd Smith, Fred Shero	Peter Mahovlich, Mon., C
1977	Wales 4, Campbell 3	Vancouver	Scotty Bowman, Fred Shero	Rick Martin, Buf., LW
1978	Wales 3, Campbell 2 (OT)	Buffalo	Scotty Bowman, Fred Shero	Billy Smith, NYI, G
1979	No game (see below)			
1980	Wales 6, Campbell 3	Detroit	Scotty Bowman, Al Arbour	Reggie Leach, Phi., RW
1981	Campbell 4, Wales 1	Los Angeles	Pat Quinn, Scotty Bowman	Mike Liut, St.L., G
1982	Wales 4, Campbell 2	Washington	Al Arbour, Glen Sonmor	Mike Bossy, NYI, RW
1983	Campbell 9, Wales 3	NY Islanders	Roger Neilson, Al Arbour	Wayne Gretzky, Edm., C
1984	Wales 7, Campbell 6	New Jersey	Al Arbour, Glen Sather	Don Maloney, NYR, LW
1985	Wales 6, Campbell 4	Calgary	Al Arbour, Glen Sather	Mario Lemieux, Pit., C
1986	Wales 4, Campbell 3 (OT)	Hartford	Mike Keenan, Glen Sather	Grant Fuhr, Edm., G
1987	No game (see below)			
1988	Wales 6, Campbell 5 (OT)	St. Louis	Mike Keenan, Glen Sather	Mario Lemieux, Pit., C
1989	Campbell 9, Wales 5	Edmonton	Glen Sather, Terry O'Reilly	Wayne Gretzky, LA, C
1990	Wales 12, Campbell 7	Pittsburgh	Pat Burns, Terry Crisp	Mario Lemieux, Pit., C
1991	Campbell 11, Wales 5	Chicago	John Muckler, Mike Milbury	Vincent Damphousse, Tor., LW
1992	Campbell 10, Wales 6	Philadelphia	Bob Gainey, Scotty Bowman	Brett Hull, St.L., RW
1993	Wales 16, Campbell 6	Montreal	Scotty Bowman, Mike Keenan	Mike Gartner, NYR, RW
1994	East 9, West 8	NY Rangers	Jacques Demers, Barry Melrose	Mike Richter, NYR, G
1995	No game (see below)			

No All-Star Game: in 1966 (moved from start of season to mid-season); in 1979 (replaced by Challenge Cup series with USSR); in 1987 (replaced by Rendez-Vous '87 series with USSR); and in 1995 (cancelled when NHL lockout shortened season to 48 games).

NHL Franchise Origins

Here is what the current 26 teams in the National Hockey League have to show for the years they have put in as members of the NHL, the early National Hockey Association (NHA) and the more recent World Hockey Association (WHA). League titles and Stanley Cup championships are noted by year won. The Stanley Cup has automatically gone to the NHL champion since the 1926-27 season. Following the 1992-93 season, the NHL renamed the Clarence Campbell Conference the Western Conference, while the Prince of Wales Conference became the Eastern Conference.

Western Conference

	First Season	League Titles	Franchise Stops
Anaheim, Mighty Ducks of	1993-94 (NHL)	None	•Anaheim, CA (1993—)
Calgary Flames	1972-73 (NHL)	1 Cup (1989)	•Atlanta (1972-80) Calgary (1980—)
Chicago Blackhawks	1926-27 (NHL)	3 Cups (1934,38,61)	•Chicago (1926—)
Colorado Avalanche	1972-73 (WHA)	1 WHA (1977)	•Quebec City (1972-95) Denver (1995—)
Dallas Stars	1967-68 (NHL)	None	•Bloomington, MN (1967-93) Dallas (1993—)
Detroit Red Wings	1926-27 (NHL)	7 Cups (1936-37,43,50, 52,54-55)	•Detroit (1926—)
Edmonton Oilers	1973-74 (WHA)	5 Cups (1984-85,87-88,90)	•Edmonton (1972—)
Los Angeles Kings	1967-68 (NHL)	None	•Inglewood, CA (1967—)
St. Louis Blues	1967-68 (NHL)	None	•St. Louis (1967—)
San Jose Sharks	1991-92 (NHL)	None	•San Francisco (1991-93) San Jose (1993—)
Toronto Maple Leafs	1916-17 (NHA)	2 NHL (1918,22) 13 Cups (1918,22,32,42,45 47-49,51,62-64,67)	•Toronto (1916—)
Vancouver Canucks	1970-71 (NHL)	None	•Vancouver (1970—)
Winnipeg Jets	1972-73 (WHA)	3 WHA (1976,78-79)	•Winnipeg (1972—)

Eastern Conference

	First Season	League Titles	Franchise Stops
Boston Bruins	1924-25 (NHL)	5 Cups (1929,39,41,70,72)	•Boston (1924—)
Buffalo Sabres	1970-71 (NHL)	None	•Buffalo (1970—)
Florida Panthers	1993-94 (NHL)	None	•Miami (1993—)

Hartford Whalers	1972-73 (WHA)	1 WHA (1973)	•Boston (1972-74)
			  W. Springfield, MA (1974-75)
			  Hartford, CT (1975-78)
			  Springfield, MA (1978-80)
			  Hartford (1980—)

Montreal Canadiens	1909-10 (NHA)	2 NHA (1916-17)
		2 NHL (1924-25)
		24 Cups (1916,24,30-31,44,46,
		  53,56-60,65-66,68-69,
		  71,73,76-79,86,93)
			•Montreal (1909—)

New Jersey Devils	1974-75 (NHL)	1 Cup (1995)	•Kansas City (1974-76)
			  Denver (1976-82)
			  E. Rutherford, NJ (1982—)

New York Islanders	1972-73 (NHL)	4 Cups (1980-83)	•Uniondale, NY (1972—)
New York Rangers	1926-27 (NHL)	4 Cups (1928,33,40,94)	•New York (1926—)
Ottawa Senators	1992-93 (NHL)	None	•Ottawa (1992—)
Philadelphia Flyers	1967-68 (NHL)	2 Cups (1974-75)	•Philadelphia (1967—)
Pittsburgh Penguins	1967-68 (NHL)	2 Cups (1991-92)	•Pittsburgh (1967—)
Tampa Bay Lightning	1992-93 (NHL)	None	•Tampa, FL (1992—93) St. Petersburg, FL (1993—)
Washington Capitals	1974-75 (NHL)	None	•Landover, MD (1974—)

Note: The Hartford Civic Center roof collapsed after a snowstorm in January 1978, forcing the Whalers to move their home games to Springfield, Mass., for two years.

The Growth of the NHL

Of the four franchises that comprised the National Hockey League (NHL) at the start of the 1917-18 season, only two remain—the Montreal Canadiens and the Toronto Maple Leafs (originally the Toronto Arenas). From 1919-26, eight new teams joined the league, but only four—the Boston Bruins, Chicago Blackhawks (originally Black Hawks), Detroit Red Wings (originally Cougars) and New York Rangers—survived.

It was 41 years before the NHL expanded again, doubling in size for the 1967-68 season with new teams in Los Angeles, Minnesota, Oakland, Philadelphia, Pittsburgh and St. Louis. The league had 16 clubs by the start of the 1972-73 season, but it also had a rival in the **World Hockey Association**, which debuted that year with 12 teams.

The NHL added two more teams in 1974 and merged the struggling Cleveland Barons (originally the Oakland Seals) and Minnesota North Stars in 1978, before absorbing four WHA clubs—the Edmonton Oilers, Hartford Whalers, Quebec Nordiques and Winnipeg Jets—in time for the 1979-80 season. Five expansion teams have joined the league so far in the 1990s, giving the NHL its current 26-team roster.

Expansion/Merger Timetable
For teams currently in NHL.

1919—Quebec Bulldogs finally take the ice after sitting out NHL's first two seasons; **1924**—Boston Bruins and Montreal Maroons; **1925**—New York Americans and Pittsburgh Pirates; **1926**—Chicago Black Hawks (now Blackhawks), Detroit Cougars (now Red Wings) and New York Rangers; **1932**—Ottawa Senators return after sitting out 1931-32 season.

1967—California Seals (later Cleveland Barons), Los Angeles Kings, Minnesota North Stars, Philadelphia Flyers, Pittsburgh Penguins and St. Louis Blues.

1970—Buffalo Sabres and Vancouver Canucks; **1972**—Atlanta Flames (now Calgary) and New York Islanders; **1974**—Kansas City Scouts (now New Jersey Devils) and Washington Capitals; **1978**—Cleveland Barons merge with Minnesota North Stars (now Dallas Stars) and team remains in Minnesota; **1979**—added WHA's Edmonton Oilers, Hartford Whalers, Quebec Nordiques (now Colorado Avalanche) and Winnipeg Jets.

1991—San Jose Sharks; **1992**—Ottawa Senators and Tampa Bay Lightning; **1993**—Mighty Ducks of Anaheim and Florida Panthers.

City and Nickname Changes

1919—Toronto Arenas renamed St. Pats; **1920**—Quebec moves to Hamilton and becomes Tigers (will fold in 1925); **1926**—Toronto St. Pats renamed Maple Leafs; **1929**—Detroit Cougars renamed Falcons.

1930—Pittsburgh Pirates move to Philadelphia and become Quakers (will fold in 1931); **1932**—Detroit Falcons renamed Red Wings; **1934**—Ottawa Senators move to St. Louis and become Eagles (will fold in 1935); **1941**—New York Americans renamed Brooklyn Americans (will fold in 1942).

1967—California Seals renamed Oakland Seals three months into first season; **1970**—Oakland Seals renamed California Golden Seals; **1976**—California Golden Seals renamed Seals; **1976**—California Seals move to Cleveland and become Barons, while Kansas City Scouts move to Denver and become Colorado Rockies; **1978**—Cleveland Barons merge with Minnesota North Stars and become Minnesota North Stars.

1980—Atlanta Flames move to Calgary; **1982**—Colorado Rockies move to East Rutherford, N.J., and become New Jersey Devils; **1986**—Chicago Black Hawks renamed Blackhawks; **1993**—Minnesota North Stars move to Dallas and become Stars. **1995**—Quebec Nordiques move to Denver and become Colorado Avalanche.

Defunct NHL Teams
Teams that once played in the NHL, but no longer exist.

Brooklyn—Americans (1941-42, formerly NY Americans from 1925-41); **Cleveland**—Barons (1976-78, originally California-Oakland Seals from 1967-76); **Hamilton (Ont.)**—Tigers (1920-25, originally Quebec Bulldogs from 1919-20); **Montreal**—Maroons (1924-38) and Wanderers (1917-18); **New York**—Americans (1925-42, later Brooklyn Americans for 1941-42); **Oakland**—Seals (1967-76, also known as California Seals and Golden Seals and later Cleveland Barons from 1976-78); **Ottawa**—Senators (1917-31 and 1932-34, later St. Louis Eagles for 1934-35); **Philadelphia**—Quakers (1930-31, originally Pittsburgh Pirates from 1925-30); **Pittsburgh**—Pirates (1925-30, later Philadelphia Quakers for 1930-31); **Quebec**—Bulldogs (1919-20, later Hamilton Tigers from 1920-25); **St. Louis**—Eagles (1934-35), originally Ottawa Senators (1917-31 and 1932-34).

WHA Teams (1972-79)

Baltimore—Blades (1975); **Birmingham**—Bulls (1976-78); **Calgary**—Cowboys (1975-77); **Chicago**—Cougars (1972-75); **Cincinnati**—Stingers (1975-79); **Cleveland**—Crusaders (1972-76, moved to Minnesota); **Denver**—Spurs (1975-76, moved to Ottawa); **Edmonton**—Oilers (1972-79, originally called Alberta Oilers in 1972-73); **Houston**—Aeros (1972-78); **Indianapolis**—Racers (1974-78).

Los Angeles—Sharks (1972-74, moved to Michigan); **Michigan**—Stags (1974-75, moved to Baltimore); **Minnesota**—Fighting Saints (1972-76) and New Fighting Saints (1976-77); **New England**—Whalers (1972-79, played in Boston from 1972-74, West Springfield, MA from 1974-75, Hartford from 1975-78 and Springfield, MA in 1979); **New Jersey**—Knights (1973-74, moved to San Diego); **New York**—Raiders (1972-73, renamed Golden Blades in 1973, moved to New Jersey).

Ottawa—Nationals (1972-73, moved to Toronto) and Civics (1976); **Philadelphia**—Blazers (1972-73, moved to Vancouver); **Phoenix**—Roadrunners (1974-77); **Quebec**—Nordiques (1972-79); **San Diego**—Mariners (1974-77); **Toronto**—Toros (1973-76, moved to Birmingham, AL); **Vancouver**—Blazers (1973-75, moved to Calgary); **Winnipeg**—Jets (1972-79).

Annual NHL Leaders
Art Ross Trophy (Scoring)

Given to the player who leads the league in points scored and named after the former Boston Bruins general manager-coach. First presented in 1947, names of prior leading scorers have been added retroactively. A tie for the scoring championship is broken three ways: 1. total goals; 2. fewest games played; 3. first goal scored.

Multiple winners: Wayne Gretzky (10); Gordie Howe (6); Phil Esposito (5); Mario Lemieux and Stan Mikita (4); Guy Lafleur (3); Max Bentley, Charlie Conacher, Bill Cook, Babe Dye, Bernie Geoffrion, Bobby Hull, Elmer Lach, Newsy Lalonde, Joe Malone, Dickie Moore, Howie Morenz, Bobby Orr and Sweeney Schriner (2).

Year	Player	Gm	G	A	Pts	Year	Player	Gm	G	A	Pts
1918	Joe Malone, Mon	20	44	0	44	1957	Gordie Howe, Det	70	44	45	89
1919	Newsy Lalonde, Mon	17	23	9	32	1958	Dickie Moore, Mon	70	36	48	84
						1959	Dickie Moore, Mon	70	41	55	96
1920	Joe Malone, Que	24	39	6	45	1960	Bobby Hull, Chi	70	39	42	81
1921	Newsy Lalonde, Mon	24	33	8	41	1961	Bernie Geoffrion, Mon	64	50	45	95
1922	Punch Broadbent, Ott	24	32	14	46	1962	Bobby Hull, Chi	70	50	34	84
1923	Babe Dye, Tor	22	26	11	37	1963	Gordie Howe, Det	70	38	48	86
1924	Cy Denneny, Ott	21	22	1	23	1964	Stan Mikita, Chi	70	39	50	89
1925	Babe Dye, Tor	29	38	6	44	1965	Stan Mikita, Chi	70	28	59	87
1926	Nels Stewart, Maroons	36	34	8	42	1966	Bobby Hull, Chi	65	54	43	97
1927	Bill Cook, NYR	44	33	4	37	1967	Stan Mikita, Chi	70	35	62	97
1928	Howie Morenz, Mon	43	33	18	51	1968	Stan Mikita, Chi	72	40	47	87
1929	Ace Bailey, Tor	44	22	10	32	1969	Phil Esposito, Bos	74	49	77	126
1930	Cooney Weiland, Bos	44	43	30	73	1970	Bobby Orr, Bos	76	33	87	120
1931	Howie Morenz, Mon	39	28	23	51	1971	Phil Esposito, Bos	78	76	76	152
1932	Busher Jackson, Tor	48	28	25	53	1972	Phil Esposito, Bos	76	66	67	133
1933	Bill Cook, NYR	48	28	22	50	1973	Phil Esposito, Bos	78	55	75	130
1934	Charlie Conacher, Tor	42	32	20	52	1974	Phil Esposito, Bos	78	68	77	145
1935	Charlie Conacher, Tor	47	36	21	57	1975	Bobby Orr, Bos	80	46	89	135
1936	Sweeney Schriner, NYA	48	19	26	45	1976	Guy Lafleur, Mon	80	56	69	125
1937	Sweeney Schriner, NYA	48	21	25	46	1977	Guy Lafleur, Mon	80	56	80	136
1938	Gordie Drillon, Tor	48	26	26	52	1978	Guy Lafleur, Mon	79	60	72	132
1939	Toe Blake, Mon	48	24	23	47	1979	Bryan Trottier, NYI	76	47	87	134
1940	Milt Schmidt, Bos	48	22	30	52	1980	Marcel Dionne, LA	80	53	84	137
1941	Bill Cowley, Bos	46	17	45	62	1981	Wayne Gretzky, Edm	80	55	109	164
1942	Bryan Hextall, NYR	48	24	32	56	1982	Wayne Gretzky, Edm	80	92	120	212
1943	Doug Bentley, Chi	50	33	40	73	1983	Wayne Gretzky, Edm	80	71	125	196
1944	Herbie Cain, Bos	48	36	46	82	1984	Wayne Gretzky, Edm	74	87	118	205
1945	Elmer Lach, Mon	50	26	54	80	1985	Wayne Gretzky, Edm	80	73	135	208
1946	Max Bentley, Chi	47	31	30	61	1986	Wayne Gretzky, Edm	80	52	163	215
1947	Max Bentley, Chi	60	29	43	72	1987	Wayne Gretzky, Edm	79	62	121	183
1948	Elmer Lach, Mon	60	30	31	61	1988	Mario Lemieux, Pit	77	70	98	168
1949	Roy Conacher, Chi	60	26	42	68	1989	Mario Lemieux, Pit	76	85	114	199
1950	Ted Lindsay, Det	69	23	55	78	1990	Wayne Gretzky, LA	73	40	102	142
1951	Gordie Howe, Det	70	43	43	86	1991	Wayne Gretzky, LA	78	41	122	163
1952	Gordie Howe, Det	70	47	39	86	1992	Mario Lemieux, Pit	64	44	87	131
1953	Gordie Howe, Det	70	49	46	95	1993	Mario Lemieux, Pit	60	69	91	160
1954	Gordie Howe, Det	70	33	48	81	1994	Wayne Gretzky, LA	81	38	92	130
1955	Bernie Geoffrion, Mon	70	38	37	75	1995	Jaromir Jagr, Pit	48	32	38	70
1956	Jean Beliveau, Mon	70	47	41	88						

Note: The three times players have tied for total points in one season the player with more goals has won the trophy. In 1961-62, Hull outscored Andy Bathgate of NY Rangers, 50 goals to 28. In 1979-80, Dionne outscored Wayne Gretzky of Edmonton, 53-51. In 1995, Jagr outscored Eric Lindros of Philadelphia, 32-29.

NHL 500-Goal Scorers

Maurice Richard of Montreal was the first NHL palyer to score 500 goals when he reached that plateau in his 863rd game. Since then he has been joined by 18 others. Of the 500-goal scorers listed below, two (Gartner and Hull) went on to score over 600 goals, two (Dionne and Esposito) scored over 700, and two (Gretzky and Howe) have scored over 800. Players who were active in 1995 are in **bold** type.

Player	Date	Game #	Player	Date	Game #
Maurice Richard, Mon vs Chi	10/19/57	863	Mike Bossy, NYI vs Bos	1/2/86	647
Gordie Howe, Det at NYR	3/14/62	1045	Gilbert Perreault, Buf vs NJ	3/9/86	1159
Bobby Hull, Chi vs NYR	2/21/70	861	**Wayne Gretzky**, Edm vs Van	11/22/86	575
Jean Beliveau, Mon vs Min	2/11/71	1101	Lanny McDonald, Calg vs NYI	3/21/89	1107
Frank Mahovlich, Mon vs Van	3/21/73	1105	Bryan Trottier, NYI vs Calg	2/13/90	1104
Phil Esposito, Bos vs Det	12/22/74	803	**Mike Gartner**, NYR vs Wash	10/14/91	936
John Bucyk, Bos vs St.L	10/30/75	1370	Michel Goulet, Chi vs Calg	2/16/92	951
Stan Mikita, Chi vs Van	2/27/77	1221	**Jari Kurri**, LA vs Bos	10/17/92	833
Marcel Dionne, LA at Wash	12/14/82	887	**Dino Ciccarelli**, Det at LA	1/8/94	946
Guy Lafleur, Mon at NJ	12/20/83	918			

Goals

Multiple winners: Bobby Hull (7); Phil Esposito (6); Charlie Conacher, Wayne Gretzky, Gordie Howe and Maurice Richard (5); Bill Cook, Babe Dye and Brett Hull (3); Jean Beliveau, Doug Bentley, Mike Bossy, Bernie Geoffrion, Bryan Hextall, Mario Lemieux, Joe Malone and Nels Stewart (2).

Year	Winner	No
1918	Joe Malone, Mon	44
1919	Odie Cleghorn, Mon	23
	& Newsy Lalonde, Mon	23
1920	Joe Malone, Que	39
1921	Babe Dye, Ham-Tor	35
1922	Punch Broadbent, Ott	32
1923	Babe Dye, Tor	26
1924	Cy Denneny, Ott	22
1925	Babe Dye, Tor	38
1926	Nels Stewart, Maroons	34
1927	Bill Cook, NYR	33
1928	Howie Morenz, Mon	33
1929	Ace Bailey, Tor	22
1930	Cooney Weiland, Bos	43
1931	Charlie Conacher, Tor	31
1932	Charlie Conacher, Tor	34
	& Bill Cook, NYR	34
1933	Bill Cook, NYR	28
1934	Charlie Conacher, Tor	32
1935	Charlie Conacher, Tor	36
1936	Charlie Conacher, Tor	23
	& Bill Thoms, Tor	23
1937	Larry Aurie, Det	23
	& Nels Stewart, Bos-NYA	23
1938	Gordie Drillon, Tor	26
1939	Roy Conacher, Bos	26
1940	Bryan Hextall, NYR	24
1941	Bryan Hextall, NYR	26
1942	Lynn Patrick, NYR	32
1943	Doug Bentley, Chi	33
1944	Doug Bentley, Chi	38
1945	Maurice Richard, Mon	50
1946	Gaye Stewart, Tor	37
1947	Maurice Richard, Mon	45
1948	Ted Lindsay, Det	33
1949	Sid Abel, Det	28
1950	Maurice Richard, Mon	43
1951	Gordie Howe, Det	43
1952	Gordie Howe, Det	47
1953	Gordie Howe, Det	49
1954	Maurice Richard, Mon	37
1955	Bernie Geoffrion, Mon	38
	& Maurice Richard, Mon	38
1956	Jean Beliveau, Mon	47
1957	Gordie Howe, Det	44
1958	Dickie Moore, Mon	36
1959	Jean Beliveau, Mon	45
1960	Bronco Horvath, Bos	39
	& Bobby Hull, Chi	39
1961	Bernie Geoffrion, Mon	50
1962	Bobby Hull, Chi	50
1963	Gordie Howe, Det	38
1964	Bobby Hull, Chi	43
1965	Norm Ullman, Tor	42
1966	Bobby Hull, Chi	54
1967	Bobby Hull, Chi	52
1968	Bobby Hull, Chi	44
1969	Bobby Hull, Chi	58
1970	Phil Esposito, Bos	43
1971	Phil Esposito, Bos	76
1972	Phil Esposito, Bos	66
1973	Phil Esposito, Bos	55
1974	Phil Esposito, Bos	68
1975	Phil Esposito, Bos	61
1976	Reggie Leach, Phi	61
1977	Steve Shutt, Mon	60
1978	Guy Lafleur, Mon	60
1979	Mike Bossy, NYI	69
1980	Danny Gare, Buf	56
	Charlie Simmer, LA	56
	& Blaine Stoughton, Hart	56
1981	Mike Bossy, NYI	68
1982	Wayne Gretzky, Edm	92
1983	Wayne Gretzky, Edm	71
1984	Wayne Gretzky, Edm	87
1985	Wayne Gretzky, Edm	73
1986	Jari Kurri, Edm	68
1987	Wayne Gretzky, Edm	62
1988	Mario Lemieux, Pit	70
1989	Mario Lemieux, Pit	85
1990	Brett Hull, St.L	72
1991	Brett Hull, St.L	86
1992	Brett Hull, St.L	70
1993	Alexander Mogilny, Buf	76
	& Teemu Selanne, Win	76
1994	Pavel Bure, Van	60
1995	Peter Bondra, Wash	34

Assists

Multiple winners: Wayne Gretzky (14); Bobby Orr (5); Frank Boucher, Bill Cowley, Phil Esposito, Gordie Howe, Elmer Lach, Stan Mikita and Joe Primeau (3); Syl Apps, Andy Bathgate, Jean Beliveau, Doug Bentley, Art Chapman, Bobby Clarke, Ted Lindsay, Bert Olmstead, Henri Richard and Bryan Trottier (2).

Year	Winner	No
1918	No official records kept.	
1919	Newsy Lalonde, Mon	9
1920	Corbett Denneny, Tor	12
1921	Louis Berlinquette, Mon	9
	Harry Cameron, Tor	9
	& Joe Matte, Ham	9
1922	Punch Broadbent, Ott	14
	& Leo Reise, Ham	14
1923	Ed Bouchard, Ham	12
1924	King Clancy, Ott	8
1925	Cy Denneny, Ott	15
1926	Frank Nighbor, Ott	13
1927	Dick Irvin, Chi	18
1928	Howie Morenz, Mon	18
1929	Frank Boucher, NYR	16
1930	Frank Boucher, NYR	36
1931	Joe Primeau, Tor	32
1932	Joe Primeau, Tor	37
1933	Frank Boucher, NYR	28
1934	Joe Primeau, Tor	32
1935	Art Chapman, NYA	34
1936	Art Chapman, NYA	28
1937	Syl Apps, Tor	29
1938	Syl Apps, Tor	29
1939	Bill Cowley, Bos	34
1940	Milt Schmidt, Bos	30
1941	Bill Cowley, Bos	45
1942	Phil Watson, NYR	37
1943	Bill Cowley, Bos	45
1944	Clint Smith, Chi	49
1945	Elmer Lach, Mon	54
1946	Elmer Lach, Mon	34
1947	Billy Taylor, Det	46
1948	Doug Bentley, Chi	37
1949	Doug Bentley, Chi	43
1950	Ted Lindsay, Det	55
1951	Gordie Howe, Det	43
	& Teeder Kennedy, Tor	43
1952	Elmer Lach, Mon	50
1953	Gordie Howe, Det	46
1954	Gordie Howe, Det	48
1955	Bert Olmstead, Mon	48
1956	Bert Olmstead, Mon	56
1957	Ted Lindsay, Det	55
1958	Henri Richard, Mon	52
1959	Dickie Moore, Mon	55
1960	Don McKenney, Bos	49
1961	Jean Beliveau, Mon	58
1962	Andy Bathgate, NYR	56
1963	Henri Richard, Mon	50
1964	Andy Bathgate, NYR-Tor	58
1965	Stan Mikita, Chi	59
1966	Jean Beliveau, Mon	48
	Stan Mikita, Chi	48
	& Bobby Rousseau, Mon	48
1967	Stan Mikita, Chi	62
1968	Phil Esposito, Bos	49
1969	Phil Esposito, Bos	77
1970	Bobby Orr, Bos	87
1971	Bobby Orr, Bos	102
1972	Bobby Orr, Bos	80
1973	Phil Esposito, Bos	75
1974	Bobby Orr, Bos	90
1975	Bobby Clarke, Phi	89
	& Bobby Orr, Bos	89
1976	Bobby Clarke, Phi	89
1977	Guy Lafleur, Mon	80
1978	Bryan Trottier, NYI	77
1979	Bryan Trottier, NYI	87
1980	Wayne Gretzky, Edm	86
1981	Wayne Gretzky, Edm	109
1982	Wayne Gretzky, Edm	120
1983	Wayne Gretzky, Edm	125
1984	Wayne Gretzky, Edm	118
1985	Wayne Gretzky, Edm	135
1986	Wayne Gretzky, Edm	163
1987	Wayne Gretzky, Edm	121
1988	Wayne Gretzky, Edm	109
1989	Wayne Gretzky, LA	114
	& Mario Lemieux, Pit	114
1990	Wayne Gretzky, LA	102
1991	Wayne Gretzky, LA	122
1992	Wayne Gretzky, LA	90
1993	Adam Oates, Bos	97
1994	Wayne Gretzky, LA	92
1995	Ron Francis, Pit	48

Annual NHL Leaders (Cont.)

Goals Against Average

Average determined by games played through 1942-43 season and by minutes played since then. Minimum of 15 games from 1917-18 season through 1925-26; minimum of 25 games since 1926-27 season. Not to be confused with the Vezina Trophy. Goaltenders who posted the season's lowest goals against average, but did not win the Vezina are in **bold** type.

Multiple winners: Jacques Plante (9); Clint Benedict and Bill Durnan (6); Johnny Bower, Ken Dryden and Tiny Thompson (4); Georges Vezina (3); Frankie Brimsek, Turk Broda, George Hainsworth, Dominik Hasek, Harry Lumley, Bernie Parent, Pete Peeters, Patrick Roy and Terry Sawchuk (2).

Year		GAA	Year		GAA	Year		GAA
1918	Georges Vezina, Mon	3.82	1944	Bill Durnan, Mon	2.18	1970	**Ernie Wakely**, St.L	2.11
1919	Clint Benedict, Ott	2.94	1945	Bill Durnan, Mon	2.42	1971	**Jacques Plante**, Tor	1.88
			1946	Bill Durnan, Mon	2.60	1972	Tony Esposito, Chi	1.77
1920	Clint Benedict, Ott	2.67	1947	Bill Durnan, Mon	2.30	1973	Ken Dryden, Mon	2.26
1921	Clint Benedict, Ott	3.13	1948	Turk Broda, Tor	2.38	1974	Bernie Parent, Phi	1.89
1922	Clint Benedict, Ott	3.50	1949	Bill Durnan, Mon	2.10	1975	Bernie Parent, Phi	2.03
1923	Clint Benedict, Ott	2.25				1976	Ken Dryden, Mon	2.03
1924	Georges Vezina, Mon	2.00	1950	Bill Durnan, Mon	2.20	1977	Bunny Larocque, Mon	2.09
1925	Georges Vezina, Mon	1.87	1951	Al Rollins, Tor	1.77	1978	Ken Dryden, Mon	2.05
1926	Alex Connell, Ott	1.17	1952	Terry Sawchuk, Det	1.90	1979	Ken Dryden, Mon	2.30
1927	**Clint Benedict**, Mon-M	1.51	1953	Terry Sawchuk, Det	1.90			
1928	Geo. Hainsworth, Mon	1.09	1954	Harry Lumley, Tor	1.86	1980	Bob Sauve, Buf	2.36
1929	Geo. Hainsworth, Mon	0.98	1955	**Harry Lumley**, Tor	1.94	1981	Richard Sevigny, Mon	2.40
			1956	Jacques Plante, Mon	1.86	1982	**Denis Herron**, Mon	2.64
1930	Tiny Thompson, Bos	2.23	1957	Jacques Plante, Mon	2.02	1983	Pete Peeters, Bos	2.36
1931	Roy Worters, NYA	1.68	1958	Jacques Plante, Mon	2.11	1984	**Pat Riggin**, Wash	2.66
1932	Chuck Gardiner, Chi	1.92	1959	Jacques Plante, Mon	2.16	1985	**Tom Barrasso**, Buf	2.66
1933	Tiny Thompson, Bos	1.83				1986	**Bob Froese**, Phi	2.55
1934	**Wilf Cude**, Det-Mon	1.57	1960	Jacques Plante, Mon	2.54	1987	**Brian Hayward**, Mon	2.81
1935	Lorne Chabot, Chi	1.83	1961	Johnny Bower, Tor	2.50	1988	Pete Peeters, Wash	2.78
1936	Tiny Thompson, Bos	1.71	1962	Jacques Plante, Mon	2.37	1989	Patrick Roy, Mon	2.47
1937	Norm Smith, Det	2.13	1963	**Jacques Plante**, Mon	2.49			
1938	Tiny Thompson, Bos	1.85	1964	Johnny Bower, Tor	2.11	1990	**Mike Liut**, Hart-Wash	2.53
1939	Frankie Brimsek, Bos	1.58	1965	Johnny Bower, Tor	2.38	1991	Ed Belfour, Chi	2.47
			1966	**Johnny Bower**, Tor	2.25	1992	Patrick Roy, Mon	2.36
1940	Dave Kerr, NYR	1.60	1967	Glenn Hall, Chi	2.38	1993	**Felix Potvin**, Tor	2.50
1941	Turk Broda, Tor	2.06	1968	Gump Worsley, Mon	1.98	1994	Dominik Hasek, Buf	1.95
1942	Frankie Brimsek, Bos	2.45	1969	Jacques Plante, St.L	1.96	1995	Dominik Hasek, Buf	2.11
1943	John Mowers, Det	2.47						

Penalty Minutes

Multiple winners: Red Horner (8); Gus Mortson and Dave Schultz (4); Bert Corbeau, Lou Fontinato and Tiger Williams (3); Billy Boucher, Carl Brewer, Red Dutton, Pat Egan, Bill Ezinicki, Joe Hall, Tim Hunter, Keith Magnuson, Chris Nilan and Jimmy Orlando (2).

Year		Min	Year		Min	Year		Min
1918	Joe Hall, Mon	60	1944	Mike McMahon, Mon	98	1970	Keith Magnuson, Chi	213
1919	Joe Hall, Mon	85	1945	Pat Egan, Bos	86	1971	Keith Magnuson, Chi	291
			1946	Jack Stewart, Det	73	1972	Bryan Watson, Pit	212
1920	Cully Wilson, Tor	79	1947	Gus Mortson, Tor	133	1973	Dave Schultz, Phi	259
1921	Bert Corbeau, Mon	86	1948	Bill Barilko, Tor	147	1974	Dave Schultz, Phi	348
1922	Sprague Cleghorn, Mon	63	1949	Bill Ezinicki, Tor	145	1975	Dave Schultz, Phi	472
1923	Billy Boucher, Mon	52				1976	Steve Durbano, Pit-KC	370
1924	Bert Corbeau, Tor	55	1950	Bill Ezinicki, Tor	144	1977	Tiger Williams, Tor	338
1925	Billy Boucher, Mon	92	1951	Gus Mortson, Tor	142	1978	Dave Schultz, LA-Pit	405
1926	Bert Corbeau, Tor	121	1952	Gus Kyle, Bos	127	1979	Tiger Williams, Tor	298
1927	Nels Stewart, Mon-M	133	1953	Maurice Richard, Mon	112			
1928	Eddie Shore, Bos	165	1954	Gus Mortson, Chi	132	1980	Jimmy Mann, Win	287
1929	Red Dutton, Mon-M	139	1955	Fern Flaman, Bos	150	1981	Tiger Williams, Van	343
			1956	Lou Fontinato, NYR	202	1982	Paul Baxter, Pit	409
1930	Joe Lamb, Ott	119	1957	Gus Mortson, Chi	147	1983	Randy Holt, Wash	275
1931	Harvey Rockburn, Det	118	1958	Lou Fontinato, NYR	152	1984	Chris Nilan, Mon	338
1932	Red Dutton, NYA	107	1959	Ted Lindsay, Chi	184	1985	Chris Nilan, Mon	358
1933	Red Horner, Tor	144				1986	Joey Kocur, Det	377
1934	Red Horner, Tor	146	1960	Carl Brewer, Tor	150	1987	Tim Hunter, Calg	361
1935	Red Horner, Tor	125	1961	Pierre Pilot, Chi	165	1988	Bob Probert, Det	398
1936	Red Horner, Tor	167	1962	Lou Fontinato, Mon	167	1989	Tim Hunter, Calg	375
1937	Red Horner, Tor	124	1963	Howie Young, Det	273			
1938	Red Horner, Tor	82	1964	Vic Hadfield, NYR	151	1990	Basil McRae, Min	351
1939	Red Horner, Tor	85	1965	Carl Brewer, Tor	177	1991	Rob Ray, Buf	350
			1966	Reg Fleming, Bos-NYR	166	1992	Mike Peluso, Chi	408
1940	Red Horner, Tor	87	1967	John Ferguson, Mon	177	1993	Marty McSorley, LA	399
1941	Jimmy Orlando, Det	99	1968	Barclay Plager, St.L	153	1994	Tie Domi, Win	347
1942	Pat Egan, NYA	124	1969	Forbes Kennedy, Phi-Tor	219	1995	Enrico Ciccone, TB	225
1943	Jimmy Orlando, Det	99						

All-Time NHL Regular Season Leaders
Through 1995 regular season.

CAREER
Players active during 1995 in **bold** type.

Points

		Yrs	Gm	G	A	Pts
1	**Wayne Gretzky**	16	1173	814	1692	2506
2	Gordie Howe	26	1767	801	1049	1850
3	Marcel Dionne	18	1348	731	1040	1771
4	Phil Esposito	18	1282	717	873	1590
5	Stan Mikita	22	1394	541	926	1467
6	**Bryan Trottier**	18	1279	524	901	1425
7	John Bucyk	23	1540	556	813	1369
	Mark Messier	16	1127	492	877	1369
9	Guy Lafleur	17	1126	560	793	1353
10	**Paul Coffey**	15	1078	358	978	1336
11	Gilbert Perreault	17	1191	512	814	1326
12	**Dale Hawerchuk**	14	1055	489	825	1314
13	**Jari Kurri**	14	1028	565	731	1296
14	Alex Delvecchio	24	1549	456	825	1281
15	Jean Ratelle	21	1281	491	776	1267
16	**Denis Savard**	15	1063	451	812	1263
17	**Peter Stastny**	15	977	450	789	1239
18	**Ray Bourque**	16	1146	323	908	1231
19	Norm Ullman	20	1410	490	739	1229
20	Jean Beliveau	20	1125	507	712	1219
21	**Mario Lemieux**	10	599	494	717	1211
22	Bobby Clarke	15	1144	358	852	1210
23	**Mike Gartner**	16	1208	629	562	1191
24	Bobby Hull	16	1063	610	560	1170
25	**Steve Yzerman**	12	862	481	679	1160
26	Michel Goulet	15	1089	548	604	1152
27	**Ron Francis**	14	1008	349	789	1138
28	Bernie Federko	14	1000	369	761	1130
29	Mike Bossy	10	752	573	553	1126
30	Darryl Sittler	15	1096	484	637	1121

Goals

		Yrs	Gm	No
1	**Wayne Gretzky**	16	1173	814
2	Gordie Howe	26	1767	801
3	Marcel Dionne	18	1348	731
4	Phil Esposito	18	1282	717
5	**Mike Gartner**	16	1208	629
6	Bobby Hull	16	1063	610
7	Mike Bossy	10	752	573
8	**Jari Kurri**	14	1028	565
9	Guy Lafleur	17	1126	560
10	John Bucyk	23	1540	556
11	Michel Goulet	15	1089	548
12	Maurice Richard	18	978	544
13	Stan Mikita	22	1394	541
14	Frank Mahovlich	18	1181	533
15	**Dino Ciccarelli**	15	1015	529
16	**Bryan Trottier**	18	1279	524
17	Gilbert Perreault	17	1191	512
18	Jean Beliveau	18	1125	507
19	Lanny McDonald	16	1111	500
20	**Mario Lemieux**	10	599	494
21	Glenn Anderson	15	1096	492
	Mark Messier	16	1127	492
23	Jean Ratelle	21	1281	491
24	Norm Ullman	20	1410	490
25	**Dale Hawerchuk**	14	1055	489
26	**Joe Mullen**	15	971	487
27	Darryl Sittler	15	1096	484
28	**Steve Yzerman**	12	862	481
29	Alex Delvecchio	24	1549	456
30	**Denis Savard**	15	1063	451

Assists

		Yrs	Gm	No
1	**Wayne Gretzky**	16	1173	1692
2	Gordie Howe	26	1767	1049
3	Marcel Dionne	18	1348	1040
4	**Paul Coffey**	15	1078	978
5	Stan Mikita	22	1394	926
6	**Ray Bourque**	16	1146	908
7	**Bryan Trottier**	18	1279	901
8	**Mark Messier**	16	1127	877
9	Phil Esposito	18	1281	873
10	Bobby Clarke	15	1144	852
11	**Dale Hawerchuk**	14	1055	825
	Alex Delvecchio	24	1549	825
13	Gilbert Perreault	17	1191	814
14	John Bucyk	23	1540	813
15	**Denis Savard**	15	1063	812
16	Guy Lafleur	17	1126	793
17	**Peter Stastny**	15	977	789
	Ron Francis	14	1008	789
19	Jean Ratelle	21	1281	776
20	Bernie Federko	14	1000	761

Penalty Minutes

		Yrs	Gm	Min
1	Tiger Williams	14	962	3966
2	**Dale Hunter**	15	1099	3106
2	Chris Nilan	13	688	3043
4	**Tim Hunter**	14	709	2889
5	**Marty McSorley**	12	707	2723
6	Willi Plett	12	834	2572
7	Basil McRae	14	550	2405
8	Garth Butcher	14	897	2302
9	Dave Schultz	9	535	2294
10	**Jay Wells**	16	1001	2279

NHL-WHA Top 15

All-Time regular season scoring leaders, including games played in World Hockey Association (1972-79). NHL players with WHA experience are listed in CAPITAL letters. Players active during 1995 are in **bold** type.

Points

		Yrs	G	A	Pts
1	**WAYNE GRETZKY**	17	860	1756	2616
2	GORDIE HOWE	32	975	1383	2358
3	BOBBY HULL	23	913	895	1808
4	Marcel Dionne	18	731	1040	1771
5	Phil Esposito	18	717	873	1590
6	Stan Mikita	22	541	926	1467
7	Bryan Trottier	18	524	901	1425
8	**MARK MESSIER**	17	493	887	1380
9	John Bucyk	23	556	813	1369
10	NORM ULLMAN	22	537	822	1359
11	Guy Lafleur	17	560	793	1353
12	Paul Coffey	15	358	978	1336
13	FRANK MAHOVLICH	22	622	713	1335
14	Gilbert Perreault	17	512	814	1326
15	Dale Hawerchuk	14	489	825	1314

WHA Totals: GRETZKY (1 yr, 60 gm, 46-64—110); HOWE (6 yrs, 419 gm, 174-334—508); HULL (7 yrs, 411 gm, 303-335—638); MAHOVLICH (4 yrs, 237 gm, 89-143—232); MESSIER (1 yr, 52 gm, 1-10—11); ULLMAN (2 yrs, 144 gm, 47-83—130).

All-Time NHL Regular Season Leaders (Cont.)

Years Played

		Yrs	Career	Gm
1	Gordie Howe	26	1946-71, 79-80	1767
2	Alex Delvecchio	24	1950-74	1549
	Tim Horton	24	1949-50, 51-74	1446
4	John Bucyk	23	1955-78	1540
5	Stan Mikita	22	1958-80	1394
	Doug Mohns	22	1953-75	1390
	Dean Prentice	22	1952-74	1378
8	Harry Howell	21	1952-73	1411
	Ron Stewart	21	1952-73	1353
	Jean Ratelle	21	1960-81	1281
	Allan Stanley	21	1948-69	1244
	Eric Nesterenko	21	1951-72	1219
	Marcel Pronovost	21	1950-70	1206
	George Armstrong	21	1949-50, 51-71	1187
	Terry Sawchuk	21	1949-70	971
	Gump Worsley	21	1952-53, 54-74	862

Note: Combined NHL-WHA years played: Howe (32); Howell (24); Bobby Hull (23); Norm Ullman, Nesterenko, Frank Mahovlich and Dave Keon (22).

Games Played

		Yrs	Career	Gm
1	Gordie Howe	26	1946-71, 79-80	1767
2	Alex Delvecchio	24	1950-74	1549
3	John Bucyk	23	1955-78	1540
4	Tim Horton	24	1949-50, 51-74	1446
5	Harry Howell	21	1952-73	1411
6	Norm Ullman	20	1955-75	1410
7	Stan Mikita	22	1958-80	1394
8	Doug Mohns	22	1953-75	1390
9	Larry Robinson	20	1972-92	1384
10	Dean Prentice	22	1952-74	1378
11	Ron Stewart	21	1952-73	1353
12	Marcel Dionne	18	1971-89	1348
13	Red Kelly	20	1947-67	1316
14	Dave Keon	18	1960-75, 79-82	1296
15	Phil Esposito	18	1963-81	1282

Note: Combined NHL-WHA games played: Howe (2,186), Keon (1,597), Howell (1,581), Ullman (1,554), Bobby Hull (1,474) and Frank Mahovlich (1,418).

Goaltending

Wins

		Yrs	Gm	W	L	T	Pct
1	Terry Sawchuk	21	971	**435**	337	188	.551
2	Jacques Plante	18	837	**434**	246	137	.615
3	Tony Esposito	16	886	**423**	307	151	.566
4	Glenn Hall	18	906	**407**	327	165	.544
5	Rogie Vachon	16	795	**355**	291	115	.542
6	Gump Worsley	21	862	**335**	353	150	.489
7	Harry Lumley	16	804	**332**	324	143	.505
8	**Andy Moog**	15	582	**313**	160	71	.641
9	Billy Smith	18	680	**305**	233	105	.556
10	Turk Broda	12	629	**302**	224	101	.562
11	Mike Liut	13	663	**293**	271	74	.517
12	**Grant Fuhr**	14	596	**290**	195	71	.585
13	Ed Giacomin	13	610	**289**	206	97	.570
14	Dan Bouchard	14	655	**286**	232	113	.543
15	Tiny Thompson	12	553	**284**	194	75	.581
16	**Patrick Roy**	10	529	**277**	166	65	.609
17	Bernie Parent	13	608	**270**	197	121	.562
	Gilles Meloche	18	788	**270**	351	131	.446
19	**Mike Vernon**	12	597	**267**	161	55	.610
20	**Tom Barrasso**	12	548	**266**	197	61	.566

Losses

		Yrs	Gm	W	L	T	Pct
1	Gump Worsley	21	862	335	**353**	150	.489
2	Gilles Meloche	18	788	270	**351**	131	.446
3	Terry Sawchuk	21	971	435	**337**	188	.551
4	Glenn Hall	18	906	407	**327**	165	.544
5	Harry Lumley	16	804	332	**324**	143	.505

Goals Against Average

Minimum of 300 games played.

Before 1950

		Gm	Min	GA	GAA
1	George Hainsworth	465	29,415	937	1.91
2	Alex Connell	416	26,030	837	2.01
3	Chuck Gardiner	316	19,687	664	2.02
4	Lorne Chabot	412	25,309	861	2.04
5	Tiny Thompson	552	34,174	1183	2.08

Since 1950

		Gm	Min	GA	GAA
1	Ken Dryden	397	23,352	870	2.24
2	Jacques Plante	837	49,633	1965	2.38
3	Glenn Hall	906	53,484	2239	2.51
4	Terry Sawchuk	971	57,205	2401	2.52
5	Johnny Bower	552	32,077	1347	2.52

Shutouts

		Yrs	Games	No
1	Terry Sawchuk	21	971	103
2	George Hainsworth	11	464	94
3	Glenn Hall	18	906	84
4	Jacques Plante	18	837	82
5	Alex Connell	12	417	81
	Tiny Thompson	12	553	81
7	Tony Esposito	16	886	76
8	Lorne Chabot	11	411	73
9	Harry Lumley	16	804	71
10	Roy Worters	12	484	66
11	Turk Broda	14	629	62
12	John Roach	14	492	58
13	Clint Benedict	13	362	57
14	Bernie Parent	13	608	55
15	Ed Giacomin	13	610	54

NHL-WHA Top 15

All-Time regular season wins leaders, including games played in World Hockey Association (1972-79). NHL goaltenders with WHA experience are listed in CAPITAL letters. Players active during 1995 are in **bold** type.

Wins

		Yrs	W	L	T	Pct
1	JACQUES PLANTE	19	449	260	138	.612
2	Terry Sawchuk	21	435	337	188	.551
3	Tony Esposito	16	423	307	151	.566
4	Glenn Hall	18	407	327	165	.544
5	Rogie Vachon	16	355	291	115	.542
6	Gump Worsley	21	335	353	150	.489
7	Harry Lumley	16	332	324	143	.505
8	GERRY CHEEVERS	16	329	172	83	.634
9	MIKE LIUT	15	324	310	78	.510
10	**Andy Moog**	15	313	160	71	.641
11	Billy Smith	18	305	233	105	.556
12	BERNIE PARENT	14	303	225	121	.560
13	Turk Broda	12	302	224	101	.562
14	**Grant Fuhr**	14	290	195	71	.585
15	Ed Giacomin	13	289	206	97	.570

WHA Totals: CHEEVERS (4 yrs, 191 gm, 99-78-9); LIUT (2 yrs, 81 gm, 31-39-4); PARENT (1 yr, 63 gm, 33-28-0); PLANTE (1 yr, 31 gm, 15-14-1).

SINGLE SEASON

Scoring

Points

		Season	G	A	Pts
1	Wayne Gretzky, Edm	1985-86	52	163	215
2	Wayne Gretzky, Edm	1981-82	92	120	212
3	Wayne Gretzky, Edm	1984-85	73	135	208
4	Wayne Gretzky, Edm	1983-84	87	118	205
5	Mario Lemieux, Pit	1988-89	85	114	199
6	Wayne Gretzky, Edm	1982-83	71	125	196
7	Wayne Gretzky, Edm	1986-87	62	121	183
8	Mario Lemieux, Pit	1987-88	70	98	168
	Wayne Gretzky, LA	1988-89	54	114	168
10	Wayne Gretzky, Edm	1980-81	55	109	164
11	Wayne Gretzky, LA	1990-91	41	122	163
12	Mario Lemieux, Pit	1992-93	69	91	160
13	Steve Yzerman, Det	1988-89	65	90	155
14	Phil Esposito, Bos	1970-71	76	76	152
15	Bernie Nicholls, LA	1988-89	70	80	150
16	Wayne Gretzky, Edm	1987-88	40	109	149
17	Pat LaFontaine, Buf	1992-93	53	95	148
18	Mike Bossy, NYI	1981-82	64	83	147
19	Phil Esposito, Bos	1973-74	68	77	145
20	Adam Oates, Bos	1992-93	45	97	142
	Wayne Gretzky, LA	1989-90	40	102	142

WHA 150 points or more: 154—Marc Tardif, Que. (1977-78).

Goals

		Season	Gm	No
1	Wayne Gretzky, Edm	1981-82	80	92
2	Wayne Gretzky, Edm	1983-84	74	87
3	Brett Hull, St.L	1990-91	78	86
4	Mario Lemieux, Pit	1988-89	76	85
5	Alexander Mogilny, Buf	1992-93	77	76
	Phil Esposito, Bos	1970-71	78	76
	Teemu Selanne, Win	1992-93	84	76
8	Wayne Gretzky, Edm	1984-85	80	73
9	Brett Hull, St.L	1989-90	80	72
10	Jari Kurri, Edm	1984-85	73	71
	Wayne Gretzky, Edm	1982-83	80	71
12	Brett Hull, St.L	1991-92	73	70
	Mario Lemieux, Pit	1987-88	77	70
	Bernie Nicholls, LA	1988-89	79	70
15	Mario Lemieux, Pit	1992-93	60	69
	Mike Bossy, NYI	1978-79	80	69
17	Phil Esposito, Bos	1973-74	78	68
	Jari Kurri, Edm	1985-86	78	68
	Mike Bossy, NYI	1980-81	79	68
20	Phil Esposito, Bos	1971-72	76	66
	Lanny McDonald, Calg	1982-83	80	66

WHA 70 goals or more: 77—Bobby Hull, Win. (1974-75); 75—Real Cloutier, Que. (1978-79); 71—Marc Tardif, Que. (1975-76); 70—Anders Hedberg, Win. (1976-77).

Assists

		Season	Gm	No
1	Wayne Gretzky, Edm	1985-86	80	163
2	Wayne Gretzky, Edm	1984-85	80	135
3	Wayne Gretzky, Edm	1982-83	80	125
4	Wayne Gretzky, LA	1990-91	78	122
5	Wayne Gretzky, Edm	1986-87	79	121
6	Wayne Gretzky, Edm	1981-82	80	120
7	Wayne Gretzky, Edm	1983-84	74	118
8	Mario Lemieux, Pit	1988-89	76	114
	Wayne Gretzky, LA	1988-89	78	114
10	Wayne Gretzky, Edm	1987-88	64	109
	Wayne Gretzky, Edm	1980-81	80	109
12	Wayne Gretzky, LA	1989-90	73	102
	Bobby Orr, Bos	1970-71	78	102
14	Mario Lemieux, Pit	1987-88	77	98
15	Adam Oates, Bos	1992-93	84	97

WHA 95 assists or more: 106—Andre Lacroix, S.Diego 1974-75).

Goaltending

Wins

		Season	Record
1	Bernie Parent, Phi	1973-74	47-13-12
2	Bernie Parent, Phi	1974-75	44-14- 9
	Terry Sawchuk, Det	1950-51	44-13-13
	Terry Sawchuk, Det	1951-52	44-14-12
5	Tom Barrasso, Pit	1992-93	43-14- 5
	Ed Belfour, Chi	1990-91	43-19- 7
7	Jacques Plante, Mon	1955-56	42-12-10
	Jacques Plante, Mon	1961-62	42-14-14
	Ken Dryden, Mon	1975-76	42-10- 8
	Mike Richter, NYR	1993-94	42-12- 6

Most WHA wins in one season: 44—Richard Brodeur, Que. (1975-76).

Losses

		Season	Record
1	Gary Smith, Cal	1970-71	19-48- 4
2	Al Rollins, Chi	1953-54	12-47- 7
3	Peter Sidorkiewicz, Ott	1992-93	8-46- 3
4	Harry Lumley, Chi	1951-52	17-44- 9
5	Harry Lumley, Chi	1950-51	12-41-10
	Craig Billington, Ott	1993-94	11-41- 4

Most WHA losses in one season: 36—Don McLeod, Van. (1974-75) and Andy Brown, Ind. (1974-75).

Shutouts

		Season	Gm	No
1	George Hainsworth, Mon	1928-29	44	22
2	Alex Connell, Ottawa	1925-26	36	15
	Alex Connell, Ottawa	1927-28	44	15
	Hal Winkler, Bos	1927-28	44	15
	Tony Esposito, Chi	1969-70	63	15

Most WHA shutouts in one season: 5—Gerry Cheevers, Cle. (1972-73) and Joe Daly, Win. (1975-76).

Goals Against Average
Before 1950

		Season	Gm	GAA
1	George Hainsworth, Mon	1928-29	44	0.98
2	George Hainsworth, Mon	1927-28	44	1.09
3	Alex Connell, Ottawa	1925-26	36	1.17
4	Tiny Thompson, Bos	1928-29	44	1.18
5	Roy Worters, NY Americans	1928-29	38	1.21

Since 1950

		Season	Gm	GAA
1	Tony Esposito, Chi	1971-72	48	1.77
2	Al Rollins, Tor	1950-51	40	1.77
3	Harry Lumley, Tor	1953-54	69	1.86
4	Jacques Plante, Mon	1955-56	64	1.86
5	Jacques Plante, Tor	1970-71	40	1.88

Penalty Minutes

		Season	Min
1	Dave Schultz, Phi	1974-75	472
2	Paul Baxter, Pit	1981-82	409
3	Mike Peluso, Chi	1991-92	408
4	Dave Schultz, LA-Pit	1977-78	405
5	Marty McSorley, LA	1992-93	399
6	Bob Probert, Det	1987-88	398
7	Basil McRae, Min	1987-88	382
8	Joey Kocur, Det	1985-86	377
9	Tim Hunter, Calg	1988-89	375
10	Steve Durbano, Pit-KC	1975-76	370
	Gino Odjick, Van	1992-93	370

WHA 355 minutes or more: 365—Curt Brackenbury, Min-Que. (1975-76).

All-Time NHL Regular Season Leaders (Cont.)
SINGLE GAME
Scoring

Points

	Date	G-A—Pts
Darryl Sittler, Tor vs Bos.	2/7/76	6-4—10
Maurice Richard, Mon vs Det	12/28/44	5-3— 8
Bert Olmstead, Mon vs Chi.	1/9/54	4-4— 8
Tom Bladon, Phi vs Cle.	12/11/77	4-4— 8
Bryan Trottier, NYI vs NYR	12/23/78	5-3— 8
Peter Stastny, Que at Wash	2/22/81	3-5— 8
Anton Stastny, Que at Wash	2/22/81	3-5— 8
Wayne Gretzky, Edm vs NJ	11/19/83	3-5— 8
Wayne Gretzky, Edm vs Min	1/4/84	4-4— 8
Paul Coffey, Edm vs Det	3/14/86	2-6— 8
Mario Lemieux, Pit vs St.L	10/15/88	2-6— 8
Bernie Nicholls, LA vs Tor	12/1/88	2-6— 8
Mario Lemieux, Pit vs NJ	12/31/88	5-3— 8

Goals

	Date	No
Joe Malone, Que vs Tor	1/31/20	7
Newsy Lalonde, Mon vs Tor	1/10/20	6
Joe Malone, Que vs Ott.	3/10/20	6
Corb Denneny, Tor vs Ham	1/26/21	6
Cy Denneny, Ott vs Ham	3/7/21	6
Syd Howe, Det vs NYR	2/3/44	6
Red Berenson, St.L at Phi	11/7/68	6
Darryl Sittler, Tor vs Bos.	2/7/76	6

Assists

	Date	No
Billy Taylor, Det at Chi.	3/16/47	7
Wayne Gretzky, Edm vs Wash	2/15/80	7
Wayne Gretzky, Edm at Chi	12/11/85	7
Wayne Gretzky, Edm vs Que	2/14/86	7

22 players tied with 6 each.

THE GREAT ONE: FOR THE RECORD

Los Angeles center Wayne Gretzky broke Gordie Howe's all-time NHL regular season goal-scoring record with his 802nd goal on Mar. 23, 1994. The record was the 60th league mark he has either tied or set outright. Gretzky will enter the 1995-96 regular season with 814 goals, 1,692 assists and 2,506 points—all league career records.

Year by Year Statistics

			Regular Season				Playoffs					Awards
Season	Age	Club	Gm	G	A	Pts	PM	Gm	G	A	Pts	PM	
1978-79	18	Indianapolis	8	3	3	6	0	—	—	—	—	—	
		Edmonton	72	43	61	104	19	13	10*	10	20*	2	WHA Top Rookie
1979-80	19	Edmonton	79	51	86*	137†	21	3	2	1	3	0	Hart & Byng
1980-81	20	Edmonton	80	55	109*	164*	28	9	7	14	21	4	Hart & Ross
1981-82	21	Edmonton	80	92*	120*	212*	26	5	5	7	12	8	Hart & Ross
1982-83	22	Edmonton	80	71*	125*	196*	59	16	12	26*	38*	4	Hart & Ross
1983-84	23	Edmonton	74	87*	118*	205*	39	19	13	22*	35*	12	Hart & Ross
1984-85	24	Edmonton	80	73*	135*	208*	52	18	17	30*	47*	4	Hart, Ross & Smythe
1985-86	25	Edmonton	80	52	163*	215*	46	10	8	11	19	2	Hart & Ross
1986-87	26	Edmonton	79	62*	121*	183*	28	21	5	29*	34*	6	Hart & Ross
1987-88	27	Edmonton	64	40	109*	149	24	19	12	31*	43*	16	Smythe
1988-89	28	Los Angeles	78	54	114†	168	26	11	5	17	22	0	Hart
1989-90	29	Los Angeles	73	40	102*	142*	42	7	3	7	10	0	Ross
1990-91	30	Los Angeles	78	41	122*	163*	16	12	4	11	15	2	Ross & Byng
1991-92	31	Los Angeles	74	31	90*	121	34	6	2	5	7	2	Byng
1992-93	32	Los Angeles	45	16	49	65	6	24	15*	25*	40*	4	—
1993-94	33	Los Angeles	81	38	92*	130*	20	—	—	—	—	—	Byng
1995	34	Los Angeles	48	11	37	48	6	—	—	—	—	—	
		WHA totals	80	46	64	110	19	13	10	10	20	2	
		NHL totals	1173	814	1692	2506	473	180	110	236	346	64	

*Led league; †Tied for league lead.

Gretzky vs. Howe

The all-time records of Wayne Gretzky and Gordie Howe, pro hockey's two most prolific scorers. Below are their career records in the NHL, the WHA and the two leagues combined. Howe played with Detroit (1946-71) and Hartford (1979-80) in the NHL and with Houston (1973-77) and New England (1977-79) in the WHA.

NHL	Regular Season					Playoffs						Stanley Cups
	Yrs	Gm	G	A	Pts	PM	Yrs	Gm	G	A	Pts	PM	
Wayne Gretzky	16	1173	814	1692	2506	473	14	180	110	236	346	64	4 (1984-85,87-88)
Gordie Howe	26	1767	801	1049	1850	1685	20	157	68	92	160	220	4 (1950,52,54-55)

WHA	Regular Season					Playoffs						AVCO World Cups
	Yrs	Gm	G	A	Pts	PM	Yrs	Gm	G	A	Pts	PM	
Gordie Howe	6	419	174	334	508	399	6	78	28	43	71	115	2 (1974-75)
Wayne Gretzky	1	80	46	64	110	19	1	13	10	10	20	2	None

NHL/WHA	Regular Season					Playoffs					
	Yrs	Gm	G	A	Pts	PM	Yrs	Gm	G	A	Pts	PM
Wayne Gretzky	17	1253	860	1756	2616	492	15	193	120	246	366	66
Gordie Howe	32	2186	975	1383	2358	2084	26	235	96	135	231	335

All-Time Winningest NHL Coaches

Top 20 NHL career victories through the 1995 season. Career, regular season and playoff records are noted along with NHL titles won. Coaches active during 1995 season in **bold** type.

		Career				Regular Season				Playoffs			
		Yrs	W	L	T	Pct	W	L	T	Pct	W	L	T	Pct	Stanley Cups
1	**Scotty Bowman**	23	1065	513	238	.652	913	421	238	.656	152	92	0	.623	6 (1973,76-79,92)
2	Al Arbour	22	902	662	246	.566	779	576	246	.563	123	86	0	.589	4 (1980-83)
3	Dick Irvin	26	790	609	228	.556	690	521	226	.559	100	88	2	.532	4 (1932,44,46,53)
4	Billy Reay	16	599	445	175	.563	542	385	175	.571	57	60	0	.487	None
5	Toe Blake	13	582	292	159	.640	500	255	159	.634	82	37	0	.689	8 (1956-60,65-66,68)
6	Glen Sather	11	553	305	110	.628	464	268	110	.616	89	37	0	.706	4 (1984-85,87-88)
7	**Mike Keenan**	10	507	330	82	.596	423	267	82	.601	84	63	0	.571	1 (1994)
8	Bryan Murray	12	501	381	115	.560	467	337	115	.571	34	44	0	.436	None
9	Punch Imlach	15	467	421	163	.522	423	373	163	.526	44	48	0	.478	4 (1962-64,67)
10	Jack Adams	21	465	442	162	.511	413	390	161	.512	52	52	1	.500	2 (1936-37)
11	Fred Shero	10	451	272	119	.606	390	225	119	.612	61	47	0	.565	2 (1974-75)
12	Emile Francis	13	433	326	112	.561	393	273	112	.577	40	53	0	.430	None
13	**Jacques Demers**	11	430	411	113	.510	375	368	113	.504	55	43	0	.561	1 (1993)
14	Roger Neilson	13	418	366	132	.528	381	326	132	.533	37	40	0	.481	None
15	Sid Abel	16	414	470	155	.473	382	426	155	.477	32	44	0	.421	None
16	Pat Quinn	11	405	328	102	.546	354	282	102	.549	51	46	0	.526	None
17	Bob Berry	11	395	377	121	.510	384	355	121	.517	11	22	0	.333	None
18	Art Ross	18	393	310	95	.552	361	277	90	.558	32	33	5	.493	1 (1939)
19	Michel Bergeron	10	369	387	104	.490	338	350	104	.492	31	37	0	.456	None
20	Bob Pulford	11	364	348	130	.510	336	305	130	.520	28	43	0	.394	None

Note: The NHL does not recognize records from the World Hockey Association (1972-79), so the following WHA overall coaching records are not included above: **Demers** (155-164-44 in 4 yrs); **Sather** (103-97-1 in 3 yrs).

Where They Coached

Abel—Chicago (1952-54), Detroit (1957-68,69-70), St. Louis (1971-72), Kansas City (1975-76); **Adams**—Toronto (1922-23), Detroit (1927-47); **Arbour**—St. Louis (1970-73), NY Islanders (1973-86,88-94); **Bergeron**—Quebec (1980-87), NY Rangers (1987-89), Quebec (1989-90); **Berry**—Los Angeles (1978-81), Montreal (1981-84), Pittsburgh (1984-87), St. Louis (1992-94); **Blake**—Montreal (1955-68); **Bowman**—St. Louis (1967-71), Montreal (1971-79), Buffalo (1979-87), Pittsburgh (1991-93), Detroit (1993—).
Demers—Quebec (1979-80), St. Louis (1983-86), Detroit (1986-90), Montreal (1992—); **Francis**—NY Rangers (1965-75), St. Louis (1976-77,81-83); **Imlach**—Toronto (1958-69), Buffalo (1970-72), Toronto (1979-81); **Irvin**—Chicago (1930-31,55-56), Toronto (1931-40), Montreal (1940-55); **Keenan**—Philadelphia (1984-88), Chicago (1988-92), NY Rangers (1993-94), St. Louis (1994—); **Murray**—Washington (1982-90), Detroit (1990-93).
Neilson—Toronto (1977-79), Buffalo (1979-81), Vancouver (1982-83), Los Angeles (1984), NY Rangers (1989-93), Florida (1993-95); **Pulford**—Los Angeles (1972-77), Chicago (1977-79,81-82,85-87); **Quinn**—Philadelphia (1978-82), Los Angeles (1984-87), Vancouver (1990-94); **Reay**—Toronto (1957-59), Chicago (1963-77); **Ross**—Montreal Wanderers (1917-18), Hamilton (1922-23), Boston (1924-28,29-34,36-39,41-45); **Sather**—Edmonton (1979-89, 93-94); **Shero**—Philadelphia (1971-78), NY Rangers (1978-81).

Top Winning Percentages

Minimum of 275 victories, including playoffs.

		Yrs	W	L	T	Pct
1	**Scotty Bowman**	23	1065	513	238	**.652**
2	Toe Blake	13	582	292	159	**.640**
3	Glen Sather	11	553	305	110	**.628**
4	Fred Shero	10	451	272	119	**.606**
5	Don Cherry	6	281	177	77	**.597**
6	**Mike Keenan**	10	507	330	82	**.596**
7	Tommy Ivan	9	324	205	111	**.593**
8	**Pat Burns**	7	335	230	61	**.584**
9	Al Arbour	22	902	662	246	**.566**
10	Billy Reay	16	599	445	175	**.563**
11	Emile Francis	13	433	326	112	**.561**
12	Bryan Murray	12	501	381	115	**.560**
13	Hap Day	10	308	237	81	**.557**
14	**Brian Sutter**	7	300	233	66	**.556**
	Dick Irvin	26	790	609	228	**.556**
16	Lester Patrick	13	312	242	115	**.552**
	Art Ross	18	393	310	95	**.552**
18	Bob Johnson	6	275	223	58	**.547**
19	Pat Quinn	11	405	328	102	**.546**
20	**Roger Neilson**	13	418	366	132	**.528**
21	Punch Imlach	15	467	421	163	**.522**
22	Jack Adams	21	465	442	162	**.511**
23	Bob Berry	11	395	377	121	**.510**
	Jacques Demers	11	430	411	113	**.510**
	Bob Pulford	11	364	348	130	**.510**

Active Coaches' Victories

Through 1995 season, including playoffs.

		Yrs	W	L	T	Pct
1	Scotty Bowman, Det	23	1065	513	238	.652
2	Mike Keenan, St.L	10	507	330	82	.596
3	Jacques Demers, Mon	11	430	411	113	.510
4	Pat Burns, Tor	7	335	230	61	.584
5	Terry Crisp, TB	6	236	203	54	.533
6	Terry Murray, Phi	6	219	176	32	.550
7	Eddie Johnston, Pit	6	200	217	70	.483
8	Bob Gainey, Dal	5	177	192	51	.482
9	Pierre Page, Calg	5	167	192	49	.469
10	Paul Holmgren, Hart	7	166	222	44	.435
11	Jacques Lemaire, NJ	4	159	105	32	.591
12	Terry Simpson, Win	6	132	139	35	.489
13	Jim Schoenfeld, Wash	6	118	118	34	.500
14	Mike Millbury, NYI	2	113	66	21	.618
15	Rick Ley, Van	3	96	104	32	.483
16	Rick Bowness, Ott	5	85	221	33	.299
17	Tim Constantine, SJ	2	63	74	20	.465
18	Ron Wilson, Ana	2	49	73	10	.409
19	Marc Crawford, Col	1	32	17	5	.639
20	Colin Campbell, NYR	1	26	29	3	.474
21	Ron Low, Edm	1	5	7	1	.423
22	Craig Hartsburg, Chi	0	0	0	0	.000
	Steve Kasper, Bos	0	0	0	0	.000
	Doug MacLean, Fla	0	0	0	0	.000
	Ted Nolan, Buf	0	0	0	0	.000
	Larry Robinson, LA	0	0	0	0	.000

Annual Awards

Hart Memorial Trophy

Awarded to the player "adjudged to be the most valuable to his team" and named after Cecil Hart, the former manager-coach of the Montreal Canadiens. Winners selected by Pro Hockey Writers Assn. (PHWA). Winners' scoring statistics or goaltender W-L records and goals against average are provided; (*) indicates led or tied for league lead.

Multiple winners: Wayne Gretzky (9); Gordie Howe (6); Eddie Shore (4); Bobby Clarke, Howie Morenz and Bobby Orr (3); Jean Beliveau, Bill Cowley, Phil Esposito, Bobby Hull, Guy Lafleur, Mario Lemieux, Mark Messier, Stan Mikita and Nels Stewart (2).

Year		G	A	Pts	Year		G	A	Pts
1924	Frank Nighbor, Ottawa, C	10	3	13	1960	Gordie Howe, Det., RW	28	45	73
1925	Billy Burch, Hamilton, C	20	4	24	1961	Bernie Geoffrion, Mon., RW	50	45	95*
1926	Nels Stewart, Maroons, C	34	8	42*	1962	Jacques Plante, Mon., G	42-14-14; 2.37*
1927	Herb Gardiner, Mon., D	6	6	12	1963	Gordie Howe, Det., RW	38	48	86*
1928	Howie Morenz, Mon., C	33	18	51*	1964	Jean Beliveau, Mon., C	28	50	78
1929	Roy Worters, NYA, G	16-13-9; 1.21			1965	Bobby Hull, Chi., LW	39	32	71
1930	Nels Stewart, Maroons, C	39	16	55	1966	Bobby Hull, Chi., LW	54	43	97*
1931	Howie Morenz, Mon., C	28	23	51*	1967	Stan Mikita, Chi., C	35	62	97*
1932	Howie Morenz, Mon., C	24	25	49	1968	Stan Mikita, Chi., C	40	47	87*
1933	Eddie Shore, Bos., D	8	27	35	1969	Phil Esposito, Bos., C	49	77	126*
1934	Aurel Joliat, Mon., LW	22	15	37	1970	Bobby Orr, Bos., D	33	87	120*
1935	Eddie Shore, Bos., D	7	26	33	1971	Bobby Orr, Bos., D	37	102	139
1936	Eddie Shore, Bos., D	3	16	19	1972	Bobby Orr, Bos., D	37	80	117
1937	Babe Siebert, Mon., D	8	20	28	1973	Bobby Clarke, Phi., C	37	67	104
1938	Eddie Shore, Bos., D	3	14	17	1974	Phil Esposito, Bos., C	68	77	145*
1939	Toe Blake, Mon., LW	24	23	47*	1975	Bobby Clarke, Phi., C	27	89	116
1940	Ebbie Goodfellow, Det., D	11	17	28	1976	Bobby Clarke, Phi., C	30	89	119
1941	Bill Cowley, Bos., C	17	45	62*	1977	Guy Lafleur, Mon., RW	56	80	136*
1942	Tommy Anderson, NYA, D	12	29	41	1978	Guy Lafleur, Mon., RW	60	72	132*
1943	Bill Cowley, Bos., C	27	45	72	1979	Bryan Trottier, NYI., C	47	87	134*
1944	Babe Pratt, Tor., D	17	40	57	1980	Wayne Gretzky, Edm., C	51	86	137*
1945	Elmer Lach, Mon., C	26	54	80*	1981	Wayne Gretzky, Edm., C	55	109	164*
1946	Max Bentley, Chi., C	31	30	61*	1982	Wayne Gretzky, Edm., C	92	120	212*
1947	Maurice Richard, Mon., RW	45	26	71	1983	Wayne Gretzky, Edm., C	71	125	196*
1948	Buddy O'Connor, NYR, C	24	36	60	1984	Wayne Gretzky, Edm., C	87	118	205*
1949	Sid Abel, Det., C	28	26	54	1985	Wayne Gretzky, Edm., C	73	135	208*
1950	Chuck Rayner, NYR, G	28-30-11; 2.62			1986	Wayne Gretzky, Edm., C	52	163	215*
1951	Milt Schmidt, Bos., C	22	39	61	1987	Wayne Gretzky, Edm., C	62	121	183*
1952	Gordie Howe, Det., RW	47	39	86*	1988	Mario Lemieux, Pit., C	70	98	168*
1953	Gordie Howe, Det., RW	49	46	95*	1989	Wayne Gretzky, LA, C	54	114	168
1954	Al Rollins, Chi., G	12-47-7; 3.23			1990	Mark Messier, Edm., C	45	84	129
1955	Ted Kennedy, Tor., C	10	42	52	1991	Brett Hull, St. L., RW	86	45	131
1956	Jean Beliveau, Mon., C	47	41	88*	1992	Mark Messier, NYR, C	35	72	107
1957	Gordie Howe, Det., RW	44	45	89*	1993	Mario Lemieux, Pit., C	69	91	160*
1958	Gordie Howe, Det., RW	33	44	77	1994	Sergei Fedorov, Det., C	56	64	120
1959	Andy Bathgate, NYR, RW	40	48	88	1995	Eric Lindros, Phi., C	29	41	70*

Calder Memorial Trophy

Awarded to the most outstanding rookie of the year and named after Frank Calder, the late NHL president (1917-43). Since the 1990-91 season, all eligible candidates must not have attained their 26th birthday by Sept. 15 of their rookie year. Winners selected by PHWA. Winners' scoring statistics or goaltender W-L record & goals against average are provided.

Year		G	A	Pts	Year		G	A	Pts
1933	Carl Voss, NYR-Det., C	8	15	23	1950	Jack Gelineau, Bos., G	22-30-15; 3.28		
1934	Russ Blinco, Maroons, C	14	9	23	1951	Terry Sawchuk, Det., G	44-13-13; 1.99		
1935	Sweeney Schriner, NYA, LW	18	22	40	1952	Bernie Geoffrion, Mon., RW	30	24	54
1936	Mike Karakas, Chi., G	21-19-8; 1.92			1953	Gump Worsley, NYR, G	13-29-8; 3.06
1937	Syl Apps, Tor., C	16	29	45	1954	Camille Henry, NYR, LW	24	15	39
1938	Cully Dahlstrom, Chi., C	10	9	19	1955	Ed Litzenberger, Mon-Chi., RW	23	28	51
1939	Frankie Brimsek, Bos., G	33-9-1; 1.58			1956	Glenn Hall, Det., G	30-24-16; 2.11
1940	Kilby MacDonald, NYR, LW	15	13	28	1957	Larry Regan, Bos., RW	14	19	33
1941	John Quilty, Mon., C	18	16	34	1958	Frank Mahovlich, Tor., LW	20	16	36
1942	Knobby Warwick, NYR, RW	16	17	33	1959	Ralph Backstrom, Mon., C	18	22	40
1943	Gaye Stewart, Tor., LW	24	23	47	1960	Billy Hay, Chi., C	18	37	55
1944	Gus Bodnar, Tor., C	22	40	62	1961	Dave Keon, Tor., C	20	25	45
1945	Frank McCool, Tor., G	24-22-4; 3.22			1962	Bobby Rousseau, Mon., RW	21	24	45
1946	Edgar Laprade, NYR, C	15	19	34	1963	Kent Douglas, Tor., D	7	15	22
1947	Howie Meeker, Tor., RW	27	18	45	1964	Jacques Laperriere, Mon., D	2	28	30
1948	Jim McFadden, Det., C	24	24	48	1965	Roger Crozier, Det., G	40-23-7; 2.42		
1949	Penny Lund, NYR, RW	14	16	30	1966	Brit Selby, Tor., LW	14	13	27

Year		G	A	Pts	Year		G	A	Pts
1967	Bobby Orr, Bos., D	13	28	41	1982	Dale Hawerchuk, Win., C	45	58	103
1968	Derek Sanderson, Bos., C	24	25	49	1983	Steve Larmer, Chi., RW	43	47	90
1969	Danny Grant, Min., LW	34	31	65	1984	Tom Barrasso, Buf., G	26-12-3;		2.84
					1985	Mario Lemieux, Pit., C	43	57	100
1970	Tony Esposito, Chi., G	38-17-8;		2.17	1986	Gary Suter, Calg., D	18	50	68
1971	Gilbert Perreault, Buf., C	38	34	72	1987	Luc Robitaille, LA, LW	45	39	84
1972	Ken Dryden, Mon., G	39-8-15;		2.24	1988	Joe Nieuwendyk, Calg., C	51	41	92
1973	Steve Vickers, NYR, LW	30	23	53	1989	Brian Leetch, NYR, D	23	48	71
1974	Denis Potvin, NYI, D	17	37	54					
1975	Eric Vail, Atl., LW	39	21	60	1990	Sergei Makarov, Calg., RW	24	62	86
1976	Bryan Trottier, NYI, C	32	63	95	1991	Ed Belfour, Chi., G	43-19-7;		2.47
1977	Willi Plett, Atl., RW	33	23	56	1992	Pavel Bure, Van., RW	34	26	60
1978	Mike Bossy, NYI, RW	53	38	91	1993	Teemu Selanne, Win., RW	76	56	132
1979	Bobby Smith, Min., C	30	44	74	1994	Martin Brodeur, NJ, G	27-11-8;		2.40
					1995	Peter Forsberg, Que., C	15	35	50
1980	Ray Bourque, Bos., D	17	48	65					
1981	Peter Stastny, Que., C	39	70	109					

Vezina Trophy

From 1927-80, given to the principal goaltender(s) on the team allowing the fewest goals during the regular season. Trophy named after 1920's goalie Georges Vezina of the Montreal Canadiens, who died of tuberculosis in 1926. Since the 1980-81 season, the trophy has been awarded to the most outstanding goaltender of the year as selected by the league's general managers.

Multiple winners: Jacques Plante (7, one of them shared); Bill Durnan (6); Ken Dryden (5, three shared); Bunny Larocque (4, all shared); Terry Sawchuk (4, one shared); Tiny Thompson (4); Tony Esposito (3, two shared); George Hainsworth (3); Glenn Hall (3, two shared); Patrick Roy (3); Ed Belfour (2); Johnny Bower (2, one shared); Frankie Brimsek (2); Turk Broda (2); Chuck Gardiner (2); Dominik Hasek (2); Charlie Hodge (2, one shared); Bernie Parent (2, one shared); Gump Worsley (2, both shared).

Year		Record	GAA	Year		Record	GAA
1927	George Hainsworth, Mon	28-14-2	1.52	1967	Glenn Hall, Chi	19-5-5	2.38
1928	George Hainsworth, Mon	26-11-7	1.09		& Denis Dejordy, Chi	22-12-7	2.46
1929	George Hainsworth, Mon	22-7-15	0.98	1968	Gump Worsley, Mon	19-9-8	1.98
					& Rogie Vachon, Mon	23-13-2	2.48
1930	Tiny Thompson, Bos	38-5-1	2.23	1969	Jacques Plante, St.L	18-12-6	1.96
1931	Roy Worters, NYA	18-16-10	1.68		& Glenn Hall, St.L	19-12-8	2.17
1932	Chuck Gardiner, Chi	18-19-11	1.92				
1933	Tiny Thompson, Bos	25-15-8	1.83	1970	Tony Esposito, Chi	38-17-8	2.17
1934	Chuck Gardiner, Chi	20-17-11	1.73	1971	Ed Giacomin, NYR	27-10-7	2.16
1935	Lorne Chabot, Chi	26-17-5	1.83		& Gilles Villemure, NYR	22-8-4	2.30
1936	Tiny Thompson, Bos	22-20-6	1.71	1972	Tony Esposito, Chi	31-10-6	1.77
1937	Norm Smith, Det	25-14-9	2.13		& Gary Smith, Chi	14-5-6	2.42
1938	Tiny Thompson, Bos	30-11-7	1.85	1973	Ken Dryden, Mon	33-7-13	2.26
1939	Frankie Brimsek, Bos	33-9-1	1.58	1974	(Tie) Bernie Parent, Phi	47-13-12	1.89
					Tony Esposito, Chi	34-14-21	2.04
1940	Dave Kerr, NYR	27-11-10	1.60	1975	Bernie Parent, Phi	44-14-10	2.03
1941	Turk Broda, Tor	28-14-6	2.06	1976	Ken Dryden, Mon	42-10-8	2.03
1942	Frankie Brimsek, Bos	24-17-6	2.45	1977	Ken Dryden, Mon	41-6-8	2.14
1943	John Mowers, Det	25-14-11	2.47		& Bunny Larocque, Mon	19-2-4	2.09
1944	Bill Durnan, Mon	38-5-7	2.18	1978	Ken Dryden, Mon	37-7-7	2.05
1945	Bill Durnan, Mon	38-8-4	2.42		& Bunny Larocque, Mon	22-3-4	2.67
1946	Bill Durnan, Mon	24-11-5	2.60	1979	Ken Dryden, Mon	30-10-7	2.30
1947	Bill Durnan, Mon	34-16-10	2.30		& Bunny Larocque, Mon	22-7-4	2.84
1948	Turk Broda, Tor	32-15-13	2.38	1980	Bob Sauve, Buf	20-8-4	2.36
1949	Bill Durnan, Mon	28-23-9	2.10		& Don Edwards, Buf	27-9-12	2.57
				1981	Richard Sevigny, Mon	20-4-3	2.40
1950	Bill Durnan, Mon	26-21-17	2.20		Denis Herron, Mon	6-9-6	3.50
1951	Al Rollins, Tor	27-5-8	1.77		& Bunny Larocque, Mon	16-9-3	3.03
1952	Terry Sawchuk, Det	44-14-12	1.90	1982	Billy Smith, NYI	32-9-4	2.97
1953	Terry Sawchuk, Det	32-15-16	1.90	1983	Pete Peeters, Bos	40-11-9	2.36
1954	Harry Lumley, Tor	32-24-13	1.86	1984	Tom Barrasso, Buf	26-12-3	2.84
1955	Terry Sawchuk, Det	40-17-11	1.96	1985	Pelle Lindbergh, Phi	40-17-7	3.02
1956	Jacques Plante, Mon	42-12-10	1.86	1986	John Vanbiesbrouck, NYR	31-21-5	3.32
1957	Jacques Plante, Mon	31-18-12	2.02	1987	Ron Hextall, Phi	37-21-6	3.00
1958	Jacques Plante, Mon	34-14-8	2.11	1988	Grant Fuhr, Edm	40-24-9	3.43
1959	Jacques Plante, Mon	38-16-13	2.16	1989	Patrick Roy, Mon	33-5-6	2.47
1960	Jacques Plante, Mon	40-17-12	2.54	1990	Patrick Roy, Mon	31-16-5	2.53
1961	Johnny Bower, Tor	33-15-10	2.50	1991	Ed Belfour, Chi	43-19-7	2.47
1962	Jacques Plante, Mon	42-14-14	2.37	1992	Patrick Roy, Mon	36-22-8	2.36
1963	Glenn Hall, Chi	30-20-16	2.55	1993	Ed Belfour, Chi	41-18-11	2.59
1964	Charlie Hodge, Mon	33-18-11	2.26	1994	Dominik Hasek, Buf	30-20-6	1.95
1965	Johnny Bower, Tor	13-13-8	2.38	1995	Dominik Hasek, Buf	19-14-7	2.11
	& Terry Sawchuk, Tor	17-13-6	2.56				
1966	Gump Worsley, Mon	29-14-6	2.36				
	& Charlie Hodge, Mon	12-7-2	2.58				

Annual Awards (Cont.)
Lady Byng Memorial Trophy

Awarded to the player "adjudged to have exhibited the best type of sportsmanship and gentlemanly conduct combined with a high standard of playing ability" and named after Lady Evelyn Byng, the wife of former Canadian Governor General (1921-26) Baron Byng of Vimy. Winners selected by PHWA.

Multiple winners: Frank Boucher (7); Wayne Gretzky and Red Kelly (4); Bobby Bauer, Mike Bossy and Alex Delvecchio (3); Johnny Bucyk, Marcel Dionne, Dave Keon, Stan Mikita, Joey Mullen, Frank Nighbor, Jean Ratelle, Clint Smith and Sid Smith (2).

Year		Year		Year	
1925	Frank Nighbor, Ott., C	1949	Bill Quackenbush, Det., D	1972	Jean Ratelle, NYR, C
1926	Frank Nighbor, Ott., C			1973	Gilbert Perreault, Buf., C
1927	Billy Burch, NYA, C	1950	Edgar Laprade, NYR, C	1974	Johnny Bucyk, Bos., LW
1928	Frank Boucher, NYR, C	1951	Red Kelly, Det., D	1975	Marcel Dionne, Det., C
1929	Frank Boucher, NYR, C	1952	Sid Smith, Tor., LW	1976	Jean Ratelle, NY-Bos., C
		1953	Red Kelly, Det., D	1977	Marcel Dionne, LA, C
1930	Frank Boucher, NYR, C	1954	Red Kelly, Det., D	1978	Butch Goring, LA, C
1931	Frank Boucher, NYR, C	1955	Sid Smith, Tor., LW	1979	Bob MacMillan, Atl., RW
1932	Joe Primeau, Tor., C	1956	Earl Reibel, Det., C		
1933	Frank Boucher, NYR, C	1957	Andy Hebenton, NYR, RW	1980	Wayne Gretzky, Edm., C
1934	Frank Boucher, NYR, C	1958	Camille Henry, NYR, LW	1981	Rick Kehoe, Pit., RW
1935	Frank Boucher, NYR, C	1959	Alex Delvecchio, Det., LW	1982	Rick Middleton, Bos., RW
1936	Doc Romnes, Chi., F			1983	Mike Bossy, NYI, RW
1937	Marty Barry, Det., C	1960	Don McKenney, Bos., C	1984	Mike Bossy, NYI, RW
1938	Gordie Drillon, Tor., RW	1961	Red Kelly, Tor., D	1985	Jari Kurri, Edm., RW
1939	Clint Smith, NYR, C	1962	Dave Keon, Tor., C	1986	Mike Bossy, NYI, RW
		1963	Dave Keon, Tor., C	1987	Joey Mullen, Calg., RW
1940	Bobby Bauer, Bos., RW	1964	Ken Wharram, Chi., RW	1988	Mats Naslund, Mon., LW
1941	Bobby Bauer, Bos., RW	1965	Bobby Hull, Chi., LW	1989	Joey Mullen, Calg., RW
1942	Syl Apps, Tor., C	1966	Alex Delvecchio, Det., LW		
1943	Max Bentley, Chi., C	1967	Stan Mikita, Chi., C	1990	Brett Hull, St.L., RW
1944	Clint Smith, Chi., C	1968	Stan Mikita, Chi., C	1991	Wayne Gretzky, LA, C
1945	Bill Mosienko, Chi., RW	1969	Alex Delvecchio, Det., LW	1992	Wayne Gretzky, LA, C
1946	Toe Blake, Mon., LW			1993	Pierre Turgeon, NYI, C
1947	Bobby Bauer, Bos., RW	1970	Phil Goyette, St.L., C	1994	Wayne Gretzky, LA, C
1948	Buddy O'Connor, NYR, C	1971	Johnny Bucyk, Bos., LW	1995	Ron Francis, Pit., C

Note: Bill Quackenbush and Red Kelly are the only defensemen to win the Lady Byng.

James Norris Memorial Trophy

Awarded to the most outstanding defenseman of the year and named after James Norris, the late Detroit Red Wings owner-president. Winners selected by PHWA.

Multiple winners: Bobby Orr (8); Doug Harvey (7); Ray Bourque (5); Paul Coffey, Pierre Pilote and Denis Potvin (3); Chris Chelios, Rod Langway and Larry Robinson (2).

Year		Year		Year	
1954	Red Kelly, Detroit	1969	Bobby Orr, Boston	1982	Doug Wilson, Chicago
1955	Doug Harvey, Montreal	1970	Bobby Orr, Boston	1983	Rod Langway, Washington
1956	Doug Harvey, Montreal	1971	Bobby Orr, Boston	1984	Rod Langway, Washington
1957	Doug Harvey, Montreal	1972	Bobby Orr, Boston	1985	Paul Coffey, Edmonton
1958	Doug Harvey, Montreal	1973	Bobby Orr, Boston	1986	Paul Coffey, Edmonton
1959	Tom Johnson, Montreal	1974	Bobby Orr, Boston	1987	Ray Bourque, Boston
		1975	Bobby Orr, Boston	1988	Ray Bourque, Boston
1960	Doug Harvey, Montreal	1976	Denis Potvin, NY Islanders	1989	Chris Chelios, Montreal
1961	Doug Harvey, Montreal	1977	Larry Robinson, Montreal		
1962	Doug Harvey, NY Rangers	1978	Denis Potvin, NY Islanders	1990	Ray Bourque, Boston
1963	Pierre Pilote, Chicago	1979	Denis Potvin, NY Islanders	1991	Ray Bourque, Boston
1964	Pierre Pilote, Chicago	1980	Larry Robinson, Montreal	1992	Brian Leetch, NY Rangers
1965	Pierre Pilote, Chicago	1981	Randy Carlyle, Pittsburgh	1993	Chris Chelios, Chicago
1966	Jacques Laperriere, Montreal			1994	Ray Bourque, Boston
1967	Harry Howell, NY Rangers			1995	Paul Coffey, Detroit
1968	Bobby Orr, Boston				

Frank Selke Trophy

Awarded to the outstanding defensive forward of the year and named after the late Montreal Canadiens general manager. Winners selected by the PHWA.

Multiple winners: Bob Gainey (4); Guy Carbonneau (3).

Year		Year		Year	
1978	Bob Gainey, Mon., LW	1984	Doug Jarvis, Wash., C	1990	Rick Meagher, St.L., C
1979	Bob Gainey, Mon., LW	1985	Craig Ramsay, Buf., LW	1991	Dirk Graham, Chi., RW
		1986	Troy Murray, Chi., C	1992	Guy Carbonneau, Mon., C
1980	Bob Gainey, Mon., LW	1987	Dave Poulin, Phi., C	1993	Doug Gilmour, Tor., C
1981	Bob Gainey, Mon., LW	1988	Guy Carbonneau, Mon., C	1994	Sergei Fedorov, Det., C
1982	Steve Kasper, Bos., C	1989	Guy Carbonneau, Mon., C	1995	Ron Francis, Pit., C
1983	Bobby Clarke, Phi., C				

Jack Adams Award

Awarded to the coach "adjudged to have contributed the most to his team's success" and named after the late Detroit Red Wings coach and general manager. Winners selected by NHL Broadcasters' Assn.; (*) indicates division champion.

Multiple winners: Jacques Demers and Pat Quinn (2).

Year		Improvement	Year		Improvement
1974	Fred Shero, Phi	37-30-11 to 50-16-12*	1985	Mike Keenan, Phi	44-26-10 to 53-20- 7*
1975	Bob Pulford, LA	41-14-23 to 37-35- 8	1986	Glen Sather, Edm	49-20-11* to 56-17- 7*
1976	Don Cherry, Bos	40-26-14 to 48-15-17*	1987	Jacques Demers, Det	17-57- 6 to 34-36-10
1977	Scotty Bowman, Mon	58-11-11* to 60- 8-12*	1988	Jacques Demers, Det	34-36-10 to 41-28-11*
1978	Bobby Kromm, Det	16-55- 9 to 32-34-14	1989	Pat Burns, Mon	45-22-13 to 53-18- 9*
1979	Al Arbour, NYI	48-17-15* to 51-15-14*			
1980	Pat Quinn, Phi	40-25-15 to 48-12-20*	1990	Bob Murdoch, Win	26-42-12 to 37-32-11
1981	Red Berenson, St.L	34-34-12 to 45-18-17*	1991	Brian Sutter, St.L	37-34- 9 to 47-22-11
1982	Tom Watt, Win	9-57-14 to 33-33-14	1992	Pat Quinn, Van	28-43- 9 to 42-26-12*
1983	Orval Tessier, Chi	30-38-12 to 47-23-10*	1993	Pat Burns, Tor	30-43-7 to 44-29-11
1984	Bryan Murray, Wash	39-25-16 to 48-27- 5	1994	Jacques Lemaire, NJ	40-37-7 to 47-25-12
			1995	Marc Crawford, Que	34-42- 8 to 30-13-5*

Lester Pearson Award

Awarded to the season's most outstanding player and named after the former diplomat, Nobel Peace Prize winner and Canadian prime minister. Winners selected by the NHL Players Assn.

Multiple winners: Wayne Gretzky (5); Guy Lafleur and Mario Lemieux (3); Marcel Dionne, Phil Esposito and Mark Messier (2).

Year		Year		Year	
1971	Phil Esposito, Bos., C	1980	Marcel Dionne, LA, C	1988	Mario Lemieux, Pit., C
1972	Jean Ratelle, NYR, C	1981	Mike Liut, St.L., G	1989	Steve Yzerman, Det., C
1973	Bobby Clarke, Phi., C	1982	Wayne Gretzky, Edm., C		
1974	Phil Esposito, Bos., C	1983	Wayne Gretzky, Edm., C	1990	Mark Messier, Edm., C
1975	Bobby Orr, Bos., D	1984	Wayne Gretzky, Edm., C	1991	Brett Hull, St.L., RW
1976	Guy Lafleur, Mon., RW	1985	Wayne Gretzky, Edm., C	1992	Mark Messier, NYR, C
1977	Guy Lafleur, Mon., RW	1986	Mario Lemieux, Pit., C	1993	Mario Lemieux, Pit., C
1978	Guy Lafleur, Mon., RW	1987	Wayne Gretzky, Edm., C	1994	Sergei Fedorov, Det., C
1979	Marcel Dionne, LA, C			1995	Eric Lindros, Phi., C

Bill Masterton Trophy

Awarded to the player who "best exemplifies the qualities of perseverance, sportsmanship and dedication to hockey" and named after the 29-year-old rookie center of the Minnesota North Stars who died of a head injury sustained in a 1968 NHL game. Presented by the PHWA.

Year		Year		Year	
1968	Claude Provost, Mon., RW	1978	Butch Goring, LA, C	1988	Bob Bourne, LA, C
1969	Ted Hampson, Oak., C	1979	Serge Savard, Mon., D	1989	Tim Kerr, Phi., C
1970	Pit Martin, Chi., C	1980	Al MacAdam, Min., RW	1990	Gord Kluzak, Bos., D
1971	Jean Ratelle, NYR, C	1981	Blake Dunlop, St.L., C	1991	Dave Taylor, LA, RW
1972	Bobby Clarke, Phi., C	1982	Chico Resch, Colo., G	1992	Mark Fitzpatrick, NYI, G
1973	Lowell MacDonald, Pit., RW	1983	Lanny McDonald, Calg., RW	1993	Mario Lemieux, Pit., C
1974	Henri Richard, Mon., C	1984	Brad Park, Det., D	1994	Cam Neely, Bos., RW
1975	Don Luce, Buf., C	1985	Anders Hedberg, NYR, RW	1995	Pat LaFontaine, Buf., C
1976	Rod Gilbert, NYR, RW	1986	Charlie Simmer, Bos., LW		
1977	Ed Westfall, NYI, RW	1987	Doug Jarvis, Hart., C		

Number One Draft Choices

Overall first choices in the NHL Draft since the league staged its first universal amateur draft in 1969. Players are listed with team that selected them; those who became Rookie of the Year are in **bold** type.

Year		Year		Year	
1969	Rejean Houle, Mon., LW	1978	**Bobby Smith**, Min., C	1987	Pierre Turgeon, Buf., C
1970	**Gilbert Perreault,** Buf., C	1979	Rob Ramage, Colo., D	1988	Mike Modano, Min., C
1971	Guy Lafleur, Mon., RW	1980	Doug Wickenheiser, Mon., C	1989	Mats Sundin, Que., RW
1972	Billy Harris, NYI, RW	1981	**Dale Hawerchuk**, Win., C	1990	Owen Nolan, Que., RW
1973	**Denis Potvin,** NYI, D	1982	Gord Kluzak, Bos., D	1991	Eric Lindros, Que., C
1974	Greg Joly, Wash., D	1983	Brian Lawton, Min., C	1992	Roman Hamrlik, TB, D
1975	Mel Bridgman, Phi., C	1984	**Mario Lemieux,** Pit., C	1993	Alexandre Daigle, Ott., C
1976	Rick Green, Wash., D	1985	Wendel Clark, Tor., LW/D	1994	Ed Jovanovski, Fla., D
1977	Dale McCourt, Det., C	1986	Joe Murphy, Det., C	1995	Bryan Berard, Ott., D

World Hockey Association
WHA Finals

The World Hockey Association began play in 1972-73 as a 12-team rival of the 56-year-old NHL. The WHA played for the Avco World Trophy in its seven playoff finals (Avco Financial Services underwrote the playoffs).

Multiple winners: Winnipeg (3); Houston (2).

Year	Winner	Head Coach	Series	Loser	Head Coach
1973	New England Whalers	Jack Kelley	4-1 (WWLWW)	Winnipeg Jets	Bobby Hull
1974	Houston Aeros	Bill Dineen	4-0	Chicago Cougars	Pat Stapleton
1975	Houston Aeros	Bill Dineen	4-0	Quebec Nordiques	Jean-Guy Gendron
1976	Winnipeg Jets	Bobby Kromm	4-0	Houston Aeros	Bill Dineen
1977	Quebec Nordiques	Marc Boileau	4-3 (LWLWWLW)	Winnipeg Jets	Bobby Kromm
1978	Winnipeg Jets	Larry Hillman	4-0	NE Whalers	Harry Neale
1979	Winnipeg Jets	Larry Hillman	4-2 (WWLWLW)	Edmonton Oilers	Glen Sather

Playoff MVPs—1973—No award; **1974**—No award; **1975**—Ron Grahame, Houston, G; **1976**—Ulf Nilsson, Winnipeg, C; **1977**—Serg Bernier, Quebec, C; **1978**—Bobby Guindon, Winnipeg, C; **1979**—Rich Preston, Winnipeg, RW.

Most Valuable Player
(Gordie Howe Trophy, 1976-79)

Year		G	A	Pts
1973	Bobby Hull, Win., LW	51	52	103
1974	Gordie Howe, Hou., RW	31	69	100
1975	Bobby Hull, Win., LW	77	65	142
1976	Marc Tardif, Que., LW	71	77	148
1977	Robbie Ftorek, Pho., C	46	71	117
1978	Marc Tardif, Que., LW	65	89	154
1979	Dave Dryden, Edm., G	41-17-2; 2.89		

Scoring Leaders

Year		Gm	G	A	Pts
1973	Andre Lacroix, Phi	78	50	74	124
1974	Mike Walton, Min	78	57	60	117
1975	Andre Lacroix, S. Diego	78	41	106	147
1976	Marc Tardif, Que.	81	71	77	148
1977	Real Cloutier, Que.	76	66	75	141
1978	Marc Tardif, Que.	78	65	89	154
1979	Real Cloutier, Que.	77	75	54	129

Note: In 1979, 18 year-old Rookie of the Year Wayne Gretzky finished third in scoring (46-64—110).

Rookie of the Year

Year		G	A	Pts
1973	Terry Caffery, N. Eng., C	39	61	100
1974	Mark Howe, Hou., LW	38	41	79
1975	Anders Hedberg, Win., RW	53	47	100
1976	Mark Napier, Tor., RW	43	50	93
1977	George Lyle, N. Eng., LW	39	33	72
1978	Kent Nilsson, Win., C	42	65	107
1979	Wayne Gretzky, Ind.-Edm., C	46	64	110

Best Goaltender

Year		Record	GAA
1973	Gerry Cheevers, Cleveland	32-20-0	2.84
1974	Don McLeod, Houston	33-13-3	2.56
1975	Ron Grahame, Houston	33-10-0	3.03
1976	Michel Dion, Indianapolis	14-15-1	2.74
1977	Ron Grahame, Houston	27-10-2	2.74
1978	Al Smith, New England	30-20-3	3.22
1979	Dave Dryden, Edmonton	41-17-2	2.89

Best Defenseman

Year	
1973	J.C. Tremblay, Quebec
1974	Pat Stapleton, Chicago
1975	J.C. Tremblay, Quebec
1976	Paul Shmyr, Cleveland
1977	Ron Plumb, Cincinnati
1978	Lars-Erik Sjoberg, Winnipeg
1979	Rick Ley, New England

Coach of the Year

Year		Improvement
1973	Jack Kelley, N. Eng	46-30-2*
1974	Billy Harris, Tor	35-39-4 to 41-33-4
1975	Sandy Hucul, Pho	Expan. to 39-31-8
1976	Bobby Kromm, Win	38-35-5 to 52-27-2*
1977	Bill Dineen, Hou	53-27-0* to 50-24-6*
1978	Bill Dineen, Hou	50-24-6* to 42-34-4
1979	John Brophy, Birm	36-41-3 to 32-42-6

*Won Division.

WHA All-Star Game

The WHA All-Star Game was an Eastern Division vs Western Division contest from 1973-75. In 1976, the league's five Canadian-based teams played the nine teams in the US. Over the final three seasons—East played West in 1977; AVCO Cup champion Quebec played a WHA All-Star team in 1978; and in 1979, a full WHA All-Star team played a three-game series with Moscow Dynamo of the Soviet Union.

Year	Result	Host	Coaches	Most Valuable Player
1973	East 6, West 2	Quebec	Jack Kelley, Bobby Hull	Wayne Carleton, Ottawa
1974	East 8, West 4	St. Paul, MN	Jack Kelley, Bobby Hull	Mike Walton, Minnesota
1975	West 6, East 4	Edmonton	Bill Dineen, Ron Ryan	Rejean Houle, Quebec
1976	Canada 6, USA 1	Cleveland	Jean-Guy Gendron, Bill Dineen	Can—Real Cloutier, Que. USA—Paul Shmyr, Cleve.
1977	East 4, West 2	Hartford	Jacques Demers, Bobby Kromm	East—L. Levasseur, Min. West—W. Lindstrom, Win.
1978	Quebec 5, WHA 4	Quebec	Marc Boileau, Bill Dineen	Quebec—Marc Tardif WHA—Mark Howe, NE
1979	WHA def. Moscow Dynamo 3 games to none (4-2, 4-2, 4-3)	Edmonton	Larry Hillman, P. Iburtovich	No awards

World Championship

The World Hockey Championship tournament has been played regularly since 1930. The International Ice Hockey Federation (IIHF), which governs both the World and Winter Olympic tournaments, considers the Olympic champions from 1920-68 to also be the World champions. However the IIHF has not recognized an Olympic champion as World champion since 1968. The IIHF has sanctioned separate World Championships in Olympic years three times—in 1972, 1976 and again in 1992. The World championship is officially vacant for the three Olympic years from 1980-88.

Multiple winners: Soviet Union/Russia (23); Canada (20); Czechoslovakia and Sweden (6); USA (2).

Year		Year		Year		Year	
1920	Canada	1949	Czechoslovakia	1965	Soviet Union	1980	Not held
1924	Canada	1950	Canada	1966	Soviet Union	1981	Soviet Union
1928	Canada	1951	Canada	1967	Soviet Union	1982	Soviet Union
1930	Canada	1952	Canada	1968	Soviet Union	1983	Soviet Union
1931	Canada	1953	Sweden	1969	Soviet Union	1984	Not held
1932	Canada	1954	Soviet Union	1970	Soviet Union	1985	Czechoslovakia
1933	United States	1955	Canada	1971	Soviet Union	1986	Soviet Union
1934	Canada	1956	Soviet Union	1972	Czechoslovakia	1987	Sweden
1935	Canada	1957	Sweden	1973	Soviet Union	1988	Not held
1936	Great Britain	1958	Canada	1974	Soviet Union	1989	Soviet Union
1937	Canada	1959	Canada	1975	Soviet Union	1990	Soviet Union
1938	Canada	1960	United States	1976	Czechoslovakia	1991	Sweden
1939	Canada	1961	Canada	1977	Czechoslovakia	1992	Sweden
1940-46	Not held	1962	Sweden	1978	Soviet Union	1993	Russia
1947	Czechoslovakia	1963	Soviet Union	1979	Soviet Union	1994	Canada
1948	Canada	1964	Soviet Union			1995	Finland

Canada vs USSR Summits

The first competition between the Soviet National Team and the NHL took place Sept. 2-28, 1972. A team of NHL All-Stars emerged as the winner of the heralded 8-game series, but just barely—winning with a record of 4-3-1 after trailing 1-3-1.

Two years later a WHA All-Star team played the Soviet Nationals and could win only one game and tie three others in eight contests. Two other Canada vs USSR series took place during NHL All-Star breaks: the three-game Challenge Cup at New York in 1979, and the two-game Rendez-Vous '87 in Quebec City in 1987.

The NHL All-Stars played the USSR in a three-game Challenge Cup series in 1979.

1972 Team Canada vs USSR

NHL All-Stars vs Soviet National Team.

Date	City	Result	Goaltenders
9/2	Montreal	USSR, 7-3	Tretiak/Dryden
9/4	Toronto	Canada, 4-1	Esposito/Tretiak
9/6	Winnipeg	Tie, 4-4	Tretiak/Esposito
9/8	Vancouver	USSR, 5-3	Tretiak/Dryden
9/22	Moscow	USSR, 5-4	Tretiak/Esposito
9/24	Moscow	Canada, 3-2	Dryden/Tretiak
9/26	Moscow	Canada, 4-3	Esposito/Tretiak
9/28	Moscow	Canada, 6-5	Dryden/Tretiak

Standings

	W	L	T	Pts	GF	GA
Team Canada (NHL)	4	3	1	9	32	32
Soviet Union	3	4	1	7	32	32

Leading Scorers

1. Phil Esposito, Canada, (7-6—13); **2.** Aleksandr Yakushev, USSR (7-4—11); **3.** Paul Henderson, Canada (7-2—9); **4.** Boris Shadrin, USSR (3-5—8); **5.** Valeri Kharlamov, USSR (3-4—7) and Vladimir Petrov, USSR (3-4—7); **7.** Bobby Clarke, Canada (2-4—6) and Yuri Liapkin, USSR (1-5—6).

1974 Team Canada vs USSR

WHA All-Stars vs Soviet National Team.

Date	City	Result	Goaltenders
9/17	Quebec City	Tie, 3-3	Tretiak/Cheevers
9/19	Toronto	Canada, 4-1	Cheevers/Tretiak
9/21	Winnipeg	USSR, 8-5	Tretiak/McLeod
9/23	Vancouver	Tie, 5-5	Tretiak/Cheevers
10/1	Moscow	USSR, 3-2	Tretiak/Cheevers
10/3	Moscow	USSR, 5-2	Tretiak/Cheevers
10/5	Moscow	Tie, 4-4	Cheevers/Tretiak
10/6	Moscow	USSR, 3-2	Sidelinkov/Cheevers

Standings

	W	L	T	Pts	GF	GA
Soviet Union	4	1	3	11	32	27
Team Canada (WHA)	1	4	3	5	27	32

Leading Scorers

1. Bobby Hull, Canada (7-2—9); **2.** Aleksandr Yakushev, USSR (6-2—8), Ralph Backstrom, Canada (4-4—8) and Valeri Kharlamov, USSR (2-6—8); **5.** Gordie Howe, Canada (3-4—7), Andre Lacroix, Canada (1-6—7) and Vladimir Petrov, USSR (1-6—7).

1979 Challenge Cup Series

NHL All-Stars vs Soviet National Team

Date	City	Result	Goaltenders
2/8	New York	NHL, 4-2	K. Dryden/Tretiak
2/10	New York	USSR, 5-4	Tretiak/K. Dryden
2/11	New York	USSR, 6-0	Myshkin/Cheevers

Rendez-Vous '87

NHL All-Stars vs Soviet National Team

Date	City	Result	Goaltenders
2/11	Quebec	NHL, 4-3	Fuhr/Belosheykhin
2/13	Quebec	USSR, 5-3	Belosheykhin/Fuhr

The Canada Cup

After organizing the historic 8-game Team Canada-Soviet Union series of 1972, NHL Players Association executive director Alan Eagleson and the NHL created the Canada Cup in 1976. For the first time, the best players from the world's six major hockey powers—Canada, Czechoslovakia, Finland, Russia, Sweden and the USA competed together in one tournament.

1976
Round Robin Standings

	W	L	T	Pts	GF	GA
Canada	4	1	0	8	22	6
Czechoslovakia	3	1	1	7	19	9
Soviet Union	2	2	1	5	23	14
Sweden	2	2	1	5	16	18
United States	1	3	1	3	14	21
Finland	1	4	0	2	16	42

Finals (Best of 3)

Date	City	Score
9/13	Toronto	Canada 6, Czechoslovakia 0
9/15	Montreal	Canada 5, Czechoslovakia 4 (OT)

Note: Darryl Sittler scored the winning goal for Canada at 11:33 in overtime to clinch the Cup, 2 games to none.

Leading Scorers

1. Victor Hluktov, USSR (5-4—9), Bobby Orr, Canada (2-7—9) and Denis Potvin, Canada (1-8—9); **4.** Bobby Hull, Canada (5-3—8) and Milan Novy, Czechoslovakia (5-3—8).

Team MVPs

Canada—Rogie Vachon   Sweden—Borje Salming
Czech.—Milan Novy   USA—Robbie Ftorek
USSR—Alexandr Maltsev   Finland—Matti Hagman
Tournament MVP—Bobby Orr, Canada

1981
Round Robin Standings

	W	L	T	Pts	GF	GA
Canada	4	0	1	9	32	13
Soviet Union	3	1	1	7	20	13
Czechoslovakia	2	1	2	6	21	13
United States	2	2	1	5	17	19
Sweden	1	4	0	2	13	20
Finland	0	4	1	1	9	31

Semifinals

Date	City	Score
9/11	Ottawa	USSR 4, Czechoslovakia 1
9/11	Montreal	Canada 4, United States 1

Finals

Date	City	Score
9/13	Montreal	USSR 8, Canada 1

Leading Scorers

1. Wayne Gretzky, Canada (5-7—12); **2.** Mike Bossy, Canada (8-3—11), Bryan Trottier, Canada (3-8—11), Guy Lafleur, Canada (2-9—11), Alexei Kasatonov, USSR (1-10—11).

All-Star Team

Goal—Vladislav Tretiak, USSR; **Defense**—Arnold Kadlec, Czech. and Alexei Kasatonov, USSR; **Forwards**—Mike Bossy, Canada, Gil Perreault, Canada, and Sergei Shepelev, USSR. **Tournament MVP**—Tretiak.

1984
Round Robin Standings

	W	L	T	Pts	GF	GA
Soviet Union	5	0	0	10	22	7
United States	3	1	1	7	21	13
Sweden	3	2	0	6	15	16
Canada	2	2	1	5	23	18
West Germany	0	4	1	1	13	29
Czechoslovakia	0	4	1	1	10	21

Semifinals

Date	City	Score
9/12	Edmonton	Sweden 9, United States 2
9/15	Montreal	Canada 3, USSR 2 (OT)

Note: Mike Bossy scored the winning goal for Canada at 12:29 in overtime.

Finals (Best of 3)

Date	City	Score
9/16	Calgary	Canada 5, Sweden 2
9/18	Edmonton	Canada 6, Sweden 5

Leading Scorers

1. Wayne Gretzky, Canada (5-7—12); **2.** Michel Goulet, Canada (5-6—11), Kent Nilsson, Sweden (3-8—11), Paul Coffey, Canada (3-8—11); **5.** Hakan Loob, Sweden (6-4—10).

All-Star Team

Goal—Vladimir Myshkin, USSR; **Defense**—Paul Coffey, Canada and Rod Langway, USA; **Forwards**—Wayne Gretzky, Canada, John Tonelli, Canada, and Sergei Makarov, USSR. **Tournament MVP**—Tonelli

1987
Round Robin Standings

	W	L	T	Pts	GF	GA
Canada	3	0	2	8	19	13
Soviet Union	3	1	1	7	22	13
Sweden	3	2	0	6	17	14
Czechoslovakia	2	2	1	5	12	15
United States	2	3	0	4	13	14
Finland	0	5	0	0	9	23

Semifinals

Date	City	Score
9/8	Hamilton	USSR 4, Sweden 2
9/9	Montreal	Canada 5, Czechoslovakia 3

Finals (Best of 3)

Date	City	Score
9/11	Montreal	USSR 6, Canada 5 (OT)
9/13	Hamilton	Canada 6, USSR 5 (2 OT)
9/15	Hamilton	Canada 6, USSR 5

Note: In Game 1, Alexander Semak of USSR scored at 5:33 in overtime. In Game 2, Mario Lemieux of Canada scored at 10:07 in the second overtime period. Lemieux also won Game 3 on a goal with 1:26 left in regulation time.

Leading Scorers

1. Wayne Gretzky, Canada (3-18—21); **2.** Mario Lemieux, Canada (11-7—18); **3.** Sergei Makarov, USSR (7-8—15); **4.** Vladimir Krutov, USSR (7-7—14); **5.** Viacheslav Bykov, USSR (2-7—9); **6.** Ray Bourque, Canada (2-6—8).

All-Star Team

Goal—Grant Fuhr, Canada; **Defense**—Ray Bourque, Canada and Viacheslav Fetisov, USSR; **Forwards**—Wayne Gretzky, Canada, Mario Lemieux, Canada, and Vladimir Krutov, USSR. **Tournament MVP**—Gretzky.

1991

Round Robin Standings

	W	L	T	Pts	GF	GA
Canada	3	0	2	8	21	11
United States	4	1	0	8	19	15
Finland	2	2	1	5	10	13
Sweden	2	3	0	4	13	17
Soviet Union	1	3	1	3	14	14
Czechoslovakia	1	4	0	2	11	18

Leading Scorers

1. Wayne Gretzky, Canada (4-8—12); **2.** Steve Larmer, Canada (6-5—11); **3.** Brett Hull, USA (2-7—9); **4.** Mike Modano, USA (2-7—9); **5.** Mark Messier, Canada (2-6—8).

Semifinals

Date	City	Score
9/11	Hamilton	United States 7, Finland 3
9/12	Toronto	Canada 4, Sweden 0

Finals (Best of 3)

Date	City	Score
9/14	Montreal	Canada 4, United States 1
9/16	Hamilton	Canada 4, United States 2

All-Star Team

Goal—Bill Ranford, Canada; **Defense**—Al MacInnis, Canada and Chris Chelios, USA; **Forwards**—Wayne Gretzky, Canada, Jeremy Roenick, USA and Mats Sundin, Sweden. **Tournament MVP**—Bill Ranford.

U.S. DIVISION I COLLEGE HOCKEY

NCAA Final Four

The NCAA Division I hockey tournament began in 1948 and was played at the Broadmoor Ice Palace in Colorado Springs from 1948-57. Since 1958, the tournament has moved around the country, stopping for consecutive years only at Boston Garden from 1972-74. Consolation games to determine third place were played from 1949-89 and discontinued in 1990.

Multiple Winners: Michigan (7); Denver, North Dakota and Wisconsin (5); Boston University (4); Lake Superior St., Michigan Tech and Minnesota (3); Colorado College, Cornell, Michigan St. and RPI (2).

Year	Champion	Head Coach	Score	Runner-up	Third Place		Fourth Place
1948	Michigan	Vic Heyliger	8-4	Dartmouth	Colorado College and Boston College		

Year	Champion	Head Coach	Score	Runner-up	Third Place	Score	Fourth Place
1949	Boston College	Snooks Kelley	4-3	Dartmouth	Michigan	10-4	Colorado Col.
1950	Colorado College	Cheddy Thompson	13-4	Boston Univ.	Michigan	10-6	Boston Col.
1951	Michigan	Vic Heyliger	7-1	Brown	Boston U.	7-4	Colorado Col.
1952	Michigan	Vic Heyliger	4-1	Colorado Col.	Yale	4-1	St. Lawrence
1953	Michigan	Vic Heyliger	7-3	Minnesota	RPI	6-3	Boston Univ.
1954	RPI	Ned Harkness	5-4*	Minnesota	Michigan	7-2	Boston Col.
1955	Michigan	Vic Heyliger	5-3	Colorado Col.	Harvard	6-3	St. Lawrence
1956	Michigan	Vic Heyliger	7-5	Michigan Tech	St. Lawrence	6-2	Boston Col.
1957	Colorado College	Tom Bedecki	13-6	Michigan	Clarkson	2-1†	Harvard
1958	Denver	Murray Armstrong	6-2	North Dakota	Clarkson	5-1	Harvard
1959	North Dakota	Bob May	4-3*	Michigan St.	Boston Col.	7-6†	St. Lawrence
1960	Denver	Murray Armstrong	5-3	Michigan Tech	Boston Univ.	7-6	St. Lawrence
1961	Denver	Murray Armstrong	12-2	St. Lawrence	Minnesota	4-3	RPI
1962	Michigan Tech	John MacInnes	7-1	Clarkson	Michigan	5-1	St. Lawrence
1963	North Dakota	Barry Thorndycraft	6-5	Denver	Clarkson	5-3	Boston Col.
1964	Michigan	Allen Renfrew	6-3	Denver	RPI	2-1	Providence
1965	Michigan Tech	John MacInnes	8-2	Boston Col.	North Dakota	9-5	Brown
1966	Michigan St.	Amo Bessone	6-1	Clarkson	Denver	4-3	Boston Univ.
1967	Cornell	Ned Harkness	4-1	Boston Univ.	Michigan St.	6-1	North Dakota
1968	Denver	Murray Armstrong	4-0	North Dakota	Cornell	6-1	Boston Col.
1969	Denver	Murray Armstrong	4-3	Cornell	Harvard	6-5†	Michigan Tech
1970	Cornell	Ned Harkness	6-4	Clarkson	Wisconsin	6-5	Michigan Tech
1971	Boston University	Jack Kelley	4-2	Minnesota	Denver	1-0	Harvard
1972	Boston University	Jack Kelley	4-0	Cornell	Wisconsin	5-2	Denver
1973	Wisconsin	Bob Johnson	4-2	Denver	Boston Col.	3-1	Cornell
1974	Minnesota	Herb Brooks	4-2	Michigan Tech	Boston Univ.	7-5	Harvard
1975	Michigan Tech	John MacInnes	6-1	Minnesota	Boston Univ.	10-5	Harvard
1976	Minnesota	Herb Brooks	6-4	Michigan Tech	Brown	8-7	Boston Univ.
1977	Wisconsin	Bob Johnson	6-5*	Michigan	Boston Univ.	6-5	New Hampshire
1978	Boston University	Jack Parker	5-3	Boston Col.	Bowling Green	4-3	Wisconsin
1979	Minnesota	Herb Brooks	4-3	North Dakota	Dartmouth	7-3	New Hampshire
1980	North Dakota	Gino Gasparini	5-2	Northern Mich.	Dartmouth	8-4	Cornell
1981	Wisconsin	Bob Johnson	6-3	Minnesota	Michigan Tech	5-2	Northern Mich.
1982	North Dakota	Gino Gasparini	5-2	Wisconsin	Northeastern	10-4	New Hampshire
1983	Wisconsin	Jeff Sauer	6-2	Harvard	Providence	4-3	Minnesota
1984	Bowling Green	Jerry York	5-4*	Minn-Duluth	North Dakota	6-5†	Michigan St.
1985	RPI	Mike Addesa	2-1	Providence	Minn-Duluth	7-6†	Boston Col.
1986	Michigan St.	Ron Mason	6-5	Harvard	Minnesota	6-4	Denver
1987	North Dakota	Gino Gasparini	5-3	Michigan St.	Minnesota	6-3	Harvard
1988	Lake Superior St.	Frank Anzalone	4-3*	St. Lawrence	Maine	5-2	Minnesota
1989	Harvard	Billy Cleary	4-3*	Minnesota	Michigan St.	7-4	Maine

†Consolation game overtimes ended in 1st OT except in 1957, '59 and '69, which all ended in 2nd OT.

NCAA Final Four (Cont.)

Year	Champion	Head Coach	Score	Runner-up	Third Place
1990	Wisconsin	Jeff Sauer	7-3	Colgate	Boston College and Boston University
1991	Northern Michigan	Rick Comley	8-7*	Boston Univ.	Maine and Clarkson
1992	Lake Superior St.	Jeff Jackson	5-3	Wisconsin	Michigan and Michigan St.
1993	Maine	Shawn Walsh	5-4	Lake Superior St.	Boston University and Michigan
1994	Lake Superior St.	Jeff Jackson	9-1	Boston Univ.	Harvard and Minnesota
1995	Boston University	Jack Parker	6-2	Maine	Michigan and Minnesota

*Championship game overtime goals: 1954—1:54; 1959—4:22; 1977—0: 23; 1984—7:11 in 4th OT; 1988—4:46; 1989—4:16; 1991—1:57 in 3rd OT.

Note: Runners-up Denver (1973) and Wisconsin (1992) had participation voided by the NCAA for using ineligible players.

Most Outstanding Player

The Most Outstanding Players of each NCAA Div. I tournament since 1948. Winners of the award who did not play for the tournament champion are in **bold** type. In 1960, three players, none on the winning team, shared the award.
Multiple winners: Lou Angotti and Marc Behrend (2).

Year		Year		Year	
1948	**Joe Riley**, Dartmouth, F	1963	Al McLean, N. Dakota, F	1980	Doug Smail, N. Dakota, F
1949	**Dick Desmond**, Dart., G	1964	Bob Gray, Michigan, G	1981	Marc Behrend, Wisc., G
		1965	Gary Milroy, Mich. Tech, F	1982	Phil Sykes, N. Dakota, F
1950	**Ralph Bevins**, Boston U., G	1966	Gaye Cooley, Mich. St., G	1983	Marc Behrend, Wisc., G
1951	**Ed Whiston**, Brown, G	1967	Walt Stanowski, Cornell, D	1984	Gary Kruzich, Bowl. Green, G
1952	**Ken Kinsley**, Colo. Col., G	1968	Gerry Powers, Denver, G	1985	**Chris Terreri**, Prov., G
1953	John Matchefts, Mich., F	1969	Keith Magnuson, Denver, D	1986	Mike Donnelly, Mich. St., F
1954	Abbie Moore, RPI, F			1987	Tony Hrkac, N. Dakota, F
1955	**Phil Hilton**, Colo. Col., D	1970	Dan Lodboa, Cornell, D	1988	Bruce Hoffort, Lk. Superior, G
1956	Lorne Howes, Mich., G	1971	Dan Brady, Boston U., G	1989	Ted Donato, Harvard, F
1957	Bob McCusker, Colo. Col., F	1972	Tim Regan, Boston, U., G		
1958	Murray Massier, Denver, F	1973	Dean Talafous, Wisc., F	1990	Chris Tancill, Wisconsin, F
1959	Reg Morelli, N. Dakota, F	1974	Brad Shelstad, Minn., G	1991	Scott Beattie, No. Mich., F
		1975	Jim Warden, Mich. Tech, G	1992	Paul Constantin, Lk. Superior, F
1960	**Lou Angotti**, Mich. Tech., F;	1976	Tom Vanelli, Minn., F	1993	Jim Montgomery, Maine, F
	Bob Marquis, Boston U., F;	1977	Julian Baretta, Wisc., G	1994	Sean Tallaire, Lk. Superior, F
	& Barry Urbanski, Boston U., G	1978	Jack O'Callahan, Boston U., D	1995	Chris O'Sullivan, Boston U., F
1961	Bill Masterton, Denver, F	1979	Steve Janaszak, Minn., G		
1962	Lou Angotti, Mich. Tech, F				

Hobey Baker Award

College hockey's Player of the Year award; voted on by a national panel of sportswriters, broadcasters, college coaches and pro scouts. First presented in 1981 by the Decathlon Athletic Club of Bloomington, Minn., in the name of the Princeton collegiate hockey and football star who was killed in World War I.

Year		Year		Year	
1981	Neal Broten, Minnesota, F	1986	Scott Fusco, Harvard, F	1991	Dave Emma, Boston College, F
1982	George McPhee, Bowl. Green, F	1987	Tony Hrkac, North Dakota, F	1992	Scott Pellerin, Maine, F
1983	Mark Fusco, Harvard, D	1988	Robb Stauber, Minnesota, G	1993	Paul Kariya, Maine, F
1984	Tom Kurvers, Minn-Duluth, D	1989	Lane MacDonald, Harvard, F	1994	Chris Marinucci, Minn-Duluth, F
1985	Bill Watson, Minn-Duluth, F	1990	Kip Miller, Michigan St., F	1995	Brian Holzinger, Bowl. Green, F

Coach of the Year

The Penrose Memorial Trophy, voted on by the American Hockey Coaches Association and first presented in 1951 in the name of Colorado gold and copper magnate Spencer T. Penrose. Penrose built the Broadmoor hotel and athletic complex in Colorado Springs, that originally hosted the NCAA hockey championship from 1948-57.
Multiple winners: Len Ceglarski and Charlie Holt (3); Rick Comley, Eddie Jeremiah, Snooks Kelly, John MacInnes, Jack Parker, Jack Riley and Cooney Weiland (2).

Year		Year		Year	
1951	Eddie Jeremiah, Dartmouth	1967	Eddie Jeremiah, Dartmouth	1983	Bill Cleary, Harvard
1952	Cheedy Thompson, Colo. Col.	1968	Ned Harkness, Cornell	1984	Mike Sertich, Minn-Duluth
1953	John Mariucci, Minnesota	1969	Charlie Holt, New Hampshire	1985	Len Ceglarski, BC
1954	Vic Heyliger, Michigan			1986	Ralph Backstrom, Denver
1955	Cooney Weiland, Harvard	1970	John MacInnes, Michigan Tech	1987	Gino Gasparini, N. Dakota
1956	Bill Harrison, Clarkson	1971	Cooney Weiland, Harvard	1988	Frank Anzalone, Lk. Superior
1957	Jack Riley, Army	1972	Snooks Kelly, BC	1989	Joe Marsh, St. Lawrence
1958	Harry Cleverly, BU	1973	Len Ceglarski, BC		
1959	Snooks Kelly, BC	1974	Charlie Holt, New Hampshire	1990	Terry Slater, Colgate
		1975	Jack Parker, BU	1991	Rick Comley, No. Michigan
1960	Jack Riley, Army	1976	John MacInnes, Michigan Tech	1992	Ron Mason, Michigan St.
1961	Murray Armstrong, Denver	1977	Jerry York, Clarkson	1993	George Gwozdecky, Miami-OH
1962	Jack Kelley, Colby	1978	Jack Parker, BU	1994	Don Lucia, Colorado Col.
1963	Tony Frasca, Colorado Col.	1979	Charlie Holt, New Hampshire	1995	Shawn Walsh, Maine
1964	Tom Eccleston, Providence				
1965	Jim Fullerton, Brown	1980	Rick Comley, No. Michigan		
1966	Amo Bessone, Michigan St.	1981	Bill O'Flaherty, Clarkson		
	& Len Ceglarski, Clarkson	1982	Fern Flaman, Northeastern		

Note: 1960 winner Jack Riley won the award for coaching the USA to its first hockey gold medal in the Winter Olympics at Squaw Valley.

A dejected Alabama head coach **Gene Stallings** faces a news conference shortly after the NCAA slapped his football program with three years' probation on Aug. 2, 1995.

COLLEGE SPORTS

Mixed Bag

Halfway through the century's last decade major college sports are flourishing, but there is no shortage of difficult times ahead.

To the casual observer, 1995 represented some of the best of times ever in college athletics. Signs were everywhere that, in the collective consciousness of the nation, college sports had never been more successful or more popular:

While there was still no Division I-A college football playoff, the evolution of the Bowl Coalition into the new Bowl Alliance had greatly increased the chances of a No. 1 vs. No. 2 game for the national championship (see page 186). That game, scheduled for Jan. 2, 1996 at the Fiesta Bowl will generate the highest payout in postseason history— $8.5 million per team. In all, the title game will generate $27 million that will be shared by all the conferences in the alliance.

College football attendance, which had sagged in recent years, was up over 1.5 million fans in 1994 and was expected to improve even more in '95 despite the fact that more games than ever were on television. The average attendance for a Division I-A game in 1994 was 41,678. In the Big Ten and Southeastern conferences, the average was well over 63,000 per game.

In basketball, the Division I men's tournament continued to grow in value. CBS, anxious to protect its most popular TV sports property, announced an eight-year contract extension with the NCAA on Dec. 6, 1994, worth $1.725 billion through the 2001-02 season.

Women's basketball, which had been increasing in popularity each year, went off the charts when undefeated University of Connecticut went 35-0 and won the NCAA championship game with a memorable, come-from-behind 70-64 win over Tennessee.

Not only did the 1996 Final Four in Charlotte sell out by June of '95, but a new TV deal with ESPN and ESPN2 guarantees better tournament TV coverage (23 games) than ever before.

Those factors and more made a prima facie case that college athletics was better and stronger than it had ever been and that the future would provide only more of the same.

But underneath the surface there were a number of troubling signs that did not bode well for the future. Signs that college athletics was in danger of degenerating into a tug of war between the Haves and Have-Nots, making the pursuit of money the most important competition in college sports today.

To understand what is taking place, one need look no further than the Southwest Conference. The SWC played its last football season in 1995, despite an 81-year tradition filled with some of the richest memories in the history of the sport. Four of its members will join the Big Eight to form the new Big 12 Conference following the 1995-96 school year.

Tony Barnhart is the national college sports writer for the *Atlanta Journal and Constitution* and a contributing reporter for ESPN.

Division I college basketball continued to thrive on all fronts in 1994-95 with UCLA regaining the men's championship and the undefeated **University of Connecticut** (above) winning the women's title. New television contracts with CBS and ESPN also guaranteed more money and coverage.

"It's a sad thing to see," said Texas A&M head coach R.C. Slocum, who has been involved with the league for over 20 years. "You wonder how after 81 years such a thing could happen."

The SWC had its problems with NCAA rules violations, particularly in the 1970s and 80s, but that's not why the conference died. It died because in the brave new world of college athletics, a league whose members all hail from the same state simply isn't financially viable. There are only so many television sets in Texas, pardner.

So Baylor, Texas, Texas A&M and Texas Tech will throw in with Nebraska, Oklahoma, Colorado and Co., thereby retaining their status as "Haves" in the college sports universe.

The future is less certain for their four soon-to-be former SWC stablemates. Rice, Southern Methodist and Texas Christian are bound for the expanded, 16-team Western Athletic Conference, while Houston will join the newly-minted Conference USA— a merger of the Metro and Great Midwest basketball conferences that will also play football (see page 440).

The fear of going from the elite to the forgotten is the primary force driving Division I college athletics in the mid-1990s. And the chilling reality is this: The stakes have become so high that for some, playing fast and loose with the rules is no longer a question of morality. It has become just one of the risks of doing business.

Alabama, which had never been on NCAA probation in its 102-year football history, was nailed with sanctions on Aug. 2, which will keep the Crimson Tide from postseason competition this year. The NCAA said Alabama played an ineligible player, defensive back Antonio Langham, during the 1993 season even though it knew Langham had signed with an agent. The penalties may cost Alabama as much as $1.1 million in revenue.

The 1990s are only half over but already five of the 12 members of the SEC—

Alabama, Auburn, Florida, Kentucky and Mississippi— have been on NCAA probation. A sixth, Mississippi State, was notified on July 25 that it was under an official investigation and could face penalties.

Miami of Florida, the dominant football program of the last 10 years, is now awash in scandals ranging from Pell Grant fraud to drug policy violations. It was determined that Warren Sapp, the 1994 Lombardi Award winner, failed a drug test prior to the 1995 Orange Bowl but was allowed to play by coach Dennis Erickson because the national championship was on the line.

Sports Illustrated reported in its Aug. 7 issue that as many as 80 NCAA schools could be involved in an investigation into a bogus quickie degree program at the Southeastern College of the Assemblies of God, a bible school in Lakeland, Fla. The violations could be severe enough to force the NCAA to completely revamp its policies on accepting junior college players into its member schools.

These examples and others paint a discouraging picture.

"The major problem with college athletics is that at times it has grown too big or gotten too hot," said Gene Corrigan, the commissioner of the ACC. "There are moments when I think we need to throw some cold water on it and just cool down for a while. I still maintain that most facets about college athletics are good and worthwhile. But sometimes it looks like a monster out of control."

Many observers believe the rest of the decade is going to be a battle over the soul of college athletics. On one side is the consuming need to win in order to generate the dollars to survive. On the other is the belief, although rarely expressed, that college athletics is still a part of the educational process in America.

Television's influence will only increase in 1996 when individual conferences begin their own football TV deals with the networks. The SEC, for example, has broken away from the College Football Association's television package with ABC to cut its own deal with CBS. Beginning next year, SEC members who agree to big nonconference games made for TV will receive an additional $125,000 per game from the league's TV revenue pool.

CBS, in turn, will enter 1996 as the pri-

The Struggle To Comply With Title IX

While college athletic departments continue to struggle with myriad problems dealing with money and credibility, yet another issue— gender equity— is one that is simply not going to go away.

Title IX, the federal statue that requires equal treatment under the law for women by educational institutions, observed its 20th anniversary in 1992. The consensus then was that while the lot of female athletes had certainly improved, they were still a far cry from getting an equal share of dollars and other resources available to male athletes.

There were a number of lawsuits filed and schools promised to do better in the future and that, many believed, would be the end of it.

That has hardly been the case, however. For many schools whose athletic departments were already financially strapped, the only way to increase opportunities for women was to decrease them for men.

With as many as 85 men on football scholarship at the big Division I-A schools, and no comparable sport for women, dropping men's sports was the only way to bring the numbers closer together. In 1995, for example, 14 colleges dropped the sport of wrestling. San Francisco State, faced with a possible lawsuit by female athletes, simply dropped football and added women's tennis.

"That denied 120 opportunities for men and added eight opportunities for women," said Grant Teaff, the former head football coach at Baylor who is now executive director of the American Football Coaches Association. "We do not believe that was ever the intent of Title IX."

Then came the bombshell court ruling of March 29 when a U.S. District Court in Rhode Island found that Brown University was in violation of Title IX despite the fact that its 17-sport women's program was twice the national average and considered the most enlightened in the country.

Senior judge Raymond Pettine's 69-page ruling ordered Brown to restructure its athletic department so that participation rates "mirrored" the student body, which is 52 percent female.

It was the first time that such a high court had ruled that "proportionality" was the component which most dictated Title IX compliance. While

Brown University president **Vartan Gregorian** (center) addressing the May 9 congressional hearing on Title IX compliance conducted by the House Subcommittee on Postsecondary Education, Training and Lifelong Learning. Also testifying were Eastern Illinois University president **David Jorns** (left) and **Norma Cantu**, the assistant education secretary for civil rights.

there were 17 women's varsity sports at Brown compared to 16 for men, the women's teams had only 342 slots while the men's teams had 555.

The ruling was hailed by women's advocates as the next step on the road to equality. Their position was that men's sports did not have to be cut to provide more opportunity for women.

"That's just a smokescreen," said Donna Lopiano, executive director of the Women's Sports Foundation, an advocacy group for female athletes. "All that has to be done is require football to operate with a different standard of living. It uses the majority of the resources and those need to be more equitably distributed."

At a standing room only House subcommittee hearing on Title IX that took place in Washington on May 9, Norma Cantu, the assistant education secretary for civil rights, explained the Office of Civil Rights' three-part test that decides if an institution is in compliance with the law:

In essence, an institution must demonstrate the following:

1. That the female-to-male-ratio of athletics participation sustantially matches the female-to-male ratio of the undergraduate student body;

2. A clear history of continual program expansion for the underrepresented gender;

3. That the program fully and effectively accommodates interests and abilities of underrepresented gender.

Brown president Vartan Gregorian defended his school's efforts to comply with Title IX, but took exception to the testing procedure for compliance.

"These rules and guidelines are so ambiguous, so inconsistent and so imprecise," said Gregorian, "that they leave judges with total discretion and rob institutions of any flexibility in meeting OCR's tests."

Responded Cantu: "I don't hear how you can be both specific and flexible. I think we have hit on the right balance."

Women's advocates say that athletic resources are finite and they want what they perceive as their fair share. Just what a "fair share" is, of course, is open to interpretation, but if football has to be cut, so be it.

The other side argues that the courts never intended for men's sports to be dismantled in order to provide opportunities for women. And football, they say, cannot take the hit because at most schools it generates the lion's share of the athletic department's resources.

The issue will never be completely resolved until a case, like Brown's, ends up in the U.S. Supreme Court.

In the meantime, the smart schools continue to add sports for women no matter what the cost in an effort to increase their numbers and avoid a lawsuit.

mary college football network with exclusive rights to the SEC, Big East and two of the three rotating national championship venues in the Bowl Alliance— the Fiesta and Orange bowls. ABC will have the remaining major Alliance bowl— the Sugar— plus the Rose Bowl, which could undercut the Alliance should a Big 10 or Pac-10 team finish the regular season ranked No. 1 or No. 2.

Conferences will also be sitting down with the networks in the spring, juggling the dates of their league games in order to maximize television exposure.

"More and more you're going to see the conferences working with the networks trying to give them the maximum amount of quality programming for their dollar," said SEC commissioner Roy Kramer. "Basketball has done it for years and now it's football's turn."

The NCAA continues to look into the murky relationship between shoe companies, coaches, schools and the recruiting of blue-chip basketball players. Nike, for example, has signed a deal with the University of North Carolina that will give the school $4.6 million in cash and equipment over the next four years. A similar deal with Duke awarded coach Mike Krzyzewski a $1 million signing bonus in 1993. Several top-name coaches receive more money from shoe companies than they get in salary from their respective schools.

The concern is that shoe companies can use their influence and resources to steer top recruits to programs and coaches who use their equipment. As of now, there is no rule against it. Even though no shoe company has ever been publicly accused of steering a prospect to one of its "schools", it is another example of the financial tail wagging the college athletics dog.

Also coming to the table in greater numbers are the corporate sponsors of college athletic events, who have their own agenda. That's why the annual Oklahoma-Texas football game, a traditional rivalry that needs no enhancing, became the "Dr. Pepper Red River Shootout" in 1995.

"Colleges are always looking for ways to raise revenues, especially in light of gender equity and non-revenue producing sports," said Jim Host, whose company, Host Communications, Inc. of Lexington, Ky., came up with this latest can't-miss marketing idea. "There are a number of college football rivalries that corporate America would like to get involved in and we're looking for different ways to help make that happen."

Corporate sponsorship of bowl games, of course, is already a time-honored tradition, although the price keeps going up and title sponsors keep changing. On Aug. 8, the Fiesta Bowl announced a three-year, $15 million deal with Frito-Lay that would rename this season's national championship game in honor of Tostitos ("You have Tostitos, You Have A Party"). The Fiesta Bowl has previously shared billing with the Sunkist Citrus Growers (1986-91) and IBM OS/2 (1993-95).

Meanwhile, the folks who run the Florida Citrus Bowl stadium guaranteed Duke $850,000 to switch its 1995 opening home game against Florida State from Durham to Orlando. Next season, another ACC member, Maryland, will get $1 million to move its home game against the FSU to Joe Robbie Stadium in Miami. No wonder the Seminoles haven't lost a conference football game since joining the ACC in 1992.

"We always have to be careful, that in trying to make our athletic departments stay in the black, that we don't sell our souls to the devil," said the ACC's Corrigan. "I don't think we've done that and I don't think we will. But that doesn't mean we don't have to think every day about what we're doing."

The negative ramifications in this unceasing drive for dollars are many but this may be the worst: If some schools will stretch the rule book in order to win, it only stands to reason that they will be less than discriminating when it comes to the kind of athlete they bring into their programs.

On Sept. 10, Nebraska running back and Heisman Trophy candidate Lawrence Phillips was suspended from the team indefinitely by coach Tom Osborne after the player's arrest for assaulting a former girlfriend and co-ed.

Osborne, who won his first national championship in 1994 with Phillips leading the team in rushing and scoring, later told the Omaha World-Herald that his star junior "has a problem with anger, and he sometimes loses control."

Phillips is just one of six members of the '94 Cornhuskers' squad who have had run-ins with the law. One teammate, junior back Riley Washington, was ordered on Sept. 8 to stand trial on a charge of attempted sec-

Charles Votaw

Former Southwest Conference boss **Steve Hatchell** (left) was named commissioner of the new Big 12 Conference on March 26. The Big 12 officially opens for business on July 1, 1996 when the SWC dissolves and Baylor, Texas, Texas A&M and Texas Tech all join the current Big Eight. Kansas State president **Jon Wefald** chaired the search committee that hired Hatchell.

ond-degree murder for his alleged involvement in a shooting on Aug. 2.

But Nebraska is only the latest Division I-A national champion to struggle with off-field problems. Florida State, Alabama, Washington, Colorado and Miami of Florida, who have combined to win or share six national titles since 1987, have all had players (and programs) investigated by the local police or the NCAA infractions committee.

"Sometimes these are bad kids [who] have no business being in anybody's program. But people want to win, so they take the chance," said a Division I athletic director who did not want to be identified. "In other cases, some kids see all the money being generated by college athletics and wonder 'Where's my share?' They think everybody is getting rich except them."

At the confluence of these financial, legal, and social pressures were the coaches. Their job, as always, was to win and in the process, make everybody happy—players, fans, alumni, athletic directors, school presidents, NCAA officials and the media.

As it turned out, 1994-1995 was not a banner year for coaches.

Michigan football coach Gary Moeller was forced to resign on May 4, six days after a brawl in a restaurant where he had become intoxicated. All parties agreed that the incident was out of character for Moeller, but Michigan had gone 8-4 each of the past two seasons without a Rose Bowl appearance and suddenly he was cut loose.

Indiana University was fined $30,000 by the NCAA on June 13 due to a tirade by basketball coach Bob Knight after an NCAA tournament game (see page 281). Knight never apologized.

Reports in *The Miami Herald* revealed that the University of Miami football coaching staff, led by head coach Erickson, condoned acts of lawlessness. There were reports that Sapp, the All-America defensive tackle, failed as many as seven drug tests, but was allowed to continue playing. In all, 12 members of the Hurricanes' 1995 Orange Bowl team had arrest records. Erickson quit on Jan. 12 to become head coach of the NFL's Seattle Seahawks.

Some coaches, like Colorado's Bill McCartney, decided to get out of the rat race. McCartney, who built the Colorado football program from scratch and won a national championship in 1990, left to administer "Promise Keepers" a national support group for Christian men.

Vivian Stringer became the highest-paid women's basketball coach in the country on July 14, when she left Iowa to take over at Rutgers for a base salary of $150,000 a year.

"I finally decided that if all I was doing with my life was winning football games, it wasn't amounting to much," he said.

But for most coaches, the lure of the national spotlight and the money that comes with it remained too strong to resist.

Where once colleges would never have contemplated competing with the pros for coaching talent, the realities of today's market place dictates that they must. To lose a top-caliber coach when the financial stakes are this high is a risk many schools cannot afford to take. Coaches know this and, more than ever in 1995, used their leverage to the utmost.

As the college football season opened, Florida State coach Bobby Bowden was negotiating a contract extension that would keep him at FSU through the 2000 season. He was expected to receive a financial package worth $1 million per year. And Florida's Steve Spurrier and Notre Dame's Lou Holtz figured to be right behind him.

Kentucky basketball coach Rick Pitino already has a commitment to stay in Lexington at $1 million per year into the next century. He'll also receive a substantial bonus— as much as $1 million— if he stays through the 2000-01 season.

And the big bucks aren't going just to the men. Until this year, Pat Summitt, the Tennessee women's basketball coach, was easily the highest paid woman in college coaching with an annual base salary of $118,000 plus incentives and endorsements that boost her take-home pay to over $200,000.

On July 14, however, Rutgers University stunned the basketball community by signing ex-Iowa coach Vivian Stringer to a six-year contract with a yearly base salary of $150,000— more than the base salaries of either men's basketball coach Bob Wenzel ($124,000) or football coach Doug Graber ($145,000). With benefits and incentives, Stringer, who has a 23-year career record of 520-135, could pocket up to $300,000 per year.

As the 1995-96 school year began, Stringer's contract was viewed as the latest piece of artillery in the ever-escalating college athletics arms race.

Finally, just when it seems college athletics is having enough problems from external forces, one of its own is questioning the entire system.

Walter Byers, the executive director of the NCAA from 1951-86 and one of the most powerful figures in its history, now believes the organization has become "tyrannical and self-righteous."

These views and many others critical of the power structure of college athletics are set forth in Byers' new book, *Unsportsmanlike Conduct*, which was published in early fall.

In the book, Byers argues for a College Athletes Bill of Rights that would, in effect, deregulate the NCAA and eliminate many of the restrictions that are now in place for student athletes. If Byers had his way, athletes would be free to transfer at any time, could hold jobs year round, and would be able to consult with agents without fear of penalty.

His most chilling recommendation, however, calls for the courts to use existing antitrust law to break up the NCAA's stranglehold on college sports.

"I believe the record clearly shows," writes Byers, "that the major hope for reform lies outside the college cartel."

Byers' book was just another sign that college athletics is in need of some significant changes if it is to survive into the next century. ❑

NCAA Division I Basketball Schools
1995-96 Season
Conferences and coaches as of Sept. 15, 1995.

New conference in 1995-96: Conference USA (11 teams)— former Great Midwest members ALABAMA-BIRMINGHAM, CINCINNATI, DEPAUL, MARQUETTE, MEMPHIS and SAINT LOUIS; former Metro members LOUISVILLE, NC-CHARLOTTE, SOUTH FLORIDA, SOUTHERN MISSISSIPPI and TULANE.

Switching conferences in 1995-96: to Atlantic 10 (5)— DAYTON from Great Midwest, FORDHAM from Patriot, LA SALLE and XAVIER-OH from Midwestern, and VIRGINIA TECH from Metro; to Big East (2)— RUTGERS and WEST VIRGINIA from Atlantic 10; to Colonial (1)— VIRGINIA COMMONWEALTH from Metro; to North Atlantic (1)— TOWSON ST. from Big South.

Independent joining conference in 1995-96: NOTRE DAME to Big East.

Moving up from Division II in 1995-96 (3): HAMPTON to Mid-Eastern; JACKSONVILLE ST. to Trans America; and WOFFORD to Independent.

Changing conference name on July 1, 1996: Big Eight becomes Big 12.

Breakup of Southwest Conference on June 30, 1996: BAYLOR, TEXAS, TEXAS A&M and TEXAS TECH to Big 12; RICE, SMU and TCU to Western Athletic; HOUSTON to Conference USA.

Joining Big 12 in 1996-97 (4): BAYLOR, TEXAS, TEXAS A&M and TEXAS TECH from Southwest.

Joining Big West in 1996-97 (4): BOISE ST. and IDAHO from Big Sky; NORTH TEXAS from Southland, CAL POLY SLO from American West.

Joining Conference USA in 1996-97: HOUSTON from Southwest.

Joining Ohio Valley in 1996-97: EASTERN ILLINOIS from Mid-Continent.

Joining WAC in 1996-97 (6): SAN JOSE ST. and UNLV from Big West; TULSA from Mo. Valley; and RICE, SMU and TCU from Southwest.

New Division I program starting in 1996-97: PORTLAND ST. to Big Sky.

Joining Mid-American in 1997-98 (2): MARSHALL from Southern and NORTHERN ILLINOIS from Midwestern.

Joining Metro Atlantic in 1997-98 (2): MARIST and RIDER from Northeast.

Joining Mid-American in 1998-99: BUFFALO from Mid-Continent.

	Nickname	Conference	Head Coach	Location	Colors
Air Force	Falcons	WAC	Reggie Minton	Colo. Springs, CO	Blue/Silver
Akron	Zips	Mid-American	Dan Hipsher	Akron, OH	Blue/Gold
Alabama	Crimson Tide	SEC-West	David Hobbs	Tuscaloosa, AL	Crimson/White
Alabama St.	Hornets	Southwestern	James Oliver	Montgomery, AL	Black/Gold
Ala-Birmingham	Blazers	USA	Gene Bartow	Birmingham, AL	Green/Gold
Alcorn St.	Braves	Southwestern	Sam Weaver	Lorman, MS	Purple/Gold
American	Eagles	Colonial	Chris Knoche	Washington, DC	Red/White/Blue
Appalachian St.	Mountaineers	Southern	Tom Apke	Boone, NC	Black/Gold
Arizona	Wildcats	Pac-10	Lute Olson	Tucson, AZ	Cardinal/Navy
Arizona St.	Sun Devils	Pac-10	Bill Frieder	Tempe, AZ	Maroon/Gold
Arkansas	Razorbacks	SEC-West	Nolan Richardson	Fayetteville, AR	Cardinal/White
Arkansas-Little Rock	Trojans	Sun Belt	Wimp Sanderson	Little Rock, AR	Maroon/Gold/White
Arkansas St.	Indians	Sun Belt	Dickey Nutt	State Univ., AR	Scarlet/Black
Army	Cadets, Black Knights	Patriot	Dino Gaudio	West Point, NY	Black/Gold/Gray
Auburn	Tigers	SEC-West	Cliff Ellis	Auburn, AL	Orange/Blue
Austin Peay St.	Governors	Ohio Valley	Dave Loos	Clarksville, TN	Red/White
Ball St.	Cardinals	Mid-American	Ray McCallum	Muncie, IN	Cardinal/White
Baylor	Bears	SWC	Harry Miller	Waco, TX	Green/Gold
Bethune-Cookman	Wildcats	Mid-Eastern	Tony Sheals	Daytona Beach, FL	Maroon/Gold
Boise St.	Broncos	Big Sky	Rod Jensen	Boise, ID	Orange/Blue
Boston College	Eagles	Big East	Jim O'Brien	Chestnut Hill, MA	Maroon/Gold
Boston University	Terriers	North Atlantic	Dennis Wolff	Boston, MA	Scarlet/White
Bowling Green	Falcons	Mid-American	Jim Larranaga	Bowling Green, OH	Orange/Brown
Bradley	Braves	Mo. Valley	Jim Molinari	Peoria, IL	Red/White
BYU	Cougars	WAC	Roger Reid	Provo, UT	Royal Blue/White
Brown	Bears	Ivy	Frank Dobbs	Providence, RI	Brown/Cardinal/White
Bucknell	Bison	Patriot	Pat Flannery	Lewisburg, PA	Orange/Blue
Buffalo	Bulls	Mid-Continent	Tim Cohane	Buffalo, NY	Blue/Red/White
Butler	Bulldogs	Midwestern	Barry Collier	Indianapolis, IN	Blue/White

NCAA Division I Basketball Schools (Cont.)

	Nickname	Conference	Head Coach	Location	Colors
California	Golden Bears	Pac-10	Todd Bozeman	Berkeley, CA	Blue/Gold
CS-Fullerton	Titans	Big West	Bob Hawking	Fullerton, CA	Blue/Orange/White
CS-Northridge	Matadors	American West	Pete Cassidy	Northridge, CA	Red/White/Black
CS-Sacramento	Hornets	American West	Don Newman	Sacramento, CA	Green/Gold
Cal Poly SLO	Mustangs	American West	Jeff Schneider	San Luis Obispo, CA	Green/Gold
Campbell	Fighting Camels	Trans Am	Billy Lee	Buies Creek, NC	Orange/Black
Canisius	Golden Griffins	Metro Atlantic	John Beilein	Buffalo, NY	Blue/Gold
Centenary	Gentlemen	Trans Am	Tommy Vardeman	Shreveport, LA	Maroon/White
Central Conn. St.	Blue Devils	Mid-Continent	Mark Adams	New Britain, CT	Blue/White
Central Florida	Golden Knights	Trans Am	Kirk Speraw	Orlando, FL	Black/Gold
Central Michigan	Chippewas	Mid-American	Leonard Drake	Mt. Pleasant, MI	Maroon/Gold
Charleston So.	Buccaneers	Big South	Gary Edwards	Charleston, SC	Blue/Gold
Chicago St.	Cougars	Mid-Continent	Craig Hodges	Chicago, IL	Green/White
Cincinnati	Bearcats	USA	Bob Huggins	Cincinnati, OH	Red/Black
The Citadel	Bulldogs	Southern	Pat Dennis	Charleston, SC	Blue/White
Clemson	Tigers	ACC	Rick Barnes	Clemson, SC	Purple/Orange
Cleveland St.	Vikings	Midwestern	Mike Boyd	Cleveland, OH	Green/White
Coastal Carolina	Chanticleers	Big South	Michael Hopkins	Myrtle Beach, SC	Scarlet/Black
Colgate	Red Raiders	Patriot	Jack Bruen	Hamilton, NY	Maroon/Gray/White
College of Charleston	Cougars	Trans Am	John Kresse	Charleston, SC	Maroon/White
Colorado	Golden Buffaloes	Big Eight	Joe Harrington	Boulder, CO	Silver/Gold/Black
Colorado St.	Rams	WAC	Stew Morrill	Ft. Collins, CO	Green/Gold
Columbia	Lions	Ivy	Armond Hill	New York, NY	Lt. Blue/White
Connecticut	Huskies	Big East	Jim Calhoun	Storrs, CT	Blue/White
Coppin St.	Eagles	Mid-Eastern	Ron Mitchell	Baltimore, MD	Royal Blue/Gold
Cornell	Big Red	Ivy	Al Walker	Ithaca, NY	Carnelian Red/White
Creighton	Bluejays	Mo. Valley	Dana Altman	Omaha, NE	Blue/White
Dartmouth	Big Green	Ivy	Dave Faucher	Hanover, NH	Green/White
Davidson	Wildcats	Southern	Bob McKillop	Davidson, NC	Red/Black
Dayton	Flyers	Atlantic 10	Oliver Purnell	Dayton, OH	Red/Blue
DePaul	Blue Demons	USA	Joey Meyer	Chicago, IL	Scarlet/Blue
Delaware	Blue Hens	North Atlantic	Mike Brey	Newark, DE	Blue/Gold
Delaware St.	Hornets	Mid-Eastern	Fred Goodman	Dover, DE	Red/Blue
Detroit Mercy	Titans	Midwestern	Perry Watson	Detroit, MI	Red/White/Blue
Drake	Bulldogs	Mo. Valley	Rudy Washington	Des Moines, IA	Blue/White
Drexel	Dragons	North Atlantic	Bill Herrion	Philadelphia, PA	Navy Blue/Gold
Duke	Blue Devils	ACC	Mike Krzyzewski	Durham, NC	Royal Blue/White
Duquesne	Dukes	Atlantic 10	Scott Edgar	Pittsburgh, PA	Red/Blue
East Carolina	Pirates	Colonial	Joe Dooley	Greenville, NC	Purple/Gold
East Tenn. St.	Buccaneers	Southern	Alan LeForce	Johnson City, TN	Blue/Gold
Eastern Illinois	Panthers	Mid-Continent	Rick Samuels	Charleston, IL	Blue/Gray
Eastern Kentucky	Colonels	Ohio Valley	Mike Calhoun	Richmond, KY	Maroon/White
Eastern Michigan	Eagles	Mid-American	Ben Braun	Ypsilanti, MI	Green/White
Eastern Washington	Eagles	Big Sky	Steve Aggers	Cheney, WA	Red/White
Evansville	Aces	Mo. Valley	Jim Crews	Evansville, IN	Purple/White
Fairfield	Stags	Metro Atlantic	Paul Cormier	Fairfield, CT	Cardinal Red
Fairleigh Dickinson	Knights	Northeast	Tom Green	Teaneck, NJ	Blue/Black
Florida	Gators	SEC-East	Lon Kruger	Gainesville, FL	Orange/Blue
Florida A&M	Rattlers	Mid-Eastern	Ron Brown	Tallahassee, FL	Orange/Green
Florida Atlantic	Owls	Trans Am	Kevin Billerman	Boca Raton, FL	Blue/Gray
Florida Int'l	Golden Panthers	Trans Am	Shakey Rodriguez	Miami, FL	Blue/Yellow
Florida St.	Seminoles	ACC	Pat Kennedy	Tallahassee, FL	Garnet/Gold
Fordham	Rams	Atlantic 10	Nick Macarchuk	Bronx, NY	Maroon/White
Fresno St.	Bulldogs	WAC	Jerry Tarkanian	Fresno, CA	Cardinal/Blue
Furman	Paladins	Southern	Joe Cantafio	Greenville, SC	Purple/White
George Mason	Patriots	Colonial	Paul Westhead	Fairfax, VA	Green/Gold
George Washington	Colonials	Atlantic 10	Mike Jarvis	Washington, DC	Buff/Blue
Georgetown	Hoyas	Big East	John Thompson	Washington, DC	Blue/Gray
Georgia	Bulldogs, 'Dawgs	SEC-East	Tubby Smith	Athens, GA	Red/Black
Georgia Southern	Eagles	Southern	Gregg Polinsky	Statesboro, GA	Blue/White
Georgia St.	Panthers	Trans Am	Carter Wilson	Atlanta, GA	Royal Blue/Crimson
Georgia Tech	Yellow Jackets	ACC	Bobby Cremins	Atlanta, GA	Old Gold/White
Gonzaga	Bulldogs, Zags	West Coast	Dan Fitzgerald	Spokane, WA	Blue/White/Red
Grambling St.	Tigers	Southwestern	Lacey Reynolds	Grambling, LA	Black/Gold
Hampton	Pirates	Mid-Eastern	Byron Samuels	Hampton, VA	Royal Blue/White
Hartford	Hawks	North Atlantic	Paul Brazeau	W. Hartford, CT	Scarlet/White
Harvard	Crimson	Ivy	Frank Sullivan	Cambridge, MA	Crimson/Black/White
Hawaii	Rainbows	WAC	Riley Wallace	Honolulu, HI	Green/White
Hofstra	Flying Dutchmen	North Atlantic	Jay Wright	Hempstead, NY	Blue/White/Gold

	Nickname	Conference	Head Coach	Location	Colors
Holy Cross	Crusaders	Patriot	Bill Raynor	Worcester, MA	Royal Purple
Houston	Cougars	SWC	Alvin Brooks	Houston, TX	Scarlet/White
Howard	Bison	Mid-Eastern	Mike McLeese	Washington, DC	Blue/White/Red
Idaho	Vandals	Big Sky	Joe Cravens	Moscow, ID	Silver/Gold
Idaho St.	Bengals	Big Sky	Herb Williams	Pocatello, ID	Orange/Black
Illinois	Fighting Illini	Big Ten	Lou Henson	Champaign, IL	Orange/Blue
Illinois-Chicago	Flames	Midwestern	Bob Hallberg	Chicago, IL	Indigo/Flame
Illinois St.	Redbirds	Mo. Valley	Kevin Stallings	Normal, IL	Red/White
Indiana	Hoosiers	Big Ten	Bob Knight	Bloomington, IN	Cream/Crimson
Indiana St.	Sycamores	Mo. Valley	Sherman Dillard	Terre Haute, IN	Blue/White
Iona	Gaels	Metro Atlantic	Tim Welsh	New Rochelle, NY	Maroon/Gold
Iowa	Hawkeyes	Big Ten	Tom Davis	Iowa City, IA	Old Gold/Black
Iowa St.	Cyclones	Big Eight	Tim Floyd	Ames, IA	Cardinal/Gold
Jackson St.	Tigers	Southwestern	Andrew Stoglin	Jackson, MS	Blue/White
Jacksonville	Dolphins	Sun Belt	George Scholtz	Jacksonville, FL	Green/Gold
Jacksonville St.	Gamecocks	Trans Am	Bill Jones	Jacksonville, AL	Red/White
James Madison	Dukes	Colonial	Lefty Driesell	Harrisonburg, VA	Purple/Gold
Kansas	Jayhawks	Big Eight	Roy Williams	Lawrence, KS	Crimson/Blue
Kansas St.	Wildcats	Big Eight	Tom Asbury	Manhattan, KS	Purple/White
Kent	Golden Flashes	Mid-American	Dave Grube	Kent, OH	Navy Blue/Gold
Kentucky	Wildcats	SEC-East	Rick Pitino	Lexington, KY	Blue/White
La Salle	Explorers	Atlantic 10	Speedy Morris	Philadelphia, PA	Blue/Gold
Lafayette	Leopards	Patriot	Fran O'Hanlon	Easton, PA	Maroon/White
Lamar	Cardinals	Sun Belt	Grey Giovanine	Beaumont, TX	Red/White
Lehigh	Engineers	Patriot	Dave Duke	Bethlehem, PA	Brown/White
Liberty	Flames	Big South	Jeff Meyer	Lynchburg, VA	Red/White/Blue
Long Beach St.	49ers	Big West	Seth Greenberg	Long Beach, CA	Black/Gold
Long Island	Blackbirds	Northeast	Ray Haskins	Brooklyn, NY	Blue/White
LSU	Fighting Tigers	SEC-West	Dale Brown	Baton Rouge, LA	Purple/Gold
Louisiana Tech	Bulldogs	Sun Belt	Jim Wooldridge	Ruston, LA	Red/Blue
Louisville	Cardinals	USA	Denny Crum	Louisville, KY	Red/Black/White
Loyola-CA	Lions	West Coast	John Olive	Los Angeles, CA	Crimson/Gray/Lt.Blue
Loyola-IL	Ramblers	Midwestern	Ken Burmeister	Chicago, IL	Maroon/Gold
Loyola-MD	Greyhounds	Metro Atlantic	Brian Ellerbe	Baltimore, MD	Green/Gray
Maine	Black Bears	North Atlantic	Rudy Keeling	Orono, ME	Blue/White
Manhattan	Jaspers	Metro Atlantic	Fran Fraschilla	Riverdale, NY	Kelly Green/White
Marist	Red Foxes	Northeast	Dave Magarity	Poughkeepsie, NY	Red/White
Marquette	Golden Eagles	USA	Mike Deane	Milwaukee, WI	Blue/Gold
Marshall	Thundering Herd	Southern	Billy Donovan	Huntington, WV	Green/White
Maryland	Terrapins, Terps	ACC	Gary Williams	College Park, MD	Red/White/Black/Gold
MD-Balt. County	Retrievers	Big South	Tom Sullivan	Baltimore, MD	Black/Old Gold
MD-Eastern Shore	Hawks	Mid-Eastern	Jeff Menday	Princess Anne, MD	Maroon/Gray
Massachusetts	Minutemen	Atlantic 10	John Calipari	Amherst, MA	Maroon/White
McNeese St.	Cowboys	Southland	Ron Everhart	Lake Charles, LA	Blue/Gold
Memphis	Tigers	USA	Larry Finch	Memphis, TN	Blue/Gray
Mercer	Bears	Trans Am	Bill Hodges	Macon, GA	Orange/Black
Miami-FL	Hurricanes	Big East	Leonard Hamilton	Miami, FL	Orange/Green/White
Miami-OH	Redskins	Mid-American	Herb Sendek	Oxford, OH	Red/White
Michigan	Wolverines	Big Ten	Steve Fisher	Ann Arbor, MI	Maize/Blue
Michigan St.	Spartans	Big Ten	Tom Izzo	East Lansing, MI	Green/White
Middle Tenn. St.	Blue Raiders	Ohio Valley	Dave Farrar	Murfreesboro, TN	Blue/White
Minnesota	Golden Gophers	Big Ten	Clem Haskins	Minneapolis, MN	Maroon/Gold
Mississippi	Ole Miss, Rebels	SEC-West	Rob Evans	Oxford, MS	Red/Blue
Mississippi St.	Bulldogs	SEC-West	Richard Williams	Starkville, MS	Maroon/White
Miss. Valley St.	Delta Devils	Southwestern	Lafayette Stribling	Itta Bena, MS	Green/White
Missouri	Tigers	Big Eight	Norm Stewart	Columbia, MO	Old Gold/Black
Missouri-KC	Kangaroos	Mid-Continent	Lee Hunt	Kansas City, MO	Blue/Gold
Monmouth	Hawks	Northeast	Wayne Szoke	W. Long Branch, NJ	Royal Blue/White
Montana	Grizzlies	Big Sky	Blaine Taylor	Missoula, MT	Copper/Silver/Gold
Montana St.	Bobcats	Big Sky	Mick Durham	Bozeman, MT	Blue/Gold
Morehead St.	Eagles	Ohio Valley	Dick Fick	Morehead, KY	Blue/Gold
Morgan St.	Bears	Mid-Eastern	Chris Fuller	Baltimore, MD	Blue/Orange
Mt. St. Mary's	Mountaineers	Northeast	Jim Phelan	Emmitsburg, MD	Blue/White
Murray St.	Racers	Ohio Valley	Mark Gottfried	Murray, KY	Blue/Gold
Navy	Midshipmen	Patriot	Don DeVoe	Annapolis, MD	Navy Blue/Gold
Nebraska	Cornhuskers	Big Eight	Danny Nee	Lincoln, NE	Scarlet/Cream
Nevada	Wolf Pack	Big West	Pat Foster	Reno, NV	Silver/Blue
New Hampshire	Wildcats	North Atlantic	Gib Chapman	Durham, NH	Blue/White
New Mexico	Lobos	WAC	Dave Bliss	Albuquerque, NM	Cherry/Silver

NCAA Division I Basketball Schools (Cont.)

	Nickname	Conference	Head Coach	Location	Colors
New Mexico St.	Aggies	Big West	Neil McCarthy	Las Cruces, NM	Crimson/White
New Orleans	Privateers	Sun Belt	Tic Price	New Orleans, LA	Royal Blue/Silver
Niagara	Purple Eagles	Metro Atlantic	Jack Armstrong	Lewiston, NY	Purple/White/Gold
Nicholls St.	Colonels	Southland	Rickey Broussard	Thibodaux, LA	Red/Gray
North Carolina	Tar Heels	ACC	Dean Smith	Chapel Hill, NC	Carolina Blue/White
North Carolina A&T	Aggies	Mid-Eastern	Roy Thomas	Greensboro, NC	Blue/Gold
North Carolina St.	Wolfpack	ACC	Les Robinson	Raleigh, NC	Red/White
NC-Asheville	Bulldogs	Big South	Randy Wiel	Asheville, NC	Royal Blue/White
NC-Charlotte	49ers	USA	Jeff Mullins	Charlotte, NC	Green/White
NC-Greensboro	Spartans	Big South	Randy Peele	Greensboro, NC	Gold/White/Navy
NC-Wilmington	Seahawks	Colonial	Jerry Wainwright	Wilmington, NC	Green/Gold
North Texas	Eagles	Southland	Tim Jankovich	Denton, TX	Green/White
NE Illinois	Golden Eagles	Mid-Continent	Rees Johnson	Chicago, IL	Royal Blue/Gold
NE Louisiana	Indians	Southland	Mike Vining	Monroe, LA	Maroon/Gold
Northeastern	Huskies	North Atlantic	Dave Leitao	Boston, MA	Red/Black
Northern Arizona	Lumberjacks	Big Sky	Ben Howland	Flagstaff, AZ	Blue/Gold
Northern Illinois	Huskies	Midwestern	Brian Hammel	De Kalb, IL	Cardinal/Black
Northern Iowa	Panthers	Mo. Valley	Eldon Miller	Cedar Falls, IA	Purple/Old Gold
Northwestern	Wildcats	Big Ten	Ricky Byrdsong	Evanston, IL	Purple/White
Northwestern St.	Demons	Southland	J.D. Barnett	Natchitoches, LA	Burnt Orange/Purple
Notre Dame	Fighting Irish	Big East	John MacLeod	South Bend, IN	Gold/Blue
Ohio University	Bobcats	Mid-American	Larry Hunter	Athens, OH	Green/White
Ohio St.	Buckeyes	Big Ten	Randy Ayers	Columbus, OH	Scarlet/Gray
Oklahoma	Sooners	Big Eight	Kelvin Sampson	Norman, OK	Crimson/Cream
Oklahoma St.	Cowboys	Big Eight	Eddie Sutton	Stillwater, OK	Orange/Black
Old Dominion	Monarchs	Colonial	Jeff Capel	Norfolk, VA	Slate Blue/Silver
Oral Roberts	Golden Eagles	Independent	Bill Self	Tulsa, OK	Navy Blue/Gold
Oregon	Ducks	Pac-10	Jerry Green	Eugene, OR	Green/Yellow
Oregon St.	Beavers	Pac-10	Eddie Payne	Corvallis, OR	Orange/Black
Pacific	Tigers	Big West	Bob Thomason	Stockton, CA	Orange/Black
Pennsylvania	Quakers	Ivy	Fran Dunphy	Philadelphia, PA	Red/Blue
Penn St.	Nittany Lions	Big Ten	Bruce Parkhill	University Park, PA	Blue/White
Pepperdine	Waves	West Coast	Tony Fuller	Malibu, CA	Blue/Orange
Pittsburgh	Panthers	Big East	Ralph Willard	Pittsburgh, PA	Gold/Blue
Portland	Pilots	West Coast	Rob Chavez	Portland, OR	Purple/White
Prairie View A&M	Panthers	Southwestern	Elwood Plummer	Prairie View, TX	Purple/Gold
Princeton	Tigers	Ivy	Pete Carril	Princeton, NJ	Orange/Black
Providence	Friars	Big East	Pete Gillen	Providence, RI	Black/White
Purdue	Boilermakers	Big Ten	Gene Keady	W. Lafayette, IN	Old Gold/Black
Radford	Highlanders	Big South	Ron Bradley	Radford, VA	Blue/Red/Green
Rhode Island	Rams	Atlantic 10	Al Skinner	Kingston, RI	Blue/White
Rice	Owls	SWC	Willis Wilson	Houston, TX	Blue/Gray
Richmond	Spiders	Colonial	Bill Dooley	Richmond, VA	Red/Blue
Rider	Broncs	Northeast	Kevin Bannon	Lawrenceville, NJ	Cranberry/White
Robert Morris	Colonials	Northeast	Jarrett Durham	Coraopolis, PA	Blue/White
Rutgers	Scarlet Knights	Big East	Bob Wenzel	New Brunswick, NJ	Scarlet
St. Bonaventure	Bonnies	Atlantic 10	Jim Baron	St. Bonaventure, NY	Brown/White
St. Francis-NY	Terriers	Northeast	Ron Ganulin	Brooklyn, NY	Red/Blue
St. Francis-PA	Red Flash	Northeast	Tom McConnell	Loretto, PA	Red/White
St. John's	Red Storm	Big East	Brian Mahoney	Jamaica, NY	Red/White
St. Joseph's-PA	Hawks	Atlantic 10	Phil Martelli	Philadelphia, PA	Crimson/Gray
Saint Louis	Billikens	USA	Charlie Spoonhour	St. Louis, MO	Blue/White
St. Mary's-CA	Gaels	West Coast	Ernie Kent	Moraga, CA	Red/Blue
St. Peter's	Peacocks	Metro Atlantic	Rodger Blind	Jersey City, NJ	Blue/White
Sam Houston St.	Bearkats	Southland	Jerry Hopkins	Huntsville, TX	Orange/White
Samford	Bulldogs	Trans Am	John Brady	Birmingham, AL	Red/Blue
San Diego	Toreros	West Coast	Brad Holland	San Diego, CA	Lt. Blue/Navy/White
San Diego St.	Aztecs	WAC	Fred Trenkle	San Diego, CA	Scarlet/Black
San Francisco	Dons	West Coast	Phil Mathews	San Francisco, CA	Green/Gold
San Jose St.	Spartans	Big West	Stan Morrison	San Jose, CA	Gold/White/Blue
Santa Clara	Broncos	West Coast	Dick Davey	Santa Clara, CA	Bronco Red/White
Seton Hall	Pirates	Big East	George Blaney	South Orange, NJ	Blue/White
Siena	Saints	Metro Atlantic	Bob Beyer	Loudonville, NY	Green/Gold
South Alabama	Jaguars	Sun Belt	Bill Musselman	Mobile, AL	Red/White/Blue
South Carolina	Gamecocks	SEC-East	Eddie Fogler	Columbia, SC	Garnet/Black
South Carolina St.	Bulldogs	Mid-Eastern	Ben Betts	Orangeburg, SC	Garnet/Blue
South Florida	Bulls	USA	Bobby Paschal	Tampa, FL	Green/Gold
SE Louisiana	Lions	Trans Am	John Lyles	Hammond, LA	Green/Gold

	Nickname	Conference	Head Coach	Location	Colors
SE Missouri St.	Indians	Ohio Valley	Ron Shumate	Cape Girardeau, MO	Red/Black
Southern Illinois	Salukis	Mo. Valley	Rich Herrin	Carbondale, IL	Maroon/White
SMU	Mustangs	Southwest	Mike Dement	Dallas, TX	Red/Blue
Southern Miss.	Golden Eagles	USA	M.K. Turk	Hattiesburg, MS	Black/Gold
Southern Utah	Thunderbirds	American West	Bill Evans	Cedar City, UT	Scarlet/Royal Blue
Southern-BR	Jaguars	Southwestern	Ben Jobe	Baton Rouge, LA	Blue/Gold
SW Missouri St.	Bears	Mo. Valley	Steve Alford	Springfield, MO	Maroon/White
SW Texas St.	Bobcats	Southland	Mike Miller	San Marcos, TX	Maroon/Gold
SW Louisiana	Ragin' Cajuns	Sun Belt	Marty Fletcher	Lafayette, LA	Vermilion/White
Stanford	Cardinal	Pac-10	Mike Montgomery	Stanford, CA	Cardinal/White
S.F. Austin St.	Lumberjacks	Southland	Ned Fowler	Nacogdoches, TX	Purple/White
Stetson	Hatters	Trans Am	Randy Brown	DeLand, FL	Green/White
Syracuse	Orangemen	Big East	Jim Boeheim	Syracuse, NY	Orange
Temple	Owls	Atlantic 10	John Chaney	Philadelphia, PA	Cherry/White
Tennessee	Volunteers	SEC-East	Kevin O'Neill	Knoxville, TN	Orange/White
Tenn-Chattanooga	Moccasins	Southern	Mack McCarthy	Chattanooga, TN	Navy Blue/Gold
Tenn-Martin	Pacers	Ohio Valley	Cal Luther	Martin, TN	Orange/White/Blue
Tennessee St.	Tigers	Ohio Valley	Frankie Allen	Nashville, TN	Blue/White
Tennessee Tech	Golden Eagles	Ohio Valley	Frank Harrell	Cookeville, TN	Purple/Gold
Texas	Longhorns	SWC	Tom Penders	Austin, TX	Burnt Orange/White
Texas A&M	Aggies	SWC	Tony Barone	College Station, TX	Maroon/White
TCU	Horned Frogs	SWC	Billy Tubbs	Ft. Worth, TX	Purple/White
Texas Southern	Tigers	Southwestern	Robert Moreland	Houston, TX	Maroon/Gray
Texas Tech	Red Raiders	SWC	James Dickey	Lubbock, TX	Scarlet/Black
TX-Arlington	Mavericks	Southland	Eddie McCarter	Arlington, TX	Royal Blue/White
TX-Pan American	Broncs	Sun Belt	Mark Adams	Edinburg, TX	Green/White
TX-San Antonio	Roadrunners	Southland	Tim Carter	San Antonio, TX	Orange/Navy Blue
Toledo	Rockets	Mid-American	Larry Gipson	Toledo, OH	Blue/Gold
Towson St.	Tigers	North Atlantic	Terry Truax	Towson, MD	Gold/White/Black
Troy St.	Trojans	Mid-Continent	Don Maestri	Troy, AL	Cardinal/Gray/Black
Tulane	Green Wave	USA	Perry Clark	New Orleans, LA	Olive Green/Sky Blue
Tulsa	Golden Hurricane	Mo. Valley	Steve Robinson	Tulsa, OK	Blue/Red/Gold
UC-Irvine	Anteaters	Big West	Rod Baker	Irvine, CA	Blue/Gold
UCLA	Bruins	Pac-10	Jim Harrick	Los Angeles, CA	Blue/Gold
UC-Santa Barbara	Gauchos	Big West	Jerry Pimm	Santa Barbara, CA	Blue/Gold
UNLV	Runnin' Rebels	Big West	Billy Bayno	Las Vegas, NV	Scarlet/Gray
USC	Trojans	Pac-10	Charlie Parker	Los Angeles, CA	Cardinal/Gold
Utah	Utes	WAC	Rick Majerus	Salt Lake City, UT	Crimson/White
Utah St.	Aggies	Big West	Larry Eustachy	Logan, UT	Navy Blue/White
UTEP	Miners	WAC	Don Haskins	El Paso, TX	Orange/White/Blue
Valparaiso	Crusaders	Mid-Continent	Homer Drew	Valparaiso, IN	Brown/Gold
Vanderbilt	Commodores	SEC-East	Jan van Breda Kolff	Nashville, TN	Black/Gold
Vermont	Catamounts	North Atlantic	Tom Brennan	Burlington, VT	Green/Gold
Villanova	Wildcats	Big East	Steve Lappas	Villanova, PA	Blue/White
Virginia	Cavaliers	ACC	Jeff Jones	Charlottesville, VA	Orange/Blue
VCU	Rams	Colonial	Sonny Smith	Richmond, VA	Black/Gold
VMI	Keydets	Southern	Bart Bellairs	Lexington, VA	Red/White/Yellow
Virginia Tech	Hokies, Gobblers	Atlantic 10	Bill Foster	Blacksburg, VA	Orange/Maroon
Wagner	Seahawks	Northeast	Tim Capstraw	Staten Island, NY	Green/White
Wake Forest	Demon Deacons	ACC	Dave Odom	Winston-Salem, NC	Old Gold/Black
Washington	Huskies	Pac-10	Bob Bender	Seattle, WA	Purple/Gold
Washington St.	Cougars	Pac-10	Kevin Eastman	Pullman, WA	Crimson/Gray
Weber St.	Wildcats	Big Sky	Ron Abegglen	Ogden, UT	Royal Purple/White
West Virginia	Mountaineers	Big East	Gale Catlett	Morgantown, WV	Old Gold/Blue
Western Carolina	Catamounts	Southern	Phil Hopkins	Cullowhee, NC	Purple/Gold
Western Illinois	Leathernecks	Mid-Continent	Jim Kerwin	Macomb, IL	Purple/Gold
Western Kentucky	Hilltoppers	Sun Belt	Matt Kilcullen	Bowling Green, KY	Red/White
Western Michigan	Broncos	Mid-American	Bob Donewald	Kalamazoo, MI	Brown/Gold
Wichita St.	Shockers	Mo. Valley	Scott Thompson	Wichita, KS	Yellow/Black
William & Mary	Tribe	Colonial	Charlie Woollum	Williamsburg, VA	Green/Gold/Silver
Winthrop	Eagles	Big South	Dan Kenney	Rock Hill, SC	Garnet/Gold
Wisconsin	Badgers	Big Ten	Dick Bennett	Madison, WI	Cardinal/White
WI-Green Bay	Phoenix	Midwestern	Mike Heideman	Green Bay, WI	Green/White/Red
WI-Milwaukee	Panthers	Midwestern	Ric Cobb	Milwaukee, WI	Black/Gold
Wofford	Terriers	Independent	Richard Johnson	Spartanburg, SC	Old Gold/Black
Wright St.	Raiders	Midwestern	Ralph Underhill	Dayton, OH	Green/Gold
Wyoming	Cowboys	WAC	Joby Wright	Laramie, WY	Brown/Yellow
Xavier	Musketeers	Atlantic 10	Skip Prosser	Cincinnati, OH	Blue/White
Yale	Bulldogs, Elis	Ivy	Dick Kuchen	New Haven, CT	Yale Blue/White
Youngstown St.	Penguins	Mid-Continent	Dan Peters	Youngstown, OH	Red/White

NCAA Division I-A Football Schools

1996 Season

Conferences and coaches as of Sept. 15, 1995.

Changing conference name on July 1, 1996: Big Eight becomes Big 12.

Breakup of Southwest Conference on June 30, 1996: BAYLOR, TEXAS, TEXAS A&M and TEXAS TECH to Big 12; RICE, SMU and TCU to Western Athletic; HOUSTON to Conference USA.

New conference in 1996: Conference USA (6 teams)— former independents CINCINNATI, LOUISVILLE, MEMPHIS, SOUTHERN MISSISSIPPI and TULANE; HOUSTON from Southwest.

Joining Big 12 in 1996 (4): BAYLOR, TEXAS, TEXAS A&M and TEXAS TECH from Southwest.

Joining Big West in 1996 (3): independent NORTH TEXAS; BOISE ST. and IDAHO from Div. I-AA Big Sky Conference.

Joining Western Athletic in 1996 (6): SAN JOSE ST. and UNLV from Big West; RICE, SMU and TCU from Southwest; independent TULSA.

Leaving Big West in 1996 (4): ARKANSAS ST., LOUISIANA TECH, NORTHERN ILLINOIS and SOUTHWESTERN LOUISIANA to become independents.

Moving up from Division I-AA in 1996 (2): independents ALABAMA-BIRMINGHAM and CENTRAL FLORIDA.

Joining Mid-American in 1997: MARSHALL from Div. I-AA Southern Conference and independent NORTHERN ILLINOIS.

Joining Mid-American in 1998: BUFFALO from Div. I-AA Mid-Continent Conference.

	Nickname	Conference	Head Coach	Location	Colors
Air Force	Falcons	WAC	Fisher DeBerry	Colo. Springs, CO	Blue/Silver
Akron	Zips	Mid-American	Lee Owens	Akron, OH	Blue/Gold
Alabama	Crimson Tide	SEC-West	Gene Stallings	Tuscaloosa, AL	Crimson/White
Alabama-Birm.	Blazers	Independent	Wastson Brown	Birmingham, AL	Green/Gold/White
Arizona	Wildcats	Pac-10	Dick Tomey	Tucson, AZ	Cardinal/Navy
Arizona St.	Sun Devils	Pac-10	Bruce Snyder	Tempe, AZ	Maroon/Gold
Arkansas	Razorbacks	SEC-West	Danny Ford	Fayetteville, AR	Cardinal/White
Arkansas St.	Indians	Big West	John Bobo	State Univ., AR	Scarlet/Black
Army	Cadets, Black Knights	Independent	Bob Sutton	West Point, NY	Black/Gold/Gray
Auburn	Tigers	SEC-West	Terry Bowden	Auburn, AL	Orange/Blue
Ball St.	Cardinals	Mid-American	Bill Lynch	Muncie, IN	Cardinal/White
Baylor	Bears	Big 12-South	Chuck Reedy	Waco, TX	Green/Gold
Boston College	Eagles	Big East	Dan Henning	Chestnut Hill, MA	Maroon/Gold
Bowling Green	Falcons	Mid-American	Gary Blackney	Bowling Green, OH	Orange/Brown
BYU	Cougars	WAC	LaVell Edwards	Provo, UT	Royal Blue/White
California	Golden Bears	Pac-10	Keith Gilbertson	Berkeley, CA	Blue/Gold
Central Florida	Golden Knights	Independent	Gene McDowell	Orlando, FL	Black/Gold
Central Michigan	Chippewas	Mid-American	Dick Flynn	Mt. Pleasant, MI	Maroon/Gold
Cincinnati	Bearcats	USA	Rick Minter	Cincinnati, OH	Red/Black
Clemson	Tigers	ACC	Tommy West	Clemson, SC	Purple/Orange
Colorado	Golden Buffaloes	Big 12-North	Rick Neuheisel	Boulder, CO	Silver/Gold/Black
Colorado St.	Rams	WAC	Sonny Lubick	Ft. Collins, CO	Green/Gold
Duke	Blue Devils	ACC	Fred Goldsmith	Durham, NC	Royal Blue/White
East Carolina	Pirates	Independent	Steve Logan	Greenville, NC	Purple/Gold
Eastern Michigan	Eagles	Mid-American	Rick Rasnick	Ypsilanti, MI	Green/White
Florida	Gators	SEC-East	Steve Spurrier	Gainesville, FL	Orange/Blue
Florida St.	Seminoles	ACC	Bobby Bowden	Tallahassee, FL	Garnet/Gold
Fresno St.	Bulldogs	WAC	Jim Sweeney	Fresno, CA	Cardinal/Blue
Georgia	Bulldogs, 'Dawgs	SEC-East	Ray Goff	Athens, GA	Red/Black
Georgia Tech	Yellow Jackets	ACC	George O'Leary	Atlanta, GA	Old Gold/White
Hawaii	Rainbow Warriors	WAC	Bob Wagner	Honolulu, HI	Green/White
Houston	Cougars	USA	Kim Helton	Houston, TX	Scarlet/White
Illinois	Fighting Illini	Big Ten	Lou Tepper	Champaign, IL	Orange/Blue
Indiana	Hoosiers	Big Ten	Bill Mallory	Bloomington, IN	Cream/Crimson
Iowa	Hawkeyes	Big Ten	Hayden Fry	Iowa City, IA	Old Gold/Black
Iowa St.	Cyclones	Big 12-North	Dan McCarney	Ames, IA	Cardinal/Gold
Kansas	Jayhawks	Big 12-North	Glen Mason	Lawrence, KS	Crimson/Blue
Kansas St.	Wildcats	Big 12-North	Bill Snyder	Manhattan, KS	Purple/White
Kent	Golden Flashes	Mid-American	Jim Corrigall	Kent, OH	Navy Blue/Gold
Kentucky	Wildcats	SEC-East	Bill Curry	Lexington, KY	Blue/White
LSU	Fighting Tigers	SEC-West	Gerry DiNardo	Baton Rouge, LA	Purple/Gold
Louisiana Tech	Bulldogs	Big West	Joe Raymond Peace	Ruston, LA	Red/Blue
Louisville	Cardinals	USA	Ron Cooper	Louisville, KY	Red/Black/White

	Nickname	Conference	Head Coach	Location	Colors
Maryland	Terrapins, Terps	ACC	Mark Duffner	College Park, MD	Red/White/Black/Gold
Memphis	Tigers	USA	Rip Scherer	Memphis, TN	Blue/Gray
Miami-FL	Hurricanes	Big East	Butch Davis	Miami, FL	Orange/Green/White
Miami-OH	Redskins	Mid-American	Randy Walker	Oxford, OH	Red/White
Michigan	Wolverines	Big Ten	Lloyd Carr	Ann Arbor, MI	Maize/Blue
Michigan St.	Spartans	Big Ten	Nick Saban	E. Lansing, MI	Green/White
Minnesota	Golden Gophers	Big Ten	Jim Wacker	Minneapolis, MN	Maroon/Gold
Mississippi	Ole Miss, Rebels	SEC-West	Tommy Tuberville	Oxford, MS	Cardinal/Navy Blue
Mississippi St.	Bulldogs	SEC-West	Jackie Sherrill	Starkville, MS	Maroon/White
Missouri	Tigers	Big 12-North	Larry Smith	Columbia, MO	Old Gold/Black
Navy	Midshipmen	Big 12-North	Charlie Weatherbie	Annapolis, MD	Navy Blue/Gold
Nebraska	Cornhuskers	Big 12-North	Tom Osborne	Lincoln, NE	Scarlet/Cream
Nevada	Wolf Pack	Big West	Chris Ault	Reno, NV	Silver/Blue
New Mexico	Lobos	WAC	Dennis Franchione	Albuquerque, NM	Cherry/Silver
New Mexico St.	Aggies	Big West	Jim Hess	Las Cruces, NM	Crimson/White
North Carolina	Tar Heels	ACC	Mack Brown	Chapel Hill, NC	Carolina Blue/White
North Carolina St.	Wolfpack	ACC	Mike O'Cain	Raleigh, NC	Red/White
North Texas	Eagles	Big West	Matt Simon	Denton, TX	Green/White
NE Louisiana	Indians	Independent	Ed Zaunbrecher	Monroe, LA	Maroon/Gold
Northern Illinois	Huskies	Big West	Charlie Sadler	De Kalb, IL	Cardinal/Black
Northwestern	Wildcats	Big Ten	Gary Barnett	Evanston, IL	Purple/White
Notre Dame	Fighting Irish	Independent	Lou Holtz	South Bend, IN	Gold/Blue
Ohio University	Bobcats	Mid-American	Jim Grobe	Athens, OH	Green/White
Ohio St.	Buckeyes	Big Ten	John Cooper	Columbus, OH	Scarlet/Gray
Oklahoma	Sooners	Big 12-South	H. Schnellenberger	Norman, OK	Crimson/Cream
Oklahoma St.	Cowboys	Big 12-South	Bob Simmons	Stillwater, OK	Orange/Black
Oregon	Ducks	Pac-10	Mike Bellotti	Eugene, OR	Green/Yellow
Oregon St.	Beavers	Pac-10	Jerry Pettibone	Corvallis, OR	Orange/Black
Pacific	Tigers	Big West	Chuck Shelton	Stockton, CA	Orange/Black
Penn St.	Nittany Lions	Big Ten	Joe Paterno	University Park, PA	Blue/White
Pittsburgh	Panthers	Big East	Johnny Majors	Pittsburgh, PA	Blue/Gold
Purdue	Boilermakers	Big Ten	Jim Colletto	W. Lafayette, IN	Old Gold/Black
Rice	Owls	WAC	Ken Hatfield	Houston, TX	Blue/Gray
Rutgers	Scarlet Knights	Big East	Doug Graber	New Brunswick, NJ	Scarlet
San Diego St.	Aztecs	WAC	Ted Tollner	San Diego, CA	Scarlet/Black
San Jose St.	Spartans	WAC	John Ralston	San Jose, CA	Gold/White/Blue
South Carolina	Gamecocks	SEC-East	Brad Scott	Columbia, SC	Garnet/Black
SMU	Mustangs	WAC	Tom Rossley	Dallas, TX	Red/Blue
Southern Miss.	Golden Eagles	USA	Jeff Bower	Hattiesburg, MS	Black/Gold
SW Louisiana	Ragin' Cajuns	Big West	Nelson Stokley	Lafayette, LA	Vermilion/White
Stanford	Cardinal	Pac-10	Tyrone Willingham	Stanford, CA	Cardinal/White
Syracuse	Orangemen	Big East	Paul Pasqualoni	Syracuse, NY	Orange
Temple	Owls	Big East	Ron Dickerson	Philadelphia, PA	Cherry/White
Tennessee	Volunteers	SEC-East	Phillip Fulmer	Knoxville, TN	Orange/White
Texas	Longhorns	Big 12-South	John Mackovic	Austin, TX	Burnt Orange/White
Texas A&M	Aggies	Big 12-South	R.C. Slocum	College Station, TX	Maroon/White
TCU	Horned Frogs	WAC	Pat Sullivan	Ft. Worth, TX	Purple/White
Texas Tech	Red Raiders	Big 12-South	Spike Dykes	Lubbock, TX	Scarlet/Black
Toledo	Rockets	Mid-American	Gary Pinkel	Toledo, OH	Blue/Gold
Tulane	Green Wave	USA	Buddy Teevens	New Orleans, LA	Olive Green/Sky Blue
Tulsa	Golden Hurricane	WAC	Dave Rader	Tulsa, OK	Blue/Gold
UCLA	Bruins	Pac-10	Terry Donahue	Los Angeles, CA	Blue/Gold
UNLV	Runnin' Rebels	WAC	Jeff Horton	Las Vegas, NV	Scarlet/Gray
USC	Trojans	Pac-10	John Robinson	Los Angeles, CA	Cardinal/Gold
Utah	Utes	WAC	Ron McBride	Salt Lake City, UT	Crimson/White
Utah St.	Aggies	Big West	John L. Smith	Logan, UT	Navy Blue/White
UTEP	Miners	WAC	Charlie Bailey	El Paso, TX	Orange/White/Blue
Vanderbilt	Commodores	SEC-East	Rod Dowhower	Nashville, TN	Black/Gold
Virginia	Cavaliers	ACC	George Welsh	Charlottesville, VA	Orange/Blue
Virginia Tech	Hokies, Gobblers	Big East	Frank Beamer	Blacksburg, VA	Orange/Maroon
Wake Forest	Demon Deacons	ACC	Jim Caldwell	Winston-Salem, NC	Old Gold/Black
Washington	Huskies	Pac-10	Jim Lambright	Seattle, WA	Purple/Gold
Washington St.	Cougars	Pac-10	Mike Price	Pullman, WA	Crimson/Gray
West Virginia	Mountaineers	Big East	Don Nehlen	Morgantown, WV	Old Gold/Blue
Western Michigan	Broncos	Mid-American	Al Molde	Kalamazoo, MI	Brown/Gold
Wisconsin	Badgers	Big Ten	Barry Alvarez	Madison, WI	Cardinal/White
Wyoming	Cowboys	WAC	Joe Tiller	Laramie, WY	Brown/Yellow

NCAA Division I-AA Football Schools

1996 Season

Conferences and coaches as of Sept. 15, 1995.

Joining Ohio Valley in 1996: EASTERN ILLINOIS from Gateway.
Joining Southland in 1996: independent TROY ST.
Moving up from Division II in 1996: PORTLAND ST. to Big Sky.
Joining Patriot League in 1997: independent TOWSON ST.
Joining Southland in 1997: independent JACKSONVILLE ST.

	Nickname	Conference	Head Coach	Location	Colors
Ala-Birmingham	Blazers	Independent	Watson Brown	Birmingham, AL	Green/Gold
Alabama St.	Hornets	Southwestern	Houston Markham	Montgomery, AL	Black/Gold
Alcorn St.	Braves	Southwestern	Cardell Jones	Lorman, MS	Purple/Gold
Appalachian St.	Mountaineers	Southern	Jerry Moore	Boone, NC	Black/Gold
Austin Peay St.	Governors	Ohio Valley	Roy Gregory	Clarksville, TN	Red/White
Bethune-Cookman	Wildcats	Mid-Eastern	Jack McClairen	Daytona Beach, FL	Maroon/Gold
Boise St.	Broncos	Big Sky	Pokey Allen	Boise, ID	Orange/Blue
Boston University	Terriers	Yankee	Dan Allen	Boston, MA	Scarlet/White
Brown	Bears	Ivy	Mark Whipple	Providence, RI	Brown/Red/White
Bucknell	Bison	Patriot	Tom Gadd	Lewisburg, PA	Orange/Blue
Buffalo	Bulls	Independent	Craig Cirbus	Buffalo, NY	Blue/White
Butler	Bulldogs	Pioneer	Ken LaRose	Indianapolis, IN	Blue/White
CS-Northridge	Matadors	American West	Dave Baldwin	Northridge, CA	Red/Black/White
CS-Sacramento	Hornets	American West	Gregg Knapp	Sacramento, CA	Green/Gold
Cal Poly SLO	Mustangs	American West	Andre Patterson	San Luis Obispo, CA	Green/Gold
Canisius	Golden Griffins	Metro Atlantic	Chuck Williams	Buffalo, NY	Blue/Gold
Central Conn. St.	Blue Devils	Independent	Sal Cintorino	New Britain, CT	Blue/White
Charleston So.	Buccaneers	Independent	David Dowd	Charleston, SC	Blue/Gold
The Citadel	Bulldogs	Southern	Charlie Taaffe	Charleston, SC	Blue/White
Colgate	Red Raiders	Patriot	Edward Sweeney	Hamilton, NY	Maroon/White
Columbia	Lions	Ivy	Ray Tellier	New York, NY	Lt. Blue/White
Connecticut	Huskies	Yankee	Skip Holtz	Storrs, CT	Blue/White
Cornell	Big Red	Ivy	Jim Hofher	Ithaca, NY	Red/White
Dartmouth	Big Green	Ivy	John Lyons	Hanover, NH	Green/White
Davidson	Wildcats	Independent	Tim Landis	Davidson, NC	Red/Black
Dayton	Flyers	Pioneer	Mike Kelly	Dayton, OH	Red/Blue
Delaware	Blue Hens	Yankee	Tubby Raymond	Newark, DE	Blue/Gold
Delaware St.	Hornets	Mid-Eastern	Bill Collick	Dover, DE	Red/Blue
Drake	Bulldogs	Pioneer	Rob Ash	Des Moines, IA	Blue/White
Duquesne	Dukes	Metro Atlantic	Greg Gattuso	Pittsburgh, PA	Red/Blue
East Tenn. St.	Buccaneers	Southern	Mike Cavan	Johnson City, TN	Blue/Gold
Eastern Illinois	Panthers	Gateway	Bob Spoo	Charleston, IL	Blue/Gray
Eastern Kentucky	Colonels	Ohio Valley	Roy Kidd	Richmond, KY	Maroon/White
Eastern Wash.	Eagles	Big Sky	Mike Kramer	Cheney, WA	Red/White
Evansville	Aces	Pioneer	Robin Cooper	Evansville, IN	Purple/White
Fairfield	Stags	Metro Atlantic	Tom Masella	Fairfield, CT	Cardinal Red
Florida A&M	Rattlers	Mid-Eastern	Billy Joe	Tallahassee, FL	Orange/Green
Fordham	Rams	Patriot	Nick Quartaro	New York, NY	Maroon/White
Furman	Paladins	Southern	Bobby Johnson	Greenville, SC	Purple/White
Georgetown	Hoyas	Metro Atlantic	Bob Benson	Washington, DC	Blue/Gray
Georgia Southern	Eagles	Southern	Tim Stowers	Statesboro, GA	Blue/White
Grambling St.	Tigers	Southwestern	Eddie Robinson	Grambling, LA	Black/Gold
Hampton	Pirates	Mid-Eastern	Joe Taylor	Hampton, VA	Royal Blue/White
Harvard	Crimson	Ivy	Tim Murphy	Cambridge, MA	Crimson/Black/White
Hofstra	Flying Dutchmen	Independent	Joe Gardi	Hempstead, NY	Blue/White/Gold
Holy Cross	Crusaders	Patriot	Peter Vaas	Worcester, MA	Royal Purple
Howard	Bison	Mid-Eastern	Steve Wilson	Washington, DC	Blue/White
Idaho	Vandals	Big Sky	Chris Tormey	Moscow, ID	Silver/Gold
Idaho St.	Bengals	Big Sky	Brian McNeely	Pocatello, ID	Orange/Black
Illinois St.	Redbirds	Gateway	Jim Heacock	Normal, IL	Red/White
Indiana St.	Sycamores	Gateway	Dennis Raetz	Terre Haute, IN	Blue/White
Iona	Gaels	Metro Atlantic	Harold Crocker	New Rochelle, NY	Maroon/Gold
Jackson St.	Tigers	Southwestern	James Carson	Jackson, MS	Blue/White
Jacksonville St.	Gamecocks	Independent	Bill Burgess	Jacksonville, AL	Red/White
James Madison	Dukes	Yankee	Alex Wood	Harrisonburg, VA	Purple/Gold
Lafayette	Leopards	Patriot	Bill Russo	Easton, PA	Maroon/White
Lehigh	Engineers	Patriot	Kevin Higgins	Bethlehem, PA	Brown/White
Liberty	Flames	Independent	Sam Rutigliano	Lynchburg, VA	Red/White/Blue

	Nickname	Conference	Head Coach	Location	Colors
Maine	Black Bears	Yankee	Kirk Ferentz	Orono, ME	Blue/White
Marist	Red Foxes	Metro Atlantic	Jim Parady	Poughkeepsie, NY	Red/White
Marshall	Thundering Herd	Southern	Jim Donnan	Huntington, WV	Green/White
Massachusetts	Minutemen	Yankee	Mike Hodges	Amherst, MA	Maroon/White
McNeese St.	Cowboys	Southland	Bobby Keasler	Lake Charles, LA	Blue/Gold
Middle Tenn. St.	Blue Raiders	Ohio Valley	Boots Donnelly	Murfreesboro, TN	Blue/White
Miss. Valley St.	Delta Devils	Southwestern	Larry Dorsey	Itta Bena, MS	Green/White
Monmouth	Hawks	Independent	Kevin Callahan	W. Long Branch, NJ	Royal Blue/White
Montana	Grizzlies	Big Sky	Don Read	Missoula, MT	Copper/Silver/Gold
Montana St.	Bobcats	Big Sky	Cliff Hysell	Bozeman, MT	Blue/Gold
Morehead St.	Eagles	Ohio Valley	Matt Ballard	Morehead, KY	Blue/Gold
Morgan St.	Bears	Mid-Eastern	Ricky Diggs	Baltimore, MD	Blue/Orange
Murray St.	Racers	Ohio Valley	Houston Nutt	Murray, KY	Blue/Gold
New Hampshire	Wildcats	Yankee	Bill Bowes	Durham, NH	Blue/White
Nicholls St.	Colonels	Southland	Darren Barbier	Thibodaux, LA	Red/Gray
North Carolina A&T	Aggies	Mid-Eastern	Bill Hayes	Greensboro, NC	Blue/Gold
Northeastern	Huskies	Yankee	Barry Gallup	Boston, MA	Red/Black
Northern Ariz.	Lumberjacks	Big Sky	Steve Axman	Flagstaff, AZ	Blue/Gold
Northern Iowa	Panthers	Gateway	Terry Allen	Cedar Falls, IA	Purple/Old Gold
Northwestern St.	Demons	Southland	Sam Goodwin	Natchitoches, LA	Purple/White
Pennsylvania	Quakers	Ivy	Al Bagnoli	Philadelphia, PA	Red/Blue
Prairie View A&M	Panthers	Southwestern	Hensley Sapenter	Prairie View, TX	Purple/Gold
Princeton	Tigers	Ivy	Steve Tosches	Princeton, NJ	Orange/Black
Rhode Island	Rams	Yankee	Bob Griffin	Kingston, RI	Blue/White
Richmond	Spiders	Yankee	Jim Reid	Richmond, VA	Red/Blue
Robert Morris	Colonials	Independent	Joe Walton	Coraopolis, PA	Blue/White
St. Francis-PA	Red Flash	Independent	Pete Mayock	Loretto, PA	Red/White
St. John's-NY	Red Storm	Metro Atlantic	Bob Ricca	Jamaica, NY	Red/White
St. Mary's-CA	Gaels	Independent	Mike Rasmussen	Moraga, CA	Red/Blue
St. Peter's	Peacocks	Metro Atlantic	Mark Collins	Jersey City, NJ	Blue/White
Sam Houston St.	Bearkats	Southland	Ron Randleman	Huntsville, TX	Orange/White/Blue
Samford	Bulldogs	Independent	Pete Hurt	Birmingham, AL	Red/Blue
San Diego	Toreros	Pioneer	Brian Fogarty	San Diego, CA	Lt. Blue/Navy/White
Siena	Saints	Metro Atlantic	Jack DuBois	Loudonville, NY	Green/Gold
South Carolina St.	Bulldogs	Mid-Eastern	Willie Jeffries	Orangeburg, SC	Garnet/Blue
SE Missouri St.	Indians	Ohio Valley	John Mumford	Cape Girardeau, MO	Red/Black
Southern-BR	Jaguars	Southwestern	Pete Richardson	Baton Rouge, LA	Blue/Gold
Southern Illinois	Salukis	Gateway	Shawn Watson	Cardondale, IL	Maroon/White
Southern Utah	Thunderbirds	American West	Jack Bishop	Cedar City, UT	Scarlet/Blue/White
SW Missouri St.	Bears	Gateway	Del Miller	Springfield, MO	Maroon/White
SW Texas St.	Bobcats	Southland	Jim Bob Helduser	San Marcos, TX	Maroon/Gold
S.F. Austin St.	Lumberjacks	Southland	John Pearce	Nacogdoches, TX	Purple/White
Tenn-Chattanooga	Moccasins	Southern	Buddy Green	Chattanooga, TN	Navy Blue/Gold
Tenn-Martin	Skyhawks	Ohio Valley	Don McLeary	Martin, TN	Orange/White/Blue
Tennessee St.	Tigers	Ohio Valley	Bill Davis	Nashville, TN	Blue/White
Tennessee Tech	Golden Eagles	Ohio Valley	Jim Ragland	Cookeville, TN	Purple/Gold
Texas Southern	Tigers	Southwestern	Bill Thomas	Houston, TX	Maroon/Gray
Towson St.	Tigers	Independent	Gordy Combs	Towson, MD	Gold/White/Black
Troy St.	Trojans	Southland	Larry Blakeney	Troy, AL	Cardinal/Gray/Black
Valparaiso	Crusaders	Pioneer	Tom Horne	Valparaiso, IN	Brown/Gold
Villanova	Wildcats	Yankee	Andy Talley	Villanova, PA	Blue/White
VMI	Keydets	Southern	Bill Stewart	Lexington, VA	Red/White/Yellow
Wagner	Seahawks	Independent	Walt Hameline	Staten Island, NY	Green/White
Weber St.	Wildcats	Big Sky	Dave Arslanian	Ogden, UT	Royal Purple/White
Western Carolina	Catamounts	Southern	Steve Hodgin	Cullowhee, NC	Purple/Gold
Western Illinois	Leathernecks	Gateway	Randy Ball	Macomb, IL	Purple/Gold
Western Kentucky	Hilltoppers	Independent	Jack Harbaugh	Bowling Green, KY	Red/White
William & Mary	Tribe	Yankee	Jimmye Laycock	Williamsburg, VA	Green/Gold
Wofford	Terriers	Independent	Mike Ayers	Spartanburg, SC	Old Gold/Black
Yale	Bulldogs, Elis	Ivy	Carmen Cozza	New Haven, CT	Yale Blue/White
Youngstown St.	Penguins	Independent	Jim Tressel	Youngstown, OH	Scarlet/White

Native American Nicknames Down to 11

As of the start of the 1995-96 academic year the number of Native American nickname variations stood at 11 in Division I basketball and football: INDIANS (3)— Arkansas St., Northeast Louisiana and Southeast Missouri St; BRAVES (2)— Alcorn St. and Bradley; CHIPPEWAS— Central Michigan; FIGHTING ILLINI— Illinois; MOCCASINS— Tennessee-Chattanooga; REDSKINS— Miami of Ohio; SEMINOLES— Florida St.; and TRIBE— William & Mary.

Oklahoma St.	Oklahoma	Fresno St.	Wisconsin
Bob Simmons	**H. Schnellenberger**	**Jerry Tarkanian**	**Dick Bennett**
Colorado to Cowboys	Louisville to Sooners	Bulldogs, Class of '56	Green Bay to Madison

Coaching Changes

New head coaches were named at 37 Division I basketball schools after the 1994-95 season while 20 Division I-A football schools and 11 Division I-AA football schools changed head coaches following the 1994 season. Coaching changes listed below are as of Sept. 15, 1995.

Division I Basketball

	Old Coach	Record	Why Left?	New Coach	Old Job
Akron	Coleman Crawford	8-18	Resigned	Dan Hipsher	Coach, Stetson
Arkansas St.	Nelson Catalina	8-20	Reassigned	Dickey Nutt	Ast., Arkansas St.
Boise St.	Bobby Dye	17-10	Retired	Rod Jensen	Ast., Boise St.
Cal Poly SLO	Steve Beason	1-26	Fired	Jeff Schneider	Ast., Washington St.
Columbia	Jack Rohan	4-22	Retired	Armond Hill	Ast., Columbia
Delaware	Steve Steinwedel	12-15	Resigned	Mike Brey	Ast., Duke
Duquesne	John Carroll	10-18	Fired	Scott Edgar	Coach, Murray St.
East Carolina	Eddie Payne	18-11	to Oregon St.*	Joe Dooley	Ast., E. Carolina
Eastern Wash.	John Wade	6-20	Resigned	Steve Aggers	Ast., Kansas St.
Florida Atlantic	Tim Loomis	9-18	named Ast. AD	Kevin Billerman	Ast., UNC-Charlotte
Florida Int'l	Bob Weltlich	11-18	Resigned	Shakey Rodriguez	Coach., Miami (Fla.) HS
Fresno St	Gary Colson	13-15	Resigned	Jerry Tarkanian	ex-UNLV coach
Georgia	Hugh Durham	18-9	Fired	Tubby Smith	Coach, Tulsa
Ga. Southern	Doug Durham#	8-20	Interim	Gregg Polinsky	Ast., Alabama
Grambling St.	Aaron James	11-17	Resigned	Lacey Reynolds	Ast., Texas Southern
Iona	Jerry Welsh#	5-12	Retired	Tim Welsh	Interim, Iona
Lafayette	John Leone	2-25	Resigned	Fran O'Hanlon	Ast., Penn
Long Island	Paul Lizzo	11-17	Resigned	Ray Haskins	Ast., Long Island
MD-Balt. County	Earl Hawkins	13-14	Fired	Tom Sullivan	Ast., Seton Hall
Michigan St	Jud Heathcote	22-6	Retired	Tom Izzo	Ast., Michigan St.
Morgan St.	Lynn Ramage	5-22	Interim	Chris Fuller	Coach, Erie CC (N.Y.)
Murray St.	Scott Edgar	21-9	to Duquesne*	Mark Gottfried	Ast., UCLA
NC-Greensboro	Mike Dement	23-6	to SMU*	Randy Peele	Ast., NC-Greensboro
Oregon St	Jim Anderson	9-18	Retired	Eddie Payne	Coach, E. Carolina
St. Peter's	Ted Fiore	19-11	Fired	Rodger Blind	Ast., St. Peter's
San Francisco	Jim Brovelli	10-19	named Ast. AD	Phil Mathews	Coach, Ventura JC (Calif.)
South Alabama	Judas Prada#	9-18	Interim	Bill Musselman	NBA scout
SMU	John Shumate	7-20	Resigned	Mike Dement	Coach, NC-Greensboro
SW Missouri St	Mark Bernsen	16-11	Resigned	Steve Alford	Coach., Manchester (Ind.)
Stetson	Dan Hipsher	15-12	to Akron*	Randy Brown	Ast., Stetson
TX-San Antonio	Stu Starner	15-13	Reassigned	Tim Carter	Coach, Nebraska-Omaha
Tulsa	Tubby Smith	24-8	to Georgia*	Steve Robinson	Ast., Kansas
UNLV	Tim Grgurich	12-16	Resigned	Billy Bayno	Ast., UMass
Western Carolina	Benny Dees	14-14	Retired	Phil Hopkins	Ast., Western Carolina
Wisconsin	Stan Van Gundy	13-14	Fired	Dick Bennett	Coach, WI-Green Bay
WI-Green Bay	Dick Bennett	22-8	to Wisconsin*	Mike Heideman	Ast., WI-Green Bay
WI-Milwaukee	Steve Antrim	3-24	Reassigned	Ric Cobb	Ast., WI-Milwaukee

* As head coach.

At Georgia Southern, Doug Durham served as interim replacement for Frank Kerns, who resigned just before the start of the 1994-95 season. At Iona, Jerry Welsh (5-12) handed day-to-day coaching duties over to his son and assistant Tim (5-5) on Feb. 4. At South Alabama, Judas Prada (8-15) served as interim replacement for Ronnie Arrow (1-3), who was fired on Dec. 16.

Note: Grgurich officially resigned as UNLV head coach on Mar. 3, 1995, after suffering from stress-related exhaustion. Grgurich served as coach from Oct. 22, 1994 through Jan. 5, 1995 and was 2-5. Assistant coach Howie Landa (5-2) succeeded Grgurich but also stepped down due to stress and was replaced by assistant Cle Edwards (5-9).

Also: At USC, George Raveling retired on Nov. 14 due to injuries suffered in a Sept. 25 auto accident. Assistant Charlie Parker, who was named interim head coach, was given the full-time job on Mar. 24, 1995.

Division I-A Football

	Old Coach	Record	Why Left?	New Coach	Old Job
Akron	Gerry Faust	1-10-0	Fired	Lee Owens	Ast., Ohio St.
Ball St	Paul Schudel	5-5-1	to Illinois†	Bill Lynch	Ast., Indiana
Colorado	Bill McCartney	11-1-0	Resigned	Rick Neuheisel	Ast., Colorado
Eastern Mich	Ron Cooper	5-6-0	to Louisville*	Rick Rasnick	Ast., Utah
Georgia Tech	Bill Lewis	1-10-0	Fired	George O'Leary	Ast., Georgia Tech
Iowa St	Jim Walden	0-10-1	Fired	Dan McCarney	Ast., Wisconsin
LSU	Curley Hallman	4-7-0	Fired	Gerry DiNardo	Coach, Vanderbilt
Louisville	H. Schnellenberger	6-5-0	to Oklahoma*	Ron Cooper	Coach, Eastern Mich.
Memphis	Chuck Stobart	6-5-0	Fired	Rip Scherer	Coach, James Madison
Miami-FL	Dennis Erickson	10-2-0	to NFL Seahawks*	Butch Davis	Ast., NFL Cowboys
Michigan St	George Perles	5-6-0	Retired	Nick Saban	Ast., NFL Browns
Mississippi	Joe Lee Dunn	4-7-0	Interim	Tommy Tuberville	Ast., Texas A&M
Navy	George Chaump	3-8-0	Fired	Charlie Weatherbie	Coach, Utah St.
Ohio Univ	Tom Lichtenberg	0-11-0	Fired	Jim Grobe	Ast., Air Force
Oklahoma	Gary Gibbs	6-6-0	Resigned	H. Schnellenberger	Coach, Louisville
Oklahoma St	Pat Jones	3-7-1	Fired	Bob Simmons	Ast., Colorado
Oregon	Rich Brooks	9-4-0	to NFL Rams*	Mike Bellotti	Ast., Oregon
Stanford	Bill Walsh	3-7-1	Resigned	Tyrone Willingham	Ast., NFL Vikings
Utah St	Charlie Weatherbie	3-8-0	to Navy*	John L. Smith	Coach, Idaho
Vanderbilt	Gerry DiNardo	5-6-0	to LSU*	Rod Dowhower	Ast., NFL Browns

*As head coach; †as an assistant.

Note: Georgia Tech was 1-7 when Lewis was fired as head coach on Nov. 7, 1994. Defensive coordinator O'Leary was named interim head coach and went 0-3. He was made the full-time head coach on Nov. 28, 1994.

Division I-AA Football

	Old Coach	Record	Why Left?	New Coach	Old Job
Ala-Birmingham	Jim Hilyer	7-4-0	to CFL Barracudas†	Watson Brown	Ast., Oklahoma
Bucknell	Lou Maranzana	5-6-0	Fired	Tom Gadd	Ast., San Jose St.
Buffalo	Jim Ward	3-8-0	Fired	Craig Cirbus	Ast., Penn St.
CS-Northridge	Bob Burt	3-7-0	to Temescal HS*	Dave Baldwin	Coach, Santa Rosa JC
CS-Sacramento	Mike Clemons	5-5-0	to Pacific†	John Volek	Coach, Fresno City Col.
Canisius	Barry Mynter	2-8-0	Resigned	Chuck Williams	Ast., Canisius
Idaho	John L. Smith	9-3-0	to Utah St.*	Chris Tormey	Ast., Washington
James Madison	Rip Scherer	10-3-0	to Memphis*	Alex Wood	Ast., Wake Forest
Nicholls St	Rick Rhoades	5-6-0	to S.F. Austin St.†	Darren Barbier	Coach, Hahnville HS
Richmond	Jim Marshall	3-8-0	Fired	Jim Reid	Ast., Boston College
SW Missouri St	Jesse Branch	4-7-0	to Ark. Assoc. AD	Del Miller	Ast., Kansas St.

*As head coach; †as an assistant.

NCAA Division I Schools on Probation

As of Sept. 1, 1995, there were 21 Division I member institutions serving NCAA probations.

School	Sport	Yrs	Penalty To End	School	Sport	Yrs	Penalty To End
Virginia Tech	M/W X-country	2	11/10/95	Nevada-Las Vegas	Basketball	3	11/9/96
Auburn	Basketball	4	11/22/95	Southwestern La	Baseball	2	4/22/97
	Tennis	4	11/22/95	West Virginia	Tennis	2	4/22/97
	& Football	4	11/22/95	Washington St	Baseball	2	6/21/97
Pittsburgh	Football	2	11/23/95		& Football	2	6/21/97
	Basketball	2	11/23/95	Alcorn St.	M/W Basketball	3	11/13/97
New Mexico	X-country	3	12/7/95		& Football	3	11/13/97
	Track	3	12/7/95	Coastal Carolina	Basketball	4	8/12/98
	W. Gym	3	12/7/95	Mississippi	Football	4	9/30/98
Oklahoma St.	Wrestling	3	1/5/96	Morgan St	M/W Basketball	4	2/3/98
Tulsa	All sports	3	1/8/96		M/W X-country	4	2/3/98
Wisconsin	Wrestling	2	1/12/96		M/W Tennis	4	2/3/98
Ball St.	Basketball	2	6/3/96		M/W Track	4	2/3/98
Drake	Basketball	1	6/4/96		& Wrestling	4	2/3/98
Washington	Football	2	6/5/96	Alabama	Football	3	6/3/98
Southwest Texas St.	Baseball	2	10/1/96	Texas A&M	Football	5	1/6/99

Note: Alabama appealed the NCAA decision shortly after sanctions were handed down on Aug. 2, 1995.

Remaining postseason and TV sanctions

No 1995 football postseason: Alabama, Mississippi and Morgan St.
No 1996 basketball postseason: Alcorn St. and Morgan St. (men and women).
Football TV restrictions: Mississippi (no games in 1995) and Washington (maximum of 4 games in 1995).

1994-95 Directors' Cup

Officially, the Sears Directors' Cup and sponsored by the National Association of Collegiate Directors of Athletics. Introduced in 1993-94 to honor the nation's best overall Division I athletic department (combining men's and women's sports).

Standings computed by NACDA with points awarded for each school's finish in 22 sports (10 core sports and one wild card sport for men and 10 core sports and one wild card sport for women). National champions in each sports get 64 points, runners-up get 63, etc., through tournament field. Division I-A football points based on final USA Today/CNN Coaches Top 25 poll. Listed below are team conferences, combined Final Four finishes (1st thru 4th place) for men's and women's programs, overall points in bold type, and rank the year before (1993-94).

	Conf	1-2-3-4	Pts	93-94 Rank			Conf	1-2-3-4	Pts	93-94 Rank
1	Stanford	Pac-10	5-2-2-1	971½	2nd	14 Georgia	SEC	0-0-4-0	561	21st
2	North Carolina	ACC	1-1-1-0	789½	1st	15 Alabama	SEC	0-1-0-0	551	15th
3	UCLA	Pac-10	3-4-2-2	736½	3rd	16 Ohio St	Big Ten	0-0-1-0	542½	23rd
4	Arizona	Pac-10	0-1-1-0	716½	6th	17 Wisconsin	Big Ten	0-0-0-0	541½	12th
5	Florida	SEC	0-1-0-0	691	4th	18 Arkansas	SEC	2-1-1-1	474½	NR
6	USC	Pac-10	0-2-0-1	668	8th	19 LSU	SEC	2-0-1-0	464	NR
7	Michigan	Big Ten	1-3-1-1	657½	9th	Virginia	ACC	1-0-1-0	464	19th
8	Penn St	Big Ten	1-2-3-0	644½	5th	21 Duke	ACC	0-0-0-0	423½	NR
9	Nebraska	Big Eight	1-1-0-0	637	18th	22 Oklahoma	Big Eight	0-0-0-1	423	20th
10	Texas	SWC	1-0-3-1	636	7th	23 Colorado	Big Eight	1-1-1-1	420½	NR
11	Tennessee	SEC	0-2-1-0	627	13th	24 Florida St	ACC	0-0-0-1	414½	25th
12	Arizona St	Pac-10	1-0-0-2	601½	10th	25 Oklahoma St	Big Eight	1-0-1-0	407	NR
13	California	Pac-10	0-0-1-0	568½	17th					

Top 25 Men's and Women's Athletic Programs

Unofficial ranking of Top 25 NCAA Division I men's and women's athletic programs in 1994-95, according to performances in 10 leading sports (based on participation). Points based on 20 for a national championship, 19 for runner-up, etc. Determining factors as follows:

Men's rankings— Cross-country (NCAA meet); Football (final AP postseason Top 25); Soccer (NCAA Final Four and final Soccer America regular season Top 20); Basketball (final USA Today/CNN Coaches postseason Top 25); Swimming (NCAA meet); Wrestling (NCAA meet); Baseball (final Baseball America postseason Top 25); Golf (NCAA tournament); Tennis (final Intercollegiate Tennis Assn. postseason Top 50); and Outdoor Track (NCAA meet).

Women's rankings— Field Hockey (NCAA Final Four and final NCAA regular season Top 20); Soccer (NCAA Final Four and final Soccer America regular season Top 20); Cross-country (NCAA meet); Volleyball (NCAA Final Four and final American Volleyball Coaches Assn. regular season Top 20); Swimming (NCAA meet); Basketball (final USA Today/CNN Coaches postseason Top 25); Tennis (final ITA postseason Top 50); Golf (NCAA tournament); Softball (final USA Today/National Softball Coaches Assn. postseason Top 25); and Outdoor Track (NCAA meet).

MEN

		Conf.	Cross-country	Football	Soccer	Basketball	Swimming	Wrestling	Baseball	Golf	Tennis	Outdoor Track	TOTAL
1	Stanford	Pac-10	15	0	0	0	19	0	11	0	20	0	84
2	USC	Pac-10	0	8	0	0	11	0	19	16	9½	17	80½
3	UCLA	Pac-10	0	0	17½	20	0	0	0	0	17	19	73½
4	Oklahoma St	Big Eight	10	0	0	17	0	14	10	20	0	0	71
5	Tennessee	SEC	9	0	0	0	15	0	16	4	4½	16	64½
6	North Carolina	ACC	0	0	9	18	0	13	0	2	0	14	56
7	Texas	SWC	0	0	0	0	17	0	0	18	11½	7½	54
8	Arkansas	SEC	11	0	0	19	0	0	0	0	0	20	50
9	Arizona	Pac-10	18	1	0	0	13	0	0	11	0	6	49
	Arizona St	Pac-10	0	0	0	8	7	17	0	17	0	0	49
	Florida St	ACC	0	17	0	0	0	0	18	14	0	0	49
12	Penn St	Big Ten	13	19	0	0	0	16	0	0	0	0	48
13	Auburn	SEC	0	12	0	0	18	0	12	4	0	0	46
14	LSU	SEC	0	0	0	0	9	0	6	0	11½	18	44½
15	Michigan	Big Ten	14	9	0	0	20	0	0	0	0	½	43½
16	Miami-FL	Big East	0	15	0	0	10	0	17	0	0	0	42
17	California	Pac-10	0	0	0	0	16	0	0	15	8	0	39
	Virginia	ACC	0	6	20	7	0	0	0	0	0	0	39
19	Florida	SEC	0	14	0	0	6	0	0	8	7	3	38
20	Colorado	Big Eight	19	18	0	0	0	0	0	0	0	0	37
21	Nebraska	Big Eight	0	20	0	0	0	15	0	0	0	0	35
22	Georgia	SEC	0	0	0	0	5	0	0	19	10½	0	34½
23	Iowa St	Big Eight	20	0	0	0	1	7	0	0	0	4	32
24	Iowa	Big Ten	0	0	0	0	8	20	0	0	0	½	28½
25	N.C. State	ACC	0	4	11	0	0	0	0	12½	0	0	27½

WOMEN

	Conf.	Field Hockey	Soccer	Cross-country	Volleyball	Swimming	Basketball	Tennis	Golf	Softball	Outdoor Track	TOTAL
1 Stanford	Pac-10	0	15	14	20	20	18	17	17	0	0	121
2 UCLA	Pac-10	0	0	0	19	11	0	15	14	20	19	98
3 Georgia	SEC	0	0	0	3	15	17	18	3	0	18	74
4 Arizona	Pac-10	0	0	11	5	16	0	13	9	19	0	73
5 North Carolina	ACC	19	20	0	0	0	10	0	13	0	5	67
6 Texas	SWC	0	0	0	0	18	0	20	11½	0	14	63½
7 Michigan	Big Ten	0	0	19	0	19	0	0	0	12	0	50
Nebraska	Big Eight	0	0	5	16	12	0	0	0	3	14	50
9 Penn St	Big 10	15	0	12	17½	0	5	0	0	0	0	49½
10 Tennessee	SEC	0	0	0	0	9	19	9	0	0	12	49
11 Arizona St	Pac-10	0	0	0	6	7	0	12	20	0	3	48
12 Colorado	Big Eight	0	0	17	8	0	16	0	0	0	6½	47½
Ohio St	Big Ten	11	0	0	17½	5	0	0	0	0	14	47½
14 Connecticut	Big East	7	17½	0	0	0	20	0	0	0	0	44½
15 Florida	SEC	0	0	1	7	13	3	19	0	0	0	43
16 Duke	ACC	0	14	0	0	0	0	4	14	10	0	42
17 Wake Forest	ACC	½	0	9	0	0	0	11	18	0	0	38½
18 Wisconsin	Big Ten	0	9	13	0	0	0	0	0	0	11	33
19 Washington	Pac-10	0	8	6	0	0	8	0	4½	6	0	32½
20 California	Pac-10	9	0	0	0	0	0	16	0	7	0	32
Iowa	Big Ten	17	0	0	0	0	0	0	0	15	0	32
USC	Pac-10	0	0	0	11	14	0	0	0	7	0	32

Others in Top 25: 23. Notre Dame and Villanova (30 pts); 25. Northwestern (28 pts).

1994-95 NCAA Team Champions

Thirteen schools won two or more national championships during the 1994-95 academic year, led by Stanford with five and UCLA and Division III Kenyon of Ohio with three each.

Multiple winners: FIVE— Stanford (Div. I men's gymnastics, men's tennis, women's swimming, women's volleyball and water polo). THREE— UCLA (Div. I men's basketball, men's volleyball and softball); Kenyon (Div. III men's and women's swimming and women's tennis). TWO— Abilene Christian (Div. II women's indoor and outdoor track); Adams St. (Div. II men's and women's cross-country); Arkansas (Div. I men's indoor and outdoor track); Cortland St. (Div. III women's cross-country and field hockey); Florida Southern (Div. II baseball and men's golf); Lincoln (Div. III men's indoor and outdoor track); LSU (Div. I women's indoor and outdoor track); St. Augustine's (Div. II men's indoor and outdoor track); Trenton St. (Div. III women's lacrosse and women's soccer); Wisconsin-Oshkosh (Div. III women's indoor and outdoor track).

Overall titles in parentheses; (*) indicates repeat champions.

FALL

Cross Country

MEN

Div.	Winner		Runner-Up	Score
I	Iowa St.	(2)	Colorado	65-88
II	Adams St., CO*	(3)	Western St., CO	55-73
III	Williams	(1)	N. Central, IL	98-110

WOMEN

Div.	Winner		Runner-Up	Score
I	Villanova*	(6)	Michigan	75-108
II	Adams St., CO*	(3)	Western St., CO	47-55
III	Cortland St., NY*	(5)	Calvin, MI	54-115

Field Hockey

Div.	Winner		Runner-Up	Score
I	James Madison	(1)	N. Carolina	2-1 (OT)†
II	Lock Haven, PA	(3)	Bloomsburg, PA*	2-1
III	Cortland St., NY*	(2)	Trenton St., NJ	2-1

†Decided on penalty strokes.

Football

Div.	Winner		Runner-Up	Score
I-A	Nebraska	(3)	Penn St.	AP poll
I-AA	Youngstown St.*	(3)	Boise St.	28-14
II	North Alabama*	(2)	TX A&M-K'ville	16-10
III	Albion, MI	(1)	Wash. & Jeff.	38-15

Note: There is no official Div. I-A playoff.

Soccer

MEN

Div.	Winner		Runner-Up	Score
I	Virginia*	(5)	Indiana	1-0
II	Tampa	(2)	Oakland, MI	3-0 (OT)
III	Bethany, WV	(1)	Johns Hopkins	1-0 (OT)

WOMEN

Div.	Winner		Runner-Up	Score
I	North Carolina*	(12)	Notre Dame	5-0
II	Franklin Pierce, NH	(1)	Regis, CO	2-0
III	Trenton St.*	(2)	UC-San Diego	2-1(OT)

Volleyball

WOMEN

Div.	Winner		Runner-Up	Score
I	Stanford	(2)	UCLA	4 sets
II	Northern Mich.*	(2)	CS-Bakersfield	4 sets
III	Washington, MO*	(5)	WI-Oshkosh	3 sets

Water Polo

Div.	Winner		Runner-Up	Score
National	Stanford*	(8)	USC	14-10

1994-95 NCAA Team Champions (Cont.)

Overall titles in parentheses; (*) indicates repeat champions.

WINTER

Basketball

MEN

Div.	Winner		Runner-Up	Score
I	UCLA	(11)	Arkansas*	89-78
II	Southern Ind.	(1)	CS-Riverside	71-63
III	WI-Platteville	(2)	Manchester, IN	69-55

WOMEN

Div.	Winner		Runner-Up	Score
I	Connecticut	(1)	Tennessee	70-64
II	North Dakota St.*	(4)	Portland St.	98-85
III	Capital, OH*	(2)	WI-Oshkosh	59-55

Fencing

Div.	Winner		Runner-Up	Score
Combined	Penn St.	(3)	St. John's	440-413

Gymnastics

Div.	Winner		Runner-Up	Score
Men	Stanford	(3)	Nebraska*	by 0.875
Women	Utah*	(9)	Alabama & Michigan	by 0.225

Ice Hockey

Div.	Winner		Runner-Up	Score
I	Boston University	(4)	Maine	6-2
II	Bemidji St., MN*	(4)	Mercyhurst, PA	6-2, 5-4
III	Middlebury, VT	(1)	Fredonia St.	1-0

Rifle

Div.	Winner		Runner-Up	Score
Combined	West Va.	(10)	Air Force	6241-6187

Skiing

Div.	Winner		Runner-Up	Score
Combined	Colorado	(13)	Utah	720½-711

Swimming & Diving

MEN

Div.	Winner		Runner-Up	Score
I	Michigan	(11)	Stanford*	561-475
II	Oakland, MI*	(3)	CS-Bakersfield	890-573
III	Kenyon, OH*	(16)	Hope, MI	687-295

WOMEN

Div.	Winner		Runner-Up	Score
I	Stanford*	(6)	Michigan	497½-478½
II	Air Force	(1)	Oakland, MI*	690-563
III	Kenyon, OH*	(12)	Williams, MA	527½-333

Indoor Track

MEN

Div.	Winner		Runner-Up	Score
I	Arkansas*	(12)	George Mason & Tennessee	59-26 -26
II	St. Augustine's	(7)	Abilene Chrst.*	87¼-84¼
III	Lincoln, PA		Albany St., NY	56-32

WOMEN

Div.	Winner		Runner-Up	Score
I	LSU*	(6)	UCLA	40-37
II	Abilene Christian*	(7)	Adams St., CO	67-38
III	WI-Oshkosh*	(2)	Cortland St., NY	42-26

Wrestling

Div.	Winner		Runner-Up	Score
I	Iowa	(15)	Oregon St.	134-77½
II	Central Oklahoma*	(4)	NE-Omaha	148-103
III	Augsburg, MN	(3)	Trenton St.	84½-76½

SPRING

Baseball

Div.	Winner		Runner-Up	Score
I	CS-Fullerton	(3)	USC	11-5
II	Fla. Southern	(8)	Georgia College	15-0
III	La Verne, CA	(1)	Methodist, NC	5-3

Golf

MEN

Div.	Winner		Runner-Up	Score
I	Oklahoma St.	(8)	Stanford	1156-1156†
II	Fla. Southern	(7)	SC-Aiken	1204-1214
III	Methodist, NC*	(5)	Otterbein	899-917

†Oklahoma St. won on 1st hole of sudden death.
Note: rain shortened Div. III tourney to 54 holes.

WOMEN

Div.	Winner		Runner-Up	Score
National	Arizona St.*	(4)	San Jose St.	1155-1181

Lacrosse

MEN

Div.	Winner		Runner-Up	Score
I	Syracuse	(6)	Maryland	13-9
II	Adelphi, NY	(4)	Springfield	12-10
III	Salisbury St., MD	(2)	Nazareth, NY	22-13

WOMEN

Div.	Winner		Runner-Up	Score
I	Maryland	(3)	Princeton* (1)	13-5
III	Trenton St., NJ*	(7)	Wm. Smith, NY	14-13

Softball

Div.	Winner		Runner-Up	Score
I	UCLA	(8)	Arizona*	4-2
II	Kennesaw St., GA	(1)	Bloomsburg, PA	3-2
III	Chapman, CA	(1)	Trenton St., NJ	4-2

Tennis

Note that both Div. II tournaments were team-only.

MEN

Div.	Winner		Runner-Up	Score
I	Stanford	(13)	Mississippi	4-0
II	Lander, SC*	(3)	North Florida	4-2
III	UC-Santa Cruz	(2)	Washington, MD	4-1

WOMEN

Div.	Winner		Runner-Up	Score
I	Texas	(2)	Florida	5-4
II	Armstrong St., GA	(1)	Grand Canyon	4-0
III	Kenyon	(2)	UC-San Diego	5-4

Outdoor Track

MEN

Div.	Winner		Runner-Up	Score
I	Arkansas*	(5)	UCLA	61½-55
II	St. Augustine's NC*	(7)	Abilene Chrst.	140½-95
III	Lincoln, PA	(3)	Williams	80-61

WOMEN

Div.	Winner		Runner-Up	Score
I	LSU*	(9)	UCLA	69-58
II	Abilene Christian	(5)	CS-Los Angeles	106½-71
III	WI-Oshkosh	(3)	St. Thomas-MN	58-52

Volleyball

MEN

Div.	Winner		Runner-Up	Score
National	UCLA	(15)	Penn St.	3 sets

Penn St.

Olga Kalinovskaya
Fencing

Kentucky

Jenny Hansen
Women's Gymnastics

UCLA

Keri Phebus
Women's Tennis

North Carolina

T. J. Jaworsky
Wrestling

1994-95 Division I Individual Champions

Repeat champions in **bold** type.

FALL
Cross-country

Men (10,000 meters)	Time
1 Martin Keino, Arizona	30:08.7
2 Adam Goucher, Colorado	30:12.0
3 Kevin Sullivan, Michigan	30:22.4

Women (5,000 meters)	Time
1 Jennifer Rhines, Villanova	16:31.2
2 Amy Rudolph, Providence	16:44.8
3 Rebecca Spies, Villanova	16:55.8

WINTER
Fencing
MEN

Event		Record
Epee	Mike Gattner, Lawrence	23-5
Foil	Sean McClain, Stanford	24-4
Sabre	Paul Palestis, NYU	23-5

WOMEN

Event		Record
Epee	Tina Loven, St. John's	24-5
Foil	**Olga Kalinovskaya**, Penn St.	29-0

Gymnastics
MEN

Event		Points
All-Around	Richard Grace, Nebraska	58.325
Horizontal Bar	Rick Kieffer, Nebraska	9.838
Parallel Bars	**Richard Grace**, Nebraska	9.800
Pommel Horse	Drew Durbin, Ohio St.	9.900
Rings	Dave Frank, Temple	9.825
Vault	Ian Bachrach, Stanford	9.713
Floor Exercise	Jay Thornton, Iowa	9.850

WOMEN

Event		Points
All-Around	**Jenny Hansen**, Kentucky	39.800
Uneven Bars	**Beth Wymer**, Michigan	9.950
Balance Beam	**Jenny Hansen**, Kentucky	10.000
Vault	**Jenny Hansen**, Kentucky	9.975
Floor Exercise (tie)	Leslie Angeles, Georgia	9.950
	Jenny Hansen, Kentucky	9.950
	& Stella Umeh, UCLA	9.950

Rifle
COMBINED
Smallbore

	Pts
1 Oleg Seleznev, Alaska-Fairbanks	1,177
2 Trevor Gathman, West Virginia	1,170
3 Ryan Meagher, West Virginia	1,169

Air Rifle

	Pts
1 Benji Belden, Murray St.	390
2 Erik Anderson, Kentucky	390
3 Jen Corindia, Norwich, VT	389

Note: Belden won in inner tens (26-24).

Skiing
MEN

Event		Time
Slalom	Scott Wither, Colorado	1:38.15
Giant Slalom	Bryan Sax, Colorado	2:10.99
10-k Classical	**Havard Solbaken**, Utah	27:24.5
20-k Freestyle	Thomas Weman, Utah	52:39.2

WOMEN

Event		Time
Slalom	Narcisa Sehovic, Denver	1:50.28
Giant Slalom	**Christl Hager**, Utah	2:08.36
5-k Classical	Heidi Selenes, Utah	15:51.8
15-k Freestyle	Heidi Selenes, Utah	45:32.4

Wrestling

Wgt	Champion	Runner-Up
108	Sam Henson, Clemson	Eric Akin, Iowa St.
118	Kelvin Jackson, Mich.St.	Eric Ivins, Okla.
126	Jeff McGinness, Iowa	Sanshiro Abe, Penn St.
134	T.J. Jaworsky, UNC	Babak Mohammadi, Ore.St.
142	John Hughes, Penn St.	Gerry Abas, Fresno St.
150	Steve Marianetti, Ill.	Lincoln McIlravy, Iowa
158	Ernest Benion, Ill.	Dan Wirnsberger, Mich.St.
167	Markus Mollica, Ariz.St.	Mark Branch, Okla.St.
177	Les Gutches, Ore.St.	Quincey Clark, Okla.
190	J.J. McGrew, Okla.St.	Joel Sharratt, Iowa
Hvy	Tolly Thompson, Neb	Justin Greenlee, No.Iowa

Defending champions (4): T.J. Jaworsky (won at 134 lbs); Lincoln McIlravy (lost at 150); Mark Branch (lost at 167); Joel Sharratt (lost at 190).

Arizona St.
Beata Kaszuba
Women's Swimming

Michigan
Tom Dolan
Men's Swimming

LSU
D'Andre Hill
Women's Track & Field

UCLA
John Godina
Men's Track and Field

Swimming & Diving

(*) indicates meet record; (†) is American record.

MEN

Event (yards)		Time
50 free	Gustavo Borges, Michigan	19.68
100 free	**Gustavo Borges**, Michigan	42.85
200 free	**Gustavo Borges**, Michigan	1:34.61
500 free	Tom Dolan, Michigan	4:08.75†
1650 free	Tom Dolan, Michigan	14:29.31†
100 back	**Brian Retterer**, Stanford	45.43†
200 back	Brian Retterer, Stanford	1:40.61
100 breast	Kurt Grote, Stanford	53.21
200 breast	**Kurt Grote**, Stanford	1:55.02
100 butterfly	Lars Frolander, SMU	46.18†
200 butterfly	**Ugur Taner**, California	1:44.39
200 IM	Kurt Jachimowski, Auburn	1:43.66
400 IM	Tom Dolan, Michigan	3:38.18†
200 free relay	**Stanford**	1:16.98
400 free relay	Stanford	2:52.57
800 free relay	**Michigan**	6:21.65
200 medley relay	**Stanford**	1:26.08
400 medley relay	**Stanford**	3:07.28†

Diving		Points
1-meter	Pat Bogart, Minnesota	593.60
3-meter	**Evan Stewart**, Tennessee	655.40
Platform	Tyce Routson, Miami-FL	785.70

WOMEN

Event (yards)		Time
50 free	Ashley Tappin, Arizona	22.34
100 free	**Jenny Thompson**, Stanford	48.38
200 free	Ashley Tappin, Arizona	1:45.23
500 free	Mimosa McNerney, Florida	4:41.86
1650 free	Mimosa McNerney, Florida	15:59.71
100 back	Alecia Humphrey, Michigan	54.10
200 back	Alecia Humphrey, Michigan	1:54.68
100 breast	**Beata Kaszuba**, Ariz. St.	59.71†
200 breast	Beata Kaszuba, Ariz. St.	2:09.71*
100 butterfly	**Jenny Thompson**, Stanford	52.77
200 butterfly	**Berit Puggaard**, SMU	1:57.86
200 IM	Jenny Thompson, Stanford	1:57.63
400 IM	Allison Wagner, Florida	4:09.04
200 free relay	Georgia	1:30.84
400 free relay	**Stanford**	3:17.17
800 free relay	SMU	7:14.31
200 medley relay	Stanford	1:40.88
400 medley relay	Michigan	3:38.40

Diving		Points
1-meter	Cheril Santini, SMU	454.80
3-meter	Tracy Bonner, Tennessee	580.20
Platform	Eileen Richetelli, Stanford	630.10

Indoor Track

(*) indicates meet record.

MEN

Event		Time
55 meters	Tim Harden, Kentucky	6.12
200 meters	Dave Dopek, DePaul	20.78
400 meters	Deon Minor, Baylor	46.00
800 meters	Michael Williams, Manhattan	1:48.12
Mile	Kevin Sullivan, Michigan	3:55.33*
3000 meters	Jason Bunston, Arkansas	8:06.81
5000 meters	Mark Carroll, Providence	13:55.15
55-m hurdles	Phillip Riley, Florida St.	7.10
4x400-m relay	North Carolina	3:06.36
Distance medley relay	Michigan	9:34.44

Event		Hgt/Dist
High Jump	Petar Malesev, Nebraska	7- 4¼
Pole Vault	Tim Mack, Tennessee	18- 4½
Long Jump	Kareem Streete-Thompson, Rice	26- 4¼
Triple Jump	Hrvoje Verzi, Georgia	54- 4½
Shot Put	**John Godina**, UCLA	66-11¼
35-lb Throw	Alex Papadimitriou, UTEP	71- 5¼

WOMEN

Event		Time
55 meters	Melinda Sergent, UTEP	6.73
200 meters	Merlene Frazer, Texas	23.14
400 meters	Youlanda Warren, LSU	52.39
800 meters	**Amy Wickus**, Wisconsin	2:04.86
Mile	Trine Pilskog, Arkansas	4:39.19
3000 meters	Sarah Schwald, Arkansas	9:19.90
5000 meters	Jennifer Rhines, Villanova	15:41.12*
55-m hurdles	Gillian Russell, Miami-FL	7.49
4x400-m relay	Texas	3:32.17
Distance medley relay	Villanova	11:11.98

Event		Hgt/Dist
High Jump	**Amy Acuff**, UCLA	6- 5½
Long Jump	Diane Guthrie-Gresha, G. Mason	21- 8¼
Triple Jump	Najuma Fletcher, Pitt	44- 2¾
Shot Put	Dawn Dumble, UCLA	57- 8½

SPRING
Golf
MEN

		Total
1 Chip Spratlin, Auburn	67-71-70-75	283
2 Ted Purdy, Arizona	74-70-70-70	284
Chris Tidland, Okla. St	69-69-72-74	284

WOMEN

	Total
1 Kristel Mourgue d'Algue, Ariz. St.	72-67-74-70—283
2 Wendy Ward, Arizona St.	72-71-71-71—285
Vibeke Stensrud, San Jose St	69-69-71-76—285

Tennis

MEN

Singles— Sargis Sargsian (Ariz. St.) def. Brett Hansen (USC), 3-6, 6-3, 6-4.

Doubles— Mahesh Bhupathi & Ali Hamadeh (Mississippi) def. Chad Clark & Trey Phillips (Texas), 7-6 (7-2), 6-2.

WOMEN

Singles— Keri Phebus (UCLA) def. Kelly Pace (Texas), 6-2, 6-3.

Doubles— Keri Phebus & Susie Starrett (UCLA) def. Kelly Pace & Cristina Moros (Texas), 6-3, 6-3.

Outdoor Track

(*) indicates meet record.

MEN

Event	Time
100 meters ....Tim Harden, Kentucky	10.05
200 meters.....................Ato Boldon, UCLA	20.24
400 meters ......Greg Haughton, Geo. Mason	44.62
800 meters ......Brandon Rock, Arkansas	1:46.37
1500 meters ....Kevin Sullivan, Michigan	3:37.57
5000 meters ....Martin Keino, Arizona	14:36.78
10,000 meters ......Godfrey Siamusiye, Ark.	28:59.60
110-m hurdles ....Duane Ross, Clemson	13.32
400-m hurdles......Ken Harnden, N.Carolina	48.72
3000-m steeple ....**Jim Svenoy**, UTEP	8:21.48
4x100-m relay..........................TCU	38.63
4x400-m relay..........................Baylor	3:02.78

Event	Hgt/Dist
High Jump ....Ray Doakes, Arkansas	7- 4½
Pole Vault.........Lawrence Johnson, Tennessee	18- 8¼
Long Jump.......Kareem Street-Thompson, Rice	27- 2
Triple Jump........Ndabe Mdhlongwa, SW La.	55- 4¾
Shot Put......................John Godina, UCLA	72- 2¼ *
Discus ....**John Godina**, UCLA	202- 4
Hammer ....**Balazs Kiss**, USC	261- 3 *
Javelin ....Greg Johnson, UCLA	244- 3
Decathlon.....................Mario Sategna, LSU	8172 pts

WOMEN

Event	Time
100 meters.......................D'Andre Hill, LSU	11.11
200 meters........Sevatheda Fynes, East. Mich.	22.63
400 meters ....Nicole Green, Kansas St.	52.01
800 meters ....**Inez Turner**, SW Texas St.	2:00.27
1500 meters ....Amy Wickus, Wisconsin	4:14.53
3000 meters ....Kathy Butler, Wisconsin	9:09.02
5000 meters ....Jennifer Rhines, Villanova	15:56.18
10,000 meters ....Katie Swords, SMU	34:28.46
100-m hurdles ....**Gillian Russell**, Miami-FL	12.99
400-m hurdles......Tonya Williams, Illinois	55.17
4x100-m relay ....LSU	43.10
4x400-m relay ....LSU	3:28.26

Event	Hgt/Dist
High Jump ....Amy Acuff, UCLA	6- 5 *
Long Jump.....................Pat Itanyi, West Va.	22- 1
Triple Jump ....**Nicola Martial**, Nebraska	45- 1
Shot Put ....Valeyta Althouse, UCLA	59-11¾*
Discus ....Dawn Dumble, UCLA	187- 2
Javelin ....**Valerie Tulloch**, Rice	192- 1
Heptathlon ....**D. Guthrie-Gresham**, G. Mason	6527 pts*

Most Outstaning Players

(*) indicates won individual or all-around NCAA championship; (†) high-point winner in NCAA track meet. There were no official Outstanding Players in the men's and women's combined sports of fencing, riflery and skiing.

MEN

Baseball ....Mark Kotsay, CS-Fullerton
Basketball ....Ed O'Bannon, UCLA
Cross-country ....Martin Keino, Arizona *
Golf...Chip Spratlin, Auburn *
Gymnastics........................Richard Grace, Nebraska *
Ice Hockey...................Chris O'Sullivan, Boston Univ.
Lacrosse ....Brian Dougherty, Maryland
Soccer: Offense....................Damian Silvera, Virginia
Defense........................Mark Peters, Virginia
Swimming & Diving ....Tom Dolan, Michigan
Tennis ....Sargis Sargsian, Ariz. St. *
Track: Indoor ....Kevin Sullivan, Michigan†
Outdoor ....John Godina, UCLA†
Volleyball..................................Jeff Nygaard, UCLA
Water Polo ....Jack Bowen, Jeremy Laster
and Frank Schneider of Stanford
Wrestling ......................T.J. Jaworsky, North Carolina

WOMEN

Basketball ....Rebecca Lobo, Connecticut
Cross-country ....Jennifer Rhines, Villanova *
Golf ....Kristel Mourgue d'Algue, Ariz. St. *
Gymnastics ....Jenny Hansen, Kentucky *
Soccer: Offense ....Tisha Venturini, North Carolina
Defense..............Staci Wilson, North Carolina
Softball ....Tanya Harding, UCLA
Swimming & Diving ....Beata Kaszuba, Ariz. St.
Tennis ....Keri Phebus, UCLA *
Track: Indoor ....Merlene Frazer, Texas†
Outdoor ....D'Andre Hill, LSU†

No awards: Field Hockey, Lacrosse and Volleyball.

1994-95 NAIA Team Champions

Total NAIA titles in parentheses.

FALL

Cross Country: MEN'S— Lubbock Christian, TX (5); WOMEN'S— Puget Sound, WA (3). **Football:** MEN'S— Division I: Northeastern St., OK (2) and Division II: Westminster, PA (6). **Soccer:** MEN'S— West Virginia Wesleyan (5); WOMEN'S— Lynn, FL (2). **Volleyball:** WOMEN'S— BYU-Hawaii (5).

WINTER

Basketball: MEN'S— Division I: Birmingham-Southern, AL (2) and Division II: Bethel, IN (1); WOMEN'S— Division I: Southern Nazarene, OK (3) and Division II: Western Oregon (1). **Swimming & Diving:** MEN'S— Puget Sound, WA (1); WOMEN'S— Simon Fraser, BC (5). **Indoor Track:** MEN'S— Lubbock Christian, TX (2); WOMEN'S— Southern-New Orleans (1). **Wrestling:** MEN'S— Findlay, OH (1).

SPRING

Baseball: MEN'S— Bellevue., NE (1); **Golf:** MEN'S— Texas Wesleyan (5); WOMEN'S— Lynn, FL (1); **Softball:** WOMEN'S— Oklahoma City (2); **Tennis:** MEN'S— Auburn-Montgomery, AL (2); WOMEN'S— Lynn, FL (2); **Outdoor Track:** MEN'S— Azusa Pacific, CA (11); WOMEN'S— Southern-New Orleans (1).

Annual NCAA Division I Team Champions

Men's and Women's NCAA Division I team champions from Cross-country to Wrestling. Rowing is included, although the NCAA does not sanction championships in the sport. Team champions in baseball, basketball, football, golf, ice hockey, soccer and tennis can be found in the appropriate chapters throughout the almanac. See pages xxx-xxx for list of 1994-95 individual champions.

CROSS-COUNTRY

Men

Iowa State ended a four-year Arkansas hold on the championship by placing five runners in the Top 22 and beating runner-up and Big Eight rival Colorado by 65-88. Arkansas, which hosted the event for the first time, was third with 172 points. Ian Robinson led the Cyclones with a ninth place finish (30:36.5) Arizona's Martin Keino won the individual title, covering the 10,000-meter course in 30:08.7. Freshman Adam Goucher of Colorado was second at 30:12.0. *(Prairie Grove, Ark.; Nov. 21, 1994.)*

Multiple winners: Michigan St. (8); Arkansas and UTEP (7); Oregon and Villanova (4); Drake, Indiana, Penn St. and Wisconsin (3); Iowa St., San Jose St. and Western Michigan (2).

Year		Year		Year		Year		Year	
1938	Indiana	1949	Michigan St.	1960	Houston	1972	Tennessee	1984	Arkansas
1939	Michigan St.	1950	Penn St.	1961	Oregon St.	1973	Oregon	1985	Wisconsin
1940	Indiana	1951	Syracuse	1962	San Jose St.	1974	Oregon	1986	Arkansas
1941	Rhode Island	1952	Michigan St.	1963	San Jose St.	1975	UTEP	1987	Arkansas
1942	Indiana	1953	Kansas	1964	Western Mich.	1976	UTEP	1988	Wisconsin
	& Penn St.	1954	Oklahoma St.	1965	Western Mich.	1977	Oregon	1989	Iowa St.
1943	Not held	1955	Michigan St.	1966	Villanova	1978	UTEP	1990	Arkansas
1944	Drake	1956	Michigan St.	1967	Villanova	1979	UTEP	1991	Arkansas
1945	Drake	1957	Notre Dame	1968	Villanova	1980	UTEP	1992	Arkansas
1946	Drake	1958	Michigan St.	1969	UTEP	1981	UTEP	1993	Arkansas
1947	Penn St.	1959	Michigan St.	1970	Villanova	1982	Wisconsin	1994	Iowa St.
1948	Michigan St.			1971	Oregon	1983	Vacated		

Women

For the sixth year in a row a Villanova runner outran the field to pace her team to the national championship. Jennifer Rhines, a junior who finished second in 1993, conquered the 5,000-meter course in 16:31.2, placing ahead of Providence's Amy Randolph (16:44.8) and Nova teammate Rebecca Spies (16:55.8). The Wildcats beat out second place Michigan, 75-108. Arkansas was third with 110 points. *(Prairie Grove, Ark.; Nov. 21, 1994.)*

Multiple winners: Villanova (6); Oregon, Virginia and Wisconsin (2).

Year		Year		Year		Year		Year	
1981	Virginia	1984	Wisconsin	1987	Oregon	1990	Villanova	1993	Villanova
1982	Virginia	1985	Wisconsin	1988	Kentucky	1991	Villanova	1994	Villanova
1983	Oregon	1986	Texas	1989	Villanova	1992	Villanova		

FENCING

Men & Women

Led by Olga Kalinovskaya's third straight title in the women's foil, Penn State won its third team championship in six years by a 27-point margin (440-413) over runner-up St. John's of New York. The Nittany Lions, who finished second to Notre Dame in 1994, took advantage of the national meet's new format which eliminated team weapon events in favor of overall performances in five individual events. St. John's, the surprise team of the meet, was led by women's epee champion Tina Loven. *(Notre Dame, Ind.; March 25-28, 1995.)*

Multiple winners: Penn St. (3); Columbia/Barnard (2). **Note:** Prior to 1990, men and women held separate championships. Men's multiple winners included: NYU (12); Columbia (11); Wayne St. (7); Navy, Notre Dame and Penn (3); Illinois (2). Women's multiple winners included: Wayne St. (3); Yale (2).

Year		Year		Year		Year		Year	
1990	Penn St.	1992	Columbia/	1993	Columbia/	1994	Notre Dame	1995	Penn St.
1991	Penn St.		Barnard		Barnard				

FIELD HOCKEY

Women

James Madison, a first-time Final Four qualifier, won the championship by defeating North Carolina 4-2 on penalty strokes after two 15-minute overtime periods failed to untie a 1-1 score. The defeat marked the fourth time in five years that UNC has reached the final and lost and the second straight year it has been beaten on penalty strokes. JMU shut out host Northeastern, 1-0, and UNC downed Iowa, 4-1, in the semifinals. *(Brookline, Mass.; Nov. 19-20, 1994.)*

Multiple winners: Old Dominion (7); Connecticut and Maryland (2).

Year		Year		Year		Year		Year	
1981	Connecticut	1984	Old Dominion	1987	Maryland	1990	Old Dominion	1993	Maryland
1982	Old Dominion	1985	Connecticut	1988	Old Dominion	1991	Old Dominion	1994	James Madison
1983	Old Dominion	1986	Iowa	1989	North Carolina	1992	Old Dominion		

GYMNASTICS

Men

The 1995 championship came down to Stanford and Nebraska for the fourth straight year with the Cardinal beating the defending champion Cornhuskers by less than a point (232.400 to 231.525). The Huskers won three of the seven events, paced by Richard Grace's victories in the parallel bars and the all-around, and Rich Kieffer's title in the horizontal bar. Vaulter Ian Bachrach captured Stanford's lone individual title. *(Columbus, Ohio; April 20-22, 1995.)*

Multiple winners: Illinois and Penn St. (9); Nebraska (8); So. Illinois (4); Iowa St., Oklahoma and Stanford (3); California, Florida St., Michigan and UCLA (2).

Year		Year		Year		Year		Year	
1938	Chicago	1954	Penn St.	1965	Penn St.	1975	California	1986	Arizona St.
1939	Illinois	1955	Illinois	1966	So.Illinois	1976	Penn St.	1987	UCLA
1940	Illinois	1956	Illinois	1967	So.Illinois	1977	Indiana St.	1988	Nebraska
1941	Illinois	1957	Penn St.	1968	California		& Oklahoma	1989	Illinois
1942	Illinois	1958	Michigan St.	1969	Iowa	1978	Oklahoma		
1943-47 Not held			& Illinois		& Michigan (T)	1979	Nebraska	1990	Nebraska
1948	Penn St.	1959	Penn St.					1991	Oklahoma
1949	Temple	1960	Penn St.	1970	Michigan	1980	Nebraska	1992	Stanford
		1961	Penn St.		& Michigan (T)	1981	Nebraska	1993	Stanford
1950	Illinois	1962	USC	1971	Iowa St.	1982	Nebraska	1994	Nebraska
1951	Florida St.	1963	Michigan	1972	So. Illinois	1983	Nebraska	1995	Stanford
1952	Florida St.	1964	So. Illinois	1973	Iowa St.	1984	UCLA		
1953	Penn St.			1974	Iowa St.	1985	Ohio St.		

(T) indicates won trampoline competition (1969 and '70).

Women

Déjà vu ruled in Georgia as defending champions Utah, Jenny Hansen of Kentucky and Beth Wymer of Michigan all repeated. Hansen was the meet's outstanding performer for the second year in a row, holding on to her titles in the all-around, vault and balance beam and adding a fourth in the floor exercise where she tied UCLA's Stella Umeh and Georgia's Leslie Angeles. Wymer won the uneven bars for the third consecutive year, while Utah took its second straight team title and ninth in the last 14 years. *(Athens, Ga.; April; 20-22, 1995.)*

Multiple winners: Utah (9); Georgia (3); Alabama (2).

Year		Year		Year		Year		Year	
1982	Utah	1985	Utah	1988	Alabama	1991	Alabama	1994	Utah
1983	Utah	1986	Utah	1989	Georgia	1992	Utah	1995	Utah
1984	Utah	1987	Georgia	1990	Utah	1993	Georgia		

LACROSSE

Men

Syracuse scored two quick goals in the last minute of the first half to take a 5-4 lead against Maryland and went on to win 13-9 in front of 26,229 at Byrd Stadium. Rob Kavovit scored four goals for the Orangemen, who have now won five titles in the last eight years. In the semifinals, Syracuse beat Virginia, 20-13, and Maryland defeated Johns Hopkins, 16-8. Maryland goalie Brian Dougherty, who stopped 46 shots in two games, was named MVP of the tournament. *(College Park, Md.; May 27-29, 1995.)*

Multiple winners: Johns Hopkins (7); Syracuse (6); North Carolina (4); Cornell (3); Maryland and Princeton (2).

Year		Year		Year		Year		Year	
1971	Cornell	1976	Cornell	1981	North Carolina	1986	North Carolina	1991	North Carolina
1972	Virginia	1977	Cornell	1982	North Carolina	1987	Johns Hopkins	1992	Princeton
1973	Maryland	1978	Johns Hopkins	1983	Syracuse	1988	Syracuse	1993	Syracuse
1974	Johns Hopkins	1979	Johns Hopkins	1984	Johns Hopkins	1989	Syracuse	1994	Princeton
1975	Maryland	1980	Johns Hopkins	1985	Johns Hopkins	1990	Syracuse	1995	Syracuse

Women

In a rematch of the 1994 final, undefeated Maryland jumped out to an 8-1 lead against defending champion Princeton and coasted to a 13-5 victory. Kelly Amonte's four goals and three more by Cathy Nelson paced the 17-0 Terrapins, who have now won three NCAA titles. UM-PU final came about after the Terps beat Penn State, 12-7, and the Tigers downed Dartmouth, 13-8, in the semifinals. *(Trenton, N.J.; May 20-21, 1995.)*

Multiple winners: Maryland (3); Penn St., Temple and Virginia (2).

Year		Year		Year		Year		Year	
1982	Massachusetts	1985	New Hampshire	1988	Temple	1991	Virginia	1994	Princeton
1983	Delaware	1986	Maryland	1989	Penn St.	1992	Maryland	1995	Maryland
1984	Temple	1987	Penn St.	1990	Harvard	1993	Virginia		

Annual NCAA Division I Team Champions (Cont.)

RIFLE

Men & Women

West Virginia set a new championship meet scoring record with 6,241 points to reclaim the title they've now won eight times in the last 10 years. The Mountaineers outshot runner-up Air Force by 54 points. Defending champion Alaska-Fairbanks set a team record with 1,563 air rifle points, but finished fifth overall. Individual champs were the Nanooks' Oleg Seleznev in the smallbore and Murray State's Benji Belden in the air rifle. *(Annapolis, Md.; March 2-4, 1995.)*

Multiple winners: West Virginia (10); Tennessee Tech (3); Murray St. (2).

Year		Year		Year		Year		Year	
1980	Tenn. Tech	1984	West Virginia	1987	Murray St.	1990	West Virginia	1993	West Virginia
1981	Tenn. Tech	1985	Murray St.	1988	West Virginia	1991	West Virginia	1994	AK-Fairbanks
1982	Tenn. Tech	1986	West Virginia	1989	West Virginia	1992	West Virginia	1995	West Virginia
1983	West Virginia								

ROWING

After sweeping the collegiate rowing triple crown in 1993 and again in '94, the Brown University varsity eight won only two of the three races in 1995. On May 21, the Bears finished third behind Princeton and Northeastern in the 50th edition of the Sprints on May 21 at Lake Quinsigamond in Worcester, Mass. Over the next three weeks, however, Brown came roaring back to win both the IRA and the Nationals with record-breaking times.

Brown crew: Bow— Rupert Roxborough; Seat 2— Dave Filippone; Seat 3— John Polansky; Seat 4— Porter Collins; Seat 5— Ben Holbrook; Seat 6— Jamie Koven; Seat 7— Dennis Zvegeli; Stroke— Nikola Stojic; Cox— Rajanya Shah; Coach— Scott Roop.

Intercollegiate Rowing Association Regatta
• VARSITY EIGHTS
Men

After its disappointing third at the Eastern Sprints, Brown came back to win the 93rd running of the IRA Regatta in record time. The Bears covered the 2,000-meter course on Camden's Cooper River in a blistering 5:31.3, outrowing a six-boat field that included runner-up Navy (5:34.9) and third place Washington (5:35.2). Harvard and Princeton finished fourth and fifth. *(Camden, N.J.; June 3, 1995.)*

The IRA was formed in 1895 by several northeastern colleges after Harvard and Yale quit the Rowing Association (established in 1871) to stage an annual race of their own. Since then the IRA Regatta has been contested over courses of varing lengths in Poughkeepsie, N.Y., Marietta, Ohio, Syracuse, N.Y. and Camden, N.J.

Distances: 4 miles (1895-97,1899-1916,1925-41); 3 miles (1898,1921-24,1947-49,1952-63,1965-67); 2 miles (1920,1950-51); 2000 meters (1964, since 1968).

Multiple winners: Cornell (24); Navy (13); California and Washington (10); Penn (9); Brown and Wisconsin (7); Syracuse (6); Columbia (4); Northeastern (2).

Year		Year		Year		Year		Year	
1895	Columbia	1915	Cornell	1936	Washington	1959	Wisconsin	1978	Syracuse
1896	Cornell	1916	Syracuse	1937	Washington	1960	California	1979	Brown
1897	Cornell	1917-19	Not held	1938	Navy	1961	California	1980	Navy
1898	Penn			1939	California	1962	Cornell	1981	Cornell
1899	Penn	1920	Syracuse			1963	Cornell	1982	Cornell
		1921	Navy	1940	Washington	1964	California	1983	Brown
1900	Penn	1922	Navy	1941	Washington	1965	Navy	1984	Navy
1901	Cornell	1923	Washington	1942-46	Not held	1966	Wisconsin	1985	Princeton
1902	Cornell	1924	Washington	1947	Navy	1967	Penn	1986	Brown
1903	Cornell	1925	Navy	1948	Washington	1968	Penn	1987	Brown
1904	Syracuse	1926	Washington	1949	California	1969	Penn	1988	Northeastern
1905	Cornell	1927	Columbia					1989	Penn
1906	Cornell	1928	California	1950	Washington	1970	Washington		
1907	Cornell	1929	Columbia	1951	Wisconsin	1971	Cornell	1990	Wisconsin
1908	Syracuse			1952	Navy	1972	Penn	1991	Northeastern
1909	Cornell	1930	Cornell	1953	Navy	1973	Wisconsin	1992	Dartmouth,
1910	Cornell	1931	Navy	1954	Navy*	1974	Wisconsin		Navy & Penn†
		1932	California	1955	Cornell	1975	Wisconsin		
1911	Cornell	1933	Not held	1956	Cornell	1976	California	1993	Brown
1912	Cornell	1934	California	1957	Cornell	1977	Cornell	1994	Brown
1913	Syracuse	1935	California	1958	Cornell			1995	Brown
1914	Columbia								

*In 1954, Navy was disqualified because of an ineligble coxwain; no trophies were given.   †First dead heat in history of IRA Regatta.

The Harvard-Yale Regatta

Harvard lengthened its current winning streak to 11 in a row on June 10, 1995, taking the 130th Harvard-Yale Regatta for varsity eights by one length over Yale on the Thames River at New London, Conn. Both crews broke the upstream course record for the third straight year in the four-mile event. The Crimson's winning time was 18 minutes, 45.5 seconds. The Harvard-Yale Regatta is the country's oldest intercollegiate sporting event and Harvard holds a 79-51 edge.

National Rowing Championships

VARSITY EIGHTS

The Brown men and Princeton women each won their third consecutive national rowing title at Hasha Lake near Cincinnati. Brown set a record pace and held off Princeton to become the first men's crew to three-peat since Harvard (1987-89). The Bears' time of 5:23.40 won the Herschede Cup by seven seats. Princeton's women's crew nipped a fast-closing University of Washington boat by less than a second to hold on to the Ferguson Bowl with a time of 6:11.98. *(Harsha Lake, Bantam, Ohio; June 10, 1995.)*

Men

National championship raced annually since 1982 in Bantam, Ohio over a 2000-meter course on Harsha Lake. Winner receives Herschede Cup.

Multiple winners: Harvard (6); Brown (3); Wisconsin (2).

Year	Champion	Time	Runner-up	Time	Year	Champion	Time	Runner-up	Time
1982	Yale	5:50.8	Cornell	5:54.15	1990	Wisconsin	5:52.5	Harvard	5:56.84
1983	Harvard	5:59.6	Washington	6:00.0	1991	Penn	5:58.21	Northeastern	5:58.48
1984	Washington	5:51.1	Yale	5:55.6	1992	Harvard	5:33.97	Dartmouth	5:34.28
1985	Harvard	5:44.4	Princeton	5:44.87	1993	Brown	5:54.15	Penn	5:56.98
1986	Wisconsin	5:57.8	Brown	5:59.9	1994	Brown	5:24:52	Harvard	5:25:83
1987	Harvard	5:35.17	Brown	5:35.63	1995	Brown	5:23:40	Princeton	5:25:83
1988	Harvard	5:35.98	Northeastern	5:37.07					
1989	Harvard	5:36.6	Washington	5:38.93					

Women

National championship held over various distances at 10 different venues since 1979. Distances—1000 meters (1979-81); 1500 meters (1982-83); 1000 meters (1984); 1750 meters (1985); 2000 meters (1986-88, since 1991); 1852 meters (1989-90). Winner receives Ferguson Bowl.

Multiple winners: Washington (7); Princeton (4); Boston University (2).

Year	Champion	Time	Runner-up	Time	Year	Champion	Time	Runner-up	Time
1979	Yale	3:06	California	3:08.6	1988	Washington	6:41.0	Yale	6:42.37
					1989	Cornell	5:34.9	Wisconsin	5:37.5
1980	California	3:05.4	Oregon St.	3:05.8					
1981	Washington	3:20.6	Yale	3:22.9	1990	Princeton	5:52.2	Radcliffe	5:54.2
1982	Washington	4:56.4	Wisconsin	4:59.83	1991	Boston Univ.	7:03.2	Cornell	7:06.21
1983	Washington	4:57.5	Dartmouth	5:03.02	1992	Boston Univ.	6:28.79	Cornell	6:32.79
1984	Washington	3:29.48	Radcliffe	3:31.08	1993	Princeton	6:40.75	Washington	6:43.86
1985	Washington	5:28.4	Wisconsin	5:32.0	1994	Princeton	6:11.38	Yale	6:14.46
1986	Wisconsin	6:53.28	Radcliffe	6:53.34	1995	Princeton	6:11.98	Washington	6:12.69
1987	Washington	6:33.8	Yale	6:37.4					

SKIING

Men & Women

Utah won five individual titles, but Colorado scored at least 80 points in each of the four men's and women's events to edge the Utes, 720½ points to 711. The team title was the Buffs' 13th and first since 1991. Colorado got two individual wins by Scott Wither in the slalom and Bryan Sax in the giant slalom. Utah swept the cross-country events with Heidi Selenes winning the women's 5-kilometer freestyle and 15-km classical, Havard Solbaken taking the men's 10-km freestyle and Thomas Weman capturing the men's 20-km classical. *(Attitash Mt. and Jackson Touring Center, Bartlett, N.H.; March 9-11, 1995.)*

Multiple winners: Denver (14); Colorado (13); Utah (7); Vermont (5); Dartmouth and Wyoming (2).

Year		Year		Year		Year		Year	
1954	Denver	1963	Denver	1972	Colorado	1980	Vermont	1988	Utah
1955	Denver	1964	Denver	1973	Colorado	1981	Utah	1989	Vermont
1956	Denver	1965	Denver	1974	Colorado	1982	Colorado		
1957	Denver	1966	Denver	1975	Colorado	1983	Utah	1990	Vermont
1958	Dartmouth	1967	Denver	1976	Colorado	1984	Utah	1991	Colorado
1959	Colorado	1968	Wyoming		& Dartmouth	1985	Wyoming	1992	Vermont
		1969	Denver	1977	Colorado	1986	Utah	1993	Utah
1960	Colorado			1978	Colorado	1987	Utah	1994	Vermont
1961	Denver	1970	Denver	1979	Colorado			1995	Colorado
1962	Denver	1971	Denver						

SOFTBALL

Women

The top two teams in the country— No. 1 UCLA and No. 2 Arizona— squared off in the final for the fourth time in five years and the Bruins won, 4-2. Transfer student and Australian national team star Tanya Harding, the 23-year-old winning pitcher in all four of UCLA's tournament games, arrived on campus March 22 and dropped out of school on May 31. *(Oklahoma City; May 25-29, 1995.)*

Multiple winners: UCLA (8); Arizona (3); Texas A&M (2).

Year		Year		Year		Year		Year	
1982	UCLA	1985	UCLA	1988	UCLA	1991	Arizona	1994	Arizona
1983	Texas A&M	1986	CS-Fullerton	1989	UCLA	1992	UCLA	1995	UCLA
1984	UCLA	1987	Texas A&M	1990	UCLA	1993	Arizona		

Annual NCAA Division I Team Champions (Cont.)

SWIMMING & DIVING

Men

Sophomore Tom Dolan set American records in the 500-yard freestyle (4:08.75), the 1,650-yd free (14:29.31) and the 400-yd individual medley (3:38.18) and added a fourth victory in the 800-yd freestyle relay to lead Michigan to its first team championship since 1961. He was helped by freestyle sprinter Gustavo Borges, who won at 50 yards and repeated as 100-yd and 200-yd champion. The Wolverines beat runner-up Stanford, 561 points to 475. The Cardinal won eight events, six of them with the help of Brian Retterer, who won the 100- and 200-yd backstrokes, led off the 200- and 400-yd medlay relays, and anchored the 200- and 400-yd freestyle relays. Retterer also set a pair of American records (Indianapolis, Ind.; March 23-25, 1995.)

Multiple winners: Michigan and Ohio St. (11); USC (9); Stanford (7); Indiana (6); Texas (5); Yale (4); California and Florida (2).

Year		Year		Year		Year		Year	
1937	Michigan	1949	Ohio St.	1960	USC	1972	Indiana	1984	Florida
1938	Michigan	1950	Ohio St.	1961	Michigan	1973	Indiana	1985	Stanford
1939	Michigan	1951	Yale	1962	Ohio St.	1974	USC	1986	Stanford
1940	Michigan	1952	Ohio St.	1963	USC	1975	USC	1987	Stanford
1941	Michigan	1953	Yale	1964	USC	1976	USC	1988	Texas
1942	Yale	1954	Ohio St.	1965	USC	1977	USC	1989	Texas
1943	Ohio St.	1955	Ohio St.	1966	USC	1978	Tennessee	1990	Texas
1944	Yale	1956	Ohio St.	1967	Stanford	1979	California	1991	Texas
1945	Ohio St.	1957	Michigan	1968	Indiana	1980	California	1992	Stanford
1946	Ohio St.	1958	Michigan	1969	Indiana	1981	Texas	1993	Stanford
1947	Ohio St.	1959	Michigan	1970	Indiana	1982	UCLA	1994	Stanford
1948	Michigan			1971	Indiana	1983	Florida	1995	Michigan

Women

Stanford rallied for victories in the final two events to beat Michigan and capture its fourth consecutive national championship. The meet was decided on wins by Eileen Richetelli in the platform dive and the 400-yard freestyle relay team anchored by Jenny Thompson. Thompson also swam on the Cardinal's winning 200-yd medley relay team and claimed individual titles in the 100-yd freestyle, 100-yd butterfly and 200-yd I.M. Arizona State's Beata Kaszuba set meet breaststroke records of 59.71 at 100 yards and 2:09.71 at 200 yards. (Austin, Texas; March 16-18, 1995.)

Multiple winners: Texas (7); Stanford (6).

Year		Year		Year		Year		Year	
1982	Florida	1985	Texas	1988	Texas	1991	Texas	1994	Stanford
1983	Stanford	1986	Texas	1989	Stanford	1992	Stanford	1995	Stanford
1984	Texas	1987	Texas	1990	Texas	1993	Stanford		

INDOOR TRACK

Men

The loss to graduation of individual-event champions Erick Walder, Calvin Davis and Niall Bruton mattered little as Arkansas scored six top-three finishes to easily win its 12th consecutive national title. Jason Bunston, who won the 5,000-meter race in 1994, was the Razorbacks' only '95 champion, taking the 3,000 meters. All 14 events in the meet were won by different schools. George Mason and Tennessee tied for second place, trailing the Hogs by 29 points, 59-26. (RCA Dome, Indianapolis; March 10-11, 1995.)

Multiple winners: Arkansas (12); UTEP (7); Kansas and Villanova (3); USC (2).

Year		Year		Year		Year		Year	
1965	Missouri	1971	Villanova	1978	UTEP	1984	Arkansas	1990	Arkansas
1966	Kansas	1972	USC	1979	Villanova	1985	Arkansas	1991	Arkansas
1967	USC	1973	Manhattan	1980	UTEP	1986	Arkansas	1992	Arkansas
1968	Villanova	1974	UTEP	1981	UTEP	1987	Arkansas	1993	Arkansas
1969	Kansas	1975	UTEP	1982	UTEP	1988	Arkansas	1994	Arkansas
1970	Kansas	1976	UTEP	1983	SMU	1989	Arkansas	1995	Arkansas
		1977	Washington St.						

Women

LSU edged UCLA, 40-37, to win its third straight championship despite only two top-three finishes. Youlanda Warren figured in both of them, winning the 400 meters and anchoring the Tigers' second place in the 4x400 relay. Three runners repeated as winners— Amy Wickus of Wisconsin in the 800 meters, Amy Acuff of UCLA in the high jump and 1994 cross-country champion Jennifer Rhines of Villanova, who added the indoor 5,000-meter title to her resume. (RCA Dome, Indianapolis; Mar. 10-11, 1995.)

Multiple winners: LSU (6); Texas (3); Nebraska (2).

Year		Year		Year		Year		Year	
1983	Nebraska	1986	Texas	1989	LSU	1992	Florida	1994	LSU
1984	Nebraska	1987	LSU	1990	Texas	1993	LSU	1995	LSU
1985	Florida St.	1988	Texas	1991	LSU				

Tom Ewart/NCAA Photos

Villanova's **Jennifer Rhines** (No. 211) ran away with three national championships in 1994–95, winning the Cross-country title and the 5,000-meter crowns in both Indoor and Outdoor Track.

OUTDOOR TRACK

Men

Trailing UCLA, 51-49½, going into the second to last event of the championships, Arkansas placed three runners in the top eight of the 5,000 meters to win its fourth consecutive national title by 6½ points. Godfrey Siamusiye placed third in the 5,000 and won the 10,000 to pace the Razorbacks along with fellow winners Brandon Rock (800 meters) and Ray Doakes (high jump). John Godina of UCLA was the meet's only double winner (discus and shot put) and Balazs Kiss of USC won the hammer throw for the third straight year. *(Knoxville, Tenn.; May 31-June 3, 1995.)*

Multiple winners: USC (26); UCLA (8); UTEP (6); Arkansas, Illinois and Oregon (5); Kansas, LSU and Stanford (3); SMU and Tennessee (2).

Year		Year		Year		Year		Year	
1921	Illinois	1937	USC	1952	USC	1967	USC	1980	UTEP
1922	California	1938	USC	1953	USC	1968	USC	1981	UTEP
1923	Michigan	1939	USC	1954	USC	1969	San Jose St.	1982	UTEP
1924	Not held	1940	USC	1955	USC	1970	BYU, Kansas	1983	SMU
1925	Stanford*	1941	USC	1956	UCLA		& Oregon	1984	Oregon
1926	USC*	1942	USC	1957	Villanova	1971	UCLA	1985	Arkansas
1927	Illinois*	1943	USC	1958	USC	1972	UCLA	1986	SMU
1928	Stanford	1944	Illinois	1959	Kansas	1973	UCLA	1987	UCLA
1929	Ohio St.	1945	Navy	1960	Kansas	1974	Tennessee	1988	UCLA
1930	USC	1946	Illinois	1961	USC	1975	UTEP	1989	LSU
1931	USC	1947	Illinois	1962	Oregon	1976	USC	1990	LSU
1932	Indiana	1948	Minnesota	1963	USC	1977	Arizona St.	1991	Tennessee
1933	LSU	1949	USC	1964	Oregon	1978	UCLA & UTEP	1992	Arkansas
1934	Stanford	1950	USC	1965	Oregon	1979	UTEP	1993	Arkansas
1935	USC	1951	USC		& USC			1994	Arkansas
1936	USC			1966	UCLA			1995	Arkansas

(*) indicates unofficial championship.

Women

Led by 100-meter champion D'Andre Hill, LSU piled up 29 points in the three sprint events and won both relays to clinch their ninth straight national title. Meet records were set by Amy Acuff of UCLA in the high jump (6-5), teammate Valeyta Althouse in the shot put (59-11¾) and George Mason's Diane Guthrie-Gresham in the heptathlon (6,527 points). Jennifer Rhines of Villanova completed her three-season sweep of the 5,000 meters, adding the outdoor title to her wins in the cross-country and the indoor. *(Knoxville, Tenn.; May 31-June 3, 1995.)*

Multiple winners: LSU (9); UCLA (2).

Year		Year		Year		Year		Year	
1982	UCLA	1985	Oregon	1988	LSU	1991	LSU	1994	LSU
1983	UCLA	1986	Texas	1989	LSU	1992	LSU	1995	LSU
1984	Florida St.	1987	LSU	1990	LSU	1993	LSU		

Annual NCAA Division I Team Champions (Cont.)

VOLLEYBALL

Men

UCLA, a five-set loser to Penn State in the 1994 final, came back to sweep the defending champions, 15-3, 15-10, 15-10, for its 15th national title. The Bruins completed the season with a 31-1 record, avenging their only loss to Ball State by routing the Cardinals in the semifinals, 15-12, 15-9, 15-10. *(Springfield, Mass.; May 5-6, 1995.)*

Multiple winners: UCLA (15); Pepperdine and USC (4).

Year		Year		Year		Year		Year	
1970	UCLA	1976	UCLA	1981	UCLA	1986	Pepperdine	1991	Long Beach St.
1971	UCLA	1977	USC	1982	UCLA	1987	UCLA	1992	Pepperdine
1972	UCLA	1978	Pepperdine	1983	UCLA	1988	USC	1993	UCLA
1973	San Diego St.	1979	UCLA	1984	UCLA	1989	UCLA	1994	Penn St.
1974	UCLA	1980	USC	1985	Pepperdine	1990	USC	1995	UCLA
1975	UCLA								

Women

With freshman Kristin Folkl leading the way with a career-high 25 kills, Stanford beat Pac-10 rival UCLA to regain the championship it first won in 1992. The Cardinal downed the Bruins in four games, 15-10, 5-15, 16-14, 15-13, to finish the season at 32-1. In the semifinals, Stanford eliminated Ohio State in three games and UCLA got past Penn State in five. *(Austin, Texas; Dec. 15-17, 1994.)*

Multiple winners: Hawaii and UCLA (3); Long Beach St., Pacific and Stanford (2).

Year		Year		Year		Year		Year	
1981	USC	1984	UCLA	1987	Hawaii	1990	UCLA	1993	Long Beach St.
1982	Hawaii	1985	Pacific	1988	Texas	1991	UCLA	1994	Stanford
1983	Hawaii	1986	Pacific	1989	Long Beach St.	1992	Stanford		

WATER POLO

Men

Defending champion Stanford scored nine goals in the final two periods to break a 5-5 halftime tie and defeat Southern Cal, 14-10. Tournament MVPs Frank Schneider, Jeremy Laster and Jack Bowen led the Cardinal, who beat UCLA, 9-5, while USC sunk California, 11-6, in the All-Pac-10 semifinals. *(Long Beach, Calif.; Nov. 25-27, 1994.)*

Multiple winners: California (11); Stanford (8); UC-Irvine and UCLA (3).

Year		Year		Year		Year		Year	
1969	UCLA	1975	California	1980	Stanford	1985	Stanford	1990	California
1970	UC-Irvine	1976	Stanford	1981	Stanford	1986	Stanford	1991	California
1971	UCLA	1977	California	1982	UC-Irvine	1987	California	1992	California
1972	UCLA	1978	Stanford	1983	California	1988	California	1993	Stanford
1973	California	1979	UC-S. Barbara	1984	California	1989	UC-Irvine	1994	Stanford
1974	California								

WRESTLING

Men

Performing in front of a record 81,028 fans in six sessions over three days, host Iowa easily won its 15th national title, beating runner-up Oregon St., 134 to 77½. The Hawkeyes came away with one champion (Jeff McGuinness at 126 lbs), two runners-up (Lincoln McIlravy at 150 and Joel Sharratt at 190) and two thirds (Mike Mena at 118 and Ray Brinzer at 177). North Carolina's T.J. Jaworsky, the 134-lb winner, was the only 1994 champion to repeat. Four others didn't, including Iowa's McIlravy, a junior who had a 55-bout win streak snapped in the final by Steve Marianetti of Illinois and Penn State heavyweight Kerry McCoy, who lost in the semifinals after 88 straight wins. *(Iowa City, Iowa; March 16-18, 1995.)*

Multiple winners: Oklahoma St. (30); Iowa (15); Iowa St. (8); Oklahoma (7).

Year		Year		Year		Year		Year	
1928	Okla. A&M*	1940	Okla. A&M	1956	Okla. A&M	1970	Iowa St.	1983	Iowa
1929	Okla. A&M	1941	Okla. A&M	1957	Oklahoma	1971	Iowa St.	1984	Iowa
1930	Okla. A&M	1942	Okla. A&M	1958	Okla. St.	1972	Iowa St.	1985	Iowa
1931	Okla. A&M*	1943-45	Not held	1959	Okla. St.	1973	Iowa St.	1986	Iowa
1932	Indiana*	1946	Okla. A&M	1960	Oklahoma	1974	Oklahoma	1987	Iowa St.
1933	Okla. A&M* & Iowa St.*	1947	Cornell Col.	1961	Okla. St.	1975	Iowa	1988	Arizona St.
		1948	Okla. A&M	1962	Okla. St.	1976	Iowa	1989	Okla. St.
1934	Okla. A&M	1949	Okla. A&M	1963	Oklahoma	1977	Iowa St.	1990	Okla. St.
1935	Okla. A&M	1950	Northern Iowa	1964	Okla. St.	1978	Iowa	1991	Iowa
1936	Oklahoma	1951	Oklahoma	1965	Iowa St.	1979	Iowa	1992	Iowa
1937	Okla. A&M	1952	Oklahoma	1966	Okla. St.	1980	Iowa	1993	Iowa
1938	Okla. A&M	1953	Penn St.	1967	Michigan St.	1981	Iowa	1994	Okla. St.
1939	Okla. A&M	1954	Okla. A&M	1968	Okla. St.	1982	Iowa	1995	Iowa
		1955	Okla. A&M	1969	Iowa St.				

(*) indicates unofficial champions. **Note:** Oklahoma A&M became Oklahoma St. in 1958.

Chris Evert with former President **George Bush** after Mr. Bush had helped install her as the International Tennis Hall of Fame's only 1995 inductee.

HALLS OF FAME & AWARDS

BASEBALL

National Baseball Hall of Fame & Museum

Established in 1935 by Major League Baseball to celebrate the game's 100th anniversary. **Address:** P.O. Box 590, Cooperstown, NY 13326. **Telephone:** (607) 547-7200.

Eligibility: Nominated players must have played at least part of 10 seasons in the Major Leagues and be retired for at least five but no more than 20 years. Voting done by Baseball Writers' Association of America. Certain nominated players not elected by the writers can become eligible via the Veterans' Committee 23 years after retirement. The Hall of Fame board of directors voted unanimously on Feb. 4, 1991, to exclude players on baseball's ineligible list from consideration. Pete Rose is the only living ex-player on that list.

Class of 1995 (5)**:** BBWAA vote— third baseman **Mike Schmidt**, Philadelphia (1972-89). VETERANS' COMMITTEE vote— outfielder **Richie Ashburn**, Philadelphia-NL (1948-59), Chicago-NL (1960-61), New York-NL (1962); pitcher **Vic Willis**, Boston-NL (1898-1905), Pittsburgh (1906-09), St. Louis-NL (1910); Negro Leagues pitcher, 2nd baseman and outfielder **Leon Day**, Baltimore (1934), Brooklyn-Newark Eagles (1935-43,46,49); executive **William Hulbert**, National League founder and president (1877-82).

1995 Top 10 vote-getters (460 BBWAA ballots cast, 345 needed to elect): 1. **Mike Schmidt** (444); 2. **Phil Niekro** (286); 3. **Don Sutton** (264); 4. **Tony Perez** (259); 5. **Steve Garvey** (196); 6. **Tony Oliva** (149); 7. **Ron Santo** (139); 8. **Jim Rice** and **Bruce Sutter** (137); 10. **Jim Kaat** (100).

Elected first year on ballot (31): Hank Aaron, Ernie Banks, Johnny Bench, Lou Brock, Rod Carew, Steve Carlton, Ty Cobb, Bob Feller, Bob Gibson, Reggie Jackson, Walter Johnson, Al Kaline, Sandy Koufax, Mickey Mantle, Christy Mathewson, Willie Mays, Willie McCovey, Joe Morgan, Stan Musial, Jim Palmer, Brooks Robinson, Frank Robinson, Jackie Robinson, Babe Ruth, **Mike Schmidt**, Tom Seaver, Warren Spahn, Willie Stargell, Honus Wagner, Ted Williams and Carl Yastrzemski.

Members are listed with years of induction; (+) indicates deceased members.

Catchers

Bench, Johnny 1989	+ Cochrane, Mickey 1947	+ Hartnett, Gabby 1955
Berra, Yogi 1972	+ Dickey, Bill 1954	+ Lombardi, Ernie 1986
+ Bresnahan, Roger 1945	+ Ewing, Buck 1939	+ Schalk, Ray 1955
+ Campanella, Roy 1969	+ Ferrell, Rick 1984	

1st Basemen

+ Anson, Cap 1939	+ Connor, Roger 1976	Killebrew, Harmon 1984
+ Beckley, Jake 1971	+ Foxx, Jimmie 1951	McCovey, Willie 1986
+ Bottomley, Jim 1974	+ Gehrig, Lou 1939	+ Mize, Johnny 1981
+ Brouthers, Dan 1945	+ Greenberg, Hank 1956	+ Sisler, George 1939
+ Chance, Frank 1946	+ Kelly, George 1973	+ Terry, Bill 1954

2nd Basemen

Carew, Rod 1991	+ Gehringer, Charley 1949	Morgan, Joe 1990
+ Collins, Eddie 1939	+ Herman, Billy 1975	+ Robinson, Jackie 1962
Doerr, Bobby 1986	+ Hornsby, Rogers 1942	Schoendienst, Red 1989
+ Evers, Johnny 1946	+ Lajoie, Nap 1937	
+ Frisch, Frankie 1947	+ Lazzeri, Tony 1991	

Shortstops

Aparicio, Luis 1984	+ Jackson, Travis 1982	+ Tinker, Joe 1946
+ Appling, Luke 1964	+ Jennings, Hugh 1945	+ Vaughan, Arky 1985
+ Bancroft, Dave 1971	+ Maranville, Rabbit 1954	+ Wagner, Honus 1936
Banks, Ernie 1977	Reese, Pee Wee 1984	+ Wallace, Bobby 1953
Boudreau, Lou 1970	Rizzuto, Phil 1994	+ Ward, Monte 1964
+ Cronin, Joe 1956	+ Sewell, Joe 1977	

3rd Basemen

+ Baker, Frank 1955	+ Lindstrom, Fred 1976	Schmidt, Mike 1995
+ Collins, Jimmy 1945	Mathews, Eddie 1978	+ Traynor, Pie 1948
Kell, George 1983	Robinson, Brooks 1983	

Left Fielders

Brock, Lou 1985	+ Kelley, Joe 1971	+ Simmons, Al 1953
+ Burkett, Jesse 1946	Kiner, Ralph 1975	Stargell, Willie 1988
+ Clarke, Fred 1945	+ Manush, Heinie 1964	+ Wheat, Zack 1959
+ Delahanty, Ed 1945	+ Medwick, Joe 1968	Williams, Billy 1987
+ Goslin, Goose 1968	Musial, Stan 1969	Williams, Ted 1966
+ Hafey, Chick 1971	+ O'Rourke, Jim 1945	Yastrzemski, Carl 1989

Center Fielders

Ashburn, Richie 1995	DiMaggio, Joe 1955	+ Roush, Edd 1962
+ Averill, Earl 1975	+ Duffy, Hugh 1945	Snider, Duke 1980
+ Carey, Max 1961	+ Hamilton, Billy 1961	+ Speaker, Tris 1937
+ Cobb, Ty 1936	+ Mantle, Mickey 1974	+ Waner, Lloyd 1967
+ Combs, Earle 1970	Mays, Willie 1979	+ Wilson, Hack 1979

Wide World Photos

Philadelphia Phillies' legends **Richie Ashburn** (left) and **Mike Schmidt** show off their new plaques following Baseball Hall of Fame induction ceremonies at Cooperstown, N.Y. on July 30.

Right Fielders

Aaron, Hank	1982	Jackson, Reggie	1993	+ Rice, Sam	1963
+ Clemente, Roberto	1973	Kaline, Al	1980	Robinson, Frank	1982
+ Crawford, Sam	1957	+ Keeler, Willie	1939	+ Ruth, Babe	1936
+ Cuyler, Kiki	1968	+ Kelly, King	1945	Slaughter, Enos	1985
+ Flick, Elmer	1963	+ Klein, Chuck	1980	+ Thompson, Sam	1974
+ Heilmann, Harry	1952	+ McCarthy, Tommy	1946	+ Waner, Paul	1952
+ Hooper, Harry	1971	+ Ott, Mel	1951	+ Youngs, Ross	1972

Pitchers

+ Alexander, Grover	1938	+ Haines, Jess	1970	+ Pennock, Herb	1948
+ Bender, Chief	1953	+ Hoyt, Waite	1969	Perry, Gaylord	1991
+ Brown, Mordecai	1949	+ Hubbell, Carl	1947	+ Plank, Eddie	1946
Carlton, Steve	1994	Hunter, Catfish	1987	+ Radbourne, Old Hoss	1939
+ Chesbro, Jack	1946	Jenkins, Ferguson	1991	+ Rixey, Eppa	1963
+ Clarkson, John	1963	+ Johnson, Walter	1936	Roberts, Robin	1976
+ Coveleski, Stan	1969	+ Joss, Addie	1978	+ Ruffing, Red	1967
+ Dean, Dizzy	1953	+ Keefe, Tim	1964	+ Rusie, Amos	1977
+ Drysdale, Don	1984	Koufax, Sandy	1972	Seaver, Tom	1992
+ Faber, Red	1964	Lemon, Bob	1976	Spahn, Warren	1973
Feller, Bob	1962	+ Lyons, Ted	1955	+ Vance, Dazzy	1955
Fingers, Rollie	1992	Marichal, Juan	1983	+ Waddell, Rube	1946
Ford, Whitey	1974	+ Marquard, Rube	1971	+ Walsh, Ed	1946
+ Galvin, Pud	1965	+ Mathewson, Christy	1936	+ Welch, Mickey	1973
Gibson, Bob	1981	+ McGinnity, Joe	1946	Wilhelm, Hoyt	1985
+ Gomez, Lefty	1972	Newhouser, Hal	1992	+ Willis, Vic	1995
+ Grimes, Burleigh	1964	+ Nichols, Kid	1949	Wynn, Early	1972
+ Grove, Lefty	1947	Palmer, Jim	1990	+ Young, Cy	1937

Baseball Hall of Fame (Cont.)

Managers

+ Alston, Walter.........................1983
+ Durocher, Leo.........................1994
+ Harris, Bucky 1975
+ Huggins, Miller 1964

Lopez, Al................................1977
+ Mack, Connie 1937
+ McCarthy, Joe........................1957
+ McGraw, John 1937

+ McKechnie, Bill 1962
+ Robinson, Wilbert 1945
+ Stengel, Casey 1966

Umpires

Barlick, Al...............................1989
+ Conlan, Jocko 1974
+ Connolly, Tom 1953

+ Evans, Billy 1973
+ Hubbard, Cal 1976

+ Klem, Bill 1953
+ McGowan, Bill 1992

From Negro Leagues

+ Bell, Cool Papa (OF)...............1974
+ Charleston, Oscar (1B-OF)......1976
+ Dandridge, Ray (3B)...............1987
+ Day, Leon (P-OF-2B)...............1995

+ Dihigo, Martin (P-OF)............1977
+ Foster, Rube (P-Mgr)..............1981
+ Gibson, Josh (C) 1972
Irvin, Monte (OF) 1973

+ Johnson, Judy (3B) 1975
Leonard, Buck (1B) 1972
+ Lloyd, Pop (SS).......................1977
+ Paige, Satchel (P) 1971

Pioneers and Executives

+ Barrow, Ed 1953
+ Bulkeley, Morgan 1937
+ Cartwright, Alexander............1938
+ Chadwick, Henry 1938
+ Chandler, Happy.....................1982
+ Comiskey, Charles...................1939
+ Cummings, Candy....................1939
+ Frick, Ford 1970

+ Giles, Warren 1979
+ Griffith, Clark 1946
+ Harridge, Will 1972
+ Hulbert, William 1995
+ Johnson, Ban 1937
+ Landis, Kenesaw 1944
+ MacPhail, Larry.......................1978
+ Rickey, Branch 1967

+ Spalding, Al 1939
+ Veeck, Bill 1991
+ Weiss, George........................1971
+ Wright, George 1937
+ Wright, Harry 1953
+ Yawkey, Tom 1980

Ford Frick Award

First presented in 1978 by Hall of Fame for meritorious contributions by baseball broadcasters. Named in honor of the late newspaper reporter, broadcaster, National League president and commissioner, the Frick Award does not constitute induction into the Hall of Fame.

Year		Year		Year	
1978	Mel Allen & Red Barber	1984	Curt Gowdy	1990	Byrum Saam
1979	Bob Elson	1985	Buck Canel	1991	Joe Garagiola
1980	Russ Hodges	1986	Bob Prince	1992	Milo Hamilton
1981	Ernie Harwell	1987	Jack Buck	1993	Chuck Thompson
1982	Vin Scully	1988	Lindsey Nelson	1994	Bob Murphy
1983	Jack Brickhouse	1989	Harry Caray	1995	Bob Wolff

J.G. Taylor Spink Award

First presented in 1962 by the Baseball Writers' Association of America for meritorious contributions by members of the BBWAA. Named in honor of the late publisher of *The Sporting News*, the Spink Award does not constitute induction into the Hall of Fame. Winners are honored in the year following their selection.

Year		Year		Year	
1962	J.G. Taylor Spink	1974	John Carmichael	1985	Earl Lawson
1963	Ring Lardner		& James Isaminger	1986	Jack Lang
1964	Hugh Fullerton	1975	Tom Meany & Shirley Povich	1987	Jim Murray
1965	Charley Dryden	1976	Harold Kaese & Red Smith	1988	Bob Hunter & Ray Kelly
1966	Grantland Rice	1977	Gordon Cobbledick	1989	Jerome Holtzman
1967	Damon Runyon		& Edgar Munzel	1990	Phil Collier
1968	H.G. Salsinger	1978	Tim Murnane & Dick Young	1991	Ritter Collett
1969	Sid Mercer	1979	Bob Broeg & Tommy Holmes	1992	Leonard Koppett
1970	Heywood C. Broun	1980	Joe Reichler & Milt Richman		& Buzz Saidt
1971	Frank Graham	1981	Bob Addie & Allen Lewis	1993	John Wendell Smith
1972	Dan Daniel, Fred Lieb	1982	Si Burick	1994	No award
	& J. Roy Stockton	1983	Ken Smith		
1973	Warren Brown, John Drebinger	1984	Joe McGuff		
	& John F. Kieran				

Major League Baseball's 100th Anniversary All-Time Team

Selected by the Baseball Writers Assn. of America and released July 21, 1969. All-Time team members in **bold** type; vote totals not released.

C **Mickey Cockrane**, Bill Dickey, Roy Campanella
1B **Lou Gehrig**, George Sisler, Stan Musial,
2B **Rogers Hornsby**, Charley Gehringer, Eddie Collins
SS **Honus Wagner**, Joe Cronin, Ernie Banks
3B **Pie Traynor**, Brooks Robinson, Jackie Robinson

OF **Babe Ruth**, **Ty Cobb**, **Joe DiMaggio**,
      Ted Williams, Tris Speaker, Willie Mays
RHP **Walter Johnson**, Christy Mathewson, Cy Young
LHP **Lefty Grove**, Sandy Koufax, Carl Hubbell
Mgr. **John McGraw**, Casey Stengel, Joe McCarthy

All-Time Outstanding Player: **Ruth**, Cobb, Wagner, DiMaggio

BASKETBALL

Naismith Memorial Basketball Hall of Fame

Established in 1949 by the National Association of Basketball Coaches in memory of the sport's inventor, Dr. James Naismith. Original Hall opened in 1968 and current Hall in 1985. **Address:** 1150 West Columbus Avenue, Springfield, MA 01105. **Telephone:** (413) 781-6500.

Eligibility: Nominated players and referees must be retired for five years, coaches must have coached 25 years or be retired for five, and contributors must have already completed their noteworthy service to the game. Voting done by 24-member honors committee made up of media representatives, Hall of Fame members and trustees. Any nominee not elected after five years becomes eligible for consideration by the Veterans' Committee after a five-year wait.

Class of 1995 (7): PLAYERS— center **Kareem Abdul-Jabbar** (born Lew Alcindor), college (UCLA, 1965-69), NBA (Milwaukee, 1969-75; LA Lakers, 1975-89); forward/center **Vern Mikkelsen**, college (Hamline, 1945-49), NBA (Minneapolis, 1949-59). COACHES— **Aleksandr Gomelsky**, Soviet national men's team (1960-88); **John Kundla**, NBA (Minneapolis, 1947-59). REFEREE— **Earl Strom**, NBA (1957-69, 1972-90), ABA (1969-72). WOMEN— center/forward **Cheryl Miller**, USC (1982-86), U.S. Olympic team (1984); center **Anne Donovan**, Old Dominion (1979-83), U.S. Olympic team (1984 and '88).

1995 finalists (nominated but not elected): PLAYERS— Arnie Risen and Tom (Satch) Sanders. FOREIGN PLAYER— Kresimir Cosic. COACH— Gene Shue.

Note: John Wooden is the only member to be honored as both a player and a coach.

Members are listed with years of induction; (+) indicates deceased members.

Men

Abdul-Jabbar, Kareem 1995	Gola, Tom 1975	Mikan, George 1959
Archibald, Nate 1991	Greer, Hal 1981	Mikkelsen, Vern....................1995
Arizin, Paul 1977	+ Gruenig, Robert 1963	Monroe, Earl 1990
+ Barlow, Thomas (Babe)...........1980	Hagan, Cliff...........................1977	Murphy, Calvin 1993
Barry, Rick 1987	+ Hanson, Victor.......................1960	+ Murphy, Charles (Stretch).......1960
Baylor, Elgin 1976	Havlicek, John 1983	+ Page, Harlan (Pat) 1962
+ Beckman, John......................1972	Hawkins, Connie 1992	Pettit, Bob 1970
Bellamy, Walt........................1993	Hayes, Elvin 1990	Phillip, Andy 1961
Belov, Sergei.........................1992	Heinsohn, Tom 1986	+ Pollard, Jim..........................1977
Bing, Dave............................1990	Holman, Nat...........................1964	Ramsey, Frank 1981
+ Borgmann, Benny 1961	Houbregs, Bob 1987	Reed, Willis 1981
Bradley, Bill..........................1982	+ Hyatt, Chuck 1959	Robertson, Oscar 1979
+ Brennan, Joe........................1974	Issel, Dan 1993	+ Roosma, John 1961
Cervi, Al...............................1984	Jeannette, Buddy 1994	Russell, Bill 1974
Chamberlain, Wilt...................1978	+ Johnson, Bill (Skinny) 1976	+ Russell, John (Honey).............1964
+ Cooper, Charles (Tarzan) 1976	Johnston, Neil 1990	Schayes, Dolph 1972
Cousy, Bob 1970	Jones, K C 1989	+ Schmidt, Ernest J 1973
Cowens, Dave........................1991	Jones, Sam 1983	+ Schommer, John 1959
Cunningham, Billy 1986	+ Krause, Edward (Moose) 1975	+ Sedran, Barney 1962
Davies, Bob 1969	Kurland, Bob 1961	Sharman, Bill 1975
+ DeBernardi, Forrest 1961	Lanier, Bob 1992	+ Steinmetz, Christian...............1961
DeBusschere, Dave 1982	+ Lapchick, Joe 1966	+ Thompson, John (Cat) 1962
Dehnert, Dutch 1968	Lovellette, Clyde 1988	Thurmond, Nate.....................1984
Endacott, Paul 1971	Lucas, Jerry 1979	Twyman, Jack 1982
Erving, Julius (Dr. J) 1993	Luisetti, Hank 1959	Unseld, Wes 1988
Foster, Bud...........................1964	Macauley, Ed 1960	+ Vandivier, Robert (Fuzzy) 1974
Frazier, Walt.........................1987	+ Maravich, Pete 1987	+ Wachter, Ed 1961
+ Friedman, Marty 1971	Martin, Slater 1981	Walton, Bill 1993
+ Fulks, Joe............................1977	+ McCracken, Branch 1960	Wanzer, Bobby 1987
Gale, Laddie..........................1976	+ McCracken, Jack 1962	West, Jerry 1979
Gallatin, Harry 1991	McDermott, Bobby 1988	Wilkens, Lenny 1989
Gates, William (Pop) 1989	McGuire, Dick 1993	Wooden, John 1960

Coaches

+ Anderson, Harold (Andy).........1984	Gomelsky, Aleksandr...............1995	McGuire, Frank......................1976
Auerbach, Red 1968	Harshman, Marv.....................1984	+ Meanwell, Walter (Doc)..........1959
+ Barry, Sam 1978	+ Hickey, Eddie 1978	Meyer, Ray 1978
+ Blood, Ernest (Prof) 1960	+ Hobson, Howard (Hobby).........1965	Miller, Ralph 1988
+ Cann, Howard.......................1967	Holzman, Red 1986	Ramsay, Jack 1992
+ Carlson, Henry (Doc) 1959	+ Iba, Hank 1968	Rubini, Cesare 1994
Carnesecca, Lou 1992	+ Julian, Alvin (Doggie) 1967	+ Rupp, Adolph 1968
Carnevale, Ben 1969	+ Keaney, Frank 1960	+ Sachs, Leonard 1961
+ Case, Everett.........................1981	+ Keogan, George 1961	Shelton, Everett 1979
Crum, Denny 1994	Knight, Bob............................1991	Smith, Dean 1982
Daly, Chuck 1994	Kundla, John 1995	Taylor, Fred 1985
Dean, Everett 1966	+ Lambert, Ward (Piggy) 1960	+ Wade, Margaret 1984
+ Diddle, Ed 1971	Litwack, Harry 1975	Watts, Stan 1985
+ Drake, Bruce 1972	+ Leoffler, Ken 1964	Wooden, John 1972
Gaines, Clarence (Bighouse) ...1981	+ Lonborg, Dutch 1972	+ Woolpert, Phil 1992
Gardner, Jack 1983	+ McCutchan, Arad 1980	
+ Gill, Amory (Slats) 1967	McGuire, Al...........................1992	

Basketball Hall of Fame (Cont.)

Women

Blazejowski, Carol	1994	Meyers, Ann	1993	Semenova, Juliana	1993
Donovan, Anne	1995	Miller, Cheryl	1995	White, Nera	1992
Harris, Lucy	1992				

Teams

Buffalo Germans	1961	New York Renaissance	1963	Original Celtics	1959
First Team	1959				

Referees

+ Enright, Jim	1978	+ Leith, Lloyd	1982	+ Shirley, J. Dallas	1979
+ Hepbron, George	1960	Mihalik, Red	1986	+ Strom, Earl	1995
+ Hoyt, George	1961	Nucatola, John	1977	Tobey, Dave	1961
+ Kennedy, Pat	1959	+ Quigley, Ernest (Quig)	1961	+ Walsh, David	1961

Contributors

+ Abbott, Senda Berenson	1984	+ Hinkle, Tony	1965	+ Porter, Henry (H.V.)	1960
+ Allen, Forrest (Phog)	1959	+ Irish, Ned	1964	+ Reid, William A	1963
+ Bee, Clair	1967	+ Jones, R. William	1964	+ Ripley, Elmer	1972
+ Brown, Walter A	1965	+ Kennedy, Walter	1980	+ St. John, Lynn W	1962
+ Bunn, John	1964	+ Liston, Emil (Liz)	1974	+ Saperstein, Abe	1970
+ Douglas, Bob	1971	McLendon, John	1978	+ Schabinger, Arthur	1961
+ Duer, Al	1981	+ Mokray, Bill	1965	+ Stagg, Amos Alonzo	1959
Fagen, Clifford B	1983	+ Morgan, Ralph	1959	Stankovic, Boris	1991
+ Fisher, Harry	1973	+ Morgenweck, Frank (Pop)	1962	+ Steitz, Ed	1983
+ Fleisher, Larry	1991	+ Naismith, James	1959	+ Taylor, Chuck	1968
+ Gottlieb, Eddie	1971	Newell, Pete	1978	+ Teague, Bertha	1984
+ Gulick, Luther	1959	+ O'Brien, John J. (Jack)	1961	+ Tower, Oswald	1959
Harrison, Les	1979	+ O'Brien, Larry	1991	+ Trester, Ather (A.L.)	1961
+ Hepp, Ferenc	1980	+ Olsen, Harold G	1959	+ Wells, Cliff	1971
+ Hickox, Ed	1959	+ Podoloff, Maurice	1973	+ Wilke, Lou	1982

Curt Gowdy Award

First presented in 1990 by the Hall of Fame Board of Trustees for meritorious contributions by the media. Named in honor of the former NBC sportscaster, the Gowdy Award does not constitute induction into the Hall of Fame.

Year		Year		Year	
1990	Curt Gowdy & Dick Herbert	1993	Leonard Lewin & Johnny Most	1995	Dick Enberg & Bob Hammel
1991	Dave Dorr & Marty Glickman	1994	Leonard Koppett		
1992	Sam Goldaper & Chick Hearn		& Cawood Ledford		

BOWLING

National Bowling Hall of Fame & Museum

The National Bowling Hall is one museum with separate wings for honorees of the American Bowling Congress (ABC), Professional Bowlers' Association (PBA) and Women's International Bowling Congress (WIBC). The museum does not include the new Ladies Pro Bowlers Tour Hall of Fame, which is located in Las Vegas (see page 467). **Address:** 111 Stadium Plaza, St. Louis, MO 63102. **Telephone:** (314) 231-6340.

Professional Bowlers Association

Established in 1975. **Eligibility:** Nominees must be PBA members and at least 35 years old. Voting done by 50-member panel that includes writers who have covered bowling for at least 12 years.

    Class of 1995 (3): PERFORMANCE— **David Ozio** and **Walter Ray Williams Jr.** MERITORIOUS SERVICE— **Roger Zeller**.

    Members are listed with years of induction; (+) indicates deceased members.

Performance

+ Allen, Bill	1983	+ Fazio, Buzz	1976	Salvino, Carmen	1975
Anthony, Earl	1986	Godman, Jim	1987	Smith, Harry	1975
Berardi, Joe	1990	Hardwick, Billy	1977	Soutar, Dave	1979
Bluth, Ray	1975	Holman, Marshall	1990	Stefanich, Jim	1980
Buckley, Roy	1992	Hudson, Tommy	1989	Voss, Brian	1994
Burton, Nelson Jr	1979	Johnson, Don	1977	Webb, Wayne	1993
Carter, Don	1975	Laub, Larry	1985	Weber, Dick	1975
Colwell, Paul	1991	Ozio, David	1995	+ Welu, Billy	1975
Cook, Steve	1993	Pappas, George	1986	Williams, Walter Ray Jr.	1995
Davis, Dave	1978	Petraglia, John	1982	Zahn, Wayne	1981
Dickinson, Gary	1988	Ritger, Dick	1978		
Durbin, Mike	1984	Roth, Mark	1987		

Veterans

Allison, Glenn	1984	+ Joseph, Joe 1985	McGrath, Mike 1988
Asher, Barry	1988	Limongello, Mike.....1994	+ St. John, Jim 1989
Foremsky, Skee	1992	Marzich, Andy........1990	Strampe, Bob..........1987
Guenther, Johnny	1986	McCune, Don 1991	

Meritorious Service

Antenora, Joe	1993	Fisher, E.A. (Bud) 1984	Pezzano, Chuck 1975
Archibald, John	1989	+ Frantz, Lou 1978	Reichert, Jack..........1992
Clemens, Chuck	1994	Golden, Harry 1983	+ Richards, Joe 1976
Elias, Eddie	1976	Hoffman, Ted Jr.......1985	Schenkel, Chris 1976
Esposito, Frank	1975	Jowdy, John 1988	Stitzlein, Lorraine 1980
Evans, Dick	1986	Kelley, Joe 1989	Thompson, Al 1991
Firestone, Raymond	1987	+ Nagy, Steve 1977	Zeller, Roger 1995

American Bowling Congress

Established in 1941 and open to professional and amateur bowlers. **Eligibility:** Nominated bowlers must have competed in at least 20 years of ABC tournaments. Voting done by 170-member panel made up of ABC officials, Hall of Fame members and media representatives.

Class of 1995 (5): PERFORMANCE— **Greg Griffo** and **Tommy Tuttle**. PIONEERS— **Rev. Charles Carow** and **Hiroto Hirashima**. MERITORIOUS SERVICE— **Al Matzelle**.

Members are listed with years of induction; (+) indicates deceased members.

Performance

Allison, Glenn	1979	Golembiewski, Billy	1979	O'Donnell, Chuck	1968
Anthony, Earl	1986	Griffo, Greg	1995	Pappas, George	1989
+ Asplund, Harold	1978	Guenther, Johnny	1988	+ Patterson, Pat	1974
Baer, Gordy	1987	Hardwick, Billy	1985	Ritger, Dick	1984
Beach, Bill	1991	Hart, Bob	1994	+ Rogoznica, Andy	1993
Benkovic, Frank	1958	Hennessey, Tom	1976	Salvino, Carmen	1979
Berlin, Mike	1994	Hoover, Dick	1974	Schissler, Les	1991
+ Billick, George	1982	Horn, Bud	1992	Schroeder, Jim	1990
+ Blouin, Jimmy	1953	Howard, George	1986	+ Schwoegler, Connie	1968
Bluth, Ray	1973	Jackson, Eddie	1988	Semiz, Teata	1991
+ Bodis, Joe	1941	Johnson, Don	1982	+ Sielaff, Lou	1968
+ Bomar, Buddy	1966	Johnson, Earl	1987	+ Sinke, Joe	1977
+ Brandt, Allie	1960	+ Joseph, Joe	1969	+ Sixty, Billy	1961
+ Brosius, Eddie	1976	+ Jouglard, Lee	1979	Smith, Harry	1978
+ Bujack, Fred	1967	+ Kartheiser, Frank	1967	+ Smith, Jimmy	1941
Bunetta, Bill	1968	+ Kawolics, Ed	1968	Soutar, Dave	1985
Burton, Nelson Jr	1981	+ Kissoff, Joe	1976	+ Sparando, Tony	1968
+ Burton, Nelson Sr	1964	Klares, John	1982	+ Spinella, Barney	1968
+ Campi, Lou	1968	+ Knox, Billy	1954	Steers, Harry	1941
+ Carlson, Adolph	1941	+ Koster, John	1941	Stefanich, Jim	1983
Carter, Don	1970	+ Krems, Eddie	1973	+ Stein, Otto Jr	1971
+ Caruana, Frank	1977	Kristof, Joe	1968	Stoudt, Bud	1991
+ Cassio, Marty	1972	+ Krumske, Paul	1968	Strampe, Bob	1977
+ Castellano, Graz	1976	+ Lange, Herb	1941	+ Thoma, Sykes	1971
+ Clause, Frank	1980	+ Lauman, Hank	1976	Toft, Rod	1991
Cohn, Alfred	1985	Lillard, Bill	1972	Tountas, Pete	1989
+ Crimmins, Johnny	1962	Lindemann, Tony	1979	Tucker, Bill	1988
Davis, Dave	1990	+ Lindsey, Mort	1941	Tuttle, Tommy	1995
+ Daw, Charlie	1941	Lippe, Harry	1989	+ Varipapa, Andy	1957
+ Day, Ned	1952	Lubanski, Ed	1971	+ Ward, Walter	1959
Dickinson, Gary	1992	Lucci, Vince Sr	1978	Weber, Dick	1970
+ Easter, Sarge	1963	+ Marino, Hank	1941	+ Welu, Billy	1975
Ellis, Don	1981	+ Martino, John	1969	+ Wilman, Joe	1951
+ Falcaro, Joe	1968	Marzich, Andy	1993	+ Wolf, Phil	1961
Faragalli, Lindy	1968	McGrath, Mike	1993	Wonders, Rich	1990
+ Fazio, Buzz	1963	+ McMahon, Junie	1967	+ Young, George	1959
Fehr, Steve	1993	+ Mercurio, Skang	1967	Zahn, Wayne	1980
+ Gersonde, Russ	1968	+ Meyers, Norm	1984	Zikes, Les	1983
+ Gibson, Therm	1965	+ Nagy, Steve	1963	+ Zunker, Gil	1941
Godman, Jim	1987	Norris, Joe	1954	

Pioneers

+ Allen, Lafayette Jr.	1994	Hall, William Sr.	1994	+ Schutte, Louis	1993
+ Carow, Rev. Charles	1995	Hirashima, Hirohito	1995	+ Thompson, William V.	1993
+ Celestine, Sydney	1993	+ Karpf, Samuel	1993	+ Timm, Dr. Henry	1993
+ Curtis, Thomas	1993	+ Pasdeloup, Frank	1993	
de Freitas, Eric	1994	+ Satow, Masao	1994	

American Bowling Congress (Cont.)

Meritorious Service

+ Allen, Harold 1966
Baker, Frank 1975
+ Baumgarten, Elmer................1963
+ Bellisimo, Lou 1986
+ Bensinger, Bob 1969
+ Chase, LeRoy 1972
+ Coker, John 1980
+ Collier, Chuck 1963
+ Cruchon, Steve....................1983
+ Ditzen, Walt 1973
+ Doehrman, Bill 1968
Elias, Eddie........................1985
Evans, Dick 1992
Franklin, Bill........................1992
+ Hagerty, Jack......................1963

+ Hattstrom, H.A. (Doc) 1980
+ Hermann, Cone 1968
+ Howley, Pete 1941
+ Kennedy, Bob 1981
+ Langtry, Abe 1963
+ Levine, Sam 1971
+ Luby, David 1969
Luby, Mort Jr....................1988
+ Luby, Mort Sr....................1974
Matzelle, Al 1995
+ McCullough, Howard 1971
+ Patterson, Morehead 1985
+ Petersen, Louie 1963

Pezzano, Chuck 1982
Picchietti, Remo 1993
Pluckhahn, Bruce..................1989
+ Raymer, Milt 1972
+ Reed, Elmer 1978
Rudo, Milt..........................1984
Schenkel, Chris 1988
+ Sweeney, Dennis 1974
Tessman, Roger 1994
+ Thum, Joe..........................1980
Weinstein, Sam 1970
+ Whitney, Eli 1975
Wolf, Fred 1976

Women's International Bowling Congress

Established in 1953. **Eligibility:** Performance nominees must have won at least one WIBC Championship Tournament title, a WIBC Queens tournament title or an international competition title and have bowled in at least 15 national WIBC Championship Tournaments (unless injury or illness cut career short).
    Class of 1995 (2): PERFORMANCE— **Patty Ann** and **Robin Romeo**.
    Members are listed with years of induction; (+) indicates deceased members.

Performance

Abel, Joy................................1984
Ann, Patty 1995
Bolt, Mae 1978
Bouvia, Gloria 1987
Boxberger, Loa....................1984
Buckner, Pam 1990
Burling, Catherine 1958
+ Burns, Nina 1977
Cantaline, Anita 1979
Carter, LaVerne 1977
Carter, Paula 1994
Coburn, Doris 1976
Costello, Pat 1986
Costello, Patty 1989
Dryer, Pat 1978
Duval, Helen 1970
Fellmeth, Catherine..............1970
Fothergill, Dotty 1980
+ Fritz, Deane 1966
Garms, Shirley 1971
Gloor, Olga 1976
Graham, Linda 1992
Graham, Mary Lou 1989
+ Greenwald, Goldie 1953
Grinfelds, Vesma..................1991

+ Harman, Janet 1985
+ Hartrick, Stella 1972
+ Hatch, Grayce 1953
Havlish, Jean 1987
+ Hoffman, Martha 1979
Holm, Joan 1974
+ Humphreys, Birdie 1979
Ignizio, Mildred 1975
Jacobson, D.D 1981
+ Jaeger, Emma 1953
Kelly, Annese 1985
+ Knechtges, Doris 1983
Kuczynski, Betty 1981
Ladewig, Marion 1964
Martin, Sylvia Wene 1966
Martorella, Millie 1975
+ Matthews, Merle 1974
+ McCutcheon, Floretta 1956
Merrick, Marge 1980
+ Mikiel, Val 1979
+ Miller, Dorothy 1954
Mivelaz, Betty 1991
Mohacsi, Mary 1994
Morris, Betty 1983
Nichols, Lorrie 1989

Norman, Edie Jo 1993
Norton, Virginia 1988
Notaro, Phyllis 1979
Ortner, Bev 1972
+ Powers, Connie 1973
Rickard, Robbie 1994
+ Robinson, Leona 1969
Romeo, Robin 1995
+ Rump, Anita 1962
+ Ruschmeyer, Addie 1961
+ Ryan, Esther 1963
+ Sablatnik, Ethel 1979
+ Schulte, Myrtle 1965
+ Shablis, Helen 1977
+ Simon, Violet (Billy) 1960
+ Small, Tess 1971
+ Smith, Grace 1968
Soutar, Judy 1976
+ Stockdale, Louise................1953
Toepfer, Elvira 1976
+ Twyford, Sally 1964
+ Warmbier, Marie 1953
Wilkinson, Dorothy 1990
+ Winandy, Cecelia 1975
Zimmerman, Donna 1982

Meritorious Service

Baetz, Helen 1977
+ Baker, Helen 1989
+ Banker, Gladys 1994
+ Bayley, Clover 1992
+ Berger, Winifred 1976
+ Bohlen, Philena 1955
Borschuk, Lo 1988
Botkin, Freda 1986
+ Chapman, Emily 1957
+ Crowe, Alberta 1982
+ Dornblaser, Gertrude..............1979
Duffy, Agnes 1987
Finke, Gertrude 1990
+ Fisk, Rae 1983

+ Haas, Dorothy 1977
+ Higley, Margaret 1969
+ Hochstadter, Bee 1967
+ Kay, Nora 1964
+ Kelly, Ellen 1979
Kelone, Theresa 1978
+ Knepprath, Jeannette..........1963
+ Lasher, Iolia 1967
Marrs, Mabel 1979
+ McBride, Bertha 1968
+ Menne, Catherine 1979
+ Mraz, Jo 1959
O'Connor, Billie 1992
+ Phaler, Emma....................1965

+ Porter, Cora 1986
+ Quin, Zoe 1979
+ Rishling, Gertrude 1972
Simone, Anne 1991
Sloan, Catherine 1985
+ Speck, Berdie 1966
Spitalnick, Mildred 1994
+ Spring, Alma 1979
+ Switzer, Pearl 1973
Todd, Trudy 1993
+ Veatch, Georgia 1974
+ White, Mildred 1975
+ Wood, Ann 1970

Ladies Pro Bowlers Tour

Established in 1995 by the Ladies Pro Bowlers Tour. **Address:** Sam's Town Hotel, Gambling Hall and Bowling Center, 5111 Boulder Highway, Las Vegas, NV 89122. **Telephone:** (815) 332-5756.

Eligibility: Nominees in performance category must have at least five titles from organizations including All-Star, World Invitational, LPBT, WPBA, PWBA, TPA and LPBA. Voting done by 10-member committee of bowling writers appointed by LPBT president John Falzone.

Class of 1995: 10 members in inaugural class (see below).

Members are listed with year of induction; (+) indicates deceased member.

Performance

Adamek, Donna	1995	Fothergill, Dotty	1995	Martorella, Millie	1995
Costello, Patty	1995	Ladewig, Marion	1995	Morris, Betty	1995

Pioneers

Carter, LaVerne	1995	Duval, Helen	1995	Garms, Shirley	1995

Builder

+Veatch, Georgia 1995

BOXING

International Boxing Hall of Fame

Established in 1989 and opened in 1990. **Address:** 1 Hall of Fame Drive, Canastota, NY 13032. **Telephone:** (315) 697-7095.

Eligibility: All nominees must be retired for five years. Voting done by 142-member panel made up of Boxing Writers' Association members and world-wide boxing historians.

Class of 1995 (15): MODERN ERA— **Wilfredo Gomez** (super bantamweight, featherweight & jr. lightweight); **Masahiko (Fighting) Harada** (flyweight, bantamweight & featherweight); **Bob Montgomery** (lightweight); **Pasqual Perez** (flyweight). OLD-TIMERS— **Max Baer** (heavyweight); **Jack Dillon** (middleweight & light heavyweight); **Johnny Kilbane** (featherweight); **Jack McAuliffe** (lightweight). PIONEERS— **Tom Johnson** (heavyweight); **Jem Ward** (heavyweight). NON-PARTICIPANTS— **Cus D'Amato** (trainer and manager); **Arthur Mercante** (referee); **Gilbert Odd** (historian and editor); **George Siler** (referee); **Jack Solomons** (British promoter).

Members are listed with year of induction; (+) indicates deceased member.

Modern Era

Ali, Muhammad	1990	+ Graham, Billy	1992	Norton, Ken	1992
Arguello, Alexis	1992	+ Graziano, Rocky	1991	Olivares, Ruben	1991
+ Armstrong, Henry	1990	Griffith, Emile	1990	Ortiz, Carlos	1991
Basilio, Carmen	1990	Hagler, Marvelous Marvin	1993	Patterson, Floyd	1991
Benvenuti, Nino	1992	Harado, Masahiko (Fighting)	1995	Pep, Willie	1990
+ Berg, Jackie (Kid)	1994	Jack, Beau	1991	+ Perez, Pasqual	1995
+ Burley, Charley	1992	Jofre, Eder	1992	+ Robinson, Sugar Ray	1990
+ Cerdan, Marcel	1991	Johnson, Harold	1993	Saddler, Sandy	1990
+ Charles, Ezzard	1990	LaMotta, Jake	1990	+ Sanchez, Salvadore	1991
+ Conn, Billy	1990	+ Liston, Sonny	1991	Schmeling, Max	1992
+ Elorde, Gabriel (Flash)	1993	+ Louis, Joe	1990	Spinks, Michael	1994
Foster, Bob	1990	+ Marciano, Rocky	1990	+ Tiger, Dick	1991
Frazier, Joe	1990	Maxim, Joey	1994	+ Walcott, Jersey Joe	1990
Fullmer, Gene	1991	Montgomery, Bob	1995	+ Williams, Ike	1990
Gavilan, Kid	1990	+ Monzon, Carlos	1990	Zale, Tony	1991
Giardello, Joey	1993	Moore, Archie	1990	Zarate, Carlos	1994
Gomez, Wilfredo	1995	Napoles, Jose	1990	+ Zivic, Fritzie	1993

Old-Timers

Ambers, Lou	1992	+ Flowers, Theodore (Tiger)	1993	+ McCoy, Charles (Kid)	1991
+ Attell, Abe	1990	+ Gans, Joe	1990	+ McFarland, Packey	1992
+ Baer, Max	1995	+ Gibbons, Mike	1992	+ McGovern, Terry	1990
+ Britton, Jack	1990	+ Gibbons, Tommy	1993	McLarnin, Jimmy	1991
+ Brown, Panama Al	1992	+ Greb, Harry	1990	+ Nelson, Battling	1992
+ Canzoneri, Tony	1990	+ Griffo, Young	1991	+ O'Brien, Philadelphia Jack	1994
+ Carpentier, Georges	1991	+ Jackson, Peter	1990	+ Rosenbloom, Maxie	1993
+ Chocolate, Kid	1991	+ Jeffries, James J	1990	+ Ross, Barney	1990
+ Corbett, James J.	1990	+ Johnson, Jack	1990	+ Ryan, Tommy	1991
+ Darcy, Les	1993	+ Ketchel, Stanley	1990	+ Sharkey, Jack	1994
+ Dempsey, Jack	1990	+ Kilbane, Johnny	1995	+ Tunney, Gene	1990
+ Dempsey, Jack (Nonpareil)	1992	+ Langford, Sam	1990	+ Villa, Pancho	1994
+ Dillon, Jack	1995	+ Leonard, Benny	1990	+ Walcott, Joe	1991
+ Dixon, George	1990	+ Lewis, John Henry	1994	+ Walker, Mickey	1990
+ Driscoll, Jem	1990	+ Lewis, Ted (Kid)	1992	+ Wilde, Jimmy	1990
+ Dundee, Johnny	1991	+ Loughran, Tommy	1991	+ Wills, Harry	1992
+ Fitzsimmons, Bob	1990	+ McAuliffe, Jack	1995	

Boxing Hall of Fame (Cont.)

Pioneers

+ Belcher, Jem 1992
+ Brain, Ben 1994
+ Broughton, Jack 1990
+ Burke, James (Deaf)..................1992
+ Cribb, Tom...............................1991
+ Duffy, Paddy 1994
+ Figg, James 1992

+ Jackson, Gentleman John........1992
+ Johnson, Tom 1995
+ King, Tom 1992
+ Langham, Nat...........................1992
+ Mace, Jem 1990
+ Mendoza, Daniel 1990
+ Pearce, Henry 1993

+ Sayers, Tom 1990
  Spring, Tom 1992
+ Sullivan, John L 1990
+ Thompson, William 1991
+ Ward, Jem 1995

Non-Participants

+ Andrews, Thomas S...............1992
+ Arcel, Ray 1991
+ Blackburn, Jack........................1992
  Brenner, Teddy 1993
+ Chambers, John Graham.......1990
  Clancy, Gil 1993
+ Coffroth, James W..................1991
+ D'Amato, Cus...........................1995
+ Donovan, Arthur 1993
  Dundee, Angelo......................1992
  Dundee, Chris..........................1994

Dunphy, Don 1993
+ Egan, Pierce 1991
+ Fleischer, Nat...........................1990
  Futch, Eddie.............................1994
+ Goldman, Charley 1992
+ Goldstein, Ruby 1994
+ Jacobs, Jimmy..........................1993
+ Jacobs, Mike............................1990
+ Kearns, Jack (Doc) 1990
+ Liebling, A.J.............................1992
+ Lonsdale, Lord..........................1990

Markson, Harry 1992
  Mercante, Arthur....................1995
  Odd, Gilbert 1995
+ Parnassus, George 1991
+ Queensberry, Marquis of........1990
+ Rickard, Tex.............................1990
+ Siler, George 1995
+ Solomons, Jack 1995
+ Taub, Sam 1994
+ Walker, James J. (Jimmy) 1992

Old *Ring* Hall Members Not in Int'l. Boxing Hall

Nat Fleischer, the late founder and editor-in-chief of *The Ring*, established his magazine's Boxing Hall of Fame in 1954, but it was abandoned after the 1987 inductions. One hundred members of the old *Ring* Hall have been elected to the International Hall since 1989. The 65 boxers and one sportswriter who have yet to be elected to the International Hall are listed below with their year of induction into the *Ring* Hall.

Modern Group

+ Apostoli, Fred 1978
+ Braddock, James J..................1964
+ Escobar, Sixto 1975
+ Garcia, Ceferino 1977

+ Jenkins, Lew............................1976
+ Lesnevich, Gus 1973
+ Petrolle, Billy 1962
+ Shirai, Yoshio...........................1977

+ Tendler, Lew 1961
+ Wright, Chalky 1976

Old-Timers

+ Berlenbach, Paul 1971
+ Britt, Jimmy 1976
+ Burns, Tommy 1960
+ Chaney, George (K.O.)...........1974
+ Choynski, Joe 1959
+ Corbett, Young II 1965
+ Coulon, Johnny 1965
+ Delaney, Jack...........................1973
+ Fields, Jackie 1977
+ Genaro, Frankie.......................1973
+ Herman, Pete 1959
+ Houck, Leo 1969

+ Jeannette, Joe 1967
+ Jeffra, Harry 1982
+ Kid, The Dixie 1975
+ Klaus, Frank.............................1974
+ LaBarba, Fidel 1972
+ Lavigne, George (Kid) 1959
+ Levinsky, Battling 1966
+ Lynch, Benny...........................1986
+ Maher, Peter 1978
+ McVey, Sam.............................1986
+ Mitchell, Charley 1957
+ Ortiz, Manuel 1985

+ Papke, Billy..............................1972
+ Ritchie, Willie...........................1962
+ Root, Jack 1961
+ Sharkey, Tom 1959
+ Smith, Jeff...............................1969
+ Stribling, Young 1985
+ Taylor, Bud..............................1986
+ Welsh, Freddie.........................1960
+ Willard, Jess............................1977
+ Williams, Kid............................1970
+ Wolgast, Ad 1958

Pioneers

+ Aaron, Barney (Young) 1967
+ Chambers, Arthur 1954
+ Chandler, Tom..........................1972
+ Clark, Nobby 1971
+ Collyer, Sam 1964
+ Donnelly, Dan 1960
+ Donovan, Prof. Mike................1970

+ Goss, Joe.................................1969
+ Gully, John 1959
+ Heenan, John C 1954
+ Hyer, Jacob 1968
+ Hyer, Tom 1954
+ Jackling, Thomas....................1985
+ Kilrain, Jack.............................1965

+ Molineaux, Tom 1958
+ Morrissey, John 1954
+ Price, Ned 1962
+ Richmond, Bill 1956
+ Ryan, Paddy 1973
+ Sam, Young Dutch 1975

Non-Participant

+ Daniel, Dan (sportswriter) 1977

FOOTBALL

College Football Hall of Fame

Established in 1955 by the National Football Foundation. **Address:** P.O. Box 11146, South Bend, IN 46634 (officially opened new building at 111 South St. Joseph Street in South Bend on Aug. 25, 1995). **Telephone:** (219) 235-9999.

Eligibility: Nominated players must be out of college 10 years and a first team All-America pick by a major selector during their careers; coaches must be retired three years. Voting done by 12-member panel of athletic directors, conference and bowl officials and media representatives.

Class of 1995 (13): PLAYERS— HB **Jim Brown**, Syracuse (1954-56); End **Chris Burford**, Stanford (1957-59); DB **Tommy Casanova** LSU (1969-71); QB **Jake Gibbs** Mississippi (1958-60); OT **Rich Glover**, Nebraska (1970-72); FB **Jim Grabowski**, Illinois (1963-65); End **Jim Martin**, Notre Dame (1946-47, 48-49); LB **Dennis Onkotz**, Penn St. (1967-69); LB **Rick Redman**, Washington (1962-64); End **Paul Robeson**, Rutgers (1915-1918); RB **Billy Sims**, Oklahoma (1975-79); LB **Mike Singletary**, Baylor (1977-80). COACH— **Frank Kush**, Arizona St. (1958-79).

Note: Bobby Dodd and **Amos Alonzo Stagg** are the only members to be honored as both players and coaches.

Players are listed with final year they played in college and coaches are listed with year of induction; (+) indicates deceased members.

Players

+ Abell, Earl-Colgate................1915
Agase, Alex-Purdue/Ill...........1946
+ Agganis, Harry-Boston U........1952
Albert, Frank-Stanford............1941
+ Aldrich, Ki-TCU....................1938
+ Aldrich, Malcolm-Yale............1921
+ Alexander, Joe-Syracuse........1920
Alworth, Lance-Arkansas.........1961
+ Ameche, Alan-Wisconsin........1954
+ Ames, Knowlton-Princeton......1889
Amling, Warren-Ohio St..........1946
Anderson, Dick-Colorado........1967
Anderson, Donny-Tex.Tech......1966
+ Anderson, Hunk-N.Dame........1921
Atkins, Doug-Tennessee..........1952

Babich, Bob-Miami-OH..........1968
+ Bacon, Everett-Wesleyan........1912
+ Bagnell, Reds-Penn..............1950
+ Baker, Hobey-Princeton........1913
+ Baker, John-USC..................1931
+ Baker, Moon-N'western........1926
Baker, Terry-Oregon St..........1962
+ Ballin, Harold-Princeton........1914
+ Banker, Bill-Tulane..............1929
Banonis, Vince-Detroit..........1941
+ Barnes, Stan-California..........1921
+ Barrett, Charles-Cornell........1915
+ Baston, Bert-Minnesota..........1916
+ Battles, Cliff-WV Wesleyan......1931
Baugh, Sammy-TCU..............1936
Baughan, Maxie-Ga.Tech........1959
+ Bausch, James-Kansas..........1930
Beagle, Ron-Navy................1955
Beban, Gary-UCLA..............1967
Bechtol, Hub-Texas..............1946
+ Beckett, John-Oregon............1916
Bednarik, Chuck-Penn...........1948
Behm, Forrest-Nebraska........1940
Bell, Bobby-Minnesota..........1962
Bellino, Joe-Navy................1960
Below, Marty-Wisconsin........1923
+ Benbrook, Al-Michigan..........1910
+ Berry, Charlie-Lafayette........1924
Bertelli, Angelo-N.Dame........1943
Berwanger, Jay-Chicago........1935
+ Bettencourt, L.-St.Mary's........1927
Biletnikoff, Fred-Fla.St...........1964
Blanchard, Doc-Army............1946
+ Blozis, Al-Georgetown..........1942
Bock, Ed-Iowa St................1938
Bomar, Lynn-Vanderbilt........1924

+ Bomeisler, Bo-Yale..............1913
+ Booth, Albie-Yale................1931
+ Borries, Fred-Navy..............1934
+ Bosley, Bruce-West Va..........1955
Bosseler, Don-Miami,FL........1956
Bottari, Vic-California............1938
+ Boynton, Ben-Williams..........1920
+ Brewer, Charles-Harvard........1895
+ Bright, Johnny-Drake............1951
Brodie, John-Stanford..........1956
+ Brooke, George-Penn............1895
Brown, Bob-Nebraska..........1963
Brown, Geo-Navy/S.Diego St.1947
+ Brown, Gordon-Yale............1900
Brown, Jim-Syracuse............1956
+ Brown, John, Jr.-Navy..........1913
+ Brown, Johnny Mack-Ala......1925
+ Brown, Tay-USC................1932
+ Bunker, Paul-Army..............1902
Burford, Chris-Stanford........1959
Burton, Ron-N'western..........1959
Butkus, Dick-Illinois............1964
+ Butler, Robert-Wisconsin......1912

Cafego, George-Tenn............1939
+ Cagle, Red-SWLa/Army........1929
+ Cain, John-Alabama............1932
Cameron, Ed-Wash.& Lee......1924
+ Campbell, David-Harvard......1901
Campbell, Earl-Texas..........1977
+ Cannon, Jack-N.Dame..........1929
Cappelletti, John-Penn St......1973
+ Carideo, Frank-N.Dame........1930
+ Carney, Charles-Illinois........1921
Caroline, J.C.-Illinois..........1954
Carpenter, Bill-Army............1959
+ Carpenter, Hunter-Va.Tech......1905
Carroll, Chas.-Washington......1928
Casanova, Tommy-LSU........1971
+ Casey, Edward-Harvard........1919
Cassady, Howard-Ohio St......1955
+ Chamberlin, Guy-Neb..........1915
Chapman, Sam-California......1938
Chappuis, Bob-Michigan......1947
+ Christman, Paul-Missouri......1940
+ Clark, Dutch-Colo. Col.........1929
Cleary, Paul-USC..............1947
+ Clevenger, Zora-Indiana......1903
Cloud, Jack-Wm. & Mary......1948
+ Cochran, Gary-Princeton......1897
+ Cody, Josh-Vanderbilt........1919
Coleman, Don-Mich.St.........1951

Conerly, Charlie-Miss............1947
Connor, George-HC/ND........1947
+ Corbin, William-Yale............1888
Corbus, William-Stanford......1933
+ Cowan, Hector-Princeton......1889
+ Coy, Edward (Tad)-Yale........1909
+ Crawford, Fred-Duke............1933
Crow, John David-Tex.A&M....1957
+ Crowley, Jim-Notre Dame......1924
Csonka, Larry-Syracuse........1967
Cutter, Slade-Navy..............1934
+ Czarobski, Ziggie-N.Dame......1947

Dale, Carroll-Va.Tech..........1959
+ Dalrymple, Gerald-Tulane......1931
+ Dalton, John-Navy..............1911
+ Daly, Chas.-Harvard/Army....1902
Daniell, Averell-Pitt............1936
+ Daniell, James-Ohio St........1941
+ Davies, Tom-Pittsburgh........1921
+ Davis, Ernie-Syracuse..........1961
Davis, Glenn-Army............1946
Davis, Robert-Ga.Tech..........1947
Dawkins, Pete-Army............1958
DeLong, Steve-Tennessee......1964
DeRogatis, Al-Duke............1948
+ DesJardien, Paul-Chicago......1914
+ Devine, Aubrey-Iowa..........1921
+ DeWitt, John-Princeton........1903
Dial, Buddy-Rice................1958
Ditka, Mike-Pittsburgh........1960
Dobbs, Glenn-Tulsa............1942
+ Dodd, Bobby-Tennessee........1930
Donan, Holland-Princeton......1950
+ Donchess, Joseph-Pitt..........1929
Dorsett, Tony-Pitt..............1976
+ Dougherty, Nathan-Tenn......1909
Drahos, Nick-Cornell..........1940
+ Driscoll, Paddy-N'western......1917
+ Drury, Morley-USC............1927
Dudley, Bill-Virginia............1941

Easley, Kenny-UCLA............1980
+ Eckersall, Walter-Chicago......1906
+ Edwards, Turk-Wash.St.........1931
+ Edwards, Wm.-Princeton......1899
Eichenlaub, Ray-N.Dame......1914
Eisenhauer, Steve-Navy........1953
Elkins, Larry-Baylor............1964
Elliott, Bump-Mich/Purdue....1947
Elliott, Pete-Michigan..........1948
Evans, Ray-Kansas..............1947
+ Exendine, Albert-Carlisle......1907

College Football Hall of Fame (Cont.)

Players

Falaschi, Nello-S.Clara..........1936
Fears, Tom-S.Clara/UCLA....1947
+ Feathers, Beattie-Tenn...........1933
Fenimore, Bob-Okla.St 1946
+ Fenton, Doc-LSU..................1909
Ferraro, John-USC 1944
Fesler, Wes-Ohio St..............1930
+ Fincher, Bill-Ga.Tech.............1920
Fischer, Bill-Notre Dame 1948
+ Fish, Hamilton-Harvard 1909
+ Fisher, Robert-Harvard 1911
+ Flowers, Allen-Ga.Tech 1920
+ Fortmann Danny-Colgate........1935
Francis, Sam-Nebraska 1936
Franco, Ed-Fordham..............1937
+ Frank, Clint-Yale..................1937
Franz, Rodney-California.........1949
Frederickson, Tucker-Auburn.....1964
+ Friedman, Benny-Michigan......1926

Gabriel, Roman-N.C. State 1961
Gain, Bob-Kentucky 1950
+ Galiffa, Arnold-Army.............1949
Gallarneau, Hugh-Stanford......1940
+ Garbisch, Edgar-W.&J./Army..1924
Garrett, Mike-USC 1965
+ Gelbert, Charles-Penn............1896
+ Geyer, Forest-Oklahoma........1915
Gibbs, Jake-Miss..................1960
Giel, Paul-Minnesota 1953
Gifford, Frank-USC 1951
+ Gilbert, Walter-Auburn...........1936
Gilmer, Harry-Alabama...........1947
+ Gipp, George-N.Dame...........1920
+ Gladchuk, Chet-Boston Col 1940
Glass, Bill-Baylor..................1956
Glover, Rich-Nebraska 1972
Goldberg, Marshall-Pitt 1938
Goodreault, Gene-BC.............1940
+ Gordon, Walter-Calif 1918
+ Governali, Paul-Columbia........1942
Grabowski, Jim-Illinois...........1965
Graham, Otto-N'western.........1943
+ Grange, Red-Illinois 1925
+ Grayson, Bobby-Stanford........1935
+ Green, Jack-Tulane/Army........1945
Greene, Joe-N.Texas St 1968
Griese, Bob-Purdue................1966
Griffin, Archie-Ohio St 1975
Groom, Jerry-Notre Dame 1950
+ Gulick, Merle-Toledo/Hobart ..1929
+ Guyon, Joe-Ga.Tech..............1918

Hadl, John-Kansas 1961
+ Hale, Edwin-Miss.College 1921
Hall, Parker-Miss..................1938
Ham, Jack-Penn St 1970
Hamilton, Bob-Stanford 1935
+ Hamilton, Tom-Navy.............1926
Hanson, Vic-Syracuse 1926
+ Harder, Pat-Wisconsin...........1942
+ Hardwick, Tack-Harvard 1914
+ Hare, T.Truxton-Penn 1900
+ Harley, Chick-Ohio St............1919
+ Harmon, Tom-Michigan 1940
+ Harpster, Howard-Carnegie......1928
+ Hart, Edward-Princeton..........1911
Hart, Leon-Notre Dame 1949
Hartman, Bill-Georgia.............1937
+ Hazel, Homer-Rutgers............1924
+ Hazeltine, Matt-Calif 1954

+ Healey, Ed.-Dartmouth...........1916
+ Heffelfinger, Pudge-Yale.........1891
+ Hein, Mel-Washington St........1930
+ Heinrich, Don-Washington.......1952
Hendricks, Ted-Miami,FL........1968
+ Henry, Pete-Wash&Jeff.........1919
+ Herschberger, C.-Chicago.......1898
+ Herwig, Robert-Calif 1937
+ Heston, Willie-Michigan.........1904
+ Hickman, Herman-Tenn..........1931
+ Hickok, William-Yale 1894
Hill, Dan-Duke 1938
+ Hillebrand, Art-Princeton........1899
+ Hinkey, Frank-Yale................1894
Hinkle, Carl-Vanderbilt............1937
+ Hinkle, Clarke-Bucknell..........1931
Hirsch, Elroy-Wisc./Mich........1943
+ Hitchcock, James-Auburn........1932
Hoffmann, Frank-N.Dame........1931
+ Hogan, James J.-Yale............1904
+ Holland, Brud-Cornell............1938
+ Holleder, Don-Army 1955
+ Hollenback, Bill-Penn.............1908
Holovak, Mike-Boston Col 1942
Holub, E.J.-Texas Tech 1960
Hornung, Paul-N.Dame..........1956
+ Horrell, Edwin-California.........1924
Horvath, Les-Ohio St 1944
+ Howe, Arthur-Yale................1911
+ Howell, Dixie-Alabama 1934
+ Hubbard, Cal-Centenary........1926
+ Hubbard, John-Amherst.........1906
+ Hubert, Pooley-Ala...............1925
Huff, Sam-West Virginia 1955
Humble, Weldon-Rice.............1946
+ Hunt, Joe-Texas A&M............1927
Huntington, Ellery-Colgate......1914
Hutson, Don-Alabama............1934

+ Ingram, Jonas-Navy 1906
+ Isbell, Cecil-Purdue...............1937

+ Jablonsky, J.-Army/Wash.......1933
Janowicz, Vic-Ohio St............1951
+ Jenkins, Darold-Missouri........1941
Jensen, Jackie-California.........1948
+ Joesting, Herbert-Minn...........1927
Johnson, Bob-Tennessee.........1967
+ Johnson, Jimmie-Carlisle/
                    N'western 1903
Johnson, Ron-Michigan...........1968
+ Jones, Calvin-Iowa 1955
+ Jones, Gomer-Ohio St 1935
Jordan, Lee Roy-Alabama........1962
+ Juhan, Frank-U.of South 1910
Justice, Charlie-N.Car 1949

+ Kaer, Mort-USC 1926
Karras, Alex-Iowa 1957
Kavanaugh, Ken-LSU............1939
+ Kaw, Edgar-Cornell...............1922
Kazmaier, Dick-Princeton........1951
+ Keck, James-Princeton...........1921
Kelley, Larry-Yale.................1936
+ Kelly, Wild Bill-Montana 1926
Kenna, Doug-Army................1944
+ Kerr, George-Boston Col 1941
+ Ketcham, Henry-Yale............1913
Keyes, Leroy-Purdue.............1968
+ Killinger, Glenn-Penn St 1921
+ Kilpatrick, John-Yale.............1910

Kimbrough, John-Tex A&M.....1940
+ Kinard, Frank-Mississippi........1937
+ King, Phillip-Princeton............1893
+ Kinnick, Nile-Iowa.................1939
+ Kipke, Harry-Michigan...........1923
+ Kirkpatrick, John-Yale............1910
+ Kitzmiller, John-Oregon..........1930
+ Koch, Barton-Baylor..............1931
+ Koppisch, Walt-Columbia........1924
Kramer, Ron-Michigan............1956
Krueger, Charlie-Tex.A&M......1957
Kutner, Malcolm-Texas...........1941
Kwalick, Ted-Penn St.............1968

+ Lach, Steve-Duke..................1941
+ Lane, Myles-Dartmouth..........1927
Lattner, Johnny-N.Dame.........1953
Lauricella, Hank-Tenn.............1952
+ Lautenschlaeger-Tulane..........1925
+ Layden, Elmer-N.Dame..........1924
+ Layne, Bobby-Texas..............1947
+ Lea, Langdon-Princeton..........1895
LeBaron, Eddie-Pacific...........1949
+ Leech, James-VMI................1920
+ Lester, Darrell-TCU...............1935
Lilly, Bob-TCU 1960
Little, Floyd-Syracuse 1966
+ Lio, Augie-Georgetown 1940
+ Locke, Gordon-Iowa 1922
+ Lourie, Don-Princeton............1921
Lucas, Richie-Penn St 1959
Luckman, Sid-Columbia 1938
Lujack, Johnny-N.Dame..........1947
+ Lund, Pug-Minnesota 1934
Lynch, Jim-Notre Dame..........1966

+ Macomber, Bart-Illinois..........1915
MacLeod, Robert-Dart. 1938
Maegle, Dick-Rice 1954
+ Mahan, Eddie-Harvard...........1915
Majors, John-Tennessee..........1956
+ Mallory, William-Yale 1923
Mancha, Vaughn-Ala.............1947
+ Mann, Gerald-SMU...............1927
Manning, Archie-Miss.............1970
Manske, Edgar-N'western........1933
Marinaro, Ed-Cornell..............1971
Markov, Vic-Washington.........1937
+ Marshall, Bobby-Minn............1906
Martin, Jim-Notre Dame 1949
Matson, Ollie-San Fran 1952
Matthews, Ray-TCU..............1927
+ Maulbetsch, John-Mich..........1914
+ Mauthe, Pete-Penn St............1912
+ Maxwell, Robert-Chicago/
                    Swarthmore ...1906
McAfee, George-Duke............1939
+ McClung, Thomas-Yale..........1891
McColl, Bill-Stanford..............1951
+ McCormick, Jim-Princeton.......1907
McDonald, Tommy-Okla.........1956
+ McDowall, Jack-N.C.State.......1927
McElhenny, Hugh-Wash..........1951
+ McEver, Gene-Tennessee........1931
+ McEwan, John-Army.............1916
McFadden, Banks-Clemson......1939
McFadin, Bud-Texas..............1950
McGee, Mike-Duke 1959
+ McGinley, Edward-Penn 1924
+ McGovern, John-Minn............1910
McGraw, Thurman-Colo.St......1949

+ McKeever, Mike-USC 1960
+ McLaren, George-Pitt 1918
+ McMillan, Dan-USC/Calif. 1922
+ McMillin, Bo-Centre 1921
+ McWhorter, Bob-Georgia 1913
+ Mercer, LeRoy-Penn 1912
Meredith, Don-SMU 1959
+ Metzger, Bert-N.Dame 1930
+ Meylan, Wayne-Nebraska 1967
Michaels, Lou-Kentucky 1957
Mickal, Abe-LSU 1935
Miller, Creighton-N.Dame 1943
+ Miller, Don-Notre Dame 1924
Miller, Eugene-Penn St 1913
+ Miller, Fred-Notre Dame 1928
Miller, Rip-Notre Dame 1924
Millner, Wayne-N.Dame 1935
+ Milstead, C.A.-Wabash/Yale .. 1923
+ Minds, John-Penn 1897
Minisi, Skip-Penn/Navy 1947
+ Modzelewski, Dick-Md. 1952
+ Moffat, Alex-Princeton 1883
+ Molinski, Ed-Tenn 1940
Montgomery, Cliff-Columbia .. 1933
Moomaw, Donn-UCLA 1952
+ Morley, William-Columbia 1902
Morris, George-Ga.Tech 1952
Morris, Larry-Ga.Tech 1954
Morton, Craig-California 1964
+ Morton, Bill-Dartmouth 1931
+ Moscrip, Monk-Stanford 1935
+ Muller, Brick-California 1922

+ Nagurski, Bronko-Minn 1929
+ Nevers, Ernie-Stanford 1925
+ Newell, Marshall-Harvard 1893
Newman, Harry-Michigan 1932
+ Newsome, Ozzie-Alabama 1977
Nielson, Gifford-BYU 1977
Nobis, Tommy-Texas 1965
Nomellini, Leo-Minnesota 1949

+ Oberlander, Andrew-Dart 1925
+ O'Brien, Davey-TCU 1938
+ O'Dea, Pat-Wisconsin 1899
Odell, Bob-Penn 1943
+ O'Hearn, Jack-Cornell 1915
Olds, Robin-Army 1942
+ Oliphant, Elmer-Army/Pur 1917
Olsen, Merlin-Utah St 1961
Onkotz, Dennis-Penn St. 1969
+ Oosterbaan, Bennie-Mich 1927
O'Rourke, Charles-BC 1940
+ Orsi, John-Colgate 1931
+ Osgood, Win-Cornell 1892
Osmanski, Bill-Holy Cross 1938
+ Owen, George-Harvard 1922
Owens, Jim-Oklahoma 1949
Owens, Steve-Oklahoma 1969

Page, Alan-Notre Dame 1966
Pardee, Jack-Texas A&M 1956
Parilli, Babe-Kentucky 1951
Parker, Ace-Duke 1936
Parker, Jackie-Miss.St 1953
Parker, Jim-Ohio St. 1956
+ Pazzetti, Vince-Lehigh 1912
+ Peabody, Chub-Harvard 1941
+ Peck, Robert-Pittsburgh 1916
+ Pennock, Stan-Harvard 1914
Pfann, George-Cornell 1923
+ Phillips, H.D.-U.of South 1904
Phillips, Loyd-Arkansas 1966
Pihos, Pete-Indiana 1946
Pingel, John-Michigan St 1938

+ Pinckert, Erny-USC 1931
Plunkett, Jim-Stanford 1970
+ Poe, Arthur-Princeton 1899
+ Pollard, Fritz-Brown 1916
Poole, B.-Miss/NC/Army 1947
Powell, Marvin-USC 1976
Pregulman, Merv-Michigan 1943
+ Price, Eddie-Tulane 1949
+ Pund, Peter-Georgia Tech 1928

Ramsey, G.-Wm&Mary 1942
Redman, Rick-Wash 1964
+ Reeds, Claude-Oklahoma 1913
Reid, Mike-Penn St 1969
Reid, Steve-Northwestern 1936
+ Reid, William-Harvard 1899
Renfro, Mel-Oregon 1963
+ Rentner, Pug-N'western 1932
+ Reynolds, Bobby-Nebraska 1952
+ Reynolds, Bob-Stanford 1935
Richter, Les-California 1951
+ Riley, Jack-Northwestern 1931
+ Rinehart, Chas.-Lafayette 1897
Roberts, J. D.-Oklahoma 1953
+ Robeson, Paul-Rutgers 1918
+ Rodgers, Ira-West Va. 1919
+ Rogers, Ed-Carlisle/Minn 1903
Romig, Joe-Colorado 1961
+ Rosenberg, Aaron-USC 1933
Rote, Kyle-SMU 1950
+ Routt, Joe-Texas A&M 1937

+ Salmon, Red-Notre Dame 1903
+ Sauer, George-Nebraska 1933
Savitsky, George-Penn 1947
Sayers, Gale-Kansas 1964
Scarbath, Jack-Maryland 1952
+ Scarlett, Hunter-Penn 1908
Schloredt, Bob-Wash 1960
+ Schoonover, Wear-Ark. 1929
+ Schreiner, Dave-Wisconsin 1942
+ Schultz, Germany-Mich 1908
+ Schwab, Dutch-Lafayette 1922
+ Schwartz, Marchy-N.Dame..... 1931
+ Schwegler, Paul-Wash 1931
Scott, Clyde-Arkansas 1948
Scott, Richard-Navy 1947
Scott, Tom-Virginia 1953
+ Seibels, Henry-Sewanee 1899
Sellers, Ron-Florida St. 1968
Selmon, Lee Roy-Okla 1975
+ Shakespeare, Bill-N.Dame 1935
+ Shelton, Murray-Cornell 1915
+ Shevlin, Tom-Yale 1905
+ Shively, Bernie-Illinois 1926
+ Simons, Monk-Tulane 1934
Simpson, O.J.-USC 1968
Sims, Billy-Oklahoma 1979
Singletary, Mike-Baylor 1980
Sington, Fred-Alabama 1930
+ Sinkwich, Frank-Georgia 1942
+ Sitko, Emil-Notre Dame 1949
+ Skladany, Joe-Pittsburgh 1933
+ Slater, Duke-Iowa 1921
+ Smith, Bruce-Minnesota 1941
Smith, Bubba-Michigan St. 1966
+ Smith, Clipper-N.Dame 1927
+ Smith, Ernie-USC 1932
Smith, Harry-USC 1939
Smith, Jim Ray-Baylor 1954
Smith, Riley-Alabama 1935
+ Smith, Vernon-Georgia 1931
+ Snow, Neil-Michigan 1901
Sparlis, Al-UCLA 1945

+ Spears, Clarence-Dart 1915
Spears, W.D.-Vanderbilt 1927
+ Sprackling, Wm.-Brown 1911
+ Sprague, Bud-Army/Texas 1928
Spurrier, Steve-Florida 1966
Stafford, Harrison-Texas 1932
+ Stagg, Amos Alonzo-Yale 1889
+ Starcevich, Max-Wash 1936
Staubach, Roger-Navy 1964
+ Steffen, Walter-Chicago 1908
Steffy, Joe-Tenn/Army 1947
+ Stein, Herbert-Pitt 1921
Steuber, Bob-Missouri 1943
+ Stevens, Mal-Yale 1923
Stillwagon, Jim-Ohio St. 1970
+ Stinchcomb, Pete-Ohio St. 1920
+ Stevenson, Vincent-Penn 1905
Strom, Brock-Air Force 1959
+ Strong, Ken-NYU 1928
+ Strupper, Ev-Ga.Tech 1917
+ Stuhldreher, Harry-N.Dame 1924
+ Sturhan, Herb-Yale 1926
+ Stydahar, Joe-West Va. 1935
+ Suffridge, Bob-Tennessee 1940
+ Suhey, Steve-Penn St 1947
Sullivan, Pat-Auburn 1971
+ Sundstrom, Frank-Cornell 1923
Swann, Lynn-USC 1973
+ Swanson, Clarence-Neb 1921
+ Swiacki, Bill-Columbia/HC 1947
Swink, Jim-TCU 1956

Taliaferro, Geo.-Indiana 1948
Tarkenton, Fran-Georgia 1960
+ Tavener, John-Indiana 1944
+ Taylor, Chuck-Stanford 1942
Thomas, Aurelius-Ohio St 1957
+ Thompson, Joe-Pittsburgh 1907
+ Thorne, Samuel-Yale 1895
+ Thorpe, Jim-Carlisle 1912
+ Ticknor, Ben-Harvard 1930
+ Tigert, John-Vanderbilt 1904
Tinsley, Gaynell-LSU 1936
Tipton, Eric-Duke 1938
Tonnemaker, Clayton-Minn 1949
+ Torrey, Bob-Pennsylvania 1905
+ Travis, Brick-Missouri 1920
Trippi, Charley-Georgia 1946
+ Tryon, Edward-Colgate 1925
Turner, Bulldog-H.Simmons 1939
Twilley, Howard-Tulsa 1965

+ Utay, Joe-Texas A&M 1907

+ Van Brocklin, Norm-Ore 1948
+ Van Sickel, Dale-Florida 1929
+ Van Surdam, H.-Wesleyan 1905
+ Very, Dexter-Penn St 1912
Vessels, Billy-Oklahoma 1952
+ Vick, Ernie-Michigan 1921

+ Wagner, Hube-Pittsburgh 1913
Walker, Doak-SMU 1949
+ Wallace, Bill-Rice 1935
+ Walsh, Adam-N.Dame 1924
+ Warburton, Cotton, USC....... 1934
Ward, Bob-Maryland 1951
+ Warner, William-Cornell 1904
+ Washington, Kenny-UCLA 1939
+ Weatherall, Jim-Okla. 1951
Webster, George-Mich.St. 1966
Wedemeyer, H.-St.Mary's 1947
+ Weekes, Harold-Columbia 1902
Weiner, Art-N.Carolina 1949
+ Weir, Ed-Nebraska 1925

College Football Hall of Fame (Cont.)

Players

+ Welch, Gus-Carlisle.................1914
+ Weller, John-Princeton 1935
+ Wendell, Percy-Harvard 1912
+ West, Belford-Colgate...............1919
+ Westfall, Bob-Michigan 1941
+ Weyand, Babe-Army 1915
+ Wharton, Buck-Penn................1896
+ Wheeler, Arthur-Princeton 1894
  White, Byron-Colorado 1938
  White, Randy-Maryland 1974
  Whitmire, Don-Navy/Ala 1944
+ Wickhorst, Frank-Navy 1926
  Widseth, Ed-Minnesota 1936

+ Wildung, Dick-Minnesota.......1942
  Williams, Bob-N.Dame 1950
  Williams, Froggie-Rice 1949
  Willis, Bill-Ohio St 1944
  Wilson, Bobby-SMU 1935
+ Wilson, George-Wash 1925
+ Wilson, Harry-Army/Penn St....1926
  Wilson, Mike-Lafayette..........1928
  Wistert, Albert-Michigan 1942
  Wistert, Alvin-Michigan 1949
+ Wistert, Whitey-Michigan 1933
+ Wojciechowicz, Alex-Fordham .1937
+ Wood, Barry-Harvard.............1931

+ Wyant, Andy-Chicago 1894
+ Wyatt, Bowden-Tenn 1938
+ Wyckoff, Clint-Cornell............1895

+ Yarr, Tommy-N.Dame.............1931
  Yary, Ron-USC 1967
+ Yoder, Lloyd-Carnegie 1926
+ Young, Buddy-Illinois.............1946
+ Young, Harry-Wash.& Lee......1916
+ Young, Waddy-Okla 1938
  Youngblood, Jack-Florida 1970

  Zarnas, Gust-Ohio State 1937

Coaches

+ Aillet, Joe............................1989
+ Alexander, Bill.....................1951
+ Anderson, Ed 1971
+ Armstrong, Ike.....................1957
+ Bachman, Charlie.................1978
+ Banks, Earl 1992
+ Baujan, Harry 1990
+ Bell, Matty 1955
+ Bezdek, Hugo 1954
+ Bible, Dana X 1951
+ Bierman, Bernie....................1955
  Blackman, Bob.....................1987
+ Blaik, Earl (Red)..................1965
  Broyles, Frank 1983
+ Bryant, Paul (Bear)...............1986
+ Caldwell, Charlie..................1961
+ Camp, Walter 1951
  Casanova, Len......................1977
+ Cavanaugh, Frank 1954
+ Colman, Dick 1990
+ Crisler, Fritz.........................1954
+ Daugherty, Duffy 1984
  Devaney, Bob 1981
  Devine, Dan 1985
+ Dobie, Gil 1951
+ Dodd, Bobby.......................1993
+ Donohue, Michael 1951
  Dooley, Vince 1994
+ Dorais, Gus..........................1954
+ Edwards, Bill 1986
+ Engle, Rip 1973
  Faurot, Don..........................1961
+ Gaither, Jake 1973
  Gillman, Sid 1989
+ Godfrey, Ernest.....................1972
  Graves, Ray 1990
+ Gustafson, Andy...................1985
+ Hall, Edward 1951
+ Harding, Jack.......................1980
+ Harlow, Richard 1954
+ Harman, Harvey....................1981

+ Harper, Jesse........................1971
+ Haughton, Percy...................1951
+ Hayes, Woody 1983
+ Heisman, John W 1954
+ Higgins, Robert.....................1954
+ Hollingberry, Babe................1979
  Howard, Frank......................1989
+ Ingram, Bill 1973
+ Jennings, Morley...................1973
+ Jones, Biff 1954
+ Jones, Howard......................1951
+ Jones, Tad 1958
+ Jordan, Lloyd.......................1978
+ Jordan, Ralph (Shug).............1982
+ Kerr, Andy...........................1951
  Kush, Frank 1995
+ Leahy, Frank.........................1970
+ Little, George.......................1955
+ Little, Lou 1960
+ Madigan, Slip 1974
  Maurer, Dave 1991
  McClendon, Charley 1986
+ McCracken, Herb..................1973
+ McGugin, Dan 1951
  McKay, John 1988
+ McKeen, Allyn 1991
+ McLaughry, Tuss 1962
+ Merritt, John.........................1994
+ Meyer, Dutch 1956
+ Mollenkopf, Jack..................1988
+ Moore, Bernie 1954
+ Moore, Scrappy 1980
+ Morrison, Ray 1954
+ Munger, Georg 1976
+ Munn, Clarence (Biggie).........1959
+ Murray, Bill 1974
+ Murray, Frank 1983
+ Mylin, Ed (Hooks).................1974
+ Neale, Earle (Greasy) 1967
+ Neely, Jess 1971
+ Nelson, David 1987

+ Neyland, Robert 1956
+ Norton, Homer 1971
+ O'Neill, Frank (Buck) 1951
+ Owen, Bennie 1951
  Parseghian, Ara 1980
+ Perry, Doyt 1988
+ Phelan, Jimmy 1973
+ Prothro, Tommy 1991
  Ralston, John 1992
+ Robinson, E.N. 1955
+ Rockne, Knute 1951
+ Romney, Dick 1954
+ Roper, Bill 1951
  Royal, Darrell 1983
+ Sanford, George 1971
  Schembechler, Bo 1993
+ Schmidt, Francis 1971
+ Schwartzwalder, Ben.............1982
+ Shaughnessy, Clark...............1968
+ Shaw, Buck 1972
+ Smith, Andy 1951
+ Snavely, Carl........................1965
+ Stagg, Amos Alonzo 1951
+ Sutherland, Jock...................1951
+ Tatum, Jim 1984
+ Thomas, Frank......................1951
+ Vann, Thad 1987
  Vaught, Johnny.....................1979
+ Wade, Wallace 1955
+ Waldorf, Lynn (Pappy)...........1966
+ Warner, Glenn (Pop).............1951
+ Wieman, E.E. (Tad)...............1956
+ Wilce, John 1954
+ Wilkinson, Bud 1969
+ Williams, Henry 1951
+ Woodruff, George 1963
  Woodson, Warren..................1989
+ Yost, Fielding (Hurry Up) 1951
+ Zuppke, Bob 1951

Pro Football Hall of Fame

Established in 1963 by National Football League to commemorate the sport's professional origins. **Address:** 2121 George Halas Drive NW, Canton, OH 44708. **Telephone:** (216) 456-8207.

Eligibility: Nominated players must be retired five years, coaches must be retired, and contributors can still be active. Voting done by 36-member panel made up of media representatives from all 30 NFL cities, one PFWA representative and five selectors-at-large.

Class of 1995 (5): PLAYERS— WR **Steve Largent**, Seattle (1976-89); DE **Lee Roy Selmon**, Tampa Bay (1976-84); TE **Kellen Winslow**, San Diego (1979-87). SENIOR— DT **Henry Jordan**, Cleveland (1957-58), Green Bay (1959-69). CONTRIBUTOR— **Jim Finks**, Minnesota GM (1964-73), Chicago president (1974-82), New Orleans president (1986-94).

1995 finalists (nominated, but not elected): PLAYERS— Dan Dierdorf, Carl Eller, L.C. Greenwood, Ray Guy, Mike Haynes, Charlie Joiner, Tom Mack, Mel Renfro, Dwight Stephenson and Lynn Swann.

Members are listed with year of induction; (+) indicates deceased members.

☞

Quarterbacks

Baugh, Sammy 1963
Blanda, George (also PK).......1981
Bradshaw, Terry 1989
+ Clark, Dutch 1963
+ Conzelman, Jimmy 1964
Dawson, Len 1987
+ Driscoll, Paddy 1965
Fouts, Dan 1993

Graham, Otto 1965
Griese, Bob 1990
+ Herber, Arnie.......................1966
Jurgensen, Sonny 1983
+ Layne, Bobby 1967
Luckman, Sid 1965
Namath, Joe 1985
Parker, Clarence (Ace)...........1972

Starr, Bart.............................1977
Staubach, Roger 1985
Tarkenton, Fran 1986
Tittle, Y.A..............................1971
Unitas, Johnny 1979
+ Van Brocklin, Norm...............1971
+ Waterfield, Bob.....................1965

Running Backs

+ Battles, Cliff 1968
Brown, Jim 1971
Campbell, Earl......................1991
Canadeo, Tony 1974
Csonka, Larry 1987
Dorsett, Tony 1994
Dudley, Bill 1966
Gifford, Frank.......................1977
+ Grange, Red.........................1963
+ Guyon, Joe............................1966
Harris, Franco 1990
+ Hinkle, Clarke........................1964

Hornung, Paul.......................1986
Johnson, John Henry 1987
Kelly, Leroy 1994
+ Leemans, Tuffy.......................1978
Matson, Ollie........................1972
McAfee, George 1966
McElhenny, Hugh 1970
+ McNally, Johnny (Blood).........1963
Moore, Lenny 1975
Motley, Marion......................1968
+ Nagurski, Bronko 1963
+ Nevers, Ernie.........................1963

Payton, Walter 1993
Perry, Joe 1969
Riggins, John 1992
Sayers, Gale 1977
Simpson, O.J 1985
+ Strong, Ken 1967
Taylor, Jim 1976
+ Thorpe, Jim...........................1963
Trippi, Charley 1968
Van Buren, Steve 1965
Walker, Doak........................1986

Ends & Wide Receivers

Alworth, Lance......................1978
Badgro, Red.........................1981
Berry, Raymond 1973
Biletnikoff, Fred.....................1988
+ Chamberlin, Guy 1965
Ditka, Mike...........................1988
Fears, Tom 1970

+ Hewitt, Bill 1971
Hirsch, Elroy (Crazylegs)........1968
Hutson, Don..........................1963
Largent, Steve 1995
Lavelli, Dante 1975
Mackey, John 1992
Maynard, Don 1987

+ Millner, Wayne.......................1968
Mitchell, Bobby 1983
Pihos, Pete 1970
Smith, Jackie.........................1994
Taylor, Charley 1984
Warfield, Paul 1983
Winslow, Kellen 1995

Linemen (pre-World War II)

+ Edwards, Turk (T) 1969
+ Fortmann, Dan (G).................1985
+ Healey, Ed (T) 1964
+ Hein, Mel (C) 1963
+ Henry, Pete (T) 1963

+ Hubbard, Cal (T) 1963
Kiesling, Walt (G)...................1966
+ Kinard, Bruiser (T).................1971
+ Lyman, Link (T).......................1964
+ Michalske, Mike (G)................1964

Musso, George (T-G)..............1982
+ Stydahar, Joe (T) 1967
+ Trafton, George (C)................1964
Turner, Bulldog (C)................1966
+ Wojciechowicz, Alex (C)........1968

Offensive Linemen

Bednarik, Chuck (C-LB) 1967
Brown, Roosevelt (T)...............1975
Gatski, Frank (C)....................1985
Gregg, Forrest (T-G)...............1977
Groza, Lou (T-PK)...................1974
Hannah, John (G) 1991

Jones, Stan (T-G-DT)...............1991
Langer, Jim (C).......................1987
Little, Larry (G)......................1993
McCormack, Mike (T) 1984
Mix, Ron (T-G).......................1979
Otto, Jim (C) 1980

Parker, Jim (G).......................1973
Ringo, Jim (C) 1981
St. Clair, Bob (T)....................1990
Shell, Art (T) 1989
Upshaw, Gene (G) 1987

Defensive Linemen

Atkins, Doug.........................1982
+ Buchanan, Buck 1990
Davis, Willie 1981
Donovan, Art.........................1968
+ Ford, Len 1976
Greene, Joe 1987
Jones, Deacon 1980

+ Jordan, Henry........................1995
Lilly, Bob..............................1980
Marchetti, Gino.....................1972
Nomellini, Leo.......................1969
Olsen, Merlin 1982
Page, Alan 1988
Robustelli, Andy 1971

Selmon, Lee Roy 1995
Stautner, Ernie.......................1969
Weinmeister, Arnie.................1984
White, Randy 1994
Willis, Bill 1977

Linebackers

Bell, Bobby 1983
Butkus, Dick 1979
Connor, George (DT-OT).........1975
+ George, Bill..........................1974

Ham, Jack 1988
Hendricks, Ted 1990
Huff, Sam 1982
Lambert, Jack........................1990

Lanier, Willie 1986
Nitschke, Ray........................1978
Schmidt, Joe 1973

Defensive Backs

Adderley, Herb 1980
Barney, Lem 1992
Blount, Mel 1989
Brown, Willie 1984

+ Christiansen, Jack 1970
Houston, Ken 1986
Johnson, Jimmy 1994
Lane, Dick (Night Train) 1974

Lary, Yale 1979
+ Tunnell, Emlen 1967
Wilson, Larry 1978
Wood, Willie.........................1989

Placekicker

Stenerud, Jan........................1991

Pro Football Hall of Fame (Cont.)

Coaches

+ Brown, Paul 1967
  Ewbank, Weeb 1978
+ Flaherty, Ray.....................1976
  Gillman, Sid 1983
  Grant, Bud 1994

+ Halas, George 1963
+ Lambeau, Curly..................1963
  Landry, Tom 1990
+ Lombardi, Vince 1971

+ Neale, Earle (Greasy)............1969
  Noll, Chuck 1993
+ Owen, Steve 1966
  Walsh, Bill 1993

Contributors

+ Bell, Bert..............................1963
+ Bidwill, Charles.....................1967
+ Carr, Joe 1963
  Davis, Al 1992
+ Finks, Jim 1995

+ Halas, George 1963
  Hunt, Lamar...........................1972
+ Mara, Tim 1963
+ Marshall, George..................1963
+ Ray, Hugh (Shorty) 1966

+ Reeves, Dan........................1967
+ Rooney, Art 1964
  Rozelle, Pete 1985
  Schramm, Tex 1991

Dick McCann Award

First presented in 1969 by the Pro Football Writers of America for long and distinguished reporting on pro football. Named in honor of the first director of the Hall, the McCann Award does not constitute induction into the Hall of Fame.

Year		Year		Year	
1969	George Strickler	1978	Murray Olderman	1987	Jerry Magee
1970	Arthur Daley	1979	Pat Livingston	1988	Gordon Forbes
1971	Joe King	1980	Chuck Heaton	1989	Vito Stellino
1972	Lewis Atchison	1981	Norm Miller	1990	Will McDonough
1973	Dave Brady	1982	Cameron Snyder	1991	Dick Connor
1974	Bob Oates	1983	Hugh Brown	1992	Frank Luska
1975	John Steadman	1984	Larry Felser	1993	Ira Miller
1976	Jack Hand	1985	Cooper Rollow	1994	Don Pierson
1977	Art Daley	1986	Bill Wallace	1995	Ray Didinger

Pete Rozelle Award

First presented in 1989 by the Hall of Fame for exceptional longtime contributions to radio and TV in pro football. Named in honor of the former NFL commissioner, who was also a publicist and GM for the LA Rams, the Rozelle Award does not constitute induction into the Hall of Fame.

Year		Year		Year	
1989	Bill McPhail	1992	Chris Schenkel	1994	Pat Summerall
1990	Lindsey Nelson	1993	Curt Gowdy	1995	Frank Gifford
1991	Ed Sabol				

NFL's 75th Anniversary All-Time Team

Selected by a 15-member panel of former players, NFL and Pro Football Hall of Fame officials and media representatives and released Sept. 1, 1994.

OFFENSE

Wide Receivers (4): Lance Alworth, Raymond Berry, Don Hutson and Jerry Rice
Tight Ends (2): Mike Ditka and Kellen Winslow
Tackles (3): Roosevelt Brown, Forrest Gregg and Anthony Munoz
Guards (3): John Hannah, Jim Parker and Gene Upshaw
Centers (2): Mel Hein and Mike Webster
Quarterbacks (4): Sammy Baugh, Otto Graham, Joe Montana and Johnny Unitas
Running Backs (6): Jim Brown, Marion Motley, Bronko Nagurski, Walter Payton, O.J. Simpson and Steve Van Buren

DEFENSE

Ends (3): Deacon Jones, Gino Marchetti and Reggie White
Tackles (3): Joe Greene, Bob Lilly and Merlin Olsen
Linebackers (7): Dick Butkus, Jack Ham, Ted Hendricks, Jack Lambert, Willie Lanier, Ray Nitschke and Lawrence Taylor
Cornerbacks (4): Mel Blount, Mike Haynes, Dick (Night Train) Lane and Rod Woodson
Safties (3): Ken Houston, Ronnie Lott and Larry Wilson

SPECIALISTS

Placekicker: Jan Stenerud
Punter: Ray Guy
Kick Returner: Gale Sayers
Punt Returner: Billy (White Shoes) Johnson

Canadian Football Hall of Fame

Established in 1963. Current Hall opened in 1972. **Address:** 58 Jackson Street West, Hamilton, Ontario, L8P 1L4. **Telephone:** (905) 528-7566.

Eligibility: Nominated players must be retired three years, but coaches and builders can still be active. Voting done by 15-member panel of Canadian pro and amateur football officials.

Class of 1995 (3): PLAYERS— QB **Dieter Brock**, Winnipeg (1974-83), Hamilton (1983-84); RB **Tom Grant**, Hamilton (1956-68), Winnipeg (1969). BUILDER— **Greg Fulton**, compiler of official CFL record manual from 1966-73; also CFL secretary-treasurer and Rules Committee chairman since 1967.

Members are listed with year of induction; (+) indicates deceased members.

Players

Atchison, Ron 1978	Griffing, Dean 1965	Parker, Jackie.........................1971
Bailey, Byron.........................1975	Hanson, Fritz 1963	Patterson, Hal 1971
Baker, Bill 1994	Harris, Wayne 1976	Perry, Gordon 1970
Barrow, John 1976	Harrison, Herm 1993	+ Perry, Norm.........................1963
+ Batstone, Harry 1963	Helton, John 1986	Ploen, Ken 1975
+ Beach, Ormond 1963	Henley, Garney 1979	+ Quilty, S.P. (Silver).............1966
Box, Ab 1965	Hinton, Tom 1991	+ Rebholz, Russ......................1963
+ Breen, Joe 1963	+ Huffman, Dick 1987	Reed, George 1979
+ Bright, Johnny 1970	+ Isbister, Bob Sr 1965	+ Reeve, Ted 1963
Brown, Tom............................1984	Jackson, Russ 1973	Rigney, Frank 1985
Brock, Dieter..........................1995	+ Jacobs, Jack 1963	+ Rodden, Mike 1964
Casey, Tom 1964	+ James, Eddie (Dynamite).........1963	+ Rowe, Paul 1964
Charlton, Ken 1992	James, Gerry 1981	Ruby, Martin 1974
Clements, Tom 1994	+ Kabat, Greg 1966	+ Russel, Jeff 1963
Coffey, Tommy Joe 1977	Kapp, Joe 1984	+ Scott, Vince..........................1982
+ Conacher, Lionel 1963	Keeling, Jerry 1989	Shatto, Dick 1975
Copeland, Royal 1988	Kelly, Brian 1991	+ Simpson, Ben 1963
Corrigall, Jim 1990	Kelly, Ellison 1992	Simpson, Bob 1976
+ Cox, Ernest 1963	Krol, Joe 1963	+ Sprague, David......................1963
+ Craig, Ross 1964	Kwong, Normie 1969	Stevenson, Art 1969
+ Cronin, Carl 1967	Lancaster, Ron 1982	Stewart, Ron 1977
+ Cutler, Wes 1968	+ Lawson, Smirle 1963	+ Stirling, Hugh (Bummer)..........1966
Dalla Riva, Peter 1993	+ Leadlay, Frank (Pep)..............1963	Sutherin, Don 1992
+ Dixon, George 1974	+ Lear, Les 1974	Thelen, Dave 1989
+ Eliowitz, Abe 1969	Lewis, Leo 1973	+ Timmis, Brian 1963
+ Emerson, Eddie 1963	Lunsford, Earl 1983	Tinsley, Bud 1982
Etcheverry, Sam 1969	Luster, Marv 1990	+ Tommy, Andy 1989
Evanshen, Terry 1984	Luzzi, Don 1986	+ Trawick, Herb 1975
Faloney, Bernie 1974	+ McCance, Ches 1976	+ Tubman, Joe 1968
+ Fear, A.H. (Cap) 1967	McGill, Frank..........................1965	Tucker, Whit 1993
Fennell, Dave 1990	McQuarters, Ed 1988	Urness, Ted 1989
+ Ferraro, John 1966	Miles, Rollie 1980	Vaughan, Kaye 1978
Fieldgate, Norm 1979	+ Molson, Percy 1963	Wagner, Virgil 1980
Fleming, Willie 1982	Morris, Frank 1983	+ Welch, Hawley (Huck) 1964
Gabriel, Tony 1985	+ Morris, Ted 1964	Wilkinson, Tom 1987
Gaines, Gene 1994	Mosca, Angelo 1987	Wylie, Harvey 1980
+ Gall, Hugh 1963	Nelson, Roger 1986	Young, Jim 1991
Golab, Tony 1964	Neumann, Peter 1979	+ Zock, Bill 1985
Grant, Tom 1995	O'Quinn, John (Red) 1981	
Gray, Herbert 1983	Pajaczkowski, Tony 1988	

Builders

+ Back, Leonard.......................1971	Gaudaur, J.G. (Jake) 1984	+ Montgomery, Ken....................1970
+ Bailey, Harold.......................1965	Grant, Bud 1983	+ Newton, Jack.........................1964
+ Ballard, Harold......................1987	+ Grey, Lord Earl 1963	+ Preston, Ken 1990
+ Berger, Sam 1993	+ Griffith, Dr. Harry 1963	+ Ritchie, Alvin 1963
+ Brook, Tom 1975	+ Halter, Sydney 1966	+ Ryan, Joe B...........................1968
+ Brown, D. Wes 1963	+ Hannibal, Frank 1963	Sazio, Ralph 1988
Chipman, Arthur 1969	+ Hayman, Lew 1975	+ Shaughnessy, Frank (Shag) 1963
Clair, Frank 1981	+ Hughes, W.P. (Billy) 1974	+ Shouldice, W.T. (Hap)............1977
+ Cooper, Ralph.......................1992	Keys, Eagle 1990	+ Simpson, Jimmie 1986
+ Crighton, Hec 1986	Kimball, Norman 1991	+ Slocomb, Karl 1989
+ Currie, Andrew 1974	+ Kramer, R.A. (Bob) 1987	+ Spring, Harry 1976
+ Davies, Dr. Andrew 1969	+ Lieberman, M.I. (Moe)............1973	Stukus, Annis 1974
+ DeGruchy, John 1963	+ McBrien, Harry 1978	+ Taylor, N.J. (Piffles)...............1963
Dojack, Paul 1978	+ McCaffrey, Jimmy 1967	+ Tindall, Frank 1985
+ Duggan, Eck 1981	+ McCann, Dave 1966	+ Warner, Clair 1965
+ DuMoulin, Seppi 1963	McNaughton, Don 1994	+ Warwick, Bert 1964
+ Foulds, Willliam 1963	+ McPherson, Don.....................1983	+ Wilson, Seymour.....................1984
Fulton, Greg 1995	+ Metras, Johnny 1980	

GOLF

A new Golf Museum and Hall of Fame is expected to open in late 1997 at World Golf Village, which is scheduled to begin construction in early 1996 at St. Johns County, Fla., between Jacksonville and St. Augustine. The new hall will incorporate the inactive PGA/World Golf Hall of Fame (formerly run by the PGA of America) and the active LPGA Hall as well as provide a role for the USGA and the Royal and Ancient Golf Club of St. Andrews. Questions concerning the new Golf Hall of Fame and Museum should be directed to the PGA Tour at (904) 273-3350.

PGA/World Golf Hall of Fame

Established in 1974, but inactive since 1993. Will become part of the PGA Tour's new Golf Museum and Hall of Fame in 1997. Members are listed with year of induction; (+) indicates deceased members.

Men

+ Anderson, Willie ... 1975	+ Hagen, Walter ... 1974	Palmer, Arnold ... 1974
+ Armour, Tommy ... 1976	+ Hilton, Harold ... 1978	Player, Gary ... 1974
+ Ball, John, Jr ... 1977	Hogan, Ben ... 1974	Runyan, Paul ... 1990
+ Barnes, Jim ... 1989	Irwin, Hale ... 1992	Sarazen, Gene ... 1974
+ Boros, Julius ... 1982	+ Jones, Bobby ... 1974	+ Smith, Horton ... 1990
+ Braid, James ... 1976	+ Little, Lawson ... 1980	Snead, Sam ... 1974
Casper, Billy ... 1978	Littler, Gene ... 1990	+ Taylor, John H ... 1975
Cooper, Lighthorse Harry ... 1992	+ Locke, Bobby ... 1977	Thomson, Peter ... 1988
+ Cotton, Thomas ... 1980	Middlecoff, Cary ... 1986	+ Travers, Jerry ... 1976
+ Demaret, Jimmy ... 1983	+ Morris, Tom, Jr ... 1975	+ Travis, Walter ... 1979
DeVicenzo, Roberto ... 1989	+ Morris, Tom, Sr ... 1976	Trevino, Lee ... 1981
+ Evans, Chick ... 1975	Nelson, Byron ... 1974	+ Vardon, Harry ... 1974
Floyd, Ray ... 1989	Nicklaus, Jack ... 1974	Watson, Tom ... 1988
+ Guldahl, Ralph ... 1981	+ Ouimet, Francis ... 1974	

Women

Berg, Patty ... 1974	Rawls, Betsy ... 1987	Whitworth, Kathy ... 1982
Carner, JoAnne ... 1985	Suggs, Louise ... 1979	Wright, Mickey ... 1976
+ Howe, Dorothy C.H ... 1978	+ Vare, Glenna Collett ... 1975	+ Zaharias, Babe Didrikson ... 1974
Lopez, Nancy ... 1989	+ Wethered, Joyce ... 1975	

Contributors

Campbell, William ... 1990	+ Graffis, Herb ... 1977	+ Roberts, Clifford ... 1978
+ Corcoran, Fred ... 1975	+ Harlow, Robert ... 1988	Rodriguez, Chi Chi ... 1992
+ Crosby, Bing ... 1978	Hope, Bob ... 1983	+ Ross, Donald ... 1977
+ Dey, Joe ... 1975	Jones, Robert Trent ... 1987	+ Tufts, Richard ... 1992

Old PGA Hall Members Not in PGA/World Hall

The original PGA Hall of Fame was established in 1940 by the PGA of America, but abandoned after the 1982 inductions in favor of the PGA/World Golf Hall of Fame. Twenty-seven members of the old PGA Hall have been elected to the PGA/World Hall since then. Players yet to make the cut are listed below with year of induction into old PGA Hall.

+ Brady, Mike ... 1960	Ford, Doug ... 1975	+ McLeod, Fred ... 1960
+ Burke, Billy ... 1966	+ Ghezzi, Vic ... 1965	+ Picard, Henry ... 1961
Burke, Jack Jr ... 1975	+ Harbert, Chick ... 1968	+ Revolta, Johnny ... 1963
+ Cruickshank, Bobby ... 1967	Harper, Chandler ... 1969	+ Shute, Denny ... 1957
+ Diegel, Leo ... 1955	+ Harrison, Dutch ... 1962	+ Smith, Alex ... 1940
+ Dudley, Ed ... 1964	+ Hutchison, Jock Sr ... 1959	+ Smith, Macdonald ... 1954
+ Dutra, Olin ... 1962	+ McDermott, John ... 1940	+ Wood, Craig ... 1956
+ Farroll, Johnny ... 1961	+ Mangrum, Lloyd ... 1964	

LPGA Hall of Fame

Established in 1967 by the LPGA to replace the old Women's Golf Hall of Fame (founded in 1950). Originally located in Augusta, GA (1967-77), the Hall has been moved to Pinehurst, NC (1977-83), Sugar Land, TX (1983-89) and Daytona Beach, FL (since 1990). Will become part of the PGA Tour's new Golf Museum and Hall of Fame in 1997. **Address:** LPGA Headquarters, 2570 Volusia Ave., Suite B, Daytona Beach, FL 32114. **Telephone:** (904) 254-8800.

Eligibility: Nominees must have played 10 years on the LPGA tour and won 30 official events, including two major championships; 35 official events and one major; or 40 official events and no majors.

Latest inductee: Betsy King (30 wins, 5 majors) became the 14th player to gain entry by capturing the ShopRite Classic in Somers Point, N.J. on June 25, 1995. **Leading candidates** (through Sept. 15, 1995): Amy Alcott (29 wins, 5 majors) and Beth Daniel (32 wins, 1 major).

Members are listed with year of induction; (+) indicates deceased members.

Players

Berg, Patty ... 1951	Lopez, Nancy ... 1987	Wright, Mickey ... 1964
Bradley, Pat ... 1991	Mann, Carol ... 1977	+ Zaharias, Babe Didrikson ... 1951
Carner, JoAnne ... 1982	Rawls, Betsy ... 1960	
Haynie, Sandra ... 1977	Sheehan, Patty ... 1993	### Contributor
Jameson, Betty ... 1951	Suggs, Louise ... 1951	+ Dinah Shore ... 1994
King, Betsy ... 1995	Whitworth, Kathy ... 1975	

HOCKEY

Hockey Hall of Fame

Established in 1945 by the National Hockey League and opened in 1961. **Address:** BCE Place, 30 Yonge Street, Toronto, Ontario, M5E 1X8. **Telephone:** (416) 360-7735.

Eligibility: Nominated players and referees must be retired three years. Voting done by 15-member panel made up of pro and amateur hockey personalities and media representatives. A 15-member Veterans Committee selects older players.

Class of 1995 (4): PLAYER—defenseman **Larry Robinson,** Montreal (1972–89), Los Angeles (1989–92). VETERAN—left wing **Bun Cook,** NY Rangers (1926–36), Boston (1936–37). BUILDERS—**Gunter Sebetzki** (International Ice Hockey Federation president, 1975–94) and NHL executive **Bill Torrey** (NY Islanders GM, 1972–92).

Members are listed with year of induction; (+) indicates deceased members.

Forwards

Abel, Sid 1969	+ Frederickson, Frank 1958	+ O'Connor, Buddy 1988
+ Adams, Jack 1959	Gainey, Bob 1992	+ Oliver, Harry 1967
Apps, Syl 1961	+ Gardner, Jimmy 1962	Olmstead, Bert 1985
Armstrong, George 1975	Geoffrion, Bernie 1972	+ Patrick, Lynn 1980
+ Bailey, Ace 1975	+ Gerard, Eddie 1945	Perreault, Gilbert 1990
+ Bain, Dan 1945	Gilbert, Rod 1982	+ Phillips, Tom 1945
+ Baker, Hobey 1945	+ Gilmour, Billy 1962	+ Primeau, Joe 1963
Barber, Bill 1990	+ Griffis, Si 1950	Pulford, Bob 1991
+ Barry, Marty 1965	+ Hay, George 1958	+ Rankin, Frank 1961
Bathgate, Andy 1978	+ Hextall, Bryan 1969	Ratelle, Jean 1985
Beliveau, Jean 1972	+ Hooper, Tom 1962	Richard, Henri 1979
+ Bentley, Doug 1964	Howe, Gordie 1972	Richard, Maurice (Rocket) 1961
+ Bentley, Max 1966	+ Howe, Syd 1965	+ Richardson, George 1950
+ Blake, Toe 1966	Hull, Bobby 1983	+ Roberts, Gordie 1971
Bossy, Mike 1991	+ Hyland, Harry 1962	+ Russel, Blair 1965
+ Boucher, Frank 1958	+ Irvin, Dick 1958	+ Russell, Ernie 1965
+ Bowie, Dubbie 1945	+ Jackson, Busher 1971	+ Ruttan, Jack 1962
+ Broadbent, Punch 1962	+ Joliat, Aurel 1947	+ Scanlan, Fred 1965
Bucyk, John (Chief) 1981	+ Keats, Duke 1958	Schmidt, Milt 1961
+ Burch, Billy 1974	Kennedy, Ted (Teeder) 1966	+ Schriner, Sweeney 1962
Clarke, Bobby 1987	Keon, Dave 1986	+ Seibert, Oliver 1961
+ Colville, Neil 1967	Lach, Elmer 1966	Shutt, Steve 1993
+ Conacher, Charlie 1961	Lafleur, Guy 1988	+ Siebert, Babe 1964
+ Cook, Bill 1952	+ Lalonde, Newsy 1950	Sittler, Darryl 1989
+ Cook, Bun 1995	Laprade, Edgar 1993	+ Smith, Alf 1962
+ Cowley, Bill 1968	Lemaire, Jacques 1984	Smith, Clint 1991
+ Crawford, Rusty 1962	+ Lewis, Herbie 1989	+ Smith, Hooley 1972
+ Darragh, Jack 1962	Lindsay, Ted 1966	+ Smith, Tommy 1973
+ Davidson, Scotty 1950	+ MacKay, Mickey 1952	+ Stanley, Barney 1962
Day, Hap 1961	Mahovlich, Frank 1981	+ Stewart, Nels 1962
Delvecchio, Alex 1977	+ Malone, Joe 1950	+ Stuart, Bruce 1961
+ Denneny, Cy 1959	+ Marshall, Jack 1965	+ Taylor, Fred (Cyclone) 1947
Dionne, Marcel 1992	+ Maxwell, Fred 1962	+ Trihey, Harry 1950
+ Drillon, Gordie 1975	McDonald, Lanny 1992	Ullman, Norm 1982
+ Drinkwater, Graham 1950	+ McGee, Frank 1945	+ Walker, Jack 1960
Dumart, Woody 1992	+ McGimsie, Billy 1962	+ Walsh, Marty 1962
+ Dunderdale, Tommy 1974	Mikita, Stan 1983	Watson, Harry 1994
+ Dye, Babe 1970	Moore, Dickie 1974	+ Watson, Harry (Moose) 1962
Esposito, Phil 1984	+ Morenz, Howie 1945	+ Weiland, Cooney 1971
+ Farrell, Arthur 1965	+ Mosienko, Bill 1965	+ Westwick, Harry (Rat) 1962
+ Foyston, Frank 1958	+ Nighbor, Frank 1947	+ Whitcroft, Fred 1962
	+ Noble, Reg 1962	

Goaltenders

+ Benedict, Clint 1965	Giacomin, Eddie 1987	Parent, Bernie 1984
Bower, Johnny 1976	+ Hainsworth, George 1961	+ Plante, Jacques 1978
Brimsek, Frankie 1966	Hall, Glenn 1975	Rayner, Chuck 1973
+ Broda, Turk 1967	+ Hern, Riley 1962	+ Sawchuk, Terry 1971
Cheevers, Gerry 1985	+ Holmes, Hap 1972	Smith, Billy 1993
+ Connell, Alex 1958	+ Hutton, J.B. (Bouse) 1962	+ Thompson, Tiny 1959
Dryden, Ken 1983	+ Lehman, Hughie 1958	Tretiak, Vladislav 1989
+ Durnan, Bill 1964	+ LeSueur, Percy 1961	+ Vezina, Georges 1945
Esposito, Tony 1988	Lumley, Harry 1980	Worsley, Gump 1980
+ Gardiner, Chuck 1945	+ Moran, Paddy 1958	+ Worters, Roy 1969

Hockey Hall of Fame (Cont.)

Defensemen

Boivin, Leo 1986	+ Hall, Joe 1961	+ Pitre, Didier 1962
+ Boon, Dickie 1952	+ Harvey, Doug 1973	Potvin, Denis 1991
Bouchard, Butch 1966	Horner, Red 1965	+ Pratt, Babe 1966
+ Boucher, George 1960	+ Horton, Tim 1977	Pronovost, Marcel 1978
+ Cameron, Harry 1962	Howell, Harry 1979	+ Pulford, Harvey 1945
+ Clancy, King 1958	+ Johnson, Ching 1958	Quackenbush, Bill 1976
+ Clapper, Dit 1947	+ Johnson, Ernie 1952	Reardon, Kenny 1966
+ Cleghorn, Sprague 1958	Johnson, Tom 1970	Robinson, Larry 1995
+ Conacher, Lionel 1994	Kelly, Red 1969	+ Ross, Art 1945
Coulter, Art 1974	Laperriere, Jacques 1987	Savard, Serge 1986
+ Dutton, Red 1958	Lapointe, Guy 1993	Seibert, Earl 1963
Flaman, Fernie 1990	+ Laviolette, Jack 1962	+ Shore, Eddie 1947
Gadsby, Bill 1970	+ Mantha, Sylvio 1960	+ Simpson, Joe 1962
+ Gardiner, Herb 1958	+ McNamara, George 1958	Stanley, Allan 1981
+ Goheen, F.X. (Moose) 1952	Orr, Bobby 1979	+ Stewart, Jack 1964
+ Goodfellow, Ebbie 1963	Park, Brad 1988	+ Stuart, Hod 1945
+ Grant, Mike 1950	+ Patrick, Lester 1947	+ Wilson, Gordon (Phat) 1962
+ Green, Wilf (Shorty) 1962	Pilote, Pierre 1975	

Referees & Linesmen

Armstrong, Neil 1991	+ Hayes, George 1988	+ Rodden, Mike 1962
Ashley, John 1981	+ Hewitson, Bobby 1963	+ Smeaton, J. Cooper 1961
Chadwick, Bill 1964	+ Ion, Mickey 1961	Storey, Red 1967
D'Amico, John 1993	Pavelich, Matt 1987	Udvari, Frank 1973
+ Elliott, Chaucer 1961		

Builders

+ Adams, Charles 1960	+ Hay, Charles 1984	Page, Fred 1993
+ Adams, Weston W. Sr 1972	+ Hendy, Jim 1968	+ Patrick, Frank 1958
+ Ahearn, Frank 1962	+ Hewitt, Foster 1965	+ Pickard, Allan 1958
+ Ahearne, J.F. (Bunny) 1977	+ Hewitt, W.A. 1945	+ Pilous, Rudy 1985
+ Allan, Sir Montagu 1945	+ Hume, Fred 1962	Poile, Bud 1990
Allen, Keith 1992	+ Imlach, Punch 1984	Pollock, Sam 1978
+ Ballard, Harold 1977	Ivan, Tommy 1964	+ Raymond, Donat 1958
+ Bauer, Fr. David 1989	+ Jennings, Bill 1975	+ Robertson, John Ross 1945
+ Bickell, J.P. 1978	+ Johnson, Bob 1992	+ Robinson, Claude 1945
Bowman, Scotty 1991	+ Juckes, Gordon 1979	+ Ross, Philip 1976
+ Brown, George 1961	+ Kilpatrick, John 1960	Sebetzki, Gunther 1995
+ Brown, Walter 1962	Knox, Seymour III 1993	+ Selke, Frank 1960
+ Buckland, Frank 1975	+ Leader, Al 1969	Sinden, Harry 1983
Butterfield, Jack 1980	LeBel, Bob. 1970	+ Smith, Frank 1962
+ Calder, Frank 1945	+ Lockhart, Tom 1965	+ Smythe, Conn 1958
+ Campbell, Angus 1964	+ Loicq, Paul 1961	Snider, Ed. 1988
+ Campbell, Clarence 1966	+ Mariucci, John 1985	+ Stanley, Lord of Preston 1945
+ Cattarinich, Joseph 1977	Mathers, Frank. 1992	+ Sutherland, James 1945
+ Dandurand, Leo 1963	+ McLaughlin, Frederic 1963	+ Tarasov, Anatoli 1974
Dilio, Frank. 1964	+ Milford, Jake 1984	Torrey, Bill 1995
+ Dudley, George 1958	Molson, Hartland 1973	+ Turner, Lloyd 1958
+ Dunn, James 1968	+ Nelson, Francis 1945	+ Tutt, William Thayer 1978
Eagleson, Alan 1989	+ Norris, Bruce 1969	Voss, Carl 1974
Francis, Emile 1982	+ Norris, James D 1962	+ Waghorne, Fred 1961
+ Gibson, Jack 1976	+ Norris, James Sr 1958	+ Wirtz, Arthur 1971
+ Gorman, Tommy 1963	+ Northey, William 1945	Wirtz, Bill 1976
+ Griffiths, Frank A. 1993	+ O'Brien, J.A. 1962	Ziegler, John 1987
+ Hanley, Bill 1986	O'Neill, Brian 1994	

Elmer Ferguson Award

First presented in 1984 by the Professional Hockey Writers' Association for meritorious contributions by members of the PHWA. Named in honor of the late Montreal newspaper reporter, the Ferguson Award does not constitute induction into the Hall of Fame and is not necessarily an annual presentation.

1984—Jacques Beauchamp, Jim Burchard, Red Burnett, Dink Carroll, Jim Coleman, Ted Damata, Marcel Desjardins, Jack Dulmage, Milt Dunnell, Elmer Ferguson, Tom Fitzgerald, Trent Frayne, Al Laney, Joe Nichols, Basil O'Meara, Jim Vipond and Lewis Walter
1985—Charlie Barton, Red Fisher, George Gross, Zotique L'Esperance, Charles Mayer & Andy O'Brien
1986—Dick Johnston, Leo Monahan & Tim Moriarty

1987—Bill Brennan, Rex MacLeod, Ben Olan & Fran Rosa
1988—Jim Proudfoot & Scott Young
1989—Claude Larochelle & Frank Orr
1990—Bertrand Raymond
1991—Hugh Delano
1992—No award
1993—Al Strachan
1994—No award
1995—Jake Gatecliff

Foster Hewitt Award

First presented in 1984 by the NHL Broadcasters' Association for meritorious contributions by members of the NHLBA. Named in honor of Canada's legendary "Voice of Hockey," the Hewitt Award does not constitute induction into the Hall of Fame and is not necessarily an annual presentation.

1984—Fred Cusick, Danny
  Gallivan, Foster Hewitt
  & Rene Lecavelier
1985—Budd Lynch & Doug Smith
1986—Wes McKnight & Lloyd Pettit

1987—Bob Wilson
1988—Dick Irvin
1989—Dan Kelly
1990—Jiggs McDonald
1991—Bruce Martyn

1992—Jim Robson
1993—Al Shaver
1994—Ted Darling
1995—Brian McFarlane

U.S. Hockey Hall of Fame

Established in 1968 by the Eveleth (Minn.) Civic Association Project H Committee and opened in 1973. **Address:** 801 Hat Trick Ave., P.O. Box 657, Eveleth, MN 55734. **Telephone:** (218) 744-5167.

 Eligibility: Nominated players and referees must be American-born and retired five years; coaches must be American-born and must have coached predominantly American teams. Voting done by 12-member panel made up of Hall of Fame members and U.S. hockey officials.

 Class of 1995 (3): PLAYERS— center **Henry Boucha** (Warroad, Minn. H.S., 1965-69; 1972 U.S. Olympic team; Detroit, Minnesota, Kansas City and Colorado in NHL, 1971-77) and defenseman **Ken Morrow** (Bowling Green, 1976-79; 1980 U.S. Olympic team; New York Islanders of NHL, 1980-89). ADMINISTRATOR— **Jim Claypool** (ex-president of Minnesota Amatuer Hockey Assn., Amateur Hockey Assn. director and manager of 1960 U.S. Olympic team).

 Members are listed with year of induction; (+) indicates deceased members.

Players

+ Abel, Clarence (Taffy) 1973	Everett, Doug 1974	McCartan, Jack......................1983
+ Baker, Hobey 1973	Ftorek, Robbie 1991	Moe, Bill 1974
Bartholome, Earl 1977	+ Garrison, John 1974	Morrow, Ken...........................1995
+ Bessone, Peter........................1978	Garrity, Jack 1986	+ Moseley, Fred 1975
Blake, Bob 1985	+ Goheen, Frank (Moose)..........1973	+ Murray, Hugh (Muzz) Sr........1987
Boucha, Henry.........................1995	Grant, Wally 1994	+ Nelson, Hub 1978
Brimsek, Frankie.....................1973	+ Harding, Austie......................1975	Olson, Eddie...........................1977
Cavanaugh, Joe......................1994	Iglehart, Stewart.....................1975	+ Owen, George.......................1973
+ Chaisson, Ray 1974	Ikola, Willard 1990	+ Palmer, Winthrop...................1973
Chase, John 1973	Johnson, Virgil........................1974	Paradise, Bob 1989
Christian, Bill 1984	+ Karakas, Mike.......................1973	Purpur, Clifford (Fido)............1974
Christian, Roger......................1989	Kirrane, Jack 1987	Riley, Bill................................1977
Cleary, Bill 1976	+ Lane, Myles 1973	+ Romnes, Elwin (Doc)..............1973
Cleary, Bob 1981	Langevin, Dave 1993	Rondeau, Dick 1985
+ Conroy, Tony 1975	+ Linder, Joe 1975	+ Williams, Tom 1981
Dahlstrom, Carl (Cully) 1973	+ LoPresti, Sam 1973	+ Winters, Frank (Coddy) 1973
+ DesJardins, Vic 1974	+ Mariucci, John 1973	+ Yackel, Ken 1986
+ Desmond, Richard 1988	Matchefts, John 1991	
+ Dill, Bob 1979	Mayasich, John.......................1976	

Coaches

+ Almquist, Oscar 1983	Heyliger, Vic 1974	Pleban, Connie 1990
Bessone, Amo 1992	Ikola, Willard 1990	Riley, Jack..............................1979
Brooks, Herb...........................1990	+ Jeremiah, Eddie 1973	+ Ross, Larry 1988
Ceglarski, Len 1992	+ Johnson, Bob 1991	+ Thompson, Cliff 1973
+ Fullerton, James 1992	Kelley, Jack 1993	+ Stewart, Bill 1982
+ Gordon, Malcolm...................1973	+ Kelly, John (Snooks)...............1974	+ Winsor, Ralph 1973
Harkness, Ned.........................1994		

Referee

Chadwick, Bill........................1974

Contributor

Schulz, Charles M. 1993

+ Brown, George 1973	
+ Brown, Walter 1973	
Bush, Walter...........................1980	
Clark, Don..............................1978	
Claypool, Jim..........................1985	

Administrators

+ Gibson, J.L. (Doc).................1973	Ridder, Bob............................1976
+ Jennings, Bill.........................1981	Trumble, Hal 1970
+ Kahler, Nick..........................1980	+ Tutt, Thayer 1973
+ Lockhart, Tom........................1973	Wirtz, Bill...............................1967
Marvin, Cal 1982	+ Wright, Lyle 1973

Members of Both Hockey and U.S. Hockey Halls of Fame

(as of Sept. 15, 1995)

Players	**Coach**	**Builders**	
Hobey Baker	Bob Johnson	George Brown	Tom Lockhart
Frankie Brimsek		Walter Brown	Thayer Tutt
Frank (Moose) Goheen	**Referee**	Doc Gibson	Bill Wirtz
John Mariucci	Bill Chadwick	Bill Jennings	

HORSE RACING

National Horse Racing Hall of Fame

Established in 1950 by the Saratoga Springs Racing Association and opened in 1955. **Address:** National Museum of Racing and Hall of Fame, Union Ave., Saratoga Springs, NY 12866. **Telephone:** (518) 584-0400.

Eligibility: Nominated horses must be retired five years; jockeys must be active at least 15 years; trainers must be active at least 25 years. Voting done by 100-member panel of horse racing media.

Class of 1995 (5): JOCKEY— **Jerry Bailey**. TRAINER—**Bobby Frankel**. HORSES— **Crusader, Foolish Pleasure** and **La Prevoyante**.

Members are listed with year of induction; (+) indicates deceased members.

Jockeys

+ Adams, Frank (Dooley)* 1970	+ Garrison, Snapper 1955	+ Parke, Ivan 1978
+ Adams, John 1965	+ Griffin, Henry 1956	+ Patrick, Gil 1970
+ Aitcheson, Joe Jr.* 1978	+ Guerin, Eric 1972	Pincay, Laffit Jr. 1975
Arcaro, Eddie 1958	Hartack, Bill 1959	+ Purdy, Sam 1970
Atkinson, Ted 1957	Hawley, Sandy 1992	+ Reiff, John 1956
Baeza, Braulio 1976	+ Johnson, Albert 1971	+ Robertson, Alfred 1971
Bailey, Jerry 1995	+ Knapp, Willie 1969	Rotz, John L. 1983
+ Bassett, Carroll* 1972	+ Kummer, Clarence 1972	+ Sande, Earl 1955
+ Blum, Walter 1987	+ Kurtsinger, Charley 1967	+ Schilling, Carroll 1970
+ Bostwick, George H.* 1968	+ Loftus, Johnny 1959	Shoemaker, Bill 1958
+ Boulmetis, Sam 1973	Longden, Johnny 1958	+ Simms, Willie........................1977
+ Brooks, Steve 1963	Maher, Danny 1955	+ Sloan, Todhunter 1955
+ Burns, Tommy 1983	+ McAtee, Linus 1956	+ Smithwick, A. Patrick* 1973
+ Butwell, Jimmy 1984	McCarron, Chris 1989	+ Stout, James 1968
Cauthen, Steve 1994	+ McCreary, Conn 1974	+ Taral, Fred 1955
+ Coltiletti, Frank 1970	+ McKinney, Rigan 1968	+ Tuckman, Bayard Jr.* 1973
Cordero, Angel Jr......................1988	+ McLaughlin, James 1955	Turcotte, Ron 1979
+ Crawford, Robert (Specs)* 1973	+ Miller, Walter 1955	+ Turner, Nash 1955
Day, Pat 1991	+ Murphy, Isaac 1955	Ussery, Robert..........................1980
Delahoussaye, Eddie 1993	+ Neves, Ralph 1960	Velasquez, Jorge 1990
+ Ensor, Lavelle (Buddy)............1962	+ Notter, Joe 1963	+ Woolfe, George 1955
+ Fator, Laverne 1955	+ O'Connor, Winnie....................1956	+ Workman, Raymond 1956
Fishback, Jerry* 1992	+ Odom, George 1955	Ycaza, Manuel..........................1977
+ Garner, Andrew (Mack)..........1969	+ O'Neill, Frank 1956	
		*Steeplechase jockey

Trainers

+ Barrera, Laz 1979	+ Hyland, John 1956	+ Parke, Burley 1986
+ Bedwell, H. Guy 1971	+ Jacobs, Hirsch........................1958	+ Penna, Angel Sr. 1988
+ Brown, Edward D...................1984	Jerkens, H. Allen 1975	+ Pincus, Jacob 1988
Burch, Elliot 1980	+ Johnson, William R. 1986	+ Rogers, John 1955
+ Burch, Preston M. 1963	+ Jolley, LeRoy 1987	+ Rowe, James Sr. 1955
+ Burch, W.P. 1955	+ Jones, Ben A. 1958	Schulhofer, Scotty 1992
+ Burlew, Fred 1973	Jones, H.A. (Jimmy) 1959	Sheppard, Jonathan 1990
+ Byers, J.D. (Dilly) 1967	+ Joyner, Andrew 1955	+ Smith, Robert A.......................1976
+ Childs, Frank E. 1968	Kelly, Tom 1993	+ Smithwick, Mike 1976
Cocks, W. Burling 1985	Laurin, Lucien 1977	Stephens, Woody 1976
Croll, Jimmy 1994	+ Lewis, J. Howard 1969	+ Thompson, H.J. 1969
+ Duke, William 1956	+ Luro, Horatio 1980	+ Trotsek, Harry 1984
+ Feustel, Louis 1964	+ Madden, John 1983	Van Berg, Jack 1985
+ Fitzsimmons, J. (Sunny Jim) 1958	+ Maloney, Jim 1989	+ Van Berg, Marion 1970
Frankel, Bobby 1995	Martin, Frank (Pancho)..........1981	+ Veitch, Sylvester 1977
+ Gaver, John M. 1966	McAnally, Ron 1990	+ Walden, Robert......................1970
+ Healey, Thomas......................1955	+ McDaniel, Henry 1956	+ Ward, Sherrill 1978
+ Hildreth, Samuel 1955	+ Miller, MacKenzie 1987	Whiteley, Frank Jr.....................1978
+ Hirsch, Max 1959	+ Molter, William, Jr. 1960	Whittingham, Charlie 1974
+ Hirsch, W.J. (Buddy)................1982	+ Mulholland, Winbert 1967	Winfrey, W.C. (Bill) 1971
+ Hitchcock, Thomas Sr..............1973	+ Neloy, Eddie............................1983	
+ Hughes, Hollie 1973	Nerud, John 1972	

Horses

Year foaled in parentheses.

+ Ack Ack (1966) 1986	+ Alsab (1939)..........................1976	+ Armed (1941).........................1963
Affectionately (1960)..............1989	+ Alydar (1975).........................1989	+ Artful (1902) 1956
Affirmed (1975).....................1980	Alysheba (1984) 1993	+ Arts and Letters (1966)............1994
All-Along (1979)....................1990	+ American Eclipse (1814) 1970	+ Assault (1943) 1964

+ Battleship (1927).................1969
+ Bed O'Roses (1947).............1976
+ Beldame (1901).....................1956
+ Ben Brush (1893)..................1955
+ Bewitch (1945).....................1977
+ Bimelech (1937)....................1990
+ Black Gold (1919)................1989
+ Black Helen (1932)...............1991
+ Blue Larkspur (1926)...........1957
+ Bold Ruler (1954)................1973
+ Bon Nouvel (1960)...............1976
+ Boston (1833).......................1955
+ Broomstick (1901)...............1956
+ Buckpasser (1963)...............1970
+ Busher (1942).......................1964
+ Bushranger (1930)...............1967

+ Cafe Prince (1970)...............1985
+ Carry Back (1958)................1975
+ Cavalcade (1931).................1993
+ Challendon (1936)...............1977
+ Chris Evert (1971)................1988
+ Cicada (1959).......................1967
+ Citation (1945).....................1959
+ Coaltown (1945)..................1983
+ Colin (1905).........................1956
+ Commando (1898).................1956
+ Count Fleet (1940)...............1961
+ Crusader (1923)....................1995

+ Dahlia (1971)........................1981
+ Damascus (1964)..................1974
+ Dark Mirage (1965)..............1974
+ Davona Dale (1976).............1985
+ Desert Vixen (1970)..............1979
+ Devil Diver (1939)................1980
+ Discovery (1931)..................1969
+ Domino (1891)......................1955
+ Dr. Fager (1964)...................1971
+ Eight 30 (1936).....................1994
+ Elkridge (1938).....................1966
+ Emperor of Norfolk (1885) 1988
+ Equipoise (1928)...................1957
+ Exterminator (1915)..............1957

+ Fairmount (1921)..................1985
+ Fair Play (1905)....................1956

+ Firenze (1885)......................1981
  Flatterer (1979).....................1994
  Foolish Pleasure (1972) 1995
+ Forego (1971)......................1979

+ Gallant Bloom (1966)...........1977
+ Gallant Fox (1927)...............1957
+ Gallant Man (1954)..............1987
+ Gallorette (1942)..................1962
+ Gamely (1964)......................1980
  Genuine Risk (1977) 1986
+ Good and Plenty (1900)........1956
+ Grey Lag (1918)....................1957

+ Hamburg (1895)...................1986
+ Hanover (1884).....................1955
+ Henry of Navarre (1891).......1985
+ Hill Prince (1947)..................1991
+ Hindoo (1878).......................1955

+ Imp (1894)...........................1965

+ Jay Trump (1957)..................1971
  John Henry (1975)..................1990
+ Johnstown (1936)..................1992
+ Jolly Roger (1922)................1965

+ Kingston (1884).....................1955
+ Kelso (1957).........................1967
+ Kentucky (1861)....................1983

  Lady's Secret (1982)..............1992
  La Prevoyante (1970).............1995
+ L'Escargot (1963)..................1977
+ Lexington (1850)...................1955
+ Longfellow (1867)..................1971
+ Luke Blackburn (1877)...........1956

+ Majestic Prince (1966)...........1988
+ Man o' War (1917)................1957
+ Miss Woodford (1880)...........1967
+ Myrtlewood (1933)................1979

+ Nashua (1952)......................1965
+ Native Dancer (1950).............1963
+ Native Diver (1959)...............1978
+ Northern Dancer (1961)..........1976
+ Neji (1950)...........................1966

+ Oedipus (1941).....................1978
+ Old Rosebud (1911)...............1968

+ Omaha (1932) 1965

+ Pan Zareta (1910)................1972
+ Parole (1873) 1984
  Personal Ensign (1984)...........1993
+ Peter Pan (1904)..................1956
  Princess Rooney (1980)..........1991

+ Real Delight (1949)...............1987
+ Regret (1912) 1957
+ Reigh Count (1925)...............1978
+ Roamer (1911)......................1981
+ Roseben (1901)......................1956
+ Round Table (1954)...............1972
+ Ruffian (1972)......................1976
+ Ruthless (1864).....................1975

+ Salvator (1886).....................1955
+ Sarazen (1921)......................1957
+ Seabiscuit (1933)..................1958
+ Searching (1952)...................1978
  Seattle Slew (1974)................1981
+ Secretariat (1970)..................1974
+ Shuvee (1966).......................1975
+ Silver Spoon (1956)...............1978
+ Sir Archy (1805)....................1955
+ Sir Barton (1916)..................1957
  Slew o'Gold (1980)................1992
+ Stymie (1941).......................1975
+ Susan's Girl (1969)................1976
+ Swaps (1952)........................1966
+ Sword Dancer (1956).............1977
+ Sysonby (1902).....................1956

+ Ta Wee (1966).....................1994
+ Tim Tam (1955)....................1985
+ Tom Fool (1949)...................1960
+ Top Flight (1929)..................1966
+ Tosmah (1961).....................1984
+ Twenty Grand (1928)............1957
+ Twilight Tear (1941)..............1963

+ War Admiral (1934)...............1958
+ Whirlaway (1938).................1959
+ Whisk Broom II (1907) 1979

  Zaccio (1976).......................1990
+ Zev (1920) 1983

+ Hanes, John W 1982
+ Jeffords, Walter M.................1973

Exemplars of Racing

Mellon, Paul 1989

Widener, George D...............1971

Harness Racing Living Hall of Fame

Established by the U.S. Harness Writers Association (USHWA) in 1958. **Address:** Trotting Horse Museum, 240 Main Street, P.O. Box 590, Goshen, NY 10924; **Telephone:** (914) 294-6330.
Eligibility: Open to all harness racing drivers, trainers and executives. Voting done by USHWA membership. There are 65 members of the Living Hall of Fame, but only the 35 drivers and trainer-drivers are listed below.
Members are listed with years of induction; (+) indicates deceased members.

Trainer-Drivers

  Abbatiello, Carmine.............1986
  Abbatiello, Tony..................1995
  Ackerman, Doug..................1995
+ Avery, Earle........................1975
+ Baldwin, Ralph 1972
  Beissinger, Howard 1975
  Bostwick, Dunbar 1989
+ Cameron, Del 1975
  Campbell, John....................1991
+ Chapman, John 1980
  Cruise, Jimmy......................1987
  Dancer, Stanley....................1970

+ Ervin, Frank........................1969
  Farrington, Bob....................1980
  Filion, Herve........................1976
+ Garnsey, Glen 1983
  Galbraith, Clint....................1990
  Gilmour, Buddy....................1990
  Harner, Levi........................1986
+ Haughton, Billy....................1969
+ Hodgins, Clint......................1973
  Insko, Del.............................1981
  Miller, Del............................1969
+ O'Brien, Joe 1971

  O'Donnell, Bill 1991
  Patterson, John Sir 1994
+ Pownall, Harry 1971
  Riegle, Gene........................1992
+ Russell, Sanders...................1971
+Shively, Bion 1968
  Sholty, George.....................1985
  Simpson, John Sr 1972
+ Smart, Curly........................1970
  Waples, Keith 1987
  Waples, Ron........................1994

MEDIA

National Sportscasters and Sportswriters Hall of Fame

Established in 1959 by the National Sportscasters and Sportswriters Association. **Mailing Address:** P.O. Box 559, Salisbury, NC 28144. A permanent museum is scheduled to open in the autumn of 1996. **Telephone:** (704) 633-4275.

Eligibility: Nominees must be active for at least 25 years. Voting done by NSSA membership and other media representatives.

Class of 1995 (4): sportscasters **Bob Elson** and **Keith Jackson** and sportswriters **Mel Durslag** and **Frank Graham Sr.**

Members are listed with year of induction; (+) indicates deceased members.

Sportscasters

Allen, Mel	1972	Glickman, Marty	1992	+ McNamee, Graham	1964
+ Barber, Walter (Red)	1973	Gowdy, Curt	1981	+ Nelson, Lindsey	1979
Brickhouse, Jack	1983	Harwell, Ernie	1989	+ Prince, Bob	1986
Buck, Jack	1990	+ Hodges, Russ	1975	Schenkel, Chris	1981
Caray, Harry	1989	+ Hoyt, Waite	1987	Scott, Ray	1982
+ Cosell, Howard	1993	+ Husing, Ted	1963	Scully, Vin	1991
+ Dean, Dizzy	1976	Jackson, Keith	1985	+ Stern, Bill	1974
Dunphy, Don	1986	+ McCarthy, Clem	1970	Summerall, Pat	1994
+ Elson, Bob	1995	McKay, Jim	1987		

Sportswriters

Anderson, Dave	1990	+ Graham, Frank Sr.	1995	Povich, Shirley	1984
Bisher, Furman	1989	+ Grimsley, Will	1987	+ Rice, Grantland	1962
Burick, Si	1985	Heinz, W.C.	1987	+ Runyon, Damon	1964
+ Cannon, Jimmy	1986	+ Kieran, John	1971	Russell, Fred	1988
+ Carmichael, John P.	1994	+ Lardner, Ring	1967	Sherrod, Blackie	1991
+ Connor, Dick	1992	+ Murphy, Jack	1988	+ Smith, Walter (Red)	1977
+ Considine, Bob	1980	Murray, Jim	1978	+ Spink, J.G. Taylor	1969
+ Daley, Arthur	1976	Olderman, Murray	1993	+ Ward, Arch	1973
Durslag, Mel	1995	+ Parker, Dan	1975	+ Woodward, Stanley	1974
+ Gould, Alan	1990	Pope, Edwin	1994		

American Sportscasters Hall of Fame

Established in 1984 by the American Sportscasters Association. **Address:** 5 Beekman Street, Suite 814, New York, NY 10038. A permanent museum site is in the planning stages. **Telephone:** (212) 227-8080.

Eligibility: nominations made by selection committee of previous winners, voting by ASA membership.

Class of 1995: Chick Hearn.

Members are listed with year of induction; (+) indicates deceased members.

Allen, Mel	1985	Glickman, Marty	1993	+ McCarthy, Clem	1987
+ Barber, Walter (Red)	1984	Gowdy, Curt	1985	McKay, Jim	1987
Brickhouse, Jack	1985	Harwell, Ernie	1991	+ McNamee, Graham	1984
Buck, Jack	1990	Hearn, Chick	1995	+ Nelson, Lindsey	1986
Caray, Harry	1989	+ Husing, Ted	1984	Scully, Vin	1992
+ Cosell, Howard	1993	Jackson, Keith	1994	+ Stern, Bill	1984
Dunphy, Don	1984				

40th Anniversary Top 40s

In 1986, *Sport* magazine celebrated its 40th anniversary by publishing a list of the 40 most significant athletes and sports figures from 1946-86. Eight years later, *Sports Illustrated* toasted its first four decades with a Top 40 of its own.

On both lists (19): Hank Aaron, Muhammad Ali, Roone Arledge, Jim Brown, Bear Bryant, Howard Cosell, Wayne Gretzky, Billie Jean King, Marvin Miller, Joe Namath, Martina Navratilova, Jack Nicklaus, Bobby Orr, Arnold Palmer, Pelé, Pete Rose, Pete Rozelle, Bill Russell and John Wooden.

Sport's "The 40 Who Changes Sports"

Selected by the editors of *Sport* for the magazine's 40th anniversary issue (December 1986). Entries were not ranked.

Aaron, Hank	Baseball	Evert, Chris	Tennis	Orr, Bobby	Hockey
Ali, Muhammad	Boxing	Flood, Curt	Baseball	Palmer, Arnold	Golf
Arledge, Roone	Television	+ France, Bill Sr	Auto Racing	Pelé	Soccer
Auerbach, Red	Baskteball	Gretzky, Wayne	Hockey	+ Rickey, Branch	Baseball
+ Bikila, Abebe	Track & Field	King, Billie Jean	Tennis	+ Robinson, Jackie	Baseball
Bouton, Jim	Literature	+ Lombardi, Vince	Football	+ Robinson, Sugar Ray	Boxing
Brown, Jim	Football	+ Mantle, Mickey	Baseball	Rose, Pete	Baseball
+ Brown, Paul	Football	Mays, Willie	Baseball	Rozelle, Pete	Football
+ Brundage, Avery	Olympics	Miller, Marvin	Baseball	Russell, Bill	Basketball
+ Bryant, Bear	Football	Namath, Joe	Football	Shoemaker, Bill	Horse Racing
Chamberlain, Wilt	Basketball	Navratilova, Martina	Tennis	+ Stengel, Casey	Baseball
+ Cosell, Howard	Television	Nicklaus, Jack	Golf	Williams, Ted	Baseball
Cousy, Bob	Basketball	+ Norris, James D.	Boxing	Wooden, John	Basketball
Davis, Al	Football				

Sports Illustrated's "40 For the Ages"

Selected by the editors of *Sports Illustrated* for the weekly magazie's 40th anniversary issue (Sept. 19, 1994). Entries were ranked (see below).

Aaron, Hank	Baseball	+ Gores, Dr. Harold	Synthetic Turf	Navratilova, Martina	Tennis
Ali, Muhammad	Boxing	Gretzky, Wayne	Hockey	Nicklaus, Jack	Golf
Arledge, Roone	Television	Jackson, Dr. Robert	Medicine	Orr, Bobby	Hockey
+ Ashe, Arthur	Tennis	Jordan, Michael	Basketball	Palmer, Arnold	Golf
Larry Bird		King, Billie Jean	Tennis	Pelé	Soccer
& Magic Johnson	Basketball	King, Don	Boxing	Petty, Richard	Auto Racing
Brown, Jim	Football	Korbut, Olga	Gymnastics	Rasmussen, Bill	Television
+ Bryant, Bear	Football	Lemond, Greg	Cycling	Rose, Pete	Baseball
+ Clemente, Roberto	Baseball	Leonard, Sugar Ray	Boxing	Rozelle, Pete	Football
+ Cosell, Howard	Television	Lewis, Carl	Track & Field	Russell, Bill	Basketball
Davidson, Gary	Business	McCormack, Mark	Business	Ryan, Nolan	Baseball
Erving, Julius	Basketball	Miller, Marvin	Baseball	+ Secretariat	Horse Racing
+ Fixx, Jim	Running	Montana, Joe	Football	Wooden, John	Basketball
Fleming, Peggy	Figure Skating	Namath, Joe	Football		

Overall Ranking (in order of importance)

1 Muhammad Ali	11 Carl Lewis	21 Bill Russell	31 Bobby Orr
2 Michael Jordan	12 Wayne Gretzky	22 Howard Cosell	32 Sugar Ray Leonard
3 Roone Arledge	13 Pete Rozelle	23 Joe Montana	33 Jim Fixx
4 Jim Brown	14 Martina Navratilova	24 Bear Bryant	34 Nolan Ryan
5 Billie Jean King	15 Hank Aaron	25 Roberto Clemente	35 Peggy Fleming
6 Pete Rose	16 John Wooden	26 Olga Korbut	36 Don King
7 Marvin Miller	17 Secretariat	27 Arthur Ashe	37 Dr. Robert Jackson
8 Larry Bird	18 Joe Namath	28 Richard Petty	38 Greg Lemond
& Magic Johnson	19 Dr. Harold Gores	29 Bill Rasmussen	39 Gary Davidson
9 Arnold Palmer	20 Jack Nicklaus	30 Pelé	40 Julius Erving
10 Mark McCormack			

MOTOR SPORTS

Motorsports Hall of Fame of America

Established in 1989. **Mailing Address:** P.O. Box 194, Novi, MI 48050. **Telephone:** (313) 349-7223.

Eligibility: Nominees must be retired at least three years or engaged in their area of motor sports for at least 20 years. Areas include: open wheel, stock car, dragster, sports car, motorcycle, off road, power boat, air racing and land speed records.

Class of 1995 (9): DRIVERS— **Peter De Paolo** (Indy cars); **Chip Hanauer** (hydroplanes); **Rex Mays** (Indy cars); **Bruce McLaren** (Formula One and Can Am, F1 car owner); **Fireball Roberts** (stock cars). CONTRIBUTORS— **Keith Black** (speed boat and drag racing engine builder); **Louis Chevrolet** (auto racing pioneer, driver, innovator, car company founder); **Bruce McLaren** (driver, Formula One race team owner, **Roger Penske** (driver, owner of IndyCar, NASCAR and Formula One race teams, CART co-founder, race track owner).

Members are listed with year of induction; (+) indicates deceased members.

Drivers

Allison, Bobby	1992	Gurney, Dan	1991	+ Oldfield, Barney	1989
Andretti, Mario	1990	Hanauer, Chip	1995	Parks, Wally	1993
Arfons, Art	1991	Hill, Phil	1989	Pearson, David	1993
+ Baker, Cannonball	1989	+ Holbert, Al	1993	+ Petrali, Joe	1992
Breedlove, Craig	1993	+ Horn, Ted	1993	Petty, Richard	1989
+ Campbell, Sir Malcolm	1994	Johnson, Junior	1991	Prudhomme, Don	1991
Cantrell, Bill	1992	Jones, Parnelli	1992	+ Roberts, Fireball	1995
+ Chenoweth, Dean	1991	Kalitta, Connie	1992	Roberts, Kenny	1990
+ Clark, Jim	1990	Leonard, Joe	1991	+ Shaw, Wilbur	1991
DeCosta, Roger	1994	+ McLaren, Bruce	1995	+ Thompson, Mickey	1990
+ DePalma, Ralph	1992	Mann, Dick	1993	+ Turner, Roscoe	1991
+ DePaolo, Peter	1995	+ Mays, Rex	1995	Unser, Bobby	1994
+ Donahue, Mark	1990	Meyer, Louis	1993	+ Vukovich, Bill Sr	1992
Foyt, A.J.	1989	Muldowney, Shirley	1990	Ward, Roger	1995
Garlits, Don	1989	+ Muncy, Bill	1989	+ Wood, Gar	1990
Glidden, Bob	1994	Musson, Ron	1993	Yarborough, Cale	1994

Pilots

+ Cochran, Jacqueline	1993				
+ Curtiss, Glenn	1990				
+ Doolittle, Jimmy	1989				
+ Earhart, Amelia	1992				
+ Falck, Bill	1994				

Contributors

+ Agajanian, J.C	1992	Hall, Jim	1994
Bignotti, George	1993	+ Hulman, Tony	1991
+ Black, Keith	1995	Little, Bernie	1994
+ Chevrolet, Louis	1995	Penske, Roger	1995
Economaki, Chris	1994	+ Rickenbacker, Eddie	1994
+ France, Bill Sr.	1990	Shelby, Carroll	1992

International Motorsports Hall of Fame

Established in 1990 by the International Motorsports Hall of Fame Commission. **Mailing Address:** P.O.Box 1018, Talladega, AL 35160. **Telephone:** (205) 362-5002.

Eligibility: Nominees must be retired from their specialty in motorsports for five years. Voting done by 150-member panel made up of the world-wide auto racing media.

Class of 1996: To be announced Sept. 17, 1995 for induction on April 25, 1996 (see Updates chapter). There was no Class of '95.

Members are listed with year of induction; (+) indicates deceased members.

Drivers

Allison, Bobby 1993	Hill, Phil.............1991	Pearson, David 1993
+ Ascari, Alberto 1992	+ Holbert, Al.............1993	Petty, Lee 1990
Baker, Buck............1990	Jarrett, Ned 1991	+ Roberts, Fireball 1990
+ Bettenhausen, Tony 1991	Johnson, Junior 1990	Roberts, Kenny 1992
Brabham, Jack............1990	Jones, Parnelli............1990	Rose, Mauri 1994
+ Campbell, Sir Malcolm 1990	Lauda, Niki 1993	+ Shaw, Wilbur 1991
+ Clark, Jim 1990	Lorenzen, Fred 1991	Stewart, Jackie 1990
+ DePalma, Ralph 1991	+ Lund, Tiny 1994	Thomas, Herb 1994
+ Donahue, Mark............1990	+ Mays, Rex 1993	+ Turner, Curtis 1992
+ Fangio, Juan Manuel............1990	+ McLaren, Bruce 1991	Unser, Bobby 1990
Flock, Tim 1991	Meyer, Louis 1992	+ Vukovich, Bill 1991
+ Gregg, Peter 1992	Moss, Stirling 1990	Ward Rodger 1992
Gurney, Dan 1990	+ Oldfield, Barney 1990	+ Weatherly, Joe 1994
+ Hill, Graham 1990	Parsons, Benny 1994	Yarborough, Cale 1993

Contributors

Bignotti, George............1993	+ France, Bill Sr 1990	Parks, Wally 1992
+ Chapman, Colin............1994	Granatelli, Andy 1992	+ Rickenbacker, Eddie 1992
+ Chevrolet, Louis............1992	+ Hulman, Tony............1990	Shelby, Carroll 1991
+ Ferrari, Enzo............1994	Marcum, John............1994	+ Thompson, Mickey 1990
+ Ford, Henry............1993	Moody, Ralph 1994	Yunick, Smokey............1990

OLYMPICS

U.S. Olympic Hall of Fame

Established in 1983 by the United States Olympic Committee. **Mailing Address:** U.S. Olympic Committee, 1750 East Boulder Street, Colorado Springs, CO 80909. Plans for a permanent museum site have been suspended due to lack of funding. **Telephone:** (719) 578-4529.

Eligibility: Nominated athletes must be five years removed from active competition. Voting done by National Sportscasters and Sportswriters Association, Hall of Fame members and the USOC board members of directors.

Class of 1995: Voting for membership in the Hall was suspended in 1993.

Members are listed with year of induction; (+) indicates deceased members.

Teams

1956 Basketball—Dick Boushka, Carl Cain, Chuck Darling, Bill Evans, Gib Ford, Burdy Haldorson, Bill Hougland, Bob Jeangerard, K.C. Jones, Bill Russell, Ron Tomsic, +Jim Walsh and coach +Gerald Tucker.

1960 Basketball—Jay Arnette, Walt Bellamy, Bob Boozer, Terry Dischinger, Burdy Haldorson, Darrall Imhoff, Allen Kelley, +Lester Lane, Jerry Lucas, Oscar Robertson, Adrian Smith, Jerry West and coach Pete Newell.

1964 Basketball—Jim Barnes, Bill Bradley, Larry Brown, Joe Caldwell, Mel Counts, Richard Davies, Walt Hazzard, Luke Jackson, John McCaffrey, Jeff Mullins, Jerry Shipp, George Wilson and coach +Hank Iba.

1960 Ice Hockey—Billy Christian, Roger Christian, Billy Cleary, Bob Cleary, Gene Grazia, Paul Johnson, Jack Kirrane, John Mayasich, Jack McCartan, Bob McKay, Dick Meredith, Weldon Olson, Ed Owen, Rod Paavola, Larry Palmer, Dick Rodenheiser, +Tom Williams and coach Jack Riley.

1980 Ice Hockey—Bill Baker, Neal Broten, Dave Christian, Steve Christoff, Jim Craig, Mike Eruzione, John Harrington, Steve Janaszak, Mark Johnson, Ken Morrow, Rob McClanahan, Jack O'Callahan, Mark Pavelich, Mike Ramsey, Buzz Schneider, Dave Silk, Eric Strobel, Bob Suter, Phil Verchota, Mark Wells and coach Herb Brooks.

The Olympic Order

Established in 1974 by the International Olympic Committee (IOC) to honor athletes, officials and media members who have made remarkable contributions to the Olympic movement. The IOC's Council of the Olympic Order is presided over by the IOC president and active IOC members are not eligible for consideration. Through 1995, only two American officials have received the Order's highest commendation—the gold medal:

Avery Brundage, president of USOC (1928-53) and IOC (1952-72), was given the award posthumously in 1975.

Peter Ueberroth, president of Los Angeles Olympic Organizing Committee, was given the award in 1984.

Alpine Skiing

Mahre, Phil............................1992

Bobsled

+ Eagan, Eddie (see Boxing)......1983

Boxing

Clay, Cassius*.........................1983
+ Eagan, Eddie (see Bobsled).....1983
Foreman, George....................1990
Frazier, Joe............................1989
Leonard, Sugar Ray................1985
Patterson, Floyd 1987

*Clay changed name to Muhammad Ali in 1964.

Cycling

Carpenter-Phinney, Connie 1992

Diving

King, Miki..............................1992
Lee, Sammy...........................1990
Louganis, Greg 1985
McCormick, Pat 1985

Figure Skating

Albright, Tenley......................1988
Button, Dick 1983
Fleming, Peggy 1983
Hamill, Dorothy......................1991
Hamilton, Scott.......................1990

Gymnastics

Conner, Bart 1991
Retton, Mary Lou....................1985
Vidmar, Peter 1991

Rowing

+ Kelly, Jack Sr. 1990

Speed Skating

Heiden, Eric...........................1983

Swimming

Babashoff, Shirley 1987
Caulkins, Tracy 1990
+ Daniels, Charles 1988
de Varona, Donna 1987
+ Kahanamoku, Duke 1984
+ Madison, Helene....................1992
Meyer, Debbie 1986
Naber, John...........................1984
Schollander, Don....................1983
Spitz, Mark............................1983
+ Weissmuller, Johnny 1983

Track & Field

Beamon, Bob 1983
Boston, Ralph.........................1985
+ Calhoun, Lee..........................1991
Campbell, Milt 1992
Davenport, Willie 1991
Davis, Glenn..........................1986
+ Didrikson, Babe 1983
Dillard, Harrison.....................1983
Evans, Lee 1989
+ Ewry, Ray 1983
Fosbury, Dick 1992
Jenner, Bruce 1986
Johnson, Rafer 1983
+ Kraenzlein, Alvin 1985
Lewis, Carl............................1985
Mathias, Bob 1983

Mills, Billy..............................1984
Morrow, Bobby 1989
Moses, Edwin 1985
O'Brien, Parry 1984
Oerter, Al 1983
+ Owens, Jesse 1983
+ Paddock, Charley...................1991
Richards, Bob 1983
+ Rudolph, Wilma 1983
+ Sheppard, Mel 1989
Shorter, Frank 1984
+ Thorpe, Jim............................1983
Toomey, Bill...........................1984
Tyus, Wyomia.........................1985
Whitfield, Mal.........................1988
+ Wykoff, Frank.........................1984

Weight Lifting

+ Davis, John 1989
Kono, Tommy..........................1990

Wrestling

Gable, Dan 1985

Contributors

Arledge, Roone......................1989
+ Brundage, Avery 1983
+ Bushnell, Asa 1990
Hull, Col. Don 1992
+ Iba, Hank 1985
+ Kane, Robert..........................1986
+ Kelly, Jack Jr..........................1992
McKay, Jim.............................1988
Miller, Don.............................1984
Simon, William 1991
Walker, LeRoy........................1987

SOCCER

National Soccer Hall of Fame

Established in 1950 by the Philadelphia Oldtimers Association. First exhibit unveiled in Oneonta, NY in 1982. Moved into present building in 1987. New Hall of Fame planned at Wright National Soccer Campus in Oneonta. **Address:** 5-11 Ford Avenue, Oneonta, NY 13820. **Telephone:** (607) 432-3351.

Eligibility: Nominated players must have represented the U.S. in international competition and be retired five years; other categories include Meritorious Service and Special Commendation.

Nominations made by state organizations and a veterans' committee. Voting done by nine-member committee made up of Hall of Famers, U.S. Soccer officials and members of the national media.

Class of 1995 (5): PLAYERS— former national team members **George Brown** (forward, 1956-59) and **Willy Schaller** (midfielder, 1952-60). CONTRIBUTORS— **Clay Berling**, the founding publisher of *Soccer America*; **Alfred Kleinaitis**, college, pro and World Cup referee (1962-91); **Al Miller**, college coach at Hartwick (1967-72) and pro coach in NASL with Philadelphia (1973-75) and Dallas (1976-80).

Members are listed with home state and year of induction; (+) indicates deceased members.

Members

Abronzino, Umberto (CA) 1971
Aimi, Milton (TX) 1991
+ Alonso, Julie (NY)...................1972
+ Andersen, William (NY)..........1956
+ Ardizzone, John (CA) 1971
+ Armstrong, James (NY) 1952
+ Auld, Andrew (RI)...................1986

Bahr, Walter (PA) 1976
Barr, George (NY) 1983
+ Barriskill, Joe (NY)..................1953
+ Beardsworth, Fred (MA)..........1965
Berling, Clay (CA) 1995
Bernabei, Ray (PA) 1978
Best, John O. (CA)..................1982
+ Bookie, Michael (PA)...............1986
+ Booth, Joseph (CT)..................1952

Borghi, Frank (MO) 1976
Boulos, Frenchy (NY) 1980
+ Boxer, Matt (CA)....................1961
+ Briggs, Lawrence E. (MA)........1978
+ Brittan, Harold (PA) 1951
+ Brock, John (MA)....................1950
+ Brown, Andrew M. (OH)..........1950
+ Brown, David (NJ)...................1951
Brown, George (NJ)................1995
Brown, James (NY)..................1986

+ Cahill, Thomas W (NY)............1950
+ Carenza, Joe (MO).................1982
+ Caraffi, Ralph (OH) 1959
Chacurian, Chico (CT) 1992
+ Chesney, Stan (NY).................1966
+ Coll, John (NY).......................1986

+ Collins, George M. (MA)..........1951
+ Colombo, Charlie (MO) 1976
+ Commander, Colin (OH) 1967
+ Cordery, Ted (CA) 1975
+ Craddock, Robert (PA) 1959
+ Craggs, Edmund (WA).............1969
Craggs, George (WA) 1981
+ Cummings, Wilfred R. (IL) 1953

+ Delach, Joseph (PA) 1973
DeLuca, Enzo (NY) 1979
+ Dick, Walter (CA)...................1989
Diorio, Nick (PA) 1974
+ Donaghy, Edward J. (NY) 1951
+ Donelli, Buff (PA) 1954
+ Donnelly, George (NY).............1989
+ Douglas, Jimmy (NJ)...............1954

National Soccer Hall of Fame (Cont.)

+ Dresmich, John W. (PA) 1968
+ Duff, Duncan (CA) 1972
+ Dugan, Thomas (NJ) 1951
+ Dunn, James (MO) 1974

Edwards, Gene (WI) 1985
+ Epperleim, Rudy (NJ) 1951

+ Fairfield, Harry (PA) 1951
Feibusch, Ernst (CA) 1984
+ Ferguson, John (PA) 1950
+ Fernley, John A. (MA) 1951
+ Ferro, Charles (NY) 1958
+ Fishwick, George E. (IL) 1974
+ Flamhaft, Jack (NY) 1964
+ Fleming, Harry G. (PA) 1967
+ Florie, Thomas (NJ) 1986
+ Foulds, Pal (MA) 1953
+ Foulds, Sam (MA) 1969
+ Fowler, Dan (NY) 1970
+ Fowler, Peg (NY) 1979
Fricker, Werner (PA) 1992
+ Fryer, William J. (NJ) 1951

+ Gaetjens, Joe (NY) 1976
+ Gallagher, James (NY) 1986
+ Garcia, Pete (MO) 1964
+ Gentle, James (PA) 1986
Getzinger, Rudy (IL) 1991
+ Giesler, Walter (MO) 1962
Glover, Teddy (NY) 1965
+ Gonsalves, Billy (MA) 1950
Gormley, Bob (PA) 1989
+ Gould, David L. (PA) 1953
+ Govier, Sheldon (IL) 1950
Greer, Don (CA) 1985
Gryzik, Joe (IL) 1973
+ Guelker, Bob (MO) 1980
Guennel, Joe (CO) 1980

Harker, Al (PA) 1979
+ Healy, George (MI) 1951
Heilpern, Herb (NY) 1988
+ Hemmings, William (IL) 1961
+ Hudson, Maurice (CA) 1966
Hunt, Lamar (TX) 1982
Hynes, John (NY) 1977

+ Iglehart, Alfredda (MD) 1951

+ Japp, John (PA) 1953
+ Jeffrey, William (PA) 1951
+ Johnson, Jack (IL) 1952

Kabanica, Mike (WI) 1987
Kehoe, Bob (MO) 1990
Kelly, Frank (NJ) 1994
+ Kempton, George (WA) 1950

Keough, Harry (MO) 1976
+ Klein, Paul (NJ) 1953
Kleinaitis, Al (IN) 1995
+ Koszma, Oscar (CA) 1964
Kracher, Frank (IL) 1983
Kraft, Granny (MD) 1984
+ Kraus, Harry (NY) 1963
+ Kunter, Rudy (NY) 1963

+ Lamm, Kurt (NY) 1979
Lang, Millard (MD) 1950
Larson, Bert (CT) 1988
+ Lewis, H. Edgar (PA) 1950
Lombardo, Joe (NY) 1984
Long, Denny (MO) 1993

+ MacEwan, John J. (MI) 1953
+ Maca, Joe (NY) 1976
+ Magnozzi, Enzo (NY) 1978
+ Maher, Jack (IL) 1970
+ Manning, Dr. Randolf (NY) 1950
+ Marre, John (MO) 1953
McBride, Pat (MO) 1994
+ McClay, Allan (MA) 1971
+ McGhee, Bart (NY) 1986
+ McGrath, Frank (MA) 1978
+ McGuire, Jimmy (NY) 1951
+ McGuire, John (NY) 1951
+ McIlveney, Eddie (PA) 1976
McLaughlin, Bennie (PA) 1977
+ McSkimming, Dent (MO) 1951
Merovich, Pete (PA) 1971
+ Mieth, Werner (NJ) 1974
+ Millar, Robert (NY) 1950
Miller, Al (OH) 1995
+ Miller, Milton (NY) 1971
+ Mills, Jimmy (PA) 1954
Monson, Lloyd (NY) 1994
Moore, James F. (MO) 1971
+ Moorehouse, George (NY) 1986
+ Morrison, Robert (PA) 1951
+ Morrissette, Bill (MA) 1967

Nanoski, Jukey (PA) 1993
+ Netto, Fred (IL) 1958
Newman, Ron (CA) 1992
+ Niotis, D.J. (IL) 1963

+ O'Brien, Shamus (NY) 1990
Olaff, Gene (NJ) 1971
+ Oliver, Arnie (MA) 1968

+ Palmer, William (PA) 1952
Pariani, Gino (MO) 1976
+ Patenaude, Bert (MA) 1971
+ Pearson, Eddie (GA) 1990
+ Peel, Peter (IL) 1951

Pelé (Brazil) 1993
Peters, Wally (NJ) 1967
Phillipson, Don (CO) 1987
+ Piscopo, Giorgio (NY) 1978
+ Pomeroy, Edgar (CA) 1955

+ Ramsden, Arnold (TX) 1957
+ Ratican, Harry (MO) 1950
Reese, Doc (MD) 1957
+ Renzulli, Pete (NY) 1951
Ringsdorf, Gene (MD) 1979
Roth, Werner (NY) 1989
+ Rottenberg, Jack (NJ) 1971
Roy, Willy (IL) 1989
+ Ryan, Hun (PA) 1958

+ Sager, Tom (PA) 1968
Saunders, Harry (NY) 1981
Schaller, Willy (IL) 1995
Schellscheidt, Mannie (NJ) 1990
Schillinger, Emil (PA) 1960
+ Schroeder, Elmer (PA) 1951
+ Scwarcz, Erno (NY) 1951
+ Shields, Fred (PA) 1968
+ Single, Erwin (NY) 1981
+ Slone, Philip (NY) 1986
+ Smith, Alfred (NY) 1951
+ Souza, Ed (MA) 1976
Souza, Clarkie (MA) 1976
+ Spalding, Dick (PA) 1951
+ Stark, Archie (NJ) 1950
+ Steelink, Nicolaas (CA) 1971
+ Steur, August (NY) 1969
+ Stewart, Douglas (PA) 1950
+ Stone, Robert T. (CO) 1971
+ Swords, Thomas (MA) 1976

+ Tintle, Joseph (NJ) 1952
+ Tracey, Ralph (MO) 1986
+ Triner, Joseph (IL) 1951

+ Vaughan, Frank (MO) 1986

+ Walder, Jimmy (PA) 1971
+ Wallace, Frank (MO) 1976
+ Washauer, Adolph (CA) 1977
+ Webb, Tom (WA) 1987
+ Weir, Alex (NY) 1975
+ Weston, Victor (WA) 1956
+ Wilson, Peter (NJ) 1950
+ Wood, Alex (MI) 1986
+ Woods, John W. (IL) 1952

Yeagley, Jerry (IN) 1989
+ Young, John (CA) 1958

+ Zampini, Dan (PA) 1963
Zerhusen, Al (CA) 1978

SWIMMING

International Swimming Hall of Fame

Established in 1965 by the U.S. College Coaches' Swim Forum. **Address**: One Hall of Fame Drive, Ft. Lauderdale, FL 33316. **Telephone**: (305) 462-6536.
Categories for induction are: swimming, diving, water polo, synchronized swimming, coaching, pioneers and contributors. Of the 445 members, 248 are from the United States. Contributors are not included in the following list.
Members are listed with year of induction; (+) indicates deceased members.

U.S. Men

+ Anderson, Miller 1967
+ Boggs, Phil 1985
Breen, George 1975
+ Browning, Skippy 1975
Bruner, Mike 1988
Burton, Mike 1977

+ Cann, Tedford 1967
Carey, Rick 1993
Clark, Earl 1972
Clark, Steve 1966
Cleveland, Dick 1991
Clotworthy, Robert 1980

+ Crabbe, Buster 1965
+ Daniels, Charlie 1965
Degener, Dick 1971
DeMont, Rick 1990
+ Desjardins, Pete 1966
+ Faricy, John 1990

+ Farrell, Jeff 1968
+ Fick, Peter 1978
+ Flanagan, Ralph 1978
Ford, Alan 1966
Furniss, Bruce 1987
Gaines, Rowdy 1995
Glancy, Harrison 1990
+ Goodwin, Budd 1971
Graef, Jed 1988
Haines, George 1977
Hall, Gary 1981
+ Harlan, Bruce 1973
+ Hebner, Harry 1968
Hencken, John 1988
Hickcox, Charles 1976
Higgins, John 1971
Holiday, Harry 1991
Irwin, Juno Stover 1980
Jastremski, Chet 1977
+ Kahanamoku, Duke 1965
+ Kealoha, Warren 1968
Kiefer, Adolph 1965
Kinsella, John 1986
Konno, Ford 1972
+ Kruger, Stubby 1986
+ Kuehn, Louis 1988
+ Langer, Ludy 1988
Larson, Lance 1980

Lee, Dr. Sammy 1968
+ LeMoyne, Harry 1988
Louganis, Greg 1993
Lundquist, Steve 1990
Mann, Thompson 1984
McCormick, Pat 1965
+ McDermott, Turk 1969
+ McGillivray, Perry 1981
McKenzie, Don 1989
McKinney, Frank 1975
McLane, Jimmy 1970
+ Medica, Jack 1966
Montgomery, Jim 1986
Mullikan, Bill 1984
Naber, John 1982
Nakama, Keo 1975
+ O'Connor, Wally 1966
Oyakawa, Yoshi 1979
+ Patnik, Al 1969
+ Riley, Mickey 1977
+ Ris, Wally 1966
Robie, Carl 1976
Ross, Clarence 1988
+ Ross, Norman 1967
Roth, Dick 1987
+ Ruddy, Joe 1986
Russell, Doug 1985
Saari, Roy 1976

+ Schaeffer, E. Carroll 1968
Scholes, Clarke 1980
Schollander, Don 1965
Shaw, Tim 1989
+ Sheldon, George 1989
+ Skelton, Robert 1988
Smith, Bill 1966
+ Smith, Dutch 1979
+ Smith, Jimmy 1992
Smith, R. Jackson 1983
Spitz, Mark 1977
Stack, Allen 1979
Stickles, Ted 1995
Stock, Tom 1989
+ Swendsen, Clyde 1991
Tobian, Gary 1978
Troy, Mike 1971
Vande Weghe, Albert 1990
+ Verdeur, Joe 1966
+ Vollmer, Hal 1990
Von Saltza, Chris 1966
Wayne, Marshall 1981
Webster, Bob 1970
+ Weissmuller, Johnny 1965
+ White, Al 1965
Wrightson, Bernie 1984
Yoryzk, Bill 1971

U.S. Women

Anderson, Terry 1986
Atwood, Sue 1992
Babashoff, Shirley 1982
Ball, Catie 1976
+ Bauer, Sybil 1967
Belote, Melissa 1983
Bliebtrey, Ethelda 1967
+ Boyle, Charlotte 1988
Burke, Lynne 1978
Bush, Lesley 1986
Callen, Gloria 1984
Caretto, Patty 1987
Carr, Cathy 1988
Caulkins, Tracy 1990
Chadwick, Florence 1970
Chandler, Jennifer 1987
+ Coleman, Georgia 1966
Cone, Carin 1984
Costie, Candy 1995
Crlenkovich, Helen 1981
Curtis, Ann 1966
de Varona, Donna 1969
+ Dorfner, Olga 1970
Draves, Vickie 1969
Duenkel, Ginny 1985
Ederle, Gertrude 1965
Ellis, Kathy 1991
Ferguson, Cathy 1978
Finneran, Sharon 1985

+ Galligan, Claire 1970
+ Garatti-Seville, Eleanor 1992
Gestring, Marjorie 1976
Gossick, Sue 1988
+ Guest, Irene 1990
Hall, Kaye 1979
Henne, Jan 1979
Holm, Eleanor 1966
Hunt-Newman, Virginia 1993
Johnson, Gail 1983
Kane, Marion 1981
+ Kaufman, Beth 1967
Kight, Lenore 1981
King, Micki 1978
Kolb, Claudia 1975
+ Lackie, Ethel 1969
Lord-Landon, Alice 1993
+ Madison, Helene 1966
Mann, Shelly 1966
McGrath, Margo 1989
McKim, Josephine 1991
Meagher, Mary T. 1993
+ Meany, Helen 1971
Meyer, Debbie 1977
Mitchell, Michele 1995
Moe, Karen 1992
Morris, Pam 1965
Neilson, Sandra 1986
+ Norelius, Martha 1967

Olsen, Zoe-Ann 1989
O'Rourke, Heidi 1980
+ Osipowich, Albina 1986
Pedersen, Susan 1995
Pinkston, Betty Becker 1967
Pope, Paula Jean Meyers 1979
Potter, Cynthia 1987
Poynton, Dorothy 1968
+ Rawls, Katherine 1965
Redmond, Carol 1989
Riggin, Aileen 1967
Ross, Anne 1984
Rothammer, Keena 1991
Ruiz-Conforto, Tracie 1993
Ruuska, Sylvia 1976
Schuler, Carolyn 1989
Seller, Peg 1988
+ Smith, Caroline 1988
Stouder, Sharon 1972
+ Vilen, Kay 1978
+ Wainwright, Helen 1972
+ Watson, Lillian (Pokey) 1984
Wehselau, Mariechen 1989
Welshons, Kim 1988
Wichman, Sharon 1991
Williams, Esther 1966
Woodbridge, Margaret 1989

U.S. Coaches

+ Armbruster, Dave 1966
+ Bachrach, Bill 1966
Hobie 1983
+ Brandsten, Ernst 1966
+ Brauninger, Stan 1972
+ Cady, Fred 1969
+ Center, George (Dad) 1991
Chavoor, Sherman 1977
+ Cody, Jack 1970
Counsilman, Dr. James 1976
+ Curtis, Katherine 1979
Daland, Peter 1977
+ Daughters, Ray 1971

Draves, Lyle 1989
Gambril, Don 1983
Haines, George 1977
Handley, L. de B. 1967
Hannula, Dick 1987
Kimball, Dick 1985
+ Kiputh, Bob 1965
Mann, Matt II 1965
McCormick, Glen 1995
Moriarty, Phil 1980
Mowerson, Robert 1986
Muir, Bob 1989
+ Neuschaufer, Al 1967

Nitzkowski, Monte 1991
O'Brien, Ron 1988
+ Papenguth, Richard 1986
+ Peppe, Mike 1966
+ Pinkston, Clarence 1966
+ Robinson, Tom 1965
Sakamoto, Soichi 1966
+ Sava, Charlie 1970
+ Schlueter, Walt 1978
Smith, Dick 1979
Stager, Gus 1982
Thornton, Nort 1995
Tinkham, Stan 1989

TENNIS

International Tennis Hall of Fame

Originally the National Tennis Hall of Fame. Established in 1953 by James Van Alen and sanctioned by the U.S. Tennis Association in 1954. Renamed the International Tennis Hall of Fame in 1976. **Address:** 194 Bellevue Ave., Newport, RI 02840. **Telephone:** (401) 849-3990.

Eligibility: Nominated players must be five years removed from being a "significant factor" in competitive tennis. Voting done by members of the international tennis media.

Class of 1995 (1): PLAYER—**Chris Evert** (pro, 1972-89).

Members are listed with year of induction; (+) indicates deceased members.

Men

+ Adee, George	1964	+ Hewitt, Bob	1992	Ralston, Dennis	1987
+ Alexander, Fred	1961	+ Hoad, Lew	1980	+ Renshaw, Ernest	1983
+ Allison, Wilmer	1963	+ Hovey, Fred	1974	+ Renshaw, William	1983
+ Alonso, Manuel	1977	+ Hunt, Joe	1966	+ Richards, Vincent	1961
+ Ashe, Arthur	1985	+ Hunter, Frank	1961	Riggs, Bobby	1967
+ Behr, Karl	1969	+ Johnston, Bill	1958	Roche, Tony	1986
Borg, Bjorn	1987	+ Jones, Perry	1970	Rosewall, Ken	1980
+ Borotra, Jean	1976	Kodes, Jan	1990	Santana, Manuel	1984
Bromwich, John	1984	Kramer, Jack	1968	Savitt, Dick	1976
+ Brookes, Norman	1977	Lacoste, Rene	1976	Schroeder, Ted	1966
+ Brugnon, Jacques	1976	+ Larned, William	1956	+ Sears, Richard	1955
Budge, Don	1964	Larsen, Art	1969	Sedgman, Frank	1979
+ Campbell, Oliver	1955	Laver, Rod	1981	Segura, Pancho	1984
+ Chace, Malcolm	1961	+ Lott, George	1964	Seixas, Vic	1971
+ Clark, Clarence	1983	Mako, Gene	1973	+ Shields, Frank	1964
+ Clark, Joseph	1955	+ McKinley, Chuck	1986	+ Slocum, Henry	1955
+ Clothier, William	1956	+ McLoughlin, Maurice	1957	Smith, Stan	1987
+ Cochet, Henri	1976	McMillan, Frew	1992	Stolle, Fred	1985
Cooper, Ashley	1991	McNeill, Don	1965	Talbert, Bill	1967
+ Crawford, Jack	1979	Mulloy, Gardnar	1972	+ Tilden, Bill	1959
+ Doeg, John	1962	+ Murray, Lindley	1958	Trabert, Tony	1970
+ Doherty, Lawrence	1980	+ Myrick, Julian	1963	Van Ryn, John	1963
+ Doherty, Reginald	1980	Nastase, Ilie	1991	Vilas, Guillermo	1991
Drobny, Jaroslav	1983	Newcombe, John	1986	+ Vines, Ellsworth	1962
+ Dwight, James	1955	+ Nielsen, Arthur	1971	+ von Cramm, Gottfried	1977
Emerson, Roy	1982	Olmedo, Alex	1987	+ Ward, Holcombe	1956
+ Etchebaster, Pierre	1978	+ Osuna, Rafael	1979	+ Washburn, Watson	1965
Falkenburg, Bob	1974	Parker, Frank	1966	+ Whitman, Malcolm	1955
Fraser, Neale	1984	+ Patterson, Gerald	1989	+ Wilding, Anthony	1978
+ Garland, Chuck	1969	Patty, Budge	1977	+ Williams, Richard 2nd	1957
+ Gonzales, Pancho	1968	+ Perry, Fred	1975	Wood, Sidney	1964
+ Grant, Bryan (Bitsy)	1972	+ Pettitt, Tom	1982	+ Wrenn, Robert	1955
+ Griffin, Clarence	1970	Pietrangeli, Nicola	1986	+ Wright, Beals	1956
+ Hackett, Harold	1961	+ Quist, Adrian	1984		

Women

+ Atkinson, Juliette	1974	Goolagong Cawley, Evonne	1988	+ Nuthall Shoemaker, Betty	1977
Austin, Tracy	1992	+ Hansell, Ellen	1965	Osborne duPont, Margaret	1967
+ Barger-Wallach, Maud	1958	Hard, Darlene	1973	Palfrey Danzig, Sarah	1963
Betz Addie, Pauline	1965	Hart, Doris	1969	+ Roosevelt, Ellen	1975
+ Bjurstedt Mallory, Molla	1958	Haydon Jones, Ann	1985	+ Round Little, Dorothy	1986
Brough Clapp, Louise	1967	Heldman, Gladys	1979	+ Ryan, Elizabeth	1972
+ Browne, Mary	1957	+ Hotchkiss Wightman, Hazel	1957	+ Sears, Eleanora	1968
Bueno, Maria	1978	Jacobs, Helen Hull	1962	Smith Court, Margaret	1979
+ Cahill, Mabel	1976	King, Billie Jean	1987	+ Sutton Bundy, May	1956
+ Connolly Brinker, Maureen	1968	+ Lenglen, Suzanne	1978	+ Townsend Toulmin, Bertha	1974
+ Dod, Charlotte (Lottie)	1983	Mandlikova, Hana	1994	Wade, Virginia	1989
+ Douglass Chambers, Dorothy	1981	+ Marble, Alice	1964	+ Wagner, Marie	1969
Evert, Chris	1995	+ McKane Godfree, Kitty	1978	Wills Moody Roark, Helen	1959
Fry Irvin, Shirley	1970	+ Moore, Elisabeth	1971		
Gibson, Althea	1971	Mortimer Barrett, Angela	1993		

Contributors

+ Baker, Lawrence Sr	1975	+ Gustaf, V (King of Sweden)	1980	+ Outerbridge, Mary	1981
Chatrier, Philippe	1992	+ Hester, W.E. (Slew)	1981	+ Pell, Theodore	1966
Collins, Bud	1994	+ Hopman, Harry	1978	+ Tingay, Lance	1982
Cullman, Joseph F. 3rd	1990	Hunt, Lamar	1993	+ Tinling, Ted	1986
+ Danzig, Allison	1968	+ Laney, Al	1979	+ Van Alen, James	1965
+ Davis, Dwight	1956	Martin, Alastair	1973		
+ Gray, David	1985	Martin, William McC	1982		

TRACK & FIELD

National Track & Field Hall of Fame

Established in 1974 by the The Athletics Congress (now USA Track & Field). Originally located in Charleston, WV, the Hall moved to Indianapolis in 1983 and reopened at the Hoosier Dome in 1986. **Address:** One Hoosier Dome, Indianapolis, IN 46225. **Telephone:** (317) 261-0500.

Eligibility: Nominated athletes must be retired three years and coaches must have coached at least 20 years, if retired, or 35 years, if still coaching. Voting done by 800-member panel made up of Hall of Fame and USA Track & Field officials, Hall of Fame members, current U.S. champions and members of the Track & Field Writers of America.

Class of 1995: To be announced Sept. 29 (see Updates chapter).

Members are listed with year of induction; (+) indicates deceased members.

Men

+ Albritton, Dave 1980
  Ashenfelter, Horace 1975
+ Bausch, James 1979
  Beamon, Bob 1977
  Beatty, Jim 1990
  Bell, Greg 1988
+ Boeckmann, Dee 1976
  Boston, Ralph...................1974
+ Calhoun, Lee...................1974
  Campbell, Milt 1989
+ Clark, Ellery 1991
  Connolly, Harold 1984
  Courtney, Tom 1978
+ Cunningham, Glenn 1974
+ Curtis, William 1979
  Davenport, Willie................1982
  Davis, Glenn 1974
  Davis, Harold 1974
  Dillard, Harrison 1974
  Dumas, Charley 1990
  Evans, Lee 1983
  Ewell, Barney 1986
+ Ewry, Ray 1974
+ Flanagan, John 1975
  Fosbury, Dick 1981
+ Gordien, Fortune 1979
  Greene, Charlie 1992
+ Hahn, Archie 1983
+ Hardin, Glenn 1978
  Hayes, Bob 1976
  Held, Bud 1987

  Hines, Jim.....................1979
+ Houser, Bud 1979
+ Hubbard, DeHart 1979
  Jenkins, Charlie................1992
  Jenner, Bruce 1980
+ Johnson, Cornelius 1994
  Johnson, Rafer 1974
  Jones, Hayes 1976
  Kelley, John 1980
  Kiviat, Abel 1985
+ Kraenzlein, Alvin 1974
  Laird, Ron 1986
  Mathias, Bob 1974
  Matson, Randy 1984
+ Meredith, Ted 1982
+ Metcalfe, Ralph 1975
  Milburn, Rod 1993
  Mills, Billy 1976
  Moore, Tom 1988
  Morrow, Bobby 1975
+ Mortensen, Jess 1992
  Moses, Edwin 1994
+ Myers, Lawrence 1974
  O'Brien, Parry 1974
  Oerter, Al 1974
+ Osborn, Harold 1974
+ Owens, Jesse 1974
+ Paddock, Charley 1976
  Patton, Mel 1985
  Peacock, Eulace 1987
+ Prefontaine, Steve..............1976

+ Ray, Joie.....................1976
+ Rice, Greg....................1977
  Richards, Bob 1975
+ Rose, Ralph 1976
  Ryun, Jim 1980
+ Scholz, Jackson 1977
  Schul, Bob 1991
  Seagren, Bob 1986
+ Sheppard, Mel 1976
+ Sheridan, Martin 1988
  Shorter, Frank 1989
  Sime, Dave 1981
+ Simpson, Robert.................1974
  Smith, Tommie 1978
+ Stanfield, Andy 1977
  Steers, Les 1974
  Thomas, John 1985
+ Thomson, Earl 1977
+ Thorpe, Jim 1975
+ Tolan, Eddie 1982
  Toomey, Bill 1975
+ Towns, Forrest (Spec) 1976
  Warmerdam, Cornelius 1974
  Whitfield, Mal..................1974
  Wilkins, Mac 1993
+ Williams, Archie 1992
  Wohlhuter, Rick 1990
  Woodruff, John 1978
  Wottle, Dave 1982
+ Wykoff, Frank...................1977
  Young, George 1981

Women

  Coachman, Alice 1975
+ Copeland, Lillian 1994
+ Didrikson, Babe 1974
  Faggs, Mae 1976
  Ferrell, Barbara................1988
+ Hall Adams, Evelyne 1988
  Heritage, Doris Brown 1990

+ Jackson, Nell 1989
  Manning, Madeline 1984
  McDaniel, Mildred 1983
  McGuire, Edith..................1979
  Robinson, Betty 1977
+ Rudolph, Wilma 1974
  Schmidt, Kate 1994

  Shiley Newhouse, Jean...........1993
+ Stephens, Helen 1975
  Tyus, Wyomia 1980
+ Walsh, Stella 1975
  Watson, Martha..................1987
  White, Willye 1981

Coaches

+ Baskin, Weems 1982
+ Beard, Percy 1981
  Bell, Sam 1992
  Botts, Tom 1983
  Bowerman, Bill..................1981
  Bush, Jim 1987
+ Cromwell, Dean 1974
  Doherty, Ken 1976
  Easton, Bill 1975
+ Elliott, Jumbo 1981
+ Giegengack, Bob 1978

+ Hamilton, Brutus................1974
+ Haydon, Ted 1975
+ Hayes, Billy 1976
+ Haylett, Ward 1979
+ Higgins, Ralph 1982
+ Hillman, Harry 1976
+ Hurt, Edward 1975
+ Hutsell, Wilbur 1977
+ Jones, Thomas 1977
  Jordan, Payton 1982
+ Littlefield, Clyde..............1981

+ Moakley, Jack 1988
+ Murphy, Michael 1974
+ Snyder, Larry 1978
  Temple, Ed 1989
+ Templeton, Dink 1976
  Walker, LeRoy 1983
+ Wilt, Fred 1981
+ Winter, Bud 1985
  Wright, Stan 1993
+ Yancy, Joseph 1984

Track & Field Hall of Fame (Cont.)

Contributors

+ Abramson, Jesse 1981
  Andersen, Roxanne 1991
+ Bakjian, Andy 1986
+ Brundage, Avery 1974

+ Ferris, Dan 1974
+ Griffith, John 1979
+ Lebow, Fred 1994

+ Nelson, Bert...........................1991
  Nelson, Cordner 1988
+ Sullivan, James 1977

WOMEN

International Women's Sports Hall of Fame

Established in 1980 by the Women's Sports Foundation. **Address:** Women's Sports Foundation, Eisenhower Park, East Meadow, NY 11554. **Telephone:** (516) 542-4700.

Eligibility: Nominees' achievements and commitment to the development of women's sports must be internationally recognized. Athletes are elected in two categories—Pioneer (before 1960) and Contemporary (since 1960). Members are divided below by sport for the sake of easy reference; (*) indicates member inducted in Pioneer category. Coaching nominees must have coached at least 10 years.

Class of 1995 (6): CONTEMPORARY— **Annichen Kringstad** (orienteering) and marathon runner **Grete Waitz** (track & field). PIONEERS—**Judy Devlin Hashman** (badminton) and **Betty Hicks** (golf). COACHES— **Jody Conradt** (basketball) and **Barbara Jacket** (track & field).

Members are listed with year of induction; (+) indicates deceased members.

Alpine Skiing

Cranz, Christl*........................1991
Lawrence, Andrea Mead*.......1983
Moser-Proell, Annemarie 1982

Auto Racing

Guthrie, Janet 1980

Aviation

+ Coleman, Bessie* 1992
+ Earhart, Amelia*....................1980
+ Marvingt, Marie* 1987

Badminton

Hashman, Judy Devlin*...........1995

Baseball

Stone, Toni* 1993

Basketball

Meyers, Ann..............................1985
Miller, Cheryl 1991

Bowling

Ladewig, Marion* 1984

Cycling

Carpenter Phinney, Connie 1990

Diving

King, Micki 1983
McCormick, Pat* 1984
Riggin, Aileen* 1988

Equestrian

Hartel, Lis 1994

Fencing

Schacherer-Elek, Ilona*...........1989

Figure Skating

Albright, Tenley* 1983
+ Blanchard, Theresa Weld* 1989
  Fleming, Peggy 1981
  Heiss Jenkins, Carol*..............1992
+ Henie, Sonja* 1982
  Protopopov, Ludmila 1992
  Rodnina, Irena 1988

Golf

Berg, Patty* 1980
Carner, JoAnne 1987
Hicks, Betty* 1995
Mann, Carol 1982
Rawls, Betsy* 1986
Suggs, Louise* 1987
+ Vare, Glenna Collett* 1981
  Whitworth, Kathy 1984
  Wright, Mickey 1981

Golf/Track & Field

+ Zaharias, Babe Didrikson*......1980

Gymnastics

Caslavska, Vera 1991
Comaneci, Nadia 1990
Korbut, Olga 1982
Latynina, Larissa*...................1985
Retton, Mary Lou....................1993
Tourischeva, Lyudmila.............1987

Shooting

Murdock, Margaret 1988

Softball

Joyce, Joan.............................1989

Speed Skating

+ Klein Outland, Kit* 1993
  Young, Sheila.........................1981

Swimming

Caulkins, Tracy 1986
Curtis Cuneo, Ann* 1985
de Varona, Donna 1983
Ederle, Gertrude*....................1980
Fraser, Dawn 1985
Holm, Eleanor* 1980
Meagher, Mary T....................1993
Meyer-Reyes, Debbie 1987

Tennis

+ Connolly, Maureen* 1987
+ Dod, Charlotte (Lottie)* 1986
  Evert, Chris.............................1981
  Gibson, Althea* 1980
  Goolagong Cawley, Evonne....1989
+ Hotchkiss Wightman, Hazel*...1986
  King, Billie Jean 1980
+ Lenglen, Suzanne* 1984
  Navratilova, Martina 1984
+ Sears, Eleanora* 1984
  Smith Court, Margaret...........1986

Track & Field

Blankers-Koen, Fanny* 1982
Cheng, Chi 1994
Coachman Davis, Alice*..........1991
Manning Mims, Madeline*.......1987
+ Rudolph, Wilma......................1980
+ Stephens, Helen*....................1983
  Szewinska, Irena 1992
  Tyus, Wyomia.........................1981
  Waitz, Grete 1995
  White, Willye 1988

Volleyball

+ Hyman, Flo.............................1986

Water Skiing

McGuire, Willa Worthington* 1990

Orienteering

Kringstad, Annichen...............1995

Coaches

Applebee, Constance 1991
Backus, Sharron 1993
Conradt, Judy 1995
Grossfeld, Muriel 1991
Jacket, Barbara........................1995
+ Jackson, Nell 1990
  Kanakogi, Rusty 1994
  Summitt, Pat Head..................1990
+ Wade, Margaret 1992

Wide World Photos

Former center **Bill Laimbeer** (left) of the two-time NBA champion Detroit Pistons is presented with his retired No. 40 jersey by former teammate **Isiah Thomas** at ceremonies in Auburn Hills on Feb. 4, 1995.

RETIRED NUMBERS

Major League Baseball

The New York Yankees have retired the most uniform numbers (13) in the Major Leagues; followed by Pittsburgh and the Brooklyn-Los Angeles Dodgers (8), the Chicago White Sox (7), the New York-San Francisco Giants (6) and the St. Louis Cardinals (5). Four players and a manager have had their numbers retired by two teams: **Hank Aaron**—#44 by the Boston-Milwaukee-Atlanta Braves and the Milwaukee Brewers; **Rod Carew**—#29 by Minnesota and California; **Rollie Fingers**—#34 by Milwaukee and Oakland; **Frank Robinson**—#20 by Cincinnati and Baltimore; and **Casey Stengel**—#37 by the New York Yankees and New York Mets.

Numbers retired in 1995 (3): CALIFORNIA— #50 worn by late conditioning coach **Jimmie Reese**, who died at age 92 in 1994; KANSAS CITY— #20 worn by 2nd baseman **Frank White** (1973-90 with Royals); MINNESOTA— #14 worn by 1st baseman **Kent Hrbek** (1981-94 with Twins).

American League

Three AL teams—the Seattle Mariners, Texas Rangers and Toronto Blue Jays—have not retired any numbers.

Baltimore
4 Earl Weaver
5 Brooks Robinson
20 Frank Robinson
22 Jim Palmer
33 Eddie Murray

Boston Red Sox
1 Bobby Doerr
4 Joe Cronin
8 Carl Yastrzemski
9 Ted Williams

California Angels
26 Gene Autry
29 Rod Carew
30 Nolan Ryan
50 Jimmie Reese

Chicago White Sox
2 Nellie Fox
3 Harold Baines
4 Luke Appling
9 Minnie Minoso
11 Luis Aparicio
16 Ted Lyons
19 Billy Pierce

Cleveland Indians
3 Earl Averill
5 Lou Boudreau
14 Larry Doby
18 Mel Harder
19 Bob Feller

Detroit Tigers
2 Charley Gehringer
5 Hank Greenberg
6 Al Kaline

Kansas City Royals
5 George Brett
10 Dick Howser
20 Frank White

Milwaukee Brewers
19 Robin Yount
34 Rollie Fingers
44 Hank Aaron

Minnesota Twins
3 Harmon Killebrew
6 Tony Oliva
20 Kent Hrbek
29 Rod Carew

New York Yankees
1 Billy Martin
3 Babe Ruth
4 Lou Gehrig
5 Joe DiMaggio
7 Mickey Mantle
8 Yogi Berra & Bill Dickey
9 Roger Maris
10 Phil Rizzuto
15 Thurman Munson
16 Whitey Ford
32 Elston Howard
37 Casey Stengel
44 Reggie Jackson

Oakland Athletics
27 Catfish Hunter
34 Rollie Fingers

Retired Numbers (Cont.)

National League

San Francisco has honored former NY Giants Christy Mathewson and John McGraw even though they played before numbers were worn.

Atlanta Braves
3 Dale Murphy
21 Warren Spahn
35 Phil Niekro
41 Eddie Mathews
44 Hank Aaron

Chicago Cubs
14 Ernie Banks
26 Billy Williams

Cincinnati Reds
1 Fred Hutchinson
5 Johnny Bench

Houston Astros
25 Jose Cruz
32 Jim Umbricht
33 Mike Scott
40 Don Wilson

Los Angeles Dodgers
1 Pee Wee Reese
4 Duke Snider
19 Jim Gilliam
24 Walter Alston
32 Sandy Koufax
39 Roy Campanella
42 Jackie Robinson
53 Don Drysdale

Montreal Expos
8 Gary Carter
10 Rusty Staub

New York Mets
14 Gil Hodges
37 Casey Stengel
41 Tom Seaver

Philadelphia Phillies
1 Richie Ashburn
20 Mike Schmidt
32 Steve Carlton
36 Robin Roberts

Pittsburgh Pirates
1 Billy Meyer
4 Ralph Kiner
8 Willie Stargell
9 Bill Mazeroski
20 Pie Traynor
21 Roberto Clemente
33 Honus Wagner
40 Danny Murtaugh

St. Louis Cardinals
6 Stan Musial
14 Ken Boyer
17 Dizzy Dean
20 Lou Brock
45 Bob Gibson
85 August (Gussie) Busch

San Diego Padres
6 Steve Garvey

San Francisco Giants
3 Bill Terry
4 Mel Ott
11 Carl Hubbell
24 Willie Mays
27 Juan Marichal
44 Willie McCovey

National Basketball Association

Boston has retired the most numbers (19) in the NBA; followed by the New York Knicks (7); Milwaukee, Portland and the Rochester-Cincinnati Royals/Kansas City-Omaha-Sacramento Kings (6); and the Los Angeles Lakers and Syracuse Nats/Philadelphia 76ers (5). Six players have had their numbers retired by two teams: **Kareem Abdul-Jabbar**—#33 by LA Lakers and Milwaukee; **Wilt Chamberlain**—#13 by the Los Angeles Lakers and Philadelphia; **Julius Erving**—#6 by Philadelphia and #32 by New Jersey; **Bob Lanier**—#16 by Detroit and Milwaukee; **Oscar Robertson**—#1 by Milwaukee and #14 by Sacramento; and **Nate Thurmond**—#42 by Cleveland and Golden State.

Numbers retired in 1995 (4): BOSTON— #35 worn by forward **Reggie Lewis** (1987-93 with Celtics); CLEVELAND— #22 worn by forward **Larry Nance** (1988-94 with Cavs); DETROIT— #40 worn by center **Bill Laimbeer** (1982-94 with Pistons); PHILADELPHIA— #10 worn by guard **Maurice Cheeks** (1978-89 with 76ers).

Eastern Conference

Four Eastern teams—the Charlotte Hornets, Miami Heat, Orlando Magic, and expansion Toronto Raptors—have not retired any numbers.

Boston Celtics
1 Walter A. Brown
2 Red Auerbach
3 Dennis Johnson
6 Bill Russell
10 Jo Jo White
14 Bob Cousy
15 Tom Heinsohn
16 Tom (Satch) Sanders
17 John Havlicek
18 Dave Cowens
19 Don Nelson
21 Bill Sharman
22 Ed Macauley
23 Frank Ramsey
24 Sam Jones
25 K.C. Jones
32 Kevin McHale
33 Larry Bird
35 Reggie Lewis
Loscy Jim Loscutoff
Radio mike Johnny Most

Atlanta Hawks
9 Bob Pettit
23 Lou Hudson

Chicago Bulls
4 Jerry Sloan
10 Bob Love
23 Michael Jordan

Cleveland Cavaliers
7 Bingo Smith
22 Larry Nance
34 Austin Carr
42 Nate Thurmond

Detroit Pistons
15 Vinnie Johnson
16 Bob Lanier
21 Dave Bing
40 Bill Laimbeer

Indiana Pacers
30 George McGinnis
34 Mel Daniels
35 Roger Brown

Milwaukee Bucks
1 Oscar Robertson
2 Junior Bridgeman
4 Sidney Moncrief
14 Jon McGlocklin
16 Bob Lanier
32 Brian Winters
33 Kareem Abdul-Jabbar

New York Knicks
10 Walt Frazier
12 Dick Barnett
15 Dick McGuire
   & Earl Monroe
19 Willis Reed
22 Dave DeBusschere
24 Bill Bradley
613 Red Holzman

New Jersey Nets
4 Wendell Ladner
11 Drazen Petrovic
23 John Williamson
25 Bill Melchionni
32 Julius Erving

Philadelphia 76ers
6 Julius Erving
10 Maurice Cheeks
13 Wilt Chamberlain
15 Hal Greer
24 Bobby Jones
32 Billy Cunningham
P.A. mike Dave Zinkoff

Washington Bullets
11 Elvin Hayes
25 Gus Johnson
41 Wes Unseld

Western Conference

Three Western teams—the Los Angeles Clippers, Minnesota Timberwolves, and expansion Vancouver Grizzlies—have not retired any numbers.

Dallas Mavericks
15 Brad Davis

Denver Nuggets
2 Alex English
33 David Thompson
40 Byron Beck
44 Dan Issel

Golden St. Warriors
14 Tom Meschery
16 Al Attles
24 Rick Barry
42 Nate Thurmond

Houston Rockets
23 Calvin Murphy
45 Rudy Tomjanovich

Los Angeles Lakers
13 Wilt Chamberlain
22 Elgin Baylor
32 Magic Johnson
33 Kareem Abdul-Jabbar
44 Jerry West

Phoenix Suns
5 Dick Van Arsdale
6 Walter Davis
33 Alvan Adams
42 Connie Hawkins
44 Paul Westphal

Portland Trail Blazers
13 Dave Twardzik
15 Larry Steele
20 Maurice Lucas
32 Bill Walton
36 Lloyd Neal
45 Geoff Petrie
77 Jack Ramsay

Sacramento Kings
6 Fans ("Sixth Man")
11 Bob Davies
12 Maurice Stokes
14 Oscar Robertson
27 Jack Twyman
44 Sam Lacey

San Antonio Spurs
13 James Silas
44 George Gervin

Seattle SuperSonics
19 Lenny Wilkens
32 Fred Brown

Utah Jazz
1 Frank Layden
7 Pete Maravich

National Football League

The Chicago Bears have retired the most uniform numbers (13) in the NFL; followed by the New York Giants (9); the Dallas Texans/Kansas City Chiefs (8); the Baltimore-Indianapolis Colts and San Francisco (7); Detroit (6); and the Boston-New England Patriots, Cleveland and Philadelphia (5). No player has ever had his number retired by more than one NFL team.

Numbers retired in 1995 (2): NY GIANTS—#11 worn by quarterback **Phil Simms** (1979–93 with Giants); SEATTLE— #80 worn by wide receiver **Steve Largent** (1976-89 with Seahawks).

NFC

Atlanta, Dallas and the expansion Carolina Panthers are the only NFC teams that haven't retired any numbers. The Falcons haven't issued uniforms #10 (Steve Bartowski), #31 (William Andrews) and #60 (Tommy Nobis) since those players retired; while the Cowboys have a "Ring of Honor" at Texas Stadium that includes nine players and one coach— Tony Dorsett, Chuck Howley, Lee Roy Jordan, Tom Landry, Bob Lilly, Don Meredith, Don Perkins, Mel Renfro, Roger Staubach and Randy White.

Arizona Cardinals
8 Larry Wilson
77 Stan Mauldin
88 J.V. Cain
99 Marshall Goldberg

Chicago Bears
3 Bronko Nagurski
5 George McAfee
7 George Halas
28 Willie Galimore
34 Walter Payton
40 Gale Sayers
41 Brian Piccolo
42 Sid Luckman
51 Dick Butkus
56 Bill Hewitt
61 Bill George
66 Bulldog Turner
77 Red Grange

Detroit Lions
7 Dutch Clark
22 Bobby Layne
37 Doak Walker
56 Joe Schmidt
85 Chuck Hughes
88 Charlie Sanders

Green Bay Packers
3 Tony Canadeo
14 Don Hutson
15 Bart Starr
66 Ray Nitschke

Minnesota Vikings
10 Fran Tarkenton
88 Alan Page

New Orleans Saints
31 Jim Taylor
81 Doug Atkins

New York Giants
1 Ray Flaherty
7 Mel Hein
11 Phil Simms
14 Y.A. Tittle
32 Al Blozis
40 Joe Morrison
42 Charlie Conerly
50 Ken Strong
56 Lawrence Taylor

Philadelphia Eagles
15 Steve Van Buren
40 Tom Brookshier
44 Pete Retzlaff
60 Chuck Bednarik
70 Al Wistert
99 Jerome Brown

St. Louis Rams
7 Bob Waterfield
74 Merlin Olsen

San Francisco 49ers
12 John Brodie
34 Joe Perry
37 Jimmy Johnson
39 Hugh McElhenny
70 Charlie Krueger
73 Lou Nomellini
87 Dwight Clark

Tampa Bay Bucs
63 Lee Roy Selmon

Wash. Redskins
33 Sammy Baugh

AFC

Four AFC teams—the Buffalo Bills, Oakland Raiders, Pittsburgh Steelers and the expansion Jacksonville Jaguars—have not retired any numbers.

Cincinnati Bengals
54 Bob Johnson

Cleveland Browns
14 Otto Graham
32 Jim Brown
45 Ernie Davis
46 Don Fleming
76 Lou Groza

Denver Broncos
18 Frank Tripucka
44 Floyd Little

Houston Oilers
34 Earl Campbell
43 Jim Norton
63 Mike Munchak
65 Elvin Bethea

Indianapolis Colts
19 Johnny Unitas
22 Buddy Young
24 Lenny Moore
70 Art Donovan
77 Jim Parker
82 Raymond Berry
89 Gino Marchetti

Kansas City Chiefs
3 Jan Stenerud
16 Len Dawson
28 Abner Haynes
33 Stone Johnson
36 Mack Lee Hill
63 Willie Lanier
78 Bobby Bell
86 Buck Buchanan

Miami Dolphins
12 Bob Griese

New England Patriots
20 Gino Cappelletti
57 Steve Nelson
73 John Hannah
79 Jim Hunt
89 Bob Dee

New York Jets
12 Joe Namath
13 Don Maynard

San Diego Chargers
14 Dan Fouts

Seattle Seahawks
12 Fans ("12th Man")
80 Steve Largent

Retired Numbers (Cont.)

National Hockey League

The Boston Bruins have retired the most uniform numbers (7) in the NHL; followed by Montreal and Detroit (6); Buffalo, Chicago, N.Y. Islanders, St. Louis and Philadelphia (4); and the Boston-New England-Hartford Whalers, Los Angeles Kings and Quebec Nordiques-Colorado Avalanche (3). Two players have had their numbers retired by two teams: Gordie Howe—#9 by Detroit and Hartford; and Bobby Hull—#9 by Chicago and Winnipeg.

Numbers retired in 1995 (8): BUFFALO—#2 worn by defenseman **Tim Horton** (1972-74 with Sabres), #7 worn by left wing **Rick Martin** (1971-81 with Sabres) and #14 worn by right wing **Rene Robert** (1972-79 with Sabres); DETROIT— #12 worn by center **Sid Abel** (1938-52 with Red Wings); LOS ANGELES— #18 worn by forward **Dave Taylor** (1977-94 with Kings); MONTREAL— #1 worn by goaltender **Jacques Plante** (1952-63 with Canaiens); NY ISLANDERS— #23 worn by right wing **Bob Nystrom** (1972-86 with Isles); QUEBEC (now Colorado)— #16 worn by left wing **Michel Goulet** (1979-90 with Nordiques).

Eastern Conference

The New Jersey Devils, Ottawa Senators, Tampa Bay Lightning and Florida Panthers are the only Eastern teams that have not retired a number.

Boston Bruins
2 Eddie Shore
3 Lionel Hitchman
4 Bobby Orr
5 Dit Clapper
7 Phil Esposito
9 John Bucyk
15 Milt Schmidt

Buffalo Sabres
2 Tim Horton
7 Rick Martin
11 Gilbert Perreault
14 Rene Robert

Hartford Whalers
2 Rick Ley
9 Gordie Howe
19 John McKenzie

Montreal Canadiens
1 Jacques Plante
2 Doug Harvey
4 Jean Beliveau
  & Aurel Joliat
7 Howie Morenz
9 Maurice Richard
10 Guy Lafleur
16 Henri Richard
  & Elmer Lach

New York Islanders
5 Denis Potvin
22 Mike Bossy
23 Bob Nystrom
31 Billy Smith

New York Rangers
1 Eddie Giacomin
7 Rod Gilbert

Philadelphia Flyers
1 Bernie Parent
4 Barry Ashbee
7 Bill Barber
16 Bobby Clarke

Pittsburgh Penguins
21 Michel Briere

Washington Capitals
7 Yvon Labre

Western Conference

The San Jose Sharks and Mighty Ducks of Anaheim are the only Western teams that have not retired a number.

Calgary Flames
9 Lanny McDonald

Chicago Blackhawks
1 Glenn Hall
9 Bobby Hull
21 Stan Mikita
35 Tony Esposito

Colorado Avalanche
3 J.C. Tremblay
8 Marc Tardif
16 Michel Goulet

Dallas Stars
8 Bill Goldsworthy
19 Bill Masterton

Detroit Red Wings
1 Terry Sawchuk
6 Larry Aurie
7 Ted Lindsay
9 Gordie Howe
10 Alex Delvecchio
12 Sid Abel

Edmonton Oilers
3 Al Hamilton

Los Angeles Kings
16 Marcel Dionne
18 Dave Taylor
30 Rogie Vachon

St. Louis Blues
3 Bob Gassoff
8 Barclay Plager
11 Brian Sutter
24 Bernie Federko

Toronto Maple Leafs
5 Bill Barilko
6 Ace Bailey

Vancouver Canucks
12 Stan Smyl

Winnipeg Jets
9 Bobby Hull

AWARDS

Sports Illustrated Sportsman of the Year

Selected annually by the editors of *Sports Illustrated* magazine since 1954.

Year		Year		Year	
1954	**Roger Bannister**, track	1972	**Billie Jean King**, tennis	1987	**"8 Athletes Who Care"**
1955	**Johnny Podres**, baseball		& **John Wooden**, basketball		**Bob Bourne**, hockey
1956	**Bobby Morrow**, track	1973	**Jackie Stewart**, auto racing		**Kip Keino**, track
1957	**Stan Musial**, baseball	1974	**Muhammad Ali**, boxing		**Judi Brown King**, track
1958	**Rafer Johnson**, track	1975	**Pete Rose**, baseball		**Dale Murphy**, baseball
1959	**Ingemar Johansson**, boxing	1976	**Chris Evert**, tennis		**Chip Rives**, football
		1977	**Steve Cauthen**, horse racing		**Patty Sheehan**, golf
1960	**Arnold Palmer**, golf	1978	**Jack Nicklaus**, golf		**Rory Sparrow**, basketball
1961	**Jerry Lucas**, basketball	1979	**Terry Bradshaw**, football		**Reggie Williams**, football
1962	**Terry Baker**, football		& **Willie Stargell**, baseball	1988	**Orel Hershiser**, baseball
1963	**Pete Rozelle**, pro football			1989	**Greg LeMond**, cycling
1964	**Ken Venturi**, golf	1980	**U.S. Olympic hockey team**		
1965	**Sandy Koufax**, baseball	1981	**Sugar Ray Leonard**, boxing	1990	**Joe Montana**, football
1966	**Jim Ryun**, track	1982	**Wayne Gretzky**, hockey	1991	**Michael Jordan**, basketball
1967	**Carl Yastrzemski**, baseball	1983	**Mary Decker**, track	1992	**Arthur Ashe**, tennis
1968	**Bill Russell**, basketball	1984	**Mary Lou Retton**, gymnastics	1993	**Don Shula**, football
1969	**Tom Seaver**, baseball		& **Edwin Moses**, track	1994	**Johan Olav Koss**, sp. skating
		1985	**Kareem Abdul-Jabbar**, basketball		& **Bonnie Blair**, sp. skating
1970	**Bobby Orr**, hockey	1986	**Joe Paterno**, football		
1971	**Lee Trevino**, golf				

Associated Press Athletes of the Year

Selected annually by AP newspaper sports editors since 1931.

Male

Boxer George Foreman, who regained the heavyweight title at age 45 on Nov. 5 with a 10th-round knockout of WBA and IBF champion Michael Moorer, was named the top male athlete of 1994 by Associated Press sports editors. His award came 20 years after Muhammad Ali won Male Athlete of the Year honors for dethroning Foreman in Zaire.

The Top 10 vote-getters (first place votes in parentheses): 1. **George Foreman**, boxing (32), 204 points; 2. **Hakeem Olajuwon**, pro basketball (16), 138 pts; 3. **Nick Price**, golf (15), 111 pts; 4. **Jerry Rice**, pro football (11), 96 pts; 5. **Emmitt Smith**, pro football (11), 95 pts; 6. **Johann Olav Koss**, speed skating (11), 85 pts; 7. **Dan Jansen**, speed skating (7), 79 pts; 8. **Barry Sanders**, pro football (6), 46 pts; 9. **Jeff Bagwell**, baseball (3), 43 pts; 10. (TIE) **Mark Messier**, pro hockey (2), 36 pts and **Greg Maddux**, baseball, 36 pts.

Multiple winners: Michael Jordan (3); Don Budge, Sandy Koufax, Carl Lewis, Joe Montana and Byron Nelson (2).

Year		Year		Year	
1931	**Pepper Martin**, baseball	1953	**Ben Hogan**, golf	1975	**Fred Lynn**, baseball
1932	**Gene Sarazen**, golf	1954	**Willie Mays**, baseball	1976	**Bruce Jenner**, track
1933	**Carl Hubbell**, baseball	1955	**Hopalong Cassady**, col. football	1977	**Steve Cauthen**, horse racing
1934	**Dizzy Dean**, baseball	1956	**Mickey Mantle**, baseball	1978	**Ron Guidry**, baseball
1935	**Joe Louis**, boxing	1957	**Ted Williams**, baseball	1979	**Willie Stargell**, baseball
1936	**Jesse Owens**, track	1958	**Herb Elliott**, track		
1937	**Don Budge**, tennis	1959	**Ingemar Johansson**, boxing	1980	**U.S. Olympic hockey team**
1938	**Don Budge**, tennis			1981	**John McEnroe**, tennis
1939	**Nile Kinnick**, college football	1960	**Rafer Johnson**, track	1982	**Wayne Gretzky**, hockey
		1961	**Roger Maris**, baseball	1983	**Carl Lewis**, track
1940	**Tom Harmon**, college football	1962	**Maury Wills**, baseball	1984	**Carl Lewis**, track
1941	**Joe DiMaggio**, baseball	1963	**Sandy Koufax**, baseball	1985	**Dwight Gooden**, baseball
1942	**Frank Sinkwich**, college football	1964	**Don Schollander**, swimming	1986	**Larry Bird**, pro basketball
1943	**Gunder Haegg**, track	1965	**Sandy Koufax**, baseball	1987	**Ben Johnson**, track
1944	**Byron Nelson**, golf	1966	**Frank Robinson**, baseball	1988	**Orel Hershiser**, baseball
1945	**Byron Nelson**, golf	1967	**Carl Yastrzemski**, baseball	1989	**Joe Montana**, pro football
1946	**Glenn Davis**, college football	1968	**Denny McLain**, baseball		
1947	**Johnny Lujack**, college football	1969	**Tom Seaver**, baseball	1990	**Joe Montana**, pro football
1948	**Lou Boudreau**, baseball			1991	**Michael Jordan**, pro basketball
1949	**Leon Hart**, college football	1970	**George Blanda**, pro football	1992	**Michael Jordan**, pro basketball
		1971	**Lee Trevino**, golf	1993	**Michael Jordan**, pro basketball
1950	**Jim Konstanty**, baseball	1972	**Mark Spitz**, swimming	1994	**George Foreman**, boxing
1951	**Dick Kazmaier**, college football	1973	**O.J. Simpson**, pro football		
1952	**Bob Mathias**, track	1974	**Muhammad Ali**, boxing		

Female

Speed skater Bonnie Blair, who won two gold medals at the Winter Olympics in Lillehammer, Norway, to push her career Olympic medal count to five golds and one bronze, was the AP sports editors' top female athlete of 1994.

The Top 10 vote-getters (first place votes in parentheses): 1. **Bonnie Blair**, speed skating (86), 492 points; 2. **Oksana Baiul**, figure skating (15), 172 pts; 3. **Steffi Graf**, tennis (6), 110 pts; 4. (TIE) **Nancy Kerrigan**, figure skating (6), 79 pts and **Jackie Joyner-Kersee**, track & field (3), 79 pts; 6. **Arantxa Sanchez Vicario**, tennis (5), 70 pts; 7. **Picabo Street**, alpine skiing (3), 53 pts; 8. **Laura Davies**, golf (2), 37 pts; 9. **Martina Navratilova**, tennis (3), 27 pts; 10. **Charlotte Smith**, college basketball (1), 18 pts.

Multiple winners: Babe Didrikson Zaharias (6); Chris Evert (4); Patty Berg and Maureen Connolly (3); Tracy Austin, Althea Gibson, Billie Jean King, Nancy Lopez, Alice Marble, Martina Navratilova, Wilma Rudolph, Monica Seles, Kathy Whitworth and Mickey Wright (2).

Year		Year		Year	
1931	**Helene Madison**, swimming	1953	**Maureen Connolly**, tennis	1975	**Chris Evert**, tennis
1932	**Babe Didrikson**, track	1954	**Babe Didrikson Zaharias**, golf	1976	**Nadia Comaneci**, gymnastics
1933	**Helen Jacobs**, tennis	1955	**Patty Berg**, golf	1977	**Chris Evert**, tennis
1934	**Virginia Van Wie**, golf	1956	**Pat McCormick**, diving	1978	**Nancy Lopez**, golf
1935	**Helen Wills Moody**, tennis	1957	**Althea Gibson**, tennis	1979	**Tracy Austin**, tennis
1936	**Helen Stephens**, track	1958	**Althea Gibson**, tennis		
1937	**Katherine Rawls**, swimming	1959	**Maria Bueno**, tennis	1980	**Chris Evert Lloyd**, tennis
1938	**Patty Berg**, golf			1981	**Tracy Austin**, tennis
1939	**Alice Marble**, tennis	1960	**Wilma Rudolph**, track	1982	**Mary Decker Tabb**, track
		1961	**Wilma Rudolph**, track	1983	**Martina Navratilova**, tennis
1940	**Alice Marble**, tennis	1962	**Dawn Fraser**, swimming	1984	**Mary Lou Retton**, gymnastics
1941	**Betty Hicks Newell**, golf	1963	**Mickey Wright**, golf	1985	**Nancy Lopez**, golf
1942	**Gloria Callen**, swimming	1964	**Mickey Wright**, golf	1986	**Martina Navratilova**, tennis
1943	**Patty Berg**, golf	1965	**Kathy Whitworth**, golf	1987	**Jackie Joyner-Kersee**, track
1944	**Ann Curtis**, swimming	1966	**Kathy Whitworth**, golf	1988	**Florence Griffith Joyner**, track
1945	**Babe Didrikson Zaharias**, golf	1967	**Billie Jean King**, tennis	1989	**Steffi Graf**, tennis
1946	**Babe Didrikson Zaharias**, golf	1968	**Peggy Fleming**, skating		
1947	**Babe Didrikson Zaharias**, golf	1969	**Debbie Meyer**, swimming	1990	**Beth Daniel**, golf
1948	**Fanny Blankers-Koen**, track			1991	**Monica Seles**, tennis
1949	**Marlene Bauer**, golf	1970	**Chi Cheng**, track	1992	**Monica Seles**, tennis
		1971	**Evonne Goolagong**, tennis	1993	**Sheryl Swoopes**, basketball
1950	**Babe Didrikson Zaharias**, golf	1972	**Olga Korbut**, gymnastics	1994	**Bonnie Blair**, speed skating
1951	**Maureen Connolly**, tennis	1973	**Billie Jean King**, tennis		
1952	**Maureen Connolly**, tennis	1974	**Chris Evert**, tennis		

UPI International Athletes of the Year

Selected annually by United Press International's European newspaper sports editors since 1974.

Male

Multiple winners: Sebastian Coe, Alberto Juantorena and Carl Lewis (2).

Year	Year	Year
1974 **Muhammad Ali**, boxing	1981 **Sebastian Coe**, track	1988 **Matt Biondi**, swimming
1975 **Joao Oliveira**, track	1982 **Daley Thompson**, track	1989 **Boris Becker**, tennis
1976 **Alberto Juantorena**, track	1983 **Carl Lewis**, track	1990 **Stefan Edberg**, tennis
1977 **Alberto Juantorena**, track	1984 **Carl Lewis**, track	1991 **Sergei Bubka**, track
1978 **Henry Rono**, track	1985 **Steve Cram**, track	1992 **Kevin Young**, track
1979 **Sebastian Coe**, track	1986 **Diego Maradona**, soccer	1993 **Miguel Induráin**, cycling
1980 **Eric Heiden**, speed skating	1987 **Ben Johnson**, track	1994 **Johan Olav Koss**, speed skating

Female

Multiple winners: Nadia Comaneci, Steffi Graf, Marita Koch and Monica Seles (2).

Year	Year	Year
1974 **Irena Szewinska**, track	1981 **Chris Evert Lloyd**, tennis	1988 **Florence Griffith Joyner**, track
1975 **Nadia Comaneci**, gymnastics	1982 **Marita Koch**, track	1989 **Steffi Graf**, tennis
1976 **Nadia Comaneci**, gymnastics	1983 **Jarmila Kratochvilova**, track	1990 **Merlene Ottey**, track
1977 **Rosie Ackermann**, track	1984 **Martina Navratilova**, tennis	1991 **Monica Seles**, tennis
1978 **Tracy Caulkins**, swimming	1985 **Mary Decker Slaney**, track	1992 **Monica Seles**, tennis
1979 **Marita Koch**, track	1986 **Heike Drechsler**, track	1993 **Wang Junxia**, track
1980 **Hanni Wenzel**, alpine skiing	1987 **Steffi Graf**, tennis	1994 **Le Jingyi**, swimming

Jesse Owens International Trophy

Presented annually by the International Amateur Athletic Association since 1981 and selected by a worldwide panel of electors. The Jesse Owens International Trophy is named after the late American Olympic champion, who won four gold medals at the 1936 Summer Games in Berlin.

Year	Year	Year
1981 **Eric Heiden**, speed skating	1986 **Said Aouita**, track	1992 **Mike Powell**, track
1982 **Sebastian Coe**, track	1987 **Greg Louganis**, diving	1993 **Vitaly Scherbo**, gymnastics
1983 **Mary Decker**, track	1988 **Ben Johnson**, track	1994 **Wang Junxia**, track
1984 **Edwin Moses**, track	1990 **Roger Kingdom**, track	1995 **Johan Olva Koss**, speed skating
1985 **Carl Lewis**, track	1991 **Greg LeMond**, cycling	

James E. Sullivan Memorial Award

Presented annually by the Amateur Athletic Union since 1930. The Sullivan Award is named after the former AAU president and given to the athlete who, "by his or her performance, example and influence as an amateur, has done the most during the year to advance the cause of sportsmanship." An athlete cannot win the award more than once.

The 1994 winner was speed skater **Dan Jansen**, the World Sprint champion whose world record time of 1:12.43 in the 1,000 meters won a gold medal at Lillehammer (his first medal in four Olympics). The other nine finalists are listed alphabetically: **Bruce Baumgartner** (wrestling), **Leroy Burrell** (track & field), **Dominique Dawes** (gymnastics), **Michael Johnson** (track & field), **Nancy Kerrigan** (figure skating), **Shannon Miller** (gymnastics), **Tommy Moe** (alpine skiing), **Glenn Robinson** (basketball) and **Tiger Woods** (golf). Vote totals were not released.

Year	Year	Year
1930 **Bobby Jones**, golf	1952 **Horace Ashenfelter**, track	1975 **Tim Shaw**, swimming
1931 **Barney Berlinger**, track	1953 **Sammy Lee**, diving	1976 **Bruce Jenner**, track
1932 **Jim Bausch**, track	1954 **Mal Whitfield**, track	1977 **John Naber**, swimming
1933 **Glenn Cunningham**, track	1955 **Harrison Dillard**, track	1978 **Tracy Caulkins**, swimming
1934 **Bill Bonthron**, track	1956 **Pat McCormick**, diving	1979 **Kurt Thomas**, gymnastics
1935 **Lawson Little**, golf	1957 **Bobby Morrow**, track	1980 **Eric Heiden**, speed skating
1936 **Glenn Morris**, track	1958 **Glenn Davis**, track	1981 **Carl Lewis**, track
1937 **Don Budge**, tennis	1959 **Parry O'Brien**, track	1982 **Mary Decker**, track
1938 **Don Lash**, track	1960 **Rafer Johnson**, track	1983 **Edwin Moses**, track
1939 **Joe Burk**, rowing	1961 **Wilma Rudolph**, track	1984 **Greg Louganis**, diving
	1963 **John Pennel**, track	1985 **Joan B. Samuelson**, track
1940 **Greg Rice**, track	1964 **Don Schollander**, swimming	1986 **Jackie Joyner-Kersee**, track
1941 **Leslie MacMitchell**, track	1965 **Bill Bradley**, basketball	1987 **Jim Abbott**, baseball
1942 **Cornelius Warmerdam**, track	1966 **Jim Ryun**, track	1988 **Florence Griffith Joyner**, track
1943 **Gilbert Dodds**, track	1967 **Randy Matson**, track	1989 **Janet Evans**, swimming
1944 **Ann Curtis**, swimming	1968 **Debbie Meyer**, swimming	
1945 **Doc Blanchard**, football	1969 **Bill Toomey**, track	1990 **John Smith**, wrestling
1946 **Arnold Tucker**, football		1991 **Mike Powell**, track
1947 **John B. Kelly, Jr.**, rowing	1970 **John Kinsella**, swimming	1992 **Bonnie Blair**, speed skating
1948 **Bob Mathias**, track	1971 **Mark Spitz**, swimming	1993 **Charlie Ward**, football
1949 **Dick Button**, skating	1972 **Frank Shorter**, track	1994 **Dan Jansen**, speed skating
	1973 **Bill Walton**, basketball	
1950 **Fred Wilt**, track	1974 **Rich Wohlhuter**, track	
1951 **Bob Richards**, track		

USOC Sportsman & Sportswoman of the Year

To the outstanding overall male and female athletes from within the U.S. Olympic Committee member organizations. Winners are chosen from nominees of the national governing bodies for Olympic and Pan American Games and affiliated organizations. Voting is done by members of the national media, USOC board of directors and Athletes' Advisory Council.

Sportsman

Multiple winners: Eric Heiden (3); Matt Biondi and Greg Louganis (2).

Year		Year		Year	
1974	**Jim Bolding**, track	1981	**Scott Hamilton**, fig. skating	1988	**Matt Biondi**, swimming
1975	**Clint Jackson**, boxing	1982	**Greg Louganis**, diving	1989	**Roger Kingdom**, track
1976	**John Naber**, swimming	1983	**Rick McKinney**, archery	1990	**John Smith**, wrestling
1977	**Eric Heiden**, speed skating	1984	**Edwin Moses**, track	1991	**Carl Lewis**, track
1978	**Bruce Davidson**, equestrian	1985	**Willie Banks**, track	1992	**Pablo Morales**, swimming
1979	**Eric Heiden**, speed skating	1986	**Matt Biondi**, swimming	1993	**Michael Johnson**, track
1980	**Eric Heiden**, speed skating	1987	**Greg Louganis**, diving	1994	**Dan Jansen**, speed skating

Sportswoman

Multiple winners: Bonnie Blair, Tracy Caulkins, Jackie Joyner-Kersee and Sheila Young Ochowicz (2).

Year		Year		Year	
1974	**Shirley Babashoff**, swimming	1982	**Melanie Smith**, equestrian	1989	**Janet Evans**, swimming
1975	**Kathy Heddy**, swimming	1983	**Tamara McKinney**, skiing	1990	**Lynn Jennings**, track
1976	**Sheila Young**, speedskating	1984	**Tracy Caulkins**, swimming	1991	**Kim Zmeskal**, gymnastics
1977	**Linda Fratianne**, fig. skating	1985	**Mary Decker Slaney**, track	1992	**Bonnie Blair**, speed skating
1978	**Tracy Caulkins**, swimming	1986	**Jackie Joyner-Kersee**, track	1993	**Gail Devers**, track
1979	**Sippy Woodhead**, swimming	1987	**Jackie Joyner-Kersee**, track	1994	**Bonnie Blair**, speed skating
1980	**Beth Heiden**, speed skating	1988	**Florence Griffith Joyner**, track		
1981	**Sheila Ochowicz**, speed skating & cycling				

Honda Broderick Cup

To the outstanding collegiate woman athlete of the year in NCAA competition. Winner is chosen from nominees in each of the NCAA's 10 competitive sports. Final voting is done by member athletic directors. Award is named after founder and sportswear manufacturer Thomas Broderick.

Multiple winner: Tracy Caulkins (2).

Year			Year		
1977	**Lucy Harris**, Delta St.	basketball	1986	**Kamie Ethridge**, Texas	basketball
1978	**Ann Meyers**, UCLA	basketball	1987	**Mary T. Meagher**, California	swimming
1979	**Nancy Lieberman**, Old Dominion	basketball	1988	**Teresa Weatherspoon**, La. Tech	basketball
1980	**Julie Shea**, N.C. State	track & field	1989	**Vicki Huber**, Villanova	track
1981	**Jill Sterkel**, Texas	swimming	1990	**Suzy Favor**, Wisconsin	track
1982	**Tracy Caulkins**, Florida	swimming	1991	**Dawn Staley**, Virginia	basketball
1983	**Deitre Collins**, Hawaii	volleyball	1992	**Missy Marlowe**, Utah	gymnastics
1984	**Tracy Caulkins**, Florida	swimming	1993	**Lisa Fernandez**, UCLA	softball
	& **Cheryl Miller**, USC	basketball	1994	**Mia Hamm**, North Carolina	soccer
1985	**Jackie Joyner**, UCLA	track & field			

Flo Hyman Award

Presented annually since 1987 by the Women's Sports Foundation for "exemplifying dignity, spirit and commitment to excellence" and named in honor of the late captain of the 1984 U.S. Women's Volleyball team. Voting by WSF members.

Year		Year		Year	
1987	**Martina Navratilova**, tennis	1990	**Chris Evert**, tennis	1993	**Lynette Woodward**, basketball
1988	**Jackie Joyner-Kersee**, track	1991	**Diana Golden**, skiing	1994	**Patty Sheehan**, golf
1989	**Evelyn Ashford**, track	1992	**Nancy Lopez**, golf	1995	**Mary Lou Retton**, gymnastics

Arthur Ashe Award for Courage

Presented since 1993 on the annual ESPN "Espys" telecast. Given to a member of the sports community who has exemplified the same courage, spirit and determination to help others despite personal hardship that characterized Arthur Ashe, the late tennis champion and humanitarian. Voting done by select 26-member committee of media and sports personalities.

Year		Year		Year	
1993	**Jim Valvano**, basketball	1994	**Steve Palermo**, baseball	1995	**Howard Cosell**, TV & radio

Time Man of the Year

Since Charles Lindbergh was named *Time* magazine's first Man of the Year for 1927, two individuals with significant sports credentials have won the honor.

Year
1984 **Peter Ueberroth**, president of the Los Angeles Olympic Organizing Committee.
1991 **Ted Turner**, owner-president of Turner Broadcasting System, founder of CNN cable news network, owner of the Atlanta Braves (NL) and Atlanta Hawks (NBA), and former winning America's Cup skipper.

The Hickok Belt

Officially known as the S. Rae Hickok Professional Athlete of the Year Award and presented by the Kickik Manufacturing Co. of Arlington, Texas, from 1950–76. The trophy was a large belt of gold, diamonds and other jewels, reportedly worth $30,000 in 1976, the last year it was handed out. Voting was done by 270 newspaper sports editors from around the country.

Multiple winner: Sandy Koufax (2).

Year	Year	Year
1950 **Phil Rizzuto**, baseball	1960 **Arnold Palmer**, golf	1970 **Brooks Robinson**, baseball
1951 **Allie Reynolds**, baseball	1961 **Roger Maris**, baseball	1971 **Lee Trevino**, golf
1952 **Rocky Marciano**, boxing	1962 **Maury Wills**, baseball	1972 **Steve Carlton**, baseball
1953 **Ben Hogan**, golf	1963 **Sandy Koufax**, baseball	1973 **O.J. Simpson**, football
1954 **Willie Mays**, baseball	1964 **Jim Brown**, football	1974 **Muhammad Ali**, boxing
1955 **Otto Graham**, football	1965 **Sandy Koufax**, baseball	1975 **Pete Rose**, baseball
1956 **Mickey Mantle**, baseball	1966 **Frank Robinson**, baseball	1976 **Ken Stabler**, football
1957 **Carmen Basilio**, boxing	1967 **Carl Yastrzemski**, baseball	1977 Discontinued
1958 **Bob Turley**, baseball	1968 **Joe Namath**, football	
1959 **Ingemar Johansson**, boxing	1969 **Tom Seaver**, baseball	

ABC's "Wide World of Sports" Athlete of the Year

Selected annually by the producers of ABC Sports since 1962.

Multiple winner: Greg Lemond (2).

Year	Year	Year
1962 **Jim Beatty**, track	1974 **Muhammad Ali**, boxing	1987 **Dennis Conner**, yachting
1963 **Valery Brumel**, track	1975 **Jack Nicklaus**, golf	1988 **Greg Louganis**, diving
1964 **Don Schollander**, swimming	1976 **Nadia Comaneci**, gymnastics	1989 **Greg Lemond**, cycling
1965 **Jim Clark**, auto racing	1977 **Steve Cauthen**, horse racing	1990 **Greg Lemond**, cycling
1966 **Jim Ryun**, track	1978 **Ron Guidry**, baseball	1991 **Carl Lewis**, track
1967 **Peggy Fleming**, figure skating	1979 **Willie Stargell**, baseball	& **Kim Zmeskal**, gymnastics
1968 **Bill Toomey**, track	1980 **U.S. Olympic hockey team**	1992 **Bonnie Blair**, speed skating
1969 **Mario Andretti**, auto racing	1981 **Sugar Ray Leonard**, boxing	1993 **Evander Holyfield**, boxing
1970 **Willis Reed**, basketball	1982 **Wayne Gretzky**, hockey	1994 **Al Unser Jr.**, auto racing
1971 **Lee Trevino**, golf	1983 **Australia II**, yachting	
1972 **Olga Korbut**, gymnastics	1984 **Edwin Moses**, track	
1973 **O.J. Simpson**, football	1985 **Pete Rose**, baseball	
& **Jackie Stewart**, auto racing	1986 **Debi Thomas**, figure skating	

The Sporting News Sportsman of the Year

Selected annually by the editors of *The Sporting News* since 1968. 'Man of the Year' changed to 'Sportsman' of the Year in 1993.

Year	Year	Year
1968 **Denny McLain**, baseball	1978 **Ron Guidry**, baseball	1988 **Jackie Joyner-Kersee**, track
1969 **Tom Seaver**, baseball	1979 **Willie Stargell**, baseball	1989 **Joe Montana**, football
1970 **John Wooden**, basketball	1980 **George Brett**, baseball	1990 **Nolan Ryan**, baseball
1971 **Lee Trevino**, golf	1981 **Wayne Gretzky**, hockey	1991 **Michael Jordan**, basketball
1972 **Charles O. Finley**, baseball	1982 **Whitey Herzog**, baseball	1992 **Mike Krzyzewski**, col. bask.
1973 **O.J. Simpson**, pro football	1983 **Bowie Kuhn**, baseball	1993 **Cito Gaston**
1974 **Lou Brock**, baseball	1984 **Peter Ueberroth**, LA Olympics	& **Pat Gillick**, baseball
1975 **Archie Griffin**, football	1985 **Pete Rose**, baseball	1994 **Emmitt Smith**, pro football
1976 **Larry O'Brien**, basketball	1986 **Larry Bird**, pro basketball	
1977 **Steve Cauthen**, horse racing	1987 No award	

Presidential Medal of Freedom

Since President John F. Kennedy established the Medal of Freedom as America's highest civilian honor in 1963, only nine sports figures have won the award. Note that (*) indicates the presentation was made posthumously.

Year		President	Year		President
1963 **Bob Kiphuth**, swimming	....	Kennedy	1986 **Earl (Red) Blaik**, football	....	Reagan
1976 **Jesse Owens**, track & field	....	Ford	1991 **Ted Williams**, baseball	....	Bush
1977 **Joe DiMaggio**, baseball	....	Ford	1992 **Richard Petty**, auto racing	....	Bush
1983 **Paul (Bear) Bryant***, football	....	Reagan	1993 **Arthur Ashe***, tennis	....	Clinton
1984 **Jackie Robinson***, baseball	....	Reagan			

TROPHY CASE

From the first organized track meet at Olympia in 776 B.C., to the Lillehammer Winter Olympics over 2,700 years later, championships have been officially recognized with prizes that are symbolically rich and eagerly pursued. Here are 15 of the most coveted trophies in America.

(Illustrations by Lynn Mercer Michaud.)

America's Cup

First presented by England's Royal Yacht Squadron to the winner of an invitational race around the Isle of Wight on Aug. 22, 1851 . . . . originally called the Hundred Guinea Cup . . . . renamed after the U.S. boat *America*, winner of the first race . . . . made of sterling silver and designed by London jewelers R. & G. Garrard . . . . measures 2 feet, 3 inches high and weighs 16 lbs . . . . originally cost 100 guineas ($500), now valued at $250,000 . . . . bell-shaped base added in 1958 . . . . challenged for every three to four years . . . . trophy held by yacht club sponsoring winning boat.

Vince Lombardi Trophy

First presented at the AFL-NFL World Championship Game (now Super Bowl) on Jan. 15, 1967 . . . . originally called the World Championship Game Trophy . . . . renamed in 1971 in honor of former Green Bay Packers GM-coach and two-time Super Bowl winner Vince Lombardi, who died in 1970 as coach of Washington . . . . made of sterling silver and designed by Tiffany & Co. of New York . . . . measures 21 inches high and weighs 7 lbs (football depicted is regulation size) . . . . valued at $12,500 . . . . competed for annually. . . . winning team keeps trophy.

Olympic Gold Medal

First presented by International Olympic Committee in 1908 (until then winners received silver medals) . . . . second and third place finishers also got medals of silver and bronze for first time in 1908 . . . . each medal must be at least 2.4 inches in diameter and 0.12 inches thick . . . . the gold medal is actually made of silver, but must be gilded with at least 6 grams (0.21 ounces) of pure gold . . . . the gold medal for the 1994 Winter Games at Lillehammer, Norway, was made of stone and metal and designed by Ingjerd Hanevold of Oslo . . . . each contains 6 grams of pure gold in the rings . . . . 155 were made for approximately $486 each . . . . competed for every two years as Winter and Summer Games alternate . . . . winners keep medals.

Stanley Cup

Donated by Lord Stanley of Preston, the Governor General of Canada and first presented in 1893 . . . . original cup was made of sterling silver by an unknown London silversmith and measured 7 inches high with an 11½-inch diameter . . . . in order to accommodate all the rosters of winning teams, the cup now measures 35½ inches high with a base 54 inches around and weighs 32 lbs . . . . originally bought for 10 guineas ($48.67), it is now insured for $75,000 . . . . actual cup retired to Hall of Fame and replaced in 1970 . . . . presented to NHL playoff champion since 1918 . . . . trophy loaned to winning team for one year.

World Cup

First presented by the Federation Internationale de Football Association (FIFA) . . . . originally called the World Cup Trophy . . . . renamed the Jules Rimet Cup (after the then FIFA president) in 1946, but retired by Brazil after that country's third title in 1970 . . . . new World Cup trophy created in 1974 . . . . designed by Italian sculptor Silvio Gazzaniga and made of solid 18 carat gold with two malachite rings inlaid at the base . . . . measures 14.2 inches high and weighs 11 lbs . . . . insured for $200,000 (U.S.) . . . . competed for every four years . . . . winning team gets gold-plated replica.

WORLD CHAMPIONSHIP TROPHY
PRESENTED BY THE COMMISSIONER OF BASEBALL

Commissioner's Trophy

First presented by the Commissioner of baseball to the winner of the 1967 World Series . . . . also known as the World Championship Trophy . . . . made of brass and gold plate with an ebony base and a baseball in the center made of pewter with a silver finish . . . . designed by Balfour & Co. of Attleboro, Mass . . . . 28 pennants represent 14 AL and 14 NL teams . . . . measures 30 inches high and 36 inches around at the base and weighs 30 lbs . . . . valued at $15,000 . . . . competed for annually . . . . winning team keeps trophy.

Larry O'Brien Trophy

First presented in 1978 to winner of NBA Finals . . . . originally called the Walter A. Brown Trophy after the league pioneer and Boston Celtics owner (an earlier NBA championship bowl was also named after Brown) . . . . renamed in 1984 in honor of outgoing commissioner O'Brien, who served from 1975-84 . . . . made of sterling silver with 24 carat gold overlay and designed by Tiffany & Co. of New York . . . . measures 2 feet high and weighs 14½ lbs (basketball depicted is regulation size) . . . . valued at $13,500 . . . . competed for annually . . . . winning team keeps trophy.

Heisman Trophy

First presented in 1935 to the best college football player east of the Mississippi by the Downtown Athletic Club of New York . . . . players across the entire country eligible since 1936 . . . . originally called the DAC Trophy . . . . renamed in 1936 following the death of DAC athletic director and former college coach John W. Heisman . . . . made of bronze and designed by New York sculptor Frank Eliscu, it measures 13½ in. high, 6½ in. wide and 14 in. long at the base and weighs 25 lbs . . . . valued at $2,000 . . . . voting done by national media and former Heisman winners . . . . awarded annually . . . . winner keeps trophy.

James E. Sullivan Memorial Award

First presented by the Amateur Athletic Union (AAU) in 1930 as a gold medal and given to the nation's outstanding amateur athlete . . . . trophy given since 1933 . . . . named after the amateur sports movement pioneer, who was a founder and past president of AAU and the director of the 1904 Olympic Games in St. Louis . . . . made of bronze with a marble base, it measures 17½ in. high and 11 in. wide at the base and weighs 13½ lbs . . . . valued at $2,500 . . . . voting done by AAU and USOC officials, former winners and selected media . . . . awarded annually . . . . winner keeps trophy.

Ryder Cup

Donated in 1927 by English seed merchant Samuel Ryder, who offered the gold cup for a biennial match between teams of golfing pros from Great Britain and the United States . . . . the format changed in 1977 to include the best players on the European PGA Tour . . . . made of 14 carat gold on a wood base and designed by Mappin and Webb of London . . . . the golfer depicted on the top of the trophy is Ryder's friend and teaching pro Abe Mitchell . . . . the cup measures 16 in. high and weighs 4 lbs . . . . insured for $50,000 . . . . competed for every two years at alternating British and U.S. sites . . . . the cup is held by the PGA headquarters of the winning side.

Davis Cup

Donated by American college student and U.S. doubles champion Dwight F. Davis in 1900 and presented by the International Tennis Federation (ITF) to the winner of the annual 16-team men's competition . . . . officially called the International Lawn Tennis Challenge Trophy . . . . made of sterling silver and designed by Shreve, Crump and Low of Boston, the cup has a matching tray (added in 1921) and a very heavy two-tiered base containing rosters of past winning teams . . . . it stands 34½ in. high and 108 in. around at the base and weighs 400 lbs . . . . insured for $150,000 . . . . competed for annually . . . . trophy loaned to winning country for one year.

Borg-Warner Trophy

First presented by the Borg-Warner Automotive Co. of Chicago in 1936 to the winner of the Indianapolis 500 . . . . replaced the Wheeler-Schebler Trophy which went to the 400-mile leader from 1911-32 . . . . made of sterling silver with bas-relief sculptured heads of each winning driver and a gold bas-relief head of Tony Hulman, the owner of the Indy Speedway from 1945-77 . . . . designed by Robert J. Hill and made by Gorham, Inc. of Rhode Island . . . . measures 51½ in. high and weighs over 80 lbs . . . . new base added in 1988 and the entire trophy restored in 1991 . . . . competed for annually . . . . insured for $1 million . . . . trophy stays at Speedway Hall of Fame . . . . winner gets a 14-in. high replica valued at $30,000.

NCAA Championship Trophy

First presented in 1952 by the NCAA to all 1st, 2nd and 3rd place teams in sports with sanctioned tournaments . . . . 1st place teams receive gold-plated awards, 2nd place award is silver-plated and 3rd is bronze . . . . replaced silver cup given to championship teams from 1939-1951 . . . . made of walnut, the trophy stands 24¾ in. high, 14⅛ in. wide and 4½ in. deep at the base and weighs 15 lbs . . . . designed by Medallic Art Co. of Danbury, Conn. and made by House of Usher of Kansas City since 1990 . . . . valued at $500 . . . . competed for annually . . . . winning teams keep trophies.

World Championship Belt

First presented in 1921 by the World Boxing Association, one of the three organizations (the World Boxing Council and International Boxing Federation are the others) generally accepted as sanctioning legitimate world championship fights . . . . belt weighs 8 lbs. and is made of hand tanned leather . . . . the outsized buckle measures 10½ in. high and 8 in. wide, is made of pewter with 24 carat gold plate and contains crystal and semi-precious stones . . . . side panels of polished brass are for engraving title bout results . . . . currently made by Phil Valentino Originals of Jersey City, N.J. . . . . champions keep belts even if they lose their title.

World Championship Ring

Rings decorated with gems and engraving date back to ancient Egypt where the wealthy wore heavy gold and silver rings to indicate social status . . . . championship rings in sports serve much the same purpose, indicating the wearer is a champion . . . . the San Francisco 49ers' ring for winning Super Bowl XXIX on Jan. 29, 1995 was designed by the Balfour Co. of North Attleboro, Mass . . . . each ring is made of 10-carat yellow gold and contains five marquis diamonds— two weighing 30 points (for the team's Super Bowl wins in 1982 and '85), two weighing 45 points (for back-to-back titles in 1989 and '90) and one weighing 65 points (for the victory in 1995) . . . .those large diamonds are surrounded by 47 smaller diamonds . . . . aproximately 200 rings were made for players and team personnel and cost in excess of $15,000 each.

Sixty years ago at the 1936 Summer Olympics in Berlin, American sprinters **Helen Stephens** (left) and **Jesse Owens**, won six gold medals between them, including both 100-meter dashes.

WHO'S WHO

Sports Personalities

Seven hundred and ninety-six entries dating back to the turn of the century. Pages updated through Sept. 15, 1995.

Hank Aaron (b. Feb. 5, 1934): Baseball OF; led NL in HRs and RBI 4 times each and batting twice with Milwaukee and Atlanta Braves; MVP in 1957; played in 24 All-Star Games, all-time leader in HRs (755) and RBI (2,297), 3rd in hits (3,771); executive with Braves and TBS, Inc.

Jim Abbott (b. Sept. 19, 1967): Baseball LHP; born without a right hand; All-America hurler at Michigan; won Sullivan Award in 1987; threw 4-0 no-hitter for NY Yankees vs. Cleveland (Sept. 4, 1993).

Kareem Abdul-Jabbar (b. Lew Alcindor, Apr. 16, 1947): Basketball C; led UCLA to 3 NCAA titles (1967-69); tourney MVP 3 times; Player of Year twice; led Milwaukee (1) and LA Lakers (5) to 6 NBA titles; playoff MVP twice (1971,85), regular season MVP 6 times (1971-72,74,76-77,80); retired in 1989 after 20 seasons as all-time leader in over 20 categories.

Andre Agassi (b. Apr. 29, 1970): Tennis; No. 1 men's player in the world as of Sept. 10, 1995 with 31 career tournament wins and 3 grand slam titles; won Wimbledon in 1992, U.S. Open as unseeded entry in '94 and Australian Open in 1995; helped U.S. win 2 Davis Cup finals (1990,92).

Troy Aikman (b. Nov. 21, 1966): Football QB; consensus All-America at UCLA (1988); 1st overall pick in 1989 NFL Draft (by Dallas); led Cowboys to 2 straight Super Bowl titles (1992 and '93 seasons); MVP in Super Bowl XXVII; entered 1995 season as second highest-paid player in NFL ($50 million over 8 years).

Tenley Albright (b. July 18, 1935): Figure skater; 2-time world champion (1953,55); won Olympic silver (1952) and gold (1956) medals; became a surgeon.

Grover Cleveland (Pete) Alexander (b. Feb. 26, 1887, d. Nov. 4, 1950): Baseball RHP; won 20 or more games 9 times; 373 career wins and 90 shutouts.

Muhammad Ali (b. Cassius Clay, Jan. 17, 1942): Boxer; 1960 Olympic light heavyweight champion; only 3-time world heavyweight champ (1964-67,1974-78,1978-79); defeated Sonny Liston (1964), George Foreman (1974) and Leon Spinks (1978) for title; fought Joe Frazier in 3 memorable bouts (1971-75), winning twice; adopted Black Muslim faith in 1964 and changed name; stripped of title in 1967 after conviction for refusing induction into U.S. Army; verdict reversed by Supreme Court in 1971; career record of 56-5 with 37 KOs and 19 successful title defenses.

Forrest (Phog) Allen (b. Nov. 18, 1885, d. Sept. 16, 1974): Basketball; college coach 48 years; directed Kansas to NCAA title (1952); 5th on all-time list with 746 career wins.

Bobby Allison (b. Dec. 3, 1937): Auto racer; 3-time winner of Daytona 500 (1978,82,88); NASCAR national champ in 1983; father of Davey.

Davey Allison (b. Feb. 25, 1961, d. July 13, 1993): Auto racer; stock car Rookie of Year (1987); winner of 19 NASCAR races including 1992 Daytona 500; killed at age 32 in helicopter accident at Talladega Superspeedway; son of Bobby.

Walter Alston (b. Dec. 1, 1911, d. Oct. 1, 1984): Baseball; managed Brooklyn-LA Dodgers 23 years, won 7 pennants and 4 World Series (1955,59,63,65); retired after 1976 season with 2,060 wins (2,040 regular season and 20 postseason).

Sparky Anderson (b. Feb. 22, 1934): Baseball; only manager to win World Series in each league—Cincinnati in NL (1975-76) and Detroit in AL (1984); 3rd-ranked skipper on all-time career list with 2,168 wins (2,134 regular season and 34 postseason).

Willie Anderson (b. May 1878, d. Oct. 25, 1910): Scottish golfer; became an American citizen and won 4 U.S. Open titles, including an unmatched 3 straight from 1903-05; also won four Western Opens from 1902-09.

Mario Andretti (b. Feb. 28, 1940): Auto racer; 4-time USAC-CART national champion (1965-66,69,84); only driver to win Daytona 500 (1967), Indy 500 (1969) and Formula One world title (1978); Indy 500 Rookie of Year (1965); retired following 1994 racing season ranked 1st in poles (67) and starts (407) and 2nd in wins (52) on all-time IndyCar list; father of Michael and Jeff, uncle of John.

Michael Andretti (b. Oct. 5, 1962): Auto racer; 1991 CART national champion with single-season record 8 wins; Indy 500 Rookie of Year (1984); left IndyCar circuit for ill-fated Formula One try in 1993; returned to IndyCar in '94; entered 1995 with 29 career wins; son of Mario.

Earl Anthony (b. Apr. 27, 1938): Bowler; 6-time PBA Bowler of Year; 41 career titles; first to earn $100,000 in 1 season (1975); first to earn $1 million in career.

Said Aouita (b. Nov. 2, 1959): Moroccan runner; won gold (5000m) and bronze (800m) in 1984 Olympics; won 5000m at 1987 World Championships; formerly held 2 world records recognized by IAAF—2000m and 5000m.

Luis Aparicio (b. Apr. 29, 1934): Baseball SS; all-time leader in most games, assists, chances and double plays by shortstop; led AL in stolen bases 9 times (1956-64); 506 career steals.

Al Arbour (b. Nov. 1, 1932): Hockey; coached NY Islanders to 4 straight Stanley Cup titles (1980-83); retired after 1993-94 season 2nd on all-time career list with 902 wins (779 regular season and 123 postseason).

Eddie Arcaro (b. Feb. 19, 1916): Jockey; 2-time Triple Crown winner (Whirlaway in 1941, Citation in '48); from 1938-52, he won Kentucky Derby 5 times, Preakness and Belmont 6 times each.

Roone Arledge (b. July 8, 1931): Sports TV innovator of live events, anthology shows, Olympic coverage and "Monday Night Football"; ran ABC Sports from 1968-86; has run ABC News since 1977.

Henry Armstrong (b. Dec. 12, 1912, d. Oct. 22, 1988): Boxer; held feather-, light- and welterweight titles simultaneously in 1938; pro record 145-20-9 with 98 KOs.

Arthur Ashe (b. July 10, 1943, d. Feb. 6, 1993): Tennis; first black man to win U.S. Championship (1968) and Wimbledon (1975); 1st U.S. player to earn $100,000 in 1 year (1970); won Davis Cup as player (1968-70) and captain (1981-82); wrote black sports history, Hard Road to Glory; announced in 1992 that he was infected with AIDS virus from a blood transfusion during 1983 heart surgery; died Feb. 6, 1993 at age 49.

Evelyn Ashford (b. Apr. 15, 1957): Track & Field; winner of 4 Olympic gold medals— 100m in 1984, and 4x100m in 1984, '88 and '92; also won silver medal in 100m in '88; member of 5 U.S. Olympic teams (1976-92).

Red Auerbach (b. Sept. 20, 1917): Basketball; winningest coach (regular season and playoffs) in NBA history; won 1,037 times in 20 years; as coach-GM, led Boston to 9 NBA titles, including 8 in a row (1959-66); also coached defunct Washington Capitols (1946-49); NBA Coach of the Year award named after him; retired as Celtics coach in 1966 and as GM in '84; club president since 1970.

Tracy Austin (b. Dec. 12, 1962): Tennis; youngest player to win U.S. Open (age 16 in 1979); won 2nd U.S. Open in '81; named AP Female Athlete of Year twice before she was 20; recurring neck and back injuries shortened career after 1983; youngest player ever inducted into Tennis Hall of Fame (age 29 in 1992).

Paul Azinger (b. Jan. 6, 1960): Golf; PGA Player of Year in 1987; entered 1995 with 11 career wins, including '93 PGA Championship; missed 1st 7 months of '94 season overcoming lymphoma (a form of cancer) in right shoulder blade.

Oksana Baiul (b. Feb. 26, 1977): Ukrainian figure skater; 1993 world champion at age 15; edged Nancy Kerrigan by a 5-4 judges' vote for 1994 Olympic gold medal.

Hobey Baker (b. Jan. 15, 1892, d. Dec 21, 1918): Football and hockey star at Princeton (1911-14); member of college football and pro hockey halls of fame; college hockey Player of Year award named after him; killed in WWI plane crash.

Seve Ballesteros (b. Apr. 9, 1957): Spanish golfer; has won British Open 3 times (1979,84,88) and Masters twice (1980,83); 3-time European Golfer of Year (1986,88,91); has led Europe to 3 Ryder Cup titles (1985,87,89); entered 1995 with 70 world-wide victories.

Ernie Banks (b. Jan. 31, 1931): Baseball SS-1B; led NL in home runs and RBI twice each; 2-time MVP (1958-59) with Chicago Cubs; 512 career HRs.

Roger Bannister (b. Mar. 23, 1929): British runner; first to run mile in less than 4 minutes (3:59.4 on May 6, 1954).

Walter (Red) Barber (b. Feb. 17, 1908, d. Oct. 22, 1992): Radio-TV; renowned baseball play-by-play broadcaster for Cincinnati, Brooklyn and N.Y. Yankees from 1934-66; won Peabody Award for radio commentary in 1991.

Charles Barkley (b. Feb. 20, 1963): Basketball F; 5-time All-NBA 1st team with Philadelphia and Phoenix; traded to Suns for 3 players (June 17, 1992); U.S. Olympic Dream Team member in '92; NBA regular season MVP in 1993.

Rick Barry (b. Mar. 28, 1944): Basketball F; only player to lead both NBA and ABA in scoring; 5-time All-NBA 1st team; playoff MVP with Golden St. in 1975.

Sammy Baugh (b. Mar. 17, 1914): Football QB-DB-P; led Washington to NFL titles in 1937 (his rookie year) and '42; led league in passing 6 times, punting 4 times and interceptions once.

Elgin Baylor (b. Sept. 16, 1934): Basketball F; MVP of NCAA tournament in 1958; led Minneapolis-LA Lakers to 8 NBA Finals; 10-time All-NBA 1st team (1959-65,67-69).

Bob Beamon (b. Aug. 29, 1946): Track & Field; won 1968 Olympic gold medal in long jump with world record (29-ft, 2½ in.) that shattered old mark by nearly 2 feet; record finally broken by 2 inches in 1991 by Mike Powell.

Franz Beckenbauer (b. Sept. 11, 1945): Soccer; captain of West German World Cup champions in 1974 then coached West Germany to World Cup title in 1990; invented sweeper position; played in U.S. for NY Cosmos (1977-80,83).

Boris Becker (b. Nov. 22, 1967): German tennis player; 3-time Wimbledon champ (1985-86,89); youngest male (17) to win Wimbledon; led country to 1st Davis Cup win in 1988; has also won U.S. (1989) and Australian (1991) Opens.

Chuck Bednarik (b. May 1, 1925): Football C-LB; 2-time All-America at Penn and 7-time All-Pro with NFL Philadelphia Eagles as both center (1950) and linebacker (1951-56); missed only 3 games in 14 seasons; led Eagles to 1960 NFL title as a 35-year-old two-way player.

Clair Bee (b. Mar. 2, 1896, d. May 20, 1983): Basketball coach who led LIU to 2 undefeated seasons (1936,39) and 2 NIT titles (1939,41); his teams won 95 percent of their games between 1931-51, including 43 in a row from 1935-37; coached NBA Baltimore Bullets from 1952-54, but was only 34-116; contributions to game include 1-3-1 zone defense, 3-second rule and NBA 24-second clock; also authored sports manuals and fictional Chip Hilton sports books for kids.

Jean Beliveau (b. Aug. 31, 1931): Hockey C; led Montreal to 10 Stanley Cups in 17 playoffs; playoff MVP (1965); 2-time regular season MVP (1956,64).

Bert Bell (b. Feb. 25, 1895, d. Oct. 11, 1959): Football; team owner and 2nd NFL commissioner (1946-59); proposed college draft in 1935 and instituted TV blackout rule.

Deane Beman (b. Apr. 22, 1938): Golf; 1st commissioner of PGA Tour (1974-94); introduced "stadium golf"; as player, won U.S. Amateur twice and British Amateur once.

Johnny Bench (b. Dec. 7, 1947): Baseball C; led NL in HRs twice and RBI 3 times; 2-time regular season MVP (1970,72) with Cincinnati, World Series MVP in 1976; 389 career HRs.

Patty Berg (b. Feb. 13, 1918): Golfer; 57 career pro wins including 15 Majors; 3-time AP Female Athlete of Year (1938,43,55).

Chris Berman (b. May 10, 1955): Radio-TV; 4-time Sportscaster of Year known for his nicknames and jovial studio anchoring on ESPN; play-by-play man only year Brown University football team won Ivy League (1976).

Yogi Berra (b. May 12, 1925): Baseball C; played on 10 World Series winners with NY Yankees; holds several WS records— games played (75), at bats (259) and hits (71); 3-time AL MVP (1951,54-55); managed both Yankees (1964) and NY Mets (1973) to pennants.

Jay Berwanger (b. Mar. 19, 1914): Football HB; University of Chicago star; won 1st Heisman Trophy in 1935.

Gary Bettman (b. June 2, 1952): Hockey; former NBA executive, who was named first commissioner of NHL on Dec. 11, 1992; took office on Feb. 1, 1993.

Abebe Bikila (b. Aug. 7, 1932, d. Oct. 25, 1973): Ethiopian runner; 1st to win consecutive Olympic marathons (1960,64).

Matt Biondi (b. Oct. 8, 1965): Swimmer; won 7 medals in 1988 Olympics, including 5 gold (2 individual, 3 relay); has won a total of 11 medals (8 gold, 2 silver and a bronze) in 3 Olympics (1984,88,92).

Larry Bird (b. Dec. 7, 1956): Basketball F; college Player of Year (1979) at Indiana St.; 1980 NBA Rookie of Year; 9-time All-NBA 1st team; 3-time regular season MVP (1984-86); led Boston to 3 NBA titles (1981,84, 86); 2-time playoff MVP (1984,86); U.S. Olympic Dream Team member in '92.

The Black Sox: Eight Chicago White Sox players who were banned from baseball for life in 1921 for allegedly throwing the 1919 World Series— RHP Eddie Cicotte (1884-1969), OF Happy Felsch (1891-1964), 1B Chick Gandil (1887-1970), OF Shoeless Joe Jackson (1889-1951), INF Fred McMullin (1891-1952), SS Swede Risberg (1894-1975), 3B-SS Buck Weaver (1890-1956), and LHP Lefty Williams (1893-1959).

Earl (Red) Blaik (b. Feb. 15, 1897, d. May 6, 1989): Football; coached Army to consecutive national titles in 1944-45; 166 career wins and 3 Heisman winners (Blanchard, Davis, Dawkins).

Bonnie Blair (b. Mar. 18, 1964): Speedskater; only American woman to win 5 Olympic gold medals in Winter or Summer Games; won 500-meters in 1988, then 500m and 1,000m in both 1992 and '94; added 1,000m bronze in 1988; Sullivan Award winner (1992); retired on 31st birthday as reigning world sprint champ.

Hector (Toe) Blake (b. Aug. 21, 1912, d. May 17, 1995): Hockey LW; led Montreal to 2 Stanley Cups as a player and 8 more as coach; regular season MVP in 1939.

Felix (Doc) Blanchard (b. Dec. 11, 1924): Football FB; 3-time All-America; led Army to national titles in 1944-45; Glenn Davis' running mate; won Heisman Trophy and Sullivan Award in 1945.

George Blanda (b. Sept. 17, 1927): Football QB-PK; NFL's all-time leading scorer (2,002 points); led Houston to 2 AFL titles (1960-61); played 26 pro seasons; retired at 48.

Fanny Blankers-Koen (b. Apr. 26, 1918): Dutch sprinter; 30-year-old mother of two, who won 4 gold medals (100m, 200m, 800m hurdles and 4x100m relay) at 1948 Olympics.

Drew Bledsoe (b. Feb. 14, 1972): Football QB; 1st overall pick in 1993 NFL draft (by New England); holds NFL single-season record for most passes attempted (691) and single-game records for most passes completed (45), attempted (70); entered 1995 season as highest-paid player in NFL ($42 million over 7 years).

Wade Boggs (b. June 15, 1958): Baseball 3B; entered 1995 season with 5 AL batting titles (1983,85-88) at Boston and .335 career average in 13 seasons.

Barry Bonds (b. July 24, 1964): Baseball OF; 3-time NL MVP, twice with Pittsburgh (1990,92) and once with San Francisco (1993); NL's HR and RBI leader in 1993; signed 6-year deal with Giants worth $43.75 million following '92 season; son of Bobby.

Bjorn Borg (b. June 6, 1956): Swedish tennis player; 2-time Player of Year (1979-80); won 6 French Opens and 5 straight Wimbledons (1976-80); led Sweden to 1st Davis Cup win in 1975; retired in 1983 at age 26; attempted unsuccessful comeback in 1991.

Mike Bossy (b. Jan. 22, 1957): Hockey RW; led NY Isles to 4 Stanley Cups; playoff MVP in 1982; scored 50 goals or more 9 straight years; 573 career goals.

Ralph Boston (b. May 9, 1939): Track & Field; medaled in 3 consecutive Olympic long jumps— gold (1960), silver (1964), bronze (1968).

Ray Bourque (b. Dec. 28, 1960): Hockey D; 11-time All-NHL 1st team, has won Norris Trophy 5 times (1987-88,1990-91,94) with Boston.

Bobby Bowden (b. Nov. 8, 1929): Football; coached Florida St. to a national title in 1993; entered '95 regular season 5th on all-time career list with 249 wins, including a 14-3-1 bowl record in 29 years as coach at Samford, West Va. and FSU; father of Terry.

Terry Bowden (b. Feb. 24, 1956): Football; led Auburn to 11-0 record in his first season as Division I-A head coach in 1993; NCAA probation earned under previous staff prevented bowl appearance; son of Bobby.

Riddick Bowe (b. Aug. 10, 1967): Boxing; won world heavyweight title with unanimous decision over champion Evander Holyfield on Nov. 13, 1992; lost title to Holyfield on majority decision Nov. 6, 1993; entered 1995 with pro record of 35-1 and 29 KOs.

Scotty Bowman (b. Sept. 18, 1933): Hockey; all-time winningest NHL coach in both regular season (913 wins) and playoffs (152) over 23 seasons; led Montreal to 5 Stanley Cups (1973,76-79) and Pittsburgh to another (1992).

Jack Brabham (b. Apr. 2, 1926): Australian auto racer; 3-time Formula One champion (1959-60,66); 14 career wins.

Bill Bradley (b. July 28, 1943): Basketball F; 3-time All-America at Princeton; Player of Year and NCAA tourney MVP in 1965; captain of gold medal-winning 1964 U.S. Olympic team; Sullivan Award winner (1965); led NY Knicks to 2 NBA titles (1970,73); U.S. Senator (D, N.J.) since 1979, but announced in 1995 he will not seek re-election in '96.

Pat Bradley (b. Mar. 24, 1951): Golfer; 2-time LPGA Player of Year (1986,91); has won all four majors on LPGA tour, including 3 du Maurier Classics; inducted into the LPGA Hall of Fame on Jan. 18, 1992; entered 1995 as all-time LPGA money leader and 13th in wins (30).

Terry Bradshaw (b. Sept. 2, 1948): Football QB; led Pittsburgh to 4 Super Bowl titles (1975-76,79-80); 2-time Super Bowl MVP (1979-80).

George Brett (b. May 15, 1953): Baseball 3B-1B; AL batting champion in 3 different decades (1976,80,90); MVP in 1980; led KC to World Series title in 1985; retired after 1993 season with 3,154 hits and .305 career average.

Lou Brock (b. June 18, 1939): Baseball OF; former all-time stolen base leader (938); led NL in steals 8 times; led St. Louis to 2 World Series titles (1964,67); had 3,023 career hits.

Herb Brooks (b. Aug. 5, 1937): Hockey; former U.S. Olympic player (1964,68) who coached 1980 team to gold medal; coached Minnesota to 3 NCAA titles (1974,76,78); also coached NY Rangers, Minnesota and New Jersey in NHL.

Jim Brown (b. Feb. 17, 1936): Football FB; All-America at Syracuse (1956) and NFL Rookie of Year (1957); led NFL in rushing 8 times; 8-time All-Pro (1957-61,63-65); 3-time MVP (1958,63,65) with Cleveland; ran for 12,312 yards and scored 756 points in just 9 seasons.

Larry Brown (b. Sept. 14, 1940): Basketball; played in ACC, AAU, 1964 Olympics and ABA; 3-time assist leader (1968-70) and 3-time Coach of Year (1973,75-76) in ABA; coached ABA's Carolina and Denver and NBA's Denver, New Jersey, San Antonio, LA Clippers and Indiana; also coached UCLA to Final Four (1980) and Kansas to NCAA title (1988).

Paul Brown (b. Sept. 7, 1908, d. Aug. 5, 1991): Football innovator; coached Ohio St. to national title in 1942; in pros, directed Cleveland Browns to 4 straight AAFC titles (1946-49) and 3 NFL titles (1950,54-55); formed Cincinnati Bengals as head coach and part-owner in 1968 (reached playoffs in '70).

Sergi Bruguera (b. Jan. 16, 1971): Spanish tennis player; won consecutive French Opens in 1993 and '94; entered '95 as decade's winningest clay court player.

Valery Brumel (b. Apr. 14, 1942): Soviet high jumper; dominated event from 1961-64; broke world record 5 times; won silver medal in 1960 Olympics and gold in 1964; highest jump was 7-5.

Avery Brundage (b. Sept. 28, 1887, d. May 5, 1975): Amateur sports czar for over 40 years as president of AAU (1928-35), U.S. Olympic Committee (1929-53) and International Olympic Committee (1952-72).

Paul (Bear) Bryant (b. Sept. 11, 1913, d. Jan. 26, 1983): Football; coached at 4 colleges over 38 years; directed Alabama to 5 national titles (1961,64-65,78-79); 323 career wins; 15 bowl wins including 8 Sugar Bowls.

Sergey Bubka (b. Dec. 4, 1963): Ukrainian pole vaulter; 1st man to clear 20 feet both indoors and out (1991); holder of indoor (20-2) and outdoor (20-1¾) world records as of Sept. 10, 1995; 5-time world champion (1983,87,91,93,95); won Olympic gold medal in 1988, but failed to clear any height in 1992 Games.

Don Budge (b. June 13, 1915): Tennis; in 1938 became 1st player to win the Grand Slam— the French, Wimbledon, U.S. and Australian titles in 1 year; led U.S. to 2 Davis Cups (1937-38); turned pro in late '38.

Maria Bueno (b. Oct. 11, 1939): Brazilian tennis player; won 4 U.S. Championships (1959,63-64,66) and 3 Wimbledons (1959-60,64).

Leroy Burrell (b. Feb. 21, 1967): Track & Field; set current world record of 9.85 in 100 meters, July 6, 1994; previously held record (9.90) in 1991; member of 4 world record-breaking 4 x 100m relay teams.

George Bush (b. June 12, 1924): 41st President of U.S. (1989-93) and avid sportsman; played 1B on 1947 and '48 Yale baseball teams that placed 2nd in College World Series; captain of 1948 team.

Susan Butcher (b. Dec. 26, 1956): Sled Dog racer; 4-time winner of Iditarod Trail race (1986-88,90).

Dick Butkus (b. Dec. 9, 1942): Football LB; 2-time All-America at Illinois (1963-64); All-Pro 7 of 9 NFL seasons with Chicago Bears.

Dick Button (b. July 18, 1929): Figure skater; 5-time world champion (1948-52); 2-time Olympic champ (1948,52); Sullivan Award winner (1949); won Emmy Award as Best Analyst for 1980-81 TV season.

Walter Byers (b. Mar. 13, 1922): College athletics; 1st executive director of NCAA, serving from 1951-88.

Frank Calder (b. Nov. 17, 1877, d. Feb. 4, 1943): Hockey; 1st NHL president (1917-43); guided league through its formative years; NHL's Rookie of the Year award named after him.

Lee Calhoun (b. Feb. 23, 1933, d. June 22, 1989): Track & Field; won consecutive Olympic gold medals in the 110m hurdles (1956,60).

Walter Camp (b. Apr. 7, 1859, d. Mar. 14, 1925): Football coach and innovator; established scrimmage line, center snap, downs, 11 players per side; elected 1st All-America team (1889).

Roy Campanella (b. Nov. 19, 1921, d. June 26, 1993): Baseball C; 3-time NL MVP (1951,53,55); led Brooklyn to 5 pennants and 1st World Series title (1955); career cut short when 1958 car accident left him paralyzed.

Clarence Campbell (b. July 9, 1905, d. June 24, 1984): Hockey; 3rd NHL president (1946-77), league tripled in size from 6 to 18 teams during his tenure.

Earl Campbell (b. Mar. 29, 1955): Football RB; won Heisman Trophy in 1977; led NFL in rushing 3 times; 3-time All-Pro; 2-time MVP (1978-79) at Houston.

John Campbell (b. Apr. 8, 1955): Harness racing; 4-time winner of Hambletonian (1987,88,90,95); 3-time Driver of Year; first driver to go over $100 million in career winnings; entered 1995 with 6,687 career wins.

Milt Campbell (b. Dec. 9, 1933): Track & Field; won silver medal in 1952 Olympic decathlon and gold medal in '56.

Jimmy Cannon (b. 1910, d. Dec. 5, 1973): Tough, opinionated New York sportswriter and essayist who viewed sports as an extension of show business; protégé of Damon Runyon; covered World War II for Stars & Stripes.

Tony Canzoneri (b. Nov. 6, 1908, d. Dec. 9, 1959): Boxer; 2-time world lightweight champion (1930-33,35-36); pro record 141-24-10 with 44 KOs.

Jennifer Capriati (b. Mar. 29, 1976): Tennis; youngest Grand Slam semifinalist ever (age 14 in 1990 French Open); also youngest to win a match at Wimbledon (1990); upset Steffi Graf to win gold medal at 1992 Olympics; left tour in '94 due to personal problems including an arrest for marijuana possession.

Harry Caray (b. Mar. 1, 1917): Radio-TV; baseball play-by-play broadcaster for St. Louis Cardinals, Oakland, Chicago White Sox and Cubs since 1945; father of sportscaster Skip and grandfather of sportscaster Chip.

Rod Carew (b. Oct. 1, 1945): Baseball 2B-1B; led AL in batting 7 times (1969,72-75,77-78) with Minnesota; MVP in 1977; had 3,053 career hits.

Steve Carlton (b. Dec. 22, 1944): Baseball LHP; won 20 or more games 6 times; 4-time Cy Young winner (1972,77,80,82) with Philadelphia; 329 career wins.

JoAnne Carner (b. Apr. 4, 1939): Golfer; 5-time U.S. Amateur champion; 2-time U.S. Open champ; 3-time LPGA Player of Year (1974,81-82); 7th in career wins (42).

Don Carter (b. July 29, 1926): Bowler; 6-time Bowler of Year (1953-54,57-58,60-61); voted Greatest of All-Time in 1970.

Joe Carter (b. Mar. 7, 1960): Baseball OF; 3-time All-America at Wichita St. (1979-81); won 1993 World Series for Toronto with 3-run HR in bottom of the 9th of Game 6; entered 1995 season with 302 HRs and 1,097 RBI in 12 years.

Alexander Cartwright (b. Apr. 17, 1820, d. July 12, 1892): Baseball; engineer and draftsman who spread gospel of baseball from New York City to California gold fields; widely regarded as the father of modern game; his guidelines included setting 3 strikes for an out and 3 outs for each half inning.

Billy Casper (b. June 4, 1931): Golfer; 2-time PGA Player of Year (1966,70); has won U.S. Open (1959,66), Masters (1970), U.S. Senior Open (1983); compiled 51 PGA wins and 9 on Senior Tour.

Tracy Caulkins (b. Jan. 11, 1963): Swimmer; won 3 gold medals (2 individual) at 1984 Olympics; set 5 world records and won 48 U.S. national titles from 1978-84; Sullivan Award winner (1978); 2-time Honda Broderick Cup winner (1982,84).

Evonne Goolagong Cawley (b. July 31, 1951): Australian tennis player; won Australian Open 4 times, Wimbledon twice (1971,79), French once.

Florence Chadwick (b. Nov. 9, 1917, d. Mar. 15, 1995): Dominant distance swimmer of 1950's; set English Channel records from France to England (1950) and England to France (1951 and '55).

Wilt Chamberlain (b. Aug. 21, 1936): Basketball C; consensus All-America in 1957 and '58 at Kansas; Final Four MVP in 1957; led NBA in scoring 7 times and rebounding 11 times; 7-time All-NBA first team; also league MVP (1960,66-68) in Philadelphia; scored 100 points vs. NY Knicks in Hershey, Pa., Mar. 2, 1962; led Philadelphia 76ers (1967) and LA Lakers (1972) to NBA titles; playoff MVP in 1972.

A.B. (Happy) Chandler (b. July 14, 1898, d. June 15, 1991): Baseball; former Kentucky governor and U.S. Senator who succeeded Judge Landis as commissioner in 1945; backed Branch Rickey's move in 1947 to make Jackie Robinson 1st black player in major leagues; deemed too pro-player and ousted by owners in 1951.

Julio Cesar Chavez (b. July 12, 1962): Mexican boxer; world jr. welterweight champ; also held titles as jr. lightweight (1984-87) and lightweight (1987-89); fought Pernell Whitaker to controversial draw for welterweight title on Sept. 10, 1993; entered 1995 with 92-1-1 record with 76 KOs; 90-bout unbeaten streak ended Jan. 29, 1994 when Frankie Randall won title on split decision; Chavez won title back four months later.

Linford Christie (b. Apr. 2, 1960): British sprinter; won 100-meter gold medals at both 1992 Olympics (9.96) and '93 World Championships (9.87); set indoor world record in 200-meters (20.25) on Feb. 19, 1995 in Lievin, France.

Jim Clark (b. Mar. 14, 1936, d. Apr. 7, 1968): Scottish auto racer; 2-time Formula One world champion (1963,65); won Indy 500 in 1965; killed in car crash.

Bobby Clarke (b. Aug. 13, 1949): Hockey C; led Philadelphia Flyers to consecutive Stanley Cups in 1974-75; 3-time regular season MVP (1973,75-76).

Ron Clarke (b. Feb. 21, 1937): Australian runner; from 1963-70 set 17 world records in races from 2 miles to 20,000 meters; never won Olympic gold medal.

Roger Clemens (b. Aug. 4, 1962): Baseball RHP; fanned MLB record 20 batters in 9-inning game (April 29, 1986); 3 Cy Young Awards (1986-87,91) with Boston; AL MVP in 1986; entered 1995 season with 172 wins in 11 seasons.

Roberto Clemente (b. Aug. 18, 1934, d. Dec. 31, 1972): Baseball OF; hit .300 or better 13 times with Pittsburgh; led NL in batting 4 times; World Series MVP in 1971; regular season MVP in 1966; had 3,000 career hits; killed in plane crash.

Ty Cobb (b. Dec. 18, 1886, d. July 17, 1961): Baseball OF; all-time highest career batting average (.367); hit .400 or better 3 times; led AL in batting 12 times and stolen bases 6 times with Detroit; MVP in 1911; had 4,191 career hits and 892 steals.

Mickey Cochrane (b. Apr. 6, 1903, d. June 28, 1962): Baseball C; led Philadelphia A's (1929-30) and Detroit (1935) to 3 World Series titles; 2-time AL MVP (1928,34).

Sebastian Coe (b. Sept. 29, 1956): British runner; won gold medal in 1500m and silver medal in 800m at both 1980 and '84 Olympics; although retired, still holds world records in 800m and 1000m; elected to Parliament as Conservative in 1992.

Paul Coffey (b. June 1, 1961): Hockey D; holds NHL record for goals (358), assists (978) and points (1,336) by a defenseman; member of four Stanley Cup championship teams at Edmonton (1984-85,87) and Pittsburgh (1991).

Eddie Collins (b. May 2, 1887, d. Mar. 25, 1951): Baseball 2B; led Philadelphia A's (1910-11) and Chicago White Sox (1917) to 3 World Series titles; AL MVP in 1914; had 3,311 career hits and 743 stolen bases.

Nadia Comaneci (b. Nov. 12, 1961): Romanian gymnast; 1st to record perfect 10 in Olympics; won 3 individual gold medals at 1976 Olympics and 2 more in '80.

Lionel Conacher (b. May 24, 1901, d. May 26, 1954): Canada's greatest all-around athlete; NHL hockey (2 Stanley Cups), CFL football (1 Grey Cup), minor league baseball, soccer, lacrosse, track, amateur boxing champion; also member of Parliament (1949-54).

Gene Conley (b. Nov. 10, 1930): Baseball and Basketball played for World Series and NBA champions with Milwaukee Braves (1957) and Boston Celtics (1959-61); winning pitcher in 1954 All-Star Game; won 91 games in 11 seasons.

Billy Conn (b. Oct. 8, 1917, d. May 29, 1993): Boxer; Pittsburgh native and world light heavyweight champion from 1939-41; nearly upset heavyweight champ Joe Louis in 1941 title bout, but was knocked out in 13th round; pro record 63-11-1 with 14 KOs.

Dennis Conner (b. Sept. 16, 1942): Sailing; 3-time America's Cup-winning skipper aboard Freedom (1980), Stars & Stripes (1987) and the Stars & Stripes catamaran (1988); only American skipper to lose Cup, first in 1983 when Australia II beat Liberty and again in '95 when New Zealand's Black Magic swept Conner and his Stars & Stripes crew aboard the borrowed Young America.

Maureen Connolly (b. Sept. 17, 1934, d. June 21, 1969): Tennis; in 1953 1st woman to win Grand Slam (at age 19); riding accident ended her career in '54; won both Wimbledon and U.S. titles 3 times (1951-53); 3-time AP Female Athlete of Year (1951-53).

Jimmy Connors (b. Sept. 2, 1952): Tennis; No.1 player in world 5 times (1974-78); won 5 U.S. Opens, 2 Wimbledons and 1 Australian; rose from No. 936 at the close of 1990 to U.S. Open semifinals in 1991 at age 39; NCAA singles champ (1971); all-time leader in pro singles titles (109) and matches won at U.S. Open (98) and Wimbledon (84).

Jack Kent Cooke (b. Oct. 25, 1912): Football; sole owner of NFL Washington Redskins since 1985; teams have won 2 Super Bowls (1987,91); also owned NBA Lakers and NHL Kings in LA; built LA Forum for $12 million in 1967.

Angel Cordero Jr. (b. Nov. 8, 1942): Jockey; third on all-time list with 7,057 wins in 38,646 starts; won Kentucky Derby 3 times (1974,76,85), Preakness twice and Belmont once; 2-time Eclipse Award winner (1982-83); set to resume career on Oct. 1, 1995 after retiring in 1992.

Howard Cosell (b. Mar. 25, 1920, d. Apr. 23, 1995): Radio-TV; former ABC commentator on "Monday Night Football" and "Wide World of Sports," who energized TV sports journalism with abrasive "tell it like it is" style.

Bob Costas (b. Mar. 22, 1952): Radio-TV; NBC anchor for NBA, NFL and Summer Olympics as well as baseball play-by-play man; 6-time Emmy winner and 5-time Sportscaster of Year.

James (Doc) Counsilman (b. Dec. 28, 1920): Swimming; coached Indiana men's swim team to 6 NCAA championships (1968-73); coached the 1964 and '76 U.S. men's Olympic teams that won a combined 21 of 24 gold medals; in 1979 became oldest person (59) to swim English Channel; retired in 1990 with dual meet record of 287-36-1.

Fred Couples (b. Oct. 3, 1959): Golfer; 2-time PGA Tour Player of the Year (1991,92); entered 1995 with 11 Tour victories, including 1992 Masters.

Jim Courier (b. Aug. 17, 1970): Tennis; No. 1 player in world in 1992, has won two Australian Opens (1992-93) and two French (1991-92); played on 1992 Davis Cup winner; Nick Bollettieri Academy classmate of Andre Agassi.

Margaret Smith Court (b. July 16, 1942): Australian tennis player; won Grand Slam in both singles (1970) and mixed doubles (1963 with Ken Fletcher); 26 Grand Slam singles titles— 11 Australian, 7 U.S., 5 French and 3 Wimbledon.

Bob Cousy (b. Aug. 9, 1928): Basketball G; led NBA in assists 8 times; 10-time All-NBA 1st team (1952-61); MVP in 1957; led Boston to 6 NBA titles (1957,59-63).

Buster Crabbe (b. Feb. 7, 1910, d. Apr. 23, 1983): Swimmer; 2-time Olympic freestyle medalist with bronze in 1928 (1500m) and gold in '32 (400m); became movie star and King of Serials as Flash Gordon and Buck Rogers.

Ben Crenshaw (b. Jan. 11, 1952): Golfer; co-NCAA champion with Tom Kite in 1972; battled Graves' disease in mid-1980's; entered 1995 with 18 career Tour victories; won Masters for second time on April 9 and dedicated it to 90-year-old mentor Harvey Penick, who had died on April 2.

Joe Cronin (b. Oct. 12, 1906, d. Sept. 7, 1984): Baseball SS; hit over .300 and drove in over 100 runs 8 times each; MVP in 1930; player-manager in Washington and Boston (1933-47); AL president (1959-73).

Ann Curtis (b. Mar. 6, 1926): Swimming; won 2 gold medals and 1 silver in 1948 Olympics; set 4 world and 18 U.S. records during career; 1st woman and swimmer to win Sullivan Award (1944).

Betty Cuthbert (b. Apr. 20, 1938): Australian runner; won gold medals in 100 and 200 meters and 4x100m relay at 1956 Olympics; also won 400m gold at 1964 Olympics.

Chuck Daly (b. July 20, 1930): Basketball; coached Detroit to two NBA titles (1989-90) before leaving in 1992 to coach New Jersey; retired after 1993-94 season with 638 career wins (including playoffs) in 12 years; coached NBA "Dream Team" to gold medal in 1992 Olympics.

John Daly (b. Apr. 28, 1966): Golfer; suprise winner of 1991 PGA Championship as unknown 25-year-old; battled through personal troubles in 1994 to return in '95 and win 2nd major at British Open, beating Italy's Constantin Rocca in 4-hole playoff.

Stanley Dancer (b. July 25, 1927): Harness racing; winner of 4 Hambletonians; trainer-driver of Triple Crown winners in Trotting (Nevele Pride in 1968 and Super Bowl in '72) and Pacing (Most Happy Fella in 1970); entered 1995 with 3,780 career wins.

Tamas Darnyi (b. June 3, 1967): Hungarian swimmer; 2-time double gold medal winner in 200m and 400m individual medley at 1988 and '92 Olympics; also won both events in 1986 and '91 world championships; set world records in both at '91 worlds; 1st swimmer to break 2 minutes in 200m IM (1:59:36).

Al Davis (b. July 4, 1929): Football; GM-coach of Oakland 1963-66; helped force AFL-NFL merger as AFL commissioner (April-July 1966); returned to Oakland as managing general partner and directed club to 3 Super Bowl wins (1977,81,84); defied fellow NFL owners and moved Raiders to LA in 1982; turned down owners' 1995 offer to build him a new stadium in LA and moved back to Oakland instead.

Dwight Davis (b. July 5, 1879, d. Nov. 28, 1945): Tennis; donor of Davis Cup; played for winning U.S. team in 1st two Cup finals (1900,02); won U.S. and Wimbledon doubles titles in 1901; Secretary of War (1925-29) under Coolidge.

Glenn Davis (b. Dec. 26, 1924): Football HB; 3-time All-America; led Army to national titles in 1944-45; Doc Blanchard's running mate; won Heisman Trophy in 1946.

John Davis (b. Jan. 12, 1921, d. July 13, 1984): Weightlifting; 6-time world champion; 2-time Olympic super-heavyweight champ (1948,52); undefeated from 1938-53.

Dizzy Dean (b. Jan. 16 1911, d. July 17, 1974): Baseball RHP; led NL in strikeouts and complete games 4 times; last NL pitcher to win 30 games (30-7 in 1934); MVP in 1934 with St. Louis; 150 career wins.

Dave DeBusschere (b. Oct. 16, 1940): Basketball F; 3-time All-America at Detroit; youngest coach in NBA history (24 in 1964); player-coach of Detroit Pistons (1964-67); played in 8 All-Star games; won 2 NBA titles as player with NY Knicks; ABA commissioner (1975-76); also pitched 2 seasons for Chicago White Sox (1962-63) with 3-4 record.

Pierre de Coubertin (b. Jan. 1, 1863, d. Sept. 2, 1937): French educator; father of the Modern Olympic Games; IOC president from 1896-1925.

Anita DeFrantz (b. Oct. 4, 1952): Olympics; attorney who is one of 2 American delegates to the International Olympic Committee (James Easton is the other); first woman to represent U.S. on IOC; member of USOC Executive Committee; member of bronze medal U.S. women's eight-oared shell at Montreal in 1976.

Cedric Dempsey (b. Apr. 14, 1932): College sports; named to succeed Dick Schultz as NCAA executive director on Nov. 5, 1993; served as athletic director at Pacific (1967-79), San Diego St. (1979), Houston (1979-82) and Arizona (1983-93).

Jack Dempsey (b. June 24, 1895, d. May 31, 1983): Boxer; world heavyweight champion from 1919-26; lost title to Gene Tunney, then lost "Long Count" rematch in 1927 when he floored Tunney in 7th round but failed to retreat to neutral corner; pro record 62-6-10 with 49 KOs.

Donna de Varona (b. Apr. 26, 1947): Swimming; won gold medals in 400 IM and 400 freestyle relay at 1964 Olympics; set 18 world records during career; co-founder of Women's Sports Foundation in 1974.

Gail Devers (b. Nov. 19, 1966): Track & Field; fastest-ever woman sprinter-hurdler; overcame thyroid disorder (Graves' disease) that sidelined her in 1989-90 and nearly resulted in having both feet amputated; won 1992 Olympic gold medal in 100 meters (10.82); 3-time world champion in 100 meters (1993) and 100-meter hurdles (1993,95).

Klaus Dibiasi (b. Oct. 6, 1947): Italian diver; won 3 consecutive Olympic gold medals in platform event (1968,72,76).

Eric Dickerson (b. Sept. 2, 1960): Football RB; led NFL in rushing 4 times (1983-84,86,88); ran for single-season record 2,105 yards in 1984; NFC Rookie of Year in 1983; All-Pro 5 times; traded from LA Rams to Indianapolis (Oct. 31, 1987) in 3-team, 10-player deal (including draft picks) that also involved Buffalo; 2nd on all-time career rushing list with 13,259 yards in 11 seasons.

Harrison Dillard (b. July 8, 1923): Track & Field; only man to win Olympic gold medals in both sprints (100m in 1948) and hurdles (110m in 1952).

Joe DiMaggio (b. Nov. 25, 1914): Baseball OF; hit safely in 56 straight games (1941); led AL in batting, HRs and RBI twice each; 3-time MVP (1939,41,47); hit .325 with 361 HRs over 13 seasons; led NY Yankees to 10 World Series titles.

Mike Ditka (b. Oct. 18, 1939): Football; All-America at Pitt (1960); NFL Rookie of Year (1961); 5-time Pro Bowl tight end for Chicago Bears; also played for Philadelphia and Dallas in 12-year career; returned to Chicago as head coach in 1982; won Super Bowl XX; compiled 112-68-0 record in 11 seasons with Bears.

Charlotte (Lottie) Dod (b. Sept. 24, 1871, d. June 27, 1960): British athlete; was 5-time Wimbledon singles champion (1887-88,91-93); youngest player ever to win Wimbledon (15 in 1887); archery silver medalist at 1908 Olympics; member of national field hockey team in 1899; British Amateur golf champ in 1904.

Tony Dorsett (b. Apr. 7, 1954): Football RB; won Heisman Trophy leading Pitt to national title in 1976; all-time NCAA Div. I-A rushing leader with 6,082 yards; led Dallas to Super Bowl title as NFC Rookie of Year (1977); NFC Player of Year (1981); ranks 3rd on all-time NFL list with 12,739 yards gained in 12 years; holds NFL record for run from scrimmage (99 yards vs. Min. in 1983).

James (Buster) Douglas (b. Apr. 7, 1960): Boxing; 50-1 shot who knocked out undefeated Mike Tyson in 10th round on Feb. 10, 1990 to win heavyweight title in Tokyo; 10 months later, lost only title defense to Evander Holyfield by KO in 3rd round.

The Dream Team: Head coach Chuck Daly's "Best Ever" 12-man NBA All-Star squad that headlined the 1992 Summer Olympics in Barcelona and easily won the basketball gold medal; co-captained by Larry Bird and Magic Johnson, with veterans Charles Barkley, Clyde Drexler, Patrick Ewing, Michael Jordan, Karl Malone, Chris Mullin, Scottie Pippen, David Robinson, John Stockton and rookie Christian Laettner.

Dream Team II: Head coach Don Nelson's 12-man NBA All-Star squad that cruised to gold medal at 1994 World Basketball Championships in Toronto— Derrick Coleman, Joe Dumars, Kevin Johnson, Larry Johnson, Shawn Kemp, Dan Majerle, Reggie Miller, Alonzo Mourning, Shaquille O'Neal, Mark Price, Steve Smith and Dominique Wilkins.

Dream Team III: Head coach Lenny Wilkens' 10-man NBA All-Star squad that will represent the U.S. at the 1996 Summer Olympics in Atlanta— Anfernee Hardaway, Grant Hill, Karl Malone, Reggie Miller, Hakeem Olajuwon, Shaquille O'Neal, Scottie Pippen, David Robinson, Glenn Robinson and John Stockton; two more players will be added in '96.

Heike Drechsler (b. Dec. 16, 1964): German long jumper and sprinter; East German before reunification in 1991; set world long jump record (24-2¼) in 1988; won long jump gold medals at 1992 Olympics and 1983 and '93 World Championships; won silver medal in long jump and bronze medals in both 100- and 200-meter sprints at 1988 Olympics.

Ken Dryden (b. Aug. 8, 1947): Hockey G; led Montreal to 6 Stanley Cup titles; playoff MVP as rookie in 1971; won or shared 5 Vezina Trophies; 2.24 career GAA.

Don Drysdale (b. July 23, 1936, d. July 3, 1993): Baseball RHP; led NL in strikeouts 3 times and games started 4 straight years; pitched and won record 6 shutouts in a row in 1968; Cy Young Award winner in 1962; won 209 games and hit 29 HRs in 14 years.

Charley Dumas (b. Feb. 12, 1937): U.S. high jumper; first man to clear 7 feet (7-0 1/2) on June 29, 1956; won gold medal at 1956 Olympics.

Margaret Osborne du Pont (b. Mar. 4, 1918): Tennis; won 5 French, 7 Wimbledon and an unprecedented 24 U.S. national titles in singles, doubles and mixed doubles from 1941-62.

Roberto Duran (b. June 16, 1951): Panamanian boxer; one of only 4 fighters to hold 4 different world titles— lightweight (1972-79), welterweight (1980), junior middleweight (1983) and middleweight (1989-90); lost famous "No Mas" welterweight title bout when he quit in 8th round against Sugar Ray Leonard (1980); pro record stood at 94-11 and 65 KOs after 12-round loss to Vinny Pazienza on Jan. 14, 1995.

Leo Durocher (b. July 27, 1905, d. Oct. 7, 1991): Baseball; managed in NL 24 years; won 2,015 games, including postseason; 3 pennants with Brooklyn (1941) and NY Giants (1951,54); won World Series in 1954.

Eddie Eagan (b. Apr. 26, 1898, d. June 14, 1967): Only athlete to win gold medals in both Summer and Winter Olympics (Boxing in 1920, Bobsled in 1932).

Alan Eagleson (b. Apr. 24, 1933): Hockey; Toronto lawyer, agent and 1st executive director of NHL Players Assn. (1967-90); midwifed Team Canada vs. Soviet series (1972) and Canada Cup; charged with racketeering and defrauding NHLPA in 32-count indictment handed down by U.S. grand jury on Mar. 3, 1994.

Dale Earnhardt (b. Apr. 29, 1952): Auto racer; 7-time NASCAR national champion (1980,86-87,90-91, 93-94); Rookie of Year in 1979; entered 1995 as all-time NASCAR money leader with $22,794,304 and 6th on career wins list with 63; in 21 years, has never won Daytona 500.

James Easton (b. July 26, 1935): Olympics; archer and sporting goods manufacturer (Easton softball bats); one of 2 American delegates to the International Olympic Committee; president of International Archery Federation (FITA); member of LA Olympic Organizing Committee in 1984.

Dick Ebersol (b. July 28, 1947): Radio-TV; protégé of ABC Sports czar Roone Arledge; key NBC exec in launching of "Saturday Night Live" in 1975; became president of NBC Sports in 1989, won U.S. TV rights to both 2000 Summer and 2002 Winter Olympics with unprecedented combined bid of $1.27 billion in August 1995.

Stefan Edberg (b. Jan. 19, 1966): Swedish tennis player; 2-time No.1 player (1990-91); 2-time winner of Australian Open (1985,87), Wimbledon (1988,90) and U.S. Open (1991-92); has never won French.

Gertrude Ederle (b. Oct. 23, 1906): Swimmer; 1st woman to swim English Channel, breaking men's record by 2 hours in 1926; won 3 medals in 1924 Olympics.

Krisztina Egerszegi (b. Aug. 16, 1974): Hungarian swimmer; 3-time gold medal winner (100m and 200m backstroke and 400m IM) in 1992 Olympics; also won a gold (200m back) and silver (100m back) in 1988 Games; youngest (age 14) ever to win swimming gold.

Bill Elliott (b. Oct. 8, 1955): Auto racer; 2-time winner of Daytona 500 (1985,87); NASCAR national champ in 1988; entered 1995 with 40 NASCAR wins.

Herb Elliott (b. Feb. 25, 1938): Australian runner; undefeated from 1958-60; ran 17 sub-4:00 miles; 3 world records; won gold medal in 1500 meters at 1960 Olympics; retired at age 22.

Roy Emerson (b. Nov. 3, 1936): Australian tennis player; won 12 Majors in singles— 6 Australian, 2 French, 2 Wimbledon and 2 U.S. from 1961-67.

Kornelia Ender (b. Oct. 25, 1958): East German swimmer; 1st woman to win 4 gold medals at one Olympics (1976), all in world-record time.

Julius Erving (b. Feb. 22, 1950): Basketball F; in ABA (1972-76)— 3-time MVP, 2-time playoff MVP, led NY Nets to 2 titles (1974-76); in NBA (1977-87)— 5-time All-NBA 1st team, MVP in 1981, led Philadelphia 76ers to title in 1983.

Phil Esposito (b. Feb. 20, 1942): Hockey C; 1st NHL player to score 100 points in a season (126 in 1969); 6-time All-NHL 1st team with Boston; 2-time MVP (1969,74); 5-time scoring champ; star of 1972 Canada-Soviet series; president-GM of NHL's Tampa Bay Lightning.

Janet Evans (b. Aug. 28, 1971): Swimmer; won 3 individual gold medals (400m & 800m freestyle, 400m IM) at 1988 Olympics; 1989 Sullivan Award winner; entered 1995 as world record-holder in 400m, 800m and 1500m freestyles; won 1 gold (800m) and 1 silver (400m) at 1992 Olympics.

Lee Evans (b. Feb. 25, 1947): Track & Field; dominant quarter-miler in world from 1966-72; world record in 400m at 1968 Olympics stood 20 years.

Chris Evert (b. Dec. 21, 1954): Tennis; No.1 player in world 5 times (1975-77,80-81); won at least 1 Grand Slam singles title every year from 1974-86; 18 Majors in all— 7 French, 6 U.S., 3 Wimbledon and 2 Australian; retired after 1989 season.

Weeb Ewbank (b. May 6, 1907): Football; only coach to win NFL and AFL titles; led Baltimore to 2 NFL titles (1958-59) and NY Jets to Super Bowl III win.

Patrick Ewing (b. Aug. 5, 1962): Basketball C; 3-time All-America; led Georgetown to 3 NCAA Finals and 1984 title; tourney MVP in '84; NBA Rookie of Year with New York in '86; All-NBA in 1990; led U.S. Olympic team to gold medals in 1984 and '92.

Ray Ewry (b. Oct. 14, 1873, d. Sept. 29, 1937): Track & Field; won 10 gold medals over 4 consecutive Olympics (1900,04,06,08); all events he won (Standing HJ, LJ and TJ) were discontinued in 1912.

Nick Faldo (b. July 18, 1957): British golfer; 3-time winner of British Open (1987,90,92) and 2-time winner of Masters (1989-90); 3-time European Golfer of Year (1989-90, 92); PGA Player of the Year in 1990.

Juan Manuel Fangio (b. June 24, 1911, d. July 17, 1995): Argentine auto racer; 5-time Formula One world champion (1951,54-57); 24 career wins, retired in 1958.

Sergei Fedorov (b. Dec. 13, 1969): Hockey C; first Russian to win NHL Hart Trophy as 1993-94 regular season MVP; 2-time All-Star with Detroit.

Donald Fehr (b. July 18, 1948): Baseball labor leader; protégé of Marvin Miller; executive director and general counsel of Major League Players Assn. since 1983; led players in 1994 "salary cap" strike that lasted eight months and resulted in first cancellation of World Series since 1904.

Bob Feller (b. Nov. 3, 1918): Baseball RHP; led AL in strikeouts 7 times and wins 6 times with Cleveland; threw 3 no-hitters and 12 one-hitters; 266 career wins.

Tom Ferguson (b. Dec. 20, 1950): Rodeo; 6-time All-Around champion (1974-79); 1st cowboy to win $100,000 in one season (1978); 1st to win $1 million in career (1986).

Cecil Fielder (b. Sept. 21, 1963): Baseball 1B; returned from one season with Hanshin Tigers in Japan to hit 51 HRs for Detroit Tigers in 1990; led MLB in RBI 3 straight years (1990-92); AL MVP runner-up in 1990 and '91.

Herve Filion (b. Feb. 1, 1940): Harness racing; 10-time Driver of Year; entered 1995 season as all-time leader in races won with 14,525 in 34 years.

Rollie Fingers (b. Aug. 25, 1946): Baseball RHP; relief ace with 341 career saves; won AL MVP and Cy Young awards in 1981 with Milwaukee; World Series MVP in 1974 with Oakland.

Charles O. Finley (b. Feb. 22, 1918): Baseball owner; moved KC A's to Oakland in 1968; won 3 straight World Series from 1972-74; also owned teams in NHL and ABA.

Bobby Fischer (b. Mar. 9, 1943): Chess; at 15, became youngest international grandmaster in chess history; only American to hold world championship (1972-75); was stripped of title in 1975 after refusing to defend against Anatoly Karpov and became recluse; re-emerged to defeat old foe and former world champion Boris Spassky in 1992.

Carlton Fisk (b. Dec. 26, 1947): Baseball C; set all-time major league record at age 45 for games caught (2,226); also all-time HR leader for catchers (376); AL Rookie of Year (1972) and 10-time All-Star; hit epic, 12th-inning Game 6 homer for Boston Red Sox in 1975 World Series.

Emerson Fittipaldi (b. Dec. 12, 1946): Brazilian auto racer; 2-time Formula One world champion (1972,74); 2-time winner of Indy 500 (1989,93); won overall IndyCar title in 1989.

Bob Fitzsimmons (b. May 26, 1863, d. Oct. 22, 1917): British boxer; held three world titles— middleweight (1881-97), heavyweight (1897-99) and light heavyweight (1903-05); pro record 40-11 with 32 KOs.

James (Sunny Jim) Fitzsimmons (b. July 23, 1874, d. Mar. 11, 1966): Horse racing; trained horses that won over 2,275 races, including 2 Triple Crown winners— Gallant Fox in 1930 and Omaha in '35.

Jim Fixx (b. Apr. 23, 1932, d. July 20, 1984): Running; author who popularized the sport of running; his 1977 bestseller The Complete Book of Running, is credited with helping start America's fitness revolution; died of a heart attack while running.

Larry Fleisher (b. Sept. 26, 1930, d. May 4, 1989): Basketball; led NBA players union from 1961-89; increased average yearly salary from $9,400 in 1967 to $600,000 without a strike.

Peggy Fleming (b. July 27, 1948): Figure skating; 3-time world champion (1966-68); won Olympic gold medal in 1968.

Curt Flood (b. Jan. 18, 1938): Baseball OF; played 15 years (1956-69,71) mainly with St. Louis; hit over .300 6 times with 7 gold gloves; refused trade to Phillies in 1969; lost challenge to baseball's reserve clause in Supreme Court in 1972 (see Peter Seitz).

Ray Floyd (b. Sept. 14, 1942): Golfer; entered 1995 with 22 PGA victories in 4 decades; joined Senior PGA Tour in 1992; has won Masters (1976), U.S. Open (1986), PGA twice (1969,82) and PGA Seniors Championship (1995); only player to ever win on PGA and Senior tours in same year (1992); member of 8 Ryder Cup teams and captain in 1989.

Doug Flutie (b. Oct. 23, 1962): Football QB; won Heisman Trophy with Boston College (1984); has played in USFL, NFL and CFL since then; 4-time CFL MVP with B.C. Lions (1991) and Calgary (1992-94); led Calgary to Grey Cup title in '92; missed 2nd half of 1995 season with injured right elbow.

Gerald Ford (b. July 14, 1913): 38th President of the U.S.; lettered as center on undefeated Michigan football teams in 1932 and '33; MVP on 1934 squad.

Whitey Ford (b. Oct. 21, 1928): Baseball LHP; all-time leader in World Series wins (10); led AL in wins 3 times; won both Cy Young and World Series MVP in 1961 with NY Yankees.

George Foreman (b. Jan. 10, 1949): Boxer; Olympic heavyweight champ (1968); world heavyweight champ (1973-74 and 94-95); lost title to Muhammad Ali (KO-8th) in '74; recaptured it on Nov. 5, 1994 at age 45 with a 1-round KO of WBA/IBF champ Michael Moorer,

becoming the oldest man to win heavyweight crown; named AP Male Athlete of Year 20 years after losing title to Ali; entered 1995 with pro record of 73-4 and 68 KOs; stripped of WBA title on Mar. 4 after declining to fight No. 1 contender; successfully defended title at age 46 against 26-year-old Axel Schultz of Germany in controversial majority decision on Apr. 22; gave up IBF title in June after refusing rematch with Schultz.

Dick Fosbury (b. Mar. 6, 1947): Track & Field; revolutionized high jump with back-first "Fosbury Flop"; won gold medal at 1968 Olympics.

Greg Foster (b. Aug. 4, 1958): Track & Field; 3-time winner of World Championship gold medal in 110-meter hurdles (1983,87,91); best Olympic performance a silver in 1984; world indoor champion in 1991; made world Top 10 rankings 15 years (a record for running events).

The Four Horsemen: Senior backfield that led Notre Dame to national collegiate football championship in 1924; put together as sophomores by Irish coach Knute Rockne; immortalized by sportswriter Grantland Rice, whose report of the Oct. 19, 1924, Notre Dame-Army game began: "Outlined against a blue, gray October sky the Four Horsemen rode again..."; HB Jim Crowley (b. Sept. 10, 1902, d. Jan. 15, 1986), FB Elmer Layden (b. May 4, 1903, d. June 30, 1973), HB Don Miller (b. May 30, 1902, d. July 28, 1979) and QB Harry Stuhldreher (b. Oct. 14, 1901, d. Jan. 26, 1965).

The Four Musketeers: French quartet that dominated men's world tennis in 1920s and '30s, winning 8 straight French singles titles (1925-32), 6 Wimbledons in a row (1924-29) and 6 consecutive Davis Cups (1927-32)— Jean Borotra (b. Aug. 13, 1898, d. July 17, 1994), Jacques Brugnon (b. May 11, 1895, d. Mar. 20, 1978), Henri Cochet (b. Dec. 14, 1901, d. Apr. 1, 1987), Rene Lacoste (b. July 2, 1905).

Jimmie Foxx (b. Oct. 22, 1907, d. July 21, 1967): Baseball 1B; led AL in HRs 4 times and batting twice; won Triple Crown in 1933; 3-time MVP (1932-33,38) with Philadelphia and Boston; hit 30 HRs or more 12 years in a row; 534 career HRs.

A.J. Foyt (b. Jan. 16, 1935): Auto racer; 7-time USAC-CART national champion (1960-61,63-64,67,75,79); 4-time Indy 500 winner (1961,64,67,77); only driver in history to win Indy 500, Daytona 500 (1972) and 24 Hours of LeMans (1967 with Dan Gurney); retired in 1993 as all-time IndyCar wins leader with 67.

Bill France Sr. (b. Sept. 26, 1909, d. June 7, 1992): Stock car pioneer and promoter; founded NASCAR in 1948; guided race circuit through formative years; built both Daytona (Fla.) Int'l Speedway and Talladega (Ala.) Superspeedway.

Dawn Fraser (b. Sept. 4, 1937): Australian swimmer; won gold medals in 100m freestyle at 3 consecutive Olympics (1956,60,64).

Joe Frazier (b. Jan. 12, 1944): Boxer; 1964 Olympic heavyweight champion; world heavyweight champ (1970-73); fought Muhammad Ali 3 times and won once; pro record 32-4-1 with 27 KOs.

Ford Frick (b. Dec. 19, 1894, d. Apr. 8, 1978): Baseball; sportswriter and radio announcer who served as NL president (1934-51) and commissioner (1951-65); convinced record-keepers to list Roger Maris' and Babe Ruth's season records separately; major leagues moved to west coast and expanded from 16 to 20 teams during his tenure.

Frankie Frisch (b. Sept. 9, 1898, d. Mar. 12, 1973): Baseball 2B; played on 8 NL pennant winners in 19 years with NY and St. Louis; hit .300 or better 11 years in a row (1921-31); MVP in 1931; player-manager from 1933-37.

Dan Gable (b. Oct. 25, 1948): Wrestling; career college wrestling record of 118-1 at Iowa St., where he was a 2-time NCAA champ (1968,69) and tourney MVP in 1969 (137 lbs); won gold medal (149 lbs) at 1972 Olympics; coached U.S. freestyle team in 1988; coached Iowa to 9 straight NCAA titles (1978-86) and has added four more since 1991.

Eddie Gaedel (b. June 8, 1925, d. June 18, 1961): Baseball pinch hitter; St. Louis Browns' midget whose career lasted one at bat (he walked) on Aug 19, 1951.

Clarence (Bighouse) Gaines (b. May 21, 1924): Basketball; retired as coach of Div. II Winston-Salem for 1992-93 season with 828-446 record in 47 years; ranks 3rd on all-time NCAA list behind Adolph Rupp (876) and Dean Smith (830).

Alonzo (Jake) Gaither (b. Apr. 11, 1903, d. Feb. 18, 1994): Football; head coach at Florida A&M for 25 years; led Rattlers to 6 national black college titles; retired after 1969 season with record of 203-36-4 and a winning percentage of .844; coined phrase, "I like my boys agile, mobile and hostile."

Cito Gaston (b. Mar. 17, 1944): Baseball; managed Toronto to consecutive World Series titles (1992-93); first black manager to win Series; shared The Sporting News 1993 Man of Year award with Blue Jays GM Pat Gillick.

Lou Gehrig (b. June 19, 1903, d. June 2, 1941): Baseball 1B; played in 2,130 consecutive games from 1923-39 a major league record until Cal Ripken Jr. surpassed it in 1995; led AL in RBI 5 times and HRs 3 times; drove in 100 runs or more 13 years in a row; 2-time MVP (1927,36); hit .340 with 493 HRs over 17 seasons; led NY Yankees to 7 World Series titles; died at age 37 of Amyotrophic lateral sclerosis (ALS), a rare and incurable disease of the nervous system better known as Lou Gehrig's disease.

Charley Gehringer (b. May 11, 1903, d. Jan. 21, 1993): Baseball 2B; hit .300 or better 13 times; AL batting champion and MVP with Detroit in 1937.

A. Bartlett Giamatti (b. Apr. 14, 1938, d. Sept. 1, 1989): Scholar and 7th commissioner of baseball; banned Pete Rose for life for betting on Major League games and associating with known gamblers and drug dealers; also served as president of Yale (1978-86) and National League (1986-89).

Joe Gibbs (b. Nov. 25, 1940): Football; coached Washington to 140 victories and 3 Super Bowl titles in 12 seasons before retiring on Mar. 5, 1993; owner of NASCAR racing team that won 1993 Daytona 500.

Althea Gibson (b. Aug. 25, 1927): Tennis; won both Wimbledon and U.S. championships in 1957 and '58; 1st black to play in either tourney and 1st to win each title.

Bob Gibson (b. Nov. 9, 1935): Baseball RHP; won 20 or more games 5 times; won 2 NL Cy Young Awards (1968,70); MVP in 1968; led St. Louis to 2 World Series titles; Series MVP twice (1964,67); 251 career wins.

Josh Gibson (b. Dec. 21, 1911, d. Jan. 20, 1947): Baseball C; the "Babe Ruth of the Negro Leagues"; Satchel Paige's battery mate with Pittsburgh Crawfords.

Kirk Gibson (b. May 28, 1957): Baseball OF; All-America flanker at Michigan St. in 1978; chose baseball career and was AL playoff MVP with Detroit in 1984 and NL regular season MVP with Los Angeles in 1988.

Frank Gifford (b. Aug. 16, 1930): Football HB; 4-time All-Pro (1955-57,59); NFL MVP in 1956; led NY Giants to 3 NFL title games; TV sportscaster since 1958, beginning career while still a player.

Sid Gillman (b. Oct. 26, 1911): Football innovator; only coach in both College and Pro Football halls of fame; led college teams at Miami-OH and Cincinnati to combined 81-19-2 record from 1944-54; coached LA Rams (1955-59) in NFL, then led LA-San Diego Chargers to 5 Western titles and 1 league championship in first six years of AFL.

George Gipp (b. Feb. 18, 1895, d. Dec. 14, 1920): Football FB; died of throat infection 2 weeks before he made All-America (Notre Dame's 1st); rushed for 2,341 yards, scored 156 points and averaged 38 yards a punt in 4 years (1917-20).

Marc Girardelli (b. July 18, 1963): Luxembourg Alpine skier; Austrian native who refused to join Austrian Ski Federation because he wanted to be coached by his father; won unprecedented 5th overall World Cup title in 1993; winless at Olympics, although he won 2 silver medals in 1992.

Tom Gola (b. Jan. 13, 1933): Basketball F; 4-time All-America and 1955 Player of Year at La Salle; MVP in 1952 NIT and '54 NCAA tournaments, leading Pioneers to both titles; won NBA title as rookie with Philadelphia Warriors in 1956; 4-time NBA All-Star.

Marshall Goldberg (b. Oct. 24, 1917): Football HB; 2-time consensus All-America at Pittsburgh (1937-38); led Pitt to national championship in 1937; played with NFL champion Chicago Cardinals 10 years later.

Lefty Gomez (b. Nov. 26, 1908, d. Feb. 17, 1989): Baseball LHP; 4-time 20-game winner with NY Yankees; holds World Series record for most wins (6) without a defeat; pitched on 5 world championship clubs in 1930s.

Pancho Gonzales (b. May 9, 1928, d. July 3, 1995): Tennis; won consecutive U.S. Championships in 1947-48 before turning pro at 21; dominated pro tour from 1950-61; in 1969 at age 41, played longest Wimbledon match ever (5:12), beating Charlie Pasarell 22-24,1-6,16-14,6-3,11-9.

Bob Goodenow (b. Oct. 29, 1952): Hockey; succeeded Alan Eagleson as executive director of NHL Players Assn. in 1990; led players out on 10-day strike (Apr. 1-10) in 1992 and during 103-day owners' lockout in 1994-95.

Jeff Gordon (b. Aug. 4, 1971): Auto racer; NASCAR Rookie of Year (1993); won inaugural Brickyard 400 in 1994; dominated '95 NASCAR season, winning 7 races and 8 poles as of Sept. 17.

Dr. Harold Gores (b. Sept. 20, 1909, d. May 28, 1993): Educator and first president of Education Facilities Laboratories in New York; in 1964 hired Monsanto Co. to produce a synthetic turf that kids could play on in city schoolyards; resulting ChemGrass proved too expensive for playground use, but it was just what the Houston Astros were looking for in 1966 to cover the floor of the Astrodome where grass refused to grow; and AstroTurf was born.

Shane Gould (b. Nov. 23, 1956): Australian swimmer; set world records in 5 different freestyle events between July 1971 and Jan. 1972; won 3 gold medals, a silver and bronze in 1972 Olympics then retired at age 16.

Alf Goullet (b. Apr. 5, 1891, d. Mar. 11, 1995): Cycling; Australian who gained fame and fortune early in century as premier performer on U.S. 6-day bike race circuit; won 8 annual races at Madison Square Garden with 6 different partners from 1913-23.

Curt Gowdy (b. July 31, 1919): Radio-TV; former radio voice of NY Yankees and then Boston Red Sox from 1949-66; TV play-by-play man for AFL, NFL and major league baseball; has broadcast World Series, All-Star Games, Rose Bowls, Super Bowls, Olympics and NCAA Final Fours for all 3 networks; also hosted "The American Sportsman."

Steffi Graf (b. June 14, 1969): German tennis player; won Grand Slam and Olympic gold medal in 1988 at age 19; won three of four majors in 1993 and 1995; has won 18 Grand Slam titles— 6 at Wimbledon, 4 Australian, French, and U.S. Opens.

Otto Graham (b. Dec. 6, 1921): Football QB and basketball All-America at Northwestern; in pro ball, led Cleveland Browns to 7 league titles in 10 years, winning 4 AAFC championships (1946-49) and 3 NFL (1950,54-55); 5-time All-Pro; 2-time NFL MVP (1953,55).

Red Grange (b. June 13, 1903, d. Jan. 28, 1991): Football HB; 3-time All-America at Illinois who brought 1st huge crowds to pro football when he signed with Chicago Bears in 1925; formed 1st AFL with manager-promoter C.C. Pyle in 1926, but league folded and he returned to NFL.

Bud Grant (b. May 20, 1927): Football and Basketball; only coach to win 100 games in both CFL and NFL and only member of both CFL and U.S. Pro Football halls of fame; led Winnipeg to 4 Grey Cup titles (1958-59,61-62) in 6 appearances, but his Minnesota Vikings lost all 4 Super Bowl attempts in 1970's; all-time rank of 3rd in CFL wins (122) and 8th in NFL wins (168); also All-Big Ten at Minnesota in both football and basketball in late 1940's; a 3-time CFL All-Star offensive end; also member of 1950 NBA champion Minneapolis Lakers.

Rocky Graziano (b. June 7, 1922, d. May 22, 1990): Boxer; world middleweight champion (1946-47); fought Tony Zale for title 3 times in 21 months, losing twice; pro record 67-10-6 with 52 KOs; movie "Somebody Up There Likes Me" based on his life.

Hank Greenberg (b. Jan. 1, 1911, d. Sept. 4, 1986): Baseball 1B; led AL in HRs and RBI 4 times each; 2-time MVP (1935,40) with Detroit; 331 career HRs.

Joe Greene (b. Sept. 24, 1946): Football DT; 5-time All-Pro (1972-74,77,79); led Pittsburgh to 4 Super Bowl titles in 1970s.

Bud Greenspan (b. Sept. 18, 1926): Filmmaker specializing in the Olympic Games; has won Emmy awards for 22-part "The Olympiad" (1976-77) and historical vignettes for ABC-TV's coverage of 1980 Winter Games; won 1994 Emmy award for edited special on Lillehammer Winter Olympics.

Wayne Gretzky (b. Jan. 26, 1961): Hockey C; 10-time NHL scoring champion; 9-time regular season MVP (1979-87,89) and 9-time All-NHL first team; has scored 200 points or more in a season 4 times; led Edmonton to 4 Stanley Cups (1984-85,87-88); 2-time playoff MVP (1985,88); traded to LA Kings (Aug. 9, 1988); broke Gordie Howe's all-time NHL goal scoring record of 801 on Mar. 23, 1994; entered 1995-96 regular season as all-time NHL leader in points (2,506), goals (814) and assists (1,692); also all-time Stanley Cup leader in points (346), goals (110) and assists (236).

Bob Griese (b. Feb. 3, 1945): Football QB; 2-time All-Pro (1971,77); led Miami to undefeated season (17-0) in 1972 and consecutive Super Bowl titles (1973-74).

Ken Griffey Jr. (b. Nov. 21, 1969): Baseball OF; overall 1st pick of 1987 Draft by Seattle; 4-time gold glove winner in 1st 5 seasons; MVP of 1992 All-Star game at age 23; hit home runs in 8 consecutive games in 1993; entered 1995 with 172 HRs; broke wrist making catch in 1995, out nearly 3 months; son of Ken Sr.

Archie Griffin (b. Aug. 21, 1954): Football RB; only college player to win two Heisman Trophies (1974-75); rushed for 5,177 yards in career at Ohio St.

Emile Griffith (b. Feb. 3, 1938): Boxer; world welterweight champion (1961,62-63,63-65); world middleweight champion (1966-67,67-68); pro record 85-24-2 with 23 KOs.

Dick Groat (b. Nov. 4, 1930): Basketball and Baseball SS; 2-time basketball All-America at Duke and college Player of Year in 1951; won NL MVP award as shortstop with Pittsburgh in 1960; won World Series with Pirates (1960) and St. Louis (1964).

Lefty Grove (b. Mar. 6, 1900, d. May 22, 1975): Baseball LHP; won 20 or more games 8 times; led AL in ERA 9 times and strikeouts 7 times; 31-4 record and MVP in 1931 with Philadelphia; 300 career wins.

Lou Groza (b. Jan. 25, 1924): Football T-PK; 6-time All-Pro; played in 13 championship games for Cleveland from 1946-67; kicked winning field goal in 1950 NFL title game; 1,608 career points (1,349 in NFL).

Janet Guthrie (b. Mar. 7, 1938): Auto racer; in 1977, became 1st woman to race in Indianapolis 500; placed 9th at Indy in 1978.

Tony Gwynn (b. May 9, 1960): Baseball OF; 4-time NL batting champion (1984,87-89) at San Diego; entered 1995 with .333 career average in 13 seasons; was hitting .394 on Aug. 12, 1994 when players' strike began.

Harvey Haddix (b. Sept. 18, 1925, d. Jan. 9, 1994): Baseball LHP; pitched 12 perfect innings for Pittsburgh, but lost to Milwaukee in the 13th, 1-0 (May 26, 1959).

Walter Hagen (b. Dec. 21, 1892, d. Oct. 5, 1969): Pro golf pioneer; won 2 U.S. Opens (1914,19), 4 British Opens (1922,24,28-29), 5 PGA Championships (1921,24-27) and 5 Western Opens; retired with 40 PGA wins; 6-time U.S. Ryder Cup captain.

Marvin Hagler (b. May 23, 1954): Boxer; world middleweight champion 1980-87; enjoyed his nickname "Marvelous Marvin" so much he would have his name legally changed; pro record 62-3-2 with 52 KOs.

George Halas (b. Feb. 2, 1895, d. Oct. 31, 1983): Football pioneer; MVP in 1919 Rose Bowl; player-coach-owner of Chicago Bears from 1920-83; signed Red Grange in 1925; coached Bears for 40 seasons and won 7 NFL titles (1932-33,40-41,43,46,63); 2nd on all-time career list with 324 wins.

Dorothy Hamill (b. July 26, 1956): Figure skater; won Olympic gold medal and world championship in 1976; Ice Capades headliner from 1977-84; bought financially-strapped Ice Capades in 1993.

Scott Hamilton (b. Aug. 28, 1958): Figure skater; 4-time world champion (1981-84); won gold medal at 1984 Olympics.

Tonya Harding (b. Nov. 12, 1970): Figure skater; 1991 U.S. women's champion; involved in bizarre plot hatched by ex-husband Jeff Gillooly to injure rival Nancy Kerrigan on Jan. 6, 1994 and keep her off Olympic team; won '94 U.S. women's title in Kerrigan's absence; denied any role in assault and sued USOC when her berth on Olympic team was threatened; finished 8th at Lillehammer (Kerrigan recovered and won silver medal); pleaded guilty on Mar. 16 to conspiracy to hinder investigation; stripped of 1994 title by U.S. Figure Skating Assn.

Tom Harmon (b. Sept. 28, 1919, d. Mar. 17, 1990): Football HB; 2-time All-America at Michigan; won Heisman Trophy in 1940; played with AFL NY Americans in 1941 and NFL LA Rams (1946-47); World War II fighter pilot who won Silver Star and Purple Heart; became radio-TV commentator.

Franco Harris (b. Mar. 7, 1950): Football RB; ran for over 1,000 yards a season 8 times; rushed for 12,120 yards in 13 years; led Pittsburgh to 4 Super Bowl titles.

Leon Hart (b. Nov. 2, 1928): Football E; only player to win 3 national championships in college and 3 more in the NFL; won his titles at Notre Dame (1946-47,49) and with Detroit Lions (1952-53,57); 3-time All-America and last lineman to win Heisman Trophy (1949); All-Pro on both offense and defense in 1951.

Bill Hartack (b. Dec. 9, 1932): Jockey; won Kentucky Derby 5 times (1957,60,62,64,69), Preakness 3 times (1956,64,69), but the Belmont only once (1960).

Doug Harvey (b. Dec. 19, 1924, d. Dec. 26, 1989): Hockey D; 10-time All-NHL 1st team; won Norris Trophy 7 times (1955-58,60-62); led Montreal to 6 Stanley Cups.

Dominik Hasek (b. Jan. 29, 1965): Czech hockey G; 2-time Vezina Trophy winner (1993-94,95); led NHL with a 1.95 GAA in 1993-94— the first sub-2.00 GAA since Bernie Parent in 1974.

Billy Haughton (b. Nov. 2, 1923, d. July 15, 1986): Harness racing; 4-time winner of Hambletonian; trainer-driver of one Pacing Triple Crown winner (1968); 4,910 career wins.

João Havelange (b. May 8, 1916): Soccer; Brazilian-born president of Federation Internationale de Football Assoc. (FIFA) since 1974; also member of International Olympic Committee.

John Havlicek (b. Apr. 8, 1940): Basketball; played in 3 NCAA Finals at Ohio St. (1960-62); led Boston to 8 NBA titles (1963-66,68-69,74,76); playoff MVP in 1974; 4-time All-NBA 1st team.

Bob Hayes (b. Dec. 20, 1942): Track & Field and Football; won gold medal in 100m at 1964 Olympics; All-Pro SE for Dallas in 1966; convicted of drug trafficking in 1979 and served 18 months of a 5-year sentence.

Woody Hayes (b. Feb. 14, 1913, d. Mar. 12, 1987): Football; coached Ohio St. to 3 national titles (1954,57,68) and 4 Rose Bowl victories; 238 career wins in 28 seasons at Denison, Miami-OH and OSU.

Thomas Hearns (b. Oct. 18, 1958): Boxer; has held recognized world titles as welterweight, light middleweight, middleweight and light heavyweight; four career losses have come against Sugar Ray Leonard, Marvin Hagler and twice Iran Barkley; entered 1995 with pro record of 53-4-1 and 42 KOs.

Eric Heiden (b. June 14, 1958): Speedskater; 3-time overall world champion (1977-79); won all 5 men's gold medals at 1980 Olympics, setting new records in each; Sullivan Award winner (1980).

Mel Hein (b. Aug. 22, 1909, d. Jan. 31, 1992): Football C; NFL All-Pro 8 straight years (1933-40); MVP in 1938 with NY Giants; didn't miss a game in 15 seasons.

John W. Heisman (b. Oct. 23, 1869, d. Oct. 3, 1936): Football; coached at 9 colleges from 1892-1927; won 185 games; Director of Athletics at Downtown Athletic Club in NYC (1928-36); DAC named Heisman Trophy after him.

Carol Heiss (b. Jan. 20, 1940): Figure skater; 5-time world champion (1956-60); won Olympic silver medal in 1956 and gold in '60; married 1956 men's gold medalist Hayes Jenkins.

Rickey Henderson (b. Dec. 25, 1958): Baseball OF; AL playoff MVP (1989) and AL regular season MVP (1990); set single-season base stealing record of 130 in 1982; has led AL in steals a record 11 times; broke Lou Brock's all-time record of 938 on May 1, 1991; entered 1995 season as all-time leader in steals (1,117) and HRs as leadoff player (66).

Sonja Henie (b. Apr. 8, 1912, d. Oct. 12, 1969): Norwegian figure skater; 10-time world champion (1927-36); won 3 consecutive Olympic gold medals (1928,32,36); became movie star.

Foster Hewitt (b. Nov. 21, 1902, d. Apr. 21, 1985): Radio-TV; Canada's premier hockey play-by-play broadcaster from 1923-81; coined phrase, "He shoots, he scores!"

Graham Hill (b. Feb. 15, 1929, d. Nov. 29, 1975): British auto racer; 2-time Formula One world champion (1962,68); won Indy 500 in 1966; killed in plane crash; father of Damon.

Phil Hill (b. Apr. 20, 1927): Auto racer; first U.S. driver to win Formula One championship (1961); 3 career wins (1958-64).

Max Hirsch (b. July 30, 1880, d. Apr. 3, 1969): Horse racing; trained 1,933 winners from 1908-68; won Triple Crown with Assault in 1946.

Tommy Hitchcock (b. Feb. 11, 1900, d. Apr. 19, 1944): Polo; world class player at 20; achieved 10-goal rating 18 times from 1922-40.

Lew Hoad (b. Nov. 23, 1934, d. July 3, 1994): Australian tennis player; 2-time Wimbledon winner (1956-57); won Australian, French and Wimbledon titles in 1956, but missed capturing Grand Slam at Forest Hills when beaten by Ken Rosewall in 4-set final.

Ben Hogan (b. Aug. 13, 1912): Golfer; 4-time PGA Player of Year; one of only four players to win all four Grand Slam titles (others are Nicklaus, Player and Sarazen); won 4 U.S. Opens, 2 Masters, 2 PGAs and 1 British Open between 1946-53; only player to win three majors in one year when he won Masters, U.S. Open and British Open in 1953; nearly killed in Feb. 13, 1949 car accident, but came back to win U.S. Open in '50; third on all-time list with 63 career wins.

Eleanor Holm (b. Dec. 6, 1913): Swimmer; won gold medal in 100m backstroke at 1932 Olympics; thrown off '36 U.S. team for drinking champagne in public and shooting craps on boat to Germany.

Nat Holman (b. Oct. 18, 1896, d. Feb. 12, 1995): Basketball pioneer; played pro with Original Celtics (1920-28); coached CCNY to both NCAA and NIT titles in 1950 (a year later, several of his players were caught up in a point-shaving scandal); 423 career wins.

Larry Holmes (b. Nov. 3, 1949): Boxer; heavyweight champion (WBC or IBF) from 1978-85; successfully defended title 20 times before losing to Michael Spinks; returned from first retirement in 1988 and was KO'd in 4th by then champ Mike Tyson; launched second comeback in 1991; fought and lost title bids against Evander Holyfield in '92 and Oliver McCall on Apr. 8, 1995; fought McCall at age 45 years and 5 months; entered 1995 with pro record of 61-4 and 40 KOs.

Lou Holtz (b. Jan. 6, 1937): Football; coached Notre Dame to national title in 1988; 2-time Coach of Year (1977,88) entered 1995 season with 199-89-7 record in 25 seasons with 5 schools— Wm. & Mary (3 years), N.C. State (4), Arkansas (7), Minnesota (2) and ND (9); also coached NFL NY Jets for 13 games (3-10) in 1976.

Evander Holyfield (b. Oct. 19, 1962): Boxer; missed shot at Olympic gold medal in 1984 when he lost controversial light heavyweight semifinal after knocking his opponent out (referee ruled it was a late hit); knocked out Buster Douglas in 3rd round to become world heavyweight champion on Oct. 25, 1990; 2 of first 4 title defenses included decisions over 42-year-old ex-champs George Foreman and Larry Holmes; lost title to Riddick Bowe by unanimous decision on Nov. 13, 1992; beat Bowe by majority decision to reclaim title on Nov. 6, 1993; lost title again to Michael Moorer by majority decision on Apr. 22, 1994; after retiring in '94 due to an apparent heart defect, he returned to the ring in 1995 with a cleaner bill of health and a pro record of 30-2 and 22 KOs.

Red Holzman (b. Aug. 10, 1920): Basketball; played for NBL and NBA champions at Rochester (1946,51); coached NY Knicks to 2 NBA titles (1970,73); Coach of Year (1970); ranks 10th on all-time NBA list with 754 wins (including playoffs).

Rogers Hornsby (b. Apr. 27, 1896, d. Jan. 5, 1963): Baseball 2B; hit .400 three times, including .424 in 1924; led NL in batting 7 times; 2-time MVP (1925,29) with St. Louis; career average of .358 over 23 years is all-time highest in NL.

Paul Hornung (b. Dec. 23, 1935): Football HB-PK; only Heisman Trophy winner to play for losing team (2-8 Notre Dame in 1956); 3-time NFL scoring leader (1959-61) at Green Bay; 176 points in 1960, an all-time record; MVP in 1961; suspended by NFL for 1963 season for betting on his own team.

Gordie Howe (b. Mar. 31, 1928): Hockey RW; played 32 seasons in NHL and WHA from 1946-80; led NHL in scoring 6 times; All-NHL 1st team 12 times; MVP 6 times in NHL (1952-53,57-58,60,63) with Detroit and once in WHA (1974) with Houston; ranks 2nd on all-time NHL list in goals (801) and points (1,850) to Wayne Gretzky; played with sons Mark and Marty at Houston (1973-77) and New England-Hartford (1977-80).

Cal Hubbard (b. Oct. 31, 1900, d. Oct. 19, 1977): Member of college football, pro football and baseball halls of fame; 9 years in NFL; 4-time All-Pro at end and tackle; AL umpire for 15 years (1936-51).

Carl Hubbell (b. June 22, 1903, d. Nov. 21, 1988): Baseball LHP; led NL in wins and ERA 3 times each; 2-time MVP (1933,36) with NY Giants; fanned Ruth, Gehrig, Foxx, Simmons and Cronin in succession in 1934 All-Star Game; 253 career wins.

Sam Huff (b. Oct. 4, 1934): Football LB; glamorized NFL's middle linebacker position with NY Giants from 1956-63; subject of "The Violent World of Sam Huff" TV special in 1961; helped lead club to 6 division titles and a world championship (1956).

Miller Huggins (b. Mar. 27, 1879, d. Sept. 25, 1929): Baseball; managed NY Yankees from 1918 until his death late in '29 season; led Yanks to 6 pennants and 3 World Series titles from 1921-28.

H. Wayne Huizenga (b. Dec. 29, 1937): Owner; vice chairman of Viacom Inc. and chairman of Blockbuster Entertainment Group; co-founded Waste Management Inc., the world's largest waste collection and disposal company in 1971; majority owner of baseball's Florida Marlins and 100-percent owner of NFL Miami Dolphins, NHL Florida Panthers and Joe Robbie Stadium, where Marlins and Dolphins play.

Bobby Hull (b. Jan. 3, 1939): Hockey LW; led NHL in scoring 3 times; 2-time MVP (1965-66) with Chicago; All-NHL first team 10 times; jumped to WHA in 1972, 2-time MVP there (1973,75) with Winnipeg; scored 913 goals in both leagues; father of Brett.

Brett Hull (b. Aug. 9, 1964): Hockey RW; named NHL MVP in 1991 with St. Louis; holds single season RW scoring record with 86 goals; he and father Bobby have both won Hart (MVP), Lady Byng (sportsmanship) and All-Star Game MVP trophies.

Jim (Catfish) Hunter (b. Apr. 8, 1946): Baseball RHP; won 20 games or more 5 times (1971-75); played on 5 World Series winners with Oakland and NY Yankees; threw perfect game in 1968; won Cy Young Award in '74.

Ibrahim Hussein (b. June 3, 1958): Kenyan distance runner; 3-time winner of Boston Marathon (1988,91-92) and 1st African runner to win in Boston; won New York Marathon in 1987.

Don Hutson (b. Jan. 31, 1913): Football E-PK; led NFL in receptions 8 times and interceptions once; 9-time All-Pro (1936,38-45) for Green Bay; 99 career TD catches.

Flo Hyman (b. July 31, 1954, d. Jan. 24, 1986): Volleyball; 3-time All-America spiker at Houston and captain of 1984 U.S. Women's Olympic team; died of heart attack caused by Marfan Syndrome during a match in Japan in 1986; Women's Sports Foundation's Hyman Award for excellence and dedication named after her.

Hank Iba (b. Aug. 6, 1904, d. Jan. 15, 1993): Basketball; coached Oklahoma A&M to 2 straight NCAA titles (1945-46); 767 career wins in 41 years; coached U.S. Olympic team to 2 gold medals (1964,68), but lost to Soviets in controversial '72 final.

Mike Ilitch (b. July 20, 1929): Baseball and Hockey owner; chairman of Little Caesar's, the international pizza chain; bought Detroit Red Wings of NHL for $8 million in 1982 and AL Detroit Tigers for $85 million in 1992.

Punch Imlach (b. Mar. 15, 1918, d. Dec. 1, 1987): Hockey; directed Toronto to 4 Stanley Cups (1962-64,67) in 11 seasons as GM-coach.

Miguel Induráin (b. July 16, 1964): Spanish cyclist; won a record 5th straight Tour de France in 1995, joining legends Jacques Anquetil and Bernard Hinault of France and Eddy Merckx of Belgium as the only 5 time winners.

Hale Irwin (b. June 3, 1945): Golfer; oldest player ever to win U.S. Open (45 in 1990); NCAA champion in 1967; entered 1995 with 20 PGA victories, including 3 U.S. Opens (1974,79,90); 5-time Ryder Cup team member.

Bo Jackson (b. Nov. 30, 1962): Baseball OF and Football RB; won Heisman Trophy in 1985 and MVP of baseball All-Star Game in 1989; starter for both baseball's KC Royals and NFL's LA Raiders in 1988 and '89; severely injured left hip Jan. 13, 1991, in NFL playoffs; waived by Royals but signed by Chicago White Sox in 1991; missed entire 1992 season recovering from hip surgery; played for White Sox in 1993 and California in '94 before retiring.

Joe Jackson (b. July 16, 1889, d. Dec. 5, 1951): Baseball OF; hit .300 or better 11 times; nicknamed "Shoeless Joe"; career average of .356 (see Black Sox).

Phil Jackson (b. Sept. 17, 1945): Basketball; NBA champion as reserve forward with New York in 1973 (injured when Knicks won in '70); coached Chicago to three straight NBA titles (1991-93); finished 1994-95 season with 408 wins (including playoffs) in just 6 seasons.

Reggie Jackson (b. May 18, 1946): Baseball OF; led AL in HRs 4 times; MVP in 1973; played on 5 World Series winners with Oakland, NY Yankees; 1977 Series MVP with 5 HRs; 563 career HRs; all-time strikeout leader (2,597).

Dr. Robert Jackson (b. Aug. 6, 1932): Surgeon; revolutionized sports medicine by popularizing the use of othroscopic surgery to treat injuries; learned technique from Japanese physician that allowed ahtletes to return quickly from potentially career-ending injuries.

Helen Jacobs (b. Aug. 6, 1908): Tennis; 4-time winner of U.S. Championship (1932-35); Wimbledon winner in 1936; lost 4 Wimbledon finals to arch-rival Helen Wills Moody.

Dan Jansen (b. June 17, 1965): Speedskater; 1993 world record-holder in 500m; fell in 500m and 1,000m in 1988 Olympics at Calgary after learning of death of sister Jane; placed 4th in 500m and didn't attempt 1,000m 4 years later in Albertville; fell in 500m at '94 Games in Lillehammer, but finally won an Olympic medal with world record (1:12.43) effort in 1,000m, then took victory lap with baby daughter Jane in his arms; won 1994 Sullivan Award.

James J. Jeffries (b. Apr. 15, 1875, d. Mar. 3, 1953): Boxer; world heavyweight champion (1899-1905); retired undefeated but came back to fight Jack Johnson in 1910 and lost (KO,15th).

David Jenkins (b. June 29, 1936): Figure skater; brother of Hayes; 3-time world champion (1957-59); won gold medal at 1960 Olympics.

Hayes Jenkins (b. Mar. 23, 1933): Figure skater; 4-time world champion (1953-56); won gold medal at 1956 Olympics; married 1960 women's gold medalist Carol Heiss.

Bruce Jenner (b. Oct. 28, 1949): Track & Field; won gold medal in 1976 Olympic decathlon.

Jackie Jensen (b. Mar. 9, 1927, d. July 14, 1982): Football RB and Baseball OF; consensus All-America at California in 1948; American League MVP with Boston Red Sox in 1958.

Ben Johnson (b. Dec. 30, 1961): Canadian sprinter; set 100m world record (9.83) at 1987 World Championships; won 100m at 1988 Olympics, but flunked drug test and forfeited gold medal; 1987 world record revoked in '89 for admitted steroid use; returned drug-free in 1991, but performed poorly; banned for life by IAAF in 1993 for testing positive after a meet in Montreal.

Bob Johnson (b. Mar. 4, 1931, d. Nov. 26, 1991): Hockey; coached Pittsburgh Penguins to 1st Stanley Cup title in 1991; led Wisconsin to 3 NCAA titles (1973,77,81) in 15 years; also coached 1976 U.S. Olympic team and NHL Calgary (1982-87).

Earvin (Magic) Johnson (b. Aug. 14, 1959): Basketball G; led Michigan St. to NCAA title in 1979 and was tourney MVP; All-NBA 1st team 9 times; 3-time MVP (1987,89-90); led LA Lakers to 5 NBA titles; 3-time playoff MVP (1980, 82, 87); 2nd all-time in NBA assists with 9,921; retired on Nov. 7, 1991 after announcing he was HIV-positive; returned to score 25 points in 1992 NBA All-Star game; U.S. Olympic Dream Team member in '92; announced NBA comeback then retired again before start of 1992-93 season; named head coach of Lakers on Mar. 23, 1994, but finished season at 5-11 and quit; later named minority owner of team.

Jack Johnson (b. Mar. 31, 1878, d. June 10, 1946): Boxer; controversial heavyweight champion (1908-15) and 1st black to hold title; defeated Tommy Burns for crown at age 30; fled to Europe in 1913 after Mann Act conviction; lost title to Jess Willard in Havana, but claimed to have taken a dive; pro record 78-8-12 with 45 KOs.

Jimmy Johnson (b. July 16, 1943): Football; All-SWC defensive lineman on Arkansas' 1964 national championship team; coached Miami-FL to national title in 1987; college record of 81-34-3 in 10 years; hired by old friend and new Dallas owner Jerry Jones to succeed Tom Landry in February 1989; went 1-15 in '89, then led Cowboys to consecutive Super Bowl victories in 1992 and '93 seasons; quit on Mar. 29, 1994 after feuding with Jones; became TV analyst.

Michael Johnson (b. Sept. 13, 1967): Track & Field; scored historic double at 1995 World Championships in Goteborg, winning 200 meters (19.79) and 400 meters (43.39) in near-world record times; also anchored winning 4x400-meter relay team; has 6 career gold medals in worlds (2nd only to Carl Lewis); member of U.S. 4x400 relay team that won Olympic gold in 1996.

Rafer Johnson (b. Aug. 18, 1934): Track & Field; won silver medal in 1956 Olympic decathlon and gold medal in 1960.

Walter Johnson (b. Nov. 6, 1887, d. Dec. 10, 1946): Baseball RHP; won 20 games or more 10 straight years; led AL in ERA 5 times, wins 6 times and strikeouts 12 times; twice MVP (1913, 24) with Washington; all-time leader in shutouts (110) and 2nd in wins (416).

Ben A. Jones (b. Dec. 31, 1882, d. June 13, 1961): Horse racing; Calumet Farm trainer (1939-47); saddled 6 Kentucky Derby champions and 2 Triple Crown winners—Whirlaway in 1941 and Citation in '48.

Bobby Jones (b. Mar. 17, 1902, d. Dec. 18, 1971): Won U.S. and British Opens plus U.S. and British Amateurs in 1930 to become golf's only Grand Slam winner ever; from 1922-30, won 4 U.S. Opens, 5 U.S. Amateurs, 3 British Opens, and played in 6 Walker Cups; founded Masters tournament in 1934.

Deacon Jones (b. Dec. 9, 1938): Football DE; 5-time All-Pro (1965-69) with LA Rams; unofficial all-time NFL sack leader with 172 in 14 years.

Jerry Jones (b. Oct. 13, 1942): Football; owner-GM of Dallas Cowboys; maverick who bought declining team (3-13) and Texas Stadium for $140 million in 1989; hired old friend Jimmy Johnson to replace legendary Tom Landry as coach; their partnership led Cowboys to Super Bowl titles in 1992 and '93 seasons; when feud developed in 1994, Jones let Johnson go and hired Barry Switzer; defied NFL owners by signing separate sponsorship deals with Pepsi and Nike in 1995, causing NFL to file a $300 million lawsuit against him on Sept. 19.

Roy Jones Jr. (b. Jan. 16, 1969): Boxing; robbed of gold medal at 1988 Summer Olympics due to an error in scoring; still voted Outstanding Boxer of the Games; won IBF middleweight crown by beating Bernard Hopkins in 1993; moved up to super middleweight and won IBF title from James Toney on Nov. 18, 1994; entered Sept. '95 with pro record of 29-0-0 with 25 KOs.

Michael Jordan (b. Feb. 17, 1963): Basketball G; College Player of Year with North Carolina in 1984; led NBA in scoring 7 years in a row (1987-93); 7-time All-NBA 1st team; 3-time regular season MVP (1988,91-92) and 3-time MVP of NBA Finals (1991-93); only 3-time AP Male Athlete of Year; led U.S. Olympic team to gold medals in 1984 and '92; stunned sports world when he retired at age 30 on Oct. 6, 1993; signed as OF with Chicago White Sox and spent summer of '94 in Double A with Birmingham; barely hit his weight with .204 average; made one of the most anticipated comebacks in sports history when he returned to the Bulls lineup on Mar. 19, 1995 and shot 7-for-28; lost first playoff series since 1990 when Bulls were eliminated by Orlando in second round.

Florence Griffith Joyner (b. Dec. 21, 1959): Track & Field; set world records in 100 and 200 meters in 1988; won 3 gold medals at '88 Olympics (100m, 200m, 4x100m relay); Sullivan Award winner (1988); retired in 1989; designed NBA Indiana Pacers uniforms (1990); named as co-chairperson of President's Council on Physical Fitness and Sports in 1993.

Jackie Joyner-Kersee (b. Mar. 3, 1962): Track & Field; 2-time world champion in both long jump (1987,91) and heptathlon (1987,93); won heptathlon gold medals at 1988 and '92 Olympics and LJ gold at '88 Games; has also won Olympic silver (1984) in heptathlon and bronze (1992) in LJ; Sullivan Award winner (1986); only woman to receive The Sporting News Man of Year award.

Alberto Juantorena (b. Nov. 21, 1950): Cuban runner; won both 400m and 800m gold medals at 1976 Olympics.

Sonny Jurgensen (b. Aug. 23, 1934): Football QB; played 18 seasons with Philadelphia and Washington; led NFL in passing twice (1967,69); All-Pro in 1961; 255 career TD passes.

Duke Kahanamoku (b. Aug. 24, 1890, d. Jan. 22, 1968): Swimmer; won 3 gold medals and 2 silver over 3 Olympics (1912,20,24); also surfing pioneer.

Al Kaline (b. Dec. 19, 1934): Baseball; youngest player (at age 20) to win batting title (led AL with .340 in 1955); had 3,007 hits, 399 HRs in 22 years with Detroit.

Anatoly Karpov (b. May 23, 1951): Chess; Russian world champion from 1975-85; regained International Chess Federation (FIDE) version of championship in 1993 when countryman Garry Kasparov was stripped of title after forming new Professional Chess Association.

Garry Kasparov (b. Apr. 13, 1963): Chess; Azerbaijani who became youngest player (22 years, 210 days) ever to win world championship as Russian in 1985; defeated countryman Anatoly Karpov for title; split with International Chess Federation (FIDE) to form Professional Chess Association (PCA) in 1993; stripped of FIDE title in '93 but successfully defended PCA title against Briton Nigel Short; began latest title defense in New York on Sept. 11 in best-of-20 game match against 25-year-old Viswanatha Anand of India; winner will get $1 million and loser half that.

Ewing Kauffman (b. Sept. 21, 1916, d. Aug. 1, 1993): Baseball; pharmaceutical billionaire and longtime owner of Kansas City Royals; Royals Stadium renamed for Kauffman on July 2, 1993, one month before his death.

Mike Keenan (b. Oct. 21, 1949): Hockey; coach who finally led NY Rangers to Stanley Cup title in 1994 after 54 unsuccessful years; quit a month later in pay dispute and signed with St. Louis as coach-GM; entered 1995-96 season with 507 wins (including playoffs); also reached Cup finals with Philadelphia (1987) and Chicago (1992); coached Team Canada to Canada Cup wins in 1987 and '91.

Kipchoge (Kip) Keino (b. Jan. 17, 1940): Kenyan runner; young policeman who beat USA's Jim Ryun to win 1,500m gold medal at 1968 Olympics; won again in steeplechase at 1972 Summer Games; his success spawned long line of international distance champions from Kenya.

Johnny Kelley (b. Sept. 6, 1907): Distance runner, ran in his 61st and final Boston Marathon at age 84 in 1992, finishing in 5:58:36; won Boston twice (1935,45) and was 2nd 7 times.

Jim Kelly (b. Feb. 14, 1960): Football QB; led Buffalo to four consecutive Super Bowl appearances, and is only QB to lose four times; named to AFC Pro Bowl team 5 times; entered 1995 season ranked 4th on all-time list with passer rating of 85.8.

Walter Kennedy (b. June 8, 1912, d. June 26, 1977): Basketball; 2nd NBA commissioner (1963-75), league doubled in size to 18 teams during his term of office.

Nancy Kerrigan (b. Oct. 13, 1969): Figure skating; 1993 U.S. women's champion and Olympic medalist in 1992 (bronze) and '94 (silver); victim of Jan. 6, 1994 assault at U.S. nationals in Detroit when Shane Stant clubbed her in right knee with metal baton after a practice session; conspiracy hatched by Jeff Gillooly, ex-husband of rival Tonya Harding; although unable to compete in nationals, she quickly recovered and was granted berth on Olympic team; finished 2nd in Lillehammer to Oksana Baiul of Ukraine by a 5-4 judges' vote.

Harmon Killebrew (b. June 29, 1936): Baseball 3B-1B; led AL in HRs 6 times and RBI 3 times; MVP in 1969 with Minnesota; 573 career HRs.

Jean-Claude Killy (b. Aug. 30, 1943): French alpine skier; 2-time World Cup champion (1967-68); won 3 gold medals at 1968 Olympics in Grenoble; co-president of 1992 Winter Games in Albertville.

Ralph Kiner (b. Oct. 27, 1922): Baseball OF; led NL in home runs 7 straight years (1946-52) with Pittsburgh; 369 career HRs.

Betsy King (b. Aug. 13, 1955): Golfer; 2-time LPGA Player of Year (1984,89), who entered 1995 as Tour's all-time money winner with $4,892,873; 2-time winner of both U.S. Open (1989,90) and Dinah Shore (1987,90); became only 14th player to qualify for LPGA Hall of Fame on June 25, 1995 when she won the ShopRite Classic for her 30th career victory since 1977.

Billie Jean King (b. Nov. 22, 1943): Tennis; women's rights pioneer; Wimbledon singles champ 6 times; U.S. champ 4 times; first woman athlete to earn $100,000 in one year (1971); beat 55-year-old Bobby Riggs 6-4, 6-3, 6-3, to win $100,000 in 1973.

Don King (b. Aug. 20, 1931): Boxing promoter; controlled heavyweight title from 1978-90 while Larry Holmes and Mike Tyson were champions; 1st major promotion was Muhammad Ali's comeback fight in 1970; former numbers operator who served 4 years for manslaughter (1967-70); acquitted of tax evasion and fraud in 1985; indicted July 14, 1994 for allegedly bilking Lloyd's of London out of $350,000 on a false insurance claim involving a training injury to Julio Cesar Chavez in June 1991; regained control of heavyweight title in 1994 with wins by Oliver McCall (WBC) and Bruce Seldon (WBA); resumed role as Tyson's promoter after ex-champion's release from prison on Mar. 25, 1995.

Tom Kite (b. Dec. 9, 1949): Golfer; entered 1995 as all-time PGA Tour money leader with over $9.1 million (Greg Norman passed him on Aug. 27); finally won 1st major with victory in 1992 U.S. Open at Pebble Beach; co-NCAA champion with Ben Crenshaw (1972); PGA Rookie of Year (1973); PGA Player of Year (1989).

Gene Klein (b. Jan. 29, 1921, d. Mar. 12, 1990): Horseman; won 3 Eclipse awards as top owner (1985-87); filly Winning Colors won 1988 Kentucky Derby; also owned San Diego Chargers football team (1966-84).

Bob Knight (b. Oct. 25, 1940): Basketball; has coached Indiana to 3 NCAA titles (1976,81,87); 3-time Coach of Year (1975-76,89); 659 career wins in 30 years; coached 1984 U.S. Olympic team to gold medal.

Phil Knight (b. Feb. 24, 1938): Founder and chairman of Nike, Inc., the $4 billion shoe and fitness company founded in 1972 and based in Beaverton, Ore.; stable of endorsees includes Michael Jordan, Andre Agassi and Sergey Bubka; named "The Most Powerful Man in Sports" by The Sporting News in 1992.

Olga Korbut (b. May 16, 1955): Soviet gymnast; 3 gold medals at 1972 Olympics; first to perform back somersault on balance beam.

Johann Olav Koss (b. Oct. 29, 1968): Norwegian speedskater; won three gold medals at 1994 Olympics in Lillehammer with world records in the 1,500m, 5,000m and 10,000m; also won 1,500m gold and 10,000m silver in 1992 Games; retired shortly after Olympics.

Sandy Koufax (b. Dec. 30, 1935): Baseball LHP; led NL in strikeouts 4 times and ERA 5 straight years; won 3 Cy Young Awards (1963,65,66) with LA Dodgers; MVP in 1963; 2-time World Series MVP (1963,65); threw perfect game against Chicago Cubs (1-0, Sept. 9, 1965) and had 3 other no-hitters in 1962, '63 and '64.

Alvin Kraenzlein (b. Dec. 12, 1876, d. Jan. 6, 1928): Track & Field; won 4 individual gold medals in 1900 Olympics (60m, long jump, 110m and 200m hurdles).

Jack Kramer (b. Aug. 1, 1921): Tennis; Wimbledon singles champ 1947; U.S. champ 1946-47; promoter and Open pioneer.

Ingrid Kristiansen (b. Mar. 21, 1956): Norwegian runner; 2-time Boston Marathon winner (1986,89); won New York City Marathon in 1989; entered 1995 holding 2 world records recognized by IAAF— 5,000m and marathon.

Julie Krone (b. July 24, 1963): Jockey; only woman to ride winning horse in a Triple Crown race when she captured Belmont Stakes aboard Colonial Affair in 1993; entered 1995 as all-time winningest female jockey with 2,869 wins.

Mike Krzyzewski (b. Feb. 13, 1947): Basketball; has coached Duke to 7 Final Four appearances in last 10 years; won consecutive NCAA titles in 1991 and '92; missed most of 1994-95 season with a back injury and stress-related exhaustion; 20-year record of 431-186.

Alan Kulwicki (b. Dec. 14, 1954, d. Apr. 1, 1993): Auto racer; 1992 NASCAR national champion; 1st college grad and Northerner to win title; NASCAR Rookie of Year in 1986; famous for driving car backwards on victory lap; killed at age 38 in plane crash near Bristol, Tenn.

Marion Ladewig (b. Oct. 30, 1914): Bowler; named Woman Bowler of the Year 9 times (1950-54,57-59,63).

Guy Lafleur (b. Sept. 20, 1951): Hockey RW; led NHL in scoring 3 times (1975-78); 2-time MVP (1977-78), played for 5 Stanley Cup winners in Montreal; playoff MVP in 1977; returned to NHL as player in 1988 after election to Hall of Fame; retired again in 1991.

Napoleon (Nap) Lajoie (b. Sept. 5, 1874, d. Feb. 7, 1959): Baseball 2B; led AL in batting 3 times (1901,03-04); batted .422 in 1901; hit .338 for career with 3,244 hits.

Jack Lambert (b. July 8, 1952): Football LB; 6-time All-Pro (1975-76,79-82); led Pittsburgh to 4 Super Bowl titles.

Kenesaw Mountain Landis (b. Nov. 20, 1866, d. Nov. 25, 1944): U.S. District Court judge who became first baseball commissioner (1920-44); banned Black Sox for life.

Tom Landry (b. Sept. 11, 1924): Football; All-Pro DB for NY Giants (1954); coached Dallas for 29 years (1960-88); won 2 Super Bowls (1972,78); 3rd on NFL all-time list with 270 wins.

Steve Largent (b. Sept. 28, 1954): Football WR; retired in 1989 after 14 years in Seattle with then NFL records in passes caught (819) and TD passes caught (100); elected to U.S. House of Representatives (R, Okla.) in 1994 and Pro Football Hall of fame in '95.

Don Larsen (b. Aug. 7, 1929): Baseball RHP; NY Yankees hurler who pitched the only perfect game in World Series history— a 2-0 victory over Brooklyn in Game 5 of the 1956 Series (Oct. 8); Series MVP that year; had career record of 81-91 in 14 seasons with 6 clubs.

Tommy Lasorda (b. Sept. 22, 1927): Baseball; has managed LA Dodgers to 2 World Series titles (1981,88) in 4 appearances; entered 1995 season with 1,480 regular-season wins in 19 years.

Larissa Latynina (b. Dec. 27, 1934): Soviet gymnast; won total of 18 medals, (9 gold) in 3 Olympics (1956,60,64).

Nikki Lauda (b. Feb. 22, 1949): Austrian auto racer; 3-time world Formula One champion (1975,77,84); 25 career wins from 1971-85.

Rod Laver (b. Aug. 9, 1938): Australian tennis player; only player to win Grand Slam twice (1962,69); Wimbledon champion 4 times; 1st to earn $1 million in prize money.

Andrea Mead Lawrence (b. Apr. 19, 1932): Alpine skier; won 2 gold medals at 1952 Olympics.

Bobby Layne (b. Dec. 19, 1926, d. Dec. 1, 1986): Football QB; college star at Texas; master of 2-minute offense; led Detroit to 4 divisional titles and 3 NFL championships in 1950's.

Frank Leahy (b. Aug. 27, 1908, d. June 21, 1973): Football; coached Notre Dame to four national titles (1943,46-47,49); career record of 107-13-9 for a winning pct. of .864.

Brian Leetch (b. Mar. 3, 1968): Hockey D; NHL Rookie of Year in 1989; won Norris Trophy as top defenseman in 1992; Conn Smythe Trophy winner as playoffs' MVP in 1994 when he helped lead NY Rangers to 1st Stanley Cup title in 54 years.

Jacques Lemaire (b. Sept. 7, 1945): Hockey C; member of 8 Stanley Cup champions in Montreal; scored 366 goals in 12 seasons; coached Canadiens from 1983-85; directed New Jersey Devils to surprising 4-game sweep of Detroit to win 1995 Stanley Cup.

Claude Lemieux (b. July 16, 1965): Hockey RW; pivotal member of Stanley Cup championship teams in Montreal (1986) and New Jersey (1995); playoff MVP with Devils in '95; no relation to Mario.

Mario Lemieux (b. Oct. 5, 1965): Hockey C; 4-time NHL scoring leader (1988-89,92-93); Rookie of Year (1985); 3-time All-NHL 1st team (1988-89,93); 2-time regular season MVP (1988,93); 3-time All-Star Game MVP; led Pittsburgh to consecutive Stanley Cup titles (1991 and '92) and was playoff MVP both years; won 1993 scoring title despite missing 24 games to undergo radiation treatments for Hodgkin's disease; missed 62 games during 1993-94 season mostly due to back injuries; sat out 1994-95 season due to fatigue but will return to play reduced schedule in 1995-96.

Greg LeMond (b. June 26, 1961): Cyclist; 3-time Tour de France winner (1986,89-90); only non-European to win the event; retired in Dec. 1994 after being diagnosed with a rare muscular disease known as mitochondrial myopathy.

Ivan Lendl (b. Mar. 7, 1960): Czech tennis player; No.1 player in world 4 times (1985-87,89); has won both French and U.S. Opens 3 times and Australian twice; owns 94 career tournament wins.

Suzanne Lenglen (b. May 24, 1899, d. July 4, 1938): French tennis player; dominated women's tennis from 1919-26; won both Wimbledon and French singles titles 6 times.

Sugar Ray Leonard (b. May 17, 1956): Boxer; light welterweight Olympic champ (1976); won world welterweight title 1979 and four more titles; retired after losing to Terry Norris on Feb. 9, 1991, with record of 36-2-1 and 25 KOs.

Marv Levy (b. Aug. 3, 1928): Football; coached Buffalo to four consecutive Super Bowls, but is one of two coaches who are 0-4 (Bud Grant is the other); won 50 games and two CFL Grey Cups with Montreal (1974,77); entered 1995 season with 127 NFL victories.

Carl Lewis (b. July 1, 1961): Track & Field; won 4 Olympic gold medals in 1984 (100m, 200m, 4x100m, LJ), 2 more in '88 (100m, LJ) and 2 more in '92 (4x100m, LJ) for a career total of 8; has record 8 World Championship titles and 9 medals in all; Sullivan Award winner (1981); entered 1995 with 71 long jumps over 28 feet.

Nancy Lieberman-Cline (b. July 1, 1958): Basketball; 3-time All-America and 2-time Player of Year (1979-80); led Old Dominion to consecutive AIAW titles in 1979 and '80; played in defunct WPBL and WABA and became 1st woman to play in men's pro league (USBL) in 1986.

Eric Lindros (b. Feb. 28, 1973): Hockey C; No. 1 pick in 1991 NHL draft by the Nordiques; sat out 1991-92 season rather than play in Quebec; traded to Philadelphia in 1992 for 6 players, 2 No. 1 picks and $15 million; elected Flyers captain at age 22; won Hart Trophy as league MVP in 1995.

Sonny Liston (b. May 8, 1932, d. Dec. 30, 1970): Boxer; heavyweight champion (1962-64), who knocked out Floyd Patterson twice in the first round, then lost title to Muhammad Ali (then Cassius Clay) in 1964; pro record of 50-4 with 39 KOs.

Rebecca Lobo (b. Oct. 6, 1973): Basketball F; women's college basketball Player of the Year in 1995; led Connecticut to undefeated season (35-0) and national title; member of 1996 U.S. Olympic team.

Vince Lombardi (b. June 11, 1913, d. Sept. 3, 1970): Football; coached Green Bay to 5 NFL titles; won first 2 Super Bowls ever played (1967-68); died as NFL's all-time winningest coach with percentage of .740 (105-35-6); Super Bowl trophy named in his honor.

Johnny Longden (b. Feb. 14, 1907): Jockey; first to win 6,000 races; rode Count Fleet to Triple Crown in 1943.

Nancy Lopez (b. Jan. 6, 1957): Golfer; 4-time LPGA Player of the Year (1978-79,85,88); Rookie of Year (1977); 3-time winner of LPGA Championship; reached Hall of Fame by age 30 with 35 victories; entered 1995 with 47 career wins.

Donna Lopiano (b. Sept. 11, 1946): Former basketball and softball star who was women's athletic director at Texas for 18 years before leaving to become executive director of Women's Sports Foundation in 1992.

Greg Louganis (b. Jan. 29, 1960): U.S. diver; won platform and springboard gold medals at both 1984 and '88 Olympics; revealed on Feb. 22, 1995 that he has AIDS.

Joe Louis (b. May 13, 1914, d. Apr. 12, 1981): Boxer; world heavyweight champion from June 22, 1937 to Mar. 1, 1949; his reign of 11 years, 8 months longest in division history; successfully defended title 25 times; retired in 1949, but returned to lose title shots against successors Ezzard Charles in 1950 and Rocky Marciano in '51; pro record of 63-3 with 49 KOs.

Sid Luckman (b. Nov. 21, 1916): Football QB; 6-time All-Pro; led Chicago Bears to 4 NFL titles (1940-41,43,46); MVP in 1943.

Hank Luisetti (b. June 16, 1916): Basketball F; 3-time All-America at Stanford (1935-38); revolutionized game with one-handed shot.

Johnny Lujack (b. Jan. 4, 1925): Football QB; led Notre Dame to three national titles (1943,46-47); won Heisman Trophy in 1947.

Darrell Wayne Lukas (b. Sept. 2, 1935): Horse racing; 4-time Eclipse Award-winning trainer who saddled Horses of Year Lady's Secret in 1988 and Criminal Type in 1990; first trainer to earn over $100 million in purses; led nation in earnings 11 times from 1983-94; Triple Crown sweep in 1995 with Thunder Gulch and Timber Country gave him five Triple Crown wins in a row; has now won Preakness four times and Kentucky Derby and Belmont twice each.

Gen. Douglas MacArthur (b. Jan. 26, 1880, d. Apr. 5, 1964): Controversial U.S. general of World War II and Korea; president of U.S. Olympic Committee (1927-28); college football devotee, National Football Foundation MacArthur Bowl (for No.1 team) named after him.

Connie Mack (b. Dec. 22, 1862, d. Feb. 8, 1956): Baseball owner; managed Philadelphia A's until he was 87 (1901-50); all-time major league wins leader with 3,755, including postseason; won 9 AL pennants and 5 World Series (1910-11,13,29-30); also finished last 18 times.

Andy MacPhail (b. Apr. 5, 1953): Baseball; Chicago Cubs president, who was GM of 2 World Series champions in Minnesota (1987,91); won first title at age 34; son of Lee, grandson of Larry.

Larry MacPhail (b. Feb. 3, 1890, d. Oct. 1, 1975): Baseball executive and innovator; introduced major leagues to night games at Cincinnati (May 24, 1935); won pennant in Brooklyn (1941) and World Series with NY Yankees (1947); father of Lee.

Lee MacPhail (b. Oct. 25, 1917): Baseball; AL president (1974-83); president of owners' Player Relations Committee (1984-85); also GM of Baltimore (1959-65) and NY Yankees (1967-74); son of Larry and father of Andy.

John Madden (b. Apr. 10, 1936): Football and Radio-TV; won 112 games and a Super Bowl (1976 season) as coach of Oakland Raiders; has won 10 Emmy Awards since 1982 as NFL analyst with CBS and Fox; signed 4-year, $32 million deal with Fox in 1994— a richer contract than any NFL player.

Greg Maddux (b. Apr. 14, 1966): Baseball RHP; won unprecedented 3 straight NL Cy Young Awards with Cubs (1992) and Atlanta (1993-94); has led NL in ERA twice (1993-94); entered 1995 with record of 131-91 in 9 seasons.

Larry Mahan (b. Nov. 21, 1943): Rodeo; 6-time All-Around world champion (1966-70,73).

Phil Mahre (b. May 10, 1957): Alpine skier; 3-time World Cup overall champ (1981-83); finished 1-2 with twin brother Steve in 1984 Olympic slalom.

Karl Malone (b. July 24, 1963): Basketball F; 7-time All-NBA 1st team (1989-95) with Utah; member of the 1992 and '96 Olympic Dream Teams.

Moses Malone (b. Mar. 23, 1955): Basketball C; signed with Utah of ABA at age 19; has led NBA in rebounding 6 times; 4-time All-NBA 1st team; 3-time NBA MVP (1979,82-83); playoff MVP with Philadelphia in 1983; played in 21st pro season in 1994-95.

Nigel Mansell (b. Aug. 8, 1953): British auto racer; won 1992 Formula One driving championship with record 9 victories and 14 poles; quit Grand Prix circuit to race Indy cars in 1993; 1st rookie to win IndyCar title; 3rd driver to win IndyCar and F1 titles; returned to F1 after 1994 IndyCar season and won '94 Australian Grand Prix; left F1 again on May 23, 1995 with 31 wins and 32 poles in 15 years.

Mickey Mantle (b. Oct. 20, 1931, d. Aug. 13, 1995): Baseball OF; named after Hall of Fame catcher Mickey Cochrane; led AL in home runs 4 times; won Triple Crown in 1956; hit 52 HRs in 1956 and 54 in '61; 3-time MVP (1956-57,62); hit 536 career HRs; played in 12 World Series with NY Yankees and won 7 times; all-time Series leader in HRs (18), RBI (40), runs (42) and strikeouts (54); underwent liver transplant on June 8, 1995 and died of cancer two months later.

Diego Maradona (b. Oct. 30, 1960): Soccer F; captain and MVP of 1986 World Cup champion Argentina; also led national team to 1990 World Cup final; consensus Player of Decade in 1980's; led Napoli to 2 Italian League titles (1987,90) and UEFA Cup (1989); tested positive for cocaine and suspended 15 months by FIFA in 1991; returned to World Cup as Argentine captain in 1994, but was kicked out of tournament after two games when doping test found 5 banned substances in his urine.

Pete Maravich (b. June 27, 1947, d. Jan. 5, 1988): Basketball; NCAA scoring leader 3 times (1968-70); averaged 44.2 points a game over career; Player of Year in 1970; NBA scoring champ in '77 with New Orleans.

Alice Marble (b. Sept. 28, 1913, d. Dec. 13, 1990): Tennis; 4-time U.S. champion (1936,38-40); won Wimbledon in 1939; swept U.S. singles, doubles and mixed doubles from 1938-40.

Gino Marchetti (b. Jan. 2, 1927): Football DE; 8-time NFL All-Pro (1957-64) with Baltimore Colts.

Rocky Marciano (b. Sept. 1, 1923, d. Aug. 31, 1969): Boxer; heavyweight champion (1952-56); retired undefeated; pro record of 49-0 with 43 KOs; killed in plane crash.

Juan Marichal (b. Oct. 20, 1938): Baseball RHP; won 21 or more games 6 times for S.F. Giants from 1963-69; ended 16-year career with 243 wins.

Dan Marino (b. Sept. 15, 1961): Football QB; 4-time leading passer in AFC (1983-84,86,89); set NFL single-season records for TD passes (48) and passing yards (5,084) with Miami in 1984; entered 1995 season ranked 2nd in career TD passes (328) and passing yards (45,173).

Roger Maris (b. Sept. 10, 1934, d. Dec. 14, 1985): Baseball OF; broke Babe Ruth's single-season HR record with 61 in 1961; 2-time AL MVP (1960-61) with NY Yankees.

Billy Martin (b. May 16, 1928, d. Dec. 25, 1989): Baseball; 5-time manager of NY Yankees; won 2 pennants and 1 World Series (1977); also managed Minnesota, Detroit, Texas and Oakland; played 2B on 4 Yankee world champions in 1950's.

Eddie Mathews (b. Oct. 13, 1931): Baseball 3B; led NL in HRs twice (1953,59); hit 30 or more home runs 9 straight years; 512 career HRs.

Christy Mathewson (b. Aug. 12, 1880, d. Oct. 7, 1925): Baseball RHP; won 22 or more games 12 straight years (1903-14); 373 career wins; pitched 3 shutouts in 1905 World Series.

Bob Mathias (b. Nov. 17, 1930): Track & Field; youngest winner of decathlon with gold medal in 1948 Olympics at age 17; first to repeat as decathlon champ in 1952; Sullivan Award winner (1948); 4-term member of U.S. Congress (R, Calif.) from 1967-74.

Ollie Matson (b. May 1, 1930): Football HB; All-America at San Francisco (1951); bronze medal winner in 400m at 1952 Olympics; 4-time All-Pro for NFL Chicago Cardinals (1954-57); traded to LA Rams for 9 players in 1959; accounted for 12,884 all-purpose yards and scored 73 TDs in 14 seasons.

Willie Mays (b. May 6, 1931): Baseball OF; led NL in HRs and stolen bases 4 times each; 2-time MVP (1954,65) with NY-SF Giants; played in 24 All-Star Games; 660 HRs and 3,283 hits in career.

Bill Mazeroski (b. Sept. 5, 1936): Baseball 2B; career .260 hitter who won the 1960 World Series for Pittsburgh with a lead-off HR in the bottom of the 9th inning of Game 7; the pitcher was Ralph Terry of the NY Yankees, the count was 1-0 and the score was tied 9-9; also a sure-fielder, Maz won 8 gold gloves in 17 seasons.

Joe McCarthy (b. Apr. 21, 1887, d. Jan. 13, 1978): Baseball; managed NY Yankees to 8 pennants and 7 World Series titles (1931-46).

Mark McCormack (b. Nov. 6, 1930): Founder and CEO of International Management Group (IMG), the sports management conglomerate who represent, among others, Joe Montana, Wayne Gretzky, Arnold Palmer, Andre Agassi and Pete Sampras.

Pat McCormick (b. May 12, 1930): U.S. diver; won women's platform and springboard gold medals in both 1952 and '56 Olympics.

Willie McCovey (b. Jan. 10, 1938): Baseball 1B; led NL in HRs 3 times and RBI twice; MVP in 1969 with SF; 521 career HRs; indicted for tax evasion in July 1995.

John McEnroe (b. Feb. 16, 1959): Tennis; No.1 player in the world 4 times (1981-84); 4-time U.S. Open singles champ (1979-81,84); 3-time Wimbledon champ (1981,83-84); has played on 5 Davis Cup winners (1978-79,81-82,92); won NCAA singles title (1978); finished career with 77 championships in singles, 77 more in doubles (including 9 Grand Slam titles), and American Davis Cup records for years played (13) and singles matches won (41).

John McGraw (b. Apr. 7, 1873, d. Feb. 25, 1934): Baseball; managed NY Giants to 9 NL pennants between 1905-24; won World Series 3 times in 1905 and 1921-22; 2nd on all-time career list with 2,810 wins in 33 seasons (2,784 regular season and 26 postseason).

Frank McGuire (b. Nov. 8, 1916, d. Oct. 11, 1994): Basketball; winner of 731 games as high school, college and pro coach; only coach to win 100 games at 3 colleges— St. John's (103), North Carolina (164) and South Carolina (283); won 550 games in 30 college seasons; 1957 UNC team went 32-0 and beat Kansas 54-53 in triple OT to win NCAA title; coached NBA Philadelphia Warriors to 49-31 record in 1961-62 season, but refused to move with team to San Francisco.

Jim McKay (b. Sept. 24, 1921): Radio-TV; host and commentator of ABC's Olympic coverage and "Wide World of Sports" show since 1961; 12-time Emmy winner; also given Peabody Award in 1988 and Life Achievement Emmy in 1990; became part owner of Baltimore Orioles in 1993.

John McKay (b. July 5, 1923): Football; coached USC to 3 national titles (1962,67,72); won Rose Bowl 5 times; reached NFL playoffs 3 times with Tampa Bay.

Tamara McKinney (b. Oct. 16, 1962): Skiing; only American woman to win overall Alpine World Cup championship (1983); won World Cup slalom (1984) and giant slalom titles twice (1981,83).

Denny McLain (b. Mar. 29, 1944): Baseball RHP; last pitcher to win 30 games (1968); 2-time Cy Young winner (1968-69) with Detroit; convicted of racketeering, extortion and drug possession in 1985, served 29 months of 25-year jail term, sentence overturned when court ruled he had not received a fair trial.

Rick Mears (b. Dec. 3, 1951): Auto racer; 3-time CART national champ (1979,81-82); 4-time winner of Indianapolis 500 (1979,84,88,91) and only driver to win 6 Indy 500 poles; Indy 500 Rookie of Year (1978); retired after 1992 season with 29 IndyCar wins and 40 poles.

Mark Messier (b. Jan. 18, 1961): Hockey C; 2-time Hart Trophy winner as MVP with Edmonton (1990) and NY Rangers (1992); captain of Rangers team that finally won 1st Stanley Cup since 1940; entered 1995-96 season with 492 regular season goals; ranked 2nd (behind Gretzky) in all-time playoff points (272) and assists (170).

Debbie Meyer (b. Aug. 14, 1952): Swimmer; 1st swimmer to win 3 individual gold medals at one Olympics (1968).

George Mikan (b. June 18, 1924): Basketball C; 3-time All-America (1944-46); led DePaul to NIT title (1945); led Minneapolis Lakers to 5 NBA titles in 6 years (1949-54); first commissioner of ABA (1967-69).

Stan Mikita (b. May 20, 1940): Hockey C; led NHL in scoring 4 times; won both MVP and Lady Byng awards in 1967 and '68 with Chicago.

Cheryl Miller (b. Jan. 3, 1964): Basketball; 3-time college Player of Year (1984-86); led USC to NCAA title and U.S. to Olympic gold medal in 1984; coached USC to 44-14 record in 2 seasons before quitting to join Turner Sports as NBA reporter.

Del Miller (b. July 5, 1913): Harness racing; driver, trainer, owner, breeder, seller and track owner; drove to 2,441 wins from 1939-90.

Marvin Miller (b. Apr. 14, 1917): Baseball labor leader; executive director of Players' Assn. from 1966-82; increased average salary from $19,000 to over $240,000; led 13-day strike in 1972 and 50-day walkout in '81.

Shannon Miller (b. Mar. 10, 1977): Gymnast; won 5 medals in 1992 Olympics; All-Around women's world champion in 1993 and '94.

Billy Mills (b. June 30, 1938): Track & Field; upset winner of 10,000m gold medal at 1964 Olympics.

Bora Milutinovic (b. Sept. 7, 1944): Soccer; Serbian who coached United States national team from 1991-95, but was fired on Apr. 14, 1995 when he refused to accept additional duties as director of player development; hired 4 months later to revive Mexican national team; known as a miracle worker, he led Mexico, Costa Rica and the U.S. into the 2nd round of the last three World Cups.

Tommy Moe (b. Feb. 17, 1970): Alpine skier; won Downhill and placed 2nd in Super-G at 1994 Winter Olympics; 1st U.S. man to win 2 Olympic alpine medals in one year.

Paul Molitor (b. Aug. 22, 1956): Baseball DH-1B; All-America SS at Minnesota in 1976; signed as free agent by Toronto on Dec. 7, 1992, after 15 years with Milwaukee; led Blue Jays to 2nd straight World Series title as MVP (1993); has hit .418 in 2 Series appearances (1982,93); holds World Series record with five hits in one game; entered 1995 season with lifetime .307 average in 17 seasons.

Joe Montana (b. June 11, 1956): Football QB; led Notre Dame to national title in 1977; led San Francisco to 4 Super Bowl titles in 1980s; only 3-time Super Bowl MVP; 2-time NFL MVP (1989-90); has led NFL in passing 5 times; missed all of 1991 season and nearly all of '92 after elbow surgery; traded to Kansas City in 1993; ranked 2nd in all-time passing efficiency (92.3), 4th in TD passes (273) and yards passing (40,551); announced retirement in San Francisco Apr. 18, 1995.

Helen Wills Moody (b. Oct. 6, 1905): Tennis; won 8 Wimbledon singles titles, 7 U.S. and 4 French from 1923-38.

Warren Moon (b. Nov. 18, 1956): Football QB; MVP of 1978 Rose Bowl with Washington; MVP of CFL with Edmonton in 1983; led Eskimos to 5 consecutive Grey Cup titles (1978-82) and was playoff MVP twice (1980,82); joined Houston of NFL in 1984; led NFL in attempts, completions and yards in 1990 and '91; picked for 8 Pro Bowls; traded to Minnesota in 1994.

Archie Moore (b. Dec. 13, 1913): Boxer; world light-heavyweight champion (1952-60); pro record 199-26-8 with 145 KOs.

Michael Moorer (b. Nov. 12, 1967): Boxer; became 1st left-hander to win heavyweight title when he scored majority decision over Evander Holyfield on Apr. 22, 1994; lost title to George Foreman on 10th round KO Nov. 5, 1994; entered '95 with pro record of 36-1 with 30 KOs.

Noureddine Morceli (b. Feb. 28, 1970): Algerian runner; 3-time world champion at 1,500 meters (1991,93, 95); set world records at mile (3:44.39) in 1993, at 3,000m (7:25.11) in '94 and at 1,500m (3:27.37) in 1995.

Howie Morenz (b. June 21, 1902, d. Mar. 8, 1937): Hockey C; 3-time NHL MVP (1928,31-32); led Montreal Canadiens to 3 Stanley Cups; voted Outstanding Player of the Half-Century in 1950.

Joe Morgan (b. Sept. 19, 1943): Baseball 2B; led NL in walks 4 times; regular-season MVP both years he led Cincinnati to World Series titles (1975-76); 3rd behind Babe Ruth and Ted Williams in career walks with 1,865.

Bobby Morrow (b. Oct. 15, 1935): Track & Field; won 3 gold medals at 1956 Olympics (100m, 200m and 4x400m relay).

Willie Mosconi (b. June 27, 1913, d. Sept. 12, 1993): Pocket Billiards; 14-time world champion from 1941-57.

Annemarie Moser-Proll (b. Mar. 27, 1953): Austrian alpine skier; won World Cup overall title 6 times (1971-75,79); all-time women's World Cup leader in career wins with 61; won Downhill in 1980 Olympics.

Edwin Moses (b. Aug. 31, 1955): Track & Field; won 400m hurdles at 1976 and '84 Olympics, bronze medal in '88; also winner of 122 consecutive races from 1977-87.

Stirling Moss (b. Sept. 17, 1929): Auto racer; won 194 of 466 career races and 16 Formula One events, but was never world champion.

Marion Motley (b. June 5, 1920): Football FB; all-time leading AAFC rusher; rushed for over 4,700 yards and 31 TDs for Cleveland Browns (1946-53).

Dale Murphy (b. Mar. 12, 1956): Baseball OF; led NL in RBI 3 times and HRs twice; 2-time MVP (1982-83) with Atlanta; also played with Philadelphia and Colorado; retired May 27, 1993, with 398 HRs.

Jack Murphy (b. Feb. 5, 1923, d. Sept. 24, 1980): Sports editor and columnist of The San Diego Union from 1951-80; instrumental in bringing AFL Chargers south from LA in 1961, landing Padres as NL expansion team in '69; and lobbying for 54,000-seat San Diego stadium that would later bear his name.

Eddie Murray (b. Feb. 24, 1956): Baseball 1B-DH; AL Rookie of Year in 1977; entered 1995 with 458 HRs and most games with switch-hit homers (11); became 20th player in history, but only 2nd switch hitter (after Pete Rose) to get 3,000 hits when he singled off Minnesota's Mike Trombley on June 30, 1995.

Jim Murray (b. Dec. 29, 1919): Sports columnist for LA Times since 1961; 14-time Sportswriter of the Year; won Pulitzer Prize for commentary in 1990.

Ty Murray (b. Oct. 11, 1969): Rodeo cowboy; 6-time All-Around world champion (1989-94); Rookie of Year in 1988; youngest (age 20) to win All-Around title; set single season earnings mark with $297,896 in 1993; missed most of 1995 season with knee injury.

Stan Musial (b. Nov. 21, 1920): Baseball OF-1B; led NL in batting 7 times; 3-time MVP (1943,46,48) with St. Louis; played in 24 All-Star Games; had 3,630 career hits and .331 average.

John Naber (b. Jan. 20, 1956): Swimmer; won 4 gold medals and a silver in 1976 Olympics.

Bronko Nagurski (b. Nov. 3, 1908, d. Jan. 7, 1990): Football FB-T; All-America at Minnesota (1929); All-Pro with Chicago Bears (1932-34); charter member of college and pro halls of fame.

James Naismith (b. Nov. 6, 1861, d. Nov. 28, 1939): Canadian physical education instructor who invented basketball in 1891 at the YMCA Training School (now Springfield College) in Springfield, Mass.

Joe Namath (b. May 31, 1943): Football QB; signed for unheard-of $400,000 as rookie with AFL's NY Jets in 1965; 2-time All-AFL (1968-69) and All-NFL (1972); led Jets to Super Bowl title as MVP in '69.

Ilie Nastase (b. July 19, 1946): Romanian tennis player; No.1 in the world twice (1972-73); won U.S. (1972) and French (1973) Opens.

Martina Navratilova (b. Oct. 18, 1956): Tennis player; No.1 player in the world 7 times (1978-79,82-86); won her record 9th Wimbledon singles title in 1990; also won 4 U.S. Opens, 3 Australian and 2 French; in all, won 18 Grand Slam singles titles and 38 Grand Slam doubles titles; all-time leader among men and women in singles titles (167) and money won ($20.3 million) over 21 years; retired from singles play after 1994 season with No. 8 ranking and appearance in 12th Wimbledon final

Cosmas Ndeti (b. Nov. 24, 1971): Kenyan distance runner; winner of three consecutive Boston Marathons (1993-95), set course record of 2:07:15 in 1994.

Earle (Greasy) Neale (b. Nov. 5, 1891, d. Nov. 2, 1973): Baseball and Football; hit .357 for Cincinnati in 1919 World Series; also played with pre-NFL Canton Bulldogs; later coached Philadelphia Eagles to 2 NFL titles (1948-49).

Primo Nebiolo (b. July 14, 1923): Italian president of International Amateur Athletic Federation (IAAF) since 1981; also an at-large member of International Olympic Committee; regarded as dictatorial, but credited with elevating track & field to world class financial status.

Byron Nelson (b. Feb. 4, 1912): Golfer; 2-time winner of both Masters (1937,42) and PGA (1940,45); also U.S. Open champion in 1939; won 19 tournaments in 1945, including 11 in a row; also set all-time PGA stroke average with 68.33 strokes per round over 120 rounds in '45.

Lindsey Nelson (b. May 25, 1919, d. June 10, 1995): Radio-TV; all-purpose play-by-play broadcaster for CBS, NBC and others; 4-time Sportscaster of the Year (1959-62); voice of Cotton Bowl for 25 years and NY Mets from 1962-78; given Life Achievement Emmy Award in 1991.

Ernie Nevers (b. July 11, 1903, d. May 3, 1976): Football FB; earned 11 letters in four sports at Stanford; played pro football, baseball and basketball; scored 40 points for Chicago Cardinals in one NFL game (1929).

Paula Newby-Fraser (b. June 2, 1962): Zimbabwean triathlete; 7-time winner of Ironman Triathlon in Hawaii; established women's record of 8:55:28 in 1992.

John Newcombe (b. May 23, 1944): Australian tennis player; No.1 player in world 3 times (1967,70-71); won Wimbledon 3 times and U.S. and Australian championships twice each.

Bob Neyland (b. Feb. 17, 1892, d. Mar. 28, 1962): Football; 3-time coach at Tennessee; had 173-31-12 record in 21 years; won national title in 1951; Vols' stadium named for him; also Army general who won Distinguished Service Cross as supply officer in World War II.

Jack Nicklaus (b. Jan. 21, 1940): Golfer; all-time leader in major tournament wins with 20— including 6 Masters, 5 PGAs, 4 U.S. Opens and 3 British Opens; oldest player to win Masters (46 in 1986); PGA Player of Year 5 times (1967,72-73,75-76); named Golfer of Century by PGA in 1988; 6-time Ryder Cup player and 2-time captain (1983,87); won NCAA title (1961) and 2 U.S. Amateurs (1959,61); entered 1995 with 70 PGA Tour wins (2nd to Sam Snead's 81); 3rd win in Tradition in '95 gave him 7 majors in 6 years on Seniors Tour.

Chuck Noll (b. Jan. 5, 1932): Football; coached Pittsburgh to 4 Super Bowl titles (1975-76,79-80); retired after 1991 season ranked 5th on all-time list with 209 wins (including playoffs) in 23 years.

Greg Norman (b. Feb. 10, 1955): Australian golfer; PGA Tour's all-time money winner ($9.5 million), passing Tom Kite on Aug. 27, 1995; entered 1995 with 65 tournament wins worldwide; 2-time British Open winner (1986,93); lost Masters by a stroke in both 1986 (to Jack Nicklaus) and '87 (to Larry Mize in sudden death).

James D. Norris (b. Nov. 6, 1906, d. Feb. 25, 1966): Boxing promoter and NHL owner; president of International Boxing Club from 1949 until U.S. Supreme Court ordered its break-up (for anti-trust violations) in 1958; only NHL owner to win Stanley Cups in two cities' Detroit (1936-37,43) and Chicago (1961).

Paavo Nurmi (b. June 13, 1897, d. Oct. 2, 1973): Finnish runner; won 9 gold medals (6 individual) in 1920, '24 and '28 Olympics; from 1921-31 broke 23 world outdoor records in events ranging from 1,500 to 20,000 meters.

Dan O'Brien (b. July 18, 1966): Track & Field; set world record in decathlon (8,891 pts) on Sept. 4-5, 1992, after failing to qualify for event at U.S. Olympic Trials; three-time gold medalist at World Championships (1991,93,95).

Larry O'Brien (b. July 7, 1917, d. Sept. 27, 1990): Basketball; former U.S. Postmaster General and 3rd NBA commissioner (1975-84), league absorbed 4 ABA teams and created salary cap during his term in office.

Parry O'Brien (b. Jan. 28, 1932): Track & Field; in 4 consecutive Olympics, won two gold medals, a silver and placed 4th in the shot put (1952-64).

Al Oerter (b. Sept. 19, 1936): Track & Field; his 4 discus gold medals in consecutive Olympics from 1956-68 is an unmatched Olympic record.

Sadaharu Oh (b. May 20, 1940): Baseball 1B; led Japan League in HRs 15 times; 9-time MVP for Tokyo Giants; hit 868 HRs in 22 years.

Hakeem Olajuwon (b. Jan. 21, 1963): Basketball C; Nigerian native who was consensus All-America in 1984 and Final Four MVP in 1983 for Houston; overall 1st pick by Houston Rockets in 1984 NBA draft; led Rockets to back-to-back NBA titles (1994,95); regular season MVP ('94) and playoff MVP ('94,'95); 6-time All-NBA 1st team (1987-89,93-95).

José Maria Olazábal (b. Feb. 5, 1966): Spanish golfer; entered 1995 season with 13 worldwide victories; won only major at '94 Masters.

Barney Oldfield (b. Jan. 29, 1878, d. Oct. 4, 1946): Auto racing pioneer; drove cars built by Henry Ford; first man to drive car a mile per minute (1903).

Walter O'Malley (b. Oct. 9, 1903, d. Aug. 9, 1979): Baseball owner; moved Brooklyn Dodgers to Los Angeles after 1957 season; won 4 World Series (1955,59,63,65).

Shaquille O'Neal (b. Mar. 6, 1972): Basketball C; 2-time All-America at LSU (1991-92); overall 1st pick (as a junior) by Orlando in 1992 NBA draft; Rookie of Year in 1993; led NBA in scoring in 1995; member of Dreams II and III.

Bobby Orr (b. Mar. 20, 1948): Hockey D; 8-time Norris Trophy winner as best defenseman; led NHL in scoring twice and assists 5 times; All-NHL 1st team 8 times; regular season MVP 3 times (1970-72); playoff MVP twice (1970,72) with Boston.

Tom Osborne (b. Feb. 23, 1937): Football; entered 1995 season with record of 219-47-3 in 22 seasons as coach at Nebraska; his win percentage of .820 is best of any active coach in Division I-A; finally won national championship in 1994.

Mel Ott (b. Mar. 2, 1909, d. Nov. 21, 1958): Baseball OF; joined NY Giants at age 16; led NL in HRs 6 times; had 511 HRs and 1,860 RBI in 22 years.

Kristin Otto (b. Feb. 7, 1966): East German swimmer; 1st woman to win 6 gold medals (4 individual) at one Olympics (1988).

Francis Ouimet (b. May 8, 1893, d. Sept. 3, 1967): Golfer; won 1913 U.S. Open as 20-year-old amateur playing on Brookline, Mass. course where he used to caddie; won U.S. Amateur twice; 8-time Walker Cup player.

Steve Owen (b. Apr. 21, 1898, d. May 17, 1964): Football; All-Pro guard (1927); coached NY Giants for 23 years (1931-53); won 153 career games and 2 NFL titles (1934,38).

Jesse Owens (b. Sept. 12, 1913, d. Mar. 31, 1980): Track & Field; broke 5 world records in one afternoon at Big Ten Championships (May 25, 1935); a year later, he won 4 gold medals (100m, 200m, 4x100m relay and long jump) at Berlin Summer Olympics.

Alan Page (b. Aug. 7, 1945): Football DE; consensus All-America at Notre Dame in 1966 and member of two national championship teams; 6-time NFL All-Pro and 1971 Player of Year with Minnesota Vikings; also a lawyer who was elected to Minnesota Supreme Court in 1992.

Satchel Paige (b. July 7, 1906, d. June 6, 1982): Baseball RHP; pitched 55 career no-hitters over 20 seasons in Negro Leagues, entered Major Leagues with Cleveland in 1948 at age 42; had 28-31 record in 5 years; returned to AL at age 59 to start 1 game for Kansas City in 1965; went 3 innings, gave up a hit and got a strikeout.

Arnold Palmer (b. Sept. 10, 1929): Golfer; winner of 4 Masters, 2 British Opens and a U.S. Open; 2-time PGA Player of Year (1960,62); 1st player to earn over $1 million in career (1968); annual PGA Tour money leader award named after him; entered 1995 with 60 wins on PGA Tour and 10 more on Senior Tour.

Jim Palmer (b. Oct. 15, 1945): Baseball RHP; 3-time Cy Young Award winner (1973,75-76); won 20 or more games 8 times with Baltimore; 1991 comeback attempt at age 45 scrubbed in spring training.

Bill Parcells (b. Aug. 22, 1941): Football; coached NY Giants to 2 Super Bowl titles (1986,90); retired after 1990 season then returned in '93 as coach of New England; entered 1995 season with 10-year record of 100-70-1.

Jack Pardee (b. Apr. 19, 1936): Football; All-America linebacker at Texas A&M; 2-time All-Pro with LA Rams (1963) and Washington (1971); 2-time NFL Coach of Year (1976,79) and winner of 87 games in 11 seasons; only man hired as head coach in NFL, WFL, USFL and CFL; also coached at University of Houston.

Bernie Parent (b. Apr. 3, 1945): Hockey G; led Philadelphia Flyers to 2 Stanley Cups as playoff MVP (1974,75); 2-time Vezina Trophy winner; posted 55 career shutouts and 2.55 GAA in 13 seasons.

Joe Paterno (b. Dec. 21, 1926): Football; has coached Penn State to 2 national titles (1982,86) and 16-8-1 bowl record in 29 years; also had three unbeaten teams that didn't finish No. 1; Coach of Year 4 times (1968,78,82,86); entered 1995 season leading all active Div. I-A coaches with 269 wins (including bowls).

Craig Patrick (b. May 20, 1946): Hockey; 3rd generation Patrick to have name inscribed on Stanley Cup; GM of 2-time Cup champion Pittsburgh Penguins (1991-92); also captain of 1969 NCAA champion at Denver; assistant coach-GM of 1980 gold medal-winning U.S. Olympic team; scored 72 goals in 8 NHL seasons and won 69 games in 3 years as coach; grandson of Lester.

Lester Patrick (b. Dec. 30, 1883, d. June 1, 1960): Hockey; pro hockey pioneer as player, coach and general manager for 43 years; led NY Rangers to Stanley Cups as coach (1928,33) and GM (1940); grandfather of Craig.

Floyd Patterson (b. Jan. 4, 1935): Boxer; Olympic middleweight champ in 1952; world heavyweight champion (1956-59,60-62); 1st to regain heavyweight crown; fought Ingemar Johansson 3 times in 22 months from 1959-61 and won last two; pro record 55-8-1 with 40 KOs; jr. lightweight champion Tracy Harris Patterson is his adopted son.

Walter Payton (b. July 25, 1954): Football RB; NFL's all-time leading rusher with 16,726 yards; scored 109 career TDs; All-Pro 7 times with Chicago; MVP in 1977; led Bears to Super Bowl title in Jan. 1986.

Pelé (b. Oct. 23, 1940): Brazilian soccer F; given name— Edson Arantes do Nascimento; led Brazil to 3 World Cup titles (1958,62,70); came to U.S. in 1975 to play for NY Cosmos in NASL; scored 1,281 goals in 22 years; currently Brazil's minister of sport.

Roger Penske (b. Feb. 20, 1937): Auto racing; national sports car driving champion (1964); established racing team in 1961; co-founder of Championship Auto Racing Teams (CART); Penske Racing entered 1995 with a record 91 IndyCar victories, including 10 Indianapolis 500s and 9 IndyCar points titles; shocked racing world by failing to qualify car for 1995 Indy 500.

Willie Pep (b. Sept. 19, 1922): Boxer; 2-time world featherweight champion (1942-48,49-50); pro record 230-11-1 with 65 KOs.

Fred Perry (b. May 18, 1909, d. Feb. 2, 1995): British tennis player; 3-time Wimbledon champ (1934-36); fist player to win all four Grand Slam singles titles, though not simultaneously; last native to win All-England men's title.

Gaylord Perry (b. Sept. 15, 1938): Baseball RHP; only pitcher to win a Cy Young Award in both leagues; retired in 1983 with 314 wins and 3,534 strikeouts over 22 years and with 8 teams; brother Jim won 215 games for family total of 529.

Bob Pettit (b. Dec. 12, 1932): Basketball F; All-NBA 1st team 10 times (1955-64); 2-time MVP (1956,59) with St. Louis Hawks; first player to score 20,000 points.

Richard Petty (b. July 2, 1937): Auto racer; 7-time winner of Daytona 500; 7-time NASCAR national champ (1964,67,71-72,74-75,79); first stock car driver to win $1 million in career; all-time NASCAR leader in races won (200), poles (127) and wins in a single season (27 in 1967); retired after 1992 season; son of Lee (54 career wins) and father of Kyle (7 wins entering 1995).

Laffit Pincay Jr. (b. Dec. 29, 1946): Jockey; 5-time Eclipse Award winner (1971,73-74,79,85); winner of 3 Belmonts and 1 Kentucky Derby (aboard Swale in 1984); entered 1995 with 8,217 career wins, trailing only Bill Shoemaker's 8,833.

Nelson Piquet (b. Aug. 17, 1952): Brazilian auto racer; 3-time Formula One world champion (1981,83, 87); left circuit in 1991 with 23 career wins.

Jacques Plante (b. Jan. 17, 1929, d. Feb. 27, 1986): Hockey G; led Montreal to 6 Stanley Cups (1953,56-60); won 7 Vezina Trophies; MVP in 1962; first goalie to regularly wear a mask; posted 82 shutouts with 2.38 GAA.

Gary Player (b. Nov. 1, 1936): South African golfer; 3-time winner of Masters and British Open; only player in 20th century to win British Open in three different decades (1959,68,74); one of only four players to win all four Grand Slam titles (others are Hogan, Nicklaus and Sarazen); has also won 2 PGAs, a U.S. Open and 2 U.S. Senior Opens; entered 1995 with 21 wins on PGA Tour and 17 more on Senior Tour.

Jim Plunkett (b. Dec. 5, 1947): Football QB; Heisman Trophy winner in 1970; AFL Rookie of the Year in 1971; led Oakland-LA Raiders to Super Bowl wins in 1981 and '84; MVP in '81.

Maurice Podoloff (b. Aug. 18, 1890, d. Nov. 24, 1985): Basketball; engineered merger of Basketball Assn. of America and National Basketball League into NBA in 1949; NBA commissioner (1949-63); league MVP trophy named after him.

Fritz Pollard (b. Jan. 27, 1894, d. May 11, 1986): Football; 1st black All-America RB (1916 at Brown); 1st black to play in Rose Bowl; 7-year NFL pro (1920-26); 1st black NFL coach, at Milwaukee and Hammond, Ind.

Sam Pollock (b. Dec. 15, 1925): Hockey GM; managed NHL Montreal Canadiens to 9 Stanley Cups in 14 years (1965-78).

Denis Potvin (b. Oct. 29, 1953): Hockey D; won Norris Trophy 3 times (1976,78-79); 5-time All-NHL 1st-team; led NY Islanders to 4 Stanley Cups.

Mike Powell (b. Nov. 10, 1963): Track & Field; broke Bob Beamon's 23-year-old long jump world record by 2 inches with leap of 29-ft., 4½ in. at the 1991 World Championships; Sullivan Award winner (1991); won long jump silver medals in 1988 and '92 Olympics; repeated as world champ in 1993.

Steve Prefontaine (b. Jan. 25, 1951, d. June 1, 1975): Track & Field; All-America distance runner at Oregon; first athlete to win same event at NCAA championships 4 straight years (5,000 meters from 1970-73); finished 4th in 5,000 at 1972 Munich Olympics; first athlete to endorse Nike running shoes; killed in a one-car accident.

Nick Price (b. Jan. 28, 1957): Zimbabwean golfer; PGA Tour Player of Year in 1993 and '94; became 1st player since Nick Faldo in 1990 to win 2 Grand Slam titles in same year when he took British Open and PGA Championship in 1994; also won PGA in '92.

Alain Prost (b. Feb. 24, 1955): French auto racer; 4-time Formula One world champion (1985-86,89,93); sat out 1992 then returned to win 4th title in 1993; retired after '93 season as all-time F1 wins leader with 51.

Kirby Puckett (b. Mar. 14, 1961): Baseball OF; led Minnesota Twins to World Series titles in 1987 and '91; entered 1995 season with a batting title (1989), 2,135 hits and a .318 career average in 11 seasons.

C.C. Pyle (b. 1882, d. Feb. 3, 1939): Promoter; known as "Cash and Carry"; hyped Red Grange's pro football debut by arranging 1925 barnstorming tour with Chicago Bears; had Grange bolt NFL for new AFL in 1926 (AFL folded in '27); also staged 2 Transcontinental Races (1928-29), known as "Bunion Derbies."

Bobby Rahal (b. Jan. 10, 1953): Auto racer; 3-time PPG Cup champ (1986,87,92); entered 1995 with 24 career IndyCar wins, including 1986 Indy 500.

Jack Ramsay (b. Feb. 21, 1925): Basketball; coach who won 239 college games with St. Joseph's-PA in 11 seasons and 906 NBA games (including playoffs) with 4 teams over 21 years; placed 3rd in 1961 Final Four; led Portland to NBA title in 1977.

Bill Rassmussen (b. Oct. 15, 1932): Radio-TV; unemployed radio broadcaster who founded ESPN, the nation's first 24-hour all-sports cable-TV network, in 1978; bought out by Getty Oil in 1981.

Willis Reed (b. June 25, 1942): Basketball C; led NY Knicks to NBA titles in 1970 and '73, playoff MVP both years; regular season MVP 1970.

Mary Lou Retton (b. Jan. 24, 1968): Gymnast; won gold medal in women's All-Around at the 1984 Olympics, also won 2 silvers and 2 bronzes.

Butch Reynolds (b. June 8, 1964): Track & Field; set current world record in 400 meters (43.29) in 1988; banned for 2½ years for allegedly failing drug test in 1990; sued IAAF and won $27.4 million judgment in 1992, but award was voided in '94; won silver medal in 400 meters and gold as member of U.S. 4x400-meter relay team at both 1993 and '95 World Championships.

Grantland Rice (b. Nov. 1, 1880, d. July 13, 1954): First celebrated American sportswriter; chronicled the Golden Age of Sport in 1920s; immortalized Notre Dame's "Four Horsemen."

Jerry Rice (b. Oct. 13, 1962): Football WR; 2-time Div. I-AA All-America at Mississippi Valley St. (1983-84); 7-time All-Pro; regular season MVP in 1987 and Super Bowl MVP in 1989 with San Francisco; entered 1995 season as NFL all-time leader in touchdowns with 139; his 820 career receptions trail only Art Monk's 934.

Henri Richard (b. Feb. 29, 1936): Hockey C; leap year baby who played on more Stanley Cup championship teams (11) than anybody else; at 5-foot-7, known as the "Pocket Rocket"; brother of Maurice.

Maurice Richard (b. Aug. 4, 1921): Hockey RW; the "Rocket"; 8-time NHL 1st team All-Star; MVP in 1947; 1st to score 50 goals in one season (1945); 544 career goals; played on 8 Stanley Cup winners in Montreal.

Bob Richards (b. Feb. 2, 1926): Track & Field; pole vaulter, ordained minister and original Wheaties pitchman, who won gold medals at 1952 and '56 Olympics; remains only 2-time Olympic pole vault champ.

Nolan Richardson (b. Dec. 27, 1941): Basketball; coached Arkansas to consecutive NCAA finals, beating Duke in 1994 and losing to UCLA in '95; entered 1995-96 season with career record of 371-119 in 15 years.

Tex Rickard (b. Jan. 2, 1870, d. Jan. 6, 1929): Promoter who handled boxing's first $1 million gate (Dempsey vs. Carpentier in 1921); built Madison Square Garden in 1925; founded NY Rangers as Garden tenant in 1926 and named NHL team after himself (Tex's Rangers); also built Boston Garden in 1928.

Eddie Rickenbacker (b. Oct. 8, 1890, d. July 23, 1973): Mechanic and auto racer; became America's top flying ace (22 kills) in World War I; owned Indianapolis Speedway (1927-45) and ran Eastern Air Lines (1938-59).

Branch Rickey (b. Dec. 20, 1881, d. Dec. 9, 1965): Baseball innovator; revolutionized game with creation of modern farm system while general manager of St. Louis Cardinals (1917-42); integrated Major Leagues in 1947 as president-GM of Brooklyn Dodgers when he brought up Jackie Robinson (whom he had signed on Oct. 23, 1945); later GM of Pittsburgh Pirates.

Leni Riefenstahl (b. Aug. 22, 1902): German filmmaker of 1930's; directed classic sports documentary "Olympia" on 1936 Berlin Summer Olympics; infamous, however, for also making 1934 Hitler propaganda film "Triumph of the Will."

Roy Riegels (b. Apr. 4, 1908, d. Mar. 26, 1993): Football; California center who picked up fumble in 2nd quarter of 1929 Rose Bowl and raced 70 yards in the wrong direction to set up a 2-point safety in 8-7 loss to Georgia Tech.

Bobby Riggs (b. Feb. 25, 1918): Tennis; won Wimbledon once (1939) and U.S. title twice (1939,41) before turning pro in 1941; legendary hustler who made his biggest score in 1973 as 55-year-old male chauvinist challenging the best women players; beat No. 1 Margaret Smith Court 6-2, 6-1, but was thrashed by No. 2 Billie Jean King, 6-4, 6-3, 6-3 in nationally-televised "Battle of the Sexes" on Sept. 20, before 30,492 at the Astrodome.

Pat Riley (b. Mar. 20, 1945): Basketball; coached LA Lakers to 4 of their 5 NBA titles in 1980s (1982,85,87-88); coached New York from 1991-95; 2-time Coach of Year (1990,93) and all-time NBA leader in playoff wins (137); quit Knicks after 1994-95 season with year left on contract; signed with Miami Heat on Sept. 2 as coach, team president and part-owner after Knicks agreed to drop tampering charges in exchange for $1 million and a conditional first round draft pick.

Cal Ripken Jr. (b. Aug. 24, 1960): Baseball SS; broke Lou Gehrig's major league Iron Man record of 2,130 consecutive games played on Sept. 6, 1995; record streak began on May 30, 1982; 2-time AL MVP (1983,91) for Baltimore; AL starting SS in All-Star Game since 1984; entered 1995 season with 310 HRs in 14 seasons, the most ever by a shortstop.

Joe Robbie (b. July 7, 1916, d. Jan. 7, 1990): Football; original owner of Miami Dolphins (1966-90); won 2 Super Bowls (1972-73); built $115-million Robbie Stadium with private funds in 1987.

Oscar Robertson (b. Nov. 24, 1938): Basketball G; 3-time college Player of Year (1958-60) at Cincinnati; led 1960 U.S. Olympic team to gold medal; NBA Rookie of Year (1961); 9-time All-NBA 1st team; MVP in 1964 with Cincinnati Royals; NBA champion in 1971 with Milwaukee Bucks; 3rd in career assists with 9,887.

Paul Robeson (b. Apr. 8, 1898, d. Jan. 23, 1976): Black 4-sport star and 2-time football All-America (1917-18) at Rutgers; 3-year NFL pro; also scholar, lawyer, singer, actor and political activist; long-tainted by Communist sympathies, he was finally inducted into College Football Hall of Fame in 1995.

Brooks Robinson (b. May 18, 1937): Baseball 3B; led AL in fielding 12 times from 1960-72 with Baltimore; regular season MVP in 1964; World Series MVP in 1970.

David Robinson (b. Aug. 6, 1965): Basketball C; college Player of Year at Navy in 1987; overall 1st pick by San Antonio in 1987 NBA draft; served in military from 1987-89; NBA Rookie of Year in 1990 and regular season MVP in '95; 2-time All-NBA 1st team (1991,92); led NBA in scoring in 1994; member of 1988, '92 and '96 U.S. Olympic teams.

Eddie Robinson (b. Feb. 13, 1919): Football; head coach at Div. I-AA Grambling State for 52 years; winningest coach in college history; has led Tigers to 8 national black college titles; entered 1995 season with career record of 397-143-15.

Frank Robinson (b. Aug. 31, 1935): Baseball OF; won MVP in NL (1961) and AL (1966); Triple Crown winner and World Series MVP in 1966 with Baltimore; 1st black manager in Major Leagues with Cleveland in 1975; also managed in SF and Baltimore.

Jackie Robinson (b. Jan. 31, 1919, d. Oct. 24, 1972): Baseball 1B-2B-3B; 4-sport athlete at UCLA; hit .387 with K.C. Monarchs of Negro Leagues in 1945; signed by Brooklyn Dodgers on Oct. 23, 1945 and broke Major League baseball's color line in 1947; Rookie of Year in 1947 and NL's MVP in '49; hit .311 over 10 seasons.

Sugar Ray Robinson (b. May 3, 1921, d. Apr. 12, 1989): Boxer; world welterweight champion (1946-51); 5-time middleweight champ; retired at age 45 after 25 years in the ring; pro record 174-19-6 with 109 KOs.

Knute Rockne (b. Mar. 4, 1888, d. Mar. 31, 1931): Football; coached Notre Dame to 3 consensus national titles (1924,29,30), all-time winningest college coach (.881) with record of 105-12-5 over 13 seasons; killed in plane crash.

Bill Rodgers (b. Dec. 23, 1947): Distance runner; won Boston and New York City marathons 4 times each from 1975-80.

Irina Rodnina (b. Sept. 12, 1949): Soviet figure skater; won 10 world championships and 3 Olympic gold medals in pairs competition from 1971-80.

Diann Roffe-Steinrotter (b. Mar. 24, 1967): Alpine skier; 2-time Olympic medalist in Super-G; won silver at Albertville in 1992, then gold at Lillehammer in '94.

Art Rooney (b. Jan. 27, 1901, d. Aug. 25, 1988): Race track legend and pro football pioneer; bought Pittsburgh Steelers franchise in 1933 for $2,500; finally won NFL title with 1st of 4 Super Bowls in 1974 season.

Theodore Roosevelt (b. Oct. 27, 1858, d. Jan. 6, 1919): 26th President of the U.S.; physical fitness buff who boxed as undergraduate at Harvard; credited with presidential assist in forming of Intercollegiate Athletic Assn. (now NCAA) in 1905-06.

Mauri Rose (b. May 26, 1906, d. Jan. 1, 1981): Auto racer; 3-time winner of Indy 500 (1941,47-48).

Murray Rose (b. Jan. 6, 1939): Australian swimmer; won 3 gold medals at 1956 Olympics; added a gold, silver and bronze in 1960.

Pete Rose (b. Apr. 14, 1941): Baseball OF-IF; all-time hits leader with 4,256; led NL in batting 3 times; regular-season MVP in 1973; World Series MVP in 1975; had 44-game hitting streak in '78; managed Cincinnati (1984-89); banned for life in 1989 for conduct detrimental to baseball; convicted of tax evasion in 1990 and sentenced to 5 months in prison; released Jan. 7, 1991.

Ken Rosewall (b. Nov. 2, 1934): Tennis; won French and Australian singles titles at age 18; U.S. champ twice, but never won Wimbledon.

Mark Roth (b. Apr. 10, 1951): Bowler; 4-time PBA Player of Year (1977-79,84); entered 1995 with 33 tournament wins; victory in Apr. 15, 1995 Foresters Open was first in 7 year; U.S. Open champ in 1984.

Alan Rothenberg (b. Apr. 10, 1939): Soccer; president of U.S. Soccer since 1990; surprised European skeptics by directing hugely successful 1994 World Cup tournament; faces challenge of getting oft-delayed outdoor Major League Soccer off ground in 1996.

Patrick Roy (b. Oct. 5, 1965): Hockey G; led Montreal to 2 Stanley Cup titles; playoff MVP as rookie in 1986 and again in '93; has won Vezina Trophy 3 times (1989-90,92).

Pete Rozelle (b. Mar. 1, 1926): Football; NFL Commissioner from 1960-89; presided over growth of league from 12 to 28 teams, merger with AFL, creation of Super Bowl and advent of huge TV rights fees.

Wilma Rudolph (b. June 23, 1940, d. Nov. 12, 1994): Track & Field; won 3 gold medals (100m, 200m and 4x400m relay) at 1960 Olympics; also won relay silver in '56 Games; 2-time AP Athlete of Year (1960-61) and Sullivan Award winner in 1961.

Damon Runyon (b. Oct. 4, 1884, d. Dec. 10, 1946): Kansas native who gained fame as New York journalist, sports columnist and short-story writer; best known for 1932 story collection, "Guys and Dolls."

Adolph Rupp (b. Sept. 2, 1901, d. Dec. 10, 1977): Basketball; all-time Div. I college wins leader with 876; coached Kentucky to 4 NCAA championships (1948-49,51,58) and an NIT title (1946).

Bill Russell (b. Feb. 12, 1934): Basketball C; won titles in college, Olympics and pros; 5-time NBA MVP; led Boston to 11 titles from 1957-69; also became first big league black head coach in 1966.

Babe Ruth (b. Feb. 6, 1895, d. Aug. 16, 1948): Baseball LHP-OF; 2-time 20-game winner with Boston Red Sox (1916-17); had a 94-46 regular season record with a 2.28 ERA, while he was 3-0 in the World Series with an ERA of 0.87; sold to NY Yankees for $100,000 in 1920; AL MVP in 1923; led AL in slugging average 13 times, HRs 12 times, RBI 6 times and batting once (.378 in 1924); hit 60 HRs in 1927 and 50 or more 3 other times; ended career with Boston Braves in 1935 with 714 HRs, 2,211 RBI and a batting average of .342; remains all-time leader in times walked (2,056) and slugging average (.690).

Johnny Rutherford (b. Mar. 12, 1938): Auto racer; 3-time winner of Indy 500 (1974,76,80); CART national champion in 1980.

Nolan Ryan (b. Jan. 31, 1947): Baseball RHP; author of record 7 no-hitters against Kansas City and Detroit (1973), Minnesota (1974), Baltimore (1975), LA Dodgers (1981), Oakland A's (1990) and Toronto (1991 at age 44); 2-time 20-game winner (1973-74); 2-time NL leader in ERA (1981,87); led AL in strikeouts 9 times and NL twice in 27 years; retired after 1993 season with 324 wins, 292 losses and all-time records for strikeouts (5,714) and walks (2,795); never won Cy Young Award.

Samuel Ryder (b. Mar. 24, 1858, d. Jan. 2, 1936): Golf; English seed merchant who donated the Ryder Cup in 1927 for competition between pro golfers from Great Britain and the U.S.; made his fortune by coming up with idea of selling seeds to public in small packages.

Toni Sailer (b. Nov. 17, 1935): Austrian skier; 1st to win 3 alpine gold medals in Winter Olympics— taking downhill, slalom and giant slalom events in 1956.

Juan Antonio Samaranch (b. July 17, 1920): Native of Barcelona, Spain; president of International Olympic Committee since 1980; reelection likely in 1996 given IOC's move in '95 to bump membership age limit to 80.

Pete Sampras (b. Aug. 12, 1971): Tennis; No.1 player in world in 1993 and '94; overtaken as No. 1 in 1995 by friend and arch-rival Andre Agassi; youngest ever U.S. Open men's champion (19 years, 28 days) in 1990; won Wimbledon and U.S. Open titles in 1993; Australian Open and Wimbledon in '94, and Wimbledon and U.S. Open in '95; won 5-set doubles match with John McEnroe to help win 1992 Davis Cup final.

Joan Benoit Samuelson (b. May 16, 1957): Distance runner; has won Boston Marathon twice (1979,83); won first women's Olympic marathon in 1984 Games at Los Angeles; Sullivan Award recipient in 1985.

Arantxa Sanchez Vicario (b. Dec. 18, 1971): Spanish tennis player; entered 1995 season with 20 tour victories, including 1989 French Open; won both French and U.S. Opens in 1994 and was finalist in three of four Slam finals in '95; teamed with Conchita Martinez to win 3 of 4 Federation Cups from 1991-94.

Earl Sande (b. Nov. 13, 1898, d. Aug. 19, 1968): Jockey; rode Gallant Fox to Triple Crown in 1930; won 5 Belmonts and 3 Kentucky Derbys.

Barry Sanders (b. July 16, 1968): Football RB; won 1988 Heisman Trophy as junior at Oklahoma St.; all-time NCAA single season leader in rushing (2,628 yards), scoring (234 points) and TDs (39); 2-time NFL rushing leader with Detroit (1990,94); NFC Rookie of Year (1988); 2-time NFL Player of Year (1991,94); NFC MVP (1994).

Deion Sanders (b. Aug. 9, 1967): Baseball OF and Football DB-KR; 2-time All-America at Florida St. in football (1987-88); 4-time NFL All-Pro with Atlanta and San Francisco (1991-94); led Major Leagues in triples (14) with Atlanta in 1992 and hit .533 in World Series the same year; signed with San Francisco 49ers as free agent in 1994 and helped Niners win Super Bowl XXIX; only athlete to play in both World Series and Super Bowl; traded from Cincinnati to S.F. Giants on July 21, 1995 and signed a 7-year, $35 million deal with Dallas Cowboys on Sept. 9.

Abe Saperstein (b. July 4, 1901, d. Mar. 15, 1966): Basketball; founded all-black, Harlem Globetrotters barnstorming team in 1927; coached sharpshooting comedians to 1940 world pro title in Chicago and established troupe as game's foremost goodwill ambassadors; also served as 1st commissioner of American Basketball League (1961-62).

Gene Sarazen (b. Feb. 27, 1902): Golfer; one of only four players to win all four Grand Slam titles (others are Hogan, Nicklaus and Player); won Masters, British Open, 2 U.S. Opens and 3 PGA titles between 1922-35; invented sand wedge in 1930.

Glen Sather (b. Sept. 2, 1943): Hockey; GM-coach of 4 Stanley Cup winners in Edmonton (1984-85,87-88) and GM-only for another in 1990; ranks 6th on all-time NHL list with 553 wins (including playoffs).

Terry Sawchuk (b. Dec. 28, 1929, d. May 31, 1970): Hockey G; recorded 103 shutouts in 21 NHL seasons; 4-time Vezina Trophy winner; played on 4 Stanley Cup winners at Detroit and Toronto; posted career 2.52 GAA.

Gale Sayers (b. May 30, 1943): Football HB; 2-time All-America at Kansas; NFL Rookie of Year (1965) and 5-time All-Pro with Chicago; scored then-record 22 TDs in rookie year.

Chris Schenkel (b. Aug. 21, 1923): Radio-TV; 4-time Sportscaster of Year; easy-going baritone who has covered basketball, bowling, football, golf and the Olympics for ABC and CBS; host of ABC's Pro Bowlers Tour for 33 years; received lifetime achievement Emmy Award in 1993.

Vitaly Scherbo (b. Jan. 13, 1972): Russian gymnast; winner of unprecedented 6 gold medals in gymnastics, including men's All-Around, for Unified Team in 1992 Olympics.

Mike Schmidt (b. Sept. 27, 1949): Baseball 3B; led NL in HRs 8 times; 3-time MVP (1980,81,86) with Philadelphia; 548 career HRs and 10 gold gloves; inducted into Hall of Fame in 1995.

Don Schollander (b. Apr. 30, 1946): Swimming; won 4 gold medals at 1964 Olympics, plus one gold and one silver in 1968; won Sullivan Award in 1964.

Dick Schultz (b. Sept. 5, 1929): Reform-minded executive director of NCAA from 1988-93; announced resignation on May 11, 1993, in wake of special investigator's report citing Univ. of Virginia with improper student-athlete loan program during Schultz's tenure as athletic director (1981-87); named executive director of the USOC on June 23, 1995.

Michael Schumacher (b. Jan. 3, 1969): Auto racer; entered 1995 with 10 career Formula One wins; world champion in 1994 with 9 victories, continued dominance in '95 with 6 more wins as of Sept. 15.

Bob Seagren (b. Oct. 17, 1946): Track & Field; won gold medal in pole vault at 1968 Olympics; broke world outdoor record 5 times.

Tom Seaver (b. Nov. 17, 1944): Baseball RHP; won 3 Cy Young Awards (1969,73,75); had 311 wins, 3,640 strikeouts and 2.86 ERA over 20 years.

George Seifert (b. Jan. 22, 1940): Football; coached San Francisco to a record 17 wins in his 1st season as head coach in 1989; guided 49ers to Super Bowl-winning seasons in 1989 and '94; entered 1995 season as NFL's winningest coach ever with 84-24 record and .778 winning pct.

Peter Seitz (b. May 17, 1905, d. Oct. 17, 1983): Baseball arbitrator; ruled on Dec. 23, 1975 that players who perform for one season without a signed contract can become free agents; decision ushered in big money era for players.

Monica Seles (b. Dec. 2, 1973): Yugoslav tennis player; No.1 in the world in 1991 and '92 after winning Australian, French and U.S. Opens both years; 3-time winner of both Australian and French; youngest to win Grand Slam title this century when she won French at age 16 in 1990; winner of 30 singles titles in just 5 years before she was stabbed in the back by Steffi Graf fan Gunter Parche on Apr. 30, 1993 during match in Hamburg, Germany; spent remainder of 1993, all of '94 and most of '95 recovering; returned to WTA Tour with win at the Canadian Open on Aug. 20, 1995; reached U.S. Open final before losing to Graf in 3 sets.

Bud Selig (b. July 30, 1934): Baseball; Milwaukee car dealer who bought the Seattle Pilots for $10.8 million in 1970 and moved team to Midwest; chairman of owners' executive council and de facto commissioner since he and colleagues forced Fay Vincent to resign on Sept. 7, 1992; presided over 232-day players' strike that resulted in cancellation of World Series for first time since 1904 and delayed opening of 1995 season until Apr. 25.

Frank Selke (b. May 7, 1893, d. July 3, 1985): Hockey; GM of 6 Stanley Cup champions in Montreal (1953,56-60).

Ayrton Senna (b. Mar. 21, 1960, d. May 1, 1994): Brazilian auto racer; 3-time Formula One champion (1988,90-91); entered 1994 season as all-time F1 leader in poles (62) and 2nd in wins (41); killed in crash at Imola, Italy during '94 San Marino Grand Prix.

Wilbur Shaw (b. Oct. 13, 1902, d. Oct. 30, 1954): Auto racer; 3-time winner and 3-time runner-up of Indy 500 from 1933-1940.

Patty Sheehan (b. Oct. 27, 1956): Golfer; LPGA Player of Year in 1983; clinched entry into LPGA Hall of Fame with 30th career win in 1993; entered 1995 season with 3 LPGA titles (1983-84,93) and 2 U.S. Opens (1992, 94).

Bill Shoemaker (b. Aug. 19, 1931): Jockey; all-time career wins leader with 8,833; 3-time Eclipse Award winner as Jockey (1981) and special award recipient (1976,81); won Belmont 5 times, Kentucky Derby 4 times and Preakness twice; oldest jockey to win Kentucky Derby (age 54, aboard Ferdinand in 1986); retired in 1990 to become trainer; paralyzed in 1991 auto accident but continues to train horses.

Eddie Shore (b. Nov. 25, 1902, d. Mar. 16, 1985): Hockey D; only NHL defenseman to win Hart Trophy as MVP 4 times (1933,35-36,38); led Boston Bruins to Stanley Cup titles in 1929 and '39; had 105 goals and 1,047 penalty mins in 14 seasons.

Frank Shorter (b. Oct. 31, 1947): Track & Field; won gold medal in marathon at 1972 Olympics, 1st American to win in 64 years.

Don Shula (b. Jan. 4, 1930): Football; one of only two NFL coaches with 300 wins (George Halas is the other); has taken 6 teams to Super Bowls and won twice with Miami (1973-74); 4-time Coach of Year, twice with Baltimore (1964,68) and twice with Miami (1970-71); entered 1995 season with NFL-record 338 career wins (including playoffs) and a winning percentage of .670; father of Cincinnati head coach David, who entered 1995 with 3-year record of 11-37.

Al Simmons (b. May 22, 1902, d. May 26, 1956): Baseball OF; led AL in batting twice (1930-31) and knocked in 100 runs or more 11 straight years (1924-34).

O.J. Simpson (b. July 9, 1947): Football RB; won Heisman Trophy in 1968 at USC; ran for 2,003 yards in NFL in 1973; All-Pro 5 times; MVP in 1973; rushed for 11,236 career yards; TV analyst and actor after career ended; arrested June 17, 1994 and held without bail as only suspect in double murder of ex-wife Nicole Brown Simpson and her friend Ronald Goldman; trial began on Jan. 24, 1995.

George Sisler (b. Mar. 24, 1893, d. Mar. 26, 1973): Baseball 1B; hit over .400 twice (1920,22); 257 hits in 1920 still a major league record.

Mary Decker Slaney (b. Aug. 4, 1958): U.S. middle distance runner; has held 7 separate American track & field records from the 800 to 10,000 meters; won both 1,500 and 3,000 meters at 1983 World Championships in Helsinki, but no Olympic medals.

Raisa Smetanina (b. Feb. 29, 1952): Russian Nordic skier; all-time Winter Olympics medalist with 10 cross-country medals (4 gold, 5 silver and a bronze) in 5 appearances (1976,80,84,88,92) for USSR and Unified Team.

Billy Smith (b. Dec. 12, 1950): Hockey G; led NY Islanders to 4 consecutive Stanley Cups (1980-83); won Vezina Trophy in 1982; Stanley Cup MVP in 1983.

Dean Smith (b. Feb. 28, 1931): Basketball; has coached North Carolina to 25 NCAA tournaments in 34 years, reaching Final Four 10 times and winning championship twice (1982,93); coached U.S. Olympic team to gold medal in 1976; entered 1995-96 season with 830 wins, 2nd only to Adolph Rupp's 876 on all-time Div. I victory list with 830.

Emmitt Smith (b. May 15, 1969): Football RB; consensus All-America (1989) at Florida; 3-time NFL rushing leader (1991-93); 3-time All-Pro (1992-94); regular season and Super Bowl MVP in 1993; played on two Super Bowl champions (1992 and '93 seasons).

John Smith (b. Aug. 9, 1965): Wrestler; 2-time NCAA champion for Oklahoma St. at 134 lbs (1987-88) and Most Outstanding Wrestler of '88 championships; 3-time world champion; gold medal winner at 1988 and '92 Olympics at 137 lbs; only wrestler ever to win Sullivan Award (1990); coached Oklahoma St. to 1994 NCAA title and brother Pat was Most Outstanding Wrestler.

Lee Smith (b. Dec. 4, 1957): Baseball RHP; 3-time NL saves leader (1983,91-92); entered 1995 season as all-time major league saves leader with 434.

Ozzie Smith (b. Dec. 26, 1954): Baseball SS; won 13 straight gold gloves (1980-92); played in 12 straight All-Star Games (1981-92); MVP of 1985 NL playoffs; entered 1995 season with all-time assist record for shortstops with 8,084.

Walter (Red) Smith (b. Sept. 25, 1905, d. Jan. 15, 1982): Sportswriter for newspapers in Philadelphia and New York from 1936-82; won Pulitzer Prize for commentary in 1976.

Conn Smythe (b. Feb. 1, 1895, d. Nov. 18, 1980): Hockey pioneer; built Maple Leaf Gardens in 1931; managed Toronto to 7 Stanley Cups before retiring in 1961.

Sam Snead (b. May 27, 1912): Golfer; won both Masters and PGA 3 times and British Open once; runner-up in U.S. Open 4 times; PGA Player of Year in 1949; oldest player (52 years, 10 months) to win PGA event with Greater Greensboro Open title in 1965; all-time PGA Tour career victory leader with 81.

Peter Snell (b. Dec. 17, 1938): Track & Field; New Zealander who won gold medal in 800m at 1960 Olympics, then won both the 800m and 1,500m at 1964 Games.

Javier Sotomayor (b. Oct. 13, 1967): Cuban high jumper; first man to clear 8 feet (8-0) on July 29, 1989; won gold medal at 1992 Olympics with jump of only 7-ft, 8-in.; broke world record with leap of 8-0½ in 1993.

Warren Spahn (b. Apr. 23, 1921): Baseball LHP; led NL in wins 8 times; won 20 or more games 13 times; Cy Young winner in 1957; most career wins (363) by a left-hander.

Tris Speaker (b. Apr. 4, 1888, d. Dec. 8, 1958): Baseball OF; all-time leader in outfield assists (449) and doubles (793); had .344 career batting average and 3,515 hits.

J.G. Taylor Spink (b. Nov. 6, 1888, d. Dec. 7, 1962): Publisher of The Sporting News from 1914-62; Baseball Writers' Assn. annual meritorious service award named after him.

Mark Spitz (b. Feb. 10, 1950): Swimmer; set 23 world and 35 U.S. records; won all-time record 7 gold medals (4 individual, 3 relay) in 1972 Olympics; also won 4 medals (2 gold, a silver and a bronze) in 1968 Games for a total of 11; comeback attempt at age 41 foundered in 1991.

Amos Alonzo Stagg (Aug. 16, 1862, d. Mar. 17, 1965): Football innovator; coached at U. of Chicago for 41 seasons and College of the Pacific for 14 more; won 314 games; elected to both college football and basketball halls of fame.

Willie Stargell (b. Mar. 6, 1940): Baseball OF-1B; led NL in home runs twice (1971,73); 475 career HRs; regular-season and World Series MVP in 1979.

Bart Starr (b. Jan. 9, 1934): Football QB; led Green Bay to 5 NFL titles and 2 Super Bowl wins from 1961-67; regular season MVP in 1966; MVP of Super Bowls I and II.

Roger Staubach (b. Feb. 5, 1942): Football QB; Heisman Trophy winner as Navy junior in 1963; led Dallas to 2 Super Bowl titles (1972,78) and was Super Bowl MVP in 1972; 5-time leading passer in NFC (1971,73,77-79).

George Steinbrenner (b. July 4, 1930): Baseball; principal owner of NY Yankees since 1973; teams have won 4 pennants and 2 World Series (1977-78); has changed managers 18 times and GMs 10 times in 22 years; ordered by baseball commissioner Fay Vincent in 1990 to surrender control of club for dealings with small-time gambler; reinstated on Mar. 1, 1993; also serves as one of 3 VPs of U.S. Olympic Committee.

Casey Stengel (b. July 30, 1890, d. Sept. 29, 1975): Baseball; player for 14 years and manager for 25; outfielder and lifetime .284 hitter with 5 clubs (1912-25); guided NY Yankees to 10 AL pennants and 7 World Series titles from 1949-60; 1st NY Mets skipper from 1962-65.

Ingemar Stenmark (b. Mar. 18, 1956): Swedish alpine skier; 3-time World Cup overall champ (1976-78); posted 86 World Cup wins in 16 years; won 2 gold medals at 1980 Olympics.

Helen Stephens (b. Feb. 3, 1918, d. Jan. 17, 1994): Track & Field; set 3 world records in 100-yard dash and 4 more in 100 meters in 1935-36; won gold medals in 100 meters and 4x100-meter relay in 1936 Olympics; retired in 1937.

Woody Stephens (b. Sept. 1, 1913): Horse racing; trainer who saddled an unprecedented 5 straight winners in Belmont Stakes (1982-86); also had two Kentucky Derby winners (1974,84); trained 1982 Horse of Year Conquistador Cielo; won Eclipse award as nation's top trainer in 1983.

David Stern (b. Sept. 22, 1942): Basketball; marketing expert and NBA commissioner since 1984; took office the year Michael Jordan turned pro; has presided over stunning artistic and financial success of NBA both nationally and internationally, best demonstrated by reception of the Dream Team at 1992 Olympics; league has grown from 23 teams to 29 during his watch; received unprecedented 5-year, $27.5 million contract extension in 1990; imposed owners' lockout on July 1 when league and players union failed to agree on new contract; ended lockout on Sept. 18 when players voted down bid to decertify their union .

Teófilo Stevenson (b. Mar. 29, 1952): Cuban boxer; won 3 consecutive gold medals as Olympic heavyweight (1972,76,80); did not turn pro.

Jackie Stewart (b. June 11, 1939): Auto racer; won 27 Formula One races and 3 world driving titles from 1965-73.

Curtis Strange (b. Jan. 30, 1955): Golfer; won consecutive U.S. Open titles (1988-89); 3-time leading money winner on PGA Tour (1985,87-88); first PGA player to win $1 million in one year (1988).

Picabo Street (b. Apr. 3, 1971): Skiing; won silver in women's downhill at 1994 Winter Olympics; her '95 World Cup downhill series title first-ever by U.S. women.

Louise Suggs (b. Sept. 7, 1923): Golfer; won 11 Majors and 50 LPGA events overall from 1949-62.

James E. Sullivan (b. Nov. 18, 1862, d. Sept. 16, 1914): Track & Field; pioneer who founded Amateur Athletic Union (AAU) in 1888; director of St. Louis Olympic Games in 1904; AAU's annual Sullivan Award for performance and sportsmanship named after him.

John L. Sullivan (b. Oct. 15, 1858, d. Feb. 2, 1918): Boxer; world heavyweight champion (1882-92); last of bare-knuckle champions.

Pat Summitt (b. June 14, 1952): Basketball; women's basketball coach at Tennessee (1974—); 2nd all-time with 564 career victories; coached Lady Vols to 3 national championships (1987,89,91).

Barry Switzer (b. Oct. 5, 1937): Football; coached Oklahoma to 3 national titles (1974-75,85); 4th on all-time winningest list with 157-29-4 record and .837 win percentage; resigned in 1989 after OU was slapped with 3-year NCAA probation and 5 players were brought up on criminal charges; hired as Dallas Cowboys head coach on Mar. 30, 1994 and led Dallas to a 12-4 regular season record and an NFC Eastern Div. title.

Paul Tagliabue (b. Nov. 24, 1940): Football; NFL attorney who was elected league's 4th commissioner in 1989; ushered in salary cap in 1994; league expanded by 2 teams in 1995 for 1st time since '76; brought $300 million suit against Dallas owner Jerry Jones on Sept. 18, 1995 for Jones' rogue sponsorship deals with Pepsi and Nike.

Anatoli Tarasov (b. 1918, d. June 23, 1995): Hockey; coached Soviet Union to 9 straight world championships and 3 Olympic gold medals (1964,68,72).

Jerry Tarkanian (b. Aug. 30, 1930): Basketball; all-time winningest college coach with .837 winning pct.; had record of 625-122 in 24 years at Long Beach St. and UNLV; led UNLV to 4 Final Fours and one national title (1990); fought 16-year battle with NCAA over purity of UNLV program; quit as coach after going 26-2 in 1991-92; fired after 20 games (9-11) as coach of NBA San Antonio Spurs in 1992; left retirement on April 5, 1995 to coach his alma mater, Fresno St.

Fran Tarkenton (b. Feb. 3, 1940): Football QB; 2-time NFL All-Pro (1973,75); Player of Year (1975); threw for 47,003 yards and 342 TDs (both NFL records) in 18 seasons with Minnesota and NY Giants.

Chuck Taylor (b. June 24, 1901, d. June 23, 1969): Converse traveling salesman whose name came to grace the classic, high-top canvas basketball sneakers known as "Chucks"; over 500 million pairs have been sold since 1917; he also ran clinics worldwide and edited Converse Basketball Yearbook from 1922-68.

Lawrence Taylor (b. Feb. 4, 1959): Football LB; All-America at North Carolina (1980); only defensive player in NFL history to be consensus Player of Year (1986); led NY Giants to Super Bowl titles in 1986 and '90 seasons; played in a record 10 Pro Bowls (1981-90); retired after 1993 season with 132½ sacks.

Gustavo Thoeni (b. Feb. 28, 1951): Italian alpine skier; 4-time World Cup overall champion (1971-73,75); won giant slalom at 1972 Olympics.

Frank Thomas (b. May 27, 1968): Baseball 1B; All-America at Auburn in 1989; 2-time AL MVP with Chicago (1993,94); batting .353 with 38 HRs and 101 RBI when 1994 players' strike began on Aug. 12.

Isiah Thomas (b. Apr. 30, 1961): Basketball; led Indiana to NCAA title as sophomore and tourney MVP in 1981; consensus All-America guard in '81; led Detroit to 2 NBA titles in 1989 and '90; NBA Finals MVP in 1990; 3-time All-NBA 1st team (1984-86); retired in 1994 at age 33 after tearing right Achilles tendon; GM of expansion Toronto Raptors.

Thurman Thomas (b. May 16, 1966): Football RB; 3-time AFC rushing leader (1990-91,93); 2-time All-Pro (1990-91); NFL Player of Year (1991); led Buffalo to 4 straight Super Bowls (1991-94).

Daley Thompson (b. July 30, 1958): British Track & Field; won consecutive gold medals in decathlon at 1980 and '84 Olympics.

John Thompson (b. Sept. 2, 1941): Basketball; has coached centers Patrick Ewing, Alonzo Mourning and Dikembe Mutombo at Georgetown; reached NCAA tourney final 3 out of 4 years with Ewing, winning title in 1984; also led Hoyas to 6 Big East tourney titles; coached 1988 U.S. Olympic team to bronze medal; entered 1995-96 season with 524 wins in 23 years.

Bobby Thomson (b. Oct. 25, 1923): Baseball OF; career .270 hitter who won the 1951 NL pennant for the NY Giants with a 1-out, 3-run HR in the bottom of the 9th inning of Game 3 of a best-of-3 playoff with Brooklyn; the pitcher was Ralph Branca, the count was 0-1 and the Dodgers were ahead 4-2; the Giants had trailed Brooklyn by 13 games on Aug. 11th.

Jim Thorpe (b. May 28, 1888, d. May 28, 1953): 2-time All-America in football; won both pentathlon and decathlon at 1912 Olympics; stripped of medals a month later for playing semi-pro baseball prior to Games; medals restored in 1982; played major league baseball (1913-19) and pro football (1920-26,28); chosen "Athlete of the Half Century" by AP in 1950.

Bill Tilden (b. Feb. 10, 1893, d. June 5, 1953): Tennis; won 7 U.S. and 3 Wimbledon titles in 1920's; led U.S. to 7 straight Davis Cup victories (1920-26).

Tinker to Evers to Chance: Chicago Cubs double play combination from 1903-08; immortalized in poem by New York sportswriter Franklin P. Adams— SS Joe Tinker (1880-1948), 2B Johnny Evers (1883-1947) and 1B Frank Chance (1877-1924); all 3 managed the Cubs and made the Hall of Fame.

Y.A. Tittle (b. Oct. 24, 1926): Football QB; played 17 years in AFC and NFL; All-Pro 4 times; league MVP with San Francisco (1957) and NY Giants (1962); passed for 28,339 career yards.

Alberto Tomba (b. Dec. 19, 1966): Italian alpine skier; all-time Olympic medalist with 5 (3 gold, 2 silver); became 1st alpine skier to win gold medals in 2 consecutive Winter Games when he won the slalom and giant slalom in 1988 then repeated in the GS in '92; also won silvers in slalom in 1992 and '94; won 1st overall World Cup championship along with slalom and giant slalom titles in 1995.

Vladislav Tretiak (b. Apr. 25, 1952): Hockey G; led USSR to Olympic gold medals in 1972 and '76; starred for Soviets against Team Canada in 1972, and again in 2 Canada Cups (1976,81).

Lee Trevino (b. Dec. 1, 1939): Golfer; 2-time winner of 3 Majors— U.S. Open (1968,71), British Open (1971-72) and PGA (1974,84); Player of Year once on PGA Tour (1971) and 3 times with Seniors (1990,92,94); entered 1995 with 27 PGA Tour wins and 24 on Senior Tour; all-time money leader on combined tours ($8.6 million).

Bryan Trottier (b. July 17, 1956): Hockey C; led NY Islanders to 4 straight Stanley Cups (1980-83); Rookie of Year (1976); scoring champion (134 points) and regular season MVP in 1979; playoff MVP (1980); added 5th and 6th Cups with Pittsburgh in 1991 and '92.

Gene Tunney (b. May 25, 1897, d. Nov. 7, 1978): Boxer; world heavyweight champion from 1926-28; beat 31-year-old champ Jack Dempsey in unanimous 10 round decision in 1926; beat him again in famous "long count" rematch in '27; quit while still champion in 1928 with 65-1-1 record and 47 KOs.

Ted Turner (b. Nov. 19, 1938): Sportsman and TV mogul, skippered Courageous to America's Cup win in 1977; owner of both Atlanta Braves and Hawks; owner of superstation WTBS, and cable stations CNN and TNT; founder of Goodwill Games; 1991 Time Man of Year.

Mike Tyson (b. June 30, 1966): Boxer; youngest (age 19) to win heavyweight title (WBC in 1986); undisputed champ from 1987 until upset loss to 50-1 shot Buster Douglas on Feb. 10, 1990, in Tokyo; found guilty on Feb. 10, 1992, of raping 18-year-old Miss Black America contestant Desiree Washington in Indianapolis on July 19, 1991; sentenced to 6-year prison term; released May 9, 1995 after serving 3 years; made return to the ring on Aug. 19 with disqualification win over Peter McNeeley at 1:29 of 1st round; has grossed $96 million worldwide and improved his pro record to 42-1-0 with 36 KOs.

Wyomia Tyus (b. Aug. 29, 1945): Track & Field; 1st woman to win consecutive Olympic gold medals in 100m (1964-68).

Peter Ueberroth (b. Sept. 2, 1937): Organizer of 1984 Summer Olympics in LA; 1984 Time Man of Year; baseball commissioner from 1984-89; headed Rebuild Los Angeles for one year after 1992 riots.

Johnny Unitas (b. May 7, 1933): Football QB; led Baltimore Colts to 2 NFL titles (1958-59) and a Super Bowl win (1971); All-Pro 5 times; 3-time MVP (1959,64,67); passed for 40,239 career yards and 290 TDs.

Al Unser Jr. (b. Apr. 19, 1962): Auto racer; 2-time CART-IndyCar national champion (1990,94); captured Indy 500 for 2nd time in 3 years in '94, giving Unser family 9 overall titles at the Brickyard; entered 1995 with 27 IndyCar wins in 13 years; son of Al and nephew of Bobby.

Al Unser Sr. (b. May 29, 1939): Auto racer; 3-time USAC-CART national champion (1970,83,85); 4-time winner of Indy 500 (1970-71,78,87); retired in 1994 ranked 3rd on all-time IndyCar list with 39 wins; younger brother of Bobby and father of Little Al.

Bobby Unser (b. Feb. 20, 1934): Auto racer; 2-time USAC-CART national champion (1968,74); 3-time winner of Indy 500 (1968,75,81); retired after 1981 season; ranks 4th on all-time IndyCar list with 35 wins.

Gene Upshaw (b. Aug. 15, 1945): Football G; 2-time All-AFL and 3-time All-NFL selection with Oakland; helped lead Raiders to 2 Super Bowl titles in 1976 and '80 seasons; executive director of NFL Players Assn. since 1987; agreed to application of salary cap in 1994.

Norm Van Brocklin (b. Mar. 15, 1926, d. May 2, 1983): Football QB-P; led NFL in passing 3 times and punting twice; led LA Rams (1951) and Philadelphia (1960) to NFL titles; MVP in 1960.

Johnny Vander Meer (b. Nov. 2, 1914): Baseball LHP; only major leaguer to pitch consecutive no-hitters (June 11 & 15, 1938).

Harold S. Vanderbilt (b. July 6, 1884, d. July 4, 1970): Sportsman; successfully defended America's Cup 3 times (1930, 34,37); also invented contract bridge in 1926.

Glenna Collett Vare (b. June 20, 1903, d. Feb. 10, 1989): Golfer; won record 6 U.S. Women's Amateur titles from 1922-35; known as "the female Bobby Jones."

Andy Varipapa (b. Mar. 31, 1891, d. Aug. 25, 1984): Bowler; trick-shot artist; won consecutive All-Star match game titles (1947-48) at age 53.

Bill Veeck (b. Feb. 9, 1914, d. Jan. 2, 1986): Maverick baseball executive; owned AL teams in Cleveland, St. Louis and Chicago from 1946-80; introduced ballpark giveaways, exploding scoreboards, and midget Eddie Gaedel; won World Series with Indians (1948) and pennant with White Sox (1959).

Jacques Villeneuve (b. Apr. 9, 1971): Canadian auto racer; Indianapolis 500 runner-up and IndyCar Rookie of Year in 1994; won 500 and IndyCar driving championship in 1995; announced plans to jump to Formula One racing in 1996.

Fay Vincent (b. May 29, 1938): Baseball; became 8th commissioner after death of A. Bartlett Giamatti in 1989; presided over World Series earthquake, owners' lockout and banishment of NY Yankees owner George Steinbrenner in his first year on the job; contentious relationship with owners resulted in his resignation on Sept. 7, 1992, four days after 18-9 "no confidence" vote; office has been vacant since.

Lasse Viren (b. July 22, 1949): Finnish runner; won gold medals at 5,000 and 10,00 meters in 1972 Munich Olympics; repeated 5,000/10,000 double in 1976 Montreal Games but added a 5th place in the marathon.

Lanny Wadkins (b. Dec. 5, 1949): Golfer; member of 8 Ryder Cup teams and captain of 1995 team; entering 1995 had 21 PGA Tour wins.

Honus Wagner (b. Feb. 24, 1874, d. Dec. 6, 1955): Baseball SS; hit .300 for 17 consecutive seasons (1897-1913) with Pittsburgh; led NL in batting 8 times; ended career with 3,418 career hits, a .327 average and 722 stolen bases.

Lisa Wagner (b. May 19, 1961): Bowler; 3-time LPBT Player of Year (1983,88,93); 1980's Bowler of Decade; first woman bowler to earn $100,000 in a season; entered 1995 season with a record 28 pro titles.

Grete Waitz (b. Oct. 1, 1953): Norwegian runner; 9-time winner of New York City Marathon from 1978-88; won silver medal at 1984 Olympics.

Doak Walker (b. Jan. 1, 1927): Football HB; won Heisman Trophy as SMU junior in 1948; led Detroit to 2 NFL titles (1952-53); All-Pro 4 times in 6 years.

Herschel Walker (b. Mar. 3, 1962): Football RB; led Georgia to national title as freshman in 1980; won Heisman in 1982 then jumped to USFL in '83; signed by Dallas after USFL folded; led NFL in rushing in 1988; traded to Minnesota in 1989 for 5 players and 6 draft picks; has since played for Philadelphia and NY Giants.

Bill Walsh (b. Nov. 30, 1931): Football; coached San Francisco to 3 Super Bowl titles (1982,85,89); retired after 1989 Super Bowl with 102 wins in 10 seasons; returned to college coaching in 1992 for his second stint at Stanford; retired again after 1994 season; entering 1995 NFL season, six former Walsh assistants were head coaches.

Bill Walton (b. Nov. 5, 1952): Basketball C; 3-time college Player of Year (1972-74); led UCLA to 2 national titles (1972-73); led Portland to NBA title as MVP in 1977; regular season MVP in 1978.

Arch Ward (b. Dec. 27, 1896, d. July 9, 1955): Promoter and sports editor of Chicago Tribune from 1930-55; founder of baseball All-Star Game (1933), Chicago College All-Star Football Game (1934) and the All-America Football Conference (1946-49).

Charlie Ward (b. Oct. 12, 1970): Football QB and Basketball G; led Florida St. to national football championship in 1993; 1st Heisman Trophy winner to play for national champs since Tony Dorsett in 1976, won Sullivan Award same year; 3-year starter for FSU basketball team; not taken in NFL Draft; 1st round pick (26th overall) of NY Knicks in 1994 NBA draft.

Glenn (Pop) Warner (b. Apr. 5, 1871, d. Sept. 7, 1954): Football innovator; coached at 7 colleges over 49 years; 319 career wins 2nd only to Bear Bryant's 323 in Div. I-A; produced 47 All-Americas, including Jim Thorpe and Ernie Nevers.

Tom Watson (b. Sept. 4, 1949): Golfer; 6-time PGA Player of the Year (1977-80,82,84); has won 5 British Opens, 2 Masters and a U.S. Open; 4-time Ryder Cup member and captain of 1993 team; entered 1995 with 32 tour wins.

Dick Weber (b. Dec. 23, 1929): Bowler; 3-time PBA Bowler of the Year (1961,63,65); won 30 PBA titles in 4 decades.

Johnny Weissmuller (b. June 2, 1904, d. Jan. 20 1984): Swimmer; won 3 gold medals at 1924 Olympics and 2 more at 1928 Games; became Hollywood's most famous Tarzan.

Jerry West (b. May 28, 1938): Basketball G; 2-time All-America and NCAA tourney MVP (1959) at West Virginia; led 1960 U.S. Olympic team to gold medal; 10-time All-NBA 1st-team; NBA finals MVP (1969); led LA Lakers to NBA title once as player (1972) and 5 times as GM in 1980's; his silhouette serves as the NBA's logo.

Pernell Whitaker (b. Jan. 2, 1964): Boxer; won Olympic gold medal as lightweight in 1984; has won 4 world championships as lightweight, jr. welterweight, welterweight and jr. middleweight; outfought but failed to beat Julio Cesar Chavez when Sept. 10, 1993 welterweight title defense ended in controversial draw; entered 1995 with pro record of 34-1-1 and 15 KOs.

Bill White (b. Jan. 28, 1934): Baseball; NL president and highest ranking black executive in sports from 1989-94; as 1st baseman, won 7 gold gloves and hit .286 with 202 HRs in 13 seasons.

Byron (Whizzer) White (b. June 8, 1917): Football; All-America HB at Colorado (1935-37); signed with Pittsburgh in 1938 for the then largest contract in pro history ($15,800); took Rhodes scholarship in 1939; returned to NFL in 1940 to lead league in rushing and retired in 1941; named to U.S. Supreme Court by President Kennedy in 1962 and stepped down in 1993.

Reggie White (b. Dec. 19, 1961): Football DE; consensus All-America in 1983 at Tennessee; 7-time All-NFL (1986-92) with Philadelphia; signed as free agent with Green Bay in 1993 for $17 million over 4 years; entered 1995 season with an official NFL-record 145 sacks.

Kathy Whitworth (b. Sept. 27, 1939): Golf; 7-time LPGA Player of the Year (1966-69,71-73); won 6 Majors; 88 tour wins, most on LPGA or PGA tour.

Hazel Hotchkiss Wightman (b. Dec. 20, 1886, d. Dec. 5, 1974): Tennis; won 16 U.S. national titles; 4-time U.S. Women's champion (1909-11,19); donor of Wightman Cup.

Hoyt Wilhelm (b. July 26, 1923): Baseball RHP; Knuckleballer who is all-time leader in games pitched (1,070), games finished (651) and games won in relief (124); had career ERA of 2.52 and 227 saves; 1st relief pitcher inducted into Hall of Fame (1985); threw no-hitter vs. NY Yankees (1958); also hit lone HR of career in first major league at bat (1952).

Lenny Wilkens (b. Oct. 28, 1937): Basketball; MVP of 1960 NIT as Providence guard; played 15 years in NBA, including 4 as player-coach; MVP of 1971 All-Star Game; coached Seattle to NBA title in 1979; Coach of Year in 1994 with Atlanta; passed Red Auerbach as NBA's all-time winningest regular-season coach with his 939th victory on Jan. 6, 1995; entered 1995-96 season with 968 regular-season wins and 1,028 wins including playoffs (2nd only to Auerbach's 1,037).

Dominique Wilkins (b. Jan. 12, 1960): Basketball F; last player to lead NBA in scoring (1986) before Michael Jordan's reign; All-NBA 1st team in '86; traded from Atlanta to LA Clippers in 1994; later signed as free agent with Boston; elder statesman of Dream Team II; signed with pro team in Greece after 1994-95 season.

Bud Wilkinson (b. Apr. 23, 1916, d. Feb. 9, 1994): Football; played on 1936 national championship team at Minnesota; coached Oklahoma to 3 national titles (1950,55,56); won 4 Orange and 2 Sugar Bowls; teams had winning streaks of 47 (1953-57) and 31 (1948-50); retired after 1963 season with 145-29-4 record in 17 years; also coached St. Louis of NFL to 9-20 record in 1978-79.

Ted Williams (b. Aug. 30, 1918): Baseball OF; led AL in batting 6 times, and HRs and RBI 4 times each; won Triple Crown twice (1942,47); 2-time MVP (1946,49); last player to bat .400 when he hit .406 in 1941; Marine Corps combat pilot who missed three full seasons during World War II (1943-45) and most of two others (1952-53) during Korean War; hit .344 lifetime with 521 HRs in 19 years with Boston Red Sox.

Walter Ray Williams Jr. (b. Oct. 6, 1959): Bowling and Horseshoes; 2-time PBA Bowler of Year (1986,93); has also won 6 World Horseshoe Pitching titles.

Dave Winfield (b. Oct. 3, 1951): Baseball OF-DH; selected in 4 major sports league drafts in 1973— NFL, NBA, ABA, and MLB; chose baseball and has played in 12 All-Star Games over 20-year career; at age 41, helped lead Toronto to World Series title in 1992; reached 3,000 hits in 1993; entered 1995 as leading active player in hits, HRs and RBI among others.

Katarina Witt (b. Dec. 3, 1965): East German figure skater; 4-time world champion (1984-85,87-88); won consecutive Olympic gold medals (1984,88).

John Wooden (b. Oct. 14, 1910): Basketball; college Player of Year at Purdue in 1932; coached UCLA to 10 national titles (1964-65,67-73,75); only member of Basketball Hall of Fame inducted as both player and coach; Bruins won first title of post-Wooden era in 1995.

Tiger Woods (b. Dec. 30, 1975): Golfer; became youngest player (age 18) and first black to win U.S. Amateur when he did it in 1995, repeated as champion in '95; has now won 3 USGA championships in as many years (Bobby Jones won 8 from 1923-30, including 4 U.S. Opens).

Mickey Wright (b. Feb. 14, 1935): Golfer; won 3 of 4 Majors (LPGA, U.S. Open, Titleholders) in 1961; 4-time winner of both U.S. Open and LPGA titles; 82 career wins including 13 Majors.

Early Wynn (b. Jan. 6, 1920): Baseball RHP; won 20 games 5 times; Cy Young winner in 1959; 300 career wins in 23 years.

Cale Yarborough (b. Mar. 27, 1940): Auto racer; 3-time NASCAR national champion (1976-78); 4-time winner of Daytona 500 (1968,77,83-84); ranks 4th on NASCAR all-time list with 83 wins.

Carl Yastrzemski (b. Aug. 22, 1939): Baseball OF; led AL in batting 3 times; won Triple Crown and MVP in 1967; had 3,419 hits and 452 HRs in 23 years with Boston.

Cy Young (b. Mar. 29, 1867, d. Nov. 4, 1955): Baseball RHP; all-time leader in wins (511), losses (315), complete games (750) and innings pitched (7,355); had career 2.63 ERA in 22 years (1890-1911); 30-game winner 5 times and 20-game winner 10 other times; threw 3 no-hitters and perfect game (1904); AL and NL pitching awards named after him.

Dick Young (b. Oct. 17, 1917, d. Aug. 31, 1987): Confrontational sportswriter for 44 years with New York tabloids; as baseball beat writer and columnist, he led change from flowery prose to hard-nosed reporting.

Sheila Young (b. Oct. 14, 1950): Speed skater and cyclist; 1st U.S. athlete to win 3 medals at Winter Olympics (1976); won speed skating overall and sprint cycling world titles in 1976.

Steve Young (b. Oct. 11, 1961): Football QB; consensus All-America at BYU (1983); NFL Player of Year (1992) with S.F. 49ers; only QB to lead NFL in passer rating 4 straight years (1991-94); rating of 112.8 in 1994 was highest ever; threw NFL playoff-record 6 TD passes in MVP performance against San Diego in Super Bowl XXIX; holds NFL career records for highest passer rating (96.8) and completion percentage (63.6).

Robin Yount (b. Sept. 16, 1955): Baseball SS-OF; AL MVP at 2 positions— as SS in 1982 and OF in '89; retired after 1993 season with 3,142 hits, 251 HRs and a major league record 123 sacrifice flies after 20 seasons with Milwaukee Brewers.

Mario Zagalo (b. Aug. 9, 1931): Soccer; Brazilian forward who is one of only two men (Franz Beckenbauer is the other) to serve as both captain (1962) and coach (1970) of World Cup champion; served as advisor for Brazil's 1994 World Cup champion.

Babe Didrikson Zaharias (b. June 26, 1914, d. Sept. 27, 1956): All-around athlete who was chosen AP Female Athlete of Year 6 times from 1932-54; won 2 gold medals (javelin and 80-meter hurdles) and a silver (high jump) at 1932 Olympics; took up golf in 1935 and went on to win 55 pro and amateur events; won 10 majors, including 3 U.S. Opens (1948,50,54); helped found LPGA in 1949; chosen female "Athlete of the Half Century" by AP in 1950.

Tony Zale (b. May 29, 1913): Boxer; 2-time world middleweight champion (1941-47,48); fought Rocky Graziano for title 3 times in 21 months in 1947-48, winning twice; pro record 67-18-2 with 44 KOs.

Frank Zamboni (b. Jan. 16, 1901, d. July 27, 1988): Mechanic, ice salesman and skating rink owner in Paramount, Calif.; invented 1st ice-resurfacing machine in 1949; over 4,000 sold in more than 33 countries since then.

Emil Zatopek (b. Sept. 19, 1922): Czech distance runner; winner of 1948 Olympic gold medal at 10,000 meters; 4 years later, won unprecedented Olympic triple crown (5,000 meters, 10,000 meters and marathon) at 1952 Games in Helsinki.

John Ziegler (b. Feb. 9, 1934): Hockey; NHL president from 1977-92; negotiated settlement with rival WHA in 1979 that led to inviting four WHA teams (Edmonton, Hartford, Quebec and Winnipeg) to join NHL; stepped down June 12, 1992, 2 months after settling 10-day players' strike.

Pirmin Zurbriggen (b. Feb. 4, 1963): Swiss alpine skier; 4-time World Cup overall champ (1984,87-88,90) and 3-time runner-up; 40 World Cup wins in 10 years; won gold and bronze medals at 1988 Olympics.

Atlanta's new $207 million **Centennial Olympic Stadium** (foreground) as it looked a year before the opening of the 1996 Summer Olympics. Atlanta-Fulton County Stadium is in the background.

BALLPARKS & ARENAS

BALLPARKS & ARENAS
by Michelle Hiskey

Built to Shrink

*Atlanta's Centennial Olympic Stadium will hold 85,000
then shed 35,000 seats as the home of the Braves in 1997.*

The Modern Olympic Games turn 100 in 1996 and Atlanta will stage much of the celebration in a new baseball park masquerading as an 85,000-seat track and field stadium.

For 17 days in July and August, Centennial Olympic Stadium will be the focal point for over three billion worldwide television viewers as primary site of the Summer Olympics, from opening to closing ceremonies.

Eight months later, it will open the 1997 baseball season as the 49,831-seat home of the Atlanta Braves.

"While it's going to be a magnificent Olympic stadium, it is first and last a baseball park," said Braves' president Stan Kasten. "The other way around wouldn't be fair."

Kasten's statement may sound a bit nervy considering Olympic organizers plan to spend $207 million to build the stadium with another $30 million earmarked to modify it for baseball and raze nearby Atlanta-Fulton County Stadium, where the Braves have played since 1966. With the old stadium out of the way, fans in the new park will have a clear view of the downtown skyline.

The Braves, who are owned by cable TV magnate Ted Turner, have played hardball with the city and Olympic officials to control the design and operation of the new stadium, which they also get to re-name once the Olympics are over.

Michelle Hiskey is a staff writer for the Olympics department of the *Atlanta Journal and Constitution*.

Long unhappy with their governmental landlords at Atlanta-Fulton County Stadium, where tractor pulls and motorcross events were often booked to make ends meet, the Braves made repeated threats to move to the suburbs. Nobody listened, however, until the team started winning pennants in 1991.

And the Braves weren't alone in wanting out. The Atlanta Falcons of the NFL entertained an offer to move to Jacksonville, Fla., before the state stepped in and built the Georgia Dome for them in 1990.

A month after the Dome opened, Atlanta won the approval of the International Olympic Committee to host the 1996 Summer Games— edging out the birthplace of the Olympics, Athens, Greece, in the process.

The winning bid included plans for an outdoor stadium to be built on the huge parking lot just south of Atlanta-Fulton County Stadium. Organizers, however, didn't want to leave the city with a monumental white elephant after the Games, so they asked the Braves to join them in designing a stadium that would suit the demands of both the IOC and the ballclub.

Realizing the degree of expertise and creativity that would be needed to make two stadiums out of one, Kasten hired wunderkind architect Janet Marie Smith to direct the operation. Smith helped craft the modern old-fashioned look of Baltimore's Oriole Park at Camden Yards which has become a classic of sports architecture since it opened in 1992.

Fans will recognize her touch in the Atlanta

A model of what Atlanta's **Olympic Stadium** will look like after it is converted into a 49,831-seat ballpark in time for the 1997 baseball season. Atlanta-Fulton County Stadium, where the Braves have played since 1966, will be torn down later to provide a clear view of the city skyline.

park's two-toned brick exterior and lacy steel sunscreen.

"When we started out, we first studied Montreal, so we could avoid all the problems they've had," said Kasten, referring to the cavernous home of the Expos which ended up costing the organizers of the 1976 Summer Olympics a staggering $770 million. "In Montreal, you're practically roofed in and there's enough room beyond the outfield to fit another stadium. That's a bad setup. We'll have an open-air design and you'll be able to see the Atlanta skyline over the outfield wall."

Los Angeles Memorial Coliseum is another former Olympic stadium-cum-baseball field that the Braves won't be emulating. Built in 1923, the 94,000-seat Coliseum was the main venue for the 1932 and '84 Summer Games. It was also the neighborhood gridiron for UCLA, Southern Cal and the Los Angeles Rams before the Dodgers became co-tenants for four seasons after moving west from Brooklyn in 1958.

It was a tight fit. With the left field foul pole only 250 feet from home plate, a 42-foot screen had to be installed to prevent 251-foot pop-ups from becoming home runs. A critical and artistic success it wasn't.

Atlanta Olympic officials studied several options for their main stadium, including a temporary facility a la Albertville's collapsible grandstands at the 1992 Winter Games. When the decision was finally made to build a convertible stadium, designers were told to make sure none of it looked temporary.

So far, so good.

"I think you'll find that in every respect we are living up to our commitment to provide the great athletes of the world with the finest sporting venues that exist anywhere in the world," said Billy Payne, the president of the Atlanta Committee for the Olympic Games (ACOG).

Decked out in colorful banners, Centennial Stadium will look and feel very Olympic and permanent in 1996. But the dressing, a pattern of quilts and leaves called "The Look of the Games," will not totally disguise the field's future as a baseball park.

The stands surrounding the field, for instance, do not form the conventional oval found in most track and field stadiums. Instead, the southwest corner of the stadium cuts into the field-level grandstand at a sharp angle to make room for home plate— a puzzling design to the eye of international observers unfamiliar with America's national pastime.

"The seating doesn't follow the logical curve of any European stadium," reported *La Vanguardia*, the largest circulation daily newspaper in Barcelona, site of the 1992 Summer Olympics. "The baseball design will keep the spectators sitting by one of the curves farther away than usual."

But Janet Marie Smith says that feature is crucial.

"No doubt the most important decision in making this stadium work was giving it that tight pinched elbow," she said. "It allows the seats to be oriented to baseball after the Olympics."

The stadium represents the biggest chunk of the $516 million ACOG plans to spend on the construction of 10 venues. As of Sept. 1, 1995 the death of one construction worker— who was killed on March 20 when a light tower at the stadium gave way and crashed onto a concrete grandstand— has been the only major setback. Through the summer, the project was on time and on budget.

After the stadium, the big ticket construction projects are the $31 million field hockey complex at the Atlanta University Center (which will later be converted to football and soccer stadiums), the $17.5 million, open-air Aquatic Center at Georgia Tech; the $16 million tennis center at Stone Mountain and the $15 million Georgia International Horse Park in suburban Conyers, Ga.

ACOG staged the first major test run of its completed facilities in August with a three-week pre-Olympic festival of 12 events called "Atlanta Sports '95." While there were clearly problems with the yachting marina in Savannah (too small), the field hockey pitch at Clark Atlanta University (the artificial turf bubbled up and didn't drain properly) and the computer software at the swimming stadium (the Pan Pacific Championships were plagued with inaccurate heat times and seeding) officials confidently pronounced all snafus fixable.

The computerized accreditation network, based on Barcelona's successful 1992 system, also malfunctioned— breaking down twice in two days much to the annoyance of athletes, officials and working media, some of whom were kept waiting in sweltering accreditation centers for as long as 10 hours.

Amid record-breaking temperatures in the 100-degree range during the festival, many

Los Angeles Loses Rams And Raiders

In one of the strangest migratory twists of fate in the history of pro football, the tiny college town of Clemson, S.C., had an NFL team in 1995 and Los Angeles didn't.

No matter that L.A. is the country's second largest television market and Clemson has an off-campus population of only 11,150, the fact is that Clemson's Memorial Stadium was the interim home of the expansion Carolina Panthers while L.A. Memorial Coliseum and Anaheim Stadium were vacant.

Clemson got the Panthers because the team needed a place to play for a year while a new $175 million stadium is being built in Charlotte. Metropolitan Los Angeles lost the Rams and Raiders because both teams got better offers.

The Rams went to St. Louis and the Raiders returned to Oakland for the same reason that most professional sports teams pull up stakes: Money.

St. Louis, desperate to return to the NFL since losing the Cardinals to Phoenix in 1988, offered Rams owner Georgia Frontiere a package that included everything but the Gateway Arch— a new $270 million domed stadium with 67,000 seats; a minimal annual lease of $250,000; her choice of three sites for a $15 million practice facility and the money needed to retire the team's $30 million debt to Anaheim. All this for the worst team in the NFC, whose record from 1990-94 was 23-57.

The deal also included an estimated $74 million from 46,000 permanent seat licenses bought by charter season ticket holders. The permanent seat license (PSL) is a perfectly legal scheme devised by the NBA's Charlotte Hornets in 1987 and employed by the Carolina Panthers to help finance their new stadium. For a payment of up to $4,500 per seat St. Louis fans were invited to purchase the right to buy a season ticket for perpetuity. The season tickets are extra. PSLs were also a major part of the deal that lured the Raiders back to Oakland.

Faced with choice of staying in Anaheim and losing a projected $6 million or moving to St. Louis and pocketing a guaranteed annual profit of $20 million, Frontiere announced on Jan. 17 that the Rams were moving to her old home town.

Construction workers installing seats at the **Trans World Dome** in St. Louis on June 27. After playing their first three home games of the regular season at outdoor Busch Stadium, the transplanted Rams were scheduled to open their new 67,000-seat, $270 million home on Oct. 22 against San Francisco.

Two months later, NFL owners denied her permission by a 21-3 vote with the Raiders' Al Davis among six owners abstaining. A month after that, on April 12, the owners changed their minds and approved the move by a 23-6 vote (Davis again abstained). The Rams got the green light after agreeing to pay the league a $30 million relocation fee in addition to handing over nearly 25 percent ($17 million) of their $74 million PSL money.

Meanwhile, that the Raiders were anxious to flee the ancient L.A. Coliseum was no secret. Built in 1923 in what is now South Central L.A., the place was a relic of a bygone era (i.e., it has no luxury boxes). Celebrated as a two-time Olympic stadium and listed as a national historic landmark, the Coliseum's age, address and vulnerability to earthquakes made Davis and Co. cringe.

With the Rams gone and the Raiders threatening to leave, NFL owners, who had fought unsuccessfully to keep Davis from moving to L.A. in 1982, now found themselves begging him to stay.

On May 24, the owners adopted a plan that would provide the Raiders with a $200 million, 67,500-seat stadium at Hollywood Park in Inglewood by 1997. Other perks included two Super Bowls in the first 10 years with Davis controlling the distribution of over 10,000 tickets and shared revenues from the eventual placement of an NFC team in the city.

Davis, who is now 65 years-old, mulled the offer over and turned it down saying he doubted the stadium would ever be done on time due to construction delays and concerns about an environmental impact study.

Enter Oakland. Always on the lookout to steal the Raiders back, Mayor Elihu Harris and Oakland Coliseum president George Vukasin came up with a $225 million package that included the following: $100 million to modernize Oakland Coliseum with up to 150 luxury suites before the 1996 NFL season, $54 million in relocation loans, $10 million for a new practice facility, $13 million to retire the debt on the L.A. Coliseum and the rest in reserve funds to cover future debt service.

On June 23, Davis announced the Raiders were returning to the Bay Area.

"For the first time, a team that has left a town has come home," said Mayor Harris.

But for how long?

visitors wondered how organizers plan to handle similar weather at outdoor venues next year.

ACOG said it planned to experiment with a water-vapor cooling system designed to reduce the air temperature at outdoor sites by up to 15 degrees.

Climate control even presented some difficulties indoors. At Georgia State University, badminton players complained that the air-conditioning system interfered with the flight of the shuttlecock.

Back to Centennial Stadium, which won't begin its limited run as a Olympic venue until 1996. With only eight months to change the stadium into a baseball park once the Olympics are over, preliminary work has already been done to streamline the conversion.

"We first had a square outfield, but after we got into it, we realized we could reuse the curved seating of the Olympic bowl for baseball," said Bill Johnson, a designer with Ellerbe Becket. "Our overall idea was not to pay for something that we had to throw away."

The idea of two stadiums in one still vexes some observers. "It's been shown conclusively that when you build a stadium for two sports, you get a mediocre stadium for both," said Bob Bluthardt, chairman of the ballparks committee of the Society for American Baseball Research. "If Atlanta can pull it off, it'll be a pretty good trick."

"I think one sport is going to be compromised, and that's probably track, because of the geometry," said Brad Schrock, who designed $215.5 million Coors Field in Denver. "But they've come up with an interesting solution."

The opening of Coors Field on March 31, accentuated the trend, which Atlanta will follow, to cram as many amenities as possible into baseball's new old-fashioned stadiums. More luxury suites, more children's areas, more automatic teller machines and more women's restrooms. It all adds up to better attractions for fans and their money, according to stadium designers and team owners.

"If it wasn't for the luxury boxes and premium seats, we wouldn't have jobs," said Schrock of Kansas City-based HOK Sport, the architects of Camden Yards and Jacobs Field in Cleveland. "We want to enhance the experience for fans, but we don't want to

World Wide Photos

The main entrance of **Coors Field,** the Colorado Rockies' new home in Denver, is meant to resemble old-time ballparks like Ebbets Field in Brooklyn and Wrigley Field in Chicago.

take it to the point of glitzy entertainment."

Coors Field opened its doors for the first time on the 232nd day of the players' strike and under overcast skies. It still attracted a near-sellout crowd of 47,563 for an exhibition game featuring replacement players. Fans wore T-shirts that said "I came to see the field, not the fielders" while vendors hawked blueprints of the ballpark for $10.

With a brewery, a kid-sized concession stand, and a special club level of roomier and costlier seats, Coors Field built in lots of money-making extras. But baseball purists say there is a fine line between paying genuine homage to ballparks of the past and building a string of quasi-amusement parks.

"Coors Field is a state-of-the-art stadium with a lot of nostalgia built into it," says Bruce Hellerstein, who has assembled a shrine to baseball parks in the basement of his suburban Denver home and sports a 12-foot replica of Coors Field in his backyard.

"Unfortunately, there's so much copycatting going on with these new parks that the nostalgia's getting to be pretty forced. It bugs me when people say Coors is old-fashioned. No way. Fenway Park and

Wrigley Field are old-fashioned. You can't compare these new parks to them."

There is nothing old-fashioned about the construction of the four new basketball and hockey arenas scheduled to open their doors in Boston, Portland, Seattle and Vancouver this fall.

The FleetCenter in Boston and General Motors Place in Vancouver are both completely new buildings and home to teams in both the NBA and NHL. Key Arena at Seattle Center and Portland's Rose Garden will house NBA clubs and, in Seattle's case, a minor league hockey team.

Other than the Celtics and Bruins, the only trappings of the old Boston Garden that will make the trip to the new FleetCenter will be the Celts' parquet playing floor and all those NBA (16) and Stanley Cup (5) championship banners that hung from the rafters of the old barn (see page 549).

The vacating of the Garden in 1995 comes a year after the Bulls and Blackhawks left Chicago Stadium for the new United Center and a little less than a year before the Canadiens are scheduled to move out of the old Montreal Forum. All three arenas were originally built in the 1920s and were lifelong stops in the NHL.

One of the National Football League's newest stadiums belonged to one of its newest teams, the expansion Jacksonville Jaguars of the AFC.

At a cost of $146 million, Jacksonville Municipal Stadium has risen from the ashes of the old Gator Bowl with a capacity of 73,000 seats— 10,000 of which remain from the old structure's west upper deck. Smaller than the original 82,000-seat Gator Bowl, the new place will still be home for the postseason Gator Bowl and the "World's Largest Cocktail Party," otherwise known as the annual Southeastern Conference showdown between Florida and Georgia.

The Jaguars' 30-year lease agreement with Jacksonville ("Jagsonville" to NFL-crazed locals) is one of the NFL's sweetest: $875,000 a year in rent and they get to keep all revenue from parking, tickets and concessions.

The league's other expansion club, the Carolina Panthers will play at Clemson University's Memorial Stadium for a year before moving into $175 million Carolinas Stadium (capacity: 72,300) in Charlotte in 1996.

New stadiums represent such a gap in revenues between the NFL Haves and Have-Nots that the league entertained a proposal to share new revenues from luxury suites and permanent seat licenses.

Stadium economics forced the Green Bay Packers to discontinue their 42-year tradition of calling Milwaukee's County Stadium their home away from home. With only 56,051 seats, no skyboxes and sightlines primarily for baseball, County Stadium cost the Packers $400,000 each time they played there compared to much fatter per game revenue at Lambeau Field in Green Bay.

The Wisconsin state legislature held hearings in September on a bill backing a new stadium in Milwaukee with a first-of-its-kind convertable roof and a price tag of $225 million. The baseball Brewers have committed $90 million to the project and will pay $33 million in rent over a 30-year lease.

In Seattle, the prospects of landing a new ballpark dimmed somewhat when a fractured wrist sidelined star outfielder Ken Griffey Jr. from May 26 to Aug. 15.

The Mariners, who entered September very much in the hunt for a wild card playoff berth, were counting on a Griffey-led march to the A.L. West division title to help convince voters to back a proposed sales tax to fund a new $270 million, retractable-roof stadium. A referendum was scheduled for Sept. 19 (see "Updates" chapter).

To meet spiraling payrolls, teams are milking as much money as they can from the buildings they play in. Bud Selig, the acting baseball commissioner and owner of the Milwaukee Brewers' warned that new ballparks were needed in 11 cities, and if the taxpayers or public-private entities don't deliver, their teams may have to move.

"You can't sugarcoat it," he said. "There are some teams that will not survive in this economic environment without new stadiums."

In Atlanta, the NBA Hawks— the other major league franchise owned by Ted Turner and run by Stan Kasten— shopped around in 1995 for a downtown or suburban location to build a new arena. The club has decided to abandon the 24-year-old Omni after their lease expires in 2002. Why? Because the luxury suites aren't luxurious or plentiful enough and most of their fans live in the suburbs.

In the meantime, the Omni will host Olympic volleyball in 1996. ❐

BALLPARKS & ARENAS
COMING ATTRACTIONS

1995

BASEBALL

Colorado (NL): Coors Field (Coors brewery is title sponsor) opened March 31 with "replacement players" exhibition game between Rockies and New York Yankees. The Rockies won, 4-1, before a crowd of 47,563. Baseball players' strike delayed regular season Opening Day until April 26 when the Rockies beat the New York Mets, 11-9 in 14 innings before 47,228. Located in downtown Denver at the corner of 20th and Blake streets; seats 50,400 for baseball only; open air and grass field; includes 58 luxury suites and cost $215.5 million.

NBA BASKETBALL

Boston (East): Grand opening of the FleetCenter (Fleet Bank is title sponsor) scheduled for Sept. 30 with musical program featuring the Boston Pops and figure skater Nancy Kerrigan. Located only nine inches from the 67-year-old Boston Garden (which will be razed in 1996); seats 18,400 for basketball and 17,200 for NHL Bruins; includes 104 luxury suites and cost $172 million. Celtics' home opener vs. Milwaukee scheduled for Nov. 3.

Portland (West): Grand opening of the Rose Garden (Portland is known as "City of Roses") scheduled for Oct. 12 with ceremony honoring Trail Blazers' fans and project construction workers. Located next to Memorial Coliseum in downtown Portland; seats 20,340 for basketball; includes 70 luxury suites and cost $262 million for new arena, office building and entertainment complex, three new garages and renovation of old Coliseum. Trail Blazers' home opener vs. Vancouver scheduled for Nov. 3.

Seattle (West): Grand opening of Key Arena at Seattle Center (Key Bank is title sponsor) scheduled for Oct. 26 with charitable concert featuring and the Seattle Symphony and tenor Jose Carreras. Located on site of old Seattle Center Coliseum which has been rebuilt; seats 17,100 for basketball and 13,000 for the Thunderbirds of the Western Hockey League; includes 58 luxury suites and cost $80 million. Sonics' home opener vs. L.A. Lakers scheduled for Nov. 4.

Vancouver (West): Grand opening of General Motors Place (GM Canada is title sponsor) scheduled for Sept. 17 with laser show and public open house. Located at downtown site adjacent to B.C. Place (home of the CFL football Lions); seats 20,004 for basketball and 19,056 for NHL Canucks; includes 88 luxury suites and cost $125 million (US). Grizzlies' home opener vs. Minnesota scheduled for Nov. 5.

NFL FOOTBALL

Jacksonville (AFC): Reopening of the renovated Gator Bowl, renamed Jacksonville Municipal Stadium, was an Aug. 18 preseason game vs. St. Louis, won by the Rams, 27-10, before a crowd of 71,884. Only west upper deck and 10,000 seats remain from old Gator Bowl; seats 73,000 for football; open air, grass field; includes 85 luxury suites and cost $146 million. Jaguars' regular season home opener vs. Houston scheduled for Sept. 3.

St. Louis (NFC): Grand opening of Trans World Dome (TWA Airlines is title sponsor) scheduled for Oct. 22 with NFL regular season game vs. San Francisco. Located on downtown site adjoining America's Center convention complex; seats 67,000 for football; indoor, artificial turf field; includes 123 luxury suites and cost $270 million. Rams will play first three regular season games at outdoor Busch Stadium.

NHL HOCKEY

Boston (East): Grand opening of the FleetCenter (Fleet Bank is title sponsor) scheduled for Sept. 30 with musical program featuring the Boston Pops and figure skater Nancy Kerrigan. Located only nine inches from the 67-year-old Boston Garden (which will be razed in 1996); seats 17,200 for hockey and 18,400 for NBA Celtics; includes 104 luxury suites and cost $172 million. Bruins' home opener vs. the New York Islanders scheduled for Oct. 7.

St. Louis (West): NHL owners' lockout delayed Blues' 1995 home opener at Kiel Center (Henry Kiel was mayor from 1913-25) until Jan. 26 when they beat Los Angeles, 3-1, before a crowd of 20,282. Located on downtown site of old Kiel Auditorium near St. Louis Arena; seats 18,500 for hockey and 20,000 for college basketball; includes 80 luxury suites and cost $170 million for new arena, razing old auditorium and construction of parking garage.

Vancouver (West): Grand opening of General Motors Place (GM Canada is title sponsor) scheduled for Sept. 17 with laser show and public open house. Located at downtown site adjacent to B.C. Place (home of the CFL Lions); seats 19,056 for hockey and 20,004 for NBA Grizzlies; includes 88 luxury suites and cost $125 million (US). Canucks' home opener vs. Detroit scheduled for Oct. 9.

1996

NBA BASKETBALL

Philadelphia (East): Construction of CoreStates Center (CoreStates Financial Corp. is title sponsor) nearing completion. Located on site of razed JFK Stadium adjacent to CoreStates Spectrum and Veterans Stadium; will seat 21,000 for basketball and 19,500 for NHL Flyers; will include 139 luxury suites; estimated cost: $217 million. Sixers' home opener scheduled for November 1996.

NFL FOOTBALL

Carolina (NFC): Construction of Carolinas Stadium nearing completion. Located in downtown Charlotte; will seat 72,300 for football; open air, grass field; will include 135 luxury suites; estimated cost: $175 million. Panthers' home opener scheduled for September 1996.

Oakland (AFC): Major renovation of Oakland-Alameda County Coliseum will begin following 1995 season. Plans call for football seating to increase to 65,000; rebuilding will include 150 luxury suites; estimated cost: $85 million, including new training and office facilities. Raiders home reopener scheduled for September 1996.

NHL HOCKEY

Buffalo (East): Construction of Crossroads Arena nearing completion. Located three blocks from Buffalo Auditorium where the waterfront meets the intersection of South Park and Main St.; will seat 19,500 for hockey and 20,500 for college basketball; will include 80 luxury suites; estimated cost: $125 million. Sabres' home opener scheduled for October 1996.

Montreal (East): Construction of the new Montreal Forum very near completion. Located at Windsor Station in downtown Montreal; will seat 21,450 for hockey; will include 136 luxury suites; estimated cost: $170 million (US). The Canadiens, who will begin the 1995-96 season at the old Montreal Forum on St. Catherine St., are scheduled to open the new building in March 1996.

Ottawa (East): Construction of Ottawa Palladium nearing completion. Located in suburban Kanata, Ontario; will seat 18,500 for hockey; will include 147 luxury suites; estimated cost: $240 million (US) for arena, office tower, hotel, roads and highway interchange. The Senators, who will begin the 1995-96 season at the Ottawa Civic Center, are scheduled to open the new building in January 1996.

Philadelphia (East): Construction of CoreStates Center (CoreStates Financial Corp. is title sponsor) nearing completion. Located on site of razed JFK Stadium adjacent to CoreStates Spectrum and Veterans Stadium; will seat 19,500 for hockey and 21,000 for NBA 76ers; will include 139 luxury suites; estimated cost: $217 million. Flyers' home opener scheduled for October 1996.

Tampa Bay (East): Construction of as yet unnamed arena nearing completion. Located on waterfront site near Tampa Aquarium; will seat 19,500 for hockey; will include 71 luxury suites; estimated cost: $130 million. Lightning's home opener scheduled for October 1996.

1997

BASEBALL

Atlanta (NL): Construction of 85,000-seat Centennial Olympic Stadium for 1996 Summer Games nearing completion. Located across from Atlanta-Fulton County Stadium; will be converted to 49,831-seat ballpark for baseball only immediately following '96 Olympics; open air, grass field; will include approximately 60 luxury suites; estimated cost $221 million to build Olympic stadium and convert to smaller ballpark. Braves' home opener scheduled for April 1997.

NBA BASKETBALL

Toronto (East): Groundbreaking for Air Canada Center (Air Canada is title sponsor) scheduled for October 1995. To be located on site of Old Canada Post Building at corner of Bay Street and Lake Shore Road; will seat 22,500 for basketball and 21,325 for hockey (the NHL Maple Leafs will not be tenants); will include 124 luxury suites; estimated cost: $172 million (US). Raptors' home opener scheduled for November 1997.

Washington (East): Groundbreaking for MCI Center (MCI is title sponsor) scheduled for October 1995. To be located above the Gallery Place Metro Station near National Mall; will seat 21,500 for basketball and 20,000 for NHL Capitals; will include 110 luxury suites; estimated cost: $175 million. Bullets' home opener scheduled for November 1997.

NFL FOOTBALL

Washington (NFC): Groundbreaking for Redskins Stadium scheduled for October 1995. To be located on site six miles east of RFK Stadium in Landover, Md.; will seat 78,400 for football; open air, grass field; will include 280 luxury suites; estimated cost: $165 million. Redskins' home opener scheduled for September 1997.

NHL HOCKEY

Washington (East): Groundbreaking for MCI Center (MCI is title sponsor) scheduled for October 1995. To be located above the Gallery Place Metro Station near National Mall; will seat 20,000 for hockey and 21,500 for NBA Bullets; will include 110 luxury suites; estimated cost: $175 million. Capitals' home opener scheduled for October 1997.

1998

BASEBALL

Arizona (expansion team): Groundbreaking for Bank One Ballpark (Bank One is title sponsor) scheduled for October 1995. To be located one block from America West Arena and feature a retracable roof; will seat 47,350 for baseball only; grass field; will include 65 luxury suites; estimated cost: $280 million. Diamondbacks' major league home opener scheduled for April 1998.

Cincinnati (NL): New ballpark in planning stages. Would be part of $540 million downtown project including separate football stadium for NFL Bengals. Earliest groundbreaking would be April 1996 near Riverfront Stadium; would seat 47,000 for baseball; open air, grass field; would include 65 luxury suites; estimated cost: $203 million. Earliest Reds' home opener would be April 1998.

Seattle (AL): New Century Park in planning stages. Would be located in parking lot across from Kingdome; seating of 45,000 for baseball only; open air, grass field; would include 70 luxury suites; estimated cost: $240 million. Earliest Mariners' home opener would be April 1998.

Tampa Bay (expansion team): Plans call for renovating the ThunderDome, which was originally called the Florida Suncoast Dome when it opened in 1990. Current tenant, the NHL Lightning, scheduled to move out after 1995-96 season. Located in St. Petersburg at the corner of 16th St. and 1st Ave. South; will seat 48,000 for baseball; indoor, artificial turf field; will include 66 luxury suites; estimated cost: $50 million. Devil Rays' major league home opener scheduled for April 1998.

NBA BASKETBALL

Denver (West): Groundbreaking for Pepsi Center (Pepsi-Cola is title sponsor) tentatively scheduled for early 1996. To be built by team owner COMSAT Inc., along with a television studio on downtown site adjacent to the new Elitch Gardens theme park; will seat 19,100 for basketball and 17,700 for NHL Avalanche; will include 84 luxury suites; estimated cost: $132 million. Nuggets' home opener planned for November 1998.

NFL FOOTBALL

Cincinnati (AFC): New stadium in planning stages. Would be part of $540 million downtown project including separate baseball park for NL Reds. Earliest groundbreaking would be April, 1996 near Riverfront Stadium; would seat 54,000 for football; open air, grass field; would include 45 luxury suites; estimated cost: $170 million. Earliest Bengals' home opener would be September 1998.

NHL HOCKEY

Colorado (West): Groundbreaking for Pepsi Center (Pepsi-Cola is title sponsor) tentatively scheduled for early 1996. To be built by team owner COMSAT Inc., along with a television studio in downtown Denver, adjacent to the new Elitch Gardens theme park; will seat 17,700 for hockey and 19,100 for NBA Nuggets; will include 84 luxury suites; estimated cost: $132 million. Avalanche home opener planned for October 1998.

Home, Sweet Home

The home fields, home courts and home ice of the AL, NL, NBA, NFL, CFL, NHL, NCAA Division I-A college football and Division I basketball. Also included are Formula One, IndyCar, Indy Racing League and NASCAR auto racing tracks.

Attendance figures for the 1994 NFL regular season and the 1994-95 NBA and NHL regular seasons are provided. See Baseball chapter for 1995 AL and NL attendance figures.

MAJOR LEAGUE BASEBALL

American League

		Built	Capacity	LF	LCF	CF	RCF	RF	Field
					—Outfield Fences—				
Baltimore Orioles	Oriole Park at Camden Yards	1992	48,262	333	410	400	373	318	Grass
Boston Red Sox	Fenway Park	1912	33,871	310	379	420	380	302	Grass
California Angels	Anaheim Stadium	1966	64,593	333	386	404	386	333	Grass
Chicago White Sox	Comiskey Park	1991	44,321	347	383	400	383	347	Grass
Cleveland Indians	Jacobs Field	1994	42,865	325	370	405	375	325	Grass
Detroit Tigers	Tiger Stadium	1912	52,416	340	365	440	375	325	Grass
Kansas City Royals	Ewing Kauffman Stadium	1973	40,625	330	375	410	375	330	Grass
Milwaukee Brewers	County Stadium	1953	53,192	315	392	402	392	315	Grass
Minnesota Twins	Hubert H. Humphrey Metrodome	1982	56,144	343	385	408	367	327	Turf
New York Yankees	Yankee Stadium	1923	57,545	318	399	408	385	314	Grass
Oakland Athletics	Oakland-Alameda County Coliseum	1966	46,942	330	375	400	375	330	Grass
Seattle Mariners	The Kingdome	1976	59,158	331	389	405	380	312	Turf
Texas Rangers	The Ballpark in Arlington	1994	49,178	334	388	400	407	325	Grass
Toronto Blue Jays	SkyDome	1989	50,516	328	375	400	375	328	Turf

National League

		Built	Capacity	LF	LCF	CF	RCF	RF	Field
					—Outfield Fences—				
Atlanta Braves	Atlanta-Fulton County Stadium	1965	52,710	330	385	402	385	330	Grass
Chicago Cubs	Wrigley Field	1914	38,765	355	368	400	368	353	Grass
Cincinnati Reds	Riverfront Stadium	1970	52,952	330	375	404	375	330	Turf
Colorado Rockies	Coors Field	1995	50,400	347	390	415	375	350	Grass
Florida Marlins	Joe Robbie Stadium	1987	46,238	330	385	434	385	345	Grass
Houston Astros	The Astrodome	1965	54,350	325	375	400	375	325	Turf
Los Angeles Dodgers	Dodger Stadium	1962	56,000	330	385	395	385	330	Grass
Montreal Expos	Olympic Stadium	1976	46,500	325	375	404	375	325	Turf
New York Mets	Shea Stadium	1964	55,601	338	371	410	371	338	Grass
Philadelphia Phillies	Veterans Stadium	1971	62,238	330	371	408	371	330	Turf
Pittsburgh Pirates	Three Rivers Stadium	1970	47,972	335	375	400	375	335	Turf
St. Louis Cardinals	Busch Stadium	1966	57,078	330	375	402	375	330	Grass
San Diego Padres	San Diego/ Jack Murphy Stadium	1967	46,510	327	370	405	370	327	Grass
San Francisco Giants	Candlestick Park	1960	63,000	335	365	400	365	328	Grass

1998 Expansion Teams

		Built	Capacity	LF	LCF	CF	RCF	RF	Field
					—Outfield Fences—				
Arizona Diamondbacks	Bank One Ballpark	1998	47,350	335	387	405	387	335	Grass
Tampa Bay Devil Rays	ThunderDome	1990	48,000	335	385	410	385	335	Turf

Rank by Capacity

AL		NL	
California	64,593	San Francisco	63,000
Seattle	59,158	Philadelphia	62,238
New York	57,545	St. Louis	57,078
Minnesota	56,144	Los Angeles	56,000
Milwaukee	53,192	New York	55,601
Detroit	52,416	Houston	54,350
Toronto	50,516	Cincinnati	52,952
Texas	49,178	Atlanta	52,710
Baltimore	48,262	Colorado	50,400
Oakland	46,942	Pittsburgh	47,972
Chicago	44,321	San Diego	46,510
Cleveland	42,865	Montreal	46,500
Kansas City	40,625	Florida	46,238
Boston	33,871	Chicago	38,765

Rank by Age

AL		NL	
Boston	1912	Chicago	1914
Detroit	1912	San Francisco	1960
New York	1923	Los Angeles	1962
Milwaukee	1953	New York	1964
California	1966	Houston	1965
Oakland	1966	Atlanta	1965
Kansas City	1973	St. Louis	1966
Seattle	1976	San Diego	1967
Minnesota	1982	Cincinnati	1970
Toronto	1989	Pittsburgh	1970
Chicago	1991	Philadelphia	1971
Baltimore	1992	Montreal	1976
Cleveland	1994	Florida	1987
Texas	1994	Colorado	1995

Note: New York's Yankee Stadium (AL) was rebuilt in 1976.

Home Fields

Listed below are the principal home fields used through the years by current American and National League teams. The NL became a major league in 1876, the AL in 1901.

The capacity figures in the right-hand column indicate the largest seating capacity of the ballpark while the club played there. Capacity figures before 1915 (and the introduction of concrete grandstands) are sketchy at best and have been left blank.

American League

Baltimore Orioles

1901	Lloyd Street Grounds (Milwaukee)	—
1902-53	Sportsman's Park II (St. Louis)	30,500
1954-91	Memorial Stadium (Baltimore)	53,371
1992—	Camden Yards......................................	48,262

Boston Red Sox

1901-11	Huntington Ave. Grounds	—
1912—	Fenway Park......................................	33,871
	(1934 capacity–27,000)	

California Angels

1961	Wrigley Field (Los Angeles)	20,457
1962-65	Dodger Stadium....................................	56,000
1966—	Anaheim Stadium................................	64,593
	(1966 capacity–43,250)	

Chicago White Sox

1901-10	Southside Park	—
1910-90	Comiskey Park I....................................	43,931
1991—	Comiskey Park II	44,321

Cleveland Indians

1901-09	League Park I	—
1910-46	League Park II	21,414
1932-93	Cleveland Stadium................................	74,483
1994—	Jacobs Field	42,865

Detroit Tigers

1901-11	Bennett Park	—
1912—	Tiger Stadium....................................	52,416
	(1912 capacity–23,000)	

Kansas City Royals

1969-72	Municipal Stadium................................	35,020
1973—	Kauffman Stadium................................	40,625
	(1973 capacity–40,762)	

Milwaukee Brewers

1969	Sick's Stadium (Seattle)...........................	25,420
1970—	County Stadium (Milwaukee)....................	53,192
	(1970 capacity–46,62)	

Minnesota Twins

1901-02	American League Park (Washington, DC)	—
1903-60	Griffith Stadium....................................	27,410
1960-81	Metropolitan Stadium (Bloomington, MN)................................	45,919
1982—	HHH Metrodome (Minneapolis)	56,144
	(1982 capacity–54,000)	

New York Yankees

1901-02	Oriole Park (Baltimore)	—
1903-12	Hilltop Park (New York)	—
1913-22	Polo Grounds II	38,000
1923-73	Yankee Stadium I	67,224
1974-75	Shea Stadium......................................	55,101
1976—	Yankee Stadium II..................................	57,545
	(1976 capacity–57,145)	

Oakland Athletics

1901-08	Columbia Park (Philadelphia)................	—
1909-54	Shibe Park	33,608
1955-67	Municipal Stadium (Kansas City)	35,020
1968—	Oakland Alameda County Coliseum	46,942
	(1968 capacity–48,621)	

Seattle Mariners

1977—	The Kingdome.....................................	59,158
	(1977 capacity–59,438)	

Texas Rangers

1961	Griffith Stadium (Washington, DC)...........	27,410
1962-71	RFK Stadium......................................	45,016
1972-93	Arlington Stadium (Texas)........................	43,521
1994—	The Ballpark in Arlington.......................	49,178

Toronto Blue Jays

1977-89	Exhibition Stadium................................	43,737
1989—	SkyDome	50,516
	(1989 capacity–49,500)	

Ballpark Name Changes: CHICAGO–**Comiskey Park I** originally White Sox Park (1910-12), then Comiskey Park in 1913, then White Sox Park again in 1962, then Comiskey Park again in 1976; CLEVELAND–**League Park** renamed Dunn Field in 1920, then League Park again in 1928; Cleveland Stadium originally Municipal Stadium (1932-74); DETROIT–**Tiger Stadium** originally Navin Field (1912-37), then Briggs Stadium (1938-60); KANSAS CITY–**Kauffman Stadium** originally Royals Stadium (1973-93); LOS ANGELES–**Dodger Stadium** referred to as Chavez Ravine by AL while Angels played there (1962-65); PHILADELPHIA–**Shibe Park** renamed Connie Mack Stadium in 1953; ST. LOUIS–**Sportsman's Park** renamed Busch Stadium in 1953; WASHINGTON–**Griffith Stadium** originally National Park (1892-20), **RFK Stadium** originally D.C. Stadium (1961-68).

National League

Atlanta Braves

1876-94	South End Grounds I (Boston)	—
1894-1914	South End Grounds II...........................	—
1915-52	Braves Field	40,000
1953-65	County Stadium (Milwaukee)................	43,394
1966—	Atlanta-Fulton County Stadium	52,710
	(1966 capacity–50,000)	

Chicago Cubs

1876-77	State Street Grounds...........................	—
1878-84	Lakefront Park	—
1885-91	West Side Park....................................	—
1891-93	Brotherhood Park	—
1893-1915	West Side Grounds	—
1916—	Wrigley Field......................................	38,765
	(1916 capacity–16,000)	

Major League Baseball (Cont.)
Home Fields

Cincinnati Reds

1876-79	Avenue Grounds	—
1880	Bank Street Grounds	—
1890-1901	Redland Field I	—
1902-11	Palace of the Fans	—
1912-70	Crosley Field	29,603
1970—	Riverfront Stadium	52,952
	(1970 capacity–52,000)	

Colorado Rockies

1993-94	Mile High Stadium (Denver)	76,100
1995—	Coors Field	50,400

Florida Marlins

1993—	Joe Robbie Stadium (Miami)	46,238

Houston Astros

1962-64	Colt Stadium	32,601
1965—	The Astrodome	54,350
	(1965 capacity–45,011)	

Los Angeles Dodgers

1890	Washington Park I (Brooklyn)	—
1891-97	Eastern Park	—
1898-1912	Washington Park II	—
1913-56	Ebbets Field	31,497
1957	Ebbets Field	31,497
	& Roosevelt Stadium (Jersey City)	24,167
1958-61	Memorial Coliseum (Los Angeles)	93,600
1962—	Dodger Stadium	56,000

Montreal Expos

1969-76	Jarry Park	28,000
1977—	Olympic Stadium	46,500
	(1977 capacity–58,500)	

New York Mets

1962-63	Polo Grounds	55,987
1964—	Shea Stadium	55,601
	(1964 capacity–55,101)	

Philadelphia Phillies

1883-86	Recreation Park	—
1887-94	Huntingdon Ave.Grounds	—
1895-1938	Baker Bowl	18,800
1938-70	Shibe Park	33,608
1971—	Veterans Stadium	62,238
	(1971 capacity–56,371)	

Pittsburgh Pirates

1887-90	Recreation Park	—
1891-1909	Exposition Park	—
1909-70	Forbes Field	35,000
1970—	Three Rivers Stadium	47,972
	(1970 capacity–50,235)	

St. Louis Cardinals

1876-77	Sportsman's Park I	—
1885-86	Vandeventer Lot	—
1892-1920	Robison Field	18,000
1920-66	Sportsman's Park II	30,500
1966—	Busch Stadium	57,078
	(1966 capacity–50,126)	

San Diego Padres

1969—	San Diego/Jack Murphy Stadium	46,510
	(1969 capacity–47,634)	

San Francisco Giants

1876	Union Grounds (Brooklyn)	—
1883-88	Polo Grounds I (New York)	—
1889-90	Manhattan Field	—
1891-1957	Polo Grounds II	55,987
1958-59	Seals Stadium (San Francisco)	22,900
1960—	Candlestick Park	63,000
	(1960 capacity–42,553)	

Ballpark Name Changes: ATLANTA–**Atlanta-Fulton County Stadium** originally Atlanta Stadium (1966-1974); CHICAGO–**Wrigley Field** originally Weeghman Park (1914-17), then Cubs Park (1918-25); CINCINNATI–**Redland Field** originally League Park (1890-93) and **Crosley Field** originally Redland Field II (1912-33); HOUSTON–**Astrodome** originally Harris County Domed Stadium before it opened in 1965; PHILADELPHIA–**Shibe Park** renamed Connie Mack Stadium in 1953; ST. LOUIS–**Robison Field** originally Vandeventer Lot, then League Park, the Cardinal Park all before becoming Robison Field in 1901, **Sportsman's Park** renamed Busch Stadium in 1953, and **Busch Stadium** originally Busch Memorial Stadium (1966-82); SAN DIEGO–**San Diego/Jack Murphy Stadium** originally San Diego Stadium (1967-81).

NATIONAL BASKETBALL ASSOCIATION
Western Conference

		Location	Built	Capacity
Dallas Mavericks	**Reunion Arena**	Dallas, Texas	1980	**17,502**
Denver Nuggets	**McNichols Arena**	Denver, Colo.	1975	**17,171**
Golden State Warriors	**Oakland Coliseum Arena**	Oakland, Calif.	1966	**15,025**
Houston Rockets	**The Summit**	Houston, Texas	1975	**16,611**
Los Angeles Clippers	**Los Angeles Sports Arena**	Los Angeles, Calif.	1959	**16,021**
	& Arrowhead Pond	Anaheim, Calif.	1993	**18,198**
Los Angeles Lakers	**Great Western Forum**	Inglewood, Calif.	1967	**17,505**
Minnesota Timberwolves	**Target Center**	Minneapolis, Minn.	1990	**19,006**
Phoenix Suns	**America West Arena**	Phoenix, Ariz.	1992	**19,023**
Portland Trail Blazers	**Rose Garden**	Portland, Ore.	1995	**20,340**
Sacramento Kings	**ARCO Arena**	Sacramento, Calif.	1988	**17,317**
San Antonio Spurs	**Alamodome**	San Antonio, Texas	1993	**20,500**
Seattle SuperSonics	**Key Arena at Seattle Center**	Seattle, Wash.	1962	**17,100**
Utah Jazz	**Delta Center**	Salt Lake City, Utah	1991	**19,911**
Vancouver Grizzlies	**General Motors Place**	Vancouver, B.C.	1995	**20,004**

Notes: Seattle's Key Arena was originally the Seattle Coliseum before being rebuilt in 1995; San Antonio's Alamodome seating is expandable to hold 32,500; and the Los Angeles Clippers are scheduled to play eight of 41 regular season home games at the Arrowhead Pond in Anaheim in 1995-96.

Eastern Conference

		Location	Built	Capacity
Atlanta Hawks	The Omni	Atlanta, Ga.	1972	**16,365**
Boston Celtics	FleetCenter	Boston, Mass.	1995	**18,400**
Charlotte Hornets	Charlotte Coliseum	Charlotte, N.C.	1988	**23,698**
Chicago Bulls	United Center	Chicago, Ill.	1994	**21,500**
Cleveland Cavaliers	Gund Arena	Cleveland, Ohio	1994	**20,562**
Detroit Pistons	The Palace of Auburn Hills	Auburn Hills, Mich.	1988	**21,454**
Indiana Pacers	Market Square Arena	Indianapolis, Ind.	1974	**16,530**
Miami Heat	Miami Arena	Miami, Fla.	1988	**15,200**
Milwaukee Bucks	Bradley Center	Milwaukee, Wisc.	1988	**18,633**
New Jersey Nets	Byrne Meadowlands Arena	E. Rutherford, N.J.	1981	**20,039**
New York Knicks	Madison Square Garden	New York, N.Y.	1968	**19,763**
Orlando Magic	Orlando Arena	Orlando, Fla.	1989	**15,998**
Philadelphia 76ers	CoreStates Spectrum	Philadelphia, Pa.	1967	**18,168**
Toronto Raptors	SkyDome	Toronto, Ont.	1989	**22,911**
Washington Bullets	USAir Arena	Landover, Md.	1973	**18,756**
	& Baltimore Arena	Baltimore, Md.	1962	**12,756**

Note: Washington is scheduled to play four of 41 regular season home games at Baltimore Arena in 1995-96.

Rank by Capacity

West

San Antonio	20,500	Charlotte	23,698
Portland	20,340	Toronto	22,911
Vancouver	20,004	Chicago	21,500
Utah	19,911	Detroit	21,454
Phoenix	19,023	Cleveland	20,562
Minnesota	19,006	New Jersey	20,039
LA Lakers	17,505	New York	19,763
Dallas	17,502	Washington	18,756
Sacramento	17,317	Milwaukee	18,633
Denver	17,171	Boston	18,400
Seattle	17,100	Philadelphia	18,168
Houston	16,611	Indiana	16,530
LA Clippers	16,005	Atlanta	16,365
Golden St.	15,025	Orlando	15,998
		Miami	15,200

Note: Alamodome seating is expandable to 32,500.

Rank by Age

West

LA Clippers	1959	Philadelphia	1967
Seattle	1962	New York	1968
Golden St.	1966	Atlanta	1972
LA Lakers	1967	Washington	1973
Denver	1975	Indiana	1974
Houston	1975	New Jersey	1981
Dallas	1980	Charlotte	1988
Sacramento	1988	Detroit	1988
Minnesota	1990	Miami	1988
Utah	1991	Milwaukee	1988
Phoenix	1992	Orlando	1989
San Antonio	1993	Toronto	1989
Portland	1995	Chicago	1994
Vancouver	1995	Cleveland	1994
		Boston	1995

Note: The Seattle Coliseum was rebuilt and renamed Key Arena in 1995.

1994-95 NBA Attendance

Official overall attendance in the NBA for the 1994-95 season was 18,516,484 for an average per game crowd of 16,727 over 1,107 games. Teams in each conference are ranked by attendance over 41 home games based on total tickets distributed; sellouts are listed in S/O column. Numbers in parentheses indicate rank in 1993-94.

Western Conference

		Attendance	S/O	Average
1	San Antonio (1)	920,413	15	22,449
2	Utah (2)	811,159	34	19,784
3	Phoenix (3)	779,943	41	19,023
4	Sacramento (5)	709,997	41	17,317
5	Denver (6)	704,011	41	17,171
6	Dallas (12)	678,433	27	16,547
7	Houston (8)	653,389	27	15,936
8	Seattle (7)	633,748	18	15,457
9	Golden St. (7)	616,025	41	15,025
10	Minnesota (4)	603,518	2	14,720
11	LA Lakers (10)	591,125	13	14,418
12	Portland (11)	529,759	41	12,921
13	LA Clippers (13)	438,254	7	10,689
	TOTAL	8,669,774	318	15,986

Notes: LA Clippers played 34 games at LA Sports Arena (four sellouts and 9,332 avg.), six at The Pond in Anaheim (two sellouts and 17,782 avg.) and one at Yokohama Arena in Japan (a sellout at 14,239); Portland played 40 games at Memorial Coliseum (40 sellouts and 12,888 avg.) and one at Yokohama Arena in Japan (a sellout at 14,239). Also, Seattle played its entire 41-game regular season at the Tacoma Dome.

Eastern Conference

		Attendance	S/O	Average
1	Charlotte (1)	971,618	41	23,698
2	Chicago (4)	926,278	41	22,592
3	Cleveland (5)	833,850	31	20,338
4	New York (2)	810,283	41	19,763
5	Detroit (3)	719,090	14	17,539
6	Washington (9)	701,094	30	17,100
7	New Jersey (6)	684,102	16	16,685
8	Milwaukee (12)	670,720	13	16,359
9	Orlando (8)	656,410	41	16,010
10	Indiana (13)	655,028	24	15,976
11	Boston (11)	606,870	39	14,802
12	Miami (10)	598,761	8	14,604
13	Philadelphia (14)	507,809	3	12,386
14	Atlanta (12)	504,807	4	12,312
	TOTAL	9,846,710	299	16,487

Note: Boston played 38 games at Boston Garden (38 sellouts and 14,890 avg.) and three at Hartford Civic Center (one sellout and 13,683 avg.); Washington played 37 games at USAir Arena (26 sellouts and 17,569 avg.) and four at Baltimore Arena (4 sellouts, 12,756 avg.).

National Basketball Association (Cont.)
Home Courts

Listed below are the principal home courts used through the years by current NBA teams. The largest capacity of each arena is noted in the right-hand column. ABA arenas (1972-76) are included for Denver, Indiana, New Jersey and San Antonio.

Western Conference

Dallas Mavericks

1980—	Reunion Arena	17,502

Denver Nuggets

1967-75	Auditorium Arena	6,841
1975—	McNichols Sports Arena	17,171
	(1975 capacity–16,700)	

Golden State Warriors

1946-52	Philadelphia Arena	7,777
1952-62	Convention Hall (Philadelphia)	9,200
	& Philadelphia Arena	7,777
1962-64	Cow Palace (San Francisco)	13,862
1964-66	Civic Auditorium	7,500
	& (USF Memorial Gym)	6,000
1966-67	Cow Palace, Civic Auditorium	
	& Oakland Coliseum Arena	15,000
1967-71	Cow Palace	14,500
1971—	Oakland Coliseum Arena	15,025
	(1971 capacity–12,905)	

Houston Rockets

1967-71	San Diego Sports Arena	14,000
1971-72	Hofheinz Pavilion (Houston)	10,218
1972-73	Hofheinz Pavilion	10,218
	& HemisFair Arena (San Antonio)	10,446
1973-75	Hofheinz Pavilion	10,218
1975—	The Summit	16,661
	(1975 capacity–15,600)	

Los Angeles Clippers

1970-78	Memorial Auditorium (Buffalo)	17,300
1978-84	San Diego Sports Arena	12,167
1985-94	Los Angeles Sports Arena	16,005
1994—	Los Angeles Sports Arena	16,021
	& Arrowhead Pond	18,198

Los Angeles Lakers

1948-60	Minneapolis Auditorium	10,000
1960-67	Los Angeles Sports Arena	14,781
1967—	Great Western Forum (Inglewood, CA)	17,505
	(1967 capacity–17,086)	

Minnesota Timberwolves

1989-90	Hubert H. Humphrey Metrodome	23,000
1990—	Target Center	19,006

Phoenix Suns

1968-92	Arizona Veterans' Memorial Coliseum	14,487
1992—	America West Arena	19,023

Portland Trail Blazers

1970-95	Memorial Coliseum	12,888
1995—	Rose Garden	20,340

Sacramento Kings

1948-55	Edgarton Park Arena (Rochester, NY)	5,000
1955-58	Rochester War Memorial	10,000
1958-72	Cincinnati Gardens	11,438
1972-74	Municipal Auditorium (Kansas City)	9,929
	& Omaha (NE) Civic Auditorium	9,136
1974-78	Kemper Arena (Kansas City)	16,785
	& Omaha Civic Auditorium	9,136
1978-85	Kemper Arena	16,785
1985-88	ARCO Arena I	10,333
1988—	ARCO Arena II	17,317
	(1988 capacity–16,517)	

San Antonio Spurs

1967-70	Memorial Auditorium (Dallas)	8,088
	& Moody Coliseum (Dallas)	8,500
1970-71	Moody Coliseum	8,500
	Tarrant Convention Center (Ft. Worth)	13,500
	& Municipal Coliseum (Lubbock)	10,400
1971-73	Moody Coliseum	9,500
	& Memorial Auditorium	8,088
1973-93	HemisFair Arena (San Antonio)	16,057
1993—	The Alamodome	20,500

Seattle SuperSonics

1967-78	Seattle Center Coliseum	14,098
1978-85	Kingdome	40,192
1985-94	Seattle Center Coliseum	14,252
1994-95	Tacoma Dome	19,000
1995—	Key Arena at Seattle Center	17,100

Utah Jazz

1974-75	Municipal Auditorium	7,853
	& Louisiana Superdome	47,284
1975-79	Superdome	47,284
1979-83	Salt Palace (Salt Lake City)	12,519
1983-84	Salt Palace	12,519
	& Thomas & Mack Center (Las Vegas)	18,500
1985-91	Salt Palace	12,616
1991—	Delta Center	19,911

Vancouver Grizzlies

1995—	General Motors Place	20,004

Eastern Conference

Atlanta Hawks

1949-51	Wheaton Field House (Moline, IL)	6,000
1951-55	Milwaukee Arena	11,000
1955-68	Kiel Auditorium (St. Louis)	10,000
1968-72	Alexander Mem. Coliseum (Atlanta)	7,166
1972—	The Omni	16,365
	(1972 capacity–16,818)	

Boston Celtics

1946-95	Boston Garden	14,890
1995—	FleetCenter	18,400

Note: From 1975-95 the Celtics played some regular season games at the Hartford Civic Center (15,418).

Charlotte Hornets

1988—	Charlotte Coliseum	23,698
	(1988 capacity–23,500)	

Chicago Bulls

1966-67	Chicago Amphitheater	11,002
1967-94	Chicago Stadium	18,676
1994—	United Center	21,500

Cleveland Cavaliers

1970-74	Cleveland Arena	11,000
1974-94	The Coliseum (Richfield, OH)	20,273
1994—	Gund Arena	20,562

Detroit Pistons

1948-52 North Side H.S. Gym (Ft. Wayne, IN) 3,800
1952-57 Memorial Coliseum (Ft. Wayne)................9,306
1957-61 Olympia Stadium (Detroit)......................14,000
1961-78 Cobo Arena...11,147
1978-88 Silverdome (Pontiac, MI) 22,366
1988—   The Palace of Auburn Hills 21,454

Indiana Pacers

1967-74 State Fairgrounds (Indianapolis) 9,479
1974—   Market Square Arena 16,530
         (1974 capacity–17,287)

Miami Heat

1988—   Miami Arena 15,200

Milwaukee Bucks

1968-88 Milwaukee Arena (The Mecca) 11,052
1988—   Bradley Center 18,633

New Jersey Nets

1967-68 Teaneck (NJ) Armory 3,500
1968-69 Long Island Arena (Commack, NY)...........6,500
1969-71 Island Garden (W. Hempstead, NY)...........5,200
1971-77 Nassau Coliseum (Uniondale, NY)...........15,500
1977-81 Rutgers Ath. Center (Piscataway, NJ)..........9,050
1981—   Meadowlands Arena (E. Rutherford, NJ) 20,039

New York Knicks

1946-68 Madison Sq. Garden III (50th St.) 18,496
1968—   Madison Sq. Garden IV (33rd St.) 19,763
         (1968 capacity–19,694)

Orlando Magic

1989—   Orlando Arena 15,998

Philadelphia 76ers

1949-51 State Fair Coliseum (Syracuse, NY) 7,500
1951-63 Onondaga County (NY) War Memorial 8,000
1963-67 Convention Hall (Philadelphia)................12,000
         & Philadelphia Arena 7,777
1967—   CoreStates Spectrum 18,168
         (1967 capacity–15,205)

Toronto Raptors

1995—   SkyDome 22,911

Washington Bullets

1961-62 Chicago Amphitheater 11,000
1962-63 Chicago Coliseum 7,100
1963-73 Baltimore Civic Center............................12,289
1973—   USAir Arena (Landover, MD) 18,756
         (1973 capacity–17,500)

Note: Since 1988-89, the Bullets have played four regular season games at Baltimore Arena (12,756).

Building Name Changes: PHILADELPHIA— **CoreStates Spectrum** originally The Spectrum (1967-94); WASHINGTON—**USAir Arena** originally Capital Centre (1973–93).

NATIONAL FOOTBALL LEAGUE

American Conference

		Location	Built	Capacity	Field
Buffalo Bills	**Rich Stadium**	Orchard Park, N.Y.	1973	**80,024**	Turf
Cincinnati Bengals	**Riverfront Stadium**	Cincinnati, Ohio	1970	**60,389**	Turf
Cleveland Browns	**Cleveland Stadium**	Cleveland, Ohio	1931	**78,512**	Grass
Denver Broncos	**Mile High Stadium**	Denver, Colo.	1948	**76,273**	Grass
Houston Oilers	**Astrodome**	Houston, Texas	1965	**59,969**	Turf
Indianapolis Colts	**RCA Dome**	Indianapolis, Ind.	1984	**60,272**	Turf
Jacksonville Jaguars	**Jacksonville Municipal Stadium**	Jacksonville, Fla.	1949	**73,000**	Grass
Kansas City Chiefs	**Arrowhead Stadium**	Kansas City, Mo.	1972	**79,101**	Grass
Oakland Raiders	**Oakland-Alameda County Coliseum**	Oakland, Calif.	1966	**54,587**	Grass
Miami Dolphins	**Joe Robbie Stadium**	Miami, Fla.	1987	**74,916**	Grass
New England Patriots	**Foxboro Stadium**	Foxboro, Mass.	1971	**60,292**	Grass
New York Jets	**Giants Stadium**	E. Rutherford, N.J.	1976	**77,716**	Turf
Pittsburgh Steelers	**Three Rivers Stadium**	Pittsburgh, Pa.	1970	**59,600**	Turf
San Diego Chargers	**San Diego/Jack Murphy Stadium**	San Diego, Calif.	1967	**60,789**	Grass
Seattle Seahawks	**Kingdome**	Seattle, Wash.	1976	**66,400**	Turf

National Conference

		Location	Built	Capacity	Field
Arizona Cardinals	**Sun Devil Stadium**	Tempe, Ariz.	1958	**73,269**	Grass
Atlanta Falcons	**Georgia Dome**	Atlanta, Ga.	1992	**71,228**	Turf
Carolina Panthers	**Memorial Stadium**	Clemson, S.C.	1942	**81,473**	Grass
Chicago Bears	**Soldier Field**	Chicago, Ill.	1924	**66,950**	Grass
Dallas Cowboys	**Texas Stadium**	Irving, Texas	1971	**63,812**	Turf
Detroit Lions	**Pontiac Silverdome**	Pontiac, Mich.	1975	**80,365**	Turf
Green Bay Packers	**Lambeau Field**	Green Bay, Wisc.	1957	**60,790**	Grass
Minnesota Vikings	**Hubert H. Humphrey Metrodome**	Minneapolis, Minn.	1982	**63,000**	Turf
New Orleans Saints	**Louisiana Superdome**	New Orleans, La.	1975	**70,120**	Turf
New York Giants	**Giants Stadium**	E. Rutherford, N.J.	1976	**77,716**	Turf
Philadelphia Eagles	**Veterans Stadium**	Philadelphia, Pa.	1971	**65,178**	Turf
St. Louis Rams	**Busch Stadium**	St. Louis, Mo.	1966	**59,022**	Turf
	& Trans World Dome	St. Louis, Mo.	1995	**67,000**	Turf
San Francisco 49ers	**3Com Park**	San Francisco, Calif.	1960	**70,207**	Grass
Tampa Bay Buccaneers	**Tampa Stadium**	Tampa, Fla.	1967	**74,301**	Grass
Washington Redskins	**Robert F. Kennedy Stadium**	Washington, D.C.	1961	**56,454**	Grass

Notes: St. Louis was scheduled to open the 1995 season at Busch Stadium and move into its new indoor stadium by late October. Also, Green Bay, which had played some home games in Milwaukee every year since 1933, ended the affiliation after the 1994 season. Carolina played the 1995 season at Clemson University's Memorial Stadium, but will move into a new, 72,300-seat stadium in downtown Charlotte in 1996. Jacksonville Municipal Stadium was originally the Gator Bowl before being rebuilt and renamed in 1995. Candlestick Park in San Francisco was renamed 3Com Park (after the computer company) for the 1995 NFL season only.

National Football League (Cont.)

Rank by Capacity

AFC		NFC	
Buffalo	80,024	Carolina	81,473
Kansas City	79,101	Detroit	80,365
Cleveland	78,512	NY Giants	77,716
NY Jets	77,716	Tampa Bay	74,301
Denver	76,273	Arizona	73,269
Miami	74,916	Atlanta	71,228
Jacksonville	73,000	San Francisco	70,207
Seattle	66,400	New Orleans	70,120
San Diego	60,789	St. Louis	67,000
Cincinnati	60,389	Chicago	66,950
New England	60,292	Philadelphia	65,178
Indianapolis	60,272	Dallas	63,812
Houston	59,969	Minnesota	63,000
Pittsburgh	59,600	Green Bay	60,790
Oakland	54,587	Washington	56,454

Rank by Age

AFC		NFC	
Cleveland	1931	Chicago	1924
Denver	1948	Carolina	1942
Jacksonville	1949	Green Bay	1957
Houston	1965	Arizona	1958
Oakland	1966	San Francisco	1960
San Diego	1967	Washington	1961
Cincinnati	1970	Tampa Bay	1967
Pittsburgh	1970	Dallas	1971
New England	1971	Philadelphia	1971
Kansas City	1972	Detroit	1975
Buffalo	1973	New England	1975
NY Jets	1976	New Orleans	1975
Seattle	1976	NY Giants	1976
Indianapolis	1984	Minnesota	1982
Miami	1987	Atlanta	1992
		St. Louis	1995

1994 NFL Attendance

Official overall paid attendance in the NFL for the 1994 season was a record 14,030,435 for an average per game crowd of 62,636 over 224 games. Cumulative announced (day of game) attendance figures listed by *The Sporting News* in its 1995 Pro Football Guide show an overall NFL attendance of 13,479,680 for an average per game crowd of 60,177. Teams in each conference are ranked by attendance over eight home games, according to *TSN* figures. Rank column indicates rank in entire league. Numbers in parentheses indicate conference rank in 1993.

AFC

		Attendance	Rank	Average
1	Kansas City (2)	610,878	1st	76,360
2	Buffalo (1)	595,543	2nd	74,443
3	Denver (3)	574,180	4th	71,773
4	Cleveland (4)	559,582	5th	69,948
5	Miami (5)	551,970	6th	68,996
6	NY Jets (6)	528,538	8th	66,067
7	San Diego (7)	479,842	13th	59,980
8	New England (13)	472,718	15th	59,090
9	Pittsburgh (10)	461,272	18th	57,659
10	Cincinnati (14)	421,964	21st	52,746
11	Seattle (8)	420,136	22nd	52,517
12	LA Raiders (12)	409,564	24th	51,196
13	Indianapolis (11)	396,462	25th	49,558
14	Houston (9)	353,514	27th	44,189
	TOTAL	6,836,163	—	61,037

NFC

		Attendance	Rank	Average
1	NY Giants (1)	583,857	3rd	72,982
2	Detroit (3)	547,977	7th	68,497
3	Philadelphia (6)	518,691	9th	64,836
4	San Francisco (5)	516,736	10th	64,592
5	Dallas (4)	516,088	11th	64,511
6	Arizona (14)	511,317	12th	63,915
7	Minnesota (9)	474,744	14th	59,343
8	New Orleans (2)	469,900	16th	58,738
9	Chicago (7)	468,015	17th	58,502
10	Atlanta (8)	458,509	19th	57,314
11	Green Bay (10)	458,074	20th	57,259
12	Washington (11)	413,669	23rd	51,709
13	Tampa Bay (12)	367,443	26th	45,930
14	LA Rams (13)	338,497	28th	42,312
	TOTAL	6,643,517	—	59,317

Note: Seattle played three games at the University of Washington's Husky Stadium (63,015 avg.) and five at the Kingdome (46,218 avg.) after the building reopened on Nov. 9.

Note: Green Bay played five games at Lambeau Field (58,637 avg.) and three at County Stadium in Milwaukee (54,964 avg.).

Home Fields

Listed below are the principal home fields used through the years by current NFL teams. The largest capacity of each stadium is noted in the right-hand column. All-America Football Conference stadiums (1946-49) are included for Cleveland and San Francisco.

AFC

Buffalo Bills

1960-72	War Memorial Stadium	45,748
1973—	Rich Stadium (Orchard Park, NY)	80,024
	(1973 capacity–80,020)	

Cincinnati Bengals

1968-69	Nippert Stadium (Univ. of Cincinnati)	26,500
1970—	Riverfront Stadium	60,389
	(1970 capacity–56,200)	

Cleveland Browns

1946—	Cleveland Stadium	78,512
	(1946 capacity–85,703)	

Denver Broncos

1960—	Mile High Stadium	76,273
	(1960 capacity–34,000)	

Houston Oilers

1960-64	Jeppesen Stadium	23,500
1965-67	Rice Stadium (Rice Univ.)	70,000
1968—	Astrodome	59,969
	(1968 capacity–52,000)	

Indianapolis Colts

1953-83	Memorial Stadium (Baltimore)	60,020
1984—	RCA Dome (Indianapolis)	60,272
	(1984 capacity–60,127)	

Jacksonville Jaguars

1995—	Jacksonville Municipal Stadium	73,000

Kansas City Chiefs

1960-62	Cotton Bowl (Dallas)	72,000
1963-71	Municipal Stadium (Kansas City)	47,000
1972—	Arrowhead Stadium	79,101
	(1972 capacity–78,097)	

Miami Dolphins

1966-86	Orange Bowl	75,206
1987—	Joe Robbie Stadium	74,916
	(1987 capacity–75,500)	

New England Patriots

1960-62	Nickerson Field (Boston Univ.)	17,369
1963-68	Fenway Park	33,379
1969	Alumni Stadium (Boston College)	26,000
1970	Harvard Stadium	37,300
1971—	Foxboro Stadium	60,292
	(1971 capacity–61,114)	

New York Jets

1960-63	Polo Grounds	55,987
1964-83	Shea Stadium	60,372
1984—	Giants Stadium (E. Rutherford, NJ)	77,716

Oakland Raiders

1960	Kesar Stadium (San Francisco)	59,636
1961	Candlestick Park	42,500
1962-65	Frank Youell Field (Oakland)	20,000
1666-81	Oakland-Alameda County Coliseum	54,587
1982-94	Memorial Coliseum (Los Angeles)	67,800
1995—	Oakland-Alameda County Coliseum	54,587

Pittsburgh Steelers

1933-57	Forbes Field	35,000
1958-63	Forbes Field	35,000
	& Pitt Stadium	54,500
1964-69	Pitt Stadium	54,500
1970—	Three Rivers Stadium	59,600
	(1970 capacity–49,000)	

San Diego Chargers

1960	Memorial Coliseum (Los Angeles)	92,604
1961-66	Balboa Stadium (San Diego)	34,000
1967—	San Diego/Jack Murphy Stadium	60,789
	(1967 capacity–54,000)	

Seattle Seahawks

1976-94	Kingdome	66,000
1994	Kingdome	66,400
	& Husky Stadium	72,500
1995—	Kingdome	66,400

Ballpark Name Changes: CLEVELAND–**Cleveland Stadium** originally Municipal Stadium (1932-74); DENVER–**Mile High Stadium** originally Bears Stadium (1948-66); INDIANAPOLIS–**RCA Dome** originally Hoosier Dome (1984-94); NEW ENGLAND–**Foxboro Stadium** originally Schaefer Stadium (1971-82), then Sullivan Stadium (1983-89); SAN DIEGO–**San Diego/Jack Murphy Stadium** originally San Diego Stadium (1967-81).

NFC

Arizona Cardinals

1920-21	Normal Field (Chicago)	7,500
1922-25	Comiskey Park	28,000
1926-28	Normal Field	7,500
1929-59	Comiskey Park	52,000
1960-65	Busch Stadium (St. Louis)	34,000
1966-87	Busch Memorial Stadium	54,392
1988—	Sun Devil Stadium (Tempe, AZ)	73,269

Atlanta Falcons

1966-91	Atlanta-Fulton County Stadium	59,643
1992—	Georgia Dome	71,228

Carolina Panthers

1995	Memorial Stadium (Clemson, SC)	81,473
1996	Carolinas Stadium	72,300

Chicago Bears

1920	Staley Field (Decatur, IL)	—
1921-70	Wrigley Field (Chicago)	37,741
1971—	Soldier Field	66,950
	(1971 capacity–55,049)	

Dallas Cowboys

1960-70	Cotton Bowl	72,132
1971—	Texas Stadium (Irving, TX)	63,812
	(1971 capacity–65,101)	

Detroit Lions

1930-33	Spartan Stadium (Portsmouth, OH)	8,200
1934-37	Univ. of Detroit Stadium	25,000
1938-74	Tiger Stadium	54,468
1975—	Pontiac Silverdome	80,365
	(1975 capacity–80,638)	

Green Bay Packers

1921-22	Hagemeister Brewery Park	—
1923-24	Bellevue Park	—
1925-56	City Stadium I	24,800
1957—	Lambeau Field	60,790
	(1957 capacity–32,150)	

Note: The Packers played some games in Milwaukee from 1933-94: at Borchert Field, State Fair Park and Marquette Stadium (1933-52), and County Stadium (1953-94).

St. Louis Rams

1937-42	Municipal Stadium (Cleveland)	85,703
1945	Suspended operations for one year.	
1944-45	Municipal Stadium	85,703
1946-79	Memorial Coliseum (Los Angeles)	92,604
1980-94	Anaheim Stadium	69,008
1995	Busch Stadium (St. Louis)	59,022
	& Trans World Dome	67,000

Minnesota Vikings

1961-81	Metropolitan Stadium (Bloomington)	48,446
1982—	HHH Metrodome (Minneapolis)	63,000
	(1982 capacity–62,220)	

New Orleans Saints

1967-74	Tulane Stadium	80,997
1975—	Louisiana Superdome	70,120
	(1975 capacity–74,472)	

New York Giants

1925-55	Polo Grounds II	55,200
1956-73	Yankee Stadium I	63,800
1973-74	Yale Bowl (New Haven, CT)	70,896
1975	Shea Stadium	60,372
1976—	Giants Stadium (E. Rutherford, NJ)	77,716
	(1976 capacity–76,800)	

Philadelphia Eagles

1933-35	Baker Bowl	18,800
1936-39	Municipal Stadium	73,702
1940	Shibe Park	33,608
1941	Municipal Stadium	73,702
1942	Shibe Park	33,608
1943	Forbes Field (Pittsburgh)	34,528
1944-57	Shibe Park	33,608
1958-70	Franklin Field (Univ. of Penn.)	60,546
1971—	Veterans Stadium	65,178
	(1971 capacity–65,000)	

San Francisco 49ers

1946-70	Kezar Stadium	59,636
1971—	3Com Park	68,491
	(1971 capacity–61,246)	

National Football League (Cont.)
Home Fields

Tampa Bay Buccaneers				Washington Redskins		

1976— Tampa Stadium 74,296
        (1976 capacity–71,951)

1932   Braves Field (Boston)..............................40,000
1933-36 Fenway Park 27,000
1937-60 Griffith Stadium (Washington, DC)...........35,000
1961— RFK Stadium 56,454
        (1961 capacity–55,004)

Ballpark Name Changes: ATLANTA–**Atlanta-Fulton County Stadium** originally Atlanta Stadium (1966-74); CHICAGO–**Wrigley Field** originally Cubs Park (1916-25), also, Comiskey Park originally White Sox Park (1910-12); DETROIT–**Tiger Stadium** originally Navin Field (1912-37), then Briggs Stadium (1938-60), also, **Pontiac Silverdome** originally Pontiac Metropolitan Stadium (1975); GREEN BAY–**Lambeau Field** originally City Stadium II (1957-64); PHILADELPHIA–**Shibe Park** renamed Connie Mack Stadium in 1953; ST. LOUIS–**Busch Memorial Stadium** renamed Busch Stadium in 1983; SAN FRANCISCO–**3Com Park** originally Candlestick Park (1960-94); WASHINGTON–**RFK Stadium** originally D.C. Stadium (1961-68).

NATIONAL HOCKEY LEAGUE

Western Conference

		Location	Built	Capacity	Rink
Anaheim, Mighty Ducks of	**Arrowhead Pond**	Anaheim, Calif.	1993	**17,250**	200 x 85
Calgary Flames........................	**Olympic Saddledome**	Calgary, Alb.	1983	**20,230**	200 x 85
Chicago Blackhawks	**United Center**	Chicago, Ill.	1994	**20,500**	200 x 85
Colorado Avalanche	**McNichols Arena**	Denver, Colo.	1975	**16,058**	200 x 85
Dallas Stars	**Reunion Arena**	Dallas, Texas	1980	**16,924**	200 x 85
Detroit Red Wings	**Joe Louis Arena**	Detroit, Mich.	1979	**19,275**	200 x 85
Edmonton Oilers	**Northlands Coliseum**	Edmonton, Alb.	1974	**17,503**	200 x 85
Los Angeles Kings	**Great Western Forum**	Inglewood, Calif.	1967	**16,005**	200 x 85
St. Louis Blues	**Kiel Center**	St. Louis, Mo.	1994	**19,260**	200 x 85
San Jose Sharks........................	**San Jose Arena**	San Jose, Calif.	1993	**17,190**	200 x 85
Toronto Maple Leafs	**Maple Leaf Gardens**	Toronto, Ont.	1931	**15,728***	200 x 85
Vancouver Canucks...................	**General Motors Place**	Vancouver, B.C.	1995	**19,056**	200 x 85
Winnipeg Jets............................	**Winnipeg Arena**	Winnipeg, Man.	1954	**15,393**	200 x 85

*Including Standing Room.

Eastern Conference

		Location	Built	Capacity	Rink
Boston Bruins	**FleetCenter**	Boston, Mass.	1995	**17,200**	200 x 85
Buffalo Sabres	**Memorial Auditorium**	Buffalo, N.Y.	1940	**16,284***	193 x 84
Florida Panthers.......................	**Miami Arena**	Miami, Fla.	1988	**14,503**	200 x 85
Hartford Whalers	**Civic Center Coliseum**	Hartford, Conn.	1975	**15,635**	200 x 85
Montreal Canadiens..................	**Montreal Forum**	Montreal, Que.	1924	**17,959***	200 x 85
	& New Montreal Forum	Montreal, Que.	1996	**21,450**	200 x 85
New Jersey Devils	**Byrne Meadowlands Arena**	E. Rutherford, N.J.	1981	**19,040**	200 x 85
New York Islanders	**Veterans' Coliseum**	Uniondale, N.Y.	1971	**16,297**	200 x 85
New York Rangers	**Madison Square Garden**	New York, N.Y.	1968	**18,200**	200 x 85
Ottawa Senators	**Ottawa Civic Center**	Ottawa, Ont.	1967	**10,755**	200 x 85
	& Ottawa Palladium	Ottawa, Ont.	1996	**18,500**	200 x 85
Philadelphia Flyers	**CoreStates Spectrum**	Philadelphia, Pa.	1967	**17,380**	200 x 85
Pittsburgh Penguins	**Civic Arena**	Pittsburgh, Pa.	1961	**17,537**	200 x 85
Tampa Bay Lightning	**ThunderDome**	St. Petersburg, Fla.	1990	**26,000**	200 x 85
Washington Capitals	**USAir Arena**	Landover, Md.	1973	**18,130**	200 x 85

*Including Standing Room.

Rank by Capacity

Western		Eastern	
Chicago 20,500		Tampa Bay 26,000	
Calgary................20,230		Montreal...............21,450	
Detroit..................19,275		New Jersey............19,040	
St. Louis................19,260		Ottawa..................18,500	
Vancouver............19,056		NY Rangers 18,200	
Edmonton.............17,503		Washington 18,130	
Anaheim 17,250		Pittsburgh 17,537	
San Jose 17,190		Philadelphia..........17,380	
Dallas...................16,924		Boston 17,200	
Colorado..............16,058		NY Islanders 16,297	
Los Angeles 16,005		Buffalo 16,284	
Toronto 15,728		Hartford 15,635	
Winnipeg..............15,393		Florida 14,503	

Rank by Age

Western		Eastern	
Toronto 1931		Buffalo 1940	
Winnipeg 1954		Pittsburgh 1961	
Los Angeles 1967		Philadelphia.............1967	
Edmonton 1974		NY Rangers...............1968	
Colorado 1975		NY Islanders.............1971	
Detroit 1979		Washington..............1973	
Dallas......................1980		Hartford....................1975	
Calgary...................1983		New Jersey...............1981	
Anaheim 1993		Florida 1988	
San Jose 1993		Tampa Bay 1990	
Chicago 1994		Boston 1995	
St. Louis 1994		Montreal 1996	
Vancouver...............1995		Ottawa 1996	

Note: Hartford Civic Center was rebuilt in 1980.

The Garden Was Boston's Bleak House

by Clark Booth

People wonder how you can be sentimental about a grimy, gothic sports emporium that had all the creature comforts of the Roman Coliseum and none of its charm.

But then we are talking about "The Garden," built by Tex Rickard during the Golden Age of Sport for the amusement of Greater Bostonians who have always prized the idiosyncratic.

The place was dank in the winter, a sauna in the spring and summer and, after the circus had come through in the fall, it invariably stunk of tigers and elephants until the season changed and it got chilly all over again. Outsiders thought it was fairly absurd but natives remained reverent because we believed the Garden had institutional heritage the equal of any pile of brick and mortar in the New World.

Rickard, the match-maker who presided over New York's Madison Square Garden, built the Boston Garden principally for boxing. Dorchester's Dick (Honeyboy) Finnegan beat French featherweight champion Andre Routis in the building's first event on Nov. 17, 1928.

But from the start, hockey was the game of choice. The Bruins of 1929, led by Eddie Shore and Dit Clapper, were the first resident champs. Five decades later, Bobby Orr regained the Stanley Cup with an airborne goal in overtime to lead the home team out of the NHL wilderness after 29 years.

That was 1970. Fancy sporting palaces were sprouting in even the backwaters of the Republic and there was a rising clamor— mainly from basketball fans— for Boston to get into the 20th century. Hockey, boxing and wrestling were better suited to the Garden's noir than basketball and the softer entertainments. It had everything to do with ambiance. The Garden was a bleak house, full of shadows and characters straight out of Dickens. The harsher the game, the better the fit.

It's illustrative that hockey's two ugliest brawls —Shore's attack on Ace Bailey in 1933 and Rocket Richard's assault on Hal Laycoe and linesman Cliff Thompson in 1955— took place there. But it was the rather more artistic works of Red Auerbach's Celtics that will be most remembered. Their 16 championship banners

Wide World Photos

The Bruins were tenants longer, but it was the Celtics' 16 NBA championship banners that gave the **Boston Garden** its international stature.

hanging from the rafters, spanning the ages from Cousy and Russell to Parish and Bird, gave the joint international stature.

There was, however, much more to the Garden. FDR, Churchill, Curley, De Valera and JFK all spoke there. Louis, Marciano, Robinson and Hagler fought there. Billy Sunday, Billy Graham, Bishop Sheen and Aimee Semple McPherson came to save souls. And Benny Goodman, Elvis, the Beatles, the Rolling Stones and Pavarotti came to make music.

At the Garden, Bill Tilden played tennis and Notre Dame played football. It accommodated six-day bike races, Beanpot college hockey, rodeos, women's softball, ski-jumping, midget auto races and opera. And old-timers still insist the greatest act of all was a wisp of a Scandinavian girl named Sonja Henie.

As luck would have it, the old barn's last official event saw a lackluster Bruins squad get eliminated from the playoffs on May 14. Afterward there were too many cops in too much of a hurry to clear the place.

Sixty-eight years of history ended with a whimper. It didn't seem right.

Clark Booth is the special projects reporter at WCVB-TV in Boston and has covered sports and politics in the city since 1962.

National Hockey League (Cont.)

1995 NHL Attendance

Official overall paid attendance for the 1995 season according to the NHL accounting office was 9,233,884 (paid tickets) for an average per game crowd of 14,798 over 624 games. Cumulative announced (day of game) attendance figures listed by *The Hockey News* in its May 19, 1995 edition show an overall NHL attendance of 9,904,462 (including standing room) for an average per game crowd of 15,873 (an increase of 250 fans per game over 1993-94). Teams in each conference are ranked by attendance over 24 home games, according to *THN* figures. There were no neutral site games. Number of sellouts are listed in S/O column. Numbers in parentheses indicate rank in 1993-94.

Western Conference

		Attendance	S/O	Average
1	Detroit (1)	474,714	24	19,780
2	Calgary (2)	456,858	4	19,036
3	Chicago (3)	499,625	22	20,818
4	St. Louis (4)	467,274	17	19,470
5	San Jose (6)	412,560	24	17,190
6	Anaheim (5)	412,176	24	17,174
7	Dallas (7)	401,489	17	16,729
8	Toronto (8)	377,596	23	15,733
9	Los Angeles (9)	369,929	14	15,414
10	Vancouver (10)	334,384	2	13,933
11	Edmonton (11)	314,972	0	13,124
12	Winnipeg (12)	312,300	4	13,013
	TOTAL	4,833,877	176	16,461

Eastern Conference

		Attendance	S/O	Average
1	Tampa Bay (1)	478,594	2	19,941
2	NY Rangers (2)	436,646	24	18,194
3	Philadelphia (3)	411,968	24	17,165
4	Montreal (4)	407,146	24	16,964
5	New Jersey (6)	393,106	6	16,379
6	Pittsburgh (5)	386,599	9	16,108
7	Buffalo (7)	361,271	9	15,053
8	Quebec (9)	345,480	8	14,395
9	Washington (8)	343,235	2	14,301
10	Boston (11)	343,218	20	14,301
11	Florida (10)	340,742	12	14,198
12	NY Islanders (12)	301,764	3	12,574
13	Hartford (13)	283,720	3	11,822
14	Ottawa (14)	237,096	5	9,879
	TOTAL	5,070,585	151	15,091

Home Ice

Listed below are the principal home buildings used through the years by current NHL teams. The largest capacity of each arena is noted in the right hand column. World Hockey Association arenas (1972-76) are included for Edmonton, Hartford, Quebec (now Colorado) and Winnipeg.

Western Conference

Anaheim, Mighty Ducks of

1993—	Arrowhead Pond	17,250

Calgary Flames

1972-80	The Omni (Atlanta)	15,278
1980-83	Calgary Corral	7,424
1983—	Olympic Saddledome	20,230
	(1983 capacity—16,674)	

Chicago Blackhawks

1926-29	Chicago Coliseum	5,000
1929-94	Chicago Stadium	17,317
1994—	United Center	20,500

Colorado Avalanche

1972-95	Le Colisée de Quebec	15,399
1995—	McNichols Arena (Denver)	16,058

Dallas Stars

1967-93	Met Center (Bloomington, MN)	15,174
1993—	Reunion Arena (Dallas)	16,942

Detroit Red Wings

1926-27	Border Cities Arena (Windsor, Ont.)	3,200
1927-79	Olympia Stadium (Detroit)	16,700
1979—	Joe Louis Arena	19,275
	(1979 capacity—19,275)	

Edmonton Oilers

1972-74	Edmonton Gardens	7,200
1974—	Northlands Coliseum	17,503
	(1974 capacity—15,513)	

Los Angeles Kings

1967—	Great Western Forum (Inglewood, CA)	16,005
	(1967 capacity—15,651)	

Note: The Kings played 17 games at Long Beach Sports Arena and LA Sports Arena at the start of the 1967-68 season.

St. Louis Blues

1967-94	St. Louis Arena	17,188
1994—	Kiel Center	19,260

San Jose Sharks

1991-93	Cow Palace (Daly City, CA)	11,100
1993—	San Jose Arena	17,190

Toronto Maple Leafs

1917-31	Mutual Street Arena	8,000
1931—	Maple Leaf Gardens	15,728
	(1931 capacity—13,542)	

Vancouver Canucks

1970-95	Pacific Coliseum	16,150
1995—	General Motors Place	19,056

Winnipeg Jets

1972—	Winnipeg Arena	15,393
	(1972 capacity—10,177)	

Building Name Changes: DALLAS—**Met Center** in Minneapolis originally Metropolitan Sports Center (1967-82); LOS ANGELES—**Great Western Forum** originally The Forum (1967-88); ST. LOUIS—**St. Louis Arena** renamed The Checkerdome in 1977, then St. Louis Arena again in 1982.

Eastern Conference

Boston Bruins

1924-28	Boston Arena	6,200
1928-95	Boston Garden	14,448
1995—	FleetCenter	17,200

Buffalo Sabres

1970—	Memorial Auditorium (The Aud)	16,284
	(1970 capacity—10,429)	

Florida Panthers

1993— Miami Arena 14,503

Hartford Whalers

1972-73 Boston Garden 14,442
1973-74 Boston Garden (regular season)...............14,442
   West Springfield (MA) Big E (playoffs) 5,513
1974-75 West Springfield Big E 5,513
   & Hartford (CT) Civic Center....................10,507
1975-76 Hartford Civic Center 10,507
1977-78 Hartford Civic Center 10,507
   & Springfield (MA) Civic Center................7,725
1978-79 Springfield Civic Center 7,725
1979-80 Springfield Civic Center 7,725
   & Hartford Civic Center II 14,250
1980— Hartford Civic Center II 15,635
   (1980 capacity–14,460)

Note: The Hartford Civic Center roof caved in January 1978, forcing the Whalers to move their home games to Springfield, MA for two years.

Montreal Canadiens

1910-20 Jubilee Arena...3,200
1913-18 Montreal Arena (Westmount)....................6,000
1918-26 Mount Royal Arena 6,750
1926-68 Montreal Forum I 15,500
1968-95 Montreal Forum II 17,959
1996— Montreal Forum III 21,450

New Jersey Devils

1974-76 Kemper Arena (Kansas City) 16,300
1976-82 McNichols Arena (Denver) 15,900
1982— Meadowlands Arena (E. Rutherford, NJ)....19,040
   (1982 capacity–19,023)

New York Islanders

1972— Nassau Veterans' Mem. Coliseum............16,297
   (1972 capacity–14,500)

New York Rangers

1925-68 Madison Square Garden III 15,925
1968— Madison Square Garden IV 18,200
   (1968 capacity–17,250)

Ottawa Senators

1992-95 Ottawa Civic Center 10,755
1996— Ottawa Palladium (Kanata) 18,500

Philadelphia Flyers

1967— CoreStates Spectrum................................17,380
   (1967 capacity–14,558)

Pittsburgh Penguins

1967— Civic Arena..17,537
   (1967 capacity–12,508)

Tampa Bay Lightning

1992-93 Expo Hall (Tampa) 10,500
1993— ThunderDome (St. Petersburg)................26,000

Washington Capitals

1974— USAir Arena (Landover, MD)...................18,130

Building Name Changes: PHILADELPHIA—**CoreStates Spectrum** originally The Spectrum (1967-94); WASHINGTON—**USAir Arena** originally Capital Centre (1974-93).

AUTO RACING

Formula One, NASCAR Winston Cup, IndyCar and the new Indy Racing League (IRL) racing circuits. Qualifying records accurate as of Sept. 1, 1995. Capacity figures for NASCAR, IndyCar and IRL tracks are approximate and pertain to grandstand seating only. Standing room and hillside terrain seating featured at most road courses are not included.

IndyCar

	Location	Miles	Qual.mph Record	Set By	Seats
Belle Isle Park	Detroit, Mich.	2.1**	108.649	Nigel Mansell (1994)	18,000
Burke Lakefront Airport	Cleveland, Ohio	2.37**	147.512	Gil de Ferran (1995)	36,000
Exhibition Place	Toronto, Ont.	1.78**	110.396	Jacques Villeneuve (1995)	60,000
Laguna Seca Raceway	Monterey, Calif.	2.21*	113.768	Paul Tracy (1994)	8,000
Long Beach	Long Beach, Calif.	1.59**	109.066	Michael Andretti (1995)	45,000
Miami	Miami, Fla.	1.84**	104.892	Michael Andretti (1995)	50,000
Michigan International Speedway	Brooklyn, Mich.	2.0	234.275	Mario Andretti (1993)	70,000
Mid-Ohio Sports Car Course	Lexington, Ohio	2.25*	119.517	Al Unser Jr. (1994)	6,000
The Milwaukee Mile	West Allis, Wisc.	1.0	165.752	Raul Boesel (1993)	36,800
Nazareth Speedway	Nazareth, Pa.	1.0	187.441	Robby Gordon (1995)	35,000
Pacific Place	Vancouver, B.C.	1.65**	110.293	Scott Goodyear (1993)	65,000
Portland International Raceway	Portland, Ore.	1.95	117.614	Jacques Villeneuve (1995)	27,000
Piquet Int'l Raceway (new course)	Rio de Janeiro, Brazil	1.3	—	First race in 1996.	80,000
Road America	Elkhart Lake, Wisc.	4.0*	142.206	Jacques Villeneuve (1995)	10,000
Surfers Paradise	Gold Coast, Australia	2.8**	106.053	Nigel Mansell (1994)	55,000

*Road courses (not ovals). **Temporary street circuits.

Indy Racing League

Founded by Indianapolis Motor Speedway president Tony George, the Indy Racing League will compete with the IndyCar circuit and field five races, anchored by the Indianapolis 500, in 1996.

	Location	Miles	Qual.mph Record	Set By	Seats
Indianapolis Motor Speedway	Indianapolis, Ind.	2.5	232.482	Roberto Guerrero (1992)	265,000
Las Vegas Motor Speedway	Las Vegas, Nev.	1.5	—	First race in 1996.	107,000
New Hampshire Intl. Speedway	Loudon, N.H.	1.06	177.436	Andre Ribeiro (1995)	60,000
Phoenix International Raceway	Phoenix, Ariz.	1.0	181.952	Bryan Herta (1995)	50,000
Walt Disney World Course	Orlando, Fla.	1.1	—	First race in 1996.	55,000

Auto Racing (Cont.)
NASCAR

	Location	Miles	Qual.mph Record	Set By	Seats
Atlanta Motor Speedway	Hampton, Ga.	1.52	185.830	Greg Sacks (1994)	78,000
Bristol International Raceway	Bristol, Tenn.	0.53	125.093	Mark Martin (1995)	65,000
Charlotte Motor Speedway	Concord, N.C.	1.5	185.759	Ward Burton (1994)	140,000
Darlington International Raceway	Darlington, N.C.	1.37	170.833	Jeff Gordon (1995)	55,000
Daytona International Speedway	Daytona Beach, Fla.	2.5	210.364	Bill Elliott (1987)	97,900
Dover Downs International Speedway	Dover, Del.	1.0	153.669	Jeff Gordon (1995)	55,000
Indianapolis Motor Speedway	Indianapolis, Ind.	2.5	172.536	Jeff Gordon (1995)	265,000
Martinsville Speedway	Martinsville, Va.	0.53	94.129	Ted Musgrave (1994)	56,000
Michigan International Speedway	Brooklyn, Mich.	2.0	186.611	Jeff Gordon (1995)	70,000
New Hampshire Int'l Speedway	Loudon, N.H.	1.06	128.815	Mark Martin (1995)	60,000
North Carolina Motor Speedway	Rockingham, N.C.	1.02	157.620	Jeff Gordon (1995)	55,000
North Wilkesboro Speedway	N. Wilkesboro, N.C.	0.63	119.016	Ernie Irvan (1994)	45,000
Phoenix International Raceway	Phoenix, Ariz.	1.0	129.833	Sterling Marlin (1994)	50,000
Pocono International Raceway	Long Pond, Pa.	2.5	164.558	Rusty Wallace (1994)	77,000
Richmond International Raceway	Richmond, Va.	0.75	124.757	Jeff Gordon (1995)	71,350
Sears Point International Raceway	Sonoma, Calif.	2.52*	92.132	Ricky Rudd (1995)	42,500
Talladega Superspeedway	Talladega, Ala.	2.66	212.809	Bill Elliott (1987)	85,000
Watkins Glen	Watkins Glen, N.Y.	2.45*	120.411	Mark Martin (1995)	35,000

*Road courses (not ovals). **Note:** Richmond sells reserved seats only (no infield) for Winston Cup races.

Formula One
Race track capacity figures unavailable.

Grand Prix	Miles	Qual.mph Record	Set By
Argentine **Autodromo de la Ciudad** (Buenos Aires)	2.64	84.131	David Coulthard (1995)
Australian **Adelaide** (South Australia)	2.347	114.680	Nigel Mansell (1992)
Belgian **Spa-Francorchamps**	4.333	141.123	Nigel Mansell (1992)
Brazilian **Interlagos** (Sao Paulo)	2.687	127.799	Nigel Mansell (1992)
British **Silverstone** (Towcester)	3.247	148.043	Nigel Mansell (1992)
Canadian **Circuit Gilles Villeneuve** (Montreal)	2.753	125.459	Alain Prost (1993)
European **Nürburgring** (Nürburg/Eifel, Germany)	2.822	131.219	Teo Fabi (1985)
French **Magny Cours** (Nevers)	2.641	128.709	Nigel Mansell (1992)
German **Hockenheimring** (Hockenheim)	4.235	156.722	Nigel Mansell (1991)
Hungarian **Hungaroring** (Budapest)	2.465	117.602	Riccardo Patrese (1992)
Italian **Autodromo di Nazionale, Monza** (Milan)	3.604	159.951	Ayrton Senna (1991)
Japanese **Suzuka** (Nagoya)	3.641	138.515	Gerhard Berger (1991)
Monaco **Monte Carlo**	2.068	94.766	Michael Schumacher (1994)
Pacific **T1 Circuit Aida** (Japan)	2.301	117.970	Ayrton Senna (1994)
Portuguese **Autodromo do Estoril**	2.703	133.224	Nigel Mansell (1992)
San Marino **Ferrari Cicuit** (Imola, Italy)	3.132	138.265	Ayrton Senna (1994)
Spanish **Catalunya** (Barcelona)	2.950	136.472	Alain Prost (1993)

SOCCER

World's Premier Soccer Stadiums
According to *The Ultimate Encyclopedia of Soccer*, compiled by the editors of *World Soccer* magazine.

Top 20 (Listed by city)

Stadium	Location	Capacity	Stadium	Location	Capacity
Nou Camp	Barcelona, Spain	130,000	Luzhniki Stadion	Moscow, Russia	100,000
Olympiastadion	Berlin, Germany	76,006	Olympiastadion	Munich, Germany	74,000
Monumental	Buenos Aires, Argentina	76,000	San Paulo	Naples, Italy	85,102
Hampden Park	Glasgow, Scotland	50,000	Parc des Princes	Paris, France	49,700
Estadio da Luz	Lisbon, Portugal	130,000	Rose Bowl	Pasadena, Calif.	102,083
Wembley	London, England	80,000	Maracana	Rio de Janeiro, Brazil	120,000
Santiago Bernabeu	Madrid, Spain	105,000	Olimpico	Rome, Italy	80,000
Azteca	Mexico City, Mexico	110,000	Morumbi	Sao Paulo, Brazil	150,000
Guiseppe Meazza	Milan, Italy	83,107	Olympic Stadium	Tokyo, Japan	62,000
Centenario	Montevideo, Uruguay	76,609	Prater	Vienna, Austria	62,958

Note: Construction is underway in Paris for an 80,000-seat stadium that will be the principle venue for the 1998 World Cup.

Major League Soccer

The long-delayed debut of Major League Soccer, the new U.S. Division I outdoor league, is scheduled to take place March 31, 1996. The 10-team MLS is sanctioned by FIFA and will end its first season with a championship game on Oct. 20. Note that as of Aug. 1, 1995, none of the teams had nicknames and all capacity figures are approximate given the adjustments of football stadium seating to soccer.

Western Conference

	Stadium	Built	Seats	Field
Dallas	Cotton Bowl	1932	47,500	Grass
Denver	Mile High	1948	38,000	Grass
Kansas City	Arrowhead	1972	29,500	Grass
Los Angeles	L.A. Coliseum	1923	47,000	Grass
San Jose	Spartan	1933	31,218	Grass

Eastern Conference

	Stadium	Built	Seats	Field
Boston	Foxboro	1971	38,482	Grass
Columbus	Ohio	1922	32,588	Grass
New Jersey	Giants	1976	34,235	Turf
Tampa	Tampa	1967	35,000	Grass
Washington, D.C.	RFK	1961	55,757	Grass

MISCELLANEOUS

Canadian Football League

North Division

		Location	Built	Capacity	Field
British Columbia Lions	B.C. Place	Vancouver, B.C.	1983	40,000	Turf
Calgary Stampeders	McMahon Stadium	Calgary, Alb.	1960	37,317	Turf
Edmonton Eskimos	Commonwealth Stadium	Edmonton, Alb.	1978	60,081	Grass
Hamilton Tiger-Cats	Ivor Wynne Stadium	Hamilton, Ont.	1932	29,123	Turf
Ottawa Rough Riders	Frank Clair Stadium	Ottawa, Ont.	1967	30,927	Turf
Saskatchewan Roughriders	Taylor Field	Regina, Sask.	1948	27,637	Turf
Toronto Argos	SkyDome	Toronto, Ont.	1989	50,377	Turf
Winnipeg Blue Bombers	Winnipeg Stadium	Winnipeg, Man.	1953	33,554	Turf

South Division

		Location	Built	Capacity	Field
Baltimore Stallions	Memorial Stadium	Baltimore, Md.	1954	54,600	Grass
Birmingham Barracudas	Legion Field	Birmingham, Ala.	1927	75,017	Grass
Memphis Mad Dogs	Liberty Bowl	Memphis, Tenn.	1965	62,380	Grass
San Antonio Texans	Alamodome	San Antonio, Tex.	1993	59,000	Turf
Shreveport Pirates	Independence Stadium	Shreveport, La.	1936	40,000	Grass

Note: Independence Stadium holds 50,460, but only 40,000 seats are available for CFL games.

Arena Football League

American Conference

		Location	Built	Capacity
Arizona Rattlers	America West Arena	Phoenix, Ariz.	1992	15,505
Iowa Barnstormers	Veterans Auditorium	Des Moines, Iowa	1955	11,500
Las Vegas Sting	Thomas & Mack Center	Las Vegas, Nev.	1993	13,000
Memphis Pharaohs	The Pyramid	Memphis, Tenn.	1992	18,500
Milwaukee Mustangs	Bradley Center	Milwaukee, Wisc.	1988	17,819
St. Louis Stampede	Kiel Center	St. Louis, Mo.	1994	18,000
San Jose SaberCats	San Jose Arena	San Jose, Calif.	1990	17,190

National Conference

		Location	Built	Capacity
Albany Firebirds	Knickerbocker Arena	Albany, NY	1990	14,080
Charlotte Rage	Charlotte Coliseum	Charlotte, N.C.	1988	21,864
Connecticut Coyotes	Hartford Civic Center	Hartford, Conn.	1975	16,500
Miami Hooters	Miami Arena	Miami, Fla.	1988	14,600
Orlando Predators	Orlando Arena	Orlando, Fla.	1989	12,680
Tampa Bay Storm	ThunderDome	Tampa Bay, Fla.	1990	20,250

Horse Racing
Triple Crown race tracks

Race	Racetrack	Seats	Infield
Kentucky Derby	Churchill Downs	48,500	100,000
Preakness	Pimlico Race Course	40,000	60,000
Belmont Sakes	Belmont Park	32,491	50,000

Record crowds: Kentucky Derby— 163,628 (1974); Preakness— 98,896 (1989); Belmont— 82,694 (1971).

Tennis
Grand Slam center courts

Event	Main Stadium	Seats
Australian Open	Flanders Park	15,000
French Open	Stade Roland Garros	16,500
Wimbledon	Centre Court	13,118
U.S. Open	Louis Armstrong Stadium	19,500

COLLEGE BASKETBALL

The 50 Largest Arenas

The 50 largest arenas in Division I for the 1995-96 NCAA regular season. Note that (*) indicates part-time home court.

		Seats	Home Team			Seats	Home Team
1	Carrier Dome	33,000	Syracuse	26	Erwin Center	16,042	Texas
2	Thompson-Boling Arena	24,535	Tennessee	27	Miami Arena	15,862	Miami
3	Rupp Arena	24,000	Kentucky	28	LA Sports Arena	15,509	USC
4	Marriott Center	22,700	BYU	29	Carver-Hawkeye Arena	15,500	Iowa
5	Dean Smith Center	21,572	N. Carolina		Knickerbocker Arena	15,500	Siena*
6	The Pyramid	20,142	Memphis	31	Memorial Gymnasium	15,317	Vanderbilt
7	Byrne Meadowlands Arena	20,029	Seton Hall*	32	Breslin Events Center	15,138	Michigan St.
8	Kiel Center	20,000	Saint Louis	33	Coleman Coliseum	15,043	Alabama
	UNI-Dome	20,000	Northern Iowa	34	Oakland Coliseum	15,039	California*
10	Bud Walton Arena	19,200	Arkansas	35	Arena-Auditorium	15,028	Wyoming
11	USAir Arena	19,035	Georgetown	36	Jordan Center	15,000	Penn St.
12	Madison Square Garden	18,876	St. John's*		Huntsman Center	15,000	Utah
13	Freedom Hall	18,865	Louisville	38	Cole Fieldhouse	14,500	Maryland
14	Bradley Center	18,592	Marquette	39	Joel Memorial Coliseum	14,407	Wake Forest
15	Thomas & Mack Center	18,500	UNLV	40	Devaney Sports Center	14,302	Nebraska
16	CoreStates Spectrum	18,060	Villanova*	41	Williams Arena	14,300	Minnesota
17	University Arena (The Pit)	18,018	New Mexico	42	University Activity Center	14,287	Arizona St.
18	San Jose Arena	18,000	San Jose St.	43	Maravich Assembly Center	14,164	LSU
19	Rosemont Horizon	17,500	DePaul*	44	McKale Center	14,140	Arizona
20	Assembly Hall	17,357	Indiana	45	Mackey Arena	14,123	Purdue
21	ARCO Arena	17,300	CS-Sacramento	46	Hilton Coliseum	14,020	Iowa St.
22	Pittsburgh Civic Arena	16,725	Pittsburgh*	47	WVU Coliseum	14,000	West Va.
23	Allen Field House	16,341	Kansas	48	CSU Convocation Center	13,610	Cleveland St.
24	Assembly Hall	16,321	Illinois	49	Crisler Arena	13,562	Michigan
25	Hartford Civic Center	16,294	UConn	50	Bramlage Coliseum	13,500	Kansas St.

Division I Conference Home Courts

NCAA Division I conferences for the 1995-96 season. Teams with home games in more than one arena are noted.

American West

	Home Floor	Seats
CS-Northridge	The Matadome	3,000
CS-Sacramento	Hornet Gym	1,800
	& ARCO Arena	17,300
Cal Poly SLO	Mott Gym	3,500
Southern Utah	Centrum	5,300

Atlantic Coast

	Home Floor	Seats
Clemson	Littlejohn Coliseum	11,020
Duke	Cameron Indoor Stadium	9,314
Florida St	Leon County Civic Center	12,500
Georgia Tech	Alexander Mem. Coliseum	10,000
Maryland	Cole Field House	14,500
North Carolina	Dean Smith Center	21,572
N.C. State	Reynolds Coliseum	12,400
Virginia	University Hall	8,457
Wake Forest	Joel Mem. Coliseum	14,407

Atlantic 10

	Home Floor	Seats
Dayton	Dayton Arena	13,455
Duquesne	Palumbo Center	6,200
Fordham	Rose Hill Gym	3,470
G. Washington	Smith Center	5,000
La Salle	Philadelphia Civic Center	10,000
Massachusetts	Mullins Center	9,493
Rhode Island	Keaney Gymnasium	4,000
	& Providence Civic Center	13,106
St. Bonaventure	Reilly Center	6,000
St. Joseph's-PA	Alumni Mem. Fieldhouse	3,200
Temple	McGonigle Hall	3,900
Virginia Tech	Cassell Coliseum	10,052
Xavier-OH	Cincinnati Gardens	10,400

Note: Former Midwestern members La Salle and Xavier-OH, along with Dayton (Great Midwest), Fordham (Patriot) and Va. Tech (Metro) all joined conference after 1994-95 season.

Big East

	Home Floor	Seats
Boston College	Conte Forum	8,606
Connecticut	Gampel Pavilion	8,241
	& Hartford Civic Center	16,294
Georgetown	USAir Arena	19,035
Miami-FL	Miami Arena	15,862
Notre Dame	Joyce Center	11,418
Pittsburgh	Fitzgerald Field House	6,798
	& Pittsburgh Civic Arena	16,725
Providence	Providence Civic Center	13,106
Rutgers	Brown Athletic Center	9,000
St. John's	Alumni Hall	6,008
	& Madison Square Garden	18,876
Seton Hall	Byrne Meadowlands Arena	20,029
Syracuse	Carrier Dome	33,000
Villanova	duPont Pavilion	6,500
	& CoreStates Spectrum	18,060
West Virginia	WVU Coliseum	14,000

Note: Former Atlantic 10 members Rutgers and West Virginia and former independent Notre Dame joined conference after 1994-95 season.

Big Eight

	Home Floor	Seats
Colorado	Coors Events Center	11,198
Iowa St	Hilton Coliseum	14,020
Kansas	Allen Fieldhouse	16,341
Kansas St	Bramlage Coliseum	13,500
Missouri	Hearnes Center	13,300
Nebraska	Devaney Sports Center	14,302
Oklahoma	Lloyd Noble Center	11,100
Oklahoma St	Gallagher-Iba Arena	6,381

Note: The Big Eight will become the Big 12 in 1996-97 with the addition of Baylor, Texas, Texas A&M and Texas Tech from the SWC which will fold after the 1995-96 school year.

Big Sky

	Home Floor	Seats
Boise St	BSU Pavilion	12,380
Eastern Wash	Reese Court	5,000
Idaho	Kibbie Dome	10,000
Idaho St	Holt Arena	7,938
Montana	Dahlberg Arena	9,029
Montana St	Worthington Arena	7,287
Northern Ariz	Walkup Skydome	9,500
Weber St	Dee Events Center	12,000

Big South

	Home Floor	Seats
Charleston So	CSU Fieldhouse	2,500
	& N. Charleston Coliseum	13,000
Coastal Carolina	Kimbel Gymnasium	1,800
	& Myrtle Beach Con. Center	5,000
Liberty	Vines Center	9,000
MD-Balt.County	UMBC Fieldhouse	4,024
NC-Asheville	Justice Center	2,500
	& Asheville Civic Center	6,800
NC-Greensboro	Fleming Gymnasium	2,320
Radford	Dedmon Center	5,000
Winthrop	Winthrop Coliseum	6,100

Big Ten

	Home Floor	Seats
Illinois	Assembly Hall	16,321
Indiana	Assembly Hall	17,357
Iowa	Carver-Hawkeye Arena	15,500
Michigan	Crisler Arena	13,562
Michigan St	Breslin Events Center	15,138
Minnesota	Williams Arena	14,300
Northwestern	Welsh-Ryan Arena	8,117
Ohio St	St. John Arena	13,276
Penn St	Rec Hall	6,846
	& Jordan Center	15,000
Purdue	Mackey Arena	14,123
Wisconsin	Wisconsin Field House	11,500

Note: There are 11 schools in the Big Ten.

Big West

	Home Floor	Seats
CS-Fullerton	Titan Gym	4,000
Long Beach St	The Pyramid	5,000
Nevada	Lawlor Events Center	11,200
New Mexico St	Pan American Center	13,071
Pacific	Spanos Center	6,150
San Jose St	The Event Center	5,000
	& San Jose Arena	18,000
UC-Irvine	Bren Events Center	5,000
UC-Santa Barbara	The Thunderdome	6,000
UNLV	Thomas & Mack Center	18,500
Utah St	The Smith Spectrum	10,270

Colonial

	Home Floor	Seats
American	Bender Arena	5,000
East Carolina	Minges Coliseum	7,500
George Mason	Patriot Center	10,000
James Madison	JMU Convocation Center	7,612
NC-Wilmington	Trask Coliseum	6,100
Old Dominion	Norfolk Scope	10,253
Richmond	Robins Center	9,171
VCU	Richmond Coliseum	12,500
Wm. & Mary	William & Mary Hall	10,000

Note: Former Metro member Virginia Commonwealth (VCU) joined conference after 1994-95 season.

Conference USA

	Home Floor	Seats
Ala-Birmingham	UAB Arena	8,500
Cincinnati	Shoemaker Center	13,176
DePaul	Rosemont Horizon	17,500
Louisville	Freedom Hall	18,865
Marquette	Bradley Center	18,592
Memphis	The Pyramid	20,142
NC-Charlotte	Independence Arena	9,575
Saint Louis	Kiel Center	20,000
South Florida	Sun Dome	10,411
Southern Miss	Green Coliseum	8,095
Tulane	Fogelman Arena	3,600

Note: Formed after 1994-95 season with six schools from Great Midwest (UAB, Cincinnati, DePaul, Marquette, Memphis and Saint Louis) and five from Metro (Louisville, NC-Charlotte, South Florida, Southern Miss and Tulane). Houston will join conference for the 1996-97 season when the SWC folds following the 1995-96 school year.

Ivy League

	Home Floor	Seats
Brown	Pizzitola Sports Center	2,800
Columbia	Levien Gymnasium	3,408
Cornell	Newman Arena	4,750
Dartmouth	Berry Sports Center	2,200
Harvard	Briggs Athletic Center	3,000
Penn	The Palestra	8,700
Princeton	Jadwin Gymnasium	7,500
Yale	Payne Whitney Gymnasium	3,100

Metro

	Home Floor	Seats
Canisius	Memorial Auditorium	11,500
	& Koessler Athletic Center	1,800
Fairfield	Alumni Hall	2,479
Iona	Mulcahy Center	3,200
Loyola-MD	Reitz Arena	3,000
Manhattan	Draddy Gymnasium	3,000
Niagara	Niagara Falls Conv. Center	6,000
	& Gallagher Center	3,200
St. Peter's	Yanitelli Center	3,200
Siena	Alumni Recreation Center	4,000
	& Knickerbocker Arena	15,500

Metro Atlantic

	Home Floor	Seats
Akron	JAR Arena	5,500
Ball St	University Arena	11,500
Bowling Green	Anderson Arena	5,000
Central Mich	Rose Arena	6,000
Eastern Mich	Bowen Field House	5,600
Kent	Memorial Athletic Center	6,327
Miami-OH	Millett Hall	9,200
Ohio Univ	Convocation Center	13,000
Toledo	Savage Hall	9,000
Western Mich	University Arena	5,800

Dome, Sweet Dome

There are 10 domes in Division I basketball (in alphabetical order): Baby Dome (Prairie View); Cajundome (SW Louisiana); Carrier Dome (Syracuse); Gold Dome (Centenary); Joe Reed Acadome (Alabama St.); Kibbie Dome (Idaho); Sun Dome (South Fla.); The Thunderdome (UC-Santa Barbara); UNI-Dome (No. Iowa) and Walkup Skydome (No. Ariz.).

College Basketball (Cont.)
Division I Conference Home Courts

Mid-Continent

	Home Floor	Seats
Buffalo	Alumni Arena	10,000
Central Conn. St.	Detrick Gym	4,000
Chicago St.	Phys. Ed. & Athletics Bldg.	2,000
Eastern Ill.	Lantz Gym	6,200
Missouri-K.C.	Municipal Auditorium	10,000
NE Illinois	Phys. Ed. Complex	2,000
Troy St.	Sartain Hall	3,500
Valparaiso	Athletics-Recreation Center	4,500
Western Ill.	Western Hall	5,139
Youngstown St.	Beeghly Center	8,000

Mid-Eastern

	Home Floor	Seats
Bethune-Cookman	Moore Gym	3,000
Coppin St.	Pullen Gym	3,000
Delaware St.	Memorial Hall	3,000
Florida A&M	Gaither Gym	3,350
Hampton	Hampton Convocation Center	7,200
Howard	Burr Gym	3,000
MD-East.Shore	Tawes Gym	1,200
Morgan St.	Hill Field House	5,500
N. Carolina A&T	Corbett Sports Center	7,500
S. Carolina St.	SHM Center	3,200

Note: Former Div. II school Hampton joined conference after the 1994-95 season.

Midwestern

	Home Floor	Seats
Butler	Hinkle Fieldhouse	11,043
Cleveland St.	CSU Convocation Center	13,610
Detroit Mercy	Cobo Arena	11,143
IL-Chicago	UIC Pavilion	8,000
Loyola-IL	Alumni Gym	2,975
Northern Illinois	Chick Evans Field House	6,044
WI-Green Bay	Brown County Arena	5,600
WI-Milwaukee	The Mecca	11,052
Wright St.	Nutter Center	10,632

Missouri Valley

	Home Floor	Seats
Bradley	Carver Arena	10,825
Creighton	Omaha Civic Auditorium	9,481
Drake	Knapp Center	7,002
Evansville	Roberts Stadium	12,300
Illinois St.	Redbird Arena	10,600
Indiana St.	Hulman Center	10,200
Northern Iowa	UNI-Dome	10-20,000
Southern Ill.	SIU Arena	10,014
SW Missouri St.	Hammons Student Center	8,858
Tulsa	Maxwell Convention Center	8,659
Wichita St.	Levitt Arena	10,656

North Atlantic

	Home Floor	Seats
Boston University	Case Center	2,500
Delaware	Bob Carpenter Center	5,058
Drexel	Phys. Education Center	2,300
Hartford	The Sports Center	4,475
Hofstra	Physical Fitness Center	3,500
Maine	Alfond Arena	6,000
New Hampshire	Lundholm Gym	3,500
Northeastern	Matthews Arena	6,000
Towson St.	Towson Center	5,000
Vermont	Patrick Gym	3,200

Note: former Big South member Towson State joined conference after 1994-95 season.

Northeast

	Home Floor	Seats
FDU-Teaneck	Rothman Center	5,000
LIU-Brooklyn	Schwartz Athletic Center	1,700
Marist	McCann Center	3,944
Monmouth	Boylan Gym	3,000
Mt. St. Mary's	Knott Arena	3,500
Rider	Alumni Gymnasium	1,650
Robert Morris	Sewall Center	3,056
St. Francis-NY	Phys. Ed. Center	1,400
St. Francis-PA	Maurice Stokes Center	3,500
Wagner	Sutter Gym	1,650

Ohio Valley

	Home Floor	Seats
Austin Peay	Dunn Center	9,000
Eastern Ky	McBrayer Arena	6,500
Middle Tenn. St	Murphy Center	11,520
Morehead St	Johnson Arena	6,500
Murray St	Racer Arena	5,550
SE Missouri St	Show Me Center	7,000
Tennessee-Martin	Skyhawk Arena	6,700
Tennessee St.	Gentry Complex	10,500
Tennessee Tech	Eblen Center	10,150

Pacific-10

	Home Floor	Seats
Arizona	McKale Center	14,140
Arizona St	Univ. Activity Center	14,287
California	Harmon Gym	6,578
	& Oakland Coliseum	15,039
Oregon	McArthur Court	10,063
Oregon St.	Gill Coliseum	10,400
Stanford	Maples Pavilion	7,500
UCLA	Pauley Pavilion	12,819
USC	LA Sports Arena	15,509
Washington	Hec Edmundson Pavilion	7,870
Washington. St.	Friel Court	12,058

Patriot League

	Home Floor	Seats
Army	Christl Arena	5,043
Bucknell	Davis Gym	2,300
Colgate	Cotterell Court	3,000
Holy Cross	Hart Recreation Center	4,000
Lafayette	Kirby Field House	3,500
Lehigh	Stabler Arena	5,600
Navy	Alumni Hall	5,710

Southeastern

EASTERN	Home Floor	Seats
Florida	O'Connell Center	12,000
Georgia	Georgia Coliseum	10,512
Kentucky	Rupp Arena	24,000
South Carolina	Carolina Coliseum	12,401
Tennessee	Thompson-Boling Arena	24,535
Vanderbilt	Memorial Gymnasium	15,317

WESTERN	Home Floor	Seats
Alabama	Coleman Coliseum	15,043
Arkansas	Bud Walton Arena	19,200
Auburn	Eaves-Memorial Coliseum	10,108
LSU	Maravich Assembly Center	14,164
Mississippi	Tad Smith Coliseum	8,135
Mississippi St	Humphrey Coliseum	10,000

Independents

Home Floor		Seats
Oral Roberts	Mabee Center	10,500
Wofford	Johnson Arena	3,500

Note: Wofford moved up from Div. II after 1994-95 season.

Southern

Home Floor		Seats
Appalachian St	Varsity Gymnasium	8,000
The Citadel	McAlister Field House	6,200
Davidson	Belk Arena	6,000
E. Tenn. St	Memorial Center	12,000
Furman	Greenville Mem. Auditorium	6,000
Ga. Southern	Hanner Fieldhouse	5,500
Marshall	Henderson Center	10,250
Tenn-Chatt	UTC Arena	11,218
VMI	Cameron Hall	5,029
W. Carolina	Ramsey Center	7,826

Southland

Home Floor		Seats
McNeese St	Burton Coliseum	8,000
Nicholls St	Stopher Gym	3,800
North Texas	UNT Super Pit	9,885
NE Louisiana	Ewing Coliseum	8,000
N'western St	Prather Coliseum	3,900
Sam Houston St	Johnson Coliseum	6,172
SW Texas St	Strahan Coliseum	7,200
S.F. Austin St	W.R. Johnson Coliseum	7,203
TX-Arlington	Texas Hall	4,200
TX-San Antonio	Convocation Center	5,100

Southwest

Home Floor		Seats
Baylor	Ferrell Center	10,084
Houston	Hofheinz Pavilion	10,245
Rice	Autry Court	5,000
SMU	Moody Coliseum	8,998
Texas	Erwin Center	16,042
Texas A&M	G. Rollie White Coliseum	7,500
TCU	Daniel-Meyer Coliseum	7,166
Texas Tech	Lubbock Municipal Coliseum	8,174

Note: The SWC will fold following the 1995-96 school year. In 1996-97, Baylor, Texas, Texas A&M, and Texas Tech will join the Big 12 (formerly the Big Eight); Rice, Southern Methodist and Texas Christian will join the WAC; and Houston will join Conference USA.

Southwestern

Home Floor		Seats
Alabama St	Joe Reed Acadome	7,000
Alcorn St	Davey L. Whitney Arena	7,500
Grambling St.	Memorial Gym	4,500
Jackson St	Williams Center	8,000
Miss.Valley	Harrison Athletic Complex	6,000
Prairie View	The Baby Dome	6,600
Southern-BR	Clark Activity Center	7,500
TX Southern	Health & P.E. Building	7,500

Sun Belt

Home Floor		Seats
Ark-Little Rock	Barton Coliseum	8,303
Arkansas St	Convocation Center	10,563
Jacksonville	Jacksonville Coliseum	10,000
Lamar	Montagne Center	10,080
Louisiana Tech	Thomas Assembly Center	8,000
New Orleans	Lakefront Arena	10,000
South Alabama	Mobile Civic Center	10,000
SW Louisiana	The Cajundome	12,000
Texas-Pan Am	UTPA Field House	5,000
Western Ky	E.A. Diddle Arena	11,300

Trans America

Home Floor		Seats
Campbell	Carter Gym	1,050
	& Cumberland County CC	5,000
Centenary	Gold Dome	5,000
Central Fla	UCF Arena	5,100
Charleston	Kresse Arena	3,052
Fla. Atlantic	FAU Gym	5,000
Florida Int'l	Golden Panther Arena	4,661
Georgia St	GSU Athletic Complex	5,500
Jacksonville St.	Mathews Coliseum	5,500
Mercer	Macon Coliseum	8,500
Samford	Seibert Hall	4,000
SE Louisiana	University Center	7,500
Stetson	Edmunds Center	5,000

Note: Div. II Jacksonville St. moved up to join conference after the 1994-95 season.

West Coast

Home Floor		Seats
Gonzaga	Martin Centre	4,000
Loyola-CA	Gersten Pavilion	4,156
Pepperdine	Firestone Fieldhouse	3,104
Portland	Chiles Center	5,000
St. Mary's-CA	McKeon Pavilion	3,500
San Diego	USD Sports Center	2,500
San Francisco	Memorial Gym	5,300
Santa Clara	Toso Pavilion	5,000

Western Athletic

Home Floor		Seats
Air Force	Clune Arena	6,000
BYU	Marriott Center	22,700
Colorado St	Moby Arena	9,000
Fresno St	Selland Arena	10,159
Hawaii	Special Events Arena	10,000
New Mexico	University Arena (The Pit)	18,018
San Diego St	Peterson Gym	3,668
UTEP	Special Events Center	12,222
Utah	Huntsman Center	15,000
Wyoming	Arena-Auditorium	15,028

Note: The WAC will add six teams for the 1996-97 season with Rice, SMU and TCU coming over from the SWC; San Jose St. and UNLV from the Big West and Tulsa from the Missouri Valley Conference.

Future NCAA Final Four Sites

MEN

Year	Arena	Seats	Location
1996	Meadowlands Arena	20,029	E. Rutherford
1997	RCA Dome	47,100	Indianapolis
1998	Alamodome	40,000	San Antonio
1999	ThunderDome	32,351	St. Petersburg
2000	RCA Dome	47,100	Indianapolis
2001	Metrodome	50,000	Minneapolis
2002	Georgia Dome	40,000	Atlanta

WOMEN

Year	Arena	Seats	Location
1996	Charlotte Coliseum	23,698	Charlotte
1997	Riverfront Coliseum	17,000	Cincinnati
1998	Kemper Arena	16,668	Kansas City
1999	San Jose Arena	17,500	San Jose
2000	CoreStates Spectrum	16,975	Philadelphia

COLLEGE FOOTBALL

The 40 Largest I-A Stadiums

The 35 largest stadiums in NCAA Division I-A college football heading into the 1996 season. Note that (*) indicates stadium not on campus.

		Location	Seats	Home Team	Conference	Built	Field
1	Michigan Stadium	Ann Arbor, Mich.	**102,501**	Michigan	Big Ten	1927	Grass
2	Rose Bowl*	Pasadena, Calif.	**102,083**	UCLA	Pac-10	1922	Grass
3	LA Memorial Coliseum*	Los Angeles, Calif.	**94,159**	USC	Pac-10	1923	Grass
4	Beaver Stadium	University Park, Pa.	**93,967**	Penn St.	Big Ten	1960	Grass
5	Neyland Stadium	Knoxville, Tenn.	**91,902**	Tennessee	SEC-East	1921	Grass
6	Ohio Stadium	Columbus, Ohio	**89,800**	Ohio St.	Big Ten	1922	Grass
7	Stanford Stadium	Stanford, Calif.	**85,500**	Stanford	Pac-10	1921	Grass
8	Sanford Stadium	Athens, Ga.	**85,434**	Georgia	SEC-East	1929	Grass
9	Jordan-Hare Stadium	Auburn, Ala.	**85,214**	Auburn	SEC-West	1939	Grass
10	Legion Field*	Birmingham, Ala.	**83,091**	Alabama	SEC-West	1927	Grass
11	Florida Field	Gainesville, Fla.	**83,000**	Florida	SEC-East	1929	Grass
12	Memorial Stadium	Clemson, S.C.	**81,474**	Clemson	ACC	1942	Grass
13	Tiger Stadium	Baton Rouge, La.	**80,150**	LSU	SEC-West	1924	Grass
14	Memorial Stadium	Austin, Texas	**77,809**	Texas	Big 12-South	1924	Turf
15	Camp Randall Stadium	Madison, Wisc.	**77,745**	Wisconsin	Big Ten	1917	Turf
16	Giants Stadium	E. Rutherford, N.J.	**77,716**	Rutgers	Big East	1976	Turf
17	Spartan Stadium	East Lansing, Mich.	**76,000**	Michigan St.	Big Ten	1957	Turf
18	Memorial Stadium	Berkeley, Calif.	**75,662**	California	Pac-10	1923	Grass
19	Owen Field	Norman, Okla.	**75,004**	Oklahoma	Big 12-South	1924	Grass
20	Doak Campbell Stadium	Tallahasse, Fla.	**75,000**	Florida St.	ACC	1950	Grass
21	Orange Bowl*	Miami, Fla.	**74,712**	Miami-FL	Big East	1935	Grass
22	Sun Devil Stadium	Tempe, Ariz.	**73,656**	Arizona St.	Pac-10	1959	Grass
23	Memorial Stadium	Lincoln, Neb.	**72,700**	Nebraska	Big 12-North	1923	Turf
24	Husky Stadium	Seattle, Wash.	**72,500**	Washington	Pac-10	1920	Turf
25	Williams-Brice Stadium	Columbia, S.C.	**72,400**	South Carolina	SEC-East	1934	Grass
26	Memorial Stadium	Champaign, Ill.	**70,904**	Illinois	Big Ten	1923	Turf
27	Kinnick Stadium	Iowa City, Iowa	**70,397**	Iowa	Big Ten	1929	Grass
28	Kyle Field	College Station, Texas	**70,210**	Texas A&M	Big 12-South	1925	Turf
29	Bryant-Denny Stadium	Tuscaloosa, Ala.	**70,123**	Alabama	SEC-West	1929	Grass
30	Rice Stadium	Houston, Tex.	**70,000**	Rice	WAC-1	1950	Turf
31	Superdome*	New Orleans, La.	**69,056**	Tulane	USA	1975	Turf
32	Cotton Bowl*	Dallas, Tex.	**68,252**	SMU	WAC-1	1932	Grass
33	Ross-Ade Stadium	W. Lafayette, Ind.	**67,861**	Purdue	Big Ten	1924	Grass
34	Veterans Stadium*	Philadelphia, Pa.	**66,592**	Temple	Big East	1971	Turf
35	Cougar Stadium	Provo, Utah	**65,000**	BYU	WAC-3	1964	Grass
36	HHH Metrodome*	Minneapolis, Minn.	**63,699**	Minnesota	Big Ten	1982	Turf
37	Mountaineer Field	Morgantown, W. Va.	**63,500**	West Virginia	Big East	1980	Turf
38	Liberty Bowl *	Memphis, Tenn.	**62,380**	Memphis	USA	1965	Grass
39	Faurot Field	Columbia, Mo.	**62,000**	Missouri	Big 12-North	1926	Grass
40	SD/Jack Murphy Stadium*	San Diego, Calif.	**61,121**	San Diego St.	WAC-4	1967	Grass

Note: Immediately following the 1995 season, construction was scheduled to begin that would increase the capacity of Notre Dame Stadium to 80,990 by the start of the 1997 season. The $50 million renovation project will not prevent the Irish from playing there in 1996.

1996 Conference Home Fields

NCAA Division I-A conference by conference listing includes member teams heading into the 1996 season. Note that (*) indicates stadium is not on campus.

Atlantic Coast

	Stadium	Built	Seats	Field
Clemson	Memorial	1942	81,474	Grass
Duke	Wallace Wade	1929	33,941	Grass
Florida St	Doak Campbell	1950	75,000	Grass
Ga. Tech	Dodd	1913	46,000	Grass
Maryland	Byrd	1950	45,000	Grass
N. Carolina	Kenan	1927	52,000	Grass
N.C. State	Carter-Finley	1966	53,500†	Grass
Virginia	Scott	1931	40,000	Grass
Wake Forest	Groves	1968	31,500	Grass

† Grass bank holds additional 10,000.

Big East

	Stadium	Built	Seats	Field
Boston Col	Alumni	1957	44,500	Turf
Miami-FL	Orange Bowl*	1935	74,712	Grass
Pittsburgh	Pitt	1925	56,500	Turf
Rutgers	Rutgers	1994	42,000	Grass
	& Giants Stadium	1976	77,716	Turf
Syracuse	Carrier Dome	1980	50,000	Turf
Temple	Veterans*	1971	66,592	Turf
Va. Tech	Lane	1965	50,000	Grass
West Va.	Mountaineer Field	1980	63,500	Turf

University of Michigan

With a seating capacity of 102,501, **Michigan Stadium** is the largest playing facility in college football. The Wolverines, who led the nation in attendance in 1994 with an average crowd of 106,217 in six games, entered 1995 with a streak of 122 consecutive 100,000-plus crowds going back to Nov. 8, 1975.

Big 12

With the breakup of the Southwest Conference on June 30, 1996, the Big Eight will become the Big 12 with the addition of Baylor, Texas, Texas A&M and Texas Tech from the SWC.

NORTH	Stadium	Built	Seats	Field
Colorado	Folsom Field	1924	51,748	Turf
Iowa St	Trice Field	1975	50,000	Turf
Kansas	Memorial	1921	50,250	Turf
Kansas St	KSU	1968	42,000	Turf
Missouri	Faurot Field	1926	62,000	Grass
Nebraska	Memorial	1923	72,700	Turf

SOUTH	Stadium	Built	Seats	Field
Baylor	Floyd Casey	1950	50,000	Turf
Oklahoma	Owen Field	1924	75,004	Grass
Oklahoma St	Lewis Field	1920	50,614	Turf
Texas	Memorial	1924	77,809	Turf
Texas A&M	Kyle Field	1925	70,210	Turf
Texas Tech	Jones	1947	50,500	Turf

Note: The annual Oklahoma-Texas game has been played at the Cotton Bowl (capacity 68,252) in Dallas since 1937.

Big Ten

	Stadium	Built	Seats	Field
Illinois	Memorial	1923	70,904	Turf
Indiana	Memorial	1960	52,354	Turf
Iowa	Kinnick	1929	70,397	Grass
Michigan	Michigan	1927	102,501	Grass
Michigan St	Spartan	1957	76,000	Turf
Minnesota	Metrodome*	1982	63,699	Turf
Northwestern	Dyche	1926	49,256	Turf
Ohio St	Ohio	1922	89,800	Grass
Penn St	Beaver	1960	93,967	Grass
Purdue	Ross-Ade	1924	67,861	Grass
Wisconsin	Camp Randall	1917	77,745	Turf

Big West

	Stadium	Built	Seats	Field
Arkansas St	Indian	1974	33,410	Grass
Louisiana Tech	Joe Aillet	1968	30,200	Grass
Nevada	Mackay	1965	31,545	Grass
New Mexico St	Aggie Memorial	1978	30,343	Grass
North Texas	Fouts Field	1952	30,500	Turf
Northern Ill	Huskie	1965	31,000	Turf
Pacific	Stagg Memorial	1950	30,000	Grass
SW Louisiana	Cajun Field	1971	31,000	Grass
Utah St	Romney	1968	30,257	Grass

Conference USA

Conference USA, which begins play in basketball in 1995, will become a football league in 1996 when '95 independents Cincinnati, Louisville, Memphis, Southern Miss and Tulane are joined by Houston of the Southwest Conference, which dissolves on June 30, 1996.

	Stadium	Built	Seats	Field
Houston	Astrodome*	1965	60,000	Turf
	& Robertson	1942	22,000	Grass
Cincinnati	Nippert	1916	35,000	Turf
Louisville	Cardinal*	1956	35,500	Turf
Memphis	Liberty Bowl*	1965	62,380	Grass
Southern Miss	Roberts	1976	33,000	Grass
Tulane	Superdome*	1975	69,056	Turf

I-A Independents

	Stadium	Built	Seats	Field
Army	Michie	1924	39,929	Turf
E. Carolina	Dowdy-Ficklen	1963	35,000	Grass
Navy	Navy-Marine Corps Memorial	1959	30,000	Grass
Notre Dame	Notre Dame	1930	59,075	Grass

Note: Notre Dame Stadium will be enlarged to hold 80,900 by the 1997 season. The Irish will still be able to play there in '96.

College Football (Cont.)
Division I-A Conference Home Fields

Mid-American

	Stadium	Built	Seats	Field
Akron	Rubber Bowl*	1940	35,202	Turf
Ball St.	Ball State	1967	16,319	Grass
Bowling Green	Doyt Perry	1966	30,599	Grass
Central Mich	Kelly/Shorts	1972	20,086	Turf
Eastern Mich	Rynearson	1969	30,200	Turf
Kent	Dix	1969	30,520	Grass
Miami-OH	Fred Yager	1983	25,183	Grass
Ohio Univ	Peden	1929	20,000	Grass
Toledo	Glass Bowl	1937	26,248	Turf
Western Mich	Waldo	1939	30,000	Grass

Pacific-10

	Stadium	Built	Seats	Field
Arizona	Arizona	1928	56,167	Grass
Arizona St	Sun Devil	1959	73,656	Grass
California	Memorial	1923	75,662	Grass
Oregon	Autzen	1967	41,698	Turf
Oregon St.	Parker	1953	35,547	Turf
Stanford	Stanford	1921	85,500	Grass
UCLA	Rose Bowl*	1922	102,083	Grass
USC	LA Coliseum*	1923	94,159	Grass
Washington	Husky	1920	72,500	Turf
Washington St	Martin	1972	40,000	Turf

Southeastern

EASTERN	Stadium	Built	Seats	Field
Florida	Florida Field	1929	83,000	Grass
Georgia	Sanford	1929	85,434	Grass
Kentucky	Commonwealth	1973	57,800	Grass
S. Carolina	Williams-Brice	1934	72,400	Grass
Tennessee	Neyland	1921	91,902	Grass
Vanderbilt	Vanderbilt	1922	41,000	Turf
WESTERN	**Stadium**	**Built**	**Seats**	**Field**
Alabama	Bryant-Denny	1929	70,123	Grass
	& Legion Field*	1927	83,091	Grass
Arkansas	Razorback	1938	51,000	Grass
	& War Memorial*	1948	53,727	Grass
Auburn	Jordan-Hare	1939	85,214	Grass
LSU	Tiger	1924	80,150	Grass
Mississippi	Vaught-Hem'way	1941	42,577	Grass
Miss. St.	Scott Field	1915	40,656	Grass

Notes: EAST— Vanderbilt Stadium was rebuilt in 1981. WEST— at Alabama, Bryant-Denny Stadium is in Tuscaloosa and Legion Field is in Birmingham.

SEC Championship Game

The first two SEC Championship Games were played at Legion Field in Birmingham, Ala., in 1992 and 1993. The game was moved to Atlanta's 71,230-seat Georgia Dome in 1994.

Western Athletic

With the breakup of the Southwest Conference on June 30, 1996, the WAC will grow to 16 teams with the addition of SWC refugees Rice, Southern Methodist and Texas Christian, plus Nevada-Las Vegas and San Jose St. from the Big West and independent Tulsa.

DIVISION A	Stadium	Built	Seats	Field
BYU	Cougar	1964	65,000	Grass
New Mexico	University	1960	31,218	Grass
Rice	Rice	1950	70,000	Turf
SMU	Cotton Bowl	1932	68,252	Grass
TCU	Amon Carter	1929	46,000	Grass
Tulsa	Skelly	1930	40,385	Turf
Utah	Robert Rice	1927	32,500	Turf
UTEP	Sun Bowl*	1963	52,000	Turf

DIVISION B	Stadium	Built	Seats	Field
Air Force	Falcon	1962	52,123	Grass
Colorado St	Hughes	1968	30,000	Grass
Fresno St	Bulldog	1980	41,031	Grass
Hawaii	Aloha*	1975	50,000	Turf
San Diego St.	SD/Murphy*	1967	61,121	Grass
San Jose St	Spartan	1933	31,218	Grass
UNLV	Sam Boyd*	1971	32,000	Turf
Wyoming	War Memorial	1950	33,500	Grass

WAC Championship Game

The first WAC championship game between division winners will take place on Dec. 7, 1996 at Sam Boyd Stadium in Las Vegas.

Bowl Games

Listed alphabetically and updated as of Aug. 1, 1995. The Bowl Alliance, which is scheduled to go into effect with the 1995 season, calls for the national championship game (No. 1-ranked alliance team vs. No. 2 alliance team) to rotate between the Fiesta Bowl (Jan. 2, 1996), Sugar Bowl (Jan. 2, 1997) and Orange Bowl (Jan. 2, 1998). See page 186.

	Stadium	Built	Seats	Field		Stadium	Built	Seats	Field
Alamo	Alamodome	1993	65,000	Turf	Independence	Independence	1936	50,460	Grass
Aloha	Aloha	1975	50,000	Turf	Sun	Sun Bowl	1963	51,120	Turf
Carquest	Joe Robbie	1986	74,915	Grass	Las Vegas	Silver Bowl	1971	33,215	Turf
Copper	Arizona	1928	56,165	Grass	Liberty	Liberty Bowl	1965	62,920	Grass
Cotton	Cotton	1932	68,250	Turf	Orange	Orange Bowl	1935	74,475	Grass
Fiesta	Sun Devil	1958	73,655	Grass	Outback	Tampa	1967	74,300	Grass
Fla. Citrus	Fla. Citrus Bowl	1936	73,300	Grass	Peach	Georgia Dome	1992	71,230	Turf
Gator	Municipal	1949	73,000	Grass	Rose	Rose Bowl	1922	100,225	Grass
Holiday	SD/Jack Murphy	1967	62,860	Grass	Sugar	Superdome	1975	77,450	Turf

Note: Old Gator Bowl stadium was rebuilt for NFL Jacksonville Jaguars in 1995 and renamed Jacksonville Municipal Stadium.

Playing Sites

Alamo— San Antonio; **Aloha**— Honolulu; **Carquest**— Miami; **Copper**— Tucson; **Cotton**— Dallas; **Fiesta**— Tempe; **Florida Citrus**— Orlando; **Gator**— Jacksonville; **Holiday**— San Diego; **Independence**— Shreveport; **Sun**— El Paso; **Las Vegas**— Las Vegas; **Liberty**— Memphis; **Orange**— Miami; **Outback**— Tampa; **Peach**— Atlanta; **Rose**— Pasadena; **Sugar**— New Orleans.

THE OFFICIAL COLA

Maverick NFL owner **Jerry Jones** of the Dallas Cowboys shows off some new custom-made footwear after announcing a $25 million deal making Pepsi the official cola of Texas Stadium.

BUSINESS & MEDIA

Big Bucks

Two billion-dollar acquisitions and an NFL loose cannon highlight one week in a year full of wheeling and dealing.

The Week That Was in the business of sports came by surprise in midsummer and actually lasted eight days.

On July 31, the Walt Disney Co. stunned the corporate world by announcing the acquisition of Capital Cities/ABC. Valued at $19 billion, the merger of these two entertainment industry giants was the second largest takeover ever and was carried off without a leak or any knowledge of how long Disney had ogled the company that owns ABC Sports, ESPN and ESPN2.

On Aug. 7, in another shocker, NBC Sports announced that it had secured the TV rights to both the 2000 Summer Olympics in Sydney, Australia, and the 2002 Winter Olympics in Salt Lake City for a combined $1.27 billion. NBC, which will broadcast its third straight Summer Games next year in Atlanta won the approval of the International Olympic Committee by offering to pay $715 million for Sydney and $555 million for Salt Lake City, which the IOC had chosen on June 16 as the 2002 cold weather site.

In between those two mega-deals, Dallas Cowboys owner and NFL loose cannon Jerry Jones announced on Aug. 3, that he had signed a 10-year, $25 million deal to make Pepsi-Cola the official soft drink of Texas Stadium. It was an audacious marketing maneuver that circumvented a league contract already in place that pronounced

Coca-Cola as the official soda pop of the NFL.

Of the three transactions, the Disney-Cap Cities merger was the biggest and the Jones-Pepsi alliance was the most controversial. But NBC's decision to jump the gun on a four-network auction for the Sydney rights and go for two Olympics at once was the slickest.

Conceived on Wednesday, Aug. 2, by NBC Sports president Dick Ebersol and NBC network boss Bob Wright with the approval of General Electric chairman Jack Welch, the plan led Ebersol on a two-day odyssey from New York to Göteborg, Sweden, to Montreal.

Thursday evening in Göteborg, Ebersol made his pitch to IOC president Juan Antonio Samaranch and placed two conditions on the offer: ABC, CBS and Fox could not be told and it had to be accepted by Sunday night, Aug. 6.

Impressed, Samaranch asked Ebersol to fly to Montreal and present the bid to Richard Pound, chairman of the IOC's TV negotiating committee. Ebersol and Pound met Friday night, after which Pound called Samaranch and advised him to take the offer. The contract was drawn up and agreed to early Saturday morning and formally announced two days later.

"This was too good a deal for us not to say yes to," said Pound, who had received a $701 million offer from Fox network for the Sydney rights alone four days before NBC's two-Olympics bid. Fox chairman

---

Richard Sandomir writes the television sports column for *The New York Times.*

Flanked by NBC Sports president **Dick Ebersol** and International Olympic Committee negotiator **Dick Pound** on Aug. 7, NBC president **Bob Wright** announces his network's $1.27 billion deal for the exclusive U.S. television rights to both the 2000 Summer Olympics and 2002 Winter Games.

Rupert Murdoch, a native Australian, had openly coveted the Sydney Games.

"What Fox would or wouldn't do is moot at this point," said Pound. "The [NBC] figures are higher than we planned."

Incredibly, NBC felt it couldn't justify paying much more than $620 million for Sydney alone, yet had no problem going $95 million higher as long as it could spend an additional $555 million on Salt Lake City.

Why? Because advertising sales were so good for next summer's Atlanta Games that packaging Sydney and Salt Lake City together, even with record Olympic price tags, began to look like a steal— especially in terms of spending 1995 dollars on an event that is seven years away. In hindsight, many industry observers felt the IOC could have gotten more for the Salt Lake Games.

With exclusive rights to three of the next four Olympics plus Emmy-winning performances at the 1988 and '92 Summer Games in Seoul and Barcelona, NBC can lay claim to being a 1990's version of ABC in its heyday: the network of the Olympics. The symmetry is perfect: Ebersol began his career as an ABC Olympics researcher, then became an assistant to Roone Arledge, the legendary president of ABC Sports.

Following NBC's coup, Ebersol couldn't help but recall how just days after wrapping up ABC's coverage of the 1972 Summer Olympics in Munich, Arledge had jetted off to Montreal to make his preemptive, "take it or leave it," offer of $25 million for the '76 Summer Games. They took it.

"Like father, like son," said Ebersol.

The boldness of NBC's Olympic strategy, which includes using the network's two cable outlets— CNBC and America's Talking— for additional coverage, was seen by many as a calculated response to the Disney-Cap Cities merger earlier in the week.

Disney's acquisition of Cap Cities and its top-rated ABC network made it the world's largest media conglomerate, a title it held outright until Sept. 22, when Time Warner Inc. and Turner Broadcasting System agreed to an even bigger merger, valued at $19.8 billion, after a tumultuous five-week courtship.

Not to worry. Time-Warner may get Ted Turner's CNN, TNT and the Atlanta Braves, but Disney gets ESPN and ESPN2.

Disney chairman Michael Eisner values ESPN's global brand name— one that is fast becoming as well known as Coca-Cola and Kodak— and the opportunity it presents to help market the Disney Channel internationally. There is also the possibility of building a chain of ESPN sports bars and perhaps even a sports theme park.

No doubt Eisner also mused over the

prospect of selling Chris Berman teddy bears and a line of Downtown Julie Brown lingerie at Disney's retail stores.

"Sometimes I do feel like a cartoon character," cracked Keith Olbermann, the acerbic, wiseguy anchor of ESPN's "SportsCenter."

But the most remarkable aspect of the sports cable giant's importance to Disney was the revelation by Cap Cities' chairman Thomas Murphy that ESPN, which is now cable's most profitable service, is worth between $4.5 billion and $5 billion.

"Think about it. That's what CBS is worth," said ESPN founder Bill Rasmussen, referring to the Aug. 2 announcement that Westinghouse had agreed to purchase the ailing "Tiffany network" for $5.4 billion.

Meanwhile, CBS Sports, which lost its NFL rights to Fox on Dec. 17, 1993, reestablished itself as a major player on Dec. 6, 1994, by extending its exclusive relationship with the NCAA men's basketball tournament through the year 2002 for a record $1.725 billion.

"We wanted to aggressively plan our future," said CBS Sports president David Kenin. "This is a fundamental building block of our sports strategy."

By 1996, CBS will be the top college football network as well, with rights to the Big East and Southeastern conferences and two of the three primary Bowl Alliance national championship bowls— the Fiesta and Orange (see "College Sports" chapter).

Back in Hollywood, Disney's Eisner, who has been a major league sports fixture since his company bought the NHL expansion Mighty Ducks of Anaheim for $50 million in 1992, expanded into baseball and auto racing among other things in '95.

On May 18, Disney bought 25 percent of the California Angels for a reported $30 million from 86-year-old owner Gene Autry. It also assumed the role of managing general partner with the option to purchase the rest of the club after the former singing cowboy and western movie star rides off into the sunset.

The Indy Racing League, which was formed by Indianapolis Motor Speedway president Tony George in 1995, debuts on Jan. 27, 1996, with the Indy 200 at Walt Disney World in Orlando.

The 1.1-mile oval is one of the attractions at a $100 million sports complex currently under construction at Disney World. The complex, which is scheduled to officially open in May 1997, will also serve as the new headquarters of the Amateur Athletic Union (AAU).

Eisner has also reportedly talked to NFL commissioner Paul Tagliabue about the possibility of bringing a team to the Los Angeles area in the wake of the 1995 departure of both the Rams and Raiders (see page 534).

Which brings us to Jerry Jones and his Coke-free stadium in Irving, Texas.

Jones, who bought the Cowboys and Texas Stadium for $140 million in 1989, started a campaign in 1994 to break up NFL Properties, the enormously successful licensing and sponsorship arm that divides all revenues equally between the league's 30 teams.

Why? Because Jones reckoned that merchandise bearing the Cowboys' name and logo accounted for 24 percent of the $90 million NFL Properties accumulated in royalties last year. Instead of an equal share of $3 million, he figured the Cowboys were entitled to around $22 million.

"If there's a team in the league right now that can't market itself better than $3 million a year," said Jones, "then they don't belong in the league."

Jones was able to make his deal with Pepsi because the NFL Properties deal with Coca-Cola cannot force individual stadiums to sell Coke.

NFL commissioner Tagliabue reacted by calling Jones greedy. Fellow owner Art Modell of Cleveland went further, stating: "There is no way we can let him get away with this."

Coca-Cola struck back on Aug. 11, by signing Cowboys quarterback Troy Aikman to an endorsement contract.

Jones thumbed his nose at the NFL again on Sept. 4 when he signed an exclusive seven-year sponsorship deal with Nike for a reported $14 million that includes building a football theme park adjacent to Texas Stadium and dressing Cowboys' players and coaches in Nike apparel. Nike's trademark swoosh logo, however, cannot be displayed on the equipment because the company doesn't have a licensing agreement with NFL Properties.

Four days later, Jones struck again outbidding the San Francsico 49ers for free agent All-Pro defensive back and Nike pitchman

Capital Cities/ABC, Inc.

Walt Disney Co. chairman **Michael Eisner** and Capital Cities/ABC president **Tom Murphy** shake hands in New York after their July 31 announcement that the two entertainment giants would merge in a deal valued at $19 billion. Cap Cities assets include ABC Sports, ESPN and ESPN2.

Deion Sanders. Pooling his Pepsi and Nike money, Jones inked the 28-year-old two-sport star to a five-year deal worth $35 million, including a record $13 million signing bonus. Only quarterback Troy Aikman, who has a $50 million contract, makes more than Prime Time in Big D.

"This contract isn't competitive, it's destructive," said San Francisco president Carmen Policy, who signed Sanders to a one-year, $1.34 million deal in 1994 that helped the 49ers win the Super Bowl (see page 220). "We wanted Deion back, but not for something like this. This is ridiculous. There was no need for it."

Said one AFC executive to *The Boston Globe's* Will McDonough, "Playing Dallas will be like playing an all-star team. Their talent is so much above the rest of us now it's not close. This guy [Jones] is dangerous. Really dangerous. The rest of us better wake up. He's changing the rules of the game."

The league finally retaliated on Sept. 18, when NFL Properties filed a $300 million lawsuit in New York federal court against Jones and the Cowboys.

"This isn't about soda pop, sneakers, do-rags or who has a logo on a wristband,"

said Tagliabue. "This is a clear attack on a philosophy. If you have a successful philosophy for 75 years, you hold it pretty sacred."

Minnesota Vikings owner Roger Headrick, who is chairman of the NFL Properties executive committee, added that without a revenue sharing agreement, "you've got chaos, you've got bedlam... you've got Major League Baseball."

Jones remained defiant at a Sept. 19 closed-door hearing with fellow owners in Atlanta. Afterward, he reiterated that he was an innocent man looking to raise money to service his debt, fix up his stadium, pay gargantuan signing bonuses, and yes, start a debate on the future of NFL Properties.

"I'm [just] sorry it got litigious," he said.

All this in the one major team sport that enjoyed labor harmony in 1995.

Elsewhere, major league baseball stumbled through a 232-day players' strike that scuttled the 1994 World Series, brought about an early spring training populated with replacement players, shortened the '95 regular season to 144 games and ended on March 31 with a court ruling rather than a new collective bargaining agreement.

Hockey fans had to put up with a 103-day NHL owners' lockout that was finally resolved on Jan. 11 with a new CBA, but which cut the regular season from 84 to 48 games and pushed the Stanley Cup final past the summer solstice.

In the NBA, owners and players agreed to play the 1994-95 season without interruption only to have chaos break out in the offseason. Dissident players, led by superstars Michael Jordan and Patrick Ewing and their agents, sought to have their union decertified just as it was agreeing to a new six-year contract with ownership. (See Updates chapter for complete review of the year in labor.)

Speaking of Jordan, he came out of retirement in 1995.

The minor league outfielder, who topped the 1994 *Forbes* magazine list of the world's 40 top-earning athletes for the third straight year with $30 million in endorsements, returned from self-imposed basketball exile in March.

His comeback, spurred in part by his reluctance to make it to the major league level in baseball as a replacement player, quickened the heartbeats of players, uniform shirtmakers and TV networks everywhere. Games starring a rusty but occasionally brilliant second-coming version of Jordan posted drastically higher ratings on NBC and TNT than non-Air fare (see page 340).

Mike Tyson also emerged from the shadows in 1995 after serving a three-year prison term in Indiana for rape.

Released on March 25, he struck it rich less than two weeks later— signing two exclusive-service contracts with MGM Grand in Las Vegas and the Showtime Entertainment Television that guaranteed him and promoter Don King a minimum of $150 million over the six-fight, 2½-year length of the deal.

On Aug. 19, Tyson's first fight since June 28, 1991, ended in just 89 seconds when he pulverized a tomato can named Peter McNeeley. The fight grossed more than $96 million worldwide, including a United States-record $63 million for pay-per-view TV.

Nevertheless, King announced on Sept. 14 that Tyson's next bout with Buster Mathis Jr. on Nov. 4 would be seen not on pay-per-view, but on Fox Network, where the rights went for about $10 million.

Baseball's Doomed TV Partnership

This could only have happened in major league baseball.

The national pastime agrees with the sports czars at ABC and NBC that the game's TV rights are worth so little that upfront cash is not requested in contract negotiations for the 1994 and '95 seasons.

Instead, baseball and the networks form a joint venture called The Baseball Network and agree to sell their own advertising. This after baseball had collected $1.06 billion from CBS the previous four seasons.

The CBS deal lost oodles of money, of course, but it was overpriced to begin with. Still, baseball grossly undervalued itself at a time when the rights fees for virtually everything else carried by TV sports divisions were soaring.

The merry partners— well, at least ABC and NBC were merry because they bought into the new baseball deal with start-up fees of just $10 million each— waited until the All-Star Game to start their prime time regular season schedules in both 1994 and '95 and killed off the Saturday afternoon Game of the Week altogether.

The Baseball Network (TBN) also chose to regionalize all its games so that viewers usually got the contests they'd normally see on their local teams' regular stations. And if that wasn't bad enough, TBN elected to regionalize the playoffs, too, thereby condemning fans everywhere to watching just one League Championship Series while both A.L. and N.L. series aired simultaneously.

And so, baseball's bold new broadcasting partnership set out in 1994 to reshape TV sports history, only to have the players ruin everything with a season-ending strike.

A financial meltdown followed. Instead of collecting as much as $170 million in anticipated revenue, TBN received only $30 million. And it was clear that unless a sales miracle occurred in 1995, it wouldn't reach its two-season sales goal of $330 million— which was contractually required to extend the venture for two more years.

And that's where the partnership ran aground.

ABC and NBC kept asking baseball officials

to extend the deal for another year or more, so that the financial targets could be met and TBN could prove itself. Moreover, ABC and NBC insisted they were promised a one-year extension should sales plummet in the wake of a strike. The only problem was they didn't get the strike protection in writing.

Baseball responded by not responding. Don't bother us now: we're thinking, we're mulling, we're musing, said interim commissioner Bud Selig.

ABC Sports president Dennis Swanson and NBC Sports boss Dick Ebersol got angry and on June 23, their patience finally ran out.

Declaring that they had been treated like "crap" and "scum," Swanson and Ebersol took the only action they felt they could take after such dreadful treatment: They gave *USA Today* TV sports columnist Rudy Martzke an exclusive on their angry divorce action.

Martzke got the story because he agreed to the odious caveats demanded by Ebersol and Swanson– mainly, don't call Selig for his side of the story and don't contact rivals CBS or Fox for their reaction.

However they chose to announce the biggest breakup in TV sports since CBS fired Brent Musberger in 1990, the two network honchos were mighty peeved. "If you're looking for someone who exhibited good faith, it was the networks," said Swanson.

Ebersol added that he felt an "utter sense of betrayal" at baseball's mistreatment of its partners and then ripped into Fox, saying that if baseball eloped with Rupert Murdoch, "they'd be trading in the No. 1 and No. 2 networks for a pushcart."

Fox, proud of its inaugural NFL and NHL telecasts in 1994 and '95 replied in kind. Said Fox Television chairman Chase Carey: "[Ebersol's] trying to create an impression that defies reality. If he weren't so paranoid about us, why is he so focused on us. He's consumed."

Selig and others responsible for not giving ABC and NBC what they wanted, were reserved in their replies. Told that his inaction meant bad faith to his former partners, Selig said sadly: "I'm grieved by that."

But baseball gave ABC and NBC no answer because it cared not to. It's revamped TV committee saw a new market opening up, with interest from both Fox and CBS, and wanted a return to guaranteed money and, perhaps, to some daytime network telecasts.

The divorce wasn't official until Aug. 15, when baseball told ABC and NBC by letter that the partnership was dissolved.

Angry as it was, ABC may be back, however. Now that Disney, which bought 25 percent of the California Angels in 1995, is acquiring ABC, the network could be interested again. It had to decide by Oct. 9. According to the TBN contract, the old partners have an exclusive renegotiating period until then to decide it they still want to play ball.

"We're sacrificing $60 to $70 million to give something back to America," said King, mindful that the McNeeley fight had been a rip-off.

It wasn't likely that Tyson would receive that much. And his charitable spirit was also blessed with Clausewitzian strategy: taking the fight off Showtime Event Television pay-per-view meant pitting a free fight in prime time against TVKO's pay-per-view telecast of the Evander Holyfield-Riddick Bowe bout.

King and Time Warner Sports, TVKO's parent, had played an acrimonious but entertaining game of scheduling chicken over Nov. 4, admitting it was economically suicidal to hold both fights on that date, but each refusing to back off.

Elsewhere, it took very serious money to buy a major league baseball expansion franchise in 1995. On March 9, three weeks *before* the end of the players strike, MLB welcomed the Arizona Diamondbacks and the Tampa Bay Devil Rays into the fold for $130 million each. Both teams will begin play in 1998.

The NFL officially fielded its first new teams in 20 years on Sept. 3, when the Carolina Panthers and Jacksonville Jaguars opened the '95 regular season. The Panthers and Jags were admitted as expansion franchises in 1993 for $140 million apiece.

The expansion entry fee for Seattle and Tampa Bay back in 1976 was $16 million. By comparison, the New England Patriots made 23-year quarterback Drew Bledsoe the highest-paid player in NFL history on July 20, signing him to a seven-year contract worth $42 million.

The NBA was set to suit up its 28th and 29th teams in November when the Toronto Raptors and Vancouver Grizzlies are scheduled to join the league. They each paid $125 million for the privilege.

All or part of several major league teams were sold in 1995, but none for more than the beleaguered Tampa Bay Buccaneers of the NFL, who were bought by West Palm Beach financier Malcolm Glazer for $192 million. The sum was a record for a pro franchise, exceeding the $185 million the NFL's Philadelphia Eagles went for in 1994.

"The Buc stops here," said Glazer, dismissing rumors that he might move the club. "Tampa Bay is going to have this team forever, as far as I'm concerned." He also said he needed local business leaders to help him line up the financing for a new stadium loaded with luxury boxes and permanent seat licenses to protect his investment.

While the Bucs were able to find a local buyer with deep enough pockets to keep the team in town, the Quebec Nordiques and Winnipeg Jets of the NHL were not as lucky.

During the hockey offseason, the Nordiques were sold for $75 million to COMSAT Entertainment Group, which also owns the NBA's Denver Nuggets. Meanwhile, a community effort in the province of Manitoba failed to raise enough money to hold on to the Jets, opening the way to a probable migration to Minneapolis for the 1996-97 season.

Sports television in 1995 had nothing scandalous to cover even remotely resembling the '94 double dip of Nancy and Tonya's ridiculous Olympic soap opera and the bizarre chase and arrest of double-murder suspect O.J. Simpson.

Unless it was the O.J. *trial.* Of course, by the time the prosecution made its opening arguments on Jan. 20, the case had long since ceased to be a sports story— except when O.J.'s bust was briefly stolen from the Pro Football Hall of Fame.

Instead, we got some genuine personal drama.

In February, four-time Olympic diving champion Greg Louganis confessed to "20/20" interviewer Barbara Walters that he had AIDS. It was the ABC magazine show's highest-rated episode. And viewers saw Mickey Mantle waste away during two sad midsummer TV appearances after his liver transplant and the subsequent discovery of a rapidly-spreading cancer.

Cal Ripken saved whatever was left of baseball's good name on Sept. 6, when he played in his 2,131st consecutive game and a packed house in Baltimore reacted with a joyous, 22-minute standing ovation when he officially passed Lou Gehrig in the bottom of the fifth.

ESPN carried the game nationally and stayed with the lovefest, including Ripken's moving victory lap, without breaking for a commercial. It was a rare moment that temporarily lifted the post-strike smog that has settled over the game.

Even Chris Berman was speechless. The talkative play-by-play man and sidekick Buck Martinez stayed mute for over 18 minutes. ❏

Carin Baer/Castle Rock Entertainment

Jerry Seinfeld (letter E, second from left) and **Michael Richards** (letter V, third from left) in the "Seinfeld" episode where Jerry and Kramer ended up having to help spell out "Devils" in order to get tickets to a hockey game. Both "Seinfeld" and the New Jersey Devils were No. 1 in 1995.

1994-95 Top 20 Prime Time TV Series

Final 1994-95 prime time network television ratings, according to Nielsen Media Research. Covers period from Sept. 20, 1994 through April 17, 1995, and includes all series of 10 episodes or more. Events are listed with ratings points and audience share; each ratings point represents 954,000 households and shares indicate percentage of TV sets in use. Note that (*) indicates new show.

Overall network standings: 1. **ABC** (12.0 rating/20 share); 2. **NBC** (11.5 rating/19 share); 3. **CBS** (11.1 rating/18 share); 4. **FOX** (7.7/12 share).

		Net	Rating	Share	93-94 Rank			Net	Rating	Share	93-94 Rank
1	Seinfeld	NBC	20.5	31	3	11	Mad About You	NBC	15.2	25	35
2	ER*	NBC	20.0	33	—	12	Madman of the People*	NBC	14.9	23	—
3	Home Improvement	ABC	19.9	29	1	13	Ellen	ABC	14.7	23	—
4	Grace Under Fire	ABC	18.8	29	5	14	Frasier	NBC	14.3	21	6
5	**Mon. Night Football**	ABC	17.8	30	9	15	Murphy Brown	CBS	14.1	21	10
6	60 Minutes	CBS	17.1	28	2	16	20/20	ABC	14.0	25	12
7	NYPD Blue	ABC	16.5	27	19†	17	CBS Sunday Movie	CBS	13.7	22	11
8	Friends*	NBC	16.1	25	—	18	NBC Monday Movie	NBC	13.6	21	26
9	Roseanne	ABC	15.6	24	4	19	Dave's World	CBS	13.4	20	18
	Murder, She Wrote	CBS	15.6	24	8	20	Me and the Boys*	ABC	13.1	20	—

Note: "Ellen" was a 1993-94 mid-season replacement called "These Friends of Mine" that only aired four times (18.7 rating and 29 share).

1994-95 Top 72 TV Sports Events

Final 1994-95 network television ratings for nationally-telecast sports events, according to Nielsen Media Research. Covers period from Sept. 19, 1994 through Aug. 31, 1995, including 17 Monday Night Football games but not including pre-game, halftime and post-game shows. Due to the players' strike there were no baseball playoffs and no World Series played in 1994. Events are listed with ratings points and audience share; each ratings point represents 954,000 households and shares indicate percentage of TV sets in use.

Multiple entries: SPORTS— NFL Football (28); NBA Basketball (16); Figure Skating (9); NCAA Basketball (8); College Football bowl games (5); Auto Racing (2); Major League Baseball, Golf and Miscellaneous (1). NETWORKS— NBC (35); CBS (13); ABC (12); FOX (11).

		Date	Net	Rtg/Sh			Date	Net	Rtg/Sh
1	**Super Bowl XXIX** (49ers vs Chargers)	1/29	ABC	41.3/62	10	**NCAA Basketball Championship** (UCLA vs Arkansas)	4/3	CBS	19.3/30
2	**NFC Championship** (Cowboys at 49ers)	1/15	FOX	34.2/57	11	**NFC Semifinal** (Bears at 49ers)	1/7	FOX	19.1/37
3	**AFC Championship** (Chargers at Steelers)	1/15	NBC	28.3/58	12	**Orange Bowl** (Nebraska vs Miami-FL)	1/1	NBC	18.9/31
4	**AFC Semifinal** (Dolphins at Chargers)	1/8	NBC	25.1/45	13	**Rose Bowl** (Penn St. vs Oregon)	1/2	ABC	18.2/30
5	**AFC Wild Card** (Chiefs at Dolphins)	12/31	ABC	24.1/48	14	**NFC Wild Card** (Lions at Packers)	12/31	ABC	18.1/42
6	**NFC Semifinal** (Packers at Dallas)	1/8	FOX	22.7/49	15	**Monday Night Football** (Various teams)	17 wks	ABC	17.7/30
7	**AFC Wild Card** (Patriots at Browns)	1/1	NBC	22.0/48	16	**NFL Christmas Eve Late Game** (4pm EST, Various teams)	12/24	NBC	16.4/41
8	**NFC Wild Card** (Bears at Vikings)	1/1	FOX	21.0/40	17	**NFL Thanksgiving, Late Game** (Packers at Cowboys)	11/24	FOX	16.0/42
9	**AFC Semifinal** (Browns at Steelers)	1/7	NBC	19.4/44	18	**NFL Thanksgiving, Early Game** (Bills at Lions)	11/24	NBC	15.8/42

1994-95 Top 72 TV Sports Events (Cont.)

	Date	Net	Rtg/Sh
NFL Late Season Saturday			
(Browns at Cowboys)............12/10	NBC	15.8/35
20 **NFL Regular Season Early Game**			
(Various teams)................7 wks	FOX	15.0/34
21 **NFL Regular Season Late Game**			
(Various teams)................6 wks	NBC	14.9/30
NBA Finals, Game 4			
(Magic at Rockets)..................6/14	NBC	14.9/26
Sugar Bowl			
(Florida St. vs Florida) 1/2	ABC	14.9/24
24 **NBA Finals, Game 1**			
(Rockets at Magic)..................6/7	NBC	14.7/26
25 **NBA Finals, Game 3**			
(Magic at Rockets)..................6/11	NBC	14.1/25
26 **Baseball All-Star Game**			
(AL vs NL at Texas) 7/11	ABC	13.9/25
27 **NCAA Basketball Semifinal**			
(Arkansas vs N. Carolina)..........4/1	CBS	13.3/25
28 **World Pro Fig. Skating Champs., Part 2**			
(from Landover, Md.)..............1/28	NBC	12.9/22
29 **NFL Late Season Saturday**			
(Broncos at 49ers)................12/17	NBC	12.7/29
30 **NFL Regular Season, Early Game**			
(Various teams)................7 wks	NBC	12.3/29
31 **NBA Eastern Semifinal, Game 1**			
(Bulls at Magic)..................5/7	NBC	12.2/24
32 **NBA Western Final, Game 6**			
(Spurs at Rockets)..................6/1	NBC	12.1/22
Ice Wars: USA vs World, Part 2			
(Figure Skating)................11/12	CBS	12.1/21
34 **NBA Finals, Game 2**			
(Rockets at Magic)..................6/9	NBC	12.0/23
35 **NFL Christmas Eve, Early Game**			
(1pm EST, Various teams).......12/24	FOX	11.9/30
NFC Regular Season Single Game			
(Various teams)................6 wks	FOX	11.9/29
37 **NFL Pro Bowl**			
(AFC vs NFC at Honolulu)..........2/5	ABC	11.8/20
38 **NCAA Basketball Semifinal**			
(UCLA vs Oklahoma St.)............4/1	CBS	11.6/27
39 **NBA Eastern Final, Game 7**			
(Pacers at Magic)..................6/4	NBC	11.5/22
40 **Rock N' Roll Skating Championships**			
(Figure Skating)................1/17	FOX	11.3/17
41 **NBA Western Final, Game 5**			
(Rockets at Spurs)..................5/30	NBC	11.2/20
42 **NFL Late Season Saturday**			
(Vikings at Lions)................12/17	FOX	11.0/31
Florida Citrus Bowl			
(Alabama vs Ohio St.)..............1/2	ABC	11.0/24
NBA Eastern Final, Game 5			
(Pacers at Magic)..................5/31	NBC	11.0/20
World Pro Fig. Skating Champs., Part 1			
(from Landover, Md.)..............1/27	NBC	11.0/18

	Date	Net	Rtg/Sh
46 **Ice Wars: USA vs the World, Part 1**			
(Figure Skating)................11/9	CBS	10.8/16
47 **NBA All-Star Game**			
(East vs West at Phoenix).........2/12	NBC	10.7/17
48 **NBA Eastern Semifinals, Game 4**			
(Magic at Bulls)................5/14	NBC	10.6/25
49 **NFL Late Season Saturday**			
(Lions at Jets)................12/10	FOX	10.3/29
50 **NFL Regular Season Late Game**			
(Various teams)................7 wks	FOX	10.0/21
51 **Masters Golf, Final Round**			
(Crenshaw wins)................4/9	CBS	9.8/23
NCAA Basketball Regional Finals			
(Arkansas vs Virginia)........3/26	CBS	9.8/22
NBA Eastern First Round, Game 2			
(Bulls at Hornets)................4/30	NBC	9.8/20
Gold Championship			
(Figure Skating)................11/19	NBC	9.8/17
55 **NBA Eastern Semifinal, Game 7**			
(Pacers at Knicks)................5/21	NBC	9.7/26
NFL Regular Season Early Game			
(Various teams)................6 wks	NBC	9.7/23
57 **NBA Eastern Final, Game 6**			
(Magic at Pacers)................6/2	NBC	9.6/19
58 **NCAA Basketball Second Round**			
(Various teams)................3/19	CBS	9.5/21
NCAA Basketball Regional Final			
(N. Carolina vs Kentucky) 3/25	CBS	9.5/21
60 **World Figure Skating Championships**			
(from Birmingham, England)...3/11	NBC	9.3/17
61 **NFL Christmas Eve Early Game**			
(1pm EST, Various teams)........12/24	NBC	9.2/23
62 **NFL 1995 Monday Night Preseason**			
(Vikings at Chargers)................8/7	ABC	8.8/16
63 **Sports Illustrated Swimsuit Special**			
(The Class of '95)................2/14	NBC	8.6/15
64 **Indianapolis 500**			
(Villeneuve wins)................5/28	ABC	8.4/26
NBA Eastern Final, Game 4			
(Magic at Pacers)................5/29	NBC	8.4/22
AT&T Skates of Gold, II			
(Figure Skating)................2/18	NBC	8.4/15
67 **1994 College Football, Late Games**			
(Colo. at Mich. & others)........9/24	ABC	8.3/22
68 **Skates X Two World Team Challenge**			
(Figure Skating)................4/27	CBS	8.1/13
69 **NCAA Basketball Regional Semifinals**			
(Various teams)................3/23	CBS	8.0/14
70 **NBA Western Semifinals, Game 4**			
(Spurs at Lakers)................5/14	NBC	7.8/24
Daytona 500			
(Marlin wins 2nd in a row) 2/19	CBS	7.8/20
72 **NCAA Basketball Regional Final**			
(UCLA vs UConn) 3/25	CBS	7.7/22

1994-95 Top-Rated Cable TV Sports Events

Final 1994-95 cable television ratings covering period from Sept. 1, 1994 through Sept. 10, 1995.

NFL Telecasts

	Date	Net	Rtg
1 Lions at Dolphins 12/25	ESPN	15.1
2 Bears at Vikings........................12/1	ESPN	13.4
Bills at Dolphins..................12/4	ESPN	13.4
4 Raiders at Chiefs..................11/6	ESPN	12.4
5 Rams at 49ers..................11/20	ESPN	11.2
6 Raiders at Seahawks................12/18	ESPN	10.6
7 Saints at Falcons..................12/11	ESPN	10.4
8 Packers at Vikings................10/20	TNT	10.2
9 Chiefs at Falcons 9/18	TNT	9.8
10 Dolphins at Bengals 10/2	TNT	9.4

Non-NFL Telecasts

	Date	Net	Rtg
1 NBA: Bulls at Magic, Game 2 .....5/10	TNT	7.9
2 CFA: Florida St. at Miami...........10/8	ESPN	7.7
3 MLB: Ripken's 2,131st................9/6	ESPN	7.5
4 NBA: Magic at Bulls, Game 3 ......5/12	TNT	6.9
5 NBA: Pacers at Magic, Game 2....5/25	TNT	6.5
6 NBA: Pacers at Magic, Game 1....5/23	TNT	6.4
NBA: Rockets at Spurs, Game 4 ...5/29	TNT	6.4
8 NBA: Rockets at Spurs, Game 1 ..5/22	TNT	6.3
9 NBA: Knicks at Pacers, Game 3 ..5/11	TNT	6.0
NBA: Magic at Bulls, Game 6 .....5/18	TBS	6.0

All-Time Top-Rated TV Programs

NFL Football dominates television's All-Time Top-Rated 50 Programs with 18 Super Bowls and the 1981 NFC Championship Game making the list. Rankings based on surveys taken from July 1960 through August 1995; include only sponsored programs seen on individual networks; and programs under 30 minutes scheduled duration are excluded. Programs are listed with ratings points, audience share and number of households watching, according to Nielsen Media Research.

Multiple entries: The Super Bowl (18); "The Beverly Hillbillies" and "Roots" (7); "The Thorn Birds" (3); "The Bob Hope Christmas Show," "The Ed Sullivan Show," "Gone With The Wind" and 1994 Winter Olympics (2).

	Program	Episode/Game	Net	Date	Rating	Share	Households
1	M*A*S*H (series)	Final episode	CBS	2/28/83	**60.2**	77	50,150,000
2	Dallas (series)	"Who Shot J.R.?"	CBS	11/21/80	**53.3**	76	41,470,000
3	Roots (mini-series)	Part 8	ABC	1/30/77	**51.1**	71	36,380,000
4	**Super Bowl XVI**	49ers 26, Bengals 21	CBS	1/24/82	**49.1**	73	40,020,000
5	**Super Bowl XVII**	Redskins 27, Dolphins 17	NBC	1/30/83	**48.6**	69	40,480,000
6	**XVII Winter Olympics**	Women's Figure Skating	CBS	2/23/94	**48.5**	64	45,690,000
7	**Super Bowl XX**	Bears 46, Patriots 10	NBC	1/26/86	**48.3**	70	41,490,000
8	Gone With the Wind (movie)	Part 1	NBC	11/7/76	**47.7**	65	33,960,000
9	Gone with the Wind (movie)	Part 2	NBC	11/8/76	**47.4**	64	33,750,000
10	**Super Bowl XII**	Cowboys 27, Broncos 10	CBS	1/15/78	**47.2**	67	34,410,000
11	**Super Bowl XIII**	Steelers 35, Cowboys 31	NBC	1/21/79	**47.1**	74	35,090,000
12	Bob Hope Special	Christmas Show	NBC	1/15/70	**46.6**	64	27,260,000
13	**Super Bowl XVIII**	Raiders 38, Redskins 9	CBS	1/22/84	**46.4**	71	38,800,000
	Super Bowl XIX	49ers 38, Dolphins 16	ABC	1/20/85	**46.4**	63	39,390,000
15	**Super Bowl XIV**	Steelers 31, Rams 19	CBS	1/20/80	**46.3**	67	35,330,000
16	ABC Theater (special)	"The Day After"	ABC	11/20/83	**46.0**	62	38,550,000
17	Roots (mini-series)	Part 6	ABC	1/28/77	**45.9**	66	32,680,000
	The Fugitive (series)	Final episode	ABC	8/29/67	**45.9**	72	25,700,000
19	**Super Bowl XXI**	Giants 39, Broncos 20	CBS	1/25/87	**45.8**	66	40,030,000
20	Roots (mini-series)	Part 5	ABC	1/27/77	**45.7**	71	32,540,000
21	**Super Bowl XXVIII**	Cowboys 30, Bills 13	NBC	1/29/94	**45.5**	66	42,860,000
	Cheers	Final episode	NBC	5/20/93	**45.5**	64	42,360,500
23	The Ed Sullivan Show	Beatles' 1st appearence	CBS	2/9/64	**45.3**	60	23,240,000
24	**Super Bowl XXVII**	Cowboys 52, Bills 17	NBC	1/31/93	**45.1**	66	41,988,100
25	Bob Hope Special	Christmas Show	NBC	1/14/71	**45.0**	61	27,050,000
26	Roots (mini-series)	Part 3	ABC	1/25/77	**44.8**	68	31,900,000
27	**Super Bowl XI**	Raiders 32, Vikings 14	NBC	1/9/77	**44.4**	73	31,610,000
	Super Bowl XV	Raiders 27, Eagles 10	NBC	1/25/81	**44.4**	63	34,540,000
29	**Super Bowl VI**	Cowboys 24, Dolphins 3	CBS	1/16/72	**44.2**	74	27,450,000
30	**XVII Winter Olympics**	Women's Figure Skating	CBS	2/25/94	**44.1**	64	41,540,000
	Roots (mini-series)	Part 2	ABC	1/24/77	**44.1**	62	31,400,000
32	The Beverly Hillbillies	Regular episode	CBS	1/8/64	**44.0**	65	22,570,000
33	Roots (mini-series)	Part 4	ABC	1/26/77	**43.8**	66	31,190,000
	The Ed Sullivan Show	Beatles' 2nd appearence	CBS	2/16/64	**43.8**	60	22,445,000
35	**Super Bowl XXIII**	49ers 20, Bengals 16	NBC	1/22/89	**43.5**	68	39,320,000
36	The Academy Awards	John Wayne wins Oscar	ABC	4/7/70	**43.4**	78	25,390,000
37	Thorn Birds (mini-series)	Part 3	ABC	3/29/83	**43.2**	62	35,990,000
38	Thorn Birds (mini-series)	Part 4	ABC	3/30/83	**43.1**	62	35,900,000
39	**NFC Championship Game**	49ers 28, Cowboys 27	CBS	1/10/82	**42.9**	62	34,940,000
40	The Beverly Hillbillies	Regular episode	CBS	1/15/64	**42.8**	62	21,960,000
41	**Super Bowl VII**	Dolphins 14, Redskins 7	NBC	1/14/73	**42.7**	72	27,670,000
42	Thorn Birds (mini-series)	Part 2	ABC	3/28/83	**42.5**	59	35,400,000
43	**Super Bowl IX**	Steelers 16, Vikings 6	NBC	1/12/75	**42.4**	72	29,040,000
	The Beverly Hillbillies	Regular episode	CBS	2/26/64	**42.4**	60	21,750,000
45	**Super Bowl X**	Steelers 21, Cowboys 17	CBS	1/18/76	**42.3**	78	29,440,000
	ABC Sunday Night Movie	"Airport"	ABC	11/11/73	**42.3**	63	28,000,000
	ABC Sunday Night Movie	"Love Story"	ABC	10/1/72	**42.3**	62	27,410,000
	Cinderella	Musical special	CBS	2/22/65	**42.3**	59	22,250,000
	Roots (mini-series)	Part 7	ABC	1/29/77	**42.3**	65	30,120,000
50	The Beverly Hillbillies	Regular episode	CBS	3/25/64	**42.2**	59	21,650,000

All-Time Top-Rated Cable TV Sports Events

All-time cable television for sports events, according to ESPN and Turner Sports research. Covers period from Sept. 1, 1980 through Sept. 10, 1995.

	NFL Telecasts	Date	Net	Rtg		Non-NFL Telecasts	Date	Net	Rtg
1	Chicago at Minnesota	12/6/87	ESPN	17.6	1	NBA: Detroit-Boston	6/1/88	TBS	8.8
2	Detroit at Miami	12/25/94	ESPN	15.1	2	NBA: Chicago-Detroit	5/31/89	TBS	8.2
3	Chicago at Minnesota	12/3/89	ESPN	14.7	3	NBA: Detroit-Boston	5/26/88	TBS	8.1
4	Cleveland at San Fran	11/29/87	ESPN	14.2	4	NCAA: G'town-St. John's	2/27/85	ESPN	8.0
5	Pittsburgh at Houston	12/30/90	ESPN	13.8	5	NBA: Chicago-Orlando	5/10/95	TNT	7.9

The Rights Stuff

The roster of major 1995-96 television rights on network and cable TV as of Sept. 15, 1995.

ABC

Auto Racing— 1996 Indianapolis 500 and four other Indy Racing League races; NASCAR Brickyard 400.

Major League Baseball— shared coverage of 1995 playoffs and World Series with NBC.

College Basketball— 1996 regular season games.

Bowling— 1996 PBA Tour.

College Football— Big Ten/Pac-10 and CFA regular season (except Notre Dame home games) for 1995 and '96; Big 12 and WAC for 1996; SEC Championship Game 1995 and '96; Aloha, Citrus, Rose and Sugar bowls for 1995 and '96 seasons; 1995 Army-Navy game.

Figure Skating— 1996 World, U.S. and European Championships.

NFL Football— ABC Monday Night Football; two 1995 season Wild Card playoff games; 1996 Pro Bowl.

Golf— 1996 British Open; British Senior Open; LPGA Dinah Shore; PGA, LPGA and Seniors Skins games.

Horse Racing— 1996 Kentucky Derby; Preakness; Belmont Stakes.

Soccer— 1996 Major League Soccer championship game.

CBS

Auto Racing— 1996 Daytona 500 and three other NASCAR races.

College Basketball— 1995-96 Big East, Big Ten and SEC regular season games and Big East and SEC conference tournaments; NCAA Men's tournament and Final Four through 2002.

College Football— Fiesta, Orange, Cotton and Sun bowls for 1995 and '96 seasons; Big East and SEC regular season games in 1996; 1996 Army-Navy game.

Golf— 1996 PGA Tour; Masters; PGA Championship, LPGA Championship.

Olympics— 1998 Winter Games at Nagano.

Tennis— 1996 U.S. Open.

ESPN (and ESPN2)

Auto Racing— 1996 IndyCar, NASCAR and Formula One.

Major League Baseball— 1996 regular season.

College Basketball— Men's 1995-96 regular season and conference tournaments and pre- and postseason NIT; Women's 1995-96 regular season and NCAA tournament and Final Four.

Bowling— 1996 PBA and LPBT tours.

Boxing— Top Rank series.

Cycling— 1996 Tour de France.

College Football— Big 10/Pac-10 and CFA regular season (except Notre Dame home games) for 1995 and '96 season; Heisman Trophy Show; Alamo, Copper, Holiday, Independence, Liberty, Outback and Peach bowls.

NFL Football— Sunday Night Football (2nd half of 1995 and '96 seasons); 1996 College Draft.

Golf— 1996 U.S. and British Open (early rounds); PGA, Senior and LPGA tour events.

NHL Hockey— 1995-96 regular season and Stanley Cup playoffs.

College Hockey— 1996 NCAA Final Four.

Soccer— 1996 Major League Soccer regular season and playoffs; U.S. National Team games.

Tennis— 1995 and '96 Davis Cup, Grand Slam Cup and Fed Cup; 1996 ATP Tour and Australian Open.

FOX

NFL Football— NFC regular season and playoffs through 1997 season; 1997 Super Bowl.

NHL Hockey— 1996 All-Star Game and selected regular season and Stanley Cup playoff games.

NBC

Major League Baseball— shared coverage of 1995 playoffs and World Series with ABC.

NBA Basketball— 1995-96 regular season and playoffs, NBA finals and All-Star Game.

College Football— Notre Dame home games for 1995 and '96 seasons; 1995 Gator Bowl.

NFL Football— AFC regular season and playoffs through 1997 season; 1996 and '98 Super Bowls.

Golf— 1996 U.S. Open, U.S. Women's Open, U.S. Senior Open, Players Championship and PGA Seniors Championship; 1997 Ryder Cup.

Horse Racing— 1996 Breeders' Cup.

Olympics— 1996 Summer Games in Atlanta; 2000 Summer Games in Sydney; 2002 Winter Games in Salt Lake City.

Tennis— 1996 French Open and Wimbledon.

Turner (TBS and TNT)

Auto Racing— 1996 Coca-Cola 600 and NASCAR circuit on TBS.

Major League Baseball— 1996 Atlanta Braves regular season on TBS.

NBA Basketball— 1995-96 regular season and playoffs on TBS and TNT; NBA Draft on TNT.

College Football— Carquest and Senior bowls for 1995 season on TBS.

NFL Football— Sunday Night Football (1st half of 1995 season) on TNT.

Golf— PGA Championship (early rounds, partial 3rd and 4th), Grand Slam of Golf and Senior Slam of Golf on TBS.

Olympics TV Rights

On Aug. 7, 1995, NBC announced it had successfully bid a record $1.27 billion for the exclusive U.S. television rights to the 2000 Summer Games in Sydney and the 2002 Winter Games in Salt Lake City.

Year	Games	Location	Rights Fee	Net	TV Hrs
1960	Winter	Squaw Valley	$ 50,000	CBS	15
	Summer	Rome	394,000	CBS	20
1964	Winter	Innsbruck	$597,000	ABC	17¼
	Summer	Tokyo	1.5 mil.	NBC	14
1968	Winter	Grenoble	$2.5 mil.	ABC	27
	Summer	Mexico City	4.5 mil.	ABC	43¾
1972	Winter	Sapporo	$6.4 mil.	NBC	37
	Summer	Munich	7.5 mil.	ABC	62¾
1976	Winter	Innsbruck	$10 mil.	ABC	43½
	Summer	Montreal	25 mil.	ABC	76½
1980	Winter	Lake Placid	$15.5 mil.	ABC	53¼
	Summer	Moscow	87 mil.	NBC	150*
1984	Winter	Sarajevo	$91.5 mil.	ABC	63
	Summer	Los Angeles	225 mil.	ABC	180
1988	Winter	Calgary	$309 mil.	ABC	94½
	Summer	Seoul	300 mil.	NBC	179½
1992	Winter	Albertville	$243 mil.	CBS	116
	Summer	Barcelona	401 mil.	NBC	161
1994	Winter	Lillehammer	$300 mil.	CBS	120
1996	Summer	Atlanta	456 mil.	NBC	168
1998	Winter	Nagano	$375 mil.	CBS	TBA
2000	Summer	Sydney	$715 mil.	NBC	TBA
2002	Winter	Salt Lake City	555 mil.	NBC	TBA

*NBC planned 150 hours of coverage for the 1980 Summer Olympics, but since the U.S. boycotted the Games, NBC did not cover them and did not pay the rights fee.

What Major League Franchises Are Worth

The estimated total market value of the 107 major league baseball, basketball, football and hockey franchises operating in the U.S. and Canada in 1993-94. Figures according to *Financial World* magazine's fourth annual survey, released May 9, 1995. Franchise values are estimates of what a team would have been worth if put up for sale in early 1995. Values are based on gate receipts, radio and TV revenues, stadium/arena income (luxury suites, concessions, parking, etc.), operating income, player salaries and other expenses. Figures are in millions of dollars.

Avg. franchise values: NFL ($160 million), **NBA** ($114 million), **Baseball** ($111 million) and **NHL** ($71 million).

BASEBALL			NBA			NFL			NHL		
	Value			Value			Value			Value	
	1994	1993		1994	1993		1994	1993		1994	1993
NY Yankees	$185	$166	Detroit	$180	$154	Dallas	$238	$190	Detroit	$124	$104
Baltimore	164	129	New York	173	136	Miami	186	161	Anaheim*	108	—
Texas	157	132	LA Lakers	169	168	San Francisco	186	167	NY Rangers	108	81
Chicago-AL	152	133	Chicago	166	149	Philadelphia	182	172	Boston	106	88
Toronto	146	150	Phoenix	156	108	Buffalo	172	164	Chicago	102	80
Boston	143	141	Cleveland	133	118	Kansas City	172	153	Toronto	90	77
LA Dodgers	143	138	Portland	132	122	New Orleans	171	154	Vancouver	87	69
Chicago-NL	135	120	Boston	127	117	NY Giants	168	176	Montreal	86	82
NY Mets	134	147	Utah	127	98	Cleveland	163	165	Philadelphia	86	69
Atlanta	120	96	Seattle	119	96	Chicago	161	160	Los Angeles	81	85
Colorado	117	110	San Antonio	110	100	Houston	158	157	Pittsburgh	75	62
St. Louis	110	105	Charlotte	110	104	Atlanta	156	148	St. Louis	69	59
Cleveland	103	100	Sacramento	108	84	Arizona	155	146	San Jose	66	52
San Francisco	102	93	Orlando	101	84	Minnesota	154	147	Buffalo	60	55
Oakland	101	114	Minnesota	99	92	Green Bay	154	141	Washington	59	47
Philadelphia	96	96	Washington	96	78	San Diego	153	142	Ottawa	56	50
Kansas City	96	94	Houston	95	84	LA Rams	153	148	Tampa Bay	55	39
Florida	92	81	Golden St	93	85	Seattle	152	148	New Jersey	54	51
Houston	92	85	Milwaukee	92	77	Washington	151	158	NY Islanders	53	53
California	88	93	New Jersey	92	79	Tampa Bay	151	142	Calgary	50	50
Cincinnati	84	86	Denver	88	69	New England	151	142	Dallas	50	46
Detroit	83	89	Miami	88	76	Denver	150	147	Quebec	49	43
Minnesota	80	83	LA Clippers	87	83	NY Jets	149	142	Florida*	47	—
Seattle	76	80	Atlanta	84	72	LA Raiders	145	146	Hartford	43	46
Montreal	76	75	Philadelphia	81	83	Pittsburgh	144	143	Edmonton	42	46
Milwaukee	75	96	Dallas	81	79	Detroit	141	138	Winnipeg	35	35
San Diego	74	85	Indiana	77	67	Cincinnati	137	142			
Pittsburgh	70	79				Indianapolis	134	141			

*Expansion teams in 1993-94.

Teams Bought in 1995

Nine major league clubs acquired new majority owners or significant minority owners from Nov. 1, 1994 through Sept. 20, 1995, while two 1998 expansion baseball franchises were awarded to well-heeled backers.

MAJOR LEAGUE BASEBALL

Arizona Diamondbacks: 1998 expansion franchise awarded on March 9, 1995, to Arizona Professional Baseball Team, Inc. for $130 million. Partnership headed by Phoenix Suns president and CEO Jerry Colangelo. Other investers include comedian Billy Crystal and Phil Knight, owner of Nike, Inc.

Tampa Bay Devil Rays: 1998 expansion franchise awarded on March 9, 1995, to local group of corporations and individuals headed by majority owner Vince Naimoli. Price tag: $130 million.

California Angels: Walt Disney Co. purchased 25 percent of the Anaheim-based club from 86-year-old owner Gene Autry and his wife Jackie for a reported $30 million on May 18, 1995. Disney, which also owns the NHL's Mighty Ducks of Anaheim, took over the day-to-day running of the Angels and has an option to buy the remaining 75 percent of the team after Autry's death. Autry, the former singing cowboy and western movie star, was awarded the club as a 1961 expansion team (originally the Los Angeles Angels) for $2.45 million on Dec. 6, 1960.

Oakland A's: Real estate developers Steve Schott and Ken Hofmann purchased 100 percent of the club from the family of 79-year-old owner Walter Haas for a reported $85 million on July 21, 1995. Hofmann is also a minority owner of the Seattle Seahawks. The Haas family, owners of the Levi-Strauss Co., bought the A's from Charles O. Finley for $12.7 million on July 23, 1980.

San Diego Padres: A limited partnership headed by computer software magnate John Moores purchased the Padres from a partnership headed by TV sitcom producer Tom Werner for a reported $80 million on Dec. 21, 1994. Werner, the former majority owner whose group bought the club from Joan Kroc for $75 million on April 2, 1990, is a minority owner in the new partnership.

NBA BASKETBALL

Miami Heat: The family of majority owner and Carnival Cruise Lines founders Ted Arison paid a reported $60 million to buy out the 30 percent interest held by minority partners Lewis Schaffel and Billy Cunningham. The league formally approved the deal on Feb. 13, 1995. The Arisons now own 88 percent of the team and four limited partners own the rest. The Heat cost $32.5 million as a 1988 expansion team.

Golden State Warriors: Minority owner Chris Cohan increased his stake in the club from 25 to 100 percent by buying out an investor group headed by Jim Fitzgerald and Dan Finnane for an estimated $105 million. The league formally approved the deal on Jan. 18, 1995. Fitzgerald and Finnane purchased the Warriors from Frank Mieuli for $18 million in May 1986.

Teams Bought in 1995 (Cont.)

NFL FOOTBALL

Tampa Bay Buccaneers: West Palm Beach financier Malcolm Glazer purchased the club from the estate of the late Hugh Culverhouse for a reported $192 million on Jan. 16, 1995. The NFL approved the deal on Mar. 12. Culverhouse bought the Bucs as a 1976 expansion team for $16 million on Dec. 5, 1974.

NHL HOCKEY

Los Angeles Kings: Denver investor Philip Anschutz and Los Angeles real estate developer Ed Roski announced on Sept. 20 that they will buy the financially-hobbled franchise from Joe Cohen and Jeffrey Sudikoff, who own 72 percent of the club. The purchase price was reported to be in the $110-to-$115 million range. Cohen and Sudikoff had already filed for bankruptcy protection when the sale was announced. Meanwhile, the remaining 28 percent of the team once owned by convicted swindler Bruce McNall is currently held by a bankruptcy trustee.

Quebec Nordiques: Majority owner Marcel Aubut sold club to COMSAT Entertainment Group of Denver on June 21, 1995, for $75 million (U.S. funds). COMSAT Entertainment Group also owns the NBA Denver Nuggets and is a subsidiary of COMSAT Corporation, a global provider of communications and entertainment products and services based in Bethesda, Md. Team was renamed the Colorado Avalanche on Aug. 10, 1995. Aubut and a group of Quebec businessmen bought the Nordiques from Carling-O'Keefe Brewery for $14.8 million (Canadian) on Nov. 29, 1988.

Vancouver Canucks: Seattle businessman and cellular phone magnate John McCaw Jr. bought controlling interest in both the Canucks and NBA Grizzlies on March 7, 1995, by increasing his stake in Orca Bay Sports & Entertainment from 30 to 60 percent while partner Arthur Griffiths' holdings were reduced from 70 to 40 percent. Orca Bay, which changed its name from Northwest Entertainment Group on Aug. 22, 1995, owns 87 percent of the Canucks and 100 percent of both the Grizzlies and the new General Motors Place arena. *Financial World* magazine estimates Orca Bay to be worth $350 million (U.S. funds), which means McCaw paid Griffiths around $116.5 million (U.S.) for 30 percent. The Griffiths family bought the Canucks as an NHL expansion team for $6 million in 1970.

The 1994 *Forbes* Top 40

The 40 highest-paid athletes of 1994 (including salary, winnings, endorsements, etc.), according to the Dec. 19, 1994 issue of *Forbes* magazine. Nationality, birth date, and each athlete's rank on the 1993 list are also given. Age refers to athlete's age as of Dec. 31, 1994.

	Sport	Salary/ Winnings	Other Income	Total	Nat	Birthdate	(Age)	1993 Rank
1 Michael Jordan	Baseball	$0.01	$30.0	$30.01	USA	Feb. 17, 1963	31	1
2 Shaquille O'Neal	Basketball	4.2	12.5	16.7	USA	Mar. 6, 1972	22	6
3 Jack Nicklaus	Golf	0.3	14.5	14.8	USA	Jan. 21, 1940	54	13
4 Arnold Palmer	Golf	0.1	13.5	13.6	USA	Sept. 10, 1929	65	11
5 Gerhard Berger	Auto Racing	12.0	1.5	13.5	AUT	Aug. 27, 1959	35	29†
6 Wayne Gretzky	Hockey	9.0*	4.5	13.5	CAN	Jan. 26, 1961	33	22
7 Michael Moorer	Boxing	12.0	0.1	12.1	USA	Nov. 12, 1967	27	NR
8 Evander Holyfield	Boxing	10.0	2.0	12.0	USA	Oct. 19, 1962	32	12
9 Andre Agassi	Tennis	1.9	9.5	11.4	USA	Apr. 29, 1970	24	20
10 Nigel Mansell	Auto Racing	9.3	2.0	11.3	GBR	Aug. 8, 1953	41	19
11 Pete Sampras	Tennis	3.6	7.0	10.6	USA	Aug. 12, 1971	23	16
12 Joe Montana	Football	3.3	7.0	10.3	USA	June 11, 1956	38	10
13 Charles Barkley	Basketball	3.3	6.0	9.3	USA	Feb. 20, 1963	31	34†
14 Greg Norman	Golf	1.3	7.5	8.8	AUS	Feb. 10, 1955	39	21
15 George Foreman	Boxing	3.5	5.0	8.5	USA	Jan. 10, 1949	45	5
Julio Cesar Chavez	Boxing	8.0	0.5	8.5	MEX	July 12, 1962	32	23
17 David Robinson	Basketball	6.1	2.3	8.4	USA	Aug. 6, 1965	29	18
18 Lennox Lewis	Boxing	8.0	0.3	8.3	GBR	Sept. 2, 1965	29	7
19 Steffi Graf	Tennis	1.5	6.5	8.0	GER	June 14, 1969	25	15
Jean Alesi	Auto Racing	7.0	1.0	8.0	FRA	June 11, 1964	30	NR
21 Emerson Fittipaldi	Auto Racing	4.0	3.5	7.5	BRA	Dec. 12, 1946	48	14
22 Boris Becker	Tennis	2.0	5.0	7.0	GER	Nov. 22, 1967	27	32
23 Stefan Edberg	Tennis	2.5	4.0	6.5	SWE	Jan. 19, 1966	28	24
24 Scott Mitchell	Football	6.4*	0.0	6.4	USA	Jan. 2, 1968	26	NR
25 Heath Shuler	Football	6.1*	0.2	6.3	USA	Dec. 31, 1971	23	NR
26 Marshall Faulk	Football	6.1*	0.1	6.2	USA	Feb. 26, 1973	21	NR
James Toney	Boxing	6.2	0.0	6.2	USA	Aug. 24, 1968	26	NR
28 Dan Wilkinson	Football	6.0*	0.1	6.1	USA	Mar. 13, 1973	21	NR
29 Patrick Ewing	Basketball	4.0	2.0	6.0	USA	Aug. 5, 1962	32	NR
Michael Schumacher	Auto Racing	5.0	1.0	6.0	GBR	Jan. 3, 1969	25	NR
31 Michael Chang	Tennis	1.8	4.0	5.8	USA	Feb. 22, 1972	22	25
32 Mario Andretti	Auto Racing	3.0	2.5	5.5	USA	Feb. 28, 1940	54	NR
Trent Dilfer	Football	5.3	0.2	5.5	USA	Mar. 13, 1972	22	NR
Dale Earnhardt	Auto Racing	3.0	2.5	5.5	USA	Apr. 29, 1952	42	NR
35 Roberto Baggio	Soccer	3.3	2.0	5.3	ITA	Feb. 18, 1967	27	NR
36 Pernell Whitaker	Boxing	5.2	0.0	5.2	USA	Jan. 2, 1964	30	NR
Will Clark	Baseball	4.9*	0.3	5.2	USA	Mar. 13, 1964	30	NR
38 Deion Sanders	Football/Baseball	3.3	1.6	4.9	USA	Aug. 9, 1967	27	NR
Gabriela Sabatini	Tennis	0.9	4.0	4.9	ARG	May 16, 1970	24	34†
40 Al Unser Jr	Auto Racing	3.8	1.0	4.8	USA	Apr. 19, 1962	32	NR

* Includes signing bonus

AWARDS

The Peabody Award

Presented annually since 1940 for outstanding achievement in radio and television broadcasting. Only 13 Peabodys have been given for sports programming. Named after Georgia banker and philanthropist George Foster Peabody, the awards are administered by the Henry W. Grady College of Journalism and Mass Communication at the University of Georgia.

Television

Year
1960 **CBS** for coverage of 1960 Winter and Summer Olympic Games
1966 ABC's **"Wide World of Sports"** (for Outstanding Achievement in Promotion of International Understanding).
1968 **ABC Sports** coverage of both the 1968 Winter and Summer Olympic Games.
1972 **ABC Sports** coverage of the 1972 Summer Olympics in Munich.
1973 **Joe Garagiola** of NBC Sports (for "The Baseball World of Joe Garagiola").
1976 **ABC Sports** coverage of both the 1976 Winter and Summer Olympic Games.
1984 **Roone Arledge**, president of ABC News & Sports (for significant contributions to news and sports programming).
1986 **WFAA-TV**, Dallas for its investigation of the Southern Methodist University football program.
1988 **Jim McKay** of ABC Sports (for pioneering efforts and career accomplishments in the world of TV sports).
1991 **CBS Sports** coverage of the 1991 Masters golf tournament
     & **HBO Sports** and Black Canyon Productions for the baseball special "When It Was A Game."

Radio

Year
1974 **WSB** radio in Atlanta for "Henry Aaron: A Man with a Mission."
1991 **Red Barber** of National Public Radio (for his six decades as a broadcaster and his 10 years as a commentator on NPR's "Morning Edition").

National Emmy Awards
Sports Programming

Presented by the Academy of Television Arts and Sciences since 1948. Eligibility period covered the calendar year from 1948-57 and since 1988.

Multiple major award winners: ABC "Wide World of Sports" (19); ABC Olympics coverage (9); NFL Films Football coverage (8); ABC "Monday Night Football and CBS NFL Football coverage (6); CBS NCAA Basketball coverage and CBS "NFL Today" (5); ESPN "Outside the Lines" series (4); ABC "The American Sportsman," ABC Indianapolis 500 coverage, ESPN "GameDay," ESPN "SportsCenter" and NBC Olympics coverage (3); ABC Kentucky Derby coverage, ABC "Sportsbeat," Bud Greenspan Olympic specials, CBS Olympics coverage, CBS Golf coverage, MTV Sports series and NBC World Series coverage (2).

1949
Coverage—"Wrestling" (KTLA, Los Angeles)

1950
Program—"Rams Football" (KNBH-TV, Los Angeles)

1954
Program—"Gillette Cavalcade of Sports" (NBC)

1965-66
Programs—"Wide World of Sports" (ABC), "Shell's Wonderful World of Golf" (NBC) and "CBS Golf Classic" (CBS)

1966-67
Program—"Wide World of Sports" (ABC)

1967-68
Program—"Wide World of Sports" (ABC)

1968-69
Program—"1968 Summer Olympics" (ABC)

1969-70
Programs—"NFL Football" (CBS) and "Wide World of Sports" (ABC)

1970-71
Program—"Wide World of Sports" (ABC)

1971-72
Program—"Wide World of Sports" (ABC)

1972-73
News Special—"Coverage of Munich Olympic Tragedy" (ABC)
Sports Programs—"1972 Summer Olympics" (ABC) and "Wide World of Sports" (ABC)

1973-74
Program—"Wide World of Sports" (ABC)

1974-75
Non-Edited Program—"Jimmy Connors vs Rod Laver Tennis Challenge" (CBS)
Edited Program—"Wide World of Sports" (ABC)

1975-76
Live Special—"1975 World Series: Cincinnati vs Boston" (NBC)
Live Series—"NFL Monday Night Football" (ABC)
Edited Specials—"1976 Winter Olympics" (ABC) and "Triumph and Tragedy: The Olympic Experience" (ABC)
Edited Series—"Wide World of Sports" (ABC)

1976-77
Live Special—"1976 Summer Olympics" (ABC)
Live Series—"The NFL Today/NFL Football" (CBS)
Edited Special—"1976 Summer Olympics Preview" (ABC)
Edited Series—"The Olympiad" (PBS)

1977-78
Live Special—"Muhammad Ali vs Leon Spinks Heavyweight Championship Fight" (CBS)
Live Series—"The NFL Today/NFL Football" (CBS)
Edited Special—"The Impossible Dream: Ballooning Across the Atlantic" (CBS)
Edited Series—"The Way It Was" (PBS)

1978-79
Live Special—"Super Bowl XIII: Pittsburgh vs Dallas" (NBC)
Live Series—"NFL Monday Night Football" (ABC)
Edited Special—"Spirit of '78: The Flight of Double Eagle II" (ABC)
Edited Series—"The American Sportsman" (ABC)

National Emmy Awards (Cont.)
Sports Programming

1979-80
Live Special—"1980 Winter Olympics" (ABC)
Live Series—"NCAA College Football" (ABC)
Edited Special—"Gossamer Albatross: Flight of Imagination" (CBS)
Edited Series—"NFL Game of the Week" (NFL Films)

1980-81
Live Special—"1981 Kentucky Derby" (ABC)
Live Series—"PGA Golf Tour" (CBS)
Edited Special—"Wide World of Sports 20th Anniversary Show" (ABC)
Edited Series—"The American Sportsman" (ABC)

1981-82
Live Special—"1982 NCAA Basketball Final: North Carolina vs Georgetown" (CBS)
Live Series—"NFL Football" (CBS)
Edited Special—"1982 Indianapolis 500" (ABC)
Edited Series—"Wide World of Sports" (ABC)

1982-83
Live Special—"1982 World Series: St. Louis vs Milwaukee" (NBC)
Live Series—"NFL Football" (CBS)
Edited Special—"Wimbledon '83" (NBC)
Edited Series—"Wide World of Sports" (ABC)
Journalism—"ABC Sportsbeat" (ABC)

1983-84
No awards given

1984-85
Live Special—"1984 Summer Olympics" (ABC)
Live Series—No award given
Edited Special—"Road to the Super Bowl '85" (NFL Films)
Edited Series—"The American Sportsman" (ABC)
Journalism—"ABC Sportsbeat" (ABC), "CBS Sports Sunday" (CBS), Dick Schaap features (ABC) and 1984 Summer Olympic features (ABC)

1985-86
No awards given

1986-87
Live Special—"1987 Daytona 500" (CBS)
Live Series—"NFL Football" (CBS)
Edited Special—"Wide World of Sports 25th Anniversary Special" (ABC)
Edited Series—"Wide World of Sports" (ABC)

1987-88
Live Special—"1987 Kentucky Derby" (ABC)
Live Series—"NFL Monday Night Football" (ABC)
Edited Special—"Paris-Roubaix Bike Race" (CBS)
Edited Series—"Wide World of Sports" (ABC)

1988
Live Special— "1988 Summer Olympics" (NBC)
Live Series—"1988 NCAA Basketball" (CBS)
Edited Special—"Road to the Super Bowl '88" (NFL Films)
Edited Series—"Wide World of Sports" (ABC)
Studio Show—"NFL GameDay" (ESPN)
Journalism—1988 Summer Olympic reporting (NBC)

1989
Live Special—"1989 Indianapolis 500" (ABC)
Live Series—"NFL Monday Night Football" (ABC)
Edited Special—"Trans-Antarctica! The International Expedition" (ABC)
Edited Series—"This is the NFL" (NFL Films)
Studio Show—"NFL Today" (CBS)
Journalism—1989 World Series Game 3 earthquake coverage (ABC)

1990
Live Special—"1990 Indianapolis 500" (ABC)
Live Series—"1990 NCAA Basketball Tournament" (CBS)
Edited Special—"Road to Super Bowl XXIV" (NFL Films)
Edited Series—"Wide World of Sports" (ABC)
Studio Show—"SportsCenter" (ESPN)
Journalism—"Outside the Lines: The Autograph Game" (ESPN)

1991
Live Special—"1991 NBA Finals: Chicago vs LA Lakers" (NBC)
Live Series—"1991 NCAA Basketball Tournament" (CBS)
Edited Special—"Wide World of Sports 30th Anniversary Special" (ABC)
Edited Series—"This is the NFL" (NFL Films)
Studio Show—"NFL GameDay" (ESPN) and "NFL Live" (NBC)
Journalism—"Outside the Lines: Steroids—Whatever It Takes" (ESPN)

1992
Live Special—"1992 Breeders' Cup" (NBC)
Live Series—"1992 NCAA Basketball Tournament" (CBS)
Edited Special—"1992 Summer Olympics" (NBC)
Edited Series—"MTV Sports" (MTV)
Studio Show—"The NFL Today" (CBS)
Journalism—"Outside the Lines: Portraits in Black and White" (ESPN)

1993
Live Special—"1993 World Series" (CBS)
Live Series—"Monday Night Football" (ABC)
Edited Special—"Road to the Super Bowl" (NFL Films)
Edited Series—"This is the NFL" (NFL Films)
Studio Show—"The NFL Today" (CBS)
Journalism (TIE)—"Outside the Lines: Mitch Ivey Feature" (ESPN) and "SportsCenter: University of Houston Football" (ESPN).
Feature—"Arthur Ashe: His Life, His Legacy" (NBC).

1994
Live Special— "NHL Stanley Cup Finals" (ESPN)
Live Series— "Monday Night Football" (ABC)
Edited Special— "Lillehammer '94: 16 Days of Glory" (Disney/Cappy Productions)
Edited Series— "MTV Sports" (MTV)
Studio Show— "NFL GameDay" (ESPN)
Journalism— "1994 Winter Olympic Games: Mossad feature" (CBS)
Feature (TIE)— "Heroes of Telemark" on Winter Olympic Games (CBS); and "Vanderbilt running back Brad Gaines" on SportsCenter (ESPN).

"Baseball" Wins Prime Time Emmy

Ken Burns's miniseries "Baseball" won the 1994 Emmy Award for Outstanding Informational Series. The nine-part documentary aired from Sept. 18-28, 1994 and ran more than 18 hours, drawing the largest audience in PBS history.

Sportscasters of the Year
National Emmy Awards

An Emmy Award for Sportscasters was first introduced in 1968 and given for Outstanding Host/Commentator for the 1967-68 TV season. Two awards, one for Outstanding Host or Play-by-Play and the other for Outstanding Analyst, were first presented in 1981 for the 1980-81 season. Three awards, for Outstanding Studio Host, Play-by-Play and Analyst, have been given since the 1993 season

Multiple winners: John Madden (10); Jim McKay (9); Bob Costas (6); Dick Enberg (4); Al Michaels (2). Note that Jim McKay has won a total of 12 Emmy awards: eight for Host/Commentator, one for Host/Play-by-Play, two for Sports Writing, and one for News Commentary.

Season	Host/Commentator	Season	Host/Play-by-Play	Season	Analyst
1967-68	Jim McKay, ABC	1980-81	Dick Enberg, NBC	1980-81	Dick Button, ABC
1968-69	No award	1981-82	Jim McKay, ABC	1981-82	John Madden, CBS
1969-70	No award	1982-83	Dick Enberg, NBC	1982-83	John Madden, CBS
1970-71	Jim McKay, ABC	1983-84	No award	1983-84	No award
	& Don Meredith, ABC	1984-85	George Michael, NBC	1984-85	No award
1971-72	No award	1985-86	No award	1985-86	No award
1972-73	Jim McKay, ABC	1986-87	Al Michaels, ABC	1986-87	John Madden, CBS
1973-74	Jim McKay, ABC	1987-88	Bob Costas, NBC	1987-88	John Madden, CBS
1974-75	Jim McKay, ABC	1988	Bob Costas, NBC	1988	John Madden, CBS
1975-76	Jim McKay, ABC	1989	Al Michaels, ABC	1989	John Madden, CBS
1976-77	Frank Gifford, ABC	1990	Dick Enberg, NBC	1990	John Madden, CBS
1977-78	Jack Whitaker, CBS	1991	Bob Costas, NBC	1991	John Madden, CBS
1978-79	Jim McKay, ABC	1992	Bob Costas, NBC	1992	John Madden, CBS
1979-80	Jim McKay, ABC				

Year	Studio Host	Year	Play-by-Play	Year	Analyst
1993	Bob Costas, NBC	1993	Dick Enberg, NBC	1993	Billy Packer, CBS
1994	Bob Costas, NBC	1994	Keith Jackson, ABC	1994	John Madden, Fox

Life Achievement Emmy Award

For outstanding work as an exemplary television sportscaster over many years.

Year		Year		Year		Year	
1989	Jim McKay	1991	Curt Gowdy	1993	Pat Summerall	1994	Howard Cosell
1990	Lindsey Nelson	1992	Chris Schenkel				

National Sportscasters and Sportswriters Assn. Award

Sportscaster of the Year presented annually since 1959 by the National Sportscasters and Sportswriters Association, based in Salisbury, N.C. Voting is done by NSSA members and selected national media.

Multiple winners: Keith Jackson and Bob Costas (5); Chris Berman, Lindsey Nelson and Chris Schenkel (4); Dick Enberg, Al Michaels and Vin Scully (3); Curt Gowdy and Ray Scott (2).

Year		Year		Year		Year	
1959	Lindsey Nelson	1969	Curt Gowdy	1979	Dick Enberg	1988	Bob Costas
						1989	Chris Berman
1960	Lindsey Nelson	1970	Chris Schenkel	1980	Dick Enberg		
1961	Lindsey Nelson	1971	Ray Scott		& Al Michaels	1990	Chris Berman
1962	Lindsey Nelson	1972	Keith Jackson	1981	Dick Enberg	1991	Bob Costas
1963	Chris Schenkel	1973	Keith Jackson	1982	Vin Scully	1992	Bob Costas
1964	Chris Schenkel	1974	Keith Jackson	1983	Al Michaels	1993	Chris Berman
1965	Vin Scully	1975	Keith Jackson	1984	John Madden	1994	Chris Berman
1966	Curt Gowdy	1976	Keith Jackson	1985	Bob Costas		
1967	Chris Schenkel	1977	Pat Summerall	1986	Al Michaels		
1968	Ray Scott	1978	Vin Scully	1987	Bob Costas		

American Sportscasters Association Award

Sportscaster of the Year presented annually from 1984-94, with the exception of 1988, by the New York-based American Sportscasters Association. Two awards presented starting in 1995 to honor top play-by-play personality and studio host. Voting done by ASA members and officials. All four-time winners become ineligible for additional awards.

Multiple winners: Bob Costas and Dick Enberg (4).

Sportscaster of the Year

Year		Year		Year	Play-by-Play	Year	Studio Host
1984	Dick Enberg	1990	Dick Enberg	1995	Al Michaels	1995	Chris Berman
1985	Vin Scully	1991	Bob Costas				
1986	Dick Enberg	1992	Bob Costas				
1987	Dick Enberg	1993	Bob Costas				
1988	No award	1994	Pat Summerall				
1989	Bob Costas						

The Pulitzer Prize

The Pulitzer Prizes for journalism, letters and music have been presented annually since 1917 in the name of Joseph Pulitzer (1847-1911), the publisher of the New York World. Prizes are awarded by the president of Columbia University on the recommendation of a board of review. Fourteen Pulitzers have been awarded for newspaper sports reporting, sports commentary and sports photography.

News Coverage

1935 **Bill Taylor,** NY Herald Tribune, for his reporting on the 1934 America's Cup yacht races.

Special Citation

1952 **Max Kase,** NY Journal-American, for his reporting on the 1951 college basketball point-shaving scandal.

Meritorious Public Service

1954 **Newsday** (Garden City, N.Y.) for its exposé of New York State's race track scandals and labor racketeering.

General Reporting

1956 **Arthur Daley,** NY Times, for his 1955 columns.

Investigative Reporting

1981 **Clark Hallas** & **Robert Lowe,** (Tucson) Arizona Daily Star, for their 1980 investigation of the University of Arizona athletic department.

1986 **Jeffrey Marx** & **Michael York,** Lexington (Ky.) Herald-Leader, for their 1985 investigation of the basketball program at the University of Kentucky and other major colleges.

Specialized Reporting

1985 **Randall Savage** & **Jackie Crosby,** Macon (Ga.) Telegraph and News, for their 1984 investigation of athletics and academics at the University of Georgia and Georgia Tech.

Commentary

1976 **Red Smith,** NY Times, for his 1975 columns.
1981 **Dave Anderson,** NY Times, for his 1980 columns.
1990 **Jim Murray,** LA Times, for his 1989 columns.

Photography

1949 **Nat Fein,** NY Herald Tribune, for his photo, "Babe Ruth Bows Out."

1952 **John Robinson** & **Don Ultang,** Des Moines (Iowa) Register and Tribune, for their sequence of six pictures of the 1951 Drake-Oklahoma A&M football game, in which Drake's Johnny Bright had his jaw broken.

1985 **The Photography Staff** of the Orange County (Calif.) Register, for their coverage of the 1984 Summer Olympics in Los Angeles.

1993 **William Snyder** & **Ken Geiger,** The Dallas Morning News, for their coverage of the 1992 Summer Olympics in Barcelona, Spain.

Sportswriter of the Year
NSSA Award

Presented annually since 1959 by the National Sportscasters and Sportswriters Association, based in Salisbury, N.C. Voting is done by NSSA members and selected national media.

Multiple winners: Jim Murray (14); Frank Deford (6); Red Smith (5); Will Grimsley (4); Peter Gammons and Rick Reilly (3).

Year		Year		Year	
1959	Red Smith, NY Herald-Tribune	1972	Jim Murray, LA Times	1984	Frank Deford, Sports Ill.
1960	Red Smith, NY Herald-Tribune	1973	Jim Murray, LA Times	1985	Frank Deford, Sports Ill.
1961	Red Smith, NY Herald-Tribune	1974	Jim Murray, LA Times	1986	Frank Deford, Sports Ill.
1962	Red Smith, NY Herald-Tribune	1975	Jim Murray, LA Times	1987	Frank Deford, Sports Ill.
1963	Arthur Daley, NY Times	1976	Jim Murray, LA Times	1988	Frank Deford, Sports Ill.
1964	Jim Murray, LA Times	1977	Jim Murray, LA Times	1989	Peter Gammons, Sports Ill.
1965	Red Smith, NY Herald-Tribune	1978	Will Grimsley, AP		
1966	Jim Murray, LA Times	1979	Jim Murray, LA Times	1990	Peter Gammons, Boston Globe
1967	Jim Murray, LA Times			1991	Rick Reilly, Sports Ill.
1968	Jim Murray, LA Times	1980	Will Grimsley, AP	1992	Rick Reilly, Sports Ill.
1969	Jim Murray, LA Times	1981	Will Grimsley, AP	1993	Peter Gammons, Boston Globe
		1982	Frank Deford, Sports Ill.	1994	Rick Reilly, Sports Ill.
1970	Jim Murray, LA Times	1983	Will Grimsley, AP		
1971	Jim Murray, LA Times				

Best Newspaper Sports Sections of 1994

Winners of the annual Associated Press Sports Editors' contest for best daily and Sunday sports sections in newspapers of 175,000 circulation or more. Selections made by a committee of APSE members and announced March 1, 1995.

Top 10 Dailies

Boston Globe
Chicago Sun-Times
Dallas Morning News
Los Angeles Times
Miami Herald
New York Daily News
New York Times
Newsday
Philadelphia Daily News
Washington Post

Honorable mention: Baltimore Sun; Chicago Tribune; Detroit Free Press; Fort Worth Star-Telegram; Houston Chronicle; Los Angeles Daily News; Orange County (Calif.) Register; Philadelphia Inquirer; St. Paul (Minn.) Pioneer Press; USA Today.

Top 10 Sunday

Atlanta Journal-Constitution
Baltimore Sun
Boston Globe
Chicago Sun-Times
Cleveland Plain Dealer
Dallas Morning News
Ft. Lauderdale Sun-Sentinal
Los Angeles Times
Miami Herald
St. Paul Pioneer Press

Honorable mention: Hartford Courant; Houston Chronicle; Minneapolis Star Tribune; New Orleans Times-Picayune; New York Times; Newsday; Orange County (Calif.) Register; Orlando Sentinel; San Jose Mercury News; Washington Post.

Directory of Organizations

Listing of the major sports organizations, teams and media addresses and officials as of Sept. 15, 1995.

AUTO RACING

IndyCar
(Championship Auto Racing Teams, Inc.)
755 W. Big Beaver Rd., Suite 800, Troy, MI 48084
(810) 362-8800
President-CEO ....Andrew Craig
Director of Publicity ....Adam Saal

Indy Racing League
4790 West 16th St., Indianapolis, ID 46222
(317) 481-8500
Exec. Director & CEO ....Jack Long
Commissioner ....Tom Binford
Director of Public Relations ....Bob Walters

FISA— Formula One
(Federation Internationale de Sport Automobile)
8 Bis Rue Boissy D'anglas 75008 Paris, France
TEL: 011-33-1-4312-4455
President ....Max Mosley
Secretary General..................................Pierre de Coninck
Director of Public Relations.................Francesco Longanesi

NASCAR
(National Assn. of Stock Car Auto Racing)
P.O. Box 2875, Daytona Beach, FL 32120
(904) 253-0611
President..Bill France Jr.
Director of Public Relations ....Andy Hall

NHRA
(National Hot Rod Association)
2035 Financial Way, Glendora, CA 91740
(818) 914-4761
President ....Dallas Gardner
Director of Communications.........................Denny Darnell

MAJOR LEAGUE BASEBALL

Office of the Commissioner
350 Park Ave., New York, NY 10022
(212) 339-7800
Commissioner..vacant
               (Fay Vincent resigned Sept. 7, 1992)
Chairman, Executive Council ....Bud Selig
General Counsel..................................Thomas Ostertag
Executive Dir. of Public Relatons...........................Rich Levin

Player Relations Committee
350 Park Ave., New York, NY 10022
(212) 339-7400
President & COO ....Randy Levine
Associate Counsels.......................................John Westhoff
                                             & Louis Melendez

Major League Baseball Players Association
12 East 49th St., 24th Floor, New York, NY 10017
(212) 826-0808
Exec. Director & General Counsel ....Donald Fehr
Special Assistant ....Mark Belanger

AL

American League Office
350 Park Ave., New York, NY 10022
(212) 339-7600
President..Gene Budig
V.P., Admin. & Media Affairs......................Phyllis Merhige

Baltimore Orioles
333 West Camden St., Baltimore, MD 21201
(410) 685-9800
Managing General Partner............................Peter Angelos
Vice Chairman, Business & Finance ....Joseph Foss
General Manager ....Roland Hemond
Director of Public Relations.............................John Maroon

Boston Red Sox
Fenway Park, 4 Yawkey Way, Boston, MA 02215
(617) 267-9440
General Partner..................................Jean R. Yawkey Trust
President-CEO ....John Harrington
Exec. V.P. & General Manager.....................Dan Duquette
V.P., Public Relations.....................................Dick Bresciani

California Angels
P. O. Box 2000, Anaheim, CA 92803
(714) 937-7200 or (213) 625-1123
Chairman..Gene Autry
Minority Owner ....Walt Disney Co.
President & CEO ....Richard Brown
V.P. & General Manager.....................................Bill Bavasi
Ast. V.P., Media Relations................................John Sevano

Chicago White Sox
Comiskey Park, 333 W. 35th St., Chicago, IL 60616
(312) 924-1000
Chairman..Jerry Reinsdorf
Vice Chairman..Eddie Einhorn
Senior V.P. & General Manager ....Ron Schueler
Director of Public Relations ....Doug Abel

Cleveland Indians
Jacobs Field, 2401 Ontario St., Cleveland, OH 44115
(216) 420-4200
Owner-Chairman-CEO ....Richard Jacobs
Exec. V.P. & General Manager ....John Hart
V.P., Public Relations.......................................Bob DiBiasio

Detroit Tigers
Tiger Stadium, 2121 Trumbull Ave., Detroit, MI 48216
(313) 962-4000
Owner-Chairman ....Mike Ilitch
Owner-Secretary-Treasurer ....Marian Ilitch
President-CEO..John McHale Jr.
Sr. Director, General Manager.............................Joe Klein
Sr. Director, Public Relations...............................Dan Ewald

Kansas City Royals
P.O. Box 419969, Kansas City, MO 64141
(816) 921-2200
Owner ....Ewing Kauffman Irrevocable Trust
Chairman-CEO..David Glass
Exec. V.P. & General Manager ....Herk Robinson
V.P., Public Relations ....Dean Vogelaar

Milwaukee Brewers
County Stadium, P.O. Box 3099, Milwaukee, WI 53201
(414) 933-4114
President-CEO ....Bud Selig
Senior V.P., Baseball Operations ....Sal Bando
V.P. & General Counsel ....Wendy Selig-Prieb
Director of Media Relations ....Jon Greenberg

Minnesota Twins
Hubert H. Humphrey Metrodome
501 Chicago Ave. South, Minneapolis, MN 55415
(612) 375-1366
Owner..Carl Pohlad
President..Jerry Bell
V.P. & General Manager..................................Terry Ryan
Director of Media Relations ....Rob Antony

New York Yankees
Yankee Stadium, Bronx, NY 10451
(718) 293-4300
Principal Owner.................................George Steinbrenner
General Partner...Joe Malloy
V.P. & General Manager................................Gene Michael
Dir. of Media Relations/Publicity.......................Rob Butcher

Oakland Athletics
Oakland-Alameda County Coliseum
Oakland, CA 94621
(510) 638-4900
Co-Owners ....Steve Schott and Ken Hofmann
President & General Manager ....Sandy Alderson
Director of Baseball Information ....Jay Alves

Seattle Mariners
P.O. Box 4100, Seattle, WA 98104
(206) 628-3555
Chairman-CEO ....John Ellis
President-COO ....Chuck Armstrong
V.P., Baseball Operations ....Woody Woodward
Director of Public Relations ....Dave Aust

Texas Rangers
1000 Ballpark Way, Arlington, TX 76011
(817) 273-5222
General Partners ....Rusty Rose and Tom Schieffer
V.P., General Manager ....Doug Melvin
V.P., Public Relations ....John Blake

Toronto Blue Jays
SkyDome, One Blue Jays Way, Suite 3200
Toronto, Ontario M5V 1J1
(416) 341-1000
Chairman...Peter Widdrington
President-CEO..Paul Beeston
Exec. V.P. & General Manager ....Gord Ash
Director of Public Relations ....Howie Starkman

NL

National League Office
350 Park Ave., New York, NY 10022
(212) 339-7700
President & Treasurer ....Leonard Coleman
Exec. Dir. of Public Relations.......................Ricky Clemons

Atlanta Braves
P.O. Box 4064, Atlanta, GA 30302
(404) 522-7630
Owner...Ted Turner
President ....Stan Kasten
Exec. V.P. & General Manager...................John Schuerholz
Director of Public Relations ....Jim Schultz

Chicago Cubs
1060 West Addison St., Chicago, IL 60613
(312) 404-2827
Owner...The Tribune Company
President-CEO ....Andy MacPhail
General Manager ....Ed Lynch
Director of Media Relations ....Sharon Pannozzo

Cincinnati Reds
100 Riverfront Stadium, Cincinnati, OH 45202
(513) 421-4510
General Partner-President-CEO ....Marge Schott
General Manager ....Jim Bowden
Director of Publicity ....Jon Braude

Colorado Rockies
Coors Field, 2001 Blake St., Denver, CO 80205
(303) 292-0200
Chairman-President-CEO ....Jerry McMorris
Senior V.P. & General Manager ....Bob Gebhard
Director of Public Relations............................Mike Swanson

Florida Marlins
2267 N.W. 199th St., Miami, FL 33056
(305) 626-7400
Chairman..Wayne Huizenga
Exec. V.P. & General Manager ....Dave Dombrowski
Director of Media Relations ....Chuck Pool

Houston Astros
The Astrodome, P.O. Box 288, Houston, TX 77001
(713) 799-9500
Chairman-CEO ....Drayton McLane Jr.
President..Tal Smith
General Manager ....Bob Watson
Director of Media Relations ....Rob Matwick

Los Angeles Dodgers
1000 Elysian Park Ave., Los Angeles, CA 90012
(213) 224-1500
President ....Peter O'Malley
Exec. V.P. & General Manager ....Fred Claire
Director of Publicity ....Jay Lucas

Montreal Expos
P.O. Box 500, Station M, Montreal, Quebec H1V 3P2
(514) 253-3434
General Partner-President.........................Claude Brochu
V.P., Baseball Operations................................Bill Stoneman
Director of Media Relations ....Peter Loyello

New York Mets
126th St. & Roosevelt Ave., Flushing, NY 11368
(718) 507-6387
Chairman...Nelson Doubleday
President-CEO...Fred Wilpon
Exec. V.P., Baseball Operations ....Joe McIlvaine
Director of Media Relations ....Jay Horwitz

Philadelphia Phillies
P.O. Box 7575, Philadelphia, PA 19101
(215) 463-6000
Managing General Partner...................................Bill Giles
Senior V.P. & General Manager ....Lee Thomas
Manager, Media Relations ....Gene Dias

Pittsburgh Pirates
P.O. Box 7000, Pittsburgh, PA 15212
(412) 323-5000
Chairman...Vincent Sarni
President-CEO...Mark Sauer
Senior V.P. & General Manager ....Cam Bonifay
Director of Media Relations ....Jim Trdinich

St. Louis Cardinals
250 Stadium Plaza, St. Louis, MO 63102
(314) 421-3060
Chairman...August A. Busch III
Vice Chairman ....Fred Kuhlmann
President...Mark Lamping
V.P. & General Manager ....Walt Jocketty
Director of Public Relations ....Brian Bartow

San Diego Padres
P.O. Box 2000, San Diego, CA 92112
(619) 283-4494
Chairman..John Moores
President-CEO..Larry Lucchino
V.P., Baseball Operations & G.M ....Randy Smith
Director, Media Relations ....Roger Riley

San Francisco Giants
Candlestick Park, San Francisco, CA 94124
(415) 468-3700
Managing General Partner........................Peter Magowan
Senior V.P. & General Manager ....Bob Quinn
Director of Public Relations.................................Bob Rose

1988 Expansion Teams

Arizona Diamondbacks
P.O. Box 2095, Phoenix, AZ 85001
(602) 514-8500
Chief Executive Officer...............................Jerry Colangelo
President..Rich Dozer
V.P. & General Manager ....Joe Garagiola Jr.
Director of Public Relations ....TBA

Tampa Bay Devil Rays
ThunderDome, One Stadium Dr., St. Petersburg, FL 33705
(813) 825-3137
Managing General Partner ....Vincent Naimoli
General Manager..Chuck Lamar
Director of Public Relations ....TBA

PRO BASKETBALL

NBA

League Office
Olympic Tower, 645 Fifth Ave., New York, NY 10022
(212) 407-8000
Commissioner...David Stern
Deputy Commissioner...................................Russell Granik
V.P., Public Relations ....Brian McIntyre
Director of Media Relations ....Jan Hubbard

NBA Players Association
1775 Broadway, Suite 2401, New York, NY 10019
(212) 333-7510
Exec. Dir. & Gen. Counsel ....Simon Gourdine
President ....Buck Williams

Atlanta Hawks
One CNN Center, South Tower, Suite 405
Atlanta, GA 30303
(404) 827-3800
Owner...Ted Turner
President..Stan Kasten
General Manager...Pete Babcock
Director of Media Relations..............................Arthur Triche

Boston Celtics
151 Merrimac St., 4th Floor, Boston, MA 02114
(617) 523-6050
Chairman..Paul Gaston
President...Red Auerbach
Exec. V.P. & General Manager ....Jan Volk
Exec. V.P. & Head Coach....................................M.L. Carr
Director of Public Relations....................................Jeff Twiss

Charlotte Hornets
100 Hive Drive, Charlotte, NC 28217
(704) 357-0252
Owner...George Shinn
President...Spencer Stolpen
V.P., Basketball Operations ....Bob Bass
Director of Media Relations ....Harold Kaufman

Chicago Bulls
United Center, 1901 West Madison St.
Chicago, IL 60612
(312) 455-4000
Chairman...Jerry Reinsdorf
V.P., Basketball Operations...........................Jerry Krause
Director of Media Services...............................Tim Hallam

Cleveland Cavaliers
One Centre Court, Cleveland, OH 44115
(216) 420-2000
Owner-Chairman...Gordon Gund
Owner-Vice Chairman ....George Gund III
President & General Manager ....Wayne Embry
Director of Media Relations ....Bob Zink

Dallas Mavericks
Reunion Arena, 777 Sports St., Dallas, TX 75207
(214) 988-0117
Owner-President...Donald Carter
COO-General Manager ....Norm Sonju
Dir. of Player Personnel ....Keith Grant
Director of Media Services ....Kevin Sullivan

Denver Nuggets
1635 Clay St., Denver, CO 80204
(303) 893-6700
Owner...........................COMSAT Entertainment Group
President-GM-Head Coach.......................Bernie Bickerstaff
Director of Media Services ....Tommy Sheppard

Detroit Pistons
The Palace of Auburn Hills
Two Championship Dr., Auburn Hills, MI 48326
(810) 377-0100
Managing Partner ....William Davidson
President..Tom Wilson
V.P. of Player Personnel ....Rick Sund
V.P. of Public Relations...Matt Dobek

Golden State Warriors
Oakland Coliseum Arena, Oakland, CA 94621
(510) 638-6300
Owner-CEO...Chris Cohan
General Manager ....Dave Twardzik
Director of Communications ....Julie Marvel

Houston Rockets
The Summit, 10 Greenway Plaza, Houston, TX 77046
(713) 627-3865
Owner ....Les Alexander
Exec. V.P. of Business Operations ....John Thomas
Director of Public Relations...........................Kathy Frietsch

Indiana Pacers
300 East Market St., Indianapolis, IN 46204
(317) 263-2100
Owners ....Melvin Simon & Herb Simon
President & General Manager......................Donnie Walsh
Director of Media Relations...........................David Benner

Los Angeles Clippers
L.A. Sports Arena
3939 S. Figueroa St., Los Angeles, CA 90037
(213) 748-8000
Owner-Chairman..Donald Sterling
V.P., Basketball Operations ....Elgin Baylor
Director of Communications ....Jesse Barkin

Los Angeles Lakers
Great Western Forum
3900 W. Manchester Blvd., Inglewood, CA 90305
(310) 419-3100
Owner ....Jerry Buss
Exec. V.P., Basketball Operations.......................Jerry West
General Manager ....Mitch Kupchak
Director of Public Relations...................................John Black

Miami Heat
Miami Arena, Miami, FL 33136
(305) 577-4328
Managing General Partner ....Micky Arison
President-Head Coach ....Pat Riley
Exec. V.P., Basketball Operations ....Dave Wohl
V.P. of Communications..Mark Pray

Milwaukee Bucks
Bradley Center, 1001 N. Fourth St., Milwaukee, WI 53203
(414) 227-0500
President ....Sen. Herb Kohl (D., Wisc.)
V.P., Basketball Ops. & Head Coach.............Mike Dunleavy
Director of Publicity ....Bill King II

Minnesota Timberwolves
Target Center, 600 First Ave. North, Minneapolis, MN 55403
(612) 673-1600
Owner ....Glen Taylor
President ....Rob Moor
V.P., Basketball Operations............................Kevin McHale
Director of Media Relations.................................Kent Wipf

New Jersey Nets
405 Murray Hill Pkwy., East Rutherford, NJ 07073
(201) 935-8888
Chairman ....Alan Aufzien
Acting President-COO....................................Jim Lampariello
Exec. V.P. & General Manager ....Willis Reed
Director of Public Relations.................................John Mertz

New York Knickerbockers
Madison Square Garden
2 Penn Plaza, 3rd Floor, New York, NY 10121
(212) 465-6471
Owner ....ITT Corp./Cablevision Systems Inc.
President (MSG) ....Dave Checketts
Exec. V.P. & General Manager ....Ernie Grunfeld
Director of Media Services ....Josh Rosenfeld

Orlando Magic
Orlando Arena, 1 Magic Place, Orlando, FL 32801
(407) 649-3200
Owner ....Rich DeVos
President ....Bob Vander Weide
General Manager & COO ....Pat Williams
Dir. of Publicity/Media Relations ....Alex Martins

Philadelphia 76ers
Veterans Stadium
Broad St. and Pattison Ave., Philadelphia, PA 19148
(215) 339-7600
Owner-President ....Harold Katz
General Manager & Head Coach ....John Lucas
Director of Public Relations ....Joe Favorito

Phoenix Suns
P.O. Box 1369, Phoenix, AZ 85001
(602) 379-7900
President-CEO...Jerry Colangelo
V.P., Administration-G.M. ....Bryan Colangelo
V.P., Dir. of Player Personnel.....................Dick Van Arsdale
Media Relations Director...Julie Fie

Portland Trail Blazers
One Center Court, Suite 200, Portland, OR 97227
(503) 234-9291
Owner-Chairman..Paul Allen
President & General Manager.........................Bob Whitsitt
Director of Communications ....John Christensen

Sacramento Kings
One Sports Parkway, Sacramento, CA 95834
(916) 928-0000
Managing General Partner...............................Jim Thomas
President...Rick Benner
V.P., Basketball Operations...............................Geoff Petrie
Director of Media Relations...........................Travis Stanley

San Antonio Spurs
Alamodome, 100 Montana St., San Antonio, TX 78203
(210) 554-7700
Chairman ....Gen. Robert McDermott
President-CEO ....John Diller
Exec. V.P., Basketball Operations................Gregg Popovich
Director of Media Relations...............................Tom James

Seattle SuperSonics
490 Fifth Ave. North, Seattle, WA 98109
(206) 281-5800
Owner-Chairman..Barry Ackerley
President & General Manager ....Wally Walker
Director of Media Relations...............................Cheri White

Toronto Raptors
20 Bay St., Suite 1702, Toronto, Ontario M5J 2N8
(416) 214-2255
President...John Bitove Jr.
V.P. Basketball Operations ....Isiah Thomas
Director of Communications ....John Lashway

Utah Jazz
Delta Center, 301 West South Temple
Salt Lake City, UT 84101
(801) 325-2500
Owner ....Larry Miller
General Manager ....Tim Howells
President ....Frank Layden
Director of Media Services.................................Kim Turner

Vancouver Grizzlies
General Motors Place, 800 Griffiths Way
Vancouver, B.C. V6B 6G1
(604) 899-4666
Owner-Vice Chaiman ....John McCaw Jr.
Chairman-CEO ....Arthur Griffiths
GM & V.P. Basketball Operations ....Stu Jackson
Director of Media Relations................................Steve Frost

Washington Bullets
One Harry S. Truman Dr., Landover, MD 20785
(301) 773-2255
Chairman..Abe Pollin
President..Susan O'Malley
V.P. & General Manager....................................John Nash
Director of Public Relations...........................Matt Williams

CBA

Continental Basketball Assocation
701 Market St., Suite 140, St. Louis, MO 63101
(314) 621-7222
Commissioner ....Tom Valdiserri
V.P. of Basketball Operations ....Clay Moser
Director of Public Relations ....Brett Meister
Member teams (14): Chicago Rockers, Ft. Wayne (IN)
Fury, Florida BeachDogs, Grand Rapids Mackers, Hartford
Hellcats, Oklahoma City Cavalry, Omaha Racers, Pittsburgh
Piranhas, Quad City (IL) Thunder, Rockford (IL) Lightning,
San Diego CBA club, Shreveport (LA) Storm, Sioux Falls
(SD) Skyforce, and Yakima (WA) Sun Kings.

BOWLING

ABC
(American Bowling Congress)
5301 South 76th St., Greendale, WI 53129
(414) 421-6400
Executive Director..Darold Dobs
Public Relations Manager ....Dave DeLorenzo

BPAA
(Bowling Proprietors' Assn. of America)
P.O. Box 5802, Arlington, TX 76005
(817) 649-5105
Chief Operating Officer ....Tim Rice
President...Kurt Brose
Director of Public Relations ....Rosie Crews

LPBT
(Ladies Professional Bowlers Tour)
7171 Cherryvale Blvd., Rockford, IL 61112
(815) 332-5756
President...John Falzone
Media Director ....Angel Tucker

PBA
(Professional Bowlers Association)
1720 Merriman Road, P.O. Box 5118, Akron, OH 44334
(216) 836-5568
Commissioner..Mike Connor
Public Relations Director.................................Kevin Shippy

WIBC
(Women's International Bowling Congress)
5301 South 76th St., Greendale, WI 53129
(414) 421-9000
President...Joyce Deitch
Public Relations Manager ....Dave DeLorenzo

BOXING

IBF
(International Boxing Federation)
134 Evergreen Place, 9th Floor,
East Orange, NJ 07018
(201) 414-0300
President..Robert (Bob) Lee
Executive Secretary ....Marian Muhammad
Champs. & Ratings Chairman ....Doug Beavers
                    P.O. Box 7577, Portsmouth, VA 23707
                                             (804) 399-6608

WBA
(World Boxing Association)
Centro Comercial Ciudad Turmero, Local #21, Piso #2
Calle Petion Cruce Con Urdaneta,
Turmero, 2115 Estado Aragua, Venezuela
TEL: 011-58-44-63-1584
President...Gilberto Mendoza
General Counsel/U.S. Spokesman ....Jimmy Binns
           1735 Market St., 39th Floor, Phila., PA 19103
                                             (215) 557-8000
Championship Chairman ....Elias Cordorba
           P.O. Box 87-1022, Panama 1, Rep. de Panama
                                       TEL: 011-507-264-5363
Ratings Chairman ....Bolivar Icaza
           P.O. Box 1833, Panama 1, Rep. de Panama
                                       TEL: 011-507-263-5167

WBC
(World Boxing Council)
Genova 33-503, Col. Juarez,
Delegacion Cuauhtemoc, MEXICO, 06600, D.F.
TEL: 011-525-533-6546
President..Jose Sulaiman
Executive Secretary ....Eduardo Lamazon
Press Information/U.S. Spokesman..................John Brister
           411 Ballentine St., Bay St. Louis, MS 39520
                                             (601) 467-3304

WBO
(World Boxing Organization)
Borinquen St. #57, Santa Rita, San Juan, P.R. 00925
(809) 765-7542
President..Francisco Valcarcel
Championship Chairman............................John Montano
                                               Phoenix, Arizona
                                               (602) 542-1417
Ratings Chairman...Louis Perez
                                               San Juan, P.R.
                                               (809) 258-0340

Don King Productions, Inc.
871 West Oakland, Park Blvd., Oakland Park, FL 33311
(305) 568-3500
President..Don King
Director of Public Relations............................Mike Marley

Top Rank
3900 Paradise Road, Suite 227, Las Vegas, NV 89102
(702) 732-2717
Chairman...Bob Arum
Director of Marketing ....Michael Malitz

Golden Gloves Assn. of America, Inc.
8801 Princess Jeanne N.E., Albuquerque, NM 87112
(505) 298-8042
Executive Director..Stan Gallup
President...Chick Paris

COLLEGE SPORTS

CCA
(Collegiate Commissioners Association)
800 South Broadway, Suite 400, Walnut Creek, CA 94596
(510) 932-4411
President..Jim Delany (Big Ten)
Exec. V.P. ....Mike Gilleran (West Coast Conf.)
Secretary-Treasurer ....David Price

CFA
(College Football Association)
6688 Gunpark Drive, Suite 201, Boulder, CO 80301
(303) 530-5566
Executive Director.....................................Charles Neinas
Director of Marketing ....Sam Baker

NAIA
(National Assn. of Intercollegiate Athletics)
6120 South Yale, Suite 1450, Tulsa, OK 74136
(918) 494-8828
President-CEO..James Chasteen
Public Relations Contact ....Kevin Henry

NCAA
(National Collegiate Athletic Association)
6201 College Blvd., Overland Park, KS 66211
(913) 339-1906
President.......................................Gene Corrigan (ACC)
                              (term expires January, 1997)
Executive Director ....Cedric Dempsey
Asst. Exec. Dir. for Enforcement........................David Berst
Director of Public Information ....Kathryn Reith

WSF
(Women's Sports Foundation)
Eisenhower Park, East Meadow, NY 11554
(516) 542-4700
Executive Director..Donna Lopiano
Communications Director...........................Lynnore Lawton

Major NCAA Conferences

See pages 435-443 for basketball coaches, football
coaches, nicknames and colors of all Division I basketball
schools and Division I-A and I-AA football schools.

ATLANTIC COAST CONFERENCE
P.O. Drawer ACC
Greensboro, NC 27419
(910) 854-8787   Founded: 1953
Commissioner ....Gene Corrigan
Director of Media Relations ....Brian Morrison
  1995-96 members: BASKETBALL & FOOTBALL (9)—
Clemson, Duke, Florida St., Georgia Tech, Maryland, North
Carolina, North Carolina St., Virginia and Wake Forest.

Clemson University
Clemson, SC 29633   Founded: 1889
SID: (803) 656-2114   Enrollment: 16,300
President..Deno Curry
Athletic Director ....Bobby Robinson
Sports Information Director ....Tim Bourret

Duke University
Durham, NC 27708   Founded: 1838
SID: (919) 684-2633   Enrollment: 6,100
President...Nannerl Keohane
Athletic Director ....Tom Butters
Sports Information Director ....Mike Cragg

Florida State University
Tallahassee, FL 32316   Founded: 1857
SID: (904) 644-1403   Enrollment: 28,500
President............................Talbot (Sandy) D'Alemberte
Athletic Director...Dave Hart Jr.
Sports Information Director...............................Rob Wilson

Georgia Tech
Atlanta, GA 30332
SID: (404) 894-5445
President ....Wayne Clough
Athletic Director ....Homer Rice
Sports Information Director ....Mike Finn

Founded: 1885
Enrollment: 13,000

University of Maryland
College Park, MD 20741
SID: (301) 314-7064
President ....William E. Kirwan
Athletic Director ....Debbi Yow
Sports Information Director ....Herb Hartnett

Founded: 1807
Enrollment: 25,900

University of North Carolina
Chapel Hill, NC 27514
SID: (919) 962-2123
Chancellor ....Michael K. Hooker
Athletic Director ....John Swofford
Sports Information Director...............Rick Brewer

Founded: 1789
Enrollment: 24,300

North Carolina State University
Raleigh, NC 27695
SID: (919) 515-2102
Chancellor ....Larry Monteith
Athletic Director ....Todd Turner
Sports Information Director ....Mark Bockelman

Founded: 1887
Enrollment: 25,500

University of Virginia
Charlottesville, VA 22903
SID: (804) 982-5500
President ....John T. Casteen III
Athletic Director ....Terry Holland
Sports Information Director ....Rich Murray

Founded: 1819
Enrollment: 18,100

Wake Forest University
Winston-Salem, NC 27109
SID: (910) 759-5640
President ....Thomas K. Hearn Jr.
Athletic Director ....Ron Wellman
Sports Information Director..............................John Justus

Founded: 1834
Enrollment: 3,600

෨

BIG EAST CONFERENCE
56 Exchange Terrace
Providence, RI 02903
(401) 272-9108
Commissioner ....Mike Tranghese
Asst. Commissioner/P.R ....John Paquette
    1995-96 members: BASKETBALL (13)— Boston College, Connecticut, Georgetown, Miami-FL, Notre Dame, Pittsburgh, Providence, Rutgers, St. John's, Seton Hall, Syracuse, Villanova and West Virginia; FOOTBALL (8)— Boston College, Miami-FL, Pittsburgh, Rutgers, Syracuse, Temple, Virginia Tech and West Virginia.

Founded: 1979

Boston College
Chestnut Hill, MA 02167
SID: (617) 552-3004
President...Rev. J. Donald Monan, SJ
Athletic Director ....Chet Gladchuk
Sports Information Director................................Reid Oslin

Founded: 1863
Enrollment: 9,000

University of Connecticut
Storrs, CT 06269
SID: (203) 486-3531
President...Harry J. Hartley
Athletic Director ....Lew Perkins
Sports Information Director..............................Tim Tolokan

Founded: 1881
Enrollment: 11,000

Georgetown University
Washington, DC 20057
SID: (202) 687-2492
President...Rev. Leo J. O'Donovan, SJ
Athletic Director ....Francis X. Rienzo
Sports Information Director ....Bill Hurd

Founded: 1798
Enrollment: 6,300

University of Miami
Coral Gables, FL 33124
SID: (305) 284-3244
President...Edward T. Foote II
Athletic Director ....Paul Dee
Sports Information Director ....John Hahn

Founded: 1926
Enrollment: 13,200

University of Notre Dame
Notre Dame, IN 46556
SID: (219) 631-7516
President...Rev. Edward (Monk) Malloy
Athletic Director ....Michael Wadsworth
Sports Information Director ....John Heisler

Founded: 1842
Enrollment: 10,100

University of Pittsburgh
Pittsburgh, PA 15213
SID: (412) 648-8240
President...J. Dennis O'Connor
Athletic Director ....Oval Jaynes
Sports Information Director ....Ron Wahl

Founded: 1787
Enrollment: 13,500

Providence College
Providence, RI 02918
SID: (401) 865-2272
President...Philip A. Smith, OP
Athletic Director ....John Marinatto
Sports Information Director ....Tim Connor

Founded: 1917
Enrollment: 3,800

Rutgers University
New Brunswick, NJ 08903
SID: (908) 445-4200
President...Francis L. Lawrence
Athletic Director ....Fred Gruninger
Sports Information Director ....Pete Kowalski

Founded: 1766
Enrollment: 34,000

St. John's University
Jamaica, NY 11439
SID: (718) 990-6367
President ....Rev. Donald J. Harrington, CM
Athletic Director ....Edward J. Manetta Jr.
Sports Information Director ....Frank Racaniello

Founded: 1870
Enrollment: 18,000

Seton Hall University
South Orange, NJ 07079
SID: (201) 761-9493
President ....Rev. Thomas R. Peterson, OP
Athletic Director ....Larry Keating
Sports Information Director ....John Wooding

Founded: 1856
Enrollment: 10,200

Syracuse University
Syracuse, NY 13244
SID: (315) 443-2608
Chancellor...Kenneth Shaw
Athletic Director ....Jake Crouthamel
Sports Information Director ....Larry Kimball

Founded: 1870
Enrollment: 10,200

Temple University
Philadelphia, PA 19122
SID: (215) 204-7445
President...Peter J. Liacouras
Athletic Director .....................................R.C. Johnson
Sports Information Director ....Jerry Emig

Founded: 1884
Enrollment: 32,000

Villanova University
Villanova, PA 19085
SID: (610) 519-4120
President ....Rev. Edmund Dobbin, OSA
Athletic Director ....Gene DeFilippo
Sports Information Director ....Karen Frascona

Founded: 1842
Enrollment: 5,900

Virginia Tech
Blacksburg, VA 24061
SID: (540) 231-6726
President...Paul Torgersen
Athletic Director ....Dave Braine
Sports Information Director ....Dave Smith

Founded: 1872
Enrollment: 22,200

West Virginia University
Morgantown, WV 26507   Founded: 1867
SID: (304) 293-2821   Enrollment: 23,000
President......................................David Hardesty
Athletic Director...............................Ed Pastilong
Sports Information Director...................Shelly Poe

ଈଔ

BIG EIGHT/BIG 12 CONFERENCE
(officially becomes Big 12 conference on July 1, 1996)
104 West 9th Street, Suite 408
Kansas City, MO 64105
(816) 471-5088   Founded: 1907
Big Eight commissioner.....................Carl James
Big 12 commissioner ....Steve Hatchell
Service Bureau Director.........................Jeff Bollig
1995-96 members: BASKETBALL & FOOTBALL (8)—
Colorado, Iowa St., Kansas, Kansas St., Missouri,
Nebraska, Oklahoma and Oklahoma St.
New in 1996-97: BASKETBALL & FOOTBALL (4)—
Baylor, Texas, Texas A&M and Texas Tech.

University of Colorado
Boulder, CO 80309   Founded: 1876
SID: (303) 492-5626   Enrollment: 25,000
President....................................Judith E.N. Albino
Athletic Director..................................Bill Marolt
Sports Information Director....................Dave Plati

Iowa State University
Ames, IA 50011   Founded: 1858
SID: (515) 294-3372   Enrollment: 25,300
President....................................Martin Jischke
Athletic Director...............................Eugene Smith
Sports Information Director..............Tom Kroeschell

University of Kansas
Lawrence, KS 66045   Founded: 1866
SID: (913) 864-3417   Enrollment: 25,200
Chancellor...............................Robert Hemenway
Athletic Director.................................Bob Frederick
Sports Information Director...................Dean Buchan

Kansas State University
Manhattan, KS 66502   Founded: 1863
SID: (913) 532-6735   Enrollment: 20,700
President..Jon Wefald
Athletic Director.................................Max Urick
Sports Information Director......................Ben Boyle

University of Missouri
Columbia, MO 65205   Founded: 1839
SID: (314) 882-3241   Enrollment: 26,200
Chancellor.....................................Charles Kiesler
Athletic Director..............................Joe Castiglione
Sports Information Director...................Bob Brendel

University of Nebraska
Lincoln, NE 68588   Founded: 1869
SID: (402) 472-2263   Enrollment: 24,000
Interim Chancellor..........................JoAnne Leitzel
Athletic Director...................................Bill Byrne
Sports Information Director...............Chris Anderson

University of Oklahoma
Norman, OK 73019   Founded: 1890
SID: (405) 325-8231   Enrollment: 24,900
President...David Boren
Athletic Director..............................Donnie Duncan
Sports Information Director.............Mike Prusinski

Oklahoma State University
Stillwater, OK 74078   Founded: 1890
SID: (405) 744-5749   Enrollment: 18,500
President......................................James Halligan
Athletic Director ....Terry Don Phillips
Sports Information Director..............Steve Buzzard

BIG TEN CONFERENCE
1500 West Higgins Road
Park Ridge, IL 60068-6300
(708) 696-1010   Founded: 1895
Commissioner....................................Jim Delany
Dir. of Information Services.........Dennis LaBissonier
1995-96 members: BASKETBALL & FOOTBALL (11)—
Illinois, Indiana, Iowa, Michigan, Michigan St., Minnesota,
Northwestern, Ohio St., Penn St., Purdue and Wisconsin.

University of Illinois
Champaign, IL 61820   Founded: 1867
SID: (217) 333-1390   Enrollment: 36,000
President....................................James J. Stukel
Athletic Director.................................Ron Guenther
Sports Information Director...................Mike Pearson

Indiana University
Bloomington, IN 47405   Founded: 1820
SID: (812) 855-9610   Enrollment: 36,000
President..Myles Brand
Athletic Director..............................Clarence Doninger
Sports Information Director...............Kit Klingelhoffer

University of Iowa
Iowa City, IA 52242   Founded: 1847
SID: (319) 335-9411   Enrollment: 28,000
Interim President................................Peter Nathan
Athletic Director.................................Bob Bowlsby
Sports Information Director....................Phil Haddy

University of Michigan
Ann Arbor, MI 48109   Founded: 1817
SID: (313) 763-1381   Enrollment: 36,800
President...................................James J. Duderstadt
Athletic Director.................................Joe Roberson
Sports Information Director...................Bruce Madej

Michigan State University
East Lansing, MI 48824   Founded: 1855
SID: (517) 355-2271   Enrollment: 39,700
President.....................................Peter McPherson
Athletic Director...............................Merritt Norvell
Sports Information Director...................Ken Hoffman

University of Minnesota
Minneapolis, MN 55455   Founded: 1851
SID: (612) 625-4090   Enrollment: 38,000
President.......................................Nils Hasselmo
Athletic Director..............................McKinley Boston
Sports Information Director....................Marc Ryan

Northwestern University
Evanston, IL 60208   Founded: 1851
SID: (708) 491-7503   Enrollment: 7,400
President....................................Henry S. Bienen
Athletic Director...................................Rick Taylor
Sports Information Director...................Brad Hurlbut

Ohio State University
Columbus, OH 43210   Founded: 1870
SID: (614) 292-6861   Enrollment: 49,500
President.....................................E. Gordon Gee
Athletic Director.................................Andy Geiger
Sports Information Director....................Steve Snapp

Big Six Doubles Size

Iowa St., Kansas, Kansas St., Missouri, Nebraska and
Oklahoma left the Missouri Valley Conference in 1928
to form the Big Six. The league grew to become the Big
Seven in 1948 with the addition of Colorado and then
the Big Eight when Oklahoma St. arrived 10 years later.

As of July 1, 1996, the conference will expand again
to become the Big 12 with the official arrival of Baylor,
Texas, Texas A&M and Texas Tech from the Southwest
Conference, which will dissolve on June 30.

Penn State University

University Park, PA 16802   Founded: 1855
SID: (814) 865-1757   Enrollment: 38,200
President ....Graham Spanier
Athletic Director ....Tim Curley
Sports Information Director..................Jeff Nelson

Purdue University

West Lafayette, IN 47907   Founded: 1869
SID: (317) 494-3202   Enrollment: 34,500
President ....Steven C. Beering
Athletic Director ....Morgan Burke
Sports Information Director................Mark Adams

University of Wisconsin

Madison, WI 53711   Founded: 1848
SID: (608) 262-1811   Enrollment: 40,300
Chancellor ....David Ward
Athletic Director ....Pat Richter
Sports Information Director...............Steve Malchow

❧

BIG WEST CONFERENCE

2 Corporate Park, Suite 206
Irvine, CA 92714
(714) 261-2525   Founded: 1969
Commissioner ....Dennis Farrell
Director of Information ....Dennis Bickmeier
   1995-96 members: BASKETBALL (10)— CS-Fullerton, Long Beach St., Nevada, New Mexico St., Pacific, San Jose St., UC-Irvine, UC-Santa Barbara, UNLV and Utah St.; FOOTBALL (10)— Arkansas St., Louisiana Tech, Nevada, New Mexico St., Northern Illinois, Pacific, San Jose St., SW Louisiana, UNLV and Utah St.
   New in 1996-97: BASKETBALL (4)— Boise St., Cal Poly-SLO, Idaho and North Texas; FOOTBALL (3)— Boise St., Idaho and North Texas.
   Out in 1996-97: BASKETBALL (2)— San Jose St., UNLV; FOOTBALL (6)— Arkansas St., Louisiana Tech, Northern Illinois, San Jose St., SW Louisiana and UNLV.

Arkansas State University

State University, AK 72467   Founded: 1909
SID: (501) 972-2541   Enrollment: 10,300
President...Les Wyatt
Athletic Director ....Brad Hovious
Sports Information Director...........Gina Bowman

Cal State-Fullerton

Fullerton, CA 92634   Founded: 1957
SID: (714) 773-3970   Enrollment: 22,500
President ....Milton A. Gordon
Athletic Director..........................John Easterbrook
Sports Information Director................Mel Franks

Long Beach State

Long Beach, CA 90840   Founded: 1949
SID: (310) 985-7978   Enrollment: 27,500
President.......................................Robert Maxson
Athletic Director................................Dave O'Brien
Sports Information Director ....Scott Cathcart

Louisiana Tech

Ruston, LA 71272   Founded: 1894
SID: (318) 257-3144   Enrollment: 10,200
President ....Dan Reneau
Athletic Director ....Jim Oakes
Interim Sports Information Director ....Hank Largin

University of Nevada

Reno, NV 89557   Founded: 1874
SID: (702) 784-4600   Enrollment: 12,400
President ....Joe Crowley
Athletic Director ....Chris Ault
Sports Information Director ....Paul Stuart

New Mexico State University

Las Cruces, NM 88003   Founded: 1888
SID: (505) 646-3929   Enrollment: 15,800
President ....Michael Orenduff
Athletic Director...................................Al Gonzales
Sports Information Director ....Steve Shutt

Northern Illinois University

De Kalb, IL 60115   Founded: 1895
SID: (815) 753-1706   Enrollment: 22,900
President ....John E. La Tourette
Athletic Director ....Cary Groth
Sports Information Director..................Mike Korcek

University of the Pacific

Stockton, CA 95211   Founded: 1851
SID: (209) 946-2479   Enrollment: 4,000
President ....Donald DeRosa
Athletic Director ....Bob Lee
Sports Information Director ....Mike Millerick

San Jose State University

San Jose, CA 95192   Founded: 1857
SID: (408) 924-1217   Enrollment: 27,000
President ....Robert Caret
Athletic Director ....Tom Brennan
Sports Information Director...................Lawrence Fan

University of Southwestern Louisiana

Lafayette, LA 70506   Founded: 1898
SID: (318) 482-6331   Enrollment: 17,000
President ....Ray Authement
Athletic Director.....................Nelson Schexnayder
Sports Information Director..................Dan McDonald

University of California, Irvine

Irvine, CA 92717   Founded: 1962
SID: (714) 824-5814   Enrollment: 15,600
Chancellor.................................Laurel Wilkening
Athletic Director ....Dan Guerrero
Sports Information Director ....Bob Olson

University of California, Santa Barbara

Santa Barbara, CA 93106   Founded: 1944
SID: (805) 893-3428   Enrollment: 18,200
Chancellor.......................................Henry Yang
Athletic Director ....Gary Cunningham
Sports Information Director ....Bill Mahoney

UNLV— University of Nevada, Las Vegas

Las Vegas, NV 89154   Founded: 1957
SID: (702) 895-3207   Enrollment: 20,200
President.......................................Carol Harter
Athletic Director ....Charles Cavagnaro
Sports Information Director ....Jim Gemma

Utah State University

Logan, UT 84322   Founded: 1888
SID: (801) 797-1361   Enrollment: 20,400
President.......................................George Emert
Athletic Director...................................Chuck Bell
Sports Information Director..................John Lewandowski

❧

CONFERENCE USA

(1995-96 is the first basketball season, football follows in '96)
35 East Wacker Drive, Suite 650, Chicago, IL 60601
(312) 553-0483   Founded: 1995
Commissioner ....Mike Slive
Director of Information.........................Erika Amstadt
   1995-96 members: BASKETBALL (11)— Alabama-Birmingham, Cincinnati, DePaul, Louisville, Marquette, Memphis, NC-Charlotte, Saint Louis, South Florida, Southern Miss and Tulane.
   New in 1996-97: BASKETBALL (1)— Houston; FOOTBALL (6)— Cincinnati, Houston, Louisville, Memphis, Southern Miss and Tulane.

University of Alabama-Birmingham
Birmingham, AL 35294 — Founded: 1969
SID: (205) 934-0722 — Enrollment: 16,252
President:...J. Claude Bennett
Athletic Director...Gene Bartow
Sports Information Director.......................Grant Shingleton

University of Cincinnati
Cincinnati, OH 45221 — Founded: 1819
SID: (513) 556-5191 — Enrollment: 36,000
President...Joseph A. Steger
Athletic Director...Gerald O'Dell
Sports Information Director..........................Tom Hathaway

DePaul University
Chicago, IL 60614 — Founded: 1898
SID: (312) 325-7525 — Enrollment: 16,747
President...Rev. John P. Minogue
Athletic Director..Bill Bradshaw
Sports Information Director...............................John Lanctot

University of Louisville
Louisville, KY 40292 — Founded: 1798
SID: (502) 852-6581 — Enrollment: 23,000
President...John W. Shumaker
Athletic Director..Bill Olsen
Sports Information Director...............................Kenny Klein

Marquette University
Milwaukee, WI 53233 — Founded: 1881
SID: (414) 288-7447 — Enrollment: 10,750
President...Rev. Albert J. DiUlio
Athletic Director...Bill Cords
Sports Information Director..........................Kathleen Hohl

Memphis University
Memphis, TN 38152 — Founded: 1912
SID: (901) 678-2337 — Enrollment: 21,500
President...V. Lane Rawlins
Interim Athletic Director...............................Donald Carson
Sports Information Director.................................Bob Winn

University of North Carolina-Charlotte
Charlotte, NC 28223 — Founded: 1946
SID: (704) 547-4937 — Enrollment: 15,650
Chancellor...J. H. Woodward
Athletic Director..Judy Rose
Sports Information Director.......................Tom Whitestone

Saint Louis University
St. Louis, MO 63103 — Founded: 1818
SID: (314) 977-2524 — Enrollment: 11,300
President...Rev. Lawrence Biondi
Athletic Director...Doug Woolard
Sport Information Director.......................Doug McIlhagga

University of South Florida
Tampa, FL 33620 — Founded: 1956
SID: (813) 974-4086 — Enrollment: 35,000
President...Betty Castor
Athletic Director..Paul Griffin
Sports Information Director...........................John Gerdes

University of Southern Mississippi
Hattiesburg, MS 39406 — Founded: 1910
SID: (601) 266-4503 — Enrollment: 13,000
President...Aubrey K. Lucas
Athletic Director...Bill McLellan
Sports Information Director..........................Regiel Napier

Tulane University
New Orleans, LA 70118 — Founded: 1834
SID: (504) 865-5506 — Enrollment: 10,800
President...Eamon M. Kelly
Athletic Director..Kevin White
Sports Information Director.......................Lenny Vangilder

MID-AMERICAN CONFERENCE
Four SeaGate, Suite 102
Toledo, OH 43604
(419) 249-7177 — Founded: 1946
Commissioner...Jerry Ippoliti
Director of Communications..............................Tom Lessig
1995-96 members: BASKETBALL & FOOTBALL (10)—
Akron, Ball St., Bowling Green, Central Michigan, Eastern
Michigan, Kent, Miami-OH, Ohio University, Toledo and
Western Michigan.

University of Akron
Akron, OH 44325 — Founded: 1870
SID: (216) 972-7468 — Enrollment: 26,000
President...Peggy Gordon Elliott
Athletic Director..Mike Bobinski
Sports Information Director.................................Mac Yates

Ball State University
Muncie, IN 47306 — Founded: 1918
SID: (317) 285-8242 — Enrollment: 20,700
President..John Worthen
Athletic Director..Andrea Seger
Sports Information Director..........................Joe Hernandez

Bowling Green State University
Bowling Green, OH 43403 — Founded: 1910
SID: (419) 372-7075 — Enrollment: 17,000
President...Sidney Ribeau
Athletic Director...Ron Zwierlein
Sports Information Director.................................Steve Barr

Central Michigan University
Mt. Pleasant, MI 48859 — Founded: 1892
SID: (517) 774-3277 — Enrollment: 16,300
President...Leonard Plachta
Athletic Director..Herb Deromedi Jr.
Sports Information Director.......................Fred Stabley Jr.

Eastern Michigan University
Ypsilanti, MI 48197 — Founded: 1849
SID: (313) 487-0317 — Enrollment: 24,000
President...William Shelton
Athletic Director...Tim Weiser
Sports Information Director...............................Jim Streeter

Kent State University
Kent, OH 44242 — Founded: 1910
SID: (216) 672-2110 — Enrollment: 28,600
President...Carol Cartwright
Athletic Director...Laing Kennedy
Sports Information Director.......................Dale Gallagher

Miami University
Oxford, OH 45056 — Founded: 1809
SID: (513) 529-4327 — Enrollment: 16,000
President...Paul Risser
Athletic Director...Eric Hyman
Sports Information Director.................................John Estes

Ohio University
Athens, OH 45701 — Founded: 1804
SID: (614) 593-1298 — Enrollment: 18,500
President...Robert Glidden
Athletic Director..Tom Boeh
Sports Information Director..........................Pam Fronko

University of Toledo
Toledo, OH 43606 — Founded: 1872
SID: (419) 530-3790 — Enrollment: 24,200
President...Frank Horton
Athletic Director..Allen Bohl
Sports Information Director...............................Rod Brandt

Western Michigan University
Kalamazoo, MI 49008 — Founded: 1903
SID: (616) 387-4138 — Enrollment: 25,600
President...Diether Haenicke
Interim Athletic Director.................................Charles Elliott
Sports Information Director..............................John Beatty

PACIFIC-10 CONFERENCE
800 South Broadway, Suite 400
Walnut Creek, CA 94596
(510) 932-4411 — Founded: 1915
Commissioner ....Thomas Hansen
Asst. Commissioner, Public Relations................Jim Muldoon
1995-96 members: BASKETBALL & FOOTBALL (10)—
Arizona, Arizona St., California, Oregon, Oregon St.,
Stanford, UCLA, USC, Washington and Washington St.

University of Arizona
Tucson, AZ 85721 — Founded: 1885
SID: (520) 621-4163 — Enrollment: 35,100
President...Manuel Pacheco
Athletic Director..Jim Livengood
Sports Information Director.........................Tom Duddleston

Arizona State University
Tempe, AZ 85287 — Founded: 1885
SID: (602) 965-6592 — Enrollment: 42,600
President...Lattie F. Coor
Interim Athletic Director.......................Christine Wilkinson
Sports Information Director ....Mark Brand

University of California
Berkeley, CA 94720 — Founded: 1868
SID: (510) 642-5363 — Enrollment: 31,000
Chancellor ....Chang-Lin Tien
Athletic Director ....John Kasser
Sports Information Director ....Kevin Reneau

University of Oregon
Eugene, OR 97401 — Founded: 1876
SID: (503) 346-5488 — Enrollment: 16,600
President...Dave Frohnmeyer
Athletic Director...Bill Moos
Sports Information Director ....Steve Hellyer

Oregon State University
Corvallis, OR 97331 — Founded: 1868
SID: (503) 737-3720 — Enrollment: 15,000
President..John Byrne
Athletic Director ....Dutch Bauchman
Sports Information Director ....Hal Cowan

Stanford University
Stanford, CA 94305 — Founded: 1891
SID: (415) 723-4418 — Enrollment: 13,100
President..Gerhard Casper
Athletic Director...Ted Leyland
Sports Information Director ....Gary Migdol

UCLA— Univ. of California, Los Angeles
Los Angeles, CA 90024 — Founded: 1919
SID: (310) 206-6831 — Enrollment: 34,000
Chancellor ....Charles Young
Athletic Director...Pete Dalis
Sports Information Director...............................Marc Dellins

USC— Univ. of Southern California
Los Angeles, CA 90089 — Founded: 1880
SID: (213) 740-8480 — Enrollment: 27,700
President..Steven Sample
Athletic Director ....Mike Garrett
Sports Information Director ....Tim Tessalone

University of Washington
Seattle, WA 98195 — Founded: 1861
SID: (206) 543-2230 — Enrollment: 34,000
President...Richard McCormick
Athletic Director.......................................Barbara Hedges
Sports Information Director ....Jim Daves

Washington State University
Pullman, WA 99164 — Founded: 1890
SID: (509) 335-0270 — Enrollment: 19,400
President...Samuel Smith
Athletic Director ....Rick Dickson
Sports Information Director...........................Rod Commons

SOUTHEASTERN CONFERENCE
2201 Civic Center Blvd.
Birmingham, AL 35203
(205) 458-3010 — Founded: 1933
Commissioner ....Roy Kramer
Director of Communications ....Charles Bloom
1995-96 members: BASKETBALL & FOOTBALL (12)—
Alabama, Arkansas, Auburn, Florida, Georgia, Kentucky,
LSU, Mississippi, Mississippi St., South Carolina, Tennessee
and Vanderbilt.

University of Alabama
Tuscaloosa, AL 35487 — Founded: 1831
SID: (205) 348-6084 — Enrollment: 20,000
President..Roger Sayers
Acting Athletic Director...................................Glen Tuckett
Sports Information Director ....Larry White

University of Arkansas
Fayetteville, AR 72701 — Founded: 1871
SID: (501) 575-2751 — Enrollment: 14,700
President...Daniel Ferritor
Athletic Director ....Frank Broyles
Sports Information Director ....Rick Schaeffer

Auburn University
Auburn, AL 36831 — Founded: 1856
SID: (334) 844-9800 — Enrollment: 21,500
President...William V. Muse
Athletic Director ....David Housel
Sports Information Director ....Kent Partridge

University of Florida
Gainesville, FL 32604 — Founded: 1853
SID: (904) 375-4683 ext. 6100 — Enrollment: 35,500
President ....John Lombardi
Athletic Director..Jeremy Foley
Sports Information Director ....John Humenik

University of Georgia
Athens, GA 30613 — Founded: 1785
SID: (706) 542-1621 — Enrollment: 29,500
President ....Charles Knapp
Athletic Director ....Vince Dooley
Sports Information Director............................Claude Felton

University of Kentucky
Lexington, KY 40506 — Founded: 1865
SID: (606) 257-3838 — Enrollment: 24,200
President.............................Charles T. Wethington Jr.
Athletic Director ....C.M. Newton
Sports Information Director ....Rena Vicini

LSU— Louisiana State University
Baton Rouge, LA 70894 — Founded: 1860
SID: (504) 388-8226 — Enrollment: 24,200
Chancellor ....William (Bud) Davis
Athletic Director ....Joe Dean
Sports Information Director............................Herb Vincent

University of Mississippi
Oxford, MS 38677 — Founded: 1848
SID: (601) 232-7522 — Enrollment: 10,400
Chancellor ....Robert C. Khayat
Athletic Director...Pete Boone
Sports Information Director ....Langston Rogers

Mississippi State University
Starkville, MS 39762 — Founded: 1878
SID: (601) 325-2703 — Enrollment: 13,400
President..Donald Zacharias
Athletic Director.......................................Larry Templeton
Sports Information Director ....Mike Nemeth

University of South Carolina
Columbia, SC 29208 — Founded: 1801
SID: (803) 777-5204 — Enrollment: 25,600
President...John Palms
Athletic Director ....Mike McGee
Sports Information Director ....Kerry Tharp

University of Tennessee
Knoxville, TN 37901   Founded: 1794
SID: (615) 974-1212   Enrollment: 25,600
President..Joe Johnson
Athletic Director.............................Doug Dickie
Sports Information Director...................Bud Ford

Vanderbilt University
Nashville, TN 37212   Founded: 1873
SID: (615) 322-4121   Enrollment: 9,300
Chancellor...................................Joe B. Wyatt
Athletic Director........................Paul Hoolahan
Sports Information Director..........Rod Williamson

2♪

SOUTHWEST CONFERENCE
(The SWC will disband on June 30, 1996)
P.O. Box 569420
Dallas, TX 75356-9420
(214) 634-7353   Founded: 1914
Commissioner.............................Kyle Kallander
Director of Information ....Bo Carter
    1995-96 members: BASKETBALL & FOOTBALL (8)—
Baylor, Houston, Rice, SMU, TCU, Texas, Texas A&M and
Texas Tech.

Baylor University
Waco, TX 76711   Founded: 1845
SID: (817) 755-2743   Enrollment: 12,500
President.................................Robert B. Sloan
Athletic Director..............................Dick Ellis
Sports Information Director..........Maxey Parrish

University of Houston
Houston, TX 77204   Founded: 1927
SID: (713) 743-9404   Enrollment: 34,000
President...................................Glenn Goerke
Athletic Director...............................Bill Carr
Sports Information Director.............Donna Turner

Rice University
Houston, TX 77005   Founded: 1912
SID: (713) 527-4034   Enrollment: 2,700
President..................................Malcolm Gillis
Athletic Director..............................Bobby May
Sports Information Director................Bill Cousins

SMU— Southern Methodist University
Dallas, TX 75275   Founded: 1911
SID: (214) 768-2883   Enrollment: 5,300
President.......................................Gerald Turner
Athletic Director..........................Jim Copeland
Sports Information Director..............Ed Wisneski

University of Texas
Austin, TX 78713   Founded: 1883
SID: (512) 471-7437   Enrollment: 49,300
President.................................Robert Berdahl
Athletic Director.........................DeLoss Dodds
Sports Information Director....................Bill Little

Texas A&M University
College Station, TX 77843   Founded: 1876
SID: (409) 845-5725   Enrollment: 43,900
President.......................................Ray Bowen
Athletic Director............................Wally Groff
Sports Information Director............Alan Cannon

TCU— Texas Christian University
Fort Worth, TX 76129   Founded: 1873
SID: (817) 921-7969   Enrollment: 7,200
Chancellor.................................William Tucker
Athletic Director......................Frank Windegger
Sports Information Director..................Glen Stone

Texas Tech University
Lubbock, TX 79409   Founded: 1923
SID: (806) 742-2770   Enrollment: 25,000
President..................................Robert Lawless
Athletic Director...........................Bob Bokrath
Sports Information Director ....Joe Hornaday

2♪

WESTERN ATHLETIC CONFERENCE
14 West Dry Creek Circle
Littleton, CO 80120
(303) 795-1962   Founded: 1962
Commissioner.................................Karl Benson
Director of Communications ....Dan Willis
    1995-96 members: BASKETBALL & FOOTBALL (10)—
Air Force, BYU, Colorado St., Fresno St., Hawaii, New
Mexico, San Diego St., Utah, UTEP and Wyoming.
    New in 1996-97: BASKETBALL & FOOTBALL (6)— Rice,
San Jose St., SMU, TCU, Tulsa and UNLV.

U.S. Air Force Academy
Colorado Springs, CO 80840   Founded: 1959
SID: (719) 472-2313   Enrollment: 4,100
Superintendent......................Lt. Gen. Paul Stein
Athletic Director ....Col. Kenneth Schweitzer
Sports Information Director ....Dave Kellogg

Brigham Young University
Provo, UT 84602   Founded: 1875
SID: (801) 378-4911   Enrollment: 26,000
President...Rex E. Lee
Athletic Director........................Rondo Fehlberg
Sports Information Director ....Ralph Zobell

Colorado State University
Fort Collins, CO 80523   Founded: 1870
SID: (970) 491-5067   Enrollment: 20,600
President.......................................Albert Yates
Athletic Director ....Tom Jurich
Sports Information Director............Gary Ozzello

Fresno State University
Fresno, CA 93740   Founded: 1911
SID: (209) 278-2509   Enrollment: 18,900
President.....................................John D. Welty
Athletic Director ....Gary Cunningham
Sports Information Director ....Scott Johnson

University of Hawaii
Honolulu, HI 96822   Founded: 1907
SID: (808) 956-7523   Enrollment: 20,000
President..................................Kenneth Mortimer
Athletic Director ....Hugh Yoshida
Interim Sports Information Director ....Lois Manin

University of New Mexico
Albuquerque, NM 87131   Founded: 1889
SID: (505) 2772026   Enrollment: 24,300
President......................................Richard Peck
Athletic Director...........................Rudy Davalos
Sports Information Director........Greg Remington

San Diego State University
San Diego, CA 92182   Founded: 1897
SID: (619) 594-5547   Enrollment: 29,000
President.......................................Thomas Day
Athletic Director ....Rick Bay
Sports Information Director ....John Rosenthal

University of Utah
Salt Lake City, UT 84112   Founded: 1850
SID: (801) 581-3510   Enrollment: 27,100
President.......................................Arthur Smith
Athletic Director ....Chris Hill
Sports Information Director........Bruce Woodbury

UTEP— University of Texas at El Paso
El Paso, TX 79968   Founded: 1913
SID: (915) 747-5330   Enrollment: 17,500
President...Diana Natalicio
Athletic Director...........................John Thompson
Sports Information Director............................Eddie Mullens

University of Wyoming
Laramie, WY 82071   Founded: 1886
SID: (307) 766-2256   Enrollment: 10,600
President..Terry Roark
Athletic Director...Paul Roach
Sports Information Director.......................Kevin McKinney

MAJOR INDEPENDENTS
Division I-A football independents in 1995.

Army— U.S. Military Academy
West Point, NY 10996   Founded: 1802
SID: (914) 938-3303   Enrollment: 4,200
Superintendent.........................Lt. Gen. Howard D. Graves
Athletic Director......................................Al Vanderbush
Sports Information Director...............................Bob Beretta

University of Cincinnati
Cincinnati, OH 45221   Founded: 1819
SID: (513) 556-5191   Enrollment: 36,000
President..Joseph A. Steger
Athletic Director..Gerald O'Dell
Sports Information Director...........................Tom Hathaway

East Carolina University
Greenville, NC 27858   Founded: 1907
SID: (919) 328-4522   Enrollment: 17,800
Chancellor...Richard Eakin
Athletic Director..Mike Hamrick
Sports Information Director................................Norm Reilly

University of Louisville
Louisville, KY 40292   Founded: 1798
SID: (502) 852-6581   Enrollment: 23,000
President..John W. Shumaker
Athletic Director...Bill Olsen
Sports Information Director...............................Kenny Klein

Memphis University
Memphis, TN 38152   Founded: 1912
SID: (901) 678-2337   Enrollment: 21,500
President...V. Lane Rawlins
Interim Athletic Director...............................Donald Carson
Sports Information Director...............................Bob Winn

Navy— U.S. Naval Academy
Annapolis, MD 21402   Founded: 1845
SID: (410) 268-6226   Enrollment: 4,000
Superintendent...............................Adm. Charles R. Larson
Athletic Director..Jack Lengyel
Sports Information Director.................................Tom Bates

University of Notre Dame
Notre Dame, IN 46556   Founded: 1842
SID: (219) 631-7516   Enrollment: 10,100
President..........................Rev. Edward (Monk) Malloy
Athletic Director...................................Michael Wadsworth
Sports Information Director..............................John Heisler

University of Southern Mississippi
Hattiesburg, MS 39406   Founded: 1910
SID: (601) 266-4503   Enrollment: 13,000
President..Aubrey K. Lucas
Athletic Director..Bill McLellan
Sports Information Director............................Regiel Napier

Tulane University
New Orleans, LA 70118   Founded: 1834
SID: (504) 865-5506   Enrollment: 10,800
President..Eamon M. Kelly
Athletic Director..Kevin White
Sports Information Director........................Lenny Vangilder

University of Tulsa
Tulsa, OK 74104   Founded: 1894
SID: (918) 631-2395   Enrollment: 4,900
President.......................................Robert Donaldson
Interim Athletic Director...................................Judy MacLeod
Sports Information Director...........................Don Tomkalski

OTHER MAJOR DIVISION I CONFERENCES
Conferences that play either Division I basketball or Division I-AA football, or both.

American West Conference
5855 Brookline Lane
San Luis Obispo, CA 93401
(805) 756-1412   Founded: 1993
Commissioner...Vic Buccola
Director of Information...............................Mike Robles
   1995-96 members: BASKETBALL & FOOTBALL (4)— Cal Poly St. Luis Obispo, CS-Northridge, CS-Sacramento and Southern Utah.
   Out in 1996–97: Cal Poly SLO.

Atlantic 10 Conference
2 Penn Center Plaza, Suite 1410
Philadelphia, PA 19102
(215) 751-0500   Founded: 1976
Commissioner..Linda Bruno
Director of Communications...............................Ray Cella
   1995-96 members: BASKETBALL (12)— Dayton, Duquesne, Fordham, George Washington, La Salle, Massachusetts, Rhode Island, St. Bonaventure, St. Joseph's-PA, Temple, Virginia Tech. and Xavier-OH.

Big Sky Conference
P.O. Box 1459
Ogden, UT 84402
(801) 392-1978   Founded: 1963
Commissioner...Douglas Fullerton
Director of Information....................................Ron Loghry
   1995-96 members: BASKETBALL & FOOTBALL (8)— Boise St., Eastern Washington, Idaho, Idaho St., Montana, Montana St., Northern Arizona and Weber St.
   New in 1996-97: Portland St.
   Out in 1996-97: Boise St. and Idaho.

Big South Conference
1551 21st Avenue North, Suite 11
Myrtle Beach, SC 29577
(803) 448-9998   Founded: 1983
Commissioner...Buddy Sasser
Director of Public Relations.........................Carl McAloose
   1995-96 members: BASKETBALL (8)— Charleston Southern, Coastal Carolina, Liberty, MD-Baltimore County, NC-Asheville, NC-Greensboro, Radford, and Winthrop.

Colonial Athletic Association
8625 Patterson Ave.
Richmond, VA 23229
(804) 754-1616   Founded: 1985
Commissioner..Tom Yeager
Director of Information...............................Tripp Sheppard
   1995-96 members: BASKETBALL (8)— American, East Carolina, George Mason, James Madison, NC-Wilmington, Old Dominion, Richmond, Virginia Commonwealth and William & Mary.

Gateway Football Conference
1000 Union Station, Suite 333
St. Louis, MO 63103
(314) 421-2268
Commissioner ....Patty Viverito
Director of Information ....Mike Kern
   1995 members (7): Eastern Illinois, Illinois St., Indiana St., Northern Iowa, Southern Illinois, SW Missouri St. and Western Illinois.
   Out in 1996: Eastern Illinois.

Ivy League
120 Alexander Street
Princeton, NJ 08544
(609) 258-6426
Executive Director ....Jeffrey Orleans
Director of Information ....Chuck Yrigoyen
   1995-96 members: BASKETBALL & FOOTBALL (8)— Brown, Columbia, Cornell, Dartmouth, Harvard, Pennsylvania, Princeton and Yale.

Metro Atlantic Athletic Conference
1090 Amboy Avenue
Edison, NJ 08837
(908) 225-0202
Commissioner ....Richard Ensor
Director of Media Relations............................Jaye Cavallo
   1995-96 members: BASKETBALL (8)— Canisius, Fairfield, Iona, Loyola-MD, Manhattan, Niagara, St. Peter's and Siena. FOOTBALL (8)— Canisius, Duquesne, Georgetown, Iona, Marist, St. John's, St. Peter's and Siena.
   New in 1996-97: FOOTBALL— Fairfield.

Mid-Continent Conference
40 Shuman Blvd., Suite 118
Naperville, IL 60563
(708) 416-7560
Commissioner ....Jon Steinbrecher
Director of Media Relations............................Sharon Pavol
   1995-96 members: BASKETBALL (10)— Buffalo, Central Connecticut St., Chicago St., Eastern Illinois, Missouri/K.C., NE Illinois, Troy St., Valparaiso, Western Illinois, Youngstown St.
   Out in 1996-97: Eastern Illinois

Mid-Eastern Athletic Conference
102 North Elm St. SE Building, Suite 401
Greensboro, NC 27401
(910) 275-9961
Commissioner ....Ken Free
Director of Service Bureau...............................Larry Barber
   1995-96 members: BASKETBALL (10)— Bethune-Cookman, Coppin St., Delaware St., Florida A&M, Hampton, Howard, MD-Eastern Shore, Morgan St., North Carolina A&T and South Carolina St.; FOOTBALL (8)— all but Coppin St. and MD-Eastern Shore.

Midwestern Collegiate Conference
201 South Capitol Ave., Suite 500
Indianapolis, IN 46225
(317) 237-5622
Commissioner...John LeCrone
Director of Communications ....Will Hancock
   1995-96 members: BASKETBALL (9)— Butler, Cleveland St., Detroit Mercy, Illinois-Chicago, Loyola-IL, Northern Illinois, Wisconsin-Green Bay, Wisconsin-Milwaukee and Wright St.

Division I Hockey Conferences
The four Division I hockey conferences are the Eastern Collegiate Athletic Conference (ECAC) in Centerville, Mass., (508) 771-5060; the Central Collegiate Hockey Assn. (CCHA) in Ann Arbor, Mich.; Hockey East in Orono, Me., (207) 866-2244; and the Western Collegiate Hockey Assn. in Madison, Wisc. (608) 251-4007.

Missouri Valley Conference
1000 St. Louis Union Station, Suite 333
St. Louis, MO 63103
(314) 421-0339
Commissioner ....Doug Elgin
Asst. Commissioner for Communications ....Jack Watkins
   1995-96 members: BASKETBALL (11)— Bradley, Creighton, Drake, Evansville, Illinois St., Indiana St., Northern Iowa, Southern Illinois, SW Missouri St., Tulsa and Wichita St.
   Out in 1996-97: Tulsa.

North Atlantic Conference
P.O. Box 69 — 28 Main Street
Orono, ME 04473
(207) 866-2383
Commissioner...Stuart Haskell
Director of Information..Julie Power
   1995-96 members: BASKETBALL (10)— Boston University, Delaware, Drexel, Hartford, Hofstra, Maine, New Hampshire, Northeastern, Towson St. and Vermont.

Northeast Conference
900 Route 9, Suite 120
Woodbridge, NJ 07095
(908) 636-9119
Commissioner...Chris Monasch
Director of Information ....Dave Siroty
   1995-96 members: BASKETBALL (10)— Fairleigh Dickinson, LIU-Brooklyn, Marist, Monmouth, Mount St. Mary's, Rider, Robert Morris, St. Francis-NY, St. Francis-PA and Wagner.

Ohio Valley Conference
278 Franklin Road, Suite 103
Brentwood, TN 37027
(615) 371-1698
Commissioner...Dan Beebe
Director of Information ....Rob Washburn
   1995-96 members: BASKETBALL & FOOTBALL (9)— Austin Peay St., Eastern Kentucky, Middle Tennessee St., Morehead St., Murray St., SE Missouri St., Tennessee-Martin, Tennessee St. and Tennessee Tech.
   New in 1996-97: Eastern Illinois.

Patriot League
3897 Adler Place, Building C, Suite 310
Bethlehem, PA 18017
(610) 691-2414
Executive Director ....Constance Hurlbut
Director of Information ....Todd Newcomb
   1995-96 members: BASKETBALL (7)— Army, Bucknell, Colgate, Holy Cross, Lafayette, Lehigh and Navy; FOOTBALL (5)— all except Army and Navy, who play independent Div. I-A schedules.
   New in 1996: Towson St. (football only).

Pioneer Football League
1000 St. Louis Union Station, Suite 333
St. Louis, MO 63103
(314) 421-0339
Commissioner ....Patty Viverito
Director of Information ....Mike Kern
   1995 members: FOOTBALL (6): Butler, Dayton, Drake, Evansville, San Diego and Valparaiso.

Southern Conference
1 West Pack Square, Suite 1508
Asheville, NC 28801
(704) 255-7872
Commissioner ....Wright Waters
Asst. Commissioner, Media Relations..............Chris Walker
   1995-96 members: BASKETBALL (10)— Appalachian St., The Citadel, Davidson, East Tennessee St., Furman, Georgia Southern, Marshall, Tennessee-Chattanooga, VMI and Western Carolina; FOOTBALL (9)—all except Davidson.

Southland Conference
1309 West 15th Street, Suite 303
Plano, TX 75075
(214) 424-4833   Founded: 1963
Executive Director ....Britton Banowski
Director of Information ....Greg Fort
   1995-96 members: BASKETBALL (10)— McNeese St., Nicholls St., North Texas, NE Louisiana, Northwestern St., Sam Houston St., Southwest Texas St., Stephen F. Austin St., Texas-Arlington and Texas-San Antonio; FOOTBALL (6)— all except North Texas, NE Louisiana, Texas-Arlington and Texas-San Antonio.
   New in 1996-97: FOOTBALL (2)— Jacksonville St. and Troy St.
   Out in 1996-97: North Texas.

Southwestern Athletic Conference
1500 Sugar Bowl Drive, Superdome
New Orleans, LA 70112
(504) 523-7574   Founded: 1920
Commissioner ....James Frank
Director of Publicity...................................Lonza Hardy Jr.
   1995-96 members: BASKETBALL & FOOTBALL (8)— Alabama St., Alcorn St., Grambling St., Jackson St., Mississippi Valley St., Prairie View A&M, Southern-Baton Rouge and Texas Southern.

Sun Belt Conference
One Galleria Boulevard, Suite 2115
Metairie, LA 70001
(504) 834-6600   Founded: 1976
Commissioner ....Craig Thompson
Director of Media Services...........................Dayna Wells
   1995-96 members: BASKETBALL (10)— Arkansas-Little Rock, Arkansas St., Jacksonville, Lamar, Louisiana Tech, New Orleans, South Alabama, SW Louisiana, Texas-Pan American and Western Kentucky.

Trans America Conference
The Commons, 3370 Vineville Ave., Suite 108-B,
Macon, GA 31204
(912) 474-3394   Founded: 1978
Commissioner...Bill Bibb
Director of Information ....Ted Gumbart
   1995-96 members: BASKETBALL (12)— Campbell, Centenary, Central Florida, College of Charleston, Florida Atlantic, Florida International, Georgia St., Jacksonville St., Mercer, Samford, SE Louisiana and Stetson.

West Coast Conference
400 Oyster Point Blvd., Suite 221
South San Francisco, CA 94080
(415) 873-8622   Founded: 1952
Commissioner ....Michael Gilleran
Director of Information ....Don Ott
   1995-96 members: BASKETBALL (8)— Gonzaga, Loyola Marymount, Pepperdine, Portland, St. Mary's, San Diego, San Francisco and Santa Clara.

Yankee Conference
University of Richmond, P.O. Box 8
Richmond, VA 23173
(804) 289-8371   Founded: 1946
Executive Director...Chuck Boone
Director of Information ....Pat McCarthy
   1996 members: FOOTBALL (12)— Boston University, Connecticut, Delaware, James Madison, Maine, Massachusetts, New Hampshire, Northeastern, Rhode Island, Richmond, Villanova and William & Mary.

⬛ **PRO FOOTBALL** ⬛

National Football League

League Office
410 Park Ave., New York, NY 10022
(212) 758-1500
Commissioner ....Paul Tagliabue
President...Neil Austrian
Exec. V.P. & League Counsel...............................Jay Moyer
Director of Information, AFC.....................Leslie Hammond
Director of Information, NFC......................Reggie Roberts

NFL Management Council
410 Park Ave., New York, NY 10022
(212) 758-1500
Chairman...Harold Henderson
V.P. & General Counsel ....Dennis Curran

NFL Players Association
2021 L Street NW, Suite 600, Washington, DC 20036
(202) 463-2200
Executive Director ....Gene Upshaw
Asst. Exec. Director ....Doug Allen
General Counsel....................................Richard Berthelsen
Director of Public Relations..........................Frank Woschitz

AFC

Buffalo Bills
One Bills Drive, Orchard Park, NY 14127
(716) 648-1800
Owner-President...Ralph Wilson
Exec. V.P. & General Manager...........................John Butler
V.P. & Head Coach ....Marv Levy
Director of Media Relations..........................Scott Berchtold

Cincinnati Bengals
200 Riverfront Stadium, Cincinnati, OH 45202
(513) 621-3550
Chairman..Austin Knowlton
President & General Manager ....Mike Brown
Public Relations Director ....Jack Brennan

Cleveland Browns
80 First Avenue, Berea, OH 44017
(216) 891-5000
Owner-President...Art Modell
Exec. V.P., Legal & Administration ....Jim Bailey
V.P., Assistant to President............................David Modell
V.P., Public Relations ....Kevin Byrne

Denver Broncos
13655 Broncos Parkway, Englewood, CO 80112
(303) 649-9000
Owner-President-CEO..Pat Bowlen
General Manager ....John Beake
Director of Media Relations........................Jim Saccomano

Houston Oilers
6910 Fannin St., Houston, TX 77030
(713) 797-9111
Owner-President..................................K.S. (Bud) Adams Jr.
Exec. V.P. & General Manager ....Floyd Reese
Director of Media Services ....Dave Pearson

Indianapolis Colts
P.O. Box 535000, Indianapolis, IN 46253
(317) 297-2658
Owner-President-Treasurer................................Robert Irsay
V.P. & General Manager.......................................Jim Irsay
V.P., Dir. Football Operations...............................Bill Tobin
Director of Public Relations ....Craig Kelley

Jacksonville Jaguars
One Stadium Place, Jacksonville, FL 32202
(904) 633-6000
Chairman-CEO ....Wayne Weaver
President-COO ....David Seldin
V.P., Football Operations ....Michael Huyghue
Exec. Director of Communications ....Dan Edwards

Kansas City Chiefs
One Arrowhead Drive, Kansas City, MO 64129
(816) 924-9300
Owner-Founder ....Lamar Hunt
Chairman...Jack Steadman
President-CEO-General Manager ....Carl Peterson
Director of Public Relations...........................Bob Moore

Miami Dolphins
7500 SW 30th St., Davie, FL 33314
(305) 452-7000
Owner-President-CEO ....Wayne Huizenga
Exec. V.P. & General Manager ....Eddie Jones
Director of Media Relations ....Harvey Greene

New England Patriots
Foxboro Stadium, 60 Washington St., Foxboro, MA 02035
(508) 543-8200
Owner-President-CEO ....Bob Kraft
General Manager & Head Coach ....Bill Parcells
Director of Public Relations............................Don Lowery

New York Jets
1000 Fulton Ave., Hempstead, NY 11550
(516) 538-6600
Owner-Chairman...Leon Hess
President...Steve Gutman
V.P. & General Manager ....Dick Steinberg
Director of Public Relations ....Frank Ramos

Oakland Raiders
332 Center St., El Segundo, CA 90245
(310) 322-3451
Managing General Partner ....Al Davis
Executive Assistant......................................Al LoCasale
Publications Director ....Mike Taylor

Pittsburgh Steelers
300 Stadium Circle, Pittsburgh, PA 15212
(412) 323-1200
Owner-President...Dan Rooney
Vice Presidents...................John McGinley & Art Rooney Jr.
Media Relations Coordinator.........................Rob Boulware

San Diego Chargers
Jack Murphy Stadium, Box 609609, San Diego, CA 92160
(619) 280-2111
Owner-Chairman...Alex Spanos
President -Vice Chairman...............................Dean Spanos
General Manager ....Bobby Beathard
Director of Public Relations ....Bill Johnston

Seattle Seahawks
11220 NE 53rd Street, Kirkland, WA 98033
(206) 827-9777
Owner ....Ken Behring
President...David Behring
Public Relations Director...............................Dave Neubert

NFC

Arizona Cardinals
P.O. Box 888, Phoenix, AZ 85001
(602) 379-0101
Owner-President..Bill Bidwill
General Manager & Head Coach....................Buddy Ryan
Public Relations Director ....Paul Jensen

Atlanta Falcons
One Falcon Place, Suwanee, GA 30174
(770) 945-1111
Owner-Chairman.....................................Rankin Smith Sr.
President ....Taylor Smith
V.P., Player Personnel ....Ken Herock
Director of Public Relations............................Charlie Taylor

Carolina Panthers
227 West Trade St., Suite 1600, Charlotte, NC 28202
(704) 358-7000
Founder-Owner ....Jerry Richardson
President ....Mike McCormack
General Manager..Bill Polian
Director of Communications...........................Charlie Dayton

Chicago Bears
Halas Hall, 250 N. Washington, Lake Forest, IL 60045
(708) 295-6600
Owner-Chairman.................................Edward McCaskey
President-CEO ....Mike McCaskey
V.P., Football Operations ....Ted Phillips
Director of Public Relations ....Bryan Harlan

Dallas Cowboys
Cowboys Center
One Cowboys Parkway, Irving, TX 75063
(214) 556-9900
Owner-President-GM..Jerry Jones
Public Relations Director ....Rich Dalrymple

Detroit Lions
Pontiac Silverdome
1200 Featherstone Rd., Pontiac, MI 48342
(810) 335-4131
Owner-President.....................................William Clay Ford
Executive V.P. & COO.................................Chuck Schmidt
Director of Media Relations ....Mike Murray

Green Bay Packers
1265 Lombardi Ave., Green Bay, WI 54304
(414) 496-5700
President-CEO ....Bob Harlan
Exec. V.P. & General Manager ....Ron Wolf
Exec. Dir. of Public Relations...........................Lee Remmel

Minnesota Vikings
9520 Viking Drive, Eden Prairie, MN 55344
(612) 828-6500
Owner-Chairman....................................John Skoglund
President-CEO ....Roger Headrick
V.P., Team Operations................................Jeff Diamond
Director of Public Relations ....David Pelletier

New Orleans Saints
6928 Saints Drive, Metairie, LA 70003
(504) 733-0255
Owner-President...Tom Benson
V.P., Football Operations..............................Bill Kuharich
V.P. & Head Coach ....Jim Mora
Director of Media Relations ....Rusty Kasmiersky

New York Giants
Giants Stadium, East Rutherford, NJ 07073
(201) 935-8111
President/co-CEO ....Wellington Mara
Chairman/co-CEO ....Preston Robert Tisch
V.P. & General Manager ....George Young
Director of Public Relations ....Pat Hanlon

Philadelphia Eagles
Veterans Stadium, Broad St. & Pattison Ave.
Philadelphia, PA 19148
(215) 463-2500
Owner ....Jeff Lurie
Director of Football Administration....................Bob Ackles
Director of Public Relations..............................Ron Howard

St. Louis Rams
Matthews-Dickey Boys Club
4245 N. Kingshighway, St. Louis, MO 63115
(314) 877-3790
Owner-Chairman ....Georgia Frontiere
President ....John Shaw
V.P., Football Operations ....Steve Ortmayer
Director of Public Relations ....Rick Smith

San Francisco 49ers
4949 Centennial Blvd., Santa Clara, CA 95054
(408) 562-4949
Owner ....Edward DeBartolo Jr.
President ....Carmen Policy
V.P., Football Operations ....Dwight Clark
Director of Public Relations..............................Rodney Knox

Tampa Bay Buccanners
1 Buccaneer Place, Tampa, FL 33607
(813) 870-2700
Owner-President ....Malcolm Glazer
General Manager ....Rich McKay
Director of Public Relations..............................Chip Namias

Washington Redskins
Redskin Park, P.O. Box 17247, Washington D.C. 20041
(703) 478-8900
Owner-Chairman-CEO ....Jack Kent Cooke
Executive V.P...John Kent Cooke
General Manager ....Charley Casserly
Director of Communications ....Rick Vaughn

Canadian Football League

League Office
CFL Building, 110 Eglinton Avenue West, 5th Floor
Toronto, Ontario M4R 1A3
(416) 322-9650
Commissioner...Larry Smith
Chairman...John Tory
V.P., Football Operations ....Ed Chalupka
Manager of Communications ....Jim Neish

CFL Players Association
467 Speers Rd., Unit 5, Oakville, Ontario L6K 3S4
(905) 844-7852
President ....Dan Ferrone
Legal Counsel ....Ed Molstad

Baltimore Stallions
Memorial Stadium, 1000 E 33rd St.
Baltimore, MD 21218
(410) 554-1010
Owner-President ....Jim Speros
General Manager & Head Coach ....Don Matthews
Director of Media Relations ....Mike Gathagan

Birmingham Barracudas
Legion Field, 401 Eighth Ave., West
Birmingham, AL 35204
(205) 323-2832
Owner...Art Williams
President...Larry Lemak
General Manager ....Roy Shivers
Director of Media Relations ....Mark Dalton

British Columbia Lions
10605 135th St., Surrey, B.C. V3T 4C8
(604) 930-5466
Owner..Bill Comrie
President...Doug Bodie
General Manager ....Eric Tillman
Dir. of Media/Public Relations...........................Roger Kelly

Calgary Stampeders
McMahon Stadium, 1817 Crowchild Trail, NW
Calgary, Alberta T2M 4R6
(403) 289-0205
Owner-President ....Larry Ryckman
General Manager & Head Coach ....Wally Buono
Media Relations Coordinator......................Tania Van Brunt

Edmonton Eskimos
9023 11th Ave., Edmonton, Alberta T5B 0C3
(403) 448-1525
Owner..Community-owned
President...John Ramsey
General Manager ....Hugh Campbell
Director of Communications ....Allan Watt

Hamilton Tiger-Cats
2 King Street West, Hamilton, Ontario L8P 1A1
(905) 521-5666
Chairman..David M. Macdonald
General Manager ....Neil Lumsden
Communications Director.................................Norm Miller

Ottawa Rough Riders
Landsdowne Park, Coliseum Bldg.
1015 Bank St., Ottawa, Ontario K1S 3W7
(613) 235-5554
Owner..Horn Chen
Director of Football Operations....................Garney Henley
Director of Media Relations ....Gary Page

Saskatchewan Roughriders
2940 — 10th Avenue, P.O. Box 1277
Regina, Saskatchewan S4P 3B8
(306) 569-2323
Owner..Community-owned
President..John Lipp
COO & General Manager ....Alan Ford
Media Coordinator..Tony Playter

Shreveport Pirates
2835 Hollywood, Fifth Floor, Shreveport, LA 71108
(318) 636-3388
Owner ....Bernie Glieberman
President ....Lonie Glieberman
General Manager & Head Coach ....Forrest Gregg
Dir. of Public/Media Relations.........................Missy Setters

Toronto Argonauts
SkyDome Gate 9, P.O. Box 2005, Station B
Toronto, Ontario M5T 3H8
(416) 341-5151
Owners..TSN Enterprises
President..Paul Beesten
General Manager & Head Coach................Bob O'Billovich
Manager of Media Relations ....Mike Cosentino

Winnipeg Blue Bombers
1465 Maroons Road, Winnipeg, Manitoba R3G 0L6
(204) 784-2583
Owner..Community-owned
President..Reg Low
General Manager & Head Coach ....Cal Murphy
Dir. of Public/Media Relations ............................J.D. Boyd

WLAF

World League of American Football
26-A Albemarle St.
London, England W1X 3FA
TEL: 011-44-171-355-1995
President..Oliver Luck
Public Relations Contact............................Alastair MacPhail
    Member teams (6): Amsterdam Admirals, Barcelona
Dragons, Frankfurt Galaxy, London Monarchs, Rhein Fire
(Dusseldorf), Scottish Claymores (Edinburgh).

GOLF

LPGA Tour
(Ladies Professional Golf Association)
2570 West International Speedway Blvd., Suite B
Daytona Beach, FL 32114
(904) 254-8800
Commissioner ....Charles Mechem
Deputy Commissioner...Jim Webb
Director of Communications...............................Elaine Scott

PGA of America
100 Avenue of the Champions
Palm Beach Gardens, FL 33410
(407) 624-8400
President ....Tom Addis III
CEO ....Jim Awtrey
Director of Communications ....Terry McSweeney

PGA European Tour
Wentworth Drive, Virginia Water
Surrey, England GU25 4LX
TEL: 011-44-1344-842881
Executive Director ....Ken Schofield
Director of Communications ....Mitchell Platts

PGA Tour
112 TPC Blvd., Ponte Vedra, FL 32082
(904) 285-3700
Commissioner ....Tim Finchem
Director of Information ....Dave Lancer

Royal & Ancient Golf Club of St. Andrews
St. Andrews, Fife, Scotland KY16 9JD
TEL: 011-44-1334-472112
Secretary...Michael Bonallack
Deputy Secretary..George Wilson

USGA
(United States Golf Association)
P.O. Box 708, Liberty Corner Road, Far Hills, NJ 07931
(908) 234-2300
President ....Reg Murphy
Executive Director ....David Fay
Director of Communications...........................Mark Carlson

PRO HOCKEY

NHL

Commissioner ....Gary Bettman
Senior V.P., Hockey Operations.........................Brian Burke
Senior V.P., COO ....Stephen Solomon
V.P., Public Relations ....Arthur Pincus

League Offices
Montreal..................1800 McGill College Ave., Suite 2600
Montreal, Quebec H3A 3J6
(514) 288-9220

New York ....1251 Sixth Ave., 47th Floor
New York, NY 10020
(212) 789-2000

Toronto ....75 International Blvd., Suite 300
Rexdale, Ontario M9W 6L9
(416) 798-0809

NHL Players' Association
1 Dundas St. West, Suite 2300
Toronto, Ontario M5G 1Z3
(416) 408-4040
Executive Director ....Bob Goodenow
Associate Counsel ....Ian Pulver

Anaheim, Mighty Ducks of
Arrowhead Pond of Anaheim, P.O. Box 61077
Anaheim, CA 92803
(714) 704-2700
Owner ....Walt Disney Co.
Governor...Michael Eisner
General Manager ....Jack Ferreira
Director of Public Relations ....Bill Robertson

Boston Bruins
FleetCenter, 150 Causeway St., Boston, MA 02114
(617) 624-1909
Owner ....Jeremy Jacobs
President & General Manager ....Harry Sinden
Director of Media Relations ....Heidi Holland

Buffalo Sabres
Memorial Auditorium, 140 Main St., Buffalo, NY 14202
(716) 856-7300
Chairman ....Seymour Knox III
President-CEO ....Doug Moss
General Manager ....John Muckler
Director of Public Relations...........................Jeff Holbrook

Calgary Flames
Canadian Airlines Saddledome, P.O. Box 1540 Station M
Calgary, Alberta T2P 3B9
(403) 777-2177
Owners......................Harley Hotchkiss, Grant A. Bartlett,
Murray Edwards, Ronald V. Joyce, Alvin G. Libin,
Allan P. Markin, J.R. McCaig, Byron and Daryl Seamen
President ....W.C. (Bill) Hay
V.P. & General Manager ....Doug Risebrough
Director of Public Relations..............................Rick Skaggs

Chicago Blackhawks
United Center, 1901 West Madison St.
Chicago, IL 60612
(312) 455-7000
Owner-President...William Wirtz
Senior V.P. & General Manager ....Bob Pulford
Director of Public Relations ....Jim DeMaria

Colorado Avalanche
1635 Clay St., Denver, CO 80204
(303) 893-6700
Owner ....COMSAT Entertainment Group
President ....Charlie Lyons
Exec. V.P., Hockey Operations & GM. ....Pierre Lacroix
Director of Media Relations.........................Jean Martineau

Dallas Stars
211 Cowboys Parkway, Irving, TX 75063
(214) 868-2890
Owner...Norman Green
General Manager & Head Coach....................Bob Gainey
Director of Public Relations................................Larry Kelly

Detroit Red Wings
Joe Louis Arena, 600 Civic Center Drive
Detroit, MI 48226
(313) 396-7544
Owner/President ....Mike Ilitch
Owner/Secretary-Treasurer ....Marian Ilitch
Senior V.P ....Jim Devellano
Dir. of Player Personnel & Head Coach ....Scotty Bowman
Director of Public Relations ....Bill Jamieson

Edmonton Oilers
Edmonton Coliseum, 7424 118th Ave.
Edmonton, Alberta, T5B 4M9
(403) 474-8561
Owner ....Peter Pocklington
President & General Manager ....Glen Sather
Exec. V.P. & Assistant GM ....Bruce MacGregor
Director of Public Relations.....................................Bill Tuele

Florida Panthers
100 North East Third Ave., 10th Floor
Fort Lauderdale, FL 33301
(305) 768-1900
Owner ....Wayne Huizenga
President..Bill Torrey
General Manager ....Bryan Murray
Dir. of Public & Media Relations ....Greg Bouris

Hartford Whalers
242 Trumbull St., 8th Floor, Hartford, CT 06103
(203) 728-3366
Owner-CEO ....Peter Karmanos Jr.
General Partner ....Thomas Thewes
President & General Manager ....Jim Rutherford
Director of Communications ....John Forslund

Los Angeles Kings
Great Western Forum, 3900 West Manchester Blvd.
Inglewood, CA 90306
(310) 419-3160
Majority Owners ....Philip Anschutz and Ed Roski
President..Rogie Vachon
General Manager ....Sam McMaster
Director of Media Relations ....Rick Minch

Montreal Canadiens
Montreal Forum, 2313 St. Catherine St. West
Montreal, Quebec H3H 1N2
(514) 932-2582
Owner...Molson Companies, Ltd.
Chairman-President ....Ronald Corey
V.P. & Managing Director ....Serge Savard
Director of Communications ....Don Beauchamp

New Jersey Devils
Meadowlands Arena
P.O. Box 504, East Rutherford, NJ 07073
(201) 935-6050
Chairman ....John McMullen
President & General Manager ....Lou Lamoriello
Director of Media Relations ....Mike Levine

New York Islanders
Nassau Veterans' Memorial Coliseum
Uniondale, NY 11553
(516) 794-4100
Owners ....Paul Greenwood, Ralph Palleschi,
            Robert Rosenthal and Stephen Walsh
V.P. & General Manager..............................Don Maloney
Director of Media Relations ....Ginger Killian

New York Rangers
2 Penn Plaza, 14th Floor, New York, NY 10121
(212) 465-6486
Owner ....ITT Corp./Cablevision Systems Inc.
President (MSG) ....Dave Checketts
President & General Manager ....Neil Smith
Director of Communications........................Brooks Thomas

Ottawa Senators
301 Moodie Dr., Suite 200, Nepean, Ontario, K2H 9C4
(613) 721-0115
Chief Operating Officer ....Rod Bryden
President & General Manager ....Randy Sexton
Director of Media Relations..........................Laurent Benoit

Philadelphia Flyers
3601 South Broad St., Philadelphia, PA 19148
(215) 465-4500
Majority Owner..Ed Snider
President & General Manager ....Bob Clarke
Director of Public Relations..............................Mark Piazza

Pittsburgh Penguins
Civic Arena, Pittsburgh, PA 15219
(412) 642-1800
Owners ....Howard Baldwin, Morris Belzberg
            and Thomas Ruta
Exec. V.P. & General Manager........................Craig Patrick
Director of Public Relations............................Cindy Himes

St. Louis Blues
Kiel Center, 1401 Clark Ave., St. Louis, MO 63103
(314) 622-2500
President-CEO ....Jack Quinn
General Manager & Head Coach ....Mike Keenan
Director of Public Relations ....Adam Fell

San Jose Sharks
525 West Santa Clara St., San Jose, CA 95113
(408) 287-7070
Owner-Chairman................................George Gund III
Co-Owner ....Gordon Gund
President-CEO ....Art Savage
Exec. V.P.& Dir. of Hockey Operations ....Dean Lombardi
Director of Media Relations..............................Ken Arnold

Tampa Bay Lightning
501 East Kennedy Blvd., Suite 175, Tampa, FL 33602
(813) 229-2658
Owners ....Lightning Partners, Inc.
President & General Manager ....Phil Esposito
Director of Hockey Operations ....Tony Esposito
V.P., Communications..................................Gerry Helper

Toronto Maple Leafs
Maple Leaf Gardens
60 Carlton Street, Toronto, Ontario M5B 1L1
(416) 977-1641
Chairman-CEO ....Steve Stavro
President-COO-GM..................................Cliff Fletcher
Public Relations Coordinator ....Pat Park

Vancouver Canucks
General Motors Place, 800 Griffiths Way
Vancouver, B.C. V6B 6G1
(604) 899-4600
Owner-Vice Chairman..............................John McCaw Jr.
Chairman-CEO ....Arthur Griffiths
President & General Manager............................Pat Quinn
Dir. of Public & Media Relations..................Steve Tambellini

Washington Capitals
USAir Arena, Landover, MD 20785
(301) 386-7000
Chairman..Abe Pollin
President..Susan O'Malley
V.P. & General Manager ....Dave Poile
V.P. of Communications..................................Matt Williams

Winnipeg Jets
1661 Portage Ave., 10th Floor
Winnipeg, Manitoba R3J 3T7
(204) 982-5387
Owner-President ....Barry Shenkarow
General Manager...John Paddock
Director of Information ....Igor Kuperman

IIHF

International Ice Hockey Federation
Todistrasse 23
CH-8002 Zurich, Switzerland
TEL: 011-411-281-1430
President ....Rene Fasel
General Secretary ....Jan-Ake Edvinsson

HORSE RACING

Breeders' Cup Limited
2525 Harrodsburg Road, Suite 500
Lexington, KY 40504
(606) 223-5444
President ....James E. (Ted) Bassett III
Executive Director.....................................D.G. Van Clief, Jr.
Director of Communications ....Dan Metzger

The Jockeys' Guild
250 West Main Street, Suite 1820, Lexington, KY 40507
(606) 259-3211
President ....Jerry Bailey
National Manager.......................................John Giovanni

TRA
(Thoroughbred Racing Associations)
420 Fair Hill Drive, Suite 1, Elkton, MD 21921
(410) 392-9200
President...Clifford C. Goodrich
Executive V.P ....Chris Scherf
Racing Commissioner..............................J. Brian McGrath
Director of Services.............................Conrad Sobkowiak

TRC
(Thoroughbred Racing Communications)
40 East 52nd Street, New York, NY 10022
(212) 371-5910
Executive Director...Tom Merritt
Director of Media Relations ....Bob Curran

USTA
(United States Trotting Association)
750 Michigan Ave., Columbus, OH 43215
(614) 224-2291
President ....Corwin Nixon
Executive V.P ....Fred Noe
Director of Public Relations............................John Pawlak

MEDIA

PERIODICALS

Sports Illustrated
Time & Life Bldg., Rockefeller Center
New York, NY 10020
(212) 586-1212
Publisher ....David Long
Managing Editor..Mark Mulvoy
Executive Editor ....Peter Carry

The Sporting News
1212 North Lindbergh Blvd., St. Louis, MO 63132
(314) 997-7111
President-CEO..Nicholas Niles
Editor..John Rawlings

USA Today
1000 Wilson Blvd., Arlington, VA 22229
(703) 276-3400
Owner ....Gannett Co.
President-Publisher ....Tom Curley
Managing Editor/Sports..............................Gene Policins

WIRE SERVICES

Associated Press
50 Rockefeller Plaza, New York, NY 10020
(212) 621-1630
Sports Editor...Terry Taylor
Deputy Sports Editor ....Ron Sirak

United Press International
1400 Eye Street NW, 8th Floor, Washington, DC 20005
(202) 898-8000
Sports Editor..Scott Zucker

The Sports Network
701 Mason's Mill Business Park
Huntington Valley, PA 19006
(215) 947-2400
President..Mickey Charles
Director of Operations ....Phil Sokol
Managing Editor ....Steve Abbott

Sportsticker
600 Plaza Two, Jersey City, NJ 07311
(201) 309-1200
President ....Peter Bavasi
Vice President ....Rick Alessandri
Managing Editor...Joe Carnicelli

TV NETWORKS

ABC Sports
47 West 66th St., 13th Floor, New York, NY 10023
(212) 456-4867
President..Dennis Swanson
Senior V.P., Production ....Dennis Lewin
Executive Producer ....Jack O'Hara
Director of Information ....Mark Mandel

CBC Sports
P.O. Box 500 Station A 5H 100
Toronto, Ontario M5W 1E6
(416) 205-6523
Head of Sports ....Alan Clark
Sr. Executive Producer ....Doug Sellars
Publicist ....Susan Proctor

Classic Sports Network
35 East 21st. St., 4th Floor, New York, NY 10010
(212) 529-8000
President ....Steve Greenberg
Executive Producer....................................Douglas Warshaw
V.P. Marketing ....Steve Merrill

CBS Sports
51 West 52nd St., 25th Floor, New York, NY 10019
(212) 975-5230
President ....David Kenin
Senior V.P., Production ....Rick Gentile
V.P., Programming ....Len DeLuca
Director of Public Relations...........................Robin Brendle

ESPN
ESPN Plaza, Bristol, CT 06010
(203) 585-2000
President-CEO...Steve Bornstein
Sr. V.P., Programming....................................John Wildhack
Executive Editor ....John Walsh
Managing Editor, ESPN2 ....Vince Doria
Director of Communications ....Mike Soltys

FOX Sports
PO Box 900, Beverly Hills, CA 90213
(213) 856-2128
President...David Hill
Exec. Producer ....Ed Goren
V.P., Media Relations (NYC).........................Vince Wladika
(212) 556-2472

The Golf Channel
7580 Commerce Center Drive, Orlando, FL 32819
(407) 363-4653
President-CEO...Joe Gibbs
V.P., Production...Mike Whelan
Director of Public Relations ....Kyle Eng

HBO Sports
1100 Ave. of the Americas, New York, NY 10036
(212) 512-1987
President-CEO..Seth Abraham
V.P., Executive Producer ....Ross Greenburg
V.P., Programming ....Bob Greenway
Director of Publicity.......................................Ray Stallone

MTV Sports
1633 Broadway, 32nd Floor, New York, NY 10024
(212) 846-4684
Executive Producer ....Carol Donovan
Publicity Contact......................................Cinnamon Boothe

NBC Sports
30 Rockefeller Plaza, New York, NY 10112
(212) 664-2160
President..Dick Ebersol
Executive Producer ....Tommy Roy
Director of Public Relations ....Ed Markey

Prime SportsChannel Networks
Prime Network: 5251 Gulfton St., Houston, TX 77081
(713) 661-0078
NewSport: 3 Crossways Park West
Woodbury, NY 11797
(516) 921-3764
CEO ....James Dolan
COO ....Josh Sapan
V.P., Programming ....Michael Lardner
Dir. of Media Relations....................................Craig Sanders

TSN-The Sports Network
2225 Shepherd Ave. East, Suite 100
Willowdale, Ontario, M2J-5C2
(416) 494-1212
President & General Manager......................Jim Thompson
Public Relations Officer ....Rosemary Pitfield

Turner Sports
One CNN Center, 13th Floor, Atlanta, GA 30303
(404) 827-1735
President..Harvey Schiller
Executive Producer ....Mike Pearl
Sr. V.P., Programming ....Kevin O'Malley
Director of Media Relations............................Greg Hughes

Univision (Spanish)
9405 NW 41st St., Miami, FL 33178
(305) 471-4008
Sports Director ....Jorge Hidalgo
Publicity Coordinator ....Rosalyn Espinosa

USA Network
1230 Ave. of the Americas, New York, NY 10020
(212) 408-9100
V.P., Executive Producer....................................Gordon Beck
V.P., Programming ....Rob Korrea
Sports Publicist..Dan Schoenberg

OLYMPICS

IOC
(International Olympic Committee)
Chateau de Vidy, CH-1007 Lausanne, Switzerland
TEL: 011-41-21-621-6111
President......................................Juan Antonio Samaranch
Director General..Francois Carrard
Secretary General ....Francoise Zweifel
Coordinator, Public Informartion ....Fekrou Kidane
Director of Information ....Michele Verdier

1996 SUMMER GAMES
Atlanta Committee for the Olympic Games
250 Williams St., Suite 6000, (P.O. Box 1996)
Atlanta, GA 30301
(404) 224-1996
President-CEO ....Billy Payne
Sr. Exec. V.P. & COO ................................A.D. Frazier Jr.
Director of Communications............................Bob Brennan
Managing Dir. of Public Relations................Dick Yarbrough
(Games of XXVIth Olympiad, July 19-Aug. 4)

1998 WINTER GAMES
Nagano Olympic Organizing Committee
KT Building, 3109-63 Kawaishinden
Nagano City 380, Japan
TEL: 011-81-262-25-1998
Time difference: 13 hours ahead of New York (EDT)
President..Eishiro Saito
Director General ....Makoto Kobayashi
Head of Media ....Akira Hashimoto
(XVIIIth Olympic Winter Games, Feb. 7-22)

2000 SUMMER GAMES
Sydney Olympic Organizing Committee
Level 14, Maritime Center, 207 Kent St.
Sydney, Australia NSW 2000
TEL: 011-612-931-2000
Time difference: 14 hours ahead of New York (EDT)
President..Gary Pemberton
Director General ....Bob Elphinston
Director of Information ....Ian Dose
(Games of XXVIIth Olympiad, Sept. 16-Oct. 1)

2002 WINTER GAMES
Salt Lake Olympic Organizing Committee
215 South State, Suite 2002, Second Floor
Salt Lake City, UT 84111
(801) 322-2002
Chairman ....Frank Joklik
President..Tom Welch
Vice President ....Dave Johnson
Dir. of Public Information ....Mike Korologos
(XIXth Olympic Winter Games, Feb. 9-24)

COA
(Canadian Olympic Association)
2380 Avenue Pierre Dupuy, Montreal, Quebec H3C-3R4
(514) 861-3371
CEO-General Secretary ....Carol Anne Letheren
President..Bill Warren
IOC members......................................Carol Anne Letheren
              & Richard Pound
Manager of Media Relations ....Lorraine Lafreniere
              (613) 748-5647

USOC
(United States Olympic Committee)
One Olympic Plaza, Colorado Springs, CO 80909
(719) 632-5551
President..LeRoy Walker
Director..Dick Schultz
IOC members..Anita DeFrantz
              & James Easton
Director of Public/Media Relations..................Mike Moran

1998 GOODWILL GAMES
New York Organizing Committee
Two World Trade Center, Suite 2164
New York, NY 10048
(212) 321-1998
Chairman ....Bob Johnson
President..Michael Rowe
V.P., Communications..Don Smith
Project Director ....Stephen Chriss
(4th Goodwill Games, July 25-Aug. 9)

1999 PAN AMERICAN GAMES
Pan American Games Society
(Winnipeg 1999, Inc.)
50 Shaftesbury Blvd., Winninpeg, Manitoba R3P 0M1
(204) 985-1999
President-CEO-Media Contact ....Don MacKenzie
(XIIIth Pan American Games, July 24-Aug. 8)

U.S. OLYMPICS TRAINING CENTERS

Colorado Springs Training Center
One Olympic Plaza, Colorado Springs, CO 80909
(719) 578-4500 ext. 5500
Director..John Smyth

Lake Placid Training Center
421 Old Military Road, Lake Placid, NY 12946
(518) 523-2600
Acting Director..Jack Favro

San Diego Training Center
c/o San Diego National Sports Training Foundation
1650 Hotel Circle N., Suite 125, San Diego, CA 92108
(619) 656-1500
Director.....................................Patrice Milkovich

U.S. OLYMPIC ORGANIZATIONS

National Archery Association
One Olympic Plaza, Colorado Springs, CO 80909
(719) 578-4576
President...............................Thomas Stevenson Jr.
Executive Director ....Robert C. Balink
Media Contact.....................................Coleen Walker Mar

U.S. Badminton Association
One Olympic Plaza, Colorado Springs, CO 80909
(719) 578-4808
President.....................................Diane Cornell
Executive Director ....Jim Hadley
Communications Director............................Paul Pawlaczyk

USA Baseball
2160 Greenwood Avenue, Trenton, NJ 08609
(609) 586-2381
President....................................Mark Marquess
Executive Director & CEO ....Richard Case
Dir. of Media Relations....................................George Doig

USA Basketball
5465 Mark Dabling Blvd., Colorado Springs, CO 80918
(719) 590-4800
President...C.M. Newton
Executive Director ....Warren Brown
Director of Public Relations................................Craig Miller

U.S. Biathlon Association
421 Old Military Rd., Lake Placid, NY 12946
(518) 523-3836
President...............................Maj. Gen. Donald E. Edwards
Exec. Director ....Duane (Dusty) Johnstone
Director of Summer Biathalon.........................Kyle Woodlief

U.S. Bobsled and Skeleton Federation
P.O. Box 828, 421 Old Military Road
Lake Placid, NY 12946
(518) 523-1842
President...Jim Morris
Executive Director ....Matt Roy

USA Boxing
One Olympic Plaza, Colorado Springs, CO 80909
(719) 578-4506
President......................................Jerry Dusenberry
Executive Director ....Bruce Mathis
Communications Director ....Kurt Stenerson

U.S. Canoe and Kayak Team
Pan American Plaza, Suite 610
201 South Capitol Avenue, Indianapolis, IN 46225
(317) 237-5690
Chairman..Lamar Sims
Executive Director ....Chuck Wielgus
Dir. of Communications/Marketing...............Craig Bohnert

U.S. Cycling Federation
One Olympic Plaza, Colorado Springs, CO 80909
(719) 578-4581
President.......................................Mike Fraysse
Executive Director ....Lisa Voight
Director of Communications ....Cheryl Kvasnicka

United States Diving, Inc.
Pan American Plaza, Suite 430,
201 South Capitol Avenue, Indianapolis, IN 46225
(317) 237-5252
President..Steve McFarland
Executive Director ....Todd Smith
Director of Communications.....................Dave Shatkowski

U.S. Equestrian Team
Pottersville Road, Gladstone, NJ 07934
(908) 234-1251
President.......................................Finn Caspersen
Executive Director ....Bob Standish
Director of Public Relations ....Marty Bauman
(508) 698-6810

U.S. Fencing Association
One Olympic Plaza, Colorado Springs, CO 80909
(719) 578-4511
President...Steve Sobel
Interim Executive Director.........................William Goering

U.S. Field Hockey Assocation
One Olympic Plaza, Colorado Springs, CO 80909
(719) 578-4567
President ....Jenepher Shillingford
Executive Director...................................Carrie Haag
Director of Media/Public Relations................Marc Whitney

U.S. Figure Skating Association
20 First Street, Colorado Springs, CO 80906
(719) 635-5200
President......................................Morry Stillwell
Executive Director ....Jerry Lace
Communications Coordinator.....................Heather Linhart

USA Gymnastics
Pan American Plaza, Suite 300
201 South Capitol Avenue, Indianapolis, IN 46225
(317) 237-5050
President-Exec. Director................................Kathy Scanlan
Director of Public Relations ....Luan Peszek

USA Hockey
4965 North 30th St., Colorado Springs, CO 80919
(719) 599-5500
President ....Walter Bush
Executive Director ....Dave Ogrean
Dir. of Public Relations & Media.....................Darryl Seibel

United States Judo, Inc.
P.O. Box 10013, El Paso, TX 79991
(915) 771-6699
President & Media Contact ....Frank Fullerton

U.S. Luge Association
P.O. Box 651, Lake Placid, NY 12946
(518) 523-2071
President...Dwight Bell
Executive Director ....Ron Rossi
Public Relations Manager ....Dmitry Feld

U.S. Modern Pentathlon Association
530 McCullough, Suite 619, San Antonio, TX 78215
(210) 246-3000
President...Robert Marbut Jr.
Executive Director ....Dean Billick

U.S. Rowing
Pan American Plaza, Suite 400
201 South Capitol Avenue, Indianapolis, IN 46225
(317) 237-5656
President ....Dave Vogel
Executive Director.................................Frank Coyle
Media Contact ....Terry Friel

U.S. Sailing Association
P.O. Box 209, Newport, RI 02840
(401) 849-5200
President ....Dave Irish
Executive Director ....Terry D. Harper
Media Contact....................................Barby MacGowan
(401) 849-0220

U.S. Shooting Team
One Olympic Plaza, Colorado Springs, CO 80909
(719) 578-4670
Program Administrator..........................Steven Ducoff
Director of Operations.....................................Joseph Berry
Public Relations Director...............................Nancy Moore

U.S. Skiing
P.O. Box 100, 1500 Kearns Blvd., Park City, UT 84060
(801) 649-9090
Chairman..Nick Badami
Interim CEO ....Chuck Dillman
President U.S. Ski Association.........................Jim McCarthy
Director of Communications...............................Tom Kelly

U.S. Soccer Federation
U.S. Soccer House
1801-1811 South Prairie Ave., Chicago, IL 60616
(312) 808-1300
President ....Alan Rothenberg
Executive Director ....Hank Steinbrecher
Director of Communications.........................Thomas Lange

Amateur Softball Association
2801 N.E. 50th Street, Oklahoma City, OK 73111
(405) 424-5266
President...Wayne Myers
Executive Director ....Don Porter
Dir. Media Relations/PR/Hall of Fame..............Bill Plummer
Director of Communications.............................Ron Babb

U.S. International Speedskating Assn.
P.O. Box 16157, Rocky River, OH 44116
(216) 899-0128
President ....Bill Cushman
Executive Director ....Katie Marquard
Media Relations Director....................Susan Polakoff Shaw

U.S. Swimming, Inc.
One Olympic Plaza, Colorado Springs, CO 80909
(719) 578-4578
President..Carol Zaleski
Executive Director ....Ray Essick
Director of Communications.........................Charlie Snyder

U.S. Synchronized Swimming, Inc.
Pan American Plaza, Suite 510
201 South Capitol Avenue, Indianapolis, IN 46225
(317) 237-5700
President..Nancy Wightman
Executive Director ....Debbie Hesse
Communications Coordinator ....Laura LaMarca

U.S. Table Tennis Association
One Olympic Plaza, Colorado Springs, CO 80909
(719) 578-4583
President ....Terry Timmins
Executive Director...Paul Montville

U.S. Team Handball Federation
One Olympic Plaza, Colorado Springs, CO 80909
(719) 578-4582
President...................................Thomas P. Rosandich
Executive Director..................................Michael Cavanaugh
Media Contact ....Frank Davis

U.S. Tennis Association
70 West Red Oak Lane, White Plains, NY 10604
(914) 696-7000
President...Lester M. Snyder Jr.
Executive Director ....M. Marshall Happer III
Dir. of Communications.........................Page Dahl Crosland

USA Track and Field
P.O. Box 120, Indianapolis, IN 46206
(317) 261-0500
President..Larry Ellis
Executive Director ....Ollan Cassell
Press Information Director ....Pete Cava

U.S. Volleyball Association
3595 East Fountain Blvd., Suite I-2
Colorado Springs, CO 80910
(719) 637-8300
President...Jerry Sherman
Executive Director-CEO ....John Carroll
Director of Media Relations ....Tony Lovitt

United States Water Polo
Pan American Plaza, Suite 520
201 South Capitol Avenue, Indianapolis, IN 46225
(317) 237-5599
President ....Richard Foster
Executive Director ....Bruce Wigo
Dir. of Media/Public Relations...................Kevin Messenger

U.S. Weightlifting Federation
One Olympic Plaza, Colorado Springs, CO 80909
(719) 578-4508
President...Jim Schmitz
Executive Director...............................George Greenway
Communications Director ....John Halpin

USA Wrestling
6155 Lehman Drive, Colorado Springs, CO 80918
(719) 598-8181
President ....Larry Sciacchetano
Executive Director ....Jim Scherr
Dir. of Communications...................................Gary Abbott

AFFILIATED ORGANIZATIONS

U.S. Curling Association
1100 Center Point Drive, Box 866
Stevens Point, WI 54481
(715) 344-1199
President ....Warren Lowe
Exec. Dir. & Media Contact ....David Garber

U.S. Amateur Confederation of Roller Skating
P.O. Box 6579, Lincoln, NE 68506
(402) 483-7551
President ....Betty Ann Danna
Executive Director ....George Pickard
Information Director ....Andy Sealey

U.S. Taekwondo Union
One Olympic Plaza, Suite 405
Colorado Springs, CO 80909
(719) 578-4632
President ....Hwa Chong
Exec. Director & Media Contact..................Robert Fujimura

Triathlon Federation USA
3595 East Fountain Blvd., Suite F-1
Colorado Springs, CO 80910
(719) 597-9090
Executive Director ....Steve Locke
Media Contact and Deputy Director ....Tim Yount

American Water Ski Association
799 Overlook Drive, S.E., Winter Haven, FL 33884
(813) 324-4341
President ....Harold Hill
Executive Director..Duke Waldrop
Director of Communications..........................Don Cullimore

SOCCER

FIFA
(Federation Internationale de Football Assn.)
P.O. Box 85, 8030 Zurich, Switzerland
TEL: 011-41-1-384-9595
President ....Joao Havelange
General Secretary ....Joseph Blatter
Director of Communications ....Keith Cooper

1998 WORLD CUP

French Organizing Committee
90 Avenue des Champs Elysees
F-75008 Paris, France
TEL: 011-33-1-44-95-1998
Time difference: five hours ahead of New York (EDT)
Co-Presidents ....Ferdnand Sastre
                                                      and Michel Platini
General Director..Jacques Lambert
Dir. of Press & Communications ....Alain Leiblang
(16th World Cup, June 10-July 12)

CONCACAF
(Confederation of North, Central American
& Caribbean Association Football)
725 Fifth Ave., 17th Floor, New York, NY 10022
(212) 308-0044
President ....Jack Austin Warner
General Secretary ....Chuck Blazer

U.S. Soccer
(United States Soccer Federation)
Soccer House, 1801-1811 South Prairie Ave.
Chicago, IL 60616
(312) 808-1300
President ....Alan Rothenberg
Exec. Director/Sec. General ....Hank Steinbrecher
Director of Communications ....Tom Lange

A-League
(American Professional Soccer League)
2 Village Rd., Suite 5, Horsham, PA 19044
(215) 657-7440
Commissioner..Richard Groff
Operations Director..................................Chris Branscome
Director of Media Relations ....Derek Aframe
   Member teams (6): Atlanta Ruckus, Colorado Foxes,
Montreal Impact, New York Centaurs, Seattle Sounders and
Vancouver 86ers.

CISL
(Continental Indoor Soccer League)
16027 Ventura Blvd., Suite 605, Encino, CA 91436
(818) 906-7627
Commissioner...Ron Weinstein
League Counsel ....Dan Grigsby
Director of Media Relations ....Dan Courtemanche

MLS
(Major League Soccer)
2049 Century Park East, Suite 4390
Los Angeles, CA 90067
(310) 772-2600
Chairman...Alan Rothenberg
COO ....Bill Sage
   Member cities (10): Boston, Columbus (OH), Dallas,
Denver, Kansas City, Los Angeles, New Jersey, Tampa Bay,
San Jose, and Washington D.C.

NPSL
(National Professional Soccer League)
229 Third Street, NW, Canton, OH 44702
(216) 455-4625
Commissioner ....Steve M. Paxos
Director of Operations..............................Paul Luchowski
   Member teams (13): American Division— Baltimore
Spirit, Buffalo Blizzard, Canton Invaders, Cincinnati
Silverbacks, Cleveland Crunch and Harrisburg Heat.
National Division— Chicago Power, Detroit Rockers,
Kansas City Attack, Milwaukee Wave, St. Louis Ambush
and Wichita Wings. Expansion— Tampa Bay Terror.

USISL
(United States Interregional Soccer League)
4322 N. Beltline Rd., Suite B-205, Irving, TX 75038
(214) 570-7575
Commissioner..Francisco Marcos
Administrative Manager ....Beverly Wright
Director of Public Relations.............................Mike Agnew

TENNIS

ATP Tour
(Association of Tennis Professionals)
200 ATP Tour Blvd., Ponte Verde Beach, FL 32082
(904) 285-8000
Chief Executive Officer ....Mark Miles
V.P., Communications ....Pete Alfano

ITF
(International Tennis Federation)
Pallisert Rd., Barons Court
London, England W14 9EN
TEL: 011-44-171-3818060
President ....Brian Tobin
General Manager...Doug Mec
Media Administrator ....Ian Barnes

TeamTennis
445 North Wells, Suite 404, Chicago, IL 60610
(312) 245-5300
Chief Executive Officer...............................Billie Jean King
Executive Director ....Ilana Kloss
Communications Director ....Kim Couch

USTA
(United States Tennis Association)
70 West Red Oak Lane, White Plains, NY 10604
(914) 696-7000
President ....Lester Snyder
Executive Director ....TBA
Dir. of Communications...............................Page Crosland

WTA Tour
(Women's Tennis Association)
133 First Street NE, St. Petersburg, FL 33701
(813) 895-5000
Executive Director & CEO...............Anne Person Worcester
V.P., Marketing & Communications ....David Fechtman

TRACK & FIELD

IAAF
(International Ameteur Athletics Federation)
17 Rue Princesse Florestine
BP 359, MC-98007, Monaco
TEL: 011-33-93-30-7070
President...Primo Nebiolo
General Secretary ....Istvan Gyulai
Director of Information..............................Giorgio Reinei

1997 WORLD CHAMPIONSHIPS

Athens Organizing Committee
Assn. Hellenique d'Athletisme Amateur (SEGAS)
137 Avenue Syngrou, Athens 17121, Greece
TEL: 011-30-1-935-8592
Time difference: Seven hours ahead of New York (EDT)
President..Stratos Molyvas
General Secretary ....Kostis Grammatikopoulos
(6th World Championships, Aug. 1-10)

AAU
(Amateur Athletic Union)
3400 West 86th St., Indianapolis, IN 46268
(317) 872-2900
President...Bobby Dodd
Director of Communications............................Tim Niemann

USA Track & Field
P.O. Box 120
Indianapolis, IN 46206
(317) 261-0500
Executive Director...Ollan Cassell
Director of Information ....Pete Cava

YACHTING

1999-2000 America's Cup

New Zealand Defense Committee
(Royal New Zealand Yacht Squadron)
P.O. Box 1927, Auckland, New Zealand
TEL: 011-64-9-357-6712
Time difference: 16 hours ahead of New York (EDT)
Exec. Director & Contact ....Alan Sefton
(Next America's Cup defense scheduled to begin in Oct. 1999 and run through Feb. 2000, off the coast of Auckland)

MISCELLANEOUS

All-American Soap Box Derby
P.O.Box 7233, Akron, OH 44306
(216) 733-8723
President ....Bob Otterman
Chairman of the Board and Dir. PR ....Bob Proyer

Arena Football League
2200 West Commercial Blvd., Suite 101
Ft. Lauderdale, FL 33309
(305) 777-2700
Commissioner ....James Drucker
Coordinator, Media Services............................Nick Gandy
    Member teams (13): American Conference— Arizona
Rattlers, Iowa Barnstormers, Las Vegas Sting, Memphis
Pharaoahs, Milwaukee Mustangs, St. Louis Stampede and
San Jose Sabrecats. National Conference— Albany (NY)
Firebirds, Charlotte Rage, Connecticut Coyotes, Miami
Hooters, Orlando Predators, and Tampa Bay Storm.

Association of Volleyball Professionals
15260 Ventura Blvd., Suite 2250, Sherman Oaks, CA 91403
(818) 386-2486
President..Jon Stevenson
Exec. Director...Jerry Solomon
Media Contact ....Steve Vanderpool

BASS, Inc.
(Bass Anglers Sportsmen Society)
5845 Carmichael Blvd., Mongomery, AL 36117
(334) 272-9530
CEO..Helen Sevier
Publicity Director...Ann Lewis

International Game Fish Association
1301 East Atlantic Blvd., Pompano Beach, FL 33060
(305) 941-3474
Chairman..George Matthews
President ....Mike Leach
Editor...Ray Crawford

Little League Baseball Incorporated
P.O. Box 3485, Williamsport, PA 17701
(717) 326-1921
CEO..C.J. Hale
President ....Steven Keener
Director of Communications ....Dennis Sullivan

Major Indoor Lacrosse League
2310 West 75th St., Prairie Village, KS 66208
(913) 384-8960
Chairman-CEO...Chris Fritz
President ....Russ Cline
Director of Public Relations ....Mary Havel
    Member teams (6): Baltimore Thunder, Boston Blazers,
Buffalo Bandits, New York Saints, Philadelphia Wings and
Rochestern Knighthawks.

National Rifle Assocation
11250 Waples Mill Road, Fairfax, VA 22030
(703) 267-1000
Executive VP...Wayne LaPierre
Public Affairs Director......................................Bill Powers

National Sports Foundation
1314 North Hayworth Ave., Suite 402
Los Angeles, CA 90046
(213) 851-1400
Executive Director ....Ed Harris

Professional Rodeo Cowboys Association
101 Pro Rodeo Drive, Colorado Springs, CO 80919
(719) 593-8840
Commissioner...Lewis Cryer
Director of Public Relations ....Steve Fleming

Roller Hockey International
5182 Katella Ave., Suite 106, Los Alamitos, CA 90720
(714) 385-1769
Commissioner ....Ralph Backstrom
COO ....David B. McLane
Public Relations Director..................................Nancy King

Special Olympics
1350 New York Ave., NW, Suite 500
Washington, DC 20005
(202) 628-3630
Founder..............................Eunice Kennedy Shriver
COB...Sargent Shriver
COO...Edgar May
Public Affairs Director...............................Jay Emmet

Wheelchair Sports USA
3595 East Fountain Blvd., Suite L-1
Colorado Springs, CO 80910
(719) 574-1150
Chairman..Paul DePace
Assoc. Exec. Director ....Patricia Long

Great Britain's **Jonathan Edwards** crashes through the 60-foot barrier on his way to a gold medal in the triple jump at the 1995 World Track & Field Championships in Göteborg, Sweden.

INTERNATIONAL SPORTS

Whistling Dixie

The year's warm weather championships all point to Atlanta and the approaching celebration of the Centennial Olympics.

The Olympics turn 100 in 1996. Over that century, they have divided into Summer and Winter Games and multiplied over 40 times in numbers of athletes and nearly 15-fold in numbers of nations.

In 1896, an estimated 245 male athletes from 14 countries competed in the first Olympics of the modern era in Athens, Greece. In 1996, over 10,000 athletes of both sexes from 197 countries will march in the opening ceremonies at the Centennial Games in Atlanta.

The Olympics were once hailed as a bulwark of amateurism. In truth, they were elitist, for the working classes could not afford time off without pay to perfect their sporting skills. As the Games have become more and more professional, they have also become more egalitarian— even if the inclusion of U.S. basketball pros served to show mainly that they have no equals in the world.

Through wars, communism, ugly competitive disputes, drug-use scandals, terrorism and boycotts, the Olympics have both grown into medal-crazy gigantism and retained the simple notion of their founder, Baron Pierre de Coubertin, that the important thing is to participate.

For a fortnight every two years, the Olympic Games briefly carry the torch for humanity. And for all their commercialism, politics and fractiousness, they provide what is likely the largest and longest assembly of diverse and often feuding peoples.

In 1995, athletes around the world prepared for Atlanta at various world, hemispheric and continental events, highlighted by the World Track & Field Championships in Göteborg, Sweden (see page 606). And even though the next Winter Olympics won't take place until 1998, there was plenty of activity in the cold weather sports as well.

A summary of the year's major Olympic event stories follows. For other sports, including America's Cup yachting and World Cup Rugby, see the Miscellaneous chapter.

Figure Skating. The wildest incident in figure skating history led to the wildest season ever in what once was the most decorous of sports.

Spurred by the stunning Olympic TV ratings that followed the 1994 attack on Nancy Kerrigan by associates of rival Tonya Harding, promoters, agents and TV networks rushed into action. There were more than 30 televised figure skating competitions in 1994-95, ranging from the ersatz ("Rock N' Roll Figure Skating Championships") to the traditional national and World Championships for Olympic-eligible skaters. CBS was an especially big player as it scrambled to fill a programming void created by the loss of NFL football.

"It's the Wild West out there," said promoter Michael Burg, referring to the free-for-all among network TV's programming gunslingers.

Philip Hersh covers international sports for the *Chicago Tribune* and has been the *Tribune's* full-time Olympics writer since 1986.

Women's gold medalist **Lu Chen** of China (center) with runner-up **Surya Bonaly** of France (left) and third place finisher **Nicole Bobek** of the United States at the 1995 World Figure Skating Championships in Birmingham, England. Chen is the first Chinese to ever win a world figure skating title.

To everyone's surprise, the glut of events and the hodgepodge of different rules governing them did not decrease spectator interest. In fact, Fox-TV's "Rock N' Roll" event, with celebrities judging Olympic champions, drew a national 11.3 rating with an audience share of 17. That prompted NBC honcho Don Ohlmeyer, to start calling around the next day to find out where he could get similar shows for the 1995-96 season.

And more there will be, starting in September and running through late spring.

Because most of the 1994-95 events were unsanctioned (open only to skaters not eligible for the Olympics), the International Skating Union saw the sport getting completely out of its control. The ISU, which governs Olympic and World Championship competitions, fought back by creating six ISU-sanctioned open events (eligibles and ineligibles) and a lucrative Grand Prix circuit for eligibles only, hoping to provide enough financial incentive for those skaters to *stay* eligible.

That wasn't enough, however, to lure back big-name pros— like Kerrigan, reigning Olympic champion Oksana Baiul and

1992 Olympic and world champion Kristi Yamaguchi— when the ISU's deadline for eligibility reinstatement passed April 1.

The only significant returnee was Japan's Midori Ito, who had turned pro after finishing second in the 1992 Olympics. Ito reportedly was subjected to substantial national pressure to compete in the 1998 Olympics in Nagano, Japan. Another announced returnee, former ice dance world champions Maya Usova and Alexandr Zhulin of Russia, apparently have reconsidered and will remain pro.

In the midst of all that chaos, there was skating— and a new national champion with a wild-child reputation not unlike that of defrocked 1994 champ Harding.

She is Nicole Bobek, 17, the former chain-smoking, practice-shunning hellion, who was tamed by her eighth coach in eight years, Richard Callaghan of the Detroit Figure Skating Club.

Bobek's reputation immediately was tarnished, however, by revelations that she had entered a conditional plea of guilty and was placed on probation (since ended due to procedural violations) prior to nationals
Continued on page 608

Gary M. Prior/Allsport

With victories at 200 and 400 meters and a third gold medal in the men's 4x400-meter relay, America's **Michael Johnson** was the center of attention at the World Track and Field Championships in August.

Twilight of the Gods In Sweden

In a land where Valhalla beckoned from as nearby as a practice track bearing that name, the 1995 World Track and Field Championships turned into the twilight of the track and field gods.

The nine-day competition at Göteborg, Sweden's Ullevi Stadium, named for the Norse god of sport and fun, will be remembered more for who didn't win than who did.

The list of those who left without a medal included many of the sport's seemingly eternal stars: Carl Lewis, Jackie Joyner-Kersee and Mike Conley of the U.S.; Linford Christie of Great Britain; and Heike Drechsler of Germany.

The question now is whether that group of thirtysomethings, which won a total of six gold medals in Barcelona, can recapture their youth before the 1996 Olympics in Atlanta. The 1995 worlds made each of them look more like relics than medal contenders on the eve of the 100th anniversary of the Summer Games.

The world meet's dominant figures included established stars like Noureddine Morceli of Algeria, Moses Kiptanui of Kenya,

Michael Johnson and Dan O'Brien of the U.S., and the evergreen pole vaulter, Sergey Bubka, of Ukraine.

Morceli (1,500 meters), Kiptanui (3,000-meter steeplechase) and O'Brien (decathlon) each won a third straight world title. Bubka, is the only athlete to win five in a row. And Johnson became the first man to win both the 200 and 400 meters in an Olympics or World Championships.

Other repeat history: a controversy involving U.S. sprinter Gwen Torrence, who has a history of putting her feet in places they don't belong (including her mouth).

And, although the overall performance level was down from the four previous world meets, the entire competition was elevated by the courage of Cuba's Ana Quirot. She won the 800 meters while bearing the scars of a 1993 kitchen accident that led to the death of the baby she was carrying and nearly killed her as well. "In my worst moments," she said later, "I never thought I could come back so strongly. This is my most beautiful victory."

Quirot's medal was one of 16 won by

Atlantic and Caribbean island neighbors of the United States. Jamaica, a nation of just 2.5 million, led the way with seven medals— third behind only the U.S. (19) and Russia (13, but just one gold).

Torrence, meanwhile, was denied a convincing victory over Jamaica's Merlene Ottey in the 200 meters because she ran out of her lane. Ottey later used the word "cheating" to describe what her longtime rival had done— an intemperate choice of words undoubtedly caused by the bad relations between Torrence and the rest of the track world.

Torrence was still a double winner, taking the 100 meters— her first individual world title— and anchoring the 4x100 relay team. Those were among the 12 gold medals won by the U.S., only one fewer than its best-ever 13 from the 1993 worlds. But the U.S. total was seven fewer than '93 and its lowest in five world meets— a drop that the failures of both Lewis and Joyner-Kersee factored into.

Lewis, 34, finished the worst season of his career by withdrawing from both the long jump and 4x100 relay with a leg injury. Joyner-Kersee, 33, finished 6th in the long jump and then withdrew from the heptathlon with nagging injuries. It was the first time Lewis has ever been shutout in a world meet and the first no-medal performance by Joyner-Kersee since 1983.

Johnson tried to make up the difference by himself, winning more gold medals than any nation except his own. Adding a third gold in the 4x400-meter relay, Johnson left Göteborg with only one regret: having barely missed breaking world records in both the 200 and 400. He clocked 43.39 seconds in the 400, second-fastest ever behind Butch Reynolds' record 43.29; and 19.79 in the 200, just 7/100ths off Pietro Mennea's mark of 19.72.

Four world records were broken in the meet, three of them in the triple jump and two by the same jumper, Jonathan Edwards of Great Britain.

Edwards surpassed two notable barriers, one metric, the other imperial. He opened with history's first legal (non wind-aided) jump past 18 meters, then followed with the first past 60 feet. The distances were 59 feet, 7 inches and 60 feet, ¼-inch, meaning Edwards had improved the world record he set two weeks before the world meet by more than a foot.

Inessa Kravets of Ukraine, the former indoor world-record holder in the triple jump, broke the outdoor mark with a leap of 50 feet, 10 ¼ inches.

Clive Brunskill/Allsport

Cuba's **Ana Quirot** was the world meet's most inspirational performer, coming back from a near-fatal accident in 1993 to win the 800 meters.

Kim Batten had no such record-breaking credentials in her resume. In fact, just being in the world meet had seemed a longshot for Batten, who had an emergency appendectomy in May. But she needed a world record to beat teammate Tonja Buford in the 400-meter hurdles. Batten clocked 52.61, Buford 52.62. Both were faster than the old mark of 52.74 set by Great Britain's Sally Gunnell, who was sidelined by an injury. Neither had ever run within a second of what each did in this race.

And then there was (or wasn't) China. The female footsoldiers of tyrannical coach Ma Junren had won six of the nine medals— including all three golds— at 1,500, 3,000 and 10,000 meters in 1993. At the start of this year, Ma's troops had disbanded amid persistent rumors of drug use and rebellion against brutal training methods.

In Göteborg, China had just one woman entrant, Dong Zhoaxia, in races of 800 meters through the marathon. She failed to make the final in the 10,000 and did not finish her qualifying heat in the 5,000.

Said 5,000-meter champion Sonia O'Sullivan of the Chinese: "They have vanished."

after a charge of felony home invasion in a Detroit suburb. That was followed by a going-over in a variety of tabloids and *People* magazine, all of whom aired allegations from a linked group of people claiming Bobek's mother, Jana, and the mother's friend, Joyce Barron, had abused Nicole. None of those allegations have been independently corroborated.

With all that hanging over her, Bobek still managed to win the bronze medal at the 1995 World Championships in Birmingham, England. She had led after the short-program phase of the competition before, literally, falling behind China's Lu Chen— the first Chinese to win a world figure skating title— and France's Surya Bonaly, runner-up three years straight.

At the nationals in Providence, another revitalized skater, Todd Eldredge, returned to the top after three years of injuries and malaise. By winning his third U.S. title since 1990, Eldredge gave Callaghan the distinction of being the first to coach both the male and female U.S. champions since Gus Lussi in 1950. Eldredge also led after the short program at the world meet and wound up second behind Canada's courageous Elvis Stojko, who won despite suffering a serious ankle injury in January.

The medals captured by Eldredge, Bobek and the bronze-winning pairs team of Jenni Meno and Todd Sand (who were married in July), ended a disastrous two-year run for U.S. skaters at the world meet. Team USA had been shut out of the medals in 1993 and '94— only the second time since World War II that had happened. The first time was the three years following the Feb. 15, 1961 plane crash that claimed the lives of the entire U.S. team on its way to the worlds in Prague.

Other 1995 world titlists included pairs champions Radka Kovarikova and Rene Novotny of the Czech Republic, and ice dance winners Oksana Gritschuk and Yevgeny Platov of Russia.

Tonya & Nancy. The never-ending saga of figure skating's fun couple— Tonya Harding and Nancy Kerrigan— continued throughout the year, with poignantly contrasting episodes a week and a continent apart.

On Sunday, Sept. 3, Harding made her singing debut before what she hoped would be a receptive hometown audience in Portland, Ore. Instead, she was showered with catcalls and plastic bottles when the crowd turned ugly at a muscular dystrophy fund-raiser where Harding and her band were the warm-up act for Kool & the Gang.

The following Saturday in Boston, Kerrigan, 25, was married to her agent, Jerry Solomon, 41, in a scene one witness compared to a Kennedy wedding— complete with hundreds of onlookers outside the church and a reception at the President's Ballroom at the local Hyatt Regency hotel.

The rest of the year was more of the same for Harding and Kerrigan, linked forever by the Jan. 6, 1994 incident in which associates of Harding hit Kerrigan on the knee in a failed attempt to keep her out of the 1994 Olympics.

Kerrigan continued to make millions in endorsements, pro shows and competitions (in which the quality of her skating was erratic at best). She also headlined a far-from-sold out skating tour with singer Aaron Neville.

Harding, meanwhile, had her breasts enlarged and unsuccessfully asked a judge to reduce her hours of community service and change the terms of the $50,000 charitable donation she made as part of her 1994 plea bargain. She also appeared as "Mrs. Santa Claus" during free-time skating at the Portland mall rink where she used to practice.

Other developments: Harding's fan club disbanded when she demanded it hand over all its funds; her ex-husband, Jeff Gillooly, the so-called mastermind of the Kerrigan hit, legally changed his name to Jeff Stone shortly after his March release from jail, where he served eight months of a two-year sentence for racketeering; hit man Shane Stant and getaway driver Derrick Smith were released from prison in late July; and roly-poly bodyguard Shawn Eckhardt was freed in September.

Speed Skating. The 1994-95 season was the Bonnie Blair Farewell Tour— a.k.a. "Bye, Bye, Miss American Pie"— and what a glorious farewell it was for the most-gilded female athlete in U.S. Olympic history.

The biggest celebration came on The Rink That Bonnie Built, the new Pettit Ice Center in Milwaukee. Three hundred members of the "Blair Bunch," her vastly extended fan club of family and friends, were among the 2,600 fans at the sold-out arena as Blair won all four races en route to her third overall title at the World Sprint Speedskating

Alpine skiing World Cup overall champions **Alberto Tomba** of Italy (right) and **Vreni Schneider** of Switzerland celebrate after clinching their titles in March. It was Tomba's first overall title and the third for Schneider, who retired from World Cup racing in April with 55 career wins.

Championships in mid-February.

Blair's 11th and last season as a world-class sprinter ended on her 31st birthday (March 18) at a low-key meet at the Olympic oval in Calgary, where she had won her first gold medal back in 1988. Fittingly, she went out with skates blazing. In the 1,000 meters, she turned in a career-best (and U.S. record) time of 1 minute, 18.05 seconds. Then she was clocked at 38.87 seconds in the 500— the second fastest time ever, second only to the world record of 38.69 she had set on the same ice in January.

Blair also won the 500- and 1,000-meter World Cup season titles, taking 10 of the 13 races at the shorter distance.

That she went out skating better than ever prompted questions about whether she might reconsider her decision to retire. "I'm sorry," she said. "It's kind of funny. People were wondering why I was still skating after the 1988 Olympics and now they want me to stick around longer."

Without Blair and Dan Jansen, who retired in August 1994 to become a millionaire endorser and corporate schmoozer, U.S. speed skating likely will return to the dol-drums of 1984. That year, in Sarajevo, Blair and Jansen made their Olympic debuts for a team that won no medals (one of only two Olympic washouts ever in the sport).

No U.S. man finished higher than sixth in a World Cup or World Championship race in 1994-95, although Chris Witty did man-age a second and a third at 1,000 meters in the World Cup and a second in one of the two 1,000s at the World Sprints.

Other world champions: Yoon-Man Kim in the men's sprints, the first world title for South Korea; Rintje Ritsma of Holland in the men's all-around; and Gunda Niemann of Germany in the women's all-around, in which she swept all four races for a fourth title.

Alpine Skiing. Alberto Tomba had his greatest season since his flamboyant debut in 1987-88, and Picabo Street became the first U.S. downhill queen as the White Circus staggered through a winter of post-ponements, venue shifts and general chaos due to warm weather.

The weather, in fact, prevented Tomba from filling the one gap on his résumé: a world championship title. The 1995 World Championships in Sierra Nevada, Spain, the southernmost major ski area in Europe, were cancelled for lack of snow. The usually biennial event was rescheduled to start in

Spain's **Miguel Induráin** after winning the Tour de France for an unprecedented fifth straight time. Only three other cyclists have won five Tours.

Sierra Nevada on Feb. 11, 1996.

On the World Cup circuit, Tomba won his first overall title with victories in seven (all in a row) of the nine slaloms and four giant slaloms, which also gave him his fourth season titles in both events. Tomba's initial giant slalom win of the season was his first in nearly three years.

The 11 victories topped his previous season-best of nine in both 1987-88 and 1990-91 and gave him 44 for his career. That moved Tomba, who turns 29 in December, to within one of Luxembourg's Marc Girardelli on an all-time victory list topped by the 86 of Sweden's Ingemar Stenmark.

Tomba, who previously had finished second in the overall standings three times, also became the first skier since Stenmark in 1978 to win the World Cup overall crown without skiing any of the speed events. His achievement actually was more difficult, since Super-G (a speed event) was not a World Cup event in Stenmark's era.

Street, the ebullient, once-undisciplined teenager from Sun Valley, Idaho, has matured at 24 into the fastest woman on the mountains. Beginning the season without a World Cup win to her credit, Street won six of nine downhills, including the final five, and took second in another downhill and a Super-G.

Her teammate, Alaskan Hilary Lindh, won two of the other downhills, giving the U.S. unprecedented World Cup speed-event success amplified by the surprising pair of downhill wins from Kyle Rasmussen, 26, who before this season had never finished higher than 7th in a World Cup race.

There was nothing new about the women's overall champion, though: it was Switzerland's Vreni Schneider, 30, who announced her retirement on April 19, after winning her third overall title, sixth slalom title and fifth giant slalom title. Schneider finishes with 55 career wins, just seven shy of all-time leader Annemarie Moser-Proell of Austria and 21 ahead of third-place Hanni Wenzel of Liechtenstein.

Biathlon. France, which never before had won an individual medal in the World Championships that began in 1958, wound up with three golds and a bronze in the four events at the 1995 meet in Anterselva, Italy. Corinne Niogret, 22, was the star, with gold in the 15-kilometer and bronze in the 7.5-kilometer races. Anne Briand won the 7.5, while Patrice Bailly-Salins took the men's 10km. Lone non-French winner: Tomas Sikora of Poland in the 20km.

Bobsled. Pierre Lueders ended a 30-year Canadian medal drought at the World Championships in Winterberg, Germany, by driving his two-man sled to silver behind defending champion Christoph Langen of the host country. Lueders also won the World Cup 2-man season title. German perennial Wolfgang Hoppe, 37, won the 4-man world title, giving him an astonishing 30 medals in world, Olympic and European championships. U.S. sleds were 7th in two-man (Brian Shimer) and 9th in 4-man (Tuffy Latour). Shimer, hurt before the 4-man race at the worlds, finished third in the World Cup 4-man standings.

Hockey. The hope of having NHL players in the 1998 Winter Olympics seems to have been lost over a four-day difference between the players union and the league's backward-thinking Board of Governors, who cannot understand the public relations value of having their best players show off before millions of TV viewers. The players want a 14-day hiatus for the Games, which will run from Feb. 7-20 in Nagano, Japan. The owners are insisting on only 10, and they will apparently not relent.

A line nicknamed "Tupu, Hupu and Lupu," for the Finnish version of Donald Duck's nephews, helped the Finns win their first World Championship with a 4-1 victory over host Sweden in Stockholm (see page 393). Center Saku Koivu and wings Jere Lehtinen and Ville Peltonen combined for six points in the gold-medal game.

Canada, minus the NHL stars who had helped it win the 1994 world title, beat the Czech Republic, 4-1, in the bronze-medal game. Team USA was unbeaten (3-0-2) in the round-robin phase of the tournament, but lost to Canada in the quarterfinals and was awarded sixth-place based on overall record.

Luge. Chris Thorpe of Marquette, Mich., and Gordy Scheer of Croton-on-Hudson, N.Y., gave the U.S. its first doubles medal (silver) at a World Championships, finishing behind Germans Stefan Krausse and Jan Behrendt in Lillehammer, Norway. That medal— only the second-ever at the worlds for the U.S.— capped a strong season for Thorpe and Scheer, whose World Cup record included one win (1st ever for a U.S. doubles team), six seconds and three thirds in 10 events, good for third in the overall standings.

U.S. singles sledders did not do nearly as well, although Cammy Myler of Lake Placid had her country's best-ever women's finish (4th) at the worlds. World Championship rookie Larry Dolan was the top men's placer at 8th, while 1993 winner Wendel Suckow was 9th. Winners were Gabi Kohlisch of Germany for the women and Armin Zoggeler of Italy for the men.

Ski Jump and **Nordic Combined.** Japan's Takanobu Okape upset World Cup champion Andreas Goldberger of Austria to win the 90-meter hill title at the World Championships in Thunder Bay, Ont. Tommy Ingebrightsen, 17, of Norway became the youngest ski jumping world champion when he beat Goldberger on the 120-meter hill. Goldberger, however, won 10 of the 20 World Cup events, including the prestigious Four Hills Tournament.

After a disappointing fifth (behind winner Fred Borre Lundberg of Norway) in the individual race, Kenji Ogiwara helped

Wide World Photos

Thirteen-year-old **Dominique Moceanu** became the youngest national all-around gymnastics champion in history at the U.S. Championships in August.

Japan to a runaway victory in the Nordic combined team event at the worlds.

Cross-Country Skiing. Vitaly Smirnov of Kazakhstan and the Russian women's team were utterly dominant at the World Championships on the slushy courses of overheated Thunder Bay, Ont. Smirnov, 31, won three of the four individual races (10km and 30km classic, 15km pursuit) and was third behind Silvio Fauner of Italy in the other (50km freestyle).

The Russian women won all five events, led by Larissa Lazhutina (5km and 15km classic, 10km pursuit) and Elena Valbe (30km freestyle). Lazhutina, 29, mother of a 4-year-old girl, ran a leg of the winning relay, making her the first to win four gold medals at a worlds. The Russian women also won three silver medals and one bronze.

Freestyle Skiing. Trace Worthington's career-long quest for a major global championship title ended when he won both the aerials and combined events at the 1995 World Championships in La Clusaz, France. Worthington, 25, of Park City, Utah, became the first freestyle skier to win two world titles in the same meet. U.S. skiers dominated the worlds with six medals, including four golds— Nikki Stone (aerials) and Kristean Porter (overall) got the others.

Baseball. A United States team, made up of likely candidates for the 1996

Olympic squad, had a historic 4-game sweep of perennial world champion Cuba during a summer barnstorming tour of the U.S. Never before had the U.S. swept Cuba in a series of any length.

Basketball. New U.S. citizen Hakeem Olajuwon of the NBA champion Houston Rockets— the world's best player at the moment— heads Dream Team III for the 1996 Olympics. Olajuwon needed a special dispensation from the international basketball federation to play for his adopted country because he had competed in an international tournament for his native Nigeria as a teenager. See pages 350 and 509 for team roster.

The 1995 European Championships in Athens ended in political and officiating controversies as Yugoslavia (now Serbia and Montenegro) reclaimed the title it had won (as six federated republics) in 1989 and 1991. The Yugoslavs were banned from defending in 1993 because of U.N. sanctions linked to the Serbs' war in Bosnia.

With two minutes remaining in Yugoslavia's 96-90 win over Lithuania in the 1995 final, the Lithuanians left the court to protest calls made by U.S. official George Tolliver. The Lakers' Vlade Divac of Yugoslavia was among those who persuaded Lithuania to finish.

In the award ceremony that followed, the bronze-medalist players from Croatia (a former Yugoslav republic) walked off the stand as a war protest when Yugoslavia was announced to get its gold.

Furthermore, convinced that International Basketball Federation (FIBA) president Boris Stankovic, a Serb, had engineered the Yugoslavs' victory over Greece in the semifinals, the Greek crowd whistled as Yugoslav players were awarded their medals. That led a crowd of celebrants in Belgrade, Yugoslavia, to break every window in the Greek embassy there.

Boxing. The U.S. managed a gold medal at the 1995 World Championships in Berlin, avoiding a duplication of its historic gold-medal shutout at the previous meet in 1993. The team's overall performance, however, was its worst ever, with just two medals. The gold came from light heavyweight Antonio Tarver of Orlando, who looks like the only U.S. championship contender for the 1996 Olympics.

Cuba led the gold medal count for the sev-enth time in eight world meets with 4, plus 2 silver and 3 bronze in the 12 weight classes. Cuban heavyweight Felix Savon won an unprecedented fifth straight world title.

Germany returned to the elite of amateur boxing with 10 medals (1 gold, 1 silver, 8 bronze), quite an improvement over the 2 bronzes it won in 1993.

Canoe/Kayak. The Hungarian team of Csaba Horvath and Gregory Kolonics won five titles (two in events on the 1996 Olympic program) in August's World Sprint Championships in Duisberg, Germany. The U.S. had only three finalists (of 108 places) in the 12 Olympic-program events, with the top finish a seventh by Mike Harbold in the single kayak 1,000.

The U.S. did significantly better in the World Whitewater Championships in England, where David Hearn won the single canoe and Scott Shipley was second in the single kayak.

Cycling. Miguel Induráin's historic fifth consecutive victory in the Tour de France was overshadowed by the tragic events of the 15th stage on July 18, when Italy's Fabio Casartelli, 24, died after hitting his helmetless head on the road when he crashed during a steep descent. Casartelli, the 1992 Olympic road race champion, was the third rider to die in the 93 years of the Tour, but the first since England's Tom Simpson in 1967.

The day after Casartelli's death, the riders turned the 16th stage into what the French sports paper, *L'Equipe*, headlined a "Tour of Dignity." The stage was contested at a funereal pace, and, near its end, Casartelli's Motorola teammates were allowed to take the lead and finish together in silent tribute.

There was another such tribute a day later, when Motorola rider Lance Armstrong pointed repeatedly toward the skies and blew kisses heavenward as he completed a winning 17-mile breakaway in the 18th stage. Armstrong would go on to complete the race for the first time in three tries, taking 36th.

Induráin, meanwhile, became the fourth man to win five Tours (joining Jacques Anquetil of France, Eddy Merckx of Belgium and Bernard Hinault of France) but the first to win five straight.

The 31-year-old Spaniard built his 4 minute, 35-second final margin over Alex Zulle of Switzerland by winning both individual time trials and was the dominant

Salt Lake City To Host 2002 Winter Games

Ravell Call/The Deseret News

Salt Lake City citizens rejoice on June 16, after hearing that the IOC had selected the capital of Utah to host the 2002 Winter Olympics.

Southeast of Salt Lake City, not far from the spot where, in 1847, Brigham Young told his bone-weary band of Mormons, "This is The Place," stands 9,026-foot-high Mount Olympus.

The peak, which is part of the Wasatch Range, was later named by Greek immigrants, who arrived in the 1860s to work on the nation's first transcontinental railroad system.

On June 16, 1995, after 30 years of climbing and four expeditions that fell short of the *summum*, Salt Lake City finally reached the top of sports' Mount Olympus. That was the day the International Olympic Committee, meeting in Budapest, Hungary, selected Utah's well-prepared capital city to host the 2002 Winter Olympics.

The technical superiority of Salt Lake's bid won 54 of the 89 votes on the first ballot, with Ostersund, Sweden and Sion, Switzerland tying for second at 14. Quebec City managed just seven votes.

It was the first time since Sapporo, Japan won the right to host the 1972 Winter Games that the IOC had chosen an Olympic host city on the first ballot.

The decision gave credibility to a revamped selection process that had been filled with political intrigue and favor-trading in the past. The voters obviously were swayed, as they should have been, by the report of the IOC's evaluation commission, which gave Salt Lake the only "excellent" rating of the finalists.

Salt Lake will be the sixth U.S. city to hold an Olympics— joining summer venues St. Louis (1904), Los Angeles (1932 and '84) and Atlanta (1996), and cold weather sites Lake Placid (1932 and '80) and Squaw Valley, Calif. (1960).

In 1970, Denver was chosen by the IOC to host the 1976 Winter Games but withdrew after Colorado voters rejected a 1972 bond issue that would have allocated $5 million to finance the effort.

The choice of Salt Lake City paid immediate dividends for the IOC, the U.S. Olympic Committee and 2000 Summer Games host Sydney, Australia, when NBC paid a stunning $1.27 billion for exclusive U.S. TV rights to both 2000 and 2002 (see page 561).

That broke down to $715 million for Sydney and $555 million for Salt Lake, approximately 40 percent more than each had budgeted for U.S. rights and a record for both Summer and Winter Games. The local organizing committee gets to keep 60 percent of that total.

It will also mean $127 million for the USOC, which gets 10 percent of U.S. rights. That should help alleviate fears that the USOC would need to make severe cuts in its next budget (1997 through 2000).

"We projected the difference in Salt Lake City's winning and losing at a $150 million swing in our budget for the next quadrennium," said USOC spokesman Mike Moran.

After narrowly losing to Nagano, Japan, in the 1991 bidding for the '98 Winter Games, Salt Lake City buckled down for what was likely its final try. The city overcame objections it was too bland, too boozeless and too Mormon-dominated by keeping a significant promise: that it would have all the major competition venues built by 1995.

Only a cover for the speedskating oval and a secondary ice arena must be added to what already is The Place.

force throughout the race, in which Bjarne Riis of Denmark was a surprising third.

Diving. To no one's surprise, China dominated the 4th FINA World Diving Cup in September at the new Olympic Aquatics Center at Georgia Tech. The Chinese fell two short of matching their previous sweep of all six individual events, although they did win nine of 12 medals.

The U.S. was shut out of the medals for the second straight time, leaving the Americans without a diving medal in Olympic-program events at major world competitions since 1992.

Doping. China's persistent disclaimers that no drug use was involved in their athletes' success began to wither in mid-November 1994 when the *Chicago Tribune* revealed that 1994 world swimming champion Yang Aihua had tested positive for steroids and several other Chinese women swimmers were being investigated as possible steroid positives.

Two weeks later, the Olympic Council of Asia announced 11 doping positives of Chinese athletes (7 swimmers, including another women's world champion, Lu Bin), at the 1994 Asian Games. All had taken the rarely-used steroid, dihydrotestosterone (DHT). That meant 13 Chinese swimmers had positive test results in 1993-94, while only seven swimmers from other nations had tested positive since the sport's first such result in 1972.

Gymnastics. Bela Karolyi's newest protégé, 13-year-old Dominique Moceanu (4-feet, 5 inches; 70 pounds) became the youngest national all-around champion in history at the 1995 meet in New Orleans. Moceanu beat 1993 champion Shannon Miller, 18, who was runnerup, and Dominique Dawes, who was fourth after having won all five events at the '94 nationals. Dawes, 18, retained her individual apparatus titles in floor exercise and uneven bars. On the men's side, John Roethlisberger won his fourth all-around title.

Without Miller, who dropped out with fatigue during compulsories, the U.S. women still placed second to Romania at the 1994 World Team Championships at Dortmund, Germany in November. China edged Russia for the men's title, its first since 1983. See the Updates chapter for results of the 1995 World Championships schedule for Oct. 1-10 in Sabae, Japan.

Marathons. The silver anniversary New York Marathon in November 1994 nearly had an ending worthy of Bonehead Merkle and Wrong Way Riegels. With seven-tenths of a mile left in the race, German Silva of Mexico made a wrong turn in Central Park, running 12 strides off course before spectators' expressions alerted him to the mistake.

Silva righted himself in time to win the race in 2 hours, 11 minutes, 21 seconds, two seconds faster than countryman Benjamin Paredes. In the women's race, Tegla Loroupe, 21, of Kenya turned her debut at the 26-mile, 385-yard distance into the first major marathon win by a black African woman with a time of 2:27:37. The entire event became a memorial to charismatic race founder Fred Lebow, who had died a month earlier of brain cancer at age 62

The 99th Boston Marathon, run in April 1995, was a day for a three-peat and a repeat. Cosmas Ndeti of Kenya (2:09:02) became the third man to win Boston three straight times, following Bill Rodgers (1978-80) and Clarence DeMar (1922-24). Uta Pippig of Germany took a second straight women's title (2:25:11), with Loroupe, bothered by dehydration, struggling home ninth.

In winning the '95 World Championships marathon, Spain's Martín Fíz became the rare athlete in recent years capable of winning both major championships and big-money invitationals. In the past two years, Fíz, 32, also has won the 1994 European Championships and the 1995 Rotterdam Marathon.

Pan American Games. Hemispheric inversion brought the XIIth Pan Am Games, a quadrennial summer event, to four Argentine cities in the middle of winter in North America. That meant the United States could not send most of its best athletes to the 34-sport, 42-country, 5,000-athlete festival.

While the U.S. ran away with the overall medal count (a record 424 to 238 for runner-up Cuba), it fared poorly in team sports.

A baseball team from St. John's University went 0-6; the men's basketball team, made up of minor league pros from the CBA, went 4-3, but won a silver medal (the U.S. hasn't won the Pan Am title since 1983); the men's soccer team arrived as defending champions and left went winless (0-3) for the first time since 1975 and failed to score a goal for the first time ever.

Ethiopia's **Haile Gebrselassie** raises his arms in victory on Aug. 16, after shattering the world record in the 5,000 meters by nearly 11 seconds at a meet in Zurich. Earlier in the year, Gebrselassie set a new world mark in the 10,000 and successfully defended his 5,000-meter title at the World Championships.

The big winner was host Argentina, which placed fourth in the overall medal standings, its best showing since 1963. The Argentines won gold in six of 13 team sports, including soccer, volleyball and basketball, and their successes were hailed by surprisingly large and joyous crowds.

The U.S. carried away a record 169 golds (a number inflated by added events), including 22 from a strong swimming team that set 11 Pan Am records. The star American swimmer was Angel Martino who won 4 golds (50-, 100-, and 400-meter free and 400 medley relay). U.S. women gymnasts swept their five events for the first time since 1963, with Shannon Miller taking the all-around, floor exercise and uneven bars.

Rowing. Ten countries won gold medals in the 14 Olympic-program events at the 1995 World Championships in Tampere, Finland, with Italy (3), Germany (2) and Canada (2) the only multiple winners. The U.S. women's eight won the only American gold.

Softball. The U.S. women's nine-year, 106-game winning streak ended in a 1-0 loss to China at August's pre-Olympic test competition, Superball '95, in Columbus, Ga. The U.S. came back to beat China 8-0 for the gold medal in the tournament that included the world's top teams.

Swimming. One of the year's presumed major events, the biennial Pan Pacific Games, gained in political substance but lost competitively when three of the Pan Pac four founder nations (U.S., Canada and Australia) voted to ban China because of its poor record on doping control. Only Japan dissented from the ban, based on the number of Chinese positives in 1993 and 1994 and strong circumstantial evidence it had a centrally organized doping program.

The U.S. (42 medals) and Australia (34) splashed into the void to dominate the watered-down test of Georgia Tech's Olympic Aquatics Center. The highlight was a world record of 3 minutes, 15.11 seconds in the 4x100-meter relay by the American team of David Fox, Joe Hudepohl, Jon Olsen and Gary Hall Jr. That broke the 7-year-old mark (3:16.53) set by the U.S. at the 1988 Olympics, which had become the second oldest record in men's swimming.

The oldest record fell a couple weeks later at the European Championships in Vienna, when Denis Pankratov of Russia won the 100-meter butterfly in 52.32 seconds, erasing the mark of 52.84 set by Pablo Morales of the U.S. in 1986. Pankratov, 21, a human Red October who has brought the submarine start method to the butterfly, also broke the 200-meter record with a 1:55.22 earlier at Canet, France, earlier in the summer. That trimmed :00.47 from the mark set by Melvin Stewart of the U.S. in 1991.

Pankratov and Germany's Franziska Van Almsick were the stars of the Europeans. Van Almsick won five gold medals, but blew a chance to equal her record 1993 haul of six when she missed the 200-meter final by one place. That was an eerie rerun of what Van Almsick had done in the 1994 World Championships. In that meet, compliant teammate Dagmar Hase was given financial incentive to relinquish her spot in the final, where Van Almsick won with a world-record time.

How had the mighty fallen? In 1993, Chinese women had 101 placings— including 7 firsts— among the world's top 25 in the 13 individual events on the Olympic program. Two years later, Chinese women had just 9 such placings, the best a second by world champion Liu Limin in the 100 butterfly.

Elsewhere, Janet Evans, winner of four Olympic gold medals, lost an 800-meter race for the first time since 1987, to 15-year-old Brooke Bennett at the U.S. Championships in Pasadena. Evans, who needed three wins to tie Tracy Caulkins' record of 48 U.S. titles, was shut out, also losing the 400 (second to Bennett) and 1,500 free (fifth to Bennett). That broke a streak of 14 straight national meets in which Evans had won at least one title.

Track & Field. A season climaxed by the 5th World Championships began to take its eventual shape in late winter, when Michael Johnson of the U.S. twice lowered the indoor world record for the 400 meters (final mark: 44.63 seconds). Johnson, of Dallas, would go on to extend his six-year winning streak in the 400 to 49 races; go unbeaten in 11 finals at 200; become the first U.S. man since 1899 to win both those races at the national championships; and the first to win both in a major global competition.

For all that, Johnson likely will lose track's Athlete of the Year honors to Haile Gebrselassie, 23, of Ethiopia, who set world records at both the 10,000 and 5,000 meters.

On June 5 in Hengelo, Holland, Gebrselassie lowered the world mark in the 10,000 by nearly nine seconds to 26:52.23. Then,

on Aug. 16 in Zurich, he took 10.35 seconds off the 5,000 world record with a clocking of 12:44.95. That was the biggest drop in the 5,000 since 1942. In between, he successively defended his 10,000-meter world title in Göteborg with a meet record time of 27:12.95.

Other world record-setters (in Olympic events) included the following: Algeria's Noureddine Morceli, taking his own mark in the 1,500 down to 3:27.37; Kenya's Moses Kiptanui, breaking his own mark and the 8-minute barrier in the 3,000 steeplechase (7:59.18); Great Britain's Jonathan Edwards, rewriting the triple jump mark three times, the first breaking the 10-year-old mark set by Willie Banks of the U.S., the last breaking the 60-foot barrier (60 feet, ¼ inch); and Ukraine's Inessa Kravets in the women's triple jump (50-10 ¼).

Left hanging more than two months after it took place was the apparent world record (29 feet, 4 ¾ inches) by Cuban long jumper Ivan Pedroso in the 6,726-foot altitude of Sestriere, Italy. The Italian Track Federation has refused to submit Pedroso's record for ratification because of irregularities in the wind-gauge reading, leaving Mike Powell's 1991 mark of 29-4 ½ as the official world record.

Weightlifting. With a team of mainly ethnic Turks from Bulgaria, Turkey (8) led the gold-medal tally at the 1994 World Championships in Istanbul. The Turks' national hero, two-time Olympic champion Naim Suleymanoglu (repatriated from Bulgaria in 1987), was best on all six lifts in the 68-kilogram class. On the women's side, China entered six women in five weight classes and won 13 of 15 available gold medals with 11 world records.

Wrestling. Showing what the home-mat advantage might be worth next year in the Olympics, the U.S. won four gold medals and its second team title in three years at the 1995 World Championships in Atlanta— the first time the event has been in the U.S. since 1979.

U.S. winners included 34-year-old Bruce Baumgartner, who won his third world title, Terry Brands and Kevin Jackson, who each won their second, and Kurt Angle, who won for the first time.

Iran, sending only its second team in any sport to the U.S. since 1978, was second in the team total. ❐

THE 1996 INFORMATION PLEASE SPORTS ALMANAC

INT'L SPORTS STATISTICS

THE SEASON IN REVIEW
1994-1995
CHAMPIONS • RECORDS

SEC A
PAGE 617

TRACK & FIELD

1995 IAAF World Championships

The 5th IAAF World Championships in Athletics at Ullevi Stadium in Göteborg, Sweden (Aug. 5-13). Note that (WR) indicates a world record, (AR) an American record and (CR) a championship meet record.

Final Medal Standings

Unofficial point totals based on three points for every gold medal, two for each silver and one for each bronze.

		G	S	B	Total	Pts			G	S	B	Total	Pts
1	United States	12	2	5	19	45	22	Australia	0	1	1	2	3
2	Russia	1	4	7	12	18		Burundi	0	1	1	2	3
3	Belarus	2	3	2	7	14		Czech Republic	1	0	0	1	3
4	Jamaica	1	4	2	7	13		Denmark	1	0	0	1	3
5	Germany	2	2	2	6	12		Ireland	1	0	0	1	3
	Italy	2	2	2	6	12		Tajikistan	1	0	0	1	3
7	Kenya	2	1	3	6	11		Syria	1	0	0	1	3
8	Great Britain	1	3	1	5	10	29	Hungary	0	0	2	2	2
	Cuba	2	2	0	4	10		Poland	0	0	2	2	2
10	Canada	2	1	1	4	9		Bermuda	0	1	0	1	2
	Portugal	2	1	1	4	9		China	0	1	0	1	2
12	Morocco	0	3	1	4	7		Kazakhstan	0	1	0	1	2
	Ukraine	2	0	1	3	7		Mexico	0	1	0	1	2
14	Bulgaria	1	1	1	3	6		Namibia	0	1	0	1	2
	Finland	1	1	1	3	6		Surinam	0	1	0	1	2
	Algeria	2	0	0	2	6		Zambia	0	1	0	1	2
17	France	1	0	2	3	5	38	Brazil	0	0	1	1	1
	Bahamas	1	1	0	2	5		Dominica	0	0	1	1	1
	Ethiopia	1	1	0	2	5		Nigeria	0	0	1	1	1
	Spain	1	1	0	2	5		Norway	0	0	1	1	1
21	Romania	0	2	0	2	4		Saudi Arabia	0	0	1	1	1
								Trinidad & Tobago	0	0	1	1	1
								TOTALS	44	44	44	132	264

MEN

Three medals: Michael Johnson, USA (3-0-0). **Two medals:** Donovan Bailey, CAN (2-0-0); Butch Reynolds, USA (1-1-0); Bruny Surin, CAN (1-1-0), Greg Haughton, JAM (0-1-1).

100 meters

		Time
1	Donovan Bailey, CAN	9.97
2	Bruny Surin, CAN	10.03
3	Ato Boldon, T&T	10.03

Top USA finalist: 5th— Mike Marsh (10.10).

200 meters

		Time	
1	Michael Johnson, USA	19.79	CR
2	Frank Fredericks, NAB	20.12	
3	Jeff Williams, USA	20.18	

400 meters

		Time	
1	Michael Johnson, USA	43.39	CR
2	Butch Reynolds, USA	44.22	
3	Greg Haughton, JAM	44.56	

Other Top 10 USA: 5th— Darnell Hall (44.83).

800 meters

		Time
1	Wilson Kipketer, DEN	1:45.08
2	Arthemon Hatungimana, BUR	1:45.64
3	Vebjorn Rodal, NOR	1:45.68

Top 10 USA: 5th— Brandon Rock (1:46.42); 6th— Jose Parrilla (1:46.44); 8th— Mark Everett (1:53.12).

1500 meters

		Time
1	Noureddine Morceli, ALG	3:33.73
2	Hicham El Guerrouj, MOR	3:35.28
3	Venuste Niyongabo, BUR	3:35.56

Top 10 USA: 10th— Paul McMullen (3:38.23).

5000 meters

		Time
1	Ismael Kirui, KEN	13:16.77
2	Khalid Boulami, MOR	13:17.15
3	Shem Kororia, KEN	13:17.59

Top 10 USA: 7th— Bob Kennedy (13:32.10).

1995 World Track & Field Championships (Cont.)

MEN

10,000 meters

	Time	
1 Haile Gebrselassie, ETH	27:12.95	CR
2 Khalid Skah, MOR	27:14.53	
3 Paul Tergat, KEN	27:14.70	

Top 10 USA: 9th— Todd Williams (27:52.87).

Marathon

	Time
1 Martin Fíz, SPA	2:11:41
2 Dionisio Ceron, MEX	2:12:13
3 Luiz Dos Santos, BRA	2:12:49

Top 10 USA: 10th— Steve Plasencia (2:16:56).

4x100-meter Relay

	Time
1 Canada	38.31
2 Australia	38.50
3 Italy	39.07

CAN— Robert Esmie, Glenroy Gilbert, Bruny Surin, Donovan Bailey; **AUS**— Henderson, Jackson, Brimacombe, March; **ITA**— Puggioni, Madonia, Cipolloni, Floris.
Note: USA was disqualified in first round on failed baton exchange.

4x400-meter Relay

	Time
1 United States	2:57.32
2 Jamaica	2:59.88
3 Nigeria	3:03.18

USA— Marlon Ramsey, Derek Mills, Butch Reynolds, Michael Johnson; **JAM**— McDonald, Clarke, McFarlane, Haughton; **NGR**— Ekpeyong, Adejuyigbe, Monye, Bada.

110-meter Hurdles

	Time
1 Allen Johnson, USA	13.00
2 Tony Jarrett, GBR	13.04
3 Roger Kingdom, USA	13.19

Other Top 8 USA: 4th— Jack Pierce (13.27).

400-meter Hurdles

	Time
1 Derrick Adkins, USA	47.98
2 Samuel Matete, ZAM	48.03
3 Stephane Diagana, FRA	48.14

3000-meter Steeplechase

	Time	
1 Moses Kiptanui, KEN	8:04.16	CR
2 Christopher Koskei, KEN	8:09.30	
3 Sa'ad Shaddad Al-Asmari, SAU	8:12.95	

20-kilometer Walk

	Time
1 Michele Didoni, ITA	1:19:59
2 Valentin Massana, SPA	1:20:23
3 Yevgeny Misyulya, BLR	1:20:48

50-kilometer Walk

	Time
1 Valentin Kononen, FIN	3:43:42
2 Giovanni Perricelli, ITA	3:45:11
3 Robert Korzeniowski, POL	3:45:57

High Jump

	Height
1 Troy Kemp, BAH	7- 9¼
2 Javier Sotomayor, CUB	7- 9¼
3 Artur Partyka, POL	7- 8½

Top 10 USA: 7th— Tony Barton (7-6).

Pole Vault

	Height
1 Sergey Bubka, UKR	19- 5
2 Maksim Tarasov, RUS	19- 2¾
3 Jean Galfione, FRA	19- 2¾

Top 10 USA: 6th— Scott Huffman (18-8¼); 8th— Dean Starkey (18-4½).

Long Jump

	Distance
1 Ivan Pedroso, CUB	28- 6½
2 James Beckford, JAM	27- 2¾
3 Mike Powell, USA	27- 2½

Triple Jump

	Distance	
1 Jonathan Edwards, GBR	60- 0¼	WR
2 Brian Wellman, BER	57- 9¾	
3 Jerome Romain, DOM	57- 8½	

Top 10 USA: 7th— Mike Conley (55-7¾).

Shot Put

	Distance
1 John Godina, USA	70- 5¼
2 Mika Halvari, FIN	68- 8
3 Randy Barnes, USA	66-11½

Other Top 10 USA: 5th— Brent Noon (66-0½).

Discus

	Distance	
1 Lars Riedel, GER	225- 7	CR
2 Vladimir Dubrovshchik, BLR	216- 6	
3 Vasiliy Kaptyukh, BLR	216- 2	

Top 10 USA: 10th— John Godina (199-7).

Hammer Throw

	Distance
1 Andrey Abduvaliyev, TAJ	267- 7
2 Igor Astapkovich, BLR	266- 1
3 Tibor Gecsek, HUN	265- 8

Top 10 USA: 5th— Lance Deal (258-1).

Javelin

	Distance
1 Jan Zelezny, CZE	293-11
2 Steve Backley, GBR	283- 2
3 Boris Henry, GER	282- 5

Decathlon

(Ten events in two days: DAY 1— 100 meters, 400 meters, Long Jump, Shot Put, High Jump; DAY 2— 110m Hurdles, Discus, Pole Vault, Javelin, 1,500 meters).

	Points
1 Dan O'Brien, USA	8,695
2 Eduard Hamalainen, BLR	8,498
3 Mike Smith, CAN	8,419

Other Top 10 USA: 8th— Chris Huffins (8,193 pts).

Mike Powell/Allsport

Gwen Torrence of the United States (right) beats out archrival **Merlene Ottey** of Jamaica to win the women's 4x100-meter relay at the World Track & Field Championships in Göteborg, Sweden.

WOMEN

Three medals: Merlene Ottey, JAM (1-2-0). **Two medals:** Gwen Torrence, USA (2-0-0); Fernanda Ribeiro, POR (1-1-0), Jearl Miles, USA (1-0-1); Kelly Holmes, GBR (0-1-1), Irina Privalova, RUS (0-1-1).

100 meters

		Time
1	Gwen Torrence, USA	10.85
2	Merlene Ottey, JAM	10.94
3	Irina Privalova, RUS	10.96

Other Top 10 USA: 4th— Carlette Guidry (11.07).

200 meters

		Time
1	Merlene Ottey, JAM	22.12
2	Irina Privalova, RUS	22.12
3	Galina Malchugina, RUS	22.37

Disqualified: unofficial winner Gwen Torrence, USA (21.77) for lane violation.

400 meters

		Time
1	Marie-José Pérec, FRA	49.28
2	Pauline Davis, BAH	49.96
3	Jearl Miles, USA	50.00

Other Top 10 USA: 7th— Maicel Malone (50.99).

800 meters

		Time
1	Ana Quirot, CUB	1:56.11
2	Letitia Vriesde, SUR	1:56.68
3	Kelly Holmes, GBR	1:56.95

Top 10 USA: Meredith Rainey (1:58.20).

1500 meters

		Time
1	Hassiba Boulmerka, ALG	4:02.42
2	Kelly Holmes, GBR	4:03.04
3	Carla Sacramento, POR	4:03.79

Top 10 USA: 7th— Ruth Wysocki (4:07.08).

5000 meters
(3000-meter race from 1983-93)

		Time	
1	Sonia O'Sullivan, IRE	14:46.47	CR
2	Fernanda Ribeiro, POR	14:48.54	
3	Zohra Ouaziz, MOR	14:53.77	

10,000 meters

		Time
1	Fernanda Ribeiro, POR	31:04.99
2	Derartu Tulu, ETH	31:08.10
3	Tecla Lorupe, KEN	31:17.66

Best USA: 12th— Lynn Jennings (32:12.82).

Marathon

		Time
1	Manuela Machado, POR	2:25:39
2	Anuta Catuna, ROM	2:26:25
3	Ornella Ferrara, ITA	2:30:11

Top 10 USA: 7th— Linda Somers (2:32:12).

Note: The day after the race it was revealed that the course was 400 meters too short (runners had been waved out of the stadium one lap too early).

4x100-meter Relay

		Time
1	United States	42.12
2	Jamaica	42.25
3	Germany	43.01

USA— Celena Monde-Milne, Carlette Guidry, Chryste Gaines, Gwen Torrence; **JAM**— Duhaney, Cuthbert, McDonald, Ottey; **GER**— Paschke, Lichtenhagen, Knoll, Becker.

4x400-meter Relay

		Time
1	United States	3:22.39
2	Russia	3:23.98
3	Australia	3:25.88

USA— Kim Graham, Rochelle Stevens, Camara Jones, Jearl Miles; **RUS**— Chebykina, Goncharenko, Sotnikova, Andreyeva; **AUS**— Naylor, Poetschka, Gainsford, Freeman.

Disqualified: unofficial 2nd place Jamaica (3:23.76) for lane violation.

100-meter Hurdles

		Time
1	Gail Devers, USA	12.68
2	Olga Shishigina, KAZ	12.80
3	Yuliya Graudyn, RUS	12.85

1995 World Track & Field Championships (Cont.)

WOMEN

400-meter Hurdles

		Time	
1	Kim Batten, USA	52.61	WR
2	Tonja Buford, USA	52.62	
3	Deon Hemmings, JAM	53.48	

10-kilometer Walk

		Time	
1	Irina Stankina, RUS	42:13	CR
2	Elisabetta Perrone, ITA	42:16	
3	Yelena Nikolayeva, RUS	42:20	

Best USA: 15th— Michelle Rohl (44.17, AR).

High Jump

		Height
1	Stefka Kostadinova, BUL	6- 7
2	Alina Astafei, GER	6- 6¼
3	Inga Babakova, UKR	6- 6¼

Top 10 USA: tie for 8th— Amy Acuff (6-4).

Long Jump

		Distance
1	Fiona May, ITA	22-10¾
2	Niurka Montalvo, CUB	22- 6¼
3	Irina Mushailova, RUS	22- 5

Top 10 USA: 6th— Jackie Joyner-Kersee (22-1½).
Note: defender Heike Drechsler of Germany was 9th (21-9½).

Triple Jump

		Distance	
1	Inessa Kravets, UKR	50-10¼	WR
2	Iva Prandzheba, BUL	49- 9¾	
3	Anna Biryukova, RUS	49- 5¾	

Shot Put

		Distance
1	Astrid Kumbernuss, GER	69- 7½
2	Huang Zhihong, CHN	65- 9
3	Svetla Mitkova, BUL	64- 2¼

Top 10 USA: 7th— Ramona Pagel (61-8½); 9th— Connie Price-Smith (61-5).

Discus

		Distance
1	Ellina Zvereva, BLR	225- 2
2	Ilke Wyludda, GER	220- 6
3	Olga Chernyavskaya, RUS	219- 4

Javelin

		Distance
1	Natalya Shikolenko, BLR	221- 8
2	Felicia Tilea, ROM	214- 0
3	Mikaela Ingberg, FIN	213- 9

Heptathlon

(Seven events in two days: DAY 1— 100m H, HJ, Shot, 200m; DAY 2— LJ, Javelin, 800m.)

		Points
1	Ghada Shouaa, SYR	6,651
2	Svetlana Moskalets, RUS	6,575
3	Rita Inancsi, HUN	6,522

Top 10 USA: 5th— Kym Carter (6,329); 8th— Dedee Nathan (6,258); 10— Kelly Blair (6,229).

Note: Two-time world champ Jackie Joyner-Kersee of the U.S. pulled out of event after finishing 6th in long jump.

World Outdoor Records Set in 1995

World outdoor records set or equaled between Oct. 1, 1994 and Sept. 15, 1995; (p) indicates record is pending.

MEN

Event		Record	Old Mark	Former Holder
1,500 meters	**Noureddine Morceli**, ALG	3:27.37	3:28.56	Noureddine Morceli, ALG (1992)
2,000 meters	**Noureddine Morceli**, ALG	4:47.88	4:50.81	Said Aouita, MOR (1987)
5,000 meters	**Moses Kiptanui**, KEN	12:55.30	12:56.96	Haile Gebrselassie, ETH (1994)
5,000 meters	**Haile Gebrselassie**, ETH	12:44.39p	12:55.30	Moses Kiptanui, KEN (1995)
10,000 meters	**Haile Gebrselassie**, ETH	26:43.53	26:52.23	William Sigei, KEN (1994)
3,000m Steeple	**Moses Kiptanui**, KEN	7:59.18p	8:02.08	Moses Kiptanui, KEN (1992)
Long Jump	**Ivan Pedroso**, CUB	29- 4¾*	29- 4½	Mike Powell, USA (1991)
Triple Jump	**Jonathan Edwards**, GBR	59- 0	58-11½	Willie Banks, USA (1985)
Triple Jump	**Jonathan Edwards**, GBR	59- 7	59- 0	Jonathan Edwards, GBR (1995)
Triple Jump	**Jonathan Edwards**, GBR	60- 0¼p	59- 7	Jonathan Edwards, GBR (1995)

*Apparent world record disallowed because of interference with wind gauge at altitude.

WOMEN

Event		Record	Old Mark	Former Holder
1,000 meters	**Maria Mutola**, MOZ	2:29.34	2:30.67	Christine Wachtel, E. Ger (1990)
5,000 meters	**Fernanda Ribiero**, POR	14:36.45p	14:37.33	Ingrid Kristiansen, NOR (1986)
400m Hurdles	**Kim Batten**, USA	52.61p	52.74	Sally Gunnell, GBR (1993)
Pole Vault	**Daniela Bartova**, CZE	13- 9¾p	13- 9¼	Daniela Bartova, CZE (1995)
Triple Jump	**Inessa Kravets**, UKR	50-10¼p	49- 6¼	Ann Biryukova, RUS (1993)
Hammer Throw	**Olga Kuzenkova**, RUS	223- 7p	220-11	Svetla Sudak, BLR (1994)
Hammer Throw	**Olga Kuzenkova**, RUS	223- 7p	223- 7	Olga Kuzenkova, RUS (1995)

Note: The women's pole vault record was broken a dozen times in 1995— eight times by Daniela Bartova of the Czech Republic and once each by Andrea Muller of Germany and Cai Weiyan, Zhong Guiqing and Sun Caiyun of China. Bartova's current mark was set on Aug. 22, 1995.

1995 IAAF Mobil Grand Prix Final

The final meeting of the International Amateur Athletic Federation's Outdoor Grand Prix season, which includes the world's 16 leading outdoor invitational meets. Athletes earn points throughout the season with the leading point winners invited to the Grand Prix Final. The 1995 final was held Sept. 9, 1995 at Louis II Stadium in Monte Carlo.

MEN

Event		Time	Event		Hgt/Dist
200m	Michael Johnson, USA	19.93	Pole Vault	Okkert Brits, SAF	19- 6½
800m	Benson Koech, KEN	1:45.27	Long Jump	Ivan Pedroso, CUB	27-10¼
3000m	Haile Gebrselassie, ETH	7:35.90	Discus	Dmitri Shevchenko, RUS	222-11
3000m Steeple	Moses Kiptanui, KEN	8:02.45	Javelin	Jan Zelezny, CZH	302- 9
110m Hurdles	Mark Crear, USA	13.07			

WOMEN

Event		Time	Event		Hgt/Dist
200m	Gwen Torrence, USA	22.20	High Jump	Inga Babakova, UKR	6- 8
800m	Maria Mutola, MOZ	1:55.72	Triple Jump	Anna Biryukova, RUS	49- 2¼
3000m	Sonia O'Sullivan, IRE	8:39.94	Shot Put	Astrid Kumberness, GER	66- 3¼
400m Hurdles	Kim Batten, USA	53.49			

Final Top 5 Standings

Overall Men's and Women's winners receive $130,000 (US) each; all ties broken by complex Grand Prix scoring system.

MEN

1. Moses Kiptanui, KEN (84 points); 2. Jan Zelezny, CZH (72 pts); 3. Mark Crear, USA (72 pts); 4. Michael Johnson, USA (72 pts); 5. Ivan Pedroso, CUB (72 pts).

WOMEN

1. Maria Mutola, MOZ (78 points); 2. Anna Biryukova, RUS (72 pts); 3. Gwen Torrence, USA (72 pts); 4. Sonia O'Sullivan, IRE (72 pts); 5. Astrid Kumberness, GER (72 pts).

1995 IAAF World Indoor Championships

The 5th IAAF World Indoor Championships at Barcelona, Spain (Mar. 10-12). Note that (WR) indicates world record.

Final Medal Standings

The unofficial point totals are based on three points for every gold medal, two for each silver and one for each bronze.

	G	S	B	Total	Pts		G	S	B	Total	Pts
1 United States	4	4	7	15	27	9 Canada	1	0	1	2	4
2 Russia	6	2	4	12	26	France	1	0	1	2	4
3 Cuba	3	1	0	4	11	Morocco	1	0	1	2	4
4 Germany	1	2	3	6	10	Kazakhstan	0	2	0	2	4
5 Jamaica	2	1	0	3	7	Spain	0	2	0	2	4
6 Bermuda	2	0	0	2	6	14 Bulgaria	0	1	1	2	3
7 Czech Republic	0	2	1	3	5	Great Britain	0	1	1	2	3
Italy	1	1	0	2	5	Slovenia	0	1	1	2	3
						Sweden	0	1	1	2	3

One gold medal (3 pts): Australia, Finland, Mozambique, Norway, Romania and Ukraine. **One silver medal** (2 pts): Bahamas, Greece, Kenya, Nigeria and Portugal. **One bronze medal** (1 pt): Chile, China, Japan, South Africa, Surinam and Yugoslavia.

MEN

Event		Time
60m	Bruny Surin, CAN	6.46
200m	Geir Moen, NOR	20.58
400m	Darnell Hall, USA	46.17
800m	Clive Terrelonge, JAM	1:47.30
1500m	Hichem El Guerrouj, MOR	3:44.54
3000m	Gennaro Di Napoli, ITA	7:50.89
60m H	Allen Johnson, USA	7.39
4x400m	USA (Rod Tolbert, Calvin Davis, Todd Long, Frankie Atwater)	3:07.37

Event		Hgt/Dist
High Jump	Javier Sotomayor, CUB	7- 9¾
Pole Vault	Sergey Bubka, UKR	19- 4¼
Long Jump	Ivan Pedroso, CUB	27-11
Triple Jump	Brian Wellman, BER	58- 1¾
Shot Put	Mika Halvari, FIN	68- 0 ½
Heptathlon	Christian Plaziat, FRA	6,246 pts

Other USA medalists: 1500m— Erik Nedeau (3rd, 3:44.91); **60m H—** Courtney Hawkins (2nd, 7.41); **HJ—** Tony Barton (3rd, 7-7¼); **LJ—** Erik Walder (3rd, 26-8½); **Shot—** C.J. Hunter (2nd, 67-6¼).

WOMEN

Event		Time
60m	Merlene Ottey, JAM	6.97
200m	Melina Gainsford, AUS	22.64
400m	Irina Privalova, RUS	50.23
800m	Maria Mutola, MOZ	1:57.62
1500m	Regina Jacobs, USA	4:12.61
3000m	Gabriela Szabo, ROM	8:54.50
60m H	Aliuska Lopez, CUB	7.92
4x400m	Russia (Chebykina, Rusina, Kulikova, Goncharenko)	3:29.29

Event		Hgt/Dist	
High Jump	Alina Astafei, GER	6- 7	
Long Jump	Lyudmila Galkina, RUS	22- 9¾	
Triple Jump	Yolanda Chen, RUS	49- 3¾	WR
Shot Put	Larisa Peleshenko, RUS	65- 4¾	
Pentathlon	Svetlana Moskalets, RUS	4,834 pts	

Other USA medalists: 60m— Carlette Guidry (3rd, 7.11); **3000m—** Lynn Jennings (2nd, 8:55.23) and Joan Nesbit (3rd, 8:56.08); **4x400m relay—** Pasha, Dooley, Graham and Harris (3rd, 3:31.43); **Shot—** Connie Price-Smith (3rd, 62-8¾); **Pentathlon—** Kym Carter (2nd, 4632 pts, AR)

Track & Field (Cont.)
World, Olympic and American Records
As of Sept. 15, 1995

World outdoor records officially recognized by the International Amateur Athletics Federation (IAAF); (p) indicates record is pending.

MEN
Running

Event		Time		Date Set	Location
100 meters:	**World**	9.85	**Leroy Burrell**, USA	July 6, 1994	Lausanne, SWI
	Olympic	9.92	Carl Lewis, USA	Sept. 24, 1988	Seoul
	American	9.85	Burrell (same as World)	—	—
200 meters:	**World**	19.72	**Pietro Mennea**, Italy	Sept. 12, 1979	Mexico City
	Olympic	19.75	Joe DeLoach, USA	Sept. 28, 1988	Seoul
	American	19.73	Mike Marsh	Aug. 5, 1992	Barcelona
400 meters:	**World**	43.29	**Butch Reynolds**, USA	Aug. 17, 1988	Zurich
	Olympic	43.50	Quincy Watts, USA	Aug. 5, 1992	Barcelona
	American	43.29	Reynolds (same as World)	—	—
800 meters:	**World**	1:41.73	**Sebastian Coe**, Great Britain	June 10, 1981	Florence
	Olympic	1:43.00	Joaquim Cruz, Brazil	Aug. 6, 1984	Los Angeles
	American	1:42.60	Johnny Gray	Aug. 28, 1985	Koblenz, W. Ger.
1000 meters:	**World**	2:12.18	**Sebastian Coe**, Great Britain	July 11, 1981	Oslo
	Olympic		Not an event		
	American	2:13.9	Rick Wohlhuter	July 30, 1974	Oslo
1500 meters:	**World**	3:27.37	**Noureddine Morceli**, Algeria	July 12, 1995	Nice, FRA
	Olympic	3:32.53	Sebastian Coe, Great Britain	Aug. 11, 1984	Los Angeles
	American	3:29.77	Sydney Maree	Aug. 25, 1985	Cologne
Mile:	**World**	3:44.39	**Noureddine Morceli**, Algeria	Sept. 5, 1993	Rieti, ITA
	Olympic		Not an event		
	American	3:47.69	Steve Scott	July 7, 1982	Oslo
2000 meters:	**World**	4:47.88	**Noureddine Morceli**, Algeria	July 3, 1995	Paris
	Olympic		Not an event		
	American	4:52.44	Jim Spivey	Sept. 15, 1987	Lausanne
3000 meters:	**World**	7:28.96	**Noureddine Morceli**, Algeria	Aug. 2, 1994	Monte Carlo
	Olympic		Not an event		
	American	7:35.33	Bob Kennedy	July 18, 1994	Nice, FRA
5000 meters:	**World**	12:44.39p	**Haile Gebrselassie**, Ethiopia	Aug. 16, 1995	Zurich
	Olympic	13:05.59	Said Aouita, Morocco	Aug. 11, 1984	Los Angeles
	American	13:01.15	Sydney Maree	July 27, 1985	Oslo
10,000 meters:	**World**	26:43.53	**Haile Gebrselassie**, Ethiopia	June 5, 1995	Hengelo, HOL
	Olympic	27:21.46	Brahim Boutaib, Morocco	Sept. 26, 1988	Seoul
	American	27:20.56	Mark Nenow	Sept. 5, 1986	Brussels
20,000 meters:	**World**	56:55.6	**Arturo Barrios**, Mexico	Mar. 30, 1991	La Fleche, FRA
	Olympic		Not an event		
	American	58:15.0	Bill Rodgers	Aug. 9, 1977	Boston
Marathon:	**World**	2:06:50	**Belayneh Densimo**, Ethiopia	Apr. 17, 1988	Rotterdam
	Olympic	2:09:21	Carlos Lopes, Portugal	Aug. 12, 1984	Los Angeles
	American	2:10:04	Pat Petersen	Apr. 23, 1989	London
		2:08:52*	Alberto Salazar	Apr. 19, 1982	Boston

Note: The **Mile** run is 1,609.344 meters and the **Marathon** is 42,194.988 meters (26 miles, 385 yards).
*Former American record no longer officially recognized.

Walking

Event		Time		Date Set	Location
20 km:	**World**	1:17:25.5	**Bernardo Segura**, Mexico	May 7, 1994	Fana, NOR
	Olympic	1:19:57	Jozef Pribilinec, Czechoslovakia	Sept. 23, 1988	Seoul
	American	1:24:26.9	Allen James	May 7, 1994	Fana, NOR
50 km:	**World**	3:41:28.2	**Rene Piller**, France	May 7, 1994	Fana, NOR
	Olympic	3:38:29	Vyacheslav Ivanenko, USSR	Sept. 30, 1988	Seoul
	American	4:04:23.8	Herm Nelson	Oct. 29, 1989	Seattle

Hurdles

Event		Time		Date Set	Location
110 meters:	**World**	12.91	**Colin Jackson**, Great Britain	Aug. 20, 1993	Stuttgart
	Olympic	12.98	Roger Kingdom, USA	Sept. 28, 1988	Seoul
	American	12.92	Roger Kingdom	Aug. 16, 1989	Zurich
400 meters:	**World**	46.78	**Kevin Young**, USA	Aug. 6, 1992	Barcelona
	Olympic	46.78	Young (same as World)	—	—
	American	46.78	Young (same as World)	—	—

Note: The hurdles at 110 meters are 3 feet, 6 inches high and the hurdles at 400 meters are 3 feet. There are 10 hurdles in both races.

Steeplechase

Event		Time		Date Set	Location
3000 meters:	**World**	7:59.18p	**Moses Kiptanui**, Kenya	Aug. 18, 1995	Zurich
	Olympic	8:05.51	Julius Kariuki, Kenya	Sept. 30, 1988	Seoul
	American	8:09.17	Henry Marsh	Aug. 28, 1985	Koblenz

Note: A steeplechase course consists of 28 hurdles (3 feet high) and seven water jumps (12 feet long).

Relays

Event		Time		Date Set	Location
4 x 100m:	**World**	37.40	**USA** (Marsh, Burrell, Mitchell, C.Lewis)	Aug. 8, 1992	Barcelona
		37.40	**USA** (Drummond, Cason, Mitchell, Burrell)	Aug. 21, 1993	Stuttgart
	Olympic	37.40	USA (same as World)	—	—
	American	37.40	USA (same as World)	—	—
4 x 200m:	**World**	1:18.68	**USA** (Marsh, Burrell, Heard, C.Lewis)	Apr. 17, 1994	Walnut, Calif.
	Olympic		Not an event	—	—
	American	1:19.11	USA (same as World)	—	—
4 x 400m:	**World**	2:54.29	**USA** (Valmon, Watts, Reynolds, Johnson)	Aug. 22, 1993	Stuttgart
		2:55.74	USA (Valmon, Watts, Johnson, S.Lewis)	Aug. 8, 1992	Barcelona
	American	2:54.29	USA (same as World)	—	—
4 x 800m:	**World**	7:03.89	**Great Britain** (Elliott, Cook, Cram, Coe)	Aug. 30, 1982	London
	Olympic		Not an event	—	—
	American	7:06.5	SMTC (J.Robinson, Mack, E.Jones, Gray)	Apr. 26, 1986	Walnut, Calif.
4 x 1500m:	**World**	14:38.8	**West Germany** (Wessinghage, Hudak, Lederer, Fleschen)	Aug. 17, 1977	Cologne
	Olympic		Not an event	—	—
	American	14:46.3	USA (Aldredge, Clifford, Harbour, Duits)	June 24, 1979	Bourges, FRA

Field Events

Event		Mark		Date Set	Location
High Jump:	**World**	8- 0½	**Javier Sotomayor**, Cuba	July 27, 1993	Salamanca, SPA
	Olympic	7- 9¾	Gennady Avdeyenko, USSR	Sept. 25, 1988	Seoul
	American	7-10½	Charles Austin	Aug. 7, 1991	Zurich
Pole Vault:	**World**	20- 1¾	**Sergey Bubka**, Ukraine	July 31, 1994	Sestriere, ITA
	Olympic	19- 4¼	Sergey Bubka, USSR	Sept. 28, 1988	Seoul
	American	19- 7	Scott Huffman	June 18, 1994	Knoxville, Tenn.
Long Jump:	**World**	29- 4¾*	**Ivan Pedroso**, CUB	July 29, 1995	Sestriere, ITA
		29- 4½	**Mike Powell**, USA	Aug. 30, 1991	Tokyo
	Olympic	29- 2½	Bob Beamon, USA	Oct. 18, 1968	Mexico City
	American	29- 4½	Powell (same as World)	—	—
Triple Jump:	**World**	60- 0¼	**Jonathan Edwards**, GBR	Aug. 7, 1995	Göteborg
	Olympic	57-10¼	Mike Conley, USA	Aug. 3, 1992	Barcelona
	American	58-11½	Willie Banks	June 16, 1985	Indianapolis
Shot Put:	**World**	75-10¼	**Randy Barnes**, USA	May 20, 1990	Los Angeles
	Olympic	73- 8¾	Ulf Timmermann, East Germany	Sept. 23, 1988	Seoul
	American	75-10¼	Barnes (same as World)	—	—
Discus:	**World**	243- 0	**Jurgen Schult**, East Germany	June 6, 1986	Neubrandenburg
	Olympic	225- 9	Jurgen Schult, East Germany	Oct. 1, 1988	Seoul
	American	237- 4	Ben Plucknett	July 7, 1981	Stockholm
Javelin:	**World**	313-10	**Jan Zelezny**, Czech Republic	Aug. 29, 1993	Sheffield, ENG
	Olympic	294- 2	Jan Zelezny, Czechoslovakia	Aug. 8, 1992	Barcelona
	American	281- 2	Tom Pukstys	June 26, 1993	Kuortane, FIN
Hammer:	**World**	284- 7	**Yuri Sedykh**, USSR	Aug. 30, 1986	Stuttgart
	Olympic	278- 2	Sergey Litvinov, USSR	Sept. 26, 1988	Seoul
	American	270- 8	Lance Deal	June 17, 1994	Knoxville, Tenn.

*Apparent world record disallowed because of interference with wind gauge at altitude.
Note: The international weights for men— **Shot** (16 lbs); **Discus** (4 lbs/6.55 oz); **Javelin** (minimum 1 lb/12¼ oz); **Hammer** (16 lbs).

Decathlon

Event		Points		Date Set	Location
Ten Events:	**World**	8891	**Dan O'Brien**, USA	Sept.4-5, 1992	Talence, FRA
	Olympic	8847	Daley Thompson, Great Britain	Aug. 8-9, 1984	Los Angeles
	American	8891	O'Brien (same as World)	—	—

Note: O'Brien's WR times and distances, in order over two days— **100m** (10.43); **LJ** (26-6¼); **Shot** (54-9¼); **HJ** (6-9½); **400m** (48.51); **110m H** (13.98); **Discus** (159-4); **PV** (16-4¾); **Jav** (205-4); **1500m** (4:42.10).

Track & Field (Cont.)
WOMEN
Running

Event		Time		Date Set	Location
100 meters:	**World**	10.49	**Florence Griffith Joyner**, USA	July 16, 1988	Indianapolis
	Olympic	10.62	Florence Griffith Joyner, USA	Sept. 24, 1988	Seoul
	American	10.49	Griffith Joyner (same as World)	—	—
200 meters:	**World**	21.34	**Florence Griffith Joyner**, USA	Sept. 29, 1988	Seoul
	Olympic	21.34	Griffith Joyner (same as World)	—	—
	American	21.34	Griffith Joyner (same as World)	—	—
400 meters:	**World**	47.60	**Marita Koch**, East Germany	Oct. 6, 1985	Canberra, AUS
	Olympic	48.65	Olga Bryzgina, USSR	Sept. 26, 1988	Seoul
	American	48.83	Valerie Brisco	Aug. 6, 1984	Los Angeles
800 meters:	**World**	1:53.28	**Jarmila Kratochvilova**, Czech.	July 26, 1983	Munich
	Olympic	1:53.42	Nadezhda Olizarenko, USSR	July 27, 1980	Moscow
	American	1:56.90	Mary Decker Slaney	Aug. 16, 1985	Bern
1000 meters:	**World**	2:29.34	**Maria Mutola**, Mozambique	Aug. 25, 1995	Brussels
	Olympic		Not an event	—	—
	American	2:33.93	Suzy Hamilton	June 4, 1995	Eugene, Ore.
1500 meters:	**World**	3:50.46	**Qu Yunxia**, China	Sept. 11, 1993	Beijing
	Olympic	3:53.96	Paula Ivan, Romania	Oct. 1, 1988	Seoul
	American	3:57.12	Mary Decker	July 26, 1983	Stockholm
Mile:	**World**	4:15.61	**Paula Ivan**, Romania	July 10, 1989	Nice
	Olympic		Not an event	—	—
	American	4:16.71	Mary Decker Slaney	Aug. 21, 1985	Zurich
2000 meters:	**World**	5:25.36	**Sonia O'Sullivan**, Ireland	July 8, 1994	Edinburgh
	Olympic		Not an event	—	—
	American	5:32.7	Mary Decker	Aug. 3, 1984	Eugene
3000 meters:	**World**	8:06.11	**Wang Junxia**, China	Sept. 13, 1993	Beijing
	Olympic	8:26.53	Tatyana Samolenko, USSR	Sept. 25, 1988	Seoul
	American	8:25.83	Mary Decker Slaney	Sept. 7, 1985	Rome
5000 meters:	**World**	14:36.45p	**Fernanda Ribiero**, Portugal	July 22, 1995	Hechtel, BEL
	Olympic		Not an event	—	—
	American	14:56.07	Annette Peters	Aug. 27, 1993	Berlin
10,000 meters:	**World**	29:31.78	**Wang Junxia**, China	Sept. 8, 1993	Beijing
	Olympic	31:05.21	Olga Bondarenko, USSR	Sept. 30, 1988	Seoul
	American	31:19.89	Lynn Jennings	Aug. 7, 1992	Barcelona
Marathon:	**World**	2:21:06	**Ingrid Kristiansen**, Norway	Apr. 21, 1985	London
	Olympic	2:24:52	Joan Benoit, USA	Aug. 5, 1984	Los Angeles
	American	2:21:21	Joan Benoit Samuelson	Oct. 20, 1985	Chicago

Note: The **Mile** run is 1,609.344 meters and the **Marathon** is 42,194.988 meters (26 miles, 385 yards).

Relays

Event		Time		Date Set	Location
4 x 100m:	**World**	41.37	**East Germany** (Gladisch, Rieger, Auerswald, Gohr)	Oct. 6, 1985	Canberra, AUS
	Olympic	41.60	East Germany (Muller, Wockel, Auerswald, Gohr)	Aug. 1, 1980	Moscow
	American	41.49	USA (Finn, Torrence, Vereen, Devers)	Aug. 22, 1993	Stuttgart
4 x 200m:	**World**	1:28.15	**East Germany** (Gohr, Muller, Wockel, Koch)	Aug. 9, 1980	Jena, E. Ger.
	Olympic		Not an event	—	—
	American	1:32.55p	LSU (Hill, Boone, Hall, Taplin)	Apr. 30, 1994	Philadelphia
4 x 400m:	**World**	3:15.17	**USSR** (Ledovskaya, Nazarova, Pinigina, Bryzgina)	Oct. 1, 1988	Seoul
	Olympic	3:15.17	USSR (same as World)	—	—
	American	3:15.51	USA (Howard, Dixon, Brisco, Griffith Joyner)	Oct. 1, 1988	Seoul

Hurdles

Event		Time		Date Set	Location
100 meters:	**World**	12.21	**Yordanka Donkova**, Bulgaria	Aug. 20, 1988	Stara Zagora, BUL
	Olympic	12.38	Yordanka Donkova, Bulgaria	Sept. 30, 1988	Seoul
	American	12.46	Gail Devers	Aug. 20, 1993	Stuttgart
400 meters:	**World**	52.61p	**Kim Batten**, USA	Aug. 11, 1995	Göteborg
	Olympic	53.17	Debra Flintoff-King, Australia	Sept. 28, 1988	Seoul
	American	52.61p	Batten (same as World)	—	—

Note: The hurdles at 110 meters are 3 feet, 6 inches high and the hurdles at 400 meters are 3 feet. There are 10 hurdles in both races.

Walking

Event	Time		Date Set	Location
5 km: **World**	20:17.19	**Kerry Saxby**, Australia	Jan. 14, 1990	Sydney, AUS
Olympic		Not an event	—	—
American	21:28.17	Teresa Vaill	Apr. 24, 1993	Philadelphia
10 km: **World**	41:37.9	**Gao Hongmiao**, China	Apr. 7, 1994	Beijing
Olympic	44:32	Chen Yueling, China	Aug. 3, 1992	Barcelona
American	44:17p	Michelle Rohl	Aug. 7, 1995	Göteborg

Field Events

Event	Mark		Date Set	Location
High Jump: **World**	6-10¼	**Stefka Kostadinova**, Bulgaria	Aug. 30, 1987	Rome
Olympic	6- 8	Louise Ritter, USA	Sept. 30, 1988	Seoul
American	6- 8	Louise Ritter	July 8, 1988	Austin
	6- 8	Ritter (see Olympic)	—	—
Pole Vault: **World**	13- 9¾p	**Daniela Bartova**, Czech Rep.	Aug. 22, 1995	Linz, AUT
Olympic		Not an event	—	—
American	13- 1¾p	Melissa Price	June 24, 1995	Walnut, Calif.
Long Jump: **World**	24- 8¼	**Galina Chistyakova**, USSR	June 11, 1988	Leningrad
Olympic	24- 3¼	Jackie Joyner-Kersee, USA	Sept. 29, 1988	Seoul
American	24- 7	Jackie Joyner-Kersee	May 22, 1994	New York
Triple Jump: **World**	50-10¼p	**Inessa Kravets**, Ukraine	Aug. 8, 1995	Göteborg
Olympic		Event as of 1996	—	—
American	46- 9p	Sheila Hudson-Strudwick	July 25, 1995	Monte Carlo
Shot Put: **World**	74- 3	**Natalya Lisovskaya**, USSR	June 7, 1987	Moscow
Olympic	73- 6¼	Ilona Slupianek, E.Germany	July 24, 1980	Moscow
American	66- 2½	Ramona Pagel	June 25, 1988	San Diego
Discus: **World**	252- 0	**Gabriele Reinsch**, E.Germany	July 9, 1988	Neubrandenburg
Olympic	237- 2½	Martina Hellmann, E.Germany	Sept. 29, 1988	Seoul
American	216-10	Carol Cady	May 31, 1986	San Jose
Javelin: **World**	262- 5	**Petra Felke**, East Germany	Sept. 9, 1988	Potsdam, E. Ger.
Olympic	245- 0	Petra Felke, East Germany	Sept. 26, 1988	Seoul
American	227- 5	Kate Schmidt	Sept. 10, 1977	Furth, W. Ger.
Hammer: **World**	223- 7p	**Olga Kuzenkova**, Russia	June 18, 1995	Moscow
Olympic		Not an event	—	—
American	193- 4	Carol Cady	June 11, 1988	Los Gatos, Calif.

Note: The international weights for women— **Shot** (8 lbs/13 oz); **Discus** (2 lbs/3.27 oz); **Javelin** (minimum 1 lb/5.16 oz); **Hammer** (16 lbs).

Heptathlon

Event	Points		Date Set	Location
Seven Events: **World**	7291	**Jackie Joyner-Kersee**, USA	Sept. 23-24, 1988	Seoul
Olympic	7291	Joyner-Kersee (same as World)	—	—
American	7291	Joyner-Kersee (same as World)	—	—

Note: Joyner-Kersee's WR times and distances, in order over two days— **100m H** (12.69); **HJ** (6-1¼); **Shot** (51-10); **200m** (22.56); **LJ** (23-10¼); **Jav** (149-10); **800m** (2:08.51).

World Indoor Records Set in 1995

World indoor records set or equaled between Oct. 1, 1994 and Sept. 15, 1995; (p) indicates record is pending.

MEN

Event		Record	Old Mark	Former Holder
200 meters	**Linford Christie**, GBR	20.25p	20.36	Bruno Marie-Rose, FRA (1987)
400 meters	**Michael Johnson**, USA	44.97	45.02	Danny Everett, USA (1992)
400 meters	**Michael Johnson**, USA	44.63p	44.97	Michael Johnson, USA (1995)
3,000 meters	**Moses Kiptanui**, KEN	7:35.15	7:37.31	Moses Kiptanui, KEN (1992)
5,000m Walk	**Mikhail Shchennikov**, RUS	18:07.08p	18:15.25	Grigoriy Kornev, RUS (1992)

WOMEN

Event		Record	Old Mark	Former Holder
50 meters	**Irina Privalova**, RUS	5.96p	6.00	Merlene Ottey, JAM (1994)
60 meters	**Irina Privalova**, RUS	=6.92p	6.92	Irina Privalova, RUS (1993)
1,000 meters	**Lyubov Kremlyova**, RUS	2:34.18p	2:34.8	Brigitte Kraus, W. Ger (1978)
Pole Vault	**Sun Caiyun**, CHN	13- 7¼p	13- 6½	Sun Caiyun, CHN (1995)
Triple Jump	**Yolanda Chen**, RUS	49- 3¾p	48-10¾	Inna Lasovskaya, RUS (1994)

Note: The women's indoor pole vault record was broken five times in 1995— all by Sun Caiyun of China. Her current mark was set on Feb. 15, 1995.

Track and Field (Cont.)
World and American Indoor Records
As of Sept. 15, 1995

World indoor records officially recognized by the International Amateur Athletics Federation (IAAF).

MEN
Running

Event		Time		Date Set	Location
50 meters:	World	5.61	**Manfred Kokot**, East Germany	Feb. 4, 1973	East Berlin
		5.61	**James Sanford**, USA	Feb. 20, 1981	San Diego
	American	5.61	Sanford (same as World)	—	—
60 meters:	World	6.41	**Andre Cason**, USA	Feb. 14, 1992	Madrid
	American	6.41	Cason (same as World)	—	—
200 meters:	World	20.25p	**Linford Christie**, Britain	Feb. 19, 1995	Lievin, FRA
	American	20.55	Michael Johnson	Jan. 26, 1991	Lievin, FRA
400 meters:	World	44.63p	**Michael Johnson**, USA	Mar. 4, 1995	Atlanta
	American	44.63p	Johnson (same as World)	—	—
800 meters:	World	1:44.84	**Paul Ereng**, Kenya	Mar. 4, 1989	Budapest
	American	1:45.00	Johnny Gray	Mar. 8, 1992	Sindelfingen, GER
1000 meters:	World	2:15.26	**Noureddine Morceli**, Algeria	Feb. 22, 1992	Birmingham, ENG
	American	2:18.19	Ocky Clark	Feb. 12, 1989	Stuttgart
1500 meters:	World	3:34.16	**Noureddine Morceli**, Algeria	Feb. 28, 1991	Seville
	American	3:38.12	Jeff Atkinson	Mar. 5, 1989	Budapest
Mile:	World	3:49.78	**Eamonn Coghlan**, Ireland	Feb. 27, 1983	E. Rutherford, N.J.
	American	3:51.8	Steve Scott	Feb. 20, 1981	San Diego
3000 meters:	World	7:35.15	**Moses Kiptanui**, Kenya	Feb. 12, 1995	Ghent, BEL
	American	7:39.94	Steve Scott	Feb. 10, 1989	E. Rutherford, N.J.
5000 meters:	World	13:20.4	**Suleiman Nyambui**, Tanzania	Feb. 6, 1981	New York
	American	13:20.55	Doug Padilla	Feb. 12, 1982	New York

Note: The **Mile** run is 1,609.344 meters.

Hurdles

Event		Time		Date Set	Location
50 meters:	World	6.25	**Mark McKoy**, Canada	Mar. 5, 1986	Kobe, JPN
	American	6.35	Greg Foster	Jan. 27, 1985	Rosemont, Ill.
		6.35	Greg Foster	Jan. 31, 1987	Ottawa
60 meters:	World	7.30	**Colin Jackson**, Britain	Mar. 6, 1994	Sindelfingen, GER
	American	7.36	Greg Foster	Jan. 16, 1987	Los Angeles

Note: The hurdles for both distances are 3 feet, 6 inches high. There are four hurdles in the 50 meters and five in the 60.

Relays

Event		Time		Date Set	Location
4x200 meters:	World	1:22.11	**Great Britain**	Mar. 3, 1991	Glasgow
	American	1:22.71	National Team	Mar. 3, 1991	Glasgow
4x400 meters:	World	3:03.05	**Germany**	Mar. 10, 1991	Seville
	American	3:03.24	National Team	Mar. 10, 1991	Seville

Field Events

Events		Mark		Date Set	Location
High Jump:	World	7-11¼	**Javier Sotomayor**, Cuba	Mar. 4, 1989	Budapest
	American	7-10½	Hollis Conway	Mar. 10, 1991	Seville
Pole Vault:	World	20- 2	**Sergey Bubka**, Ukraine	Feb. 21, 1993	Donyetsk, UKR
	American	19- 3¾	Billy Olson	Jan. 25, 1986	Albuquerque
Long Jump:	World	28-10¼	**Carl Lewis**, USA	Jan. 27, 1984	New York
	American	28-10¼	Lewis (same as World)	—	—
Triple Jump:	World	58- 3¾	**Leonid Voloshin**, Russia	Feb. 6, 1994	Grenoble, FRA
	American	58- 3¼	Mike Conley	Feb. 27, 1987	New York
Shot Put:	World	74- 4¼	**Randy Barnes**, USA	Jan. 20, 1989	Los Angeles
	American	74- 4¼	Barnes (same as World)	—	—

Note: The international shot put weight for men is 16 lbs.

Heptathlon

		Points		Date Set	Location
Seven Events:	World	6476	**Dan O'Brien**, USA	Mar. 13-14, 1993	Toronto
	American	6476	O'Brien (same as World)	—	—

Note: O'Brien's WR times and distances, in order over two days— **60m** (6.67); **LJ** (25-8¾); **SP** (52-6¾); **HJ** (6-11¾); **60m H** (7.85); **PV** (17-0¾); **1000m** (2:57.96).

WOMEN

Running

Event	Time		Date Set	Location
50 meters:	**World** 5.96p	**Irina Privalova**, Russia	Feb. 9, 1995	Madrid
	American 6.10	Gail Devers	Feb. 20, 1993	Los Angeles
60 meters:	**World** 6.92	**Irina Privalova**, Russia	Feb. 11, 1993	Madrid
	6.92	**Irina Privalova**, Russia	Feb. 9, 1995	Madrid
	American 6.95	Gail Devers	Mar. 12, 1993	Toronto
200 meters:	**World** 21.87	**Merlene Ottey**, Jamaica	Feb. 13, 1993	Lievin, FRA
	American 22.73	Carlette Guidry	Mar. 4, 1995	Atlanta
400 meters:	**World** 49.59	**Jarmila Kratochvilova**, Czech.	Mar. 7, 1982	Milan
	American 50.64	Diane Dixon	Mar. 10, 1991	Seville
800 meters:	**World** 1:56.40	**Christine Wachtel**, E. Germany	Feb. 13, 1988	Vienna
	American 1:58.9	Mary Decker	Feb. 22, 1980	San Diego
1000 meters:	**World** 2:34.18p	**Lyubov Kremlyova**, Russia	Feb. 15, 1995	Erfurt, GER
	American 2:37.6	Mary Decker Slaney	Jan. 21, 1989	Portland
1500 meters:	**World** 4:00.27	**Doina Melinte**, Romania	Feb. 9, 1990	E. Rutherford, N.J.
	American 4:00.8	Mary Decker	Feb. 8, 1980	New York
1500 meters:	**World** 4:00.27	**Doina Melinte**, Romania	Feb. 9, 1990	E. Rutherford, N.J.
	American 4:20.5	Mary Decker	Feb. 19, 1982	San Diego
3000 meters:	**World** 8:33.82	**Elly van Hulst**, Holland	Mar. 4, 1989	Budapest
	American 8:40.45	Lynn Jennings	Feb. 23, 1990	New York
5000 meters:	**World** 15:03.17	**Liz McGolgan**, Great Britain	Feb. 22, 1992	Birmingham, ENG
	American 15:22.64	Lynn Jennings	Jan. 7, 1990	Hanover, N.H.

Note: The **Mile** run is 1,609.344 meters.

Hurdles

Event	Time		Date Set	Location
50 meters:	**World** 6.58	**Cornelia Oschkenat**, E. Ger.	Feb. 20, 1988	East Berlin
	American 6.67	Jackie Joyner-Kersee	Feb. 10, 1995	Reno, Nev.
60 meters:	**World** 7.69	**Lyudmila Narozhilenko**, USSR	Feb. 4, 1990	Chelyabinsk, USSR
	American 7.81	Jackie Joyner-Kersee	Feb. 5, 1989	Fairfax, Va.

Note: The hurdles for both distances are 2 feet, 9 inches high. There are four hurdles in the 50 meters and five in the 60.

Walking

Event	Time		Date Set	Location
3000 meters:	**World** 11:44.00	**Alina Ivanova**, RUS	Feb. 7, 1992	Moscow
	American 12:20.79	Debbi Lawrence	Mar. 12, 1993	Toronto

Relays

Event	Time		Date Set	Location
4x200 meters:	**World** 1:32.55	**West Germany**	Feb. 20, 1988	Dortmund, W. Ger.
	American 1:33.24	National Team	Feb. 12, 1994	Glasgow
4x400 meters:	**World** 3:27.22	**Germany**	Mar. 10, 1991	Seville
	American 3:29.0	National Team	Mar. 10, 1991	Seville
4x800 meters:	**World** 8:18.71	**Russia**	Feb. 4, 1994	Moscow
	American 8:25.5	Villanova	Feb. 7, 1987	Gainesville, Fla.

Field Events

Event	Mark		Date Set	Location
High Jump:	**World** 6- 9½	**Heike Henkel**, Germany	Feb. 9, 1992	Karlsruhe, GER
	American 6- 6¾	Coleen Sommer	Feb. 13, 1982	Ottawa
Pole Vault:	**World** 13- 7¼p	**Sun Caiyun**, China	Feb. 15, 1995	Erfurt, GER
	American 12- 2	Melissa Price	Feb. 11, 1995	Los Angeles
Long Jump:	**World** 24- 2¼	**Heike Drechsler**, E. Germany	Feb. 13, 1988	Vienna
	American 23- 4¾	Jackie Joyner-Kersee	Mar. 5, 1992	Atlanta
Triple Jump:	**World** 49- 3¾p	**Yolanda Chen**, Russia	Mar. 11, 1995	Barcelona
	American 46- 8¼	Sheila Hudson-Strudwick	Mar. 4, 1995	Atlanta
Shot Put:	**World** 73-10	**Helena Fibingerova**, Czech.	Feb. 19, 1977	Jablonec, CZE
	American 65- 0¾	Ramona Pagel	Feb. 20, 1987	Inglewood, Calif.

Note: The international shotput weight for women is 8 lbs. and 13 oz.

Pentathlon

Event	Points		Date Set	Location
Five Events:	**World** 4991	**Irina Byelova**, Russia	Feb. 14-15, 1993	Berlin
	American 4632	Kym Carter	Mar. 10, 1995	Barcelona

Note: Byelova's WR times and distances, in order over two days— **60m H** (8.22); **HJ** (6-4); **SP** (43-5¾); **LJ** (21-10¾); **800m** (2:10.26).

SWIMMING

1995 Pan Pacific Championships

Winners in the 1995 Pan Pacific Swimming Championships at the Georgia Tech Aquatic Center in Atlanta (Aug. 9-13). The Chinese national team was banned from the meet due to positive drug test results at the Asian Games meet in November 1994. Note that (WR) indicates a world record, (AR) an American record and (CR) a championship meet record.

MEN

Event		Time	
50m free	Gary Hall Jr., USA	22.30	
100m free	Gary Hall Jr., USA	49.47	
200m free	Danyon Loader, NZE	1:48.72	
400m free	Daniel Kowalski, AUS	3:50.01	
800m free	Daniel Kowalski, AUS	7:50.28	
1500m free	Kieren Perkins, AUS	14:58.92	
100m back	Jeff Rouse, USA	54.99	
200m back	Tripp Schwenk, USA	1:58.87	CR
100m breast	Eric Wunderlich, USA	1:01.80	
200m breast	Akira Hayashi, JPN	2:13.60	
100m fly	Scott Miller, AUS	53.07	CR
200m fly	Scott Miller, AUS	1:57.86	CR
200 I.M.	Tom Dolan, USA	2:00.89	
400 I.M.	Tom Dolan, USA	4:14.77	CR
4x100m free	USA (David Fox, Joe Hudepohl, Jon Olsen, Gary Hall Jr.)	3:15.11	WR
4x200m free	AUS (Malcolm Allen, Glen Housman, Matthew Dunn, Daniel Kowalski)	7:17.52	CR
4x100m mdly	USA (Jeff Rouse, Eric Wunderlich, Mark Henderson, Gary Hall Jr.)	3:37.04	CR

WOMEN

Event		Time	
50m free	Amy Van Dyken, USA	25.03	AR
100m free	Jenny Thompson, USA	55.31	
200m free	Suzu Chiba, JPN	2:00.00	
400m free	Brooke Bennett, USA	4:10.46	
800m free	Haley Lewis, AUS	8:28.78	
1500m free	Brooke Bennett, USA	16:15.58	
100m back	Noriko Inada, JPN	1:02.02	
200m back	Nicole Stevenson, AUS	2:11.26	
100m breast	Penelope Heyns, SAF	1:08.09	CR
200m breast	Samantha Riley, AUS	2:24.81	CR
100m fly	Susan O'Neill, AUS	59.58	
200m fly	Susan O'Neill, AUS	2:07.29	CR
200 I.M.	Ellinora Overton, AUS	2:14.68	
400 I.M.	Fumie Kurotori, JPN	4:44.22	
4x100m free	USA (Amy Van Dyken, Angel Martino, Melanie Valerio, Jenny Thompson)	3:41.59	CR
4x200m free	USA (Cristina Teuscher, Melanie Valerio, Trina Jackson, Jenny Thompson)	8:02.68	CR
4x100m mdly	AUS (Nicole Stevenson, Samantha Riley, Susan O'Neill, Sarah Ryan)	4:02.93	CR

1995 European Championships

Winners in the 1995 European Swimming Championships at Vienna (Aug. 17-24). Note that (WR) indicates a world record.

MEN

Event		Time	
50m free	Aleksandr Popov, RUS	22.25	
100m free	Aleksandr Popov, RUS	49.10	
200m free	Jani Sievinen, FIN	1:48.98	
400m free	Steffan Zesner, GER	3:50.35	
1500m free	Jorg Hoffmann, GER	15:11.25	
100m back	Vladimir Selkov, RUS	55.48	
200m back	Vladimir Selkov, RUS	1:58.48	
100m breast	Frederick Deburghgraeve, BEL	1:01.12	
200m breast	Andrei Korneev, RUS	2:12.62	
100m fly	Denis Pankratov, RUS	52.32	WR
200m fly	Denis Pankratov, RUS	1:56.34	
200 I.M.	Jani Sievinen, FIN	1:58.61	
400 I.M.	Jani Sievinen, FIN	4:14.75	
4x100m free	Russia	3:18.84	
4x200m free	Germany	7:18.22	
4x100m mdly	Russia	3:38.11	

WOMEN

Event		Time	
50m free	Linda Olofsson, SWE	25.76	
100m free	Franziska Van Almsick, GER	55.34	
200m free	Kerstin Kielgass, GER	2:00.56	
400m free	Franziska Van Almsick, GER	4:08.37	
800m free	Julia Jung, GER	8:36.08	
100m back	Mette Jacobson, DEN	1:02.46	
200m back	Krisztina Egerszegi, HUN	2:07.24	
100m breast	Brigitte Becue, BEL	1:09.30	
200m breast	Brigitte Becue, BEL	2:27.66	
100m fly	Mette Jacobson, DEN	1:00.64	
200m fly	Michelle Smith, IRE	2:11.60	
200 I.M.	Michelle Smith, IRE	2:15.27	
400 I.M.	Krisztina Egerszegi, HUN	4:40.33	
4x100m free	Germany	3:43.22	
4x200m free	Germany	8:06.11	

1995 FINA World Cup Diving Championships

Major event winners in the 9th FINA World Cup Diving Championships at the Georgia Tech's Olympic Aquatic Center in Atlanta (Sept. 5-9, 1995).

MEN

Event		Points
1-meter Springboard	Yu Zhuocheng, CHN	418.50
3-meter Springboard	Dimitri Sautin, RUS	684.21
Platform	Sun Shuwei, CHN	681.48

WOMEN

Event		Points
1-meter Springboard	Vera Ilyina, RUS	287.49
3-meter Springboard	Fu Mingxia, CHN	540.63
Platform	Chi Bin, CHN	512.82

1995 FINA Water Polo World Cup

Winners in the 9th FINA Water Polo World Cup at the Georgia Tech Aquatic Center in Atlanta (Sept. 12-17, 1995).

Final .... Hungary over Italy, 11-10   **Third Place** .... Russia over USA, 10-8 (OT)

Agence Presse France

The United States men's 4x100-meter freestyle relay team of **Gary Hall Jr.**, **David Fox**, **Joe Hudepohl** and **Jon Olsen** after setting a new world record of 3:15.11 at the Pan Pacific Games.

World, Olympic and American Records
As of Sept. 15, 1995

World long course records officially recognized by the Federation Internationale de Natation Amateur (FINA). Note that (ph) indicates preliminary heat; (r) relay lead-off split; and (s) indicates split time.

MEN

Freestyle

Distance		Time		Date Set	Location
50 meters:	**World**	21.81	**Tom Jager**, USA	Mar. 24, 1990	Nashville
	Olympic	21.91	Aleksandr Popov, Unified Team	July 30, 1992	Barcelona
	American	21.81	Jager (same as World)	—	—
100 meters:	**World**	48.21	**Aleksandr Popov**, Russia	June 18, 1994	Monte Carlo
	Olympic	48.63	Matt Biondi, USA	Sept. 22, 1988	Seoul
	American	48.42	Matt Biondi	Aug. 10, 1988	Austin, Tex.
200 meters:	**World**	1:46.69	**Giorgio Lamberti**, Italy	Aug. 15, 1989	Bonn, W. Ger.
	Olympic	1:46.70	Yevgeny Sadovyi, Unified Team	July 26, 1992	Barcelona
	American	1:47.72ph	Matt Biondi	Aug. 8, 1988	Austin, Tex.
400 meters:	**World**	3:43.80	**Kieren Perkins**, Australia	Sept. 9, 1994	Rome
	Olympic	3:45.00	Yevgeny Sadovyi, Unified Team	July 29, 1992	Barcelona
	American	3:48.06	Matt Cetlinski	Aug. 11, 1988	Austin, Tex.
800 meters:	**World**	7:46.00s	**Kieren Perkins**, Australia	Aug. 24, 1994	Victoria, CAN
	Olympic		Not an event	—	—
	American	7:52.45	Sean Killion	July 27, 1987	Clovis, Calif.
1500 meters:	**World**	14:41.66	**Kieren Perkins**, Australia	Aug. 24, 1994	Victoria, CAN
	Olympic	14:43.48	Kieren Perkins, Australia	July 31, 1992	Barcelona
	American	15:01.51	George DiCarlo	June 30, 1984	Indianapolis

Backstroke

Distance		Time		Date Set	Location
100 meters:	**World**	53.86r	**Jeff Rouse**, USA	July 31, 1992	Barcelona
	Olympic	53.98	Mark Tewksbury, Canada	July 30, 1992	Barcelona
	American	53.86r	Rouse (same as World)	—	—
200 meters:	**World**	1:56.57	**Martin Zubero**, Spain	Nov. 23, 1991	Tuscaloosa, Ala.
	Olympic	1:58.47	Martin Zubero, Spain	July 28, 1992	Barcelona
	American	1:58.33	Tripp Schwenk	Aug. 1, 1995	Pasadena

Breaststroke

Distance		Time		Date Set	Location
100 meters:	**World**	1:00.95ph	**Karoly Guttler**, Hungary	Aug. 5, 1993	Sheffield, ENG
	Olympic	1:01.50	Nelson Diebel, USA	July 26, 1992	Barcelona
	American	1:01.40	Nelson Diebel,	Mar. 1, 1992	Indianapolis
		1:01.40	Seth van Neerden	Aug. 14, 1994	Indianapolis

Swimming (Cont.)

MEN
Breaststroke

Distance	Time		Date Set	Location
200 meters:	**World**............2:10.16	**Mike Barrowman**, USA	July 29, 1992	Barcelona
	Olympic.............2:10.16	Barrowman (same as World)	—	—
	American...........2:10.16	Barrowman (same as World)	—	—

Butterfly

Distance	Time		Date Set	Location
100 meters:	**World**............52.32	**Denis Pankratov**, Russia	Aug. 23, 1995	Vienna
	Olympic.............53.00	Anthony Nesty, Suriname	Sept. 21, 1988	Seoul
	American...........52.84	Pablo Morales	June 23, 1986	Orlando
200 meters:	**World**............1:55.22	**Denis Pankratov**, Russia	June 14, 1995	Canet, FRA
	Olympic.............1:56.26	Melvin Stewart, USA	July 30, 1992	Barcelona
	American...........1:55.69	Melvin Stewart	Jan. 12, 1991	Perth, AUS

Individual Medley

Distance	Time		Date Set	Location
200 meters:	**World**............1:58.16	**Jani Sievinen**, Finland	Sept. 11, 1994	Rome
	Olympic.............2:00.17	Tamas Darnyi, Hungary	Sept. 25, 1988	Seoul
	American...........2:00.11	David Wharton	Aug. 20, 1989	Tokyo
400 meters:	**World**............4:12.30	**Tom Dolan**, USA	Sept. 6, 1994	Rome
	Olympic.............4:14.23	Tamas Darnyi, Hungary	July 27, 1992	Barcelona
	American...........4:12.30	Dolan (same as World)	—	—

Relays

Distance	Time		Date Set	Location
4x100m free:	**World**............3:15.11	**USA** (Fox, Hudepohl, Olsen, Hall)	Aug. 12, 1995	Atlanta
	Olympic.............3:16.53	USA (Jacobs, Dalbey, Jager, Biondi)	Sept. 25, 1988	Seoul
	American...........3:15.11	USA (same as World)	—	—
4x200m free:	**World**............7:11.95	**Unified Team** (Lepikov, Pychnenko, Taianovitch, Sadovyi)	July 27, 1992	Barcelona
	Olympic.............7:11.95	Unified Team (same as World)	—	—
	American...........7:12.51	USA (Dalbey, Cetlinski, Gjertsen, Biondi)	Sept. 21, 1988	Seoul
4x100m medley:	**World**............3:36.93	**USA** (Berkoff, Schroeder, Biondi, Jacobs)	Sept. 25, 1988	Seoul
	3:36.93	**USA** (Rouse, Diebel, Morales, Olsen)	July 31, 1992	Barcelona
	Olympic.............3:36.93	USA (same as World)	—	—
	American...........3:36.93	USA (same as World)	—	—

WOMEN
Freestyle

Distance	Time		Date Set	Location
50 meters:	**World**............24.51	**Le Jingyi**, China	Sept. 11, 1994	Rome
	Olympic.............24.79	Yang Wenyi, China	July 31, 1992	Barcelona
	American...........25.03	Amy Van Dyken	Aug. 13, 1995	Atlanta
100 meters:	**World**............54.01	**Le Jingyi**, China	Sept. 5, 1994	Rome
	Olympic.............54.65	Zhaung Yong, China	July 26, 1992	Barcelona
	American...........54.48	Jenny Thompson	Mar. 1, 1992	Indianapolis
200 meters:	**World**............1:56.78	**Franziska Van Almsick**, Ger.	Sept. 6, 1994	Rome
	Olympic.............1:57.65	Heike Friedrich, East Germany	Sept. 21, 1988	Seoul
	American...........1:57.90	Nicole Haislett	July 27, 1992	Barcelona
400 meters:	**World**............4:03.85	**Janet Evans**, USA	Sept. 22, 1988	Seoul
	Olympic.............4:03.85	Evans (same as World)	—	—
	American...........4:03.85	Evans (same as World)	—	—
800 meters:	**World**............8:16.22	**Janet Evans**, USA	Aug. 20, 1989	Tokyo
	Olympic.............8:20.20	Janet Evans, USA	Sept. 24, 1988	Seoul
	American...........8:16.22	Evans (same as World)	—	—
1500 meters:	**World**............15:52.10	**Janet Evans**, USA	Mar. 26, 1988	Orlando
	Olympic..................	Not an event	—	—
	American...........15:52.10	Evans (same as World)	—	—

Backstroke

Distance		Time		Date Set	Location
100 meters:	**World**	1:00.16	**He Cihong**, China	Sept. 10, 1994	Rome
	Olympic	1:00.68	Krisztina Egerszegi, Hungary	July 28, 1992	Barcelona
	American	1:00.82r	Lea Loveless	July 30, 1992	Barcelona
200 meters:	**World**	2:06.62	**Krisztina Egerszegi**, Hungary	Aug. 26, 1991	Athens
	Olympic	2:07.06	Krisztina Egerszegi, Hungary	July 31, 1992	Barcelona
	American	2:08.60	Betsy Mitchell	June 27, 1986	Orlando

Breaststroke

Distance		Time		Date Set	Location
100 meters:	**World**	1:07.69	**Samantha Riley**, Australia	Sept. 9, 1994	Rome
	Olympic	1:07.95	Tania Dangalakova, Bulgaria	Sept. 23, 1988	Seoul
	American	1:08.17	Anita Nall	July 29, 1992	Barcelona
200 meters:	**World**	2:24.76	**Rebecca Brown**, Australia	Mar. 16, 1994	Queensland, AUS
	Olympic	2:26.65	Kyoko Iwasaki, Japan	July 27, 1992	Barcelona
	American	2:25.35	Anita Nall	Mar. 2, 1992	Indianapolis

Butterfly

Distance		Time		Date Set	Location
100 meters:	**World**	57.93	**Mary T. Meagher**, USA	Aug. 16, 1981	Brown Deer, Wisc.
	Olympic	58.62	Qian Hong, China	July 29, 1992	Barcelona
	American	57.93	Meagher (same as World)	—	—
200 meters:	**World**	2:05.96	**Mary T. Meagher**, USA	Aug. 13, 1981	Brown Deer, Wisc.
	Olympic	2:06.90	Mary T. Meagher, USA	Aug. 4, 1984	Los Angeles
	American	2:05.96	Meagher (same as World)	—	—

Individual Medley

Distance		Time		Date Set	Location
200 meters:	**World**	2:11.65	**Lin Li**, China	July 28, 1992	Barcelona
	Olympic	2:11.65	Li (same as World)	—	—
	American	2:11.91	Summer Sanders	July 28, 1992	Barcelona
400 meters:	**World**	4:36.10	**Petra Schneider**, East Germany	Aug. 1, 1982	Guayaquil, ECU
	Olympic	4:36.29	Petra Schneider, East Germany	July 26, 1980	Moscow
	American	4:37.58	Summer Sanders	July 26, 1992	Barcelona

Relays

Distance		Time		Date Set	Location
4x100m free:	**World**	3:37.91	**China** (Jingyi, S.Ying, L.Ying, Lu)	Sept. 7, 1994	Rome
	Olympic	3:39.46	USA (Haislett, Torres, Martino, Thompson)	July 28, 1992	Barcelona
	American	3:39.46	USA (same as Olympic)	—	—
4x200m free:	**World**	7:55.47	**E. Germany** (Stellmach, Strauss, Mohring, Friedrich)	Aug. 18, 1987	Strasbourg, FRA
	Olympic		Not an event	—	—
	American	8:02.12	**USA** (Mitchell, Meagher, Brown, Wayte)	Aug. 22, 1986	Madrid
4x100m medley:	**World**	4:01.67	**China** (Cihong, Guohong, Limin, Jingyi)	Sept. 10, 1994	Rome
	Olympic	4:02.54	USA (Loveless, Nall, Ahmann-Leighton, Thompson)	July 30, 1992	Barcelona
	American	4:02.54	USA (same as Olympic)	—	—

World Records Set in 1995

World long course records set between Oct. 1, 1994 and Sept. 15, 1995. There were no women's world records set.

MEN

Event		Record	Old Mark	Former Holder
100-meter butterfly	**Denis Pankratov**, Russia	52.32	52.84	Pablo Morales, USA, 1986
200-meter butterfly	**Denis Pankratov**, Russia	1:55.22	1:55.69	Melvin Stewart, USA, 1991
4x100m freestyle	**USA Pan Pacific Team** (David Fox, Joe Hudepohl, Jon Olsen, Gary Hall Jr.)	3:15.11	3:16.53	USA (Chris Jacobs, Troy Dalbey, Tom Jager, Matt Biondi), 1988

WINTER SPORTS

Alpine Skiing

World Cup Champions

MEN

Overall...Alberto Tomba, ITA
Downhill...Luc Alphand, FRA
Slalom...Alberto Tomba, ITA
Giant Slalom ....Alberto Tomba, ITA
Super G ....Peter Runggaldier, ITA
Combined ....Marc Girardelli, LUX
Nation's Cup ....Austria

Top Five Standings

Overall (32 races): 1. Alberto Tomba, ITA (1150 pts); 2. Gunther Mader, AUT (775); 3. Jure Kosir, SLO (760); 4. Marc Girardelli, LUX (744); 5. Kjetil Andre Aamodt, NOR (708). *Best USA*— Kyle Rasmussen (17th, 436 pts).
Downhill (9 races)— 1. Luc Alphand, FRA (484 pts); 2. Kristian Ghedina, ITA (473); 3. Patrick Ortlieb, AUT (426); 4. Armin Assinger, AUT (419); 5. Josef Strobl, AUT (307). *Best USA*— Kyle Rasmussen (6th, 288 pts).
Slalom (9 races): 1. Alberto Tomba , ITA (700 pts); 2. Michael Tritscher, AUT (477); 3. Jure Kosir, SLO (405); 4. Ole Kristian Furuseth, NOR (401); 5. Mario Reiter, AUT (341). *Best USA*— Matt Grosjean (33rd, 32 pts).
Giant Slalom (7 races): 1. Alberto Tomba, ITA (450 pts); 2. Jure Kosir, SLO (355); 3. Harald Strand Nilsen, NOR (322); 4. Kjetil Andre Aamodt, NOR (307); 5. Michael von Gruenigen, SWI (296). *Best USA*— Jeremy Nobis (33rd, 26 pts).
Super G (5 races): 1. Peter Runggaldier, ITA (332 pts); 2. Gunther Mader, AUT (250); 3. Werner Perathoner, ITA (237); 4. Richard Kroell, AUT (170); 5. Kyle Rasmussen, USA (148).
Combined (2 events): 1. Marc Girardelli, LUX (200 pts); 2. Harald Christian Strand Nilsen, NOR (140); 3. Lasse Kjus, NOR (125); 4. Kjetil Andre Aamodt, NOR (100); 5. Espen Hellerud, NOR (72). *Best USA*— Tommy Moe (12th, 26 pts).
Nation's Cup (32 races): 1. Austria (5,884 pts); 2. Italy (3,756); 3. Norway (3,139); 4. Switzerland (2,158); 5. France (1,976); 6. United States (1,233).

WOMEN

Overall...Vreni Schneider, SWI
Downhill...Picabo Street, USA
Slalom..Vreni Schneider, SWI
Giant Slalom ....Vreni Schneider, SWI
Super G ....Katja Seizinger, GER
Combined...Pernilla Wiberg, SWE
Nation's Cup...Switzerland

Top Five Standings

Overall (32 races): 1. Vreni Schneider, SWI (1,248 pts); 2. Katja Seizinger, GER (1,242); 3. Heidi Zeller Baehler, SWI (1,044); 4. Martina Ertl (985); 5. Picabo Street, USA (905). *Other Top 10 USA*— Hilary Lindh (9th, 549 pts).
Downhill (9 races)— 1. Picabo Street, USA (709 pts); 2. Hilary Lindh, USA (493); 3. Katja Seizinger, GER (445); 4. Warwara Zelenskaja, RUS (416); 5. Isolde Kostner, ITA (310).
Slalom (7 races): 1. Vreni Schneider, SWI (560 pts); 2. Pernilla Wiberg, SWE (355); 3. Martina Ertl, GER (278); 4. Urska Hrovat, SLO (275); 5. Kristina Andersson, SWE (247). *Best USA*— Kristina Koznick (26th, 46 pts).
Giant Slalom (8 races): 1. Vreni Schneider, SWI (450 pts); 2. Heidi Zeller Baehler, SWI (420); 3. Spela Pretnar, SLO (352); 4. Martina Ertl, GER (333); 5. Deborah Compagnoni, ITA (325). *Best USA*— Eva Twardokens (13th, 143 pts).

Super G (7 races): 1. Katja Seizinger, GER (446 pts); 2. Heidi Zeller Baehler, SWI (366); 3. Heidi Zurbriggen, SWI (251); 4. Renate Goetschl, AUT (245); 5. Martina Ertl, GER (237). *Best USA*— Picabo Street (8th, 196 pts).
Combined (1 event): 1. Pernilla Wiberg, SWE (100 pts); 2. Vreni Schneider, SWI (80); 3. Martina Ertl, GER (60); 4. Katja Seizinger, GER (50); 5. Marianne Kjoerstad, NOR (45).
Nation's Cup (32 races): 1. Switzerland (3,857 pts); 2. Germany (3,508); 3. Austria (2,978); 4. Italy (2,206); 5. United States (2,081).

U.S. Championships

at Park City/Snowbasin, Utah (Mar. 20-28)

MEN

Downhill ....AJ Kitt, Rochester, N.Y.
Slalom..................Matt Grosjean, Steamboat Springs, Colo.
Giant Slalom ....Daron Rahlves, Truckee, Calif.
Super G ....(cancelled)
Combined ....Casey Puckett, Crested Butte, Colo.

WOMEN

Downhill.......................Megan Gerety, Anchorage, Alaska
Slalom...................Kristina Koznick, Burnsville, Minn.
Giant Slalom ....Heidi Voelker, Park City, Utah
Super G ....(cancelled)
Combined.........Carrie Sheinberg, Port Washington, N.Y.

Biathlon

World Cup Champions

Men's Overall ....Jon Age Tyldum, NOR
Women's Overall.....................................Anne Briand, FRA

U.S. Championships

at Lake Placid, N.Y. (Jan. 3-4)

MEN

10-km ....Curt Schreiner, Saratoga Springs, N.Y.
20-km ....Duncan Douglas, Lake Placid, N.Y.

WOMEN

7.5 km ....Kara Salmela, Lake Placid, N.Y.
15-km ....Beth Coats, Breckenridge, Colo.

Bobsled

World Cup Champion Drivers

Two-Man ....Pierre Lueders, Canada I
Four-Man.....................................Pierre Lueders, Canada II
Combined ....Pierre Lueders

U.S. Championship Drivers

Lake Placid, N.Y. (Feb. 22-25)

Two-Man ....Tuffy Latour, Schenectady, N.Y.
Four-Man ....Jim Herberich, Winchester, Mass.

Luge

World Cup Champions

Men's Singles ....Armin Zoggeler, ITA
Men's Doubles ....Jan Behrendt & Stefan Krause, GER
Women's Singles ....Gabi Kohlisch, GER

U.S. Championships

Lake Placid, N.Y. (Jan. 4)

Men's Singles ....Robert Pipkins, Staten Island, N.Y.
Women's Singles....................B. Calcaterra-McMahon, Waterford, Conn.

Freestyle Skiing

World Cup Champions

MEN

Overall ....Jonny Moseley, USA
Aerials..Trace Worthington, USA
Moguls...............................Sergey Shupletsov, RUS
Ballet.....................................Rune Kristiansen, NOR
Combined...................................Trace Worthington, USA

WOMEN

Overall ....Kristean Porter, USA
Aerials......................................Nikki Stone, USA
Moguls ....Raphaelle Monod, FRA
Ballet ....Ellen Breen, USA
Combined ....Maja Schmid, SWI

U.S. Championships

at Park City, Utah (Mar. 19-25)

MEN

Invert. Aerials ....Trace Worthington, Park City, Utah
Uprgt. Aerials ....Toby Dawson, Vail, Colo.
Moguls ....Troy Benson, Evergreen, Colo.
Ballet ....Jason Bodnar, Colchester, Vt.
Invert. Combined................................Trace Worthington
Uprgt. Combined ....Tony Basile, Squaw Valley, Calif.

WOMEN

Invert. Aerials ....Nikki Stone, Westboro, Mass.
Uprgt. Aerials.........Hannah Hardaway, Moultonboro, N.H.
Moguls ....Ann Battelle, Steamboat Springs, Colo.
Ballet......................................Ellen Breen, West Hills, Calif.
Invert. Combined ....Kristean Porter, Greenland, N.H.
Uprgt. Combined...................Tracy Jolles, Wellesley, Mass.

Nordic Skiing

World Cup Champions

MEN

Cross-country ....Bjorn Dahlie, NOR
Ski Jumping ....Andreas Goldberger, AUS
Nordic Combined ....Kenji Ogiwara, JPN

WOMEN

Cross-country ....Elena Valbe, RUS

U.S. Championships

Cross-country

at Lake Placid, N.Y. (Feb. 22-25)

MEN

10-km classical....................Justin Wadsworth, Bend, Ore.
15-km freestyle ....Carl Swensen, North Conway, N.H.
30-km freestyle...Justin Wadsworth
50-km freestyle...........Luke Bodensteiner, West Bend, Wisc.
(at Royal Gorge, Calif., Mar. 26)

WOMEN

5-km classical ....Leslie Thompson, Stowe, Vt.
10-km freestyle...Leslie Thompson
15-km fresstyle..............Nina Kemppel, Anchorage, Alaska
30-km freestyle...Leslie Thompson
(at Royal Gorge, Calif., Mar. 26)

Ski Jumping

at Park City, Utah (Jan. 14)

Large Hill..no event
Normal Hill ....Randy Weber, Steamboat Springs, Colo.

Nordic Combined

at Steamboat Springs, Colo. (Nov. 25, 1994)
Individual............Ryan Heckman, Steamboat Springs, Colo.

Figure Skating

World Championships

at Birmingham, England (Mar. 6-12)

Men's— 1. Elvis Stojko, Canada; 2. Todd Eldredge, USA; 3. Philippe Candeloro, France.

Women's— 1. Lu Chen, China; 2. Surya Bonaly, France; 3. Nicole Bobek, USA.

Pairs— 1. Radka Kovarikova & Rene Novotny, Czech Republic; 2. Yevgenia Shishkova & Naumov, Russia; 3. Jenni Meno & Todd Sand, USA.

Ice Dance— 1. Oksana Gritschuk & Yevgeny Platov, Russia; 2. Susanna Rahkamo & Petri Kokko, Finland; 3. Sophie Moniotte & Pascal Lavanchy, France.

U.S. Championships

at Providence, R.I. (Feb. 6-11)

Men's ....Todd Eldredge, South Chatham, Mass.
Women's ....Nicole Bobek, Chicago
Pairs ....Jenni Meno, Westlake, Ohio
& Todd Sand, Thousand Oakes, Calif.
Ice Dance ....Renee Roca, Rochester, N.Y.
& Gorsha Sur, Colorado Springs, Colo.

European Championships

at Dortmund, Germany (Jan. 30-Feb. 4)

Men's..Ilya Kulik, RUS
Women's...............................Surya Bonaly, FRA
Pairs ....Mandy Woetzel & Ingo Steuer, GER
Ice Dance...........Susanna Rahkamo & Petri Kokko, FIN

Speed Skating

World Cup Champions

MEN

500 meters ....Hiroyasu Shimizu, JPN
1000 meters.......................................Yukinori Miyabe, JPN
1500 meters ....Neal Marshall, CAN
5000 meters ....Rintje Ritsma, HOL

WOMEN

500 meters ....Bonnie Blair, USA
1000 meters ....Bonnie Blair, USA
1500 meters ....Gunda Niemann, GER
3000 meters ....Gunda Niemann, GER

World Long Track Championships

MEN

at Baselga, Italy (Feb. 11-12)

500 meters...Hiroyuki Noake, JPN
1500 meters ....Rintje Ritsma, HOL
5000 meters ....Frank Dittrich, GER
10,000 meters ....Rintje Ritsma, HOL
All-Around...Rintje Ritsma, HOL

WOMEN

at Savalen, Norway (Mar. 4-5)

500 meters ....Gunda Niemann, GER
1500 meters ....Gunda Niemann, GER
3000 meters ....Gunda Niemann, GER
5000 meters ....Gunda Niemann, GER
All-Around..Gunda Niemann, GER
Note: Bonnie Blair of the USA did not compete.

World Sprint Championships

at West Allis, Wisc. (Feb. 18-19)

Men: 500 meters ....Yoon-Man Kim, S. Korea
1000 meters ....Yoon-Man Kim, S. Korea
Overall........................Yoon-Man Kim, S. Korea
Women: 500 meters ....Bonnie Blair, USA
1000 Meters ....Bonnie Blair, USA
Overall ....Bonnie Blair, USA

SUMMER SPORTS

Basketball

Pan Am Games

at Buenos Aires, Argentina (Mar. 9-26)
Men's Final ....Argentina over USA, 90-86

CBA

Finals ....Yakima Sun Kings over Pittsburgh Piranahs
(4 games to 2)

Europe

Continental Championships

National Final.................Yugoslavia over Lithuania, 96-90
Club Final ....Real Madrid over Olympiakos, 73-61

National Club Champions

French League ....Olympique d'Antibes
German League ....Bayer-Leverkusen
Greek League...Olympiakos Piraeus
Italian League ....Buckler Bologna
Spanish League ....FC Barcelona

Cross-country

IAAF World Championships

at Durham, England (Mar. 25)
Men (7.53 miles)......................1. Paul Tergat, KEN 34:05
2. Ismael Kirui, KEN 34:13
3. Salah Hissou, MAR 34:14
Best USA— Todd Williams, 9th 34:47
Women (4.02 miles.)..................1. Derartu Tulu, ETH 20:21
2. Catherina McKiernan, IRL 20:29
3. Sally Barsosio, KEN 20:39
Best USA— Joan Nesbit, 6th 20:50

Cycling

Tour de France

82nd Tour de France (July 1-23); 20 stages plus prologue covering 2,270 miles from Brittany to Paris; 115 out of 189 riders finished the race.
Winning time: 92 hours, 44 minutes, 59 seconds (an average hourly speed of 24 mph). **Winner's share:** 2,200,200 francs ($455,440).

		Team	Behind
1	Miguel Induráin, SPA	Banesto	—
2	Alex Zulle, SWI	ONCE	4:35
3	Bjarne Riis, DEN	Gewiss	6:47
4	Laurent Jalabert, FRA	ONCE	8:24
5	Ivan Gotti, ITA	Gewiss	11:33
6	Melchor Mauri, SPA	ONCE	15:20
7	Fernado Escartin, SPA	Mapei	15:49
8	Tony Rominger, SWI	Mapei	16:46
9	Richard Virenque, FRA	Festina	17:31
10	Hernan Buenahora, COL	Kelme	18:51

Best USA: 36th— Lance Armstrong, Austin, Texas, Team Motorola, 1:28:06 behind.

Other Worldwide Champions

MEN

Giro d'Italia (ITA) ....Tony Rominger, SWI
Vuelta de Espana (SPA) ....Laurent Jalabert, FRA
World Pro Road Race ....ends Oct. 8
World Time Trial ....ends Oct. 4
Paris-to-Roubaix ....Franco Ballerini, ITA
Tour du Pont (USA)............................Lance Armstrong, USA
CoreStates U.S. Pro ....Norm Alvis, USA

WOMEN

PowerBar Challenge (USA)*....................Dede Demet, USA
Tour Cycliste Feminin (FRA)...............Fabiana Luperini, ITA
Giro d'Italia Femminile (ITA)...............Fabiana Luperini, ITA
*formerly, the Ore-ida Challenge.

Gymnastics

World Championships

at Sabae, Japan (Oct. 1-10)
See Updates chapter.

U.S. Championships

at New Orleans (Aug. 16-19)

MEN

All-Around.....................John Roethlisberger, Minneapolis
Horizontal Bar ....John Roethlisberger
Parallel Bars ....John Roethlisberger
Vault ....David St. Pierre, Culver City, Calif.
Pommel Horse ....Mark Sohn, Arlington Hgts., Ill.
Rings ....Paul O'Neill, Mandan, N.D.
Floor Exercise ....Daniel Stover, Oklahoma City

WOMEN

All-Around.........................Dominique Moceanu, Houston
Vault ....Shannon Miller, Edmond, Okla.
Uneven Bars ....Dominique Dawes, Silver Spring, Md.
Balance Beam ....Doni Thompson, Colorado Springs
& Monica Flammer, Houston
Floor Exercise ....Dominique Dawes

Marathons

1995 Winners

Los Angeles

Mar. 5	Men	Rolando Vera, ECU	2:11:39
	Women	Nadia Prasad, FRA	2:29:50

London

Apr. 2	Men	Dionisio Ceron, MEX	2:08:30
	Women	Malgorzata Sobanska, POL	2:27:43

IAAF World Cup (Athens)

Apr. 9	Men	Douglas Wakihuri, KEN	2:12:01
	Women	Anuta Catuna, ROM	2:31:10

Boston

Apr.17	Men	Cosmas Ndeti, KEN	2:09:22
	Women	Uta Pippig, GER	2:25:11

Rotterdam

Apr. 23	Men	Martin Fíz, SPA	2:08:57
	Women	Monica Pont, SPA	2:30:34

IAAF World Championship (Göteborg)

Aug. 12	Men	Martin Fíz, SPA	2:11:41
5	Women	Manuela Machado, POR	2:25:39

Late 1994

New York City

Nov. 6	Men	German Silva, MEX	2:11:21
	Women	Tegla Loroupe, KEN	2:27:37

Fukuoka

Dec. 4	Men	Boay Akonay, TAN	2:09:45

(No women's division)

Rowing

World Championships

at Tampere, Finland (Aug. 21-27)

MEN

Coxed Fours.................USA (Ben Holbrook, Porter Collins,
Scott Munn, Christian Ahrens)
Single Sculls...Iztok Cop, SLO
Eights...Germany (USA 3rd)

WOMEN

Single Sculls ....Maria Brandin, SWE
Eights.................USA (Anne Kakela, Mary McCagg, Laurel
Korholz, Monica Tranel-Michini, Betsy
McCagg, Catriona Fallon, Amy Fuller,
Jennifer Dore and cox Yasmin Farooq)

THE 1996 INFORMATION PLEASE SPORTS ALMANAC

INT'L SPORTS STATISTICS

THROUGH THE YEARS
1896-1995
WINNERS • RECORDS

SEC B

PAGE 635

TRACK & FIELD

IAAF World Championships

While the Summer Olympics have served as the unofficial world outdoor championships for track and field throughout the century, a separate World Championship meet was started in 1983 by the International Amateur Athletic Federation (IAAF). The meet was held every four years from 1983-91, but began an every-other-year cycle in 1993. World Championship sites include Helsinki (1983), Rome (1987), Tokyo (1991), Stuttgart (1993) and Göteborg, Sweden (1995). Note that (WR) indicates world record and (CR) indicates championship meet record.

MEN

Multiple gold medals (including relays): Carl Lewis (8); Michael Johnson (6); Sergey Bubka (5); Calvin Smith (4); Greg Foster, Werner Gunthor, Moses Kiptanui, Noureddine Morceli, Dan O'Brien, Butch Reynolds and Lars Riedel (3); Andrey Abduvaliyev, Donovan Bailey, Leroy Burrell, Andre Cason, Maurizio Damilano, Haile Gebrselassie, Ismael Kirui, Billy Konchellah, Sergey Litvinov, Dennis Mitchell, Edwin Moses, Mike Powell and Jan Zelezny (2).

100 meters

Year		Time	
1983	Carl Lewis, USA	10.07	
1987	Carl Lewis, USA	9.93	
1991	Carl Lewis, USA	9.86	WR
1993	Linford Christie, GBR	9.87	
1995	Donovan Bailey, CAN	9.97	

Note: Ben Johnson was the original winner in 1987, but was stripped of his title and world record time (9.83) following his 1989 admission of drug taking.

200 meters

Year		Time	
1983	Calvin Smith, USA	20.14	
1987	Calvin Smith, USA	20.16	
1991	Michael Johnson, USA	20.01	
1993	Frank Fredericks, NAM	19.85	
1995	Michael Johnson, USA	19.79	CR

400 meters

Year		Time	
1983	Bert Cameron, JAM	45.05	
1987	Thomas Schonlebe, E.Ger	44.33	
1991	Antonio Pettigrew, USA	44.57	
1993	Michael Johnson, USA	43.65	
1995	Michael Johnson, USA	43.39	CR

800 meters

Year		Time	
1983	Willi Wülbeck, W.Ger	1:43.65	
1987	Billy Konchellah, KEN	1:43.06	CR
1991	Billy Konchellah, KEN	1:43.99	
1993	Paul Ruto, KEN	1:44.71	
1995	Wilson Kipketer, DEN	1:45.08	

1500 meters

Year		Time	
1983	Steve Cram, GBR	3:41.59	
1987	Abdi Bile, SOM	3:36.80	
1991	Noureddine Morceli, ALG	3:32.84	CR
1993	Noureddine Morceli, ALG	3:34.24	
1995	Noureddine Morceli, ALG	3:33.73	

5000 meters

Year		Time	
1983	Eammon Coghlan, IRE	13:28.53	
1987	Said Aoutia, MOR	13:26.44	
1991	Yobes Ondieki, KEN	13:14.45	
1993	Ismael Kirui, KEN	13:02.75	CR
1995	Ismael Kirui, KEN	13:16.77	

10,000 meters

Year		Time	
1983	Alberto Cova, ITA	28:01.04	
1987	Paul Kipkoech, KEN	27:38.63	
1991	Moses Tanui, KEN	27:38.74	
1993	Haile Gebrselassie, ETH	27:46.02	
1995	Haile Gebrselassie, ETH	27:12.95	CR

Marathon

Year		Time	
1983	Rob de Castella, AUS	2:10:03	CR
1987	Douglas Wakiihuri, KEN	2:11:48	
1991	Hiromi Taniguchi, JPN	2:14:57	
1993	Mark Plaatjes, USA	2:13:57	
1995	Martin Fiz, SPA	2:11:41	

110-meter Hurdles

Year		Time	
1983	Greg Foster, USA	13.42	
1987	Greg Foster, USA	13.21	
1991	Greg Foster, USA	13.06	
1993	Colin Jackson, GBR	12.91	WR
1995	Allen Johnson, USA	13.00	

400-meter Hurdles

Year		Time	
1983	Edwin Moses, USA	47.50	
1987	Edwin Moses, USA	47.46	
1991	Samuel Matete, ZAM	47.64	
1993	Kevin Young, USA	47.18	CR
1995	Derrick Adkins, USA	47.98	

Track & Field Championships (Cont.)
Men

3000-meter Steeplechase

Year		Time	
1983	Patriz Ilg, W. Ger	8:15.06	
1987	Francesco Panetta, ITA	8:08.57	
1991	Moses Kiptanui, KEN	8:12.59	
1993	Moses Kiptanui, KEN	8:06.36	
1995	Moses Kiptanui, KEN	8:04.16	CR

4x100-meter Relay

Year		Time	
1983	United States	37.86	WR
1987	United States	37.90	
1991	United States	37.50	WR
1993	United States	37.48	CR
1995	Canada	38.31	

4x400-meter Relay

Year		Time	
1983	Soviet Union	3:00.79	
1987	United States	2:57.29	
1991	Great Britain	2:57.53	
1993	Great Britain	2:54.29	WR
1995	United States	2:57.32	

20-kilometer Walk

Year		Time	
1983	Ernesto Canto, MEX	1:20:49	
1987	Maurizio Damilano, ITA	1:20:45	
1991	Maurizio Damilano, ITA	1:19:37	CR
1993	Valentin Massana, SPA	1:22.31	
1995	Michele Didoni, ITA	1:19.59	

50-kilometer Walk

Year		Time	
1983	Ronald Weigel, E. Ger	3:43:08	
1987	Hartwig Gauder, E. Ger	3:40:53	CR
1991	Aleksandr Potashov, USSR	3:53:09	
1993	Jesus Angel Garcia, SPA	3:41:41	
1995	Valentin Kononen, FIN	3:43.42	

High Jump

Year		Height	
1983	Gennedy Avdeyenko, USSR	7- 7¼	
1987	Patrik Sjoberg, SWE	7- 9¾	
1991	Charles Austin, USA	7- 9¾	
1993	Javier Sotomayor, CUB	7-10½	CR
1995	Troy Kemp, BAH	7- 9¼	

Pole Vault

Year		Height	
1983	Sergey Bubka, USSR	18- 8¼	
1987	Sergey Bubka, USSR	19- 2¼	
1991	Sergey Bubka, USSR	19- 6¼	CR
1995	Sergey Bubka, UKR	19- 5	

Long Jump

Year		Distance	
1983	Carl Lewis, USA	28- 0¾	
1987	Carl Lewis, USA	28- 0¼	
1991	Mike Powell, USA	29- 4½	WR
1993	Mike Powell, USA	28- 2¼	
1995	Ivan Pedroso, CUB	28- 6½	

Triple Jump

Year		Distance	
1983	Zdzislaw Hoffmann, POL	57- 2	
1987	Khristo Markov, BUL	58- 9	
1991	Kenny Harrison, USA	58- 4	
1993	Mike Conley, USA	58- 7¼	
1995	Jonathan Edwards, GBR	60- 0¼	WR

Shot Put

Year		Distance	
1983	Edward Sarul, POL	70- 2¼	
1987	Werner Günthör, SWI	72-11¼	CR
1991	Werner Günthör, SWI	71- 1¼	
1993	Werner Günthör, SWI	72- 1	
1995	John Godina, USA	70- 5¼	

Discus

Year		Distance	
1983	Imrich Bugar, CZE	222- 2	
1987	Jurgen Schult, E. Ger	225- 6	
1991	Lars Riedel, GER	217- 2	
1993	Lars Riedel, GER	222- 2	
1995	Lars Riedel, GER	225- 7	CR

Hammer Throw

Year		Distance	
1983	Sergey Litvinov, USSR	271- 3	
1987	Sergey Litvinov, USSR	272- 6	CR
1991	Yuri Sedykh, USSR	268- 0	
1993	Andrey Abduvaliyev, TAJ	267-10	
1995	Andrey Abduvaliyev, TAJ	267- 7	

Javelin

Year		Distance	
1983	Detlef Michel, E. Ger	293- 7	
1987	Seppo Raty, FIN	274- 1	
1991	Kimmo Kinnunen, FIN	297-11	CR
1993	Jan Zelezny, CZE	282- 1	
1995	Jan Zelezny, CZE	293-11	

Decathlon

Year		Points	
1983	Daley Thompson, GBR	8714	
1987	Torsten Voss, E. Ger	8680	
1991	Dan O'Brien, USA	8812	
1993	Dan O'Brien, USA	8817	CR
1995	Dan O'Brien, USA	8695	

Wide World Photos

Carl Lewis of the U.S. is the all-time winningest athlete in the World Championships with five individual gold medals and three more in relays.

WOMEN

Multiple gold medals (including relays): Jackie Joyner-Kersee (4); Gail Devers, Tatyana Samolenko Dorovskikh, Silke Gladisch, Marita Koch, Jearl Miles, Merlene Ottey and Gwen Torrence (3); Hassiba Boulmerka, Olga Bryzgina, Mary Decker, Heike Daute Drechsler, Martina Optiz Hellmann, Stefka Kostadinova, Katrin Krabbe, Jarmila Kratochvilova, Marie-Rose Perec and Huang Zhihong (2).

100 meters

Year		Time	
1983	Marlies Gohr, E. Ger	10.97	
1987	Silke Gladisch, E. Ger	10.90	
1991	Katrin Krabbe, GER	10.99	
1993	Gail Devers, USA	10.81	CR
1995	Gwen Torrence, USA	10.85	

200 meters

Year		Time	
1983	Marita Koch, E. Ger	22.13	
1987	Silke Gladisch, E. Ger	21.74	CR
1991	Katrin Krabbe, GER	22.09	
1993	Merlene Ottey, JAM	21.98	
1995	Merlene Ottey, JAM	22.12	

400 meters

Year		Time	
1983	Jarmila Kratochvilova, CZE	47.99	WR
1987	Olga Bryzgina, USSR	49.38	
1991	Marie-José Pérec, FRA	49.13	
1993	Jearl Miles, USA	49.82	
1995	Marie-José Pérec, FRA	49.28	

800 meters

Year		Time	
1983	Jarmila Kratochvilova, CZE	1:54.68	CR
1987	Sigrun Wodars, E. Ger	1:55.26	
1991	Lilia Nurutdinova, USSR	1:57.50	
1993	Maria Mutola, MOZ	1:55.43	
1995	Ana Quirot, CUB	1:56.11	

1500 meters

Year		Time	
1983	Mary Decker, USA	4:00.90	
1987	Tatiana Samolenko, USSR	3:58.56	CR
1991	Hassiba Boulmerka, ALG	4:02.21	
1993	Liu Dong, CHN	4:00.50	
1995	Hassiba Boulmerka, ALG	4:02.42	

5000 meters

Held as 3000-meter race from 1983–93

Year		Time	
1983	Mary Decker, USA	8:34.62	
1987	Tatyana Samolenko, USSR	8:38.73	
1991	T. Samolenko Dorovskikh, USSR	8:35.82	
1993	Qu Yunxia, CHN	8:28.71	CR
1995	Sonia O'Sullivan, IRE	14:46.47	CR

10,000 meters

Year		Time	
1983	Not held		
1987	Ingrid Kristiansen, NOR	31:05.85	
1991	Liz McColgan, GBR	31:14.31	
1993	Wang Junxia, CHN	30:49.30	CR
1995	Fernanda Ribeiro, POR	31:04.99	

Marathon

Year		Time	
1983	Grete Waitz, NOR	2:28:09	
1987	Rose Mota, POR	2:25:17	CR
1991	Wanda Panfil, POL	2:29:53	
1993	Junko Asari, JPN	2:30:03	
1995	Manuela Machado, POR	2:25.39	

100-meter Hurdles

Year		Time	
1983	Bettine Jahn, E. Ger	12.35 w	
1987	Ginka Zagorcheva, BUL	12.34	CR
1991	Lyudmila Narozhilenko, USSR	12.59	
1993	Gail Devers, USA	12.46	
1995	Gail Devers, USA	12.68	

w indicates wind-aided.

400-meter Hurdles

Year		Time	
1983	Yekaterina Fesenko, USSR	54.14	
1987	Sabine Busch, E. Ger	53.62	
1991	Tatiana Ledovskaya, USSR	53.11	
1993	Sally Gunnell, GBR	52.74	WR
1995	Kim Batten, USA	52.61	WR

4x100-meter Relay

Year		Time	
1983	East Germany	41.76	
1987	United States	41.58	
1991	Jamaica	41.94	
1993	Russia	41.49	CR
1995	United States	42.12	

4x400-meter Relay

Year		Time	
1983	East Germany	3:19.73	
1987	East Germany	3:18.63	
1991	Soviet Union	3:18.43	
1993	United States	3:16.71	CR
1995	United States	3:22.39	

10-kilometer Walk

Year		Time	
1983	Not held		
1987	Irina Strakhova, USSR	44:12	
1991	Alina Ivanova, USSR	42:57	
1993	Sari Essayah, FIN	42:59	
1995	Irina Stankina, RUS	42:13	CR

High Jump

Year		Height	
1983	Tamara Bykova, USSR	6- 7	
1987	Stefka Kostadinova, BUL	6-10¼	WR
1991	Heike Henkel, GER	6- 8¾	
1993	Ioamnet Quintero, CUB	6- 6¼	
1995	Stefka Kostadinova, BUL	6- 7	

Long Jump

Year		Distance	
1983	Heike Daute, E. Ger	23-10¼ w	
1987	Jackie Joyner-Kersee, USA	24- 1¾	CR
1991	Jackie Joyner-Kersee, USA	24- 0¼	
1993	Heike Drechsler, GER	23- 4	
1995	Fiona May, ITA	22-10¾ w	

w indicates wind-aided.

Triple Jump

Year		Distance	
1983	Not held		
1987	Not held		
1991	Not held		
1993	Ana Biryukova, RUS	46- 6¼	WR
1995	Inessa Kravets, UKR	50-10¾	WR

Track & Field Championships (Cont.)
Women

Shot Put

Year		Distance	
1983	Helena Fibingerova, CZE	69- 0	
1987	Natalia Lisovskaya, USSR	69- 8	CR
1991	Huang Zhihong, CHN	68- 4	
1993	Huang Zhihong, CHN	67- 6	
1995	Astrid Kumbernuss, GER	69- 7½	

Javelin

Year		Distance	
1983	Tiina Lillak, FIN	232- 4	
1987	Fatima Whitbread, GBR	251- 5	CR
1991	Xu Demei, CHN	225- 8	
1993	Trine Hattestad, NOR	227- 0	
1995	Natalya Shikolenko, BLR	221- 8	

Discus

Year		Distance	
1983	Martina Opitz, E. Ger	226- 2	
1987	Martina Opitz Hellmann, E. Ger	235- 0	CR
1991	Tsvetanka Khristova, BUL	233- 0	
1993	Olga Burova, RUS	221- 1	
1995	Ellina Zvereva, BLR	225- 2	

Heptathlon

Year		Points	
1983	Ramona Neubert, E. Ger	6770	
1987	Jackie Joyner-Kersee, USA	7128	CR
1991	Sabine Braun, GER	6672	
1993	Jackie Joyner-Kersee, USA	6837	
1995	Ghada Shouaa, SYR	6651	

Marathons

Boston

America's oldest regularly contested foot race, the Boston Marathon is held on Patriots' Day every April and will be run for the 100th time in 1996. It has been run at four different distances: 24 miles, 1232 yards (1897-1923); 26 miles, 209 yards (1924-26); 26 miles, 385 yards (1927-52); 25 miles, 958 yards (1953-56); and 26 miles, 385 yards (since 1957).

MEN

Multiple winners: Clarence DeMar (7); Gerard Cote and Bill Rodgers (4); Ibrahim Hussein, Cosmas Ndeti and Leslie Pawson (3); Tarzan Brown, Jim Caffrey, John A. Kelley, John Miles, Eino Oksanen, Toshihiko Seko, Geoff Smith and Aurele Vandendriessche (2).

Year		Time
1897	John McDermott, New York	2:55:10
1898	Ronald McDonald, Massachusetts	2:42:00
1899	Lawrence Brignolia, Massachusetts	2:54:38
1900	Jim Caffrey, Canada	2:39:44
1901	Jim Caffrey, Canada	2:29:23
1902	Sam Mellor, New York	2:43:12
1903	J.C. Lorden, Massachusetts	2:41:29
1904	Mike Spring, New York	2:38:04
1905	Fred Lorz, New York	2:38:25
1906	Tim Ford, Massachusetts	2:45:45
1907	Tom Longboat, Canada	2:24:24
1908	Tom Morrissey, New York	2:25:43
1909	Henri Renaud, New Hampshire	2:53:36
1910	Fred Cameron, Nova Scotia	2:28:52
1911	Clarence DeMar, Massachusetts	2:21:39
1912	Mike Ryan, Illinois	2:21:18
1913	Fritz Carlson, Minnesota	2:25:14
1914	James Duffy, Canada	2:25:01
1915	Edouard Fabre, Canada	2:31:41
1916	Arthur Roth, Massachusetts	2:27:16
1917	Bill Kennedy, New York	2:28:37
1918	World War relay race	
1919	Carl Linder, Massachusetts	2:29:13
1920	Peter Trivoulidas, New York	2:29:31
1921	Frank Zuna, New Jersey	2:18:57
1922	Clarence DeMar, Massachusetts	2:18:10
1923	Clarence DeMar, Massachusetts	2:23:37
1924	Clarence DeMar, Massachusetts	2:29:40
1925	Charles Mellor, Illinois	2:33:00
1926	John Miles, Nova Scotia	2:25:40
1927	Clarence DeMar, Massachusetts	2:40:22
1928	Clarence DeMar, Massachusetts	2:37:07
1929	John Miles, Nova Scotia	2:33:08
1930	Clarence DeMar, Massachusetts	2:34:48
1931	James Henigan, Massachusetts	2:46:45

Year		Time
1932	Paul deBruyn, Germany	2:33:36
1933	Leslie Pawson, Rhode Island	2:31:01
1934	Dave Komonen, Canada	2:32:53
1935	John A. Kelley, Massachusetts	2:32:07
1936	Ellison (Tarzan) Brown, Rhode Island	2:33:40
1937	Walter Young, Canada	2:33:20
1938	Leslie Pawson, Rhode Island	2:35:34
1939	Ellison (Tarzan) Brown, Rhode Island	2:28:51
1940	Gerard Cote, Canada	2:28:28
1941	Leslie Pawson, Rhode Island	2:30:38
1942	Joe Smith, Massachusetts	2:26:51
1943	Gerard Cote, Canada	2:28:25
1944	Gerard Cote, Canada	2:31:50
1945	John A. Kelley, Massachusetts	2:30:40
1946	Stylianos Kyriakides, Greece	2:29:27
1947	Yun Bok Suh, Korea	2:25:39
1948	Gerard Cote, Canada	2:31:02
1949	Karle Leandersson, Sweden	2:31:50
1950	Kee Yonh Ham, Korea	2:32:39
1951	Shigeki Tanaka, Japan	2:27:45
1952	Doroteo Flores, Guatemala	2:31:53
1953	Keizo Yamada, Japan	2:18:51
1954	Veiko Karvonen, Finland	2:20:39
1955	Hideo Hamamura, Japan	2:18:22
1956	Antti Viskari, Finland	2:14:14
1957	John J. Kelley, Connecticut	2:20:05
1958	Franjo Mihalic, Yugoslavia	2:25:54
1959	Eino Oksanen, Finland	2:22:42
1960	Paavo Kotila, Finland	2:20:54
1961	Eino Oksanen, Finland	2:23:39
1962	Eino Oksanen, Finland	2:23:48
1963	Aurele Vandendriessche, Belgium	2:18:58
1964	Aurele Vandendriessche, Belgium	2:19:59
1965	Morio Shigematsu, Japan	2:16:33
1966	Kenji Kimihara, Japan	2:17:11
1967	David McKenzie, New Zealand	2:15:45

Year		Time
1968	Amby Burfoot, Connecticut	2:22:17
1969	Yoshiaki Unetani, Japan	2:13:49
1970	Ron Hill, England	2:10:30
1971	Alvaro Mejia, Colombia	2:18:45
1972	Olavi Suomalainen, Finland	2:15:39
1973	Jon Anderson, Oregon	2:16:03
1974	Neil Cusack, Ireland	2:13:39
1975	Bill Rodgers, Massachusetts	2:09:55
1976	Jack Fultz, Pennsylvania	2:20:19
1977	Jerome Drayton, Canada	2:14:46
1978	Bill Rodgers, Massachusetts	2:10:13
1979	Bill Rodgers, Massachusetts	2:09:27
1980	Bill Rodgers, Massachusetts	2:12:11
1981	Toshihiko Seko, Japan	2:09:26
1982	Alberto Salazar, Oregon	2:08:52
1983	Greg Meyer, New Jersey	2:09:00
1984	Geoff Smith, England	2:10:34
1985	Geoff Smith, England	2:14:05
1986	Rob de Castella, Australia	2:07:51
1987	Toshihiko Seko, Japan	2:11:50
1988	Ibrahim Hussein, Kenya	2:08:43
1989	Abebe Mekonnen, Ethiopia	2:09:06
1990	Gelindo Bordin, Italy	2:08:19
1991	Ibrahim Hussein, Kenya	2:11:06
1992	Ibrahim Hussein, Kenya	2:08:14
1993	Cosmas Ndeti, Kenya	2:09:33
1994	Cosmas Ndeti, Kenya	2:07:15*
1995	Cosmas Ndeti, Kenya	2:09.22

*Course record.

Wide World Photos

Germany's **Uta Pippig** won her second straight Boston Marathon in 1995 and plans to return for the 100th running of the race on April 15, 1996.

WOMEN

Multiple winners: Rosa Mota (3); Joan Benoit, Miki Gorman, Ingrid Kristiansen, Olga Markova and Uta Pippig (2).

Year		Time	Year		Time
1972	Nina Kuscsik, New York	3:08:58	1984	Lorraine Moller, New Zealand	2:29:28
1973	Jacqueline Hansen, California	3:05:59	1985	Lisa Larsen Weidenbach, Mass	2:34:06
1974	Miki Gorman, California	2:47:11	1986	Ingrid Kristiansen, Norway	2:24:55
1975	Liane Winter, West Germany	2:42:24	1987	Rosa Mota, Portugal	2:25:21
1976	Kim Merritt, Wisconsin	2:47:10	1988	Rosa Mota, Portugal	2:24:30
1977	Miki Gorman, California	2:48:33	1989	Ingrid Kristiansen, Norway	2:24:33
1978	Gayle Barron, Georgia	2:44:52			
1979	Joan Benoit, Maine	2:35:15	1990	Rosa Mota, Portugal	2:25:23
			1991	Wanda Panfil, Poland	2:24:18
1980	Jacqueline Gareau, Canada	2:34:28	1992	Olga Markova, CIS	2:23:43
1981	Allison Roe, New Zealand	2:26:46	1993	Olga Markova, Russia	2:25:27
1982	Charlotte Teske, West Germany	2:29:33	1994	Uta Pippig, Germany	2:21:45*
1983	Joan Benoit, Maine	2:22:43	1995	Uta Pippig, Germany	2:25:11

*Course record.

New York City

Started in 1970, the New York City Marathon is run in the fall, usually on the first Sunday in November. The route winds through all of the city's five boroughs and finishes in Central Park.

MEN

Multiple winners: Bill Rodgers (4); Alberto Salazar (3); Tom Fleming and Orlando Pizzolato (2).

Year		Time	Year		Time
1970	Gary Muhrcke, USA	2:31:38	1980	Alberto Salazar, USA	2:09:41
1971	Norman Higgins, USA	2:22:54	1981	Alberto Salazar, USA	2:08:13
1972	Sheldon Karlin, USA	2:27:52	1982	Alberto Salazar, USA	2:09:29
1973	Tom Fleming, USA	2:21:54	1983	Rod Dixon, New Zealand	2:08:59
1974	Norbert Sander, USA	2:26:30	1984	Orlando Pizzolato, Italy	2:14:53
1975	Tom Fleming, USA	2:19:27	1985	Orlando Pizzolato, Italy	2:11:34
1976	Bill Rodgers, USA	2:10:09	1986	Gianni Poli, Italy	2:11:06
1977	Bill Rodgers, USA	2:11:28	1987	Ibrahim Hussein, Kenya	2:11:01
1978	Bill Rodgers, USA	2:12:12	1988	Steve Jones, Wales	2:08:20
1979	Bill Rodgers, USA	2:11:42	1989	Juma Ikangaa, Tanzania	2:08:01*

Marathons (Cont.)
New York City
MEN

Year		Time	Year		Time
1990	Douglas Wakiihuri, Kenya	2:12:39	1993	Andres Espinosa, Mexico	2:10:04
1991	Salvador Garcia, Mexico	2:09:28	1994	German Silva, Mexico	2:11:21
1992	Willie Mtolo, South Africa	2:09:29		*Course record.	

WOMEN

Multiple winners: Grete Waitz (9); Miki Gorman and Nina Kuscsik (2).

Year		Time	Year		Time
1970	No Finisher		1984	Grete Waitz, Norway	2:29:30
1971	Beth Bonner, USA	2:55:22	1985	Grete Waitz, Norway	2:28:34
1972	Nina Kuscsik, USA	3:08:41	1986	Grete Waitz, Norway	2:28:06
1973	Nina Kuscsik, USA	2:57:07	1987	Priscilla Welch, Britain	2:30:17
1974	Katherine Switzer, USA	3:07:29	1988	Grete Waitz, Norway	2:28:07
1975	Kim Merritt, USA	2:46:14	1989	Ingrid Kristiansen, Norway	2:25:30
1976	Miki Gorman, USA	2:39:11			
1977	Miki Gorman, USA	2:43:10	1990	Wanda Panfil, Poland	2:30:45
1978	Grete Waitz, Norway	2:32:30	1991	Liz McColgan, Scotland	2:27:23
1979	Grete Waitz, Norway	2:27:33	1992	Lisa Ondieki, Australia	2:24:40*
			1993	Uta Pippig, Germany	2:26:24
1980	Grete Waitz, Norway	2:25:41	1994	Tegla Laroupe, Kenya	2:27:37
1981	Allison Roe, New Zealand	2:25:29			
1982	Grete Waitz, Norway	2:27:14		*Course record.	
1983	Grete Waitz, Norway	2:27:00			

Annual Awards

Track & Field News Athletes of the Year

Voted on by an international panel of track and field experts and presented since 1959 for men and 1974 for women.

MEN

Multiple winners: Carl Lewis (3); Sergey Bubka, Sebastian Coe, Alberto Juantorena, Noureddine Morceli, Jim Ryun and Peter Snell (2).

Year		Event	Year		Event
1959	Martin Lauer, W. Germany	110H/Decathlon	1977	Alberto Juantorena, Cuba	400/800
			1978	Henry Rono, Kenya	5000/10,000/Steeplechase
1960	Rafer Johnson, USA	Decathlon	1979	Sebastian Coe, Great Britain	800/1500
1961	Ralph Boston, USA	Long Jump/110 Hurdles			
1962	Peter Snell, New Zealand	800/1500	1980	Edwin Moses, USA	400 Hurdles
1963	C.K. Yang, Taiwan	Decathlon/Pole Vault	1981	Sebastian Coe, Great Britain	800/1500
1964	Peter Snell, New Zealand	800/1500	1982	Carl Lewis, USA	100/200/Long Jump
1965	Ron Clarke, Australia	5000/10,000	1983	Carl Lewis, USA	100/200/Long Jump
1966	Jim Ryun, USA	800/1500	1984	Carl Lewis, USA	100/200/Long Jump
1967	Jim Ryun, USA	1500	1985	Said Aouita, Morocco	1500/5000
1968	Bob Beamon, USA	Long Jump	1986	Yuri Sedykh, USSR	Hammer Throw
1969	Bill Toomey, USA	Decathlon	1987	Ben Johnson, Canada	100
			1988	Sergey Bubka, USSR	Pole Vault
1970	Randy Matson, USA	Shot Put	1989	Roger Kingdom, USA	110 Hurdles
1971	Rod Milburn, USA	110 Hurdles			
1972	Lasse Viren, Finland	5000/10,000	1990	Michael Johnson, USA	200/400
1973	Ben Jipcho, Kenya	1500/5000/Steeplechase	1991	Sergey Bubka, USSR	Pole Vault
1974	Rick Wohlhuter, USA	800/1500	1992	Kevin Young, USA	400 Hurdles
1975	John Walker, New Zealand	800/1500	1993	Noureddine Morceli, Algeria	Mile/1500/3000
1976	Alberto Juantorena, Cuba	400/800	1994	Noureddine Morceli, Algeria	Mile/1500/3000

WOMEN

Multiple winners: Marita Koch (4); Jackie Joyner-Kersee (3); Evelyn Ashford (2).

Year		Event	Year		Event
1974	Irena Szewinska, Poland	100/200/400	1985	Marita Koch, E. Germany	100/200/400
1975	Faina Melnik, USSR	Shot Put/Discus	1986	Jackie Joyner-Kersee, USA	Heptathlon/Long Jump
1976	Tatiana Kazankina, USSR	800/1500	1987	Jackie Joyner-Kersee, USA	100H/Heptathlon/LJ
1977	Rosemarie Ackermann, E. Germany	High Jump	1988	Florence Griffith Joyner, USA	100/200
1978	Marita Koch, E. Germany	100/200/400	1989	Ana Quirot, Cuba	400/800
1979	Marita Koch, E. Germany	100/200/400			
			1990	Merlene Ottey, Jamaica	100/200
1980	Ilona Briesenick, E. Germany	Shot Put	1991	Heike Henkel, Germany	High Jump
1981	Evelyn Ashford, USA	100/200	1992	Heike Drechsler, Germany	Long Jump
1982	Marita Koch, E. Germany	100/200/400	1993	Wang Junxia, China	1500/3000/10,000
1983	Jarmila Kratochvilova, Czech	200/400/800	1994	Jackie Joyner-Kersee, USA	100H/Heptathlon/LJ
1984	Evelyn Ashford, USA	100			

SWIMMING & DIVING
FINA World Championships

While the Summer Olympics have served as the unofficial world championships for swimming and diving throughout the century, a separate World Championship meet was started in 1973 by the International Amateur Swimming Federation (FINA). The meet was held three times between 1973-78, then every four years since then. Sites have included Belgrade (1973); Cali, COL (1975); West Berlin (1978); Guayaquil, ECU (1982); Madrid (1986); Perth (1991) and Rome (1994).

Swimming
MEN

Most gold medals (including relays): Jim Montgomery (7); Matt Biondi (6); Rowdy Gaines (5); Joe Bottom, Tamas Darnyi, Michael Gross, Tom Jager, David McCagg, Vladimir Salnikov and Tim Shaw (4); Billy Forrester, Andras Hargitay, Roland Matthes, John Murphy, Jeff Rouse, Norbert Rozsa and David Wilkie (3).

50-meter Freestyle

Year		Time	
1973-82 Not held			
1986	Tom Jager, USA	22.49	
1991	Tom Jager, USA	22.16	CR
1994	Aleksandr Popov, RUS	22.17	

100-meter Freestyle

Year		Time	
1973	Jim Montgomery, USA	51.70	
1975	Tim Shaw, USA	51.25	
1978	David McCagg, USA	50.24	
1982	Jorg Woithe, E. Ger	50.18	
1986	Matt Biondi, USA	48.94	CR
1991	Matt Biondi, USA	49.18	
1994	Aleksandr Popov, RUS	49.12	

200-meter Freestyle

Year		Time	
1973	Jim Montgomery, USA	1:53.02	
1975	Tim Shaw, USA	1:52.04	
1978	Billy Forrester, USA	1:51.02	
1982	Michael Gross, W. Ger	1:49.84	
1986	Michael Gross, W. Ger	1:47.92	
1991	Giorgio Lamberti, ITA	1:47.27	
1994	Antti Kasvio, FIN	1:47.32	CR

400-meter Freestyle

Year		Time	
1973	Rick DeMont, USA	3:58.18	
1975	Tim Shaw, USA	3:54.88	
1978	Vladimir Salnikov, USSR	3:51.94	
1982	Vladimir Salnikov, USSR	3:51.30	
1986	Rainer Henkel, W. Ger	3:50.05	
1991	Jorg Hoffman, GER	3:48.04	
1994	Kieren Perkins, AUS	3:43.80	WR

1500-meter Freestyle

Year		Time	
1973	Stephen Holland, AUS	15:31.85	
1975	Tim Shaw, USA	15:28.92	
1978	Vladimir Salnikov, USSR	15:03.99	
1982	Vladimir Salnikov, USSR	15:01.77	
1986	Rainer Henkel, W. Ger	15:05.31	
1991	Jorg Hoffman, GER	14:50.36	WR
1994	Kieren Perkins, AUS	14:50.52	

100-meter Backstroke

Year		Time	
1973	Roland Matthes, E. Ger	57.47	
1975	Roland Matthes, E. Ger	58.15	
1978	Bob Jackson, USA	56.36	
1982	Dirk Richter, E. Ger	55.95	
1986	Igor Polianski, USSR	55.58	
1991	Jeff Rouse, USA	55.23	
1994	Martin Lopez-Zubero, SPA	55.17	CR

200-meter Backstroke

Year		Time	
1973	Roland Matthes, E. Ger	2:01.87	
1975	Zoltan Varraszto, HUN	2:05.05	
1978	Jesse Vassallo, USA	2:02.16	
1982	Rick Carey, USA	2:00.82	
1986	Igor Polianski, USSR	1:58.78	CR
1991	Martin Zubero, SPA	1:59.52	
1994	Vladimir Selkov, RUS	1:57.42	

100-meter Breaststroke

Year		Time	
1973	John Hencken, USA	1:04.02	
1975	David Wilkie, GBR	1:04.26	
1978	Walter Kusch, W. Ger	1:03.56	
1982	Steve Lundquist, USA	1:02.75	
1986	Victor Davis, CAN	1:02.71	
1991	Norbert Rozsa, HUN	1:01.45	WR
1994	Norbert Rozsa, HUN	1:01.24	

200-meter Breaststroke

Year		Time	
1973	David Wilkie, GBR	2:19.28	
1975	David Wilkie, GBR	2:18.23	
1978	Nick Nevid, USA	2:18.37	
1982	Victor Davis, CAN	2:14.77	WR
1986	Jozsef Szabo, HUN	2:14.27	
1991	Mike Barrowman, USA	2:11.23	WR
1994	Norbert Rozsa, HUN	2:12.81	

100-meter Butterfly

Year		Time	
1973	Bruce Robertson, CAN	55.69	
1975	Greg Jagenburg, USA	55.63	
1978	Joe Bottom, USA	54.30	
1982	Matt Gribble, USA	53.88	
1986	Pablo Morales, USA	53.54	
1991	Anthony Nesty, SUR	53.29	CR
1994	Rafal Szukala, POL	53.51	

200-meter Butterfly

Year		Time	
1973	Robin Backhaus, USA	2:03.32	
1975	Billy Forrester, USA	2:01.95	
1978	Mike Bruner, USA	1:59.38	
1982	Michael Gross, W. Ger	1:58.85	
1986	Michael Gross, W. Ger	1:56.53	
1991	Melvin Stewart, USA	1:55.69	WR
1994	Denis Pankratov, RUS	1:56.54	

200-meter Individual Medley

Year		Time	
1973	Gunnar Larsson, SWE	2:08.36	
1975	Andras Hargitay, HUN	2:07.72	
1978	Graham Smith, CAN	2:03.65	WR
1982	Alexander Sidorenko, USSR	2:03.30	
1986	Tamás Darnyi, HUN	2:01.57	
1991	Tamás Darnyi, HUN	1:59.36	WR
1994	Janis Sievinen, FIN	1:58.16	WR

FINA Swimming Championships (Cont.)
MEN

400-meter Individual Medley

Year		Time	
1973	Andras Hargitay, HUN	4:31.11	
1975	Andras Hargitay, HUN	4:32.57	
1978	Jesse Vassallo, USA	4:20.05	WR
1982	Ricardo Prado, BRA	4:19.78	WR
1986	Tamás Darnyi, HUN	4:18.98	
1991	Tamás Darnyi, HUN	4:12.36	WR
1994	Tom Dolan, USA	4:12.30	WR

4 x 200-meter Freestyle Relay

Year		Time	
1973	United States	7:33.22	WR
1975	West Germany	7:39.44	
1978	United States	7:20.82	
1982	United States	7:21.09	
1986	East Germany	7:15.91	
1991	Germany	7:13.50	CR
1994	Sweden	7:17.34	

4 x 100-meter Freestyle Relay

Year		Time	
1973	United States	3:27.18	
1975	United States	3:24.85	
1978	United States	3:19.74	
1982	United States	3:19.26	WR
1986	United States	3:19.98	
1991	United States	3:17.15	
1994	United States	3:16.90	CR

4 x 100-meter Medley Relay

Year		Time	
1973	United States	3:49.49	
1975	United States	3:49.00	
1978	United States	3:44.63	
1982	United States	3:40.84	WR
1986	United States	3:41.25	
1991	United States	3:39.66	
1994	United States	3:37.74	CR

WOMEN

Most gold medals (including relays): Kornelia Ender (8); Kristin Otto (7); Tracy Caulkins, Heike Friedrich, Le Jingyi, Rosemarie Kother and Ulrike Richter (4); Hannalore Anke, Lu Bin, He Cihong, Janet Evans, Nicole Haislett, Lui Limin, Birgit Meineke, Joan Pennington, Manuela Stellmach, Renate Vogel and Cynthia Woodhead (3).

50-meter Freestyle

Year		Time	
1973-82 Not held			
1986	Tamara Costache, ROM	25.28	WR
1991	Zhuang Yong, CHN	25.47	
1994	Le Jingyi, CHN	24.51	WR

100-meter Freestyle

Year		Time	
1973	Kornelia Ender, E. Ger	57.54	
1975	Kornelai Ender, E. Ger	56.50	
1978	Barbara Krause, E. Ger	55.68	
1982	Birgit Meineke, E. Ger	55.79	
1986	Kristin Otto, E. Ger	55.05	
1991	Nicole Haislett, USA	55.17	
1994	Le Jingyi, CHN	54.01	WR

200-meter Freestyle

Year		Time	
1973	Keena Rothhammer, USA	2:04.99	
1975	Shirley Babashoff, USA	2:02.50	
1978	Cynthia Woodhead, USA	1:58.53	WR
1982	Annemarie Verstappen, HOL	1:59.53	
1986	Heike Friedrich, E. Ger	1:58.26	
1991	Hayley Lewis, AUS	2:00.48	
1994	Franziska Van Almsick, GER	1:56.78	WR

400-meter Freestyle

Year		Time	
1973	Heather Greenwood, USA	4:20.28	
1975	Shirley Babashoff, USA	4:22.70	
1978	Tracey Wickham, AUS	4:06.28	WR
1982	Carmela Schmidt. E. Ger	4:08.98	
1986	Heike Friedrich, E. Ger	4:07.45	
1991	Janet Evans, USA	4:08.63	
1994	Yang Aihua, CHN	4:09.64	

800-meter Freestyle

Year		Time	
1973	Novella Calligaris, ITA	8:52.97	
1975	Jenny Turrall, AUS	8:44.75	
1978	Tracey Wickham, AUS	8:25.94	
1982	Kim Linehan, USA	8:27.48	
1986	Astrid Strauss, E. Ger	8:28.24	
1991	Janet Evans, USA	8:24.05	CR
1994	Janet Evans, USA	8:29.85	

100-meter Backstroke

Year		Time	
1973	Ulrike Richter, E. Ger	1:05.42	
1975	Ulrike Richter, E. Ger	1:03.30	
1978	Linda Jezek, USA	1:02.55	
1982	Kristin Otto, E. Ger	1:01.30	
1986	Betsy Mitchell, USA	1:01.74	
1991	Krisztina Egerszegi, HUN	1:01.78	
1994	He Cihong, CHN	1:00.57	WR

200-meter Backstroke

Year		Time	
1973	Melissa Belote, USA	2:20.52	
1975	Birgit Treiber, E. Ger	2:15.46	WR
1978	Linda Jezek, USA	2:11.93	WR
1982	Cornelia Sirch, E. Ger	2:09.91	WR
1986	Cornelia Sirch, E. Ger	2:11.37	
1991	Krisztina Egerszegi, HUN	2:09.15	
1994	He Cihong, CHN	2:07.40	CR

100-meter Breaststroke

Year		Time	
1973	Renate Vogel, E. Ger	1:13.74	
1975	Hannalore Anke, E. Ger	1:12.72	
1978	Julia Bogdanova, USSR	1:10.31	WR
1982	Ute Geweniger, E. Ger	1:09.14	
1986	Sylvia Gerasch, E. Ger	1:08.11	WR
1991	Linley Frame, AUS	1:08.81	
1994	Samantha Riley, AUS	1:07.69	WR

200-meter Breaststroke

Year		Time	
1973	Renate Vogel, E. Ger	2:40.01	
1975	Hannalore Anke, E. Ger	2:37.25	
1978	Lina Kachushite, USSR	2:31.42	WR
1982	Svetlana Varganova, USSR	2:28.82	
1986	Silke Hoerner, E. Ger	2:27.40	WR
1991	Elena Volkova, USSR	2:29.53	
1994	Samantha Riley, AUS	2:26.87	CR

100-meter Butterfly

Year		Time	
1973	Kornelia Ender, E. Ger	1:02.53	
1975	Kornelia Ender, E. Ger	1:01.24	WR
1978	Joan Pennington, USA	1:00.20	
1982	Mary T. Meagher, USA	59.41	
1986	Kornelai Gressler, E. Ger	59.51	
1991	Qian Hong, CHN	59.68	
1994	Liu Limin, CHN	58.98	CR

200-meter Butterfly

Year		Time	
1973	Rosemarie Kother, E. Ger	2:13.76	
1975	Rosemarie Kother, E. Ger	2:15.92	
1978	Tracy Caulkins, USA	2:09.78	WR
1982	Ines Geissler, E. Ger	2:08.66	
1986	Mary T. Meagher, USA	2:08.41	
1991	Summer Sanders, USA	2:09.24	
1994	Liu Limin, CHN	2:07.25	CR

200-meter Individual Medley

Year		Time	
1973	Andre Huebner, E. Ger	2:20.51	
1975	Kathy Heddy, USA	2:19.80	
1978	Tracy Caulkins, USA	2:19.80	WR
1982	Petra Schneider, E. Ger	2:11.79	CR
1986	Kristin Otto, E. Ger	2:15.56	
1991	Lin Li, CHN	2:13.40	
1994	Lu Bin, CHN	2:12.34	

400-meter Individual Medley

Year		Time	
1973	Gudrun Wegner, E. Ger	4:57.71	
1975	Ulrike Tauber, E. Ger	4:52.76	
1978	Tracy Caulkins, USA	4:40.83	WR
1982	Petra Schneider, E. Ger	4:36.10	WR
1986	Kathleen Nord, E. Ger	4:43.75	
1991	Lin Li, CHN	4:41.45	
1994	Dai Guohong, CHN	4:39.14	

4 x 100-meter Freestyle Relay

Year		Time	
1973	East Germany	3:52.45	
1975	East Germany	3:49.37	
1978	United States	3:43.43	WR
1982	East Germany	3:43.97	
1986	East Germany	3:40.57	
1991	United States	3:43.26	
1994	China	3:37.91	WR

4 x 200-meter Freestyle Relay

Year		Time	
1973-82	Not held		
1986	East Germany	7:59.33	WR
1991	Germany	8:02.56	
1994	China	7:57.96	CR

4 x 100-meter Medley Relay

Year		Time	
1973	East Germany	4:16.84	
1975	East Germany	4:14.74	
1978	United States	4:08.21	
1982	East Germany	4:05.8	WR
1986	East Germany	4:04.82	
1991	United States	4:06.51	
1994	China	4:01.67	CR

Diving

Multiple Gold Medals: MEN— Greg Louganis (5); Phil Boggs (3); Klaus Dibiasi (2). WOMEN— Irina Kalinina and Gao Min (3); Fu Mingxia (2).

MEN

1-meter Springboard

Year		Pts
1991	Edwin Jongejans, HOL	588.51
1994	Evan Stewart, ZIM	382.14

3-meter Springboard

Year		Pts
1973	Phil Boggs, USA	618.57
1975	Phil Boggs, USA	597.12
1978	Phil Boggs, USA	913.95
1982	Greg Louganis, USA	752.67
1986	Greg Louganis, USA	750.06
1991	Kent Ferguson, USA	650.25
1994	Yu Zhuocheng, CHN	655.44

Platform

Year		Pts
1973	Klaus Dibiasi, ITA	559.53
1975	Klaus Dibiasi, ITA	547.98
1978	Greg Louganis, USA	844.11
1982	Greg Louganis, USA	634.26
1986	Greg Louganis, USA	668.58
1991	Sun Shuwei, CHN	626.79
1994	Dmitri Sautin, RUS	634.71

WOMEN

1-meter Springboard

Year		Pts
1991	Gao Min, CHN	478.26
1994	Chen Lixia, CHN	279.30

3-meter Springboard

Year		Pts
1973	Christa Koehler, E. Ger	442.17
1975	Irina Kalinina, USSR	489.81
1978	Irina Kalinina, USSR	691.43
1982	Megan Neyer, USA	501.03
1986	Gao Min, CHN	582.90
1991	Gao Min, CHN	539.01
1994	Tan Shuping, CHN	548.49

Platform

Year		Pts
1973	Ulrike Knape, SWE	406.77
1975	Janet Ely, USA	403.89
1978	Irina Kalinina, USSR	412.71
1982	Wendy Wyland, USA	438.79
1986	Chen Lin, CHN	449.67
1991	Fu Mingxia, CHN	426.51
1994	Fu Mingxia, CHN	434.04

ALPINE SKIING
World Cup Overall Champions

World Cup Overall Champions (downhill and slalom events combined) since the tour was organized in 1967.

MEN

Multiple winners: Marc Girardelli (5), Gustavo Thoeni and Pirmin Zurbriggen (4); Phil Mahre, and Ingemar Stenmark (3); Jean-Claude Killy and Karl Schranz (2).

Year		Year		Year	
1967	Jean-Claude Killy, France	1977	Ingemar Stenmark, Sweden	1987	Pirmin Zurbriggen, Switzerland
1968	Jean-Claude Killy, France	1978	Ingemar Stenmark, Sweden	1988	Pirmin Zurbriggen, Switzerland
1969	Karl Schranz, Austria	1979	Peter Luescher, Switzerland	1989	Marc Girardelli, Luxembourg
1970	Karl Schranz, Austria	1980	Andreas Wenzel, Lichtenstein	1990	Pirmin Zurbriggen, Switzerland
1971	Gustavo Thoeni, Italy	1981	Phil Mahre, USA	1991	Marc Girardelli, Luxembourg
1972	Gustavo Thoeni, Italy	1982	Phil Mahre, USA	1992	Paul Accola, Switzerland
1973	Gustavo Thoeni, Italy	1983	Phil Mahre, USA	1993	Marc Girardelli, Luxembourg
1974	Piero Gros, Italy	1984	Pirmin Zurbriggen, Switzerland	1994	Kjetil Andre Aamodt, Norway
1975	Gustavo Thoeni, Italy	1985	Marc Girardelli, Luxembourg	1995	Alberto Tomba, Italy
1976	Ingemar Stenmark, Sweden	1986	Marc Girardelli, Luxembourg		

WOMEN

Multiple winners: Annemarie Moser-Proell (6); Petra Kronberger and Vreni Schneider (3); Michela Figini, Nancy Greene, Erika Hess, Maria Walliser and Hanni Wenzel (2).

Year		Year		Year	
1967	Nancy Greene, Canada	1977	Lise-Marie Morerod, Switzerland	1987	Maria Walliser, Switzerland
1968	Nancy Greene, Canada	1978	Hanni Wenzel, Lichtenstein	1988	Michela Figini, Switzerland
1969	Gertrud Gabi, Austria	1979	Annemarie Moser-Proell, Austria	1989	Vreni Schneider, Switzerland
1970	Michele Jacot, France	1980	Hanni Wenzel, Lichtenstein	1990	Petra Kronberger, Austria
1971	Annemarie Proell, Austria	1981	Marie-Theres Nadig, Switzerland	1991	Petra Kronberger, Austria
1972	Annemarie Proell, Austria	1982	Erika Hess, Switzerland	1992	Petra Kronberger, Austria
1973	Annemarie Proell, Austria	1983	Tamara McKinney, USA	1993	Anita Wachter, Austria
1974	Annemarie Proell, Austria	1984	Erika Hess, Switzerland	1994	Vreni Schneider, Switzerland
1975	Annemarie Moser-Proell, Austria	1985	Michela Figini, Switzerland	1995	Vreni Schneider, Switzerland
1976	Rosi Mittermaier, W. Germany	1986	Maria Walliser, Switzerland		

TOUR DE FRANCE

The world's premier cycling event, the Tour de France is staged throughout the country (sometimes passing through neighboring countries) over four weeks. The 1946 Tour, however, the first after World War II, was only a five-day race.

Multiple winners: Jacques Anquetil, Bernard Hinault, Miguel Induráin and Eddy Merckx (5); Louison Bobet, Greg LeMond and Philippe Thys (3); Gino Bartali, Ottavio Bottecchia, Fausto Coppi, Laurent Fignon, Nicholas Frantz, Firmin Lambot, André Leducq, Sylvere Maes, Antonin Magne, Lucien Petit-Breton and Bernard Thevenet (2).

Year		Year		Year	
1903	Maurice Garin, France	1935	Romain Maes, Belgium	1969	Eddy Merckx, Belgium
1904	Henri Cornet, France	1936	Sylvere Maes, Belgium	1970	Eddy Merckx, Belgium
1905	Louis Trousselier, France	1937	Roger Lapebie, France	1971	Eddy Merckx, Belgium
1906	René Pottier, France	1938	Gino Bartali, Italy	1972	Eddy Merckx, Belgium
1907	Lucien Petit-Breton, France	1939	Sylvere Maes, Belgium	1973	Luis Ocana, Spain
1908	Lucien Petit-Breton, France			1974	Eddy Merckx, Belgium
1909	Francois Faber, Luxembourg	1940-45	Not held	1975	Bernard Thevenet, France
1910	Octave Lapize, France	1946	Jean Lazarides, France	1976	Lucien van Impe, Belgium
1911	Gustave Garrigou, France	1947	Jean Robic, France	1977	Bernard Thevenet, France
1912	Odile Defraye, Belgium	1948	Gino Bartali, Italy	1978	Bernard Hinault, France
1913	Philippe Thys, Belgium	1949	Fausto Coppi, Italy	1979	Bernard Hinault, France
1914	Philippe Thys, Belgium	1950	Ferdinand Kubler, Switzerland	1980	Joop Zoetemelk, Holland
1915-18	Not held	1951	Hugo Koblet, Switzerland	1981	Bernard Hinault, France
1919	Firmin Lambot, Belgium	1952	Fausto Coppi, Italy	1982	Bernard Hinault, France
1920	Philippe Thys, Belgium	1953	Louison Bobet, France	1983	Laurent Fignon, France
1921	Léon Scieur, Belgium	1954	Louison Bobet, France	1984	Laurent Fignon, France
1922	Firmin Lambot, Belgium	1955	Louison Bobet, France	1985	Bernard Hinault, France
1923	Henri Pelissier, France	1956	Roger Walkowiak, France	1986	Greg LeMond, USA
1924	Ottavio Bottecchia, Italy	1957	Jacques Anquetil, France	1987	Stephen Roche, Ireland
1925	Ottavio Bottecchia, Italy	1958	Charly Gaul, Luxembourg	1988	Pedro Delgado, Spain
1926	Lucien Buysse, Belgium	1959	Federico Bahamontes, Spain	1989	Greg LeMond, USA
1927	Nicholas Frantz, Luxembourg	1960	Gastone Nencini, Italy	1990	Greg LeMond, USA
1928	Nicholas Frantz, Luxembourg	1961	Jacques Anquetil, France	1991	Miguel Induráin, Spain
1929	Maurice Dewaele, Belgium	1962	Jacques Anquetil, France	1992	Miguel Induráin, Spain
1930	André Leducq, France	1963	Jacques Anquetil, France	1993	Miguel Induráin, Spain
1931	Antonin Magne, France	1964	Jacques Anquetil, France	1994	Miguel Induráin, Spain
1932	André Leducq, France	1965	Felice Gimondi, Italy	1995	Miguel Induráin, Spain
1933	Georges Speicher, France	1966	Lucien Aimar, France		
1934	Antonin Magne, France	1967	Roger Pingeon, France		
		1968	Jan Janssen, Holland		

FIGURE SKATING

World Champions

Skaters who won World and Olympic championships in the same year are listed in **bold** type.

MEN

Multiple winners: Ulrich Salchow (10); Karl Schafer (7); Dick Button (5); Willy Bockl, Kurt Browning, Scott Hamilton and Hayes Jenkins (4); Emmerich Danzor, Gillis Grafstrom, Gustav Hugel, David Jenkins, Fritz Kachler and Ondrej Nepela (3); Brian Boitano, Gilbert Fuchs, Jan Hoffmann, Felix Kaspar, Vladimir Kovalev, Elvis Stojko and Tim Wood (2).

Year		Year		Year	
1896	Gilbert Fuchs, Germany	1932	**Karl Schafer**, Austria	1968	Emmerich Danzer, Austria
1897	Gustav Hugel, Austria	1933	Karl Schafer, Austria	1969	Tim Wood, USA
1898	Henning Grenander, Sweden	1934	Karl Schafer, Austria		
1899	Gustav Hugel, Austria	1935	Karl Schafer, Austria	1970	Tim Wood, USA
		1936	**Karl Schafer**, Austria	1971	Ondrej Nepela, Czechoslovakia
1900	Gustav Hugel, Austria	1937	Felix Kaspar, Austria	1972	**Ondrej Nepela**, Czechoslovakia
1901	Ulrich Salchow, Sweden	1938	Felix Kaspar, Austria	1973	Ondrej Nepela, Czechoslovakia
1902	Ulrich Salchow, Sweden	1939	Graham Sharp, Britain	1974	Jan Hoffmann, E. Germany
1903	Ulrich Salchow, Sweden			1975	Sergie Volkov, USSR
1904	Ulrich Salchow, Sweden	1940-46	Not held	1976	**John Curry**, Britain
1905	Ulrich Salchow, Sweden	1947	Hans Gerschwiler, Switzerland	1977	Vladimir Kovalev, USSR
1906	Gilbert Fuchs, Germany	1948	**Dick Button**, USA	1978	Charles Tickner, USA
1907	Ulrich Salchow, Sweden	1949	Dick Button, USA	1979	Vladimir Kovalev, USSR
1908	**Ulrich Salchow**, Sweden				
1909	Ulrich Salchow, Sweden	1950	Dick Button, USA	1980	Jan Hoffmann, E. Germany
		1951	Dick Button, USA	1981	Scott Hamilton, USA
1910	Ulrich Salchow, Sweden	1952	**Dick Button**, USA	1982	Scott Hamilton, USA
1911	Ulrich Salchow, Sweden	1953	Hayes Jenkins, USA	1983	Scott Hamilton, USA
1912	Fritz Kachler, Austria	1954	Hayes Jenkins, USA	1984	**Scott Hamilton**, USA
1913	Fritz Kachler, Austria	1955	Hayes Jenkins, USA	1985	Alexander Fadeev, USSR
1914	Gosta Sandhal, Sweden	1956	**Hayes Jenkins**, USA	1986	Brian Boitano, USA
1915-21	Not held	1957	David Jenkins, USA	1987	Brian Orser, Canada
		1958	David Jenkins, USA	1988	**Brian Boitano**, USA
1922	Gillis Grafstrom, Sweden	1959	David Jenkins, USA	1989	Kurt Browning, Canada
1923	Fritz Kachler, Austria				
1924	**Gillis Grafstrom**, Sweden	1960	Alan Giletti, France	1990	Kurt Browning, Canada
1925	Willy Bockl, Austria	1961	Not held	1991	Kurt Browning, Canada
1926	Willy Bockl, Austria	1962	Donald Jackson, Canada	1992	**Viktor Petrenko**, CIS
1927	Willy Bockl, Austria	1963	Donald McPherson, Canada	1993	Kurt Browning, Canada
1928	Willy Bockl, Austria	1964	**Manfred Schneldorfer**, W. Ger	1994	Elvis Stojko, Canada
1929	Gillis Grafstrom, Sweden	1965	Alain Calmat, France	1995	Elvis Stojko, Canada
		1966	Emmerich Danzer, Austria		
1930	Karl Schafer, Austria	1967	Emmerich Danzer, Austria		
1931	Karl Schafer, Austria				

WOMEN

Multiple winners: Sonja Henie (10); Carol Heiss and Herma Planck Szabo (5); Lily Kronberger and Katarina Witt (4); Sjoukje Dijkstra, Peggy Fleming, Meray Horvath (3); Tenley Albright, Linda Fratianne, Anett Poetzsch, Beatrix Schuba, Barbara Ann Scott, Gabriele Seyfert, Megan Taylor, Alena Vrzanova, and Kristi Yamaguchi (2).

Year		Year		Year	
1906	Madge Syers, Britain	1934	Sonja Henie, Norway	1962	Sjoukje Dijkstra, Holland
1907	Madge Syers, Britian	1935	Sonja Henie, Norway	1963	Sjoukje Dijkstra, Holland
1908	Lily Kronberger, Hungary	1936	**Sonja Henie**, Norway	1964	**Sjoukje Dijkstra**, Holland
1909	Lily Kronberger, Hungary	1937	Cecilia Colledge, Britain	1965	Petra Burka, Canada
1910	Lily Kronberger, Hungary	1938	Megan Taylor, Britain	1966	Peggy Fleming, USA
1911	Lily Kronberger, Hungary	1939	Megan Taylor, Britain	1967	Peggy Fleming, USA
1912	Meray Horvath, Hungary			1968	**Peggy Fleming**, USA
1913	Meray Horvath, Hungary	1940-46	Not held	1969	Gabriele Seyfert, E. Germany
1914	Meray Horvath, Hungary	1947	Barbara Ann Scott, Canada		
1915-21	Not held	1948	**Barbara Ann Scott**, Canada	1970	Gabriele Seyfert, E. Germany
		1949	Alena Vrzanova, Czechoslovakia	1971	Beatrix Schuba, Austria
1922	Herma Planck-Szabo, Austria	1950	Alena Vrzanova, Czechoslovakia	1972	**Beatrix Schuba**, Austria
1923	Herma Planck-Szabo, Austria	1951	Jeannette Altwegg, Britain	1973	Karen Magnussen, Canada
1924	**Herma Planck-Szabo**, Austria	1952	Jacqueline Du Bief, France	1974	Christine Errath, E. Germany
1925	Herma Planck-Szabo, Austria	1953	Tenley Albright, USA	1975	Dianne DeLeeuw, Holland
1926	Herma Planck-Szabo, Austria	1954	Gundi Busch, W. Germany	1976	**Dorothy Hamill**, USA
1927	Sonja Henie, Norway	1955	Tenley Albright, USA	1977	Linda Fratianne, USA
1928	**Sonja Henie**, Norway	1956	Carol Heiss, USA	1978	Anett Poetzsch, E. Germany
1929	Sonja Henie, Norway	1957	Carol Heiss, USA	1979	Linda Fratianne, USA
1930	Sonja Henie, Norway	1958	Carol Heiss, USA	1980	**Anett Poetzsch**, E. Germany
1931	Sonja Henie, Norway	1959	Carol Heiss, USA	1981	Denise Biellmann, Switzerland
1932	**Sonja Henie**, Norway	1960	**Carol Heiss**, USA	1982	Elaine Zayak, USA
1933	Sonja Henie, Norway	1961	Not held	1983	Rosalyn Sumners, USA
				1984	**Katarina Witt**, E. Germany

Figure Skating (Cont.)
World Champions
WOMEN

Year		Year		Year	
1985	Katarina Witt, E. Germany	1989	Midori Ito, Japan	1993	Oksana Baiul, Ukraine
1986	Debi Thomas, USA	1990	Jill Trenary, USA	1994	Yuka Sato, Japan
1987	Katarina Witt, E. Germany	1991	Kristi Yamaguchi, USA	1995	Lu Chen, China
1988	**Katarina Witt, E. Germany**	1992	**Kristi Yamaguchi, USA**		

U.S. Champions

Skaters who won U.S., World and Olympic championships in same year are in **bold** type.

MEN

Multiple winners: Dick Button and Roger Turner (7); Sherwin Badger and Robin Lee (5); Brian Boitano, Scott Hamilton, David Jenkins, Hayes Jenkins and Charles Tickner (4); Todd Eldredge, Gordon McKellen, Nathaniel Niles and Tim Wood (3); Scott Allen, Christopher Bowman, Scott Davis, Eugene Turner and Gary Visconti (2).

Year		Year		Year		Year	
1914	Norman Scott	1936	Robin Lee	1957	David Jenkins	1977	Charles Tickner
1915-17	Not held	1937	Robin Lee	1958	David Jenkins	1978	Charles Tickner
1918	Nathaniel Niles	1938	Robin Lee	1959	David Jenkins	1979	Charles Tickner
1919	Not held	1939	Robin Lee	1960	David Jenkins	1980	Charles Tickner
1920	Sherwin Badger	1940	Eugene Turner	1961	Bradley Lord	1981	Scott Hamilton
1921	Sherwin Badger	1941	Eugene Turner	1962	Monty Hoyt	1982	Scott Hamilton
1922	Sherwin Badger	1942	Robert Specht	1963	Thomas Litz	1983	Scott Hamilton
1923	Sherwin Badger	1943	Arthur Vaughn	1964	Scott Allen	1984	**Scott Hamilton**
1924	Sherwin Badger	1944-45	Not held	1965	Gary Visconti	1985	Brian Boitano
1925	Nathaniel Niles	1946	Dick Button	1966	Scott Allen	1986	Brian Boitano
1926	Chris Christenson	1947	Dick Button	1967	Gary Visconti	1987	Brian Boitano
1927	Nathaniel Niles	1948	**Dick Button**	1968	Tim Wood	1988	**Brian Boitano**
1928	Roger Turner	1949	Dick Button	1969	Tim Wood	1989	Christopher Bowman
1929	Roger Turner	1950	Dick Button	1970	Tim Wood	1990	Todd Eldredge
1930	Roger Turner	1951	Dick Button	1971	John (Misha) Petkevich	1991	Todd Eldredge
1931	Roger Turner	1952	**Dick Button**	1972	Ken Shelley	1992	Christopher Bowman
1932	Roger Turner	1953	Hayes Jenkins	1973	Gordon McKellen	1993	Scott Davis
1933	Roger Turner	1954	Hayes Jenkins	1974	Gordon McKellen	1994	Scott Davis
1934	Roger Turner	1955	Hayes Jenkins	1975	Gordon McKellen	1995	Todd Eldredge
1935	Robin Lee	1956	**Hayes Jenkins**	1976	Terry Kubicka		

WOMEN

Multiple winners: Maribel Vinson (9); Theresa Weld Blanchard and Gretchen Merrill (6); Tenley Albright, Peggy Fleming, and Janet Lynn (5); Linda Fratianne and Carol Heiss (4); Dorothy Hamill, Beatrix Loughran, Rosalyn Summers, Joan Tozzer and Jill Trenary (3); Yvonne Sherman and Debi Thomas (2).

Year		Year		Year		Year	
1914	Theresa Weld	1936	Maribel Vinson	1956	Tenley Albright	1976	**Dorothy Hamill**
1915-17	Not held	1937	Maribel Vinson	1957	Carol Heiss	1977	Linda Fratianne
1918	Rosemary Beresford	1938	Joan Tozzer	1958	Carol Heiss	1978	Linda Fratianne
1919	Not held	1939	Joan Tozzer	1959	Carol Heiss	1979	Linda Fratianne
1920	Theresa Weld	1940	Joan Tozzer	1960	**Carol Heiss**	1980	Linda Fratianne
1921	Theresa Blanchard	1941	Jane Vaughn	1961	Laurence Owen	1981	Elaine Zayak
1922	Theresa Blanchard	1942	Jane Sullivan	1962	Barbara Pursley	1982	Rosalyn Sumners
1923	Theresa Blanchard	1943	Gretchen Merrill	1963	Lorraine Hanlon	1983	Rosalyn Sumners
1924	Theresa Blanchard	1944	Gretchen Merrill	1964	Peggy Fleming	1984	Rosalyn Sumners
1925	Beatrix Loughran	1945	Gretchen Merrill	1965	Peggy Fleming	1985	Tiffany Chin
1926	Beatrix Loughran	1946	Gretchen Merrill	1966	Peggy Fleming	1986	Debi Thomas
1927	Beatrix Loughran	1947	Gretchen Merrill	1967	Peggy Fleming	1987	Jill Trenary
1928	Maribel Vinson	1948	Gretchen Merrill	1968	**Peggy Fleming**	1988	Debi Thomas
1929	Maribel Vinson	1949	Yvonne Sherman	1969	Janet Lynn	1989	Jill Trenary
1930	Maribel Vinson	1950	Yvonne Sherman	1970	Janet Lynn	1990	Jill Trenary
1931	Maribel Vinson	1951	Sonya Klopfer	1971	Janet Lynn	1991	Tonya Harding
1932	Maribel Vinson	1952	Tenley Albright	1972	Janet Lynn	1992	**Kristi Yamaguchi**
1933	Maribel Vinson	1953	Tenley Albright	1973	Janet Lynn	1993	Nancy Kerrigan
1934	Suzanne Davis	1954	Tenley Albright	1974	Dorothy Hamill	1994	vacated*
1935	Maribel Vinson	1955	Tenley Albright	1975	Dorothy Hamill	1995	Nicole Bobek

* Tonya Harding was stripped of the 1994 women's title and banned from membership in the U.S. Figure Skating Assn. for life on June 30, 1994 for violating the USFSA Code of Ethics after she pleaded guilty to a charge of conspiracy to hinder the prosecution related to the Jan. 6, 1994 attack on Nancy Kerrigan.

Tony Duffy/Allsport

Twelve years ago in Los Angeles, the last time the Summer Games were held in the United States, America's **Joan Benoit** (center) won the gold medal in the first-ever Olympic women's marathon.

OLYMPIC GAMES

THE 1996 INFORMATION PLEASE SPORTS ALMANAC — OLYMPICS STATISTICS — THROUGH THE YEARS 1896-1992 SUMMER GAMES — SEC A PAGE 648

Modern Olympic Games

The modern Olympic movement will celebrate its centennial anniversary in 1996 at the Summer Games in Atlanta. This special 70-page section reviews all 23 editions of the Summer Olympics that have been held, including the previous three occasions the Games were hosted by the United States— St. Louis in 1904 and Los Angeles in 1932 and '84. This chapter also includes an event-by-event recap of all major Olympic champions since 1896 in the Summer Games and since 1924 in the Winter Games, as well as All-Time medal-winner lists in both Games. Further information on the Olympics can be found in the "Ballparks & Arenas" and "Timeout" chapters.

The Summer Olympics

Year	No	Location	Dates	Nations	Most medals	USA Medals
1896	I	Athens, GRE	Apr. 6-15	14	Greece (10-19-18—47)	11- 6- 2— 19 (2nd)
1900	II	Paris, FRA	May 20-Oct. 28	26	France (26-37-32—95)	18-14-15— 47 (2nd)
1904	III	St. Louis, USA	July 1-Nov. 23	13	USA (78-84-82—244)	78-84-82—244 (1st)
1906-a	—	Athens, GRE	Apr. 22-May 2	20	France (15-9-16—40)	12- 6- 6— 24 (3rd)
1908	IV	London, GBR	Apr. 27-Oct. 31	22	Britain (54-46-38—138)	23-12-12— 47 (2nd)
1912	V	Stockholm, SWE	May 5-July 22	28	Sweden (23-24-17—64)	25-18-20— 63 (2nd)
1916	VI	Berlin, GER	Cancelled (WWI)			
1920	VII	Antwerp, BEL	Apr. 20-Sept. 12	29	USA (41-27-27—95)	41-27-27— 95 (1st)
1924	VIII	Paris, FRA	May 4-July 27	44	USA (45-27-27—99)	45-27-27— 99 (1st)
1928	IX	Amsterdam, HOL	May 17-Aug. 12	46	USA (22-18-16—56)	22-18-16— 56 (1st)
1932	X	Los Angeles, USA	July 30-Aug. 14	37	USA (41-32-30—103)	41-32-30—103 (1st)
1936	XI	Berlin, GER	Aug. 1-16	49	Germany (33-26-30-89)	24-20-12— 56 (2nd)
1940-b	XII	Tokyo, JPN	Cancelled (WWII)			
1944	XIII	London, GBR	Cancelled (WWII)			
1948	XIV	London, GBR	July 29-Aug. 14	59	USA (38-27-19—84)	38-27-19— 84 (1st)
1952-cd	XV	Helsinki, FIN	July 19-Aug. 3	69	USA (40-19-17—76)	40-19-17— 76 (1st)
1956-e	XVI	Melbourne, AUS	Nov. 22-Dec .8	72	USSR (37-29-32—98)	32-25-17— 74 (2nd)
1960	XVII	Rome, ITA	Aug. 25-Sept. 11	83	USSR (43-29-31—103)	34-21-16— 71 (2nd)
1964	XVIII	Tokyo, JPN	Oct. 10-24	93	USA (36-26-28—90)	36-26-28— 90 (1st)
1968-f	XIX	Mexico City, MEX	Oct. 12-27	113	USA (45-28-34—107)	45-28-34—107 (1st)
1972	XX	Munich, W. GER	Aug. 26-Sept. 10	122	USSR (50-27-22—99)	33-31-30— 94 (2nd)
1976-g	XXI	Montreal, CAN	July 17-Aug. 1	88	USSR (49-41-35—125)	34-35-25— 94 (3rd)
1980-h	XXII	Moscow, USSR	July 19-Aug. 3	81	USSR (80-69-46—195)	Boycotted Games
1984-i	XXIII	Los Angeles, USA	July 28-Aug. 12	140	USA (83-61-30—174)	83-61-30—174 (1st)
1988	XXIV	Seoul, S. KOR	Sept. 17-Oct. 2	160	USSR (55-31-46—132)	36-31-27— 94 (3rd)
1992-j	XXV	Barcelona, SPA	July 25-Aug. 9	172	UT (45-38-29—112)	37-34-37—108 (2nd)
1996	XXVI	Atlanta, USA	July 20-Aug. 4	197		
2000	XXVII	Sydney, AUS	Sept. 16-Oct. 1			

a—The 1906 Intercalated Games in Athens are considered unofficial by the IOC because they did not take place in the four-year cycle established in 1896. However, most record books include these interim games with the others.

b—The 1940 Summer Games are originally scheduled for Tokyo, but Japan resigns as host after the outbreak of the Sino-Japanese war in 1937. Helsinki is the next choice, but the IOC cancels the Games after Russian troops invade Finland in 1939.

c—Germany and Japan are allowed to rejoin Olympic community for first Summer Games since 1936. Though a divided country, the Germans send a joint East-West team.

d—The Soviet Union (USSR) participates in its first Olympics, Winter or Summer, since the Russian revolution in 1917 and takes home the second most medals (22-30-19—71).

e—Due to Australian quarantine laws, the equestrian events for the 1956 Games are held in Stockholm, June 10-17.

f—East Germany and West Germany send separate teams for the first time and will continue to do so through 1988.

g—The 1976 Games are boycotted by 32 nations, most of them from black Africa, because the IOC will not ban New Zealand. Earlier that year, a rugby team from New Zealand had toured racially-segregated South Africa.

h—The 1980 Games are boycotted by 64 nations, led by the USA, to protest the Russian invasion of Afghanistan on Dec. 27, 1979.

i—The 1984 Games are boycotted by 14 Eastern Bloc nations, led by the USSR, to protest America's overcommercialization of the Games, inadequate security and an anti-Soviet attitude by the U.S. government. Most believe, however, the communist walkout is simply revenge for 1980.

j—Germany sends a single team after East and West German reunification in 1990 and the USSR competes as the Unified Team after the breakup of the Soviet Union in 1991.

1896

Athens

The ruins of ancient Olympia were excavated by the German archaeologist Ernst Curtius from 1875-81.

Among the remains uncovered was the ancient stadium where the original Olympic Games were celebrated from 776 B.C. to 393 A.D., when Roman emperor Theodosius I banned all pagan festivals.

Athletics played an important role in the religious festivals of the ancient Greeks, who believed competitive sports pleased the spirits of the dead. The festivals honoring gods like Zeus were undertaken by many Greek tribes and cities and usually held every four years.

During the first 13 Olympiads (an Olympiad is an interval of four years between celebrations of the Olympic Games), the only contested event was a footrace of 200 yards (180 meters). Longer races were gradually introduced and by 708 B.C., field events like the discus and javelin throws and the long jump were part of the program. Wrestling and boxing followed and in 640 B.C., four-horse chariot races became a fixture at the Games.

During the so-called Golden Age of Greece, which most historians maintain lasted from 477 to 431 B.C., Olympia was considered holy ground. Victorious athletes gave public thanks to the gods and were revered as heroes. Three-time winners had statues erected in their likeness and received various gifts and honors, including exemption from taxation.

Eventually, however, winning and the rewards that went with victory corrupted the original purpose of the Ancient Games. Idealistic amateurs gave way to skilled foreign athletes, who were granted the citizenship needed to compete and were paid handsomely by rich Greek gamblers.

There is evidence to suggest that the Games continued until the temples of Olympia were physically demolished in 426 A.D. by a Roman army sent by Theodosius II. Over the next 15 centuries, earthquakes and floods buried the site, until its discovery in 1875.

On June 23, 1894, French educator Baron Pierre de Coubertin, speaking at the Sorbonne in Paris to a gathering of international sports leaders from nine nations— including the United States and Russia— proposed that the ancient Games be revived on an international scale. The idea was enthusiastically received and the Modern Olympics, as we know them, were born.

The first Olympiad was celebrated two years later in Athens, where an estimated 245 athletes (all men) from 14 nations competed in the ancient Panathenaic stadium before large and enthusiastic crowds.

Americans won nine of the 12 track and field events, but Greece won the most medals with 47. The highlight was the victory by native peasant Spiridon Louis in the first marathon race, which was run over the same course covered by the Greek hero Pheidippides after the battle of Marathon in 490 B.C.

Top 10 Standings

National medal standings are not recognized by the IOC. The unofficial point totals are based on 3 points for a gold medal, 2 for a silver and 1 for a bronze.

		Gold	Silver	Bronze	Total	Pts
1	Greece	10	19	18	47	86
2	USA	11	6	2	19	47
3	Germany	7	5	3	15	34
4	France	5	4	2	11	25
5	Great Britain	3	3	1	7	16
6	Denmark	1	2	4	7	11
	Hungary	2	1	3	6	11
8	Austria	2	0	3	5	9
9	Switzerland	1	2	0	3	7
10	Australia	2	0	0	2	6

Leading Medal Winners

Number of individual medals won on the left; gold, silver and bronze breakdown to the right.

No		Sport	G-S-B
6	Hermann Weingärtner, GER	Gymnastics	3-2-1
4	Karl Schuman, GER	Gymnastics & Wrestling	4-0-0
4	Alfred Flatow, GER	Gymnastics	3-1-0
4	Bob Garrett, USA	Track/Field	2-1-1
4	Viggo Jensen, DEN	Shooting & Weightlifting	1-2-1
3	Paul Masson, FRA	Cycling	3-0-0
3	Teddy Flack, AUS	Track/Field & Tennis	2-0-1
3	Jules Zutter, SWI	Gymnastics	1-2-0
3	James Connolly, USA	Track/Field	1-1-1
3	Leon Flameng, FRA	Cycling	1-1-1
3	Adolf Schmal, AUT	Cycling	1-0-2
3	Efstathios Choraphas, GRE	Swimming	0-1-2
3	Holger Nielsen, DEN	Shooting	0-1-2

Track & Field

Event		Time
100m	Tom Burke, USA	12.0
400m	Tom Burke, USA	54.2
800m	Teddy Flack, AUS	2:11.0
1500m	Teddy Flack, AUS	4:33.2
Marathon	Spiridon Louis, GRE	2:58:50
110m H	Tom Curtis, USA	17.6

Event		Mark
High Jump	Ellery Clark, USA	5-11¼
Pole Vault	William Hoyt, USA	10-10
Long Jump	Ellery Clark, USA	20-10
Triple Jump	James Connolly, USA	44-11¾
Shot Put	Bob Garrett, USA	36- 9¾
Discus	Bob Garrett, USA	95- 7½

Swimming

Event		Time
100m Free	Alfréd Hajós, HUN	1:22.2
500m Free	Paul Neumann, AUT	8:12.6
1200m Free	Alfréd Hajós, HUN	18:22.2

Other		Time
Sailors'		
100m Free	Ioannis Malokinis, GRE	2:20.4

Team Sports

None

Also Contested

Cycling, Fencing, Gymnastics, Shooting, Tennis, Weightlifting and Greco-Roman Wrestling.

1900

Paris

The success of the revived Olympics moved Greece to declare itself the rightful host of all future Games, but de Coubertin and the International Olympic Committee were determined to move the athletic feast around. In France, however, the Games were overshadowed by the brand new Eiffel Tower and all but ignored by the organizers of the 1900 Paris Exposition.

Despite their sideshow status, the Games attracted 1,330 athletes from 22 nations and enjoyed more publicity, if not bigger crowds, than in Athens.

University of Pennsylvania roommates Alvin Kraenzlein, Irving Baxter and John Tewksbury and Purdue grad Ray Ewry dominated the 23 track and field events, winning 11 and taking five seconds and a third. Kraenzlein remains the only track and fielder to win four individual titles in one year. Women were invited to compete for the first time and Britain's Charlotte Cooper won the singles and mixed doubles in tennis.

No gold medals were given out in Paris. Winners received silver medals with bronze for second place.

Top 10 Standings

National team medal standings are not recognized by the IOC. The unofficial point totals are based on 3 points for a gold medal, 2 for a silver and 1 for a bronze.

	Gold	Silver	Bronze	Total	Pts
1 France	26	37	32	95	184
2 USA	18	14	15	47	97
3 Great Britain	16	6	8	30	68
4 Belgium	6	5	5	16	33
5 Switzerland	6	1	1	8	21
6 Germany	3	2	2	7	15
7 Denmark	1	3	2	6	11
Hungary	1	3	2	6	11
9 Australia	2	0	4	6	10
Holland	1	2	3	6	10

Leading Medal Winners

Number of individual medals won on the left; gold, silver and bronze breakdown to the right.

MEN

No		Sport	G-S-B
5	Irving Baxter, USA	Track/Field	2-3-0
5	John W. Tewksbury, USA	Track/Field	2-2-1
4	Alvin Kraenzlein, USA	Track/Field	4-0-0
4	Konrad Stäheli, SWI	Shooting	3-0-1
4	Achille Paroche, FRA	Shooting	1-2-1
4	Stan Rowley, AUS	Track/Field	1-0-3
4	Ole Östmo, NOR	Shooting	0-2-2
3	Ray Ewry, USA	Track/Field	3-0-0
3	Charles Bennett, AUS	Track/Field	2-1-0
3	Emil Kellenberger, SWI	Shooting	2-1-0

No		Sport	G-S-B
3	Laurie Doherty, GBR	Tennis	2-0-1
3	Reggie Doherty, GBR	Tennis	2-0-1
3	E. Michelet, FRA	Yachting	1-0-2
3	F. Michelet, FRA	Yachting	1-0-2
3	Anders Nielsen, DEN	Shooting	0-3-0
3	Zoltán Halmay, HUN	Swimming	0-2-1
3	Léon Moreaux, FRA	Shooting	0-2-1

WOMEN

No		Sport	G-S-B
2	Charlotte Cooper, GBR	Tennis	2-0-0
2	Marion Jones, USA	Tennis	0-0-2

Track & Field

Event			Time	
60m	Alvin Kraenzlein, USA		7.0	WR
100m	Frank Jarvis, USA		11.0	OR
200m	John W. Tewksbury, USA		22.2	
400m	Maxey Long, USA		49.4	OR
800m	Alfred Tysoe, GBR		2:01.2	
1500m	Charles Bennett, GBR		4:06.2	WR
Marathon	Michel Théato, FRA		2:59:45	
110m H	Alvin Kraenzlein, USA		15.4	OR
200m H	Alvin Kraenzlein, USA		25.4	
400m H	John W. Tewksbury, USA		57.6	
3000m Steeple	George Orton, CAN		7:34.4	
4000m Steeple	John Rimmer, GBR		12:58.4	
5000m Team	GBR (Charles Bennett, John Rimmer, Sidney Robinson, Alfred Tysoe, Stanley Rowley)		26 pts	

Event		Mark	
High Jump	Irving Baxter, USA	6- 2¾	OR
Pole Vault	Irving Baxter, USA	10-10	
Long Jump	Alvin Kraenzlein, USA	23- 6¾	OR
Triple Jump	Meyer Prinstein, USA	47- 5¾	OR
Shot Put	Richard Sheldon, USA	46- 3	OR
Discus	Rudolf Bauer, HUN	118- 3	OR
Hammer	John Flanagan, USA	163- 1	

Standing		Mark	
High Jump	Ray Ewry, USA	5- 5	WR
Long Jump	Ray Ewry, USA	10- 6¼	
Triple Jump	Ray Ewry, USA	34- 8½	

Swimming

Event		Time
220yd Free	Frederick Lane, AUS	2:25.2
1000m Free	John Jarvis, GBR	13:40.2
4000m Free	John Jarvis, GBR	58:24.0
200m Back	Ernst Hoppenberg, GER	2:47.0
200m Team	GER (Ernst Hoppenberg, Max Hainle, Max Schone, Julius Frey, Herbert von Petersdorff)	32 pts

Team Sports

Sport	Champion
Cricket	Great Britain
Polo	Great Britain/USA
Rugby	France
Soccer	Great Britain
Tug-of-War	Sweden/Norway
Water Polo	Great Britain

Note: In Polo, Foxhunters Hurlingham defeated Club Rugby in a contest of teams made up of British and American players. A combined 6-man team of Swedes and Norwegians won the Tug-of-War.

Also Contested

Archery, Croquet, Cycling, Equestrian, Fencing, Golf, Gymnastics, Rowing, Shooting, Tennis and Yachting.

1904

St. Louis

Originally scheduled for Chicago, the Games were moved to St. Louis and held in conjunction with the centennial celebration of the Louisiana Purchase.

The program included more sports than in Paris, but with only 11 nations sending athletes, the first Olympics to be staged in the United States had a decidedly All-American flavor—over 500 of the 681 competitors were Americans. Little wonder the home team won 80 percent of the medals.

The rout was nearly total in track and field where the U.S.—led by triple-winners Ray Ewry, Archie Hahn, Jim Lightbody and Harry Hillman—took 23 of 25 gold medals and swept 20 events.

The marathon, which was run over dusty roads in brutally hot weather, was the most bizarre event of the Games. Thomas Hicks of the U.S. won, but only after his handlers fed him painkillers during the race. And an impostor nearly stole the victory when Fred Lorz, who dropped out after nine miles, was seen trotting back to the finish line to retrieve his clothes. Amused that officials thought he had won the race, Lorz played along until he was found out shortly after the medal ceremony. Banned for life by the AAU, Lorz was reinstated a year later and won the 1905 Boston Marathon.

Top 10 Standings

National medal standings are not recognized by the IOC. The unofficial point totals are based on 3 points for a gold medal, 2 for a silver and 1 for a bronze.

		Gold	Silver	Bronze	Total	Pts
1	USA	78	84	82	244	484
2	Germany	4	4	4	12	24
3	Canada	4	1	1	6	15
4	Hungary	2	1	1	4	9
	Cuba	3	0	0	3	9
6	Austria	1	1	1	3	6
	Britian/Ireland	1	1	1	3	6
8	Greece	1	0	1	2	4
	Switzerland	1	0	1	2	4
10	Cuba/USA	1	0	0	1	3

Leading Medal Winners

Number of individual medals won on the left; gold, silver and bronze breakdown to the right.

MEN

No		Sport	G-S-B
6	Anton Heida, USA	Gymnastics	5-1-0
6	George Eyser, USA	Gymnastics	3-2-1
6	Burton Downing, USA	Cycling	2-3-1
5	Marcus Hurley, USA	Cycling	4-0-1
5	Charles Daniels, USA	Swimming	3-1-1
5	Albertson Van Zo Post, USA	Fencing	2-1-2
5	William Merz, USA	Gymnastics	0-1-4
4	Jim Lightbody, USA	Track/Field	3-1-0
4	Francis Gailey, USA	Swimming	0-3-1
4	Teddy Billington, USA	Cycling	0-1-3
4	Frank Kungler, USA	Weightlifting, Wrestling & Tug of War	0-1-3
3	Ray Ewry, USA	Track/Field	3-0-0
3	Ramón Fonst, CUB	Fencing	3-0-0
3	Archie Hahn, USA	Track/Field	3-0-0
3	Harry Hillman, USA	Track/Field	3-0-0
3	Julius Lenhart, AUT	Gymnastics	2-1-0
3	George Bryant, USA	Archery	2-0-1
3	Emil Rausch, GER	Swimming	2-0-1
3	Robert Williams, USA	Archery	1-2-0
3	Ralph Rose, USA	Track/Field	1-1-1
3	William Thompson, USA	Archery	1-0-2
3	Charles Tatham, USA	Fencing	0-2-1
3	William Hogenson, USA	Track/Field	0-1-2
3	Emil Voigt, USA	Gymnastics	0-1-2

WOMEN

No		Sport	G-S-B
2	Lida Howell, USA	Archery	2-0-0
2	Emma Cooke, USA	Archery	0-2-0
2	Jessie Pollack, USA	Archery	0-0-2

Track & Field

Event		Time	
60m	Archie Hahn, USA	7.0	=WR
100m	Archie Hahn, USA	11.0	
200m	Archie Hahn, USA	21.6	OR
400m	Harry Hillman, USA	49.2	OR
800m	Jim Lightbody, USA	1:56.0	OR
1500m	Jim Lightbody, USA	4:05.4	WR
Marathon	Thomas Hicks, USA	3:28:53	
110m H	Frederick Schule, USA	16.0	
200m H	Harry Hillman, USA	24.6	OR
400m H	Harry Hillman, USA	53.0	
3000m Steeple	Jim Lightbody, USA	7:39.6	
4-mile Team	New York AC (Arthur Newton, George Underwood, Paul Pilgrim, Howard Valentine, David Munson)	27 pts	

Event		Mark	
High Jump	Sam Jones, USA	5-11	
Pole Vault	Charles Dvorak, USA	11- 5¾	
Long Jump	Meyer Prinstein, USA	24- 1	OR
Triple Jump	Meyer Prinstein, USA	47- 1	
Shot Put	Ralph Rose, USA	48- 7	WR
56-lb Throw	Étienne Desmarteau, CAN	34- 4	
Discus	Martin Sheridan, USA	128-10½	OR
Hammer	John Flanagan, USA	168- 1	OR
Triathlon	Max Emmerich, USA	35.7 pts	
Decathlon	Tom Kiely, IRL	6036 pts	

Note: Sheridan won Discus throw-off after tying with Rose for 1st.

Standing		Mark	
High Jump	Ray Ewry, USA	5- 3	
Long Jump	Ray Ewry, USA	11- 4⅞	WR
Triple Jump	Ray Ewry, USA	34- 7¼	

1904 (Cont.)
Swimming

Event		Time
50yd Free	Zoltán Halmay, HUN	28.0
100yd Free	Zoltán Halmay, HUN	1:02.8
220yd Free	Charles Daniels, USA	2:44.2
440yd Free	Charles Daniels, USA	6:16.2
880yd Free	Emil Rausch, GER	13:11.4
Mile Free	Emil Rausch, GER	27:18.2
100yd Back	Walter Brack, GER	1:16.8
400yd Brst	Georg Zacharias, GER	7:23.6
4x50yd Free	USA (Joe Ruddy, Leo Goodwin, Louis Handle, Charles Daniels)	2:04.6

Note: Halmay won 50-Free in swim-off with Scott Leary of USA.

Diving		Points
Platform	George Sheldon, USA	12.66
Plunge		**Mark**
for Distance	William Dickey, USA	62-6

Team Sports

Sport	Champion
Lacrosse	Canada (Shamrock-Winnipeg)
Soccer	Canada (Galt Football Club)
Tug-of-War	USA (Milwaukee AC)
Water Polo	USA (New York AC)

Also Contested

Archery, Boxing, Cycling, Fencing, Golf, Gymnastics, Roque (Croquet), Rowing, Tennis, Weightlifting and Freestyle Wrestling.

1906

Athens

After disappointing receptions in Paris and St. Louis, the Olympic movement returned to Athens for the Intercalated Games of 1906. The mutual desire of Greece and Baron de Coubertin to recapture the spirit of the 1896 Games led to an understanding that the Greeks would host an interim games every four years between Olympics.

Nearly 900 athletes from 20 countries came to Athens, including, for the first time, an official American team picked by the USOC.

As usual, the U.S. dominated track and field, taking 11 of 21 events, including double wins by Martin Sheridan (shot put and freestyle discus), Ray Ewry (standing high and long jumps) and Paul Pilgrim (400 and 800 meters). The previously unknown Pilgrim had been an 11th-hour addition to the team.

Verner Järvinen, the first Finn to compete in the Olympics, won the Greek-style discus throw and placed second in the freestyle discus. He returned home a national hero and inspired Finland to become a future Olympic power.

The Intercalated Games were cancelled due to political unrest in 1910 and never reappeared. Medals won are considered unofficial by the IOC.

Top 10 Standings

National medal standings are not recognized by the IOC. The unofficial point totals are based on 3 points for a gold medal, 2 for a silver and 1 for a bronze.

		Gold	Silver	Bronze	Total	Pts
1	France	15	9	16	40	79
2	Greece	8	13	12	33	62
3	USA	12	6	6	24	54
4	Great Britain	8	11	5	24	51
5	Italy	7	6	3	16	36
6	Switzerland	5	6	4	15	31
7	Germany	4	6	5	15	29
8	Sweden	2	5	7	14	23
9	Hungary	2	5	3	10	19
10	Austria	3	3	2	8	17
	Norway	4	2	1	7	17

Leading Medal Winners

Number of individual medals won on the left; gold, silver and bronze breakdown to the right.

MEN

No		Sport	G-S-B
6	Louis Richardet, SWI	Shooting	4-2-0
5	Martin Sheridan, USA	Track/Field	2-3-0
5	Konrad Stäheli, SWI	Shooting	2-2-1
5	Léon Moreaux, FRA	Shooting	2-1-2
5	Jean Reich, SWI	Shooting	1-1-3
4	Gudbrand Skatteboe, NOR	Shooting	3-1-0
4	Gustav Casmir, GER	Fencing	2-2-0
4	Eric Lemming, SWE	Track/Field & Tug of War	1-0-0
3	Francesco Verri, ITA	Cycling	3-0-0
3	Enrico Bruna, ITA	Rowing	3-0-0
3	Georgio Cesana, ITA	Rowing	3-0-0
3	Max Decugis, FRA	Tennis	3-0-0
3	Emilio Fontanella, ITA	Rowing	3-0-0
3	Georges Dillon-Cavanaugh, FRA	Fencing	2-1-0
3	Henry Taylor, GBR	Swimming	1-1-1
3	Fernand Vast, FRA	Cycling	1-0-2
3	Raoul de Boigne, FRA	Shooting	0-1-2
3	John Jarvis, GBR	Swimming	0-1-2

WOMEN

No		Sport	G-S-B
2	Sophia Marinou, GRE	Tennis	0-2-0

Track & Field

Event		Time
100m	Archie Hahn, USA	11.2
400m	Paul Pilgrim, USA	53.2
800m	Paul Pilgrim, USA	2:01.5
1500m	Jim Lightbody, USA	4:12.0
5 Miles	Henry Hawtrey, GBR	26:11.8
Marathon	Billy Sherring, CAN	2:51:23.6
110m H	Robert Leavitt, USA	16.2
500mWalk	George Bonhag, USA	7:12.6
3000mWalk	György Sztantics, HUN	15:13.2
Event		**Mark**
High Jump	Con Leahy, GBR/IRL	5- 10
Pole Vault	Fernand Gonder, FRA	11- 5¾
Long Jump	Meyer Prinstein, USA	23- 7½
Triple Jump	Peter O'Connor, GBR/IRL	46- 2¼
Shot Put	Martin Sheridan, USA	40- 5¼
Stone Throw	Nicolaos Georgantas, GRE	65- 4½
Discus	Martin Sheridan, USA	136- 0
Greek Discus	Verner Järvinen, FIN	115- 4½
Freestyle Javelin	Eric Lemming, SWE	176-10 **WR**
Pentathlon	Hjalmar Mellander, SWE	24 pts

Notes: Weight in Stone Throw was 14.08 lbs; spinning not allowed in Greek-style Discus.

Standing		Mark
High Jump	Ray Ewry, USA	5- 1¼
Long Jump	Ray Ewry, USA	10-10

Swimming

Event		Time
100m Free	Charles Daniels, USA	1:13.4
400m Free	Otto Scheff, AUT	6:23.8
Mile Free	Henry Taylor, GBR	28:28.0
4x250m Free	HUN (József Onody, Henrik Hajós, Geza Kiss, Zoltán Halmay)	16:52.4

Diving		Points
Platform	Gottlob Walz, GER	156.0

Team Sports

Sport	Champion
Soccer	Denmark
Tug-of-War	Germany

Also Contested

Canoeing, Cycling, Fencing, Gymnastics, Rowing, Shooting, Tennis, Weightlifting and Greco-Roman Wrestling.

1908

London

The fourth Olympic Games were certainly the wettest and probably the most contentious in history.

Held at a new 68,000-seat stadium in the Shepherds Bush section of London, the 1908 Games were played out under continually rainy skies and suffered from endless arguments between British officials and many of the other countries involved—especially the United States.

"The Battle of Shepherds Bush" began almost immediately, when the U.S. delegation noticed that there was no American flag among the national flags decorating the stadium for the opening ceremonies. U.S. flag bearer and discus champion Martin Sheridan responded by refusing to dip the Stars and Stripes when he passed King Edward VII's box in the parade of athletes. "This flag dips to no earthly king," Sheridan said. And it hasn't since.

The Americans, at least, got to march with their flag. Finland, then ruled by Russia, could not. Informed they would have to use a Russian flag, the furious Finns elected to march with no flag at all.

Once again the marathon proved to be the Games' most memorable event. Laid out over a 26-mile, 365-yard course that stretched from Windsor Castle to the royal box at Shepherds Bush, the race ended in controversy when leader Dorando Pietri of Italy staggered into the packed stadium, took a wrong turn, collapsed, was helped up by doctors, wobbled and fell three more times before being half-carried across the finish line by race officials. Caught up in the drama of Pietri's agony, the cheering crowd hardly noticed that he was declared the winner just as second place runner, Johnny Hayes of the U.S., entered the stadium.

Pietri was later disqualified in favor of Hayes, but only after British and U.S. officials argued for an hour and fights had broken out in the stands.

Top 10 Standings

National medal standings are not recognized by the IOC. The unofficial point totals are based on 3 points for a gold medal, 2 for a silver and 1 for a bronze

		Gold	Silver	Bronze	Total	Pts
1	Great Britain	54	46	38	138	292
2	USA	23	12	12	47	105
3	Sweden	8	6	11	25	47
4	France	5	5	9	19	34
5	Canada	3	3	10	16	25
6	Germany	3	5	5	13	24
7	Hungary	3	4	2	9	19
8	Norway	2	3	3	8	15
	Belgium	1	5	2	8	15
10	Italy	2	2	0	4	10

Leading Medal Winners

Number of individual medals won on the left; gold, silver and bronze breakdown to the right.

MEN

No		Sport	G-S-B
3	Mel Sheppard, USA	Track/Field	3-0-0
3	Henry Taylor, GBR	Swimming	3-0-0
3	Benjamin Jones, GBR	Cycling	2-1-0
3	Martin Sheridan, USA	Track/Field	2-0-1
3	Oscar Swahn, SWE	Shooting	2-0-1
3	Josiah Ritchie, GBR	Tennis	1-1-1
3	Ted Ranken, GBR	Shooting	0-3-0

WOMEN

No		Sport	G-S-B
2	Madge Syers, GBR	Figure Skating	1-0-1

Note: Figure Skating was part of the Summer Olympics in 1908 and '20.

Track & Field

Event		Time	
100m	Reggie Walker, SAF	10.8	=OR
200m	Bobby Kerr, CAN	22.6	
400m	Wyndham Halswelle, GBR	50.0	
800m	Mel Sheppard, USA	1:52.8	WR
1500m	Mel Sheppard, USA	4:03.4	OR
5 Miles	Emil Voigt, GBR	25:11.2	
Marathon	Johnny Hayes, USA	2:55:18.4	OR
110m H	Forrest Smithson, USA	15.0	WR
400m H	Charley Bacon, USA	55.0	WR
3200m Steeple	Arthur Russell, GBR	10:47.8	
3500m Walk	George Larner, GBR	14:55.0	
10-mi Walk	George Larner, GBR	1:15:57.4	
Medley Relay	USA (William Hamilton, Nathaniel Cartmell, John Taylor, Mel Sheppard)	3:29.4	
3-mile Relay	GBR (Joseph Deakin, Archie Robertson, Wilfred Coales)	6 pts	

Note: Medley Relay made up of two 200m runs, a 400m and an 800m.

1908 (Cont.)

Event		Mark	
High Jump	Harry Porter, USA	6- 3	OR
Pole Vault	Edward Cooke, USA	12- 2	OR
Long Jump	Frank Irons, USA	24- 6½	OR
Triple Jump	Timothy Ahearne, GBR/IRL	48-11½	OR
Shot Put	Ralph Rose, USA	46- 7½	
Discus	Martin Sheridan, USA	134- 2	
Greek Discus	Martin Sheridan, USA	128- 4	OR
Hammer	John Flanagan, USA	170- 4	OR
Javelin	Eric Lemming, SWE	179-10	WR
Freestyle Javelin	Eric Lemming, SWE	178- 7½	

Note: Spinning not allowed in Greek-style Discus.

Standing		Mark
High Jump	Ray Ewry, USA	5- 2
Long Jump	Ray Ewry, USA	10-11¼

Swimming
MEN

Event		Time	
100m Free	Charles Daniels, USA	1:05.6	WR
400m Free	Henry Taylor, GBR	5:36.8	
1500m Free	Henry Taylor, GBR	22:48.4	WR
100m Back	Arno Bieberstein, GER	1:24.6	WR
200m Brst	Frederick Holman, GBR	3:09.2	WR
4x200m Free	GBR (John Derbyshire, Paul Radmilovic, William Foster, Henry Taylor)	10:55.6	WR

Diving		Points
Platform	Hjalmar Johansson, SWE	83.75
Spring	Albert Zürner, GER	85.5

Team Sports

Sport	Champion
Field Hockey	Great Britain (England)
Lacrosse	Canada
Polo	Great Britain (Roehampton)
Rugby	Australia
Soccer	Great Britain
Tug-of-War	Great Britain (City Police)
Water Polo	Great Britain

Also Contested
Archery, Boxing, Cycling, Fencing, Figure Skating, Gymnastics, Jeu de Paume (court tennis), Racquets, Rowing, Shooting, Tennis, Freestyle Wrestling, Greco-Roman Wrestling and Yachting.

1912
Stockholm

The belligerence of 1908 was replaced with benevolence four years later, as Sweden provided a well-organized and pleasant haven for the troubled Games.

And then there were Jim Thorpe and Hannes Kolehmainen.

Thorpe, a 24-year-old American Indian who was a two-time consensus All-America football player at Carlisle (Pa.) Institute, won the two most demanding events in track and field—the pen-tathlon and decathlon. And he did it with ease. "You sir," said the Swedes' King Gustav V at the medal ceremony, "are the greatest athlete in the world." To which Thorpe is said to have replied, "Thanks, King."

Kolehmainen, a 22-year-old Finnish vegetarian, ran away with three distance events being run for the first time—the 5,000- and 10,000-meter races and the 12,000-meter cross-country run. He also picked up a silver medal in the 12,000-meter team race.

Ralph Craig of the U.S. was the only other winner of two individual track gold medals, taking both the 100 and 200-meter runs. The 100 final had seven false starts, one with Craig sprinting the entire distance before being called back.

Although Thorpe returned to the U.S. a hero, a year later it was learned that he had played semi-pro baseball for $25 a week in 1910. The IOC, with the full support of the American Olympic Committee, stripped him of his medals and erased his records.

The medals and records were returned in 1982—30 years after Thorpe's death.

Top 10 Standings
National medal standings are not recognized by the IOC. The unofficial point totals are based on 3 points for a gold medal, 2 for a silver and 1 for a bronze.

		Gold	Silver	Bronze	Total	Pts
1	Sweden	23	24	17	64	134
2	USA	25	18	20	63	131
3	Great Britain	10	15	16	41	76
4	Finland	9	8	9	26	52
5	Germany	5	13	7	25	48
6	France	7	4	3	14	32
7	Denmark	1	6	5	12	20
8	Norway	3	2	5	10	18
9	Canada	3	2	3	8	16
	Hungary	3	2	3	8	16
	South Africa	4	2	0	6	16

Leading Medal Winners
Number of individual medals won on the left; gold, silver and bronze breakdown to the right.

MEN

No		Sport	G-S-B
6	Louis Richardet, SWI	Shooting	4-2-0
5	Wilhelm Carlberg, SWE	Shooting	3-2-0
4	Hannes Kolehmainen, FIN	Track/Field	3-1-0
4	Eric Carlberg, SWE	Shooting	2-2-0
4	Johan von Holst, SWE	Shooting	2-1-1
4	Carl Osburn, USA	Shooting	1-2-1
3	Alfred Lane, USA	Shooting	3-0-0
3	Åke Lundeberg, SWE	Shooting	2-1-0
3	Frederick Hird, USA	Shooting	2-0-1
3	Jean Cariou, FRA	Equestrian	1-1-1
3	Charles Dixon, GBR	Tennis	1-1-1
3	Harold Hardwick, AUS	Swimming	1-0-2
3	Jack Hatfield, GBR	Swimming	0-2-1
3	Charles Stewart, GBR	Shooting	0-0-3

WOMEN

No		Sport	G-S-B
2	Edith Hannam, GBR	Tennis	2-0-0
2	Jennie Fletcher, GBR	Swimming	1-0-1
2	Sigrid Fick, SWE	Tennis	0-1-1

Track & Field

Event		Time
100m	Ralph Craig, USA 10.8	=OR
200m	Ralph Craig, USA 21.7	
400m	Charlie Reidpath, USA 48.2	OR
800m	Ted Meredith, USA................1:51.9	WR
1500m	Arnold Jackson, GBR.............3:56.8	OR
5000m	Hannes Kolehmainen, FIN....14:36.6	WR
10,000m	Hannes Kolehmainen, FIN....31:20.8	
X-country		
(12,000m)	Hannes Kolehmainen, FIN ...45:11.6	
Marathon	Kenneth McArthur, SAF ...2:36:54.8	
110m H	Frederick Kelly, USA..............15.1	
10k Walk	George Goulding, CAN 46:28.4	
4x100m	GBR (David Jacobs, Harold	
	Macintosh, Victor d'Arcy,	
	William Applegarth) 42.4	OR
4x400m	USA (Mel Sheppard, Edward	
	Lindberg, Ted Meredith,	
	Charlie Reidpath) 3:16.6	WR
3000m Team	USA (Tel Berna, Norman Taber,	
	George Bonhag) ....9 pts	
X-country	SWE (Hjalmar Andersson, John	
(12,000m)	Eke, Josef Ternström) ....10 pts	

Event		Mark
High Jump	Alma Richards, USA..................6- 4	OR
Pole Vault	Harry Babcock, USA 12-11½	OR
Long Jump	Albert Gutterson, USA............24-11¼	OR
Triple Jump	Gustaf Lindblom, SWE............48- 5¼	
Shot Put	Babe McDonald, USA..............50- 4	OR
Discus	Armas Taipale, FIN................148- 3	OR
Hammer	Matt McGrath, USA...............179- 7	OR
Javelin	Eric Lemming, SWE 198-11	WR
Pentathlon	Jim Thorpe, USA ....7 pts	
Decathlon	Jim Thorpe, USA ....8412 pts	WR

Standing		Mark
High Jump	Platt Adams, USA...................5- 4¼	
Long Jump	Constantin Tsiklitiras, GRE 11- 0¾	

Both Hands		Mark
Shot Put	Ralph Rose, USA 90-10½	
Discus	Armas Taipale, FIN.................271-10	
Javelin	Juho Saaristo, FIN 359- 0	

Swimming
MEN

Event		Time
100m Free	Duke Kahanamoku, USA.........1:03.4	
400m Free	George Hodgson, CAN 5:24.4	
1500m Free	George Hodgson, CAN 22:00.0	WR
100m Back	Harry Hebner, USA 1:21.2	
200m Brst	Walter Bathe, GER................3:01.8	OR
400m Brst	Walter Bathe, GER................6:29.6	OR
4x200m Free	AUS (Cecil Healy, Malcolm	
	Champion, Leslie Boardman,	
	Harold Hardwick)..............10:11.6	WR

Diving		Points
Spring	Paul Günther, GER..................79.23	
Platform	Erik Adlerz, SWE 73.94	
Plain High	Erik Adlerz, SWE 40.0	

WOMEN

Event		Time
100m Free	Fanny Durack, AUS 1:22.2	
4x100m Free	GBR (Bella Moore, Jennie	
	Fletcher, Annie Speirs,	
	Irene Steer) 5:52.8	WR

Diving		Points
Platform	Greta Johansson, SWE 39.9	

Team Sports

Sports	Champion
Soccer..Great Britain	
Tug-of-War ....Sweden	
Water Polo ....Great Britain	

Also Contested

Cycling, Equestrian, Fencing, Gymnastics, Modern Pentathlon, Rowing, Shooting, Tennis, Greco-Roman Wrestling and Yachting.

1920

Antwerp

The Olympic quadrennial, scheduled for Berlin in 1916, was interrupted by World War I—the so-called "War to End All Wars," which had involved 28 countries and killed nearly 10 million troops in four years.

The four-year cycle of Olympiads—Berlin would have been the sixth—is still counted, however, even though the Games were not played.

Less than two years after the armistice, the Olympics resumed in Belgium, a symbolic and austere choice considering it had been occupied for four years by enemy forces. Still, 29 countries (one more than participated in the war) sent a record 2,600 athletes to the Games. Germany and Austria, the defeated enemy of Belgium and the Allies, were not invited.

The United States turned in the best overall team performance, winning 41 gold medals, but the talk of the Games was 23-year-old distance runner Paavo Nurmi of Finland. Nurmi won the 10,000-meter run and 8,000-meter cross-country, took a third gold in the team cross-country and silver in the 5,000-meter run. In all, Finland won nine track and field gold medals to break the U.S. dominance in the sport.

Elsewhere, Albert Hill of Britain made his Olympic debut at age 36 and won both the 800- and 1,500-meter runs. World record holder Charley Paddock of the U.S. won the 100 meters, but was upset in the 200 by teammate Allan Woodring, who was a last-minute addition to the team. And in swimming, the U.S. won 11 of 15 events, led by triple gold medalists Norman Ross and Ethelda Bleibtrey, defending men's 100-meter freestyle champion Duke Kahanamoku and 14-year-old springboard diving champion Aileen Riggin.

The Antwerp Games were also noteworthy for the introduction of the Olympic oath—uttered for the first time by Belgium fencer Victor Bion—and the Olympic flag, with its five multicolored, intersecting rings.

1920 (Cont.)

Top 10 Standings

National medal standings are not recognized by the IOC. The unofficial point totals are based on 3 points for a gold medal, 2 for a silver and 1 for a bronze.

		Gold	Silver	Bronze	Total	Pts
1	USA	41	27	27	95	204
2	Sweden	19	20	25	64	122
3	Great Britain	14	15	13	42	85
4	France	9	19	13	41	78
5	Finland	15	10	9	34	74
	Belgium	13	11	11	35	72
7	Norway	13	9	9	31	66
8	Italy	13	5	5	23	54
9	Denmark	3	9	1	13	28
10	Holland	4	2	5	11	21

Leading Medal Winners

Number of individual medals won on the left; gold, silver and bronze breakdown to the right.

MEN

No		Sport	G-S-B
7	Willis Lee, USA	Shooting	5-1-1
7	Lloyd Spooner, USA	Shooting	4-1-2
6	Hubert van Innis, BEL	Archery	4-2-0
6	Carl Osburn, USA	Shooting	4-1-1
5	Nedo Nadi, ITA	Fencing	5-0-0
5	Otto Olsen, NOR	Shooting	3-2-0
5	Larry Nuesslein, USA	Shooting	2-1-2
5	Julien Brulé, FRA	Archery	1-3-1
4	Dennis Fenton, USA	Shooting	3-0-1
4	Aldo Nadi, ITA	Fencing	3-1-0
4	Paavo Nurmi, FIN	Track/Field	3-1-0
4	Harold Natvig, NOR	Shooting	2-1-1
4	Östen Östensen, NOR	Shooting	0-2-2
4	Erik Backman, SWE	Track/Field	0-1-3
4	Fritz Kuchen, SWI	Shooting	0-0-4
3	Norman Ross, USA	Swimming	3-0-0
3	Albert Hill, GBR	Track/Field	2-1-0
3	Morris Kirksey, USA	Track/Field & Rugby	2-1-0
3	Charley Paddock, USA	Track/Field	2-1-0
3	Bevil Rudd, SAF	Track/Field	1-0-2
3	Ettore Caffaratti, ITA	Equestrian	0-1-2

Fourteen shooters tied with 3 each.

WOMEN

No		Sport	G-S-B
3	Ethelda Bleibtrey, USA	Swimming	3-0-0
3	Suzanne Lenglen, FRA	Tennis	2-0-1
3	Kitty McKane, GBR	Tennis	1-1-1
3	Frances Schroth, USA	Swimming	1-0-2
2	Irene Guest, USA	Swimming	1-1-0
2	Margaret Woodbridge, USA	Swimming	1-1-0
2	Dorothy Holman, GBR	Tennis	0-2-0

Track & Field

Event		Time	
200m	Allen Woodring, USA	22.0	
400m	Bevil Rudd, SAF	49.6	
800m	Albert Hill, GBR	1:53.4	
1500m	Albert Hill, GBR	4:01.8	
5000m	Joseph Guillemot, FRA	14:55.6	
10,000m	Paavo Nurmi, FIN	31:45.8	
X-country (8000m)	Paavo Nurmi, FIN	27:15.0	
Marathon	Hannes Kolehmainen, FIN	2:32:35.8	WB
110m H	Earl Thomson, CAN	14.8	WR
400m H	Frank Loomis, USA	54.0	WR

Event		Time	
3000m Steeple	Percy Hodge, GBR	10:00.4	OR
3k Walk	Ugo Frigerio, ITA	13:14.2	OR
10k Walk	Ugo Frigerio, ITA	48:06.2	
4x100m	USA (Charley Paddock, Jackson Scholz, Loren Murchison, Morris Kirksey)	42.2	WR
4x400m	GBR (Cecil Griffiths, Robert Lindsay, John Ainsworth-Davis, Guy Butler)	3:22.2	
3000m Team	USA (Horace Brown, Arlie Schardt, Ivan Dresser)	10 pts	
X-country (8000m)	FIN (Paavo Nurmi, Heikki Liimatainen, Teudor Koskenniemi)	10 pts	

Event		Mark	
High Jump	Richmond Landon, USA	6- 4	=OR
Pole Vault	Frank Foss, USA	13- 5	WR
Long Jump	William Petersson, SWE	23- 5½	
Triple Jump	Vilho Tuulos, FIN	47- 7	
Shot Put	Ville Pörhölä, FIN	48- 7¼	
56-lb Throw	Babe McDonald, USA	36-11½	OR
Discus	Elmer Niklander, FIN	146- 7	
Hammer	Pat Ryan, USA	173- 5	
Javelin	Jonni Myyrä, FIN	215-10	OR
Pentathlon	Eero Lehtonen, FIN	14 pts	
Decathlon	Helge Lövland, NOR	6803 pts	

Swimming

MEN

Event			Time	
100m Free	Duke Kahanamoku, USA		1:01.4	
400m Free	Norman Ross, USA		5:26.8	
1500m Free	Norman Ross, USA		22:23.2	
100m Back	Warren Kealoha, USA		1:15.2	
200m Brst	Håkan Malmroth, SWE		3:04.4	
400m Brst	Håkan Malmroth, SWE		6:31.8	
4x200m Free	USA (Perry McGillivray, Pua Kealoha, Norman Ross, Duke Kahanamoku)		10:04.4	WR

Diving		Points
Plain High	Arvid Wallman, SWE	183.5
Platform	Clarence Pinkston, USA	100.67
Spring	Louis Kuehn, USA	675.4

WOMEN

Event		Time	
100m Free	Ethelda Bleibtrey, USA	1:13.6	WR
300m Free	Ethelda Bleibtrey, USA	4:34.0	WR
4x100m Free	USA (Margaret Woodbridge, Frances Schroth, Irene Guest, Ethelda Bleibtrey)	5:11.6	WR

Diving		Points
Platform	Stefani Fryland-Clausen, DEN	34.6
Spring	Aileen Riggin, USA	539.9

Team Sports

Sport	Champion
Field Hockey	Great Britain
Ice Hockey	Canada
Polo	Great Britain
Soccer	Belgium
Rugby	United States
Tug-of-War	Great Britain
Water Polo	Great Britain/Ireland

Also Contested

Archery, Boxing, Cycling, Equestrian, Fencing, Figure Skating, Gymnastics, Modern Pentathlon, Rowing, Shooting, Tennis, Weightlifting, Freestyle Wrestling, Greco-Roman Wrestling and Yachting.

1924

Paris

Paavo Nurmi may have been the talk of Antwerp in 1920, but he was the sensation of Paris four years later.

It wasn't just that the "Flying Finn" won five gold medals, it was the way he did it. Running with a stopwatch on his wrist, Peerless Paavo captured the 1,500 and 5,000-meter finals within an hour of each other and set Olympic records in both. Two days later, he blew away the field in the 10,000-meter cross-country run where the heat and an unusually difficult course combined to knock out 23 of 38 starters (Finland also won the team gold in the event). And finally, the next day he led the Finns to victory in the 3,000-meter team race. His performance overshadowed the four gold medals of teammate Ville Ritola.

The gold medals won by British runners Harold Abrahams in the 100 meters and Eric Liddell in the 400 were chronicled in the 1981 Academy Award-winning film *Chariots of Fire*. The movie, however, was not based on fact. Liddell, a devout Christian, knew months in advance that the preliminary for the 100 (his best event) was on a Sunday, so he had plenty of time to change plans and train for the 400. Also, he and Abrahams never competed against each other in real life.

Speaking of the movies, Johnny Weissmuller of the U.S. won three swimming gold medals in the 100- and 400-meter freestyles and water polo. He would later become Hollywood's most famous Tarzan.

Top 10 Standings

National medal standings are not recognized by the IOC. The unofficial point totals are based on 3 points for a gold medal, 2 for a silver and 1 for a bronze.

		Gold	Silver	Bronze	Total	Pts
1	USA	45	27	27	99	216
2	France	13	15	10	38	79
3	Finland	14	13	10	37	78
4	Great Britain	9	13	12	34	65
5	Sweden	4	13	12	29	50
6	Switzerland	7	8	10	25	47
7	Italy	8	3	5	16	35
8	Belgium	3	7	3	13	26
9	Norway	5	2	3	10	22
10	Holland	4	1	5	10	19

Leading Medal Winners

Number of individual medals won on the left; gold, silver and bronze breakdown to the right.

MEN

No		Sport	G-S-B
6	Ville Ritola, FIN	Track/Field	4-2-0
5	Paavo Nurmi, FIN	Track/Field	5-0-0
5	Roger Ducret, FRA	Fencing	3-2-0
4	Johnny Weissmuller, USA	Swimming & Water Polo	3-0-1
3	Ole Lilloe-Olsen, NOR	Shooting	2-1-0
3	Vincent Richards, USA	Tennis	2-1-0
3	Albert Séquin, FRA	Gymnastics	1-2-0
3	Boy Charlton, AUS	Swimming	1-1-1
3	August Güttinger, SWI	Gymnastics	1-0-2
3	Robert Prazák, CZE	Gymnastics	0-3-0
3	Arne Borg, SWE	Swimming	0-2-1
3	Jean Gutweniger, SWI	Gymnastics	0-2-1
3	Henri Hoevenaers, BEL	Cycling	0-2-1

WOMEN

No		Sport	G-S-B
3	Gertrude Ederle, USA	Swimming	1-0-2
2	Ethel Lackie, USA	Swimming	2-0-0
2	Hazel Wightman, USA	Tennis	2-0-0
2	Helen Wills, USA	Tennis	2-0-0
2	Betty Becker, USA	Diving	1-1-0
2	Mariechen Wehselau, USA	Swimming	1-1-0
2	Kitty McKane, GBR	Tennis	0-1-1
2	Aileen Riggin, USA	Swimming & Diving	0-1-1

Track & Field

Event			Time
100m	Harold Abrahams, GBR	10.6	=OR
200m	Jackson Scholz, USA	21.6	
400m	Eric Liddell, GBR	47.6	OR
800m	Douglas Lowe, GBR	1:52.4	
1500m	Paavo Nurmi, FIN	3:53.6	OR
5000m	Paavo Nurmi, FIN	14:31.2	OR
10,000m	Ville Ritola, FIN	30:23.2	WR
X-country (10,000m)	Paavo Nurmi, FIN	32:54.8	
Marathon	Albin Stenroos, FIN	2:41:22.6	
110m H	Daniel Kinsey, USA	15.0	
400m H	Morgan Taylor, USA	52.6	
3000m Steeple	Ville Ritola, FIN	9:33.6	OR
10k Walk	Ugo Frigerio, ITA	47:49.0	
4x100m	USA (Francis Hussey, Louis Clarke, Loren Murchison, Alfred Leconey)	41.0	=WR
4x400M	USA (C.S. Cochrane, Alan Helffrich, J.O. MacDonald, William Stevenson)	3:16.0	WR
3000m Team	FIN (Paavo Nurmi, Ville Ritola, Elias Katz)	8 pts	
X-country (10,000m)	FIN (Paavo Nurmi, Ville Ritola, Hekki Liimatainen)	11 pts	

Event		Mark	
High Jump	Harold Osborn, USA	6- 6	OR
Pole Vault	Lee Barnes, USA	12-11½	
Long Jump	De Hart Hubbard, USA	24- 5	
Triple Jump	Nick Winter, AUS	50-11¼	WR
Shot Put	Bud Houser, USA	49- 2¼	
Discus	Bud Houser, USA	151- 4	
Hammer	Fred Tootell, USA	174-10	
Javelin	Jonni Myyrä, FIN	206- 7	
Pentathlon	Eero Lehtonen, FIN	14 pts	
Decathlon	Harold Osborn, USA	7711 pts	WR

Swimming

MEN

Event			Time
100m Free	Johnny Weissmuller, USA	59.0	OR
400m Free	Johnny Weissmuller, USA	5:04.2	OR
1500m Free	Boy Charlton, AUS	20:06.6	WR
100m Back	Warren Kealoha, USA	1:13.2	OR
200m Brst	Robert Skelton, USA	2:56.6	

1924 (Cont.)

Event		Time	
4x200mFree	USA (Wallace O'Connor, Harry Glancy, Ralph Breyer, Johnny Weissmuller)...............9:53.4		WR

Diving		Points
Plain High	Richmond Eve, AUS	160.0
Platform	Albert White, USA	97.46
Spring	Albert White, USA	696.4

WOMEN

Event		Time	
100mFree	Ethel Lackie, USA.....................1:12.4		
400mFree	Martha Norelius, USA...............6:02.2		OR
100mBack	Sybil Bauer, USA......................1:23.2		OR
200m Brst	Lucy Morton, GBR.....................3:33.2		OR
4x100mFree	USA (Gertrude Ederle, Euphrasia Donnelly, Ethel Lackie, Mariechen Wehselau) 4:58.8		WR

Diving		Points
Platform	Caroline Smith, USA 33.2
Spring	Elizabeth Becker, USA 474.5

Team Sports

Sport	Champion
Polo	............................Argentina
Rugby	.....................United States
Soccer	...........................Uruguay
Water Polo	..............................France

Also Contested

Boxing, Cycling, Equestrian, Fencing, Gymnastics, Modern Pentathlon, Rowing, Shooting, Tennis, Weightlifting, Freestyle Wrestling, Greco-Roman Wrestling and Yachting.

1928
IX OLYMPIADE
AMSTERDAM

1928

Amsterdam

"We are here to represent the greatest country on earth. We did not come here to lose gracefully. We came here to win—and win decisively."

So ordered American Olympic Committee president Gen. Douglas Mac-Arthur before the start of the 1928 Games and his athletes delivered, easily winning the unofficial national standings for the third Olympiad in a row.

The U.S. men won eight gold medals in track and field, but were victorious in only one individual running race (Ray Barbuti in the 400 meters). In the sprints, Canada's Percy Williams became the first non-American to win both the 100 and 200. Finland claimed four running titles, including Paavo Nurmi's victory in the 10,000 meters—his ninth overall gold medal in three Olympic Games. Teammate and arch-rival Ville Ritola placed second in the 10,000 and outran Nurmi in the 5,000.

These Games marked Germany's return to the Olympic fold after serving a 10-year probation for its "aggressiveness" in World War I. It was also the first Olympics that women were allowed to participate in track and field (despite objections from Pope Pius IX). And in swimming, the U.S. got double gold performances from Martha Norelius, Albina Osipowich and Johnny Weissmuller, and diver Pete Desjardins.

Top 10 Standings

National medal standings are not recognized by the IOC. The unofficial point totals are based on 3 points for a gold medal, 2 for a silver and 1 for a bronze.

		Gold	Silver	Bronze	Total	Pts
1	USA............................	22	18	16	56	118
2	Germany	10	7	14	31	58
3	Finland.....................	8	8	9	25	49
4	Sweden.....................	7	6	12	25	45
5	France	6	10	5	21	43
6	Holland.....................	6	9	4	19	40
7	Italy.........................	7	5	7	19	38
8	Great Britain	3	10	7	20	36
9	Switzerland	7	4	4	15	33
10	Canada	4	4	7	15	27

Leading Medal Winners

Number of individual medals won on the left; gold, silver and bronze breakdown to the right.

MEN

No		Sport	G-S-B
4	Georges Miez, SWI ....Gymnastics		3-1-0
4	Hermann Hänggi, SWI ....Gymnastics		2-1-1
3	Lucien Gaudin, FRA ....Fencing		2-1-0
3	Eugen Mack, SWI ....Gymnastics		2-0-1
3	Paavo Nurmi, FIN ....Track/Field		1-2-0
3	Ladislav Vácha, CZE ....Gymnastics		1-2-0
3	Leon Stukelj, YUG ....Gymnastics		1-0-2
3	Emanuel Löffler, CZE ....Gymnastics		0-2-1

WOMEN

No		Sport	G-S-B
3	Joyce Cooper, GBR.......................Swimming		0-1-2
2	Martha Norelius, USA ....Swimming		2-0-0
2	Albina Osipowich, USA ....Swimming		2-0-0
2	Maria Braun, HOL ....Swimming		1-1-0
2	Eleanor Garatti, USA....................Swimming		1-1-0
2	Betty Robinson, USA....................Track/Field		1-1-0
2	Fanny Rosenfeld, CAN ....Track/Field		1-1-0
2	Ethel Smith, CAN ....Track/Field		1-0-1
2	Ellen King, GBR...........................Swimming		0-2-0
2	Georgia Coleman, USA.....................Diving		0-1-1

Track & Field
MEN

Event		Time	
100m	Percy Williams, CAN 10.8		
200m	Percy Williams, CAN 21.8		
400m	Ray Barbuti, USA...........................47.8		
800m	Douglas Lowe, GBR 1:51.8		OR
1500m	Harri Larva, FIN 3:53.2		OR
5000m	Ville Ritola, FIN.........................14:38.0		
10,000m	Paavo Nurmi, FIN....................30:18.8		OR
Marathon	Mohamed El Ouafi, FRA 2:32:57.0		
110m H	Syd Atkinson, SAF 14.8		
400m H	David Burghley, GBR....................53.4		OR
3000m Steeple	Toivo Loukola, FIN 9:21.8		WR
4x100m	USA (Frank Wykoff, Jimmy Quinn, Charley Borah, Hank Russell).......41.0		WR
4x400m	USA (George Baird, Bud Spencer, Fred Alderman, Ray Barbuti) 3:14.2		WR

Event		Mark	
High Jump	Bob King, USA	6- 4½	
Pole Vault	Sabin Carr, USA	13- 9¼	OR
Long Jump	Ed Hamm, USA	25- 4½	OR
Triple Jump	Mikio Oda, JPN	49-11	
Shot Put	Johnny Kuck, USA	52- 0¾	WR
Discus	Bud Houser, USA	155- 3	OR
Hammer	Pat O'Callaghan, IRL	168- 7	
Javelin	Erik Lundkvist, SWE	218- 6	OR
Decathlon	Paavo Yrjölä, FIN	8053 pts	WR

WOMEN

Event		Time	
100m	Betty Robinson, USA	12.2	=WR
800m	Lina Radke, GER	2:16.8	WR
4x100m	CAN (Fanny Rosenfeld, Ethel Smith, Florence Bell, Myrtle Cook)	48.4	WR

Event		Mark	
High Jump	Ethel Catherwood, CAN	5- 2½	
Discus	Halina Konopacka, POL	129-11¾	WR

Swimming

MEN

Event		Time	
100m Free	Johnny Weissmuller, USA	58.6	OR
400m Free	Alberto Zorilla, ARG	5:01.6	OR
1500m Free	Arne Borg, SWE	19:51.8	OR
100m Back	George Kojac, USA	1:08.2	WR
200m Brst	Yoshiyuki Tsuruta, JPN	2:48.8	OR

Event		Time	
4x200m Free	USA (Austin Clapp, Walter Laufer, Gorge Kojac, Johnny Weissmuller)	9:36.2	WR

Diving		Points
Platform	Pete Desjardins, USA	98.74
Spring	Pete Desjardins, USA	185.04

WOMEN

Event		Time	
100m Free	Albina Osipowich, USA	1:11.0	OR
400m Free	Martha Norelius, USA	5:42.8	WR
100m Back	Maria Braun, HOL	1:22.0	
200m Brst	Hilde Schrader, GER	3:12.6	
4x100m Free	USA (Adelaide Lambert, Eleanor Garatti, Albina Osipowich, Martha Norelius)	4:47.6	WR

Diving		Points
Platform	Elizabeth Becker Pinkston, USA	31.6
Spring	Helen Meany, USA	78.62

Team Sports

Sport	Champion
Field Hockey	India
Soccer	Uruguay
Water Polo	Germany

Also Contested

Boxing, Cycling, Equestrian, Fencing, Gymnastics, Modern Pentathlon, Rowing, Weightlifting, Freestyle Wrestling, Greco-Roman Wrestling and Yachting.

1932

Los Angeles

Despite a world-wide economic depression and predictions that the 1932 Summer Olympics were doomed to failure, 37 countries sent over 1,300 athletes to southern California and the Games were a huge success.

Energized by perfect weather and the buoyant atmosphere of the first Olympic Village, the competition was fierce. Sixteen world and Olympic records fell in men's track and field alone.

In women's track, 18-year-old Babe Didrikson, who had set world records in the 80-meter hurdles, javelin and high jump at the AAU Olympic Trials three weeks before, came to L.A. and announced, "I am out to beat everybody in sight." She almost did, too—winning the hurdles and javelin, but taking second in the high jump (despite tying teammate Jean Shiley for first) when her jumping style was ruled illegal.

Didrikson's heroics, along with American Eddie Tolan's double in the 100 and 200 meters and Italian Luigi Beccali's upset victory in the 1,500, were among the Games' highlights, but they didn't quite make up for the absence of Finland's famed distance runner Paavo Nurmi.

Just before the Games, the IOC said that Nurmi would not be allowed to participate in his fourth Olympics because he had received excessive expense money on a trip to Germany in 1929. The ruling came as no surprise in the track world where it was said, "Nurmi has the lowest heartbeat and the highest asking price of any athlete in the world."

The Japanese men and American women dominated in swimming, each winning five of six events. Helene Madison of the U.S. won two races and anchored the winning relay team.

Top 10 Standings

National medal standings are not recognized by the IOC. The unofficial point totals are based on 3 points for a gold medal, 2 for a silver and 1 for a bronze.

		Gold	Silver	Bronze	Total	Pts
1	USA	41	32	30	103	217
2	Italy	12	12	12	36	72
3	Sweden	9	5	9	23	46
4	France	10	5	4	19	44
5	Finland	5	8	12	25	43
6	Germany	3	12	5	20	38
7	Japan	7	7	4	18	39
8	Great Britain	4	7	5	16	31
	Hungary	6	4	5	15	31
10	Canada	2	5	8	15	24

Leading Medal Winners

Number of individual medals won on the left; gold, silver and bronze breakdown to the right.

MEN

No		Sport	G-S-B
4	István Pelle, HUN	Gymnastics	2-2-0
4	Giulio Gaudini, ITA	Fencing	0-3-1
4	Heikki Savolainen, FIN	Gymnastics	0-1-3
3	Romeo Neri, ITA	Gymnastics	3-0-0
3	Alex Wilson, CAN	Track/Field	0-1-2
3	Philip Edwards, CAN	Track/Field	0-0-3

1932 (Cont.)
WOMEN

No		Sport	G-S-B
3	Helene Madison, USA ....Swimming		3-0-0
3	Babe Didrikson, USA...................Track/Field		2-1-0
2	Georgia Coleman, USA.......................Diving		1-1-0
2	Eleanor Garatti, USA...................Swimming		1-0-1
2	Willy den Ouden, HOL ....Swimming		0-2-0
2	Valerie Davies, GBR ....Swimming		0-0-2

Track & Field
MEN

Event		Time	
100m	Eddie Tolan, USA 10.3		OR
200m	Eddie Tolan, USA 21.2		OR
400m	Bill Carr, USA 46.2		WR
800m	Tommy Hampson, GBR.............1:49.7		WR
1500m	Luigi Beccali, ITA 3:51.2		OR
5000m	Lauri Lehtinen, FIN 14:30.0		OR
10,000m	Janusz Kusocinski, POL 30:11.4		OR
Marathon	Juan Carlos Zabala, ARG.....2:31:36.0		OR
110m H	George Saling, USA 14.6		
400m H	Bob Tisdall, IRL 51.7		
3000m Steeple	Volmari Iso-Hollo, FIN 10:33.4		
50k Walk	Thomas Green, GBR...............4:50:10		
4x100m	USA (Bob Kiesel, Emmett Toppino, Hector Dyer, Frank Wykoff) 40.0		WR
4x400m	USA (Ivan Fuqua, Edgar Ablowich, Karl Warner, Bill Carr) 3:08.2		WR

Note: Due to a lap count error, the 3000-meter steeplechase actually went 3460 meters, or one lap too many.

Event		Mark	
High Jump	Duncan McNaughton, CAN.......6- 5½		
Pole Vault	Bill Miller, USA..........................14- 1¾		OR
Long Jump	Edward Gordon, USA 25- 0¾		
Triple Jump	Chuhei Nambu, JPN 51- 7		WR
Shot Put	Leo Sexton, USA 52- 6		OR
Discus	John Anderson, USA 162- 4		OR
Hammer	Pat O'Callaghan, IRL 176-11		
Javelin	Matti Järvinen, FIN 238- 6		OR
Decathlon	Jim Bausch, USA.................8462 pts		WR

WOMEN

Event		Time	
100m	Stella Walsh, POL 11.9		=WR
80m H	Babe Didrikson, USA 11.7		WR
4x100m	USA (Mary Carew, Evelyn Furtsch, Annette Rogers, Wilhelmina Von Bremen)............46.9		WR

Event		Mark	
High Jump	Jean Shiley, USA......................5- 5¼		WR
Discus	Lillian Copeland, USA 133- 2		OR
Javelin	Babe Didrikson, USA 143- 4		OR

Swimming
MEN

Event		Time	
100m Free	Yasuji Miyazaki, JPN..................58.2		
400m Free	Buster Crabbe, USA 4:48.4		OR
1500m Free	Kusuo Kitamura, JPN.............19:12.4		OR
100m Back	Masaji Kiyokawa, JPN.............1:08.6		
200m Brst	Yoshiyuki Tsuruta, JPN 2:45.4		
4x200m Free	JPN (Yasuji Miyazaki, Masonori Yusa, Takashi Yokoyama, Hisakichi Toyoda)..................8:58.4		WR

Diving		Points
Platform	Harold Smith, USA.................124.80	
Spring	Michael Galitzen, USA 161.38	

WOMEN

Event		Time	
100m Free	Helene Madison, USA 1:06.8		OR
400m Free	Helene Madison, USA 5:28.5		WR
100m Back	Eleanor Holm, USA 1:19.4		
200m Brst	Clare Dennis, AUS 3:06.3		OR
4x100m Free	USA (Josephine McKim, Helen Johns, Eleanor Saville-Garatti, Helene Madison)..................4:38.0		WR

Diving		Points
Platform	Dorothy Poynton, USA.............40.26	
Spring	Georgia Coleman, USA...........87.52	

Team Sports

Sport		Champion
Field Hockey ....India		
Water Polo ....Hungary		

Also Contested

Boxing, Cycling, Equestrian, Fencing, Gymnastics, Modern Pentathlon, Rowing, Shooting, Weightlifting, Freestyle Wrestling, Greco-Roman Wrestling and Yachting.

GERMANY BERLIN 1936 1-16 AUGUST
OLYMPIC GAMES

1936

Berlin

At the Big Ten track and field championships of 1935, Ohio State's Jesse Owens equaled or set world records in four events: the 100 and 220-yard dashes, 200-yard low hurdles and the long jump. He was also credited with world marks in the 200-meter run and 200-meter hurdles. That's six world records in one afternoon, and he did it all in 45 minutes!

The following year, he swept the 100 and 200 meters and long jump at the Olympic Trials and headed for Germany favored to win all three.

In Berlin, dictator Adolf Hitler and his Nazi followers felt sure that the Olympics would be the ideal venue to demonstrate Germany's oft-stated racial superiority. He directed that $25 million be spent on the finest facilities, the cleanest streets and the temporary withdrawal of all outward signs of the state-run anti-Jewish campaign. By the time over 4,000 athletes from 49 countries arrived for the Games, the stage was set.

Then Jesse Owens, a black sharecropper's son from Alabama, stole the show—winning his three individual events and adding a fourth gold medal in the 400-meter relay. The fact that four other American blacks also won did little to please Herr Hitler, but the applause from the German crowds, especially for Owens, was thunderous. As it was for New Zealander Jack Lovelock's thrilling win over Glenn Cunningham and defending champ Luigi Beccali in the 1,500 meters.

Germany won only five combined gold medals in men's and women's track and field, but saved face for the "master race" in the overall medal count with an 89-56 margin over the United States.

The top female performers in Berlin were 17-year-old Dutch swimmer Rie Mastenbroek, who won three gold medals, and 18-year-old American runner Helen Stephens, who captured the 100 meters and anchored the winning 4x100-meter relay team.

Basketball also made its debut as a medal sport and was played outdoors. The U.S. men easily won the first gold medal championship game with a 19-8 victory over Canada, in the rain.

Top 10 Standings

National medal standings are not recognized by the IOC. The unofficial point totals are based on 3 points for a gold medal, 2 for a silver and 1 for a bronze.

		Gold	Silver	Bronze	Total	Pts
1	Germany	33	26	30	89	181
2	USA	24	20	12	56	124
3	Italy	8	9	5	22	47
4	Finland	7	6	6	19	39
	France	7	6	6	19	39
6	Sweden	6	5	9	20	37
	Hungary	10	1	5	16	37
8	Japan	6	4	8	18	34
9	Holland	6	4	7	17	33
10	Great Britain	4	7	3	14	29

Leading Medal Winners

Number of individual medals won on the left; gold, silver and bronze breakdown to the right.

MEN

No		Sport	G-S-B
6	Konrad Frey, GER	Gymnastics	3-1-2
5	Alfred Schwarzmann, GER	Gymnastics	3-0-2
5	Eugen Mack, SWI	Gymnastics	0-4-1
4	Jesse Owens, USA	Track/Field	4-0-0
3	Robert Charpentier, FRA	Cycling	3-0-0
3	Guy Lapébie, FRA	Cycling	2-1-0
3	Jack Medica, USA	Swimming	1-2-0
3	Matthias Volz, GER	Gymnastics	1-0-2

WOMEN

No		Sport	G-S-B
4	Rie Mastenbroek, HOL	Swimming	3-1-0
2	Helen Stephens, USA	Track/Field	2-0-0
2	Dorothy Poynton Hill, USA	Diving	1-0-1
2	Gisela Arendt, GER	Swimming	0-1-1

Track & Field

MEN

Event		Time	
100m	Jesse Owens, USA	10.3	
200m	Jesse Owens, USA	20.7	OR
400m	Archie Williams, USA	46.5	
800m	John Woodruff, USA	1:52.9	
1500m	Jack Lovelock, NZE	3:47.8	WR
5000m	Gunnar Höckert, FIN	14:22.2	OR
10,000m	Ilmari Salminen, FIN	30:15.4	
Marathon	Sohn Kee-chung, JPN	2:29:19.2	OR
110m H	Forrest Towns, USA	14.2	
400m H	Glenn Hardin, USA	52.4	
3000m Steeple	Volmari Iso-Hollo, FIN	9:03.8	WR
50k walk	Harold Whitlock, GBR	4:30:41.4	OR

Note: Marathon winner Sohn was a Korean, but was forced to run for Japan which occupied his country.

Event		Time	
4x100m	USA (Jesse Owens, Ralph Metcalfe, Foy Draper, Frank Wykoff)	39.8	WR
4x400m	GBR (Frederick Wolff, Godfrey Rampling, William Roberts, A.G. Brown)	3:09.0	

Event		Mark	
High Jump	Cornelius Johnson, USA	6-8	OR
Pole Vault	Earle Meadows, USA	14-3¼	OR
Long Jump	Jesse Owens, USA	26-5½	OR
Triple Jump	Naoto Tajima, JPN	52-6	WR
Shot Put	Hans Woellke, GER	53-1¾	OR
Discus	Ken Carpenter, USA	165-7	OR
Hammer	Karl Hein, GER	185-4	OR
Javelin	Gerhard Stöck, GER	235-8	
Decathlon	Glenn Morris, USA	7900 pts	WR

WOMEN

Event		Time	
100m	Helen Stephens, USA	11.5w	
80m H	Trebisonda Valla, ITA	11.7	
4x100m	USA (Harriet Bland, Annette Rogers, Betty Robinson, Helen Stephens)	46.9	

w indicates wind-aided.

Event		Mark	
High Jump	Ibolya Csák, HUN	5-3	
Discus	Gisela Mauermayer, GER	156-3	OR
Javelin	Tilly Fleischer, GER	148-3	OR

Swimming

MEN

Event		Time	
100m Free	Ferenc Csík, HUN	57.6	
400m Free	Jack Medica, USA	4:44.5	OR
1500m Free	Noboru Terada, JPN	19:13.7	
100m Back	Adolf Kiefer, USA	1:05.9	OR
200m Brst	Tetsuo Hamuro, JPN	2:41.5	OR
4x200m Free	JPN (Masanori Yusa, Shigeo Sugiura, Masaharu Taguchi, Shigeo Arai)	8:51.5	WR

Diving		Points
Platform	Marshall Wayne, USA	113.58
Spring	Richard Degener, USA	163.57

WOMEN

Event		Time	
100m Free	Rie Mastenbroek, HOL	1:05.9	OR
400m Free	Rie Mastenbroek, HOL	5:26.4	OR
100m Back	Nida Senff, HOL	1:18.9	
200m Brst	Hideko Maehata, JPN	3:03.6	
4x100m Free	HOL (Johanna Selbach, Catherina Wagner, Willemijntje den Ouden, Rie Mastenbroek)	4:36.0	

Diving		Points
Platform	Dorothy Poynton Hill, USA	33.93
Spring	Marjorie Gestring, USA	89.27

Team Sports

Sport	Champion
Basketball	United States
Field Hockey	India
Handball	Germany
Polo	Argentina
Soccer	Italy
Water Polo	Hungary

Note: In Water Polo, both Hungary and Germany finished with records of 8-0-1. The Hungarians were awarded the gold medal on total goals (57-56).

Also Contested

Boxing, Canoeing, Cycling, Equestrian, Fencing, Gymnastics, Modern Pentathlon, Rowing, Shooting, Weightlifting, Freestyle Wrestling, Greco-Roman Wrestling and Yachting.

1948

London

The Summer Olympics were scheduled for Tokyo in 1940, but by mid-1938, Japan was at war with China and withdrew as host. The IOC immediately transferred the Games to Helsinki and the Finns eagerly began preparations only to be invaded by Russia in 1939.

By then, of course, Germany had marched into Poland and World War II was on. The Japanese attacked Pearl Harbor two years later, and the bombs didn't stop falling until 1945. Against this backdrop of global conflict, the Olympic Games were cancelled again in 1940 and '44. Many of the participants in the 1936 Games died in the war.

Eager to come back after two dormant Olympiads, the IOC offered the 1948 Games to London. Much of the British capital had been reduced to rubble in the blitz, but the offer was accepted and the Games went on—successfully, without frills, and without invitations extended to Germany and Japan. The Soviet Union was invited, but chose not to show.

The United States reclaimed its place at the top of the overall medal standings, but the primary individual stars were a 30-year-old Dutch mother of two and a 17-year-old kid from California.

Fanny Blankers-Koen duplicated Jesse Owens' track and field grand slam of 12 years before by winning the 100-meter run and 200-meter run, the 80-meter hurdles, and anchoring the women's 400-meter relay.

And Bob Mathias, just two months after graduating from Tulare High School, won the gold medal in the decathlon, an event he had taken up for the first time during the summer.

Top 10 Standings

National medal standings are not recognized by the IOC. The unofficial point totals are based on 3 points for a gold medal, 2 for a silver and 1 for a bronze.

		Gold	Silver	Bronze	Total	Pts
1	USA	38	27	19	84	187
2	Sweden	16	11	17	44	87
3	Italy	8	12	9	29	57
4	France	10	6	13	29	55
5	Hungary	10	5	12	27	52
6	Great Britain	3	14	6	23	43
	Finland	8	7	5	20	43
8	Switzerland	5	10	5	20	40
9	Denmark	5	7	8	20	37
10	Holland	5	2	9	16	28
	Turkey	6	4	2	12	28

Leading Medal Winners

Number of individual medals won on the left; gold, silver and bronze breakdown to the right.

MEN

No		Sport	G-S-B
5	Veikko Huhtanen, FIN	Gymnastics	3-1-1
4	Paavo Aaltonen, FIN	Gymnastics	3-0-1
3	Jimmy McLane, USA	Swimming	2-1-0
3	Humberto Mariles, MEX	Equestrian	2-0-1
3	Mal Whitfield, USA	Track/Field	2-0-1
3	Barney Ewell, USA	Track/Field	1-2-0
3	Michael Reusch, SWI	Gymnastics	1-2-0
3	Josef Stalder, SWI	Gymnastics	1-1-1
3	Ferenc Pataki, HUN	Gymnastics	1-0-2
3	Walter Lehmann, SWI	Gymnastics	0-3-0
3	Edoardo Mangiarotti, ITA	Fencing	0-2-1
3	János Mogyorósi, HUN	Gymnastics	0-1-2

WOMEN

No		Sport	G-S-B
4	Fanny Blankers-Koen, HOL	Track/Field	4-0-0
3	Ann Curtis, USA	Swimming	2-1-0
3	Micheline Ostermeyer, FRA	Track/Field	2-0-1
3	Karen-Margrete Harup, DEN	Swimming	1-2-0
3	Shirley Strickland, AUS	Track/Field	0-1-2

Track & Field

MEN

Event		Time	
100m	Harrison Dillard, USA	10.3	=OR
200m	Mel Patton, USA	21.1	
400m	Arthur Wint, JAM	46.2	
800m	Mal Whitfield, USA	1:49.2	OR
1500m	Henri Eriksson, SWE	3:49.8	
5000m	Gaston Reiff, BEL	14:17.6	OR
10,000m	Emil Zátopek, CZE	29:59.6	OR
Marathon	Delfo Cabrera, ARG	2:34:51.6	
110m H	Bill Porter, USA	13.9	OR
400m H	Roy Cochran, USA	51.1	OR
3000m Steeple	Thore Sjöstrand, SWE	9:04.6	
10k Walk	John Mikaelsson, SWE	45:13.2	
50k Walk	John Ljunggren, SWE	4:41:52	
4x100m	USA (Barney Ewell, Lorenzo Wright, Harrison Dillard, Mel Patton)	40.6	
4x400m	USA (Art Harnden, Cliff Bourland, Roy Cochran, Mal Whitfield)	3:10.4	

Event		Mark	
High Jump	John Winter, AUS	6- 6	
Pole Vault	Guinn Smith, USA	14- 1¼	
Long Jump	Willie Steele, USA	25- 8	
Triple Jump	Arne Åhman, SWE	50- 6¼	
Shot Put	Wilbur Thompson, USA	56- 2	OR
Discus	Adolfo Consolini, ITA	173- 2	OR
Hammer	Imre Németh, HUN	183-11	
Javelin	Tapio Rautavaara, FIN	228-10	
Decathlon	Bob Mathias, USA	7139 pts	

WOMEN

Event		Time	
100m	Fanny Blankers-Koen, HOL	11.9	
200m	Fanny Blankers-Koen, HOL	24.4	
80m H	Fanny Blankers-Koen, HOL	11.2	OR
4x100m	HOL (Xenia Stad-de Jong, Jeanette Witziers-Timmer, Gerda van der Kade-Koudijs, Fanny Blankers-Koen)	47.5	

Event		Mark	
High Jump	Alice Coachman, USA	5-6	OR
Long Jump	Olga Gyarmati, HUN	18-8¼	
Shot Put	Micheline Ostermeyer, FRA	45-1½	
Discus	Micheline Ostermeyer, FRA	137-6	
Javelin	Herma Bauma, AUT	149-6	

Note: Coachman and Dorothy Odam of Britain tied for 1st place, but Coachman was awarded gold medal for making height on first try.

Swimming
MEN

Event		Time	
100m Free	Wally Ris, USA	57.3	OR
400m Free	Bill Smith, USA	4:41.0	OR
1500m Free	Jimmy McLane, USA	19:18.5	
100m Back	Allen Stack, USA	1:06.4	
200m Brst	Joe Verdeur, USA	2:39.3	OR
4x200mFree	USA (Wally Ris, Jimmy McLane, Wally Wolf, Bill Smith)	8:46.0	WR
Diving		**Points**	
Platform	Sammy Lee, USA	130.05	
Spring	Bruce Harlan, USA	163.64	

WOMEN

Event		Time	
100m Free	Greta Andersen, DEN	1:06.3	
400m Free	Ann Curtis, USA	5:17.8	OR
100m Back	Karen M. Harup, DEN	1:14.4	OR
200m Brst	Nel van Vliet, HOL	2:57.2	
4x100mFree	USA (Marie Corridon, Thelma Kalama, Brenda Helser, Ann Curtis)	4:29.2	OR
Diving		**Points**	
Platform	Vicki Draves, USA	68.87	
Spring	Vicki Draves, USA	108.74	

Team Sports

Sport	Champion
Basketball	United States
Field Hockey	India
Soccer	Sweden
Water Polo	Italy

Also Contested
Boxing, Canoeing, Cycling, Equestrian, Fencing, Gymnastics, Modern Pentathlon, Rowing, Shooting, Weightlifting, Freestyle Wrestling, Greco-Roman Wrestling and Yachting.

IOCURILE OLIMPICE
HELSINKI FINLANDA

1952
Helsinki

The Soviet Union returned to the Olympic fold in 1952 after a 40-year absence, a period of time that included a revolution and two world wars. Ironically, the Soviets chose to make their comeback in Finland, a country they had invaded twice during World War II.

This time it was the United States that was surprised by the Russians, and the USA had to scramble on the last day of competition to hold off the USSR's assault on first place in the overall standings. It was the beginning of an all-consuming 36-year Cold War rivalry.

Despite the Soviets' impressive debut, it was a Communist from another Iron Curtain country who turned in the most memorable individual performance of the Games. Emil Zátopek of Czechoslovakia, the 10,000-meter champion in London, not only repeated at 10,000 meters, but also won at 5,000 and in the marathon—an event he had never run before. He also set Olympic records in each race and topped it off by watching his wife Dana Zátopková win the women's javelin.

Zátopek's unique triple was wildly applauded by the distance-minded Finns, but their greatest outburst came in the opening ceremonies when legendary countryman Paavo Nurmi, now 56, ran into the stadium with the Olympic torch and handed it off to another native legend Hannes Kolehmainen, now 62, who lit the flame to start the Games.

Also, Harrison Dillard of the U.S. won the 110-meter hurdles. In 1948, Dillard, the world's best hurdler, failed to qualify for the hurdles and won the 100-meter dash instead.

Top 10 Standings
National medal standings are not recognized by the IOC. The unofficial point totals are based on 3 points for a gold medal, 2 for a silver and 1 for a bronze.

		Gold	Silver	Bronze	Total	Pts
1	USA	40	19	17	76	175
2	USSR	21	30	18	69	141
3	Hungary	16	10	16	42	84
4	Sweden	12	13	10	35	72
5	Italy	8	9	4	21	46
6	Finland	6	3	13	22	37
7	France	6	6	6	18	36
8	Germany	0	7	17	24	31
9	Czechoslovakia	7	3	3	13	30
10	Australia	6	2	3	11	25

Leading Medal Winners
Number of individual medals won on the left; gold, silver and bronze breakdown to the right.

MEN

No		Sport	G-S-B
6	Viktor Chukarin, USSR	Gymnastics	4-2-0
4	Edoardo Mangiarotti, ITA	Fencing	2-2-0
4	Grant Shaginyan, USSR	Gymnastics	2-2-0
4	Josef Stalder, SWI	Gymnastics	0-2-2
3	Emil Zátopek, CZE	Track/Field	3-0-0
3	Ford Konno, USA	Swimming	2-1-0
3	Herb McKenley, JAM	Track/Field	1-2-0
3	Hans Eugster, SWI	Gymnastics	1-1-1

WOMEN

No		Sport	G-S-B
7	Maria Gorokhovskaya, USSR	Gymnastics	2-5-0
6	Margit Korondi, HUN	Gymnastics	1-1-4
4	Nina Bocharova, USSR	Gymnastics	2-2-0
4	Ágnes Keleti, HUN	Gymnastics	1-1-2
3	Yekaterina Kalinchuk, USSR	Gymnastics	2-1-0
3	Éva Novák, HUN	Swimming	1-2-0
3	Galina Minaicheva, USSR	Gymnastics	1-1-1
3	Aleksandra Chudina, USSR	Track/Field	0-2-1

1952 (Cont.)
Track & Field
MEN

Event		Time	
100m	Lindy Remigino, USA	10.4	
200m	Andy Stanfield, USA	20.7	
400m	George Rhoden, JAM	45.9	OR
800m	Mal Whitfield, USA	1:49.2	=OR
1500m	Josy Barthel, LUX	3:45.1	OR
5000m	Emil Zátopek, CZE	14:06.6	OR
10,000m	Emil Zátopek, CZE	29:17.0	OR
Marathon	Emil Zátopek, CZE	2:23:03.2	OR
110m H	Harrison Dillard, USA	13.7	OR
400m H	Charley Moore, USA	50.8	OR
3000m Steeple	Horace Ashenfelter, USA	8:45.4	WR
10k Walk	John Mikaelsson, SWE	45:02.8	OR
50k Walk	Giuseppe Dordoni, ITA	4:28:07.8	OR
4x100m	USA (Dean Smith, Harrison Dillard, Lindy Remigino, Andy Stanfield)	40.1	
4x400m	JAM (Arthur Wint, Leslie Laing, Herb McKenley, George Rhoden)	3:03.9	WR

Event		Mark	
High Jump	Walt Davis, USA	6- 8½	OR
Pole Vault	Bob Richards, USA	14-11	OR
Long Jump	Jerome Biffle, USA	24-10	
Triple Jump	Adhemar da Silva, BRA	53- 2¾	WR
Shot Put	Parry O'Brien, USA	57- 1½	OR
Discus	Sim Iness, USA	180- 6	OR
Hammer	József Csérmák, HUN	197-11	OR
Javelin	Cy Young, USA	242- 1	OR
Decathlon	Bob Mathias, USA	7887 pts	WR

WOMEN

Event		Time	
100m	Marjorie Jackson, AUS	11.5	WR
200m	Marjorie Jackson, AUS	23.7	
80m H	Shirley Strickland, AUS	10.9	WR
4x100m	USA (Mae Faggs, Barbara Jones, Janet Moreau, Catherine Hardy)	45.9	WR

Event		Mark	
High Jump	Esther Brand, SAF	5- 5¾	
Long Jump	Yvette Williams, NZE	20- 5¾	OR
Shot Put	Galina Zybina, USSR	50- 1¾	WR
Discus	Nina Romaschkova, USSR	168- 8	OR
Javelin	Dana Zátopková, CZE	165- 7	

Swimming
MEN

Event		Time	
100m Free	Clarke Scholes, USA	57.4	
400m Free	Jean Boiteux, FRA	4:30.7	OR
1500m Free	Ford Konno, USA	18:30.3	OR
100m Back	Yoshi Oyakawa, USA	1:05.4	OR
200m Brst	John Davies, AUS	2:34.4	OR
4x200mFree	USA (Wayne Moore, Bill Woolsey, Ford Konno, Jimmy McLane)	8:31.1	OR

Diving		Points
Platform	Sammy Lee, USA	156.28
Spring	Skippy Browning, USA	205.29

WOMEN

Event		Time	
100m Free	Katalin Szöke, HUN	1:06.8	
400m Free	Valéria Gyenge, HUN	5:12.1	OR
100m Back	Joan Harrison, SAF	1:14.3	
200m Brst	Éva Székely, HUN	2:51.7	OR
4x100mFree	HUN (Ilona Novák, Judit Temes, Éva Novák, Katalin Szöke)	4:24.4	WR

Diving		Points
Platform	Pat McCormick, USA	79.37
Spring	Pat McCormick, USA	147.30

Team Sports

Sport	Champion
Basketball	United States
Field Hockey	India
Soccer	Hungary
Water Polo	Hungary

Also Contested

Boxing, Canoeing, Cycling, Equestrian, Fencing, Gymnastics, Modern Pentathlon, Rowing, Shooting, Weightlifting, Freestyle Wrestling, Greco-Roman Wrestling and Yachting.

1956
Melbourne

Armed conflicts in Egypt and Hungary threatened to disrupt the 1956 Games, which were scheduled to begin on Nov. 22 (during the summer Down Under).

In July, Egypt seized the Suez Canal from British and French control. In October, Britain and France invaded Egypt in an attempt to retake the canal. Then in November, Russian tanks rolled into Hungary to crush an anti-Communist revolt.

The only direct bearing these events had in Melbourne came when the Soviet water polo team met the Hungarians in the semifinals. Hungary won 4-0, but the match turned ugly after a Hungarian player was pulled bleeding from the pool with a deep gash over his eye from a Russian head butt. A brawl quickly ensued involving both players and spectators and the police had to step in to prevent a riot.

Otherwise, the Soviets outmedaled the U.S. for the first time, cleaning up in gymnastics and winning their first track and field titles when Vladimir Kuts ran off with the 5,000 and 10,000 meters.

The American men won 15 track and field titles, including three golds for sprinter Bobby Morrow and Al Oerter's first victory in the discus.

Harold Connolly of the U.S. won the hammer throw and the heart of the women's discus champion, Olga Fikotová of Czechoslovakia. Their romance captured the imagination of the world and three months after the Games they were married.

Emil Zátopek, the Czech hero of Helsinki, returned to defend his marathon title and came in sixth. Winner Alain Mimoun, of France, had finished second to Zátopek three times in previous Olympics.

Top 10 Standings

National medal standings are not recognized by the IOC. The unofficial point totals are based on 3 points for a gold medal, 2 for a silver and 1 for a bronze.

		Gold	Silver	Bronze	Total	Pts
1	USSR	37	29	32	98	201
2	USA	32	25	17	74	163
3	Australia	13	8	14	35	69
4	Hungary	9	10	7	26	54
5	Germany	6	13	7	26	51
6	Italy	8	8	9	25	49
7	Great Britain	6	7	11	24	43
8	Sweden	8	5	6	19	40
9	Japan	4	10	5	19	37
10	Romania	5	3	5	13	26
	France	4	4	6	14	26

Leading Medal Winners

Number of individual medals won on the left; gold, silver and bronze breakdown to the right.

MEN

No		Sport	G-S-B
5	Viktor Chukarin, USSR	Gymnastics	3-1-1
5	Takashi Ono, JPN	Gymnastics	1-3-1
4	Valentin Muratov, USSR	Gymnastics	3-1-0
4	Yuriy Titov, USSR	Gymnastics	1-1-2
4	Masao Takemoto, JPN	Gymnastics	0-1-3
3	Bobby Morrow, USA	Track/Field	3-0-0
3	Murray Rose, AUS	Swimming	3-0-0
3	Edoardo Mangiarotti, ITA	Fencing	2-0-1
3	Thane Baker, USA	Track/Field	1-1-1
3	Masami Kubota, JPN	Gymnastics	0-2-1
3	George Breen, USA	Swimming	0-1-2

WOMEN

No		Sport	G-S-B
6	Ágnes Keleti, HUN	Gymnastics	4-2-0
6	Larissa Latynina, USSR	Gymnastics	4-1-1
4	Tamara Manina, USSR	Gymnastics	1-2-1
3	Sofiya Muratova, USSR	Gymnastics	1-0-3
3	Betty Cuthbert, AUS	Track/Field	3-0-0
3	Lorraine Crapp, AUS	Swimming	2-1-0
3	Dawn Fraser, AUS	Swimming	2-1-0
3	Olga Tass, HUN	Gymnastics	1-1-1

Track & Field
MEN

Event		Time	
100m	Bobby Morrow, USA	10.5	
200m	Bobby Morrow, USA	20.6	OR
400m	Charley Jenkins, USA	46.7	
800m	Tom Courtney, USA	1:47.7	OR
1500m	Ron Delany, IRL	3:41.2	OR
5000m	Vladimir Kuts, USSR	13:39.6	OR
10,000m	Vladimir Kuts, USSR	28:45.6	OR
Marathon	Alain Mimoun, FRA	2:25:00.0	
110m H	Lee Calhoun, USA	13.5	OR
400m H	Glenn Davis, USA	50.1	=OR
3000m Steeple	Chris Brasher, GBR	8:41.2	OR
20k Walk	Leonid Spirin, USSR	1:31:27.4	
50k Walk	Norman Read, NZE	4:30:42.8	
4x100m	USA (Ira Murchison, Leamon King, Thane Baker, Bobby Morrow)	39.5	WR
4x400m	USA (Lou Jones, Jesse Mashburn, Charlie Jenkins, Tom Courtney)	3:04.8	

Event		Mark	
High Jump	Charley Dumas, USA	6-11½	OR
Pole Vault	Bob Richards, USA	14-11½	OR
Long Jump	Greg Bell, USA	25-8¼	OR
Triple Jump	Adhemar da Silva, BRA	53-7¾	OR
Shot Put	Parry O'Brien, USA	60-11¼	OR
Discus	Al Oerter, USA	184-11	OR
Hammer	Harold Connolly, USA	207-3	OR
Javelin	Egil Danielson, NOR	281-2	WR
Decathlon	Milt Campbell, USA	7937 pts	OR

WOMEN

Event		Time	
100m	Betty Cuthbert, AUS	11.5	
200m	Betty Cuthbert, AUS	23.4	=OR
80m H	Shirley Strickland, AUS	10.7	OR
4x100m	AUS (Shirley Strickland, Norma Croker, Fleur Mellor, Betty Cuthbert)	44.5	WR

Event		Mark	
High Jump	Mildred McDaniel, USA	5-9¼	WR
Long Jump	Elzbieta Krzesinska, POL	20-10	=WR
Shot Put	Tamara Tyshkevich, USSR	54-5	OR
Discus	Olga Fikotová, CZE	176-1	OR
Javelin	Inese Jaunzeme, USSR	176-8	

Swimming
MEN

Event		Time	
100m Free	Jon Henricks, AUS	55.4	OR
400m Free	Murray Rose, AUS	4:27.3	OR
1500m Free	Murray Rose, AUS	17:58.9	
100m Back	David Theile, AUS	1:02.2	OR
200m Brst	Masaru Furukawa, JPN	2:34.7	OR
200m Fly	Bill Yorzyk, USA	2:19.3	OR
4x200m Free	AUS (Kevin O'Halloran, John Devitt, Murray Rose, Jon Henricks)	8:23.6	WR

Diving		Points
Platform	Joaquin Capilla, MEX	152.44
Spring	Bob Clotworthy, USA	159.56

WOMEN

Event		Time	
100m Free	Dawn Fraser, AUS	1:02.0	WR
400m Free	Lorraine Crapp, AUS	4:54.6	OR
100m Back	Judy Grinham, GBR	1:12.9	OR
200m Brst	Ursula Happe, GER	2:53.1	OR
100m Fly	Shelly Mann, USA	1:11.0	OR
4x100m Free	AUS (Dawn Fraser, Faith Leech, Sandra Morgan, Lorraine Crapp)	4:17.1	WR

Diving		Points
Platform	Pat McCormick, USA	84.85
Spring	Pat McCormick, USA	142.36

Team Sports

Sport	Champion
Basketball	United States
Field Hockey	India
Soccer	Soviet Union
Water Polo	Hungary

Also Contested

Boxing, Canoeing, Cycling, Equestrian, Fencing, Gymnastics, Modern Pentathlon, Rowing, Shooting, Weightlifting, Freestyle Wrestling, Greco-Roman Wrestling and Yachting.

Note: Equestrian events were held in Stockholm, Sweden, June 10-17, due to Australian quarantine laws.

JEUX DE LA XVII OLYMPIADE
ROMA 25.VIII-11.IX

1960

Rome

Free of political entanglements, save the ruling that Nationalist China had to compete as Formosa, the 1960 Games attracted a record 5,348 athletes from 83 countries. More importantly, it was the first Summer Games covered by U.S. television. CBS bought the rights for $394,000.

Rome was a coming-out party for 18-year-old Louisville boxer Cassius Clay. The brash but engaging Clay, who would later change his name to Muhammad Ali and hold the world heavyweight title three times, won the Olympic light heavyweight crown, pummeling Polish opponent Zbigniew Pietryskowsky in the final. Clay was so proud of his gold medal he didn't take it off for two days.

Sprinter Wilma Rudolph and swimmer Chris von Saltza each won three gold medals for the U.S. Rudolph, who was one of 19 children and who couldn't walk without braces until she was 11, struck gold at 100 and 200 meters and anchored the winning 400-meter relay team. Von Saltza won the 400-meter freestyle, placed second in the 100-free and anchored the winning 400-free and medley relays.

The U.S. men won nine track and field titles, including repeat gold medals for Lee Calhoun, Glenn Davis and Al Oerter. Rafer Johnson and C.K. Yang of Formosa, college teammates at UCLA, finished 1-2 in the decathlon.

Among the other stars in Rome were barefoot Ethiopian marathoner Abebe Bikila, Australia's Herb Elliott in the 1,500 meters, Russian gymnasts Boris Shakhlin and Larissa Latynina.

Finally, the greatest amateur basketball team ever assembled represented the U.S. and won easily. The 12-man roster included Oscar Robertson, Jerry West, Jerry Lucas, Walt Bellamy and Terry Dischinger–four of whom would become NBA Rookies of the Year from 1961-64.

Top 10 Standings

National medal standings are not recognized by the IOC. The unofficial point totals are based on 3 points for a gold medal, 2 for a silver and 1 for a bronze.

	Gold	Silver	Bronze	Total	Pts
1 USSR	43	29	31	103	218
2 USA	34	21	16	71	160
3 Germany	12	19	11	42	85
4 Italy	13	10	13	36	72
5 Australia	8	8	6	22	46
6 Hungary	6	8	7	21	41
7 Poland	4	6	11	21	35
8 Japan	4	7	7	18	33
9 Great Britain	2	6	12	20	30
10 Turkey	7	2	0	9	25

Leading Medal Winners

Number of individual medals won on the left; gold, silver and bronze breakdown to the right.

MEN

No		Sport	G-S-B
7	Boris Shakhlin, USSR	Gymnastics	4-2-1
6	Takashi Ono, JPN	Gymnastics	3-1-2
3	Murray Rose, AUS	Swimming	1-1-1
3	John Konraads, AUS	Swimming	1-0-2
3	Yuri Titov, USSR	Gymnasitcs	0-2-1

WOMEN

No		Sport	G-S-B
6	Larissa Latynina, USSR	Gymnastics	3-2-1
4	Chris von Saltza, USA	Swimming	3-1-0
4	Polina Astakhova, USSR	Gymnastics	2-1-1
4	Sofia Muratova, USSR	Gymnastics	1-2-1
3	Wilma Rudolph, USA	Track/Field	3-0-0
3	Dawn Fraser, AUS	Swimming	1-2-0
3	Tamara Lyukhina, USSR	Gymnastics	1-0-2

Track & Field

MEN

Event		Time	
100m	Armin Hary, GER	10.2	OR
200m	Livio Berruti, ITA	20.5	=WR
400m	Otis Davis, USA	44.9	WR
800m	Peter Snell, NZE	1:46.3	OR
1500m	Herb Elliott, AUS	3:35.6	WR
5000m	Murray Halberg, NZE	13:43.4	
10,000m	Pyotr Bolotnikov, USSR	28:32.2	OR
Marathon	Abebe Bikila, ETH	2:15:16.2	WB
110m H	Lee Calhoun, USA	13.8	
400m H	Glenn Davis, USA	49.3	=OR
3000m Steeple	Zdzislaw Krzyszkowiak, POL	8:34.2	OR
20k Walk	Vladimir Golubnichiy, USSR	1:34:07.2	
50k Walk	Don Thompson, GBR	4:25:30.0	OR
4x100m	GER (Bernd Cullmann, Armin Hary, Walter Mahlendorf, Martin Lauer)	39.5	=WR
4x400m	USA (Jack Yerman, Earl Young, Glenn Davis, Otis Davis)	3:02.2	WR

Event		Mark	
High Jump	Robert Shavlakadze, USSR	7- 1	OR
Pole Vault	Don Bragg, USA	15- 5	OR
Long Jump	Ralph Boston, USA	26- 7¾	OR
Triple Jump	József Schmidt, POL	55- 2	OR
Shot Put	Bill Nieder, USA	64- 6¾	OR
Discus	Al Oerter, USA	194- 2	OR
Hammer	Vasily Rudenkov, USSR	220- 2	OR
Javelin	Viktor Tsibulenko, USSR	277- 8	
Decathlon	Rafer Johnson, USA	8392 pts	OR

WOMEN

Event		Time	
100m	Wilma Rudolph, USA	11.0 ^{w}	
200m	Wilma Rudolph, USA	24.0	
800m	Lyudmila Shevtsova, USSR	2:04.3	=WR
80m H	Irina Press, USSR	10.8	
4x100m	USA (Martha Hudson, Lucinda Williams, Barbara Jones, Wilma Rudolph)	44.5	

^{w} indicates wind-aided.

Event		Mark	
High Jump	Iolanda Balas, ROM	6- 0¾	OR
Long Jump	Vyera Krepkina, USSR	20-10¾	OR
Shot Put	Tamara Press, USSR	56-10	OR
Discus	Nina R. Ponomaryeva, USSR	180- 9	OR
Javelin	Elvira Ozolina, USSR	183- 8	OR

Boxing

Weight Class	Champion
Flyweight (112 lbs)	Gyula Török, HUN
Bantamweight (119)	Oleg Grigoryev, USSR
Featherweight (125)	Francesco Musso, ITA
Lightweight (132)	Kazimierz Pazdzior, POL
Lt. Welterweight (139)	Bohumil Nemecek, CZE
Welterweight (148)	Nino Benvenuti, ITA
Lt. Middleweight (156)	Skeeter McClure, USA
Middleweight (165)	Eddie Crook, USA
Lt. Heavyweight (178)	Cassius Clay, USA
Heavyweight (178+)	Franco De Piccoli, ITA

Gymnastics

MEN

Individual		Points
All-Around	Boris Shakhlin, USSR	115.95
Floor	Nobuyuki Aihara, JPN	19.45
Horiz.Bar	Takashi Ono, JPN	19.60
Paral.Bars	Boris Shakhlin, USSR	19.40
Rings	Albert Azaryan, USSR	19.725
Side Horse	Boris Shakhlin, USSR & Eugen Ekman, FIN	19.375
Vault	Boris Shakhlin, USSR & Takashi Ono, JPN	19.35

Team		Points
All-Around	JPN (Ono, Tsurumi, Aihara, Endo, Takemoto, Mitsukuri)	575.20

WOMEN

Individual		Points
All-Around	Larissa Latynina, USSR	77.031
Bal.Beam	Eva Bosáková, CZE	19.283
Floor	Larissa Latynina, USSR	19.583
Uneven Bars	Polina Astakhova, USSR	19.616
Vault	Margarita Nikolayeva, USSR	19.316

Team		Points
All-Around	USSR (Latynina, Muratova, Astakhova, Nikolayeva, Ivanova, Lyukhina)	382.320

Swimming

MEN

Event		Time	
100m Free	John Devitt, AUS	55.2	OR
400m Free	Murray Rose, AUS	4:18.3	OR
1500m Free	John Konrads, AUS	17:19.6	OR
100m Back	David Theile, AUS	1:09.9	OR
200m Brst	Bill Mulliken, USA	2:37.4	
200m Fly	Mike Troy, USA	2:12.8	WR
4x200mFree	USA (George Harrison, Dick Blick, Mike Troy, Jeff Farrell)	8:10.2	WR
4x100m Mdly	USA (Frank McKinney, Paul Hait, Lance Larson, Jeff Farrell)	4:05.4	WR

Diving		Points
Platform	Bob Webster, USA	165.56
Spring	Gary Tobian, USA	170.00

WOMEN

Event		Time	
100m Free	Dawn Fraser, AUS	1:01.2	OR
400m Free	Chris von Saltza, USA	4:50.6	OR
100m Back	Lynn Burke, USA	1:09.3	OR
200m Brst	Anita Lonsbrough, GBR	2:49.5	WR
100m Fly	Carolyn Schuler, USA	1:09.5	OR
4x100mFree	USA (Joan Spillane, Shirley Stobs, Carolyn Wood, Chris von Saltza)	4:08.9	WR
4x100m Mdly	USA (Lynn Burke, Patty Kempner, Carolyn Schuler, Chris von Saltza)	4:41.1	WR

Diving

		Points
Platform	Ingrid Krämer, GER	91.28
Spring	Ingrid Krämer, GER	155.81

Team Sports

Men	Champion
Basketball	United States
Field Hockey	Pakistan
Soccer	Yugoslavia
Water Polo	Italy

Also Contested

Canoeing, Cycling, Equestrian, Fencing, Modern Pentathlon, Rowing, Shooting, Weightlifting, Freestyle Wrestling, Greco-Roman Wrestling and Yachting.

1964

Tokyo

Twenty-six years after Japan's wartime government forced the Japanese Olympic Committee to resign as hosts of the 1940 Summer Games, Tokyo welcomed the world to the first Asian Olympics. The new Japan spared no expense—a staggering $3 billion was spent to rebuild the city—and was rewarded with a record-breaking fortnight.

Twelve world and six Olympic records fell in swimming, with Americans accounting for 13. Eighteen-year-old Don Schollander led the way, winning two individual and two relay gold medals to become the first swimmer to win four events in one Games. Sharon Stouder collected three golds and a silver for the U.S. women, but the most remarkable performance of all belonged to Australian Dawn Fraser, who won the 100-meter freestyle for the third straight Olympics.

In track and field, Al Oerter of the U.S. won the discus for the third straight time. His record toss was one of 25 world and Olympic marks broken. Another fell when Billy Mills of the U.S. electrified the Games by coming from behind for an upset win in the 10,000 meters. New Zealander Peter Snell, the defending 800-meter champion, won both the 800 and 1,500 (last done in 1920).

Sprinter Bob Hayes of the U.S. equaled the world record of 10 seconds flat in the 100 meters, but stunned the crowd with a sub-9 second, come-from-behind anchor leg to lead the U.S. to set a new world record in the 4 x 100 meters.

Abebe Bikila of Ethiopia became the first runner to win consecutive marathons. The remarkable Betty Cuthbert of Australia, who won three sprint gold medals in Melbourne, came back eight years later at age 26 to win the 400. And Russian gymnast Larissa Latynina won six medals for the second Olympics in a row.

1964 (Cont.)
Top 10 Standings

National medal standings are not recognized by the IOC. The unofficial point totals are based on 3 points for a gold medal, 2 for a silver and 1 for a bronze.

		Gold	Silver	Bronze	Total	Pts
1	USA	36	26	28	90	188
2	USSR	30	31	35	96	187
3	Germany	10	22	18	50	92
4	Japan	16	5	8	29	66
5	Italy	10	10	7	27	57
6	Hungary	10	7	5	22	49
7	Poland	7	6	10	23	43
8	Great Britain	4	12	2	18	38
9	Australia	6	2	10	18	32
10	Czechoslovakia	5	6	3	14	30

Leading Medal Winners

Number of individual medals won on the left; gold, silver and bronze breakdown to the right.

MEN

No		Sport	G-S-B
4	Don Schollander, USA	Swimming	4-0-0
4	Yukio Endo, JPN	Gymnastics	3-1-0
4	Shuji Tsurumi, JPN	Gymnastics	1-3-0
4	Boris Shakhlin, USSR	Gymnastics	1-2-1
4	Viktor Lisitsky, USSR	Gymnastics	0-4-0
4	Hans-Joachim Klein, GER	Swimming	0-3-1
3	Steve Clark, USA	Swimming	3-0-0
3	Franco Menichelli, ITA	Gymnastics	1-1-1
3	Frank Wiegard, GER	Swimming	0-3-0

WOMEN

No		Sport	G-S-B
6	Larissa Latynina, USSR	Gymnastics	2-2-2
4	Vera Cáslavská, CZE	Gymnastics	3-1-0
4	Polina Astakhova, USSR	Gymnastics	2-1-1
4	Sharon Stouder, USA	Swimming	3-1-0
4	Kathy Ellis, USA	Swimming	2-0-2
4	Irena Kirszenstein, POL	Track/Field	1-2-0
3	Ada Kok, HOL	Swimming	1-2-0
3	Edith Maguire, USA	Track/Field	1-2-0
3	Mary Rand, GBR	Track/Field	1-1-1

Track & Field
MEN

Event		Time	
100m	Bob Hayes, USA	10.0	=WR
200m	Henry Carr, USA	20.3	OR
400m	Mike Larrabee, USA	45.1	
800m	Peter Snell, NZE	1:45.1	OR
1500m	Peter Snell, NZE	3:38.1	
5000m	Bob Schul, USA	13:48.8	
10,000m	Billy Mills, USA	28:24.4	OR
Marathon	Abebe Bikila, ETH	2:12:11.2	WB
110m H	Hayes Jones, USA	13.6	
400m H	Rex Cawley, USA	49.6	
3000m Steeple	Gaston Roelants, BEL	8:30.8	OR
20k Walk	Ken Matthews, GBR	1:29:34.0	OR
50k Walk	Abdon Pamich, ITA	4:11:12.4	OR
4x100m	USA (Paul Drayton, Gerald Ashworth, Richard Stebbins, Bob Hayes)	39.0	WR
4x400m	USA (Ollan Cassell, Mike Larrabee, Ulis Williams, Henry Carr)	3:00.7	WR

Event		Mark	
High Jump	Valery Brumel	7- 1¾	OR
Pole Vault	Fred Hansen, USA	16- 8¾	OR
Long Jump	Lynn Davies, GBR	26- 5¾	
Triple Jump	Józef Schmidt, POL	55- 3½	OR
Shot Put	Dallas Long, USA	66- 8½	OR
Discus	Al Oerter, USA	200- 1	OR
Hammer	Romuald Klim, USSR	228-10	OR
Javelin	Pauli Nevala, FIN	271- 2	
Decathlon	Willi Holdorf, GER	7887 pts	

WOMEN

Event		Time	
100m	Wyomia Tyus, USA	11.4	
200m	Edith McGuire, USA	23.0	OR
400m	Betty Cuthbert, AUS	52.0	OR
800m	Ann Packer, GBR	2:01.1	OR
80m H	Karin Balzer, GER	10.5w	
4x100m	POL (Teresa Ciepla, Irena Kirszenstein, Halina Górecka, Ewa Klobukowska)	43.6	

w indicates wind-aided.

Event		Mark	
High Jump	Iolanda Balas, ROM	6- 2¾	OR
Long Jump	Mary Rand GBR	22- 2¼	WR
Shot Put	Tamara Press, USSR	59- 6¼	OR
Discus	Tamara Press, USSR	187-10	OR
Javelin	Mihaela Penes, ROM	198- 7	
Pentathlon	Irina Press, USSR	5246 pts	WR

Boxing

Weight Class	Champion
Flyweight (112 lbs)	Fernando Atzori, ITA
Bantamweight (119)	Takao Sakurai, JPN
Featherweight (125)	Stanislav Stepashkin, USSR
Lightweight (132)	Józef Grudzien, POL
Lt. Welterweight (139)	Jerzy Kulej, POL
Welterweight (148)	Marian Kasprzyk, POL
Lt. Middleweight (156)	Boris Lagutin, USSR
Middleweight (165)	Valery Popenchenko, USSR
Lt. Heavyweight (178)	Cosimo Pinto, ITA
Heavyweight (178+)	Joe Frazier, USA

Gymnastics
MEN

Individual		Points
All-Around	Yukio Endo, JPN	115.95
Floor	Franco Menichelli, ITA	19.45
Horiz.Bar	Boris Shakhlin, USSR	19.625
Paral.Bars	Yukio Endo, JPN	19.675
Rings	Takuji Haytta, JPN	19.475
Side Horse	Miroslav Cerar, YUG	19.525
Vault	Haruhiro Yamashita, JPN	19.60

Team		Points
All-Around	JPN (Endo, Tsurumi, Yamashita, Hayata, Mitsukuri, Ono)	577.95

WOMEN

Individual		Points
All-Around	Vera Cáslavská, CZE	77.564
Bal.Beam	Vera Cáslavská, CZE	19.449
Floor	Larissa Latynina, USSR	19.599
Uneven Bars	Polina Astakhova, USSR	19.332
Vault	Vera Cáslavská, CZE	19.483

Team		Points
All-Around	USSR (Latynina, Astakhova, Volchetskaya, Zamotailova, Manina, Gromova)	280.890

Swimming

MEN

Event		Time	
100m Free	Don Schollander, USA	53.4	OR
400m Free	Don Schollander, USA	4:12.2	WR
1500m Free	Robert Windle, AUS	17:01.7	OR
200m Back	Jed Graef, USA	2:10.3	WR
200m Brst	Ian O'Brien, AUS	2:27.8	WR
200m Fly	Kevin Berry, AUS	2:06.6	WR
400m I.M.	Dick Roth, USA	4:45.4	WR
4x100mFree	USA (Steve Clark, Mike Austin, Gary Ilman, Don Schollander)	3:32.3	WR
4x200mFree	USA (Steve Clark, Roy Saari, Gary Ilman, Don Schollander)	7:52.1	WR
4x100mMdly	USA (Thompson Mann, Bill Craig, Fred Schmidt, Steve Clark)	3:58.4	WR

Diving		Points
Platform	Bob Webster, USA	148.58
Spring	Ken Sitzberger, USA	159.90

WOMEN

Event		Time	
100m Free	Dawn Fraser, AUS	59.5	OR
400m Free	Ginny Duenkel, USA	4:43.3	OR
100m Back	Cathy Ferguson, USA	1:07.7	WR
200m Brst	G. Prozumenshikova, USSR	2:46.4	OR
100m Fly	Sharon Stouder, USA	1:04.7	WR
400m Mdly	Donna de Varona, USA	5:18.7	OR
4x100m Free	USA (Sharon Stouder, Donna de Varona, Pokey Watson, Kathy Ellis)	4:03.8	WR
4x100m Mdly	USA (Cathy Ferguson, Cynthia Goyette, Sharon Stouder, Kathy Ellis)	4:33.9	WR

Diving		Points
Platform	Lesley Bush, USA	99.80
Spring	Ingrid Engel-Krämer, GER	145.00

Team Sports

Men	Champion
Basketball	United States
Field Hockey	India
Soccer	Hungary
Volleyball	Soviet Union
Water Polo	Hungary
Women	**Champion**
Volleyball	Japan

Also Contested

Canoeing, Cycling, Equestrian, Fencing, Judo, Modern Pentathlon, Rowing, Shooting, Weightlifting, Freestyle Wrestling, Greco-Roman Wrestling and Yachting.

1968

Mexico City

The Games of the Nineteenth Olympiad were the highest and most controversial ever held.

Staged at 7,349 feet above sea level where the thin air was a major concern to many competing countries, the Mexico City Olympics were another chapter in a year buffeted by the Vietnam War, the assassinations of Martin Luther King and Robert Kennedy, the Democratic Convention in Chicago, and the Russian invasion of Czechoslovakia.

Ten days before the Olympics were scheduled to open on Oct. 12, over 30 Mexico City university students were killed by army troops when a campus protest turned into a riot. Still, the Games began on time and were free of discord until black Americans Tommy Smith and John Carlos, who finished 1-3 in the 200-meter run, bowed their heads and gave the Black Power salute during the national anthem as a protest against racism in the U.S.

They were immediately thrown off the team by the USOC.

The thin air helped shatter records in every men's and women's race up to 1,500 meters and played a role in U.S. long jumper Bob Beamon's incredible gold medal leap of 29-feet, 2½ inches —beating the existing world mark by nearly two feet.

Other outstanding American performances included Al Oerter's record fourth consecutive discus title, Debbie Meyer's three individual swimming gold medals, the innovative Dick Fosbury winning the high jump with his backwards "flop," and Wyomia Tyus becoming the first woman to win back-to-back golds in the 100 meters.

Top 10 Standings

National medal standings are not recognized by the IOC. The unofficial point totals are based on 3 points for a gold medal, 2 for a silver and 1 for a bronze.

		Gold	Silver	Bronze	Total	Pts
1	USA	45	28	34	107	225
2	USSR	29	32	30	91	181
3	Hungary	10	10	12	32	62
4	Japan	11	7	7	25	54
5	E. Germany	9	9	7	25	52
6	W. Germany	5	10	10	25	45
7	Australia	5	7	5	17	34
8	France	7	3	5	15	32
9	Poland	5	2	11	18	30
10	Czechoslovakia	7	2	4	13	29
	Romania	4	6	5	15	29

Leading Medal Winners

Number of individual medals won on the left; gold, silver and bronze breakdown to the right.

MEN

No		Sport	G-S-B
7	Mikhail Voronin, USSR	Gymnastics	2-4-1
6	Akinori Nakayama, JPN	Gymnastics	4-1-1
4	Charles Hickcox, USA	Swimming	3-1-0
4	Sawao Kato, JPN	Gymnastics	3-0-1
4	Mark Spitz, USA	Swimming	2-1-1
4	Mike Wenden, AUS	Swimming	2-1-1
3	Roland Matthes, E. Ger	Swimming	2-1-0
3	Ken Walsh, USA	Swimming	2-1-0
3	Pierre Trentin, FRA	Cycling	2-0-1
3	Vladimir Kosinski, USSR	Swimming	0-2-1
3	Leonid Ilyichev, USSR	Swimming	0-1-2

1968 (Cont.)

WOMEN

No		Sport	G-S-B
6	Vera Cáslavská, CZE	Gymnastics	4-2-0
4	Sue Pedersen, USA	Swimming	2-2-0
4	Natalya Kuchinskaya, USSR	Gymnastics	2-0-2
4	Jan Henne, USA	Swimming	2-1-1
4	Zinaida Voronina, USSR	Gymnastics	1-1-2
3	Debbie Meyer, USA	Swimming	3-0-0
3	Kaye Hall, USA	Swimming	2-0-1
3	Larissa Petrik, USSR	Gymnastics	2-0-1
3	Ellie Daniel, USA	Swimming	1-1-1
3	Linda Gustavson, USA	Swimming	1-1-1
3	Elaine Tanner, CAN	Swimming	0-2-1

Track & Field

MEN

Event		Time	
100m	Jim Hines, USA	9.95	WR
200m	Tommie Smith, USA	19.83	WR
400m	Lee Evans, USA	43.86	WR
800m	Ralph Doubell, AUS	1:44.3	=WR
1500m	Kip Keino, KEN	3:34.9	
5000m	Mohamed Gammoudi, TUN	14:05.0	
10,000m	Naftali Temu, KEN	29:27.4	
Marathon	Mamo Wolde, ETH	2:20:26.4	
110m H	Willie Davenport, USA	13.3	OR
400m H	David Hemery, GBR	48.12	WR
3000m Steeple	Amos Biwott, KEN	8:51.0	
20k Walk	Vladimir Golubnichiy, USSR	1:33:58.4	
50k Walk	Christoph Höhne, E. Ger	4:20:13.6	
4x100m	USA (Charlie Greene, Mel Pender, Ronnie Ray Smith, Jim Hines)	38.2	WR
4x400m	USA (Vince Matthews, Ron Freeman, Larry James, Lee Evans)	2:56.16	WR

Event		Mark	
High Jump	Dick Fosbury, USA	7- 4¼	OR
Pole Vault	Bob Seagren, USA	17- 8½	OR
Long Jump	Bob Beamon, USA	29- 2½	WR
Triple Jump	Viktor Saneyev, USSR	57- 0¾	WR
Shot Put	Randy Matson, USA	67- 4¾	
Discus	Al Oerter, USA	212- 6	OR
Hammer	Gyula Zsivóyzky, HUN	240- 8	OR
Javelin	Janis Lusis, USSR	295- 7	OR
Decathlon	Bill Toomey, USA	8193 pts	OR

WOMEN

Event		Time	
100m	Wyomia Tyus, USA	11.0	WR
200m	Irena K. Szewinska, POL	22.5	WR
400m	Colette Besson, FRA	52.0	=OR
800m	Madeline Manning, USA	2:00.9	OR
80m H	Maureen Caird, AUS	10.3	OR
4x100m	USA (Barbara Ferrell, Margaret Bailes, Mildrette Netter, Wyomia Tyus)	42.8	WR

Event		Mark	
High Jump	Miloslava Rezková, CZE	5-11½	
Long Jump	Viorica Viscopoleanu, ROM	22- 4½	WR
Shot Put	Margitta Gummel, E. Ger	64- 4	WR
Discus	Lia Manoliu, ROM	191- 2	OR
Javelin	Angéla Németh, HUN	198- 0	
Pentathlon	Ingrid Becker, GER	5098 pts	

Boxing

Weight Class	Champion
Lt. Flyweight (106 lbs)	Francisco Rodriquez, VEN
Flyweight (112)	Ricardo Delgado, MEX
Bantamweight (119)	Valery Sokolov, USSR
Featherweight (125)	Antonio Roldan, MEX
Lightweight (132)	Ron Harris, USA
Lt. Welterweight (139)	Jerzy Kulej, POL
Welterweight (148)	Manfred Wolke, E. Ger
Lt. Middleweight (156)	Boris Lagutin, USSR
Middleweight (165)	Chris Finnegan, GBR
Lt. Heavyweight (178)	Dan Pozniak, USSR
Heavyweight (178+)	George Foreman, USA

Gymnastics

MEN

Individual		Points
All-Around	Sawao Kato, JPN	115.9
Floor	Sawao Kato, JPN	19.475
Horiz.Bar	Akinori Nakayama, JPN & Mikhail Voronin, USSR	19.55
Paral.Bars	Akinori Nakayama, JPN	19.475
Rings	Akinori Nakayama, JPN	19.45
Side Horse	Miroslav Cerar, YUG	19.325
Vault	Mikhail Voronin, USSR	19.00

Team		Points
All-Around	JPN (Kato, Nakayama, Kenmotsu, Kato, Endo, Tsukahara)	575.90

WOMEN

Individual		Points
All-Around	Vera Cáslavská, CZE	78.25
Bal.Beam	Natayla Kuchinskaya, USSR	19.65
Floor	Vera Cáslavská, CZE & Larissa Petrik, USSR	19.675
Uneven Bars	Vera Cáslavská, CZE	19.65
Vault	Vera Cáslavská, CZE	19.775

Team		Points
All-Around	USSR (Voronina, Kuchinskaya, Petrik, Karasseva, Tourischeva, Burda)	382.85

Swimming

MEN

Event		Time	
100m Free	Mike Wenden, AUS	52.2	WR
200m Free	Mike Wenden, AUS	1:55.2	OR
400m Free	Mike Burton, USA	4:09.0	OR
1500m Free	Mike Burton, USA	16:38.9	OR
100m Back	Roland Matthes, E. Ger	58.7	OR
200m Back	Roland Matthes, E. Ger	2:09.6	OR
100m Brst	Don McKenzie, USA	1:07.7	OR
200m Brst	Felipe Muñoz, MEX	2:28.7	
100m Fly	Doug Russell, USA	55.9	OR
200m Fly	Carl Robie, USA	2:08.7	
200m I.M.	Charles Hickcox, USA	2:12.0	OR
400m I.M.	Charles Hickcox, USA	4:48.4	
4x100mFree	USA (Zack Zorn, Steve Rerych, Mark Spitz, Ken Walsh)	3:31.7	WR
4x200mFree	USA (John Nelson, Steve Rerych, Mark Spitz, Don Schollander)	7:52.33	
4x100m Mdly	USA (Charles Hickcox, Don McKenzie, Doug Russell, Ken Walsh)	3:54.9	WR

Diving		Points
Platform	Klaus Dibiasi, ITA	164.18
Spring	Bernie Wrightson, USA	170.15

WOMEN

Event		Time	
100m Free	Jan Henne, USA	1:00.0	
200m Free	Debbie Meyer, USA	2:10.5	OR
400m Free	Debbie Meyer, USA	4:31.8	OR
800m Free	Debbie Meyer, USA	9:24.0	OR
100m Back	Kaye Hall, USA	1:06.2	WR
200m Back	Pokey Watson, USA	2:24.8	OR
100m Brst	Djurdjica Bjedov, YUG	1:15.8	OR
200m Brst	Sharon Wichman, USA	2:44.4	OR

Event		Time	
100m Fly	Lyn McClements, AUS	1:05.5	
200m Fly	Ada Kok, HOL	2:24.7	OR
200m I.M.	Claudia Kolb, USA	2:24.7	OR
400m I.M.	Claudia Kolb, USA	5:08.5	OR
4x100m Free	USA (Jane Barkman, Linda Gustavson, Sue Pedersen, Jan Henne)	4:02.5	OR
4x100m Mdly	USA (Kaye Hall, Catie Ball, Ellie Daniel, Sue Pedersen)	4:28.3	OR

Diving		Points
Platform	Milena Duchková, CZE	109.59
Spring	Sue Gossick, USA	150.77

Team Sports

Men	Champion
Basketball	United States
Field Hockey	Pakistan
Soccer	Hungary
Volleyball	Soviet Union
Water Polo	Yugoslavia

Women	Champion
Volleyball	Soviet Union

Also Contested

Canoeing, Cycling, Equestrian, Fencing, Modern Pentathlon, Rowing, Shooting, Weightlifting, Freestyle Wrestling, Greco-Roman Wrestling and Yachting.

1972

Munich

On Sept. 5, with six days left in the Games, eight Arab commandos slipped into the Olympic Village, killed two Israeli team members and seized nine others as hostages. Later that night, all nine were killed in a shootout between the terrorists and West German police at a military airport.

The tragedy stunned the world and stopped the XXth Olympiad in its tracks. But after suspending competition for 24 hours and holding a memorial service attended by 80,000 at the main stadium, 84-year-old outgoing IOC president Avery Brundage and his committee ordered the Games to continue.

They went on without 22-year-old swimmer Mark Spitz, who had set an Olympic gold medal record by winning four individual and three relay events, all in world record times. Spitz, an American Jew, was an inviting target for further terrorism and agreed with West German officials when they advised him to leave the country.

The pall that fell over Munich quieted an otherwise boisterous Games that saw American swimmer Rick DeMont stripped of a gold medal for taking asthma medication and track medalists Vince Matthews and Wayne Collett of the U.S. banned for life for fooling around on the victory stand during the American national anthem.

The United States also lost an Olympic basketball game for the first time ever (they were 62-0) when the Russians were given three chances to convert a last-second inbound pass and finally won, 51-50. The U.S. refused the silver medal.

Munich was also where 17-year-old Soviet gymnast Olga Korbut and 16-year-old swimmer Shane Gould of Australia won three gold medals each and Britain's 33-year-old Mary Peters won the pentathlon.

Top 10 Standings

National medal standings are not recognized by the IOC. The unofficial point totals are based on 3 points for a gold medal, 2 for a silver and 1 for a bronze.

		Gold	Silver	Bronze	Total	Pts
1	USSR	50	27	22	99	226
2	USA	33	31	30	94	191
3	E. Germany	20	23	23	66	129
4	W. Germany	13	11	16	40	77
5	Japan	13	8	8	29	63
6	Hungary	6	13	16	35	60
7	Bulgaria	6	10	5	21	43
8	Australia	8	7	2	17	40
	Poland	7	5	9	21	40
10	Italy	5	3	10	18	31
	Great Britain	4	5	9	18	31

Leading Medal Winners

Number of individual medals won on the left; gold, silver and bronze breakdown to the right.

MEN

No		Sport	G-S-B
7	Mark Spitz, USA	Swimming	7-0-0
5	Sawao Kato, JPN	Gymnastics	3-2-0
4	Jerry Heidenreich, USA	Swimming	2-1-1
4	Roland Matthes, E. Ger	Swimming	2-1-1
4	Akinori Nakayama, JPN	Gymnastics	2-1-1
4	Shigeru Kasamatsu, JPN	Gymnastics	1-1-2
4	Eizo Kenmotsu, JPN	Gymnastics	1-1-2
3	Valery Borsov, USSR	Track/Field	2-1-0
3	Mitsuo Tsukahara, JPN	Gymnastics	2-0-1
3	Steve Genter, USA	Swimming	1-2-0
3	Viktor Klimenko, USSR	Gymnastics	1-2-0
3	Mike Stamm, USA	Swimming	1-2-0
3	Vladimir Bure, USSR	Swimming	0-1-2

WOMEN

No		Sport	G-S-B
5	Shane Gould, AUS	Swimming	3-1-1
5	Karin Janz, E. Ger	Gymnastics	2-2-1
4	Olga Korbut, USSR	Gymnastics	3-1-0
4	Lyudmila Tourischeva, USSR	Gymnastics	2-1-1
4	Tamara Lazakovitch, USSR	Gymnastics	1-1-2

Track & Field
MEN

Event		Time	
100m	Valery Borzov, USSR	10.14	
200m	Valery Borzov, USSR	20.00	
400m	Vince Matthews, USA	44.66	
800m	Dave Wottle, USA	1:45.9	
1500m	Pekka Vasala, FIN	3:36.3	
5000m	Lasse Viren, FIN	13:26.4	OR
10,000m	Lasse Viren, FIN	27:38.4	WR
Marathon	Frank Shorter, USA	2:12:19.8	
110m H	Rod Milburn, USA	13.24	=WR
400m H	John Akii-Bua, UGA	47.82	WR
3000m Steeple	Kip Keino, KEN	8:23.6	OR

1972 (Cont.)

Event		Time	
20k Walk	Peter Frenkel, E. Ger	1:26:42.4	OR
50k Walk	Bernd Kannenberg, W. Ger	3:56:11.6	OR
4x100m	USA (Larry Black, Robert Taylor, Gerald Tinker, Eddie Hart)	38.19	=WR
4x400m	KEN (Charles Asati, Hezaklah Nyamau, Robert Ouko, Julius Sang)	2:59.8	

Event		Mark	
High Jump	Yuri Tarmak, USSR	7- 3¾	
Pole Vault	Wolfgang Nordwig, E. Ger	18- 0½	OR
Long Jump	Randy Williams, USA	27- 0½	
Triple Jump	Viktor Saneyev, USSR	56-11¼	
Shot Put	Wladyslaw Komar, POL	69- 6	OR
Discus	Ludvik Danek, CZE	211- 3	
Hammer	Anatoly Bondarchuk, USSR	247- 8	OR
Javelin	Klaus Wolfermann, W. Ger	296-10	OR
Decathlon	Nikolai Avilov, USSR	8454 pts	WR

WOMEN

Event		Time	
100m	Renate Stecher, E. Ger	11.07	
200m	Renate Stecher, E. Ger	22.40	=WR
400m	Monika Zehrt, E. Ger	51.08	OR
800m	Hildegard Falck, W. Ger	1:58.55	OR
1500m	Lyudmila Bragina, USSR	4:01.4	WR
100m H	Annelie Ehrhardt, E. Ger	12.59	WR
4x100m	W. Ger. (Christiane Krause, Ingrid Mickler, Annegret Richter, Heidemarie Rosendahl)	42.81	=WR
4x400m	E. Ger. (Dägmar Käsling, Rita Kühne, Helga Seidler, Monika Zehrt)	3:23.0	WR

Event		Mark	
High Jump	Ulrike Meyfarth, W. Ger	6- 3½	=WR
Long Jump	Heidemarie Rosendahl, W. Ger	22- 3	
Shot Put	Nadezhda Chizhova, USSR	69- 0	WR
Discus	Faina Melnik, USSR	218- 7	OR
Javelin	Ruth Fuchs, E. Ger	209- 7	OR
Pentathlon	Mary Peters, GBR	4801 pts	WR

Boxing

Weight Class	Champion
Lt. Flyweight (106 lbs)	György Gedó, HUN
Flyweight (112)	Georgi Kostadinov, BUL
Bantamweight (119)	Orlando Martinez, CUB
Featherweight (125)	Boris Kousnetsov, USSR
Lightweight (132)	Jan Szczepanski, POL
Lt. Welterweight (139)	Ray Seales, USA
Welterweight (148)	Emilio Correa, CUB
Lt. Middleweight (156)	Dieter Kottysch, W. Ger
Middleweight (165)	Vyacheslav Lemechev, USSR
Lt. Heavyweight (178)	Mate Parlov, YUG
Heavyweight (178+)	Teófilo Stevenson, CUB

Gymnastics

MEN

Individual		Points
All-Around	Sawao Kato, JPN	114.650
Floor	Nikolai Andrianov, USSR	19.175
Horiz.Bar	Mitsuo Tsukahara, JPN	19.725
Paral.Bars	Sawao Kato, JPN	19.475
Rings	Akinori Nakayama, JPN	19.35
Side Horse	Viktor Klimenko, USSR	19.125
Vault	Klaus Köste, E. Ger	18.85

Team		Points
All-Around	JPN (Kato, Kenmotsu, Kasamatsu, Nakayama, Tsukahara, Okamura)	571.25

WOMEN

Individual		Points
All-Around	Lyudmila Tourischeva, USSR	77.025
Bal.Beam	Olga Korbut, USSR	19.40
Floor	Olga Korbut, USSR	19.575
Uneven Bars	Karin Janz, E. Ger	19.675
Vault	Karin Janz, E. Ger	19.525

Team		Points
All-Around	USSR (Tourischeva, Korbut, Lazakovitch, Burda, Saadi, Koshel)	380.50

Swimming

MEN

Event		Time	
100m Free	Mark Spitz, USA	51.22	WR
200m Free	Mark Spitz, USA	1:52.78	WR
400m Free	Brad Cooper, USA	4:00.27	OR
1500m Free	Mike Burton, USA	15:52.58	WR
100m Back	Roland Matthes, E. Ger	56.58	OR
200m Back	Roland Matthes, E. Ger	2:02.82	=WR
100m Brst	Nobutaka Taguchi, JPN	1:04.94	WR
200m Brst	John Hencken, USA	2:21.55	WR
100m Fly	Mark Spitz, USA	54.27	WR
200m Fly	Mark Spitz, USA	2:00.70	WR
200m I.M.	Gunnar Larsson, SWE	2:07.17	WR
400m I.M.	Gunnar Larsson, SWE	4:31.98	WR
4x100m Free	USA (Dave Edgar, John Murphy, Jerry Heidenreich, Mark Spitz)	3:26.42	WR
4x200m Free	USA (John Kinsella, Fred Tyler, Steve Genter, Mark Spitz)	7:35.78	WR
4x100m Mdly	USA (Mike Stamm, Tom Bruce, Mark Spitz, Jerry Heidenreich)	3:48.16	WR

Diving		Points
Platform	Klaus Dibiasi, ITA	504.12
Spring	Vladimir Vasin, USSR	594.09

WOMEN

Event		Time	
100m Free	Sandra Neilson, USA	58.59	OR
200m Free	Shane Gould, AUS	2:03.56	WR
400m Free	Shane Gould, AUS	4:19.44	WR
800m Free	Keena Rothhammer, USA	8:53.68	WR
100m Back	Melissa Belote, USA	1:05.78	OR
200m Back	Melissa Belote, USA	2:19.19	WR
100m Brst	Cathy Carr, USA	1:13.58	WR
200m Brst	Beverly Whitfield, AUS	2:41.71	OR
100m Fly	Mayumi Aoki, JPN	1:03.34	WR
200m Fly	Karen Moe, USA	2:15.57	WR
200m I.M.	Shane Gould, AUS	2:23.07	WR
400m I.M.	Gail Neall, AUS	5:02.97	WR
4x100m Free	USA (Sandra Neilson, Jennifer Kemp, Jane Barkman, Shirley Babashoff)	3:55.19	WR
4x100m Mdly	USA (Melissa Belote, Cathy Carr, Deena Deardurff, Sandra Neilson)	4:20.75	WR

Diving		Points
Platform	Ulrika Knape, SWE	390.00
Spring	Micki King, USA	450.03

Team Sports

Men	Champion
Basketball	Soviet Union
Field Hockey	West Germany
Handball	Yugoslavia
Soccer	Poland
Volleyball	Japan
Water Polo	Soviet Union

Women	Champion
Volleyball	Soviet Union

Also Contested

Archery, Canoeing, Cycling, Equestrian, Fencing, Judo, Modern Pentathlon, Rowing, Shooting, Weightlifting, Freestyle Wrestling, Greco-Roman Wrestling and Yachting.

1976

Montreal

In 1970, when Montreal was named to host the Summer Olympics '76, organizers estimated it would cost $310 million to stage the Games. However, due to political corruption, mismanagement, labor disputes, inflation and a $100 million outlay for security to prevent another Munich, the final bill came to more than $1.5 billion.

Then, right before the Games were scheduled to open in July, 32 nations, most of them from black Africa, walked out when the IOC refused to ban New Zealand because its national rugby team was touring racially-segregated South Africa. Taiwan also withdrew when Communist China pressured trading partner Canada to deny the Taiwanese the right to compete as the Republic of China.

When the Games finally got started they were quickly stolen by 14-year-old Romanian gymnast Nadia Comaneci, who scored seven perfect 10s on her way to three gold medals.

East Germany's Kornelia Ender did Comaneci one better, winning four times as the GDR captured 11 of 13 events in women's swimming. John Naber (4 gold) and the U.S. men did the East German women one better when they won 12 of 13 in swimming.

In track and field, Cuba's Alberto Juantorena won the 400- and 800-meter runs, and Finland's Lasse Viren took the 5,000 and 10,000. Viren missed a third gold when he placed fifth in the marathon.

Four Americans who became household names during the Games were decathlon winner Bruce Jenner and three future world boxing champions—Ray Leonard and the Spinks brothers, Michael and Leon.

Top 10 Standings

National medal standings are not recognized by the IOC. The unofficial point totals are based on 3 points for a gold medal, 2 for a silver and 1 for a bronze.

		Gold	Silver	Bronze	Total	Pts
1	USSR	49	41	35	125	264
2	USA	34	35	25	94	197
3	E. Germany	40	25	25	90	195
4	W. Germany	10	12	17	39	71
5	Japan	9	6	10	25	49
6	Poland	7	6	13	26	46
7	Romania	4	9	14	27	44
8	Bulgaria	6	9	7	22	43
9	Cuba	6	4	3	13	29
10	Hungary	4	5	13	22	35

Leading Medal Winners

Number of individual medals won on the left; gold, silver and bronze breakdown to the right.

MEN

No		Sport	G-S-B
7	Nikolai Andrianov, USSR	Gymnastics	4-2-1
5	John Naber, USA	Swimming	4-1-0
5	Mitsuo Tsukahara, JPN	Gymnastics	2-1-2
4	Jim Montgomery, USA	Swimming	3-0-1
3	John Hencken, USA	Swimming	2-1-0
3	Sawao Kato, JPN	Gymnastics	2-1-0
3	Eizo Kenmotsu, JPN	Gymnastics	1-2-0
3	Rüdiger Helm, E. Ger	Canoeing	1-0-2

WOMEN

No		Sport	G-S-B
5	Kornelia Ender, E. Ger	Swimming	4-1-0
5	Nadia Comaneci, ROM	Gymnastics	3-1-1
5	Shirley Babashoff, USA	Swimming	1-4-0
4	Nelli Kim, USSR	Gymnastics	3-1-0
4	Andrea Pollack, E. Ger	Swimming	2-2-0
4	Lyudmila Tourischeva, USSR	Gymnastics	1-2-1
3	Ulrike Richter, E. Ger	Swimming	3-0-0
3	Annagret Richter, W. Ger	Track/Field	1-2-0
3	Renate Stecher, E. Ger	Track/Field	1-1-1
3	Teodora Ungureanu, ROM	Gymnastics	0-2-1

Track & Field

MEN

Event		Time	
100m	Hasely Crawford, TRI	10.06	
200m	Donald Quarrie, JAM	20.23	
400m	Alberto Juantorena, CUB	44.26	
800m	Alberto Juantorena, CUB	1:43.50	WR
1500m	John Walker, NZE	3:39.17	
5000m	Lasse Viren, FIN	13:24.76	
10,000m	Lasse Viren, FIN	27:40.38	
Marathon	Waldemar Cierpinski, E. Ger	2:09:55	OR
110m H	Guy Drut, FRA	13.30	
400m H	Edwin Moses, USA	47.64	WR
3000m Steeple	Anders Gärdeud, SWE	8:08.2	WR
20k Walk	Daniel Bautista, MEX	1:24:40.6	OR
4x100m	USA (Harvey Glance, Johnny Jones, Millard Hampton, Steve Riddick)	38.33	
4x400m	USA (Herman Frazier, Benjamin Brown, Fred Newhouse, Maxie Parks)	2:58.65	

Event		Mark	
High Jump	Jacek Wszola, POL	7- 4½	OR
Pole Vault	Tadeusz Slusarski, POL	18- 0½	=OR
Long Jump	Arnie Robinson, USA	27- 4¾	
Triple Jump	Viktor Saneyev, USSR	56- 8¾	
Shot Put	Udo Beyer, E. Ger	69- 0¾	
Discus	Mac Wilkins, USA	221- 5	
Hammer	Yuri Sedykh, USSR	254- 4	OR
Javelin	Miklos Nèmeth, HUN	310- 4	WR
Decathlon	Bruce Jenner, USA	8617 pts	WR

WOMEN

Event		Time	
100m	Annegret Richter, W. Ger	11.08	
200m	Bärbel Eckert, E. Ger	22.37	OR
400m	Irena K. Szewinska, POL	49.29	WR
800m	Tatyana Kazankina, USSR	1:54.94	WR
1500m	Tatyana Kazankina, USSR	4:05.48	
100m H	Johanna Schaller, E. Ger	12.77	

1976 (Cont.)

Event		Time
4x100m	E. Ger. (Marlies Oelsner, Renate Stecher, Carla Bodendorf, Bärbel Eckert)	42.55 OR
4x400m	E. Ger. (Doris Maletzki, Brigitte Rohde, Ellen Streidt, Christina Brehmer)	3:19.23 WR

Event		Mark
High Jump	Rosemarie Ackermann, E. Ger.	6- 4 OR
Long Jump	Angela Voigt, E. Ger.	22- 0¾
Shot Put	Ivanka Hristova, BUL	69- 5¼ OR
Discus	Evelin Schlaak, E. Ger.	226- 4 OR
Javelin	Ruth Fuchs, E. Ger.	216- 4 OR
Pentathlon	Siegrun Siegl, E. Ger.	4745 pts

Boxing

Weight Class	Champion
Lt. Flyweight (106 lbs)	Jorge Hernandez, CUB
Flyweight (112)	Leo Randolph, USA
Bantamweight (119)	Gu Yong-Ju, N. Kor
Featherweight (125)	Angel Herrera, CUB
Lightweight (132)	Howard Davis, USA
Lt. Welterweight (139)	Ray Leonard, USA
Welterweight (148)	Jochen Bachfeld, E. Ger
Lt. Middleweight (156)	Jerzy Rybicki, POL
Middleweight (165)	Michael Spinks, USA
Lt. Heavyweight (178)	Leon Spinks, USA
Heavyweight (178+)	Teófilo Stevenson, CUB

Gymnastics
MEN

Individual		Points
All-Around	Nikolai Andrianov, USSR	116.65
Floor	Nikolai Andrianov, USSR	19.45
Horiz.Bar	Mitsuo Tsukahara, JPN	19.675
Paral.Bars	Sawao Kato, JPN	19.675
Rings	Nikolai Andrianov, USSR	19.65
Side Horse	Zoltàn Magyar, HUN	19.70
Vault	Nikolai Andrianov, USSR	19.45

Team		Points
All-Around	JPN (Kato, Tsukahara, Kajiyama, Kenmotsu, Igarashi, Fujimoto)	576.85

WOMEN

Individual		Points
All-Around	Nadia Comaneci, ROM	79.275
Bal.Beam	Nadia Comaneci, ROM	19.95
Floor	Nelli Kim, USSR	19.85
Uneven Bars	Nadia Comaneci, ROM	20.00
Vault	Nelli Kim, USSR	19.80

Team		Points
All-Around	USSR (Kim, Tourischeva, Korbut, Saadi, Filatova, Grozdova)	466.00

Swimming
MEN

Event		Time	
100m Free	Jim Montgomery, USA	49.99	WR
200m Free	Bruce Furniss, USA	1:50.29	WR
400m Free	Brian Goodell, USA	3:51.93	WR
1500m Free	Brian Goodell, USA	15:02.40	WR
100m Back	John Naber, USA	55.49	WR
200m Back	John Naber, USA	1:59.19	WR
100m Brst	John Hencken, USA	1:03.11	WR
200m Brst	David Wilkie, GBR	2:15.11	WR
100m Fly	Matt Vogel, USA	54.35	
200m Fly	Mike Bruner, USA	1:59.23	WR
400m I.M.	Rod Strachan, USA	4:23.68	WR
4x200m Free	USA (Mike Bruner, Bruce Furniss, John Naber, Jim Montgomery)	7:23.22	WR

Event		Time	
4x100m Mdly	USA (John Naber, John Hencken, Matt Vogel, Jim Montgomery)	3:42.22	WR

Diving		Points
Platform	Klaus Dibiasi, ITA	600.51
Spring	Phil Boggs, USA	619.05

WOMEN

Event		Time	
100m Free	Kornelia Ender, E. Ger	55.65	WR
200m Free	Kornelia Ender, E. Ger	1:59.26	WR
400m Free	Petra Thümer, E. Ger	4:09.89	WR
800m Free	Petra Thümer, E. Ger	8:37.14	WR
100m Back	Ulrike Richter, E. Ger	1:01.83	OR
200m Back	Ulrike Richter, E. Ger	2:13.43	WR
100m Brst	Hannelore Anke, E. Ger	1:11.16	
200m Brst	Marina Koshevaia, USSR	2:33.35	WR
100m Fly	Kornelia Ender, E. Ger	1:00.13	WR
200m Fly	Andrea Pollack, E. Ger	2:11.41	OR
400m I.M.	Ulrike Tauber, E. Ger	4:42.77	WR
4x100m Free	USA (Kim Peyton, Wendy Boglioli, Jill Sterkel, Shirley Babashoff)	3:44.82	WR
4x100m Mdly	GDR (Ulrike Richter, Hannelore Anke, Andrea Pollack, Kornelia Ender)	4:07.95	WR

Diving		Points
Platform	Elena Vaytsekhovskaya, USSR	406.59
Spring	Jennifer Chandler, USA	506.19

Team Sports

Men		Champion
Basketball		United States
Field Hockey		New Zealand
Handball		Soviet Union
Soccer		East Germany
Volleyball		Poland
Water Polo		Hungary

Women		Champion
Basketball		Soviet Union
Handball		Soviet Union
Volleyball		Japan

Also Contested

Archery, Canoeing, Cycling, Equestrian, Fencing, Judo, Modern Pentathlon, Rowing, Shooting, Weightlifting, Freestyle Wrestling, Greco-Roman Wrestling and Yachting.

OLYMPIAD 80 MOSCOU Moscow МОСКВА

1980
Moscow

Four years after 32 nations walked out of the Montreal Games, twice that many chose to stay away from Moscow—many in support of an American-led boycott to protest the December, 1979, Russian invasion of Afghanistan.

Unable to persuade the IOC to cancel or move the Summer Games, U.S. President Jimmy Carter pressured the USOC to officially withdraw in April. Many western governments, like West Germany and Japan, followed suit and withheld their athletes. But others, like Britain and France, while supporting the boycott, allowed their Olympic committees to participate if they wished.

The first Games to be held in a Communist country opened in July with 81 nations in attendance and were dominated by the USSR and East Germany. They were also plagued by charges of rigged judging and poor sportsmanship by Moscow fans who, without the Americans around, booed the Poles and East Germans unmercifully.

Otherwise, Soviet gymnast Aleksandr Dityatin became the first athlete to win eight medals in one year; the belle of Montreal, Nadia Comaneci of Romania, returned to win two more gold medals; and Cuban heavyweight Teofilo Stevenson became the first boxer to win three golds in the same weight division.

In track and field, Miruts Yifter of Ethiopia won at 5,000 and 10,000 meters, but the most thrilling moment of the Games came in the last lap of the 1,500 meters where Sebastian Coe of Great Britain outran countryman Steve Ovett and Jurgen Straub of East Germany for the gold.

Top 10 Standings

National medal standings are not recognized by the IOC. The unofficial point totals are based on 3 points for a gold medal, 2 for a silver and 1 for a bronze.

		Gold	Silver	Bronze	Total	Pts
1	USSR	80	69	46	195	424
2	E. Germany	47	37	42	126	257
3	Bulgaria	8	16	17	41	73
4	Hungary	7	10	15	32	56
5	Poland	3	14	15	32	52
6	Cuba	8	7	5	20	43
	Romania	6	6	13	25	43
8	Great Britain	5	7	9	21	38
9	Italy	8	3	4	15	34
10	France	6	5	3	14	31

Leading Medal Winners

Number of individual medals won on the left; gold, silver and bronze breakdown to the right.

MEN

No		Sport	G-S-B
8	Aleksandr Dityatin, USSR	Gymnastics	3-4-1
5	Nikolai Andrianov, USSR	Gymnastics	2-2-1
4	Roland Brückner, E. Ger	Gymnastics	1-1-2
3	Vladimir Parfenovich, USSR	Canoeing	3-0-0
3	Vladimir Salnikov, USSR	Swimming	3-0-0
3	Sergei Kopliakov, USSR	Swimming	2-1-0
3	Aleksandr Tkachyov, USSR	Gymnastics	2-1-0
3	Andrei Krylov, USSR	Swimming	1-2-0
3	Arsen Miskarov, USSR	Swimming	0-2-1

WOMEN

No		Sport	G-S-B
5	Ines Diers, E. Ger	Swimming	2-2-1
4	Caren Metschuck, E. Ger	Swimming	3-1-0
4	Nadia Comaneci, ROM	Gymnastics	2-2-0
4	Natalya Shaposhnikova, USSR	Gymnastics	2-0-2
4	Maxi Gnauck, E. Ger	Gymnastics	1-1-2
3	Barbara Krause, E. Ger	Swimming	3-0-0
3	Rica Reinisch, E. Ger	Swimming	3-0-0
3	Yelena Davydova, USSR	Gymnastics	2-1-0
3	Steffi Kraker, E. Ger	Gymnastics	0-1-2
3	Melita Ruhn, ROM	Gymnastics	0-1-2

Track & Field

MEN

Event		Time
100m	Allan Wells, GBR	10.25
200m	Pietro Mennea, ITA	20.19
400m	Viktor Markin, USSR	44.60
800m	Steve Ovett, GBR	1:45.4
1500m	Sebastian Coe, GBR	3:38.4
5000m	Miruts Yifter, ETH	13:21.0
10,000m	Miruts Yifter, ETH	27:42.7
Marathon	Waldemar Cierpinski, E. Ger	2:11:03
110m H	Thomas Munkelt, E. Ger	13.39
400m H	Volker Beck, E. Ger	48.70
3000m Steeple	Bronislaw Malinowski, POL	8:09.7
20k Walk	Maurizio Damilano, ITA	1:23:35.5 OR
50k Walk	Hartwig Gauder, E. Ger	3:49:24.0
4x100m	USSR (Vladimir Muravyov, Nikolai Sidorov, Aleksandr Aksinin, Andrei Prokofiev)	38.26
4x400m	USSR (Remigius Valiulis, Mikhail Linge, Nikolai Chernetsky, Viktor Markin)	3:01.1

Event		Mark
High Jump	Gerd Wessig, E. Ger	7- 8¾ WR
Pole Vault	Wladyslaw Kozakiewicz, POL	18-11½ WR
Long Jump	Lutz Dombrowski, E. Ger	28- 0¼
Triple Jump	Jaak Uudmäe, USSR	56-11¼
Shot Put	Vladimir Kiselyov, USSR	70- 0½ OR
Discus	Viktor Rashchupkin, USSR	218- 8
Hammer	Yuri Sedykh, USSR	268- 4 WR
Javelin	Dainis Kula, USSR	299- 2
Decathlon	Daley Thompson, GBR	8495 pts

WOMEN

Event		Time
100m	Lyudmila Kondratyeva, USSR	11.06
200m	Bärbel E. Wöckel, E. Ger	22.03 OR
400m	Marita Koch, E. Ger	48.88 OR
800m	Nadezhda Olizarenko, USSR	1:53.42 WR
1500m	Tatyana Kazankina, USSR	3:56.6 OR
100m H	Vera Komisova, USSR	12.56 OR
4x100m	E. Ger. (Romy Müller, Bärbel E. Wöckel, Ingrid Auerswald, Marlies O. Göhr)	41.60 WR
4x400m	USSR (Tatyana Prorochenko, Tatyana Goistschik, Nina Zyuskova, Irina Nazarova)	3:20.2

Event		Mark
High Jump	Sara Simeoni, ITA	6- 5½ OR
Long Jump	Tatiana Kolpakova, USSR	23- 2 OR
Shot Put	Ilona Slupianke, E. Ger	73- 6¼
Discus	Evelin S. Jahl, E. Ger	229- 6 OR
Javelin	Maria Colon, CUB	224- 5 OR
Pentathlon	Nadezhda Tkachenko, USSR	5083 pts WR

Boxing

Weight Class	Champion
Lt. Flyweight (106 lbs)	Shamil Sabyrov, USSR
Flyweight (112)	Peter Lessov, BUL
Bantamweight (119)	Juan Hernandez, CUB
Featherweight (125)	Rudi Fink, E. Ger
Lightweight (132)	Angel Herrera, CUB
Lt. Welterweight (139)	Patrizio Oliva, ITA
Welterweight (148)	Andrès Aldama, CUB
Lt. Middleweight (156)	Armando Martinez, CUB
Middleweight (165)	José Gomez, CUB
Lt. Heavyweight (178)	Slobodan Kacar, YUG
Heavyweight (178+)	Teófilo Stevenson, CUB

1980 (Cont.)
Gymnastics
MEN

Individual		Points
All-Around	Aleksandr Dityatin, USSR	118.65
Floor	Roland Brückner, E. Ger	19.75
Horiz.Bar	Stoyan Deltchev, BUL	19.825
Paral.Bars	Aleksandr Tkachyov, USSR	19.775
Rings	Aleksandr Dityatin, USSR	19.875
Side Horse	Zoltán Magyar, HUN	19.925
Vault	Nikolai Andrianov, USSR	19.825

Team		Points
All-Around	USSR (Dityatin, Andrianov, Azaryan, Tkachyov, Makuts, Markelov)	598.60

WOMEN

Individual		Points
All-Around	Yelena Davydova, USSR	79.15
Bal.Beam	Nadia Comaneci, ROM	19.80
Floor	Nadia Comaneci, ROM & Nelli Kim, USSR	19.875
Uneven Bars	Maxi Gnauk, E. Ger	19.875
Vault	Natalya Shaposhnikova, USSR	19.725

Team		Points
All-Around	USSR (Shaposhnikova, Davydova, Kim, Filatova, Zakharova, Naimuschina)	394.90

Swimming
MEN

Event		Time	
100m Free	Jörg Woithe, E. Ger	50.40	
200m Free	Sergei Kopliakov, USSR	1:49.91	OR
400m Free	Vladimir Salnikov, USSR	3:51.31	OR
1500m Free	Vladimir Salnikov, USSR	14:58.27	WR
100m Back	Bengt Baron, SWE	56.33	
200m Back	Sándor Wladár, HUN	2:01.93	
100m Brst	Duncan Goodhew, GBR	1:03.44	
200m Brst	Robertas Zhulpa, USSR	2:15.85	
100m Fly	Pär Arvidsson, SWE	54.92	
200m Fly	Sergei Fesenko, USSR	1:59.76	
400m I.M.	Aleksandr Sidorenko, USSR	4:22.89	OR
4x200m Free	USSR (Sergei Kopliakov, Vladimir, Salnikov, Ivar Stukolkin, Andrei Krylov)	7:23.50	
4x100m Mdly	AUS (Mark Kerry, Peter Evans, Mark Tonelli, Neil Brooks)	3:45.70	

Diving		Points
Platform	Falk Hoffmann, E. Ger	835.650
Spring	Aleksandr Portnov, USSR	905.025

WOMEN

Event		Time	
100m Free	Barbara Krause, E. Ger	54.79	WR
200m Free	Barbara Krause, E. Ger	1:58.33	OR
400m Free	Ines Diers, E. Ger	4:08.76	OR
800m Free	Michelle Ford, AUS	8:28.90	OR
100m Back	Rica Reinisch, E. Ger	1:00.86	WR
200m Back	Rica Reinisch, E. Ger	2:11.77	WR
100m Brst	Ute Geweniger, E. Ger	1:10.22	
200m Brst	Lina Kaciusytė, USSR	2:29.54	OR
100m Fly	Caren Metschuck, E. Ger	1:00.42	
200m Fly	Ines Geissler, E. Ger	2:10.44	OR
400m I.M.	Petra Schneider, E. Ger	4:36.29	WR
4x100m Free	E. Ger. (Barbara Krause, Caren Metschuck, Ines Diers, Sarina Hülsenbeck)	3:42.71	WR
4x100m Mdly	E. Ger. (Rica Reinisch, Ute Geweniger, Andrea Pollack, Caren Metschuck)	4:06.67	WR

Diving		Points
Platform	Martina Jäschke, E. Ger	596.25
Spring	Irina Kalinina, USSR	725.91

Team Sports

Men	Champion
Basketball	Yugoslavia
Field Hockey	India
Handball	East Germany
Soccer	Czechoslovakia
Volleyball	Soviet Union
Water Polo	Soviet Union

Women	Champion
Basketball	Soviet Union
Field Hockey	Zimbabwe
Handball	Soviet Union
Volleyball	Soviet Union

Also Contested

Archery, Canoeing, Cycling, Equestrian, Fencing, Judo, Modern Pentathlon, Rowing, Shooting, Weightlifting, Freestyle Wrestling, Greco-Roman Wrestling and Yachting.

1984

Los Angeles

For the third consecutive Olympiad, a boycott prevented all member nations from attending the Summer Games. This time, the Soviet Union and 13 Communist allies stayed home in an obvious payback for the West's snub of Moscow in 1980. Romania was the only Warsaw Pact country to come to L.A.

While a record 141 nations did show up, the level of competition was hardly what it might have been had the Soviets and East Germans made the trip. As a result, the United States won a record 83 gold medals in the most lopsided Summer Games since St. Louis 80 years before.

The American gold rush was led by 23-year-old Carl Lewis, who duplicated Jesse Owens' 1936 track and field grand slam by winning the 100 and 200 meters and the long jump, and anchoring the 400-meter relay. Teammate Valerie Brisco-Hooks won three times, taking the 200, 400 and 1,600 relay.

Sebastian Coe of Britain became the first repeat winner of the 1,500 meters since Jim Lightbody of the U.S. in 1906. Other repeaters were Briton Daley Thompson in the decathlon and U.S. hurdler Edwin Moses, who won in 1976 but was not allowed to defend his title in '80.

Romanian gymnast Ecaterina Szabó matched Lewis' four gold medals and added a silver, but the darling of the Games was little (4-foot-8 ¾), 16-year-old Mary Lou Retton, who won the women's All-Around with a pair of 10s in her last two events.

The L.A. Olympics were the first privately financed Games ever and made an unheard of profit of $215 million. *Time* magazine was so impressed it made Organizing president Peter Ueberroth its Man of the Year.

Top 10 Standings

National medal standings are not recognized by the IOC. The unofficial point totals are based on 3 points for a gold medal, 2 for a silver and 1 for a bronze.

		Gold	Silver	Bronze	Total	Pts
1	USA	83	61	30	174	401
2	W. Germany	17	19	23	59	112
3	Romania	20	16	17	53	109
4	Canada	10	18	16	44	82
5	China	15	8	9	32	70
6	Italy	14	6	12	32	66
7	Japan	10	8	14	32	60
8	Great Britain	5	11	21	37	58
9	France	5	7	16	28	45
10	Australia	4	8	12	24	40

Leading Medal Winners

Number of individual medals won on the left; gold, silver and bronze breakdown to the right.

MEN

No		Sport	G-S-B
6	Li Ning, CHN	Gymnastics	3-2-1
5	Koji Gushiken, JPN	Gymnastics	2-1-2
4	Carl Lewis, USA	Track/Field	4-0-0
4	Mike Heath, USA	Swimming	3-1-0
4	Michael Gross, W. Ger	Swimming	2-2-0
4	Mitch Gaylord, USA	Gymnastics	1-1-2
3	Rick Carey, USA	Swimming	3-0-0
3	Ian Ferguson, NZE	Canoeing	3-0-0
3	Rowdy Gaines, USA	Swimming	3-0-0
3	Peter Vidmar, USA	Gymnastics	2-1-0
3	Victor Davis, CAN	Swimming	1-2-0
3	Pablo Morales, USA	Swimming	1-2-0
3	Lou Yun, CHN	Gymnastics	1-2-0
3	Shinji Morisue, JPN	Gymnastics	1-1-1
3	Lars-Erik Moberg, SWE	Canoeing	0-3-0
3	Mark Stockwell, AUS	Swimming	0-2-1

WOMEN

No		Sport	G-S-B
5	Ecaterina Szabó, ROM	Gymnastics	4-1-0
5	Mary Lou Retton, USA	Gymnastics	1-2-2
4	Nancy Hogshead, USA	Swimming	3-1-0
3	Valerie Brisco-Hooks, USA	Track/Field	3-0-0
3	Tracy Caulkins, USA	Swimming	3-0-0
3	Mary T. Meagher, USA	Swimming	3-0-0
3	Agneta Andersson, SWE	Canoeing	2-1-0
3	Chandra Cheeseborough, USA	Track/Field	2-1-0
3	Simona Pauca, ROM	Gymnastics	2-0-1
3	Julie McNamara, USA	Gymnastics	1-2-0
3	Anne Ottenbrite, CAN	Swimming	1-1-1
3	Karin Seick, W. Ger	Swimming	0-1-2
3	Annemarie Verstappen, HOL	Swimming	0-1-2

Track & Field

MEN

Event		Time	
100m	Carl Lewis, USA	9.99	
200m	Carl Lewis, USA	19.80	OR
400m	Alonzo Babers, USA	44.27	
800m	Joaquim Cruz, BRA	1:43.00	OR
1500m	Sebastian Coe, GBR	3:32.53	OR
5000m	Said Aouita, MOR	13:05.59	OR
10,000m	Alberto Cova, ITA	27:47.54	
Marathon	Carlos Lopes, POR	2:09:21	OR
110m H	Roger Kingdom, USA	13.20	OR
400m H	Edwin Moses, USA	47.75	
3000m Steeple	Julius Korir, KEN	8:11.80	
20k Walk	Ernesto Canto, MEX	1:23:13.0	OR
50k Walk	Raúl González, MEX	3:47:26.0	OR

Event		Time	
4x100m	USA (Sam Graddy, Ron Brown, Calvin Smith, Carl Lewis)	37.83	WR
4x400m	USA (Sunder Nix, Ray Armstead, Alonzo Babers, Antonio McKay)	2:57.91	

Event		Mark	
High Jump	Dietmar Mögenburg, W. Ger	7- 8 ½	
Pole Vault	Pierre Quinon, FRA	18-10 ¼	
Long Jump	Carl Lewis, USA	28- 0 ¼	
Triple Jump	Al Joyner, USA	56- 7 ½	
Shot Put	Alessandro Andrei, ITA	69- 9	
Discus	Rolf Danneberg, W. Ger	218- 6	
Hammer	Juha Tiainen, FIN	256- 2	
Javelin	Arto Härkönen, FIN	284- 8	
Decathlon	Daley Thompson, GBR	8798 pts	=WR

WOMEN

Event		Time	
100m	Evelyn Ashford, USA	10.97	OR
200m	Valerie Brisco-Hooks, USA	21.81	OR
400m	Valerie Brisco-Hooks, USA	48.83	OR
800m	Doina Melinte, ROM	1:57.60	
1500m	Gabriella Dorio, ITA	4:03.25	
3000m	Maricica Puica, ROM	8:35.96	OR
Marathon	Joan Benoit, USA	2:24.52	
100m H	Benita Fitzgerald-Brown, USA	12.84	
400m H	Nawal El Moutawakel, MOR	54.61	OR
4x100m	USA (Alice Brown, Jeanette Bolden, Chandra Cheeseborough, Evelyn Ashford)	41.65	
4x400m	USA (Lillie Leatherwood, Sherri Howard, Valerie Brisco-Hooks, Chandra Cheeseborough)	3:18.29	OR

Event		Mark	
High Jump	Ulrike Meyfarth, W. Ger	6- 7 ½	OR
Long Jump	Anisoara Stanciu, ROM	22-10	
Shot Put	Claudia Losch, W. Ger	67- 2 ¼	
Discus	Ria Stalman, HOL	214- 5	
Javelin	Tessa Sanderson, GBR	228- 2	OR
Heptathlon	Glynis Nunn, AUS	6390 pts	OR

Boxing

Weight Class	Champion
Lt. Flyweight (106 lbs)	Paul Gonzales, USA
Flyweight (112)	Steve McCrory, USA
Bantamweight (119)	Maurizio Stecca, ITA
Featherweight (125)	Meldrick Taylor, USA
Lightweight (132)	Pernell Whitaker, USA
Lt. Welterweight (139)	Jerry Page, USA
Welterweight (148)	Mark Breland, USA
Lt. Middleweight (156)	Frank Tate, USA
Middleweight (165)	Shin Joon-Sup, S. Kor
Lt. Heavyweight (178)	Anton Josipovic, YUG
Heavyweight (200)	Henry Tillman, USA
Super Heavyweight (200+)	Tyrell Biggs, USA

Gymnastics

MEN

Individual		Points
All-Around	Koji Gushiken, JPN	118.7
Floor	Li Ning, CHN	19.925
Horiz.Bar	Shinji Morisue, JPN	20.00
Paral.Bars	Bart Conner, USA	19.95
Rings	Koji Gushiken, JPN & Li Ning, CHN	19.85
Side Horse	Li Ning, CHN & Peter Vidmar, USA	19.95 19.95
Vault	Lou Yun, CHN	19.95

Team		Points
All-Around	USA (Peter Vidmar, Bart Conner, Mitch Gaylord, Tim Daggett, James Hartung, Scott Johnson)	591.40

1984 (Cont.)
WOMEN

Individual		Points
All-Around	Mary Lou Retton, USA	79.175
Bal.Beam	Simona Pauco, ROM	
	& Ecaterina Szabó, ROM	19.80
Floor	Ecaterina Szabó, ROM	19.975
Uneven Bars	Julie McNamara, USA	
	& Ma Yanhong, CHN	19.95
Vault	Ecaterina Szabó, ROM	19.875

Team		Points
All-Around	ROM (Szabó, Cutina, Pauca,	
	Grigoras, Stanulet, Agache)	392.02

Rhythmic		Points
All-Around	Lori Fung, CAN	57.950

Swimming
MEN

Event		Time	
100m Free	Rowdy Gaines, USA	49.80	OR
200m Free	Michael Gross, W. Ger.	1:47.44	WR
400m Free	George DiCarlo, USA	3:51.23	OR
1500m Free	Mike O'Brien, USA	15:05.20	
100m Back	Rick Carey, USA	55.79	
200m Back	Rick Carey, USA	2:00.23	
100m Brst	Steve Lundquist, USA	1:01.65	WR
200m Brst	Victor Davis, CAN	2:13.34	WR
100m Fly	Michael Gross, W. Ger.	53.08	WR
200m Fly	Jon Sieben, AUS	1:57.04	WR
200m I.M.	Alex Baumann, CAN	2:01.42	WR
400m I.M.	Alex Baumann, CAN	4:17.41	WR
4x100m Free	USA (Chris Cavanaugh, Mike		
	Heath, Matt Biondi,		
	Rowdy Gaines)	3:19.03	WR
4x200m Free	USA (Mike Heath, David Larson,		
	Jeff Float, Bruce Hayes)	7:15.69	WR
4x100m Mdly	USA (Rick Carey, Steve		
	Lundquist, Pablo Morales,		
	Rowdy Gaines)	3:39.30	WR

Diving		Points
Platform	Greg Louganis, USA	710.91
Spring	Greg Louganis, USA	754.41

WOMEN

Event		Time	
100m Free	Nancy Hogshead, USA	55.92	
200m Free	Mary Wayte, USA	1:59.23	
400m Free	Tiffany Cohen, USA	4:07.10	OR
800m Free	Tiffany Cohen, USA	8:24.95	OR
100m Back	Theresa Andrews, USA	1:02.55	
200m Back	Jolanda de Rover, HOL	2:12.38	
100m Brst	Petra van Staveren, HOL	1:09.88	OR
200m Brst	Anne Ottenbrite, CAN	2:30.38	
100m Fly	Mary T. Meagher, USA	59.26	
200m Fly	Mary T. Meagher, USA	2:06.90	OR
200m I.M.	Tracy Caulkins, USA	2:12.64	OR
400m I.M.	Tracy Caulkins, USA	4:39.24	

Event		Time
4x100m Free	USA (Jenna Johnson, Carrie	
	Steinseifer, Dara Torres,	
	Nancy Hogshead)	3:43.43
4x100m Mdly	USA (Theresa Andrews, Tracy	
	Caulkins, Mary T. Meagher,	
	Nancy Hogshead)	4:08.34

Diving		Points
Platform	Zhou Jihong, CHN	435.51
Spring	Sylvie Bernier, CAN	530.70

Team Sports

Men	Champion
Basketball	United States
Field Hockey	Pakistan

Team Sports

Men	Champion
Handball	Yugoslavia
Soccer	France
Volleyball	United States
Water Polo	Yugoslavia
Women	**Champion**
Basketball	United States
Field Hockey	Holland
Handball	Yugoslavia
Volleyball	China

Also Contested

Archery, Canoeing, Cycling, Equestrian, Fencing, Judo, Modern Pentathlon, Rowing, Shooting, Synchronized Swimming, Weightlifting, Freestyle Wrestling, Greco-Roman Wrestling and Yachting.

SÉOUL 1988

1988
Seoul

For the first time since Munich in 1972, there was no organized boycott of the Summer Olympics. Cuba and Ethiopia stayed away in support of North Korea (the IOC turned down the North Koreans' demand to co-host the Games, so they refused to participate), but that was about it.

More countries (160) sent more athletes (9,627) to South Korea than to any previous Olympics. There were also more security personnel (100,000) than ever before given Seoul's proximity (30 miles) to the North and the possibility of student demonstrations for reunification.

Ten days into the Games, Canadian Ben Johnson beat defending champion Carl Lewis in the 100-meter dash with a world record time of 9.79. The next day, however, Johnson was stripped of his gold medal and sent packing by the IOC when his post-race drug test indicated steroid use.

Lewis, who finished second in the 100, was named the winner. He also repeated in the long jump, but was second in the 200 and did not run the 400 relay. Teammate Florence Griffith Joyner claimed four medals—gold in the 100, 200 and 400-meter relay, and silver in the 1,600 relay. Her sister-in-law Jackie Joyner-Kersee won the long jump and heptathlon.

The most gold medals were won by swimmers—Kristin Otto of East Germany (6) and American Matt Biondi (5). Otherwise, Steffi Graf added an Olympic gold medal to her Grand Slam sweep in tennis, Greg Louganis won both men's diving events for the second straight time, and the U.S. men's basketball team had to settle for third place after losing to the gold medal-winning Soviets, 82-76, in the semifinals.

Top 10 Standings

National medal standings are not recognized by the IOC. The unofficial point totals are based on 3 points for a gold medal, 2 for a silver and 1 for a bronze.

		Gold	Silver	Bronze	Total	Pts
1	USSR	55	31	46	132	273
2	E. Germany	37	35	30	102	211
3	USA	36	31	27	94	197
4	W. Germany	11	14	15	40	76
5	Bulgaria	10	12	13	35	67
	South Korea	12	10	11	33	67
7	Hungary	11	6	6	23	51
8	China	5	11	12	28	49
	Romania	7	11	6	24	49
10	Great Britain	5	10	9	24	44

Leading Medal Winners

Number of individual medals won on the left; gold, silver and bronze breakdown to the right.

MEN

No		Sport	G-S-B
7	Matt Biondi, USA	Swimming	5-1-1
5	Vladimir Artemov, USSR	Gymnastics	4-1-0
4	Dmitri Bilozerchev, USSR	Gymnastics	3-0-1
4	Valeri Lyukin, USSR	Gymnastics	2-2-0
3	Chris Jacobs, USA	Swimming	2-1-0
3	Carl Lewis, USA	Track/Field	2-1-0
3	Holger Behrendt, E. Ger	Gymnastics	1-1-1
3	Uwe Dassler, E. Ger	Swimming	1-1-1
3	Paul McDonald, NZE	Canoeing	1-1-1
3	Igor Polianski, USSR	Swimming	1-0-2
3	Gennadi Prigoda, USSR	Swimming	0-1-2
3	Sven Tippelt, E. Ger	Gymnastics	0-1-2

WOMEN

No		Sport	G-S-B
6	Kristin Otto, E. Ger	Swimming	6-0-0
6	Daniela Silivas, ROM	Gymnastics	3-2-1
4	Florence Griffith Joyner, USA	Track/Field	3-1-0
4	Svetlana Boguinskaya, USSR	Gymnastics	2-1-1
4	Elena Shushunova, USSR	Gymnastics	2-1-1
3	Janet Evans, USA	Swimming	3-0-0
3	Silke Hörner, E. Ger	Swimming	2-0-1
3	Daniela Hunger, E. Ger	Swimming	2-0-1
3	Katrin Meissner, E. Ger	Swimming	2-0-1
3	Birgit Schmidt, E. Ger	Canoeing	2-1-0
3	Birte Weigang, E. Ger	Swimming	1-2-0
3	Vania Guecheva, BUL	Canoeing	1-1-1
3	Gabriela Potorac, ROM	Gymnastics	0-2-1
3	Heike Drechsler, E. Ger	Track/Field	0-1-2

Track & Field

MEN

Event		Time	
100m	Carl Lewis, USA	9.92	OR
200m	Joe DeLoach, USA	19.75	OR
400m	Steve Lewis, USA	43.87	
800m	Paul Ereng, KEN	1:43.45	
1500m	Peter Rono, KEN	3:35.96	
5000m	John Ngugi, KEN	13:11.70	
10,000m	Brahim Boutaib, MOR	27:21.46	OR
Marathon	Gelindo Bordin, ITA	2:10:32	
110m H	Roger Kingdom, USA	12.98	OR
400m H	Andre Phillips, USA	47.19	OR
3000m Steeple	Julius Kariuki, KEN	8:05.51	OR
20k Walk	Jozef Pribilinec, CZE	1:19:57	OR
50k Walk	Viacheslav Ivanenko, USSR	3:38:29	OR
4x100m	USSR (Victor Bryzgine, Vladimir Krylov, Vladimir Mouraviev, Vitaly Savine)	38.19	
4x400m	USA (Danny Everett, Steve Lewis, Kevin Robinzine, Butch Reynolds)	2:56.16	=WR

Event		Mark	
High Jump	Guennadi Avdeenko, USSR	7- 9¾	OR
Pole Vault	Sergey Bubka, USSR	19- 4¼	OR
Long Jump	Carl Lewis, USA	28- 7¼	
Triple Jump	Hristo Markov, BUL	57- 9¼	OR
Shot Put	Ulf Timmermann, E. Ger	73- 8¾	OR
Discus	Jürgen Schult, E. Ger	225- 9	OR
Hammer	Sergey Litvinov, USSR	278- 2	OR
Javelin	Tapio Korjus, FIN	276- 6	
Decathlon	Christian Schenk, E. Ger	8488 pts	

WOMEN

Event		Time	
100m	Florence Griffith Joyner, USA	10.54	OR
200m	Florence Griffith Joyner, USA	21.34	WR
400m	Olga Bryzgina, USSR	48.65	OR
800m	Sigrun Wodars, E. Ger	1:56.10	
1500m	Paula Ivan, ROM	3:53.96	OR
3000m	Tatiana Samolenko, USSR	8:26.53	OR
10,000m	Olga Bondarenko, USSR	31:05.21	OR
Marathon	Rosa Mota, POR	2:25:40	
100m H	Yordanka Donkova, BUL	12.38	OR
400m H	Debra Flintoff-King, AUS	53.17	OR
4x100m	USA (Alice Brown, Sheila Echols, Florence Griffith Joyner, Evelyn Ashford)	41.98	
4x400m	USSR (Tatyana Ledovskaia, Olga Nazarova, Maria Piniguina, Olga Bryzgina)	3:15.18	WR

Event		Mark	
High Jump	Louise Ritter, USA	6- 8	OR
Long Jump	Jackie Joyner-Kersee, USA	24- 3¼	OR
Shot Put	Natalya Lisovskaya, USSR	72-11¼	
Discus	Martina Hellmann, E. Ger	237- 2½	OR
Javelin	Petra Felke, E. Ger	245- 0	OR
Heptathlon	Jackie Joyner-Kersee, USA	7291 pts	WR

Boxing

Weight Class	Champion
Lt. Flyweight (106 lbs)	Ivailo Hristov, BUL
Flyweight (112)	Kim Kwang-Sun, S. Kor
Bantamweight (119)	Kennedy McKinney, USA
Featherweight (125)	Giovanni Parisi, ITA
Lightweight (132)	Andreas Zuelow, E. Ger
Lt. Welterweight (139)	Vyacheslav Yanovsky, USSR
Welterweight (148)	Robert Wangila, KEN
Lt. Middleweight (156)	Park Si-Hun, S. Kor
Middleweight (165)	Henry Maske, E. Ger
Lt. Heavyweight (178)	Andrew Maynard, USA
Heavyweight (200)	Ray Mercer, USA
Super Heavyweight (200+)	Lennox Lewis, CAN

Gymnastics

MEN

Individual		Points
All-Around	Vladimir Artemov, USSR	119.125
Floor	Sergey Kharkov, USSR	19.925
Horiz.Bar	Vladimir Artemov, USSR & Valeri Lyukin, USSR	19.900
Paral.Bars	Vladimir Artemov, USSR	19.925
Rings	Dmitri Bilozerchev, USSR & Holger Behrendt, E. Ger	19.925
Side Horse	Dmitri Bilozerchev, USSR, Lyubomir Geraskov, BUL & Zsolt Borkai, HUN	19.950
Vault	Lou Yun, CHN	19.875

Team		Points
All-Around	USSR (Artemov, Bilozerchev, Kharkov, Lyukin, Gogoladze, Nouvikov)	593.350

1988 (Cont.)
WOMEN

Individual		Points
All-Around	Yelena Shushunova, USSR	79.662
Bal.Beam	Daniela Silivas, ROM	19.924
Floor	Daniela Silivas, ROM	19.937
Uneven Bars	Daniela Silivas, ROM	20.000
Vault	Svetlana Boguinskaya, USSR	19.905

Team		Points
All-Around	USSR (Shushunova, Boguinskaya, Baitova, Chevtchenko, Strajeva, Lachtchenova)	395.475

Rhythmic		Points
All-Around	Marina Lobatch, USSR	60.0

Swimming
MEN

Event		Time	
50m Free	Matt Biondi, USA	22.14	WR
100m Free	Matt Biondi, USA	48.63	OR
200m Free	Duncan Armstrong, AUS	1:47.25	WR
400m Free	Uwe Dassler, E. Ger	3:46.95	WR
1500m Free	Vladimir Salnikov, USSR	15:00.04	
100m Back	Daichi Suzuki, JPN	55.05	
200m Back	Igor Polianski, USSR	1:59.37	
100m Brst	Adrian Moorhouse, GBR	1:02.04	
200m Brst	József Szabó, HUN	2:13.52	
100m Fly	Anthony Nesty, SUR	53.00	OR
200m Fly	Michael Gross, W. Ger	1:56.94	OR
200m I.M.	Tamás Darnyi, HUN	2:00.17	WR
400m I.M.	Tamás Darnyi, HUN	4:14.75	WR
4x100m Free	USA (Chris Jacobs, Troy Dalbey, Tom Jager, Matt Biondi)	3:16.53	WR
4x200m Free	USA (Troy Dalbey, Matt Cetlinski, Doug Gjertsen, Matt Biondi)	7:12.51	WR

Event		Time	
4x100m Med	USA (David Berkoff, Rich Schroeder, Matt Biondi, Chris Jacobs)	3:36.93	WR

Diving		Points
Platform	Greg Louganis, USA	638.61
Spring	Greg Louganis, USA	730.80

WOMEN

Event		Time	
50m Free	Kristin Otto, E. Ger	25.49	OR
100m Free	Kristin Otto, E. Ger	54.93	
200m Free	Heike Freidrich, E. Ger	1:57.65	OR
400m Free	Janet Evans, USA	4:03.85	WR
800m Free	Janet Evans, USA	8:20.20	OR
100m Back	Kristin Otto, E. Ger	1:00.89	
200m Back	Krisztina Egerszegi, HUN	2:09.29	OR
100m Brst	Tania Dangalakova, BUL	1:07.95	OR
200m Brst	Silke Hörner, E. Ger	2:26.71	WR
100m Fly	Kristin Otto, E. Ger	59.00	OR
200m Fly	Kathleen Nord, E. Ger	2:09.51	
200m I.M.	Daniela Hunger, E. Ger	2:12.59	OR
400m I.M.	Janet Evans, USA	4:37.76	
4x100m Free	E. Ger. (Kristin Otto, Katrin Meissner, Daniela Hunger, Manuela Stellmach)	3:40.63	OR
4x100m Med	E. Ger. (Kristin Otto, Silke Hörner, Birte Weigang, Katrin Meissner)	4:03.74	OR

Diving		Points
Platform	Xu Yanmei, CHN	445.20
Spring	Gao Min, CHN	580.23

Tennis
MEN

Singles:	Miloslav Mecir, CZE, def. Tim Mayotte, USA, 3-6,6-2,6-4,6-2
Doubles:	Ken Flach & Robert Seguso, USA, def. Emilio Sanchez & Sergio Casal, SPA, 6-3,6-4,6-7,6-7,9-7

WOMEN

Singles:	Steffi Graf, W. Ger, def. Gabriela Sabatini, ARG, 6-3,6-3
Doubles:	Pam Shriver and Zina Garrison, USA, def. Jana Novotna and Helena Sukova, CZE, 4-6,6-2,10-8

Team Sports

Men	Champion
Basketball	Soviet Union
Field Hockey	Great Britain
Handball	Soviet Union
Soccer	Soviet Union
Volleyball	United States
Water Polo	Yugoslavia

Women	Champion
Basketball	United States
Field Hockey	Australia
Handball	South Korea
Volleyball	Soviet Union

Also Contested

Archery, Canoeing, Cycling, Equestrian, Fencing, Judo, Modern Pentathlon, Shooting, Synchronized Swimming, Table Tennis, Weightlifting, Freestyle Wrestling, Greco-Roman Wrestling and Yachting.

Barcelona'92

1992

Barcelona

The year IOC president Juan Antonio Samaranch brought the Olympics to his native Spain marked the first renewal of the Summer Games since the fall of communism in Eastern Europe and the reunification of Germany in 1990.

A record 10,563 athletes from 172 nations gathered without a single country boycotting the Games. Both Cuba and North Korea returned after 12 years and South Africa was welcomed back after 32, following the national government's denunciation of apartheid racial policies.

While Germany competed under one flag and ideology for the first time since 1936, 12 nations from the former Soviet Union joined forces one last time as the Unified Team.

This was also the year the IOC threw open the gates to professional athletes after 96 years of high-minded opposition. Basketball was the chief beneficiary as America's popular "Dream Team" of NBA All-Stars easily won the gold.

Carl Lewis earned his seventh and eighth career gold medals with a third consecutive Olympic win in the long jump, and an anchor-leg performance on the American 400-meter relay team that helped establish a world record. Gail Devers of the U.S., whose feet had nearly been amputated by doctors in 1990 as a result of radiation treatment for Graves' disease, won the women's 100 meters.

Other track and field athletes stumbled, however. After Olympic favorite and world champion Dan O'Brien failed to even make the U.S. team, Dave Johnson, the new favorite, settled for the bronze. Ukrainian pole vaulter Sergey Bubka, who had dominated the sport for the past decade was the heavy favorite but failed to clear any height.

China's Fu Mingxia, 13, won the women's platform diving gold, becoming the second-youngest person to win an individual gold medal. In gymnastics, Vitaly Scherbo of Belarus, competing for the Unified Team, won six golds. Cuba made their Olympic return rewarding, capturing seven boxing golds as well as the gold in baseball.

Top 10 Standings

National medal standings are not recognized by the IOC. The unofficial point totals are based on 3 points for a gold medal, 2 for a silver and 1 for a bronze.

		Gold	Silver	Bronze	Total	Pts
1	Unified Team	45	38	29	112	240
2	United States	37	34	37	108	216
3	Germany	33	21	28	82	169
4	China	16	22	16	54	108
5	Cuba	14	6	11	31	65
6	Hungary	11	12	7	30	64
7	South Korea	12	5	12	29	58
8	Spain	13	7	2	22	55
9	France	8	5	16	29	50
	Australia	7	9	11	27	50

Leading Medal Winners

Number of individual medals won on the left; gold, silver and bronze breakdown to the right.

MEN

No		Sport	G-S-B
6	Vitaly Scherbo, UT	Gymnastics	6-0-0
5	Grigory Misiutin, UT	Gymnastics	1-4-0
4	Aleksandr Popov, UT	Gymnastics	2-2-0
4	Yevgeny Sadovyi, UT	Swimming	3-0-0
3	Matt Biondi, USA	Swimming	2-1-0
3	Jon Olsen, USA	Swimming	2-0-1
3	Mel Stewart, USA	Swimming	2-0-1
3	Vladimir Pychnenko, UT	Swimming	1-2-0
3	Li Xiaosahuang, CHN	Gymnastics	1-1-1
3	Li Jing, CHN	Gymnastics	0-3-0
3	Anders Holmertz, SWE	Swimming	0-2-1
3	Andreas Wecker, GER	Gymnastics	0-1-2

WOMEN

No		Sports	G-S-B
5	Shannon Miller, USA	Gymnastics	0-2-3
4	Tatiana Gutsu, UT	Gymnastics	2-1-1
4	Lavinia Milosovici, ROM	Gymnastics	2-1-1
4	Summer Sanders, USA	Swimming	2-1-1
4	Franziska van Almsick, GER	Swimming	0-2-2
3	Krisztina Egerszegi, HUN	Swimming	3-0-0
3	Nicole Haislett, USA	Swimming	3-0-0
3	Crissy Ahmann-Leighton, USA	Swimming	2-1-0

WOMEN

No		Sports	G-S-B
3	Jenny Thompson, USA	Swimming	2-1-0
3	Gwen Torrence, USA	Track/Field	2-1-0
3	Tatyana Lysenko, UT	Gymnastics	2-0-1
3	Lin Li, CHN	Swimming	1-2-0
3	Dagmar Hase, GER	Swimming	1-2-0
3	Zhuang Yong, CHN	Swimming	1-2-0
3	Rita Koban, HUN	Kayaking	1-1-1
3	Anita Hall, USA	Swimming	1-1-1
3	Daniela Hunger, GER	Swimming	0-1-2

Track & Field

MEN

Event		Time
100m	Linford Christie, GBR	9.96
200m	Mike Marsh, USA	20.01
400m	Quincy Watts, USA	43.50 OR
800m	William Tanui, KEN	1:43.66
1500m	Fermin Cacho, SPA	3:40.12
5000m	Dieter Baumann, GER	13:12.52
10,000m	Khalid Skah, MOR	27:46.70
Marathon	Hwang Young-Cho, S. Kor	2:13.23
110m H	Mark McKoy, CAN	13.12
400m H	Kevin Young, USA	46.78 WR
3000m Steeple	Matthew Birir, KEN	8:08.84
20k Walk	Daniel Plaza Montero, SPA	1:21:45
50k Walk	Andrei Perlov, UT	3:50:13
4x100m	USA (Mike Marsh, Leroy Burrell, Dennis Mitchell, Carl Lewis)	37.40 WR
4x400m	USA (Andrew Valmon, Quincy Watts, Michael Johnson, Steve Lewis)	2:55.74 WR

Event		Mark
High Jump	Javier Sotomayor, CUB	7-8
Pole Vault	Maksim Tarasov, UT	19-0¼
Long Jump	Carl Lewis, USA	28-5½
Triple Jump	Mike Conley, USA	59-7½ᵂ
Shot Put	Michael Stulce, USA	71-2½
Discus	Romas Ubartas, LIT	213-8
Hammer	Andrei Abduvaliyev, UT	270-9
Javelin	Jan Zelezny, CZE	294-2 OR
Decathlon	Robert Zmelik, CZE	8611 pts

W indicates wind-aided.

WOMEN

Event		Time
100m	Gail Devers, USA	10.82
200m	Gwen Torrence, USA	21.81
400m	Marie-Jose Perec, FRA	48.83
800m	Ellen van Langen, HOL	1:55.54
1500m	Hassiba Boulmerka, ALG	3:55.30
3000m	Elena Romanova, UT	8:46.04
10,000m	Derartu Tulu, ETH	31:06.02
Marathon	Valentina Yegorova, UT	2:32:41
100m H	Paraskevi Patoulidou, GRE	12.64
400m H	Sally Gunnell, GBR	53.23
10K Walk	Chen Yueling, CHN	44.32
4x100m	USA (Evelyn Ashford, Esther Jones, Carlette Guidry-White, Gwen Torrence)	42.11
4x400m	UT (Yelena Ruzina, Lyudmila Dzhigalova, Olga Nazarova, Olga Bryzgina)	3:20.20

Event		Mark
High Jump	Heike Henkel, GER	6-7½
Long Jump	Heike Drechsler, GER	23-5¼
Shot Put	Svetlana Krivaleva, UT	69-1¼
Discus	Maritza Marten, CUB	229-10
Javelin	Silke Renk, GER	224-2
Heptathlon	Jackie Joyner-Kersee, USA	7044 pts

1992 (Cont.)
Boxing

Weight Class	Champion
Lt. Flyweight (106 lbs)	Rogelio Marcelo, CUB
Flyweight (112)	Su Choi-Chol, N. Kor
Bantamweight (119)	Joel Casamayor, CUB
Featherweight (125)	Andreas Tews, GER
Lightweight (132)	Oscar De La Hoya, USA
Lt. Welterweight (139)	Hector Vinent, CUB
Welterweight (147)	Michael Carruth, IRE
Lt. Middleweight (156)	Juan Lemus, CUB
Middleweight (165)	Ariel Hernandez, CUB
Lt. Heavyweight (178)	Torsten May, GER
Heavyweight (200)	Felix Savon, CUB
Super Heavyweight (200+)	Roberto Balado, CUB

Gymnastics
MEN

Individual		Points
All-Around	Vitaly Scherbo, UT	59.025
Floor	Li Xiaoshuang, CHN	9.925
Horiz.Bar	Trent Dimas, USA	9.875
Paral.Bars	Vitaly Scherbo, UT	9.900
Rings	Vitaly Scherbo, UT	9.937
Side Horse	Vitaly Scherbo, UT & Pae Gil-Su, N. Kor	9.925
Vault	Vitaly Scherbo, UT	9.856
Team		Points
All Around	UT (Scherbo, Belenki, Misiutin, Korobchinski, Voropayev, Sharipov)	585.450

WOMEN

Individual		Points
All-Around	Tatiana Gutsu, UT	39.737
Bal.Beam	Tatiana Lyssenko, UT	9.975
Floor	Lavinia Milosovici, ROM	10.000
Uneven Bars	Lu Li, CHN	10.000
Vault	Henrietta Onodi, HUN & Lavinia Milosovici, ROM	9.925
Team		Points
All Around	UT (Boginskaya, Lyssenko, Galiyeva, Goutsou, Grudneva, Chusovitina)	395.666
Rythmic		Points
All Around	Aleksandra Timoshenko, UT	59.037

Swimming
MEN

Event		Time	
50m Free	Aleksandr Popov, UT	21.91	OR
100m Free	Aleksandr Popov, UT	49.02	
200m Free	Yevgeny Sadovyi, UT	1:46.70	OR
400m Free	Yevgeny Sadovyi, UT	3:45.00	WR
1500m Free	Kieren Perkins, AUS	14:43.48	WR
100m Back	Mark Tewksbury, CAN	53.98	OR
200m Back	Martin Lopez-Zubero, SPA	1:58.47	OR
100m Brst	Nelson Diebel, USA	1:01.50	OR
200m Brst	Mike Barrowman, USA	2:10.16	WR
100m Fly	Pablo Morales, USA	53.32	
200m Fly	Mel Stewart, USA	1:56.26	OR
200m I.M.	Tamás Darnyi, HUN	2:00.76	
400m I.M.	Tamás Darnyi, HUN	4:14.23	OR
4x100m Free	USA (Joe Hudepohl, Matt Biondi, Tom Jager, Jon Olsen)	3:16.74	
4x200m Free	UT (Dmitri Lepikov, Vladimir Pychnenko, Veniamin Taianovitch, Yevgeny Sadovyi)	7:11.95	WR
Diving		Points	
Platform	Sun Shuwei, CHN	677.31	
Spring	Mark Lenzi, USA	676.53	

WOMEN

Event		Time	
50m Free	Yang Wenyi, CHN	24.79	WR
100m Free	Zhuang Yong, CHN	54.64	OR
200m Free	Nicole Haislett, USA	1:57.90	
400m Free	Dagmar Hase, GER	4:07.18	
800m Free	Janet Evans, USA	8:25.52	
100m Back	Krisztina Egerszegi, HUN	1:00.68	OR
200m Back	Krisztina Egerszegi, HUN	2:07.06	OR
100m Brst	Yelena Rudkovskaya, UT	1:08.00	
200m Brst	Kyoko Iwasaki, JPN	2:26.65	OR
100m Fly	Qian Hong, CHN	58.62	OR
200m Fly	Summer Sanders, USA	2:08.67	
200m I.M.	Lin Li, CHN	2:11.65	WR
400m I.M.	Krisztina Egerszegi, HUN	4:36.54	
4x100m Free	USA (Nicole Haislett, Dara Torres, Angel Martino, Jenny Thompson)	3:39.46	WR
4x100m Med	USA (Lea Loveless, Anita Nall, Crissy Ahmann-Leighton, Jenny Thompson)	4:02.54	WR
Diving		Points	
Platform	Fu Mingxia, CHN	461.43	
Spring	Gao Min, CHN	572.40	

Tennis
MEN

Singles:	Marc Rosset, SWI, def. Jordi Arrese, SPA, 7-6,6-4,3-6,4-6,8-6.
Doubles:	Boris Becker and Michael Stich, GER, def. Wayne Ferreira and Piet Norval, SAF, 7-6,4-6,7-6,6-3.
Singles:	Jennifer Capriati, USA, def. Steffi Graf, GER, 3-6,6-3,6-4.
Doubles:	Gigi Fernandez and Mary Joe Fernandez, USA, def. Conchita Martinez and Arantxa Sanchez Vicario, SPA, 7-5,2-6,6-2.

Team Sports

Men	Champion
Baseball	Cuba
Basketball	United States
Field Hockey	Germany
Handball	Unified Team
Soccer	Spain
Volleyball	Brazil
Water Polo	Italy

Women	Champion
Basketball	Unified Team
Field Hockey	Spain
Handball	South Korea
Volleyball	Cuba

Also Contested
Archery, Badminton, Canoeing, Cycling, Equestrian, Fencing, Judo, Modern Pentathlon, Shooting, Table Tennis, Weightlifting, Freestyle Wrestling, Greco-Roman Wrestling and Yachting.

New Events for 1996
Women's soccer and softball as well as men's and women's beach volleyball and mountain biking will make their Summer Olympic debuts in Atlanta. Overall, events have been added in 16 sports–including track and field, where the women's triple jump begins and the 5,000-meter race replaces the 3,000. In swimming, the women's 4x200 freestyle relay will be added.

Georgia On The Minds of 197 Nations

by Philip Hersh

Budget problems. Fights with international sports federations. Price gouging. Racial flashpoints. The Bubba factor.

The Centennial Olympic Games isn't just 16 days of glory.

That's what Atlanta has learned in the 18 months leading up to July 19, 1996, when the capital of Georgia will play host to 10,000 athletes from 197 invited nations in the Games of the XXVIth Olympiad.

There seems little doubt the city will overcome the organizational, logistical, political, and budgetary hassles that have dogged its preparations since Sept. 18, 1990, when it won the International Olympic Committee nod over sentimental favorite Athens, Greece.

The question of how these Games will be perceived from Afghanistan to Zimbabwe is far less certain than Atlanta's claim to have them "on time and on budget." Will the world see the integrated New South or the racially divided Old South, where the Georgia state flag still harkens back to the Confederacy?

But there are more compelling questions to be answered in Atlanta:

• *What kind of team will China send?*

In 1992, the Chinese seemed on the verge of filling the sports superpower vacuum created by the disappearance of the Soviet Bloc. In the next two years, its women swimmers and women distance runners utterly dominated their events. By 1995, those athletes virtually had disappeared and few expect them to return before Atlanta.

Banned from the 1995 Pan Pacific Games because of repeated positive drug tests in 1993 and '94, the Chinese swimmers were expected to make something of a splash in the 1995 World University Games. Instead, they sent a five-woman team that barely stayed afloat.

After winning six of the nine women's medals in the 1,500, 3,000 and 10,000 meters at the 1993 World Track and Field Championships, China did not even have a finalist at those distances in this year's world meet.

"I don't think we can draw any conclusions from what we are seeing right now," said Dennis Pursley, U.S. swimming's national team director.

Atlanta 1996

Atlanta Committe for the Olympic Games

• *Michael Who?*

Even with his historic triumphs at 200 and 400 meters in both the national and world championships in 1995, Michael Johnson remains the least-known exceptional athlete in the United States. He hopes a track schedule change will enable him to win the same two events in Atlanta and earn some of the superstar status attached to another MJ.

• *Which pixie will win in Dixie?*

In Barcelona four years ago, the women's gymnastics all-around final came down to a battle between Tatiana Gutsu of Ukraine (4 feet, 6 inches, 69 pounds) and Shannon Miller (4-6, 70 lbs.) of the United States. Gutsu won and the sport lost. While gymnastics officials have tried to give grown women a chance in the event, the U.S. crowned 13-year-old Dominique Moceanu (4-5, 70 lbs.) as its youngest national champion ever in 1995.

• *Is Dream Team III necessary?*

Not really, but after 26 years of rooting for the lowly Hawks of the NBA, Atlanta is ready for a winner—and having Hakeem Olajuwon and Shaquille O'Neal on the home team should be a hoot.

Otherwise, as the third American city (after St. Louis and Los Angeles) to host the Summer Olympics, Atlanta is set to celebrate the 100th anniversary of the Modern Games with all the southern hospitality it can muster.

Philip Hersh is the Olympics writer for the *Chicago Tribune.* His report on The Year in International Sports begins on page 603.

Event-by-Event

Gold medal winners from 1896-1992 in the following events: Baseball, Basketball, Boxing, Diving, Field Hockey, Gymnastics, Soccer, Swimming, Tennis, and Track & Field.

BASEBALL

Year
1992 **Cuba**, Taiwan, Japan

BASKETBALL

MEN

Multiple gold medals: USA (10); USSR (2).

Year		Year	
1936	**United States**, Canada, Mexico	1972	**Soviet Union**, United States, Cuba
1948	**United States**, France, Brazil	1976	**United States**, Yugoslavia, Soviet Union
1952	**United States**, Soviet Union, Uruguay	1980	**Yugoslavia**, Italy, Soviet Union
1956	**United States**, Soviet Union, Uruguay	1984	**United States**, Spain, Yugoslavia
1960	**United States**, Soviet Union, Brazil	1988	**Soviet Union**, Yugoslavia, United States
1964	**United States**, Soviet Union, Brazil	1992	**United States**, Croatia, Lithuania
1968	**United States**, Yugoslavia, Soviet Union		

U.S. Medal-Winning Men's Basketball Teams

1936 (gold medal): Sam Balter, Ralph Bishop, Joe Fortenberry, Tex Gibbons, Francis Johnson, Carl Knowles, Frank Lubin, Art Mollner, Don Piper, Jack Ragland, Carl Shy, Willard Schmidt, Duane Swanson and William Wheatley. Coach—Jim Needles; Assistant—Gene Johnson. Final: USA over Canada, 19-8.

1948 (gold medal): Cliff Barker, Don Barksdale, Ralph Beard, Louis Beck, Vince Boryla, Gordon Carpenter, Alex Groza, Wallace Jones, Bob Kurland, Ray Lumpp, R.C. Pitts, Jesse Renick, Robert (Jackie) Robinson and Ken Rollins. Coach—Omar Browning; Assistant—Adolph Rupp. Final: USA over France, 65-21.

1952 (gold medal): Ron Bontemps, Mark Freiberger, Wayne Glasgow, Charlie Hoag, Bill Hougland, John Keller, Dean Kelley, Bob Kenney, Bob Kurland, Bill Lienhard, Clyde Lovellette, Frank McCabe, Dan Pippin and Howie Williams. Coach—Warren Womble; Assistant—Forrest (Phog) Allen. Final: USA over USSR, 36-25.

1956 (gold medal): Dick Boushka, Carl Cain, Chuck Darling, Bill Evans, Gib Ford, Burdy Haldorson, Bill Hougland, Bob Jeangerard, K.C. Jones, Bill Russell, Ron Tomsic, Jim Walsh. Coach—Gerald Tucker; Assistant—Bruce Drake. Final: USA over USSR, 89-55.

1960 (gold medal): Jay Arnette, Walt Bellamy, Bob Boozer, Terry Dischinger, Jerry Lucas, Oscar Robertson, Adrian Smith, Burdy Haldorson, Darrall Imhoff, Allen Kelley, Lester Lane and Jerry West. Coach—Pete Newell; Assistant—Warren Womble. Final round: USA defeated USSR (81-57), Italy (112-81) and Brazil (90-63) in round robin.

1964 (gold medal): Jim (Bad News) Barnes, Bill Bradley, Larry Brown, Joe Caldwell, Mel Counts, Dick Davies, Walt Hazzard, Lucius Jackson, Pete McCaffrey, Jeff Mullins, Jerry Shipp and George Wilson. Coach—Hank Iba; Assistant—Henry Vaughn. Final: USA over USSR, 73-59.

1968 (gold medal): Mike Barrett, John Clawson, Don Dee, Cal Fowler, Spencer Haywood, Bill Hosket, Jim King, Glynn Saulters, Charlie Scott, Mike Silliman, Ken Spain, and JoJo White. Coach—Hank Iba; Assistant—Henry Vaughn. USA over Yugoslavia, 65-50.

1972 (silver medal refused): Mike Bantom, Jim Brewer, Tom Burleson, Doug Collins, Kenny Davis, Jim Forbes, Tom Henderson, Bobby Jones, Dwight Jones, Kevin Joyce, Tom McMillen and Ed Ratleff. Coach—Hank Iba; Assistants— John Bach and Don Haskins. Final: USSR over USA, 51-50.

1976 (gold medal): Tate Armstrong, Quinn Buckner, Kenny Carr, Adrian Dantley, Walter Davis, Phil Ford, Ernie Grunfeld, Phil Hubbard, Mitch Kupchak, Tommy LaGarde, Scott May and Steve Sheppard. Coach—Dean Smith; Assistants— Bill Guthridge and John Thompson. Final: USA over Yugoslavia, 95-74.

1980 (no medal): USA boycotted Moscow Games. Final: Yugoslavia over Italy, 86-77.

1984 (gold medal): Steve Alford, Patrick Ewing, Vern Fleming, Michael Jordan; Joe Kleine, Jon Koncak, Chris Mullin, Sam Perkins, Alvin Robertson, Wayman Tisdale, Jeff Turner and Leon Wood. Coach—Bobby Knight; Assistants— Don Donoher and George Raveling. Final: USA over Spain, 96-65.

1988 (bronze medal): Stacey Augmon, Willie Anderson, Bimbo Coles, Jeff Grayer, Hersey Hawkins, Dan Majerle, Danny Manning, Mitch Richmond, J.R. Reid, David Robinson, Charles D. Smith and Charles E. Smith. Coach—John Thompson; Assistants—George Raveling and Mary Fenlon. Final: USSR over Yugoslavia, 76-63.

1992 (gold medal): Charles Barkley, Larry Bird, Clyde Drexler, Patrick Ewing, Magic Johnson, Michael Jordan, Christian Laettner, Karl Malone, Chris Mullin, Scottie Pippen, David Robinson and John Stockton. Coach—Chuck Daly; Assistants— Lenny Wilkens, Mike Krzyzewski and P.J. Carlesimo. Final: USA over Croatia, 117-85.

WOMEN

Multiple gold medals: USSR/UT (3); USA (2).

Year		Year	
1976	**Soviet Union**, United States, Bulgaria	1988	**United States**, Yugoslavia, Soviet Union
1980	**Soviet Union**, Bulgaria, Yugoslavia	1992	**Unified Team**, China, United States
1984	**United States**, South Korea, China		

U.S. Gold Medal-Winning Women's Basketball Teams

1984: Cathy Boswell, Denise Curry, Anne Donovan, Teresa Edwards, Lea Henry, Janice Lawrence, Pamela McGee, Carol Menken-Schaudt, Cheryl Miller, Kim Mulkey, Cindy Noble, Lynette Woodard. Coach—Pat Summitt; Assistant—Kay Yow. Final: USA over South Korea, 85–55.

1988: Cindy Brown, Vicky Bullett, Cynthia Cooper, Anne Donovan, Teresa Edwards, Kamie Ethridge, Jennifer Gillom, Bridgette Gordon, Andrea Lloyd, Katrina McClain, Suzie McConnell, Teresa Weatherspoon. Coach—Kay Yow; Assistants— Sylvia Hatchell and Susan Yow. Final: USA over Yugoslavia, 77–70.

BOXING

Multiple gold medals: László Papp and Teófilo Stevenson (3); Angel Herrera, Oliver Kirk, Jerzy Kulej, Boris Lagutin and Harry Mallin (2). All fighters won titles in consecutive Olympics, except Kirk, who won both the bantamweight and featherweight titles in 1904 (he only had to fight once in each division).

Light Flyweight (106 lbs)

Year		Final Match	Year		Final Match
1968	Francisco Rodriguez, VEN	Decision, 3-2	1984	Paul Gonzales, USA	Default
1972	György Gedó, HUN	Decision, 5-0	1988	Ivailo Hristov, BUL	Decision, 5-0
1976	Jorge Hernandez, CUB	Decision, 4-1	1992	Rogelio Marcelo, CUB	Decision, 24-10
1980	Shamil Sabyrov, USSR	Decision, 3-2			

Flyweight (112 lbs)

Year		Final Match	Year		Final Match
1904	George Finnegan, USA	Stopped, 1st	1960	Gyula Török, HUN	Decision, 3-2
1920	Frank Di Gennara, USA	Decision	1964	Fernando Atzori, ITA	Decision, 4-1
1924	Fidel LaBarba, USA	Decision	1968	Ricardo Delgado, MEX	Decision, 5-0
1928	Antal Kocsis, HUN	Decision	1972	Georgi Kostadinov, BUL	Decision, 5-0
1932	István Enekes, HUN	Decision	1976	Leo Randolph, USA	Decision, 3-2
1936	Willi Kaiser, GER	Decision	1980	Peter Lessov, BUL	Stopped, 2nd
1948	Pascual Perez, ARG	Decision	1984	Steve McCrory, USA	Decision, 4-1
1952	Nate Brooks, USA	Decision, 3-0	1988	Kim Kwang-Sun, S. Kor	Decision, 4-1
1956	Terence Spinks, GBR	Decision	1992	Su Choi-Chol, N. Kor	Decision, 12-2

Bantamweight (119 lbs)

Year		Final Match	Year		Final Match
1904	Oliver Kirk, USA	Stopped, 3rd	1960	Oleg Grigoryev, USSR	Decision
1908	Henry Thomas, GBR	Decision	1964	Takao Sakurai, JPN	Stopped, 2nd
1920	Clarence Walker, SAF	Decision	1968	Valery Sokolov, USSR	Stopped, 2nd
1924	William Smith, SAF	Decision	1972	Orlando Martinez, CUB	Decision, 5-0
1928	Vittorio Tamagnini, ITA	Decision	1976	Gu Yong-Ju, N. Kor	Decision, 5-0
1932	Horace Gwynne, CAN	Decision	1980	Juan Hernandez, CUB	Decision, 5-0
1936	Ulderico Sergo, ITA	Decision	1984	Maurizio Stecca, ITA	Decision, 4-1
1948	Tibor Csik, HUN	Decision	1988	Kennedy McKinney, USA	Decision, 5-0
1952	Pentti Hämäläinen, FIN	Decision, 2-1	1992	Joel Casamayor, CUB	Decision, 14-8
1956	Wolfgang Behrendt, GER	Decision			

Featherweight (125 lbs)

Year		Final Match	Year		Final Match
1904	Oliver Kirk, USA	Decision	1960	Francesco Musso, ITA	Decision, 4-1
1908	Richard Gunn, GBR	Decision	1964	Stanislav Stepashkin, USSR	Decision, 3-2
1920	Paul Fritsch, FRA	Decision	1968	Antonio Roldan, MEX	Won on Disq.
1924	John Fields, USA	Decision	1972	Boris Kousnetsov, USSR	Decision, 3-2
1928	Lambertus van Klaveren, HOL	Decision	1976	Angel Herrera, CUB	KO, 2nd
1932	Carmelo Robledo, ARG	Decision	1980	Rudi Fink, E. Ger	Decision, 4-1
1936	Oscar Casanovas, ARG	Decision	1984	Meldrick Taylor, USA	Decision, 5-0
1948	Ernesto Formenti, ITA	Decision	1988	Giovanni Parisi, ITA	Stopped, 1st
1952	Jan Zachara, CZE	Decision, 2-1	1992	Andreas Tews, GER	Decision, 16-7
1956	Vladimir Safronov, USSR	Decision			

Lightweight (132 lbs)

Year		Final Match	Year		Final Match
1904	Harry Spanger, USA	Decision	1960	Kazimierz Pazdzior, POL	Decision, 4-1
1908	Frederick Grace, GBR	Decision	1964	József Grudzien, POL	Decision
1920	Samuel Mosberg, USA	Decision	1968	Ronnie Harris, USA	Decision, 5-0
1924	Hans Nielsen, DEN	Decision	1972	Jan Szczepanski, POL	Decision, 5-0
1928	Carlo Orlandi, ITA	Decision	1976	Howard Davis, USA	Decision, 5-0
1932	Lawrence Stevens, SAF	Decision	1980	Angel Herrera, CUB	Stopped, 3rd
1936	Imre Harangi, HUN	Decision	1984	Pernell Whitaker, USA	Foe quit, 2nd
1948	Gerald Dreyer, SAF	Decision	1988	Andreas Zuelow, E. Ger	Decision, 5-0
1952	Aureliano Bolognesi, ITA	Decision, 2-1	1992	Oscar De La Hoya, USA	Decision, 7-2
1956	Richard McTaggart, GBR	Decision			

Light Welterweight (139 lbs)

Year		Final Match	Year		Final Match
1952	Charles Adkins, USA	Decision, 2-1	1976	Ray Leonard, USA	Decision, 5-0
1956	Vladimir Yengibaryan, USSR	Decision	1980	Patrizio Oliva, ITA	Decision, 4-1
1960	Bohumil Nemecek, CZE	Decision, 5-0	1984	Jerry Page, USA	Decision, 5-0
1964	Jerzy Kulej, POL	Decision, 5-0	1988	Vyacheslav Yanovsky, USSR	Decision, 5-0
1968	Jerzy Kulej, POL	Decision, 3-2	1992	Hector Vinent, CUB	Decision, 11-1
1972	Ray Seales, USA	Decision, 3-2			

Boxing (Cont.)
Welterweight (147 lbs)

Year		Final Match	Year		Final Match
1904	Albert Young, USA	Decision	1960	Nino Benvenuti, ITA	Decision, 4-1
1920	Bert Schneider, CAN	Decision	1964	Marian Kasprzyk, POL	Decision, 4-1
1924	Jean Delarge, BEL	Decision	1968	Manfred Wolke, E. Ger	Decision, 4-1
1928	Edward Morgan, NZE	Decision	1972	Emilio Correa, CUB	Decision, 5-0
1932	Edward Flynn, USA	Decision	1976	Jochen Bachfeld, E. Ger	Decision, 3-2
1936	Sten Suvio, FIN	Decision	1980	Andrés Aldama, CUB	Decision, 4-1
1948	Julius Torma, CZE	Decision	1984	Mark Breland, USA	Decision, 5-0
1952	Zygmunt Chychla, POL	Decision, 3-0	1988	Robert Wangila, KEN	KO, 2nd
1956	Nicolae Linca, ROM	Decision, 3-2	1992	Michael Carruth, IRE	Decision, 13-10

Light Middleweight (156 lbs)

Year		Final Match	Year		Final Match
1952	László Papp, HUN	Decision, 3-0	1976	Jerzy Rybicki, POL	Decision, 5-0
1956	László Papp, HUN	Decision	1980	Armando Martinez, CUB	Decision, 4-1
1960	Skeeter McClure, USA	Decision, 4-1	1984	Frank Tate, USA	Decision, 5-0
1964	Boris Lagutin, USSR	Decision, 4-1	1988	Park Si-Hun, S. Kor	Decision, 3-2
1968	Boris Lagutin, USSR	Decision, 5-0	1992	Juan Lemus, CUB	Decision, 6-1
1972	Dieter Kottysch, W.Ger	Decision, 3-2			

Middleweight (165 lbs)

Year		Final Match	Year		Final Match
1904	Charles Mayer, USA	Stopped, 3rd	1960	Eddie Crook, USA	Decision, 3-2
1908	John Douglas, GBR	Decision	1964	Valery Popenchenko, USSR	Stopped, 1st
1920	Harry Mallin, GBR	Decision	1968	Christopher Finnegan, GBR	Decision, 3-2
1924	Harry Mallin, GBR	Decision	1972	Vyacheslav Lemechev, USSR	KO, 1st
1928	Piero Toscani, ITA	Decision	1976	Michael Spinks, USA	Stopped, 3rd
1932	Carmen Barth, USA	Decision	1980	José Gomez, CUB	Decision, 4-1
1936	Jean Despeaux, FRA	Decision	1984	Shin Joon-Sup, S. Kor	Decision, 3-2
1948	László Papp, HUN	Decision	1988	Henry Maske, E. Ger	Decision, 5-0
1952	Floyd Patterson, USA	KO, 1st	1992	Ariel Hernandez, CUB	Decision, 12-7
1956	Gennady Schatkov, USSR	KO, 1st			

Light Heavyweight (178 lbs)

Year		Final Match	Year		Final Match
1920	Eddie Eagan, USA	Decision	1964	Cosimo Pinto, ITA	Decision, 3-2
1924	Harry Mitchell, GBR	Decision	1968	Dan Poznjak, USSR	Default
1928	Victor Avendaño, ARG	Decision	1972	Mate Parlov, YUG	Stopped, 2nd
1932	David Carstens, SAF	Decision	1976	Leon Spinks, USA	Stopped, 3rd
1936	Roger Michelot, FRA	Decision	1980	Slobodan Kacar, YUG	Decision, 4-1
1948	George Hunter, SAF	Decision	1984	Anton Josipovic, YUG	Default
1952	Norvel Lee, USA	Decision, 3-0	1988	Andrew Maynard, USA	Decision, 5-0
1956	Jim Boyd, USA	Decision	1992	Torsten May, GER	Decision, 8-3
1960	Cassius Clay, USA	Decision, 5-0			

Note: Cassius Clay changed his name to Muhammad Ali after winning the world heavyweight championship in 1964.

Heavyweight (201 lbs)

Year		Final Match	Year		Final Match
1984	Henry Tillman, USA	Decision, 5-0	1992	Felix Savon, CUB	Decision, 14-1
1988	Ray Mercer, USA	KO, 1st			

Super Heavyweight (Unlimited)

Year		Final Match	Year		Final Match
1904	Samuel Berger, USA	Decision	1960	Franco De Piccoli, ITA	KO, 1st
1908	Albert Oldham, GBR	KO, 1st	1964	Joe Frazier, USA	Decision, 3-2
1920	Ronald Rawson, GBR	Decision	1968	George Foreman, USA	Stopped, 2nd
1924	Otto von Porat, NOR	Decision	1972	Teófilo Stevenson, CUB	Default
1928	Arturo Rodriguez Jurado, ARG	Stopped, 1st	1976	Teófilo Stevenson, CUB	KO, 3rd
1932	Santiago Lovell, ARG	Decision	1980	Teófilo Stevenson, CUB	Decision, 4-1
1936	Herbert Runge, GER	Decision	1984	Tyrell Biggs, USA	Decision, 4-1
1948	Rafael Iglesias, ARG	KO, 2nd	1988	Lennox Lewis, CAN	Stopped, 2nd
1952	Ed Sanders, USA	Won on Disq.*	1992	Roberto Balado, CUB	Decision, 13-2
1956	Pete Rademacher, USA	Stopped, 1st			

* Sanders' opponent, Ingemar Johansson was disqualified in 2nd round for not trying.

Future World Heavyweight Champions
Seven Olympic gold medal winners eventually went on to win the heavyweight championship of the world.

Middleweights	Light Heavyweights	Heavyweights	Super Heavyweight
Floyd Patterson	Cassius Clay	Joe Frazier	Lennox Lewis
Michael Spinks	Leon Spinks	George Foreman	

DIVING

MEN

Multiple gold medals: Greg Louganis (4); Klaus Dibiasi (3); Pete Desjardins, Sammy Lee, Bob Webster and Albert White (2).

Springboard

Year		Points	Year		Points
1908	Albert Zürner, GER	85.5	1960	Gary Tobian, USA	170.00
1912	Paul Günther, GER	79.23	1964	Ken Sitzberger, USA	159.90
1920	Louis Kuehn, USA	675.4	1968	Bernie Wrightson, USA	170.15
1924	Albert White, USA	696.4	1972	Vladimir Vasin, USSR	594.09
1928	Pete Desjardins, USA	185.04	1976	Phil Boggs, USA	619.05
1932	Michael Galitzen, USA	161.38	1980	Aleksandr Portnov, USSR	905.03
1936	Richard Degener, USA	163.57	1984	Greg Louganis, USA	754.41
1948	Bruce Harlan, USA	163.64	1988	Greg Louganis, USA	730.80
1952	David Browning, USA	205.29	1992	Mark Lenzi, USA	676.53
1956	Bob Clotworthy, USA	159.56			

Platform

Year		Points	Year		Points
1904	George Sheldon, USA	12.66	1956	Joaquin Capilla, MEX	152.44
1906	Gottlob Walz, GER	156.0	1960	Bob Webster, USA	165.56
1908	Hjalmar Johansson, SWE	83.75	1964	Bob Webster, USA	148.58
1912	Erik Adlerz, SWE	73.94	1968	Klaus Dibiasi, ITA	164.18
1920	Clarence Pinkston, USA	100.67	1972	Klaus Dibiasi, ITA	504.12
1924	Albert White, USA	97.46	1976	Klaus Dibiasi, ITA	600.51
1928	Pete Desjardins, USA	98.74	1980	Falk Hoffmann, E. Ger	835.65
1932	Harold Smith, USA	124.80	1984	Greg Louganis, USA	710.91
1936	Marshall Wayne, USA	113.58	1988	Greg Louganis, USA	638.61
1948	Sammy Lee, USA	130.05	1992	Sun Shuwei, CHN	677.31
1952	Sammy Lee, USA	156.28			

WOMEN

Multiple gold medals: Pat McCormick (4); Ingrid Engel-Krämer (3); Vicki Draves, Dorothy Poynton Hill and Gao Min (2).

Springboard

Year		Points	Year		Points
1920	Aileen Riggin, USA	539.9	1964	Ingrid Engel-Krämer, GER	145.00
1924	Elizabeth Becker, USA	474.5	1968	Sue Gossick, USA	150.77
1928	Helen Meany, USA	78.62	1972	Micki King, USA	450.03
1932	Georgia Coleman, USA	87.52	1976	Jennifer Chandler, USA	506.19
1936	Marjorie Gestring, USA	89.27	1980	Irina Kalinina, USSR	725.91
1948	Vicki Draves, USA	108.74	1984	Sylvie Bernier, CAN	530.70
1952	Pat McCormick, USA	147.30	1988	Gao Min, CHN	580.23
1956	Pat McCormick, USA	142.36	1992	Gao Min, CHN	572.40
1960	Ingrid Krämer, GER	155.81			

Platform

Year		Points	Year		Points
1912	Greta Johansson, SWE	39.9	1960	Ingrid Krämer, GER	91.28
1920	Stefani Fryland-Clausen, DEN	34.6	1964	Lesley Bush, USA	99.80
1924	Caroline Smith, USA	33.2	1968	Milena Duchková, CZE	109.59
1928	Elizabeth Becker Pinkston, USA	31.6	1972	Ulrika Knape, SWE	390.00
1932	Dorothy Poynton, USA	40.26	1976	Elena Vaytsekhovskaya, USSR	406.59
1936	Dorothy Poynton Hill, USA	33.93	1980	Martina Jäschke, E. Ger	596.25
1948	Vicki Draves, USA	68.87	1984	Zhou Jihong, CHN	435.51
1952	Pat McCormick, USA	79.37	1988	Xu Yanmei, CHN	445.20
1956	Pat McCormick, USA	84.85	1992	Fu Mingxia, CHN	461.43

FIELD HOCKEY

MEN

Multiple gold medals: India (8); Great Britain and Pakistan (3); West Germany/Germany (2).

Year		Year	
1908	**Great Britain**, Ireland, Scotland	1964	**India**, Pakistan, Australia
1920	**Great Britain**, Denmark, Belgium	1968	**Pakistan**, Australia, India
1928	**India**, Holland, Germany	1972	**West Germany**, Pakistan, India
1932	**India**, Japan, United States	1976	**New Zealand**, Australia, Pakistan
1936	**India**, Germany, Holland	1980	**India**, Spain, Soviet Union
1948	**India**, Great Britain, Holland	1984	**Pakistan**, West Germany, Great Britain
1952	**India**, Holland, Great Britain	1988	**Great Britain**, West Germany, Holland
1956	**India**, Pakistan, Germany	1992	**Germany**, Australia, Pakistan
1960	**Pakistan**, India, Spain		

Field Hockey (Cont.)
WOMEN

Year		Year	
1980	**Zimbabwe**, Czechoslovakia, Soviet Union	1988	**Australia**, South Korea, Holland
1984	**Holland**, West Germany, United States	1992	**Spain**, Germany, Great Britain

GYMNASTICS

MEN

At least 4 gold medals (including team events): Sawao Kato (8); Nikolai Andrianov, Viktor Chukarin and Boris Shakhlin (7); Akinori Nakayama and Vitaly Scherbo (6); Yukio Endo, Anton Heida, Mitsuo Tsukahara and Takashi Ono (5); Vladimir Artemov, Georges Miez and Valentin Muratov (4).

All-Around

Year		Points	Year		Points
1900	Gustave Sandras, FRA	302.0	1952	Viktor Chukarin, USSR	115.7
1904	Julius Lenhart, AUT	69.80	1956	Viktor Chukarin, USSR	114.25
1906	Pierre Payssé, FRA	97.0	1960	Boris Shakhlin, USSR	115.95
1908	Alberto Braglia, ITA	317.0	1964	Yukio Endo, JPN	115.95
1912	Alberto Braglia, ITA	135.0	1968	Sawao Kato, JPN	115.9
1920	Giorgio Zampori, ITA	88.35	1972	Sawao Kato, JPN	114.650
1924	Leon Stukelj, YUG	110.340	1976	Nikolai Andrianov, USSR	116.65
1928	Georges Miez, SWI	247.500	1980	Aleksandr Dityatin, USSR	118.65
1932	Romeo Neri, ITA	140.625	1984	Koji Gushiken, JPN	118.7
1936	Alfred Schwarzmann, GER	113.100	1988	Vladimir Artemov, USSR	119.125
1948	Veikko Huhtanen, FIN	229.7	1992	Vitaly Scherbo, UT	59.025

Horizontal Bar

Year		Points	Year		Points
1896	Hermann Weingartner, GER	—	1964	Boris Shakhlin, USSR	19.625
1904	(TIE) Anton Heida, USA	40.0	1968	(TIE) Akinori Nakayama, JPN	19.55
	& Edward Hennig, USA	40.0		& Mikhail Voronin, USSR	19.55
1924	Leon Stukelj, YUG	19.73	1972	Mitsuo Tsukahara, JPN	19.725
1928	Georges Miez, SWI	19.17	1976	Mitsuo Tsukahara, JPN	19.675
1932	Dallas Bixler, USA	18.33	1980	Stoyan Deltchev, BUL	19.825
1936	Aleksanteri Saarvala, FIN	19.367	1984	Shinji Morisue, JPN	20.00
1948	Josef Stalder, SWI	19.85	1988	(TIE) Vladimir Artemov, USSR	19.900
1952	Jack Günthard, SWI	19.55		& Valeri Lyukin, USSR	19.900
1956	Takashi Ono, JPN	19.60	1992	Trent Dimas, USA	9.875
1960	Takashi Ono, JPN	19.60			

Parallel Bars

Year		Points	Year		Points
1896	Alfred Flatow, GER	—	1960	Boris Shakhlin, USSR	19.40
1904	George Eyser, USA	44.0	1964	Yukio Endo, JPN	19.675
1924	August Güttinger, SWI	21.63	1968	Akinori Nakayama, JPN	19.475
1928	Ladislav Vácha, CZE	18.83	1972	Sawao Kato, JPN	19.475
1932	Romeo Neri, ITA	18.97	1976	Sawao Kato, JPN	19.675
1936	Konrad Frey, GER	19.067	1980	Aleksandr Tkachyov, USSR	19.775
1948	Michael Reusch, SWI	19.75	1984	Bart Conner, USA	19.95
1952	Hans Eugster, SWI	19.65	1988	Vladimir Artemov, USSR	19.925
1956	Viktor Chukarin, USSR	19.20	1992	Vitaly Scherbo, UT	9.900

Vault

Year		Points	Year		Points
1896	Karl Schumann, GER	—	1960	(TIE) Takashi Ono, JPN	19.35
1904	(TIE) George Eyser, USA	36.0		& Boris Shakhlin, USSR	19.35
	& Anton Heida, USA	36.0	1964	Haruhiro Yamashita, JPN	19.60
1924	Frank Kriz, USA	9.98	1968	Mikhail Voronin, USSR	19.00
1928	Eugen Mack, SWI	9.58	1972	Klaus Köste, E. Ger	18.85
1932	Savino Guglielmetti, ITA	18.03	1976	Nikolai Andrianov, USSR	19.45
1936	Alfred Schwarzmann, GER	19.20	1980	Nikolai Andrianov, USSR	19.825
1948	Paavo Aaltonen, FIN	19.55	1984	Lou Yun, CHN	19.95
1952	Viktor Chukarin, USSR	19.20	1988	Lou Yun, CHN	19.875
1956	(TIE) Helmut Bantz, GER	18.85	1992	Vitaly Scherbo, UT	9.856
	& Valentin Muratov, USSR	18.85			

Pommel Horse

Year		Points	Year		Points
1896	Louis Zutter, SWI	—	1964	Miroslav Cerar, YUG	19.525
1904	Anton Heida, USA	.42	1968	Miroslav Cerar, YUG	19.325
1924	Josef Wilhelm, SWI	21.23	1972	Viktor Klimenko, SOV	19.125
1928	Hermann Hänggi, SWI	19.75	1976	Zoltán Magyar, HUN	19.70
1932	István Pelle, HUN	19.07	1980	Zoltán Magyar, HUN	19.925
1936	Konrad Frey, GER	19.333	1984	(TIE) Li Ning, CHN	19.95
1948	(TIE) Paavo Aaltonen, FIN	19.35		& Peter Vidmar, USA	19.95
	Veikko Huhtanen, FIN	19.35	1988	(TIE) Dmitri Bilozerchev, USSR	19.95
	& Heikki Savolainen, FIN	19.35		Zsolt Borkai, HUN	19.95
1952	Viktor Chukarin, USSR	19.50		& Lyubomir Geraskov, BUL	19.95
1956	Boris Shakhlin, USSR	19.25	1992	(TIE) Pae Gil-Su, N. Kor	9.925
1960	(TIE) Eugen Ekman, FIN	19.375		& Vitaly Scherbo, UT	9.925
	& Boris Shakhlin, USSR	19.375			

Rings

Year		Points	Year		Points
1896	Ioannis Mitropoulos, GRE	—	1968	Akinori Nakayama, JPN	19.45
1904	Hermann Glass, USA	.45	1972	Akinori Nakayama, JPN	19.35
1924	Francesco Martino, ITA	21.553	1976	Nikolai Andrianov, USSR	19.65
1928	Leon Stukelj, YUG	19.25	1980	Aleksandr Dityatin, USSR	19.875
1932	George Gulack, USA	18.97	1984	(TIE) Koji Gushiken, JPN	19.85
1936	Alois Hudec, CZE	19.433		& Li Ning, CHN	19.85
1948	Karl Frei, SWI	19.80	1988	(TIE) Holger Behrendt, E. Ger	19.925
1952	Grant Shaginyan, USSR	19.75		& Dmitri Bilozerchev, USSR	19.925
1956	Albert Azaryan, USSR	19.35	1992	Vitaly Scherbo, UT	9.937
1960	Albert Azaryan, USSR	19.725			
1964	Takuji Haytta, JPN	19.475			

Floor Exercise

Year		Points	Year		Points
1932	Istvän Pelle, HUN	9.60	1968	Sawao Kato, JPN	19.475
1936	Georges Miez, SWI	18.666	1972	Nikolai Andrianov, USSR	19.175
1948	Ferenc Pataki, HUN	19.35	1976	Nikolai Andrianov, USSR	19.45
1952	William Thoresson, SWE	19.25	1980	Roland Brückner, E. Ger	19.75
1956	Valentin Muratov, USSR	19.20	1984	Li Ning, CHN	19.925
1960	Nobuyuki Aihara, JPN	19.45	1988	Sergei Kharkov, USSR	19.925
1964	Franco Menichelli, ITA	19.45	1992	Li Xiaosahuang, CHN	9.925

Team Combined Exercises

Year		Points	Year		Points
1904	United States	374.43	1956	Soviet Union	568.25
1906	Norway	19.00	1960	Japan	575.20
1908	Sweden	438	1964	Japan	577.95
1912	Italy	265.75	1968	Japan	575.90
1920	Italy	359.855	1972	Japan	571.25
1924	Italy	839.058	1976	Japan	576.85
1928	Switzerland	1718.625	1980	Soviet Union	598.60
1932	Italy	541.850	1984	United States	591.40
1936	Germany	657.430	1988	Soviet Union	593.35
1948	Finland	1358.30	1992	Unified Team	585.45
1952	Soviet Union	574.40			

WOMEN

At least 4 gold medals (including team events): Larissa Latynina (9); Vera Cáslavská (7); Polina Astakhova, Nadia Comaneci, Agnes Keleti and Nelli Kim (5); Olga Korbut, Ecaterina Szabó and Lyudmila Tourischeva (4).

All-Around

Year		Points	Year		Points
1952	Maria Gorokhovskaya, USSR	76.78	1976	Nadia Comaneci, ROM	79.275
1956	Larissa Latynina, USSR	74.933	1980	Yelena Davydova, USSR	79.15
1960	Larissa Latynina, USSR	77.031	1984	Mary Lou Retton, USA	79.175
1964	Vera Cáslavská, CZE	77.564	1988	Yelena Shushunova, USSR	79.662
1968	Vera Cáslavská, CZE	78.25	1992	Tatiana Gutsu, UT	39.737
1972	Lyudmila Tourischeva, USSR	77.025			

Vault

Year		Points	Year		Points
1952	Yekaterina Kalinchuk, USSR	19.20	1976	Nelli Kim, USSR	19.80
1956	Larissa Latynina, USSR	18.833	1980	Natalia Shaposhnikova, USSR	19.725
1960	Margarita Nikolayeva, USSR	19.316	1984	Ecaterina Szabó, ROM	19.875
1964	Vera Cáslavská, CZE	19.483	1988	Svetlana Boginskaya, USSR	19.905
1968	Vera Cáslavská, CZE	19.775	1992	(TIE) Henrietta Onodi, HUN	9.925
1972	Karin Janz, E. Ger	19.525		& Lavinia Milosovici, ROM	9.925

Gymnastics (Cont.)
WOMEN
Uneven Bars

Year		Points	Year		Points
1952	Margit Korondi, HUN	19.40	1976	Nadia Comaneci, ROM	20.00
1956	Agnes Keleti, HUN	18.966	1980	Maxi Gnauck, E. Ger	19.875
1960	Polina Astakhova, USSR	19.616	1984	(TIE) Julianne McNamora, USA	19.95
1964	Polina Astakhova, USSR	19.332		& Ma Yanhong, CHN	19.95
1968	Vera Cáslavská, CZE	19.65	1988	Daniela Silivas, ROM	20.00
1972	Karin Janz, E. Ger	19.675	1992	Lu Li, CHN	10.00

Balance Beam

Year		Points	Year		Points
1952	Nina Bocharova, USSR	19.22	1976	Nadia Comaneci, ROM	19.95
1956	Agnes Keleti, HUN	18.80	1980	Nadia Comaneci, ROM	19.80
1960	Eva Bosáková, CZE	19.283	1984	(TIE) Simona Pauca, ROM	19.80
1964	Vera Cáslavská, CZE	19.449		& Ecaterina Szabó, ROM	19.80
1968	Natalya Kuchinskaya, USSR	19.65	1988	Daniela Silivas, ROM	19.924
1972	Olga Korbut, USSR	19.40	1992	Tatiana Lyssenko, UT	9.975

Floor Exercise

Year		Points	Year		Points
1952	Agnes Keleti, HUN	19.36	1972	Olga Korbut, USSR	19.575
1956	(TIE) Agnes Keleti, HUN	18.733	1976	Nelli Kim, USSR	19.85
	& Larissa Latynina, USSR	18.733	1980	(TIE) Nadia Comaneci, ROM	19.875
1960	Larissa Latynina, USSR	19.583		& Nelli Kim, USSR	19.875
1964	Larissa Latynina, USSR	19.599	1984	Ecaterina Szabó, ROM	19.975
1968	(TIE) Vera Cáslavská, CZE	19.675	1988	Daniela Silivas, ROM	19.937
	& Larissa Petrik, USSR	19.675	1992	Lavinia Milosovici, ROM	10.000

Team Combined Exercises

Year		Points	Year		Points
1928	Holland	316.75	1968	Soviet Union	382.85
1936	Germany	506.50	1972	Soviet Union	380.50
1948	Czechoslovakia	445.45	1976	Soviet Union	466.00
1952	Soviet Union	527.03	1980	Soviet Union	394.90
1956	Soviet Union	444.800	1984	Romania	392.02
1960	Soviet Union	382.320	1988	Soviet Union	395.475
1964	Soviet Union	280.890	1992	Unified Team	395.666

SOCCER

Multiple gold medals: Great Britain and Hungary (3); Uruguay and USSR (2).

Year		Year	
1900	**Great Britain**, France, Belgium	1956	**Soviet Union**, Yugoslavia, Bulgaria
1904	**Canada**, USA I, USA II	1960	**Yugoslavia**, Denmark, Hungary
1906	**Denmark**, Smyrna (Int'l entry), Greece	1964	**Hungary**, Czechoslovakia, Germany
1908	**Great Britain**, Denmark, Holland	1968	**Hungary**, Bulgaria, Japan
1912	**Great Britain**, Denmark, Holland	1972	**Poland**, Hungary, East Germany & Soviet Union
1920	**Belgium**, Spain, Holland	1976	**East Germany**, Poland, Soviet Union
1924	**Uruguay**, Switzerland, Sweden	1980	**Czechoslovakia**, East Germany, Soviet Union
1928	**Uruguay**, Argentina, Italy	1984	**France**, Brazil, Yugoslavia
1936	**Italy**, Austria, Norway	1988	**Soviet Union**, Brazil, West Germany
1948	**Sweden**, Yugoslavia, Denmark	1992	**Spain**, Poland, Ghana
1952	**Hungary**, Yugoslavia, Sweden		

SWIMMING

World and Olympic records below that appear to be broken or equalled by winning times in subsequent years, but are not so indicated, were all broken in preliminary heats leading up to the finals. Some events were not held at every Olympics.

MEN

At least 4 gold medals (including relays): Mark Spitz (9); Matt Biondi (8); Charles Daniels, Tom Jager, Don Schollander, and Johnny Weissmuller (5); Tamás Darnyi, Roland Matthes, John Naber, Murray Rose, Vladimir Salnikov and Henry Taylor (4).

50-meter Freestyle

Year		Time		Year		Time	
1904	Zoltán Halmay, HUN (50 yds)	28.0		1988	Matt Biondi, USA	22.14	**WR**
1906-84 Not held				1992	Aleksandr Popov, UT	21.91	**OR**

100-meter Freestyle

Year		Time		Year		Time	
1896	Alfréd Hajós, HUN	1:22.2		1952	Clarke Scholes, USA	57.4	
1904	Zoltán Halmay, HUN (100 yds)	1:02.8		1956	Jon Henricks, AUS	55.4	OR
1906	Charles Daniels, USA	1:13.4		1960	John Devitt, AUS	55.2	OR
1908	Charles Daniels, USA	1:05.6	WR	1964	Don Schollander, USA	53.4	OR
1912	Duke Kahanamoku, USA	1:03.4		1968	Michael Wenden, AUS	52.2	WR
1920	Duke Kahanamoku, USA	1:00.4	WR	1972	Mark Spitz, USA	51.22	WR
1924	Johnny Weissmuller, USA	59.0	OR	1976	Jim Montgomery, USA	49.99	WR
1928	Johnny Weissmuller, USA	58.6	OR	1980	Jorg Woithe, E. Ger	50.40	
1932	Yasuji Miyazaki, JPN	58.2		1984	Rowdy Gaines, USA	49.80	OR
1936	Ferenc Csik, HUN	57.6		1988	Matt Biondi, USA	48.63	OR
1948	Wally Ris, USA	57.3	OR	1992	Aleksandr Popov, UT	49.02	

200-meter Freestyle

Year		Time		Year		Time	
1900	Frederick Lane, AUS (220 yds)	2:25.2	OR	1980	Sergei Kopliakov, USSR	1:49.81	OR
1904	Charles Daniels, USA (220 yds)	2:44.2		1984	Michael Gross, W. Ger	1:47.44	WR
1968	Michael Wenden, AUS	1:55.2	OR	1988	Duncan Armstrong, AUS	1:47.25	OR
1972	Mark Spitz, USA	1:52.78	WR	1992	Yevgeny Sadovyi, UT	1:46.70	OR
1976	Bruce Furniss, USA	1:50.29	WR				

400-meter Freestyle

Year		Time		Year		Time	
1896	Paul Neumann, AUT (550m)	8:12.6		1952	Jean Boiteux, FRA	4:30.7	OR
1904	Charles Daniels, USA (440 yds)	6:16.2		1956	Murray Rose, AUS	4:27.3	OR
1906	Otto Scheff, AUT	6:23.8		1960	Murray Rose, AUS	4:18.3	OR
1908	Henry Taylor, GBR	5:36.8		1964	Don Schollander, USA	4:12.2	WR
1912	George Hodgson, CAN	5:24.4		1968	Mike Burton, USA	4:09.0	OR
1920	Norman Ross, USA	5:26.8		1972	Bradford Cooper, AUS*	4:00.27	OR
1924	Johnny Weissmuller, USA	5:04.2		1976	Brian Goodell, USA	3:51.93	WR
1928	Alberto Zorilla, ARG	5:01.6	OR	1980	Vladimir Salnikov, USSR	3:51.31	OR
1932	Buster Crabbe, USA	4:48.4	OR	1984	George DiCarlo, USA	3:51.23	OR
1936	Jack Medica, USA	4:44.5	OR	1988	Uwe Dassler, E. Ger	3:46.95	WR
1948	Bill Smith, USA	4:41.0	OR	1992	Yevgeny Sadovyi, UT	3:45.00	WR

*Australian Cooper finished second to Rick DeMont of the U.S., who was disqualified when he flunked the post-race drug test (his asthma medication was on the IOC's banned list).

1500-meter Freestyle

Year		Time		Year		Time	
1896	Alfréd Hajós, HUN (1200m)	18:22.2	OR	1952	Ford Konno, USA	18:30.3	OR
1900	John Arthur Jarvis, GBR (1000m)	13:40.2		1956	Murray Rose, AUS	17:58.9	
1904	Emil Rausch, GER (1 mile)	27:18.2		1960	Jon Konrads, AUS	17:19.6	OR
1906	Henry Taylor, GBR (1 mile)	28:28.0		1964	Robert Windle, AUS	17:01.7	OR
1908	Henry Taylor, GBR	22:48.4	WR	1968	Mike Burton, USA	16:38.9	OR
1912	George Hodgson, CAN	22:00.0	WR	1972	Mike Burton, USA	15:52.58	WR
1920	Norman Ross, USA	22:23.2		1976	Brian Goodell, USA	15:02.40	WR
1924	Andrew (Boy) Charlton, AUS	20:06.6	WR	1980	Vladimir Salnikov, USSR	14:58.27	WR
1928	Arne Borge, SWE	19:51.8	OR	1984	Mike O'Brien, USA	15:05.20	
1932	Kusuo Kitamura, JPN	19:12.4	OR	1988	Vladimir Salnikov, USSR	15:00.40	
1936	Noboru Terada, JPN	19:13.7		1992	Kieren Perkins, AUS	14:43.48	WR
1948	James McLane, USA	19:18.5					

100-meter Backstroke

Year		Time		Year		Time	
1904	Walter Brack, GER (100 yds)	1:16.8		1956	David Theile, AUS	1:02.2	OR
1908	Arno Bieberstein, GER	1:24.6	WR	1960	David Theile, AUS	1:01.9	OR
1912	Harry Hebner, USA	1:21.2		1968	Roland Matthes, E. Ger	58.7	OR
1920	Warren Kealoha, USA	1:15.2		1972	Roland Matthes, E. Ger	56.58	OR
1924	Warren Kealoha, USA	1:13.2	OR	1976	John Naber, USA	55.49	WR
1928	George Kojac, USA	1:08.2	WR	1980	Bengt Baron, SWE	56.33	
1932	Masaji Kiyokawa, JPN	1:08.6		1984	Rick Carey, USA	55.79	
1936	Adolf Kiefer, USA	1:05.9	OR	1988	Daichi Suzuki, JPN	55.05	
1948	Allen Stack, USA	1:06.4		1992	Mark Tewksbury, CAN	53.98	OR
1952	Yoshinobu Oyakawa, USA	1:05.4	OR				

200-meter Backstroke

Year		Time		Year		Time	
1900	Ernst Hoppenberg, GER	2:47.0		1980	Sándor Wladár, HUN	2:01.93	
1964	Jed Graef, USA	2:10.3	WR	1984	Rick Carey, USA	2:00.23	
1968	Roland Matthes, E. Ger	2:09.6	OR	1988	Igor Poliansky, USSR	1:59.37	
1972	Roland Matthes, E. Ger	2:02.82	=WR	1992	Martin Lopez-Zubero, SPA	1:58.47	OR
1976	John Naber, USA	1:59.19	WR				

Swimming (Cont.)
MEN
100-meter Breaststroke

Year		Time		Year		Time	
1968	Don McKenzie, USA	1:07.7	OR	1984	Steve Lundquist, USA	1:01.65	WR
1972	Nobutaka Taguchi, JPN	1:04.94	WR	1988	Adrian Moorhouse, GBR	1:02.04	
1976	John Hencken, USA	1:03.11	WR	1992	Nelson Diebel, USA	1:01.50	OR
1980	Duncan Goodhew, GBR	1:03.44					

200-meter Breaststroke

Year		Time		Year		Time	
1908	Frederick Holman, GBR	3:09.2	WR	1960	Bill Mulliken, USA	2:37.4	
1912	Walter Bathe, GER	3:01.8	OR	1964	Ian O'Brien, AUS	2:27.8	WR
1920	Hakan Malmroth, SWE	3:04.4		1968	Felipe Múñoz, MEX	2:28.7	
1924	Robert Skelton, USA	2:56.6		1972	John Hencken, USA	2:21.55	WR
1928	Yoshiyuki Tsuruta, JPN	2:48.8	OR	1976	David Wilkie, GBR	2:15.11	WR
1932	Yoshiyuki Tsuruta, JPN	2:45.4		1980	Robertas Zhulpa, USSR	2:15.85	
1936	Tetsuo Hamuro, JPN	2:41.5	OR	1984	Victor Davis, CAN	2:13.34	WR
1948	Joseph Verdeur, USA	2:39.3	OR	1988	József Szabó, HUN	2:13.52	
1952	John Davies, AUS	2:34.4	OR	1992	Mike Barrowman, USA	2:10.16	WR
1956	Masaru Furukawa, JPN	2:34.7*	OR				

*In 1956, the butterfly stroke and breaststroke were separated into two different events.

100-meter Butterfly

Year		Time		Year		Time	
1968	Doug Russell, USA	55.9	OR	1984	Michael Gross, W. Ger	53.08	WR
1972	Mark Spitz, USA	54.27	WR	1988	Anthony Nesty, SUR	53.0	OR
1976	Matt Vogel, USA	54.35		1992	Pablo Morales, USA	53.32	
1980	Pär Arvidsson, SWE	54.92					

200-meter Butterfly

Year		Time		Year		Time	
1956	Bill Yorzyk, USA	2:19.3	OR	1976	Mike Bruner, USA	1:59.23	WR
1960	Mike Troy, USA	2:12.8	WR	1980	Sergei Fesenko, USSR	1:59.76	
1964	Kevin Berry, AUS	2:06.6	WR	1984	Jon Sieben, AUS	1:57.04	WR
1968	Carl Robie, USA	2:08.7		1988	Michael Gross, W. Ger	1:56.94	OR
1972	Mark Spitz, USA	2:00.70	WR	1992	Melvin Stewart, USA	1:56.26	OR

200-meter Individual Medley

Year		Time		Year		Time	
1968	Charles Hickcox, USA	2:12.0	OR	1988	Tamás Darnyi, HUN	2:00.17	WR
1972	Gunnar Larsson, SWE	2:07.17	WR	1992	Tamás Darnyi, HUN	2:00.76	
1984	Alex Baumann, CAN	2:01.42	WR				

400-meter Individual Medley

Year		Time		Year		Time	
1964	Richard Roth, USA	4:45.4	WR	1980	Aleksandr Sidorenko, USSR	4:22.89	OR
1968	Charles Hickcox, USA	4:48.4		1984	Alex Baumann, CAN	4:17.41	WR
1972	Gunnar Larsson, SWE	4:31.98	OR	1988	Tamás Darnyi, HUN	4:14.75	WR
1976	Rod Strachan, USA	4:23.68	WR	1992	Tamás Darnyi, HUN	4:14.23	OR

4x100-meter Freestyle Relay

Year		Time		Year		Time	
1964	United States	3:32.2	WR	1984	United States	3:19.03	WR
1968	United States	3:31.7	WR	1988	United States	3:16.53	WR
1972	United States	3:26.42	WR	1992	United States	3:16.74	
1976-80	Not held						

4x200-meter Freestyle Relay

Year		Time		Year		Time	
1906	Hungary (x250m)	16:52.4		1956	Australia	8:23.6	WR
1908	Great Britain	10:55.6	WR	1960	United States	8:10.2	WR
1912	Australia/New Zealand	10:11.6	WR	1964	United States	7:52.1	WR
1920	United States	10:04.4	WR	1968	United States	7:52.33	
1924	United States	9:53.4	WR	1972	United States	7:35.78	WR
1928	United States	9:36.2	WR	1976	United States	7:23.22	WR
1932	Japan	8:58.4	WR	1980	Soviet Union	7:23.50	
1936	Japan	8:51.5	WR	1984	United States	7:15.69	WR
1948	United States	8:46.0	WR	1988	United States	7:12.51	WR
1952	United States	8:31.1	OR	1992	Unified Team	7:11.95	WR

4x100-meter Medley Relay

Year		Time		Year		Time	
1960	United States	4:05.4	WR	1980	Australia	3:45.70	
1964	United States	3:58.4	WR	1984	United States	3:39.30	WR
1968	United States	3:54.9	WR	1988	United States	3:36.93	WR
1972	United States	3:48.16	WR	1992	United States	3:36.93	=WR
1976	United States	3:42.22	WR				

WOMEN

At least 4 gold medals (including relays): Kristin Otto (6); Krisztina Egerszegi, Kornelia Ender, Janet Evans and Dawn Fraser (4).

50-meter Freestyle

Year		Time		Year		Time	
1988	Kristin Otto, E. Ger	25.49	OR	1992	Yang Wenyi, CHN	24.79	WR

100-meter Freestyle

Year		Time		Year		Time	
1912	Fanny Durack, AUS	1:22.2		1964	Dawn Fraser, AUS	59.5	OR
1920	Ethelda Bleibtrey, USA	1:13.6	WR	1968	Jan Henne, USA	1:00.0	
1924	Ethel Lackie, USA	1:12.4		1972	Sandra Neilson, USA	58.59	OR
1928	Albina Osipowich, USA	1:11.0	OR	1976	Kornelia Ender, E. Ger	55.65	WR
1932	Helene Madison, USA	1:06.8	OR	1980	Barbara Krause, E. Ger	54.79	WR
1936	Rie Mastenbroek, HOL	1:05.9	OR	1984	(TIE) Nancy Hogshead, USA	55.92	
1948	Greta Andersen, DEN	1:06.3			& Carrie Steinseifer, USA	55.92	
1952	Katalin Szöke, HUN	1:06.8		1988	Kristin Otto, E. Ger	54.93	
1956	Dawn Fraser, AUS	1:02.0	WR	1992	Zhuang Yong, CHN	54.65	OR
1960	Dawn Fraser, AUS	1:01.2	OR				

200-meter Freestyle

Year		Time		Year		Time	
1968	Debbie Meyer, USA	2:10.5		1984	Mary Wayte, USA	1:59.23	
1972	Shane Gould, AUS	2:03.56	WR	1988	Heike Friedrich, E. Ger	1:57.65	OR
1976	Kornelia Ender, E. Ger	1:59.26	WR	1992	Nicole Haislett, USA	1:57.90	
1980	Barbara Krause, E. Ger	1:58.33	OR				

400-meter Freestyle

Year		Time		Year		Time	
1920	Ethelda Bleibtrey, USA (300m)	4:34.0	WR	1964	Ginny Duenkel, USA	4:43.3	OR
1924	Martha Norelius, USA	6:02.2	OR	1968	Debbie Meyer, USA	4:31.8	OR
1928	Martha Norelius, USA	5:42.8	WR	1972	Shane Gould, AUS	4:19.44	WR
1932	Helene Madison, USA	5:28.5	OR	1976	Petra Thümer, E. Ger	4:09.89	WR
1936	Rie Mastenbroek, HOL	5:26.4	OR	1980	Ines Diers, E. Ger	4:08.76	OR
1948	Ann Curtis, USA	5:17.8	OR	1984	Tiffany Cohen, USA	4:07.10	OR
1952	Valéria Gyenge, HUN	5:12.1	OR	1988	Janet Evans, USA	4:03.85	WR
1956	Lorraine Crapp, AUS	4:54.6	OR	1992	Dagmar Hase, GER	4:07.18	
1960	Chris von Saltza, USA	4:50.6	OR				

800-meter Freestyle

Year		Time		Year		Time	
1968	Debbie Meyer, USA	9:24.0	OR	1984	Tiffany Cohen, USA	8:24.95	OR
1972	Keena Rothhammer, USA	8:53.68	WR	1988	Janet Evans, USA	8:20.20	OR
1976	Petra Thümer, E. Ger	8:37.14	WR	1992	Janet Evans, USA	8:25.52	
1980	Michelle Ford, AUS	8:28.90	OR				

100-meter Backstroke

Year		Time		Year		Time	
1924	Sybil Bauer, USA	1:23.2	OR	1964	Cathy Ferguson, USA	1:07.7	WR
1928	Maria Braun, HOL	1:22.0		1968	Kaye Hall, USA	1:06.2	WR
1932	Eleanor Holm, USA	1:19.4		1972	Melissa Belote, USA	1:05.78	OR
1936	Dina Senff, HOL	1:18.9		1976	Ulrike Richter, E. Ger	1:01.83	OR
1948	Karen-Margrete Harup, DEN	1:14.4	OR	1980	Rica Reinisch, E. Ger	1:00.86	WR
1952	Joan Harrison, SAF	1:14.3		1984	Theresa Andrews, USA	1:02.55	
1956	Judy Grinham, GBR	1:12.9	OR	1988	Kristin Otto, E. Ger	1:00.89	
1960	Lynn Burke, USA	1:09.3	OR	1992	Krisztina Egerszegi, HUN	1:00.68	OR

200-meter Backstroke

Year		Time		Year		Time	
1968	Pokey Watson, USA	2:24.8	OR	1984	Jolanda de Rover, HOL	2:12.38	
1972	Melissa Belote, USA	2:19.19	WR	1988	Krisztina Egerszegi, HUN	2:09.29	OR
1976	Ulrike Richter, E. Ger	2:13.43	OR	1992	Krisztina Egerszegi, HUN	2:07.06	OR
1980	Rica Reinisch, E. Ger	2:11.77	WR				

Swimming (Cont.)
WOMEN
100-meter Breaststroke

Year		Time		Year		Time	
1968	Djurdjica Bjedov, YUG	1:15.8	OR	1984	Petra van Staveren, HOL	1:09.88	OR
1972	Cathy Carr, USA	1:13.58	WR	1988	Tania Dangalakova, BUL	1:07.95	OR
1976	Hannelore Anke, E. Ger	1:11.16		1992	Yelena Rudkovskaya, UT	1:08.00	
1980	Ute Geweniger, E. Ger	1:10.22					

200-meter Breaststroke

Year		Time		Year		Time	
1924	Lucy Morton, GBR	3:33.2	OR	1964	Galina Prozumenshikova, USSR	2:46.4	OR
1928	Hilde Schrader, GER	3:12.6		1968	Sharon Wichman, USA	2:44.4	OR
1932	Clare Dennis, AUS	3:06.3	OR	1972	Beverley Whitfield, AUS	2:41.71	OR
1936	Hideko Maehata, JPN	3:03.6		1976	Marina Koshevaya, USSR	2:33.35	WR
1948	Petronella van Vliet, HOL	2:57.2		1980	Lina Kaciusyte, USSR	2:29.54	OR
1952	Éva Székely, HUN	2:51.7	OR	1984	Anne Ottenbrite, CAN	2:30.38	
1956	Ursula Happe, GER	2:53.1	OR	1988	Silke Hörner, E. Ger	2:26.71	WR
1960	Anita Lonsbrough, GBR	2:49.5	WR	1992	Kyoko Iwasaki, JPN	2:26.65	OR

100-meter Butterfly

Year		Time		Year		Time	
1956	Shelly Mann, USA	1:11.0	OR	1976	Kornelia Ender, E. Ger	1:00.13	=WR
1960	Carolyn Schuler, USA	1:09.5	OR	1980	Caren Metschuck, E. Ger	1:00.42	
1964	Sharon Stouder, USA	1:04.7	WR	1984	Mary T. Meagher, USA	59.26	
1968	Lynn McClements, AUS	1:05.5		1988	Kristin Otto, E. Ger	59.00	OR
1972	Mayumi Aoki, JPN	1:03.34		1992	Qian Hong, CHN	58.62	OR

200-meter Butterfly

Year		Time		Year		Time	
1968	Ada Kok, HOL	2:24.7	OR	1984	Mary T. Meagher, USA	2:06.90	OR
1972	Karen Moe, USA	2:15.57	WR	1988	Kathleen Nord, E. Ger	2:09.51	
1976	Andrea Pollack, E. Ger	2:11.41	OR	1992	Summer Sanders, USA	2:08.67	
1980	Ines Geissler, E. Ger	2:10.44	OR				

200-meter Individual Medley

Year		Time		Year		Time	
1968	Claudia Kolb, USA	2:24.7	OR	1988	Daniela Hunger, E. Ger	2:12.59	OR
1972	Shane Gould, AUS	2:23.07	WR	1992	Lin Li, CHN	2:11.65	WR
1984	Tracy Caulkins, USA	2:12.64	OR				

400-meter Individual Medley

Year		Time		Year		Time	
1964	Donna de Varona, USA	5:18.7	OR	1980	Petra Schneider, E. Ger	4:36.29	WR
1968	Claudia Kolb, USA	5:08.5	OR	1984	Tracy Caulkins, USA	4:39.24	
1972	Gail Neall, AUS	5:02.97	WR	1988	Janet Evans, USA	4:37.76	
1976	Ulrike Tauber, E. Ger	4:42.77	WR	1992	Krisztina Egerszegi, HUN	4:36.54	

4x100-meter Freestyle Relay

Year		Time		Year		Time	
1912	Great Britain	5:52.8	WR	1960	United States	4:08.9	WR
1920	United States	5:11.6	WR	1964	United States	4:03.8	WR
1924	United States	4:58.8	WR	1968	United States	4:02.5	OR
1928	United States	4:47.6	WR	1972	United States	3:55.19	WR
1932	United States	4:38.0	WR	1976	United States	3:44.82	WR
1936	Holland	4:36.0	OR	1980	East Germany	3:42.71	WR
1948	United States	4:29.2	OR	1984	United States	3:43.43	
1952	Hungary	4:24.4	WR	1988	East Germany	3:40.63	OR
1956	Australia	4:17.1	WR	1992	United States	3:39.46	WR

4x100-meter Medley Relay

Year		Time		Year		Time	
1960	United States	4:41.1	WR	1980	East Germany	4:06.67	WR
1964	United States	4:33.9	WR	1984	United States	4:08.34	
1968	United States	4:28.3	OR	1988	East Germany	4:03.74	OR
1972	United States	4:20.75	WR	1992	United States	4:02.54	WR
1976	East Germany	4:07.95	WR				

TENNIS
MEN

Multiple gold medals (including doubles): John Boland, Max Decugis, Laurie Doherty, Reggie Doherty, Arthur Gore, André Grobert, Vincent Richards, Charles Winslow and Beals Wright (2).

Singles

Year			Year		
1896	John Boland	Great Britain/Ireland	1920	Louis Raymond	South Africa
1900	Laurie Doherty,	Great Britain	1924	Vincent Richards	United States
1904	Beals Wright	United States	1928-84	Not held	
1906	Max Decugis	France	1988	Miloslav Mecir	Czechoslovakia
1908	Josiah Ritchie	Great Britain	1992	Marc Rosset	Switzerland
	(Indoor) Arthur Gore	Great Britain			
1912	Charles Winslow	South Africa			
	(Indoor) André Gobert	France			

Doubles

Year		Year	
1896	John Boland, IRL & Fritz Traun, GER	1920	Noel Turnbull & Max Woosnam, GBR
1900	Laurie and Reggie Doherty, GBR	1924	Vincent Richards & Frank Hunter, USA
1904	Edgar Leonard & Beals Wright, USA	1928-84	Not held
1906	Max Decugis & Maurice Germot, FRA	1988	Ken Flach & Robert Seguso, USA
1908	George Hillyard & Reggie Doherty, GRB	1992	Boris Becker & Michael Stich, GER
	(Indoor) Arthur Gore & Herbert Barrett, GBR		
1912	Charles Winslow & Harold Kitson, SAF		
	(Indoor) André Gobert & Maurice Germot, FRA		

WOMEN

Multiple gold medals (including doubles): Helen Wills (2).

Singles

Year			Year		
1900	Charlotte Cooper	Great Britain	1920	Suzanne Lenglen	France
1906	Esmee Simiriotou	Greece	1924	Helen Wills	United States
1908	Dorothea Chambers	Great Britain	1928-84	Not held	
	(Indoor) Gwen Eastlake-Smith	Great Britain	1988	Steffi Graf	West Germany
1912	Marguerite Broquedis	France	1992	Jennifer Capriati	USA
	(Indoor) Edith Hannam	Great Britain			

Doubles

Year		Year	
1920	Winifred McNair & Kitty McKane, GBR	1988	Pam Shriver & Zina Garrison, USA
1924	Hazel Wightman & Helen Wills, USA	1992	Gigi Fernandez & Mary Joe Fernandez, USA
1928-84	Not held		

TRACK & FIELD

World and Olympic records below that appear to be broken or equalled by winning times, heights and distances in subsequent years, but are not so indicated, were all broken in preliminary races and field events leading up to the finals.

MEN

At least 4 gold medals (including relays and discontinued events): Ray Ewry (10); Paavo Nurmi (9); Carl Lewis (8); Ville Ritola and Martin Sheridan (5); Harrison Dillard, Archie Hahn, Hannes Kolehmainen, Alvin Kraenzlein, Eric Lemming, Jim Lightbody, Al Oerter, Jesse Owens, Meyer Prinstein, Mel Sheppard, Lasse Viren and Emil Zátopek (4). Note that all of Ewry's gold medals came before 1912, in the Standing High Jump, Standing Long Jump and Standing Triple Jump.

100 meters

Year		Time			Year		Time		
1896	Tom Burke, USA	12.0			1952	Lindy Remigino, USA	10.4		
1900	Frank Jarvis, USA	11.0			1956	Bobby Morrow, USA	10.5		
1904	Archie Hahn, USA	11.0			1960	Armin Hary, GER	10.2	OR	
1906	Archie Hahn, USA	11.2			1964	Bob Hayes, USA	10.0	=WR	
1908	Reggie Walker, SAF	10.8	=OR		1968	Jim Hines, USA	9.95	WR	
1912	Ralph Craig, USA	10.8			1972	Valery Borzov, USSR	10.14		
1920	Charley Paddock, USA	10.8			1976	Hasely Crawford, TRI	10.06		
1924	Harold Abrahams, GBR	10.6	=OR		1980	Allan Wells, GBR	10.25		
1928	Percy Williams, CAN	10.8			1984	Carl Lewis, USA	9.99		
1932	Eddie Tolan, USA	10.3	OR		1988	Carl Lewis, USA*	9.92	WR	
1936	Jesse Owens, USA	10.3[w]			1992	Linford Christie, GBR	9.96		
1948	Harrison Dillard, USA	10.3	=OR						

[w] indicates wind-aided.

*Lewis finished second to Ben Johnson of Canada, who set a world record of 9.79 seconds. A day later, Johnson was stripped of his gold medal and his record when he tested positive for steroid use in a post-race drug test.

Track & Field (Cont.)
MEN
200 meters

Year		Time		Year		Time	
1900	John Walter Tewksbury, USA	22.2		1956	Bobby Morrow, USA	20.6	OR
1904	Archie Hahn, USA	21.6	OR	1960	Livio Berruti, ITA	20.5	=WR
1908	Bobby Kerr, CAN	22.6		1964	Henry Carr, USA	20.3	OR
1912	Ralph Craig, USA	21.7		1968	Tommie Smith, USA	19.83	WR
1920	Allen Woodring, USA	22.0		1972	Valery Borzov, USSR	20.00	
1924	Jackson Scholz, USA	21.6		1976	Donald Quarrie, JAM	20.23	
1928	Percy Williams, CAN	21.8		1980	Pietro Mennea, ITA	20.19	
1932	Eddie Tolan, USA	21.2	OR	1984	Carl Lewis, USA	19.80	OR
1936	Jesse Owens, USA	20.7	OR	1988	Joe DeLoach, USA	19.75	OR
1948	Mel Patton, USA	21.1		1992	Mike Marsh, USA	20.01	
1952	Andy Stanfield, USA	20.7					

400 meters

Year		Time		Year		Time	
1896	Tom Burke, USA	54.2		1952	George Rhoden, JAM	45.9	OR
1900	Maxey Long, USA	49.4	OR	1956	Charley Jenkins, USA	46.7	
1904	Harry Hillman, USA	49.2	OR	1960	Otis Davis, USA	44.9	WR
1906	Paul Pilgrim, USA	53.2		1964	Mike Larrabee, USA	45.1	
1908	Wyndham Halswelle, GBR	50.0		1968	Lee Evans, USA	43.86	WR
1912	Charlie Reidpath, USA	48.2	OR	1972	Vince Matthews, USA	44.66	
1920	Bevil Rudd, SAF	49.6		1976	Alberto Juantorena, CUB	44.26	
1924	Eric Liddell, GBR	47.6	OR	1980	Viktor Markin, USSR	44.60	
1928	Ray Barbuti, USA	47.8		1984	Alonzo Babers, USA	44.27	
1932	Bill Carr, USA	46.2	WR	1988	Steve Lewis, USA	43.87	
1936	Archie Williams, USA	46.5		1992	Quincy Watts, USA	43.50	OR
1948	Arthur Wint, JAM	46.2					

800 meters

Year		Time		Year		Time	
1896	Teddy Flack, AUS	2:11.0		1952	Mal Whitfield, USA	1:49.2	=OR
1900	Alfred Tysoe, GBR	2:01.2		1956	Tom Courtney, USA	1:47.7	OR
1904	Jim Lightbody, USA	1:56.0	OR	1960	Peter Snell, NZE	1:46.3	OR
1906	Paul Pilgrim, USA	2:01.5		1964	Peter Snell, NZE	1:45.1	OR
1908	Mel Sheppard, USA	1:52.8	WR	1968	Ralph Doubell, AUS	1:44.3	=WR
1912	Ted Meredith, USA	1:51.9	WR	1972	Dave Wottle, USA	1:45.9	
1920	Albert Hill, GBR	1:53.4		1976	Alberto Juantorena, CUB	1:43.50	WR
1924	Douglas Lowe, GBR	1:52.4		1980	Steve Ovett, GBR	1:45.4	
1928	Douglas Lowe, GBR	1:51.8	OR	1984	Joaquim Cruz, BRA	1:43.00	OR
1932	Tommy Hampson, GBR	1:49.7	WR	1988	Paul Ereng, KEN	1:43.45	
1936	John Woodruff, USA	1:52.9		1992	William Tanui, KEN	1:43.66	
1948	Mal Whitfield, USA	1:49.2	OR				

1500 meters

Year		Time		Year		Time	
1896	Teddy Flack, AUS	4:33.2		1952	Josy Barthel, LUX	3:45.1	OR
1900	Charles Bennett, GBR	4:06.2	WR	1956	Ron Delany, IRL	3:41.2	OR
1904	Jim Lightbody, USA	4:05.4	WR	1960	Herb Elliott, AUS	3:35.6	WR
1906	Jim Lightbody, USA	4:12.0		1964	Peter Snell, NZE	3:38.1	
1908	Mel Sheppard, USA	4:03.4	OR	1968	Kip Keino, KEN	3:34.9	OR
1912	Arnold Jackson, GBR	3:56.8	OR	1972	Pekka Vasala, FIN	3:36.3	
1920	Albert Hill, GBR	4:01.8		1976	John Walker, NZE	3:39.17	
1924	Paavo Nurmi, FIN	3:53.6	OR	1980	Sebastian Coe, GBR	3:38.4	
1928	Harry Larva, FIN	3:53.2	OR	1984	Sebastian Coe, GBR	3:32.53	OR
1932	Luigi Beccali, ITA	3:51.2	OR	1988	Peter Rono, KEN	3:35.96	
1936	John Lovelock, NZE	3:47.8	WR	1992	Fermin Cacho, SPA	3:40.12	
1948	Henry Eriksson, SWE	3:49.8					

5000 meters

Year		Time		Year		Time	
1912	Hannes Kolehmainen, FIN	14:36.6	WR	1960	Murray Halberg, NZE	13:43.4	
1920	Joseph Guillemot, FRA	14:55.6		1964	Bob Schul, USA	13:48.8	
1924	Paavo Nurmi, FIN	14:31.2		1968	Mohamed Gammoudi, TUN	14:05.0	
1928	Ville Ritola, FIN	14:38.0		1972	Lasse Viren, FIN	13:26.4	OR
1932	Lauri Lehtinen, FIN	14:30.0	OR	1976	Lasse Viren, FIN	13:24.76	
1936	Gunnar Höckert, FIN	14:22.2	OR	1980	Miruts Yifter, ETH	13:21.0	
1948	Gaston Reiff, BEL	14:17.6	OR	1984	Said Aouita, MOR	13:05.59	OR
1952	Emil Zátopek, CZE	14:06.6	OR	1988	John Ngugi, KEN	13:11.70	
1956	Vladimir Kuts, USSR	13:39.6	OR	1992	Dieter Baumann, GER	13:12.52	

10,000 meters

Year		Time		Year		Time	
1912	Hannes Kolehmainen, FIN	31:20.8		1960	Pyotr Bolotnikov, USSR	28:32.2	OR
1920	Paavo Nurmi, FIN	31:45.8		1964	Billy Mills, USA	28:24.4	OR
1924	Ville Ritola, FIN	30:23.2	WR	1968	Naftali Temu, KEN	29:27.4	
1928	Paavo Nurmi, FIN	30:18.8	OR	1972	Lasse Viren, FIN	27:38.4	WR
1932	Janusz Kusocinski, POL	30:11.4	OR	1976	Lasse Viren, FIN	27:40.38	
1936	Ilmari Salminen, FIN	30:15.4		1980	Miruts Yifter, ETH	27:42.7	
1948	Emil Zátopek, CZE	29:59.6	OR	1984	Alberto Cova, ITA	27:47.54	
1952	Emil Zátopek, CZE	29:17.0	OR	1988	Brahim Boutaib, MOR	27:21.46	OR
1956	Vladimir Kuts, USSR	28:45.6	OR	1992	Khalid Skah, MOR	27:46.70	

Marathon

Year		Time		Year		Time	
1896	Spiridon Louis, GRE	2:58:50		1952	Emil Zátopek, CZE	2:23:03.2	OR
1900	Michel Théato, FRA	2:59:45		1956	Alain Mimoun, FRA	2:25:00.0	
1904	Thomas Hicks, USA	3:28:53		1960	Abebe Bikila, ETH	2:15:16.2	WB
1906	Billy Sherring, CAN	2:51:23.6		1964	Abebe Bikila, ETH	2:12:11.2	WB
1908	Johnny Hayes, USA*	2:55:18.4	OR	1968	Mamo Wolde, ETH	2:20:26.4	
1912	Kenneth McArthur, SAF	2:36:54.8		1972	Frank Shorter, USA	2:12:19.8	
1920	Hannes Kolehmainen, FIN	2:32:35.8	WB	1976	Waldemar Cierpinski, E. Ger	2:09:55.0	OR
1924	Albin Stenroos, FIN	2:41:22.6		1980	Waldemar Cierpinski, E. Ger	2:11:03.0	
1928	Boughèra El Ouafi, FRA	2:32:57.0		1984	Carlos Lopes, POR	2:09:21.0	OR
1932	Juan Carlos Zabala, ARG	2:31:36.0	OR	1988	Gelindo Bordin, ITA	2:10:32	
1936	Sohn Kee-Chung, JPN†	2:29:19.2	OR	1992	Hwang Young-Cho, S. Kor	2:13:23	
1948	Delfo Cabrera, ARG	2:34:51.6					

*Dorando Pietri of Italy placed first, but was disqualified for being helped across the finish line.
†Sohn was a Korean, but he was forced to compete under the name Kitei Son by Japan, which occupied Korea at the time.
Note: Marathon distances—40,000 meters (1896,1904); 40,260 meters (1900); 41,860 meters (1906); 42,195 meters (1908 and since 1924); 40,200 meters (1912); 42,750 meters (1920). Current distance of 42,195 meters measures 26 miles, 385 yards.

110-meter Hurdles

Year		Time		Year		Time	
1896	Tom Curtis, USA	17.6		1952	Harrison Dillard, USA	13.7	OR
1900	Alvin Kraenzlein, USA	15.4	OR	1956	Lee Calhoun, USA	13.5	OR
1904	Frederick Schule, USA	16.0		1960	Lee Calhoun, USA	13.8	
1906	Robert Leavitt, USA	16.2		1964	Hayes Jones, USA	13.6	
1908	Forrest Smithson, USA	15.0	WR	1968	Willie Davenport, USA	13.3	OR
1912	Frederick Kelly, USA	15.1		1972	Rod Milburn, USA	13.24	=WR
1920	Earl Thomson, CAN	14.8	WR	1976	Guy Drut, FRA	13.30	
1924	Daniel Kinsey, USA	15.0		1980	Thomas Munkelt, E. Ger	13.39	
1928	Syd Atkinson, SAF	14.8		1984	Roger Kingdom, USA	13.20	OR
1932	George Saling, USA	14.6		1988	Roger Kingdom, USA	12.98	OR
1936	Forrest (Spec) Towns, USA	14.2		1992	Mark McKoy, CAN	13.12	
1948	William Porter, USA	13.9	OR				

400-meter Hurdles

Year		Time		Year		Time	
1900	John Walter Tewksbury, USA	57.6		1956	Glenn Davis, USA	50.1	=OR
1904	Harry Hillman, USA	53.0		1960	Glenn Davis, USA	49.3	OR
1908	Charley Bacon, USA	55.0	WR	1964	Rex Cawley, USA	49.6	
1920	Frank Loomis, USA	54.0	WR	1968	David Hemery, GBR	48.12	WR
1924	Morgan Taylor, USA	52.6		1972	John Akii-Bua, UGA	47.82	WR
1928	David Burghley, GBR	53.4	OR	1976	Edwin Moses, USA	47.64	WR
1932	Bob Tisdall, IRL	51.7		1980	Volker Beck, E. Ger	48.70	
1936	Glenn Hardin, USA	52.4		1984	Edwin Moses, USA	47.75	
1948	Roy Cochran, USA	51.1	OR	1988	Andre Phillips, USA	47.19	OR
1952	Charley Moore, USA	50.8	OR	1992	Kevin Young, USA	46.78	WR

3000-meter Steeplechase

Year		Time		Year		Time	
1900	George Orton, CAN	7:34.4		1956	Chris Brasher, GBR	8:41.2	OR
1904	Jim Lightbody, USA	7:39.6		1960	Zdzislaw Krzyszkowiak, POL	8:34.2	OR
1908	Arthur Russell, GBR	10:47.8		1964	Gaston Roelants, BEL	8:30.8	OR
1920	Percy Hodge, GBR	10:00.4	OR	1968	Amos Biwott, KEN	8:51.0	
1924	Ville Ritola, FIN	9:33.6	OR	1972	Kip Keino, KEN	8:23.6	OR
1928	Toivo Loukola, FIN	9:21.8	WR	1976	Anders Gärderud, SWE	8:08.2	WR
1932	Volmari Iso-Hollo, FIN*	10:33.4		1980	Bronislaw Malinowski, POL	8:09.7	
1936	Volmari Iso-Hollo, FIN	9:03.8	WR	1984	Julius Korir, KEN	8:11.80	
1948	Thore Sjöstrand, SWE	9:04.6		1988	Julius Kariuki, KEN	8:05.51	OR
1952	Horace Ashenfelter, USA	8:45.4	WR	1992	Matthew Birir, KEN	8:08.84	OR

*Iso-Hollo ran one extra lap due to lap counter's mistake.
Note: Other steeplechase distances—2500 meters (1900); 2590 meters (1904); 3200 meters (1908) and 3460 meters (1932).

Track & Field (Cont.)
MEN
4x100-meter Relay

Year		Time		Year		Time	
1912	Great Britain	42.4		1960	Germany	39.5	=WR
1920	United States	42.2	WR	1964	United States	39.0	WR
1924	United States	41.0	=WR	1968	United States	38.23	WR
1928	United States	41.0	=WR	1972	United States	38.19	WR
1932	United States	40.0	WR	1976	United States	38.33	
1936	United States	39.8	WR	1980	Soviet Union	38.26	
1948	United States	40.6		1984	United States	37.83	WR
1952	United States	40.1		1988	Soviet Union	38.19	
1956	United States	39.5	WR	1992	United States	37.40	WR

4x400-meter Relay

Year		Time		Year		Time	
1908	United States	3:29.4		1960	United States	3:02.2	WR
1912	United States	3:16.6	WR	1964	United States	3:00.7	WR
1920	Great Britain	3:22.2		1968	United States	2:56.16	WR
1924	United States	3:16.0	WR	1972	Kenya	2:59.8	
1928	United States	3:14.2	WR	1976	United States	2:58.65	
1932	United States	3:08.2	WR	1980	Soviet Union	3:01.1	
1936	Great Britain	3:09.0		1984	United States	2:57.91	
1948	United States	3:10.4		1988	United States	2:56.16	=WR
1952	Jamaica	3:03.9	WR	1992	United States	2:55.74	WR
1956	United States	3:04.8					

20-kilometer Walk

Year		Time		Year		Time	
1956	Leonid Spirin, USSR	1:31:27.4		1976	Daniel Bautista, MEX	1:24:40.6	OR
1960	Vladimir Golubnichiy, USSR	1:34:07.2		1980	Maurizio Damilano, ITA	1:23:35.5	OR
1964	Ken Matthews, GBR	1:29:34.0	OR	1984	Ernesto Canto, MEX	1:23:13	OR
1968	Vladimir Golubnichiy, USSR	1:33:58.4		1988	Jozef Pribilinec, CZE	1:19:57	OR
1972	Peter Frenkel, E.Ger	1:26:42.4	OR	1992	Daniel Plaza Montero, SPA	1:21:45	

50-kilometer Walk

Year		Time		Year		Time	
1932	Thomas Green, GBR	4:50:10		1968	Christoph Höhne, E. Ger	4:20:13.6	
1936	Harold Whitlock, GBR	4:30:41.4	OR	1972	Bernd Kannenberg, W. Ger	3:56:11.6	OR
1948	John Ljunggren, SWE	4:41:52		1976	Not held		
1952	Giuseppe Dordoni, ITA	4:28:07.8	OR	1980	Hartwig Gauder, E. Ger	3:49:24.0	OR
1956	Norman Read, NZE	4:30:42.8		1984	Raúl González, MEX	3:47:26	OR
1960	Don Thompson, GBR	4:25:30.0	OR	1988	Vyacheslav Ivanenko, USSR	3:38:29	OR
1964	Abdon Pamich, ITA	4:11:12.4	OR	1992	Andrei Perlov, UT	3:50:13	

High Jump

Year		Height		Year		Height	
1896	Ellery Clark, USA	5-11¼		1952	Walt Davis, USA	6- 8½	OR
1900	Irving Baxter, USA	6- 2¾	OR	1956	Charley Dumas, USA	6-11½	OR
1904	Sam Jones, USA	5-11		1960	Robert Shavlakadze, USSR	7- 1	OR
1906	Cornelius Leahy, GBR/IRL	5-10		1964	Valery Brumel, USSR	7- 1¾	OR
1908	Harry Porter, USA	6- 3	OR	1968	Dick Fosbury, USA	7- 4¼	OR
1912	Alma Richards, USA	6- 4	OR	1972	Yuri Tarmak, USSR	7- 3¾	
1920	Richmond Landon, USA	6- 4	=OR	1976	Jacek Wszola, POL	7- 4½	OR
1924	Harold Osborn, USA	6- 6	OR	1980	Gerd Wessig, E. Ger	7- 8¾	WR
1928	Bob King, USA	6- 4½		1984	Dietmar Mögenburg, W. Ger	7- 8½	
1932	Duncan McNaughton, CAN	6- 5½		1988	Gennady Avdeyenko, USSR	7- 9¾	OR
1936	Cornelius Johnson, USA	6- 8	OR	1992	Javier Sotomayor, CUB	7- 8	
1948	John Winter, AUS	6- 6					

Pole Vault

Year		Height		Year		Height	
1896	William Hoyt, USA	10-10		1948	Guinn Smith, USA	14- 1¼	
1900	Irving Baxter, USA	10-10		1952	Bob Richards, USA	14-11	OR
1904	Charles Dvorak, USA	11- 5¾		1956	Bob Richards, USA	14-11½	OR
1906	Fernand Gonder, FRA	11- 5¾		1960	Don Bragg, USA	15- 5	OR
1908	(TIE) Edward Cooke, USA	12- 2		1964	Fred Hansen, USA	16- 8¾	OR
	& Alfred Gilbert, USA	12- 2	OR	1968	Bob Seagren, USA	17- 8½	OR
1912	Harry Babcock, USA	12-11½		1972	Wolfgang Nordwig, E. Ger	18- 0½	OR
1920	Frank Foss, USA	13- 5	WR	1976	Tadeusz Slusarski, POL	18- 0½	=OR
1924	Lee Barnes, USA	12-11½		1980	Wladyslaw Kozakiewicz, POL	18-11½	WR
1928	Sabin Carr, USA	13- 9¼		1984	Pierre Quinon, FRA	18-10¼	
1932	Bill Miller, USA	14- 1¾		1988	Sergey Bubka, USSR	19- 4¼	OR
1936	Earle Meadows, USA	14- 3¼	OR	1992	Maksim Tarasov, UT	19- 0¼	

Long Jump

Year		Distance		Year		Distance	
1896	Ellery Clark, USA	20-10		1952	Jerome Biffle, USA	24-10	
1900	Alvin Kraenzlein, USA	23- 6¾	OR	1956	Greg Bell, USA	25- 8¼	
1904	Meyer Prinstein, USA	24- 1	OR	1960	Ralph Boston, USA	26- 7¾	OR
1906	Meyer Prinstein, USA	23- 7½		1964	Lynn Davies, GBR	26- 5¾	
1908	Frank Irons, USA	24- 6½	OR	1968	Bob Beamon, USA	29- 2½	WR
1912	Albert Gutterson, USA	24-11¼	OR	1972	Randy Williams, USA	27- 0½	
1920	William Petersson, SWE	23- 5½		1976	Arnie Robinson, USA	27- 4¾	
1924	De Hart Hubbard, USA	24- 5		1980	Lutz Dombrowski, E. Ger	28- 0¼	
1928	Ed Hamm, USA	25- 4½	OR	1984	Carl Lewis, USA	28- 0¼	
1932	Ed Gordon, USA	25- 0¾		1988	Carl Lewis, USA	28- 7¼	
1936	Jesse Owens, USA	26- 5½	OR	1992	Carl Lewis, USA	28- 5½	
1948	Willie Steele, USA	25- 8					

Triple Jump

Year		Distance		Year		Distance	
1896	James Connolly, USA	44-11¾		1952	Adhemar da Silva, BRA	53- 2¾	WR
1900	Meyer Prinstein, USA	47- 5¾	OR	1956	Adhemar da Silva, BRA	53- 7¾	OR
1904	Meyer Prinstein, USA	47- 1		1960	József Schmidt, POL	55- 2	
1906	Peter O'Connor, GBR/IRL	46- 2¼		1964	József Schmidt, POL	55- 3½	OR
1908	Timothy Ahearne, GBR/IRL	48-11¼	OR	1968	Viktor Saneyev, USSR	57- 0¾	WR
1912	Gustaf Lindblom, SWE	48- 5¼		1972	Viktor Saneyev, USSR	56-11¼	
1920	Vilho Tuulos, FIN	47- 7		1976	Viktor Saneyev, USSR	56- 8¾	
1924	Nick Winter, AUS	50-11¼	WR	1980	Jaak Uudmäe, USSR	56-11¼	
1928	Mikio Oda, JPN	49-11		1984	Al Joyner, USA	56- 7½	
1932	Chuhei Nambu, JPN	51- 7	WR	1988	Khristo Markov, BUL	57- 9¼	OR
1936	Naoto Tajima, JPN	52- 6	WR	1992	Mike Conley, USA	57-10¼	OR
1948	Arne Ahman, SWE	50- 6¼					

Shot Put

Year		Distance		Year		Distance	
1896	Bob Garrett, USA	36- 9¾		1952	Parry O'Brien, USA	57- 1½	OR
1900	Richard Sheldon, USA	46- 3¼	OR	1956	Parry O'Brien, USA	60-11¼	OR
1904	Ralph Rose, USA	48- 7	WR	1960	Bill Nieder, USA	64- 6¾	OR
1906	Martin Sheridan, USA	40- 5¼		1964	Dallas Long, USA	66- 8½	OR
1908	Ralph Rose, USA	46- 7½		1968	Randy Matson, USA	67- 4¾	
1912	Patrick McDonald, USA	50- 4	OR	1972	Wladyslaw Komar, POL	69- 6	OR
1920	Ville Pörhölä, FIN	48- 7¼		1976	Udo Beyer, E. Ger	69- 0¾	
1924	Bud Houser, USA	49- 2¼		1980	Vladimir Kiselyov, USSR	70- 0½	OR
1928	John Kuck, USA	52- 0¾	WR	1984	Alessandro Andrei, ITA	69- 9	
1932	Leo Sexton, USA	52- 6	OR	1988	Ulf Timmermann, E. Ger	73- 8¾	OR
1936	Hans Woellke, GER	53- 1¾	OR	1992	Mike Stulce, USA	71- 2½	
1948	Wilbur Thompson, USA	56- 2	OR				

Discus Throw

Year		Distance		Year		Distance	
1896	Bob Garrett, USA	95- 7½		1952	Sim Iness, USA	180- 6	OR
1900	Rudolf Bauer, HUN	118- 3	OR	1956	Al Oerter, USA	184-11	OR
1904	Martin Sheridan, USA	128-10½	OR	1960	Al Oerter, USA	194- 2	OR
1906	Martin Sheridan, USA	136- 0		1964	Al Oerter, USA	200- 1	OR
1908	Martin Sheridan, USA	134- 2	OR	1968	Al Oerter, USA	212- 6	OR
1912	Armas Taipale, FIN	148- 3	OR	1972	Ludvik Danek, CZE	211- 3	
1920	Elmer Niklander, FIN	146- 7		1976	Mac Wilkins, USA	221- 5	
1924	Bud Houser, USA	151- 4	OR	1980	Viktor Rashchupkin, USSR	218- 8	
1928	Bud Houser, USA	155- 3	OR	1984	Rolf Danneberg, W. Ger	218- 6	
1932	John Anderson, USA	162- 4	OR	1988	Jürgen Schult, E. Ger	225- 9	OR
1936	Ken Carpenter, USA	165- 7	OR	1992	Romas Ubartas, LIT	213- 8	
1948	Adolfo Consolini, ITA	173- 2	OR				

Hammer Throw

Year		Distance		Year		Distance	
1900	John Flanagan, USA	163- 1		1956	Harold Connolly, USA	207- 3	OR
1904	John Flanagan, USA	168- 1	OR	1960	Vasily Rudenkov, USSR	220- 2	OR
1908	John Flanagan, USA	170- 4	OR	1964	Romuald Klim, USSR	228-10	OR
1912	Matt McGrath, USA	179- 7	OR	1968	Gyula Zsivótzky, HUN	240- 8	OR
1920	Pat Ryan, USA	173- 5		1972	Anatoly Bondarchuk, USSR	247- 8	OR
1924	Fred Tootell, USA	174-10		1976	Yuri Sedykh, USSR	254- 4	OR
1928	Pat O'Callaghan, IRL	168- 7		1980	Yuri Sedykh, USSR	268- 4	WR
1932	Pat O'Callaghan, IRL	176-11		1984	Juha Tiainen, FIN	256- 2	
1936	Karl Hein, GER	185- 4	OR	1988	Sergey Litvinov, USSR	278- 2	OR
1948	Imre Németh, HUN	183-11		1992	Andrei Abduvaliyev, UT	270- 9	
1952	József Csérmák, HUN	197-11	WR				

Track & Field (Cont.)

MEN

Javelin Throw

Year		Distance		Year		Distance	
1908	Eric Lemming, SWE	179-10	WR	1960	Viktor Tsibulenko, USSR	277- 8	
1912	Eric Lemming, SWE	198-11	OR	1964	Pauli Nevala, FIN	271- 2	
1920	Jonni Myyrä, FIN	215-10	OR	1968	Jänis Lüsis, USSR	295- 7	OR
1924	Jonni Myyrä, FIN	206- 7		1972	Klaus Wolfermann, W. Ger	296-10	OR
1928	Erik Lundkvist, SWE	218- 6	OR	1976	Miklos Németh, HUN	310- 4	WR
1932	Matti Järvinen, FIN	238- 6	OR	1980	Dainis Kūla, USSR	299- 2	
1936	Gerhard Stöck, GER	235- 8		1984	Arto Härkönen, FIN	284- 8	
1948	Kai Tapio Rautavaara, FIN	228-10		1988	Tapio Korjus, FIN	276- 6	
1952	Cy Young, USA	242- 1	OR	1992	Jan Zelezny, CZE	294- 2*	OR
1956	Egil Danielson, NOR	281- 2	WR				

*In 1986 the balance point of the javelin was modified and new records have been kept since.

Decathlon

Year		Points		Year		Points	
1904	Thomas Kiely, IRL	6036		1956	Milt Campbell, USA	7937	OR
1906-08	Not held			1960	Rafer Johnson, USA	8392	OR
1912	Jim Thrope, USA	8412	WR	1964	Willi Holdorf, GER	7887	
1920	Helge Lövland, NOR	6803		1968	Bill Toomey, USA	8193	OR
1924	Harold Osborn, USA	7711	WR	1972	Nikolai Avilov, USSR	8454	WR
1928	Paavo Yrjölä, FIN	8053	WR	1976	Bruce Jenner, USA	8617	WR
1932	Jim Bausch, USA	8462	WR	1980	Daley Thompson, GBR	8495	
1936	Glenn Morris, USA	7900	WR	1984	Daley Thompson, GBR	8798	=WR
1948	Bob Mathias, USA	7139		1988	Christian Schenk, E. Ger	8488	
1952	Bob Mathias, USA	7887	WR	1992	Robert Zmelik, CZE	8611	

WOMEN

At least 3 gold medals (including relays): Evelyn Ashford, Fanny Blankers-Koen, Betty Cuthbert and Bärbel Eckert Wöckel (4); Valerie Brisco-Hooks, Olga Bryzgina, Florence Griffith Joyner, Jackie Joyner-Kersee, Tamara Press, Wilma Rudolph, Renate Stecher, Shirley Strickland, Irena Kirszenstein Szewinska and Wyomia Tyus (3).

100 meters

Year		Time		Year		Time	
1928	Betty Robinson, USA	12.2	=WR	1968	Wyomia Tyus, USA	11.08	WR
1932	Stella Walsh, POL*	11.9	=WR	1972	Renate Stecher, E. Ger	11.07	
1936	Helen Stephens, USA	11.5^w		1976	Annegret Richter, W. Ger	11.08	
1948	Fanny Blankers-Koen, HOL	11.9		1980	Lyudmila Kondratyeva, USSR	11.06	
1952	Marjorie Jackson, AUS	11.5	=WR	1984	Evelyn Ashford, USA	10.97	OR
1956	Betty Cuthbert, AUS	11.5		1988	Florence Griffith Joyner, USA	10.54^w	
1960	Wilma Rudolph, USA	11.0^w		1992	Gail Devers, USA	10.82	OR
1964	Wyomia Tyus, USA	11.4					

*An autopsy performed after Walsh's death in 1980 revealed that she was a man.
^{w} indicates wind-aided.

200 meters

Year		Time		Year		Time	
1948	Fanny Blankers-Koen, HOL	24.4		1972	Renate Stecher, E. Ger	22.40	=WR
1952	Marjorie Jackson, AUS	23.7	OR	1976	Bärbel Eckert, E. Ger	22.37	OR
1956	Betty Cuthbert, AUS	23.4	=OR	1980	Bärbel Eckert Wöckel, E. Ger	22.03	OR
1960	Wilma Rudolph, USA	24.0		1984	Valerie Brisco-Hooks, USA	21.81	OR
1964	Edith McGuire, USA	23.0	OR	1988	Florence Griffith Joyner, USA	21.34	WR
1968	Irena Szewinska, POL	22.5	WR	1992	Gwen Torrence, USA	21.81	

400 meters

Year		Time		Year		Time	
1964	Betty Cuthbert, AUS	52.0		1980	Marita Koch, E. Ger	48.88	OR
1968	Colette Besson, FRA	52.03	=OR	1984	Valerie Brisco-Hooks, USA	48.83	OR
1972	Monika Zehrt, E. Ger	51.08	OR	1988	Olga Bryzgina, USSR	48.65	OR
1976	Irena Szewinska, POL	49.29	WR	1992	Marie-Jose Perec, FRA	48.83	

800 meters

Year		Time		Year		Time	
1928	Lina Radke, GER	2:16.8	WR	1976	Tatyana Kazankina, USSR	1:54.94	WR
1932-56	Not held			1980	Nadezhda Olizarenko, USSR	1:53.42	WR
1960	Lyudmila Shevtsova, USSR	2:04.3	=WR	1984	Doina Melinte, ROM	1:57.60	
1964	Ann Packer, GBR	2:01.1	OR	1988	Sigrun Wodars, E. Ger	1:56.10	
1968	Madeline Manning, USA	2:00.9	OR	1992	Ellen van Langen, HOL	1:55.54	
1972	Hildegard Falck, W. Ger	1:58.55	OR				

1500 meters

Year		Time		Year		Time	
1972	Lyudmila Bragina, USSR	4:01.4	WR	1984	Gabriella Dorio, ITA	4:03.25	
1976	Tatyana Kazankina, USSR	4:05.48		1988	Paula Ivan, ROM	3:53.96	OR
1980	Tatyana Kazankina, USSR	3:56.6	OR	1992	Hassiba Boulmerka, ALG	3:55.30	

3000 meters

Year		Time		Year		Time
1984	Maricica Puica, ROM	8:35.96		1992	Elena Romanova, UT	8:46.04
1988	Tatyana Samolenko, USSR	8:26.53	OR			

10,000 meters

Year		Time		Year		Time
1988	Olga Bondarenko, USSR	31:05.21	OR	1992	Derartu Tulu, ETH	31:06.02

Marathon

Year		Time	Year		Time
1984	Joan Benoit, USA	2:24:52	1992	Valentina Yegorova, UT	2:32:41
1988	Rosa Mota, POR	2:25:40			

100-meter Hurdles

Year		Time		Year		Time	
1932	Babe Didrikson, USA	11.7	WR	1968	Maureen Caird, AUS	10.3	OR
1936	Trebisonda Valla, ITA	11.7		1972	Annelie Ehrhardt, E. Ger	12.59	WR
1948	Fanny Blankers-Koen, HOL	11.2	OR	1976	Johanna Schaller, E. Ger	12.77	
1952	Shirley Strickland, AUS	10.9	WR	1980	Vera Komisova, USSR	12.56	OR
1956	Shirley Strickland, AUS	10.7	OR	1984	Benita Fitzgerald-Brown, USA	12.84	
1960	Irina Press, USSR	10.8		1988	Yordanka Donkova, BUL	12.38	OR
1964	Karin Balzer, GER	10.5^w		1992	Paraskevi Patoulidou, GRE	12.64	

^{w} indicates wind-aided.   **Note:** Event held over 80 meters from 1932-68.

400-meter Hurdles

Year		Time		Year		Time
1984	Nawal El Moutawakel, MOR	54.61	OR	1992	Sally Gunnell, GBR	53.23
1988	Debra Flintoff-King, AUS	53.17	OR			

4x100-meter Relay

Year		Time		Year		Time	
1928	Canada	48.4	WR	1968	United States	42.87	WR
1932	United States	46.9	WR	1972	West Germany	42.81	WR
1936	United States	46.9		1976	East Germany	42.55	WR
1948	Holland	47.5		1980	East Germany	41.60	WR
1952	United States	45.9	WR	1984	United States	41.65	
1956	Australia	44.5	WR	1988	United States	41.98	
1960	United States	44.5		1992	United States	42.11	
1964	Poland	43.6					

4x400-meter Relay

Year		Time		Year		Time	
1972	East Germany	3:23.0	WR	1984	United States	3:18.29	OR
1976	East Germany	3:19.23	WR	1988	Soviet Union	3:15.18	WR
1980	Soviet Union	3:20.2		1992	Unified Team	3:20.20	

10-kilometer Walk

Year		Time
1992	Chen Yueling, CHN	44.32

High Jump

Year		Height		Year		Height	
1928	Ethel Catherwood, CAN	5- 2½		1968	Miloslava Režková, CZE	5-11½	
1932	Jean Shiley, USA	5- 5¼		1972	Ulrike Meyfarth, W. Ger	6- 3½	=WR
1936	Ibolya Csák, HUN	5- 3		1976	Rosemarie Ackermann, E. Ger	6- 4	OR
1948	Alice Coachman, USA	5- 6	OR	1980	Sara Simeoni, ITA	6- 5½	OR
1952	Esther Brand, SAF	5- 5¾		1984	Ulrike Meyfarth, W. Ger	6- 7½	OR
1956	Mildred McDaniel, USA	5- 9¼	WR	1988	Louise Ritter, USA	6- 8	OR
1960	Iolanda Balas, ROM	6- 0¾	OR	1992	Heike Henkel, GER	6- 7½	
1964	Iolanda Balas, ROM	6- 2¾	OR				

Long Jump

Year		Distance		Year		Distance	
1948	Olga Gyarmati, HUN	18- 8¼		1972	Heidemarie Rosendahl, W. Ger	22- 3	
1952	Yvette Williams, NZE	20- 5¾		1976	Angela Voigt, E. Ger	22- 0¾	
1956	Elzbieta Krzesinska, POL	20-10	=WR	1980	Tatyana Kolpakova, USSR	23- 2	OR
1960	Vyera Krepkina, USSR	20-10¾	OR	1984	Anisoara Cusmir-Stanciu, ROM	22-10	
1964	Mary Rand, GBR	22- 2¼	WR	1988	Jackie Joyner-Kersee, USA	24- 3¼	OR
1968	Viorica Viscopoleanu, ROM	22- 4½	WR	1992	Heike Drechsler, GER	23- 5¼	

Track & Field (Cont.)
WOMEN
Shot Put

Year		Distance		Year		Distance	
1948	Micheline Ostermeyer, FRA	45- 1½		1972	Nadezhda Chizhova, USSR	69- 0	WR
1952	Galina Zybina, USSR	50- 1¾	WR	1976	Ivanka Hristova, BUL	69- 5¼	OR
1956	Tamara Tyshkevich, USSR	54- 5	OR	1980	Ilona Slupianek, E. Ger	73- 6¼	OR
1960	Tamara Press, USSR	56-10	OR	1984	Claudia Losch, W. Ger	67- 2¼	
1964	Tamara Press, USSR	59- 6¼	OR	1988	Natalia Lisovskaya, USSR	72-11¾	
1968	Margitta Gummel, E. Ger	64- 4	WR	1992	Svetlana Krivaleva, UT	69- 1¼	

Discus Throw

Year		Distance		Year		Distance	
1928	Halina Konopacka, POL	129-11¾	WR	1968	Lia Manoliu, ROM	191- 2	OR
1932	Lillian Copeland, USA	133- 2	OR	1972	Faina Melnik, USSR	218- 7	OR
1936	Gisela Mauermayer, GER	156- 3	OR	1976	Evelin Schlaak, E. Ger	226- 4	OR
1948	Micheline Ostermeyer, FRA	137- 6		1980	Evelin Schlaak Jahl, E. Ger	229- 6	OR
1952	Nina Romaschkova, USSR	168- 8	OR	1984	Ria Stalman, HOL	214- 5	
1956	Olga Fikotová, CZE	176- 1	OR	1988	Martina Hellmann, E. Ger	237- 2½	OR
1960	Nina Ponomaryeva, USSR	180- 9	OR	1992	Maritza Marten, CUB	229-10	
1964	Tamara Press, USSR	187-10	OR				

Javelin Throw

Year		Distance		Year		Distance	
1932	Babe Didrikson, USA	143- 4		1968	Angéla Németh, HUN	198- 0	
1936	Tilly Fleischer, GER	148- 3	OR	1972	Ruth Fuchs, E. Ger	209- 7	OR
1948	Herma Bauma, AUT	149- 6	OR	1976	Ruth Fuchs, E. Ger	216- 4	OR
1952	Dana Zátopková, CZE	165- 7	OR	1980	Maria Colon Rueñes, CUB	224- 5	OR
1956	Ineze Jaunzeme, USSR	176- 8	OR	1984	Tessa Sanderson, GBR	228- 2	OR
1960	Elvira Ozolina, USSR	183- 8	OR	1988	Petra Felke, E. Ger	245- 0	OR
1964	Mihaela Penes, ROM	198- 7	OR	1992	Silke Renk, GER	224- 2	

Heptathlon

Year		Points		Year		Points	
1964	Irina Press, USSR	5246	WR	1980	Nadezhda Tkachenko, USSR	5083	WR
1968	Ingrid Becker, W. Ger	5098		1984	Glynis Nunn, AUS	6390	OR
1972	Mary Peters, GBR	4801	WR	1988	Jackie Joyner-Kersee, USA	7291	WR
1976	Siegrun Siegl, E. Ger	4745		1992	Jackie Joyner Kersee, USA	7044	

Note: Seven-event Heptathlon replaced five-event Pentathlon in 1984.

All-Time Leading Medal Winners — Single Games

Athletes who have won the most medals in a single Summer Olympics through Barcelona in 1992. Note that totals include individual, relay and team medals. U.S. athletes are in **bold** type.

MEN

No		Sport	G-S-B
8	Aleksandr Dityatin, USSR (1980)	Gym	3-4-1
7	**Mark Spitz**, USA (1976)	Swim	7-0-0
7	**Willis Lee**, USA (1920)	Shoot	5-1-1
7	**Matt Biondi**, USA (1988)	Swim	5-1-1
7	Boris Shakhlin, USSR (1960)	Gym	4-2-1
7	**Lloyd Spooner**, USA (1920)	Shoot	4-1-2
7	Mikhail Voronin, USSR (1968)	Gym	2-4-1
7	Nikolai Andrianov, USSR (1976)	Gym	2-4-1
6	Vitaly Scherbo, UT (1992)	Gym	6-0-0
6	Li Ning, CHN (1984)	Gym	3-2-1
6	Akinori Nakayama, JPN (1968)	Gym	4-1-1
6	Takashi Ono, JPN (1960)	Gym	3-1-2
6	Viktor Chukarin, USSR (1956)	Gym	4-2-0
6	Konrad Frey, GER (1936)	Gym	3-1-2
6	Ville Ritola, FIN (1924)	Track	4-2-0
6	Hubert Van Innis, BEL (1920)	Arch	4-2-0
6	**Carl Osburn**, USA (1920)	Shoot	4-1-1
6	Louis Richardet, SWI (1906)	Shoot	3-3-0
6	**Anton Heida**, USA (1904)	Gym	5-1-0
6	**George Eyser**, USA (1904)	Gym	3-2-1
10	**Burton Downing**, USA (1904)	Cycle	2-3-1

WOMEN

No		Sport	G-S-B
7	Maria Gorokhovskaya, USSR (1952)	Gym	2-5-0
6	Kristin Otto, E. Ger (1988)	Swim	6-0-0
6	Agnes Keleti, HUN (1956)	Gym	4-2-0
6	Vera Caslavska, CZE (1968)	Gym	4-2-0
6	Larisa Latynina, USSR (1956)	Gym	4-1-1
6	Larisa Latynina, USSR (1960)	Gym	3-2-1
6	Daniela Silivas, ROM (1988)	Gym	3-2-1
6	Larisa Latynina, USSR (1964)	Gym	2-2-2
6	Margit Korondi, HUN, (1956)	Gym	1-1-4
5	Kornelia Ender, E. Ger (1976)	Swim	4-1-0
5	Ecaterina Szabo, ROM (1984)	Gym	4-1-0
5	Shane Gould, AUS (1972)	Swim	3-1-1
5	Nadia Comaneci, ROM (1976)	Gym	3-1-1
5	Karin Janz, E. Ger (1972)	Gym	2-2-1
5	Ines Diers, E. Ger (1980)	Swim	2-2-1
5	**Shirley Babashoff**, USA (1976)	Swim	1-4-0
5	**Mary Lou Retton**, USA (1984)	Gym	1-2-2
5	**Shannon Miller**, USA (1992)	Gym	0-2-3

All-Time Leading Medal Winners — Career
All Nations

Most Overall Medals
MEN

No		Sport	G-S-B
15	Nikolai Andrianov, USSR	Gymnastics	7-5-3
13	Boris Shakhlin, USSR	Gymnastics	7-4-2
13	Edoardo Mangiarotti, ITA	Fencing	6-5-2
13	Takashi Ono, JPN	Gymnastics	5-4-4
12	Paavo Nurmi, FIN	Track/Field	9-3-0
12	Sawao Kato, JPN	Gymnastics	8-3-1
11	Mark Spitz, USA	Swimming	9-1-1
11*	Matt Biondi, USA	Swimming	8-2-1
11	Viktor Chukarin, USSR	Gymnastics	7-3-1
11	Carl Osburn, USA	Shooting	5-4-2
10	Ray Ewry, USA	Track/Field	10-0-0
10	Aladár Gerevich, HUN	Fencing	7-1-2
10	Akinori Nakayama, JPN	Gymnastics	6-2-2
10	Aleksandr Dityatin, USSR	Gymnastics	3-6-1
9	Carl Lewis, USA	Track/Field	8-1-0
9	Martin Sheridan, USA	Track/Field	5-3-1
9	Zoltán Halmay, HUN	Swimming	3-5-1
9	Giulio Gaudini, ITA	Fencing	3-4-2
9	Mikhail Voronin, USSR	Gymnastics	2-6-1
9	Heikki Savolainen, FIN	Gymnastics	2-1-6
9	Yuri Titov, USSR	Gymnastics	1-5-3

*Includes gold medal as preliminary member of 1st-place relay team.

Games Participated In
Andrianov (1972,76,80); **Biondi** (1984,88,92); **Chukarin** (1952,56); **Dityatin** (1976,80); **Ewry** (1900,04,06,08); **Gerevich** (1932,36,48,52,56,60); **Gaudini** (1928,32,36); **Halmay** (1900,04,06,08); **Kato** (1968,72,76); **Lewis** (1984,88,92); **Mangiarotti** (1936,48,52,56,60); **Nakayama** (1968,72); **Nurmi** (1920,24,28); **Ono** (1952,56,60,64); **Osburn** (1912,20, 24); **Savolainen** (1928,32,36,48,52); **Shakhlin** (1956,60,64); **Sheridan** (1904,06,08); **Spitz** (1968,72); **Titov** (1956,60,64); **Voronin** (1968,72).

WOMEN

No		Sport	G-S-B
18	Larissa Latynina, USSR	Gymnastics	9-5-4
11	Vera Cáslavská, CZE	Gymnastics	7-4-0
10	Agnes Keleti, HUN	Gymnastics	5-3-2
10	Polina Astaknova, USSR	Gymnastics	5-2-3
9	Nadia Comaneci, ROM	Gymnastics	5-3-1
9	Lyudmila Tourischeva, USSR	Gymnastics	4-3-2
8	Kornelia Ender, E. Ger	Swimming	4-4-0
8	Dawn Fraser, AUS	Swimming	4-4-0
8	Shirley Babashoff, USA	Swimming	2-6-0
8	Sofia Muratova, USSR	Gymnastics	2-2-4
7	Irena Kirzenstein Szewinska, POL	Track/Field	3-2-2
7	Shirley Strickland, AUS	Track/Field	3-1-3
7	Maria Gorokhovskaya, USSR	Gymnastics	2-5-0
7	Ildikó Ságiné-Ujlaki-Rejtö, HUN	Fencing	2-3-2

Games Participated In
Astaknova (1956,60,64); **Babashoff** (1972,76); **Cáslavská** (1960,64,68); **Comaneci** (1976,80); **Ender** (1972,76); **Fraser** (1956,60,64); **Gorokhovskaya** (1952); **Keleti** (1952,56); **Latynina** (1956,60,64); **Muratova** (1956,60); **Ságiné-Rejtö** (1960,64, 68,72,76); **Strickland** (1948,52,56); **Szewinska** (1964,68,72,76,80); **Tourischeva** (1968, 72,76).

Most Individual Medals
Not including team competition.

	Sport	G-S-B
Men: 12-Nikolai Andrianov, USSR	Gym	6-3-3
Women: 14-Larissa Latynina, USSR	Gym	7-4-3

Most Gold Medals
MEN

No		Sport	G-S-B
10	Ray Ewry, USA	Track/Field	10-0-0
9	Paavo Nurmi, FIN	Track/Field	9-3-0
9	Mark Spitz, USA	Swimming	9-1-1
8	Sawao Kato, JPN	Gymnastics	8-3-1
8*	Matt Biondi, USA	Swimming	8-2-1
8	Carl Lewis, USA	Track/Field	8-1-0
7	Nikolai Andrianov, USSR	Gymnastics	7-5-3
7	Boris Shakhlin, USSR	Gymnastics	7-4-2
7	Viktor Chukarin, USSR	Gymnastics	7-3-1
7	Aladar Gerevich, HUN	Fencing	7-1-2

*Includes gold medal as preliminary member of 1st-place relay team.

WOMEN

No		Sport	G-S-B
9	Larissa Latynina, USSR	Gymnastics	9-5-4
7	Vera Cáslavská, CZE	Gymnastics	7-4-0
6	Kristin Otto, E. Ger	Swimming	6-0-0
5	Agnes Keleti, HUN	Gymnastics	5-3-2
5	Nadia Comaneci, ROM	Gymnastics	5-3-1
5	Polina Astaknova, USSR	Gymnastics	5-2-3
4	Kornelia Ender, E. Ger	Swimming	4-4-0
4	Dawn Fraser, AUS	Swimming	4-4-0
4	Lyudmila Tourischeva, USSR	Gymnastics	4-3-2
4	Evelyn Ashford, USA	Track/Field	4-1-0
4	Krisztina Egerszegi, HUN	Swimming	4-1-0
4	Janet Evans, USA	Swimming	4-1-0
4	Fanny Blankers-Koen, HOL	Track/Field	4-0-0
4	Betty Cuthbert, AUS	Track/Field	4-0-0
4	Pat McCormick, USA	Diving	4-0-0
4	Bärbel Eckert Wöckel, E. Ger.	Track/Field	4-0-0

Most Silver Medals
MEN

No		Sport	G-S-B
6	Alexandr Dityatin, USSR	Gymnastics	3-6-1
6	Mikhail Voronin, USSR	Gymnastics	2-6-1
5	Nikolai Andrianov, USSR	Gymnastics	7-5-3
5	Edoardo Mangiarotti, ITA	Fencing	6-5-2
5	Zoltán Halmay, HUN	Swimming	3-5-1
5	Gustavo Marzi, ITA	Fencing	2-5-0
5	Yuri Titov, USSR	Gymnastics	1-5-3
5	Viktor Lisitsky, USSR	Gymnastics	0-5-0

WOMEN

No		Sport	G-S-B
6	Shirley Babashoff, USA	Swimming	2-6-0
5	Larissa Latynina, USSR	Gymnastics	9-5-4
5	Maria Gorokhovskaya, USSR	Gymnastics	2-5-0
4	Vera Cáslavská, CZE	Gymnastics	7-4-0
4	Kornelia Ender, E. Ger	Swimming	4-4-0
4	Dawn Fraser, AUS	Swimming	4-4-0
4	Erica Zuchold, E. Ger	Gymnastics	0-4-1

Most Bronze Medals
MEN

No		Sport	G-S-B
6	Heikki Savolainen, FIN	Gymnastics	2-1-6
5	Daniel Revenu, FRA	Fencing	1-0-5
5	Philip Edwards, CAN	Track/Field	0-0-5
5	Adrianus Jong, HOL	Fencing	0-0-5

WOMEN

No		Sport	G-S-B
4	Larissa Latynina, USSR	Gymnastics	9-5-4
4	Sofia Muratova, USSR	Gymnastics	2-2-4
4	Merlene Ottey, JAM	Track/Field	0-0-4

All-Time Leading USA Medal Winners

Most Overall Medals
MEN

No		Sport	G-S-B
11	Mark Spitz	Swimming	9-1-1
11*	Matt Biondi	Swimming	8-2-1
11	Carl Osburn	Shooting	5-4-2
10	Ray Ewry	Track/Field	10-0-0
9	Carl Lewis	Track/Field	8-1-0
9	Martin Sheridan	Track/Field	5-3-1
8	Charles Daniels	Swimming	5-1-2
7†	Tom Jager	Swimming	5-1-1
7	Willis Lee	Shooting	5-1-1
7	Lloyd Spooner	Shooting	4-1-2
6	Anton Heida	Gymnastics	5-1-0
6	Don Schollander	Swimming	5-1-0
6	Johnny Weissmuller	Swim/Water Polo	5-0-1
6	Alfred Lane	Shooting	5-0-1
6	Jim Lightbody	Track/Field	4-2-0
6	George Eyser	Gymnastics	3-2-1
6	Michael Plumb	Equestrian	2-4-0
6	Burton Downing	Cycling	2-3-1
6	Bob Garrett	Track/Field	2-2-2

*Includes gold medal as prelim. member of 1st-place relay team.
†Includes 3 gold medals as prelim. member of 1st-place relay teams.

Games Participated In

Biondi (1984,88,92); **Daniels** (1904,06,08); **Downing** (1904); **Ewry** (1900,04,06,08); **Eyser** (1904); **Garrett** (1896,1900); **Heida** (1904); **Jager** (1984,88,92); **Lane** (1912,20); **Lee** (1920); **Lewis** (1984,88,92); **Lightbody** (1904,06); **Osburn** (1912,20,24); **Plumb** (1960, 64,68,72,76,84); **Schollander** (1964, 68); **Sheridan** (1904,06,08); **Spitz** (1968,72); **Spooner** (1920); **Weissmuller** (1924,28).

WOMEN

No		Sport	G-S-B
8	Shirley Babashoff	Swimming	2-6-0
5	Evelyn Ashford	Track/Field	4-1-0
5	Janet Evans	Swimming	4-1-0
5*	Mary T. Meagher	Swimming	3-1-1
5	Florence Griffith Joyner	Track/Field	3-2-0
5	Jackie Joyner-Kersee	Track/Field	3-1-1
5	Mary Lou Retton	Gymnastics	1-2-2
5	Shannon Miller	Gymnastics	0-2-3
4	Pat McCormick	Diving	4-0-0
4	Valerie Brisco-Hooks	Track/Field	3-1-0
4	Nancy Hogshead	Swimming	3-1-0
4	Sharon Stouder	Swimming	3-1-0
4	Wyomia Tyus	Track/Field	3-1-0
4	Wilma Rudolph	Track/Field	3-0-1
4	Chris von Saltza	Swimming	3-1-0
4	Sue Pederson	Swimming	2-2-0
4	Jan Henne	Swimming	2-1-1
4	Dorothy Poynton Hill	Diving	2-1-1
4*	Summer Sanders	Swimming	2-1-1
4*	Dara Torres	Swimming	2-1-1
4	Kathy Ellis	Swimming	2-0-2
4	Georgia Coleman	Diving	1-2-1

*Includes silver medal as prelim. member of 2nd-place relay team.

Games Participated In

Ashford (1976,84,88,92); **Babashoff** (1972,76); **Brisco-Hooks** (1984,88); **Coleman** (1928,32); **Ellis** (1964); **Evans** (1988,92); **Griffith Joyner** (1984,88); **Henne** (1968); **Hogshead** (1984); **Joyner-Kersee** (1984,88,92); **McCormick** (1952,56); **Meagher** (1984,88); **Miller** (1992); **Pederson** (1968); **Poynton Hill** (1928,32,36); **Retton** (1984); **Rudolph** (1956,60); **Sanders** (1992); **Stouder** (1964); **Torres** (1984,88,92); **Tyus** (1964,68); **von Saltza** (1960).

Most Gold Medals
MEN

No		Sport	G-S-B
10	Raymond Ewry	Track/Field	10-0-0
9	Mark Spitz	Swimming	9-1-1
8	Carl Lewis	Track/Field	8-1-0
8*	Matt Biondi	Swimming	8-2-1
5	Carl Osburn	Shooting	5-4-2
5	Martin Sheridan	Track/Field	5-3-1
5	Charles Daniels	Swimming	5-1-2
5†	Tom Jager	Swimming	5-1-1
5	Willis Lee	Shooting	5-1-1
5	Anton Heida	Gymnastics	5-1-0
5	Don Schollander	Swimming	5-1-0
5	Johnny Weissmuller	Swim/Water Polo	5-0-1
5	Alfred Lane	Shooting	5-0-1
5	Morris Fisher	Shooting	5-0-0
4	Jim Lightbody	Track/Field	4-2-0
4	Lloyd Spooner	Shooting	4-1-2
4	Greg Louganis	Diving	4-1-0
4	John Naber	Swimming	4-1-0
4	Meyer Prinstein	Track/Field	4-1-0
4	Mel Sheppard	Track/Field	4-1-0
4	Marcus Hurley	Cycling	4-0-1
4	Harrison Dillard	Track/Field	4-0-0
4	Archie Hahn	Track/Field	4-0-0
4	Alvin Kraenzlein	Track/Field	4-0-0
4	Al Oerter	Track/Field	4-0-0
4	Jesse Owens	Track/Field	4-0-0

*Includes gold medal as prelim. member of 1st-place relay team.
†Includes 3 gold medals as prelim. member of 1st-place relay teams.

WOMEN

No		Sport	G-S-B
4	Evelyn Ashford	Track/Field	4-1-0
4	Janet Evans	Swimming	4-1-0
4	Pat McCormick	Diving	4-0-0
3	Florence Griffith Joyner	Track/Field	3-2-0
3	Jackie Joyner-Kersee	Track/Field	3-1-1
3*	Mary T. Meagher	Swimming	3-1-1
3	Valerie Brisco-Hooks	Track/Field	3-1-0
3	Nancy Hogshead	Swimming	3-1-0
3	Sharon Stouder	Swimming	3-1-0
3	Wyomia Tyus	Track/Field	3-1-0
3	Chris von Saltza	Swimming	3-1-0
3	Wilma Rudolph	Track/Field	3-0-1
3	Melissa Belote	Swimming	3-0-0
3	Ethelda Bleibtrey	Swimming	3-0-0
3	Tracy Caulkins	Swimming	3-0-0
3*	Nicole Haislett	Swimming	3-0-0
3	Helen Madison	Swimming	3-0-0
3	Debbie Meyer	Swimming	3-0-0
3	Sandra Neilson	Swimming	3-0-0
3	Martha Norelius	Swimming	3-0-0
3*	Carrie Steinseifer	Swimming	3-0-0

*Includes gold medal as prelim. member of 1st-place relay team.

Most Silver Medals
MEN

No		Sport	G-S-B
4	Carl Osburn	Shooting	5-4-2
4	Michael Plumb	Equestrian	2-4-0
3	Martin Sheridan	Track/Field	5-3-1
3	Burton Downing	Cycling	2-3-1
3	Irving Baxter	Track/Field	2-3-0
3	Earl Thomson	Equestrian	2-3-0

WOMEN

No		Sport	G-S-B
6	Shirley Babashoff	Swimming	2-6-0

All-Time Medal Standings, 1896-1992

All-time Summer Games medal standings, according to *The Golden Book of the Olympic Games*. Medal counts include the 1906 Intercalated Games which are not recognized by the IOC.

	G	S	B	Total
1 **United States**	788	602	528	1918
2 USSR (1952-88)	395	319	296	1010
3 Great Britain	168	215	212	595
4 France	160	172	191	523
5 Sweden	130	147	172	449
6 East Germany (1956-88)	159	150	136	445
7 Italy	153	125	132	410
8 Hungary	135	125	145	405
9 Germany (1896-36,92—)	104	103	107	314
10 West Germany (1952-88)	77	104	120	301
11 Finland	98	78	112	288
12 Japan	89	83	92	264
13 Australia	77	76	98	251
14 Romania	59	70	90	219
15 Poland	43	62	105	210
16 Canada	45	67	82	194
17 Holland	45	53	71	169
18 Switzerland	42	66	59	167
Bulgaria	40	69	58	167
20 Denmark	34	59	56	149
21 Czechoslovakia (1924-92)	49	49	44	142
22 Belgium	35	47	47	129
23 Norway	43	39	35	117
24 China	36	41	37	114
25 Unified Team (1992)	45	38	29	112
26 Greece	24	38	43	105
27 South Korea	31	27	41	99
28 Yugoslavia (1924-88)	26	30	30	86
29 Cuba	35	25	23	83
30 Austria	18	30	32	80
31 New Zealand	26	10	28	64
32 Turkey	26	15	12	53
South Africa	16	17	20	53
34 Spain	17	19	11	47
Argentina	13	19	15	47
36 Mexico	9	13	18	40
37 Kenya	13	13	13	39
Brazil	9	10	20	39
39 Iran	4	12	17	33
40 Jamaica	4	13	7	24
41 Estonia	7	6	10	23
42 North Korea	6	5	10	21
43 Great Britain/Ireland	6	11	3	20
44 Egypt	6	5	5	16
45 Ireland	5	5	5	15
46 India	8	3	3	14
47 Ethiopia	6	1	6	13
Portugal	2	4	7	13
Mongolia	0	5	8	13
50 Pakistan	3	3	4	10
51 Morocco	4	2	3	9
Uruguay	2	1	6	9
53 Venezuela	1	2	5	8
Chile	0	6	2	8
Nigeria	0	4	4	8
Philippines	0	1	7	8
57 Trinidad & Tobago	1	2	4	7
58 Indonesia	2	3	1	6
Latvia	0	4	2	6
Colombia	0	2	4	6
Bohemia	0	1	5	6
62 Uganda	1	3	1	5
Tunisia	1	2	2	5
Russia	0	3	2	5

	G	S	B	Total
Puerto Rico	0	1	4	5
66 Peru	1	3	0	4
Algeria	1	0	3	4
Chinese Taipei	0	2	2	4
Lebanon	0	2	2	4
Ghana	0	1	3	4
Thailand	0	1	3	4
72 Luxembourg	2	1	0	3
Bahamas	1	0	2	3
Croatia	0	1	2	3
75 Japan/Korea	1	0	1	2
Lithuania	1	0	1	2
Surinam	1	0	1	2
Namibia	0	2	0	2
Tanzania	0	2	0	2
Cameroon	0	1	1	2
Great Britain/USA	0	1	1	2
Haiti	0	1	1	2
Iceland	0	1	1	2
Israel	0	1	1	2
Russia/Estonia	0	1	1	2
United Arab Republic	0	1	1	2
The Antilles	0	0	2	2
Panama	0	0	2	2
Slovenia	0	0	2	2
90 Australia/New Zealand	1	0	0	1
Cuba/USA	1	0	0	1
Denmark/Sweden	1	0	0	1
Gr. Britain/Ireland/Germany	1	0	0	1
Gr. Britain/Ireland/USA	1	0	0	1
Ireland/USA	1	0	0	1
Zimbabwe	1	0	0	1
Belgium/Greece	0	1	0	1
Ceylon	0	1	0	1
Costa Rica	0	1	0	1
France/USA	0	1	0	1
France/Gr. Britain/Ireland	0	1	0	1
Ivory Coast	0	1	0	1
Netherlands Antilles	0	1	0	1
Senegal	0	1	0	1
Singapore	0	1	0	1
Smyrna	0	1	0	1
Syria	0	1	0	1
Virgin Islands	0	1	0	1
Australia/Great Britain	0	0	1	1
Bermuda	0	0	1	1
Bohemia/Great Britain	0	0	1	1
Djibouti	0	0	1	1
Dominican Republic	0	0	1	1
France/Great Britain	0	0	1	1
Guyana	0	0	1	1
Iraq	0	0	1	1
Malaysia	0	0	1	1
Mexico/Spain	0	0	1	1
Niger	0	0	1	1
Qatar	0	0	1	1
Scotland	0	0	1	1
Thessalonika	0	0	1	1
Wales	0	0	1	1
Zambia	0	0	1	1

Combined totals:	G	S	B	Total
USSR/UT/Russia	440	360	327	1127
Germany/E. Ger/W. Ger	340	357	363	1060

Notes: Athletes from the USSR participated in the Summer Games from 1952-88, returned as the Unified Team in 1992 after the breakup of the Soviet Union (in 1991) and then competed for the independent republics of Belarus, Kazakhstan, Russia, Ukraine, Uzbekistan and three others in the 1994 Winter Games. Yugoslavia divided into Croatia and Bosnia-Herzegovina in 1991, while Czechoslovakia split into Slovenia and the Czech Republic the same year. Germany was barred from the Olympics in 1924 and '48 following World Wars I and II. Divided into East and West Germany after WWII, both countries competed together from 1952-64, then separately from 1968-88. Germany was reunified in 1990.

THE 1996 INFORMATION PLEASE SPORTS ALMANAC — OLYMPICS STATISTICS — THROUGH THE YEARS 1924-1994 WINTER GAMES — SEC B PAGE 706

The Winter Olympics

The move toward a winter version of the Olympics began in 1908 when figure skating made an appearance at the Summer Games in London. Ten-time world champion Ulrich Salchow of Sweden, who originated the backwards, one revolution jump that bears his name, and Madge Syers of Britain were the first singles champions. Germans Anna Hubler and Heinrich Berger won the pairs competition.

Organizers of the 1916 Summer Games in Berlin planned to introduce a "Skiing Olympia," featuring nordic events in the Black Forest, but the Games were cancelled after the outbreak of World War I in 1914.

The Games resumed in 1920 at Antwerp, Belgium, where figure skating returned and ice hockey was added as a medal event. Sweden's Gillis Grafstrom and Magda Julin took individual honors, while Ludovika and Walter Jakobsson were the top pair. In hockey, Canada won the gold medal with the United States second and Czechoslovakia third.

Despite the objections of Modern Olympics' founder Baron Pierre de Coubertin and the resistance of the Scandinavian countries, which had staged their own Nordic championships every four or five years from 1901-26 in Sweden, the International Olympic Committee sanctioned an "International Winter Sports Week" at Chamonix, France, in 1924. The 11-day event, which included nordic skiing, speed skating, figure skating, ice hockey and bobsledding, was a huge success and was retroactively called the First Olympic Winter Games.

Seventy years after those first cold weather Games, the 17th edition of the Winter Olympics took place in Lillehammer, Norway, in 1994. The event ended the four-year Olympic cycle of staging both Winter and Summer Games in the same year and began a new schedule that calls for the two Games to alternate every two years.

Year	No	Location	Dates	Nations	Most medals	USA Medals
1924	I	Chamonix, FRA	Jan. 25-Feb. 4	16	Norway (4-7-6—17)	1-2-1— 4 (3rd)
1928	II	St. Moritz, SWI	Feb. 11-19	25	Norway (6-4-5—15)	2-2-2— 6 (2nd)
1932	III	Lake Placid, USA	Feb. 4-15	17	USA (6-4-2—12)	6-4-2—12 (1st)
1936	IV	Garmisch-Partenkirchen, GER	Feb. 6-16	28	Norway (7-5-3—15)	1-0-3— 4 (T-5th)
1940-a	—	Sapporo, JPN	Cancelled (WWII)			
1944	—	Cortina d'Ampezzo, ITA	Cancelled (WWII)			
1948	V	St. Moritz, SWI	Jan. 30-Feb. 8	28	Norway (4-3-3—10), Sweden (4-3-3—10) & Switzerland (3-4-3—10)	3-4-2— 9 (4th)
1952-b	VI	Oslo, NOR	Feb. 14-25	30	Norway (7-3-6—16)	4-6-1—11 (2nd)
1956-c	VII	Cortina d'Ampezzo, ITA	Jan. 26-Feb. 5	32	USSR (7-3-6—16)	2-3-2— 7 (T-4th)
1960	VIII	Squaw Valley, USA	Feb. 18-28	30	USSR (7-5-9—21)	3-4-3—10 (2nd)
1964	IX	Innsbruck, AUT	Jan. 29-Feb. 9	36	USSR (11-8-6—25)	1-2-3— 6 (7th)
1968-d	X	Grenoble, FRA	Feb. 6-18	37	Norway (6-6-2—14)	1-5-1— 7 (T-7th)
1972	XI	Sapporo, JPN	Feb. 3-13	35	USSR (8-5-3—16)	3-2-3— 8 (6th)
1976-e	XII	Innsbruck, AUT	Feb. 4-15	37	USSR (13-6-8—27)	3-3-4—10 (T-3rd)
1980	XIII	Lake Placid, USA	Feb. 14-23	37	E. Germany (9-7-7—23)	6-4-2—12 (3rd)
1984	XIV	Sarajevo, YUG	Feb. 7-19	49	USSR (6-10-9—25)	4-4-0— 8 (T-5th)
1988	XV	Calgary, CAN	Feb. 13-28	57	USSR (11-9-9—29)	2-1-3— 6 (T-8th)
1992-f	XVI	Albertville, FRA	Feb. 8-23	63	Germany (10-10-6—26)	5-4-2—11 (6th)
1994-g	XVII	Lillehammer, NOR	Feb. 12-27	67	Norway (10-11-5—26)	6-5-2—13 (T-5th)
1998	XVIII	Nagano, JPN	Feb. 7-22			
2002	XIX	Salt Lake City, USA	Feb. 9-24			

a—The 1940 Winter Games are originally scheduled for Sapporo, but Japan resigns as host in 1937 when the Sino-Japanese war breaks out. St. Moritz is the next choice, but the Swiss feel that ski instructors should not be considered professionals and the IOC withdraws its offer. Finally, Garmisch-Partenkirchen is asked to serve again as host, but the Germans invade Poland in 1939 and the Games are eventually cancelled.
b—Germany and Japan are allowed to rejoin the Olympic community for the first time since World War II. Though a divided country, the Germans send a joint East-West team.
c—The Soviet Union (USSR) participates in its first Winter Olympics and takes home the most medals, including the gold medal in ice hockey.
d—East Germany and West Germany officially send separate teams for the first time and will continue to do so through 1988.
e—The IOC grants the 1976 Winter Games to Denver in May 1970, but in 1972 Colorado voters reject a $5 million bond issue to finance the undertaking. Denver immediately withdraws as host and the IOC selects Innsbruck, the site of the 1964 Games, to take over.
f—Germany sends a single team after East and West German reunification in 1990 and the USSR competes as the Unified Team after the breakup of the Soviet Union in 1991.
g—The IOC moves the Winter Games' four-year cycle ahead two years in order to separate them from the Summer Games and alternate Olympics every two years.

Event-by-Event

Gold medal winners from 1924-94 in the following events: Alpine Skiing, Biathlon, Bobsled, Cross-country Skiing, Figure Skating, Ice Hockey, Luge, Nordic Combined, Ski Jumping and Speed Skating.

ALPINE SKIING

MEN

Multiple gold medals: Jean-Claude Killy, Toni Sailer and Alberto Tomba (3); Henri Oreiller, Ingemar Stenmark and Markus Wasmeier (2).

Downhill

Year		Time	Year		Time
1948	Henri Oreiller, FRA	2:55.0	1976	Franz Klammer AUT	1:45.73
1952	Zeno Colò, ITA	2:30.8	1980	Leonhard Stock, AUS	1:45.50
1956	Toni Sailer, AUT	2:52.2	1984	Bill Johnson, USA	1:45.59
1960	Jean Vuarnet, FRA	2:06.0	1988	Pirmin Zurbriggen, SWI	1:59.63
1964	Egon Zimmermann, AUT	2:18.16	1992	Patrick Ortlieb, AUT	1:50.37
1968	Jean-Claude Killy, FRA	1:59.85	1994	Tommy Moe, USA	1:45.75
1972	Bernhard Russi, SWI	1:51.43			

Slalom

Year		Time	Year		Time
1948	Edi Reinalter, SWI	2:10.3	1976	Piero Gros, ITA	2:03.29
1952	Othmar Schneider, AUT	2:00.0	1980	Ingemar Stenmark, SWE	1:44.26
1956	Toni Sailer, AUT	3:14.7	1984	Phil Mahre, USA	1:39.41
1960	Ernst Hinterseer, AUT	2:08.9	1988	Alberto Tomba, ITA	1:39.47
1964	Pepi Stiegler, AUT	2:11.13	1992	Finn Christian Jagge, NOR	1:44.39
1968	Jean-Claude Killy, FRA	1:39.73	1994	Thomas Stangassinger, AUT	2:02.02
1972	Francisco Ochoa, SPA	1:49.27			

Giant Slalom

Year		Time	Year		Time
1952	Stein Eriksen, NOR	2:25.0	1976	Heini Hemmi, SWI	3:26.97
1956	Toni Sailer, AUS	3:00.1	1980	Ingemar Stenmark, SWE	2:40.74
1960	Roger Staub, SWI	1:48.3	1984	Max Julen, SWI	2:41.18
1964	Francois Bonlieu, FRA	1:46.71	1988	Alberto Tomba, ITA	2:06.37
1968	Jean-Claude Killy, FRA	3:29.28	1992	Alberto Tomba, ITA	2:06.98
1972	Gustav Thöni, ITA	3:09.62	1994	Markus Wasmeier, GER	2:52.46

Super Giant Slalom

Year		Time	Year		Time
1988	Frank Piccard, FRA	1:39.66	1994	Markus Wasmeier, GER	1:32.53
1992	Kjetil Andre Aamodt, NOR	1:13.04			

Alpine Combined

Year		Points	Year		Points
1936	Franz Pfnür, GER	99.25	1992	Josef Polig, ITA	14.58
1948	Henri Oreiller, FRA	3.27	**Year**		**Time**
1952-84 Not held			1994	Lasse Kjus, NOR	3:17.53
1988	Hubert Strolz, AUT	36.55			

WOMEN

Multiple gold medals: Vreni Schneider (3); Deborah Compagnoni, Marielle Goitschel, Trude Jochum-Beiser, Petra Kronberger, Andrea Mead Lawrence, Rosi Mittermaier, Marie-Theres Nadig, Hanni Wenzel and Pernilla Wiberg (2).

Downhill

Year		Time	Year		Time
1948	Hedy Schlunegger, SWI	2:28.3	1976	Rosi Mittermaier, W. Ger	1:46.16
1952	Trude Jochum-Beiser, AUT	1:47.1	1980	Annemarie Moser-Pröll, AUT	1:37.52
1956	Madeleine Berthod, SWI	1:40.7	1984	Michela Figini, SWI	1:13.36
1960	Heidi Biebl, GER	1:37.6	1988	Marina Kiehl, W. Ger	1:25.86
1964	Christl Haas, AUT	1:55.39	1992	Kerrin Lee-Gartner, CAN	1:52.55
1968	Olga Pall, AUT	1:40.87	1994	Katja Seizinger, GER	1:35.93
1972	Marie-Theres Nadig, SWI	1:36.68			

Slalom

Year		Time	Year		Time
1948	Gretchen Fraser, USA	1:57.2	1976	Rosi Mittermaier, W. Ger	1:30.54
1952	Andrea Mead Lawrence, USA	2:10.6	1980	Hanni Wenzel, LIE	1:25.09
1956	Renée Colliard, SWI	1:52.3	1984	Paoletta Magoni, ITA	1:36.47
1960	Anne Heggtveit, CAN	1:49.6	1988	Vreni Schneider, SWI	1:36.69
1964	Christine Goitschel, FRA	1:29.86	1992	Petra Kronberger, AUT	1:32.68
1968	Marielle Goitschel, FRA	1:25.86	1994	Vreni Schneider, SWI	1:56.01
1972	Barbara Cochran, USA	1:31.24			

Alpine Skiing (Cont.)
WOMEN
Giant Slalom

Year		Time	Year		Time
1952	Andrea Mead Lawrence, USA	2:06.8	1976	Kathy Kreiner, CAN	1:29.13
1956	Ossi Reichert, GER	1:56.5	1980	Hanni Wenzel, LIE	2:41.66
1960	Yvonne Rügg, SWI	1:39.9	1984	Debbie Armstrong, USA	2:20.98
1964	Marielle Goitschel, FRA	1:52.24	1988	Vreni Schneider, SWI	2:06.49
1968	Nancy Greene, CAN	1:51.97	1992	Pernilla Wiberg, SWE	2:12.74
1972	Marie-Theres Nadig, SWI	1:29.90	1994	Deborah Compagnoni, ITA	2:30.97

Super Giant Slalom

Year		Time	Year		Time
1988	Sigrid Wolf, AUT	1:19.03	1994	Diann Roffe-Steinrotter, USA	1:22.15
1992	Deborah Compagnoni, ITA	1:21.22			

Alpine Combined

Year		Points	Year		Points
1936	Christl Cranz, GER	97.06	1992	Petra Kronberger, AUT	2.55
1948	Trude Beiser, AUT	6.58	Year		Time
1952-84	Not held		1994	Pernilla Wiberg, SWE	3:05.16
1988	Anita Wachter, AUT	29.25			

BIATHLON

MEN

Multiple gold medals (including relays): Aleksandr Tikhonov (4); Mark Kirchner (3); Anatoly Alyabyev, Ivan Biakov, Sergei Chepikov, Viktor Mamatov, Frank-Peter Roetsch, Magnar Solberg and Dmitri Vasilyev (2).

10 kilometers

Year		Time	Year		Time
1980	Frank Ullrich, E. Ger	32:10.69	1992	Mark Kirchner, GER	26:02.3
1984	Erik Kvalfoss, NOR	30:53.8	1994	Sergei Chepikov, RUS	28:07.0
1988	Frank-Peter Roetsch, E. Ger	25:08.1			

20 kilometers

Year		Time	Year		Time
1960	Klas Lestander, SWE	1:33:21.6	1980	Anatoly Alyabyev, USSR	1:08:16.31
1964	Vladimir Melanin, USSR	1:20:26.8	1984	Peter Angerer, W. Ger	1:11:52.7
1968	Magnar Solberg, NOR	1:13:45.9	1988	Frank-Peter Roetsch, E. Ger	56:33.3
1972	Magnar Solberg, NOR	1:15:55.50	1992	Yevgeny Redkine, UT	57:34.4
1976	Nikolai Kruglov, USSR	1:14:12.26	1994	Sergei Tarasov, RUS	57:25.3

4x7.5-kilometer Relay

Year		Time	Year		Time	Year		Time
1968	Soviet Union	2:13:02.4	1980	Soviet Union	1:34:03.27	1992	Germany	1:24:43.5
1972	Soviet Union	1:51:44.92	1984	Soviet Union	1:38:51.7	1994	Germany	1:30:22.1
1976	Soviet Union	1:57:55.64	1988	Soviet Union	1:22:30.0			

WOMEN

Multiple gold medals (including relays): Myriam Bedard and Anfisa Reztsova (2). Note that Reztsova won a third gold medal in 1988 in the Cross-country 4x5-kilometer Relay.

7.5 kilometers

Year		Time	Year		Time
1992	Anfisa Reztsova, UT	24:29.2	1994	Myriam Bedard, CAN	26:08.8

15 kilometers

Year		Time	Year		Time
1992	Antje Misersky, GER	51:47.2	1994	Myriam Bedard, CAN	52:06.6

4 x 7.5 kilometer Relay

Year		Time	Year		Time
1992	France	1:15:55.6	1994	Russia	1:47:19.5

Note: Event featured three skiers per team in 1992.

Youngest and Oldest Gold Medalists in an Individual Event

Youngest: MEN— Toni Nieminen, Finland, Large Hill Ski Jumping, 1992 (16 years, 261 days); WOMEN—Sonja Henie, Norway, Figure Skating, 1928 (15 years, 315 days).

Oldest: MEN— Magnar Solberg, NOR, 20-km Biathlon, 1972 (35 years, 4 days); WOMEN— Christina Baas-Kaiser, Holland, 3,000m Speed Skating, 1972 (33 years, 268 days).

BOBSLED

Multiple gold medals: DRIVERS—Meinhard Nehmer (3); Billy Fiske, Wolfgang Hoppe, Eugenio Monti, Andreas Ostler and Gustav Weder (2). CREW—Bernard Germeshausen (3); Donat Acklin, Luciano De Paolis, Cliff Gray, Lorenz Nieberl and Dietmar Schauerhammer (2).

Two-Man

Year		Time	Year		Time
1932	United States (Hubert Stevens)	8:14.74	1972	West Germany (Wolfgang Zimmerer)	4:57.07
1936	United States (Ivan Brown)	5:29.29	1976	East Germany (Meinhard Nehmer)	3:44.42
1948	Switzerland (Felix Endrich)	5:29.2	1980	Switzerland (Erich Schärer)	4:09.36
1952	Germany (Andreas Ostler)	5:24.54	1984	East Germany (Wolfgang Hoppe)	3:25.56
1956	Italy (Lamberto Dalla Costa)	5:30.14	1988	Soviet Union (Jānis Kipurs)	3:54.19
1960	Not held		1992	Switzerland I (Gustav Weder)	4:03.26
1964	Great Britain (Anthony Nash)	4:21.90	1994	Switzerland I (Gustav Weder)	3:30.81
1968	Italy (Eugenio Monti)	4:41.54			

Four-Man

Year		Time	Year		Time
1924	Switzerland (Eduard Scherrer)	5:45.54	1968	Italy (Eugenio Monti)	2:17.39
1928	United States (Billy Fiske)	3:20.5	1972	Switzerland (Jean Wicki)	4:43.07
1932	United States (Billy Fiske)	7:53.68	1976	East Germany (Meinhard Nehmer)	3:40.43
1936	Switzerland (Pierre Musy)	5:19.85	1980	East Germany (Meinhard Nehmer)	3:59.92
1948	United States (Francis Tyler)	5:20.1	1984	East Germany (Wolfgang Hoppe)	3:20.22
1952	Germany (Andreas Ostler)	5:07.84	1988	Switzerland (Ekkehard Fasser)	3:47.51
1956	Switzerland (Franz Kapus)	5:10.44	1992	Austria I (Ingo Appelt)	3:53.90
1960	Not held		1994	Germany II (Harald Czudaj)	3:27.78
1964	Canada (Vic Emery)	4:14.46			

Note: Five-man sleds were used in 1928.

CROSS-COUNTRY SKIING

There have been two significant changes in men's and women's Cross-country racing since the end of the 1984 Winter Games in Sarajevo. First, the classical and freestyle (i.e., skating) techniques were designated for specific events beginning in 1988, and the Pursuit race was introduced in 1992.

MEN

Multiple gold medals (including relays): Bjorn Dählie (5); Sixten Jernberg, Gunde Svan, Thomas Wassberg and Nikolai Zimyatov (4); Veikko Hakulinen, Eero Mäntyranta and Vegard Ulvang (3); Hallgeir Brenden, Harald Grönningen, Thorlief Haug, Jan Ottoson, Pål Tyldum and Vyacheslav Vedenine (2).
Multiple gold medals (including Nordic Combined): Johan Gröttumsbråten and Thorlief Haug (3).

10-kilometer Classical

Year		Time	Year		Time
1924-88	Not held		1994	Bjorn Dählie, NOR	24:20.1
1992	Vegard Ulvang, NOR	27:36.0			

15-kilometer Freestyle Pursuit

A 15-km Freestyle race in which the starting order is determined by order of finish in the 10-km Classical race. Time given is combined time of both events.

Year		Time	Year		Time
1924-88	Not held		1994	Bjorn Dählie, NOR	1:00.08.8
1992	Bjorn Dählie, NOR	1:05:37.9			

15-kilometer Classical (Discont.)

Discontinued in 1992 and replaced by 15-km Freestyle Pursuit. Event was held over 18 kilometers from 1924-52.

Year		Time	Year		Time
1924	Thorleif Haug, NOR	1:14:31.0	1964	Eero Mäntyranta, FIN	50:54.1
1928	Johan Gröttumsbråten, NOR	1:37:01.0	1968	Harald Grönningen, NOR	47:54.2
1932	Sven Utterström, SWE	1:23:07.0	1972	Sven-Ake Lundbäck, SWE	45:28.24
1936	Erik-August Larsson, SWE	1:14:38.0	1976	Nikolai Bazhukov, USSR	43:58.47
1948	Martin Lundström, SWE	1:13:50.0	1980	Thomas Wassberg, SWE	41:57.63
1952	Hallgeir Brenden, NOR	1:01:34.0	1984	Gunde Svan, SWE	41:25.6
1956	Hallgeir Brenden, NOR	49:39.0	1988	Mikhail Devyatyarov, USSR	41:18.9
1960	Håkon Brusveen NOR	51:55.5			

30-kilometer Freestyle

Year		Time	Year		Time
1924-52	Not held		1976	Sergei Saveliev, USSR	1:30:29.38
1956	Veikko Hakulinen, FIN	1:44:06.0	1980	Nikolai Zimyatov, USSR	1:27:02.80
1960	Sixten Jernberg, SWE	1:51:03.9	1984	Nikolai Zimyatov, USSR	1:28:56.3
1964	Eero Mäntyranta, FIN	1:30:50.7	1988	Alexi Prokurorov, USSR	1:24:26.3
1968	Franco Nones, ITA	1:35:39.2	1992	Vegard Ulvang, NOR	1:22:27.8
1972	Vyacheslav Vedenine, USSR	1:36:31.15	1994	Thomas Alsgaard, NOR	1:12:26.4

Cross-country Skiing (Cont.)
MEN
50-kilometer Classical

Year		Time	Year		Time
1924	Thorleif Haug, NOR	3:44:32.0	1968	Ole Ellefsaeter, NOR	2:28:45.8
1928	Per Erik Hedlund, SWE	4:52:03.0	1972	Pål Tyldum, NOR	2:43:14.75
1932	Veli Saarinen, FIN	4:28:00.0	1976	Ivar Formo, NOR	2:37:30.05
1936	Elis Wiklund, SWE	3:30:11.0	1980	Nikolai Zimyatov, USSR	2:27:24.60
1948	Nils Karlsson, SWE	3:47:48.0	1984	Thomas Wassberg, SWE	2:15:55.8
1952	Veikko Hakulinen, FIN	3:33:33.0	1988	Gunde Svan, SWE	2:04:30.9
1956	Sixten Jernberg, SWE	2:50:27.0	1992	Bjorn Dählie, NOR	2:03:41.5
1960	Kalevi Hämäläinen, FIN	2:59:06.3	1994	Vladimir Smirnov, KAZ	2:07:20.3
1964	Sixten Jernberg, SWE	2:43:52.6			

4x10-kilometer Mixed Relay
Two Classical and two Freestyle legs.

Year		Time	Year		Time	Year		Time
1936	Finland	2:41:33.0	1964	Sweden	2:18:34.6	1984	Sweden	1:55:06.3
1948	Sweden	2:32:08.0	1968	Norway	2:08:33.5	1988	Sweden	1:43:58.6
1952	Finland	2:20:16.0	1972	Soviet Union	2:04:47.94	1992	Norway	1:39:26.0
1956	Soviet Union	2:15:30.0	1976	Finland	2:07:59.72	1994	Italy	1:41:15.0
1960	Finland	2:18:45.6	1980	Soviet Union	1:57:03.46			

WOMEN

Multiple gold medals (including relays): Lyubov Egorova (6); Galina Kulakova and Raisa Smetanina (4); Claudia Boyarskikh and Marja-Liisa Hämäläinen (3); Manuela Di Centa, Toini Gustafsson, Larisa Lazutina, Barbara Petzold and Elena Valbe (2).
Multiple gold medals (including relays and Biathlon): Anfisa Reztsova (2).

5-kilometer Classical

Year		Time	Year		Time
1952-60 Not held			1980	Raisa Smetanina, USSR	15:06.92
1964	Claudia Boyarskikh, USSR	17:50.5	1984	Marja-Liisa Hämäläinen, FIN	17:04.0
1968	Toini Gustafsson, SWE	16:45.2	1988	Marjo Matikainen, FIN	15:04.0
1972	Galina Kulakova, USSR	17:00.50	1992	Marjut Lukkarinen, FIN	14:13.8
1976	Helena Takalo, FIN	15:48.69	1994	Lyubov Egorova, RUS	14:08.8

10-kilometer Freestyle Pursuit
A 10-km Freestyle race in which the starting order is determined by order of finish in the 5-km Classical race. Time given is combined time of both events.

Year		Time	Year		Time
1952-88 Not held			1994	Lyubov Egorova, RUS	41:38.1
1992	Lyubov Egorova, UT	40:07.7			

10-kilometer Classical (Discont.)
Discontinued in 1992 and replaced by 10-km Freestyle Pursuit. Event was held over 18 kilometers from 1924-52.

Year		Time	Year		Time
1952	Lydia Wideman, FIN	41:40.0	1972	Galina Kulakova, USSR	34:17.82
1956	Lyubov Kosyreva, USSR	38:11.0	1976	Raisa Smetanina, USSR	30:13.41
1960	Maria Gusakova, USSR	39:46.6	1980	Barbara Petzold, E. Ger	30:31.54
1964	Claudia Boyarskikh, USSR	40:24.3	1984	Marja-Liisa Hämäläinen, FIN	31:44.2
1968	Toini Gustafsson, SWE	36:46.5	1988	Vida Venciene, USSR	30:08.3

15-kilometer Freestyle

Year		Time	Year		Time
1952-88 Not held			1994	Manuela Di Centa, ITA	39:44.5
1992	Lyubov Egorova, UT	42:20.8			

30-kilometer Classical
Event was held over 20 kilometers from 1984-88.

Year		Time	Year		Time
1984	Marja-Liisa Hämäläinen, FIN	1:01:45.0	1992	Stefania Belmondo, ITA	1:22:30.1
1988	Tamara Tikhonova, USSR	55:53.6	1994	Manuela Di Centa, ITA	1:25:41.6

4x5-kilometer Mixed Relay
Two Classical and two Freestyle legs. Event featured three skiers per team from 1956-72.

Year		Time	Year		Time	Year		Time
1956	Finland	1:09:01.0	1972	Soviet Union	48:46.15	1988	Soviet Union	59:51.1
1960	Sweden	1:04:21.4	1976	Soviet Union	1:07:49.75	1992	Unified Team	59:34.8
1964	Soviet Union	59:20.2	1980	East Germany	1:02:11.10	1994	Russia	57:12.5
1968	Norway	57:30.0	1984	Norway	1:06:49.7			

FIGURE SKATING

MEN

Multiple gold medals: Gillis Grafström (3); Dick Button and Karl Schäfer (2).

Year		Year		Year	
1908	Ulrich Salchow...............SWE	1948	Dick Button.....................USA	1976	John Curry ....GBR
1912	Not held	1952	Dick Button.....................USA	1980	Robin Cousins.................GBR
1920	Gillis Grafström ....SWE	1956	Hayes Alan Jenkins.........USA	1984	Scott Hamilton ....USA
1924	Gillis Grafström ....SWE	1960	David Jenkins ....USA	1988	Brian Boitano ....USA
1928	Gillis Grafström ....SWE	1964	Manfred Schnelldorfer......GER	1992	Victor Petrenko ....UT
1932	Karl Schäfer ....AUT	1968	Wolfgang Schwarz ....AUT	1994	Alexei Urmanov ....RUS
1936	Karl Schäfer ....AUT	1972	Ondrej Nepela................CZE		

WOMEN

Multiple gold medals: Sonja Henie (3); Katarina Witt (2).

Year		Year		Year	
1908	Madge Syers ....GBR	1948	Barbara Ann Scott ....CAN	1976	Dorothy Hamill ....USA
1912	Not held	1952	Jeanette Altwegg.............GBR	1980	Anett Pötzsch...............E. Ger
1920	Magda Julin-Mauroy.......SWE	1956	Tenley Albright ....USA	1984	Katarina Witt...............E. Ger
1924	Herma Planck-Szabö........AUT	1960	Carol Heiss ....USA	1988	Katarina Witt...............E. Ger
1928	Sonja Henie ....NOR	1964	Sjoukje Dijkstra ....HOL	1992	Kristi Yamaguchi ....USA
1932	Sonja Henie ....NOR	1968	Peggy Fleming.................USA	1994	Oksana Baiul..................UKR
1936	Sonja Henie ....NOR	1972	Beatrix Schuba ....AUT		

Pairs

Multiple gold medals: MEN—Pierre Brunet, Sergei Grinkov, Oleg Protopopov and Aleksandr Zaitsev (2). WOMEN—Irina Rodnina (3); Ludmila Belousova, Ekaterina Gordeeva and Andrée Joly Brunet (2).

Year		Year	
1908	Anna Hübler & Heinrich Burger................Germany	1960	Barbara Wagner & Robert Paul..................Canada
1912	Not held	1964	Ludmila Belousova & Oleg Protopopov ....USSR
1920	Ludovika & Walter Jakobsson......................Finland	1968	Ludmila Belousova & Oleg Protopopov ....USSR
1924	Helene Engelmann & Alfred Berger..............Austria	1972	Irina Rodnina & Aleksei Ulanov ....USSR
1928	Andrée Joly & Pierre Brunet ....France	1976	Irina Rodnina & Aleksandr Zaitsev ....USSR
1932	Andrée & Pierre Brunet................................France	1980	Irina Rodnina & Aleksandr Zaitsev ....USSR
1936	Maxi Herber & Ernst Baier ....Germany	1984	Elena Valova & Oleg Vasiliev.......................USSR
1948	Micheline Lannoy & Pierre Baugniet.............Belgium	1988	Ekaterina Gordeeva & Sergei Grinkov...............USSR
1952	Ria & Paul Falk ....Germany	1992	Natalya Mishkutienok & Arthur Dmitriev.............UT
1956	Elisabeth Schwartz & Kurt Oppelt ....Austria	1994	Ekaterina Gordeeva & Sergei Grinkov...............RUS

Ice Dancing

Year		Year	
1976	Lyudmila Pakhomova & Aleksandr Gorshkov....USSR	1988	Natalia Bestemianova & Andrei Bukin ....USSR
1980	Natalia Linichuk & Gennady Karponosov ....USSR	1992	Marina Klimova & Sergei Ponomarenko ....UT
1984	Jayne Torvill & Christopher Dean..........Great Britain	1994	Oksana Gritschuk & Yevgeny Platov ....RUS

ICE HOCKEY

Multiple gold medals: Soviet Union/Unified Team (8); Canada (6); United States (2).

Year		Year	
1920	**Canada**, United States Czechoslovakia	1964	**Soviet Union**, Sweden, Czechoslovakia
1924	**Canada**, United States, Great Britain	1968	**Soviet Union**, Czechoslovakia, Canada
1928	**Canada**, Sweden, Switzerland	1972	**Soviet Union**, United States, Czechoslovakia
1932	**Canada**, United States, Germany	1976	**Soviet Union**, Czechoslovakia, West Germany
1936	**Great Britain**, Canada, United States	1980	**United States**, Soviet Union, Sweden
1948	**Canada**, Czechoslovakia, Switzerland	1984	**Soviet Union**, Czechoslovakia, Sweden
1952	**Canada**, United States, Sweden	1988	**Soviet Union**, Finland, Sweden
1956	**Soviet Union**, United States, Canada	1992	**Unified Team**, Canada, Czechoslovakia
1960	**United States**, Canada, Soviet Union	1994	**Sweden**, Canada, Finland

U.S. Gold Medal Hockey Teams

1960

Forwards: Billy Christian, Roger Christian, Billy Cleary, Gene Grazia, Paul Johnson, Bob McVey, Dick Meredith, Weldy Olson, Dick Rodenheiser and Tom Williams. **Defensemen:** Bob Cleary, Jack Kirrane (captain), John Mayasich, Bob Owen and Rod Paavola. **Goaltenders:** Jack McCartan and Larry Palmer. **Coach:** Jack Riley.

1980

Forwards: Neal Broten, Steve Christoff, Mike Eruzione (captain), John Harrington, Mark Johnson, Rob McClanahan, Mark Pavelich, Buzz Schneider, Dave Silk, Eric Strobel, Phil Verchota and Mark Wells. **Defensemen:** Bill Baker, Dave Christian, Ken Morrow, Jack O'Callahan, Mike Ramsey and Bob Suter. **Goaltenders:** Jim Craig and Steve Janaszak. **Coach:** Herb Brooks.

LUGE

MEN

Multiple gold medals: (including doubles): Norbert Hahn, Georg Hackl, Paul Hildgartner, Thomas Köhler and Hans Rinn (2).

Singles

Year		Time	Year		Time
1964	Thomas Köhler, GER	3:26.77	1984	Paul Hildgartner, ITA	3:04.258
1968	Manfred Schmid, AUT	2:52.48	1988	Jens Müller, E. Ger	3:05.548
1972	Wolfgang Scheidel, E.Ger	3:27.58	1992	Georg Hackl, GER	3:02.363
1976	Dettlef Günther, E.Ger	3:27.688	1994	Georg Hackl, GER	3:21.571
1980	Bernhard Glass, E.Ger	2:54.796			

Doubles

Year		Time	Year		Time	Year		Time
1964	Austria	1:41.62	1976	East Germany	1:25.604	1988	East Germany	1:31.940
1968	East Germany	1:35.85	1980	East Germany	1:19.331	1992	Germany	1:32.053
1972	(TIE) East Germany & Italy	1:28.35 1:28.35	1984	West Germany	1:23.620	1994	Italy	1:36.720

WOMEN

Multiple gold medals: Steffi Martin Walter (2).

Singles

Year		Time	Year		Time
1964	Ortrun Enderlein, GER	3:24.67	1984	Steffi Martin, E. Ger	2:46.570
1968	Erica Lechner, ITA	2:28.66	1988	Steffi Martin Walter, E. Ger	3:03.973
1972	Anna-Maria Müller, E. Ger	2:59.18	1992	Doris Neuner, AUT	3:06.696
1976	Margit Schumann, E. Ger	2:50.621	1994	Gerda Weissensteiner, ITA	3:15.517
1980	Vera Zozulya, USSR	2:36.537			

NORDIC COMBINED

Multiple gold medals: Ulrich Wehling (3); Johan Gröttumsbräten (2).

Individual

Year		Points	Year		Points
1924	Thorleif Haug, NOR	18.906	1968	Franz Keller, W. Ger	449.04
1928	Johan Gröttumsbräten, NOR	17.833	1972	Ulrich Wehling, E. Ger	413.340
1932	Johan Gröttumsbräten, NOR	446.00	1976	Ulrich Wehling, E. Ger	423.39
1936	Oddbjörn Hagen, NOR	430.3	1980	Ulrich Wehling, E. Ger	432.200
1948	Heikki Hasu, FIN	448.80	1984	Tom Sandberg, NOR	422.595
1952	Simon Slattvik, NOR	451.621	1988	Hippolyt Kempf, SWI	432.230
1956	Sverre Stenersen, NOR	455.000	1992	Fabrice Guy, FRA	426.470
1960	Georg Thoma, GER	457.952	1994	Fred Borre Lundberg, NOR	457.970
1964	Tormod Knutsen, NOR	469.28			

Team

Year		Points	Year		Points
1924-84	Not held		1992	Japan	1247.180
1988	West Germany	792.08	1994	Japan	1368.860

SKI JUMPING

Multiple gold medals (including team jumping): Matti Nykänen (4); Jens Weissflog (3); Birger Ruud and Toni Nieminen (2).

Normal Hill—70 Meters

Year		Points	Year		Points
1924-60	Not held		1980	Anton Innauer, AUT	266.3
1964	Veikko Kankkonen, FIN	229.9	1984	Jens Weissflog, E. Ger	215.2
1968	Jiri Raska, CZE	216.5	1988	Matti Nykänen, FIN	229.1
1972	Yukio Kasaya, JPN	244.2	1992	Ernst Vettori, AUT	222.8
1976	Hans-Georg Aschenbach, E.Ger	252.0	1994	Espen Bredesen, NOR	282.0

Large Hill—90 Meters

Year		Points	Year		Points
1924	Jacob Tullin Thams, NOR	18.960	1968	Vladimir Beloussov, USSR	231.3
1928	Alf Andersen, NOR	19.208	1972	Wojciech Fortuna, POL	219.9
1932	Birger Ruud, NOR	228.1	1976	Karl Schnabl, AUT	234.8
1936	Birger Ruud, NOR	232.0	1980	Jouko Törmänen, FIN	271.0
1948	Petter Hugsted, NOR	228.1	1984	Matti Nykänen, FIN	231.2
1952	Arnfinn Bergmann, NOR	226.0	1988	Matti Nykänen, FIN	224.0
1956	Antti Hyvärinen, FIN	227.0	1992	Toni Nieminen, FIN	239.5
1960	Helmut Recknagel, GER	227.2	1994	Jens Weissflog, GER	274.5
1964	Toralf Engan, NOR	230.7			

Note: Jump held at various lengths from 1924-56; at 80 meters from 1960-64; at 90 meters from 1968-88; and at 120 meters in 1992.

Team Large Hill

Year		Points	Year		Points
1924-84	Not held		1992	Finland	644.4
1988	Finland	634.4	1994	Germany	970.1

SPEED SKATING

MEN

Multiple gold medals: Eric Heiden and Clas Thunberg (5); Ivar Ballangrud, Yevgeny Grishin and Johann Olav Koss (4); Hjalmar Andersen, Tomas Gustafson, Irving Jaffee and Ard Schenk (3); Gaétan Boucher, Knut Johannesen, Erhard Keller, Uwe-Jens Mey and Jack Shea (2). Note that Thunberg's total includes the All-Around, which was contested for the only time in 1924.

500 meters

Year		Time		Year		Time	
1924	Charles Jewtraw, USA	44.0		1964	Terry McDermott, USA	40.1	OR
1928	(TIE) Bernt Evensen, NOR	43.4	OR	1968	Erhard Keller, W. Ger	40.3	
	& Clas Thunberg, FIN	43.4	OR	1972	Erhard Keller, W. Ger	39.44	OR
1932	Jack Shea, USA	43.4	=OR	1976	Yevgeny Kulikov, USSR	39.17	OR
1936	Ivar Ballangrud, NOR	43.4	=OR	1980	Eric Heiden, USA	38.03	OR
1948	Finn Helgesen, NOR	43.1	OR	1984	Sergei Fokichev, USSR	38.19	
1952	Ken Henry, USA	43.2		1988	Uwe-Jens Mey, E. Ger	36.45	WR
1956	Yevgeny Grishin, USSR	40.2	=WR	1992	Uwe-Jens Mey, GER	37.14	
1960	Yevgeny Grishin, USSR	40.2	=WR	1994	Aleksandr Golubev, RUS	36.33	OR

1000 meters

Year		Time		Year		Time	
1924-72	Not held			1988	Nikolai Gulyaev, USSR	1:13.03	OR
1976	Peter Mueller, USA	1:19.32		1992	Olaf Zinke, GER	1:14.85	
1980	Eric Heiden, USA	1:15.18	OR	1994	Dan Jansen, USA	1:12.43	WR
1984	Gaétan Boucher, CAN	1:15.80					

1500 meters

Year		Time		Year		Time	
1924	Clas Thunberg, FIN	2:20.8		1964	Ants Antson, USSR	2:10.3	
1928	Clas Thunberg, FIN	2:21.1		1968	Kees Verkerk, HOL	2:03.4	OR
1932	Jack Shea, USA	2:57.5		1972	Ard Schenk, HOL	2:02.96	OR
1936	Charles Mathisen, NOR	2:19.2	OR	1976	Jan Egil Storholt, NOR	1:59.38	OR
1948	Sverre Farstad, NOR	2:17.6	OR	1980	Eric Heiden, USA	1:55.44	OR
1952	Hjalmar Andersen, NOR	2:20.4		1984	Gaétan Boucher, CAN	1:58.36	
1956	(TIE)Yevgeny Grishin, USSR	2:08.6	WR	1988	André Hoffman, E. Ger	1:52.06	WR
	& Yuri Mikhailov, USSR	2:08.6	WR	1992	Johann Olav Koss, NOR	1:54.81	
1960	(TIE) Roald Aas, NOR	2:10.4		1994	Johann Olav Koss, NOR	1:51.29	WR
	& Yevgeny Grishin, USSR	2:10.4					

5000 meters

Year		Time		Year		Time	
1924	Clas Thunberg, FIN	8:39.0		1968	Fred Anton Maier, NOR	7:22.4	WR
1928	Ivar Ballangrud, NOR	8:50.5		1972	Ard Schenk, HOL	7:23.61	
1932	Irving Jaffee, USA	9:40.8		1976	Sten Stensen, NOR	7:24.48	
1936	Ivar Ballangrud, NOR	8:19.6	OR	1980	Eric Heiden, USA	7:02.29	OR
1948	Reidar Liaklev, NOR	8:29.4		1984	Tomas Gustafson, SWE	7:12.28	
1952	Hjalmar Andersen, NOR	8:10.6	OR	1988	Tomas Gustafson, SWE	6:44.63	WR
1956	Boris Shilkov, USSR	7:48.7	OR	1992	Geir Karlstad, NOR	6:59.97	
1960	Viktor Kosichkin, USSR	7:51.3		1994	Johann Olav Koss, NOR	6:34.96	WR
1964	Knut Johannesen, NOR	7:38.4	OR				

Speed Skating (Cont.)

MEN

10,000 meters

Year		Time		Year		Time	
1924	Julius Skutnabb, FIN	18:04.8		1968	Johnny Höglin, SWE	15:23.6	OR
1928	Irving Jaffee, USA*	18:36.5		1972	Ard Schenk, HOL	15:01.35	OR
1932	Irving Jaffee, USA	19:13.6		1976	Piet Kleine, HOL	14:50.59	OR
1936	Ivar Ballangrud, NOR	17:24.3	OR	1980	Eric Heiden, USA	14:28.13	WR
1948	Ake Seyffarth, SWE	17:26.3		1984	Igor Malkov, USSR	14:39.90	
1952	Hjalmar Andersen, NOR	16:45.8	OR	1988	Tomas Gustafson, SWE	13:48.20	WR
1956	Sigvard Ericsson, SWE	16:35.9	OR	1992	Bart Veldkamp, HOL	14:12.12	
1960	Knut Johannesen, NOR	15:46.6	WR	1994	Johann Olav Koss, NOR	13:30.55	WR
1964	Jonny Nilsson, SWE	15:50.1					

*Unofficial, according to the IOC. Jaffee recorded the fastest time, but the event was called off in progress due to thawing ice.

WOMEN

Multiple gold medals: Lydia Skoblikova (6); Bonnie Blair (5); Karin Enke and Yvonne van Gennip (3); Tatiana Averina, Gunda Niemann and Christa Rothenburger (2).

500 meters

Year		Time		Year		Time	
1960	Helga Haase, GER	45.9		1980	Karin Enke, E. Ger	41.78	OR
1964	Lydia Skoblikova, USSR	45.0	OR	1984	Christa Rothenburger, E. Ger	41.02	OR
1968	Lyudmila Titova, USSR	46.1		1988	Bonnie Blair, USA	39.10	WR
1972	Anne Henning, USA	43.33	OR	1992	Bonnie Blair, USA	40.33	
1976	Sheila Young, USA	42.76	OR	1994	Bonnie Blair, USA	39.25	

1000 meters

Year		Time		Year		Time	
1960	Klara Guseva, USSR	1:34.1		1980	Natalia Petruseva, USSR	1:24.10	OR
1964	Lydia Skoblikova, USSR	1:33.2	OR	1984	Karin Enke, E. Ger	1:21.61	OR
1968	Carolina Geijssen, HOL	1:32.6	OR	1988	Christa Rothenburger, E. Ger	1:17.65	WR
1972	Monika Pflug, W. Ger	1:31.40	OR	1992	Bonnie Blair, USA	1:21.90	
1976	Tatiana Averina, USSR	1:28.43	OR	1994	Bonnie Blair, USA	1:18.74	

1500 meters

Year		Time		Year		Time	
1960	Lydia Skoblikova, USSR	2:25.2	WR	1980	Annie Borckink, HOL	2:10.95	OR
1964	Lydia Skoblikova, USSR	2:22.6	OR	1984	Karin Enke, E. Ger	2:03.42	WR
1968	Kaija Mustonen, FIN	2:22.4	OR	1988	Yvonne van Gennip, HOL	2:00.68	OR
1972	Dianne Holum, USA	2:20.85	OR	1992	Jacqueline Börner, GER	2:05.87	
1976	Galina Stepanskaya, USSR	2:16.58	OR	1994	Emese Hunyady, AUT	2:02.19	

3000 meters

Year		Time		Year		Time	
1960	Lydia Skoblikova, USSR	5:14.3		1980	Bjorg Eva Jensen, NOR	4:32.13	OR
1964	Lydia Skoblikova, USSR	5:14.9		1984	Andrea Schöne, E. Ger	4:24.79	OR
1968	Johanna Schut, HOL	4:56.2	OR	1988	Yvonne van Gennip, HOL	4:11.94	WR
1972	Christina Baas-Kaiser, HOL	4:52.14	OR	1992	Gunda Niemann, GER	4:19.90	
1976	Tatiana Averina, USSR	4:45.19	OR	1994	Svetlana Bazhanova, RUS	4:17.43	

5000 meters

Year		Time		Year		Time	
1960-84 Not held				1992	Gunda Niemann, GER	7:31.57	
1988	Yvonne van Gennip, HOL	7:14.13	WR	1994	Claudia Pechstein, GER	7:14.37	

Athletes with Winter and Summer Medals

Only three athletes have won medals in both the Winter and Summer Olympics:

Eddie Eagan, USA— Light Heavyweight Boxing gold (1920) and Four-man Bobsled gold (1932).

Jacob Tullin Thams, Norway— Ski Jumping gold (1924) and 8-meter Yachting silver (1936).

Christa Luding-Rothenburger, East Germany— Speed Skating gold at 500 meters (1984) and 1,000m (1988), silver at 500m (1988) and bronze at 500m (1992) and Match Sprint Cycling silver (1988). Luding-Rothenburger is the only athlete to ever win medals in both Winter and Summer Games in the same year.

All-Time Leading Medal Winners

MEN

No		Sport	G-S-B
9	Sixten Jernberg, SWE	Cross-country	4-3-2
8	Bjorn Dählie, NOR	Cross-country	5-3-0
7	Clas Thunberg, FIN	Speed Skating	5-1-1
7	Ivar Ballangrud, NOR	Speed Skating	4-2-1
7	Veikko Hakulinen, FIN	Cross-country	3-3-1
7	Eero Mäntyranta, FIN	Cross-country	3-2-2
7	Bogdan Musiol, E. Ger/GER	Bobsled	1-5-1
6	Gunde Svan, SWE	Cross-country	4-1-1
6	Vegard Ulvang, NOR	Cross-country	3-2-1
6	Johan Gröttumsbraten, NOR	Nordic	3-1-2
6	Wolfgang Hoppe, E. Ger/GER	Bobsled	2-3-1
6	Eugenio Monti, ITA	Bobsled	2-2-2
6	Roald Larsen, NOR	Speed Skating	0-2-4
5	**Eric Heiden, USA**	Speed Skating	5-0-0
5	Yevgeny Grishin, USSR	Speed Skating	4-1-0
5	Johann Olav Koss, NOR	Speed Skating	4-1-0
5	Matti Nykänen, FIN	Ski Jumping	4-1-0
5	Aleksandr Tikhonov, USSR	Biathlon	4-1-0
5	Nikolai Zimyatov, USSR	Cross-country	4-1-0
5	Alberto Tomba, ITA	Alpine	3-2-0
5	Harald Grönningen, NOR	Cross-country	2-3-0
5	Pål Tyldum, NOR	Cross-country	2-3-0
5	Knut Johannesen, NOR	Speed Skating	2-2-1
5	Vladimir Smirnov, USSR/UT/KAZ	X-country	1-4-0
5	Kjetil André Aamodt, NOR	Alpine	1-2-2
5	Peter Angerer, W. Ger/GER	Biathlon	1-2-2
5	Juha Mieto, FIN	Cross-country	1-2-2
5	Fritz Feierabend, SWI	Bobsled	0-3-2

WOMEN

No		Sport	G-S-B
10	Raisa Smetanina, USSR/UT	Cross-country	4-5-1
9	Lyubov Egorova, UT/RUS	Cross-country	6-3-0
8	Galina Kulakova, USSR	Cross-country	4-2-2
8	Karin (Enke) Kania, E. Ger	Speed Skating	3-4-1
7	Marja-Liisa (Hämäläinen) Kirvesniemi, FIN	Cross-country	3-0-4
7	Andrea (Mitscherlich, Schöne) Ehrig, E. Ger	Speed Skating	1-5-1
6	Lydia Skoblikova, USSR	Speed Skating	6-0-0
6	**Bonnie Blair, USA**	Speed Skating	5-0-1
6	Manuela Di Centa, ITA	Cross-country	2-2-2
6	Elena Valbe, UT/RUS	Cross-country	2-0-4
5	Anfisa Reztsova, USSR/UT	CC/Biathlon	3-1-1
5	Vreni Schneider, SWI	Alpine	3-1-1
5	Gunda Neimann, GER	Speed Skating	2-2-1
5	Helena Takalo, FIN	Cross-country	1-3-1
5	Stefania Belmondo, ITA	Cross-country	1-1-3
5	Alevtina Kolchina, USSR	Cross-country	1-1-3

Games Medaled In

MEN— Aamodt (1992,94); **Angerer** (1980,84,88); **Ballangrud** (1928,32,36); **Dählie** (1992,94); **Feierabend** (1936,48,52); **Grishin** (1956,60,64); **Gröttumsbraten** (1924,28,32); **Grönningen** (1960,64,68); **Hakulinen** (1952,56,60); **Heiden** (1980); **Hoppe** (1984,88,92,94); **Jernberg** (1956,60,64); **Johannesen** (1956,60,64); **Koss** (1992,94). **Larsen** (1924,28); **Mäntyranta** (1960,64,68); **Mieto** (1976,80,84); **Monti** (1956,60,64,68); **Musiol** (1980,84,88,92); **Nykänen** (1984,88); **Smirnov** (1988,92,94); **Svan** (1984,88); **Thunberg** (1924,28); **Tikhonov** (1968,72,76,80); **Tomba** (1988,92,94); **Tyldum** (1968,72,76); **Ulvang** (1988,92,94); **Zimyatov** (1980,84).

WOMEN— Belmondo (1992,94); **Blair** (1988,92,94); **Di Centa** (1992,94); **Egorova** (1992,94); **Ehrig** (1976,80,84,88); **Kania** (1980,84,88); **Kirvesniemi** (1984,88,94); **Kolchina** (1956,64,68); **Kulakova** (1968,72,76,80); **Niemann** (1992-94); **Reztsova** (1988,92,94); **Schneider** (1988,92,94); **Skoblikova** (1960,64); **Smetanina** (1976,80,84,88,92); **Takalo** (1972,76,80); **Valbe** (1992,94).

Most Gold Medals

MEN

No		Sport	G-S-B
5	Bjorn Dählie, NOR	Cross-country	5-3-0
5	Clas Thunberg, FIN	Speed Skating	5-1-1
5	**Eric Heiden, USA**	Speed Skating	5-0-0
4	Sixten Jernberg, SWE	Cross-country	4-3-2
4	Ivar Ballangrud, NOR	Speed Skating	4-2-1
4	Gunde Svan, SWE	Cross-country	4-1-1
4	Yevgeny Grishin, USSR	Speed Skating	4-1-0
4	Johann Olav Koss, NOR	Speed Skating	4-1-0
4	Matti Nykänen, FIN	Ski Jumping	4-1-0
4	Aleksandr Tikhonov, USSR	Biathlon	4-1-0
4	Nikolai Zimyatov, USSR	Cross-country	4-1-0
4	Thomas Wassberg, SWE	Cross-country	4-0-0
3	Veikko Hakulinen, FIN	Cross-country	3-3-1
3	Eero Mäntyranta, FIN	Cross-country	3-2-2
3	Vegard Ulvang, NOR	Cross-country	3-2-1
3	Alberto Tomba, ITA	Alpine	3-2-0
3	Johan Gröttumsbräten, NOR	Nordic	3-1-2
3	Bernhard Germeshausen, E. Ger	Bobsled	3-1-0
3	Gillis Grafström, SWE	Figure Skating	3-1-0
3	Tomas Gustafson, SWE	Speed Skating	3-1-0
3	Vladislav Tretiak, USSR	Ice Hockey	3-1-0
3	Jens Weissflog, E. Ger/GER	Ski Jumping	3-1-0
3	Meinhard Nehmer, E. Ger	Bobsled	3-0-1
3	Hjalmar Andersen, NOR	Speed Skating	3-0-0
3	Vitaly Davydov, USSR	Ice Hockey	3-0-0
3	Anatoly Firsov, USSR	Ice Hockey	3-0-0
3	Thorleif Haug, NOR	Cross-country	3-0-0
3	**Irving Jaffee, USA**	Speed Skating	3-0-0
3	Andrei Khomoutov, USSR/UT	Ice Hockey	3-0-0
3	Jean-Claude Killy, FRA	Alpine	3-0-0
3	Viktor Kuzkin, USSR	Ice Hockey	3-0-0
3	Aleksandr Ragulin, USSR	Ice Hockey	3-0-0
3	Toni Sailer, AUT	Alpine	3-0-0
3	Ard Schenk, HOL	Speed Skating	3-0-0
3	Ulrich Wehling, E. Ger	Ski Jumping	3-0-0

WOMEN

No		Sport	G-S-B
6	Lyubov Egorova, UT/RUS	Cross-country	6-3-0
6	Lydia Skoblikova, USSR	Speed Skating	6-0-0
5	**Bonnie Blair, USA**	Speed Skating	5-0-1
4	Raisa Smetanina, USSR/UT	Cross-country	4-5-1
4	Galina Kulakova, USSR	Cross-country	4-2-2
3	Karin (Enke) Kania, E. Ger	Speed Skating	3-4-1
3	Anfisa Reztsova, USSR/UT	CC/Biathlon	3-1-1
3	Vreni Schneider, SWI	Alpine	3-1-1
3	Marja-Liisa (Hämäläinen) Kirvesniemi, FIN	Cross-country	3-0-4
3	Claudia Boyarskikh, USSR	Cross-country	3-0-0
3	Sonja Henie, NOR	Figure Skating	3-0-0
3	Irina Rodnina, USSR	Figure Skating	3-0-0
3	Yvonne van Gennip, HOL	Speed Skating	3-0-0

All-Time Leading USA Medalists

MEN

No		Sport	G-S-B
5	Eric Heiden	Speed Skating	5-0-0
3*	Irving Jaffee	Speed Skating	3-0-0
3	Pat Martin	Bobsled	1-2-0
3	John Heaton	Bobsled/Cresta	0-2-1
2	Dick Button	Figure Skating	2-0-0
2†	Eddie Eagan	Boxing/Bobsled	2-0-0
2	Billy Fiske	Bobsled	2-0-0
2	Cliff Gray	Bobsled	2-0-0
2	Jack Shea	Speed Skating	2-0-0
2	Billy Cleary	Ice Hockey	1-1-0
2	Jennison Heaton	Bobsled/Cresta	1-1-0
2	John Mayasich	Ice Hockey	1-1-0
2	Terry McDermott	Speed Skating	1-1-0
2	Dick Meredith	Ice Hockey	1-1-0
2	Tommy Moe	Alpine	1-1-0
2	Weldy Olson	Ice Hockey	1-1-0
2	Dick Rodenheiser	Ice Hockey	1-1-0
2	David Jenkins	Figure Skating	1-1-0
2	Stan Benham	Bobsled	0-2-0
2	Herb Drury	Ice Hockey	0-2-0
2	Eric Flaim	Sp. Skate/ST Sp. Skate	0-2-0
2	Frank Synott	Ice Hockey	0-2-0
2	John Garrison	Ice Hockey	0-1-1

WOMEN

No		Sport	G-S-B
6	Bonnie Blair	Speed Skating	5-0-1
4	Cathy Turner	ST Sp. Skating	2-1-1
4	Dianne Holum	Speed Skating	1-2-1
3	Sheila Young	Speed Skating	1-1-1
3	Leah Poulos Mueller	Speed Skating	0-3-0
3	Beatrix Loughran	Figure Skating	0-2-1
3	Amy Peterson	ST Sp. Skating	0-2-1
2	Andrea Mead Lawrence	Alpine	2-0-0
2	Tenley Albright	Figure Skating	1-1-0
2	Gretchen Fraser	Alpine	1-1-0
2	Carol Heiss	Figure Skating	1-1-0
2	Diann Roffe-Steinrotter	Alpine	1-1-0
2	Anne Henning	Speed Skating	1-0-1
2	Penny Pitou	Alpine	0-2-0
2	Nancy Kerrigan	Figure Skating	0-1-1
2	Jean Saubert	Alpine	0-1-1
2	Nikki Ziegelmeyer	ST Sp. Skating	0-1-1

Notes: The Cresta run is undertaken on a heavy sled ridden head first in the prone position and has only been held at St. Moritz in 1928 and '48. Also, the term ST Sp. Skating refers to Short Track (or pack) Speed Skating.

*Jaffee is generally given credit for a third gold medal in the 10,000-meter Speed Skating race of 1928. He had the fastest time before the race was cancelled due to thawing ice. The IOC considers the race unofficial.

†Eagan won the Light Heavyweight boxing title at the 1920 Summer Games in Antwerp and the four-man Bobsled at the 1932 Winter Games in Lake Placid. He is the only athlete ever to win gold medals in both the Winter and Summer Olympics.

All-Time Medal Standings, 1924-94

All-time Winter Games medal standings, according to *The Golden Book of the Olympic Games* and updated through 1994. Medal counts include figure skating medals (1908 and '20) and hockey medals (1920) awarded at the Summer Games. National medal standings for the Winter and Summer Games are not recognized by the IOC.

		G	S	B	Total
1	Norway	73	77	64	214
2	Soviet Union (1956-88)	78	57	59	194
3	**United States**	53	56	37	146
4	Austria	36	48	44	128
5	East Germany (1956-88)	43	39	36	118
6	Finland	36	45	42	123
7	Sweden	39	26	34	99
8	Switzerland	27	29	29	85
9	Italy	25	21	21	67
10	Germany (1928-36,92—)	23	21	17	61
11	Canada	19	20	25	64
12	West Germany (1952-88)	18	20	19	57
13	France	16	16	21	53
14	Holland	14	19	17	50
15	Russia (1994—)	12	8	4	24
16	Unified Team (1992)	9	6	8	23
17	Great Britain	7	4	12	23
18	Czechoslovakia (1924-92)	2	8	16	26
19	Japan	3	8	8	19
20	South Korea	6	2	2	10
21	Liechtenstein	2	2	5	9

		G	S	B	Total
22	China	0	4	2	6
23	Hungary	0	2	4	6
24	Belgium	1	1	2	4
	Poland	1	1	2	4
	Yugoslavia (1924-88)	0	3	1	4
	Kazakhstan (1994—)	1	2	0	3
28	Spain	1	0	1	2
	Ukraine (1994—)	1	0	1	2
	Belarus (1994—)	0	2	0	2
	Luxembourg	0	2	0	2
32	Slovenia (1992—)	0	0	3	3
	North Korea	0	1	1	2
	Uzbekistan (1994—)	1	0	0	1
35	New Zealand	0	1	0	1
36	Australia	0	0	1	1
	Bulgaria	0	0	1	1
	Romania	0	0	1	1

Combined totals	G	S	B	Total
USSR/UT/Russia	99	71	71	241
Germany/E. Ger/W. Ger	84	80	72	236

Notes: Athletes from the USSR participated in the Winter Games from 1956-88, returned as the Unified Team in 1992 after the breakup of the Soviet Union (in 1991) and then competed for the independent republics of Belarus, Kazakhstan, Russia, Ukraine, Uzbekistan and three others in 1994. Yugoslavia divided into Croatia and Bosnia-Herzegovina in 1991, while Czechoslovakia split into Slovenia and the Czech Republic the same year.

Germany was barred from the Olympics in 1924 and 1948 as an aggressor nation in both World Wars I and II. Divided into East and West Germany after WWII, both countries competed under one flag from 1952-64, then as separate teams from 1968-88. Germany was reunified in 1990.

Midfielders **Cobi Jones** (left) and **John Harkes** were major players in the United States national team's stunning 3-0 victory over Argentina in the 1995 Copa America tournament in Uruguay.

SOCCER

Boom Times

Money, sleaze and free agency dominate the game in Europe,
while closer to home the U.S. national team stars at the Copa.

Money. Whether Italian lire or German marks or Spanish pesetas or English pounds— or, yes, even in Yankee dollars— money poured into soccer in 1995.

The game itself seemed to fade into the background after the World Cup high of 1994. Money became the dominant theme. Memories of the games and players of World Cup '94 were replaced by a new set of images. The financial figures were in, and they were sensational. The tournament, hosted by the United States, turned in a profit of $100 million. Each of the 24 teams that had participated would receive $670,000 for each game that it had played.

World Cup '98, to be played in France, kept up the pace. The organizers announced an initial operating budget of $300 million, plus the building of a new stadium in Paris, the Grand Stade, at a cost of $400 million. Calling it the "greatest mass media event of the 20th century," the French organizers predicted a cumulative total of 37 billion television viewers for the tournament (World Cup '94 had managed only a mere 32 billion).

It was the same story at the club level. The German league announced that its income had tripled in the past decade, up to a record $360 million in 1994. England's

Paul Gardner has been the columnist for *Soccer America* since 1982 and is the author of four books on the sport, including *The Simplest Game* (Collier Books).

Manchester United announced a record profit of over $15 million at the halfway point of the 1994-95 season.

There were a few dark spots— but even when clubs got seriously into debt, no one seemed too concerned, such was the faith in soccer. One of the most famous of all clubs, Real Madrid, was reported to be on the verge of bankruptcy, with debts of nearly $86 million. "Nonsense," said its treasurer. "An exaggeration. The true figure is $53 million. But we are the richest club in Spain, we have no problems with the banks or anyone."

The situation was somewhat grimmer for Tony Wood, owner of the English 2nd division club Leyton Orient. After losing his coffee-growing business in the Rwandan civil war, he offered the club for sale at a bargain price: "I will hand over the keys to anyone who gives me five pounds ($7.50)."

Olympique Marseille, the pride of France when it won the 1993 European Cup, was reportedly $50 million in debt. Its problems had started when its chairman, former French government minister Bernard Tapie, was accused of trying to bribe an opposing team to lose. He was then accused of trying to silence witnesses at his trial, during which he spat abuse and threats at judge, prosecutors and witnesses alike.

Found guilty and sentenced to one year in jail, Tapie protested that he was to blame "only for not being rich enough to go on." If he had lied during the trial, he said, "I lied in good faith." Marseille was sent down to the second division.

After many years with AC Milan in Italy, Holland's **Ruud Gullit** (right) could be found elevating his game with Chelsea of the English Premier League in 1995. He is one of several top foreign players, including countryman Denis Bergkamp, to sign with suddenly free-spending clubs in England.

The combination of money and corruption was nowhere more evident than in England. Suddenly England was up there with Italy and Spain as the sport's big spenders. Top foreign players— among them Germany's Jurgen Klinsmann, France's Eric Cantona and the Dutch duo of Ruud Gullit and Denis Bergkamp— made the move to the English Premier League. Spending on players escalated dramatically. Liverpool broke the English record when it bought forward Stan Collymore from Nottingham Forest for a fee of $13 million.

But the most commonly used word during the English season was "sleaze." It really did seem as though there was too much money around. How else to account for the extraordinary goings-on at Arsenal? Coach George Graham was accused by the press of pocketing money paid by Arsenal for the purchase of players.

The specific accusation was that he and a Norwegian agent, Rune Hauge, negotiated the purchase of two Danish players, told Arsenal that the fee was substantially higher than that agreed, then split the difference between them.

The pay-off— known as a "bung" in England— was substantial. As soon as the accusations surfaced the English tax authorities started an investigation and Graham— while denying any wrongdoing— turned over some $430,000 to Arsenal. Surprisingly, Arsenal expressed confidence in Graham, and did not fire him until an independent investigation found him guilty of misconduct. He was suspended for one year from all soccer activity.

There was plenty more on the sleaze front. Bruce Grobbelaar, for years the goalkeeper with top club Liverpool, was arrested and charged with match-fixing. Arsenal player Paul Merson admitted to a gambling and drug addiction, and was suspended while he underwent rehab.

The dreaded English hooligans made a formidable re-appearance at England's Feb.

Wide World Photos

The British tabloids were quick to condemn the return of hooliganism at the international friendly between England and Ireland at Dublin on Feb. 16. The match had to be abandoned when fan violence resulted in over 50 injuries and 40 arrests.

15 exhibition game with Ireland in Dublin, where they rained bottles, chairs and other missiles on to the field. There more than 50 injuries and 40 arrests, and the game had to be suspended after 23 minutes.

The violence was particularly worrying since England is scheduled to host Euro '96, the 10th quadrennial European Championship from June 8-30. Guarantees of a trouble-free tournament began to look rather doubtful.

But it was a foreigner who provided the sleaziest episode of the English season. Manchester United's French star Eric Cantona, a striker equally famous for his goal-scoring prowess and his short fuse, leaped into the stands during a game with Crystal Palace on Jan. 25 and delivered a spectacular kung-fu kick at a spectator who was abusing him.

Manchester United immediately suspended him and added a fine of $30,000, and the Football Association followed with a seven-month ban. But this one went further. Cantona was also found guilty of assault in the criminal courts and given a two week jail sentence— later commuted to 120 hours of community service.

The 29-year-old Cantona, a tempestuous, brooding man with a penchant for writing poetry, commented: "When the seagulls follow the trawler, it is because they think sardines will be thrown into the sea." Less cryptically, a 13-year-old fan penned an ode to Cantona: "Eric is an idol, Eric is a star. If my mother had her way, he would also be my Pa."

Cantona returned to action with a flourish before the hometown fans on Oct. 1, assisting on a goal in the second minute of play and tying the game on a penalty kick in the second half as Manchester United tied Liverpool, 2-2.

The dean of soccer rebels, 34-year-old Diego Maradona, continued his troubled saga in Argentina. After FIFA had confirmed his 15-month worldwide ban following a positive dope-test during World Cup '94, Maradona announced: "They killed me. I'm completely dead. I don't know where I stand now. I can't find myself."

In 1995, Maradona took over as head coach at Mandiyu, quit after only two months and moved on to coach Racing at a reported $750,000 a year.

Next he turned up in Cuba to visit his pal Fidel Castro ("I would give my life for Fidel," he said.), then went on to France to receive an award. There, he announced that he would not play again.

After receiving a $1,400 fine for insulting a referee, Maradona was then ejected from a game for throwing water over a linesman. "I was only trying to get his attention to make a substitution," he said. Two days later, he resigned as Racing's coach.

In May, Maradona was said to be on the verge of signing, as a player, for Pelé's old club, Santos of Brazil. "It would be another chance for him," said Pelé, now Minister of Sport in the Brazilian government, "We all make mistakes. Nobody is perfect."

Instead, Maradona reached an agreement to play for his old club, Boca Juniors, at a reported $20,000 a month. In preparation for his return to the playing field, he underwent liposuction treatment to get rid of his double chin.

He finally returned to the playing field on Oct. 1, before a crowd of 70,000 at the Olympic Stadium in Seoul. Sluggish but sporting a new blond streak in his black hair, Maradona set up a goal with a corner kick in the 42nd minute as Boca Juniors

Alexi Lalas (No. 22) and **Eric Wynalda** (left center) join mob of players congratulating midfielder **Frank Klapas** (hidden) after his goal gave the United States national team a 1-0 lead over Argentina in the first half of their July 14 Copa America match. Lalas and Wynalda also scored in the 3-0 upset.

beat the South Korean national team, 2-1.

The comeback was such an big event back in Argentina that President Carlos Menem flew in to see the game.

Amidst the mountains of money, the mayhem and the madness, there were serious attempts to actually play the sport of soccer.

FIFA staged three of its own tournaments during 1995: the Women's World Championship in Sweden (see page 723), and the Men's Under-20 and Under-17 World Cups.

The U-20 championship was in trouble before a ball was even kicked. It was supposed to be played in Nigeria in March, but months beforehand rumors were circulating that Nigeria would not be able to handle it. "It'll be the eighth wonder of the world if they're ready by March," said Jack Warner of FIFA's executive committee.

In February, FIFA announced that it was postponing the tournament because of the "health situation" in Nigeria.

Cries of foul and discrimination quickly followed. "Nigeria and black Africa have been insulted," said Babasola Rhodes of the Nigerian National Sports Commission. Samson Omeruah, president of the Nigerian Football Association, denied that there was a health crisis in Nigeria. FIFA backed off, and said it would reconsider its decision.

On March 16, FIFA confirmed that it was withdrawing the tournament from Nigeria. This time the reason given was worry over security. With only one month to prepare, Qatar was named host and the tournament was rescheduled for April 13-28. Nigeria refused to participate and tried, unsuccessfully, to organize a boycott by the other African qualifiers, Burundi and Cameroon.

The championship, with semifinal pairings of Portugal-Brazil and Spain-Argentina, turned into a triumph for Latin soccer. Victories for Brazil and Argentina set up an all-South American final which ended in a 2-0 win for Argentina.

Staged in Ecuador in August, the U-17 World Cup also saw Argentina and Brazil reach the Final Four again, but it was Ghana that claimed the title.

Ghana's 3-2 win over Brazil in the final suggests a close game, but it was never that. Indeed, such was Ghana's superiority over every other team in the tournament, that many doubted its players could possibly be the right age.

One of the few who made his suspicions public was the Portuguese coach, Rui Cacador: "The players of Ghana cannot be the age they say they are," he said. "No team of 16-year-olds can play constantly on the offensive, as this team does, or possess this level of ball control."

FIFA continued to use the U-17 tournament as a testing ground for rule changes. In Ecuador, the experiment was with time-outs— one per team per half. The coaches, said FIFA, have asked us to try it. Yet most of the 16 coaches in Ecuador expressed only lukewarm support for the idea. In the 32 games of the tournament, 44 time-outs were called— only one third of the 128 that could have been taken.

In 1995, there were two major tournaments at the senior professional level: the Intercontinental Cup in January and the Copa America in July.

The Intercontinental, played in Saudi Arabia, featured the hosts plus the reigning champion national teams of Europe (Denmark), South America (Argentina), Africa (Nigeria), Asia (Japan) and North America (Mexico). Denmark defeated Argentina, 2-0, in the final.

Uruguay staged the Copa America, the South American Championship, which included two invited North American teams: Mexico and the United States.

In what turned out to be a mediocre tournament, a rather ordinary Uruguayan team tied Brazil, 1-1, in the final and then won, 5-3, on penalty kicks for their 14th Copa title. Winning coach Hector Nunez was at pains to point out that the victory had been obtained without the gamesmanship that Uruguay has so often been accused of in the past: "We don't win games by poking other players' eyes and grabbing their testicles," said Nunez.

The surprise team of the tournament— the "revelation" according to the Uruguayan press— was the United States, which stunned Argentina, 3-0, and reached the semifinals before losing, 1-0, to Brazil.

After demolishing Chile, 4-0, and beating Bolivia, 2-1, to clinch a berth in the second round, Argentine coach Daniel Passarella— he of the no-long-hair, no-earrings, no-gays-on-the-team stance— decided to rest virtually everyone against the U.S. and started *nine* substitutes

Beyond any shadow of a doubt Passarella massively underestimated the Americans and quickly paid for it as Frank Klopas scored in the 21st minute and long-haired Alexi Lalas scored in the 32nd minute to give the U.S. a 2-0 lead at halftime.

Passarella put his big attacking guns back on the field in the second in the second half, but it didn't work. A third U.S. goal by Eric Wynalda in the 59th minute ended the scoring.

"We knew the risk we were taking with the decision to rest players," said Passarella later. "But we never considered that we were going to lose."

The Argentine press called it, "The Black Night" and "An historic slap in the face."

On the other hand, interim American head coach Steve Sampson said, "I think it's the second most important U.S. win in history. The first was against Colombia, because that was in the World Cup."

Interim coach? On April 14, three months before the Copa America, the United States Soccer Federation announced that coach Bora Milutinovic had resigned. Bora piped up a day later, denied the resignation, and said he'd been fired. Whatever happened, it was an embarrassment for USSF president Alan Rothenberg, who had been going around publicly declaring his faith in Bora.

Rothenberg, executing a sudden U-turn, now said that a new coach was needed and it would have to be a foreigner because "they have the international experience that we lack."

The USSF announced that it was negotiating with Carlos Queiroz of Portugal, highly respected for his work in developing young players. Queiroz elected to stay in Portugal. Then the USSF went after Carlos Alberto Parreira, Brazil's 1994 World Cup-winning coach. But Parreira accepted a $1 million-plus contract with Turkish club Fenerbahce.

All of which left the U.S. national team without a coach on the eve of its own tournament, U.S. Cup '95. Sampson, a former Division I college coach and Bora's only American-born assistant, was hurriedly given the interim job.

The team responded immediately to Sampson's leadership, beating Nigeria (3-2) and Mexico (4-0), and tying Colombia (0-0) to win U.S. Cup '95. His part-time status was extended through Copa America, where the Americans beat Chile and Argentina in the round robin, then eliminated Mexico in the quarterfinals before bowing to the Brazilians, just as they had in the Round of the 16 in World Cup '94.

In the third-place game, the U.S. badly ran out of steam, and was beaten, 4-1, by

U.S. Women Place 3rd in World Cup

by Dean Caparaz

Team captain **Gro Espeseth** raises the winner's trophy after Norway's 2-0 victory over Germany in the final of the Women's World Championship.

There was no storybook ending for the United States women this time.

Unlike 1991, when the U.S. beat Norway to win the inaugural Women's World Championship in China on a last-minute goal by its best player, things just didn't go the Americans' way in the '95 World Cup in Sweden.

Norway gained sweet revenge by knocking the USA off, 1-0, in this year's semifinals. The Scandinavians scored in the 11th minute and dominated the game until there were 13 minutes remaining to play. That's when their All-World midfielder Heidi Stoere was sent off with her second yellow card for tripping U.S. forward Mia Hamm.

The Americans, who entered the tournament as favorites to win it all again, rallied down the stretch, but fell short as two Joy Fawcett kicks hit the crossbar and Norwegian goalkeeper Bente Nordby made several sensational saves.

"You don't forget things like that, how it feels," said U.S. midfielder Julie Foudy. "Like someone snatched away your dream. All the sweat and the tears you put into all this. Just half an inch off that crossbar."

The loss was a devastating one for head coach Tony DiCicco and his defending champs, who had trained full-time for several months prior to the World Cup and then battled through injuries and other adversity in Sweden.

The major setback was the loss of star striker Michelle Akers for most of the tournament. Akers, considered the top player in the world, suffered a concussion and a sprained right knee in a disappointing 3-3 tie with China in the opening game and didn't return to action until the semifinal. Forward Carin Gabarra was also ailing, beset by back spasms as soon as the team arrived in Sweden.

The sending off of goalkeeper Briana Scurry in the second game against Denmark didn't help matters, either. With no substitutions left, the U.S. was forced to put Hamm in goal and held on to a 2-0 victory.

Scurry was unavailable for the next game against Australia and DiCicco rested several other starters as well. When the Aussies took a surprising 1-0 lead in the 54th minute, a few starters came off the bench and the U.S. rallied to win, 4-1, and clinch Group C by goal differential over China.

In the quarterfinals of the medal round, the Americans routed Japan in what turned out to be their only dominating game of the tournament.

After eliminating the U.S. in the semifinals, Norway faced Germany in a rain-swept final and thoroughly outplayed the Germans for a 2-0 victory. Midfielder Hege Riise, who was later named the tournament MVP, scored the winning goal in the 37th minute.

The U.S. gained some revenge of its own by blanking China, 2-0, in the third-place game. But that was small consolation.

"This was a World Cup of adversities for the U.S.," said Akers after the semifinal loss, which was the only full game she played. "It was one thing after another, and we lost today for a reason.

"Maybe it was to remind us that we aren't going to win anymore just because we're the United States. We're going to have work harder now."

Dean Caparaz is an associate editor at *Soccer America*.

Wide World Photos

Mexican goalkeeper **Jorge Campos** at the June 6 press conference in New York announcing the 10 franchise cities in the new Major League Soccer pro league. Campos will play for Los Angeles when the league begins play on April 6, 1996.

Colombia. Still, fourth place was much better than anyone had expected.

Back home, Rothenberg was maneuvering into yet another U-turn. The necessity for a foreign coach was forgotten, and a three-year contract was given to Sampson, making him the man who would guide the USA through the qualifying games for World Cup '98 and, if successful, into the final, 32-team tournament in France.

Rothenberg was also hard at work putting together the promised new Major League Soccer. On June 6, he announced with much fanfare that the 10-team MLS would begin play on April 6, 1996 (a year behind schedule) in 10 cities: Boston, Columbus (Ohio), Dallas, Denver, Kansas City, Los Angeles, New York/New Jersey, San Jose, Tampa Bay and Washington, D.C.

The league itself, under its single-entity structure, was responsible for signing players, who would then be put into a draft. Big name signings included Mexicans Jorge Campos and Hugo Sanchez.

Also on the MLS target list were top international stars Roberto Donadoni (Italy), Rene Higuita and Carlos Valderrama (Colombia), and Ronnie Whelan (Ireland). U.S. national team members who had already signed MLS contracts included Tab Ramos, John Harkes, Roy Lassiter, Jurgen Sommer, Mike Burns and Mike Lapper.

The whole business of players' contracts in international soccer came up for review— or possible revolution— in 1995.

In most countries, the tradition was that even when a contract had expired, the player's club continued to own the rights to that player. This is the basis under which clubs pay enormous amounts of money to other clubs in the form of "transfer fees" to sign up star players. The system also gives a club substantial power in deciding whether, and to which other team, a player could be traded.

Jean-Marc Bosman, a little-known player from Belgium, was denied a move to the French team Dunkerque from FC Liege after his contract expired in 1990. Rather than accept his fate, Bosman took the matter to the European Court of Justice, asking that the transfer system be declared illegal, and that players be allowed to become free agents when their contracts run out. The basis of his case was that, under European law, restrictions on employment are illegal.

While the soccer world held its breath waiting for Court advocate general Carl Otto Lenz to deliver his verdict, speculation ran wild.

The doomsayers declared that if transfer fees were declared illegal, it would mean the end of pro soccer. Or at least of the small clubs who live by developing young players and selling them to the big clubs.

The opposite point of view was that the abolition of transfer fees would be the best thing that ever happened— freeing the players from slavery and forcing the sport to measure up to market values.

On Sept. 20, Herr Lenz duely delivered his opinion. He would recommend to the full court that the transfer system be declared illegal and the full court usually accepted his recommendations.

Bosman had won. When the verdict had sunk in, reason returned and the feeling was that this was *not*, after all, the end of soccer. Something would be worked out.

Meanwhile, another voice was heard on the matter of contracts. It was that of Argentine coach Alfio Basile, who had just been fired after only three months in charge of Atletico Madrid.

"My contract?" he told journalists, "You ask about my contract? I s--- on my contract." □

THE 1996 INFORMATION PLEASE SPORTS ALMANAC

SOCCER STATISTICS

SEC A

THE SEASON IN REVIEW
1994-1995
WORLD • EUROPE • AMERICA

PAGE 725

FIFA Top 50 World Rankings

FIFA announced a new monthly world ranking system on Aug. 13, 1993, designed to "provide a constant international comparison of national team performances." The rankings are based on a mathematical formula that weighs strength of schedule, importance of matches and goals scored for and against. Games considered include World Cup qualifying and final rounds, Continental championship qualifying and final rounds, and friendly matches. At the end of the year, FIFA designates a Team of the Year. Teams of the Year so far have been Germany (1993) and Brazil (1994).

FINAL 1994

World Cup Final Four teams in **bold** type.

	Points	1993 Rank		Points	1993 Rank		Points	1993 Rank
1 **Brazil** (1st)	67.18	3	18 England	52.48	11	35 South Korea	40.60	41
2 Spain	61.80	5	19 France	52.30	15	36 Japan	40.41	43
3 **Sweden** (3rd)	61.41	9	20 Portugal	50.87	20	37 Uruguay	39.18	17
4 **Italy** (2nd)	61.35	2	21 Zambia	49.18	27	38 Finland	38.67	45
5 Germany	61.25	1	22 Egypt	48.25	26	39 Iceland	38.66	47
6 Holland	59.91	7	23 United States	47.84	22	40 China	37.76	53
7 Switzerland	58.30	12	24 Belgium	47.15	25	41 Wales	37.73	29
8 Norway	58.11	4	25 Ivory Coast	47.06	33	42 Israel	37.40	57
9 Ireland	57.63	10	26 Ghana	46.96	37	43 Slovakia	37.14	—
10 Argentina	56.67	8	27 Saudi Arabia	44.76	38	44 Bolivia	37.03	58
11 Romania	56.61	13	28 Greece	44.55	34	45 No. Ireland	36.79	39
12 Nigeria	54.39	18	29 Poland	43.86	28	46 UAE	36.54	51
13 Russia	54.35	14	30 Tunesia	43.61	32	47 Chile	36.29	55
14 Denmark	54.26	6	31 Cameroon	43.56	23	48 Turkey	35.90	52
15 Mexico	53.68	16	32 Scotland	43.04	24	49 Austria	35.56	36
16 **Bulgaria** (4th)	53.53	31	33 Morocco	42.98	30	50 Senegal	35.27	56
17 Colombia	52.74	21	34 Czech Republic	41.49	—			

Note: The Czech Republic and Slovakia were part of the former Czechoslovakia before declaring their independence in 1993.

1995 (as of Sept. 19)

	Points	1994 Rank		Points	1994 Rank		Points	1994 Rank
1 Brazil	68.42	1	18 United States	50.09	23	35 Morocco	42.52	33
2 Spain	59.69	2	19 Czech Republic	49.32	34	36 Saudi Arabia	42.44	27
3 Germany	59.28	5	20 Ireland	49.26	9	37 Slovakia	42.25	43
4 Norway	58.86	8	21 Egypt	48.97	22	38 Finland	41.74	38
5 Italy	58.10	4	22 Uruguay	48.68	37	39 Cameroon	41.42	31
6 Argentina	57.80	10	23 Zambia	47.57	21	40 Chile	40.64	47
7 Denmark	57.51	14	24 Scotland	47.56	32	41 Austria	40.26	49
8 Russia	56.75	13	25 Ghana	47.53	26	42 South Korea	39.43	35
9 Mexico	54.93	15	26 England	47.04	18	43 Senegal	39.08	50
10 Switzerland	54.41	7	27 Tunesia	46.83	30	44 Iceland	38.95	39
11 Bulgaria	54.40	16	28 Poland	46.75	29	45 Israel	38.44	42
12 Portugal	54.17	20	29 Turkey	46.43	48	46 Bolivia	37.97	44
13 Colombia	53.53	17	30 Greece	46.30	28	47 Mali	37.66	52
14 Romania	53.14	11	31 Ivory Coast	45.49	25	48 Croatia	37.31	62
15 Sweden	52.84	3	32 Japan	44.58	36	49 Lithuania	37.16	59
16 France	52.83	19	33 Belgium	43.89	24	50 UAE	37.12	46
17 Holland	51.25	6	34 Nigeria	43.32	12			

Countdown to World Cup France '98

Date	Activity	Date	Activity
Dec. 12, 1995	Group draw for preliminary competition	Nov. 30, 1997	Completion of any necessary playoffs
Mar. 1, 1996	Start of preliminary competition	June 10, 1998	Final 32-team tournament begins in France
Nov. 16, 1997	End of preliminary competition	July 12, 1998	Championship game at Grand Stade in Paris

National Team Competition
WORLDWIDE
Intercontinental Cup

Contested for the second time since 1992 by the five reigning continental champions of Africa, Asia, Europe, North America and South America. Hosted by Saudi Arabia, whose national team is also in the field of six. Top side in each three-team group advances to the one-game final.

ROUND ROBIN STANDINGS

Group A	Gm	W	L	T	Pts	GF	GA
*Denmark	2	1	0	1	4	3	1
Mexico	2	1	0	1	4	3	1
Saudi Arabia	2	0	2	0	0	0	4

Note: Denmark defeated Mexico 4-2 on penalty kicks after their final Group A match ended in a 1-1 draw.

Group B	Gm	W	L	T	Pts	GF	GA
*Argentina	2	1	0	1	4	5	1
Nigeria	2	1	0	1	4	3	0
Japan	2	0	2	0	0	1	8

Note: Argentina and Nigeria played to a 0-0 draw, but Argentina advanced on a 4-3 goal differential.

THIRD PLACE

Jan. 13 (Riyadh)...........................Mexico 1, Nigeria 1*
*Mexico won shootout, 5-4.

FINAL

Jan. 13 (Riyadh) ....Denmark 2, Argentina 0
Scoring: DEN— Michael Laudrup (pen 10), Peter Rasmussen (74).
Att: 30,000.

1995 World Youth Championship

April 13-28 at Doha, Qatar. Originally scheduled for March 11-26 in Nigeria, FIFA withdrew the event on Feb. 10 for security, insurance and medical reasons.

FIRST ROUND

Round Robin; each team played the other three teams in its group once. Note that three points were awarded for a win and one point for a tie and (*) indicates team advanced to second round.

Group A	Gm	W	L	T	Pts	GF	GA
*Brazil	3	2	0	1	7	8	0
*Russia	3	1	0	2	5	3	1
Syria	3	1	2	0	3	1	8
Qatar	3	0	2	1	1	1	4

Group B	Gm	W	L	T	Pts	GF	GA
*Spain	3	3	0	0	9	13	5
*Japan	3	1	1	1	4	5	4
Chile	3	0	1	2	2	6	9
Burundi	3	0	2	1	1	2	8

Group C	Gm	W	L	T	Pts	GF	GA
*Portugal	3	3	0	0	9	7	2
*Argentina	3	2	1	0	6	5	3
Holland	3	1	2	0	3	7	5
Honduras	3	0	3	0	0	5	14

Group D	Gm	W	L	T	Pts	GF	GA
*Cameroon	3	2	0	1	7	7	4
*Australia	3	1	1	1	4	5	4
Costa Rica	3	1	2	0	3	3	6
Germany	3	0	1	2	2	3	4

QUARTERFINALS

Brazil 2 ....Japan 1
Spain 4 ....Russia 1
Portugal 2 ....OT...................Australia 1
Argentina 2..Cameroon 0

SEMIFINALS

Brazil 1 ....Portugal 0
Argentina 3..Spain 0

THIRD PLACE

Portugal 3 ....Spain 2

FINAL
Apr. 28 at Khalifa Stadium (Att— 50,000)

Argentina 2...Brazil 0
Golden Ball (MVP)— Caio, Brazil.
Golden Foot (Leading scorers)— 1. Joseba, Spain (7-3— 14 pts); 2. Dani, Portugal (4-5—13 pts); 3. Caio, Brazil (5-2—12 pts).

1995 Under-17 World Championship
Aug. 3-20 at Ecuador

FIRST ROUND

Round Robin; each team played the other three teams in its group once. Note that three points were awarded for a win and one point for a tie and (*) indicates team advanced to second round.

Group A	Gm	W	L	T	Pts	GF	GA
*Ghana	3	3	0	0	9	5	1
*Ecuador	3	1	1	1	4	3	2
Japan	3	1	1	1	4	2	2
United States	3	0	3	0	0	1	6

USA results: Aug. 3— Ecuador, 2-0; Aug. 5— Japan, 1-2; Aug. 8— Ghana, 0-2.

Group B	Gm	W	L	T	Pts	GF	GA
*Argentina	3	3	0	0	9	7	0
*Portugal	3	1	2	0	3	5	6
Guinea	3	1	2	0	3	3	6
Costa Rica	3	1	2	0	3	2	5

Group C	Gm	W	L	T	Pts	GF	GA
*Nigeria	3	2	0	1	7	5	2
*Australia	3	1	1	1	4	5	4
Spain	3	1	1	1	4	4	4
Qatar	3	0	2	1	1	1	5

Group D	Gm	W	L	T	Pts	GF	GA
*Brazil	3	2	0	1	7	5	0
*Oman	3	2	0	1	7	5	1
Germany	3	1	2	0	3	3	6
Canada	3	0	3	0	0	1	7

QUARTERFINALS

Ghana 2 ....Portugal 1
Oman 2 ....Nigeria 1
Brazil 3 ....Australia 1
Argentina 3...Ecuador 1

SEMIFINALS

Ghana 3 ....Oman 1
Brazil 3 ....Argentina 0

THIRD PLACE

Argentina 2...Oman 0

FINAL
Aug. 20 at Guayaquil (Att— 25,000)

Ghana 3 ....Brazil 2
Golden Ball (MVP)— Mohammed Kathiri, Oman.
Golden Foot (Leading scorers)— 1. Daniel Allsop, Australia (5-1—11 pts in 4 games); 2. Kathiri, Oman (5-1—11 pts in 6 games); 3. Fernando Gatti, Argentina (4-1—9 pts).

U.S. National Team
1995 Schedule and Results

Through Sept. 16, 1995. All U.S. Cup '95 (June 11-25) and Parmalat Cup (Aug. 4-6) matches are noted. Copa America match opponents are in **bold** type. U.S. Cup and Copa America matches were against national teams, while Parmalat Cup matches were against two European club teams— 1995 UEFA Cup champion Parma of Italy and 1995 European Cup quarterfinalist Benfica of Portugal. All other matches are international friendlies.

Date		Result	USA Goals	Site	Crowd
Mar. 25	Uruguay*	T, 2-2	John Kerr and Ernie Stewart	Dallas	12,242
Apr. 22	Belgium	L, 0-1	—	Brussels, Belgium	14,000
May 28	Costa Rica	L, 1-2	Paul Caligiuri	Tampa	7,415
June 11	Nigeria (U.S. Cup)	W, 3-2	John Harkes, Marcelo Balboa and Cobi Jones	Foxboro, Mass.	22,576
June 18	Mexico (U.S. Cup)	W, 4-0	Roy Wegerle, Thomas Dooley, Harkes and Claudio Reyna	Washington, D.C.	38,615
June 25	Colombia (U.S. Cup)	T, 0-0	—	Piscataway, N.J.	36,126
July 8	**Chile**	W, 2-1	Eric Wynalda (2)	Paysandu, Uruguay	22,000
July 11	**Bolivia**	L, 0-1	—	Paysandu, Uruguay	22,000
July 14	**Argentina**	W, 3-0	Frank Klopas, Alexi Lalas and Wynalda	Paysandu, Uruguay	21,000
July 17	**Mexico**	T, 0-0	(U.S. wins shootout, 4-1)	Paysandu, Uruguay	9,000
July 20	**Brazil**	L, 0-1	—	Maldonado, Uruguay	9,000
July 22	**Colombia**	L, 1-4	Joe-Max Moore	Maldonado, Uruguay	3,000
Aug. 4	Parma (Parmalat)	L, 1-2	Mike Lapper	East Rutherford, N.J.	34,826
Aug. 6	Benfica (Parmalat)	W, 2-1	Klopas and Roy Lassiter	East Rutherford, N.J.	32,854
Sept. 16	Sweden	L, 0-1	—	Norrkoping, Sweden	14,200

*Game suspended due to rain storm (83 minutes played).

Overall record: 5-7-3. **US Cup record:** 2-0-1. **Copa America record:** 2-3-1. **Parmalat Cup record:** 1-1-0. **Team scoring:** Goals for— 19; Goals against— 18. **Individual scoring:** Wynalda (3); Harkes and Klopas (2); Balboa, Caligiuri, Dooley, Jones, Kerr, Lalas, Lapper, Reyna, Lassiter, Moore, Stewart and Wegerle.

1995 Copa America Roster

Individual records for entire season through Sept. 16, 1995. Note that the column labeled "Career C/G" refers to career caps and goals.

Forwards	GP	GS	Mins	G	A	Pts	Career C/G
John Kerr	5	3	320	1	1	2	17/2
Jovan Kirovski	7	4	287	0	0	0	11/2
Joe-Max Moore	6	5	495	1	1	2	41/10
Ernie Stewart	9	9	763	1	2	3	30/4
Eric Wynalda	8	8	568	3	1	4	65/18

Note: Roy Wegerle missed Copa America with injured left foot.

Defenders	GP	GS	Mins	G	A	Pts	Career C/G
Marcelo Balboa	6	6	466	1	0	1	105/11
Gregg Berhalter	1	0	31	0	0	0	2/0
Brian Bliss	3	1	93	0	0	0	43/2
Paul Caligiuri	13	13	1160	1	0	0	104/5
Alexi Lalas	11	10	938	1	0	1	62/6
Mike Lapper	4	4	315	0	0	0	44/1

Midfielders	GP	GS	Mins	G	A	Pts	Career C/G
Mike Burns	13	12	1082	0	1	1	34/0
Thomas Dooley	9	9	786	1	0	1	53/5
John Harkes	8	8	720	2	1	3	60/6
Cobi Jones	12	6	758	1	4	5	68/6
Frank Klopas	9	7	452	1	0	1	44/13
Tab Ramos	7	1	271	0	0	0	61/3
Claudio Reyna	8	7	541	1	2	3	27/3
Mike Sorber	8	6	445	0	0	0	53/2

Goalkeepers	GP	GS	Mins	Record	SO	Career Caps
Brad Friedel	8	8	720	2-5-1	8	35
Kasey Keller	4	4	360	3-1-0	5	12
Juergen Sommer	1	1	83	0-0-1	2	3

Shutouts: Friedel and Keller (2).

Yellow cards: Stewart (4); Harkes, Klopas and Wynalda (3); Burns, Lalas and Reyna (2); Balboa, Dooley, Jones and Lapper. **Red cards:** none. **Copa America games/minutes:** Caligiuri and Lalas (6 games/540 minutes); Stewart (6/518); Burns (6/482); Dooley and Harkes (5/450); Moore (5/405); Wynalda (5/388); Jones (6/337); Friedel and Keller (3/270); Ramos (6/263); Klopas (5/252); Reyna (4/230); Balboa (3/196); Sorber (5/193); Lapper (1/90); Kerr and Kirovski (1/45).

Head coaches: Bora Milutinovic (resigned Apr. 14) and Steve Sampson (interim coach from Apr. 14 to Aug. 1, named head coach on Aug. 2); **Assistant coach:** Clive Charles; **Goal coach:** Milutin Soskic; **General Manager:** Tom King; **Captain:** Marcelo Balboa.

U.S. Cup '95

Third U.S. Cup hosted by the United States, June 11-25, 1995. Match results listed with city and attendance.

Round Robin Standings

Group B	Gm	W	L	T	Pts	GF	GA
United States	3	2	0	1	7	7	2
Colombia	3	1	0	2	5	1	0
Mexico	3	1	1	1	4	2	5
Nigeria	3	0	3	0	0	3	6

Leading scorer: John Harkes, USA (2-1— 5 pts).

Match Results

6/11	Foxboro, Mass. (22,578)	USA 3, Nigeria 2
6/17	Piscataway, N.J. (15,216)	Colombia 1, Nigeria 0
6/18	Wash., D.C. (38,615)	USA 4, Mexico 0
6/21	Wash., D.C. (20,432)	Colombia 0, Mexico 0
6/24	Dallas (27,166)	Mexico 2, Nigeria 1
6/25	Piscataway, N.J. (36,126)	USA 0, Colombia 0

National Team Competition (Cont.)
1995 Copa America

Regarded as the Championship of South America since its inception in 1916, the Copa America began extending invitations to Central and North American teams in 1993. CONCACAF champion Mexico and the United States participated in 1995. Held July 5-23 in Uruguay.

FIRST ROUND

Round Robin; each team played the other three teams in its group once. Note that three points were awarded for a win and one point for a tie and (*) indicates team advanced to second round.

Group A	Gm	W	L	T	Pts	GF	GA
*Uruguay	3	2	0	1	7	6	2
*Paraguay	3	2	1	0	6	5	4
*Mexico	3	1	1	1	4	5	4
Venezuela	3	0	3	0	0	4	10

RESULTS: **July 5**— Uruguay 4, Venezuela 1. **July 6**— Paraguay 2, Mexico 1. **July 9**— Uruguay 1, Paraguay 0; Mexico 3, Venezuela 1. **July 12**— Paraguay 3, Venezuela 2. **July 13**— Mexico 1, Uruguay 1

Group B	Gm	W	L	T	Pts	GF	GA
*Brazil	3	3	0	0	9	6	0
*Colombia	3	1	1	1	4	2	4
Ecuador	3	1	2	0	3	2	3
Peru	3	0	2	1	1	2	5

RESULTS: **July 7**— Colombia 1, Peru 1; Brazil 1, Ecuador 0. **July 10**— Colombia 1, Ecuador 0; Brazil 2, Peru 0. **July 13**— Ecuador 2, Peru 1; Brazil 3, Colombia 0.

Group C	Gm	W	L	T	Pts	GF	GA
*United States	3	2	1	0	6	5	2
*Argentina	3	2	1	0	6	6	4
*Bolivia	3	1	1	1	4	4	4
Chile	3	0	2	1	1	3	8

RESULTS: **July 8**— USA 2, Chile 1; Argentina 2, Bolivia 1. **July 11**— Bolivia 1, USA 0; Argentina 4, Chile 0. **July 14**— Bolivia 2, Chile 2; USA 3, Argentina 0.

QUARTERFINALS

7/16	Montevideo (50,000)	Colombia 1, Paraguay 1*
7/16	Montevideo (50,000)	Uruguay 2, Bolivia 1
7/17	Paysandu (9,000)	USA 0, Mexico 0*
7/17	Rivera (27,000)	Brazil 2, Argentina 2*

*Shootout wins: Colombia, 5-4; USA, 4-1; Brazil, 4-2.

SEMIFINALS

7/19	Montevideo (30,000)	Uruguay 2, Colombia 0
7/20	Maldonado (9,000)	Brazil 1, USA 0

THIRD PLACE

7/22	Maldonado (2,500)	Colombia 4, USA 1

FINAL

July 23 at Centenario Stadium

7/23	Montevideo (65,000)	Uruguay 1, Brazil 1*

*Uruguay wins shootout, 5-3.

Copa America All-Star Team

Selected by *Soccer America.*

G—Kasey Keller, USA
D—Aldair, BRA
D—Paul Caligiuri, USA
D—Roberto Carlos, BRA
D—Javier Zanetti, ARG
M—Dunga, BRA

M—Marco Etcheverry, BOL
M—Enzo Francescoli, URU
M—John Harkes, USA
F—Gabriel Batistuta, ARG
F—Edmundo, ARG

Leading Goal Scorers

4 goals— Gabriel Batistuta, ARG; Luis Garcia, MEX. **3 goals**— Abel Balbo, ARG; Marcelo Otero, URU; Tulio, BRA; Eric Wynalda, USA.

Club Team Competition
1994 Toyota Cup

Formerly the Intercontinental Cup; a year-end match for the World Club Championship between the European Cup and Copa Libertadores winners. Played Dec. 1, 1994, before 60,000 at Tokyo's National Stadium.

FINAL

Velez Sarsfield (ARG) 2 .... AC Milan (Italy) 0
Scoring: Velez Sarsfield— Roberto Trotta (penalty kick at 50 minutes); Asad (57 minutes). **Man of the Match:** Asad.

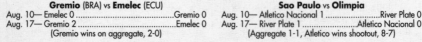

1995 Copa Liberatadores

Contested by the league champions of South America's football union. Two-leg Semifinals and two-leg Final; home teams listed first. Winner Gremio of Brazil plays European Cup champion Ajax Amsterdam of Holland in 1995 Toyota Cup, Dec. 14 in Tokyo.

Final Four: Atletico Nacional (Colombia), Emelec (Ecuador), Gremio (Brazil) and River Plate (Argentina).

SEMIFINALS

Gremio (BRA) vs **Emelec** (ECU)
Aug. 10— Emelec 0 .... Gremio 0
Aug. 17— Gremio 2 .... Emelec 0
(Gremio wins on aggregate, 2-0)

Sao Paulo vs **Olimpia**
Aug. 10— Atletico Nacional 1 .... River Plate 0
Aug. 17— River Plate 1 .... Atletico Nacional 0
(Aggregate 1-1, Atletico wins shootout, 8-7)

FINAL

Aug. 24— Gremio 3 .... Atletico Nacional 1
Aug. 30— Atletico Nacional 1 .... Gremio 1
(Gremio wins on aggregate, 4-2)

EUROPE

There are three European club competitions sanctioned by the Union of European Football Associations (UEFA). The **European Cup** (officially, the Champions' Cup) is a knockout contest between national league champions of UEFA member countries; the **Cup Winners' Cup** is between winners of domestic cup competitions (note that a double winner— league and cup titles— would play for the European Cup and be replaced in the Cup Winners' Cup by the team it defeated in the domestic cup final); and the **UEFA Cup** is between the so-called "best of the rest," usually the national league runners-up. Note that home teams are listed first.

1995 European Cup

Champions League: Six-game double round-robin in four 4-team groups (Sept. 14-Dec. 7, 1994); top two teams in each group advance to quarterfinal round. Winner Ajax Amsterdam of Holland plays Copa Libertadores champion Gremio of Brazil in the 1995 Toyota Cup, Dec. 14 in Tokyo.

ROUND ROBIN STANDINGS

Group A

	W	L	T	Pts	GF	GA
*IFK Göteborg (SWE)	4	1	1	9	10	7
*Barcelona (SPA)	2	2	2	6	11	8
Manchester United (ENG)	2	2	2	6	11	11
Galatasaray (TUR)	1	4	1	3	3	9

Note: Barcelona advances based on head-to-head results with Manchester United.

Group B

	W	L	T	Pts	GF	GA
*Paris St. Germain (FRA)	6	0	0	12	12	3
*Bayern Munich (GER)	2	2	2	6	8	7
Spartak Moscow (RUS)	1	3	2	4	8	12
Dinamo Kiev (UKR)	1	5	0	2	5	11

Group C

	W	L	T	Pts	GF	GA
*Benfica (POR)	3	0	3	9	9	5
*Hajduk Split (CRO)	2	2	2	6	5	7
Steaua Bucharest (HUN)	1	2	3	5	7	6
Anderlecht (BEL)	0	2	4	4	4	7

Group D

	W	L	T	Pts	GF	GA
*Ajax Amsterdam (HOL)	4	0	2	10	9	2
*AC Milan (ITA)	3	2	1	7	6	5
Austria Salzburg	1	2	3	5	4	6
AEK Athens (GRE)	0	4	2	2	3	9

National Champions

Twenty-five 1995 league champions and cup winners.

League Champion		Cup Winner
SV Salzburg	Austria	Rapid Vienna
Anderlecht	Belgium	Club Bruges
Levski Sofia	Bulgaria	Lokomotiv Sofia
Hajduk Split	Croatia	Hajduk Split
Sparta Prague	Czech Rep.	Hradec Kralove
Aalborg	Denmark	FC Copenhagen
Blackburn Rovers	England	Everton
Nantes	France	Paris St. Germain
Borussia Dortmund	Germany	Borussia M'gladbach
Panathinaikos	Greece	Panathinaikos
Ajax	Holland	Feyenoord
Ferencvaros	Hungary	Ferencvaros
Dundalk	Ireland	Derry City
Juventus	Italy	Juventus
Crusaders	No. Ireland	Linfield
Legia Warsaw	Poland	Legia Warsaw
FC Porta	Portugal	Sporting Lisbon
Steaua Bucharest	Romania	Petrolul Ploiesti
Spartak Moscow*	Russia	Dinamo Moscow
Rangers	Scotland	Celtic
Slovan Bratislava	Slovakia	Inter Bratislava
Real Madrid	Spain	Deportivo Coruna
IFK Gothenburg*	Sweden	Halmstads
Grasshoppers	Switzerland	FC Sion
Besiktas	Turkey	Trabzonspor

*1994 champion; Russia and Sweden play spring-fall seasons.

QUARTERFINALS

Two legs, total goals; home team listed first.

Bayern Munich vs. IFK Goteborg

Mar. 1 — Bayern Munich 0 .... IFK Göteborg 0
Mar. 15 — IFK Göteborg 2 .... Bayern Munich 2
(Aggregate 2-2; Bayern wins on away goals)

Barcelona vs. Paris St. Germain

Mar. 1 — Barcelona 1 .... Paris SG 1
Mar. 15 — Paris SG 2 .... Barcelona 1
(Paris SG wins on aggregate, 3-2)

AC Milan vs. Benfica

Mar. 1 — AC Milan 2 .... Benfica 0
Mar. 15 — Benfica 0 .... AC Milan 0
(Milan wins on aggregate, 2-0)

Hajduk Split vs. Ajax Amsterdam

Mar. 1 — Hajduk Split 0 .... Ajax 0
Mar. 15 — Ajax 3 .... Hajduk Split 0
(Ajax wins on aggregate, 3-0)

SEMIFINALS

Two legs, total goals; home team listed first.

Bayern Munich vs. Ajax Amsterdam

Apr. 5 — Bayern Munich 0 .... Ajax Amsterdam 0
Apr. 19 — Ajax Amsterdam 5 .... Bayern Munich 2
(Ajax wins on aggregate, 5-2)

Paris St. Germain vs. AC Milan

Apr. 5 — Paris St. Germain 0 .... AC Milan 1
Apr. 19 — AC Milan 2 .... Paris St. Germain 0
(Milan wins on aggregate, 3-0)

FINAL

(May 24 at Vienna; Att— 49,730)

Ajax Amsterdam 1 .... AC Milan 0
Scoring: Ajax— Patrick Kluivert (85th minute).

1995 Cup Winners' Cup

Two-leg Semifinals one-game Final; home team listed first.
Final Four: Arsenal (England), Chelsea (England), Real Zaragoza (Spain) and Sampdoria (Italy).

SEMIFINALS

Arsenal vs. Sampdoria

Apr. 6 — Arsenal 3 .... Sampdoria 2
Apr. 20 — Sampdoria 3 .... Arsenal 2
(Aggregate 5-5, Arsenal wins on PKs, 3-2)

Real Zaragoza vs. Chelsea

Apr. 6 — Real Zaragoza 3 .... Chelsea 0
Apr. 20 — Chelsea 3 .... Real Zaragoza 1
(Zaragoza wins on aggregate, 4-3)

FINAL

(May 10 at Paris; Att— 42,424)

Real Zaragoza 2 .... OT .... Arsenal 1
Scoring: Zaragoza— Juan Esnaider (68th minute) and Nayim (120th); Arsenal— John Hartson (75th).

Club Team Competition (Cont.)

1995 UEFA Cup

Two-leg Semifinals, two-game Final; home team listed first.
Final Four: Bayer Leverkusen (Germany), Borussia Dortmund (Germany), Juventus (Italy) and Parma (Italy).

SEMIFINALS

Bayer Leverkusen vs. Parma

Apr. 4 — Bayer Leverkusen 1 ....Parma 2
Apr. 18 — Parma 3 ....Bayer Leverkusen 0
(Parma wins on aggregate, 5-1)

Juventus vs. Borussia Dortmund

Apr. 4 — Juventus 2 ....Borussia Dortmund 2
Apr. 18 — Borussia Dortmund 1 ....Juventus 2
(Juventus wins on aggregate, 4-3)

FINAL

May 3 (29,000)— Parma 1 ....Juventus 0
Scoring: Parma— Dino Baggio (5th minute).

May 17 (80,750)— Juventus 1 ....Parma 1
Scoring: Juventus— Gianluca Vialli (33rd minute); Parma— Dino Baggio (53rd).

Note: Match was moved to Milan's San Siro Stadium after Juventus and Turin city officials were unable to resolve disagreement over advertising revenues.

(Parma wins on aggregate, 2-1)

U.S. Foreign Legion

U.S. National Team members playing for teams overseas as of Sept. 7, 1995.

	Foreign Club	Div.
Marcelo Balboa	Leon (Mexico)	1st
Gregg Berhalter	FC Zwolle (Holland)	2nd
Brian Bliss	Carl-Zeiss Jena (Germany)	2nd
Mike Burns	Viborg (Denmark)	1st
Paul Caligiuri	St. Pauli (Germany)	Bund.
Tom Dooley	Schalke 04 (Germany)	Bund.
Brad Friedel	Galatasaray (Turkey)	1st
John Harkes	Derby County (England)	1st
John Kerr	Millwall (England)	1st
Jovan Kirovski	Manchester United (England)	Prem.*
Alexi Lalas	Padova (Italy)	Serie A
Mike Lapper	Southend (England)	1st
Joe-Max Moore	Nuernberg (Germany)	2nd
Steve Pittman	Partick Thistle (Scotland)	1st
Tab Ramos	Tigres (Mexico)	1st
Claudio Reyna	Bayer Leverkusen (Germany)	Bund.
Juergen Sommer	Queen's Park (England)	Prem.
Mike Sorber	UNAM (Mexico)	1st
Ernie Stewart	Willem II (Holland)	1st
Eric Wynalda	VFB Bochum (Germany)	Bund.

*On reserve team.

U.S. Pro Leagues

Division champions (*) and playoff qualifiers (†) are noted.

NPSL Final Standings (Indoor)

American Division

	W	L	Pct.	GB	GF	GA
* Cleveland Crunch	30	10	.750	—	742	524
†Baltimore Spirit	23	17	.575	7	615	572
†Harrisburg Heat	23	17	.575	7	594	526
†Buffalo Blizzard	20	20	.500	10	579	552
Dayton Dynamo	15	25	.375	15	548	671
Canton Invaders	6	34	.150	24	443	752

National Division

	W	L	Pct.	GB	GF	GA
* St. Louis Ambush	30	10	.750	—	711	465
†Kansas City Attack	29	11	.725	4	641	460
†Milwaukee Wave	23	17	.575	7	535	459
†Detroit Rockers	18	22	.450	12	508	546
Wichita Wings	17	23	.425	13	480	583
Chicago Power	6	34	.150	24	420	706

Playoffs

Division Semifinals (Best of 3): Cleveland over Buffalo (2-1); Harrisburg over Baltimore (2-1); St. Louis over Detroit (2-0); Kansas City over Milwaukee (2-1).

Division Finals (Best of 5): Harrisburg over Cleveland (3-0); St. Louis over Kansas City (3-2).

Championship (Best of 7): St. Louis over Harrisburg (4-0).

A-League Final Standings (Outdoor)

	W	L	Pts	GF	GA
* Montreal Impact	17	7	51	47	27
†Seattle Sounders	18	6	51	40	24
†Vancouver 86ers	10	14	33	38	43
†Atlanta Ruckus	13	11	32	29	41
Colorado Foxes	8	16	29	35	41
New York Centaurs	6	18	20	21	39

Note: Montreal wins regular season title on goal differential.
Also: Teams earn three points for a regulation win, two points for a shootout win and one point for a shootout loss.

Playoffs

Began Sept. 14 (see Updates chapter).

CISL Final Standings (Indoor)

Eastern Division

	W	L	Pct.	GB	GF	GA
* Monterrey La Raza	23	5	.821	—	242	169
†Dallas Sidekicks	18	10	.643	5	215	169
Wash. Warthogs	13	15	.464	10	190	207
Pittsburgh Stingers	10	18	.357	13	140	184
Detroit Neon	5	23	.179	18	143	236

Southern Division

	W	L	Pct.	GB	GF	GA
* Anaheim Splash	17	11	.607	—	188	167
†Mexico Toros	17	11	.607	—	200	147
†San Diego Sockers	17	11	.607	—	185	167
Ariz. Sandsharks	11	17	.393	6	176	222
Houston Hotshots	8	20	.286	9	156	201

Western Division

	W	L	Pct.	GB	GF	GA
* Sacramento Knights	20	8	.714	—	200	163
†San Jose Grizzlies	15	13	.536	5	206	180
†L. Vegas Dustdevils	13	15	.464	7	215	208
Seattle SeaDogs	12	16	.429	8	175	202
Portland Pride	11	17	.393	9	218	227

Playoffs

Began Oct. 5 (see Update chapter).

Major Soccer League Debuts in 1996

Major League Soccer, the new 10-team outdoor soccer league will open its inaugural season on April 6, 1996, and play a 32-game schedule concluding with a neutral-site championship game on Oct. 20.

The 10 teams will be divided into two conferences:

Eastern Conference: Boston, Columbus (Ohio), New York/New Jersey, Tampa and Washington, D.C.

Western Conference: Dallas, Denver, Kansas City, Los Angeles and San Jose.

1995 Women's World Cup

Officially, the Women's World Championship. Held from June 5-18 in Sweden. The United States was defending champion

FIRST ROUND

Round Robin; each team played the other three teams in its group once. Note that three points were awarded for a win and one point for a tie and (*) indicates team advanced to second round.

Group A	Gm	W	L	T	Pts	GF	GA
*Germany	3	2	1	0	6	9	4
*Sweden	3	2	1	0	6	5	3
*Japan	3	1	2	0	3	2	4
Brazil	3	1	2	0	3	3	8

Group B	Gm	W	L	T	Pts	GF	GA
*Norway	3	3	0	0	9	17	0
*England	3	2	1	0	6	6	6
Canada	3	0	2	1	1	5	13
Nigeria	3	0	2	1	1	5	14

Group C	Gm	W	L	T	Pts	GF	GA
*United States	3	2	0	1	7	9	4
*China	3	2	0	1	7	10	6
*Denmark	3	1	2	0	3	6	5
Australia	3	0	3	0	0	3	13

USA results: June 6— China, 3-3; June 8—Denmark, 2-0; June 10— Australia, 4-1.

QUARTERFINALS

6/13 Vaesteras (2,317) ....Germany 3, England 0
6/13 Helsingborg (7,937) ....China 1, Sweden 1*
6/13 Gaevle (3,537) ....USA 4, Japan 0
6/13 Karlstad (4,655) ....Norway 3, Denmark 1
*China wins shootout, 4-3.

SEMIFINALS

6/15 Helsingborg (3,629) ....Germany 1, China 0
6/15 Vaesteras (2,893) ....Norway 1, USA 0

THIRD PLACE

6/17 Gaevle (4,335) ....USA 2, China 0

FINAL
at Stromvallen Stadium
6/18 Stockholm (17,158)...........Norway 2, Germany 0

Golden Ball (MVP)— Hege Riise, Norway (midfielder). **Golden Foot** (Leading scorers)— 1. Ann Kristin Aarones, Norway (6-0—12 pts); 2. Hege Riise, Norway (5-5—15 pts); 3. Guihong Shi, CHN (3-2—8 pts) and Wen Sun, CHN (3-2—8 pts).

U.S. Women's National Team

1995 World Championship roster: G— Mary Harvey, Briana Scurry and Saskia Webber; D— Joy Fawcett, Linda Hamilton, Carla Overbeck, Thori Staples; M— Amanda Cromwell, Julie Foudy, Jen Lalor, Kristine Lilly, Holly Manthei, Tiffany Roberts, Tisha Venturini; F— Michelle Akers, Carin Gabarra, Mia Hamm, Debbie Keller, Tiffany Milbrett, Sarah Rafanelli; **Coach**— Tony DiCicco; **Captain:** Carla Overbeck.

1995 Schedule and Results

Through Aug. 6, 1995. All Algarve Cup (AC), Tournoi International Feminin (TIF) and U.S. Women's Cup '95 matches are noted. Women's World Championship match opponents are in **bold** type. All other opponents are international friendly matches.

Date		Result	USA Goals	Site	Crowd
Feb. 24	Denmark	W, 7-0	Akers (3), Hamm (2), Lilly, Roberts	Winter Park, Fla.	2,238
Mar. 14	Finland (AC)	W, 2-0	Lilly, Hamm	Faro, Portugal	N/A
Mar. 16	Portugal (AC)	W, 3-0	Milbrett, Gabarra, Lilly	Portimao, Portugal	N/A
Mar. 17	Denmark (AC)	L, 0-2	—	Lagos, Portugal	N/A
Mar. 19	Norway (AC)	T, 3-3	Akers, Gabarra, Lilly (Norway won shootout, 4-2)	Quarteira, Portugal	N/A
Apr. 11	Italy (TIF)	W, 3-0	Akers, Venturini, Gabarra	Poissy, France	N/A
Apr. 12	Canada (TIF)	W, 5-0	Hamm (3), Akers, Milbrett	St. Maur, France	N/A
Apr. 15	France (TIF)	W, 3-0	Gabarra, Lilly, Hamm	Strasbourg, France	N/A
Apr. 28	Finland	W, 2-0	Akers, Venturini	Decatur, Ga.	5,432
Apr. 30	Finland	W, 6-0	Lilly, Akers, own goal, Neaton, Foudy, Hamm	Davidson, N.C.	3,295
May 12	Brazil	W, 3-0	Hamm (2), Venturini	Tacoma, Wash.	3,291
May 14	Brazil	W, 4-1	Akers (2), Gabarra, Milbrett	Portland, Ore.	4,911
May 19	Canada	W, 9-1	Akers (2), Hamm (2), Gabarra (2), Lilly (2), Milbrett	Dallas	6,145
May 22	Canada	W, 2-1	Milbrett, Neaton	Edmonton	500
June 6	**China**	T, 3-3	Venturini, Milbrett, Hamm	Gaevle, Sweden	4,635
June 8	**Denmark**	W, 2-0	Lilly, Milbrett	Gaevle, Sweden	2,704
June 10	**Australia**	W, 4-1	Foudy, Facett, Overbeck, Keller	Helsingborg, Sweden	1,105
June 13	**Japan**	W, 4-0	Lilly (2), Milbrett, Venturini	Gaevle, Sweden	3,537
June 15	**Norway**	L, 0-1	—	Vasteras, Sweden	2,893
June 17	**China**	W, 2-0	Venturini, Hamm	Gaevle, Sweden	4,335
July 30	CHN-Taipei (US)	W, 9-0	Venturini (3), Hamm (2), Akers (2), Overbeck (2)	New Britain, Conn.	3,782
Aug. 3	Australia (US)	W, 4-2	Hamm (2), Akers, Lilly	New Brunswick, N.J.	3,352
Aug. 6	Norway (US)	W, 2-1	Hamm, Pearman	Washington, D.C.	7,083

Overall record: 19-2-2. **World Championship record:** 4-1-1. **U.S. Cup '95 record:** 3-0-0. **Team scoring:** Goals for— 82 (includes own goal by Finland); Goals against— 16. **Individual scorers:** Mia Hamm (19); Michelle Akers (15); Kristine Lilly (12); Tisha Venturini (9); Tiffany Milbrett (8); Carin Gabarra (7); Carla Overbeck (3); Julie Foudy and Natalie Neaton (2); Joy Fawcett, Debbie Keller, Tammy Pearman and Tiffany Roberts.

Colleges

MEN

1994 Final *Soccer America* Top 20

Final 1994 regular season poll including games through Nov. 13th. Conducted by the national weekly *Soccer America* and released in the Nov. 28th issue. Listing includes records through conference playoffs as well as NCAA tournament record and team lost to. Teams in **bold** type went on to reach NCAA Final Four. All tournament games decided by penalty kicks are considered ties.

		Nov. 12 Record	NCAA Recap
1	**Indiana**	19-2-0	4-1 (Virginia)
2	Boston Univ.	18-0-1	1-1 (Brown)
3	South Carolina	16-3-0	0-1 (N.C. State)
4	**Virginia**	17-3-1	5-0
5	Fresno St	17-2-1	0-0-1 (San Fran.)
6	Duke	14-6-1	1-1 (J. Madison)
7	**UCLA**	15-4-1	3-1 (Indiana)
8	NC-Charlotte	16-3-0	0-1 (Charleston)
9	N.C. State	13-6-0	1-1 (Charleston)
10	James Madison	18-2-2	2-1 (Virginia)
11	North Carolina	13-6-0	0-1 (J. Madison)
12	SMU	14-3-1	1-1 (UCLA)
13	CS-Fullerton	12-6-2	2-1 (Indiana)
14	Georgetown	18-3-0	0-1 (Maryland)
15	Florida Int'l	16-3-1	0-1 (Duke)
16	St. John's	14-4-3	0-1 (Rutgers)
17	William & Mary	18-3-1	Did not play
18	Ala-Birmingham	15-3-1	0-1 (UCLA)
19	San Jose St	15-4-0	Did not play
20	Penn St	15-5-1	1-1 (Rutgers)

Note: Unranked **Rutgers**, 11-9-3 during the regular season and 3-1 (Virginia) in the NCAA tournament, was the 4th entry in the Final Four.

NCAA Division I Tournament

First Round (Nov. 19-20)

Boston Univ. 2		at Harvard 0
at Brown 3	2 OT	New Hampshire 2
at CS-Fullerton 3	2 OT	San Diego 1
Col. of Charleston 1	4 OT	at NC-Charlotte 0
Creighton 2		at Saint Louis 1
Duke 2	2 OT	at Florida Int'l 1
at Indiana 1	2 OT	Notre Dame 0
James Madison 3		at North Carolina 0
Maryland 4	2 OT	at Georgetown 3
N.C. State 1		at South Carolina 0
at Penn St. 3		Robert Morris 0
at Rutgers 1		St. John's 0
San Francisco 1	4 OT	at Fresno St. 1

(USF wins shootout, 4-2)

at SMU 2		Wisconsin 1
at UCLA 3	2 OT	Ala-Birmingham 2
at Virginia 3		NC-Greensboro 0

Second Round (Nov. 27)

Brown 3		at Boston Univ. 2
at CS-Fullerton St. 1	3 OT	San Francisco 0
Charleston 5	3 OT	at N.C. State 4
at Indiana 1		Creighton 0
at James Madison 2		Duke 1
at Rutgers 3	2 OT	Penn St. 2
UCLA 4		at SMU 2
at Virginia 2		Maryland 1

Quarterfinals (Dec. 4)

at Indiana 2	CS-Fullerton 1
at Rutgers 3	Brown 1
at UCLA 3	Charleston 2
at Virginia 4	James Madison 1

FINAL FOUR

at Davidson, N.C. (Dec. 9-11)

Semifinals

Virginia 2	Rutgers 1
Indiana 4	UCLA 1

Championship

Virginia 1	Indiana 0

Scoring: UVa— A.J. Wood (Brandon Pollard and Tain Nix) 20:06. **Attendance:** 12,033.

Final records: Virginia (22-3-1); Indiana (23-3); UCLA (18-5); Rutgers (14-10-3).

Most Outstanding Players: OFFENSE— Damian Silvera, Virginia midfielder; DEFENSE— Mark Peters, Virginia, goaltender.

Coaches: Bruce Arena, Virginia and Jerry Yeagley, Indiana.

WOMEN

1994 Final *Soccer America* Top 20

Final 1994 regular season poll including games through Nov. 6th. Conducted by the national weekly *Soccer America* and released in the Nov. 21st issue. Listing includes records through conference playoffs as well as NCAA tournament record and team lost to. Teams in **bold** type went on to reach NCAA Final Four. All tournament games decided by penalty kicks are considered ties.

		Nov. 6 Record	NCAA Recap
1	**Notre Dame**	20-0-1	4-1 (N. Carolina)
2	**North Carolina**	21-1-1	5-0
3	William & Mary	16-3-0	1-1 (Notre Dame)
4	Stanford	16-1-1	0-1-1 (Portland)
5	Duke	16-4-1	1-1 (N. Carolina)
6	**Connecticut**	17-3-0	2-1 (N. Carolina)
7	Hartford	15-3-1	1-1 (UConn)
8	**Portland**	14-5-0	2-1 (Notre Dame)
9	Santa Clara	14-4-1	0-1 (St. Mary's)
10	George Mason	15-2-2	1-1 (Notre Dame)
11	Massachusetts	15-5-0	1-1 (Hartford)
12	Wisconsin	16-5-0	0-1 (Wash. St.)
13	Washington	12-6-1	0-0-1 (Stanford)
14	Virginia	13-4-3	0-1 (Geo. Mason)
15	Clemson	15-4-0	0-0-1 (N.C. St.)
16	Brown	10-4-1	1-1 (UConn)
17	Dartmouth	11-3-1	0-1 (Brown)
18	Oregon St	13-4-0	0-1 (Washington)
19	Washington St	11-6-1	1-1 (Wm.& Mary)
20	Vanderbilt	16-4-0	1-1 (Duke)

NCAA Division I Tournament

After eight first round games.

East Regional

at Hartford, Conn. (Nov. 12-13)

Semifinals:	Connecticut 1		Brown 0
	Hartford 2		Massachusetts 0
Final:	Connecticut 2	3 OT	Hartford 1

South Regional

at Chapel Hill, N.C. (Nov. 12-13)

Semifinals:	Duke 2	Vanderbilt 1
	North Carolina 4	N.C. State 2
Final:	North Carolina 3	Duke 1

Cavs, Heels Keep NCAA Titles Coming

by Mike Woitalla

If, as coaches claim, parity has increased in college soccer, it is evident only in that an array of teams have challenged the dynasties.

The Virginia Cavaliers won their fourth straight NCAA Division I championship on Dec. 11, 1994, with a 1-0 victory over Indiana. The Hoosiers thus joined South Carolina (1993), San Diego (1992) and Santa Clara (1991) as unsuccessful contenders.

The 32-team field in the 1994 NCAA playoffs included four first-time qualifiers and emerging powers like Creighton, Maryland and NC-Charlotte. But nobody could stop UVA.

"We're a greedy group of people," said Cavaliers coach Bruce Arena, "and we want to keep this championship in Virginia." Since the NCAA tournament began in 1959, no other team has won even three straight titles.

Senior forward A.J. Wood, who had a hat trick in the Cavs' 4-1 quarterfinal win over James Madison, scored the winning goal of the final to finish the season with a school record 23 goals.

Midfielder Claudio Reyna, the 1993 Player of the Year as a junior, left school with three championship rings to join the U.S. national team and play professionally with Bayer Leverkusen in the German first division. No problem. Juniors Damian Silvera and Mike Fisher stepped in and the juggernaut rolled on.

Fisher, who registered 15 goals and 13 assists in 25 games, missed the final against Indiana due to a yellow-card suspension. This brought out even more industrious play from Silvera, who helped shut down the Hoosiers' two Player-of-the-Year forwards Brian Maisonneuve (Hermann Award) and Todd Yeagley (MAC Award).

Virginia, a team known for its attack-minded play, resorted to tough defense in the final after Wood's 23rd minute goal.

The 1994 Final Four drew wide praise for displaying a sophisticated, skillful level of soccer not usually associated with the college game.

The final crowd of 12,033 was the highest paid attendance in NCAA history. After three years at Davidson, N.C., the Final Four moved to Richmond in 1995.

The U.S. Olympic team in Atlanta could have a distinct Cavalier look to it given that Reyna, Fisher,

Phil Stephens

Virginia midfielder **Mike Fisher** in action against Rutgers during 1994 NCAA Final Four semifinal.

Wood, Silvera, Billy Walsh, Brandon Pollard and Clint Peay have all been invited to camp.

Meanwhile, the North Carolina women's team won its ninth straight NCAA Division I championship on Nov. 18, 1994, blanking Notre Dame, 5-0.

When North Carolina won the first NCAA women's title in 1982, only 25 teams participated at the Division I level. By 1994, 154 schools were on board and 24 were invited to the playoffs.

The added competition, however, has had only a minor effect on UNC. During the regular season, Notre Dame tied the Tar Heels 0-0 to break the their 92-game winning streak, and Duke later handed them their first loss (3-2) in 101 games.

Coach Anson Dorrance's women avenged both blemishes in the playoffs— beating Duke, 3-1, in the quarterfinals and, after a 3-0 semifinal win over Connecticut, thumping Notre Dame in the final at Portland, Ore.

UNC has now won 12 of 13 NCAA titles and its impact is felt not only on the U.S. women's national team— six Tar Heels were on the 1995 World Cup squad— but also in the college coaching ranks, where 10 former Tar Heels were head coaches in '94.

Mike Woitalla is a senior editor at *Soccer America*.

Colleges (Cont.)
WOMEN

NCAA Division I Tournament

Central Regional

at South Bend, Ind. (Nov. 12-13)

Semifinals: Notre Dame 3 ....George Mason 1
Wm. & Mary 4.....................Washington St. 0
Final: Notre Dame 2 ....Wm. & Mary 1

West Regional

at Portland, Ore. (Nov. 12-13)

Semifinals: Portland 6.............................St. Mary's-CA 0
Stanford 0.............2 OT ....Washington 0
(Stanford wins shootout, 6-5)
Final: Portland 2 ....3 OT...............Stanford 1

1994 Annual Awards

Men's Players of the Year

Hermann Trophy ....Brian Maisonneuve, Indiana, M
MAC Award ....Todd Yeagley, Indiana, M
Soccer America................................A.J. Wood, Virginia, F

Women's Player of the Year

Hermann Trophy ....Tisha Venturini, N. Carolina, M
MAC Award...Tisha Venturini
Soccer America...Tisha Venturini

NSCAA Coaches of the Year

Division I: Men's.............................Jerry Yeagley, Indiana
Women's...............Chris Petrucelli, Notre Dame

Division I All-America Teams
MEN

As selected by the National Soccer Coaches Assn. of America (NSCAA). Holdovers from the 1993 All-America team are in **bold** type.

First Team

Pos		Cl	Hgt	Wgt
G	David Kramer, Fresno St ....Sr.	6-2	180
D	Matt McKeon, Saint Louis ....Jr.	6-2	190
D	Brandon Pollard, Virginia ....Jr.	5-11	168
D	Eddie Pope, North Carolina................Jr.	6-0	175
M	**Jason Kreis**, Duke ....Sr.	5-7	155
M	Brian Maisonneuve, Indiana...............Sr.	5-11	168
M	Todd Yeagley, Indiana.......................Sr.	6-0	170
F	Brent Bennett, J. Madison ....Sr.	5-8	137
F	Mac Cozier, NC-Charlotte ....Jr.	5-8	165
F	Darren Eales, Brown ....Sr.	5-8	160
F	**Staale Soebye**, San Francisco ....Sr.	6-1	170

WOMEN

As selected by the National Soccer Coaches Assn. of America (NSCAA). Most schools do not list heights and weights of women athletes. Holdovers from the 1993 All-America team are in **bold** type.

First Team

GOALKEEPER— Jen Renola, Notre Dame, So. DEFENDERS— **Jessica Fischer**, Stanford, Jr.; Heidi Kocer, Massachusetts, Sr.; Thori Staples, N.C. State. MIDFIELDERS— **Cindy Daws**, Notre Dame, So.; **Jennifer Lalor**, Santa Clara, Jr.; Jessica Reifer, Hartford, Sr.; **Tisha Venturini**, North Carolina, Sr. FORWARDS— Shannon MacMillan, Portland, Jr.; Tiffeny Milbrett, Portland, Sr.; Natalie Neaton, Wm. & Mary, Jr.; **Kelly Walbert**, Duke, Jr.

FINAL FOUR

at Portland, Ore. (Nov. 18-20)

Semifinals

North Carolina 3 ....Connecticut 0
Notre Dame 1 ....Portland 0

Championship

North Carolina 5 ....Notre Dame 0

Scoring: UNC— Angela Kelly (Keri Sanchez amd Sarah Dacey), 14:22; Tisha Venturini, 55:09; Robin Confer (Sanchez), 72:16; Venturini (Kelly), 82:25; Dacey, 88:40. **Attendance:** 5,000.

Final records: North Carolina (25-1-1); Notre Dame (22-1-1); Connecticut (19-4); Portland (16-6).

Most Outstanding Players: OFFENSE— Tisha Venturini, North Carolina, midfielder; DEFENSE— Staci Wilson, North Carolina, defender.

Other Tournaments
MEN

NCAA Division II

Semifinals: Oakland (Mich.) over Seattle Pacific, 6-4 (2 OT); Tampa over Southern Conn. St., 0-0 (4 OT, Tampa wins shootout, 5-4).
Championship: Tampa over Oakland, 3-0 (2 OT). Final records: Tampa (15-2-1) and Oakland (17-2-2)

NCAA Division III

Semifinals: Bethany (W. Va.) over Wisconsin-Oshkosh, 0-0 (2 OT, Bethany wins shootout, 4-2); Johns Hopkins over Trenton St., 1-0.
Championship: Bethany over Johns Hopkins, 1-0 (OT). Final records: Bethany (18-5-1) and Johns Hopkins (17-3-3).

NAIA

Semifinals: West Va. Wesleyan over Lynn (Fla.), 2-1; Mobile (Ala.) over Lindsey Wilson (Ky.), 2-0.
Championship: West Va. Wesleyan over Mobile, 4-2. Final records: West Va. Wesleyan (20-3-4) and Mobile (21-4-0).

WOMEN

NCAA Division II

Semifinals: Franklin Pierce (N.H.) over Mercyhurst (Pa.), 2-1; Regis (Colo.) over Quincy (Ill.), 3-1.
Championship: Franklin Pierce over Regis, 2-0. Final records: Franklin Pierce (19-0-0) and Regis (14-8-1).

NCAA Division III

Semifinals: Trenton St. (N.J.) over Geneseo St. (N.Y.), 6-0; UC-San Diego over North Carolina Wesleyan, 2-0.
Championship: Trenton St. over UC-San Diego, 4-3 (3 OT). Final records: Trenton St. (22-1-0) and UC-San Diego (14-1-3).

NAIA

Semifinals: Park (Mo.) over Westmont (Calif.), 2-1; Lynn (Fla.) over Georgian Court (N.J.), 3-1.
Championship: Lynn over Park, 3-1. Final records: Lynn (24-0-1) and Park (25-4-0).

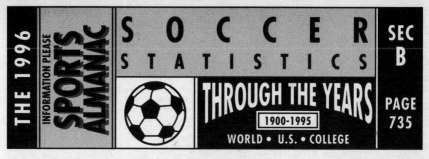

THE 1996 INFORMATION PLEASE SPORTS ALMANAC

SOCCER STATISTICS

SEC B

THROUGH THE YEARS
1900-1995
WORLD • U.S. • COLLEGE

PAGE 735

The World Cup

The Federation Internationale de Football Association (FIFA) began the World Cup championship tournament in 1930 with a 13-team field in Uruguay. Sixty-four years later, 138 countries competed in qualifying rounds to fill 24 berths in the 1994 World Cup finals. FIFA has increased the World Cup '98 tournament field from 24 to 32 teams, including automatic berths for defending champion Brazil and host France. The other 30 slots are allotted by region: Europe (14), Africa (5), South America (4), CONCACAF (3), Asia (3), and the one remaining position to the winner of a playoff between the fourth place team in Asia and the champion of Oceania.

The United States hosted the World Cup for the first time in '94 and American crowds shattered tournament attendance records (see page 739). Tournaments have now been played three times in North America (Mexico 2 and U.S.), four times in South America (Argentina, Chile, Brazil and Uruguay) and eight times in Europe (Italy 2, England, France, Spain, Sweden, Switzerland and West Germany).

Brazil retired the first World Cup (called the Jules Rimet Trophy after FIFA's first president) in 1970 after winning it for the third time. The new trophy, first presented in 1974, is known as simply the World Cup.

Multiple winners: Brazil (4); Italy and West Germany (3); Argentina and Uruguay (2).

Year	Champion	Manager	Score	Runner-up	Host Country	Third Place
1930	Uruguay	Alberto Suppici	4-2	Argentina	Uruguay	No game
1934	Italy	Vittório Pozzo	2-1*	Czechoslovakia	Italy	Germany 3, Austria 2
1938	Italy	Vittório Pozzo	4-2	Hungary	France	Brazil 4, Sweden 2
1942-46	Not held					
1950	Uruguay	Juan Lopez	2-1	Brazil	Brazil	No game
1954	West Germany	Sepp Herberger	3-2	Hungary	Switzerland	Austria 3, Uruguay 1
1958	Brazil	Vicente Feola	5-2	Sweden	Sweden	France 6, W. Ger. 3
1962	Brazil	Aimoré Moreira	3-1	Czechoslovakia	Chile	Chile 1, Yugoslavia 0
1966	England	Alf Ramsey	4-2*	W. Germany	England	Portugal 2, USSR 1
1970	Brazil	Mario Zagalo	4-1	Italy	Mexico	W. Ger. 1, Uruguay 0
1974	West Germany	Helmut Schoen	2-1	Holland	W. Germany	Poland 1, Brazil 0
1978	Argentina	Cesar Menotti	3-1*	Holland	Argentina	Brazil 2, Italy 1
1982	Italy	Enzo Bearzot	3-1	W. Germany	Spain	Poland 3, France 2
1986	Argentina	Carlos Bilardo	3-2	W. Germany	Mexico	France 4, Belgium 2*
1990	West Germany	Franz Beckenbauer	1-0	Argentina	Italy	Italy 2, England 1
1994	Brazil	Carlos Parreira	0-0†	Italy	USA	Sweden 4, Bulgaria 0
1998	at France (June 10–July 12)					

*Winning goals scored in overtime (no sudden death); †Brazil defeated Italy in shootout (3-2) after scoreless overtime period (30 minutes).

All-Time World Cup Leaders

Career Goals

World Cup scoring leaders through 1994. Years listed are years played in World Cup.

	No
Gerd Müller, West Germany (1970, 74)	14
Just Fontaine, France (1958)	13
Pelé, Brazil (1958, 62, 66, 70)	12
Sandor Kocsis, Hungary (1954)	11
Helmut Rahn, West Germany (1954, 58)	11
Teofilo Cubillas, Peru (1970, 78)	10
Gregorz Lato, Poland (1974, 78, 82)	10
Gary Lineker, England (1986, 90)	10

Most Valuable Player

Officially, the Golden Ball Award, the Most Valuable Player of the World Cup tournament has been selected since 1982 by a panel of international soccer journalists.

Year		Year	
1982	Paolo Rossi, Italy	1990	Toto Schillaci, Italy
1986	Diego Maradona, Arg.	1994	Romario, Brazil

Single Tournament Goals

World Cup tournament scoring leaders through 1994.

Year		Gm	No
1930	Guillermo Stabile, Argentina	4	8
1934	Angelo Schiavio, Italy	3	4
	Oldrich Nejedly, Czechoslovakia	4	4
	& Edmund Conen, Germany	4	4
1938	Leônidas, Brazil	3	8
1950	Ademir, Brazil	6	7
1954	Sandor Kocsis, Hungary	5	11
1958	Just Fontaine, France	6	13
1962	Drazen Jerkovic, Yugoslavia	6	5
1966	Eusébio, Portugal	6	9
1970	Gerd Müller, West Germany	6	10
1974	Grzegorz Lato, Poland	7	7
1978	Mario Kempes, Argentina	7	6
1982	Paolo Rossi, Italy	7	6
1986	Gary Lineker, England	5	6
1990	Toto Schillaci, Italy	7	6
1994	Oleg Salenko, Russia	3	6
	Hristo Stoichkov, Bulgaria	7	6

All-Time World Cup Ranking Table

Since the first World Cup in 1930, Brazil is the only country to play in all 15 final tournaments and win the championship four times. The FIFA All-Time Table below ranks all nations that have ever qualified for a World Cup final tournament by points earned through 1994. Victories, which earned two points from 1930-90, were awarded three points starting in 1994. Note that Germany's appearances include 10 made by West Germany from 1954-90. Participants in the 1994 World Cup final are in **bold** type.

		App	Gm	W	L	T	Pts	GF	GA
1	**Brazil**	15	73	49	11	13	111	159	68
2	**Germany**	13	73	42	15	16	100	154	97
3	**Italy**	13	61	35	12	14	84	97	59
4	**Argentina**	11	52	26	17	9	61	90	65
5	**England**	9	41	18	11	12	48	55	38
6	**Spain**	9	37	15	13	9	39	53	44
7	Uruguay	9	37	15	14	8	38	61	52
	Russia	8	34	16	12	6	38	60	40
9	**Sweden**	9	38	14	15	9	37	66	60
10	France	9	34	15	14	5	35	71	56
	Yugoslavia	8	33	14	12	7	35	55	42
12	Hungary	9	32	15	14	3	33	87	57
13	Poland	5	23	13	7	5	31	39	29
14	**Holland**	6	25	11	8	6	28	43	29
15	Czech Rep.	8	30	11	14	5	27	44	45
16	Austria	6	26	12	12	2	26	40	43
17	**Mexico**	10	33	7	18	8	22	31	68
	Belgium	9	29	9	16	4	22	37	53
19	Chile	6	21	7	11	3	17	26	32
20	**Romania**	6	17	6	7	4	16	26	29
21	**Switzerland**	7	22	6	13	3	15	33	51
22	Scotland	7	20	4	10	6	14	23	35
23	**Bulgaria**	6	23	3	13	7	13	21	46
24	Portugal	2	9	6	3	0	12	19	12
25	Peru	4	15	4	8	3	11	19	31
	No. Ireland	3	13	3	5	5	11	13	23
27	Paraguay	4	11	3	4	4	10	16	25
	Cameroon	3	11	3	4	4	10	11	21
29	**USA**	5	14	4	9	1	9	17	33
30	**Ireland**	2	9	1	3	5	7	4	7
31	**Colombia**	3	10	2	6	2	6	13	20
	Denmark	1	4	3	1	0	6	10	6
	East Germany	1	6	2	2	2	6	5	5
34	**Morocco**	3	10	1	6	3	5	7	13
	Algeria	2	6	2	3	1	5	6	10
	Wales	1	5	1	1	3	5	4	4
37	Costa Rica	1	4	2	2	0	4	4	6
	Nigeria	1	4	2	2	0	4	7	4
	Saudi Arabia	1	4	2	2	0	4	5	6
40	**South Korea**	4	11	0	8	3	3	9	34
	Norway	2	4	1	2	1	3	2	3
	Cuba	1	3	1	1	1	3	5	12
	North Korea	1	4	1	2	1	3	5	9
	Tunisia	1	3	1	1	1	3	3	2
45	Egypt	2	4	0	2	2	2	3	6
	Honduras	1	3	0	1	2	2	2	3
	Israel	1	3	0	1	2	2	1	3
	Turkey	1	3	1	2	0	2	10	11
49	**Bolivia**	3	6	0	5	1	1	1	20
	Australia	1	3	0	2	1	1	0	5
	Iran	1	3	0	2	1	1	2	8
	Kuwait	1	3	0	2	1	1	2	6
53	El Salvador	2	6	0	6	0	0	1	22
	Canada	1	3	0	3	0	0	0	5
	East Indies	1	1	0	1	0	0	0	6
	Greece	1	3	0	3	0	0	0	10
	Haiti	1	3	0	3	0	0	2	14
	Iraq	1	3	0	3	0	0	1	4
	New Zealand	1	3	0	3	0	0	2	12
	UAE	1	3	0	3	0	0	2	11
	Zaire	1	3	0	3	0	0	0	14

The United States in the World Cup

While the United States has fielded a national team every year of the World Cup, only four of those teams have been able to make it past the preliminary competition and qualify for the final World Cup tournament. The 1994 national team automatically qualified because the U.S. served as host of the event for the first time. The U.S. has played in three of the first four World Cups (1930, '34 and '50) and each of the last two (1990, '94). The Americans have a record of 4-9-1 in 14 World Cup matches, with two victories in 1930, a 1-0 upset of England in 1950, and a 2-1 shocker over Colombia in 1994.

1930

1st Round Matches

United States 3 .... Belgium 0
United States 3 .... Paraguay 0

Semifinals

Argentina 6 .... United States 1
U.S. Scoring—Bert Patenaude (3), Bart McGhee (2), James Brown, Thomas Florie.

1934

1st Round Match

Italy 7 .... United States 1
U.S. Scoring—Buff Donelli (who later became a noted college and NFL football coach).

1950

1st Round Matches

Spain 3 .... United States 1
United States 1 .... England 0
Chile 5 .... United States 2
U.S. Scoring—Joe Gaetjens, Joe Maca, John Souza, Frank Wallace.

1990

1st Round Matches

Czechoslovakia 5 .... United States 1
Italy 1 .... United States 0
Austria 2 .... United States 1
U.S. Scoring—Paul Caligiuri, Bruce Murray.

1994

1st Round Matches

United States 1 .... Switzerland 1
United States 2 .... Colombia 1
Romania 1 .... United States 0

Round of 16

Brazil 1 .... United States 0
Overall U.S. Scoring— Eric Wynalda, Ernie Stewart, own goal (Colombia defender Andres Escobar).

World Cup Finals

Current World Cup champion Brazil and finalist Italy each appeared in their fifth Cup championship game in 1994 and played to the first scoreless overtime draw in the history of the Cup final. The match was also the first decided by a shootout (Brazil winning, 3-2). West Germany (now Germany) has played in the most Cup finals with six. Note that a four-team round robin determined the 1950 championship—the deciding game turned out to be the last one of the tournament between Uruguay and Brazil.

1930

Uruguay 4, Argentina 2

(at Montevideo, Uruguay)

	1	2—T
July 30 Uruguay (4-0)	1	3—4
Argentina (4-1)	2	0—2

Goals: Uruguay—Pablo Dorado (12th minute), Pedro Cea (54th), Santos Iriarte (68th), Castro (89th); Argentina—Carlos Peucelle (20th), Guillermo Stabile (37th).

Uruguay—Ballesteros, Nasazzi, Mascheroni, Andrade, Fernandez, Gestido, Dorado, Scarone, Castro, Cea, Iriarte.

Argentina—Botasso, Della Torre, Paternoster, J. Evaristo, Monti, Suarez, Peucelle, Varallo, Stabile, Ferreira, M. Evaristo.

Attendance: 90,000. **Referee:** Langenus (Belgium).

1934

Italy 2, Czechoslovakia 1 (OT)

(at Rome)

	1	2	OT—T
June 10 Italy (4-0-1)	0	1	1—2
Czechoslovakia (3-1)	0	1	0—1

Goals: Italy—Raimondo Orsi (80th minute), Angelo Schiavio (95th); Czechoslovakia—Puc (70th).

Italy—Combi, Monzeglio, Allemandi, Ferraris IV, Monti, Bertolini, Guaita, Meazza, Schiavio, Ferrari, Orsi.

Czechoslovakia—Planicka, Zenisek, Ctyroky, Kostalek, Cambal, Krcil, Junek, Svoboda, Sobotka, Nejedly, Puc.

Attendance: 55,000. **Referee:** Eklind (Sweden).

1938

Italy 4, Hungary 2

(at Paris)

	1	2—T
June 19 Italy (4-0)	3	1—4
Hungary (3-1)	1	1—2

Goals: Italy—Gino Colaussi (5th minute), Silvio Piola (16th), Colassi (35th), Piola (82nd); Hungary—Titkos (7th), Georges Sarosi (70th).

Italy—Olivieri, Foni, Rava, Serantoni, Andreolo, Locatelli, Biavati, Meazza, Piola, Ferrari, Colaussi.

Hungary—Szabo, Polgar, Biro, Szalay, Szucs, Lazar, Sas, Vincze, G. Sarosi, Szengeller, Titkos.

Attendance: 65,000. **Referee:** Capdeville (France).

1950

Uruguay 2, Brazil 1

(at Rio de Janeiro)

	1	2—T
July 16 Uruguay (3-0-1)	0	2—2
Brazil (4-1-1)	0	1—1

Goals: Uruguay—Juan Schiaffino (66th minute), Chico Ghiggia (79th); Brazil—Friaça (47th).

Uruguay—Maspoli, M. Gonzales, Tejera, Gambetta, Varela, Andrade, Ghiggia, Perez, Miguez, Schiaffino, Moran.

Brazil—Barbosa, Augusto, Juvenal, Bauer, Danilo, Bigode, Friaça, Zizinho, Ademir, Jair, Chico.

Attendance: 199,854. **Referee:** Reader (England).

1954

West Germany 3, Hungary 2

(at Berne, Switzerland)

	1	2—T
July 4 West Germany (4-1)	2	1—3
Hungary (4-1)	2	0—2

Goals: West Germany—Max Morlock (10th minute), Helmut Rahn (18th), Rahn (84th); Hungary—Ferenc Puskas (4th), Zoltan Czibor (9th).

West Germany—Turek, Posipal, Liebrich, Kohlmeyer, Eckel, Mai, Rahn, Morlock, O. Walter, F. Walter, Schaefer.

Hungary—Grosics, Buzansky, Lorant, Lantos, Bozsik, Zakarias, Czibor, Kocsis, Hidegkuti, Puskas, J. Toth.

Attendance: 60,000. **Referee:** Ling (England).

1958

Brazil 5, Sweden 2

(at Stockholm)

	1	2—T
June 29 Brazil (5-0-1)	2	3—5
Sweden (4-1-1)	1	1—2

Goals: Brazil—Vavà (9th minute), Vavà (32nd), Pelé (55th), Mario Zagalo (68th), Pelé (90th); Sweden—Nils Liedholm (3rd), Agne Simonsson (80th).

Brazil—Gilmar, D. Santos, N. Santos, Zito, Bellini, Orlando, Garrincha, Didi, Vavà, Pelé, Zagalo.

Sweden—Svensson, Bergmark, Axbom, Boerjesson, Gustavsson, Parling, Hamrin, Gren, Simonsson, Liedholm, Skoglund.

Attendance: 49,737. **Referee:** Guigue (France).

1962

Brazil 3, Czechoslovakia 1

(at Santiago, Chile)

	1	2—T
June 17 Brazil (5-0-1)	1	2—3
Czechoslovakia (3-2-1)	1	0—1

Goals: Brazil—Amarildo (17th minute), Zito (68th), Vavà (77th); Czechoslovakia—Josef Masopust (15th).

Brazil—Gilmar, D. Santos, N. Santos, Zito, Mauro, Zozimo, Garrincha, Didi, Vavà, Amarildo, Zagalo.

Czechoslovakia—Schroiff, Tichy, Novak, Pluskal, Popluhar, Masopust, Pospichal, Scherer, Kvasniak, Kadraba, Jelinek.

Attendance: 68,679. **Referee:** Latishev (USSR).

1966

England 4, West Germany 2 (OT)

(at London)

	1	2	OT—T
July 30 England (5-0-1)	1	1	2—4
West Germany (4-1-1)	1	1	0—2

Goals: England—Geoff Hurst (18th minute), Martin Peters (78th), Hurst (101st), Hurst (120th); West Germany—Helmut Haller (12th), Wolfgang Weber (90th).

England—Banks, Cohen, Wilson, Stiles, J. Charlton, Moore, Ball, Hurst, B. Charlton, Hunt, Peters.

West Germany—Tilkowski, Höttges, Schnellinger, Beckenbauer, Schulz, Weber, Haller, Seeler, Held, Overath, Emmerich.

Attendance: 93,802. **Referee:** Dienst (Switzerland).

World Cup Finals (Cont.)

1970

Brazil 4, Italy 1

(at Mexico City)

	1	2—T
June 21 Brazil (6-0)	1	3—4
Italy (3-1-2)	1	0—1

Goals: Brazil—Pelé (18th minute), Gerson (65th), Jairzinho (70th), Carlos Alberto (86th); Italy—Roberto Boninsegna (37th).

Brazil—Felix, C. Alberto, Everaldo, Clodoaldo, Brito, Piazza, Jairzinho, Gerson, Tostão, Pelé, Rivelino.

Italy—Albertosi, Burgnich, Facchetti, Bertini (Juliano, 73rd), Rosato, Cera, Domenghini, Mazzola, Boninsegna (Rivera, 84th), De Sisti, Riva.

Attendance: 107,412. **Referee:** Glockner (E. Germany).

1974

West Germany 2, Holland 1

(at Munich)

	1	2—T
July 7 West Germany (6-1)	2	0—2
Holland (5-1-1)	1	0—1

Goals: West Germany—Paul Breitner (25th minute, penalty kick), Gerd Müller (43rd); Holland—Johan Neeskens (1st, penalty kick).

West Germany—Maier, Beckenbauer, Vogts, Breitner, Schwarzenbeck, Overath, Bonhof, Hoeness, Grabowski, Müller, Holzenbein.

Holland—Jongbloed, Suurbier, Rijsbergen (De Jong, 58th), Krol, Haan, Jansen, Van Hanegem, Neeskens, Rep, Cruyff, Rensenbrink (R. Van de Kerkhof, 46th).

Attendance: 77,833. **Referee:** Taylor (England).

1978

Argentina 3, Holland 1 (OT)

(at Buenos Aires)

	1	2	OT—T
June 25 Argentina (5-1-1)	1	0	2—3
Holland (3-2-2)	1	0	1—1

Goals: Argentina—Mario Kempes (37th minute), Kempes (104th), Daniel Bertoni (114th); Holland—Dirk Nanninga (81st).

Argentina—Fillol, Olguin, L. Galvan, Passarella, Tarantini, Ardiles (Larrosa, 65th), Gallego, Kempes, Luque, Bertoni, Ortiz (Houseman, 77th).

Holland—Jongbloed, Jansen (Suurbier, 72nd), Brandts, Krol, Poortvliet, Haan, Neeskens, W. Van de Kerkhof, R. Van de Kerkhof, Rep (Nanninga, 58th), Rensenbrink.

Attendance: 77,260. **Referee:** Gonella (Italy).

1982

Italy 3, West Germany 1

(at Madrid)

	1	2—T
July 11 Italy (4-0-3)	0	3—3
West Germany (4-2-1)	0	1—1

Goals: Italy—Paolo Rossi (57th minute), Marco Tardelli (68th), Alessandro Altobelli (81st); West Germany—Paul Breitner (83rd).

Italy—Zoff, Scirea, Gentile, Cabrini, Collovati, Bergomi, Tardelli, Oriali, Conti, Rossi, Graziani (Altobelli, 8th, and Causio, 89th).

West Germany—Schumacher, Stielike, Kaltz, Briegel, K.H. Forster, B. Forster, Breitner, Dremmler (Hrubesch, 61st), Littbarski, Fischer, Rummenigge (Müller, 69th).

Attendance: 90,080. **Referee:** Coelho (Brazil).

1986

Argentina 3, West Germany 2

(at Mexico City)

	1	2—T
June 29 Argentina (6-0-1)	1	2—3
West Germany (4-2-1)	0	2—2

Goals: Argentina—Jose Brown (22nd minute), Jorge Valdano (55th), Jorge Burruchaga (83rd); West Germany—Karl-Heinz Rummenigge (73rd), Rudi Völler (81st).

Argentina—Pumpido, Cuciuffo, Olarticoechea, Ruggeri, Brown, Batista, Burruchaga (Trobbiani, 89th), Giusti, Enrique, Maradona, Valdano.

West Germany—Schumacher, Jakobs, B. Forster, Berthold, Briegel, Eder, Brehme, Matthäus, Rummenigge, Magath (Hoeness, 61st), Allofs (Völler, 46th).

Attendance: 114,590. **Referee:** Filho (Brazil).

1990

West Germany 1, Argentina 0

(at Rome)

	1	2—T
July 8 West Germany (6-0-1)	0	1—1
Argentina (4-2-1)	0	0—0

Goals: West Germany—Andreas Brehme (85th minute, penalty kick).

West Germany—Illgner, Berthold (Reuter, 73rd), Kohler, Augenthaler, Buchwald, Brehme, Haessler, Matthäus, Littbarski, Klinsmann, Völler.

Argentina: Goycoechea, Ruggeri (Monzon, 46th), Simon, Serrizuela, Lorenzo, Basualdo, Troglio, Burruchaga (Calderon, 53rd), Sensini, Dezotti, Maradona.

Attendance: 73,603. **Referee:** Codesal (Mexico).

1994

Brazil 0, Italy 0 (SO)

(at Pasadena, Calif.)

	1	2	OT—T
July 17 Brazil (6-0-1)	0	0	0—0*
Italy (4-2-1)	0	0	0—0

*Brazil wins shootout, 3-2.

Shootout (five shots each, alternating): ITA— Baresi (miss, 0-0); BRA— Santos (blocked, 0-0); ITA— Albertini (goal, 1-0); BRA—Romario (goal, 1-1); ITA— Evani (goal, 2-1); BRA— Branco (goal, 2-2); ITA— Massaro (blocked, 2-2); BRA— Dunga (goal, 2-3); ITA—R. Baggio (miss, 2-3).

Brazil— Taffarel, Jorginho (Cafu, 21st minute), Branco, Aldair, Santos, Mazinho, Silva, Dunga, Zinho (Viola, 106th), Bebeto, Romario.

Italy— Pagliuca, Mussi (Apolloni, 35th minute), Baresi, Benarrivo, Maldini, Albertini, D. Baggio (Evani, 95th), Berti, Donadoni, R. Baggio, Massaro.

Attendance: 94,194. **Referee:** Puhl (Hungary).

World Cup Shootouts

Introduced in 1982; winning sides in **bold** type.

Year	Round			Final	SO
1982	Semi	**W. Germany**	vs France	3-3	(5-4)
1986	Quarter	**Belgium**	vs Spain	1-1	(5-4)
	Quarter	**France**	vs Brazil	1-1	(4-3)
	Quarter	**W. Germany**	vs Mexico	0-0	(4-1)
1990	Second	**Ireland**	vs Romania	0-0	(5-4)
	Quarter	**Argentina**	vs Yugoslavia	0-0	(3-2)
	Semi	**Argentina**	vs Italy	1-1	(4-3)
	Semi	**W. Germany**	vs England	1-1	(4-3)
1994	Second	**Bulgaria**	vs Mexico	1-1	(3-1)
	Quarter	**Sweden**	vs Romania	2-2	(5-4)
	Final	**Brazil**	vs Italy	0-0	(3-2)

Year-by-Year Comparisons

How the 15 World Cup tournaments have compared in nations qualifying, matches played, players participating, goals scored, average goals per game, overall attendance and attendance per game.

Year	Host	Continent	Nations	Matches	Players	Goals Scored	Goals Per Game	Attendance Overall	Attendance Per Game
1930	Uruguay	So. America	13	18	189	70	3.8	434,500	24,138
1934	Italy	Europe	16	17	208	70	4.1	395,000	23,235
1938	France	Europe	15	18	210	84	4.7	483,000	26,833
1942-46	Not held								
1950	Brazil	So. America	13	22	192	88	4.0	1,337,000	60,772
1954	Switzerland	Europe	16	26	233	140	5.3	943,000	36,270
1958	Sweden	Europe	16	35	241	126	3.6	868,000	24,800
1962	Chile	So. America	16	32	252	89	2.8	776,000	24,250
1966	England	Europe	16	32	254	89	2.8	1,614,677	50,458
1970	Mexico	No. America	16	32	270	95	3.0	1,673,975	52,311
1974	West Germany	Europe	16	38	264	97	2.6	1,774,022	46,684
1978	Argentina	So. America	16	38	277	102	2.7	1,610,215	42,374
1982	Spain	Europe	24	52	396	146	2.8	1,856,277	33,967
1986	Mexico	No. America	24	52	414	132	2.5	2,402,951	46,211
1990	Italy	Europe	24	52	413	115	2.2	2,517,348	48,411
1994	United States	No. America	24	52	437	140	2.7	3,567,415	68,102
1998	France	Europe	32	—	—	—	—	—	—

OTHER WORLDWIDE COMPETITION

The Olympic Games

Held every four years since 1896, except during World War I (1916) and World War II (1940-44). Soccer was not a medal sport in 1896 at Athens or in 1932 at Los Angeles. By agreement between FIFA and the IOC, Olympic soccer competition is currently limited to players 23 years old and under.

Multiple winners: England and Hungary (3); Soviet Union and Uruguay (2).

Year		Year	
1900	**England,** France, Belgium	1956	**Soviet Union,** Yugoslavia, Bulgaria
1904	**Canada,** USA I, USA II	1960	**Yugoslavia,** Denmark, Hungary
1906	**Denmark,** Smyrna (Int'l entry), Greece	1964	**Hungary,** Czechoslovakia, East Germany
1908	**England,** Denmark, Holland	1968	**Hungary,** Bulgaria, Japan
1912	**England,** Denmark, Holland	1972	**Poland,** Hungary, East Germany
1920	**Belgium,** Spain, Holland	1976	**East Germany,** Poland, Soviet Union
1924	**Uruguay,** Switzerland, Sweden	1980	**Czechoslovakia,** East Germany, Soviet Union
1928	**Uruguay,** Argentina, Italy	1984	**France,** Brazil, Yugoslavia
1936	**Italy,** Austria, Norway	1988	**Soviet Union,** Brazil, West Germany
1948	**Sweden,** Yugoslavia, Denmark	1992	**Spain,** Poland, Ghana
1952	**Hungary,** Yugoslavia, Sweden		

The Under-20 World Cup

Held every two years since 1977. Officially, The World Youth Championship for the FIFA/Coca-Cola Cup.
Multiple winners: Brazil (3); Argentina and Portugal (2).

Year		Year	
1977	Soviet Union	1987	Yugoslavia
1979	Argentina	1989	Portugal
1981	West Germany	1991	Portugal
1983	Brazil	1993	Brazil
1985	Brazil	1995	Argentina

The Under-17 World Cup

Held every two years since 1985. Officially, The U-17 World Tournament for the FIFA/JVC Cup.
Multiple winners: Ghana and Nigeria (2).

Year		Year	
1985	Nigeria	1991	Ghana
1987	Soviet Union	1993	Nigeria
1989	Saudi Arabia	1995	Ghana

Indoor World Championship

First held in 1989. FIFA's only Five-a-Side tournament.
Multiple winners: Brazil (2).

Year		Year	
1989	Brazil	1996	(at Spain)
1992	Brazil		

Women's World Cup

First held in 1991. Officially, the FIFA Women's World Championship.

Year		Year	
1991	United States	1995	Norway

Intercontinental Cup

First held in 1992. Contested by the Continental champions of Africa, Asia, Europe, North America and South America.

Year		Year	
1992	Argentina	1995	Denmark

CONTINENTAL COMPETITION

European Championship

Held every four years since 1960. Officially, the European Football Championship.
Multiple winner: West Germany (2).

Year		Year		Year		Year	
1960	Soviet Union	1972	West Germany	1984	France	1992	Denmark
1964	Spain	1976	Czechoslovakia	1988	Holland	1996	(at England)
1968	Italy	1980	West Germany				

Copa America

Held irregularly since 1916. Unofficially, the Championship of South America.
Multiple winners: Argentina and Uruguay (14); Brazil (4); Paraguay and Peru (2).

Year		Year		Year		Year	
1916	Uruguay	1927	Argentina	1947	Argentina	1967	Uruguay
1917	Uruguay	1929	Argentina	1949	Brazil	1975	Peru
1919	Brazil	1935	Uruguay	1953	Paraguay	1979	Paraguay
1920	Uruguay	1937	Argentina	1955	Argentina	1983	Uruguay
1921	Argentina	1939	Peru	1956	Uruguay	1987	Uruguay
1922	Brazil	1941	Argentina	1957	Argentina	1989	Brazil
1923	Uruguay	1942	Uruguay	1958	Argentina	1991	Argentina
1924	Uruguay	1945	Argentina	1959	Uruguay	1993	Argentina
1925	Argentina	1946	Argentina	1963	Bolivia	1995	Uruguay
1926	Uruguay						

African Nations' Cup

Contested since 1957 and held every two years since 1968.
Multiple winners: Ghana (4); Congo/Zaire and Egypt (3); Cameroon and Nigeria (2).

Year		Year		Year		Year	
1957	Egypt	1968	Zaire	1978	Ghana	1988	Cameroon
1959	Egypt	1970	Sudan	1980	Nigeria	1990	Algeria
1962	Ethiopia	1972	Congo	1982	Ghana	1992	Ivory Coast
1963	Ghana	1974	Zaire	1984	Cameroon	1994	Nigeria
1965	Ghana	1976	Morocco	1986	Egypt		

CONCACAF Gold Cup

The Confederation of North, Central American and Caribbean Football Championship. Contested irregularly from 1963-81 and revived as CONCACAF Gold Cup in 1991.
Multiple winners: Mexico (4); Costa Rica (2).

Year		Year		Year		Year	
1963	Costa Rica	1969	Costa Rica	1977	Mexico	1991	United States
1965	Mexico	1971	Mexico	1981	Honduras	1993	Mexico
1967	Guatemala	1973	Haiti				

CLUB COMPETITION

Toyota Cup

Also known as the World Club Championship. Contested annually in December between the winners of the European Cup and South America's Copa Libertadores. Four European Cup winners refused to participate in the championship match in the 1970s and were replaced each time by the European Cup runner-up: Panathinaikos (Greece) for Ajax Amsterdam (Holland) in 1971; Juventus (Italy) for Ajax in 1973; Atlético Madrid (Spain) for Bayern Munich (West Germany) in 1974; and Malmo (Sweden) for Nottingham Forest (England) in 1979. Another European Cup winner, Marseille of France, was prohibited by the Union of European Football Associations (UEFA) from playing for the 1993 Toyota Cup because of its involvement in the match-rigging scandal.

Best-of-three game format from 1960-68, then a two-game/total goals format from 1969-79. Toyota became Cup sponsor in 1980, changed the format to a one-game championship and moved it to Toyko.

Multiple winners: AC Milan, Nacional and Peñarol (3); Independiente, Inter-Milan, Santos and São Paulo (2).

Year		Year		Year	
1960	Real Madrid (Spain)	1972	Ajax Amsterdam (Holland)	1984	Independiente (Argentina)
1961	Peñarol (Uruguay)	1973	Independiente (Argentina)	1985	Juventus (Italy)
1962	Santos (Brazil)	1974	Atlético Madrid (Spain)	1986	River Plate (Argentina)
1963	Santos (Brazil)	1975	Not held	1987	FC Porto (Portugal)
1964	Inter-Milan (Italy)	1976	Bayern MunichW.Germany)	1988	Nacional (Uruguay)
1965	Inter-Milan (Italy)	1977	Boca Juniors (Argentina)	1989	AC Milan (Italy)
1966	Peñarol (Uruguay)	1978	Not held	1990	AC Milan (Italy)
1967	Racing Club (Argentina)	1979	Olimpia (Paraguay)	1991	Red Star (Yugoslavia)
1968	Estudiantes (Argentina)	1980	Nacional (Uruguay)	1992	São Paulo (Brazil)
1969	AC Milan (Italy)	1981	Flamengo (Brazil)	1993	São Paulo (Brazil)
1970	Feyenoord (Holland)	1982	Peñarol (Uruguay)	1994	Velez Sarsfield (Argentina)
1971	Nacional (Uruguay)	1983	Gremio (Brazil)		

European Cup

Contested annually since the 1955-56 season by the league champions of the member countries of the Union of European Football Associations (UEFA).

Multiple winners: Real Madrid (6); AC Milan (5); Ajax Amsterdam and Liverpool (4); Bayern Munich (3); Benfica, Inter-Milan and Nottingham Forest (2).

Year		Year		Year	
1956	Real Madrid (Spain)	1970	Feyenoord (Holland)	1983	SV Hamburg (W. Germany)
1957	Real Madrid (Spain)	1971	Ajax Amsterdam (Holland)	1984	Liverpool (England)
1958	Real Madrid (Spain)	1972	Ajax Amsterdam (Holland)	1985	Juventus (Italy)
1959	Real Madrid (Spain)	1973	Ajax Amsterdam (Holland)	1986	Steaua Bucharest (Romania)
1960	Real Madrid (Spain)	1974	Bayern Munich (W. Germany)	1987	FC Porto (Portugal)
1961	Benfica (Portugal)	1975	Bayern Munich (W. Germany)	1988	PSV Eindhoven (Holland)
1962	Benfica (Portugal)	1976	Bayern Munich (W. Germany)	1989	AC Milan (Italy)
1963	AC Milan (Italy)	1977	Liverpool (England)	1990	AC Milan (Italy)
1964	Inter-Milan (Italy)	1978	Liverpool (England)	1991	Red Star Belgrade (Yugo.)
1965	Inter-Milan (Italy)	1979	Nottingham Forest (England)	1992	Barcelona (Spain)
1966	Real Madrid (Spain)	1980	Nottingham Forest (England)	1993	Marseille (France)
1967	Glasgow Celtic (Scotland)	1981	Liverpool (England)	1994	AC Milan (Italy)
1968	Manchester United (England)	1982	Aston Villa (England)	1995	Ajax Amsterdam (Holland)
1969	AC Milan (Italy)				

European Cup Winners' Cup

Contested annually since the 1960-61 season by the cup winners of the member countries of the Union of European Football Associations (UEFA).

Multiple winners: Barcelona (3); AC Milan, RSC Anderlecht and Dinamo Kiev (2).

Year		Year		Year	
1961	Fiorentina (Italy)	1973	AC Milan (Italy)	1985	Everton (England)
1962	Atlético Madrid (Spain)	1974	FC Magdeburg (E. Germany)	1986	Dinamo Kiev (USSR)
1963	Tottenham Hotspur (England)	1975	Dinamo Kiev (USSR)	1987	Ajax Amsterdam (Holland)
1964	Sporting Lisbon (Portugal)	1976	RSC Anderlecht (Belgium)	1988	Mechelen (Belgium)
1965	West Ham United (England)	1977	SV Hamburg (W. Germany)	1989	Barcelona (Spain)
1966	Borussia Dortmund (W. Germany)	1978	RSC Anderlecht (Belgium)	1990	Sampdoria (Italy)
1967	Bayern Munich (W. Germany)	1979	Barcelona (Spain)	1991	Manchester United (England)
1968	AC Milan (Italy)	1980	Valencia (Spain)	1992	Werder Bremen (Germany)
1969	Slovan Bratislava (Czech.)	1981	Dinamo Tbilisi (USSR)	1993	Parma (Italy)
1970	Manchester City (England)	1982	Barcelona (Spain)	1994	Arsenal (England)
1971	Chelsea (England)	1983	Aberdeen (Scotland)	1995	Real Zaragoza (Spain)
1972	Glasgow Rangers (Scotland)	1984	Juventus (Italy)		

UEFA Cup

Contested annually since the 1957-58 season by teams other than league champions and cup winners of the Union of European Football Associations (UEFA). Teams selected by UEFA based on each country's previous performance in the tournament. Teams from England were banned from UEFA Cup play from 1985-90 for the criminal behavior of their supporters.

Multiple winners: Barcelona and Juventus (3); Borussia Mönchengladbach, IFK Göteborg, Leeds United, Liverpool, Real Madrid, Tottenham Hotspur and Valencia (2).

Year		Year		Year	
1958	Barcelona (Spain)	1972	Tottenham Hotspur (England)	1983	RSC Anderlecht (Belgium)
1959	Not held	1973	Liverpool (England)	1984	Tottenham Hotspur (England)
1960	Barcelona (Spain)	1974	Feyenoord (Holland)	1985	Real Madrid (Spain)
1961	AS Roma (Italy)	1975	Borussia Mönchen-	1986	Real Madrid (Spain)
1962	Valencia (Spain)		gladbach (W. Germany)	1987	IFK Göteborg (Sweden)
1963	Valencia (Spain)	1976	Liverpool (England)	1988	Bayer Leverkusen
1964	Real Zaragoza (Spain)	1977	Juventus (Italy)		(W. Germany)
1965	Ferencvaros (Hungary)	1978	PSV Eindhoven (Holland)	1989	Napoli (Italy)
1966	Barcelona (Spain)	1979	Borussia Mönchen-	1990	Juventus (Italy)
1967	Dinamo Zagreb (Yugoslavia)		gladbach (W. Germany)	1991	Inter-Milan (Italy)
1968	Leeds United (England)	1980	Eintracht Frankfurt	1992	Ajax Amsterdam (Holland)
1969	Newcastle United (England)		(W. Germany)	1993	Juventus (Italy)
1970	Arsenal (England)	1981	Ipswich Town (England)	1994	Inter-Milan (Italy)
1971	Leeds United (England)	1982	IFK Göteborg (Sweden)	1995	Parma (Italy)

Club Competition (Cont.)
Copa Libertadores

Contested annually since the 1955-56 season by the league champions of South America's football union.

Multiple winners: Independiente (7); Peñarol (5); Estudiantes and Nacional-Uruguay (3); Boca Juniors, Gremio, Olimpia, Santos and São Paulo (2).

Year		Year		Year	
1960	Peñarol (Uruguay)	1972	Independiente (Argentina)	1984	Independiente (Argentina)
1961	Peñarol (Uruguay)	1973	Independiente (Argentina)	1985	Argentinos Jrs. (Argentina)
1962	Santos (Brazil)	1974	Independiente (Argentina)	1986	River Plate (Argentina)
1963	Santos (Brazil)	1975	Independiente (Argentina)	1987	Peñarol (Uruguay)
1964	Independiente (Argentina)	1976	Cruzeiro (Brazil)	1988	Nacional (Uruguay)
1965	Independiente (Argentina)	1977	Boca Juniors (Argentina)	1989	Nacional Medellin (Colombia)
1966	Peñarol (Uruguay)	1978	Boca Juniors (Argentina)		
1967	Racing Club (Argentina)	1979	Olimpia (Paraguay)	1990	Olimpia (Paraguay)
1968	Estudiantes de la Plata (Argentina)			1991	Colo Colo (Chile)
1969	Estudiantes de la Plata (Argentina)	1980	Nacional (Uruguay)	1992	São Paulo (Brazil)
		1981	Flamengo (Brazil)	1993	São Paulo (Brazil)
1970	Estudiantes de la Plata (Argentina)	1982	Peñarol (Uruguay)	1994	Velez Sarsfield (Argentina)
1971	Nacional (Uruguay)	1983	Gremio (Brazil)	1995	Gremio (Brazil)

Annual Awards

World Player of the Year

Presented by FIFA, the European Sports Magazine Association (ESM) and Adidas, the sports equipment manufacturer, since 1991. Winners are selected by national team coaches from around the world.

Year		Nat'l Team	Year		Nat'l Team
1991	Lothar Matthäus, Inter-Milan	Germany	1993	Roberto Baggio, Juventus	Italy
1992	Marco Van Basten, AC Milan	Holland	1994	Romario, Barcelona	Brazil

European Player of the Year

Officially, the "Ballon d'Or" and presented by *France Football* magazine since 1956. Candidates are limited to European players in European leagues and winners are selected by a panel of 49 European soccer journalists.

Multiple winners: Johan Cruyff, Michel Platini and Marco Van Basten (3); Franz Beckenbauer, Alfredo di Stéfano, Kevin Keegan and Karl-Heinz Rummenigge (2).

Year		Nat'l Team	Year		Nat'l Team
1956	Stanley Matthews, Blackpool	England	1976	Franz Beckenbauer, Bayern Munich	W. Ger.
1957	Alfredo di Stéfano, Real Madrid	Arg./Spain	1977	Allan Simonsen, B. Mönchengladbach	Denmark
1958	Raymond Kopa, Real Madrid	France	1978	Kevin Keegan, SV Hamburg	England
1959	Alfredo di Stéfano, Real Madrid	Arg./Spain	1979	Kevin Keegan, SV Hamburg	England
1960	Luis Suarez, Barcelona	Spain	1980	K.H. Rummenigge, Bayern Munich	W. Ger.
1961	Enrique Sivori, Juventus	Arg./Italy	1981	K.H. Rummenigge, Bayern Munich	W. Ger.
1962	Josef Masopust, Dukla Prague	Czech.	1982	Paolo Rossi, Juventus	Italy
1963	Lev Yashin, Dinamo Moscow	Soviet Union	1983	Michel Platini, Juventus	France
1964	Denis Law, Manchester United	Scotland	1984	Michel Platini, Juventus	France
1965	Eusébio, Benfica	Portugal	1985	Michel Platini, Juventus	France
1966	Bobby Charlton, Manchester United	England	1986	Igor Belanov, Dinamo Kiev	Soviet Union
1967	Florian Albert, Ferencvaros	Hungary	1987	Ruud Gullit, AC Milan	Holland
1968	George Best, Manchester United	No. Ireland	1988	Marco Van Basten, AC Milan	Holland
1969	Gianni Rivera, AC Milan	Italy	1989	Marco Van Basten, AC Milan	Holland
1970	Gerd Müller, Bayern Munich	W. Ger.	1990	Lothar Matthäus, Inter-Milan	W. Ger.
1971	Johan Cruyff, Ajax Amsterdam	Holland	1991	Jean-Pierre Papin, Marseille	France
1972	Franz Beckenbauer, Bayern Munich	W. Ger.	1992	Marco Van Basten, AC Milan	Holland
1973	Johan Cruyff, Barcelona	Holland	1993	Roberto Baggio, Juventus	Italy
1974	Johan Cruyff, Barcelona	Holland	1994	Hristo Stoitchkov, Barcelona	Bulgaria
1975	Oleg Blokhin, Dinamo Kiev	Soviet Union			

South American Player of the Year

Presented by *El Pais* of Uruguay since 1971. Candidates are limited to South American players in South American leagues and winners are selected by a panel of 80 Latin American sports editors.

Multiple winners: Elias Figueroa and Zico (3); Diego Maradona and Carlos Valderrama (2).

Year		Nat'l Team	Year		Nat'l Team
1971	Tostão, Cruzeiro	Brazil	1978	Mario Kempes, Valencia	Argentina
1972	Teofilo Cubillas, Alianza Lima	Peru	1979	Diego Maradona, Argentinos Juniors	Argentina
1973	Pelé, Santos	Brazil	1980	Diego Maradona, Boca Juniors	Argentina
1974	Elias Figueroa, Internacional	Chile	1981	Zico, Flamengo	Brazil
1975	Elias Figueroa, Internacional	Chile	1982	Zico, Flamengo	Brazil
1976	Elias Figueroa, Internacional	Chile	1983	Socrates, Corinthians	Brazil
1977	Zico, Flamengo	Brazil	1984	Enzo Francescoli, River Plate	Uruguay

Year		Nat'l Team	Year		Nat'l Team
1985	Julio Cesar Romero, Fluminense	Paraguay	1990	Raul Amarilla, Olimpia	Paraguay
1986	Antonio Alzamendi, River Plate	Uruguay	1991	Oscar Ruggeri, Velez Sarsfield	Argentina
1987	Carlos Valderrama, Deportivo Cali	Colombia	1992	Rai, São Paulo	Brazil
1988	Ruben Paz, Racing Buenos Aires	Uruguay	1993	Carlos Valderrama, Atl. Junior	Colombia
1989	Bebeto, Vasco da Gama	Brazil	1994	Cafu, São Paulo	Brazil

African Player of the Year

Officially, the African "Ballon d'Or" and presented by *France Football* magazine since 1970. All African players are eligible for the award and winners are selected by a panel of 52 African soccer journalists.

Multiple winners: Abedi Pele (3); Roger Milla and Thomas N'kona (2).

Year		Year		Year	
1970	Salif Keita, Mali	1979	Thomas N'Kono, Cameroon	1987	Rabah Madjer, Algeria
1971	Ibrahim Sunday, Ghana	1980	Jean Manga Onguene, Cameroon	1988	Kalusha Bwalya, Zambia
1972	Cherif Souleymane, Guinea	1981	Lakhdar Belloumi, Algeria	1989	George Weah, Liberia
1973	Tshimimu Bwanga, Zaire	1982	Thomas N'Kono, Cameroon		
1974	Paul Moukila, Congo	1983	Mahmoud Al-Khatib, Egypt	1990	Roger Milla, Cameroon
1975	Ahmed Faras, Morocco	1984	Theophile Abega, Cameroon	1991	Abedi Pele, Ghana
1976	Roger Milla, Cameroon	1985	Mohamed Timoumi, Morocco	1992	Abedi Pele, Ghana
1977	Dhiab Tarak, Tunisia	1986	Badou Zaki, Morocco	1993	Abedi Pele, Ghana
1978	Abdul Razak, Ghana			1994	George Weah, Liberia

U.S. Player of the Year

Presented by Honda and the Spanish-speaking radio show "Futbol de Primera" since 1991. Candidates are limited to American players who have played at least five games in the APSL or with the U.S. National Team and winners are selected by a panel of U.S. soccer journalists.

Year		Year		Year		Year	
1991	Hugo Perez	1992	Eric Wynalda	1993	Thomas Dooley	1994	Marcelo Balboa

U.S. PRO LEAGUES

OUTDOOR

National Professional Soccer League (1967)

Not sanctioned by FIFA, the international soccer federation. The NPSL recruited individual players to fill the rosters of its 10 teams. The league lasted only one season.

	Playoff Final			Regular Season			
Year	Winner	Score(s)	Loser	Leading Scorer	G	A	Pts
1967	Oakland Clippers	0-1, 4-1	Baltimore Bays	Yanko Daucik, Toronto	20	8	48

United Soccer Association (1967)

Sanctioned by FIFA. Originally called the North American Soccer League, it became the USA to avoid being confused with the National Professional Soccer League (see above). Instead of recruiting individual players, the USA imported 12 entire teams from Europe to represent its 12 franchises. It, too, only lasted a season. The league champion Los Angeles Wolves were actually Wolverhampton of England and the runner-up Washington Whips were Aberdeen of Scotland.

	Playoff Final			Regular Season			
Year	Winner	Score	Loser	Leading Scorer	G	A	Pts
1967	Los Angeles Wolves	6-5 (OT)	Washington Whips	Roberto Boninsegna, Chicago	10	1	21

North American Soccer League (1968-84)

The NPSL and USA merged to form the NASL in 1968 and the new league lasted until 1985. The NASL championship was known as the Soccer Bowl from 1975-84. One game decided the NASL title every year but five. There were no playoffs in 1969; a two-game/aggregate goals format was used in 1968 and '70; and a best-of-three games format was used in 1971 and '84; (*) indicates overtime and (†) indicates game decided by shootout.

Multiple winners: NY Cosmos (5); Chicago (2).

	Playoff Final			Regular Season			
Year	Winner	Score(s)	Loser	Leading Scorer	G	A	Pts
1968	Atlanta Chiefs	0-0,3-0	San Diego Toros	John Kowalik, Chicago	30	9	69
1969	Kansas City Spurs	No game	Atlanta Chiefs	Kaiser Motaung, Atlanta	16	4	36
1970	Rochester Lancers	3-0,1-3	Washington Darts	Kirk Apostolidis, Dallas	16	3	35
1971	Dallas Tornado	1-2*,4-1,2-0	Atlanta Chiefs	Carlos Metidieri, Rochester	19	8	46
1972	New York Cosmos	2-1	St. Louis Stars	Randy Horton, New York	9	4	22
1973	Philadelphia Atoms	2-0	Dallas Tornado	Kyle Rote, Jr., Dallas	10	10	30
1974	Los Angeles Aztecs	3-3†	Miami Toros	Paul Child, San Jose	15	6	36
1975	Tampa Bay Rowdies	2-0	Portland Timbers	Steve David, Miami	23	6	52
1976	Toronto Metros	3-0	Minnesota Kicks	Giorgio Chinaglia, New York	19	11	49

Note: In 1969, Kansas City won the NASL regular season championship with 110 points to 109 for Atlanta. There were no playoffs.

U.S. Pro Leagues (Cont.)

Playoff Final

Year	Winner	Score(s)	Loser
1977	New York Cosmos	2-1	Seattle Sounders
1978	New York Cosmos	3-1	Tampa Bay Rowdies
1979	Vancouver Whitecaps	2-1	Tampa Bay Rowdies
1980	New York Cosmos	3-0	Ft. Laud. Strikers
1981	Chicago Sting	0-0†	New York Cosmos
1982	New York Cosmos	1-0	Seattle Sounders
1983	Tulsa Roughnecks	2-0	Toronto Blizzard
1984	Chicago Sting	2-1,3-2	Toronto Blizzard

Regular Season

Leading Scorer	G	A	Pts
Steve David, Los Angeles	26	6	58
Giorgio Chinaglia, New York	34	11	79
Oscar Fabbiani, Tampa Bay	25	8	58
Giorgio Chinaglia, New York	32	13	77
Giorgio Chinaglia, New York	29	16	74
Giorgio Chinaglia, New York	20	15	55
Roberto Cabanas, New York	25	16	66
Steve Zungul, Golden Bay	20	10	50

Regular Season MVP

Regular season Most Valuable Player as designated by the NASL.
Multiple winner: Carlos Metidieri (2).

Year		Year		Year	
1967	Rueben Navarro, Phila (NPSL)	1973	Warren Archibald, Miami	1979	Johan Cruyff, Los Angeles
1968	John Kowalik, Chicago	1974	Peter Silvester, Baltimore	1980	Roger Davies, Seattle
1969	Cirilio Fernandez, KC	1975	Steve David, Miami	1981	Giorgio Chinaglia, New York
1970	Carlos Metidieri, Rochester	1976	Pelé, New York	1982	Peter Ward, Seattle
1971	Carlos Metidieri, Rochester	1977	Franz Beckenbauer, New York	1983	Roberto Cabanas, New York
1972	Randy Horton, New York	1978	Mike Flanagan, New England	1984	Steve Zungul, Golden Bay

A-League (American Professional Soccer League)

The American Professional Soccer League was formed in 1990 with the merger of the Western Soccer League and the New American Soccer League. The APSL was officially sanctioned as an outdoor pro league in 1992 and changed its name to the A-League in 1995.
Multiple winner: Colorado (2).

Year		Year		Year		Year	
1990	Maryland Bays	1992	Colorado Foxes	1993	Colorado Foxes	1994	Montreal Impact
1991	SF Bay Blackhawks						

INDOOR

Major Soccer League (1978-92)

Originally the Major Indoor Soccer League from 1978-79 season through 1989-90. The MISL championship was decided by one game in 1980 and 1981; a best-of-three games series in 1979, best-of-five games in 1982 and 1983; and best-of-seven games since 1984. The MSL folded after the 1991-92 season.
Multiple winners: San Diego (8); New York (4).

Playoff Final

Year	Winner	Series	Loser
1979	New York Arrows	2-0 (WW)	Philadelphia
1980	New York Arrows	7-4 (1 game)	Houston
1981	New York Arrows	6-5 (1 game)	St. Louis
1982	New York Arrows	3-2 (LWWLW)	St. Louis
1983	San Diego Sockers	3-2 (WWLLW)	Baltimore
1984	Baltimore Blast	4-1 (LWWWW)	St. Louis
1985	San Diego Sockers	4-1 (WWLWW)	Baltimore
1986	San Diego Sockers	4-3 (WLLLWWW)	Minnesota
1987	Dallas Sidekicks	4-3 (LLWWLWW)	Tacoma
1988	San Diego Sockers	4-0	Cleveland
1989	San Diego Sockers	4-3 (LWWWLLW)	Baltimore
1990	San Diego Sockers	4-2 (LWWLW)	Baltimore
1991	San Diego Sockers	4-2 (WLWLWW)	Cleveland
1992	San Diego Sockers	4-2 (WWWLLW)	Dallas

Regular Season

Leading Scorer	G	A	Pts
Fred Grgurev, Philadelphia	46	28	74
Steve Zungul, New York	90	46	136
Steve Zungul, New York	108	44	152
Steve Zungul, New York	103	60	163
Steve Zungul, NY/Golden Bay	75	47	122
Stan Stamenkovic, Baltimore	34	63	97
Steve Zungul, San Diego	68	68	136
Steve Zungul, Tacoma	55	60	115
Tatu, Dallas	73	38	111
Eric Rasmussen, Wichita	55	57	112
Preki, Tacoma	51	53	104
Tatu, Dallas	64	49	113
Tatu, Dallas	78	66	144
Zoran Karic, Cleveland	39	63	102

Playoff MVPs

MSL playoff Most Valuable Players, selected by a panel of soccer media covering the playoffs.
Multiple winners: Zungul (4); Quinn (2).

Year		Year	
1979	Shep Messing, NY	1986	Brian Quinn, SD
1980	Steve Zungul, NY	1987	Tatu, Dallas
1981	Steve Zungul, NY	1988	Hugo Perez, SD
1982	Steve Zungul, NY	1989	Victor Nogueira, SD
1983	Juli Veee, SD	1990	Brian Quinn, SD
1984	Scott Manning, Bal.	1991	Ben Collins, SD
1985	Steve Zungul, SD	1992	Thompson Usiyan, SD

Regular Season MVPs

MSL regular season Most Valuable Players, selected by a panel of soccer media from every city in the league.
Multiple winner: Zungul (6); Nogueira and Tatu (2)

Year		Year	
1979	Steve Zungul, NY	1986	Steve Zungul, SD/Tac.
1980	Steve Zungul, NY	1987	Tatu, Dallas
1981	Steve Zungul, NY	1988	Erik Rasmussen, Wich.
1982	Steve Zungul, NY & Stan Terlecki, Pit.	1989	Preki, Tacoma
1983	Alan Mayer, SD	1990	Tatu, Dallas
1984	Stan Stamenkovic, Bal.	1991	Victor Nogueira, SD
1985	Steve Zungul, SD	1992	Victor Nogueira, SD

NASL Indoor Champions (1980-84)

The North American Soccer League started an indoor league in the fall of 1979. The indoor NASL, which featured many of the same teams and players who played in the outdoor NASL, crowned champions from 1980-82 before suspending play. It was revived for the 1983-84 indoor season but folded for good in 1984.

Multiple winners: San Diego (2).

Year		Year		Year		Year	
1980	Memphis Rogues	1982	San Diego Sockers	1983	Play suspended	1984	San Diego Sockers
1981	Edmonton Drillers						

National Professional Soccer League

The winter indoor NPSL began as the American Indoor Soccer Association in 1984-85, then changed its name in 1989-90.

Multiple winner: Canton (5).

Year		Year		Year		Year	
1985	Canton (OH) Invaders	1988	Canton Invaders	1991	Chicago Power	1994	Cleveland Crunch
1986	Canton Invaders	1989	Canton Invaders	1992	Detroit Rockers	1995	St. Louis Ambush
1987	Louisville Thunder	1990	Canton Invaders	1993	Kansas City Attack		

Continental Indoor Soccer League

The summer indoor CISL played its first season in 1993.

Year		Year	
1993	Dallas Sidekicks	1994	Las Vegas Dustdevils

U.S. COLLEGES

NCAA Men's Division I Champions

NCAA Division I champions since the first title was contested in 1959. The championship has been shared three times—in 1967, 1968 and 1989. There was a playoff for third place from 1974-81.

Multiple winners: Saint Louis (10); San Francisco and Virginia (5); Indiana (3); Clemson, Howard, and Michigan St. (2).

Year	Winner	Head Coach	Score	Runner-up	Host/Site	Semifinalists
1959	Saint Louis	Bob Guelker	5-2	Bridgeport	UConn	West Chester, CCNY
1960	Saint Louis	Bob Guelker	3-2	Maryland	Brooklyn	West Chester, UConn
1961	West Chester	Mel Lorback	2-0	Saint Louis	Saint Louis	Bridgeport, Rutgers
1962	Saint Louis	Bob Guelker	4-3	Maryland	Saint Louis	Mich. St., Springfield
1963	Saint Louis	Bob Guelker	3-0	Navy	Rutgers	Army, Maryland
1964	Navy	F.H. Warner	1-0	Michigan St.	Brown	Army, Saint Louis
1965	Saint Louis	Bob Guelker	1-0	Michigan St.	Saint Louis	Army, Navy
1966	San Francisco	Steve Negoesco	5-2	LIU-Brooklyn	California	Army, Mich. St.
1967-a	Michigan St. & Saint Louis	Gene Kenney Harry Keough	0-0	—	Saint Louis	LIU-Bklyn, Navy
1968-b	Michigan St. & Maryland	Gene Kenney Doyle Royal	2-2 (2 OT)	—	Ga. Tech	Brown, San Jose St.
1969	Saint Louis	Harry Keough	4-0	San Francisco	San Jose St.	Harvard, Maryland
1970	Saint Louis	Harry Keough	1-0	UCLA	SIU-Ed'sville	Hartwick, Howard
1971-c	Howard	Lincoln Phillips	3-2	Saint Louis	Miami	Harvard, San Fran.
1972	Saint Louis	Harry Keough	4-2	UCLA	Miami	Cornell, Howard
1973	Saint Louis	Harry Keough	2-1 (OT)	UCLA	Miami	Brown, Clemson

Year	Winner	Head Coach	Score	Runner-up	Host/Site	Third Place
1974	Howard	Lincoln Phillips	2-1 (4OT)	Saint Louis	Saint Louis	Hartwick 3, UCLA 1
1975	San Francisco	Steve Negoesco	4-0	SIU-Ed'sville	SIU-Ed'sville	Brown 2, Howard 0
1976	San Francisco	Steve Negoesco	1-0	Indiana	Penn	Hartwick 4, Clemson 3
1977	Hartwick	Jim Lennox	2-1	San Francisco	California	SIU-Ed'sville 3, Brown 2
1978-d	San Francisco	Steve Negoesco	4-3 (OT)	Indiana	Tampa	Clemson 6, Phi. Textile 2
1979	SIU-Ed'sville	Bob Guelker	3-2	Clemson	Tampa	Penn St. 2, Columbia 1
1980	San Francisco	Steve Negoesco	4-3 (OT)	Indiana	Tampa	Ala. A&M 2, Hartwick 0
1981	Connecticut	Joe Morrone	2-1 (OT)	Alabama A&M	Stanford	East. Ill. 4, Phi. Textile 2

Year	Winner	Head Coach	Score	Runner-up	Host/Site	Semifinalists
1982	Indiana	Jerry Yeagley	2-1 (8 OT)	Duke	Ft. Lauderdale	UConn, SIU-Ed'sville
1983	Indiana	Jerry Yeagley	1-0 (2 OT)	Columbia	Ft. Lauderdale	UConn, Virginia
1984	Clemson	I.M. Ibrahim	2-1	Indiana	Seattle	Hartwick, UCLA
1985	UCLA	Sigi Schmid	1-0 (8 OT)	American	Seattle	Evansville, Hartwick
1986	Duke	John Rennie	1-0	Akron	Tacoma	Fresno St., Harvard
1987	Clemson	I.M. Ibrahim	2-0	San Diego St.	Clemson	Harvard, N. Carolina
1988	Indiana	Jerry Yeagley	1-0	Howard	Indiana	Portland, S. Carolina
1989-e	Santa Clara & Virginia	Steve Sampson Bruce Arena	1-1 (2 OT)	—	Rutgers	Indiana, Rutgers

Notes: a—game declared a draw due to inclement weather after regulation time; b—game declared a draw after two overtimes; c—Howard vacated title for using ineligible player; d—San Francisco vacated title for using ineligible player; e—game declared a draw due to inclement weather after two overtimes.

U.S. Colleges (Cont.)

Year	Winner	Head Coach	Score	Runner-up	Host/Site	Semifinalists
1990-f	UCLA	Sigi Schmid	0-0 (PKs)	Rutgers	South Fla.	Evansville, N.C. State
1991-g	Virginia	Bruce Arena	0-0 (PKs)	Santa Clara	Tampa	Indiana, Saint Louis
1992	Virginia	Bruce Arena	2-0	San Diego	Davidson	Davidson, Duke
1993	Virginia	Bruce Arena	2-0	South Carolina	Davidson	CS-Fullerton, Princeton
1994	Virginia	Bruce Arena	1-0	Indiana	Davidson	Rutgers, UCLA

Notes: f—UCLA wins on penalty kicks (4-3) after four overtimes; **g**—Virginia wins on penalty kicks (3-1) after four overtimes.

Women's NCAA Division I Champions

NCAA Division I women's champions since the first tournament was contested in 1982. The University of North Carolina has won the title every year but 1985 when they lost the final to George Mason.
    Multiple winner: North Carolina (12).

Year	Winner	Score	Runner-up	Year	Winner	Score	Runner-up
1982	North Carolina	2-0	Central Florida	1989	North Carolina	2-0	Colorado College
1983	North Carolina	4-0	George Mason	1990	North Carolina	6-0	Connecticut
1984	North Carolina	2-0	Connecticut	1991	North Carolina	3-1	Wisconsin
1985	George Mason	2-0	North Carolina	1992	North Carolina	9-1	Duke
1986	North Carolina	2-0	Colorado College	1993	North Carolina	6-0	George Mason
1987	North Carolina	1-0	Massachusetts	1994	North Carolina	5-0	Notre Dame
1988	North Carolina	4-1	N.C. State				

Annual Awards
MEN
Hermann Trophy

College Player of the Year. Voted on by Division I college coaches and selected sportswriters and first presented in 1967 in the name of Robert Hermann, one of the founders of the North American Soccer League.
    Multiple winners: Mike Seerey, Ken Snow and Al Trost (2).

Year		Year		Year	
1967	Dov Markus, LIU	1977	Billy Gazonas, Hartwick	1987	Bruce Murray, Clemson
1968	Manuel Hernandez, San Jose St.	1978	Angelo DiBernardo, Indiana	1988	Ken Snow, Indiana
1969	Al Trost, Saint Louis	1979	Jim Stamatis, Penn St.	1989	Tony Meola, Virginia
1970	Al Trost, Saint Louis	1980	Joe Morrone, Jr. UConn	1990	Ken Snow, Indiana
1971	Mike Seerey, Saint Louis	1981	Armando Betancourt, Indiana	1991	Alexi Lalas, Rutgers
1972	Mike Seerey, Saint Louis	1982	Joe Ulrich, Duke	1992	Brad Friedel, UCLA
1973	Dan Counce, Saint Louis	1983	Mike Jeffries, Duke	1993	Claudio Reyna, Virginia
1974	Farrukh Quraishi, Oneonta St.	1984	Amr Aly, Columbia	1994	Brian Maisonneuve, Indiana
1975	Steve Ralbovsky, Brown	1985	Tom Kain, Duke		
1976	Glenn Myernick, Hartwick	1986	John Kerr, Duke		

Missouri Athletic Club Award

College Player of the Year. Voted on by men's team coaches around the country from Division I to junior college level and first presented in 1986 by the Missouri Athletic Club of St. Louis.
    Multiple winner: Claudio Reyna and Ken Snow (2).

Year		Year		Year	
1986	John Kerr, Duke	1989	Tony Meola, Virginia	1992	Claudio Reyna, Virginia
1987	John Harkes, Virginia	1990	Ken Snow, Indiana	1993	Claudio Reyna, Virginia
1988	Ken Snow, Indiana	1991	Alexi Lalas, Rutgers	1994	Todd Yeagley, Indiana

WOMEN
Hermann Trophy

Women's College Player of the year. Voted on by Division I college coaches and selected sportswriters and first presented in 1988 in the name of Robert Hermann, one of the founders of the North American Soccer League.
    Multiple winner: Mia Hamm (2).

Year		Year		Year	
1988	Michelle Akers, Central Fla.	1991	Kristine Lilly, N. Carolina	1993	Mia Hamm, N. Carolina
1989	Shannon Higgins, N. Carolina	1992	Mia Hamm, N. Carolina	1994	Tisha Venturini, N. Carolina
1990	April Kater, Massachusetts				

Missouri Athletic Club Award

Women's College Player of the Year. Voted on by women's team coaches around the country from Division I to junior college level and first presented in 1991 by the Missouri Athletic Club of St. Louis.
    Multiple winner: Mia Hamm (2).

Year		Year		Year	
1991	Kristine Lilly, N. Carolina	1993	Mia Hamm, N. Carolina	1994	Tisha Venturini, N. Carolina
1992	Mia Hamm, N. Carolina				

Brunswick Corporation

Mike Aulby leaps into the air after winning the Tournament of Champions on April 22. The victory made him the fourth bowler in PBA history to win all of the tour's Triple Crown events.

BOWLING

Grand Slam

Mike Aulby finally wins Tournament of Champions after 16 tries, becoming first player to win all four of bowling's major events.

Mike Aulby became professional bowling's ultimate champion at the Tournament of Champions on April 22.

By winning the PBA Tour's premier event, the 35-year-old Hoosier not only became the fourth player in history to win all three Triple Crown tournaments, but is now the only man to capture bowling's Grand Slam— the T of C, the U.S. Open, the PBA National Championship and the ABC Masters.

Aulby, who won the PBA National in 1979 (as a rookie) and again in '85 and captured both the Open and Masters in 1989, joined Billy Hardwick, Johnny Petraglia and Pete Weber as members of the Triple Crown club.

"I don't know how many times I've been asked, 'Do you think you can win the Triple Crown?' or 'When are you going to win the Tournament of Champions?'" said Aulby, who beat Bob Spaulding for the title in a thrilling, 237-232 final. "Thankfully, that's something I don't have to deal with anymore."

One thing he didn't have to deal with going into the 1995 Tournament of Champions was a career-long run of bad luck at the Riviera Lanes in Akron, the city where the PBA is headquartered and the T of C had been held every year since its inception in 1965. Sponsored by the Firestone Tire and Rubber Company for 29 years and taken over by cross-town rival General Tire Inc. in 1994, the T of C left Akron for suburban Chicago in '95 after General Tire unexpectedly decided to buy out the remaining two years of its three-year contract.

"It seems like the only luck I ever had in the Tournament of Champions was bad," said Aulby. "Every time I came to Akron, I'd be thinking that this was the year. But the TV lanes [Nos. 27 and 28] at Riviera were never my friends. Having the tournament somewhere else definitely made me more relaxed and I didn't feel the pressure as much."

Evacuating Akron was prompted by the Brunswick Corporation, the recreational sports supplier, which insisted on two concessions before signing on as the T of C's new sponsor: the event had to be moved closer to the company's Chicago headquarters and it had to be merged with the Brunswick World Open tournament.

Renamed the Brunswick World Tournament of Champions, the first three days of the event were held at the Deer Park Lanes in Lake Zurich, Ill., with the televised finals played out at Harper Community College in nearby Palatine.

The finals were held in an arena setting that is becoming very popular in PBA championship rounds. An announced crowd of 3,030 packed the Harper Fieldhouse and many fans who arrived

Tom Gaffney has covered bowling, golf and college sports for the *Akron Beacon Journal* since 1987.

After failing to win the Tournament of Champions in Akron, **Mike Aulby** finally captured the title in Palatine, Ill., before a crowd of over 3,000 at Harper Community College. The T of C was moved to suburban Chicago in 1995 to be near the headquarters of Brunswick Corp., the events's new sponsor.

without tickets were turned away at the door.

Aulby, who was seeded second going into the stepladder playoff, threw eight consecutive strikes against amateur champion Pat Healey Jr., to win their semifinal match, 265-177. That set up a final with the top-seeded Spaulding, 33, who had won the first PBA title of his career at the Quaker State 250 in Grand Prairie, Texas on Feb. 4. Aulby went into the match with 22 career wins.

Spaulding, the top seed, held a narrow advantage throughout the match until the ninth frame when he left the 7-10 split and failed to convert. "The ball skidded too long on the oil," Spaulding said afterward. "It was just a bad break. Up until then, I thought I was going to win."

But the pride of Greenville, S.C., rallied by getting three strikes in the 10th frame to put pressure on Aulby, who was last up.

Aulby, who needed two strikes and a count of four to prevail, got a double and eight pins, although his second strike was shaky. Shaky or not, he reacted with an impressive vertical leap triggered, no doubt, by the realization that, finally, the Triple Crown was his. And so was the Tour's biggest winner's check of $60,000 plus a motorboat and trailer.

After the victory, Aulby immediately hugged his wife Tami and his 4-year-old son Christopher and then looked up to pay tribute to his father, Jim, who died on July 4, 1994.

Parker Bohn III, a 10-time tour winner who finished fifth in the T of C, summed up Aulby's achievement this way: "There are some great bowlers in this game, but Mike Aulby is one of the greatest bowlers of all time."

Aulby proved it again on May 6 by winning the ABC Masters (and $50,600) for the

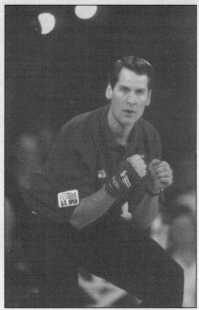

Scott Alexander (left) and **Dave Husted** won the two major championships that Mike Aulby didn't in 1995. Alexander picked up his first tour victory at the PBA National in Toledo, while Husted notched his second U.S. Open title before a record crowd of 7,212 at Joe Louis Arena in Detroit.

second time— claiming his sixth major with a 200-187 victory over Mark Williams at the National Bowling Stadium in Reno, Nev.

By the end of the Summer Tour on Aug. 22, Aulby appeared headed for his second Player of the Year award as the PBA leader in both winnings with $188,753 and average at 225.89.

His main competition was 14th-year pro Dave D'Entremont, who won back to back tournaments in February at the Choice Hotels and Greater Peoria Opens, led the tour in championship round appearances with seven and was second in winnings with $133,110.

D'Entremont, who beat Aulby, 203-190, in the final at Peoria, also won a showdown with Senior Tour champion Gene Stus as part of the Choice Hotels event. His earnings over the eight-day period between Feb. 11-18 came to $90,000.

The three other double winners through the summer were Jess Stayrook, Dave Husted and Norm Duke.

Stayrook won the first and 10th stops on the Winter Tour— the AC-Delco Classic and the Bud Light Championship.

Husted, who went into semi-retirement in 1994, took the Showboat Invitational in Las Vegas on Jan. 28 then followed it up on April 8 by winning the U.S. Open for the second time (he first won it in 1982).

In front of a PBA-record crowd of 7,212 at Joe Louis Arena in Detroit, the 35-year-old Husted gained the 12th title of his career by defeating first-time finalist Paul Koehler, 266-245, to earn $46,000.

Duke, the defending Player of the Year who won five titles in 1994 as well as leading the PBA in earnings and scoring average, continued his winning ways in 1995, becoming the PBA's 12th millionaire with a July 18 victory at the Oregon Open in Portland.

A month later, he won the Cleveland Open at the Ambassador Lanes in Bedford, Ohio, marking the third time and the third different bowling center he has won that title. Those victories, plus a win at the last Tournament of Champions held in Akron in '94 means that four of Duke's 11 career titles have come in the northeast corner of the Buckeye State.

The year's remaining major, the PBA

National Championship was won by 28-year-old Scott Alexander of Seattle, who had been a semi-regular on the tour since 1986 but hadn't won anything.

This time, he shocked everyone at the Imperial Lanes in Toledo by finishing as the top seed and then beating PBA Hall of Famer and fifth-seeded Wayne Webb in the championship match, 246-210.

Alexander is the ninth bowler to win his first championship at the PBA National. Webb, meanwhile, who made the PBA Hall in 1993 as a 17-time winner, hasn't titled since 1989.

Age was the story in two other PBA tournaments held during the year.

On April 15, the legendary Mark Roth, a four-time Player of the Year from 1977-84, won his first tour event in seven years at age 45. He beat Walter Ray Williams Jr., 233-189, in the nationally televised title game of the IOF Foresters Open in Toronto. It was Roth's 34th career title— seven behind all-time PBA leader Earl Anthony.

"The [television] lights seemed extra bright today, but then it's been a long time since I'd seen them in person," quipped Roth afterward.

John Handegard, the Senior Tour's Player of the Year in 1991, tried the regular tour as a 57-year-old in 1995 and became the oldest player to win a regular PBA tour stop by taking the Northwest Classic in Kennewick, Wash., on July 11. The previous oldest winner had been Hall of Famer Buzz Fazio, who was 56 years and 307 days old when he won the Northern California Open in 1965.

Handegard needed a strike on the final ball of the position round to sneak past Walter Ray Williams Jr. and into the championship round. Once there all he had to do was beat four of the biggest names in bowling— Aulby (215-205), Duke (239-225), Bryan Goebel (237-235) and, in the title match, Mark Williams (278-247). Those four players had combined for 44 national titles.

"Unimaginable...unbelievable...this is the biggest win of my career," said a stunned Handegard. "Getting through this field was tough. I'm not sure if the pressure was on me or them, because I'm sure they didn't want to lose to a senior."

Handegard made more pro bowling history on Aug. 29 when he won the Jackson,

Senior tour veteran **John Handegard** won the Northwest Classic on July 11 and became, at age 57, the oldest player to ever win a championship on the regular PBA tour. He is also the only player to win tournaments in both tours in the same year.

Mich., stop on the Senior Tour, becoming the first player to win titles on both tours in the same year. His 246-185 victory over top-seeded Avery LeBlanc was his 11th as a Senior.

Elsewhere, Tommy Evans set the early pace with back-to-back victories in January, while Dave Davis won the ABC Senior Masters in Reno. Davis defeated Handegard in the championship match, 223-216.

Gary Dickinson, 52, the Senior Player of the Year in both 1993 and '94, won two titles through the summer and led the tour in earnings with $54,095.

The highlight of the 1995 LPBT women's season came on May 18 when Sandy Postma, a 48-year-old grandmother and part-time player, won the WIBC Queens in Tucson.

Postma rolled through two qualifying rounds and five matches before defeating Carolyn Dorin, 226-187, in the final. It was her first major title after never having finished better than eighth in 11 years on the tour.

"You always go into a tournament think-

The highlight of the 1995 women's pro bowling season was the WIBC Queens title won by 48-year-old grandmother **Sandy Postma** on May 18 in Tucson. The victory was Postma's first in 11 years on the circuit.

ing it would be nice to win, but it hardly ever happens," said Postma. "Winning a tournament has been a lifelong dream, but winning the Queens is beyond comprehension."

Tish Johnson, who won the Sam's Town Invitational for the third time in six years on Nov. 21, 1994, became the fourth player in LPBT history to win 20 championships when she took the Alexandria (La.) Open on March 2, 1995. On that date she joined Lisa Wagner (28), Patty Costello (25) and Aleta Sill (24) in the 20-win club.

Johnson and Wagner each added another title to their totals in July, Wagner winning the Old Dominion Open and Johnson taking the Tunica Classic.

The 1994 LPBT Player of the Year award was won by Anne Marie Duggan, who won three championships, placed first in scoring average (213.47), first in the Merit rankings and second in earnings with $124,722— just behind Sill's $126,325.

Otherwise, 1995 witnessed the eagerly-awaited opening of the National Bowling Stadium in Reno. The 330,000-square foot stadium cost about $35 million and has 80 Brunswick lanes and 1,200 permanent seats. The bowling area has a 44-foot ceiling, which is about 30 feet higher than most bowling centers.

The first major event in the facility was the American Bowling Congress Tournament, which drew a record number of individuals (92,000) and teams (17,285) from all around the country from Feb. 4 through July 1.

The J. W. All-Stars won the team all-events title. Team members were 1985 ABC Masters champion Steve Wunderlich and John Weltzien, Storm DeVincent, Dave Olm and Robert Comito.

Other champions included two from Washington state— Seattle's Arden Lanes in the regular team event and Spokane's Matt Surina in singles.

The ABC will be holding its annual tournament at the National Bowling Stadium four more times in the next 14 years. The 1996 ABC Tournament will be held in Salt Lake City, Utah.

The Women's International Bowling Congress, which will hold its annual tournament at the National Bowling Stadium in 1997, held its 1995 event in Tucson, Ariz., from April 1 through June 12. A total of 43,400 individuals and 8,422 teams competed.

Beth Owen of Dallas, Tex. was the dominant woman bowler in the WIBC tournament, winning both the Classic Division singles and all-event titles.

At the Pan American Games in Buenos Aires, Argentina, in March, the United States bowling team, coached by Fred Borden of Akron, came away with five gold medals, two silvers and one bronze.

Pat Healey, who went on to finish third in the PBA Tournament of Champions a month later, took home three gold medals and a silver, winning the masters finals, doubles (with Chris Barnes) and team competition and placing second in men's singles.

At the Intercollegiate Bowling Championships at Knoxville, Tenn., in April, Wichita State won its third consecutive men's title and Nebraska won the women's championship.

Finally, Drew Hylen beat Chris Barnes, 219-191, and Lynda Norry Adams beat Kendra Cameron, 223-197, to capture the men's and women's titles at the U.S. Amateur Championships at Reno's Hilton Lanes in September. ❑

Tournament Results

Winners of stepladder finals in all PBA, Seniors and LPBT tournaments from Nov. 2, 1994, through the Summer Tour of 1995; major tournaments in **bold** type. Note that (*) indicates winner was top seeded player entering championship round. See Updates Chapter for later results.

PBA

Late 1994 Fall Tour

Final	Event	Winner	Earnings	Score	Runner-up
Nov. 3	Touring Players Championship	Jason Couch	$27,000	238-214	Parker Bohn III
Nov. 2	Great Lakes Classic	Dave Ferraro	16,000	279-256	Norm Duke
Nov. 9	Brunswick World Open	Eric Forkel*	45,492	225-212	David Ozio
Dec. 11	Merit Mixed Doubles	Aleta Sill/	20,000	458-432	Tammy Turner/
		Bryan Goebel	20,000		Bob Spaulding
Dec. 11	National Resident Pro	Dale Traber*	6,000	288-246	Gary Shultis

1995 Winter Tour

Final	Event	Winner	Earnings	Score	Runner-up
Jan. 14	AC-Delco Classic	Jess Stayrook*	$45,000	247-215	Bob Learn Jr.
Jan. 21	Hilton Hotels Classic	Justin Hromek	35,000	213-190	Mike Scroggins
Jan. 28	Showboat Invitational	Dave Husted	37,000	254-196	Ricky Ward
Feb. 4	Quaker State 250	Bob Spaulding*	48,000	231-183	Kelly Coffman
Feb. 11	Choice Hotels Open	Dave D'Entremont*	45,000†	242-214	Tommy Evans
Feb. 18	Greater Peoria Open	Dave D'Entremont	20,000	203-190	Mike Aulby
Feb. 25	**PBA National Championship**	Scott Alexander*	35,000#	246-210	Wayne Webb
Mar. 4	Greater Baltimore Open	David Traber	18,000	217-214	Eric Forkel
Mar.11	Johnny Petraglia Open	John Gant	34,000	234-216	Ken McNeely
Mar.18	Bud Light Championship	Jess Stayrook	37,000	237-236	Philip Ringener
Mar.25	Tums Classic	Jack Jurek*	25,000	231-228	David Traber
Apr. 1	SplitFire Spark Plug Open	Danny Wiseman	39,000	231-224	Steve Jaros
Apr. 8	**BPAA U.S. Open**	Dave Husted*	46,000	266-245	Paul Koehler
Apr. 15	IOF Foresters Open	Mark Roth	45,000	233-189	W.R. Williams Jr.
Apr. 22	**Tournament of Champions**	Mike Aulby	60,000	237-232	Bob Spaulding
May 6	**ABC Masters**	Mike Aulby	50,600	200-187	Mark Williams

†Does not include $25,000 D'Entremont won by beating PGA Senior Tour representative Gene Stus, 268-245, in the "Winning Never Gets Old" Challenge match.
#Does not include 1995 Chevrolet Lumina awarded to winner.
Note: The American Bowling Congress Masters tournament is not a PBA Tour event.

1995 Summer Tour

Final	Event	Winner	Earnings	Score	Runner-up
July 11	Northwest Classic	John Handegard	$18,000	278-247	Mark Williams
July 18	Oregon Open	Norm Duke	18,000	230-193	Justin Hromek
July 25	Tucson Open	Bryan Goebel	16,000	212-190	Bob Belmont
Aug. 1	Columbia 300 Open	Parker Bohn III*	19,000	248-218	Jason Couch
Aug. 8	Ebonite Kentucky Classic	Randy Pedersen*	19,000	244-203	Mark Williams
Aug.15	Cleveland Open	Norm Duke*	16,000	278-259	Bob Learn Jr.
Aug.22	*Bowlers Journal Classic*	Jason Couch*	18,500	202-190	Dave D'Entremont

Aulby Fourth to Win Triple Crown

By winning the 1995 Tournament of Champions, Mike Aulby joined Billy Hardwick, Johnny Petraglia and Pete Weber as the only players to win each of the PBA's three Triple Crown events— the U.S. Open, the PBA National and the T of C. Aulby won the Open in 1989 and the PBA in both 1979 and '85. Combined with his 1989 victory in the American Bowling Congress (ABC) Masters, Aulby is now the only player to ever win bowling's Grand Slam.

SENIOR PBA
1995 Winter Tour

Final	Event	Winner	Earnings	Score	Runner-up
Jan. 11	Tri-Cities Senior Classic	Tommy Evans*	$7,500	279-246	Dave Soutar
Jan. 18	Northwest Senior Open	Tommy Evans*	7,500	230-221	John Handegard

1995 Spring/Summer Tour

Final	Event	Winner	Earnings	Score	Runner-up
Jan. 11	Tri-Cities Senior Classic	Tommy Evans*	$7,500	279-246	Dave Soutar
Apr. 27	Ladies and Legends	Jim Brenner/	9,000	235-225	Larry Laub/
		Cheryl Daniels	9,000		Dede Davidson
June 8	Greater Providence Senior Open	Gary Dickinson*	8,000	267-207	Allie Clarke
June 30	ABC Senior Masters	Dave Davis	38,000	216-209	John Handegard
July 6	Twin Falls Senior Open	Hobo Boothe*	6,500	223-217	Bobby Knipple
Aug. 3	Rocky Mountain Senior Open	Barry Gurney*	10,000	216-187	Avery LeBlanc
Aug.12	Showboat Senior Invitational	Denny Torgerson	20,000	229-226	Gene Stus
Aug.21	South Bend Hoosier Classic	Dan Roche	8,000	279-257	Les Zikes
Aug.29	Jackson Senior Championship	John Handegard	16,500	246-185	Avery LeBlanc

LPBT
Late 1994 Fall Tour

Final	Event	Winner	Earnings	Score	Runner-up
Nov. 3	Hammer Eastern Open	Carol Gianotti	$13,500	224-223	Anne Marie Duggan
Nov.10	South Bend Open	Sandra Jo Shiery	9,000	247-225	Carol Gianotti
Nov.21	**Sam's Town Invitational**	Tish Johnson*	18,000	178-172	Carol Gianotti
Dec. 11	Merit Mixed Doubles	Aleta Sill/	20,000	458-432	Tammy Turner/
		Bryan Goebel	20,000		Bob Spaulding

1995 Winter Tour

Final	Event	Winner	Earnings	Score	Runner-up
Feb. 9	Texas Border Shoot-Out	Aleta Sill	$10,800	204-203	Tish Johnson
Feb. 16	South Texas Open	Sandra Jo Shiery*	10,800	216-203	Rachel Perez
Feb. 23	Claremore Classic	Kim Canady*	10,800	256-201	Michelle Mullen
Mar. 2	Alexandria Louisiana Open	Tish Johnson	10,800	215-184	Anne Marie Duggan
Mar. 9	New Orleans Classic	Robin Romeo*	10,800	223-215	Carolyn Dorin
Mar.16	AMF XS Challenge	Anne Marie Duggan*	12,600	269-212	Carolyn Dorin

1995 Spring/Summer Tour

Final	Event	Winner	Earnings	Score	Runner-up
Apr. 27	Ladies & Legends	Cheryl Daniels/	$9,000	235-225	Dede Davidson/
		Jim Brenner	9,000		Larry Laub
May 4	Storm Doubles	Kim Adler/	7,000	190-190*	Anne Marie Duggan/
		Nancy Fehr*	7,000		Stacy Rider
May 10	California Classic	Robin Romeo	10,800	214-205	Cheryl Daniels
May 18	**WIBC Queens**	Sandy Postma	12,525	226-187	Carolyn Dorin
May 25	Omaha Lancers Open	Wendy Macpherson	13,500	225-179	Kim Straub
July 13	Old Dominion Open	Lisa Wagner	13,500	226-220	Carol Norman
July 20	Rocket City Challenge	Tammy Turner	10,800	214-181	Michelle Mullen
July 27	Tunica Classic	Tish Johnson	10,800	210-203	Sandra Jo Shiery

Note: The Women's International Bowling Congress Queens tournament is not an LPBT Tour event.
*****Roll-off:** Adler/Fehr defeated Duggan/Rider in second two-frame, 40-38.

1995 Fall Tour Schedules

PBA

Events (7): Japan Cup in Tokyo (Sept. 21-24); Indianapolis Open (Sept. 29-Oct. 4); Greater Detroit Open (Oct. 6-11); Great Lakes Classic (Oct. 14-18); Rochester Open (Oct. 21-25); AMF Dick Weber Classic (Oct. 28-Nov. 1); Touring Players Championship (Nov. 4-8).

SENIOR PBA

Events (3): Naples Open (Sept. 15-19); St. Petersburg/Clearwater Open (Sept. 22-26); Palm Beach Classic (Sept. 30-Oct. 4).

LPBT

Events (7): **BPAA U.S. Open** (Sept. 29-Oct. 6); Brunswick Three Rivers Open (Oct. 8-12); Columbia 300 Delaware Open (Oct 14-19); Hammer Eastern Open (Oct. 21-26); Lady Ebonite Classic (Oct. 29-Nov. 2); Hammer Players Championship (Nov. 4-9); **Sam's Town Invitational** (Nov. 12-18).

Tour Leaders

Official standings for 1994 and unofficial standings (through summer tours) for 1995. Note that (TB) indicates Tournaments Bowled; (CR) Championship Rounds as Stepladder Finalist; and (1st) Titles Won. Men's PBA earnings include ABC Masters and Women's LPBT earnings include WIBC Queens.

Final 1994

PBA

Top 10 Money Winners

		TB	CR	1st	Earnings
1	Norm Duke	21	8	5	$273,753
2	Walter Ray Williams Jr.	28	11	2	189,745
3	Bryan Goebel	30	6	4	173,992
4	Eric Forkel	23	5	1	138,639
5	John Mazza	23	2	2	129,500
6	Parker Bohn III	28	5	0	127,385
7	Brian Voss	27	5	1	121,378
8	Pete Weber	28	6	0	120,973
9	Johnny Petraglia	19	1	0	115,070
10	Justin Hromek	27	3	1	110,731

Top 10 Averages

		Gm	Pins	Avg
1	Norm Duke	808	180,050	222.83
2	Walter Ray Williams Jr.	1062	236,397	222.60
3	Amleto Monacelli	760	167,669	220.62
4	Parker Bohn III	896	196,414	219.21
5	Bryan Goebel	988	216,474	219.10
6	Eric Forkel	713	156,033	218.84
7	John Mazza	697	152,097	218.22
8	David Ozio	786	171,507	218.20
9	Dave Arnold	868	189,138	217.90
10	Randy Pederson	840	182,992	217.85

SENIOR PBA

Top 5 Money Winners

		TB	CR	1st	Earnings
1	Gary Dickinson	13	6	1	$54,095
2	Delano Boothe	13	1	1	48,048
3	John Handegard	12	6	2	46,980
4	Tommy Evans	13	3	1	42,033
5	Rich Moores	12	3	0	38,567

Top 5 Averages

		Gm	Pins	Avg
1	John Handegard	459	101,956	222.13
2	Dave Davis	376	83,172	221.20
3	Gene Stus	511	112,985	221.11
4	Larry Laub	344	75,866	220.54
5	Gary Dickinson	451	99,325	220.23

LPBT

Top 10 Money Winners

		TB	CR	1st	Earnings
1	Aleta Sill	21	8	4	$126,325
2	Anne Marie Duggan	22	7	3	124,722
3	Tish Johnson	21	3	1	82,756
4	Marianne DiRupo	21	3	1	72,369
5	Carol Gianotti	20	3	1	68,039
6	Tammy Turner	19	3	1	65,023
7	Carolyn Dorin	21	1	1	62,117
8	Kim Couture	19	2	1	61,979
9	Leanne Barrette	21	1	1	61,349
10	Sandra Jo Shiery	21	2	2	51,358

Top 5 Averages

		Gm	Pins	Avg
1	Anne Marie Dugan	762	162,664	213.47
2	Dana Miller-Mackie	480	101,131	210.69
3	Tish Johnson	806	169,736	210.59
4	Marianne DiRupo	661	139,048	210.36
5	Kim Couture	716	150,417	210.08

1995 (through Aug. 29)

PBA

Top 10 Money Winners

		TB	CR	1st	Earnings
1	Mike Aulby	20	5	1	$188,753
2	David D'Entremont	22	7	2	133,110
3	Jess Stayrook	22	4	2	116,355
4	Dave Husted	13	2	2	106,515
5	Robert Spaulding	18	2	1	104,495
6	Mark Williams	21	4	0	95,602
7	Walter Ray Williams Jr.	18	5	0	80,595
8	Parker Bohn III	21	5	1	78,855
9	Norm Duke	20	5	2	76,055
10	Bob Learn Jr.	19	3	0	66,525

Top 10 Averages

		Gm	Pins	Avg
1	Mike Aulby	702	158,577	225.89
2	Walter Ray Williams Jr.	619	138,071	223.05
3	Dave Husted	367	81,780	222.83
4	Norm Duke	642	142,598	222.11
5	Mark Williams	745	165,148	221.67
6	Bryan Goebel	650	143,633	220.97
7	Parken Bohn III	719	158,605	220.59
8	Dave D'Entremont	760	167,543	220.45
9	Joe Firpo	587	128,918	219.62
10	David Traber	592	129,896	219.41

SENIOR PBA

Top 5 Money Winners

		TB	CR	1st	Earnings
1	John Handegard	9	5	1	$54,450
2	Dave Davis	6	1	1	46,450
3	Tommy Evans	8	4	2	36,226
4	Gene Stus	10	3	0	32,775
5	Pete Couture	7	3	0	32,175

Top 5 Averages

		Gm	Pins	Avg
1	Tommy Evans	319	71,434	223.93
2	John Handegard	388	85,732	220.96
3	Larry Laub	338	74,465	220.31
4	Pete Couture	314	69,146	220.21
5	Gene Stus	335	73,295	218.79

LPBT

Top 10 Money Winners

		TB	CR	1st	Earnings
1	Tish Johnson	14	4	2	$71,162
2	Anne Marie Duggan	14	5	1	60,147
3	Cheryl Daniels	14	5	1	55,366
4	Carolyn Dorin	14	5	0	53,409
5	Kim Canady	14	3	0	47,885
6	Kim Adler	14	5	1	45,026
7	Robin Romeo	10	2	2	41,411
8	Carol Norman	14	3	0	40,290
9	Aleta Sill	14	3	1	37,201
10	Tammy Turner	14	1	1	36,326

Top 5 Averages

		Gm	Pins	Avg
1	Anne Marie Duggan	501	108,219	216.01
2	Tish Johnson	529	113,719	214.97
3	Carol Norman	525	112,376	214.05
4	Cheryl Daniels	501	106,684	212.94
5	Robin Romeo	363	76,934	211.94

THE 1996 INFORMATION PLEASE SPORTS ALMANAC

BOWLING STATISTICS

THROUGH THE YEARS
1942-1995
CHAMPIONS • AWARDS

SEC B

PAGE 756

Major Championships
MEN
BPAA U.S. Open

Started in 1941 by the Bowling Proprietors' Association of America, 18 years before the founding of the Professional Bowlers Association. Originally the BPAA All-Star Tournament, it became the U.S. Open in 1971. There were two BPAA All-Star tournaments in 1955, in January and December.

Multiple winners: Don Carter and Dick Weber (4); Del Ballard, Jr., Marshall Holman, Dave Husted, Junie McMahon, Connie Schwoegler, Andy Varipapa and Pete Weber (2).

Year		Year		Year		Year	
1942	John Crimmons	1956	Bill Lillard	1970	Bobby Cooper	1984	Mark Roth
1943	Connie Schwoegler	1957	Don Carter	1971	Mike Limongello	1985	Marshall Holman
1944	Ned Day	1958	Don Carter	1972	Don Johnson	1986	Steve Cook
1945	Buddy Bomar	1959	Billy Welu	1973	Mike McGrath	1987	Del Ballard Jr.
1946	Joe Wilman	1960	Harry Smith	1974	Larry Laub	1988	Pete Weber
1947	Andy Varipapa	1961	Bill Tucker	1975	Steve Neff	1989	Mike Aulby
1948	Andy Varipapa	1962	Dick Weber	1976	Paul Moser		
1949	Connie Schwoegler	1963	Dick Weber	1977	Johnny Petraglia	1990	Ron Palombi Jr.
1950	Junie McMahon	1964	Bob Strampe	1978	Nelson Burton Jr.	1991	Pete Weber
1951	Dick Hoover	1965	Dick Weber	1979	Joe Berardi	1992	Robert Lawrence
1952	Junie McMahon	1966	Dick Weber			1993	Del Ballard Jr.
1953	Don Carter	1967	Les Schissler	1980	Steve Martin	1994	Justin Hromek
1954	Don Carter	1968	Jim Stefanich	1981	Marshall Holman	1995	Dave Husted
1955	Steve Nagy	1969	Billy Hardwick	1982	Dave Husted		
				1983	Gary Dickinson		

PBA National Championship

The Professional Bowlers Association was formed in 1958 and its first national championship tournament was held in Memphis in 1960. The tournament has been held in Toledo, Ohio, since 1981.

Multiple winners: Earl Anthony (6); Mike Aulby, Dave Davis, Mike McGrath and Wayne Zahn (2).

Year		Year		Year		Year	
1960	Don Carter	1970	Mike McGrath	1980	Johnny Petraglia	1990	Jim Pencak
1961	Dave Soutar	1971	Mike Limongello	1981	Earl Anthony	1991	Mike Miller
1962	Carmen Salvino	1972	Johnny Guenther	1982	Earl Anthony	1992	Eric Forkel
1963	Billy Hardwick	1973	Earl Anthony	1983	Earl Anthony	1993	Ron Palombi Jr.
1964	Bob Strampe	1974	Earl Anthony	1984	Bob Chamberlain	1994	David Traber
1965	Dave Davis	1975	Earl Anthony	1985	Mike Aulby	1995	Scott Alexander
1966	Wayne Zahn	1976	Paul Colwell	1986	Tom Crites		
1967	Dave Davis	1977	Tommy Hudson	1987	Randy Pedersen		
1968	Wayne Zahn	1978	Warren Nelson	1988	Brian Voss		
1969	Mike McGrath	1979	Mike Aulby	1989	Pete Weber		

Brunswick World Tournament of Champions

Originally the Firestone Tournament of Champions (1965-93), the tournament has also been sponsored by General Tire (1994) and Brunswick Corp. (since 1995). Held annually in Akron, Ohio from 1965-94, the T of C was moved to suburban Chicago in 1995.

Multiple winners: Mike Durbin (3); Earl Anthony, Jim Godman, Marshall Holman and Mark Williams (2).

Year		Year		Year		Year	
1965	Billy Hardwick	1973	Jim Godman	1981	Steve Cook	1990	Dave Ferraro
1966	Wayne Zahn	1974	Earl Anthony	1982	Mike Durbin	1991	David Ozio
1967	Jim Stefanich	1975	Dave Davis	1983	Joe Berardi	1992	Marc McDowell
1968	Dave Davis	1976	Marshall Holman	1984	Mike Durbin	1993	George Branham III
1969	Jim Godman	1977	Mike Berlin	1985	Mark Williams	1994	Norm Duke
1970	Don Johnson	1978	Earl Anthony	1986	Marshall Holman	1995	Mike Aulby
1971	Johnny Petraglia	1979	George Pappas	1987	Pete Weber		
1972	Mike Durbin	1980	Wayne Webb	1988	Mark Williams		
				1989	Del Ballard Jr.		

ABC Masters Tournament

Sponsored by the American Bowling Congress. The Masters is not a PBA event, but is considered one of the four major tournaments on the men's tour and is open to qualified pros and amateurs.

Multiple winners: Earl Anthony, Mike Aulby, Billy Golembiewski, Dick Hoover and Billy Welu (2).

Year		Year		Year		Year	
1951	Lee Jouglard	1963	Harry Smith	1975	Eddie Ressler	1987	Rick Steelsmith
1952	Willard Taylor	1964	Billy Welu	1976	Nelson Burton Jr.	1988	Del Ballard Jr.
1953	Rudy Habetler	1965	Billy Welu	1977	Earl Anthony	1989	Mike Aulby
1954	Red Elkins	1966	Bob Strampe	1978	Frank Ellenburg		
1955	Buzz Fazio	1967	Lou Scalia	1979	Doug Myers	1990	Chris Warren
1956	Dick Hoover	1968	Pete Tountas			1991	Doug Kent
1957	Dick Hoover	1969	Jim Chestney	1980	Neil Burton	1992	Ken Johnson
1958	Tom Hennessey			1981	Randy Lightfoot	1993	Norm Duke
1959	Ray Bluth	1970	Don Glover	1982	Joe Berardi	1994	Steve Fehr
		1971	Jim Godman	1983	Mike Lastowski	1995	Mike Aulby
1960	Billy Golembiewski	1972	Bill Beach	1984	Earl Anthony		
1961	Don Carter	1973	Dave Soutar	1985	Steve Wunderlich		
1962	Billy Golembiewski	1974	Paul Colwell	1986	Mark Fahy		

WOMEN

BPAA U.S. Open

Started by the Bowling Proprietors' Association of America in 1949, 11 years before the founding of the Professional Women's Bowling Association. Originally the BPAA Women's All-Star Tournament, it became the U.S. Open in 1971. There were two BPAA All-Star tournaments in 1955, in January and December. Note that (a) indicates amateur.

Multiple winners: Marion Ladewig (8); Donna Adamek, Paula Sperber Carter, Pat Costello, Dotty Fothergill, Dana Miller-Mackie and Sylvia Wene (2).

Year		Year		Year		Year	
1949	Marion Ladewig	1960	Sylvia Wene	1972	a-Lorrie Koch	1984	Karen Ellingsworth
		1961	Phyllis Notaro	1973	Millie Martorella	1985	Pat Mercatanti
1950	Marion Ladewig	1962	Shirley Garms	1974	Pat Costello	1986	Wendy Macpherson
1951	Marion Ladewig	1963	Marion Ladewig	1975	Paula Sperber Carter	1987	Carol Norman
1952	Marion Ladewig	1964	LaVerne Carter	1976	Patty Costello	1988	Lisa Wagner
1953	Not held	1965	Ann Slattery	1977	Betty Morris	1989	Robin Romeo
1954	Marion Ladewig	1966	Joy Abel	1978	Donna Adamek		
1955	Sylvia Wene	1967	Gloria Simon	1979	Diana Silva	1990	Dana Miller-Mackie
1955	Anita Cantaline	1968	Dotty Fothergill			1991	Anne Marie Duggan
1956	Marion Ladewig	1969	Dotty Fothergill	1980	Pat Costello	1992	Tish Johnson
1957	Not held			1981	Donna Adamek	1993	Dede Davidson
1958	Merle Matthews	1970	Mary Baker	1982	Shinobu Saitoh	1994	Aleta Sill
1959	Marion Ladewig	1971	a-Paula Sperber	1983	Dana Miller	1995	ends Oct. 6

WIBC Queens

Sponsored by the Women's International Bowling Congress, the Queens is a double elimination, match play tournament. It is not an LPBT event, but is open to qualified pros and amateurs. Note that (a) indicates amateur.

Multiple winners: Millie Martorella (3); Donna Adamek, Dotty Fothergill, Aleta Sill and Katsuko Sugimoto (2).

Year		Year		Year		Year	
1961	Janet Harman	1970	Millie Martorella	1980	Donna Adamek	1990	a-Patty Ann
1962	Dorothy Wilkinson	1971	Millie Martorella	1981	Katsuko Sugimoto	1991	Dede Davidson
1963	Irene Monterosso	1972	Dotty Fothergill	1982	Katsuko Sugimoto	1992	Cindy Coburn-Carroll
1964	D.D. Jacobson	1973	Dotty Fothergill	1983	Aleta Sill	1993	Jan Schmidt
1965	Betty Kuczynski	1974	Judy Soutar	1984	Kazue Inahashi	1994	Anne Marie Duggan
1966	Judy Lee	1975	Cindy Powell	1985	Aleta Sill	1995	Sandra Postma
1967	Millie Martorella	1976	Pam Rutherford	1986	Cora Fiebig		
1968	Phyllis Massey	1977	Dana Stewart	1987	Cathy Almeida		
1969	Ann Feigel	1978	Loa Boxberger	1988	Wendy Macpherson		
		1979	Donna Adamek	1989	Carol Gianotti		

Sam's Town Invitational

Originally held in Milwaukee as the Pabst Tournament of Champions, but discontinued after one year (1981). The event was revived in 1984, moved to Las Vegas and renamed the Sam's Town Tournament of Champions. Since then it has been known as the LPBT Tournament of Champions (1985), the Sam's Town National Pro/Am (1986-88) and the Sam's Town Invitational (since 1989).

Multiple winners: Tish Johnson (3); Aleta Sill (2).

Year		Year		Year		Year	
1981	Cindy Coburn	1986	Aleta Sill	1990	Wendy Macpherson	1994	Tish Johnson
1982-83	Not held	1987	Debbie Bennett	1991	Lorrie Nichols	1995	ends Nov. 18
1984	Aleta Sill	1988	Donna Adamek	1992	Tish Johnson		
1985	Patty Costello	1989	Tish Johnson	1993	Robin Romeo		

Major Championships (Cont.)
WOMEN
WPBA National Championship (1960-1980)

The Women's Professional Bowling Association National Championship tournament was discontinued when the WPBA broke up in 1981. The WPBA changed its name from the Professional Women Bowlers Association (PWBA) in 1978.

Multiple winners: Patty Costello (3); Dotty Fothergill (2).

Year		Year		Year		Year	
1960	Marion Ladewig	1966	Judy Lee	1971	Patty Costello	1976	Patty Costello
1961	Shirley Garms	1967	Betty Mivelaz	1972	Patty Costello	1977	Vesma Grinfelds
1962	Stephanie Balogh	1968	Dotty Fothergill	1973	Betty Morris	1978	Toni Gillard
1963	Janet Harman	1969	Dotty Fothergill	1974	Pat Costello	1979	Cindy Coburn
1964	Betty Kuczynski	1970	Bobbe North	1975	Pam Buckner	1980	Donna Adamek
1965	Helen Duval						

Annual Leaders
Average
PBA Tour

The George Young Memorial Award, named after the late ABC Hall of Fame bowler. Based on at least 16 national PBA tournaments from 1959-78, and at least 400 games of tour competition since 1979.

Multiple winners: Mark Roth (6); Earl Anthony (5); Marshall Holman (3); Norm Duke, Billy Hardwick, Don Johnson and Wayne Zahn (2).

Year		Avg	Year		Avg	Year		Avg
1962	Don Carter	212.84	1973	Earl Anthony	215.80	1984	Marshall Holman	213.91
1963	Bill Hardwick	210.35	1974	Earl Anthony	219.34	1985	Mark Baker	213.72
1964	Ray Bluth	210.51	1975	Earl Anthony	219.06	1986	John Gant	214.38
1965	Dick Weber	211.90	1976	Mark Roth	215.97	1987	Marshall Holman	216.80
1966	Wayne Zahn	208.63	1977	Mark Roth	218.17	1988	Mark Roth	218.04
1967	Wayne Zahn	212.14	1978	Mark Roth	219.83	1989	Pete Weber	215.43
1968	Jim Stefanich	211.90	1979	Mark Roth	221.66			
1969	Billy Hardwick	212.96				1990	Amleto Monacelli	218.16
			1980	Earl Anthony	218.54	1991	Norm Duke	218.21
1970	Nelson Burton Jr	214.91	1981	Mark Roth	216.70	1992	Dave Ferraro	219.70
1971	Don Johnson	213.98	1982	Marshall Holman	216.15	1993	Walter R. Williams Jr.	222.98
1972	Don Johnson	215.29	1983	Earl Anthony	216.65	1994	Norm Duke	222.83

LPBT Tour

Based on at least 282 games of tour competition.

Multiple winners: Leanne Barrette, Nikki Gianulias and Lisa Rathgeber Wagner (3); and Aleta Sill (2).

Year		Avg	Year		Avg	Year		Avg
1981	Nikki Gianulias	213.71	1986	Nikki Gianulias	213.89	1991	Leanne Barrette	211.48
1982	Nikki Gianulias	210.63	1987	Wendy Macpherson	211.11	1992	Leanne Barrette	211.36
1983	Lisa Rathgeber	208.50	1988	Lisa Wagner	213.02	1993	Tish Johnson	215.39
1984	Aleta Sill	210.68	1989	Lisa Wagner	211.87	1994	Anne Marie Daggan	213.47
1985	Aleta Sill	211.10	1990	Leanne Barrette	211.53			

Money Won
PBA Tour

Multiple winners: Earl Anthony (6); Dick Weber and Mark Roth (4); Mike Aulby, Don Carter and Walter Ray Williams Jr. (2).

Year		Earnings	Year		Earnings	Year		Earnings
1959	Dick Weber	$ 7,672	1972	Don Johnson	$56,648	1985	Mike Aulby	$201,200
			1973	Don McCune	69,000	1986	W.R. Williams Jr.	145,550
1960	Don Carter	22,525	1974	Earl Anthony	99,585	1987	Pete Weber	179,516
1961	Dick Weber	26,280	1975	Earl Anthony	107,585	1988	Brian Voss	225,485
1962	Don Carter	49,972	1976	Earl Anthony	110,833	1989	Mike Aulby	298,237
1963	Dick Weber	46,333	1977	Mark Roth	105,583			
1964	Bob Strampe	33,592	1978	Mark Roth	134,500	1990	Amleto Monacelli	204,775
1965	Dick Weber	47,675	1979	Mark Roth	124,517	1991	David Ozio	225,585
1966	Wayne Zahn	54,720				1992	Marc McDowell	176,215
1967	Dave Davis	54,165	1980	Wayne Webb	116,700	1993	W.R. Williams Jr	296,370
1968	Jim Stefanich	67,375	1981	Earl Anthony	164,735	1994	Norm Duke	273,753
1969	Billy Hardwick	64,160	1982	Earl Anthony	134,760			
			1983	Earl Anthony	135,605			
1970	Mike McGrath	52,049	1984	Mark Roth	158,712			
1971	Johnny Petraglia	85,065						

WPBA and LPBT Tours

WPBA leaders through 1980; LPBT leaders since 1981.

Multiple winners: Aleta Sill (5); Donna Adamek (4); Patty Costello and Betty Morris (3); Dotty Fothergill, Tish Johnson and Aleta Sill (2).

Year		Earnings	Year		Earnings	Year		Earnings
1965	Betty Kuczynski	$ 3,792	1975	Judy Soutar	$20,395	1985	Aleta Sill	$ 52,655
1966	Joy Abel	5,795	1976	Patty Costello	39,585	1986	Aleta Sill	36,962
1967	Shirley Garms	4,920	1977	Betty Morris	23,802	1987	Betty Morris	63,735
1968	Dotty Fothergill	16,170	1978	Donna Adamek	31,000	1988	Lisa Wagner	105,500
1969	Dotty Fothergill	9,220	1979	Donna Adamek	26,280	1989	Robin Romeo	113,750
1970	Patty Costello	9,317	1980	Donna Adamek	31,907	1990	Tish Johnson	94,420
1971	Vesma Grinfelds	4,925	1981	Donna Adamek	41,270	1991	Leanne Barrette	87,618
1972	Patty Costello	11,350	1982	Nikki Gianulias	45,875	1992	Tish Johnson	96,872
1973	Judy Cook	11,200	1983	Aleta Sill	42,525	1993	Aleta Sill	57,995
1974	Betty Morris	30,037	1984	Aleta Sill	81,452	1994	Aleta Sill	126,325

All-Time Leaders

All-time leading money winners on the PBA and LPBT tours, through 1994. PBA figures date back to 1959, while LPBT figures include Women's Pro Bowlers Association (WPBA) earnings through 1980. National tour titles are also listed.

Money Won

PBA Top 20

		Titles	Earnings
1	Pete Weber	26	$1,706,246
2	Marshall Holman	21	1,631,273
3	Mike Aulby	22	1,437,013
4	Mark Roth	33	1,427,678
5	Walter Ray Williams Jr	15	1,424,909
6	Earl Anthony	41	1,361,931
7	Amleto Monacelli	15	1,317,676
8	Brian Voss	14	1,304,522
9	Dave Husted	10	1,237,556
10	Wayne Webb	17	1,084,641
11	Del Ballard Jr	12	1,022,912
12	David Ozio	10	1,000,944
13	Dave Ferraro	9	1,000,631
14	Gary Dickinson	8	977,471
15	Parker Bohn III	10	961,073
16	Norm Duke	9	958,406
17	Dick Weber	26	895,906
18	Tom Baker	7	831,679
19	Steve Cook	15	826,176
20	Joe Berardi	10	825,185

WPBA-LPBT Top 12

		Titles	Earnings
1	Aleta Sill	23	$656,931
2	Tish Johnson	19	585,605
3	Lisa Wagner	28	575,442
4	Robin Romeo	14	512,540
5	Nikki Gianulias	18	477,558
6	Donna Adamek	19	473,984
7	Lorrie Nichols	15	460,841
8	Leanne Barrette	15	454,015
9	Anne Marie Duggan	11	413,929
10	Cindy Coburn-Carroll	14	389,516
11	Jeanne Naccarato	9	373,050
12	Dana Miller-Mackie	12	362,794

Senior PBA Top 5

		Titles	Earnings
1	John Handegard	10	$262,162
2	Teata Semiz	7	225,037
3	Gene Stus	6	217,440
4	Dick Weber	6	201,861
5	John Hricsina	4	191,027

Annual Awards

MEN

BWAA Bowler of the Year

Winners selected by Bowling Writers Association of America.

Multiple winners: Earl Anthony and Don Carter (6); Mark Roth (4); Dick Weber (3); Mike Aulby, Buddy Bomar, Ned Day, Billy Hardwick, Don Johnson, Steve Nagy and Walter Ray Williams Jr. (2).

Year		Year		Year		Year	
1942	Johnny Crimmins	1956	Bill Lillard	1970	Nelson Burton Jr.	1984	Mark Roth
1943	Ned Day	1957	Don Carter	1971	Don Johnson	1985	Mike Aulby
1944	Ned Day	1958	Don Carter	1972	Don Johnson	1986	Walter Ray Williams Jr.
1945	Buddy Bomar	1959	Ed Lubanski	1973	Don McCune	1987	Marshall Holman
1946	Joe Wilman	1960	Don Carter	1974	Earl Anthony	1988	Brian Voss
1947	Buddy Bomar	1961	Dick Weber	1975	Earl Anthony	1989	Mike Aulby
1948	Andy Varipapa	1962	Don Carter	1976	Earl Anthony		
1949	Connie Schwoegler	1963	Dick Weber	1977	Mark Roth	1990	Amleto Monacelli
1950	Junie McMahon	1964	Billy Hardwick	1978	Mark Roth	1991	David Ozio
1951	Lee Jouglard	1965	Dick Weber	1979	Mark Roth	1992	Marc McDowell
1952	Steve Nagy	1966	Wayne Zahn			1993	Walter Ray Williams Jr.
1953	Don Carter	1967	Dave Davis	1980	Wayne Webb	1994	Norm Duke
1954	Don Carter	1968	Jim Stefanich	1981	Earl Anthony		
1955	Steve Nagy	1969	Billy Hardwick	1982	Earl Anthony		
				1983	Earl Anthony		

Annual Awards (Cont.)

MEN
PBA Player of the Year

Winners selected by members of Professional Bowlers Association. The PBA Player of the Year has differed from the BWAA Bowler of the Year four times—in 1963, '64, '89 and '92.

Multiple winners: Earl Anthony (6); Mark Roth (4); Billy Hardwick, Don Johnson, Amleto Monacelli and Walter Ray Williams Jr. (2).

Year		Year		Year		Year	
1963	Billy Hardwick	1972	Don Johnson	1980	Wayne Webb	1988	Brian Voss
1964	Bob Strampe	1973	Don McCune	1981	Earl Anthony	1989	Amleto Monacelli
1965	Dick Weber	1974	Earl Anthony	1982	Earl Anthony	1990	Amleto Monacelli
1966	Wayne Zahn	1975	Earl Anthony	1983	Earl Anthony	1991	David Ozio
1967	Dave Davis	1976	Earl Anthony	1984	Mark Roth	1992	Dave Ferraro
1968	Jim Stefanich	1977	Mark Roth	1985	Mike Aulby	1993	Walter Ray Williams Jr.
1969	Billy Hardwick	1978	Mark Roth	1986	Walter Ray Williams Jr.	1994	Norm Duke
1970	Nelson Burton Jr.	1979	Mark Roth	1987	Marshall Holman		
1971	Don Johnson						

PBA Rookie of the Year

Winners selected by members of Professional Bowlers Association.

Year		Year		Year		Year	
1964	Jerry McCoy	1972	Tommy Hudson	1980	Pete Weber	1988	Rick Steelsmith
1965	Jim Godman	1973	Steve Neff	1981	Mark Fahy	1989	Steve Hoskins
1966	Bobby Cooper	1974	Cliff McNealy	1982	Mike Steinbach	1990	Brad Kiszewski
1967	Mike Durbin	1975	Guy Rowbury	1983	Toby Contreras	1991	Ricky Ward
1968	Bob McGregor	1976	Mike Berlin	1984	John Gant	1992	Jason Couch
1969	Larry Lichstein	1977	Steve Martin	1985	Tom Crites	1993	Mark Scroggins
1970	Denny Krick	1978	Joseph Groskind	1986	Marc McDowell	1994	Tony Ament
1971	Tye Critchlow	1979	Mike Aulby	1987	Ryan Shafer		

WOMEN
BWAA Bowler of the Year

Winners selected by Bowling Writers Association of America.

Multiple winners: Marion Ladewig (9); Donna Adamek and Lisa Rathgeber Wagner (4); Betty Morris (3); Patty Costello, Dotty Forthergill, Shirley Garms, Tish Johnson, Val Mikiel, Aleta Sill, Judy Soutar and Sylvia Wene (2).

Year		Year		Year		Year	
1948	Val Mikiel	1960	Sylvia Wene	1972	Patty Costello	1984	Aleta Sill
1949	Val Mikiel	1961	Shirley Garms	1973	Judy Soutar	1985	Aleta Sill
1950	Marion Ladewig	1962	Shirley Garms	1974	Betty Morris	1986	Lisa Wagner
1951	Marion Ladewig	1963	Marion Ladewig	1975	Judy Soutar	1987	Betty Morris
1952	Marion Ladewig	1964	LaVerne Carter	1976	Patty Costello	1988	Lisa Wagner
1953	Marion Ladewig	1965	Betty Kuczynski	1977	Betty Morris	1989	Robin Romeo
1954	Marion Ladewig	1966	Joy Abel	1978	Donna Adamek	1990	Tish Johnson
1955	Sylvia Wene	1967	Millie Martorella	1979	Donna Adamek	1991	Leanne Barrette
1956	Anita Cantaline	1968	Dotty Fothergill	1980	Donna Adamek	1992	Tish Johnson
1957	Marion Ladewig	1969	Dotty Fothergill	1981	Donna Adamek	1993	Lisa Wagner
1958	Marion Ladewig	1970	Mary Baker	1982	Nikki Gianulias	1994	Anne Marie Duggan
1959	Marion Ladewig	1971	Paula Sperber	1983	Lisa Rathgeber		

LPBT Player of the Year

Winners selected by members of Ladies Professional Bowlers Tour. The LPBT Player of the Year has differed from the BWAA Bowler of the Year twice—in 1985 and '86.

Multiple winners: Lisa Rathgeber Wagner (3); Leanne Barrette (2).

Year		Year		Year		Year	
1983	Lisa Rathgeber	1986	Jeanne Maiden	1989	Robin Romeo	1992	Tish Johnson
1984	Aleta Sill	1987	Betty Morris	1990	Leanne Barrette	1993	Lisa Wagner
1985	Patty Costello	1988	Lisa Wagner	1991	Leanne Barrette	1994	Anne Marie Duggan

WPBA and LPBT Rookie of the Year

Winners selected by members of Women's Professional Bowlers Association (1978–80) and the Ladies Professional Bowlers Tour (since 1981).

Year		Year		Year		Year	
1978	Toni Gillard	1983	Anne Marie Pike	1987	Paula Drake	1991	Kim Kahrman
1979	Nikki Gianulias	1984	Paula Vidad	1988	Mary Martha Cerniglia	1992	Marianne DiRupo
1980	Lisa Rathgeber	1985	Dede Davidson	1989	Kim Terrell	1993	Kathy Zielke
1981	Cindy Mason	1986	Wendy Macpherson	1990	Debbie McMullen	1994	Tammy Turner
1982	Carol Norman						

Trainer **D. Wayne Lukas** hoists the winner's trophy after Thunder Gulch's surprise victory in the Kentucky Derby. It was the third of a record-breaking five straight Triple Crown wins for Lukas.

HORSE RACING

Wayne's World

*A Triple Crown sweep by two Lukas horses and the arrival
of Cigar highlight a very good year for thoroughbred racing.*

D. Wayne Lukas did something in 1995 that no thoroughbred racing trainer had ever done before: He won the Triple Crown with two different horses— Thunder Gulch in the Kentucky Derby and Belmont Stakes and Timber Country in the Preakness.

In addition, Lukas also stretched his personal Triple Crown winning streak to an unprecedented five straight, going back to Tabasco Cat's victories in the 1994 Preakness and Belmont.

Nick Zito, whose horses finished second in three of the five races during Lukas' streak, told *Sports Illustrated*, "I guess I'll have to get Pegasus to beat him. What he's done is tremendous, unbelievable."

Whether Thunder Gulch would be back in the Belmont winner's circle come the Breeders' Cup on Oct. 28 remained to be decided (see Update chapter). But just as Lukas entries prosper in Triple Crown races, so do they thrive in the Breeders' Cup, where he has sent 12 winners to the post in 87 starts since the series began in 1984.

The Breeders' Cup is always as much a prelude as a climax, and the 11th running of racing's "Day of Days" at Churchill Downs in Louisville was essentially where the 1995 racing season began.

By sunset on Nov. 5, 1994, we knew who

the champions were going to be, and we knew even more surely that '95 promised to be a very good year. After all, Holy Bull was coming back.

Although the big gray star was kept out of the Breeders' Cup so he would be fresh for winter racing in Florida, he was a sure thing for 1994 Horse of the Year. An impressive win by Concern in the Classic threatened the Bull's title not at all, but it did give fans the hope that somebody might be able to press the champion at least a little in 1995.

Three-year-old filly champion Heavenly Prize, although second to longshot One Dreamer in the Distaff, was due back, as was the champion colt and Juvenile winner Timber Country. The coming year looked very promising indeed.

But optimism must be tempered when creatures of flesh and bone are involved. The most outstanding single individual of Breeders' Cup Day '94, the two-year-old filly Flanders, would *not* be back. The crowd was first surprised to see the previously unchallenged filly driven to a narrow win over fellow D. Wayne Lukas-trainee Serena's Song, then stunned to see her leave the track in a horse ambulance. The entire racing world was amazed to hear later that Flanders had won a million-dollar race on a fractured right foreleg.

"We'll never know how good she really was," said Flanders' owner William T. Young upon accepting her Eclipse Award. Actually, we do know. She was just about

Sharon Smith has covered horse racing for ESPN, NBC and *Horse Illustrated* and is the author of *The Performance Mare* and *The Affordable Horse* (Howell Book House).

Jockey **Gary Stevens** exults as 24-to-1 shot **Thunder Gulch** wins the 121st running of the Kentucky Derby by more than two lengths over Tejano Run and Timber Country at Churchill Downs. Thunder Gulch went on to win the Belmont Stakes after finishing third in the Preakness.

as good as it is possible to be. Flanders was retired, but 1995 still looked like it would be a very good year. Serena's Song would be back, hoping this time for a championship of her own.

No such luck for the year's champion steeplechaser. On November 13, Warm Spell broke a shoulder in a fall in the Colonial Cup and was destroyed. His bold jumping probably contributed to his death.

"He thought he could do anything," said Warm Spell's owner John Griggs. He was able to do enough to earn an Eclipse Award, although it had to be awarded posthumously.

The death of a champion in action hurts the entire sport, but racing could point with some pride to its avoidance of labor strife. Members of the Jockeys' Guild threatened to stay home on Jan. 1, 1995, if their organization failed to reach a contract agreement with the major racetracks. Strictly speaking, the Guild is not a union and a walkout would not be a strike, but it

could have been disastrous nonetheless.

Fortunately, the two sides reached an agreement on Dec. 30 and the jockeys rode as scheduled on New Year's Day. Guild president Jerry Bailey wasn't entirely satisfied with improvements in payments for disabled jockeys and health insurance for riders, but he noted that jockeys' problems were finally getting the attention they deserved.

As was Bailey himself. He was inducted into the racing Hall of Fame later in the year, along with trainer Bobby Frankel and horses Crusader, Foolish Pleasure and La Prevoyante.

Mike Smith, who won his second straight Eclipse Award-as 1994's top jockey, was certainly happy to be in action in January when Holy Bull returned to the races as a four-year-old. Their easy win in the Olympic Handicap at Gulfstream Park was the eagerly-awaited kickoff for the year that was going to be so good for racing.

But a horse is a fragile creature to carry

Wide World Photos

Cigar and jockey **Jerry Bailey** enter the winner's circle at Suffolk Downs in Boston after their victory in the Massachusetts Handicap on June 3. The four-year-old was unbeaten in eight races through September.

so much hope, and February's Donn Handicap at Gulfstream proved that inescapable fact. Six furlongs into the race, Smith heard a popping sound, felt something wrong, shouted "Oh, no!" and pulled Holy Bull up. The horse had injured a tendon and ligament in his left foreleg and his racing career was over.

"It's a terrible blow," said trainer Bill Mott after the race. The lament came from the man who trained not Holy Bull but the race's ultimate winner, four-year-old Cigar, who had just won his a Grade 1 race and $180,000. The superstars of the sport are cherished that much.

They are cherished because they are so rare, but you couldn't prove that with Cigar. Perhaps due to feelings of guilt for winning the race that sent Holy Bull off to early retirement, Cigar went on to march back and forth across the country, laying waste to six major handicaps at six different tracks on both coasts and in between.

"He makes my job look very easy," jockey Jerry Bailey said after Cigar's win in the

Massachusetts Handicap in June.

The three-year-olds who make up thoroughbred racing's showcase division took a little more time to live up to the standards of the year. They hadn't quite done it when the gate opened for the Kentucky Derby.

During the first four months of 1995, the returning champion Timber Country wasn't exactly bad, but he wasn't exactly good either. He had earned over a hundred thousand dollars but was winless in three starts prior to his arrival at Churchill Downs the first week in May.

Afternoon Deelites had been unbeaten going into the Santa Anita Derby in April, but he had lost that nine furlong race in the worst way possible for a horse looking towards the ten furlongs of the Kentucky Derby a month later. He was caught in the last furlong at Santa Anita by Larry the Legend, who didn't stay sound long enough to make the trip to Louisville.

Talkin Man won two big races in New York, including the Wood Memorial on April 15, and he had his trainer Roger Attfield nervously considering the possibility of being the trainer of the Derby favorite. "I'm very skeptical about that," Attfield said after the Wood. "But it does look pretty good for the Derby."

Attfield didn't have to worry about being favored, since the one horse who had fully lived up to expectations took to the track on Derby Day. That was Serena's Song, who had won four straight races early in 1995. Lukas called her the "Princess" and thought that she and entry mate Timber Country deserved their roles as favorites— although a favorite hadn't won the Derby since Spectacular Bid in 1979.

Lukas was less enthusiastic about his third entry, Thunder Gulch, the Florida Derby winner, who was coming off a fourth place finish in the Blue Grass Stakes. But Lukas and anybody else who took a good look at the odds board had to agree that Thunder Gulch, running as an individual entry because of different ownership, did not deserve to go off in the Kentucky Derby at nearly 25-1.

It was the last time in his life that Thunder Gulch would start a race at such odds. Jockey Gary Stevens set him perfectly just off the pace, moved him into third place at the top of the stretch, and then turned him loose.

Lammtarra, with jockey **Frankie Dettori** aboard, winning the Prix de l'Arc de Triomphe at Longchamp racetrack in Paris on Oct. 1. The three-year-old British horse also won the English Derby and the King George VI and Queen Elizabeth Diamond Stakes in 1995.

"He absolutely accelerated," Stevens said after the race. "It was an unbelievable feeling."

Tejano Run finished well for second, Timber Country even better for third. Serena's Song, who had set a quick pace for a mile, faded to finish 16th, but jockey Corey Nakatani wisely saved her to fight another day. Two weeks later she was back in her own division, winning the Black Eyed Susan at Pimlico, and went on to dominate three-year-old fillies in New York during the rest of the summer.

As for Timber Country, the Pimlico crowd still believed in him, making the slightly tarnished champion the Preakness favorite.

Their faith was not misplaced. With five horses across the track at the eighth pole, one emerged in the final furlong. Timber Country became the first two-year-old champion since Spectacular Bid and the first Breeders' Cup Juvenile winner ever to win the Preakness. Oliver's Twist was second, and Thunder Gulch was a thoroughly respectable— if slightly overlooked— third.

The trip to the Preakness winners' circle was the fourth for jockey Pat Day, but it was his first victory aboard Timber Country in over six months. "He was more responsive, more competitive and more enthusiastic about the work than he has been," Day said.

He was also back on top of the horse racing world, along with trainer Lukas, who had now won four Triple Crown races in a row— a feat matched only by the legendary Lucien Laurin, who had done it with Riva Ridge in the 1972 Belmont and Triple Crown winner Secretariat in '73.

Five in a row seemed likely, given the fact that Timber Country had raced like a horse who would like the mile and a half of the Belmont. But Lukas knows as well as anybody not to place too much hope on flesh and bone. The day before the Belmont Stakes Timber Country came down with a fever and had to be withdrawn. "It's a major disappointment," Lukas said.

Harness Racing Communications

Harness racing's all-time money-winning horse **Peace Corps** and her foal in June. The bay filly's sire, Mack Lobell, ranks third on the all-time list and won the 1987 Hambletonian.

But how disappointed does a trainer have a right to be when he can start a Kentucky Derby winner in the Belmont Stakes? Not at all, as it turned out. Thunder Gulch broke well, lay just off Star Standard's pace, and went on to pass that horse in the final quarter mile. Thunder Gulch gave himself undisputed leadership of his division and gave Lukas the record five Triple Crown races in a row.

"Everything fell into place," Lukas said. "I'm a little overwhelmed."

So was the rest of the three-year-old division as summer came and went. Thunder Gulch traveled to Hollywood Park in California and followed his Belmont win with a victory in the Swaps Stakes in July. When the matchless Seattle Slew tried that in 1977, he lost his first race ever.

In August, Thunder Gulch traveled to Saratoga, where he won the Travers Stakes. "We're excited," Lukas said. "We're looking forward to Cigar." So was everybody else who knew that there was such a thing as horse racing.

Another division lived up to expectations, when Heavenly Prize, the three-year-old filly champion of 1994, returned to win five Grade 1 races in a row over the spring and summer. She carried weight, ran fast and won big.

"She is as good as I've ever had," said trainer Shug McGaughey after her win in the John A. Morris Handicap at Saratoga in August. That is considerable praise from the man who trained the unbeaten Personal Ensign.

Overseas, the year's top performer was undefeated British three-year-old Lammtarra, who became the first horse since Mill Reef in 1971 to win the English Derby at Epsom, the King George VI and Queen Elizabeth Diamond Stakes at Ascot, and the Prix de l'Arc de Triomphe at Longchamp in Paris.

In harness racing, the big story of the summer was the brilliant trotting filly CR Kay Suzie, who became only the second filly to win the Yonkers Trot. She entered the Hambletonian as the heavy and deserving favorite. But she unaccountably broke stride in her elimination and failed to make the finals.

Tagliabue took the honors at the Meadowlands, but Suzie made up for it a month later when she beat him easily in the two heats of the World Trotting Derby at DuQuoin. Her world record-tying time of 1:52.4 restored her reputation and placed her in the company of previous Trotting Derby filly winners Panty Raid and Peace Corps.

CR Kay Suzie is set to race in 1996, allowing still more anticipation, and after that is likely to follow in the hoofprints of Peace Corps, whose first foal was born in May in Kentucky. The bay filly was announced as the richest foal ever, being the daughter of the $4.9 million winner Peace Corps and the $3.9 million winner Mack Lobell. That's nearly $9 million in parental earnings for the new baby.

Finally, three years and eight months after he retired following multiple injuries in a spill at Aqueduct Racetrack in New York, Hall of Fame jockey Angel Cordero Jr. returned to racing on Oct. 1 at age 52.

Appearing at El Commandante Race Track in San Juan, Puerto Rico, where he rode his first winner 35 years ago, Cordero rode Bandit Bomber to victory in a $22,000 allowance race. Cordero ranks third on the all-time list with 7,057 wins. ❑

THE 1996 SPORTS ALMANAC — INFORMATION PLEASE

HORSE RACING STATISTICS

THE SEASON IN REVIEW
1994-1995
THOROUGHBRED • HARNESS

SEC A

PAGE 767

Thoroughbred Racing
Major Stakes Races

Winners of major stakes races from Oct. 15, 1994 through Sept. 23; (T) indicates turf race course; (F) indicates furlongs.
See Updates for later results.

LATE 1994

Date	Race	Track	Miles	Winner	Jockey	Purse
Oct. 15	My Dear Girl Stakes	Calder	1¹⁄₁₆	Fortune Pending	Jorge Velasquez	$400,000
Oct. 15	In Reality Stakes	Calder	1¹⁄₁₆	Sea Emperor	Wigberto Ramos	400,000
Oct. 15	Wash., D.C. Int'l Mile	Laurel	1¼ (T)	Paradise Creek	Pat Day	600,000
Oct. 15	Goodwood Handicap	Santa Anita	1⅛	Bertrando	Gary Stevens	200,000
Oct. 16	Rothman's International	Woodbine	1½ (T)	Raintrap	Robbie Davis	1,000,000
Oct. 16	Spinster Stakes	Keeneland	1⅛	Dispute	Pat Day	300,000
Nov. 5	Breeders' Cup Classic	Churchill Downs	1¼	Concern	Jerry Bailey	3,000,000
Nov. 5	Breeders' Cup Turf	Churchill Downs	1½ (T)	Tikkanen	Mike Smith	2,000,000
Nov. 5	Breeders' Cup Distaff	Churchill Downs	1⅛	One Dreamer	Gary Stevens	1,000,000
Nov. 5	Breeders' Cup Mile	Churchill Downs	1 (T)	Barathea (IRE)	Lanfranco Dettori	1,000,000
Nov. 5	Breeders' Cup Juvenile	Churchill Downs	1¹⁄₁₆	Timber Country	Pat Day	1,000,000
Nov. 5	Breeders' Cup Juv. Fil	Churchill Downs	1¹⁄₁₆	Flanders	Pat Day	1,000,000
Nov. 5	Breeders' Cup Sprint	Churchill Downs	6 F	Cherokee Run	Mike Smith	1,000,000
Nov. 19	Hawthorne Cup Gold	Hawthorne	1¼	Recoup the Cash	Juvenal Diaz	400,000
Nov. 27	Japan Cup	Tokyo Racecourse	1½ (T)	Marvelous Crown (JPN)	Katsumi Minai	3,475,345
Dec. 11	Hollywood Turf Cup	Hollywood	1½ (T)	Frenchpark (GB)	Corey Black	500,000
Dec. 17	Hollywood Starlet	Hollywood	1¹⁄₁₆	Serena's Song	Corey Nakatani	250,000
Dec. 18	Hollywood Futurity	Hollywood	1¹⁄₁₆	Afternoon Deelites	Kent Desormeaux	500,000

1995 (through Sept. 23)

Date	Race	Track	Miles	Winner	Jockey	Purse
Jan. 14	El Camino Real Derby	Bay Meadows	1¹⁄₁₆	Jumron (GB)	Joncalino Almeida	$200,000
Feb. 5	Charles H. Strub Stakes	Santa Anita	1¼	Dare and Go	Alex Solis	500,000
Feb. 11	Donn Handicap	Gulfstream	1⅛	Cigar	Jerry Bailey	300,000
Feb. 18	Fountain of Youth	Gulfstream	1¹⁄₁₆	Thunder Gulch	Mike Smith	200,000
Mar. 5	Gulfstream Park Handi.	Gulfstream	1¼	Cigar	Jerry Bailey	500,000
Mar. 11	Santa Anita Handicap	Santa Anita	1¼	Urgent Request (IRE)	Gary Stevens	1,000,000
Mar. 11	Florida Derby	Gulfstream	1⅛	Thunder Gulch	Mike Smith	500,000
Mar. 25	Gotham Stakes	Aqueduct	1	Talkin Man	Mike Smith	250,000
Mar. 26	San Luis Rey Stakes	Santa Anita	1½ (T)	Sandpit (BRA)	Corey Nakatani	250,000
Apr. 1	Jim Beam Stakes	Turfway	1⅛	Serena's Song	Corey Nakatani	600,000
Apr. 1	Flamingo Stakes	Hialeah	1⅛	Pyramid Peak	Herb McCauley	200,000
Apr. 8	Santa Anita Derby	Santa Anita	1⅛	Larry The Legend	Gary Stevens	500,000
Apr. 15	Blue Grass Stakes	Keeneland	1⅛	Wild Syn	Randy Romero	500,000
Apr. 15	California Derby	Golden Gate	1¹⁄₁₆ (T)	Fine n' Majestic	Eddie Delahoussaye	200,000
Apr. 15	Oaklawn Handicap	Oaklawn	1⅛	Cigar	Jerry Bailey	750,000
Apr. 15	Wood Memorial	Aqueduct	1⅛	Talkin Man	Shane Sellers	500,000
Apr. 21	Apple Blossom Handicap	Oaklawn	1¹⁄₁₆	Heavenly Prize	Pat Day	500,000
Apr. 22	Arkansas Derby	Oaklawn	1⅛	Dazzling Falls	Garrett Gomez	500,000
Apr. 23	San Juan Capistrano	Santa Anita	1¾ (T)	Red Bishop	Mike Smith	400,000
May 5	Kentucky Oaks	Churchill Downs	1⅛	Gal in a Ruckus	Herb McCauley	300,000
May 6	**Kentucky Derby**	Churchill Downs	1¼	Thunder Gulch	Gary Stevens	500,000
May 6	2,000 Guineas Stakes	Newmarket	1	Pennekamp	Thierry Jarret	£ 230,000
May 7	Acorn Stakes	Belmont	1	Cat's Cradle	Chris Antley	150,000
May 13	Pimlico Special	Pimlico	1³⁄₁₆	Cigar	Jerry Bailey	600,000
May 13	Illinois Derby	Sportsman's Park	1⅛	Peaks and Valleys	Julie Krone	500,000
May 19	Black-Eyed Susan Stakes	Pimlico	1⅛	Serena's Song	Gary Stevens	200,000
May 20	**Preakness Stakes**	Pimlico	1³⁄₁₆	Timber Country	Pat Day	687,400

Thoroughbred Racing (Cont.)
Major Stakes Races
1995 (through Sept. 23)

Date	Race	Track	Miles	Winner	Jockey	Purse
May 27	Jersey Derby	Garden State	1 1/16 (T)	Da Hoss	Julie Krone	150,000
May 29	Metropolitan Handicap	Belmont	1	You and I	Jorge Chavez	500,000
May 29	Hollywood Turf Handicap	Hollywood Park	1 1/4 (T)	Earl of Barking (IRE)	Goncalino Almeida	500,000
June 3	Massachusetts Handicap	Suffolk Downs	1 1/8	Cigar	Jerry Bailey	250,000
June 9	Mother Goose Stakes	Belmont	1 1/8	Serena's Song	Gary Stevens	200,000
June 10	**Belmont Stakes**	Belmont	1 1/2	Thunder Gulch	Gary Stevens	500,000
June 10	Vodafone English Derby	Epsom Downs	1 1/2 (T)	Lammtarra	Walter Swinburn	1,317,841
June 11	Californian Stakes	Hollywood Park	1 1/4	Concern	Mike Smith	250,000
June 25	Caesars Int'l Handicap	Atlantic City	1 3/16 (T)	Sandpit (BRA)	Corey Nakatani	500,000
July 2	Irish Derby	Curragh	1 1/2 (T)	Winged Love	Oliver Peslier	£ 960,000
July 2	Hollywood Gold Cup	Hollywood Park	1 1/4	Cigar	Jerry Bailey	750,000
July 4	Suburban Handicap	Belmont	1 1/4	Key Contender	Jerry Bailey	350,000
July 8	Coaching Club Am. Oaks	Belmont	1 1/4	Golden Bri	Jose Santos	250,000
July 9	Queen's Plate	Woodbine	1 1/4	Regal Discovery	Tod Kabel	400,000
July 22	King George VI and Queen Elizabeth Diamond Stakes	Ascot	1 1/2 (T)	Lammtarra	Frankie Dettori	£ 742,131
July 30	Prince of Wales Stakes	Fort Erie	1 3/16	Kiridashi	Larry Attard	203,000
July 30	Haskell Invitational	Monmouth	1 1/8	Serena's Song	Gary Stevens	500,000
Aug. 5	Whitney Handicap	Saratoga	1 1/8	Unaccounted For	Pat Day	350,000
Aug. 12	Alabama Stakes	Saratoga	1 1/4	Pretty Discreet	Mike Smith	200,000
Aug. 13	Pacific Classic	Del Mar	1 1/4	Tinners Way	Eddie Delahoussaye	1,000,000
Aug. 19	Travers Stakes	Saratoga	1 1/4	Thunder Gulch	Gary Stevens	750,000
Aug. 20	Breeders' Stakes	Fort Erie	1 1/2 (T)	Charlie's Dewan	Craig Perret	250,000
Aug. 20	Philip Iselin Handicap	Monmouth	1 1/8	Schossberg	Dave Penna	300,000
Aug. 26	Beverly D. Stakes	Arlington	1 3/16 (T)	Possibly Perfect	Corey Nakatani	500,000
Aug. 27	Arlington Million	Arlington	1 1/4 (T)	Awad	Eddie Maple	1,000,000
Sept. 16	Woodward Stakes	Belmont	1 1/8	Cigar	Jerry Bailey	500,000
Sept. 16	Man o' War Stakes	Belmont	1 3/8 (T)	Millkom	Gary Stevens	400,000
Sept. 16	Ruffian Handicap	Belmont	1 1/16	Inside Information	Mike Smith	200,000
Sept. 17	Molson Export Million	Woodbine	1 1/8	Peaks and Valleys	Julie Krone	1,000,000
Sept. 23	Kentucky Cup Classic	Turfway	1 1/8	Thunder Gulch	Gary Stevens	400,000
Sept. 23	Budweiser Breeders' Cup	Turfway	1 1/16	Mariah's Storm	Robert Lester	200,000

TRC National Thoroughbred Poll
(Sept. 25, 1995)

Through Week 29 of the 1995 racing season. Poll taken by Thoroughbred Racing Communications, Inc., and based on the votes of sports and Thoroughbred racing media. First place votes are in parentheses.

	Pts	Owner (Trainer)	'95 Record Sts—1-2-3	Earnings	Last Start (Date, Distance)
1 Cigar (30)	309	Allen Paulson (Bill Mott)	8—8-0-0	$2,809,800	1st— Woodward Stakes (Sept. 16, 1 1/8 mi.)
2 Thunder Gulch (1)	279	Michael Tabor (D. Wayne Lukas)	9—7-0-1	2,621,580	1st— Kentucky Cup Classic (Sept. 23, 1 1/8 mi.-T)
3 Heavenly Prize	221	Ogden Phipps (Shug McGaughey)	5—4-1-0	645,900	1st— John A. Morris Stakes (Aug. 20, 1 1/4 mi.)
4 Serena's Song	202	Beverley & Robert Lewis (D. Wayne Lukas)	11—8-2-0	1,354,920	2nd— Turfway Bud B.C. (Sept. 23, 1 1/16 mi.-T)
5 Inside Information	147	Ogden Mills Phipps (Shug McGaughey)	6—5-1-0	439,642	1st— Ruffian Stakes (Sept. 16, 1 1/16 mi.)
6 Sandpit (BRA)	141	Sierra Thoroughbreds (Richard Mandella)	7—4-2-0	1,282,700	2nd— Arlington Million (Aug. 27, 1 1/4 mi.)
7 Possibly Perfect	131	Blue Vista Inc. (Bobby Frankel)	6—5-1-0	743,100	1st— Beverly D. Stakes (Aug. 26, 1 3/16 mi.)
8 Awad	82	Ryehill Farm (David Donk)	12—4-3-0	1,040,810	1st— Arlington Million (Aug. 27, 1 1/4 mi.)
9 Tinners Way	36	Juddmonte Farm (Bobby Frankel)	4—1-1-1	817,500	5th— Arlington Million (Aug. 27, 1 1/4 mi.)
10 Hennessy	35	Robert & Beverly Lewis (D. Wayne Lukas)	5—4-1-0	322,900	1st—Hopeful Stakes (Aug. 27, 7 furlongs)

Others receiving votes: 11. French Deputy (20 points); **12.** Concern (19); **13.** Not Surprising (18); **14.** Peaks and Valleys (16); **15.** Mariah's Storm (14); **16.** You and I (12); **17.** Millkom and Timber Country (7); **19.** L'Carriere (4); **20.** Lord Carson (3); **21.** Golden Attraction and Poor But Honest (1).

The 1995 Triple Crown

121st KENTUCKY DERBY

Grade I for three-year olds; 8th race at Churchill Downs in Louisville. **Date**— May 6, 1995; **Distance**— 1¼ miles; **Stakes Purse**— $957,400 ($707,400 to winner; $145,000 for 2nd; $70,000 for 3rd; $35,000 for 4th); **Track**— Fast; **Off**— 5:33 p.m. EDT; **Favorites**— Serena's Song and Timber Country (7-2 odds).
Winner— Thunder Gulch; **Field**— 19 horses; **Time**— 2:01⅕; **Start**— Good; **Won**— Driving; **Sire**— Gulch (by Mr. Prospector); **Dam**— Line of Thunder (by Storm Bird); **Record** (going into race): 9 starts, 4 wins, 2 seconds, 1 third; **Last start:** 4th in Blue Grass Stakes (Apr. 15); **Breeder**— Peter M. Brant (Ky.).

Order of Finish	Jockey	PP	1/4	1/2	3/4	1-Mile	Stretch	Finish	To $1
Thunder Gulch	Gary Stevens	16	6-1½	5-½	5-½	3-1½	1-1½	**1**-2¼	24.50
Tejano Run	Jerry Bailey	14	13-head	12-1	10-head	6-head	3-head	**2**-head	8.60
Timber Country	Pat Day	15	14-½	13-head	12-head	11-head	10-head	**3**-¾	3.40
Jumron	Goncalino Almeida	10	8-head	9-1½	9-1½	4-½	5-½	**4**-head	5.60
Mecke	Robbie Davis	18	16-½	16-1½	19	13-1½	8-½	**5**-½	11.60
Eltish	Eddie Delahoussaye	7	10-1	10-head	11-head	9-2	6-½	**6**-3	10.90
Knockadoon	Chris McCarron	2	19	19	18-head	14-½	12-½	**7**-neck	11.60
Afternoon Deelites	Kent Desormeaux	12	7-head	6-head	6-½	5-head	7-head	**8**-neck	8.70
Citadeed	Eddie Maple	19	3-½	7-½	2-head	7-½	9-½	**9**-¾	11.60
In Character	Chris Antley	9	17-1	15-head	17-head	12-1½	13-2	**10**-½	11.60
Suave Prospect	Julie Krone	6	9-1½	11-4	14-1	8-½	11-½	**11**-½	13.10
Talkin Man	Mike Smith	11	4-1½	3-head	4-head	2-head	2-1	**12**-½	4.00
Dazzling Falls	Garrett Gomez	1	12-head	14-½	13-1½	19	15-1	**13**-neck	27.60
Ski Captain	Yutaka Take	17	18-½	17-head	16-1	15-1½	14-1	**14**-1½	11.60
Jambalaya Jazz	Craig Perret	5	15-½	18-1½	15-head	16-head	16-2	**15**-neck	18.00
Serena's Song	Corey Nakatani	13	1-head	1-1½	1-½	1-head	4-1	**16**-1½	3.40
Pyramid Peak	Herb McCauley	3	5-1	8-head	8-head	17-1	17-6	**17**-6	18.00
Lake George	Shane Sellers	8	11-1	4-1	7-1	10-head	18-12	**18**-21	11.60
Wild Syn	Randy Romero	4	2-½	2-1½	3-½	18-½	19	**19**	18.80

Times— 0:22⅖; 0:45⅘; 1:10⅕; 1:35⅗; 2:01⅕.

$2 Mutual Prices— #11 Thunder Gulch ($51.00, $24.20, $12.20); #10 Tejano Run ($10.20, $6.80); #2b Timber Country ($3.80). **Exacta**— (11-10) for $480.00; **Trifecta**— (11-10-2) for $2,099.20; **Pick Six**— (9-5-2-4-9-11) five correct for $17,641.80; **Scratched**— none. **Overweights**— none. **Attendance**— 144,110; **TV Rating**— 6.0/20 share (ABC).

Trainers & Owners (by finish): **1**— D. Wayne Lukas & Michael Tabor; **2**— Kenneth McPeak & Roy Monroe; **3**— D. Wayne Lukas & Robert and Beverly Lewis, W.T. Young and Overbrook Farm, and Graham J. Beck and Gainesway Farm; **4**— Gary Lewis & Charles Dunn; **5**— Manny Tortora & James R. Lewis; **6**— Henry Cecil & Juddmonte Farms (Khalid Abdullah); **7**— Tony Reinstedler & William K. Warren; **8**— Richard Mandella & Burt Bacharach; **9**— Peter Chapple-Hyam & Ivan Allen; **10**— Bruce Jackson & Jackson, Dave Farr and Vince Baker; **11**— Nick Zito & William J. Condre and Mike Sherman; **12**— Roger Attfield & Kinghaven Farms, Helen G. Stollery and Peter Wall; **13**— Chuck Turco & Chateau Ridge Farm (Donald G. Kroeger); **14**— Hideyuki Mori & Shadai Racehorse Co.; **15**— John Ward & John C. Oxley; **16**— D. Wayne Lukas & Robert and Beverly Lewis; **17**— John Ward & John C. Oxley; **18**— Mike Orman & Stonehenge Stable and David Lavin; **19**— Thomas Arnemann & Jurgen Arnemann.

120th PREAKNESS STAKES

Grade I for three-year olds; 10th race at Pimlico in Baltimore. **Date**— May 20, 1995; **Distance**— 1 3/16 miles; **Stakes Purse**— $687,400 ($446,810 to winner; $137,480 for 2nd; $68,740 for 3rd; $34,370 for 4th); **Track**— Fast; **Off**— 5:33 p.m. EDT; **Favorite**— Timber Country (9-5).
Winner— Timber Country; **Field**— 11 horses; **Time**— 1:54⅖; **Start**— Good; **Won**— Driving; **Sire**— Woodman (by Mr. Prospector); **Dam**— Fall Aspen (by Pretense); **Record** (going into race): 11 starts, 4 wins, 1 second, 4 thirds; **Last start:** 3rd in Kentucky Derby (May 6); **Breeder**— Lowquest Ltd. (Ky.)

Order of Finish	Jockey	PP	1/4	1/2	3/4	Stretch	Finish	To $1
Timber Country	Pat Day	7	6-1	6-1½	6-3	3-head	**1**-½	1.90
Oliver's Twist	Albert Delagado	10	4-½	4-½	4-1	5-3½	**2**-neck	25.20
Thunder Gulch	Gary Stevens	11	5-1	5-1	5-2	4-head	**3**-4	3.80
Star Standard	Chris McCarron	8	2-1½	2-1	2-1½	1-head	**4**-½	29.50
Mecke	Robbie Davis	9	10-8	10-8	7-2	6-1½	**5**-neck	28.60
Talkin Man	Mike Smith	4	3-1	3-2	3-1½	2-½	**6**-5¾	3.20
Our Gatsby	Kent Desormeaux	2	11	11	11	8-3	**7**-neck	10.90
Mystery Storm	Craig Perret	3	1-1½	1-head	1-head	7-5	**8**-9	25.00
Tejano Run	Jerry Bailey	5	8-head	7-head	8-2	9-5	**9**-2¾	4.70
Pana Brass	Eddie Maple	6	9-1½	8-2	9-5	10-10	**10**-17	64.30
Itron	Ricky Frazier	1	7-1	9-head	10-1½	11	**11**	81.00

Times— 0:23⅕; 0:47⅕; 1:10⅘; 1:35⅖; 1:54⅖.

$2 Mutual Prices— #7 Timber Country ($5.80, $4.20, $2.80); #10 Oliver's Twist ($16.80, $6.40); #11 Thunder Gulch ($3.60). **Exacta**— (7-10) for $266.00; **Trifecta**— (7-10-11) for $909.60; **Pick Six**—none ; **Scratched**— none. **Overweights**— none. **Attendance**— 87,707; **TV Rating**—3.7/11share (ABC).

Trainers & Owners (by finish): **1**— D. Wayne Lukas & Robert and Beverly Lewis, W.T. Young and Overbrook Farm, Graham J. Beck and Gainesway Farm; **2**— Bill Boniface Jr. & Charles Oliver; **3**— D. Wayne Lukas & Michael Tabor; **4**— Nick Zito & William Condren & Joseph Cornacchia; **5**— Emanuel "Manny" Tortora & James R. Lewis; **6**— Roger Attfield & Kinghaven Farms, Helen G. Stollery and Peter Wall; **7**— Donnie Von Hemel & Charles F. Heider; **8**— Larry Robideaux & David Beard; **9**— Kenneth McPeek & Roy Monroe; **10**— Alfredo Callejas & Robert Perez; **11**— Roy Frazier & David Albert.

127th BELMONT STAKES

Grade I for three-year olds; 9th race at Belmont Park in Elmont, N.Y. **Date**— June 10, 1995; **Distance**— 1½ miles; **Stakes Purse**— $692,400 ($415,440 to winner; $138,480 for 2nd; $76,164 for 3rd; $41,544 for 4th); **Track**— Fast; **Off**— 5:33 p.m. EDT; **Favorite**—Thunder Gulch (6-5).
Winner— Thunder Gulch. Timber Country was the early favorite at 6-5 before he was withdrawn on June 9 with 104-degree fever; **Field**— 11 horses; **Time**— 2:32; **Start**— Good; **Won**— Driving; **Sire**— Gulch (by Mr. Prospector); **Dam**—Line of Thunder (by Storm Bird); **Record** (going into race): 11 starts, 5 wins, 2 second, 2 thirds **Last Start**— 3rd in Preakness Stakes (May 20); **Breeder**— Peter M. Brant (Ky.)

Order of Finish	Jockey	PP	1/4	1/2	1-Mile	1 1/4-M	Stretch	Finish	To $1
Thunder Gulch	Gary Stevens	10	4-½	3-1½	2-1	2-3	1-head	**1**-2	1.50
Star Standard	Julie Krone	11	1-1	1-½	1-½	1-½	2-5	**2**-3½	6.30
Citadeed	Eddie Maple	1	2-head	4-1	5-½	3-½	3-½	**3**-1½	6.30
Knockadoon	Chris McCarron	9	6-½	6-1½	6-1	4-1½	4-6	**4**-4½	5.70
Pana Brass	Wigberto Ramos	3	11	10-½	8-½	7-2	5-½	**5**-5	79.25
Off'n'away	Mike Smith	2	10-½	11	7-3½	5-2	6-4	**6**-1	5.40
Ave's Flag	John Velasquez	5	9-head	9-1	9-4	9-3	7-1	**7**-4	29.75
Composer	Jerry Bailey	6	5-1½	5-1½	4-½	6-2	8-5	**8**-7½	10.50
Colonial Secretary	Jose Santos	8	8-½	7-head	10-head	11	9-2	**9**-3	52.00
Is Sveikatas	Jorge Chavez	4	7-½	8-head	11	10-½	10-3	**10**-6½	67.75
Wild Syn	Randy Romero	7	3-½	2-½	3-head	8-head	11	**11**	13.30

Times— 0:24⅗; 0:50⅕; 1:15⅕; 1:40⅗; 2:05⅗; 2:32.
$2 Mutual Prices— #01 Thunder Gulch ($5.00, $3.70, $2.49); #12 Star Standard ($5.80, $4.30); #1 Citadeed ($4.40).
Exacta— (10-12) for $25.20; **Trifecta**— (10-12-1) for $81.50; **Pick Six**—none **Scratched**— Timber Country.
Overweights— None. **Attendance**—37,171; **TV Rating**— 3.8/12 share (ABC)
Trainers & Owners (by finish): **1**— D. Wayne Lukas & Michael Tabor; **2**— Nick Zito & William Condren and Joseph Cornacchia; **3**— Richard Violette & Ivan Allen; **4**— Anthony Reinstedler & William K. Warren; **5**— Alfredo Callejas & Robert Perez; **6**— Dermot Weld & Moyglare Stud; **7**— Leo O'Brien & David McNulty; **8**— Bill Mott & Henryk deKwiatkowski, **9**— Gene Weymouth & Buckland Farm; **10**— Clarke Whitaker & Clarke Whitaker; **11**— Thomas Arnemann & Jurgen Arnemann.

1994-95 Money Leaders

Official Top 10 standings for 1994 and unofficial Top 10 for 1995, through Sept. 24, as compiled by *The Daily Racing Form.*

FINAL 1994

HORSES	Age	Sts	1-2-3	Earnings
Paradise Creek	5	11	8-2-1	$2,610,187
Concern	3	14	3-5-6	2,541,670
Tabasco Cat	3	12	5-3-1	2,164,334
Holy Bull	3	10	8-0-0	2,095,000
Tikkanen	3	9	3-1-2	1,508,344
Dramatic Gold	3	10	4-2-2	1,294,850
Go for Gin	3	11	2-4-1	1,178,596
Devil His Due	5	12	3-6-1	1,142,000
Cherokee Run	4	9	3-3-3	943,690
Timber Country	2	7	4-0-2	927,025

JOCKEYS	Mts	1st	Earnings
Mike Smith	1484	317	$15,979,820
Pat Day	1147	316	14,543,715
Gary Stevens	1402	258	12,651,291
Jerry Bailey	1221	255	11,515,912
Kent Desormeaux	1163	251	11,275,077
Chris McCarron	870	156	10,921,495
Corey Nakatani	1015	194	9,676,658
Eddie Delahoussave	1012	184	8,609,179
Jose Santos	1249	208	8,329,940
Alex Solis	1372	222	7,685,647

TRAINERS	Sts	1st	Earnings
D. Wayne Lukas	693	147	$9,247,457
Bill Mott	575	137	7,043,317
Richard Mandella	350	68	4,984,977
H. Allen Jerkens	454	111	4,940,476
Ron McAnallay	461	80	4,736,496
Robert Frankel	280	52	4,692,793
Shug McGaughey	258	80	4,453,376
Richard Small	268	49	4,273,199
Gary Jones	301	66	4,160,037
Scotty Schulhofer	411	74	3,753,869

1995 (through Sept. 24)

HORSES	Age	Sts	1-2-3	Earnings
Cigar	5	8	8-0-0	$2,809,800
Thunder Gulch	3	9	7-0-1	2,621,580
Serena's Song	3	11	8-2-0	1,354,920
Sandpit (BRA)	6	7	4-2-0	1,282,700
Awad	5	12	4-3-0	1,040,810
Peaks and Valleys	3	6	4-2-0	1,023,750
Tinners Way	5	4	1-1-1	817,500
Possible Perfect	5	6	5-1-0	743,100
Petionville	3	9	5-0-1	723,275
Dazzling Falls	3	8	3-2-1	698,000

JOCKEYS	Mts	1st	Earnings
Corey Nakatani	1,072	240	$12,185,788
Jerry Bailey	1,026	237	10,893,487
Gary Stevens	671	142	9,921,674
Mike Smith	1,085	208	8,350,185
Pat Day	902	198	8,106,755
Kent Desormeaux	917	187	7,823,719
Chris McCarron	698	124	7,392,745
Eddie Delahoussaye	785	125	7,005,033
Alex Solis	1,056	148	6,160,410
Shane Sellers	843	158	6,085,419

TRAINERS	Sts	1st	Earnings
D. Wayne Lukas	531	127	$9,397,852
William I. Mott	486	128	7,384,734
Richard E. Mandella	237	49	4,898,576
Robert J. Frankel	244	51	4,494,667
Ronald L. McAnally	319	53	3,809,220
Claude McGaughey III	226	52	3,242,077
Jerrry Hollendorfer	679	145	2,717,811
H. A. Jerkens	350	60	2,695,309
Roger L. Attfield	238	45	2,446,419
Gary F. Jones	234	42	2,341,925

Harness Racing

1994-95 Major Stakes Races

Winners of major stakes races from Oct. 15, 1994 through Sept. 21, 1995; all paces and trots cover one mile; (BC) indicates year-end Breeders' Crown series.

LATE 1994

Date	Race	Raceway	Winner	Time	Driver	Purse
Oct. 15	BC Horse/Gelding Pace	Freehold	Village Jiffy	1:52⅖	Paul MacDonell	$334,000
Oct. 15	BC Mare Pace	Freehold	Shady Daisy	1:53⅕	Michel Lachance	250,000
Oct. 15	BC Horse/Gelding Trot	Freehold	Pine Chip	1:55⅖	John Campbell	300,000
Oct. 15	BC Mare Trot	Freehold	Ambro Keepsake	1:57⅘	Stig Johansson	250,000
Oct. 21	BC 3-Yr-Old Colt Pace	Garden St.	Magical Mike	1:51⅗	Michel Lachance	400,000
Oct. 21	BC 3-Yr-Old Filly Pace	Garden St.	Hardie Hanover	1:51⅘	Tim Twaddle	325,000
Oct. 21	BC 3-Yr-Old Colt Trot	Garden St.	Incredible Abe	1:54⅕	Italo Tamborrino	400,000
Oct. 21	BC 3-Yr-Old Filly Trot	Garden St.	Imageofa Clear Day	1:55⅖	Bill O'Donnell	325,000
Oct. 28	BC 2-Yr-Old Colt Trot	Woodbine	Eager Seelster	1:58⅗	Teddy Jacbos	384,500
Oct. 28	BC 2-Yr-Old Filly Trot	Woodbine	Lookout Victory	1:57⅗	John Patterson Jr.	334,000
Oct. 28	BC 2-Yr-Old Colt Pace	Woodbine	Jenna's Beach Boy	1:51⅘	Bill Fahy	670,700
Oct. 28	BC 2-Yr-Old Filly Pace	Woodbine	Yankee Cashmere	1:56	Peter Wrenn	501,400
Nov. 19	Governor's Cup	Garden St.	CA Connection	1:54⅕	Joe Anderson	616,400
Nov. 24	Goldsmith Maid	Garden St.	CR Kay Suzie	1:56	Rod Allen	300,000
Dec. 4	Provincial Cup	Windsor	Pacific Rockey	1:52¾	Jack Moiseyeu	200,000

1995 (through Sept. 21)

Date	Race	Raceway	Winner	Time	Driver	Purse
June 24	North America Cup	Woodbine	David's Pass	1:52⅕	John Campbell	$1,000,000
July 1	Messenger Stakes	Ladbroke	David's Pass	1:52⅘	John Campbell	328,825
July 8	Yonkers Trot	Yonkers	CR Kay Suzie	1:56	Rod Allen	276,564
July 15	Meadowlands Pace	Meadowlands	David's Pass	1:50⅘	John Campbell	1,000,000
Aug. 5	**Hambletonian**	Meadowlands	Tagliabue	1:54⅘	John Campbell	1,200,000
Aug. 12	Sweetheart Pace	Meadowlands	On Her Way	1:54⅘	Cat Manzi	571,100
Aug. 12	Woodrow Wilson Pace	Meadowlands	A Stud Named Sue	1:52⅘	George Brennan Jr.	585,500
Aug. 26	Cane Pace	Yonkers	Mattgilla Gorilla	1:54⅖	David Ingraham	384,375
Sept. 2	World Trotting Derby	Du Quoin	CR Kay Suzie	1:52⅘	Rod Allen	585,000
Sept. 21	Little Brown Jug	Delaware	Nick's Fantasy	1:51⅖	John Campbell	543,670

1994-95 Money Leaders

Official Top 10 standings for 1994 and unofficial Top 10 for 1995 through Sept. 22, as compiled by the U.S. Trotting Assn.

FINAL 1994

HORSES	Age	Sts	1-2-3	Earnings
Cam's Card Shark	3pc	18	15-2-0	$2,264,714
Pacific Rocket	3pc	27	11-11-2	1,418,325
Victory Dream	3tc	17	9-4-1	992,662
Magical Mike	3pc	18	9-3-4	912,677
Falcons Future	3pc	29	12-6-1	848,334
Bullville Victory	3tc	24	9-4-4	724,812
Electric Slide	3pf	21	13-2-2	659,007
Donerail	2tc	15	13-0-1	636,925
Dontgetinmyway	2pc	16	6-6-1	610,018
Mr Lavec	3tc	15	6-4-5	590,529

DRIVERS	Sts	1st	Earnings
John Campbell	1848	379	$9,834,113
Jack Moiseyev	2788	541	7,108,020
Michel Lachance	2166	301	6,255,284
Ron Waples	2514	311	4,913,926
Doug Brown	2042	429	4,701,237
Cat Manzi	3034	407	4,569,712
Dave Magee	2742	360	4,358,819
Steve Condren	1670	263	3,460,635
Luc Ouellette	2313	551	3,301,289
Bill Fahy	1199	145	3,141,330

1995 (through Sept. 22)

HORSES	Age	Sts	1-2-3	Earnings
David's Pass	3pc	13	5-2-1	$1,452,362
CR Kay Suzie	3tf	13	10-0-1	910,353
Tagliabue	3tc	12	4-5-2	865,850
A Stud Named Sue	2pc	9	8-0-0	669,887
Pacific Rocket	4ph	26	16-3-2	649,555
Ball and Chain	5ph	27	8-7-8	612,044
Village Connection	3pc	20	12-3-3	561,170
Neutrality	3pc	11	3-4-2	487,447
Jenna's Beach Boy	3pc	9	8-1-0	465,093
She's A Great Lady	3pf	20	11-4-1	447,480

DRIVERS	Sts	1st	Earnings
John Campbell	1587	291	$7,700,669
Michel Lachance	1812	272	5,219,792
Jack Moiseyev	2318	389	5,172,133
Cat Manzi	2250	299	4,088,328
Doug Brown	1626	318	4,035,672
Luc Ouellette	1835	529	3,695,801
Tony Morgan	2540	575	3,250,239
David Magee	2042	410	3,131,832
Ron Pierce	1997	255	3,029,723
Bill Fahy	1091	152	3,001,734

Thoroughbred Racing
The Triple Crown

The term "Triple Crown" was coined by sportswriter Charles Hatton while covering the 1930 victories of Gallant Fox in the Kentucky Derby, Preakness Stakes and Belmont Stakes. Before then, only Sir Barton (1919) had won all three races in the same year. Since then, nine horses have won the Triple Crown. Two trainers, James (Sunny Jim) Fitzsimmons and Ben A. Jones, have saddled two Triple Crown champions, while Eddie Arcaro is the only jockey to ride two champions.

Year		Jockey	Trainer	Owner	Sire/Dam
1919	**Sir Barton**	Johnny Loftus	H. Guy Bedwell	J.K.L. Ross	Star Shoot/Lady Sterling
1930	**Gallant Fox**	Earl Sande	J.E. Fitzsimmons	Belair Stud	Sir Gallahad III/Marguerite
1935	**Omaha**	Willie Saunders	J.E. Fitzsimmons	Belair Stud	Gallant Fox/Flambino
1937	**War Admiral**	Charley Kurtsinger	George Conway	Samuel Riddle	Man o' War/Brushup
1941	**Whirlaway**	Eddie Arcaro	Ben A. Jones	Calumet Farm	Blenheim II/Dustwhirl
1943	**Count Fleet**	Johnny Longden	Don Cameron	Mrs. J.D. Hertz	Reigh Count/Quickly
1946	**Assault**	Warren Mehrtens	Max Hirsch	King Ranch	Bold Venture/Igual
1948	**Citation**	Eddie Arcaro	Ben A. Jones	Calumet Farm	Bull Lea/Hydroplane II
1973	**Secretariat**	Ron Turcotte	Lucien Laurin	Meadow Stable	Bold Ruler/Somethingroyal
1977	**Seattle Slew**	Jean Cruguet	Billy Turner	Karen Taylor	Bold Reasoning/My Charmer
1978	**Affirmed**	Steve Cauthen	Laz Barrera	Harbor View Farm	Exclusive Native/Won't Tell You

Note: Gallant Fox (1930) is the only Triple Crown winner to sire another Triple Crown winner, Omaha (1935). Wm. Woodward Sr., owner of Belair Stud, was breeder-owner of both horses and both were trained by Sunny Jim Fitzsimmons.

Triple Crown Near Misses

Forty-one horses have won two legs of the Triple Crown. Of those, a dozen won the Kentucky Derby (KD) and Preakness Stakes (PS) only to be beaten in the Belmont Stakes (BS). Two others, Burgoo King (1932) and Bold Venture (1936), each won the Derby and Preakness but were forced out of the Belmont with the same injury—a bowed tendon—that effectively ended their racing careers. In 1978, Alydar finished second to Affirmed in all three races, the only time that has happened. Note that the Preakness preceeded the Kentucky Derby in 1922, '23 and '31; (*) indicates won on disqualification.

Year		KD	PS	BS	Year		KD	PS	BS
1877	**Cloverbrook**	DNS	won	won	1961	**Carry Back**	won	won	7th
1878	**Duke of Magenta**	DNS	won	won	1963	**Chateaugay**	won	2nd	won
1880	**Grenada**	DNS	won	won	1964	**Northern Dancer**	won	won	3rd
1881	**Saunterer**	DNS	won	won	1966	**Kauai King**	won	won	4th
1895	**Belmar**	DNS	won	won	1967	**Damascus**	3rd	won	won
1920	**Man o'War**	DNS	won	won	1968	**Forward Pass**	won*	won	2nd
1922	**Pillory**	DNS	won	won	1969	**Majestic Prince**	won	won	2nd
1923	**Zev**	won	12th	won	1971	**Canonero II**	won	won	4th
1931	**Twenty Grand**	won	2nd	won	1972	**Riva Ridge**	won	4th	won
1932	**Burgoo King**	won	won	DNS	1974	**Little Current**	5th	won	won
1936	**Bold Venture**	won	won	DNS	1976	**Bold Forbes**	won	3rd	won
1939	**Johnstown**	won	5th	won	1979	**Spectacular Bid**	won	won	3rd
1940	**Bimelech**	2nd	won	won	1981	**Pleasant Colony**	won	won	3rd
1942	**Shut Out**	won	5th	won	1984	**Swale**	won	7th	won
1944	**Pensive**	won	won	2nd	1987	**Alysheba**	won	won	4th
1949	**Capot**	2nd	won	won	1988	**Risen Star**	3rd	won	won
1950	**Middleground**	won	2nd	won	1989	**Sunday Silence**	won	won	2nd
1953	**Native Dancer**	2nd	won	won	1991	**Hansel**	10th	won	won
1955	**Nashua**	2nd	won	won	1994	**Tabasco Cat**	6th	won	won
1956	**Needles**	won	2nd	won	1995	**Thunder Gulch**	won	3rd	won
1958	**Tim Tam**	won	won	2nd					

The Triple Crown Challenge (1987-93)

Seeking to make the Triple Crown more than just a media event and to insure that owners would not be attracted to more lucrative races, officials at Churchill Downs, the Maryland Jockey Club and the New York Racing Association created Triple Crown Productions in 1985 and announced that a $1 million bonus would be given to the horse that performs best in the Kentucky Derby, Preakness Stakes and Belmont Stakes. Furthermore, a bonus of $5 million would be presented to any horse winning all three races.

Revised in 1991, the rules stated that the winning horse must: 1. finish all three races; 2. earn points by finishing first, second, third or fourth in at least one of the three races; and 3. earn the highest number of points based on the following system—10 points to win, five to place, three to show and one to finish fourth. In the event of a tie, the $1 million is distributed equally among the top point-getters. From 1987-90, the system was five points to win, three to place and one to show. The Triple Crown Challenge was discontinued in 1994.

Year		KD	PS	BS	Pts	Year		KD	PS	BS	Pts
1987	1 **Bet Twice**	2nd	2nd	1st — 11		1991	1 **Hansel**	10th	1st	1st — 20	
	2 Alysheba	1st	1st	4th — 10			2 Strike the Gold	1st	6th	2nd — 15	
	3 Cryptoclearance	4th	3rd	2nd — 4			3 Mane Minister	3rd	3rd	3rd — 9	
1988	1 **Risen Star**	3rd	1st	1st — 11		1992	1 **Pine Bluff**	5th	1st	3rd — 13	
	2 Winning Colors	1st	3rd	6th — 6			2 Casual Lies	2nd	3rd	5th — 8	
	3 Brian's Time	6th	2nd	3rd — 4			(No other horses ran all three races.)				
1989	1 **Sunday Silence**	1st	1st	2nd — 13		1993	1 **Sea Hero**	1st	5th	7th — 10	
	2 Easy Goer	2nd	2nd	1st — 11			2 Wild Gale	3rd	8th	3rd — 6	
	3 Hawkster	5th	5th	5th — 0			(No other horses ran all three races.)				
1990	1 **Unbridled**	1st	2nd	4th — 8							
	2 Summer Squall	2nd	1st	DNR — 8							
	3 Go and Go	DNR	DNR	1st — 5							
	(Unbridled was only horse to run all three races.)										

Kentucky Derby

For three-year-olds. Held the first Saturday in May at Churchill Downs in Louisville, Ky. Inaugurated in 1875.
Originally run at 1½ miles (1875-95), shortened to present 1¼ miles in 1896.
Trainers with most wins: Ben Jones (6); Dick Thompson (4); Sunny Jim Fitzsimmons and Max Hirsch (3).
Jockeys with most wins: Eddie Arcaro and Bill Hartack (5); Bill Shoemaker (4); Angel Cordero Jr., Issac Murphy and Earl Sande (3).
Winning fillies: Regret (1915), Genuine Risk (1980) and Winning Colors (1988).

Year		Time	Jockey	Trainer	2nd place	3rd place
1875	**Aristides**	2:37¾	Oliver Lewis	Ansel Anderson	Volcano	Verdigris
1876	**Vagrant**	2:38¼	Bobby Swim	James Williams	Creedmore	Harry Hill
1877	**Baden-Baden**	2:38	Billy Walker	Ed Brown	Leonard	King William
1878	**Day Star**	2:37¼	Jimmy Carter	Lee Paul	Himyar	Leveler
1879	**Lord Murphy**	2:37	Charlie Shauer	George Rice	Falsetto	Strathmore
1880	**Fonso**	2:37½	George Lewis	Tice Hutsell	Kimball	Bancroft
1881	**Hindoo**	2:40	Jim McLaughlin	James Rowe Sr.	Lelex	Alfambra
1882	**Apollo**	2:40¼	Babe Hurd	Green Morris	Runnymede	Bengal
1883	**Leonatus**	2:43	Billy Donohue	John McGinty	Drake Carter	Lord Raglan
1884	**Buchanan**	2:40¼	Isaac Murphy	William Bird	Loftin	Audrain
1885	**Joe Cotton**	2:37¼	Babe Henderson	Alex Perry	Bersan	Ten Booker
1886	**Ben Ali**	2:36½	Paul Duffy	Jim Murphy	Blue Wing	Free Knight
1887	**Montrose**	2:39¼	Isaac Lewis	John McGinty	Jim Gore	Jacobin
1888	**MacBeth II**	2:38¼	George Covington	John Campbell	Gallifet	White
1889	**Spokane**	2:34½	Thomas Kiley	John Rodegap	Proctor Knott	Once Again
1890	**Riley**	2:45	Isaac Murphy	Edward Corrigan	Bill Letcher	Robespierre
1891	**Kingman**	2:52¼	Isaac Murphy	Dud Allen	Balgowan	High Tariff
1892	**Azra**	2:41½	Lonnie Clayton	John Morris	Huron	Phil Dwyer
1893	**Lookout**	2:39¼	Eddie Kunze	Wm. McDaniel	Plutus	Boundless
1894	**Chant**	2:41	Frank Goodale	Eugene Leigh	Pearl Song	Sigurd
1895	**Halma**	2:37½	Soup Perkins	Byron McClelland	Basso	Laureate
1896	**Ben Brush**	2:07¾	Willie Simms	Hardy Campbell	Ben Eder	Semper Ego
1897	**Typhoon II**	2:12½	Buttons Garner	J.C. Cahn	Ornament	Dr. Catlett
1898	**Plaudit**	2:09	Willie Simms	John E. Madden	Lieber Karl	Isabey
1899	**Manuel**	2:12	Fred Taral	Robert Walden	Corsini	Mazo
1900	**Lieut. Gibson**	2:06¼	Jimmy Boland	Charles Hughes	Florizar	Thrive
1901	**His Eminence**	2:07¾	Jimmy Winkfield	F.B. Van Meter	Sannazarro	Driscoll
1902	**Alan-a-Dale**	2:08¾	Jimmy Winkfield	T.C. McDowell	Inventor	The Rival
1903	**Judge Himes**	2:09	Hal Booker	J.P. Mayberry	Early	Bourbon
1904	**Elwood**	2:08½	Shorty Prior	C.E. Durnell	Ed Tierney	Brancas
1905	**Agile**	2:10¾	Jack Martin	Robert Tucker	Ram's Horn	Layson
1906	**Sir Huon**	2:08⅘	Roscoe Troxler	Pete Coyne	Lady Navarre	James Reddick
1907	**Pink Star**	2:12⅗	Andy Minder	W.H. Fizer	Zal	Ovelando

Kentucky Derby (Cont.)

Year		Time	Jockey	Trainer	2nd place	3rd place
1908	**Stone Street**	2:15⅕	Arthur Pickens	J.W. Hall	Sir Cleges	Dunvegan
1909	**Wintergreen**	2:08⅕	Vincent Powers	Charles Mack	Miami	Dr. Barkley
1910	**Donau**	2:06⅖	Fred Herbert	George Ham	Joe Morris	Fighting Bob
1911	**Meridian**	2:05	George Archibald	Albert Ewing	Governor Gray	Colston
1912	**Worth**	2:09⅖	C.H. Shilling	Frank Taylor	Duval	Flamma
1913	**Donerail**	2:04⅘	Roscoe Goose	Thomas Hayes	Ten Point	Gowell
1914	**Old Rosebud**	2:03⅖	John McCabe	F.D. Weir	Hodge	Bronzewing
1915	**Regret**	2:05⅖	Joe Notter	James Rowe Sr.	Pebbles	Sharpshooter
1916	**George Smith**	2:04	Johnny Loftus	Hollie Hughes	Star Hawk	Franklin
1917	**Omar Khayyam**	2:04⅗	Charles Borel	C.T. Patterson	Ticket	Midway
1918	**Exterminator**	2:10⅘	William Knapp	Henry McDaniel	Escoba	Viva America
1919	**SIR BARTON**	2:09⅘	Johnny Loftus	H. Guy Bedwell	Billy Kelly	Under Fire
1920	**Paul Jones**	2:09	Ted Rice	Billy Garth	Upset	On Watch
1921	**Behave Yourself**	2:04⅕	Charles Thompson	Dick Thompson	Black Servant	Prudery
1922	**Morvich**	2:04⅗	Albert Johnson	Fred Burlew	Bet Mosie	John Finn
1923	**Zev**	2:05⅖	Earl Sande	David Leary	Martingale	Vigil
1924	**Black Gold**	2:05⅕	John Mooney	Hanly Webb	Chilhowee	Beau Butler
1925	**Flying Ebony**	2:07⅗	Earl Sande	William Duke	Captain Hal	Son of John
1926	**Bubbling Over**	2:03⅘	Albert Johnson	Dick Thompson	Bagenbaggage	Rock Man
1927	**Whiskery**	2:06	Linus McAtee	Fred Hopkins	Osmand	Jock
1928	**Reigh Count**	2:10⅖	Chick Lang	Bert Michell	Misstep	Toro
1929	**Clyde Van Dusen**	2:10⅘	Linus McAtee	Clyde Van Dusen	Naishapur	Panchio
1930	**GALLANT FOX**	2:07⅗	Earl Sande	Jim Fitzsimmons	Gallant Knight	Ned O.
1931	**Twenty Grand**	2:01⅘	Charley Kurtsinger	James Rowe Jr.	Sweep All	Mate
1932	**Burgoo King**	2:05⅕	Eugene James	Dick Thompson	Economic	Stepenfetchit
1933	**Brokers Tip**	2:06⅘	Don Meade	Dick Thompson	Head Play	Charley O.
1934	**Cavalcade**	2:04	Mack Garner	Bob Smith	Discovery	Agrarian
1935	**OMAHA**	2:05	Willie Saunders	Jim Fitzsimmons	Roman Soldier	Whiskolo
1936	**Bold Venture**	2:03⅗	Ira Hanford	Max Hirsch	Brevity	Indian Broom
1937	**WAR ADMIRAL**	2:03⅕	Charley Kurtsinger	George Conway	Pompoon	Reaping Reward
1938	**Lawrin**	2:04⅘	Eddie Arcaro	Ben Jones	Dauber	Can't Wait
1939	**Johnstown**	2:03⅖	James Stout	Jim Fitzsimmons	Challedon	Heather Broom
1940	**Gallahadion**	2:05	Carroll Bierman	Roy Waldron	Bimelech	Dit
1941	**WHIRLAWAY**	2:01⅖	Eddie Arcaro	Ben Jones	Staretor	Market Wise
1942	**Shut Out**	2:04⅖	Wayne Wright	John Gaver	Alsab	Valdina Orphan
1943	**COUNT FLEET**	2:04	Johnny Longden	Don Cameron	Blue Swords	Slide Rule
1944	**Pensive**	2:04⅕	Conn McCreary	Ben Jones	Broadcloth	Stir Up
1945	**Hoop Jr**	2:07	Eddie Arcaro	Ivan Parke	Pot O'Luck	Darby Dieppe
1946	**ASSAULT**	2:06⅗	Warren Mehrtens	Max Hirsch	Spy Song	Hampden
1947	**Jet Pilot**	2:06⅘	Eric Guerin	Tom Smith	Phalanx	Faultless
1948	**CITATION**	2:05⅖	Eddie Arcaro	Ben Jones	Coaltown	My Request
1949	**Ponder**	2:04⅕	Steve Brooks	Ben Jones	Capot	Palestinian
1950	**Middleground**	2:01⅗	William Boland	Max Hirsch	Hill Prince	Mr. Trouble
1951	**Count Turf**	2:02⅗	Conn McCreary	Sol Rutchick	Royal Mustang	Ruhe
1952	**Hill Gail**	2:01⅗	Eddie Arcaro	Ben Jones	Sub Fleet	Blue Man
1953	**Dark Star**	2:02	Hank Moreno	Eddie Hayward	Native Dancer	Invigorator
1954	**Determine**	2:03	Raymond York	Willie Molter	Hasty Road	Hasseyampa
1955	**Swaps**	2:01⅘	Bill Shoemaker	Mesh Tenney	Nashua	Summer Tan
1956	**Needles**	2:03⅖	David Erb	Hugh Fontaine	Fabius	Come On Red
1957	**Iron Liege**	2:02⅕	Bill Hartack	Jimmy Jones	Gallant Man	Round Table
1958	**Tim Tam**	2:05	Ismael Valenzuela	Jimmy Jones	Lincoln Road	Noureddin
1959	**Tomy Lee**	2:02⅕	Bill Shoemaker	Frank Childs	Sword Dancer	First Landing
1960	**Venetian Way**	2:02⅖	Bill Hartack	Victor Sovinski	Bally Ache	Victoria Park
1961	**Carry Back**	2:04	John Sellers	Jack Price	Crozier	Bass Clef
1962	**Decidedly**	2:00⅖	Bill Hartack	Horatio Luro	Roman Line	Ridan
1963	**Chateaugay**	2:01⅘	Braulio Baeza	James Conway	Never Bend	Candy Spots
1964	**Northern Dancer**	2:00	Bill Hartack	Horatio Luro	Hill Rise	The Scoundrel
1965	**Lucky Debonair**	2:01⅕	Bill Shoemaker	Frank Catrone	Dapper Dan	Tom Rolfe
1966	**Kauai King**	2:02	Don Brumfield	Henry Forrest	Advocator	Blue Skyer
1967	**Proud Clarion**	2:00⅗	Bobby Ussery	Loyd Gentry	Barbs Delight	Damascus
1968	**Forward Pass***	—	Ismael Valenzuela	Henry Forrest	Francie's Hat	T.V. Commercial
1969	**Majestic Prince**	2:01⅘	Bill Hartack	Johnny Longden	Arts and Letters	Dike
1970	**Dust Commander**	2:03⅖	Mike Manganello	Don Combs	My Dad George	High Echelon
1971	**Canonero II**	2:03⅕	Gustavo Avila	Juan Arias	Jim French	Bold Reason
1972	**Riva Ridge**	2:01⅘	Ron Turcotte	Lucien Laurin	No Le Hace	Hold Your Peace

*Dancer's Image finished first (in 2:02½), but was disqualified after traces of prohibited medication were found in his system.

Year		Time	Jockey	Trainer	2nd place	3rd place
1973	**SECRETARIAT**	1:59⅖	Ron Turcotte	Lucien Laurin	Sham	Our Native
1974	**Cannonade**	2:04	Angel Cordero Jr.	Woody Stephens	Hudson County	Agitate
1975	**Foolish Pleasure**	2:02	Jacinto Vasquez	LeRoy Jolley	Avatar	Diabolo
1976	**Bold Forbes**	2:01⅗	Angel Cordero Jr.	Laz Barrera	Honest Pleasure	Elocutionist
1977	**SEATTLE SLEW**	2:02⅕	Jean Cruguet	Billy Turner	Run Dusty Run	Sanhedrin
1978	**AFFIRMED**	2:01⅕	Steve Cauthen	Laz Barrera	Alydar	Believe It
1979	**Spectacular Bid**	2:02⅖	Ron Franklin	Bud Delp	General Assembly	Golden Act
1980	**Genuine Risk**	2:02	Jacinto Vasquez	LeRoy Jolley	Rumbo	Jaklin Klugman
1981	**Pleasant Colony**	2:02	Jorge Velasquez	John Campo	Woodchopper	Partez
1982	**Gato Del Sol**	2:02⅖	E. Delahoussaye	Eddie Gregson	Laser Light	Reinvested
1983	**Sunny's Halo**	2:02⅕	E. Delahoussaye	David Cross Jr.	Desert Wine	Caveat
1984	**Swale**	2:02⅖	Laffit Pincay Jr.	Woody Stephens	Coax Me Chad	At The Threshold
1985	**Spend A Buck**	2:00⅕	Angel Cordero Jr.	Cam Gambolati	Stephan's Odyssey	Chief's Crown
1986	**Ferdinand**	2:02⅘	Bill Shoemaker	Chas.Whittingham	Bold Arrangement	Broad Brush
1987	**Alysheba**	2:03⅗	Chris McCarron	Jack Van Berg	Bet Twice	Avies Copy
1988	**Winning Colors**	2:02⅕	Gary Stevens	D. Wayne Lukas	Forty Niner	Risen Star
1989	**Sunday Silence**	2:05	Pat Valenzuela	Chas. Whittingham	Easy Goer	Awe Inspiring
1990	**Unbridled**	2:02	Craig Perret	Carl Nafzger	Summer Squall	Pleasant Tap
1991	**Strike the Gold**	2:03	Chris Antley	Nick Zito	Best Pal	Mane Minister
1992	**Lil E. Tee**	2:03	Pat Day	Lynn Whiting	Casual Lies	Dance Floor
1993	**Sea Hero**	2:02⅖	Jerry Bailey	Mack Miller	Prairie Bayou	Wild Gale
1994	**Go For Gin**	2:03⅗	Chris McCarron	Nick Zito	Strodes Creek	Blumin Affair
1995	**Thunder Gulch**	2:01⅕	Gary Stevens	D. Wayne Lukas	Tejano Run	Timber Country

Preakness Stakes

For three-year-olds. Held two weeks after the Kentucky Derby at Pimlico Race Course in Baltimore, Md. Inaugurated 1873. Originally run at 1½ miles (1873-88), then at 1¼ miles (1889), 1½ miles (1890), 1 1/16 miles (1894-1900), 1 mile & 70 yards (1901-07), 1 1/16 miles (1908), 1 mile (1909-10), 1⅛ miles (1911-24), and the present 13/16 miles since 1925

Trainers with most wins: Robert W. Walden (7); T.J. Healey (5); Sunny Jim Fitzsimmons, Jimmy Jones and D. Wayne Lukas (4); and J. Whalen (3).

Jockeys with most wins: Eddie Arcaro (6); Pat Day (4); G. Barbee, Bill Hartack and Lloyd Hughes (3).

Winning fillies: Flocarline (1903), Whimsical (1906), Rhine Maiden (1915) and Nellie Morse (1924).

Year		Time	Jockey	Trainer	2nd place	3rd place
1873	**Survivor**	2:43	G. Barbee	A.D. Pryor	John Boulger	Artist
1874	**Culpepper**	2:56½	W. Donohue	H. Gaffney	King Amadeus	Scratch
1875	**Tom Ochiltree**	2:43½	L. Hughes	R.W. Walden	Viator	Bay Final
1876	**Shirley**	2:44¾	G. Barbee	W. Brown	Rappahannock	Compliment
1877	**Cloverbrook**	2:45½	C. Holloway	J. Walden	Bombast	Lucifer
1878	**Duke of Magenta**	2:41¾	C. Holloway	R.W. Walden	Bayard	Albert
1879	**Harold**	2:40½	L. Hughes	R.W. Walden	Jericho	Rochester
1880	**Grenada**	2:40½	L. Hughes	R.W. Walden	Oden	Emily F.
1881	**Saunterer**	2:40½	T. Costello	R.W. Walden	Compensation	Baltic
1882	**Vanguard**	2:44½	T. Costello	R.W. Walden	Heck	Col. Watson
1883	**Jacobus**	2:42½	G. Barbee	R. Dwyer	Parnell	(2-horse race)
1884	**Knight of Ellerslie**	2:39½	S. Fisher	T.B. Doswell	Welcher	(2-horse race)
1885	**Tecumseh**	2:49	Jim McLaughlin	C. Littlefield	Wickham	John C.
1886	**The Bard**	2:45	S. Fisher	J. Huggins	Eurus	Elkwood
1887	**Dunboyne**	2:39½	W. Donohue	W. Jennings	Mahoney	Raymond
1888	**Refund**	2:49	F. Littlefield	R.W. Walden	Bertha B.*	Glendale
1889	**Buddhist**	2:17½	W. Anderson	J. Rogers	Japhet	(2-horse race)
1890	**Montague**	2:36¾	W. Martin	E. Feakes	Philosophy	Barrister
1891-93	Not held					
1894	**Assignee**	1:49¼	F. Taral	W. Lakeland	Potentate	Ed Kearney
1895	**Belmar**	1:50½	F. Taral	E. Feakes	April Fool	Sue Kittie
1896	**Margrave**	1:51	H. Griffin	Byron McClelland	Hamilton II	Intermission
1897	**Paul Kauvar**	1:51¼	T. Thorpe	T.P. Hayes	Elkins	On Deck
1898	**Sly Fox**	1:49¾	W. Simms	H. Campbell	The Huguenot	Nuto
1899	**Half Time**	1:47	R. Clawson	F. McCabe	Filigrane	Lackland
1900	**Hindus**	1:48⅖	H. Spencer	J.H. Morris	Sarmatian	Ten Candles
1901	**The Parader**	1:47⅕	F. Landry	T.J. Healey	Sadie S.	Dr. Barlow
1902	**Old England**	1:45⅘	L. Jackson	G.B. Morris	Maj. Daingerfield	Namtor
1903	**Flocarline**	1:44⅘	W. Gannon	H.C. Riddle	Mackey Dwyer	Rightful
1904	**Bryn Mawr**	1:44⅕	E. Hildebrand	W.F. Presgrave	Wotan	Dolly Spanker
1905	**Cairngorm**	1:45⅘	W. Davis	A.J. Joyner	Kiamesha	Coy Maid
1906	**Whimsical**	1:45	Walter Miller	T.J. Gaynor	Content	Larabie
1907	**Don Enrique**	1:45⅗	G. Mountain	J. Whalen	Ethon	Zambesi

* Later named Judge Murray.

Preakness Stakes (Cont.)

Year		Time	Jockey	Trainer	2nd place	3rd place
1908	**Royal Tourist**	1:46⅖	Eddie Dugan	A.J. Joyner	Live Wire	Robert Cooper
1909	**Effendi**	1:39⅘	Willie Doyle	F.C. Frisbie	Fashion Plate	Hill Top
1910	**Layminster**	1:40⅗	R. Estep	J.S. Healy	Dalhousie	Sager
1911	**Watervale**	1:51	Eddie Dugan	J. Whalen	Zeus	The Nigger
1912	**Colonel Holloway**	1:56⅗	C. Turner	D. Woodford	Bwana Tumbo	Tipsand
1913	**Buskin**	1:53⅖	James Butwell	J. Whalen	Kleburne	Barnegat
1914	**Holiday**	1:53⅘	A. Schuttinger	J.S. Healy	Brave Cunarder	Defendum
1915	**Rhine Maiden**	1:58	Douglas Hoffman	F. Devers	Half Rock	Runes
1916	**Damrosch**	1:54⅘	Linus McAtee	A.G. Weston	Greenwood	Achievement
1917	**Kalitan**	1:54⅖	E. Haynes	Bill Hurley	Al M. Dick	Kentucky Boy
1918	**War Cloud**	1:53⅗	Johnny Loftus	W.B. Jennings	Sunny Slope	Lanius
1918	**Jack Hare Jr**	1:53⅖	Charles Peak	F.D. Weir	The Porter	Kate Bright
1919	**SIR BARTON**	1:53	Johnny Loftus	H. Guy Bedwell	Eternal	Sweep On
1920	**Man o' War**	1:51⅗	Clarence Kummer	L. Feustel	Upset	Wildair
1921	**Broomspun**	1:54⅕	F. Coltiletti	James Rowe Sr.	Polly Ann	Jeg
1922	**Pillory**	1:51⅗	L. Morris	Thomas Healey	Hea	June Grass
1923	**Vigil**	1:53⅗	B. Marinelli	Thomas Healey	General Thatcher	Rialto
1924	**Nellie Morse**	1:57⅕	John Merimee	A.B. Gordon	Transmute	Mad Play
1925	**Coventry**	1:59	Clarence Kummer	William Duke	Backbone	Almadel
1926	**Display**	1:59⅘	John Maiben	Thomas Healey	Blondin	Mars
1927	**Bostonian**	2:01⅗	Whitey Abel	Fred Hopkins	Sir Harry	Whiskery
1928	**Victorian**	2:00⅕	Sonny Workman	James Rowe Jr.	Toro	Solace
1929	**Dr. Freeland**	2:01⅗	Louis Schaefer	Thomas Healey	Minotaur	African
1930	**GALLANT FOX**	2:00⅗	Earl Sande	Jim Fitzsimmons	Crack Brigade	Snowflake
1931	**Mate**	1:59	George Ellis	J.W. Healy	Twenty Grand	Ladder
1932	**Burgoo King**	1:59⅘	Eugene James	Dick Thompson	Tick On	Boatswain
1933	**Head Play**	2:02	Charley Kurtsinger	Thomas Hayes	Ladysman	Utopian
1934	**High Quest**	1:58⅕	Robert Jones	Bob Smith	Cavalcade	Discovery
1935	**OMAHA**	1:58⅖	Willie Saunders	Jim Fitzsimmons	Firethorn	Psychic Bid
1936	**Bold Venture**	1:59	George Woolf	Max Hirsch	Granville	Jean Bart
1937	**WAR ADMIRAL**	1:58⅖	Charley Kurtsinger	George Conway	Pompoon	Flying Scot
1938	**Dauber**	1:59⅘	Maurice Peters	Dick Handlen	Cravat	Menow
1939	**Challedon**	1:59⅘	George Seabo	Louis Schaefer	Gilded Knight	Volitant
1940	**Bimelech**	1:58⅗	F.A. Smith	Bill Hurley	Mioland	Gallahadion
1941	**WHIRLAWAY**	1:58⅘	Eddie Arcaro	Ben Jones	King Cole	Our Boots
1942	**Alsab**	1:57	Basil James	Sarge Swenke	Requested & Sun Again (dead heat)	
1943	**COUNT FLEET**	1:57⅖	Johnny Longden	Don Cameron	Blue Swords	Vincentive
1944	**Pensive**	1:59⅕	Conn McCreary	Ben Jones	Platter	Stir Up
1945	**Polynesian**	1:58⅘	W.D. Wright	Morris Dixon	Hoop Jr.	Darby Dieppe
1946	**ASSAULT**	2:01⅖	Warren Mehrtens	Max Hirsch	Lord Boswell	Hampden
1947	**Faultless**	1:59	Doug Dodson	Jimmy Jones	On Trust	Phalanx
1948	**CITATION**	2:02⅖	Eddie Arcaro	Jimmy Jones	Vulcan's Forge	Bovard
1949	**Capot**	1:56	Ted Atkinson	J.M. Gaver	Palestinian	Noble Impulse
1950	**Hill Prince**	1:59⅕	Eddie Arcaro	Casey Hayes	Middleground	Dooly
1951	**Bold**	1:56⅖	Eddie Arcaro	Preston Burch	Counterpoint	Alerted
1952	**Blue Man**	1:57⅖	Conn McCreary	Woody Stephens	Jampol	One Count
1953	**Native Dancer**	1:57⅘	Eric Guerin	Bill Winfrey	Jamie K.	Royal Bay Gem
1954	**Hasty Road**	1:57⅖	Johnny Adams	Harry Trotsek	Correlation	Hasseyampa
1955	**Nashua**	1:54⅗	Eddie Arcaro	Jim Fitzsimmons	Saratoga	Traffic Judge
1956	**Fabius**	1:58⅖	Bill Hartack	Jimmy Jones	Needles	No Regrets
1957	**Bold Ruler**	1:56⅕	Eddie Arcaro	Jim Fitzsimmons	Iron Liege	Inside Tract
1958	**Tim Tam**	1:57⅕	Ismael Valenzuela	Jimmy Jones	Lincoln Road	Gone Fishin'
1959	**Royal Orbit**	1:57	William Harmatz	R. Cornell	Sword Dancer	Dunce
1960	**Bally Ache**	1:57⅗	Bobby Ussery	Jimmy Pitt	Victoria Park	Celtic Ash
1961	**Carry Back**	1:57⅗	Johnny Sellers	Jack Price	Globemaster	Crozier
1962	**Greek Money**	1:56⅕	John Rotz	V.W. Raines	Ridan	Roman Line
1963	**Candy Spots**	1:56⅕	Bill Shoemaker	Mesh Tenney	Chateaugay	Never Bend
1964	**Northern Dancer**	1:56⅘	Bill Hartack	Horatio Luro	The Scoundrel	Hill Rise
1965	**Tom Rolfe**	1:56⅕	Ron Turcotte	Frank Whiteley	Dapper Dan	Hail To All
1966	**Kauai King**	1:55⅖	Don Brumfield	Henry Forrest	Stupendous	Amberoid
1967	**Damascus**	1:55⅕	Bill Shoemaker	Frank Whiteley	In Reality	Proud Clarion
1968	**Forward Pass**	1:56⅘	Ismael Valenzuela	Henry Forrest	Out Of the Way	Nodouble
1969	**Majestic Prince**	1:55⅗	Bill Hartack	Johnny Longden	Arts and Letters	Jay Ray
1970	**Personality**	1:56⅕	Eddie Belmonte	John Jacobs	My Dad George	Silent Screen
1971	**Canonero II**	1:54	Gustavo Avila	Juan Arias	Eastern Fleet	Jim French
1972	**Bee Bee Bee**	1:55⅗	Eldon Nelson	Red Carroll	No Le Hace	Key To The Mint

Year		Time	Jockey	Trainer	2nd place	3rd place
1973	**SECRETARIAT**	1:54⅖	Ron Turcotte	Lucien Laurin	Sham	Our Native
1974	**Little Current**	1:54⅗	Miguel Rivera	Lou Rondinello	Neapolitan Way	Cannonade
1975	**Master Derby**	1:56⅖	Darrel McHargue	Smiley Adams	Foolish Pleasure	Diabolo
1976	**Elocutionist**	1:55	John Lively	Paul Adwell	Play The Red	Bold Forbes
1977	**SEATTLE SLEW**	1:54⅖	Jean Cruguet	Billy Turner	Iron Constitution	Run Dusty Run
1978	**AFFIRMED**	1:54⅖	Steve Cauthen	Laz Barrera	Alydar	Believe It
1979	**Spectacular Bid**	1:54⅕	Ron Franklin	Bud Delp	Golden Act	Screen King
1980	**Codex**	1:54⅕	Angel Cordero Jr.	D. Wayne Lukas	Genuine Risk	Colonel Moran
1981	**Pleasant Colony**	1:54⅗	Jorge Velasquez	John Campo	Bold Ego	Paristo
1982	**Aloma's Ruler**	1:55⅖	Jack Kaenel	John Lenzini Jr.	Linkage	Cut Away
1983	**Deputed Testamony**	1:55⅖	Donald Miller Jr.	Bill Boniface	Desert Wine	High Honors
1984	**Gate Dancer**	1:53⅗	Angel Cordero Jr.	Jack Van Berg	Play On	Fight Over
1985	**Tank's Prospect**	1:53⅖	Pat Day	D. Wayne Lukas	Chief's Crown	Eternal Prince
1986	**Snow Chief**	1:54⅘	Alex Solis	Melvin Stute	Ferdinand	Broad Brush
1987	**Alysheba**	1:55⅘	Chris McCarron	Jack Van Berg	Bet Twice	Cryptoclearance
1988	**Risen Star**	1:56⅕	E. Delahoussaye	Louie Roussel III	Brian's Time	Winning Colors
1989	**Sunday Silence**	1:53⅘	Pat Valenzuela	Chas. Whittingham	Easy Goer	Rock Point
1990	**Summer Squall**	1:53⅗	Pat Day	Neil Howard	Unbridled	Mister Frisky
1991	**Hansel**	1:54	Jerry Bailey	Frank Brothers	Corporate Report	Mane Minister
1992	**Pine Bluff**	1:55⅗	Chris McCarron	Tom Bohannan	Alydeed	Casual Lies
1993	**Prairie Bayou**	1:56⅗	Mike Smith	Tom Bohannon	Cherokee Run	El Bakan
1994	**Tabasco Cat**	1:56⅖	Pat Day	D. Wayne Lukas	Go For Gin	Concern
1995	**Timber Country**	1:54⅖	Pat Day	D. Wayne Lukas	Oliver's Twist	Thunder Gulch

Belmont Stakes

For three-year-olds. Held three weeks after Preakness Stakes at Belmont Park in Elmont, N.Y. Inaugurated in 1867 at Jerome Park, moved to Morris Park in 1890 and Belmont Park in 1905.

Originally run at 1 mile and 5 furlongs (1867-89), then 1¼ miles (1890-1905), 1⅜ miles (1906-25), and the present 1½ miles since 1926.

Trainers with most wins: James Rowe, Sr. (8); Sam Hildreth (7); Sunny Jim Fitzsimmons (6); Woody Stephens (5); Max Hirsch and Robert W. Walden (4); Elliott Burch, Lucien Laurin, F. McCabe and D. McDaniel (3).

Jockeys with most wins: Eddie Arcaro and Jim McLaughlin (6); Earl Sande and Bill Shoemaker (5); Braulio Baeza, Laffit Pincay, Jr and James Stout (3).

Winning fillies: Ruthless (1867) and Tanya (1905).

Year		Time	Jockey	Trainer	2nd place	3rd place
1867	**Ruthless**	3:05	J. Gilpatrick	A.J. Minor	DeCourcey	Rivoli
1868	**General Duke**	3:02	Bobby Swim	A. Thompson	Northumberland	Fanny Ludlow
1869	**Fenian**	3:04¼	C. Miller	J. Pincus	Glenelg	Invercauld
1870	**Kingfisher**	2:59½	W. Dick	R. Colston	Foster	Midday
1871	**Harry Bassett**	2:56	W. Miller	D. McDaniel	Stockwood	By the Sea
1872	**Joe Daniels**	2:58¼	James Roe	D. McDaniel	Meteor	Shylock
1873	**Springbok**	3:01¾	James Roe	D. McDaniel	Count d'Orsay	Strachino
1874	**Saxon**	2:39½	G. Barbee	W. Prior	Grinstead	Aaron Pennington
1875	**Calvin**	2:42¼	Bobby Swim	A. Williams	Aristides	Milner
1876	**Algerine**	2:40½	Billy Donohue	Major Doswell	Fiddlesticks	Barricade
1877	**Cloverbrook**	2:46	C. Holloway	J. Walden	Loiterer	Baden-Baden
1878	**Duke of Magenta**	2:43½	L. Hughes	R.W. Walden	Bramble	Sparta
1879	**Spendthrift**	2:42¾	George Evans	T. Puryear	Monitor	Jericho
1880	**Grenada**	2:47	L. Hughes	R.W. Walden	Ferncliffe	Turenne
1881	**Saunterer**	2:47	T. Costello	R.W. Walden	Eole	Baltic
1882	**Forester**	2:43	Jim McLaughlin	L. Stuart	Babcock	Wyoming
1883	**George Kinney**	2:42½	Jim McLaughlin	James Rowe Sr.	Trombone	Renegade
1884	**Panique**	2:42	Jim McLaughlin	James Rowe Sr.	Knight of Ellerslie	Himalaya
1885	**Tyrant**	2:43	Paul Duffy	W. Claypool	St. Augustine	Tecumseh
1886	**Inspector B**	2:41	Jim McLaughlin	F. McCabe	The Bard	Linden
1887	**Hanover**	2:43½	Jim McLaughlin	F. McCabe	Oneko	(2-horse race)
1888	**Sir Dixon**	2:40¼	Jim McLaughlin	F. McCabe	Prince Royal	(2-horse race)
1889	**Eric**	2:47¼	W. Hayward	J. Huggins	Diablo	Zephyrus
1890	**Burlington**	2:07¾	Pike Barnes	A. Cooper	Devotee	Padishah
1891	**Foxford**	2:08¾	Ed Garrison	M. Donavan	Montana	Laurestan
1892	**Patron**	2:12	W. Hayward	L. Stuart	Shellbark	(2-horse race)
1893	**Commanche**	1:53¼	Willie Simms	G. Hannon	Dr. Rice	Rainbow
1894	**Henry of Navarre**	1:56½	Willie Simms	B. McClelland	Prig	Assignee
1895	**Belmar**	2:11½	Fred Taral	E. Feakes	Counter Tenor	Nanki Poo
1896	**Hastings**	2:24½	H. Griffin	J.J. Hyland	Handspring	Hamilton II
1897	**Scottish Chieftain**	2:23¼	J. Scherrer	M. Byrnes	On Deck	Octagon
1898	**Bowling Brook**	2:32	F. Littlefield	R.W. Walden	Previous	Hamburg
1899	**Jean Beraud**	2:23	R. Clawson	Sam Hildreth	Half Time	Glengar

Belmont Stakes (Cont.)

Year		Time	Jockey	Trainer	2nd place	3rd place
1900	**Ildrim**	2:21¼	Nash Turner	H.E. Leigh	Petruchio	Missionary
1901	**Commando**	2:21	H. Spencer	James Rowe Sr.	The Parader	All Green
1902	**Masterman**	2:22⅗	John Bullman	J.J. Hyland	Renald	King Hanover
1903	**Africander**	2:21¾	John Bullman	R. Miller	Whorler	Red Knight
1904	**Delhi**	2:06⅗	George Odom	James Rowe Sr.	Graziallo	Rapid Water
1905	**Tanya**	2:08	E. Hildebrand	J.W. Rogers	Blandy	Hot Shot
1906	**Burgomaster**	2:20	Lucien Lyne	J.W. Rogers	The Quail	Accountant
1907	**Peter Pan**	N/A	G. Mountain	James Rowe Sr.	Superman	Frank Gill
1908	**Colin**	N/A	Joe Notter	James Rowe Sr.	Fair Play	King James
1909	**Joe Madden**	2:21⅗	E. Dugan	Sam Hildreth	Wise Mason	Donald MacDonald
1910	**Sweep**	2:22	James Butwell	James Rowe Sr.	Duke of Ormonde	(2-horse race)
1911-12	Not held					
1913	**Prince Eugene**	2:18	Roscoe Troxler	James Rowe Sr.	Rock View	Flying Fairy
1914	**Luke McLuke**	2:20	Merritt Buxton	J.F. Schorr	Gainer	Charlestonian
1915	**The Finn**	2:18⅖	George Byrne	E.W. Heffner	Half Rock	Pebbles
1916	**Friar Rock**	2:22	E. Haynes	Sam Hildreth	Spur	Churchill
1917	**Hourless**	2:17⅘	James Butwell	Sam Hildreth	Skeptic	Wonderful
1918	**Johren**	2:20⅖	Frank Robinson	A. Simons	War Cloud	Cum Sah
1919	**SIR BARTON**	2:17⅖	John Loftus	H. Guy Bedwell	Sweep On	Natural Bridge
1920	**Man o' War**	2:14⅕	Clarence Kummer	L. Feustel	Donnacona	(2-horse race)
1921	**Grey Lag**	2:16⅘	Earl Sande	Sam Hildreth	Sporting Blood	Leonardo II
1922	**Pillory**	2:18⅘	C.H. Miller	T.J. Healey	Snob II	Hea
1923	**Zev**	2:19	Earl Sande	Sam Hildreth	Chickvale	Rialto
1924	**Mad Play**	2:18⅘	Earl Sande	Sam Hildreth	Mr. Mutt	Modest
1925	**American Flag**	2:16⅘	Albert Johnson	G.R. Tompkins	Dangerous	Swope
1926	**Crusader**	2:32⅕	Albert Johnson	George Conway	Espino	Haste
1927	**Chance Shot**	2:32⅖	Earl Sande	Pete Coyne	Bois de Rose	Flambino
1928	**Vito**	2:33⅕	Clarence Kummer	Max Hirsch	Genie	Diavolo
1929	**Blue Larkspur**	2:32⅘	Mack Garner	C. Hastings	African	Jack High
1930	**GALLANT FOX**	2:31⅗	Earl Sande	Jim Fitzsimmons	Whichone	Questionnaire
1931	**Twenty Grand**	2:29⅗	Charley Kurtsinger	James Rowe Jr.	Sun Meadow	Jamestown
1932	**Faireno**	2:32⅘	Tom Malley	Jim Fitzsimmons	Osculator	Flag Pole
1933	**Hurryoff**	2:32⅗	Mack Garner	H. McDaniel	Nimbus	Union
1934	**Peace Chance**	2:29⅕	W.D. Wright	Pete Coyne	High Quest	Good Goods
1935	**OMAHA**	2:30⅗	Willie Saunders	Jim Fitzsimmons	Firethorn	Rosemont
1936	**Granville**	2:30	James Stout	Jim Fitzsimmons	Mr. Bones	Hollyrood
1937	**WAR ADMIRAL**	2:28⅗	Charley Kurtsinger	George Conway	Sceneshifter	Vamoose
1938	**Pasteurized**	2:29⅖	James Stout	George Odom	Dauber	Cravat
1939	**Johnstown**	2:29⅗	James Stout	Jim Fitzsimmons	Belay	Gilded Knight
1940	**Bimelech**	2:29⅗	Fred Smith	Bill Hurley	Your Chance	Andy K.
1941	**WHIRLAWAY**	2:31	Eddie Arcaro	Ben Jones	Robert Morris	Yankee Chance
1942	**Shut Out**	2:29⅕	Eddie Arcaro	John Gaver	Alsab	Lochinvar
1943	**COUNT FLEET**	2:28⅕	Johnny Longden	Don Cameron	Fairy Manhurst	Deseronto
1944	**Bounding Home**	2:32⅕	G.L. Smith	Matt Brady	Pensive	Bull Dandy
1945	**Pavot**	2:30⅕	Eddie Arcaro	Oscar White	Wildlife	Jeep
1946	**ASSAULT**	2:30⅘	Warren Mehrtens	Max Hirsch	Natchez	Cable
1947	**Phalanx**	2:29⅖	R. Donoso	Syl Veitch	Tide Rips	Tailspin
1948	**CITATION**	2:28⅕	Eddie Arcaro	Jimmy Jones	Better Self	Escadru
1949	**Capot**	2:30⅕	Ted Atkinson	John Gaver	Ponder	Palestinian
1950	**Middleground**	2:28⅗	William Boland	Max Hirsch	Lights Up	Mr. Trouble
1951	**Counterpoint**	2:29	David Gorman	Syl Veitch	Battlefield	Battle Morn
1952	**One Count**	2:30⅕	Eddie Arcaro	Oscar White	Blue Man	Armageddon
1953	**Native Dancer**	2:28⅗	Eric Guerin	Bill Winfrey	Jamie K.	Royal Bay Gem
1954	**High Gun**	2:30⅘	Eric Guerin	Max Hirsch	Fisherman	Limelight
1955	**Nashua**	2:29	Eddie Arcaro	Jim Fitzsimmons	Blazing Count	Portersville
1956	**Needles**	2:29⅘	David Erb	Hugh Fontaine	Career Boy	Fabius
1957	**Gallant Man**	2:26⅗	Bill Shoemaker	John Nerud	Inside Tract	Bold Ruler
1958	**Cavan**	2:30⅕	Pete Anderson	Tom Barry	Tim Tam	Flamingo
1959	**Sword Dancer**	2:28⅖	Bill Shoemaker	Elliott Burch	Bagdad	Royal Orbit
1960	**Celtic Ash**	2:29⅕	Bill Hartack	Tom Barry	Venetian Way	Disperse
1961	**Sherluck**	2:29⅕	Braulio Baeza	Harold Young	Globemaster	Guadalcanal
1962	**Jaipur**	2:28⅘	Bill Shoemaker	B. Mulholland	Admiral's Voyage	Crimson Satan
1963	**Chateaugay**	2:30⅕	Braulio Baeza	James Conway	Candy Spots	Choker
1964	**Quadrangle**	2:28⅖	Manuel Ycaza	Elliott Burch	Roman Brother	Northern Dancer
1965	**Hail to All**	2:28⅖	John Sellers	Eddie Yowell	Tom Rolfe	First Family
1966	**Amberoid**	2:29⅗	William Boland	Lucien Laurin	Buffle	Advocator

Wide World Photos

Jockey **Ron Turcotte** glances back at the field as **Secretariat** rounds the turn en route to a 31-length victory and the Triple Crown in the 1973 Belmont Stakes. The winning time of 2:24 is still a world record for a mile and a half on dirt.

Year		Time	Jockey	Trainer	2nd place	3rd place
1967	**Damascus**	2:28⅘	Bill Shoemaker	F.Y. Whiteley Jr.	Cool Reception	Gentleman James
1968	**Stage Door Johnny**	2:27⅕	Gus Gustines	John Gaver	Forward Pass	Call Me Prince
1969	**Arts and Letters**	2:28⅘	Braulio Baeza	Elliott Burch	Majestic Prince	Dike
1970	**High Echelon**	2:34	John Rotz	John Jacobs	Needles N Pens	Naskra
1971	**Pass Catcher**	2:30⅖	Walter Blum	Eddie Yowell	Jim French	Bold Reason
1972	**Riva Ridge**	2:28	Ron Turcotte	Lucien Laurin	Ruritania	Cloudy Dawn
1973	**SECRETARIAT**	2:24	Ron Turcotte	Lucien Laurin	Twice A Prince	My Gallant
1974	**Little Current**	2:29⅕	Miguel Rivera	Lou Rondinello	Jolly Johu	Cannonade
1975	**Avatar**	2:28⅕	Bill Shoemaker	Tommy Doyle	Foolish Pleasure	Master Derby
1976	**Bold Forbes**	2:29	Angel Cordero Jr.	Laz Barrera	McKenzie Bridge	Great Contractor
1977	**SEATTLE SLEW**	2:29⅗	Jean Cruguet	Billy Turner	Run Dusty Run	Sanhedrin
1978	**AFFIRMED**	2:26⅘	Steve Cauthen	Laz Barrera	Alydar	Darby Creek Road
1979	**Coastal**	2:28⅗	Ruben Hernandez	David Whiteley	Golden Act	Spectacular Bid
1980	**Temperence Hill**	2:29⅘	Eddie Maple	Joseph Cantey	Genuine Risk	Rockhill Native
1981	**Summing**	2:29	George Martens	Luis Barerra	Highland Blade	Pleasant Colony
1982	**Conquistador Cielo**	2:28⅕	Laffit Pincay Jr.	Woody Stephens	Gato Del Sol	Illuminate
1983	**Caveat**	2:27⅘	Laffit Pincay Jr.	Woody Stephens	Slew o' Gold	Barberstown
1984	**Swale**	2:27⅕	Laffit Pincay Jr.	Woody Stephens	Pine Circle	Morning Bob
1985	**Creme Fraiche**	2:27	Eddie Maple	Woody Stephens	Stephan's Odyssey	Chief's Crown
1986	**Danzig Connection**	2:29⅘	Chris McCarron	Woody Stephens	Johns Treasure	Ferdinand
1987	**Bet Twice**	2:28⅕	Craig Perret	Jimmy Croll	Cryptoclearance	Gulch
1988	**Risen Star**	2:26⅖	E. Delahoussaye	Louie Roussel III	Kingpost	Brian's Time
1989	**Easy Goer**	2:26	Pat Day	Shug McGaughey	Sunday Silence	Le Voyageur
1990	**Go And Go**	2:27⅕	Michael Kinane	Dermot Weld	Thirty Six Red	Baron de Vaux
1991	**Hansel**	2:28	Jerry Bailey	Frank Brothers	Strike the Gold	Mane Minister
1992	**A.P. Indy**	2:26	E. Delahoussaye	Neil Drysdale	My Memoirs	Pine Bluff
1993	**Colonial Affair**	2:29⅘	Julie Krone	Scotty Schulhofer	Kissin Kris	Wild Gale
1994	**Tabasco Cat**	2:26⅘	Pat Day	D. Wayne Lukas	Go For Gin	Strodes Creek
1995	**Thunder Gulch**	2:32	Gary Stevens	D. Wayne Lukas	Star Standard	Citadeed

Breeders' Cup Championship

(See Update chapter for 1995 results)

Inaugurated on Nov. 10, 1984, the Breeders' Cup Championship consists of seven races on one track on one day late in the year to determine Thoroughbred racing's principle champions.

The Breeders' Cup has been held at the following tracks (in alphabetical order): Aqueduct Racetrack (N.Y.) in 1985; Belmont Park (N.Y.) in 1990 and '95 (see Updates chapter); Churchill Downs (Ky.) in 1988, '91 and '94; Gulfstream Park (Fla.) in 1989 and '92; Hollywood Park (Calif.) in 1984 and '87; and Santa Anita Park (Calif.) in 1986 and '93.

Trainers with most wins: D. Wayne Lukas (12); Neil Drysdale and Shug McGaughey (5); Francois Boutin and Ron McAnally (3).

Jockeys with most wins: Pat Day (8); Eddie Delahoussaye and Laffit Pincay Jr. (7); Pat Valenzuela (6); Chris McCarron and Jose Santos (5); Angel Cordero (4); Jerry Bailey, Craig Perret, Randy Romero, Mike Smith and Gary Stevens (3).

Juvenile

Distances: one mile (1984-85, 87); 1$\frac{1}{16}$ miles (1986 and since 1988).

Year		Time	Jockey	Trainer	2nd place	3rd place
1984	**Chief's Crown**	1:36⅕	Don MacBeth	Roger Laurin	Tank's Prospect	Spend A Buck
1985	**Tasso**	1:36⅕	Laffit Pincay Jr.	Neil Drysdale	Storm Cat	Scat Dancer
1986	**Capote**	1:43⅘	Laffit Pincay Jr.	D. Wayne Lukas	Qualify	Alysheba
1987	**Success Express**	1:35⅕	Jose Santos	D. Wayne Lukas	Regal Classic	Tejano
1988	**Is It True**	1:46⅗	Laffit Pincay Jr.	D. Wayne Lukas	Easy Goer	Tagel
1989	**Rhythm**	1:43⅗	Craig Perret	Shug McGaughey	Grand Canyon	Slavic
1990	**Fly So Free**	1:43⅖	Jose Santos	Scotty Schulhofer	Take Me Out	Lost Mountain
1991	**Arazi**	1:44⅗	Pat Valenzuela	Francois Boutin	Bertrando	Snappy Landing
1992	**Gilded Time**	1:43⅖	Chris McCarron	Darrell Vienna	It'sali'lknownfact	River Special
1993	**Brocco**	1:42⅘	Gary Stevens	Randy Winick	Blumin Affair	Tabasco Cat
1994	**Timber Country**	1:44⅖	Pat Day	D. Wayne Lukas	Eltish	Tejano Run

Juvenile Fillies

Distances: one mile (1984-85, 87); 1$\frac{1}{16}$ miles (1986 and since 1988).

Year		Time	Jockey	Trainer	2nd place	3rd place
1984	**Outstandingly**	1:37⅘	Walter Guerra	Pancho Martin	Dusty Heart	Fine Spirit
1985	**Twilight Ridge**	1:35⅘	Jorge Velasquez	D. Wayne Lukas	Family Style	Steal A Kiss
1986	**Brave Raj**	1:43⅕	Pat Valenzuela	Melvin Stute	Tappiano	Saros Brig
1987	**Epitome**	1:36⅖	Pat Day	Phil Hauswald	Jeanne Jones	Dream Team
1988	**Open Mind**	1:46⅗	Angel Cordero Jr.	D. Wayne Lukas	Darby Shuffle	Lea Lucinda
1989	**Go for Wand**	1:44⅕	Randy Romero	Wm. Badgett, Jr.	Sweet Roberta	Stella Madrid
1990	**Meadow Star**	1:44	Jose Santos	LeRoy Jolley	Private Treasure	Dance Smartly
1991	**Pleasant Stage**	1:46⅖	Eddie Delahoussaye	Chris Speckert	La Spia	Cadillac Women
1992	**Liza**	1:42⅘	Pat Valenzuela	Alex Hassingfer	Educated Risk	Boots 'n Jackie
1993	**Phone Chatter**	1:43	Laffit Pincay Jr.	Richard Mandella	Sardula	Heavenly Prize
1994	**Flanders**	1:45⅕	Pat Day	D. Wayne Lukas	Serena's Song	Stormy Blues

Note: In 1984, winner Fran's Valentine was disqualified for interference in the stretch and placed 10th.

Sprint

Distance: six furlongs (since 1984).

Year		Time	Jockey	Trainer	2nd place	3rd place
1984	**Eillo**	1:10⅕	Craig Perret	Budd Lepman	Commemorate	Fighting Fit
1985	**Precisionist**	1:08⅖	Chris McCarron	L.R. Fenstermaker	Smile	Mt. Livermore
1986	**Smile**	1:08⅖	Jacinto Vasquez	Scotty Schulhofer	Pine Tree Lane	Bedside Promise
1987	**Very Subtle**	1:08⅘	Pat Valenzuela	Melvin Stute	Groovy	Exclusive Enough
1988	**Gulch**	1:10⅖	Angel Cordero Jr.	D. Wayne Lukas	Play The King	Afleet
1989	**Dancing Spree**	1:09	Angel Cordero Jr.	Shug McGaughey	Safely Kept	Dispersal
1990	**Safely Kept**	1:09⅗	Craig Perret	Alan Goldberg	Dayjur	Black Tie Affair
1991	**Sheikh Albadou**	1:09⅕	Pat Eddery	Alexander Scott	Pleasant Tap	Robyn Dancer
1992	**Thirty Slews**	1:08⅕	Eddie Delahoussaye	Bob Baffert	Meafara	Rubiano
1993	**Cardmania**	1:08⅗	Eddie Delahoussaye	Derek Meredith	Meafara	Gilded Time
1994	**Cherokee Run**	1:09⅖	Mike Smith	Frank Alexander	Soviet Problem	Cardmania

Mile

Year		Time	Jockey	Trainer	2nd place	3rd place
1984	**Royal Heroine**	1:32⅗	Fernando Toro	John Gosden	Star Choice	Cozzene
1985	**Cozzene**	1:35	Walter Guerra	Jan Nerud	Al Mamoon	Shadeed
1986	**Last Tycoon**	1:35⅕	Yves St.-Martin	Robert Collet	Palace Music	Fred Astaire
1987	**Miesque**	1:32⅘	Freddie Head	Francois Boutin	Show Dancer	Sonic Lady
1988	**Miesque**	1:38⅗	Freddie Head	Francois Boutin	Steinlen	Simply Majestic
1989	**Steinlen**	1:37⅕	Jose Santos	D. Wayne Lukas	Sabona	Most Welcome
1990	**Royal Academy**	1:35⅕	Lester Piggott	M.V. O'Brien	Itsallgreektome	Priolo
1991	**Opening Verse**	1:37⅖	Pat Valenzuela	Dick Lundy	Val des Bois	Star of Cozzene
1992	**Lure**	1:32⅘	Mike Smith	Shug McGaughey	Paradise Creek	Brief Truce
1993	**Lure**	1:33⅖	Mike Smith	Shug McGaughey	Ski Paradise	Fourstars Allstar
1994	**Barathea**	1:34⅖	Frankie Dettori	Luca Cumani	Johann Quatz	Unfinished Symph

Note: In 1985, 2nd place finisher Palace Music was disqualified for interference and placed 9th.

Distaff

Distances: 1¼ miles (1984-87); 1⅛ miles (since 1988).

Year		Time	Jockey	Trainer	2nd place	3rd place
1984	**Princess Rooney**	2:02⅖	Eddie Delahoussaye	Neil Drysdale	Life's Magic	Adored
1985	**Life's Magic**	2:02	Angel Cordero Jr.	D. Wayne Lukas	Lady's Secret	DontstopThemusic
1986	**Lady's Secret**	2:01⅕	Pat Day	D. Wayne Lukas	Fran's Valentine	Outstandingly
1987	**Sacahuista**	2:02⅘	Randy Romero	D. Wayne Lukas	Clabber Girl	Oueee Bebe
1988	**Personal Ensign**	1:52	Randy Romero	Shug McGaughey	Winning Colors	Goodbye Halo
1989	**Bayakoa**	1:47⅖	Laffit Pincay Jr.	Ron McAnally	Gorgeous	Open Mind
1990	**Bayakoa**	1:49⅕	Laffit Pincay Jr.	Ron McAnally	Colonial Waters	Valay Maid
1991	**Dance Smartly**	1:50⅘	Pat Day	Jim Day	Versailles Treaty	Brought to Mind
1992	**Paseana**	1:48	Chris McCarron	Ron McAnally	Versailles Treaty	Magical Maiden
1993	**Hollywood Wildcat**	1:48⅕	Eddie Delahoussaye	Neil Drysdale	Paseana	Re Toss
1994	**One Dreamer**	1:50⅗	Gary Stevens	Thomas Proctor	Heavenly Prize	Miss Dominique

Turf

Distance: 1½ miles (since 1984).

Year		Time	Jockey	Trainer	2nd place	3rd place
1984	**Lashkari**	2:25⅕	Yves St.-Martin	de Royer-Dupre	All Along	Raami
1985	**Pebbles**	2:27	Pat Eddery	Clive Brittain	Strawberry Road II	Mourjane
1986	**Manila**	2:25⅖	Jose Santos	Leroy Jolley	Theatrical	Estrapade
1987	**Theatrical**	2:24⅖	Pat Day	Bill Mott	Trempolino	Village Star II
1988	**Gt. Communicator**	2:35⅕	Ray Sibille	Thad Ackel	Sunshine Forever	Indian Skimmer
1989	**Prized**	2:28	Eddie Delahoussaye	Neil Drysdale	Sierra Roberta	Star Lift
1990	**In The Wings**	2:29⅗	Gary Stevens	Andre Fabre	With Approval	El Senor
1991	**Miss Alleged**	2:30⅘	Eric Legrix	Pascal Bary	Itsallgreektome	Quest for Fame
1992	**Fraise**	2:24	Pat Valenzuela	Bill Mott	Sky Classic	Quest for Fame
1993	**Kotashaan**	2:25	Kent Desormeaux	Richard Mandella	Bien Bien	Luazur
1994	**Tikkanen**	2:26⅖	Mike Smith	Jonathan Pease	Hatoof	Paradise Creek

Classic

Distance: 1¼ miles (since 1984).

Year		Time	Jockey	Trainer	2nd place	3rd place
1984	**Wild Again**	2:03⅖	Pat Day	Vincent Timphony	Slew o' Gold	Gate Dancer
1985	**Proud Truth**	2:00⅘	Jorge Velasquez	John Veitch	Gate Dancer	Turkoman
1986	**Skywalker**	2:00⅖	Laffit Pincay Jr.	M. Whittingham	Turkoman	Precisionist
1987	**Ferdinand**	2:01⅖	Bill Shoemaker	C. Whittingham	Alysheba	Judge Angelucci
1988	**Alysheba**	2:04⅘	Chris McCarron	Jack Van Berg	Seeking the Gold	Waquoit
1989	**Sunday Silence**	2:00⅕	Chris McCarron	C. Whittingham	Easy Goer	Blushing John
1990	**Unbridled**	2:02⅕	Pat Day	Carl Nafzger	Ibn Bey	Thirty Six Red
1991	**Black Tie Affair**	2:02⅘	Jerry Bailey	Ernie Poulos	Twilight Agenda	Unbridled
1992	**A.P. Indy**	2:00⅕	Eddie Delahoussaye	Neil Drysdale	Pleasant Tap	Jolypha
1993	**Arcangues**	2:00⅘	Jerry Bailey	Andre Fabre	Bertrando	Kissin Kris
1994	**Concern**	2:02⅖	Jerry Bailey	Richard Small	Tabasco Cat	Dramatic Gold

Note: In 1984, 2nd place finisher Gate Dancer was disqualified for interference and placed 3rd.

Breeders' Cup Leaders

The all-time money-winning horses and race winning jockeys in the history of the Breeders' Cup through 1994.

Top 10 Horses

		Sts	1-2-3	Earnings
1	Alysheba	3	1-1-1	$2,133,000
2	Unbridled	2	1-0-1	1,710,000
3	Black Tie Affair (IRE)	3	1-0-1	1,668,000
4	A.P. Indy	1	1-0-0	1,560,000
	Arcangues	1	1-0-0	1,560,000
	Concern	1	1-0-0	1,560,000
7	Ferdinand	1	1-0-0	1,350,000
	Proud Truth	1	1-0-0	1,350,000
	Skywalker	2	1-0-0	1,350,000
	Sunday Silence	1	1-0-0	1,350,000
	Theatrical (IRE)	3	1-1-0	1,350,000
	Wild Again	1	1-0-0	1,350,000

Top 10 Jockeys

		Sts	1-2-3	Earnings
1	Pat Day	59	8-9-6	$11,631,000
2	Chris McCarron	60	5-11-5	9,002,000
3	Eddie Delahoussaye	54	7-3-5	7,479,000
4	Laffit Pincay Jr	60	7-4-9	6,811,000
5	Angel Cordero Jr	48	4-7-7	6,020,000
6	Gary Stevens	44	3-7-5	5,613,000
7	Jerry Bailey	27	3-3-1	5,611,000
8	Jose Santos	37	5-1-4	4,415,000
9	Pat Valenzuela	32	6-0-1	4,202,000
10	Pat Edderly	27	2-3-3	3,570,000

Top 10 Trainers

		Sts	1-2-3	Earnings
1	D. Wayne Lukas	87	12-13-8	$10,844,000
2	Shug McGaughey	33	5-7-1	5,183,000
3	Neil Drysdale	14	5-2-0	4,580,000
4	Andre Fabre	21	2-3-3	4,504,000
5	Charlie Whittingham	23	2-2-3	4,298,000
6	Jack Van Berg	14	1-3-3	3,600,000
7	Bill Mott	16	2-3-1	3,002,000
8	Bobby Frankel	23	0-4-3	2,463,000
9	Scotty Schulhofer	19	2-2-3	2,366,000
10	Leroy Jolley	16	2-1-0	2,145,000

Annual Money Leaders
Horses

Annual money-leading horses since 1910, according to *The American Racing Manual*.
Multiple leaders: Round Table, Buckpasser and Alysheba (2).

Year		Age	Sts	1st	Earnings	Year		Age	Sts	1st	Earnings
1910	Novelty	2	16	11	$ 72,630	1953	Native Dancer	3	10	9	$513,425
1911	Worth	2	13	10	16,645	1954	Determine	3	15	10	328,700
1912	Star Charter	4	17	6	14,655	1955	Nashua	3	12	10	752,550
1913	Old Rosebud	2	14	12	19,057	1956	Needles	3	8	4	440,850
1914	Roamer	3	16	12	29,105	1957	Round Table	3	22	15	600,383
1915	Borrow	7	9	4	20,195	1958	Round Table	4	20	14	662,780
1916	Campfire	2	9	6	49,735	1959	Sword Dancer	3	13	8	537,004
1917	Sun Briar	2	9	5	59,505						
1918	Eternal	2	8	6	56,173	1960	Bally Ache	3	15	10	445,045
1919	Sir Barton	3	13	8	88,250	1961	Carry Back	3	16	9	565,349
						1962	Never Bend	2	10	7	402,969
1920	Man o' War	3	11	11	166,140	1963	Candy Spots	3	12	7	604,481
1921	Morvich	2	11	11	115,234	1964	Gun Bow	4	16	8	580,100
1922	Pillory	3	7	4	95,654	1965	Buckpasser	2	11	9	568,096
1923	Zev	3	14	12	272,008	1966	Buckpasser	3	14	13	669,078
1924	Sarzen	3	12	8	95,640	1967	Damascus	3	16	12	817,941
1925	Pompey	2	10	7	121,630	1968	Forward Pass	3	13	7	546,674
1926	Crusader	3	15	9	166,033	1969	Arts and Letters	3	14	8	555,604
1927	Anita Peabody	2	7	6	111,905						
1928	High Strung	2	6	5	153,590	1970	Personality	3	18	8	444,049
1929	Blue Larkspur	3	6	4	153,450	1971	Riva Ridge	2	9	7	503,263
						1972	Droll Role	4	19	7	471,633
1930	Gallant Fox	3	10	9	308,275	1973	Secretariat	3	12	9	860,404
1931	Gallant Flight	2	7	7	219,000	1974	Chris Evert	3	8	5	551,063
1932	Gusto	3	16	4	145,940	1975	Foolish Pleasure	3	11	5	716,278
1933	Singing Wood	2	9	3	88,050	1976	Forego	6	8	6	401,701
1934	Cavalcade	3	7	6	111,235	1977	Seattle Slew	3	7	6	641,370
1935	Omaha	3	9	6	142,255	1978	Affirmed	3	11	8	901,541
1936	Granville	3	11	7	110,295	1979	Spectacular Bid	3	12	10	1,279,334
1937	Seabiscuit	4	15	11	168,580						
1938	Stagehand	3	15	8	189,710	1980	Temperence Hill	3	17	8	1,130,452
1939	Challedon	3	15	9	184,535	1981	John Henry	6	10	8	1,798,030
						1982	Perrault (GB)	5	8	4	1,197,400
1940	Bimelech	3	7	4	110,005	1983	All Along (FRA)	4	7	4	2,138,963
1941	Whirlaway	3	20	13	272,386	1984	Slew o' Gold	4	6	5	2,627,944
1942	Shut Out	3	12	8	238,872	1985	Spend A Buck	3	7	5	3,552,704
1943	Count Fleet	3	6	6	174,055	1986	Snow Chief	3	9	6	1,875,200
1944	Pavot	2	8	8	179,040	1987	Alysheba	3	10	3	2,511,156
1945	Busher	3	13	10	273,735	1988	Alysheba	4	9	7	3,808,600
1946	Assault	3	15	8	424,195	1989	Sunday Silence	3	9	7	4,578,454
1947	Armed	6	17	11	376,325						
1948	Citation	3	20	19	709,470	1990	Unbridled	3	11	4	3,718,149
1949	Ponder	3	21	9	321,825	1991	Dance Smartly	3	8	8	2,876,821
						1992	A.P. Indy	3	7	5	2,622,560
1950	Noor	5	12	7	346,940	1993	Kotashaan (FRA)	5	10	6	2,619,014
1951	Counterpoint	3	15	7	250,525	1994	Paradise Creek	5	11	8	2,610,187
1952	Crafty Admiral	4	16	9	277,225						

Jockeys

Annual money-leading jockeys since 1910, according to *The American Racing Manual*.
Multiple leaders: Bill Shoemaker (10); Laffit Pincay Jr. (7); Eddie Arcaro (6); Braulio Baeza (5); Chris McCarron and Jose Santos (4); Angel Cordero Jr. and Earl Sande (3); Ted Atkinson, Laverne Fator, Mack Garner, Bill Hartack, Charles Kurtsinger, Johnny Longden, Mike Smith, Sonny Workman and Wayne Wright (2).

Year		Mts	Wins	Earnings	Year		Mts	Wins	Earnings
1910	Carroll Shilling	506	172	$176,030	1924	Ivan Parke	844	205	$290,395
1911	Ted Koerner	813	162	88,308	1925	Laverne Fator	315	81	305,775
1912	Jimmy Butwell	684	144	79,843	1926	Laverne Fator	511	143	361,435
1913	Merritt Buxton	887	146	82,552	1927	Earl Sande	179	49	277,877
1914	J. McCahey	824	155	121,845	1928	Linus McAtee	235	55	301,295
1915	Mack Garner	775	151	96,628	1929	Mack Garner	274	57	314,975
1916	John McTaggart	832	150	155,055					
1917	Frank Robinson	731	147	148,057	1930	Sonny Workman	571	152	420,438
1918	Lucien Luke	756	178	201,864	1931	Charley Kurtsinger	519	93	392,095
1919	John Loftus	177	65	252,707	1932	Sonny Workman	378	87	385,070
					1933	Robert Jones	471	63	226,285
1920	Clarence Kummer	353	87	292,376	1934	Wayne Wright	919	174	287,185
1921	Earl Sande	340	112	263,043	1935	Silvio Coucci	749	141	319,760
1922	Albert Johnson	297	43	345,054	1936	Wayne Wright	670	100	264,000
1923	Earl Sande	430	122	569,394	1937	Charley Kurtsinger	765	120	384,202

Year		Mts	Wins	Earnings	Year		Mts	Wins	Earnings
1938	Nick Wall	658	97	$ 385,161	1967	Braulio Baeza	1064	256	3,088,888
1939	Basil James	904	191	353,333	1968	Braulio Baeza	1089	201	2,835,108
					1969	Jorge Velasquez	1442	258	2,542,315
1940	Eddie Arcaro	783	132	343,661					
1941	Don Meade	1164	210	398,627	1970	Laffit Pincay Jr.	1328	269	2,626,526
1942	Eddie Arcaro	687	123	481,949	1971	Laffit Pincay Jr.	1627	380	3,784,377
1943	Johnny Longden	871	173	573,276	1972	Laffit Pincay Jr.	1388	289	3,225,827
1944	Ted Atkinson	1539	287	899,101	1973	Laffit Pincay Jr.	1444	350	4,093,492
1945	Johnny Longden	778	180	981,977	1974	Laffit PincayJr.	1278	341	4,251,060
1946	Ted Atkinson	1377	233	1,036,825	1975	Braulio Baeza	1190	196	3,674,398
1947	Douglas Dodson	646	141	1,429,949	1976	Angel Cordero Jr.	1534	274	4,709,500
1948	Eddie Arcaro	726	188	1,686,230	1977	Steve Cauthen	2075	487	6,151,750
1949	Steve Brooks	906	209	1,316,817	1978	Darrel McHargue	1762	375	6,188,353
					1979	Laffit Pincay Jr.	1708	420	8,183,535
1950	Eddie Arcaro	888	195	1,410,160					
1951	Bill Shoemaker	1161	257	1,329,890	1980	Chris McCarron	1964	405	7,666,100
1952	Eddie Arcaro	807	188	1,859,591	1981	Chris McCarron	1494	326	8,397,604
1953	Bill Shoemaker	1683	485	1,784,187	1982	Angel Cordero Jr.	1838	397	9,702,520
1954	Bill Shoemaker	1251	380	1,876,760	1983	Angel Cordero Jr.	1792	362	10,116,807
1955	Eddie Arcaro	820	158	1,864,796	1984	Chris McCarron	1565	356	12,038,213
1956	Bill Hartack	1387	347	2,343,955	1985	Laffit Pincay Jr.	1409	289	13,415,049
1957	Bill Hartack	1238	341	3,060,501	1986	Jose Santos	1636	329	11,329,297
1958	Bill Shoemaker	1133	300	2,961,693	1987	Jose Santos	1639	305	12,407,355
1959	Bill Shoemaker	1285	347	2,843,133	1988	Jose Santos	1867	370	14,877,298
					1989	Jose Santos	1459	285	13,847,003
1960	Bill Shoemaker	1227	274	2,123,961					
1961	Bill Shoemaker	1256	304	2,690,819	1990	Gary Stevens	1504	283	13,881,198
1962	Bill Shoemaker	1126	311	2,916,844	1991	Chris McCarron	1440	265	14,456,073
1963	Bill Shoemaker	1203	271	2,526,925	1992	Kent Desormeaux	1568	361	14,193,006
1964	Bill Shoemaker	1056	246	2,649,553	1993	Mike Smith	1510	343	14,024,815
1965	Braulio Baeza	1245	270	2,582,702	1994	Mike Smith	1484	317	15,979,820
1966	Braulio Baeza	1341	298	2,951,022					

Annual Money-Leading Female Jockeys

Annual money-leading female jockeys since 1979, according to *The American Racing Manual*.
Multiple leaders: Julie Krone (10); Patty Cooksey and Karen Rogers (2).

Year		Mts	Wins	Earnings	Year		Mts	Wins	Earnings
1979	Karen Rogers	550	77	$ 590,469	1987	Julie Krone	1698	324	$4,522,191
1980	Karen Rogers	622	65	894,878	1988	Julie Krone	1958	363	7,770,314
1981	Patty Cooksey	1469	197	895,951	1989	Julie Krone	1673	368	8,031,445
1982	Mary Russ	952	84	1,319,363	1990	Julie Krone	649	144	2,846,237
1983	Julie Krone	1024	151	1,095,622	1991	Julie Krone	1414	230	7,748,077
1984	Patty Cooksey	955	116	803,189	1992	Julie Krone	1462	282	9,220,824
1985	Abby Fuller	883	145	1,452,576	1993	Julie Krone	1012	212	6,415,462
1986	Julie Krone	1442	199	2,357,136	1994	Julie Krone	571	101	3,968,337

Trainers

Annual money-leading trainers since 1908, according to *The American Racing Manual*.
Multiple leaders: D. Wayne Lukas (11); Sam Hildreth (9), Charlie Whittingham (7); Sunny Jim Fitzsimmons and Jimmy Jones (5); Laz Barrera, Ben Jones and Willie Molter (4); Hirsch Jacobs, Eddie Neloy and James Rowe Sr. (3); H. Guy Bedwell, Jack Gaver, John Schorr, Humming Bob Smith, Silent Tom Smith, and Mesh Tenney (2).

Year		Wins	Earnings	Year		Wins	Earnings
1908	James Rowe Sr.	50	$284,335	1925	G.R. Tompkins	30	$199,245
1909	Sam Hildreth	73	123,942	1926	Scott Harlan	21	205,681
1910	Sam Hildreth	84	148,010	1927	W.H. Bringloe	63	216,563
1911	Sam Hildreth	67	49,418	1928	John Schorr	65	258,425
1912	John Schorr	63	58,110	1929	James Rowe Jr.	25	314,881
1913	James Rowe Sr.	18	45,936	1930	Sunny Jim Fitzsimmons	47	397,355
1914	R.C. Benson	45	59,315	1931	Big Jim Healy	33	297,300
1915	James Rowe Sr.	19	75,596	1932	Sunny Jim Fitzsimmons	68	266,650
1916	Sam Hildreth	39	70,950	1933	Humming Bob Smith	53	135,720
1917	Sam Hildreth	23	61,698	1934	Humming Bob Smith	43	249,938
1918	H. Guy Bedwell	53	80,296	1935	Bud Stotler	87	303,005
1919	H. Guy Bedwell	63	208,728	1936	Sunny Jim Fitzsimmons	42	193,415
1920	Louis Feustal	22	186,087	1937	Robert McGarvey	46	209,925
1921	Sam Hildreth	85	262,768	1938	Earl Sande	15	226,495
1922	Sam Hildreth	74	247,014	1939	Sunny Jim Fitzsimmons	45	266,205
1923	Sam Hildreth	75	392,124	1940	Silent Tom Smith	14	269,200
1924	Sam Hildreth	77	255,608	1941	Ben Jones	70	475,318

Annual Money Leaders (Cont.)
Trainers

Year		Wins	Earnings	Year		Sts	Wins	Earnings
1942	Jack Gaver	48	$ 406,547	1970	Charlie Whittingham	551	82	$1,302,354
1943	Ben Jones	73	267,915	1971	Charlie Whittingham	393	77	1,737,115
1944	Ben Jones	60	601,660	1972	Charlie Whittingham	429	79	1,734,020
1945	Silent Tom Smith	52	510,655	1973	Charlie Whittingham	423	85	1,865,385
1946	Hirsch Jacobs	99	560,077	1974	Pancho Martin	846	166	2,408,419
1947	Jimmy Jones	85	1,334,805	1975	Charlie Whittingham	487	3	2,437,244
1948	Jimmy Jones	81	1,118,670	1976	Jack Van Berg	2362	496	2,976,196
1949	Jimmy Jones	76	978,587	1977	Laz Barrera	781	127	2,715,848
1950	Preston Burch	96	637,754	1978	Laz Barrera	592	100	3,307,164
1951	Jack Gaver	42	616,392	1979	Laz Barrera	492	98	3,608,517
1952	Ben Jones	29	662,137	1980	Laz Barrera	559	99	2,969,151
1953	Harry Trotsek	54	1,028,873	1981	Charlie Whittingham	376	74	3,993,302
1954	Willie Molter	136	1,107,860	1982	Charlie Whittingham	410	63	4,587,457
1955	Sunny Jim Fitzsimmons	66	1,270,055	1983	D. Wayne Lukas	595	78	4,267,261
1956	Willie Molter	142	1,227,402	1984	D. Wayne Lukas	805	131	5,835,921
1957	Jimmy Jones	70	1,150,910	1985	D. Wayne Lukas	1140	218	11,155,188
1958	Willie Molter	69	1,116,544	1986	D. Wayne Lukas	1510	259	12,345,180
1959	Willie Molter	71	847,290	1987	D. Wayne Lukas	1735	343	17,502,110
				1988	D. Wayne Lukas	1500	318	17,842,358
Year		Sts	Wins	Earnings	1989	D. Wayne Lukas	1398	305	16,103,998
1960	Hirsch Jacobs	—	97	$ 748,349	1990	D. Wayne Lukas	1396	267	14,508,871
1961	Jimmy Jones	—	62	759,856	1991	D. Wayne Lukas	1497	289	15,942,223
1962	Mesh Tenney	—	58	1,099,474	1992	D. Wayne Lukas	1349	230	9,806,436
1963	Mesh Tenney	192	40	860,703	1993	Bobby Frankel	345	79	8,933,252
1964	Bill Winfrey	287	61	1,350,534	1994	D. Wayne Lukas	693	147	9,247,457
1965	Hirsch Jacobs	610	91	1,331,628					
1966	Eddie Neloy	282	93	2,456,250					
1967	Eddie Neloy	262	72	1,776,089					
1968	Eddie Neloy	212	52	1,233,101					
1969	Elliott Burch	156	26	1,067,936					

Trainer **Jimmy Jones** (center) in the Kentucky Derby winner's circle with 1948 Triple Crown winner **Citation** and jockey **Eddie Arcaro**. All three led their divisions in money won that year.

All-Time Leaders

The all-time money-winning horses and race-winning jockeys of North America through 1994, according to *The American Racing Manual*. Records include all available information on races in foreign countries.

Top 35 Horses—Money Won

Note that horses who raced in 1994 are in **bold** type; and (f) indicates female.

		Sts	1st	2nd	3rd	Earnings
1	Alysheba	26	11	8	2	$6,679,242
2	John Henry	83	39	15	9	6,597,947
3	**Best Pal**	38	16	9	4	5,129,645
4	Sunday Silence	14	9	5	0	4,968,554
5	Easy Goer	20	14	5	1	4,837,770
6	Unbridled	24	8	6	6	4,489,475
7	Spend A Buck	15	10	3	2	4,220,689
8	Creme Fraiche	64	17	12	13	4,024,727
9	Ferdinand	29	8	9	6	3,777,978
10	**Devil His Due**	38	11	10	3	3,769,485
11	Slew o' Gold	21	12	5	1	3,533,534
12	Precisionist	46	20	10	4	3,485,396
13	Strike the Gold	31	6	8	5	3,457,026
14	**Paradise Creek**	25	14	7	1	3,386,925
15	Snow Chief	24	13	3	5	3,383,210
16	Cryptoclearance	44	12	10	7	3,376,327
17	Black Tie Affair	45	18	9	6	3,370,694
18	Bet Twice	26	10	6	4	3,308,599
19	Steinlen	45	20	10	7	3,300,100
20	Dance Smartly (f)	17	12	2	3	3,263,836
21	Sky Classic	29	15	6	1	3,240,398
22	**Bertrando**	22	9	6	2	3,185,510
23	Gulch	32	13	8	4	3,095,521
24	Lady's Secret (f)	45	25	9	3	3,021,425
25	All Along (f)	21	9	4	2	3,015,764
26	A.P. Indy	11	8	0	1	2,979,815
27	Theatrical	22	10	4	2	2,943,627
28	Hansel	14	7	2	3	2,936,586
29	**Paseana** (f)	30	16	7	1	2,930,403
30	**Sea Hero**	24	6	3	4	2,929,869
31	Great Communicator	56	14	10	7	2,922,615
32	Symboli Rudolf	16	13	1	1	2,909,593
33	Farma Way	23	6	5	1	2,897,176
34	With Approval	23	13	5	1	2,863,540
35	Marquetry	36	10	9	4	2,856,811

Top 35 Jockeys—Races Won

Note that jockeys active in 1994 are in **bold** type.

		Yrs	Wins	Earnings
1	Bill Shoemaker	42	8833	$123,375,524
2	**Laffit Pincay Jr.**	29	8213	183,910,301
3	Angel Cordero Jr.	31	7057	164,526,217
4	**Jorge Velasquez**	31	6682	123,252,413
5	**David Gall**	38	6611	20,837,406
6	**Larry Snyder**	35	6388	47,207,289
7	**Carl Gambardella**	39	6349	29,389,041
8	**Pat Day**	23	6308	149,339,825
9	**Sandy Hawley**	27	6205	81,863,406
10	**Chris McCarron**	19	6074	177,686,860
11	Johnny Longden	40	6032	24,665,800
12	**Earlie Fires**	30	5678	66,450,725
13	**Eddie Delahoussaye**	25	5375	138,120,927
14	**Jacinto Vasquez**	35	5153	78,464,935
15	Eddie Arcaro	31	4779	30,039,543
16	**Russell Baze**	21	4749	63,733,355
17	Don Brumfield	37	4573	43,567,861
18	Steve Brooks	34	4451	18,239,817
19	Walter Blum	22	4382	26,497,189
20	Bill Hartack	22	4272	26,466,758
21	**Eddie Maple**	27	4227	97,382,914
22	Avelino Gomez	34	4081	11,777,297
23	Hugo Dittfach	33	4000	13,506,052
24	**Craig Perret**	29	3946	84,805,894
25	**Philip Grove**	28	3907	15,720,989
26	**Ronald Ardoin**	22	3851	35,782,406
27	**Randy Romero**	21	3829	63,445,527
28	Ted Atkinson	22	3795	17,449,360
29	David Whited	36	3784	25,067,466
30	Ralph Neves	21	3772	13,786,239
31	Leroy Moyers	34	3770	21,491,585
32	Bobby Baird	39	3749	12,592,611
33	Ron Hansen	16	3693	42,635,184
34	**Daniel Weiler**	38	3692	12,216,012
35	**Steve Neff**	24	3685	15,522,684

Retired: Arcaro (1961), Atkinson (1959), Baird (1982), Blum (1975), Brooks (1975), Brumfield (1989), Cordero (1992), Dittfach (1989), Gomez (1980), Hartack (1974), Hansen (1993), Longden (1966), Moyers (1992), Neves (1964), Shoemaker (1990) and Whited (1993).

Horse of the Year (1936-70)

In 1971, the *Daily Racing Form*, the Thoroughbred Racing Associations, and the National Turf Writers Assn. joined forces to create the Eclipse Awards. Before then, however, the *Racing Form* (1936-70) and the TRA (1950-70) issued separate selections for Horse of the Year. Their picks differed only four times from 1950-70 and are so noted. Horses listed in CAPITAL letters are Triple Crown winners; (f) indicates female.

Multiple winners: Kelso (5); Challedon, Native Dancer and Whirlaway (2).

Year		Year		Year		Year	
1936	Granville	1946	ASSAULT	1955	Nashua	1964	Kelso
1937	WAR ADMIRAL	1947	Armed	1956	Swaps	1965	Roman Brother (DRF)
1938	Seabiscuit	1948	CITATION	1957	Bold Ruler (DRF)		Moccasin (TRA)
1939	Challedon	1949	Capot		Dedicate (TRA)	1966	Buckpasser
1940	Challedon	1950	Hill Prince	1958	Round Table	1967	Damascus
1941	WHIRLAWAY	1951	Counterpoint	1959	Sword Dancer	1968	Dr. Fager
1942	Whirlaway	1952	One Count (DRF)	1960	Kelso	1969	Arts and Letters
1943	COUNT FLEET		Native Dancer (TRA)	1961	Kelso	1970	Fort Marcy (DRF)
1944	Twilight Tear (f)	1953	Tom Fool	1962	Kelso		Personality (TRA)
1945	Busher (f)	1954	Native Dancer	1963	Kelso		

Eclipse Awards

The Eclipse Awards, honoring the Horse of the Year and other champions of the sport, are sponsored by the *Daily Racing Form*, the Thoroughbred Racing Associations and the National Turf Writers Assn.

The awards are named after the 18th century racehorse and sire, Eclipse, who began racing at age five and was unbeaten in 18 starts (eight wins were walkovers). As a stallion, Eclipse sired winners of 344 races, including three Epsom Derby champions.

Horses listed in CAPITAL letters won the Triple Crown that year. Age of horse in parentheses where necessary.

Multiple winners (horses): Forego (8); John Henry (7); Affirmed and Secretariat (5); Flatterer, Seattle Slew and Spectacular Bid (4); Ack Ack, Susan's Girl and Zaccio (3); All Along, Alysheba, Bayakoa, Black Tie Affair, Cafe Prince, Conquistador Cielo, Desert Vixen, Ferdinand, Flawlessly, Go for Wand, Holy Bull, Housebuster, Kotashaan, Lady's Secret, Life's Magic, Lonesome Glory, Miesque, Morley Street, Open Mind, Paseana, Riva Ridge, Slew o'Gold and Spend A Buck (2).

Multiple winners (people): Laffit Pincay Jr. (5); Laz Barrera, Pat Day, John Franks and D. Wayne Lukas (4); Steve Cauthen, Pat Day, Harbor View Farm, Fred W. Hooper, Nelson Bunker Hunt, Mr. & Mrs. Gene Klein, Dan Lasater, Ogden Phipps, Bill Shoemaker, Edward Taylor and Charlie Whittingham (3); Braulio Baeza, C.T. Chenery, Claiborne Farm, Angel Cordero Jr., Kent Desormeaux, John W. Galbreath, Chris McCarron, Paul Mellon and Mike Smith (2).

Horse of the Year

Year		Year		Year		Year	
1971	Ack Ack (5)	1977	SEATTLE SLEW (3)	1983	All Along (4)	1989	Sunday Silence (3)
1972	Secretariat (2)	1978	AFFIRMED (3)	1984	John Henry (9)	1990	Criminal Type (5)
1973	SECRETARIAT (3)	1979	Affirmed (4)	1985	Spend A Buck (3)	1991	Black Tie Affair (5)
1974	Forego (4)	1980	Spectacular Bid (4)	1986	Lady's Secret (4)	1992	A.P. Indy (3)
1975	Forego (5)	1981	John Henry (6)	1987	Ferdinand (4)	1993	Kotashaan (5)
1976	Forego (6)	1982	Conquistador Cielo (3)	1988	Alysheba (4)	1994	Holy Bull (3)

Older Male

Year		Year		Year		Year	
1971	Ack Ack (5)	1977	Forego (7)	1983	Bates Motel (4)	1989	Blushing John (4)
1972	Autobiography (4)	1978	Seattle Slew (4)	1984	Slew o' Gold (4)	1990	Criminal Type (5)
1973	Riva Ridge (4)	1979	Affirmed (4)	1985	Vanlandingham (4)	1991	Black Tie Affair (5)
1974	Forego (4)	1980	Spectacular Bid (4)	1986	Turkoman (4)	1992	Pleasant Tap (5)
1975	Forego (5)	1981	John Henry (6)	1987	Ferdinand (4)	1993	Bertrando (4)
1976	Forego (6)	1982	Lemhi Gold (4)	1988	Alysheba (4)	1994	The Wicked North (4)

Older Filly or Mare

Year		Year		Year		Year	
1971	Shuvee (5)	1977	Cascapedia (4)	1983	Amb. of Luck (4)	1989	Bayakoa (5)
1972	Typecast (6)	1978	Late Bloomer (4)	1984	Princess Rooney (4)	1990	Bayakoa (6)
1973	Susan's Girl (4)	1979	Waya (5)	1985	Life's Magic (4)	1991	Queena (5)
1974	Desert Vixen (4)	1980	Glorious Song (4)	1986	Lady's Secret (4)	1992	Paseana (5)
1975	Susan's Girl (6)	1981	Relaxing (5)	1987	North Sider (5)	1993	Paseana (6)
1976	Proud Delta (4)	1982	Track Robbery (6)	1988	Personal Ensign (4)	1994	Sky Beauty (4)

3-Year-Old Colt or Gelding

Year		Year		Year		Year	
1971	Canonero II	1977	SEATTLE SLEW	1983	Slew o' Gold	1989	Sunday Silence
1972	Key to the Mint	1978	AFFIRMED	1984	Swale	1990	Unbridled
1973	SECRETARIAT	1979	Spectacular Bid	1985	Spend A Buck	1991	Hansel
1974	Little Current	1980	Temperence Hill	1986	Snow Chief	1992	A.P. Indy
1975	Wajima	1981	Pleasant Colony	1987	Alysheba	1993	Prairie Bayou
1976	Bold Forbes	1982	Conquistador Cielo	1988	Risen Star	1994	Holy Bull

3-Year-Old Filly

Year		Year		Year		Year	
1971	Turkish Trousers	1977	Our Mims	1983	Heartlight No. One	1989	Open Mind
1972	Susan's Girl	1978	Tempest Queen	1984	Life's Magic	1990	Go for Wand
1973	Desert Vixen	1979	Davona Dale	1985	Mom's Command	1991	Dance Smartly
1974	Chris Evert	1980	Genuine Risk	1986	Tiffany Lass	1992	Saratoga Slew
1975	Ruffian	1981	Wayward Lass	1987	Sacahuista	1993	Hollywood Wildcat
1976	Revidere	1982	Christmas Past	1988	Winning Colors	1994	Heavenly Prize

2-Year-Old Colt or Gelding

Year		Year		Year		Year	
1971	Riva Ridge	1977	Affirmed	1983	Devil's Bag	1989	Rhythm
1972	Secretariat	1978	Spectacular Bid	1984	Chief's Crown	1990	Fly So Free
1973	Protagonist	1979	Rockhill Native	1985	Tasso	1991	Arazi
1974	Foolish Pleasure	1980	Lord Avie	1986	Capote	1992	Gilded Time
1975	Honest Pleasure	1981	Deputy Minister	1987	Forty Niner	1993	Dehere
1976	Seattle Slew	1982	Roving Boy	1988	Easy Goer	1994	Timber Country

2-Year-Old Filly

Year		Year		Year		Year	
1971	Numbered Account	1978	(tie) Candy Eclair	1983	Althea	1989	Go for Wand
1972	La Prevoyante		& It's in the Air	1984	Outstandingly	1990	Meadow Star
1973	Talking Picture	1979	Smart Angle	1985	Family Style	1991	Pleasant Stage
1974	Ruffian	1980	Heavenly Cause	1986	Brave Raj	1992	Eliza
1975	Dearly Precious	1981	Before Dawn	1987	Epitome	1993	Phone Chatter
1976	Sensational	1982	Landaluce	1988	Open Mind	1994	Flanders
1977	Lakeville Miss						

Champion Turf Horse

Year		Year		Year		Year	
1971	Run the Gantlet (3)	1973	SECRETARIAT (3)	1975	Snow Knight (4)	1977	Johnny D (3)
1972	Cougar II (6)	1974	Dahlia (4)	1976	Youth (3)	1978	Mac Diarmida (3)

Champion Male Turf Horse

Year		Year		Year		Year	
1979	Bowl Game (5)	1983	John Henry (8)	1987	Theatrical (5)	1991	Tight Spot (4)
1980	John Henry (5)	1984	John Henry (9)	1988	Sunshine Forever (3)	1992	Sky Classic (5)
1981	John Henry (6)	1985	Cozzene (4)	1989	Steinlen (6)	1993	Kotashaan (5)
1982	Perrault (5)	1986	Manila (3)	1990	Itsallgreektome (3)	1994	Paradise Creek (5)

Champion Female Turf Horse

Year		Year		Year		Year	
1979	Trillion (5)	1983	All Along (4)	1987	Miesque (3)	1991	Miss Alleged (4)
1980	Just A Game II (4)	1984	Royal Heroine (4)	1988	Miesque (4)	1992	Flawlessly (4)
1981	De La Rose (3)	1985	Pebbles (4)	1989	Brown Bess (7)	1993	Flawlessly (5)
1982	April Run (4)	1986	Estrapade (6)	1990	Laugh and Be Merry (5)	1994	Hatoof (5)

Sprinter

Year		Year		Year		Year	
1971	Ack Ack (5)	1977	What a Summer (4)	1983	Chinook Pass (4)	1989	Safely Kept (3)
1972	Chou Croute (4)	1978	(tie) Dr. Patches (4)	1984	Eillo (4)	1990	Housebuster (3)
1973	Shecky Greene (3)		& J.O. Tobin (4)	1985	Precisionist (4)	1991	Housebuster (4)
1974	Forego (4)	1979	Star de Naskra (4)	1986	Smile (4)	1992	Rubiano (5)
1975	Gallant Bob (3)	1980	Plugged Nickle (3)	1987	Groovy (4)	1993	Cardmania (7)
1976	My Juliet (4)	1981	Guilty Conscience (5)	1988	Gulch (4)	1994	Cherokee Run (4)
		1982	Gold Beauty (3)				

Steeplechase or Hurdle Horse

Year		Year		Year		Year	
1971	Shadow Brook (7)	1977	Cafe Prince (7)	1983	Flatterer (4)	1989	Highland Bud (4)
1972	Soothsayer (5)	1978	Cafe Prince (8)	1984	Flatterer (5)	1990	Morley Street (6)
1973	Athenian Idol (5)	1979	Martie's Anger (4)	1985	Flatterer (6)	1991	Morley Street (7)
1974	Gran Kan (8)	1980	Zaccio (4)	1986	Flatterer (7)	1992	Lonesome Glory (4)
1975	Life's Illusion (4)	1981	Zaccio (5)	1987	Inlander (6)	1993	Lonesome Glory (5)
1976	Straight and True (6)	1982	Zaccio (6)	1988	Jimmy Lorenzo (6)	1994	Warm Spell (6)

Outstanding Jockey

Year		Year		Year		Year	
1971	Laffit Pincay Jr.	1977	Steve Cauthen	1983	Angel Cordero Jr.	1989	Kent Desormeaux
1972	Braulio Baeza	1978	Darrel McHargue	1984	Pat Day	1990	Craig Perret
1973	Laffit Pincay Jr.	1979	Laffit Pincay Jr.	1985	Laffit Pincay Jr.	1991	Pat Day
1974	Laffit Pincay Jr.	1980	Chris McCarron	1986	Pat Day	1992	Kent Desormeaux
1975	Braulio Baeza	1981	Bill Shoemaker	1987	Pat Day	1993	Mike Smith
1976	Sandy Hawley	1982	Angel Cordero Jr.	1988	Jose Santos	1994	Mike Smith

Outstanding Apprentice Jockey

Year		Year		Year		Year	
1971	Gene St. Leon	1977	Steve Cauthen	1983	Declan Murphy	1989	Michael Luzzi
1972	Thomas Wallis	1978	Ron Franklin	1984	Wesley Ward	1990	Mark Johnston
1973	Steve Valdez	1979	Cash Asmussen	1985	Art Madrid Jr.	1991	Mickey Walls
1974	Chris McCarron	1980	Frank Lovato Jr.	1986	Allen Stacy	1992	Rosemary Homeister
1975	Jimmy Edwards	1981	Richard Migliore	1987	Kent Desormeaux	1993	Juan Umana
1976	George Martens	1982	Alberto Delgado	1988	Steve Capanas	1994	Dale Beckner

Eclipse Awards (Cont.)
Outstanding Trainer

Year		Year		Year		Year	
1971	Charlie Whittingham	1977	Laz Barrera	1983	Woody Stephens	1989	Charlie Whittingham
1972	Lucien Laurin	1978	Laz Barrera	1984	Jack Van Berg	1990	Carl Nafzger
1973	H. Allen Jerkens	1979	Laz Barrera	1985	D. Wayne Lukas	1991	Ron McAnally
1974	Sherill Ward	1980	Bud Delp	1986	D. Wayne Lukas	1992	Ron McAnally
1975	Steve DiMauro	1981	Ron McAnally	1987	D. Wayne Lukas	1993	Bobby Frankel
1976	Laz Barrera	1982	Charlie Whittingham	1988	Shug McGaughey	1994	D. Wayne Lukas

Outstanding Owner

Year		Year		Year		Year	
1971	Mr. & Mrs. E.E. Fogleson	1978	Harbor View Farm	1983	John Franks	1989	Ogden Phipps
1972-73	No award	1979	Harbor View Farm	1984	John Franks	1990	Frances Genter
1974	Dan Lasater	1980	Mr. & Mrs. Bertram Firestone	1985	Mr. & Mrs. Gene Klein	1991	Sam-Son Farms
1975	Dan Lasater	1981	Dotsam Stable	1986	Mr. & Mrs. Gene Klein	1992	Juddmonta Farms
1976	Dan Lasater	1982	Viola Sommer	1987	Mr. & Mrs. Gene Klein	1993	John Franks
1977	Maxwell Gluck			1988	Ogden Phipps	1994	John Franks

Outstanding Breeder

Year		Year		Year		Year	
1971	Paul Mellon	1977	Edward P. Taylor	1983	Edward P. Taylor	1989	North Ridge Farm
1972	C.T. Chenery	1978	Harbor View Farm	1984	Claiborne Farm	1990	Calumet Farm
1973	C.T. Chenery	1979	Claiborne Farm	1985	Nelson Bunker Hunt	1991	Mr. & Mrs. John Mabee
1974	John W. Galbreath	1980	Mrs. Henry Paxson	1986	Paul Mellon	1992	William S. Farish
1975	Fred W. Hooper	1981	Golden Chance Farm	1987	Nelson Bunker Hunt	1993	Allan Paulson
1976	Nelson Bunker Hunt	1982	Fred W. Hooper	1988	Ogden Phipps	1994	William T. Young

Outstanding Achievement

Year		Year	
1971	Charles Engelhard*	1972	Arthur B. Hancock Jr.*

*Awarded posthumously.

Man of the Year

Year		Year	
1972	John W. Galbreath	1974	William L. McKnight
1973	Edward P. Taylor	1975	John A. Morris

Award of Merit

Year		Year		Year		Year	
1976	Jack J. Dreyfus	1980	John D. Shapiro	1986	Herman Cohen	1990	Warner L. Jones
1977	Steve Cauthen	1981	Bill Shoemaker	1987	J.B. Faulconer	1991	Fred W. Hooper
1978	Dinny Phipps	1984	John Gaines	1988	John Forsythe	1992	Joe Hirsch
1979	Jimmy Kilroe	1985	Keene Daingerfield	1989	Michael Sandler		& Robert P. Strub

Special Award

Year		Year		Year		Year	
1971	Robert J. Kleberg	1980	John T. Landry & Pierre E. Bellocq	1985	Arlington Park	1988	Edward J. DeBartolo Sr.
1974	Charles Hatton	1984	C.V. Whitney	1987	Anheuser-Busch	1989	Richard Duchossois
1976	Bill Shoemaker						

HARNESS RACING

Triple Crown Winners
PACERS

Seven 3-year-olds have won the Cane Pace, Little Brown Jug and Messenger Stakes in the same year since the Pacing Triple Crown was established in 1956. No trainer or driver has won it more than once.

Year		Driver	Trainer	Owner
1959	**Adios Butler**	Clint Hodgins	Paige West	Paige West & Angelo Pellillo
1965	**Bret Hanover**	Frank Ervin	Frank Ervin	Richard Downing
1966	**Romeo Hanover**	Bill Myer & George Sholty*	Jerry Silverman	Lucky Star Stables & Morton Finder
1968	**Rum Customer**	Billy Haughton	Billy Haughton	Kennilworth Farms & L.C. Mancuso
1970	**Most Happy Fella**	Stanley Dancer	Stanley Dancer	Egyptian Acres Stable
1980	**Niatross**	Clint Galbraith	Clint Galbraith	Niagara Acres, Niatross Stables & Clint Galbraith
1983	**Ralph Hanover**	Ron Waples	Stew Firlotte	Waples Stable, Pointsetta Stable, Grant's Direct Stable & P.J. Baugh

*Myer drove Romeo Hanover in the Cane, Sholty in the other two races.

TROTTERS

Six 3-year-olds have won the Yonkers Trot, Hambletonian and Kentucky Futurity in the same year since the Trotting Triple Crown was established in 1955. Stanley Dancer is the only driver/trainer to win it twice.

Year		Driver/Trainer	Owner
1955	**Scott Frost**	Joe O'Brien	S.A. Camp Farms
1963	**Speedy Scot**	Ralph Baldwin	Castleton Farms
1964	**Ayres**	John Simpson Sr.	Charlotte Sheppard
1968	**Nevele Pride**	Stanley Dancer	Nevele Acres & Lou Resnick
1969	**Lindy's Pride**	Howard Beissinger	Lindy Farms
1972	**Super Bowl**	Stanley Dancer	Rachel Dancer & Rose Hild Breeding Farm

Triple Crown Near Misses

PACERS

Seven horses have won the first two legs of the Triple Crown, but not the third. The Cane Pace (CP), Little Brown Jug (LBJ), and Messenger Stakes (MS) have not always been run in the same order so numbers after races won indicate sequence for that year.

Year		CP	LBJ	MS
1957	**Torpid**	won, 1	won, 2	DNF
1960	**Countess Adios**	won, 2	NE	won, 1
1971	**Albatross**	won, 2	2nd*	won, 1
1976	**Keystone Ore**	won, 1	won, 2	2nd*
1986	**Barberry Spur**	won, 1	won, 2	2nd*
1990	**Jake and Elwood**	won, 1	NE	won, 2
1992	**Western Hanover**	won, 1	2nd*	won, 2
1993	**Rijadh**	won, 1	2nd*	won, 2

*Winning horses: Nansemond (1971), Windshield Wiper (1976), Amity Chef (1986), Fake Left (1992), Life Sign (1993).
Note: Torpid (1957) scratched before the final heat; Countess Adios (1960) not eligible for Messenger; Jake and Elwood (1990) not eligible for Little Brown Jug.

TROTTERS

Six horses have won the first two legs of the Triple Crown—the Yonkers Trot (YT) and the Hambletonian (Ham)—but not the third. The eventual winner of the Ky. Futurity (KF) is listed.

Year		YT	Ham	KF
1962	**A.C.'s Viking**	won	won	Safe Mission
1976	**Steve Lobell**	won	won	Quick Pay
1977	**Green Speed**	won	won	Texas
1978	**Speedy Somolli**	won	won	Doublemint
1987	**Mack Lobell**	won	won	Napoletano
1993	**American Winner**	won	won	Pine Chip

Note: Green Speed (1977) not eligible for Ky. Futurity.

The Hambletonian

For three-year-old trotters. Inaugurated in 1926 and has been held in Syracuse, N.Y.; Lexington, Ky.; Goshen, N.Y.; Yonkers, N.Y.; Du Quoin, Ill.; and, since 1981 at The Meadowlands in East Rutherford, N.J.
Run at one mile since 1947. Winning horse must win two heats.
Drivers with most wins: John Campbell, Stanley Dancer, Billy Haughton and Ben White (4); Howard Beissinger, Del Cameron, and Henry Thomas (3).

Year	Horse	Driver	Fastest Heat	Year	Horse	Driver	Fastest Heat
1926	**Guy McKinney**	Nat Ray	2:04¾	1957	**Hickory Smoke**	John Simpson Sr.	2:00½
1927	**Iosola's Worthy**	Marvin Childs	2:03¾	1958	**Emily's Pride**	Flave Nipe	1:59⅗
1928	**Spencer**	W.H. Lessee	2:02½	1959	**Diller Hanover**	Frank Ervin	2:01⅕
1929	**Walter Dear**	Walter Cox	2:02¾	1960	**Blaze Hanover**	Joe O'Brien	1:59⅗
1930	**Hanover's Bertha**	Tom Berry	2:03	1961	**Harlan Dean**	James Arthur	1:58⅗
1931	**Calumet Butler**	R.D. McMahon	2:03¼	1962	**A.C.'s Viking**	Sanders Russell	1:59⅗
1932	**The Marchioness**	Will Caton	2:01¼	1963	**Speedy Scot**	Ralph Baldwin	1:57⅗
1933	**Mary Reynolds**	Ben White	2:03¾	1964	**Ayres**	John Simpson Sr.	1:56⅗
1934	**Lord Jim**	Doc Parshall	2:02¾	1965	**Egyptian Candor**	Del Cameron	2:03⅗
1935	**Greyhound**	Sep Palin	2:02¼	1966	**Kerry Way**	Frank Ervin	1:58⅗
1936	**Rosalind**	Ben White	2:01¾	1967	**Speedy Streak**	Del Cameron	2:00
1937	**Shirley Hanover**	Henry Thomas	2:01½	1968	**Nevele Pride**	Stanley Dancer	1:59⅗
1938	**McLin Hanover**	Henry Tomas	2:02¼	1969	**Lindys Pride**	Howard Beissinger	1:57⅗
1939	**Peter Astra**	Doc Parshall	2:04¼	1970	**Timothy T**	John Simpson Jr.	1:58⅗
1940	**Spencer Scott**	Fred Egan	2:02	1971	**Speedy Crown**	Howard Beissinger	1:57⅗
1941	**Bill Gallon**	Lee Smith	2:05	1972	**Super Bowl**	Stanley Dancer	1:56⅗
1942	**The Ambassador**	Ben White	2:04	1973	**Flirth**	Ralph Baldwin	1:57½
1943	**Volo Song**	Ben White	2:02½	1974	**Christopher T**	Billy Haughton	1:58⅗
1944	**Yankee Maid**	Henry Thomas	2:04	1975	**Bonefish**	Stanley Dancer	1:59
1945	**Titan Hanover**	Harry Pownall Sr.	2:04	1976	**Steve Lobell**	Billy Haughton	1:56⅗
1946	**Chestertown**	Thomas Berry	2:02½	1977	**Green Speed**	Billy Haughton	1:55⅗
1947	**Hoot Mon**	Sep Palin	2:00	1978	**Speedy Somolli**	Howard Beissinger	1:55
1948	**Demon Hanover**	Harrison Hoyt	2:02	1979	**Legend Hanover**	George Sholty	1:56½
1949	**Miss Tilly**	Fred Egan	2:01⅖	1980	**Burgomeister**	Billy Haughton	1:56⅗
1950	**Lusty Song**	Del Miller	2:02	1981	**Shiaway St. Pat**	Ray Remmen	2:01⅕
1951	**Mainliner**	Guy Crippen	2:02⅖	1982	**Speed Bowl**	Tommy Haughton	1:56⅗
1952	**Sharp Note**	Bion Shively	2:02⅗	1983	**Duenna**	Stanley Dancer	1:57⅗
1953	**Helicopter**	Harry Harvey	2:01⅗	1984	**Historic Freight**	Ben Webster	1:56⅗
1954	**Newport Dream**	Del Cameron	2:02⅗	1985	**Prakas**	Bill O'Donnell	1:54⅗
1955	**Scott Frost**	Joe O'Brien	2:00⅗	1986	**Nuclear Kosmos**	Ulf Thoresen	1:55⅗
1956	**The Intruder**	Ned Bower	2:01⅗	1987	**Mack Lobell**	John Campbell	1:53⅗

The Hambletonian (Cont.)

Year		Driver	Fastest Heat	Year		Driver	Fastest Heat
1988	**Armbro Goal**	John Campbell	1:54⅘	1992	**Alf Palema**	Mickey McNichol	1:56⅗
1989	**Park Avenue Joe**	Ron Waples	1:54⅘	1993	**American Winner**	Ron Pierce	1:53⅕
	& Probe	Bill Fahy		1994	**Victory Dream**	Michel Lachance	1:54⅕
1990	**Harmonious**	John Campbell	1:54⅕	1995	**Tagliabue**	John Campbell	1:54⅘
1991	**Giant Victory**	Jack Moiseyev	1:54⅘				

Note: In 1989, Park Avenue Joe and Probe finished in a dead heat in the race-off. They were later declared co-winners, but Park Avenue Joe was awarded 1st place money because his three-race summary (2-1-1) was better than Probe's (1-9-1).

All-Time Leaders

The all-time winning trotters, pacers and drivers through 1994 according to *The Trotting and Pacing Guide*. Purses for horses include races in foreign countries. Earnings and wins for drivers include only races held in North America.

Top 15 Horses—Money Won

Note that (*) indicates horse raced in 1994.

		T/P	Sts	1st	Earnings
1	Peace Corps*	T	42	35	$4,907,307
2	Ourasi (FRA)	T	N/A	32	4,010,105
3	Mack Lobell	T	86	65	3,917,594
4	Reve d'Udon*	T	23	18	3,611,351
5	Nihilator	P	38	35	3,225,653
6	Artsplace*	P	49	37	3,085,083
7	Presidential Ball	P	38	26	3,021,363
8	Matt's Scooter	P	61	37	2,944,591
9	On the Road Again	P	61	44	2,819,102
10	Ideal du Gazeau (FRA)	T	N/A	21	2,744,777
11	Vrai Lutin (FRA)	T	N/A	N/A	2,612,429
12	Grades Singing	T	101	66	2,607,552
13	Beach Towel	P	36	29	2,570,357
14	Embassy Lobell (FRA)	T	21	8	2,566,370
15	Western Hanover*	P	42	27	2,541,647

Top 15 Drivers — Races Won

All drivers were active in 1994.

		Yrs	1st	Earnings
1	Herve Filion	34	14,525	$83,485,489
2	Carmine Abbatiello	39	7,132	49,705,424
3	Michel Lachance	27	7,041	76,330,321
4	John Campbell	23	6,687	128,787,234
5	Dave Magee	22	6,519	44,998,965
6	Walter Case Jr	18	6,481	24,765,382
7	Cat Manzi	27	6,284	50,767,140
8	Jack Moiseyev	19	5,969	50,784,611
9	Ron Waples	29	5,959	59,366,938
10	Eddie Davis	31	5,844	20,052,611
11	Doug Brown	22	5,832	50,164,511
12	Leigh Fitch	33	5,816	5,608,922
13	Bill Gale	24	5,760	32,715,825
14	Joe Marsh Jr	40	5,760	35,347,295
15	Walter Paisley	37	5,712	34,655,715

Annual Awards

Harness Horse of the Year

Selected since 1947 by U.S. Trotting Association and the U.S. Harness Writers Association; age of winning horse is noted; (t) indicates trotter and (p) indicates pacer. USTA added Trotter and Pacer of the Year awards in 1970.

Multiple winners: Bret Hanover and Nevele Pride (3); Adios Butler, Albatross, Cam Fella, Good Time, Mack Lobell, Niatross and Scott Frost (2).

Year		Year		Year		Year	
1947	Victory Song (4t)	1960	Adios Butler (4p)	1972	Albatross (4p)	1984	Fancy Crown (3t)
1948	Rodney (4t)	1961	Adios Butler (5p)	1973	Sir Dalrai (4p)	1985	Nihilator (3p)
1949	Good Time (3p)	1962	Su Mac Lad (8t)	1974	Delmonica Hanover(5t)	1986	Forrest Skipper (4p)
1950	Proximity (8t)	1963	Speedy Scot (3t)	1975	Savoir (7t)	1987	Mack Lobell (3t)
1951	Pronto Don (6t)	1964	Bret Hanover (2p)	1976	Keystone Ore (3p)	1988	Mack Lobell (4t)
1952	Good Time (6t)	1965	Bret Hanover (3p)	1977	Green Speed (3t)	1989	Matt's Scooter (4p)
1953	Hi Lo's Forbes (5p)	1966	Bret Hanover (4p)	1978	Abercrombie (3p)		
1954	Stenographer (3t)	1967	Nevele Pride (2t)	1979	Niatross (2p)	1990	Beach Towel (3p)
1955	Scott Frost (3t)	1968	Nevele Pride (3t)	1980	Niatross (3p)	1991	Precious Bunny (3p)
1956	Scott Frost (4t)	1969	Nevele Pride (4t)	1981	Fan Hanover (3p)	1992	Artsplace (4p)
1957	Torpid (3p)			1982	Cam Fella (3p)	1993	Staying Together (4p)
1958	Emily's Pride (3t)	1970	Fresh Yankee (7t)	1983	Cam Fella (4p)	1994	Cam's Card Chark (3p)
1959	Bye Bye Byrd (4p)	1971	Albatross (3p)				

Driver of the Year

Determined by Universal Driving Rating System (UDR) and presented by the Harness Tracks of America since 1968. Eligible drivers must have at least 1,000 starts for the season.

Multiple winners: Herve Filion (10); John Campbell and Michel Lachance (3); Walter Case Jr., Bill O'Donnell and Ron Waples (2).

Year		Year		Year		Year	
1968	Stanley Dancer	1976	Herve Filion	1983	John Campbell	1990	John Campbell
1969	Herve Filion	1977	Donald Dancer	1984	Bill O'Donnell	1991	Walter Case Jr.
		1978	Carmine Abbatiello	1985	Michel Lachance	1992	Walter Case Jr.
1970	Herve Filion		& Herve Filion	1986	Michel Lachance	1993	Jack Moiseyeu
1971	Herve Filion	1979	Ron Waples	1987	Michel Lachance	1994	Dave Magee
1972	Herve Filion			1988	John Campbell		
1973	Herve Filion	1980	Ron Waples	1989	Herve Filion		
1974	Herve Filion	1981	Herve Filion				
1975	Joe O'Brien	1982	Bill O'Donnell				

Monica Seles (left) and **Steffi Graf** embrace after the U.S. Open womens' final. Although Graf won, the match marked the return of Seles to Grand Slam play after being stabbed in 1993.

TENNIS

Doubles

Tennis enjoys a revival as Seles returns to challenge Graf and Americans Agassi and Sampras battle for No. 1.

This is what we had been missing for 28 months.

We had missed Steffi Graf hitting that slice backhand low, lower, lowest and Monica Seles bending so that her knees almost scraped the ground to hit the ball back.

We had missed Seles and her grunt— the "unh...eeee" filling the stadium as she hit a forehand or backhand so hard that it whistled in the wind. And the sight of Graf in full flight— running down balls no one else even tries for in long, smooth strides similar to those of a world class sprinter.

On Sept. 9, under a bright Saturday afternoon sun and in front of a standing-room-only U.S. Open crowd of 19,883 at Louis Armstrong Stadium, Graf and Seles opposed each other in the final of a Grand Slam tournament for the first time in over 31 months.

The two best women tennis players in the world played for an hour and 52 minutes. They each ran until they couldn't catch their breath. They pumped their fists and yelled at the sky and even broke down and giggled at three noisy seagulls who were squawking at them from the cheap seats.

Finally, Seles, lunged and punched a forehand into the net and Graf was the winner, 7-6 (8-6), 6-0, 6-3.

It was the tennis match of the year and it

capped a wacky, wonderful, emotional, sad and thrilling 12 months that made tennis popular again.

The television ratings for the U.S. Open semifinals and finals were over 50 percent higher than in 1994 and the Sunday men's final between top-ranked Americans Pete Sampras and Andre Agassi pushed NFL football for top-rated sports program of the weekend.

The highlights of the year in the tennis begin with Monica's return to active duty.

On April 30, 1993, she had been stabbed in the back by an unemployed German lathe operator named Gunter Parche at a tournament in Hamburg, Germany. Parche attacked Seles during a changeover and said he did it so Graf could be No. 1 again.

He got his wish. With Seles out of the way, Graf won six of the next 10 Grand Slams and was No. 1 for 1993 and '94. Parche also got away with it— receiving a two-year suspended sentence from a Hamburg judge on Oct. 14, 1993 and having the sentence upheld in another court on April.

Seles was 19-years-old and the No. 1 player in the world at the time of the assault, having won seven of the last eight Grand Slam tournaments she had played in.

Traumatized by the assault, Seles was treated by Nevada sports psychologist Jerry Russel May and avoided competition (and crowds) for over two years. She returned to public view on July 29 in an Atlantic City

Diane Pucin is a columnist for the *The Philadelphia Inquirer* where she has covered international tennis since 1988.

Wide World Photos

Pete Sampras (left) and **Andre Agassi** shake hands at the net following Sampras' four-set victory at the U.S. Open on Sept. 10. While Agassi took the Australian Open and held the No. 1 ranking most of the year, Sampras walked off with two Grand Slam titles, including his third straight at Wimbledon.

exhibition match with Martina Navratilova that she won, 6-3, 6-2.

Two weeks later, she won the du Maurier Open at Toronto in her first tournament back— routing Gabriela Sabatini (6-1, 6-0) and Amanda Coetzer (6-0, 6-1) in the semifinals and finals.

"I wasn't sure I'd ever be back to play tennis again," she said. "It's been such a struggle to get to this point, but from that day [of the stabbing] to this day, what a difference."

Graf, meanwhile, came to New York with a bad back, a sore left foot and the knowledge that her father— and manager— Peter was imprisoned in Germany on charges of income tax evasion.

It was with all this baggage that Graf and Seles walked onto center court at the U.S. Open. They then proceeded to play a brand of hard-hitting, well-executed and daring tennis that ended with Graf winning her third Grand Slam singles championship of the year. It was also the 18th singles title of her career, tying her with Martina Navratilova and Chris Evert.

When it was over, Graf called the victory, "the biggest win I have ever achieved. There is nothing that even comes close to this one."

And it was only the second-most emotional match of the year.

The most emotional happened 10 months earlier, in the men's quarterfinals at the Australian Open.

Sampras, then the No. 1 player in the world and seeded first, was playing his good friend and long-time rival Jim Courier. What nobody knew, however, was that he had entered the match on Tuesday shortly after going through the most stressful 24 hours of his life.

His coach and friend, Tim Gullikson, had collapsed following a practice session with Sampras the previous Friday. This was the second time in four months that Gullikson had collapsed and a doctor at the Melbourne hospital gave the 43-year-old Gullikson grim news. There was a brain tumor and Gullikson might have only six months to live. Sampras was told about the diagnosis, helped get his coach on a flight home to Wheaton, Ill. and then went to play Courier.

After losing the first two sets, Sampras had come back to win the second two. Early in the fifth set, with Sampras serving, someone in the crowd yelled, "Win it for Tim." Sampras broke down. He sobbed and served, sobbed and hit groundstrokes, sobbed and volleyed and it was only when Courier, the friend, yelled, "You okay Pete?" that Sampras collected himself and went on to win the match, 6-7 (4-7), 6-7 (3-7), 6-3, 6-4, 6-3.

Sampras kept himself together long enough to get to the final where he would meet Agassi and lose in four sets. Their year-long rivalry— from Flinders Park to Flushing Meadow— was the second great storyline of 1995.

Sampras and Agassi. No. 1 and No. 2. The best All-America tennis rivalry since John McEnroe and Jimmy Connors. Sampras on top as the world's best player in 1993 and '94, and Agassi on the rise as the second best player in 1994 after ranking 24th at the end of '93.

Beating Sampras in Melbourne gave Agassi his second straight Grand Slam title, following the 1994 U.S. Open. He lost their rematch at Indian Wells, Calif., on March 13, but regained the edge two weeks later by winning their final in the Lipton Championships at Key Biscayne, Fla., 3-6, 6-2, 7-6 (7-3).

That victory gave Agassi the computer points he needed to replace Sampras as No. 1 on April 10, ending Pete's 101-week stay at the top.

Meanwhile, they helped get the United States into the 1995 Davis Cup final by teaming up in singles for victories over Italy in April and Sweden in September. The U.S. was scheduled to meet Russia in the Cup final in Moscow Dec. 1-3.

Back in the spring, both Agassi and Sampras had prepared grimly for the French Open. While they both had Australian, Wimbledon and U.S. Open titles, neither had won the French. Sampras had planned a grueling clay court season of playing the entire circuit in Europe. Agassi chose to play sparingly, come to Europe late and hope to be ready.

Sampras's plan backfired when he sprained an ankle badly in Monte Carlo in late April and missed the rest of the season.

He came to Paris ill-prepared and lost in the first round to Gilbert Schaller, a dirtballer from Austria.

Agassi, on the other hand, arrived healthy and blew through the first three rounds as he looked forward to a semifinal appointment with Austria's Thomas Muster. It didn't happen. In the quarters, Agassi pulled a thigh muscle and could barely move in a straight-set loss to Yevgeny Kafelnikov of Russia.

Muster, who needed five sets to dispose of Spain's pesky Alberto Costa in the quarters, routed Kafelnikov in their semifinal and then beat Michael Chang in the final, 7-5, 6-2, 6-4, for his first major title. Muster went on to win 70 straight matches and 10 tournaments on clay over the spring and summer, but shied away from grass and passed up Wimbledon.

Shaking off their injuries Sampras and Agassi arrived in England anxious to resume their rivalry. Sampras, the two-time defending champion, was trying to become the first American man to win three straight (or, "three-Pete," as the headline writers hoped). Agassi, the 1992 champ, just wanted his title back.

Little did No. 1 and No. 2 know that the headlines of this fortnight would be stolen early by No. 80— Jeff Tarango, a little-known Californian with a short fuse and pugnacious wife.

Tarango, who had finally gotten past the first round at Wimbledon in his seventh try, walked off the court in the middle of his third round match with Germany's Alexander Mronz, whose only previous brush with notoriety was being Steffi Graf's first boyfriend. Down a set and losing 1-3 in the second, Tarango took exception to a serving call by chair umpire Bruno Rebeuh and became unhinged when Rebeuh issued a code violation warning when Tarango yelled "Shut up!" to a spectator, who had urged him to get on with the match.

The enraged Tarango then called Rebeuh "the most corrupt official in the game" and quit the match— something no one had ever done in 109 years at Wimbledon. After Tarango had taken his leave and been defaulted, his French wife, Benedicte, took off after Rebeuh and slapped him.

What followed was one of the weirdest press conferences ever at the All-England Club. Neither Tarango was apologetic. Said

Steffi Graf (right) and **Arantxa Sanchez Vicario** squared off in the finals of the French Open and Wimbledon with Graf winning both championships in three sets. Their battle at Wimbledon was exhausting, but reached epic proportions when the 11th game of the third set went on for 32 points.

Benedicte: "I slap him and I slap him again if I get the chance." Her husband then gave a rambling diatribe accusing Rebeuh of favoring certain players and throwing calls their way.

Sanity was restored when Sampras and Agassi and Boris Becker and Goran Ivanisevic made it to the men's semifinals while Graf and Arantxa Sanchez Vicario advanced to the women's finals.

Sanchez Vicario had already reached the finals of the Australian Open, where she'd lost to hard-hitting Mary Pierce; and the French Open, where Graf beat her 6-0 in the third and deciding set. Even though she and Graf had exchanged the No. 1 ranking six times in 1995, no one was prepared for their thrilling third set at Wimbledon— a set that included the most exciting single game in a big women's match in recent memory.

It was the 11th game of the third set and for over 20 minutes it exposed the heart and soul of its two combatants. With Sanchez-Vicario serving, the game went on for 32 points, 13 deuces and six break-point opportunities. It was a masterpiece of lunging volleys, topspin passing shots, mes-

merizing aces and wicked forehands. And when it was over, the crowd at centre court delivered a standing ovation.

Graf won the game to take a 6-5 lead, then served out the match with signature forehand bullets deep into the corner that Sanchez Vicario could only wave at.

After 2 hours and 2 minutes of enthralling and draining tennis, Graf had her sixth Wimbledon championship with a 4-6, 6-1, 7-5 triumph.

With Seles expected back during the summer, the Women's Tennis Association met behind closed doors at Wimbledon to decide what ranking she should hold upon her return. Should she be anointed No. 1, her rank when she was stabbed? If so, should this ranking be protected for a week, a month, six months, a year? And what of players like Sanchez Vicario, who would be pushed into semifinal meetings with Graf? Ultimately, it was decided that Seles would be ranked co-No. 1 with Graf but there were hard feelings.

It took Martina Navratilova, the president of the WTA, to put the arguments into perspective.

"What's frustrating to me," Navratilova

American **Jeff Tarango** and his wife
Benedicte were the fun couple of the fortnight at Wimbledon when he quit his
third-round match in a huff and she slapped
the umpire who riled her husband.

said, "is that the players benefited from
Monica's absence. They won more money,
they won more Grand Slams because she
wasn't around and now they're not willing
to give back to her a little of what perhaps
they gained by her absence."

As for the men at Wimbledon, there
would be no epic 11th game in the deciding set of the final and Agassi and Sampras
would not renew hostilities at center court.

Agassi built a 6-2, 4-1 lead over Becker in
the semis then inexplicably collapsed. After
dropping only one set in his first five
matches, Agassi lost a few points, got rattled,
and was bounced in four sets by Becker.

Sampras needed five sets to defeat
Ivanisevic in the semis, after which
Ivanisevic used the word "unlucky" 16 times
to describe his loss. But luck had nothing to
do with it.

In the final, Sampras rallied from one set
down to beat Becker, 6-7 (5-7), 6-2, 6-4, 6-
2. Afterward, Becker, a three-time
champion in the 1980s, called Sampras,
the new three-time champion of the '90s,
"clearly the best player in the world."
Sampras dedicated the victory to Gullikson,
his ailing coach.

Seven weeks later, Agassi, Sampras,
Muster and Becker entered the U.S. Open
as the top four seeds. Three made it to the
final four— Muster lost his fourth-round
match to Courier.

Agassi faced Becker with a score to settle
in the semifinals and this time he didn't fall
apart, winning in four sets. At Wimbledon,
Becker had complained that Nike, the athletic wear company which represents
Agassi and Sampras, had too much influence in player scheduling and court
placement. He also said that a lot of players
on the tour don't like Agassi.

In New York, Becker reiterated his
thoughts about Nike and at the end of his
match with Agassi the two barely
exchanged handshakes.

Afterward, Agassi spoke of how he'd lost
respect for Becker. "After Wimbledon," he
said, "Boris said some things that bothered
me on a very personal level. It's hard for me
to respect anybody who's going to beat me
and say things that are not only wrong, but
meant to hurt. I don't understand that and I
don't respect it."

Sampras beat Courier in four sets in their
semifinal, then downed Agassi, 6-4, 6-3, 4-
6, 7-5, in a 2-hour and 28-minute final that
didn't seem that close or that long.

The highlight of the match was a 21-shot
point in the 10th game of the opening set
and Sampras up 5-4. The point demonstrated the ferocity of the Agassi-Sampras
rivalry at its best and marked Sampras as
the greatest athlete playing men's tennis
today.

It was a rally of power and angles, of
depth and finesse. There were drop shots
and smashes, lobs and bombardments. It
was a set point and a break point. And
finally, after nearly two dozen shots,
Sampras swung with that looping, one-
handed backhand that is so feared and
made an X on the court where the ball
zipped one way and Agassi went the other.
The ball kissed the sideline and Agassi
kissed the match good-bye.

The win left little doubt who the best
player in the world was, no matter what the
computer said.

"Pete has won two Slams, so I'd have to
say that, come December 31st, he's going
to feel better about the year than I am,"
said Agassi, who likely will end the year
ranked No. 1.   ❏

Tournament Results

Winners of men's and women's pro singles championships from Oct. 30, 1994 through Sept. 17, 1995. See Updates chapter for later results.

Men's ATP Tour

LATE 1994

Finals	Tournament	Winner	Earnings	Loser	Score
Oct. 30	Stockholm Open	Boris Becker	$244,000	G. Ivanisevic	46 64 63 76
Oct. 30	Hellmann's Cup (Santiago)	Alberto Berasategui	27,000	F. Clavet	63 64
Nov. 6	Paris Indoor	Andre Agassi	330,000	M. Rosset	63 63 46 75
Nov. 6	Topper Open (Montevideo)	Alberto Berasategui	27,000	F. Clavet	64 60
Nov. 13	European Community Champs. (Antwerp)	Pete Sampras	156,000	M. Larsson	76 64
Nov. 13	Kremlin Cup (Moscow)	Alexander Volkov	156,000	C. Adams	62 64
Nov. 13	South American Open (Buenos Aires)	Alex Corretja	42,000	J. Frana	63 57 76
Nov. 20	ATP World Championship (Frankfurt)	Pete Sampras	1,225,000	B. Becker	46 63 75 64
Nov. 27	ATP Doubles Champs. (Jakarta)	Jan Apell/ Jonas Bjorkman	137,500 137,500	T. Woodbridge/ M. Woodforde	64 46 46 76 76
Dec. 11	ITF Grand Slam Cup (Munich)	Magnus Larsson	1,500,000	P. Sampras	76 46 76 64

Note: The Grand Slam Cup, sponsored by the International Tennis Federation, is not an ATP Tour event.

1995 (through Sept. 17)

Finals	Tournament	Winner	Earnings	Loser	Score
Jan. 8	Qatar Open (Doha)	Stefan Edberg	$84,000	M Larsson	76 61
Jan. 8	Australian Hardcourt (Adelaide)	Jim Courier	43,000	A. Boetsch	62 75
Jan. 16	The Peters N.S.W. Open T.O.C. (Sydney)	Patrick McEnroe	43,000	R. Fromberg	62 76
Jan. 16	Indonesian Open (Jakarta)	Paul Haarhuis	43,000	R. Vasek	75 75
Jan. 16	Benson & Hedges Open (Auckland)	Thomas Enqvist	43,000	C. Adams	62 61
Jan. 30	**Australian Open** (Melbourne)	Andre Agassi	480,000	P. Sampras	46 61 76 64
Feb. 12	Sybase Open (San Jose)	Andre Agassi	43,000	M. Chang	62 16 63
Feb. 12	Open 13 (Marseille)	Boris Becker	72,000	D. Vacek	67 64 75
Feb. 12	Dubai Open (UAE)	Wayne Ferreira	142,000	A. Gaudenzi	63 63
Feb. 19	Kroger/St. Jude International (Memphis)	Todd Martin	117,000	P. Haarhuis	76 64
Feb. 19	Muratti Time Indoor (Milan)	Yevgeny Kafelnikov	128,000	B. Becker	75 57 76
Feb. 26	Eurocard Open (Stuttgart)	Richard Krajicek	395,000	M. Stich	76 63 67 16 63
Feb. 26	Comcast U.S.Indoor (Philadelphia)	Thomas Enqvist	110,000	M. Chang	06 64 60
Mar. 5	ABN/AMRO World (Rotterdam)	Richard Krajicek	80,000	P. Haarhuis	76 64
Mar. 5	Mass Mutual Championships (Scottsdale)	Jim Courier	43,000	M. Philippoussis	76 64
Mar. 5	Abierto Mexicano (Mexico City)	Thomas Muster	43,200	F. Meligeni	76 75
Mar. 12	Copenhagen Open	Martin Sinner	29,000	A. Olhovskiy	67 76 63
Mar. 13	Newsweek Champions Cup (Indian Wells)	Pete Sampras	225,000	A. Agassi	75 63 75
Mar. 19	St. Petersburg Open (Russia)	Yevgeny Kafelnikov	42,500	G. Raoux	62 62
Mar. 26	Lipton Championships (Key Biscayne)	Andre Agassi	330,000	P. Sampras	36 62 76
Mar. 26	Grand Prix Hassan II (Casablanca)	Gilbert Schaller	29,000	A. Costa	64 62
Apr. 9	Estoril Open (Lisbon)	Thomas Muster	77,000	A. Costa	64 62
Apr. 9	South African Open (Johannesburg)	Martin Sinner	43,000	G. Raoux	61 64
Apr. 16	Japan Open (Tokyo)	Jim Courier	154,000	A. Agassi	64 63
Apr. 16	Trofeo Conde de Godo (Barcelona)	Thomas Muster	128,000	M. Larsson	62 61 64
Apr. 23	Salem Open (Hong Kong)	Michael Chang	43,000	J. Bjorkman	63 61
Apr. 23	Philips Open (Nice)	Marc Rosset	43,000	Y. Kafelnikov	64 60
Apr. 30	Volvo Monte Carlo Open	Thomas Muster	254,000	B. Becker	46 57 61 76 60
Apr. 30	KAL Cup Korea Open (Seoul)	Greg Rusedski	29,000	L. Rehmann	64 31 (ret.)
May 7	BMW Open (Munich)	Wayne Ferreira	57,000	M. Stich	75 76
May 7	AT&T Challenge (Atlanta)	Michael Chang	43,000	A. Agassi	61 67 64

Tournament Results (Cont.)

Men's ATP Tour

Finals	Tournament	Winner	Earnings	Loser	Score
May 14	Panasonic German Open (Hamburg)	Andrei Medvedev	$254,000	G. Ivanisevic	63 62 61
May 14	US Clay Court Champ. (Pinehurst, NC)	Thomas Enqvist	37,500	J. Frana	63 36 63
May 21	Nokia Italian Open (Rome)	Thomas Muster	277,000	S. Brugera	36 76 62 63
May 21	America's Red Clay Champ. (Coral Sprgs.)	Todd Woodbridge	32,600	G. Rusedski	64 62
May 28	Peugeot World Team Cup (Dusseldorf)	Sweden	450,000	Croatia	2-1
May 28	Internazionali di Tennis (Bologna)	Marcelo Rios	43,000	M. Filippini	62 64
June 11	**French Open** (Paris)	Thomas Muster	620,560	M. Chang	75 62 64
June 18	Stella Artois Grass Court (London)	Pete Sampras	71,000	G. Forget	76 76
June 18	Ordina Open (Rosmalen)	Karol Kucera	43,000	A. Jarryd	76 76
June 18	Maia Open/Oporto Cup (Oporto)	Alberto Berasategui	43,000	C. Costa	36 63 64
June 24	The Nottingham Open	Javier Frana	43,000	T. Woodbridge	76 63
June 25	Gerry Weber Open (Halle)	Marc Rossett	98,000	M. Stich	36 76 76
June 25	Internationaler Raiffeisen Grand Prix	Thomas Muster	50,000	B. Ulihrach	63 36 61
July 9	**Wimbledon** (London)	Pete Sampras	573,050	B. Becker	67 62 64 62
July 16	Hall of Fame Championships (Newport)	David Prinosil	32,600	D. Wheaton	76 57 62
July 16	Swedish Open (Bastad)	Fernando Meligeni	43,000	C. Ruud	64 64
July 16	Rado Swiss Open (Gstaad)	Yevgeny Kafelnikov	73,000	J. Hlasek	63 64 36 63
July 24	Mercedes Cup (Stuttgart)	Thomas Muster	157,000	J. Apell	62 62
July 24	Legg Mason Classic (Washington, D.C.)	Andre Agassi	90,000	S. Edberg	64 26 75
July 30	du Maurier Ltd. Open (Montreal)	Andre Agassi	254,000	P. Sampras	36 62 63
July 30	Grolsch Open (Amsterdam)	Marcelo Rios	43,000	J. Siemerink	64 75 64
Aug. 6	EA Generali Open (Kitzbühel)	Alberto Costa	51,000	T. Muster	46 64 76 26 64
Aug. 6	Skoda Czech Open (Prague)	Bohdan Ulihrach	48,200	J. Sanchez	62 62
Aug. 6	Infiniti Open (Los Angeles)	Michael Stich	43,000	T. Enqvist	67 76 62
Aug. 13	San Marino Open	Thomas Muster	39,000	A. Gaudenzi	62 60
Aug. 13	Thriftway ATP Championship (Cincinnati)	Andre Agassi	254,000	M. Chang	75 62
Aug. 20	RCA/U.S. Hardcourts (Indianapolis)	Thomas Enqvist	150,000	B. Karbacher	64 63
Aug. 20	Volvo International (New Haven)	Andre Agassi	150,000	R. Krajicek	36 76 63
Aug. 27	Croatia Open (Umag)	Thomas Muster	54,000	C. Costa	36 76 64
Aug. 28	Genovese Hamlet Cup (Long Island)	Yevgeny Kafelnikov	43,000	J. Siemerink	76 62
Sept. 10	**U.S. Open** (New York)	Pete Sampras	575,000	A. Agassi	64 63 46 75
Sept. 17	Colombia Tennis World Series	Nicholas Lapentti	43,000	M. Tobon	26 61 64
Sept. 17	Romanian Open (Bucharest)	Thomas Muster	189,000	G. Schaller	64 63
Sept. 17	Grand Prix Passing Shot (Bordeaux)	Yahiya Doumbia	54,000	J. Hlasek	64 64

Women's WTA Tour

LATE 1994

Finals	Tournament	Winner	Earnings	Loser	Score
Oct. 30	Nokia Grand Prix (Germany)	Jana Novotna	$80,000	I. Majoli	62 64
Nov. 6	Bank of the West Classic (Oakland)	A. Sanchez Vicario	80,000	M. Navratilova	16 76 76
Nov. 6	Bell Challenge (Quebec City)	Katerina Maleeva	27,000	B. Schultz	63 63
Nov. 13	Va. Slims of Philadelphia	Anke Huber	150,000	M. Pierce	60 67 75
Nov. 20	Va. Slims Doubles Champs. (New York)	Gigi Fernandez/ Natalia Zvereva	90,000	J. Novotna/ A. Sanchez Vicario	63 67 63
Nov. 20	Va. Slims Championships (New York)	Gabriela Sabatini	250,000	L. Davenport	63 62 64

1995 (through Sept. 24)

Finals	Tournament	Winner	Earnings	Loser	Score
Jan. 15	Tasmanian International Open (Hobart)	Leila Meskhi	$17,000	L. Fang	62 63
Jan. 16	New South Wales Open (Sydney)	Gabriela Sabatini	59,500	L. Davenport	63 63
Jan. 30	**Australian Open** (Melbourne)	Mary Pierce	351,120	A. Sanchez Vicario	63 62
Feb. 5	Toray Pan Pacific Open (Tokyo)	Kimiko Date	148,500	L. Davenport	61 62
Feb. 5	Amway Classic (Auckland)	Nicol Bradtke	17,500	G. Helgeson-Nielsen	36 62 61
Feb. 12	Ameritech Cup (Chicago)	Magdalena Maleeva	79,000	L. Raymond	63 75
Feb. 19	Open Gaz de France (Paris)	Steffi Graf	79,000	M. Pierce	62 62
Feb. 19	IGA Classic (Oklahoma City)	Brenda Schultz	26,500	E. Likhovtseva	61 62
Feb. 26	EA Generali (Linz)	Jana Novotna	26,500	B. Rittner	67 63 64
Mar. 6	The Evert Cup (Indian Wells)	Mary Joe Fernandez	79,000	N. Zvereva	64 63
Mar. 6	Puerto Rico Open	Joannette Kruger	25,000	K. Nagatsuka	76 63
Mar. 12	Delray Beach Championships	Steffi Graf	79,000	C. Martinez	62 64
Mar. 20	Lipton Championships (Key Biscayne)	Steffi Graf	205,000	K. Date	61 64
Apr. 3	Family Circle Cup (Hilton Head)	Conchita Martinez	148,500	M. Maleeva	61 61
Apr. 9	Bausch & Lomb Champs. (Amelia Island)	Conchita Martinez	79,000	G. Sabatini	61 64
Apr. 16	Japan Open (Tokyo)	Amy Frazier	26,500	K. Date	76 75
Apr. 16	Gallery Furniture Champs (Houston)	Steffi Graf	79,000	A. Carlsson	61 61

Finals	Tournament	Winner	Earnings	Loser	Score
Apr. 30	Internat'l Champ. of Spain (Barcelona)	A. Sanchez Vicario	$79,000	I. Majoli	57 60 62
Apr. 30	Croation Open (Zagreb)	Sabine Appelmans	25,000	S. Meier	64 63
May 7	Citizen Cup (Hamburg)	Conchita Martinez	79,000	M. Hingis	61 60
May 14	Nokia Italian Open (Rome)	Conchita Martinez	148,500	A. Sanchez Vicario	63 61
May 14	Prague Open (Prague)	Juile Halard	17,000	L. Richterova	64 64
May 21	German Open (Berlin)	A. Sanchez Vicario	148,500	M. Maleeva	64 61
May 28	Internationaux de Strasbourg	Lindsay Davenport	25,000	K. Date	36 61 62
June 11	**French Open** (Paris)	Steffi Graf	503,740	A. Sanchez Vicario	75 46 60
June 18	DFS Classic (Birmingham)	Zina Garrison Jackson	26,500	L. McNeil	63 63
June 24	Direct Line Insurance Int'l. (Eastbourne)	Nathalie Tauziat	79,000	C. Rubin	36 60 75
July 3	**Wimbledon** (London)	Steffi Graf	525,000	A. Sanchez Vicario	46 61 75
July 16	Torneo Internazionale (Palermo)	Irina Spinea	17,500	S. Hack	76 62
July 30	Styrian Open (Austria)	Judith Wiesner	17,500	R. Dragomir	76 63
Aug. 7	Toshiba Classic (San Diego)	Conchita Martinez	79,500	L. Raymond	62 60
Aug. 14	Acura Classic (Los Angeles)	Conchita Martinez	79,500	C. Rubin	46 61 63
Aug. 20	du Maurier Ltd. Open (Toronto)	Monica Seles	148,500	A. Coetzer	60 61
Sept. 9	**U.S. Open** (New York)	Steffi Graf	575,000	M. Seles	76 06 63
Sept. 17	TVA Cup (Nagoya)	Linda Wild	17,500	S. Kleinova	64 62
Sept. 17	Warsaw Cup	Barbara Paulus	25,000	A. Fusai	76 46 61
Sept. 23	Moscow Open	Magdalena Maleeva	26,500	E. Makarova	64 62
Sept. 24	Nichirei Open (Tokyo)	Mary Pierce	79,000	A. Sanchez Vicario	63 63

1995 Grand Slam Tournaments

Australian Open
MEN'S SINGLES

FINAL EIGHT— #1 Pete Sampras; #2 Andre Agassi; #5 Michael Chang; #9 Jim Courier; #10 Yevgeny Kafelnikov; #13 Andrei Medvedev; plus undseeded Jacco Eltingh and Aaron Krickstein.

Quarterfinals

Sampras def. Courier	......	67(4-7) 67 (3-7) 63 64 63
Chang def. Medvedev	......	76 (9-7) 75 63
Agassi def. Kafelnikov	......	62 75 60
Krickstein def. Eltingh	......	76 (7-3) 64 57 64

Semifinals

Sampras def. Chang	......	67 (6-8) 63 64 64
Agassi def. Krickstein	......	64 64 30 (Ret.)

Final

Agassi def. Sampras	......	46 61 76 (8-6) 64

WOMEN'S SINGLES

FINAL EIGHT— #1 Arantxa Sanchez Vicario; # 2 Conchita Martinez; #4 Mary Pierce; #6 Lindsay Davenport; #8 Natasha Zvereva; plus undseeded Angelica Gavaldon, Naoko Sawamatsu and Marianne Werdel Witmeyer.

Quarterfinals

Sanchez Vicario def. Sawamatsu	......	61 63
Werdel Witmeyer def. Gavaldon	......	61 62
Pierce def. Zvereva	......	61 64
Martinez def. Davenport	......	63 46 63

Semifinals

Sanchez Vicario def. Werdel Witmeyer	......	64 61
Pierce def. Martinez	......	63 61

Final

Pierce def. Sanchez Vicario	......	63 62

DOUBLES FINALS

Men— #13 Jared Palmer & Richey Reneberg def. Mark Knowles & Danile Nestor, 6-3, 3-6, 6-3, 6-2.

Women— #2 Jana Novotna & Arantxa Sanchez Vicario def. #1 Gigi Fernandez & Natasha Zvereva, 6-3, 6-7 (3-7), 6-4.

Mixed— Natasha Zvereva & Rick Leach def. #5 Cyril Suk & Gigi Fernandez, 7-6 (7-4), 6-7 (3-7), 6-4.

French Open
MEN'S SINGLES

FINAL EIGHT— #1 Andre Agassi; #5 Thomas Muster; #6 Michael Chang; #7 Sergei Brugera; #9 Yevgeny Kafelnikov; plus unseeded Alberto Costa, Renzo Furlan and Adrian Voinea.

Quarterfinals

Kafelnikov def. Agassi	......	64 63 75
Muster def. Costa	......	62 36 67 75 62
Chang def. Voinea	......	75 60 61
Brugera def. Furlan	......	75 61 75

Semifinals

Chang def. Brugera	......	64 76 76
Muster def. Kafelnikov	......	64 60 64

Final

Muster def. Chang	......	75 62 64

WOMEN'S SINGLES

FINAL EIGHT— #1 Arantxa Sanchez Vicario; #2 Steffi Graf; #4 Conchita Martinez; #8 Gabriela Sabatini; #9 Kimiko Date; #12 Iva Majoli; plus unseeded Virginia Ruano-Pascal and Chanda Rubin.

Quarterfinals

Sanchez Vicario def. Rubin	......	63 61
Graf def. Sabatini	......	61 60
Martinez def. Ruano-Pascal	......	60 64
Date def. Majoli	......	75 61

Semifinals

Sanchez Vicario def. Date	......	75 63
Graf def. Martinez	......	63 67 63

Final

Graf def. Sanchez Vicario	......	75 46 60

DOUBLES FINALS

Men— #2 Jacco Eltingh & Paul Haarhuis def. (unseeded) Nicklaus Kulti & Magnus Larsson, 6-7, 6-4, 6-1.

Women— #2 Gigi Fernandez & Natalia Zvereva def. #1 Jana Novotna & Arantxa Sanchez Vicario, 6-7 (6-8), 6-4, 7-5.

Mixed— #1 Larisa Neiland & Mark Woodforde def. (unseeded) Hetherington & John-Lafinne de Jager, 7-6 (10-8), 7-6 (7-4).

1994 Grand Slam Tournaments (Cont.)

Wimbledon

MEN'S SINGLES

FINAL EIGHT— #1 Andre Agassi; #2 Pete Sampras; #3 Boris Becker; #4 Goran Ivanisevic; #6 Yevgeny Kafelnikov; plus unseeded Jacco Eltingh, Cedric Pioline and Shuzo Matsuoka.

Quarterfinals

Sampras def. Matsuoka	67 (5-7) 63 64 62
Agassi def. Eltingh	62 63 64
Becker def. Pioline	63 61 67 (6-8) 67 (10-12) 97
Ivanisevic def. Kafelnikov	75 76 (13-11) 63

Semifinals

Sampras def. Ivanisevic	76 (9-7) 46 63 46 63
Becker def. Agassi	26 76 (7-1) 64 76 (7-1)

Final

Sampras def. Becker	67 (5-7) 62 64 62

WOMEN'S SINGLES

FINAL EIGHT— #1 Steffi Graf; #2 Aranxta Sanchez Vicario; #3 Conchita Martinez; #4 Jana Novotna; #6 Kimiko Date; #8 Gabriela Sabatini; #13 Mary Jo Fernandez; #15 Brenda Schultz-McCarthy.

Quarterfinals

Graf def. Fernandez	63 60
Novotna def. Date	62 63
Martinez def. Sabatini	75 76 (7-5)
Sanchez Vicario def. Schultz-McCarthy	64 76 (7-4)

Semifinals

Graf def. Novotna	57 64 62
Sanchez Vicario def. Martinez	63 67 (5-7) 61

Final

Graf def. Sanchez Vicario	46 61 75

DOUBLES FINALS

Men— #2 Todd Woodbridge & Mark Woodforde def. (unseeded) Rick Leach & Scott Melville 7-5, 7-6 (10-8), 7-6 (7-5).

Women— #2 Jana Novotna & Arantxa Sanchez Vicario def. #1 Gigi Fernandez & Natasha Zvereva, 5-7, 7-5, 6-4.

Mixed— #3 Jonathan Stark & Martina Navratilova def. #4 Cyril Suk & Gigi Fernandez, 6-4, 6-4.

U.S. Open

MEN'S SINGLES

FINAL EIGHT— #1 Andre Agassi; #2 Pete Sampras; #4 Boris Becker; #5 Michael Chang; #14 Jim Courier; plus unseeded Petr Korda, Pat McEnroe and Bud Black.

Quarterfinals

Agassi def. Korda	64 62 16 75
Becker def. McEnroe	64 76 67 76
Courier def. Chang	76 76 75
Sampras def. Black	76 64 60

Semifinals

Agassi def. Becker	76 (6-4) 76 (6-2) 46 64
Sampras def. Courier	75 46 64 75

Final

Sampras def. Agassi	64 63 46 75

WOMEN'S SINGLES

FINAL EIGHT— #1 Steffi Graf; #2 Monica Seles; #4 Conchita Martinez; #5 Jana Novotna; #9 Gabriela Sabatini; #14 Mary Joe Fernandez; #16 Brenda Schultz-McCarthy; plus unseeded Amy Frazier.

Quarterfinals

Graf def. Frazier	62 63
Sabatini def. Fernandez	61 63
Martinez def. Schultz-McCarthy	36 76 (6-3) 62
Seles def. Novotna	76 (7-5)62

Semifinals

Graf def. Sabatini	64 76 (7-5)
Seles def. Martinez	62 62

Final

Graf def. Seles	76 (8-6) 06 63

DOUBLES FINALS

Men— #2 Todd Woodbridge & Mark Woodforde def. #15 Alex O'Brien & Sandon Stolle, 6-3, 6-3.

Women— #2 Gigi Fernandez & Natasha Zvereva def. Brenda Schultz-McCarthy & Rennae Stubbs, 7-6 (7-3), 6-2.

Mixed— unseeded Meredith McGrath & M. Lucena def. #3 Gigi Fernandez & Cyril Suk, 6-4 6-4.

1995 Fed Cup

Originally the Federation Cup and started in 1963 by the International Tennis Federation as the Davis Cup of women's tennis. Played by 32 teams over one week at one site through 1994. Tournament changed in 1995 to Davis Cup-style format of four rounds and home sites.

Quarterfinals
(Apr. 22-23)

Winner		Loser
at USA 5		Austria 0
Spain 3		at Bulgaria 2
at Germany 4		Japan 1
at France 3		South Africa 2

Semifinals

United States 3, France 2
at Wilmington, N.C. (July 22-23)

Day One— Lindsay Davenport (USA) def. Julie Halard (FRA), 7-6 (6-0), 7-5; Mary Pierce (FRA) def. Mary Joe Fernandez (USA), 7-6 (7-1), 6-3.

Day Two— Davenport (USA) def. Pierce (FRA), 6-3, 4-6, 6-0; Halard (FRA) def. M.J. Fernandez (USA), 1-6, 7-5, 6-1; Davenport & Gigi Fernandez (USA) def. Halard & Nathalie Tauziat (FRA), 6-1, 7-6 (7-1).

Spain 3, Germany 2
at Santander, Spain (July 22-23)

Day One— Conchita Martinez (SPA) def. Anke Huber (GER), 6-2, 2-6, 6-0; Sabine Hack (GER) def. Arantxa Sanchez Vicario (SPA), 6-4, 6-2.

Day Two— Sanchez Vicario (SPA) def. Huber (GER), 6-3, 1-6, 6-2; Martinez (SPA) def. Hack (GER), 6-0, 6-0; Huber & Claudia Porwik (GER) def. Maria Antonia Sanchez & Virginia Ruano (SPA), 6-2, 6-2.

Finals
at Valencia, Spain (Nov. 25-26)

Singles Leaders

Official Top 20 computer rankings and money leaders of men's and women's tours for 1994 and unofficial rankings and money leaders for 1995 (through Sept. 24), as compiled by the ATP (Association of Tennis Professionals) and WTA (Women's Tennis Association). Note that money list includes doubles earnings.

Final 1994 Computer Rankings and Money Won

Listed are events won and times a finalist and semifinalist (Finish, 1-2-SF), match record (W-L), and earnings for the year.

MEN

	Finish 1-2-SF	W-L	Earnings
1 Pete Sampras	10-1-1	74-11	$3,607,812
2 Andre Agassi	5-1-2	51-13	1,941,667
3 Boris Becker	4-3-3	48-16	2,029,756
4 Sergi Bruguera	3-3-4	65-24	3,031,874
5 Goran Ivanisevic	2-4-4	63-26	2,060,278
6 Michael Chang	6-3-1	65-20	1,789,495
7 Stefan Edberg	3-1-4	60-25	2,489,161
8 Alberto Berasategui	7-2-1	65-25	939,651
9 Michael Stich	3-2-4	60-24	2,033,623
10 Todd Martin	2-3-3	51-19	888,342
11 Yevgeny Kafelnikov	3-1-5	67-28	1,011,563
12 Wayne Ferreira	5-2-2	69-25	1,063,341
13 Jim Courier	0-2-5	47-19	1,921,584
14 Marc Rosset	2-2-3	49-26	768,004
15 Andrei Medvedev	2-2-1	34-17	1,211,134
16 Thomas Muster	3-0-3	58-24	654,829
17 Richard Krajicek	3-0-1	33-14	555,116
18 Petr Korda	0-3-1	38-22	612,012
19 Magnus Larsson	2-2-1	35-22	639,105
20 Jason Stoltenberg	1-2-2	38-25	498,842

Note: ITF Grand Slam Cup statistics are considered unofficial by the ATP and not included here.

WOMEN

	Finish 1-2-SF	W-L	Earnings
1 Steffi Graf	7-3-1	58-6	$1,487,980
2 A. Sanchez Vicario	8-4-0	74-9	2,943,665
3 Conchita Martinez	4-0-3	55-15	1,540,167
4 Jana Novotna	3-0-3	43-11	876,119
5 Mary Pierce	0-5-3	45-18	768,614
6 Lindsay Davenport	2-1-4	48-15	600,745
7 Gabriela Sabatini	1-2-5	42-17	874,470
8 Martina Navratilova	1-4-1	33-14	851,082
9 Kimiko Date	2-0-4	33-14	376,904
10 Natasha Zvereva	1-3-2	30-12	874,592
11 Magdalena Maleeva	2-0-3	33-12	324,347
12 Anke Huber	3-0-2	41-17	456,731
13 Iva Majoli	0-3-3	39-19	318,152
14 Mary Joe Fernandez	1-1-0	25-10	193,411
15 Brenda Schultz	1-4-3	49-23	334,046
16 Amy Frazier	1-2-2	28-15	244,767
17 Lori McNeil	1-0-2	26-15	337,046
18 Amanda Coetzer	1-1-2	38-19	361,791
19 Sabine Hack	1-0-2	35-18	291,296
20 Ines Gorrochategui	0-1-0	23-10	186,971

1995 Computer Rankings (through Sept. 24)

For Men's Tour, listed are tournaments won and times a finalist and semifinalist (Finish, 1-2-SF), match record (W-L), and computer points earned (Pts). For Women's Tour, listed are tournaments won and times a finalist and semifinalist (Finish, 1-2-SF), match record (W-L), and average computer points per game (Avg).

MEN

ATP/IBM singles rankings based on total computer points from each player's 14 best tournaments covering the last 12 months. Tournaments, titles and match won-lost records, however, are for 1995 only.

Rank 95 (94)	Finish 1-2-SF	W-L	Pts
1 (2) Andre Agassi	7-4-2	72-8	5400
2 (1) Pete Sampras	4-3-3	55-12	4959
3 (16) Thomas Muster	11-1-0	76-11	4072
4 (3) Boris Becker	1-3-1	40-14	3420
5 (6) Michael Chang	2-4-1	50-14	3015
6 (11) Yevgeny Kafelnikov	4-1-4	62-22	2670
7 (5) Goran Ivanisevic	0-1-7	41-20	2608
8 (60) Thomas Enqvist	4-1-2	52-18	2073
9 (13) Jim Courier	3-0-3	44-14	1964
10 (4) Sergi Bruguera	0-1-4	36-15	1953
11 (14) Marc Rosset	2-0-2	32-16	1940
12 (9) Michael Stich	1-3-2	45-18	1933
13 (17) Richard Krajicek	2-1-1	32-21	1906
14 (12) Wayne Ferreira	2-0-2	43-24	1842
15 (19) Magnus Larsson	0-2-3	32-19	1824
16 (8) Alberto Berasategui	1-0-0	28-26	1409
17 (15) Andrei Medvedev	1-0-1	36-21	1385
18 (24) Andrea Gaudenzi	0-2-3	32-24	1288
19 (10) Todd Martin	1-0-3	37-19	1263
20 (7) Stefan Edberg	1-1-2	37-16	1257

WOMEN

WTA Tour Media Information System singles rankings based on average computer points awarded for each tournament played during the last 12 months. Tournaments, titles and match won-lost records, however, are for 1995 only.

Rank 95 (94)	Finish 1-2-SF	W-L	Avg
1 (1) Steffi Graf	7-0-0	39-1	357.2
1 (NR) Monica Seles	1-1-0	11-1	0.0
2 (2) A. Sanchez-Vicario	2-5-2	49-13	240.4
3 (3) Conchita Martinez	6-1-4	59-7	226.2
4 (4) Jana Novotna	1-0-4	28-8	185.9
5 (5) Mary Pierce	2-1-2	33-12	181.1
6 (9) Kimiko Date	1-3-2	40-11	169.4
7 (7) Gabriela Sabatini	1-1-5	39-14	156.4
8 (11) Magdalena Maleeva	2-2-3	25-9	148.5
9 (6) Lindsay Davenport	1-2-0	31-10	144.5
10 (12) Anke Huber	0-0-2	30-13	122.5
11 (14) Mary Joe Fernandez	1-0-1	24-11	104.2
12 (10) Natasha Zvereva	0-1-3	26-13	98.7
13 (13) Iva Majoli	0-1-2	19-11	92.3
14 (15) B. Schultz-McCarthy	1-1-1	28-11	88.7
15 (23) Chanda Rubin	1-2-0	36-14	79.6
16 (87) Martina Hingis	0-2-0	20-10	79.1
17 (26) Naoko Sawamatsu	0-0-1	24-12	74.9
18 (22) Helena Sukova	0-0-1	12-10	71.3
19 (16) Amy Frazier	1-0-1	26-12	69.9
20 (35) Nathalie Tauziat	1-0-0	24-14	64.7

Note: Seles was restored to her No. 1 ranking by the WTA on July 20. She will be co-No. 1 with Graf for her first six events or 12 months, whichever comes first. Seles was forced to leave the tour after being stabbed in the back on April 30, 1993.

Singles Leaders (Cont.)
1995 Money Winners
Amounts include singles and doubles earnings through Sept. 24, 1995.

MEN

	Earnings		Earnings		Earnings
1 Andre Agassi	$2,279,741	8 Richard Krajicek	$777,702	15 Magnus Larsson	$652,560
2 Pete Sampras	2,170,666	9 Michael Stich	770,407	16 Mark Woodforde	648,581
3 Thomas Muster	2,087,129	10 Wayne Ferriera	746,186	17 Jacco Eltingh	645,441
4 Yevgeny Kafelnikov	1,716,511	11 Paul Haarhuis	707,812	18 Jim Courier	638,262
5 Boris Becker	1,036,658	12 Thomas Enqvist	691,546	19 Andrei Medvedev	594,317
6 Michael Chang	971,140	13 Sergi Bruguera	671,769	20 Jonas Bjorkman	569,867
7 Goran Ivanisevic	943,382	14 Todd Woodbridge	670,146		

WOMEN

	Earnings		Earnings		Earnings
1 Steffi Graf	$1,888,050	8 Kimiko Date	$542,113	15 Larisa Neiland	$293,345
2 A. Sanchez Vicario	1,326,256	9 Gigi Fernandez	495,773	16 Chanda Rubin	271,942
3 Conchita Martinez	1,171,318	10 Monica Seles	397,010	17 Eva Majoli	248,150
4 Natasha Zvereva	651,262	11 Lindsay Davenport	383,522	18 Amanda Coetzer	246,586
5 Jana Novotna	621,736	12 Mary Joe Fernandez	348,357	19 Nathalie Tauziat	237,556
6 Mary Pierce	584,718	13 B. Schultz-McCarthy	348,034	20 Anke Huber	234,364
7 Gabriela Sabatini	574,108	14 Magdalena Maleeva	322,283		

Davis Cup

Sweden defeated Russia, 4-1, in Moscow to capture the 1994 Davis Cup. It was the fifth championship for the Swedes, but their first since winning three out of four years from 1984-87. Yevgeny Kafelnikov kept the Russians from being shut out in their first appearance in the Cup final, beating Stefan Edberg in reverse singles after Sweden had clinched the title.

1994 Final
Sweden 4, Russia 1
(at Moscow, Dec. 2-4)
Day One— Stefan Edberg (SWE) def. Alexander Volkov (RUS), 6-4, 6-2, 6-7 (2-7), 0-6, 8-6; Magnus Larsson (SWE) def. Yevgeny Kafelnikov (RUS), 6-0, 6-2, 3-6, 2-6, 6-3.
Day Two— Jonas Bjorkman & Jan Apell (SWE) def. Kafelnikov & Andrei Olhovskiy (RUS), 6-7 (4-7), 6-2, 6-3, 1-6, 8-6.
Day Three— Larsson def. Volkov, 7-6 (7-4), 6-4; Kafelnikov def. Edberg, 4-6, 6-4, 6-0.

1995 Early Rounds

Moscow will host the Davis Cup final for the second straight year, as Russia plays the United States, Dec. 1-3. The Russians reached the final by upsetting Boris Becker and Germany, 3-2, while the Americans eliminated Cup holder Sweden, 4-1. The U.S. has won the Cup 30 times since play began in 1900. Russia has never won.

First ROUND
(Feb. 3-5)

Winner	Loser
at Austria 4	Spain 1
at Germany 4	Croatia 1
Holland 4	at Switzerland 1
at Italy 4	Czech Republic 1
Russia 4	at Belgium 1
at South Africa 3	Australia 2
Sweden 3	at Denmark 2
at USA 4	France 1

QUARTERFINALS
(Mar. 31-Apr. 2)

Winner	Loser
Germany 4	at Holland 1
USA 5	at Italy 0
at Russia 4	South Africa 1
at Sweden 5	Austria 0

SEMIFINALS
United States 4, Sweden 1
at Las Vegas (Sept. 22-24)
Day One— Pete Sampras (USA) def. Thomas Enqvist (SWE), 6-3, 6-4, 3-6, 6-3; Andre Agassi (USA) def. Mats Wilander (SWE), 7-6 (7-5), 6-2, 6-2.
Day Two— Stefan Edberg & Jonas Bjorkman (SWE) def. Todd Martin & Jonathan Stark (USA), 6-3, 6-4, 6-4.
Day Three— Martin (USA) def. Enqvist (SWE), 7-5, 7-5, 7-6 (7-2); Sampras (USA) def. Wilander (SWE), 2-6, 7-6 (7-4), 6-3.

Russia 3, Germany 2
at Moscow (Sept. 22-24)
Day One— Boris Becker (GER) def. Andrei Chesnokov (RUS), 6-7 (4-7), 6-3, 7-6 (7-3), 7-5; Michael Stich (GER) def. Yevgeny Kafelnikov (RUS), 6-1, 4-6, 6-3, 6-4
Day Two— Kafelnikov & Andrei Olhovskiy (RUS) def. Becker & Stich (GER), 7-6 (7-3), 6-4, 2-6, 6-7 (5-7), 7-5.
Day Three— Kafelnikov (RUS) def. Bernd Karbacher (GER), 6-1, 7-6 (7-5), 6-2; Chesnokov (RUS) def. Stich (GER), 6-4, 1-6, 1-6, 6-3, 14-12.

Agassi vs. Sampras
From the 1992 French Open to the '95 U.S. Open, Davis Cup teammates Pete Sampras and Andre Agassi have met 11 times with Sampras winning six. Sampras also leads their all-time series, 9-8.

Tourney (Rd.)	Winner	Score
'92 French Open (QF)	Agassi	76 62 61
'93 Wimbledon (QF)	Sampras	62 62 36 36 64
'94 Key Biscayne (F)	Sampras	57 63 63
'94 Osaka (SF)	Sampras	63 61
'94 Paris-Indoor (QF)	Agassi	76 75
'94 ATP Champ. (SF)	Sampras	46 76 63
'95 Australian Open (F)	Agassi	46 61 76 64
'95 Indian Wells (F)	Sampras	75 63 75
'95 Key Biscayne (F)	Agassi	36 62 76
'95 Canadian Open (F)	Agassi	36 62 63
'95 U.S. Open (F)	Sampras	64 63 46 75

THE 1996 INFORMATION PLEASE SPORTS ALMANAC

TENNIS STATISTICS

THROUGH THE YEARS
1877-1995
MAJOR TITLES • LEADERS

SEC B

PAGE 803

Grand Slam Championships
Australian Open
MEN

Became an Open Championship in 1969. Two tournaments were held in 1977; the first in January, the second in December. Tournament moved back to January in 1987, so no championship was decided in 1986.

Surface: Synpave Rebound Ace (hardcourt surface composed of polyurethane and synthetic rubber).

Multiple winners: Roy Emerson (6); Jack Crawford and Ken Rosewall (4); James Anderson, Rod Laver, Adrian Quist, Mats Wilander and Pat Wood (3); Jack Bromwich, Ashley Cooper, Jim Courier, Stefan Edberg, Rodney Heath, Johan Kriek, Ivan Lendl, John Newcombe, Frank Sedgman, Guillermo Vilas and Tony Wilding (2).

Year	Winner	Loser	Score
1905	Rodney Heath	A. Curtis	46 63 64 64
1906	Tony Wilding	H. Parker	60 64 64
1907	Horace Rice	H. Parker	63 64 64
1908	Fred Alexander	A. Dunlop	36 36 60 62 63
1909	Tony Wilding	E. Parker	61 75 62
1910	Rodney Heath	H. Rice	64 63 62
1911	Norman Brookes	H. Rice	61 62 63
1912	J. Cecil Parke	A. Beamish	36 63 16 61 75
1913	Ernie Parker	H. Parker	26 61 62 63
1914	Pat Wood	G. Patterson	64 63 57 61
1915	Francis Lowe	H. Rice	46 61 61 64
1916-18	Not held	World War I	
1919	A.R.F. Kingscote	E. Pockley	64 60 63
1920	Pat Wood	R. Thomas	63 46 68 61 63
1921	Rhys Gemmell	A. Hedeman	75 61 64
1922	James Anderson	G. Patterson	60 36 36 63 62
1923	Pat Wood	C.B. St. John	61 61 63
1924	James Anderson	R. Schlesinger	63 64 36 57 63
1925	James Anderson	G. Patterson	11-9 26 62 63
1926	John Hawkes	J. Willard	61 63 61
1927	Gerald Patterson	J. Hawkes	36 64 36 18-16 63
1928	Jean Borotra	R.O. Cummings	64 61 46 57 63
1929	John Gregory	R. Schlesinger	62 62 57 75
1930	Gar Moon	H. Hopman	63 61 63
1931	Jack Crawford	H. Hopman	64 62 26 61
1932	Jack Crawford	H. Hopman	46 63 36 63 61
1933	Jack Crawford	K. Gledhill	26 75 63 62
1934	Fred Perry	J. Crawford	63 75 61
1935	Jack Crawford	F. Perry	26 64 64 64
1936	Adrian Quist	J. Crawford	62 63 46 36 97
1937	Viv McGrath	J. Bromwich	63 16 60 26 61
1938	Don Budge	J. Bromwich	64 62 61
1939	Jack Bromwich	A. Quist	64 61 63
1940	Adrian Quist	J. Crawford	63 61 62
1941-45	Not held	World War II	
1946	Jack Bromwich	D. Pails	57 63 75 36 62
1947	Dinny Pails	J. Bromwich	46 64 36 75 86
1948	Adrian Quist	J. Bromwich	64 36 63 26 63
1949	Frank Sedgman	J. Bromwich	63 63 62
1950	Frank Sedgman	K. McGregor	63 64 46 61
1951	Dick Savitt	K. McGregor	63 26 63 61
1952	Ken McGregor	F. Sedgman	75 12-10 26 62
1953	Ken Rosewall	M. Rose	60 63 64

Year	Winner	Loser	Score
1954	Mervyn Rose	R. Hartwig	62 06 64 62
1955	Ken Rosewall	L. Hoad	97 64 64
1956	Lew Hoad	K. Rosewall	64 36 64 75
1957	Ashley Cooper	N. Fraser	63 9-11 64 62
1958	Ashley Cooper	M. Anderson	75 63 64
1959	Alex Olmedo	N. Fraser	61 62 36 63
1960	Rod Laver	N. Fraser	57 36 63 86 86
1961	Roy Emerson	R. Laver	16 63 75 64
1962	Rod Laver	R. Emerson	86 06 64 64
1963	Roy Emerson	K. Fletcher	63 63 61
1964	Roy Emerson	F. Stolle	63 64 62
1965	Roy Emerson	F. Stolle	79 26 64 75 61
1966	Roy Emerson	A. Ashe	64 68 62 63
1967	Roy Emerson	A. Ashe	64 61 61
1968	Bill Bowrey	J. Gisbert	75 26 97 64
1969	Rod Laver	A. Gimeno	63 64 75
1970	Arthur Ashe	D. Crealy	64 97 62
1971	Ken Rosewall	A. Ashe	61 75 63
1972	Ken Rosewall	M. Anderson	76 63 75
1973	John Newcombe	O. Parun	63 67 75 61
1974	Jimmy Connors	P. Dent	76 64 46 63
1975	John Newcombe	J. Connors	75 36 64 75
1976	Mark Edmondson	J. Newcombe	67 63 76 61
1977	Roscoe Tanner	G. Vilas	63 63 63
	Vitas Gerulaitis	J. Lloyd	63 76 57 36 62
1978	Guillermo Vilas	J. Marks	64 64 36 63
1979	Guillermo Vilas	J. Sadri	76 63 62
1980	Brian Teacher	K. Warwick	75 76 63
1981	Johan Kriek	S. Denton	62 76 67 64
1982	Johan Kriek	S. Denton	63 63 62
1983	Mats Wilander	I. Lendl	61 64 64
1984	Mats Wilander	K. Curren	67 64 76 62
1985	Stefan Edberg	M. Wilander	64 63 63
1986	Not held		
1987	Stefan Edberg	P. Cash	63 64 36 57 63
1988	Mats Wilander	P. Cash	63 67 36 61 86
1989	Ivan Lendl	M. Mecir	62 62 62
1990	Ivan Lendl	S. Edberg	46 76 52 (ret.)
1991	Boris Becker	I. Lendl	16 64 64 64
1992	Jim Courier	S. Edberg	63 36 64 62
1993	Jim Courier	S. Edberg	62 61 26 75
1994	Pete Sampras	T. Martin	76 64 64
1995	Andre Agassi	P. Sampras	46 61 76 64

Grand Slam Championships (Cont.)
Australian Open
WOMEN

Became an Open Championship in 1969. Two tournaments were held in 1977, the first in January, the second in December. Tournament moved back to January in 1987, so no championship was decided in 1986.

Multiple winners: Margaret Smith Court (11); Nancye Wynne Bolton (6); Daphne Akhurst (5); Evonne Goolagong Cawley and Steffi Graf (4); Jean Hartigan, Martina Navratilova and Monica Seles (3); Coral Buttsworth, Chris Evert Lloyd, Thelma Long, Hana Mandlikova, Mall Molesworth and Mary Carter Reitano (2).

Year	Winner	Loser	Score	Year	Winner	Loser	Score
1922	Mall Molesworth	E. Boyd	63 10-8	1962	Margaret Smith	J. Lehane	60 62
1923	Mall Molesworth	E. Boyd	61 75	1963	Margaret Smith	J. Lehane	62 62
1924	Sylvia Lance	E. Boyd	63 36 64	1964	Margaret Smith	L. Turner	63 62
1925	Daphne Akhurst	E. Boyd	16 86 64	1965	Margaret Smith	M. Bueno	57 64 52 (ret)
1926	Daphne Akhurst	E. Boyd	61 63	1966	Margaret Smith	N. Richey	walkover
1927	Esna Boyd	S. Harper	57 61 62	1967	Nancy Richey	L. Turner	61 64
1928	Daphne Akhurst	E. Boyd	75 62	1968	Billie Jean King	M. Smith	61 62
1929	Daphne Akhurst	L. Bickerton	61 57 62	1969	Margaret Court	B.J. King	64 61
1930	Daphne Akhurst	S. Harper	10-8 26 75	1970	Margaret Court	K. Melville	61 63
1931	Coral Buttsworth	M. Crawford	16 63 64	1971	Margaret Court	E. Goolagong	26 76 75
1932	Coral Buttsworth	K. Le Messurier	97 64	1972	Virginia Wade	E. Goolagong	64 64
1933	Joan Hartigan	C. Buttsworth	64 63	1973	Margaret Court	E. Goolagong	64 75
1934	Joan Hartigan	M. Molesworth	61 64	1974	Evonne Goolagong	C. Evert	76 46 60
1935	Dorothy Round	N. Lyle	16 61 63	1975	Evonne Goolagong	M. Navratilova	63 62
1936	Joan Hartigan	N. Bolton	64 64	1976	Evonne Cawley	R. Tomanova	62 62
1937	Nancye Wynne	E. Westacott	63 57 64	1977	Kerry Reid	D. Balestrat	75 62
1938	Dorothy Bundy	D. Stevenson	63 62		Evonne Cawley	H. Gourlay	63 60
1939	Emily Westacott	N. Hopman	61 62	1978	Chris O'Neill	B. Nagelsen	63 76
				1979	Barbara Jordan	S. Walsh	63 63
1940	Nancye Wynne	T. Coyne	57 64 60				
1941-45	Not held	World War II		1980	Hana Mandlikova	W. Turnbull	60 75
1946	Nancye Bolton	J. Fitch	64 64	1981	Martina Navratilova	C. Evert Lloyd	67 64 75
1947	Nancye Bolton	N. Hopman	63 62	1982	Chris Evert Lloyd	M. Navratilova	63 26 63
1948	Nancye Bolton	M. Toomey	63 61	1983	Martina Navratilova	K. Jordan	62 76
1949	Doris Hart	N. Bolton	63 64	1984	Chris Evert Lloyd	H. Sukova	67 61 63
				1985	Martina Navratilova	C. Evert Lloyd	62 46 62
1950	Louise Brough	D. Hart	64 36 64	1986	Not held		
1951	Nancye Bolton	T. Long	61 75	1987	Hana Mandlikova	M. Navratilova	75 76
1952	Thelma Long	H. Angwin	62 63	1988	Steffi Graf	C. Evert	61 76
1953	Maureen Connolly	J. Sampson	63 62	1989	Steffi Graf	H. Sukova	64 64
1954	Thelma Long	J. Staley	63 64				
1955	Beryl Penrose	T. Long	64 63	1990	Steffi Graf	M.J. Fernandez	63 64
1956	Mary Carter	T. Long	36 62 97	1991	Monica Seles	J. Novotna	57 63 61
1957	Shirley Fry	A. Gibson	63 64	1992	Monica Seles	M.J. Fernandez	62 63
1958	Angela Mortimer	L. Coghlan	63 64	1993	Monica Seles	S. Graf	46 63 62
1959	Mary Reitano	T. Schuurman	62 63	1994	Steffi Graf	A.S. Vicario	60 62
				1995	Mary Pierce	A.S. Vicario	63 62
1960	Margaret Smith	J. Lehane	75 62				
1961	Margaret Smith	J. Lehane	61 64				

French Open
MEN

Prior to 1925, entry was restricted to members of French clubs. Became an Open Championship in 1968, but closed to contract pros in 1972.

Surface: Red clay.

First year: 1891. **Most wins:** Max Decugis (8).

Multiple winners (since 1925): Bjorn Borg (6); Henri Cochet (4); Rene Lacoste, Ivan Lendl and Mats Wilander (3); Sergi Bruguera, Jim Courier, Jaroslav Drobny, Roy Emerson, Jan Kodes, Rod Laver, Frank Parker, Nicola Pietrangeli, Ken Rosewall, Manuel Santana, Tony Trabert and Gottfried von Cramm (2).

Year	Winner	Loser	Score	Year	Winner	Loser	Score
1925	Rene Lacoste	J. Borotra	75 61 64	1935	Fred Perry	G. von Cramm	63 36 61 63
1926	Henri Cochet	R. Lacoste	62 64 63	1936	Gottfried von Cramm	F. Perry	60 26 62 26 60
1927	Rene Lacoste	B. Tilden	64 46 57 63 11-9	1937	Henner Henkel	H. Austin	61 64 63
1928	Henri Cochet	R. Lacoste	57 63 61 63	1938	Don Budge	R. Menzel	63 62 64
1929	Rene Lacoste	J. Borotra	63 26 60 26 86	1939	Don McNeill	B. Riggs	75 60 63
1930	Henri Cochet	B. Tilden	36 86 63 61	1940-45	Not held	World War II	
1931	Jean Borotra	C. Boussus	26 64 75 64	1946	Marcel Bernard	J. Drobny	36 26 61 64 63
1932	Henri Cochet	G. de Stefani	60 64 46 63	1947	Joseph Asboth	E. Sturgess	86 75 64
1933	Jack Crawford	H. Cochet	86 61 63	1948	Frank Parker	J. Drobny	64 75 57 86
1934	Gottfried von Cramm	J. Crawford	64 79 36 75 63	1949	Frank Parker	B. Patty	63 16 61 64

Year	Winner	Loser	Score	Year	Winner	Loser	Score
1950	Budge Patty	J. Drobny	61 62 36 57 75	1973	Ilie Nastase	N. Pilic	63 63 60
1951	Jaroslav Drobny	E. Sturgess	63 63 63	1974	Bjorn Borg	M. Orantes	26 67 60 61 61
1952	Jaroslav Drobny	F. Sedgman	62 60 36 64	1975	Bjorn Borg	G. Vilas	62 63 64
1953	Ken Rosewall	V. Seixas	63 64 16 62	1976	Adriano Panatta	H. Solomon	61 64 46 76
1954	Tony Trabert	A. Larsen	64 75 61	1977	Guillermo Vilas	B. Gottfried	60 63 60
1955	Tony Trabert	S. Davidson	26 61 64 62	1978	Bjorn Borg	G. Vilas	61 61 63
1956	Lew Hoad	S. Davidson	64 86 63	1979	Bjorn Borg	V. Pecci	63 61 67 64
1957	Sven Davidson	H. Flam	63 64 64				
1958	Mervyn Rose	L. Ayala	63 64 64	1980	Bjorn Borg	V. Gerulaitis	64 61 62
1959	Nicola Pietrangeli	I. Vermaak	36 63 64 61	1981	Bjorn Borg	I. Lendl	61 46 62 36 61
				1982	Mats Wilander	G. Vilas	16 76 60 64
1960	Nicola Pietrangeli	L. Ayala	36 63 64 46 63	1983	Yannick Noah	M. Wilander	62 75 76
1961	Manuel Santana	N. Pietrangeli	46 61 36 60 62	1984	Ivan Lendl	J. McEnroe	36 26 64 75 75
1962	Rod Laver	R. Emerson	36 26 63 97 62	1985	Mats Wilander	I. Lendl	36 64 62 62
1963	Roy Emerson	P. Darmon	36 61 64 64	1986	Ivan Lendl	M. Pernfors	63 62 64
1964	Manuel Santana	N. Pietrangeli	63 61 46 75	1987	Ivan Lendl	M. Wilander	75 62 36 76
1965	Fred Stolle	T. Roche	36 60 62 63	1988	Mats Wilander	H. Leconte	75 62 61
1966	Tony Roche	I. Gulyas	61 64 75	1989	Michael Chang	S. Edberg	61 36 46 64 62
1967	Roy Emerson	T. Roche	61 64 26 62				
1968	Ken Rosewall	R. Laver	63 61 26 62	1990	Andres Gomez	A. Agassi	63 26 64 64
1969	Rod Laver	K. Rosewall	64 63 64	1991	Jim Courier	A. Agassi	36 64 26 61 64
				1992	Jim Courier	P. Korda	75 62 61
1970	Jan Kodes	Z. Franulovic	62 64 60	1993	Sergi Bruguera	J. Courier	64 26 62 36 63
1971	Jan Kodes	I. Nastase	86 62 26 75	1994	Sergi Bruguera	A. Berasategui	63 75 26 61
1972	Andres Gimeno	P. Proisy	46 63 61 61	1995	Thomas Muster	M. Chang	75 62 64

WOMEN

Prior to 1925, entry was restricted to members of French clubs. Became an Open Championship in 1968, but closed to contract pros in 1972.

First year: 1897. **Most wins:** Chris Evert Lloyd (7) and Suzanne Lenglen (6).

Multiple winners (since 1920): Chris Evert Lloyd (7); Margaret Smith Court (5); Steffi Graf and Helen Wills Moody (4); Monica Seles and Hilde Sperling (3); Maureen Connolly, Margaret Osborne duPont, Doris Hart, Ann Haydon Jones, Suzanne Lenglen, Simone Mathieu, Margaret Scriven, Martina Navratilova, Lesley Turner and Arantxa Sanchez Vicario (2).

Year	Winner	Loser	Score	Year	Winner	Loser	Score
1925	Suzanne Lenglen	K. McKane	61 62	1963	Lesley Turner	A. Jones	26 63 75
1926	Suzanne Lenglen	M. Browne	61 60	1964	Margaret Smith	M. Bueno	57 61 62
1927	Kea Bouman	I. Peacock	62 64	1965	Lesley Turner	M. Smith	63 64
1928	Helen Wills	E. Bennett	61 62	1966	Ann Jones	N. Richey	63 61
1929	Helen Wills	S. Mathieu	63 64	1967	Francoise Durr	L. Turner	46 63 64
				1968	Nancy Richey	A. Jones	57 64 61
1930	Helen Moody	H. Jacobs	62 61	1969	Margaret Court	A. Jones	61 46 63
1931	Cilly Aussem	B. Nuthall	86 61				
1932	Helen Moody	S. Mathieu	75 61	1970	Margaret Court	H. Niessen	62 64
1933	Margaret Scriven	S. Mathieu	62 46 64	1971	Evonne Goolagong	H. Gourlay	63 75
1934	Margaret Scriven	H. Jacobs	75 46 61	1972	Billie Jean King	E. Goolagong	63 63
1935	Hilde Sperling	S. Mathieu	62 61	1973	Margaret Court	C. Evert	67 76 64
1936	Hilde Sperling	S. Mathieu	63 64	1974	Chris Evert	O. Morozova	61 62
1937	Hilde Sperling	S. Mathieu	62 64	1975	Chris Evert	M. Navratilova	26 62 61
1938	Simone Mathieu	N. Landry	60 63	1976	Sue Barker	R. Tomanova	62 06 62
1939	Simone Mathieu	J. Jedrzejowska	63 86	1977	Mima Jausovec	F. Mihai	62 67 61
				1978	Virginia Ruzici	M. Jausovec	62 62
1940-45	Not held	World War II		1979	Chris Evert Lloyd	W. Turnbull	62 60
1946	Margaret Osborne	P. Betz	16 86 75				
1947	Patricia Todd	D. Hart	63 36 64	1980	Chris Evert Lloyd	V. Ruzici	60 63
1948	Nelly Landry	S. Fry	62 06 60	1981	Hana Mandlikova	S. Hanika	62 64
1949	Margaret duPont	N. Adamson	75 62	1982	Martina Navratilova	A. Jaeger	76 61
				1983	Chris Evert Lloyd	M. Jausovec	61 62
1950	Doris Hart	P. Todd	64 46 62	1984	Martina Navratilova	C. Evert Lloyd	63 61
1951	Shirley Fry	D. Hart	63 36 63	1985	Chris Evert Lloyd	M. Navratilova	63 67 75
1952	Doris Hart	S. Fry	64 64	1986	Chris Evert Lloyd	M. Navratilova	26 63 63
1953	Maureen Connolly	D. Hart	62 64	1987	Steffi Graf	M. Navratilova	64 46 86
1954	Maureen Connolly	G. Bucaille	64 61	1988	Steffi Graf	N. Zvereva	60 60
1955	Angela Mortimer	D. Knode	26 75 10-8	1989	A. Sanchez Vicario	S. Graf	76 36 75
1956	Althea Gibson	A. Mortimer	60 12-10				
1957	Shirley Bloomer	D. Knode	61 63	1990	Monica Seles	S. Graf	76 64
1958	Susi Kormoczi	S. Bloomer	64 16 62	1991	Monica Seles	A.S. Vicario	63 64
1959	Christine Truman	S. Kormoczi	64 75	1992	Monica Seles	S. Graf	62 36 10-8
				1993	Steffi Graf	M.J. Fernandez	46 62 64
1960	Darlene Hard	Y. Ramirez	63 64	1994	A. Sanchez Vicario	M. Pierce	64 64
1961	Ann Haydon	Y. Ramirez	62 61	1995	Steffi Graff	A.S. Vicario	76 46 60
1962	Margaret Smith	L. Turner	63 36 75				

Grand Slam Champions (Cont.)

Wimbledon
MEN

Officially called "The Lawn Tennis Championships" at the All England Club, Wimbledon. Challenge round system (defending champion qualified for following year's final) used from 1877–1921. Became an Open Championship in 1968, but closed to contract pros in 1972.

Surface: Grass.

Multiple winners: Willie Renshaw (7); Bjorn Borg and Laurie Doherty (5); Reggie Doherty, Rod Laver and Tony Wilding (4); Wilfred Baddeley, Boris Becker, Arthur Gore, John McEnroe, John Newcombe, Fred Perry, Pete Sampras and Bill Tilden (3); Jean Borotra, Norman Brookes, Don Budge, Henri Cochet, Jimmy Connors, Stefan Edberg, Roy Emerson, John Hartley, Lew Hoad, Rene Lacoste, Gerald Patterson and Joshua Pim (2).

Year	Winner	Loser	Score	Year	Winner	Loser	Score
1877	Spencer Gore	W. Marshall	61 62 64	1936	Fred Perry	G. von Cramm	61 61 60
1878	Frank Hadow	S. Gore	75 61 97	1937	Don Budge	G. von Cramm	63 64 62
1879	John Hartley	V. St. L. Gould	62 64 62	1938	Don Budge	H. Austin	61 60 63
				1939	Bobby Riggs	E. Cooke	26 86 36 63 62
1880	John Hartley	H. Lawford	60 62 26 63	1940–45	Not held	World War II	
1881	Willie Renshaw	J. Hartley	60 62 61	1946	Yvon Petra	G. Brown	62 64 79 57 64
1882	Willie Renshaw	E. Renshaw	61 26 46 62 62	1947	Jack Kramer	T. Brown	61 63 62
1883	Willie Renshaw	E. Renshaw	26 63 63 46 63	1948	Bob Falkenburg	J. Bromwich	75 06 62 36 75
1884	Willie Renshaw	H. Lawford	60 64 97	1949	Ted Schroeder	J. Drobny	36 60 63 46 64
1885	Willie Renshaw	H. Lawford	75 62 46 75	1950	Budge Patty	F. Sedgman	61 8-10 62 63
1886	Willie Renshaw	H. Lawford	60 57 63 64	1951	Dick Savitt	K. McGregor	64 64 64
1887	Herbert Lawford	E. Renshaw	16 63 36 64 64	1952	Frank Sedgman	J. Drobny	46 62 63 62
1888	Ernest Renshaw	H. Lawford	63 75 60	1953	Vic Seixas	K. Nielsen	97 63 64
1889	Willie Renshaw	E. Renshaw	64 61 36 60	1954	Jaroslav Drobny	K. Rosewall	13-11 46 62 97
1890	William Hamilton	W. Renshaw	68 62 36 61 61	1955	Tony Trabert	K. Nielsen	63 75 61
1891	Wilfred Baddeley	J. Pim	64 16 75 60	1956	Lew Hoad	K. Rosewall	62 46 75 64
1892	Wilfred Baddeley	J. Pim	46 63 63 62	1957	Lew Hoad	A. Cooper	62 61 62
1893	Joshua Pim	W. Baddeley	36 61 63 62	1958	Ashley Cooper	N. Fraser	36 63 64 13-11
1894	Joshua Pim	W. Baddeley	10-8 62 86	1959	Alex Olmedo	R. Laver	64 63 64
1895	Wilfred Baddeley	W. Eaves	46 26 86 62 63	1960	Neale Fraser	R. Laver	64 36 97 75
1896	Harold Mahony	W. Baddeley	62 68 57 86 63	1961	Rod Laver	C. McKinley	63 61 64
1897	Reggie Doherty	H. Mahony	64 64 63	1962	Rod Laver	M. Mulligan	62 62 61
1898	Reggie Doherty	L. Doherty	63 63 26 57 61	1963	Chuck McKinley	F. Stolle	97 61 64
1899	Reggie Doherty	A. Gore	16 46 62 63 62	1964	Roy Emerson	F. Stolle	64 12-10 46 63
1900	Reggie Doherty	S. Smith	68 63 61 62	1965	Roy Emerson	F. Stolle	64 11-9 64
1901	Arthur Gore	R. Doherty	46 75 64 64	1966	Manuel Santana	D. Ralston	64 11-9 64
1902	Laurie Doherty	A. Gore	64 63 36 60	1967	John Newcombe	W. Bungert	63 61 61
1903	Laurie Doherty	F. Riseley	75 63 60	1968	Rod Laver	T. Roche	63 64 62
1904	Laurie Doherty	F. Riseley	-61 75 86	1969	Rod Laver	J. Newcombe	64 57 64 64
1905	Laurie Doherty	N. Brookes	86 62 64	1970	John Newcombe	K. Rosewall	57 63 62 36 61
1906	Laurie Doherty	F. Riseley	64 46 62 63	1971	John Newcombe	S. Smith	63 57 26 64 64
1907	Norman Brookes	A. Gore	64 62 62	1972	Stan Smith	I. Nastase	46 63 63 46 75
1908	Arthur Gore	R. Barrett	63 62 46 36 64	1973	Jan Kodes	A. Metreveli	61 98 63
1909	Arthur Gore	M. Ritchie	68 16 62 62 62	1974	Jimmy Connors	K. Rosewall	61 61 64
1910	Tony Wilding	A. Gore	64 75 46 62	1975	Arthur Ashe	J. Connors	61 61 57 64
1911	Tony Wilding	R. Barrett	64 46 26 62 (ret)	1976	Bjorn Borg	I. Nastase	64 62 97
1912	Tony Wilding	A. Gore	64 64 46 64	1977	Bjorn Borg	J. Connors	36 62 61 57 64
1913	Tony Wilding	M. McLoughlin	86 63 10-8	1978	Bjorn Borg	J. Connors	62 62 63
1914	Norman Brookes	T. Wilding	64 64 75	1979	Bjorn Borg	R. Tanner	67 61 36 63 64
1915–18	Not held	World War I		1980	Bjorn Borg	J. McEnroe	16 75 63 67 86
1919	Gerald Patterson	N. Brookes	63 75 62	1981	John McEnroe	B. Borg	46 76 76 64
1920	Bill Tilden	G. Patterson	26 63 62 64	1982	Jimmy Connors	J. McEnroe	36 63 67 76 64
1921	Bill Tilden	B. Norton	46 26 61 60 75	1983	John McEnroe	C. Lewis	62 62 62
1922	Gerald Patterson	R. Lycett	63 64 62	1984	John McEnroe	J. Connors	61 61 62
1923	Bill Johnston	F. Hunter	60 63 61	1985	Boris Becker	K. Curren	63 67 76 64
1924	Jean Borotra	R. Lacoste	61 36 61 36 64	1986	Boris Becker	I. Lendl	64 63 75
1925	Rene Lacoste	J. Borotra	63 63 46 86	1987	Pat Cash	I. Lendl	76 62 75
1926	Jean Borotra	H. Kinsey	86 61 63	1988	Stefan Edberg	B. Becker	46 76 64 62
1927	Henri Cochet	J. Borotra	46 46 63 64 75	1989	Boris Becker	S. Edberg	60 76 64
1928	Rene Lacoste	H. Cochet	61 46 64 62	1990	Stefan Edberg	B. Becker	62 62 36 36 64
1929	Henri Cochet	J. Borotra	64 63 64	1991	Michael Stich	B. Becker	64 76 64
1930	Bill Tilden	W. Allison	63 97 64	1992	Andre Agassi	G. Ivanisevic	67 64 64 16 64
1931	Sidney Wood	F. Shields	walkover	1993	Pete Sampras	J. Courier	76 76 36 63
1932	Ellsworth Vines	H. Austin	64 62 60	1994	Pete Sampras	G. Ivanisevic	76 76 60
1933	Jack Crawford	E. Vines	46 11-9 62 26 64	1995	Pete Sampras	B. Becker	67 62 64 62
1934	Fred Perry	J. Crawford	63 60 75				
1935	Fred Perry	G. von Cramm	62 64 64				

WOMEN

Officially called "The Lawn Tennis Championships" at the All England Club, Wimbledon. Challenge round system (defending champion qualified for following year's final) used from 1886-1921. Became an Open Championship in 1968, but closed to contract pros in 1972.

Multiple winners: Martina Navratilova (9); Helen Wills Moody (8); Dorothea Douglass Chambers (7); Steffi Graf, Blanche Bingley Hillyard, Billie Jean King and Suzanne Lenglen (6); Lottie Dod and Charlotte Cooper Sterry (5); Louise Brough (4); Maria Bueno, Maureen Connolly, Margaret Smith Court and Chris Evert Lloyd (3); Evonne Goolagong Cawley, Althea Gibson, Dorothy Round, May Sutton and Maud Watson (2).

Year	Winner	Loser	Score	Year	Winner	Loser	Score
1884	Maud Watson	L. Watson	68 63 63	1940-45	Not held	World War II	
1885	Maud Watson	B. Bingley	61 75	1946	Pauline Betz	L. Brough	62 64
1886	Blanche Bingley	M. Watson	63 63	1947	Margaret Osborne	D. Hart	62 64
1887	Lottie Dod	B. Bingley	62 60	1948	Louise Brough	D. Hart	63 86
1888	Lottie Dod	B. Hillyard	63 63	1949	Louise Brough	M. duPont	10-8 16 10-8
1889	Blanche Hillyard	L. Rice	46 86 64				
				1950	Louise Brough	M. duPont	61 36 61
1890	Lena Rice	M. Jacks	64 61	1951	Doris Hart	S. Fry	61 60
1891	Lottie Dod	B. Hillyard	62 61	1952	Maureen Connolly	L. Brough	75 63
1892	Lottie Dod	B. Hillyard	61 61	1953	Maureen Connolly	D. Hart	86 75
1893	Lottie Dod	B. Hillyard	68 61 64	1954	Maureen Connolly	L. Brough	62 75
1894	Blanche Hillyard	E. Austin	61 61	1955	Louise Brough	B. Fleitz	75 86
1895	Charlotte Cooper	H. Jackson	75 86	1956	Shirley Fry	A. Buxton	63 61
1896	Charlotte Cooper	W. Pickering	62 63	1957	Althea Gibson	D. Hard	63 62
1897	Blanche Hillyard	C. Cooper	57 75 62	1958	Althea Gibson	A. Mortimer	86 62
1898	Charlotte Cooper	L. Martin	64 64	1959	Maria Bueno	D. Hard	64 63
1899	Blanche Hillyard	C. Cooper	62 63				
				1960	Maria Bueno	S. Reynolds	86 60
1900	Blanche Hillyard	C. Cooper	46 64 64	1961	Angela Mortimer	C. Truman	46 64 75
1901	Charlotte Sterry	B. Hillyard	62 62	1962	Karen Susman	V. Sukova	64 64
1902	Muriel Robb	C. Sterry	75 61	1963	Margaret Smith	B.J. Moffitt	63 64
1903	Dorothea Douglass	E. Thomson	46 64 62	1964	Maria Bueno	M. Smith	64 79 63
1904	Dorothea Douglass	C. Sterry	60 63	1965	Margaret Smith	M. Bueno	64 75
1905	May Sutton	D. Douglass	63 64	1966	Billie Jean King	M. Bueno	63 36 61
1906	Dorothea Douglass	M. Sutton	63 97	1967	Billie Jean King	A. Jones	63 64
1907	May Sutton	D. Chambers	61 64	1968	Billie Jean King	J. Tegart	97 75
1908	Charlotte Sterry	A. Morton	64 64	1969	Ann Jones	B.J. King	36 63 62
1909	Dora Boothby	A. Morton	64 46 86				
				1970	Margaret Court	B.J. King	14-12 11-9
1910	Dorothea Chambers	D. Boothby	62 62	1971	Evonne Goolagong	M. Court	64 61
1911	Dorothea Chambers	D. Boothby	60 60	1972	Billie Jean King	E. Goolagong	63 63
1912	Ethel Larcombe	C. Sterry	63 61	1973	Billie Jean King	C. Evert	60 75
1913	Dorothea Chambers	R. McNair	60 64	1974	Chris Evert	O. Morzova	60 64
1914	Dorothea Chambers	E. Larcombe	75 64	1975	Billie Jean King	E. Cawley	60 61
1915-18	Not held	World War I		1976	Chris Evert	E. Cawley	63 46 86
1919	Suzanne Lenglen	D. Chambers	10-8 46 97	1977	Virginia Wade	B. Stove	46 63 61
				1978	Martina Navratilova	C. Evert	26 64 75
1920	Suzanne Lenglen	D. Chambers	63 60	1979	Martina Navratilova	C. Evert Lloyd	64 64
1921	Suzanne Lenglen	E. Ryan	62 60				
1922	Suzanne Lenglen	M. Mallory	62 60	1980	Evonne Cawley	C. Evert Lloyd	61 76
1923	Suzanne Lenglen	K. McKane	62 62	1981	Chris Evert Lloyd	H. Mandlikova	62 62
1924	Kathleen McKane	H. Wills	46 64 64	1982	Martina Navratilova	C. Evert Lloyd	61 36 62
1925	Suzanne Lenglen	J. Fry	62 60	1983	Martina Navratilova	A. Jaeger	60 63
1926	Kathleen Godfree	L. de Alvarez	62 46 63	1984	Martina Navratilova	C. Evert Lloyd	76 62
1927	Helen Wills	L. de Alvarez	62 63	1985	Martina Navratilova	C. Evert Lloyd	46 63 62
1928	Helen Wills	L. de Alvarez	62 63	1986	Martina Navratilova	H. Mandlikova	76 63
1929	Helen Wills	H. Jacobs	61 62	1987	Martina Navratilova	S. Graf	75 63
				1988	Steffi Graf	M. Navratilova	57 62 61
1930	Helen Moody	E. Ryan	62 62	1989	Steffi Graf	M. Navratilova	62 67 61
1931	Cilly Aussem	H. Kranwinkel	62 75				
1932	Helen Moody	H. Jacobs	63 61	1990	Martina Navratilova	Z. Garrison	64 61
1933	Helen Moody	D. Round	64 68 63	1991	Steffi Graf	G. Sabatini	64 36 86
1934	Dorothy Round	H. Jacobs	62 57 63	1992	Steffi Graf	M. Seles	62 61
1935	Helen Moody	H. Jacobs	63 36 75	1993	Steffi Graf	J. Novotna	76 16 64
1936	Helen Jacobs	H.K. Sperling	62 46 75	1994	Conchita Martinez	M. Navratilova	64 36 63
1937	Dorothy Round	J. Jedrzejowska	62 26 75	1995	Steffi Graf	A.S. Vicario	46 61 75
1938	Helen Moody	H. Jacobs	64 60				
1939	Alice Marble	K. Stammers	62 60				

Wimbledon Mourns Passing of Perry and Gonzales

Wimbledon legends Fred Perry and Pancho Gonzales, died in 1995. Perry, who won three straight men's singles titles from 1934-36, remains the last Englishman to win the championship. Gonzales, who never won Wimbledon, did win the longest match ever played there— a 5-hour and 12-minute marathon in the first round of the 1969 tournament against Charlie Pasarell. The 41-year-old Gonzales took the 112-game match, 22-24, 1-6, 16-14, 6-3, 11-9.

Grand Slam Champions (Cont.)

U.S. Open
MEN

Challenge round system (defending champion qualified for following year's final) used from 1884-1911. Known as the Patriotic Tournament in 1917 during World War I. Amateur and Open Championships held in 1968 and '69. Became an exclusively Open Championship in 1970.
Surface: Decoturf II (acrylic cement).
Multiple winners: Bill Larned, Richard Sears and Bill Tilden (7); Jimmy Connors (5); John McEnroe and Robert Wrenn (4); Oliver Campbell, Ivan Lendl, Fred Perry, Pete Sampras and Malcolm Whitman (3); Don Budge, Stefan Edberg, Roy Emerson, Neale Fraser, Pancho Gonzales, Bill Johnston, Jack Kramer, Rene Lacoste, Rod Laver, Maurice McLoughlin, Lindley Murray, John Newcombe, Frank Parker, Bobby Riggs, Ken Rosewall, Frank Sedgman, Henry Slocum Jr., Tony Trabert, Ellsworth Vines and Dick Williams (2).

Year	Winner	Loser	Score
1881	Richard Sears	W. Glyn	60 63 62
1882	Richard Sears	C. Clark	61 64 60
1883	Richard Sears	J. Dwight	62 60 97
1884	Richard Sears	H. Taylor	60 16 60 62
1885	Richard Sears	G. Brinley	63 46 60 63
1886	Richard Sears	R. Beeckman	46 61 63 64
1887	Richard Sears	H. Slocum Jr.	61 63 62
1888	Henry Slocum Jr.	H. Taylor	64 61 60
1889	Henry Slocum Jr.	Q. Shaw	63 61 46 62
1890	Oliver Campbell	H. Slocum Jr.	62 46 63 61
1891	Oliver Campbell	C. Hobart	26 75 79 61 62
1892	Oliver Campbell	F. Hovey	75 36 63 75
1893	Robert Wrenn	F. Hovey	64 36 64 64
1894	Robert Wrenn	M. Goodbody	68 61 64 64
1895	Fred Hovey	R. Wrenn	63 62 64
1896	Robert Wrenn	F. Hovey	75 36 60 16 61
1897	Robert Wrenn	W. Eaves	46 86 63 26 62
1898	Malcolm Whitman	D. Davis	36 62 62 61
1899	Malcolm Whitman	P. Paret	61 62 36 75
1900	Malcolm Whitman	B. Larned	64 16 62 62
1901	Bill Larned	B. Wright	62 68 64 64
1902	Bill Larned	R. Doherty	46 63 64 86
1903	Laurie Doherty	B. Larned	60 63 10-8
1904	Holcombe Ward	B. Clothier	10-8 64 97
1905	Beals Wright	H. Ward	62 61 11-9
1906	Bill Clothier	B. Wright	63 60 64
1907	Bill Larned	R. LeRoy	62 62 64
1908	Bill Larned	B. Wright	61 62 86
1909	Bill Larned	B. Clothier	61 62 57 16 61
1910	Bill Larned	T. Bundy	61 57 60 68 61
1911	Bill Larned	M. McLoughlin	64 64 62
1912	Maurice McLoughlin	W.F. Johnson	36 26 62 64 62
1913	Maurice McLoughlin	R. Williams	64 57 63 61
1914	Dick Williams	M. McLoughlin	63 86 10-8
1915	Bill Johnston	M. McLoughlin	16 60 75 10-8
1916	Dick Williams	B. Johnston	46 64 06 62 64
1917	Lindley Murray	N. Niles	57 86 63 63
1918	Lindley Murray	B. Tilden	63 61 75
1919	Bill Johnston	B. Tilden	64 64 63
1920	Bill Tilden	B. Johnston	61 16 75 57 63
1921	Bill Tilden	W. Johnson	61 63 61
1922	Bill Tilden	B. Johnston	46 36 62 63 64
1923	Bill Tilden	B. Johnston	64 61 64
1924	Bill Tilden	B. Johnston	61 97 62
1925	Bill Tilden	B. Johnston	46 11-9 63 46 63
1926	Rene Lacoste	J. Borotra	64 60 64
1927	Rene Lacoste	B. Tilden	11-9 63 11-9
1928	Henri Cochet	F. Hunter	46 64 36 75 63
1929	Bill Tilden	F. Hunter	36 63 46 62 64
1930	John Doeg	F. Shields	10-8 16 64 16-14
1931	Ellsworth Vines	G. Lott Jr.	79 63 97 75
1932	Ellsworth Vines	H. Cochet	64 64 64
1933	Fred Perry	J. Crawford	63 11-13 46 60 61
1934	Fred Perry	W. Allison	64 63 16 86
1935	Wilmer Allison	S. Wood	62 62 63
1936	Fred Perry	D. Budge	26 62 86 16 10-8
1937	Don Budge	G. von Cramm	61 79 61 36 61
1938	Don Budge	G. Mako	63 68 62 61
1939	Bobby Riggs	S.W. van Horn	64 62 64
1940	Don McNeill	B. Riggs	46 68 63 63 75
1941	Bobby Riggs	F. Kovacs	57 61 63 63
1942	Fred Schroeder	F. Parker	86 75 36 46 62
1943	Joe Hunt	J. Kramer	63 68 10-8 60
1944	Frank Parker	B. Talbert	64 36 63 63
1945	Frank Parker	B. Talbert	14-12 61 62
1946	Jack Kramer	T. Brown, Jr.	97 63 60
1947	Jack Kramer	F. Parker	46 26 61 60 63
1948	Pancho Gonzales	E. Sturgess	62 63 14-12
1949	Pancho Gonzales	F. Schroeder	16-18 26 61 62 64
1950	Arthur Larsen	H. Flam	63 46 57 64 63
1951	Frank Sedgman	V. Seixas	64 61 61
1952	Frank Sedgman	G. Mulloy	61 62 63
1953	Tony Trabert	V. Seixas	63 62 63
1954	Vic Seixas	R. Hartwig	36 62 64 64
1955	Tony Trabert	K. Rosewall	97 63 63
1956	Ken Rosewall	L. Hoad	46 62 63 63
1957	Mal Anderson	A. Cooper	10-8 75 64
1958	Ashley Cooper	M. Anderson	62 36 46 10-8 86
1959	Neale Fraser	A. Olmedo	63 57 62 64
1960	Neale Fraser	R. Laver	64 64 97
1961	Roy Emerson	R. Laver	75 63 62
1962	Rod Laver	R. Emerson	62 64 57 64
1963	Rafael Osuna	F. Froehling	75 64 62
1964	Roy Emerson	F. Stolle	64 62 64
1965	Manuel Santana	C. Drysdale	62 79 75 61
1966	Fred Stolle	J. Newcombe	46 12-10 63 64
1967	John Newcombe	C. Graebner	64 64 86
1968	Am-Arthur Ashe	B. Lutz	46 63 8-10 60 64
	Op-Arthur Ashe	T. Okker	14-12 57 63 36 63
1969	Am-Stan Smith	B. Lutz	97 63 61
	Op-Rod Laver	T. Roche	79 61 63 62
1970	Ken Rosewall	T. Roche	26 64 76 63
1971	Stan Smith	J. Kodes	36 63 62 76
1972	Ilie Nastase	A. Ashe	36 63 67 64 63
1973	John Newcombe	J. Kodes	64 16 46 62 63
1974	Jimmy Connors	K. Rosewall	61 60 61
1975	Manuel Orantes	J. Connors	64 36 76 64
1976	Jimmy Connors	B. Borg	64 36 76 64
1977	Guillermo Vilas	J. Connors	26 63 76 60
1978	Jimmy Connors	B. Borg	64 62 62
1979	John McEnroe	V. Gerulaitis	75 63 63
1980	John McEnroe	B. Borg	76 61 67 57 64
1981	John McEnroe	B. Borg	46 62 64 63
1982	Jimmy Connors	I. Lendl	63 62 46 64
1983	Jimmy Connors	I. Lendl	63 67 75 60
1984	John McEnroe	I. Lendl	63 64 61
1985	Ivan Lendl	J. McEnroe	76 63 64
1986	Ivan Lendl	M. Mecir	64 62 60
1987	Ivan Lendl	M. Wilander	67 60 76 64
1988	Mats Wilander	I. Lendl	64 46 63 57 64
1989	Boris Becker	I. Lendl	76 16 63 76

Year	Winner	Loser	Score	Year	Winner	Loser	Score
1990	Pete Sampras	A. Agassi	64 63 62	1993	Pete Sampras	C. Pioline	64 64 63
1991	Stefan Edberg	J. Courier	62 64 60	1994	Andre Agassi	M. Stich	61 76 75
1992	Stefan Edberg	P. Sampras	36 64 76 62	1995	Pete Sampras	A. Agassi	64 63 46 75

WOMEN

Challenge round system used from 1887-1918. Five set final played from 1887-1901. Amateur and Open Championships held in 1968 and '69. Became an exclusively Open Championship in 1970.

Multiple winners: Molla Mallory Bjurstedt (8); Helen Wills Moody (7); Chris Evert Lloyd (6); Margaret Smith Court (5); Pauline Betz, Mario Bueno, Steffi Graf, Helen Jacobs, Billie Jean King, Alice Marble, Elisabeth Moore, Martina Navratilova and Hazel Hotchkiss Wightman (4); Juliette Atkinson, Mary Browne, Maureen Connolly and Margaret Osborne duPont (3); Tracy Austin, Mabel Cahill, Sarah Palfrey Cooke, Darlene Hard, Doris Hart, Althea Gibson, Monica Seles and Bertha Townsend (2).

Year	Winner	Loser	Score	Year	Winner	Loser	Score
1887	Ellen Hansell	L. Knight	61 60	1943	Pauline Betz	L. Brough	63 57 63
1888	Bertha Townsend	E. Hansell	63 65	1944	Pauline Betz	M. Osborne	63 86
1889	Bertha Townsend	L. Voorhes	75 62	1945	Sarah Cooke	P. Betz	36 86 64
1890	Ellen Roosevelt	B. Townsend	62 62	1946	Pauline Betz	P. Canning	11-9 63
1891	Mabel Cahill	E. Roosevelt	64 61 46 63	1947	Louise Brough	M. Osborne	86 46 61
1892	Mabel Cahill	E. Moore	57 63 64 46 62	1948	Margaret duPont	L. Brough	46 64 15-13
1893	Aline Terry	A. Schultz	61 63	1949	Margaret duPont	D. Hart	64 61
1894	Helen Hellwig	A. Terry	75 36 60 36 63	1950	Margaret duPont	D. Hart	64 63
1895	Juliette Atkinson	H. Hellwig	64 62 61	1951	Maureen Connolly	S. Fry	63 16 64
1896	Elisabeth Moore	J. Atkinson	64 46 62 62	1952	Maureen Connolly	D. Hart	63 75
1897	Juliette Atkinson	E. Moore	63 63 46 36 63	1953	Maureen Connolly	D. Hart	62 64
1898	Juliette Atkinson	M. Jones	63 57 64 26 75	1954	Doris Hart	L. Brough	68 61 86
1899	Marion Jones	M. Banks	61 61 75	1955	Doris Hart	P. Ward	64 62
1900	Myrtle McAteer	E. Parker	62 62 60	1956	Shirley Fry	A. Gibson	63 64
1901	Elizabeth Moore	M. McAteer	64 36 75 26 62	1957	Althea Gibson	L. Brough	63 62
1902	Marion Jones	E. Moore	61 10(ret)	1958	Althea Gibson	D. Hard	36 61 62
1903	Elizabeth Moore	M. Jones	75 86	1959	Maria Bueno	C. Truman	61 64
1904	May Sutton	E. Moore	61 62	1960	Darlene Hard	M. Bueno	64 10-12 64
1905	Elizabeth Moore	H. Homans	64 57 61	1961	Darlene Hard	A. Haydon	63 64
1906	Helen Homans	M. Barger-Wallach	64 63	1962	Margaret Smith	D. Hard	97 64
1907	Evelyn Sears	C. Neely	63 62	1963	Maria Bueno	M. Smith	75 64
1908	Maud B. Wallach	Ev. Sears	63 16 63	1964	Maria Bueno	C. Graebner	61 60
1909	Hazel Hotchkiss	M. Wallach	60 61	1965	Margaret Smith	B.J. Moffitt	86 75
1910	Hazel Hotchkiss	L. Hammond	64 62	1966	Maria Bueno	N. Richey	63 61
1911	Hazel Hotchkiss	F. Sutton	8-10 61 97	1967	Billie Jean King	A. Jones	11-9 64
1912	Mary Browne	E. Sears	64 62	1968	Am-Margaret Court	M. Bueno	62 62
1913	Mary Browne	D. Green	62 75		Op-Virginia Wade	B.J. King	64 62
1914	Mary Browne	M. Wagner	62 16 61	1969	Am-Margaret Court	V. Wade	46 63 60
1915	Molla Bjurstedt	H. Wightman	46 62 60		Op-Margaret Court	N. Richey	62 62
1916	Molla Bjurstedt	L. Raymond	60 61	1970	Margaret Court	R. Casals	62 26 61
1917	Molla Bjurstedt	M. Vanderhoef	46 60 62	1971	Billie Jean King	R. Casals	64 76
1918	Molla Bjurstedt	E. Goss	64 63	1972	Billie Jean King	K. Melville	63 75
1919	Hazel Wightman	M. Zinderstein	61 62	1973	Margaret Court	E. Goolagong	76 57 62
1920	Molla Mallory	M. Zinderstein	63 61	1974	Billie Jean King	E. Goolagong	36 63 75
1921	Molla Mallory	M. Browne	46 64 62	1975	Chris Evert	E. Cawley	57 64 62
1922	Molla Mallory	H. Wills	63 61	1976	Chris Evert	E. Cawley	63 60
1923	Helen Wills	M. Mallory	62 61	1977	Chris Evert	W. Turnbull	76 62
1924	Helen Wills	M. Mallory	61 63	1978	Chris Evert	P. Shriver	75 64
1925	Helen Wills	K. McKane	36 60 62	1979	Tracy Austin	C. Evert Lloyd	64 63
1926	Molla Mallory	E. Ryan	46 64 97	1980	Chris Evert Lloyd	H. Mandlikova	57 61 61
1927	Helen Wills	B. Nuthall	61 64	1981	Tracy Austin	M. Navratilova	16 76 76
1928	Helen Wills	H. Jacobs	62 61	1982	Chris Evert Lloyd	H. Mandlikova	63 61
1929	Helen Wills	P. Watson	64 62	1983	Martina Navratilova	C. Evert Lloyd	61 63
1930	Betty Nuthall	A. Harper	61 64	1984	Martina Navratilova	C. Evert Lloyd	46 64 64
1931	Helen Moody	E. Whitingstall	64 61	1985	Hana Mandlikova	M. Navratilova	76 16 76
1932	Helen Jacobs	C. Babcock		1986	Martina Navratilova	H. Sukova	63 62
1933	Helen Jacobs	H. Moody	86 36 30(ret)	1987	Martina Navratilova	S. Graf	76 61
1934	Helen Jacobs	S. Palfrey	61 64	1988	Steffi Graf	G. Sabatini	63 36 61
1935	Helen Jacobs	S. Fabyan	62 64	1989	Steffi Graf	M. Navratilova	36 75 61
1936	Alice Marble	H. Jacobs	46 63 62	1990	Gabriela Sabatini	S. Graf	62 76
1937	Anita Lizana	J. Jedrzejowska	64 62	1991	Monica Seles	M. Navratilova	76 61
1938	Alice Marble	N. Wynne	60 62	1992	Monica Seles	A.S. Vicario	63 63
1939	Alice Marble	H. Jacobs	60 8-10 64	1993	Steffi Graf	H. Sukova	63 63
1940	Alice Marble	H. Jacobs	62 63	1994	A. Sanchez Vicario	S. Graf	16 76 64
1941	Sarah Cooke	P. Betz	75 62	1995	Steffi Graf	M. Seles	76 06 63
1942	Pauline Betz	L. Brough	46 61 64				

Grand Slam Summary

Singles winners of the four Grand Slam tournaments—Australian, French, Wimbledon and United States—since the French was opened to all comers in 1925. Note that there were two Australian Opens in 1977 and none in 1986.

MEN

Three wins in one year: Jack Crawford (1933); Fred Perry (1934); Tony Trabert (1955); Lew Hoad (1956); Ashley Cooper (1958); Roy Emerson (1964); Jimmy Connors (1974); Mats Wilander (1988).

Two wins in one year: Roy Emerson (4 times); Bjorn Borg and Pete Sampras (3 times); Rene Lacoste, Ivan Lendl, John Newcombe and Fred Perry (twice); Boris Becker, Don Budge, Henri Cochet, Jimmy Connors, Jim Courier, Neale Fraser, Jack Kramer, John McEnroe, Alex Olmedo, Budge Patty, Bobby Riggs, Ken Rosewall, Dick Savitt, Frank Sedgman and Guillermo Vilas (once).

Year	Australia	French	Wimbledon	U.S.	Year	Australia	French	Wimbledon	U.S.
1925	Anderson	Lacoste	Lacoste	Tilden	1962	**Laver**	**Laver**	**Laver**	**Laver**
1926	Hawkes	Cochet	Borotra	Lacoste	1963	Emerson	Emerson	McKinley	Osuna
1927	Patterson	Lacoste	Cochet	Lacoste	1964	Emerson	Santana	Emerson	Emerson
1928	Borotra	Cochet	Lacoste	Cochet	1965	Emerson	Stolle	Emerson	Santana
1929	Gregory	Lacoste	Cochet	Tilden	1966	Emerson	Roche	Santana	Stolle
					1967	Emerson	Emerson	Newcombe	Newcombe
1930	Moon	Cochet	Tilden	Doeg	1968	Bowrey	Rosewall	Laver	Ashe
1931	Crawford	Borotra	Wood	Vines	1969	**Laver**	**Laver**	**Laver**	**Laver**
1932	Crawford	Cochet	Vines	Vines					
1933	Crawford	Crawford	Crawford	Perry	1970	Ashe	Kodes	Newcombe	Rosewall
1934	Perry	von Cramm	Perry	Perry	1971	Rosewall	Kodes	Newcombe	Smith
1935	Crawford	Perry	Perry	Allison	1972	Rosewall	Gimeno	Smith	Nastase
1936	Quist	von Cramm	Perry	Perry	1973	Newcombe	Nastase	Kodes	Newcombe
1937	McGrath	Henkel	Budge	Budge	1974	Connors	Borg	Connors	Connors
1938	**Budge**	**Budge**	**Budge**	**Budge**	1975	Newcombe	Borg	Ashe	Orantes
1939	Bromwich	McNeill	Riggs	Riggs	1976	Edmondson	Panatta	Borg	Connors
					1977	Tanner	Vilas	Borg	Vilas
1940	Quist	—	—	McNeill		& Gerulaitis			
1941	—	—	—	Riggs	1978	Vilas	Borg	Borg	Connors
1942	—	—	—	Schroeder	1979	Vilas	Borg	Borg	McEnroe
1943	—	—	—	Hunt					
1944	—	—	—	Parker	1980	Teacher	Borg	Borg	McEnroe
1945	—	—	—	Parker	1981	Kriek	Borg	McEnroe	McEnroe
1946	Bromwich	Bernard	Petra	Kramer	1982	Kriek	Wilander	Connors	Connors
1947	Pails	Asboth	Kramer	Kramer	1983	Wilander	Noah	McEnroe	Connors
1948	Quist	Parker	Falkenburg	Gonzales	1984	Wilander	Lendl	McEnroe	McEnroe
1949	Sedgman	Parker	Schroeder	Gonzales	1985	Edberg	Wilander	Becker	Lendl
					1986	—	Lendl	Becker	Lendl
1950	Sedgman	Patty	Patty	Larsen	1987	Edberg	Lendl	Cash	Lendl
1951	Savitt	Drobny	Savitt	Sedgman	1988	Wilander	Wilander	Edberg	Wilander
1952	McGregor	Drobny	Sedgman	Sedgman	1989	Lendl	Chang	Becker	Becker
1953	Rosewall	Rosewall	Seixas	Trabert					
1954	Rose	Trabert	Drobny	Seixas	1990	Lendl	Gomez	Edberg	Sampras
1955	Rosewall	Trabert	Trabert	Trabert	1991	Becker	Courier	Stich	Edberg
1956	Hoad	Hoad	Hoad	Rosewall	1992	Courier	Courier	Agassi	Edberg
1957	Cooper	Davidson	Hoad	Anderson	1993	Courier	Bruguera	Sampras	Sampras
1958	Cooper	Rose	Cooper	Cooper	1994	Sampras	Bruguera	Sampras	Agassi
1959	Olmedo	Pietrangeli	Olmedo	Fraser	1995	Agassi	Muster	Sampras	Sampras
1960	Laver	Pietrangeli	Fraser	Fraser					
1961	Emerson	Santana	Laver	Emerson					

The Calendar Year Grand Slam

The tennis Grand Slam has only been accomplished nine times in the same calendar year in either singles or doubles. And only two players have managed to do it twice— Rod Laver in singles (1962 and '69) and Margaret Smith Court in singles (1970) and doubles (1963).

Men's Singles

1938 ....Don Budge, USA
1962 ....Rod Laver, Australia
1969 ....Rod Laver, Australia

Men's Doubles

1951 ....Frank Sedgman, Australia
& Ken McGregor, Australia

Mixed Doubles

1963 ....Ken Fletcher, Australia
& Margaret Smith, Australia
1967 ....Owen Davidson and two partners

Women's Singles

1953 ....Maureen Connolly, USA
1970 ....Margaret Smith Court, Australia
1988 ....Steffi Graf, West Germany*

*Also won gold medal at Seoul Olympics.

Women's Doubles

1960 ....Maria Bueno, Brazil & two partners
1984 ....Martina Navratilova, USA
& Pam Shriver, USA

Note: In women's doubles, Bueno won Australia with Christine Truman, then took the French, Wimbledon and the U.S. with Darlene hard. In mixed Doubles—Davidson won Australia with Lesley Turner, then took the French, Wimbledon and the U.S. with Billie Jean King.

WOMEN

Three in one year: Helen Wills Moody (1928 and '29); Margaret Smith Court (1962, '65, '69 and '73); Billie Jean King (1972); Martina Navratilova (1983 and '84); Steffi Graf (1989, '93 and '95); and Monica Seles (1991 and '92).

Two in one year: Chris Evert Lloyd (5 times); Helen Wills Moody and Martina Navratilova (3 times); Maria Bueno, Maureen Connolly, Margaret Smith Court, Althea Gibson, Billie Jean King (twice); Cilly Aussem, Pauline Betz, Louise Brough, Evonne Goolagong Cawley, Shirley Fry, Darlene Hard, Margaret Osborne duPont, Suzanne Lenglen, Alice Marble and Arantxa Sanchez Vicario (once).

Year	Australia	French	Wimbledon	U.S.
1925	Akhurst	Lenglen	Lenglen	Wills
1926	Akhurst	Lenglen	Godfree	Mallory
1927	Boyd	Bouman	Wills	Wills
1928	Akhurst	Wills	Wills	Wills
1929	Akhurst	Wills	Wills	Wills
1930	Akhurst	Moody	Moody	Nuthall
1931	Buttsworth	Aussem	Aussem	Moody
1932	Buttsworth	Moody	Moody	Jacobs
1933	Hartigan	Scriven	Moody	Jacobs
1934	Hartigan	Scriven	Round	Jacobs
1935	Round	Sperling	Moody	Jacobs
1936	Hartigan	Sperling	Jacobs	Marble
1937	Bolton	Sperling	Round	Lizana
1938	Bundy	Mathieu	Moody	Marble
1939	Westacott	Mathieu	Marble	Marble
1940	Bolton	—	—	Marble
1941	—	—	—	Cooke
1942	—	—	—	Betz
1943	—	—	—	Betz
1944	—	—	—	Betz
1945	—	—	—	Cooke
1946	Bolton	Osborne	Betz	Betz
1947	Bolton	Todd	Osborne	Brough
1948	Bolton	Landry	Brough	du Pont
1949	Hart	du Pont	Brough	du Pont
1950	Brough	Hart	Brough	du Pont
1951	Bolton	Fry	Hart	Connolly
1952	Long	Hart	Connolly	Connolly
1953	**Connolly**	**Connolly**	**Connolly**	**Connolly**
1954	Long	Connolly	Connolly	Hart
1955	Penrose	Mortimer	Brough	Hart
1956	Carter	Gibson	Fry	Fry
1957	Fry	Bloomer	Gibson	Gibson
1958	Mortimer	Kormoczi	Gibson	Gibson
1959	Reitano	Truman	Bueno	Bueno
1960	Smith	Hard	Bueno	Hard
1961	Smith	Haydon	Mortimer	Hard
1962	Smith	Smith	Susman	Smith
1963	Smith	Turner	Smith	Bueno
1964	Smith	Smith	Bueno	Bueno
1965	Smith	Turner	Smith	Smith
1966	Smith	Jones	King	Bueno
1967	Richey	Durr	King	King
1968	King	Richey	King	Wade
1969	Court	Court	Jones	Court
1970	**Court**	**Court**	**Court**	**Court**
1971	Court	Goolagong	Goolagong	King
1972	Wade	King	King	King
1973	Court	Court	King	Court
1974	Goolagong	Evert	Evert	King
1975	Goolagong	Evert	King	Evert
1976	Cawley	Barker	Evert	Evert
1977	Reid & Cawley	Jausovec	Wade	Evert
1978	O'Neil	Ruzici	Navratilova	Evert
1979	Jordan	Evert Lloyd	Navratilova	Austin
1980	Mandlikova	Evert Lloyd	Cawley	Evert Lloyd
1981	Navratilova	Mandlikova	Evert Lloyd	Austin
1982	Evert Lloyd	Navratilova	Navratilova	Evert Lloyd
1983	Navratilova	Evert Lloyd	Navratilova	Navratilova
1984	Evert Lloyd	Navratilova	Navratilova	Navratilova
1985	Navratilova	Evert Lloyd	Navratilova	Mandlikova
1986	—	Evert Lloyd	Navratilova	Navratilova
1987	Mandlikova	Graf	Navratilova	Navratilova
1988	**Graf**	**Graf**	**Graf**	**Graf**
1989	Graf	Vicario	Graf	Graf
1990	Graf	Seles	Navratilova	Sabatini
1991	Seles	Seles	Graf	Seles
1992	Seles	Seles	Graf	Seles
1993	Seles	Graf	Graf	Graf
1994	Graf	Vicario	Martinez	Vicario
1995	Pierce	Graf	Graf	Graf

All-Time Grand Slam Singles Titles

Men and women with the most singles championships in the Australian, French, Wimbledon and U.S. championships, through 1995. Note that (*) indicates player never played in that particular Grand Slam event; and players active in 1995 are in **bold** type.

Top 15 Men

		Aus	Fre	Wim	US	Total
1	Roy Emerson	6	2	2	2	12
2	Bjorn Borg	0	6	5	0	11
	Rod Laver	3	2	4	2	11
4	Bill Tilden	*	0	3	7	10
5	Jimmy Connors	1	0	2	5	8
6	Ivan Lendl	2	3	0	3	8
7	Fred Perry	1	1	3	3	8
8	Ken Rosewall	4	2	0	2	8
9	Henri Cochet	*	4	2	1	7
	Rene Lacoste	*	3	2	2	7
	Bill Larned	*	0	*	7	7
	John McEnroe	0	0	3	4	7
	John Newcombe	2	0	3	2	7
	Willie Renshaw	*	*	7	*	7
	Pete Sampras	1	0	3	3	7
	Dick Sears	*	*	0	7	7

Top 15 Women

		Aus	Fre	Wim	US	Total
1	Margaret Smith Court	11	5	3	5	24
2	Helen Wills Moody	*	4	8	7	19
3	**Steffi Graf**	4	4	6	4	19
	Chris Evert	2	7	3	6	18
	Martina Navratilova	3	2	9	4	18
6	Billie Jean King	1	1	6	4	12
	Suzanne Lenglen	*	6	6	0	12
8	Maureen Connolly	1	2	3	3	9
9	Molla Bjurstedt Mallory	*	*	0	8	8
	Monica Seles	3	3	0	2	8
11	Maria Bueno	0	0	3	5	7
	Evonne Goolagong	4	1	2	0	7
13	Dorothea D. Chambers	*	*	7	0	7
14	Nancy Bolton	6	0	0	0	6
	Louise Brough	1	0	4	1	6
	Margaret duPont	*	2	1	3	6
	Doris Hart	1	2	1	2	6
	Blanche Bingley Hillyard	*	*	6	*	6

Grand Slam Summary (Cont.)

Overall Leaders

All-Time Grand Slam titlists including all singles and doubles championships at the four major tournaments. Titles listed under each heading are singles, doubles and mixed doubles. Players active in 1995 are in bold type.

MEN

		Career	Australian	French	Wimbledon	U.S.	Titles S-D-M	Titles
1	Roy Emerson	1959-71	6-3-0	2-6-0	2-3-0	2-4-0	12-16-0	28
2	John Newcombe	1965-76	2-5-0	0-3-0	3-6-0	2-3-1	7-17-1	25
3	Frank Sedgman	1949-52	2-2-2	0-2-2	1-3-2	2-2-2	5-9-8	22
4	Bill Tilden	1913-30	*	0-0-1	3-1-0	7-5-4	10-6-5	21
5	Rod Laver	1959-71	3-4-0	2-1-1	4-1-2	2-0-0	11-6-3	20
6	Jack Bromwich	1938-50	2-8-1	0-0-0	0-2-2	0-3-1	2-13-4	19
7	Ken Rosewall	1953-72	4-3-0	2-2-0	0-2-0	2-2-1	8-9-1	18
	Neale Fraser	1957-62	0-3-1	0-3-0	1-2-0	2-3-3	3-11-4	18
	Jean Borotra	1925-36	1-1-1	1-5-2	2-3-1	0-0-1	4-9-5	18
	Fred Stolle	1962-69	0-3-1	1-2-0	0-2-3	1-3-2	2-10-6	18
11	John McEnroe	1977-93	0-0-0	0-0-1	3-5-0	4-4-0	7-9-1	17
	Jack Crawford	1929-35	4-4-3	1-1-1	1-1-1	0-0-0	6-6-5	17
	Adrian Quist	1936-50	3-10-0	0-1-0	0-2-0	0-1-0	3-14-0	17
14	Laurie Doherty	1897-1906	*	*	5-8-0	1-2-0	6-10-0	16
15	Henri Cochet	1922-32	*	4-3-2	2-2-0	1-0-1	7-5-3	15
	Vic Seixas	1952-56	0-1-0	0-2-1	1-0-4	1-2-3	2-5-8	15
	Bob Hewitt	1961-79	0-2-1	0-1-2	0-5-2	0-1-1	0-9-6	15

WOMEN

		Career	Australian	French	Wimbledon	U.S.	S-D-M	Total Titles
1	Margaret Court Smith	1960-75	11-8-2	5-4-4	3-2-5	5-5-8	24-19-19	62
2	**Martina Navratilova**	1974—	3-8-0	2-7-2	9-7-3	4-9-2	18-31-7	56
3	Billie Jean King	1961-81	1-0-1	1-1-2	6-10-4	4-5-4	12-16-11	39
4	Margaret du Pont	1941-60	*	2-3-0	1-5-1	3-13-9	6-21-10	37
5	Louise Brough	1942-57	1-1-0	0-3-0	4-5-4	1-12-4	6-21-8	35
	Doris Hart	1948-55	1-1-2	2-5-3	1-4-5	2-4-5	6-14-15	35
7	Helen Wills Moody	1923-38	*	4-2-0	8-3-1	7-4-2	19-9-3	31
8	Elizabeth Ryan	1914-34	*	0-4-0	0-12-7	0-1-2	0-17-9	26
9	Suzanne Lenglen	1919-26	*	6-2-2	6-6-3	0-0-0	12-8-5	25
10	**Pam Shriver**	1981—	0-7-0	0-4-1	0-5-0	0-5-0	0-21-1	22
11	Chris Evert	1974-89	2-0-0	7-2-0	3-1-0	6-0-0	18-3-0	21
	Darlene Hard	1958-69	*	1-3-2	0-4-3	2-6-0	3-13-5	21
13	Nancye Wynne Bolton	1935-52	6-10-4	0-0-0	0-0-0	0-0-0	6-10-4	20
14	Maria Bueno	1958-68	0-1-0	0-1-1	3-5-0	4-4-0	7-11-1	19
	Steffi Graf	1982—	4-0-0	4-0-0	6-1-0	4-0-0	18-1-0	19
	Thelma Coyne Long	1936-58	2-12-4	0-0-1	0-0-0	0-0-0	2-12-5	19

Annual Number One Players

Unofficial world rankings for men and women determined by the *London Daily Telegraph* from 1914-72. Since then, official world rankings computed by men's and women's tours. Rankings included only amateur players from 1914 until the arrival of open (professional) tennis in 1968. No rankings were released during World Wars I and II.

MEN

Multiple winners: Bill Tilden (6); Jimmy Connors (5); Henri Cochet, Rod Laver, Ivan Lendl and John McEnroe (4); John Newcombe and Fred Perry (3); Bjorn Borg, Don Budge, Ashley Cooper, Stefan Edberg, Roy Emerson, Neale Fraser, Jack Kramer, Rene Lacoste, Ilie Nastase, Pete Sampras, Frank Sedgman and Tony Trabert (2).

Year		Year		Year		Year	
1914	Maurice McLoughlin	1932	Ellsworth Vines	1952	Frank Sedgman	1968	Rod Laver
1915-18	No rankings	1933	Jack Crawford	1953	Tony Trabert	1969	Rod Laver
1919	Gerald Patterson	1934	Fred Perry	1954	Jaroslav Drobny		
		1935	Fred Perry	1955	Tony Trabert	1970	John Newcombe
1920	Bill Tilden	1936	Fred Perry	1956	Lew Hoad	1971	John Newcombe
1921	Bill Tilden	1937	Don Budge	1957	Ashley Cooper	1972	Ilie Nastase
1922	Bill Tilden	1938	Don Budge	1958	Ashley Cooper	1973	Ilie Nastase
1923	Bill Tilden	1939	Bobby Riggs	1959	Neale Fraser	1974	Jimmy Connors
1924	Bill Tilden			1960	Neale Fraser	1975	Jimmy Connors
1925	Bill Tilden	1940-45	No rankings	1961	Rod Laver	1976	Jimmy Connors
1926	Rene Lacoste	1946	Jack Kramer	1962	Rod Laver	1977	Jimmy Connors
1927	Rene Lacoste	1947	Jack Kramer	1963	Rafael Osuna	1978	Jimmy Connors
1928	Henri Cochet	1948	Frank Parker	1964	Roy Emerson	1979	Bjorn Borg
1929	Henri Cochet	1949	Pancho Gonzales	1965	Roy Emerson		
				1966	Manuel Santana	1980	Bjorn Borg
1930	Henri Cochet	1950	Budge Patty	1967	John Newcombe	1981	John McEnroe
1931	Henri Cochet	1951	Frank Sedgman			1982	John McEnroe

Year		Year		Year		Year	
1983	John McEnroe	1987	Ivan Lendl	1990	Stefan Edberg	1993	Pete Sampras
1984	John McEnroe	1988	Mats Wilander	1991	Stefan Edberg	1994	Pete Sampras
1985	Ivan Lendl	1989	Ivan Lendl	1992	Jim Courier		
1986	Ivan Lendl						

WOMEN

Multiple winners: Helen Wills Moody (9); Margaret Smith Court and Martina Navratilova (7); Steffi Graf (6); Chris Evert Lloyd (5); Margaret Osborne duPont and Billie Jean King (4); Maureen Connolly (3); Maria Bueno, Althea Gibson, Suzanne Lenglen and Monica Seles (2).

Year		Year		Year		Year	
1925	Suzanne Lenglen	1947	Margaret Osborne	1963	Margaret Smith	1979	Martina Navratilova
1926	Suzanne Lenglen	1948	Margaret duPont	1964	Margaret Smith	1980	Chris Evert Lloyd
1927	Helen Wills	1949	Margaret duPont	1965	Margaret Smith	1981	Chris Evert Lloyd
1928	Helen Wills	1950	Margaret duPont	1966	Billie Jean King	1982	Martina Navratilova
1929	Helen Wills Moody	1951	Doris Hart	1967	Billie Jean King	1983	Martina Navratilova
1930	Helen Wills Moody	1952	Maureen Connolly	1968	Billie Jean King	1984	Martina Navratilova
1931	Helen Wills Moody	1953	Maureen Connolly	1969	Margaret Court	1985	Martina Navratilova
1932	Helen Wills Moody	1954	Maureen Connolly	1970	Margaret Court	1986	Martina Navratilova
1933	Helen Wills Moody	1955	Louise Brough	1971	Evonne Goolagong	1987	Steffi Graf
1934	Dorothy Round	1956	Shirley Fry	1972	Billie Jean King	1988	Steffi Graf
1935	Helen Wills Moody	1957	Althea Gibson	1973	Margaret Court	1989	Steffi Graf
1936	Helen Jacobs	1958	Althea Gibson	1974	Billie Jean King	1990	Steffi Graf
1937	Anita Lizana	1959	Maria Bueno	1975	Chris Evert	1991	Monica Seles
1938	Helen Wills Moody	1960	Maria Bueno	1976	Chris Evert	1992	Monica Seles
1939	Alice Marble	1961	Angela Mortimer	1977	Chris Evert	1993	Steffi Graf
1940-45	No rankings	1962	Margaret Smith	1978	Martina Navratilova	1994	Steffi Graf
1946	Pauline Betz						

Annual Top 10 World Rankings (since 1968)

Year by year Top 10 world computer rankings for Men (ATP Tour) and Women (WTA Tour) since the arrival of open tennis in 1968. Rankings from 1968-72 made by Lance Tingay of the *London Daily Telegraph*. Since 1973, computerized rankings by ATP Tour (men) and WTA Tour (women).

MEN

1968	1971	1974	1977
1 Rod Laver	1 John Newcombe	1 Jimmy Connors	1 Jimmy Connors
2 Arthur Ashe	2 Stan Smith	2 John Newcombe	2 Guillermo Vilas
3 Ken Rosewall	3 Rod Laver	3 Bjorn Borg	3 Bjorn Borg
4 Tom Okker	4 Ken Rosewall	4 Rod Laver	4 Vitas Gerulaitis
5 Tony Roche	5 Jan Kodes	5 Guillermo Vilas	5 Brian Gottfried
6 John Newcombe	6 Arthur Ashe	6 Tom Okker	6 Eddie Dibbs
7 Clark Graebner	7 Tom Okker	7 Arthur Ashe	7 Manuel Orantes
8 Dennis Ralston	8 Marty Riessen	8 Ken Rosewall	8 Raul Ramirez
9 Cliff Drysdale	9 Cliff Drysdale	9 Stan Smith	9 Ilie Nastase
10 Pancho Gonzales	10 Ilie Nastase	10 Ilie Nastase	10 Dick Stockton

1969	1972	1975	1978
1 Rod Laver	1 Stan Smith	1 Jimmy Connors	1 Jimmy Connors
2 Tony Roche	2 Ken Rosewall	2 Guillermo Vilas	2 Bjorn Borg
3 John Newcombe	3 Ilie Nastase	3 Bjorn Borg	3 Guillermo Vilas
4 Tom Okker	4 Rod Laver	4 Arthur Ashe	4 John McEnroe
5 Ken Rosewall	5 Arthur Ashe	5 Manuel Orantes	5 Vitas Gerulaitis
6 Arthur Ashe	6 John Newcombe	6 Ken Rosewall	6 Eddie Dibbs
7 Cliff Drysdale	7 Bob Lutz	7 Ilie Nastase	7 Brian Gottfried
8 Pancho Gonzales	8 Tom Okker	8 John Alexander	8 Raul Ramirez
9 Andres Gimeno	9 Marty Riessen	9 Roscoe Tanner	9 Harold Solomon
10 Fred Stolle	10 Andres Gimeno	10 Rod Laver	10 Corrado Barazzutti

1970	1973	1976	1979
1 John Newcombe	1 Ilie Nastase	1 Jimmy Connors	1 Bjorn Borg
2 Ken Rosewall	2 John Newcombe	2 Bjorn Borg	2 Jimmy Connors
3 Tony Roche	3 Jimmy Connors	3 Ilie Nastase	3 John McEnroe
4 Rod Laver	4 Tom Okker	4 Manuel Orantes	4 Vitas Gerulaitis
5 Arthur Ashe	5 Stan Smith	5 Raul Ramirez	5 Roscoe Tanner
6 Ilie Nastase	6 Ken Rosewall	6 Guillermo Vilas	6 Guillermo Vilas
7 Tom Okker	7 Manuel Orantes	7 Adriano Panatta	7 Arthur Ashe
8 Roger Taylor	8 Rod Laver	8 Harold Solomon	8 Harold Solomon
9 Jan Kodes	9 Jan Kodes	9 Eddie Dibbs	9 Jose Higueras
10 Cliff Richey	10 Arthur Ashe	10 Brian Gottfried	10 Eddie Dibbs

Annual Top 10 World Rankings (Cont.)

MEN

1980	1984	1988	1992
1 Bjorn Borg	1 John McEnroe	1 Mats Wilander	1 Jim Courier
2 John McEnroe	2 Jimmy Connors	2 Ivan Lendl	2 Stefan Edberg
3 Jimmy Connors	3 Ivan Lendl	3 Andre Agassi	3 Pete Sampras
4 Gene Mayer	4 Mats Wilander	4 Boris Becker	4 Goran Ivanisevic
5 Guillermo Vilas	5 Andres Gomez	5 Stefan Edberg	5 Boris Becker
6 Ivan Lendl	6 Anders Jarryd	6 Kent Carlsson	6 Michael Chang
7 Harold Solomon	7 Henrik Sundstrom	7 Jimmy Connors	7 Petr Korda
8 Jose-Luis Clerc	8 Pat Cash	8 Jakob Hlasek	8 Ivan Lendl
9 Vitas Gerulaitis	9 Eliot Teltscher	9 Henri Leconte	9 Andre Agassi
10 Eliot Teltscher	10 Yannick Noah	10 Tim Mayotte	10 Richard Krajicek

1981	1985	1989	1993
1 John McEnroe	1 Ivan Lendl	1 Ivan Lendl	1 Pete Sampras
2 Ivan Lendl	2 John McEnroe	2 Boris Becker	2 Michael Stich
3 Jimmy Connors	3 Mats Wilander	3 Stefan Edberg	3 Jim Courier
4 Bjorn Borg	4 Jimmy Connors	4 John McEnroe	4 Sergi Bruguera
5 Jose-Luis Clerc	5 Stefan Edberg	5 Michael Chang	5 Stefan Edberg
6 Guillermo Vilas	6 Boris Becker	6 Brad Gilbert	6 Andrei Medvedev
7 Gene Mayer	7 Yannick Noah	7 Andre Agassi	7 Goran Ivanisevic
8 Eliot Teltscher	8 Anders Jarryd	8 Aaron Krickstein	8 Michael Chang
9 Vitas Gerulaitis	9 Miloslav Mecir	9 Alberto Mancini	9 Thomas Muster
10 Peter McNamara	10 Kevin Curren	10 Jay Berger	10 Cedric Pioline

1982	1986	1990	1994
1 John McEnroe	1 Ivan Lendl	1 Stefan Edberg	1 Pete Sampras
2 Jimmy Connors	2 Boris Becker	2 Boris Becker	2 Andre Agassi
3 Ivan Lendl	3 Mats Wilander	3 Ivan Lendl	3 Boris Becker
4 Guillermo Vilas	4 Yannick Noah	4 Andre Agassi	4 Sergi Brugera
5 Vitas Gerulaitis	5 Stefan Edberg	5 Pete Sampras	5 Goran Ivanisevic
6 Jose-Luis Clerc	6 Henri Leconte	6 Andres Gomez	6 Michael Chang
7 Mats Wilander	7 Joakim Nystrom	7 Thomas Muster	7 Stefan Edberg
8 Gene Mayer	8 Jimmy Connors	8 Emilio Sanchez	8 Alberto Berasategui
9 Yannick Noah	9 Miloslav Mecir	9 Goran Ivanisevic	9 Michael Stich
10 Peter McNamara	10 Andres Gomez	10 Brad Gilbert	10 Todd Martin

1983	1987	1991
1 John McEnroe	1 Ivan Lendl	1 Stefan Edberg
2 Ivan Lendl	2 Stefan Edberg	2 Jim Courier
3 Jimmy Connors	3 Mats Wilander	3 Boris Becker
4 Mats Wilander	4 Jimmy Connors	4 Michael Stich
5 Yannick Noah	5 Boris Becker	5 Ivan Lendl
6 Jimmy Arias	6 Miloslav Mecir	6 Pete Sampras
7 Jose Higueras	7 Pat Cash	7 Guy Forget
8 Jose-Luis Clerc	8 Yannick Noah	8 Karel Novacek
9 Kevin Curren	9 Tim Mayotte	9 Petr Korda
10 Gene Mayer	10 John McEnroe	10 Andre Agassi

WOMEN

1968	1969	1970	1971
1 Billie Jean King	1 Margaret Court	1 Margaret Court	1 Evonne Goolagong
2 Virginia Wade	2 Ann Jones	2 Billie Jean King	2 Billie Jean King
3 Nancy Richey	3 Billie Jean King	3 Rosie Casals	3 Margaret Court
4 Maria Bueno	4 Nancy Richey	4 Virginia Wade	4 Rosie Casals
5 Margaret Court	5 Julie Heldman	5 Helga Niessen	5 Kerry Melville
6 Ann Jones	6 Rosie Casals	6 Kerry Melville	6 Virginia Wade
7 Judy Tegart	7 Kerry Melville	7 Julie Heldman	7 Judy Tagert
8 Annette du Plooy	8 Peaches Bartkowicz	8 Karen Krantzcke	8 Francoise Durr
9 Leslie Bowrey	9 Virginia Wade	9 Francoise Durr	9 Helga N. Masthoff
10 Rosie Casals	10 Leslie Bowrey	10 Nancy R. Gunter	10 Chris Evert

Connors and Navratilova Rule Top 10

Jimmy Connors and Martina Navratilova have been the world's top-ranked players more often than anyone else since the advent of open tennis in 1968. Connors was the No. 1 men's player five consecutive years from 1974-78, while Navratilova was the No. 1 women's player seven times from 1978 to 1986, including five years in a row from 1982-86.

1972
1 Billie Jean King
2 Evonne Goolagong
3 Chris Evert
4 Margaret Court
5 Kerry Melville
6 Virginia Wade
7 Rosie Casals
8 Nancy R. Gunter
9 Francoise Durr
10 Linda Tuero

1973
1 Margaret S. Court
2 Billie Jean King
3 Evonne G. Cawley
4 Chris Evert
5 Rosie Casals
6 Virginia Wade
7 Kerry Reid
8 Nancy Richey
9 Julie Heldman
10 Helga Masthoff

1974
1 Billie Jean King
2 Evonne G. Cawley
3 Chris Evert
4 Virginia Wade
5 Julie Heldman
6 Rosie Casals
7 Kerry Reid
8 Olga Morozova
9 Lesley Hunt
10 Francoise Durr

1975
1 Chris Evert
2 Billie Jean King
3 Evonne G. Cawley
4 Martina Navratilova
5 Virginia Wade
6 Margaret S. Court
7 Olga Morozova
8 Nancy Richey
9 Francoise Durr
10 Rosie Casals

1976
1 Chris Evert
2 Evonne G. Cawley
3 Virginia Wade
4 Martina Navratilova
5 Sue Barker
6 Betty Stove
7 Dianne Balestrat
8 Mima Jausovec
9 Rosie Casals
10 Francoise Durr

1977
1 Chris Evert
2 Billie Jean King
3 Martina Navratilova
4 Virginia Wade
5 Sue Barker
6 Rosie Casals
7 Betty Stove
8 Dianne Balestrat
9 Wendy Turnbull
10 Kerry Reid

1978
1 Martina Navratilova
2 Chris Evert Lloyd
3 Evonne G. Cawley
4 Virginia Wade
5 Billie Jean King
6 Tracy Austin
7 Wendy Turnbull
8 Kerry Reid
9 Betty Stove
10 Dianne Balestrat

1979
1 Martina Navratilova
2 Chris Evert Lloyd
3 Tracy Austin
4 Evonne G. Cawley
5 Billie Jean King
6 Dianne Balestrat
7 Wendy Turnbull
8 Virginia Wade
9 Kerry Reid
10 Sue Barker

1980
1 Chris Evert Lloyd
2 Tracy Austin
3 Martina Navratilova
4 Hana Mandlikova
5 Evonne G. Cawley
6 Billie Jean King
7 Andrea Jaeger
8 Wendy Turnbull
9 Pam Shriver
10 Greer Stevens

1981
1 Chris Evert Lloyd
2 Tracy Austin
3 Martina Navratilova
4 Andrea Jaeger
5 Hana Mandlikova
6 Sylvia Hanika
7 Pam Shriver
8 Wendy Turnbull
9 Bettina Bunge
10 Barbara Potter

1982
1 Martina Navratilova
2 Chris Evert Lloyd
3 Andrea Jaeger
4 Tracy Austin
5 Wendy Turnbull
6 Pam Shriver
7 Hana Mandlikova
8 Barbara Potter
9 Bettina Bunge
10 Sylvia Hanika

1983
1 Martina Navratilova
2 Chris Evert Lloyd
3 Andrea Jaeger
4 Pam Shriver
5 Sylvia Hanika
6 Jo Durie
7 Bettina Bunge
8 Wendy Turnbull
9 Tracy Austin
10 Zina Garrison

1984
1 Martina Navratilova
2 Chris Evert Lloyd
3 Hana Mandlikova
4 Pam Shriver
5 Wendy Turnbull
6 Manuela Maleeva
7 Helena Sukova
8 Claudia Kohde-Kilsch
9 Zina Garrison
10 Kathy Jordan

1985
1 Martina Navratilova
2 Chris Evert Lloyd
3 Hana Mandlikova
4 Pam Shriver
5 Claudia Kohde-Kilsch
6 Steffi Graf
7 Manuela Maleeva
8 Zina Garrison
9 Helena Sukova
10 Bonnie Gadusek

1986
1 Martina Navratilova
2 Chris Evert Lloyd
3 Steffi Graf
4 Hana Mandlikova
5 Helena Sukova
6 Pam Shriver
7 Claudia Kohde-Kilsch
8 M. Maleeva-Fragniere
9 Zina Garrison
10 Claudia Kohde-Kilsch

1987
1 Steffi Graf
2 Martina Navratilova
3 Chris Evert
4 Pam Shriver
5 Hana Mandlikova
6 Gabriela Sabatini
7 Helena Sukova
8 M. Maleeva-Fragniere
9 Zina Garrison
10 Claudia Kohde-Kilsch

1988
1 Steffi Graf
2 Martina Navratilova
3 Chris Evert
4 Gabriela Sabatini
5 Pam Shriver
6 M. Maleeva-Fragniere
7 Natalia Zvereva
8 Helena Sukova
9 Zina Garrison
10 Barbara Potter

1989
1 Steffi Graf
2 Martina Navratilova
3 Gabriela Sabatini
4 Z. Garrison-Jackson
5 A. Sanchez Vicario
6 Monica Seles
7 Conchita Martinez
8 Helena Sukova
9 M. Maleeva-Fragniere
10 Chris Evert

1990
1 Steffi Graf
2 Monica Seles
3 Martina Navratilova
4 Mary Joe Fernandez
5 Gabriela Sabatini
6 Katerina Maleeva
7 A. Sanchez Vicario
8 Jennifer Capriati
9 M. Maleeva-Fragniere
10 Z. Garrison-Jackson

1991
1 Monica Seles
2 Steffi Graf
3 Gabriela Sabatini
4 Martina Navratilova
5 A. Sanchez Vicario
6 Jennifer Capriati
7 Jana Novotna
8 Mary Joe Fernandez
9 Conchita Martinez
10 M. Maleeva-Fragniere

1992
1 Monica Seles
2 Steffi Graf
3 Gabriela Sabatini
4 A. Sanchez Vicario
5 Martina Navratilova
6 Mary Joe Fernandez
7 Jennifer Capriati
8 Conchita Martinez
9 M. Maleeva-Fragniere
10 Jana Novotna

1993
1 Steffi Graf
2 A. Sanchez Vicario
3 Martina Navratilova
4 Conchita Martinez
5 Gabriela Sabatini
6 Jana Novotna
7 Mary Joe Fernandez
8 Monica Seles
9 Jennifer Capriati
10 Anke Huber

1994
1 Steffi Graf
2 A. Sanchez Vicario
3 Conchita Martinez
4 Jana Novotna
5 Mary Pierce
6 Lindsay Davenport
7 Gabriela Sabatini
8 Martina Navratilova
9 Kimiko Date
10 Natasha Zvereva

All-Time Singles Leaders

Tournaments Won

All-time tournament wins from the arrival of open tennis in 1968 through 1994. Men's totals include ATP Tour, Grand Prix and WCT tournaments. Players active in 1995 are in **bold** type.

MEN

	Total			Total			Total
1 Jimmy Connors	109	11 Arthur Ashe	33	21 **Andre Agassi**	24
2 Ivan Lendl	94	**Mats Wilander**	33	22 **Thomas Muster**	23
3 John McEnroe	77	13 John Newcombe	32	Yannick Noah	23
4 Bjorn Borg	62	Manuel Orantes	32	24 Eddie Dibbs	22
5 Guillermo Vilas	61	Ken Rosewall	32	Harold Solomon	22
6 Ilie Nastase	57	16 Tom Okker	31	26 Andres Gomez	21
7 Rod Laver	47	17 **Pete Sampras**	30	27 **Brad Gilbert**	20
8 Boris Becker	42	18 Vitas Gerlaitius	27	28 **Michael Chang**	19
9 **Stefan Edberg**	40	19 Jose-Luis Clerc	25	29 Raul Ramirez	17
10 Stan Smith	39	Brian Gottfried	25	30 Vijay Amritraj	16

WOMEN

	Total			Total			Total
1 Martina Navratilova	167	11 Tracy Austin	29	21 D. Fromholtz Balestrat.	19
2 Chris Evert	157	12 Hana Mandlikova	27	M. Maleeva-Fragniere	19
3 E. Goolagong Cawley	88	13 **Gabriela Sabatini**	26	23 Rosie Casals	18
4 **Steffi Graf**	86	14 Nancy Richey	25	24 Virginia Rizici	17
5 Margaret Court	79	15 **Conchita Martinez**	23	Regina Marsikova	17
6 Billie Jean King	67	16 Kerry Melville Reid	22	26 Sue Barker	15
7 Virginia Wade	55	17 Sue Barker	21	27 Peaches Bartkowicz	14
8 Helga Masthoff	37	Pam Shriver	21	Andrea Jaeger	14
9 **Monica Seles**	32	19 Julie Heldman	20	**Sandra Cecchini**	14
10 Olga Morozova	31	**A. Sanchez Vicario**	20	30 **Z. Garrison Jackson**	13
				Wendy Turnbull	13

Money Won

All-time money winners from the arrival of open tennis in 1968 through 1994. Totals include doubles earnings.

MEN

	Earnings			Earnings			Earnings
1 Ivan Lendl	$20,512,417	11 Goran Ivanisevic	$6,787,433	21 Jakob Hlasek	$4,119,912
2 Stefan Edberg	18,137,745	12 Michael Chang	6,210,840	22 Tomas Smid	3,699,738
3 Boris Becker	15,466,037	13 Sergi Brugera	6,129,516	23 Bjorn Borg	3,655,751
4 John McEnroe	12,239,622	14 Anders Jarryd	5,061,947	24 Thomas Muster	3,410,589
5 Pete Sampras	11,813,112	15 Guillermo Vilas	4,923,882	25 Mark Woodforde	3,351,141
6 Jim Courier	10,352,364	16 Emilio Sanchez	4,785,166	26 Yannick Noah	3,295,395
7 Jimmy Connors	8,513,840	17 Brad Gilbert	4,486,097	27 Karel Novacek	3,159,239
8 Andre Agassi	7,700,705	18 Petr Korda	4,291,863	28 Henri Laconte	3,153,428
9 Mats Wilander	7,581,092	19 Andres Gomez	4,284,725	29 John Fitzgerald	3,096,936
10 Michael Stich	7,363,147	20 Guy Forget	4,228,145	30 Kevin Curren	2,955,060

WOMEN

	Earnings			Earnings			Earnings
1 Martina Navratilova	$20,283,727	11 Natasha Zvereva	$4,095,581	21 Katerina Maleeva	$2,146,055
2 Steffi Graf	14,641,990	12 Conchita Martinez	3,971,307	22 Tracy Austin	1,992,380
3 Chris Evert	8,896,195	13 Hana Mandlikova	3,340,959	23 Billie Jean King	1,966,487
4 A. Sanchez Vicario	8,318,016	14 Gigi Fernandez	3,285,302	24 Nathalie Tauziat	1,861,373
5 Gabriela Sabatini	7,888,822	15 M. Maleeva-Fragniere	3,244,811	25 Elizabeth Smylie	1,623,032
6 Monica Seles	7,408,981	16 Mary Joe Fernandez	3,058,613	26 Rosalyn Nideffer	1,617,857
7 Pam Shriver	5,286,382	17 Wendy Turnbull	2,769,024	27 Kathy Jordan	1,592,111
8 Helena Sukova	5,274,586	18 Lori McNeil	2,705,378	28 Virginia Wade	1,542,278
9 Jana Novotna	4,430,422	19 Larisa Neiland	2,456,451	29 Jennifer Capriati	1,496,398
10 Z. Garrison Jackson	4,249,006	20 C. Kohde-Kilsch	2,225,837	30 Patty Fendick	1,456,982

Longest Matches

Singles

126 Games— Roger Taylor (GBR) def. Wieslaw Gasiorek (POL), 27-29, 31-29, 6-4; King's Cup, Warsaw, 1966.

Doubles

147 Games— Dick Leach and Dick Dell (USA) def. Len Schloss and and Tom Mozu (USA), 3-6, 49-47, 22-20, 2nd round, Newport Casino, Newport, R.I., 1967.

Year-end Tournaments
MEN
Masters/ATP Tour World Championship

The year-end championship of the ATP men's tour since 1970. Contested by the year's top eight players. Originally a round-robin, the Masters was revised in 1972 to include a round-robin to decide the four semifinalists then a single elimination format after that. The tournament switched from December to January in 1977–78, then back to December in 1986. Held at Madison Square Garden in New York from 1978-89. Replaced by ATP Tour World Championship in 1990 and held in Frankfurt, Germany since then.

Multiple Winners: Ivan Lendl (5); Ilie Nastase (4); John McEnroe (3); Boris Becker, Bjorn Borg and Pete Sampras (2).

Year	Winner		Runner-Up	Year	Winner	Loser	Score
1970	Stan Smith (4-1)		Rod Laver (4-1)	1983	Ivan Lendl	J. McEnroe	64 64 62
1971	Ilie Nastase (6-0)		Stan Smith (4-2)	1984	John McEnroe	I. Lendl	63 64 64

Year	Winner	Loser	Score	Year	Winner	Loser	Score
				1985	John McEnroe	I. Lendl	75 60 64
1972	Ilie Nastase	S. Smith	63 62 36 26 63	1986	Ivan Lendl	B. Becker	62 76 63
1973	Ilie Nastase	T. Okker	63 75 46 63	1986	Ivan Lendl	B. Becker	64 64 64
1974	Guillermo Vilas	I. Nastase	76 62 36 36 64	1987	Ivan Lendl	M. Wilander	62 62 63
1975	Ilie Nastase	B. Borg	62 62 61	1988	Boris Becker	I. Lendl	57 76 36 62 76
1976	Manuel Orantes	W. Fibak	57 62 06 76 61	1989	Stefan Edberg	B. Becker	46 76 63 61
1978	Jimmy Connors	B. Borg	64 16 64				
1979	John McEnroe	A. Ashe	67 63 75	1990	Andre Agassi	S. Edberg	57 76 75 62
				1991	Pete Sampras	J. Courier	36 76 63 64
1980	Bjorn Borg	V. Gerulaitis	62 62	1992	Boris Becker	J. Courier	64 63 75
1981	Bjorn Borg	I. Lendl	64 62 62	1993	Michael Stich	P. Sampras	76 26 76 62
1982	Ivan Lendl	V. Gerulaitis	67 26 76 62 64	1994	Pete Sampras	B. Becker	46 63 75 64

Note: In 1970, Smith was declared the winner because he beat Laver in their round-robin match (4-6, 6-3, 6-4).

WCT Championship (1971-89)

World Championship Tennis was established in 1967 to promote professional tennis and led the way into the open era. It's major singles and doubles championships were held every May among the top eight regular season finishers on the circuit from 1971 until the WCT folded in 1989.

Mutliple winners: John McEnroe (5), Jimmy Connors, Ivan Lendl and Ken Rosewall (2).

Year	Winner	Loser	Score	Year	Winner	Loser	Score
1971	Ken Rosewall	R. Laver	64 16 76 76	1981	John McEnroe	J. Kriek	61 62 64
1972	Ken Rosewall	R. Laver	46 60 63 67 76	1982	Ivan Lendl	J. McEnroe	62 36 63 63
1973	Stan Smith	A. Ashe	63 63 46 64	1983	John McEnroe	I. Lendl	62 46 63 67 76
1974	John Newcombe	B. Borg	46 63 63 62	1984	John McEnroe	J. Connors	61 62 63
1975	Arthur Ashe	B. Borg	36 64 64 60	1985	Ivan Lendl	T. Mayotte	76 64 61
1976	Bjorn Borg	G. Vilas	16 61 75 61	1986	Anders Jarryd	B. Becker	67 61 61 64
1977	Jimmy Connors	D. Stockton	67 61 64 63	1987	Miloslav Mercir	J. McEnroe	60 36 62 62
1978	Vitas Gerulaitis	E. Dibbs	63 62 61	1988	Boris Becker	S. Edberg	64 16 75 62
1979	John McEnroe	B. Borg	75 46 62 76	1989	John McEnroe	B. Gilbert	63 63 76
1980	Jimmy Connors	J. McEnroe	26 76 61 62				

WOMEN

WTA Tour Championship

Originally the Virginia Slims Championships from 1971-94. The WTA Tour's year-end tournament took place in March from 1972 until 1986 when the WTA decided to adopt a January-to-November playing season. Given the changeover, two championships were held in 1986. Held every year since 1979 at Madison Square Garden in New York.

Multiple winners: Martina Navratilova (8); Chris Evert (4); Steffi Graf and Monica Seles (3); Evonne Goolagong and Gabriela Sabatini (2).

Year	Winner	Loser	Score	Year	Winner	Loser	Score
1972	Chris Evert	K. Reid	75 64	1984	M. Navratilova	C. Evert	63 75 61
1973	Chris Evert	N. Richey	63 63	1985	M. Navratilova	H. Sukova	63 75 64
1974	Evonne Goolagong	C. Evert	63 64	1986	M. Navratilova	H. Mandlikova	62 60 36 61
1975	Chris Evert	M. Navratilova	64 62	1986	M. Navratilova	S. Graf	76 63 62
1976	Evonne Goolagong	C. Evert	63 57 63	1987	Steffi Graf	G. Sabatini	46 64 60 64
1977	Chris Evert	S. Barker	26 61 61	1988	Gabriela Sabatini	P. Shriver	75 62 62
1978	M. Navratilova	E. Goolagong	76 64	1989	Steffi Graf	M. Navratilova	64 75 26 62
1979	M. Navratilova	T. Austin	63 36 62	1990	Monica Seles	G. Sabatini	64 57 36 64 62
1980	Tracy Austin	M. Navratilova	62 26 62	1991	Monica Seles	M. Navratilova	64 36 75 60
1981	M. Navratilova	A. Jaeger	63 76	1992	Monica Seles	M. Navratilova	75 63 61
1982	Sylvia Hanika	M. Navratilova	16 63 64	1993	Steffi Graf	A. S. Vicario	61 64 36 61
1983	M. Navratilova	C. Evert	62 60	1994	Gabriela Sabatini	L. Davenport	63 62 64

Mike Powell/Ilsport

The 1992 U.S. Davis Cup team that beat Switzerland in the final at Fort Worth, Texas (from left to right): singles players **Andre Agassi** and **Jim Courier**, doubles partners **John McEnroe** and **Pete Sampras**, and non-playing captain **Tom Gorman**. The Americans beat the Swiss, 3–1, for their 30th Davis Cup title since 1900.

Davis Cup

Established in 1900 as an annual international tournament by American player Dwight Davis. Originally called the International Lawn Tennis Challenge Trophy. Challenge round system until 1972. Since 1981, the top 16 nations in the world have played a straight knockout tournament over the course of a year. The format is a best-of-five match of two singles, one doubles and two singles over three days. Note that from 1900–24 Australia and New Zealand competed together as Australasia.

Multiple winners: USA (30); Australia (20); France (7); Australasia (6); British Isles and Sweden (5); Britain (4); Germany (3).

Challenge Rounds

Year	Winner	Loser	Score	Site	Year	Winner	Loser	Score	Site
1900	USA	British Isles	3-0	Boston	1924	USA	Australia	5-0	Philadelphia
1901	Not held				1925	USA	France	5-0	Philadelphia
1902	USA	British Isles	3-2	New York	1926	USA	France	4-1	Philadelphia
1903	British Isles	USA	4-1	Boston	1927	France	USA	3-2	Philadelphia
1904	British Isles	Belgium	5-0	Wimbledon	1928	France	USA	4-1	Paris
1905	British Isles	USA	5-0	Wimbledon	1929	France	USA	3-2	Paris
1906	British Isles	USA	5-0	Wimbledon	1930	France	USA	4-1	Paris
1907	Australasia	British Isles	3-2	Wimbledon	1931	France	Britain	3-2	Paris
1908	Australasia	USA	3-2	Melbourne	1932	France	USA	3-2	Paris
1909	Australasia	USA	5-0	Sydney	1933	Britain	France	3-2	Paris
1910	Not held				1934	Britain	USA	4-1	Wimbledon
1911	Australasia	USA	5-0	Christchurch,NZ	1935	Britain	USA	5-0	Wimbledon
1912	British Isles	Australasia	3-2	Melbourne	1936	Britain	Australia	3-2	Wimbledon
1913	USA	British Isles	3-2	Wimbledon	1937	USA	Britain	4-1	Wimbledon
1914	Australasia	USA	3-2	New York	1938	USA	Australia	3-2	Philadelphia
1915-18	Not held	World War I			1939	Australia	USA	3-2	Philadelphia
1919	Australasia	British Isles	4-1	Sydney	1940-45	Not held	World War II		
1920	USA	Australasia	5-0	Auckland, NZ	1946	USA	Australia	5-0	Melbourne
1921	USA	Japan	5-0	New York	1947	USA	Australia	4-1	New York
1922	USA	Australasia	4-1	New York	1948	USA	Australia	5-0	New York
1923	USA	Australasia	4-1	New York	1949	USA	Australia	4-1	New York

Year	Winner	Loser	Score	Site	Year	Winner	Loser	Score	Site
1950	Australia	USA	4-1	New York	1960	Australia	Italy	4-1	Sydney
1951	Australia	USA	3-2	Sydney	1961	Australia	Italy	5-0	Melbourne
1952	Australia	USA	4-1	Adelaide	1962	Australia	Mexico	5-0	Brisbane
1953	Australia	USA	3-2	Melbourne	1963	USA	Australia	3-2	Adelaide
1954	USA	Australia	3-2	Sydney	1964	Australia	USA	3-2	Cleveland
1955	Australia	USA	5-0	New York	1965	Australia	Spain	4-1	Sydney
1956	Australia	USA	5-0	Adelaide	1966	Australia	India	4-1	Melbourne
1957	Australia	USA	3-2	Melbourne	1967	Australia	Spain	4-1	Brisbane
1958	USA	Australia	3-2	Brisbane					
1959	Australia	USA	3-2	New York					

Final Rounds

Year	Winner	Loser	Score	Site	Year	Winner	Loser	Score	Site
1968	USA	Australia	4-1	Adelaide	1982	USA	France	4-1	Grenoble
1969	USA	Romania	5-0	Cleveland	1983	Australia	Sweden	3-2	Melbourne
1970	USA	W. Germany	5-0	Cleveland	1984	Sweden	USA	4-1	Göteborg
1971	USA	Romania	3-2	Charlotte	1985	Sweden	W. Germany	3-2	Munich
1972	USA	Romania	3-2	Bucharest	1986	Australia	Sweden	3-2	Melbourne
1973	Australia	USA	5-0	Cleveland	1987	Sweden	India	5-0	Göteborg
1974	So. Africa	India	walkover	Not held	1988	W. Germany	Sweden	4-1	Göteborg
1975	Sweden	Czech.	3-2	Stockholm	1989	W. Germany	Sweden	3-2	Stuttgart
1976	Italy	Chile	4-1	Santiago	1990	USA	Australia	3-2	St. Petersburg
1977	Australia	Italy	3-1	Sydney	1991	France	USA	3-1	Lyon
1978	USA	Britain	4-1	Palm Springs	1992	USA	Switzerland	3-1	Ft. Worth
1979	USA	Italy	5-0	San Francisco	1993	Germany	Australia	4-1	Dusseldorf
1980	Czech.	Italy	4-1	Prague	1994	Sweden	Russia	4-1	Moscow
1981	USA	Argentina	3-1	Cincinnati					

Note: In 1974, India refused to play the final as a protest against the South African government's policies of apartheid.

Fed Cup

Originally the Federation Cup and started in 1963 by the International Tennis Federation as the Davis Cup of women's tennis. Played by 32 teams over one week at one site through 1994. Tournament changed in 1995 to Davis Cup-style format of four rounds and home sites.

Multiple winners: USA (14); Australia (7); Czechoslovakia (5); Spain (3); Germany (2).

Year	Winner	Loser	Score	Site	Year	Winner	Loser	Score	Site
1963	USA	Australia	2-1	London	1980	USA	Australia	3-0	W. Germany
1964	Australia	USA	2-1	Philadelphia	1981	USA	Britain	3-0	Tokyo
1965	Australia	USA	2-1	Melbourne	1982	USA	W. Germany	3-0	Santa Clara
1966	USA	W. Germany	3-0	Italy	1983	Czech.	W. Germany	2-1	Zurich
1967	USA	Britain	2-0	W. Germany	1984	Czech.	Australia	2-1	Brazil
1968	Australia	Holland	3-0	Paris	1985	Czech.	USA	2-1	Japan
1969	USA	Australia	2-1	Athens	1986	USA	Czech.	3-0	Prague
1970	Australia	Britain	3-0	W. Germany	1987	W. Germany	USA	2-1	Vancouver
1971	Australia	Britain	3-0	Perth	1988	Czech.	USSR	2-1	Melbourne
1972	So. Africa	Britain	2-1	Africa	1989	USA	Spain	3-0	Tokyo
1973	Australia	So. Africa	3-0	W. Germany	1990	USA	USSR	2-1	Atlanta
1974	Australia	USA	2-1	Italy	1991	Spain	USA	2-1	Nottingham
1975	Czech.	Australia	3-0	France	1992	Germany	Spain	2-1	Frankfurt
1976	USA	Australia	2-1	Philadelphia	1993	Spain	Australia	3-0	Frankfurt
1977	USA	Australia	2-1	Eastbourne	1994	Spain	USA	3-0	Frankfurt
1978	USA	Australia	2-1	Melbourne					
1979	USA	Australia	3-0	Spain					

Maiden and Married Names of Women's Champions

Maiden Name	Married Name	Maiden Name	Married Name
Blanche Bingley	Blanche Hillyard	Hazel Hotchkiss	Hazel Wightman
Molla Bjurstedt	Molla Mallory	Hilde Krahwinkel	Hilde Sperling
Patricia Canning	Patricia Todd	Kerry Melville	Kerry Reid
Mary Carter	Mary Raitano	Kathleen McKane	Kathleen Godfrey
Charlotte Cooper	Charlotte Sterry	Billie Jean Moffitt	Billie Jean King
Thelma Coyne	Thelma Long	Margaret Osborne	Margaret duPont
Dorothea Douglass	Dorothea Lambert Chambers	Sarah Palfrey	Sarah Fabyan Cooke
Chris Evert	Chris Evert Lloyd	Margaret Smith	Margaret Smith Court
Evonne Goolagong	Evonne Cawley	Helen Wills	Helen Wills Moody
Louise Hammond	Louise Raymond	Nancye Wynne	Nancye Bolton
Ann Haydon	Ann Haydon Jones		

COLLEGES

NCAA team titles were not sanctioned until 1946. NCAA women's individual and team championships started in 1982.

Men's NCAA Individual Champions (1883-1945)

Multiple winners: Malcolm Chace and Pancho Segura (3); Edward Chandler, George Church, E.B. Dewhurst, Fred Hovey, Frank Guernsey, W.P. Knapp, Robert LeRoy, P.S. Sears, Cliff Sutter, Ernest Sutter and Richard Williams (2).

Year		Year		Year	
1883	J. Clark, Harvard (spring)	1903	E.B. Dewhurst, Penn	1925	Edward Chandler, Calif.
	H. Taylor, Harvard (fall)	1904	Robert LeRoy, Columbia	1926	Edward Chandler, Calif.
1884	W.P. Knapp, Yale	1905	E.B. Dewhurst, Penn	1927	Wilmer Allison, Texas
1885	W.P. Knapp, Yale	1906	Robert LeRoy, Columbia	1928	Julius Seligson, Lehigh
1886	G.M. Brinley, Trinity, CT	1907	G.P. Gardner Jr, Harvard	1929	Berkeley Bell, Texas
1887	P.S. Sears, Harvard	1908	Nat Niles, Harvard		
1888	P.S. Sears, Harvard	1909	Wallace Johnson, Penn	1930	Cliff Sutter, Tulane
1889	R.P. Huntington Jr, Yale			1931	Keith Gledhill, Stanford
		1910	R.A. Holden Jr, Yale	1932	Cliff Sutter, Tulane
1890	Fred Hovey, Harvard	1911	E.H. Whitney, Harvard	1933	Jack Tidball, UCLA
1891	Fred Hovey, Harvard	1912	George Church, Princeton	1934	Gene Mako, USC
1892	William Larned, Cornell	1913	Richard Williams, Harv.	1935	Wilbur Hess, Rice
1893	Malcolm Chace, Brown	1914	George Church, Princeton	1936	Ernest Sutter, Tulane
1894	Malcolm Chace, Yale	1915	Richard Williams, Harv.	1937	Ernest Sutter, Tulane
1895	Malcolm Chace, Yale	1916	G.C. Caner, Harvard	1938	Frank Guernsey, Rice
1896	Malcolm Whitman, Harvard	1917-1918	Not held	1939	Frank Guernsey, Rice
1897	S.G. Thompson, Princeton	1919	Charles Garland, Yale		
1898	Leo Ware, Harvard			1940	Don McNeill, Kenyon
1899	Dwight Davis, Harvard	1920	Lascelles Banks, Yale	1941	Joseph Hunt, Navy
		1921	Philip Neer, Stanford	1942	Fred Schroeder, Stanford
1900	Ray Little, Princeton	1922	Lucien Williams, Yale	1943	Pancho Segura, Miami-FL
1901	Fred Alexander, Princeton	1923	Carl Fischer, Phi. Osteo.	1944	Pancho Segura, Miami-FL
1902	William Clothier, Harvard	1924	Wallace Scott, Wash.	1945	Pancho Segura, Miami-FL

NCAA Men's Division I Champions

Multiple winners (Teams): UCLA and USC (15); Stanford (13); Georgia and William & Mary (2). (Players): Alex Olmedo, Mikael Pernfors, Dennis Ralston and Ham Richardson (2).

Year	Team winner	Individual Champion	Year	Team winner	Individual Champion
1946	USC	Bob Falkenburg, USC	1972	Trinity-TX	Dick Stockton, Trinity-TX
1947	Wm. & Mary	Garner Larned, Wm.& Mary	1973	Stanford	Alex Mayer, Stanford
1948	Wm. & Mary	Harry Likas, San Francisco	1974	Stanford	John Whitlinger, Stanford
1949	San Francisco	Jack Tuero, Tulane	1975	UCLA	Bill Martin, UCLA
			1976	USC & UCLA	Bill Scanlon, Trinity-TX
1950	UCLA	Herbert Flam, UCLA	1977	Stanford	Matt Mitchell, Stanford
1951	USC	Tony Trabert, Cincinati	1978	Stanford	John McEnroe, Stanford
1952	UCLA	Hugh Stewart, USC	1979	UCLA	Kevin Curren, Texas
1953	UCLA	Ham Richardson, Tulane			
1954	UCLA	Ham Richardson, Tulane	1980	Stanford	Robert Van't Hof, USC
1955	USC	Jose Aguero, Tulane	1981	Stanford	Tim Mayotte, Stanford
1956	UCLA	Alex Olmedo, USC	1982	UCLA	Mike Leach, Michigan
1957	Michigan	Barry MacKay, Michigan	1983	Stanford	Greg Holmes, Utah
1958	USC	Alex Olmedo, USC	1984	UCLA	Mikael Pernfors, Georgia
1959	Tulane & Notre Dame	Whitney Reed, San Jose St.	1985	Georgia	Mikael Pernfors, Georgia
			1986	Stanford	Dan Goldie, Stanford
1960	UCLA	Larry Nagler, UCLA	1987	Georgia	Andrew Burrow, Miami-FL
1961	UCLA	Allen Fox, UCLA	1988	Stanford	Robby Weiss, Pepperdine
1962	USC	Rafael Osuna, USC	1989	Stanford	Donni Leaycraft, LSU
1963	USC	Dennis Ralston, USC			
1964	USC	Dennis Ralston, USC	1990	Stanford	Steve Bryan, Texas
1965	UCLA	Arthur Ashe, UCLA	1991	USC	Jared Palmer, Stanford
1966	USC	Charlie Pasarell, UCLA	1992	Stanford	Alex O'Brien Stanford
1967	USC	Bob Lutz, USC	1993	USC	Chris Woodruff, Tennessee
1968	USC	Stan Smith, USC	1994	USC	Mark Merklein, Florida
1969	USC	Joaquin Loyo-Mayo, USC	1995	Stanford	Sargis Sargisian, Ariz. St.
1970	UCLA	Jeff Borowiak, UCLA			
1971	UCLA	Jimmy Connors, UCLA			

Women's NCAA Champions

Multiple winners (Teams): Stanford (8); USC and Texas (2). (Players): Sandra Birch, Patty Fendick and Lisa Raymond (2).

Year	Team winner	Individual Champion	Year	Team winner	Individual Champion
1982	Stanford	Alycia Moulton, Stanford	1989	Stanford	Sandra Birch, Stanford
1983	USC	Beth Herr, USC	1990	Stanford	Debbie Graham, Stanford
1984	Stanford	Lisa Spain, Georgia	1991	Stanford	Sandra Birch, Stanford
1985	USC	Linda Gates, Stanford	1992	Florida	Lisa Raymond, Florida
1986	Stanford	Patty Fendick, Stanford	1993	Texas	Lisa Raymond, Florida
1987	Stanford	Patty Fendick, Stanford	1994	Georgia	Angela Lettiere, Georgia
1988	Stanford	Shaun Stafford, Florida	1995	Texas	Keri Phoebus, UCLA

A gleeful European captain **Bernard Gallacher** clutches the Ryder Cup trophy during award ceremonies in Rochester, N.Y., following Europe's upset win over the United States on Sept. 24.

GOLF

by Marino Parascenzo

Choke Hill

*The United States blows a 2-point lead on the final day
as the Europeans take back the Ryder Cup, 14½ to 13½.*

The Ryder Cup, that golfing orphan-turned-international hot ticket, has achieved such prominence in recent years that stateside media types can't resist giving each new edition a Don King-style moniker of mayhem.

In 1991, at Kiawah Island, N.C., it was "The War on the Shore." Two years ago, at Sutton Coldfield, England, it was "The Battle at the Belfry."

The United States won both of those matches, so the phrasing was heroic. Unfortunately for the heavily favored Americans, the 1995 matches were held at Oak Hill Country Club in Rochester, N.Y. Naturally, when the U.S. blew a two-point lead on the final day, the debacle became known as "The Choke at the Oak."

The underdog Europeans, a grand collection of aging stars, retreads and neophytes, charged from behind on Sept. 24, and whipped the Yanks at their own game, the singles matches. They won seven of the 12 singles and tied one to wrest the Cup from their hosts by a score of 14½ to 13½.

What lit up the critics, however, was how the Americans lost. Five matches went to the 18th hole. The Euros won four of them, and in three, the Americans bogeyed. They hit trees, they hit rough and they hit sand. What they didn't hit were greens.

Marino Parascenzo has been the *Pittsburgh Post-Gazette's* golf writer since 1975. He is also a contributing editor to *Golf Digest* magazine.

The biggest surprise was Curtis Strange, who led Nick Faldo 1-up with three holes to play in their pivotal match and then bogeyed all three, handing Faldo a 1-up win.

At the 18th, Faldo did his best to hand it back as he drove into the deep left rough and could only chop out down the fairway. He then recovered by lobbing a magnificent wedge snug to the pin.

"I left myself a lovely little four-footer just outside the left edge," Faldo said. "Everything was shaking but the putter, so I made it."

Strange had been a wild-card pick (along with Fred Couples) by U.S. captain and old pal, Lanny Wadkins. The selection, however, had been a controversial one since Strange hadn't posted a victory on the PGA Tour since winning his second straight U.S. Open in 1989 on this same course.

"Eleven guys played their hearts out," said Strange, who was winless in three matches, "and I let them down terribly." In five Ryder Cup appearances, Strange has had the misfortune of playing on four U.S. teams that failed to beat the Europeans.

America's Corey Pavin was the top point-getter on either side, going 4-1, and U.S. rookie Phil Mickelson (3-0) was the only entrant to go unbeaten. Ben Crenshaw, like Strange, lost all three of his matches.

On the European side, David Gilford, Sam Torrance and Constantino Rocca each won three matches, while their nine team-mates all won at least once.

The happiest man in Rochester was the

Stephen Munday/Allsport

Curtis Strange of the U.S. hides his face in his hands as teammates applaud the European side following the final round of the Ryder Cup. Strange could have clinched the Cup for the Americans by winning or halving his singles match with Nick Faldo. Instead, he bogeyed the final three holes and lost.

European captain Bernard Gallacher, who finally won the Cup after seven tries as a player and two as captain.

"I don't think anybody thought we could do it, but I did," he said. "Finally won in the 10th time. I can't tell you how good it feels."

Looking around the raucous European locker room, he added: "We needed a good performance out of the whole team and we got it. They played majestically. We had such a very, very strong desire to win this trophy back and we just kept at it."

The United States still owns a 23-6-2 record in the biennial matches, but the Euros, who won for only the second time on American soil (the first was 1987), hold a lead of 3-2-1 in the past six matches.

Elsewhere in the world of golf in 1995: Fred Couples had a bad back, Jose-Maria Olazabal a bad right foot, John Daly a bad haircut and Ben Wright a bad rap (he said).

Couples had to take time off, and Olazabal limped all year long and had to pass up his Ryder Cup berth.

Daly shaved his head the week after he won the British Open. "People kept telling me it was too long," he explained. It was the second time he'd done that. The first time, it was because he was trying to break a spell of poor play. He'd try anything he said. "But I'm sure as hell not going to wear knickers."

The year began with what many considered a grave threat to pro tours in the United States, Europe, and elsewhere— Greg Norman's proposed World Tour. The new supertour, underwritten by fellow Aussie Rupert Murdoch's Fox television network, would feature eight $3 million events for the elite 30 or 40 golfers around the globe.

Fox announced the tour on Nov. 17, 1994. A few weeks later, at the $2.5 million Johnnie Walker World Championship in Jamaica, the best players in the world were ridiculing the idea and mocking Norman.

The Johnnie Walker was just the kind of tournament Norman had in mind and he had qualified for the exclusive field. Yet, he didn't show up.

"If he wants to play the best," scoffed Scotland's Colin Montgomerie, "why isn't he here?"

Wide World Photos

Ben Crenshaw is comforted by caddy Carl Jackson after winning his second Masters on April 9. Three days before the tournament started Crenshaw's friend and mentor Harvey Penick died and Crenshaw held back his grief until he sank his winning putt.

In the opinion of most players, the proposal hadn't been well thought out.

"It doesn't make sense," said Nick Faldo. "There's no way [this tour] is going to happen."

And it didn't.

Norman himself backpedalled as fast as he could. At a news conference in February, he stunned his audience. "Remember, I had nothing to do with it," he said. "Yes, I favored it and I supported it, but I had nothing to do with organizing it."

The general feeling was that a world tour would hurt the existing tours by drawing away players and sponsors. As far as anyone could tell, his tour had no players, no sites, no sponsors, and the Fox money was iffy at best. It was dead.

The flap of the year— one of the hottest in the history of the game, in fact— hit the LPGA Tour on the eve of the LPGA Championship in May. CBS Sports golf commentator Ben Wright was asked by a local newspaper interviewer why it seems sponsors and television were reluctant to support women's golf.

"Let's face facts here," Wright was quoted as saying in *The News Journal* of Wilmington, Del. "Lesbians in the sport hurt women's golf." And so it went.

Wright was also quoted as saying that women golfers are handicapped by their breasts interfering with their swing.

Wright proclaimed his innocence. "I am disgusted at the pack of lies and distortions attributed to me..." he said.

Apart from whether Wright did or did not make the statements, what made the episode so surprising is that both subjects were old hat in golf circles. Tom Watson, for one, made a similar observation on LPGA lesbianism in a *Golf Digest* article years before. And earlier in 1995, *Golf Digest* carried a one-page lesson in which a woman pro, addressing a fact of life and anatomy, advised women how to adjust their arms around their breasts in order to improve their swings.

Despite calls for Wright's removal from the telecast, CBS stuck with him and the firestorm burned itself out.

When the golf world got around to playing golf in 1995, it produced some memorable moments.

Ben Crenshaw won the most emotional Masters since Jack Nicklaus in 1986, although Crenshaw's was probably more poignant.

Harvey Penick, his beloved golf coach since his student days back University of Texas, died at age 90 on April 2, the Sunday before the start of the tournament. Crenshaw was tense and solemn all week, and when he dropped the winning putt, he bent over with his head in his hands and sobbed.

Crenshaw hadn't won in a year. His game was in pieces. But he had pulled it all together that week.

"It was like someone put their hand on my shoulder...and guided me through," he said.

Crenshaw held off Davis Love III and Norman in the final round, holing a 5-footer for a birdie at the 16th to regain the lead, and a 13-footer at the 17th to pad it. He then two-putted the 18th for a bogey and his second green jacket.

The 1995 Masters also marked the coming-out of amateur phenom Tiger Woods into the world of grown-up golf. Woods, who was invited to Augusta as the 1994 U.S. Amateur champion, showed a breathtaking long game and an erratic approach game. The only amateur to make the cut, he shot 72-72-77-72—293, and tied for 41st, four shots out of last place.

But if he impressed the Masters, the Masters didn't impress him.

Are you intimidated by all this? someone asked. "No," he said. "It's just another tournament." Were you impressed by the drive up Magnolia Lane? "Was that it?" he asked back.

Woods also informed the international media corps that he is not black, as was commonly believed.

"I'm Indian, black, Asian, and white," Woods said. "It's an injustice to all my heritages to just single me out as black."

A week later, he announced he would be granting no more interviews until after the NCAA championship in early June. He tied for fifth there, and Oklahoma State beat his Stanford team for the team title.

Woods, at 19, was named to the U.S. Walker Cup team, which fared no better. He went 2-2 in his matches and the underdog amateurs from Great Britain and Ireland upset the Yanks, 14-10.

But Woods' season was far from a bust. On Aug. 27, he won his second straight U.S. Amateur, beating Philadelphia-area auto dealer Buddy Marucci 2-up in the 36-hole final at Newport (R.I.) C.C.

The U.S. Open returned to historic Shinnecock Hills, in Southampton, N.Y., site of the second Open in 1896. And in a field loaded with heavyweights, it was a junior middleweight— 5-foot-9, 150-pound Corey Pavin— who jabbed and finessed Shinnecock into submission.

Pavin trailed Norman and Tom Lehman by three at the start of the final round. He tied for the lead with a birdie at the 12th, took the lead with a birdie at the 15th, and then locked up the win at the 18th with an electrifying 228-yard 4-wood to within five feet of the hole.

"That was the greatest shot I ever hit under pressure," he said after finishing with a par-280 total for a two-stroke win. The Open victory earned Pavin $350,000 in prize money and freed him forever from being referred to as "the best player never to have won a major."

The British Open returned to St. Andrews, Scotland in '95 and boiled down to a duel between the big-hitting John Daly and

Corey Pavin gives the United States Open trophy a kiss after winning his first major championship on June 18 at Shinnecock Hills in Southampton, N.Y.

Constantino Rocca, the first Italian with a real shot at winning the title.

Rocca, goat of the 1993 Ryder Cup after missing a short putt, almost got another set of horns at St. Andrews when he choked on a short chip shot at the final hole and chunked it into the Valley of Sin, a swale in front of the green. He then became an international hero by sinking a 65-foot putt to tie Daly, who went on to win the aggregate four-hole playoff.

Steve Elkington, the Houston-based Australian, prevented an American sweep of the four majors when he beat Scotland's Colin Montgomerie in a sudden-death playoff for the PGA Championship at raggedy-greened Riviera, in Los Angeles.

Almost lost in the heat was Ernie Els, the 1994 U.S. Open champ from South Africa, who is often billed as unflappable, Els was a tournament-record 13-under-par going into the final round when he flapped and ended up third with a 72.

Elkington shot a final-round 7-under 64, and Monty put on a blistering finish, getting birdies at the last three holes for a 65 to tie at 17-under 267 and force the playoff.

Betsy King earned her way into the LPGA Hall of Fame on June 25 with a victory at the ShopRite Classic in New Jersey. The win was the 30th of her 19-year career but the first since Nov. 7, 1993.

It lasted one hole, at the 18th. Elkington was looking at a 20-footer that was about identical to one he just watched Monty make for a third straight bird in regulation. Elkington followed the same line, and dropped it for his own birdie. And when Monty couldn't match him, Elkington had his first major.

In women's golf, three of the LPGA's four majors were captured by first-time winners, beginning with Nanci Bowen at the Dinah Shore.

Bowen didn't know she was leading until she reached the final hole. She bogeyed, then watched as Tammie Green, Nancy Lopez, and Laura Davies all fell short, leaving her with a one-shot victory.

Davies, incidentally, inquired about entering the British Open during the year, but was informed by the Royal and Ancient Golf Club of St. Andrews that the Open is a men's tournament, just as the application blank says. The U. S. Golf Association, however, has no such restrictions against female participants— provided they can qualify— and some golf observers are waiting to see whether Davies takes a shot at 1996 U.S. Open.

Davies was beaten by a stroke at the LPGA Championship where Kelly Robbins caught her down the final stretch. "This was my week," said Robbins, a fourth-year pro with two career wins. "But Laura's definitely the dominant player in the world right now."

At the U.S. Women's Open, Annika Sorenstam, the 1994 Rookie of the Year, came from five shots back to win after Meg Mallon went bogey-triple bogey. Sorenstam, the seventh first-time winner of the season, was leading the tour's money list with over $542,000 by late September.

Lidback became the 10th first-timer with her win at the du Maurier. A dual citizen of Peru and Sweden, she defeated full Swede, Liselotte Neumann, by a stroke.

On June 25, three-time Player of the Year Betsy King, finally earned her way into the LPGA Hall of Fame with career victory No. 30 at the ShopRite Classic in Somers Point, N.J. It had taken her 1 year, 7 months, and 18 days from her 29th victory to make it— a span in which the questions and well-wishing were as tough as the wait. "I used to count the days that went by without someone mentioning it," King said.

The LPGA will enter 1996 with a new commissioner. Charlie Mechem had announced before the Ben Wright uproar that '95 would be his last year. It remains to be seen whether his successor, 41-year-old Jim Ritts, a former TV executive, inherited damaged goods.

On the Senior PGA Tour, Jack Nicklaus, who keeps hinting that he'll retire, continued to push back the date by placing well in the big tournaments. He started the year by winning The Tradition in April for his sixth Senior major since joining the tour in 1990.

After that he placed eighth in the PGA Seniors' Championship, and second in both the Seniors Players Championship and the U.S. Senior Open.

Ray Floyd won the PGA Seniors' Championship by five strokes. J.C. Snead defeated Nicklaus in a playoff to win the Senior Players Championship. And Tom Weiskopf, the former "Towering Inferno," beat Nicklaus by four-shots in the U.S. Senior Open at Congressional. It was his first national title.

"Finally," Weiskopf said, "I'm part of USGA history." ❑

THE 1996 INFORMATION PLEASE SPORTS ALMANAC

GOLF STATISTICS

THE SEASON IN REVIEW
1994-1995
PGA • SENIORS • LPGA

SEC A

PAGE 827

Tournament Results

Winners of PGA, European PGA, PGA Seniors and LPGA tournaments from Oct. 30, 1994 through Sept. 24, 1995.

PGA Tour

Late 1994

Last Rd	Tournament	Winner	Earnings	Runner-Up
Oct. 30	The Tour Championship	Mark McCumber (274)*	$540,000	F. Zoeller (274)
Nov. 6	Kapalua International	Fred Couples (279)	180,000	B. Gilder (281)
Nov. 9	PGA Grand Slam	Greg Norman (136)	400,000	N. Price (139)
Nov. 13	World Cup of Golf	USA —Fred Couples/	150,000	ZIM— M. McNulty/
		Davis Love III (536)	(each)	T. Johnstone (550)
Nov. 20	Franklin Funds Shark Shootout	Fred Couples/	150,000	C. Strange/
		Brad Faxon (190)	(each)	M. O'Meara (192)
Nov. 27	The Skins Game	Paul Azinger (4)	80,000	P. Stewart (3)
Dec. 4	JC Penney Classic	M. Figueras-Dotti/	150,000	H. Alfredsson/
		Brad Bryant (262)*	(each)	R. Gamez (262)

World Cup teams: USA (Fred Couples 65-63-68-69—265; and Davis Love III 67-66-69-69—271), Zimbabwe (Mark McNulty 68-67-67-70—272, and Tony Johnstone 67-72-66-73—278)

*Playoffs (1): **Tour Championship—** McCumber won on the 1st hole; **JC Penney—** Figueras-Dotti and Bryant won on the 4th hole.

1995 (through Sept. 24)

Last Rd	Tournament	Winner	Earnings	Runner-Up
Jan. 8	Mercedes Championship	Steve Elkington (278)*	$180,000	B. Lietzke (278)
Jan. 15	United Airlines Hawaiian Open	John Morse (269)	216,000	D. Waldorf
				& T. Lehman (272)
Jan. 22	Northern Telecom Open	Phil Mickelson (269)	225,000	S. Simpson
				& J. Gallagher (270)
Jan. 29	Phoenix Open	Vijay Singh (269)*	234,000	B. Mayfair (269)
Feb. 5	AT&T Pebble Beach National Pro-Am	Peter Jacobsen (271)	252,000	D. Duval (273)
Feb. 12	Buick Invitational of California	Peter Jacobsen (269)	216,000	M. Calcavecchia (273)
Feb. 19	Bob Hope Chrysler Classic	Kenny Perry (335)	216,000	D. Duval (336)
Feb. 26	Nissan Open	Corey Pavin (268)	216,000	J. Don Blake
				& K. Perry (271)
Mar. 5	Doral Ryder Open	Nick Faldo (273)	270,000	P. Jacobsen
				& G. Norman (274)
Mar. 12	Honda Classic	Mark O'Meara (275)	216,000	N. Faldo (276)
Mar. 19	Nestle Invitational	Loren Roberts (272)	216,000	B. Faxon (274)
Mar. 26	The Players Championship	Lee Janzen (283)	540,000	B. Langer (284)
Apr. 2	Freeport-McMoRan Classic	Davis Love III (274)*	216,000	M. Heinen (274)
Apr. 9	**The Masters** (Augusta)	Ben Crenshaw (274)	396,000	D. Love III (275)
Apr. 16	MCI Classic	Bob Tway (275)*	234,000	N. Henke
				& D. Frost (275)
Apr. 23	Kmart Greater Greensboro Open	Jim Gallagher (274)	270,000	P. Jacobsen
				& J. Sluman (275)
Apr. 30	Shell Houston Open	Payne Stewart (276)*	252,000	S. Hoch (276)
May 7	BellSouth Classic	Mark Calcavecchia (271)	234,000	J. Gallagher (273)
May 14	GTE Byron Nelson Classic	Ernie Els (263)	234,000	3-way tie (266)
May 21	Buick Classic	Vijay Singh (278)*	216,000	D. Martin (278)
May 28	Colonial National Invitation	Tom Lehman (271)	252,000	C. Parry (272)
June 4	Memorial Tournament	Greg Norman (269)	306,000	3-way tie (273)
June 11	Kemper Open	Lee Janzen (272)*	252,000	Corey Pavin (272)
June 18	**U.S. Open** (Shinnecock Hills)	Corey Pavin (280)	350,000	Greg Norman (282)
June 25	Canon Greater Hartford Open	Greg Norman (267)	216,000	3-way tie (269)

Tournament Results (Cont.)
PGA Tour

Last Rd	Tournament	Winner	Earnings	Runner-Up
July 23	Deposit Guaranty Golf Classic	Ed Dougherty (272)	$126,000	G. Morgan (274)
July 23	**British Open** (St. Andrews)	John Daly (282)*	200,000	C. Rocca (282)
July 30	Ideon Classic at Pleasant Valley	Fred Funk (268)	180,000	J. McGovern (269)
Aug. 6	Buick Open	Woody Austin (270)*	216,000	M. Brisky (270)
Aug. 13	**PGA Championship** (Pacific Palisades)	Steve Elkington (267)*	360,000	C. Montgomerie (267)
Aug. 20	The Sprint International	Lee Janzen (34)†	270,000	E. Els (33)
Aug. 27	NEC World Series of Golf	Greg Norman (278)*	360,000	B. Mayfair & N. Price (278)
Sept. 3	Greater Milwaukee Open	Scott Hoch (269)	180,000	M. Dawson (272)
Sept. 10	Bell Canadian Open	Mark O'Meara (274)*	234,000	B. Lohr (274)
Sept. 17	B.C. Open	Hal Sutton (269)	180,000	J. McGovern (270)
Sept. 24	Quad Cities Open	D.A. Weibring (197)	180,000	J. Kaye (198)
Sept. 24	**The Ryder Cup** (Rochester)	Europe (14½)	(none)	United States (13½)

(See Updates Chapter for later results.)
Rain-shortened.
†The scoring for the Sprint International was based on a modified Stableford system (8 points for a double eagle, 5 for an eagle, 2 for a birdie, 0 for a par, -1 for bogey, -3 for double bogey or worse).

*Playoffs (12): **Mercedes**— Elkington won on 2nd hole; **Phoenix**— Singh won on 1st hole; **Freeport-McMoRan**— Love III won on 2nd hole; **MCI**— Tway won on 2nd hole; **Houston**— Stewart won on 1st hole; **Buick**— Singh won on 5th hole; **Kemper**— Janzen won on 1st hole; **British**— Daly won 4-hole playoff; **Buick**— Austin won on 2nd hole; **PGA Championship**— Elkington won on 1st hole; **NEC World Series**— Norman won on 1st hole; **Bell Canadian Open**— O'Meara won on 1st hole;

Second place ties (3 players or more): 3-WAY— **Byron Nelson** (D.A. Weibring, M. Heinen and R. Lee Freeman), **Memorial** (S. Elkington, M. Calcavecchia, D. Duval); **Greater Hartford** (K. Triplett, D. Stockton, G. Waite), 4-WAY— **Motorola Western** (J. Maggert, J. Leonard, S. Simpson, J. Haas),

PGA Majors

The Masters

Edition: 59th   **Dates:** April 6-9
Site: Augusta National GC, Augusta, Ga.
Par: 36-36—72 (6925 yards)

		1	2	3	4	Tot	Earnings
1	Ben Crenshaw	70	67	69	68	274	$396,000
2	Davis Love III	69	69	71	66	275	237,600
3	Greg Norman	73	68	68	68	277	127,600
	Jay Haas	71	64	72	70	277	127,600
5	David Frost	66	71	71	71	279	83,600
	Steve Elkington	73	67	67	72	279	83,600
7	Phil Mickelson	66	71	70	73	280	70,950
	Scott Hoch	69	67	71	73	280	70,950
9	Curtis Strange	72	71	65	73	281	63,800
10	Fred Couples	71	69	67	75	282	57,200
	Brian Henninger	70	68	68	76	282	57,200

Early round leaders: 1st— Frost, Mickelson, and Jose Maria Olazabal (66); 2nd— Haas (135); 3rd— Henninger and Crenshaw (206).
Top amateur: Tiger Woods (293).

British Open

Edition: 124th   **Dates:** July 20-23
Site: Fife, Scotland
Par: 36-36—72 (6933 yards)   **Purse:** $1,989,375 (US)

		1	2	3	4	Tot	Earnings
1	John Daly	67	71	73	71	282	$200,000
2	Constantino Rocca	69	70	70	73	282	160,000
3	Michael Campbell	71	71	65	76	283	105,065
	Steven Bottomley	70	72	72	69	283	105,065
	Mark Brooks	70	69	73	71	283	105,065
6	Vijay Singh	68	72	73	71	284	64,800
	Steve Elkington	72	69	69	74	284	64,800
8	Corey Pavin	69	70	72	74	285	53,333
	Bob Estes	72	70	71	72	285	53,333
	Mark James	72	75	68	70	285	53,333

Playoff: Daly (3-4-4-4— 15) def. Constantino Rocca (4-5-7-3— 19) in 4-hole playoff.
Early round leaders: 1st— Ben Crenshaw, Daly, Mark McNulty and Tom Watson (67); 2nd— Daly, Brad Faxon and Katsuyoshi Tomori (138); 3rd— Campbell (207).
Top amateur: Gordon Sherry (291).

U.S. Open

Edition: 95th   **Dates:** June 15-18
Site: Shinnecock Hills GC, Southampton, N.Y.
Par: 35-35—70 (6944 yards)   **Purse:** $2,000,000

		1	2	3	4	Tot	Earnings
1	Corey Pavin	72	69	71	68	280	$350,000
2	Greg Norman	68	67	74	73	282	207,000
3	Tom Lehman	70	72	67	74	283	131,974
4	Davis Love III	72	68	73	71	284	66,634
	Phil Mickelson	68	70	72	74	284	66,634
	Bill Glasson	69	70	76	69	284	66,634
	Jay Haas	70	73	72	69	284	66,634
	Neal Lancaster	70	72	77	65	284	66,634
	Jeff Maggert	69	72	77	66	284	66,634
10	Frank Nobilo	72	72	70	71	285	44,184
	Vijay Singh	70	71	72	72	285	44,184
	Bob Tway	69	69	72	75	285	44,184

Early round leaders: 1st— Nick Price (66); 2nd— Norman (135); 3rd— Lehman and Norman (209).
Top amateur: none.

PGA Championship

Edition: 77th   **Dates:** Aug. 10-13
Site: Riviera CC, Pacific Palisades, Calif.
Par: 35-36—71 (6956 yards)   **Purse:** $2,000,000

		1	2	3	4	Tot	Earnings
1	Steve Elkington	68	67	68	64	267	$360,000
2	Colin Montgomerie	68	67	67	65	267	216,000
3	Ernie Els	66	65	66	72	269	116,000
	Jeff Maggert	66	69	65	69	269	116,000
5	Brad Faxon	70	67	71	63	271	80,000
6	Mark O'Meara	64	67	69	73	273	68,500
	Bob Estes	69	68	68	68	273	68,500
8	Craig Stadler	71	66	66	71	274	50,000
	Steve Lowery	69	68	68	69	274	50,000
	Justin Leonard	68	66	70	70	274	50,000
	Jay Haas	69	71	64	70	274	50,000
	Jeff Sluman	69	67	68	70	274	50,000

Playoff: Elkington won on 1st hole of sudden death.
Early round leaders: 1st— Michael Bradley (63); 2nd— Els, O'Meara (131); 3rd— Els (197).
Top amateur: none.

1995 Ryder Cup

The 31st Ryder Cup matches, Sept. 22-24, at Oak Hill Country Club in Rochester, N.Y.

ROSTERS

Selections for both the U.S. and Europe teams were determined by a special Ryder Cup points system that ranked players from the beginning of the 1994 season through the '95 PGA Championship. On Aug. 13, the Top 10 players on the PGA and European PGA tours automatically qualified for their Ryder Cup teams with non-playing captains Lanny Wadkins of the U.S. and Bernard Gallacher of Europe each rounding out their 12-man rosters with two wild card picks. Players are listed alphabetically with previous Ryder Cup appearances in parentheses; countries of European players are also noted.

United States: Qualifiers— Ben Crenshaw (3); Brad Faxon (none); Jay Haas (1); Peter Jacobsen (1); Tom Lehman (none); Davis Love III (1); Jeff Maggert (none); Phil Mickelson (none); Corey Pavin (2); Loren Roberts (none); Wild cards— Fred Couples (3) and Curtis Strange (4).

Europe: Qualifiers— Seve Ballesteros (Spain, 7); Howard Clark (England, 5); David Gilford (England, 1); Mark James (England, 6); Per-Ulrik Johansson (Sweden, none); Bernhard Langer (Germany, 7); Colin Montgomerie (Scotland, 2); Constantino Rocca (Italy, 1); Sam Torrance (Scotland, 7); Philip Walton (Ireland, none). Wild cards—Nick Faldo (England, 9) and Ian Woosnam (Wales, 6). Woosnam replaced José Marie Olazabal, who withdrew due to an injury to his right foot.

First Day
Morning Alternate Shots

Winner	Score	Loser
Pavin/Lehman	1-up	Faldo/Montgomerie
Torrance/Rocca	3&2	Haas/Couples
Love/Maggert	4&3	Clark/James
Langer/Johansson	1-up	Crenshaw/Strange
Even, 2-2		

Afternoon Best Ball

Winner	Score	Loser
Gilford/Ballesteros	4&3	Faxon/Jacobsen
Maggert/Roberts	6&5	Torrance/Rocca
Couples/Love	3&2	Faldo/Montgomerie
Pavin/Mickelson	6&4	Langer/Johansson
USA wins, 3-1		
(USA leads, 5-3)		

Second Day
Morning Alternate Shots

Winner	Score	Loser
Faldo/Montgomerie	4&2	Strange/Haas
Torrance/Rocca	6&5	Maggert/Love
Roberts/Jacobsen	1-up	Woosnam/Walton
Langer/Gilford	4&3	Pavin/Lehman
Europe wins, 3 to 1		
(Even, 6-6)		

Afternoon Fourball

Winner	Score	Loser
Faxon/Couples	4&2	Montgomerie/Torrance
Woosnam/Rocca	3&2	Crenshaw/Love
Mickelson/Haas	3&2	Gilford/Ballesteros
Pavin/Roberts	1-up	Faldo/Langer
USA wins, 3 to 1		
(USA leads, 9-7)		

Third Day
Individual Match Play

Winner	Score	Loser
Tom Lehman	4&3	Seve Ballesteros
Mark James	4&3	Jeff Maggert
Howard Clark	1-up	Peter Jacobsen
Ian Woosnam	halved	Fred Couples
Davis Love III	3&2	Constantino Rocca
David Gilford	1-up	Brad Faxon
Colin Montgomerie	3&1	Ben Crenshaw
Nick Faldo	1-up	Curtis Strange
Sam Torrance	2&1	Loren Roberts
Corey Pavin	3&2	Bernhard Langer
Philip Walton	1-up	Jay Haas
Phil Mickelson	2&1	Per-Ulrik Johansson
Europe wins day, 7½ to 4½		
(Europe wins Ryder Cup, 14½ to 13½)		

Overall Records

Team and individual match play combined.

Europe W-L-H	Pts	United States W-L-H	Pts
Gilford 3-1-0	3	Pavin 4-1-0	4
Rocca 3-2-0	3	Mickelson 3-0-0	3
Torrance 3-2-0	3	Roberts 3-1-0	3
Faldo 2-3-0	2	Love 3-2-0	3
Langer 2-3-0	2	Couples 2-1-1	2½
Montgomerie 2-3-0	2	Lehman 2-1-0	2
Woosnam 1-1-1	1½	Maggert 2-2-0	2
Clark 1-1-0	1	Faxon 1-2-0	1
James 1-1-0	1	Jacobsen 1-2-0	1
Walton 1-1-0	1	Haas 1-3-0	1
Ballesteros 1-2-0	1	Crenshaw 0-3-0	0
Johansson 1-2-0	1	Strange 0-3-0	0

Sony World Rankings
Through Sept. 24, 1995.

Begun in 1986, the Sony World Rankings combine the best golfers on the PGA and European PGA tours. Rankings are based on a rolling three-year period and weighted in favor of more recent results. Points are awarded after each worldwide tournament according to finish. Final point averages are determined by dividing a player's total points by the number of tournaments played in 1995.

		Avg			Avg			Avg
1	Greg Norman	22.32	8	Fred Couples	11.67	15	Sam Torrance	8.18
2	Nick Price	16.15	9	Masashi Ozaki	10.99	16	Seve Ballesteros	8.15
3	Ernie Els	15.47	10	José Maria Olazabal	10.46	17	Lee Janzen	8.09
4	Nick Faldo	15.04	11	Steve Elkington	9.92	18	David Frost	8.08
5	Bernhard Langer	14.67	12	Tom Lehman	9.55	19	Davis Love III	8.07
6	Colin Montgomerie	14.08	13	Vijay Singh	9.29	20	Peter Jacobsen	7.34
7	Corey Pavin	12.32	14	Mark McCumber	8.62			

European PGA Tour

Earnings listed in pounds sterling (£) unless otherwise indicated.

Late 1994

Last Rd	Tournament	Winner	Earnings	Runner-Up
Oct. 30	Volvo Masters	Bernhard Langer (276)	£125,000	S. Ballesteros
		& V. Singh (277)		
Nov. 13	World Cup of Golf	USA —Fred Couples/	92,966	ZIM— M. McNulty/
		Davis Love III (536)	(each)	T. Johnstone (550)
Dec. 18	Johnnie Walker World Championship	Ernie Els (268)	351,932	M. McCumber
				& N. Faldo (274)

1995 (through Sept. 24)

Last Rd	Tournament	Winner	Earnings	Runner-Up
Jan. 22	Dubai Desert Classic	Fred Couples (268)	£ 75,000	C. Montgomerie (271)
Jan. 29	Johnny Walker Classic (Manila)	Fred Couples (277)	100,000	N. Price (279)
Feb. 5	Madeira Island Open	Santiago Luna (272)	41,660	C. Cevaer (276)
Feb. 12	Canary Islands Open	Jarmo Sandelin (282)	40,719	S. Ballesteros
				& P. Eales (283)
Feb. 19	Lexington South Africa PGA	Ernie Els (271)	39,479	R. Wessels (273)
Feb. 26	Open Mediterriana	Robert Karlsson (276)	50,000	4-way tie (279)
Mar. 5	Andalucia Open	Alex Cejka (278)	49,345	C. Rocca (281)
Mar. 12	Moroccan Open	Mark James (275)	58,330	D. Gilford (276)
Mar. 19	Portuguese Open	Adam Hunter (277)*	50,000	D. Clarke (277)
Mar. 26	Baleares Open	Greg Turner (274)	40,478	C. Rocca (276)
Apr. 17	Catalonia Open	Philip Walton (281)	50,000	A. Coltart (284)
Apr. 23	Air France Cannes Open	Andre Bossert (132)#	37,500	J. Van de Velde
				& O. Rojahn (134)
Apr. 30	European Four Ball	Seve Ballesteros/	35,000	M. Clayton/
		Jose Olazabal (256)	35,000	P. O'Malley (259)
May 7	Italian Open	Sam Torrance (269)	61,717	J. Rivero (271)
May 14	Benson & Hedges Intl. Open	Peter O'Malley (280)	108,330	C. Rocca
				& M. James (281)
May 21	Spanish Open	Seve Ballesteros (274)	91,660	I. Garrido
				& J. Rivero (276)
May 29	Volvo PGA Championship	Bernhard Langer (279)	150,000	P. Johansson
				& M. Campbell (280)
June 4	Murphy's English Open	Philip Walton (274)*	108,330	C. Montgomerie (274)
June 11	Deutsche Bank Open	Bernhard Langer (270)	108,330	J. Spence (276)
June 18	DHL Jersey Open	Andrew Oldcorn (273)	50,000	D. Robertson (276)
June 25	Peugeot French Open	Paul Broadhurst (274)	91,660	N. Briggs (282)
July 2	BMW International Open	Frank Nobilo (272)	91,660	J. Sandelin
				& B. Langer (274)
July 9	Murphy's Irish Open	Sam Torrance (277)*	111,108	H. Clark
				& S. Cage (277)
July 15	The Scottish Open	Wayne Riley (276)	108,330	N. Faldo (278)
July 23	**British Open**	John Daly (282)*	125,000	C. Rocca (282)
July 30	Heineken Dutch Open	Scott Hoch (269)	108,330	S. Torrance
				& M. Jonzon (271)
Aug. 6	Scandinavian Masters	Jesper Parnevik (270)	108,330	C. Montgomerie (275)
Aug. 13	Austrian Open	Alexander Cejka (267)	41,660	3-way tie (271)
Aug. 20	Chemapol Trophy Czech Open	Peter Tervaninen (268)	125,000	H. Clark (269)
Aug. 27	Volvo German Open	Colin Montgomerie (268)	108,330	S. Torrance
				& N. Fasth (269)
Sept. 3	European Masters	Mathais Groenberg (270)	116,660	C. Rocca
				& B. Lane (272)
Sept. 10	Lancome Trophy	Colin Montgomerie (269)	100,000	S. Torrance (270)
Sept. 17	British Masters	Sam Torrance (270)	108,330	M. Campbell (271)
Sept. 24	**The Ryder Cup** (Rochester, N.Y.)	Europe (14½)	(none)	United States (13 ½)

(See Updates Chapter for later results.)
Rain-shortened.

*Playoffs (4): **Portugese**— Hunter won on 1st hole; **English**— Walton won on 2nd hole; **Irish**— Torrance won on 2nd hole; **British**— Daly won 4-hole playoff.

Second place ties (3 players or more): 3-WAY— **Austrian Open** (R. Muntz, R. Rafferty, I. Garrido, P. Linhart); 4-WAY— **Mediterranean Open** (A. Forsbrand, M. Angel Jimenez, J. Sandelin, S. Torrance).

Tournament Results (Cont.)

Senior PGA Tour

LATE 1994

Last Rd	Tournament	Winner	Earnings	Runner-Up
Oct. 30	Kaanapali Classic	Bob Murphy (195)	$82,500	J. Kiefer (197)
Nov. 13	Senior Tour Championship	Ray Floyd (273)*	240,000	J. Albus (273)
Dec. 11	Diners Club Matches	Dave Eichelberger/	125,000	J. Nicklaus/
		Ray Floyd (19 holes)	(each)	A. Palmer

*Playoffs (1): **Senior Championship**— Floyd won on 5th hole.

1995 (through Sept. 24)

Last Rd	Tournament	Winner	Earnings	Runner-Up
Jan. 15	Senior Tournament of Champions	Jim Colbert (209)*	$148,400	J. Albus (209)
Jan. 29	Senior Skins Game	Ray Floyd (14)	420,000	J. Nicklaus (4)
Feb. 5	Royal Caribbean Classic	J.C. Snead (209)*	127,500	R. Floyd (209)
Feb. 12	The Intellinet Challenge	Bob Murphy (137)	90,500	R. Floyd (138)
Feb. 19	GTE Suncoast Classic	Dave Stockton (204)	112,500	3-way tie (206)
Feb. 26	Chrysler Cup	USA (11)	50,000	International Team (5)
Mar. 5	FHP Health Care Classic	Bruce Devlin (130)*#	112,500	D. Eichelberger (130)
Mar. 7	Senior Slam at Los Cabos	Ray Floyd (139)	250,000	D. Stockton (145)
Mar. 12	SBC Dominion Seniors	Jim Albus (205)	97,500	J. Sigel
				& R. Floyd (208)
Mar. 19	Toshiba Senior Classic	George Archer (199)	120,000	D. Stockton
				& T. Wargo (200)
Mar. 26	American Express Grand Slam (Japan)	Isao Aoki (173)#	90,000	G. Gilbert
				& G. Marsh (175)
Apr. 2	**The Tradition** (Scottsdale)	Jack Nicklaus (276)*	150,000	I. Aoki (276)
Apr. 16	**PGA Seniors** (Palm Beach Gardens)	Ray Floyd (277)	180,000	3-way tie (282)
Apr. 23	Liberty Mutual Legends of Golf	Mike Hill/	100,000	G. Gilbert/
		Lee Trevino (195)	100,000	J.C. Snead (197)
Apr. 30	Las Vegas Senior Classic	Jim Colbert (205)	150,000	3-way tie (207)
May 7	PaineWebber Invitational	Bob Murphy (203)	120,000	R. Floyd
				& L. Ziegler (205)
May 14	Cadillac NFL Classic	George Archer (205)	142,500	R. Floyd
				& B. Murphy (206)
May 21	Bell Atlantic Classic	Jim Colbert (207)	135,000	J.C. Snead (208)
May 28	Quicksilver Classic	Dave Stockton (208)	165,000	I. Aoki (209)
June 4	Bruno's Memorial Classic	Graham Marsh (201)	157,500	J.C. Snead (206)
June 11	BellSouth Classic at Opryland	Jim Dent (203)	165,000	B. Murphy (205)
June 18	Dallas Reunion Pro-Am	Tom Wargo (197)	82,500	D. Eichelberger
				& D. Stockton (204)
June 25	Nationwide Championship	Bob Murphy (203)	180,000	B. Summerhays
				& H. Irwin (205)
July 2	**U.S. Senior Open** (Bethesda)	Tom Weiskopf (275)	175,000	J. Nicklaus (279)
July 9	Kroger Classic	Mike Hill (196)	135,000	I. Aoki (197)
July 16	**Senior Players Champs.** (Dearborn)	J.C. Snead (272)*	225,000	J. Nicklaus (272)
July 23	First of America Classic	Jimmy Powell (201)	105,000	B. Hiskey (206)
July 30	Ameritech Open	Hale Irwin (195)	127,500	K. Zarley (202)
Aug. 6	VFW Senior Championship	Bob Murphy (195)	135,000	J. Colbert (196)
Aug. 13	Burnet Classic	Ray Floyd (201)	165,000	G. Marsh (202)
Aug. 20	Northville Long Island Classic	Lee Trevino (202)	120,000	B. Allin (206)
Aug. 27	Bank of Boston Classic	Isao Aoki (204)	120,000	B. Charles
				& H. Irwin (205)
Sept. 3	Franklin Quest Classic	Tony Jacklin (206)	90,000	6-way tie (207)
Sept. 10	GTE Northwest Classic	Walt Morgan (203)	90,000	D. Stockton (206)
Sept. 17	Brickyard Crossing Championship	Simon Hobday (204)	112,500	5-way tie (205)
Sept. 24	Bank One Classic	Gary Player (211)	90,000	J. Kiefer (213)

(See Updates Chapter for later results.)
#Rain-shortened.

*Playoffs (5): **Tournament of Champions**— Colbert won on 3rd hole; **Royal Carribean**— Snead won 1st hole; **Health Care**— Devlin won on 2nd hole. **The Tradition**— Nicklaus won on 3rd hole; **Players Championship**— Snead won on 1st hole.
　　Second place ties (3 players or more): 3-WAY— **PGA Seniors** (J.P. Cain, L. Gilbert, L. Trevino); **Las Vegas** (J. Dent, R. Thompson, R. Floyd); **GTE Suncoast** (J. Colbert, B. Charles, J.C. Snead); 5-WAY— **Brickyard Crossing** (K. Zarley, I. Aoki, H. Irwin, L. Trevino, B. Murphy); 6-WAY— **Franklin Quest** (T. Weiskopf, D. Stockton, J.P. Cain, R. McBee, B. Summerhays, S. Hobday).

Senior PGA Majors

The Tradition

Edition: 7th   **Dates:** Mar. 30-Apr. 2
Site: Desert Mt. Cochise Course, Scottsdale, Ariz.
Par: 36-36—72 (6869 yards)   **Purse:** $1,000,000

		1	2	3	4	Tot	Earnings
1	Jack Nicklaus	69	71	69	67	276	$150,000
2	Isao Aoki	71	66	72	67	276	88,000
3	Jim Ferree	67	74	69	67	277	72,000
4	Jim Colbert	76	64	70	70	280	60,000
5	Jimmy Powell	75	68	69	69	281	48,000
6	Ray Floyd	70	72	71	69	282	38,000
	Jay Sigel	70	69	71	72	282	38,000
8	Tom Weiskopf	75	74	67	67	283	27,500
	Dale Douglass	74	74	67	68	283	27,500
	Bruce Summerhays	71	77	66	69	283	27,500
	Bob Murphy	73	71	69	70	283	27,500

Playoff: Nicklaus won on 3rd hole of sudden death.
Early round leaders: 1st— Ferree (67); 2nd— Aoki (137); 3rd— Aoki, Nicklaus (209).

PGA Seniors' Championship

Edition: 58th   **Dates:** April 13-16
Site: PGA National GC, Palm Beach Gardens, Fla.
Par: 36-36—72 (6702 yards)   **Purse:** $1,000,000

		1	2	3	4	Tot	Earnings
1	Ray Floyd	70	70	67	70	277	$180,000
2	John Paul Cain	72	71	70	69	282	75,000
	Larry Gilbert	71	70	72	69	282	75,000
	Lee Trevino	72	70	69	71	282	75,000
5	Graham Marsh	71	71	70	71	283	40,000
	Isao Aoki	70	69	73	71	283	40,000
	Bob Charles	70	75	68	70	283	40,000
8	Jack Nicklaus	76	66	68	74	284	30,000
9	Jim Colbert	69	69	71	76	285	25,000
10	Bob Murphy	71	73	70	72	286	17,883
	Jim Albus	69	73	69	75	286	17,883
	George Archer	73	71	68	74	286	17,883

Early round leaders: 1st— Calvin Peete, DeWitt Weaver, and Harry Toscano (66); 2nd— Colbert (138); 3rd— Floyd (207).

U.S. Senior Open

Edition: 16th   **Dates:** June 26-July 2
Site: Congressional CC, Bethesda, Md.
Par: 36-36—72 (6945 yards)   **Purse:** $1,000,000

		1	2	3	4	Tot	Earnings
1	Tom Weiskopf	69	69	69	68	275	$175,000
2	Jack Nicklaus	71	71	70	67	279	103,500
3	Bob Murphy	69	70	71	70	280	51,998
	Isao Aoki	70	70	68	72	280	51,998
5	J.C. Snead	68	73	70	71	282	32,625
	Hale Irwin	72	68	71	71	282	32,625
7	Lee Trevino	73	68	74	68	283	28,073
8	Graham Marsh	69	70	74	71	284	24,811
	Ray Floyd	70	72	69	73	284	24,811
10	DeWitt Weaver	73	71	70	71	285	22,043

Early round leaders: 1st—Larry Ringer and Snead (68); 2nd— Weiskopf and Tommy Aaron (138); 3rd— Weiskopf (207).

Sr. Players Championship

Edition: 13th   **Dates:** July 13-16
Site: TPC of Michigan, Dearborn, Mich.
Par: 36-36—72 (6970 yards)   **Purse:** $1,500,000

		1	2	3	4	Tot	Earnings
1	J.C. Snead	69	68	66	69	272	$225,000
2	Jack Nicklaus	71	68	66	67	272	132,000
3	Jim Colbert	70	63	75	68	276	90,000
	Jerry McGee	68	73	67	68	276	90,000
	Ben Smith	73	67	67	68	276	90,000
6	Isao Aoki	71	68	68	70	277	60,000
7	Don Bies	74	71	68	65	278	48,000
	Bob Murphy	71	68	69	70	278	48,000
	Dave Stockton	69	69	66	74	278	48,000
10	Hale Irwin	74	69	72	64	279	34,500
	Tom Weiskopf	70	71	69	69	279	34,500
	Al Geiberger	70	70	69	70	279	34,500
	Ray Floyd	69	70	66	74	279	34,500

Playoff: Snead won on 1st hole of sudden death.
Early round leaders: 1st— McGee, Bob Charles, and Bob Zimmerman (68); 2nd— Colbert (133) 3rd—J.C. Snead (203).

LPGA Tour

LATE 1994

Last Rd	Tournament	Winner	Earnings	Runner-Up
Oct. 30	Nichirei International (Japan)	USA (22.5 pts)	$550,000	Japan (13.5)
Nov. 6	Toray Japan Queens Cup	Woo-Son Ko (206)*	105,000	B. King (206)
Dec. 4	JCPenney Classic	Marta Figueras-Dotti/ Brad Bryant*	150,000 (each)	H. Alfredsson/ R. Gamez
Dec. 11	Diner's Club Matches	Kelly Robbins & Tammie Green (2 &1)	125,000	J. Inkster & P. Sheehan
Dec. 18	Wendy's Three-Tour Challenge	PGA Tour (206)@	450,000	Senior PGA & LPGA (218)

@Three-Tour Teams: PGA (Greg Norman, Fred Couples, Paul Azinger); Senior PGA (Jack Nicklaus, Dave Stockton, Raymond Floyd); LPGA (Patty Sheehan, Nancy Lopez, Laura Davies).
*Playoffs (2): **Toray Japan Queens**— Ko won on the 1st hole; **JCPenny Classic**— Dotti/Bryant won on 4th hole.

1995 (through Sept. 24)

Last Rd	Tournament	Winner	Earnings	Runner-Up
Jan. 15	Chrysler-Plymouth Tournament of Champions	Dawn Coe-Jones (281)	$115,000	B. Daniel (287)
Jan. 22	HealthSouth Inaugural	Pat Bradley (211)	67,500	B. Daniel (212)
Feb. 19	Cup Noodles Hawaiian Open	Barb Thomas (204)	82,500	3-way tie (209)
Mar. 12	Ping/Welch's Championship	Dottie Mochrie (278)	67,500	A. Sorenstam & C. Rarick (283)
Mar. 19	Standard Register Ping	Laura Davies (280)	105,000	Beth Daniel (281)
Mar. 26	**Nabisco Dinah Shore** (Rancho Mirage)	Nanci Bowen (285)	127,500	S. Redman (286)
Apr. 16	Pinewild Championship	Rosie Jones (211)*	97,500	D. Mochrie (211)
Apr. 23	Chick-fil-A Charity Championship	Laura Davies (201)	75,000	K. Robbins (205)
Apr. 30	Sprint Championship	Val Skinner (273)	180,000	K. Tschetter (275)

Tournament Results (Cont.)
LPGA

Last Rd	Tournament	Winner	Earnings	Runner-Up
May 7	Sara Lee Classic	Michelle McGann (202)	$78,750	3-way tie (203)
May 14	**LPGA Championship** (Wilmington)	Kelly Robbins (274)	180,000	L. Davies (275)
May 21	Star Bank Classic	Chris Johnson (210)	75,000	J. Inkster (211)
May 28	Corning Classic	Alison Nicholas (275)	82,500	D. Ammaccapane & B. Mucha (278)
May 28	JC Penney Skins Game	Dottie Mochrie (8)	290,000	L. Davies (6)
June 4	Oldsmobile Classic	Dale Eggeling (274)	90,000	3-way tie (276)
June 11	Edina Realty Classic (Minnesota)	Julie Larsen (205)	75,000	L. A. Mills (206)
June 18	Rochester International	Patty Sheehan (278)	82,500	S. Steinhauer (282)
June 25	ShopRite Classic	Betsy King (204)	97,500	R. Jones & B. Daniel (206)
July 2	Youngstown-Warren Classic	Michelle McGann (205)*	82,500	K. Peterson-Parker (205)
July 9	Jamie Farr Toledo Classic	Kathryn Marshall (205)	75,000	S. Steinhauer (206)
July 16	**U.S. Women's Open** (Colo. Springs)	Annika Sorenstam (278)	175,000	M. Mallon (279)
July 23	JAL Big Apple Classic	Tracy Kerdyk (273)	105,000	4-way tie (277)
July 30	Friendly's Classic	Becky Iverson (276)	75,000	H. Alfredsson & K. Robbins (278)
Aug. 6	McCall's Classic at Stratton Mt.	Dottie Mochrie (204)	75,000	K. Robbins (207)
Aug. 13	Ping/Welch's Championship	Beth Daniel (271)	67,500	M. Mallon & C. Walker (274)
Aug. 20	Women's British Open	Karrie Webb (278)	92,400	A. Sorenstam & J. McGill (284)
Aug. 27	**du Maurier Ltd. Classic** (Que.)	Jenny Lidback (280)	150,000	L. Neumann (281)
Sept. 4	State Farm Rail Classic	Mary Beth Zimmerman (206)*	82,500	E. Klein (206)
Sept. 10	Ping-AT&T Championship	Alison Nicholas (207)	75,000	K. Robbins (210)
Sept. 17	Safeco Classic	Patty Sheehan (274)	75,000	E. Klein (276)
Sept. 24	GHP Heartland Classic	Annika Sorenstam (278)	78,750	J. Stephenson (288)

(See Updates Chapter for later results.)

*Playoffs (3): Pinewild— Jones won on 1st hole; **Youngstown-Warren**— McGann won on the 3rd hole; **State Farm Rail**— Zimmerman won on 2nd hole.

Second Place ties: (3 players or more): 3-WAY— **Hawaiian Open** (H. Kobayashi, K. Tschetter, C. Johnson); **Sara Lee** (D. Morchrie, K. Robbins, L. Davies); **Oldsmobile** (M. Mallon, A. Sorenstam, E. Crosby); 4-WAY— **JAL Big Apple** (E. Crosby, C. Pierce, M. McGann and C. Hjalmarsson).

LPGA Majors

Dinah Shore

Edition: 24th   **Dates:** March 23-26
Site: Mission Hills CC, Rancho Mirage, Calif.
Par: 36-36—72 (6446 yards)   **Purse:** $850,000

	1	2	3	4	Tot	Earnings
1 Nanci Bowen	69	75	71	70	285	$127,500
2 Susie Redman	75	70	70	71	286	79,129
3 Brandie Burton	75	71	69	—	287	42,237
Sherri Turner	72	74	71	70	287	42,237
Laura Davies	75	69	70	73	287	42,237
Nancy Lopez	74	71	68	74	287	42,237

Early round leaders: 1st— Muffin Spencer-Devlin, Penny Hammel and Bowen (69); 2nd— Green (141); 3rd— Green (211)
Top amateur: None.

LPGA Championship

Edition: 41st   **Dates:** May 11-14
Site: Du Pont CC, Wilmington, Del.
Par: 35-36—71 (6386 yards)   **Purse:** $1,200,000

	1	2	3	4	Tot	Earnings
1 Kelly Robbins	66	68	72	68	274	$180,000
2 Laura Davies	68	68	69	70	275	111,711
3 Julie Larsen	71	68	70	71	280	65,416
Marianne Morris	67	71	70	71	280	65,416
Patty Sheehan	67	68	72	73	280	65,416

Early round leaders: 1st—Robbins (66); 2nd— Robbins (134); 3rd—Davies (205).
Top amateur: None.

U.S. Women's Open

Edition: 50th   **Dates:** July 13-16
Site: The Broadmoor GC, Colorado Springs, Colo.
Par: 35-35—70 (6398 yards)   **Purse:** $1,000,000

	1	2	3	4	Tot	Earnings
1 Annika Sorenstam	67	71	72	68	278	$175,000
2 Meg Mallon	70	69	66	74	279	103,500
3 Betsy King	72	69	72	67	280	56,238
Pat Bradley	67	71	72	70	280	56,238
5 Leta Lindley	70	68	74	69	281	35,285
Rosie Jones	69	70	70	72	281	35,285

Early round leaders: 1st— Jill Briles-Hinton (66); 2nd— Eight tied at 138; 3rd— Mallon (205).
Top amateur: Sarah Lebrun Ingram (294).

du Maurier Classic

Edition: 23rd   **Dates:** August 24-27
Site: Beaconsfield GC, Pointe-Claire, Quebec
Par: 36-36—72 (6261 yards)   **Purse:** $1,000,000

	1	2	3	4	Tot	Earnings
1 Jenny Lidback	71	69	68	72	280	$150,000
2 Liselotte Neumann	71	66	72	72	281	93,093
3 Juli Inkster	72	71	70	70	283	67,933
4 Tammie Green	75	71	68	70	284	52,837
5 Betsy King	76	70	67	72	285	38,998
Jane Geddes	71	73	69	72	285	38,998

Early round leaders: 1st— Patty Sheehan (66); 2nd— Neumann (137); 3rd—Lidback (205).
Top amateur: Mary Ann Lapointe (293).

Money Leaders

Official money leaders of PGA, European PGA, Senior PGA and LPGA tours for 1994 and unofficial money leaders for 1995 (through Sept. 24), as compiled by the PGA, European PGA and LPGA. All European amounts are in pound sterling (£).

PGA

Arnold Palmer Award standings: listed are tournaments played (TP); cuts made (CM); 1st, 2nd and 3rd place finishes; and earnings for the year.

	Final 1994	TP	CM	Finish 1-2-3	Earnings		1995 (through Sept. 24)	TP	CM	Finish 1-2-3	Earnings
1	Nick Price	19	14	5-1-0	$1,499,927	1	Greg Norman	14	13	3-2-1	$1,555,709
2	Greg Norman	16	16	1-3-0	1,330,307	2	Lee Janzen	26	20	3-0-0	1,311,561
3	Mark McCumber	20	18	3-0-0	1,208,209	3	Corey Pavin	20	16	2-1-1	1,071,793
4	Tom Lehman	23	21	1-1-1	1,031,144	4	Peter Jacobsen	23	21	2-2-1	1,014,157
5	Fuzzy Zoeller	19	16	0-5-0	1,016,804	5	Davis Love III	22	20	1-1-1	1,004,349
6	Loren Roberts	22	19	1-2-1	1,015,671	6	Jim Gallagher Jr.	24	19	2-2-1	991,805
7	José Marie Olazabal	8	6	2-1-0	969,900	7	Steve Elkington	19	14	2-1-0	988,852
8	Corey Pavin	20	15	1-3-1	906,305	8	Vijay Singh	21	16	2-0-0	910,713
9	Jeff Maggert	26	21	0-2-2	814,475	9	Billy Mayfair	25	18	1-2-0	839,032
10	Hale Irwin	22	18	1-1-1	814,436	10	David Duval	23	18	0-3-1	791,158

EUROPEAN PGA

Volvo Order of Merit standings: listed are tournaments played (TP); cuts made (CM); 1st, 2nd and 3rd place finishes; and earnings for the year. Note that 1994 totals do not include Johnnie Walker World Championship.

	Final 1994	TP	CM	Finish 1-2-3	Earnings		1995 (through Sept. 24)	TP	CM	Finish 1-2-3	Earnings
1	Colin Montgomerie	21	19	3-2-0	£762,720	1	Sam Torrance	23	19	3-4-0	£619,139
2	Berhard Langer	18	18	2-1-4	635,483	2	Colin Montgomerie	17	15	2-3-2	590,056
3	Seve Ballesteros	17	14	2-3-0	590,101	3	Costantino Rocca	22	21	0-5-1	432,415
4	José Maria Olazabal	16	16	2-2-2	516,108	4	Bernhard Langer	12	12	2-1-0	389,634
5	Miguel Angel Jimenez	26	22	1-2-0	437,403	5	Michael Campbell	18	14	0-2-2	355,339
6	Vijay Singh	11	10	2-1-0	364,314	6	Mark James	24	20	1-1-0	256,666
7	David Gilford	26	21	2-1-0	326,629	7	Peter O'Malley	18	16	1-0-0	234,377
8	Nick Faldo	11	10	1-1-0	321,256	8	Wayne Riley	24	20	1-0-2	232,687
9	Mark Roe	25	22	1-1-1	312,540	9	Philip Walton	22	13	2-0-0	218,056
10	Ernie Els	12	10	1-2-0	311,850	10	Howard Clark	19	12	0-2-1	211,789

SENIOR PGA

	Final 1994	TP	CM	Finish 1-2-3	Earnings		1995 (through Sept. 24)	TP	CM	Finish 1-2-3	Earnings
1	Dave Stockton	32	32	3-3-5	$1,402,519	1	Dave Stockton	27	27	2-4-2	$1,041,564
2	Ray Floyd	20	20	4-5-2	1,382,762	2	Jim Colbert	27	27	3-2-1	1,036,735
3	Jim Albus	35	35	2-6-3	1,237,128	3	Bob Murphy	21	21	4-3-1	1,032,741
4	Lee Trevino	23	23	6-1-3	1,202,369	4	Ray Floyd	18	18	2-6-0	1,010,545
5	Jim Colbert	33	33	2-5-2	1,012,115	5	Isao Aoki	20	20	1-4-2	900,033
6	Tom Wargo	36	36	1-3-0	1,005,344	6	J.C. Snead	22	22	2-3-1	879,756
7	Jim Dent	30	30	1-0-5	950,891	7	Graham Marsh	20	20	1-1-1	681,623
8	Bob Murphy	30	30	2-4-3	855,862	8	Lee Trevino	23	23	1-2-0	675,424
9	Larry Gilbert	31	31	2-2-0	848,544	9	George Archer	24	24	2-0-3	648,007
10	George Archer	30	30	0-1-2	717,578	10	Jim Albus	27	27	1-1-1	594,193

LPGA

	Final 1994	TP	CM	Finish 1-2-3	Earnings		1995 (through Sept. 24)	TP	CM	Finish 1-2-3	Earnings
1	Laura Davies	22	21	3-3-2	$687,201	1	Annika Sorenstam	17	17	2-3-1	$542,724
2	Beth Daniel	25	21	4-1-1	659,426	2	Kelly Robbins	23	18	1-5-0	527,655
3	Liselotte Neumann	21	18	3-1-3	505,701	3	Dottie Mochrie	22	20	2-2-0	481,000
4	Dottie Mochrie	27	27	1-1-2	472,728	4	Betsy King	24	23	1-0-3	464,149
5	Donna Andrews	23	22	3-0-0	429,015	5	Laura Davies	15	14	2-2-1	462,995
6	Tammie Green	24	20	1-3-1	418,969	6	Beth Daniel	22	21	1-4-0	443,305
7	Sherri Steinhauer	27	24	1-0-1	413,398	7	Michelle McGann	22	19	2-1-3	436,484
8	Kelly Robins	25	20	1-1-0	396,778	8	Val Skinner	23	21	1-0-1	401,489
9	Betsy King	27	27	0-2-2	390,239	9	Meg Mallon	22	20	0-3-0	393,534
10	Meg Mallon	27	24	0-1-1	353,385	10	Rosie Jones	23	20	1-1-1	390,906

THE 1996 SPORTS ALMANAC · INFORMATION PLEASE

GOLF STATISTICS

THROUGH THE YEARS 1860-1995

MAJOR TITLES • LEADERS

SEC B

PAGE 835

Major Championships
MEN
The Masters

The Masters has been played every year since 1934 at the Augusta National Golf Club in Augusta, GA. Both the course (6905 yards, par 72) and the tournament were created by Bobby Jones; (*) indicates playoff winner.

Multiple winners: Jack Nicklaus (6); Arnold Palmer (4); Jimmy Demaret, Gary Player and Sam Snead (3); Seve Ballesteros, Ben Crenshaw, Nick Faldo, Ben Hogan, Bernhard Langer, Byron Nelson, Horton Smith and Tom Watson (2).

Year	Winner	Score	Runner-up
1934	Horton Smith	284	Craig Wood (285)
1935	Gene Sarazen*	282	Craig Wood (282)
1936	Horton Smith	285	Harry Cooper (286)
1937	Byron Nelson	283	Ralph Guldahl (285)
1938	Henry Picard	285	Ralph Guldahl & Harry Cooper (287)
1939	Ralph Guldahl	279	Sam Snead (280)
1940	Jimmy Demaret	280	Lloyd Mangrum (284)
1941	Craig Wood	280	Byron Nelson (283)
1942	Byron Nelson*	280	Ben Hogan (280)
1943-45	Not held		World War II
1946	Herman Keiser	282	Ben Hogan (283)
1947	Jimmy Demaret	281	Frank Stranahan & Byron Nelson (283)
1948	Claude Harmon	279	Cary Middlecoff (284)
1949	Sam Snead	282	Lloyd Mangrum & Johnny Bulla (285)
1950	Jimmy Demaret	283	Jim Ferrier (285)
1951	Ben Hogan	280	Skee Riegel (282)
1952	Sam Snead	286	Jack Burke Jr. (290)
1953	Ben Hogan	274	Ed Oliver (279)
1954	Sam Snead*	289	Ben Hogan (289)
1955	Cary Middlecoff	279	Ben Hogan (286)
1956	Jack Burke Jr.	289	Ken Venturi (290)
1957	Doug Ford	283	Sam Snead (286)
1958	Arnold Palmer	284	Doug Ford, & Fred Hawkins (285)
1959	Art Wall Jr.	284	Cary Middlecoff (285)
1960	Arnold Palmer	282	Ken Venturi (283)
1961	Gary Player	280	Arnold Palmer & Charles R. Coe (281)
1962	Arnold Palmer*	280	Dow Finsterwald & Gary Player (280)
1963	Jack Nicklaus	286	Tony Lema (287)
1964	Arnold Palmer	276	Jack Nicklaus & Dave Marr (282)
1965	Jack Nicklaus	271	Arnold Palmer & Gary Player (280)
1966	Jack Nicklaus*	288	Gay Brewer Jr. & Tommy Jacobs (288)
1967	Gay Brewer Jr.	280	Bobby Nichols (281)
1968	Bob Goalby	277	Roberto DeVicenzo (278)
1969	George Archer	281	Billy Casper, George Knudson & Tom Weiskopf (282)
1970	Billy Casper*	279	Gene Littler (279)
1971	Charles Coody	279	Jack Nicklaus & Johnny Miller (281)
1972	Jack Nicklaus	286	Bruce Crampton, Bobby Mitchell & Tom Weiskopf (289)
1973	Tommy Aaron	283	J.C. Snead (284)
1974	Gary Player	278	Tom Weiskopf, & Dave Stockton (280)
1975	Jack Nicklaus	276	Johnny Miller & Tom Weiskopf (277)
1976	Ray Floyd	271	Ben Crenshaw (279)
1977	Tom Watson	276	Jack Nicklaus (278)
1978	Gary Player	277	Hubert Green, Rod Funseth & Tom Watson (278)
1979	Fuzzy Zoeller*	280	Ed Sneed & Tom Watson (280)
1980	Seve Ballesteros	275	Gibby Gilbert & Jack Newton (279)
1981	Tom Watson	280	Jack Nicklaus & Johnny Miller (282)
1982	Craig Stadler*	284	Dan Pohl (284)
1983	Seve Ballesteros	280	Ben Crenshaw, & Tom Kite (284)
1984	Ben Crenshaw	277	Tom Watson (279)
1985	Bernhard Langer	282	Curtis Strange, Seve Ballesteros & Ray Floyd (284)
1986	Jack Nicklaus	279	Greg Norman (280)
1987	Larry Mize*	285	Seve Ballesteros & Greg Norman (285)
1988	Sandy Lyle	281	Mark Calcavecchia (282)
1989	Nick Faldo*	283	Scott Hoch (283)
1990	Nick Faldo*	278	Ray Floyd (278)
1991	Ian Woosnam	277	J.M. Olazabal (278)
1992	Fred Couples	275	Ray Floyd (277)
1993	Bernhard Langer	277	Chip Beck (281)
1994	J.M. Olazabal	279	Tom Lehman (281)
1995	Ben Crenshaw	274	Davis Love III (275)

Major Championships (Cont.)
The Masters
*PLAYOFFS

1935: Gene Sarazen (144) def. Craig Wood (149) in 36 holes. **1942:** Byron Nelson (69) def. Ben Hogan (70) in 18 holes. **1954:** Sam Snead (70) def. Ben Hogan (71) in 18 holes. **1962:** Arnold Palmer (68) def. Gary Player (71) and Dow Finsterwald (77) in 18 holes. **1966:** Jack Nicklaus (70) def. Tommy Jacobs (72) and Gay Brewer (78) in 18 holes. **1970:** Billy Casper (69) def. Gene Littler (74) in 18 holes. **1979:** Fuzzy Zoeller (4-3) def. Ed Sneed (4-4) and Tom Watson (4-4) on 2nd hole of sudden death. **1982:** Craig Stadler (4) def. Dan Pohl (5) on 1st hole of sudden death. **1987:** Larry Mize (4-3) def. Greg Norman (4-4) and Seve Ballesteros (5) on 2nd hole of sudden death. **1989:** Nick Faldo (5-3) def. Scott Hoch (5-4) on 2nd hole of sudden death. **1990:** Nick Faldo (4-4) def. Raymond Floyd (4-x) on second hole of sudden death.

U.S. Open

Played at a different course each year, the U.S. Open was launched by the new U.S. Golf Association in 1895. The Open was a 36-hole event from 1895-97 and has been 72 holes since then. It switched from a 3-day, 36-hole Saturday finish to 4 days of play in 1965. Note that (*) indicates playoff winner and (a) indicates amateur winner.

Multiple winners: Willie Anderson, Ben Hogan, Bobby Jones and Jack Nicklaus (4); Hale Irwin (3); Julius Boros, Billy Casper, Ralph Guldahl, Walter Hagen, John McDermott, Cary Middlecoff, Andy North, Gene Sarazen, Alex Smith, Curtis Strange and Lee Trevino (2).

Year	Winner	Score	Runner-up	Course	Location
1895	Horace Rawlins	173	Willie Dunn (175)	Newport GC	Newport, R.I.
1896	James Foulis	152	Horace Rawlins (155)	Shinnecock Hills GC	Southampton, N.Y.
1897	Joe Lloyd	162	Willie Anderson (163)	Chicago GC	Wheaton, Ill.
1898	Fred Herd	328	Alex Smith (335)	Myopia Hunt Club	Hamilton, Mass.
1899	Willie Smith	315	George Low, W.H. Way & Val Fitzjohn (326)	Baltimore CC	Baltimore
1900	Harry Vardon	313	J.H. Taylor (315)	Chicago GC	Wheaton, Ill.
1901	Willie Anderson*	331	Alex Smith (331)	Myopia Hunt Club	Hamilton, Mass.
1902	Laurie Auchterlonie	307	Stewart Gardner (313)	Garden City GC	Garden City, N.Y.
1903	Willie Anderson*	307	David Brown (307)	Baltusrol GC	Springfield, N.J.
1904	Willie Anderson*	303	Gil Nicholls (308)	Glen View Club	Golf, Ill.
1905	Willie Anderson	314	Alex Smith (316)	Myopia Hunt Club	Hamilton, Mass.
1906	Alex Smith	295	Willie Smith (302)	Onwentsia Club	Lake Forest, Ill.
1907	Alec Ross	302	Gil Nicholls (304)	Phila. Cricket Club	Chestnut Hill, Pa.
1908	Fred McLeod*	322	Willie Smith (322)	Myopia Hunt Club	Hamilton, Mass.
1909	George Sargent	290	Tom McNamara (294)	Englewood GC	Englewood, N.J.
1910	Alex Smith*	298	Macdonald Smith & John McDermott (298)	Phila. Cricket Club	Chestnut Hill, Pa.
1911	John McDermott*	307	George Simpson & Mike Brady (307)	Chicago GC	Wheaton, Ill.
1912	John McDermott	294	Tom McNamara (296)	CC of Buffalo	Buffalo
1913	a-Francis Ouimet*	304	Harry Vardon & Ted Ray (304)	The Country Club	Brookline, Mass.
1914	Walter Hagen	290	a-Chick Evans (291)	Midlothian CC	Blue Island, Ill.
1915	a-John Travers	297	Tom McNamara (298)	Baltusrol GC	Springfield, N.J.
1916	a-Chick Evans	286	Jock Hutchinson (288)	Minikahda Club	Minneapolis
1917-18	Not held		World War I		
1919	Walter Hagen*	301	Mike Brady (301)	Brae Burn CC	West Newton, Mass.
1920	Ted Ray	295	Jock Hutchison, Jack Burke, Leo Diegel & Harry Vardon (296)	Inverness Club	Toledo, Ohio
1921	Jim Barnes	289	Walter Hagen & Fred McLeod (298)	Columbia CC	Chevy Chase, Md.
1922	Gene Sarazen	288	a-Bobby Jones & John Black (289)	Skokie CC	Glencoe, Ill.
1923	a-Bobby Jones*	296	Bobby Cruickshank (296)	Inwood CC	Far Rockaway, N.Y.
1924	Cyril Walker	297	a-Bobby Jones (300)	Oakland Hills CC	Birmingham, Mich.
1925	Willie Macfarlane*	291	a-Bobby Jones (291)	Worcester CC	Worcester, Mass.
1926	a-Bobby Jones	293	Joe Turnesa (294)	Scioto CC	Columbus, Ohio
1927	Tommy Armour*	301	Harry Cooper (301)	Oakmont CC	Oakmont, Pa.
1928	Johnny Farrell*	294	a-Bobby Jones (294)	Olympia Fields CC	Matteson, Ill.
1929	a-Bobby Jones*	294	Al Espinosa (294)	Winged Foot CC	Mamaroneck, N.Y.
1930	a-Bobby Jones	287	Macdonald Smith (289)	Interlachen CC	Hopkins, Minn.
1931	Billy Burke*	292	George Von Elm (292)	Inverness Club	Toledo, Ohio
1932	Gene Sarazen	286	Bobby Cruickshank & Phil Perkins (289)	Fresh Meadow CC	Flushing, N.Y.
1933	a-Johnny Goodman	287	Ralph Guldahl (288)	North Shore GC	Glenview, Ill.
1934	Olin Dutra	293	Gene Sarazen (294)	Merion Cricket Club	Ardmore, Pa.
1935	Sam Parks Jr.	299	Jimmy Thomson (301)	Oakmont CC	Oakmont, Pa.

Major Championships (Cont.)
U.S. Open

Year	Winner	Score	Runner-up	Course	Location
1936	Tony Manero	282	Harry E. Cooper (284)	Baltusrol GC	Springfield, N.J.
1937	Ralph Guldahl	281	Sam Snead (283)	Oakland Hills CC	Birmingham, Mich.
1938	Ralph Guldahl	284	Dick Metz (290)	Cherry Hills CC	Denver
1939	Byron Nelson*	284	Craig Wood & Denny Shute (284)	Philadelphia CC	Philadelphia
1940	Lawson Little*	287	Gene Sarazen (287)	Canterbury GC	Cleveland
1941	Craig Wood	284	Denny Shute (287)	Colonial Club	Ft. Worth
1942-45	Not held		World War II		
1946	Lloyd Mangrum*	284	Byron Nelson & Vic Ghezzi (284)	Canterbury GC	Cleveland
1947	Lew Worsham*	282	Sam Snead (282)	St. Louis CC	Clayton, Mo.
1948	Ben Hogan	276	Jimmy Demaret (278)	Riviera CC	Los Angeles
1949	Cary Middlecoff	286	Clayton Heafner & Sam Snead (287)	Medinah CC	Medinah, Ill.
1950	Ben Hogan*	287	Lloyd Mangrum & George Fazio (287)	Merion Golf Club	Ardmore, Pa.
1951	Ben Hogan	287	Clayton Heafner (289)	Oakland Hills CC	Birmingham, Mich.
1952	Julius Boros	281	Ed Oliver (285)	Northwood Club	Dallas
1953	Ben Hogan	283	Sam Snead (289)	Oakmont CC	Oakmont, Pa.
1954	Ed Furgol	284	Gene Littler (285)	Baltusrol GC	Springfield, N.J.
1955	Jack Fleck*	287	Ben Hogan (287)	Olympic CC	San Francisco
1956	Cary Middlecoff	281	Ben Hogan & Julius Boros (282)	Oak Hill CC	Rochester, N.Y.
1957	Dick Mayer*	282	Cary Middlecoff (282)	Inverness Club	Toledo, Ohio
1958	Tommy Bolt	283	Gary Player (287)	Southern Hills CC	Tulsa
1959	Billy Casper	282	Bob Rosburg (283)	Winged Foot GC	Marmaroneck, N.Y.
1960	Arnold Palmer	280	Jack Nicklaus (282)	Cherry Hills CC	Denver
1961	Gene Littler	281	Doug Sanders & Bob Goalby (282)	Oakland Hills CC	Birmingham, Mich.
1962	Jack Nicklaus*	283	Arnold Palmer (283)	Oakmont CC	Oakmont, Pa.
1963	Julius Boros*	293	Arnold Palmer & Jacky Cupit (293)	The Country Club	Brookline, Mass.
1964	Ken Venturi	278	Tommy Jacobs (282)	Congressional CC	Bethesda, Md.
1965	Gary Player*	282	Kel Nagle (282)	Bellerive CC	St. Louis
1966	Billy Casper*	278	Arnold Palmer (278)	Olympic CC	San Francisco
1967	Jack Nicklaus	275	Arnold Palmer (279)	Baltusrol GC	Springfield, N.J.
1968	Lee Trevino	275	Jack Nicklaus (279)	Oak Hill CC	Rochester, N.Y.
1969	Orville Moody	281	Al Geiberger, Deane Beman & Bob Rosburg (282)	Champions GC	Houston
1970	Tony Jacklin	281	Dave Hill (288)	Hazeltine National GC	Chaska, Minn.
1971	Lee Trevino*	280	Jack Nicklaus (280)	Merion GC	Ardmore, Pa.
1972	Jack Nicklaus	290	Bruce Crampton (293)	Pebble Beach GL	Pebble Beach, Calif.
1973	Johnny Miller	279	John Schlee (280)	Oakmont CC	Oakmont, Pa.
1974	Hale Irwin	287	Forest Fezler (289)	Winged Foot GC	Mamaroneck, N.Y.
1975	Lou Graham*	287	John Mahaffey (287)	Medinah CC	Medinah, Ill.
1976	Jerry Pate	277	Al Geiberger & Tom Weiskopf (279)	Atlanta AC	Duluth, Ga.
1977	Hubert Green	278	Lou Graham (279)	Southern Hills CC	Tulsa
1978	Andy North	285	Dave Stockton & J.C. Snead (286)	Cherry Hills CC	Denver
1979	Hale Irwin	284	Gary Player & Jerry Pate (286)	Inverness Club	Toledo, Ohio
1980	Jack Nicklaus	272	Isao Aoki (274)	Baltusrol GC	Springfield, N.J.
1981	David Graham	273	George Burns & Bill Rogers (276)	Merion GC	Ardmore, Pa.
1982	Tom Watson	282	Jack Nicklaus (284)	Pebble Beach GL	Pebble Beach, Calif.
1983	Larry Nelson	280	Tom Watson (281)	Oakmont CC	Oakmont, Pa.
1984	Fuzzy Zoeller*	276	Greg Norman (276)	Winged Foot GC	Mamaroneck, N.Y.
1985	Andy North	279	Dave Barr, T.C. Chen & Denis Watson (280)	Oakland Hills CC	Birmingham, Mich.
1986	Ray Floyd	279	Lanny Wadkins & Chip Beck (281)	Shinnecock Hills GC	Southampton, N.Y.
1987	Scott Simpson	277	Tom Watson (278)	Olympic Club	San Francisco
1988	Curtis Strange*	278	Nick Faldo (278)	The Country Club	Brookline, Mass.
1989	Curtis Strange	278	Chip Beck, Ian Woosnam & Mark McCumber (279)	Oak Hill CC	Rochester, N.Y.

Major Championships (Cont.)
U.S. Open

Year	Winner	Score	Runner-up	Course	Location
1990	Hale Irwin*	280	Mike Donald (280)	Medinah CC	Medinah, Ill.
1991	Payne Stewart*	282	Scott Simpson (282)	Hazeline National GC	Chaska, Minn.
1992	Tom Kite	285	Jeff Sluman (287)	Pebble Beach GL	Pebble Beach, Calif.
1993	Lee Janzen	272	Payne Stewart (274)	Baltusrol GC	Springfield, N.J.
1994	Ernie Els*	279	Colin Montgomerie (279) & Loren Roberts (279)	Oakmont CC	Oakmont, Pa.
1995	Corey Pavin	280	Greg Norman (282)	Shinnecock Hills GC	Southampton, N.Y.

*PLAYOFFS

1901: Willie Anderson (85) def. Alex Smith (86) in 18 holes. **1903:** Willie Anderson (82) def. David Brown (84) in 18 holes. **1908:** Fred McLeod (77) def. Willie Smith (83) in 18 holes. **1910:** Alex Smith (71) def. John McDermott (75) and Macdonald Smith (77) in 18 holes. **1911:** John McDermott (80) def. Mike Brady (82) and George Simpson (85) in 18 holes. **1913:** Francis Ouimet (72) def. Harry Vardon (77) and Ted Ray (78) in 18 holes. **1919:** Walter Hagen (77) def. Mike Brady (78) in 18 holes. **1923:** Bobby Jones (76) def. Bobby Cruickshank (78) in 18 holes. **1925:** Willie Macfarlane (75-72—147) def. Bobby Jones (75-73—148) in 36 holes. **1927:** Tommy Armour (76) def. Harry Cooper (79) in 18 holes. **1928:** Johnny Farrell (70-73—143) def. Bobby Jones (73-71—144) in 36 holes. **1929:** Bobby Jones (141) def. Al Espinosa (164) in 36 holes. **1931:** Billy Burke (149-148) def. George Von Elm (149-149) in 72 holes. **1939:** Byron Nelson (68-70) def. Craig Wood (68-73) and Denny Shute (76) in 36 holes. **1940:** Lawson Little (70) def. Gene Sarazen (73) in 18 holes. **1946:** Lloyd Mangrum (72-72—144) def. Byron Nelson (72-73—145) and Vic Ghezzi (72-73—145) in 36 holes. **1947:** Lew Worsham (69) def. Sam Snead (70) in 18 holes. **1950:** Ben Hogan (69) def. Lloyd Mangrum (73) and George Fazio (75) in 18 holes. **1955:** Jack Fleck (69) def. Ben Hogan (72) in 18 holes. **1957:** Dick Mayer (72) def. Cary Middlecoff (79) in 18 holes. **1962:** Jack Nicklaus (71) def. Arnold Palmer (74) in 18 holes. **1963:** Julius Boros (70) def. Jacky Cupit (73) and Arnold Palmer (76) in 18 holes. **1965:** Gary Player (71) def. Kel Nagle (74) in 18 holes. **1966:** Billy Casper (69) def. Arnold Palmer (73) in 18 holes. **1971:** Lee Trevino (68) def. Jack Nicklaus (71) in 18 holes. **1975:** Lou Graham (71) def. John Mahaffey (73) in 18 holes. **1984:** Fuzzy Zoeller (67) def. Greg Norman (75) in 18 holes. **1988:** Curtis Strange (71) def. Nick Faldo (75) in 18 holes. **1990:** Hale Irwin (74-3) def. Mike Donald (74-4) on 1st hole of sudden death after 18 holes. **1991:** Payne Stewart (75) def. Scott Simpson (77) in 18 holes. **1994:** Ernie Els (74-4-4) def. Loren Roberts (74-4-5) and Colin Montgomerie (78-x-x) on 2nd hole of sudden death after 18 holes.

British Open

The oldest of the Majors, The Open began in 1860 to determine "the champion golfer of the world." While only professional golfers participated in the first year of the tournament, amateurs have been invited ever since. Competition was extended from 36 to 72 holes in 1892. Conducted by the Royal and Ancient Golf Club of St. Andrews, The Open is rotated among select golf courses in England and Scotland. Note that (*) indicates playoff winner and (a) indicates amateur winner.

Multiple winners: Harry Vardon (6); James Braid, J.H. Taylor, Peter Thomson and Tom Watson (5); Walter Hagen, Bobby Locke, Tom Morris Sr., Tom Morris Jr., and Willie Park (4); Jamie Anderson, Seve Ballesteros, Henry Cotton, Nick Faldo, Robert Ferguson, Bobby Jones, Jack Nicklaus and Gary Player (3); Harold Hilton, Bob Martin, Greg Norman, Arnold Palmer, Willie Park Jr., and Lee Trevino (2).

Year	Winner	Score	Runner-up	Course	Location
1860	Willie Park	174	Tom Morris Sr. (176)	Prestwick Club	Ayrshire, Scotland
1861	Tom Morris Sr.	163	Willie Park (167)	Prestwick Club	Ayrshire, Scotland
1862	Tom Morris Sr.	163	Willie Park (176)	Prestwick Club	Ayrshire, Scotland
1863	Willie Park	168	Tom Morris Sr. (170)	Prestwick Club	Ayrshire, Scotland
1864	Tom Morris Sr.	167	Andrew Strath (169)	Prestwick Club	Ayrshire, Scotland
1865	Andrew Strath	162	Willie Park (164)	Prestwick Club	Ayrshire, Scotland
1866	Willie Park	169	David Park (171)	Prestwick Club	Ayrshire, Scotland
1867	Tom Morris Sr.	170	Willie Park (172)	Prestwick Club	Ayrshire, Scotland
1868	Tom Morris Jr.	157	Robert Andrew (159)	Prestwick Club	Ayrshire, Scotland
1869	Tom Morris Jr.	154	Tom Morris Sr. (157)	Prestwick Club	Ayrshire, Scotland
1870	Tom Morris Jr.	149	Bob Kirk (161)	Prestwick Club	Ayrshire, Scotland
1871	Not held				
1872	Tom Morris Jr.	166	David Strath (169)	Prestwick Club	Ayrshire, Scotland
1873	Tom Kidd	179	Jamie Anderson (180)	St. Andrews	St. Andrews, Scotland
1874	Mungo Park	159	Tom Morris Jr. (161)	Musselburgh	Musselburgh, Scotland
1875	Willie Park	166	Bob Martin (168)	Prestwick Club	Ayrshire, Scotland
1876	Bob Martin*	176	David Strath (176)	St. Andrews	St. Andrews, Scotland
1877	Jamie Anderson	160	Bob Pringle (162)	Musselburgh	Musselburgh, Scotland
1878	Jamie Anderson	157	Bob Kirk (159)	Prestwick Club	Ayrshire, Scotland
1879	Jamie Anderson	169	Andrew Kirkaldy & James Allan (172)	St. Andrews	St. Andrews, Scotland
1880	Bob Ferguson	162	Peter Paxton (167)	Musselburgh	Musselburgh, Scotland
1881	Bob Ferguson	170	Jamie Anderson (173)	Prestwick Club	Ayrshire, Scotland
1882	Bob Ferguson	171	Willie Fernie (174)	St. Andrews	St. Andrews, Scotland
1883	Willie Fernie*	159	Bob Ferguson (159)	Musselburgh	Musselburgh, Scotland
1884	Jack Simpson	160	David Rollan & Willie Fernie (164)	Prestwick Club	Ayrshire, Scotland

Major Championships (Cont.)
British Open

Year	Winner	Score	Runner-up	Course	Location
1885	Bob Martin	171	Archie Simpson (172)	St. Andrews	St. Andrews, Scotland
1886	David Brown	157	Willie Campbell (159)	Musselburgh	Musselburgh, Scotland
1887	Willie Park Jr.	161	Bob Martin (162)	Prestwick Club	Ayrshire, Scotland
1888	Jack Burns	171	David Anderson & Ben Sayers (172)	St. Andrews	St. Andrews, Scotland
1889	Willie Park Jr.*	155	Andrew Kirkaldy (155)	Musselburgh	Musselburgh, Scotland
1890	a-John Ball	164	Willie Fernie (167) & A. Simpson (167)	Prestwick Club	Ayrshire, Scotland
1891	Hugh Kirkaldy	166	Andrew Kirkaldy & Willie Fernie (168)	St. Andrews	St. Andrews, Scotland
1892	a-Harold Hilton	305	John Ball, Sandy Herd & Hugh Kirkaldy (308)	Muirfield	Gullane, Scotland
1893	Willie Auchterlonie	322	Johnny Laidlay (324)	Prestwick Club	Ayrshire, Scotland
1894	J.H. Taylor	326	Douglas Rolland (331)	Royal St. George's	Sandwich, England
1895	J.H. Taylor	322	Sandy Herd (326)	St. Andrews	St. Andrews, Scotland
1896	Harry Vardon*	316	J.H. Taylor (316)	Muirfield	Gullane, Scotland
1897	a-Harold Hilton	314	James Braid (315)	Hoylake	Hoylake, England
1898	Harry Vardon	307	Willie Park Jr. (308)	Prestwick Club	Ayrshire, Scotland
1899	Harry Vardon	310	Jack White (315)	Royal St. George's	Sandwich, England
1900	J.H. Taylor	309	Harry Vardon (317)	St. Andrews	St. Andrews, Scotland
1901	James Braid	309	Harry Vardon (312)	Muirfield	Gullane, Scotland
1902	Sandy Herd	307	Harry Vardon (308)	Hoylake	Hoylake, England
1903	Harry Vardon	300	Tom Vardon (306)	Prestwick Club	Ayrshire, Scotland
1904	Jack White	296	James Braid (297)	Royal St. George's	Sandwich, England
1905	James Braid	318	J.H. Taylor (323) & Rolland Jones (323)	St. Andrews	St. Andrews, Scotland
1906	James Braid	300	J.H. Taylor (304)	Muirfield	Gullane, Scotland
1907	Arnaud Massy	312	J.H. Taylor (314)	Hoylake	Hoylake, England
1908	James Braid	291	Tom Ball (299)	Prestwick Club	Ayrshire, Scotland
1909	J.H. Taylor	295	James Braid (299)	Deal	Deal, England
1910	James Braid	299	Sandy Herd (303)	St. Andrews	St. Andrews, Scotland
1911	Harry Vardon*	303	Arnaud Massy (303)	Royal St. George's	Sandwich, England
1912	Ted Ray	295	Harry Vardon (299)	Muirfield	Gullane, Scotland
1913	J.H. Taylor	304	Ted Ray (312)	Hoylake	Hoylake, England
1914	Harry Vardon	306	J.H. Taylor (309)	Prestwick Club	Ayrshire, Scotland
1915-19	Not held		World War I		
1920	George Duncan	303	Sandy Herd (305)	Deal	Deal, England
1921	Jock Hutchison*	296	Roger Wethered (296)	St. Andrews	St. Andrews, Scotland
1922	Walter Hagen	300	George Duncan & Jim Barnes (301)	Royal St. George's	Sandwich, England
1923	Arthur Havers	295	Walter Hagen (296)	Troon	Troon, Scotland
1924	Walter Hagen	301	Ernest Whitcombe (302)	Hoylake	Hoylake, England
1925	Jim Barnes	300	Archie Compston & Ted Ray (301)	Prestwick Club	Ayrshire, Scotland
1926	a-Bobby Jones	291	Al Watrous (293)	Royal Lytham	Lytham, England
1927	a-Bobby Jones	285	Aubrey Boomer (291)	St. Andrews	St. Andrews, Scotland
1928	Walter Hagen	292	Gene Sarazen (294)	Royal St. George's	Sandwich, England
1929	Walter Hagen	292	Johnny Farrell (298)	Muirfield	Gullane, Scotland
1930	a-Bobby Jones	291	Macdonald Smith & Leo Diegel (293)	Hoylake	Hoylake, England
1931	Tommy Armour	296	Jose Jurado (297)	Carnoustie	Carnoustie, Scotland
1932	Gene Sarazen	283	Macdonald Smith (288)	Prince's	Prince's, England
1933	Denny Shute*	292	Craig Wood (292)	St. Andrews	St. Andrews, Scotland
1934	Henry Cotton	283	Sid Brews (288)	Royal St. George's	Sandwich, England
1935	Alf Perry	283	Alf Padgham (287)	Muirfield	Gullane, Scotland
1936	Alf Padgham	287	Jimmy Adams (288)	Hoylake	Hoylake, England
1937	Henry Cotton	290	Reg Whitcombe (292)	Carnoustie	Carnoustie, Scotland
1938	Reg Whitcombe	295	Jimmy Adams (297)	Royal St. George's	Sandwich, England
1939	Dick Burton	290	Johnny Bulla (292)	St. Andrews	St. Andrews, Scotland
1940-45	Not held		World War II		
1946	Sam Snead	290	Bobby Locke (294) & Johnny Bulla (294)	St. Andrews	St. Andrews, Scotland
1947	Fred Daly	293	Frank Stranahan & Reg Horne (294)	Hoylake	Hoylake, England
1948	Henry Cotton	284	Fred Daly (289)	Muirfield	Gullane, Scotland
1949	Bobby Locke*	283	Harry Bradshaw (283)	Royal St. George's	Sandwich, England

Major Championships (Cont.)
British Open

Year	Winner	Score	Runner-up	Course	Location
1950	Bobby Locke	279	Roberto de Vicenzo (281)	Royal Troon	Troon, Scotland
1951	Max Faulkner	285	Tony Cerda (287)	Royal Portrush	Portrush, Ireland
1952	Bobby Locke	287	Peter Thomson (288)	Royal Lytham	Lytham, England
1953	Ben Hogan	282	Frank Stranahan Dai Rees, Tony Cerda & Peter Thomson (286)	Carnoustie	Carnoustie, Scotland
1954	Peter Thomson	283	Sid Scott, Dai Rees & Bobby Locke (284)	Royal Birkdale	Southport, England
1955	Peter Thomson	281	Johny Fallon (283)	St. Andrews	St. Andrews, Scotland
1956	Peter Thomson	286	Flory Van Donck (289)	Hoylake	Hoylake, England
1957	Bobby Locke	279	Peter Thomson (282)	St. Andrews	St. Andrews, Scotland
1958	Peter Thomson*	278	Dave Thomas (278)	Royal Lytham	Lytham, England
1959	Gary Player	284	Flory Van Donck & Fred Bullock (286)	Muirfield	Gullane, Scotland
1960	Kel Nagle	278	Arnold Palmer (279)	St. Andrews	St. Andrews, Scotland
1961	Arnold Palmer	284	Dai Rees (285)	Royal Birkdale	Southport, England
1962	Arnold Palmer	276	Kel Nagle (282)	Royal Troon	Troon, Scotland
1963	Bob Charles*	277	Phil Rodgers (277)	Royal Lytham	Lytham, England
1964	Tony Lema	279	Jack Nicklaus (284)	St. Andrews	St. Andrews, Scotland
1965	Peter Thomson	285	Christy O'Connor & Brian Huggett (287)	Royal Birkdale	Southport, England
1966	Jack Nicklaus	282	Doug Sanders & Dave Thomas (283)	Muirfield	Gullane, Scotland
1967	Roberto de Vicenzo	278	Jack Nicklaus (280)	Hoylake	Hoylake, England
1968	Gary Player	289	Jack Nicklaus & Bob Charles (291)	Carnoustie	Carnoustie, Scotland
1969	Tony Jacklin	280	Bob Charles (282)	Royal Lytham	Lytham, England
1970	Jack Nicklaus*	283	Doug Sanders (283)	St. Andrews	St. Andrews, Scotland
1971	Lee Trevino	278	Lu Liang Huan (279)	Royal Birkdale	Southport, England
1972	Lee Trevino	278	Jack Nicklaus (279)	Muirfield	Gullane, Scotland
1973	Tom Weiskopf	276	Johnny Miller & Neil Coles (279)	Royal Troon	Troon, Scotland
1974	Gary Player	282	Peter Oosterhuis (286)	Royal Lytham	Lytham, England
1975	Tom Watson*	279	Jack Newton (279)	Carnoustie	Carnoustie, Scotland
1976	Johnny Miller	279	Seve Ballesteros & Jack Nicklaus (285)	Royal Birkdale	Southport, England
1977	Tom Watson	268	Jack Nicklaus (269)	Turnberry	Turnberry, Scotland
1978	Jack Nicklaus	281	Tom Kite, Ray Floyd, Ben Crenshaw & Simon Owen (283)	St. Andrews	St. Andrews, Scotland
1979	Seve Ballesteros	283	Jack Nicklaus & Ben Crenshaw (286)	Royal Lytham	Lytham, England
1980	Tom Watson	271	Lee Trevino (275)	Muirfield	Gullane, Scotland
1981	Bill Rogers	276	Bernhard Langer (280)	Royal St. George's	Sandwich, England
1982	Tom Watson	284	Peter Oosterhuis & Nick Price (285)	Royal Troon	Troon, Scotland
1983	Tom Watson	275	Hale Irwin & Andy Bean (276)	Royal Birkdale	Southport, England
1984	Seve Ballesteros	276	Bernhard Langer & Tom Watson (278)	St. Andrews	St. Andrews, Scotland
1985	Sandy Lyle	282	Payne Stewart (283)	Royal St. George's	Sandwich, England
1986	Greg Norman	280	Gordon J. Brand (285)	Turnberry	Turnberry, Scotland
1987	Nick Faldo	279	Paul Azinger & Rodger Davis (280)	Muirfield	Gullane, Scotland
1988	Seve Ballesteros	273	Nick Price (275)	Royal Lytham	Lytham, England
1989	Mark Calcavecchia*	275	Greg Norman & Wayne Grady (275)	Royal Troon	Troon, Scotland
1990	Nick Faldo	270	Payne Stewart & Mark McNulty (275)	St. Andrews	St. Andrews, Scotland
1991	Ian Baker-Finch	272	Mike Harwood (274)	Royal Birkdale	Southport, England
1992	Nick Faldo	272	John Cook (273)	Muirfield	Gullane, Scotland
1993	Greg Norman	267	Nick Faldo (269)	Royal St. George's	Sandwich, England
1994	Nick Price	268	Jesper Parnevik (269)	Turnberry	Turnberry, Scotland
1995	John Daly*	282	Constantino Rocca (282)	St. Andrews	St. Andrews, Scotland

*PLAYOFFS

1876: Bob Martin awarded title when David Strath refused playoff. **1883:** Willie Fernie (158) def. Bob Ferguson (159) in 36 holes. **1889:** Willie Park Jr. (158) def. Andrew Kirkaldy (163) in 36 holes. **1896:** Harry Vardon (157) def. John H.

Taylor (161) in 36 holes. **1911:** Harry Vardon won when Arnaud Massy conceded at 35th hole. **1921:** Jock Hutchison (150) def. Roger Wethered (159) in 36 holes. **1933:** Denny Shute (149) def. Craig Wood (154) in 36 holes. **1949:** Bobby Locke (135) def. Harry Bradshaw (147) in 36 holes. **1958:** Peter Thomson (139) def. Dave Thomas (143) in 36 holes. **1963:** Bob Charles (140) def. Phil Rodgers (148) in 36 holes. **1970:** Jack Nicklaus (72) def. Doug Sanders (73) in 18 holes. **1975:** Tom Watson (71) def. Jack Newton (72) in 18 holes. **1989:** Mark Calcavecchia (4-3-3-3—13) def. Wayne Grady (4-4-4-4—16) and Greg Norman (3-3-4-x) in 4 holes. **1995:** John Daly (3-4-4-4—15) def. Constantino Rocca (4-5-7-3—19) in 4 holes.

PGA Championship

The PGA Championship began in 1916 as a professional golfers match play tournament, but switched to stroke play in 1958. Conducted by the PGA of America, the tournament is played on a different course each year.

Multiple winners: Walter Hagen and Jack Nicklaus (5); Gene Sarazen and Sam Snead (3); Jim Barnes, Leo Diegel, Raymond Floyd, Ben Hogan, Byron Nelson, Larry Nelson, Gary Player, Paul Runyan, Denny Shute, Dave Stockton and Lee Trevino (2).

Year	Winner	Score	Runner-up	Course	Location
1916	Jim Barnes	1-up	Jock Hutchison	Siwanoy CC	Bronxville, N.Y.
1917-18	Not held		World War I		
1919	Jim Barnes	6 & 5	Fred McLeod	Engineers CC	Roslyn, N.Y.
1920	Jock Hutchison	1-up	J. Douglas Edgar	Flossmoor CC	Flossmoor, Ill.
1921	Walter Hagen	3 & 2	Jim Barnes	Inwood CC	Far Rockaway, N.Y.
1922	Gene Sarazen	4 & 3	Emmet French	Oakmont CC	Oakmont, Pa.
1923	Gene Sarazen*	1-up/38	Walter Hagen	Pelham CC	Pelham, N.Y.
1924	Walter Hagen	2-up	Jim Barnes	French Lick CC	French Lick, Ind.
1925	Walter Hagen	6 & 5	Bill Mehlhorn	Olympia Fields CC	Matteson, Ill.
1926	Walter Hagen	5 & 3	Leo Diegel	Salisbury GC	Westbury, N.Y.
1927	Water Hagen	1-up	Joe Turnesa	Cedar Crest CC	Dallas
1928	Leo Diegel	6 & 5	Al Espinosa	Five Farms CC	Baltimore
1929	Leo Diegel	6 & 4	John Farrell	Hillcrest CC	Los Angeles
1930	Tommy Armour	1-up	Gene Sarazen	Fresh Meadow CC	Flushing, N.Y.
1931	Tom Creavy	2 & 1	Denny Shute	Wannamoisett CC	Rumford, R.I.
1932	Olin Dutra	4 & 3	Frank Walsh	Keller GC	St. Paul, Minn.
1933	Gene Sarazen	5 & 4	Willie Goggin	Blue Mound CC	Milwaukee
1934	Paul Runyan*	1-up/38	Craig Wood	Park CC	Williamsville, N.Y.
1935	Johnny Revolta	5 & 4	Tommy Armour	Twin Hills CC	Oklahoma City
1936	Denny Shute	3 & 2	Jimmy Thomson	Pinehurst CC	Pinehurst, N.C.
1937	Denny Shute*	1-up/37	Harold McSpaden	Pittsburgh FC	Aspinwall, Pa.
1938	Paul Runyan	8 & 7	Sam Snead	Shawnee CC	Shawnee-on-Del, Pa.
1939	Henry Picard*	1-up/37	Byron Nelson	Pomonok CC	Flushing, N.Y.
1940	Byron Nelson	1-up	Sam Snead	Hershey CC	Hershey, Pa.
1941	Vic Ghezzi*	1-up/38	Byron Nelson	Cherry Hills CC	Denver
1942	Sam Snead	2 & 1	Jim Turnesa	Seaview CC	Atlantic City, N.J.
1943	Not held		World War II		
1944	Bob Hamilton	1-up	Byron Nelson	Manito G & CC	Spokane, Wash.
1945	Byron Nelson	4 & 3	Sam Byrd	Morraine CC	Dayton, Ohio
1946	Ben Hogan	6 & 4	Porky Oliver	Portland CC	Portland, Ore.
1947	Jim Ferrier	2 & 1	Chick Harbert	Plum Hollow CC	Detroit
1948	Ben Hogan	7 & 6	Mike Turnesa	Norwood Hills CC	St. Louis
1949	Sam Snead	3 & 2	John Palmer	Hermitage CC	Richmond, Va.
1950	Chandler Harper	4 & 3	Henry Williams Jr.	Scioto CC	Columbus, Ohio
1951	Sam Snead	7 & 6	Walter Burkemo	Oakmont CC	Oakmont, Pa.
1952	Jim Turnesa	1-up	Chick Harbert	Big Spring CC	Louisville
1953	Walter Burkemo	2 & 1	Felice Torza	Birmingham CC	Birmingham, Mich.
1954	Chick Harbert	4 & 3	Walter Burkemo	Keller GC	St. Paul, Minn.
1955	Doug Ford	4 & 3	Cary Middlecoff	Meadowbrook CC	Detroit
1956	Jack Burke	3 & 2	Ted Kroll	Blue Hill CC	Boston
1957	Lionel Hebert	2 & 1	Dow Finsterwald	Miami Valley GC	Dayton, Ohio
1958	Dow Finsterwald	276	Billy Casper (278)	Llanerch CC	Havertown, Pa.
1959	Bob Rosburg	277	Jerry Barber & Doug Sanders (278)	Minneapolis GC	St. Louis Park, Minn.
1960	Jay Hebert	281	Jim Ferrier (282)	Firestone CC	Akron, Ohio
1961	Jerry Barber**	277	Don January (277)	Olympia Fields CC	Matteson, Ill.
1962	Gary Player	278	Bob Goalby (279)	Aronimink CC	Newtown Square, Pa.
1963	Jack Nicklaus	279	Dave Ragan (281)	Dallas AC	Dallas
1964	Bobby Nichols	271	Jack Nicklaus & Arnold Palmer (274)	Columbus CC	Columbus, Ohio
1965	Dave Marr	280	Jack Nicklaus & Billy Casper (282)	Laurel Valley GC	Ligonier, Pa.

*While the PGA Championship was a match play tournament from 1916–57, the two finalists played 36 holes for the title. In the five years that a playoff was necessary, the match was decided on the 37th or 38th hole.

PGA Championships

Year	Winner	Score	Runner-up	Course	Location
1966	Al Geiberger	280	Dudley Wysong (284)	Firestone CC	Akron, Ohio
1967	Don January**	281	Don Massengale (281)	Columbine CC	Littleton, Colo.
1968	Julius Boros	281	Arnold Palmer & Bob Charles (282)	Pecan Valley CC	San Antonio
1969	Ray Floyd	276	Gary Player (277)	NCR GC	Dayton, Ohio
1970	Dave Stockton	279	Arnold Palmer & Bob Murphy (281)	Southern Hills CC	Tulsa
1971	Jack Nicklaus	281	Billy Casper (283)	PGA National GC	Palm Beach Gardens, Fla.
1972	Gary Player	281	Jim Jamieson & Tommy Aaron (283)	Oakland Hills GC	Birmingham, Mich.
1973	Jack Nicklaus	277	Bruce Crampton (281)	Canterbury GC	Cleveland
1974	Lee Trevino	276	Jack Nicklaus (277)	Tanglewood GC	Winston-Salem, N.C.
1975	Jack Nicklaus	276	Bruce Crampton (278)	Firestone CC	Akron, Ohio
1976	Dave Stockton	281	Don January & Ray Floyd (282)	Congressional CC	Bethesda, Md.
1977	Lanny Wadkins**	282	Gene Littler (282)	Pebble Beach GL	Pebble Beach, Calif.
1978	John Mahaffey**	276	Jerry Pate & Tom Watson (276)	Oakmont CC	Oakmont, Pa.
1979	David Graham**	272	Ben Crenshaw (272)	Oakland Hills CC	Birmingham, Mich.
1980	Jack Nicklaus	274	Andy Bean (281)	Oak Hill CC	Rochester, N.Y.
1981	Larry Nelson	273	Fuzzy Zoeller (277)	Atlanta AC	Duluth, Ga.
1982	Ray Floyd	272	Lanny Wadkins (275)	Southern Hills CC	Tulsa
1983	Hal Sutton	274	Jack Nicklaus (275)	Riviera CC	Los Angeles
1984	Lee Trevino	273	Lanny Wadkins & Gary Player (277)	Shoal Creek	Birmingham, Ala.
1985	Hubert Green	278	Lee Trevino (280)	Cherry Hills CC	Denver
1986	Bob Tway	276	Greg Norman (278)	Inverness Club	Toledo, Ohio
1987	Larry Nelson**	287	Lanny Wadkins (287)	PGA National	Palm Beach Gardens, Fla.
1988	Jeff Sluman	272	Paul Azinger 275)	Oak Tree GC	Edmond, Okla.
1989	Payne Stewart	276	Andy Bean, Mike Reid & Curtis Strange (277)	Kemper Lakes GC	Hawthorn Woods, Ill.
1990	Wayne Grady	282	Fred Couples (285)	Shoal Creek	Birmingham, Ala.
1991	John Daly	276	Bruce Lietzke (279)	Crooked Stick GC	Carmel, Ind.
1992	Nick Price	278	Nick Faldo, John Cook, Jim Gallagher & Gene Sauers (281)	Bellerive CC	St. Louis
1993	Paul Azinger**	272	Greg Norman (272)	Inverness Club	Toledo, Ohio
1994	Nick Price	269	Corey Pavin (275)	Southern Hills CC	Tulsa
1995	Steve Elkington**	267	Colin Montgomerie	Riviera CC	Pacific Palisades, Calif.

**PLAYOFFS

1961: Jerry Barber (67) def. Don January (68) in 18 holes. **1967:** Don January (69) def. Don Massengale (71) in 18 holes. **1977:** Lanny Wadkins (4-4-4) def. Gene Littler (4-4-5) on 3rd hole of sudden death. **1978:** John Mahaffey (4-3) def. Jerry Pate (4-4) and Tom Watson (4-5) on 2nd hole of sudden death. **1979:** David Graham (4-4-2) def. Ben Crenshaw (4-4-4) on 3rd hole of sudden death. **1987:** Larry Nelson (4) def. Lanny Wadkins (5) on 1st hole of sudden death. **1993:** Paul Azinger (4-4) def. Greg Norman (4-5) on 2nd hole of sudden death. **1995:** Steve Elkington (3) def. Colin Montgomerie (4) on 1st hole of sudden death.

Major Championship Leaders

Through 1995; active players in **bold** type.

	US Open	British Open	PGA	Masters	US Am	British Am	Total
Jack Nicklaus	4	3	5	6	2	0	**20**
Bobby Jones	4	3	0	0	5	1	**13**
Walter Hagen	2	4	5	0	0	0	**11**
Ben Hogan	4	1	2	2	0	0	**9**
Gary Player	1	3	2	3	0	0	**9**
John Ball	0	1	0	0	0	8	**9**
Arnold Palmer	1	2	0	4	1	0	**8**
Tom Watson	1	5	0	2	0	0	**8**
Harold Hilton	0	2	0	0	1	4	**7**
Gene Sarazen	2	1	3	1	0	0	**7**
Sam Snead	0	1	3	3	0	0	**7**
Harry Vardon	1	6	0	0	0	0	**7**
Lee Trevino	2	2	2	0	0	0	**6**

Tournaments: U.S. Open, British Open, PGA Championship, Masters, U.S. Amateur, and British Amateur.

Grand Slam Summary

The only golfer ever to win a recognized Grand Slam—four major championships in a single season—was Bobby Jones in 1930. That year, Jones won the U.S. and British Opens as well as the U.S. and British Amateurs.

The men's professional Grand Slam—the Masters, U.S. Open, British Open and PGA Championship—did not gain acceptance until 30 years later when Arnold Palmer won the 1960 Masters and U.S. Open. The media wrote that the popular Palmer was chasing the "new" Grand Slam and would have to win the British Open and the PGA to claim it. He did not, but then nobody has before or since.

Three wins in one year: Ben Hogan (1953). **Two wins in one year** (15): Jack Nicklaus (5 times); Ben Hogan, Arnold Palmer and Tom Watson (twice); Nick Faldo, Gary Player, Nick Price, Sam Snead, Lee Trevino and Craig Wood (once).

Year	Masters	US Open	Brit.Open	PGA
1934	H. Smith	Dutra	Cotton	Runyan
1935	Sarazen	Parks	Perry	Revolta
1936	H. Smith	Manero	Padgham	Shute
1937	B. Nelson	Guldahl	Cotton	Shute
1938	Picard	Guldahl	Whitcombe	Runyan
1939	Guldahl	B. Nelson	Burton	Picard
1940	Demaret	Little	—	B. Nelson
1941	Wood	Wood	—	Ghezzi
1942	B. Nelson	—	—	Snead
1943	—	—	—	—
1944	—	—	—	Hamilton
1945	—	—	—	B. Nelson
1946	Keiser	Mangrum	Snead	Hogan
1947	Demaret	Worsham	F. Daly	Ferrier
1948	Harmon	Hogan	Cotton	Hogan
1949	Snead	Middlecoff	Locke	Snead
1950	Demaret	Hogan	Locke	Harper
1951	Hogan	Hogan	Faulkner	Snead
1952	Snead	Boros	Locke	Turnesa
1953	Hogan	Hogan	Hogan	Burkemo
1954	Snead	Furgol	Thomson	Harbert
1955	Middlecoff	Fleck	Thomson	Ford
1956	Burke	Middlecoff	Thomson	Burke
1957	Ford	Mayer	Locke	L. Hebert
1958	Palmer	Bolt	Thomson	Finsterwald
1959	Wall	Casper	Player	Rosburg
1960	Palmer	Palmer	Nagle	J. Hebert
1961	Player	Littler	Palmer	J. Barber
1962	Palmer	Nicklaus	Palmer	Player
1963	Nicklaus	Boros	Charles	Nicklaus
1964	Palmer	Venturi	Lema	Nichols
1965	Nicklaus	Player	Thomson	Marr
1966	Nicklaus	Casper	Nicklaus	Geiberger
1967	Brewer	Nicklaus	DeVicenzo	January
1968	Goalby	Trevino	Player	Boros
1969	Archer	Moody	Jacklin	Floyd
1970	Casper	Jacklin	Nicklaus	Stockton
1971	Coody	Trevino	Trevino	Nicklaus
1972	Nicklaus	Nicklaus	Trevino	Player
1973	Aaron	J. Miller	Weiskopf	Nicklaus
1974	Player	Irwin	Player	Trevino
1975	Nicklaus	L. Graham	T. Watson	Nicklaus
1976	Floyd	J. Pate	Miller	Stockton
1977	T. Watson	H. Green	T. Watson	L. Wadkins
1978	Player	North	Nicklaus	Mahaffey
1979	Zoeller	Irwin	Ballesteros	D. Graham
1980	Ballesteros	Nicklaus	T. Watson	Nicklaus
1981	T. Watson	D. Graham	Rogers	L. Nelson
1982	Stadler	T. Watson	T. Watson	Floyd
1983	Ballesteros	L. Nelson	T. Watson	Sutton
1984	Crenshaw	Zoeller	Ballesteros	Trevino
1985	Langer	North	Lyle	H. Green
1986	Nicklaus	Floyd	Norman	Tway
1987	Mize	S. Simpson	Faldo	L. Nelson
1988	Lyle	Strange	Ballesteros	Sluman
1989	Faldo	Strange	Calcavecchia	Stewart
1990	Faldo	Irwin	Faldo	Grady
1991	Woosnam	Stewart	Baker-Finch	J. Daly
1992	Couples	Kite	Faldo	Price
1993	Langer	Janzen	Norman	Azinger
1994	Olazabal	Els	Price	Price
1995	Crenshaw	Pavin	Daly	Elkington

Vardon Trophy

Awarded since 1937 by the PGA of America to the PGA Tour regular with the lowest scoring average. The award is named after Harry Vardon, the six-time British Open champion, who won the U.S. Open in 1900. A point system was used from 1937-41.

Multiple winners: Billy Casper and Lee Trevino (5); Arnold Palmer and Sam Snead (4); Ben Hogan, Greg Norman and Tom Watson (3); Fred Couples, Bruce Crampton, Tom Kite and Lloyd Mangrum (2).

Year	Pts
1937 Harry Cooper	500
1938 Sam Snead	520
1939 Byron Nelson	473
1940 Ben Hogan	423
1941 Ben Hogan	494
1942-46 No award	

Year	Avg
1947 Jimmy Demaret	69.90
1948 Ben Hogan	69.30
1949 Sam Snead	69.37
1950 Sam Snead	69.23
1951 Lloyd Mangrum	70.05
1952 Jack Burke	70.54
1953 Lloyd Mangrum	70.22
1954 E.J. Harrison	70.41
1955 Sam Snead	69.86
1956 Cary Middlecoff	70.35
1957 Dow Finsterwald	70.30
1958 Bob Rosburg	70.11
1959 Art Wall	70.35
1960 Billy Casper	69.95
1961 Arnold Palmer	69.85
1962 Arnold Palmer	70.27
1963 Billy Casper	70.58
1964 Arnold Palmer	70.01
1965 Billy Casper	70.85
1966 Billy Casper	70.27
1967 Arnold Palmer	70.18
1968 Billy Casper	69.82
1969 Dave Hill	70.34
1970 Lee Trevino	70.64
1971 Lee Trevino	70.27
1972 Lee Trevino	70.89
1973 Bruce Crampton	70.57
1974 Lee Trevino	70.53
1975 Bruce Crampton	70.51
1976 Don January	70.56
1977 Tom Watson	70.32
1978 Tom Watson	70.16
1979 Tom Watson	70.27
1980 Lee Trevino	69.73
1981 Tom Kite	69.80
1982 Tom Kite	70.21
1983 Ray Floyd	70.61
1984 Calvin Peete	70.56
1985 Don Pooley	70.36
1986 Scott Hoch	70.08
1987 Dan Pohl	70.25
1988 Chip Beck	69.46
1989 Greg Norman	69.49
1990 Greg Norman	69.10
1991 Fred Couples	69.59
1992 Fred Couples	69.38
1993 Nick Price	69.11
1994 Greg Norman	68.81

U.S. Amateur

Match play from 1895-64, stroke play from 1965-72, match play since 1972.
Multiple winners: Bobby Jones (5); Jerry Travers (4); Walter Travis (3); Deane Beman, Charles Coe, Gary Cowan, H. Chandler Egan, Chick Evans, Lawson Little, Jack Nicklaus, Francis Ouimet, Jay Sigel, William Turnesa, Bud Ward, Harvie Ward, H.J. Whigham and Tiger Woods (2).

Year		Year		Year		Year	
1895	Charles Macdonald	1922	Jess Sweetser	1950	Sam Urzetta	1975	Fred Ridley
1896	H.J. Whigham	1923	Max Marston	1951	Billy Maxwell	1976	Bill Sander
1897	H.J. Whigham	1924	Bobby Jones	1952	Jack Westland	1977	John Fought
1898	Findlay Douglas	1925	Bobby Jones	1953	Gene Littler	1978	John Cook
1899	H.M. Harriman	1926	George Von Elm	1954	Arnold Palmer	1979	Mark O'Meara
		1927	Bobby Jones	1955	Harvie Ward		
1900	Walter Travis	1928	Bobby Jones	1956	Harvie Ward	1980	Hal Sutton
1901	Walter Travis	1929	Harrison Johnston	1957	Hillman Robbins	1981	Nathaniel Crosby
1902	Louis James			1958	Charles Coe	1982	Jay Sigel
1903	Walter Travis	1930	Bobby Jones	1959	Jack Nicklaus	1983	Jay Sigel
1904	H. Chandler Egan	1931	Francis Ouimet			1984	Scott Verplank
1905	H. Chandler Egan	1932	Ross Somerville	1960	Deane Beman	1985	Sam Randolph
1906	Eben Byers	1933	George Dunlap	1961	Jack Nicklaus	1986	Buddy Alexander
1907	Jerry Travers	1934	Lawson Little	1962	Labron Harris	1987	Billy Mayfair
1908	Jerry Travers	1935	Lawson Little	1963	Deane Beman	1988	Eric Meeks
1909	Robert Gardner	1936	John Fischer	1964	Bill Campbell	1989	Chris Patton
		1937	John Goodman	1965	Bob Murphy		
1910	W.C. Fownes Jr.	1938	William Turnesa	1966	Gary Cowan	1990	Phil Mickelson
1911	Harold Hilton	1939	Bud Ward	1967	Bob Dickson	1991	Mitch Voges
1912	Jerry Travers			1968	Bruce Fleisher	1992	Justin Leonard
1913	Jerry Travers	1940	Richard Chapman	1969	Steve Melnyk	1993	John Harris
1914	Francis Ouimet	1941	Bud Ward			1994	Tiger Woods
1915	Robert Gardner	1942-45	Not held	1970	Lanny Wadkins	1995	Tiger Woods
1916	Chick Evans	1946	Ted Bishop	1971	Gary Cowan		
1917-18	Not held	1947	Skee Riegel	1972	Vinny Giles		
1919	Davidson Herron	1948	William Turnesa	1973	Craig Stadler		
		1949	Charles Coe	1974	Jerry Pate		
1920	Chick Evans						
1921	Jesse Guilford						

British Amateur

Match play since 1885.
Multiple winners: John Ball (8); Michael Bonallack (5); Harold Hilton (4); Joe Carr (3); Horace Hutchinson, Ernest Holderness, Trevor Homer, Johnny Laidley, Lawson Little, Peter McEvoy, Dick Siderowf, Frank Stranahan, Freddie Tait and Cyril Tolley (2).

Year		Year		Year		Year	
1885	Allen MacFie	1912	John Ball	1948	Frank Stranahan	1975	Vinny Giles
1886	Horace Hutchinson	1913	Harold Hilton	1949	Samuel McCready	1976	Dick Siderowf
1887	Horace Hutchinson	1914	J.L.C. Jenkins			1977	Peter McEvoy
1888	John Ball	1915-19	Not held	1950	Frank Stranahan	1978	Peter McEvoy
1889	Johnny Laidley			1951	Richard Chapman	1979	Jay Sigel
1890	John Ball	1920	Cyril Tolley	1952	Harvie Ward		
1891	Johnny Laidley	1921	William Hunter	1953	Joe Carr	1980	Duncan Evans
1892	John Ball	1922	Ernest Holderness	1954	Douglas Bachli	1981	Phillipe Ploujoux
1893	Peter Anderson	1923	Roger Wethered	1955	Joe Conrad	1982	Martin Thompson
1894	John Ball	1924	Ernest Holderness	1956	John Beharrell	1983	Philip Parkin
1895	Leslie Balfour-Melville	1925	Robert Harris	1957	Reid Jack	1984	Jose-Maria Olazabal
1896	Freddie Tait	1926	Jesse Sweetser	1958	Joe Carr	1985	Garth McGimpsey
1897	Jack Allan	1927	William Tweddell	1959	Deane Beman	1986	David Curry
1898	Freddie Tait	1928	Thomas Perkins			1987	Paul Mayo
1899	John Ball	1929	Cyril Tolley	1960	Joe Carr	1988	Christian Hardin
				1961	Michael Bonallack	1989	Stephen Dodd
1900	Harold Hilton	1930	Bobby Jones	1962	Richard Davies		
1901	Harold Hilton	1931	Eric Smith	1963	Michael Lunt	1990	Rolf Muntz
1902	Charles Hutchings	1932	John deForest	1964	Gordon Clark	1991	Gary Wolstenholme
1903	Robert Maxwell	1933	Michael Scott	1965	Michael Bonallack	1992	Stephen Dundas
1904	Walter Travis	1934	Lawson Little	1966	Bobby Cole	1993	Ian Pyman
1905	Arthur Barry	1935	Lawson Little	1967	Bob Dickson	1994	Lee James
1906	James Robb	1936	Hector Thomson	1968	Michael Bonallack	1995	Gordon Sherry
1907	John Ball	1937	Robert Sweeny Jr.	1969	Michael Bonallack		
1908	E.A. Lassen	1938	Charles Yates				
1909	Robert Maxwell	1939	Alexander Kyle	1970	Michael Bonallack		
				1971	Steve Melnyk		
1910	John Ball	1940-45	Not held	1972	Trevor Homer		
1911	Harold Hilton	1946	James Bruen	1973	Dick Siderowf		
		1947	William Turnesa	1974	Trevor Homer		

Major Championships
WOMEN
U.S. Women's Open

The U.S. Women's Open began under the direction of the defunct Women's Professional Golfers Assn. in 1946, passed to the LPGA in 1949 and to the USGA in 1953. The tournament used a match play format its first year then switched to stroke play; (*) indicates playoff winner and (a) indicates amateur winner.

Multiple winners: Betsy Rawls and Mickey Wright (4); Susie Maxwell Berning, Hollis Stacy and Babe Zaharias (3); JoAnne Carner, Donna Caponi, Betsy King, Patty Sheehan and Louise Suggs (2).

Year		Year		Year		Year	
1946	Patty Berg	1959	Mickey Wright	1971	JoAnne Carner	1984	Hollis Stacy
1947	Betty Jameson	1960	Betsy Rawls	1972	Susie M. Berning	1985	Kathy Baker
1948	Babe Zaharias	1961	Mickey Wright	1973	Susie M. Berning	1986	Jane Geddes*
1949	Louise Suggs	1962	Murle Lindstrom	1974	Sandra Haynie	1987	Laura Davies*
1950	Babe Zaharias	1963	Mary Mills	1975	Sandra Palmer	1988	Liselotte Neumann
1951	Betsy Rawls	1964	Mickey Wright*	1976	JoAnne Carner*	1989	Betsy King
1952	Louise Suggs	1965	Carol Mann	1977	Hollis Stacy	1990	Betsy King
1953	Betsy Rawls*	1966	Sandra Spuzich	1978	Hollis Stacy	1991	Meg Mallon
1954	Babe Zaharias	1967	a-Catherine Lacoste	1979	Jerilyn Britz	1992	Patty Sheehan*
1955	Fay Crocker	1968	Susie M. Berning	1980	Amy Alcott	1993	Lauri Merten
1956	Kathy Cornelius*	1969	Donna Caponi	1981	Pat Bradley	1994	Patty Sheehan
1957	Betsy Rawls	1970	Donna Caponi	1982	Janet Anderson	1995	Annika Sorenstam
1958	Mickey Wright			1983	Jan Stephenson		

*PLAYOFFS

1953: Betsy Rawls (71) def. Jackie Pung (77) in 18 holes. **1956:** Kathy Cornelius (75) def. Barbara McIntire (82) in 18 holes. **1964:** Mickey Wright (70) def. Ruth Jessen (72) in 18 holes. **1976:** JoAnne Carner (76) def. Sandra Palmer (78) in 18 holes. **1986:** Jane Geddes (71) def. Sally Little (73) in 18 holes. **1987:** Laura Davies (71) def. Ayako Okamoto (73) and JoAnne Carner (74) in 18 holes. **1992:** Patty Sheehan (72) def. Juli Inkster (74) in 18 holes.

LPGA Championship

Officially the McDonald's LPGA Championship since 1994 (Mazda sponsored from 1987-93), the tournament began in 1955 and has had extended stays at the Stardust CC in Las Vegas (1961-66), Pleasant Valley CC in Sutton, Mass. (1967-68, 70-74); the Jack Nicklaus Sports Center at Kings Island, Ohio (1978-89) and Bethesda CC in Maryland (since 1990); (*) indicates playoff winner.

Multiple winners: Mickey Wright (4); Nancy Lopez, Patty Sheehan and Kathy Whitworth (3); Donna Caponi, Sandra Haynie, Mary Mills and Betsy Rawls (2).

Year		Year		Year		Year	
1955	Beverly Hanson	1966	Gloria Ehret	1976	Betty Burfeindt	1986	Pat Bradley
1956	Marlene Hagge*	1967	Kathy Whitworth	1977	Chako Higuchi	1987	Jane Geddes
1957	Louise Suggs	1968	Sandra Post*	1978	Nancy Lopez	1988	Sherri Turner
1958	Mickey Wright	1969	Betsy Rawls	1979	Donna Caponi	1989	Nancy Lopez
1959	Betsy Rawls	1970	Shirley Englehorn*	1980	Sally Little	1990	Beth Daniel
1960	Mickey Wright	1971	Kathy Whitworth	1981	Donna Caponi	1991	Meg Mallon
1961	Mickey Wright	1972	Kathy Ahern	1982	Jan Stephenson	1992	Betsy King
1962	Judy Kimball	1973	Mary Mills	1983	Patty Sheehan	1993	Patty Sheehan
1963	Mickey Wright	1974	Sandra Haynie	1984	Patty Sheehan	1994	Laura Davies
1964	Mary Mills	1975	Kathy Whitworth	1985	Nancy Lopez	1995	Kelly Robbins
1965	Sandra Haynie						

*PLAYOFFS

1956: Marlene Hagge def. Patti Berg in sudden death. **1968:** Sandra Post (68) def. Kathy Whitworth (75) in 18-holes. **1970:** Shirley Englehorn def. Kathy Whitworth in sudden death.

Nabisco Dinah Shore

Formerly known as the Colgate Dinah Shore from 1972-81, the tournament became the LPGA's fourth designated major championship in 1983. Named after the entertainer, this tourney has been played at Mission Hills CC in Rancho Mirage, Calif., since it began; (*) indicates playoff winner.

Multiple winners (as a major): Amy Alcott (3); Juli Inkster and Betsy King (2).

Year		Year		Year		Year	
1972	Jane Blalock	1978	Sandra Post	1984	Juli Inkster*	1990	Betsy King
1973	Mickey Wright	1979	Sandra Post	1985	Alice Miller	1991	Amy Alcott
1974	Jo Ann Prentice	1980	Donna Caponi	1986	Pat Bradley	1992	Dottie Mochrie*
1975	Sandra Palmer	1981	Nancy Lopez	1987	Betsy King*	1993	Helen Alfredsson
1976	Judy Rankin	1982	Sally Little	1988	Amy Alcott	1994	Donna Andrews
1977	Kathy Whitworth	1983	Amy Alcott	1989	Juli Inkster	1995	Nanci Bowen

*PLAYOFFS

1984: Juli Inkster def. Pat Bradley in sudden death. **1987:** Betsy King def. Patty Sheehan in sudden death. **1992:** Dottie Mochrie def. Juli Inkster in sudden death.

Major Championships (cont.)
WOMEN
du Maurier Classic

Formerly known as La Canadienne in 1973 and the Peter Jackson Classic from 1974-83, this Canadian stop on the LPGA Tour became the third designated major championship in 1979; (*) indicates playoff winner.

Multiple winners (as a major): Pat Bradley (3); JoAnne Carner (2).

Year		Year		Year		Year	
1973	Jocelyne Bourassa	1979	Amy Alcott	1985	Pat Bradley	1991	Nancy Scranton
1974	Carole Jo Skala			1986	Pat Bradley*	1992	Sherri Steinhaur
1975	JoAnne Carner	1980	Pat Bradley	1987	Jody Rosenthal	1993	Brandie Burton*
1976	Donna Caponi	1981	Jan Stephenson	1988	Sally Little	1994	Martha Nause
1977	Judy Rankin	1982	Sandra Haynie	1989	Tammie Green	1995	Jenny Lidback
1978	JoAnne Carner	1983	Hollis Stacy	1990	Cathy Johnston		
		1984	Juli Inkster				

*PLAYOFF

1986: Pat Bradley def. Ayako Okamoto in sudden death. **1993:** Brandie Burton def. Betsy King in sudden death.

Titleholders Championship (1937-72)

The Titleholders was considered a major title on the women's tour until it was discontinued after the 1972 tournament.

Multiple winners: Patty Berg (7); Louise Suggs (4); Babe Zaharias (3); Dorothy Kirby, Marilynn Smith, Kathy Whitworth and Mickey Wright (2).

Year		Year		Year		Year	
1937	Patty Berg	1947	Babe Zaharias	1955	Patty Berg	1963	Marilynn Smith
1938	Patty Berg	1948	Patty Berg	1956	Louise Suggs	1964	Marilynn Smith
1939	Patty Berg	1949	Peggy Kirk	1957	Patty Berg	1965	Kathy Whitworth
				1958	Beverly Hanson	1966	Kathy Whitworth
1940	Betty Hicks	1950	Babe Zaharias	1959	Louise Suggs	1967-71	Not held
1941	Dorothy Kirby	1951	Pat O'Sullivan				
1942	Dorothy Kirby	1952	Babe Zaharias	1960	Fay Crocker	1972	Sandra Palmer
1943-45	Not held	1953	Patty Berg	1961	Mickey Wright		
1946	Louise Suggs	1954	Louise Suggs	1962	Mickey Wright		

Western Open (1930-67)

The Western Open was considered a major title on the women's tour until it was discontinued after the 1967 tournament.

Multiple winners: Patty Berg (7); Louise Suggs and Babe Zaharias (4); Mickey Wright (3); June Beebe; Opal Hill; Betty Jameson and Betsy Rawls (2).

Year		Year		Year		Year	
1930	Mrs. Lee Mida	1940	Babe Zaharias	1950	Babe Zaharias	1960	Joyce Ziske
1931	June Beebe	1941	Patty Berg	1951	Patty Berg	1961	Mary Lena Faulk
1932	Jane Weiller	1942	Betty Jameson	1952	Betsy Rawls	1962	Mickey Wright
1933	June Beebe	1943	Patty Berg	1953	Louise Suggs	1963	Mickey Wright
1934	Marian McDougall	1944	Babe Zaharias	1954	Betty Jameson	1964	Carol Mann
1935	Opal Hill	1945	Babe Zaharias	1955	Patty Berg	1965	Susie Maxwell
1936	Opal Hill	1946	Louise Suggs	1956	Beverly Hanson	1966	Mickey Wright
1937	Betty Hicks	1947	Louise Suggs	1957	Patty Berg	1967	Kathy Whitworth
1938	Bea Barrett	1948	Patty Berg	1958	Patty Berg		
1939	Helen Dettweiler	1949	Louise Suggs	1959	Betsy Rawls		

Major Championship Leaders

Through 1994; active players in **bold** type.

	US Open	LPGA	duM	Dinah	Title-holders	Western	US Am	Brit Am	Total
Patty Berg	1	0	0	0	7	7	1	0	16
Mickey Wright	4	4	0	0	2	3	0	0	13
Louise Suggs	2	1	0	0	4	4	1	1	13
Babe Zaharias	3	0	0	0	3	4	1	1	12
Betsy Rawls	4	2	0	0	0	2	0	0	8
JoAnne Carner	2	0	0	0	0	0	5	0	7
Kathy Whitworth	0	3	0	0	2	1	0	0	6
Pat Bradley	1	1	3	1	0	0	0	0	6
Juli Inkster	0	0	1	2	0	0	3	0	6
Glenna C. Vare	0	0	0	0	0	0	6	0	6

Tournaments: U.S. Open, LPGA Championship, du Maurier Classic, Nabisco Dinah Shore, Titleholders (1937-72), Western Open (1937-67), U.S. Amateur, and British Amateur.

Grand Slam Summary

The Women's Grand Slam has consisted of four tournaments only 19 years. From 1955-66, the U.S. Open, LPGA Championship, Western Open and Titleholders tournaments served as the major events. Since 1983, the U.S. Open, LPGA, du Maurier Classic in Canada and Nabisco Dinah Shore have been the major events. No one has won a four-event Grand Slam on the women's tour.

Three wins in one year (3): Babe Zaharias (1950), Mickey Wright (1961) and Pat Bradley (1986).

Two wins in one year (14): Patty Berg and Mickey Wright (3 times); Louise Suggs (twice); Sandra Haynie, Juli Inkster, Betsy King, Meg Mallon, Betsy Rawls and Kathy Whitworth (once).

Year	LPGA	US Open	T'holders	Western
1937	—	—	Berg	Hicks
1938	—	—	Berg	Barrett
1939	—	—	Berg	Dettweiler
1940	—	—	Hicks	Zaharias
1941	—	—	Kirby	Berg
1942	—	—	Kirby	Jameson
1943	—	—	—	Berg
1944	—	—	—	Zaharias
1945	—	—	—	Zaharias
1946	—	Berg	Suggs	Suggs
1947	—	Jameson	Zaharias	Suggs
1948	—	Zaharias	Berg	Suggs
1949	—	Suggs	Kirk	Suggs
1950	—	Zaharias	Zaharias	Zaharias
1951	—	Rawls	O'Sullivan	Berg
1952	—	Suggs	Zaharias	Rawls
1953	—	Rawls	Berg	Suggs
1954	—	Zaharias	Suggs	Jameson
1955	Hanson	Crocker	Berg	Berg
1956	Hagge	Cornelius	Suggs	Hanson
1957	Suggs	Rawls	Berg	Berg
1958	Wright	Wright	Hanson	Berg
1959	Rawls	Wright	Suggs	Rawls
1960	Wright	Rawls	Crocker	Ziske
1961	Wright	Wright	Wright	Faulk
1962	Kimball	Lindstrom	Wright	Wright
1963	Wright	Mills	M.Smith	Wright
1964	Mills	Wright	M.Smith	Mann
1965	Haynie	Mann	Whitworth	Maxwell
1966	Ehret	Spuzich	Whitworth	Wright
1967	Whitworth	a-LaCoste	—	Whitworth

Year	LPGA	US Open	T'holders	Western
1968	Post	Berning	—	—
1969	Rawls	Caponi	—	—
1970	Englehorn	Caponi	—	—
1971	Whitworth	Carner	—	—
1972	Ahern	Berning	Palmer	—
1973	Mills	Berning	—	—
1974	Haynie	Haynie	—	—
1975	Whitworth	Palmer	—	—
1976	Burfeindt	Carner	—	—
1977	Higuchi	Stacy	—	—
1978	Lopez	Stacy	—	—

Year	LPGA	US Open	duMaurier	D. Shore
1979	Caponi	Britz	Alcott	
1980	Little	Alcott	Bradley	—
1981	Caponi	Bradley	Stephenson	—
1982	Stephenson	Anderson	Haynie	—
1983	Sheehan	Stephenson	Stacy	Alcott
1984	Sheehan	Stacy	Inkster	Inkster
1985	Lopez	Baker	Bradley	Miller
1986	Bradley	Geddes	Bradley	Bradley
1987	Geddes	Davies	Rosenthal	King
1988	Turner	Neumann	Little	Alcott
1989	Lopez	King	Green	Inkster
1990	Daniel	King	Johnston	King
1991	Mallon	Mallon	Scranton	Alcott
1992	King	Sheehan	Steinhaur	Mochrie
1993	Sheehan	Merten	Burton	Alfredsson
1994	Davies	Sheehan	Nause	Andrews
1995	Robbins	Sorenstam	Lidback	Bowen

Vare Trophy

The Vare Trophy for best scoring average by a player on the LPGA Tour has been awarded since 1937 by the LPGA. The award is named after Glenna Collett Vare, winner of six U.S. women's amateur titles from 1922-35.

Multiple winners: Kathy Whitworth (7); JoAnne Carner and Mickey Wright (5); Patty Berg, Beth Daniel, Nancy Lopez and Judy Rankin (3); Pat Bradley and Betsy King (2).

Year		Avg	Year		Avg	Year		Avg
1953	Patty Berg	75.00	1968	Carol Mann	72.04	1982	JoAnne Carner	71.49
1954	Babe Zaharias	75.48	1969	Kathy Whitworth	72.38	1983	JoAnne Carner	71.41
1955	Patty Berg	74.47	1970	Kathy Whitworth	72.26	1984	Patty Sheehan	71.40
1956	Patty Berg	74.57	1971	Kathy Whitworth	72.88	1985	Nancy Lopez	70.73
1957	Louise Suggs	74.64	1972	Kathy Whitworth	72.38	1986	Pat Bradley	71.10
1958	Beverly Hanson	74.92	1973	Judy Rankin	73.08	1987	Betsy King	71.14
1959	Betsy Rawls	74.03	1974	JoAnne Carner	72.87	1988	Colleen Walker	71.26
1960	Mickey Wright	73.25	1975	JoAnne Carner	72.40	1989	Beth Daniel	70.38
1961	Mickey Wright	73.55	1976	Judy Rankin	72.25	1990	Beth Daniel	70.54
1962	Mickey Wright	73.67	1977	Judy Rankin	72.16	1991	Pat Bradley	70.66
1963	Mickey Wright	72.81	1978	Nancy Lopez	71.76	1992	Dottie Mochrie	70.80
1964	Mickey Wright	72.46	1979	Nancy Lopez	71.20	1993	Betsy King	70.85
1965	Kathy Whitworth	72.61	1980	Amy Alcott	71.51	1994	Beth Daniel	70.90
1966	Kathy Whitworth	72.60	1981	JoAnne Carner	71.75			
1967	Kathy Whitworth	72.74						

U.S. Women's Amateur

Stroke play in 1895, match play since 1896.

Multiple winners: Glenna Collett Vare (6); JoAnne Gunderson Carner (5); Margaret Curtis, Beatrix Hoyt, Dorothy Campbell Hurd, Juli Inkster, Alexa Stirling, Virginia Van Wie, Anne Quast Decker Welts (3); Kay Cockerill, Beth Daniel, Vicki Goetze, Katherine Harley, Genevieve Hecker, Betty Jameson and Barbara McIntire (2).

Year		Year		Year		Year	
1895	Mrs. C.S. Brown	1922	Glenna Collett	1950	Beverly Hanson	1975	Beth Daniel
1896	Beatrix Hoyt	1923	Edith Cummings	1951	Dorothy Kirby	1976	Donna Horton
1897	Beatrix Hoyt	1924	Dorothy C. Hurd	1952	Jacqueline Pung	1977	Beth Daniel
1898	Beatrix Hoyt	1925	Glenna Collett	1953	Mary Lena Faulk	1978	Cathy Sherk
1899	Ruth Underhill	1926	Helen Stetson	1954	Barbara Romack	1979	Carolyn Hill
1900	Frances Griscom	1927	Miriam Burns Horn	1955	Patricia Lesser	1980	Juli Inkster
1901	Genevieve Hecker	1928	Glenna Collett	1956	Marlene Stewart	1981	Juli Inkster
1902	Genevieve Hecker	1929	Glenna Collett	1957	JoAnne Gunderson	1982	Juli Inkster
1903	Bessie Anthony	1930	Glenna Collett	1958	Anne Quast	1983	Joanne Pacillo
1904	Georgianna Bishop	1931	Helen Hicks	1959	Barbara McIntire	1984	Deb Richard
1905	Pauline Mackay	1932	Virginia Van Wie	1960	JoAnne Gunderson	1985	Michiko Hattori
1906	Harriot Curtis	1933	Virginia Van Wie	1961	Anne Quast Decker	1986	Kay Cockerill
1907	Margaret Curtis	1934	Virginia Van Wie	1962	JoAnne Gunderson	1987	Kay Cockerill
1908	Katherine Harley	1935	Glenna Collett Vare	1963	Anne Quast Welts	1988	Pearl Sinn
1909	Dorothy Campbell	1936	Pamela Barton	1964	Barbara McIntire	1989	Vicki Goetze
1910	Dorothy Campbell	1937	Estelle Lawson	1965	Jean Ashley	1990	Pat Hurst
1911	Margaret Curtis	1938	Patty Berg	1966	JoAnne G. Carner	1991	Amy Fruhwirth
1912	Margaret Curtis	1939	Betty Jameson	1967	Mary Lou Dill	1992	Vicki Goetze
1913	Gladys Ravenscroft	1940	Betty Jameson	1968	JoAnne G. Carner	1993	Jill McGill
1914	Katherine Harley	1941	Elizabeth Hicks	1969	Catherine Lacoste	1994	Wendy Ward
1915	Florence Vanderbeck	1942-45	Not held	1970	Martha Wilkinson	1995	Kelli Kuehne
1916	Alexa Stirling	1946	Babe D. Zaharias	1971	Laura Baugh		
1917-18	Not held	1947	Louise Suggs	1972	Mary Budke		
1919	Alexa Stirling	1948	Grace Lenczyk	1973	Carol Semple		
1920	Alexa Stirling	1949	Dorothy Porter	1974	Cynthia Hill		
1921	Marion Hollins						

British Women's Amateur Championship

Match play since 1893.

Multiple winners: Cecil Leitch and Joyce Wethered (4); May Hezlet, Lady Margaret Scott, Brigitte Varangot and Enid Wilson (3); Rhona Adair, Pam Barton, Dorothy Campbell, Elizabeth Chadwick, Julie Wade Hall, Helen Holm, Marley Spearman, Frances Stephens, Jessie Valentine and Michelle Walker (2).

Year		Year		Year		Year	
1893	Lady Margaret Scott	1922	Joyce Wethered	1952	Moira Paterson	1977	Angela Uzielli
1894	Lady Margaret Scott	1923	Doris Chambers	1953	Marlene Stewart	1978	Edwina Kennedy
1895	Lady Maraaret Scott	1924	Joyce Wethered	1954	Frances Stephens	1979	Maureen Madill
1896	Amy Pascoe	1925	Joyce Wethered	1955	Jessie Valentine	1980	Anne Quast Sander
1897	Edith Orr	1926	Cecil Leitch	1956	Wiffi Smith	1981	Belle Robertson
1898	Lena Thomson	1927	Simone de la Chaume	1957	Philomena Garvey	1982	Kitrina Douglas
1899	May Hezlet	1928	Nanette le Blan	1958	Jessie Valentine	1983	Jill Thornhill
1900	Rhona Adair	1929	Joyce Wethered	1959	Elizabeth Price	1984	Jody Rosenthal
1901	Mary Graham	1930	Diana Fishwick	1960	Barbara McIntire	1985	Lillian Behan
1902	May Hezlet	1931	Enid Wilson	1961	Marley Spearman	1986	Marnie McGuire
1903	Rhona Adair	1932	Enid Wilson	1962	Marley Spearman	1987	Janet Collingham
1904	Lottie Dod	1933	Enid Wilson	1963	Brigitte Varangot	1988	Joanne Furby
1905	Bertha Thompson	1934	Helen Holm	1964	Carol Sorenson	1989	Helen Dobson
1906	Mrs. W. Kennion	1935	Wanda Morgan	1965	Brigitte Varangot	1990	Julie Wade Hall
1907	May Hezlet	1936	Pam Barton	1966	Elizabeth Chadwick	1991	Valerie Michaud
1908	Maud Titterton	1937	Jessie Anderson	1967	Elizabeth Chadwick	1992	Bernille Pedersen
1909	Dorothy Campbell	1938	Helen Holm	1968	Brigitte Varangot	1993	Emma Duggleby
1910	Elsie Grant-Suttie	1939	Pam Barton	1969	Catherine Lacoste	1994	Emma Duggleby
1911	Dorothy Campbell	1940-45	Not held	1970	Dinah Oxley	1995	Julie Wade Hall
1912	Gladys Ravenscroft	1946	Jean Hetherington	1971	Michelle Walker		
1913	Muriel Dodd	1947	Babe Zaharias	1972	Michelle Walker		
1914	Cecil Leitch	1948	Louise Suggs	1973	Ann Irvin		
1915-19	Not held	1949	Frances Stephens	1974	Carol Semple		
1920	Cecil Leitch	1950	Lally de St. Sauveur	1975	Nancy Roth Syms		
1921	Cecil Leitch	1951	Catherine MacCann	1976	Cathy Panton		

Major Championships (Cont.)
SENIOR PGA
PGA Seniors' Championship

First played in 1937. Two championships played in 1979 and 1984.
Multiple winners: Sam Snead (6); Gary Player, Al Watrous and Eddie Williams (3); Julius Boros, Jock Hutchison, Don January, Arnold Palmer, Paul Runyan, Gene Sarazen and Lee Trevino (2).

Year		Year		Year		Year	
1937	Jock Hutchison	1953	Harry Schwab	1969	Tommy Bolt	1983	Not held
1938	Fred McLeod*	1954	Gene Sarazen	1970	Sam Snead	1984	Arnold Palmer
1939	Not held	1955	Mortie Dutra	1971	Julius Boros	1984	Peter Thomson
1940	Otto Hackbarth*	1956	Pete Burke	1972	Sam Snead	1985	Not held
1941	Jack Burke	1957	Al Watrous	1973	Sam Snead	1986	Gary Player
1942	Eddie Williams	1958	Gene Sarazen	1974	Robert de Vicenzo	1987	Chi Chi Rodriguez
1943-44	Not held	1959	Willie Goggin	1975	Charlie Sifford*	1988	Gary Player
1945	Eddie Williams	1960	Dick Metz	1976	Pete Cooper	1989	Larry Mowry
1946	Eddie Williams*	1961	Paul Runyan	1977	Julius Boros	1990	Gary Player
1947	Jock Hutchison	1962	Paul Runyan	1978	Joe Jiminez*	1991	Jack Nicklaus
1948	Charles McKenna	1963	Herman Barron	1979	Jack Fleck*	1992	Lee Trevino
1949	Marshall Crichton	1964	Sam Snead	1979	Don January	1993	Tom Wargo*
1950	Al Watrous	1965	Sam Snead	1980	Arnold Palmer*	1994	Lee Trevino
1951	Al Watrous*	1966	Fred Haas	1981	Miller Barber	1995	Ray Floyd
1952	Ernest Newnham	1967	Sam Snead	1982	Don January		
		1968	Chandler Harper				

*PLAYOFFS

1938: Fred McLeod def. Otto Hackbarth in 18 holes. **1940:** Otto Hackbarth def. Jock Hutchison in 36 holes. **1946:** Eddie Williams def. Jock Hutchison in 18 holes. **1951:** Al Watrous def. Jock Hutchison in 18 holes. **1975:** Charlie Sifford def. Fred Wampler on 1st extra hole. **1978:** Joe Jiminez def. Joe Cheves and Manuel de la Torre on 1st extra hole. **1979:** Jack Fleck def. Bill Johnston on 1st extra hole. **1980:** Arnold Palmer def. Paul Harney on 1st extra hole. **1993:** Tom Wargo def. Bruce Crampton on 2nd extra hole.

U.S. Senior Open

Established in 1980 for senior players 55 years old and over, the minimum age was dropped to 50 (the PGA Seniors Tour entry age) in 1981. Arnold Palmer, Billy Casper, Orville Moody, Jack Nicklaus and Lee Trevino are the only golfers who have won both the U.S. Open and U.S. Senior Open.
Multiple winners: Miller Barber (3); Jack Nicklaus and Gary Player (2).

Year		Year		Year		Year	
1980	Roberto deVicenzo	1984	Miller Barber	1988	Gary Player*	1992	Larry Laoretti
1981	Arnold Palmer*	1985	Miller Barber	1989	Orville Moody	1993	Jack Nicklaus
1982	Miller Barber	1986	Dale Douglass	1990	Lee Trevino	1994	Simon Hobday
1983	Bill Casper*	1987	Gary Player	1991	Jack Nicklaus*	1995	Tom Weiskopf

*PLAYOFFS

1981: Arnold Palmer (70) def. Bob Stone (74) and Billy Casper (77) in 18 holes. **1983:** Tied at 75 after 18-hole playoff, Casper def. Rod Funseth with a birdie on the 1st extra hole. **1988:** Gary Player (68) def. Bob Charles (70) in 18 holes. **1991:** Jack Nicklaus (65) def. Chi Chi Rodriguez (69) in 18 holes.

Senior Players Championship

First played in 1983 and contested in Cleveland (1983-86), Ponte Vedra, Fla. (1987-89), and Dearborn, Mich. (since 1990).
Multiple winner: Arnold Palmer and Dave Stockton (3).

Year		Year		Year		Year	
1983	Miller Barber	1987	Gary Player	1990	Jack Nicklaus	1993	Jim Colbert
1984	Arnold Palmer	1988	Billy Casper	1991	Jim Albus	1994	Dave Stockton
1985	Arnold Palmer	1989	Orville Moody	1992	Dave Stockton	1995	J.C. Snead*
1986	Chi Chi Rodriguez						

*PLAYOFF

1995: J.C. Snead def. Jack Nicklaus on 1st extra hole.

The Tradition

First played in 1989 and played every year since at the Golf Club at Desert Mountain in Scottsdale, Ariz.
Multiple winner: Jack Nicklaus (3).

Year		Year		Year		Year	
1989	Don Bies	1991	Jack Nicklaus	1993	Tom Shaw	1995	Jack Nicklaus*
1990	Jack Nicklaus	1992	Lee Trevino	1994	Ray Floyd*		

*PLAYOFF

1994: Ray Floyd def. Dale Douglass on 1st extra hole. **1995:** Jack Nicklaus def. Isao Aoki on 3rd extra hole.

Major Senior Championship Leaders

Through 1995. All players are still active.

	PGA Sr.	US Open	Senior Players	Trad	Total		PGA Sr.	US Open	Senior Players	Trad	Total
1 Jack Nicklaus	1	2	1	3	6	6 Billy Casper	0	1	1	0	2
2 Gary Player	3	2	1	0	6	Ray Floyd	0	0	1	1	2
3 Lee Trevino	2	1	0	1	4	Orville Moody	0	1	1	0	2
4 Arnold Palmer	1	0	2	0	3	Chi Chi Rodriguez	1	0	1	0	2
Miller Barber	0	2	1	0	3	Dave Stockton	0	0	2	0	2

Grand Slam Summary

The Senior Grand Slam has officially consisted of The Tradition, the PGA Senior Championship, the Senior Players Championship and the U.S. Senior Open since 1990. Jack Nicklaus won three of the four events in 1991, but no one has won all four in one season.

Three wins in one year: Jack Nicklaus (1991).

Two wins in one year: Gary Player (twice); Orville Moody, Jack Nicklaus, Arnold Palmer and Lee Trevino (once).

Year	Tradition	PGA Sr.	Players	US Open	Year	Tradition	PGA Sr.	Players	US Open
1983	—	—	M. Barber	Casper	1990	Nicklaus	Player	Nicklaus	Trevino
1984	—	Palmer	Palmer	M. Barber	1991	Nicklaus	Nicklaus	Albus	Nicklaus
1985	—	Thomson	Palmer	M. Barber	1992	Trevino	Trevino	Stockton	Laoretti
1986	—	Player	Rodriguez	Douglass	1993	Shaw	Wargo	Colbert	Nicklaus
1987	—	Rodriguez	Player	Player	1994	Floyd	Trevino	Stockton	Hobday
1988	—	Player	Casper	Player	1995	Nicklaus	Floyd	Snead	Weiskopf
1989	Bies	Mowry	Moody	Moody					

Annual Money Leaders

Official annual money leaders on the PGA, European PGA, Senior PGA and LPGA tours. European PGA earnings listed in pounds sterling (£).

PGA

Multiple leaders: Jack Nicklaus (8); Ben Hogan and Tom Watson (5); Arnold Palmer (4); Sam Snead and Curtis Strange (3); Julius Boros, Billy Casper, Tom Kite, Byron Nelson and Nick Price (2).

Year	Earnings	Year	Earnings	Year	Earnings
1934 Paul Runyan	$ 6,767	1955 Julius Boros	$ 63,122	1975 Jack Nicklaus	$ 298,149
1935 Johnny Revolta	9,543	1956 Ted Kroll	72,836	1976 Jack Nicklaus	266,439
1936 Horton Smith	7,682	1957 Dick Mayer	65,835	1977 Tom Watson	310,653
1937 Harry Cooper	14,139	1958 Arnold Palmer	42,608	1978 Tom Watson	362,429
1938 Sam Snead	19,534	1959 Art Wall	53,168	1979 Tom Watson	462,636
1939 Henry Picard	10,303				
1940 Ben Hogan	10,655	1960 Arnold Palmer	75,263	1980 Tom Watson	530,808
1941 Ben Hogan	18,358	1961 Gary Player	64,540	1981 Tom Kite	375,699
1942 Ben Hogan	13,143	1962 Arnold Palmer	81,448	1982 Craig Stadler	446,462
1943 No records kept		1963 Arnold Palmer	128,230	1983 Hal Sutton	426,668
1944 Byron Nelson	37,968	1964 Jack Nicklaus	113,285	1984 Tom Watson	476,260
1945 Byron Nelson	63,336	1965 Jack Nicklaus	140,752	1985 Curtis Strange	542,321
1946 Ben Hogan	42,556	1966 Billy Casper	121,945	1986 Greg Norman	653,296
1947 Jimmy Demaret	27,937	1967 Jack Nicklaus	188,998	1987 Curtis Strange	925,941
1948 Ben Hogan	32,112	1968 Billy Casper	205,169	1988 Curtis Strange	1,147,644
1949 Sam Snead	31,594	1969 Frank Beard	164,707	1989 Tom Kite	1,395,278
1950 Sam Snead	35,759	1970 Lee Trevino	157,037	1990 Greg Norman	1,165,477
1951 Lloyd Mangrum	26,089	1971 Jack Nicklaus	244,491	1991 Corey Pavin	979,430
1952 Julius Boros	37,033	1972 Jack Nicklaus	320,542	1992 Fred Couples	1,344,188
1953 Lew Worsham	34,002	1973 Jack Nicklaus	308,362	1993 Nick Price	1,478,557
1954 Bob Toski	65,820	1974 Johnny Miller	353,022	1994 Nick Price	1,499,927

Note: In 1944-45, Nelson's winnings were in War Bonds.

Senior PGA

Multiple leaders: Don January (3); Miller Barber, Bob Charles, Dave Stockton and Lee Trevino (2).

Year	Earnings	Year	Earnings	Year	Earnings
1980 Don January	$44,100	1985 Peter Thomson	$386,724	1990 Lee Trevino	$1,190,518
1981 Miller Barber	83,136	1986 Bruce Crampton	454,299	1991 Mike Hill	1,065,657
1982 Miller Barber	106,890	1987 Chi Chi Rodriguez	509,145	1992 Lee Trevino	1,027,002
1983 Don January	237,571	1988 Bob Charles	533,929	1993 Dave Stockton	1,175,944
1984 Don January	328,597	1989 Bob Charles	725,887	1994 Dave Stockton	1,402,519

European PGA

Multiple leaders: Seve Ballesteros (6); Sandy Lyle (3); Gay Brewer, Nick Faldo, Bernard Hunt, Bernhard Langer, Colin Montgomerie, Peter Thomson and Ian Woosnam (2).

Year		Earnings	Year		Earnings	Year		Earnings
1961	Bernard Hunt	£ 4,492	1973	Tony Jacklin	£ 24,839	1985	Sandy Lyle	£ 199,020
1962	Peter Thomson	5,764	1974	Peter Oosterhuis	32,127	1986	Seve Ballesteros	259,275
1963	Bernard Hunt	7,209	1975	Dale Hayes	20,507	1987	Ian Woosnam	439,075
1964	Neil Coles	7,890	1976	Seve Ballesteros	39,504	1988	Seve Ballesteros	502,000
1965	Peter Thomson	7,011	1977	Seve Ballesteros	46,436	1989	Ronan Rafferty	465,981
1966	Bruce Devlin	13,205	1978	Seve Ballesteros	54,348			
1967	Gay Brewer	20,235	1979	Sandy Lyle	49,233	1990	Ian Woosnam	737,977
1968	Gay Brewer	23,107				1991	Seve Ballesteros	744,236
1969	Billy Casper	23,483	1980	Greg Norman	74,829	1992	Nick Faldo	871,777
			1981	Bernhard Langer	95,991	1993	Colin Montgomerie	710,897
1970	Christy O'Connor	31,532	1982	Sandy Lyle	86,141	1994	Colin Montgomerie	762,720
1971	Gary Player	11,281	1983	Nick Faldo	140,761			
1972	Bob Charles	18,538	1984	Bernhard Langer	160,883			

LPGA

Multiple leaders: Kathy Whitworth (8); Mickey Wright (4); Patty Berg, JoAnne Carner, Betsy King and Nancy Lopez (3); Pat Bradley, Beth Daniel, Judy Rankin, Betsy Rawls, Louise Suggs and Babe Zaharias (2).

Year		Earnings	Year		Earnings	Year		Earnings
1950	Babe Zaharias	$14,800	1965	Kathy Whitworth	$ 28,658	1980	Beth Daniel	$231,000
1951	Babe Zaharias	15,087	1966	Kathy Whitworth	33,517	1981	Beth Daniel	206,998
1952	Betsy Rawls	14,505	1967	Kathy Whitworth	32,937	1982	JoAnne Carner	310,400
1953	Louise Suggs	19,816	1968	Kathy Whitworth	48,379	1983	JoAnne Carner	291,404
1954	Patty Berg	16,011	1969	Carol Mann	49,152	1984	Betsy King	266,771
1955	Patty Berg	16,492				1985	Nancy Lopez	416,472
1956	Marlene Hagge	20,235	1970	Kathy Whitworth	30,235	1986	Pat Bradley	492,021
1957	Patty Berg	16,272	1971	Kathy Whitworth	41,181	1987	Ayako Okamoto	466,034
1958	Beverly Hanson	12,639	1972	Kathy Whitworth	65,063	1988	Sherri Turner	350,851
1959	Betsy Rawls	26,774	1973	Kathy Whitworth	82,864	1989	Betsy King	654,132
			1974	JoAnne Carner	87,094			
1960	Louise Suggs	16,892	1975	Sandra Palmer	76,374	1990	Beth Daniel	863,578
1961	Mickey Wright	22,236	1976	Judy Rankin	150,734	1991	Pat Bradley	763,118
1962	Mickey Wright	21,641	1977	Judy Rankin	122,890	1992	Dottie Mochrie	693,335
1963	Mickey Wright	31,269	1978	Nancy Lopez	189,814	1993	Betsy King	595,992
1964	Mickey Wright	29,800	1979	Nancy Lopez	197,489	1994	Laura Davies	687,201

All-Time Leaders

PGA, Senior PGA and LPGA leaders through 1994.

Tournaments Won

	PGA	No		Senior PGA	No		LPGA	No
1	Sam Snead	81	1	Miller Barber	24	1	Kathy Whitworth	88
2	Jack Nicklaus	70		Lee Trevino	24	2	Mickey Wright	82
3	Ben Hogan	63	3	Don January	22	3	Patty Berg	57
4	Arnold Palmer	60		Chi Chi Rodriguez	22	4	Betsy Rawls	55
5	Byron Nelson	52	5	Bob Charles	21	5	Louise Suggs	50
6	Billy Casper	51	6	Bruce Crampton	19	6	Nancy Lopez	47
7	Walter Hagen	40	7	Gary Player	17	7	JoAnne Carner	42
	Cary Middlecoff	40	8	Mike Hill	16	8	Sandra Haynie	42
9	Gene Sarazen	38	9	George Archer	15	9	Carol Mann	38
10	Lloyd Mangrum	36	10	Peter Thomson	11	10	Patty Sheehan	32
11	Horton Smith	32		Orville Moody	11	11	Babe Zaharias	31
	Tom Watson	32	12	Dale Douglass	10		Beth Daniel	31
13	Harry Cooper	31		Arnold Palmer	10	13	Pat Bradley	30
	Jimmy Demaret	31	14	Billy Casper	9	14	Amy Alcott	29
15	Leo Diegel	30		Jim Colbert	9		Jane Blalock	29
16	Gene Littler	29		Raymond Floyd	9		Betsy King	29
	Paul Runyan	29		Al Geiberger	9	17	Judy Rankin	26
18	Lee Trevino	27		Dave Stockton	9	18	Marlene Hagge	25
19	Henry Picard	26	19	Jim Dent	8	19	Donna Caponi	24
20	Tommy Armour	24		Lee Elder	8	20	Marilynn Smith	22
	Macdonald Smith	24		Gene Littler	8	21	Sandra Palmer	21
	Johnny Miller	24	22	Jack Nicklaus	7	22	Hollis Stacey	18
23	Johnny Farrell	22	23	Don Bies	6	23	Ayako Okamoto	17
	Ray Floyd	22		Dave Hill	6	24	Jan Stephenson	16
25	Five tied with 21.		25	Larry Mowry	5	25	Juli Inkster	15
							Sally Little	15

Note: Patty Berg's total includes 13 official pro wins prior to formation of LPGA in 1950.

All-Time Leaders (Cont.)
Money Won

PGA

		Earnings
1	Tom Kite	$9,159,418
2	Greg Norman	7,937,869
3	Fred Couples	6,889,149
4	Paul Azinger	6,774,728
5	Tom Watson	6,751,328
6	Nick Price	6,726,418
7	Payne Stewart	6,523,260
8	Curtis Strange	6,433,442
9	Ben Crenshaw	6,107,759
10	Lanny Wadkins	5,931,370
11	Corey Pavin	5,835,444
12	Hale Irwin	5,654,063
13	Craig Stadler	5,606,436
14	Chip Beck	5,585,763
15	Bruce Lietzke	5,440,868
16	Jack Nicklaus	5,372,176
17	Mark O'Meara	5,212,337
18	Ray Floyd	5,129,013
19	David Frost	5,100,514
20	Mark Calcavecchia	5,023,163
21	Fuzzy Zoeller	4,748,065
22	Gil Morgan	4,735,868
23	Scott Hoch	4,673,254
24	Jay Haas	4,604,562
25	Davis Love III	4,511,891

Senior PGA

		Earnings
1	Bob Charles	$5,201,105
2	Chi Chi Rodriguez	5,110,722
3	Lee Trevino	5,108,902
4	Mike Hill	4,554,599
5	George Archer	4,352,085
6	Dale Douglass	4,113,377
7	Jim Dent	3,618,605
8	Bruce Crampton	3,604,534
9	Jim Colbert	3,498,521
10	Gary Player	3,466,026
11	Miller Barber	3,393,652
12	Dave Stockton	3,247,885
13	Al Geiberger	3,101,060
14	Orville Moody	3,057,323
15	Harold Henning	2,942,073
16	Don January	2,827,192
17	Charles Coody	2,692,028
18	Jim Albus	2,585,543
19	Ray Floyd	2,532,920
20	Walter Zembriski	2,374,070
21	Rocky Thompson	2,295,704
22	Jim Ferree	2,126,146
23	Dave Hill	2,067,259
24	Simon Hobday	2,056,175
25	Gene Littler	2,044,991

PGA/Seniors Combined

		Earnings
1	Lee Trevino	$8,587,352
2	Ray Floyd	7,661,933
3	Jack Nicklaus	6,615,764
4	George Archer	6,234,327
5	Chi Chi Rodriguez	6,147,827
6	Bob Charles	5,740,223
7	Gary Player	5,280,977
8	Mike Hill	5,128,323
9	Jim Colbert	5,051,657
10	Miller Barber	4,996,060
11	Bruce Crampton	4,980,727
12	Dale Douglass	4,691,328
13	Dave Stockton	4,527,184
14	Al Geiberger	4,366,248
15	Jim Dent	4,183,850
16	J.C. Snead	4,025,014
17	Don January	3,968,117
18	Charles Coody	3,904,018
19	Gene Littler	3,623,617
20	Orville Moody	3,447,239
21	Arnold Palmer	3,439,915
22	Billy Casper	3,316,756
23	Bob Murphy	3,267,466
24	Dave Hill	3,197,688
25	Harold Henning	3,159,120

European PGA

		Earnings
1	Nick Faldo	£4,585,771
2	Bernhard Langer	4,210,525
3	Seve Ballesteros	4,019,915
4	Ian Woosnam	3,981,488
5	Colin Montgomerie	3,077,727
6	José Maria Olazabal	3,048,582
7	Sam Torrance	2,425,738
8	Sandy Lyle	2,312,570
9	Mark McNulty	2,311,724
10	Ronan Rafferty	£2,301,359
11	Gordon Brand Jr.	2,158,823
12	Mark James	2,143,602
13	Anders Forsbrand	1,955,805
14	Rodger Davis	1,916,134
15	Howard Clark	1,691,478
16	Barry Lane	1,659,968
17	Greg Norman	1,598,746
18	Fred Couples	1,586,443
19	David Feherty	£1,568,604
20	José Rivero	1,539,050
21	Vijay Singh	1,497,308
22	Eduardo Romero	1,385,116
23	Steven Richardson	1,378,995
24	David Gilford	1,318,173
25	Frank Nobilo	1,285,515

LPGA

		Earnings
1	Betsy King	$4,892,874
2	Pat Bradley	4,772,115
3	Beth Daniel	4,492,092
4	Patty Sheehan	4,455,399
5	Nancy Lopez	4,064,803
6	Amy Alcott	3,064,889
7	JoAnne Carner	2,840,072
8	Ayako Okamoto	2,715,679
9	Dottie Mochrie	2,574,716
10	Jan Stephenson	$2,275,075
11	Jane Geddes	2,269,254
12	Rosie Jones	2,193,049
13	Juli Inkster	2,070,418
14	Hollis Stacy	2,005,088
15	Colleen Walker	1,991,324
16	Judy Dickinson	1,990,808
17	Meg Mallon	1,862,059
18	Kathy Whitworth	1,726,597
19	Tammie Green	$1,715,863
20	Laura Davies	1,685,657
21	Deb Richard	1,674,690
22	Sally Little	1,648,211
23	D. Ammaccapane	1,631,836
24	Chris Johnson	1,553,667
25	Dawn Coe-Jones	1,529,176

The Skins Game

The Skins Game is a made-for-TV, $450,000 shootout between four premier golfers playing 18 holes over two days (nine each day). Each hole is counted as a skin with the first six skins worth $15,000 apiece, the second six worth $25,000, and the last six worth $35,000. If a hole is tied, the money is added to the worth of the next hole. The PGA Skins Game was started in late November 1983, followed by the Senior Skins in late January 1988 and the LPGA Skins in late May 1990. Due to scheduling conflicts, the LPGA Skins was not played in 1991.

PGA Skins

Total winnings: 1. Payne Stewart ($840,000); 2. Fuzzy Zoeller ($695,000); 3. Jack Nicklaus ($650,000); 4. Fred Couples ($640,000); 5. Curtis Strange ($605,000); 6. Tom Watson ($440,000); 7. Lee Trevino ($435,000); 8. Ray Floyd ($350,000); 9. Arnold Palmer ($245,000); 10. Greg Norman ($200,000); 11. Gary Player ($170,000); 12. John Daly ($160,000); 13. Paul Azinger ($80,000); 14. Nick Faldo ($70,000); 15. Tom Kite ($0).

Year	Winner	Earnings	Outskinned	
1983	Gary Player	$170,000	Palmer	$140,000
			Nicklaus	40,000
			Watson	10,000
1984	Jack Nicklaus	$240,000	Watson	$120,000
			Palmer	0
			Player	0

Year	Winner	Earnings	Outskinned		Year	Winner	Earnings	Outskinned	
1985	Fuzzy Zoeller	$255,000	Watson	$100,000	1990	Curtis Strange	$220,000	Norman	$90,000
			Palmer	80,000				Faldo	70,000
			Nicklaus	15,000				Nicklaus	70,000
1986	Fuzzy Zoeller	$370,000	Trevino	$55,000	1991	Payne Stewart	$260,000	Daly	$160,000
			Palmer	25,000				Strange	120,000
			Nicklaus	0				Nicklaus	0
1987	Lee Trevino	$310,000	Nicklaus	$70,000	1992	Payne Stewart	$220,000	Couples	$210,000
			Zoeller	70,000				Norman	110,000
			Palmer	0				Kite	0
1988	Ray Floyd	$290,000	Nicklaus	$125,000	1993	Payne Stewart	$280,000	Couples	$260,000
			Trevino	35,000				Palmer	0
			Strange	0				Azinger	0
1989	Curtis Strange	$265,000	Nicklaus	$90,000	1994	Tom Watson	$210,000	Couples	$170,000
			Floyd	60,000				Azinger	80,000
			Trevino	35,000				Stewart	80,000

Senior Skins

Total winnings: 1. Arnold Palmer ($855,000); 2. Jack Nicklaus (735,000); 3. Ray Floyd ($720,000); 4. Chic Chi Rodriguez ($685,000); 5. Lee Trevino ($305,000); 6. Gary Player ($130,00); 7. Billy Casper ($80,000); 8. Sam Snead ($0).

Year	Winner	Earnings	Outskinned		Year	Winner	Earnings	Outskinned	
1988	C.C. Rodriguez	$300,000	Player	$40,000	1992	Arnold Palmer	$205,000	Rodriguez	$120,000
			Palmer	20,000				Nicklaus	95,000
			Snead	0				Trevino	30,000
1989	C.C. Rodriguez	$120,000	Player	$90,000	1993	Arnold Palmer	$190,000	Rodriguez	$145,000
			Casper	80,000				Floyd	60,000
			Palmer	70,000				Nicklaus	55,000
1990	Arnold Palmer	$240,000	Nicklaus	$140,000	1994	Ray Floyd	$240,000	Palmer	$115,000
			Trevino	70,000				Trevino	80,000
			Player	0				Nicklaus	15,000
1991	Jack Nicklaus	$310,000	Trevino	$125,000	1995	Ray Floyd	$420,000	Nicklaus	$120,000
			Palmer	15,000				Trevino	0
			Player	0				Palmer	0
			Rodriguez	0					

LPGA Skins

Total winnings: 1. Betsy King and Patty Sheehan ($395,000); 3. Dottie Mochrie ($360,000); 4. Nancy Lopez ($320,000); 5. Pat Bradley ($285,000); 6. Jan Stephenson ($270,000); 7. Laura Davies ($140,000); 8. JoAnne Carner ($110,000); 9. Meg Mallon ($65,000); 10. Brandie Burton ($0).

Year	Winner	Earnings	Outskinned		Year	Winner	Earnings	Outskinned	
1990	Jan Stephenson	$200,000	Carner	$110,000	1994	Patty Sheehan	$285,000	King	$165,000
			Lopez	95,000				Burton	0
			King	45,000				Lopez	0
1991	Not held				1995	Dottie Mochrie	$290,000	Davies	$140,000
1992	Pat Bradley	$200,000	Lopez	$115,000				Sheehan	110,000
			Stephenson	70,000				Lopez	0
			Mallon	65,000					
1992	Betsy King	$185,000	Lopez	$110,000					
			Bradley	85,000					
			Mochrie	70,000					

Annual Awards
PGA of America Player of the Year

Awarded by the PGA of America; based on points scale that weighs performance in major tournaments, regular events, money earned and scoring average.

Multiple winners: Tom Watson (6); Jack Nicklaus (5); Ben Hogan (4); Julius Boros, Billy Casper, Arnold Palmer and Nick Price (2).

Year		Year		Year		Year	
1948	Ben Hogan	1960	Arnold Palmer	1972	Jack Nicklaus	1984	Tom Watson
1949	Sam Snead	1961	Jerry Barber	1973	Jack Nicklaus	1985	Lanny Wadkins
1950	Ben Hogan	1962	Arnold Palmer	1974	Johnny Miller	1986	Bob Tway
1951	Ben Hogan	1963	Julius Boros	1975	Jack Nicklaus	1987	Paul Azinger
1952	Julius Boros	1964	Ken Venturi	1976	Jack Nicklaus	1988	Curtis Strange
1953	Ben Hogan	1965	Dave Marr	1977	Tom Watson	1989	Tom Kite
1954	Ed Furgol	1966	Billy Casper	1978	Tom Watson		
1955	Doug Ford	1967	Jack Nicklaus	1979	Tom Watson	1990	Nick Faldo
1956	Jack Burke	1968	No award			1991	Corey Pavin
1957	Dick Mayer	1969	Orville Moody	1980	Tom Watson	1992	Fred Couples
1958	Dow Finsterwald			1981	Bill Rogers	1993	Nick Price
1959	Art Wall	1970	Billy Casper	1982	Tom Watson	1994	Nick Price
		1971	Lee Trevino	1983	Hal Sutton		

Annual Awards (Cont.)

PGA Tour Player of the Year

Awarded by the PGA Tour starting in 1990. Winner voted on by tour members from list of nominees.

Multiple winner: Fred Couples and Nick Price (2).

Year	Year	Year	Year
1990 Wayne Levi	1992 Fred Couples	1993 Nick Price	1994 Nick Price
1991 Fred Couples			

PGA Tour Rookie of the Year

Awarded by the PGA Tour starting in 1990. Winner voted on by tour members from list of first-year nominees.

Year	Year	Year	Year
1990 Robert Gamez	1992 Mark Carnevale	1993 Vijay Singh	1994 Ernie Els
1991 John Daly			

PGA Senior Player of the Year

Awarded by the PGA Seniors Tour starting in 1990. Winner voted on by tour members from list of nominees.

Multiple winner: Lee Trevino (3).

Year	Year	Year	Year
1990 Lee Trevino	1991 George Archer	1992 Lee Trevino	1994 Lee Trevino
	& Mike Hill	1993 Dave Stockton	

PGA Senior Tour Rookie of the Year

Awarded by the PGA Tour starting in 1990. Winner voted on by tour members from list of first-year nominees.

Year	Year	Year	Year
1990 Lee Trevino	1992 Dave Stockton	1993 Bob Murphy	1994 Jay Sigel
1991 Jim Colbert			

European Golfer of the Year

Officially, the Johnnie Walker Trophy; voting done by panel of European golf writers and tour members.

Multiple winners: Seve Ballesteros and Nick Faldo (3); Bernhard Langer (2).

Year	Year	Year	Year
1985 Bernhard Langer	1988 Seve Ballesteros	1991 Seve Ballesteros	1993 Bernhard Langer
1986 Seve Ballesteros	1989 Nick Faldo	1992 Nick Faldo	1994 Ernie Els
1987 Ian Woosnam	1990 Nick Faldo		

LPGA Player of the Year

Awarded by the LPGA; based on performance points accumulated during the year.

Multiple winners: Kathy Whitworth (7); Nancy Lopez (4); JoAnne Carner, Beth Daniel and Betsy King (3); Pat Bradley, Beth Daniel and Judy Rankin (2).

Year	Year	Year	Year
1966 Kathy Whitworth	1974 JoAnne Carner	1982 JoAnne Carner	1990 Beth Daniel
1967 Kathy Whitworth	1975 Sandra Palmer	1983 Patty Sheehan	1991 Pat Bradley
1968 Kathy Whitworth	1976 Judy Rankin	1984 Betsy King	1992 Dottie Mochrie
1969 Kathy Whitworth	1977 Judy Rankin	1985 Nancy Lopez	1993 Betsy King
	1978 Nancy Lopez	1986 Pat Bradley	1994 Beth Daniel
1970 Sandra Haynie	1979 Nancy Lopez	1987 Ayako Okamoto	
1971 Kathy Whitworth	1980 Beth Daniel	1988 Nancy Lopez	
1972 Kathy Whitworth	1981 JoAnne Carner	1989 Betsy King	
1973 Kathy Whitworth			

Sony World Rankings

Begun in 1986, the Sony World Rankings combine the best golfers on the PGA and European PGA tours. Rankings are based on a rolling three-year period and weighed in favor of more recent results. While annual winners are not announced, certain players reaching No. 1 have dominated each year.

Multiple winners (at year's end): Greg Norman (4); Nick Faldo (3); Seve Ballesteros (2).

Year	Year	Year	Year
1986 Seve Ballesteros	1989 Seve Ballesteros	1991 Ian Woosnam	1993 Nick Faldo
1987 Greg Norman	& Greg Norman	1992 Fred Couples	1994 Nick Price
1988 Greg Norman	1990 Nick Faldo	& Nick Faldo	
	& Greg Norman		

National Team Competition
MEN
Ryder Cup

The Ryder Cup was presented by British seed merchant and businessman Samuel Ryder in 1927 for competition between professional golfers from Great Britain and the United States. The British team was expanded to include Irish players in 1973 and the rest of Europe in 1979. The United States leads the series 23-6-2 after 31 matches.

Year		Year		Year	
1927	United States, 9½-2½	1955	United States, 8-4	1977	United States, 12½-7½
1929	Great Britain, 7-5	1957	Great Britain, 7½-4½	1979	United States, 17-11
1931	United States, 9-3	1959	United States, 8½-3½	1981	United States, 18½-9½
1933	Great Britain, 6½-5½	1961	United States, 14½-9½	1983	United States, 14½-13½
1935	United States, 9-3	1963	United States, 23-9	1985	Europe, 16½-11½
1937	United States, 8-4	1965	United States, 19½-12½	1987	Europe, 15-13
1939-45	Not held	1967	United States, 23½-8½	1989	Draw, 14-14
1947	United States, 11-1	1969	Draw, 16-16	1991	United States, 14½-13½
1949	United States, 7-5	1971	United States, 18½-13½	1993	United States, 15-13
1951	United States, 9½-2½	1973	United States, 19-13	1995	Europe, 14½-13½
1953	United States, 6½-5½	1975	United States, 21-11		

Playing Sites

1927—Worcester CC (Mass.); **1929**—Moortown, England; **1931**—Scioto CC (Ohio); **1933**—Southport & Ainsdale, England; **1935**—Ridgewood CC (N.J.); **1937**—Southport & Ainsdale, England; **1939-45**—Not held.

1947—Portland CC (Ore.); **1949**—Ganton GC, England; **1951**—Pinehurst CC (N.C.); **1953**—Wentworth, England; **1955**—Thunderbird Ranch & CC (Calif.); **1957**—Lindrick GC, England; **1959**—Eldorado CC (Calif.).

1961—Royal Lytham & St. Annes, England; **1963**—East Lake CC (Ga.); **1965**—Royal Birkdale, England; **1967**—Champions GC (Tex.); **1969**—Royal Birkdale, England; **1971**—Old Warson CC (Mo.); **1973**—Muirfield, Scotland; **1975**—Laurel Valley GC (Pa.); **1977**—Royal Lytham & St. Annes, England; **1979**—Greenbrier (W.Va.).

1981—Walton Heath GC, England; **1983**—PGA National GC (Fla.); **1985**—The Belfry, England; **1987**—Muirfield Village GC (Ohio); **1989**—The Belfry, England; **1991**—Ocean Course (S.C.); **1993**—The Belfry, England; **1995**—Oak Hill CC (N.Y.)

Walker Cup

The Walker Cup was presented by American businessman George Herbert Walker in 1922 for competition between amateur golfers from Great Britain and the United States. The U.S. leads the series with a 30-4-1 record after 35 matches.

Year		Year		Year	
1922	United States, 8-4	1949	United States, 10-2	1973	United States, 14-10
1923	United States, 6½-5½	1951	United States, 7½-4½	1975	United States, 15½-8½
1924	United States, 9-3	1953	United States, 9-3	1977	United States, 16-8
1926	United States, 6½-5½	1955	United States, 10-2	1979	United States, 15½-8½
1928	United States, 11-1	1957	United States, 8½-3½	1981	United States, 15-9
1930	United States, 10-2	1959	United States, 9-3	1983	United States, 13½-10½
1932	United States, 9½-2½	1961	United States, 11-1	1985	United States, 13-11
1934	United States, 9½-2½	1963	United States, 14-10	1987	United States, 16½-7½
1936	United States, 10½-1½	1965	Draw, 12-12	1989	Britain-Ireland, 12½-11½
1938	Britain-Ireland, 7½-4½	1967	United States, 15-9	1991	United States, 14-10
1940-46	Not held	1969	United States, 13-11	1993	United States, 19-5
1947	United States, 8-4	1971	Britain-Ireland, 13-11	1995	Britain-Ireland, 14-10

WOMEN
Solheim Cup

The Solheim Cup was presented by the Karsten Manufacturing Co. in 1990 for competition between women professional golfers from Europe and the United States. The U.S. leads the series with a 2-1 record after three matches.

Year		Year		Year	
1990	United States, 11½-4½	1992	Europe, 11½-6½	1994	United States, 13-7

Curtis Cup

Named after British golfing sisters Harriot and Margaret Curtis, the Curtis Cup was first contested in 1932 between teams of women amateurs from the United States and the British Isles.

Competed for every other year since 1932 (except during World War II). The U.S. leads the series with a 20-5-3 record after 27 matches.

Year		Year		Year	
1932	United States, 5½-3½	1958	Draw, 4½-4½	1978	United States, 12-6
1934	United States, 6½-2½	1960	United States, 6½-2½	1980	United States, 13-5
1936	Draw, 4½-4½	1962	United States, 8-1	1982	United States, 14½-3½
1938	United States, 5½-3½	1964	United States, 10½-7½	1984	United States, 9½-8½
1940-46	Not held	1966	United States, 13-5	1986	British Isles, 13-5
1948	United States, 6½-2½	1968	United States, 10½-7½	1988	British Isles, 11-7
1950	United States, 7½-1½	1970	United States, 11½-6½	1990	United States, 14-4
1952	British Isles, 5-4	1972	United States, 10-8	1992	British Isles, 10-8
1954	United States, 6-3	1974	United States, 13-5	1994	Draw, 9-9
1956	British Isles, 5-4	1976	United States, 11½-6½		

COLLEGES

Men's NCAA Division I Champions

College championships decided by match play from 1897-1964, and stroke play since 1965.
Multiple winners (Teams): Yale (21); Houston (16); Princeton (12); Oklahoma St. (8); Stanford (7); Harvard (6); LSU and North Texas (4); Florida and Wake Forest (3); Michigan, Ohio St. and Texas (2). (Individuals): Ben Crenshaw and Phil Mickelson (3); Dick Crawford, Dexter Cummings, G.T. Dunlop, Fred Lamprecht, and Scott Simpson (2).

Year	Team winner	Individual champion	Year	Team winner	Individual champion
1897	Yale	Louis Bayard, Princeton	1947	LSU	Dave Barclay, Michigan
1898	Harvard (spring)	John Reid, Yale	1948	San Jose St.	Bob Harris, San Jose St.
1898	Yale (fall)	James Curtis, Harvard	1949	North Texas	Harvie Ward, N.Carolina
1899	Harvard	Percy Pyne, Princeton	1950	North Texas	Fred Wampler, Purdue
1900	Not held		1951	North Texas	Tom Nieporte, Ohio St.
1901	Harvard	H. Lindsley, Harvard	1952	North Texas	Jim Vichers, Oklahoma
1902	Yale (spring)	Chas. Hitchcock Jr., Yale	1953	Stanford	Earl Moeller, Oklahoma St.
1902	Harvard (fall)	Chandler Egan, Harvard	1954	SMU	Hillman Robbins, Memphis St.
1903	Harvard	F.O. Reinhart, Princeton	1955	LSU	Joe Campbell, Purdue
1904	Harvard	A.L. White, Harvard	1956	Houston	Rick Jones, Ohio St.
1905	Yale	Robert Abbott, Yale	1957	Houston	Rex Baxter Jr., Houston
1906	Yale	W.E. Clow Jr., Yale	1958	Houston	Phil Rodgers, Houston
1907	Yale	Ellis Knowles, Yale	1959	Houston	Dick Crawford, Houston
1908	Yale	H.H. Wilder, Harvard	1960	Houston	Dick Crawford, Houston
1909	Yale	Albert Seckel, Princeton	1961	Purdue	Jack Nicklaus, Ohio St.
1910	Yale	Robert Hunter, Yale	1962	Houston	Kermit Zarley, Houston
1911	Yale	George Stanley, Yale	1963	Oklahoma St.	R.H. Sikes, Arkansas
1912	Yale	F.C. Davison, Harvard	1964	Houston	Terry Small, San Jose St.
1913	Yale	Nathaniel Wheeler, Yale	1965	Houston	Marty Fleckman, Houston
1914	Princeton	Edward Allis, Harvard	1966	Houston	Bob Murphy, Florida
1915	Yale	Francis Blossom, Yale	1967	Houston	Hale Irwin, Colorado
1916	Princeton	J.W. Hubbell, Harvard	1968	Florida	Grier Jones, Oklahoma St.
1917-18	Not held		1969	Houston	Bob Clark, Cal St.-LA
1919	Princeton	A.L. Walker Jr., Columbia	1970	Houston	John Mahaffey, Houston
1920	Princeton	Jess Sweetster, Yale	1971	Texas	Ben Crenshaw, Texas
1921	Dartmouth	Simpson Dean, Princeton	1972	Texas	Ben Crenshaw, Texas
1922	Princeton	Pollack Boyd, Dartmouth			& Tom Kite, Texas
1923	Princeton	Dexter Cummings, Yale	1973	Florida	Ben Crenshaw, Texas
1924	Yale	Dexter Cummings, Yale	1974	Wake Forest	Curtis Strange, W.Forest
1925	Yale	Fred Lamprecht, Tulane	1975	Wake Forest	Jay Haas, Wake Forest
1926	Yale	Fred Lamprecht, Tulane	1976	Oklahoma St.	Scott Simpson, U.S.C
1927	Princeton	Watts Gunn, Georgia Tech	1977	Houston	Scott Simpson, U.S.C
1928	Princeton	Maurice McCarthy, G'town	1978	Oklahoma St.	David Edwards, Okla. St.
1929	Princeton	Tom Aycock, Yale	1979	Ohio St.	Gary Hallberg, Wake Forest
1930	Princeton	G.T. Dunlap Jr., Princeton	1980	Oklahoma St.	Jay Don Blake, Utah St.
1931	Yale	G.T. Dunlap Jr., Princeton	1981	Brigham Young	Ron Commans, U.S.C
1932	Yale	J.W. Fischer, Michigan	1982	Houston	Billy Ray Brown, Houston
1933	Yale	Walter Emery, Oklahoma	1983	Oklahoma St.	Jim Carter, Arizona St.
1934	Michigan	Charles Yates, Ga.Tech	1984	Houston	John Inman, N.Carolina
1935	Michigan	Ed White, Texas	1985	Houston	Clark Burroughs, Ohio St.
1936	Yale	Charles Kocsis, Michigan	1986	Wake Forest	Scott Verplank, Okla. St.
1937	Princeton	Fred Haas Jr., LSU	1987	Oklahoma St.	Brian Watts, Oklahoma St.
1938	Stanford	John Burke, Georgetown	1988	UCLA	E.J. Pfister, Oklahoma St.
1939	Stanford	Vincent D'Antoni, Tulane	1989	Oklahoma	Phil Mickelson, Ariz. St.
1940	Princeton & LSU	Dixon Brooke, Virginia	1990	Arizona St.	Phil Mickelson, Ariz. St.
1941	Stanford	Earl Stewart, LSU	1991	Oklahoma St.	Warren Schuette, UNLV
1942	LSU & Stanford	Frank Tatum Jr., Stanford	1992	Arizona	Phil Mickelson, Ariz. St.
1943	Yale	Wallace Ulrich, Carleton	1993	Florida	Todd Demsey, Ariz. St.
1944	Notre Dame	Louis Lick, Minnesota	1994	Stanford	Justin Leonard, Texas
1945	Ohio State	John Lorms, Ohio St.	1995	Oklahoma St.	Chip Spratlin, Auburn
1946	Stanford	George Hamer, Georgia			

Women's NCAA Champions

Decided by stroke play since 1982. **Multiple winners** (Teams): Arizona St. (4); Florida, San Jose St. and Tulsa (2).

Year	Team winner	Individual champion	Year	Team winner	Individual champion
1982	Tulsa	Kathy Baker, Tulsa	1989	San Jose St.	Pat Hurst, San Jose St.
1983	TCU	Penny Hammel, Miami	1990	Arizona St.	Susan Slaughter, Arizona
1984	Miami-FL	Cindy Schreyer, Georgia	1991	UCLA	Annika Sorenstam, Arizona
1985	Florida	Danielle Ammaccapane, Ariz.St.	1992	San Jose St.	Vicki Goetze, Georgia
1986	Florida	Page Dunlap, Florida	1993	Arizona St.	Charlotta Sorenstam, Ariz. St.
1987	San Jose St.	Caroline Keggi, New Mexico	1994	Arizona St.	Emilee Klein, Ariz. St.
1988	Tulsa	Melissa McNamara, Tulsa	1995	Arizona St.	K. Mourgue d'Algue, Ariz. St.

Canadian driver **Jacques Villeneuve** acknowledges the cheers in Victory Lane after winning the Indianapolis 500 on May 28. Villeneuve went on to capture the IndyCar season championship.

AUTO RACING

Off Road

Any season in which Team Penske fails to qualify at Indy can safely be called unusual, but 1995 went way beyond that.

The 1995 auto racing season could best be characterized as quirky. Or maybe bizarre. It was certainly unusual.

First, you had an Indianapolis 500 without a car fielded by Team Penske, winner of a record 10 Indy classics.

The 500, the world's richest and most prestigious racing event, was won by 24-year-old Jacques Villeneuve— who wasn't listed among the prerace favorites and had to make up a two-lap penalty to do it.

Even at that, Villeneuve only won because fellow Canadian Scott Goodyear had an incredible brain fade and was penalized for passing the pace car while leading the race with only a handful of laps remaining.

The beginning of the race was also memorable, but in a horrifying way. A first lap collision sent Stan Fox into the outside wall with such force that his car was sliced in half and he was sent to the hospital with serious head injuries (see page 63). Released on July 6, he began intense physical, occupational and speech therapies at a 24-hour rehabilitation center in Indianapolis.

In Formula One, 1994 world champion Michael Schumacher and archrival Damon Hill kept running into each other while battling for the '95 title. And former F1 champion Nigel Mansell, who only three

seasons ago crossed the Atlantic to conquer the IndyCar series, first couldn't fit into his new McLaren's cars, then drove in only a handful of races and then faded into sudden obscurity.

NASCAR also joined in the weirdness, with a season-long spotlight on the comeback of Ernie Irvan, who was nearly killed in an Aug. 20, 1994, accident at Michigan International Speedway. Still hampered by double vision and sporting a Jolly Roger eyepatch to cover his left eye, Irvan returned to the track first to test and then to race.

IndyCar racing, more competitive than ever in 1995 with eight different winners in 17 races, was thrown into a political battle of immense significance when Tony George, the president of Indianapolis Motor Speedway, announced the formation of the Indy Racing League. The IRL will begin its first season in January 1996 with the Indy 500 as its keystone race and a TV contract with ABC Sports.

The IndyCar circuit was further disrupted just when it appeared that Villeneuve would run away with the PPG driving championship. A long-delayed protest hearing came into play that took the title chase right down to the final race.

Despite all the strange goings-on, however, it was a great season on the race tracks.

It opened in January with a German privateer team putting a Porsche back in Victory Lane for the 19th time at the 24 Hours of Daytona sports car race. The little-

---

Mike Harris covered his first Indianapolis 500 in 1969 and has been Motorsports Editor for the Associated Press since 1980.

A stunned **Al Unser Jr.** (left) leaves the pit area area with his father **Al Sr.** (right) after failing to make the starting field of the Indianapolis 500 on the final day of qualifying. For Unser, the defending champion, it marked the first time since 1962 that no one from his family had qualified for the race.

known quartet of Germans Jurgen Lassig and Marco Werner, Frenchman Christophe Bouchut and Italian Giovanni Lavaggi outdid the feared Ferraris, which all succumbed to problems in their V12 engines.

With that out of the way, NASCAR stock cars descended on Daytona and Dale Earnhardt did everything he could think of to finally win a Daytona 500— the one big event he had never captured in his remarkable 17-year career.

For the second straight year, however, the seven-time Winston Cup champion was beaten by Tennessee farmboy Sterling Marlin, who held off a furious Earnhardt charge. Marlin has won only twice in his career, both times in NASCAR's biggest race.

Earnhardt, the two-time defending series champion, came up two car-lengths short after a dramatic run from 14th in the final 11 laps. His frustration showed afterward when he muttered, "I reckon I'm not supposed to win this damn thing."

And the season didn't get any less frustrating for the 44-year-old Earnhardt, whose leading role in stock car racing came under a serious challenge from 24-year-old Jeff Gordon.

By late in the Winston Cup season, Gordon was leading in just about every important category, including points, poles, laps led and races won. With the season winding down, he held a solid lead over runner-up Earnhardt.

Earnhardt, a master at psyching out his rivals, did his best to get to Gordon, calling him "Wonder Boy," a nickname the youngster hates, every chance he got. He also talked about how much pressure there is when the championship battle gets down to the end.

But Gordon didn't seem to notice any pressure, riding a string of 14 straight Top-10 finishes as the season neared its end.

Both Gordon and Earnhardt drove new Chevrolet Monte Carlos, the model that the General Motors division brought in this season to replace the Luminas that had been in service since the middle of the 1989 season.

Before the Lumina came along, the old

Wide World Photos

Jeff Gordon celebrates his first NASCAR win of the season at Rockingham, N.C., on Feb. 26. By October, he held a solid lead over Dale Earnhardt in the Winston Cup point standings.

Monte Carlo was the most successful car model in NASCAR history. It appears that the new Monte Carlo will carry on the tradition.

Another one of the newer Winston Cup stars, Bobby Labonte, also jumped into the limelight in '95. He won the Coca-Cola 600 at Charlotte Motor Speedway and two other events to join older brother Terry, the 1984 series champ, in the upper echelon of the sport.

Meanwhile, the 36-year-old Irvan finally got medical clearance from NASCAR late in the season and quickly made arrangements to get back in a Winston Cup car.

His appearance at North Wilkesboro Speedway on Oct. 1 ended a nearly 14-month hiatus and completed a near-miraculous recovery from the head and chest injuries that came close to taking his life.

In his first time back behind the wheel in one of Robert Yates's Ford Thunderbirds, Irvan qualified seventh, led for 31 laps early in the race and wound up sixth— just ahead of Dale Jarrett, the man who took his place and will now be his teammate.

"Normally, we wouldn't be happy with a sixth-place finish, but this is like winning," Irvan said. "This really answered a lot of people's questions. It answered a lot of my questions, too. I didn't know if I could do it. I thought I could, but it's just something you have to go out and do."

Nobody cashed in on the Winston Select Million, the prize that goes to any driver who can win two of NASCAR's Big Four events. After Marlin won at Daytona, Mark Martin won the Winston Select 500 at Talladega, the younger Labonte won the Charlotte event and Gordon earned his first Southern 500 win at Darlington, S.C.

The Brickyard 400, NASCAR's richest race, was a walkaway for Earnhardt, who earned $565,600 and was awed by the experience.

"Joining the names who have won here like [A.J.] Foyt and [Mario] Andretti and the rest of them, is something to be proud of," Earnhardt said. "It's a special feeling."

The winner of the Indy 500 was just as happy, but his youth didn't lend itself to reverence for the place.

Jacques Villeneuve's bloodlines flow from Formula One not Gasoline Alley. His father Gilles was an F1 star when he crashed and died at age 30 during practice sessions at the 1982 Belgium Grand Prix.

"I don't really remember much about my father, so it was not him who got me interested in racing," said the serious-minded Villeneuve. "But racing is in my blood and there was nothing else I really wanted to do."

Canadian-born but raised in Europe, Villeneuve won four races, six poles and held on to beat two-time series champion Al Unser Jr., who had probably the craziest season of them all.

Unser, who won Indy and seven other races on the way to the 1994 IndyCar title, got off to a bad start in '95— after he won his sixth Toyota GP of Long Beach, that is. With his favorite street circuit behind him, Little Al wasn't competitive anywhere else in the first half of the year.

At Indianapolis, a place where the Unsers had qualified at least one family member every year since 1962— and where Al Sr., Al Jr. and Uncle Bobby had combined for nine victories— there was no Unser in the 1995 field.

Roger Penske's team, struggling with a Penske-built car that refused to handle in the corners at high speed, could not find the

Mike Hewitt/Allsport

Defending Formula One driving champion **Michael Schumacher** of Germany (left) and archrival **Damon Hill** of Britain renewed their points battle in 1995, but were rarely on speaking terms.

speed to get either Unser or teammate Emerson Fittipaldi, another two-time winner, in the race.

They even borrowed Lolas from Bobby Rahal's team, but couldn't get them up to speed in time to make the race.

"This just breaks my heart," said Unser.

"I accept full blame for our not being prepared," said Penske, who failed to get a car into the race for the first time since 1968.

"I feel most sorry for Al and Emerson," he added. "Both are great drivers and deserve to be in this race. But we'll just have to try again next year. It's going to be a long 12 months."

It might even be longer if the political infighting between IndyCar and the new Indy Racing League doesn't get sorted out.

Shortly before the season came to a close, the IRL announced that 25 qualifying positions in the 33-car field would be reserved for the Top 25 leaders in IRL points after the first two races— at Orlando and Phoenix— of its five-race schedule.

The other eight slots would be at-large berths, open to all comers, including the teams that chose to stick with IndyCar and

not race in the IRL.

That infuriated powerful IndyCar-owners like Penske, Rahal, Carl Haas and Chip Ganassi, who were all toying with the idea of boycotting the 500 and running their own race the same day at Michigan— a track owned by Penske.

"I hope that people come to their senses and strike a deal," said car owner Dick Simon, who planned to run in both series because of sponsorship demands. "But there is a big chasm between the two groups. There are a lot of egos, a lot of power and a lot of money at stake."

After sitting out Indy, Unser suddenly regained his competitive edge and began to stalk Villeneuve.

He easily won a race at Portland, Ore., in June, but was disqualified by IndyCar officials several hours after the race for a technical violation that involved the required clearance between the bottom of his Penske racer and the bottom of the car's sidepods.

Runner-up Jimmy Vasser was handed the victory, his first.

After IndyCar quickly turned down

Penske's protest, the matter was left to fester for nearly two months before a special three-man panel was put in place to hear a final protest.

Villeneuve increased his lead in championship points, but couldn't clinch the title early— not as long as Unser had a chance to regain the 21 points that had been taken from him. With the points restored, Unser would still have a chance to catch Villeneuve in the final two races.

The matter remained in doubt until the final race of the season at Monterey, Calif., where Villeneuve finished 11th and Unser came in sixth. That gave Villeneuve enough points to wrap up the title no matter how the protest was decided.

Two weeks later, the panel overturned IndyCar's ruling and gave Unser back his Portland win because of what were termed inconsistencies in the way the car was measured. That made Unser the leading active Indy-car race winner with 31. He had been tied with Michael Andretti with 30.

Meanwhile, Villeneuve announced he would follow in the footsteps of his famous father and compete next season in Formula One. There, the young charger will team with British star Hill on the Williams-Renault team.

"It was not an easy decision to make because the IndyCar series is a great, competitive series," Villeneuve said. "But, in the business of auto racing, you must take your opportunities when you get them. You may not get another chance."

He will be stepping into a series in the midst of major changes and seemingly ready-made for some new star-qualify performers.

Schumacher, who had all but clinched his second straight world driving championship by early October, is the only real megastar in the European-based series.

But Schumacher isn't staying put either, having already announced that he will leave Benetton and join Ferrari for a reported two-year contract worth $48 million. His departure started a chain reaction that has just about every top-echelon driver except Hill changing teams in 1996.

That is not likely to calm down the feud between Schumacher and Hill, who seem to be drawn to each other on a racetrack like a moths to a flame.

"Sometimes, he is not a thinking driver," Schumacher has said of Hill. "Schumacher drives like there is nobody else on the race track," says Hill, returning the compliment.

Schumacher won seven of the first 14 races in the 17-race season to build a lead over Hill that was almost insurmountable. Those wins included the first victory by a German driver in the German Grand Prix on July 30. Schumacher also came back home late in the season to win the European Grand Prix at Nurburgring in the first race at the traditional German track in 10 years.

In some special events in 1995, a McLaren BMW1 GTR driven by Yannick Dalmas of France, J.J. Lehto of Finland and Masanori Sekiya of Japan, scored a hard-fought victory in the 24 Hours of LeMans.

Mario Andretti, the former Formula One and Indy-car champion, who retired from open-wheel racing at the end of the 1994 season, came out of his retirement just long enough to help his team finish second at LeMans.

Early in the rain-hampered race, Andretti ran through some mud thrown onto the track by a spinning car and slid into a concrete barrier. It took 30 minutes in the pits to repair the damage, but the Courage Porsche co-driven by Frenchmen Bob Wollek and Eric Helary made an incredible comeback on the 8.46-mile course and wound up losing by only three minutes.

"I never said I was retired from racing, only from Indy cars," Andretti said afterward. "I've won the Daytona 500 and the Indianapolis 500 and a lot of other big races, but I've never won LeMans. That's one I'd like to get before I'm completely done with driving."

Finally, the NHRA's drag racing season was highlighted by John Force's strong run toward a record-setting fifth Funny Car title. By late in the season, Force had won six times and held a big edge over runner-up Al Hofmann.

Scott Kalitta, winner of five events, was well ahead of Cory McClenathan in the Top Fuel standings, while Warren Johnson, winner of six events, was far out front in the Pro Stock division.

Competition in Pro Stock was considerably weaker after all the engines and spare parts for Darrell Alderman and Scott Geoffrion were smashed during a May break-in at their Team Mopar shop in Michigan. Both missed most of the season. ❑

THE 1996 INFORMATION PLEASE SPORTS ALMANAC

AUTO RACING STATISTICS

THE SEASON IN REVIEW
1994-1995
NASCAR • INDYCAR • FORMULA 1

SEC **A**

PAGE **863**

NASCAR RESULTS

Winners of NASCAR Winston Cup races through Oct. 1 (see Updates chapter for later results).

1995 SEASON (through Oct. 1)

Date		Location	Winner (Pos.)	Avg.mph	Earnings	Pole	Qual.mph
Feb. 19	**Daytona 500**	Daytona	Sterling Marlin (3)	141.710	$300,460	D. Jarrett	193.498
Feb. 26	Goodwrench 500	Rockingham	Jeff Gordon (1)	125.305	167,600*	J. Gordon	157.620†
Mar. 5	Pontiac 400	Richmond	Terry Labonte (24)	106.425	82,950	J. Gordon	124.757†
Mar. 12	Purolator 500	Atlanta	Jeff Gordon (3)	150.115	104,950	D. Earnhardt	185.077
Mar. 26	TranSouth 400	Darlington	Sterling Marlin (5)	111.392	86,185	J. Gordon	170.833†
Apr. 2	Food City 500	Bristol	Jeff Gordon (2)	92.011	67,645	M. Martin	124.605
Apr. 9	First Union 400	N. Wilkesboro	Dale Earnhardt (5)	102.424	77,400	J. Gordon	118.765
Apr. 23	Hanes 500	Martinsville	Rusty Wallace (15)	72.145	61,945	B. Labonte	93.308
Apr. 30	**Winston 500**	Talladega	Mark Martin (3)	178.902	98,565	T. Labonte	196.532
May 7	Save Mart 300	Sonoma	Dale Earnhardt (4)	70.681	74,860	R. Rudd	92.132†
May 20	*The Winston Select*	Charlotte	Jeff Gordon (7)	148.410	300,000	B. Labonte	139.817
May 28	**Coca-Cola 600**	Charlotte	Bobby Labonte (2)	151.952	163,850	J. Gordon	183.861
June 4	Miller Draft 500	Dover	Kyle Petty (37)	119.880	77,655	J. Gordon	153.669†
June 11	UAW-GM 500	Pocono	Terry Labonte (27)	137.720	71,175	K. Schrader	163.375
June 18	Miller Draft 400	Michigan	Bobby Labonte (19)	134.141	84,080	J. Gordon	186.611†
July 1	Pepsi 400	Daytona	Jeff Gordon (3)	166.976	96,580	D. Earnhardt	191.355
July 9	Slick 50 300	Loudon	Jeff Gordon (21)	107.029†	160,300	M. Martin	128.815†
July 16	Miller Draft 500	Pocono	Dale Jarrett (15)	134.038	72,970	B. Elliott	162.496
July 23	DieHard 500	Talladega	Sterling Marlin (1)	173.187	219,425*	S. Marlin	194.212
Aug. 5	Brickyard 400	Indianapolis	Dale Earnhardt (13)	155.218*	565,600	J. Gordon	172.536†
Aug. 13	Bud at the Glen	Watkins Glen	Mark Martin (1)	103.030†	95,290*	M. Martin	120.411†
Aug. 26	GM Goodwrench 400	Michigan	Bobby Labonte (1)	157.739	97,445*	B. Labonte	184.403
Aug. 26	Goody's 500	Bristol	Terry Labonte (9)	81.979	66,940	M. Martin	125.093†
Sept. 3	**Southern 500**	Darlington	Jeff Gordon (5)	121.231	70,630	J. Andretti	167.379
Sept. 9	Miller Draft 400	Richmond	Rusty Wallace (7)	104.459	64,515	D. Earnhardt	122.543
Sept. 17	Delaware 500	Dover	Jeff Gordon (2)	124.740	74,655	R. Mast	153.446
Sept. 24	Goody's 500	Martinsville	Dale Earnhardt (2)	73.946	78,150	J. Gordon#	
Oct. 1	Tyson Holly Farms 400	N. Wilkesboro	Mark Martin (2)	102.998	71,590	T. Musgrave	118.396

Note: *The Winston Select* (May 20) is a 105-mile, non-points race.
†Track record.
*Includes carryover Unocal 76 bonus for winning race from the pole: **Goodwrench 500**— Gordon ($91,200); **DieHard 500**— Marlin ($121,600); **Bud at the Glen**— Martin ($15,200); **GM Goodwrench 400**— B. Labonte ($7,600).
#Time trials were not held due to inclement weather, but Gordon was awarded the pole because he was the Winston Cup points leader.
Winning Cars: CHEVY MONTE CARLO (20)— Gordon 7, Earnhardt 4, B. Labonte 3, T. Labonte 3, Marlin 3; FORD THUNDERBIRD (6)— Martin 3, R. Wallace 2, Jarrett; PONTIAC GRAND PRIX (1)— Petty.

1995 Race Locations

February— DAYTONA 500 at Daytona International Speedway in Daytona Beach, Fla.; GOODWRENCH 500 at North Carolina Motor Speedway in Rockingham, N.C. **March**— PONTIAC EXCITEMENT 400 at Richmond (Va.) International Raceway; PUROLATOR 500 at Atlanta International Speedway in Atlanta, Ga.; TRANSOUTH FINANCIAL 500 at Darlington (S.C.) International Raceway. **April**— FOOD CITY 500 at Bristol (Tenn.) International Raceway; FIRST UNION 400 at North Wilkesboro (N.C.) Speedway; HANES 500 at Martinsville (Va.) Speedway; WINSTON SELECT 500 at Talladega (Ala.) Superspeedway. **May**— SAVEMART SUPERMARKETS 300 at Sears Point International Raceway in Sonoma, Calif.; THE WINSTON SELECT at Charlotte Motor Speedway in Concord, N.C.; COCA-COLA 600 at Charlotte.
June— DOVER 500 at Dover (Del.) Downs International Speedway; UAW-GM TEAMWORK 500 at Pocono International Raceway in Pocono, Pa.; MILLER GENUINE DRAFT 400 at Michigan International Speedway in Brooklyn, Mich. **July**— PEPSI 400 at Daytona; SLICK 50 300 at New Hampshire International Speedway in Loudon, N.H.; MILLER GENUINE DRAFT 500 at Pocono; DIEHARD 500 at Talladega. **August**— BRICKYARD 400 at Indianapolis Motor Speedway; BUD AT THE GLEN at Watkins Glen, (N.Y.) International; GM GOODWRENCH DEALER 400 at Brooklyn, Mich.; GOODY'S 500 at Bristol.
September— MOUNTAIN DEW SOUTHERN 500 at Darlington; MILLER GENUINE DRAFT 400 at Richmond; DELAWARE 500 at Dover; GOODY'S 500 at Martinsville. **October**— TYSON HOLLY FARMS 400 at North Wilkesboro; UAW-GM QUALITY 500 at Charlotte; AC DELCO 400 at Rockingham; SLICK 50 500 at Phoenix International Raceway. **November**— NAPA 500 at Atlanta.

NASCAR Results (Cont.)

1995 Daytona 500

Date— Sunday, Feb. 19, 1995, at Daytona International Speedway. **Distance**— 500 miles; **Course**— 2.5 miles; **Field**— 42 cars; **Average speed**— 141.710 mph; **Margin of victory**— 0.61 seconds; **Time of race**— 3 hours, 31 minutes, 42 seconds (does not count 1-hour, 44-minute rain delay on 71st lap); **Caution flags**— 10 for 41 laps; **Lead changes**— 12 among 8 drivers; **Lap leaders**— Sterling Marlin (112 laps), Jeff Gordon (61), Dale Earnhardt (23), Michael Waltrip (2), Geoff Bodine (1), Dave Marcis (1); **Pole sitter**— Dale Jarrett at 193.498 mph; **Attendance**— 150,000 (estimated); **TV Rating**— 7.8/20 share (CBS). Note that (r) indicates circuit rookie driver.

	Driver (Pos.)	Hometown	Car	Laps	Ended	Earnings
1	Sterling Marlin (3)	Columbia, Tenn.	Chevy Monte Carlo	200	Running	$300,460
2	Dale Earnhardt (2)	Kannapolis, N.C.	Chevy Monte Carlo	200	Running	212,250
3	Mark Martin (6)	Batesville, Ark.	Ford Thunderbird	200	Running	153,700
4	Ted Musgrave (12)	Troutman, N.C.	Ford Thunderbird	200	Running	111,200
5	Dale Jarrett (1)	Hickory, N.C.	Ford Thunderbird	200	Running	119,855
6	Michael Waltrip (15)	Owensboro, Ky.	Pontiac Grand Prix	200	Running	86,205
7	Steve Grissom (35)	Liberty, N.C.	Chevy Monte Carlo	200	Running	72,065
8	Terry Labonte (11)	Archdale, N.C.	Chevy Monte Carlo	200	Running	78,940
9	Ken Schrader (9)	Concord, N.C.	Chevy Monte Carlo	200	Running	70,140
10	Morgan Shepherd (30)	Conover, N.C.	Ford Thunderbird	200	Running	66,690
11	Dick Trickle (17)	Wisconsin Rapids, Wisc.	Ford Thunderbird	200	Running	61,990
12	Kyle Petty (13)	High Point, N.C.	Pontiac Grand Prix	200	Running	58,865
13	Ricky Rudd (18)	Lake Norman, N.C.	Chevy Monte Carlo	200	Running	60,620
14	Lake Speed (16)	Concord, N.C.	Ford Thunderbird	200	Running	48,830
15	Ward Burton (21)	Scottsburg, Va.	Chevy Monte Carlo	200	Running	45,015
16	r-Ricky Craven (14)	Newburgh, Me.	Chevy Monte Carlo	200	Running	47,795
17	Loy Allen Jr. (37)	Raleigh, N.C.	Ford Thunderbird	200	Running	48,975
18	Bobby Hamilton (25)	Nashville	Pontiac Grand Prix	200	Running	40,255
19	Joe Ruttman (27)	Franklin, Tenn.	Ford Thunderbird	200	Running	39,135
20	Geoff Bodine (40)	Julian, N.C.	Ford Thunderbird	200	Running	56,175
21	Rick Mast (41)	Rockbridge Baths, Va.	Ford Thunderbird	200	Running	46,270
22	Jeff Gordon (4)	Huntersville, N.C.	Chevy Monte Carlo	199	Running	67,915
23	Bill Elliott (10)	Dawsonville, Ga.	Ford Thunderbird	199	Running	42,060
24	Jeff Burton (28)	South Boston, Va.	Ford Thunderbird	199	Running	45,655
25	Brett Bodine (39)	Harrisburg, N.C.	Ford Thunderbird	199	Running	49,150
26	r-Robert Pressley (31)	Asheville, N.C.	Chevy Monte Carlo	199	Running	44,765
27	John Andretti (38)	Indianapolis	Ford Thunderbird	197	Running	35,690
28	Ben Hess (26)	Mooresville, N.C.	Ford Thunderbird	196	Running	35,785
29	r-Randy LaJoie (24)	Norwalk, Conn.	Pontiac Grand Prix	195	Running	43,955
30	Bobby Labonte (20)	Trinity, N.C.	Chevy Monte Carlo	185	Accident	45,300
31	Derrike Cope (22)	Charlotte, N.C.	Ford Thunderbird	184	Accident	35,145
32	Darrell Waltrip (5)	Franklin, Tenn.	Chevy Monte Carlo	180	Running	60,090
33	r-Davy Jones (33)	Atlanta	Ford Thunderbird	166	Running	34,290
34	Rusty Wallace (7)	Charlotte, N.C.	Ford Thunderbird	158	Accident	54,205
35	Jeremy Mayfield (29)	Goodlettsville, Tenn.	Ford Thunderbird	155	Engine	34,050
36	Dave Marcis (19)	Wausau, Wisc.	Chevy Monte Carlo	129	Engine	31,045
37	Todd Bodine (8)	Harrisburg, N.C.	Ford Thunderbird	105	Engine	49,015
38	Jeff Purvis (34)	Clarksville, Tenn.	Chevy Monte Carlo	57	Accident	33,205
39	Mike Wallace (36)	Concord, N.C.	Ford Thunderbird	57	Accident	32,955
40	r-Steve Kinser (42)	Bloomington, Ind.	Ford Thunderbird	27	Accident	40,455
41	Phil Parsons (32)	Detroit	Ford Thunderbird	27	Accident	33,005
42	Joe Nemechek (23)	Mooresville, N.C.	Chevy Monte Carlo	8	Accident	34,180

Winston Cup Point Standings

Official Top 10 NASCAR Winston Cup point leaders and Top 15 money leaders for 1994 and unofficial Top 10 point leaders and Top 15 money leaders for 1995 (through Oct. 1). Points awarded for all qualifying drivers (winner receives 175) and lap leaders. Earnings include bonuses. Listed are starts (Sts), Top 5 finishes (1-2-3-4-5), poles won (PW) and points (Pts).

FINAL 1994

		Sts	Finishes 1-2-3-4-5	PW	Pts
1	Dale Earnhardt	31	4-7-6-1-2	2	4694
2	Mark Martin	31	2-4-2-4-3	1	4250
3	Rusty Wallace	31	8-3-1-4-1	2	4207
4	Ken Schrader	31	0-1-2-4-2	0	4060
5	Ricky Rudd	31	1-0-0-3-2	1	4050
6	Morgan Shepherd	31	0-2-2-1-4	0	4029
7	Terry Labonte	31	3-1-1-0-1	0	3876
8	Jeff Gordon	31	2-1-1-2-1	1	3776
9	Darrell Waltrip	31	0-0-2-2-0	0	3688
10	Bill Elliott	31	1-1-3-0-1	1	3617

1995 SEASON (through Oct. 1)

		Sts	Finishes 1-2-3-4-5	PW	Pts
1	Jeff Gordon	27	7-4-5-0-0	8*	4201
2	Dale Earnhardt	27	4-5-4-1-2	3	3899
3	Sterling Marlin	27	3-1-0-2-1	1	3749
4	Mark Martin	27	3-1-3-1-3	4	3716
5	Rusty Wallace	27	2-3-4-1-1	0	3597
6	Terry Labonte	27	3-4-1-2-2	1	3568
7	Ted Musgrave	27	0-2-2-2-1	1	3514
8	Bobby Labonte	27	3-3-0-0-1	2	3329
9	Michael Waltrip	27	0-0-1-0-1	0	3252
10	Bill Elliott	27	0-0-0-1-2	1	3218

Other wins (10): Geoff Bodine and Ernie Irvan (3); Jimmy Spencer (2); Dale Jarrett and Sterling Marlin.

*Doesn't include pole awarded at Goody's 500 (see page 863). **Other wins** (2): Dale Jarrett and Kyle Petty.

Top 5 Finishing Order + Pole
1995 SEASON (through Oct. 1)

No.		Winner	2nd	3rd	4th	5th	Pole
1	Daytona 500	S. Marlin	D. Earnhardt	M. Martin	T. Musgrave	D. Jarrett	D. Jarrett
2	Goodwrench 500	J. Gordon	B. Labonte	D. Earnhardt	R. Rudd	D. Jarrett	J. Gordon
3	Pontiac 400	T. Labonte	D. Earnhardt	R. Wallace	K. Schrader	S. Marlin	J. Gordon
4	Purolator 500	J. Gordon	B. Labonte	T. Labonte	D. Earnhardt	D. Jarrett	D. Earnhardt
5	TranSouth 400	S. Marlin	D. Earnhardt	T. Musgrave	T. Bodine	D. Cope	J. Gordon
6	Food City 500	J. Gordon	R. Wallace	D. Waltrip	B. Hamilton	R. Rudd	M. Martin
7	First Union 400	D. Earnhardt	J. Gordon	M. Martin	R. Wallace	S. Grissom	J. Gordon
8	Hanes 500	R. Wallace	T. Musgrave	J. Gordon	D. Waltrip	M. Martin	B. Labonte
9	Winston 500	M. Martin	J. Gordon	M. Shepard	D. Waltrip	B. Labonte	T. Labonte
10	Save Mart 300	D. Earnhardt	M. Martin	J. Gordon	R. Rudd	T. Labonte	R. Rudd
11	Coca-Cola 600	B. Labonte	T. Labonte	M. Waltrip	S. Marlin	R. Rudd	J. Gordon
12	Genuine Draft 500	K. Petty	B. Labonte	T. Musgrave	H. Stricklin	D. Earnhardt	J. Gordon
13	UAW-GM 500	T. Labonte	T. Musgrave	K. Schrader	S. Marlin	H. Stricklin	K. Schrader
14	Miller 400	B. Labonte	J. Gordon	R. Wallace	J. Andretti	M. Shepherd	J. Gordon
15	Pepsi 400	J. Gordon	S. Marlin	D. Earnhardt	M. Martin	T. Musgrave	D. Earnhardt
16	Slick 50 300	J. Gordon	M. Shepherd	M. Martin	T. Labonte	R. Rudd	M. Martin
17	Miller 500	D. Jarrett	J. Gordon	R. Rudd	T. Musgrave	B. Elliott	B. Elliott
18	DieHard 500	S. Marlin	D. Jarrett	D. Earnhardt	M. Shepherd	B. Elliott	S. Marlin
19	Brickyard 400	D. Earnhardt	R. Wallace	D. Jarrett	B. Elliott	M. Martin	J. Gordon
20	Bud at the Glen	M. Martin	W. Dallenbach	J. Gordon	R. Rudd	T. Labonte	M. Martin
21	Goodwrench 400	B. Labonte	T. Labonte	J. Gordon	S. Marlin	R. Wallace	B. Labonte
22	Goody's 500	T. Labonte	D. Earnhardt	D. Jarrett	D. Waltrip	M. Martin	M. Martin
23	Southern 500	J. Gordon	D. Earnhardt	R. Wallace	W. Burton	M. Waltrip	J. Andretti
24	Miller 400	R. Wallace	T. Labonte	D. Earnhardt	D. Jarrett	B. Hamilton	D. Earnhardt
25	Delaware 500	J. Gordon	B. Hamilton	R. Wallace	J. Nemechek	D. Earnhardt	R. Mast
26	Goody's 500	D. Earnhardt	T. Labonte	R. Wallace	B. Hamilton	G. Bodine	J. Gordon
27	Holly Farms 400	M. Martin	R. Wallace	J. Gordon	T. Labonte	R. Rudd	T. Musgrave

Money Leaders
FINAL 1994

		Earnings			Earnings			Earnings
1	Dale Earnhardt	$3,300,733	6	Geoff Bodine	$1,276,126	11	Ricky Rudd	$1,044,441
2	Rusty Wallace	1,914,072	7	Ken Schrader	1,171,062	12	Bill Elliott	936,779
3	Jeff Gordon	1,779,523	8	Sterling Marlin	1,127,683	13	Dale Jarrett	881,754
4	Mark Martin	1,628,906	9	Terry Labonte	1,125,921	14	Darrell Waltrip	835,680
5	Ernie Irvan	1,311,522	10	Morgan Shepherd	1,089,038	15	Lake Speed	832,463

1995 SEASON (through Oct. 1)

		Earnings			Earnings			Earnings
1	Jeff Gordon	$2,325,440	6	Bobby Labonte	$1,188,560	11	Geoff Bodine	$830,785
2	Dale Earnhardt	2,066,495	7	Terry Labonte	1,168,300	12	Morgan Shepherd	781,891
3	Sterling Marlin	1,551,185	8	Dale Jarrett	1,135,714	13	Ken Schrader	747,445
4	Mark Martin	1,332,266	9	Ricky Rudd	933,689	14	Michael Waltrip	739,295
5	Rusty Wallace	1,215,210	10	Ted Musgrave	873,000	15	Brett Bodine	732,611

INDYCAR RESULTS

1995 SEASON

Date		Location	Winner (Pos)	Time	Avg.mpg	Pole	Qual.mph
Mar. 5	GP of Miami	Miami	Jacques Villeneuve (8)	1:59:16.863	82.801	M. Andretti	104.892†
Mar. 19	Australian GP	Queensland	Paul Tracy (9)	1:58:26.054	92.335	M. Andretti	104.313
Apr. 2	Slick-50 200	Phoenix	Robby Gordon (9)	1:29:33.930	133.980	B. Herta	181.952†
Apr. 9	GP of Long Beach	Long Beach	Al Unser Jr. (4)	1:49:32.667	91.442	M. Andretti	109.066
Apr. 23	Bosch GP	Nazareth	Emerson Fittipaldi (4)	1:31:23.410	131.305	R. Gordon	187.441†
May 28	**Indianapolis 500**	Indianapolis	Jacques Villeneuve (5)	3:15:17.561	153.616	S. Brayton	231.604
June 4	Miller 200	Milwaukee	Paul Tracy (7)	1:27:23.853	137.304	T. Fabi	162.456
June 11	Detroit GP	Belle Isle	Robby Gordon (1)	1:56:11.607	83.499	R. Gordon	108.318
June 25	Bud/GI Joe's 200	Portland	Al Unser Jr. (3)	1:54:49.410	103.933	J. Villeneuve	117.614†
July 9	Texaco/Havoline 200	Elkhart Lake	Jacques Villeneuve (1)	1:55:29.659	103.901	J. Villeneuve	142.206
July 16	Molson Indy	Toronto	Michael Andretti (6)	1:50:25.202	94.787	J. Villeneuve	110.396†
July 23	GP of Cleveland	Cleveland	Jacques Villeneuve (2)	1:38:19.151	130.113	G. de Ferran	147.512†
July 30	Marlboro 500	Michigan	Scott Pruett (12)	3:07:52.826	159.676	P. Johnstone	230.458
Aug. 13	Miller 200	Mid-Ohio	Al Unser Jr. (4)	1:44:04.774	107.110	J. Villeneuve	121.192
Aug. 20	New England 200	Loudon	Andre Ribeiro (1)	1:34:36.192	134.203	A. Ribeiro	177.436†
Sept. 3	Molson Indy	Vancouver	Al Unser Jr. (9)	1:46:54.900	95.571	J. Villeneuve	111.013
Sept. 10	Toyota GP	Monterey	Gil de Ferran (3)	1:53:17.579	98.493	J. Villeneuve	114.476

†Track record.
Winning cars: REYNARD/FORD-COSWORTH (6)— Villeneuve 4, Gordon 2; PENSKE/MERCEDES-BENZ (5)— Unser 4, Fittipaldi; LOLA/FORD COSWORTH (4)— Tracy 2, Andretti, Pruett; REYNARD/HONDA (1)— Ribeiro; REYNARD/MERCEDES-BENZ (1)— de Ferran.

IndyCar Results (Cont.)

1995 Race Locations

March— MARLBORO GRAND PRIX OF MIAMI at Bicentennial Park; INDYCAR AUSTRALIAN at Surfers Paradise, Queensland. **April**— SLICK-50 200 at Phoenix International Raceway; TOYOTA GP OF LONG BEACH at Long Beach, Calif.; BOSCH SPARK PLUG GP at Nazareth (Pa.) Speedway. **May**— INDIANAPOLIS 500 at Indianapolis Motor Speedway. **June**— MILLER GENUINE DRAFT 200 at Wisconsin State Fair Park Speedway in West Allis; ITT AUTOMOTIVE DETROIT GP at Belle Isle Park; BUDWEISER/G.I. JOE'S 200 Presented by Texaco/Havoline at Portland (Ore.) International Raceway.

July— TEXACO/HAVOLINE 200 at Road America in Elkart Lake, Wisc.; MOLSON INDY TORONTO at Exhibition Place; MEDIC DRUG GP OF CLEVELAND Presented by Dairy Mart at Burke Lakefront Airport; MARLBORO 500 at Michigan International Speedway in Brooklyn. **August**— MILLER GENUINE DRAFT 200 at Mid-Ohio Sports Car Course in Lexington; NEW ENGLAND 200 at New Hampshire International Speedway in Loudon. **September**— MOLSON INDY VANCOUVER at Pacific Place; TOYOTA GRAND PRIX OF MONTEREY at Laguna Seca (Calif.) Raceway.

1995 Indianapolis 500

Date— Sunday, May 28, 1995, at Indianapolis Motor Speedway. **Distance**— 500 miles; **Course**— 2.5 mile oval; **Field**—33 cars; **Winner's average speed**— 153.616 mph; **Margin of victory**— 2.481 seconds; **Time of race**— 3 hours, 15 minutes, 17.561 seconds; **Caution flags**— 9 for 68 laps; **Lead changes**— 23 by 10 drivers; **Lap leaders**— Gugelmin (59 laps), Goodyear (43), Andretti (41), Vasser (20), Villeneuve (19), Pruett (8), Luyendyk (7), Boesel (2), Rahal (1). **Pole sitter**— Scott Brayton at 231.604 mph; **Attendance**— 400,000 (estimated); **TV Rating**— 8.4 share (26). Note that (r) indicates rookie driver.

Driver (Pos.)	Residence	Car	Laps	Ended	Earnings
1 Jacques Villeneuve (5)	Montreal, Canada	Reynard-Ford	200	Running	$1,312,019
2 r-Christian Fittipaldi (27)	São Paulo, Brazil	Reynard-Ford	200	Running	594,668
3 Bobby Rahal (21)	Dublin, Ohio	Lola-Mercedes	200	Running	373,267
4 r-Eliseo Salazar (24)	Indianapolis, Ind.	Lola-Ford	200	Running	302,417
5 Robby Gordon (7)	Orange, Calif.	Reynard-Ford	200	Running	247,917
6 Mauricio Gugelmin (6)	Ft. Lauderdale, Fla.	Reynard-Ford	200	Running	284,667
7 Arie Luyendyk (2)	Scottsdale, Ariz.	Lola-Menard	200	Running	247,417
8 Teo Fabi (15)	Monte Carlo	Reynard-Ford	199	Running	206,853
9 Danny Sullivan (18)	Aspen, Colo.	Reynard-Ford	199	Running	193,453
10 Hiro Matsushita (10)	San Clemente, Calif.	Reynard-Ford	199	Running	196,053
11 r-Alessandro Zampedri (17)	Brescia, Italy	Lola-Ford	198	Running	199,153
12 Roberto Guerrero (13)	S.J. Capistrano, Calif.	Reynard-Mercedes	198	Running	181,203
13 Bryan Herta (33)	Indianapolis, Ind.	Reynard-Ford	198	Running	175,903
14 Scott Goodyear (3)	Carmel, Ind.	Reynard-Honda	195	Running	246,403
15 Hideshi Matsuda (20)	Japan	Lola-Ford	194	Running	200,503
16 Stefan Johansson (31)	Indianapolis, Ind.	Reynard-Ford	192	Running	182,703
17 Scott Brayton (1)	Coldwater, Mich.	Lola-Menard	190	Running	306,503
18 r-Andre Ribeiro (12)	São Paulo, Brazil	Reynard-Honda	187	Running	176,753
19 Scott Pruett (8)	Crystal Bay, Nev.	Lola-Ford	184	Crash	164,953
20 Raul Boesel (22)	Key Biscayne, Fla.	Lola-Mercedes	184	Running	169,053
21 Adrian Fernandez (25)	La Jolla, Calif.	Lola-Mercedes	176	Running	183,903
22 Jimmy Vasser (9)	Discovery Bay, Calif.	Reynard-Ford	170	Crash	162,003
23 Davy Jones (32)	Tahoe, Nev.	Lola-Ford	161	Crash	182,303
24 Paul Tracy (16)	Paradise Valley, Ariz.	Lola-Ford	136	Throttle	149,703
25 Michael Andretti (4)	Nazareth, Pa.	Lola-Ford	77	Suspension	192,053
26 Scott Sharp (30)	East Norwalk, Conn.	Lola-Ford	74	Crash	158,003
27 Buddy Lazier (23)	Vail, Colo.	Lola-Menard	45	Fuel System	145,903
28 Eric Bachelart (26)	Belgium	Lola-Ford	6	Mechanical	155,003
29 r-Gil de Ferran (19)	Indianapolis, Ind.	Reynard-Mercedes	1	Crash	149,453
30 Stan Fox (11)	Janesville, Wisc.	Reynard-Ford	0	Crash	143,603
31 Eddie Cheever (14)	Aspen, Colo.	Lola-Ford	0	Crash	144,103
32 Lyn St. James (28)	Daytona Beach, Fla.	Lola-Ford	0	Crash	127,500
33 r-Carlos Guerrero (29)	Mexico City, Mexico	Lola-Ford	0	Crash	172,853

PPG World Series Point Standings

Official Top 10 PPG Cup point leaders and Top 15 money leaders for 1993 and 1994. Points awarded for places 1 to 12, fastest qualifier and overall lap leader. Listed are starts (Sts), Top 5 finishes, poles won (PW) and points (Pts).

		Finishes					Finishes		
FINAL 1994	Sts	1-2-3-4-5	PW	Pts	**FINAL 1995**	Sts	1-2-3-4-5	PW	Pts
1 Al Unser Jr	16	8-3-0-0-0	4	225	1 Jacques Villeneuve	17	4-1-1-1-1	6	173
2 Emerson Fittipaldi	16	1-4-5-1-0	2	178	2 Al Unser Jr	15	4-2-1-0-1	0	140
3 Paul Tracy	16	3-2-3-0-1	4	152	3 Bobby Rahal	17	0-2-3-1-2	0	130
4 Michael Andretti	16	2-0-1-1-3	0	118	4 Michael Andretti	17	1-2-1-3-0	3	125
5 Robby Gordon	16	0-1-2-2-1	2	104	5 Robby Gordon	16	2-0-1-1-3	1	122
6 Jacques Villeneuve	15	1-1-1-1-0	0	94	6 Paul Tracy	17	2-3-0-1-0	0	115
7 Raul Boesel	16	0-1-0-3-0	1	90	7 Scott Pruett	17	1-1-1-1-0	0	113
8 Nigel Mansell	16	0-2-1-0-2	3	88	8 Jimmy Vasser	17	0-2-2-0-0	0	96
9 Teo Fabi	16	0-0-0-3-0	0	79	9 Teo Fabi	17	0-0-1-3-0	1	83
10 Bobby Rahal	16	0-1-1-0-0	0	59	10 Mauricio Gugelmin	17	0-1-1-1-1	0	82

Top 5 Finishing Order + Pole
1995 Season

No.		Winner	2nd	3rd	4th	5th	Pole
1	Miami GP	J. Villeneuve	M. Gugelmin	B. Rahal	S. Pruett	C. Fittipaldi	M. Andretti
2	Australian GP	P. Tracy	B. Rahal	S. Pruett	M. Gugelmin	D. Sullivan	M. Andretti
3	Phoenix	R. Gordon	M. Andretti	E. Fittipaldi	P. Tracy	J. Villeneuve	B. Herta
4	Long Beach	A. Unser Jr.	S. Pruett	T. Fabi	E. Cheever	M. Gugelmin	M. Andretti
5	Bosch GP	E. Fittipaldi	J. Villeneuve	S. Johansson	R. Gordon	E. Cheever	R. Gordon
6	Indianapolis	J. Villeneuve	C. Fittipaldi	B. Rahal	E. Salazar	R. Gordon	S. Brayton
7	Milwaukee	P. Tracy	A. Unser Jr.	M. Andretti	T. Fabi	R. Gordon	T. Fabi
8	Detroit	R. Gordon	J. Vasser	S. Pruett	M. Andretti	A. Unser Jr.	R. Gordon
9	Portland	A. Unser Jr.	J. Vasser	B. Rahal	M. Andretti	R. Boesel	J. Villeneuve
10	Road America	J. Villeneuve	P. Tracy	J. Vasser	A. Ribeiro	B. Rahal	J. Villeneuve
11	Toronto	M. Andretti	B. Rahal	J. Villeneuve	T. Fabi	R. Gordon	J. Villeneuve
12	Cleveland	J. Villeneuve	B. Herta	J. Vasser	B. Rahal	D. Sullivan	G. de Ferran
13	Michigan	S. Pruett	A. Unser Jr.	A. Fernandez	T. Fabi	E. Fittipaldi	P. Johnstone
14	Mid-Ohio	A. Unser Jr.	P. Tracy	J. Villeneuve	A. Fernandez	B. Herta	J. Villeneuve
15	New Hampshire	A. Ribiero	M. Andretti	A. Unser Jr.	J. Villeneuve	E. Fittipaldi	A. Ribeiro
16	Vancouver	A. Unser Jr.	G. de Ferran	R. Gordon	S. Johansson	B. Rahal	J. Villeneuve
17	Monterey	G. de Ferran	P. Tracy	M. Gugelmin	M. Andretti	S. Pruett	J. Villeneuve

Money Leaders
FINAL 1994

	Earnings			Earnings			Earnings
1 Al Unser Jr.	$3,535,813	6 Michael Andretti	$1,037,063		11 Jimmy Vasser	$753,163
2 Emerson Fittipaldi	1,604,163	7 Bobby Rahal	978,413		12 Scott Goodyear	724,062
3 Paul Tracy	1,267,862	8 Raul Boesel	881,612		13 Stefan Johansson	710,613
4 Robby Gordon	1,135,063	9 Teo Fabi	875,813		14 Mauricio Gugelmin	694,563
5 Jacques Villeneuve	1,101,463	10 Nigel Mansell	866,562		15 Adrian Fernandez	676,112

FINAL 1995

	Earnings			Earnings			Earnings
1 Jacques Villeneuve	$2,996,269	6 Christian Fittipaldi	$1,109,918		11 Gil de Ferran	$800,453
2 Bobby Rahal	1,390,017	7 Mauricio Gugelmin	1,022,667		12 Eliseo Salazar	790,417
3 Al Unser Jr.	1,369,000	8 Paul Tracy	1,012,953		13 Adrian Fernandez	782,903
4 Robby Gordon	1,235,667	9 Teo Fabi	991,603		14 Stefan Johansson	749,453
5 Michael Andretti	1,143,303	10 Jimmy Vasser	940,003		15 Raul Boesel	724,303

FORMULA ONE RESULTS

Winners of Formula One races through Oct. 1 (see Updates chapter for later results).

1995 SEASON (through Oct. 1)

Date	Grand Prix	Location	Winner (Pos.)	Time	Avg. mpg	Pole	Qual.mph
Mar. 26	Brazilian	São Paulo	M. Schumacher (2)	1:38:34.154	116.150	D. Hill	120.812
Apr. 9	Argentine	Buenos Aires	Damon Hill (2)	1:53:14.532	100.901	D. Coulthard	84.131†
Apr. 30	San Marino	Imola	Damon Hill (4)	1:41:42.552	113.041	M. Schumacher	125.465
May 14	Spanish	Barcelona	M. Schumacher (1)	1:34:20.507	121.366	M. Schumacher	129.819
May 28	Monaco	Monte Carlo	M. Schumacher (2)	1:53:11.258	85.503	D. Hill	90.840
June 12	Canadian	Montreal	Jean Alesi (5)	1:46:31.333	106.747	M. Schumacher	113.045
July 2	French	Magny-Cours	M. Schumacher (2)	1:38:28.429	115.806	D. Hill	123.107
July 16	British	Silverstone	Johnny Hebert (5)	1:34:35.093	128.367	D. Hill	128.367
July 30	German	Hockenheim	M. Schumacher (2)	1:22:56.043	138.019	D. Hill	146.214
Aug. 13	Hungarian	Budapest	Damon Hill (1)	1:46:25.721	107.047	D. Hill	115.302
Aug. 27	Belgian	Spa-Fran'champs	M. Schumacher (16)	1:36:47.875	118.878	G. Berger	136.377
Sept. 10	Italian	Monza	Johnny Hebert (8)	1:18:27.916	146.134	D. Coulthard	152.816
Sept. 24	Portuguese	Estoril	David Coulthard (1)	1:40:52.145	113.293	D. Coulthard	121.100
Oct. 1	European	Nurburgring	M. Schumacher (3)	1:39:59.044	109.908	D. Coulthard	129.435

†Track record.

Winning Constructors: BENETTON-FORD (9)— Schumacher 7, Hebert 2; WILLIAMS-RENAULT (4)— Hill 3; Coulthard; FERRARI (1)— Alesi (1).

1995 Race Locations

March— BRAZILIAN GP at Interlagos in São Paulo. **April**— ARGENTINE GP at Buenos Aires; SAN MARINO GP at Imola, Italy. **May**— SPANISH GP at Catalunya in Barcelona; GP of MONACO at Monte Carlo. **June**— CANADIAN GP at Circuit Gilles Villeneuve in Montreal. **July**— FRENCH GP at Magny-Cours; BRITISH GP at Silverstone in Towcester; GERMAN GP at Hockenheimring in Hockenheim. **August**— HUNGARIAN GP at Hungaroring in Budapest; BELGIAN GP at Spa-Francorchamps. **September**— ITALIAN GP at Monza in Milan; PORTUGUESE GP at Estoril. **October**— EUROPEAN GP at Nurburgring in Germany; PACIFIC GP at T1 Circuit in Aida, Japan; JAPANESE GP at Suzuka. **November**— AUSTRALIAN GP at Adelaide.

Formula One Results (Cont.)

World Championship Point Standings

Official Top 10 Formula One World Championship point leaders for 1994 and unofficial Top 10 point leaders for 1995 (through Oct. 1). Points awarded for places 1 through 6 only (i.e., 10-6-4-3-2-1). Listed are starts (Sts), Top 6 finishes, poles won (PW) and points (Pts).

Note: Formula One does not keep Money Leader standings.

FINAL 1994

		Sts	Finishes 1-2-3-4-5-6	PW	Pts
1	Michael Schumacher	14	8-2-0-0-0-0	6	92
2	Damon Hill	16	6-5-0-0-0-1	2	91
3	Gerhard Berger	16	1-3-2-1-1-0	2	41
4	Mika Hakkinen	15	0-1-5-0-0-0	0	26
5	Jean Alesi	14	0-1-3-1-1-1	1	24
6	Rubens Barrichello	15	0-0-1-5-0-0	1	19
7	Martin Brundle	16	0-1-1-1-1-1	0	16
8	David Coulthard	8	0-1-0-1-2-1	0	14
9	Nigel Mansell	4	1-0-0-1-0-0	1	13
10	Joos Verstappen	10	0-0-2-0-1-0	0	10

1995 SEASON (through Oct. 1)

		Sts	Finishes 1-2-3-4-5-6	PW	Pts
1	Michael Schumacher	14	7-1-1-0-1-0	3	82
2	Damon Hill	14	3-3-1-1-0-0	6	55
3	David Coulthard	14	1-3-3-1-0-0	3	43
4	Johnny Hebert	14	2-1-0-4-1-0	0	40
	Jean Alesi	14	1-4-0-0-3-0	0	40
6	Gerhard Berger	14	0-0-6-1-0-1	1	28
7	Heinz-Harald Frentzen	14	0-0-1-1-2-4	0	15
8	Mika Hakkinen	14	0-1-0-1-1-0	0	11
	Rubens Barrichello	14	0-1-0-1-0-2	0	11
10	Mark Blundell	12	0-0-0-1-3-1	0	10

Top 5 Finishing Order + Pole

1995 SEASON (through Oct. 1)

No.		Winner	2nd	3rd	4th	5th	Pole
1	Brazil	M. Schumacher	D. Coulthard	G. Berger	M. Hakkinen	J. Alesi	D. Hill
2	Argentina	D. Hill	J. Alesi	M. Schumacher	J. Hebert	H. Frentzen	D. Coulthard
3	San Marino	D. Hill	J. Alesi	G. Berger	D. Coulthard	M. Hakkinen	M. Schumacher
4	Spain	M. Schumacher	J. Herbert	G. Berger	D. Hill	E. Irvine	M. Schumacher
5	Monaco	M. Schumacher	D. Hill	G. Berger	J. Hebert	M. Blundell	D. Hill
6	Canada	J. Alesi	R. Barrichello	E. Irvine	O. Panis	M. Schumacher	M. Schumacher
7	France	M. Schumacher	D. Hill	D. Coulthard	M. Brundle	J. Alesi	D. Hill
8	Britain	J. Hebert	J. Alesi	D. Coulthard	O. Panis	M. Blundell	D. Hill
9	Germany	M. Schumacher	D. Coulthard	G. Berger	J. Hebert	J. Boullion	D. Hill
10	Hungary	D. Hill	D. Coulthard	G. Berger	J. Hebert	H. Frentzen	D. Hill
11	Belgium	M. Schumacher	D. Hill	M. Brundle	H. Frentzen	M. Blundell	G. Berger
12	Italy	J. Hebert	M. Hakkinen	H. Frentzen	M. Blunell	M. Salo	D. Coulthard
13	Portugal	D. Coulthard	M. Schumacher	D. Hill	G. Berger	J. Alesi	D. Coulthard
14	European	M. Schumacher	J. Alesi	D. Coulthard	R. Barrichello	J. Hebert	D. Coulthard

---

1995 Endurance Races

24 Hours of Daytona

at Daytona Beach, Fla. (Feb. 4-5).

Officially the Rolex 24 Hours at Daytona and first held in 1962 (as a 3-hour race). An IMSA Camel GT race for exotic prototype sports cars and contested over a 3.56-mile road course at Daytona International Speedway. Listed are qualifying position, drivers, chassis, and laps completed.

1 (17) Jurgen Lassig, Christophe Bouchut, Giovanni Lavaggi and Marco Werner; PORSCHE SPYDER K8; 690 laps (2,456.4 miles) at 102.280 mph; 5-lap margin of victory (2:55.54).

2 (4) Jeremy Dale, Price Cobb, Jay Cochran and Fredrick Ekblom; OLDS SPICE BDG 02; 685 laps.

3 (15) Paul Newman, Michael Brockman, Tommy Kendall and Mark Martin; FORD MUSTANG; 682 laps.

4 (21) Jochen Rohr, Hurley Haywood, Dave Murry and Berno Maylaender; PORSCHE 911 RSR; 655 laps.

5 (36) Lilian Bryner, Enzo Calderari, Renato Mastropleto and Ulrich Richter; PORSCHE 911 RSR; 654 laps.

Fastest lap: Fermin Velez, FERRARI 333SP; 121.520 mph. **Top qualifier:** Mauro Baldi, FERRARI 333SP; 124.03 mph (1:43.326).

Weather: cold and clear. **Attendance:** 45,000 (est.).

24 Hours of Le Mans

at LeMans, France (June 17-18).

Officially the Le Mans Grand Prix d'Endurance and first held in 1923. Contested over the 8.457-mile Circuit de la Sarthe in Le Mans, France. Listed are drivers, countries, car, and laps completed.

1 Yannick Dalmas (FRA), J.J. Lehto (FIN) and Masanori Sekiya (JPN); McLaren BMW F1 GTR; 298 laps (2,520.16 miles) at 105 mph

2 Bob Wollek (FRA), Mario Andretti (USA) and Eric Helary (FRA); Courage Porsche C34; 297 laps.

3 Andy Wallace (GBR), Justin Bell (GBR) and Derrick Bell (GBR); McLaren BMW F1 GTR; 296 laps.

4 Ray Bellm (GBR), Maurizio Sala (ITA) and Mark Blundell (GBR); McLaren BMW F1 GTR; 291 laps

5 Fabien Giroix (FRA), Olivier Grouillard (FRA) and Jean Deletraz (SWI); McLaren BMW F1 GTR; 290 laps.

Fastest lap: William David, WR Peugeot 41LT; 131.563 mph (3:46:.05). **Top qualifier:** William David, WR Peugeot 41LT; 134.683 mph (3:46.05).

Weather: mostly wet. **Attendance:** 160,000 (est.).

NHRA RESULTS

National Hot Rod Association Drag Racing champions in the Top Fuel, Funny Car and Pro Stock divisions from Feb. 5 through Oct. 1, 1995. All times are based on two cars racing head-to-head from a standing start over a straight line, quarter-mile course. Differences in reaction time account for apparently faster losing times.

1995 SEASON (through Oct. 1)

Date	Event		Winner	Time	MPH	2nd Place	Time	MPH
Feb. 5	Winternationals	Top Fuel	Eddie Hill	4.859	299.50	S. Kalitta	11.879	77.31
		Funny Car	Cruz Pedregon	5.304	278.72	C. Etchells	broke	—
		Pro Stock	Darrell Alderman	7.054	196.03	S. Geoffrion	7.105	195.18
Feb. 19	ATSCO Nationals	Top Fuel	Larry Dixon	4.821	300.00	S. Anderson	8.378	89.48
		Funny Car	John Force	5.057	298.30	T. Hoover	5.404	238.28
		Pro Stock	Darrell Alderman	7.073	194.46	J. Eckman	7.626	144.92
Mar. 12	Slick 50 Nationals	Top Fuel	Mike Dunn	4.857	296.34	K. Bernstein	8.292	87.67
		Funny Car	Al Hofmann	5.207	293.15	M. Oswald	5.315	284.53
		Pro Stock	Scott Geoffrion	7.062	196.03	J. Yates	7.096	195.22
Apr. 2	Gatornationals	Top Fuel	Connie Kalitta	4.794	290.79	S. Kalitta	4.954	271.65
		Funny Car	John Force	5.347	263.00	K.C. Spurlock	6.372	149.80
		Pro Stock	Warren Johnson	7.136	195.14	D. Alderman	7.119*	195.27
Apr. 24	Fram Nationals	Top Fuel	Cory McClenathan	4.806	298.90	R. Capps	5.079	236.34
		Funny Car	John Force	5.174	297.22	C. Pedregon	13.321	73.14
		Pro Stock	Mark Osborne	7.141	194.17	D. Alderman	broke	—
May 7	Mid-South Nationals	Top Fuel	Cory McClenathan	4.810	307.48	M. Dunn	4.997	288.27
		Funny Car	Gary Clapshaw	5.339	286.89	G. Densham	5.457	276.66
		Pro Stock	Mark Pawuk	7.195	192.80	J. Eckman	7.213	192.84
May 21	Mopar Nationals	Top Fuel	Larry Dixon	4.991	281.77	S. Kalitta	5.020	290.79
		Funny Car	Cruz Pedregon	5.246	294.31	D. Skuza	7.407	121.11
		Pro Stock	Bob Glidden	7.117	194.42	J. Yates	7.123	194.67
June 4	Virginia Nationals	Top Fuel	Cory McClenathan	4.962	293.82	B. Johnson	4.980	282.39
		Funny Car	John Force	5.193	270.59	K.C. Spurlock	5.570	246.23
		Pro Stock	Warren Johnson	7.062	196.03	J. Yates	7.190	195.18
June 12	Springnationals	Top Fuel	Scott Kalitta	4.772	305.18	E. Hill	4.884	287.53
		Funny Car	Al Hofmann	5.125	299.90	J. Force	9.542	85.39
		Pro Stock	Steve Schmidt	7.125	193.21	W. Johnson	7.121	192.47
July 2	West. Auto Nationals	Top Fuel	Scott Kalitta	4.820	295.27	K. Bernstein	9.548	88.85
		Funny Car	Cruz Pedregon	5.192	273.39	K.C. Spurlock	9.434	98.25
		Pro Stock	Warren Johnson	7.069	194.46	J. Yates	7.128	193.54
July 23	Mile-High Nationals	Top Fuel	Scott Kalitta	4.813	298.30	B. Johnson	5.022	261.17
		Funny Car	John Force	5.258	291.16	A. Hofmann	10.175	82.36
		Pro Stock	Kurt Johnson	7.491	183.29	J. Yates	7.465	183.00
July 30	Autolight Nationals	Top Fuel	Mike Dunn	5.107	276.83	P. Austin	6.432	141.37
		Funny Car	Al Hofmann	5.302	281.07	J. Force	5.330	286.44
		Pro Stock	Jim Yates	7.143	193.79	W. Johnson	7.138	194.55
Aug. 8	Northwest Nationals	Top Fuel	Ron Capps	4.930	295.76	C. McClenathan	12.367	77.64
		Funny Car	Al Hofmann	5.200	285.80	G. Densham	5.299	279.93
		Pro Stock	Warren Johnson	7.022	197.23	B. Glidden	7.056	195.73
Aug. 20	Champion Nationals	Top Fuel	Mike Dunn	4.952	291.63	T. Johnson Jr.	6.243	160.68
		Funny Car	John Force	5.284	291.92	G. Densham	5.850	231.06
		Pro Stock	Warren Johnson	7.202	193.05	J. Yates	7.194	191.24
Sept. 4	U.S. Nationals	Top Fuel	Larry Dixon	4.931	293.25	B. Vendorgriff Jr.	5.330	181.59
		Funny Car	Cruz Pedregon	5.075	304.67	J. Force	5.228	290.60
		Pro Stock	Warren Johnson	7.059	197.02	L. Warden	7.126	192.51
Sept. 17	Keystone Nationals	Top Fuel	Scott Kalitta	4.801	298.90	L. Dixon	5.937	150.88
		Funny Car	Chuck Etchells	6.121	264.31	J. Force	6.350	242.19
		Pro Stock	Warren Johnson	7.060	195.43	M. Pawuk	8.980	101.63
Oct. 1	Sears Nationals	Top Fuel	Scott Kalitta	4.756	295.46	M. Dunn	5.143	214.43
		Funny Car	Cruz Pedregon	5.068	301.81	A. Hofmann	5.148	296.05
		Pro Stock	Steve Schmidt	7.076	194.67	J. Eckman	10.867	83.36

*False start.

Winston Point Standings

1995 (through Oct. 1)

First place finishes in parentheses.

Top Fuel

		Pts
1	Scott Kalitta (5)	1,381
2	Cory McClenathan (3)	1,233
3	Mike Dunn (3)	1,189
4	Larry Dixon (4)	1,169
5	Blaine Johnson	1,025

Funny Car

		Pts
1	John Force (6)	1,517
2	Al Hofmann (4)	1,320
3	Cruz Pedregon (5)	1,217
4	Chuck Etchells (1)	1,031
5	Dean Skuza	874

Pro Stock

		Pts
1	Warren Johnson (6)	1,479
2	Jim Yates (1)	1,262
3	Kurt Johnson (1)	1,009
4	Jerry Eckman	916
5	Steve Schmidt (2)	902

THE 1996 SPORTS ALMANAC — INFORMATION PLEASE

AUTO RACING STATISTICS

THROUGH THE YEARS 1911-1995

MAJOR RACES • LEADERS

SEC **B**

PAGE **870**

NASCAR Circuit
The Crown Jewels

The four biggest races on the NASCAR circuit are the Daytona 500, the Winston Select 500, the Coca-Cola 600 and the Mountain Dew Southern 500. The Winston Cup Media Guide lists them as the richest (Daytona), the fastest (Winston), the longest (Coca-Cola) and the oldest (Southern). Winston has offered a $1 million bonus since 1985 to any driver who can win three of the four races. The only drivers to win three of the races in a single year are Lee Roy Yarbrough (1969), David Pearson (1976) and Bill Elliott (1985).

Daytona 500

Held early in the NASCAR season; 200 laps around a 2.5-mile high-banked oval at Daytona International Speedway in Daytona Beach, FL. First race in 1959, although stock car racing at Daytona dates back to 1936. Winning drivers who started from pole positions are in **bold** type.

Multiple winners: Richard Petty (7); Cale Yarborough (4); Bobby Allison (3); Bill Elliott and Sterling Marlin (2).

Multiple poles: Buddy Baker and Cale Yarborough (4); Bill Elliott, Fireball Roberts and Ken Schrader (3); Donnie Allison (2).

Year	Winner	Car	Owner	MPH	Pole Sitter	MPH
1959	Lee Petty	Oldsmobile	Petty Enterprises	135.521	Bob Welborn	140.121
1960	Junior Johnson	Chevrolet	Ray Fox	124.740	Cotton Owens	149.892
1961	Marvin Panch	Pontiac	Smokey Yunick	149.601	Fireball Roberts	155.709
1962	**Fireball Roberts**	Pontiac	Smokey Yunick	152.529	Fireball Roberts	156.999
1963	Tiny Lund	Ford	Wood Brothers	151.566	Fireball Roberts	160.943
1964	Richard Petty	Plymouth	Petty Enterprises	154.334	Paul Goldsmith	174.910
1965-a	Fred Lorenzen	Ford	Holman-Moody	141.539	Darel Dieringer	171.151
1966-b	**Richard Petty**	Plymouth	Petty Enterprises	160.627	Richard Petty	175.165
1967	Mario Andretti	Ford	Holman-Moody	149.926	Curtis Turner	180.831
1968	**Cale Yarborough**	Mercury	Wood Brothers	143.251	Cale Yarborough	189.222
1969	Lee Roy Yarbrough	Ford	Junior Johnson	157.950	Buddy Baker	188.901
1970	Pete Hamilton	Plymouth	Petty Enterprises	149.601	Cale Yarborough	194.015
1971	Richard Petty	Plymouth	Petty Enterprises	144.462	A.J. Foyt	182.744
1972	A.J. Foyt	Mercury	Wood Brothers	161.550	Bobby Issac	186.632
1973	Richard Petty	Dodge	Petty Enterprises	157.205	Buddy Baker	185.662
1974-c	Richard Petty	Dodge	Petty Enterprises	140.894	David Pearson	185.017
1975	Benny Parsons	Chevrolet	L.G. DeWitt	153.649	Donnie Allison	185.827
1976	David Pearson	Mercury	Wood Brothers	152.181	Ramo Stott	183.456
1977	Cale Yarborough	Chevrolet	Junior Johnson	153.218	Donnie Allison	188.048
1978	Bobby Allison	Ford	Bud Moore	159.730	Cale Yarborough	187.536
1979	Richard Petty	Oldsmobile	Petty Enterprises	143.977	Buddy Baker	196.049
1980	**Buddy Baker**	Oldsmobile	Ranier Racing	177.602*	Buddy Baker	194.099
1981	Richard Petty	Buick	Petty Enterprises	169.651	Bobby Allison	194.624
1982	Bobby Allison	Buick	DiGard Racing	153.991	Benny Parsons	196.317
1983	Cale Yarborough	Pontiac	Ranier Racing	155.979	Ricky Rudd	198.864
1984	**Cale Yarborough**	Chevrolet	Ranier Racing	150.994	Cale Yarborough	201.848
1985	**Bill Elliott**	Ford	Melling Racing	172.265	Bill Elliott	205.114
1986	Geoff Bodine	Chevrolet	Hendrick Motorsports	148.124	Bill Elliott	205.039
1987	**Bill Elliott**	Ford	Melling Racing	176.263	Bill Elliott	210.364†
1988	Bobby Allison	Buick	Stavola Brothers	137.531	Ken Schrader	198.823
1989	Darrell Waltrip	Chevrolet	Hendrick Motorsports	148.466	Ken Schrader	196.996
1990	Derrike Cope	Chevrolet	Bob Whitcomb	165.761	Ken Schrader	196.515
1991	Ernie Irvan	Chevrolet	Morgan-McClure	148.148	Davey Allison	195.955
1992	Davey Allison	Ford	Robert Yates	160.256	Sterling Martin	192.213
1993	Dale Jarrett	Chevrolet	Joe Gibbs Racing	154.972	Kyle Petty	189.426
1994	Sterling Marlin	Chevrolet	Morgan-McClure	156.931	Loy Allen	190.158
1995	Sterling Marlin	Chevrolet	Morgan-McClure	141.710	Dale Jarrett	193.498

*Track and race record for Winning Speed.   †Track and race record for Qualifying Speed.

Notes: a—rain shortened 1965 to 332+ miles; **b**—rain shortened 1966 race to 495 miles; **c**—in 1974, race shortened 50 miles due to energy crisis. **Also:** Pole sitters determined by pole qualifying race (1959-65); by two-lap average (1966-68); by fastest single lap (since 1969).

NASCAR Circuit (Cont.)

Winston Select 500

Held at Talladega (Ala.) Superspeedway. **Multiple winners:** Bobby Allison, Davey Allison, Buddy Baker and David Pearson (3); Dale Earnhardt, Darrell Waltrip and Cale Yarborough (2).

Year		Year		Year		Year	
1970	Pete Hamilton	1977	Darrell Waltrip	1983	Richard Petty	1990	Dale Earnhardt
1971	Donnie Allison	1978	Cale Yarborough	1984	Cale Yarborough	1991	Harry Gant
1972	David Pearson	1979	Bobby Allison	1985	Bill Elliott	1992	Davey Allison
1973	David Pearson			1986	Bobby Allison	1993	Ernie Irvan
1974	David Pearson	1980	Buddy Baker	1987	Davey Allison	1994	Dale Earnhardt
1975	Buddy Baker	1981	Bobby Allison	1988	Phil Parsons	1995	Mark Martin
1976	Buddy Baker	1982	Darrell Waltrip	1989	Davey Allison		

Coca-Cola 600

Held at Charlotte (N.C.) Motor Speedway. **Multiple winners:** Darrell Waltrip (5); Bobby Allison, Buddy Baker, Dale Earnhardt and David Pearson (3); Neil Bonnett, Fred Lorenzen, Jim Paschal and Richard Petty (2).

Year		Year		Year		Year	
1960	Joe Lee Johnson	1969	Lee Roy Yarbrough	1978	Darrell Waltrip	1987	Kyle Petty
1961	David Pearson			1979	Darrell Waltrip	1988	Darrell Waltrip
1962	Nelson Stacy	1970	Donnie Allison			1989	Darrell Waltrip
1963	Fred Lorenzen	1971	Bobby Allison	1980	Benny Parsons		
1964	Jim Paschal	1972	Buddy Baker	1981	Bobby Allison	1990	Rusty Wallace
1965	Fred Lorenzen	1973	Buddy Baker	1982	Neil Bonnett	1991	Davey Allison
1966	Marvin Panch	1974	David Pearson	1983	Neil Bonnett	1992	Dale Earnhardt
1967	Jim Paschal	1975	Richard Petty	1984	Bobby Allison	1993	Dale Earnhardt
1968	Buddy Baker	1976	David Pearson	1985	Darrell Waltrip	1994	Jeff Gordon
		1977	Richard Petty	1986	Dale Earnhardt	1995	Bobby Labonte

Southern 500

Held at Darlington (S.C.) International Raceway. **Multiple winners:** Cale Yarborough (5); Bobby Allison (4); Buck Baker, Dale Earnhardt, Bill Elliott, David Pearson and Herb Thomas (3); Harry Gant and Fireball Roberts (2).

Year		Year		Year		Year	
1950	Johnny Mantz	1962	Larry Frank	1974	Cale Yarborough	1985	Bill Elliott
1951	Herb Thomas	1963	Fireball Roberts	1975	Bobby Allison	1986	Tim Richmond
1952	Fonty Flock	1964	Buck Baker	1976	David Pearson	1987	Dale Earnhardt
1953	Buck Baker	1965	Ned Jarrett	1977	David Pearson	1988	Bill Elliott
1954	Herb Thomas	1966	Darel Dieringer	1978	Cale Yarborough	1989	Dale Earnhardt
1955	Herb Thomas	1967	Richard Petty	1979	David Pearson		
1956	Curtis Turner	1968	Cale Yarborough			1990	Dale Earnhardt
1957	Speedy Thompson	1969	Lee Roy Yarbrough	1980	Terry Labonte	1991	Harry Gant
1958	Fireball Roberts			1981	Neil Bonnett	1992	Darrell Waltrip
1959	Jim Reed	1970	Buddy Baker	1982	Cale Yarborough	1993	Mark Martin
		1971	Bobby Allison	1983	Bobby Allison	1994	Bill Elliott
1960	Buck Baker	1972	Bobby Allison	1984	Harry Gant	1995	Jeff Gordon
1961	Nelson Stacy	1973	Cale Yarborough				

All-Time Leaders

NASCAR's all-time Top 20 drivers in victories, pole positions and earnings based on records through 1994. Drivers active in 1995 are in **bold** type.

Victories

1	Richard Petty	200
2	David Pearson	105
3	**Darrell Waltrip**	84
	Bobby Allison	84
5	Cale Yarborough	83
6	**Dale Earnhardt**	63
7	Lee Petty	54
8	Ned Jarrett	50
	Junior Johnson	50
10	Herb Thomas	48
11	Buck Baker	46
12	**Bill Elliott**	40
	Tim Flock	40
14	**Rusty Wallace**	39
15	Bobby Isaac	37
16	Fireball Roberts	34
17	Rex White	28
18	Fred Lorenzen	26
19	Jim Paschal	25
20	Joe Weatherly	24

Pole Positions

1	Richard Petty	127
2	David Pearson	113
3	Cale Yarborough	70
4	**Darrell Waltrip**	58
5	Bobby Allison	57
6	Bobby Isaac	51
7	Junior Johnson	47
8	**Bill Elliott**	46
9	Buck Baker	44
10	Buddy Baker	40
11	Herb Thomas	38
12	Tim Flock	37
	Fireball Roberts	37
14	Ned Jarrett	36
	Rex White	36
16	**Geoff Bodine**	35
17	Fred Lorenzen	33
18	Fonty Flock	30
19	Marvin Panch	25
20	**Mark Martin**	24
	Jack Smith	24
	Alan Kulwicki	24

Earnings

1	**Dale Earnhardt**	$22,794,304
2	**Bill Elliott**	14,543,663
3	**Darrell Waltrip**	13,591,234
4	**Rusty Wallace**	11,111,883
5	**Terry Labonte**	8,096,096
6	**Ricky Rudd**	8,685,611
7	**Harry Gant**	8,438,104
8	**Geoff Bodine**	8,401,698
9	**Mark Martin**	8,137,293
10	Richard Petty	7,755,409
11	Bobby Allison	7,102,233
12	**Ken Schrader**	6,816,617
13	Davey Allison	6,726,974
14	**Kyle Petty**	6,488,824
15	**Morgan Shepherd**	5,715,816
16	**Ernie Irvin**	5,599,121
17	**Sterling Marlin**	5,098,735
18	Alan Kulwicki	5,061,202
19	Cale Yarborough	5,003,616
20	**Dave Marcis**	4,277,429

Wide World Photos   Wide World Photos

Richard Petty (left) and **Dale Earnhardt** are both NASCAR Rookies of the Year who went on to win a record seven Winston Cup driving championships. Earnhardt, who claimed his seventh title in 1994, is also the circuit's all-time money winner. Petty retired in 1992 with a record 200 victories, including seven wins in the Daytona 500.

Winston Cup Champions

Originally the Grand National Championship, 1949-70, and based on official NASCAR (National Association for Stock Car Auto Racing) records.

Multiple winners: Dale Earnhardt and Richard Petty (7); David Pearson, Lee Petty, Darrell Waltrip and Cale Yarborough (3); Buck Baker, Tim Flock, Ned Jarrett, Herb Thomas and Joe Weatherly (2).

Year		Year		Year		Year	
1949	Red Byron	1960	Rex White	1972	Richard Petty	1984	Terry Labonte
		1961	Ned Jarrett	1973	Benny Parsons	1985	Darrell Waltrip
1950	Bill Rexford	1962	Joe Weatherly	1974	Richard Petty	1986	Dale Earnhardt
1951	Herb Thomas	1963	Joe Weatherly	1975	Richard Petty	1987	Dale Earnhardt
1952	Tim Flock	1964	Richard Petty	1976	Cale Yarborough	1988	Bill Elliott
1953	Herb Thomas	1965	Ned Jarrett	1977	Cale Yarborough	1989	Rusty Wallace
1954	Lee Petty	1966	David Pearson	1978	Cale Yarborough		
1955	Tim Flock	1967	Richard Petty	1979	Richard Petty	1990	Dale Earnhardt
1956	Buck Baker	1968	David Pearson			1991	Dale Earnhardt
1957	Buck Baker	1969	David Pearson	1980	Dale Earnhardt	1992	Alan Kulwicki
1958	Lee Petty			1981	Darrell Waltrip	1993	Dale Earnhardt
1959	Lee Petty	1970	Bobby Issac	1982	Darrell Waltrip	1994	Dale Earnhardt
		1971	Richard Petty	1983	Bobby Allison		

NASCAR Rookie of the Year

Award presented to rookie driver who accumulates the most Winston Cup points based on his best 15 finishes.

Year		Year		Year		Year	
1958	Shorty Rollins	1968	Pete Hamilton	1977	Ricky Rudd	1986	Alan Kulwicki
1959	Richard Petty	1969	Dick Brooks	1978	Ronnie Thomas	1987	Davey Allison
				1979	Dale Earnhardt	1988	Ken Bouchard
1960	David Pearson	1970	Bill Dennis			1989	Dick Trickle
1961	Woodie Wilson	1971	Walter Ballard	1980	Jody Ridley		
1962	Tom Cox	1972	Larry Smith	1981	Ron Bouchard	1990	Rob Moroso
1963	Billy Wade	1973	Lennie Pond	1982	Geoff Bodine	1991	Bobby Hamilton
1964	Doug Cooper	1974	Earl Ross	1983	Sterling Marlin	1992	Jimmy Hensley
1965	Sam McQuagg	1975	Bruce Hill	1984	Rusty Wallace	1993	Jeff Gordon
1966	James Hylton	1976	Skip Manning	1985	Ken Schrader	1994	Jeff Burton
1967	Donnie Allison						

IndyCar Circuit

Indianapolis 500

Held every Memorial Day weekend; 200 laps around a 2.5-mile oval at Indianapolis Motor Speedway. First race was held in 1911. Winning drivers are listed with starting positions. Winners who started from pole position are in **bold** type.

Multiple wins: A.J. Foyt, Rick Mears and Al Unser (4); Louis Meyer, Mauri Rose, Johnny Rutherford, Wilbur Shaw and Bobby Unser (3); Emerson Fittipaldi, Gordon Johncock, Tommy Milton, Al Unser Jr., Bill Vukovich and Rodger Ward (2).

Multiple poles: Rick Mears (6); Mario Andretti and A.J. Foyt (4); Rex Mays, Duke Nalon and Tom Sneva (3); Billy Arnold, Bill Cummings, Ralph DePalma, Leon Duray, Walt Faulkner, Parnelli Jones, Jack McGrath, Jimmy Murphy, Johnny Rutherford, Eddie Sachs and Jimmy Snyder (2).

Year	Winner (Pos.)	Car	MPH	Pole Sitter	MPH
1911	Ray Harroun (28)	Marmon Wasp	74.602	Lewis Strang	—
1912	Joe Dawson (7)	National	78.719	Gil Anderson	—
1913	Jules Goux (7)	Peugeot	75.933	Caleb Bragg	—
1914	Rene Thomas (15)	Delage	82.474	Jean Chassagne	—
1915	Ralph DePalma (2)	Mercedes	89.840	Howard Wilcox	98.90
1916-a	Dario Resta (4)	Peugeot	84.001	John Aitken	96.69
1917-18	Not held	World War I			
1919	Howdy Wilcox (2)	Peugeot	88.050	Rene Thomas	104.78
1920	Gaston Chevrolet (6)	Monroe	88.618	Ralph DePalma	99.15
1921	Tommy Milton (20)	Frontenac	89.621	Ralph DePalma	100.75
1922	**Jimmy Murphy** (1)	Murphy Special	94.484	Jimmy Murphy	100.50
1923	**Tommy Milton** (1)	H.C.S. Special	90.954	Tommy Milton	108.17
1924	L.L. Corum & Joe Boyer (21)	Duesenberg Special	98.234	Jimmy Murphy	108.037
1925	Peter DePaolo (2)	Duesenberg Special	101.127	Leon Duray	113.196
1926-b	Frank Lockhart (20)	Miller Special	95.904	Earl Cooper	111.735
1927	George Souders (22)	Duesenberg	97.545	Frank Lockhart	120.100
1928	Louie Meyer (13)	Miller Special	99.482	Leon Duray	122.391
1929	Ray Keech (6)	Simplex Piston Ring Special	97.585	Cliff Woodbury	120.599
1930	**Billy Arnold** (1)	Miller-Hartz Special	100.448	Billy Arnold	113.268
1931	Louis Schneider (13)	Bowes Seal Fast Special	96.629	Russ Snowberger	112.796
1932	Fred Frame (27)	Miller-Hartz Special	104.144	Lou Moore	117.363
1933	Louie Meyer (6)	Tydol Special	104.162	Bill Cummings	118.530
1934	Bill Cummings (10)	Boyle Products Special	104.863	Kelly Petillo	119.329
1935	Kelly Petillo (22)	Gilmore Speedway Special	106.240	Rex Mays	120.736
1936	Louie Meyer (28)	Ring Free Special	109.069	Rex Mays	119.644
1937	Wilbur Shaw (2)	Shaw-Gilmore Special	113.580	Bill Cummings	123.343
1938	**Floyd Roberts** (1)	Burd Piston Ring Special	117.200	Floyd Roberts	125.681
1939	Wilbur Shaw (3)	Boyle Special	115.035	Jimmy Snyder	130.138
1940	Wilbur Shaw (2)	Boyle Special	114.277	Rex Mays	127.850
1941	Floyd Davis & Mauri Rose (17)	Noc-Out Hose Clamp Special	115.117	Mauri Rose	128.691
1942-45	Not held	World War II			
1946	George Robson (15)	Thorne Engineering Special	114.820	Cliff Bergere	126.471
1947	Mauri Rose (3)	Blue Crown Spark Plug Special	116.338	Ted Horn	126.564
1948	Mauri Rose (3)	Blue Crown Spark Plug Special	119.814	Duke Nalon	131.603
1949	Bill Holland (4)	Blue Crown Spark Plug Special	121.327	Duke Nalon	132.939
1950-c	Johnnie Parsons (5)	Wynn's Friction Proofing	124.002	Walt Faulkner	134.343
1951	Lee Wallard (2)	Belanger Special	126.244	Duke Nalon	136.498
1952	Troy Ruttman (7)	Agajanian Special	128.922	Fred Agabashian	138.010
1953	**Bill Vukovich** (1)	Fuel Injection Special	128.740	Bill Vukovich	138.392
1954	Bill Vukovich (19)	Fuel Injection Special	130.840	Jack McGrath	141.033
1955	Bob Sweikert (14)	John Zink Special	128.213	Jerry Hoyt	140.045
1956	**Pat Flaherty** (1)	John Zink Special	128.490	Pat Flaherty	145.596
1957	Sam Hanks (13)	Belond Exhaust Special	135.601	Pat O'Connor	143.948
1958	Jimmy Bryan (7)	Belond AP Parts Special	133.791	Dick Rathmann	145.974
1959	Rodger Ward (6)	Leader Card 500 Roadster	135.857	Johnny Thomson	145.908
1960	Jim Rathmann (2)	Ken-Paul Special	138.767	Eddie Sachs	146.592
1961	A.J. Foyt (7)	Bowes Seal Fast Special	139.130	Eddie Sachs	147.481
1962	Rodger Ward (2)	Leader Card 500 Roadster	140.293	Parnelli Jones	150.370
1963	**Parnelli Jones** (1)	Agajanian-Willard Special	143.137	Parnelli Jones	151.153
1964	A.J. Foyt (5)	Sheraton-Thompson Special	147.350	Jim Clark	158.828
1965	Jim Clark (2)	Lotus Ford	150.686	A.J. Foyt	161.233
1966	Graham Hill (15)	American Red Ball Special	144.317	Mario Andretti	165.899
1967-d	A.J. Foyt (4)	Sheraton-Thompson Special	151.207	Mario Andretti	168.982
1968	Bobby Unser (3)	Rislone Special	152.882	Joe Leonard	171.559
1969	Mario Andretti (2)	STP Oil Treatment Special	156.867	A.J. Foyt	170.568

IndyCar Circuit (Cont.)
Indianapolis 500

Year	Winner (Pos.)	Car	MPH	Pole Sitter	MPH
1970	**Al Unser** (1)	Johnny Lightning Special	155.749	Al Unser	170.221
1971	Al Unser (5)	Johnny Lightning Special	157.735	Peter Revson	178.696
1972	Mark Donohue (3)	Sunoco McLaren	162.962	Bobby Unser	195.940
1973-e	Gordon Johncock (11)	STP Double Oil Filters	159.036	Johnny Rutherford	198.413
1974	Johnny Rutherford (25)	McLaren	158.589	A.J. Foyt	191.632
1975-f	Bobby Unser (3)	Jorgensen Eagle	149.213	A.J. Foyt	193.976
1976-g	**Johnny Rutherford** (1)	Hy-Gain McLaren/Goodyear	148.725	Johnny Rutherford	188.957
1977	A.J. Foyt (4)	Gilmore Racing Team	161.331	Tom Sneva	198.884
1978	Al Unser (5)	FNCTC Chaparral Lola	161.363	Tom Sneva	202.156
1979	**Rick Mears** (1)	The Gould Charge	158.899	Rick Mears	193.736
1980	**Johnny Rutherford** (1)	Pennzoil Chaparral	142.862	Johnny Rutherford	192.256
1981-h	**Bobby Unser** (1)	Norton Spirit Penske PC-9B	139.084	Bobby Unser	200.546
1982	Gordon Johncock (5)	STP Oil Treatment	162.029	Rick Mears	207.004
1983	Tom Sneva (4)	Texaco Star	162.117	Teo Fabi	207.395
1984	Rick Mears (3)	Pennzoil Z-7	163.612	Tom Sneva	210.029
1985	Danny Sullivan (8)	Miller American Special	152.982	Pancho Carter	212.583
1986	Bobby Rahal (4)	Budweiser/Truesports/March	170.722	Rick Mears	216.828
1987	Al Unser (20)	Cummins Holset Turbo	162.175	Mario Andretti	215.390
1988	**Rick Mears** (1)	Pennzoil Z-7/Penske Chevy V-8	144.809	Rick Mears	219.198
1989	Emerson Fittipaldi (3)	Marlboro/Penske Chevy V-8	167.581	Rick Mears	223.885
1990	Arie Luyendyk (3)	Domino's Pizza Chevrolet	185.981*	Emerson Fittipaldi	225.301
1991	**Rick Mears** (1)	Marlboro Penske Chevy	176.457	Rick Mears	224.113
1992	Al Unser Jr. (12)	Valvoline Galmer '92	134.477	Roberto Guerrero	232.482†
1993	Emerson Fittipaldi (9)	Marlboro Penske Chevy	157.207	Arie Luyendyk	223.967
1994	**Al Unser Jr.** (1)	Marlboro Penske Mercedes	160.872	Al Unser Jr.	228.011
1995	Jacques Villeneuve (5)	Player's Ltd. Reynard Ford	153.616	Scott Brayton	231.604

*Track record for Winning Time. †Track record for Qualifying Time.
Notes: a—1916 race scheduled for 300 miles; **b**—rain shortened 1926 race to 400 miles; **c**—rain shortened 1950 race to 345 miles; **d**—1967 race postponed due to rain after 18 laps (May 30), resumed next day (May 31); **e**—rain shortened 1973 race to 332.5 miles; **f**—rain shortened 1975 race to 435 miles; **g**—rain shortened 1976 race to 255 miles; **h**—in 1981, runner-up Mario Andretti was awarded 1st place when winner Bobby Unser was penalized a lap after the race was completed for passing cars illegally under the caution flag. Unser and car-owner Roger Penske appealed the race stewards' decision to the U.S. Auto Club. Four months later, USAC overturned the ruling, saying that the penalty was too harsh and Unser should be fined $40,000 rather than stripped of his championship.

All-Time Leaders

IndyCar's all-time Top 20 drivers in victories, pole positions and earnings, based on records through 1994. Drivers active in 1995 are in **bold** type.

Victories

1	A.J. Foyt	67
2	Mario Andretti	52
3	Al Unser	39
4	Bobby Unser	35
5	**Michael Andretti**	29
	Rick Mears	29
7	Johnny Rutherford	27
	Al Unser Jr.	27
9	Roger Ward	26
10	Gordon Johncock	25
11	Ralph DePalma	24
	Bobby Rahal	24
13	Tommy Milton	23
14	Tony Bettenhausen	22
15	**Emerson Fittipaldi**	21
16	Earl Cooper	20
17	Jimmy Bryan	19
	Jimmy Murphy	19
19	Ralph Mulford	17
	Danny Sullivan	17

Pole Positions

1	Mario Andretti	67
2	A.J. Foyt	53
3	Bobby Unser	49
4	Rick Mears	38
5	Al Unser	27
	Michael Andretti	27
7	Johnny Rutherford	23
8	Gordon Johncock	20
9	Rex Mays	19
	Danny Sullivan	19
11	**Bobby Rahal**	18
12	**Emerson Fittipaldi**	17
13	Tony Bettenhausen	14
	Don Branson	14
	Tom Sneva	14
16	Parnelli Jones	12
17	Rodger Ward	11
	Danny Ongais	11
19	Johnny Thompson	10
	Dan Gurney	10
	Nigel Mansell	10

Earnings

1	Al Unser Jr.	$15,379,906
2	Emerson Fittipaldi	13,272,875
3	**Bobby Rahal**	13,003,241
4	Mario Andretti	11,552,154
5	**Michael Andretti**	11,332,566
6	Rick Mears	11,050,807
7	**Danny Sullivan**	8,254,673
8	**Arie Luyendyk**	7,124,771
9	Al Unser	6,740,843
10	A.J. Foyt	5,357,589
11	Raul Boesel	5,273,584
12	Scott Brayton	4,500,711
13	Tom Sneva	4,392,993
14	Roberto Guerrero	4,275,163
15	Scott Goodyear	4,212,298
16	Johnny Rutherford	4,209,232
17	Teo Fabi	3,991,278
18	Gordon Johncock	3,431,414
19	**Paul Tracy**	3,389,817
20	Nigel Mansell	3,393,515

Indy Racing League Debuts in 1996

The Indy Racing League, a five-race campaign anchored by the Indianapolis 500 and boasting a TV contract with ABC, will open for business in 1996. The brainchild of Indianapolis Motor Speedway president Tony George, the IRL has announced that 25 qualifying opositions in the 33-car Indianapolis 500 field will go to the Top 25 IRL leaders after two races— at Orlando and Phoenix— leaving only eight at large berths for rival IndyCar teams.

PPG Cup Champions

Officially the PPG Indy Car World Series Championship since 1979 and based on official AAA (American Automobile Assn., 1909-55), USAC (U.S. Auto Club, 1956-79), and CART (Championship Auto Racing Teams, 1979-91). CART was renamed IndyCar in 1992.

Multiple titles: A.J. Foyt (7); Mario Andretti (4); Jimmy Bryan, Earl Cooper, Ted Horn, Rick Mears, Louie Meyer, Bobby Rahal, Al Unser (3); Tony Bettenhausen, Ralph DePalma, Peter DePaolo, Joe Leonard, Rex Mays, Tommy Milton, Jimmy Murphy, Wilbur Shaw, Tom Sneva, Al Unser Jr., Bobby Unser and Rodger Ward (2).

AAA

Year		Year		Year		Year	
1909	George Robertson	1920	Tommy Milton	1931	Louis Schneider	1942-45	No racing
1910	Ray Harroun	1921	Tommy Milton	1932	Bob Carey	1946	Ted Horn
1911	Ralph Mulford	1922	Jimmy Murphy	1933	Louie Meyer	1947	Ted Horn
1912	Ralph DePalma	1923	Eddie Hearne	1934	Bill Cummings	1948	Ted Horn
1913	Earl Cooper	1924	Jimmy Murphy	1935	Kelly Petillo	1949	Johnnie Parsons
1914	Ralph DePalma	1925	Peter DePaolo	1936	Mauri Rose		
1915	Earl Cooper	1926	Harry Hartz	1937	Wilbur Shaw	1950	Henry Banks
1916	Dario Resta	1927	Peter DePaolo	1938	Floyd Roberts	1951	Tony Bettenhausen
1917	Earl Cooper	1928	Louie Meyer	1939	Wilbur Shaw	1952	Chuck Stevenson
1918	Ralph Mulford	1929	Louie Meyer			1953	Sam Hanks
1919	Howard Wilcox	1930	Billy Arnold	1940	Rex Mays	1954	Jimmy Bryan
				1941	Rex Mays	1955	Bob Sweikert

USAC

Year		Year		Year		Year	
1956	Jimmy Bryan	1962	Rodger Ward	1968	Bobby Unser	1974	Bobby Unser
1957	Jimmy Bryan	1963	A.J. Foyt	1969	Mario Andretti	1975	A.J. Foyt
1958	Tony Bettenhausen	1964	A.J. Foyt	1970	Al Unser	1976	Gordon Johncock
1959	Rodger Ward	1965	Mario Andretti	1971	Joe Leonard	1977	Tom Sneva
1960	A.J. Foyt	1966	Mario Andretti	1972	Joe Leonard	1978	A.J. Foyt
1961	A.J. Foyt	1967	A.J. Foyt	1973	Roger McCluskey		

CART/IndyCar

Year		Year		Year		Year	
1979	Rick Mears	1984	Mario Andretti	1988	Danny Sullivan	1992	Bobby Rahal
1980	Johnny Rutherford	1985	Al Unser	1989	Emerson Fittipaldi	1993	Nigel Mansell
1981	Rick Mears	1986	Bobby Rahal	1990	Al Unser Jr.	1994	Al Unser Jr.
1982	Rick Mears	1987	Bobby Rahal	1991	Michael Andretti	1995	Jacques Villeneuve
1983	Al Unser						

Indy 500 Rookie of the Year

Voted on by a panel of auto racing media. Award does not necessarily go to highest-finishing first-year driver. Graham Hill won the race on his first try in 1966, but the rookie award went to Jackie Stewart, who led with 10 laps to go only to lose oil pressure and finish 6th.

Father and son winners: Mario and Michael Andretti (1965 and 1984); Bill and Billy Vukovich (1968 and 1988).

Year		Year		Year		Year	
1952	Art Cross	1963	Jim Clark	1975	Bill Puterbaugh	1985	Arie Luyendyk
1953	Jimmy Daywalt	1964	Johnny White	1976	Vern Schuppan	1986	Randy Lanier
1954	Larry Crockett	1965	Mario Andretti	1977	Jerry Sneva	1987	Fabrizio Barbazza
1955	Al Herman	1966	Jackie Stewart	1978	Rick Mears	1988	Billy Vukovich III
1956	Bob Veith	1967	Denis Hulme		& Larry Rice	1989	Bernard Jourdain
1957	Don Edmunds	1968	Bill Vukovich	1979	Howdy Holmes		& Scott Pruett
1958	George Amick	1969	Mark Donohue			1990	Eddie Cheever
1959	Bobby Grim	1970	Donnie Allison	1980	Tim Richmond	1991	Jeff Andretti
1960	Jim Hurtubise	1971	Denny Zimmerman	1981	Josele Garza	1992	Lyn St. James
1961	Parnelli Jones	1972	Mike Hiss	1982	Jim Hickman	1993	Nigel Mansell
	& Bobby Marshman	1973	Graham McRae	1983	Teo Fabi	1994	Jacques Villeneuve
1962	Jimmy McElreath	1974	Pancho Carter	1984	Michael Andretti	1995	Christian Fittipaldi
					& Roberto Guerrero		

CART/IndyCar Rookie of the Year

Award presented to rookie who accumulates the most PPG Cup points among first year drivers. Originally the CART Rookie of the Year; CART was renamed IndyCar in 1992.

Year		Year		Year		Year	
1979	Bill Alsup	1984	Roberto Guerrero	1988	John Jones	1992	Stefan Johansson
1980	Dennis Firestone	1985	Arie Luyendyk	1989	Bernard Jourdain	1993	Nigel Mansell
1981	Bob Lazier	1986	Dominic Dobson	1990	Eddie Cheever	1994	Jacques Villeneuve
1982	Bobby Rahal	1987	Fabrizio Barbazza	1991	Jeff Andretti	1995	Gil de Ferran
1983	Teo Fabi						

Formula One Circuit
United States Grand Prix

There have been 54 official Formula One races held in the United States since 1950, including the Indianapolis 500 from 1950-60. FISA sanctioned two annual U.S. Grand Prix—USA/East and USA/West—from 1976-80 and 1983. Phoenix was the site of the U.S. Grand Prix from 1989-91.

Indianapolis 500

Officially sanctioned as Grand Prix race from 1950-60 only. See page 873 for details.

U.S. Grand Prix—East

Held from 1959-80 and 1981-88 at the following locations: Sebring, Fla. (1959); Riverside, Calif. (1960); Watkins Glen, N.Y. (1961-80); and Detroit (1982-88). There was no race in 1989.
Multiple winners: Jim Clark, Graham Hill and Ayrton Senna (3); James Hunt, Carlos Reutemann and Jackie Stewart (2).

Year		Car	Year		Car
1959	Bruce McLaren, NZE	Cooper Climax	1974	Carlos Reutemann, ARG	Brabham Ford
			1975	Niki Lauda, AUT	Ferrari
1960	Stirling Moss, GBR	Lotus Climax	1976	James Hunt, GBR	McLaren Ford
1961	Innes Ireland, GBR	Lotus Climax	1977	James Hunt, GBR	McLaren Ford
1962	Jim Clark, GBR	Lotus Climax	1978	Carlos Reutemann, ARG	Ferrari
1963	Graham Hill, GBR	BRM	1979	Gilles Villeneuve, CAN	Ferrari
1964	Graham Hill, GBR	BRM			
1965	Graham Hill, GBR	BRM	1980	Alan Jones, AUS	Williams Ford
1966	Jim Clark, GBR	Lotus BRM	1981	Not held	
1967	Jim Clark, GBR	Lotus Ford	1982	John Watson, GBR	McLaren Ford
1968	Jackie Stewart, GBR	Matra Ford	1983	Michele Alboreto, ITA	Tyrrell Ford
1969	Jochen Rindt, AUT	Lotus Ford	1984	Nelson Piquet, BRA	Brabham BMW Turbo
1970	Emerson Fittipaldi, BRA	Lotus Ford	1985	Keke Rosberg, FIN	Williams Honda Turbo
1971	Francois Cevert, FRA	Tyrrell Ford	1986	Ayrton Senna, BRA	Lotus Renault Turbo
1972	Jackie Stewart, GBR	Tyrrell Ford	1987	Ayrton Senna, BRA	Lotus Honda Turbo
1973	Ronnie Peterson, SWE	Lotus Ford	1988	Ayrton Senna, BRA	McLaren Honda Turbo

U.S. Grand Prix—West

Held from 1976-83 at Long Beach, Calif. Races also held in Las Vegas (1981-82), Dallas (1984) and Phoenix (1989-91). Race discontinued in 1992.
Multiple winners: Alan Jones and Ayrton Senna (2).

Long Beach

Year		Car
1976	Clay Regazzoni, SWI	Ferrari
1977	Mario Andretti, USA	Lotus Ford
1978	Carlos Reutemann, ARG	Ferrari
1979	Gilles Villeneuve, CAN	Ferrari
1980	Nelson Piquet, BRA	Brabham Ford
1981	Alan Jones, AUS	Williams Ford
1982	Niki Lauda, AUT	McLaren Ford
1983	John Watson, GBR	McLaren Ford

Las Vegas

Year		Car
1981	Alan Jones, AUS	Williams Ford
1982	Michele Alboreto, ITA	Tyrrell Ford

Dallas

Year		Car
1984	Keke Rosberg, FIN	Williams Honda Turbo

Phoenix

Year		Car
1989	Alain Prost, FRA	McLaren Honda
1990	Ayrton Senna, BRA	McLaren Honda
1991	Ayrton Senna, BRA	McLaren Honda

All-Time Leaders

The all-time Top 20 Grand Prix winning drivers, based on records through 1994. Listed are starts (Sts), poles won (Pole), wins (1st), second place finishes (2nd), and thirds (3rd). Drivers active in 1995 and career victories are in **bold** type.

		Sts	Pole	1st	2nd	3rd			Sts	Pole	1st	2nd	3rd
1	Alain Prost	199	33	51	35	20	13	Alberto Ascari	32	14	13	4	0
2	Ayrton Senna	161	65	41	23	16	14	Mario Andretti	128	18	12	2	5
3	**Nigel Mansell**	185	32	31	17	11		Alan Jones	116	6	12	7	5
4	Jackie Stewart	99	17	27	11	5		Carlos Reutemann	146	6	12	13	20
5	Jim Clark	72	33	25	1	6	17	James Hunt	92	14	10	6	7
	Niki Lauda	171	24	25	20	9		Ronnie Peterson	123	14	10	10	6
7	Juan-Manuel Fangio	51	28	24	10	1		Jody Scheckter	112	3	10	14	9
8	Nelson Piquet	204	24	23	20	17		**Michael Schumacher**	52	6	10	10	7
9	Stirling Moss	66	16	16	5	3	21	Gerhard Berger	163	10	9	15	14
10	Jack Brabham	126	13	14	10	7		**Damon Hill**	34	4	9	9	3
	Emerson Fittipaldi	144	6	14	13	8							
	Graham Hill	176	13	14	15	7							

Note: The following five drivers either died or were killed in their final year of competition—Clark in a Formula Two race in West Germany in 1968; Hill in a plane crash in 1975; Ascari in a private practice run in 1955; Peterson following a crash in the 1978 Italian GP; and Senna following a crash in the 1994 San Marino GP.

World Champions

Officially called the World Championship of Drivers and based on Formula One (Grand Prix) records through the 1994 racing season.

Multiple winners: Juan-Manuel Fangio (5); Alain Prost (4); Jack Brabham, Niki Lauda, Nelson Piquet, Ayrton Senna and Jackie Stewart (3); Alberto Ascari, Jim Clark, Emerson Fittipaldi and Graham Hill (2).

Year		Car
1950	Guiseppe Farina, ITA	Alfa Romeo
1951	Juan-Manuel Fangio, ARG	Alfa Romeo
1952	Alberto Ascari, ITA	Ferrari
1953	Alberto Ascari, ITA	Ferrari
1954	Juan-Manuel Fangio, ARG	Maserati/Mercedes
1955	Juan-Manuel Fangio, ARG	Mercedes
1956	Juan-Manuel Fangio, ARG	Ferrari
1957	Juan-Manuel Fangio, ARG	Maserati
1958	Mike Hawthorn, GBR	Ferrari
1959	Jack Brabham, AUS	Cooper Climax
1960	Jack Brabham, AUS	Cooper Climax
1961	Phil Hill, USA	Ferrari
1962	Graham Hill, GBR	BRM
1963	Jim Clark, GBR	Lotus Climax
1964	John Surtees, GBR	Ferrari
1965	Jim Clark, GBR	Lotus Climax
1966	Jack Brabham, AUS	Brabham Repco
1967	Denis Hulme, NZE	Brabham Repco
1968	Graham Hill, GBR	Lotus Ford
1969	Jackie Stewart, GBR	Matra Ford
1970	Jochen Rindt, AUT	Lotus Ford
1971	Jackie Stewart, GBR	Tyrrell Ford
1972	Emerson Fittipaldi, BRA	Lotus Ford
1973	Jackie Stewart, GBR	Tyrrell Ford
1974	Emerson Fittipaldi, BRA	McLaren Ford
1975	Niki Lauda, AUT	Ferrari
1976	James Hunt, GBR	McLaren Ford
1977	Niki Lauda, AUT	Ferrari
1978	Mario Andretti, USA	Lotus Ford
1979	Jody Scheckter, SAF	Ferrari
1980	Alan Jones, AUS	Williams Ford
1981	Nelson Piquet, BRA	Brabham Ford
1982	Keke Rosberg, FIN	Williams Ford
1983	Nelson Piquet, BRA	Brabham BMW Turbo
1984	Niki Lauda, AUT	McL. TAG Porsche Turbo
1985	Alain Prost, FRA	McL. TAG Porsche Turbo
1986	Alain Prost, FRA	McL. TAG Porsche Turbo
1987	Nelson Piquet, BRA	Williams Honda Turbo
1988	Ayrton Senna, BRA	McLaren Honda Turbo
1989	Alain Prost, FRA	McLaren Honda
1990	Ayrton Senna, BRA	McLaren Honda
1991	Ayrton Senna, BRA	McLaren Honda
1992	Nigel Mansell, GBR	Williams Renault
1993	Alain Prost, FRA	Williams-Renault
1994	Michael Schumacher, GER	Benetton Ford

ENDURANCE RACES

The 24 Hours at Le Mans

Officially, the Le Mans Grand Prix d'Endurance. First run May 22-23, 1923, and won by Andre Lagache and Rene Leonard in a 3-litre Chenard & Walcker. All subsequent races have been held in June, except in 1956 (July) and 1968 (September). Originally contested over a 10.73-mile track, the circuit was shortened to its present 8.451-mile distance in 1932. The original start of Le Mans, where drivers raced across the track to their unstarted cars, was discontinued in 1970.

Multiple winners: Jacky Ickx (6); Derek Bell (5); Oliver Gendebien and Henri Pescarolo (4); Woolf Barnato, Luigi Chinetti, Yannick Dalmas, Hurley Haywood, Phil Hill, Al Holbert and Klaus Ludwig (3); Sir Henry Birkin, Ivoe Bueb, Ron Flockhart, Jean-Pierre Jaussaud, Gerard Larrousse, Andre Rossignol, Raymond Sommer, Hans Stuck, Gijs van Lennep and Jean-Pierre Wimille (2).

Year	Drivers	Car	MPH
1923	Andre Lagache & Rene Leonard	Chenard & Walcker	57.21
1924	John Duff & Francis Clement	Bentley	53.78
1925	Gerard de Courcelles & Andre Rossignol	La Lorraine	57.84
1926	Robert Bloch & Andre Rossignol	La Lorraine	66.08
1927	J.D. Benjafield & Sammy Davis	Bentley	61.35
1928	Woolf Barnato & Bernard Rubin	Bentley	69.11
1929	Woolf Barnato & Sir Henry Birkin	Bentley Speed 6	73.63
1930	Woolf Barnato & Glen Kidston	Bentley Speed 6	75.88
1931	Earl Howe & Sir Henry Birkin	Alfa Romeo	78.13
1932	Raymond Sommer & Luigi Chinetti	Alfa Romeo	76.48
1933	Raymond Sommer & Tazio Nuvolari	Alfa Romeo	81.40
1934	Luigi Chinetti & Philippe Etancelin	Alfa Romeo	74.74
1935	John Hindmarsh & Louis Fontes	Lagonda	77.85
1936	Not held		
1937	Jean-Pierre Wimille & Robert Benoist	Bugatti 57G	85.13
1938	Eugene Chaboud & Jean Tremoulet	Delahaye	82.36
1939	Jean-Pierre Wimille & Pierre Veyron	Bugatti 57G	86.86
1940-48	Not held	World War II	
1949	Luigi Chinetti & Lord Selsdon	Ferrari	82.28
1950	Louis Rosier & Jean-Louis Rosier	Talbot-Lago	89.71
1951	Peter Walker & Peter Whitehead	Jaguar C	93.50
1952	Hermann Lang & Fritz Reiss	Mercedes-Benz	96.67
1953	Tony Rolt & Duncan Hamilton	Jaguar C	98.65
1954	Froilan Gonzalez & Maurice Trintignant	Ferrari 375	105.13
1955	Mike Hawthorn & Ivor Bueb	Jaguar D	107.05

Wide World Photos

Mario Andretti (center), who retired from IndyCar racing after the 1994 season, with French teammates **Bob Wollek** (right) and **Eric Helary** (left) after their second place finish in the 1995 running of the 24 Hours of Le Mans. The 55-year-old Andretti has already won the Indy 500, Daytona 500 and 24 Hours of Daytona in addition to driving championships in IndyCar and Formula One racing.

Endurance Races (Cont.)
The 24 Hours at Le Mans

Year	Drivers	Car	MPH	Year	Drivers	Car	MPH
1956	Ron Flockhart & Ninian Sanderson	Jaguar D	104.47	1972	Graham Hill & Henri Pescarolo	Matra-Simca	121.45
1957	Ron Flockhart & Ivor Bueb	Jaguar D	113.83	1973	Henri Pescarolo & Gerard Larrousse	Matra-Simca	125.67
1958	Oliver Gendebien & Phil Hill	Ferrari 250	106.18	1974	Henri Pescarolo & Gerard Larrousse	Matra-Simca	119.27
1959	Roy Salvadori & Carroll Shelby	Aston Martin	112.55	1975	Derek Bell & Jacky Ickx	Mirage-Ford	118.98
1960	Oliver Gendebien & Paul Fräre	Ferrari 250	109.17	1976	Jacky Ickx & Gijs van Lennep	Porsche 936	123.49
1961	Oliver Gendebien & Phil Hill	Ferrari 250	115.88	1977	Jacky Ickx, Jurgen Barth & Hurley Haywood	Porsche 936	120.95
1962	Oliver Gendebien & Phil Hill	Ferrari 250	115.22	1978	Jean-Pierre Jaussaud & Didier Pironi	Renault-Alpine	130.60
1963	Lodovico Scarfiotti & Lorenzo Bandini	Ferrari 250	118.08	1979	Klaus Ludwig, Bill Whittington & Don Whittington	Porsche 935	108.10
1964	Jean Guichet & Nino Vaccarella	Ferrari 275	121.54				
1965	Masten Gregory & Jochen Rindt	Ferrari 250	121.07	1980	Jean-Pierre Jaussaud & Jean Rondeau	Rondeau-Cosworth	119.23
1966	Bruce McLaren & Chris Amon	Ford Mk. II	125.37	1981	Jacky Ickx & Derek Bell	Porsche 936	124.94
1967	A.J. Foyt & Dan Gurney	Ford Mk. IV	135.46	1982	Jacky Ickx & Derek Bell	Porsche 956	126.85
1968	Pedro Rodriguez & Lucien Bianchi	Ford GT40	115.27	1983	Vern Schuppan, Hurley Haywood & Al Holbert	Porsche 956	130.70
1969	Jacky Ickx & Jackie Oliver	Ford GT40	129.38	1984	Klaus Ludwig & Henri Pescarolo	Porsche 956	126.88
1970	Hans Herrmann & Richard Attwood	Porsche 917	119.28	1985	Klaus Ludwig, Paolo Barilla & John Winter	Porsche 956	131.75
1971	Gijs van Lennep & Helmut Marko	Porsche 917	138.13				

Endurance Races (Cont.)
The 24 Hours at Le Mans

Year	Drivers	Car	MPH
1986	Derek Bell, Hans Stuck & Al Holbert	Porsche 962	128.75
1987	Derek Bell, Hans Stuck & Al Holbert	Porsche 962	124.06
1988	Jan Lammers, Johnny Dumfries & Andy Wallace	Jaguar XJR	137.75
1989	Jochen Mass, Manuel Reuter & Stanley Dickens	Sauber-Mercedes	136.39
1990	John Nielsen, Price Cobb & Martin Brundle	Jaguar XJR-12	126.71
1991	Volker Weider, Johnny Herbert & Bertrand Gachof	Mazda 787B	127.31
1992	Derek Warwick, Yannick Dalmas & Mark Blundell	Peugeot 905B	123.89
1993	Geoff Brabham, Christophe Bouchut & Eric Helary	Peugeot 905	132.58
1994	Yannick Dalmas, Hurley Haywood & Mauro Baldi	Porsche 962LM	129.82
1995	Yannick Dalmas, J.J. Lehto & Masanori Sekiya	McLaren BMW	105.00

The 24 Hours of Daytona

Officially, the Rolex 24 at Daytona. First run in 1962 as a three-hour race and won by Dan Gurney in a Lotus 19 Ford. Contested over a 3.56-mile course at Daytona (Fla.) International Speedway. There have been several distance changes since 1962: the event was a three-hour race (1962-63); a 2,000-kilometer race (1964-65); a 24-hour race (1966-71); a six-hour race (1972) and a 24-hour race again since 1973. The race was canceled in 1974 due to a national energy crisis.

Multiple winners: Hurley Haywood (5); Peter Gregg, Pedro Rodriguez and Bob Wollek (4); Derek Bell and Rolf Stommelen (3); A.J. Foyt, Al Holbert, Ken Miles, Brian Redman, Lloyd Ruby and Al Unser Jr. (2).

Year	Drivers	Car	MPH
1962	Dan Gurney	Lotus Ford	104.101
1963	Pedro Rodriguez	Ferrari GTO	102.074
1964	Pedro Rodriguez & Phil Hill	Ferrari GTO	98.230
1965	Ken Miles & Lloyd Ruby	Ford GT	99.944
1966	Ken Miles & Lloyd Ruby	Ford Mk. II	108.020
1967	Lorenzo Bandini & Chris Amon	Ferrari 330	105.688
1968	Vic Elford & Jochen Neerpasch	Porsche 907	106.697
1969	Mark Donohue & Chuck Parsons	Lola Chevrolet	99.268
1970	Pedro Rodriguez & Leo Kinnunen	Porsche 917	114.866
1971	Pedro Rodriguez & Jackie Oliver	Porsche 917K	109.203
1972	Mario Andretti & Jacky Ickx	Ferrari 312P	122.573
1973	Peter Gregg & Hurley Haywood	Porsche Carrera	106.225
1974	Not held		
1975	Peter Gregg & Hurley Haywood	Porsche Carrera	108.531
1976	Peter Gregg, Brian Redman & John Fitzpatrick	BMW CSL	104.040
1977	Hurley Haywood, John Graves & Dave Helmick	Porsche Carrera	108.801
1978	Peter Gregg, Rolf Stommelen & Antoine Hezemans	Porsche Turbo	108.743
1979	Hurley Haywood, Ted Field & Danny Ongais	Porsche Turbo	109.249
1980	Rolf Stommelen, Volkert Merl & Reinhold Joest	Porsche Turbo	114.303
1981	Bobby Rahal, Brian Redman & Bob Garretson	Porsche Turbo	113.153
1982	John Paul Sr., John Paul Jr. & Rolf Stommelen	Porsche Turbo	114.794
1983	A.J. Foyt, Preston Henn, Bob Wollek & Claude Ballot-Lena	Porsche Turbo	98.781
1984	Sarel van der Merwe, Tony Martin & Graham Duxbury	March Porsche	103.119
1985	A.J. Foyt, Bob Wollek, Al Unser Sr. & Thierry Boutsen	Porsche 962	104.162
1986	Al Holbert, Derek Bell & Al Unser Jr.	Porsche 962	105.484
1987	Al Holbert, Derek Bell, Chip Robinson & Al Unser Jr.	Porsche 962	111.599
1988	Raul Boesel, Martin Brundle & John Nielsen	Jaguar XJR-9	107.943
1989	John Andretti, Derek Bell & Bob Wollek	Porsche 962	92.009
1990	Davy Jones, Jan Lammers & Andy Wallace	Jaguar XJR-12	112.857
1991	Hurley Haywood, John Winter, Frank Jelinski, Henri Pescarolo & Bob Wollek	Porsche 962-C	106.633
1992	Masahiro Hasemi, Kazuyoshi Hoshino & Toshio Suzuki	Nissan R-91	112.897
1993	P.J. Jones, Mark Dismore & Rocky Moran	Toyota Eagle	103.537
1994	Paul Gentilozzi, Scott Pruett, Butch Leitzinger & Steve Millen	Nissan 300 ZXT	104.80
1995	Jurgen Lassig, Christophe Bouchut, Giovanni Lavaggi & Marco Werner	Porsche Spyder	102.280

NHRA Drag Racing
NHRA Winston Champions

Based on points earned during the NHRA Winston Drag Racing series. The series began for Top Fuel, Funny Car and Pro Stock in 1975.

Top Fuel

Multiple winners: Joe Amato (5); Don Garlits and Shirley Muldowney (3).

Year		Year		Year		Year	
1975	Don Garlits	1980	Shirley Muldowney	1985	Don Garlits	1990	Joe Amato
1976	Richard Tharp	1981	Jeb Allen	1986	Don Garlits	1991	Joe Amato
1977	Shirley Muldowney	1982	Shirley Muldowney	1987	Dick LaHaie	1992	Joe Amato
1978	Kelly Brown	1983	Gary Beck	1988	Joe Amato	1993	Eddie Hill
1979	Rob Bruins	1984	Joe Amato	1989	Gary Ormsby	1994	Scott Kalitta

Funny Car

Multiple winners: Don Prudhomme, Kenny Bernstein, John Force (4); Raymond Beadle (3); Frank Hawley (2).

Year		Year		Year		Year	
1975	Don Prudhomme	1980	Raymond Beadle	1985	Kenny Bernstein	1990	John Force
1976	Don Prudhomme	1981	Raymond Beadle	1986	Kenny Bernstein	1991	John Force
1977	Don Prudhomme	1982	Frank Hawley	1987	Kenny Bernstein	1992	Cruz Pedregon
1978	Don Prudhomme	1983	Frank Hawley	1988	Kenny Bernstein	1993	John Force
1979	Raymond Beadle	1984	Mark Oswald	1989	Bruce Larson	1994	John Force

Pro Stock

Multiple winners: Bob Glidden (9); Lee Shepherd (4); Darrell Alderman and Warren Johnson (2).

Year		Year		Year		Year	
1975	Bob Glidden	1980	Bob Glidden	1985	Bob Glidden	1990	John Myers
1976	Larry Lombardo	1981	Lee Shepherd	1986	Bob Glidden	1991	Darrell Alderman
1977	Don Nicholson	1982	Lee Shepherd	1987	Bob Glidden	1992	Warren Johnson
1978	Bob Glidden	1983	Lee Shepherd	1988	Bob Glidden	1993	Warren Johnson
1979	Bob Glidden	1984	Lee Shepherd	1989	Bob Glidden	1994	Darrell Alderman

All-Time Leaders
Career Victories

Top Fuel		Funny Car		Pro Stock	
1 Don Garlits	35	1 John Force	42	1 Bob Glidden	84
2 Joe Amato	34	2 Don Prudhomme	35	2 Warren Johnson	47
3 Gary Beck	19	3 Kenny Bernstein	30	3 Lee Shepherd	26
4 Shirley Muldowney	18	4 Ed McCulloch	18	4 Darrell Alderman	23
Darrell Gwynn	18	Mark Oswald	18	5 Bruce Allen	12

National-Event Victories (pro categories)

Drivers active in 1994 season are in **bold** type.

1	**Bob Glidden**	84	12 Ed McCulloch	22		**Mike Dunn**	12
2	**Don Prudhomme**	49	13 **Mark Oswald**	20		Billy Meyer	12
3	**Warren Johnson**	47	14 **John Myers**	19	24	**Cruz Pedregon**	11
4	**Kenny Bernstein**	42	Gary Beck	19		**Frank Iaconio**	11
	John Force	42	16 Shirley Muldowney	18		**Eddie Hill**	11
6	Don Garlits	35	Darrell Gwynn	18		Bill Jenkins	11
7	**Joe Amato**	34	18 Dick LaHaie	15	28	**Connie Kalitla**	10
	David Schultz	34	19 Gary Ormsby	14	29	**Gordie Bonin**	9
9	Lee Shepherd	26	20 Raymond Beadle	13		Ronnie Sox	9
10	Terry Vance	24	21 **Bruce Allen**	12		Frank Hawley	9
11	**Darrell Alderman**	23				Jeb Allen	9

Fastest Mile-Per-Hour Speeds

Fastest performances in NHRA major event history through 1994 season.

Top Fuel		Funny Car		Pro Stock	
MPH		**MPH**		**MPH**	
314.46	Kenny Bernstein, 10/30/94	303.95	John Force, 10/30/94	197.80	Darrell Alderman, 7/30/94
311.85	Kenny Bernstein, 10/30/94	303.74	John Force, 10/30/94	197.49	Warren Johnson, 4/8/94
308.95	Scott Kalitta, 9/18/94	302.82	John Force, 10/29/94	197.15	Warren Johnson, 4/23/94
308.64	Scott Kalitta, 10/3/93	302.11	John Force, 9/18/94	196.97	Warren Johnson, 4/8/94
307.90	Scott Kalitta, 9/18/94	301.40	John Force, 10/28/94	196.93	Scott Geoffrion, 5/20/94
		301.40	John Force, 10/29/94		

Mike Tyson watches **Peter McNeeley** fall to the canvas early in the first round of their Aug. 19 fight in Las Vegas. The bout was Tyson's first after being released from prison in March.

BOXING

King Tyson

With the ex-champion out of prison and back with his old promoter, none of the other heavyweights seem to matter.

Early in the morning on March 25, the day Mike Tyson was released from an Indiana prison after doing three years for rape, boxing's heavyweight division went from being a quilting bee to a three-ring circus.

Six days later, the former champion, who will turn 30 in mid-1996, announced that he would continue to use ringmaster Don King as his promoter.

Shortly after that he signed a pair of exclusive-service contracts with the MGM Grand in Las Vegas and Showtime Entertainment Television that guaranteed him and King at least $150 million over the next 2½ years or the first six fights of the former champion's comeback, whichever came first.

Who says crime doesn't pay? Tyson was worth more than ever now that he was an ex-con.

On May 25, Peter McNeeley, the 24-year-old son of former heavyweight contender Tom McNeeley, was plucked from well-deserved obscurity to be Tyson's first opponent on Aug. 19.

McNeeley, who signed for a guarantee of $700,000, earned his money promoting the fight as he utilized a staccato, New England-accented voice that sounded like Jay Leno mimicking John F. Kennedy.

"I'm Hurricane Peter McNeeley, from Medfield, Mass.," McNeeley said in the final prefight press conference. "On Saturday night, I'm going to kick Mike Tyson's ass."

Not that he didn't try.

When the bell sounded, McNeeley, rushed at Tyson, all bravado and left feet, but he was rolling around on the canvas after only seven seconds, having been tagged squarely on the chin by Tyson's first punch, an overhand right.

The hopelessly overmatched McNeeley scrambled to his feet and attempted to fight back. He again rushed at Tyson and, briefly, succeeded in driving him into the ropes. But McNeeley's counter-attack was brief; Tyson responded with two left hooks, neither of which landed flush, and a ripping right uppercut, which did. McNeeley again went down and, when he arose— still seemingly in the mood to mix it up— it was on unsteady legs. The end, it was plain to see, was near.

Nearer than anyone might have imagined, as it turned out. Before referee Mills Lane could wave Tyson back to finish the job, McNeeley's manager-trainer, Vinny Vecchione, scrambled into the ring, offering himself as a human towel toss. Lane had no choice but to award Tyson a victory by disqualification.

King, spin-doctoring like crazy, said spectators, some of whom had paid up to $1,500 for a ringside seat, had no cause for complaint.

"It's not an outrage," King insisted. "The people might be disappointed that the manager jumped into the ring, but they can't say they didn't get their money's worth. We had

---

Bernard Fernandez has been a sports reporter at *The Philadelphia Daily News* for 21 years and the boxing writer since 1987.

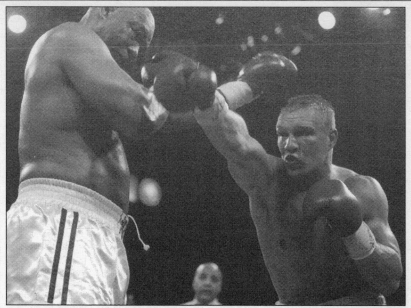

Heavyweight champion **George Foreman** (left) wards off a straight right hand from German challenger Axel Schulz during their April 22 IBF championship fight in Las Vegas. Foreman won a controversial decision, but was later stripped of the title when he declined to give Schulz a rematch.

quite a spectacle this evening. No one can say Peter McNeeley didn't come to fight. We saw a terrific altercation for the time that it lasted."

Vecchione said he didn't want to see his fighter suffer a worse fate than mere defeat. "I remember Jimmy Garcia and Gerald McClellan," he said.

The ring death of Garcia, a Colombian super featherweight, in May and the career-ending beating absorbed by WBC super middleweight champion McClellan in February haunted boxing in 1995.

The power-punching McClellan appeared to be on his way to another first-round romp when he sent challenger Nigel Benn tumbling through the ropes in their Feb. 25 fight in London. But Benn scrambled to his feet, and the two ferociously slugged it out until McClellan sagged to the canvas in the 10th round.

Shortly after the fight, McClellan collapsed in his corner and was rushed to the hospital where emergency surgery was needed to remove a blood clot from his brain. He has since returned to his Freeport, Ill., home, but he is blind and he cannot walk without assistance.

Garcia, who had to lose 30 pounds to get down to the 130-pound super featherweight limit, suffered a severe 11-round pounding at the hands of WBC champion Gabriel Ruelas in their May 6 title bout in Las Vegas. He collapsed shortly after the fight, lost consciousness by the time he reached the ambulance and was in surgery within 40 minutes. But there would be not even a slight recovery; Garcia died 13 days later.

Back to Tyson and King.

The McNeeley debacle was only a prelude to even more outrageous twists of fate. King scheduled Tyson's second post-incarceration fight for Nov. 4 against another son of a former contender, Buster Mathis Jr.

At least people had heard of Mathis, but it wasn't a big deal fight. The date, however, was. It was the same night as the long-awaited rubber match between another couple of former heavyweight champions, Riddick Bowe and Evander Holyfield, to be staged just down the Strip at Caesars Palace.

The prospect of two major pay-per-view boxing events scheduled for the same date at the same time in the same city, and competing for the same audience, would have been a huge story in any case. But the crafty King took the drama to another level with his surprise announcement on Sept. 14, that Tyson-Mathis would be aired on free TV, as the centerpiece of a three-hour block of boxing on the Fox network.

It would mark the first time a big-ticket fight will be shown on an over-the-air network in prime time since Sept. 15, 1978, when Muhammad Ali reacquired the heavyweight title from Leon Spinks, and Tyson's first exposure on network TV since he destroyed Marvis Frazier in one round on July 26, 1986, in an ABC matinee.

King's coup, of course, put media giant Time Warner, the parent corporation of HBO, in the unenviable position of having to go forward with Bowe-Holyfield III on pay-per-view in direct competition with a free Tyson fight. The stakes thus have been raised in the increasingly bitter war between Time Warner and Showtime Entertainment Television, which, as King's ally, lists Tyson as its premier attraction.

HBO sports chief Seth Abraham, in fact, already has said that King is intent on creating similar scheduling conflicts, and that his company has no choice but to load up for a high-stakes, TV version of the Gunfight at the O.K. Corral.

"HBO has Roy Jones Jr., Pernell Whitaker, George Foreman, Riddick Bowe, Evander Holyfield, Oscar De La Hoya, Lennox Lewis and Tommy Morrison," Abraham said. "I regard them as missiles, very expensive missiles. If [SET and King] start messing with our dates, I'll start messing with their dates and launch those missiles. We'll bomb them to the peace table if that's what they want."

Wow, what next?

How about King's trial for insurance fraud, where jury selection began on Sept. 27 at the new federal courthouse in Manhattan. The 64-year-old high priest of hyperbole is charged with submitting a fake contract to Lloyd's of London in order to receive $350,000 in non-refundable training fees after a June 1991 fight between Julio Cesar Chavez and Harold Brazier was canceled due to a nose injury suffered by Chavez while sparring.

If convicted, King could face a maximum sentence of five years in prison and a $250,000 fine on each of the nine counts in the indictment against him.

Although the adventures of Tyson and King dominated the year in boxing, other stories commanded attention.

Foreman, the only active fighter whose visibility level approaches Tyson's, etched his legend in granite when, on November 5, 1994, he captured the WBA and IBF heavyweight championships by knocking out Michael Moorer with a single, crushing right hand in the 10th round. Foreman was 45 years old at the time, two decades removed from the end of his first title reign.

"Given the circumstances, that probably was the greatest punch in boxing history," Foreman's promoter, Bob Arum, said with typical hyperbole. "For him to lose his title 20 years ago in Zaire (to Muhammad Ali), to come back and to throw a punch like that to regain it...it's amazing. It's beyond amazing."

Nearly as amazing as his second rise to power was the brevity of Foreman the Elder's reign. First Big George was stripped of his WBA crown for refusing to make a mandatory defense against that organization's top-rated contender, Tony Tucker, to take an IBF-sanctioned fight against unknown German Axel Schulz.

On April 22, Foreman's face was punched lopsided by Schulz, but he escaped with a controversial majority decision, whereupon the IBF also stripped him for declining to participate in an IBF-mandated rematch with the no-longer-unknown Deutschlander.

Foreman, as is his wont, laughed off the enforced removal of his titles and many of his fans laughed with him. The suspicion is that Big George can't fight much any more, but he is beloved and a good storyteller, so he undoubtedly will get big bucks to enter the ring at least one more time, probably in a spring rematch with Moorer. Oh, and Foreman is lobbying for a date with Tyson, as are most heavyweights with a fondness for large sums of money.

Bowe, who is perhaps the best heavyweight in the world when he is focused and in shape, which has not always been the case, emerged from a year-long fog to post impressive blowouts of Herbie Hide and Jorge Luis Gonzales. Holyfield, who briefly retired following a title-relinquishing loss to Moorer and the subsequent diagnosis of a noncompliant left ventricle, or "stiff heart," got a

Roy Jones Jr. (left), the IBF super middleweight champion, connects with a punch against **Vinny Pazienza** on the way to a sixth-round TKO on June 24 in Atlantic City. It was the second successful title defense by Jones after winning the championship from James Toney on Nov. 18, 1994.

clean bill of health from the Mayo Clinic and looked to be his old self in a unanimous decision over former contender Ray Mercer.

With Tyson and Foreman opting to follow their own curious agendas, Bowe and Holyfield had no recourse but to gravitate toward each other again for the third and presumably final bout in a series that has been called the Ali-Frazier of the '90s.

"We're the two best fighters out there now until somebody stands up and proves otherwise," Holyfield said of himself and Bowe. "Michael Moorer didn't want to fight Bowe. George Foreman didn't want to fight him. None of the other champions want to fight him. So here I am. We'll settle this thing among ourselves."

Other principal figures in the heavyweight division include former WBC champion Lennox Lewis, whose stock rose when he knocked Tommy Morrison down four times en route to a sixth-round TKO victory Oct. 7 in Atlantic City, and Moorer, who sued the IBF when the Newark, N.J.-based organization vaulted a South African stiff named Francois Botha ahead of him into the No. 1 spot in its ratings. An out-of-court settlement assures Moorer of first crack at the winner of a Schulz-Botha fight for the IBF title taken from Foreman. Moorer also

has the option of taking an interim bout with Foreman if he so chooses.

Also figuring prominently in the heavyweight pecking order, if for no other reason than the fact they are custodians of the moment, are WBA champion Bruce Seldon and WBC titlist Frank Bruno, who won his portion of the title with a Sept. 2 unanimous decision over Oliver McCall.

And then there's former champion Larry Holmes, the heavyweight division's other elder statesman, who is only 10 months younger than Foreman. He lost a bid to regain his title on April 8 when he lost a 12-round unanimous decision to McCall in Las Vegas. He retired (again) after the fight, then came back a few months later.

On the non-heavyweight front, there was the continued excellence of WBC welterweight titlist Pernell Whitaker; the emergence of IBF super middleweight champ Roy Jones Jr. and WBO lightweight champ Oscar De La Hoya as full-fledged superstars; the decline of Chavez, the WBC super lightweight champion, and assorted oddities involving Terry Norris, Luis Santana, Merqui Sosa, "Prince" Charles Williams, Vincent Pettway and Simon Brown.

Jones stunned super middleweight champion James Toney on Nov. 18, 1994 in Las

Gerald McClellan grimaces moments before collapsing in his corner after a 10th-round knockout loss to WBC super middleweight champion Nigel Benn on Feb. 25. Later that night, McClellan underwent brain surgery to remove a blood clot. He recovered, but is now blind and can't walk without assistance.

Vegas, taking the crown by unanimous decision. He followed up that breakthrough performance by dominating Antoine Byrd, Vinny Pazienza and Tony Thornton in 1995. The 26-year-old, Pensacola, Fla., native has shown himself to be so superior that attorney-adviser Fred Levin has allowed himself the luxury of a big, big daydream.

"Roy definitely has an interest in fighting Tyson," Levin said after Jones took care of Pazienza in six rounds on June 24 in Atlantic City. "He told me he'd weigh whatever he needed to weigh. If a middleweight can't hit him, you know a heavyweight won't be able to."

Whitaker has no heavyweight fantasies, but the WBC welterweight champ amused himself by stepping up to junior middleweight on March 4 and wresting the WBA title on a unanimous decision over Argentina's Julio Cesar Vasquez.

"I tip my hat to myself," said Whitaker, who immediately renounced the 154-pound crown and returned to welterweight. "I think Pernell Whitaker has reached another milestone. I've done everything a boxer can do, and had great fun doing it."

The Julio Cesar Whitaker most would like to get his hands on, WBC super lightweight champion Julio Cesar Chavez, last December announced plans to press on until he had achieved 100 victories. But that timetable might be altered after Chavez' most recent outing, a close but unanimous decision over Kenya's David Kamau Sept. 16 in Las Vegas. Depending upon which set of numbers you choose to believe, the Mexican standout's record now is 96-1-1, with 81 knockouts (promoter Don King's version) or 95-1-1, with 77 KOs (respected statistician Phill Marder's version).

In either case, a tired-sounding Chavez said he isn't sure if he'll hang around much past his scheduled May 5, 1996, matchup with Oscar De La Hoya, or even keep going until then.

"Now, I don't know about 100 victories," Chavez said he had held off Kamau. "I am exhausted and I'm not sure how much longer I will be fighting."

With or without Chavez, De La Hoya, the sole American gold medalist in the 1992 Barcelona Olympics, figures to keep on fighting and winning for quite a spell. His impressive list of '95 conquests already includes John-John Molina, Rafael Ruelas and Genaro Hernandez, with Jesse James Leija down for a Dec. 15 bout in Madison Square Garden.

Merqui Sosa and "Prince" Charles Williams engaged in two memorable light heavyweight battles. The first, on Jan. 13, ended in a technical draw after seven rounds when ring physician Frank B. Doggett ruled neither man was in condition to continue; the second, on June 30, saw Sosa win on a 10th-round TKO.

Terry Norris and Luis Santana fought three times from Nov. 12, 1994, to Aug. 19, and Santana was knocked down and out all three times. But he was awarded victories by disqualification the first two times when Norris was ruled to have, respectively, hit him behind the head and after the bell.

Last but not least, Vincent Pettway retained his IBF junior middleweight title (since won by Paul Vaden) by knocking out Simon Brown in six rounds of their April 29 bout in Landover, Md. But Brown's fighting instincts were such that, even while unconscious and lying flat on his back, he continued to throw jabs. ❑

THE 1996 SPORTS ALMANAC · INFORMATION PLEASE

BOXING STATISTICS

SEC A

THE SEASON IN REVIEW
1994-1995
CHAMPIONS · TITLE BOUTS

PAGE 887

Current Champions

WBA, WBC and IBF Titleholders (through Oct. 15, 1995)

The champions of professional boxing's 17 principal weight divisions, as recognized by the Word Boxing Association (WBA), World Boxing Council (WBC) and International Boxing Federation (IBF).

	Weight Limit	WBA Champion	WBC Champion	IBF Champion
Heavyweight	—	Bruce Seldon 33-3-0, 29 KO	Frank Bruno 39-4-0, 37 KO	Vacant
Cruiserweight	190 lbs	Nate Miller 26-4-0, 21 KO	Anaclet Wamba 43-2-1, 20 KO	Al Cole 25-1-0, 12 KO
Light Heavyweight	175 lbs	Virgil Hill 41-1-0, 20 KO	Fabrice Tiozzo 31-1-0, 20 KO	Henry Maske 28-0-0, 10 KO
Super Middleweight	168 lbs	Frankie Liles 27-1-0, 17 KO	Nigel Benn 42-2-1, 35 KO	Roy Jones Jr. 30-0-0, 26 KO
Middleweight	160 lbs	Jorge Castro 98-4-1, 69 KO	Quincy Taylor 26-3-0, 22 KO	Bernard Hopkins 26-2-1, 19 KO
Jr. Middleweight	154 lbs	Carl Daniels 35-1-0, 22 KO	Terry Norris 40-6-0, 25 KO	Paul Vaden 24-0-0, 12 KO
Welterweight	147 lbs	Ike Quartey 30-0-0, 26 KO	Pernell Whitaker 36-1-1, 15 KO	Felix Trinidad 26-0-0, 22 KO
Jr. Welterweight	140 lbs	Frankie Randall 52-3-1, 40 KO	Julio Cesar Chavez 95-1-1, 77 KO	Kostya Tszyu 15-0-0, 11 KO
Lightweight	135 lbs	Gussie Nazarov 21-0-0, 16 KO	Miguel A. Gonzalez 38-0-0, 29 KO	Phillip Holiday 25-0-0, 14 KO
Jr. Lightweight	130 lbs	Genaro Hernandez 31-0-1, 15 KO	Gabriel Ruelas 41-2-0, 23 KO	Tracy Patterson 52-3-1, 37 KO
Featherweight	126 lbs	Eloy Rojas 32-1-1, 25 KO	Manuel Medina 51-6-0, 23 KO	Tom Johnson 40-2-1, 24 KO
Jr. Featherweight	122 lbs	Antonio Cermeno 22-1-0, 15 KO	Hector Acero-Sanchez 32-2-3, 20 KO	Vuyani Bungu 28-2-0, 17 KO
Bantamweight	118 lbs	Daorung Chuvatana 55-4-2, 31 KO	Wayne McCullough 17-0-0, 13 KO	Mbulelo Botile 16-0-0, 10 KO
Jr. Bantamweight	115 lbs	Alimi Goitia 11-0-0, 8 KO	Hiroshi Kawashima 17-2-1, 12 KO	Carlos Salazar 38-6-1, 14 KO
Flyweight	112 lbs	Saen Sow Ploenchit 22-0-0, 6 KO	Yuri Arbachakov 21-0-0, 15 KO	Danny Romero 24-0-0, 22 KO
Jr. Flyweight	108 lbs	Hi-Yong Choi 19-1-0, 8 KO	Saman Sorjaturong 27-2-1, 22 KO	Saman Sorjaturong 27-2-1, 22 KO
Minimumweight	105 lbs	Chana Porpaoin 34-0-0, 14 KO	Ricardo Lopez 40-0-0, 30 KO	Ratanapol Vorapin 22-2-1, 17 KO

Note: the following weight divisions are also known by these names— **Cruiserweight** as Jr. Heavyweight; **Jr. Middleweight** as Super Welterweight; **Jr. Welterweight** as Super Lightweight; **Jr. Lightweight** as Super Featherweight; **Jr. Featherweight** as Super Bantamweight; **Jr. Bantamweight** as Super Flyweight; **Jr. Flyweight** as Light Flyweight; and **Minimumweight** as Strawweight.

Foreman and Tyson

The career pro records of George Foreman and Mike Tyson as of Oct. 15, 1995

George Foreman

Pro record: 74-4-0, 68 KO

No	Date	Opponent, location	Result
1	6/23/69	Don Waldhelm, New York	KO 3
2	7/1/69	Fred Ashew, Houston	KO 1
3	7/14/69	Sylvester Dullaire, Wash., D.C.	KO 1
4	8/18/69	Chuck Wepner, New York	TKO 3
5	9/18/69	John Carroll, Seattle	KO 1
6	9/23/69	Cookie Wallace, Houston	KO 2
7	10/7/69	Vernon Clay, Houston	TKO 2
8	10/31/69	Roberto Davila, New York	Wu 8
9	11/5/69	Leo Peterson, Scranton	KO 4
10	11/18/69	Max Martinez, Houston	KO 2
11	12/6/69	Bob Hazelton, Las Vegas	KO 1
12	12/16/69	Levi Forte, Miami Beach	Wu 10
13	12/18/69	Gary Wilder, Seattle	TKO 1
14	1/6/70	Charley Polite, Houston	KO 4
15	1/26/70	Jack O'Halloran, New York	KO 5
16	2/16/70	Gregorio Peralta, New York	Wu 10
17	3/31/70	Rufus Brassell, Houston	KO 1
18	4/17/70	James J. Woody, New York	TKO 3
19	4/29/70	Aaron Easting, Cleveland	TKO 4
20	5/16/70	George Johnson, Inglewood	TKO 7
21	7/20/70	Roger Russell, Philadelphia	TKO 1
22	8/4/70	George Chuvalo, New York	TKO 3
23	11/3/70	Lou Bailey, Oklahoma City	KO 3
24	11/18/70	Boone Kirkman, New York	TKO 2
25	12/19/70	Mel Turnbow, Seattle	KO 1
26	2/8/71	Charlie Boston, St. Paul, Minn.	KO 1
27	4/3/71	Stanford Harris, Lake Geneva	KO 2
28	5/10/71	Gregorio Peralta, Oakland	TKO 10
29	9/14/91	Vic Scott, El Paso	KO 1
30	9/21/71	Leroy Caldwell, Beaumont, Tex.	KO 2
31	10/7/71	Ollie Wilson, San Antonio	TKO 2
32	10/29/71	Luis F. Pires, New York	TKO 5
33	2/29/72	Murphy Goodwin, Austin, Tex.	KO 2
34	3/7/72	Clarence Boone, Beaumont, Tex.	TKO 2
35	4/10/72	Ted Gullick, Inglewood	KO 2
36	5/11/72	Miguel A. Paez, Oakland	KO 2
37	10/10/72	Terry Sorrels, Salt Lake City	KO 2
38	1/22/73	Joe Frazier, Kingston, Jamaica	TKO 2
		(won World Heavyweight title)	
39	9/1/73	Jose Roman, Tokyo	KO 1
40	3/26/74	Ken Norton, Caracus, Venezuela	TKO 2
41	10/30/74	Muhammad Ali, Kinshasa, Zaire	KO by 8
		(lost World Heavyweight title)	
42	1/24/76	Ron Lyle, Las Vegas	KO 5
43	6/15/76	Joe Frazier, Uniondale, N.Y.	TKO 5
44	8/14/76	Scott Le Doux, Utica, N.Y.	KO 3
45	10/15/76	Dino Denis, Hollywood, Fla.	KO 4
46	1/22/77	Pedro Agosto, Pensacola, Fla.	TKO 4
47	3/17/77	Jimmy Young, Hato Rey, P.R.	Lu 12
		(retired after fight)	
48	3/9/87	Steve Zouski, Sacramento	TKO 4
		(first fight of comeback)	
49	7/9/87	Charles Hostetter, Oakland	KO 3
50	9/15/87	Bobby Crabree, Springfield, Mo.	TKO 6
51	11/21/87	Tim Anderson, Orlando	TKO 4
52	12/18/87	Rocky Sekorski, Las Vegas	TKO 3
53	1/23/88	Tom Trimm, Orlando	TKO 1
54	2/5/88	Guido Trane, Las Vegas	TKO 5
55	3/19/88	Dwight Qawi, Las Vegas	TKO 7
56	5/21/88	Frank Williams, Anchorage	KO 3
57	6/26/88	Carlos Hernandez, Atlantic City	TKO 4
58	8/25/88	Ladislao Mijangos, Ft. Myers	TKO 3
59	9/10/88	Bobby Hitz, Auburn Hills, Mich.	KO 1
60	10/27/88	Tony Fulilangi, Marshall, Tex.	TKO 2
61	12/28/88	David Jaco, Bakersfield, Calif.	KO 1
62	1/26/89	Mark Young, Rochester, N.Y.	TKO 7
63	2/16/89	Manuel de Almeida, Orlando	TKO 3
64	4/30/89	J.B. Williamson, Galveston, Tex.	TKO 5
65	6/1/89	Bert Cooper, Phoenix	TKO 3
66	7/20/89	Everett Martin, Tucson	Wu 10
67	1/15/90	Gerry Cooney, Atlantic City	KO 2
68	4/17/90	Mike Jameson, Stateline, Nev.	TKO 4
69	6/16/90	Adilson Rodrigues, Las Vegas	KO 2
70	7/31/90	Ken Lakusta, Edmonton	KO 3
71	9/25/90	Terry Anderson, Millwall, England	KO 1
72	4/19/91	Evander Holyfield, Atlantic City	Lu 12
		(for World Heavyweight title)	
73	12/7/91	Jimmy Ellis, Reno, Nev.	TKO 3
74	4/11/92	Alex Stewart, Las Vegas	Wm 10
75	1/16/93	Pierre Coetzer, Reno, Nev.	TKO 8
76	6/7/93	Tommy Morrison, Las Vegas	Lu 12
77	11/5/94	Michael Moorer, Las Vegas	KO 10
		(won WBA/IBF Heavyweight titles)	
78	4/22/95	Axel Schulz, Las Vegas	Wm 12

Mike Tyson

Pro record: 42-1-0, 36 KO

No	Date	Opponent, location	Result
1	3/6/85	Hector Mercedes, Albany, N.Y.	KO 1
2	4/10/85	Trent Singleton, Albany, N.Y.	TKO 1
3	5/23/85	Don Halpin, Albany, N.Y.	KO 4
4	6/20/85	Rick Spain, Atlantic City	KO 1
5	7/11/85	John Anderson, Atlantic City	TKO 2
6	7/19/85	Larry Sims, Poughkeepsie, N.Y.	KO 3
7	8/15/85	Lorenzo Canady, Atlantic City	TKO 1
8	9/5/85	Michael Johnson, Atlantic City	KO 1
9	10/9/85	Donnie Long, Atlantic City	KO 1
10	10/25/85	Robert Colay, Atlantic City	KO 1
11	11/1/85	Sterling Benjamin, Latham, N.Y.	TKO 1
12	11/13/85	Eddie Richardson, Houston	KO 1
13	11/22/85	Conroy Nelson, Latham, N.Y.	KO 2
14	12/6/85	Sammy Scaff, New York City	KO 1
15	12/27/85	Mark Young, Latham, N.Y.	KO 1
16	1/10/86	Dave Jaco, Albany, N.Y.	KO 1
17	1/24/86	Mike Jameson, Atlantic City	TKO 5
18	2/16/86	Jesse Ferguson, Troy, N.Y.	TKO 6
19	3/10/86	Steve Zouski, Uniondale, N.Y.	KO 3
20	5/3/86	James Tillis, Glens Falls, N.Y.	Wu 10
21	5/20/86	Mitchell Green, New York City	Wu 10
22	6/13/86	Reggie Gross, New York City	TKO 1
23	6/28/86	William Hosea, Troy, N.Y.	KO 1
24	7/11/86	Lorenzo Boyd, Swan Lake, N.Y.	KO 2
25	7/26/86	Marvis Frazier, Glens Falls, N.Y.	KO 1
26	8/17/86	Jose Ribalta, Atlantic City	TKO 10
27	9/6/86	Alfonzo Ratliff, Las Vegas	KO 2
28	11/22/86	Trevor Berbick, Las Vegas	KO 2
		(won WBC heavyweight title)	
29	3/7/87	Bonecrusher Smith, Las Vegas	Wu 12
		(won WBA heavyweight title)	
30	5/30/87	Pinklon Thomas, Las Vegas	TKO 6
31	8/1/87	Tony Tucker, Las Vegas	Wu 12
		(won IBF heavyweight title)	
32	10/16/87	Tyrell Biggs, Atlantic City	TKO 7
33	1/22/88	Larry Holmes, Atlantic City	KO 4
34	3/21/88	Tony Tubbs, Tokyo	TKO 2
35	6/27/88	Michael Spinks, Atlantic City	KO 1
36	2/25/89	Frank Bruno, Las Vegas	TKO 5
37	7/21/89	Carl Williams, Atlantic City	TKO 1
38	2/10/90	Buster Douglas, Tokyo	KO by 10
		(lost world heavyweight title)	
39	6/16/90	Henry Tillman, Las Vegas	KO 1
40	12/8/90	Alex Stewart, Atlantic City	TKO 1
41	3/18/91	Razor Ruddock, Las Vegas	TKO 7
42	6/28/91	Razor Ruddock, Las Vegas	Wu 12
43	8/19/95	Peter McNeeley, Las Vegas	W disq. 1
		(first fight since release from prison)	

Major Bouts

Division by division, from Oct. 1, 1994 through Oct. 15, 1995.

WBA, WBC and IBF champions are listed in **bold** type. Note the following Result column abbreviations (in alphabetical order): **Disq.** (won by disqualification); **KO** (knockout); **MDraw** (majority draw); **NC** (no contest); **SDraw** (split draw); **TDraw** (technical draw); **TKO** (technical knockout); **TWs** (won by technical split decision); **TWu** (won by technical unanimous decision); **Wm** (won by majority decision); **Ws** (won by split decision) and **Wu** (won by unanimous decision).

Heavyweights

Date	Winner	Loser	Result		Title	Site
Oct. 22	John Carlo	Leon Spinks	KO	1	Non-title	Washington, D.C.
Nov. 1	Joe Hipp	Rodolfo Marin	Ws	10	Non-title	Las Vegas
Nov. 5	George Foreman	**Michael Moorer**	KO	10	**IBF/WBA**	Las Vegas
Nov. 5	Buster Mathis Jr.	Lyle McDowell	TKO	5	Non-title	Lake Tahoe
Nov. 11	Peter McNeeley	Lorenzo Boyd	TKO	1	Non-title	Foxboro, Mass.
Dec. 3	Riddick Bowe	Larry Donald	Wu	12	Non-title	Las Vegas
Dec. 6	Jimmy Thunder	Tony Tubbs	Wm	12	Non-title	Auburn Hills
Dec. 17	Bruce Seldon	Bill Corrigan	KO	1	Non-title	Quito, Ecuador
Dec. 17	Tim Witherspoon	Nathaniel Fitch	TKO	6	Non-title	Atlantic City
Jan. 20	Peter McNeeley	Kevin Wyrick	TKO	1	Non-title	Foxboro, Mass.
Feb. 4	Buster Mathis Jr.	Kenny Smith	Wu	10	Non-title	Las Vegas
Feb. 7	Tommy Morrison	Ken Merritt	KO	1	Non-title	Oklahoma City
Feb. 10	Peter McNeeley	Joe Barnes	KO	1	Non-title	Ft. Smith, Ark.
Feb. 18	Frank Bruno	Rodolfo Marin	KO	1	Non-title	Shepton Mallet, Eng.
Mar. 1	Lionel Butler	James Flowers	TKO	2	Non-title	Ft. Lauderdale
Mar. 5	Tommy Morrison	Marcellus Brown	TKO	3	Non-title	Muskogee, Okla.
Mar. 5	Jeremy Williams	Jesse Ferguson	TKO	7	Non-title	Palm Springs, Calif.
Mar. 7	Jimmy Thunder	Trevor Berbick	Wu	10	Non-title	Prior Lake, Minn.
Mar. 11	Riddick Bowe	Herbie Hide	KO	6	(WBO)	Las Vegas
Mar. 11	Jorge Luis Gonzalez	Bryan Scott	TKO	2	Non-title	Las Vegas
Mar. 17	Peter McNeeley	Danny Lee Wofford	TKO	1	Non-title	Worcester, Mass.
Mar. 24	Tim Witherspoon	Jesse Shelby	TKO	1	Non-title	Philadelphia
Apr. 7	Ron Lyle	Bruce Johnson	TKO	4	Non-title	Erlanger, Ky.
Apr. 8	**Oliver McCall**	Larry Holmes	Wu	12	**WBC**	Las Vegas
Apr. 8	Bruce Seldon	Tony Tucker	TKO	7	vacant **WBA**	Las Vegas
Apr. 17	Joe Hipp	Phil Brown	TKO	3	Non-title	Molina, Ill.
Apr. 18	Buster Mathis Jr.	Alex Garcia	Wu	12	Non-title	Las Vegas
Apr. 22	**George Foreman**	Axel Schulz	Wm	12	**IBF**	Las Vegas
May 1	Tommy Morrison	Terry Anderson	KO	7	Non-title	Tulsa
May 9	Jimmy Thunder	Daniel Dancuta	TKO	2	Non-title	Las Vegas
May 9	Alex Stewart	Tyrone Evans	TKO	4	Non-title	Las Vegas
May 12	Ron Lyle	Tim Pollard	KO	2	Non-title	Erlanger, Ky.
May 13	Lennox Lewis	Lionel Butler	TKO	6	Non-title	Sacramento
May 13	Michael Moorer	Melvin Foster	Wu	10	Non-title	Sacramento
May 13	Frank Bruno	Mike Evans	KO	2	Non-title	Glasgow, Scotland
May 20	Evander Holyfield	Ray Mercer	Wu	10	Non-title	Atlantic City
June 10	Tommy Morrison	Razor Ruddock	TKO	6	Non-title	Kansas City
June 17	Riddick Bowe	Jorge Luis Gonzalez	KO	6	(WBO)	Las Vegas
June 17	Jimmy Thunder	Bomani Parker	TKO	1	Non-title	Las Vegas
June 19	Leon Spinks	Ray Kipping	Wu	8	Non-title	Maryland Hgts., Mo.
June 21	Mike Weaver	George Omara	Wu	12	Non-title	Woodland Hills, Calif.
June 23	Alexander Zolkin	Bert Cooper	TKO	9	Non-title	Atlantic City
July 2	Lennox Lewis	Justin Fortune	TKO	4	Non-title	Dublin
Aug. 5	Buster Mathis Jr.	Mike Acklie	TKO	1	Non-title	Albuquerque
Aug. 8	Jimmy Thunder	Ray Anis	KO	7	Non-title	Coachella, Calif.
Aug. 8	Alex Stewart	Jesse Ferguson	Wu	10	Non-title	Coachella, Calif.
Aug. 19	Mike Tyson	Peter McNeeley	TKO	1	Non-title	Las Vegas
Aug 19	**Bruce Seldon**	Joe Hipp	TKO	10	**WBA**	Las Vegas
Aug. 25	Alex Zolkin	Tony Tubbs	Wm	12	Non-title	Atlantic City
Sept. 2	Frank Bruno	**Oliver McCall**	Wu	12	**WBC**	London
Sept. 19	Larry Holmes	Eddie Donaldson	Wu	10	Non-title	Biloxi, Miss.
Sept. 19	Earnie Shavers	Brian Morgan	Wu	8	Non-title	Omaha, Neb.
Sept. 22	Joe Bugner	Vince Cervi	Wu	12	Non-title	Gold Coast, Australia
Oct. 3	Jimmy Thunder	Melvin Foster	TKO	8	Non-title	Ledyard, Conn.
Oct. 3	Alex Stewart	Darren Hayden	TKO	5	Nontitle	Ledyard, Conn.
Oct. 7	Lennox Lewis	Tommy Morrison	TKO	6	Non-title	Atlantic City

November fights: WBO champion Riddick Bowe vs. Evander Holyfield and Mike Tyson vs. Buster Mathis Jr., both on Nov. 4 in Las Vegas.

Note: The WBA officially stripped Foreman of its title on Mar. 4, 1995, after refusing his request to sanction the bout against Germany's Axel Schulz on Apr. 22. Because Foreman was unranked when he knocked out champion Michael Moorer on Nov. 5, 1994, he was obligated to fight the WBA's No. 1 contender Tony Tucker within four months. Two months after defeating Schulz in a controversial majority decision, Foreman relinquished the IBF title rather than give Schulz a rematch as mandated by the IBF. Schulz is scheduled to fight South African Franz Botha for the vacant IBF title on Dec. 9 in Stuttgart, Germany.

Major Bouts (Cont.)
Cruiserweights (190 lbs)
(Jr. Heavyweights)

Date	Winner	Loser	Result	Title	Site
Nov. 12	**Orlin Norris**	James Heath	TKO 2	**WBA**	Mexico City
Dec. 3	**Anaclet Wamba**	Marcelo Dominguez	Wm 12	**WBC**	Salta, Argentina
Dec. 30	**Anaclet Wamba**	Perfecto Gonzalez	TKO 1	**WBC**	Pointe-a-Pitre, France
Mar. 17	**Orlin Norris**	Adolpho Washington	Wu 12	**WBA**	Worcester, Mass.
Mar. 31	Thomas Hearns*	Lenny Lapaglia	TKO 1	Non-title	Detroit
June 24	**Al Cole**	Uriah Grant	Wu 12	**IBF**	Atlantic City
July 22	Nate Miller	**Orlin Norris**	KO 8	**WBA**	London
July 25	Marcelo Dominguez**	Akim Tafer	KO 9	interim **WBC**	St. Jean, France
Sept. 2	**Marcelo Dominguez**	Reynaldo Gimenez	TKO 12	interim **WBC**	Gualeguaychu, Arg.
Sept. 26	Thomas Hearns	Earl Butler	Wu 12	Non-title	Auburn Hills, Mich.

*For unrecognized World Boxing Union championship. Hearns has now won five legitimate titles— WBA welterweight, WBC jr. middleweight, WBC light heavyweight, WBC middleweight and WBA light heavyweight— and two not so legit— WBO super middleweight and WBU cruiserweight.

**WBC champion Wamba injured himself training for a July 8 defense against Tafer and was granted a medical absence. Dominguez fought Tafer instead and won the interim title, which he will defend until Wamba can return and fight him for the unified title.

Light Heavyweights (175 lbs)

Date	Winner	Loser	Result	Title	Site
Oct. 8	**Henry Maske**	Iran Barkley	TKO 9	**IBF**	Düsseldorf, Germany
Dec. 17	Dariusz Michalczewski	Nestor Giovannini	KO 10	(WBO)	Hamburg, Germnay
Feb. 11	**Henry Maske**	Egerton Marcus	Wu 12	**IBF**	Frankfurt, Germany
Feb. 18	Montell Griffin	James Toney*	Wm 12	Non-title	Las Vegas
Feb. 25	**Mike McCallum**	Carl Jones	TKO 7	**WBC**	London
Mar. 5	Fabrice Tiozzo	Noel Magee	TKO 4	Non-title	Vitrolles, France
Mar. 11	Dariusz Michalczewski	Robert Dominguez	TKO 2	(WBO)	Cologne, Germany
Mar. 20	James Toney	Karl Willis	TKO 8	Non-title	Auburn Hills, Mich.
Apr. 1	**Virgil Hill**	Crawford Ashley	Wu 12	**WBA**	Jean, Nev.
Apr. 30	James Toney	Anthony Hembrick	TKO 6	Non-title	Las Vegas
May 20	Dariusz Michalczewski	Paul Carlo	KO 4	(WBO)	Hamburg, Germany
May 27	**Henry Maske**	Graciano Rocchigiani	Wu 12	**IBF**	Dortmund, Germany
June 16	Fabrice Tiozzo	**Mike McCallum**	Wu 12	**WBC**	Lyon, France
June 18	James Toney	Fred Delgado	TKO 5	Non-title	New Orleans
Aug. 19	Dariusz Michalczewski	Everardo Armenta	KO 5	(WBO)	Düsseldorf, Germany
Sept. 2	**Virgil Hill**	Drake Thadzi	Wu 12	**WBA**	London
Sept. 9	James Toney	Ernest Mateen	Disq. 5	Non-title	Las Vegas
Oct. 7	Dariusz Michalczewski	Philippe Michel	Wu 12	(WBO)	Frankfurt, Germany
Oct. 14	**Henry Maske**	Graciano Rocchigiani	Wu 12	**IBF**	Munich

*Toney stepped up after losing IBF super middleweight title to Roy Jones Jr. on Nov. 18, 1994.

Super Middleweights (168 lbs)

Date	Winner	Loser	Result	Title	Site
Oct. 15	Chris Eubank	Dan Schommer	Wu 12	(WBO)	Sun City, S.A.
Oct. 18	Roberto Duran	Heath Todd	TKO 6	Non-title	Bay St. Louis, Miss.
Nov. 8	Vinny Pazienza	Rafael Williams	Wu 10	Non-title	Ledyard, Conn.
Nov. 18	Roy Jones Jr.*	**James Toney**	Wu 12	**IBF**	Las Vegas
Dec. 10	Chris Eubank	Henry Wharton	Wu 12	(WBO)	Manchester, England
Dec. 17	**Frankie Liles**	Michael Nunn	Wu 12	**WBA**	Quito, Ecuador
Jan. 14	Vinny Pazienza	Roberto Duran	Wu 12	Non-title	Atlantic City
Feb. 25	**Nigel Benn**	Gerald McClellan**	KO 10	**WBC**	London
Mar. 18	**Roy Jones Jr.*****	Antoine Byrd	TKO 1	**IBF**	Pensacola, Fla.
Mar. 18	Steve Collins	Chris Eubank	Wu 12	(WBO)	Millstreet, Ireland
May 27	**Frankie Liles**	Frederic Seillier	TKO 6	**WBA**	Ft. Lauderdale
May 27	Chris Eubank	Bruno Godoy	TKO 1	Non-title	Belfast
June 10	Roberto Duran	Roni Martinez	TKO 7	Non-title	Kansas City
June 24	**Roy Jones Jr.**	Vinny Pazienza	TKO 6	**IBF**	Atlantic City
July 22	**Nigel Benn**	Vincenzo Nardiello	TKO 8	**WBC**	London
July 29	Chris Eubank	Jose Barruetabena	TKO 1	Non-title	Whitley Bay, England
Sept. 2	**Nigel Benn**	Danny Perez	KO 7	**WBC**	London
Sept. 9	Steve Collins	Chris Eubank	Ws 12	(WBO)	Millstreet, Ire.
Sept. 30	**Roy Jones Jr.**	Tony Thornton	TKO 3	**IBF**	Pensacola, Fla.

November fight: WBA champion Frankie Liles vs. Mauricio Amara in Las Vegas (Nov. 4).

*Jones renounced the IBF middleweight crown to fight Toney.

**McClellan renounced the WBC middleweight crown to fight Benn. His 10th round knockout by Benn resulted in a one-hour operation to remove a large blood clot from his brain and ended his boxing career at age 27 (record: 31-3-0, 28 KOs).

***Jones gave 5% of the gate from the March 18 Byrd fight to McClellan and his family.

Middleweights (160 lbs)

Date	Winner	Loser	Result	Title	Site
Nov. 5	**Jorge Castro**	Alex Ramos	KO 2	**WBA**	Caleta, Argentina
Dec. 10	**Jorge Castro**	John David Jackson*	TKO 9	**WBA**	Monterrey, Mexico
Dec. 14	Steve Collins	Lonny Beasley	P'poned	(WBO)	Boston
Dec. 17	Bernard Hopkins	Segundo Mercado	Draw 12	vacant **IBF**	Quito, Ecuador
Mar. 17	Julian Jackson	Agostino Cardamone	TKO 2	vacant **WBC**	Worcester, Mass.
Apr. 29	Bernard Hopkins	Segundo Mercado	TKO 7	vacant **IBF**	Landover, Md.
May 6	Dana Rosenblatt	Chad Parker	KO 1	Non-title	Las Vegas
May 19	Lonnie Bradley	David Mendez	TKO 12	(vacant WBO)	Jean, Nev.
May 27	**Jorge Castro**	Anthony Andrews	TKO 12	**WBA**	Ft. Lauderdale
May 27	Julio C. Vasquez	Ruben Ruiz	TKO 3	Non-title	Ft. Lauderdale
Aug. 19	Qunicy Taylor	**Julian Jackson**	TKO 6	**WBC**	Las Vegas
Sept. 16	Aaron Davis	Simon Brown	Wu 10	Non-title	Atlantic City
Oct. 13	**Jorge Castro**	Reggie Johnson	Ws 12	**WBA**	Comodoro, Argentina

*John David Jackson was stripped of the WBA championship in 1994 after not paying a sanctioning fee for a May 6 non-title bout and avoiding Castro, the mandatory challenger. However, on Aug. 11, 1994, a federal court in New Jersey ordered the WBA to return the title to Jackson. A further settlement resulted in Jackson fighting Castro for his old title.
Note: Gerald McClellan relinquished the WBC title on Nov. 15, 1994, in order to challenge WBC super middleweight champion Nigel Benn on Feb. 25, 1995. Roy Jones Jr. gave up the IBF middleweight title in 1994 to fight IBF super middle champ James Toney.

Junior Middleweights (154 lbs)

(Super Welterweights)

Date	Winner	Loser	Result	Title	Site
Nov. 11	**Julio C. Vasquez**	Tony Marshall	Wu 12	**WBA**	Tucuman, Argentina
Nov. 12	Luis Santana	**Terry Norris**	Disq 5*	**WBC**	Mexico City
Dec. 17	Simon Brown	Frank Newton	TKO 2	Non-title	Quito, Ecuador
Jan. 10	Buddy McGirt	Buck Smith	Wu 10	Non-title	Kenner, La.
Mar. 4	Pernell Whitaker†	**Julio C. Vasquez**	Wu 12	**WBA**	Atlantic City
Apr. 8	**Luis Santana**	Terry Norris	Disq 3**	**WBC**	Las Vegas
Apr. 29	**Vincent Pettway**	Simon Brown	KO 6	**IBF**	Landover, Md.
May 7	Buddy McGirt	Joe Gatti	TKO 5	Non-title	Biloxi, Miss.
May 19	Gianfranco Rosi	Verno Phillips	Wu 12	(WBO)	Perugia, Italy
June 10	Roberto Duran	Roni Martinez	TKO 7	Non-title	Kansas City
June 16	Carl Daniels	Julio Cesar Green	Wu 12	vacant **WBA**	Lyon, France
July 18	Buddy McGirt	John Stewart	TKO 5	Non-title	Lyndhurst, N.J.
Aug. 12	Paul Vaden	**Vincent Pettway**	TKO 12	**IBF**	Las Vegas
Aug. 19	**Terry Norris**	Luis Sanatana	TKO 2	**WBC**	Las Vegas
Sept. 16	**Terry Norris**	David Gonzales	TKO 9	Non-title	Las Vegas
Sept. 30	Andrew Council	Buddy McGirt	TKO 9	Non-title	Atlantic City

November fights: Terry Norris vs. Paul Vaden in WBC-IBF unification bout and WBA champion Carl Daniels vs. former champion Julio Cesar Vasquez, both at Las Vegas (Nov. 4).

*Santana, who was losing the fight, was declared the winner and new champion after being fouled when he was knocked down by a Norris punch to the back of the head at 2:02 of the 5th round.
†Whitaker, the WBC welterweight champion, stepped up in weight to fight Vasquez. After defeating Vasquez, he relinquished the title on March 8, 1995 and returned to the welterweight division.
**For the second time in four months, Norris was disqualified for a major rules violation, this time knocking down Santana five seconds after the bell ending the third round.

Welterweights (147 lbs)

Date	Winner	Loser	Result	Title	Site
Oct. 1	**Pernell Whitaker**	Buddy McGirt	Wu 12	**WBC**	Norfolk, Va.
Oct. 1	**Ike Quartey**	Alberto Cortes	TKO 5	**WBA**	Carpentras, France
Nov. 15	Hector Camacho	Rusty Derouen	TKO 4	Non-title	Erie, Pa.
Dec. 10	**Felix Trinidad**	Oba Carr	TKO 8	**IBF**	Monterrey, Mexico
Jan. 14	Hector Camacho	Todd Foster	TKO 5	Non-title	Atlantic City
Feb. 28	Hector Camacho	Luis Maysonet	TKO 7	Non-title	Ledyard, Conn.
Mar. 4	**Ike Quartey**	Jung-Ho Park	TKO 4	**WBA**	Atlantic City
Apr. 8	**Felix Trinidad**	Roger Turner	TKO 2	**IBF**	Las Vegas
Apr. 30	Roger Mayweather	Mike Mungin	Wu 10	Non-title	Las Vegas
May 20	Hector Camacho	Homer Gibbons	Wu 12	Non-title	Atlantic City
May 27	Eammon Loughran	Angel Beltre	NC 3	(WBO)	Belfast
June 27	Hector Camacho	Juan Arroyo	TKO 7	Non-title	Ft. Lauderdale
Aug. 6	Hector Camacho	Gary Kirkland	TKO 9	Non-title	Ledyard, Conn.
Aug. 23	**Ike Quartey**	Andrew Murray	TKO 4	**WBA**	Le Cannet, France
Aug. 23	**Pernell Whitaker**	Gary Jacobs	Wu 12	**WBC**	Atlantic City
Aug. 26	Eammon Loughran	Tony Gannarelli	TKO 6	(WBO)	Belfast
Oct. 7	Eammon Loughran	Angel Beltre	Wu 12	(WBO)	Belfast
Oct. 12	Hector Camacho	Richie Hess	TKO 4	Non-title	Washington, D.C.

November fights: WBC champion Pernell Whitaker vs. former jr. welterweight champion Jake Rodriguez and IBF champion Felix Trinidad vs Larry Barnes, both at Atlantic City (Nov. 18).

Major Bouts (Cont.)

Junior Welterweights (140 lbs)
(Super Lightweights)

Date	Winner	Loser	Result	Title	Site
Oct. 5	Ray Oliveira	Charles Murray	Wu 10	Non-title	Atlantic City
Dec. 10	**Julio Cesar Chavez**	Tony Lopez	TKO 10	**WBC**	Monterrey, Mexico
Dec. 10	**Frankie Randall**	Rodney Moore	TKO 7	**WBA**	Monterrey, Mexico
Jan. 21	Scott Walker	Alexis Arguello	Wu 12	Non-title	Las Vegas
Jan. 28	Kostya Tszyu	**Jake Rodriguez**	TKO 6	**IBF**	Las Vegas
Apr. 8	**Julio Cesar Chavez**	Giovanni Parisi	Wu 12	**WBC**	Las Vegas
Apr. 8	Juan Martin Coggi	Idelmar Paisan	Wu 10	Non-title	Buenos Aires
Apr. 28	Jake Rodriguez	Jaime Balboa	Wu 10	Non-title	Bushkill, Pa.
Apr. 29	Fred Pendleton	Darryl Tyson	TKO 10	Non-title	Landover, Md.
May 6	Juan Martin Coggi	Hiroyuki Sakamoto	Wu 10	Non-title	Tokyo
June 16	**Frankie Randall**	Jose Barboza	Ws 12	**WBA**	Lyon, France
June 25	**Kostya Tszyu**	Roger Mayweather	Wu 12	**IBF**	Newcastle, Aus.
July 29	**Julio Cesar Chavez**	Craig Houk	TKO 1	Non-title	Chicago
Aug. 12	Fred Pendleton	Tony Lopez	TKO 8	Non-title	Las Vegas
Sept. 16	**Julio Cesar Chavez**	David Kamau	Wu 12	**WBC**	Las Vegas

November fight: WBA champion Frankie Randall vs. former champion Juan Martin Coggi in Las Vegas (Nov. 4).

Lightweights (135 lbs)

Date	Winner	Loser	Result	Title	Site
Nov. 9	Billy Schwer	Manuel Hernandez	KO 6	Non-title	London
Nov. 18	Oscar De La Hoya	Carl Griffith	TKO 3	(WBO)	Las Vegas
Dec. 8	**Rafael Ruelas**	Omar Pacheco	KO 3	**IBF**	Albuquerque
Dec. 10	**Gussie Nazarov**	Joey Gamache	KO 2	**WBA**	Portland, Me.
Dec. 10	Oscar De La Hoya	John Avila	TKO 9	(WBO)	Los Angeles
Dec. 13	**Miguel A. Gonzalez**	Calvin Grove	TKO 6	**WBC**	Albuquerque
Jan. 28	**Rafael Ruelas**	Billy Schwer	TKO 8	**IBF**	Las Vegas
Feb. 18	Oscar De La Hoya	John-John Molina*	Wu 12	(WBO)	Las Vegas
Apr. 25	**Miguel A. Gonzalez**	Ricardo Silva	Wu 12	**WBC**	So. Padre Is., Tex.
May 6	Oscar De La Hoya	**Rafael Ruelas**	TKO 2	**IBF**/(WBO)	Las Vegas
May 6	Dingaan Thobela	Kenny Vice	TKO 2	Non-title	Durban, S.A.
May 7	Jesse James Leija	Jeff Mayweather	Wu 12	Non-title	Las Vegas
May 8	John-John Molina	Mark Reels	Wu 10	Non-title	San Juan, P.R.
May 12	Billy Schwer	Stephen Chungu	TKO 11	Non-title	London
May 15	**Gussie Nazarov**	Won Park	KO 2	**WBA**	Tokyo
June 2	**Miguel A. Gonzalez**	Marty Jakubowski	Wu 12	**WBC**	Ledyard, Conn.
Aug. 19	**Miguel A. Gonzalez**	Lamar Murphy	Wm 12	**WBC**	Las Vegas
Aug. 19	Phillip Holiday	Miguel Julio	TKO 10	vacant **IBF**	Sun City, S.A.
Sept. 9	Oscar De La Hoya	Genaro Hernandez**	TKO 7	(WBO)***	Las Vegas

*Molina, the IBF junior lightweight champion, stepped up in weight to fight Gonzalez.
**Hernandez, the WBA junior lightweight champion, stepped up in weight to fight De La Hoya.
***De La Hoya renounced the IBF lightweight crown on July 12 before IBF could strip him for fighting Hernandez on Sept. 9 instead of IBF No. 1 contender Miguel Julio.

Junior Lightweights (130 lbs)
(Super Featherweights)

Date	Winner	Loser	Result	Title	Site
Nov. 12	**Genaro Hernandez**	Jimmy Garcia	Wu 12	**WBA**	Mexico City
Nov. 26	**John-John Molina**	Wilson Rodriguez	KO 10	**IBF**	San Juan, P.R.
Jan. 28	**Gabriel Ruelas**	Freddie Liberatore	TKO 2	**WBC**	Las Vegas
Mar. 31	**Genaro Hernandez**	Jorge Paez	TKO 8	Non-title	Anaheim
Apr. 22	Eddie Hopson	Moises Pedroza	KO 7	vacant **IBF**	Atlantic City
Apr. 26	Tom Johnson†	Victor Laureano	TKO 3	Non-title	Auburn Hills
May 2	Jesse James Leija	Jeff Mayweather	Wu 10	Non-title	Las Vegas
May 6	**Gabriel Ruelas**	Jimmy Garcia*	TKO 11	**WBC**	Las Vegas
July 8	Jose Vida Ramos	Jorge Paez	Disq. 5	Non-title	Las Vegas
June 17	Regilio Tuur	Pete Taliaferro	TKO 5	(WBO)	New Orleans
July 9	Tracy Patterson	**Eddie Hopson**	TKO 2	**IBF**	Reno
Sept. 16	Regilio Tuur	Luis Mendoza	TKO 11	(WBO)	Arnheim, Holland

*Garcia, 23, collapsed after the fight, suffering from a blood clot on the brain. He was carried from the ring on a stretcher, rushed to University Medical Center and operated on immediately. After showing some signs of recovery, Garcia died on May 19 when doctors, after finding no brain activity, disconnected life support systems that had kept his heart beating for 13 days.
†IBF featherweight champion Johnson stepped up in weight to fight Laureano on April 26.
Notes: IBF champion Molina renounced title in January to step up and challenge Oscar De La Hoya for the WBO junior lightweight crown. The WBA stripped Genaro Hernandez of his title when he opted to move up in weight to fight Oscar De La Hoya for the IBF/WBO lightweight crown on Sept. 9.

Featherweights (126 lbs)

Date	Winner	Loser	Result	Title	Site
Oct. 22	**Tom Johnson**	Francisco Segura	Wu 12	**IBF**	Atlantic City
Nov. 2	Kevin Kelley	Pete Taliaferro	TKO 10	Non-title	Tunica, Miss.
Nov. 29	Tracy Patterson	Daryl Pinckney	Wu 10	Non-title	Atlantic City
Dec. 3	**Eloy Rojas**	Luis Mendoza	Wu 12	**WBA**	Bogota, Colombia
Jan. 7	Alejandro Gonzalez	**Kevin Kelley**	TKO 10	**WBC**	San Antonio
Jan. 28	**Tom Johnson**	Manuel Medina	Wu 12	**IBF**	Atlantic City
Mar. 29	Tracy Patterson	Jose Luis Madrid	TKO 3	Non-title	New York City
Mar. 31	**Alejandro Gonzalez**	Louie Espinoza	Wu 12	**WBC**	Anaheim
Mar. 31	Kevin Kelley	Ricardo Rivera	TKO 9	Non-title	Chester, W. Va.
May 27	**Eloy Rojas**	Yung-Kyun Park	Ws 12	**WBA**	Kwangju, S. Korea
May 28	**Tom Johnson**	Eddie Croft	Wu 12	**IBF**	So. Padre Is., Texas
June 2	**Alejandro Gonzalez**	Tony Green	TKO 9	**WBC**	Ledyard, Conn.
Aug. 13	**Eloy Rojas**	Nobutoshi Hiranaka	Wu 12	**WBA**	Tagawa, Japan
Sept. 9	Kevin Kelley	Clarence Adams	Draw 12	Non-title	Las Vegas
Sept. 23	Manuel Medina	**Alejandro Gonzalez**	Ws 12	**WBC**	Sacramento

Junior Featherweights (122 lbs)
(Super Bantamweights)

Date	Winner	Loser	Result	Title	Site
Oct. 13	**Wilfredo Vazquez**	Juan Polo Perez	Wu 12	**WBA**	Paris
Oct. 26	Hector Acero-Sanchez	Barrington Francis	Wu 10	Non-title	Bushkill, Pa.
Nov. 19	**Vuyani Bungu**	Felix Camacho	Wu 12	**IBF**	Johannesburg, S.A.
Jan. 7	**Wilfredo Vazquez**	Orlando Canizales*	Wm 12	**WBA**	San Antonio
Mar. 4	**Vuyani Bungu**	Mohammed Nurhuda	Wu 12	**IBF**	Pretoria, S.A.
Mar. 11	**Hector Acero-Sanchez**	Julio Gervacio	Wu 12	**WBC**	Atlantic City
Mar. 31	Marco Barrera	Daniel Jiminez	Wu 12	(WBO)	Anaheim
Apr. 29	**Vuyani Bungu**	Victor Llerena	Wu 12	**IBF**	Johannesburg
May 13	Antonio Cermeno	**Wilfredo Vazquez**	Wu 12	**WBA**	Bayamon, P.R.
June 2	**Hector Acero-Sanchez**	Daniel Zaragoza	MDraw 12	**WBC**	Ledyard, Conn.
July 15	Orlando Canizales	John Lewus	Wu 12	Non-title	Lake Tahoe
June 2	Marco Barrera	Frankie Toledo	TKO 2	(WBO)	Ledyard, Conn.
July 15	Marco Barrera	Maui Diaz	KO 1	(WBO)	Inglewood
Aug. 22	Marco Barrera	Agapito Sanchez	Wu 12	(WBO)	So. Padre Is., Texas
Sept. 12	Orlando Canizales	Danny Aponte	TKO 7	Non-title	Biloxi, Miss.
Sept. 26	**Vuyani Bungu**	Laureano Ramirez	Wu 12	**IBF**	Hammanskraal, S.A.

*Canizales, the IBF bantamweight champion, stepped up in weight to fight Vasquez.

Bantamweights (118 lbs)

Date	Winner	Loser	Result	Title	Site
Oct. 15	**Orlando Canizales**	Sergio Reyes	Wu 12	**IBF**	Laredo, Texas
Nov. 20	**Daorung Chuvatana**	In-Sik Koh	TWu 5	**WBA**	Bangkok
Dec. 4	**Yasuei Yakushiji**	Joichiro Tatsuyoshi*	Wm 12	**WBC**	Nagoya, Japan
Jan. 21	Harold Mestre	Juvenal Berrio	TKO 8	vacant **IBF**	Cartagena, Colombia
Apr. 2	**Yasuei Yakushiji**	Cuauhtemoc Gomez	Wm 12	**WBC**	Nagoya, Japan
Apr. 29	Mbulelo Botile	**Harold Mestre**	TKO 2	**IBF**	Johannesburg
May 27	**Daorung Chuvatana**	Lakhin CP Gym	SDraw 12	**WBA**	Bangkok
July 4	**Mbulelo Botile**	Sammy Stewart	Wu 12	**IBF**	Johannesburg
July 30	Wayne McCullough	**Yasuei Yakushiji**	Ws 12	**WBC**	Nagoya, Japan
Sept. 17	Veeraphol Sahaprom	**Daorung Chuvatana**	Ws 12	**WBA**	Bangkok

*Interim champion Tatsuyoshi, received special permission from the Japan Boxing Commission to fight after surgery after corrective surgery for detached retinas.
Note: IBF champion Canizales gave up title in November 1994 when he agreed to step up in weight to fight Wilfredo Vasquez on Jan. 7.

Junior Bantamweights (115 lbs)
(Super Flyweights)

Date	Winner	Loser	Result	Title	Site
Oct. 12	Johnny Tapia	Henry Martinez	TKO 11	(WBO)	Albuquerque
Dec. 17	**Harold Grey**	Vincenzo Balcastro	Ws 12	**IBF**	Rome
Jan. 18	**Hiroshi Kawashima**	Jose Luis Bueno	Wu 12	**WBC**	Yokohama
Feb. 25	**Hyung-Chul Lee**	Tomonori Tamura	KO 12	**WBA**	Seoul
Mar. 18	**Harold Grey**	Orlando Tobon	Wu 12	**IBF**	Cartagena, Col.
Apr. 6	Julio Borboa	Ventura Mendevil	KO 2	Non-title	Los Angeles
May 6	Johnny Tapia	Ricardo Vargas	TDraw 12	(WBO)	Las Vegas
May 24	**Hiroshi Kawashima**	Seung-Koo Lee	Wu 12	**WBC**	Yokohama
June 24	**Harold Grey**	Julio Borboa	Ws 12	**IBF**	Cartagena, Col.
July 2	Johnny Tapia	Arthur Johnson	Wm 12	(WBO)	Albuquerque
July 22	Alimi Goitia	**Hyung-Chul Lee**	KO 4	**WBA**	Seoul
Sept. 9	Johnny Tapia	Jesse Miranda	Wu 10	non-title	Las Vegas
Oct. 7	Carlos Salazar	**Harold Grey**	Ws 12	**IBF**	Mar del Plata, Arg.

Major Bouts (Cont.)

Flyweights (112 lbs)

Date	Winner	Loser	Result	Title	Site
Dec. 25	**Saen Sow Ploenchit**	Danny Nunez	TKO 11	**WBA**	Rayong, Thailand
Jan. 30	**Yuri Arbachakov**	Oscar Arciniega	Wu 12	**WBC**	Sapporo, Japan
Feb. 18	Francisco Tejedor	Jose Luis Zepeda	TKO 6	vacant **IBF**	Cartagena, Colombia
Apr. 22	Danny Romero	**Francisco Tejedor**	Wu 12	IBF	Las Vegas
May 7	**Saen Sow Ploenchit**	Evangelio Perez	Wu 12	**WBA**	Hat Yai, Thailand
June 20	Michael Carbajal*	Andre Cazarez	TKO 10	Non-title	Bakersfield, Calif.
July 29	**Danny Romero**	Miguel Martinez	TKO 7	IBF	San Antonio
Sept. 8	Willy Salazar	Danny Romero	TKO 7	Non-title	Las Vegas
Sept. 25	**Yuri Arbachakov**	Chatchai Sasakul	Wu 12	**WBC**	Tokyo

*Junior Flyweight Carbajal stepped up in weight to fight Cazarez.
Note: Phichit Sithbangprachan relinquished the IBF title on Nov. 25, 1994, rather than fight top-ranked challenger Jose Luis Zepeda. Sithbangprachan won a split decision over Zepeda on May 8, 1994.

Junior Flyweights (108 lbs)

(Light Flyweights)

Date	Winner	Loser	Result	Title	Site
Nov. 12	**Chiquita Gonzalez**	Michael Carbajal	Wm 12	**IBF/WBC**	Mexico City
Feb. 4	Hi-Yong Choi	**Leo Gamez**	Wu 12	**WBA**	Seoul
Mar. 31	**Chiquita Gonzalez**	Jesus Zuniga	KO 5	**IBF/WBC**	Anaheim
Apr. 1	Michael Carbajal	Armando Diaz	Wu 10	Non-title	Jean, Nev.
May 24	Michael Carbajal	Francisco Carrasco	TKO 4	Non-title	Bakersfield, Calif.
June 20	Michael Carbajal	Andre Cazarez	TKO 10	Non-title	Bakersfield, Calif.
July 15	Saman Sorjaturong	**Chiquita Gonzalez**	KO 7	**IBF/WBC**	Inglewood
Aug. 12	Michael Carbajal	Jose Quirino	KO 1	Non-title	Las Vegas
Sept. 5	**Hi-Yong Choi**	Keiji Yamaguchi	Ws 12	**WBA**	Osaka, Japan
Sept. 16	Michael Carbajal	Gregorio Garcia	KO 3	Non-title	Las Vegas

Minimumweights (105 lbs)

(Strawweights or Mini-Flyweights)

Date	Winner	Loser	Result	Title	Site
Nov. 12	**Ratanapol Vorapin**	Carlos Rodrigues	TKO 3	**IBF**	Bangkok
Nov. 12	**Ricardo Lopez**	Javier Varquez	TKO 8	**WBC**	Mexico City
Dec. 10	**Ricardo Lopez**	Yamil Caraballo	KO 1	**WBC**	Monterrey, Mexico
Jan. 28	**Chana Porpaoin**	Jin-Ho Kim	Wu 12	**WBA**	Bangkok
Feb. 25	**Ratanapol Vorapin**	Jerry Pahayahay	KO 3	**IBF**	Bangkok
Apr. 1	**Ricardo Lopez**	Andy Tabanas	TKO 12	**WBC**	Jean, Nev.
May 19	**Ratanapol Vorapin**	Oscar Flores	TKO 2	**IBF**	Chiang Mai, Thailand
Aug. 6	**Chana Porpaoin**	Ernesto Rubillar Jr.	KO 6	**WBA**	Bangkok

World Amateur Championships

at Berlin, May 8-13, 1995
Finals

Wgt		Result
106	**Daniel Petrov**, Bulgaria	
	def. Bernard Inom, France	11-5
112	**Zoltan Lunka**, Germany	
	def. Bolat Yumadilov, Kazakhstan	11-6
119	**Raimkul Malachbekov**, Russia	
	def. Robert Ciba, Poland	5-3
125	**Serafim Todorov**, Bulgaria	
	def. Noureddine Medjihoud, Algeria	10-4
132	**Leonard Doroftei**, Romania	
	def. Bruno Wartelle, France	12-4
139	**Hector Vinent**, Cuba	
	def. Nurhan Suelmanoglu, Turkey	7-4
147	**Juan Hernandez**, Cuba	
	def. Oleg Saitov, Russia	4-2
156	**Francisc Vastag**, Romania	
	def. Alfredo Duvergel, Cuba	12-4
165	**Ariel Hernandez**, Cuba	
	def. Tomasz Borowski, Poland	6-2
178	**Antonio Tarver**, USA	
	def. Diosvani Vega, Cuba	7-3
Heavy	**Felix Savon**, Cuba	
	def. Luan Krasniqi, Germany	TKO 2
Super	**Alexei Lezin**, Russia	
	def. Vitali Klitschko, Ukraine	12-3

U.S. National Golden Gloves

at Lowell, Mass., May 1-6, 1995
Finals

Wgt		Result
106	**Jauquin Gallardo**, Southern Calif.	
	def. Gerald Tucker, Cincinnati	5-0
112	**Kelly Wright**, St. Louis	
	def. Robert Guillen, Nevada	4-1
119	**Jorge Munoz**, Texas	
	def. Evaristo Rodriguez, Chicago	5-0
125	**Frank Carmona**, Southern Calif.	
	def. Jorge Barajas, Rocky Mountain	4-1
132	**Dante Craig**, Cincinnati	
	def. Brian Adams, New York Metro	5-0
139	**DeMarcus Corley**, Washington	
	def. Chantel Stanciel, St. Louis	4-1
147	**David Palac**, Detroit	
	def. Raul Diaz, Chicago	5-0
156	**Randie Carver**, Kansas City	
	def. Darnell Wilson, Indiana	5-0
165	**Jose Spearman**, Cincinnati	
	def. Ralph Moncrief III, Cleveland	3-2
178	**Glenn Robinson**, New York Metro	
	def. Sean Dishman, Washington	5-0
Heavy	**Nate Jones**, Illinois	
	def. David Washington, Knoxville	4-1
Super	**Tom Martin**, Sunshine State	
	def. Joseph Mesi, Syracuse	3-2

THE 1996 SPORTS ALMANAC · INFORMATION PLEASE

BOXING STATISTICS

THROUGH THE YEARS
1884-1995
WORLD CHAMPIONS

SEC B

PAGE 895

World Heavyweight Championship Fights

Widely accepted world champions in **bold** type. Note following result abbreviations: KO (knockout), TKO (technical knockout), Wu (unanimous decision), Wm (majority decision), Ws (split decision), Ref (referee's decision), ND (no decision), Disq (won on disqualification).

Year	Date	Winner	Age	Wgt	Loser	Wgt	Result	Location
1892	Sept. 7	James J. Corbett	26	178	John L. Sullivan	212	KO 21	New Orleans
1894	Jan. 25	**James J. Corbett**	27	184	Charley Mitchell	158	KO 3	Jacksonville, Fla.
1897	Mar. 17	Bob Fitzsimmons	34	167	**James J. Corbett**	183	KO 14	Carson City, Nev.
1899	June 9	James J. Jeffries	24	206	**Bob Fitzsimmons**	167	KO 11	Coney Island, N.Y.
1899	Nov. 3	**James J. Jeffries**	24	215	Tom Sharkey	183	Ref 25	Coney Island, N.Y.
1900	Apr. 6	**James J. Jeffries**	24	NA	Jack Finnegan	NA	KO 1	Detroit
1900	May 11	**James J. Jeffries**	25	218	James J. Corbett	188	KO 23	Coney Island, N.Y.
1901	Nov. 15	**James J. Jeffries**	26	211	Gus Ruhlin	194	TKO 6	San Francisco
1902	July 25	**James J. Jeffries**	27	219	Bob Fitzsimmons	172	KO 8	San Francisco
1903	Aug. 14	**James J. Jeffries**	28	220	James J. Corbett	190	KO 10	San Francisco
1904	Aug. 25	**James J. Jeffries***	29	219	Jack Munroe	186	TKO 2	San Francisco
1905	July 3	Marvin Hart	28	190	Jack Root	171	KO 12	Reno, Nev.
1906	Feb. 23	Tommy Burns	24	180	**Marvin Hart**	188	Ref 20	Los Angeles
1906	Oct. 2	**Tommy Burns**	25	NA	Jim Flynn	NA	KO 15	Los Angeles
1906	Nov. 28	**Tommy Burns**	25	172	Phila. Jack O'Brien	163½	Draw 20	Los Angeles
1907	May 8	**Tommy Burns**	25	180	Phila. Jack O'Brien	167	Ref 20	Los Angeles
1907	July 4	**Tommy Burns**	26	181	Bill Squires	180	KO 1	Colma, Calif.
1907	Dec. 2	**Tommy Burns**	26	177	Gunner Moir	204	KO 10	London
1908	Feb. 10	**Tommy Burns**	26	NA	Jack Palmer	NA	KO 4	London
1908	Mar. 17	**Tommy Burns**	26	NA	Jem Roche	NA	KO 1	Dublin
1908	Apr. 18	**Tommy Burns**	26	NA	Jewey Smith	NA	KO 5	Paris
1908	June 13	**Tommy Burns**	26	184	Bill Squires	183	KO 8	Paris
1908	Aug. 24	**Tommy Burns**	27	181	Bill Squires	184	KO 13	Sydney
1908	Sept. 2	**Tommy Burns**	27	183	Bill Lang	187	KO 6	Melbourne
1908	Dec. 26	Jack Johnson	30	192	**Tommy Burns**	168	TKO 14	Sydney
1909	Mar. 10	**Jack Johnson**	30	NA	Victor McLaglen	NA	ND 6	Vancouver
1909	May 19	**Jack Johnson**	31	205	Phila. Jack O'Brien	161	ND 6	Philadelphia
1909	June 30	**Jack Johnson**	31	207	Tony Ross	214	ND 6	Pittsburgh
1909	Sept. 9	**Jack Johnson**	31	209	Al Kaufman	191	ND 10	San Francisco
1909	Oct. 16	**Jack Johnson**	31	205½	Stanley Ketchel	170¼	KO 12	Colma, Calif.
1910	July 4	**Jack Johnson**	32	208	James J. Jeffries	227	KO 15	Reno, Nev.
1912	July 4	**Jack Johnson**	34	195½	Jim Flynn	175	TKO 9	Las Vegas, N.M.
1913	Dec. 19	**Jack Johnson**	35	NA	Jim Johnson	NA	Draw 10	Paris
1914	June 27	**Jack Johnson**	36	221	Frank Moran	203	Ref 20	Paris
1915	Apr. 5	Jess Willard	33	230	**Jack Johnson**	205½	KO 26	Havana
1916	Mar. 25	**Jess Willard**	34	225	Frank Moran	203	ND 10	NYC (Mad. Sq. Garden)
1919	July 4	Jack Dempsey	24	187	**Jess Willard**	245	TKO 4	Toledo, Ohio
1920	Sept. 6	**Jack Dempsey**	25	185	Billy Miske	187	KO 3	Benton Harbor, Mich.
1920	Dec. 14	**Jack Dempsey**	25	188¼	Bill Brennan	197	KO 12	NYC (Mad. Sq. Garden)
1921	July 2	**Jack Dempsey**	26	188	Georges Carpentier	172	KO 4	Jersey City, N.J.

*James J. Jeffries retired as champion on May 13, 1905, then came out of retirement to fight Jack Johnson for the title in 1910.

World Heavyweight Championship Fights (Cont.)

Year	Date	Winner	Age	Wgt	Loser	Wgt	Result	Location
1923	July 4	**Jack Dempsey**	28	188	Tommy Gibbons	175½	Ref 15	Shelby, Montana
1923	Sept. 14	**Jack Dempsey**	28	192½	Luis Firpo	216½	KO 2	NYC (Polo Grounds)
1926	Sept. 23	Gene Tunney	29	189½	**Jack Dempsey**	190	Wu 10	Philadelphia
1927	Sept. 22	**Gene Tunney**	30	189½	Jack Dempsey	192½	Wu 10	Chicago
1928	July 26	**Gene Tunney***	31	192	Tom Heeney	203	TKO 11	NYC (Yankee Stadium)
1930	June 12	Max Schmeling	24	188	Jack Sharkey	197	Foul 4	NYC (Yankee Stadium)
1931	July 3	**Max Schmeling**	25	189	Young Stribling	186½	TKO 15	Cleveland
1932	June 21	Jack Sharkey	29	205	**Max Schmeling**	188	Ws 15	Long Island City, N.Y.
1933	June 29	Primo Carnera	26	260½	**Jack Sharkey**	201	KO 6	Long Island City, N.Y.
1933	Oct. 22	**Primo Carnera**	26	259½	Paulino Uzcudun	229¼	Wu 15	Rome
1934	Mar. 1	**Primo Carnera**	27	270	Tommy Loughran	184	Wu 15	Miami
1934	June 14	Max Baer	25	209½	**Primo Carnera**	263¼	TKO 11	Long Island City, N.Y.
1935	June 13	James J. Braddock	29	193¾	**Max Baer**	209½	Wu 15	Long Island City, N.Y.
1937	June 22	Joe Louis	23	197¼	**James J. Braddock**	197	KO 8	Chicago
1937	Aug. 30	Joe Louis	23	197	Tommy Farr	204¼	Wu 15	NYC (Yankee Stadium)
1938	Feb. 23	**Joe Louis**	23	200	Nathan Mann	193½	KO 3	NYC (Mad. Sq. Garden)
1938	Apr. 1	**Joe Louis**	23	202½	Harry Thomas	196	KO 5	Chicago
1938	June 22	**Joe Louis**	24	198¾	Max Schmeling	193	KO 1	NYC (Yankee Stadium)
1939	Jan. 25	**Joe Louis**	24	200¼	John Henry Lewis	180¾	KO 1	NYC (Mad. Sq. Garden)
1939	Apr. 17	**Joe Louis**	24	201¼	Jack Roper	204¾	KO 1	Los Angeles
1939	June 28	**Joe Louis**	25	200¾	Tony Galento	233¾	TKO 4	NYC (Yankee Stadium)
1939	Sept. 20	**Joe Louis**	25	200	Bob Pastor	183	KO 11	Detroit
1940	Feb. 9	**Joe Louis**	25	203	Arturo Godoy	202	Ws 15	NYC (Mad. Sq. Garden)
1940	Mar. 29	**Joe Louis**	25	201½	Johnny Paychek	187½	KO 2	NYC (Mad. Sq. Garden)
1940	June 20	**Joe Louis**	26	199	Arturo Godoy	201¼	TKO 8	NYC (Yankee Stadium)
1940	Dec. 16	**Joe Louis**	26	202¼	Al McCoy	180¾	TKO 6	Boston
1941	Jan. 31	**Joe Louis**	26	202½	Red Burman	188	KO 5	NYC (Mad. Sq. Garden)
1941	Feb. 17	**Joe Louis**	26	203½	Gus Dorazio	193½	KO 2	Philadelphia
1941	Mar. 21	**Joe Louis**	26	202	Abe Simon	254½	TKO 13	Detroit
1941	Apr. 8	**Joe Louis**	26	203½	Tony Musto	199½	TKO 9	St. Louis
1941	May 23	**Joe Louis**	27	201½	Buddy Baer	237½	Disq 7	Washington, D.C.
1941	June 18	**Joe Louis**	27	199½	Billy Conn	174	KO 13	NYC (Polo Grounds)
1941	Sept. 29	**Joe Louis**	27	202¼	Lou Nova	202½	TKO 6	NYC (Polo Grounds)
1942	Jan. 9	**Joe Louis**	27	206¾	Buddy Baer	250	KO 1	NYC (Mad. Sq. Garden)
1942	Mar. 27	**Joe Louis**	27	207½	Abe Simon	255½	KO 6	NYC (Mad. Sq. Garden)
1942-45	World War II							
1946	June 9	**Joe Louis**	32	207	Billy Conn	187	KO 8	NYC (Yankee Stadium)
1946	Sept. 18	**Joe Louis**	32	211	Tami Mauriello	198½	KO 1	NYC (Yankee Stadium)
1947	Dec. 5	**Joe Louis**	33	211½	Jersey Joe Walcott	194½	Ws 15	NYC (Mad. Sq. Garden)
1948	June 25	**Joe Louis****	34	213½	Jersey Joe Walcott	194¾	KO 11	NYC (Yankee Stadium)
1949	June 22	**Ezzard Charles**	27	181¾	Jersey Joe Walcott	195½	Wu 15	Chicago
1949	Aug. 10	**Ezzard Charles**	28	180	Gus Lesnevich	182	TKO 8	NYC (Yankee Stadium)
1949	Oct. 14	**Ezzard Charles**	28	182	Pat Valentino	188½	KO 8	San Francisco
1950	Aug. 15	**Ezzard Charles**	29	183¼	Freddie Beshore	184½	TKO 14	Buffalo
1950	Sept. 27	**Ezzard Charles**	29	184½	Joe Louis	218	Wu 15	NYC (Yankee Stadium)
1950	Dec. 5	**Ezzard Charles**	29	185	Nick Barone	178½	KO 11	Cincinnati
1951	Jan. 12	**Ezzard Charles**	29	185	Lee Oma	193	TKO 10	NYC (Mad. Sq. Garden)
1951	Mar. 7	**Ezzard Charles**	29	186	Jersey Joe Walcott	193	Wu 15	Detroit
1951	May 30	**Ezzard Charles**	29	182	Joey Maxim	181½	Wu 15	Chicago
1951	July 18	Jersey Joe Walcott	37	194	**Ezzard Charles**	182	KO 7	Pittsburgh
1952	June 5	**Jersey Joe Walcott**	38	196	Ezzard Charles	191½	Wu 15	Philadelphia
1952	Sept. 23	Rocky Marciano	29	184	**Jersey Joe Walcott**	196	KO 13	Philadelphia
1953	May 15	**Rocky Marciano**	29	184½	Jersey Joe Walcott	197¾	KO 1	Chicago
1953	Sept. 24	**Rocky Marciano**	30	185	Roland LaStarza	184¾	TKO 11	NYC (Polo Grounds)
1954	June 17	**Rocky Marciano**	30	187½	Ezzard Charles	185½	Wu 15	NYC (Yankee Stadium)
1954	Sept. 17	**Rocky Marciano**	31	187	Ezzard Charles	192½	KO 8	NYC (Yankee Stadium)

*Gene Tunney retired as undefeated champion in 1928.
**Joe Louis retired as undefeated champion on Mar. 1, 1949, then came out of retirement to fight Ezzard Charles for the title in 1950.

Year	Date	Winner	Age	Wgt	Loser	Wgt	Result	Location
1955	May 16	**Rocky Marciano**	31	189	Don Cockell	205	TKO 9	San Francisco
1955	Sept. 21	**Rocky Marciano***	32	188¼	Archie Moore	188	KO 9	NYC (Yankee Stadium)
1956	Nov. 30	Floyd Patterson	21	182¼	Archie Moore	187¾	KO 5	Chicago
1957	July 29	**Floyd Patterson**	22	184	Tommy Jackson	192½	TKO 10	NYC (Polo Grounds)
1957	Aug. 22	**Floyd Patterson**	22	187¼	Pete Rademacher	202	KO 6	Seattle
1958	Aug. 18	**Floyd Patterson**	23	184½	Roy Harris	194	TKO 13	Los Angeles
1959	May 1	**Floyd Patterson**	24	182½	Brian London	206	KO 11	Indianapolis
1959	June 26	Ingemar Johansson	26	196	**Floyd Patterson**	182	TKO 3	NYC (Yankee Stadium)
1960	June 20	Floyd Patterson	25	190	**Ingemar Johansson**	194¾	KO 5	NYC (Polo Grounds)
1961	Mar. 13	**Floyd Patterson**	26	194¾	Ingemar Johansson	206½	KO 6	Miami Beach
1961	Dec. 4	**Floyd Patterson**	26	188½	Tom McNeeley	197	KO 4	Toronto
1962	Sept. 25	Sonny Liston	30	214	**Floyd Patterson**	189	KO 1	Chicago
1963	July 22	**Sonny Liston**	31	215	Floyd Patterson	194½	KO 1	Las Vegas
1964	Feb. 25	Cassius Clay**	22	210½	**Sonny Liston**	218	TKO 7	Miami Beach
1965	Mar. 5	Ernie Terrell WBA	25	199	Eddie Machen	192	Wu 15	Chicago
1965	May 25	**Muhammad Ali**	23	206	Sonny Liston	215¼	KO 1	Lewiston, Me.
1965	Nov. 1	Ernie Terrell WBA	26	206	George Chuvalo	209	Wu 15	Toronto
1965	Nov. 22	**Muhammad Ali**	23	210	Floyd Patterson	196¾	TKO 12	Las Vegas
1966	Mar. 29	**Muhammad Ali**	24	214½	George Chuvalo	216	Wu 15	Toronto
1966	May 21	**Muhammad Ali**	24	201½	Henry Cooper	188	TKO 6	London
1966	June 28	Ernie Terrell WBA	27	209½	Doug Jones	187½	Wu 15	Houston
1966	Aug. 6	**Muhammad Ali**	24	209½	Brian London	201½	KO 3	London
1966	Sept. 10	**Muhammad Ali**	24	203½	Karl Mildenberger	194¼	TKO 12	Frankfurt, W. Ger.
1966	Nov. 14	**Muhammad Ali**	24	212¾	Cleveland Williams	210½	TKO 3	Houston
1967	Feb. 6	**Muhammad Ali**	25	212¼	Ernie Terrell WBA	212½	Wu 15	Houston
1967	Mar. 22	**Muhammad Ali**	25	211½	Zora Folley	202½	KO 7	NYC (Mad. Sq. Garden)
1968	Mar. 4	Joe Frazier	24	204½	Buster Mathis	243½	TKO 11	NYC (Mad. Sq. Garden)
1968	Apr. 27	Jimmy Ellis	28	197	Jerry Quarry	195	Wm 15	Oakland
1968	June 24	Joe Frazier NY	24	203½	Manuel Ramos	208	TKO 2	NYC (Mad. Sq. Garden)
1968	Aug. 14	Jimmy Ellis WBA	28	198	Floyd Patterson	188	Ref 15	Stockholm
1968	Dec. 10	Joe Frazier NY	24	203	Oscar Bonavena	207	Wu 15	Philadelphia
1969	Apr. 22	Joe Frazier NY	25	204½	Dave Zyglewicz	190½	KO 1	Houston
1969	June 23	Joe Frazier NY	25	203½	Jerry Quarry	198½	TKO 8	NYC (Mad. Sq. Garden)
1970	Feb. 16	Joe Frazier NY	26	205	Jimmy Ellis WBA	201	TKO 5	NYC (Mad. Sq. Garden)
1970	Nov. 18	Joe Frazier	26	209	Bob Foster	188	KO 2	Detroit
1971	Mar. 8	Joe Frazier	27	205½	**Muhammad Ali**	215	Wu 15	NYC (Mad. Sq. Garden)
1972	Jan. 15	**Joe Frazier**	28	215½	Terry Daniels	195	TKO 4	New Orleans
1972	May 26	**Joe Frazier**	28	217½	Ron Stander	218	TKO 5	Omaha, Neb.
1973	Jan. 22	George Foreman	24	217½	**Joe Frazier**	214	TKO 2	Kingston, Jamaica
1973	Sept. 1	**George Foreman**	24	219½	Jose (King) Roman	196½	KO 1	Tokyo
1974	Mar. 26	**George Foreman**	25	224¾	Ken Norton	212¾	TKO 2	Caracas, Venezuela
1974	Oct. 30	Muhammad Ali	32	216½	**George Foreman**	220	KO 8	Kinshasa, Zaire
1975	Mar. 24	**Muhammad Ali**	33	223½	Chuck Wepner	225	TKO 15	Cleveland
1975	May 16	**Muhammad Ali**	33	224½	Ron Lyle	219	TKO 11	Las Vegas
1975	July 1	**Muhammad Ali**	33	224½	Joe Bugner	230	Wu 15	Kuala Lumpur, Malaysia
1975	Oct. 1	**Muhammad Ali**	33	224½	Joe Frazier	215	TKO 15	Manila, Philippines
1976	Feb. 20	**Muhammad Ali**	34	226	Jean Pierre Coopman	206	KO 5	San Juan, P.R.
1976	Apr. 30	**Muhammad Ali**	34	230	Jimmy Young	209	Wu 15	Landover, Md.
1976	May 24	**Muhammad Ali**	34	220	Richard Dunn	206½	TKO 5	Munich, W. Ger.
1976	Sept. 28	**Muhammad Ali**	34	221	Ken Norton	217½	Wu 15	NYC (Yankee Stadium)
1977	May 16	**Muhammad Ali**	35	221¼	Alfredo Evangelista	209¼	Wu 15	Landover, Md.
1977	Sept. 29	**Muhammad Ali**	35	225	Earnie Shavers	211¼	Wu 15	NYC (Mad. Sq. Garden)
1978	Feb. 15	Leon Spinks	24	197¼	**Muhammad Ali**	224¼	Ws 15	Las Vegas
1978	June 9	Larry Holmes	28	209	Ken Norton WBC‡	220	Ws 15	Las Vegas
1978	Sept. 15	Muhammad Ali†	36	221	**Leon Spinks**	201	Wu 15	New Orleans
1978	Nov. 10	Larry Holmes WBC	29	214	Alfredo Evangelista	208¼	KO 7	Las Vegas

*Rocky Marciano retired as undefeated champion on Apr. 27, 1956.
**After defeating Liston, Cassius Clay announced that he had changed his name to Muhammad Ali. He was later stripped of his title by the WBA and most state boxing commissions after refusing induction into the U.S. Army on Apr. 28, 1967.
†Muhammad Ali retired as champion on June 27, 1979, then came out of retirement to fight Larry Holmes for the title in 1980.
‡WBC recognized Ken Norton as world champion when Leon Spinks refused to meet Norton before Spinks' rematch with Muhammad Ali. Norton had scored a 15-round split decision over Jimmy Young on Nov. 5, 1977 in Las Vegas.

World Heavyweight Championship Fights (Cont.)

Year	Date	Winner	Age	Wgt	Loser	Wgt	Result	Location
1979	Mar. 23	Larry Holmes WBC	29	214	Osvaldo Ocasio	207	TKO 7	Las Vegas
1979	June 22	Larry Holmes WBC	29	215	Mike Weaver	202	TKO 12	NYC (Mad. Sq. Garden)
1979	Sept. 28	Larry Holmes WBC	29	210	Earnie Shavers	211	TKO 11	Las Vegas
1979	Oct. 20	John Tate	24	240	Gerrie Coetzee	222	Wu 15	Pretoria, S. Africa
1980	Feb. 3	Larry Holmes WBC	30	213½	Lorenzo Zanon	215	TKO 6	Las Vegas
1980	Mar. 31	Mike Weaver	27	232	John Tate WBA	232	KO 15	Knoxville, Tenn.
1980	Mar. 31	Larry Holmes WBC	30	211	Leroy Jones	254½	TKO 8	Las Vegas
1980	July 7	Larry Holmes WBC	30	214¼	Scott LeDoux	226	TKO 7	Minneapolis
1980	Oct. 2	Larry Holmes WBC	30	211½	Muhammad Ali	217½	TKO 11	Las Vegas
1980	Oct. 25	Mike Weaver WBA	28	210	Gerrie Coetzee	226½	KO 13	Sun City, Boph'swana
1981	Apr. 11	**Larry Holmes**	31	215	Trevor Berbick	215½	Wu 15	Las Vegas
1981	June 12	**Larry Holmes**	31	212¼	Leon Spinks	200¼	TKO 3	Detroit
1981	Oct. 3	Mike Weaver WBA	29	215	Quick Tillis	209	Wu 15	Rosemont, Ill.
1981	Nov. 6	**Larry Holmes**	32	213¼	Renaldo Snipes	215¾	TKO 11	Pittsburgh
1982	June 11	**Larry Holmes**	32	212½	Gerry Cooney	225½	TKO 13	Las Vegas
1982	Nov. 26	**Larry Holmes**	33	217½	Randall (Tex) Cobb	234¼	Wu 15	Houston
1982	Dec. 10	Michael Dokes	24	216	Mike Weaver WBA	209¾	TKO 1	Las Vegas
1983	Mar. 27	**Larry Holmes**	33	221	Lucien Rodriguez	209	Wu 12	Scranton, Pa.
1983	May 20	Michael Dokes WBA	24	223	Mike Weaver	218½	Draw 15	Las Vegas
1983	May 20	**Larry Holmes**	33	213	Tim Witherspoon	219½	Ws 12	Las Vegas
1983	Sept. 10	**Larry Holmes**	33	223	Scott Frank	211¼	TKO 5	Atlantic City
1983	Sept. 23	Gerrie Coetzee	28	215	Michael Dokes WBA	217	KO 10	Richfield, Ohio
1983	Nov. 25	**Larry Holmes**	34	219	Marvis Frazier	200	TKO 1	Las Vegas
1984	Mar. 9	Tim Witherspoon*	26	220¼	Greg Page	239½	Wm 12	Las Vegas
1984	Aug. 31	Pinklon Thomas	26	216	Tim Witherspoon WBC	217	Wm 12	Las Vegas
1984	Nov. 9	**Larry Holmes** IBF	35	221½	Bonecrusher Smith	227	TKO 12	Las Vegas
1984	Dec. 1	Greg Page	26	236½	Gerrie Coetzee WBA	218	KO 8	Sun City, Boph'swana
1985	Mar. 15	**Larry Holmes**	35	223½	David Bey	233¼	TKO 10	Las Vegas
1985	Apr. 29	Tony Tubbs	26	229	Greg Page WBA	239½	Wu 15	Buffalo
1985	May 20	**Carl Williams**	35	222¼	Carl Williams	215	Wu 15	Las Vegas
1985	June 15	Pinklon Thomas	27	220¼	Mike Weaver	221¼	KO 8	Las Vegas
1985	Sept. 21	Michael Spinks	29	200	**Larry Holmes** IBF	221½	Wu 15	Las Vegas
1986	Jan. 17	Tim Witherspoon	28	227	Tony Tubbs WBA	229	Wm 15	Atlanta
1986	Mar. 22	Trevor Berbick	33	218½	Pinklon Thomas WBC	222¾	Wu 15	Las Vegas
1986	Apr. 19	**Michael Spinks**	29	205	Larry Holmes	223	Ws 15	Las Vegas
1986	July 19	Tim Witherspoon WBA	28	234¾	Frank Bruno	228	TKO 11	Wembley, England
1986	Sept. 6	**Michael Spinks**	30	201	Steffen Tangstad	214¾	TKO 4	Las Vegas
1986	Nov. 22	Mike Tyson	20	221¼	Trevor Berbick WBC	218½	TKO 2	Las Vegas
1986	Dec. 12	Bonecrusher Smith	33	228½	Tim Witherspoon WBA	233½	TKO 1	NYC (Mad. Sq. Garden)
1987	Mar. 7	Mike Tyson WBC	20	219	Bonecrusher Smith WBA	233	Wu 12	Las Vegas
1987	May 30	Mike Tyson	20	218¾	Pinklon Thomas	217¾	TKO 6	Las Vegas
1987	May 30	Tony Tucker**	28	222¼	Buster Douglas	227¼	TKO 10	Las Vegas
1987	June 15	**Michael Spinks**	30	208¾	Gerry Cooney	238	TKO 5	Atlantic City
1987	Aug. 1	Mike Tyson	21	221	Tony Tucker IBF	221	Wu 12	Las Vegas
1987	Oct. 16	Mike Tyson	21	216	Tyrell Biggs	228¾	TKO 7	Atlantic City
1988	Jan. 22	Mike Tyson	21	215¾	Larry Holmes	225¾	TKO 4	Atlantic City
1988	Mar. 20	Mike Tyson	21	216¼	Tony Tubbs	238¼	KO 2	Tokyo
1988	June 27	Mike Tyson	21	218¼	**Michael Spinks**	212¼	KO 1	Atlantic City
1989	Feb. 25	**Mike Tyson**	22	218	Frank Bruno	228	TKO 5	Las Vegas
1989	July 21	**Mike Tyson**	23	219¼	Carl Williams	218	TKO 1	Atlantic City
1990	Feb. 10	Buster Douglas	29	231½	**Mike Tyson**	220½	KO 10	Tokyo
1990	Oct. 25	Evander Holyfield	28	208	**Buster Douglas**	246	KO 3	Las Vegas
1991	Apr. 19	**Evander Holyfield**	28	208	George Foreman	257	Wu 12	Atlantic City
1991	Nov. 23	**Evander Holyfield**	29	210	Bert Cooper	215	TKO 7	Atlanta
1992	June 19	**Evander Holyfield**	29	210	Larry Holmes	233	Wu 12	Las Vegas
1992	Nov. 13	Riddick Bowe	25	235	**Evander Holyfield**	205	Wu 12	Las Vegas
1993	Feb. 6	**Riddick Bowe**	25	243	Michael Dokes	244	TKO 1	NYC (Mad. Sq. Garden)
1993	May 8	Lennox Lewis WBC†	27	235	Tony Tucker	235	Wu 12	Las Vegas

*WBC recognized winner of Mar. 9, 1984 fight between Tim Witherspoon and Greg Page as world champion after Larry Holmes relinquished title in dispute. IBF then recognized Holmes.

**IBF recognized winner of May 30, 1987 fight between Tony Tucker and James (Buster) Douglas as world champion after Michael Spinks relinquished title in dispute.

†WBC recognized Lennox Lewis as world champion when Riddick Bowe gave up that portion of his title on Dec. 14, 1992, rather than fight Lewis, the WBC's mandatory challenger.

Year	Date	Winner	Age	Wgt	Loser	Wgt	Result	Location
1993	May 22	**Riddick Bowe**	25	244	Jesse Ferguson	224	TKO 2	Washington, D.C.
1993	Oct. 1	Lennox Lewis WBC	28	233	Frank Bruno	238	TKO 7	Cardiff, Wales
1993	Nov. 6	Evander Holyfield	31	217	**Riddick Bowe**	246	Wm 12	Las Vegas
1994	Apr. 22	Michael Moorer	26	214	**Evander Holyfield**	214	Wm 12	Las Vegas
1994	May 6	Lennox Lewis WBC	28	235	Phil Jackson	218	TKO 8	Atlantic City
1994	Sept. 25	Oliver McCall	29	231¼	**Lennox Lewis** WBC	238	TKO 2	London
1994	Nov. 5	George Foreman*	45	250	**Michael Moorer**	222	KO 10	Las Vegas
1995	Apr. 8	Oliver McCall WBC	29	231	Larry Holmes	236	Wu 12	Las Vegas
1995	Apr. 8	Bruce Seldon	28	236	Tony Tucker	240	TKO 7	Las Vegas
1995	Apr. 22	**George Foreman***	46	256	Axel Schulz	221	Wm 12	Las Vegas
1995	Aug. 19	Bruce Seldon WBA	28	234	Joe Hipp	223	TKO 10	Las Vegas
1995	Sept. 2	Frank Bruno	33	248	Oliver McCall WBC	235	Wu 12	London

*George Foreman won WBA and IBF championships when he beat Michael Moorer on Nov. 5, 1994. He was stripped of WBA title on Mar. 4, 1995, when he refused to fight No. 1 contender Tony Tucker, and he relinquished IBF title on June 29, 1995, rather than give Axel Schulz a rematch. Tucker lost to Bruce Seldon in their April 8 fight for vacant WBA title.

Wide World Photos

Cassius Clay (left) stunned the boxing world in 1964 when he beat champion **Sonny Liston** in a seventh round TKO. Clay changed his name to **Muhammad Ali** after winning the title.

All-Time Heavyweight Upsets

Buster Douglas was a 50-1 underdog when he defeated previously-unbeaten heavyweight champion Mike Tyson on Feb. 10, 1990. That 10th-round knockout ranks as the biggest upset in boxing history. By comparison, 45-year-old George Foreman was only a 3-1 underdog before he unexpectedly won the title from Michael Moorer on Nov. 5, 1994.

Here are the best-known upsets in the annals of the heavyweight division. All fights were for the world championship except the Max Schmeling-Joe Louis bout.

Date	Winner	Loser	Result	KO Time	Location
9/7/1892	James J. Corbett	John L. Sullivan	KO 21	1:30	Olympic Club, New Orleans
4/5/1915	Jess Willard	Jack Johnson	KO 26	1:26	Mariano Race Track, Havana
9/23/26	Gene Tunney	Jack Dempsey	Wu 10	—	Sesquicentennial Stadium, Phila.
6/13/35	James J. Braddock	Max Baer	Wu 15	—	Mad.Sq.Garden Bowl, L.I.City
6/19/36	Max Schmeling	Joe Louis	KO 12	2:29	Yankee Stadium, New York
7/18/51	Jersey Joe Walcott	Ezzard Charles	KO 7	0:55	Forbes Field, Pittsburgh
6/26/59	Ingemar Johansson	Floyd Patterson	TKO 3	2:03	Yankee Stadium, New York
2/25/64	Cassius Clay	Sonny Liston	TKO 7	*	Convention Hall, Miami Beach
10/30/74	Muhammad Ali	George Foreman	KO 8	2:58	20th of May Stadium, Zaire
2/15/78	Leon Spinks	Muhammad Ali	Ws 15	—	Hilton Pavilion, Las Vegas
9/21/85	Michael Spinks	Larry Holmes	Wu 15	—	Riviera Hotel, Las Vegas
2/10/90	Buster Douglas	Mike Tyson	KO 10	1:23	Tokyo Dome, Tokyo
11/5/94	George Foreman	Michael Moorer	KO 10	2:03	MGM Grand, Las Vegas

*Liston failed to answer bell for Round 7.

Muhammad Ali's Career Pro Record

Born Cassius Marcellus Clay, Jr. on Jan. 17, 1942, in Louisville; Amateur record of 100-5; won light-heavyweight gold medal at 1960 Olympic Games; Pro record of 56-5-0 with 37 KOs in 61 fights.

1960

Date	Opponent (location)	Result
Oct. 29	Tunney Hunsaker, Louisville	Wu 6
Dec. 27	Herb Siler, Miami Beach	TKO 4

1961

Date	Opponent (location)	Result
Jan. 17	Tony Esperti, Miami Beach	TKO 3
Feb. 7	Jim Robinson, Miami Beach	TKO 1
Feb. 21	Donnie Fleeman, Miami Beach	TKO 7
Apr. 19	Lamar Clark, Louisville	KO 2
June 26	Duke Sabedong, Las Vegas	Wu 10
July 22	Alonzo Johnson, Louisville	Wu 10
Oct. 7	Alex Miteff, Louisville	TKO 6
Nov. 29	Willi Besmanoff, Louisville	TKO 7

1962

Date	Opponent (location)	Result
Feb. 10	Sonny Banks, New York	TKO 4
Feb. 28	Don Warner, Miami Beach	TKO 4
Apr. 23	George Logan, Los Angeles	TKO 4
May 19	Billy Daniels, Los Angeles	TKO 7
July 20	Alejandro Lavorante, Los Angeles	KO 5
Nov. 15	Archie Moore, Los Angeles	KO 4

1963

Date	Opponent (location)	Result
Jan. 24	Charlie Powell, Pittsburgh	KO 3
Mar. 13	Doug Jones, New York	Wu 10
June 18	Henry Cooper, London	TKO 5

1964

Date	Opponent (location)	Result
Feb. 25	Sonny Liston, Miami Beach	TKO 7

(won World Heavyweight title)
After the fight, Clay announces he is a member of the Black Muslim religious sect and has changed his name to Muhammad Ali.

1965

Date	Opponent (location)	Result
May 25	Sonny Liston, Lewiston, Me.	KO 1
Nov. 22	Floyd Patterson, Las Vegas	TKO 12

1966

Date	Opponent (location)	Result
Mar. 29	George Chuvalo, Toronto	Wu 15
May 21	Henry Cooper, London	TKO 6
Aug. 6	Brian London, London	KO 3
Sept. 10	Karl Mildenberger, Frankfurt	TKO 12
Nov. 12	Cleveland Williams, Houston	TKO 3

1967

Date	Opponent (location)	Result
Feb. 6	Ernie Terrell, Houston	Wu 15
Mar. 22	Zora Folley, New York	KO 7
Apr. 28	Refuses induction into U.S. Army and is stripped of world title by WBA and most state commissions the next day.	
June 20	Found guilty of draft evasion in Houston; fined $10,000 and sentenced to 5 years; remains free pending appeals, but is barred from the ring.	

1968-69
(Inactive)

1970

Date	Opponent (location)	Result
Feb. 3	Announces retirement.	
Oct. 26	Jerry Quarry, Atlanta	TKO 3
Dec. 7	Oscar Bonavena, New York	TKO 15

1971

Date	Opponent (location)	Result
Mar. 8	Joe Frazier, New York	Lu 15

(for World Heavyweight title)

June 28	U.S. Supreme Court reverses Ali's 1967 conviction saying he had been drafted improperly.	
July 26	Jimmy Ellis, Houston	TKO 12

(won vacant NABF Heavyweight title)

Nov. 17	Buster Mathis, Houston	Wu 12
Dec. 26	Jurgen Blin, Zurich	KO 7

1972

Date	Opponent (location)	Result
Apr. 1	Mac Foster, Tokyo	Wu 15
May 1	George Chuvalo, Vancouver	Wu 12
June 27	Jerry Quarry, Las Vegas	TKO 7
July 19	Al (Blue) Lewis, Dublin, Ire	TKO 11
Sept. 20	Floyd Patterson, New York	TKO 7
Nov. 21	Bob Foster, Stateline, Nev	TKO 8

1973

Date	Opponent (location)	Result
Feb. 14	Joe Bugner, Las Vegas	Wu 12
Mar. 31	Ken Norton, San Diego	Ls 12

(lost NABF Heavyweight title)

Sept. 10	Ken Norton, Inglewood, Calif.	Ws 12

(regained NABF Heavyweight title)

Oct. 20	Rudi Lubbers, Jakarta, Indonesia	Wu 12

1974

Date	Opponent (location)	Result
Jan. 28	Joe Frazier, New York	Wu 12
Oct. 30	George Foreman, Kinshasa, Zaire	KO 8

(regained World Heavyweight title)

1975

Date	Opponent (location)	Result
Mar. 24	Chuck Wepner, Cleveland	TKO 15
May 16	Ron Lyle, Las Vegas	TKO 11
June 30	Joe Bugner, Kuala Lumpur, Malaysia	Wu 15
Sept. 30	Joe Frazier, Manila	TKO 14

1976

Date	Opponent (location)	Result
Feb. 20	Jean-Pierre Coopman, San Juan	KO 5
Apr. 30	Jimmy Young, Landover, Md	Wu 15
May 24	Richard Dunn, Munich	TKO 5
Sept. 28	Ken Norton, New York	Wu 15

1977

Date	Opponent (location)	Result
May 16	Alfredo Evangelista, Landover	Wu 15
Sept. 29	Earnie Shavers, New York	Wu 15

1978

Date	Opponent (location)	Result
Feb. 15	Leon Spinks, Las Vegas	Ls 15

(lost World Heavyweight title)

Sept. 15	Leon Spinks, New Orleans	Wu 15

(regained World Heavyweight title)

1979

Date		
June 27	Announces retirement.	

1980

Date	Opponent (location)	Result
Oct. 2	Larry Holmes, Las Vegas	TKO by 11

1981

Date	Opponent (location)	Result
Dec. 11	Trevor Berbick, Nassau	Lu 10

(retires after fight)

Major Titleholders

Note the following sanctioning body abbreviations: NBA (National Boxing Association), WBA (World Boxing Association), WBC (World Boxing Council), GBR (Great Britain), IBF (International Boxing Federation), plus other national and state commissions. Fighters who retired as champion are indicated by (*) and champions who abandoned or relinquished their titles are indicated by (†).

Heavyweights

Widely accepted champions in CAPITAL letters. Current champions (as of Oct. 15, 1995) in **bold** type. Note that Muhammad Ali was stripped of his world title in 1967 after refusing induction into the Army (see page 900). George Foreman was stripped of his WBA and IBF titles in 1995, but remained active as consensus champion (see page 889).

Champion	Held Title	Champion	Held Title
JOHN L. SULLIVAN	1885-92	LEON SPINKS	1978
JAMES J. CORBETT	1892-97	Ken Norton (WBC)	1978
BOB FITZSIMMONS	1897-99	Larry Holmes (WBC)	1978-80
JAMES J. JEFFRIES	1899-1905*	MUHAMMAD ALI	1978-79*
MARVIN HART	1905-06	John Tate (WBA)	1979-80
TOMMY BURNS	1906-08	Mike Weaver (WBA)	1980-82
JACK JOHNSON	1908-15	LARRY HOLMES	1980-85
JESS WILLARD	1915-19	Michael Dokes (WBA)	1982-83
JACK DEMPSEY	1919-26	Gerrie Coetzee (WBA)	1983-84
GENE TUNNEY	1926-28*	Tim Witherspoon (WBC)	1984
MAX SCHMELING	1930-32	Pinklon Thomas (WBC)	1984-86
JACK SHARKEY	1932-33	Greg Page (WBA)	1984-85
PRIMO CARNERA	1933-34	MICHAEL SPINKS	1985-87
MAX BAER	1934-35	Tim Witherspoon (WBA)	1986
JAMES J. BRADDOCK	1935-37	Trevor Berbick (WBC)	1986
JOE LOUIS	1937-49*	Mike Tyson (WBC)	1986-87
EZZARD CHARLES	1949-51	James (Bonecrusher) Smith (WBA)	1986-87
JERSEY JOE WALCOTT	1951-52	Tony Tucker (IBF)	1987
ROCKY MARCIANO	1952-56*	MIKE TYSON (WBC, WBA, IBF)	1987-90
FLOYD PATTERSON	1956-59	BUSTER DOUGLAS (WBC, WBA, IBF)	1990
INGEMAR JOHANSSON	1959-60	EVANDER HOLYFIELD (WBC, WBA, IBF)	1990-92
FLOYD PATTERSON	1960-62	RIDDICK BOWE (WBA, IBF)	1992-93
SONNY LISTON	1962-64	Lennox Lewis (WBC)	1992-94
CASSIUS CLAY (MUHAMMAD ALI)	1964-70	EVANDER HOLYFIELD (WBA, IBF)	1993-94
Ernie Terrell (WBA)	1965-67	MICHAEL MOORER (WBA, IBF)	1994
Joe Frazier (NY)	1968-70	Oliver McCall (WBC)	1994-95
Jimmy Ellis (WBA)	1968-70	GEORGE FOREMAN (WBA, IBF)	1994-95
JOE FRAZIER	1970-73	**Bruce Seldon** (WBA)	1995—
GEORGE FOREMAN	1973-74	**GEORGE FOREMAN**	1995—
MUHAMMAD ALI	1974-78	**Frank Bruno** (WBC)	1995—

Note: John L. Sullivan held the Bare Knuckle championship from 1882-85.

Light Heavyweights

Widely accepted champions in CAPITAL letters. Current champions in **bold** type.

Champion	Held Title	Champion	Held Title
JACK ROOT	1903	MAXIE ROSENBLOOM	1930-34
GEORGE GARDNER	1903	George Nichols (NBA)	1932
BOB FITZSIMMONS	1903-05	Bob Godwin (NBA)	1933
PHILADELPHIA JACK O'BRIEN	1905-12*	BOB OLIN	1934-35
JACK DILLON	1914-16	JOHN HENRY LEWIS	1935-38
BATTLING LEVINSKY	1916-20	MELIO BETTINA (NY)	1939
GEORGES CARPENTIER	1920-22	Len Harvey (GBR)	1939-42
BATTLING SIKI	1922-23	BILLY CONN	1939-40†
MIKE McTIGUE	1923-25	ANTON CHRISTOFORIDIS (NBA)	1941
PAUL BERLENBACH	1925-26	GUS LESNEVICH	1941-48
JACK DELANEY	1926-27†	Freddie Mills (GBR)	1942-46
Jimmy Slattery (NBA)	1927	FREDDIE MILLS	1948-50
TOMMY LOUGHRAN	1927-29	JOEY MAXIM	1950-52
JIMMY SLATTERY	1930	ARCHIE MOORE	1952-62

Former Champions Who Have Won Back Heavyweight Title

Only six times since 1892 has the heavyweight championship been lost by a fighter who was able to win it back. Five men have done it and Muhammad Ali did it twice.

	Lost To	Won Back From		Lost To	Won Back From
Floyd Patterson	Johansson (1959)	Johansson (1960)	Tim Witherspoon	Thomas (1984)	Tubbs (1986)
Muhammad Ali	Frazier (1970)	Foreman (1974)	Evander Holyfield	Bowe (1992)	Bowe (1993)
Muhammad Ali	L. Spinks (1978)	L. Spinks (1978)	George Foreman	Ali (1974)	Moorer (1994)

Major Titleholders (Cont.)
Light Heavyweights

Champion	Held Title	Champion	Held Title
Harold Johnson (NBA)	1961	J.B. Williamson (WBC)	1985-86
HAROLD JOHNSON	1962-63	Slobodan Kacar (IBF)	1985-86
WILLIE PASTRANO	1963-65	Marvin Johnson (WBA)	1986-87
Eddie Cotton (Mich.)	1963-64	Dennis Andries (WBC)	1986-87
JOSE TORRES	1965-66	Bobby Czyz (IBF)	1986-87
DICK TIGER	1966-68	Leslie Stewart (WBA)	1987
BOB FOSTER	1968-74*	Virgil Hill (WBA)	1987-91
Vicente Rondon (WBA)	1971-72	Prince Charles Williams (IBF)	1987-93
John Conteh (WBC)	1974-77	Thomas Hearns (WBC)	1987
Victor Galindez (WBA)	1974-78	Donny Lalonde (WBC)	1987-88
Miguel A. Cuello (WBC)	1977-78	Sugar Ray Leonard (WBC)	1988
Mate Parlov (WBC)	1978	Dennis Andries (WBC)	1989
Mike Rossman (WBA)	1978-79	Jeff Harding (WBC)	1989-90
Marvin Johnson (WBC)	1978-79	Dennis Andries (WBC)	1990-91
Matthew (Franklin) Saad Muhammad (WBC)	1979-81	Jeff Harding (WBC)	1991-94
Marvin Johnson (WBA)	1979-80	Thomas Hearns (WBA)	1991-92
Eddie (Gregory)		Iran Barkley (WBA)	1992†
Mustapha Muhammad (WBA)	1980-81	**Virgil Hill** (WBA)	1992—
Michael Spinks (WBA)	1981-83	**Henry Maske** (IBF)	1993—
Dwight (Braxton) Muhammad Qawi (WBC)	1981-83	Mike McCallum (WBC)	1994-95
MICHAEL SPINKS	1983-85†	**Fabrice Tiozzo** (WBC)	1995—

Middleweights

Widely accepted champions in CAPITAL letters. Current champions in **bold** type.

Champion	Held Title	Champion	Held Title
JACK (NONPAREIL) DEMPSEY	1884-91	TONY ZALE	1948
BOB FITZSIMMONS	1891-97	MARCEL CERDAN	1948-49
CHARLES (KID) McCOY	1897-98	JAKE LA MOTTA	1949-51
TOMMY RYAN	1898-1907	SUGAR RAY ROBINSON	1951
STANLEY KETCHEL	1908	RANDY TURPIN	1951
BILLY PAPKE	1908	SUGAR RAY ROBINSON	1951-52*
STANLEY KETCHEL	1908-10	CARL (BOBO) OLSON	1953-55
FRANK KLAUS	1913	SUGAR RAY ROBINSON	1955-57
GEORGE CHIP	1913-14	GENE FULLMER	1957
AL McCOY	1914-17	SUGAR RAY ROBINSON	1957
Jeff Smith (AUS)	1914	CARMEN BASILIO	1957-58
Mick King (AUS)	1914	SUGAR RAY ROBINSON	1958-60
Jeff Smith (AUS)	1914-15	Gene Fullmer (NBA)	1959-62
Lee Darcy (AUS)	1915-17	PAUL PENDER	1960-61
MIKE O'DOWD	1917-20	TERRY DOWNES	1961-62
JOHNNY WILSON	1920-23	PAUL PENDER	1962-63
Wm. Bryan Downey (Ohio)	1921-22	Dick Tiger (WBA)	1962-63
Dave Rosenberg (NY)	1922	DICK TIGER	1963
Jock Malone (Ohio)	1922-23	JOEY GIARDELLO	1963-65
Mike O'Dowd (NY)	1922	DICK TIGER	1965-66
Lou Bogash (NY)	1923	EMILE GRIFFITH	1966-67
HARRY GREB	1923-26	NINO BENVENUTI	1967
TIGER FLOWERS	1926	EMILE GRIFFITH	1967-68
MICKEY WALKER	1926-31†	NINO BENVENUTI	1968-70
GORILLA JONES	1931-32	CARLOS MONZON	1970-77*
MARCEL THIL	1932-37	Rodrigo Valdez (WBC)	1974-76
Ben Jeby (NY)	1932-33	RODRIGO VALDEZ	1977-78
Lou Brouillard (NBA, NY)	1933	HUGO CORRO	1978-79
Vince Dundee (NBA, NY)	1933-34	VITO ANTUOFERMO	1979-80
Teddy Yarosz (NBA, NY)	1934-35	ALAN MINTER	1980
Babe Risko (NBA, NY)	1935-36	MARVELOUS MARVIN HAGLER	1980-87
Freddie Steele (NBA, NY)	1936-38	SUGAR RAY LEONARD	1987
FRED APOSTOLI	1937-39	Frank Tate (IBF)	1987-88
Al Hostak (NBA)	1938	Sumbu Kalambay (WBA)	1987-89
Solly Krieger (NBA)	1938-39	Thomas Hearns (WBC)	1987-88
Al Hostak (NBA)	1939-40	Iran Barkley (WBC)	1988-89
CEFERINO GARCIA	1939-40	Michael Nunn (IBF)	1988-91
KEN OVERLIN	1940-41	Roberto Duran (WBC)	1989-90*
Tony Zale (NBA)	1940-41	Mike McCallum (WBA)	1989-91
BILLY SOOSE	1941	Julian Jackson (WBC)	1990-93
TONY ZALE	1941-47	James Toney (IBF)	1991-93†
ROCKY GRAZIANO	1947-48	Reggie Johnson (WBA)	1992-93

Roy Jones Jr. (IBF)	1993-94†
Gerald McClellan (WBC)	1993-95†
John David Jackson (WBA)	1993-94
Jorge Castro (WBA)	1994—

Julian Jackson (WBC)	1995
Bernard Hopkins (IBF)	1995—
Quincy Taylor (WBC)	1995—

Welterweights

Widely accepted champions in CAPITAL letters. Current champions in **bold** type.

Champion	Held Title	Champion	Held Title
PADDY DUFFY	1888-90	CARMEN BASILIO	1955-56
MYSTERIOUS BILLY SMITH	1892-94	JOHNNY SAXTON	1956
TOMMY RYAN	1894-98	CARMEN BASILIO	1956-57†
MYSTERIOUS BILLY SMITH	1898-1900	VIRGIL AKINS	1958
MATTY MATTHEWS	1900	DON JORDAN	1958-60
EDDIE CONNOLLY	1900	BENNY (KID) PARET	1960-61
JAMES (RUBE) FERNS	1900	EMILE GRIFFITH	1961
MATTY MATHEWS	1900-01	BENNY (KID) PARET	1961-62
JAMES (RUBE) FERNS	1901	EMILE GRIFFITH	1962-63
JOE WALCOTT	1901-04	LUIS RODRIGUEZ	1963
THE DIXIE KID	1904-05	EMILE GRIFFITH	1963-66†
HONEY MELLODY	1906-07	Charlie Shipes (Calif.)	1966-67
MIKE (TWIN) SULLIVAN	1907-08†	CURTIS COKES	1966-69
Harry Lewis	1908-11	JOSE NAPOLES	1969-70
Jimmy Gardner	1908	BILLY BACKUS	1970-71
Jimmy Clabby	1910-11	JOSE NAPOLES	1971-75
WALDEMAR HOLBERG	1914	Hedgemon Lewis (NY)	1972-73
TOM McCORMICK	1914	Angel Espada (WBA)	1975-76
MATT WELLS	1914-15	JOHN H. STRACEY	1975-76
MIKE GLOVER	1915	CARLOS PALOMINO	1976-79
JACK BRITTON	1915	Pipino Cuevas (WBA)	1976-80
TED (KID) LEWIS	1915-16	WILFREDO BENITEZ	1979
JACK BRITTON	1916-17	SUGAR RAY LEONARD	1979-80
TED (KID) LEWIS	1917-19	ROBERTO DURAN	1980
JACK BRITTON	1919-22	Thomas Hearns (WBA)	1980-81
MICKEY WALKER	1922-26	SUGAR RAY LEONARD	1980-82
PETE LATZO	1926-27	Donald Curry (WBA)	1983-85
JOE DUNDEE	1927-29	Milton McCrory (WBC)	1983-85
JACKIE FIELDS	1929-30	DONALD CURRY	1985-86
YOUNG JACK THOMPSON	1930	LLOYD HONEYGHAN	1986-87
TOMMY FREEMAN	1930-31	JORGE VACA (WBC)	1987-88
YOUNG JACK THOMPSON	1931	LLOYD HONEYGHAN (WBC)	1988-89
LOU BROUILLARD	1931-32	Mark Breland (WBA)	1987
JACKIE FIELDS	1932-33	Marlon Starling (WBA)	1987-88
YOUNG CORBETT III	1933	Tomas Molinares (WBA)	1988-89
JIMMY McLARNIN	1933-34	Simon Brown (IBF)	1988-91
BARNEY ROSS	1934	Mark Breland (WBA)	1989-90
JIMMY McLARNIN	1934-35	MARLON STARLING (WBC)	1989-90
BARNEY ROSS	1935-38	Aaron Davis (WBA)	1990-91
HENRY ARMSTRONG	1938-40	Maurice Blocker (WBC)	1990-91
FRITZIE ZIVIC	1940-41	Meldrick Taylor (WBA)	1991-92
Izzy Jannazzo (Md.)	1940-41	Simon Brown (WBC)	1991
FREDDIE (RED) COCHRANE	1941-46	Maurice Blocker (IBF)	1991-93
MARTY SERVO	1946*	Buddy McGirt (WBC)	1991-93
SUGAR RAY ROBINSON	1946-51†	Crisanto Espana (WBA)	1992-94
Johnny Bratton	1951	**Pernell Whitaker** (WBC)	1993—
KID GAVILAN	1951-54	**Felix Trinidad** (IBF)	1993—
JOHNNY SAXTON	1954-55	**Ike Quartey** (WBA)	1994—
TONY DeMARCO	1955		

Lightweights

Widely accepted champions in CAPITAL letters. Current champions in **bold** type.

Champion	Held Title	Champion	Held Title
JACK McAULIFFE	1886-94	FREDDIE WELSH	1915-17
GEORGE (KID) LAVIGNE	1896-99	BENNY LEONARD	1917-25*
FRANK ERNE	1899-02	JIMMY GOODRICH	1925
JOE GANS	1902-04	ROCKY KANSAS	1925-26
JIMMY BRITT	1904-05	SAMMY MANDELL	1926-30
BATTLING NELSON	1905-06	AL SINGER	1930
JOE GANS	1906-08	TONY CANZONERI	1930-33
BATTLING NELSON	1908-10	BARNEY ROSS	1933-35†
AD WOLGAST	1910-12	TONY CANZONERI	1935-36
WILLIE RITCHIE	1912-14	LOU AMBERS	1936-38

Major Titleholders (Cont.)
Lightweights

Champion	Held Title	Champion	Held Title
HENRY ARMSTRONG	1938-39	Ernesto Espana (WBA)	1979-80
LOU AMBERS	1939-40	Hilmer Kenty (WBA)	1980-81
Sammy Angott (NBA)	1940-41	Sean O'Grady (WBA,WAA)	1981
LEW JENKINS	1940-41	Alexis Arguello (WBC)	1981-82
SAMMY ANGOTT	1941-42	Claude Noel (WBA)	1981
Beau Jack (NY)	1942-43	Andrew Ganigan (WAA)	1981-82
Slugger White (Md.)	1943	Arturo Frias (WBA)	1981-82
Bob Montgomery (NY)	1943	Ray Mancini (WBA)	1982-84
Sammy Angott (NBA)	1943-44	ALEXIS ARGUELLO	1982-83
Beau Jack (NY)	1943-44	Edwin Rosario (WBC)	1983-84
Bob Montgomery (NY)	1944-47	Choo Choo Brown (IBF)	1984
Juan Zurita (NBA)	1944-45	Livingstone Bramble (WBA)	1984-86
IKE WILLIAMS	1947-51	Harry Arroyo (IBF)	1984-85
JAMES CARTER	1951-52	Jose Luis Ramirez (WBC)	1984-85
LAURO SALAS	1952	Jimmy Paul (IBF)	1985-86
JAMES CARTER	1952-54	Hector Camacho (WBC)	1985-86
PADDY DeMARCO	1954	Edwin Rosario (WBA)	1986-87
JAMES CARTER	1954-55	Greg Haugen (IBF)	1986-87
WALLACE (BUD) SMITH	1955-56	Julio Cesar Chavez (WBA)	1987-88
JOE BROWN	1956-62	Jose Luis Ramirez (WBC)	1987-88
CARLOS ORTIZ	1962-65	JULIO CESAR CHAVEZ (WBC,WBA)	1988-89
Kenny Lane (Mich.)	1963-64	Vinny Pazienza (IBF)	1987-88
ISMAEL LAGUNA	1965	Greg Haugen (IBF)	1988-89
CARLOS ORTIZ	1965-68	Pernell Whitaker (IBF,WBC)	1989-90
CARLOS TEO CRUZ	1968-69	Edwin Rosario (WBA)	1989-90
MANDO RAMOS	1969-70	Juan Nazario (WBA)	1990
ISMAEL LAGUNA	1970	PERNELL WHITAKER (IBF, WBC, WBA)	1990-92†
KEN BUCHANAN	1970-72	Joey Gamache (WBA)	1992
Pedro Carrasco (WBC)	1971-72	**Miguel A. Gonzalez** (WBC)	1992—
Mando Ramos (WBC)	1972	Tony Lopez (WBA)	1992-93
ROBERTO DURAN	1972-79†	Dingaan Thobela (WBA)	1993
Chango Carmona (WBC)	1972	Fred Pendleton (IBF)	1993-94
Rodolfo Gonzalez (WBC)	1972-74	**Gussie Nazarov** (WBA)	1993—
Ishimatsu Suzuki (WBC)	1974-76	Rafael Ruelas (IBF)	1994-95
Esteban De Jesus (WBC)	1976-78	Oscar De La Hoya (IBF)	1995†
Jim Watt (WBC)	1979-81	**Phillip Holiday** (IBF)	1995—

Featherweights

Widely accepted champions in CAPITAL letters. Current champions in **bold** type.

Champion	Held Title	Champion	Held Title
TORPEDO BILLY MURPHY	1890	Baby Arizmendi (MEX)	1935-36
YOUNG GRIFFO	1890-92	Mike Belloise (NY)	1936-37
GEORGE DIXON	1892-97	Petey Sarron (NBA)	1936-37
SOLLY SMITH	1897-98	HENRY ARMSTRONG	1937-38†
Ben Jordan (GBR)	1898-99	Joey Archibald (NY)	1938-39
Eddie Santry (GBR)	1899-1900	Leo Rodak (NBA)	1938-39
DAVE SULLIVAN	1898	JOEY ARCHIBALD	1939-40
GEORGE DIXON	1898-1900	Petey Scalzo (NBA)	1940-41
TERRY McGOVERN	1900-01	Jimmy Perrin (La.)	1940-41
YOUNG CORBETT II	1901-04	HARRY JEFFRA	1940-41
JIMMY BRITT	1904	JOEY ARCHIBALD	1941
ABE ATTELL	1904	Richie Lemos (NBA)	1941
BROOKLYN TOMMY SULLIVAN	1904-05	CHALKY WRIGHT	1941-42
ABE ATTELL	1906-12	Jackie Wilson (NBA)	1941-43
JOHNNY KILBANE	1912-23	WILLIE PEP	1942-48
Jem Driscoll (GBR)	1912-13	Jackie Callura (NBA)	1943
EUGENE CRIQUI	1923	Phil Terranova (NBA)	1943-44
JOHNNY DUNDEE	1923-24†	Sal Bartolo (NBA)	1944-46
LOUIS (KID) KAPLAN	1925-26†	SANDY SADDLER	1948-49
Dick Finnegan (Mass.)	1926-27	WILLIE PEP	1949-50
BENNY BASS	1927-28	SANDY SADDLER	1950-57*
TONY CANZONERI	1928	HOGAN (KID) BASSEY	1957-59
ANDRE ROUTIS	1928-29	DAVEY MOORE	1959-63
BATTLING BATTALINO	1929-32†	ULTIMINIO (SUGAR) RAMOS	1963-64
Tommy Paul (NBA)	1932-33	VICENTE SALDIVAR	1964-67*
Kid Chocolate (NY)	1932-33	Howard Winstone (GBR)	1968
Freddie Miller (NBA)	1933-36	Raul Rojas (WBA)	1968

Jose Legra (WBC)....................1968-69	Min-Keun Oh (IBF)...................1984-85
Shozo Saijyo (WBA)...................1968-71	Azumah Nelson (WBC)................1984-88
JOHNNY FAMECHON (WBC)..........1969-70	Barry McGuigan (WBA)...............1985-86
VICENTE SALDIVAR (WBC)................1970	Ki-Young Chung (IBF).................1985-86
KUNIAKI SHIBATA (WBC)..............1970-72	Steve Cruz (WBA)....................1986-87
Antonio Gomez (WBA).................1971-72	Antonio Rivera (IBF).................1986-88
CLEMENTE SANCHEZ (WBC) 1972	Antonio Esparragoza (WBA) 1987-91
Ernesto Marcel (WBA).................1972-74	Calvin Grove (IBF)......................1988
JOSE LEGRA (WBC)....................1972-73	Jorge Paez (IBF)....................1988-91†
EDER JOFRE (WBC)....................1973-74	Jeff Fenech (WBC)..................1988-90†
Ruben Olivares (WBA)....................1974	Marcos Villasana (WBC)..............1990-91
Bobby Chacon (WBC)..................1974-75	Yung-Kyun Park (WBA)...............1991-93
ALEXIS ARGUELLO (WBA)............1974-76†	Troy Dorsey (IBF)......................1991
Ruben Olivares (WBA)....................1975	Manuel Medina (IBF).................1991-93
David (Poison) Kotey (WBC)..........1975-76	Paul Hodkinson (WBC)...............1991-93
DANNY (LITTLE RED) LOPEZ (WBC)...1976-80	**Tom Johnson** (IBF)....................1993—
Rafael Ortega (WBA).....................1977	Goyo Vargas (WBC)....................1993
Cecilio Lastra (WBA)...................1977-78	Kevin Kelley (WBC)...................1993-95
Eusebio Pedroza (WBA)................1978-85	**Eloy Rojas** (WBA)....................1993—
SALVADOR SANCHEZ (WBC)...........1980-82	Alejandro Gonzalez (WBC) 1995
Juan LaPorte (WBC)...................1982-84	**Manuel Medina** (WBC) ....1995—
Wilfredo Gomez (WBC)...................1984	

Bantamweights

Widely accepted champions in CAPITAL letters. Current champions in **bold** type.

Champion	Held Title	Champion	Held Title
TOMMY (SPIDER) KELLY.............1887		SIXTO ESCOBAR 1936-37	
HUGHEY BOYLE...................1887-88		HARRY JEFFRA 1937-38	
TOMMY (SPIDER) KELLY.............1889		SIXTO ESCOBAR 1938-39*	
CHAPPIE MORAN..................1889-90		Georgie Pace (NBA)................1939-40	
Tommy (Spider) Kelly..............1890-92		LOU SALICA 1940-42	
GEORGE DIXON 1890-91		MANUEL ORTIZ 1942-47	
Billy Plummer.....................1892-95		HAROLD DADE 1947	
JIMMY BARRY.....................1894-99		MANUEL ORTIZ 1947-50	
Pedlar Palmer....................1895-99		VIC TOWEEL 1950-52	
TERRY McGOVERN 1899-1900		JIMMY CARRUTHERS 1952-54*	
HARRY HARRIS....................1901-02		ROBERT COHEN 1954-56	
DANNY DOUGHERTY...............1900-01		Raul Macias (NBA).................1955-57	
HARRY FORBES....................1901-03		MARIO D'AGATA 1956-57	
FRANKIE NEIL.....................1903-04		ALPHONSE HALIMI 1957-59	
JOE BOWKER......................1904-05		JOE BECERRA 1959-60*	
JIMMY WALSH ....1905-06†		Johnny Caldwell (EBU) 1961-62	
OWEN MORAN 1907-08		EDER JOFRE 1961-65	
MONTE ATTELL 1909-10		MASAHIKO FIGHTING HARADA 1965-68	
FRANKIE CONLEY 1910-11		LIONEL ROSE 1968-69	
JOHNNY COULON 1911-14		RUBEN OLIVARES 1969-70	
Digger Stanley (GBR)..............1910-12		CHUCHO CASTILLO 1970-71	
Charles Ledoux (GBR)..............1912-13		RUBEN OLIVARES 1971-72	
Eddie Campi (GBR)................1913-14		RAFAEL HERRERA 1972	
KID WILLIAMS 1914-17		ENRIQUE PINDER 1972-73	
Johnny Ertle.....................1915-18		ROMEO ANAYA 1973	
PETE HERMAN.....................1917-20		Rafael Herrera (WBC)..............1973-74	
Memphis Pal Moore...............1918-19		ARNOLD TAYLOR 1973-74	
JOE LYNCH.......................1920-21		SOO-HWAN HONG 1974-75	
PETE HERMAN........................1921		Rodolfo Martinez (WBC)............1974-76	
JOHNNY BUFF 1921-22		ALFONSO ZAMORA 1975-77	
JOE LYNCH.......................1922-24		Carlos Zarate (WBC)...............1976-79	
ABE GOLDSTEIN......................1924		JORGE LUJAN 1977-80	
CANNONBALL EDDIE MARTIN........1924-25		Lupe Pintor (WBC).................1979-83	
PHIL ROSENBERG 1925-27		JULIAN SOLIS 1980	
Teddy Baldock (GBR)................1927		JEFF CHANDLER 1980-84	
BUD TAYLOR (NBA)...............1927-28†		Albert Davila (WBC)...............1983-85	
Willie Smith (GBR)................1927-28		RICHARD SANDOVAL 1984-86	
Bushy Graham (NY)................1928-29		Satoshi Shingaki (IBF).............1984-85	
PANAMA AL BROWN................1929-35		Jeff Fenech (IBF)....................1985	
Sixto Escobar (NBA)...............1934-35		Daniel Zaragoza (WBC)..............1985	
BALTAZAR SANGCHILLI.............1935-36		Miguel (Happy) Lora (WBC).........1985-88	
Lou Salica (NBA)....................1935		GABY CANIZALES 1986	
Sixto Escobar (NBA)...............1935-36		BERNARDO PINANGO................1986-87	
TONY MARINO 1936		Wilfredo Vasquez (WBA)............1987-88	

Major Titleholders (Cont.)
Bantamweights

Champion	Held Title	Champion	Held Title
Kevin Seabrooks (IBF)	1987-88	Victor Rabanales (WBC)	1992-93
Kaokor Galaxy (WBA)	1988	Jorge Julio (WBA)	1992-93
Moon Sung-Kil (WBA)	1988-89	Jung-Il Byun (WBC)	1993
Kaokor Galaxy (WBA)	1989	Junior Jones (WBA)	1993-94
Raul Perez (WBC)	1988-91	Yasuei Yakushiji (WBC)	1993-95
Orlando Canizales (IBF)	1988-94†	John M. Johnson (WBA)	1994
Luisito Espinosa (WBA)	1989-91	Daorung Chuvatana (WBA)	1994-95
Greg Richardson	1991	Harold Mestre (IBF)	1995
Joichiro Tatsuyoshi (WBC)	1991-92	**Mbulelo Botile** (IBF)	1995—
Israel Contreras (WBA)	1991-92	**Wayne McCullough** (WBC)	1995—
Eddie Cook (WBA)	1992	**Veeraphol Sahaprom** (WBA)	1995—

Flyweights

Widely accepted champions in CAPITAL letters. Current champions in **bold** type.

Champion	Held Title	Champion	Held Title
Sid Smith (GBR)	1913	Susumu Hanagata (WBA)	1974-75
Bill Ladbury (GBR)	1913-14	Miguel Canto (WBC)	1975-79
Percy Jones (GBR)	1914	Erbito Salavarria (WBA)	1975-76
Joe Symonds (GBR)	1914-16	Alfonso Lopez (WBA)	1976
JIMMY WILDE	1916-23	Guty Espadas (WBA)	1976-78
PANCHO VILLA	1923-25	Betulio Gonzalez (WBA)	1978-79
FIDEL LaBARBA	1925-27*	Chan-Hee Park (WBC)	1979-80
FRENCHY BELANGER (NBA,IBU)	1927-28	Luis Ibarra (WBA)	1979-80
IZZY SCHWARTZ (NY)	1927-29	Tae-Shik Kim (WBA)	1980
Johnny McCoy (Calif.)	1927-28	Shoji Oguma (WBC)	1980-81
Newsboy Brown (Calif.)	1928	Peter Mathebula (WBA)	1980-81
FRANKIE GENARO (NBA,IBU)	1928-29	Santos Laciar (WBA)	1981
Johnny Hill (GBR)	1928-29	Antonio Avelar (WBC)	1981-82
SPIDER PLADNER (NBA,IBU)	1929	Luis Ibarra (WBA)	1981
FRANKIE GENARO (NBA,IBU)	1929-31	Juan Herrera (WBA)	1981-82
Willie LaMorte (NY)	1929-30	Prudencio Cardona (WBC)	1982
Midget Wolgast (NY)	1930-35	Santos Laciar (WBA)	1982-85
YOUNG PEREZ (NBA,IBU)	1931-32	Freddie Castillo (WBC)	1982
JACKIE BROWN (NBA,IBU)	1932-35	Eleoncio Mercedes (WBC)	1982-83
BENNY LYNCH	1935-38†	Charlie Magri (WBC)	1983
Small Montana (NY,Calif.)	1935-37	Frank Cedeno (WBC)	1983-84
PETER KANE	1938-43	Soon-Chun Kwon (IBF)	1983-85
Little Dado (NBA,Calif.)	1938-40	Koji Kobayashi (WBC)	1984
JACKIE PATERSON	1943-48	Gabriel Bernal (WBC)	1984
RINTY MONAGHAN	1948-50*	Sot Chitalada (WBC)	1984-88
TERRY ALLEN	1950	Hilario Zapate (WBA)	1985-87
SALVADOR (DADO) MARINO	1950-52	Chong-Kwan Chung (IBF)	1985-86
YOSHIO SHIRAI	1953-54	Bi-Won Chung (IBF)	1986
PASCUAL PEREZ	1954-60	Hi-Sup Shin (IBF)	1986-87
PONE KINGPETCH	1960-62	Dodie Penalosa (IBF)	1987
MASAHIKO (FIGHTING) HARADA	1962-63	Fidel Bassa (WBA)	1987-89
PONE KINGPETCH	1963	Choi Chang-Ho (IBF)	1987-88
HIROYUKI EBIHARA	1963-64	Rolando Bohol (IBF)	1988
PONE KINGPETCH	1964-65	Yong-Kang Kim (WBC)	1988-89
SALVATORE BURRINI	1965-66	Duke McKenzie (IBF)	1988-89
Horacio Accavallo (WBA)	1966-68	Dave McAuley (IBF)	1989-92
WALTER McGOWAN	1966	Sot Chitalada (WBC)	1989-91
CHARTCHAI CHIONOI	1966-69	Jesus Rojas (WBA)	1989-90
EFREN TORRES	1969-70	Yul-Woo Lee (WBA)	1990
Hiroyuki Ebihara (WBA)	1969	Leopard Tamakuma (WBA)	1990-91
Bernabe Villacampo (WBA)	1969-70	Muangchai Kittikasem (WBC)	1991-92
CHARTCHAI CHIONOI	1970	Yong-Kang Kim (WBA)	1991-92
Berkrerk Chartvanchai (WBA)	1970	Rodolfo Blanco (IBF)	1992
Masao Ohba (WBA)	1970-73	**Yuri Arbachakov** (WBC)	1992—
ERBITO SALAVARRIA	1970-73	Aquiles Guzman (WBA)	1992
Betulio Gonzalez (WBC)	1972	Phichit Sithbangprachan (IBF)	1992-94†
Venice Borkorsor (WBC)	1972-73	David Griman (WBA)	1992-94
VENICE BORKORSOR	1973	**Saen Sow Ploenchit** (WBA)	1994—
Chartchai Chionoi (WBA)	1973-74	Francisco Tejedor (IBF)	1995
Betulio Gonzalez (WBA)	1973-74	**Danny Romero** (IBF)	1995—
Shoji Oguma (WBC)	1974-75		

Wide World Photos

The middleweight championship fights between **Carmen Basilio** (left) and **Sugar Ray Robinson** in 1957 and '58 both earned Fight of the Year honors. Above, the two trade blows in the closing moments of their 15-round bout at Yankee Stadium on Sept. 23, 1957. Basilio won the title that night on a split decision. Robinson came back six months later at Chicago Stadium to reclaim the crown on a unanimous decision.

Annual Awards

Ring Magazine Fight of the Year

First presented in 1945 by Nat Fleischer, who started *The Ring* magazine in 1922.

Multiple matchups: Muhammad Ali vs. Joe Frazier, Carmen Basilio vs. Sugar Ray Robinson and Graziano vs. Tony Zale (2).

Multiple fights: Muhammad Ali (6); Carmen Basilio (5); George Foreman and Joe Frazier (4); Rocky Graziano, Rocky Marciano and Tony Zale (3); Nino Benvenuti, Bobby Chacon, Ezzard Charles, Marvin Hagler, Thomas Hearns, Sugar Ray Leonard, Floyd Patterson, Sugar Ray Robinson and Jersey Joe Walcott (2).

Year	Winner	Loser	Result	Year	Winner	Loser	Result
1945	Rocky Graziano	Red Cochrane	KO 10	1970	Carlos Monzon	Nino Benvenuti	KO 12
1946	Tony Zale	Rocky Graziano	KO 6	1971	Joe Frazier	Muhammad Ali	W 15
1947	Rocky Graziano	Tony Zale	KO 6	1972	Bob Foster	Chris Finnegan	KO 14
1948	Marcel Cerdan	Tony Zale	KO 12	1973	George Foreman	Joe Frazier	KO 2
1949	Willie Pep	Sandy Saddler	W 15	1974	Muhammad Ali	George Foreman	KO 8
				1975	Muhammad Ali	Joe Frazier	KO 14
1950	Jake LaMotta	Laurent Dauthuille	KO 15	1976	George Foreman	Ron Lyle	KO 4
1951	Jersey Joe Walcott	Ezzard Charles	KO 7	1977	Jimmy Young	George Foreman	W 12
1952	Rocky Marciano	Jersey Joe Walcott	KO 13	1978	Leon Spinks	Muhammad Ali	W 15
1953	Rocky Marciano	Roland LaStarza	KO 11	1979	Danny Lopez	Mike Ayala	KO 15
1954	Rocky Marciano	Ezzard Charles	KO 8				
1955	Carmen Basilio	Tony DeMarco	KO 12	1980	Saad Muhammad	Yaqui Lopez	KO 14
1956	Carmen Basilio	Johnny Saxton	KO 9	1981	Sugar Ray Leonard	Thomas Hearns	KO 14
1957	Carmen Basilio	Sugar Ray Robinson	W 15	1982	Bobby Chacon	Rafael Limon	W 15
1958	Sugar Ray Robinson	Carmen Basilio	W 15	1983	Bobby Chacon	C. Boza-Edwards	W 12
1959	Gene Fullmer	Carmen Basilio	KO 14	1984	Jose Luis Ramirez	Edwin Rosario	KO 4
				1985	Marvin Hagler	Thomas Hearns	KO 3
1960	Floyd Patterson	Ingemar Johansson	KO 5	1986	Stevie Cruz	Barry McGuigan	W 15
1961	Joe Brown	Dave Charnley	W 15	1987	Sugar Ray Leonard	Marvin Hagler	W 12
1962	Joey Giardello	Henry Hank	W 10	1988	Tony Lopez	Rocky Lockridge	W 12
1963	Cassius Clay	Doug Jones	W 10	1989	Roberto Duran	Iran Barkley	W 12
1964	Cassius Clay	Sonny Liston	KO 7				
1965	Floyd Patterson	George Chuvalo	W 12	1990	Julio Cesar Chavez	Meldrick Taylor	KO 12
1966	Jose Torres	Eddie Cotton	W 15	1991	Robert Quiroga	Akeem Anifowoshe	W 12
1967	Nino Benvenuti	Emile Griffith	W 15	1992	Riddick Bowe	Evander Holyfield	W 12
1968	Dick Tiger	Frank DePaula	W 10	1993	Michael Carbajal	Humberto Gonzalez	KO 7
1969	Joe Frazier	Jerry Quarry	KO 7	1994	Jorge Castro	John David Jackson	TKO 9

Annual Awards (Cont.)

Ring Magazine Fighter of the Year

First presented in 1928 by Nat Fleischer, who started *The Ring* magazine in 1922.

Multiple winners: Muhammad Ali (5); Joe Louis (4); Joe Frazier and Rocky Marciano (3); Ezzard Charles, George Foreman, Marvin Hagler, Thomas Hearns, Ingemar Johansson, Sugar Ray Leonard, Tommy Loughran, Floyd Patterson, Sugar Ray Robinson, Barney Ross, Dick Tiger and Mike Tyson (2).

Year		Year		Year		Year	
1928	Gene Tunney	1945	Willie Pep	1963	Cassius Clay	1980	Thomas Hearns
1929	Tommy Loughran	1946	Tony Zale	1964	Emile Griffith	1981	Sugar Ray Leonard
1930	Max Schmeling	1947	Gus Lesnevich	1965	Dick Tiger		& Salvador Sanchez
1931	Tommy Loughran	1948	Ike Williams	1966	No award	1982	Larry Holmes
1932	Jack Sharkey	1949	Ezzard Charles	1967	Joe Frazier	1983	Marvin Hagler
1933	No award	1950	Ezzard Charles	1968	Nino Benvenuti	1984	Thomas Hearns
1934	Tony Canzoneri	1951	Sugar Ray Robinson	1969	Jose Napoles	1985	Donald Curry
	& Barney Ross	1952	Rocky Marciano				& Marvin Hagler
1935	Barney Ross	1953	Carl (Bobo) Olson	1970	Joe Frazier	1986	Mike Tyson
1936	Joe Louis	1954	Rocky Marciano	1971	Joe Frazier	1987	Evander Holyfield
1937	Henry Armstrong	1955	Rocky Marciano	1972	Muhammad Ali	1988	Mike Tyson
1938	Joe Louis	1956	Floyd Patterson		& Carlos Monzon	1989	Pernell Whitaker
1939	Joe Louis	1957	Carmen Basilio	1973	George Foreman		
		1958	Ingemar Johansson	1974	Muhammad Ali	1990	Julio Cesar Chavez
1940	Billy Conn	1959	Ingemar Johansson	1975	Muhammad Ali	1991	James Toney
1941	Joe Louis			1976	George Foreman	1992	Riddick Bowe
1942	Sugar Ray Robinson	1960	Floyd Patterson	1977	Carlos Zarate	1993	Michael Carbajal
1943	Fred Apostoli	1961	Joe Brown	1978	Muhammad Ali	1994	Roy Jones Jr.
1944	Beau Jack	1962	Dick Tiger	1979	Sugar Ray Leonard		

Note: Cassius Clay changed his name to Muhammad Ali after winning the heavyweight title in 1964.

All-Time Knockout Leaders

As compiled by *The Ring Record Book and Encyclopedia*.

		Division	Career	No			Division	Career	No
1	Archie Moore	Lt. Heavy	1936-63	130	6	Sandy Saddle	Feather	1944-56	103
2	Young Stribling	Heavy	1921-33	126	7	Sam Langford	Middle	1902-26	102
3	Billy Bird	Welter	1920-48	125	8	Henry Armstrong	Welter	1931-45	100
4	George Odwel	Welter	1930-45	114	9	Jimmy Wilde	Fly	1911-23	98
5	Sugar Ray Robinson	Middle	1940-65	110	10	Len Wickwar	Lt. Heavy	1928-47	93

Triple Champions

Fighters who have won widely-accepted world titles in more than one division. Henry Armstrong is the only fighter listed to hold three titles simultaneously. Note that (*) indicates title claimant.

Sugar Ray Leonard (5)—WBC Welterweight (1979-80,80-82); WBA Jr. Middleweight (1981); WBC Middleweight (1987); WBC Super Middleweight (1988-90); WBC Light Heavyweight (1988).

Roberto Duran (4)—Lightweight (1972-79); WBC Welterweight (1980); WBA Jr. Middleweight (1983-84); WBC Middleweight (1989-90).

Thomas Hearns (4)—WBA Welterweight (1980-81); WBC Jr. Middleweight (1982-84); WBC Light Heavyweight (1987); WBA Light Heavyweight (1991);.WBC Middleweight (1987-88).

Pernell Whitaker (4)—IBF/WBC/WBA Lightweight (1989-92); IBF Jr. Lightweight (1992-93); WBC Welterweight (1993—); WBC Jr. Middleweight (1995).

Alexis Arguello (3)—WBA Featherweight (1974-77); WBC Jr. Lightweight (1978-80); WBC Lightweight (1981-83).

Henry Armstrong (3)—Featherweight (1937-38); Welterweight (1938-40); Lightweight (1938-39).

Iran Barkley (3)—WBC Middleweight (1988-89); IBF Super Middleweight (1992-93); WBA Light Heavyweight (1992).

Wilfredo Benitez (3)—Jr. Welterweight (1976-79); Welterweight (1979); WBC Jr. Middleweight (1981-82).

Tony Canzoneri (3)—Featherweight (1928); Lightweight (1930-33); Jr. Welterweight (1931-32,33).

Julio Cesar Chavez (3)—WBC Jr. Lightweight (1984-87); WBA/WBC Lightweight (1987-89); WBC/IBF Jr. Welterweight (1989-91); WBC Jr. Welterweight (1991-94, 1994—).

Jeff Fenech (3)—IBF Bantamweight (1985); WBC Jr. Featherweight (1986-88); WBC Featherweight (1988-90).

Bob Fitzsimmons (3)—Middleweight (1891-97); Light Heavyweight (1903-05); Heavyweight (1897-99).

Wilfredo Gomez (3)—WBC Super Bantamweight (1977-83); WBC Featherweight (1984); WBA Jr. Lightweight (1985-86).

Emile Griffith (3)—Welterweight (1961,62-63,63-66); Jr. Middleweight (1962-63); Middleweight (1966-67,67-68).

Terry McGovern (3)—Bantamweight (1889-1900); Featherweight (1900-01); Lightweight* (1900-01).

Barney Ross (3)—Lightweight (1933-35); Jr. Welterweight (1933-35); Welterweight (1934, 35-38).

New Zealand's **Frank Bunce** carries the ball against South Africa in the rugby World Cup final at Johannesburg on June 24. The underdog South Africans won, 15-12, in extra time. See page 914.

MISCELLANEOUS SPORTS

Black Magic

New Zealand takes America's Cup home to Auckland after sweeping to victory over Dennis Conner and crew.

It was appropriate that a boat called *Black Magic* would dominate the 1995 America's Cup.

From the start of the trials in January to the end of Team New Zealand's 5-0 sweep of Dennis Conner's borrowed *Young America* in May, the 29th defense of the world's oldest, continuous international sporting event seemed to be sailed under a spell.

In addition to the Kiwis' phenomenal run off San Diego, America's Cup '95 featured the first all-women's crew (which later added a man); the first sinking in the event's 144-year history (plus a half dozen near-calamities) the first participation by an aircraft carrier, and only the second loss of the Cup by a United States defender.

And that was just the action on the water. America's Cup XXIX was also spiced by a series of backroom deals that enabled the defending San Diego Yacht Club to send all three of its candidates to the defense finals and then allow the winner, Conner, to make a last-minute boat switch. He chose to sail into battle against New Zealand aboard the rival PACT 95 syndicate's *Young America* rather than his own *Stars & Stripes*.

And then there was the weather. In 1992, the last time the races were held, not a single day of racing was lost to the weather. Three years later, a series of unseasonable winter storms forced 19 days of weather-related disruptions.

America's Cup '95 was the third defense by the SDYC. The first, after Conner went Down Under in 1987 to win the Cup back, was against New Zealand in 1988. That was the infamous match-race series, in which a New Zealand syndicate led by Michael Fay pointed out that the Cup's century-old Deed of Gift stated that every challenge to the holder had to be honored.

When New Zealand announced it would race a 133-foot mono-hull, the angry San Diegians found a loophole of their own and defended in a 60-foot catamaran. The Americans won easily.

Fay protested and the whole thing ended up in court, giving the sport a black eye less than a year after Conner's inspirational victory in Fremantle, Australia.

This time around, there was no catamaran to save the SDYC. And Conner, the only U.S. sailor to ever lose the America's Cup, became the only U.S. sailor to lose it twice.

Not only did *Black Magic* sweep the best five-of-nine Cup final, skipper Russell Coutts and his crew led after each of the 30 legs and had an average winning margin of two minutes and 52 seconds— the widest margin since *Courageous* swept Australian challenger *Southern Cross* in 1974. Only once in the five races did *Young America* cross ahead of Black Magic's bow.

The margins of victory in the five 18.55-mile races over a six-leg, windward-leeward course were 2:45, 4:14, 1:51, 3:37 and 1:50.

Even the Kiwis were startled by the ease of their victory. "Man, did we slaughter these guys or what?" said American-born Team New Zealand co-designer Doug Peterson. "I thought we'd win, but I thought it would

New Zealand challenger **Black Magic** sails to victory on May 9 in the third race of the America's Cup final. The Kiwis, skippered by Russell Coutts, had U.S. defender *Young America* in their wake for all 30 legs of the final, which they won in five straight races in waters off San Diego.

be something like 5-3," added *Black Magic* tactician Brad Butterworth.

Said Young America helsman Paul Cayard: "I'd been in some uphill battles in my life. But I'd never been in a race before where I really felt I had so little control over the outcome. I really didn't feel we were in the race. It was the largest discrepancy in boat speed that I've seen."

The defenders had learned the hard lesson that the indomitable New Zealanders had already impressed upon six other challengers from five nations. "That black boat is some boat," *oneAustralia* skipper John Bertrand said after losing 5-1 to *Black Magic* in the finals of the challenger trials. The *oneAustralia* victory— by a margin of 15 seconds— was *Black Magic's* only on-the-water defeat in four months and 38 match races.

But it was four months that included much more than racing. Here is a chronological listing of events that helped shaped America's Cup '95:

Dec. 7, 1994: A new $3 million, 75-foot sloop belonging to France's Defi '95 syndicate falls 20 feet from its lift and crashes into the Mission Bay dock as it is being lowered into the water in for the first time. It will take one month and $1 million to repair the damage.

Jan. 4, 1995: Tornado-like winds hit the PACT 95 defense compound, destroying the team's sail loft and hospitality tent and causing $600,000 damage to *Young America*.

Feb. 4: The 1,092-foot, 94,000-ton aircraft carrier U.S.S. *Abraham Lincoln* ghosts out of the fog and parks in the middle of the challengers' starting line.

Feb. 20: The keel falls off *France 2* and the boat falls over on its side, but does not sink.

March 5: *OneAustralia* becomes the first boat in America's Cup history to sink. During a challenger trials race against Team New Zealand, a crack suddenly appears just behind *oneAustralia's* mast. The boat folds in two and disappears in two minutes. No one is hurt.

March 12: While being towed, *Young America* hits a rogue, 12-foot wave which breaks a 16-foot by 4-foot section of its hull just forward of the keel.

March 26: The keel almost falls off Conner's *Stars & Stripes* during a race.

America³ syndicate head **Bill Koch** on board *Mighty Mary* with his all-women's crew before he decided to bring in tactician Dave Dellenbaugh at the start of the America's Cup defender finals on March 18.

Fearing the boat might sink, the crew breaks out lifejackets as pumps are put aboard.

The story that got the most media attention, however, was the presence of the first all-women's team. Sixty weeks before *Black Magic* won America's Cup '95, successful 1992 defender Bill Koch announced his America³ organization would field the first all-women's bid in 1995. Until then no women had ever sailed in an America's Cup race as a working crew member.

More than 600 women applied for berths on the America³ team, from which Koch invited 120 to three tryout camps in San Diego in May 1992.

Thirty-two women were selected to fill two crews and trained for eight months off San Diego prior to the start of the defense trials. Many of the women had never raced on a sailboat before the trials began and a few had never been on a sailboat. In addition to the corps of small boat sailors, the America coaches recruited international-class rowers and weightlifters to fill some of the more physically-demanding crew positions.

Led by skipper-helmsman Leslie Egnot and *Mighty Mary* crew captain Dawn Riley, the women earned deserved accolades. But there was controversy, too. On March 18, the day of the first race in the semifinals, Koch added a man to the mix— putting 1992 tactician and starting helmsman Dave Dellenbaugh aboard the boat in place of J.J. Isler. The "all-women's crew" became the "women's team."

According to America³ spokesman Will Robinson, it was the women's idea. "I think they really wanted to win." said Robinson. "They needed experience they didn't have," so they asked Koch for some outside help.

Going into the last scheduled race of the defense finals, *Mighty Mary* needed a victory over Conner's *Stars & Stripes* to reach a one-race sail-off against the Kevin Mahaney-skippered *Young America* to determine which boat would go on to meet New Zealand. A *Stars & Stripes* victory would send Conner's crew to the America's Cup.

With a lead of 4:08 entering the final three-mile run to the finish *Mighty Mary* appeared to be comfortably in front, until Conner's boat staged the greatest last-leg comeback in America's Cup history— gaining five minutes— to win by 52 seconds.

Coming around the mark, *Mighty Mary* sailed into a windless hole and lost its momentum. *Star & Stripes*, on the other hand, was fortunate to come around in a puff of wind and gradually overtook the women to win by three boat lengths.

"Not to take anything away from their win,"

continued on page 914

YACHTING

The America's Cup

International yacht racing was launched in 1851 when England's Royal Yacht Squadron staged a 60-mile regatta around the Isle of Wight and offered a silver trophy to the winner. The 101-foot schooner *America*, sent over by the New York Yacht Club, won the race and the prize. Originally called the Hundred-Guinea Cup, the trophy was renamed The America's Cup after the winning boat's owners deeded it to the NYYC with instructions to defend it whenever challenged.

From 1870-1980, the NYYC successfully defended the Cup 25 straight times; first in large schooners and J-class boats that measured up to 140 feet in overall length, then in 12-meter boats. A foreign yacht finally won the Cup in 1983 when *Australia II* beat defender *Liberty* in the seventh and deciding race off Newport, R.I. Four years later, the San Diego Yacht Club's *Stars & Stripes* won the Cup back, sweeping the four races of the final series off Fremantle, Australia.

Then in 1988, New Zealand's Mercury Bay Boating Club, unwilling to wait the usual three- to four-year period between Cup defenses, challenged the SDYC to a match race, citing the Cup's 102-year-old Deed of Gift, which clearly stated that every challenge had to be honored. Mercury Bay announced it would race a 133-foot monohull. San Diego countered with a 60-foot catamaran. The resulting best-of-three series (Sept. 7-8) was a mismatch as the SDYC's catamaran *Stars & Stripes* won two straight by margins of better than 18 and 21 minutes. Mercury Bay syndicate leader Michael Fay protested the outcome and took the SDYC to court in New York State (where the Deed of Gift was first filed) claiming San Diego had violated the spirit of the deed by racing a catamaran instead of a monohull. N.Y. State Supreme Court judge Carmen Ciparick agreed and on March 28, 1989, ordered the SDYC to hand the Cup over to Mercury Bay. The SDYC refused, but did consent to the court's appointment of the New York Yacht Club as custodian of the Cup until an appeal was ruled on.

On Sept. 19, 1989, the Appellate Division of the N.Y. Supreme Court overturned Ciparick's decision and awarded the Cup back to the SDYC. An appeal by Mercury Bay was denied by the N.Y. Court of Appeals on April 26, 1990, ending three years of legal wrangling. To avoid the chaos of 1988-90, a new class of boat—75-foot monohulls with 110-foot masts—has been used by all competing countries since 1992.

Note that (*) indicates skipper was also owner of the boat.

Schooners and J-Class Boats

Year	Winner	Skipper	Series	Loser	Skipper
1851	*America*	Richard Brown	—	—	—
1870	*Magic*	Andrew Comstock	1-0	*Cambria*, GBR	J. Tannock
1871	*Columbia* (2-1) & *Sappho* (2-0)	Nelson Comstock Sam Greenwood	4-0	*Livonia*, GBR	J.R. Woods
1876	*Madeleine*	Josephus Williams	2-0	*Countess of Dufferin*, CAN	J.E. Ellsworth
1881	*Mischief*	Nathanael Clock	2-0	*Atalanta*, CAN	Alexander Cuthbert*
1885	*Puritan*	Aubrey Crocker	2-0	*Genesta*, GBR	John Carter
1886	*Mayflower*	Martin Stone	2-0	*Galatea*, GBR	Dan Bradford
1887	*Volunteer*	Henry Haff	2-0	*Thistle*, GBR	John Barr
1893	*Vigilant*	William Hansen	3-0	*Valkyrie II*, GBR	Wm. Granfield
1895	*Defender*	HenryHaff	3-0	*Valkyrie III*, GBR	Wm. Granfield
1899	*Columbia*	Charles Barr	3-0	*Shamrock I*, GBR	Archie Hogarth
1901	*Columbia*	Charles Barr	3-0	*Shamrock II*, GBR	E.A. Sycamore
1903	*Reliance*	Charles Barr	3-0	*Shamrock III*, GBR	Bob Wringe
1920	*Resolute*	Charles F. Adams	3-2	*Shamrock IV*, GBR	William Burton
1930	*Enterprise*	Harold Vanderbilt*	4-0	*Shamrock V*, GBR	Ned Heard
1934	*Rainbow*	Harold Vanderbilt*	4-2	*Endeavour*, GBR	T.O.M. Sopwith
1937	*Ranger*	Harold Vanderbilt*	4-0	*Endeavour II*, GBR	T.O.M. Sopwith

12-Meter Boats

Year	Winner	Skipper	Series	Loser	Skipper
1958	*Columbia*	Briggs Cunningham	4-0	*Sceptre*, GBR	Graham Mann
1962	*Weatherly*	Bus Mosbacher	4-1	*Gretel*, AUS	Jock Sturrock
1964	*Constellation*	Bob Bavier & Eric Ridder	4-0	*Sovereign*, AUS	Peter Scott
1967	*Intrepid*	Bus Mosbacher	4-0	*Dame Pattie*, AUS	Jock Sturrock
1970	*Intrepid*	Bill Ficker	4-1	*Gretel II*, AUS	Jim Hardy
1974	*Courageous*	Ted Hood	4-0	*Southern Cross*, AUS	John Cuneo
1977	*Courageous*	Ted Turner	4-0	*Australia*	Noel Robins
1980	*Freedom*	Dennis Conner	4-1	*Australia*	Jim Hardy
1983	*Australia II*	John Bertrand	4-3	*Liberty*, USA	Dennis Conner
1987	*Stars & Stripes*	Dennis Conner	4-0	*Kookaburra III*, AUS	Iain Murray

60-ft Catamaran vs 133-ft Monohull

Year	Winner	Skipper	Series	Loser	Skipper
1988	*Stars & Stripes*	Dennis Conner	2-0	*New Zealand*, NZE	David Barnes

75-ft International America's Cup Class

Year	Winner	Skipper	Series	Loser	Skipper
1992	*America*[3]	Bill Koch* & Buddy Melges	4-1	*Il Moro di Venezia*, ITA	Paul Cayard
1995	*Black Magic*, NZE	Russell Coutts	5-0	*Young America*, USA	Dennis Conner & Paul Cayard

said a disappointed Riley, "but it was so weird and puffy out there. I don't want to say they were lucky. But there was some of that."

Added backup *Mighty Mary* navigator Annie Nelson said: "We didn't lose because we're women. We lost because that's the way it was."

Immediately after his come-from-behind victory, Conner took advantage of a loophole in the mutual consent rules governing the America's Cup and announced he would sail *Young America* in the final instead of *Stars & Stripes*, which most experts considered the slowest of the three defense candidates. *Young America* had the best overall record among the U.S. boats, but had struggled in the defender finals.

In the end, the America's Cup was a rout. Conner's crew had too little practice time aboard *Young America* and the Kiwis never looked back.

1995 America's Cup
All races off coast of San Diego

CHALLENGER FINAL

Best of nine races for the Louis Vuitton Cup (April 11-19); overall elimination record in parentheses.
Syndicates: Team New Zealand (*Black Magic*); One Australia (*oneAustralia*).

	W-L	Pts	Skipper
Black Magic (36-4)	5-1	5	Russell Coutts
oneAustralia (25-15)	1-5	1	John Bertrand

DEFENDER FINAL

Round robin of 12 races for the Citizen Cup (April 10-25); the first boat eliminated stops racing, leaving the other two boats to compete; overall elimination record in parentheses. According to the unprecedented agreement reached before the series, a three-way tie would have eliminated *Stars & Stripes* and set up a one-race sailoff between *Young America* and *Mighty Mary*.
Syndicates: America³ (*Mighty Mary*); PACT 95 (*Young America*); Teams Dennis Conner (*Stars & Stripes*)

	W-L	Pts	Skipper
Stars & Stripes (19-18)	6-2	6	Dennis Conner & Paul Cayard
Young America (24-12)	3-5	5*	Kevin Mahaney
Mighty Mary (12-25)	3-5	4*	Leslie Egnot

*Young America carried over 2 points from the semifinals and Mighty Mary one point.
Note: Team Conner elected to sail *Young America* rather than the slower *Stars & Stripes* in the America's Cup final against New Zealand.

FINAL

Best of nine races; six legs over 18.55-mile course.

	W	L	Skipper
Black Magic (NZE)	5		Russell Coutts
Young America (USA)	0	5	Dennis Conner & Paul Cayard

Date	Winner	Time	Margin
May 6	*Black Magic*	2:17:43	2:45
May 8	*Black Magic*	2:37:37	4:14
May 9	*Black Magic*	2:17:28	1:51
May 11	*Black Magic*	2:34:58	3:37
May 13	*Black Magic*	2:22:35	1:50

South Africa Wins Rugby World Cup

by Ian Thomsen

The most important sports image of the year didn't feature Mike Tyson, Michael Jordan, Monica Seles or Cal Ripken Jr. Their games seemed incidental when compared to the sight of the 76-year-old black man, a former political prisoner for 27 years, celebrating with a green cap pulled down to his ears and a green jersey buttoned up to his neck.

That man was Nelson Mandela, the president of South Africa.

On June 24, Mandela was at sold-out Ellis Park in Johannesburg cheering on the green-clad Springboks— South Africa's national rugby team. While in prison from 1964 to 1990, Mandela hated rugby, which had long embodied the goals of the former white government. He and millions of other blacks used to cheer *against* the national team.

South Africa had been banned politically from participating in the rugby World Cups of 1987 and '91— not to mention the Olympic Games entirely from 1970 on— because of the former government's apartheid policies of racial separation.

Mandela's release from prison in 1990 began the process that eventually brought South Africa back into the mainstream of international politics and sports. His election as president in 1994, unthinkable only five years before, followed by two years South Africa's return to the Olympic fold in Barcelona.

Which is not to say that the Springboks were fully integrated. They weren't. When the tournament opened, the team was all-white, pending the return from injury of its lone black player, Chester Williams— the closest South Africa has come ro realizing their own Jackie Robinson.

Knowing that the rugby World Cup was the world's fifth largest tournament— behind the Winter and Summer Olympics, the soccer World Cup and the World Track and Field Championships— and assured by national team officials that the Springboks would diligently pursue integration, Mandela threw his support and credibility behind the team and his country's efforts to successfully host the World Cup.

"Out loyalties have completely changed,"

South African president **Nelson Mandela** (left) congratulates national team captain **Francois Pienaar** after the Springboks defeated New Zealand, 15-12, to win their first rugby World Cup championship.

said Mandela. "We have adopted these young men as our boys."

The Springboks' motto was "One team, One Country" and they took as their theme song a working hymn of black miners called "Shosholoza." At the opening ceremonies on May 25, they belted out the new South African anthem— one verse in Xhosa (Mandela's native tongue) and the other in Afrikaans (the white man's language) — and then, as if to confirm the new spirit, applied a dramatic 27-18 whipping to Australia, the defending champion.

Thirty days later, after 31 games and the elimination of 14 nations, South Africa reached the Cup final against heavily-favored New Zealand. Known as the All-Blacks because of their black uniforms, New Zealand came into the match with the most talked-about player in the tournament— 20-year-old wing Jonah Lomu, who had the body of a NFL tight end (6-feet-3, 230 lbs) and the speed to cover 100 yards in 10.7 seconds. Lomu was also black.

"The sins of apartheid are beginning to catch up with us," warned Khehla Mthembu, a black business leader. "Had we trained enough Zulus, we would not be worrying about who is going to take care of Jonah Lomu."

As it turned out, an inspired South African defense allowed Lomu gains of only 10 and 20 yards instead of his usual 50-yard romps and kept New Zealand out of the end zone altogether. All of the points in the game were scored by kicking, with a 30-yard drop-goal by Joel Stransky winning the game, 15-12, with seven minutes left in extra time. The victory was South Africa's first world championship in a major team sport.

The victory ceremony may have been more important than the game itself.

When Springboks' captain Francois Pienaar stepped up on the podium to accept the World Cup trophy he was met by a delighted Mandela, who was wearing a jersey identical to Pienaar's, right down to the No. 6 on the back.

The white rugby player shook hands with the sworn enemy of apartheid. Their joy was sincere. After centuries of civil war, it was a public truce.

"He told me thanks for all we've done for South Africa," Pienaar recalled. "I reciprocated, telling him we could never have done as much as he's done for South Africa."

The team may not have had the overwhelming support that would have been taken for granted in almost any other country. But the absence of political protest, which had always greeted rugby, was like a silent cheer.

The old man celebrated the Springboks' victory. It was a beginning.

Ian Thomsen is a sports columnist, based in London for the *International Herald Tribune*.

Wide World Photos   Wide World Photos   Wide World Photos

World champion **Garry Kasparov** of Russia is a study of meditation, intimidation and concentration during his PCA world championship match with India's Viswanathan Anand in New York. Kasparov retained the title on Oct. 10, winning the 20-game match 10½ to 7½ and taking home the $900,000 winner's purse.

CHESS

World Champions

Garry Kasparov of Russia, the youngest man to win the world chess championship when he beat Anatoly Karpov in 1985 at age 22, retained his title on Oct. 10 against 25-year-old Viswanathan Anand of India. Staged on the 107th-floor observation deck of New York's World Trade Center, the scheduled 20-game match lasted 18 games with Kasparov defeating Anand, 10½ to 7½, to capture the $900,000 winner's prize. Anand received half that amount. The match for the Professional Chess Association championship opened on Sept. 11 and began with an unprecedented eight consecutive draws. Anand stunned the champion by winning Game 9 to take a 5-4 lead, but Kasparov quickly recovered to win four of the next five games for a commanding 8½ to 5½ advantage. The match ended with four straight draws.

In 1993, Kasparov and then-No. 1 challenger Nigel Short of England broke away from the established International Chess Federation (FIDE) to form the PCA. The FIDE retaliated by stripping Kasparov of their world title and arranging a playoff that was won by Karpov, the former title-holder. Karpov is scheduled to meet 21-year-old Russian emigre Gata Kamsky of Brooklyn in late 1995 or early '96, depending on when FIDE can line up a sponsor for the match. Kasparov has agreed to meet the winner in a 1996 match to unify the two championships.

Years		Years		Years	
1866-94	Wilhelm Steinitz, Austria	1937-46	Alexander Alekhine, France	1963-69	Tigran Petrosian, USSR
1894-		1948-57	Mikhail Botvinnik, USSR	1969-72	Boris Spassky, USSR
1921	Emanuel Lasker, Germany	1957-58	Vassily Smyslov, USSR	1972-75	Bobby Fischer, USA*
1921-27	Jose Capablanca, Cuba	1958-59	Mikhail Botvinnik, USSR	1975-85	Anatoly Karpov, USSR
1927-35	Alexander Alekhine, France	1960-61	Mikhail Tal, USSR	1985—	Garry Kasparov, RUS
1935-37	Max Euwe, Holland	1961-63	Mikhail Botvinnik, USSR		*Fischer defaulted championship in 1975

U.S. Champions (since 1900)

Boris Gulko of Fair Lawn, N.J. won the 1994 U. S. Championships in the 14-player, round robin tournament that ran Oct. 10-26 at Key West, Fla. Gulko beat out runner-up and two-time national champion Yasser Seirawan, 9½ points to 8. The 1995 U.S. title was scheduled to be decided Nov. 18 to Dec. 6 in Modesto, Calif.

Years		Years		Years	
1857-71	Paul Morphy	1948-51	Herman Steiner	1983	Roman Dzindzichashvili,
1871-76	George Mackenzie	1951-54	Larry Evans		Larry Christiansen
1876-80	James Mason	1954-57	Arthur Bisguier		& Walter Browne
1880-89	George Mackenzie	1957-61	Bobby Fischer	1984-85	Lev Alburt
1889-90	Samuel Lipschutz	1961-62	Larry Evans	1986	Yasser Seirawan
1890	Jackson Showalter	1962-68	Bobby Fischer	1987	Joel Benjamin
1890-91	Max Judd	1968-69	Larry Evans		& Nick DeFirmian
1891-92	Jackson Showalter	1969-72	Samuel Reshevsky	1988	Michael Wilder
1892-94	Samuel Lipschutz	1972-73	Robert Byrne	1989	Roman Dzindzichashvili,
1894	Jackson Showalter	1973-74	Lubomir Kavalek		Stuart Rachels
1894-95	Albert Hodges		& John Grefe		& Yasser Seirawan
1895-97	Jackson Showalter	1974-77	Walter Browne	1990	Lev Alburt
1897-1906	Harry Pillsbury	1978-80	Lubomir Kabalek	1991	Gata Kamsky
1906-09	Vacant	1980-81	Larry Evans,	1992	Patrick Wolff
1909-36	Frank Marshall		Larry Christiansen	1993	Alexander Shabalov
1936-44	Samuel Reshevsky		& Walter Browne		& Alex Yermolinsky
1944-46	Arnold Denker	1981-83	Walter Browne	1994	Boris Gulko
1946-48	Samuel Reshevsky		& Yasser Seirawan		

DOGS

Iditarod Trail Sled Dog Race

Doug Swingley, a 41-year-old rancher from Simms, Mont., became the first non-Alaskan to win the Iditarod Trail Sled Dog Race on Mar. 14. He and his team also set a new course record, covering the 1,100-mile route in 9 days, 2 hours, 42 minutes and 19 seconds. Martin Buser, the 1994 winner, placed second. Racers were timed from the restart in Wasilla, rather than the ceremonial start in Anchorage, but the winning pace was still a half-day faster than the old record. Swingley, who won $52,500 and a new pickup, credited his lead dog Elmer with the win, saying: "If I had 15 more dogs like Elmer, we could make it in 7½ days."

Multiple winners: Rick Swenson (5); Susan Butcher (4); Martin Buser and Rick Mackey (2).

Year		Elapsed Time	Year		Elapsed Time
1973	Dick Wilmarth	20 days, 00:49:41	1985	Libby Riddles	18 days, 00:20:17
1974	Carl Huntington	20 days, 15:02:07	1986	Susan Butcher	11 days, 15:06:00
1975	Emmitt Peters	14 days, 14:43:45	1987	Susan Butcher	11 days, 02:05:13
1976	Gerald Riley	18 days, 22:58:17	1988	Susan Butcher	11 days, 11:41:40
1977	Rick Swenson	16 days, 16:27:13	1989	Joe Runyan	11 days, 05:24:34
1978	Dick Mackey	14 days, 18:52:24			
1979	Rick Swenson	15 days, 10:37:47	1990	Susan Butcher	11 days, 01:53:23
			1991	Rick Swenson	12 days, 16:34:39
1980	Joe May	14 days, 07:11:51	1992	Martin Buser	10 days, 19:17:00
1981	Rick Swenson	12 days, 08:45:02	1993	Jeff King	10 days, 15:38:15
1982	Rick Swenson	16 days, 04:40:10	1994	Martin Buser	10 days, 13:02:39
1983	Rick Mackey	12 days, 14:10:44	1995	Doug Swingley	9 days, 02:42:19*
1984	Dean Osmar	12 days, 15:07:33			

*Course record.

Westminster Kennel Club

Best in Show

Ch. Gaelforce Post Script, a perky Scottish terrier who answers to the name Peggy Sue, won best in show at the 119th annual Westminster Kennel Club show on Feb. 14 at Madison Square Garden in New York. The 4-year-old bitch, who is owned by Joe Kinnarney of Apex, N.C., and Vandra Huber of Seattle, and handled by Maripi Wooldridge, beat out 1,340 other canine champions. The judge was Jacklyn Hungerland. In addition to being the most prestigious dog show in the America, the Westminster show is also one of the oldest annual sporting events in the country.

Multiple winners: Ch. Warren Remedy (3); Ch. Chinoe's Adamant James, Ch. Comejo Wycollar Boy, Ch. Flornell Spicy Piece of Halleston; Ch. Matford Vic, Ch. My Own Brucie, Ch. Pendley Calling of Blarney, Ch. Rancho Dobe's Storm (2).

Year		Breed	Year		Breed
1907	Warren Remedy	Fox Terrier	1938	Daro of Maridor	English Setter
1908	Warren Remedy	Fox Terrier	1939	Ferry v.Rauhfelsen of Giralda	Doberman
1909	Warren Remedy	Fox Terrier			
			1940	My Own Brucie	Cocker Spaniel
1910	Sabine Rarebit	Fox Terrier	1941	My Own Brucie	Cocker Spaniel
1911	Tickle Em Jock	Scottish Terrier	1942	Wolvey Pattern of Edgerstoune	W. Highland Terrier
1912	Kenmore Sorceress	Airedale	1943	Pitter Patter of Piperscroft	Miniature Poodle
1913	Strathway Prince Albert	Bulldog	1944	Flornell Rarebit of Twin Ponds	Welsh Terrier
1914	Brentwood Hero	Old English Sheepdog	1945	Shieling's Signature	Scottish Terrier
1915	Matford Vic	Old English Sheepdog	1946	Hetherington Model Rhythm	Fox Terrier
1916	Matford Vic	Old English Sheepdog	1947	Warlord of Mazelaine	Boxer
1917	Comejo Wycollar Boy	Fox Terrier	1948	Rock Ridge Night Rocket	Bedling. Terrier
1918	Haymarket Faultless	Bull Terrier	1949	Mazelaine's Zazarac Brandy	Boxer
1919	Briergate Bright Beauty	Airedale			
			1950	Walsing Winning Trick of Edgerstoune	Scot. Terrier
1920	Comejo Wycollar Boy	Fox Terrier	1951	Bang Away of Sirrah Crest	Boxer
1921	Midkiff Seductive	Cocker Spaniel	1952	Rancho Dobe's Storm	Doberman
1922	Boxwood Barkentine	Airedale	1953	Rancho Dobe's Storm	Doberman
1923	No best-in-show award		1954	Carmor's Rise and Shine	Cocker Spaniel
1924	Barberryhill Bootlegger	Sealyham	1955	Kippax Fearnought	Bulldog
1925	Governor Moscow	Pointer	1956	Wilber White Swan	Toy Poodle
1926	Signal Circuit	Fox Terrier	1957	Shirkhan of Grandeur	Afghan Hound
1927	Pinegrade Perfection	Sealyham	1958	Puttencove Promise	Standard Poodle
1928	Talavera Margaret	Fox Terrier	1959	Fontclair Festoon	Miniature Poodle
1929	Land Loyalty of Bellhaven	Collie			
			1960	Chick T'Sun of Caversham	Pekingese
1930	Pendley Calling of Blarney	Fox Terrier	1961	Cappoquin Little Sister	Toy Poodle
1931	Pendley Calling of Blarney	Fox Terrier	1962	Elfinbrook Simon	W. Highland Terrier
1932	Nancolleth Markable	Pointer	1963	Wakefield's Black Knight	English Springer Spaniel
1933	Warland Protector of Shelterock	Airedale	1964	Courtenay Fleetfoot of Pennyworth	Whippet
1934	Flornell Spicy Bit of Halleston	Fox Terrier	1965	Carmichaels Fanfare	Scottish Terrier
1935	Nunsoe Duc de la Terrace of Blakeen	Standard Poodle	1966	Zeloy Mooremaides Magic	Fox Terrier
1936	St. Margaret Magnificent of Clairedale	Sealyham	1967	Bardene Bingo	Scottish Terrier
1937	Flornell Spicy Bit of Halleston	Fox Terrier	1968	Stingray of Derryabah	Lakeland Terrier

Dogs (Cont.)
Westminster Kennel Club
Best in Show

Year		Breed	Year		Breed
1969	Glamoor Good News	Skye Terrier	1983	Kabik's The Challenger	Afghan Hound
1970	Arriba's Prima Donna	Boxer	1984	Seaward's Blackbeard	Newfoundland
1971	Chinoe's Adamant James	E.S. Spaniel	1985	Braeburn's Close Encounter	Scottish Terrier
1972	Chinoe's Adamant James	E.S. Spaniel	1986	Marjetta National Acclaim	Pointer
1973	Acadia Command Performance	Standard Poodle	1987	Covy Tucker Hill's Manhattan	German Shepherd
1974	Gretchenhof Columbia River	German SH Pointer	1988	Great Elms Prince Charming II	Pomeranian
1975	Sir Lancelot of Barvan	Old Eng. Sheepdog	1989	Royal Tudor's Wild As The Wind	Doberman
1976	Jo Ni's Red Baron of Crofton	Lakeland Terrier			
1977	Dersade Bobby's Girl	Sealyham	1990	Wendessa Crown Prince	Pekingese
1978	Cede Higgens	Yorkshire Terrier	1991	Whisperwind on a Carousel	Stan. Poodle
1979	Oak Tree's Irishtocrat	Irish Water Spaniel	1992	Lonesome Dove	Fox Terrier
			1993	Salilyn's Condor	E.S. Spaniel
1980	Sierra Cinnar	Siberian Husky	1994	Chidley Willum	Norwich Terrier
1981	Dhandy Favorite Woodchuck	Pug	1995	Gaelforce Post Script	Scottish Terrier
1982	St. Aubrey Dragonora of Elsdon	Pekingese			

FISHING

IGFA All-Tackle World Records

All-tackle records are maintained for the heaviest fish of any species caught on any line up to 130-lb (60 kg) class and certified by the International Game Fish Association. Records logged through Oct. 1, 1995. **Address:** 3000 East Las Olas Blvd., Ft. Lauderdale, FL, 33316. **Telephone:** 305-941-3474.

FRESHWATER FISH

Species	Lbs-Oz	Where Caught	Date	Angler
Barramundi	63- 2	Queensland, Australia	Apr. 28,1991	Scott Barnsley
Bass, Guadalupe	3-11	Lake Travis, TX	Sept. 25, 1983	Allen Christenson Jr.
Bass, largemouth	22- 4	Montgomery Lake, GA	June 2,1932	George W. Perry
Bass, peacock	27- 0	Rio Negro, Brazil	Dec. 4, 1994	Gerald (Doc) Lawson
Bass, peacock butterfly	9- 8	Kendale Lakes, FL	Mar. 11, 1993	Jerry Gomez
Bass, redeye	8- 3	Flint River, GA	Oct. 23, 1977	David A. Hubbard
Bass, Roanoke	1- 5	Nottoway River, VA	Nov. 11, 1991	Tom Elkins
Bass, rock	3- 0	York River, Ontario	Aug. 1,1974	Peter Gulgin
Bass, smallmouth	11-15	Dale Hollow Lake, KY	July 9,1955	David L. Hayes
Bass, spotted	9- 7	Pine Flat Lake, CA	Feb. 25, 1994	Bob E. Shelton
Bass, striped (landlocked)	67- 8	O'Neill Forebay, San Luis, CA	May 7,1992	Hank Ferguson
Bass, Suwannee	3-14	Suwannee River, FL	Mar. 2,1985	Ronnie Everett
Bass, white	6-13	Lake Orange, VA	July 31,1989	Ronald L. Sprouse
Bass, whiterock	24- 3	Leesville Lake, VA	May 12,1989	David N. Lambert
Bass, yellow	2- 4	Lake Monroe, IN	Mar. 27,1977	Donald L. Stalker
Bass, yellow hybrid	2- 5	Kiamichi River, OK	Mar. 26, 1991	George Edwards
Bluegill	4-12	Ketona Lake, AL	Apr. 9,1950	T.S. Hudson
Bowfin	21- 8	Florence, SC	Jan. 29,1980	Robert L. Harmon
Buffalo, bigmouth	70- 5	Bussey Brake, Bastrop, LA	Apr. 21,1980	Delbert Sisk
Buffalo, black	55- 8	Cherokee Lake, TN	May 3,1984	Edward H. McLain
Buffalo, smallmouth	68- 8	Lake Hamilton, AR	May 16,1984	Jerry L. Dolezal
Bullhead, black	8- 0	Lake Waccabuc, NY	Aug. 1,1951	Kani Evans
Bullhead, brown	5- 11	Cedar Creek, FL	Mar. 28, 1995	Robert Bengis
Bullhead, yellow	4- 4	Mormon Lake, AZ	May 11,1984	Emily Williams
Burbot	18- 4	Pickford, MI	Jan. 31,1980	Tom Courtemanche
Carp	75- 11	Lac de St. Cassien, France	May 21,1987	Leo van der Gugten
Catfish, blue	109- 4	Cooper River, SC	Mar. 14,1991	George Lijewski
Catfish, channel	58- 0	Santee-Cooper Res., SC	July 7,1964	W.B. Whaley
Catfish, flathead	91- 4	Lake Lewisville, TX	Mar. 28,1982	Mike Rogers
Catfish, flatwhiskered	5-13	Cuiaba River, Brazil	June 28, 1992	Sergio Roberto Rothier
Catfish, gilded	85- 8	Amazon River, Brazil	Nov. 15, 1986	Gilberto Fernandes
Catfish, redtail	97- 7	Amazon River, Brazil	July 16, 1988	Gilberto Fernandes
Catfish, sharptoothed	79- 5	Orange River, S. Africa	Dec. 5, 1992	Hennie Moller
Catfish, white	18-14	Inverness, FL	Sept. 21,1991	Jim Miller
Char, Arctic	32- 9	Tree River, Canada	July 30,1981	Jeffery Ward
Crappie, black	4- 8	Kerr Lake, VA	Mar. 1,1981	L. Carl Herring Jr.
Crappie, white	5- 3	Enid Dam, MS	July 31,1957	Fred L. Bright
Dolly Varden	18- 9	Mashutuk River, AK	July 13,1993	Richard B. Evans
Dorado	51- 5	Corrientes, Argentina	Sept. 27,1984	Armando Giudice
Drum, freshwater	54- 8	Nickajack Lake, TN	Apr. 20,1972	Benny E. Hull

Species	Lbs-Oz	Where Caught	Date	Angler
Gar, alligator	279- 0	Rio Grande, TX	Dec. 2,1951	Bill Valverde
Gar, Florida	21- 3	Boca Raton, FL	June 3,1981	Jeff Sabol
Gar, longnose	50- 5	Trinity River, TX	July 30,1954	Townsend Miller
Gar, shortnose	5- 0	Sally Jones Lake, OK	Apr. 26,1985	Buddy Croslin
Gar, spotted	9-12	Lake Mevia, TX	Apr. 7, 1994	Rick Rivard
Goldfish	3- 0	Southland Pk., Livingston, TX	May 8,1988	Kenneth R. Kinsey
Grayling, Arctic	5-15	Katseyedie River, N.W.T.	Aug. 16,1967	Jeanne P. Branson
Inconnu	53- 0	Pah River, AK	Aug. 20,1986	Lawrence E. Hudnall
Kokanee	9- 6	Okanagan Lake, Brit.Columbia	June 18,1988	Norm Kuhn
Muskellunge	67- 8	Hayward, WI	July 24, 1949	Cal Johnson
Muskellunge, tiger	51- 3	Lac Vieux-Desert, WI-MI	July 16,1919	John A. Knobla
Perch, Nile	191- 8	Lake Victoria, Kenya	Sept. 5,1991	Andy Davison
Perch, white	4-12	Messalonskee Lake, ME	June 4,1949	Mrs. Earl Small
Perch, yellow	4- 3	Bordentown, NJ	May, 1865	Dr. C.C. Abbot
Pickerel, chain	9- 6	Homerville, GA	Feb. 17,1961	Baxley McQuaig Jr.
Pickerel, grass	1- 0	Dewart Lake, Indiana	June 9, 1990	Mike Berg
Pickerel, redfin	1-15	Redhook, NY	Oct. 16, 1988	Bill Stagias
Pike, northern	55- 1	Lake of Grefeern, W.Germany	Oct.16,1986	Lothar Louis
Redhorse, greater	9- 3	Salmon River, Pulaski, NY	May 11,1985	Jason Wilson
Redhorse, silver	11- 7	Plum Creek, WI	May 29,1985	Neal D.G. Long
Salmon, Atlantic	79- 2	Tana River, Norway	1928	Henrik Henriksen
Salmon, chinook	97- 4	Kenai River, AK	May 17,1985	Les Anderson
Salmon, chum	32- 0	Behm Canal, AK	June 7,1985	Fredrick Thynes
Salmon, coho	33- 4	Salmon River, Pulaski, NY	Sept. 27,1989	Jerry Lifton
Salmon, lake	18- 4	Lake Tanganyika, Zambia	Dec. 1, 1987	Steve Robinson
Salmon, pink	13- 1	St. Mary's River, Ontario	Sept. 23,1992	Ray Higaki
Salmon, sockeye	15- 3	Kenai River, AK	Aug. 9,1987	Stan Roach
Sauger	8-12	Lake Sakakawea, ND	Oct. 6,1971	Mike Fischer
Shad, American	11- 4	Conn.River, S.Hadley, MA	May 19,1986	Bob Thibodo
Shad, gizzard	4- 0	Lake Michigan, IN	Jan. 15, 1993	Mike Berg
Sturgeon, lake	92- 4	Kettle River, MN	Sept. 11,1986	James M. DeOtis
Sturgeon, white	468- 0	Benicia, CA	July 9,1983	Joey Pallotta 3rd
Tigerfish, giant	97- 0	Zaire River, Kinshasa, Zaire	July 9,1988	Raymond Houtmans
Tilapia	6- 0	Lake Okeechobee, FL	June 24,1989	Joseph M. Tucker
Trout, Apache	5- 3	White Mountain, AZ	May 29,1991	John Baldwin
Trout, brook	14- 8	Nipigon River, Ontario	July, 1916	Dr. W.J. Cook
Trout, brown	40- 4	Little Red River, AR	May 9,1992	Rip Collins
Trout, bull	32- 0	Lake Pond Orielle, ID	Oct. 27,1949	N.L. Higgins
Trout, cutthroat	41- 0	Pyramid Lake, NV	Dec., 1925	John Skimmerhorn
Trout, golden	11- 0	Cooks Lake, WY	Aug. 5,1948	Charles S. Reed
Trout, lake	66- 8	Great Bear Lake, N.W.T.	July 19,1991	Rodney Harback
Trout, rainbow	42- 2	Bell Island, AK	June 22,1970	David Robert White
Trout, tiger	20-13	Lake Michigan, WI	Aug. 12,1978	Peter M. Friedland
Walleye	25- 0	Old Hickory Lake, TN	Apr. 1,1960	Mabry Harper
Warmouth	2- 7	Guess Lake, Holt, FL	Oct. 19,1985	Tony D. Dempsey
Whitefish, lake	14- 6	Meaford, Ontario	May 21,1984	Dennis M.Laycock
Whitefish, mountain	5- 6	Rioh River, Saskatchewan	June 15,1988	John R. Bell
Whitefish, lake	14- 6	Meaford, Ontario	May 21, 1984	Dennis Laycock
Whitefish, round	6- 0	Putahow River, Manitoba	June 14,1984	Allan J. Ristori
Zander	25- 2	Trosa, Sweden	June 12,1986	Harry Lee Tennison

SALTWATER FISH

Species	Lbs-Oz	Where Caught	Date	Angler
Albacore	88- 2	Gran Canaria, Canary Islands	Nov. 19,1977	Siegfried Dickemann
Amberjack, greater	155-10	Challenger Bank, Bermuda	June 24,1981	Joseph Dawson
Amberjack, pacific	104- 0	Baja Calif., Mexico	July 4,1984	Richard Cresswell
Barracuda, great	85- 0	Christmas Is., Rep. of Kiribati	Apr. 11,1992	John W. Helfrich
Barracuda, Mexican	21- 0	Phantom Island, Costa Rica	Mar. 27,1987	E. Greg Kent
Barracuda, pickhandle	17- 4	Sitra Channel, Bahrain	Nov. 21,1985	Roger Cranswick
Bass, barred sand	13- 3	Huntington Beach, CA	Aug. 29,1988	Robert Halal
Bass, black sea	9- 8	Virginia Beach, VA	Jan. 9,1987	Joe Mizelle Jr.
Bass, European	20-11	Stes Maries de la Mer, France	May 6,1986	Jean Baptiste Bayle
Bass, giant sea	563- 8	Anacapa Island, CA	Aug. 20,1968	J.D. McAdam Jr.
Bass, striped	78- 8	Atlantic City, NJ	Sept. 21,1982	Albert R. McReynolds
Bluefish	31-12	Hatteras, NC	Jan. 30,1972	James M. Hussey
Bonefish	19- 0	Zululand, South Africa	May 26,1962	Brian W. Batchelor
Bonito, Atlantic	18- 4	Faial Island, Azores	July 8,1953	D. Gama Higgs
Bonito, Pacific	14-12	San Benitos Is., Baja Calif., Mexico	Oct. 12,1980	Jerome H. Rilling
Cabezon	23- 0	Juan de Fuca Strait, WA	Aug. 4,1990	Wesley Hunter
Cobia	135- 9	Shark Bay, W. Australia	July 9,1985	Peter W. Goulding
Cod, Atlantic	98-12	Isle of Shoals, NH	June 8,1969	Alphonse Bielevich

Fishing (Cont.)
IGFA All-Tackle World Records

SALTWATER FISH

Species	Lbs-Oz	Where Caught	Date	Angler
Cod, Pacific	30- 0	Andrew Bay, AK	July 7,1984	Donald R. Vaughn
Conger	133- 4	South Devon, England	June 5, 1995	Vic Evans
Dolphin	87- 0	Papagallo Gulf, Costa Rica	Sept. 25,1976	Manuel Salazar
Drum, black	113- 1	Lewes, DE	Sept. 15,1975	Gerald M. Townsend
Drum, red	94- 2	Avon, NC	Nov. 7,1984	David G. Deuel
Eel, marbled	36- 1	Durban, S. Africa	June 10,1984	Ferdie van Nooten
Eel, American	8- 8	Cliff Pond, Brewster, MA	May 17,1992	Gerald G. Lapierre Sr.
Flounder, southern	20- 9	Nassau Sound, FL	Dec. 23,1983	Larenza Mungin
Flounder, summer	22- 7	Montauk, NY	Sept. 15,1975	Charles Nappi
Grouper, warsaw	436-12	Gulf of Mexico, Destin, FL	Dec. 22,1985	Steve Haeusler
Haddock	11-11	Perkins Cove, Ogunquit, ME	Sept. 12,1991	Jim Mailea
Halibut, Atlantic	255- 4	Gloucester, MA	July 28,1989	Sonny Manley
Halibut, California	53- 4	Santa Rosa Island, CA	July 7,1988	Russell J. Harmon
Halibut, Pacific	368- 0	Gustavus, AL	July 5,1991	Celia H. Dueitt
Jack, almaco (Pacific)	132- 0	La Paz, Baja Calif., Mexico	July 21,1964	Howard H. Hahn
Jack, crevalle	57- 5	Barra do Bwanza, Angola	Oct. 10,1992	Cam Nicolson
Jack, horse-eye	24- 8	Miami, FL	Dec. 20,1982	Tito Schnau
Jewfish	680- 0	Fernandina Beach, FL	May 20,1961	Lynn Joyner
Kawakawa	29- 0	Clarion Island, Mexico	Dec. 17,1986	Ronald Nakamura
Lingcod	69- 0	Langara Is., Brit. Columbia	June 16,1992	Murray M.Romer
Mackerel, cero	17- 2	Islamorada, FL	Apr. 5,1986	G. Michael Mills
Mackerel, king	90- 0	Key West, FL	Feb. 16,1976	Norton I. Thomton
Mackerel, Spanish	13- 0	Ocracoke Inlet, NC	Nov. 4,1987	Robert Cranton
Marlin, Atlantic blue	1402- 2	Vitoria, Brazil	Feb. 29,1992	Paulo R.A. Amorim
Marlin, Black	1560- 0	Cabo Blanco, Peru	Aug. 4,1953	A.C. Glassell Jr.
Marlin, Pacific blue	1376- 0	Kaaiwi Point, Kona, HI	May 31,1982	Jay W. deBeaubien
Marlin, striped	494- 0	Tutakaka, New Zealand	Jan. 16,1986	Bill Boniface
Marlin, white	181-14	Vitoria, Brazil	Dec. 8,1979	Evandro Luiz Coser
Permit	53- 4	Lake Worth, FL	Mar. 25, 1994	Roy Brooker
Pollack	27- 6	Salcombe, Devon, England	Jan. 16,1986	Robert S. Milkins
Pollock	46-10	Perkins Cove, Ogunquit, ME	Oct. 24,1990	Linda M. Paul
Pompano, African	50- 8	Daytona Beach, FL	Apr. 21,1990	Tom Sargent
Roosterfish	114- 0	La Paz, Baja Calif., Mexico	June 1,1960	Abe Sackheim
Runner, blue	8- 7	Port Arkansas, TX	Feb. 13, 1995	Allen E. Windecker
Runner, rainbow	37- 9	Clarion Island, Mexico	Nov. 21,1991	Tom Pfleger
Sailfish, Atlantic	135- 5	Lago, Nigeria	Nov. 10,1991	Ron King
Sailfish, Pacific	221- 0	Santa Cruz Is., Ecuador	Feb. 12,1947	C.W. Stewart
Seabass, white	83-12	San Felipe, Mexico	Mar. 31,1953	L.C. Baumgardner
Seatrout, spotted	16- 0	Mason's Beach, VA	May 28,1977	William Katko
Shark, blue	437- 0	Catherine Bay, NSW, Australia	Oct. 2,1976	Peter Hyde
Shark, great white	2664- 0	Ceduna, S. Australia	Apr. 21,1959	Alfred Dean
Shark, greenland	1708- 9	Trondheimsfjord, Norway	Oct.18,1987	Terje Nordtvedt
Shark, hammerhead	991- 0	Sarasota, FL	May 30,1982	Allen Ogle
Shark, shortfin mako	1115- 0	Black River, Mauritius	Nov. 16,1988	Patrick Guillanton
Shark, porbeagle	507- 0	Pentland Firth, Scotland	Mar. 9, 1993	Christopher Bennet
Shark, bigeye thresher	802- 0	Tutakaka, New Zealand	Feb. 8,1981	Dianne North
Shark, tiger	1780- 0	Cherry Grove, SC	June 14,1964	Walter Maxwell
Snapper, cubera	121- 8	Cameron, LA	July 5,1982	Mike Hebert
Snapper, red	46- 8	Destin, FL	Oct. 1,1985	E. Lane Nichols III
Snook	53-10	Parismina Ranch, Costa Rica	Oct. 18,1978	Gilbert Ponzi
Spearfish, Mediterranean	90-13	Madeira Island, Portugal	June 2,1980	Joseph Larkin
Swordfish	1182- 0	Iquique, Chile	May 7,1953	L. Marron
Tarpon	283- 0	Sherbro Is., Sierra Leone	Apr. 16, 1991	Yvon Victor Sebag
Tautog	24- 0	Wachapreague, VA	Aug. 25,1987	Gregory R. Bell
Tuna, Atlantic bigeye	375- 8	Ocean City, MD	Aug. 26,1977	Cecil Browne
Tuna, blackfin	42- 0	Bermuda	June 2,1978	Alan J. Card
	42- 0	Challenger Bank, Bermuda	July 18,1989	Gilbert C. Pearman
Tuna, bluefin	1496- 0	Aulds Cove, Nova Scotia	Oct. 26,1979	Ken Fraser
Tuna, longtail	79- 2	Montague Is., NSW, Australia	Apr. 12,1982	Tim Simpson
Tuna, Pacific bigeye	435- 0	Cabo Blanco, Peru	Apr. 17,1957	Dr. Russell Lee
Tuna, skipjack	41-14	Pearl Banks, Mauritius	Nov. 12,1985	Edmund Heinzen
Tuna, southern bluefin	348- 5	Whakatane, New Zealand	Jan. 16,1981	Rex Wood
Tuna, yellowfin	388-12	San Benedicto Island, Mexico	Apr. 1,1977	Curt Wiesenhutter
Tunny, little	35- 2	Cape de Garde, Algeria	Dec. 14,1988	Jean Yves Chatard
Wahoo	155- 8	San Salvador, Bahamas	Apr. 3,1990	William Bourne
Weakfish	19- 2	Jones Beach, Long Island, NY	Oct. 11,1984	Dennis R. Rooney
	19- 2	Delaware Bay, DE	May 20,1989	William E. Thomas

Mark Davis of Mount Ida, Ark., shows off some of his championship catch to the 23,000 fans who packed Greensboro (N.C.) Coliseum on Aug. 5 for the weigh-in of the BASS Masters Classic fishing tournament. Davis won his first Masters title with combined weight of 47 pounds and 14 ounces.

Davis Wins BASS Classic and Angler of the Year

Mark Davis made tournament fishing history on Aug. 5, when he became the first pro to capture both the BASS Masters Classic and the BASS Angler of the Year award in the same season. Fishing on High Rock Lake near Greensboro, N.C., the 35-year-old from Mount Ida, Ark., won the Classic with a three-day total of 15 largemouth bass weighing 47 pounds-14 ounces. His primary fishing lures were a 1-lb. Strike King spinnerbait and a Bomber Fat Free Shad. Mark Hardin of Canton, Ga., was second with 14 bass weighing 46 pounds.

Davis, who missed qualifying for the Masters in 1993 and '94, accepted the winner's check of $50,000 from the Bass Anglers Sportsman Society president Ray Scott in front of over 23,000 spectators at Greensboro Coliseum, the site of the weight-in. He can expect to earn as much as $1 million more in endorsements and speaking engagements.

BASS Masters Classic

The BASS Masters Classic is fishing's version of the Masters golf tournament. Invitees to the three-day event include the 36 top-ranked pros on the BASS tour and five top-ranked amateurs. Anglers may weigh only seven bass per day and each bass must be at least 12 inches long. Competitors are allowed only seven rods and reels and are limited to the tackle they can pack into two tournament-approved tackleboxes. Only artificial lures are permitted. The first Classic, held at Lake Mead, Nevada in 1971, was a $10,000 winner-take-all event.

Multiple winners: Rick Clunn (4); Bobby Murray and Hank Parker (2).

Year		Weight	Year		Weight
1971	Bobby Murray, Hot Springs, Ark	43 -11	1984	Rick Clunn, Montgomery, Tex	75 - 9
1972	Don Butler, Tulsa, Okla	38 -11	1985	Jack Chancellor, Phenix City, Ala	45 - 0
1973	Rayo Breckenridge, Paragould, Ark	52 - 8	1986	Charlie Reed, Broken Bow, Okla	23 - 9
1974	Tommy Martin, Hemphill, Tex.	33 - 7	1987	George Cochran, N. Little Rock, Ark	15 - 5
1975	Jack Hains, Rayne, La	45 - 4	1988	Guido Hibdon, Gravois Mills, Mo	28 - 8
1976	Rick Clunn, Montgomery, Tex	59 -15	1989	Hank Parker, Denver, N.C	31 - 6
1977	Rick Clunn, Montgomery, Tex	27 - 7			
1978	Bobby Murray, Nashville, Tenn	37 - 9	1990	Rick Clunn, Montgomery, Tex	34 - 5
1979	Hank Parker, Clover, S.C	31 - 0	1991	Ken Cook, Meers, Okla	33 - 2
			1992	Robert Hamilton Jr., Brandon, Miss	59 - 6
1980	Bo Dowden, Natchitoches, La	54 -10	1993	David Fritts, Lexington, N.C	48 - 6
1981	Stanley Mitchell, Fitzgerald, Ga	35 - 2	1994	Bryan Kerchal, Newtown, Conn	36 - 7
1982	Paul Elias, Laurel, Miss	32 - 8	1995	Mark Davis, Mount Ida, Ark.	47-14
1983	Larry Nixon, Hemphill, Tex	18 - 1			

LITTLE LEAGUE BASEBALL

World Series

After a three-year absence, Taiwan returned to the top of the Little League Baseball world on Aug. 27, when a team representing the city of Tainan routed Spring, Texas, 17-4, in the World Series final. The game was called after four innings because of the 10-run mercy rule. Tainan outscored their tournament opposition, 47-6.

Multiple winners: Taiwan (16); California (5); Connecticut and Pennsylvania (4); Japan and New Jersey (3); Mexico, New York, South Korea and Texas (2).

Year	Winner	Score	Loser	Year	Winner	Score	Loser
1947	Williamsport, PA	16-7	Lock Haven, PA	1973	Tainan City, Taiwan	12-0	Tucson, AZ
1948	Lock Haven, PA	6-5	St. Petersburg, FL	1974	Kao Hsiung, Taiwan	12-1	Red Bluff, CA
1949	Hammonton, NJ	5-0	Pensacola, FL	1975	Lakewood, NJ	4-3*	Tampa, FL
				1976	Tokyo, Japan	10-3	Campbell, CA
1950	Houston, TX	2-1	Bridgeport, CT	1977	Li-Teh, Taiwan	7-2	El Cajon, CA
1951	Stamford, CT	3-0	Austin, TX	1978	Pin-Tung, Taiwan	11-1	Danville, CA
1952	Norwalk, CT	4-3	Monongahela, PA	1979	Hsien, Taiwan	2-1	Campbell, CA
1953	Birmingham, AL	1-0	Schenectady, NY				
1954	Schenectady, NY	7-5	Colton, CA	1980	Hua Lian, Taiwan	4-3	Tampa, FL
1955	Morrisville, PA	4-3	Merchantville, NJ	1981	Tai-Chung, Taiwan	4-2	Tampa, FL
1956	Roswell, NM	3-1	Merchantville, NJ	1982	Kirkland, WA	6-0	Hsien, Taiwan
1957	Monterrey, Mexico	4-0	La Mesa, CA	1983	Marietta, GA	3-1	Barahona, D. Rep.
1958	Monterrey, Mexico	10-1	Kankakee, IL	1984	Seoul, S. Korea	6-2	Altamonte, FL
1959	Hamtramck, MI	12-0	Auburn, CA	1985	Seoul, S. Korea	7-1	Mexicali, Mex.
				1986	Tainan Park, Taiwan	12-0	Tucson, AZ
1960	Levittown, PA	5-0	Ft. Worth, TX	1987	Hua Lian, Taiwan	21-1	Irvine, CA
1961	El Cajon, CA	4-2	El Campo, TX	1988	Tai Ping, Taiwan	10-0	Pearl City, HI
1962	San Jose, CA	3-0	Kankakee, IL	1989	Trumbull, CT	5-2	Kaohsiung, Taiwan
1963	Granada Hills, CA	2-1	Stratford, CT				
1964	Staten Island, NY	4-0	Monterrey, Mex.	1990	Taipei, Taiwan	9-0	Shippensburg, PA
1965	Windsor Locks, CT	3-1	Stoney Creek, Can.	1991	Taichung, Taiwan	11-0	Danville, CA
1966	Houston, TX	8-2	W. New York, NJ	1992	Long Beach, CA	6-0	Zamboanga, Phil.
1967	West Tokyo, Japan	4-1	Chicago, IL	1993	Long Beach, CA	3-2	Panama
1968	Osaka, Japan	1-0	Richmond, VA	1994	Maracaibo, Venezuela	4-3	Northridge, CA
1969	Taipei, Taiwan	5-0	Santa Clara,CA	1995	Tainan, Taiwan	17-3	Spring, TX
1970	Wayne, NJ	2-0	Campbell, CA				
1971	Tainan, Taiwan	12-3	Gary, IN				
1972	Taipei, Taiwan	6-0	Hammond, IN				

*Foreign teams were banned from the tournament in 1975, but allowed back in the following year.

Note: In 1992, Zamboanga City of the Philippines beat Long Beach, 15-4, but was stripped of the title a month later when it was discovered that the team had used several players from outside the city limits. Long Beach was then awarded the title by forfeit, 6-0 (one run for each inning of the game).

POWER BOAT RACING

APBA Gold Cup

Overcoming mechanical problems that plagued his boat right up to the start of the race, Chip Hanauer became the first 10-time winner of the APBA Gold Cup championship on June 4, when he piloted *Miss Budweiser* to victory before an estimated 400,000 spectators on the Detroit River. Hanauer, who averaged 149.160 mph over the 2.5-mile course, beat runner-up Dave Villwock aboard *Pico-American Dream* by half a lap in the six-boat final.

The American Power Boat Association Gold Cup for unlimited hydroplane racing is the oldest active motor sports trophy in North America. The first Gold Cup was competed for on the Hudson River in New York in June and September of 1904. Since then several cities have hosted the race, led by Detroit (28 times, including 1990) and Seattle (14). Note that (*) indicates driver was also owner of the winning boat.

Drivers with multiple wins: Chip Hanauer (10); Bill Muncey (8); Gar Wood (5); Dean Chenoweth (4); Caleb Bragg, Tom D'Eath, Lou Fageol, Ron Musson, George Reis and Jonathon Wainwright (3); Danny Foster, George Henley, Vic Kliesrath, E.J. Schroeder, Bill Schumacher, Zalmon G.Simmons Jr., Joe Taggart, Mark Tate, and George Townsend (2).

Year	Boat	Driver	Avg.MPH	Year	Boat	Driver	Avg.MPH
1904	*Standard* (June)	Carl Riotte*	23.160	1915	*Miss Detroit*	Johnny Milot & Jack Beebe	37.656
1904	*Vingt-Et-Un II* (Sept.)	W. Sharpe Kilmer*	24.900	1916	*Miss Minneapolis*	Bernard Smith	48.860
1905	*Chip I*	J. Wainwright*	15.000	1917	*Miss Detroit II*	Gar Wood*	54.410
1906	*Chip II*	J. Wainwright*	25.000	1918	*Miss Detroit II*	Gar Wood	51.619
1907	*Chip II*	J. Wainwright*	23.903	1919	*Miss Detroit III*	Gar Wood*	42.748
1908	*Dixie II*	E.J. Schroede*	29.938				
1909	*Dixie II*	E.J. Schroeder*	29.590	1920	*Miss America I*	Gar Wood*	62.022
1910	*Dixie III*	F.K. Burnham*	32.473	1921	*Miss America I*	Gar Wood*	52.825
1911	*MIT II*	J.H. Hayden*	37.000	1922	*Packard Chriscraft*	J.G. Vincent*	40.253
1912	*P.D.Q. II*	A.G. Miles*	39.462	1923	*Packard Chriscraft*	Caleb Bragg	43.867
1913	*Ankle Deep*	Cas Mankowski*	42.779	1924	*Baby Bootlegger*	Caleb Bragg*	45.302
1914	*Baby Speed Demon II*	Jim Blackton & Bob Edgren	48.458	1925	*Baby Bootlegger*	Caleb Bragg*	47.240
				1926	*Greenwich Folly*	George Townsend*	47.984
				1927	*Greenwich Folly*	George Townsend*	47.662

Year	Boat	Driver	Avg.MPH	Year	Boat	Driver	Avg.MPH
1928	Not held			1963	Miss Bardahl	Ron Musson	105.124
1929	Imp	Richard Hoyt*	48.662	1964	Miss Bardahl	Ron Musson	103.433
				1965	Miss Bardahl	Ron Musson	103.132
1930	Hotsy Totsy	Vic Kliesrath*	52.673	1966	Tahoe Miss	Mira Slovak	93.019
1931	Hotsy Totsy	Vic Kliesrath*	53.602	1967	Miss Bardahl	Bill Shumacher	101.484
1932	Delphine IV	Bill Horn	57.775	1968	Miss Bardahl	Bill Shumacher	108.173
1933	El Lagarto	George Reis*	56.260	1969	Miss Budweiser	Bill Sterett	98.504
1934	El Lagarto	George Reis*	55.000				
1935	El Lagarto	George Reis*	55.056	1970	Miss Budweiser	Dean Chenoweth	99.562
1936	Impshi	Kaye Don	45.735	1971	Miss Madison	Jim McCormick	98.043
1937	Notre Dame	Clell Perry	63.675	1972	Atlas Van Lines	Bill Muncey	104.277
1938	Alagi	Theo Rossi*	64.340	1973	Miss Budweiser	Dean Chenoweth	99.043
1939	My Sin	Z.G. Simmons Jr.*	66.133	1974	Pay 'n Pak	George Henley	104.428
1940	Hotsy Totsy III	Sidney Allen*	48.295	1975	Pay 'n Pak	George Henley	108.921
1941	My Sin	Z.G. Simmons Jr.*	52.509	1976	Miss U.S.	Tom D'Eath	100.412
1942-45	Not held			1977	Atlas Van Lines	Bill Muncey*	111.822
1946	Tempo VI	Guy Lombardo*	68.132	1978	Atlas Van Lines	Bill Muncey*	111.412
1947	Miss Peps V	Danny Foster	57.000	1979	Atlas Van Lines	Bill Muncey*	100.765
1948	Miss Great Lakes	Danny Foster	46.845				
1949	My Sweetie	Bill Cantrell	73.612	1980	Miss Budweiser	Dean Chenoweth	106.932
1950	Slo-Mo-Shun IV	Ted Jones	78.216	1981	Miss Budweiser	Dean Chenoweth	116.932
1951	Slo-Mo-Shun IV	Lou Fageol	90.871	1982	Atlas Van Lines	Chip Hanauer	120.050
1952	Slo-Mo-Shun IV	Stan Dollar	79.923	1983	Atlas Van Lines	Chip Hanauer	118.507
1953	Slo-Mo-Shun IV	Joe Taggart & Lou Fageol	99.108	1984	Atlas Van Lines	Chip Hanauer	130.175
				1985	Miller American	Chip Hanauer	120.643
1954	Slo-Mo-Shun IV	Joe Taggart & Lou Fageol	92.613	1986	Miller American	Chip Hanauer	116.523
				1987	Miller American	Chip Hanauer	127.620
1955	Gale V	Lee Schoenith	99.552	1988	Miss Circus Circus	Chip Hanauer & Jim Prevost	123.756
1956	Miss Thriftaway	Bill Muncey	96.552				
1957	Miss Thriftaway	Bill Muncey	101.787	1989	Miss Budweiser	Tom D'Eath	131.209
1958	Hawaii Kai III	Jack Regas	103.000	1990	Miss Budweiser	Tom D'Eath	143.176
1959	Maverick	Bill Stead	104.481	1991	Winston Eagle	Mark Tate	137.771
1960	Not held			1992	Miss Budweiser	Chip Hanauer	136.282
1961	Miss Century 21	Bill Muncey	99.678	1993	Miss Budweiser	Chip Hanauer	141.296
1962	Miss Century 21	Bill Muncey	100.710	1994	Smokin' Joe's	Mark Tate	145.532
				1995	Miss Budweiser	Chip Hanauer	149.160

PRO RODEO

All-Around Champion Cowboy

Ty Murray joined legends Larry Mahan and Tom Ferguson as the only cowboys to win six world All-Around championships on Dec. 10, 1994. The 25-year-old Murray, who has only been riding professionally since 1988, won his sixth consecutive title at the National Finals Rodeo in Las Vegas with earnings of $246,170. Hopes of a seventh straight All-Around title ended on June 17, 1995 when he tore the posterior cruciate ligament in his right knee while bull riding at a rodeo in Rancho Murieta, Calif.

The Professional Rodeo Cowboys Association (PRCA) title of All-Around World Champion Cowboy goes to the rodeo athlete who wins the most prize money in a single year in two or more events. Only prize money earned in sanctioned PRCA rodeos is counted. From 1929-44, All-Around champions were named by the Rodeo Association of America (earnings for those years is not available).

Multiple winners: Tom Ferguson, Larry Mahan and Ty Murray (6); Jim Shoulders (5); Lewis Feild and Dean Oliver (3); Everett Bowman, Louis Brooks, Clay Carr, Bill Linderman, Phil Lyne, Gerald Roberts, Casey Tibbs and Harry Tompkins (2).

Year		Year		Year		Year	
1929	Earl Thode	1934	Leonard Ward	1938	Burel Mulkey	1942	Gerald Roberts
1930	Clay Carr	1935	Everett Bowman	1939	Paul Carney	1943	Louis Brooks
1931	John Schneider	1936	John Bowman	1940	Fritz Truan	1944	Louis Brooks
1932	Donald Nesbit	1937	Everett Bowman	1941	Homer Pettigrew	1945-46	No award
1933	Clay Carr						

Year		Earnings	Year		Earnings	Year		Earnings
1947	Todd Whatley	$18,642	1958	Jim Shoulders	$32,212	1969	Larry Mahan	$57,726
1948	Gerald Roberts	21,766	1959	Jim Shoulders	32,905	1970	Larry Mahan	41,493
1949	Jim Shoulders	21,495	1960	Harry Tompkins	32,522	1971	Phil Lyne	49,245
1950	Bill Linderman	30,715	1961	Benny Reynolds	31,309	1972	Phil Lyne	60,852
1951	Casey Tibbs	29,104	1962	Tom Nesmith	32,611	1973	Larry Mahan	64,447
1952	Harry Tompkins	30,934	1963	Dean Oliver	31,329	1974	Tom Ferguson	66,929
1953	Bill Linderman	33,674	1964	Dean Oliver	31,150	1975	Tom Ferguson	50,300
1954	Buck Rutherford	40,404	1965	Dean Oliver	33,163	1976	Tom Ferguson	87,908
1955	Casey Tibbs	42,065	1966	Larry Mahan	40,358	1977	Tom Ferguson	65,981
1956	Jim Shoulders	43,381	1967	Larry Mahan	51,996	1978	Tom Ferguson	83,734
1957	Jim Shoulders	33,299	1968	Larry Mahan	49,129	1979	Tom Ferguson	96,272

Pro Rodeo (Cont.)
All Around Cowboy

Year		Earnings	Year		Earnings	Year		Earnings
1980	Paul Tierney	$105,568	1985	Lewis Feild	$130,347	1990	Ty Murray	$213,772
1981	Jimmie Cooper	105,861	1986	Lewis Feild	166,042	1991	Ty Murray	244,231
1982	Chris Lybbert	123,709	1987	Lewis Feild	144,335	1992	Ty Murray	225,992
1983	Roy Cooper	153,391	1988	Dave Appleton	121,546	1993	Ty Murray	297,896
1984	Dee Pickett	122,618	1989	Ty Murray	134,806	1994	Ty Murray	246,170

SOAP BOX DERBY

All-American Soap Box Derby

Three 11-year-olds won their divisions in the 1995 All-American Soap Box Derby at Akron on Aug. 5. Johnathan Fensterbush of Kingman, Ariz., won the Masters division in 28.69 seconds; Karen Thomas of Jamestown, N.Y., won the Stock division in 29.18; and Darcie Davisson of Kingman, Ariz., took the new Super Stock (formerly Kit) division in 28.90.

The All-American Soap Box Derby is a coasting race for small gravity-powered cars built by their drivers and assembled within strict guidelines on size, weight and cost. The Derby got its name in the 1930s when most cars were built from wooden soap boxes. Held every summer on the second Saturday of August at Derby Downs in Akron, the Soap Box Derby is open to all boys and girls from 9 to 16 years old who qualify.

There are three competitive divisions: 1. Stock (ages 9-16)— made up of generic, prefab racers that come from Derby-approved kits, can be assembled in four hours and don't exceed 200 pounds when driver, car and wheels are weighed together; 2. Super Stock (ages 10-16)— the same as Stock only with a weight limit of 220 pounds; 3. Masters (ages 11-16)— made up of racers designed by the drivers, but constructed with Derby-approved hardware. The racing ramp at Derby Downs is 953.75 feet with an 11 percent grade.

One champion reigned at the All-American Soap Box Derby each year from 1934-75; Junior and Senior division champions from 1976-87; Kit and Masters champions from 1988-91; and Stock, Kit and Masters champions starting in 1992.

Year		Hometown	Age	Year		Hometown	Age
1934	Robert Turner	Muncie, IN	11	1978	JR: Darren Hart	Salem, OR	11
1935	Maurice Bale Jr.	Anderson, IN	13		SR: Greg Cardinal	Flint, MI	13
1936	Herbert Muench Jr.	St. Louis	14	1979	JR: Russell Yurk	Flint, MI	10
1937	Robert Ballard	White Plains, NY	12		SR: Craig Kitchen	Akron, OH	14
1938	Robert Berger	Omaha, NE	14	1980	JR: Chris Fulton	Indianapolis	11
1939	Clifton Hardesty	White Plains, NY	11		SR: Dan Porul	Sherman Oaks, CA	12
1940	Thomas Fisher	Detroit	12	1981	JR: Howie Fraley	Portsmouth, OH	11
1941	Claude Smith	Akron, OH	14		SR: Tonia Schlegel	Hamilton, OH	13
1942-45	Not held			1982	JR: Carol A. Sullivan	Rochester, NH	10
1946	Gilbert Klecan	San Diego	14		SR: Matt Wolfgang	Lehigh Val., PA	12
1947	Kenneth Holmboe	Charleston, WV	14	1983	JR: Tony Carlini	Del Mar, CA	10
1948	Donald Strub	Akron, OH	13		SR: Mike Burdgick	Flint, MI	14
1949	Fred Derks	Akron, OH	15	1984	JR: Chris Hess	Hamilton, OH	11
1950	Harold Williamson	Charleston, WV	15		SR: Anita Jackson	St. Louis	15
1951	Darwin Cooper	Williamsport, PA	15	1985	JR: Michael Gallo	Danbury, CT	12
1952	Joe Lunn	Columbus, GA	11		SR: Matt Sheffer	York, PA	14
1953	Fred Mohler	Muncie, IN	14	1986	JR: Marc Behan	Dover, NH	9
1954	Richard Kemp	Los Angeles	14		SR: Tami Jo Sullivan	Lancaster, OH	13
1955	Richard Rohrer	Rochester, NY	14	1987	JR: Matt Margules	Danbury, CT	11
1956	Norman Westfall	Rochester, NY	14		SR: Brian Drinkwater	Bristol, CT	14
1957	Terry Townsend	Anderson, IN	14	1988	KIT: Jason Lamb	Des Moines, IA	10
1958	James Miley	Muncie, IN	15		MAS: David Duffield	Kansas City	13
1959	Barney Townsend	Anderson, IN	13	1989	KIT: David Schiller	Dayton, OH	12
1960	Fredric Lake	South Bend, IN	11		MAS: Faith Chavarria	Ventura, CA	12
1961	Dick Dawson	Wichita, KS	13	1990	KIT: Mark Mihal	Valparaiso, IN	12
1962	David Mann	Gary, IN	14		MAS: Sami Jones	Salem, OR	13
1963	Harold Conrad	Duluth, MN	12	1991	KIT: Paul Greenwald	Saginaw, MI	13
1964	Gregory Schumacher	Tacoma, WA	14		MAS: Danny Garland	San Diego, CA	14
1965	Robert Logan	Santa Ana, CA	12	1992	KIT: Carolyn Fox	Sublimity, OR	11
1966	David Krussow	Tacoma, WA	12		MAS: Bonnie Thornton	Redding, CA	12
1967	Kenneth Cline	Lincoln, NE	13		STK: Loren Hurst	Hudson, OH	10
1968	Branch Lew	Muncie, IN	11	1993	KIT: D.M. Del Ferraro	Stow, OH	12
1969	Steve Souter	Midland, TX	12		MAS: Dean Lutton	Delta, OH	14
1970	Samuel Gupton	Durham, NC	13		STK: Owen Yuda	Boiling Springs, PA	10
1971	Larry Blair	Oroville, CA	13	1994	KIT: Joel Endres	Akron, OH	14
1972	Robert Lange Jr.	Boulder, CO	14		MAS: D.M. Del Ferraro	Akron, OH	13
1973	Bret Yarborough	Elk Grove, CA	11		STK: Kristina Damond	Jamestown, NY	13
1974	Curt Yarborough	Elk Grove, CA	11	1995	SS: Darcie Davisson	Kingman, AZ	11
1975	Karren Stead	Lower Bucks, PA	11		MAS: J. Fensterbush	Kingman, AZ	11
1976	JR: Phil Raber	Sugarcreek, OH	11		STK: Karen Thomas	Jamestown, NY	11
	SR: Joan Ferdinand	Canton, OH	14				
1977	JR: Mark Ferdinand	Canton, OH	10				
	SR: Steve Washburn	Bristol, CT	15				

SOFTBALL

Men's and women's national champions since 1933 in Major Fast Pitch, Major Slow Pitch and Super Slow Pitch (men only). Sanctioned by the Amateur Softball Association of America.

MEN
Major Fast Pitch

Multiple winners: Clearwater Bombers (10); Raybestos Cardinals (5); Sealmasters (4); Briggs Beautyware, Pay'n Pak and Zollner Pistons (3); Billard Barbell, Decatur Pride, Hammer Air Field, Kodak Park, National Health Care, Penn Corp and Peterbilt Western (2).

Year		Year		Year	
1933	J.L. Gill Boosters, Chicago	1955	Raybestos Cardinals, Stratford, CT	1977	Billard Barbell, Reading, PA
1934	Ke-Nash-A, Kenosha, WI			1978	Billard Barbell
1935	Crimson Coaches, Toledo, OH	1956	Clearwater Bombers	1979	McArdle Pontiac/Cadillac, Midland, MI
1936	Kodak Park, Rochester, NY	1957	Clearwater Bombers		
1937	Briggs Body Team, Detroit	1958	Raybestos Cardinals	1980	Peterbilt Western, Seattle
1938	The Pohlers, Cincinnati	1959	Sealmasters, Aurora, IL	1981	Archer Daniels Midland, Decatur, IL
1939	Carr's Boosters, Covington, KY	1960	Clearwater Bombers		
1940	Kodak Park	1961	Sealmasters	1982	Peterbilt Western
1941	Bendix Brakes, South Bend, IN	1962	Clearwater Bombers	1983	Franklin Cardinals, Stratford, CT
1942	Deep Rock Oilers, Tulsa, OK	1963	Clearwater Bombers		
1943	Hammer Air Field, Fresno, CA	1964	Burch Tool, Detroit	1984	California Kings, Merced, CA
1944	Hammer Air Field	1965	Sealmasters	1985	Pay'n Pak, Seattle
1945	Zollner Pistons, Ft. Wayne, IN	1966	Clearwater Bombers	1986	Pay'n Pak
1946	Zollner Pistons	1967	Sealmasters	1987	Pay'n Pak
1947	Zollner Pistons	1968	Clearwater Bombers	1988	TransAire, Elkhart, IN
1948	Briggs Beautyware, Detroit	1969	Raybestos Cardinals	1989	Penn Corp, Sioux City, IA
1949	Tip Top Tailors, Toronto	1970	Raybestos Cardinals	1990	Penn Corp
1950	Clearwater (FL) Bombers	1971	Welty Way, Cedar Rapids, IA	1991	Gianella Bros., Rohnert Park, CA
1951	Dow Chemical, Midland, MI	1972	Raybestos Cardinals	1992	National Health Care, Sioux City, IA
1952	Briggs Beautyware	1973	Clearwater Bombers		
1953	Briggs Beautyware	1974	Gianella Bros., Santa Rosa, CA	1993	National Health Care
1954	Clearwater Bombers	1975	Rising Sun Hotel, Reading, PA	1994	Decatur (IL) Pride
		1976	Raybestos Cardinals	1995	Decatur Pride

Major Slow Pitch

Multiple winners: Gatliff Auto Sales, Riverside Paving and Skip Hogan A.C. (3); Campbell Carpets, Hamilton Tailoring and Howard's Furniture (2).

Year		Year		Year	
1953	Shields Construction, Newport, KY	1966	Michael's Lounge, Detroit	1981	Elite Coating, Gordon, CA
		1967	Jim's Sport Shop, Pittsburgh	1982	Triangle Sports, Minneapolis
1954	Waldneck's Tavern, Cincinnati	1968	County Sports, Levittown, NY	1983	No.1 Electric & Heating, Gastonia, NC
1955	Lang Pet Shop, Covington, KY	1969	Copper Hearth, Milwaukee		
1956	Gatliff Auto Sales, Newport, KY	1970	Little Caesar's, Southgate, MI	1984	Lilly Air Systems, Chicago
		1971	Pile Drivers, Va. Beach, VA	1985	Blanton's Fayetteville, NC
1957	Gatliff Auto Sales	1972	Jiffy Club, Louisville, KY	1986	Non-Ferrous Metals, Cleveland
1958	East Side Sports, Detroit	1973	Howard's Furniture, Denver, NC	1987	Stapath, Monticello, KY
1959	Yorkshire Restaurant, Newport, KY	1974	Howard's Furniture	1988	Bell Corp/FAF, Tampa, FL
		1975	Pyramid Cafe, Lakewood, OH	1989	Ritch's Salvage, Harrisburg, NC
1960	Hamilton Tailoring, Cincinnati	1976	Warren Motors, J'ville, FL	1990	New Construction, Shelbyville,IN
1961	Hamilton Tailoring	1977	Nelson Painting, Okla. City	1991	Riverside Paving, Louisville
1962	Skip Hogan A.C., Pittsburgh	1978	Campbell Carpets, Concord, CA	1992	Vernon's, Jacksonville, FL
1963	Gatliff Auto Sales	1979	Nelco Mfg. Co., Okla. City	1993	Back Porch/Destin (FL) Roofing
1964	Skip Hogan A.C.	1980	Campbell Carpets	1994	Riverside Paving, Louisville
1965	Skip Hogan A.C.			1995	Riverside Paving

Super Slow Pitch

Multiple winners: Howard's/Western Steer and Steele's Sports (3); Rich's/Superior (2).

Year		Year		Year	
1981	Howard's/Western Steer, Denver, NC	1986	Steele's Sports	1992	Rich's/Superior, Windsor Locks, CT
1982	Jerry's Catering, Miami	1987	Steele's Sports		
1983	Howard's/Western Steer	1988	Starpath, Monticello, KY	1993	Rich's/Superior
1984	Howard's/Western Steer	1989	Ritch's Salvage, Harrisburg, NC	1994	Bellcorp., Tampa
1985	Steele's Sports, Grafton, OH	1990	Steele's Silver Bullets	1995	Lighthouse/Worth, Stone Mt., GA
		1991	Sun Belt/Worth, Atlanta		

Softball (Cont.)

WOMEN
Major Fast Pitch

Multiple winners: Raybestos Brakettes (21); Orange Lionettes (9); Jax Maids (5); Arizona Ramblers and Redding Rebels (3); Hi-Ho Brakettes, J.J. Krieg's and National Screw & Manufacturing (2).

Year		Year		Year	
1933	Great Northerns, Chicago	1955	Orange Lionettes	1977	Raybestos Brakettes
1934	Hart Motors, Chicago	1956	Orange Lionettes	1978	Raybestos Brakettes
1935	Bloomer Girls, Cleveland	1957	Hacienda Rockets, Fresno, CA	1979	Sun City (AZ) Saints
1936	Nat'l Screw & Mfg., Cleveland	1958	Raybestos Brakettes,	1980	Raybestos Brakettes
1937	Nat'l Screw & Mfg.		Stratford, CT	1981	Orlando (FL) Rebels
1938	J.J. Krieg's, Alameda, CA	1959	Raybestos Brakettes	1982	Raybestos Brakettes
1939	J.J. Krieg's			1983	Raybestos Brakettes
		1960	Raybestos Brakettes	1984	Los Angeles Diamonds
1940	Arizona Ramblers, Phoenix	1961	Gold Sox, Whittier, CA	1985	Hi-Ho Brakettes, Stratford, CT
1941	Higgins Midgets, Tulsa, OK	1962	Orange Lionettes	1986	So. California Invasion, LA
1942	Jax Maids, New Orleans	1963	Raybestos Brakettes	1987	Orange County Majestics,
1943	Jax Maids	1964	Erv Lind Florists, Portland, OR		Anaheim, CA
1944	Lind & Pomeroy, Portland, OR	1965	Orange Lionettes	1988	Hi-Ho Brakettes
1945	Jax Maids	1966	Raybestos Brakettes	1989	Whittier (CA) Raiders
1946	Jax Maids	1967	Raybestos Brakettes		
1947	Jax Maids	1968	Raybestos Brakettes	1990	Raybestos Brakettes
1948	Arizona Ramblers	1969	Orange Lionettes	1991	Raybestos Brakettes
1949	Arizona Ramblers			1992	Raybestos Brakettes
		1970	Orange Lionettes	1993	Redding (CA) Rebels
1950	Orange (CA) Lionettes	1971	Raybestos Brakettes	1994	Redding Rebels
1951	Orange Lionettes	1972	Raybestos Brakettes	1995	Redding Rebels
1952	Orange Lionettes	1973	Raybestos Brakettes		
1953	Betsy Ross Rockets, Fresno, CA	1974	Raybestos Brakettes		
1954	Leach Motor Rockets,	1975	Raybestos Brakettes		
	Fresno, CA	1976	Raybestos Brakettes		

Major Slow Pitch

Multiple winners: Dana Gardens and Spooks (4); Universal Plastics (3); Cannan's Illusions, Bob Hoffman's Dots and Marks Brothers Dots (2).

Year		Year		Year	
1959	Pearl Laundry, Richmond, VA	1973	Sweeney Chevrolet, Cincinnati	1984	Spooks
		1974	Marks Brothers Dots, Miami	1985	Key Ford Mustangs,
1960	Carolina Rockets, High Pt., NC	1975	Marks Brothers Dots		Pensacola, FL
1961	Dairy Cottage, Covington, KY	1976	Sorrento's Pizza, Cincinnati	1986	Sur-Way Tomboys, Tifton, GA
1962	Dana Gardens, Cincinnati	1977	Fox Valley Lassies,	1987	Key Ford Mustangs
1963	Dana Gardens		St. Charles, IL	1988	Spooks
1964	Dana Gardens	1978	Bob Hoffman's Dots, Miami	1989	Cannan's Illusions, Houston
1965	Art's Acres, Omaha, NE	1979	Bob Hoffman's Dots		
1966	Dana Gardens			1990	Spooks
1967	Ridge Maintenance, Cleveland	1980	Howard's Rubi-Otts,	1991	Cannan's Illusions, San Antonio
1968	Escue Pontiac, Cincinnati		Graham, NC	1992	Universal Plastics, Cookeville, TN
1969	Converse Dots, Hialeah, FL	1981	Tifton (GA) Tomboys	1993	Universal Plastics
		1982	Richmond (VA) Stompers	1994	Universal Plastics
1970	Rutenschruder Floral, Cincinnati	1983	Spooks, Anoka, MN	1995	Armed Forces, Sacramento
1971	Gators, Ft. Lauderdale, FL				
1972	Riverside Ford, Cincinnati				

TRIATHLON

World Championship

Contested since 1989, the Triathlon World Championship consists of a 1.5 kilometer swim, a 40-kilometer bike ride and a 10-kilometer run. The 1995 championship was scheduled for Nov. 11-12 at Cancun, Mexico.

	MEN			WOMEN	
Year		**Time**	**Year**		**Time**
1989	Mark Allen, United States	1:58:46	1989	Erin Baker, New Zealand	2:10:01
1990	Greg Welch, Australia	1:51:37	1990	Karen Smyers, United States	2:03:33
1991	Miles Stewart, Australia	1:48:20	1991	Joanne Ritchie, Canada	2:02:04
1992	Simon Lessing, Great Britain	1:49:04	1992	Michellie Jones, Australia	2:02:08
1993	Spencer Smith, Great Britain	1:51:20	1993	Michellie Jones, Australia	2:07:41
1994	Spencer Smith, Great Britain	1:51:04	1994	Emma Carney, Australia	2:03:19

Wide World Photos

Mark Allen of Boulder, Colo., crosses the finish line at the Ironman World Triathlon Championship on Oct. 7 in Kailua-Kona, Hawaii. Allen, 37, has won the event six times in the last seven years.

Ironman Championship

Contested in Hawaii since 1978, the Ironman Triathlon Championship consists of a 2.4-mile swim, a 112-mile bike ride and 26.2-mile run. The race begins at 7 A.M. and continues all day until the course is closed at midnight.

MEN

Multiple winners: Mark Allen and Dave Scott (6); Scott Tinley (2).

Year	Date	Winner	Time	Runner-up	Margin	Start	Finish	Location
I	2/18/78	Gordon Haller	11:46	John Dunbar	34:00	15	12	Waikiki Beach
II	1/14/79	Tom Warren	11:15:56	John Dunbar	48:00	15	12	Waikiki Beach
III	1/10/80	Dave Scott	9:24:33	Chuck Neumann	1:08	108	95	Ala Moana Park
IV	2/14/81	John Howard	9:38:29	Tom Warren	26:00	326	299	Kailua-Kona
V	2/6/82	Scott Tinley	9:19:41	Dave Scott	17:16	580	541	Kailua-Kona
VI	10/9/82	Dave Scott	9:08:23	Scott Tinley	20:05	850	775	Kailua-Kona
VII	10/22/83	Dave Scott	9:05:57	Scott Tinley	0:33	964	835	Kailua-Kona
VIII	10/6/84	Dave Scott	8:54:20	Scott Tinley	24:25	1036	903	Kailua-Kona
IX	10/25/85	Scott Tinley	8:50:54	Chris Hinshaw	25:46	1018	965	Kailua-Kona
X	10/18/86	Dave Scott	8:28:37	Mark Allen	9:47	1039	951	Kailua-Kona
XI	10/10/87	Dave Scott	8:34:13	Mark Allen	11:06	1380	1284	Kailua-Kona
XII	10/22/88	Scott Molina	8:31:00	Mike Pigg	2:11	1277	1189	Kailua-Kona
XIII	10/15/89	Mark Allen	8:09:15	Dave Scott	0:58	1285	1231	Kailua-Kona
XIV	10/6/90	Mark Allen	8:28:17	Scott Tinley	9:23	1386	1255	Kailua-Kona
XV	10/19/91	Mark Allen	8:18:32	Greg Welch	6:01	1386	1235	Kailua-Kona
XVI	10/10/92	Mark Allen	8:09:08	Cristian Bustos	7:21	1364	1298	Kailua-Kona
XVII	10/30/93	Mark Allen	8:07:45	Paulli Kiuru	6:37	1438	1353	Kailua-Kona
XVIII	10/15/94	Greg Welch	8:20:27	Dave Scott	4:05	1405	1290	Kailua-Kona
XIX	10/7/95	Mark Allen	8:20:34	Thomas Hellriegel	2:25	1487	1323	Kailua-Kona

WOMEN

Multiple winners: Paula Newby-Fraser (7); Erin Baker and Sylviane Puntous (2).

Year	Winner	Time	Runner-up	Year	Winner	Time	Runner-up
1978	No finishers			1987	Erin Baker	9:35:25	Sylviane Puntous
1979	Lyn Lemaire	12:55.00	None	1988	Paula Newby-Fraser	9:01:01	Erin Baker
				1989	Paula Newby-Fraser	9:00:56	Sylviane Puntous
1980	Robin Beck	11:21:24	Eve Anderson	1990	Erin Baker	9:13:42	P. Newby-Fraser
1981	Linda Sweeney	12:00:32	Sally Edwards	1991	Paula Newby-Fraser	9:07:52	Erin Baker
1982	Kathleen McCartney	11:09:40	Julie Moss	1992	Paula Newby-Fraser	8:55:28	Julie Anne White
1982	Julie Leach	10:54:08	Joann Dahlkoetter	1993	Paula Newby-Fraser	8:58:23	Erin Baker
1983	Sylviane Puntous	10:43:36	Patricia Puntous	1994	Paula Newby-Fraser	9:20:14	Karen Smyers
1984	Sylviane Puntous	10:25:13	Patricia Puntous	1995	Karen Smyers	9:16:46	Isabelle Mouthon
1985	Joanne Ernst	10:25:22	Liz Bulman				
1986	Paula Newby-Fraser	9:49:14	Sylviane Puntous				

Other Champions

Championships decided in 1995, unless otherwise indicated.

ARCHERY

World Target Championship

at Jakarta, Indonesia (Aug. 1-6)

MEN

Olympic Bow ....Kyung-Chul Lee, South Korea
Compound Bow ....Gary Broadhead, USA

WOMEN

Olympic Bow ....Natalia Valveeva, Moldavia
Compound Bow ....Angela Moscarelli, USA

World Indoor Championship

Birmingham, England (Mar. 23-26)

MEN

Olympic Bow ....Megnus Pettersson, Sweden
Compound Bow ....Michael Hendrikse, USA

WOMEN

Olympic Bow ....Natalia Valveeva, Moldavia
Compound Bow..................................Glenda Penaz, USA

ARENA FOOTBALL

Final AFL Standings

(*) indicates Conference champion; (†) indicates playoff wild card.

American Conference

Central Division	W	L	Pct	PF	PA
* St. Louis Stampede	9	3	.750	519	533
†Iowa Barnstromers	7	5	.583	593	511
†Memphis Pharaohs	6	6	.500	459	491
Milwaukee Mustangs	4	8	.333	541	619

Western Division	W	L	Pct	PF	PA
* San Jose SaberCats	8	4	.667	524	412
†Arizona Rattlers	7	5	.583	599	587
Las Vegas Sting	6	6	.500	532	498

National Conference

Eastern Division	W	L	Pct	PF	PA
* Albany Firebirds	7	5	.583	649	560
Charlotte Rage	5	7	.417	446	519
Connecticut Coyotes	1	11	.083	409	591

Southern Division	W	L	Pct	PF	PA
* Tampa Bay Storm	10	2	.833	605	378
†Orlando Predators	7	5	.583	542	471
Miami Hooters	1	11	.083	361	609

Quarterfinals

at Tampa Bay 53 ....Memphis 41
Albany 51 ....at St. Louis 49
Orlando 55 ....at San Jose 37
Iowa 56 ....at Arizona 52

Semifinals

at Tampa Bay 56 ....Albany 49
Orlando 56 ....at Iowa 49

Arena Bowl VIII

at Tampa Bay (Att— 25,087)

Tampa Bay 48 ....Orlando 35

BILLIARDS

PBT World Championships

Pro 8-Ball ....Efren Reyes, Philippines
Pro 9-Ball ....at Winston-Salem, N.C. (Dec. 12-17)
U.S. Open 9-Ball ....Reed Pierce, USA

WPA 9-Ball Championships

1994 Mosconi Cup (Team)...USA
Challenge of Champions ....Fong-Pang Chao, Taiwan
World Championship ....at Taipai, Taiwan (Nov. 15-19)

CRICKET

1996 World Cup Final

at India, Pakistan & Sri Lanka (Feb. 14–Mar. 17)

Australia at West Indies

4-Test Series (March–May)
1st— Australia (346 & 39-0) ....West Indies (195 & 185)
2nd— Australia (216 & 300-7).....West Indies (260 & 80-2) (match drawn)
3rd— West Indies (136 & 98-1)....Australia (128 & 105)
4th— Australia (531)...................West Indies (265 & 213)
(Australia wins, 2-1. Defeat is West Indies first series loss since 1980)

West Indies at England

6-Test Series (June–August)
1st— West Indies (282 & 129-1)...England (199 & 208)
2nd— England (283 & 336).........West Indies (324 & 223)
3rd— West Indies (300) ....England (147 & 89)
4th— England (437 & 94-4) ....West Indies (216 & 314)
5th— England (440 & 269-9) ....West Indies (417 & 42-2) (match drawn)
6th— England (454 & 223-4) ....West Indies (692) (match drawn and series drawn, 2-2)

South Africa at Zimbabwe

Single 5-Day Test match, (Oct. 13–16)
South Africa (346 & 108-3) ....Zimbabwe (170 & 283)
(South Africa wins by 7 wickets)

CURLING

World Champions

Men..Canada (skip: Kerry Burtnyk)
Women ....Sweden (skip: Elisabet Gustafson)

U.S. Champions

Men.................................Superior, Wisc. (skip: Tim Somerville)
Women..................Madison, Wisc. (skip: Lisa Schoeneberg)

FIELD HOCKEY

World Cup

1994 Men's final ....Pakistan def. Holland, 4-3
1995 Women's final ....Australia def Argentina, 2-0
(USA won bronze medal, 2-1 over Holland)

1995 Pan American Games

Men's Final ....Argentina def. Canada, 1-0
(USA won bronze medal, 3-2 over Cuba)
Women's Final ....Argentina def. USA, 3-2

HANDBALL

World Four-Wall Championships
1997 in Winnipeg, Manitoba

U.S. Four-Wall Championships

Men	David Chapman, Springfield, Mo.
Women	Anna Engele, St. Paul, Minn.
Open doubles	David Chapman, Springfield, Mo. & Naty Alvarado, Hesperia, Calif.

HORSESHOE PITCHING

World Champions

Men	Alan Francis, Blythedale, Md.
Women	Sue Snyder, Harrisonville, Ky.

LACROSSE

Major Indoor Lacrosse
(*) indicates Conference champion; (†) indicates playoff wild card.

	W	L	GB	Pct	GR	GA
* Phila. Wings	7	1	—	.875	115	94
†Boston Blazers	5	3	2	.625	93	91
†Rochester Knighthawks	4	4	3	.500	98	94
†Buffalo Bandits	3	5	4	.375	109	108
Baltimore Thunder	3	5	4	.375	98	117
New York Saints	2	6	5	.250	85	93

Playoffs

Philadelphia 19	at Buffalo 16
at Rochester 10	Boston 8

Championship
(at Philadelphia, Att— 14,824)

Philadelphia 15	Rochester 14 OT

MOTORCYCLE RACING

ROAD RACING
Grand Prix Champions

125 cc	Haruchika Aoki, Japan
250 cc	Max Biaggi, Italy
500 cc	Michael Doohan, Australia
Super Bike	Carl Fogarty, England

MOTOCROSS
Motorcross des Nations

Team	Belgium (Stefan Everts, Marnicq Bervoets and Joel Smets)

Grand Prix Champions

125 cc	Alessandro Puzar, Italy
250 cc	Stefan Everts, Belgium
500 cc	Joel Smets, Belgium

RACQUETBALL

U.S. Amateur Champions

Men	Michael Bronfeld, Monterey, Calif.
Women	Michelle Gould, Boise, Idaho

IRT Pro Tour Champions

Men	Cliff Swain, Braintree, Mass.
Women	Michelle Gould, Boise, Idaho

RUGBY LEAGUE

Pro World Championship
at England (Oct. 7–28)

Semifinals

England 25	Wales 10
Australia 30	New Zealand 20

Finals

Australia 16	England 8

RUGBY UNION

Amateur World Cup
Third World Cup tournament, at Johannesburg, South Africa, from May 25 to June 24. Note that (*) indicates teams that advanced to quarterfinals.

Group A	W	L	T	Pts	PF	PA
*South Africa	3	0	0	9	69	25
*Australia	2	1	0	7	87	41
Canada	1	2	0	4	45	50
Romania	0	3	0	2	14	97

Group B	W	L	T	Pts	PF	PA
*England	3	0	0	9	95	60
*Western Somoa	2	1	0	6	96	88
Italy	1	2	0	4	69	94
Argentina	0	3	0	2	69	87

Group C	W	L	T	Pts	PF	PA
*New Zealand	3	0	0	9	222	45
*Ireland	2	1	0	6	93	94
Wales	1	2	0	4	89	64
Japan	0	3	0	2	47	252

Group D	W	L	T	Pts	PF	PA
*France	3	0	0	9	114	47
*Scotland	2	1	0	6	149	27
Tonga	1	2	0	5	44	90
Ivory Coast	0	3	0	2	29	172

Quarterfinals

France 36	Ireland 12
South Africa 42	Western Somoa 14
England 25	Australia 22
New Zealand 48	Scotland 30

Semifinals

South Africa 19	France 15
New Zealand 45	England 29

Third Place

France 19	England 9

Championship

South Africa 15	New Zealand 12

U.S. CHAMPIONS

Club:	Men	Potomac A.C., Washington, D.C.
	Women	Bay Area Shehawks, San Francisco
College:	Men	California (Berkeley)
	Women	Princeton

Australian Rules Football
AFL Grand Final
at Melbourne Cricket Ground (Sept. 30)

Carlton Blues 141	Geelong Cats 80

Other Champions (Cont.)

SHOOTING

U.S. Nationals (Pistol, Rifle)
at Chino, Calif. (July 1-9)

MEN

Air Pistol	Ben Amonette, Radford, Va.
Center Fire Pistol	Darius Young, Republic, Wash.
Free Pistol	Daryl Szarenski, Saginaw, Mich.
Rapid Fire Pistol	Dan Iuga, Brentwood, Calif.
Standard Pistol	George Ross, Santa Clarita, Calif.
Air Rifle	Ken Johnson, Marchfield, Mass.
Free Rifle, Prone	Tom Tamas, Columbus, Ga.
3-Position Rifle	Bob Foth, Colo. Springs
10m Running Target	Adam Saathoff, Hereford, Ariz.
10m Run Target, Mixed	Michael E. Johnson, USAMU
50m Running Target	Lonn Saunders, Billings, Mont.
50m Run Target, Mixed	Lonn Saunders

WOMEN

Air Pistol	Connie Petracek, Nashville
Sport Pistol	Connie Petracek
Air Rifle	Jayne Dickman, South Bend, Ind.
Standard Rifle, Prone	Elizabeth Bourland
3-Position Rifle	Stephanie Thomson, Salem, Ore.
10m Running Target	Kelly Miltner, Pueblo, Colo.
10m Run Target, Mixed	Shane Buffa, Chiloquin, Ore.

U.S. Nationals (Shotgun)
at Fort Carson, Colo. (July 29-Aug. 5)

MEN

Skeet	Bill Roy, Alamogordo, N.M.
Trap	Joshua Lakatos, Pasadena
Double Trap	Lance Bade, Ridgefield, Wash.

WOMEN

Skeet	Connie Schiller, College Station, Tex.
Trap	Deena Julin, Omaha, Neb.
Double Trap	Kim Rhode, El Monte, Calif.

SURFING

1994 Assn. of Surfing Professionals
World Tour Champions

MEN

Men	Kelly Slater, Cocoa Beach, Fla.
Women	Lisa Andersen, Ormond, Fla.

TABLE TENNIS

World Championships
at Tianjin, China (May 1-14)

Men's Singles	Kong Linghui, China
Men's Doubles	Wang Tao & Lu Lin, China
Women's Singles	Deng Yaping, China
Women's Doubles	Deng Yaping & Qiao Hong, China
Mixed Doubles	Wang Tao & Liu Wei, China

1994 U.S. Nationals
at Las Vegas (Dec. 14-18)

Men's Singles	David Zhuang, New Brunswick, N.J.
Men's Doubles	David Zhuang & Dan Seemiller, Pittsburgh
Women's Singles	Amy Feng, Martinez, Ga.
Women's Doubles	Amy Feng & Lily Yip, Metuchen, N.J.
Mixed Doubles	David Zhuang & Amy Feng

VOLLEYBALL

1994 World Championships
(Next Men's and Women's World Championships in 1998)

Men's Final	Italy def. Holland
	(15-11, 11-15, 15-11, 15-1)
Women's Finall	Cuba def. Brazil
	(15-2, 15-10, 15-5)

U.S. Open Champions

Men's Gold Div	Shakter, Belogorod, Ukraine
Women's Gold Div	Kittleman Assoc./Rudi's/
	Nick's, Chicago

Pro Beach Tours

MEN (AVP)

Manhattan Beach Open	Adam Johnson/Jose Loiola
Hermosa Beach Tournament	Karch Kiraly/Kent Steffes

WOMEN (WPVA)

Newport Shoot-out	Karolyn Kirby/Liz Masakayan
Bally's Total Fitness National	Holly McPeak/Nancy Reno
U.S. Open	Karolyn Kirby/Liz Masakayan

WATER SKIING

1995 World Championships
at Roquebrune, France (Sept. 13-17)

MEN

Slalom	Andy Mapple, England
Tricks	Americ Benet, France
Jump	Bruce Neville, Australia
Overall	Patrice Martin, France

WOMEN

Slalom	Helena Kjellander, Sweden
Tricks	Tawn Larson, USA
Jump	Brenda Nichols-Baldwin, USA
Overall	Judy Messer, Canada

U.S. Open Champions

Overall: Men	Patrice Martin, France
Women	Rhoni Barton, Winter Park, Fla.

Bud Water Ski Tour

Men's Slalom	Wade Cox, Orlando, Fla.
Men's Freestyle	Dave Reinhart, Delray Beach, Fla.
Men's Jump	Carl Roberge, Orlando, Fla.
Women's Slalom	Kristi Overton, Greenville, N.C.

WLAF FOOTBALL

World League of American Football
World Bowl '95
at Amsterdam, Holland (Att— 23,847)

Frankfurt Galaxy 26	Amsterdam Admirals 22

Darts

World Cup Champions

Men	Martin Adams, England
Women	Mandy Solomons, England

U.S. Champions

Men	Rudy Hernandez, New York
Women	Lori Verrier, Salem, Ore.

Mickey Mantle meets the press in Dallas a month after receiving a liver transplant at Baylor University Medical Center. He died on Aug. 13 at age 63 after a two-month fight with cancer.

DEATHS

Wide World Photos

Johnny Adams

Wide World Photos

Bob Allison

UPI/Bettmann

Gus Bell

Harry Abrams, 87; twice ran between New York and Los Angeles in the 1920's; in 1928, at age 21, Abrams raced 3,422 miles over 84 days in what would become known as the Bunion Derby, a feat which earned him a mention in "Ripley's Believe It or Not"; known as a showman, Abrams outran horses and participated in dance marathons in Madison Square Garden; cause of death not reported; in Briarcliff Manor, N.Y., Nov. 27, 1994.

Johnny Adams, 79; jockey and Hall of Fame trainer; won the Preakness Stakes in the former capacity; rode 3,270 winners that earned over $9.7 million; Preakness victory occurred in 1954 aboard Hasty Road; became a trainer at the end of his riding career in 1958; J.O. Tobin, one of the horses Adams trained, defeated the previously undefeated Seattle Slew, a Triple Crown winner, in the 1977 Swaps Stakes; inducted in the Racing Hall of Fame in 1965; after a long illness; in Arcadia, Calif., Aug. 19.

Jack Agness, 74; spent 35 years at one paper— The Houston Post— as a sports writer and golf columnist; graduated from the University of Houston in 1952 with a journalism degree after serving with the Marines during WWII; co-founder and former director of the Texas Golf Hall of Fame; in his sleep; in Austin, Texas, Nov. 12, 1994.

Morris (Morrie) Alhadeff, 79; spent 18 years as president and chairman of the board of Longacres Race Course Inc. in Washington state; Longacres was western Washington's premier thoroughbred racing facility for 60 years; began working at Longacres in 1947 and didn't leave until his retirement in 1989; past president of the Thoroughbred Racing Association of North America; cause of death not reported; in Seattle, Nov. 8, 1994.

Bob Allison, 60; two-time AL All-Star outfielder who hit the game-winning home run for the Minnesota Twins in Game 6 of the 1965 World Series; voted AL Rookie of the Year in 1959 as a member of the Washington Senators, compiling 30 homers, 85 RBI and a league-high 9 triples; finished his 13-year career (1958-1970) with a .255 average, 256 home runs and 796 RBI; led the AL in runs scored in 1963 with 99; from complications due to ataxia; in Rio Verde, Ariz., April 9.

Elvis Alvarez, 30; former junior bantamweight champion who captured the WBA title in 1991; left-hander lost that title less than three months after earning it; turned pro in 1983 and also won titles in the WBO and the North American Boxing Federation; shot to death by several gunmen who approached him while he was on his motorcycle; in Bogota, Colombia, July 16.

John Ayers, 42; West Texas State grad and 10-year NFL veteran, who was the starting left guard for the San Francisco 49ers first two Super Bowl championship teams in 1981 and '84; known for his outstanding one-on-one pass protection; of liver cancer; in Canyon, Tex., Oct. 2.

Francis (Reds) Bagnell, 66; chairman of the National Football Foundation, past president of the Maxwell Cluband member of the College Football Hall of Fame; dominated at single-wing tailback position for Penn between 1947-50; regularly played before crowds of 80,000 at Franklin Field; the former Penn water boy placed third in the 1950 Heisman Trophy voting behind Vic Janowicz of Ohio State and Kyle Rote of SMU; in his 1950 All-American season, Bagnell amassed a then NCAA single-game record 490 yards of total offense and completed 14 straight passes; of cardiac arrest; in Philadelphia, July 10.

Sally Bailie, 58; horse trainer who was the first woman to train a thoroughbred to victory in $100,000 and $200,000 stakes races; her best-known horse was Win, who nearly upset two-time Horse of the Year John Henry in the 1984 Turf Classic; of cancer; in Mineola, N.Y., Aug. 22.

Dick Bartell, 87; shortstop who started for the NL in baseball's first All-Star Game in 1933; played in three World Series; the career .284 hitter broke in with the Pirates and later played for the Phillies, Giants, Cubs and Tigers; helped the Giants to pennants in 1936-37; in the 1936 World Series, he hit .381 and knocked in a team-high five runs in the six-game loss to the N.Y. Yankees; following a battle with Alzheimer's disease; in Alameda, Calif., Aug. 4.

Gus Bell, 66; outfielder who spent nine of his 15 seasons in the majors with Cincinnati; patriarch of a three-generation major league family: son Buddy was an outstanding third baseman with Cleveland and Texas and grandson David played with Cleveland in 1995; a .281 career hitter for four clubs between 1950-1964; in 1953, batted .300 with 30 home runs, and in 1955 batted .308 with 27 homers; knocked in more than 100 runs in a season four times; of a heart attack; in Cincinnati, May 7.

August Belmont IV, 86; horseman who carried on family tradition when his colt Caveat won the 1983 Belmont Stakes; grandson of August Belmont II, the founder of Belmont Park and breeder of Man o' War; former chairman of The Jockey Club and the American Kennel Club; of a massive stroke; in Easton, Md., July 10.

Tom Bender, 70; long-time sportscaster who called play-by-play for Duquesne, Penn State and Pittsburgh; also called Pittsburgh Steeler games; began his career in 1955, retired in 1974; hosted a radio sports-talk show in Pittsburgh; in his sleep; in Fort Myers, Fla., Jan. 29.

Phil Bengtson, 81; Vince Lombardi's defensive coordinator during Green Bay dynasty of 1960s; Packers allowed opponents only 15.6 points per game under his direction from 1960-69; took over as head coach when Lombardi retired in 1968; posted 20-21-1 record in three seasons; an All-America tackle at the University of Minnesota in the 1930's; after a long illness; in San Diego, Dec. 18, 1994.

Hockey Hall of Fame

Wide World Photos

Motorola Cycling Team

Toe Blake

Bruce Bosley

Fabio Casartelli

Toe Blake, 82; coached the Montreal Canadiens to a record eight Stanley Cup championships, including five straight between 1955-68; also won three Cups during his 15-year playing career; played on the Canadiens' famed Punch line, with Maurice (Rocket) Richard and Elmer Lach; was the NHL's leading scorer and MVP in the 1938-39 season; won the 1946 Lady Byng Trophy and scored the Stanley Cup-winning goal in the finals that year; 13-year career coaching record, including playoffs, was 582-292-159 for a winning percentage of .640; known for the signature fedora always on his head; of Alzheimer's disease; in Montreal, May 17.

Bruce Bosley, 61; played 13 years with the San Francisco 49ers; the four-time Pro Bowl lineman was the former executive director of the NFL Alumni Association; starred in college for West Virginia where he was known for his incredible strength; helped the Mountaineers to a 31-7 record and a berth in the 1954 Sugar Bowl; member of the College Football Hall of Fame; of complications from heart disease; in San Francisco, April 26.

Charley Boswell, 78; star college athlete at Alabama who lost his sight in World War II when a German artillery shell exploded near him as he was pulling a fellow soldier from a damaged tank; gained fame later as a golfer when he shot an 81 and won numerous tournaments for blind players; hosted an annual celebrity tournament that raised $1.5 million for Birmingham's Eye Foundation Hospital; after a long illness; in Birmingham, Ala., Oct. 22.

Mikhail Botvinnik, 83; Russian grandmaster who spent most of the 1950's as world chess champion and dominated play for 15 years; had unique, scientific approach to the game; influenced a generation of Russian players including Garry Kasparov and Anatoly Karpov; did not begin play until age 12, unusual for such an accomplished player; cause of death not reported; in Moscow, May 5.

François Boutin, 58; the leading horse trainer in France 11 times; began career in 1964 and won nearly every major French race; some of his horses had notable performances on U.S. soil: April Run won the Grade I Turf Classic at Aqueduct in 1981 and 1982; the filly Miesque became the first horse to win two Breeders Cup races after beating males in 1987 and 1988, leading to Eclipse Awards both years; and Arazi captured an Eclipse after cruising to victory in the 1991 Breeders Cup Juvenile; of liver cancer; in Paris, Feb. 1.

Henry P. Bowman, 74; the first black man to referee football and basketball in the Big Ten conference; past president of the Tuskeegee Airmen veterans group and one of the first black U.S. combat pilots; cause of death not reported; in Los Angeles, Sept. 16.

Angelo Brovelli, 84; quarterback of the Pittsburgh Steelers when they were known as the Pittsburgh Pirates; played in 1933-34, playing the single-wing position and earning $400 a game; of a heart attack; in Acampo, Calif., Aug. 5.

Juan Burciaga, 65; Judge whose 1982 ruling left the National Collegiate Athletic Association (NCAA) out of the business of televised football; felt the NCAA violated anti-trust laws and acted like a "classic cartel" with its TV football contracts, ending 30 years of NCAA control and allowing schools and conferences to compete for the TV rights; of an aortic aneurysm; in Albuquerque, N.M., March 5.

Glenn Burke, 42; former center fielder who is best known for being the only professional baseball player to ever admit his homosexuality; as a top prospect in the late 70's with the Dodgers he was compared favorably to Willie Mays because of his ability to run, throw and hit; credited with originating the "high-five" while celebrating a home run by teammate Dusty Baker; later traded to Oakland; four-year totals included 35 stolen bases and a .237 average; felt he was blackballed in baseball because of his sexual orientation and wrote an autobiography, "Out At Home: The Glenn Burke Story" published just after his death; of AIDS; in San Leandro, Calif., May 30.

Bill Callahan, 74; spent 38 years as sports information director at the University of Missouri; member of the school's Athletics Hall of Fame; in 1974 received the Arch Ward Award, the highest honor awarded by the College Sports Information Directors of America; former chairman of the NCAA Public Relations Committee; of cancer; in Columbia, Mo., March 2.

Charlie Callahan, 79; sports information director at Notre Dame from 1946 to 1965; publicity chief for the Miami Dolphins from 1966 to 1984; noted storyteller of Notre Dame's glory days; publicized five Heisman Trophy winners— Johnny Lujack, Paul Hornung, John Huarte, John Lattner and Leon Hart— during his tenure at ND; of heart failure; in Bradenton, Fla., Jan. 12.

Fabio Casartelli, 24; Italian cyclist who was the 1992 Olympic road race champion; his first professional season (1983) was spent racing with Ariostea and his second with GB MG/Boy; joined Motorola Cycling Team in 1995; died from injuries sustained in a high-speed bicycle crash during a mountain descent in the 15th stage of the Tour de France— only the third time since he swam the race began in 1903 that a cyclist died while competing; in Cauterets, France, July 18.

Florence Chadwick, 76; swimmer who set a women's record for crossing the English Channel (from France to England) in 1950, completing the feat in 14 hours, 20 minutes; the next year, became the first women to cross in both directions when she swam the more challenging England-to-France route in a record time of 16:22; swam the Channel a total of four times; after a long illness; in San Diego, March 15.

Gloria Chadwick, 63; member of the United States National Ski Hall of Fame; director of the U.S. Olympic Training Center in Lake Placid since 1985 and was executive director of the U.S. Ski Association from 1961–68; of cancer; in Lake Placid, N.Y., July 30.

UPI/Bettmann   Wide World Photos   Wide World Photos

Florence Chadwick   **Harry Craft**   **Edward DeBartolo**

Bob Chandler, 45; wide receiver for Southern Cal, who led the Trojans in receiving from 1968-70; teammate and close friend of O.J. Simpson at USC; reunited with Simpson in 1971 when the Buffalo Bills drafted him with their seventh pick; traded to Oakland in 1980, just in time to play for the Raider squad that became the only team to win the Super Bowl as a wild card; caught four passes for 77 yards in Super Bowl XV; retired after 1982 season with 370 career catches and 48 touchdowns; of cancer; in Los Angeles, Jan. 27.

Marty Cohen, 97; creator of the Intercontinental Boxing Council in 1990; was a fighter, trainer, manager, promoter, judge and referee during his career; also possessed a fondness for harness racing and maintained a stable of about 20 horses; after a short illness; in Miami, May 3.

Joseph E. Cole, 80; minority owner of the Cleveland Indians in the 1950's who made two unsuccessful attempts to buy the club outright; was the last owner of *The Cleveland Press*, an afternoon newspaper he bought in 1980, that closed in 1982 after 103 years; active in the Democratic Party: chaired John F. Kennedy's Ohio campaign in 1960, major supporter of Hubert H. Humphrey's campaign for President in 1968, was treasurer of Democratic Party in 1973 and also served on the Democratic National Committee; of complications from a stroke; in Palm Beach, Fla., Jan. 7.

David Condon, 70; retired *Chicago Tribune* sports columnist; began his career at that paper in 1944 and took over the "In the Wake of the News" column in 1955, a position he held before retiring in 1982; after a long illness; in Chicago, Dec. 5, 1994.

James Whitney Cook, 90; became president of the Chicago Bulls in 1972 after a group of investors he was involved with purchased the team; spent 40 years with AT&T and its subsidiaries; of heart failure; in Naples, Fla., Nov. 27, 1994.

Howard Cosell, 75; controversial broadcaster who helped make ABC's "Monday Night Football" a national institution; born Howard Cohen; forged a memorable relationship with Cassius Clay, sticking by the new heavyweight champion when he changed his name to Muhammad Ali in 1964 and later when he refused to enter military service and was stripped of his title; voice was distinctive not only on football broadcasts but boxing matches as well; later divorced himself from both sports, disgusted with how each had evolved; voice of ABC radio and television from 1953-92; anchored ABC's Emmy Award-winning "Sportsbeat" show; also a lawyer, author and lecturer; received posthumous Lifetime Achievement Emmy in 1995; of a heart embolism; in New York, April 23.

Kresimir Cosic, 46; European basketball star who became one of the first foreigners to have an impact on U.S. basketball by starring at Brigham Young University in the 1970's; the 6-foot-11-inch center was a crowd-favorite and

All-WAC each season between 1971-1973; led BYU to a pair of conference titles and averaged 19.1 points per game; was drafted by the NBA but returned to Yugoslavia, where he was a hero as a player and coach; a four-time Olympian, led Yugoslavia to a gold medal in 1980 and a silver in 1968; of cancer; in Baltimore, May 25.

Harry Craft, 80; first skipper of the Houston Colt .45s and later the Astros; began that stint in 1962, Houston's first season in the National League; previously had managed the Kansas City Athletics and the Chicago Cubs; was Mickey Mantle's first professional manager at Independence, Kan., in the Kansas-Oklahoma-Missouri League in 1949 and in the Western Association in 1950; credited by Roger Maris, also a minor league pupil, as having helped the Yankee slugger with his hitting; after a long illness; in Conroe, Tex., Aug. 4.

Tony Cuccinello, 87; Chicago White Sox infielder who lost the 1945 AL batting title by a single point to New York's Snuffy Stirnweiss on a controversial scoring decision that cost him a hit on the final day of the season; never played another game in the majors after Chicago released him following the 1945 season in which he hit .308; played with five teams during his 15-year major-league career; career batting average of .280; of congestive hear failure; in Tampa, Fla., Sept. 21.

J. William Davis, 86; former head of the government department at Texas Tech who served on many NCAA committees and is recognized as the father of the National Letter of Intent; former NCAA Council member; vice-president and president of the Southwest Conference during his 29-years as chair of the athletics council at Texas Tech; chaired the NCAA Eligibility Committee; cause of death not reported; May 21.

Leon Day, 78; former Negro leagues baseball star who died one week after earning induction into the Baseball Hall of Fame; career flourished during the 1930's and 1940's, a time when blacks were forbidden to play in the major leagues; in the early 1950's toward the end of his career, Day played minor league ball in the International and Eastern Leagues; as a pitcher, Day is often compared to another Hall of Famer and fellow Negro leagues star, Satchel Paige, who Day defeated three of four times; known for a no-windup delivery; played center field and second base when not pitching; after a long illness; in Baltimore, March 13.

Edward J. DeBartolo Sr., 85; real estate titan whose family owns the San Francisco 49ers and once owned the Pittsburgh Penguins; born Anthony Paonessa; also owned three horse racing tracks: Louisiana Downs, Remington Park and Thistledown; net worth last listed at $850 million; one of the best-known developers of shopping malls, office towers, office parks, hotels, supermarkets and condominiums; his son, Edward, Jr., runs the 49ers; of complications from pneumonia; in Youngstown, Ohio, Dec. 19, 1994.

Howard Cosell

1920-95

by Richard Sandomir

Arrogant, truculent, brilliant, bombastic, obnoxious, trailblazing, unique. Howard Cosell would have said he was all of these, and more.

When he died at age 77 of the myriad ailments that had made him a recluse in his Manhattan apartment, Cosell had been gone from TV sportscasting for a decade and radio for 3 years.

But he was an indelible presence in a profession that hasn't seen his like before or since.

Born Howard Cohen on March 25, 1920, Cosell grew up in Brooklyn wanting to be a newspaper reporter before his family insisted that he get a law degree. After military service in World War II, he practiced law for 10 years, but did some sportswriting and part-time radio work. In 1956, he joined ABC Radio as a full-time boardcaster.

On the air, he blended his grating Brooklyn accent with a unique "Don't-give-me-that-crap" interviewing style that both upset and delighted his listeners. Later, in television, he developed a booming cadence for his narration of the halftime highlights on "Monday Night Football" that made his the most imitated voice in America.

And for sports fans it still is.

Cosell, who wore a toupee, prided himself on "telling it like it is". He relished rushing in, microphone in hand, where other reporters—especially in television— feared to tread. On his "Speaking of Sports" radio reports and later his "Sportsbeat" TV show, he forced a sports-worshipping country to confront issues like as racism, antitrust law and drugs.

He stood up for outcasts like Muhammad Ali and Curt Flood when the rest of the media looked the other way.

Roone Arledge, who loosed Cosell on America in the 1960's, first as a boxing commentator and then as the articulate, tart-tongued know-it-all on "Monday Night Football," appreciated Cosell's ability to create controversy.

"Pete Rozelle wanted announcer approval on 'Monday Night Football,'" said Arledge, the former president of ABC Sports. Rozelle backed down "never knowing I wanted Howard. [When he found out] Pete was beside himself. Bowie Kuhn wanted to get out of out of our

Wide World Photos

Howard Cosell in the broadcast booth during the early days of ABC-TV's "Monday Night Football."

baseball contract because I put Howard on. And the Montreal Olympic Committee asked us as a condition of buying the rights that we not use Howard."

Cosell was a peculiar, contradictory, ornery, passionate man. As good at hyping an event as anyone, he was also paranoid about print reporters, occasionally cruel and prone to believing that he was bigger than the events he covered.

Yet he doted on his grandchildren, worshipped his wife and wept at the mention of Jackie Robinson's courage. He was equally capable of bestowing high praise or bitter invective. Arledge, the recipient of some of both, said: "He had a strange relationship with everybody. Some days he loved you, others, he had some deep-seated resentment of you."

Added ABC's Al Michaels: "As he got older, he seemed frustrated to be in a business that didn't get the respect he felt necessary. He had to be part of a business that was respected, like being a doctor or a physicist."

Two nights after Cosell died, Arledge accepted a posthumous lifetime achievement award on his behalf at the annual Sports Emmy Award ceremonies in New York. "Of all the tributes that can be paid to Howard Cosell and his work, a moment of silence doesn't leap to mind."

Richard Sandomir writes the television sports column for *The New York Times*.

Dartmouth College

Basketball Hall of Fame

Wide World Photos

Sarah Devens   **Charley Eckman**   **Don Elston**

Sarah Devens, 21; All-Ivy League selection in field hockey, ice hockey and lacrosse for Dartmouth College; elected captain of all three teams in 1994-95; first team All-America in lacrosse; slated to attend the Olympic Festival; Devens was arguably Dartmouth's most accomplished female athlete ever; of a self-inflicted gunshot wound; in Essex, Mass., July 10.

Manfred Donike, 61; biochemist prominent in developing procedures to detect performance-enhancing drugs in international athletic competition; developed one of the first sports labs in anticipation of the 1972 Munich Olympics; member of the International Olympic Committee and the International Amateur Athletic Federation; developed procedure that refuted claims by Canadian sprinter Ben Johnson— who was stripped of his 1988 gold medal because of drug use— that his urine test was sabotaged; of a heart attack; while en route to Johannesburg, South Africa, Aug. 21.

Spencer J. Drayton, 84; former FBI agent who introduced the Thoroughbred Racing Protective Bureau in 1946, a security agency he ran for 33 years; the development of that bureau stemmed from the practice of switching horses and jockey bribes; initiated protective measure of identifying thoroughbreds through lip tattoos; of congestive heart failure; in Stuart, Fla., Nov. 27, 1994.

Mark Eaton, 45; former NCAA gymnast and nationally-known coach; 1971 NCAA titlest in floor exercise while at New Mexico; led Lobos to WAC team titles in 1968, '70 and '71; chosen as national women's coach of the year in 1989; in a plane crash; in Winslow, Ariz., March 15.

Charley Eckman, 73; former professional and college basketball referee who later coached the Fort Wayne Pistons to the championship finals in his first two seasons, 1955-56; also coached the Pistons during their first season in Detroit (1957-58), but was fired after a poor start; of colon cancer; in Glen Burnie, Md., July 3.

Melvin Eggers, 78; chancellor of Syracuse University from 1971 to 1991; credited with strengthening the university academically and athletically; the 50,000-seat Carrier Dome was built on campus during his tenure; after a long illness; in DeWitt, N.Y., Nov. 20, 1994.

Don Elston, 65; relief pitcher for the Chicago Cubs in 1950's and early 1960's; twice led the National League in appearances, with 69 in 1958 and 65 in 1959; made a total of 450 appearances, compiling 49 wins, 54 losses, 63 saves and an ERA of 3.70 during his nine-year career; of heart failure; in Evanston, Ill., Jan. 2.

Terry Elston, 37; former University of Houston quarterback who was the most valuable player in the 1980 Cotton Bowl where the eighth-ranked Cougars beat seventh-ranked Nebraska, 17-14 to end the season at No. 5; of injuries sustained after being hit by a car; in Alabama, Aug. 23.

Restituto Espineli, 19; Filipino flyweight who took up boxing to help earn a decent income for his family; one of two fighters to die from ring-related injuries on Oct. 15 (see James Murray); lapsed into coma 20 minutes after losing a unanimous 10-round decision to Marlon Carillo; of brain hemmorage; in Makati, Philippines, Oct. 15.

Bill Esposito, 67; sports information director at St. John's University in New York from 1961-84; served as the president of CoSIDA from 1976-77; elected to CoSIDA Hall of Fame in 1984; earned a bronze star in Korea; noted expert on jazz; cause on death unknown; in East Patchogue, N.Y., Sept. 9.

Dernell Every, 88; fencing champion who was a bronze medalist for the United States in the 1932 Olympics as a member of the foil team that upset the French; member of Olympic fencing teams in 1928, 1932 and 1948; won national foil individual titles in 1938, 1940 and 1945; cause of death not reported; in Mount Kisco, N.Y., July 16.

Jack Falls, 32; an ironworker who was working on the construction of Atlanta's Olympic Stadium; had been interviewed in Feb. 1995, about the perils of working and walking on small metal beams suspended in midair, saying it took, "A little bit of nerve and a lack of common sense"; in a fall after the light tower he was working on at Olympic Stadium collapsed; in Atlanta, March 20.

Juan Manuel Fangio, 84; auto racing's only five-time Formula One world champion; his 24 victories rank him seventh all-time; world championships occurred in 1951 and between 1954-57; raced in the days of leather helmets, goggles and no seat belts; known for his uncanny anticipation and reflexes; of pneumonia and kidney problems; in Buenos Aires, Argentina, July 17.

Don Faurot, 93; college football coach who created the split-T offense at Missouri, where he coached the Tigers to a record of 101-79-10 from 1935-42 and 46-56; won three Big Six (now Big Eight) conference titles in 1939, '41 and '42; lost all four bowl appearances; best college-age team he coached was Iowa Pre-Flight squad that went 9-1 and ended 1943 season ranked No. 2 behind Notre Dame; Missouri's football stadium Faurot Field is named after him; elected to College Football Hall of Fame in 1961; retired as Mizzou athletic director in 1967; of congestive heart failure; in Columbia, Mo., Oct. 19.

Rick Ferrell, 89; Hall of Fame catcher who held the American League record for games caught for 41 years; played in the majors from 1929 to 1947 for the St. Louis Browns and then with his brother and batterymate, Wes, for the Boston Red Sox and Washington Senators; voted into the Hall of Fame in 1984 by the veteran's committee; record of 1,806 games caught was broken by Carlton Fisk in 1988; caught all nine innings of the first All-Star game in 1933; served as an executive with the Detroit Tigers from 1950 to 1992; of arrhythmia; in Bloomfield Hills, Mich., July 27.

UPI/Bettmann · UPI/Bettmann · UPI/Bettmann

Juan Manuel Fangio · **Rick Ferrell** · **Pancho Gonzales**

Foolish Pleasure, 22; stallion that was the winner of the 1975 Kentucky Derby; career winnings listed at $1,216,705; best remembered for his $350,000 match race with undefeated filly Ruffian at Belmont Park on July 6, 1975 (Ruffian broke down in the race and had to be humanely destroyed); of a ruptured stomach; at Horseshoe Ranch, Dayton, Wyo., Nov. 17, 1994.

John (Frosty) Forristall, 51; trainer for the Boston Bruins for 20 years, including 1970 and 1972, the last years Boston won the Stanley Cup; trainer for the first Team Canada; later worked with the Toronto Blue Jays and the Tampa Bay Lightning; of cancer; in Boston, May 30.

Dan Fortmann, 79; member of the Pro Football Hall of Fame who was a six-time All-Pro guard for the Chicago Bears between 1936 and 1943; team physician for the Los Angeles Rams between 1947 and 1963; won three NFL championships with the Bears; of Alzheimer's disease; in Los Angeles, May 24.

Daniel M. Galbreath, 67; millionaire sportsman and son of John W. Galbreath; inherited Pittsburgh Pirates of National League after his father's death; served as the director of Churchill Downs and the National Football Foundation and Hall of Fame; family owns Darby Dan Farms, producer of Kentucky Derby winners Chateaugay in 1963 and Proud Clarion in '67; of cancer; in Columbus, Ohio, Sept. 3.

Richard Ganslen, 78; pole-vaulter whose book, "Mechanics of the Pole Vault," is now in its ninth edition and has been translated into German and Russian; won the national indoor championship in 1938, the Penn Relays 1938 and 1939 and the Millrose Games in 1939 and 1940; of a heart attack; in Denton, Texas, May 12.

Richard Garber, 66; longtime lacrosse coach at the University of Massachusetts; retired in 1990 as the only collegiate lacrosse coach with 300 victories; member of the Lacrosse Hall of Fame; after a long illness; in Northampton, Mass., Dec. 7, 1994.

Jimmy Garcia, 23; Colombian boxer who took an 11-round beating from Gabriel Ruelas during his challenge for the WBC super featherweight title on May 6; lost 32 pounds in two months to make the 130-pound limit for the fight which he lost by TKO; of brain damage suffered during the Ruelas fight; in Las Vegas, May 19.

Howard Gentry, 73; former AD and head football coach at Tennessee State; went undefeated in 1956 when the Tigers won the black college national championship; career record was 42-10-1; of cancer; Feb. 14.

Ray George, 78; star lineman for Southern Cal in the 1930's who later became head coach at Texas A&M in the early 1950's; as a senior at USC in 1938, George played on the team which upset top-ranked Notre Dame and defeated previously unbeaten and unscored-upon Duke in the Rose Bowl; the second USC player ever taken in the NFL draft; played with Detroit in 1939 and Philadelphia in

1940; coached the line at USC from 1946-50, coached Texas A&M before returning to USC in 1958 for seven more seasons as an assistant; served as assistant AD at USC from 1971-85, and also coached there again from 1972-74; of complications from a stroke; in Costa Mesa, Calif., Jan. 12.

Richard (Pancho) Gonzales, 67; was national tennis champion twice, in 1948 and 1949; turned pro in 1949— at age 21— and dominated the game between 1954 and 1962, despite never winning a singles title at Wimbledon; at age 41, won a five-hour, 12-minute match with 25-year-old Charlie Pasarell in an opening round match at Wimbledon, the longest in tournament history; known as an intense competitor; some felt he would have won more titles if he hadn't turned pro at such a young age; married and divorced six times to five different women— most recently to Rita Agassi, older sister of Andre; of stomach cancer; in Las Vegas, July 3.

Alfred Goullet, 103; champion professional bicycle racer whose top years were between 1910 and 1920; known as "the Babe Ruth of six-day bike racing;" set a world record of 1 hour, 49 minutes, 8 seconds in the 50-mile race, a mark that still stands; competed at the Velodrome in Newark, N.J., where he set six world records and won more than 400 races; competed in several Madison Square Garden six-day races (in which teams of two riders would alternate sleeping with bicycling), most notably in 1914 when he logged over 2,759 miles; member of Madison Square Garden Hall of Fame, the New York Sports Hall of Fame, the Australian Sports Hall of Fame and the U.S. Bicycling Hall of Fame; of natural causes in a retirement home; in Toms River, N.J., March 11.

David Griggs, 28; starting linebacker for the 1994 AFC champion San Diego Chargers; played five seasons with Miami before being signed as a free agent by San Diego in March 1994; attended Virginia from 1985-88 and was a three-year starter; drafted by the Saints in the seventh round in 1989; in a car crash; in Davie, Fla., June 19.

Alex Groza, 68; All-American center for Kentucky in the late 1940's who was a member of the "Fabulous Five" and whose Wildcat teams won two NCAA titles (1948 and '49) and an Olympic gold medal as the U.S. representative in 1948 Games; finished with 1,744 career points, a mark that led Kentucky for 15 years after his departure and still ranks seventh today; played for two seasons in the NBA with the Indianapolis Olympians, averaging 23.4 and 21.7 points per game from 1949-51; admitted his involvement in a point-shaving scandal while at Kentucky, an act that led to the end of his professional playing career; later became general manager and coach of the Kentucky Colonels and then became general manager of the San Diego Conquistadors, both ABA squads; of cancer; in San Diego, Jan. 21.

Wide World Photos
Alf Goullet

Natl. Cowboy Hall of Fame
Alice Greenough

UPI/Bettmann
Alex Groza

Harry Gumbert, 85; pitcher who spent 15 years in the majors hurling for the New York Giants, St. Louis Cardinals, Cincinnati Reds and Pittsburgh Pirates; played in a total of three World Series: two with the Giants (1936-37) and one with the Cardinals (1942); finished career with a record of 143-113 and a 3.68 ERA; after a long illness; in Wimberley, Texas, Jan. 4.

Walter Haas Jr., 79; heir to Levi Strauss Co. and long-time CEO of world's leading producer of blue jeans; bought Oakland Athletics from Charles O. Finley for $12.7 million in 1980 in order to keep team in Bay Area; sold franchise for only $85 million in 1995 with the condition that the new owners keep club in town; of prostate cancer; in San Francisco, Sept. 20.

William Hackett, 71; guard on Ohio State's 1942 national championship football team; All-America in 1944; co-founder in 1968 of the Cincinnati Bengals with his former OSU coach Paul Brown; following a brief illness; June 2.

Pat Haggerty, 67; spent 28 years as an NFL referee; officiated in three Super Bowls; taught and coached at Denver's Lincoln High School with another former NFL referee, Ben Dreith; made it to Triple A ball in the Detroit Tigers organization following a stint in the Navy during WWII; also officiated basketball in the Western Athletic and Big Eight conferences; of prostate and bone cancer; in Denver, Dec. 9, 1994.

Jack Hand, 82; Associated Press sports reporter who covered numerous championship boxing fights, as well as the World Series and football championships; retired from the AP in 1971 and worked for the NFL as an information and editorial coordinator; later contributed to "Game Day," a weekly NFL program; cause of death not reported; in New Milford, Pa., May 7.

Larry (Butch) Hartman, 54; stock car driver who was a five-time U.S. Auto Club champion in the 1970's; of a heart attack while driving; in Zanesville, Ohio, Dec. 21, 1994.

Thelma Griffith Haynes, 82; former co-owner of the Minnesota Twins; adopted with older brother Calvin by their uncle Clark Griffith, the Hall of Fame pitcher and owner of the Washington Senators; Calvin became president of the Senators when Clark Griffith died in 1955; when her brother moved the newly-renamed Twins to Minnesota in 1961, Thelma became executive vice president and assistant treasurer of the team; after a long illness; in Orlando, Oct. 15.

Joe Heinsen, 79; only man in uniform for each of the last two Chicago baseball pennant-winners; coached for the Cubs in 1945 and the White Sox in 1959, when both teams won their last pennants; Heinsen was associated with baseball for the last seven decades, beginning in 1930 as a semi-professional player and ending in 1994 as the pitching coach at the College of St. Francis; of a heart attack; in Joliet, Ill., July 12.

Billy Hill, 47; head football trainer at Ohio State for the past 21 years; joined the OSU football staff as an assistant trainer in 1971; became head trainer in 1974; former president of the Ohio Athletic Trainers Association and was appointed to the U.S. Olympic Committee's Sports Medicine Council last year; head trainer of the United States' men's track team at the 1984 Olympics; member of the Ohio Athletic Trainers Association Hall of Fame; of a heart attack; in Columbus, Ohio, Feb. 20.

Nat Holman, 98; billed as "the world's greatest basketball player" in the 1920's; New York native who played for New York University and professional teams such as the original Celtics; in 1921 authored the book "Scientific Basketball," a textbook for coaches everywhere that is still referred to today; highly-respected coach for City College of New York, Holman had a 37-year coaching career before retiring with a record of 421-190; his 1950 CCNY team made history by winning both the NCAA and NIT championships; in 1951, several of his players were arrested for point-shaving; he was suspended by the NYC Board of Higher Education before being vindicated and reinstated two years later; his fast-paced collegiate offense became known as "New York style" basketball; elected to Basketball Hall of Fame in 1964; of natural causes; in Riverdale, Bronx, Feb. 12.

Jim Lee Howell, 80; coached the New York Giants to one National Football League title (1956) in three championship game appearances, including the 1958 title game which they lost in overtime to the Baltimore Colts, 23-17, in what is widely considered as pro football's greatest game; compiled a record of 55-29-4 in seven seasons as head coach of the Giants; with assistants like Vince Lombardi and Tom Landry he often said, "I just blow up the footballs and keep order"; also played end on four NFL championship teams with the Giants from 1937 to 1948; played football and basketball at Arkansas in the 1930's; first inductee into the Arkansas Hall of Fame; assistant football coach at Arkansas in 1936; head coach at Wagner from 1947-53; after a long illness; in Lonoke, Ark., Jan. 4.

Vern Huffman, 80; All-America quarterback and basketball guard at Indiana in 1936; named MVP of the Big 10 in football the fall after he lead the Hoosier basketball team to the Big 10 title; third round pick by Detroit in 1937 NFL draft and played with Lions through 1939 season; worked for the FBI following pro football; after a long illness; in Bloomington, Ind., March 18.

Roy Hughes, 84; infielder who played for Cleveland, St. Louis, Philadelphia and the Chicago Cubs over eight seasons; hit .273 with five homers during that time; played for the Cubs in the 1945 World Series, hitting .294 with 3 RBI in six games at shortstop; cause of death not reported; in Asheville, N.C., March 5.

Oakland Athletics

Walter Haas Jr.

Wide World Photos

Nat Holman

Wide World Photos

Jim Lee Howell

Hideko Hyodo, 80; swimmer who became the first Japanese woman to win an Olympic gold medal with a victory in the 200-meter breaststroke at the 1936 Berlin Olympics; that win came in a world-record time of 3 minutes, 3.6 seconds; earned a silver in the same event at the 1932 Los Angeles Olympics, missing the gold by just 0.1 second; first Japanese woman to earn induction into the International Swimming Hall of Fame; of kidney failure; in Tokyo, Feb. 24.

Jamal Jackson, 22; Cleveland State forward who led his squad in scoring (16 ppg) and rebounding (8 pg); was a second team All-Midwestern Collegiate Conference member; slick-playing 6-foot-6-inch forward was a Massachusetts High School legend, having led East Boston High to a state championship in 1992 and his AAU team to a pair of national championships; of a stab wound; in Boston, Aug. 18.

Sidney Jacobs, 87; thoroughbred trainer; began training horses following World War II, in which he was wounded during the Battle of the Bulge; brother of Hall of Fame trainer Hirsch Jacobs; of complications from heart and liver disease; in Queens, N.Y., April 9.

Willie James III, 21 and **Henry Wallace III, 21**; members of Jackson State baseball team who were both killed in June 3 car crash in Jackson, Miss; James was a second baseman and Wallace was an outfielder; their deaths bring to number the number of Jackson State athletes who have been killed in auto accidents in the last seven years.

Vernal (Nippy) Jones, 70; Milwaukee Braves first-baseman who in his final at-bat helped the Braves win a World Series game in 1957; pinch hitting in the 10th inning of Game 4 and the Braves down, 5-4, he was hit in the left foot by a pitch and proved it to doubting umpire Augie Donatelli by showing him the smudge of shoe polish on the ball; he was allowed to take first base and the Braves rallied to win the game and the Series in seven games; hit .267 over eight-year career; of a heart attack; in Sacramento, Calif., Oct. 3.

Sergei Kapustin, 42; member of eight Soviet World Championship hockey teams; played for Moscow Red Army, Spartak and the Soviet Wings, and was a tournament All-Star in the 1976 and '81 Canada Cups; scored 199 goals in 208 games with the Soviet nationals; of a heart attack; in Moscow, July 15.

Jim Katcavage, 60; three-time All-Pro defensive end for the New York Giants who played on its 1956 championship team; the Giants hadn't won a title in 18 years and wouldn't win another for 30 more; 13-year pro who began his career as a fourth-round pick out of the University of Dayton; of a heart attack; in Maple Glen, Pa., Feb. 22.

Henry (Lon) Alonzo Keller, 87; designed the New York Yankees' top hat emblem; created the design shortly after WWII, when teams began to use advertising as a symbol of the end of war-time hardships; noted athletic artist designed thousands of baseball and football program covers; inducted into the New York Sports Museum and Hall of Fame in 1991; cause of death not reported; in De Land, Fla., June 26.

Bryan Kerchal, 23; Connecticut-born winner of the 1994 BASS Masters Classic; first amateur and youngest person ever to win the most prestigious event on the Bass Anglers Sportsman Society Circuit; regarded as one of the up-and-coming stars in the sport of fishing; in a plane crash in Morrisville, N.C., Dec. 13, 1994.

Paul Kipoech, 33; world champion in the 10,000-meter run in 1987; part of the dominating new-breed of Kenya's cross-country runners; finished second at the 1984, '87 and '88 world cross-country championships; quit serious running in 1988 after feuding with Kenyan officials over prize money; after a short illness; in Eldoret, Kenya, March 13.

Bjorn Kjellstrom, 84; native of Sweden who invented the modern compass and was a national champion in ski orienteering and would later introduce North America to the sport of orienteering, which involves the use of a map and a compass to move quickly over unknown parts of a forest—either on foot in warm weather or on skis in the cold; sold his compass with the slogan, "Read this or get lost;" shrewd businessman started the Silva Compass Company in Indiana in 1946; from complications of Parkinson's Disease; in Stockholm, Sept. 14.

Irving Kosloff, 82; bought the NBA's Syracuse Nationals in 1963 after Philadelphia Warriors moved to San Francisco; brought Nats to Philadelphia for 1963-64 season and renamed them the 76ers; owned the club until 1976; during that span the Sixers made the playoffs nine times, brought Wilt Chamberlain back to town and won an NBA title in 1967; the 1972-73 team went 9-73, an NBA record for futility that still stands; sold team to F. Eugene Dixon for $8 million in 1976; of leukemia; in Merion, Pa., Feb. 19.

Jack Kramer, 77; pitcher who played for four different teams during a career that began in 1939; had his best season in 1948 when he went 18-5 for the Boston Red Sox; in 1944, he went 17-13 for the St. Louis Browns and won a World Series decision against the St. Louis Cardinals; three-time all-star held a career record of 95-103; of a brain hemorrhage; in Metairie, La., May 18.

Bill Lange, 67; offensive guard who helped the Los Angeles Rams win the 1951 NFL championship; also played with the Baltimore Colts and the Chicago Cardinals; six-year NFL career cut short by knee injuries; starred for the University of Dayton in the late 1940s; of a heart attack; in Dayton, Ohio, April 5.

Karle Leandersson, 77; three-time Swedish cross-country champion who ran off with the 1949 Boston Marathon in a time of 2 hours, 31 minutes, 50 seconds; preferred to train barefoot over golf courses saying it strengthened his feet; of injuries suffered after being hit by a car while riding his bike; in Sweden, February.

Bobby Lewis, 65; head baseball coach at Pitt for 36 years; his Panther teams compiled a 438-389 record during his tenure; retired as coach in 1990 and as assistant athletic director in 1993; of cancer; in Pittsburgh, Feb. 22.

Cleveland St.

UPI/Bettmann

B.A.S.S.

Jamal Jackson   **Jim Katcavage**   **Bryan Kerchal**

Luis Lopez, 26; former University of New Mexico gymnast and member of 1992 Mexican Olympic team; one of three ex-Lobo gymnasts to die in 1995 (Mark Eaton and Tim Collins were the others); 1991 NCAA high bar champion; withdrew as student at New Mexico in 1991 after being declared ineligible for a monthly $500 stipend he received from the Mexican Gymnastics Federation; of leukemia, in Mexico City, Oct. 10.

Diego Lucero, 93; Uruguayan journalist who was only known scribe to have covered all 15 soccer World Cup finals; an amateur soccer player during the 1920's, covered the first World Cup finals in 1930 in Uruguay; of a heart attack; in Buenos Aires, Argentina, June 4.

Ron Luciano, 57; former Syracuse lineman who stood 6-foot-4 and weight 300 pounds, who became popular and flamboyant AL umpire for 11 years; retired in 1980 and later worked as a television commentator for NBC and authored four books, including, "The Umpire Strikes Back" and "Strike Two;" known for his confrontational nature on the diamond; engaged in memorable battles with Baltimore manager Earl Weaver; worked one World Series and three AL championship series; of a suicide; in Endicott, N.Y., Jan. 18.

Gary MacGregor, 41; World Hockey Association veteran who skated for seven WHA teams over five years; drafted on the second round by the Montreal Canadiens in 1974 but chose to play for the WHA's Chicago Cougars instead; best year was for Chicago in 1974-75 when he accumulated 44 goals and 34 assists; of a heart attack; in Kingston, Ontario, April 20.

Mickey Mantle, 63; Hall of Fame outfielder for the New York Yankees from 1951-68, who retired as the most powerful switch-hitter in baseball history; born in Spavinaw, Okla., on Oct. 20, 1931, and raised in nearby Commerce; named after All-Star catcher Mickey Cochrane; succeeded Joe DiMaggio as Yankee centerfielder in 1952; hit 536 home runs, including nine grand slams, during his 18-year career; also knocked in 1,509 runs and batted .298; hit homers from both sides of the plate in the same game a major league-record 10 times; helped introduce "tape measure home run" into baseball vernacular when he slugged a 565-foot homer off Washington pitcher Chuck Stobbs at Griffith Stadium on Apr. 17, 1953; played in 12 World Series and helped Yankees win title seven times (1951-53,56,58,61-62); still holds all-time Series records for HRs (18), RBI (40), runs scored (42), walks (43) and strikeouts (54); won AL Triple Crown in 1956 with 52 HRs, 130 RBI and .353 batting average; hit 54 HRs in 1961 when he and teammate Roger Maris chased Babe Ruth's single season record of 60 and Maris got 61; finished first or second in AL Most Valuable Player voting six times between 1955 and '64, winning the award in 1956, '57 and '62; slowed by numerous knee injuries which began

when he tore a cartilage in his left knee in Game 2 of 1951 World Series; played in a record 2,401 games for the Yankees and hit a record 266 HRs at Yankee Stadium; club retired uniform No. 7 on June 8, 1969; inducted into Hall of Fame in 1974; of cancer ("the most aggressive anyone on our medical team has ever seen," according to Dr. Goran Klintmalm of the Baylor University Medical Center) following a June 8 liver transplant; in Dallas, Aug. 13.

Tim Mara, 59; former co-owner of NFL New York Giants as well as grandson and namesake of franchise founder; as V.P. and treasurer he paved the way for construction of Giants Stadium and the team's 1976 move to New Jersey; in 1979, after six straight losing seasons, he feuded with uncle and 50-50 co-owner Wellington Mara over whether the club would be better served by naming a new head coach or a new general manager first (Tim wanted a new GM); they finally asked commissioner Pete Rozelle to intervene and Rozelle recommended they hire George Young as GM; Tim sold his half of team to billionaire Robert Tisch for $75 million in 1991 after the Giants won their second Super Bowl; of cancer; in Jupiter, Fla., May 31.

Pierre Marquette, 27; French runner who collapsed shortly after finishing the 1994 New York City Marathon and was pronounced dead on arrival at St. Luke's Hospital; in New York City, Nov. 6, 1994.

Eddie Mast, 46; former Temple and New York Knicks forward; led the Owls to the 1969 NIT championship, and later that year was picked in the third round of the NBA draft by the Knicks; played most of two seasons with New York and finished his career with the Atlanta Hawks; of heart attack; in Easton, Pa., Oct. 18, 1994.

Buster Mathis, 51; rotund boxer who fought former sparring partner Joe Frazier for the so-called New York World Heavyweight Title in 1968 and was knocked out in the 11th round; the fight was staged to crown a successor to Muhammad Ali, who had been stripped of his world title after refusing induction into the military; Mathis later lost a 12-round decision to Ali in a non-title bout in 1971; gained fame as a 300-lb Olympic hopeful in 1964 when he beat Frazier to win the U.S. Trials at the New York World's Fair; went to the Tokyo Games with Frazier in tow as his backup and sparring partner, but when he broke an index finger sparring with Frazier, Mathis had to step aside and Frazier went on to win the gold medal; father of Buster Mathis Jr., who was scheduled to fight Mike Tyson on Nov. 4, 1995; of heart failure, in Grand Rapids, Mich., Sept. 6.

Herb McCracken, 95; former college football player and coach who invented the huddle in 1924 after he realized an opposing team had memorized his squad's signals; ordered his team to gather before each down instead of immediately going to line of scrimmage following each play; of renal impairment; in Boynton Beach, Fla., March 11.

Mickey Mantle

1931–95

by George Vecsey

NEW YORK, Aug. 14— People will mourn the tortured man with the hollow eyes and the prematurely wrinkled face, whose liver went fast, just as his knees had done. But the real reason they are mourning Mickey Mantle today is that he was once a young lion who prowled green urban pastures, sleekly, powerfully, unpredictably.

Before he was Mickey Mantle the flawed Southwestern folk hero, he was Mickey Mantle the athlete. People of a certain age are going around with sad expressions today because of the young Mantle, the one who first captivated them, the one who gave them the intense pleasure of watching an imperfect athletic deity perform extraordinary acts.

There was nobody quite like Mantle in a baseball uniform. Even before fans grew to like him, and then adore him, they were awed by his speed and power. They loved to watch as he bounded toward first base after hitting a simple ground ball to shortstop. Williams and Musial and Killebrew never beat out grounders to short. Mantle did. The hitters who could leg out an infield single were "whippets" or "jack rabbits." Mickey Mantle was leonine. That was the part that turned fans on.

The greatest black players of the era had to keep their psychic lids on. Jackie Robinson nearly had a nervous breakdown containing his anger at racial slurs. Hank Aaron and Frank Robinson and Roberto Clemente had to worry about offending white America with their achievements and competitive personalities. But Mantle, the blond Oklahoman who called Dallas home, could act like a bruiser, like a dude, like a jock.

It's important to remember that the crowd didn't always adore Mantle. He was the heir to the most aloof and elegant Yankee, Joe DiMaggio, who would leave behind one of the great statistics in all of sports: 361 home runs and only 369 strikeouts in his career, a sensational combination of power and self-control.

Mantle would hit 536 homers and strike out 1,710 times, and when he struck out, he hurled his helmet to the ground, exposing his light hair and his crimson complexion. The crowd picked up on his fury and it booed, loud and long.

Wide World Photos

Nineteen-year-old rookie **Mickey Mantle** at spring training camp with the New York Yankees in 1951.

But not as loud and long as the cheering. So many great years and games come to mind (see facing page). Everybody has got a favorite.

A lot of people watched Mantle slug baseballs to the far corners of the American League. These forty-somethings and fifty-somethings became the emotional base of Mickey's status as a legend

But there was a downside to the legend. Some of the young sportswriters in the 1960's broke the omertà, the unspoken code, by suggesting that Mantle drank too much, caroused too much and was destroying his body.

Most fans did not want to know. I called it the "Aw-no, not-the-Mick" syndrome. And a reporter who dwelled on Mantle's self-destructive, boorish side had to remind himself that Mantle's teammates thought he was not only a great player but also a great teammate.

After retirement, Mantle made a living off being the celebrity drunk golfer. Few people worried about his dangerous excesses and his broken family, until Mantle got scared and got sober. And then he was forgiven immediately with a great rush of public sympathy.

It's too bad he didn't have more time to enjoy the affection.

George Vecsey is a sports columnist for *The New York Times*.

Wide World Photos

UPI/Bettmann

Wide World Photos

Ron Luciano   **Buster Mathis**   **Carlos Monzón**

Jay McCreary, 77; guard for Indiana's 1940 NCAA champion basketball team; later coached Louisiana State's basketball team from 1957 to 1965 amassing an 82-115 record; prior to coaching the Tigers, spent several years coaching Muncie (Ind.) High School basketball, and in 1954 his state runner-up squad played in the championship game depicted in the movie "Hoosiers"; after a long illness; in Baton Rouge, La., April 17.

Von McDaniel, 56; had a 7-5 record and a 3.22 ERA in 1957 pitching for the St. Louis Cardinals, where he combined with his brother, Lindy, a pitcher who was a big-leaguer for 21 years; appeared in just two games the following season; following a heart attack and stroke; in Lawton, Okla., Aug. 22.

Dennis Meggs, 54; inventor of revolutionary mooring device, dubbed Megg-Nets, for hockey goal nets that was used in the NHL from 1984 to 1991; net was held in place with magnetic devices but was designed to give upon slight contact; his invention was eventually replaced with Marsh Pegs a flexible insert which requires more bumping to dislodge; of an infection; in Waterloo, Ont., early July.

Louis Meyer, 91; first three-time winner of the Indianapolis 500, winning in 1928, '33 and '36; seven other drivers have since matched his feat; initiated long-standing Indy tradition of drinking milk in Victory Lane; later co-owned Offenhauser engine business whose engines won every Indy 500 from 1947-64; cause of death not reported; in Las Vegas, Oct. 7.

Leo Miles, 64; NFL's supervisor of officials since 1991; served as a game official for 22 years; worked 15 playoff games and three Super Bowls; former athletic director of Howard University; of a heart attack; in Washington, D.C., Sept. 21.

Art Mollner, 82; despite never playing college basketball, earned a spot on the U.S. team that won the first Olympic basketball gold medal at the 1936 Berlin Games; the 6-foot guard earned recognition by playing on AAU teams in the Los Angeles area; of cancer; in the San Fernando Valley, March 16.

Carlos Monzón, 52; former middleweight champion who was regarded as a hero in his native Argentina before he was convicted of killing his girlfriend in 1989; won the title on Nov. 7, 1970, with a 12th-round knockout of Nino Benvenuti in Rome; made a record 14 title defenses before his retirement in 1977; record was 89 wins (61 by knockout), 3 losses, 8 draws and one no-contest in 101 bouts; in a car accident while on furlough from prison; in Santa Rosa de Calchines, Argentina, Jan. 8.

John J. Mooney, 70; highly-regarded horse racing executive, who spent nearly a quarter century as president of the Ontario Jockey Club; resigned in 1976 to run National Stud Farm in Kleinburg, Ontario; son of jockey J.D. Mooney who won the 1924 Kentucky Derby aboard Black Gold; of a heart attack; in Toronto, Dec. 3.

Terry Moore, 82; defensive outfielder who was a member of the St. Louis Cardinals' Gas House Gang in the 1930s and two Cardinal World Series championship teams in 1942 and '46; played entire 11-year major league career in St. Louis and retired in 1948 with a batting average of .280; played in same outfield with Hall of Famers Stan Musial and Enos Slaughter; after a long illness; in Collinsville, Ill., March 29.

Francis (Hap) Moran, 93; former NFL All-Pro who was thought to be the second-oldest living veteran of the NFL; had a 91-yard run from scrimmage that is the oldest team record for the New York Giants; played for several professional teams in the 1920's and 30's including the 1926 NFL Champion Frankford Yellow Jackets, where he served as the team's starting running back and placekicker; cause of death not reported; in New Milford, Conn., Dec. 30, 1994.

James Murray, 25; Scottish boxer who underwent brain surgery following his final round knockout loss to British bantamweight champion Drew Docherty; one of two boxers to die on Oct. 15 (see Restituto Espineli); his death came eight months after American super middleweight Gerald McClellan suffered brain damage in a WBC title fight with champion Nigel Benn in London; from injuries suffered in the ring; in Glasgow, Scotland, Oct. 15.

Lindsey Nelson, 76; Tennessee native who became well-known in New York as one of the Mets' original announcers with Ralph Kiner and Bob Murphy from 1962-78; spent 17 years in New York; covered major events in the NFL, NBA, college basketball and college football (including 26 Cotton Bowls); in his early days with the expansion Mets, decided that he could attract attention away from the popular Yankees by amassing a ghastly collection of colorful sportcoats; one of those jackets rests in the broadcasters wing of the baseball Hall of Fame, where Nelson was enshrined in 1988; went on to teach broadcasting seminars at the University of Tennessee; of a bacterial infection; in Atlanta, June 10.

Ralph Neves, 78; Hall of Fame jockey who, in 1936, walked out of a mortuary after being declared dead; the close-to-fatal accident occurred at Bay Meadows in San Mateo, Calif., where he was pronounced dead after he was thrown into a rail by his mount then trampled by other horses— yet at the morgue he was given a shot of adrenaline in the heart by a doctor friend, a shot that revived him and allowed him to race the next day; he won 3,771 races before retiring in 1964; following a battle with lung cancer; in San Marcos, Calif., July 7.

Chet Nichols, 64; left-handed rookie pitcher with the Boston Braves in 1951 when he went 11-8 and led the National League with an ERA of 2.88; it was the best season of his career; injured his shoulder in the Army and became an off-speed pitcher; finished nine-year career with 34-36 record; of cancer; in Lincoln, R.I., March 27.

UPI/Bettmann

Lindsey Nelson

Wide World Photos

Ralph Neves

Wide World Photos

Harvey Penick

Ichiro Ogimura, 62; Japanese table tennis champion who captured 12 world titles in singles, mixed doubles and team competitions; won his first single and team title in 1954 while a student at Nihon University; beginning that year, he led Japan to five straight championships; was president of the International Table Tennis Federation; of lung cancer; in Tokyo, Dec. 4, 1994.

Alice Greenough Orr, 93; member of the Cowboy and Cowgirl Halls of Fame; rodeo Queen of the Bronc Riders, who went from riding horses on a mail route to performing at Madison Square Garden and on European tours; often performed as a stunt-woman in films; specialty was bronc riding but could perform virtually all rodeo tricks; helped form the Professional Rodeo Cowboys Association in 1936; married rodeo business partner Joe Orr in 1967 after working together over 40 years; cause of death not reported; in Tucson, Ariz., Aug. 20.

Gary Palmisano, 42; Bowling Green soccer coach for 16 seasons; career victory leader at the school with a record of 172-97-25; was a goalie and later an assistant coach for the Falcons before becoming their head coach in 1978; led Bowling Green to a final ranking of 12 at the end of the 1992 season; member of the 1994 World Cup organizing committee; of a heart attack; in Bowling Green, Ohio, Dec. 8, 1994.

Rick (Elvis) Parker, 39; fight promoter who was being investigated by the FBI for fixing boxing matches; promoted some of George Foreman's comeback bouts in the late 1980's; of eight gunshot wounds delivered by boxer Tim Anderson, one of his former fighters who contends Parker attempted to get him to fix fights, and who also contends that he secretly drugged him prior to a Dec., 1993 fight with former NFL lineman Mark Gastineau after he refused to take a dive; in Lake Buena Vista, Fla., April 28.

Harvey Penick, 90; legendary golf instructor who helped launch the careers of Tom Kite and Ben Crenshaw; Kite sent his 1992 U.S. Open championship trophy to Penick; head golf pro at Austin (Tex.) Country Club for 48 years; coached the University of Texas golf team from 1931-1963; teamed with former *Sports Illustrated* writer Bud Shrake to author "Harvey Penick's Little Red Book," which became the biggest-selling sports book in history with over one million copies sold; also wrote "And If You Play Golf, You're My Friend" and "For All Who Love The Game"; one week before his death the bed-ridden Penick gave Crenshaw, who would go on to win the Masters on Apr. 9, one final lesson; after a long illness; in Austin, Tex., April 2.

Fred Perry, 85; last British man to win a Wimbledon singles title, which he captured in 1934, 1935 and 1936; considered the finest male tennis player in Britain's history; typically prevailed no matter what the playing surface or locale; won eight Grand Slam titles, including three U.S. Championships, before turning pro in 1937; led Great Britain to four straight Davis Cup titles from 1933-36; started Fred Perry Sportswear in 1949; member of the International Tennis Hall of Fame since 1975; of complications suffered after a fall; in Melbourne, Australia, Feb. 2.

Rudy Pilous, 80; member of the Hockey Hall of Fame who coached the Chicago Blackhawks from 1957-63 and led that franchise to its most recent Stanley Cup, in 1961; remarkably successful junior hockey coach who guided 75 former players into the NHL, including Stan Mikita and Bobby Hull; played professionally in England, New York and in St. Catharines; of a heart attack; in St. Catharines, Ontario, Dec. 5.

Vada Pinson, 57; two-time All-Star centerfielder for the Cincinnati Reds, who twice led the National League in hits (1961 and '63) and doubles (1959 and '60); hit .343 in 1961 to help lead Reds to NL pennant; one of only six major leaguers to hit 250 home runs and steal 300 bases; the others are Bobby and Barry Bonds, Andre Dawson Willie Mays and Joe Morgan; retired after 1975 season with 2,757 hits and a .286 career average; from the effects of a stroke suffered on Oct. 5; in Oakland; Oct. 21.

Jim (Buster) Poole, 79; three-time All-Pro end for the New York Giants; first University of Mississippi player to be drafted by the NFL; his career, which was interrupted by WWII, spanned through 1937-41 and 1946; was an assistant coach at Ole Miss from 1947-70; lettered each year in three seasons at Mississippi in football, basketball and baseball; of cancer; in Oxford, Miss., Nov. 16, 1994.

Jimmy Powers, 92; long-time sports editor of *The New York Daily News*; attended Marquette and worked for papers in the midwest before landing in New York in 1936; retired in 1959; wrote "Powerhouse" boxing column and was also a commentator for NBC on its Gillette "Friday Night Fights" program; of natural causes; in Bal Harbour, Fla., Feb. 11.

Jack Price, 87; owner of Carry Back, the colt who won the 1961 Kentucky Derby and Preakness Stakes, but failed to capture the Triple Crown when he finished seventh in the Belmont; of congestive heart failure; in Miami, June 7.

Tommy Prothro, 74; football coach who took Oregon State and UCLA to successive Rose Bowls (1965 and '66); coached the NFL's LA Rams in 1971-72 and San Diego Chargers from 1973-78, finishing with a pro record of 35-51-2; spent ten years at Oregon State after taking command in 1955 and compiled a 63-37-2 record; had a 41-18-3 record for UCLA from 1966-70; of cancer; in Memphis, Tenn., May 14.

Rambling Willie, 25; pacing gelding that was one of harness racing's most durable champions; earned $2,038,219 in 305 starts, 128 of which he won; retired as the richest standardbred of all time; paced a long-time record 79 two-minute miles; was humanely destroyed after suffering from laminitis, a hoof inflammation; in Lexington, Ky., Aug. 24.

UPI/Bettmann   UCLA   Wide World Photos

Fred Perry   **Tommy Prothro**   **Bobby Riggs**

Dale Ramsburg, 53; coached West Virginia's baseball team to the most victories in school history, compiling a 540-387-9 record over 27 seasons; won four Atlantic 10 titles; led squad to berth in NCAA tournament in 1994; played shortstop for WVU in 1963 and 1964, leading it to a 54-8 record and two NCAA berths; of cancer; in Morgantown, W.Va., Nov. 3.

Allie (Chief) Reynolds, 79; ace right-hander on six World Series champions with the New York Yankees; described as "two ways great" by Casey Stengel due to his skills as a starter and reliever; in 13 seasons he compiled a record of 182-107 with 49 saves and a 3.30 ERA; went 17-8 in 1951 with no-hitters against Cleveland and Boston; retired in 1954 after suffering an injury in a team bus accident; served as the president of the National Hall of Fame for Famous American Indians; attended Oklahoma A&M (now Okla. St.) on a track scholarship but was discovered as a pitcher by basketball coach Hank Iba after being asked to throw batting practice and then striking out the first four batters he faced; Oklahoma State's baseball stadium bears his name; of complications from lymphoma and diabetes; in Okla. City, Okla., Dec. 26, 1994.

Charlie Richard, 53; football coach and athletic director at Baker University in Kansas; led Baker to the NAIA playoffs each year since 1986; compiled a 123-28-1 record in 15 seasons; returned to coaching just one month after quadruple bypass surgery in 1987; of a heart attack; in Baldwin City, Kan., Dec. 12, 1994.

Robert Riger, 70; artist and photographer who first worked for *Sports Illustrated* and who later won nine Emmy awards for his television work as a producer, director and cinematographer; copyrighted more than 90,000 photos of sporting events between 1950 and 1994; compiled 13 books; of glandular cancer; in Huntington Beach, Calif., May 20.

Bobby Riggs, 77; former No. 1 player in the world and renowned tennis hustler, who gained his greatest fame at age 55 when he lost to 29-year-old Billie Jean King in their "Battle of the Sexes" match at the Astrodome on Sept. 20, 1973; King won in straight sets, 6-4, 6-3, 6-3, before a crowd of 30,472 and a national prime time TV audience; Riggs was the world's top-ranked men's player in 1939 after winning Wimbledon and the U.S. Championships; he won the U.S. title again in 1941; he turned pro in 1942 and starred on the tour until 1950; he was inducted into the International Tennis Hall of Fame in 1967; after a seven-year battle with prostate cancer; in Leucadia, Calif., Oct. 25.

John Rodolph, 31; Olympic wheelchair racer who set world record of 18 minutes, 55 seconds for 10 kilometers at Salt Lake City in August; served as an alternate on the 1984 U.S. Olympic team; of injuries suffered when a dump truck and pickup truck collided and slid into him while he was training; in Rio Rancho, N.M., Oct. 10.

Saul Rogovin, 71; right-hander who led the American League with an ERA of 2.78 with both the Detroit Tigers and Chicago White Sox in 1951; pitched 16 innings during one game against the Boston Red Sox in 1952; also hurled for Baltimore and Philadelphia before a sore arm ended his career in 1957; went 14-9 with White Sox in 1952 and was 48-48 lifetime; later became a high school teacher; of cancer; in New York City, Jan. 23.

Bernard Rollin, 50; Staten Island runner who collapsed during the 1994 New York City marathon and was pronounced dead on arrival at St. Luke's Hospital; in New York City, Nov. 6, 1994.

Wilma Rudolph, 54; called "the Jesse Owens of women's track and field"; stricken with polio as a child and did not walk until age 8; became an Olympic gold medalist at age 20; in 1960, at Rome, she became the first American woman to win three track and field golds in one Olympics; captured the 100-meter and 200-meter dashes and the 4x100-meter relay; also won bronze medal in 1956 4x100-meter relay; won Sullivan Award in 1961; member of the National Track and Field, Women's Sports Foundation and Black Athletes Halls of Fame; of brain cancer; in Brentwood, Tenn., Nov. 12, 1994.

Archie San Romani, 82; overcame a badly-mangled right leg from a car accident as a boy to become one of the world's leading milers; went to Kansas State Teachers College in the 1930's, broke several world relay and collegiate mile and 1,500-meter records; made the 1936 Olympic team, placing fourth behind winner John Lovelock of New Zealand and medalists Glen Cunningham of the U.S. and Luigi Beccali of Italy in epic 1,500 meters; of a heart attack; in Auberry, Calif., Nov. 8, 1994.

Jack Shepard, 63; All-America catcher for Stanford in 1953, and his .362 career average is still a Cardinal record; later played for the Pittsburgh Pirates, where he hit .304 in 82 games as a rookie in 1954; major league career ended in 1956 after 12 homers, 75 RBI and a career .260 average; of pneumonia; in Atherton, Calif., Dec. 31, 1994.

David Shotkoski, 30; replacement pitcher in 1995 for the Atlanta Braves; originally signed out of high school by the Braves after being a fourth round selection in 1985; in six minor league season he was 18-24 with a 5.07 ERA; of a gunshot wound suffered during an apparent robbery attempt; in West Palm Beach, Fla., March 24.

John C. (Hi) Simmons, 89; University of Missouri baseball coach from 1937 to 1973, where he compiled a career record of 481-294-3; won an NCAA title in 1954 and 11 conference championships between 1952 and 1964; member of the State of Missouri Sports Hall of Fame and the American Baseball Coaches Association Hall of Fame; cause of death not reported; in Columbia, Mo., Jan. 12.

Wide World Photos

Hockey Hall of Fame

Wide World Photos

Bill Spivey   **Anatoli Tarasov**   **J.C. Tremblay**

James Smiddy, 71; nation's winningest high school basketball coach, recorded 1,216 wins in 44 years; the girl's coach guided Charleston (Tenn.) High for eight years and Bradley (Tenn.) Central for 36; final record was 1,216-201; of a heart attack; in Chattanooga, Tenn., July 19.

Brian Smith, 54; scored 10 goals in two NHL seasons with Minnesota and Los Angeles from 1967-69; became the sports director and a broadcaster for CJOH television in Ottawa; studio host for Ottawa Senators hockey games; of a gunshot wound to the head; in Ottawa, Aug. 2.

Charley Smith, 57; journeyman infielder who was traded by the St. Louis Cardinals to the New York Yankees for Roger Maris on Dec. 8, 1966; also played for two major league teams in both New York and Chicago; otherwise, he hit .239 with 69 HRs over 10 seasons; cause of death not reported; in Washoe, Nev., Nov. 29, 1994.

Bill Spivey, 66; seven-foot Kentucky star in the early 1950's who never realized his dream to play in the NBA because of his alleged involvement in a point shaving scandal; acquitted of perjury charges and never found guilty of any wrongdoing, yet he was thrown off the Kentucky team and then banned from the NBA for life; considered to be the best big man of his era; scored 1,213 points during his college career and had 22 points and 21 rebounds in the 1951 NCAA title game; played minor league basketball; of natural causes; in Quepos, Costa Rica, May 8.

Enoch Staley, 77; stock car racing promoter who co-founded North Wilkesboro Speedway in 1947; was chief steward for NASCAR events after its inception in 1948; drove the pace car at races in what is now the Winston Cup Series; after suffering a stroke; in Winston-Salem, N.C., May 22.

Franz Stampfl, 81; Austrian-born running coach who used the principles of interval training to guide Roger Bannister to the first sub-4:00 mile (3:59.4) on May 6, 1954; later emigrated to Australia where coached several runners, including future world record-holder Ron Clarke and Ralph Doubell; of natural causes; in Melbourne, Australia, Mar. 19.

Dick Steinberg, 60; general manager of NFL's New York Jets since 1990; previously worked with the Los Angeles Rams and New England Patriots as a scout and personnel director and helped lead both teams to Super Bowl appearances in the 1980's; known for his skills in drafting collegiate players, knowledge of football and strong work ethic; of stomach cancer; in New York City, Sept. 25.

Gil Steinke, 76; coached Texas A&I (now Texas A&M-Kingsville) to six NAIA football championships; credited with helping to integrate football in Texas; spent four seasons with the Philadelphia Eagles after playing halfback and defensive back at Texas A&I; coached from 1954 to 1977 and went 182-61-4; had only two losing seasons and retired with a 39-game winning streak; after a long illness; in Austin, Tex., May 10.

Roderick Stephens, 85; yachtsman and boating innovator who sailed in three America's Cup defense campaigns; helped design three America's Cup yachts: *Ranger* in 1937, *Columbia* in 1958 and *Constellation* in 1964; earned the U.S. Medal of Freedom for his work in developing the DUKW amphibious Army vehicle in World War II; of natural causes; in Scarsdale, N.Y., Jan. 10.

Arthur Stoner, 25; the first black cowboy to win the International Professional Rodeo Association's bronc riding championship; won the IPRA bareback bronc riding championship in 1991, 1992 and 1994; of meningitis; in Nashville, Tenn., March 17.

Woody Strode, 80; former UCLA football star who, along with college teammate Kenny Washington, signed with the Los Angeles Rams 1946, breaking the NFL's long-time color barrier by becoming the first blacks to play in the NFL in 12 years; later became an accomplished actor, earning supporting and starring roles in several films, including "Spartacus" and "The Man Who Shot Liberty Valance"; of lung cancer; in Glendora, Calif., Dec. 31, 1994.

Rev. Robert Sunderland, 66; athletic director at the University of San Francisco from 1984 to 1990 who reintroduced USF to basketball in 1985 after it had been dropped in 1982 following recruiting violations and player payoffs; helped restore dignity to a program that had won two NCAA championships in the 1950's; became commissioner of the West Coast Athletic Conference in the 70's; of cancer; in San Francisco, Jan. 5.

Rick Talley, 61; sports columnist and author; also hosted a sports talk radio show in Las Vegas; journalist for three newspapers between 1968-1987: *Chicago Today*, the *Chicago Tribune* and the *Los Angeles Daily News*; honored in 1987 by the Associated Press Sports Editors as the country's top sports columnist; was Illinois sportswriter of the year in 1973 and 1976; co-authored three books with former major leaguer Jay Johnstone; of brain cancer; in Las Vegas, Aug. 8.

Anatoly Tarasov, 76; head coach of the Soviet national hockey team for 24 years and CSKA, a Soviet hockey club, for 29 years; led the Soviet national team to a world championship every year between 1963-71; also coached teams to 11 European world championships and gold medals in the Olympics at the 1964, 1968 and 1972 games; developed Russia's distinctive finesse style of play; first European coach inducted into the Hockey Hall of Fame; after a long illness; in Moscow, June 23.

Brent Thurman, 25; one of the nation's top rodeo cowboys; bull rider and two-time National Finals Rodeo qualifier who earned nearly $70,000 in 1993 and posted career earnings of better than $160,000; first bull rider to die from injuries sustained in the NFR since the rodeo began in 1959; of injuries suffered on Dec. 11 when a bull stepped on his neck; in Las Vegas, Dec. 17, 1994.

NCAA

Jim Van Valkenburg

UPI/Bettmann

Zoilo Versalles

Basketball Hall of Fame

Margaret Wade

J.C. Tremblay, 55; defenseman for the Montreal Canadiens on five Stanley Cup champions from 1965-71; considered a great rushing defenseman, he scored 57 goals and had 306 assists through his 794-game career, which lasted from 1959 to 1974; played in seven All-Star games; one of the first NHL players to jump to the rival World Hockey Association in 1972, when he went to the Quebec Nordiques; of kidney cancer; in Montreal, Dec. 7, 1994.

Cecil Upshaw, 53; right-hander who had 27 saves for Atlanta in 1969, helping the Braves to an NL West title; spent nine years and 348 games in the majors, accumulating a 34-36 record, 86 saves and a 3.13 ERA; also pitched for the Astros, Indians, Yankees and White Sox; of a heart attack; in Lawrenceville, Ga., Feb. 7.

Tommy Valando, 72; race horse owner whose first horse, Fly So Free, won the Breeders' Cup Juvenile and the Eclipse Award as the 2-year-old champion; over a four-year career, Fly So Free won $2.5 million before retiring as a stallion; his horses always wore light-blue-and-white silks; became famous as a music publisher; of pneumonia; in West Palm Beach, Fla., Feb. 14.

Jim Van Valkenburg, 67; NCAA statistician who helped create the ratings formula for picking teams to play in the Div. I men's basketball championship tournament; worked as a sports writer for The Associated Press from 1954-68; wrote the first history of women's college basketball for the centennial edition of the NCAA basketball records book; of complications from illness; in Merriam, Kan., Sept. 11.

Zoilo Versalles, 55; shortstop who led the Minnesota Twins to the pennant in 1965, the same year he became the first Latin-American player to win the American League MVP award; hit .273 with 19 homers and 77 RBI's, led the league in doubles (45), triples (12) and runs (126) and won a Gold Glove; was never able to duplicate those feats over his 12 major league seasons, in which he averaged .242 and accumulated 95 home runs; fell on hard times later in life, and was forced to sell his MVP trophy, All-Star rings and Gold Glove award; cause of death not reported; in Bloomington, Minn., June 9.

Joe Vetrano, 76; the San Francisco 49ers first placekicker when the team played in the All-America Football Conference in 1946; at one point kicked an AAFC record 108 consecutive extra points; four-year career ended in 1950 when the struggling league reduced its roster size, limiting the luxury of having specialty players; of heart failure; in San Francisco, May 10.

Margaret Wade, 82; the first woman inducted into the Basketball Hall of Fame after her election in 1986; coached Delta State to three consecutive AIAW national titles from 1975-77; in her six seasons as coach, Delta State went 157-23 and set a record 51-game winning streak from 1974-76; the Wade Trophy for academics and community service as well as player performance has been presented in her name every year since 1978; before moving up to Delta State, Wade coached for 21 years at Cleveland (Miss.) High School where she compiled a 453-89-6 record; of cancer; in Cleveland, Miss., Feb. 16.

James L. (Bud) Walton, 73; billionaire retailer who earned his wealth with brother Sam through Wal-Mart stores; made a $15 million donation that helped construct the 19,200-seat University of Arkansas basketball arena that bears his name for him; of an aneurysm; in Miami, March 21.

Norris Weese, 43; former quarterback for the Denver Broncos who backed up Craig Morton from 1976-1979; started six games in 1979 before injuring his knee; career totals: completed 143 of 251 passes for 1,887 and 7 touchdowns, placing him third on the all-time Broncos proficiency list; played baseball and football at the University of Mississippi also played in the World Football League; of bone cancer; in Denver, Jan. 20.

Woody Williams, 82; former Cincinnati Reds infielder who, in 1943, tied a National League record when he got a hit in 10 consecutive at-bats; career .250 hitter who hit one big league home run in four seasons; also played for the Brooklyn Dodgers; from a virus infection; in Appomattox, Va., Feb. 24.

Peter Wisher, 84; Gallaudet University coach and athletic director who developed a new dance genre for the deaf and founded the Gallaudet Dance Company; was an assistant basketball coach at the University of Maryland before going to Gallaudet as a coach and physical education professor; of complications from injuries suffered in an car accident; in Washington, D.C., Oct. 8.

Bob Young, 53; former coach with the Houston Oilers, the University of Houston and the Houston Gamblers of the United States Football League; coached the Oilers' offensive line from 1990-1994; played 11 seasons in the NFL for St. Louis, Houston and New Orleans; earned All-Pro twice; played five seasons in the AFL with Denver Broncos; of a heart attack; in Houston, June 17.

Harold O. Zimman, 78; member of the U.S. Olympic Committee; owned H.O. Zimman Inc., a publishing company that produced, among other things, magazines and programs for athletic events; was on the executive board and was vice-chair of the United States Tennis Association Olympic tennis committee; awarded the Olympic Order for meritorious service to the Olympic movement in 1994; the football field at his alma mater, Tufts University, is named in his honor; of heart failure; in Beverly, Mass., Dec. 14, 1994.

Whitey Zimmerman, 65; equipment manager for the Atlanta Falcons; began as an NFL equipment manager in 1962 with the St. Louis Cardinals before joining the Falcons in 1966; twice named NFL's Equipment Manager of the Year; cause of death not reported; in Suwanee, Ga., Nov. 3, 1994.

French writer and educator **Baron Pierre de Coubertin** saw his vision of a Modern Olympic Games become reality a century ago when over 300 athletes from 14 nations competed peacefully in Athens.

TIME-OUT

Greek Revival

*The Modern Olympics began 100 years ago in Athens
thanks mainly to the efforts of an idealistic Frenchman.*

The greatest amateur athletic contests in fifteen centuries were conceived and staged by a small international group led by the French writer and educational thinker Baron Pierre de Coubertin, who thought a revival of the games of the ancient Greeks might soothe what ailed the modern world. Even if they didn't end military conflict, wrote Coubertin, the games might produce "an army of sportsmen [that] would be more human, more pitying in the struggle and more calm and gentle afterward."

Coubertin was a man of many influences— a historian, the son of an artist, and an enthusiastic oarsman and fencer, though a small one. He also, according to the writer Peter Andrews, even "dabbled in nudism."

Born in 1863, Coubertin was profoundly affected by the French defeat in the Franco-Prussian War of 1870-71. Having read the works of the headmaster of England's Rugby school he thought that French youth should be educated in something close to the English and American traditions that combined school studies with character-building athletics. By the late 1880s, he was championing these fields of valor and deploring the commercial instinct that turned the amateur athlete into a "paid gladiator."

Coubertin had visited Greece to view the sensational discoveries made there by German archeologists unearthing the ancient ruins of Olympia. In Paris in 1892, he put forward his idea for a second coming of the Olympiad before the Athletic Sports Union. But his dreamy call to "export oarsmen, runners, fencers" in "the cause of peace" did not win over the gathering.

Two years later, he brought together the first International Athletic Congress, at the Sorbonne, where representatives from nine countries struggled to produce a workable definition of amateurism, a search that would continue to elude Athletic Congresses for decades.

The Baron proposed that his native city host the reborn Olympic Games in 1900. But his pitch failed to convince the assembled delegates who, taken with their mystical connection to the ancients, sang the Greek "Hymn to Apollo" and voted on June 23, 1894 to put on Coubertin's amateur pageant in Athens, not Paris, and in two years, not six. The burden moved quickly back to Coubertin to convince the Greek government to host the world's athletes.

Over the centuries, several efforts to revive the Olympics had failed. The biggest problem facing this attempt was the lack of a finished site. Coubertin had generated the necessary international momentum to bring the Games back to Greece, but if the merchant Georgios Averoff hadn't offered to fund the entire restoration of the Olympic stadium (originally built in 143 B.C.) it is questionable whether the Games would have come off as scheduled. But they did open— on April 6, 1896, by the Roman calendar.

Nathan Ward is an associate editor at *American Heritage* magazine. He also writes about boxing and other sports.

A crowd of 40,000 filled the newly-rebuilt **Olympic Stadium** in Athens for the opening ceremonies of the first Modern Olympic Games on April 6, 1986. The United States team, which arrived the night before, performed well in their new surroundings, winning nine of 12 track and field events during the Games.

The American team that would prove so dominant at Athens arrived only the night before the opening ceremony, not realizing the Greeks were still on the old Julian calendar.

In the stadium, 40,000 Greeks and a number of American sailors watched the opening proceedings, with perhaps 40,000 more looking on from the surrounding hills. The King of Greece made a speech, there was a tremendous launching of doves, and the track and field events began.

Despite the fact they trained little during their 12-day boat ride from New York, the Americans did surprisingly well— winning seven of nine events on the first day.

James Connolly had wrenched his back so badly at his bon voyage party that his teammates had to help him in and out of chairs during the journey. By landfall he had recovered enough to become the first gold medalist of the Modern Olympics when he won the "hop, step, and jump" (now triple jump). Connolly had trained for the American "hop, *skip*, and jump," but added a second hop, as the olympic version required.

"I had not jumped the two hops since I was 12-years-old," he recalled. "I seemed to soar, and as I landed in the pit a tremendous cheer went up..." He had leaped 44-feet, 11¾ inches, a yard better than anyone else. His teammate Bob Garrett had a similarly lucky experience with the discus, which he had never seen in regulation size before winning the event on that strange, magnificent day. For more information on the 1896— and subsequent— Olympiads, see the Olympic Games chapter starting on page 247.

Baron de Coubertin, who had brought more than 300 of the world's athletes from 14 different countries together in Athens, would head the International Olympic Committee until 1925. He died in his adopted home of Geneva in 1937, and his body was buried in that international city.

His heart, however, was brought back to Olympia for burial, as he had wished.

1921
75 years ago

When asked about it decades later, Jack Dempsey remembered his "Fight of the Century" against the Frenchman Georges Carpentier as "probably the worst mismatch in the history of the heavyweight division."

But even if the July 2 bout at Boyle's Thirty Acres should never have been made, it did earn the first million dollar gate— twice that of any previous prizefight— and drew nearly 90,000 spectators, also a record. News reporters claimed the fight's crowd was the largest gathering of famous Americans in history, from Rockefellers, Astors, Vanderbilts and Roosevelts to Al Jolson, George M. Cohan, and Henry

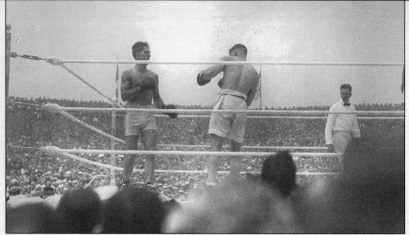

Georges Carpentier (left) evades heavyweight champion **Jack Dempsey** in the early going of their July 2, 1921, championship fight at Boyle's Thirty Acres in Jersey City, N.J. Dempsey caught up with the challenger in the fourth round and knocked him out in front of an outdoor crowd of 90,000.

Ford. In France, a squad of six Army airplanes waited to flash the outcome to Parisians: red lights for a Carpentier victory, white for the American.

On paper, the two fighters might not have belonged together, but Carpentier's slender build (he weighed only 172 pounds) and tendency to claim low blows in fights he was losing were overlooked by smitten sportswriters, who eagerly swallowed the good guy vs. bad guy hype put out by promoter Tex Rickard. Carpentier, after all, had fought in The Great War while Dempsey had only recently been acquitted of trying to avoid service.

Carpentier was the world light heavyweight champion, a title he had taken from Battling Levinsky the year before. He was also exotic and undeniably handsome— his blond hair often slicked back as he entered the ring, looking like F. Scott Fitzgerald having an after-dinner cigarette. "George sure was a beautiful-looking guy," observed the man who later flattened him.

The Dempsey-Carpentier fight was one of the first to attract large numbers of women to the sport. And even the English playwright George Bernard Shaw, who had seen the graceful Frenchman knock out the British heavyweight champion, thought style would prevail and Carpentier might somehow beat the meaner, heavier Dempsey.

Rickard spent $250,000 to build an all-pine outdoor arena in the Jersey marsh near Jersey City, N.J. As it was being constructed, Carpentier caused a considerable commotion by training in secret. He's perfecting a "secret" punch, said his handlers. More like he's practicing "ten-second naps," wrote the skeptical Ring Lardner after his third attempt to enter the Long Island training grounds.

On the day of the fight, Rickard supposedly asked Dempsey not to kill the Frenchman, who made his heroic entrance to the accompaniment of the "Marseillaise." Carpentier's eccentric trainer then went to the champion's corner and tried to put the evil eye on Dempsey, who had a good laugh.

The columnist Sophie Treadwell wrote that as he entered the square of his execution Carpentier wore "a strange, strained and crooked smile" as if he knew "the jig was up."

It was. After making Dempsey chase him awkwardly for several rounds, landing some jabs and one good right hand, Carpentier went down under a series of vicious blows in the fourth. French planes flashed the glum news over Paris. The same American reporters who had favored the game foreigner now wrote of his brave effort against the savage champion.

Dempsey, who would fight in all five million-dollar gates in the Twenties, also praised Carpentier's courage: "He fought until unconscious. That's all you can ask of anybody."

On Sept. 6, 1920, Detroit radio station WWJ had made the first broadcast of a sporting event by calling the three-round Dempsey-Billy Miske fight from Benton Harbor, Mich.

Ten months later, WJZ in Newark, N.J., aired the Dempsey-Carpentier fight—the first truly big sports event on radio. Technically, it was a live broadcast, but it certainly wasn't instantaneous. Not when you consider that Major J. Andrew White, called in his descriptions of the action from a ringside telephone to J.O. Smith, who was sitting at a desk in a railroad porters' tin shed. Smith copied down White's account, and read the words to a spellbound radio audience, thousands of whom had purchased their sets just for this event.

On Aug. 5, baseball at last debuted on the air, when KDKA's Harold Arlen gave a play-by-play account of the National League game between the visiting Philadelphia Phillies and the Pittsburgh Pirates at Forbes Field.

The 26-year-old Arlen, who was a Westinghouse foreman and nighttime studio announcer, called the game over a converted telephone, sitting in a field-level box as the Bucs beat the Phils, 8-5. "Our guys at KDKA didn't even think that baseball would last on radio," admitted Arlin, who also narrated the first tennis and football contests over the air that year, just in case.

But even if the on-air banter was often inaudible, the fit was immediately evident between baseball— with its dramatic pauses, cracking bats, and bellowing umpires— and the homey new medium. By the end of the following year over three million American households had at least one radio with which to invite baseball in.

1946
50 years ago

The first New Year's Day since the end of World War II belonged to a 20-year-old Merchant Marine veteran named Bobby Layne.

Layne, the quarterback of the University of Texas, not only led the 10th-ranked Longhorns to a 40-27 Cotton Bowl victory over Missouri, he was also personally responsible for every point his team scored.

Layne had been able to make the team as a freshman in 1944 because of wartime rules. He went into the U.S. merchant marine in '45 and when the war ended he was discharged the last weekend of October— the day Texas lost its only game of the season, a 7-6 squeaker to Rice.

The Cotton Bowl, which was celebrating its 10th year as a postseason classic, was like Homecoming Day for Layne, a Dallas native who had starred with SMU's Doak Walker at Highland Park High School.

Layne's afternoon on the gridiron went like this: he passed for two touchdowns, ran for three more and caught a 50-yard scoring strike from halfback Ralph Ellsworth. He also kicked four extra points.

Otherwise, he hit All-America end Hub Bechtol with eight passes, and completed 11 of 12 attempts for 158 yards. The game set Cotton Bowl team records for points scored (67), yards rushing (610), yards passing (340), total yards gained (950) and most first downs (41). It remained the highest scoring Cotton Bowl game until 1985.

Layne quarterbacked Texas to an 8-2 record in 1946 and a 10-1 mark in '47, the year he made Consensus All-America. Later, as one of the most colorful stars in the NFL of the 1950s, he led the Detroit Lions to three league championships.

A notorious drinker who lived life hard and died when his liver gave out in 1986, Layne once said, "If I'd have known I was going to live this long, I'd have taken better care of myself."

That line was quoted in the summer of 1995 by another Dallas resident (by way of Oklahoma), Mickey Mantle.

1971
25 years ago

Before the flimsy concept of the "Superfight" there was the incredible first meeting of Muhammad Ali and Joe Frazier on March 8, 1971. It was simply called "The Fight."

Their bout was a first for boxing on a number of fronts: each man claimed the undivided heavyweight championship and neither had suffered a professional loss.

Ali had been champion from 1964 to 1967, when he was stripped of his title for refusing induction into the army on religious grounds. After a three and a half year exile,

A stunned **Muhammad Ali** finds himself on the canvas after **Joe Frazier** connected with a left to the jaw in the 15th round of "The Fight" at Madison Square Garden on March 8, 1971. Frazier triumphed that night by unanimous decision, but Ali won their second and third meetings in 1974 and '75.

he won the right to box again and scored technical knockouts in two sloppy fights with Jerry Quarry and Oscar Bonavena. Thus revived, Ali challenged Frazier, the man who had torn through the division in his absence and claimed his crown.

The bout at the brand new Madison Square Garden was big enough before it turned into a referendum on the U.S. war in Vietnam. Ali brought the rest of the country into "The Fight" which he saw as a battle between the fast, outspoken "People's Champ" and the Establishment's "Uncle Tom."

This pointed bit of promotion pushed the match beyond its conventional sports boundaries as no fight since the second Louis-Schmeling bout in 1938— and just as unfairly. Schmeling was no Nazi, and Frazier, a hard-working Olympic gold medalist from a poor South Carolina Baptist family, was no apologist for the Pentagon.

When the two men actually got into the ring before a packed Garden and millions of pay-TV customers in theaters around the world, the most-hyped fight in history somehow lived up to its billing.

Frazier, bobbing and moving relentlessly forward, was "the human equivalent of a war machine," wrote Norman Mailer for *Life* magazine.

Ali wore red tassels on his white shoes for the bout, designed to show off his footwork.

Instead they became a symbol of his declining legs, especially when he was obliged to stand and trade punches or hold the pounding Frazier on the ropes.

Ali landed the majority of blows, but played costly games in the middle rounds. Frazier drove the action and led going into the last round, when the plan Yank Durham and Eddie Futch had devised for him finally paid off. Futch had trained his man to throw the left hook over Ali's uppercut; it landed hard in the 11th and in the 15th it brought him down. Ali, who hadn't been dropped in over seven years, was up at the count of four and rallied before time ran out.

"That round showed me that Muhammad Ali was the most valiant fighter I've ever seen," the bout's referee Arthur Mercante told Thomas Hauser. He nevertheless scored it 8-6-1 for Frazier. Ali immediately wanted a rematch and through his high-spirited alter-ego, Bundini Brown, reportedly said, "Get the gun ready— we're going to set traps."

The fight was decisive enough to throw even the sagest observers off their game. "If they fought a dozen times," Red Smith claimed afterward, "Joe Frazier would whip Muhammad Ali a dozen times; and it would get easier as they went along."

In fact, Frazier was never again as good as that night, and Ali, who won their two subsequent meetings, may have fought his best fight, too, even in losing. ❐

Other Milestones

1896
(100 years ago)

On Feb. 14, Yale beats Johns Hopkins, 2-1, in the **first intercollegiate ice hockey game**. Nine months later, several Yale graduates organize the country's first amateur ice hockey league in New York.

The first **World Figure Skating Championship** is held in St. Petersburg, Russia, with Gilbert Fuchs of Germany taking the gold medal in the men's-only competition. There are no American competitors. While women would first apply to compete by 1902, a ladies event was not introduced until 1906.

1921
(75 years ago)

Judge Kenesaw Mountain Landis begins his stormy 24-year tenure as baseball's first commissioner on Jan. 21. Landis replaces the three-man national commission that had ruled the game since the American and National Leagues merged in 1903.

The **first NCAA track and field championships** are held June 17-18 at the University of Chicago. The meet, which attracts athletes from 62 schools, is won by Illinois with Notre Dame second and Iowa third.

On June 25, **Jock Hutchison**, a British-born golf pro from Chicago, becomes the first American citizen to win the British Open. He defeats amateur Roger Wethered by nine strokes in a 36-hole playoff at St. Andrews, where he was born in 1994.

The eight baseball players known as **the Chicago Black Sox**, who were accused of throwing the 1919 World Series, are acquitted by a Chicago jury on Aug. 2, and freed on a technicality (signed confessions of several players had mysteriously disappeared). Nevertheless, baseball commissioner Landis immediately bans them all from the game for life.

Ty Cobb becomes, at 34, the youngest player ever to amass 3,000 career hits when he singles off Boston's Elmer Myers on Aug. 19th.

1936
(60 years ago)

The **Baseball Hall of Fame** announces on Feb. 2 that Ty Cobb, Babe Ruth, Honus Wagner, Christy Mathewson and Walter Johnson are the new hall's charter members. Cobb, who is named on 222 of 226 ballots, is the leading vote-getter in the nationwide poll of players and sportswriters.

University of Chicago halfback **Jay Berwanger**, who won the first Heisman Trophy in 1935, becomes the first player ever selected in the NFL's college draft when the Philadelphia Eagles pick him on Feb. 8. He declined to sign with either the Eagles or the Chicago Bears, who acquired his rights later in the year.

In the **longest game in NHL history**, the Detroit Red Wings and Montreal Maroons play eight full 20-minute periods before their scoreless tie is broken at 16:30 of the ninth period at the Montreal Forum. Maroons rookie right winger Mud Brunteau beats Detroit goalie Lorne Chabot at 2:20 a.m. on March 24 for the win.

America's **Jesse Owens** dominates the Summer Olympics in Berlin, winning an unprecedented four gold medals in track and field. With the start of World War II in 1939, the next Olympiad would not take place until London in 1948.

1946
(50 years ago)

With World War II over for a year, international **grand slam tournaments resume** in tennis and golf. Back on the calendar are Australia, France and Wimbledon in tennis, and the Masters, U.S. Open and British Open in golf. Elsewhere, the Tour de France resumes after a six-year absence and the Indianapolis 500 returns after four.

On Jan. 12, the National Football League gives owner Dan Reeves permission to move his league champion **Cleveland Rams** to Los Angeles. In the fall, the NFL is challenged for the public's attention by the new, innovative **All-America Football Conference**. The brainchild of *Chicago Tribune* sports editor Arch Ward, who originated baseball's All-Star Game and football's annual Chicago College All-Star Game, the AAFC fielded eight teams in two divisions—the Brooklyn Dodgers, Buffalo Bisons, Miami Seahawks and New York Yankees in the East; and the Chicago Rockets, Cleveland Browns, Los Angeles Dons and San Francisco 49ers in the West. The Browns would win all four AAFC championships before the league folded following the 1949 season.

Jackie Robinson debuts as organized baseball's first recognized black player on April 18 as a 2nd baseman for the International League's Montreal Royals. Robinson would finish the season as the league's top hitter (.349) and leader of the Royals' Junior World Series champions. In 1947, he would break major league baseball's color line with Brooklyn.

Assault becomes the seventh horse to win thoroughbred racing's Triple Crown, taking the Belmont Stakes by three lengths over Natchez on June 1.

Brooklyn and **St. Louis** both finish with identical 96-58 records in the National League to force the first regular season pennant playoff in major league history. The Cardinals win the best-of-3-game series, 2-0, then defeat Boston in Game 7 of the World Series as Enos Slaughter scores the winning run from first on a double by Harry Walker while Red Sox 2nd baseman Johnny Pesky holds the ball.

No. 1 Army and **No. 2 Notre Dame** meet in a battle of unbeatens before 74,000 at Yankee Stadium on Nov. 9 and come away with a scoreless tie. Three weeks later, on Dec. 2, the final Associated Press poll votes the Irish (8-0-1) the national championship over the Cadets (9-0-1). The difference comes down to Navy, their only common opponent. Notre Dame routed the Midshipmen, 28-0, while Army struggled to a 21-18 victory.

1951
(45 years ago)

A major **basketball scandal** shakes college sports on Feb. 18 when three star players for defending NCAA and NIT champion City College of New York (CCNY) are arrested for fixing games. Investigators soon find that the crookedness is widespread. Before the ordeal is over, 35 student-athletes from seven schools are found guilty of fixing 86 games in 22 cities.

Boston center Ed Macauley scores 20 points to lead the East over the West, 111-94, at Boston Garden in the **first NBA All-Star Game**. The contest is witnessed by a crowd of 10,094 on March 2.

Jersey Joe Walcott, a 37-year-old four-time loser in heavyweight title fights, finally wins the championship on July 18, knocking out champion Ezzard Charles in the 7th round at Forbes Field in Pittsburgh.

Bobby Thompson hits the **"shot heard 'round the world"** on Oct. 3, winning Game 3 of a regular season playoff series against Brooklyn. The "shot" is a 3-run homer off the Dodgers Ralph Branca in the bottom of the ninth inning at the Polo Grounds. The Giants had trailed the Dodgers by 13½ games in the NL standings on Aug. 11.

1961
(35 years ago)

The **American League expands** for the first time since becoming a major league in 1901. The Los Angeles Angels and the new Washington Senators are added while the old Senators franchise moves to Minneapolis-St. Paul and becomes the Minnesota Twins. The National League will expand by two teams— the Houston Colt .45s and New York Mets— in 1962.

Other Milestones (Cont.)

AL expansion and a longer 162-game schedule benefit New York's **Roger Maris** as he breaks Babe Ruth's single season home run record on Oct. 1. Maris belts No. 61 off Boston rookie Tracy Stallard in the fourth inning of the final game of the season. The ball is caught by fan Sal Durante, who sells it for $5,000. On July 18, commissioner Ford Frick had announced that Ruth's record "cannot be broken unless some batter hits 61 or more within his club's first 154 games."

1966
(30 years ago)

Baseball's Players Association elects 48-year-old **Marvin Miller** to be its first full time executive director on March 5. Miller was previously the assistant to the president of the United Steelworkers union.

All-black **Texas Western** (now UTEP) shocks all-white Kentucky, 72-65, in the finals of the NCAA basketball tournament at College Park, Md., on March 19. Led by guard Bobby Joe Hill and center David (Big Daddy) Lattin, the unsung Miners make 28 of 34 free throw attempts and end the season at 28-1.

The **Atlanta Braves** play their first regular season home game at Atlanta Stadium. A crowd of 50,761 turns out on the evening of April 12 to see their new heroes lose to Pittsburgh, 3-2 in 13 innings.

On June 8, the **NFL** and **AFL** announce plans to merge by the start of the 1970 pro football season. There will also be an AFL-NFL World Championship Game (now the Super Bowl) beginning after the 1966 season.

England, the nation that invented soccer, wins its only World Cup title on July 30, beating West Germany, 4-2, in extra time before a crowd of over 93,000 at Wembley Stadium in London.

Frank Robinson of the world champion Baltimore Orioles, who won the AL Triple Crown during the regular season is named the league's Most Valuable Player on Nov. 8. The honor makes him the only player to win MVP awards in both leagues.

College football's **"Game of the Decade"** is played on Nov. 19 between No. 1 Notre Dame (8-0) and No. 2 Michigan State (9-0) at East Lansing. The contest ends in a 10-10 tie after Notre Dame gets the ball on its own 30 yard line with 1:24 left and coach Ara Parseghian elects to run out the clock with four straight run plays. Two weeks later, the final AP poll ranks the Irish No. 1 for the year.

1971
(25 years ago)

Third-ranked **Nebraska** wins its first national football championship by defeating LSU, 17-12, on New Year's Night at the Orange Bowl. The Cornhuskers entered the game knowing that earlier in the day No. 1 Texas had lost to Notre Dame (24-11) in the Cotton Bowl and No. 2 Ohio State had been beaten by Stanford (27-17) in the Rose Bowl.

Lew Alcindor, who would change his name to Kareem Abdul-Jabbar in 1971, teams with veteran guard Oscar Robertson as the Milwaukee Bucks complete a four-game sweep of the Baltimore Bullets in the NBA Finals on April 30. Alcindor, 24, leads the NBA in scoring and is the playoff and regular season MVP.

Goaltender **Ken Dryden** becomes the first rookie to win the Conn Smythe Award as he backstops the Montreal Canadiens to a seven-game victory over the Chicago Black Hawks in the Stanley Cup finals on May 18. Henri Richard, the Habs' 35-year-old captain scores twice in the finale to win his 10th Cup.

In the baseball All-Star Game at Detroit's Tiger Stadium, Oakland's **Reggie Jackson** hits a soaring 520-foot home run off Pittsburgh pitcher Dock Ellis and stands at the plate to admire the shot as it strikes the light tower on the right field roof. Five other homers are hit in the game as the American League beats the National, 6-4.

Bob Short, who owned the Minneapolis Lakers of the NBA when he moved them to Los Angeles in 1960, becomes the first owner to move two teams in two different major league sports. He receives permission from the American League on Sept. 20, to relocate his Washington Senators to Arlington, Texas for the 1972 season. On Nov. 23, he renames them the Texas Rangers.

Jim Palmer of Baltimore wins his 20th game on Sept. 26, making the Orioles the first team with **four 20-game winners** in the same season since the 1920 Chicago White Sox. The three other Oriole hurlers are Mike Cueller, Dave McNally and Pat Dobson.

Steve Blass fires a 4-hitter and **Roberto Clemente** homers in Game 7 as the Pittsburgh Pirates win their first World Series since 1960. Clemente, the Series MVP after hitting .414, ended the regular season just 118 hits shy of 3,000.

The **World Hockey Association** announces plans on Nov. 1 to challenge the established NHL with a 10-team league beginning in October 1972. The WHA actually debuted with 12 teams in '72 and lasted for seven seasons.

The **longest game in NFL history** is played on Christmas Day at Municipal Stadium in Kansas City. Garo Yepremian kicks a 37-yard field goal with 7:40 remaining in the second period of sudden death overtime to give the Miami Dolphins a 27-24 victory over the Kansas City Chiefs in the opening round of the AFC playoffs.

1976
(20 years ago)

Undefeated **Indiana** beats Michigan, 86-68, to win the NCAA basketball championship on March 29 in Philadelphia. Six unbeaten teams had won NCAA titles before coach Bob Knight's Hoosiers (32-0), but none since.

Boston defeats Phoenix, 128-126, in **triple overtime** at the Boston Garden to win the most thrilling game in the history of the NBA Finals. Two days later, on June 6, the Celtics win their 13th NBA title in 20 years, beating the Suns, 87-80 in Game 6.

The **NBA** and **ABA** announce on June 17 that they will merge after nine years as rivals. Four ABA teams— the Denver Nuggets, Indiana Pacers, New York Nets and San Antonio Spurs join the NBA, while players with the Kentucky Colonels and Spirits of St. Louis will be made available in a dispersal draft.

On Nov. 4, baseball holds its **first free agent re-entry draft** in New York. Teams can pick as many players as they want, but any one player can only be selected by 12 teams. Baltimore 2nd baseman Bobby Grich is the first player picked, but his former teammate Reggie Jackson will be the biggest winner. On Nov. 29, the Yankees sign Jackson to a five-year contract worth $2.9 million.

1986
(10 years ago)

Jack Nicklaus shoots a 279 to win his sixth Masters championship. The victory also makes him the oldest player, at age 46, to win at Augusta.

Boston pitcher **Roger Clemens** sets the major league record for strikeouts in a game by fanning 20 Seattle Mariners on April 29 at Fenway Park.

Ferdinand, a 17-1 long shot, wins the Kentucky Derby on May 3. Jockey Bill Shoemaker, 54, guides his overlooked mount from last to first for his fourth and final Derby victory.

The **New York Mets** come back from the brink of elimination in the World Series to defeat Boston in seven games. The Red Sox, who haven't won the Series since 1918, are one out away from winning the title in Game 6 when a Mookie Wilson grounder goes through the legs of 1st basemen Bill Buckner allowing Ray Knight to score the winning run.

Twenty-year-old **Mike Tyson** becomes the youngest heavyweight champion in history with a 2nd-round TKO over WBC champion Trevor Berbick on Nov. 22 in Las Vegas.

RESEARCH MATERIAL

Many sources were used in the gathering of information for this almanac. Day to day material was almost always found in copies of *USA Today, The Boston Globe,* and *The New York Times.*

Several weekly and bi-weekly periodicals were also used in the past year's pursuit of facts and figures, among them— *Amusement Business, Baseball America, Boxing Illustrated, The European, FIFA News* (Soccer), *The Hockey News, The NCAA News, On Track, Soccer America, Sports Illustrated, The Sporting News, Track & Field News,* and *USA Today Baseball Weekly.*

In addition, the following books provided background material for one or more chapters of the almanac.

Arenas & Ballparks

The Ballparks, by Bill Shannon and George Kalinsky; Hawthorn Books, Inc. (1975); New York.

Diamonds, by Michael Gershman; Houghton Mifflin Co. (1993); Boston.

Green Cathedrals (Revised Edition), by Philip Lowry; Addison-Wesley Publishing Co. (1992); Reading, Mass.

The NFL's Encyclopedic History of Professional Football, Macmillan Publishing Co. (1977); New York.

Take Me Out to the Ballpark, by Lowell Reidenbaugh; The Sporting News Publishing Co. (1983); St. Louis.

24 Seconds to Shoot (An Informal History of the NBA), by Leonard Koppett; Macmillan Publishing Co. (1968); New York.

Plus many major league baseball, NBA, NFL, NHL league and team guides, and major college football and basketball guides.

Auto Racing

1995 IndyCar Media Guide, edited by Bob Andrew; Championship Auto Racing Teams; Troy, Mich.

1995 Indianapolis 500 Media Fact Book, compiled Bob Laycock, Jan Shaffer and Lee Driggers; Indianapolis Motor Speedway; Indianapolis.

Indy: 75 Years of Racing's Greatest Spectacle, by Rich Taylor; St. Martin's Press (1991); New York.

Marlboro Grand Prix Guide, 1950-94 (1995 Edition), compiled by Jacques Deschenaux; Charles Stewart & Company Ltd; Brentford, England.

1995 Winston Cup Media Guide, compiled and edited by Chris Powell; NASCAR Winston Cup Series; Winston-Salem, N.C.

Baseball

The All-Star Game (A Pictorial History, 1933 to Present), by Donald Honig; The Sporting News Publishing Co. (1987); St. Louis.

Baseball America's 1995 Almanac, edited by Allan Simpson; Baseball America, Inc.; Durham, N.C.

Baseball America's 1995 Directory, edited by Allan Simpson; Baseball America, Inc.; Durham, N.C.

The Baseball Chronology, edited by James Charlton; Macmillan Publishing Co. (1991); New York.

The Baseball Encyclopedia (Ninth Edition), editorial director, Rick Wolff; Macmillan Publishing Co. (1993); New York.

The Complete 1995 Baseball Record Book, edited by Craig Carter; The Sporting News Publishing Co.; St. Louis.

Daguerreotypes (Eighth Edition), edited by Craig Carter; The Sporting News Publishing Co.; St. Louis.

1995 NCAA Baseball and Softball, compiled by John Painter, Sean Straziscar and James Wright; edited by Ted Breidenthal; NCAA Books; Overland Park, Kan.

The Scrapbook History of Baseball by Jordan Deutsch, Richard Cohen, Roland Johnson and David Neft; Bobbs-Merrill Company, Inc. (1975); Indianapolis/New York.

1995 Sporting News Official Baseball Guide, edited by Craig Carter and Dave Sloan; The Sporting News Publishing Co.; St. Louis.

1995 Sporting News Official Baseball Register, edited by George Puro and Kyle Veltrop; The Sporting News Publishing Co.; St. Louis.

The Sports Encyclopedia: Baseball (1995 Edition), edited by David Neft and Richard Cohen; St. Martin's Press; New York.

Total Baseball (Fourth Edition), edited by John Thorn and Pete Palmer; Harper Perennial (1995); New York.

College Basketball

All the Moves (A History of College Basketball), by Neil D. Issacs; J.B. Lippincott Company (1975); New York.

1994-95 Blue Ribbon College Basketball Yearbook, edited by Chris Wallace; Christopher Publishing; Buckhannon, W.Va.

College Basketball, U.S.A. (Since 1892), by John D. McCallum; Stein and Day (1978); New York.

Collegiate Basketball: Facts and Figures on the Cage Sport, by Edwin C. Caudle; The Paragon Press (1960); Montgomery, Ala.

The Encyclopedia of the NCAA Basketball Tournament, written and compiled by Jim Savage; Dell Publishing (1990); New York.

The Final Four (Reliving America's Basketball Classic), compiled by Billy Reed; Host Communications, Inc. (1988); Lexington, Ky.

1995 NCAA Final Four Records Book, compiled by Gary Johnson; edited by Steven Hagwell; NCAA Books; Overland Park, Kan.

The Modern Encyclopedia of Basketball (Second Revised Edition), edited by Zander Hollander; Dolphins Books (1979); Doubleday & Company, Inc.; Garden City, N.Y.

1995 NCAA College Basketball Records Book, compiled by Gary Johnson, Richard Campbell, John Painter, Sean Straziscar and James Wright; edited by Laura Bollig; NCAA Books; Overland Park, Kan.

1995 NIT Tournament Guide, Madison Square Garden; New York.

Plus many 1994-95 NCAA Division I conference guides from the American West to the WAC.

Pro Basketball

The Encyclopedia of Pro Basketball Team Histories, by Peter C. Bjarkman; Carroll & Graf Publishers (1994); New York.

The Official NBA Basketball Encyclopedia (Second Edition), edited by Alex Sachare; Villard Books (1994); New York.

1994-95 Philadelphia 76ers Statistical Yearbook, edited by Harvey Pollack; Philadelphia 76ers; Philadelphia.

1994-95 Sporting News Official NBA Guide, edited by Craig Carter and Alex Sachare; The Sporting News Publishing Co.; St. Louis.

1994-95 Sporting News Official NBA Register, edited by George Puro, Alex Sachare and Kyle Veltrop; The Sporting News Publishing Co.; St. Louis.

Bowling

1995 Bowlers Journal Annual & Almanac; Luby Publishing; Chicago.

1995 LPBT Guide, Ladies Pro Bowlers Tour; Rockford, Ill.

1995 PBA Media Guide; Professional Bowlers Association; Akron, Ohio.

Boxing

The Boxing Record Book (1995), edited by Phill Marder; Fight Fax Inc.; Sicklerville, N.J.

The Ring 1985 Record Book & Boxing Encyclopedia, edited by Herbert G. Goldman; The Ring Publishing Corp.; New York.

The Ring: Boxing, The 20th Century, Steven Farhood, editor-in-chief; BDD Illustrated Books (1993); New York.

College Sports

1993-94 National Collegiate Championships, edited by Ted Breidenthal; NCAA Books; Overland Park, Kan.

1995 NCAA College Basketball Records Book, compiled by Gary Johnson, Richard Campbell, John Painter, Sean Straziscar and James Wright; edited by Laura Bollig; NCAA Books; Overland Park, Kan.

1994 NCAA College Football Records Book, compiled by Richard Campbell, John Painter and Sean Straziscar; edited by J. Gregory Summers; NCAA Books; Overland Park, Kan.

1993-94 NAIA Championships History and Records Book; National Assn. of Intercollegiate Athletics; Tulsa, Okla.

1994-95 National Directory of College Athletics, edited by Kevin Cleary; Collegiate Directories, Inc.; Cleveland.

College Football

Football: A College History, by Tom Perrin; McFarland & Company, Inc. (1987); Jefferson, N.C.

Football: Facts & Figures, by Dr. L.H. Baker; Farrar & Rinehart, Inc. (1945); New York.

Great College Football Coaches of the Twenties and Thirties, by Tim Cohane; Arlington House (1973); New Rochelle, N.Y.

1994 NCAA College Football Records Book, compiled by Richard Campbell, John Painter and Sean Straziscar; edited by J. Gregory Summers; NCAA Books; Overland Park, Kan.

Saturday Afternoon, by Richard Whittingham; Workman Publishing Co., Inc. (1985); New York.

Saturday's America, by Dan Jenkins; Sports Illustrated Books; Little, Brown & Company (1970); Boston.

Tournament of Roses, The First 100 Years, by Joe Hendrickson; Knapp Press (1989); Los Angeles.

   Plus many Division I-A and Division I-AA team and conference guides.

Pro Football

1994 Canadian Football League Guide, compiled by the CFL Communications Dept.; Toronto.

The Football Encyclopedia (The Complete History of NFL Football from 1892 to the Present), compiled by David Neft and Richard Cohen; St. Martin's Press (1994); New York.

The Official NFL Encyclopedia, by Beau Riffenburgh; New American Library (1986); New York.

Official NFL 1994 Record and Fact Book, edited by Chris Hardart and Chuck Garrity Jr.; produced by NFL Properties, Inc.; New York.

The Scrapbook History of Pro Football, by Richard Cohen, Jordan Deutsch, Roland Johnson and David Neft; Bobbs-Merrill Company, Inc. (1976); Indianapolis/New York.

1994 Sporting News Football Guide, edited by Craig Carter; The Sporting News Publishing Co.; St. Louis.

1994 Sporting News Football Register, edited George Puro and Kyle Veltrop; The Sporting News Publishing Co.; St. Louis.

1995 Sporting News Super Bowl Book, edited by Tom Dienhart, Joe Hoppel and Dave Sloan; The Sporting News Publishing Co.; St. Louis.

Golf

The Encyclopedia of Golf (Revised Edition), compiled by Nevin H. Gibson; A.S. Barnes and Company (1964); New York.

Guinness Golf Records: Facts and Champions, by Donald Steel; Guinness Superlatives Ltd. (1987); Middlesex, England.

The History of the PGA Tour, by Al Barkow; Doubleday (1989); New York.

The Illustrated History of Women's Golf, by Rhonda Glenn, Taylor Publishing Co. (1991); Dallas.

1995 LPGA Player Guide, produced by LPGA Communications Dept.; Ladies Professional Golf Assn. Tour; Daytona Beach, Fla.

1995 PGA Tour Guide, produced by PGA Tour Creative Services; Professional Golfers Assn. Tour; Ponte Vedra, Fla.

Official Guide of the PGA Championships; Triumph Books (1994); Chicago.

The PGA World Golf Hall of Fame Book, by Gerald Astor, Prentice Hall Press (1991); New York.

1995 Senior PGA Tour Guide, produced by PGA Tour Creative Services; Professional Golfers Assn. Tour; Ponte Vedra, Fla.

Pro-Golf 1995, PGA European Tour Media Guide, Virginia Water, Surrey, England.

The Random House International Encyclopedia of Golf, by Malcolm Campbell; Random House (1991); New York.

USGA Record Books (1895-1959, 1960-80 and 1981-90); U.S. Golf Association; Far Hills, N.J.

Hockey

Canada Cup '87: The Official History, No.1 Publications Ltd.; Toronto.

The Complete Encyclopedia of Hockey; edited by Zander Hollander; Visible Ink Press (1993); Detroit.

The Hockey Encyclopedia, by Stan Fischler and Shirley Walton Fischler; research editor, Bob Duff; Macmillan Publishing Co. (1983); New York.

Hockey Hall of Fame (The Official History of the Game and Its Greatest Stars), by Dan Diamond and Joseph Romain; Doubleday (1988); New York.

The National Hockey League, by Edward F. Dolan Jr.; W H Smith Publishers Inc. (1986); New York.

The Official National Hockey League 75th Anniversary Commemorative Book, edited by Dan Diamond; McClelland & Stewart, Inc. (1991); Toronto.

1994-95 Official NHL Guide & Record Book, compiled by the NHL Public Relations Dept.; New York/Montreal/Toronto.

1994-95 Sporting News Complete Hockey Book, edited by Craig Carter, George Puro and Kyle Veltrop; The Sporting News Publishing Co.; St. Louis.

The Stanley Cup, by Joseph Romain and James Duplacey; Gallery Books (1989); New York.

The Trail of the Stanley Cup (Volumes I-III), by Charles L. Coleman; Progressive Publications Inc. (1969); Sherbrooke, Quebec.

Horse Racing

1995 American Racing Manual, compiled by the Daily Racing Form; Hightstown, N.J.

1995 Breeders' Cup Statistics; Breeders' Cup Limited; Lexington, Ky.

1995 Directory and Record Book, Thoroughbred Racing Associations of North America Inc.; Elkton, Md.

1995 Kentucky Derby Media Guide, compiled by Churchill Downs Public Relations Dept.; Louisville, Ky.

1995 NYRA Media Guide, The New York Racing Association Inc.; Jamaica, N.Y.

1995 Preakness Press Guide, compiled and edited by Dale Austin, Craig Sculos and Joe Kelly; Maryland Jockey Club; Baltimore, Md.

1995 Trotting and Pacing Guide, compiled and edited by John Pawlak; United States Trotting Association; Columbus, Ohio.

International Sports

Athletics: A History of Modern Track and Field (1860-1990, Men and Women), by Roberto Quercetani; Vallardi & Associati (1990); Milan, Italy.

1995 International Track & Field Annual, Association of Track & Field Statisticians; edited by Peter Matthews; SportsBooks Ltd.; Surrey, England.

Track & Field News' Little Blue Book; Metric conversion tables; From the editors of Track & Field News (1989); Los Altos, Calif.

Miscellaneous

The America's Cup 1851-1987 (Sailing for Supremacy), by Gary Lester and Richard Sleeman; Lester-Townsend Publishing (1986); Sydney, Australia.

The Encyclopedia of Sports (Fifth Revised Edition), by Frank G. Menke; revisions by Suzanne Treat; A.S. Barnes and Co., Inc. (1975); Cranbury, N.J.

The Great American Sports Book, by George Gipe; Doubleday & Company, Inc. (1978); Garden City, N.Y.

The 1995 Information Please Almanac, edited by Otto Johnson; Houghton Mifflin Co.; Boston.

1995 Official PRCA Media Guide, edited by Steve Fleming; Professional Rodeo Cowboys Association; Colorado Springs.

The Sail Magazine Book of Sailing, by Peter Johnson; Alfred A. Knopf (1989); New York.

"Ten Years of the Ironman," Triathlete Magazine; October, 1988; Santa Monica, Calif.

The 1995 World Almanac and Book of Facts, edited by Robert Famighetti; Funk & Wagnalls; Mahwah, N.J.

Olympics

All That Glitters Is Not Gold (An Irreverent Look at the Olympic Games; by William O. Johnson, Jr.; G.P. Putnam's Sons (1972); New York.

Barcelona/Albertville 1992; edited by Lisa H. Albertson; for U.S. Olympic Committee by Commemorative Publications; Salt Lake City.

Chamonix to Lillehammer (The Glory of the Olympic Winter Games); edited by Lisa H. Albertson; for U.S. Olympic Committee by Commemorative Publication (1994); Salt Lake City.

The Complete Book of the Olympics (1992 Edition); by David Wallechinsky; Little, Brown and Co.; Boston.

The Games Must Go On (Avery Brundage and the Olympic Movement), by Allen Guttmann; Columbia University Press (1984); New York.

The Golden Book of the Olympic Games, edited by Erich Kamper and Bill Mallon; Vallardi & Associati (1992); Milan, Italy.

Hitler's Games (The 1936 Olympics), by Duff Hart-Davis; Harper & Row (1986); New York/London.

An Illustrated History of the Olympics (Third Edition); by Dick Schaap; Alfred A. Knopf (1975); New York.

The Nazi Olympics, by Richard D. Mandell; Souvenir Press (1972); London.

The Official USOC Book of the 1984 Olympic Games, by Dick Schaap; Random House/ABC Sports; New York.

The Olympics: A History of the Games, by William Oscar Johnson; Oxmoor House (1992); Birmingham, Ala.

Pursuit of Excellence (The Olympic Story), by The Associated Press and Grolier; Grolier Enterprises Inc. (1979); Danbury, Conn.

The Story of the Olympic Games (776 B.C. to 1948 A.D.), by John Kieran and Arthur Daley; J.B. Lippincott Company (1948); Philadelphia/New York.

United States Olympic Books (Seven Editions): 1936 and 1948-88; U.S. Olympic Association; New York.

The USA and the Olympic Movement, produced by the USOC Information Dept.; edited by Gayle Plant; U.S. Olympic Committee (1988); Colorado Springs.

Plus official IOC and USOC records from the 1994 Winter Olympics in Lillehammer, Norway.

Soccer

The American Encyclopedia of Soccer, edited by Zander Hollander; Everest House Publishers (1980); New York.

The European Football Yearbook (1994-95 Edition), edited by Mike Hammond; Sports Projects Ltd; West Midlands, England.

The Guinness Book of Soccer Facts & Feats, by Jack Rollin; Guinness Superlatives Ltd. (1978); Middlesex, England.

History of Soccer's World Cup, by Michael Archer; Chartwell Books, Inc. (1978); Secaucus, N.J.

The Simplest Game, by Paul Gardner; Collier Books (1994); New York.

The Story of the World Cup, by Brian Glanville; Faber and Faber Limited (1993); London/Boston.

1991-92 MSL Official Guide, Major (Indoor) Soccer League; Overland Park, Kan.

U.S. Soccer 1995 Media Guide, edited by Tom Lang; U.S. Soccer Federation; Chicago.

Tennis

Bud Collins' Modern Encyclopedia of Tennis, edited by Bud Collins and Zander Hollander; Visible Ink Press (1994); Detroit.

The Illustrated Encyclopedia of World Tennis, by John Haylett and Richard Evans; Exeter Books (1989); New York.

Official Encyclopedia of Tennis, edited by the staff of the U.S. Lawn Tennis Assn.; Harper & Row (1972); New York.

1995 ATP Tour Player Guide, compiled by ATP Tour Communications Dept.; Association of Tennis Professionals; Ponte Vedra Beach, Fla.

1995 WTA Tour Media Guide, compiled by WTA Public Relations staff; edited by Renee Bloch Shallouf; St. Petersburg, Fla.

Who's Who

The Guiness International Who's Who of Sport, edited by Peter Mathews, Ian Buchanan and Bill Mallon; Guiness Publishing (1993); Middlesex, England

101 Greatest Athletes of the Century, by Will Grimsley and the Associated Press Sports Staff; Bonanza Books (1987); Crown Publishers, Inc.; New York.

The New York Times Book of Sports Legends, edited by Joseph Vecchione; Simon & Shuster (1991); New York.

Superstars, by Frank Litsky; Vineyard Books, Inc. (1975); Secaucus, N.J.

A Who's Who of Sports Champions (Their Stories and Records), by Ralph Hicock; Houghton Mifflin Co. (1995); Boston.

Other Reference Books

Facts & Dates of American Sports, by Gorton Carruth & Eugene Ehrlich; Harper & Row, Publishers, Inc. (1988); New York.

Sports Market Place 1995 (July Edition), edited by Richard A. Lipsey; Sportsguide Inc.; Princeton N.J.

The World Book Encyclopedia (1988 Edition); World Book, Inc.; Chicago.

The World Book Yearbook (Annual Supplements, 1954-95); World Book, Inc.; Chicago.

Olympics
Winter Games

Year	No.	Host City	Dates
1998	XVIII	Nagano, Japan	Feb. 7-22
2002	XIX	Salt Lake City, Utah	Feb. 9-24

Summer Games

Year	No.	Host City	Dates
1996	XXVI	Atlanta, Georgia	July 19-Aug. 4
2000	XXVII	Sydney, Australia	Sept. 16-Oct. 1

All-Star Games
Baseball

Year	Site	Date
1996	Veterans Stadium, Philadelphia	July 9
1997	Jacobs Field, Cleveland	July 8
1998	Coors Field, Denver	July 7

NBA Basketball

Year	Site	Date
1996	Alamodome, San Antonio	Feb. 11
1997	Gund Arena, Cleveland	Feb. 9

NFL Pro Bowl

Year	Site	Date
1996	Aloha Stadium, Honolulu	Feb. 4
1997	Aloha Stadium, Honolulu	Feb. 2
1998	Aloha Stadium, Honolulu	Feb. 1

NHL Hockey

Year	Site	Date
1996	FleetCenter, Boston	Jan. 21
1997	San Jose Arena, San Jose	Jan. 18

Auto Racing

The Daytona 500 stock car race is usually held on the Sunday before the third Monday in February, while the Indianapolis 500 is usually held on the Sunday of Memorial Day weekend in May. Except for 1996, the following dates are tentative.

Year	Daytona 500	Indianapolis 500
1996	Feb. 18	May 26
1997	Feb. 16	May 25
1998	Feb. 15	May 24

NCAA Basketball
Men's Final Four

Year	Site	Date
1996	Meadowlands (N.J.) Arena	Mar. 30-Apr. 1
1997	RCA Dome, Indianapolis	March 29-31
1998	Alamodome, San Antonio	March 28-30
1999	ThunderDome, St. Petersburg	March 27-29
2000	RCA Dome, Indianapolis	April 1-3
2001	Metrodome, Minneapolis	Mar. 31-Apr. 2
2002	Georgia Dome, Atlanta	Mar. 30-Apr. 1

Women's Final Four

Year	Site	Date
1996	Charlotte (N.C.) Coliseum	March 29-31
1997	Riverfront Coliseum, Cincinnati	March 28-29
1998	Kemper Arena, Kansas City	March 28-29

NFL Football
Super Bowl

No.	Site	Date
XXX	Sun Devil Stadium, Tempe	Jan. 28, 1996
XXXI	Superdome, New Orleans	Jan. 26, 1997
XXXII	Jack Murphy Stadium, San Diego	Jan. 25, 1998
XXXIII	3Com Park, San Francisco	Jan. 24, 1999
XXXIV	Hollywood Park, Los Angeles	Jan. 23, 2000

Golf
The Masters

Year	Site	Date
1996	Augusta National Ga	April 11-14
1997	Augusta National Ga	April 10-13
1998	Augusta National Ga	April 9-12

U.S. Open

Year	Site	Date
1996	Oakland Hills CC, Birmingham, Mich.	June 13-16
1997	Congressional CC, Bethesda, Md.	June 12-15
1998	Olympic Club, San Francisco	June 18-21
1999	Pinehurst CC, Pinehurst, N.J.	June 17-20
2000	Pebble Beach (Calif.) Golf Links.	June 15-18

U.S. Women's Open

Year	Site	Date
1996	Pine Needles Resort, So. Pines, N.C.	May 30-June 2
1997	Pumpkin Ridge GC, Cornelius, Ore.	July 10-13
1998	Blackwolf Run GC, Kohler, Wisc.	July 2-5
1999	Merit Club, Libertyville, Ill.	July 22-25

U.S. Senior Open

Year	Site	Date
1996	Canterbury GC, Cleveland	July 4-7
1997	Olympia Fields GC, Olympia Field, Ill.	June 26-29
1998	Riviera CC, Pacific Palisades, Calif.	July 23-26
1999	Des Moines GC, W. Des Moines, Iowa	July 8-11

PGA Championship

Year	Site	Date
1996	Valhalla GC, Louisville	Aug. 8-11
1997	Winged Foot GC, Mamaroneck, N.Y.	Aug. 14-17
1998	Sahalee CC, Seattle	Aug. 13-16

British Open

Year	Site	Date
1996	Royal Lytham & St. Annes, England	July 18-21
1997	Royal Troon, Scotland	July 17-20

Ryder Cup

Year	Site	Date
1997	Valderrama, Spain	Sept. 20-28
1999	The Country Club, Brookline, Mass.	TBA

Horse Racing
Triple Crown

The Kentucky Derby is always held at Churchill Downs in Louisville on the first Saturday in May, followed two weeks later by the Preakness Stakes at Pimlico Race Course in Baltimore and three weeks after that by the Belmont Stakes at Belmont Park in Elmont, N.Y.

Year	Ky Derby	Preakness	Belmont
1996	May 4	May 18	June 8
1997	May 3	May 17	June 7
1998	May 2	May 16	June 6
1999	May 1	May 15	June 5

Tennis
U.S. Open

Usually held from the last Monday in August through the second Sunday in September, with Labor Day weekend the midway point in the tournament.

Year	Site	Dates
1996	U.S. Tennis Center, NYC	Aug. 26-Sept. 8
1997	U.S. Tennis Center, NYC	Aug. 25-Sept. 7
1998	U.S. Tennis Center, NYC	Aug. 24-Sept. 6
1999	U.S. Tennis Center, NYC	Aug. 23-Sept. 5